MANU'S CODE OF LAW

SOUTH ASIA RESEARCH

SERIES EDITOR

Patrick Olivelle

A Publication Series of
The University of Texas South Asia Institute
and
Oxford University Press

THE EARLY UPANIṢADS
Annotated Text and Translation

Patrick Olivelle

INDIAN EPIGRAPHY
A Guide to the Study of Inscriptions in Sanskrit, Prakrit,
and the Other Indo-Aryan Languages

Richard Salomon

A DICTIONARY OF OLD MARATHI

S. G. Tulpule and Anne Feldhaus

DONORS, DEVOTEES, AND DAUGHTERS OF GOD
Temple Women in Medieval Tamilnadu

Leslie C. Orr

JĪMŪTAVĀHANA'S *DĀYABHĀGA*
The Hindu Law of Inheritance in Bengal
Edited and Translated with an Introduction and Notes by

Ludo Rocher

A PORTRAIT OF THE HINDUS
Balthazar Solvyns and the European Image of India 1740–1824

Robert L. Hardgrave, Jr.

DIVINE TESTIMONY
A Study and Translation of the Rajasthani Oral Narrative of Devnarayan

Aditya Malik

MANU'S CODE OF LAW

A Critical Edition and Translation of the *Mānava-Dharmaśāstra*

PATRICK OLIVELLE

With the editorial assistance of
Suman Olivelle

OXFORD
UNIVERSITY PRESS

2005

OXFORD
UNIVERSITY PRESS

Oxford New York
Auckland Bangkok Buenos Aires Cape Town Chennai
Dar es Salaam Delhi Hong Kong Istanbul Karachi Kolkata
Kuala Lumpur Madrid Melbourne Mexico City Mumbai Nairobi
São Paulo Shanghai Taipei Tokyo Toronto

Published by Oxford University Press, Inc.
198 Madison Avenue, New York, New York 10016

www.oup.com

Library of Congress Cataloging-in-Publication Data
Manu (Lawgiver).
[Mānavadharmáśāstra. English & Sanskirt]
Manu's code of law : a critical edition and translation of the Mānava-dharmáśāstra / Patrick Olivelle ; with the editorial assistance of Suman Olivelle
p. cm. — (South Asia research)
Includes bibliographical references and index.
ISBN 0-19-517146-2
1. Mānavadharmáśāstra. 2. Hindu law—Sources. 3. Law—India—Sources. 4. Law—India—History. I. Olivelle, Patrick.
II. Olivelle, Suman.
III. Title. IV. Series: South Asia research (New York, N.Y.)
KNS127.3.A4 2004
294.5'94—dc22 2003070152

2 4 6 8 9 7 5 3 1

Printed in the United States of America
on acid-free paper

Preface

It was in 1991, soon after I joined the University of Texas, that I first thought about preparing a critical edition of the *Mānava-Dharmaśāstra*. I first envisaged it as a collaborative project between me and my colleague Richard Lariviere, who had then just completed the first-ever critical edition of the *Nāradasmṛti*. Little did I realize that it would take a dozen years to complete the project, nor did I have any idea how complex, labor-intensive, and time-consuming it would be. I am glad that I did not have the foresight to know then what I know now in hindsight; if I did I would never have undertaken it.

Over these past thirteen years many individuals and institutions have helped me in numerous ways; without their help this work would never have been completed. At the end of this long road, I now have the pleasant task of expressing my gratitude to all of them publicly. First and foremost, Suman Olivelle has been a full partner in the editorial work for the past seven years. She collated most of the manuscripts, learning eight different scripts in the process; proofread the entire document several times; and in general kept this complex project involving several collators organized. Richard Lariviere took on major administrative responsibilities over the years; although he could not collaborate directly in this edition, he has assisted this project in ways too numerous to mention. Albrecht Wezler read several chapters of my translation and gave valuable and insightful criticism and suggestions. During the eight months that I spent at Harvard in 2000–01, Stephanie Jamison gave unstintingly of her time and knowledge and helped me work through obscure passages of the text. During the same period Michael Witzel also assisted in a variety of ways in coming to terms with this difficult text and in the dating of some manuscripts. Several of my students helped me in collating the manuscripts: Don Davis, Robert Fulton, Robert Goodding, and Mark McClish. Other students assisted the project in numerous ways: Stephen Lindquist, Lisa Edwin, and Roger Conant. David Brick helped with the Dharma Parallels, and Elliott MacGregor with the Pāda Index. Ludo Rocher, Anne Feldhaus, and Gregory Schopen read the introduction and gave valuable comments and suggestions. Wendy Doniger, Martha Selby, and Dominik Wujastyk provided guidance especially in medical and gynecological matters. Officers of the American Institute of Indian Studies were immensely helpful in obtaining manuscripts: Pradeep Mehendiratta, Madhav Bhandare, Venugopala Rao, and Jagdish Yadav. Likewise, Karan Singh, Arlo Griffith, Cynthia Talbot, Ulrich Kragh,

Anne Feldhaus, and V. L. Manjul obtained manuscripts from Jammu, Orissa, Rajasthan, Calcutta, and Nagpur. Allen Thrasher was very helpful in giving me access to the Library of Congress in Washington, D.C. at the very beginning of this project, and Mammata Misra helped with the reading of difficult passages of an Oriya manuscript.

Many institutions assisted me in various ways. The Smithsonian Institution, the National Endowment for the Humanities, and the University of Texas gave generous grants, without which this edition would never have been completed. The Bhandarkar Oriental Research Institute in Pune obtained numerous manuscripts and did a pilot collation of a few manuscripts under a grant from the Smithsonian. I want to thank especially Dr. S. D. Laddu, who supervised that collation.

Finally, a big thank you to my daughter, Meera, who has endured this project that has absorbed both her father and mother both during her high-school years and through her four years of college! Thanks also to Cynthia Read and Theodore Calderara of the Oxford University Press, New York, who, as usual, have supported this project enthusiastically.

This is a long and complex volume with several scripts and fonts. I produced the camera-ready copy, and even with the most careful attention and proofreading there are bound to be errors for which I beg the indulgence of the readers.

Austin, Texas P.O.
June, 2004

Contents

Abbreviations

AB	*Aitareya Brāhmaṇa*
AĀ	*Aitareya Āraṇyaka*
Apa	Aparāditya, *Aparārka* com. on *YDh*
ĀpDh	*Āpastamba Dharmasūtra*
ĀpGṛ	*Āpastamba Gṛhyasūtra*
ĀpŚr	*Āpastamba Śrautasūtra*
AŚ	Kauṭalya's *Arthaśāstra*
ĀśGṛ	*Āśvalāyana Gṛhyasūtra*
ĀśŚr	*Āśvalāyana Śrautasūtra*
AU	*Aitareya Upaniṣad*
AV	*Atharvaveda*
BauŚr	*Baudhāyana Śrautasūtra*
BDh	*Baudhāyana Dharmasūtra*
Bh	Bhāruci
BhG	*Bhagavad Gītā*
BhP	*Bhaviṣya Purāṇa*
B-R	Böhtlingk and Roth, *Sanskrit-Wörterbuch*
BṛSm	*Bṛhaspati Smṛti*
BṛU	*Bṛhadāraṇyaka Upaniṣad*
cr. ap.	critical apparatus to the edition
ChU	*Chāndogya Upaniṣad*
Dev	Devaṇṇabhaṭṭa, *Smṛticandrikā*
fh	first hand
GDh	*Gautama Dharmasūtra*
Go	Govindarāja
GobhGṛ	*Gobhila Gṛhyasūtra*
haplo	haplography
Har-A	Haradatta, com. on the *ĀpDh*
Har-G	Haradatta, com. on the *GDh*
Hem	Hemādri, *Caturvargacintāmaṇi*
JaiGṛ	*Jaiminīya Gṛhyasūtra*
JAOS	*Journal of the American Oriental Society*
JB	*Jaiminīya Brāhmaṇa*
JIP	*Journal of Indian Philosophy*
Jmv	Jīmūtavāhana, *Dāyabhāga*
KātŚr	Kātyāyana Śrautasūtra
KB	*Kāṭhaka Brāhmaṇa*

KhGṛ	*Khadira Gṛhyasūtra*
KS	*Kāṭhaka Saṃhitā*
KSS	Kashi Sanskrit Series
Ku	Kullūka
Kum	Kumārila, *Tantravārttika*
Lakṣ	Lakṣmīdhara, *Kṛtyakalpataru*
ma	marginal addition
Mādh	Mādhava, *Pārāśaramādhavīya*
MBh	*Mahābhārata*
mc	marginal correction
MDh	*Mānava Dharmaśāstra*
Me	Medhātithi
Mr	Maṇirāma
MS	*Maitrāyaṇīya Saṃhitā*
M-W	Monier-Williams, *Sanskrit-English Dictionary*
Nā	Nārāyaṇa
Nd	Nandana
NSm	*Nārada Smṛti*
NT	Northern Transmission of the *MDh*
om	omission, omitted
PārGṛ	*Pāraskara Gṛhyasūtra*
PMS	*Pūrva Mīmāṃsā Sūtra*
Rām	*Rāmāyaṇa*
Rc	Rāmacandra
Rn	Rāghavānanda
ṚV	*Ṛgveda*
Śab	Śabara's commentary on *PMS*
ŚāṅkhGṛ	*Śāṅkhāyana Gṛhyasūtra*
ŚB	*Śatapatha Brāhmaṇa*
sh	second hand
ST	Southern Transmission of the *MDh*
TB	*Taittirīya Brāhmaṇa*
TS	*Taittirīya Saṃhitā*
TU	*Taittirīya Upaniṣad*
VaDh	*Vasiṣtha Dharmasūtra*
VeS	*Vedānta Sūtra*
ViDh	*Viṣnu-Darmasūtra*
Vij	Vijñāneśvara, *Mitākṣarā* com. on the *YDh*
Viś	Viśveśvara, *Bālakrīḍā* com. on the *YDh*
vl	variant reading
VkhGṛ	*Vaikhānasa Gṛhyasūtra*
WZKM	*Wiener Zeitschrift für die Kunde Morgenlandes*
WZKS	*Wiener Zeitschrift für die Kunde Südasiens*
YDh	*Yājñavakya Dharmaśāstra*
ZDMG	*Zeitschrift der Deutschen Morganländischen Gessellschaft*

MANU'S CODE OF LAW

Introduction

The pre-eminent position of the *Mānava Dharmaśāstra* (*MDh*) among the ancient Indian treatises on *dharma* was clearly established by the 5th century CE and possibly as early as the 3rd. Compliments are most meaningful when they are given by one's peers. Sometime toward the middle of the first millennium, Bṛhaspati, one of Manu's successors and himself a composer of a *Dharmaśāstra*, pays Manu the ultimate compliment: Manu is the authority, and any text contradicting Manu has no validity.[1] A couple of centuries earlier, Vātsyāyana, the author of the *Kāmasūtra* (1.1.5–10), refers to the origin of the *MDh* in words reminiscent of the first chapter of the *MDh*. And Yājñavalkya (1.4), another author of an early *Dharmaśāstra*, places Manu at the head of his list of the authors of *Dharmaśāstras*.

The fame of Manu did not diminish through the next fifteen centuries right up to the time when the administration of law was taken over by the colonial power Britain. More commentaries—nine are extant—were written on the *MDh* than on any other *Dharmaśāstra*. Even though in some areas of *dharma*—legal procedure (*vyavahāra*), for example—other texts, such as those of Nārada and Kātyāyana, became prominent, the *MDh* nevertheless remained pre-eminent throughout the long and distinguished history of Dharmaśāstric literature during the Middle Ages. I had to examine closely several prominent texts for citations from the *MDh* for this critical edition. It is clear that the *MDh* is by far the most cited Dharmaśāstric text in the medieval *Nibandhas*.

The fame of Manu, however, had spread outside of India long before the arrival of the British. The first king in the Buddhist myth of origins codified in the *Aggaññasutta*[2] is called Mahāsammata. The figure of this first king becomes identified with that of Manu in the Buddhist countries of Southeast Asia, especially Burma and Thailand, where the Buddhistic law codes are ascribed to Manu.[3]

It is no surprise, then, that the first text on *dharma* that Sir William Jones, the great pioneer of Sanskrit studies, chose to translate into English in 1794 was the *MDh*. Its translation opened for the first time the world of non-European law and religion to a western audience. Georg Bühler's translation and study, which has remained the standard for over a century, appeared in the famous Oxford University

1. See below, pp. 69.

2. For a detailed study of this myth, see Steven Collins, "The Discourse on What is Primary," *Journal of Indian Philosophy* 21(1993): 301–93.

3. For discussions of this issue, see Lingat 1973, 266–72; Steven Collins and Andrew Huxley, "The Post-Canonical Adventures of Mahāsammata," *Journal of Indian Philosophy* 24(1996): 624–48; Steven Collins, "The Lion's Roar on the Wheel-turning King: A Response to Andrew Huxley's 'The Buddha and the Social Contract'," *Ibid.*, 422–46.

Press series, *Sacred Books of the East*, edited by Max Müller, in 1886. With the establishment of Indo-European linguistics and the discovery of the Sanskrit of the Vedas as one of the earliest extant members of the family of languages to which Greek, Latin, and most modern European languages belonged, there was excitement even among non-Indologists about the cultural heritage of ancient India. During the critical 19th century, which set the agenda for much of scholarship on ancient India, the *MDh* was for better or for worse the lens through which most European scholars viewed India's past. Nietzsche, for example, regarded the *MDh* as a life-affirming representation of the Aryan religion, in contrast to the nay-saying Buddhism.[4] Passages from this text are found in every collection of readings given to students of Indian culture, history, or religion in western universities.

Fame invites controversy, and in India itself during the 20th century Manu became a lightning rod for both the conservative elements of the Hindu tradition and the liberal movements intent on alleviating the plight of women and low-caste and outcaste individuals. For the latter, Manu became the symbol of oppression. His verses were cited as the source of legitimation for such oppression, even though the same or similar passages are found in other and older documents. The first conference by untouchables at Yeola under the leadership of Dr. B. R. Ambedkar in 1935, in which it was resolved to reject Hinduism, passed a resolution with the title "To the Untouchable Community: A New Message of a New Manu." Within a month a group of young untouchable men gathered in Nasik to burn a copy of Manu ceremonially.[5] Even the prominent women's rights advocate, Madhu Kishwar, had to do battle with Manu.[6] Kishwar refers to the burning of copies of the *MDh* in the precincts of the Rajasthan High Court on March 25, 2000, and observes: "The protesters believed that the ancient text is the defining document of Brahmanical Hinduism, and also the key source of gender and caste oppression in India."

In spite of all the attention, including burning, that the *MDh* has received over the past two centuries, the study of the text itself has been neglected. More heat, literal and metaphorical, has been generated than light. Until now, even a close examination of the numerous extant manuscripts of this work, manuscripts written in nine scripts and spread all over the Indian subcontinent, has not been undertaken. Without taking any position about the social value of the *MDh*, I would hope that we would take the trouble to read the text with the attention it deserves before we praise, condemn, or burn it. I also hope that this translation and study will be of some help in understanding this controversial but important document from India's past.

4. For a fine examination of the influence of India and the *MDh* on thinkers such as Schegel, Schopenhauer, Hegel, Nietzsche, and others, see Wilhelm Halbfass, *India and Europe: An Essay in Understanding*, Albany, NY: State University of New York Press, 1988.

5. See Eleanor Zelliot, "The Psychological Dimension of the Buddhist Movement in India," in *Religion in South Asia: Religious Conversion and Revival Movements in South Asia in Medieval and Modern Times*, ed. G. A. Oddie, pp. 119–44 (Columbia, Missouri: South Asia Books, 1977). The burning of the *MDh* was advocated also by other reform activists, such as E. V. Ramasami: see M. R. Barnett, *The Politics of Cultural Nationalism in South India* (Princeton: Princeton University Press, 1976), p. 37.

6. "Manu and the Brits," *Hinduism Today*, January–February 2001, pp. 56–59.

I. Authorship and Composition

Scholars traditionally have regarded the composition of the *MDh* as a gradual process at the hands of anonymous and successive compilers, editors, and copyists lasting for several centuries, the same sort of agentless process that many have thought lies behind the composition of the great epic *Mahābhārata*. These compilers and editors, we are told, did nothing more than gather together proverbial sayings, moral maxims, and legal axioms that were floating in the mouths of people and handed down from generation to generation. The composition of the text is thus divorced from authorial intent and agency and from social, political, and economic context. The first to propose such a hypothesis was E. Washburn Hopkins (1885, 268):

> I draw the conclusion that the Çāstram [*MDh*] was in great part collated between the time when the bulk of the epic [*MBh*] was composed and its final completion, that previous to its collation there had existed a vast number of sententious remarks, proverbial wisdom, rules of morality etc. which were ascribed, not to this treatise of Manu at all, but to the ancient hero Manu as a type of godly wisdom. These I conceive to have floated about in the mouths of the people, not brought together but all loosely quoted as laws or saying of Manu and these sayings were afterwards welded into one with the laws of a particular text [sect?] called the Mānavas—a union natural enough, as the two bodies of law would then bear the same title, although the sect had no connection with Manu except in name. . . . According to my theory, these Manu-verses found in the Mānava treatise were simply caught up and drawn from the hearsay of the whole Brahman world, keeping their form after incorporation with the Mānavas' text.

In the introduction to his influential translation of the *MDh*, Bühler agreed substantially with the hypothesis of Hopkins. Bühler (1886, xc) thought that the composers of both the *MDh* and the *Mahābhārata* drew on a common stock of *Spruchweisheit* that, at the hands of the teachers of specialized schools, had spread to all legal topics. Modern scholarship by and large has accepted this view regarding the creation of the *MDh*, as well as of other ancient legal documents. Lariviere (2003, 3) expressed this widely shared view: "I doubt whether such texts as the Nāradasmṛti or the Manusmṛti were composed by a single individual." Hiltebeitel (2001, 5) cites Gitomer's view regarding the composition of the *Mahābhārata*, a view that is common with regard to ancient Indian textual formation in general: "epic textual growth and redaction proceeded in an unconscious, mechanical fashion."[7]

I want to challenge this view regarding the composition of ancient texts in general and of the *MDh* in particular. This vision of composition in the case of the *Mahābhārata* has recently been rejected, rightly I believe, by several leading epic

7. David Gitomer, "King Duryodhana: The Mahābhārata Discourse of Sinning and Virtue in Epic and Drama," *JAOS* 112 (1992): 225.

scholars.[8] That there were proverbs and legal maxims, principally composed in *śloka* verses, outside of fixed texts is beyond doubt. Indeed, it is probably such verse maxims that are cited by the authors of *Dharmasūtras* to support their judgments rendered in aphoristic prose, often with the introductory remark: *athāpy udāharanti* — "Now they also quote." The term *udāharanti* probably means that these verses were recited by experts when questions about some point arose or when circumstances warranted.[9] It would have been natural for authors of texts in almost any field, but most especially those, such as the *Dharmaśāstras*, dealing with morality and human relationships, to draw upon these maxims. Indeed, the example of the *Dharmasūtras* indicates that they clearly did so. These verse maxims, however, are easily detectable in the *Dharmasūtras*, because they are surrounded by the author's own prose. In the metrical *śāstras* it is more difficult to separate the cited maxims from the author's own composition. Let me offer a couple of examples of such maxims in the *MDh*: "When an older person comes near, the life breaths of a younger person rise up, and as he rises up and greets him, he retrieves them" (2.120). This must have been a proverbial saying concerning respect for older persons; it is cited by Patañjali and given twice in the *Mahābhārata*.[10] The verse at *MDh* 4.57 is likewise clearly a proverbial saying about inappropriate actions: "He must not sleep alone in an abandoned house, awaken a sleeping superior, speak with a menstruating woman, or go to a sacrifice uninvited."[11]

The authors of legal treatises clearly drew upon such maxims—and, indeed, on previous scholarship—in composing their texts. My point, however, is that the composition of these texts did not happen as an unconscious and gradual accumulation at different hands and at different times and places; these texts were *authored* by individuals with clear authorial intent. They gave their texts a particular structure; they argued for particular positions in law and morality; they disagreed with other experts, both their contemporaries and their predecessors; and they had particular social, economic, and political axes to grind. In all this they are not much different from modern authors.

The unitary authorship of the *MDh* was proposed over a century ago by Bühler (1886, xcii), who answered the objections of the proponents of a gradual

8. See Alf Hiltebeitel, *Rethinking the Mahābhārata: A Reader's Guide to the Education of the Dharma King* (Chicago: University of Chicago Press, 2001); Madeleine Biardeau, cited by Hiltebeitel, p. 165 ("I prefer to suppose the creation of a sole Brahman of genius"). James Fitzgerald offers a more complicated compositional history, with a final Gupta redaction (see Hiltebeitel 2001, 25–6).

9. Indeed, as one of my students, David Brick, has pointed out, the term *smṛti* in its earliest usage may have referred precisely to such memorable maxims to which attention (*smṛti*) is drawn in particular circumstances and which, of course, reside in the collective memory of the community at large or, in the case of law or grammar, in the memory of a community of experts. The citation of a maxim (*nyāya*), now mostly in prose, is also a feature of later medieval texts. For a collection such maxims, see Appendix E of V. S. Apte's *The Practical Sanskrit-English Dictionary*.

10. Patañjali's *Mahābhāṣya* on Pāṇini 6.1.84 (Kielhorn, III: 58); *MBh* 5.38.1; 13.107.32. Especially in the case of Patañjali, it is more likely that he would cite a well-known saying to illustrate a grammatical rule than a verse from a specialized text.

11. For a historical analysis of this verse and its vedic precedents, see Jamison 2000.

textual evolution, objections based on such criteria as the contradictions in the extant text. My argument for the unitary authorship of the *MDh* is based primarily on the structure of the text, a structure that has thus far gone unnoticed, perhaps because it was obscured by the chapter divisions to which the text was subjected, probably at the hand of a redactor, after its initial composition. I do not propose that the original text of the author, whom I will call "Manu" for convenience, has remained unaltered through the ages. Through a form of higher textual criticism, I will propose that certain sections are later additions (see part III) reflecting ongoing redactoral activities. Indeed, when these additions are removed, the structure I have uncovered becomes more transparent. My argument, then, is that such a unique and symmetrical structure could not have been given to this text except by a conscious plan created by a single gifted individual. A deep structure that runs through the entire book—a structure that is not apparent at first glance and that remained undetected even by the commentators—could not have simply happened over time as the text was being put together by different individuals separated by centuries. If not by an individual, then it must have been composed by a "strong chairman of a committee" with the help of research assistants who carried out his plan.

I.1 The Structure

The manuscript tradition of the *MDh* divides the text into 12 *adhyāyas* (lessons or chapters). This appears to be an old division; it is followed by all the commentators. I believe, however, that this division is not original. It was probably imposed on the text when it was subjected to a revision that added several sections (see part III), most notably the table of contents given at the conclusion of the first chapter.[12] Although several of the chapters follow the natural sequence of topics, a close reading of the text shows that they are artificial divisions. The chapters also contain different topics that the author, as I will demonstrate, intended to be separate: ch. 2 contains the sources of *dharma*, rites of passage, and the duties of a student; the duties of a king are spread over chapters 7, 8, and 9; the single topic of judicial procedure and the grounds for litigation is spread over chapters 8 and 9; and ch. 9 contains the final discussion of the king's *dharma* and the *dharma* of Vaiśyas and Śūdras. More importantly, however, the division into chapters obscures the latent and deeper structure of the text, a structure that spans the entire corpus and must go back to the author himself.

Manu uses the technique of "transitional verse" to mark the conclusion of one subject and the beginning of another. Here is an example (2.25):

> *eṣā dharmasya vo yoniḥ samāsena prakīrtitā* ǀ
> *saṃbhavaś cāsya sarvasya varṇadharmān nibodhata* ǁ
>
> I have described to you above succinctly this source of the Law, as also the origin of this whole world. Learn now the Laws of the social classes.

12. Note the parallel imposition of chapters onto the *Arthaśāstra* discussed by Scharfe 1993.

This verse marks the transition from the two introductory topics, creation of the world and the sources of *dharma*, to the main body of the text, the *dharma* of the four *varṇas*. Such a technique is unique to Manu; it is not used in the *Dharmasūtras* and sparingly, if at all, in the later *Dharmaśāstras*. Note also the use of the verb *nibodhata* in most transitional verses; this manner of expression becomes a signature of Manu. This device was, I believe, an innovation conceived by Manu and provides an insight into the plan he had for his book. By following the trail of these transitional verses, we can uncover the overall plan and structure of the *MDh*. The chart below presents schematically the structure that emerges through this method together with the transitional verses at the beginning and/or end of topics, verses that provide the clues to uncovering that structure.

The structure that emerges from tracing the transitional verses consists of four major divisions of uneven length and importance:

1) Creation of the world.
2) Sources of *dharma*.
3) The *dharma* of the four social classes.
4) Law of *karma*, rebirth, and final liberation.

Obviously, the main section in terms of both length and importance is the third, dealing with the four *varṇas*. The other three are presented as a preamble, an introduction, and a concluding postscript. The preamble and the introduction are mentioned at the end of the second section (2.25) in the transitional verse that also introduces the central third section on the four *varṇas*. The third section is mentioned also at its conclusion (12.1) in the transitional verse that also introduces the final section on *karma*.[13]

The central third section has two major sub-divisions, the first called *dharmavidhi* (rule relating to *dharma*) and the second called *prāyaścittavidhi* (rules relating to penance). These two sections—3.1 and 3.2 in the chart—are mentioned only once, at the conclusion of the first of them (10.131): "I have described above the entire set of rules pertaining to the Law of the four classes. Next, I will explain the splendid rules pertaining to penance."[14]

The first subsection (3.1) called *dharmavidhi* is the longest in the entire book and is further subdivided into two: rules of action in normal times (*anāpadi karmavidhiḥ*) and rules of action in times of adversity (*āpadi karmavidhi*). These two subdivisions—3.1.1 and 3.1.2 in the chart—are also introduced just once in the transitional verse at the conclusions of the first of them (9.336): "I have described above the splendid rules of action for the social classes outside times of adversity. Listen now to the rules for them in the proper order for times of adversity."

13. After the final section, there is a transitional verse (12.107) that introduces the secret doctrine of Manu's treatise. I think this verse as well as the section on the secret doctrine is a later addition: see below part III, chapter 12.

14. Manu may have found a precedent for this division of the book in one of his primary sources, the *Gautama Dharmasūtra*. Gautama (19.1) begins his section on penance with the statement that he has completed his discussion of the *varṇas:* "The Law pertaining to the social classes and the Law pertaining to the orders of life has been stated" (*ukto varṇadharmaś cāśramadharmaś ca*).

THE STRUCTURE OF MANU

1) SARVASYA SAṂBHAVAḤ [Origin of the World] 1.1–119

2) DHARMASYA YONIḤ [Sources of Dharma] 2.1–24

eṣā dharmasya vo yoniḥ samāsena prakīrtitā ।
sambhavaś cāsya sarvasya varṇadharmān nibodhata ॥ 2.25
I have described to you above succinctly this source of the Law, as also the origin of this whole world. Learn now the Laws of the social classes.

3) CĀTURVARṆYASYA DHARMAḤ [Dharma of the Four Varṇas] 2.25—11.266

3.1) DHARMAVIDHIḤ [Rules Relating to Dharma] 2.25—10.131

3.1.1) Anāpadi Karmavidhiḥ [Rules of Action in Normal Times] 2.26—9.336

3.1.1.1) Brāhmaṇasya Caturvidhaḥ Dharmaḥ [Fourfold Dharma of a Brahmin] 2.26—6.97

eṣa vo 'bhihito dharmo brāhmaṇasya caturvidhaḥ ।
puṇyo 'kṣayaphalaḥ pretya rājñāṃ dharmaṃ nibodhata ॥ 6.97
I have explained to you above the fourfold Law of Brahmins, a Law that is holy and brings imperishable rewards after death. Listen now to the Law of kings.

3.1.1.2) Rājñaḥ Karmavidhiḥ [Rules of Action for King] 7.1 — 9325

eṣo 'khilaḥ karmavidhir ukto rājñaḥ sanātanaḥ ।
imaṃ karmavidhiṃ vidyāt kramaśo vaiśyaśūdrayoḥ ॥ 9.325
I have described above in its entirety the eternal rules of action for the king. What follows, one should understand, are the rules of action for the Vaiśya and the Śūdra in their proper order.

3.1.1.3) Vaiśya-Śūdrayoḥ Karmavidhiḥ [Rules of Action for Vaiśyas & Śūdras] 9.326–36

eṣo 'nāpadi varṇānām uktaḥ karmavidhiḥ śubhaḥ ।
āpady api hi yas teṣāṃ kramaśas tan nibodhata ॥ ॥ 9.336
I have described above the splendid rules of action for the social classes outside times of adversity. Listen now to the rules for them in the proper order for times of adversity.

3.1.2) Āpadi Karmavidhiḥ [Rules of Action in Times of Adversity] 10.1–129

eṣa dharmavidhiḥ kṛtsnaś cāturvarṇyasya kīrtitaḥ ।
ataḥ paraṃ pravakṣyāmi prāyaścittavidhiṃ śubham ॥ 10.131
I have described above the entire set of rules pertaining to the Law of the four classes. Next, I will explain the splendid rules pertaining to penance.

3.2) PRĀYAŚCITTAVIDHIḤ [Rule Relating to Penance] 11.1–265

cāturvarṇyasya kṛtsno 'yam ukto dharmas tvayānagha ।
karmaṇāṃ phalanirvṛttiṃ śaṃsa nas tattvataḥ parām ॥ 12.1
You have described this Law for the four classes in its entirety, O Sinless One! Teach us accurately the ultimate consummation of the fruits of actions.

4) KARMAYOGASYA NIRṆAYAḤ [Determination of Karmayoga] 12.3–116

sa tān uvāca dharmātmā maharṣīn mānavo bhṛguḥ ।
asya sarvasya śṛṇuta karmayogasya nirṇayam ॥ 12.2
Bhṛgu, the son of Manu and the very embodiment of the Law, said to those great seers: "Listen to the determination with respect to engagement in action."

4.1) KARMAṆĀṂ PHALODAYAḤ [Fruits of Action] 12.3–81

eṣa sarvaḥ samuddiṣṭaḥ karmaṇāṃ vaḥ phalodayaḥ ।
naiḥśreyasaṃ karmavidhiṃ viprasyedaṃ nibodhata ॥ 12.82
I have declared to you above all the fruits arising from actions. Listen now to these rules of action for a Brahmin, rules that secure the supreme good.

4.2) NAIḤŚREYASAḤ KARMAVIDHIḤ [Rules of Action for Supreme Good] 12.83–115

etad vo 'bhihitaṃ sarvaṃ niḥśreyasakaraṃ param ।
asmād apracyuto vipraḥ prāpnoti paramāṃ gatim ॥ 12.116
I have explained to you above all the best means of securing the supreme good. A Brahmin who does not deviate from them obtains the highest state.

There is a fourth level of division in section 3.1.1 on rules for normal times. This section has three further sub-sections. The first—3.1.1.1 in the chart—is called *brāhmaṇasya caturvidhaḥ dharmaḥ* ("The Fourfold Dharma of a Brahmin") and its conclusion (6.97) also introduces the next subsection—3.1.1.2 in the chart—dealing with the king: "I have explained to you above the fourfold Law of Brahmins. . . . Listen now to the Law of kings." The third subdivision—3.1.1.3 in the chart—deals with the remaining two *varṇas*, the Vaiśya and the Śūdra; it is introduced at the conclusion of the section on kings (9.325): "I have described . . . the eternal rules of action for the king. What follows . . . are the rules of action for the Vaiśya and the Śūdra."

The final postscript dealing with *karma*, rebirth, and liberation, which is introduced in 12.1, also has two subdivisions: the first (12.3–82) is on the fruits of actions (*karmaṇāṃ phalodayaḥ*) and the second (12.83–115) is on achieving the highest bliss (*naiḥśreyasaḥ karmavidhiḥ*). These two are introduced in the transitional verse at the end of the first subsection (12.82): "I have declared to you above all the fruits arising from actions. Listen now to these rules of action for a Brahmin, rules that secure the supreme good."

An objection may perhaps be raised to my analysis, because the transitional verses I have identified above are not the only verses that introduce a topic. This is no doubt true, but all such verses simply signal the passage to a new topic within the broad structure I have outlined. In these verses, Manu does not say that he has finished one topic and is about to begin another; rather, with a few exceptions I will consider below, they simply indicate the new topic. Here is an example (2.89):

> *ekādaśendriyāṇy āhur yāni pūrve manīṣiṇaḥ* |
> *tāni samyak pravakṣyāmi yathāvad anupūrvaśaḥ* ||
>
> I will explain precisely and in their proper order the eleven organs described by wise men of old.

This is part of a long list that uses the word *pravakṣyāmi* to introduce a new topic.[15] There are other verses using this term that both introduce a new topic and mark the end of the previous topic, in a manner similar to the transitional verses I have listed within the structure. In each of these cases, however, the topics are not broad themes but specific sub-themes within the structure I have identified. Verse 5.26 is an example:

> *etad uktaṃ dvijātīnāṃ bhakṣyābhakṣyam aśeṣataḥ* |
> *māṃsasyātaḥ pravakṣyāmi vidhiṃ bhakṣaṇavarjane* ||
>
> I have described above completely what foods are forbidden and what permitted to the twice-born. I will now explain the rule on eating and on avoiding meat.

Here the author introduces the minor topic of meat-eating after his long disquisition on permitted and forbidden foods. Most such verses occur in the long section dealing with the eighteen grounds for litigation (*vyavahārapada*). At 8.214 the

15. Variants of the verb include *vakṣyāmi* and *sampravakṣyāmi*. These introductory verses are found at: 2.89; 3.22; 3.124, 169, 266; 5.57; 7.1, 36; 8.61, 119, 131, 229; 9.1; 10.25; 11.211; 12.30, 39.

passage is from the non-delivery of gifts to the non-payment of wages; at 8.218, from the non-payment of wages to breach of contract; at 8.266, from boundary disputes to verbal assault; at 8.278, from verbal assault to physical assault; and at 8.301, from physical assault to theft. In the section on inheritance, at 9.56 there is a transition from the discussion of the relative importance of the seed (man) and the womb (woman) in procreation to the *dharma* of women in a time of adversity. At 11.99 there is a transition from penances for drinking liquor to those for stealing gold.

There is another group of verses that uses the verb *nibodhata*, the verb of choice in the transitional verses within the structure I have identified. Beyond such transitional verses, however, Manu uses verses with this verb to mark the passage from one minor topic to another. Thus at 2.68 the transition is from the rite of vedic initiation to the duties of an initiated student; at 5.100, from the purification following a death for those of the same ancestry (*sapiṇḍa*) to the purification for other individuals (*asapiṇḍa*); at 5.146 from purification to the *dharma* of women; at 6.86, from ascetics (*yati*) to holy retirees (*vedasaṃnyāsika*); at 9.25, from the duties of husband and wife to a discussion of children; at 9.103, from the duties of husband and wife to partition of inheritance; at 9.148, from partition among children by wives of the same caste to that among children by wives of different castes; at 9.220, from partition of inheritance to gambling, the last ground for litigation; at 11.71, from the list of sins to the penances for their expiation; at 11.248, from penances for public sins to those for secret sins.[16] The verb √*śru* is used a few times in introductory verses: at 3.286 the transition is from the five sacrifices to the livelihood of Brahmins; at 5.110, from bodily purification to purification of articles; and at 11.180, from penances for sinners to penances for those who associate with them.

Taken collectively, all these other uses of transitional verses merely indicate smaller subdivisions of the text. They uniformly refer only to the topics dealt with just before and just after the verse. With regard to such transitions Manu is not consistent in his use of verses; sometimes he uses them, but most often he does not. Such usages, however, do not impinge on the broad structure I have outlined above. Those verses stand out from the rest both because of their consistency and because they refer back not to the topic immediately preceding them but often to a broad theme introduced hundreds of verses before. In the case of the duties of the king, for example, introduced at 6.97 and concluded at 9.325 there are 960 verses that intervene; and in the largest section within the text, the *dharma* of the four *varṇas*, there are 2415 verses between its introduction at 2.25 and its conclusion at 12.1. No text that grew "in an unconscious, mechanical fashion" can account for such a deliberate structure.

The *dharma* of a Brahmin

The largest portion of the central section on the four *varṇas* is devoted to the four-

16. At the following places, *nibodhata* simply introduces a minor topic or is an invitation to the audience to be attentive: 1.68, 119; 2.1; 3.20, 183, 193; 9.31; 12.53. The verb √*śru* is also used in similar contexts: 1.4, 60

fold *dharma* of a Brahmin encompassing much of chapter 2 and all of chapters 3–6. This section is explicitly organized around the four *āśramas.*[17] All the traditional material, however, could not be contained within the scheme of the four *āśramas*, especially the sections on the childhood rites of passage, rules of a bath-graduate (*snātaka*), and holy life styles falling outside the *āśramas* of forest hermit and wandering mendicant. Manu, however, attempts to squeeze these within his overall *āśrama* structure.

Chapter 4, on the *snātaka,* is sandwiched between chapters 3 and 5, dealing with various aspects of a householder's life. We see the difficulty Manu had with blending the *snātaka* into the *āśrama* framework when we look at the beginnings of chapters 3 and 4. chapter 3 begins quite naturally with the return home of a student who has completed his vedic studies. The author deals with the selection of a bride and marriage, with a long disquisition on the various kinds of marriage. Much of the material dealt with in chapter 3, including the *śrāddhas,* however, is organized around the five great sacrifices. For Manu, what distinguishes the householder and what makes him the epitome of religious life is his daily commitment to the five great sacrifices. Then, at the beginning of chapter 4, Manu has to repeat this within the context of the *āśrama* system: after dwelling at the teacher's house during the first part of his life, a man should return home, get married, and lead a householder's life during the second part. The fifth chapter is introduced with a question from the seers to Bhṛgu about how a Brahmin could be subject to death. This opens the way to a discussion of permitted and forbidden foods and means of bodily purification. The theme of the four *āśramas* is taken up again at the beginning of chapter 6: after living as a householder a man may become a hermit and live in a forest; and again at 6.33: after living the third part of his life as a forest hermit, he should become a wandering mendicant during the fourth and final period of his life.

Even though this section (3.1.1.1) is explicitly said to deal with the *dharma* of Brahmins, a close examination shows that Manu is here following a practice common in ritual texts. They describe fully the ritual procedure only for the archetypal rite of a group of related rites; the description of the other rites (ectypes) consists of pointing out only those ritual elements unique to each and different from the archetype. For Manu, the *dharma* of Brahmins constitutes the archetype, and he describes it fully. *Mutatis mutandis* these rules are applicable to all *varṇas*. Indeed, within this section itself Manu often points out how the *dharma* is modified for other *varṇas.* For example, under initiation he points out the different times for the different *varṇas*, the different ways of manufacturing the girdle, different kinds of staffs, and the like (2.41–7). Likewise, he enumerates the kinds of marriages and the number of wives permitted for the different *varṇas* (3.13). Manu is often explicit about the applicability of the rules in this section to all four *varṇas*. At 5.57, for example, he says that the rules on purification are applicable to all four *varṇas*. This principle of descriptive parsimony permits Manu to deal with the other *varṇas*, especially Vaiśyas and Śūdras, briefly. Only the *dharmas* specific to them are discussed.

17. For the history of this institution, see Olivelle 1993.

The Rules for a King

As I will note below (II.2), the section devoted to the king, statecraft, and law in the *MDh* is disproportionately large in comparison to Manu's predecessors within the expert tradition of *dharma*. The disproportion becomes even more striking when we take into account the fact that this section deals with matters specific to the king and the *kṣatriya* class, whereas the section on the Brahmin includes issues common to all *varṇas*.

A close reading of the section on the king reveals that Manu organized his material around a simple structure in three parts. The first part, spanning 7.1–142, deals with the origin of the king; the organization of the state machinery, including the appointment of officials; the construction of the fort; the king's marriage; the conduct of foreign policy, including war; and finally taxation. It appears that Manu's narrative scheme here envisages a new king occupying a virgin territory. He is unmarried, he has to settle the land and build a capital, and he has to organize the state apparatus. This structure suited Manu's purpose well, because it enabled him to discuss all the points associated with statecraft. Real life, however, is quite another matter; most kings would gain a kingdom either through inheritance or conquest. In either case there would be pre-existing cities, forts, and a state bureaucracy.

In the second part, Manu changes his narrative scheme to span a single day, from the morning when the king wakes up until nightfall when he goes to bed. Manu squeezes into a single day the description of all the duties of a king spread over 182 verses. The morning routine extends from 7.145 to 7.215; the afternoon routine from 7.216 to 7.222; and the evening routine from 7.223 to 7.226. This part concludes with the king going "to bed at the proper time and rise up refreshed."

The third part deals with the justice system and comprises the 18 grounds for litigation (*vyavahārapada*, often translated as "Titles of Law"). After dealing briefly with the organization of the court, Manu arranges his material on law and the dispensation of justice under the 18 grounds for litigation, commonly called titles of law (8.47–9.251). The issues relating to evidence and the interrogation of witnesses are dealt with not separately but under the first ground for litigation, the non-payment of debts. This appears to have been a convention borrowed from the *artha* tradition, to which Manu is indebted for the material relating to the king (see II.2).

Manu's organization of the 18 *vyavahārapadas* is based on a few clear principles and, I believe, is superior to the structure given to them in any other text. Manu's structure is significantly different from that of the extant *Arthaśāstra*, as well as from the other two major *Dharmaśāstras*, Nārada and Yājñavalkya. The chart below presents the organization of the *vyavahārapadas* in the four texts.

The three *Dharmaśāstras* have *ṛṇādāna* ("non-payment of debt") as the first. This is only to be expected, because disputes regarding debts, both personal and commercial, must have been the most common reason for litigants to come before a court. It is also within the context of this first ground for litigation that these authors deal with judicial procedure, including rules of evidence and the examination of witnesses. Only the *Arthaśāstra* departs from this practice; it begins the discussion

The Organization of *vyavahārapadas*

Manu	*Arthaśāstra*	Yājñavalkya	Nārada
1. *ṛṇādāna:* non-payment of debt	**strīpuṃdharma*[18]: law concering husband and wife	*ṛṇādāna:* non-payment of debt	*ṛṇādāna:* non-payment of debt
2. *nikṣepa:* deposits	*dāyavibhāga:* partition	*upanidhi:* deposits	*nikṣepa:* deposits
3. *asvāmivikraya:* sale without ownership	*vāstuvivāda:* property disputes	*dāyavibhāga:* partition	*saṃbhūyasamutthāna:* partnerships
4. *saṃbhūyasamutthāna:* partnerships	*samayasyānapākarma:* breach of contract	*sīmāvivāda:* boundary disputes	*dattāpradānika:* non-delivery of gifts
5. *dattasyānapākarma:* non-delivery of gifts	*ṛṇādāna:* non-payment of debt	*svāmipālavivāda:* disputes between owners and hersmen	*abhyupetyāśuśrūṣā:* breach of contract of service
6. *vetanādāna:* non-payment of wages	*aupanidhikam:* deposits	*asvāmivikraya:* sale without ownership	*vetanasyānapākarma:* non-payment of wages
7. *saṃvidvyatikrama:* breach of contract	*dāsakarmakalpa:* rules regarding workers	*dattāpradānika:* non-delivery of gifts	*asvāmivikraya:* sale without ownership
8. *krayavikrayānuśaya:* cancellation of sale or purchase	*saṃbhūyasamutthāna:* partnerships	*krītānuśaya:* cancellaion of purchase	*vikrīyāsaṃpradāna:* non-delivery after sale
9. *svāmipālavivāda:* disputes between owners and herdsmen	*vikrītakrītānuśaya:* cancellation of purchase or sale	*abhyupetyāśuśrūṣā:* breach of contract of service	*krītānuśaya:* cancellation of purchase
10. *sīmāvivāda:* bound-ary disputes	*dattasyānapākarma:* non-delivery of gifts	*saṃvidvyatikrama:* breach of contract	*samayasyānapākarma:* breach of conventions
11. *vākpāruṣya:* verbal assault	*asvāmivikraya:* sale without ownership	*vetanādāna:* non-payment of wages	*kṣetrajavivāda:* land disputes
12. *daṇḍapāruṣya:* physical assault	*sāhasa:* violence	*dyūtasamāhvaya:* gambling and betting	*strīpuṃsaṃyoga:* relations between husband and wife
13. *steya:* theft	*vākpāruṣya:* verbal assault	*vākpāruṣya:* verbal assault	*dāyabhāga:* partition
14. *sāhasa:* violence	*daṇḍapāruṣya:* physical assault	*daṇḍapāruṣya:* physical assualt	*sāhasa:* violence
15. *strīsaṃgrahaṇa:* sexual crimes against women	*dyūtasamāhvaya:* gambling and betting	*sāhasa:* violence	*vākpāruṣya:* verbal assault
16. *strīpuṃdharma:* law concerning husband and wife	*prakīrṇaka:* miscellaneous	*vikrīyāsaṃpradāna:* non-delivery after sale	*daṇḍapāruṣya:* physical assault
17. *vibhāga:* partition		*saṃbhūyasamutthāna:* partnerships	*dyūtasamāhvaya:* gambling and betting
18. *dyūtasamāhvaya:* gambling and betting		*steya:* theft	*prakīrṇaka:* miscellaneous
		strīsaṃgrahaṇa: sexual crimes against women	
		prakīrṇaka: miscellaneous	

18. This term is not given in the *Arthaśāstra* but the topic is treated at the very outset.

with marriage and the partition of the paternal estate. The reason for this appears to be stated in the opening *sūtra:* "All legal transactions begin with marriage" (*vivāha-pūrvo vyavahāraḥ: AŚ* 3.2.1). The other convergence in these lists is *vākpāruṣya* (verbal assault) and *daṇḍapāruṣya* (physical assault), which always go together, with *sāhasa* (violence) coming very close. Other than these, the order of the lists diverges markedly, making it clear that there was no traditionally fixed order for the *vyavahārapadas*. The order of enumeration in the *MDh*, therefore, was probably the creation of Manu himself, and we get a glimpse into his systematic way of thinking also in his arrangement of these topics. His arrangement, I think, is far superior to and more systematic than any of the others and can be presented schematically:

A. Individual and group disputes (= 1–10)
B. Criminal law (= 11–15)
C. Personal law (= 16–17)
D. Public order and safety (= 18)

Manu begins with disputes between individuals and between groups. Such disputes must have been the most common reason for litigation and cover the first ten grounds. The first nine for the most part deal with individual disputes, with the possible exception of the fourth, on partnerships, where the dispute is between an individual and a partnership of which he is a member. Likewise, disputes in the seventh, on breach of contract, may happen between individuals and between an individual and a corporate body. Disputes over boundaries—the tenth— can happen between individual land owners, but the typical dispute discussed by Manu concerns boundaries between villages.

The next category is criminal law, involving verbal and physical assault, theft, robbery/violence, and sexual crimes. Unlike in modern law, however, lawsuits for such crimes were not initiated by the state but by the injured parties.

The third category is personal or family law. The first ground for litigation under this rubric is disputes between a husband and a wife, although much of what is discussed relates to laws and conventions governing marital relationships. The second and clearly the more significant is the partition of inheritance. It is in these two topics that there is often an overlap with material covered under marriage, especially in chapter 5. This was probably inevitable when the *dharma* tradition incorporated strictly legal matters and, therefore, had to deal with marriage and family in two places, under proper conduct (*ācāra*) and law (*vyavahāra*).

The final category is gambling and betting. One would have expected Manu to present rules for the orderly conduct of these practices, as is done in other texts.[19] Manu, however, was strictly opposed to gambling and betting. For him, these areas of social practice should be suppressed rather than regulated. It is, therefore, natural for him to follow his brief discussion of gambling with the important topic of the "eradication of thorns" (*kaṇṭakaśodhana*), that is, the suppression of criminal activities, especially theft, in the kingdom. This is a topic found in all *artha* and *dharma* texts, but it falls outside the grounds for litigation. Litigation, according to ancient Indian jurisprudence, is initiated by private individuals; the king and his officials are explicitly barred from initiating law suits. The eradication of thorns, on

19. See, for example the *Āpastamba Dharmasūtra*, 2.2512–4.

the other hand, is one of the principal duties of a king; it is a police activity and falls outside the judicial process. Nevertheless, Manu sees the eradication of thorns and the suppression of gambling as part of the same administrative process.

The section on the duties of the king concludes with this pithy statement typical of Manu (9.324): "Conducting himself in this manner and always devoted to the Laws pertaining to kings, the king should direct all his servants to work for the good of his people."

The Rules for Vaiśyas and Śūdras

Manu's discussion of Vaiśyas and Śūdras, the last two of the *varṇas*, is extraordinarily brief. Eight verses are devoted to the Vaiśya and just two to the Śūdra. Even granting that, according to the ritual principle of parsimony I have discussed earlier, much of the material for these two classes was included in the discussion of the Brahmin, one would have expected something more than just ten verses.

The reason for this brevity is unclear, but I think it must be understood within the context of the socio-political motives behind Manu's composition, an issue I will address later (I.4). Simply put, Manu's interest lay not in the lower classes of society, which he considered to be an ever-present threat to the dominance of the upper classes, but in the interaction between the political power and Brahmanical priestly interests, interests that were under constant threat ranging from the Aśokan imperial polity to the foreign invasions around the turn of the millennium.

On Sin and Penance

The methodical approach demonstrated in the sections on Brahmin and king is evident also in the chapter on sin and penance (*prāyaścitta*).[20] Manu begins the topic with a discussion on the efficacy of penance, on whether penance can actually remove sins. After justifying the efficacy of and the need for penance, he divides his inquiry into two sections: public sins (11.55–189), which occupy much of the discussion, and private or secret sins (11.227).

Manu first presents the major classifications of sins: 1) the five grievous sins that cause the loss of caste (*mahāpātaka:* 11.55–9); 2) a large group of secondary sins that also cause the loss of caste called *upapātaka:* (11.60–7); and 3) four further classes of sins (11.68–71) that cause a man a) to be excluded from caste (*jātibhraṃśakara*), b) to become mixed caste (*saṃkīrṇakara*), c) to be unworthy of receiving gifts (*apātrīkaraṇa*), and d) to be impure (*malāvaha*). He concludes the classification of sins with this transitional verse: "Listen now attentively to the specific penances by which all these sins individually enumerated above may be removed" (11.72).

Manu then goes on to discuss the appropriate penances for each of the categories of sins: 1) the first four of the grievous sins (11.73–108), 2) secondary sins (11.109–24), and 3) the four further classes of sins (11.125–6). Finally, he turns from

20. There are, of course, some inconsistencies and extraneous material in this chapter. I will deal with them later in part III.

sins personally committed to association with sinners who have become outcastes as a result of their sins, a category that forms the fifth grievous sin (11.181–90). Manu introduces the last discussion with the transitional verse: "I have described above the expiation for all four kinds of sinners. Listen now to the following expiations for those who associate with outcastes" (11.180). The mention of the four kinds of sinners has caused some confusion. Grievous and secondary sins make two. The third category consists of four sins, but the penances for the four are dealt with in two verses. I think Manu viewed the first (*jātibhraṃśakara*) as one class and presented the penances for it in a single verse (11.125). He appears to have viewed the other three as forming a single class, dealing with their penances in a single verse (11.126). So, we have four categories of penances relating to the sins listed previously. The attempt to come up with four sinners as indicated in verse 11.180 may have led a redactor to insert the four offenses listed in 11.127–79. I will deal with these interpolations more extensively below (III).

The discussion of penance for publicly known sins concludes with two crisp statements. First: "No one should transact any business with uncleansed sinners; and under no circumstances should anyone abhor those who have been cleansed" (11.190). There follows an excursus containing miscellaneous items on sins and penances, which is clearly an interpolation. Manu concludes the section on penances for public sins with the transitional verse (227), which also gives the penances for private sins: "By these observances should twice-born persons cleanse themselves of public sins; they may cleanse themselves of secret sins, however, through ritual formulas and burnt offerings."

When we take out the accretions in this chapter, the clear and impressive structure of the original composition emerges. That this section on penance concludes the central portion of the treatise dealing with the *dharma* of the four *varṇas*—number 3 in the structure I have outlined above—is evident in the opening verse of the last chapter: "You have described this Law for the four classes in its entirety, O Sinless One! Teach us accurately the ultimate consummation of the fruits of actions" (12.1).

On *karma*

Chapter 12, dealing with actions and their consequences, as well as with the attainment of ultimate happiness beyond the realm of rebirth, is quite different in style and substance from the rest of the book. I am not willing to call this chapter a later addition; sufficient evidence does not exist to draw that conclusion. The entire chapter is taken up with the theme of action (*karma*), both the consequences of good and bad actions (*karmavipāka*) and the final triumph over action and the attainment of the supreme good beyond the process of rebirth. Broadly this discussion falls into two sections, the one dealing with the fruits of action (12.3–81) and the other dealing with actions leading to the supreme good (12.83–106). These two sections are divided by Manu's signature transitional verse (12.82):

> *eṣa sarvaḥ samuddiṣṭaḥ karmaṇāṃ vaḥ phalodayaḥ* |
> *naiḥśreyasakaraṃ karma viprasyedaṃ nibodhata* ||

> I have declared to you above the fruits arising from actions. Listen now to these rules of action for a Brahmin, rules that secure the supreme good.

This chapter has also undergone redactorial interventions, which I will address below in the section on the work of redactors (see III).

I.2 Author, Title, and Date

Most modern scholars know the work of Manu under the title *Manu Smṛti.* In the introduction to his influential translation, Bühler uniformly uses the title *Manu-smṛti.* The term *smṛti* is often used by scholars as a general term to cover all the *Dharmaśāstras* composed in verse, which are called "metrical *smṛtis.*" "Manusmṛti" is the term used also by Kane (1962–75) in his encyclopedic work on *Dharmaśāstra,* by Lingat (1973), and by Dave (1972–84). The exceptions are the editions of Mandlik (1886) and Jolly (1887), both of whom give the title as *Mānava-Dharmaśāstra.*

It is unclear when the word *smṛti* came to be used to designate *Dharmaśāstras* composed in verse and in particular the *MDh.*[21] In the manuscripts, the colophons at the end of each chapter and at the end of the entire work refer to it as *mānavadharmaśāstra.* The title of *śāstra* is confirmed by the self-references found in the *MDh,* which repeatedly calls itself *śāstra.*[22] It is, therefore, clear that the original title of the work, the title by which it was known to the manuscript tradition, was *mānavadharmaśāstra.* The title *manusmṛti* appears to have been a rather late innovation.

The colophon at the end of each chapter reads: *mānave dharmaśāstre bhṛguproktāyāṃ saṃhitāyām,* that is, the *Dharmaśāstra* of Manu as arranged or compiled by Bhṛgu. The use of the term *saṃhitā* is clearly intentional and connects the *MDh* to the *saṃhitās* of the Veda. It also hints at the possibility that there may be other *saṃhitās* of Manu's work than that of Bhṛgu.[23]

The *MDh* (1.58) presents a textual history of itself, ascribing the original treatise to the creator, the Imperishable One (*avyaya,* 1.57) and the Self-existent (*svayaṃbhū,* 1.3, 6). According to the *MDh,* the creator taught this treatise to his son, Manu, and he in turn taught it to his pupils, including Bhṛgu. It is Bhṛgu who becomes the spokesman and recites the treatise to the gathered seers. The view that the creator should have produced a text for the governance of his creatures is found also in other texts. In the *Mahābhārata,* Bhīṣma recounts the beginning of the world, the Kṛta age, when everything was perfect and laws were unnecessary. When

21. Medieval authors who cite the *MDh* and other *Dharmaśāstras* are of little help, because they simply say "*manuḥ*" or "*yājñavalkyaḥ.*" The earliest datable use of the term *manusmṛti* that I find in the manuscripts is in the colophon of the ms. NNg dated 1503 CE.

22. See 1.58, 59, 102, 104, 118, 119; 11.243; 12.107, 126.

23. The significance of Bhṛgu in the formation of the *Mahābhārata* has received considerable attention both from Sukthankar, the chief editor of its critical edition, and a series of subsequent scholars. For an overview, see Hiltebeitel 2001, 105–18.

things began to deteriorate, however, the creator composed a treatise in one thousand chapters dealing with the three areas of human enterprise (*trivarga*), including *dharma* (12.59.29).[24]

Later tradition picks up on the theme of *saṃhitā* in the sense of editions of the original text of Manu. At the very beginning of the *Nāradasmṛti*, it is said that Manu Prajāpati created a text containing 1080 chapters and 100,000 verses. Nārada abridged it to 12,000 verses; the latter was further abridged by Mārkaṇḍeya, which was further condensed by Sumati Bhārgava to 4,000 verses.[25] The tradition that the original composition of Manu was subjected to repeated editorial revisions and abridgments appears to have been old. Medhātithi, the 9th-century commentator on the *MDh* (on 1.58), refers to Nārada's statement that the original composition in 100,000 verses of Prajāpati, the creator, was abridged by Manu and others. The *Skandapurāṇa* has preserved the tradition that there are four versions of the original treatise, those edited by Bhṛgu, Nārada, Bṛhaspati, and Aṅgiras.[26]

My own close examination of the *MDh* and its exquisite structure makes me agree with Bühler (1886, xcii) that the text we have under the title *Mānavadharmaśāstra* ascribed to Bhṛgu is not an edition or version of a preexisting text but an original composition. I further believe that this text was authored by a single individual or at least by a strong chairman with a committee of research assistants. The kind of deep structure, so subtle yet so clear, that I have discovered in the *MDh* makes it impossible to have been composed either through unconscious accumulation or through a series of editorial interventions spanning long intervals of time. It was conceived and put together by a single individual with extraordinary ability and a systematic mind.

The eponym "Manu," of course, is not the name of the historical author of this text. The name, however, was an astute choice. The *Taittirīya Saṃhitā* (2.2.10.2) records what appears to have been a proverbial saying: "Whatever Manu has said is medicine." It is possible that numerous legal maxims were handed down ascribed to Manu, some of which, as Bühler (1886, lxxv-xcii) has pointed out, are recorded in the *Mahābhārata*. Further, Manu was regarded not just as the first human being but, at least according to one tradition, as the first king.[27] With the rise of urban centers and large kingdoms in northern India around the middle of the first millennium BCE, the significance of royalty with regard to various aspects of social life appears to have increased. In religion, leaders of new sects and ascetic communities were given royal pedigrees, including the Buddha and the Mahāvīra. "King as teacher" is a motif in the Upaniṣads, where numerous significant doctrines are ascribed to kings.

24. The motif of a large treatise composed *in illo tempore* and subsequently abridged for the use of humans is a recurrent one in Indian literature. Such claims are made for their textual histories by the *Kāmasūtra* (1.1.5–10), and Āyurvedic texts (*Suśrutasaṃhitā*, Sūtrasthāna, 1.3). See also the *Nāṭyaśāstra* (1.15–24), whose origin is ascribed to Brahman.

25. Lariviere (1989, II: 2) has shown that this passage did not belong to the original *Nāradasmṛti*. Bühler also had entertained this view, which he later rejected (Bühler 1886, xvii, n. 2). Jolly (1885, 44) also takes this to be part of Nārada. Given that this section of the *NSm* is referred to by Medhātithi, it must have been an old tradition.

26. Cited by Jolly (1889, 274) in the introduction to his translation of the *Bṛhaspatismṛti*.

27. For a survey of the myths surrounding the figure of Manu, see Bühler 1886, lvii–lxii.

With the rise of devotional religions toward the end of the first millennium BCE, we have the figures of Rāma and Kṛṣṇa, the divine *avatāras*, who are kings and not Brahmins.[28] Historically, the rise of the Maurya empire and the overwhelming presence of Aśoka and his imperial reforms must have loomed large. That a treatise on *dharma* with universal application should be ascribed not just to any king but to the first king, therefore, should come as no surprise. The clear intent was to make the work more authoritative by connecting it to both the sage responsible for the famous proverbial sayings and to the first king of humankind. The historical and political reasons for the writing of this text makes this ascription even more significant. I will examine these reasons presently.

I have used "Manu" here as a shorthand term for the historical author of the *MDh*. The name of this author is unknown, as are any details of his life: his date, his geographical location, influences that may have shaped his life and thought, and a host of biographical questions that would shed light on the text itself.[29] The most we can say is that he was a learned Brahmin from somewhere in northern India. Some of the socio-political influences that shaped his thought and that perhaps motivated the writing on the book, however, may at least be surmised by looking at the possible date of its composition.[30]

With regard to the dating of the *MDh* we do not fare much better. Its relative chronology, however, has widespread scholarly consensus. The *MDh* was undoubtedly composed after the *Dharmasūtras;* it shows clear advances in thinking on many fronts, especially in the sections relating to statecraft, royal functions, and judicial procedure. These were probably borrowed from the *artha* tradition (see II.2). The *MDh* is older than any of the other metrical *Dharmaśāstras*, especially the four old ones ascribed to Yājñavalkya, Nārada, Bṛhaspati, and Kātyāyana. Bühler has discussed the relative chronology at length in the introduction to his translation of the *MDh*, and I will not repeat all his arguments here. A couple of observations will suffice. Unlike the later texts, Manu has very little to say about documentary evidence in a court of law; he does not use the later word for a document, *lekhya,* referring to such documents by the terms *karaṇa* and *deśa* (see II.2). Manu is also less concerned with ordeals as means of proving the guilt or innocence of an accused. The term *divya,* which becomes common in later texts, is absent; Manu uses instead the word *śapatha*, which he uses both for an ordeal proper and for an oath (8.109–16).[31] The *MDh*, therefore, occupies the middle position at the point of transition from the prose and scholastic *Dharmasūtras* to the metrical *Dharmaśāstras* ascribed to authoritative divine beings.[32]

28. See Olivelle (1993, 61) for a discussion of this issue.

29. Jayaswal's (1930, 51) conclusion that the "real author" of the *MDh* was Sumati Bhārgava on the basis of the *NSm* evidence, and that it was a Śuṅga code is speculative and without firm evidence.

30. Another issue that cannot be fully resolved is whether the text was composed orally. That scholars in ancient India learned their texts by heart and that instruction involved memorizing is beyond doubt. However, I think that the *MDh* was originally composed in writing, especially in view of the mention of manuscripts at 12.103.

31. I will discuss below (V.1) the influence of the *MDh* on the later *Dharmaśāstras*.

32. The dating of the four extant *Dharmasūtras* is also problematic. In my earlier work

Setting an absolute chronology is a more difficult task. After analyzing all the data available to him, Bühler (1886, cxvii) concluded that the *MDh* must have existed by the 2nd century CE. and that it must have been composed between that date and the 2nd century BCE. Both Kane, in his monumental *History of Dharmaśāstra* (I: 344), and Lingat (1973, 96), in his influential study, broadly agree with Bühler's dating. Jayaswal (1930, 29) has gone the farthest in narrowing the upper and lower limits of the *MDh*. He considers it to be a work of the Śuṅga period during a time of Brahmanical revival after the Aśokan reforms. Jayaswal places the *MDh* during the last 170 years before the common era, but thinks it was written closer to the upper than the lower limit.

The issue is whether these upper and lower limits can be further refined and narrowed through internal and external evidence. The lower limit is totally dependent on internal evidence and on the relative chronology of the *MDh* and other ancient texts, especially the *Dharmasūtras*. For the upper limit we have a few pieces of external evidence.

Given my arguments for the unitary authorship and composition of the *MDh*, we can take more seriously than in the past the few internal references within the text that would help us determine a lower limit. In his discussion of mixed classes, Manu (10.44) refers to several ethnic groups that are identifiable.[33] They are Yavana, Kāmboja, Śaka, Pahlava, and Cīna. These are all viewed by Manu to be Kṣatriyas who have fallen to the level of Śūdras by neglecting rites and failing to honor Brahmins properly. Given that they are considered in some sense Kṣatriyas, it is clear that Manu viewed these peoples as having military power and political authority, although he found them less than exemplary. Yavana, a common Indian term for Greeks and for north-western border people of Greek heritage, is already used in Aśokan inscriptions and by Pāṇini (4.1.49) and does not help us in narrowing the date. The same is true of Kāmboja; the term is already found in Pāṇini (4.1.175). The term Pahlava, an Indian formation from the middle Persian *pahlav* (Parthian), although absent in both Patañjali and the *Dharmasūtras*, does not help much in narrowing the lower limit of the *MDh*.

The Śakas were the central Asian tribes who conquered parts of Persia and the northwestern parts of the Indian subcontinent. Their appearance in this region can be dated to around the middle of the 2nd century BCE. The first Śaka king in India

(Olivelle 2000, 9–10) I placed Āpastamba in the first half of the 3rd century BCE and Gautama toward the middle of that century. I still think this is reasonable, but because of my further exploration of the semantic development of the term *dharma* (Olivelle, forthcoming a and c), I am inclined now to place them somewhat later. The earliest literary reference to the *Dharmasūtras* as a class of literature is in Patañjali's *Mahābhāṣya:* (*dharmasūtrakārāḥ*) in 1.1.47; 5.1.119. The word *dharmaśāstra* already occurs in Kātyāyana's *Vārttika* on Pāṇini 1.2.64 (39).

33. Even this piece of internal evidence is not altogether reliable. The verse in question comes at the end of the section dealing with mixed classes. This section contains several discourses, some repeating what was stated in earlier discourses. Some doubt, therefore, is cast on the authenticity of the later discourses; they may have been the result of redactors attempting to incorporate different interpretations of the mixed classes and to take into account new ethnic groups. Lingat (1973, 94) also considers the verse in question to be an interpolation.

proper, Maues, has been dated from 94 BCE to 22 BCE. It is difficult to estimate when the presence of the Śakas as a military or political elite would have drawn the attention of an Indian scholar like Manu. They are absent in the *Dharmasūtras* in general and significantly in the parallel list of mixed *varṇas* in the *Gautama Dharmasūtra* (4.16–28), which contains the word Yavana. We do have, however, the mention of *śaka* in the compound *śakayavana* by Patañjali (on Pāṇini 2.4.10). So, the word must have been in circulation by the middle of the 2nd century BCE. Interestingly, we have the progression from *yavana* in Pāṇini, to *yavana* and *śaka* in Patañjali, to *yavana, śaka,* and *cīna* in the *MDh* and the *Mahābhārata.*

The reference to the Chinese with the word *cīna* is problematic. The term is not used by Patañjali or the *Dharmasūtras*. The word was probably derived from a central Asian language and is related to the Qin (Chin) dynasty (221–206 BCE), which, although short lived, was the first to unify China. The term itself, however, may have been older, because the Qin was a state in Northwest China prior to that time with strong trade connections with Central Asia. The term "China," like "India" itself, is not a term of self-identification by the Chinese. The term came back to China probably from India via Buddhist monks and texts.[34] When a people known as *cīna* came to be known in India is difficult to estimate. The term's absence in the earlier literature, however, makes it likely that it could not have been known before the 1st century BCE. It was during this time or a little earlier under the Han dynasty that Chinese trade with the west began to flourish.[35]

This date also fits well with the broad relative chronology of texts belonging roughly to this period. Patañjali probably lived in the middle of the 2nd century BCE. He is the first to use the expression *āryāvarta* with reference to the middle country of north India. The term is found also in the *Dharmasūtras* of Baudhāyana and Vasiṣṭha. All three define the region in almost identical words.[36] Significantly, the expression is absent in the older *Dharmasūtras* of Āpastamba and Gautama. The *MDh* is clearly posterior to Patañjali, Baudhāyana, and Vasiṣṭha. A lower limit of the 1st century BCE, thus, fits with this relative chronology as well.

External evidence for the upper date of Manu comes from sources several centuries later.[37] Thus, for example, we have possibly the earliest citation of the

34. I thank the many colleagues who responded to my e-mail request for information on *cīna*. The migration of the term back into China and into Japan (under the form *Shina*) has been studied by Joshua A. Fogel in "The Sino-Japanese Controversy over *Shina* as a Toponym for China" in his book *The Cultural Dimension of Sino-Japanese Relations: Essays on the Nineteenth and Twentieth Centuries* (Armonk, NY: M. E. Sharpe, 1995), pp. 66–76. There he cites the work of a Chinese scholar, Su Zhongxiang, who argues that *cīna* may be related not to the Qin but to the ancient state of Jing. The issue becomes even more complex when the possibility of a southern route to India via Assam is considered. However, the *MDh* appears to place the *cīna*, as well as the other foreigners, in the northwest.

35. Parallel to the *MDh*, we find the use of *cīna* in the *MBh* along with the terms *śaka* and *hūna:* see 2.23.29; 2.47.19; 3.48.21;5.19.15; 5.72.14;6.10.65; 12.65.13; 12120.15. We also have the compounds *cīnapaṭṭa* and *cīnabhūmija* in *AŚ* 2.11.114.

36. For a discussion of this point, see Olivelle 2000, 10.

37. Unfortunately, inscriptional references to the *MDh* do not appear until at least the 6th century CE. Bühler (1886, cxiii) refers to the Vallabhī inscriptions of Dhruvasena I etc., which date from 526 CE. For a survey of the inscriptional evidence, see Hopkins 1885.

MDh in Śabara's commentary on the *Pūrvamīmāṃsāsūtra* (6.1.12), where *MDh* 8.299 is cited with the simple *evaṃ smarati*. Śabara is generally dated to the 5th century CE. The clearest reference to the *MDh* in the early classical literature comes from the play *Mṛcchakaṭikā* of Śūdraka. In Act IX, the judge notes that according to Manu a Brahmin is exempt from capital punishment; he should be sent into exile instead.[38] The date of Śūdraka, however, is not certain, but the consensus appears to place him broadly during the Gupta period, although some make him a contemporary of Kālidāsa. Kālidāsa's date is also controversial, but the 4–5th centuries CE is probably the best we can do. He does not refer to the *MDh* directly. His description of the penance of following a cow in the *Raghuvaṃśa*, however, appears to be based on the *MDh* 11.109–17. In a special way, *Raghuvaṃśa* 1.89 is clearly an adaptation of Manu 11.112.[39]

The *Kāmasūtra* (1.1.5–10), in presenting its own mythical origins, claims that the creator, Prajāpati, produced a treatise of 100,000 chapters dealing with the three aims of life. The *dharma* portion of this treatise was made into a separate edition by Manu Svāyambhū.[40] All this recalls the introductory verses of the *MDh*. If we place the *Kāmasūtra* roughly in the 3rd century CE, then the fame of the *MDh* must have reached some prominence by that time.

The relationship between the *MDh* and the *Mahābhārata* has been a topic of discussion ever since Hopkins's (1885) study. Hopkins (1885, 268) concluded that the *MDh* was put together "between the time when the bulk of the epic was composed and its final completion." Bühler, after a lengthy discussion of the parallel passages in the two works, concluded that the *MDh* has not drawn on the *Mahābhārata* and that both drew on the same stock of "floating proverbial wisdom." The references and citations collected by Hopkins, I think, make a compelling case that the author(s) of the epic knew of and drew upon material from the *MDh*. It is more likely, I think, that a narrative epic would draw on expert *śāstras* for its discussions of legal matters than the other way round.[41] The issue for dating the *MDh*, however, is the date of the *Mahābhārata* itself. The latest estimate is by Hiltebeitel (2001, 18–20): "I suggest, then, that the *Mahābhārata* was composed between the mid-second century BCE and the year zero." He also suggests that the epic was written by a committee or team over a relatively brief period of time spanning "at most a couple

38. *ayaṃ hi pātakī vipro na vadhyo manur abravīt | rāṣṭrād asmāt tu nirvāsyo vibhavair akṣatair saha ||* Act IX, verse 39. This provision is found in the *MDh* 8.380.

39. The *MDh* 11.112 reads *tiṣṭhantīṣv anutiṣṭhet tu vrajantīṣv apy anuvrajet | āsīnāsu tathāsīta niyato vītamatsaraḥ ||* The *Raghuvaṃśa* 1.89 reads: *prasthitāyāṃ pratiṣṭhethāḥ sthitāyāṃ sthitim ācareḥ | niṣaṇṇāyāṃ niṣīdāsyāṃ pītāmbhasi piber apaḥ ||* Some of the divergence is caused by the fact that in the *Raghuvaṃśa* Dilīpa is told to follow just a single cow, the divine Nandinī, whereas in the *MDh* the penitent follows a herd of ordinary cows.

40. *prajāpatir hi prajāḥ sṛṣṭvā tāsāṃ sthitinibandhanaṃ trivargasya sādhanam adhyāyānāṃ śatasahasreṇāgre provāca | tasyaikadeśikaṃ manuḥ svāyaṃbhuvo dharmādhikārikaṃ pṛthak cakāra |*

41. Bühler is quite skeptical about the citations, because they do not exactly replicate the verses of the extant *MDh*. I think the differences and confusions can easily be ascribed to the team of workers engaged in the epic enterprise. The work of committees often creates confusions, misquotations, and misidentifications, especially in a work of such enormous proportions.

of generations." Fitzgerald offers a more conservative view, acknowledging several redactions, the last taking place during the Gupta period.[42] If we accept that the *MDh* was known to the writers of the *Mahābhārata*, then, even with a more conservative dating than Hiltebeitel's, the *MDh* must have been in existence by about the 2nd century CE.

Scholars as far back as Jolly thought they had found what appeared to be a solid piece of external evidence in Aśvaghoṣa, a Brahmin convert to Buddhism, who is generally assigned to the 1st–2nd centuries CE. A work ascribed to him, the *Vajrasūci*, repeatedly cites the *MDh* by name.[43] Johnston had already cast serious doubts on the authenticity of this work, calling it "a clever piece of polemics arguing against Brahman claims" and concluding that it "shows no trace of Aśvaghoṣa's style or mentality."[44] A close examination of the *Vajrasūci* supports Johnston's conclusion. It is probably a quite late Buddhist polemical pamphlet against Brahmins and cannot be dated even close to the 2nd century CE.

All this, unfortunately, does not permit us to narrow the dating as much as we would like. There is a further piece of evidence, however, that may help us in establishing a more secure lower limit. At *MDh* 8.213 a fine of "one Suvarṇa" is assessed for the non-delivery of a gift. At *MDh* 8.361 a man who talks with a woman after he is explicitly forbidden to do so is fined "one Suvarṇa."[45] Now, fines in the *MDh* is assessed in currency and there is no reason to doubt that Suvarṇa here means a gold coin. At *MDh* 8.393 a man who fails to feed a vedic scholar at a rite is forced to give twice that amount of food and a gold Māṣaka. Here also I think the reference is to a gold coin.[46] It is significant that the *Arthaśāstra*, which has a section on the minting of copper and silver coins, does not refer to the minting of gold coins.[47] There is also no unambiguous reference to gold coins (as opposed to gold articles and ornaments) in the *Arthaśāstra*.[48] There is a scholarly consensus that the minting of gold currency did not take place until the Kushans. P. L. Gupta (1969, 28) notes with reference to the Gupta king Vima Kadphises that "his most notable contribution is the

42. See Hiltebeitel 2001, 25–26.

43. See Jolly 1885, 44; Jayaswal 1930,26; Kane (1962–75) I: 330. The false ascription of this text to Aśvaghoṣa is perpetuated in the recent study by Sarla Khosla, *Aśvaghoṣa and his Times*, New Delhi: Intellectual Publishing House, 1986.

44. E. H. Johnston, *Aśvaghoṣa's Buddhacarita or Acts of the Buddha* (1936; reprint, Delhi: Motilal Banarsidass, 1984), II: xxii. As Johnston observes, the Chinese translation ascribes this text to Dharmakīrti. See also de Jong 1988.

45. At *MDh* 8.220 the fine imposed on a man breaking an agreement is said to be *catuḥsuvarṇān ṣaṇniṣkān*, which I have taken to mean "6 Niṣkas each weighing 4 Suvarṇas." Commentators, however, take the fine to be cumulative: 4 Suvarṇas and 6 Niṣkas. In any case, it appears that here also a fine assessed in gold coins is meant. A fine of 6 Niṣkas is also imposed at *MDh* 8.284.

46. The first two occurrences are in sections about whose authenticity there cannot be any doubt. They are solidly within the discussion of the eighteen grounds for litigation (*vyavāhapada*), which must go back to the original composition. Verse 8.393, on the other hand, occurs in what I call an *excursus*, and it is likely to come from later redactoral activities.

47. See D. C. Sircar, *Studies in Indian Coins* (Delhi: Motilal Banarsidass, 1968), p. 78.

48. This supports the possibility that Manu may have borrowed some of his material from the *Arthaśāstra*; see section II.2

introduction of extensive gold coins for the first time in India."[49] Vima Kadphises probably reigned the end of the first and beginning of the second century CE.[50] Vima's successors also issued gold coins; and so did the Guptas.[51] If this was the first time that gold coins were minted in any numbers in India proper, then lower limit for the composition of the *MDh* must be pushed further forward to at least the 2nd century CE. It is unlikely that the socio-political conditions during which the *MDh* was composed reflects those of the indigenous Gupta empire (see I.4). If this hypothesis is accepted, the likely period for the composition of the *MDh* would be 2nd–3rd centuries CE. Indeed, this corresponds to the date of 3rd century CE assigned to the *MDh* by the great Indian scholar of epigraphy and numismatics, D. C. Sircar (1968, 52).

I.3 Narrative Structure and Composition

Manu introduced two major innovations in comparison to the previous literature of the *dharma* tradition. First, he composed his text entirely in *ślokas*. Second, he set his text within a narrative structure that consists of a dialogue between an exalted being in the role of teacher and others desiring to learn from him.

Late vedic texts, especially the early prose Upaniṣads, regularly cite verses in support of statements and viewpoints.[52] It appears that these verses were somehow viewed as having greater authority and, therefore, able to lend greater support to the author's views, much like citations from scripture. The *Bṛhadāraṇyaka Upaniṣad*, for example, frequently cites supporting verses with the introduction *tad eṣa śloko bhavati* ("In this connection there is this verse").[53] The significance of these verses in the eyes of the authors is indicated by the fact that they write commentaries on some of them, as in *Bṛhadāraṇyaka* 1.5. We see this practice continued by the authors of the *Dharmasūtras*.[54] They also present verses as providing support for or confirmation of views they have already presented in prose and introduce them with *athāpy udāharanti* ("Now, they also quote"), indicating that these verses were well-known sayings that experts would cite in support of a particular practice or view-point.[55] In the later *Dharmasūtras*, however, we find increasing use of verses not

49. There were gold coins issued by the Graeco-Bactrian kings of the north-west and the Scythian dynasties. It is, however, unlikely that fines would be assessed in a coin that must have been rare in the Indian heartland.

50. See H. Kulke and D. Rothermund, *A History of India* (London: Routledge, 1986), p. 81.

51. "The coins of these Gupta emperors are known chiefly in gold. They issued gold coins so profusely that a contemporary poet has allegorically termed the phenomenon 'rain of gold'" (Gupta 1969, 52).

52. For a study of verses in the vedic corpus, see Paul Horsch, *Die vedische Gāthā- und Śloka-Literatur*. Bern: Francke Verlag, 1966.

53. See 2.2.3; 4.3.11; 4.4.6, 7, 8. See also *ChU*, 3.11.2; 5.2.9; 5.10.9; 5.24.5; 7.26.2; 8.6.6.

54. The exception is Gautama. For a discussion, see Olivelle 2000.

55. See *ĀpDh* 1.19.15; 1.25.9; 1.31.23; 1.32.23; 2.9.13; 2.13.6; 2.17.7. At 2.23.3 two verses are cited with the introduction *atha purāṇe ślokāv udāharanti* ("Now, they quote a couple of verses in a Purāṇa") indicating that such verses may have been found in the genre Purāṇa, although this probably does not refer to any extant Purāṇa. See *BDh* 1.1.8; 1.2.11, 15, 17; 1.7.1;

simply as citations but integrated into the composition.[56] This strategy is used with increasing frequency by Vasiṣṭha, the author of the latest *Dharmasūtra*; chapters 25–7, for example, are completely in verse.

It appears that during the last few centuries prior to the common era *ślokas* had assumed an aura of authority, and proverbial wisdom was transmitted as memorable verses. The logical outcome of this tendency was for authoritative texts themselves to be composed in verse, lending authority to the text by its very literary genre. We see this already in some of the earliest Buddhist texts, such as the anthologies of the *Suttanipāta* and the *Dhammapada* and in the verses of the *Jātakas*. The same process was probably responsible for the fact that the early prose Upaniṣads, such as the *Bṛhadāraṇyaka* and the *Chāndogya*, are followed by a series of Upaniṣads composed entirely in verse, such as the *Kaṭha*, the *Muṇḍaka*, and the *Śvetāśvatara*.

The parallel between the older and the later Upaniṣads is true of the *dharma* literature as well. Whereas the earlier texts are in prose with verse citations, the later ones are composed entirely in verse. The first such text was that of Manu. His use of verse for the composition of his *Dharmaśāstra*, therefore, must have been part of a deliberate plan to lend the kind of authority to his text that would come only through this literary genre. We have, of course, the parallel examples of the epics *Mahābhārata* and *Rāmāyaṇa* composed in verse and claiming religious authority. This move away from prose to verse continues especially in religious compositions such as the Purāṇas. In what could be regarded as expert traditions, however, the picture is mixed. The *artha* and *kāma* traditions continued to produce prose works, as did the ritual, philosophical, and grammatical traditions. The *dharma* tradition followed the trail blazed by Manu; all later *Dharmaśāstras* are written in verse, prose entering the tradition only in commentaries and medieval digests (*nibandha*).

The second innovation in the composition of the *MDh* is its narrative structure. The *Dharmasūtras* are not only written in prose but are also presented as nothing more than scholarly works.[57] There is no literary introduction; the author gets right down to business. He presents his material in a straightforward manner, and on points of controversy and debate he presents opposing viewpoints. All this is eliminated by Manu. Here the real author is presented not as a scholar but as the primeval lawgiver, the Creator Svayaṃbhū, and his intermediaries, his son Manu and the latter's disciple Bhṛgu. The law is promulgated authoritatively; there cannot be any debate, dissension, or scholarly give and take.

An anonymous group of seers approaches Manu and asks him to teach them *dharma*. Manu accedes to their wishes. He narrates the creation of the world up to the emergence of human society hierarchically arranged into the four *varṇas*. Then he asks his pupil Bhṛgu to teach them the rest (1.59), reminding me of a busy professor letting his graduate assistant do the dirty work of teaching an undergraduate

1.8.23, 25, 53; 1.10.6, 23; 1.11.16, 14; 1.21.2; 2.1.6, 17, 21; 2.2.26; 2.3.14, 16, 19, 31, 45; 2.4.1, 10, 14, 18; 2.5.4, 7, 9; *VaDh* 1.22, 38; 2.6, 27, 30, 31, 41, 48; etc.

56. For a discussion see Olivelle 2000, 6–7. For such verses, see *BDh* 1.10.26; 1.19.8; 2.6.32–42.

57. In this they parallel the older ritual texts, the *Śrautasūtras* and the *Gṛhyasūtras*.

class. Bhṛgu takes up the task in earnest; the rest of the book is the oral teaching of Bhṛgu. The seers reappear only twice—once at the beginning of chapter 5 when they ask how Brahmins can be subject to death, a question that leads to a discussion of food practices, purification, and duties of women; and a second time at the beginning of chapter 12 when they ask Bhṛgu to teach them the effects of actions (*karma*). The narrative structure given prominence at the opening of the text fizzles out; there is no conclusion to the narrative. A similar structure is found in the *Pañcatantra*, where the original setting—Viṣṇuśarman's instruction of princes in statecraft and policy under the guise of animal stories—is lost sight of in the conclusion.

We have no way of knowing all the reasons for Manu's strategy of departing from the tradition of textual composition found in the earlier *dharma* tradition. The tradition of dialogue where a teacher instructs a pupil, a son, or a king goes back to the Brāhmaṇas and the Upaniṣads. The literary structure of these dialogues, however, places these individuals within human history. The transition into divine instruction is found already in the *Chāndogya Upaniṣad*, where we have the instruction of Nārada by Sanatkumāra (7.1) and of Indra and Virocana by Prajāpati (8.7). Nevertheless, I think the example of the Buddhist texts was also a likely factor. Hiltebeitel (2001, 167) has argued that the Mahāyāna literature, especially the *Lotus Sūtra*, offers a parallel to the narrative structure of the *Mahābhārata*. For the first time in India, the words of a single charismatic individual were taken as the sole fountain of authority in a religious tradition. The doctrine of *buddhavacana*, that the sole form of textual authority is the words of the Buddha, governed the production of texts both in the early forms of Buddhism and in the Mahāyāna.[58] All texts begin with the preamble "Thus have I heard," placing the text in the mouth of the Buddha and making the function of the "author" merely that of a transcriber or re-teller of what he had heard. The narrator narrating what he had heard and placing his narrative in the distant past is also at the heart of the *Mahābhārata* structure.[59]

Although its narrative structure is much simpler, the same is true of the *MDh* as well. We have here five layers of "telling," "hearing," and re-telling. At the most remote level, we have the creator himself soon after his creative activity composing a treatise and reciting it to his son Manu (1.58). Manu is the first "hearer." He transmits it to Marīci and the other sages (1.58), who form the second tier of "hearers." At Manu's command, one of these sages, Bhṛgu, teaches the seers who had come to Manu with the mission of learning *dharma*. Bhṛgu's first word (1.60), significantly, is "Listen" (*śrūyatām*). This group of seers, still placed *in illo tempore*, constitutes the third tier of "hearers." The narrator of the entire text makes only a fleeting and implicit appearance in the very first verse of the text: "As Manu was seated, absorbed in contemplation, the great seers came up to him, paid him homage in the proper manner, and said to him." Here we have the voice of the

58. For an interesting study on ancient instructions on how to "produce" a new Buddhist text, see Gregory Schopen, "If You Can't Remember, How to Make it Up: Some Monastic Rules for Redacting Canonical Texts," in *Bauddhavidyāsudhākaraḥ: Studies in Honour of Heinz Bechert on the Occasion of his 65th Birthday*, ed. P. Kieffer-Pülz and Jens-Uwe Hartmann, Indica et Tibetica 30 (Swisttal-Odendorf, 1997), pp. 571–82.

59. C. Minkowski, "Snakes, *Sattras*, and the *Mahābhārata*," in A. Sharma, ed., *Essays on the Mahābhārata* (Leiden: Brill, 1991), 384–400; Hiltebeitel 2001.

narrator introducing the first group of characters; then he becomes silent except for two other fleeting appearances to introduce the seers' further request at 5.1–2 and to introduce Bhṛgu's final discourse at 12.2. Evidently the narrator himself, who at one level can be identified with the historical author of the text, heard the text presumably from the seers; or he has been eavesdropping on Bhṛgu's instruction of the seers. This narrator is the fourth "hearer." There is then the implied fifth "hearer", that is, all those who listen to or read this text, including modern scholars. The last verse of the book, possibly part of an interpolated section (see III), is directed at this audience: "When a twice-born recites this Treatise of Manu proclaimed by Bhṛgu, he will always follow the proper conduct and obtain whatever state he desires."

Although mediated by a series of tellers and hearers, the ultimate authority of the text lies in its original promulgator, the Creator himself.[60] Paralleling the Buddhist doctrine of *buddhavacana* and doing one better than that, the *MDh* grounds its authority (*pramāṇa*) on the *svayambhūvacana*, the words of the Self-existent One, the very ground of creation. This appeal to a single source of authority stands in sharp contrast to the traditional source of authority for and means of knowing *dharma*, namely the Veda supplemented by traditional texts (*smṛti*) and the conduct of the virtuous (*ācāra*).[61] Indeed, the *MDh* itself presents the latter doctrine when it discusses the sources of *dharma* in chapter 2. There is thus a disjuncture between the narrative structure of chapter 1 and the body of the text. The author is a traditional pandit, and his habitual methods of reasoning, argumentation, and public presentation take over in the substantive parts of the text.[62] One may ignore the references to "that is the teaching of Manu" or "so said Manu,"[63] which are peculiar in a text that was composed by Manu's father and perhaps edited by Manu. The whole text, after all, constitutes the "sayings of Manu." But such self-referential statements occur also in other Sanskrit texts. More revealing are the following.

"Whatever Law Manu has proclaimed with respect to anyone, all that has been taught in the Veda, for it contains all knowledge" (2.7). This assertion is strange within a text that is Manu's own composition. It appears that the author is trying here to reconcile the authority of Manu with the authority of the Veda as the source of *dharma*. "Tradition holds that the various groups of ancestors are the sons of all the seers headed by Marīci, seers who are the children of Manu, the son of Hiraṇyagarbha" (3.194): why ascribe to tradition (*smṛtāḥ*) a view when the creator himself is the speaker? "Because of discipline, on the other hand, Pṛthu, as well as Manu, obtained a kingdom; Kubera, lordship over wealth; and the son of Gādhi, the rank of a Brahmin" (7.42). Here Manu, along with other traditional heroes, is treated in the third person. "Bed, seat, ornaments, lust, hatred, behavior unworthy of an

60. We, of course, have parallels in other religious traditions for divinely authored law, such as the Pentateuch in the Jewish tradition and the Koran (and derivatively, Sharia) in Islam.

61. This contrasts even more with the "community standards" (*sāmayācārika*) espoused in the *ĀpDh* (1.1.1–2).

62. We find similar forgetfulness in other texts as well. See, for example, Bṛhaspati's reference to the contradictions in the *MDh* cited below in section V.1.

63. *iti manor anuśāsanam:* 8.139, 279; 9.239; *abravīn manuḥ, manur āha:* 3.150, 222; 4.103; 5.41, 131; 6.54; 8.124, 168, 204, 242, 292, 339; 9.158, 182; 10.63, 78.

Ārya, malice, and bad conduct—Manu assigned these to women" (9.17). Again, Manu appears here in the third person. At 2.16, moreover, a view is ascribed to Bhṛgu, even though Bhṛgu is the narrator! There are also verses that appear to be commentaries on a previous verse, making it likely that the verse on which the comments are based has been incorporated into the text from a different source.[64]

The author of the *MDh* does not, indeed cannot, openly present diverse opinions of scholars both due to metrical reasons, as Bühler (1886, xciii) has already pointed out, and because it would violate his narrative structure; how can the creator present diverse opinions on points of law? Yet, the pandit mentality is hard to suppress, and our author repeatedly forgets his narrative and engages in ordinary scholarly give and take (see II.1). The most obvious is the expression *iti cet* ("if you argue thus"), which marks an objection or a doubt, occurring at 9.122; 10.66, 82; 12.108. At 8.140 we have a particular interest rate set by Vasiṣṭha, and at 8.110 an appeal to the practice of former sages and gods with reference to the legitimacy of oaths.[65] The author sometimes refers to the opinions of others with the common *iti kecit* ("some say"). At 3.53 the opinion of some that a bull and a cow are given as a bride price at a seer's type of marriage is refuted; at 3.261 the author refers to different customs regarding the disposal of ancestral offerings; and at 9.32 he introduces two opinions about the person to whom a son belongs, the biological father or the husband of the mother.

Contradictions in the *MDh*

The text of the *MDh* as it has come down to us contains numerous contradictory statements. This feature has drawn the attention not only of modern scholars[66] but also of ancient commentators. The author of the *Bṛhaspati Smṛti*, a text written a few centuries after the *MDh*, had the same problem with Manu. In his section on *niyoga* (levirate), Bṛhaspati comments (1.25.16):

> *uktvā niyogo manunā niṣiddhaḥ svayam eva tu* |
> *yugahrāsād aśakyo 'yaṃ kartuṃ sarvair vidhānataḥ* ||
>
> Manu has prescribed leviratic union, and then he himself has forbidden it. Because of the shortening in each age, no one can carry it out in accordance with the prescriptions.[67]

Bṛhaspati provides a traditional solution to the problem; the contradictory rules apply to different ages. So there is no true contradiction.

Modern scholars cannot accept the traditional hermeneutical solution. Many have seen these contradictions as proof that the text had multiple authors over a long period of time; the contradictions represent changing customs and norms. Bühler

64. See for example, *MDh* 3.171–4; 4.147–9, 195–6, 254–6.

65. There are also historical references: *MDh* 8.110, 116; 10.105–8.

66. For further discussion and other viewpoints, see Bühler 1886, xcii–xcv; Doniger 1991, xliv–lviii.

67. The "shortening" has multiple meanings: the ages themselves become shorter in duration, the life span of humans become correspondingly shorter, and their proclivity to virtue also becomes weaker (See, *MDh* 1.83–84).

(1886, xcii–xciii), the first scholar to posit the unitary authorship of the *MDh*, sought to answer these critics. His answer was two-fold:

> Thus in weighing the value of the argument drawn from the occurrence of contradictory passages, two circumstances, which mostly have been left out of account, must be kept in mind: first, that it is a common habit of Indian authors to place conflicting opinions, supported by authorities of equal weight, side by side, and to allow an option, or to mention time-honoured rules, legal customs, and social institutions, and afterwards to disapprove of them; and secondly, that, as our Smṛti is in any case a recast of an earlier Sūtra, that fact alone is sufficient to account for contradictions.

The second point is based on Bühler's assumption of a pre-existing *Mānava Dharmasūtra* and must be ignored (see II.1). In my view, the author's work cannot be limited to that of an editor; even though he used older sources, as all authors do, he created a new work, and one would have to assume that a good author would seek to avoid contradictions, especially contradictions that sit side by side. Bühler's first point, however, is well taken. Manu was unable to demarcate various views with the traditional *iti* followed by the name of the authority both because the treatise was composed by the creator and because it was difficult to incorporate such attributions into a verse composition. The various views are here woven into the very fabric of Manu's narrative.[68]

Manu does, indeed, cite conflicting opinions.[69] This is demonstrated by the fact that sometimes he ascribes differing views to different factions. So, for example, the conflicting opinions about the relative superiority of the seed and the field in determining the person to whom a son belongs are stated clearly (9.32–44). Although stated less clearly, two views on primogeniture are presented at *MDh* 9.105–110 and 9.111f. Here the presence of the particle *vā* ("or," "or rather") at the beginning of 9.111, indicating an alternative that the author himself prefers, shows that we are dealing with two opinions.[70] The clearest attribution of opinions to authorities is found at 3.16:

> According to Atri and the son of Utathya, a man falls from his caste by marrying a Śūdra woman; according to Śaunaka, by fathering a son through her; and according to Bhṛgu, by producing all his offspring through her.

A clear example of an apparent contradiction where two viewpoints are juxtaposed is found at 9.97–100:

68. See my discussion below (p. 44–46) of the three views presented in *MDh* 5.61–2.

69. See the various opinions on lawful marriages (3.23–6), on meat eating (5.28–56), levirate (9.57–70), division of property and primogeniture (9.105–56), whether brothers should live together or separately (9.104–11), and shares of a son by a Śūdra wife (9.150–5). See also Manu's denunciation of bride-price at 9.98–100 and its acceptance at 8.366, 369; 9.93–7, 204–5.

70. For this use of *vā* as the preferred option, see Paul Kiparsky, *Pāṇini as a Variationist* (Cambridge, Mass.: MIT Press, 1979).

> 97 If, after the bride-price has been paid for the girl, the man who paid the price dies, she should be given to the brother-in-law, if she consents to it. 98 Even a Śūdra should not take a bride-price when he gives his daughter; for by accepting a bride-price, he is engaging in a covert sale of his daughter.
>
> 99 That after promising her to one man, she is then given to another—such a deed was never done by good people of ancient or recent times. 100 The covert sale of a daughter for a payment under the name "bride-price"—we have never heard of such a thing even in former generations.

We see here that verse 97 assumes the payment of a bride-price, a view rejected in the very next verse. In verse 99, likewise, the bride-price is assumed; the father takes money from one man and then gives the girl to another, thus getting two payments. The next verse again inveighs against the practice of bride-price. One cannot but assume that Manu is here deliberately pairing the two views.[71] Contradictory positions on marrying a Śūdra woman are, likewise, placed side by side at 3.13–4:

> 13 A Śūdra may take only a Śūdra woman as wife; a Vaiśya, the latter and a woman of his own class; a Kṣatriya, the latter two and a woman of his own class; and a Brahmin, the latter three and a woman of his own class. 14 Not a single story alludes to a Brahmin or a Kṣatriya taking a Śūdra wife even when they are going through a time of adversity.

Here, we may have not merely a juxtaposition of views but Manu actually siding with the latter view. From the verses that follow, it becomes clear that Manu did not approve of a Brahmin marrying a Śūdra, even though this view is backed by ancient authorities who permit hypergamous marriages to all classes.

We may be able here and in other instances to distinguish two voices of Manu, the legal and the moral, which may also have contributed to apparent contradictions. As a jurist he has to deal with the reality of social life and accepted custom; he has to decide whether certain actions are legal or not. It is apparent that he accepted upper-class men marrying lower-class women, even Śūdra women, as a social fact. At 9.149–57, for example, in dealing with the practical matter of dividing the paternal estate, Manu states what share the son born of a Śūdra wife should receive. Nevertheless, *dharma* is not just law but also right living, and when he uses the moral voice Manu often contradicts what he may have said within a legal context. Even today, for example, opposition to birth out of wedlock (the moral position) can exist side by side with legal and social provisions for the welfare and legal status of illegitimate children. We see such a bifurcation in Manu's discussion of permitted foods (5.4–26), where meat-eating is taken for granted. His discussion of food at an ancestral offering (3.267–72) also presupposes meat. His discussion of

71. We see a similar juxtaposition of views at 9.122–26. The first view permits seniority among sons born to wives of equal status, whereas the second view denies this and treats all of them equally.

permitted foods, however, is followed by a long statement about the evils of meat (5.27–55). Clearly, Manu here is not so much contradicting himself as providing two sets of guidelines, the one traditional that includes meat, within which he provides rules on permitted and prohibited animals, and the other reflecting the new morality of vegetarianism. The moral tone is clearly brought out at the end of Manu's long discussion on food (5.56):

> There is no fault in eating meat, in drinking liquor, or in having sex; that is the natural activity of creatures. Abstaining from such activity, however, brings great rewards.

The most famous instance of contradiction is Manu's position on leviratic union (*niyoga*), that is, the fathering of a son by a younger brother upon his dead brother's widow,[72] a contradiction already noted by Bṛhaspati. *Niyoga* was a long-established practice in India and is recorded in all the *Dharmasūtras*. Manu himself presupposes this practice, for example, in his discussion of partition (9.143–7, 190). At 9.57–63, moreover, he not only admits this practice but also lays down rules as to how it should be carried out. In the very next breath, however, he opposes this practice vehemently (9.64–8). This contradiction does not lend itself to an easy resolution, but I think here also Manu is talking in two voices. He acknowledges the traditional practice, provides rules for its proper implementation, and deals with the legal rights of children born from such a union. Nevertheless, he abhors this custom and calls it a bestial practice. He also preaches chastity to young widows; they do not need children to attain happiness here or in the hereafter (5.158–60):

> Aspiring to that unsurpassing Law of women devoted to a single husband, she should remain patient, controlled, and celibate until her death. Untold thousands of Brahmins who have remained celibate from their youth have gone to heaven without producing offspring to continue their family line. Just like these celibates, a good woman, though she be sonless, will go to heaven when she steadfastly adheres to the celibate life after her husband's death.

One other reason for apparent contradictions is the practice of using the best argument to win a debate. We see Kṛṣṇa using this sort of argumentation in the *Bhagavad Gītā;* you should do this for reason X, and if not for that then for reason Y, even if X and Y are incompatible. Thus, with reference to the question "To whom does a son belong?" Manu clearly sides with those who argue that a son belongs to the husband of the mother, just as the crop belongs not to the owner of the seed but to the owner of the field (9.41–55). Manu, however, dislikes obtaining children through surrogate fathers—a practice recognized within the doctrine of the twelve kinds of son (9.158–60)—as demonstrated by his denunciation of leviratic

72. Although it is generally the younger brother, an older brother begetting a son on a younger brother's widow is also recorded (see *MDh* 9.62). In the absence of a brother it is possible for a close relative to be appointed for fathering a son. That this practice was extended beyond the context of a person dying without issue is made clear in MDh 9.137, where *niyoga* is permitted even when a husband is impotent or sick.

union. All except the natural-born son, that is, a man's own biological son through his legitimate wife, are viewed by Manu as surrogates. Within this context, the argument that a son belongs to (or takes after) the biological father, that the seed is stronger than the field because different plants and trees grow in the same field from different seeds, is a convenient argument, and Manu uses this at 9.181: "Those who are designated here as sons because of congruity but who are born from another man's seed belong only to the one from whose seed they were born and to no one else."

In both ritual and legal texts, there are often two sets of rules, the one primary (*kalpa*) and the other secondary (*anukalpa*). The primary rules are seen as the normal and the normative. In times of emergency and when it is impossible to follow the primary rule due to lack of resources or ability, it is permitted to follow the secondary mode. Frequently, the secondary mode is associated with what has come to be known as the "Law in times of adversity" (*āpaddharma*). Sometimes, as at 3.147, Manu clearly identifies the primary and the secondary methods. Indeed, at 11.30 Manu condemns a man who follows the secondary rule when he is able to follows the primary: "When someone, though able to follow the principal mode, yet lives according to the secondary mode, that fool will obtain no reward for it after death." The two modes, however, are not always so clearly distinguished, and in those situations the differing rules may seem to be contradictory.

A major reason for apparent contradiction, as well as for the many *non-sequiturs*, that we detect in ancient Indian texts such as the *MDh* is the technique of text production that I will call "anthologizing." Hacker (1961, 80) refers to the "practice of juxtaposition, which is a primitive method of redaction, caused by the desire to do equal justice to different traditions." In anthologizing, the author opts to place material drawn from different sources side by side without much editorial intervention or any serious attempt at reconciling differences among these textual extracts.[73] I think the anthologizing technique without editorial comment is most evident in texts composed in verse; in prose compositions, such as the *Dharmasūtras*, we see greater use of ascriptions and authorial intervention either to accept or reject various views presented in the textual extracts. When textual extracts are presented in an anthological format, not only do contradictions among the sources of these extracts become apparent; it is also difficult to interpret a particular verse within the context of the surrounding verses which may come from different sources.

A final reason for apparent contradictions may be found in the frequent use of hyperbole in didactic literature. Early western scholars of the Vedas encountered what they perceived as a problem: the vedic hymns take different gods to be the highest. This went against their monotheistic presuppositions, as also against common logic. How could several gods in a pantheon be supreme at the same time? Max Müller coined the word "henotheism" to account for this phenomenon. A quick glance at the royal panegyrics (*praśastis*) of a millennium later is instructive. All

73. Doniger (1991, lv) also thinks that Manu presents the traditions he has inherited, "juxtaposing conflicting views and then adjudicating between them." Manu, however, juxtaposes far more frequently than he adjudicates.

kings, from petty chieftains to Gupta emperors, are eulogized as conquerors of the whole world. One would hardly expect the panegyrist to be accurate—he is a petty king, a tributary to king X; he managed a couple of small-scale victories! That would hardly do. Neither can you go to god X and say "You are in the third rank below Y and Z. And by the way, will you give me a thousand cows?" Even in the Catholic faith, where theological orthodoxy takes center stage, devotees of the Virgin or St. Jude do not give theologically accurate descriptions of the powers of their favorite saint; hyperbole is the norm. The vedic poets were no exception. This form of rhetoric was recognized as an *alaṅkāra*, a poetic ornament, in Sanskrit aesthetics under the name *atiśayokti*, hyperbole. In hyperbole, the literal is the enemy of the true. As Gerow observes, a hyperbole contains a falsity but is so framed as to open the door to a deeper truth:

> A "skyscraper is so tall they had to put hinges on the two top stories so to let the moon go by" [Carl Sandburg]. But of course it is not a falsity that is capable of being detected in truth tables; for the falsity, the 'exaggeration' is only apparent, only for effect. For the lie in the hyperbole is so framed as to conceal a greater truth, and a truth urgently required by the context; as these skyscrapers are the tallest things that man ever built.[74]

The use of hyperbole in religious and didactic literature is clearly different from its use in poetry. There is, however, one thing in common; neither can be taken at face value or read literally without distorting the language, misunderstanding the meaning, and producing interpretive monstrosities like "henotheism." In religious literature we have statements that giving a cow to a learned Brahmin is worth one thousand horse sacrifices, or bathing in a particular river is better than bathing ten thousand times in the Ganges at Benares. In attempting to inculcate the virtue of abstention from meat, Manu (5.53) says: "A man who abstains from meat and a man who offers the horse sacrifice every year for a hundred years—the reward for their meritorious acts is the same." In praising the life of a vedic student, Āpastamba (1.4.29) says: "A student who totally dedicates himself in this manner accomplishes in that very state all the rites carrying rewards, as well as those that pertain to a householder." An ascetic text wishes to promote the importance of giving food to ascetics: "Even if a man gives the entire earth, it would not equal the merit of preparing almsfood and giving it to a mendicant."[75] No one expects such statements to be taken literally; they are meant to eulogize certain lesser known practices and to recommend their performance. Likewise, in didactic and legal literature a sin or crime or a virtue or a good act is said to be the worst or the best. "Lack of generosity is the gravest sin; generosity is the highest austerity," says Baudhāyana (*BDh* 1.10.6). And Manu (4.224–5):

> The gods once evaluated the food of a miserly vedic scholar and that of a generous usurer and pronounced the two to be equal. Prajāpati came

74. E. Gerow, *Indian Poetics* (Wiesbaden: Harrassowitz, 1977), p. 242.

75. Cited in Yādava Prakāśa, *Yatidharmasamuccaya*, ed. P. Olivelle (Albany, NY: State University of New York Press, 1995), 6.314.

> up to them and said, "Don't make equal what is unequal. The food of the generous man is cleansed by the spirit of generosity, whereas the other food is defiled by the lack of generosity."

When the topic is generosity, even a usurer is said to be better than a miser. But when the topic is usury, it is a sin worse than even abortion: "Usury and abortion were once weighed in a balance. The abortionist rose to the top, while the usurer trembled" (*BDh* 1.10.23). It is impossible to think that these authors intended their statements to be taken as literally true, just as it is not possible to think that there is a device in the skyscrapers to let the moon pass. As in literature and poetry, so in religious, didactic, and legal literature hyperbole is simply a literary device. Failure to recognize this can only cause serious misinterpretation of texts. So, it is not a contradiction when Manu (9.14–6), in warning husbands to guard their wives, waxes eloquent on the evil tendencies inherent in women:

> They pay no attention to beauty, they pay no heed to age; whether he is handsome or ugly, they make love to him with the single thought, "He's a man!" Lechery, fickleness of mind, and hard-heartedness are innate in them; even when they are carefully guarded in this world, therefore, they become hostile towards their husbands. Recognizing thus the nature produced in them at creation by Prajāpati, a man should make the utmost effort at guarding them.

and in urging men to respect women, he eulogizes them (9.26–8):

> On account of offspring, a wife is the bearer of many blessings, worthy of honor, and the light within a home; indeed, in a home no distinction at all exists between a wife (*strī*) and Śrī, the Goddess of Fortune. She begets children; and when they are born, she brings them up—day in, day out, the wife, evidently, is the linchpin of domestic affairs. Offspring, rites prescribed by Law, obedient service,* the highest sensuous delights, and procuring heaven for oneself and one's forefathers—all this depends on the wife.

and warns against abusing them (3.56–8):

> Where women are revered, there the gods rejoice; but where they are not, no rite bears any fruit. Where female relatives grieve, that family soon comes to ruin; but where they do not grieve, it always prospers. When female relatives, not receiving due reverence, curse any house, it comes to total ruin, as if struck down by witchcraft.

That some texts fall into the literary genre of hyperbole is not merely a modern and anachronistic interpretation is demonstrated by an observation made by the commentator Medhātithi. Commenting on *MDh* 1.107, which says that the Law in its entirely is given in this text of Manu, Medhātithi remarks: "Therefore, to obtain the knowledge of the Law there is no need to refer to any other texts. This is an hyperbolic eulogy."

I do not propose that *all* apparent contradictions in the *MDh* can be resolved in these ways. Authors, even modern ones, do contradict themselves occasionally. Further, the work of redactors down the centuries, which I discuss below (III), cannot be completely detected. Changing norms and mores may have prompted some of them to introduce opinions at variance with those expressed in the original text.

Language and Meter

There is nothing remarkable about the language of the *MDh*; it is mostly simple and classical Sanskrit. The meter is the traditional *śloka*. There are, however, some linguistic and metrical peculiarities that are of interest for the history of both the language and the text.

In language, the area of greatest interest is the vocabulary. I will draw attention to the technical use of the two terms *deśa*, as documentary evidence, and *pravāsayati*, as the execution of a criminal (see II.2). These terms do not occur in any other *dharma* text and were probably borrowed from the Arthaśāstric vocabulary. Manu also uses the word *avicārayan* frequently. I think the usual meaning given to it, "without hesitation," is correct in many contexts; it probably was used in the sense of "not giving something a second thought." There are contexts, however, especially within criminal justice, when it may have a more technical meaning of inflicting a punishment without any judicial inquiry or process.[76]

A term not given in any standard Sanskrit dictionary is *bhaktaka*, found at *MDh* 7.126. It appears that even some scribes had problems with this term and changed it to the common *vetana;* but the critical edition has adopted the former for strong reasons, including the support of ancient commentators. It was probably a technical term for a particular kind of wages given to a class of people in royal service. It is derived in all likelihood from "food" or "rice" in the sense of the modern Indo-Āryan word *bhāt* "rice" and referred to wages paid in rice or other foodstuffs, a meaning attested also in inscriptions.[77]

Another term with possible Prakritic influence is *yāpya*, found at 9.4 with the meaning "to be reprimanded or censured." Here also the scribes have introduced the easier term *vācya*. How *yāpya* came to acquire this meaning is unclear, but we have modern Indo-Āryan terms such as *jābo* "worthless, contemptible" in Nepali and *zābar* in Assamese.[78]

Manu also uses the interesting term *pracāra*, which, as Scharfe (1993, 195–200) has demonstrated, means not land or pasture but activities, especially in the Arthaśāstric vocabulary. In addition to the evidence presented by Scharfe, the meaning of "activities" is apparent in the juxtaposition of *pracāra* and *ceṣṭita* at *MDh* 7.153 and 155. The old meaning of *pracāra* was forgotten early on; even Kātyāyana

76. See, for example, *MDh* 8.283; 9.270, 280.

77. D. C. Sircar's *Indian Epigraphical Glossary* (Delhi: Motilal Banarsidass, 1966) p. 49, gives *bhaktagrāma* as a village granted to someone for his maintenance and *bhaktādāya* as revenue in the form of rice.

78. See R. L. Turner, *A Comparative Dictionary of the Indo-Āryan Languages* (London: Oxford University Press, 1969), 10476. For other occurrences of this term, see *GDh* 13.23; 19.2; *BDh* 3.10.2; *VaDh* 15.19.

(884), in commenting on *MDh* 9.219, takes it to mean *gopracāra*, the grazing ground for cattle; this interpretation is followed by most medieval commentators.

Occasionally we come across sandhi irregularities, especially double sandhi resorted to for metrical reasons: see 3.47b; 11.59d; 12.59d.

In most verses Manu follows the typical Pathyā form of the Śloka meter; only occasionally does a Vipulā form intervene (see, for example, 9.196–7). Nevertheless, on several occasions we have hypermetric *pādas*, most frequently the first and the third; hypermeter never occurs in the second or fourth *pādas*, which maintain their regular iambic cadence. Hypermetric third *pādas* are found in 3.10, 270, 284; 11.118; 12.32, and hypermetric first *pādas* in 2.156; 6.93; 8.133; 9.121, 225; 10.35; 11.199, 249 (also 3.228 in most mss.). In all these instances, we have several variant readings where scribes have attempted to rectify the meter. In verse 2.201, both first and third *pādas* are hypermetric. There and in 2.156, I think, the *pādas* are only apparently hypermetric. These *pādas* read:

> *parivādāt kharo bhavati* (2.201a)
> *paribhoktā kṛmir bhavati* (2.201c)
> *na tena sthaviro bhavati* (2.156a)

I believe that *bhavati* in these verses should be pronounced in the Prakritic manner as *bhoti* with just two syllables. When so pronounced, the meter becomes a perfect Pathyā.[79] Manu uses the word *bhavati* frequently even as the final word of the first or third *pādas*, and the meter scans without having to use Prakritic pronunciation.[80] This may point to the fact that such hypermetric verses were actually common proverbs, where Prakritic influence is more likely, cited by Manu, and not his own composition.

Other metrical irregularities are encountered occasionally. At 5.163 we have *pāda*-c ending in *loke bhavati* with a wrong cadence This irregularity appears to have prompted several scribes to correct it with the reading *sā bhavel loke* and all editors to adopt this reading. At 9.238b we have possibly a case of double sandhi.

I.4 The Socio-Political Background

If we assume that the *MDh* was composed during the first couple of centuries CE—and I think this is a plausible assumption—then we may be able at least to speculate about the social and political environment of the author and perhaps the motivations for its composition. Recently similar questions have been raised with reference to the *Mahābhārata*, especially by Hiltebeitel (2001) in his new and significant book. Fitzgerald (2004, 120–1), in the introduction to his translation of the *Śānti Parvan*, also sees the epic as a response to the times not too favorable to Brahmanical privilege:

79. See the similar metrical problems created in the *Kaṭha Upaniṣad* 3.5, 6, 7, 8. The reading of *bhoti* in these passages was first suggested by L. Alsdorf, "Contributions to the Textual Criticism of the Kaṭhopaniṣad," *ZDMG* 100 (1950): 621–37.

80. See *MDh* 3.50, 275; 5.163; 6.80; 8.164; 9.22, 173, 302; 10.92; 11.38; 12.72.

> It seems fair to conjecture that the emergence of the Mauryan empire generally and Aśoka's dharma campaign in particular were profound challenges to many pious brahmins; and that these events may well have been a strong stimulus to the creation, development, redaction, and spreading of the apocalyptic *Mahābhārata* narrative. This narrative depicted violent resistance to the kind "illegitimate" political power that the Nandas, the Mauryans, and Aśoka must have represented to some, and it depicted a restoration of proper, *brāhmaṇya* kingship, which undertakes to use violence for the protection and support of brahmins.

I think the socio-political environment that prompted the composition of the great epic was not too different from that of the *MDh*. The time frame and the geography are more or less the same, and the authors of both works probably came from the class of educated and somewhat conservative Brahmins intent on protecting the rights and privileges of their class. They were composed after the collapse of the Maurya empire in the 2nd century BCE. The last Maurya emperor, Bṛhadratha, was assassinated by Puṣyamitra, who inaugurated the Śuṅga dynasty.[81] Historical memory considers Puṣyamitra to have been a Brahmin, and his dynasty was viewed as partial to Brahmin interests. The last Śuṅga was assassinated around 73 BCE. There followed the short-lived Kāṇva dynasty, also partial to Brahmin interests, that collapsed in 28 BCE. Roughly during this period, the north-western border region of the subcontinent was ruled by Greek-Bactrian kings. Although the history is somewhat murky, around the turn of the millennium, possibly a bit earlier, a new political force, the Śakas of Central Asian origin, emerged in the north-western borders and swept across the north-western region of India proper. The Śakas were displaced by the Kuśānas, also from Central Asia, who extended their empire well into the Gangetic heartland.

We can isolate at least three socio-political elements that provide the background to the composition of the *MDh*. 1) The major element is certainly the historical reality and especially the historical memory of two or three centuries later of the Maurya state and especially of the Aśokan political, social, and religious reforms.[82] Aśoka was certainly a Buddhist; whether he was anti-Brahmanical is debatable. One thing that his reforms did was to displace the Brahmin from his privileged position within the social structure. The special relationship between the political power (*kṣatra*) and the religious establishment (*brahma*) was broken. The Sanskrit compound *śramaṇa-brāhmaṇa* used frequently by Aśoka in his inscriptions indicates that his social philosophy envisaged a dual class of religious people worthy of respect and support: the newly formed ascetic communities and the old Brahmin class.

81. The historical accuracy of a "Śuṅga dynasty" has been cast into some doubt recently based on numismatic evidence by Shailendra Bhandare in his presentation to the conference "Between the Empires" held at the University of Texas at Austin, April 10–12, 2003.

82. That such a memory continued to exist long after the demise of Aśoka and the Maurya empire is demonstrated by the Buddhist literature devoted to Aśoka. See John Strong, *The Legend of King Asoka: A Study and Translation of the Asokavadana*. Princeton: Princeton University Press, 1983.

His prohibition of animal sacrifices,[83] furthermore, undercut the very raison d'être of Brahmanical privilege: the Brahmin's ability to perform sacrifices for the well-being of society and for the furtherance of royal power symbolized principally in the royal horse sacrifice. The very creation of a Brahmanical genre of literature dedicated to *dharma* was possibly due to the elevation of this word to the level of imperial ideology by Aśoka (see II.1).

2) To add insult to injury, the Mauryas, as well as the Nandas who preceded them, were considered at least within Brahmanical historical memory as Śūdras. The usurpation of Kṣatriya royal privileges by Śūdras and the ensuing suppression of Brahmins are presented as the sure signals of the corrupt times of the Kali age. Such a political situation creates the mixture of *varṇas* (*varṇasaṃkara*), the most serious social and moral corruption within Brahmanical ideology.

3) Finally, there was the contemporary political reality. There were the foreign invasions first in the border regions of the northwest and then within the heartland that established foreign rule (Parasher 1991). If we are correct in thinking that the *MDh* was written during the Kushana period, then Manu was faced with almost a new Maurya rule with the added dimension that these were also foreigners, Mlecchas. The Kushanas ruled a wide swath of northern India, and they also favored Buddhism.

Reading the *MDh* one cannot fail to see and to feel the intensity and urgency with which the author defends Brahmanical privilege. A major aim of Manu was to reestablish the old alliance between *brahma* and *kṣatra*, an alliance that in his view would benefit both the king and the Brahmin, thereby reestablishing the Brahmin in his unique and privileged position within society. We hear the repeated emphasis on the inviolability of the Brahmin in his person and in his property. He has immunity from the death penalty, from taxes, and from the confiscation of his property. The king is advised repeatedly that a Brahmin's property is poison. Stealing a Brahmin's gold is one of the five grievous sins, and the death penalty is imposed on the perpetrator. Devotion to Brahmins is a cardinal virtue of kings: "Refusal to turn back in battle, protecting the subjects, and obedient service to Brahmins—for kings, these are the best mean of securing happiness" (7.88). The reason why foreign ruling classes, such as the Greeks, Śakas, Persians, and Chinese, have fallen to the level of Śūdras, once again, is their lack of devotion to Brahmins: "By neglecting rites and by failing to visit Brahmins, however, these men of Kṣatriya birth have gradually reached in the world the level of Śūdras" (10.43).

Brahmanical privilege is threatened from two quarters: the Śūdra, within which class Manu often lumps all the lower classes of society, and the Mlecchas. Now, it is true that even the *Dharmasūtras* contain passages that are anti-Śūdra. It is taken for granted that the sole duty of Śūdras is to serve the upper classes; penalties for killing a Śūdra are much less than for killing people of the upper classes; likewise, penalties are increased for guilty Śūdras; the list could go on. Yet we also see that Śūdras acted as cooks in Brahmin households. Āpastamba (2.28.11, 15) even

83. See Rock Edict 1: *hidā nā kichi jive ālabhitu pajohitaviye;* Sanskrit: *iha na kaścit jīvaḥ ālabhya prahotavyaḥ*. The term *prahotavya* has clear reference to Brahmanical sacrifice.

says that one may learn aspects of *dharma* from Śūdras. There is a virulence in Manu's rhetoric vis-à-vis Śūdras that appears to indicate that there must be a subtext to it. How could the lowest class of society with little access to material resources pose such a threat to social order and to Brahmanical hegemony? The fear of the Śūdra contrasts sharply with Manu's view of Vaiśyas. These are dealt with in a dispassionate and straightforward way. Why were Vaiśyas, who are depicted as agriculturists and traders, that is, people with resources, not a threat to the *brahma-kṣatra* alliance that Manu was attempting to forge and strengthen? At one level, I think, historical memory is at work here; Śūdras were once in power and posed a real threat to Brahmanical hegemony, and history can always repeat itself. There is also the belief highlighted in the *Mahābhārata* with the story of Paraśu-Rāma that there are no true Kṣatriyas in the world any more; they are all Śūdras.[84]

"Śūdra" for Manu, I think, is often a code word; it identifies the enemy and it encompasses a wide cross-section of society, both past and present. It evoked the memories of bad old days; it heightened the anxiety that what happened under the Mauryas could be repeated. I also think that there was a contemporary threat to Brahmanical supremacy not so much from political power but from rival religious establishments, especially the Buddhist and the Jain monks. I think Manu includes these within his code "Śūdra." The connection between Śūdras and non-Brahmanical ascetic sects is drawn by Manu himself. In his advice regarding a Brahmin's residence, Manu (4.61) says:

> *na śūdrarājye nivasen nādhārmikajanāvṛte* |
> *na pāṣaṇḍijanākrānte nopasṛṣṭe 'ntyajair nṛbhiḥ* ||
>
> He should not live in a kingdom ruled by a Śūdra, teeming with unrighteous people, overrun by people belonging to heretical ascetic sects, or swamped by lowest-born people.[85]

Here we have a clear juxtaposition between a kingdom ruled by a Śūdra king and a region populated by *pāṣaṇḍins*, a generic term that refers to heterodox ascetics, principally Buddhist and Jain, by lowest-born people, and by unrighteous men. Indeed, Manu's instruction (9.225) to the king about cleansing his kingdom of dangerous people includes men who belong to heretical sects (*pāṣaṇḍa*). The strength of Buddhism in the northwestern regions during this period and the patronage offered to them by what for Manu were Mleccha kings may also have influenced the connection between heretic and Śūdra/Mleccha.

Alongside Śūdras, we have the Mlecchas. Manu is cognizant of the regions occupied by the foreign barbarians, for at 2.23 he defines the areas outside the central Āryāvarta as the region of Mlecchas. Manu, however, does not have much to say about the Mlecchas in the rest of the book; his focus is on the Śūdras. Or, is the code "Śūdra" meant also to encompass these other outsiders as well? Note that at

84. See also 10.129 (against Śūdras accumulating wealth); 8.22 (against having too many Śūdras in a kingdom); and 3.178 (against Brahmins who do ritual work for Śūdras). That some Śūdras (possibly foreign ruling classes) were wealthy is hinted at by Manu's adage at 11.34 that a Śūdra's power lies in wealth.

85. According to a variant reading, he should not live in a region overrun by ascetic organizations or groups (*pāṣaṇḍigaṇa*).

10.44 Manu presents the Mleccha groups such as Yavana, Śaka, and Cīna as sunk to the level of Śūdras, although they were Kṣatriyas by birth.

The ideology that drives Manu, I think, explains the plan of his book. As we will see (II.2), he devotes 1034 verses (38.6%) to the discussion of the Brahmin and 971 verses (36%) to matters relating to the king; these two take up 74.8% of the entire text.[86] Manu's agenda is two-fold: he wants to tell Brahmins how to behave as true Brahmins devoted to vedic learning and virtue, and he wants to tell kings how to behave as true kings, devoted to Brahmins and ruling the people justly. For this agenda he brings the authority of no less a person than the Creator himself, who is presented as the absent author of the text.

II. Sources of Manu

The Traditions of *dharma* and *artha*

The *MDh* presents itself as a *śāstra* both in the prelude to the work at 1.58–9 and in the colophons that conclude each chapter: *iti mānave dharmaśāstre*. The term *śāstra* has no exact parallel in English (see IV). It may refer to a system or tradition of expert knowledge in a particular field, that is, to a science. It refers especially, however, to the textualized form of that science, that is, to an authoritative compendium of knowledge signaling a breakthrough achievement within the history of that tradition and serving as a point of reference to subsequent investigations within that tradition. To use Pollock's (1989b, 301) felicitous expression, *śāstras* are "cultural grammars" that both reflect and regulate practice (*prayoga*). Examples of such written *śāstras* are found in almost every field, such as grammar, medicine, politics, erotics, dramaturgy, and poetics.[87] A *śāstra* may present new material and present the material in new ways; but essentially it is a crystallization of a long tradition of accumulated knowledge. Consequently, the author of any *śāstra* drew on materials from his predecessors. The *MDh* was no exception.

Given the elasticity of the concept of *dharma* and its broad semantic compass, the *MDh* drew on not one but at least two expert traditions: the one relating the *dharma* proper and the other centered on *artha*, viz., statecraft, polity, and the legal process.

An identifiable expert tradition of reflection, teaching, and textual composition focused on the broad and somewhat ill-defined field represented by *dharma* existed in India for a period of at least three to four centuries prior to the composition of the *MDh*. The earliest texts of this tradition, composed in prose aphorisms, were the *Dharmasūtras*. The four extant texts of this tradition,[88] the *sūtras* ascribed to Āpastamba, Baudhāyana, Gautama, and Vasiṣṭha, contain the names of numerous other experts and their conflicting views on a variety of issues. This evidence points

86. The percentage will be even higher if we exclude what I believe are sections that are later interpolations (below part III).

87. A lucid and penetrating study of the idea of *śāstra* is given in Pollock 1989a.

88. For the edition and translation, with a discussions of their dates, see Olivelle 1999b and 2000.

both to a vibrant and contentious intellectual tradition and to a rich literature, much of which, unfortunately, is now lost. The composition of the *MDh* has to be located within this tradition.

That a similar expert tradition relating to *artha* existed prior to the *MDh* is also certain. It is, however, more difficult to delineate the early history of *artha*, because only one text that has any claim to antiquity, Kauṭalya's *Arthaśāstra*, has survived. It is clear that for his discussion of statecraft and law in chapters 7–9 Manu depended on the *artha* tradition; much of this material has no precedent in the older *Dharmasūtras*.

II.1 The *dharma* Tradition

It is impossible to determine with any degree of accuracy the early chronology of the expert tradition on *dharma*. The term itself is very old, occurring in the *Ṛgveda* and other early vedic texts. Its precise meaning within those contexts, especially in the hymns of the *Ṛgveda*, is not altogether clear.[89] That some speculation about rules of ethical behavior, conventions regarding social conduct, and the judicial process should have taken place during the vedic times is clear.[90] What is less clear is when an identifiable expert tradition came into being. Some of the dates proposed by Kane (1962–75) and others for the *Dharmasūtras*, I think, are far too early.

As I have shown elsewhere (Olivelle, forthcoming-a, -c), *dharma* was not a central term in the ritual or theological vocabulary of the middle and late vedic texts. It occurs less frequently in the Brāhmaṇas and Upaniṣads than we would have predicted for a term that was to become the central concept of Indian civilization. Its semantic range is also restricted, occurring mostly within the royal vocabulary and relating to the king's function of maintaining law and order in society. The term does not play a central role even in the post-vedic ritual texts, the *Śrautasūtras* and *Gṛhyasūtras*. My hypothesis is that the term gained popularity and was given a new theological definition when it was taken over by the new religions emerging in the Gangetic valley, especially by Buddhism; *dharma* became the central concept within these religions, defining the essence of their theology and way of life. The term was given even a greater boost when it was made the defining concept in the political ideology of the Maurya empire, certainly by Aśoka and possibly by his father and grandfather, in the first half of the third century BCE.

I think that the Brahmanical focus on the same term should be seen against this background and as a response to its appropriation by their rivals for religious authority and political patronage. After Aśoka no one could ignore the term.

If this time-line is correct, then the earliest Brahmanical works on *dharma* could not have been composed long before 300 BCE, most probably after that date.

89. For the best study thus far of the early history of the term *dharma*, see Horsch 1967. A collection of studies on the history of *dharma* in various intellectual and religious traditions and in different time periods is being edited by me and is forthcoming in the *Journal of Indian Philosophy*.

90. See, for example, Stephanie Jamison's several studies on the vedic precedents of Dharmaśāstric prescriptions: 1997, 1998, 2000.

That still leaves roughly three, may be even four, centuries for the tradition to develop and mature before we come to Manu; that is a long period of time. It need not take, as some early Indologists appear to assume, two hundred years for anything new and significant to come about in ancient India.

The first products of Brahmanical reflections on *dharma* were closely connected to the vedic *śākhās*. After the composition of the middle and late vedic texts, literary activities of the *śākhās* focused on the ritual, both on the solemn vedic sacrifices (*śrauta*), which were probably becoming increasingly rare, and on the more common domestic rites (*gṛhya*). These productions adopted the aphoristic *sūtra* style that was in vogue. It was natural for the Brahmanical scholars to apply the same genre to its literature on *dharma*, a term that also had ritual connotations within Brahmanical thought. Collectively, the *Śrauta-*, *Gṛhya-*, and *Dharma-sūtras* were included in the new category of texts, the *Kalpasūtra*.[91] It is, however, unclear whether every *Dharmasūtra* was attached to a *Kalpa*. In the post-Mauryan period, it appears that the production of knowledge within Brahmanism with its strong apologetic dimensions became less confined to *śākhās*. The *sūtras* of a particular *śākhā* was authoritative only within its confines. The post-Mauryan world brought theological and political challenges that needed united efforts rather than the splintered responses of the *śākhā* system.[92] The notion of a single *dharma* for all Brahmins was taking hold; several developments within the *dharma* tradition itself bear witness to this.

One such development related to sacred geography. As Jayaswal (1930, 29–32) has observed, the origin of the notion of *Āryāvarta* probably goes back to the time of Puṣyamitra, the founder of the Śuṅga dynasty, in the middle of the second century BCE, and possibly coincided with his realm (but see above fn. 81). *Āryāvarta* was the region where Brahmins followed the *dharma* in an exemplary manner and where correct Sanskrit was spoken. The practices of this regions become normative for all. This concept does not occur in the early *Dharmasūtras* of Āpastamba and Gautama, appearing for the first time in Patañjali's *Mahābhāṣya* and the *Dharmasūtras* of Baudhāyana and Vasiṣṭha.[93] It is taken over and expanded by Manu, with the addition of further and more restricted sacred geographies labeled *brahmāvarta*, *brahmarṣideśa*, and *madhyadeśa* (*MDh* 2.17–24). More importantly, as we have seen, it was this period following the Maurya political ideology—an ideology that displaced the Brahmins from their privileged position and placed them on an equal footing with other religious virtuosi, the *Śramaṇas*—that saw a re-assertion of the unique position of the Brahmins and their special relationship to the king and the political authority. The symbiotic relationship

91. It is unclear when the term Kalpasūtra first came to be used with reference to these three classes of texts. Böhtlingk and Roth do not give any reference in their dictionary.

92. Later Mīmāṃsā developed the theory that texts of each *śākhā* is authoritative with respect to all *śākhās*, thus providing the basis for the supra-*śākhā* Veda. This theory is articulated in the maxim *śākhāntarādhikaraṇanyāya* or *sarvaśākhāpratyayanyāya*, and presented in the *Pūrva-Mīmāṃsāsūtra*, 2.4.9. See, Kane (1962–75) IV: 453.

93. See, Patañjali on Pāṇini 2.4.20 and 6.3.109; *BDh* 1.2.9; *VaDh* 1.8–12. For a discussion of these passages, see Olivelle 2000, 10.

between *brahma* and *kṣatra* was being reestablished.[94] This was the time, as Hiltebeitel (2001) and Fitzgerald (2004) have shown, that saw the creation of the two epics, a new genre of literature in India with a universal and supra-*śākhā* appeal.

One *Dharmasūtra* that was conceived as a *śāstra* with a universal application and unattached to a *śākhā* was the *Gautama Dharmasūtra*. Unattached as it was to a larger Kalpasūtra, Gautama's *sūtra* may have been conceived as a true *śāstra* in the manner of Pāṇini's grammar, another *śāstra* that was not confined to a particular *śākhā*. As I have argued elsewhere (Olivelle, 2000), Gautama is not the oldest extant *Dharmasūtra*. It shows clear signs of a maturing tradition, especially in its handling of legal procedure. I have also shown (Olivelle, forthcoming-b) that Gautama exerted strong influence on Manu; the numerous textual parallels between the two texts could not be accidental.[95] It is clear that the *Gautama Dharmasūtra* was an important source in the composition of the *MDh*. I will present here just two examples of Manu's dependence on Gautama.

MDh 2.6	GDh 1.1–2
vedo 'khilo dharmamūlaṃ smṛtiśīle ca tadvidām I *MDh*	*vedo dharmamūlaṃ tadvidāṃ ca smṛtiśīle* I
The root of *dharma* is the entire Veda, and the tradition and practice of those who know the Veda.	The root of *dharma* is the Veda, and the tradition and practice of those who know the Veda.

The dependence of Manu on Gautama here is evident; the addition of *(a)khilo* in *pāda-a* and the change in word order in *pāda-b* convert the prose into a *śloka*. What is less clear, however, is whether the *sūtra* of Gautama itself is a prose rendering of a verse original. No other *dharma* text has a formulation quite like this.

One of the most significant parallels occurs in the section on impurity caused by the birth of a child. The vulgate version of the *MDh* 5.61–2 contains two verses, and they are supported by most manuscripts:

> *yathedaṃ śāvam āśaucaṃ sapiṇḍeṣu vidhīyate* I
> ***janane 'py evam eva syān*** *nipuṇāṃ śuddhim icchatām* II 61 II
> *sarveṣāṃ śāvam āśaucaṃ* ***mātāpitros tu sūtakam*** I
> ***sūtakaṃ mātur eva syād upaspṛśya pitā śuciḥ*** II 62 II
>
> As this period of death-impurity is prescribed for those who belong to the same ancestry, so the same holds true at a birth for those who desire perfect purity. Death-impurity affects all, but birth-impurity affects only the mother and the father. The mother alone is subject to the period of birth-impurity; the father becomes pure by bathing.

94. Gautama is explicit: "The Brahma united with the Kṣatra upholds the gods, ancestors, and human beings" (*brahma kṣatreṇa pṛktaṃ devapitṛmanuṣyān dhārayati*).

95. See, for example: *GDh* 1.28 =*MDh* 5.143; *GDh* 2.11 = *MDh* 2.101; *GDh* 2.46 = *MDh* 2.73; *GDh* 10.36–7 = *MDh* 8.30; *GDh* 12.15–7 = *MDh* 8.337–8; *GDh* 12.30, 34–5 = *MDh* 8.153; *GDh* 12.37 = *MDh* 8.147–8; *GDh* 14.22 = *MDh* 5.81; *GDh* 15.16 = 3.150; *GDh* 15.18 = *MDh* 3.158; *GDh* 28.1–3 = *MDh* 9.104–5. See also the use of the term *uddhāra* for both the preemptive share of the oldest brother in partitioning ancestral property and the king's preemptive share when dividing war booty: *MDh* 7.97 and *GDh* 10.21.

In the critical edition, the *pādas* given in bold are retained and the rest is omitted, resulting in a single verse:

> *janane 'py evam eva syān mātāpitros tu sūtakam* |
> *sūtakaṃ mātur eva syād upaspṛśya pitā śuciḥ* ||
>
> The same holds true at a birth. The birth-impurity, however, affects only the mother and the father. The mother alone is subject to the period of birth-impurity; the father becomes pure by bathing.

The first half-verse of 61 was probably introduced by a later editor into the text of Manu. The likely reason for its introduction was the intervention of verse 60, which defines *sapiṇḍa*, between verses 59 and 61, thus breaking the natural continuity between the latter two. The significant *pādas* a-b of verse 59 define the period of impurity at the death of a relative: *daśāhaṃ śāvam āśaucaṃ sapiṇḍeṣu vidhīyate* —"a ten-day period of death-impurity is prescribed for those who belong to the same ancestry." If this verse came immediately before, then *evam* in the phrase *janane 'py evam* of verse 61 becomes clear; the period of impurity after a birth is the *same* as that after a death. The intervention of verse 60 prompted a later editor to insert *pādas* a-b of verse 61, making the connection between 61 and 59 explicit. A similar commentarial intrusion occurs in the parallel passage of the *Vasiṣṭha Dharmasūtra* (4.16–22) between *sūtra* 16 (which is identical to Manu 5.59 *pādas* a-b) and *sūtra* 20 (which is identical to Manu 61 *pādas* c-d). But in Vasiṣṭha, because the commentarial portion is in prose, the connection between the verses 16 and 20 remains transparent.

Both Manu and Vasiṣṭha, however, are dependent on Gautama 14.14–6. This section of Gautama on impurity begins with the determination of the time of impurity following a death (4.1–12). The section begins: *śāvam āśaucaṃ daśarātram anṛtvigdīkṣitabrahmacāriṇāṃ sapiṇḍānām*—"there is a ten-night period of death-impurity for those belonging to the same ancestry, except an officiating priest, one consecrated for a sacrifice, and a vedic student"—a provision that parallels Manu 5.59 and Vasiṣṭha 4.16. This section in Gautama concludes (4.13) with a brief definition of *sapiṇḍa*. Then Gautama (14.14–6) deals with impurity resulting from the birth of a child, two causes of impurity generally treated together in the *śāstras*:

janane 'py evam |	The same holds true at a birth.
mātāpitros tat |	It affects the father and the mother.
mātur vā |	Or just the mother.

It is evident that Gautama is giving here three opinions regarding impurity resulting from childbirth. The first treats it exactly the same as impurity resulting from a death. The second restricts it to the parents of the newborn child. The third restricts it even further to just the mother. That these were opposing views is made clear in the parallel version of Vasiṣṭha (4.20–2), which adds reasons for the three opinions (given below in italics):

> janane 'py evam eva syān *nipuṇāṃ śuddhim icchatām* |
> mātāpitror vā *bījanimittatvāt* |
> mātur ity eke — [after which a verse is cited in support of this view]

> The same holds true at a birth for those who desire perfect purity.
> Or it affects the father and the mother, because [the birth] is caused by the seed.
> Or just the mother, according to some.

The same three opinions are found in Manu 5.61–2, but they are difficult to discern because of the expansion of an original single verse into two. When we look at the single verse of the critical edition, we see the same three opinions clearly stated:

> *janane 'py evaṃ eva syān*
> *mātāpitros tu sūtakam* ǀ
> *sūtakaṃ mātur eva syād upaspṛśya pitā śuciḥ* ǁ

Stripped of their commentarial accretions, the textual dependence of both Manu and Vasiṣṭha on Gautama becomes clear.

The inquiry into the possible connections between the *MDh* and the *Dharma-sūtras* has a long history. It was Max Müller, in a letter to one Mr. Morley on July 29, 1849, who suggested for the first time that the *MDh* may have been a recast in verse of an ancient prose *Mānava Dharmasūtra*. The hypothesis received strong support from Georg Bühler (1879–82, 1886), the renowned translator of the four *Dharmasūtras* and of the *MDh* in the influential series *Sacred Books of the East*. Even though there was a Mānava ritual tradition and we have a *Śrauta-* and a *Gṛhya-sūtra* of the Mānavas, there is no evidence that a *Mānava Dharmasūtra* ever existed. After strong opposition from Jayaswal (1930) and especially from Kane (1962–75, I: 143–49, 317)), the hypothesis of an early *Mānava Dharmasūtra* has been largely abandoned by scholars (Lingat 1973, 89). Whether the author of the *MDh* belonged to the Mānava tradition, however, is unclear; there does not appear to be any direct link between the *MDh* and the ritual *sūtras* of that tradition. That there was a connection between the *MDh* and the Maitrāyaṇa *śākhā*, to which the Mānava tradition belongs, appears more likely and has been recently argued by Jamison (2000). The *MDh*, as I have attempted to show, was an original work of a gifted author; it was neither a recast nor a text that evolved through numerous and progressive accretions. However, it is also clear that Manu used the material found in the *Dharmasūtra* tradition, especially the text of Gautama, in composing his text.

II.2 The *artha* Tradition

Unlike the *Dharmasūtras*, the *MDh* devotes a proportionately larger segment to matters relating to statecraft (*rājadharma*), law, and legal procedure (*vyavahāra*), topics generally viewed as falling within the purview of *Arthaśāstra*. The *Āpastamba Dharmasūtra*, for example, devotes 83 (6%) of its 1364 *sūtras* to statecraft and law, and the *Gautama Dharmasūtra* 115 (11.8%) of its 973 *sūtras*.[96] The *MDh*, on the other hand, allots 971 (36%) of its 2680 verses to statecraft and law,

96. The *Dharmasūtras* deal with sons and inheritance separately, whereas the *MDh* includes this topic within its section on legal procedure. If we include these sections, still Āpastamba's section rises to only 115 *sūtras* (8.4%) and Gautama's to 162 (17.7%).

only slightly smaller than the section devoted to the Brahmin, which consists of 1034 verses (38.6%). The difference shrinks even further when we account for the fact that much of what is discussed in the section on the Brahmin (chapters 2–6) applies equally to other twice-born individuals. The *MDh* thus represented a watershed in the development of the expert tradition of *dharma*, as it co-opted material that belonged to the expert tradition of *artha*.

The tradition of *artha*, then, is a second textual source in the composition of the *MDh*. Although only one treatise of the *artha* tradition has survived, the one ascribed to Kauṭalya, it refers to opinions of several other schools, including one referred to as Mānava. What, if any, connection there was between the *artha* school of the Mānavas and the author of the *MDh* is impossible to determine.[97] What is clear, however, is the connection between some verses of the *MDh* and the extant *Arthaśāstra*.[98] Given the problems inherent in the dating of these two texts, it is not possible to assert with high degree of confidence who is borrowing from whom. I do agree with Kangle, however, that it is most likely that at least sections of the *Arthaśāstra* are older than Manu and are the source for some of the passages and vocabulary I will discuss below.[99] The vocabulary analysis does not support Jolly's (1923) and Fezas's (1996) contention that the *AŚ* is contemporaneous with the late *smṛti* texts of Yājñavalkya and Nārada.[100]

We find a close parallel, both textual and with regard to vocabulary, between *MDh* 8.52–7 and *Arthaśāstra* 3.1.19, especially in the use of the term *deśa* for documentary evidence (italicized in the translation):

Manu

apahnave 'dhamarṇasya dehīty uktasya saṃsadi ।
abhiyoktā diśed deśaṃ karaṇaṃ vānyad uddiśet ॥ 52 ॥
adeśaṃ yaś ca diśati nirdiśyāpahnute ca yaḥ ।
yaś cādharottarān arthān vigītān nāvabudhyate ॥ 53 ॥
apadiśyāpadeśyaṃ ca punar yas tv apadhāvati ।
samyak praṇihitaṃ cārthaṃ pṛṣṭaḥ san nābhinandati ॥ 54 ॥
asaṃbhāṣye sākṣibhiś ca deśe saṃbhāṣate mithaḥ ।
nirucyamānaṃ praśnaṃ ca necched yaś cāpi niṣpatet ॥ 55 ॥
brūhīty uktaś ca na brūyād uktaṃ ca na vibhāvayet ।
na ca pūrvāparaṃ vidyāt tasmād arthāt sa hīyate ॥ 56 ॥
jñātāraḥ santi mety uktvā diśety ukto diśen na yaḥ ।
dharmasthaḥ kāraṇair etair hīnaṃ tam api nirdiśet ॥ 57 ॥

97. Jayaswal (193, 23) thinks that there was no connection, because opinions contrary to those ascribed to the Mānavas in the *Arthaśāstra* and the *MBh* are recorded in the *MDh*.

98. For discussions of the relationship between the two texts, see Sternbach 1959, 1963; Derrett 1973, 11; 1976–78, I: 120–39.

99. For the dating of the *AŚ*, see Trautmann 1971, 185-86; Kangle 1964, and 1963–65, III: 80–83. See also my earlier comments (I.2) about the absence of reference to gold coins in the AŚ, making it likely that it is earlier than the MDh.

100. For example, the *AŚ* does not use the term *divya* for ordeal or *lekhya* for a legal document, terms common in the *YDh* and *NSm*.

52 When the debtor, told in court to pay up, denies the charge, the plaintiff should produce a *document* or offer some other evidence. 53 When the plaintiff produces something that is not *documentary evidence* [or a false *document*]; produces and then disavows it; does not realize that his earlier points contradict the ones he makes subsequently; 54 states his case and then backs away from it; does not acknowledge under questioning a point that has been clearly established; 55 secretly discusses with witnesses a *document* which is prohibited from being discussed; objects to a question clearly articulated; retreats; 56 does not speak when he is ordered "Speak!"; does not prove what he asserts; and does not understand what goes before and what after—such a plaintiff loses his suit. 57 When a plaintiff says "I have people who know," but when told "Produce them" does not produce them, the judge should declare him also the loser for these very reasons.

Arthaśāstra

(a) *nibaddhaṃ vādam utsṛjyānyaṃ vādaṃ saṃkrāmati,* (b) *pūrvoktaṃ paścimenārthena nābhisaṃdhatte,* (c) *paravākyam anabhigrāhyam abhigrāhyāvatiṣṭhate,* (d) *pratijñāya deśaṃ nirdiśetyukte na nirdiśati,* (e) *hīnadeśam adeśaṃ vā nirdiśati,* (f) *nirdiṣṭād deśād anyaṃ deśam upasthāpayati,* (g) *upasthite deśe 'rthavacanaṃ naivam ity apavyayate,* (h) *sākṣibhir avadhṛtaṃ necchati,* (i) *asaṃbhāṣye deśe sākṣibhir mithaḥ saṃbhāṣate,* (j) *iti paroktahetavaḥ* ‖ 3.1.19

(a) When someone casts aside the plaint as recorded and moves on to another plaint; (b) does not make a point made later accord with what was stated before; (c) after challenging an unchallengeable statement of the opponent, remains (stubborn); (d) promises to produce a *document,* but when told "Produce it," does not produce it; (e) produces a defective *document* or something that is not *documentary* evidence [or a false *document*]; (f) puts forward a *document* different from the *document* specified; (g) denies a significant statement in the *document* he has put forward, saying "It is not so"; (h) does not accept what has been ascertained through witnesses; (i) secretly discusses with witnesses a *document* which is prohibited from being discussed; (j) these are the reasons for loss of suit.

Both the passages contain the obscure and obsolete word *deśa*. As I have shown in the notes to the translation of *MDh* 5.53–5, this was probably an ancient term for documentary evidence presented in a court of law, a term that was later displaced by the more common *lekhya*. Manu's discussion is longer and includes items not noted by the *Arthaśāstra*; but the connection between the two passages is unmistakable. The closest parallels are Manu 52–3 and *AŚ* (d)-(f), Manu 54 (*pādas* c-d) and *AŚ* (g), and Manu 55 (*pādas* a-b) and *AŚ* (i). As Kangle (1964) has pointed out, it is only in this passage that Manu uses the term *dharmastha* for a judge; elsewhere, he consistently uses the term *prāḍvivāka*.

Kangle (1964) gives further examples of textual parallels. The definition of *sāhasa* (robbery) is nearly identical in the two, and it is obvious that Manu has borrowed this either from Kauṭalya or from another text of the *artha* tradition:

> *sāhasaṃ tv anvayavat prasabhaṃ karma yat kṛtam* ||
> *niranvayaṃ bhavet steyaṃ hṛtvāpavyayate ca yat* || *MDh* 8.332
>
> When an act is committed with force and in the presence of the victim, it is "violence"; when it is committed outside his presence, it is "theft," and so is an act that someone commits and then denies.

> *sāhasam anvayavat prasabhakarma niranvaye steyam apavyayane ca* || *AŚ* 3.17.1–2
>
> When an act is committed with force and in the presence (of the victim), it is "violence"; when it is committed outside his presence, it is "theft," and also when it is denied.

Another significant parallel in the vocabularies of the *MDh* and the *AŚ* is the term *pravāsayet*. Its normal meaning is to send someone into exile. As I have shown in the note to *MDh* 8.123, Manu frequently uses this term in its technical Arthaśāstric meaning of putting someone to death; the term may have been used first as an euphemism for executing ("getting rid of") a criminal, a kind of euphemism common in even modern military vocabulary.[101] There is also the unusual term *prakṛta* for an appointed official of the king, a term that is likely borrowed from the Arthaśāstric vocabulary.[102]

The most important influence of the *artha* tradition on the *MDh* is the incorporation of the "Grounds for Litigations" (*vyavahārapada*). Legal matters were dealt with in a disorganized manner in the *Dharmasūtras*. Hence, it is highly unlikely that the organizing of the material under 18 *vyavahārapadas* was accomplished within the *dharma* tradition. It is much more probable that this classification was achieved by the scholars of the *artha* tradition, law and legal procedure being a central focus of their labors. The author of the *MDh* probably borrowed this classificatory system, as well as the material presented within it, from the *artha* tradition. The classification of the *vyavahārapadas* in the *MDh* and the extant *Arthaśāstra*, however, are so different from each other that it is unlikely that the former borrowed from the latter. The first two *vyavahārapadas* in the *Arthaśāstra*, for example, deal with the rules governing the relationship between husband and wife and the partition of property, whereas in the *MDh* family law is treated last. The *Arthaśāstra*, moreover, has as the final category the "Miscellaneous" (*prakīrṇaka*), which is

101. See *MDh* 8.123, 332; 9.242, 289. For the *Arthaśāstra* references, see 1.18.21; 4.13.8, 20; 11.1.33, 47; 12.4.4. See also Kangle's comment on 4.13.8. Kangle correctly interprets this term to mean execution. Indeed, Medhātithi (on 8.284) calls this meaning an Arthaśāstric usage (*arthaśāstrayā*). Given the double meaning of the term, it is unclear which of the two is applicable in some places: see, for example, *MDh* 7.124; 10.96. See also 9.242d where both Bhāruci and Medhātithi gloss *pravāsana* with *vadha*.

102. See my note to the translation of *MDh* 8.11.

absent in the *MDh* but found in the later *Dharmaśāstras*, such as those of Yājñavalkya and Nārada.[103]

The *Dharmasūtras* deal with the relationship between husband and wife, the classification of sons, and the partition of property within their sections on marriage. The *MDh* is the first text to include these discussions within the section of judicial procedure and litigation, clearly indicating the influence of the *artha* tradition. This is, moreover, one reason why the *MDh* deals with matters relating to family and women in two places, once under marriage in chapter 5, and again under the 16th *vyavahārapada* in chapter 9.[104]

III. The Work of Redactors

After it leaves the hands of the author, every text assumes an independent life. This is especially true in the case of texts published before the advent of printing. These pre-modern texts continue their life as they are copied by hand, read, studied, interpreted, and commented on by succeeding generations of scribes, readers, and scholars. It is this after-life of a text that a critical edition uncovers through the collation of manuscripts and presents to the reader in its critical apparatus. This aspect of a critical edition is as important as its better known feature of attempting to reconstruct the text as composed by the author.[105]

Both these aspects—the original text and the after-life—laid out in the text and the critical apparatus of the edition presuppose that changes are introduced into the author's text by those responsible for its after-life. Some of these changes are inadvertent, such as scribal errors and misreadings; others are deliberate, such as the different but equally cogent and intelligible readings found in different recensions and the additional verses found in numerous manuscripts. These changes introduced into the text and detectable through the examination of the extant manuscripts and commentaries can be identified and moved to the critical apparatus, thus restoring the text. The manuscript and other evidence we possess, however, often do not cover the entire period from today to the time of the author. In the case of the *MDh*, we pick up the textual history midstream, at least several centuries after its composition.

Native scholars as far back as Bhāruci challenged the authenticity of individual verses. Bhāruci, for example, rejects the authenticity of 9.93, calling it a verse

103. See above p. 14 for a comparison of the *vyavahārapadas* in these four texts.

104. For other parallels between the *MDh* and *AŚ* see: *MDh* 7.99, 101 and *AŚ* 1.4.3 (see Scharfe 1993, 46–7); *MDh* 7.105 and *AŚ* 1.15.60; *MDh* 7.205 and *AŚ* 6.2.6–12; *MDh* 7.161 and *AŚ* 7.4.4–7; *MDh* 8.87–101 and *AŚ* 3.11.34–37; *MDh* 8.242 and *AŚ* 3.10.24; *MDh* 8.279 and *AŚ* 3.19.8; *MDh* 8.299–300 and *AŚ* 3.3.8–9; *MDh* 9.153 and *AŚ* 3.6.17; *MDh* 8.224 and *AŚ* 3.15.14; *MDh* 8.159 and *AŚ* 3.16.9; *MDh* 8.332 and *AŚ* 3.17.1–2; *MDh* 8.367 and *AŚ* 4.12.3; *MDh* 9.271 and *AŚ* 4.11.9; *MDh* 9.277 and *AŚ* 4.10.1; *MDh* 9.280 and *AŚ* 4.11.7; *MDh* 9.282 and *AŚ* 2.36.26–7; *MDh* 9.294–5 and *AŚ* 8.1.19; *MDh* 11.14 and *AŚ* 3.14.37; *MDh* 11.14 and *AŚ* 3.14.37.

105. For a discussion, see the Introduction to the Critical Edition in Part II of this book under "Constitution of the Text."

from another *smṛti*. Medhātithi also records this opinion: *kecid āhuḥ amānavo 'yaṃ ślokaḥ*. Clearly there were ongoing debates with regard to the authentic text of Manu. We also find that scribes or scholars introduced deliberate changes into the text. At 9.299, for example, the reading *ārabheta tataḥ kāryaṃ saṃcintya gurulāghavam* is deliberately changed in the manuscripts of the ST into *gurulāghavato jñātvā tataḥ kāryaṃ samācaret*.

If the later tradition of readers and copyists introduced changes, it is fair to assume that earlier generations did so too. Any such changes that were taken over by the extant manuscript tradition cannot be identified by the normal methods employed in the critical constitution of texts. These methods are thus called "lower criticism"; they are dependent on extant manuscripts, citations, commentaries, and the like. The text constituted by these methods can only be an approximation to the original text as written by the author.

I agree with Lariviere's (1989, xii) hypothesis that the *Dharmaśāstras* continued to expand with the addition of new materials "until a commentary on the collection was composed. A commentary would have served to fix the text, and the expansion of the text would have been more difficult after that." Because I consider the *MDh* to have a single author, I take these emendations as produced by redactors working on the original text. Such activities were made more difficult after the text was "fixed" by early commentators such as Bhāruci and Medhātithi, but they did not cease completely. Changes after that period, however, were limited to the addition of individual verses and minor changes in the wording of verses detectable through "lower criticism."

Methods of identifying early changes undetectable by manuscript evidence fall into the category of "higher criticism" and are not as sure-footed as methods employed in "lower criticism." In the former some amount of conjecture is inevitable. In Biblical studies higher criticism has been used profitably especially with regard to the Pentateuch, but there the criticism was used not to construct the original text of the author but to uncover the sources he used in constructing his text. It has, therefore, been called "source criticism."

Bühler's (1886, lxv-lxxiv) attempt to separate the ancient portions from later additions within the *MDh* was, likewise, an exercise in source criticism. His aim was to distinguish the passages going back to his hypothetical *Mānava Dharmasūtra* from those added by the editor of the versified version. His criteria were somewhat crude. He accepted sections that had parallels in other *Dharmasūtras* as part of the ancient *sūtra*, and took sections without such parallels to be the work of the editor.

My aim is different. Mine is not a source criticism but a criticism aimed at identifying possible additions and interpolations into the text composed by Manu between the time of its composition and the earliest manuscript and other evidence that we possess. The criterion I use is based on Manu's overall plan for and organization of his work, which I have outlined above in detail. We saw that Manu is careful to let his reader know that he has completed one subject and is moving on to another through "transitional verses." The structure of his work shows that Manu had a very methodical mind and a systematic work plan. It is highly unlikely, I think, that he would have introduced extraneous material right in the middle of his carefully crafted plan, thus ruining the work's organization. In the following examination of the entire text, I will follow Manu's organizational scheme and identify sections that fall outside that scheme.

Most, if not all, extraneous material is found at the interstices of his plan, at the junctures between two topics. Clearly, it was easier to introduce new material at these fault lines than within the discussion of a given topic. In the translation, I have identified these passages as "Excursus"; even if someone does not accept my contention that these are interpolations, they must at best be viewed as parenthetical statements. Even though I think that the chapter division is a later innovation, in the following discussion I will follow the chapter sequence for easy reference to the text.

Chapter One

Why would a treatise on *dharma* begin with the story of creation? Bühler (1886, lxvi) in fact remarks: "The whole first chapter must be considered as a later addition. No Dharma-sūtra begins with a description of its own origin, much less with an account of creation." Long before Bühler, the 9th-century commentator Medhātithi expressed a similar concern:

> Where did we start? And where have we ended? He [Manu] was asked the *dharmas* prescribed in the *śāstras,* and he indeed promised to explain them. To then describe the world in its unmanifest state is both irrelevant and serves no human purpose. This truly exemplifies the common saying: "Asked about the mango trees, he talked about the Kovidāra trees." With regard to this matter, there is neither an authoritative basis nor does it serve any purpose. Therefore, this entire chapter should not be studied.[106]

There is, however, a cogent defense of Manu's introductory statements found in the first chapter. I have already dealt with why Manu begins with the origin of the text, thereby investing it with supreme authority. Why he gives an account of creation is less obvious. I think the clue is found in the manner the first account of creation ends (*MDh* 1.31): "For the growth of these worlds, moreover, he produced from his mouth, arms, thighs, and feet, the Brahmin, the Kṣatriya, the Vaiśya, and the Śūdra," evoking the conclusion of the creation story in the Puruṣa Hymn (*Ṛgveda* 10.90). The seers questioned Manu not simply about *dharma* but about the *dharmas* of all social classes (1.2: *sarvavarṇānāṃ dharmān*). I think the creation account is intended to show how the four *varṇas* came into being; they are not contingent and temporary social phenomena but part of the very fabric of creation.

106. Medhātithi on *MDh* 1.5: *kva asthāḥ kva nipatitāḥ / śāstroktanipatitadharmān pṛṣṭas tān eva vaktavyatayā pratijñāya jagato 'vyākṛtāvasthāvarṇanam aprakṛtam apuruṣārthaṃ ca / so 'yaṃ satyo janapravādaḥ "āmrān pṛṣṭaḥ kovidārān ācaṣṭa" iti / na cāsmin vastuni pramāṇaṃ na ca prayojanam astīty ataḥ sarva evāyam adhyāyo nādhyetavyaḥ /*

The clarity of Manu's presentation is obscured at this point by three "excursus" containing a quite superfluous second account of creation (1.32–41), a classification of fauna and flora (1.42–50), and an account of cosmic cycles (1.51–57).[107] I believe these are interpolations introduced at the interstice between creation of the *varṇas* and the composition of the *śāstra* (1.58). In the second account of creation, for example, we have humans coming into being in verse 39, while the human race divided into the four classes already appear in verse 31!

If we eliminate the intervening 26 verses, we see an elegant transition from the creation account culminating in the production of the four *varṇas* to the composition of the treatise by the Creator and its transmission to Manu, culminating in Manu's instruction to Bhṛgu to transmit it to the sages thereby publishing it to the world:

> For the growth of these worlds, moreover, he produced from his mouth, arms, thighs, and feet, the Brahmin, the Kṣatriya, the Vaiśya, and the Śūdra. (1.31)
>
> After composing this treatise,[108] he himself imparted it first only to me according to rule; and I, in turn, taught it to Marīci and the other sages. Bhṛgu here will recite that treatise to you in its entirety, for this sage has learnt the whole of it completely from me. (1.58–9)

As the initial dialogue between the seers and Manu ends (1.4) with Manu's command "Listen!" (*śrūyatām*), so the entire preliminary narrative ends (1.60) with Bhṛgu's command "Listen!"

At this point we should have expected Bhṛgu to get on with his task and to expound the *dharmas* of the *varṇas*. That, however, is not the case. Here at this interstice between the introductory material and the body of the text, there are five "excursus" containing an account of time and cosmology (61–86), the occupations of the *varṇas* (87–91), and the excellence of Brahmins (92–101); a eulogy of Manu's treatise (102–10); and a table of contents (111–18). This material takes up the rest of chapter 1. Most scholars have taken the table of contents to be a later addition. I think this entire section represents redactorial interventions and is quite out of place here. Even though the origin of the *śāstra* and its transmission to Manu and Bhṛgu had already been stated, the eulogy of the treatise ascribes its composition not to the creator but to Manu himself (1.102). This section ends with the instruction of Bhṛgu (1.119): "Just as, upon my request, Manu formerly taught me this treatise, so you too must learn it from me today." This duplicates Bhṛgu's command "Listen!" and does not have the same force or elegance. I think the authentic voice of the author is

107. Hacker (1978) also has drawn attention to the discrepancy between the first and the second account. My argument does not exclude the possibility that some verses in the first account, especially 28–30 dealing with the repeated creation, are also interpolations, as argued by Hacker 1978. Another point worthy of note is that the Sāṃkhya terminology, dominant in the first account, is totally absent in the second account of creation.

108. The introduction of this treatise appears to be abrupt, but it was actually introduced at the very beginning 1.3: "For you alone, Master, know the true meaning of the duties contained in this entire ordinance (*vidhāna*) of the Self-existent One, an ordinance beyond the powers of thought or cognition."

heard in this imperious "Listen!" which is repeated in the two other answers to the seers' queries at 5.3 and 12.2 later in the text.

If we place the first verse of chapter 2 immediately after verse 60 of chapter 1, we see the smooth transition from the preliminary narrative to the body of the text that the author accomplished:

> *tatas tathā sa tenokto maharṣir manunā bhṛguḥ* |
> *tān abravīd ṛṣīn sarvān prītātmā śrūyatām iti* ||
> *vidvadbhiḥ sevitaḥ sadbhir nityam adveṣarāgibhiḥ* |
> *hṛdayenābhyanujñāto yo dharmas taṃ nibodhata* ||
>
> When Manu had spoken to him in this manner, the great sage Bhṛgu was delighted; he then said to all those seers: "Learn the Law always adhered to by people who are erudite, virtuous, and free from love and hate, the Law assented to by the heart."

Here we have two signature expressions of Manu: *śrūyatām* ("listen") concluding the first verse, and *nibodhata* ("learn") concluding the second. I think these two verses followed each other in the original composition of Manu, the first concluding the preamble and the second opening the main body of the work.[109]

Chapters Two to Seven

I find few if any identifiable interpolations in the central chapters of the book, 2–7. It may well be that the opportunity and/or the impulse to add new material were present at the beginning and in the concluding chapters.

Suspicion was already raised by Bühler (1886, lxvii) regarding the first eleven verses of chapter 2. I think his doubts about verses 6–11 are unfounded; he considers these to be repetitions. We would have to eliminate a lot of verses throughout the text if we were to eliminate all duplications and repetitions; an author surely has the right to repeat and reiterate. So, for example, Manu deals with women both in his treatment of marriage and household life (chapters 3–5) and under grounds for litigation (chapter 9). The only doubt I have focuses on verses 2–5 of chapter 2 that deal with desire. This section stands outside the flow of the discussion in the rest of the chapter. The kind of certainty I have with regard to the interpolations I have identified in the first chapter, however, is lacking here.

The second passage identified by Bühler is 2.88–100. This deals with the control of organs and includes an enumeration of the eleven organs. I agree with Bühler's (1886, lxvii) assessment that this passage "interrupts the continuity of the text very needlessly, and has nothing whatsoever to do with the matter treated of." Although such assessments often contain a heavy dose of subjectivity, in this particular case it is backed by textual evidence. The *Bhaviṣya Purāṇa* contains much of

109. Note further that, for example, the term *yuga* occurs in the sense of a world age only in these interpolated sections of the first chapter (1.68f) and in an interpolated section of chapter 9 (9.301–2). In the other places where the term occurs, it has the meaning of a new birth or a succeeding generation (10.42, 64), even though these sections are also not above suspicion.

the early chapter of the *MDh* (Laszlo 1971; Sternbach 1974). *Bhaviṣya* 1.2.5–27a-b reproduces the entire section on the student *MDh* 2.69–87. Immediately after this section at 1.2.27c-d, the *Bhaviṣya* gives the verse *MDh* 2.101, thus omitting the section 2.88–100, precisely the passage that we have suspected of being an interpolation (Sternbach 1974, 7). It is a possibility that the author of the *Bhaviṣya* had before him a copy of the *MDh* in which this section was missing.

Furthermore, the very wording of verses 2.87 and 2.101 indicates that they probably followed each other in the original text; the transition here is smooth, with verse 101 picking up the word *japa* from verse 87:

> *japyenaiva tu saṃsidhyed brāhmaṇo nātra saṃśayaḥ* |
> *kuryād anyan na vā kuryān maitro brāhmaṇa ucyate* || 2.87 ||
> *pūrvāṃ sandhyāṃ japaṃs tiṣṭhet sāvitrīm ārkadarśanāt* |
> *paścimāṃ tu samāsīta samyag ṛkṣavibhāvanāt* || 2.101 ||
>
> Only by soft recitation does a Brahmin achieve success; on this there is no doubt. Whether he does anything else or not, a Maitra, they say, is the true Brahmin.
>
> At the morning twilight, he should stand reciting softly the Sāvitrī verse until the sun comes into view; at the evening twilight, however, he should remain properly seated until the Big Dipper becomes clearly visible.

Medhātithi also, commenting on 2.88, appears to consider this section an appendix (*pariśiṣṭa*) to the section on twilight worship and lacking injunctive force (*arthavāda*).

On the whole, however, these central chapters are remarkably free of tampering or interpolations. One may quibble about this verse or that, but there is no sure way of determining the authenticity of individual verses.[110]

Chapter Eight

I think there are several identifiable interpolations within this chapter. I will list them first and offer explanations for my decisions: 20–2 (Śūdras as legal interpreters), 27–9 (property of minors and women), 30–40 (lost and stolen property), 386–420 (miscellanea).

Chapter 8 begins with the king entering the court to adjudicate a law suit. This is in keeping with Manu's penchant for placing his discourse in concrete situations, as, for example, discussing the king's duties by following him through a regular day from getting up in the morning to going to bed at night (7.145–226). So here Manu places his discussion of the system of justice within the context of the king coming into the court. After enumerating the 18 grounds for litigation (*vyavahārapada*; 4–8), he opens his discussion on legal proceedings. In this section he deals with a) the

110. I also think that verses 3.171–5, which look very much like a commentary explaining several technical terms, are either parenthetical remarks or interpolations. The theme of individual alongside whom one should not eat, introduced in verses 169–70, is continued after the interruption in verse 176.

judges, who substitute for the king (9–11), b) the demands of Justice that the law be administered impartially (12–9), and c) the beginning of the trial proper with a brief summary of judicial conduct and reasoning (23–6, 41–6). This admirable structure is marred by three "excursus." The first (20–2) is a diatribe against a king employing a Śūdra to interpret the law, a topic having little to do with matters at hand, coming between sections (b) and (c). Likewise, section (c) on judicial conduct and reasoning is cut in two by the intervention of some totally extraneous material having to do with property: the property of minors and women (27–9) and stolen and lost property (30–40). These matters have little to do with litigation or court proceedings. Indeed, once we remove these two "excursus" the section on judicial conduct reads smoothly: the judge should infer the truthfulness of litigants and witnesses by their external demeanor (25–6), find out the special laws of the region, caste, and family of the litigants (41–2), never initiate a law suit *suo moto* or try to suppress an action brought before him (43), apply correct judicial reasoning (44–5), and stick to the norms recognized by the cultured elite but only if they are not in conflict with those of particular regions, castes, and families (46). I think it is most probable that the three sections I have identified—verses 20–2, 27–9, and 30–40—are the work of later redactors.

The rest of the chapter moves smoothly and there are no obvious interpolations that interfere with the flow of the text. The next interpolation comes right at the end of the chapter after the section on sexual crimes against women. This "excursus" contains a motley group of topics including the control of trade, ferries and tolls, and the occupations of the *varṇas*, topics that have nothing to do with the administration of justice or law suits and belongs to chapter 7 that deals with state administration. This section is so out of place and so obviously the work of redactors that it is unnecessary to argue the point at length. It is also instructive that this long section of 35 verses comes at the end of the chapter, indicating that the addition was made after the *MDh* was subjected to the chapter division.

Chapter Nine

This chapter addresses the last three grounds for litigation: marital law, inheritance, and gambling. The sections on marital law and inheritance are remarkably free of obvious redactoral interventions. As I have already noted, the section on gambling and betting does not regulate this practice but rather seeks to abolish it. For Manu gambling and betting are a social curse and the source of many social ills. Although, following tradition, Manu lists it under grounds for litigation, in his eyes it is properly a police function. This naturally leads to the final topic under the duties of a king, namely the eradication of thorns, that is, the elimination of social parasites. Unlike law suits, which are brought before the king by private litigants, the eradication of thorns is to be initiated by the king himself and his officials.

Immediately after the section on gambling (221–8), we should have expected some concluding statement wrapping up Manu's discussion of the 18 grounds for litigation. And we find precisely such a statement in verse 250:

udito 'yaṃ vistaraśo mitho vivadamānayoḥ |

aṣṭādaśasu mārgeṣu vyavahārasya nirṇayaḥ ||

I have described above in great detail how lawsuits brought by litigants and falling within the eighteen avenues of litigation are to be decided.

After this Manu turns his attention back to the king and his duties with the statement (251):

evaṃ dharmyāṇi kāryāṇi kurvan samyaṅ mahīpatiḥ |
deśān alabdhāṃl lipseta labdhāṃś ca paripālayet ||

Carrying out properly in this manner his duties flowing from the Law, the king should both seek to acquire territories not yet acquired and protect well those that have been acquired.

after which he proceeds with the subject of the eradication of thorns (252):

samyaṅ niviṣṭadeśas tu kṛtadurgaś ca śāstrataḥ |
kaṇṭakoddharaṇe nityam ātiṣṭhed yatnam uttamam ||

After properly settling the country and building a fort according to textual norms, he should direct his maximum effort constantly at the eradication of thorns.

This admirable and methodical discussion is marred and interrupted by two section that have little to do with the subject and that have all the marks of redactorial activity.

The first comes between the conclusion of the section on gambling (228) and the closing statement on judicial procedure (250). This section (229–49) of 21 verses contains various materials dealing with punishments and grievous sins, topics that are dealt with elsewhere in the book. The natural flow of Manu's discourse is restored when we eliminate this section.

The next "excursus" (294–311) deals with various subjects including the constituents of a kingdom and the activities of the king, topics belonging to chapter 7. This interpolation is inserted between the section on the eradication of thorns (252–93) and the statement that closes this section (312). This statement finds its natural place immediately after verse 293; the intervening verses makes the closing statement out of place.

The final "excursus" (313–23) instructs the king never to offend a Brahmin and comes between the closing statement on the eradication of thorns (312) and the concluding statement that brings the entire section on the king to a close (324–5). Again this interpolated section stands out like a sore thumb next to the finely flowing narrative. See how the flow is restored once this section is eliminated:

In this and other ways should the king, always alert and tireless, suppress thieves within his own realm and even in others. (312)

Conducting himself in this manner and always devoted to the Laws pertaining to kings, the king should direct all his servants to work for the good of his people. (324)

I have described above in its entirety the eternal rules of action for the king. What follows, one should understand, are the rules of action of the Vaiśya and the Śūdra in their proper order. (325)

Chapter Ten

Chapter 9 concludes with the transitional verse that introduces the section on *āpaddharma* (the law in times of adversity):

> *eṣo 'nāpadi varṇānām uktaḥ karmavidhiḥ śubhaḥ* ।
> *āpady api hi yas teṣāṃ kramaśas tan nibodhata* ॥
>
> I have described above the splendid rules of action for the social classes outside times of adversity. Listen now to the rules for them in the proper order for times of adversity.

Chapter 10, however, begins with a long discourse on mixed *varṇas* (1–73) that appears to have little to do with how one must act in a time of adversity.

At first sight, this section also appears to have resulted from the work of later redactors who were unable to understand how Manu could have omitted a discussion on mixed classes.[111] Nevertheless, I think this section is part of the original treatise. For Manu, I think, a time of adversity was not just a temporary emergency but also a permanent state of affairs, given the decadent state of contemporary society. This enduring period of adversity is signaled by the intermixture of the *varṇas* giving rise to several intermediate and lower castes (*jāti*). This was probably the reason why Manu deals with the mixture of *varṇas* at the start of his discussion of *āpaddharma*.

Other reasons also support this conclusion. The initial request (1.2) of the seers that prompted the narration of the text included the *dharmas* of not just the four *varṇas* but also of those that are in between:[112]

> *bhagavan sarvavarṇānāṃ yathāvad anupūrvaśaḥ* ।
> *antaraprabhavānāṃ ca dharmān no vaktum arhasi* ॥
>
> Please, Lord, tell us precisely and in the proper order the Laws of all the social classes, as well as of those born in between.

It would be unlikely that a methodical writer like Manu, having introduced this issue at the very beginning, would fail to address it in the body of his text. There is no other place in the text that deals with mixed *varṇas*.

Furthermore, the *Gautama Dharmasūtra*, which was one of the sources Manu used (see II.1), has a similar section on mixed *varṇas* (4.16–28). Likewise, the *Arthaśāstra* (3.7.20–37) treats this topic in the course of its discussion of sons. With these examples in his own sources, it is unlikely that Manu would have neglected to treat this topic.

There are, however, not one but three discourses on mixed classes, and they are not always in agreement. Some suspicion, therefore, may be directed at the second and third re-tellings of the origin of the mixed classes.[113]

111. Sharma (1990, 225), indeed, considers the entire chapter 10 to be a later interpolation carried out about the 5th century CE. This is pure speculation, and there is no evidence internal or external for such a conclusion.

112. See also MDh 2.18, which also speak of *antarāla*, those born between the four regular *varṇas*.

113. Also to be noted is that the term *bāhya* with reference to excluded groups or out-

The rest of the chapter flows smoothly, and I see no section that raises suspicions of redactory intervention.

Chapter Eleven

Chapter 10 concludes with the transitional verse that introduces the new topic of penance (*MDh* 10.131):

> *eṣa dharmavidhiḥ kṛtsnaś cāturvarṇyasya kīrtitaḥ* |
> *ataḥ paraṃ pravakṣyāmi prāyaścittavidhiṃ śubham* ||
> I have described above the entire set of rules pertaining to the Law of the four classes. Next, I will explain the splendid rules pertaining to penance.

One would have expected Manu to open the topic of penance immediately, that is, at the beginning of chapter 11. That, however, is not the case. We have to wait until verse 44 for the introduction of penance. Bhāruci, the earliest commentator on Manu, also saw this as a problem. Bhāruci begins his commentary on chapter 11 with the objection that after promising to deal with penance we should have expected Manu to begin this chapter with verse 44.

When he finally gets to penance, Manu is as usual lucid and methodical. He begins with a clear and succinct introductory verse (44):

> *akurvan vihitaṃ karma ninditaṃ ca samācaran* |
> *prasajaṃś cendriyārtheṣu prāyaścittīyate naraḥ* ||
> When a man fails to carry out prescribed acts, performs disapproved acts, and is attached to the sensory objects, he is subject to a penance.

Then he discusses the significant issue of whether penance does any good. Can a person erase sins through penance? He devotes the next eight verses to this discussion, and concludes in the affirmative (54): "Therefore, one should always do penances to purify oneself; for individuals whose sins have not been expiated are born with detestable characteristics."[114] After this Manu proceeds to a methodical treatment of sins and their respective penances (see I.1).

Before we come to this lucid presentation of penance, however, there is a long (43 verses) section dealing with a gamut of topics unrelated either to penance or to each other. First is a section on occasions for giving and begging (1–26) followed by verses dealing with times of adversity (27–30), the power of Brahmins (31–5), and sacrifices (36–43). I am convinced that this entire section added at the beginning of the chapter represents not the original work of Manu but the supervening activities of redactors.

castes is found only in these later sections dealing with mixed classes: 10.28, 29, 30, 31, 39, 62. This term is unique to the *MDh*, except for what appears to be a citation of *MDh* 10.62 in *ViDh* 16.18.

114. In this case also, Manu is probably following the example set by Gautama (19.3–10), who introduces his discussion with the explicit statement: "With regard to this [i.e., penance] people raise the question: Should (a sinner) perform a penance or not" (*tatra prāyaścittaṃ kuryān na kuryād iti mīmāṃsante*).

The discussion of sins and the appropriate penances for them takes up verses 55–126. Manu then turns from personally committed sins to association with outcaste sinners, within which he deals with both excommunication from caste and readmission to it (181–9). The entire section on penance concludes with the nice and pithy statement (190):

> *enasvibhir anirṇiktair nārthaṃ kiṃcit samācaret* |
> *kṛtanirṇejanāṃś caiva na jugupseta karhi cit* ||
> No one should transact any business with uncleansed sinners; and under no circumstances should anyone abhor those who have been cleansed.

At the interstice between the sections on penances for sins (73–126) and association with outcaste sinners (181–9), however, we have a long interruption that is attributable to redactorial activity. This "excursus" (127–79) deals with penances for a) injury to living beings, b) eating forbidden food, c) theft, and d) sexual offenses. As I have already noted (I.1), the reason or opportunity for this interpolation is probably to make up the four sins that Manu mentions in his transitional verse introducing the topic of association with sinners (180): "I have described above the expiation for all four kinds of sinners. Listen now to the following expiations for those who associate with outcastes." These four kinds of sinners, however, were already presented in the previous authentic segment of the text on the classification of sins. There follows a long excursus of 126 verses (191–247) containing miscellaneous expiations for a motley list of sins and infractions. Although it is not possible to dismiss this entire section as an interpolation, yet I think the entire discourse on penance would have come to a fine close if it ended with verse 190: "No one should transact any business with uncleansed sinners; and under no circumstances should anyone abhor those who have been cleansed." The suspicion that what follows is redactoral reworking is strengthened by the very first verse of the long excursus (191): "One must not live together with people who have killed children, women, or those who come to them for protection, or with people who are ingrates, even if they have been purified in accordance with the Law." This is obviously an attempt to modify the provisions of the previous verse.

Chapter Twelve

Chapter 12 poses unique problems because it is so very different from the rest of the work. It begins with the seers making one final request of Bhṛgu to teach them the law of *karma*. One is tempted to see this entire chapter as deriving from the work of redactors. There is, however, no clear evidence that it did not belong to the original work of Manu; we cannot detect the breaks in the line of discussion that we detected in other interpolated passages or the violation of the structure that Manu has laid out.

Broadly this discussion on *karma* falls into two section, the one dealing with the fruits of action (3–81) and the other dealing with actions leading to the supreme good (83–106). These two sections are divided by one of Manu's signature transitional verses (82). It is after these two central sections of the chapter that one begins to suspect redactorial intervention. At the conclusion of the section on actions leading to the supreme good there is what appears to be the usual transitional verse (107):

> *naiḥśreyasam idaṃ karma yathoditam aśeṣataḥ* |
> *mānavasyāsya śāstrasya rahasyam upadiśyate* ||
>
> This is the totality of activities leading to the supreme good as prescribed. The secret doctrine of this Treatise of Manu will now be taught.

There follows a section (108–15) on how to resolve matters relating to *dharma* that are not covered by Manu's treatise. The language of this verse is quite different from all the other transitional verses. The passive verb *upadiśyate* is not found elsewhere; Manu prefers the active *nibodhata* and *pravakṣyāmi*. The expression *yathoditam* in the first line is also absent in other transitional verses. The expression *mānavaśāstra* is also uncharacteristic. Although the issue of how to resolve matters not covered by the text is addressed at the conclusion of the *Dharmasūtras* as well,[115] nowhere are these rules called *rahasya*. My best guess is that the text of Manu concluded with the closing verse 116:

> *etad vo 'bhihitaṃ sarvaṃ niḥśreyasakaraṃ param* |
> *asmād apracyuto vipraḥ prāpnoti paramāṃ gatim* ||
>
> I have explained to you above all the best means of securing the supreme good. A Brahmin who does not deviate from them obtains the highest state.

The "excursus" on secret teaching contains material such as the legal assembly (*pariṣad*), however, that is found also in the *Dharmasūtras* and thus has some claim to authenticity. One possibility is that this section formed the concluding statement of Manu and that the introductory verse was put there by a not very competent redactor, especially because the word *rahasya* does not occur in the body of this section. Nevertheless, the concluding verse 116 appears out of place after this section, because it refers back to the major theme of this chapter, namely, the attainment of the highest good (*niḥśreyasa*), which was the topic covered by verses 83–106. If verse 116 came directly after 106 it would have provided a fitting and elegant conclusion to the entire book.

As it is, this verse is followed by another "excursus." It appears that a redactor wanted to bring back the voice of Bhṛgu, because this section begins with Bhṛgu reflecting on the origin of the text (117): "In this manner, the blessed god, desiring to do what is beneficial for the people, revealed to me in its entirety this highest secret of the Law." There follow several verses recommending the contemplation of the Self with a strong Advaita tinge. The final verse in the extant text is an eulogy of the text itself where the voice is not that of Bhṛgu but of a third person (126): "When a twice-born recites this Treatise of Manu proclaimed by Bhṛgu, he will always follow the proper conduct and obtain whatever state he desires." This entire section is in all likelihood a later addition to bring the text to a close. I for one think that Manu's original closure is much better; it is strong and pithy, without unnecessary emotion.

115. See *ĀpDh* 2.29.13–15; *GDh* 28.48–51.

In total, then, the sections I have identified as possible interpolations through the activities on one or more redactors contain 329 verses. Out of a total of 2680 verses in my critical edition, those verses amount to just 12% of the text.

IV. Nature and Purpose of the Treatise

The year was 1794. The renowned orientalist William Jones published his English translation of the *MDh* and made the *Dharmaśāstra* tradition of India known to the rest of the world for the first time. This translation was not spurred simply by scholarly interest; it had also a practical purpose. In 1772 Warren Hastings, the British Governor General, had proposed a plan for the administration of justice in which the Hindu law based on *Dharmaśāstra* was to play a key role. British judges needed access to the original legal texts of India to implement the British policy of "administering native law to the natives" (Rocher 1969). So was born what Lariviere (1989) has called a "well-intentioned misunderstanding."[116]

What is the relationship between the provisions of the *Dharmaśāstras*, such as the *MDh*, and real law administered by courts in India down the centuries? Lariviere (1997b, 98) presents three positions held by scholars since the time of Hastings: a) the *Dharmaśāstras* are concerned with real law, b) they are merely pious wishes with no political sanction, and c) they are purely panditic commentaries with no relation to custom. Beyond the administration of law, the issues also relate to the link between *Dharmaśāstra* and the social life in India through the centuries. Lariviere (1997b, 97) asks: "What is its relationship to 'law'? Does it represent the law of the land? What is its value for the history of Indian society? What does this literature tell us about how people actually lived?"

Lariviere (1997b, 98), contrary to accepted wisdom, has boldly articulated his position: "I believe that the *dharmaśāstra* literature represents a peculiarly Indian record of local social norms and traditional standards of behavior. It represents in very definite terms the law of the land. . . . What I mean is that the whole of the *dharma* corpus can be viewed as a record of custom."[117] I am in broad agreement with Lariviere, but with some caveats. The *Dharmaśāstra* represents an expert tradition and, therefore, presents not a "record" of custom but a jurisprudential, or in Indian terms, a śāstric *reflection* on custom. Custom is taken here to a second order of discourse.

The relation between *Dharmaśāstra* and real life—whether it is law, social norms, or morality—can best be analyzed, I think, by taking the self-presentation of *Dharmaśāstra* as a *śāstra* seriously and asking the broader question: What is the

116. Scholars have questioned the position accorded to Manu by early Indologists and the British administrators. Doniger (1991, lxi) asks: "Were the British right to privilege Manu? Did they do it to advance their own interests, or because they found that this text was really in use?" More recently Dirks (2001, 34) has taken an extreme, and for me an untenable, position about the position of the *MDh* and it British appropriation. As I have shown in this introduction, the treatise of Manu had attained the preminence and prestige that few texts in India did long before the arrival of the British.

117. This view has been strongly defended and extended further by Wezler 1999b.

connection between *śāstra* and practice? Pollock's (1989a, 1989b) fine studies on the nature and history of *śāstra* have done much to illuminate this uniquely Indian form of discourse. Pollock (1989a, 18) offers the following definition derived from native reflections on the term: "*śāstra* was thought of generally as a verbal codification of rules, whether of divine or human provenance, for the positive and negative regulation of particular cultural practices." Toward the end of this study Pollock identifies the question at the heart of the relation between *Dharmaśāstra* and real life (1989a, 25): "It is the task of the cultural historian to determine what precisely may be the relationship between the learned discourse identified (or generically identifiable) as *śāstra* and the actual cultural practices of traditional India."[118]

It is impossible to deal with this issue in detail within the limits of this introduction. Nevertheless, I think it is important at least to sketch the outlines of a solution in order to grapple with the nature and purpose of *Dharmaśāstra*. Pollock (1989a, 25) himself presents some thoughts on the possible relationship between *śāstra* and practice: "(1) *śāstra* could be viewed as offering a real blueprint for practice; (2) as merely describing, *ex post facto*, a cultural product and thereby explicating its components for the benefit of a cultivated public; (3) as providing, in the guise of normative injunctions, something like a standard of taste and judgment to critics, that is, as defining the 'classic'; (4) even as functioning in some cases to 'invent' a tradition; (5) as constituting, in the hegemonic manner of high cultures elsewhere, practices as 'sciences' for theoretical or actual control; (6) or—last in order but perhaps first in importance—as endowing a practice with status, legitimacy, and authority directly conferred by any 'Vedic' charter, something most *śāstras* aspire to become" (my numbering). Clearly, these are not mutually exclusive characteristics. Indeed, several of them may and often do coexist in the same *śāstra*.

The native reflections on *śāstra* come closest to #1 and some elements of #6. That is, *śāstra* is viewed as in some sense eternal and providing the pre-existing blueprint for a particular practice. This is clearly so for the pre-eminent *śāstra*, the Veda, and its relationship to the vedic ritual. Jayanta, in his *Nyāyamañjarī*,[119] extends this to all *śāstras*: "All these sciences have existed, like the Vedas, from the beginning of time; when people ascribe them to one or another author, they are merely acknowledging someone who has sought to give them concise or detailed expression." Clearly, the *MDh* presents itself as just such an eternal *śāstra*, even though its present shape was given by Manu and Bhṛgu. Vātsyāyana in his *Kāmasūtra* (1.3.1–10), likewise, affirms the priority of *śāstra* over practice (*prayoga*). There are people who perform a practice without knowing the corresponding *śāstra*, but that practice would not have existed without the norms provided by the *śāstra*. So, courtesans practice the art of love without studying the *Kāmasūtra*, handlers of horses and elephants do so without knowing the *śāstras*

118. Pollock answers some aspects of the connection between *śāstra* (theory) and *prayoga* (practice) in other articles: 1989b, 1990, especially 1985, where he discusses in greater detail the priority of theory over practice.

119. Cited and translated by Pollock 1989a, 23.

dealing with these animals, and Brahmins speak Sanskrit without necessarily knowing Pāṇini. Manu (10.56) himself insists that even Cāṇḍāla executioners, who could hardly expected to learn *śāstras*, should carry out there task *yathāśāstram*, in accordance with śāstric provisions. Yet, Vātsyāyana insists, these rule-governed activities would not have existed but for their respective *śāstras: prayogasya ca dūrastham api śāstram eva hetuḥ* "The *śāstra* alone, however removed it may be, is the cause of practice." He concludes the discussion with an example: *tathāsti rājeti dūrasthā api janapadā na maryādām ativartante tadvat etat* "As people in the provinces do not transgress the bounds, knowing, 'The king is there', so it is in this case."[120] As the absent king is the reason for people far away to observe the bounds of law and propriety, so the *śāstra*, though unlearned, is the reason why people engage in rule-bound activities.

At a philosophical level, one may argue whether rules come before practice or practice before rules. Does grammar come before language, or vice versa? The question, however, is not rules and practice but codified rules in *śāstras* and practice. From a historical point of view, it is evident that such codes are posterior to the practices from which the rules are derived, and this is reflected in #2 of Pollock's list and in Lariviere's view of *Dharmaśāstra* as codifying custom. This, however, is only one part of the question. It deals with the origin of *śāstra*.

The second, and for us the more important question, is how a *śāstra*, once it is produced, relates to ongoing practice. I take a *śāstra* to be the outcome of an expert tradition; it is both a repository of received knowledge and a tool of instruction. Many authors no doubt attempted to write *śāstras;* only the successful ones, those that the later tradition found worth preserving in the form of memorizing and copying, have survived. Lariviere (1997b, 98) attributes the disconnect between the provisions of *Dharmaśāstra* and lived reality to the obfuscation created "by the fact that the idiom of all the *dharma* literature is one of eternality and timelessness." This is no doubt true; but I think the disconnect not just in *Dharmaśāstra* but in all *śāstras* lies deeper in the very nature of a *śāstra*. All *śāstras* represent a metadiscourse; they deal with reality but always once removed. They are blueprints, but you cannot construct a building with them!

Let us take the Vedas, the pre-eminent *śāstra*. You cannot perform a vedic sacrifice properly even if you know them all by heart. Take the *Śrautasūtras*, the treatises that are supposed to fill this vacuum. They provide just a skeleton; a vedic priest knowing just the *Śrautasūtras* would be totally lost in the nitty-gritty of the ritual activities. Take grammar, the queen of the *śāstras*. Knowing Pāṇini backwards and forwards will not permit someone to speak or read Sanskrit. Knowing the *Carakasaṃhitā* or the *Suśrutasaṃhitā* will not make someone a good doctor. The native tradition itself admits this character of *śāstra* with its emphasis on a live teacher to impart śāstric knowledge and its tradition of commentaries that elucidated the *śāstras* and frequently updated and modified their content.

120. Doniger's translation "In the same way, even citizens far away from the king do not step across the moral bounds he sets" does not account for the "iti" or capture accurately Vātsyāyana's reasoning here. Doniger, *Kāma Sūtra* (Oxford: Oxford University Press, 2002), p. 14.

Śāstras exercised control over practice not directly but through the mediation of experts (*śiṣṭa*), who were instructed in the *śāstras* in their youth and who, as adults, continued to read, reflect, and debate the *śāstras* among themselves.[121] If we take the case of drama, playwrights and directors would not be able to engage in their craft merely by knowing Bharata's *Nāṭyaśāstra;* they would have been instructed in the specifics of their craft by their teachers. Yet, their professional life and work would bear the stamp of the great *śāstra*, which they learned from their teachers and from which they drew inspiration and guidance. Manu (7.54) insists that the king's ministers should be *śāstravidaḥ*, experts in *śāstra*. It is the *śāstra* that makes a *śiṣṭa*. But the *śāstra* provides only a skeleton; it is the *śiṣṭa*, the expert, who provides the living guidance in a variety of human activities.

Turning to *Dharmaśāstra*, the experts were the Brahmins knowledgeable in these treatises, Brahmins whom the *MDh* calls *dharmapāṭhaka* (12.111). Although it is possible that passages from the *Dharmaśāstras* may have been cited in courts of law, these texts did not have a function similar to civil and criminal codes of modern states within the administration of justice. The administration of justice is mediated by the expert judges, who are conversant both with the *śāstras* and with the laws and customs of the particular region, caste, guild, or family involved in the dispute. The *Dharmaśāstras* never pretend to present all the laws and norms that govern the behavior of people. Manu (8.41) clearly spells out the extra-śāstric knowledge required to judge lawsuits: "A king who knows the Law should examine the Laws of castes, regions, guilds, and families, and only then settle the Law specific to each." There certainly is more to law than what is given in the *śāstra*, and it was unwise of the British to equate *Dharmaśāstra* with Hindu law.

It is equally unwise to consider *Dharmaśāstras* as "purely panditic commentaries" with no relation to law or real life, just as it is silly to consider Pāṇini as having no relationship to spoken Sanskrit or the *Carakasaṃhitā* as having no connection to the practice of medicine or the *Nāṭyaśāstra* as having nothing to do with the production of plays. The relationship of *śāstra* to practice in all these areas is more nuanced than envisaged by either of these extremes.[122]

Turning to the *MDh*, it is clear that it seeks to present itself as an eternal document parallel to the Vedas and composed by the creator himself. Its "hegemonic" character is evident in its aim to present a blueprint for a properly ordered society under the sovereignty of the king and the guidance of Brahmins. Although it presents the "should" more often than the "is" and may occasionally

121. The etymologies of the two terms also support their connection: *śāstra* is derived from the verbal root √*śās* (to train, teach, educate) with the suffix *tra* giving the meaning of "an instrument of training," while *śiṣṭa* is the past participle, "a trained or educated" person. One can, thus, think of *śāstra* as the instrument for creating a *śiṣṭa*.

122. Maxwell (1989, 10) dwells on the disconnect between *śilpaśāstra* and actual specimens of iconography and architecture, citing D. D. Kosambi: "The traditional Sanskrit books on architecture and iconography are contradicted by the specimens actually found." Maxwell may be correct in his assessment that those who wrote the *śāstras* were not practitioners of the craft. This is certainly true in *śilpa*, and probably also in other *śāstras* such as medicine. This may parallel the modern distinction between the creative artists, whether in literature, music, or fine arts, and the critics.

engage in pious wishes and wishful thinking, the amount of detail it presents with regard to diverse areas of human activity—ritual, food, marriage, inheritance, adoption, judicial procedure, taxation, punishment, penance—shows that it was not divorced from reality. The long literary tradition of *Dharmaśāstra*, the longest such tradition in India spanning over two millennia, shows that the *śāstras* were used continuously in the education of young Brahmins and perhaps even princes. It was this training in the *Dharmaśāstra* that the Brahmins selected as judges, lawyers, and arbiters brought to their judicial reasoning, deliberation, and judgments.[123]

The purpose of a central document such as the *MDh* is multifaceted and hard to pin down. First, there are the aims of the author when he undertook the project. These are impossible to discern except when they are reflected in the composition itself (see I.4). Second, there are the purposes to which the text was employed by succeeding generations of scholars, readers, and politicians. These are bound to be varied depending on time, place, and the varying goals of the individuals and institutions concerned. As a *śāstra*, however, and the premier *Dharmaśāstra* in Indian history, we can discern some of the roles it may have played both in learned discourse and in everyday life. The *MDh* was clearly not a "how to" book; it was neither a *Handbook of Manners* nor a *Law Code*, although it contains aspects of both. Its connection with lived reality was not immediate but mediate. I have identified two significant aspects of this mediation. First, a central *śāstra* such as this would have been used in the instruction of budding scholars, principally young Brahmins; it must have been part of the standard curriculum for aspiring *dharmapāṭhakas* in Brahmanical colleges such as *ghaṭikāsthānas* in southern India.[124] Second, it was a point of reference for the ongoing scholarly conversations, debates, and literary production in the field of *Dharmaśāstra* (see V). Some of these debates and interpretations may indeed sound panditic pedantry. But they also had a serious and often practical purposes. After all, many of the medieval Nibandhas and commentaries were commissioned by kings and others were carried out under royal patronage.

V. Manu and the Later *Dharma* Tradition

The composition of new *Dharmaśāstras* appears to have flourished in the four or five centuries following the composition of the *MDh*, that is, approximately 300–600 CE. Most of these are now lost; we only have fragments of them cited in medieval commentaries and *Nibandhas*. Only three have survived in more or less complete form: those ascribed to Viṣṇu, Yājñavalkya, and Nārada. Two others, Bṛhaspati and Kātyāyana, have been reconstructed on the basis of medieval fragments by Rangaswami Aiyangar and P. V. Kane.

123. On the existence of professional lawyers who gave advice to litigants, see Jayaswal 1930, 288–92.

124. See C. Minakshi, *Administration and Social Life under the Pallavas* (Madras: University of Madras 1938), pp. 186–212; K. A. Nilakantha Sastri. *The Colas* (Madras: University of Madras 1955), pp. 629–33. Sastri shows that *Dharmaśāstra* was part of the curriculum in colleges such as Eṇṇāriyam and Tribhuvani.

V.1 Manu and the *Dharmaśāstras*

Manu was a pioneer, and he set the standard for the literary activities of his successors. All followed Manu in composing their works in verse. Viṣṇu is the only exception, but this text was a recast of an original *sūtra* composition; indeed, the entire first chapter, which is clearly the work of the redactor, is in verse. Both Viṣṇu and Yājñavalkya follow Manu in the introductory frame of their works. Like Manu, Viṣṇu begins with the story of creation. It is the Earth personified as a woman who requests the creator, Viṣṇu, to teach her *dharma* (*ViDh* 1.48): "Tell me, Eternal One, the *dharmas* of the social classes and orders of life" (*varṇānām āśramāṇāṃ ca dharmān vada sanātana*). Yājñavalkya's frame is brief. The sages approach Yājñavalkya in Mithilā and ask him to teach them *dharma* (*YDh* 1.1): "Tell us completely the Laws of the social classes, of the orders of life, and of others" (*varṇāśrametarāṇāṃ no brūhi dharmān aśeṣataḥ*). In all these we hear the echo of the early verses of the *MDh*. After Manu, the *śāstra* is no longer simply a scholarly production as in the *Dharmasūtras* but a teaching by a god or an exalted being.

The influence of Manu on the later literature, I think, runs deeper. I have already made reference to the tradition of several redactions (*saṃhitā*) of the original composition of Manu, that of Bhṛgu being only one. The third extant *Dharmaśāstra*, that of Nārada, is explicitly viewed by the tradition to be just such a redaction.[125] The text proper is preceded by an introduction in prose that claims to be part of the text itself, although rejected as a later addition in Lariviere's (1989) critical edition. Irrespective of its provenance, this introduction claims that the text is a segment of an abbreviation of Manu's original work carried out by Nārada. Clearly, the connection to Manu must have been an old one.

Yājñavalkya (1.4) places Manu at the head of his list of the authors of *Dharmaśāstras*, the first such list in existence. Yājñavalkya's dependence on the *MDh* has been considered in detail by Kane (1962–75, I: 430) and I agree fully with his conclusion:[126] "The correspondence of Yājñavalkya's words with the text of Manu is in most cases very close, so much so that one cannot help feeling that Yāj. had the Manusmṛti before him and purposely made an attempt to abridge the somewhat loose expressions of Manu." Indeed, the abridgment and the tighter organization of the material are the main features of Yājñavalkya. He has between 1003 and 1010 verses depending on the recension, as opposed to the 2680 in the *MDh*. We have clear examples of Yājñavalkya making a single pithy verse out of several prolix ones of Manu:[127]

> *kusūladhānyako vā syāt kumbhīdhānyaka eva vā* |
> *tryahaihiko vāpi bhaved aśvasthanika eva vā* ||
> *caturṇām api caiteṣāṃ dvijānāṃ gṛhamedhinām* |
> *jyāyān paraḥ paro jñeyo dharmato lokajittamaḥ* || *MDh* 4.7–8

125. See above, p. 19. For a discussion, see also Lingat 1973, 91, 100–1.

126. See also Jayaswal 1930, 59; Lingat 1973, 99.

127. For other parallels and condensations, see *YDh* 3.26 (= *MDh* 5.103–4); *YDh* 3.27–8 (= *MDh* 5.93–8). See also *MDh* 5.8–9 and *YDh* 1.170; *MDh* 5.24–5 and *YDh* 1.169.

> Let him be a man who stores grain sufficient to fill a granary; a man who stores grain sufficient to fill a jar; a man who has sufficient grain to last three days, or a man who keeps nothing for the next day. Among all these four types of twice-born householders, each should be recognized as superior to the ones preceding it and better at winning the heavenly world, according to the Law.

This rambling discussion is abridged by Yājñavalkya to a single condensed verse using the same technical terms:

> *kusūlakumbhīdhānyo vā tryāhiko 'śvastano 'pi vā* |
> *jīved vāpi śiloñchena śreyān eṣāṃ paraḥ paraḥ* || *YDh* 1.128
>
> Let him be a man who stores grain sufficient to fill a granary; a man who stores grain sufficient to fill a jar; a man who has sufficient grain to last three days, or a man who keeps nothing for the next day. Or let him live by gleaning. Each later mode is superior to the one preceding it.

Note the compression of the two verses of Manu 4.85–6 into a single condensed one in *YDh* 1.141:

> *na rājñaḥ pratigṛhṇīyād arājanyaprasūtitaḥ* |
> *sūnācakradhvajavatāṃ veśenaiva ca jīvatām* ||
> *daśa sūnāsahasrāṇi yo vāhayati saunikaḥ* |
> *tena tulyaḥ smṛto rājā ghoras tasya pratigrahaḥ* || *MDh* 4.84–85
>
> He must never accept gifts from a king who is not from a royal lineage; from people who operate abattoirs, oil-presses, or taverns; or from people who gain their living by keeping brothels. One oil-press equals ten abattoirs; one tavern equals ten oil-presses; one brothel equals ten taverns; and one king equals ten brothels.

> *pratigrahe sūnicakridhvajiveśyānarādhipāḥ* |
> *duṣṭā daśaguṇaṃ pūrvāt pūrvād ete yathākramam* || *YDh* 1.141
>
> With regarding to accepting gifts, each later one of the following is ten times worse than each preceding in due order: butcher, oil-presser, tavern keeper, prostitute, and king.

Yājñavalkya also introduced a new organization of the Dharmaśāstric material, dividing it into three broad chapters (*adhyāya*) dealing with proper conduct (*ācāra*), law (*vyavahāra*), and penance (*prāyaścitta*). To some degree this division was already accomplished by Manu; but the division is not as clear in the *MDh* and these topics are subsumed under the overall plan of the book that we examined. The threefold division introduced by Yājñavalkya became standard in later Dharmaśāstric literature. Yājñavalkya, then, represents both an abridgment of the *MDh* and several key advances in the developing genre of *Dharmaśāstra*.

As Jolly has already discussed in detail,[128] Bṛhaspati follows the *MDh* so

128. Jolly 1889, 271–5. See also Kane (1962-75) I: 328–30. Lingat (1973,104) observes that "Bṛhaspati follows the *Manu-smṛti* very closely. He considers it as the highest authority.

closely that it appears likely that he had a copy of the *MDh* before him while he composed his text. Several verses of Bṛhaspati are actually commentaries on passages of the *MDh*. Indeed, later tradition recorded in the *Skanda Purāṇa* (Jolly 1889, 274) takes Bṛhaspati as one of the redactors of Manu. Bṛhaspati pays the ultimate tribute to Manu and his authority:[129]

> *vedārthapratibaddhatvāt prāmāṇyaṃ manoḥ smṛtam* |
> *manvarthaviparītā tu yā smṛtiḥ sā na śasyate* ||
>
> Manu, however, is the authority, the tradition declares, because he is firmly anchored to the meaning of the Vedas. Any *smṛti* opposed to the tenor of Manu is not approved.

Kātyāyana is probably later than all the authors we have discussed. Kane (1962–75, I: 496)) thinks that Kātyāyana took Nārada and Bṛhaspati as his models. It is also clear that the *MDh* was also close at hand while he was writing. Kane (1962–75, I: 499) has pointed out numerous places where Kātyāyana refers to or cites the opinions of Manu. Like Bṛhaspati, Kātyāyana also appears to comment on verses of the *MDh*. In his discussion of women's property, for example, Kātyāyana (895–901) has seven verses explaining the technical terms for the six types of such property, technical terms that are given without explanation in *MDh* 9.194.

In some sense, we can extend what Lingat (1973, 104) says about Bṛhaspati to all the authors of *Dharmaśāstras* subsequent to Manu—they are all commentators on the *MDh*, which is their exemplar and model. They are certainly not commentators in the traditional sense; but their works can be viewed as commentaries in the sense that they are drawing inspiration from and responding to the work of Manu. It is certainly at the back of their minds and perhaps in front of their eyes as they tried to both emulate it and to surpass it. Bṛhaspati, however, was prescient in his observation that no other *smṛti* will ever measure up to, much less surpass, the *śāstra* of Manu. This is demonstrated by the influence of Manu on the medieval production of texts on *dharma*.

V.2 Manu and Medieval Literature

From around the 8th century CE, the literary activities of legal experts turned from the production of *śāstras* to commenting upon them. Some of the earliest such commentaries were on the *MDh*, Bhāruci's (assigned to the 7th century by Derrett) and Medhātithi's (9th century) being the oldest surviving ones. Altogether nine such commentaries have survived, the most on any single *Dharmaśāstra*.

Probably by the 10th or 11th century a new genre of literature enters the picture. These literary productions are called *Nibandha*. They differ from commentaries in that they are not tied to a single text and explore the topics of *dharma* in a systematic way. Although original compositions of authors whose names are recorded, the *Nibandhas* consist for the most part of citations from older *Dharma-*

He refers to it and quotes it often, and in many contexts he seems to be merely a commentator on Manu."

129. Aiyangar, Saṃskārakāṇḍa, 13; Jolly 1889, XXVII, 3.

śāstras. Some *Nibandhas* are voluminous, such as the *Kṛtyakalpataru* of Lakṣmīdhara and the *Caturvargacintāmaṇi* of Hemadri. Several of these texts were produced under royal patronage.

One gauge of the influence of the *MDh* on these medieval authors is the frequency of citations, especially when compared to other *Dharmaśāstras*. As a pilot project I compared the citations of the *MDh* in three well-known *Nibandhas*, four Kāṇḍas of Lakṣmīdhara's *Kṛtyakalpataru* (*KKT*)[130] Jīmūtavāhana's *Dāyabhaga* (*Db*) and Mādhava's *Pārāśaramādhavīya* (*Pm*)[131] with those of the other major *dharma* texts. I give below the statistics:

	KKT	*Db*	*Pm*
Manu	589	101	621
Āpastamba	141	4	86
Gautama	54	20	107
Baudhāyana	101	19	109
Vasiṣṭha	114	7	123
Yājñavalkya	324	41	461
Viṣṇu	207	45	145
Nārada	384	41	309
Bṛhaspati	342	64	316
Kātyāyana	447	47	333

Only in the *Vyavahārakāṇḍa* of the KKT and the Pm are the citations from the three texts dealing solely with *vyavahāra* greater than those from Manu. In the *KKT*: Nārada 342, Bṛhaspati 301, Kātyāyana 411, and Manu 288. In the *Pm*: Nārada 282, Bṛhaspati 243, Kātyāyana 262, and Manu 190.

The centrality of Manu to the *dharma* tradition, then, is not simply because it was given prominence by western Orientalitsts, as some have charged. Long before Sir William Jones entered the scene, Manu was the dominant voice on *dharma* for close to two millennia.

Manu has cast a long shadow over the literary activities of experts in the *dharma* tradition from the early centuries of the common era right up to medieval and modern times. It is fitting, then, that, by chance or by design, the *Mānavadharmaśāstra* was the first legal text to be translated into a foreign language.

130. The Kāṇḍas are: *Brahmacāri*, *Gṛhastha*, *Rājadharma*, and *Vyavahāra*.

131. Although strictly a commentary on the *Parāśarasmṛti*, for all intents and purposes this is clearly an independent work more akin to a *Nibandha*.

Note on the Translation

The Italians say "traduttori traditori"—translators are traitors—and with some justification. It is simply not possible to capture the full import of a statement when rendering it into another language, especially a language separated from the original by a cultural and temporal chasm. Such are Sanskrit and English. Yet, translation is not only possible; it is also a cultural imperative. One can become less of a traitor by understanding the cultural, historical, and linguistic world of the source text and the target language, and this I have attempted to do.

Mine is not a "literal" translation but, hopefully, an accurate one. Literal translations, often requiring frequent parenthetical intrusions, may serve the function of a crib for those who know the original Sanskrit; they offer little to the reader without access to the original. If this was simply a translation to accompany the edition, I could have presupposed a certain knowledge of Sanskrit in my readers. This translation, however, is intended for a general readership.

Several Sanskrit terms cause special difficulties in translation, some because of their wide semantic range and others because of difficulties in determining their precise meanings. The first and the most obvious is *dharma*. In general, I have translated the term as "Law." Although *dharma* means both more and less than law in contemporary usage, I think "Law" can accurately capture a wide slice of its semantic spectrum, especially if we take into account the use of "law" in such contexts as natural law, divine law, law of gravity, and Jewish law. In some contexts, however, "Law" does not make sense. In 8.12f, for example, *dharma* is better translated as "Justice"; in other contexts it means "merit" (see 4.238; 7.79; 8.83; 11.23; 12.19); in 11.129–30 *adharma* means sin (see 11.131 where *pāpa*, "sin," is used).

Guru is another difficult term. In a few cases it refers to the teacher (2.131, 231), but most frequently it does not. The general meaning is that of an elder, frequently the father, who deserves special respect. A good example of the multiple meanings of this term occurring in a single verse is 2.205. This term is context sensitive and I have translated it by a word that approximates its contextual meaning.

In most contexts *daṇḍa* means punishment. Frequently, however, especially when used with *dāpyaḥ* ("should be made to give"), it means a fine (e.g. 8.297). The two terms *jñāti* and *bandhu* are often used interchangeably for a relative. They are also used, however, with technical meanings. Then *jñāti* refers to paternal relatives and *bandhu* to maternal relatives. The term *indriya* may refer to the senses, but in some contexts this is misleading; in the context of controlling the senses, for example, the stomach and the sexual organs are also included. Within the context of caste, *sadṛśa* appears to indicate not simply someone who is similar to another but also one of the same caste, although it may also suggest a broader meaning of someone of the same station or status. The term *antya* indicates a person of a low caste. Most frequently such a person is below a Śūdra (see 8.68, 385); he is sometimes the same as an outcaste or Cāṇḍāla and sometimes distinguished from the latter (see 11.176). The Sanskrit uses many terms for a Brāhmaṇa and a Kṣatriya. Attempting to duplicate these would have created confusion to the reader. I have used "Brahmin" and "Kṣatriya" uniformly, except when *dvija* is used. This term in the *MDh* regularly refers to a Brahmin, but not always. In some contexts the meaning is ambivalent. I have, therefore, translated it as "twice-born." The term *vadha* normally means killing and is used for judicial execution. But frequently the term refers not to killing but to physical violence or corporal punishment.

Consistency in translation is often achieved at the expense of accuracy. I have not tried to be consistent beyond reason in translating a particular word. I have already referred to the various nuances of *dharma*. A good example of different meanings of the same word is *dasyu*. In many contexts the word means a bandit, a lowlife, or a low-born person (5.131; 7.143; 8.66). In other contexts, the term has a technical meaning, referring to a particular mixed caste (10.32, 45).

Departing from the usual practice, I have translated also the additional verses given in the critical apparatus to the edition so long as they are attested in a significant number of manuscripts; these are given in the endnotes and signaled by a plus (+) sign in the translation. I have also given the alternate translations of the text if we follow variant readings, again limiting myself to significant variants that both affect the meaning and are found in a large number of manuscripts. These, as well as explanatory notes, are signaled by an asterisk in the translation.

There are nine commentaries on Manu. They are described in the Introduction to the Critical Edition, pp. 381–83. These represent the native tradition's own attempts to understand and to interpret the text. They forms an integral part of the life of Manu within India and are significant even if we may disagree with them with regard to the original meaning of a particular verse. I have, therefore, cited their views extensively in the notes.

Finally, I have been asked by friends and colleagues, including one reviewer of this work for Oxford University Press, to spell out my philosophy and methodology of translation. This is something I find difficult to do, even though volumes have been written precisely on this topic.[1] One can present qualities—deep knowl-

---

[1] See, for example, the recent volume edited by Enrica Garzilli, *Translating, Translations, Translators from India to the West*. Harvard Oriental Series, Opera Minora, 1. Cambridge, Mass., 1996. Sheldon Pollock, writing in the same volume (p. 112), expresses the feelings of real translators when confronted by armchair philosophers of translation: "Years ago I had the privilege to attend a conference with George Steiner, whose landmark book, *After Babel*, had just been published. The entire panel of philosophers and theoreticians agreed that, yes, translation was really quite impossible. The fine translator from the Dutch,

edge of the two languages, of the literary genre of the source text, of its cultural and historical background, and so on—that a good translator should possess. But we know of many atrocious translations made by very competent scholars. Reading a good translation is like listening to a fine pianist playing a difficult piece of music. He or she makes it look easy. When the reader does not notice that the original is a difficult text; that the translator had to struggle many hours and sleepless nights with a single line; that sometimes he despaired of ever making sense of a passage—then the translation has achieved its purpose. To discuss the process of translation is as counterproductive as to discuss how sausage is made; neither is a pretty sight. In both cases the proof is in the final product. A good translation should stand alone as a good piece of literature within the language of the translation. This is goal we aspire to but never fully realized; the umbilical cord that binds the translation to the original text is difficult to sever.

---

the late James Holmes, was there, and he looked at me, and I at him, in the secure knowledge that we were going to go home and somehow do the impossible. . . . translation is as philosophically problematic, stylistically individual, and practically hard as life, and as we keep on living we keep on translating, with the inevitable singular imperfections that define being human."

TRANSLATION

Editor's Outline

CHAPTER ONE

CHAPTER TWO

CHAPTER THREE

CHAPTER FOUR

CHAPTER FIVE

Prologue 5.1–3
Forbidden Food 5.3–25
Eating Meat 5.27–56
Bodily Purification 5.58–109
  Death or Birth of a Person Belonging to the Same Ancestry 5.58–99
    Death in a Distant Region 5.74–77
    Overlapping Period of Impurity 5.79
    Death of Significant Others 5.80–82
    Periods of Impurity for Different Classes 5.85–87
    Impurity from Touch 5.85–87
    Libations for the Dead 5.88–91
    Funeral Path 5.92
    Instant Purification of Kings 5.93–99
  Death of a Person Belonging to a Different Ancestry 5.101–104
  Means of Purification 5.105–109
Purification of Articles 5.111–133
  Statutory Purity of Things 5.128–133
Purification of the Body 5.134–145
Law with Respect to Women 5.147–167
  Lack of Independence 5.147–150
  Duties towards Husband 5.151–166
  Funeral 5.167–168
Concluding Statement on the Householder 5.169

CHAPTER SIX

Forest Hermit 6.1–32
  Time and Procedure 6.2–4
  Mode of Life 6.5–28
    Great Sacrifices 6.7–11
    Food 6.12–21
    Austerities 6.22–24
    Homeless Ascetic 6.25–28
  Conclusion 6.29–32
Wandering Ascetic 6.33–85
  Qualification 6.35–37
  Initiation 6.38–41
  Mode of Life 6.42–49
  Begging and Food 6.50–60
  Yogic Meditation 6.61–85
    Conduct 6.66–69
    Breath Control 6.70–71

CHAPTER SEVEN

CHAPTER EIGHT

CHAPTER NINE

CHAPTER TEN

CHAPTER ELEVEN

CHAPTER TWELVE

CHAPTER ONE

PROLOGUE

+[1]Manu was seated, absorbed in contemplation, when the great seers came up to him, paid homage to him in the appropriate manner, and addressed him in these words: [2]"Please, Lord, tell us precisely and in the proper order* the Laws of all the social classes, as well as of those born in between;* [3]for you alone, Master, know the true meaning of the duties contained in this entire ordinance* of the Self-existent One, an ordinance beyond the powers of thought or cognition."*

[4]So questioned in the proper manner* by those noble ones, that Being of boundless might paid honor to all those great seers and replied: "Listen!"

CREATION

[5]"There was this world*—pitch-dark,* indiscernible, without distinguishing marks, unthinkable, incomprehensible, in a kind of deep sleep all over. [6]Then the Self-existent Lord appeared—the Unmanifest manifesting this world beginning with the elements,* projecting his might, and dispelling the darkness. [7]That One—who is beyond the range of senses; who cannot be grasped;* who is subtle, unmanifest, and eternal; who contains all beings; and who transcends thought—it is he who shone forth* on his own.

[8]"As he focused his thought with the desire of bringing forth diverse creatures from his own body, it was the waters* that he first brought forth; and into them he poured forth his semen. [9]That became a golden egg, as bright as the sun; and in it he himself took birth as Brahmā, the grandfather of all the worlds.

[10]"The waters are called "Nārā"; the waters, clearly, are the offspring of Nara. Because his first sojourn (*ayana*) was in them, tradition calls him "Nārāyaṇa."* [11]That cause which is unmanifest and eternal, which has the nature of both the existent and the non-existent—the Male produced from it is celebrated in the world as Brahmā.*

[12]"After residing in that egg for a full year,* that Lord on his own split the egg in two by brooding on his own body. [13]From those two halves, he formed the sky and the earth, and between them the mid-space, the eight directions, and the eternal place of the waters.*

[14]"From his body, morevoer, he drew out the mind having the nature of both the existent and the non-existent; and from the mind, the ego—producer of self-awareness and ruler—[15]as also the great self (12.14), all things composed of the three attributes (12.24), and gradually the five sensory organs that grasp the sense objects. [16]By merging the subtle parts of these six* possessing boundless might into particles of his

own body, moreover, he formed all beings. [17]Because the six parts of his physical frame become attached (*ā-śri*) to these beings, the wise call his physical frame "body" (*śarīra*). [18]The great elements enter it accompanied by their activities, as also the mind, the imperishable producer of all beings, accompanied by its subtle particles.

[19]"From the subtle particles of the physical frames of these seven males* of great might, this world comes into being, the perishable from the imperishable. [20]Of these, each succeeding element acquires the quality specific to each preceding. Thus, each element, tradition tells us, possesses the same number of qualities as the number of its position in the series.* [21]In the beginning through the words of the Veda alone, he fashioned for all of them specific names and activities, as also specific stations.*

[22]"The Lord brought forth the group of gods who are endowed with breath and whose nature is to act, the subtle group of Sādhyas, and the eternal sacrifice.* [23]From fire, wind, and sun, he squeezed out* the eternal triple Veda characterized by the Ṛg verses, the Yajus formulas, and the Sāman chants, for the purpose of carrying out the sacrifice. [24]Time, divisions of time, constellations, planets, rivers, oceans, mountains, flat and rough terrain, [25]austerity, speech, sexual pleasure, desire, and anger—he brought forth this creation in his wish to bring forth these creatures.*

[26]"To establish distinctions among activities, moreover, he distinguished the Right (*dharma*) from the Wrong (*adharma*) and afflicted these creatures with the pairs of opposites such as pleasure and pain. [27]Together with the perishable atomic particles of the five elements given in tradition, this whole world comes into being in an orderly sequence. [28]As they are brought forth again and again, each creature follows on its own the very activity assigned to it in the beginning by the Lord. [29]Violence or non-violence, gentleness or cruelty, righteousness (*dharma*) or unrighteousness (*adharma*), truthfulness or untruthfulness—whichever he assigned to each at the time of creation, it stuck automatically to that creature. [30]As at the change of seasons each season automatically adopts its own distinctive marks, so do embodied beings adopt their own distinctive acts.

[31]"For the growth of these worlds, moreover, he produced from his mouth, arms, thighs, and feet, the Brahmin, the Kṣatriya, the Vaiśya, and the Śūdra.

Excursus: Second Account of Creation

[32]"Dividing his body into two, he became a man with one half and a woman with the other. By that woman the Lord brought forth Virāj.* [33]By heating himself with ascetic toil, that man, Virāj, brought forth a being by himself—know, you best of the twice-born, that I am that being, the creator of this whole world.

[34]"Desiring to bring forth creatures, I heated myself with the most arduous ascetic toil and brought forth in the beginning the ten great seers, the lords of creatures: [35]Marīci, Atri, Aṅgiras, Pulastya, Pulaha, Kratu, Pracetas, Vasiṣṭha, Bhṛgu, and Nārada. [36]They, in turn, brought forth seven other Manus of immense energy (1.61–62); the gods and the classes of gods; and the great sages of boundless might; [37]Yakṣas, Rākṣasas, Piśācas, Gandharvas, Apsarases, Asuras, Nāgas, Sarpas, and Suparṇas; the different groups of ancestors (3.192–201); [38]lightnings, thunderbolts, clouds, rainbow streaks, rainbows, meteors, storms, comets, and the manifold heavenly lights; [39]pseudo-humans,* monkeys, fish, birds of various kind, farm animals, wild animals,

humans, predatory animals, and animals with incisors in both jaws (5.18 n.); [40]worms, insects, moths, lice, flies, bugs, all creatures that sting and bite, and immobile creatures of various kind.

[41]"In this manner through ascetic toil, those noble ones brought forth at my command this whole world, the mobile and the immobile, each creature in accordance with its activity.

Excursus: Classification of Fauna and Flora

[42]"I will now explain to you exactly which type of activity is ascribed here* to which type of creature, and also their relative order with respect to birth. [43]Those born from placentas are farm animals, wild animals, predatory animals, animals with incisors in both jaws (5.18 n.), Rākṣasas, Piśācas, and humans.

[44]"Those born from eggs are birds, snakes, crocodiles, fish, and turtles, as well as other similar land and aquatic animals.

[45]"Those born from warm moisture are creatures that sting and bite; lice, flies, and bugs; those born through heat; as well as other similar creatures.

[46]"Those born from sprouts are all flora propagated through seeds or cuttings. Those that bear copious flowers and fruits and die after their fruits mature are "plants" (*oṣadhi*); [47]those that bear fruits without flowers, tradition calls "forest lords" (*vanaspati*); and those that bear both flowers and fruits, tradition calls "trees" (*vṛkṣa*). [48]Various kinds of shrubs and thickets and different types of grasses, as also creepers and vines—all these also grow from either seeds or cuttings. [49]Wrapped in a manifold darkness caused by their past deeds (12.8–9), these come into being with inner awareness,* able to feel pleasure and pain. [50]In this dreadful transmigratory cycle of beings, a cycle that rolls on inexorably for ever, these are said to represent the lowest condition, and Brahmā the highest.

Excursus: Cosmic Cycles

[51]"After bringing forth in this manner this whole world and me, that One of inconceivable prowess once again disappeared into his own body, striking down time with time.* [52]When that god is awake, then this creation is astir; but when he is asleep in deep repose, then the whole world lies dormant. [53]When he is soundly asleep, embodied beings, whose nature is to act, withdraw from their respective activities, and their minds become languid. [54]When they dissolve together into that One of immense body, then he, whose body contains all beings, sleeps tranquil and at ease. [55]Plunging himself into darkness, he lingers there for a long time together with his sense organs and ceases to perform his own activities. Then he emerges from that bodily frame. [56]When, after becoming a minute particle, he enters, conjoined, the seminal form of mobile and immobile beings, then he discharges the bodily frame.*

[57]"In this manner, by waking and sleeping, that Imperishable One incessantly brings to life and tears down this whole world, both the mobile and the immobile.

Transmission of the Law

[58]"After composing this treatise,* he himself in the beginning imparted it according to rule to me alone; and I, in turn, to Marīci* and the other sages. [59]Bhṛgu here will relate

that treatise to you completely, for this sage has learnt the whole treatise in its entirety from me."

[60]When Manu had spoken to him in this manner, the great sage Bhṛgu was delighted. He then said to all those seers: "Listen!"

Excursus: Time and Cosmology

[61–62]There are six further Manus* in the lineage of this Manu, the son of the Self-existent One: Svārociṣa, Auttami, Tāmasa, Raivata, Cākṣuṣa of great energy, and the son of Vivasvat. Possessing great nobility and might, they each have brought forth their own progeny. [63]These seven Manus of immense energy, with the son of the Self-existent One at their head, gave rise to and secured* this whole world, the mobile and the immobile, each in his own Epoch (1.61 n).

[64]Eighteen Nimeṣas ("winks") make a Kāṣṭha ("second"), thirty Kāṣṭhas a Kalā ("minute"), thirty Kalās a Muhūrta ("hour"),* and thirty Muhūrtas a day-and-night. [65]The sun divides the day and the night, both the human and the divine. The night is meant for creatures to sleep, and the day to engage in activities.

[66]For ancestors, a month constitutes a day and a night, divided into the two fortnights. The dark fortnight is the day for engaging in activities, and the bright fortnight is the night for sleeping.* [67]For gods, a year is a day and a night and their division is this: the day is the northward passage of the sun, and the night is its southward passage.

[68]Listen now to a concise account of the duration of a day-and-night of Brahmā and of each Age in proper sequence. [69]The Kṛta Age is said to last 4,000 years. It is preceded by a twilight lasting 400 years and followed by a twilight of the same length. [70]For each of the three subsequent Ages, as also for the twilights that precede and follow them, the first number of the thousands and the hundreds is progressively diminished by one.* [71]These four Ages, computed at the very beginning as lasting 12,000 years, are said to constitute a single Age of the gods.* [72]The sum total of 1,000 divine Ages should be regarded as a single day of Brahmā, and his night as having the very same duration. [73]Those who know this propitious day of Brahmā lasting 1,000 Ages, as also his night with the same duration—they are people who truly know day and night.

[74]At the end of that day-and-night, he awakens from his sleep; and when he has woken up, he brings forth the mind, which is both existent and non-existent. [75]The mind, driven by the desire to create, transmutes the creation. From the mind is born ether, whose distinctive quality is said to be sound. [76]From ether, as it is being transmuted, is born wind—powerful, pure, and bearing all odors—whose distinctive quality is thought to be touch. [77]From the wind, as it is being transmuted, is produced light—shining, brilliant, and dispelling darkness—whose distinctive quality, tradition says, is visible appearance. [78]From light, as it is being transmuted comes water, with taste as its distinctive quality; and from water, earth, with smell as its distinctive quality. That is how this creation was at the beginning.

[79]The divine Age mentioned previously as lasting 12,000—that multiplied 71 times is here referred to as an "Epoch of a Manu" (1.71 n.). [80]The countless Epochs of

Manus, as also creation and dissolution—the Supreme Lord does this again and again as a kind of sport.

[81]In the Kṛta Age, the Law is whole, possessing all four feet;* and so is truth. People never acquire any property through unlawful means. [82]By acquiring* such property, however, the Law is stripped of one foot in each of the subsequent Ages; through theft, falsehood, and fraud,* the Law disappears a foot at a time.

[83]In the Kṛta Age, people are free from sickness, succeed in all their pursuits, and have a life span of 400 years. In the Tretā and each of the subsequent Ages, however, their life span is shortened by a quarter.* [84]The life span of mortals given in the Veda, the benefits of rites, and the power of embodied beings—they all come to fruition in the world in conformity with each Age.

[85]There is one set of Laws for men in the Kṛta Age, another in the Tretā, still another in the Dvāpara, and a different set in the Kali, in keeping with the progressive shortening taking place in each Age.* [86]Ascetic toil, they say, is supreme in the Kṛta Age; knowledge in Tretā; sacrifice in Dvāpara; and gift-giving alone in Kali.

Excursus: Occupations of Social Classes

[87]For the protection of this whole creation, that One of dazzling brilliance assigned separate activities for those born from the mouth, arms, thighs, and feet. [88]To Brahmins, he assigned reciting and teaching the Veda, offering and officiating at sacrifices, and receiving and giving gifts. [89]To the Kṣatriya, he allotted protecting the subjects, giving gifts, offering sacrifices, reciting the Veda, and avoiding attachment to sensory objects; [90]and to the Vaiśya, looking after animals, giving gifts, offering sacrifices, reciting the Veda, trade, moneylending, and agriculture. [91]A single activity did the Lord allot to the Śudra, however: the ungrudging service of those very social classes (10.74–80).

Excursus: Excellence of the Brahmin

[92]A man is said to be purer above the navel. Therefore, the Self-existent One has declared, the mouth is his purest part.* [93]Because he arose from the loftiest part of the body, because he is the eldest, and because he retains the Veda,* the Brahmin is by Law the lord of this whole creation. [94]For, in the beginning, the Self-existent One heated himself with ascetic toil and brought him forth from his own mouth to convey divine oblations and ancestral offerings and to protect this whole world. [95]What creature can surpass him through whose mouth the denizens of the triple heaven always eat their oblations, and the forefathers their offerings (7.84)?

[96]Among creatures, living beings are the best; among living beings, those who subsist by intelligence; among those who subsist by intelligence,* human beings; and among human beings, Brahmins—so the tradition declares. [97]Among Brahmins, the learned are the best; among the learned, those who have made the resolve;* among those who have made the resolve, the doers; and among doers, the Vedic savants.+

[98]A Brahmin's birth alone represents the everlasting physical frame of the Law; for, born on account of the Law, he is fit for becoming Brahman. [99]For when a Brahmin is born, a preeminent birth takes place on earth—a ruler of all creatures to guard the storehouse of Laws.* [100]This whole world—whatever there is on earth—is the

property of the Brahmin. Because of his eminence and high birth, the Brahmin has a clear right to this whole world. [101]The Brahmin eats only what belongs to him, wears what belongs to him, and gives what belongs to him; it is by the kindness of the Brahmin that other people eat.*

Excursus: Treatise of Manu

[102]To determine which activities are proper to him and which to the remaining classes in their proper order, Manu, the wise son of the Self-existent, composed this treatise. [103]It should be studied diligently and taught to his pupils properly by a learned Brahmin, and by no one else.+

[104]When a Brahmin who keeps to his vows studies this treatise, he is never sullied by faults arising from mental, oral, or physical activities; [105]he purifies those alongside whom he eats (3.183–86), as also seven generations of his lineage before him and seven after him; he alone, moreover, has a right to this entire earth.

[106]This treatise is the best good-luck incantation; it expands the intellect; it procures everlasting fame;* and it is the ultimate bliss.+ [107]In this, the Law has been set forth in full—the good and the bad qualities of actions and the timeless norms of proper conduct—for all four social classes.*

[108]Proper conduct is the highest Law, as well as what is declared the Veda and given in traditional texts. Applying himself always to this treatise,* therefore, let a twice-born man remain constantly self-possessed. [109]When a Brahmin has fallen away from proper conduct, he does not reap the fruit of the Veda; but when he holds fast to proper conduct, tradition says, he enjoys its full reward. [110]Seeing thus that the Law proceeds from proper conduct, the sages understood proper conduct to be the ultimate root of all ascetic toil.

Excursus: Synopsis

[111]Origin of the world [1.6–110].
Rules for consecratory rites [2.26–67].
Observance of the vow [2.69–139].
Service [2.140–244].
The most excellent rule regarding the final bath [2.245–46].
[112]Marrying a wife [3.4–19].
Characteristics of the different types of marriage [3.20–44].
Rules regarding the great sacrifices [3.67–121, 285–86].
The timeless ordinance on ancestral rites [3.122–284].
[113]Characteristics of the different occupations [4.2–12].
Observances of a bath-graduate [4.13–257].
Permitted and forbidden food [5.4–56].
Purification [5.57–109].
Cleansing of articles [5.111–145].
[114]Law pertaining to women [5.147–168].
Hermit's life [6.1–32].
Renunciation* [6.33–85].
Retirement* [6.87–96].

The entire Law pertaining to the king [7.1–226].
Adjudication of lawsuits [8.1–46].
115Rules concerning the questioning of witnesses [8.62–123].
Law with respect to husbands and wives [9.1–102].
Law on partitioning of estates [9.104–219].
Gambling [9.221–228].
Eradication of thorns [9.232–293].
116Conduct of Vaiśyas and Śūdras [9.326–335].
Origin of mixed classes [10.1–73].
Law in times of adversity for social classes [10.81–129].
Rules on penances [11.44–266].
117The three passages into the transmigratory cycle resulting from action [12.1–81].
Final bliss [12.83–106].
Examination of the good and bad qualities of actions.
118The timeless Laws of regions, of hereditary groups, and of families.
Laws of heretical ascetic groups and guilds.*
All that Manu has set forth in this treatise.

119Just as, upon my request, Manu formerly taught me this treatise, so you too must learn it from me today.

CHAPTER TWO

THE LAW

[1]Learn the Law always adhered to by people who are erudite, virtuous, and free from love and hate, the Law assented to by the heart.*

Excursus: Desire*

[2]To be motivated by desire* is not commended, but it is impossible here to be free from desire; for it is desire that prompts vedic study and the performance of vedic rites. [3]Intention is the root of desire;* intention is the wellspring of sacrifices; and intention triggers every religious observance and every rule of restraint—so the tradition declares. [4]Nowhere in this world do we see any activity done by a man free from desire; for whatever at all that a man may do, it is the work of someone who desired it.* [5]By engaging in them* properly, a man attains the world of the immortals and, in this world, obtains all his desires just as he intended.+

Sources of Law

[6]The root of the Law is the entire Veda; the tradition and practice of those who know the Veda; the conduct of good people; and what is pleasing to oneself.* [7]Whatever Law Manu has proclaimed with respect to anyone, all that has been taught in the Veda, for it contains all knowledge.* [8]After subjecting all this* to close scrutiny with the eye of knowledge, a learned man should apply himself to the Law proper to him on the authority of the scriptures; [9]for by following the Law proclaimed in scripture and tradition, a man achieves fame in this world and unsurpassed happiness after death.

[10]"Scripture"* should be recognized as "Veda," and "tradition" as "Law Treatise." These two should never be called into question in any matter,* for it is from them that the Law has shined forth. [11]If a twice-born disparages these two* by relying on the science of logic, he ought to be ostracized by good people as an infidel and a denigrator of the Veda.

Knowledge of the Law

[12]Veda, tradition, the conduct of good people, and what is pleasing to oneself—these, they say, are the four visible marks of the Law. [13]The knowledge of the Law is prescribed for people who are unattached to wealth or pleasures; and for people who seek to know the Law, scripture is the highest authority.*

Contradictions in Law

14When there are two contradictory scriptural provisions on some issue, however, tradition takes them both to be the Law with respect to it; for wise men have correctly pronounced them both to be the Law. 15After sunrise, before sunrise, and at daybreak—the sacrifice takes place at any of these times; so states a vedic scripture.*+

Competence to Study the Law

16A man for whom it is prescribed that the rites beginning with the impregnation ceremony and ending with the funeral are to be performed with the recitation of vedic formulas—no one but he is to be recognized as entitled to study this treatise.*

The Sacred Land

17The land created by the gods and lying between the divine rivers Sarasvatī and Dṛṣadvatī is called "Brahmāvarta"—the region of Brahman.* 18The conduct handed down from generation to generation among the social classes and the intermediate classes of that land is called the "conduct of good people."

19Kurukṣetra and the lands of the Matsyas, Pañcālas, and Śūrasenakas constitute the "land of Brahmin seers," which borders on the Brahmāvarta. 20All the people on earth should learn their respective practices from a Brahmin born in that land.

21The land between the Himalaya and Vindhya ranges, to the east of Vinaśana and west of Prayāga, is known as the "Middle Region."

22The land between the same mountain ranges extending from the eastern to the western sea is what the wise call "Āryāvarta"—the region of the Āryas.

23The natural range of the black buck is to be recognized as the land fit for sacrifice; beyond that is the land of foreigners.*

24Twice-born people should diligently settle in these lands; but a Śūdra, when he is when starved for a livelihood, may live in any region at all.

> 25I have described to you above succinctly the source of the Law, as also the origin of this whole world. Learn now the Laws of the social classes.

CONSECRATORY RITES

26The consecration of the body, beginning with the ceremony of impregnation, should be performed for twice-born men by means of the sacred vedic rites, a consecration that cleanses a man both here and in the hereafter. 27The fire offerings for the benefit of the fetus, the birth rite, the first cutting of hair, and the tying of the Muñja-grass cord*—by these rites the taint of semen and womb is wiped off from twice-born men. 28Vedic recitation, religious observances, fire offerings, study of the triple Veda, ritual offerings, sons, the five great sacrifices, and sacrifices—by these a man's body is made "brāhmic."*

Childhood Rites

[29]The rule is that the birth rite of a male child* must be performed before his umbilical cord is cut; he is fed gold, honey, and ghee* to the accompaniment of vedic formulas.

[30]One should see to it that the child's naming ceremony is performed on the tenth or the twelfth day after birth, on a day or at a time that is auspicious, or under a favorable constellation. [31]For a Brahmin, the name should connote auspiciousness; for a Kṣatriya, strength; for a Vaiśya, wealth; and for a Śūdra, disdain. [32]For a Brahmin, the name should connote happiness; for a Kṣatriya, protection; for a Vaiśya, prosperity; and for a Śūdra, service. [33]For girls, the name should be easy to pronounce and without fierce connotations, have a clear meaning, be charming and auspicious, end in a long final syllable, and contain a word for blessing.*

[34]In the fourth month, one should perform the ceremony of taking the child out of the house; and in the sixth month, the feeding with rice, as also any other auspicious ceremony cherished in the family.

[35]The first cutting of hair, according to the Law, should be performed for all twice-born children in the first or the third year, in accordance with the dictates of scripture.

Vedic Initiation

Time for Initiation [36]For a Brahmin, the vedic initiation should be carried out in the eighth year from conception; for a Kṣatriya, in the eleventh year from conception; and for a Vaiśya, in the twelfth year from conception. [37]For a Brahmin desiring eminence in vedic knowledge, it should be carried out in the fifth year; for a Kṣatriya aspiring for power, in the sixth year; and for a Vaiśya aspiring for a spirit of enterprise, in the seventh year.

Failure to be Initiated [38]For a Brahmin, the time for Sāvitrī* does not lapse until the sixteenth year;* for a Kṣatriya, until the twenty-second; and for a Vaiśya, until the twenty-fourth. [39]If, after those times, any of these three has not undergone consecration at the proper time, he becomes a Vrātya (10.20–23), fallen from Sāvitrī (2.38 n.) and spurned by Āryas. [40]Even in a time of adversity, a Brahmin should never establish vedic or matrimonial links* with such people, unless they have been cleansed according to rule.

Insignia: I [41]Students should wear the skin of a black antelope, a Ruru deer, or a male goat, and clothes of hemp, flax, or wool, according to the direct order of classes.

[42]For a Brahmin, the girdle should be made with a triple cord of Muñja grass, smooth and soft; for a Kṣatriya, with a bowstring of Mūrvā hemp; and for a Vaiśya, with a string of hemp. [43]When Muñja grass is unavailable, they should be made with Kuśa grass, the Aśmantaka plant, or Balvaja grass.* One should wrap the girdle around the waist three times and make one, three, or five knots.*

[44]For a Brahmin, the sacrificial cord is made with a triple strand of cotton thread twisted upwards;* for a Kṣatriya, with strands of hemp; and for a Vaiśya, with woolen strands.

[45]A Brahmin, according to the Law, is entitled to a wood-apple or Palāśa staff; a Kṣatriya, to a banyan or Khadira staff; and a Vaiśya, to a Pīlu or Udumbara staff. [46]In terms of length, a Brahmin's staff should reach the hair; a Kṣatriya's the forehead; and a Vaiśya's the nose. [47]Every staff should be straight, without blemishes, pleasing to the eye, not liable to alarm people, with the bark intact, and undamaged by fire.

Food [48]Taking his chosen staff, he should worship the sun, walk around the fire clockwise, and go on his begging round according to rule. [49]An initiated Brahmin should beg placing the word "Madam" at the beginning; a Kṣatriya, in the middle; and a Vaiśya, at the end.* [50]The very first time, he should beg from his mother, his sister, or his own mother's sister, or from some other woman who would not snub him.

[51]After collecting as much almsfood as he needs without guile,* he should present it to his teacher, purify himself by sipping some water, and eat it facing the east. [52]Facing the east while eating procures long life; facing the south procures fame; facing the west procures prosperity; and facing the north procures truth.*+ [53]A twice-born should always eat food after sipping* some water and with a collected mind; after eating also he should sip water in the proper manner and rub water on the orifices.*

[54]He must always revere his food and eat it without disdain. When he sees the food, he should rejoice, look pleased, and receive it joyfully in every way. [55]For when food is revered, it always bestows strength and vigor; but when it is eaten without being revered, it destroys them both.

[56]He must not give his leftovers to anyone, eat between meals,* engage in overeating, or go anywhere while he is sullied with remnants.* [57]Eating too much harms his health, reduces his life expectancy, impedes heaven, hinders merit, and is despised by people; therefore, he should avoid it.

Sipping [58]A Brahmin should sip water at all times with the part of the palm linked to Brahmā, Prajāpati, or gods, but never with the part linked to ancestors.* [59]They call the flat surface at the base of the thumb the part linked to Brahmā; the base of the fingers, the part linked to Prajāpati; the finger tips, the part linked to gods; and the area beneath these two,* the part linked to ancestors.

[60]He should first sip water three times, then wipe his mouth twice, and finally rub water on his orifices, body, and head (2.53 n.). [61]A man who knows the Law and desires to become pure should always do the sipping in a secluded place, using water that is not warm or frothy, employing the appropriate part of the palm, and facing east or north. [62]A Brahmin is purified by water reaching the heart; a Kṣatriya, by water reaching the throat; a Vaiśya, by water taken into the mouth; and a Śūdra, by water wetting the lips.

Insignia: II [63]When the right hand is raised, a twice-born man is called "*upavītin*"—wearing the cord in the sacrificial mode; when the left hand is raised, he is called "*prācīnāvītin*"—wearing the cord toward the east; and when it is worn around the neck, he is called "*nivītin*"—wearing the cord down.*

[64]When the girdle, antelope skin, staff, sacrificial cord, or water pot is damaged, he should throw it in water and take a new one with the appropriate ritual formula.

Shaving Ceremony

[65]The rule is that for a Brahmin the shaving ceremony* is to be performed in the sixteenth year; for a Kṣatriya, in the twenty-second; and for a Vaiśya, in the twenty-fourth (2.38 n.).

Consecretory Rites for Women

[66]For females, on the other hand, this entire series should be performed at the proper time and in the proper sequence, but without reciting any vedic formula, for the purpose of consecrating their bodies.

[67]For females, tradition tells us, the marriage ceremony equals the rite of vedic consecration; serving the husband equals living with the teacher; and care of the house equals the tending of the sacred fires.*+

> [68]I have explained above the initiatory rite of twice-born men, a rite that signals a new birth and is sanctifying. Learn now the activities connected with it.

THE STUDENT

Instruction

[69]After initiating a pupil, the teacher should at the outset train him in purification, proper conduct, fire rituals, and twilight worship.

[70]When the pupil is ready for vedic recitation, he should sip water in the prescribed manner, dress in light clothing,* bring his organs under control, face the north, and join his palms in "*brahmāñjali*"—then should he be taught. [71]At the beginning and at the end of a vedic lesson, he should always clasp his teacher's feet and recite the Veda with joined palms—tradition calls this "*brahmāñjali*," the vedic joining of palms. [72]He should clasp his teacher's feet by crossing his hands, touching the teacher's right foot with his right hand and the teacher's left with his left.

[73]When he is ready for vedic recitation, he should say to the teacher, "Teach, Sir (*bho*)!", without being lazy at any time; and when commanded "Stop!", he should cease.* [74]At the beginning and at the end of vedic recitation, the student should always recite the syllable OṂ. If it is not recited at the beginning, the Veda slips away; if it is not recited at the end, the Veda wastes away. [75]When he is seated on sacred grass with the tips toward the east, cleansed by the purificatory blades of grass,* and purified by controlling his breath three times—then he becomes competent to recite OṂ.

The Syllable OṂ [76]The phonemes "a," "u," and "m"—Prajāpati extracted these from the three Vedas, as also "*bhū*," earth; "*bhuvaḥ*," mid-space; and "*svar*," heaven. [77]Also from the three Vedas, Prajāpati, the Supreme Lord, squeezed out foot by foot the Sāvitrī verse:* "That. . . ."

[78]By softly reciting this syllable and this verse preceded by the Calls during the two twilights, a Brahmin who knows the Veda wins the merit of reciting the Veda

itself. [79]By reciting these three one thousand times outside the village, a Brahmin is freed from even a grievous sin within a month, like a snake from its slough. [80]Someone who is a Brahmin, a Kṣatriya, or a Vaiśya by birth invites the censure of good people by cutting himself off from this verse and from the timely performance of his rite.*

[81]The three inexhaustible Great Calls preceded by OṂ and the three-footed Sāvitrī verse should be recognized as the mouth of the Veda. [82]When a man recites this verse tirelessly for three years, becoming wind and assuming an ethereal form, he reaches the highest Brahman.* [83]The highest Brahman is the monosyllable OṂ; the highest ascetic toil is the control of breath; nothing is higher than the Sāvitrī; and truth is better than ascetic silence. [84]Offering ghee while seated, offering oblations while standing*—all such vedic rites perish. The syllable (*akṣara*) OṂ should be recognized as imperishable (*akṣara*);* it is Brahman, it is Prajāpati.

Soft Recitation [85]The sacrifice consisting of soft recitation is ten times better than the sacrifice consisting of prescribed rites—a hundred times, if the recitation is done inaudibly; and a thousand times, if it is done mentally. [86]The four types of cooked oblations* along with the sacrifices consisting of prescribed rites—all these are not worth a sixteenth part of the sacrifice consisting of soft recitation. [87]Only by soft recitation does a Brahmin achieve success; on this there is no doubt. Whether he does anything else or not, a Maitra,* they say, is the true Brahmin.

Excursus: Control of the Organs

[88]As his organs meander amidst the alluring sense objects, a learned man should strive hard to control them, like a charioteer his horses.

[89]I will explain precisely and in their proper order the eleven organs described by wise men of old: [90]ear, skin, eyes, tongue, and the fifth, nostrils; anus, sexual organ, hands, feet, and speech, listed by tradition as the tenth. [91]Of these, the five in order beginning with the ear are called the organs of perception; and the five beginning with the anus, the organs of action. [92]Know that the eleventh is the mind, which, by virtue of its own distinctive quality, belongs to both groups. So, by mastering it, one masters both those quintets.

[93]By attachment to the organs, a man undoubtedly becomes corrupted; but by bringing them under control, he achieves success. [94]Desire is never quenched by enjoying desires; like a fire fed with ghee, it only waxes stronger. [95]Between a man who obtains all these and a man who gives them all up—giving up all desires is far better than obtaining them all. [96]Corrupted as these organs are* by sensory objects, one cannot bring them under control as effectively by abstinence as by constant insight. [97]Vedas, gifts,* sacrifices, constraints,* and ascetic toils—none of these is ever successful for a man with a corrupt heart.

[98]When a man feels neither elation nor revulsion at hearing, touching, seeing, eating, or smelling anything, he should be recognized as a man who has mastered his organs. [99]Of all these organs, however, if a single one slips away, through that his wisdom slips away, like water through the foot of a skin.* [100]By bringing the full range of his organs under control and by restraining his mind, a man will achieve all his goals without having to shrivel up his body through yoga.

Twilight Worship

[101]At the morning twilight, he should stand reciting softly the Sāvitrī verse until the sun comes into view; at the evening twilight, however, he should remain properly seated* until the Big Dipper becomes clearly visible. [102]When he stands reciting softly at the morning twilight, he banishes any sin committed during the night; and when he sits at the evening twilight, he removes any taint contracted during the day. [103]A man who neither stands at the morning twilight nor sits at the evening twilight should be excluded like a Śūdra from all rites of the twice-born.

Vedic Recitation

[104]Intent on carrying out the ritual of daily recitation,* he should go into the wilderness and, controlled* and composed, recite at least the Sāvitrī verse near a place of water.

[105]Rules regarding the suspension of vedic recitation (4.101–27) have no bearing on Vedic Supplements,* on daily vedic recitation, and on ritual formulas used in fire offerings. [106]The daily vedic recitation is not subject to suspension, for tradition calls it a sacrificial session consisting of vedic recitation; it is a meritorious rite at which the vedic recitation takes the place of the burnt oblation and the factors causing a suspension act as the oblatory exclamation Vaṣaṭ.*

[107]When someone, after purifying and controlling himself, performs his vedic recitation for a year according to rule, that recitation will rain milk, curd, ghee, and honey on him every single day.*

Persons Competent to Receive Vedic Instruction

[108]Kindling the sacred fire, begging almsfood, sleeping on the floor, and doing what is beneficial to his teacher—a twice-born who has undergone vedic initiation should do these until he has performed the rite of returning home.*

[109]The son of his teacher, a person who offers obedient service, a person who has given him knowledge, a virtuous person, an honest person,* someone close to him,* a capable man, someone who gives him money, a good man, and one who is his own*—these ten may be taught the Veda in accordance with the Law. [110]He must never impart instruction to anyone who has not requested it or who has requested it in an improper way; for in this world, a wise man, though learned, should conduct himself like an idiot.* [111]A man who imparts in violation of the Law and a man who requests in violation of the Law—of these two, the one or the other will incur death or enmity.

[112]Do not sow knowledge where there is no merit or money, or at least proportionate service; you don't sow good seed on brackish soil. [113]Even in a time of dreadful adversity, a vedic savant should rather die with his knowledge; let him not sow it on barren soil.

[114]Vedic knowledge came up to the Brahmin and said,* "I am your treasure. Guard me! Do not hand me over to a malcontent. I shall thus become supremely strong. [115]A man you know to be honest, restrained, and chaste—only to such a Brahmin should you disclose me, as to a vigilant guardian of your treasure."*

[116]If, however, a man learns the Veda without permission by listening to someone who is reciting it, he is guilty of stealing the Veda and will go to hell.

Salutation

[117]He should greet first* the person from whom he received knowledge—whether it is the knowledge of worldly matters, of the Veda, or of the inner self. [118]A well-disciplined Brahmin, although he knows just the Sāvitrī verse, is far better than an undisciplined one who eats all types of food and deals in all types of merchandise, though he may know all three Vedas.

[119]He should not sit on a bed or seat occupied by a superior, and he should rise from the bed or seat he is occupying before he greets such a person; [120]for when an older person comes near, the life breaths of a younger person rise up, and as he rises up and greets him, he retrieves them.* [121]When someone is conscientious about greeting and always renders assistance to the elderly, he obtains an increase in these four: life span, wisdom, fame, and power.

[122]When a Brahmin is greeting an older person, he must state his name after the greeting, saying, "I am so-and-so." [123]When greeting people who are ignorant of the greeting containing the proper name, as also any woman, a wise man should simply say "I."* [124]When he uses the greeting containing his own name, he should say "*bho*" at the end; the meaning of "*bho*"* contains the essential meanings of all proper names—that is the tradition handed down by the seers. [125]In greeting a Brahmin, he should say, "May you live long, gentle Sir!"; and at the end of the name, he should pronounce "a" and prolate the previous syllable.* [126]A learned man should not greet a Brahmin who does not know how to return a greeting; he is no better than a Śūdra.

[127]When he meets a Brahmin, he should ask him whether he is doing well (*kuśala*); a Kṣatriya, whether he is all right (*anāmaya*); a Vaiśya, whether his property is secure (*kṣema*); and a Śūdra, whether he is in good health (*ārogya*). [128]A person consecrated for sacrifice should not be addressed by name even if he is younger; a man conversant with the Law should address such a person using the words "*bho*" or "Sir" (*bhavat*). [129]He should address a woman who is another man's wife and who is not a blood relative of his using the words "Madam," "Dear Lady," or "Sister." [130]He should rise up and say, "I am so-and-so" to his maternal and paternal uncles, fathers-in-law, officiating priests, and elders who are younger than he. [131]He should honor a maternal aunt, a wife of a maternal uncle, a mother-in-law, and a paternal aunt as he would his teacher's wife; they are equal to his teacher's wife.*

[132]The feet of his brother's wife of the same social class, he should clasp every day; but the feet of the wives of his paternal and maternal relatives,* only after returning from a journey. [133]Towards a sister of his father and mother and towards his own older sister, he should behave as towards his own mother; but the mother is more venerable than they.

Precedence

[134]Among fellow citizens, people with an age difference of ten years are regarded as friends; among fellow artisans, people with an age difference of five years; among vedic scholars, people with an age difference of three years; and among blood relatives, only people with a slight age difference.

[135]A 10-year-old Brahmin and a 100-year-old king, one should know, stand with respect to each other as a father to a son; but of the two, the Brahmin is the father.

[136]Wealth, kin, age, ritual life, and the fifth, knowledge—these are the grounds for respect; and each subsequent one carries greater weight than each preceding. [137]Among persons of the three classes, one who possesses more of and to a higher degree these five grounds is more deserving of respect; and so is a Śūdra who is in his nineties.+

[138]One should give way to people in vehicles or in their nineties, the sick, people carrying loads, women, bath-graduates, kings, and bridegrooms. [139]When such people encounter each other, however, a bath-graduate and a king are to receive greater honor; but when a king and a bath-graduate encounter each other, the king pays honor to the bath-graduate.

Teacher

[140]The twice-born man who initiates a pupil and teaches him the Veda together with the ritual books and the secret texts* is called "Teacher." [141]A man who teaches a section of the Veda or else the Vedic Supplements (2.105 n.) for a living is called "Tutor." [142]The Brahmin who performs the rites beginning with the ceremony of impregnation according to rule and nourishes with food is called "Elder."* [143]The person who, after he has been chosen by someone, sets up the sacred fires and performs the cooked oblations and sacrifices such as the Agniṣṭoma offering on his behalf is called here his "Officiating Priest."

[144]He should consider the man who fills both his ears* faithfully with the Veda as his father and mother and never show hostility towards him. [145]The teacher is ten times greater* than the tutor; the father is a hundred times greater than the teacher; but the mother is a thousand times greater than the father. [146]Between the man who gave life and the man who gave the Veda, the man who gave the Veda is the more venerable father; for a Brahmin's birth in the Veda is everlasting, both here and in the hereafter. [147]When, through lust for each other, his father and mother engender him and he is conceived in the womb, he should consider that as his mere coming into existence. [148]But the birth that a teacher who has fathomed the Veda brings about according to rule by means of the Sāvitrī verse—that is his true birth, that is not subject to old age and death.

[149]A man who assists someone with vedic knowledge, be it a little or a lot, is also acknowledged here as his elder in recognition of that assistance with vedic knowledge.

[150]Even a younger Brahmin who brings about the vedic birth of an older individual and trains him in the Law proper to him becomes his father according to the Law. [151]The child sage, son of Aṅgiras, gave vedic instruction to his fathers; and having excelled them in knowledge, he called them "Little Children." [152]They became infuriated and raised the issue with the gods. The gods convened and told them: "The child addressed you properly. [153]An ignorant man, surely, is the child, and the man who imparts the Veda is the father; for they address an ignorant man as 'Child' and a man who imparts the Veda as 'Father'."

[154]The seers have established this Law: "In our eyes, only a vedic savant is an eminent man"; eminence does not come from age, gray hairs, wealth, or kin. [155]For Brahmins, seniority depends on knowledge, for Kṣatriyas on valor, and for Vaiśyas on grain and wealth; for Śūdras alone does it depends on age. [156]A man does not become a

"senior" simply because his hair has turned gray. Gods call a man with vedic learning a "senior," even though he may be young.

[157]Like an elephant made of wood, like a deer made of leather, is a Brahmin without vedic learning; these three only bear the name. [158]As fruitless as a eunuch* with women, as fruitless as a cow with a cow, and as fruitless as a gift given to an ignorant man, is a Brahmin ignorant of the Veda.

[159]A man who wishes to promote the Law should instruct creatures about what is best without hurting them, employing pleasant and gentle words. [160]Only a man whose mind and speech have been purified and are always well-guarded acquires the entire fruit of reaching the end of the Veda.* [161]Though deeply hurt, let him never use cutting words, show hostility to others in thought or deed, or use aberrant language* that would alarm people.

[162]Let a Brahmin always shrink from praise, as he would from poison; let him ever yearn for scorn, as he would for ambrosia—[163]for, a man who is scorned sleeps at ease, wakes up at ease, goes about in this world at ease; but the man who scorned him perishes.

Vedic Study

[164]A twice-born whose body has been consecrated following this orderly sequence should gradually amass the riches of ascetic toil consisting of vedic study* while he resides with his teacher. [165]A twice-born should study the entire Veda together with the secret texts (2.140 n.), as he carries out the various observances and special ascetic practices enjoined by vedic injunctions. [166]A Brahmin planning on undergoing ascetic toil should simply recite the Veda constantly; for vedic recitation is recognized here as the highest ascetic toil for a Brahmin. [167]When a twice-born, even while wearing a garland, performs his vedic recitation every day according to his ability, he is surely practising the fiercest ascetic toil down to the very tips of his nails. [168]When a Brahmin expends great effort in other matters without studying the Veda, while still alive he is quickly reduced to the status of a Śūdra, together with his children.

[169]According to a scriptural injunction, the first birth of a Brahmin is from his mother; the second takes place at the tying of the Muñja-grass girdle (2.27 n.), and the third at the consecration for a sacrifice. [170]Of these, the one signaled by the tying of the Muñja-grass girdle is his birth from the Veda. At this birth, the Sāvitrī verse is said to be his mother, and the teacher his father. [171]The teacher is called the father because he imparts the Veda, for a man does not become competent to perform any rite until the tying of the Muñja-grass girdle. [172]Such a man should not pronounce any vedic text, except when he offers a funerary oblation, for he is equal to a Śūdra until he is born from the Veda.

Observances

[173]After he has undergone vedic initiation, he is to be instructed in the observances and then taught the Veda in the proper order and according to rule. [174]The very same skin, cord, girdle, staff, and garment prescribed for him after his initiation* are prescribed for him also during the observances.

[175]Bringing all his organs under control, a vedic student living with his teacher should observe these restrictions in order to increase his ascetic toil. [176]Every day, after purifying himself by bathing, he should offer quenching libations to gods, seers, and ancestors; worship the gods; and put firewood into the sacred fire. [177]He should avoid honey, meat, perfumes, garlands, savory foods, women, all foods that have turned sour, causing injury to living beings, [178]rubbing oil on the body, putting collyrium on the eyes, using footwear or an umbrella, lust, hatred, greed, dancing, singing, playing musical instruments, [179]gambling, gossiping, slander, lies, looking at and touching women, and hurting others.

[180]He should always sleep alone and never ejaculate his semen; for when he voluntarily ejaculates his semen, he breaks his vow. [181]When a Brahmin student ejaculates his semen involuntarily in sleep, he should bathe, worship the sun, and softly recite three times the verse: "May the virile strength return again to me. . . ."

Begging and Daily Duties [182]He should fetch a pot of water, flowers, cow dung, loose soil, and Kuśa grass—as much as required—and beg for food every day.

[183]Having made himself pure, a vedic student should gather almsfood every day from the houses of persons who do not neglect the Veda or sacrifices and who have distinguished themselves in the activities proper to them. [184]He should not beg from his teacher's family or from the families of his paternal or maternal relatives. When houses of other people are unavailable, however, he may beg from these, avoiding those listed earlier when those listed later are available.* [185]When the kinds of persons mentioned above are not available, he may beg from the entire village after purifying himself and curbing his speech; but he should avoid heinous sinners.*

[186]Having fetched firewood from afar, he should stack it above ground;* and using that firewood, he should make offerings in the fire diligently morning and evening.

[187]If he fails to beg food or to put firewood into the sacred fire for seven nights without being sick, he should perform the penitential observance prescribed for a student who has broken his vow of chastity (see 11.119–24).

[188]Subsisting on almsfood every day, a votary should never eat a meal given by one person; tradition says that for a votary subsisting on almsfood is equal to a fast.+ [189]When he is invited, however, he may freely eat at an offering to the gods while keeping to his vow, and at an offering to ancestors, conducting himself like a seer; doing so does not violate his vow. [190]Wise men sanction this activity only for Brahmins; this kind of activity is not commended at all for Kṣatriyas and Vaiśyas.

Conduct towards the Teacher

[191]When he is ordered by the teacher—or even when he is not—he should apply himself every day to vedic recitation and to activities beneficial to his teacher.

[192]Bringing his body, speech, organs of perception, and mind under control, he should stand with joined palms looking at his teacher's face. [193]He must always keep his right arm uncovered,* comport himself properly, cover himself well,* and, when he is told "Be seated," sit down facing the teacher.

[194]In his teacher's presence, his food, clothes, and apparel should always be of a

lesser quality than his teacher's. He should wake up before his teacher and go to bed after him.

[195]He must never answer or converse with his teacher while lying down, seated, eating, standing,* or facing away; [196]he should do so standing up if the teacher is seated, approaching him if he is standing, going up to meet him if he is walking towards him, running after him if he is running, [197]going around to face him if he is turned away from him, coming close to him if he is far away, and bending down if he is lying down or standing at a lower level. [198]In his teacher's presence, he should always occupy a lower couch or seat; and, within his teacher's sight, he must not sit as he pleases.

[199]Even out of sight, he must not refer to his teacher by just his name or mimic his walk, speech, or mannerisms. [200]Wherever his teacher is slandered or reviled, he should either cover his ears or go someplace else.* [201]By slandering his teacher, he becomes an ass; by reviling him, a dog; by living off him, a worm; and by being jealous of him, an insect.

[202]When he is far away or angry, he must not pay his respects to his teacher; nor should he do so in the presence of a woman. When he is riding in a vehicle or seated on a chair, he should greet his teacher only after getting down. [203]He must not sit down with his teacher in such a way that the wind blows from the teacher towards him or from him towards the teacher; nor should he talk about anything out of his teacher's hearing. [204]He may sit by his teacher on a cart drawn by an ox, horse, or camel; on a terrace or a spread of grass;* or on a mat, rock, bench, or boat.

Teacher's Teacher and Other Instructors [205]In the presence of his teacher's teacher, he should behave towards him as towards his own teacher; and he must not greet his own elders* unless he is permitted by his teacher.

[206]He should always behave in the very same manner towards his vedic instructors and his own blood relatives, as also towards those who keep him from what is unrighteous and who teach him what is beneficial.

Members of Teacher's Family [207]Towards distinguished persons, as well as towards the teacher's Ārya sons* and the teacher's own relatives, he should always behave just as he does towards his teacher.

[208]A teacher's son who teaches him—whether that son is younger than or of the same age as himself, or even if he is only a student of the ritual—is entitled to the same respect as his teacher. [209]He must not massage the limbs of his teacher's son, assist him at his bath, eat his leftovers, or wash his feet.

[210]The teacher's wives of equal class should receive the same honor as the teacher, but wives of unequal class should be honored by rising up and greeting them. [211]He must not apply oil on his teacher's wife, assist her at her bath, massage her limbs, or do her hair. [212]Anyone who is over 20 and able to distinguish between the attractive and the unattractive* should not greet here a young wife of his teacher by clasping her feet. [213]It is the very nature of women here to corrupt men. On that account, prudent men are never off guard in the presence of alluring young women. [214]For an alluring young woman is capable of leading astray not only the ignorant but even learned men under

the sway of anger and lust. [215]He must not sit alone with his mother, sister, or daughter; the array of sensory organs is powerful and overpowers even a learned man. [216]A young man may freely pay his respects to the young wives of his teacher, however, by prostrating himself on the ground according to rule and saying: "I am so-and-so." [217]Recalling the Law followed by good people, he should clasp the feet of his teacher's wives upon his return from a journey and greet them every day.

[218]As a man discovers water by digging with a spade, so a student, offering obedient service, discovers the knowledge contained in his teacher.

Rules of Conduct

[219]A student may shave his head or keep his hair matted; or else he may keep just his topknot matted.

He should never let the sun rise or set while he is asleep in a village. [220]If the sun should rise or set while he is asleep, whether deliberately or inadvertently, he should fast for one day while engaging in soft recitation.* [221]If, after he had been asleep at sunrise or sunset, he does not perform the penance, he becomes saddled with a great sin. [222]After purifying himself by sipping water and becoming self-possessed, he should worship both twilights every day, softly reciting the prescribed formula in a clean spot and according to rule (2.103).

[223]If he sees a woman or a low-born man doing something conducive to welfare, he should do all of that diligently, or anything else that he is fond of. [224]Some say that Law and Wealth are conducive to welfare; others, Pleasure and Wealth; and still others, Law alone or Wealth alone. But the settled rule is this: the entire triple set* is conducive to welfare.

Mother, Father, Teacher [225]Teacher, father, mother, and older brother—these should never be treated with contempt especially by a Brahmin, even though he may be deeply hurt. [226]The teacher is the embodiment of Brahman; the father is the embodiment of Prajāpati; the mother is the embodiment of Earth; and one's brother is the embodiment of oneself. [227]The tribulations that a mother and a father undergo when humans are born cannot be repaid even in hundreds of years.

[228]He should do what is pleasing to these two every day, and always what is pleasing to his teacher. When these three are gratified, he obtains the fullness of ascetic toil. [229]Obedient service to these three is said to be the highest form of ascetic toil. Without their consent, he should not follow any other rule of conduct.* [230]For they alone are the three worlds; they alone are the three orders of life;* they alone are the three Vedas;* and they alone are called the three sacred fires. [231]The householder's fire is clearly the father; the southern fire, tradition says, is the mother; and the offertorial fire is the teacher—this is the most excellent triad of sacred fires.

[232]A householder* who does not neglect these three will win the three worlds; and, shining with his own body, he will rejoice in heaven like a god. [233]He obtains this world by devotion to his mother, and the middle world by devotion to his father; but he obtains the world of Brahman only by obedient service to his teacher. [234]When someone has attended to these three, he has attended to all his duties; should someone

not attend to them, all his rites bear him no fruit. [235]So long as these three are alive, he should not follow another rule of conduct;* taking delight in what is pleasing and beneficial to them, he should always render them obedient service. [236]Whenever he undertakes any mental, verbal, or physical activity for the sake of the next world without inconveniencing them, he should inform them of it.

[237]When these three are gratified,* a man has done all he has to do. This is the highest Law itself in person; all else is called subsidiary Law.

Non-Brahmin Teachers [238]A man with faith should accept fine learning even from a low-caste man; the highest Law even from a man of the lowest caste; and a splendid woman even from a bad family. [239]One should take ambrosia even from poison; words of wisdom even from a child; a good example even from an enemy; and gold even from filth. [240]Women, gems, learning, Law, purification, and words of wisdom, as well as crafts of various kinds, may be accepted from anyone.

[241]In a time of adversity, the rules allow a man to study the Veda under a person who is not a Brahmin; and, as long as he is studying, he should walk after that teacher and serve him obediently. [242]If he desires to attain the highest state, a pupil should not live all his life with a teacher who is not a Brahmin or who is a Brahmin but not a vedic scholar.

Life-long Student: I

[243]If he wishes to live with his teacher's family all his life, however, he should diligently serve the teacher until he is freed from his body. [244]When a Brahmin obediently serves his teacher until his body comes to an end, he goes immediately to the eternal abode of Brahman.*

Conclusion of Study

[245]Knowing the Law, he must not give any present to his teacher beforehand; but when, with his teacher's permission, he is ready to take his final bath, he should present the teacher with a gift according to his ability— [246]land, gold, a cow, or a horse; or at least an umbrella or footwear; or grain, vegetables,* or clothes—and thus gladden his teacher.

Life-long Student: II

[247]If his teacher happens to die, he should maintain the same conduct towards his teacher's son possessing the right qualities—or towards his teacher's wife, or towards a person belonging to his teacher's ancestry (5.60 n.)—as he did towards his teacher. [248]If none of these is available, he should end his life by serving the sacred fire faithfully, standing during the day and seated at night (6.22 n.). [249]When a Brahmin lives the life of a vedic student in this manner without breaking his vow, he will go to the highest station and will not be reborn on earth again.

CHAPTER THREE

MARRIAGE

Conclusion of Study

[1]He should carry out the observance relating to the three Vedas at his teacher's house, an observance lasting thirty-six years, or one-half or one-quarter of that time, or else until he has learnt them.

[2]After he has learnt in the proper order the three Vedas* or two of them, or at least one, without violating his chastity,* he should undertake the householder's order of life. [3]When he has returned in accordance with the Law proper to him and received his vedic inheritance from his father, he should be honored at the outset with the gift of a cow, as he sits on a couch wearing a garland.*

Selection of a Bride

[4]After he has taken the concluding bath with his teacher's permission and performed the rite of returning home according to rule, the twice-born should marry a wife belonging to the same class and possessing the right bodily characteristics.

[5]A girl who belongs to an ancestry (5.60 n.) different from his mother's and to a lineage* different from his father's, and who is unrelated to him by marriage,* is recommended for marriage by a twice-born man.

[6]He should avoid these ten families when contracting a marriage alliance, even though they may be prominent and rich in cattle, goats, sheep, money, and grain: [7]families negligent about rites, deficient in male issue, without vedic learning, and with hairy bodies, as well as families prone to hemorrhoids, tuberculosis, dyspepsia, epilepsy, leukoderma, or leprosy.

[8]He must not marry a girl who has red hair or an extra limb; who is sickly; who is without or with too much bodily hair;* who is a blabbermouth or jaundiced-looking;* [9]who is named after a constellation, a tree, a river, a very low caste, a mountain, a bird, a snake, or a servant; or who has a frightening name.+ [10]He should marry a woman who is not deficient in any limb; who has a pleasant name; who walks like a goose or an elephant; and who has fine body and head hair, small teeth, and delicate limbs.

[11]A wise man must not marry a girl who has no brother or whose father is unknown, for fear that the Law of "female-son" may be in force.*

[12]At the first marriage, a woman of equal class is recommended for twice-born men; but for those who proceed further through lust, these are, in order, the preferable women.* [13]A Śūdra may take only a Śūdra woman as wife; a Vaiśya, the latter and a woman of his own class; a Kṣatriya, the latter two and a woman of his own class; and a Brahmin, the latter three and a woman of his own class.

Prohibition of a Śūdra Wife [14]Not a single story* mentions a Brahmin or a Kṣatriya taking a Śūdra wife even when they were going through a time of adversity. [15]When twice-born men foolishly marry low-caste wives, they quickly reduce even their families and children to the rank of Śūdras.

[16]According to Atri and the son of Utathya, a man falls from his caste by marrying a Śūdra woman; according to Śaunaka, by fathering a son through her; and according to Bhṛgu, by producing all his offspring through her.* [17]By taking a Śūdra woman to bed, a Brahmin will descend along the downward course; and by begetting a son through her, he falls from the very rank of a Brahmin. [18]When such a woman plays the leading role in his divine, ancestral, and hospitality rites, gods and ancestors do not partake of them, and he will not go to heaven. [19]No expiation is prescribed for a man who drinks the saliva from the lips of a Śūdra woman, who is tainted by her breath, and who begets himself in her.*

Types of Marriage

[20]Listen now in brief to these eight types of marriage for all four classes, some beneficial both here and in the hereafter, and some not. [21]They are the Brāhma, the Divine, the Seer's, the Prājāpatya, the Demonic, the Gāndharva, the Fiendish, and the Ghoulish, which is the eighth and the worst. [22]Which of these is lawful for which class, their respective merits and defects, the merits and demerits of each with respect to procreation—I will explain all this to you.

[23]The first six in the order enumerated should be considered lawful for Brahmins; the last four for Kṣatriyas; the same four, with the exception of the Fiendish, for Vaiśyas and Śūdras.* [24]The first four, sages say, are recommended for Brahmins; the Fiendish alone for Kṣatriyas; and the Demonic for Vaiśyas and Śūdras. [25]The tradition recorded here, however, considers three of the last five as lawful and two as unlawful; the Demonic and the Ghoulish should never be carried out. [26]The two marriages proclaimed earlier, the Gāndharva and the Fiendish, whether undertaken separately or conjointly,* are viewed by tradition as lawful for Kṣatriyas.

[27]When a man dresses a girl up, honors her, invites on his own a man of learning and virtue, and gives her to him, it is said to be the "Brāhma" Law. [28]When a man, while a sacrifice is being carried out properly, adorns his daughter and gives her to the officiating priest as he is performing the rite, it is called the "Divine" Law. [29]When a man accepts a bull and a cow, or two pairs of them, from the bridegroom in accordance with the Law and gives a girl to him according to rule, it is called the "Seer's" Law. [30]When a man honors the girl and gives her after exhorting them with the words: "May you jointly fulfill the Law," tradition calls it the "Prājāpatya" procedure. [31]When a girl is given* after the payment of money to the girl's relatives and to the girl herself according to the man's ability and out of his own free will, it is called the "Demonic" Law. [32]When the girl and the groom have sex with each other voluntarily, that is the "Gāndharva" marriage based on sexual union* and originating from love. [33]When someone violently abducts a girl from her house as she is shrieking and weeping by causing death, mayhem, and destruction, it is called the "Fiendish" procedure.*

[34]When someone secretly rapes a woman who is asleep, drunk, or mentally deranged, it is the eighth known as "Ghoulish," the most evil of marriages.

[35]Giving a girl away by simply pouring water is recommended for Brahmins, while among the other classes it may be done through mutual love.

Sons from Different Types of Marriage [36]Brahmins, listen now as I describe accurately all that Manu has said regarding the merits of each of these marriages.

[37]A son who is born to a woman married according to the "Brāhma" rite and who does good deeds* rescues from evil* ten generations of forefathers before him and ten generations after him, with himself as the twenty-first; [38]a son born to a woman married according to the "Divine" rite rescues seven generations before him and seven after him; a son born to a woman married according to the "Seer's" rite, three before and three after; and a son born to a woman married according to "Prājāpatya" marriage, six before and six after.

[39]From all four types of marriage beginning, in order, with "Brāhma" are born sons who are eminent in vedic knowledge and respected by cultured people. [40]Endowed with beauty, spirit, and virtue,* possessing wealth and fame, furnished with every delight, and righteous to the highest degree, they will live a hundred years. [41]But in the others—the remaining wicked types of marriage—are born sons whose speech is cruel and false and who hate the Veda and the Law.

[42]From irreproachable marriages are born children beyond reproach; from reproachable marriages are born children inviting people's reproach.* Therefore, a man should avoid reproachable marriages.

Marriage Rite [43]The consecratory rite of taking the hand in marriage is prescribed only for brides of equal class. The following should be recognized as the procedure for the rite of marriage when brides are of unequal class. [44]When marrying an upper-class man, a Kṣatriya bride should take hold of an arrow, a Vaiśya bride a goad, and a Śūdra bride the hem of his garment.

Sexual Union

[45]Finding his gratification always in his wife, he should have sex with her during her season.* Devoted solely to her, he may go to her also when he wants sexual pleasure, except on the days of the moon's change.*

[46]The natural* season of women, according to tradition, consists of sixteen nights, together with the other four days* proscribed by good people. [47]Of these nights, the first four as well as the eleventh and the thirteenth are disapproved; the remaining ten nights are recommended.*

[48]Sons are born when he has sex on even nights, and girls on odd nights. Desiring a son, therefore, he should have sex with his wife on even nights during her season. [49]When the man's semen is dominant, it turns out to be a boy; when the woman's is dominant, a girl; and when both are equal, a hermaphrodite or a twin boy and girl. When both are weak or scanty, no conception takes place.*

[50]Regardless of the order of life in which a man lives,* if he avoids women during the forbidden nights and during the other eight nights,* he becomes a true celibate.

Purchasing a Wife

[51]A learned father must never accept even the slightest bride-price for his daughter; for by greedily accepting a bride-price, a man becomes a trafficker in his offspring. [52]When relatives foolishly live off a woman's wealth—slave women, vehicles, or clothes—those evil men will descend along the downward course.*

[53]At a "Seer's" marriage, some say, the bull and cow constitute the bride-price. That is totally false. Whether the amount is great or small, it is still a sale.*+ [54]When the women's relatives do not take the bride-price for themselves, it does not constitute a sale. It is an act of respect to the women, a simple token of benevolence.

Honoring Women

[55]If they desire an abundance of good fortune, fathers, brothers, husbands, and brothers-in-law should revere their women and provide them with adornments.

[56]Where women are revered,* there the gods rejoice; but where they are not, no rite bears any fruit. [57]Where female relatives grieve, that family soon comes to ruin; but where they do not grieve, it always prospers. [58]When female relatives, not receiving due reverence, curse any house, it comes to total ruin, as if struck down by witchcraft.

[59]If men want to become prosperous, therefore, they should always honor the women on joyful occasions and festive days with gifts of adornments, clothes, and food.

Marital Harmony

[60]Good fortune smiles incessantly on a family where the husband always finds delight in his wife, and the wife in her husband.

[61]For, if the wife does not sparkle, she does not arouse her husband. And if the husband is not aroused, there will be no offspring. [62]When the wife sparkles, so does the entire household; but when she ceases to sparkle, so does the entire household.

Degradation of Families

[63]By contracting aberrant marriages, by neglecting rites, and by failing to study the Veda, respectable families quickly come to ruin;* as also by disregarding Brahmins. [64]By practicing crafts, by engaging in trade, by having children only from a Śūdra wife, by dealing in cattle, horses, and vehicles, by engaging in agriculture, by entering a king's service, [65]by officiating at sacrifices of people at whose sacrifices one is forbidden to officiate, and by denying the efficacy of rites, respectable families fall into disrepute; as also those families bereft of vedic knowledge.*

[66]When they are rich in vedic knowledge, however, even poor families attain the status of "respectable family" and achieve great fame.

THE HOUSEHOLDER

[67]A householder should perform the domestic rites in his nuptial fire according to rule, as also the five great sacrifices and the daily cooking.

Great Sacrifices

[68]A householder has five slaughter-houses: fireplace, grindstone, broom,* mortar and pestle, and water pot. By his use of them, he is fettered. [69]To expiate successively for each of these, the great seers devised the five great sacrifices to be carried out daily by householders.

[70]The sacrifice to the Veda is teaching; the sacrifice to ancestors is the quenching libation; the sacrifice to gods is the burnt offering; the sacrifice to beings is the Bali offering; and the sacrifice to humans is the honoring* of guests. [71]If a man never fails to offer these five great sacrifices to the best of his ability, he remains unsullied by the taints of his slaughter-houses in spite of living permanently at home. [72]Gods, guests, dependents, ancestors, and oneself—when someone does not make offerings to these five, he has breath but no life at all.

[73]The five sacrifices are called Ahuta, Huta, Prahuta, Brāhmya-Huta, and Prāśita. [74]The Ahuta—"not offered in the fire"—is soft recitation. The Huta—"offered in the fire"—is a burnt offering. The Prahuta—"offered by scattering"—is the Bali offering to beings. The Brāhmya-Huta—"offered in Brahmins"—is the worship of Brahmins. The Prāśita—"consumed"—is the quenching libation to ancestors.

[75]He should apply himself here* daily to his vedic recitation and to making offerings to gods; for by applying himself to making offerings to gods, he upholds this world, both the mobile and the immobile. [76]An oblation duly consigned to the fire reaches the sun; from the sun comes rain; from rain, food; and from food, offspring.*

[77]As all living beings exist dependent on air, so people in other orders of life* exist dependent on the householder. [78]Because it is householders who sustain people in all three orders of life every day by giving them knowledge and food, the householder represents the most senior order of life.* [79]This is the order that must be shouldered* assiduously by anyone who desires undecaying heaven and absolute happiness, an order that cannot be shouldered by people with feeble faculties.

[80]Seers, ancestors, gods, beings, and guests seek favors from the householder, which a wise man should grant them. [81]He should duly honor the seers by private vedic recitation, gods with burnt oblations, ancestors with an ancestral offering, humans with food, and beings with a Bali offering.

Ancestral Offerings [82]He should make an ancestral offering every day with food or water, or even with milk, roots, and fruits, gladdening his ancestors thereby. [83]He should feed at least a single Brahmin for the benefit of his ancestors as part of the five great sacrifices; at this,* he should never feed even a single Brahmin* in connection with the offering to the All-gods.

Divine Offerings [84]From the oblation to All-gods* that has been cooked, a Brahmin should offer portions in the domestic fire to the following deities every day and according to rule: [85]first to Fire and to Soma; then to both of them together; to the All-gods; to Dhanvantari; [86]to Kuhū—the goddess of the new moon; to Anumati—the goddess of the full moon; to Prajāpati; to heaven and earth together; and finally to Sviṣṭakṛt—Fire who makes the offering flawless.

Bali Offerings [87]In this manner, having offered the burnt oblation properly, he should make the Bali offerings to Indra, Death, Lord of the waters (Varuṇa), and Moon, together with their attendants, making the offerings clockwise in the direction of each quarter. [88]He should make an offering by the door, saying: "To the Maruts!"; by the water pot, saying: "To the waters!"; and by the mortar and pestle, saying "To trees!" [89]He should make a Bali offering to Śrī—the goddess of prosperity—by the head of the bed; to Bhadrakālī—the auspicious black goddess—by the foot of the bed; and to Brahman and the Lord of the house in the middle of the house.

[90]He should throw into the air a Bali offering to All-gods, as well as to beings that roam during the day and to those that roam at night.* [91]In the back house,* he should make a Bali offering to Sarvānnabhūti*—the power of all food. The remainder of the Bali oblation he should offer towards the south for the ancestors. [92]He should also gently place on the ground offerings for dogs, outcastes, dog-cookers, persons with evil diseases,* crows, and worms.

[93]When a Brahmin honors all beings in this manner every day, he takes on a body of effulgence and goes by the direct route to the supreme abode.

Honoring Guests [94]After completing in this manner the Bali offering, he should feed a guest before anyone else and give almsfood to a mendicant student of the Veda* according to rule. [95]By giving almsfood, a twice-born householder obtains as much merit as he does by giving a cow to a poor man* according to rule.

[96]He should garnish* some almsfood or a pot of water and present it in accordance with the rules to a Brahmin who knows the true meaning of the Veda. [97]Divine and ancestral oblations of ignorant men come to naught when the donors offer them foolishly to Brahmins who are the equivalent of ashes.* [98]Oblations offered in the fires that are the mouths of Brahmins, fires set ablaze by knowledge and ascetic toil, rescue a man from danger and from grievous sin.+

[99]When a guest arrives, he should offer him a seat and water and give him food as well according to rule, after garnishing it according to his ability.+ [100]When a Brahmin resides without being treated with respect, he takes away all the good works of even a man who lives by gleaning ears of grain (4.5 n.) or who makes daily offerings in the five sacred fires (3.185 n.). [101]Some straw, a place on the floor, water, and fourth, a pleasant word of welcome—at least these are never wanting in the houses of good people.

[102]Tradition defines a guest as a Brahmin who spends just one night. He is called "guest" because his stay is brief.* [103]A Brahmin living in the same village or on a social visit cannot be considered a guest even when he comes to a house which has a wife or even sacred fires.* [104]When foolish householders become attached to other people's cooking, the result is that after death they are born as the cattle of those who gave them food.+

[105]A householder must never turn away a guest led there by the sun in the evening; and whether he arrives at the proper time or not, he should not let him remain in his house without food. [106]Nor should he eat anything that he does not serve his guest. Honoring (3.70 n.) a guest* leads to wealth, fame, long life, and heaven.

[107]Guests of the highest status should receive the highest treatment with respect to seat, room, bed, accompanying them as they leave,* and paying honor to them; those of equal status should receive equal treatment; and those of inferior status should receive inferior treatment. [108]If another guest arrives after he has completed the offering to All-gods, however, he should provide him also with food according to his ability; but he need not make a fresh Bali offering.*

[109]A Brahmin must not advertise his family and lineage for the sake of a meal; for the wise call a man who flaunts these for a meal "an eater of vomit."

[110]A Kṣatriya is not called a "guest" in the house of a Brahmin; nor is a Vaiśya, a Śūdra, a friend, a relative, or an elder.* [111]If, however, a Kṣatriya comes to his house fulfilling the conditions of a guest,* he may freely feed him also after the Brahmins have finished their meal. [112]Even when a Vaiśya or a Śūdra arrives at his house fulfilling the conditions of a guest, he should show kindness and feed him along with his servants. [113]Even when others, such as his friends, visit his house out of mutual affection, he should make as special a preparation of food as he can and feed them along with his wife.* [114]Newly married women, young girls, the sick, and pregnant women—these he may feed without hesitation right after* the guests.

[115]When a fool eats before he gives food to these persons, as he eats he is unaware that he is being eaten by dogs and vultures. [116]Once the Brahmins, the dependents, and the servants have finished their meal, only then should the husband and wife eat what is left over. [117]After he has honored (3.70 n.) the gods, seers, humans, ancestors, and the guardian deities of the house, the householder should eat what remains. [118]A man who cooks only for his own sake eats nothing but sin; for the food prescribed for good men is this—eating the leftovers of a sacrifice.

[119]He should honor a king, an officiating priest, a bath-graduate, an elder, a friend,* a father-in-law, and a maternal uncle with a honey-mixture* when they visit him after the lapse of one year. [120]The rule is that a king and a vedic scholar should be honored with a honey-mixture when a sacrifice is about to take place, but never outside the context of a sacrifice.

[121]When the evening meal is cooked, the wife should make a Bali offering without reciting vedic formulas. This is called "offering to All-gods," and it is prescribed both in the evening and in the morning.

Ancestral Offerings

[122]After he has offered the sacrifice to ancestors,* a Brahmin who possesses a sacred fire should perform the monthly ancestral rite called the "supplementary offering of rice balls"* on the new-moon day. [123]The wise call the monthly offering to ancestors the "supplementary offering," and it should be performed diligently using the recommended kinds of meat (cf. 3.266–72).

[124]Who are the Brahmins to be fed at this rite and who are to be avoided? How many? And with what kinds of food?—I will explain all that completely.

Number of Invitees [125]Even if he is rich, he should feed two at an offering to gods, three at an offering to ancestors, or one at either offering; he should not indulge in feeding a large number. [126]A large number is detrimental to five things: offering proper hospitality,* doing things at the right place and the right time, carrying out purifications, and finding Brahmins of quality. Therefore, he must not try to get a large number.

Quality of Invitees [127]This rite for the deceased performed at the new moon is well known by the name "ancestral offering." When a man is devoted to it, the same non-vedic rite for the deceased benefits him always.*

[128]Donors should present a divine or ancestral offering only to a vedic scholar; what is given to such an eminently worthy Brahmin yields abundant fruit. [129]He should feed even a single learned man at each rite to gods or ancestors rather than a lot of men ignorant of the Veda; he reaps thereby copious fruit. [130]He should search far and wide* for a Brahmin who has mastered the Veda; such a man is the proper recipient of divine and ancestral offerings, and tradition calls him a "guest." [131]For when one man who knows the Veda is gratified there, in terms of the Law he is worth all the men ignorant of the Veda who may eat there, be they in their millions. [132]Divine and ancestral offerings should be given to a man renowned for his knowledge, for hands smeared with blood cannot be cleansed with more blood. [133]A man will have to eat as many red-hot spikes, spears, and iron balls as the rice balls that someone ignorant of the Veda eats at his divine or ancestral offerings.

[134]Some Brahmins apply themselves to knowledge, some to ascetic toil, others to both ascetic toil and vedic recitation, and still others to ritual activities.* [135]He should diligently present divine offerings only to those who apply themselves to knowledge, but he may present ancestral offerings to any of the four according to rule. [136]Between a man whose father is not a vedic savant but whose son has mastered the Veda and a man whose father has mastered the Veda but whose the son is not vedic savant, [137]the man whose father is a vedic savant should be considered as superior.* The other deserves honor for the sake of venerating the Veda.

[138]A friend must not be fed at an ancestral offering; he is to be courted with presents. A twice-born who is deemed neither friend nor foe is the one who should be fed at an ancestral offering. [139]When a friend takes center stage* at his divine or ancestral offerings, he reaps no fruit from them after death. [140]When a man foolishly strikes up friendships by means of an ancestral offering, that lowest of twice-born, using ancestral offerings to make friends, will fall from heaven. [141]Such a sacrificial gift is ghoulish and twice-born people call it "feeding-one-another." It remains in this very world, like a blind cow in a single stall.*

[142]As a sower reaps no harvest when he sows his seeds on barren soil, so a giver earns no reward when he gives his oblation to a man ignorant of the Veda. [143]A sacrificial gift given to a learned man according to rule makes both the givers and the receivers partake of its rewards both here and in the hereafter.

[144]He may, if he so wishes, honor a friend at an ancestral offering but never a foe even if he is quite handsome;* for an oblation is fruitless in the hereafter when it is eaten by an enemy. [145]He should make every effort to feed at his ancestral offering either a scholar of the Ṛgveda who has mastered that Veda, or an Adhvaryu priest who has mastered that vedic branch, or a scholar of the Sāmaveda who has learnt it completely.

[146]When any one of these is received with honor and eats the ancestral offering of someone, his ancestors up to the seventh generation derive unending satisfaction.

[147]This, clearly, is the primary method in presenting divine and ancestral offerings. What follows, on the other hand, should be considered a secondary method that has always been followed by good people. [148]One may feed the following: maternal grandfather, maternal uncle, sister's son, father-in-law, teacher, daughter's son, son-in-law, and relative, as also one's officiating priest and a person for whom one officiates as a priest.

[149]A man who knows the Law must never probe into the qualifications of a Brahmin at a rite to the gods; when he undertakes an ancestral rite, however, he should diligently probe into his qualifications.+

Unfit Invitees [150]Brahmins who are thieves, fallen from their caste, or impotent,* or who follow the livelihood of infidels—Manu has declared these unfit to participate at divine or ancestral offerings. [151]Men who have matted hair, who do not recite the Veda, who are bald-headed,* who are gamblers, and who officiate at sacrifices offered by groups of people—these also must not be fed at an ancestral offering. [152]Physicians, temple priests, meat sellers, and those who live by trade—these should be avoided at divine and ancestral offerings.

[153]A servant of a village or a king; someone with bad nails or black teeth; someone who opposes his teacher or has abandoned the sacred fire; an usurer; [154]someone suffering from consumption; a cattle herder; a man who sets up a household before his older brother (cf. 3.171); someone who neglects his ritual duties* or hates the Veda; a man who sets up a household after his younger brother; someone linked to an association;* [155]a performer; a vedic student who has broken his vow of chastity; a husband of a Śūdra woman; a son of a remarried woman (9.175 n.); a one-eyed man; someone who lets his wife's paramour live in his house; [156]someone who teaches for a fee, as also the person taught by such a teacher; a pupil or teacher of a Śūdra; a man of uncouth speech; a son of an adultress (3.174); a son of a widow (3.174); [157]someone who repudiates his father, mother, or teacher without good reason; someone who has established vedic or matrimonial links with people fallen from their caste; [158]an arsonist; a poisoner; someone who eats from the son of an adulteress; a seller of Soma; a seafarer; a panegyrist; an oil-miller; a suborner of perjury; [159]someone who wrangles with his father; a gambler; a man who drinks liquor; someone with an evil disease (3.92 n.); a heinous sinner (2.185 n.); a hypocrite; a poison vendor;* [160]someone who manufactures bows and arrows; a lover of one's sister-in-law (3.173); a treacherous friend; a man who lives by gambling; someone whose teacher is his son; [161]an epileptic; someone with scrofula or leukoderma; a slanderer; an insane person; a blind man; and someone who scoffs at the Vedas—these persons should be avoided.

[162]A trainer of elephants, oxen, horses, or camels; an astrologer by profession; a bird breeder; a combat trainer; [163]someone who breaches canals or takes delight in obstructing them;* an architect; a messenger; a tree planter; [164]someone who uses dogs for sport; a professional falconer; a man who rapes virgins; a cruel man; someone who adopts a Śūdra occupation; a man who officiates at sacrifices of corporate bodies;* [165]someone lacking in proper conduct; an impotent man (3.150 n.); someone who is

always asking for things; a farmer by profession; a club-footed man; someone condemned by good people; [166]a man who keeps sheep or buffaloes; a husband of a woman who has had a man before (5.163 n.); someone who carries corpses—these persons should be diligently avoided.

[167]At both divine and ancestral offerings, a man who is wise and the highest of the twice-born should avoid these lowest of the twice-born, men of despicable conduct alongside whom it is unfit to eat. [168]For a Brahmin who does not recite the Veda becomes extinguished like a grass-fire, and he should not be given a divine offering; no one pours an offering in the ashes (3.97 n.).

[169]I will explain in full detail the fruit a donor reaps in the hereafter when he feeds at a divine or ancestral offering a man alongside whom it is unfit to eat. [170]What is eaten by Brahmins who do not keep to their vows, by people such as those who set up a household before their older brothers, and by other individuals alongside whom it is unfit to eat—all that is undoubtedly eaten by fiends.

[171]When someone gets married or begins to perform the daily fire sacrifice before his older brother, he is to be considered a Parivettṛ—"a man who sets up a household before his older brother"; and that older brother is a Parivitti—"a man who sets up a household after his younger brother." [172]A man who sets up a household before his older brother, a man who sets up a household after his younger brother, the woman who marries such a man, the man who gives her away, and, fifth, the priest who performs the wedding—they all go to hell. [173]When a man has a lustful affair with the wife of his deceased brother, even if she has been legally appointed for leviratic union (9.57–70), he should be considered a Didhiṣūpati—"lover of his sister-in-law." [174]Two types of sons, Kuṇḍa and Golaka, are born from someone else's wife. If her husband is alive, he is a Kuṇḍa—"son of an adulteress"; and if her husband is dead, he is a Golaka—"son of a widow." [175]These two creatures, born in someone else's field (9.33), make the divine or ancestral offering given to them futile to the donor both here and in the hereafter.

[176]When a man alongside whom it is unfit to eat looks at persons alongside whom it is fit to eat as they are taking their meal, the foolish donor fails to reap the reward of feeding as many of them as have been looked at by that man. [177]When a blind man looks at them, he destroys the fruit of feeding ninety of them; a one-eyed man, sixty; a man suffering from leukoderma, one hundred; and a man with an evil disease, one thousand. [178]When a man who officiates at sacrifices of Śūdras touches the Brahmins with a limb of his, the donor fails to reap the fruit of giving non-sacrificial offerings to as many Brahmins as have been touched by that man. [179]When even a Brahmin learned in the Veda greedily accepts anything from such a man, he quickly comes to ruin, like an unbaked clay pot in water.

[180]What is given to a seller of Soma turns into excrement; what is given to a physician turns into pus and blood; what is given to a temple priest perishes; what is given to a usurer lacks stability; [181]what is given to a trader has no effect either in this world or the next; and what is given to a twice-born man born to a remarried woman is like an oblation offered in ashes (3.97 n.). [182]The wise declare that the food given to other evil men enumerated above (3.150–66), men alongside whom it is unfit to eat, turn into fat, blood, flesh, marrow, and bone.

Persons Who Purify Those Alongside Whom They Eat [183]Brahmins who purify a row of eaters defiled by someone alongside whom it is unfit to eat—listen to a complete enumeration of such Brahmins, who purify those alongside whom they eat. [184]Men of preeminence in all the Vedas and in all the expository texts,* as also descendants in a line of vedic scholars, should be regarded as persons who purify those alongside whom they eat. [185]An expert in the three Nāciketa* fire altars; a man who maintains the five sacred fires;* a man who knows the Trisuparṇa verse; a man who knows the six Vedic Supplements (2.105 n.); a son of a woman married according to the "Brāhma" procedure (3.27); a man who sings the Jyeṣṭha Sāmans; [186]a man who knows the meaning of the Veda, as also one who teaches it; a vedic student; a man who has given a 1,000;* a 100-year-old man—these should be regarded as Brahmins who purify those alongside whom they eat.

Invitations [187]When an ancestral offering is about to take place, he should duly invite the kind of Brahmins mentioned above, a minimum of three, either on the preceding day or on the very day of the offering.

[188]When a twice-born has been invited to an ancestral rite, both he and the person performing the rite should constantly keep themselves controlled and refrain from vedic recitation; [189]for the ancestors stand by those twice-born who have been invited, follow them like the wind, and sit by them as they sit.+

[190]If a Brahmin who has been invited to a divine or ancestral offering according to rule becomes delinquent in any way, that evil man will become a pig. [191]If someone invited to an ancestral offering has a sexual encounter with a Śūdra woman, he will assume all the sins committed by the donor of that offering.

Classes of Ancestors [192]The ancestors are the primeval deities*—they are free from anger, devoted to purification, and always chaste; they have laid down their arms; and they are highly exalted. [193]From whom do they all originate; who should be worshipped and according to what specific rules—listen to an account of all that.

[194]Tradition holds that the various groups of ancestors are the sons of all the seers headed by Marīci, seers who are the children of Manu, the son of Hiraṇyagarbha (1.34–35). [195]Somasads, the sons of Virāj, are known in tradition as the ancestors of the Sādhyas. Agniṣvāttas, the sons of Marīci, are widely known in the world as the ancestors of the gods. [196]Barhiṣads, the sons of Atri, are known in tradition as the ancestors of Daityas, Dānavas, Yakṣas, Gandharvas, Serpents, Rākṣasas, Suparṇas, and Kinnaras. [197]The ancestors of Brahmins are called Somapas; of Kṣatriyas, Havirbhujs; of Vaiśyas, Ājyapas; and of Śūdras, Sukālins. [198]Somapas are the sons of Kavi; Haviṣmats, the sons of Aṅgiras; Ājyapas, the sons of Pulastya; and Sukālins, the sons of Vasiṣṭha. [199]Anagnidagdhas, Agnidagdhas, Kāvyas, Barhiṣads, Agniṣvāttas, and Saumyas—these should be regarded as the ancestors only of Brahmins. [200]It should be understood, however, that these principal classes of ancestors we have enumerated have also here countless sons and grandsons.

[201]From the seers were born the ancestors; from the ancestors, the gods and demons;* and from the gods, the whole world, the mobile and the immobile, in due order.

[202]Even some water offered to them with a generous spirit* using vessels made of silver or inlaid with silver leads to an imperishable reward.

Preparatory Rites [203]Ancestral offerings are far more significant for twice-born persons than divine offerings; for, according to tradition, a divine offering is a preliminary rite confering vigor upon the ancestral offering. [204]He should perform at the outset an offering to gods, which provides protection to ancestral rites; for fiends plunder an ancestral offering lacking such protection. [205]He should seek to begin and end an ancestral offering with offerings to gods; it should never begin or end with offerings to ancestors. Should he, instead, seek to begin or end with offerings to ancestors, he will quickly come to ruin together with his offspring.

[206]He should daub a clean and secluded area with cow dung and carefully make that area slope towards the south; [207]ancestors are always gratified by offerings made in places that are clean, secluded, in the open, and by the water's edge.+

[208]On separate seats properly arranged and spread with sacred grass, he should seat the Brahmins after they have sipped water.* [209]After seating those irreproachable Brahmins on their seats, he should honor them with fragrant perfumes and garlands, beginning with the ones associated with the divine offering.

[210]Having brought water and sesame seeds along with purificatory Kuśa blades for them, the Brahmin should make an offering in the sacred fire with the collective consent of those Brahmins.* [211]At the outset he should offer to Agni, Soma, and Yama oblations that confer vigor, and then satisfy the ancestors by offering them sacrificial food according to rule. [212]If a sacred fire is not available, however, he should offer the oblation simply in the hand of a Brahmin; for Brahmins who have seen the vedic formulas declare that the sacred fire is a twice-born.

[213]They call these highest of twice-born men the ancient* gods of the ancestral offering, free from anger, totally serene, and devoted to invigorating the world.

Principal Offerings [214]He should perform in the fire the entire series of rites so that they end in the south;* pour water on the ground with his right hand; [215]make three balls from the remainder of the sacrificial food with a collected mind; face the south and lay them down following the same procedure as at the pouring of water; [216]offer those balls in accordance with the rules, while keeping himself ritually pure; wipe his hand on those blades of sacred grass as the share of those who partake of leavings;* [217]sip some water; turn around towards the north; control his breath slowly three times; worship the six seasons and the ancestors while reciting ritual formulas; [218]once again pour the remaining water gently near the balls; smell those balls with a collected mind in the order they were laid down; [219]remove a small portion from each ball in the proper order; and get those seated Brahmins to eat them first according to rule.

[220]If his father is alive, however, he should lay down the balls only for the preceding ancestors; or he may get his own father to eat the ancestral offering like one of the Brahmins.* [221]If his father is dead but his grandfather is alive, on the other hand, he should first recite his father's name and then his great-grandfather's. [222]Manu has declared that either his grandfather may eat that ancestral offering or he may freely perform it on his own with his grandfather's permission.

[223]After pouring water mixed with sesame seeds along with purificatory Kuśa blades into their hands, he should offer a piece of those balls to each, saying, "Svadhā be to them!"

Feeding the Brahmins [224]Carrying with both his hands and by himself the vessel heaped with food, he should set it down gently in front of the Brahmins while thinking of his ancestors. [225]When food is brought without being held with both hands, evil-minded demons forcibly snatch it away. [226]Keeping himself ritually pure and with a collected mind, he should set down on the ground properly the side dishes,* such as sauces and vegetables; milk, curd, ghee, and honey; [227]various kinds of foods and delicacies; roots and fruits; and delicious meats and fragrant drinks.

[228]After bringing all these, he should dish them out gradually with a collected mind and keeping himself ritually pure, pressing all the side dishes on them.* [229]He must never shed a tear, become angry, tell a lie, touch the food with his foot, or flip it around. [230]A tear makes the food go to ghosts;* anger, to enemies; a lie, to dogs; touching with the foot, to fiends; and flipping around, to evil-doers.

[231]He should give ungrudgingly anything that the Brahmins may wish. He should narrate vedic disputations; it is pleasing to the ancestors. [232]At a rite for ancestors, he should make them listen to recitations of the Veda, legal treatises, stories, epic narratives, Purāṇas, and ancillary texts.* [233]He should cheerfully gratify the Brahmins and feed them at a leisurely pace, pressing on them repeatedly the main and the side dishes.

[234]He should diligently feed a son of his daughter at an ancestral offering, even if he is only a vedic student; place a goat's wool blanket* on each seat; and scatter sesame seeds on the ground. [235]At an ancestral offering, three things confer purity: daughter's son, goat-wool blanket, and sesame seeds; and three things are commended: purification, absence of anger, and doing things unhurriedly. [236]All the food should be very warm, and they should eat it in silence; and even when the donor inquires about it, the Brahmins should not comment on the quality of the sacrificial food. [237]As long as the food is warm, as long as they eat it in silence, and as long as they do not comment on the quality of the sacrificial food, the ancestors partake of it. [238]What is eaten wearing a turban on the head, what is eaten facing the south, or what is eaten wearing sandals, is undoubtedly eaten by fiends.

[239]A Cāṇḍāla, a pig, a cock, a dog, a menstruating woman, or a eunuch must not look at the Brahmins while they are eating. [240]What is seen by any of these during a fire offering, the giving of a gift, a ritual feeding, or a divine or ancestral oblation, becomes inefficacious. [241]A pig spoils with its breath, a cock with the waft from its wings, a dog with its gaze, and a low-caste man with his touch. [242]If someone is lame or one-eyed, lacks a limb, or has an excess limb, he should also be removed from that place, even if he is a servant of the donor.

[243]Should a Brahmin or a mendicant come there for food, he should honor him according to his ability with the permission of those Brahmins.

[244]Mixing all the varieties of food together, he should drench it with water and deposit it in front of the diners after they have finished their meal, scattering it on the ground. [245]The remnants of food and what has been scattered on the sacred grass are the

share of those who have died before their initiation or committed suicide,* and of young women of the family. [246]The fragments fallen on the ground at an ancestral offering are declared to be the share of all the deceased servants who have not been dishonest or crooked.

Rite for the Newly Deceased [247]For a deceased twice-born, he should perform the rite without the Sapiṇḍa offerings; omitting the offering to gods, he should feed the ancestral offering to one person and lay down one rice ball.* [248]Once the rite of Sapiṇḍa has been performed for him in accordance with the Law, his sons should offer the balls exactly in the above manner.*

Conclusion of the Meal [249]After eating an ancestral offering, if someone gives his leftovers to a Śūdra, that foolish man will fall down head first into the Kālasūtra hell. [250]If a man who has eaten an ancestral offering gets into bed with a Śūdra woman that day, his ancestors will lie in her feces during that month.

[251]He should ask them "Have you eaten well?"; when they are sated, he should give them water for sipping; and when they have sipped water, he should give them leave to go, saying "Please, stay around!"* [252]Immediately thereafter, the Brahmins should simply say to him: "May there be Svadhā!", for the exclamation "Svadhā" is the highest benediction in all ancestral offerings.

[253]Then, after they have finished eating, he should inform those Brahmins of the leftover food and, with their permission, do exactly as they instruct.

[254]At an offering to ancestors, one should say, "Have you eaten well?"; at a cow-pen offering,* "Was it well cooked?"; at an offering for prosperity,* "Was it delicious?"; and at a divine offering, "Was it tasty?"

[255]The afternoon, Darbha grass, proper preparation of the location, sesame seeds, liberal outlay, proper preparation of food, and excellent twice-born men—these are what ensures success at ancestral rites. [256]Darbha grass, purifier, forenoon, sacrificial foods of every kind, purifier, and what was stated above*—these should be regarded as what ensures success at divine rites. [257]Food of sages,* milk, Soma, meat, food without elaborate preparation,* and natural salt are, by their very nature, called "sacrificial food."

Concluding Rites [258]After he has dismissed those Brahmins, he should make himself pure and collected, control his speech, turn towards the south, and implore his ancestors for these favors: [259]"May donors amidst us thrive, may the Vedas and progeny! May the generous spirit never abandon us! And may we have a lot to give!"

[260]Immediately after he has laid down the balls in this manner, he should feed them to a cow, a Brahmin, a goat, or the fire, or else throw them in water. [261]Some perform the laying down of the balls towards the east;* others feed them to birds or throw them in fire or water.

[262]The wife who is wedded according to the Law, devoted to her husband, and intent on worshipping the ancestors may eat the middlemost of those balls in the proper manner, if she wants to have a son. [263]She will give birth to a son endowed with long life, fame, intelligence, wealth, progeny, righteousness, and goodness.

[264]After he has washed his hands and sipped some water, he should prepare food for his paternal relatives; give that well-garnished food to his paternal relatives; honor (3.70 n.) also his maternal relatives;* [265]let the scattered fragments remain until the Brahmins have been dismissed; and then perform the domestic Bali offering—that is the settled Law.

Food at Ancestral Rites [266]I will explain exhaustively the types of sacrificial food that are efficacious for a long time and those that are efficacious in perpetuity, when they are offered to the ancestors according to rule.

[267]By offering sesame seeds, rice, barley, beans, water, roots, and fruits according to rule, ancestors of men rejoice for one month;* [268]by offering fish, for two months; by offering the meat of the common deer, for three months; by offering sheep meat, for four months; by offering here the meat of birds, for five months; [269]by offering goat meat, for six months; by offering the meat of the spotted deer, for seven months; by offering the meat of the Eṇa antelope, for eight months; by offering the meat of the Ruru deer, for nine months; [270]by offering boar or buffalo meat, they are satisfied for ten months; by offering rabbit or turtle meat, for eleven months; [271]and by offering beef, milk,* or milk-rice, for one year. The satisfaction from the meat of a Vārdhrīṇasa horn-bill lasts for twelve years. [272]The Kālaśāka herb, Mahāśalka crustacean, the meat of the rhinoceros and the red goat, and honey, as well as every type of sage's food (3.257 n.) are efficacious in perpetuity.

Times for Ancestral Rites [273]When someone mixes any kind of food with honey and offers it on the thirteenth day of a fortnight during the rainy season and under the Magha* constellation, that also is clearly inexhaustible. [274]"Would that a man be born in our family who would offer us milk-rice with honey and ghee on the thirteenth day during the elephant's eastern shadow."* [275]Whatever a man gives properly, with a generous spirit, and according to rule, in the other world it becomes eternal and inexhaustible for his ancestors.+

[276]The lunar days in the dark fortnight beginning with the tenth but excluding the fourteenth are commended for ancestral offerings; the other days are unlike these. [277]As the later fortnight is better for an ancestral offering than the earlier fortnight,* so the afternoon is better than the forenoon. [278]When a man performs them on even days and constellations, he obtains all his wishes; whereas when he worships the ancestors on uneven days and constellations, he obtains distinguished children.

[279]He should carry out the ancestral offering tirelessly, correctly, and according to rule until its completion, wearing the sacrificial cord over the right shoulder and under the left arm, carrying blades of Darbha grass in his hand, and performing each rite so as to end in the south (3.214 n.). [280]He must not perform an ancestral offering at night—for the night belongs to fiends—or during the two twilights, or soon after sunrise.

[281]Following this procedure, he should perform here an ancestral offering three times a year—in the winter, in the summer, and in the rainy season—but the five sacrifices, every day.

[282]The rule is that the fire oblation at an ancestral rite must not be offered in the ordinary fire. A twice-born man who maintains the three sacred fires shall not perform an

ancestral offering except on a new-moon day. [283]Even if a Brahmin simply satiates his ancestors with water after he has bathed, he obtains thereby the full reward of performing an ancestral rite.

[284]The fathers, they say, are the Vasus; the grandfathers are the Rudras; and the great-grandfathers are the Ādityas—this is an ancient scriptural statement.*

Conclusion

[285]He should become a man who always eats "residue" and who always partakes of "ambrosia." "Residue" is what remains after people have eaten, and "ambrosia" is the leftovers of a sacrifice.

> [286]I have explained to you all the rules relating to the five sacrifices.
> Listen now to the rules relating to the livelihood of Brahmins.

CHAPTER FOUR

THE BATH-GRADUATE

[1]After spending the first quarter of his life at his teacher's, a twice-born man should marry a wife and spend the second quarter of his life at home.*

Right Livelihood

[2]Except during a time of adversity, a Brahmin ought to sustain himself by following a livelihood that causes little or no harm* to creatures. [3]He should gather wealth just sufficient for his subsistence through irreproachable activities that are specific to him, without fatiguing his body.*

[4]Let him sustain himself by means of "true" and "immortal," or by means of "mortal" and "fatal," or even by means of "truth-cum-falsehood"; but under no circumstances by means of the "dog's life." [5]Gleaning and picking* should be considered the "true"; what is received unasked is the "immortal"; almsfood that is begged is the "mortal"; and agriculture, tradition says, is the "fatal." [6]Trade is the "truth-cum-falsehood," and he may sustain himself even by that. Service is called the "dog's life"; therefore, he should avoid it altogether.

[7]Let him be a man who stores grain sufficient to fill a granary, a man who stores grain sufficient to fill a jar,* a man who has sufficient grain to last three days, or a man who keeps nothing for the next day. [8]Among all these four types of twice-born householders, each should be recognized as superior to the ones preceding it and better at winning the heavenly world, according to the Law.* [9]One of these may engage in the six activities; another may live by three; yet another by two; and a fourth may subsist through the sacrificial session of the Veda.* [10]A man who lives by gleaning and picking should be totally dedicated to the daily fire sacrifice and always offer only the sacrifices at the new- and full-moon days and at the solstices. [11]He must never follow a worldly occupation for the sake of livelihood, but subsist by means of a pure, upright, and honest livelihood proper to a Brahmin.

[12]One who seeks happiness should become supremely content and self-controlled, for happiness is rooted in contentment and its opposite is the root of unhappiness.

Observances

[13]Subsisting by one of these means of livelihood, a twice-born who is a bath-graduate should follow these observances, which procure heaven, long life, and fame.

[14]He should perform diligently the daily rituals specific to him prescribed in the Veda; for, by performing them according to his ability, he attains the highest state.

[15]He must never seek to obtain wealth (*artha*) with excessive passion,* through forbidden activities, when he already has sufficient wealth, or from just anyone even in a time of adversity; [16]nor shall he be passionately attached to any of the sensory objects (*artha*) out of lust, but using his mind he should stamp out any excessive attachment to them. [17]He should forsake all pursuits (*artha*) that interfere with his vedic recitation, eking out a living* some way or other, for that recitation constitutes the fulfillment of all his obligations. [18]He should comport himself here in such a way that his attire, speech, and mind are in harmony with his age, occupation, wealth (*artha*), learning, and family background.

Study

[19]Every day, he should explore the treatises*—those that aid in the quick development of one's mind, those that facilitate the acquisition of wealth, and those that promote well-being—as well as ancillary texts* of the Veda; [20]for, the more a man studies treatises, the more he comes to understand and the more brightly shines his understanding.+

Ritual Duties

[21]He must never fail to offer every day and according to his ability the sacrifices to seers, gods, beings, humans, and ancestors (see 3.70 f.).

[22]Some individuals who are experts in the sacrificial science and free from striving offer these great sacrifices incessantly in just their organs. [23]Others offer breath in speech and speech in breath every day, recognizing that the sacrifice reaches its inexhaustible consummation in speech and breath. [24]Still other Brahmins offer these sacrifices daily through knowledge alone, recognizing by the eye of knowledge that the execution of those sacrifices is rooted in knowledge.*

[25]A twice-born man, moreover, should always offer the fire sacrifice at the beginning and end of each day and night; the new-moon and the full-moon sacrifice at the end of each fortnight; [26]the new-harvest sacrifice at the end of each harvest;* the seasonal sacrifices at the end of each season; an animal sacrifice at the end of each half-year;* and Soma sacrifices at the end of each year. [27]A twice-born who has established the sacred fires, if he wants to live a long life, must never eat a new crop without offering the new-harvest sacrifice, or meat without offering an animal sacrifice; [28]for his sacred fires crave for the new crop and meat and, if they have not been honored with an offering of the new crop and an animal oblation, yearn to eat his very lifebreaths.

Reception of Guests

[29]No guest should stay at his house without being honored with a seat, food, and a bed, or with water, roots, and fruits, according to his ability. [30]He must never honor the following even with a word of welcome: ascetics of heretical sects; individuals engaging in improper activities, observing the "cat vow," or following the way of herons (4.195–6); hypocrites; and sophists. [31]At rites for gods and ancestors, he should honor (3.70 n.) individuals who have bathed after completing the Vedas, vedic learning, or vedic vows,* who are vedic scholars, or who are householders, but avoid

individuals different from these. [32]As far as he is able, a householder should give to those who do not cook* and share with all beings without causing hardship to himself.

Rules of Conduct: I

[33]If a bath-graduate is tormented by hunger, he may request money from the king, from a client at whose sacrifices he officiates, or from a resident pupil, but from no one else—that is the settled rule. [34]If he has the capacity, a Brahmin bath-graduate should never torment himself with hunger or, if he has the means, wear dirty or worn-out clothes.

[35]He shall keep his nails clipped, his hair and beard trimmed, and himself restrained; wear white clothes; remain pure; and apply himself every day to his vedic recitation and to activities conducive to his own welfare. [36]He shall carry a bamboo staff, a waterpot filled with water, and a broom of sacred grass, and wear a sacrificial cord and a pair of bright gold earrings.

[37]He must never look at the sun as it rises or sets, when it is eclipsed or reflected in water, or when it is in the middle of the sky. [38]He must not step over a rope to which a calf is tied, run in the rain, or look at his reflection in water—that is the fixed rule. [39]A mound of earth,* a cow, a god, a Brahmin, ghee, honey, and a crossroads—he should circumambulate these clockwise, as also notable trees.

Relationship with Women

[40]Though aroused, he must never have sex with his wife after the onset of her menstrual period, or even lie on the same bed with her; [41]for when a man has sex with a woman besmirched with menstrual blood, his wisdom, energy, strength, sight, and life-force waste away. [42]When he avoids a woman besmirched with menstrual blood, his wisdom, energy, strength, sight, and life-force* will wax stronger.

[43]He must never eat with his wife or look at her while she is eating, sneezing, yawning, or seated at ease; [44]nor should the Brahmin,* if he wants energy, look at her while she is applying collyrium to her eyes or oil on her body, or when she is undressed or giving birth.+

Voiding Urine and Excrement

[45]He must never eat food wearing just a single garment; bathe naked; or urinate on a road, on ashes, in a cow pen, [46]on plowed land, into water, onto a mound* or a hill, in a dilapidated temple, onto an anthill, [47]into occupied animal holes, while walking or standing, by a river bank, or at the top of a hill. [48]He must never void urine or excrement facing the wind, a fire, a Brahmin, the sun, water, or cows.

[49]Restraining his voice, remaining steadfastly attentive,* covering his body, and wrapping his head, he should ease himself after strewing the ground with sticks, clods, leaves, or grass. [50]During the day, he should void urine and excrement facing the north, at night facing the south, and at the two twilights in the same way as during the day. [51]Under a shadow or in a place that is pitch-dark, a Brahmin may do so during the day or at night facing any direction he pleases, as also when he fears for his life.

[52]When someone urinates towards a fire, the sun, the moon, water, a twice-born man, a cow, or the wind, his wisdom perishes.*

Rules of Conduct: II

[53]He must never blow on a fire with his mouth; look at a woman when she is naked; throw anything filthy into a fire; warm his feet over it; [54]place it under his bed; step over it; place it by his feet; hurt living creatures; [55]eat, travel, or sleep during the time of twilight; scribble on the ground; take off his own garland;* [56]deposit urine, excrement, sputum, blood, poison, or anything smeared with filth in water; [57]sleep alone in an abandoned house; awaken a sleeping superior;* speak with a menstruating woman; or go to a sacrifice uninvited.+

[58]Within an enclosure for the sacred fire, in a cow pen, in the presence of Brahmins, during his vedic recitation, and while eating, he shall keep his right arm uncovered (2.193 n.). [59]He must never prevent a cow from suckling her calf or report it to anyone. When he sees a rainbow in the sky, he should wisely refrain from pointing it out to anyone.

[60]He must never reside in a village full of unrighteous people or where diseases run rampant;* go on a journey alone; stay long on a mountain; [61]or live in a kingdom ruled by a Śūdra, teeming with unrighteous people, overrun by people belonging to heretical ascetic sects, or swamped by lowest-born people.

[62]He must never eat anything from which the oil has been extracted; eat beyond capacity; eat very early in the morning or very late in the evening; eat again in the evening after taking his meal in the morning; [63]undertake useless activities; drink water from his cupped hands; eat food placed on his lap; be in any way inquisitive; [64]dance; sing; play a musical instrument; clap; whistle;* make noises when sexually excited; [65]wash his feet in a brass vessel at any time; eat from a broken plate or from one that looks repulsive to him; [66]or use footwear, a garment, a sacrificial cord, an ornament, a garland, or a waterpot previously used by others.

[67]He must never travel with draft animals that are untrained, hungry, or sick, or that have broken horns, bad eyes, damaged hoofs, or deformed tails. [68]He should always travel with ones that are well trained and swift and possess good marks, color, and appearance, without driving them too hard with the whip.

[69]He should avoid the morning sun, the smoke from a funeral pyre, and broken seats. He must never cut his nails or hair;* bite off his nails with his teeth; [70]crush clods of earth; tear off grass with his fingernails; or engage in activities that are fruitless or have unpleasant future consequences. [71]A man who crushes clods, tears off grass, or bites his nails will quickly come to ruin, as also an informant and one who neglects purifications.

[72]He must never engage in a combative discussion or wear a garland outdoors.* Riding on the back of cattle is altogether reprehensible. [73]He must not enter an enclosed village or house by any passage other than the door; and at night, he should keep far away from the foot of any tree.

[74]He must never play with dice; fetch his sandals by himself; eat while lying in bed; eat anything placed in his hand or on a seat; [75]eat anything containing sesame after sunset; sleep here naked; or go anywhere while he is sullied with remnants (2.56 n.).

[76]He should eat with his feet wet, but never go to sleep with wet feet; by eating with wet feet, he obtains a long life.

[77]He must never enter a place difficult of access and hidden from sight; look at urine or excrement; cross a river swimming; [78]or, if he wishes to live long, step on hair, ash, bones, shards, cotton seeds, or chaff.

[79]He must never live in the company of outcastes, Cāṇḍālas, Pulkasas, fools, arrogant men, lowest-born people, or Antyāvasāyins. [80]He must never give a Śūdra advice, leftovers, or anything offered to the gods; teach him the Law; or prescribe an observance to him. [81]Whoever teaches him the Law or whoever prescribes an observance to him will plunge along with him into that darkness called Asaṃvṛta.

[82]He must never scratch his head with both hands together; touch his head while he is sullied with remnants (2.56 n.); or take a bath excluding the head. [83]He should refrain from pulling the hair or striking the head;* and after taking a bath including the head, he should not apply oil to any part of his body.

People from Whom Gifts May Not Be Accepted

[84]He must never accept gifts from a king who is not from a royal lineage; from people who operate abattoirs, oil-presses, or taverns; or from people who gain their living by keeping brothels. [85]One oil-press equals ten abattoirs; one tavern equals ten oil-presses; one brothel equals ten taverns; and one king equals ten brothels. [86]A king, tradition tells us, is equal to a butcher who operates ten thousand abattoirs; to accept a gift from him is a horrendous deed.

[87]When someone accepts a gift from a king who is greedy and who deviates from the provisions of the authoritative texts,* he will go in turn to these twenty hells: [88]Tāmisra, Andha-Tāmisra, Mahā-Raurava, Raurava, Kālasūtra-Naraka, Mahā-Naraka, [89]Saṃjīvana, Mahā-Vīci, Tapana, Saṃpratāpana, Saṃghāta, Sakākola, Kuḍmala, Pūtimṛttika, [90]Lohaśaṅku, Ṛjīṣa, Pathin, Sālmalī, Nadī, Asipatravana, and Loha-cāraka.*

[91]Knowing this and yearning for well-being after death, Brahmins who are learned and vedic savants do not accept gifts from a king.

Morning Duties

[92]He should wake up at the time sacred to Brahman* and reflect on matters relating to Law and Wealth, on the bodily discomforts (4.3 n.) they cause, and on the true meaning of the Veda.

[93]After getting up and answering the call of nature, he should perform the purifications and, with a collected mind, stand for a long time engaged in soft recitation during the morning twilight and, at its proper time, also during the evening twilight (2.101–3). [94]Because they performed their twilight devotions for a long time, the seers obtained long life, wisdom, fame, renown, and eminence in vedic knowledge.

Vedic Study

[95]On the full-moon day of Śrāvaṇa (July–August) or Prauṣṭhapada (August–September), a Brahmin should commence his annual course of study according to rule

and intently study the Vedas for four and a half months. [96]In the forenoon of the first day of the bright fortnight of either Puṣya (December–January) or Māgha* (January–February), a twice-born should perform the rite of terminating his vedic study outside the village.

[97]After performing in this manner the rite of terminating his vedic study outside the village in accordance with the authoritative texts, he should suspend recitation for two days and the intervening night, or just during that single day and night. [98]After that time, however, he should recite the Vedas intently during the bright fortnights and all the Vedic Supplements (2.105 n.) during the dark fortnights.

[99]He must never recite indistinctly or in the presence of Śūdras. After reciting the Veda during the last part of the night, he must not go back to sleep even if he is worn out. [100]In accordance with the aforementioned rule, he must recite the metrical sections of the Veda every day; outside a time of adversity, a twice-born must intently recite both the metrical sections of the Veda and the Brāhmaṇas.

Suspension of Vedic Recitation

[101]Anyone engaged in vedic recitation should always abstain on the following occasions when vedic recitation is to be suspended, as also should anyone engaged in teaching vedic recitation to students in the prescribed manner.

[102]When the wind becomes audible at night or kicks up the dust during the day—experts in recitation regard these as two occasions for suspending vedic recitation during the rainy season. [103]When there is lightning, thunder, and rain,* and when there is a shower of large meteors, Manu has enjoined the suspension of vedic recitation until the same time the following day. [104]It should be noted that vedic recitation is to be suspended only when these occur after the fires have been kindled, and also when clouds appear out of season. [105]When a noise erupts* in the sky, when there is an earthquake, or when halos surround the heavenly lights—even if these happen in season—one should know that vedic recitation is to be suspended until the same time the following day. [106]When lightning and the rumbling of thunder occur after the fires have been kindled, however, the suspension of recitation lasts as long as the heavenly lights are visible; if the other event also occurs, then the recitation is suspended at night as during the day.*

[107]Those who want to adhere strictly to the Law should suspend vedic recitation permanently in villages and towns and wherever there is a foul smell. [108]Vedic recitation is to be suspended in a village where there is a corpse, in the presence of a Śūdra, at the sound of weeping, and near a gathering of people.

[109]In water, in the middle of the night, after voiding urine or excrement, when he is sullied with remnants (2.56 n.), or after he has eaten an ancestral offering, a man should not even review it in his mind. [110]After accepting an invitation to an offering on behalf of a newly deceased person, a learned twice-born should not recite the Veda for three days, as also during the period of birth-impurity (5.58 f.) affecting the king and during an eclipse. [111]As long as the smell and stain of an offering on behalf of a newly deceased person lingers on the body of a learned Brahmin, he should not recite the Veda.

112He must not recite the Veda lying down, putting his feet up, or squatting with a band tied around his waist and knees;* after eating meat; after eating any food given by someone in a period of birth-impurity (5.58 f.); 113when there is fog; at the sound of arrows; during both twilights; on the new-moon day; on the fourteenth day of a fortnight; on the full-moon day; and on the eighth day of a fortnight. 114The new-moon day destroys the teacher; the fourteenth day destroys the pupil; and the eighth and full-moon days destroy the Veda. Therefore, he should avoid them altogether.

115A twice-born must not recite during a dust storm, when the horizons have turned crimson, at the howling of jackals or the cry of dogs, donkeys, and camels, and when he is seated in a row.*

116He must never recite the Veda near a cemetery, in the outskirts of a village, in a cow pen, wearing the same clothes he had on during sexual intercourse, or after accepting something at an ancestral offering. 117After accepting anything at all, whether animate or inanimate, given at an ancestral offering, he should suspend vedic recitation; for the hand of a twice-born, tradition tells us, is his mouth.

118After robbers have raided the village, after a turmoil caused by fire, and after anything out of the ordinary has happened, he should know that vedic recitation is to be suspended until the same time the following day.

119The suspension, tradition tells us, lasts for three nights both after commencing and after concluding the annual course of study; for a day and a night, however, on the eighth day of a fortnight and on the final night of every season.

120He must never recite the Veda while he is on a horse, tree, elephant, donkey, or camel; in a ship or vehicle; on arid land; 121during an altercation or a brawl; in the midst of a military unit or a battle; soon after eating; when he has indigestion; after vomiting or having an acidic belch; 122without obtaining the consent of any guest of his; when there is a strong wind; when blood is flowing from his body; or when he has been wounded by a weapon.

123He must never recite Ṛc-verses or Yajus-formulas within earshot of Sāman chanting, after reciting the conclusion of a Veda, and after reciting an Āraṇyaka.* 124The Ṛgveda is connected with the gods and the Yajurveda with humans; but the Sāmaveda, tradition tells us, is connected with ancestors. Its sound, therefore, is impure. 125Knowing this, learned men recite first the extract of the triple Veda daily and in the proper order and then the Veda.*

126When a farm animal, frog, cat, dog, snake, mongoose, or rat passes in between,* he should know that vedic recitation is to be suspended for a day and a night.

127These alone are the two occasions for suspending vedic recitation which a twice-born should diligently avoid every day: when his place of recitation has not been cleansed and when his body has not been purified.*

Rules of Conduct: III

128The new-moon day, the eighth day of a fortnight, the full-moon day, and the fourteenth day of a fortnight—on these days, a twice-born who is a bath-graduate should always remain chaste, even if his wife is in her season (3.45 n.).

[129]He must never take a bath after eating, when he is sick, in the dead of the night, regularly with his clothes on,* or in an unknown body of water.

[130]He must never tread deliberately on the shadow of these: god,* elder, king, bath-graduate, teacher, reddish-brown cow,* and a man consecrated for a sacrifice. [131]At midday and midnight, after eating an ancestral offering containing meat, and during both twilights, he should not tarry at a crossroads. [132]He must not step deliberately on used bath-powders, water from a bath, urine, excrement, blood, phlegm, spittle, or vomit.

[133]He must not consort with an enemy, a friend of an enemy, an unrighteous person, or a thief—as also with another man's wife; [134]for there is nothing in this world as sure to shorten a man's life as consorting with someone else's wife. [135]A Kṣatriya, a snake, and a learned Brahmin—however feeble these may be, he must never treat them with contempt, if he wants to prosper; [136]for when a man treats these three persons with contempt, they will reduce him to ashes. A wise man, therefore, should not treat these three with contempt. [137]He must not hold himself in contempt for his past failures; he should pursue prosperity until death, never deeming it too difficult to achieve.

[138]He should say what is true, and he should say what is pleasant; he should not say what is true but unpleasant, and he should not say what is pleasant but untrue—that is the eternal Law.* [139]He should call a lucky thing "Lucky"; or rather he should call everything "Lucky."* He should never start a senseless feud or an argument with anyone.

[140]He must never travel very early in the morning, very late in the evening, at high noon, with an unknown person, alone, or with Śūdras.

[141]He must not ridicule people who have too few or too many limbs, who are uneducated, who are very old, who lack beauty or wealth, or who are of low birth.

[142]When a Brahmin is sullied with remnants (2.56 n.), he must never touch with his hand a cow, a Brahmin, or a fire; nor, if he is healthy, should he look at the heavenly lights in the sky while he is impure. [143]If he touches any of these while he is impure, he should always touch his organs and all his limbs with water, and his navel with his palm.* [144]Unless he is sick, he must not touch his orifices without a good reason, and he should refrain from touching the hair on any of his private parts.

[145]He should apply himself to auspicious rites and good conduct, control his self, subdue his senses, and tirelessly perform soft recitations and fire offerings every day.+ [146]No misfortune befalls those who apply themselves to auspicious rites and good conduct, control their selves evey day, and perform soft recitations and fire offerings. [147]It is the soft recitation of the Veda that he should tirelessly perform every day at the proper time—for this is his highest Law, they say; others are called secondary Laws. [148]By reciting the Veda constantly, by performing purifications, by engaging in ascetic toil, and by showing no hostility to any creature, he gets to remember his former birth. [149]When, while recalling his former birth, a twice-born recites the Veda,* by that constant recitation of the Veda, he obtains unending bliss. [150]He should always make Sāvitra and pacificatory offerings on the days of the moon's change (3.45 n.) and always worship the ancestors on the eighth and the day following the eighth of each fortnight.*

[151]Urine, water from washing the feet, remnants of food, and dirty water—he

should dispose of all these far away from his house. [152]Voiding excrement, adorning oneself, bathing, brushing the teeth, applying collyrium, and the worship of gods—all these should be done only in the morning.

[153]He should visit gods and righteous Brahmins; the ruler for the sake of protection; and elders on the days of the moon's change (3.45 n.).* [154]He should greet elderly persons, offer them his seat, pay them obeisance with joined palms, and follow behind them as they leave (3.107 n.).

[155]He should tirelessly follow the root of the Law, namely, the conduct of good people, which is well set forth in scripture and tradition and is closely tied to the activities proper to him (1.107 n.)— [156]for by good conduct he obtains long life; by good conduct he obtains the kind of offspring he desires; by good conduct he obtains inexhaustible wealth; and good conduct neutralizes unlucky marks.* [157]A man of evil conduct becomes an object of reproach in the world, is always miserable, is afflicted with disease, and lives a very short life. [158]Even if he has no lucky marks at all, a man who follows the conduct of good people, who has a generous spirit (3.202 n.), and who is free from resentment, lives a hundred years.

[159]He should carefully avoid all activities that are under someone else's control, and diligently pursue those that are under his own control. [160]Whatever is under someone else's control—that is suffering; whatever is under one's own control—that is happiness. He should know that this, in a nutshell, is the definition of suffering and happiness. [161]He should diligently engage in those activities that give him inner joy and avoid those that do not.

Avoiding Violence

[162]He must never cause harm to his teacher, instructor, father, mother, elder, Brahmins, cows, and all who are given to austerities. [163]He should eschew infidelity, denigrating the Vedas, disparaging the gods, hatred, arrogance,* pride, anger, and harshness.

[164]He must not raise a stick against another person or bring it down on anyone in anger, except a son or a pupil; these he may beat in order to discipline them (8.299). [165]If a twice-born merely threatens a Brahmin with murderous intent, he will meander in the Tāmisra hell for one hundred years. [166]If he strikes him deliberately in anger with even a blade of grass, he will be reborn in evil wombs* for twenty-one births. [167]If a man foolishly draws blood from the body of a Brahmin who is not attacking him, he will experience intense suffering after death. [168]A man who draws blood will be eaten by others in the next world for as many years as the number of dust particles from the earth that the spilled blood lumps together (see 11.208).

[169]A wise man, therefore, must never threaten a twice-born person, strike him even with a blade of grass, or draw blood from his body.

Following the Path of Righteousness

[170]A man who is unrighteous, who has gained his wealth dishonestly, and who always takes delight in causing injury will never achieve happiness in this world. [171]Even when he has been brought low as a result of his righteous conduct, let him never turn to

unrighteous ways, seeing how quickly the fortunes of unrighteous and evil men are reversed.

[172]Like the earth,* practicing unrighteousness does not produce instant results in this world; but turning around gradually, it cuts off its perpetrator by his roots. [173]If not himself, then his sons; if not his sons, then his grandsons—an unrighteous act once committed never fails to repay its perpetrator. [174]Through unrighteous ways a man first prospers; then he experiences good fortune; next he vanquishes his opponents; but in the end he is destroyed root* and all.

[175]He should always take delight in speaking the truth, in following the Law, in conforming to the Ārya ways, and in purifying himself. With his speech, hands, and stomach controlled, he should discipline his disciples* according to the Law. [176]He should abandon any activity relating to Wealth or Pleasure that is in violation of Law, and even activities sanctioned by Law when they will result in future unhappiness or are repugnant to the world (2.224 n.).

[177]He must never conduct himself in a fickle manner with his hands, feet, eyes, or speech; follow crooked ways; or show hostility to others in thought or deed. [178]The path trodden by his fathers, the path trodden by his grandfathers—let him tread along that path of good people; no harm will befall him when he travels by that path.

Family and Social Relations

[179]Officiating priests; family priests; teachers; maternal uncles; guests; dependents; children; the aged; the sick; doctors;* paternal, affinal, and maternal relatives;* [180]father; mother; sisters; brother; son; wife; daughter; and slaves—he should not get into arguments with any of these. [181]By forswearing arguments with them, he is freed from all sins; and when he is conquered by them,* the householder conquers all these worlds.

[182]The teacher is the ruler of Brahman's world; the father, of Prajāpati's world; the guest, of Indra's world; the officiating priests, of the world of gods; [183]the sisters, of the world of Apsarases; maternal relatives, of the world of the Viśvedevas; affinal relatives, of the world of the waters; and the mother and maternal uncles, of the earth. [184]The children, the aged, the feeble, and the sick are to be regarded as the rulers of space. His older brother is equal to his father, and his wife and son are his own body. [185]His slaves are his own shadow, and his daughter is the object of supreme compassion. When he is assailed by any of these, therefore, he should always bear it without losing his temper.

Accepting and Giving Gifts

[186]Even if he is qualified to accept gifts, he should avoid becoming addicted to that practice, for by accepting gifts his vedic energy is quickly extinguished. [187]Without knowing the procedure prescribed by Law for accepting things, a wise man should never accept a gift even if he is racked by hunger.

[188]When an ignorant man accepts gold, land, a horse, a cow, food, clothes, sesame seeds, or ghee, he is reduced to ashes like a piece of wood.* [189]Gold and food burn up his life-force; a cow and land, his body; a horse, his sight; clothes, his skin;

ghee, his energy; and sesame seeds, his offspring. [190]When a twice-born neither engages in ascetic toil nor recites the Veda and yet loves to receive gifts, he will sink along with the donor, as a man would sink in water along with his stone float. [191]An ignorant man, therefore, should fear any kind of gift; for by acccpting even a trifling gift, an ignorant man sinks like a cow in the mud.

[192]A man who knows the Law should not give even water to a twice-born observing the "cat-vow", to an evil man observing* the "heron-vow," or to one who does not know the Veda; [193]for an object of value given to any of these three, even if it has been acquired in accordance with the rules, affects both the giver and the receiver adversely after death. [194]As a man making a crossing with a stone float sinks in the water, so will the ignorant beseecher and the ignorant donor sink to the bottom.

Hypocrisy

[195]A man who always displays the banner of righteousness and yet is greedy and deceitful, who deludes the world, who is given to violence, and who beguiles everybody should be viewed as one who observes the "cat-vow."* [196]A twice-born who goes around with downcast eyes but is cruel,* given to furthering his own ends, crooked, and being falsely sanctimonious, is a man who is observing the "heron-vow." [197]Brahmins who observe the "heron-vow" and those who display the marks of a cat fall into the Andha-Tāmisra hell as a result of that evil act.

[198]After committing a sin, he must never perform a penitential observance under the pretext that he is doing it as a meritorious act, thus covering up his sin with his observance and deceiving women and Śūdras. [199]Such Brahmins are denounced by vedic savants both here and in the hereafter, and that observance, carried out covertly, goes to the fiends.

[200]When someone earns his livelihood by wearing the insignia of a religious profession* to which he does not belong, he takes upon himself the sins of those belonging to that religious profession and is reborn in the womb of an animal.

Using What Belongs to Others

[201]He must never bathe in a reservoir that belongs to someone else. By doing so, he will be tainted with a portion of the evils committed by the man who constructed that reservoir. [202]When a man uses someone's vehicle, bed, seat, well, garden, or house without permission, he gets a quarter of the owner's sins. [203]He should always bathe in rivers, natural ponds,* lakes, pools, and springs.

[204]A wise man should always practice the central virtues and not busy himself constantly with the secondary observances. A man falls when he devotes himself to the secondary observances while neglecting the central virtues.*+

Unfit Food

[205]A Brahmin must never partake of food* at a sacrifice offered by someone who is not a vedic scholar or who officiates as a priest for a large number of people, or at one offered by a woman or an effeminate man (3.150 n.). [206]When such persons offer an

oblation, it is unpropitious for virtuous people and disagreeable to gods; therefore, he should avoid it.

207He must also never eat the following: food given by someone who is drunk, angry, or sick;* food contaminated with hair or insects or touched deliberately with the foot; 208food looked at by a murderer of a Brahmin,* touched by a menstruating woman, pecked by a bird, or touched by a dog; 209food smelled by a cow; in a special way, food given after a public announcement; food given by a group or by a prostitute; food that is despised by learned men; 210food given by a thief, a musician, a carpenter, a usurer, a man consecrated for a sacrifice, a miser, a prisoner, a shackled man,* 211a heinous sinner (2.185 n.), a eunuch, a promiscuous woman, or a hypocrite; food that has turned sour or is stale; food of a Śūdra; leftovers* (2.56 n.); 212food given by a physician, a hunter, a cruel man, someone who eats leftovers, or an Ugra; food of a woman impure by reason of childbirth; food served at a meal where someone sips water during the meal; food given during the ten days of impurity resulting from a birth;*+ 213food given without respect; meat procured capriciously (5.27); food given by a woman without a husband; food of an enemy, the chief of a town,* or an outcaste; food someone has sneezed upon; 214food given by a slanderer, a liar, a trafficker in rituals, an actor, a tailor, an ingrate, 215a blacksmith, a Niṣāda, a theatrical performer, a goldsmith, a basket-weaver, an arms merchant, 216those who raise dogs, liquor merchants, a washerman, a dyer, a heartless man, someone who lets his wife's paramour live in his house 217or who condones a paramour, or someone who is bossed by his wife in every way; food of persons during the first ten days after a death in their family; food offered to a newly deceased person,* and unappetizing food.

218The food of a king robs his energy; the food of a Śūdra, his eminence in vedic knowledge; the food of a goldsmith, his life-force; and the food of a leather-worker, his fame. 219The food of an artisan destroys his offspring, and the food of a dyer, his strength. The food of a group or of a prostitute cuts him off from the worlds. 220The food of a physician is pus; the food of a promiscuous woman is semen; the food of a usurer is excrement; and the food of an arms merchant is filth. 221The food of those others who have been listed in order as people whose food is unfit to be eaten—the wise declare that to be skin, bones, and hair.

222If someone eats the food of any one of them* unintentionally, he should fast for three days; if he eats intentionally—as also when he consumes semen, urine, or excrement—he should perform an arduous penance (11.212).+

223A learned twice-born must never eat cooked food given by a Śūdra who lacks a spirit of generosity (3.202 n.). If he is without sustenance, he may accept from such a man only raw provisions sufficient for a single day.*

224The gods once evaluated the food of a miserly vedic scholar and that of a generous usurer and pronounced the two to be equal. 225Prajāpati came up to them and said, "Don't make equal what is unequal. The food of the generous man is cleansed by the spirit of generosity, whereas the other food is defiled by the lack of generosity."

Gifts and Their Rewards

226He should tirelessly make sacrificial offerings and give gifts every day in a spirit of generosity; for, when done with a generous spirit and using justly earned wealth, they become inexhaustible.+ [227]Finding a suitable recipient, he should practice daily the Law of giving comprising sacrificial offerings and gifts, according to his ability and with a cheerful heart.+ [228]When he is asked, he should give ungrudgingly at least something, for one day he may encounter that special recipient who will rescue him from all.*

[229]One who gives water obtains satiety; one who gives food, inexhaustible happiness; one who gives sesame seeds, the kind of offspring one desires; one who gives a lamp, the finest eyesight. [230]One who gives land, obtains land; one who gives gold, long life; one who gives a house, superb dwellings; one who gives silver (*rūpya*), peerless beauty (*rūpa*); [231]one who gives clothes, residence in the same world as the Moon; one who gives a horse (*aśva*), residence in the same world as the Aśvins; one who gives an ox, bounteous prosperity; one who gives a cow, the summit of the sun; [232]one who gives a vehicle or bed, a wife; one who gives security, lordship; one who gives grain, eternal happiness; and one who gives the Veda (*brahman*), equality with Brahman.* [233]The gift of the Veda far exceeds every other gift, whether it is the gift of water, food, cows, land, clothes, sesame seeds, gold, or ghee.

[234]With whatever disposition a man makes a particular gift, he will be received with honor and obtain that very thing* with the very same disposition. [235]When due respect is shown in accepting and in giving a gift, both the receiver and the giver go to heaven; but when the opposite happens, both go to hell.

[236]He must not flaunt his austerities, lie about a sacrifice* he has performed, revile Brahmins even though aggrieved, or brag about a gift he has given. [237]A sacrifice is lost by telling a lie about it, austerity by flaunting it, longevity by reviling Brahmins, and a gift by bragging about it.

Accumulating Merit

[238]Gradually and without hurting any creature, he should pile up merit (*dharma*) like termites an anthill, so as to secure an escort in the next world; [239]for in the next world, neither father nor mother stands by him as his escort; nor does son, wife, or relative. Only merit stands by him. [240]Alone a creature is born, and alone it dies. Alone it enjoys the fruits of its good deeds, alone also the fruits of its evil deeds. [241]While his relatives discard the dead body on earth as if it were a piece of wood or a clod of earth and depart with averted faces, his merit accompanies him. [242]To secure an escort, therefore, let him gradually pile up merit every day; for with merit as his escort, he will cross over the darkness that is difficult to cross. [243]The escort quickly leads that man, who is devoted to the Law (*dharma*) and whose sins have been erased by ascetic toil, to the next world, glittering with an ethereal body.

[244]He should always build relationships with people of the highest possible rank and avoid anyone of a lower rank, if he wants to raise his family to a higher rank. [245]By going to people of the highest possible rank and by avoiding those who are lower, a Brahmin achieves distinction; by doing the opposite, he is reduced to the level of a Śūdra.

[246]A man who adheres to these observances—a man who is resolute in his undertakings, who is gentle and controlled, and who does not associate with people of

cruel conduct or cause harm to anyone—wins heaven by controlling himself and giving gifts.

Acceptance of Gifts and Food

[247]Fire wood, water, roots, fruits, food spontaneously given, honey, and the gift of freedom from fear (6.39 n.)—he may accept these from anyone. [248]Prajāpati has determined that almsfood that is brought and presented without being requested beforehand may be accepted even from a man of evil conduct. [249]If a man spurns such almsfood, his ancestors will not eat from him for fifteen years, and the sacred fire will not convey his offerings.

[250]Bed, house, Kuśa grass, perfumes, water, flowers, gems, curd, grain, fish, milk, meat, or vegetables—these he should never reject. [251]He may accept a gift from anyone for the purpose of supporting his elders and dependents and honoring gods and guests; but he may not use it to gratify himself.

[252]At a time when his elders have passed away or he is living at home without them and he is seeking a means of sustenance, he may always accept gifts from good people.

[253]A sharecropper, a friend of the family, and one's cowherd, slave, and barber—among Śūdras, these are the ones whose food is fit to be eaten, as also a person who has presented himself.*

[254]He should present himself accurately in all this: what sort of a person he is, what sort of work he wants to perform, and in what manner he will serve that person. [255]A man who misrepresents himself to good people is the worst sinner in the world; he is a thief, a man who steals his very self. [256]All things are founded on speech; speech is their root; and from speech they proceed. A man who steals speech is guilty of stealing everything.

Old Age and Retirement

[257]After he has freed himself according to rule from his debts* to the great seers, ancestors, and gods, he should hand over everything to his son and live in complete equanimity. [258]Living alone in a secluded place, he should always reflect on what is beneficial to himself; for, by reflecting alone, he attains supreme bliss.

> [259]I have explained above the invariable means of livelihood for a Brahmin householder, as also the splendid set of observances for a bath-graduate which enhances his spirit (3.40 n.). [260]When a Brahmin, knowing the vedic teachings, follows this mode of life, he frees himself always from sins and is exalted in heaven.

CHAPTER FIVE

PROLOGUE

[1]After they had heard the Laws of a bath-graduate described in this manner, the seers said this to the noble-minded Bhṛgu born from the fire:* [2]"How, O Lord, does Death prevail over Brahmins, who know the vedic teachings and follow the Law specific to them described in this manner?"

[3]Bhṛgu, the embodiment of the Law and the son of Manu, said to those great seers: "Listen to the fault because of which Death seeks to kill Brahmins."

FORBIDDEN FOOD

[4]Death seeks to kill Brahmins because of the failure to recite the Vedas, the dereliction of the rules of proper conduct, laziness, and faults with respect to food.

[5]Garlic, leeks, onions, and mushrooms are foods forbidden* to twice-born persons; and so is anything growing in an impure medium. [6]He should scrupulously eschew the following: the red sap of trees; juices flowing from incisions on trees; Śelu fruit; cow's colostrum; [7]Kṛsara porridge, Saṃyāva cake,* milk-rice, or cake prepared for no good reason; meat of an unconsecrated animal (5.27–57); food offered to deities; and sacrificial oblations.

[8]The milk of a cow within ten days after giving birth; milk of camels, single-hoofed animals, and sheep; milk of a cow that is in heat or has lost its calf; [9]milk of all wild animals except buffaloes; and milk of women—these he should eschew, as also anything that has turned sour. [10]Among foods turned sour, he may eat curd and all curd products, as well as the extracts of wholesome flowers, roots, and fruits.

[11]He should eschew all carnivorous birds, as also those that live in villages; single-hoofed animals, except those explicitly permitted;* plovers; [12]Kalaviṅka sparrows; Plava herons; Haṃsa geese; Cakra sheldrakes; village fowl; Sārasa cranes; Rajjuvāla fowl; Dātyūha waterfowl; parrots; mynahs; [13]birds that feed by pecking; web-footed birds; Koyaṣṭhi cranes; birds that feed by scratching with their feet; birds that catch fish by diving; meat from a slaughter-house; dried meat; [14]Baka egrets; Balāka ibis; Kākola ravens; Khañjarīṭaka wagtails; fish eaters; village hogs; and every kind of fish.

[15]A man who eats the meat of some animal is called "eater of that animal's meat," whereas a fish-eater is an "eater of every animal's meat." Therefore, he should eschew fish. [16]The Pāṭhīna and the Rohita fish may be eaten when they are used in an offering to gods or ancestors; Rājīva, Siṃhatuṇḍa, and Saśalka fish may be eaten at any time.

[17]He must never eat those that wander alone; unknown animals or birds, even if they are listed among those that are permitted; as also all animals with five nails.* [18]Among animals with five nails, they say, the porcupine, the hedgehog, the monitor lizard, the rhinoceros, the tortoise, and the rabbit may be eaten; as also animals with incisors in only one jaw,* with the exception of the camel.

[19]By eating mushrooms, a village hog, garlic, a village fowl, onion, or leek intentionally, a twice-born falls from his caste. [20]If he eats one of these six unwittingly, he shall perform the Sāntapana or the ascetics' lunar penance (11.213, 219). If he eats any of the others, he shall fast for one day. [21]To cleanse himself of what he may have eaten unwittingly, a Brahmin should perform at least one arduous penance (11.212) each year; but he is cleansed of what he has eaten intentionally through the specified penance.

[22]To perform sacrifices Brahmins may kill sanctioned animals and birds, as also to feed their dependents; Agastya did that long ago. [23]For, at the ancient sacrifices of seers and at the Soma offerings* of Brahmins and Kṣatriyas, the sacrificial cakes were prepared with the meat of permitted animals and birds.

[24]Any nonforbidden food or delicacy infused with oil* may be eaten even if it is stale, as also any leftovers from a sacrificial oblation. [25]Though they have not been infused with oil, however, dishes made with barley or wheat, as well as milk preparations, may be eaten by the twice-born, even if they have stood for a long time.

> [26]I have described above completely what foods are forbidden and what permitted to the twice-born. I will now explain the rule on eating and on avoiding meat.

EATING MEAT

[27]He may eat meat when it is sacrificially consecrated, at the behest of Brahmins, when he is ritually commissioned according to rule, and when his life is at risk.*

[28]Prajāpati created* this whole world as food for lifebreath; all beings, the mobile and the immobile, are nourishment for lifebreath. [29]The immobile are food for the mobile; the fangless for the fanged; the handless for the handed; and the timid for the brave. [30]The eater is not defiled by eating living beings suitable for eating, even if he eats them day after day; for the creator himself fashioned both the eaters and the living beings suitable for eating.

[31]"The sacrifice is the reason for eating meat"—this, the tradition says, is the rule of gods. Doing it for any other purpose is called the rule of fiends.* [32]When a man eats meat—whether it was purchased, procured by himself, or offered by someone else—after making an offering to gods and ancestors, he does not become defiled. [33]Except in a time of adversity, a twice-born man who knows the rules must never eat meat in contravention of the rules; if he eats meat in contravention of the rules, after death he will be eaten forcibly by those very animals. [34]In the afterlife, the sin of someone who hunts animals for profit is not as great as that of a man who eats meat procured capriciously. [35]If a man refuses to eat meat after he has been ritually commissioned

according to rule (5.27 n.), after death he will become an animal for twenty-one lifetimes. [36]A Brahmin must never eat animals that have not been consecrated with ritual formulas. Abiding by the eternal rule,* however, he must eat those that have been consecrated with ritual formulas.

[37]If he gets the urge, let him make an animal out of butter or flour; but he must never entertain the desire to kill an animal for a futile reason. [38]When a man kills an animal for a futile reason, after death he will be subject in birth after birth to being slain as many times as the number of hairs on that animal.

[39]The Self-existent One himself created domestic animals for sacrifice,* and the sacrifice is for the prosperity of this whole world. Within the sacrifice, therefore, killing is not killing. [40]When plants, domestic animals, trees, beasts, and birds die for the sake of a sacrifice, they will in turn earn superior births. [41]The honey-mixture (3.119 n.), a sacrifice, an offering to gods or ancestors—at no other occasion than these, Manu has declared, may animals be killed. [42]When a twice-born man who knows the true meaning of the Veda kills animals for these purposes, he leads himself and those animals to the highest state. [43]Whether he lives at home, at his teacher's, or in the wilderness, a twice-born man who is self-possessed must never, even in a time of adversity, carry out a killing that is not sanctioned by the Veda. [44]When a killing is sanctioned by the Veda and well-established in this mobile and immobile creation,* it should be regarded definitely as a non-killing; for it is from the Veda that the Law has shined forth.

[45]If someone, craving his own pleasure, harms harmless creatures, he will not find happiness anywhere while he is still alive or after death. [46]When someone has no desire to tie up, kill, or cause pain* to living creatures and seeks the welfare of all beings, he obtains endless bliss. [47]Whatever a man contemplates, whatever a man undertakes, whatever a man takes a liking to*—all that he obtains without effort, when he does no harm to any creature.

[48]One can never obtain meat without causing injury to living beings, and killing living beings is an impediment to heaven; he should, therefore, abstain from meat. [49]Reflecting on how meat is obtained and on how embodied creatures are tied up and killed, he should quit eating any kind of meat. [50]When a man refrains from eating meat like a goblin, except when the rules prescribe it,* he is loved by the world and is not tormented by diseases.

[51]The man who authorizes, the man who butchers, the man who slaughters, the man who buys or sells, the man who cooks, the man who serves, and the man who eats—these are all killers. [52]There is no greater sinner than a man who, outside of an offering to gods or ancestors, wants to make his own flesh thrive at the expense of someone else's.

[53]A man who abstains from meat and a man who offers the horse sacrifice every year for a hundred years—the reward for their meritorious acts* is the same. [54]Even by living on pure fruits and roots and by eating the food of sages, a man fails to obtain as great a reward as he would by abstaining completely from meat.

[55]"Me he (*māṃ sa*) will eat in the next world, whose meat (*māṃsa*) I eat in this world"—this, the wise declare, is what gave the name to and discloses the true nature of "meat" (*māṃsa*).*

[56]There is no fault in eating meat, in drinking liquor, or in having sex; that is the natural activity of creatures. Abstaining from such activity, however, brings great rewards.

> [57]I will now explain the purification after a death, as well as the purification of things, precisely and in their proper order for all four classes.

BODILY PURIFICATION

Death or Birth of a Person Belonging to the Same Ancestry

[58]Someone who has teethed, someone younger, or someone who has had his first cutting of hair* (2.35)—when any of these dies, all his relatives become impure; the same is prescribed after the birth of a child. [59]A ten-day period of impurity following a death is prescribed for those who belong to the same ancestry; alternatively, that period may last until the collection of bones,* or for three days, or for a single day.

[60]The relationship based on common ancestry* stops with the seventh generation; the relationship based on offering libations,* on the other hand, stops only when someone's birth and name are no longer remembered.

[61]The same holds true at a birth. The birth-impurity, however, affects only the mother and the father. The mother alone is subject to the period of birth-impurity; the father becomes pure by bathing [verse number 62 omitted in critical edition].+ [63]On the contrary, it is after spilling his seed that a man is purified by simply bathing; the impurity resulting from a seminal relationship adheres to him for three days.*

[64]Those who touch the corpse are purified in ten days, but those who offer libations in three.* [65]A pupil who performs the funerary rites of his deceased teacher, on the other hand, is on a par with those who carry a corpse* and is purified in ten days.

[66]After a miscarriage, a woman is purified after the same number of days as the months of her pregnancy. A menstruating woman becomes wholesome by taking a bath after her menstrual flow has ceased.

[67]When males die before the first cutting of their hair (2.35), tradition tells us, the impurity lasts a single night;* but when they die after the cutting of their hair, purity is considered to be restored after three nights. [68]When a child under two dies, its relatives should decorate its corpse and lay it down* in a clean spot outside the village; the ceremony of collecting its bones is omitted. [69]Neither the consecration with fire nor the offering of water is done for such a child; after leaving it behind in the wilderness like a piece of wood, one should keep the observances* for just three days. [70]Relatives should not offer libations of water for a child under 3; they may do so optionally if it has teethed or if its naming ceremony has been performed.

[71]When someone who had been a fellow student dies, tradition prescribes the observances for one day. In the event of a birth, the purity of those related through offering libations (5.60 n.) is considered to be restored after three days. [72]The relations

of unmarried women are purified in three days, but her siblings* are purified exactly according to the prescribed rule.*

[73]For three days* they are to eat food without artificial salt, bathe by immersion, abstain from eating meat, and sleep separately on the floor.

Death in a Distant Region [74]The above set of rules concerning impurity after death is prescribed only when a death has occurred close by; when it has happened far away, kinsmen and relatives* should know that the procedure is as follows.

[75]When someone living in a far-away place dies and one hears of it within ten days of his death, one becomes impure only for the remainder of that ten-day period. [76]If one hears of it after the lapse of ten days, one becomes impure for three days; but if it is after a year, one is purified simply by bathing. [77]When a man hears about the death of a paternal relative or the birth of a son after the lapse of ten days, he becomes pure by immersing himself in water with his clothes on. [78]When a child or someone belonging to a different ancestry* dies in a far-away place, one is purified instantly by immersing oneself in water with one's clothes on.

Overlapping Periods of Impurity [79]If during one ten-day period of impurity another death or birth occurs, a Brahmin remains impure only until the end of the initial ten-day period.

Death of Significant Others [80]At the death of one's teacher, they prescribe a three-day period of impurity; and at the death of the teacher's son or wife, the settled rule is a day and a night. [81]One becomes impure for three days at the death of a vedic scholar living near by,* and for two days plus the intervening night at the death of one's maternal uncle, pupil, officiating priest, or maternal relative. [82]At the death of a king, anyone residing within his realm* remains impure that day from dawn to dusk or that night from dusk to dawn (4.106 n.). At the death of someone who is not a vedic scholar, a vedic savant, or an elder,* one remains impure for a full day.

Periods of Impurity for Different Classes [83]A Brahmin is purified in ten days, a Kṣatriya in twelve, a Vaiśya in fifteen, and a Śūdra in a month.* [84]One should not prolong the days of impurity or postpone one's fire rituals; while performing that rite, even a uterine brother (5.72 n.) becomes immune to impurity.*

Impurity from Touch [85]When someone touches a Divākīrti,* a menstruating woman, an outcaste, a woman who has given birth, or a corpse—as also a person who has touched any of these—he is purified by bathing. [86]At the sight of an impure person, he should make himself ritually pure by sipping water and then softly recite the Solar formulas according to his capacity, and the Pāvamānī verses to the best of his ability. [87]After touching a human bone, a Brahmin is purified by bathing if the bone was greasy, but simply by sipping water, touching a cow, or gazing at the sun, if the bone was dry.

Libations for the Dead [88]A votary* shall not offer a libation until he has completed his vow; but once he has completed his vow and offered the libation, he is purified in just three days.* [89]Libations are omitted in the case of people born through capricious caste mingling;* those living in ascetic orders; suicides; [90]and women who have joined heretical sects, roam about at will, harm their fetus or husband, or drink liquor. [91]By carrying his own deceased teacher, tutor (2.141), father, mother, or elder, a votary (5.88 n.) does not break his vow.

Funeral Path [92]A dead Śūdra should be carried out through the southern gate of the city, and a twice-born person through the western, the northern, or the eastern gate, as appropriate.*

Instant Purification of Kings [93]The taint of impurity does not affect kings, votaries, and those engaged in a sacrificial session; for they are seated on the seat of Indra and are ever one with *brahman.** [94]Instant purification is prescribed for a king on the seat of majesty—the reason for this is that he is seated for the protection of his subjects—[95]as also for people killed in a riot or battle, by lightning or the king, or in defense of cows or Brahmins, and for anyone the king wants.*

[96]Soma, Fire, Sun, Wind, Indra, the Lords of wealth and water, and Yama—the king is the embodiment of these eight guardians of the world (see 7.4). [97]The lords of the world abide within the king, and no period of impurity is prescribed for him; for it is the lords of the world who both bring about and erase purity and impurity in mortal beings.*

[98]When a man is killed in battle with upraised weapons according to the Kṣatriya law, the settled rule is that for him both sacrifice and purification are accomplished instantly.*

[99]After completing the required rite,* a Brahmin is purified by touching water, a Kṣatriya his conveyance (7.75 n.) or weapon, a Vaiśya his goad or reins, and a Śūdra his staff (see 8.113).

> [100]I have explained to you above, O Brahmins, the purification in the case of people belonging to the same ancestry (5.60 n.). Listen now to the purification after death in the case of all those belonging to different ancestries.

Death of a Person Belonging to a Different Ancestry

[101]If a Brahmin carries the corpse of a twice-born person unrelated to him by ancestry as if he were a relative, or if he carries a close (2.109 n.) relative of his mother, he is purified in three days. [102]If he eats their food, on the other hand, his purification takes ten full days; but if he neither eats their food nor stays at their house, it takes just one day.+ [103]If someone willingly follows a corpse, whether it is that of a paternal relative or of someone else, he is purified after he has bathed with his clothes on, touched the fire, and eaten some ghee.

[104]When one's own people are present, one should never let a Śūdra carry a Brahmin's corpse, for a sacrificial offering defiled by a Śūdra's touch does not lead a person to heaven.*

Means of Purification

105Knowledge, austerity, fire, food, earth, mind, water, smearing with cow dung, wind, rites, sun, time*—these are the agents of purification for embodied beings.+

106Purifying oneself with respect to wealth, tradition tells us, is the highest of all purifications; for the truly pure man is the one who is pure with respect to wealth, not the one who becomes pure by using earth and water.

107Learned men are purified by forbearance; those who do forbidden things, by giving gifts; those who commit secret sins, by soft recitation; and pre-eminent experts in the Veda, by ascetic toil. 108What needs cleaning is cleansed by using earth and water, a river by its current, a woman defiled in thought by her menstrual flow, and Brahmins by renunciation.* 109The body is cleansed with water, the mind by truth, the elemental self (12.12-13 n.) by learning and austerity, and the intellect by knowledge.

> 110I have explained to you above the determination with regard to bodily purification. Listen now to the determination with regard to the purification of different kinds of articles.

PURIFICATION OF ARTICLES

111The wise have determined that metal objects, jewels, and anything lapidary* are cleaned with ash, water, and earth. 112When they are unstained,* gold vessels are cleaned with water alone, as also the aquatic, the lapidary,* or any silver article that is unembellished. 113Gold and silver issued from the union of fire and water; they are best cleaned, therefore, using their very sources. 114The cleaning of copper, iron, brass, pewter, tin, and lead is done using as appropriate alkali, acid, and water.

115All liquids,* tradition tells us, are cleaned by straining;* solids, by sprinkling water; and wooden articles, by planing.+

116During a sacrificial rite, sacrificial vessels are rubbed with the hand; the Camasa-cups and Graha-ladles, on the other hand, are cleaned by washing;* 117the Caru-pots, Sruk-spoons, and Sruva-spoons are cleaned with warm water, as are Sphya-swords, Śūrpa-winnows, Śakaṭa-carts, pestles, and mortars.

118The rule is that large quantities of grain or clothes are cleaned by sprinkling them with water, whereas small quantities are cleaned by washing them with water.+ 119Skin and wicker are to be cleaned the same way as cloth; and vegetables, roots, and fruits, the same way as grain. 120Silk and wool are cleaned with saline earth, goat's wool blankets (3.234 n.) with ground Ariṣṭa fruit, fine fabric with Bel fruit, and linen with yellow mustard. 121A discerning man should clean conch and horn, as well as articles made of bone and ivory, the same way as linen, or else with cow's urine or water. 122Grass, wood, and straw are cleaned by sprinkling water on them, a house by scrubbing it or by smearing it with cow dung (5.105 n.), and earthenware by firing it again [verse 123 is omitted].+ 124Scrubbing, smearing with cow dung, sprinkling, scraping, and letting cows stay in it—by these five means a plot of land is purified.+

125Anything that birds have pecked, cows have sniffed, or hair or insects have fouled, or over which someone has shaken* or sneezed, is cleaned by spreading some earth over it. [126]Whenever anything is being cleaned, one should keep applying earth and water until the smell and stain are gone from the article smeared with a foul substance.

[127]Gods invented three means of purification for Brahmins: being unaware that something is impure, sprinkling it with water, and getting it verbally declared as suitable.*

Statutory Purity of Things

[128]Water collected on the ground is pure if it is sufficient to slake the thirst of a cow, is uncontaminated with foul substances, and has the right odor, color, and taste. [129]The hand of an artisan is always pure, as are goods displayed for sale; the almsfood received by a student is always ritually clean—that is the settled rule. [130]A woman's mouth is always pure; so is a bird when it makes a fruit to fall, a calf when it makes the milk to flow, and a dog when it catches a deer. [131]The meat of an animal that has been killed by a dog or some other predator, or by a Cāṇḍāla or some other lowlife, is pure—that is the judgment of Manu.+

[132]All orifices above the navel are ritually clean; those below are ritually unclean, as are the foul substances that shed from the body.

[133]Flies, droplets of water,* shadows, cows, horses, rays of the sun, dust, earth, wind, and fire—these should be regarded as ritually clean to the touch.

PURIFICATION OF THE BODY

[134]To purify oneself after voiding urine or excrement and to clean any of the twelve bodily impurities, one should use a sufficient amount of earth and water. [135]Body oil, semen, blood, marrow,* urine, feces, ear-wax, nails, phlegm,* tears, discharge of the eyes, and sweat—these are the twelve impurities of man.

[136]A man intent on purifying himself should apply one lump of earth on the penis, three on the anus, ten on one hand,* and seven on both. [137]This is the purification for householders. It is twice that much for students, three times for forest hermits, and four times for ascetics. [138]After he voids urine or excrement, he must sip water and touch the orifices with water (2.53 n.); he must do so every time he prepares to recite the Veda or to eat his food.

[139]A man who desires bodily purification should first sip water three times and then wipe the mouth with water twice; but a woman or a Śūdra sips and wipes just once. [140]Śūdras who abide by the proper mode of conduct should shave their heads once a month, follow the rules of purification laid down for Vaiśyas, and eat the leftover food of twice-born persons.

[141]Drool spattering from the mouth does not make someone sullied if it does not fall on his body; nor does hair from the beard getting into the mouth or anything stuck between the teeth. [142]Drops falling on a man's feet while he is pouring water for someone else to sip are to be considered similar to water on the ground and do not make him ritually impure. [143]If a sullied person touches a man carrying something in his hand, he becomes pure by sipping some water without laying that thing down.*

[144]After vomiting or purging, one should bathe and consume some ghee; after eating food,* one should simply sip some water; and after sexual intercourse tradition requires one to take a bath. [145]After sleeping, sneezing, eating, spitting, telling a lie, and drinking water, as also when one is about to recite the Veda, one should sip some water even though one is already ritually pure.

> [146]I have explained to you above all the rules of purification, as well as the cleaning of articles, applicable to all the social classes. Listen now to the Law with respect to women.

LAW WITH RESPECT TO WOMEN

Lack of Independence

[147]Even in their own homes, a female—whether she is a child, a young woman, or an old lady—should never carry out any task independently.* [148]As a child, she must remain under her father's control; as a young woman, under her husband's; and when her husband is dead, under her sons'. She must never seek to live independently. [149]She must never want to separate herself from her father, husband, or sons; for by separating herself from them, a woman brings disgrace on both families.*

[150]She should be always cheerful, clever at housework, careful in keeping the utensils clean, and frugal in her expenditures.

Duties towards Husband

[151]The man to whom her father or, with her father's consent, her brother gives her away—she should obey him when he is alive and not be unfaithful to him when he is dead. [152]The invocation of blessings and the sacrifice to Prajāpati are performed during marriage to procure her good fortune; the act of giving away* is the reason for his lordship over her. [153]In season and out of season, in this world and in the next, the husband who performed the marriage consecration with ritual formulas always gives happiness to his woman.

[154]Though he may be bereft of virtue, given to lust, and totally devoid of good qualities, a good woman should always worship her husband like a god. [155]For women, there is no independent sacrifice, vow, or fast; a woman will be exalted in heaven by the mere fact that she has obediently served her husband.[156]A good woman, desiring to go to the same world as her husband, should never do anything displeasing to the man who took her hand, whether he is alive or dead.

[157]After her husband is dead, she may voluntarily emaciate her body by eating pure flowers, roots, and fruits; but she must never mention even the name of another man. [158]Aspiring to that unsurpassed Law of women devoted to a single husband, she should remain patient, controlled, and celibate until her death. [159]Untold thousands of Brahmins who have remained celibate from their youth have gone to heaven without producing offspring to continue their family line. [160]Just like these celibates, a good

woman, though she be sonless, will go to heaven when she steadfastly adheres to the celibate life after her husband's death.* [161]When a woman is unfaithful to her husband because of her strong desire for children, she is disgraced in this world and excluded from the husband's world.* [162]No recognition is given here to offspring fathered by another man or begotten on another's wife; nor is it taught anywhere that a good woman should take a second husband.

[163]When a woman abandons her own husband of lower rank and unites with a man of higher rank, she only brings disgrace upon herself in the world and is called "a woman who has had a man before."* [164]By being unfaithful to her husband, a woman becomes disgraced in the world, takes birth in a jackal's womb, and is afflicted with evil diseases (3.92 n.).

[165]A woman who controls her mind, speech, and body and is never unfaithful to her husband attains the worlds of her husband, and virtuous people call her a "good woman." [166]By following this conduct, a woman who controls her mind, speech, and body obtains the highest fame in this world and the world of her husband in the next.

Funeral

[167]When a wife who has conducted herself in this manner and who belongs to the same class as her husband dies before him, a twice-born man who knows the Law should cremate her with his sacred fire and sacrificial implements. [168]After he has given his sacred fires to his predeceased wife at her funeral, he should marry a wife again and establish anew his sacred fires.

CONCLUDING STATEMENT ON THE HOUSEHOLDER

[169]In accordance with these rules, he should never neglect the five sacrifices; and, marrying a wife, he should live at home during the second quarter of his life.*

CHAPTER SIX

FOREST HERMIT

+1After living this way in the householder's order according to rule, a twice-born bath-graduate should duly live in the forest, controlling his self and mastering his organs.*

Time and Procedure

2When a householder sees his skin wrinkled, his hair turned gray, and his children's children, he should take to the wilderness. 3Giving up village food and all his belongings, he should go to the forest, entrusting his wife to his sons or accompanied by her.

4Taking with him his sacrificial fires and the implements required for his domestic fire rituals, he should depart from the village to the wilderness and live there with his organs controlled.

Mode of Life

5Using various kinds of ritually clean sage's food (3.257 n.), or vegetables, roots, and fruits, he should continue to offer the same great sacrifices (3.68–70) according to rule. 6He should wear a garment of skin or tree bark;* bathe in the morning and evening; always wear matted hair; and keep his beard, body hair, and nails uncut.

Great Sacrifices 7He should give Bali offerings and almsfood to the best of his ability with whatever food he eats and honor those who visit his hermitage with water, roots, fruits, and almsfood. 8He should be always diligent in his vedic recitation; remain controlled, friendly, and collected; be always a giver and never a receiver of gifts; be compassionate towards all creatures; 9offer the daily fire sacrifice in his three sacred fires according to rule, without neglecting the new-moon and full-moon sacrifices at their proper time; 10and offer the constellation-sacrifice,* the sacrifice of first fruits (4.26), the seasonal sacrifices, the Turāyaṇa sacrifice* and the Dākṣāyaṇa sacrifice,* in their proper sequence. 11With ritually clean sage's foods that grow in spring and autumn and that he has gathered himself, he should offer separately the sacrificial cakes and oblations of milk-rice according to rule.

Food 12After he has offered that most ritually clean oblation of forest produce to the gods, he may avail himself of what remains, as also of salt that he has manufactured himself.

13He may eat vegetables growing on land or in water; flowers, roots, and fruits coming from ritually clean trees;* and oils extracted from fruits. 14He must avoid honey, meat, the Bhauma plant, mushrooms,* the Bhūstṛṇa plant, the Śigruka horse-radish, and the Śleṣmātaka fruit.

[15]In the month of Āśvayuja (September–October), he must throw away the sage's food that he had previously collected, as also vegetables, roots, fruits, and old garments.

[16]He must never eat anything grown on plowed land, even if it has been thrown away by someone; or flowers and fruits* grown in a village, even if he is in dire straits.

[17]He may eat food that has been cooked with fire or ripened by time; he may use a grindstone or use his teeth as a mortar; [18]he may clean up immediately* after eating or maintain a supply of food sufficient for a month, six months, or a year.

[19]Having gathered food to the best of his ability, he may eat it at night, during the day, at every fourth mealtime, or at every eighth mealtime;* [20]or he may maintain himself during the bright and dark halves of the month according to the lunar rule (11.217), or eat boiled barley-gruel once at the end of each half month; [21]or he may subsist permanently on just flowers, roots, and fruits that have ripened by time and wilted on their own*—abiding by the Vaikhānasa doctrine.*

Austerities [22]He should roll on the ground or stand on tiptoes all day; spend the day standing and the night seated,* bathing at dawn, midday, and dusk; [23]surround himself with the five fires* in the summer; live in the open air during the rainy season; and wear wet clothes in the winter—gradually intensifying his ascetic toil. [24]Bathing at dawn, noon, and dusk, he should offer quenching libations to ancestors and gods, and engaging in ever harsher ascetic toil, he should inflict punishment* on his body.

Homeless Ascetic [25]After depositing his sacred fires in his body* according to rule, he should become a sage without house or fire, subsisting on roots and fruits, [26]making no effort to obtain pleasurable things, remaining celibate, sleeping on the ground, showing no attachment to any place of shelter, and making his home at the foot of a tree.

[27]He should beg for almsfood just sufficient to sustain life only from Brahmin ascetics and from other twice-born householders living in the forest. [28]Or, while continuing to live in the forest, he may collect almsfood from a village and eat eight mouthfuls, receiving the almsfood in a leaf-cone, in a potsherd, or in the hand.

Conclusion

[29]To attain the full perfection of his self,* a Brahmin living in the forest must pursue these and other observances, as also the various Upaniṣadic scriptures, [30]and, to enhance his knowledge and ascetic toil and to purify his body, also those pursued* by seers, Brahmins, and householders.*

[31]Or he may set out in a north-easterly direction and, subsisting on water and air, walk straight on steadfastly until his body drops dead. [32]When a Brahmin has discarded his body through any one of these means employed by the great seers, freed from sorrow and fear, he will be exalted in the world of Brahman.

WANDERING ASCETIC

33After spending the third quarter of his life this way in the forest, he should cast off his attachments and wander about as an ascetic during the fourth.* 34When a man goes forth as an ascetic after he has moved from order to order, offered sacrifices, subdued his senses, and become worn out by giving alms and oblations, he will prosper after death.

Qualification

35Only after he has paid his three debts (4.257 n.), should a man set his mind on renunciation (1.114 n.); if he devotes himself to renunciation without paying them, he will proceed downward.* 36Only after he has studied the Vedas according to rule, fathered sons in keeping with the Law, and offered sacrifices according to his ability, should a man set his mind on renunciation; 37if a twice-born seeks renunciation without studying the Vedas, without fathering sons, and without offering sacrifices, he will proceed downward (6.35 n.).

Initiation

38Only after he has offered a sacrifice to Prajāpati at which all his possessions are given as the sacrificial gift and after he has deposited the sacred fires within himself (6.25 n.), should a Brahmin go forth from his home as an ascetic.

39Worlds of resplendent energy await a vedic savant who goes forth from his home as an ascetic after bestowing freedom from fear* on all creatures. 40Because that twice-born has not been the cause of even the slightest fear to creatures, he has nothing to fear from anyone after he is freed from his body.

41After departing from home with a cloth for straining water, the sage should wander about, ignoring the sensual delights presented to him.

Mode of Life

42To achieve success, he must always wander alone, without any companions; recognizing that success comes to the solitary man, he will forsake no one and no one will forsake him. 43He should live without fire or house, enter a village to obtain food, be dispassionate, keep no store,* and remain a silent sage and mentally composed. 44A bowl, the foot of a tree,* a ragged piece of cloth, a solitary life, and equanimity towards all—these are the marks of a renouncer.*

45He should long neither for death nor for life, but simply await his appointed time, as a servant his wages.*+ 46He should place his foot on a spot purified by his sight,* drink water purified by a cloth, speak words purified by truth, and follow a conduct purified by the mind.

47He must bear harsh words with patience; never treat anyone with contempt; never start a feud with anyone merely for the sake of this body; 48never show ire at anyone who is irate with him; bless those who curse him; and never utter an untrue word scattered across the seven gates.*

[49]Taking delight in what pertains to the self, he should remain seated without longings or sensual attachments. With himself as his only companion, he should walk about here, seeking felicity.*

Begging and Food

[50]He must never try to obtain almsfood by interpreting portents or omens, by his knowledge of astrology or palmistry,* by giving counsel, or by engaging in debates.

[51]He should never visit a house crowded with ascetics, Brahmins, birds, dogs, or other beggars; [52]and always go about with his head and beard shaved, with his nails clipped, carrying a bowl, a staff, and a water-pot, and without causing harm to any creature.

[53]His bowls must be non-metallic and undamaged; and tradition says that they are to be cleaned with just water, like Camasa-cups at a sacrifice (5.116). [54]A gourd, a wooden bowl, a clay bowl, and a wicker bowl—Manu, the son of the Self-existent One, has proclaimed these as the bowls of ascetics.

[55]He may go on his begging round only once a day. He must not be overly attached to getting a lot; for when an ascetic is overly attached to almsfood, he becomes attached also to sensual objects. [56]An ascetic should go on his daily begging round only when the smoke has cleared, the pestles are at rest, the embers are extinguished, the people have finished their meal, and the dishes have been put away.

[57]When he receives nothing, he must not become dejected; when he receives something, it must not make him elated. He should gather food just sufficient to sustain his life and become free from attachment to his belongings.* [58]He should hold anything received with a show of reverence in total disdain; even an ascetic who has freed himself is shackled by what is received with a show of reverence.* [59]By eating little and by spending the day standing and the night seated (6.22 n.) in solitude, he should pull his organs back as they are being drawn away by sensory objects. [60]By restraining his organs, by stamping out love and hatred, and by ceasing to harm creature, he becomes fit for immortality.

Yogic Meditation

[61]He should reflect on the diverse paths humans take as a result of their evil deeds; on how they fall into hell; on the tortures they endure in the abode of Yama; [62]on how they are separated from the ones they love and united with the ones they hate; on how they are overcome by old age and tormented by diseases; [63]on how the inner self departs from this body, takes birth again in a womb, and migrates through tens of billions of wombs; [64]and on how embodied beings become linked with pain as a result of pursuing what is against the Law and with imperishable happiness as a result of pursuing the Law as one's goal.

[65]By yogic meditation, he should also reflect on the subtle nature of the highest self and on its appearance in the highest and the lowest of bodies (6.73).

Conduct [66]Though decked in finery,* he should pursue the Law in whichever order he may live, treating all creatures alike; an emblem does not accomplish the Law.*

[67]Although the fruit of the Kataka tree makes water clear, yet the water does not become clear by mere mention of its name.

[68]To protect living creatures, he should walk always—whether at night or during the day—only after inspecting the ground even at the cost of bodily discomfort. [69]To purify himself of killing living creatures unintentionally during the day or at night, an ascetic should bathe and control his breath six times.

Breath Control [70]Controlling the breath* even three times according to rule while reciting the Calls and the syllable OṂ is to be considered the highest type of ascetic toil for a Brahmin. [71]As the impurities of metallic ores are burnt away when they are blasted in a furnace, so the faults of the organs are burnt away by suppressing the breath.

Meditation [72]He should burn away his faults by suppressing his breath, his taints by concentration, his attachments by the withdrawal of senses, and his base qualities by meditation. [73]Through the practice of meditation,* he should discern the course of this inner self through the highest and the lowest of creatures (6.65), a difficult course to grasp for persons with uncultivated minds.

[74]When a man possesses right understanding, he is not fettered by actions; but when he lacks understanding, he enters the transmigratory cycle. [75]By ceasing to harm living creatures, by withdrawing the organs from their attachments, by performing vedic rites, and by practicing fierce austerities, individuals do attain that state* here on earth.

Meditation on the Body [76]Constructed with beams of bones, fastened with tendons, plastered with flesh and blood, covered with skin, foul-smelling, filled with urine and excrement, [77]infested with old age and sorrow, the abode of sickness, full of pain, covered with dust, and impermanent—he must abandon this dwelling place of ghosts.* [78]When a tree falls from a river bank, the bird leaves the tree; when he abandons this body in like manner, he escapes the alligator's painful grasp.*

Final Goal [79]Consigning his good deeds to people he likes and his evil deeds to people he dislikes, he attains the eternal Brahman through the practice of meditation. [80]When by the passion of his spirit he frees himself from attachment to every object of passion,* then he wins eternal happiness both here and in the hereafter. [81]When he gives up all attachments gradually in this manner, freed from all the pairs of opposites, he comes to rest in Brahman alone.

[82]Everything prescribed here is contingent on meditation; for no one ignorant of the highest self can reap the fruits of his rites. [83]He should practice the soft recitation of vedic texts relating to sacrifice, gods, and self, as also those named "Vedānta"*—[84]this is the refuge of the ignorant, as indeed of the learned; this is the refuge of those who seek heaven, as of those who yearn for the infinite.

[85]If a twice-born lives as a wandering ascetic following the above sequence of practices,* he will cast off his sins in this world and attain the highest Brahman.

[86]I have explained to you above the Law pertaining to self-controlled ascetics. Listen now to the ritual discipline of vedic retirees (1.114 n.).

VEDIC RETIREE

Superiority of the Householder

[87]Student, householder, forest hermit, and ascetic: these four distinct orders have their origin in the householder. [88]All of these, when they are undertaken in their proper sequence as spelled out in the sacred texts, lead a Brahmin who acts in the prescribed manner to the highest state. [89]Among all of them, however, according to the dictates of vedic scripture,* the householder is said to be the best, for he supports the other three. [90]As all rivers and rivulets ultimately end up* in the ocean, so people of all the orders ultimately end up in the householder.

The Ten-Point Law

[91]Twice-born men belonging to all these four orders must always observe the ten-point Law diligently. [92]Resolve, forbearance, self-control, refraining from theft, performing purifications, mastering the organs, understanding, learning, truthfulness, and suppressing anger: these are the ten points of the Law. [93]Those Brahmins who learn the ten points of the Law and, after learning, follow them, attain the highest state.

Retirement

[94]When a twice-born man has followed the ten-point Law with a collected mind, learned the Vedānta according to rule, and freed himself from debt (4.257 n.), he may retire (1.114 n.). [95]Casting off the inherent evil of rites by retiring from all ritual activities, being self-controlled, and reciting the Veda, he should live at ease under the care of his son.

[96]When a man retires from ritual activities in this manner and, free from attachments, devotes himself completely to his duties, he erases his sins by this retirement and attains the highest state.

[97]I have explained to you above the fourfold Law of Brahmins, a Law that is holy and brings imperishable rewards after death. Listen now to the Law of kings.

CHAPTER SEVEN

THE LAW FOR THE KING

[1]I will explain the Laws pertaining to kings—how a king should conduct himself, how he came into being, and how he can attain the highest success.

Origin of the King

[2]A Kṣatriya who has received the vedic consecration* according to rule has the obligation to protect this whole world in accordance with the norms; [3]for when people here were without a king and fleeing in all directions out of fear, to protect this whole world the Lord created the king [4]by extracting eternal particles from Indra, Wind, Yama, Sun, Fire, Varuṇa, Moon, and the Lord of wealth.*

[5]Because the king was fashioned out of particles from these chiefs of the gods, he overpowers* all beings by reason of his energy. [6]Like the sun, indeed, he burns eyes and minds; no one on earth can bear to gaze upon him. [7]He is Fire, he is Wind, he is the Sun, he is the Moon, he is the King of the Law [Yama], he is Kubera, he is Varuṇa, and he is the Great Indra—by reason of his power.

[8]A king, though a mere child, must never be treated with disrespect, thinking he is just a human being; for it is a great deity who stands here in human form. [9]When approached recklessly, a fire burns only that single man, but the fire that is the king burns his family, together with all his livestock and wealth.

[10]After examining truthfully the task to be accomplished, his own strength, the time, and the place, he assumes in turn every aspect* in order to fully implement the Law; [11]he, in whose* benevolence lies Padmā, the goddess of prosperity, in whose valor lies victory, and in whose anger lies death—for he is made from the energies of them all.*

[12]The man who in his folly hates him perishes without doubt; for the king makes up his mind to destroy him quickly.* [13]When the king issues a Law favorable to those he favors or unfavorable to those out of favor, therefore, no one should transgress that Law.*

Punishment [14]For the king's sake, the Lord formerly created Punishment,* his son—the Law and protector of all beings—made from the energy of Brahman. [15]It is the fear of him that makes all beings, both the mobile and the immobile, accede to being used* and do not deviate from the Law proper to them.

[16]The king should administer appropriate Punishment on men who behave improperly, after examining truthfully the place and the time,* as well as their strength and learning. [17]Punishment is the king; he is the male; he is the leader; he is the ruler; and, tradition tells us, he stands as the surety for the Law with respect to the four orders

of life. [18]Punishment disciplines all the subjects, Punishment alone protects them, and Punishment watches over them as they sleep—Punishment is the Law, the wise declare. [19]When he is wielded properly after careful examination,* he gives delight to all the subjects; but when he is administered without careful examination, he wreaks total havoc.

[20]If the king fails to administer Punishment tirelessly on those who ought to be punished, the stronger would grill the weak like fish on a spit; [21]crows would devour the sacrificial cakes; dogs would lap up* the sacrificial offerings; no one would have any right of ownership; and everything would turn topsy-turvy.* [22]The whole world is subdued through Punishment, for an honest man is hard to find; clearly, it is the fear of Punishment that makes the whole creation accede to being used (7.15 n.). [23]Gods, demons, Gandharvas, fiends, birds, and snakes—even these accede to being used only when coerced by Punishment. [24]All the social classes would become corrupted, all boundaries would be breached, and all the people would revolt, as a result of blunders committed with respect to Punishment. [25]Wherever Punishment, dark-hued and red-eyed, prowls about as the slayer of evil-doers, there the subjects do not go astray—so long as its administrator* ascertains correctly.

[26]The proper administrator of Punishment, they say, is a king who speaks the truth, acts after careful examination (7.19 n.), is wise, and has a masterly grasp of Law, Wealth, and Pleasure. [27]When a king administers Punishment properly, he flourishes with respect to the triple set (2.224 n.); but the king who is lustful, partial, and vile is slain by that very Punishment. [28]For Punishment is immense energy, and it cannot be wielded by those with uncultivated selves. It assuredly slays a king who deviates from the Law, along with his relatives; [29]then he oppresses the fort, the realm, and the mobile and the immobile world, as well as sages and gods dwelling in mid-space.* [30]Punishment cannot be justly administered by someone who is without assistants, who is foolish or greedy, who is irresolute (1.97 n.), or who is attached to sensual objects. [31]Punishment can only be administered by someone who is honest and true to his word, who acts in conformity with the Treatises, who has good assistants, and who is wise.

Proper Behavior [32]Within his realm, he should act in accordance with the rules; upon his enemies, he should impose harsh punishments; towards his friends and loved ones,* he should behave without guile; and to Brahmins, he should show compassion. [33]When a king behaves in this manner, though he may eke out a living by gleaning, his fame spreads in the world like a drop of oil on water. [34]When a king, with no control over himself, behaves in the opposite way, his fame contracts in the world like a drop of ghee on water.

[35]The king was created as the protector of people belonging to all social classes and orders of life who, according to their rank, are devoted to the Law specific to them.*

> [36]I will explain to you precisely and in their proper order all that he,
> along with his deputies, should do as he protects his subjects.

Cultivating Virtue and Learning

[37]After getting up in the morning,* the king should pay his respects to learned Brahmins who are experts in the triple Veda and follow their admonitions; [38]and every day he should render assistance to old and upright Brahmins who know the Veda, for even fiends always honor a man who renders assistance to the elderly. [39]Even if he is a disciplined man, he should always learn the rules of discipline from them; for a disciplined king never comes to ruin.

[40]Because they lacked discipline, numerous kings came to ruin along with their possessions; and because of discipline, even those residing in the forest* gained kingdoms. [41]Because he lacked discipline, Vena came to ruin; and so did King Nahuṣa, Sudas Paijavana, Sumukha, and Nimi. [42]Because of discipline, on the other hand, Pṛthu, as well as Manu, obtained a kingdom; Kubera, lordship over wealth; and the son of Gādhi, the rank of a Brahmin.*

[43]From experts in the three Vedas, he should learn the triple Veda, the timeless science of government, logical reasoning, and the philosophy of self; and from the common people, commercial enterprises.*

[44]Day and night he should strive vigorously to subdue his organs; for when he has subdued his own organs, he is able to bring his subjects under his control.

[45]He must strenuously steer clear of the vices that result in grief: the ten stemming from pleasure and the eight arising from wrath; [46]for when a king is addicted to vices stemming from pleasure, he is cut off from Law and Wealth, but when he is addicted to those arising from wrath, he is cut off from his very life.

[47]Hunting, gambling, sleeping during the day, disparaging others, women, liquor, music, song, dance, and useless travel—this is the set of ten stemming from pleasure. [48]Slander, violence, hostility, envy, resentment, plunder, verbal abuse, and physical assault—this is the set of eight arising from wrath.

[49]Wise men identify the root of both these sets, and it is greed. He should diligently overcome it; for both these sets originate from it. [50]Drinking, gambling, women, and hunting—one should recognize these four in the order enumerated as the most harmful of the set stemming from pleasure. [51]Physical assault, verbal abuse, and plunder—one should recognize these three as always the most harmful of the set stemming from wrath. [52]Within the latter group of seven, which run rampant everywhere, a self-composed man should recognize that each preceding vice is more perilous than each subsequent.*

[53]Between vice and death, they say, vice is far worse; a man given to vice sinks to the very bottom (6.35 n.), whereas a man free of vice goes to heaven after death.

Appointment of Counselors

[54]The king should appoint seven or eight counselors.* They must be individuals who are natives of the land,* well-versed in the Treatises, brave, well-accomplished,* and coming from illustrious families, individuals who have been thoroughly investigated. [55]Even an easy task becomes difficult when undertaken by a single individual, especially if he has no associates; how much harder a kingdom yielding great revenue?

[56]He should confer with them daily on general matters relating to alliance and war, and about the state,* revenue, and security, as also the pacification of acquisitions.* [57]After ascertaining their views about his affairs,* first from each individually and then from all of them as a group, he should do what is in his best interest. [58]From the most distinguished and sagacious Brahmin among them, however, the king should seek the most important counsel, the one relating to the sixfold strategy (7.160). [59]Trusting him completely, he should always entrust all his affairs to him and proceed with any task only after reaching a decision jointly with him.

Appointment of Officials

[60]He should also appoint other officials.* They must be individuals who are honest, intelligent, steadfast, and able to collect revenues properly, individuals who have been thoroughly investigated. [61]He should appoint as many tireless, clever, and wise men as are required to carry out his obligations, [62]employing the brave and the clever amongst them, individuals coming from illustrious families, in financial affairs; the honest in mines and factories; and the timid in the interior of his residence.*

Appointment of an Envoy

[63]He should also appoint an envoy. He must be an expert in all the Treatises; able to grasp a hint, bearing, or gesture;* be honest and clever; and come from an illustrious family. [64]A man who is loyal, honest, and clever; who has a sharp memory and knows the right time and place; and who is handsome, fearless, and eloquent—such a man is recommended as a king's envoy.

[65]The army depends on the official; the enforcement of order, on the army; the treasury and the realm,* on the king; and alliance and its reverse on the envoy. [66]For an envoy is the one who forges an alliance; and he is the one who splits allies apart. An envoy does the kind of work that splits people apart.

[67]By means of concealed hints and gestures, he should decode the bearing, hints, and gestures of the rival king with the help of seducible men* in his service and uncover his plans with the help of his servants.*

[68]After finding out all the plans of the rival king accurately, he should take* the kinds of measures that would prevent damage to himself.

Constructing the Royal Fort

[69]He should settle in a region that is dry, abounding in grain, populated mainly by Āryas, healthy,* beautiful, with submissive neighbors, and providing a comfortable living.

[70]A fortress secured by a desert, a fortress with an earthen rampart, a fortress surrounded by water, a fortress protected by a forest, a fortress guarded by soldiers, and a fortress protected by a hill—finding safety in such a fortress, he should settle in a fort.* [71]He should try his very best to find safety in a hill fortress; for the hill fortress,

because of its numerous superior features, is the most excellent of them. [72]Animals, creatures living in holes, and fish find safety in the first three of them; and monkeys, humans, and gods in the last three, respectively. [73]As their enemies do not harm these when they have found safety in a fortress, so his foes do not harm a king who has found safety in a fortress.

[74]One archer positioned on a rampart can fight off a hundred, and one hundred can fight off ten thousand. On account of this, a fortress is most excellent.*+ [75]It should be well supplied with weapons, money, grain, conveyances,* Brahmins, artisans, machines, fodder, and water.

[76]At its center, he should have a house built for himself, a house that is spacious, secure, and bright, suitable for all seasons, and provided with pools and groves.*

Marriage

[77]After establishing his residence there, he should marry a wife who belongs to the same class, has the right bodily characteristics (3.8–10), comes from a prominent family, is charming, and possesses beauty and fine qualities.

Appointment of Chaplain and Priests

[78]He should also appoint a chaplain and choose his officiating priests. They are to perform on his behalf the domestic rites, as well as those requiring three sacred fires.*

[79]The king should perform various sacrifices accompanied by generous sacrificial gifts; and to acquire merit, he should distribute luxuries and money to Brahmins.

Collectors and Supervisors

[80]He should employ trusted officials to collect annual taxes from his realm, strictly follow tradition in his dealings with the population, and behave like a father towards his people.

[81]He should appoint perspicacious supervisors of various kinds to oversee different areas, and they should inspect all the activities of the men responsible for his affairs.

Devotion to Brahmins

[82]He should pay honor to Brahmins who have returned from their teacher's house; for this is the inexhaustible treasure deposited with Brahmins decreed for kings. [83]Neither thief nor enemy can steal it, and it never perishes. Therefore, the king should deposit this inexhaustible treasure with Brahmins.

[84]It never spills, it never falls, it never perishes at all—an offering made in the mouth of a Brahmin is far superior to oblations made in the fire. [85]A gift to a non-Brahmin brings an equal reward; to a Brahmin by name, a double reward; to one who is advanced in vedic study, a thousandfold reward;* and to a man who has completely mastered the Veda, an infinite reward. [86]For, whether the reward a man receives after death is large or small is contingent on his spirit of generosity (3.202 n.) and on the excellence of the recipient.+

War and Warrior Ethic

[87]When challenged by rivals—whether they are stronger, weaker, or of equal strength—as he protects his subjects, a king must never back away from battle, recalling the Law of Kṣatriyas. [88]Refusal to turn back in battle, protecting the subjects, and obedient service to Brahmins—for kings, these are the best mean of securing happiness. [89]When kings fight each other in battles with all their strength, seeking to kill each other and refusing to turn back, they go to heaven.

[90]When he is engaged in battle, he must never slay his enemies with weapons that are treacherous,* barbed, or laced with poison, or whose tips are ablaze with fire. [91]He must never slay a man standing on the ground,* an effeminate man (3.150 n.), a man with joined palms, a man with loose hair, a seated man, a man declaring "I am yours," [92]a sleeping man, a man without his armor, a naked man, a man without his weapons, a non-fighting spectator, a man engaging someone else, [93]a man with damaged weapons, a man in distress, a badly wounded man, a frightened man, or a man who has turned tail—recalling the Law followed by good people.

[94]When a man is killed in battle by the enemy as he turns tail frightened, he takes upon himself all the evil deeds committed by his master;* [95]while any good deeds that a man killed as he turns tail has stored up for the hereafter, all of that his master takes from him.

War Booty [96]Whatever a man wins—chariot, horse, elephant, parasol, money, grain, livestock, women, all goods, and base metal—all that belongs to him. [97]A pre-emptive share,* however, should be given to the king—so states the vedic scripture;* and the king should distribute among the soldiers anything that has not been won in single combat.+

> [98]I have set forth above the eternal Law of warriors without elaboration. A Kṣatriya must never deviate from this Law, as he kills his enemies in battle.

Policies for Good Government

[99]The king should seek to acquire what he has not acquired, preserve diligently what he has acquired, augment what he has preserved, and distribute what he has augmented on worthy recipients.* [100]These he should recognize as the four means of securing the goals of man (2.224 n.); and he should execute them properly and tirelessly every day. [101]What he has not acquired, he should seek to acquire with military force; what he has acquired, he should preserve with vigilance; what he has preserved, he should augment through profitable investments; and what he has augmented, he should distribute through gifts.*

[102]He should keep his military force in constant readiness,* constantly display his might, constantly guard his secrets, and constantly probe his enemy's weaknesses. [103]The whole world stands in awe of the man who keeps his military force in constant readiness; it is with military force, therefore, that he should subdue all creatures. [104]He should always act without guile and never with guile; and, guarding himself well at all

times, he should detect the guile employed by his enemies. [105]He must not let the enemy discover any weakness of his, but discover any weakness of the enemy; he should hide his limbs like a tortoise* and conceal his own weak points.

[106]He should ponder over his affairs like a heron, dart off like a rabbit, snatch like a wolf, and attack like a lion.*

[107]As he thus engages in conquest, he should bring under his control all the adversaries he encounters by the use of the strategies beginning with conciliation.*+ [108]If, after the employment of the first three strategies, they still do not submit, then he should undoubtedly subdue them by military force and in due course bring them under his control. [109]Among all four strategies beginning with conciliation, experts always recommend conciliation and military force for the enhancement of his realm.

[110]As a weeder plucks the weeds and protects the corn, so the king should protect his realm and kill his adversaries. [111]When a king in his folly oppresses his own realm indiscriminately, he is soon deprived of his kingdom and his life, along with his relatives. [112]As living beings destroy their lives by oppressing their bodies, so kings too destroy their lives by oppressing their realms.

[113]He should observe this rule always in managing his realm, for when his realm is well managed,* the king prospers* with ease.

Organization of the State

Governance of Villages and Towns [114]He should station well-supervised constabularies in the middle of two, three, and five villages, as also in the middle of one hundred villages for the protection of his realm. [115]He should appoint superintendents responsible for one village, for ten villages, for twenty villages, for one hundred villages, and for one thousand villages.

[116]When troubles* arise in a village, the superintendent of that village should, in due course, report them personally to the superintendent of ten villages, and he in turn, to the superintendent of twenty village. [117]The superintendent of twenty villages should report all that to the superintendent of a hundred villages, and he in turn should report them personally to the superintendent of a thousand villages.

[118]The superintendent of a village shall avail himself of the food, drink, firewood, and the like that the villagers are required to supply daily to the king. [119]The superintendent of ten villages shall enjoy benefits from one "family";* the superintendent of twenty villages, from five "families"; the superintendent of a hundred villages, from one village; the superintendent of a thousand villages, from one town.

Supervision of Officials [120]Their activities pertaining to the villages, as well as those undertaken by each individually,* should be overseen vigilantly by another loyal officer of the king.

[121]In each city he should appoint a general manager of all affairs, a man of high stature* and fierce appearance, like a planet among the stars.

[122]He should always make the circuit of all those officials personally and investigate their conduct within their jurisdictions* thoroughly through resident spies; [123]for the king's officials, appointed to protect the people, often become swindlers

seizing the property of others—he must protect his subjects from them. [124]When these evil-minded men extort money from people who have business* with them, the king should confiscate all their property and send them into exile.*

Wages [125]He should fix* a daily allowance for women in the royal service and for menial servants in accordance with their rank and duties. [126]One Paṇa should be given as maintenance* for those at the bottom and six Paṇas for those at the top, as also a set of clothes every six months and one Droṇa of grain every month.

Taxes and Duties

[127]The king should levy taxes on traders after taking into consideration the price of purchase and sale, the distance of transport, maintenance* and other expenses, and the cost of security.

[128]The king should always assess taxes in his realm after careful consideration so that both he and those who do the work get their fair reward. [129]As leeches, calves, and bees eat their food a little at a time, so a king should gather annual taxes from his realm a little at a time. [130]Of livestock and gold, the king shall take a one-fiftieth share;* and of grains, an eighth share, or a sixth or twelfth. [131]He shall also take a sixth share of trees, meat, honey, ghee, perfumes, herbs, condiments, flowers, roots, fruits, [132]leaves, vegetables, grass, skins, cane, earthen vessels, and everything made of stone.

[133]Even at the point of death, he shall never extract a tax from a vedic scholar, nor shall a vedic scholar living within his realm languish from hunger. [134]When a vedic scholar languishes from hunger within the domain of a king, before long his own realm will also languish from hunger. [135]After ascertaining the man's learning and conduct, he should provide him with a means of subsistence consistent with the Law and protect him in every way, as a father his own natural son (9.166). [136]When such a person practices the Law every day under the protection of the king, it augments the king's life span, wealth, and realm.

[137]He should make the common people in his realm who live by trade pay at least something annually under the rubric of a tax. [138]The king should make artisans and craftsmen, as also self-employed* Śūdras, contribute one day's work each month.

[139]He must not cut off his own root and that of others through excessive greed; for by cutting off his own root, he does harm both to himself and to them.*

Adjudicating Lawsuits

[140]After he has tried a lawsuit,* the king should be both harsh and gentle; a king who is both harsh and gentle earns high esteem.

[141]When he becomes tired of trying lawsuits filed by people, he should install on that seat a leading minister who knows the Law, is wise and self-disciplined, and comes from an illustrious family.

Protection of the Subjects

[142]Arranging in this manner for the discharge of all his obligations, he should protect these subjects with care and vigilance. [143]When bandits abduct from his realm subjects

screaming for help, while he and men in his service stand by—he is surely dead, he is not alive.+ [144]For a Kṣatriya, the protection of his subjects is the highest Law; the enjoyment of the specified rewards* binds the king to this Law.

Morning Routine

[145]He should rise in the last watch of the night (4.92 n.), perform his personal purifications with a collected mind, make the fire offering, pay his respects to Brahmins, and enter his splendid assembly hall.

[146]Standing there, he should greet all his subjects cheerfully and then dismiss them. After dismissing all his subjects, he should confer with his counselors.

Meeting with Counselors [147]Climbing up to a hilltop or a terrace, retiring to a solitary spot, or withdrawing to a wild area or a bare tract, he should confer with them unobserved.* [148]When common people, as they conspire, do not discover a king's plans, he will enjoy the entire earth, even though his treasury is empty.

[149]Idiots, the dumb, the blind, the deaf, animals, old people, women, foreigners (2.23 n.), the sick, and the crippled—he should have these removed when he confers with his counselors. [150]He should pay special attention to this, because these wretched people and animals, but women in particular, betray secret plans.

[151]At midday or midnight, when he is not tired or worn out, he should reflect on these matters either in consultation with his counselors or alone—on Law, Wealth, and Pleasure (7.100), [152]and on how they may be acquired all together when they are in mutual opposition; on giving his young girls in marriage; on protecting his young boys; [153]on dispatching ambassadors; on tying up the remaining loose ends of his undertakings;* on the activities* within the women's quarters; on the conduct of his spies; [154]on the entire eightfold agenda,* as also the set of five,* meticulously; on the affection and disaffection towards him; on the activities in the circle of neighboring kingdoms;*+ [155]on the activities of the buffer king;* on the conduct of the power-hungry king; and on the activities of the neutral king and, with great diligence, of the enemy king.

Constituents of the Circle [156]The above constituents, in brief, form the root of the circle of neighboring kings; eight others also have been enumerated, bringing the total, according to the tradition, to twelve.* [157]There are also five others and they are called official, realm, fort, treasury, and army. These are enumerated with reference to each of the above, the total coming to seventy-two.*

[158]He should recognize that his immediate neighbor is his enemy, as also anyone rendering assistance to the enemy; that his enemy's immediate neighbor is an ally; and that the one beyond these two is neutral.+ [159]He should prevail over them by conciliation and the other strategies (7.107 n.), employed both separately and collectively, and by valor and policy.

Political Strategy: I [160]He should constantly think about the sixfold strategy: forging alliances, waging war, marching into battle, remaining stationary, pursuing a double stratagem,* and seeking asylum. [161]After forging an alliance or waging war,* he should carefully examine the state of affairs and adopt the tactic of remaining stationary, marching into battle, pursuing a double stratagem, or seeking asylum.

[162]The king should realize that there are two ways to forge an alliance, to wage war, to march into battle, to remain stationary, to pursue a double strategem,* and to seek asylum. [163]He should know that there are two kinds of alliance: the one is when both parties march together into battle with the same objective—it is of immediate significance; the other is its opposite—and it looks to the future.* [164]Tradition records two types of war: the one is waged on one's own and for one's own ends, whether it is at a proper time or not; the other is occasioned when an ally has initiated the offensive.* [165]Marching into battle is said to be of two types: the one is undertaken alone when an urgent situation has suddenly arisen; the other is undertaken in coalition with an ally. [166]Tradition records two types of remaining stationary: the one is undertaken when he is gradually weakened either by fate or due to his past deeds; and the other is undertaken as a favor to an ally. [167]Experts in the relative merits of the sixfold strategy present two types of the double stratagem: the one is when the army remains stationary and the other is when the ruler remains stationary, for the success of his undertakings (7.160 n.). [168]Tradition records two types of seeking asylum: the one is intended to attain his objective when he is harassed by enemies; the other is to gain renown among good people.*

[169]When he is convinced that his future dominance is certain and that any immediate disadvantage is slight, then he should resort to an alliance. [170]When he believes that all his subjects are exceedingly content and that he himself is overwhelmingly powerful, then he should consider waging war.* [171]When he believes in his heart that his own army is in high spirit* and prosperous and that the opposite is true of his adversary, then he should march into battle against his enemy. [172]When he is weak in terms of mounted units* and infantry, then he should diligently remain stationary, while gradually appeasing the enemy. [173]When the king believes that the enemy is stronger in every respect, then he should divide his army in two and accomplish his objective (7.160 n.). [174]When he has become extremely vulnerable to his enemy's forces, then he should quickly seek asylum with a strong and righteous king. [175]Should that king keep both his own subjects and the forces of his enemy in check, he should always serve him like a teacher with all his strength. [176]Even in that case, however, if he notices a liability resulting from his asylum, he should, even in that condition, resort to the good war* without hesitation. [177]A politically astute king should employ all the strategies in such a way that his allies, neutrals, or enemies do not prevail over him.

[178]He should probe closely into the current status and the future shape of all his undertakings, as well as the positives and the negatives of all his past undertakings. [179]When a man knows the positives and the negatives with respect to the future, takes quick decisions with respect to the present, and knows the remaining loose ends of his past undertakings, he will not be overpowered by his enemies.

[180]He should arrange everything in such a way that his allies, neutrals, or enemies never prevail over him—that is political strategy in a nutshell.

War [181]When the king launches a military expedition against the realm of an enemy, he should advance at a measured pace towards the enemy's fort according to the following plan.

[182]The king should start a military expedition during the auspicious month of Mārgaśīrṣa (November–December), or towards the months of Phālguna (February–March) or Caitra (March–April), depending on the shape of his armed forces. [183]Even at other times when he foresees certain victory, he should undoubtedly declare war and launch the expedition,* as also when a calamity has struck the enemy.

[184]He should first make the necessary arrangements for his home territory, gather provisions for the expedition according to rule, secure a base for military operations, deploy spies suitably, [185]secure the three types of roads,* and inspect the six divisions of his army*—and only then march in battle formation at a measured pace against the enemy's fort.*

[186]He should be extremely vigilant about an ally who is secretly in league with the enemy, as well as about someone who has returned after going over to the enemy's side; for such a man is a very dangerous foe.

[187]He should march along his road arrayed in one of the following battle formations: staff, wagon, boar, crocodile, needle, and eagle.* [188]He should deploy his troops in the direction from which he expects danger; always set up his own camp arrayed in the lotus formation;* [189]post the commander-in-chief and the general of the army in every direction;* designate the direction from which he expects danger as the frontal direction; [190]deploy on all sides platoons of reliable soldiers with whom signals have been arranged, who are adept both at holding their ground and at pressing an attack, and who are fearless and unwavering; [191]deploy a small group to fight in close quarters and freely spread out a large group; send them into battle arrayed in the needle (7.187 n.) and the thunderbolt* formations; [192]fight with chariots and horses on level ground, with boats and elephants in marshy lands, with bows in areas covered with trees and shrubs, and with swords and shields on flat land; [193]and deploy men from the lands of the Kurus, Matsyas, Pañcālas, and Śūrasenas, as well as tall and agile men, on the front lines. [194]After arraying the troops in battle formation, he should rouse them and inspect them closely; and he should monitor their behavior even when they are engaged in combat with enemy troops.

[195]After laying siege to the enemy, he shall remain stationary—he should plunder his realm; constantly ruin his supplies of fodder, food, water, and fuel; [196]demolish reservoirs, ramparts, and moats; launch surprise assaults* against him; frighten him at night; [197]foment sedition among the seditious; keep close watch over enemy activity;* and when omens are propitious, fearlessly launch the attack with the determination to win.

[198]He should strive to triumph over his enemies through conciliation, gifts, and fomenting dissension, employed collectively or separately, but never through war. [199]Victory and defeat in battle are uncertain for the two combatants; he should, therefore, avoid war. [200]When the aforementioned three strategies fail, then let him, always on guard, pursue war in such a manner that he will triumph over his enemies.

Conduct in Victory [201]After the victory, he should pay homage to gods and righteous Brahmins; grant exemptions; and issue proclamations of amnesty.*

[202]After ascertaining the collective wishes of them all, he should install there a relation of the enemy king and draw up a treaty; [203]make the Laws commonly held among them authoritative; and honor the new ruler, together with his chief officials, with precious gifts. [204]When carried out at the appropriate time, the unwelcome seizure of desirable property and their welcome distribution are both commendable.

[205]All activities here depend on divine and human dispensations. Of these, however, the divine is inscrutable; action is possible only with respect to the human.*+

Political Strategy: II [206]Alternatively, he may leave after diligently working out an alliance with him,* recognizing that ally, gold, and land are the three rewards.* [207]After taking into consideration the foe at his heel and his rescuer from the rear* within the circle of kings, he should secure the rewards of his campaign from his opponent either as ally or as foe.

[208]A king does not prosper as much by getting gold and land as by securing a firm ally who, although currently weak, has future potential. [209]A man who knows the Law and is mindful of favors received, whose subjects are content, and who is loyal, steadfast in his undertakings, and agile,* is commended as an ally.

[210]The wise consider a man who is intelligent, brave, clever, generous, mindful of favors received, and steadfast, and who comes from an illustrious family, to be a very dangerous foe. [211]Conduct worthy of an Ārya, sound judgment with regard to men, valor, compassion, and constant generosity*—these represent the qualities of a neutral.

[212]For his own well-being, a king may abandon without hesitation even a land that is safe and always yields abundant crops and on which livestock thrive. [213]A man should save his wealth for a time of adversity, save his wife even at the cost of his wealth, and always save himself even at the cost of his wife and wealth. [214]When he sees every kind of adversity rising up fiercely in unison, a wise man should employ all the strategies collectively and individually. [215]The one who employs the strategies, the goal to be achieved through the strategies, and all the strategies in their entirety—relying on these three, he should strive for his own success.

Afternoon Routine

[216]After conferring about all this with his counselors in this manner,* he should do his exercises and take his bath at midday, and go to his private quarters to take his meal.

[217]There he should eat food that has been thoroughly examined by servants who are completely loyal, knowledgeable about time, and incorruptible, while reciting ritual formulas that remove poison.* [218]He should cleanse everything with antidotes that neutralize poison* and always carefully wear on his body gems that counteract poison. [219]Women who have been thoroughly examined and whose clothing and jewelry have been searched shall wait on him attentively with fans, water, and perfumes.

[220]He should take similar care of his vehicles (7.75 n.), beds, seats, and food, as well as of his bath, grooming, and all his ornaments.

[221]After his meal, he should relax in his private quarters with his women, and after relaxing, once again turn his attention at the proper time to his affairs. [222]Dressed in his regalia, he should again inspect his armed forces, all his conveyances, and his weapons and trappings.

Evening Routine

[223]After performing the evening twilight worship, he should arm himself and receive reports in his inner chambers from secret informants and spies about their activities.

[224]After withdrawing to another secure chamber and dismissing those people, he should again enter his private quarters to take his meal escorted by women.* [225]After eating something there once again while he is being entertained with music, he should go to bed at the proper time and rise up refreshed.

[226]A king should follow this schedule when he is healthy; but when he is unwell, he may delegate all this to his officials.

CHAPTER EIGHT

THE JUSTICE SYSTEM

Court

[1]When the king is going to try a case, he should enter the court modestly accompanied by Brahmins and counselors who are experts in policy.* [2]Seated or standing there, dressed in modest clothes and ornaments, and raising his right hand,* he should look into the cases of the plaintiffs [3]every day in accordance with the standards of the region and those specified in the legal texts, lawsuits that fall individually* under the eighteen avenues of litigation.

Grounds for Litigation

[4]Of these, (i) the first is non-payment of debts; (ii) deposits; (iii) sale without ownership; (iv) partnerships; (v) non-delivery of gifts; [5](vi) non-payment of wages; (vii) breach of contract; (viii) cancellation of a sale or purchase; (ix) disputes between owners and herdsmen; [6](x) the Law on boundary disputes; (xi) verbal assault; (xii) physical assault; (xiii) theft; (xiv) violence; (xv) sexual crimes against women;* [7](xvi) Law concerning husband and wife; (xvii) partition of inheritance; and (xviii) gambling and betting. These are the eighteen grounds on which litigation may be instituted in this world.

[8]These are the areas in which, for the most part, disputes among people arise; and the king should decide their cases based on the eternal Law.

Legal Proceedings

Judges [9]When the king does not try a case personally, however, he should appoint a learned Brahmin to do so.* [10]Entering the main court itself accompanied by three assessors, he should try the cases brought before the king, either seated or standing. [11]The place where three Brahmins versed in the Vedas and a learned officer* of the king sit, they call the court of Brahman.

Pursuit of Justice [12]When Justice (*dharma*), pierced by Injustice (*adharma*),* comes to the court for redress and the court officials do not pluck out that dart from him, then they are themselves pierced by it. [13]A man must either not enter the court or speak candidly; by refusing to speak or by speaking deceitfully, he commits a sin. [14]When Justice is struck by Injustice, and Truth by Untruth, while the court offcials remain idle onlookers, then they are themselves struck down. [15]Stricken, Justice surely strikes back; defended, Justice defends. Therefore, never strike at Justice, lest Justice, stricken, wipes us out. [16]Lord Justice is truly the bull (*vṛṣa*), and a man who impedes (*alaṁ*) him the gods call a low-born (*vṛṣa-la*). Therefore, one should never trample Justice. [17]Justice is the only friend who follows a man even in death; for all else perishes along with the body.*

[18]One-quarter of an Injustice goes to the perpetrator, one-quarter to the witness, one-quarter to all the court officials, and one-quarter to the king. [19]The king, on the other hand, becomes sinless, the court officials are freed, and the sin falls squarely on the perpetrator, when a man deserving condemnation is condemned.

***Excursus:* Śūdras as Legal Interpreters** [20]Let a king, if he so wishes, get someone who is a Brahmin only by name to interpret the Law, or even someone who simply uses his birth to make a living, but under no circumstances a Śūdra. [21]When a Śūdra interprets the Law for a king, his realm sinks like a cow in mud, as he looks on helplessly. [22]The entire realm, stricken with famine and pestilence, quickly perishes, when it is teeming with Śūdras, overrun by infidels, and devoid of twice-born people.

Judicial Conduct and Reasoning–I [23]Ascending the throne of justice with his body covered and his mind composed, he should pay homage to the guardian deities of the world and open the trial. [24]Paying attention only to these two—what is and what is not in accord with the provisions of polity (*artha*), and what is and what is not in accord with the Law (*dharma*)—he should try all the cases brought by litigants in the order of their social class.*

[25]He should discover the internal disposition of men by external signs—voice, color, expression, bearing, eyes, and gestures. [26]Inner thoughts are discerned by the bearing, expressions, gait, gestures, and manner of speaking, and by changes in the eyes and face.

***Excursus:* Property of Minors and Women** [27]The king should protect the estate inherited by a child until he has returned home after his studentship or until he is no longer a minor.*

[28]The same protection must be extended to barren women, women without sons or bereft of family, women devoted to their husbands, widows, and women in distress. [29]If their in-laws (2.132 n.) usurp their property while they are alive, a righteous king should discipline them with the punishment laid down for thieves.

***Excursus:* Lost and Stolen Property** [30]Any property that is lost and without an owner* should be kept in deposit by the king for three years. Before the lapse of three years, the owner can claim it; after that the king may take it. [31]A man who claims "This is mine" and, when questioned according to rule, identifies its physical appearance, number, and the like correctly, is the owner and deserves to have that property; [32]but if he is ignorant of the exact place and time when it was lost and its color, physical appearance, and size, he deserves a fine equal in value to that property.

[33]The king may take one-sixth of any lost property that is recovered, or else one-tenth or one-twelfth, calling to mind the Law practiced by good people. [34]Lost property that is recovered shall remain in the care of competent officials, and the king should have any thieves caught in connection with its disappearance executed by an elephant.

[35]When a man states truthfully in regard to a treasure-trove "This is mine," the king may take one-sixth or one-twelfth of it. [36]If he lies, however, he should be fined one-eighth of his wealth or, after reckoning the value of the treasure, a smaller portion.

[37]When a learned Brahmin finds a treasure-trove that had been buried by his ancestors, however, he may take the whole of it; for a Brahmin is the supreme lord of all.+ [38]When the king discovers an ancient treasure-trove buried in the ground, he should give one-half of it to Brahmins and deposit one-half in the treasury; [39]the king, by proving protection, is entitled to one-half of all ancient treasure-troves and of minerals in the ground, for he is the supreme lord of the earth.

[40]The king must restore to individuals of all classes any property of theirs stolen by thieves; if the king retains it for himself, he incurs the sin of its thief.

Judicial Conduct and Reasoning–II [41]He who knows the Law should examine the Laws of castes, regions, guilds, and families, and only then settle the Law specific to each. [42]Even men living far away endear themselves to the world when they stick to the activity specific to each and carry out their specific activities.

[43]Neither the king nor any official of his shall initiate a lawsuit* independently; nor shall he in any way suppress an action brought before him by someone else.*

[44]As a hunter traces the location of an animal by the trail of blood, so a king should trace the location of justice by deductive reasoning. [45]When he is conducting a judicial proceeding, he should pay close attention to the truth, the object of the suit, himself, the witnesses, the place, the time, and the appearance.*

[46]He should ratify the acknowledged practices of virtuous men and righteous twice-born individuals, if such practices do not conflict with those of a particular region, family, or caste.*

Grounds for Litigation: I Non-payment of Debts

[47]When a creditor petitions for the recovery of his money from a debtor and the facts are established,* the king should compel the debtor to return the money to the creditor.

[48]He should constrain the debtor and force him to pay, using any means by which the creditor may recover his money. [49]Money loaned may be recovered by invoking the Law, by litigation, by cunning, by traditional strategies,* and fifth, by force. [50]Should a creditor recover his money from the debtor on his own, he must not be prosecuted by the king simply for recovering his own money.

[51]If a man denies that he took a loan when it has been established by evidence, he should compel that man to return the money to the creditor and in addition impose a small fine proportionate to his means. [52]When the debtor, told in court to pay up, denies the charge, the plaintiff should produce a document* or offer some other evidence.

[53]When the plaintiff produces something that is not documentary evidence; produces and then disavows it;* does not realize that his earlier points contradict the ones he makes subsequently;* [54]states his case and then backs away from it;* does not acknowledge under questioning a point that has been clearly established;* [55]secretly discusses with witnesses a document which is prohibited from being discussed;* objects to a question clearly articulated;* retreats;* [56]does not speak when he is ordered

"Speak!"; does not prove what he asserts; and does not understand what goes before and what after—such a plaintiff loses his suit. 57When a plaintiff says "I have people who know,"* but when told "Produce them" does not produce them, the judge should declare him also the loser for these very reasons.

58If the plaintiff fails to present his case, he is subject to corporal punishment and a fine in accordance with the Law; and if the defendant fails to respond within three fortnights, he loses the case in the eyes of the Law.* 59The amount that one man falsely denies and the amount that the other falsely claims—the king should impose a fine equal to double those amounts on those two men ignorant of the Law.

60When a man is summoned to court by a creditor and denies the charge under questioning, he may be convicted through the testimony of at least three witnesses given in the presence of the king and Brahmins.

> 61I will now explain what sorts of individuals creditors may call as witnesses in lawsuits and how they should be made to speak* the truth.

Qualifications of Witnesses 62Householders, men with sons, natives of the region (7.54 n.), Kṣatriyas, Vaiśyas, and Śūdras, when they are called by the plaintiff, are competent to give testimony, and not just anybody, except in an emergency. 63Trustworthy men of all social classes may be called as witnesses in lawsuits, men who know the Law in its entirety and are free from greed; individuals different from these should be excluded.

64Individuals who have a stake in the suit; individuals close to the litigants; their associates and enemies; individuals with a criminal record; the very sick; and men of ill repute—these must not be called as witnesses. 65The king may not be called as a witness, nor should the following: an artisan; a performer; a vedic scholar; an individual bearing the insignia of a religious profession (4.200 n.); one who has severed all attachments; 66a totally subservient individual; a reprehensible person;* a bandit; a criminal; an old person; a child; a single person;* an individual of the lowest birth or with impaired organs; 67someone in distress; an intoxicated or insane person; someone tormented by hunger or thirst, or suffering from fatigue; a lovesick or angry person; and a thief.

68For women, women shall give testimony; for the twice-born, twice-born individuals of equal rank; for Śūdras, upright Śūdras; and for the lowest-born, those of the lowest birth. 69Anyone who has personal knowledge may give testimony for litigants when the event has taken place inside a house or in the wilderness, or in a case involving bodily harm.* 70When there is no one else, even a woman, a child, an old man, a pupil, a relative, a slave, or a servant may give testimony.

71He should recognize the trembling in the voices of children, old men, and sick persons, as also of individuals with deranged minds, when they give false testimony.*

72He must not investigate* the witnesses in all cases of violence, theft, sexual crimes, and verbal and physical assault.

Assessing Testimony 73When witnesses are in disagreement, the king should accept the testimony of the majority; when they are equally divided, the testimony of those distinguished by superior qualities; and when men with superior qualities are in disagreement, the testimony of Brahmins.

[74]Testimony is valid when it is based on what the witness himself has seen or heard. When a witness speaks truthfully with respect to that, he does not suffer any loss of merit or wealth. [75]If, in a court of Āryas, a witness says something deceitfully contrary to what he has seen or heard, after death he will plunge headlong into hell and suffer the loss of heaven.

[76]When a person, even though he is not listed as a witness* in the plaint, has seen or heard anything pertaining to the trial and he is questioned during the trial,* he also should testify in accordance with what he saw or heard.

[77]Even one man free from greed may be appointed as a witness, but never women, even if they are many and honest,* because the female mind is unsteady; nor even other men tainted with defects.

[78]Only what witnesses testify to in a forthright manner should be accepted as valid in a trial; anything different that they may testify to deceitfully for the sake of the Law has no validity.*

Questioning of Witnesses [79]When the witnesses have gathered in the court, the judge should examine them in the presence of the plaintiff and the defendant, exhorting the witnesses in the following manner:*

> [80]What you know about any mutual transaction between these two individuals pertaining to this lawsuit—state all that truthfully; for you are the witnesses in this matter. [81]If a witness speaks the truth when he testifies, he will obtain magnificent worlds, as well as unsurpassing fame here below; such speech is honored by Brahman. [82]If he speaks an untruth when he testifies, he will be bound tightly by the fetters of Varuṇa and lie helplessly for one hundred lifetimes; therefore, he should speak the truth when he testifies. [83]By truth, the witness is purified; by truth, merit is increased. Witnesses of all social classes,* therefore, should speak only the truth. [84]For the self alone is the witness of the self; the self, likewise, is the refuge of the self. Do not disdain your own self, the supreme witness of men. [85]Evil doers undoubtedly think "No one sees us";* yet gods see them clearly, and so does their own inner self. [86]Heaven, earth, waters, heart, moon, sun, fire, Yama, wind, night, the two twilights, and the Law—these know the conduct of all embodied beings.

[87]In the presence of gods and Brahmins* and in the forenoon, the judge, after purifying himself, should ask the twice-born individuals, who have purified themselves and are facing the north or the east,* to give truthful testimony. [88]He should question a Brahmin, saying "Speak"; a Kṣatriya, saying "Speak the truth"; a Vaiśya, with a reference to cows, seeds, and gold;* but a Śūdra, with a reference to these sins that cause loss of caste.*

> [89]The worlds to which tradition consigns a murderer of a Brahmin, a killer of a woman or child, a betrayer of a friend, and an ingrate—those worlds will be yours, if you testify falsely. [90]Whatever good deeds you have done

since birth, dear man, all that will go to the dogs, if you testify dishonestly. [91]"I am all alone"—should you think like that about yourself, good man; there dwells always in your heart this sage, who observes your good and evil deeds! [92]This god, Yama the son of Vivasvat, dwells in your heart. If you have no quarrel with him, then you do not have to go to the Ganges or the Kuru land.* [93]Naked, blind, shaven-headed, and racked with hunger and thirst, a man who gives false testimony will have to go to his enemy's house carrying a skull-bowl to beg for almsfood. [94]If anyone gives a false answer when questioned at a judicial investigation, in blind darkness that sinner will fall headlong into hell. [95]A person who goes to a court and testifies to what is contrary to the facts or to what he has not seen is like a blind man, eating fish along with the bones. [96]When his discerning Kṣetrajña, "the knower of the field" (12.12–3 n.), remains unperturbed as a man is giving testimony—gods know of no man superior to him in this world. [97]Listen, my friend, to an orderly enumeration of how many relatives of his a man kills* when he gives false testimony in a particular case. [98]He kills five by false testimony concerning livestock; ten, by false testimony concerning cows; one hundred, by false testimony concerning horses; and one thousand, by false testimony concerning a human being. [99]He kills the born and yet to be born by giving false testimony concerning gold; and he kills all by false testimony concerning land—never give false testimony concerning land. [100]False testimony concerning water,* they say, is similar to that concerning land; the same is true of false testimony concerning the sexual enjoyment of women and concerning all gems, whether they are aquatic or lapidary (5.111–2 n.).+ [101]After taking careful note of all these evils resulting from false testimony, tell the truth forthrightly just as you saw or heard.*

[102]He should treat Brahmins who are cattle herders, traders, artisans, performers, servants, or money lenders, just like Śūdras.+

Excusable False Testimony [103]When a man, even though he knows the truth, gives evidence in lawsuits contrary to the facts for a reason relating to the Law, he does not fall from the heavenly world; that, they say, is divine speech. [104]When telling the truth will result in the execution of a Śūdra, Vaiśya, Kṣatriya, or a Brahmin, a man may tell a lie; for that is far better than the truth.

[105]Such persons, performing the highest expiation for the sin of false testimony, should offer to the goddess Sarasvatī oblations of milk-rice dedicated to the goddess Speech. [106]Alternatively, such a person may offer an oblation of ghee in the fire according to rule, reciting the Kūṣmāṇḍa formulas, the verse to Varuṇa: "Untie, Varuṇa . . . ," or the three formulas addressed to water.*

Failure to Give Evidence [107]When a man who is not sick fails to testify for three fortnights in cases pertaining to debts and the like, he becomes liable for the entire debt and is fined one-tenth of the total.*

Signs of False Testimony 108When an illness, a fire, or the death of a relative is seen to afflict a witness within seven days of his testimony, he should be compelled to pay the debt and a fine.

Oaths and Ordeals 109When two persons are litigating matters for which there are no witnesses and the judge is unable to discern the truth, he should discover it even by means of an oath.* 110Great sages, as well as gods, have taken oaths to settle a case. Vasiṣṭha* also made an oath before King Paijavana.

111A wise man must not take an oath falsely even with regard to a trifling matter; for by taking an oath falsely, he comes to ruin here and in the hereafter. 112Taking an oath is not a sin causing loss of caste when it is made in connection with lovers, marriages, fodder for cows, or firewood, or to protect a Brahmin.*

113He should make a Brahmin swear by the truth; a Kṣatriya by his conveyance (7.75 n.) and weapons; a Vaiśya by his cattle, seeds, and gold; and a Śūdra by all the sins causing loss of caste.*

114Alternatively, he may make the person carry fire, stay submerged in water, or touch separately the heads of his sons and wife. 115When the blazing fire does not burn a man, the water does not push him up to the surface, and no misfortune quickly strikes him,* he should be judged innocent by reason of his oath. 116Long ago when Vatsa was accused by his younger brother, Fire, the world's spy, did not burn a single hair of his because he told the truth.*

False Testimony 117Every case where perjured testimony has been given should be declared a mistrial, and any judgment rendered there should be annulled.

118Testimony given through greed, delusion, fear, friendship, lust, anger, ignorance, or immaturity is considered false.

> 119I will explain in order the specific punishments for a person who
> gives false testimony for any one of these reasons.

Punishment for Perjury 120For giving false testimony through greed, he should be fined 1,000;* through delusion, the lowest fine (8.138); through fear, double the middle fine; through friendship, four times the lowest fine; 121through lust, ten times the lowest fine; through anger, three times the highest fine; through ignorance, a full 200; and through immaturity, just 100. 122These are said to be the punishments for false testimony prescribed by the wise in order to prevent the miscarriage of justice and to arrest injustice.

123When individuals of the three classes give false testimony, a righteous king should first fine them and then execute them; a Brahmin, on the other hand, should be sent into exile.*

Varieties of Punishment 124Manu, the son of the Self-existent One, has proclaimed ten places upon which punishment may be inflicted. They are applicable to the three classes; a Brahmin shall depart unscathed. 125They are: genitals, stomach, tongue, and hands; feet are the fifth; and then, eyes, nose, ears, wealth, and body.

[126]He should inflict punishment on those deserving punishment only after he has fully ascertained the proclivity,* as also the time and place, accurately, and considered carefully the ability of the criminal and the severity of the crime. [127]Unjust punishment shatters* his fame and destroys his reputation in this world, and it is also an obstacle to heaven in the next; therefore, he should avoid it completely. [128]When a king punishes those who do not deserve to be punished and neglects to punish those who deserve, he brings great infamy upon himself and he will also go to hell.

[129]He should employ first the punishment of verbal reprimand; next a public denunciation; third, a fine; and finally, corporal punishment. [130]If he is unable to restrain them even with corporal punishment, then he should impose on them all these four.*

> [131]I will explain fully the terms spread across the world relating to copper, silver, and gold for use in commercial transactions among people.

Weights [132]The fleck of dust seen when the sun shines through a lattice is called Trasareṇu,* the primary weight. [133]One should know that eight Trasareṇus make one Likṣā in weight; three Likṣās, one Rājasarṣapa; three Rājasarṣapas, one Gaurasarṣapa;* [134]six Gaurasarṣapas, one middling Yava; three Yavas, one Kṛṣṇala; five Kṛṣṇalas, one Māṣa; sixteen Māṣas, one Suvarṇa;* [135]four Suvarṇas, one Pala; and ten Palas, one Dharaṇa.

One should know that two Kṛṣṇalas weighed together make one silver Māṣaka, [136]and sixteen Māṣakas, one silver Dharaṇa, as also a Purāṇa. A copper Kārṣika, however, should be known as a Kārṣāpaṇa, or simply Paṇa; [137]ten Dharaṇas, as one silver Śatamāna; and four Suvarṇas, as one Niṣka in weight.

Fines [138]Tradition has determined 250 Paṇas as the lowest fine; 500 Paṇas should be considered the middle fine; and 1,000 Paṇas, the highest. [139]If the debtor admits that he owes the debt, he ought to be fined 500; but if he denies, twice as much—that is Manu's decree.

Rates of Interest: I [140]A money-lender may assess the rate of interest decreed by Vasiṣṭha (cf. *VaDh* 2.50) for the increase of capital and charge 1.25 per cent per month. [141]Alternatively, he may charge 2 per cent, keeping in mind the Law followed by good men; for by charging 2 per cent he does not become guilty of a sin involving money. [142]He may charge exactly 2, 3, 4, or 5 per cent interest per month, according to the descending order of the classes.*

[143]If a pledge together with any profits it may yield has been furnished, however, the creditor shall not receive any interest on the loan; nor shall the pledge be alienated or sold because the time has lapsed.* [144]He must not make use of a pledge by force; if he makes use of it, he forfeits the interest and must reimburse the owner the original value of the pledge. Otherwise, the creditor becomes guilty of stealing the pledge.

Pledges [145]Neither a pledge nor a deposit is liable to forfeiture due to the passage of time; they may be recovered even after they have been held for a long time.* [146]The owner never loses his title to anything enjoyed through his benevolence, or to cows, camels, draft animals,* horses, and animals delivered for breaking in.

[147]When an owner looks on silently as something is being enjoyed by others in his presence for ten years, he is not entitled to recover it. [148]If something is enjoyed within his own locality* and he is neither mentally incapacitated nor a minor, he loses any legal right to it; the user is entitled to that property.

[149]Pledges, boundaries, assets of minors, open deposits, sealed deposits, women, and the possessions of the king and of vedic scholars are never lost on account of enjoyment.

Rates of Interest: II [150]When a foolhardy man makes use of a pledge without the consent of its owner, he shall refund half the interest as compensation for that use.

[151]Interest on a loan shall never exceed twice the principal when fixed at one time; and on grain, fruits, wool, and draft animals, it shall not exceed five times.* [152]An interest rate set above the legal limit is exorbitant and cannot be enforced; that is called the path of usury—he is entitled to only 5 per cent.

[153]He must not charge interest beyond one year or an unauthorized rate. [Authorized forms of interest are] cyclical interest, periodic interest, contractual interest, and interest paid by manual labor.*

[154]When someone is unable to repay a debt and wants to redo the contract, he should first pay the accrued interest and then renew the evidentiary instrument. [155]If he cannot come up with the money at that time, he should renew the instrument; he is obliged to pay as much interest as is due.*

[156]When someone has entered into a contract accruing cyclical interest with a specified place and time, he shall not obtain its reward if he disregards that place and time.*

[157]When experts in sea voyages capable of forecasting profits with respect to particular places and times fix an interest rate, that is exactly the rate for repayment.

Surety [158]When a man stands here* as a surety to produce someone and fails to produce him, he must pay the man's debt from his own funds.

[159]A son is not obliged to pay a debt related to being a surety, vain gifts,* gambling debts, what is owed for liquor, or any remaining portions of fines and duties. [160]The above rule applies only to someone who stands as surety for appearance; when a man who has stood as surety for repayment dies, even his heirs can be compelled to pay it.*

[161]When someone who was a surety other than for repayment dies and the circumstances under which he became a surety are fully known, on what grounds can the creditor later demand payment of the debt? [162]If the money had been consigned to the surety and he has sufficient money, the rule is that the consignee should pay the debt from his own funds.*

Validity of Transactions [163]Transactions carried out by persons who are intoxicated, insane, distressed, or totally subservient, by children or the aged, or by unauthorized persons, are invalid. [164]Agreements, even if they are well substantiated, are void if their provisions are contrary to settled Law based on established usage.*

165A fraudulent mortgage or sale, a fraudulent gift or receipt, and wherever deceit is detected—all that must be annulled.

166If the person who took the loan is lost and the loan was used for the family, it should be paid by the relatives from their own funds even if they are living separately after the partitioning of the estate.* 167A transaction carried out for the benefit of the family even by someone totally subservient, whether it is in one's own or in a distant region, must not be rescinded by his superior.*

168What is given under the threat of force, what is enjoyed under the threat of force, and any document prepared under the threat of force—all transactions executed under the threat of force Manu has declared to be null and void.

169Three suffer for the sake of others: witnesses, surety, and family;* but four prosper: Brahmin, moneylender, merchant, and king.

Impartiality of the King 170A king must never take what he ought not to take, even if he is impoverished; nor must he forgo what he ought to take—be it an amount ever so little—even if he is rich. 171By taking what he ought not to take and by eschewing what he ought to take, the king's weakness is broadcasted; and he comes to ruin here and in the hereafter. 172By taking what is due to him, by bringing together the social classes,* and by protecting the weak, the king enhances his power;* and he prospers here and in the hereafter.

173Like Yama, therefore, the ruler should lay aside his own likes and dislikes and follow Yama's pattern of behavior (9.307), suppressing his anger and mastering his organs.

174When a king foolishly judges cases in a manner contrary to the Law, his enemies will soon bring that evil man under their dominion. 175When he controls love and hatred and looks into cases in accordance with the Law, his subjects follow him, like rivers the ocean.

Recovery of Debt 176When a debtor reports a creditor seeking to recover a debt on his own initiative, the king should compel him to pay the money to the creditor and in addition a fine equal to a quarter of the debt.

177A debtor belonging to the same or a lower caste should settle with his creditor even through manual labor (8.153 n.); but a debtor who is superior should repay it in installments.

Conclusion 178In this manner, the king should adjudicate equitably lawsuits filed by litigants, lawsuits whose outcome is based on witnesses and evidence.

Grounds for Litigation: II Deposits

179A wise man should entrust a deposit to a man who is born in an illustrious family, has an impeccable character, knows the Law, speaks the truth, has a large following, is wealthy, and is an Ārya.

180A man should recover an article in exactly the same condition as when he deposited it in the hand of another person—as the delivery, so the recovery.

181–2When a man refuses to hand over a deposit to the depositor upon request and no witnesses are available, the judge should do the following outside the presence of the depositor. He should have spies of proper age and appearance actually deposit gold with that man under some pretext and then get them to request it.* [183]If he returns it in the same manner and condition as deposited, then there is nothing to the charges that the adversaries have brought against him. [184]If, however, he does not duly return that gold to them, he should be arrested and compelled to return both*—that is the fixed rule of the Law.

[185]An open or a sealed deposit should never be returned to a next-of-kin. In the event of a mishap, they both perish; although if there is no mishap, they do not perish.* [186]When he gives them of his own accord to the next-of-kin of a deceased depositor, neither the king nor the depositor's relatives should press charges against him.

[187]One should seek to obtain that article by friendly means, without resorting in any way to subterfuge; or, after probing closely into the character of the depositary, he should settle the matter peacefully.

[188]That is the rule for the settlement of all open deposits; in the case of a sealed deposit, he is in the clear, unless he has removed something from it.* [189]He is not obliged to return a deposit that is stolen by thieves, washed away in a flood, or burnt up in a fire, unless he had removed something from it.

[190]Using all the investigative methods as well as vedic oaths, the judge should examine anyone accused of appropriating a deposit or of demanding a deposit that has not been made. [191]A man who does not hand over a deposit and a man who requests the return of a deposit he has not made—both these should be punished like thieves and fined an amount equal to the deposit. [192]A man who has appropriated an open deposit, as well as a man who has appropriated a sealed deposit—the king should compel both without distinction to pay a fine equal to its value. [193]If a man appropriates the property of others by fraudulent means, however, he and his accomplices should be put to death publicly using diverse modes of execution.

[194]When a man makes an open deposit having a specific quality and quantity in the presence of the community, it should be acknowledged to have that very quality and quantity; if someone testifies falsely with regard to it, he ought to be punished. [195]If a deposit is given or received privately, then it should be returned privately—as the delivery, so the recovery.*

> [196]Thus shall the king make judgments regarding property that has been handed over as an open deposit or entrusted out of affection as a sealed deposit, without maltreating the person holding the deposit.

Grounds for Litigation: III Sale Without Ownership

[197]When a man who is neither the owner nor authorized by the owner sells someone else's property, the king should not let that man, a thief pretending not to be a thief, offer testimony;* [198]and the man should also be fined—if he did it in the owner's presence, he should be made to pay a fine of 600; if he did it outside his presence and has no excuse, his liability is the same as for theft.*

[199]When a gift or sale is made* by someone other than the owner, it should be considered null and void in accordance with the firm principle of legal process.+

[200]In a case where a man is seen to enjoy something without any evidence of legal title to it, title is the proof of ownership and not enjoyment—that is the settled rule. [201]When a man acquires some property through a sale* in the presence of the community, he obtains that property with a clear title through legal purchase. [202]If, however, the initial seller* cannot be produced but the property is cleared by the public purchase, he must not be punished; he is released by the king and the man who lost the property gets it back.

Fraudulent Sales [203]It is improper to sell one commodity mixed with another, a flawed product, or something that measures less than claimed, located far away, or is concealed.

[204]If a man shows one girl to the bridegroom and gives another, the groom may marry both for the same price—so has Manu decreed (3.53 n.). [205]When a man gives a girl who is insane, suffers from leprosy, or has lost her virginity, he should not be punished if he has disclosed the defects beforehand.+

Grounds for Litigation: IV Partnerships

[206]If one officiating priest chosen for a sacrifice quits his work, his partners should give him a share proportionate to the work he has performed.* [207]If a priest quits his work after the sacrificial fees have been distributed, he should receive the full share but get someone else to complete the work.

[208]At a ritual where sacrificial fees are specified for each component, the priest performing a given component should receive the specified fee or all should share the entire fee.* [209]At the establishment of the sacred fires, the Adhvaryu priest should take the chariot, the Brahman priest the steed, the Hotṛ priest the horse, and the Udgātṛ priest the cart used for the purchase of Soma. [210]Among all the priests, half of the fee goes to the principals; one-half of that to those in the next rank; one-third of that to those entitled to a third; and one-quarter of that to those entitled to a quarter.*

[211]Men who carry out their activities in this world by forming partnerships should allocate shares by applying these principles.

Grounds for Litigation: V Non-delivery of Gifts

[212]When someone has pledged a monetary gift to a man who begs in order to fulfill the Law but who later does not follow through, he is not obliged to deliver that gift.* [213]If that man proceeds to enforce payment out of pride or greed, however, the king should fine him one Suvarṇa to atone for that theft.

> [214]I have described above accurately the non-delivery of a gift that accords with the Law. Next, I will explain the non-payment of wages.

Grounds for Litigation: VI Non-payment of Wages

[215]When a servant who is not sick fails to perform his stipulated work out of pride, he should be fined eight Kṛṣṇalas, and he should not be paid his wages. [216]If he was sick,

however, he should perform the work stipulated at the outset after he has recovered his health; and he should receive his wages even if a very long time has elapsed. [217]Whether he is sick or well, if he does not have the stipulated work carried out, he should not be paid his wages, even if only a small portion of the work remains undone.

> [218]I have described above completely the Law relating to the non-payment of wages. Next, I will explain the Law relating to persons who breach a contract.

Grounds for Litigation: VII Breach of Contract

[219]When a man belonging to a village, region, or corporate entity enters into a contract truthfully and then breaks it out of greed, the king should banish that man from his realm.* [220]He should arrest that man who has violated the compact and fine him 6 Niṣkas, each weighing 4 Suvarṇas, and a silver Śatamāna.*

[221]In this manner, a righteous king should apply the rules of punishment to individuals who violate compacts within a village, caste, or association.

Grounds for Litigation: VIII Cancellation of Sale or Purchase

[222]After buying or selling anything, if someone here regrets his decision, he may return or take back that article within ten days. [223]After ten days, however, he may neither return nor make someone return; if someone does take back or return, the king shall fine him 600 (see 8.120 n.).

[224]When a man gives away a defective girl without disclosing her defects (8.205), the king shall personally impose on him a fine of 96 Paṇas. [225]When a man maliciously asserts that a girl is not a virgin, he should be fined 100 (see 8.120 n.) if he cannot demonstrate her defect. [226]The ritual formulas of marriage are applicable only to virgin girls and nowhere among any people to non-virgins, for they are excluded from the rituals prescribed by Law. [227]The ritual formulas of marriage are a sure sign that she is the wife, and learned men should recognize that they reach their completion at the seventh step.*

[228]After a given transaction has been completed, if someone here regrets his decision, the king should place him on the path of the Law in accordance with the above rules.

Grounds for Litigation: IX Disputes between Owners and Herdsmen

> [229]I will explain accurately and in strict accordance with the Law the disputes between owners and herdsmen over transgressions with respect to farm animals.

Safety of the Herd [230]During the day the liability for their safety lies with the herdsman, and during the night with the owner, provided they are at his house; otherwise, the herdsman becomes liable.

[231]When a herdsman is paid in milk, he may milk the best cow out of ten with the consent of the owner; that is the payment for an uncompensated herdsman.

[232]If an animal is lost, is ravaged by worms, is killed by dogs, or perishes in a dangerous place because of inadequate effort, it is the herdsman who must pay compensation. [233]If an animal is seized by robbers, the herdsman is not required to pay compensation, provided he raised the alarm and informs his master at the proper time and place.

[234]When animals die, the herdsman should give their owners both ears, skin, tails, bladders, tendons, and yellow bile,* and point out their distinguishing marks.

[235]If goats or sheep are cornered by wolves, however, and the herdsman fails to come to their assistance, the herdsman shall be culpable for any that a wolf may attack and kill. [236]As they are roaming the woods while being kept under check in a single group, if a wolf pounces upon and kills one, the herdsman is not culpable for that.

Damage to Crops [237]An open field extending one hundred "bows" or three rod's throws* shall be left around a village; three times as large around a town. [238]If farm animals damage unfenced crops within that area, the king must not punish the herdsman for that.

[239]One should erect there a fence over which a camel cannot look and cover every hole through which a dog or pig could poke its head.

[240]When damage is done to a fenced field* alongside a road or at the edge of a village, a fine of 100 (see 8.120 n.) should be imposed if a herdsman was present; if the animals are without a herdsman, they should be impounded. [241]When damage is done in other fields, one and a half Paṇas should be assessed for each animal; and in every case, the owner of the field ought to be compensated for the crop—that is the fixed rule.

[242]Manu has declared that a cow within ten days after giving birth, bulls, and animals dedicated to gods are not subject to punishment, whether they are attended by a herdsman or not.*

[243]For an offense committed by the owner of a field, the fine shall be ten times his share; half that amount, if the offense was committed by the servants without the knowledge of the owner.*

> [244]A righteous king should follow these rules with regard to transgressions committed by owners, by animals, and by herdsmen.

Grounds for Litigation: X Boundary Disputes

[245]When a dispute arises between two villages with respect to a boundary, the king should ascertain the boundary in the month of Jyeṣṭha (May–June) when landmarks are most clearly visible.*

Boundary Markers [246]He should establish boundary trees: banyan, pipal, Kiṃśuka, cotton-tree, Sāla, palm, and trees with milky sap; [247]as also thickets, different kinds of bamboo, Śamī, creepers, mounds, reeds, and thickets of Kubjaka. In this way, the boundary will not disappear. [248]Reservoirs, wells, ponds, and waterways should be constructed at the intersection of boundaries, as also temples of gods.

[249]Seeing that in the world controversies constantly arise due to people's ignorance of boundaries, he should also have other concealed boundary markers

ensconced—[250]stones, bones, cow's hair, chaff, ashes, potsherds, dried cow dung, bricks, coal, pebbles, and sand. [251]He should also have other similar substances that the soil would not decay over time ensconced as hidden markers at the intersection of boundaries.

Settling Boundary Disputes [252]By means of these markers, the king should ascertain the boundary between two litigants, as also by continuous prior possession and by a watercourse. [253]If doubt persists even after seeing the markers, the resolution of a boundary dispute will have to rely solely on witnesses.

[254]Witnesses to a boundary should be questioned about the boundary markers in the presence of the village communities and the two litigants. [255]In accordance with the unanimous decision regarding the boundary they render upon questioning, he should make a record of the boundary, as well as of all their names. [256]Putting earth on their heads, wearing garlands and red clothes, and being made to swear each by his good deeds (8.90), they shall render a truthful decision. [257]When they render a decision in the above manner, they remain untainted as truthful witnesses; but when they render a contrary decision, they should be fined 200 (8.120 n.).

[258]When witnesses are unavailable, however, four villagers resident in the vicinity, after making themselves ritually pure, should determine the boundary in the presence of the king. [259]When native inhabitants (7.54 n.) of neighboring villages are unavailable as witnesses to a boundary, however, he may even question* the following men who roam the forest: [260]hunters, fowlers, herdsmen, fishermen, root-diggers, snake-catchers, gleaners, and others who inhabit the forest. [261]When, upon questioning, they identify a particular landmark at the intersection of the boundaries, he should establish it as the landmark between the two villages according to the Law.

[262]It should be recognized that the determination of boundary markers between fields, wells, reservoirs, gardens, and houses depends on the evidence of neighbors. [263]If neighbors give false evidence when people are litigating boundary markers, the king should impose the middle fine (8.138) on each of them individually.

[264]If someone appropriates a house, reservoir, garden, or field through intimidation, he should be fined 500; the fine is 200 if it was done inadvertently (8.120 n.).

[265]When it is impossible to ascertain the boundary, a king who knows the Law should apportion land between them on his own on the basis of utility*—that is the settled rule.

> [266]I have described above the entire Law relating to decisions regarding boundaries. Next, I will explain how cases of verbal assault are to be decided.

Grounds for Litigation: XI Verbal Assault

[267]For assailing a Brahmin, a Kṣatriya ought to be fined 100, and a Vaiśya 150 or 200; but a Śūdra ought to suffer corporal punishment (8.120 n.). [268]A Brahmin should be fined 50 for abusing a Kṣatriya, 25 for abusing a Vaiśya, and 12 for abusing a Śūdra.+

[269]For a violation by a twice-born against a person of the same social class, the fine is 12; the fine is doubled when extremely foul language is used.

[270]If a once-born man hurls grossly abusive words at twice-born men, his tongue shall be cut off, for he originated from the lowest part.* [271]If he invokes their names and castes with disdain, a red-hot iron nail ten fingers* long should be driven into his mouth. [272]If he arrogantly gives instruction on the Law to Brahmins, the king should pour hot oil into his mouth and ears.

[273]If a man arrogantly makes false statements about someone's learning, country, caste, occupation, or physical features, he should be fined 200.* [274]If a man calls someone "one-eyed," "lame," or some other similar name, he should be fined at least 1 Kārṣāpaṇa, even if what he says is true.

[275]If a man hurls accusations* at his mother, father, wife, brother, child, or elder, he should be fined 100, as also a man who fails to give way to an elder.

[276]In cases involving a Brahmin and a Kṣatriya, a discerning king should impose the following punishment: the lowest fine on the Brahmin and the middle fine on the Kṣatriya (8.138). [277]On a Vaiśya and a Śūdra also, exactly the same punishment,* except the cutting of the tongue, should be imposed according to their respective class—that is the firm conclusion.+

> [278]I have described above accurately the rules concerning the punishment for verbal assault. Next, I will explain how cases of physical assault are to be decided.

Grounds for Litigation: XII Physical Assault

Personal Injury [279]When a lowest-born man uses a particular limb to injure a superior person, that very limb of his should be cut off—that is Manu's decree. [280]If he charges with his hand or with a stick, his hand ought to be cut off; if he strikes with his foot in anger, his foot ought to be cut off. [281]If a low-born man attempts to occupy the same seat as a man of a high rank, the king should brand him on the hip and send him into exile or have his buttocks slashed. [282]If he arrogantly spits at such a person, the king should cut off both his lips; if he urinates at him, his penis; and if he breaks wind at him, his anus. [283]If he grabs him by the hair, the king should cut off both his hands without a second thought, as also if he grabs him by the feet, the beard, the neck,* or the testicles.

[284]One who bruises the skin, as also one who draws blood, is to be fined 100; and one who wounds the flesh, 6 Niṣkas. One who breaks a bone, however, should be sent into exile.* [285]For injuring any kind of tree, a fine should be imposed proportionate to its utility—that is the fixed rule. [286]If someone strikes humans or animals in order to inflict pain, the king should impose a punishment proportionate to the severity of the pain.

[287]For doing severe harm to a limb, and likewise to vigor* and blood, a man should be compelled to defray the expenses of the recovery or to pay a total fine.*

Damage to Property [288]When someone damages the property of another, whether it is deliberate or inadvertent, he should pay reparation to the other and give an equal amount to the king.

[289]In the case of leather, leather utensils, or wooden or clay products, the fine is five times their value; so also in the case of flowers, roots, and fruits.

Injuries Caused by Vehicles [290]With respect to a vehicle, its driver, and its owner, they posit ten exemptions; in other cases punishment is decreed. [291]When the nose-rope snaps; when the yoke breaks; when the vehicle skids to one side; when it slides backwards; when the axle of the vehicle breaks; when a wheel breaks; [292]when bindings, halters, or reins snap; and when the driver cries out "Get out of the way!"—in these cases Manu has declared that there should be no punishment.

[293]When the vehicle veers off due to the driver's incompetence, however, and it results in injury, the owner should be fined 200; [294]but if the driver is skilled, then it is the driver who ought to be fined; and if he is unskilled, all the riders should be fined 100 each.

[295]In a case where the driver kills living creatures when his path is obstructed by farm animals or a vehicle,* the punishment shall be enforced without hesitation. [296]If a human being is killed, he becomes immediately subject to the same liability as a thief; half that much for a large animal, such as a cow, elephant, camel, or horse.* [297]For injuring a small farm animal, the fine is 200; for a beautiful animal or bird, 50; [298]for a donkey, goat, or sheep, five Māṣas; and for killing a dog or a pig, one Māṣa.

Corporal Punishment [299]When they misbehave, a wife, son, slave, pupil, or uterine brother* may be beaten with a rope or a bamboo strip [300]on the back of their bodies and never on the head. If he beats them in any other way, his liability is the same as for theft.

> [301]I have described above completely how to decide cases of physical assault. Next, I will explain the rules for deciding the punishment for theft.

Grounds for Litigation: XIII Theft

Suppression of Thieves [302]The king should exert utmost effort at suppressing thieves. Suppressing thieves will expand both his fame and his realm; [303]for the king who gives security is always worthy of worship, and his sacrificial session* will continuously expand with the granting of safety (6.39 n.) as its sacrificial fee.

Obligation to Offer Protection [304]A sixth portion of everyone's merits goes to the king who protects; a sixth portion of their demerits likewise goes to him when he fails to protect. [305]When one studies, sacrifices, gives gifts, and performs worship, the king takes a sixth portion of it as his share by providing proper protection.

[306]By protecting creatures according to the Law and by putting to death those who merit execution, the king offers day after day sacrifices with sacrificial fees of one hundred thousand.

[307]When a king gathers levies, taxes, duties, gifts, and fines without providing protection, he will immediately go to hell. [308]They call a king who gathers a sixth

portion as levy without providing protection "one who gathers all the filth of the entire population." [309]When a king disregards proper bounds, is an infidel, is rapacious, fails to provide protection, and is predatory, one should know that he is headed along the downward course.*

[310]He should strenuously suppress the wicked by three means: imprisonment, shackling, and diverse forms of corporal punishment (8.320 n.);* [311]for by suppressing the wicked and by gratifying the virtuous kings are always purified, just as twice-born men by sacrifices.

[312]The king should always forgive litigants, children, the aged, and the sick who may insult him, if he wants to do what is beneficial to himself. [313]He who bears patiently when those in anguish insult him will be exalted in heaven for it, but he who does not forgive because of his royal status will go to hell for it.

Punishment of Thieves [314]A wise thief, with his hair loose, should go to the king* confessing his theft: "I have done this. Punish me," [315] and carrying on his shoulder a pestle, a club of Khadira wood, a spear with both ends sharpened, or an iron rod.

[316]Whether he is punished or released, the thief is released from the theft; but if the king fails to punish him, he takes upon himself the thief's guilt. [317]The murderer of a learned Brahmin (4.208 n.) rubs his sin off on the man who eats his food, an adulterous wife on her husband, a pupil and a patron of a sacrifice on the teacher, and a thief on the king. [318]When men who have committed sins are punished by kings, they go to heaven immaculate, like virtuous men who have done good deeds.

[319]A man who steals a rope or a bucket from a well or tears down a place for distributing water should pay a fine of one Māṣa and restore that article. [320]A man who steals more than ten Kumbha-measures of grain is subject to corporal punishment;* even in lesser cases he should be fined eleven times the amount and made to restitute that property to the owner. [321]The same goes for articles sold by weight. When it is more than 100 of gold, silver, and the like, and of the most excellent clothes, he is subject to capital punishment;* [322]but when it is more than 50, his hand ought to be cut off. In lesser cases, on the other hand, the king should set a fine of eleven times the value of the property.

[323]For abducting men from illustrious families and especially women, and for stealing gems of great value, a man merits the death penalty.

[324]For stealing large farm animals, as also weapons and medicine, the king should set a punishment after taking into account its time and purpose;* [325]in the case of cows belonging to Brahmins, the cleaving of the heel;* and for stealing farm animals, half his foot should be cut off immediately.

[326]For stealing thread, cotton, liquor-yeast, cow dung, molasses, curd, milk, buttermilk, water, grass, [327]vessels made of bamboo or cane, any kind of salt, clay vessels, earth, ash, [328]fish, birds, oil, ghee, meat, honey, other animal products, [329]other similar kinds of food,* boiled rice, and all kinds of cooked food—the fine is twice the value of the stolen property. [330]For flowers, green grain, shrubs, creepers, trees, and small quantities of unhusked grain, the fine is 5 Kṛṣṇalas. [331]For husked

grain, vegetables, roots, and fruits, the fine is 100 if it is committed outside the owner's presence, and 50 if it is committed in his presence (8.332 n.).

[332]When an act is committed with force and in the presence of the victim, it is "violence"; when it is committed outside his presence,* it is "theft," and so is an act that someone commits and then denies.

[333]When a man steals these articles after they have been prepared for use, the king should fine him 100,* as also a man who steals fire from a house.

[334]The king should deprive a thief of the very limb with which he commits a crime against men, to serve as a deterrent.

[335]A king should never fail to punish even his father, teacher, friend, mother, wife, son, or personal priest when they deviate from the Law proper to them. [336]In a case where an ordinary person is fined 1 Kārṣāpaṇa, the king should be fined 1,000—that is the fixed rule.* [337]With respect to theft, the liability for a Śūdra is eight times; for a Vaiśya, sixteen times; for a Kṣatriya, thirty-two times; [338]and for a Brahmin, sixty-four times, or fully 100 times, or twice sixty-four times; for he knows whether it is good or bad.*

[339]Roots and fruits from trees, wood for a fire, and grass to feed cows—Manu has declared that these do not constitute theft.

[340]If a Brahmin desires to obtain money from the hands of a man who takes what is not given—even if he does so by means of officiating at that man's sacrifices or teaching him—that Brahmin is equal to a thief. [341]When a twice-born is on the road and his provisions are exhausted, he ought not to be punished for taking two roots or two stalks of sugar-cane from the field of another man.

[342]When someone ties up those that are not tied, releases those that are tied, or takes away a slave, horse, or carriage, his liability is the same as for theft.*

> [343]A king who undertakes the suppression of thieves in this manner
> obtains fame in this world and unsurpassing happiness after death.

Grounds for Litigation: XIV Violence

[344]If a king desires to obtain the seat of Indra and inexhaustible and imperishable fame, he should never ignore even for a moment a man who perpetrates violence.* [345]A man who perpetrates violence should be considered far more evil than someone who is offensive in speech, who steals, or who assaults with a rod.* [346]A king who condones a man who engages in violence is quickly brought to ruin and becomes the object of hatred.

[347]The king must never release violent men who strike terror in all creatures eyeing either friendship or a large monetary gain.

Permissible Violence [348]Twice-born men may take up arms when the Law is thwarted or when the vicissitudes of time bring calamity upon twice-born classes. [349]When a man kills in accordance with the Law to protect his life, in a conflict over sacrificial fees,* or in defense of women or Brahmins, he remains untainted.

[350]When an assailant attacks with the intent to kill—whether he is an elder, a child, an old person, or a learned Brahmin—one may surely kill him without

hesitation. [351]In killing an assailant, the killer incurs no fault; whether it is done openly or in secret, wrath there recoils on wrath.

Grounds for Litigation: XV Sexual Crimes Against Women

Sexual Crimes against Married Women [352]When men violate the wives of others, the king should disfigure their bodies with punishments that inspire terror and then execute them* (8.6 n.; 8.284 n.); [353]for such violations give rise to the mixing of social classes among the people, creating deviation from the Law that tears out the very root* and leads to the destruction of everything.

[354]When a man carries on a conversation secretly with another man's wife, he is subject to the lowest fine (8.138) if he has been previously accused of similar offenses. [355]If someone who has not been previously accused engages in such conversation for a good reason, however, no guilt attaches to him, for he has committed no transgression.

[356]If a man converses with the wife of another at a sacred ford, in a wild tract, in a forest, or at the confluence of rivers, he is guilty of adultery. [357]Doing favors, dallying, touching the ornaments or clothes, and sitting together on a bed—all this, tradition tells us, constitutes adultery. [358]When a man touches a woman at an inappropriate place or permits her to touch him—all such acts done with mutual consent, tradition tells us, constitute adultery.

[359]In the case of adultery, everyone other than a Brahmin merits the death penalty; women of all four classes are to be guarded always with the utmost care.

[360]Mendicants, bards, men consecrated for sacrifice,* and artisans may converse with women, unless they have been explicitly banned.* [361]A man should never converse with women* when he has been forbidden to do so; when someone speaks after being forbidden, he ought to be fined 1 Suvarṇa.

[362]The above rule does not apply to wives of traveling performers or to wives who earn a living on their own,* for such men get their women to attach themselves to men and, concealing themselves, get them to have sexual liaisons. [363]When someone engages in secret conversations with such women, as also with female slaves serving a single master and with female wandering ascetics, he shall be compelled to pay a small fine.

Male Sexual Assault [364]A man who defiles a virgin against her will merits immediate execution. When a man of equal status defiles a willing virgin, however, he is not subject to execution.* [365]No fine should be imposed on a virgin who falls in love with a man superior to herself; but if she makes love to a man inferior to herself, she should be put under restraint and confined to her house. [366]When a man of inferior status makes love to a superior woman, however, he merits execution; if he makes love to a woman of equal status, he should pay a bride-price* if her father so desires.

[367]If a man arrogantly violates a virgin by force, two of his fingers* should be cut off immediately, and he should also be fined 600. [368]A man of equal status who defiles a willing girl shall not be subject to the cutting of his fingers, but he should be compelled to pay a fine of 200 to deter repetition.

Female Sexual Assault [369]If a virgin violates another virgin, she should be fined 200, pay three times the bride-price,* and receive ten lashes. [370]When a woman violates a virgin, however, her head ought to be shaved immediately—alternatively, two of her fingers should be cut off—and she should be paraded on a donkey.

Adultery [371]When a woman, arrogant because of the eminence of her relatives and her own feminine qualities, becomes unfaithful to her husband, the king should have her devoured by dogs in a public square frequented by many. [372]He should have the male offender burnt upon a heated iron bed; they should stack logs and burn up that villain there.

[373]When a convict is accused again within a year, the fine is doubled; likewise when a man has sex with a Vrātya* or a Caṇḍāla woman. [374]When a Śūdra has sex with a guarded or unguarded woman of a twice-born class—he loses a limb and all his possessions, if she was unguarded. If she was guarded, a Śūdra loses everything;* [375]a Vaiśya is imprisoned for a year and all his property is confiscated; and a Kṣatriya is fined 1,000 and his head is shaved using urine. [376]If a Vaiśya or a Kṣatriya has sex with an unguarded Brahmin woman, the Vaiśya is fined 500 and the Kṣatriya 1,000 (see 8.120 n.). [377]If any of these two has sex with a guarded Brahmin woman, he should be punished in the same way as a Śūdra or he should be burnt with a straw-fire. [378]A Brahmin who has forcible sex with a guarded Brahmin woman should be fined 1,000; for sex with a willing partner, he should be fined 500.

[379]Shaving the head is prescribed as the death penalty for Brahmins; but the other social classes are actually subject to the death penalty. [380]The king should never put a Brahmin to death, even if he has committed every sort of crime; he should banish such a Brahmin from his kingdom along with all his property, without causing him hurt. [381]There is no greater violation of the Law on earth than killing a Brahmin; therefore, a king should not even think of killing a Brahmin.

[382]If a Vaiśya has sex with a guarded Kṣatriya woman or a Kṣatriya with a guarded Vaiśya woman, both ought to receive the same punishment as a man who has sex with an unguarded Brahmin woman.+ [383]When a Brahmin has sex with those two types of guarded women, however, he should be compelled to pay a fine of 1,000; likewise, when a Kṣatriya or a Vaiśya has sex with a Śūdra woman, the fine is 1,000. [384]For sex with an unguarded Kṣatriya woman, a Vaiśya is fined 500, but a Kṣatriya has his head shaved using urine or is levied the same fine. [385]When a Brahmin has sex with an unguarded Kṣatriya or Vaiśya woman or with a Śūdra woman, he shall be fined 500, but 1,000 for sex with a lowest-born woman.*

[*Excursus*]

Miscellanea [386]The king in whose capital there is no thief, no adulterer, no person who uses offensive speech, no person who uses violence, and no person who commits physical assault, will attain the world of Indra.* [387]The suppression of these five within his territory secures for the king paramountcy among his peers and fame among his people.

[388]If the patron of a sacrifice gets rid of an officiating priest or an officiating priest the patron when both are capable of performing the rite and are untainted by any fault, each is fined 100.

[389]A mother, father, wife, or son ought never to be abandoned. Anyone who abandons these when they have not fallen from their caste shall be fined 600 by the king.

[390]When twice-born men living in hermitages* are arguing with each other about any duty, the king should never pronounce on the Law, if he cares for his own welfare. [391]Accompanied by Brahmins, the king should first pay them due reverence, pacify them initially with soothing words, and then teach them the Law specific to them.

[392]When a Brahmin fails to feed his two worthy neighbors—the one living in front of his house and the one behind—at a festival attended by twenty Brahmins, he ought to be fined 1 Māṣaka. [393]When a vedic scholar fails to feed another virtuous vedic scholar at auspicious rites, he should be compelled to give twice that amount of food and a gold Māṣaka.

[394]A blind man, an idiot, a cripple, a man over 70, and someone who takes care of vedic scholars—no one should compel these to pay any tax.

[395]The king should always honor* vedic scholars, the sick and the afflicted, children, the aged, the poor, men from illustrious families, and Āryas.

[396]A washerman shall wash clothes thoroughly and gently on a smooth cotton-wood board. He must not use some clothes to carry the other clothes or let others wear those clothes.*

[397]A weaver receiving thread weighing 10 Palas must return cloth weighing 1 Pala more; if he does otherwise, he should be compelled to pay a fine of 12.*

Control of Trade [398]When men who have experience in offices for levying duties and expertise in all types of merchandise have fixed the value of each commodity, the king should take one-twentieth of that. [399]When someone exports goods that are designated a royal monopoly* or that are forbidden out of greed, the king should confiscate all his property. [400]When a man bypasses an office for levying duties, buys or sells at forbidden times, or falsifies the enumeration of goods, he should be fined eight times what he tried to hide.

[401]After investigating the provenance of every commodity, its destination, and how long it is held by the vendor, as well as gain and loss, he should fix the sale and purchase prices. [402]Every five days or every fortnight the king should publicly fix the prices of commodities. [403]All balances, measures,* and weights should be stamped with the proper mark and should be re-inspected every six months.

Ferries and Tolls [404]A vehicle should be assessed 1 Paṇa at a ferry; a porter's load, half a Paṇa; an animal or woman, a quarter Paṇa; and a porter without a load, one-eighth of a Paṇa. [405]Vehicles loaded with goods should be assessed a toll according to the value of the goods; empty vehicles and porters without loads should be assessed some small amount.

[406]For long voyages the toll should correspond to the place and the time. It should be understood that this applies to voyages along rivers; for sea voyages, there is no set rate (8.157).

[407]Women over two months pregnant, wandering ascetics, sages, Brahmins, and those wearing the insignia of a religious profession (4.200 n.) should not be forced to pay tolls on a ferry.

[408]Whenever anything within a boat is damaged due to the negligence of the boatsmen, it is the boatsmen who should pay reparation collectively, each according to his share.

> [409]I have described above how to decide a lawsuit brought by passengers in a boat relating to the negligence of boatsmen on the water; when it is an act of god, there shall be no punishment.

Occupations of Social Classes [410]The king should make Vaiśyas pursue trade, moneylending, agriculture, and cattle herding, and make Śūdras engage in the service of twice-born people.

[411]A Brahmin should support a Kṣatriya or a Vaiśya who is starved for a livelihood out of compassion and employ them in activities proper to them. [412]If a Brahmin makes twice-born men who have undergone vedic initiation do slave labor against their will through greed and to show off his power, the king should fine him 600. [413]He may, however, make a Śūdra, whether he is bought or not, do slave labor; for the Śūdra was created by the Self-existent One solely to do slave labor for the Brahmin.

[414]Even when he is released by his master, a Śūdra is not freed from his slave status; for that is innate in him and who can remove it from him? [415]There are seven kinds of slaves: a man captured in war, a man who makes himself a slave to receive food, a slave born in the house, a purchased slave, a gifted slave, a hereditary slave, and a man enslaved for punishment.

[416]Wife, son, and slave—all these three, tradition tells us, are without property. Whatever they may earn becomes the property of the man to whom they belong.

[417]A Brahmin may confidently seize property from a Śūdra, because there is nothing that he owns; for he is a man whose property may be taken by his master.

[418]The king should strenuously make Vaiśyas and Śūdras perform the activities specific to them; for when they deviate from their specific activities, they throw this world into confusion.

[419]Every day the king should pay attention to his administrative centers,* conveyances (7.75 n.), daily income and expenditure, mines, and treasury. [420]When the king thus brings to a satisfactory conclusion all these legal matters, he gets rid of all sins and attains the highest state.

CHAPTER NINE

Grounds for Litigation: XVI Law Concerning Husband and Wife

[1]For a husband and wife who stay on the path pointed out by the Law, I shall declare the eternal Laws for both when they are together and when they are apart.*

Guarding the Wife [2]Day and night men should keep their women from acting independently; for, attached as they are to sensual pleasures, men should keep them under their control. [3]Her father guards her in her childhood, her husband guards her in her youth, and her sons guard her in her old age; a woman is not qualified to act independently (5.147–9).

[4]A father is reprehensible,* if he does not give her away at the proper time; a husband, if he does not have sex with her at the right time (3.45 n.); and a son, if he fails to guard his mother when her husband is dead. [5]Women in particular should be guarded against even the slightest evil inclination, for when they are left unguarded, they bring grief to both families (5.149 n.).+ [6]Seeing that this is clearly the highest Law of all social classes, even weak husbands strive to guard their wives; [7]for by carefully guarding his wife, a man guards his offspring, his character, his family, himself, and the Law specific to him.

[8]The husband enters the wife, becomes a fetus, and is born in this world. This, indeed, is what gives the name to and discloses the true nature of "wife" (*jāyā*)—that he is born (*jāyate*) again in her.* [9]For, a wife bears a son resembling the man she loves; to insure the purity of his offspring, therefore, he should carefully guard his wife.

[10]No man is able to thoroughly guard women by force; but by using the following strategies, he will be able to guard them thoroughly. [11]He should employ her in the collection and the disbursement of his wealth, in cleaning, in meritorious activity, in cooking food, and in looking after household goods.* [12]When they are kept confined within the house by trusted men, they are not truly guarded; only when they guard themselves by themselves are they truly well guarded.

[13]Drinking, associating with bad people, living away from the husband, travel, sleep, and staying in the houses of others—these are the six things that corrupt women. [14]They pay no attention to beauty, they pay no heed to age; whether he is handsome or ugly, they make love to him with the single thought, "He's a man!" [15]Lechery, fickleness of mind, and hard-heartedness are innate in them; even when they are carefully guarded in this world, therefore, they become hostile towards their husbands. [16]Recognizing thus the nature produced in them at creation by Prajāpati, a man should make the utmost effort at guarding them. [17]Bed, seat, ornaments, lust, hatred, behavior unworthy of an Ārya, malice, and bad conduct—Manu assigned these to women.*

[18]No rite is performed for women with the recitation of ritual formulas—that is well-established Law. "Without strength or ritual formula, women are the untruth"*—that is the fixed rule. [19]There are, likewise, numerous scriptural passages recited in the sacred books. Listen to a sample of these* intended to expose the true character of women. [20]Here is an illustration of it:* "May my father keep from me the seed that my mother, roaming about unfaithful to her husband, craved!" [21]When a woman contemplates anything harmful to her husband in her mind, this is said to be a thorough expiation of that infidelity.*

Elevation of Wife to Husband's Status [22]When a wife unites with her husband according to rule, she takes on the qualities he has, like a river uniting with the ocean. [23]Akṣamālā, a woman of the lowest birth, when she united with Vasiṣṭha—as also Śārṅgī with Mandapāla—became worthy of great respect.* [24]These and other women of low birth attained high status in this world by reason of the eminent qualities of their respective husbands.

> [25]I have described above the splendid conduct of a husband and wife commonly practiced in the world. Next, listen to the Laws that pertain to progeny, Laws that bring happiness here and in the hereafter.

Importance of Wife [26]On account of offspring, a wife is the bearer of many blessings, worthy of honor, and the light within a home; indeed, in a home no distinction at all exists between a wife (*strī*) and Śrī, the Goddess of Fortune. [27]She begets children; and when they are born, she brings them up—day in, day out, the wife,* evidently, is the linchpin of domestic affairs. [28]Offspring, rites prescribed by Law, obedient service,* the highest sensuous delights, and procuring heaven for oneself and one's forefathers—all this depends on the wife.

[29]A woman who controls her mind, speech, and body and is never unfaithful to her husband attains the worlds of her husband, and virtuous people call her a "good woman" (= 5.165). [30]By being unfaithful to her husband, on the other hand, a woman becomes disgraced in the world, takes birth in a jackal's womb, and is afflicted with evil diseases (= 5.164).

> [31]Listen now to this holy disquisition, profitable to all, carried out by virtuous people and by great ancient sages with regard to a son.

To Whom Belongs a Son? [32]It is acknowledged that a son belongs to the husband; but scripture is divided with respect to the sire—some argue for the man who fathered the child, others for the "owner of the field."*

[33]Tradition holds that the woman represents the field and the man the seed; all embodied beings spring from the union of field and seed. [34]Sometimes the seed is preeminent, at other times the female womb; but when both are equal, that offspring is greatly esteemed.*

[FIRST OPINION] [35]Between the seed and the womb, the seed is considered dominant; for the offspring of all creatures is marked by the characteristics of the seed (10.70–2). [36]When someone sows a particular kind of seed in a field prepared at the proper time, the very same kind sprouts in that field displaying its own qualities. [37]This earth, indeed, is called the eternal womb of creatures; yet the seed, as it develops, does not manifest any of the qualities associated with the womb. [38]Even when different kinds of seeds are sown by farmers in the very same plot at the right time, they are seen in the world to sprout differently, each according to its nature. [39]Vrīhi-rice, Śāla-rice, mung beans, sesame seeds, beans, barley, garlic, and sugar-cane—all these sprout according to their seed. [40]For one kind to be sown and quite another to be produced—that is simply impossible. Whatever kind of seed is sown, that same kind sprouts forth.*

[SECOND OPINION] [41]A wise and well-trained man, therefore, possessing knowledge and discrimination* and desiring a long life, should never sow his seed in the wife of another man. [42]In this connection, those who know the past relate verses sung by Wind showing that a man must never sow his seed in someone else's wife. [43]"When someone shoots an arrow at the vitals of an animal that has already been pierced, his arrow is wasted; in like manner a seed is wasted when discharged in someone else's wife." [44]Even as those who know the past regard this earth as the wife of Pṛthu, so they say that a field belongs to the man who cleared the stumps and the deer to the man who owns the arrow.*

[45]Wife, self, and offspring—that is the full extent of "man." Brahmins, likewise, proclaim this: "The husband, tradition says, is the wife."* [46]Neither sale nor dismissal cuts the wife loose from her husband; this we consider the Law established formerly by Prajāpati. [47]Once is a partition made; once is a virgin given away; once is it said "I give"—these three are done only once each.

[48]As in the case of cows, mares, female camels, slave women, female buffaloes, female goats, and ewes, the sire does not own the offspring, so is it also in the case of women. [49]When men who have seeds but no fields sow them in someone else's field, once the crop has grown they do not receive any of the harvest. [50]Even if a bull fathers a hundred calves on someone else's cows, the calves belong to the owner of the cows; the bull has spilled his semen in vain. [51]Likewise, when men without fields sow their seed in someone else's field, they create profits for the owner of the field; the owner of the seed reaps no fruit.

[52]If an agreement* has not been reached between the owner of the field and the owner of the seed with respect to the fruit, the owner of the field clearly reaps the profit; the womb is mightier than the seed. [53]When a field is handed over by contractual agreement to someone for sowing the seed, however, we see in the world that both the owner of the seed and the owner of the field receive shares from it. [54]When a seed, carried by flood or wind, sprouts in someone's field, it belongs solely to the owner of the field; the sower does not reap its fruit.*

[55]This is the Law with regard to the offspring of cows, mares, slave women, female camels, female goats, ewes, female birds, and female buffaloes.*

[56]I have described to you above the relative importance of the seed and the womb. Next, I shall explain the Law pertaining to women during a time of adversity.

Levirate [57]Tradition holds that for a younger brother, the wife of his older brother is the same as the wife of an elder;* and for an older brother, the wife of his younger brother is the same as a daughter-in-law. [58]Except in a time of adversity, if an older brother has sex with his younger brother's wife or a younger brother with his older brother's wife, they become outcastes, even if they have been duly appointed.

[59]If the line is about to die out, a wife who is duly appointed may obtain the desired progeny through a brother-in-law or a relative belonging to the same ancestry (5.60 n.). [60]The appointed man should smear himself with ghee, approach the widow at night in silence, and beget a single son, never a second. [61]Some who are knowledgeable in these matters, seeing that this leaves the purpose of the couple's appointment unfulfilled in terms of the Law, endorse begetting a second son in such women.* [62]When the purpose of his appointment to the widow has been fulfilled according to rule, however, they should behave towards each other as an elder and a daughter-in-law. [63]If, on the contrary, the appointed couple disregard the rules and behave lustfully with one another, both become outcastes, he as a molester of a daughter-in-law, and she as a violator of an elder's bed.

[64]Twice-born men should never appoint a widowed woman to another man, for in appointing her to another man, they assail the eternal Law.* [65]The nuptial formulas nowhere mention appointment, nor do injunctions relating to marriage sanction the remarriage of widows. [66]This Law of beasts, despised by learned twice-born men, was extended to humans also during the reign of Vena (7.41–2 n.). [67]He was a preeminent royal sage, who once ruled the entire earth and, his mind overcome by lust, created the intermixing of classes. [68]Since that time, good people denounce anyone who is senseless enough to appoint a woman to have children after her husband dies.

[69]If the husband of a virgin dies after their betrothal, her brother-in-law should take* her in the following manner. [70]Obtaining* her according to rule, as she is dressed in white* and devoted to pure observances, he should have sex with her once every time she is in season (3.45 n.) until she bears a child.

Contract of Betrothal [71]After giving away a virgin to someone, a prudent man must never give her away again, for in giving what has already been given, he becomes guilty of a lie with respect to a human being (8.98). [72]Even after he has accepted a virgin according to rule, he may reject her if she is found to be dishonorable, diseased, or defiled,* or if she had been given deceptively. [73]If a man gives a virgin with defects without revealing them, one may break the contract with that evil man who gave the virgin (8.205, 224–7).*

Absence of Husband [74]A man should provide for his wife before he goes away on business, for even a steadfast woman will go astray when starved for a livelihood. [75]If he provides for her before going away, she should live a life of restraint; but if he leaves without providing for her, she may maintain herself by engaging in respectable crafts.

[76]A wife should wait* for eight years when her husband has gone away for a purpose specified by Law, for six years when he has gone for learning or fame, and for three years when he has gone for pleasure.

Repudiation of a Wife [77]For one year let a husband tolerate a wife who loathes him; after one year, he should confiscate her inheritance and stop cohabiting with her. [78]If a wife commits a transgression against her husband who is deranged, drunk, or sick, deprived of her ornaments and belongings, she should be cast out for three months. [79]If a wife loathes a husband who has become insane, fallen from caste, or impotent (3.150 n.), who is without semen,* or who has contracted an evil disease (3.92 n.), she must neither be abandoned nor deprived of her inheritance.

[80]When a wife drinks liquor or is dishonest,* cantankerous, sick, vicious, or wasteful, she may be superseded at any time by marriage to another wife. [81]A barren wife may be superseded in the eighth year; a wife whose children die, in the tenth; a wife who bears girls, in the eleventh; but a foul-mouthed wife, at once. [82]If a wife is sickly but affectionate and rich in virtue, he may marry a wife to supersede her with her consent; she should never be treated with disrespect.

[83]If a wife who has been superseded storms out of the house incensed, however, she should be locked up immediately or repudiated in the presence of the family.

[84]If, after she is forbidden, a wife drinks liquor, albeit at festivals, or visits shows and fairs,* she should be fined 6 Kṛṣṇalas.

Seniority among Wives [85]If twice-born men marry women of their own class as well as others, the order of their class determines their seniority, as also how they are honored and where they reside. [86]Among all these, only the wife of equal class may care for her husband's physical needs* or participate in his daily rites prescribed by Law, never a wife belonging to a different class. [87]If he foolishly gets another wife to carry these out while a wife of equal class is available, he becomes exactly like a Brahmin-Cāṇḍāla described by the ancients.

Marriage of Daughters [88]When there is a suitor who is eminent, handsome, and of equal status, one should give the girl to him according to rule, even if she has not attained the proper age.* [89]Even if she has reached puberty, a girl should rather remain at home until death; one should never give her to a man bereft of good qualities.

[90]For three years shall a girl wait after the onset of her puberty; after that time, she may find for herself a husband of equal status. [91]If a woman who has not been given in marriage finds a husband on her own, she does not incur any sin, and neither does the man she finds. [92]A girl who chooses a husband on her own must not take with her any ornament coming from her father or mother or given by her brothers; if she takes, it is theft.*

[93]A man who takes a girl after she has reached puberty shall not pay a bride-price, for the father has lost his ownership of her by frustrating her menses.*

[94]A 30-year-old man should marry a charming girl of 12 years, or an 18-year-old, a girl of 8 years—sooner, if his fulfilling the Law would suffer. [95]A husband marries a wife given to him by gods, not from his own desire. He should always support that good woman, thereby doing what is pleasing to the gods.

[96]Women were created to bear children, and men to extend the line; therefore, scriptures have prescribed that the Law is to be carried out in common with the wife.

[97]If, after the bride-price has been paid for the girl, the man who paid the price dies, she should be given to the brother-in-law, if she consents to it. [98]Even a Śūdra should not take a bride-price when he gives his daughter; for by accepting a bride-price, he is engaging in a covert sale of his daughter. [99]That after promising her to one man, she is then given to another*—such a deed was never done by good people of ancient or recent times. [100]The covert sale of a daughter for a payment under the name "bride-price"—we have never heard of such a thing even in former generations.

[101]"Fidelity to each other should be observed until death"—this should be recognized as the highest Law between husband and wife put in a nutshell. [102]A husband and wife, after they have completed the marriage rite, should always work hard so as to prevent them from being unfaithful to each other and thus being split apart.*

> [103]I have described above the Law concerning husband and wife based on love, as well as the way to obtain offspring in times of adversity. Listen now to the Law of inheritance.

Grounds for Litigation: XVII Partition of Inheritance

[104]After the father and mother have passed on,* the brothers should gather together and partition the paternal inheritance evenly; for they are incompetent while those two are alive.

Primogeniture [105]The eldest alone, on the contrary, ought to take the entire paternal estate, and the others should live as his dependents just as they did under their father.

[106]As soon as the eldest is born, a person becomes a "man with a son" and is released from his debt to the ancestors (4.257 n.); that son, therefore, is entitled to the entire amount. [107]Only that son to whom he passes on his debt and through whom he obtains immortality is born through the Law; others, they say, are born through lust.*

[108]The eldest brother should look after the younger ones as a father his sons; and they should behave towards their eldest brother as towards their father, in accordance with the Law. [109]It is the eldest who makes the family prosper, the eldest who brings it to ruin; the eldest receives the highest honor in the world, and the eldest is never treated with disrespect by good people. [110]When the eldest behaves the way the eldest should, he is like a mother, he is like a father; but when he fails to behave the way the eldest should, he should receive the same honor as a relative.

Partition and Seniority [111]They should either live together in this manner, or rather, separately with a desire for merit. Living separately increases merit; therefore, the act of separation is meritorious.*

[112]The preemptive share of the eldest is one-twentieth, as well as the best item in the entire estate; the middle son gets one-half of that; and the youngest, one-quarter. [113]The eldest and the youngest shall take what has been prescribed; the shares of the

sons other than the eldest and the youngest are the same as that of the middle son. [114]Within each category of property, the first-born shall take the finest item, as well as anything exceedingly special and the best out of each ten. [115]When the brothers are equally accomplished in what they do, there is no preemptive share out of each ten; a little something should be given to the eldest, however, as a token of respect.

[116]Once the preemptive share has been subtracted in the above manner, the rest should be apportioned in equal shares. If, on the other hand, the preemptive share has not been subtracted, the apportioning of shares should be carried out as follows: [117]the eldest son gets a double share; the son born next gets one and a half; and the younger ones gets a single share each—that is the settled Law.

[118]From their shares, however, the brothers shall give individually to the unmarried girls—one-quarter from the share of each. Those unwilling to give will become outcastes.

[119]A single goat, sheep, or one-hoofed animal left over after the distribution should never be divided; the rule is that a single goat or sheep left over goes to the eldest.

Seniority of Leviratic Sons [120]If a younger brother begets a son on the wife of the eldest, then the division is equal—that is the settled Law. [121]That the principal should become the subordinate is impossible according to the Law; in procreation, the father is the principal. Therefore, one should allocate a share to that son in accordance with the Law.*

Seniority among Sons of Different Wives [122]How is the partition done when the youngest son is born to the seniormost wife and the first-born son to the juniormost wife? If such a doubt arises, [123]the first-born* should take one bull as his preemptive share; thereafter, the other inferior bulls* are taken by those junior to him according to the seniority of their mothers. [124]The eldest son born to the seniormost wife, on the other hand, shall take fifteen cows together with a bull; thereafter, the others receive shares according to seniority of their mothers—that is the fixed rule.

[125]Among sons born uniformly to wives of equal status, seniority is not based on their mothers; they declare seniority to be based on birth. [126]In the Subrahmaṇyā* texts also, tradition tells us, it is the eldest by birth who makes the invocation. Tradition also tells us that even between twins in the same womb seniority is based on birth.

"Female-Son" and Her Sons [127]A man without a son should make his daughter a "female-son"* in the following manner: "The child this girl bears will be the one who performs my ancestral rites."+

[128]In ancient times, Dakṣa himself, the lord of creatures, made "female-sons" in the above manner for the multiplication of his lineage. [129]After adorning them and with a joyful heart, he gave ten of them to Dharma, thirteen to Kaśyapa, and twenty-seven to King Soma.*

[130]A son is the same as one's self, and a daughter is equal to a son; while she stands there as his very self, how can someone else take his property?

[131]Anything that is part of a mother's separate property* becomes the share of her unmarried daughters; and the daughter's son shall take the entire property of a man

without a son. [132]The daughter's son shall indeed take the entire estate of the father who is without a son, and he shall offer two rice-balls, one to his father and one to his maternal grandfather. [133]The world does not recognize any difference between a son's son and a daughter's son with respect to the Law, for both the father of the one and the mother of the other sprang from his own body (9.139). [134]If, however, a son is born after a "female-son" has been appointed, the division in that case is equal; for a woman has no claim to primogeniture (9.120–1 n.).

[135]If a "female-son" somehow dies sonless, the husband of that "female-son" shall indeed take the property without hesitation. [136]When a daughter, whether she is appointed or not, bears a son by a man of equal status*—by that son his maternal grandfather becomes a man who has a son's son, and the latter shall offer him the rice-ball and inherit his property.

[137]Through a son a man gains the worlds; through a son's son he obtains eternal life; but through the son's grandson he attains the crest of the sun. [138]The Self-existent One himself has called him "son" (*putra*) because he rescues (*trā*) his father from the hell named Put. [139]The world does not acknowledge any difference between a son's son and a daughter's son, for a daughter's son also rescues him in the hereafter, just like a son's son (9.133).

[140]The son of a "female-son" shall offer the first rice-ball to his mother, the second to her father, and the third to her father's father.*

Adopted Son [141]When a man's adopted son is endowed with all the fine qualities, he may indeed inherit his estate, even if that son has been obtained from a different lineage. [142]Under no circumstances shall an adopted son inherit his biological father's lineage or estate. The offering of the rice-ball is consequent upon inheriting the lineage and estate; so when a man gives a son for adoption, the son's obligation to perform his funerary rites comes to an end.*

Leviratic Sons [143]The son of an unappointed woman and a son fathered by a brother-in-law on a woman who already has a son—neither of these is entitled to a share; the former is born to a prostitute and the latter is born of lust. [144]If the rules have not been followed, a male born even to an appointed woman is not entitled to inherit the paternal estate; for he was begotten by an outcaste (9.58, 63).

[145]A son born to an appointed woman shall inherit it, just as a natural son; that seed and its issue belong by Law to the owner of the field (9.48–51). [146]The man who keeps* his deceased brother's property and wife should produce an offspring for his brother and hand over the brother's property to him.

[147]When an unappointed woman obtains a son either through her brother-in-law or someone else, that son, born through lust, is not entitled to the estate; he is said to have been wrongly begotten.

> [148]These should be recognized as the rules for partition when the wives belong to the same caste. Listen now to the rules regarding sons of the same man born to several wives belonging to different castes.

Sons by Wives of Different Castes [149]If a Brahmin has four wives in the proper order, tradition lays down the following rule regarding partition among sons born to those wives. [150]The plowman, the stud bull, the vehicle, the ornament,* and the house is to be given to the Brahmin as his preemptive share, as well as one share from the best property.* [151]The Brahmin shall take three shares of the inheritance; the son by a Kṣatriya wife, two shares; the son by a Vaiśya wife, one and a half shares; and the son by a Śūdra wife, one share.

[152]Alternatively, a man who knows the Law may divide his entire estate into ten shares and carry out a partition consistent with the Law according to the following rule: [153]the Brahmin shall take four shares; the son by a Kṣatriya wife, three; the son by a Vaiśya wife, two; and the son by a Śūdra wife, one. [154]Whether he has a proper son or no son at all,* the Law requires that he give no more than one-tenth to a son by a Śūdra wife.

[155]The son of a Brahmin, Kṣatriya, or Vaiśya by a Śūdra wife does not share in the inheritance; his only property is whatever his father may give him.

[156]Alternatively, when all the sons of a twice-born man are born from wives of equal class, after giving a preemptive share to the eldest, the rest should take equal shares.*

[157]A Śūdra, however, has only a wife of his own class; no other wife is prescribed for him (3.13). All the sons born to such a wife, even if there are a hundred of them, shall receive equal shares.

Twelve Types of Sons [158]Of the twelve types of sons that Manu, the son of the Self-existent, has decreed for men, six are both relatives and heirs and six are relatives but not heirs.* [159]A natural son, a son begotten on the wife, a son given in adoption, a constituted son, a son born in secret, and a son adopted after being abandoned—these are the six who are both relatives and heirs. [160]A son born to an unmarried woman, a son received with marriage, a purchased son, a son born to a remarried woman, a son given in adoption by himself, and a son by a Śūdra wife—these are the six who are relatives but not heirs.

[161]A man gains the same distinction* by crossing the darkness with the aid of bad sons as he does by crossing the water with the aid of bad boats.

[162]If a natural son and a son begotten on the wife are heirs to the estate of the same man, the one whose paternal estate it is shall take it, and not the other.* [163]The natural son is the sole master of his father's wealth; nevertheless, so as not to be unkind, he should provide maintenance for the others. [164]When the natural son divides the paternal inheritance, he should give a one-sixth or one-fifth share of the paternal property to the son begotten on the wife. [165]The natural son and the son begotten on the wife receive shares of the paternal estate; but the other ten according to their order share in the lineage and the estate.*

[166]When a man fathers a son by himself through his own duly wedded wife, he should be recognized as a *natural son*—the principal son.* [167]When a wife of someone who is dead, impotent, or sick bears a son after she has been appointed in accordance with the Law specific to her, tradition calls him a *son begotten on the wife*. [168]When during a time of adversity a mother or a father joyfully gives their son in adoption with

the ceremonial pouring of water, a son belonging to the same class as the recipient, he should be known as a *son given in adoption.* [169]When someone installs a boy of equal class as his son, a boy who knows right from wrong and is endowed with filial qualities, he should be recognized as a *constituted son.* [170]When in someone's house is born a son whose father is unknown, he is a *son born in secret* within the house; and he belongs to the man whose wife gave birth to him. [171]When a boy has been abandoned by his mother and father or by one of them and he is taken by someone as his son, he is called a *son adopted after being abandoned.* [172]When an unmarried girl gives birth to a son secretly in her father's house, one should call him by the name *son born to an unmarried woman*; the offspring of an unmarried girl belongs to the man who marries her. [173]When a pregnant woman is married off, whether her condition is disclosed or not, the child in the womb belongs to the man who marries her and is called *son received with marriage.* [174]When someone purchases a boy directly from his mother and father so he may have a child, whether that child is of the same class or not, he is his *purchased son.* [175]When a woman who has been abandoned by her husband or is a widow marries again* and begets a son of her own will, he is called *son of a remarried woman.* [176]Such a woman or one who has gone away and returned, so long as she has not been deflowered, is fit to perform the marriage ceremony once again with her husband according to the rite of remarriage.* [177]When someone who has no mother or father or who has been abandoned without cause offers himself up to a man, tradition calls him a *son given in adoption by himself.* [178]When a Brahmin fathers a son by a Śūdra woman out of lust, tradition calls him a *Pāraśava* (10.8), because while still able (*pārayan*) he is a corpse (*śava*).

[179]The son a Śūdra begets by a slave woman or by a slave woman married to a slave* may take a share with his father's permission—that is the settled Law.

[180]The eleven sons enumerated above beginning with the *son begotten on the wife*—wise men call these the surrogates of a son necessitated by the possible interruption of rites (9.166 n.). [181]Those who are designated here as sons because of congruity but who are born from another man's seed belong only to the one from whose seed they were born and to no one else (9.35–40).

[182]If among several brothers born to the same father one gets a son, Manu has declared that through that son they all become men who have sons. [183]If among all the wives* of the same husband one gets a son, Manu has declared that through that son they all become women who have sons.*

[184]In the absence of each superior son each son inferior to him is entitled to the estate; but if several of them are of equal rank, all of them share the estate. [185]The sons inherit the father's estate—not the brothers, not the fathers. The estate of a man who has no son, however, is inherited by his father or by his brothers.

Alternative Heirs [186]To three water is offered; to three rice-balls are given; and the fourth offers them—there is no room for a fifth.* [187]The closest relative of a person belonging to the same ancestry shall take his property; beyond such a relative, a man belonging to the same family, the teacher, or a pupil.* [188]When none of these is available, pure and disciplined Brahmins learned in the triple Veda share the estate; in this way, the Law is not hurt. [189]The king must never take the property of a Brahmin—

that is the rule; but, in the absence of any heir, the king may take the property of persons belonging to the other classes.

190When a man has died childless, a son should be procured for him through a man of the same lineage, and any estate the deceased may have should be handed over to that son. 191When two individuals fathered by two men litigate over the property held by the wife, each shall take the estate of his own biological father to the exclusion of the other.*

Women's Property 192When their mother dies, all the uterine brothers and sisters should divide the maternal estate equally among themselves. 193If those sisters have any daughters, one should joyfully give them also, as is proper, something from their maternal grandmother's property.

194Tradition presents six types of women's property: what a woman receives at the nuptial fire, what she receives when she is taken away, what she is given as a token of love, and what she receives from her brothers, mother, and father. 195What she receives subsequent to the marriage and what her husband gives her out of affection—upon her death that property goes to her children even if her husband is alive.

196In a "Brāhma," "Divine," "Seer's," "Gāndharva," or "Prājāpatya" marriage, the property of a woman is awarded to her husband alone, if she dies childless. 197In a "Demonic" or a subsequent form of marriage, on the other hand, any property given to a woman is awarded to her mother and father, if she dies childless (see 3.20–34).

198Any property given somehow to a woman by her father goes to the unmarried Brahmin daughter, or to that daughter's offspring.*

199Women must never alienate* common property of the family or even her own private property without the consent of her husband.

200Any ornaments worn by a woman while her husband was alive shall not be partitioned by his heirs; if they do, they fall from their caste.

Disqualification from Inheritance 201The following receive no shares: the impotent (3.150 n.), outcastes, those born blind or deaf, the insane, the mentally retarded, mutes, and anyone lacking manly strength.* 202It is right, however, that a wise man should provide all of them with food and clothing according to his ability until the end; if he does not, he will become an outcaste. 203If, on the other hand, any of these, the impotent and so forth, somehow want to have wives and do have issue, their offspring is entitled to a share.

Partition of Non-ancestral Property 204If the eldest acquires any assets after his father's death, a share of it goes to his younger brothers, provided they are pursuing their studies. 205If all of them are uneducated, however, and they acquire assets by their own labor, then the division is equal, given that it is not part of the paternal estate—that is the fixed rule. 206Assets that someone acquires through learning, on the other hand, belong to him alone, as do presents from friends, wedding gifts, and anything given with the honey-mixture (3.119 n.).

207If one of the brothers, quite able to live by his own activity, does not want any property, he may be stripped of his share after giving something for his maintenance.

208If one of them earns anything by his own labor without utilizing the paternal property, he need not share it against his will, as it was acquired by his own effort.

209If the father recovers any missing ancestral property, he need not share it with his sons against his will, as it was acquired by himself.

Miscellaneous Rules of Partition 210If parties to a partition again live together and subsequently undertake a new partition, then the division is equal; primogeniture is inoperative there.

211If the oldest or the youngest among them is debarred from the distribution of shares or if either of them dies, his share is not lost.* 212Having assembled together, the uterine brothers, as well as reunited brothers and uterine sisters, should jointly divide it equally among themselves.*

213When the eldest defrauds his younger brothers through greed, he shall no longer be the eldest. Stripped of his share, he should be punished by the king. 214All brothers who pursue improper activities are unfit to inherit the property. The eldest, morevoer, must not establish his own separate property without first giving to his younger brothers.

215If prior to partition the brothers undertake a joint enterprise, on no account shall the father give unequal shares to his sons.

216A son born after partition shall inherit the entire paternal property; or, if he has brothers who have reunited, he shall share it with them.*

217The mother shall receive the inheritance of a childless son; and if the mother is also dead, the father's mother shall inherit that property.

218If something is uncovered after all debts and assets have been divided according to rule, it shall be divided equally. 219A garment, a vehicle, an ornament, prepared food, water, women, and security measures are declared to be exempt from partition.*

> 220I have described above the division of property and the ritual procedure for sons* beginning in due order with the son begotten on the wife. Listen now to the Law pertaining to gambling.

Grounds for Litigation—XVIII Gambling and Betting

221The king shall suppress gambling and betting within his realm; they are the two vices of rulers that devastate a kingdom.* 222Gambling and betting amount to open theft; the king should make constant effort at eradicating them both.

223When it is done with inanimate things, people call it "gambling"; when it is done with living beings, on the other hand, it is known as "betting."

224The king should have anyone who engages in or facilitates gambling or betting executed, as also Śūdras wearing marks of twice-born men. 225He should quickly banish from his capital gamblers, performers, entertainers,* men belonging to heretical sects, individuals engaging in illicit activities, and liquor vendors. 226When these clandestine thieves remain in a king's realm, they constantly harass his decent subjects with their illicit activities.

227In a former age* gambling was seen to create great enmity; therefore, an intelligent man should never engage in gambling even for fun. 228When a man engages in it openly or in secret, the kind of punishment to be imposed on him is left to the discretion of the king.

Excursus: Types of Punishment

229When a Kṣatriya, a Vaiśya, or a Śūdra is unable to pay a fine, he should acquit himself of the debt through work; a Brahmin, on the other hand, should pay it off in installments.

230The king should punish women, children, the insane, the elderly, the poor, those without guardians, and the sick with a lash, a cane, a rope, and the like.

231When those appointed to adjudicate lawsuits, inflamed by the heat of money,* undermine cases brought by litigants, the king should confiscate all their property. 232He should put to death those who forge royal edicts, corrupt the constituents of the realm,* or kill women, children, or Brahmins, as also those who give aid to his enemies.

233Whenever something has been adjudicated and a judgment issued,* he should recognize it as executed according to the Law and not bring it back again.* 234If an official or a judge settles a case wrongly, the king himself should settle it and fine him 1,000 (8.120 n.).

Grievous Sins Causing Loss of Caste 235A murderer of a Brahmin, a man who drinks liquor, a thief, and a man who has sex with an elder's wife—all these men should be considered individually* as guilty of a grievous sin causing loss of caste (11.55 n.).

236If any of these four fails to perform the penance, the king should determine for them a punishment, both corporal and pecuniary, that accords with the Law. 237For sex with an elder's wife, the man should be branded with the mark of a vagina; for drinking liquor, with the sign of a tavern (11.93 n.); for stealing, with the figure of a dog's foot; and for killing a Brahmin, with the figure of a headless man. 238These wretched men—with whom one is not permitted to eat, to participate at a sacrifice, to recite the Veda, or to contract marriages—shall roam the earth, excluded from all activities relating to the Law. 239Branded with marks, they shall be forsaken by their paternal and maternal relations; they should be shown no compassion and paid no reverence—that is Manu's decree.

240If they do perform the prescribed penance, on the other hand, the king should not brand the higher classes* on the forehead, but make them pay the highest fine (8.138). 241For these offenses, the middle fine should be imposed on a Brahmin, or he should be exiled from the realm along with his property and belongings. 242When others commit these sins, however, they deserve to have all their property confiscated, if they did them thoughtlessly, or to be executed,* if they did them willfully.+

243A good king must never take the property of someone guilty of a grievous sin causing loss of caste; if he takes it out of greed, he becomes tainted with the same sin. 244He should offer that fine to Varuṇa by casting it into water, or present it to a Brahmin endowed with learning and virtue. 245Varuṇa is the lord of punishment, for he holds the rod of punishment over kings; and a Brahmin who has mastered the Veda is the lord of the entire world. [246]When a king refrains from taking the fines of evil-doers, in that land are born in due course men with long lives; [247]the farmers' crops ripen, each as it was sown; children do not die; and no deformed child is born.

[248]If a man of a lower class deliberately torments Brahmins, the king should kill him using graphic modes of execution (9.279 n.) that strike terror into men. [249]A king incurs as great a sin by releasing someone who ought to be executed as by executing someone who ought not to be executed; but he gains merit by its proper exercise.

Conclusion of Grounds for Litigation

[250]I have described above in great detail how lawsuits brought by litigants and falling within the eighteen avenues of litigation are to be decided (see 8.3).

[251]Carrying out properly in this manner his duties flowing from the Law, the king should both seek to acquire territories not yet acquired and protect well those that have been acquired.*

Eradication of Thorns

[252]After properly settling the country and building a fort according to textual norms, he should direct his maximum effort constantly at the eradication of thorns.* [253]By protecting those who follow the Ārya way of life and by clearing the thorns, kings devoted to the protection of their subjects reach the highest heaven. [254]When a king collects taxes without suppressing thieves, on the other hand, it will cause an upheaval in his realm and he will be cut off from heaven. [255]When his realm, sheltered by the power of his arm, is made secure, it will always thrive, like a regularly watered tree.

[256]The king, using spies as his eyes, should identify the two kinds of thieves who steal the property of others: those who operate overtly and those who operate covertly. [257]Of these, the overt cheats are those who live by trading in various merchandise, and the covert cheats are people such as thieves and bandits of the wild.*

[258]Bribe-takers, frauds, cheats, gamblers, those who live by adjuring good luck, fortunetellers,* [259]high officials and physicians who act crookedly, those engaged in exhibiting their artistic skills, skilled prostitutes—[260]people such as these should be recognized as open thorns on his people's side, and others, the non-Āryas wearing Ārya marks,* as operating in secret. [261]After identifying these through honest undercover agents practicing those same occupations and instigating them through mobile agents posted in various spy establishments, he should lure them into his power. [262]After publicizing accurately the crimes they have committed in their respective activities, the king should duly punish them, each in proportion to his capacity and his crime. [263]For without punishment, it is impossible to suppress the crimes of evil-minded thieves who prowl the land in secret.

[264]Assembly halls, water-booths, sweetmeat-shops, brothels, taverns, restaurants, crossroads, memorial trees, fairs, theaters, [265]dilapidated parks, wild tracts,

artisans' workshops, abandoned houses, groves, and parks—[266]the king should have these types of places patrolled by mobile and stationary squads and by mobile agents* in order to interdict thieves.

[267]By means of clever former thieves who had been their associates and companions and who are adept at their various activities, he should identify and instigate them. [268]Under the pretext of attending a banquet, seeing Brahmins, or watching feats of valor, they should assemble these people in one place. [269]Those who do not gather there and those who have become suspicious of the source,* the king should forcibly attack and kill, along with their friends and paternal and maternal relatives (2.132 n.).

[270]A righteous king must never execute a thief unless he is caught with the stolen goods; if he is caught with the stolen goods and the tools of his trade, the king should execute him without hesitation. [271]He should also execute every individual within any village who gives food, implements, or shelter* to thieves.

[272]When individuals appointed to guard the provinces* and rulers of border districts who have been summoned remain uninvolved during raids, he should promptly punish them like thieves. [273]When a man who gains his livelihood by the Law deviates from the conventions of the Law, the king should make him also suffer a punishment, for he has deviated from the Law specific to him.* [274]When a village is being raided, a dike is being breached, or a highway robbery is taking place, whoever fails to hasten there with help according to his ability should be banished along with his belongings.

[275]Those who rob the king's treasury, those who act contrary to his interests, and those who conspire with his enemies—he should inflict diverse kinds of capital punishment on them.

[276]When robbers cut through walls and commit theft at night, the king should cut off their hands and impale them on sharp stakes. [277]After the first offense, he should have two fingers* of a pickpocket cut off; after the second, the hands and the feet; and after the third, he ought to be executed. [278]Those who provide fire, food, weapons, or shelter (9.271 n.), and those who receive stolen goods—the king should punish* these like thieves.

[279]Someone who breaks a reservoir should be killed by drowning or clean execution;* or else, he should repair it and be made to pay the highest fine (8.138). [280]He should kill without hesitation those who break into the treasury, the armory, or a temple, and those who steal elephants, horses, or chariots.*

[281]Someone who steals water from a reservoir constructed long ago or cuts off its water intake should be made to pay the lowest fine (8.138). [282]Anyone who drops filth on a royal highway, except in an emergency, should pay a fine of 2 Kārṣapaṇas and promptly clean up that filth;* [283]but if it was an individual with an emergency, an old man, a pregnant woman, or a child, that person merits a reprimand and should be made to clean it up—that is the settled rule.

[284]Any physician guilty of malpractice is subject to a fine, the lowest in the case of non-humans and the middle in the case of humans (8.138). [285]Anyone who destroys a bridge, a flag, a pole, or a statue should repair the entire damage and pay a fine of 500 (8.120 n.).

[286]For adulterating unadulterated substances, and for breaking or improperly boring gems, the punishment is the lowest fine.* [287]If a man deals with equivalent commodities as if they were unequal, even if he does so in terms of value, he shall receive the lowest or the middle fine.*

[288]He should locate all prisons along the royal highway where people will see the criminals, grieving and mutilated.

[289]He should promptly execute (8.123 n.) anyone who breaches the rampart, fills the moat, or breaks the gates.

[290]For all types of black magic, a fine of 200 should be imposed, as also for root-witchcraft (11.64 n.) when done by an unrelated person, and for various types of sorcery. [291]Anyone who sells infertile seed corn or jacks up the price of seed corn,* or who destroys boundary marks, shall be executed with mutilation.*

[292]A goldsmith who operates dishonestly, however, is the most wicked of all thorns, and the king should have him cut to pieces with razor knives.

[293]For stealing agricultural implements, weapons, and medicine, the king should impose a punishment taking into account the time and the purpose.*

***Excursus:* Constituents of a Kingdom** [294]Lord, official, capital, realm, treasury, army, and ally—these seven basic constituents are said to form a complete kingdom.*

[295]Among these seven basic constituents of a kingdom in the order enumerated, a grave evil affecting each preceding one must be considered the more serious. [296]In this world, a kingdom is propped up by the seven limbs like a tripod* and no single one of them is superfluous, because of their mutual dependence on the special quality of each. [297]For each limb is specially suited to carry out specific tasks; the one that accomplishes a particular task is said to be the most important with respect to it.

***Excursus:* Activities of the King** [298–9]By means of spies, by a display of strength, and by engaging in enterprises, he should identify his own and his enemy's relative strength and ascertain the relative gravity of all the adversities and evils affecting his enemy and himself; and only then should he embark on any operation. [300]Indeed, he must embark on his operations repeatedly, though repeatedly exhausted; for Fortune devotes herself only to a man who embarks on his operations.

[301]Kṛta-age, Tretā-age, Dvāpara-age, and Kali-age—the king's activities constitute all these; for the king is said to be the age. [302]When he is asleep, he is Kali; when he is awake, he is Dvāpara; when he is ready to undertake operations, he is Tretā; and when he is on the march, he is Kṛta.

[303]The king should follow the energetic activity of Indra, Sun, Wind, Yama, Varuṇa, Moon, Fire, and Earth.* [304]As Indra showers rain during the four months* of the rainy season, so the king, following the Indra-vow, should shower delights upon his realm. [305]As Sun extracts water through its rays during the eight months,* so the king should constantly extract taxes from his realm; for this is the Sun-vow. [306]As Wind moves about infiltrating all creatures, so the king should infiltrate with his mobile spies; for that is the Wind-vow. [307]As Yama, when the time has come, holds friend and foe alike in his grip, so the king should hold his subjects in his grip; for that

is the Yama-vow. [308]As we see people bound with fetters by Varuṇa, so the king should capture criminals; for that is the Varuṇa-vow. [309]When his subjects are as delighted in him as are people when they see the full moon, that king is observing the Moon-vow. [310]When the king is always inflamed and ablaze against evil-doers and crushes evil rulers of border districts, tradition calls it the Fire-vow. [311]The Earth supports all creatures equally; when a king supports all creatures in the same manner, he is observing the Earth-vow.

> [312]In this and other ways should the king, always alert and tireless,
> suppress thieves within his own realm and even in others.*

***Excursus* on Brahmins** [313]Even in the face of the deepest adversity, he must never anger Brahmins; for when they are angered, they will destroy him instantly along with his army and conveyances (7.75 n.). [314]They made the fire a consumer of everything, the ocean undrinkable, and the moon to wane and wax*—who would not be destroyed when he angers these? [315]When angered, they could create other worlds and other guardians of the world, they could convert gods into non-gods—who would prosper when he injures these? [316]The worlds and the gods always exist by taking refuge in them, and their wealth is the Veda—who would injure them if he wishes to live?

[317]Whether he is learned or not, a Brahmin is a great deity, just as Fire is a great deity, whether it is consecrated or not. [318]Even in cemeteries, the Fire, full of energy, is never tainted; and when it is offered with oblations at sacrifices, it flares up again. [319]Similarly, even if they engage in every undesirable act, Brahmins should be honored in every way; for they are the highest deity.

[320]When a Kṣatriya becomes haughty in any way in his behavior towards Brahmins, the Brahmin himself must become their controller, for the Kṣatriya sprang from the Brahmin. [321]Fire sprang from water, Kṣatriya from Brahmin,* and metal from stone; their all-pervasive energy is quenched when confronting their own source. [322]The Kṣatriya does not flourish without the Brahmin, and the Brahmin does not prosper without the Kṣatriya; but when Brahmin and Kṣatriya are united, they prosper here and in the hereafter.

[323]After giving to Brahmins the money collected from all the fines and handing over the kingdom to his son, the king should meet his death in battle.

Conclusion of the Rules for Kings

[324]Conducting himself in this manner and always devoted to the Laws pertaining to kings, the king should direct all his servants to work for the good of his people.

> [325]I have described above in its entirety the eternal rules of action for
> the king. What follows, one should understand, are the rules of
> action for the Vaiśya and the Śūdra in their proper order.

RULES OF ACTION FOR VAIŚYAS AND ŚŪDRAS

Rules for Vaiśyas

[326]After undergoing initiatory consecration and getting married, a Vaiśya should devote himself constantly to trade and to looking after farm animals; [327]for, after creating them, Prajāpati handed over to the Vaiśya the farm animals, and to the Brahmin and the king, all creatures.

[328]"I don't want to look after farm animals"—a Vaiśya should never entertain such a wish, and when there is a willing Vaiśya, under no circumstances shall anyone else look after them. [329]He shall acquaint himself with the relative values of gems, pearls, coral, metals, threads, perfumes, and condiments. [330]He should be knowledgeable about sowing seeds, the good and bad qualities of farmland, all the various ways of weighing and measuring, [331]the desirable and undesirable properties of goods, the good and bad aspects of regions, the probable profit and loss of merchandise, and how best to raise farm animals. [332]He should be well-informed about the wages to be paid to servants, the different languages of people, the manner of storing goods, and the procedures of buying and selling.

[333]He should make the utmost effort at making his assets grow in accordance with the Law and diligently distribute food to all creatures.

Rules for Śūdras

[334]For the Śūdra, on the other hand, the highest Law leading to bliss is simply to render obedient service to distinguished Brahmin householders who are learned in the Veda. [335]When he keeps himself pure, obediently serves the highest class, is soft-spoken and humble, and always takes refuge in Brahmins, he obtains a higher birth.

CONCLUSION OF THE LAW OUTSIDE TIMES OF ADVERSITY

> [336]I have described above the splendid rules of action for the social classes outside times of adversity. Listen now to the rules for them in the proper order for times of adversity.

CHAPTER TEN

RULES FOR TIMES OF ADVERSITY

Mixed Classes

The Four Classes 1Devoted to their respective activities, the three twice-born classes should study the Veda; but it is the Brahmin who should teach them, not the other two—that is the firm principle. 2The Brahmin must know the means of livelihood of all according to rule, and he should both teach them to the others and follow them himself.

3Because of his distinctive qualities, the eminence of his origin, his observance of restrictive practices, and the distinctive nature of his consecration, the Brahmin is the lord of all the classes.

4Three classes—Brahmin, Kṣatriya, and Vaiśya—are twice-born; the fourth, Śūdra, has a single birth. There is no fifth.

5In all the classes, children born in the direct order of class* to wives who are of equal class and married as virgins should be recognized as belonging to the same class by birth. 6Sons fathered by twice-born men on wives of the class immediately below theirs are considered only "similar," disdained as they are due to their mother's defect.

7That is the eternal rule with respect to those born from women of the class immediately below. The following should be recognized as the righteous rule with respect to those born from women two or three classes below.

Mixed Classes: First Discourse 8From a Brahmin man by a Vaiśya girl* is born a son called Ambaṣṭha; and by a Śūdra girl, a Niṣāda, also called Pāraśava. 9From a Kṣatriya man by a Śūdra girl is born a son called Ugra, who is cruel in his behavior and in his dealings, a being with the physical characteristics of both a Kṣatriya and a Śūdra.

10A Brahmin's children by the three lower classes, a Kṣatriya's by the two lower classes, and a Vaiśya's by the one lower class—tradition calls these six "low-born" (10.46 n.).

11From a Kṣatriya man by a Brahmin girl is born a Sūta by caste; sons of a Vaiśya by Kṣatriya and Brahmin women are a Māgadha and a Vaideha, respectively; 12and from a Śūdra by Vaiśya, Kṣatriya, and Brahmin women are born respectively an Āyogava, a Kṣattṛ, and a Cāṇḍāla, the worst of all men—so originate the intermixture of classes.

13As when there is a difference of two classes in a birth, tradition calls them Ambaṣṭha and Ugra if the difference is in the direct order, in like manner they are Kṣatṛ and Vaideha, if it is in the inverse order. 14The sons of twice-born men by women of the class immediately below theirs that have been enumerated in their proper order—they are given the name "Promixate," because of their mother's defect.*

Mixed Classes: Second Discourse [15]From a Brahmin man by an Ugra girl is born a son called Āvṛta; by an Ambaṣṭha girl, an Ābhīra; and by an Āyogava girl, a Dhigvaṇa.

[16]From a Śūdra man are born in the inverse order three "low-borns": Āyogava, Kṣattṛ, and Cāṇḍāla, the worst of all men. [17]Three further "low-borns" (10.46 n.) are born in the inverse order: from a Vaiśya man, a Māgadha and a Vaideha; and from a Kṣatriya man, a Sūta.*

[18]From a Niṣāda man by a Śūdra woman is born a Pulkasa by caste; a son born from a Śūdra man by a Niṣāda woman, tradition tells us, is a Kukkuṭa. [19]A child born from a Kṣattṛ man by an Ugra woman is said to be a Śvapāka; and from a Vaidehaka man by an Ambaṣṭha woman, a Veṇa.

[20]When children fathered by twice-born men on women of equal class do not keep the observances and have fallen from the Sāvitrī (2.38 n.), they should be called by the name Vrātya (2.39). [21]From a Vrātya of the Brahmin class are born the evil-natured Bhṛjjakaṇṭaka, the Āvantya, the Vāṭadhāna, the Puṣpadha, and the Śaikha. [22]From a Vrātya of the Kṣatriya class are born the Jhalla, the Malla, the Licchivi, the Naṭa, the Karaṇa, the Khasa, and the Draviḍa. [23]From a Vrātya of the Vaiśya class are born the Sudhanvan, the Ācārya, the Kāruṣa, the Vijanman, the Maitra, and the Sātvata.*

Mixed Classes: Third Discourse [24]By adultery among the classes, by marrying forbidden women, and by abandoning the activities proper to them, arise the intermixture of classes.* [25]I will enumerate completely those who are of mixed origin, born in the direct and in the inverse order and mutually connected.

[26]Sūta, Vaidehaka, Caṇḍāla, the worst of men, Māgadha, Kṣatṛ, and Āyogava—[27]these six beget children similar in class to themselves by women of their own class, by women of their mother's caste, and by women of higher castes.* [28]As from two of the three classes is born a child that is one's own self—being born from a woman of his own class because of the contiguity—so the same process applies to excluded men.* [29]These same men beget on each other's wives large numbers of excluded children even more vile than they and despicable. [30]Just as a Śūdra man begets an excluded child from a Brahmin woman, so also an excluded man begets from women of the four classes a child subject to even greater exclusion.

[31]Having sex in the inverse order, excluded men beget children subject to even greater exclusion, the low-born beget low-born children, generating as many as fifteen classes. [32]On an Āyogava woman—a Dasyu man begets a Sairandra, who, although not a slave, gains his livelihood as a slave, is skilled at adorning and personal attendance, and lives by trapping animals; [33]a Vaideha man begets a Maitreyaka, who has a sweet voice, eulogizes men constantly, and rings the bell at dawn; [34]and a Niṣāda man begets a Mārgava, that is, a Dāśa, who lives by working on ships and whom people living in Āryāvarta (2.22) call a Kaivarta. [35]By Āyogava women, who are non-Āryas, wear the clothes of the dead, and eat despicable food, are born severally these three low-borns.*

[36]From a Niṣāda man is born a Kārāvara, who works on leather; from a Vaidehaka, an Andhra and a Meda, both of whom dwell outside the village. [37]On a Vaideha woman—a Cāṇḍāla man begets a Pāṇḍusopāka, who deals in bamboo; and a Niṣāda man begets an Āhiṇḍika. [38]On a Pulkasa woman, a Cāṇḍāla man begets a Sopāka, a wicked man who gains his living as an executioner and is despised by good people.* [39]A son born to a Niṣāda woman by a Cāṇḍāla man is an Antyāvasāyin, who operates in cemeteries and is despised even by excluded people.

[40]These castes arising from intermixture and described above according to their fathers and mothers—whether they conceal their caste or are open about it—should be recognized by their respective activities (10.57).*

[41]The six types of sons born to women belonging to one's own or the class immediately below have characteristics of a twice-born; but tradition regards all the "delinquent-born" (10.46 n.) as having the same characteristics as Śūdras. [42]By the power of austerity and semen, in each succeeding generation* they attain here among men a higher or a lower status by birth.

[43]By neglecting rites and by failing to visit Brahmins,* however, these men of Kṣatriya birth have gradually reached in the world the level of Śūdras—[44]Puṇḍrakas, Coḍas, Draviḍas, Kāmbojas, Yavanas, Śakas, Pāradas, Pahlavas, Cīnas, Kirātas, and Daradas.* [45]All the castes in the world that are outside those born from the mouth, arms, thighs, and feet—whether they speak foreign or Ārya languages—tradition calls Dasyus.

Occupations, Residence, and Dress [46]The "low-born" among the twice-born, as well as those that tradition calls "delinquent-born,"* should live by occupations despised by the twice-born—[47]to Sūtas, management of horses and chariots; to Ambaṣṭhas, medicine; to Vaidehakas, taking care of women; to Māgadhas, trade; [48]to Niṣādas, fishing; to Āyogavas, carpentry; to Medas, Andras, Cuñcus, and Madgus, hunting wild animals; [49]to Kṣattṛs, Ugras, and Pulkasas, trapping and killing animals living in burrows; to Dhigvaṇas, working in leather; and to Veṇas, playing drums.

[50]These should live by memorial trees and in cemeteries, hills, and groves, well-recognizable* and living by the occupations specific to them.

Cāṇḍālas and Śvapacas [51]Cāṇḍālas and Śvapacas, however, must live outside the village and they should be made Apapātras.* Their property consists of dogs and donkeys, [52]their garments are the clothes of the dead; they eat in broken vessels; their ornaments are of iron; and they constantly roam about.

[53]A man who follows the Law should never seek any dealings with them. All their transactions shall be among themselves, and they must marry their own kind. [54]They depend on others for their food, and it should be given in a broken vessel. They must not go about in villages and towns at night; [55]they may go around during the day to perform some task at the command of the king, wearing distinguishing marks. They should carry away the corpses of those without relatives—that is the settled rule. [56]They should always execute those condemned to death in the manner prescribed by authoritative texts and at the command of the king; and they may take the clothes, beds, and ornaments of those condemned to death.

Further Discourse on Mixed Classes [57]An unknown man without the proper complexion,* born from a squalid womb, a non-Ārya with some measure of Ārya features—one should detect such a man by his activities (10.40). [58]Un-Ārya conduct, harshness, cruelty, and the neglect of rites reveal in this world a man who is born from a squalid womb. [59]He will possess the character of either his father or his mother, or of both; a man born from an evil womb is never able to conceal his nature. [60]If he is the result of a mixed union, even a man born in a prominent family will undoubtedly partake of his parents' character to a greater or a lesser extent.

[61]Wherever these "delinquent-born" (10.46 n.) individuals, who corrupt the social classes, are born, that realm quickly comes to ruin together with its inhabitants.

Advance to Higher Classes [62]For excluded individuals, giving up their life without artifice* for the sake of a Brahmin or a cow, or in the defense of women or children is the means for achieving success.

[63]Abstention from injuring, truthfulness, refraining from anger,* purification, and mastering the organs+—this, Manu has declared, is the gist of the Law for the four classes.

[64]If an offspring of a Brahmin man from a Śūdra woman were to bear children from a superior partner, within seven generations the inferior attains the superior caste; [65]a Śūdra thus attains the rank of a Brahmin, and so does a Brahmin the rank of a Śūdra*—one should understand that this rule holds good also for offspring born from a Kṣatriya or a Vaiśya man.

[66]If it be asked: who is superior? A child born accidentally to a Brahmin man by a non-Ārya woman or a child of a non-Ārya man by a Brahmin woman? [67]This is the resolution: a child born to an Ārya man by a non-Ārya woman becomes an Ārya by reason of his attributes, while a child born to a non-Ārya man by an Ārya woman is a non-Ārya. [68]Neither of these should be permitted to receive vedic initiation—that is the settled Law; the former because of the inferiority of his birth and the latter because he was born in the inverse order of class. [69]As a good seed sprouting in a good field grows vigorously, so a child born to an Ārya man by an Ārya woman is worthy of receiving all the consecratory rites.

[70]Some wise men extol the seed, others the field, and yet others both the seed and the field. In this regard, the settled rule is as follows. [71]A seed planted in a bad field dies midstream; a field without seed also is just bare land. [72]By the power of the seed, children born from animals became seers, receiving honor and acclaim; therefore, they extol the seed (9.32–55).

[73]The creator evaluated a non-Ārya who acts like an Ārya and an Ārya who acts like a non-Ārya and declared: "They are neither equal nor unequal."

Occupations of the Four Classes

[74]Brahmins who are established in that whose source is the Veda* and are devoted to the activities specific to them should duly live by the six occupations in their proper order: [75]teaching and studying, offering sacrifices and officiating at sacrifices, and giving and accepting gifts are the six occupations of a highest-born person.

[76]Of these six activities, however, three provide him with a livelihood: officiating at sacrifices, teaching, and accepting gifts from a completely pure person.

[77]From the Brahmin, three Laws are suspended with respect to the Kṣatriya: teaching and officiating at sacrifices, and the third, accepting gifts; [78]the same are suspended also with respect to the Vaiśya—that is the settled rule; for Manu, the Prajāpati, has not prescribed these Laws with respect to these two.

[79]Use of arms and weapons has been prescribed as the livelihood for the Kṣatriya; and trade, animal husbandry, and agriculture for the Vaiśya. Their Law, however, is giving gifts, studying, and offering sacrifices. [80]Among the activities specific to each, the most admirable are: studying the Veda for the Brahmin, protecting the people for a Kṣatriya, and trade alone for the Vaiśya.

Occupations in Times of Adversity

Brahmins [81]When a Brahmin is unable to earn a living by means of the activities specific to him given above, he may live by means of the Kṣatriya Law, for the latter is the one right below him. [82]If it be asked: what happens if he is unable to earn a living by either of these two means? Taking up agriculture or cattle-herding, he should earn a living by the occupation of a Vaiśya.

[83]A Brahmin, or even a Kṣatriya, who earns a living by the Vaiśya occupation, should try his best to avoid agriculture, which involves injury to living beings and dependence on others.* [84]People think that agriculture is something wholesome. Yet it is an occupation condemned by good people; the plow with an iron tip lacerates the ground as well as creatures living in it.

[85]When someone, deprived of livelihood, is forced to abandon this strict adherence to the Law, he may sell goods traded by Vaiśyas to increase his wealth, with the following exceptions. [86]He should avoid condiments of every kind; cooked food; sesame seeds; stones; salt; farm animals; human beings; [87]every type of dyed cloth; cloth made of hemp, flax, or wool even if they are undyed; fruits; roots; medicines; [88]water; weapons; poison; meat; Soma; all types of perfume; milk; honey; curd; ghee; oil; bees-wax;* molasses; Kuśa grass; [89]all wild animals; fanged animals; birds; liquor; indigo; lac; and all one-hoofed animals.+

[90]An individual engaged in agriculture may freely sell pure* sesame seeds that he has cultivated himself, provided they are to be used for purposes relating to the Law and have not been stored for long. [91]If someone uses sesame seeds for purposes other than eating, anointing the body, and giving as a gift, he will become a worm and plunge into the excrement of dogs together with his ancestors.

[92]By selling meat, lac, or salt, a Brahmin falls immediately from his caste; by selling milk, he becomes a Śūdra in three days; [93]but by selling here the other commodities deliberately, a Brahmin is reduced in seven days to the rank of a Vaiśya.

[94]Condiments may be bartered for condiments—but never salt for condiments*—cooked food for uncooked food, and sesame seeds for an equal amount of grain.*

Kṣatriyas [95]A Kṣatriya who has fallen on hard times may earn his living by all the above means; but under no circumstances should he even think of living by a superior occupation. [96]If a man of inferior birth out of greed lives by activities specific to his superiors, the king shall confiscate all his property and promptly send him into exile (8.123 n.). [97]Far better to carry out one's own Law imperfectly than that of someone else's perfectly; for a man who lives according to someone else's Law falls immediately from his caste.

Vaiśyas [98]When a Vaiśya is unable to sustain himself through the Law proper to him, he may live by the occupation of even a Śūdra, refraining, however, from forbidden acts; and he should discontinue it when he is able.

Śūdras [99]When a Śūdra is unable to enter into the service of twice-born men and is faced with the loss of his sons and wife, he may earn a living by the activities of artisans—[100]that is, the activities of artisans and various kinds of crafts the practice of which best serves the twice-born.

Further Occupations for Brahmins [101]A Brahmin firmly committed to his way of life and unwilling to follow the Vaiśya occupations may pursue the following Law when he is languishing through lack of a livelihood. [102]A Brahmin who has fallen on hard times may accept gifts from anybody; that something pure can be sullied is impossible according to the Law. [103]By teaching, officiating at the sacrifices of, and accepting gifts from despicable individuals, Brahmins do not incur any sin, for they are like fire and water.*

[104]When someone facing death eats food given by anyone at all, he remains unsullied by sin, as the sky by mud. [105]Ajīgarta, tormented by hunger, went up to his son to kill him; and he was not tainted with sin, as he was seeking to allay his hunger. [106]Vāmadeva, a man with a clear vision of what accords with and what is against the Law, finding himself in dire straits and trying to save his life, wanted to eat dog's meat, and yet remained unsullied. [107]Bharadvāja, a man of great austerities, when he and his sons were tormented by hunger in a desolate forest, accepted many cows from the carpenter Bṛbu. [108]Viśvāmitra, a man with a clear vision of what accords with and what is against the Law, when he was tormented by hunger, came to eat the rump of a dog, taking it from the hand of a Cāṇḍāla.*

[109]Accepting gifts, officiating at sacrifices, and teaching—among these, accepting gifts is the worst and the most reprehensible for a Brahmin with respect to the hereafter. [110]Officiating at sacrifices and teaching always pertain to those who have undergone consecratory rites, whereas accepting pertains even to a lowest-born Śūdra. [111]A sin committed by teaching or officiating at a sacrifice is removed by soft recitation and oblations, but a sin incurred by accepting a gift is removed only by discarding it and performing ascetic toil. [112]A Brahmin without a livelihood may even glean or pick single grains (4.5 n.) from anywhere; gleaning is superior to accepting gifts, and picking single grains is superior to even that.

[113]When Brahmin bath-graduates are in dire straits and want wares or money, they should petition the king; it he refuses to give, they ought to abandon him.

[114]Unplowed land is less tainted than plowed land; and among a cow, a goat, a sheep, gold, grain, and cooked food, each preceding one is less tainted than each subsequent.

Acquisition of Property [115]Seven means of acquiring wealth are in accordance with the Law: inheritance, finding, purchase, conquest, investment, work, and acceptance of gifts from good people. [116]The ten means of livelihood are: learning, craft, employment, service, cattle-herding, trade, agriculture, fortitude,* begging, and lending on interest.

[117]A Brahmin or a Kṣatriya must never lend money on interest; to pursue activities dictated by the Law, however, he may lend to an evil man at a small interest.*

[118]Even if a Kṣatriya collects 25 per cent as his share (7.130 n.) during a time of adversity, he is freed from that taint by protecting his subject to the best of his ability. [119]The Law specific to him is conquest, and he must not turn back in the face of danger;* when he protects Vaiśyas with his weapons, he may collect a levy in accordance with the Law: [120]from Vaiśyas, a one-sixth share of the grain crop and a duty of one-twentieth on other commodities, with a minimum of 1 Kārṣāpaṇa; and from Śūdras, artisans, and craftsmen, the contribution of their services (7.128–32).

Livelihood of Śūdras [121]If a Śūdra desires to earn a living, he may serve a Kṣatriya, or he may seek to earn a living by serving even a wealthy Vaiśya. [122]He should serve Brahmins for the sake of heaven or for the sake of both, for when he has the name "Brahmin" attached to him,* he has done all there is to do. [123]The service of a Brahmin alone is declared to be the pre-eminent activity of a Śūdra, for whatever other work he may do brings him no reward.

[124]They* must allocate a suitable livelihood for him from their own family resources, taking into account his ability and skill, and the number of his dependents. [125]They should give him leftover food, old clothes, grain that has been cast aside, and the old household items.

[126]A Śūdra is not affected by any sin causing loss of caste, nor is he entitled to any consecretory rite. He has no qualification with regard to the Law, but he is not prohibited from following the Law.* [127]Those who know the Law and yearn to follow it, however, incur no sin and receive praise when they imitate the practices of good men, without reciting any ritual formulas; [128]for a Śūdra obtains this world and the next without enduring disdain to the extent that he imitates the practices of good men without giving way to envy.

[129]Even a capable Śūdra must not accumulate wealth; for when a Śūdra becomes wealthy, he harasses Brahmins.

Conclusion

> [130]I have described above the Laws for the four classes during times of adversity; when they are properly followed, people attain the highest state.
>
> [131]I have described above the entire set of rules pertaining to the Law of the four classes. Next, I will explain the splendid rules pertaining to penance.

CHAPTER ELEVEN

PENANCE

Excursus: Occasions for Giving and Begging

[1]A man seeking* to extend his line; a man preparing to perform a sacrifice; a traveler; a man who has performed the sacrifice at which all his possessions are given away; a man who begs for the sake of his teacher, father, or mother; a student of the Veda; and a sick man—[2]these nine should be known as "bath-graduates," Brahmins who are beggars pursuant to the Law. Gifts must be given to these destitutes in proportion to their eminence in vedic learning.

[3]To these Brahmins food should be given along with the sacrificial fees; to others, it is said, cooked food should be given outside the sacrificial arena.* [4]The king should bestow all sorts of precious gifts on Brahmins learned in the Veda according to their merits, as well as fees for the purpose of sacrifices.

[5]When a married man marries another wife after begging for the expenses, his reward is only sensual pleasure; the resultant offspring belongs to the man who defrayed the expenses.+ [verse 6 of the vulgate is omitted in critical edition]

[7]A man who has sufficient resources to maintain his dependents for three years, or someone who has more than that, is entitled to drink Soma. [8]If a twice-born man who possesses less resources than that drinks Soma, he will not reap its reward, even though he may never have drunk Soma before.* [9]When a man of means gives to outsiders while his own people live in misery, that is counterfeit Law, dripping with honey but poisonous to taste. [10]If a man does anything for his welfare after death to the detriment of his dependents, it will make him unhappy both when he is alive and after he is dead.

[11]While a righteous king is ruling, if a man offering a sacrifice finds that his sacrifice is interrupted for want of a single item, he may, especially if he is a Brahmin, [12]take that article from the house of a Vaiśya who has a large herd of animals but has failed to perform rites or to drink Soma, in order to complete the sacrifice.* [13]He may freely take two or three items from the house of a Śūdra; for a Śūdra has nothing to do with sacrifices. [14]He may also take it without a second thought even from the house of a man who has a hundred cows but has not established his sacred fires or from that of a man who has a thousand cows but has not offered a sacrifice. [15]He may also take it from a man who is always a taker* and never a giver, if he refuses to give it; thus his fame will spread and his merits will increase.

[16]Likewise, when a man has not eaten during six mealtimes (6.19 n.), at the seventh mealtime he may take from someone who performs no rites, keeping to the rule of leaving no provisions for the next day,* [17]and taking it from his threshing floor, field, or house, or from any place where he can find something. If the man questions him, however, he should confess it to him.

[18]A Kṣatriya must never take anything belonging to a Brahmin; if he has no sustenance, however, he may take what belongs to a Dasyu or a man who neglects his rites. [19]When a man takes money from evil persons and gives them to the virtuous, he makes himself a raft and carries them both* to the other side. [20]The wise call the wealth of those devoted to sacrifice the property of gods; the possessions of those who do not offer sacrifice, on the contrary, is called the property of demons.

[21]A righteous king should never punish such a man,* for it is because of the Kṣatriya's foolishness that the Brahmin is languishing with hunger. [22]After finding out who his dependents are and inquiring into his learning and virtue, the king should provide him with provisions for a righteous livelihood from his own house. [23]After providing him with a livelihood, he should protect him in every way, for by protecting him the king receives from him one-sixth of his merits.*

[24]A man who knows the Law should never beg money from a Śūdra to perform a sacrifice; for when the patron of a sacrifice begs in this way, after death he is reborn a Cāṇḍāla. [25]If a Brahmin begs money for a sacrifice and does not devote all of it for that purpose, he will become a Bhāsa-vulture or a crow for one hundred years.

[26]If a man seizes what belongs to a god or a Brahmin out of greed, in the next world that evil man will live on the leftovers of vultures.

Excursus: Miscellaneous Topics

Times of Adversity [27]If he is unable to perform the prescribed animal and Soma sacrifices, he should offer as an expiation the Vaiśvānara oblation at the turn of the year.*

[28]When during a normal time a twice-born follows the Law according to the mode for a time of adversity, he will not receive its reward after death—that is indisputable.* [29]All the gods, the Sādhyas, and the great Brahmin sages, afraid of death during times of adversity, created a substitute for the rule. [30]When someone, though able to follow the principal mode, yet lives according to the secondary mode, that fool will obtain no reward for it after death.

Power of Brahmins [31]A Brahmin who knows the Law shall not inform the king about any matter; solely with his own power should he chastise men who do him harm. [32]Between the king's power and his own, his own power is far more potent. A twice-born, therefore, should punish enemies solely with his own power, [33]and make use of vedic texts of Atharva-Āṅgīrasa—that is indisputable. Clearly, speech is the Brahmin's weapon; with that a twice-born should strike down his enemies.+

[34]A Kṣatriya overcomes his adversities by the power of his arms; a Vaiśya and a Śūdra, by means of wealth; and a Brahmin, through soft recitation and sacrifices. [35]A Brahmin is called the creator, the chastiser, the teacher, and the benefactor; one should never say anything unpleasant to him or use harsh words against him.

Sacrifices [36]A girl, a young woman, an uneducated man, or a fool should never act as the officiant at the daily fire sacrifice, nor should a man who is in great anguish or who has not undergone initiatory consecration; [37]for, when these perform the offering, both they and the person to whom the fire sacrifice belongs fall into hell. Therefore, only a man who has mastered the Veda and is an expert in the vedic rituals should be an officiant.

38When a Brahmin fails to give a horse dedicated to Prajāpati as a sacrificial fee at the rite for establishing the sacred fires in spite of having the resources to do so, he is reduced to the level of one who has not established his sacred fires. 39A man who has mastered his organs and has a spirit of generosity (3.202 n.) may perform other meritorious acts; but under no circumstances should he offer sacrifices here with inadequate sacrificial fees. 40Organs, honor, heaven, life span, fame, offspring and livestock—a sacrifice with inadequate sacrificial fees destroys all these; a man with inadequate resources, therefore, should not offer a sacrifice (11.7–8).+

41If a Brahmin who has established his sacred fires abandons his fires deliberately, he should perform the lunar penance (11.217) for one month; for it is equal to killing a hero.*

42Those who perform their daily fire sacrifice by obtaining money from a Śūdra are considered reprehensible among vedic savants, for they are the officiating priests of Śūdras. 43Stepping with his foot on the heads of these ignorant men who serve the fires of Śūdras, the giver crosses over difficulties.

Justification of Penance

44When a man fails to carry out prescribed acts, performs disapproved acts, and is attached to the sensory objects, he is subject to a penance.

45The wise acknowledge a penance for a sin committed unintentionally; some, on the basis of vedic evidence, admit it even for a deliberately committed sin. 46A sin committed unintentionally is cleansed by vedic recitation, whereas a sin committed deliberately through folly is cleansed with various types of penance. 47When a twice-born, either by fate or by what he did in a previous life, finds himself in a condition requiring the performance of a penance, he should not associate with good people before performing that penance.*+

48Some evil men become disfigured because of the bad deeds committed in this world, and some because of deeds done in a previous life. 49A man who steals gold gets rotten nails; a man who drinks liquor, black teeth; the murderer of a Brahmin, consumption; a man who has sex with his elder's wife, skin disease; 50a slanderer, a smelly nose; an informant, a smelly mouth; a man who steals grain, the loss of a limb; a man who adulterates grain, an excess limb; 51a man who steals food, dyspepsia; a man who steals speech,* smelly breath; a man who steals clothes, leukoderma; and a man who steals horses, lame legs.+ [verse 52 omitted in critical edition] 53In this way, as a result of the remnants of their past deeds,* are born individuals despised by good people: the mentally retarded, the mute, the blind, and the deaf, as well as those who are deformed.

54Therefore, one should always do penances to purify oneself; for individuals whose sins have not been expiated are born with detestable characteristics.

Categories of Sin

Grievous Sins Causing Loss of Caste 55Killing a Brahmin, drinking liquor, stealing,* and having sex with an elder's wife—they call these "grievous sins causing loss of caste"; and so is establishing any links with such individuals (11.181–2).

[56]A lie concerning one's superiority,* a slander that reaches the king's ear, and false accusations against an elder are equal to killing a Brahmin. [57]Abandoning the Veda, reviling the Veda, giving false testimony, killing a friend,* eating unfit food or forbidden food*—these six are equal to drinking liquor. [58]Stealing deposits, men, horses, silver, land, diamonds, or gems, tradition tells us, is equal to stealing gold. [59]Sexual intercourse with uterine sisters, unmarried girls, lowest-born women, and the wives of a friend or son, they say, is equal to sex with an elder's wife.

Secondary Sins Causing Loss of Caste [60]Killing a cow; officiating at the sacrifice of an individual at whose sacrifice one is forbidden to officiate; adultery; selling oneself; forsaking one's teacher, mother, father, vedic recitation, sacred fire, or son; [61]an elder brother permitting a younger brother to marry before him; a younger brother marrying before his older brother (3.171); giving a girl in marriage to or officiating at a sacrifice of either of these; [62]deflowering a virgin; usury; breaking the vow;* selling a reservoir, park, wife, or son; [63]remaining as a Vrātya (2.39); abandoning a relative; giving instruction as a paid teacher; receiving instruction from a paid teacher; selling proscribed commodities; [64]supervising any kind of mine; constructing large equipment; injuring plants; living off one's wife; sorcery; root-witchcraft;* [65]cutting down live trees for firewood; undertaking activities solely for one's own sake; eating reprehensible food; [66]remaining without establishing the sacred fires; acting like a woman;* non-payment of debts; studying fallacious treatises; living a corrupt life; engaging in vices;* [67]stealing grain, base metals, and livestock; sex with women who drink; killing a woman, a Śūdra, a Vaiśya, or a Kṣatriya; and being an infidel—these are secondary sins causing loss of caste.

Further Categories of Sin [68]Making a Brahmin cry, smelling liquor or substances that should not be smelt, cheating, and sexual intercourse with a man—tradition calls these sins that cause exclusion from caste.*

[69]Killing donkeys, horses, camels, deer, elephants, goats, sheep, fish, snakes, or buffaloes—these should be known as sins that cause a man to be of a mixed caste (10.8–45).

[70]Accepting wealth from despicable men, trade, serving a Śūdra, and telling lies—these should be recognized as sins that make a man unworthy of receiving gifts.

[71]Killing worms, insects, or birds; eating anything that has come into contact with liquor; stealing fruits, firewood, or flowers; and lack of steadfastness—these make a man impure.

> [72]Listen now attentively to the specific observances by which all these sins individually enumerated above may be removed.

Penances for Grievous Sins Causing Loss of Caste

Killing a Brahmin [73]A man who has killed a Brahmin should construct a hut and live in the forest for twelve years, eating almsfood and making the head of a corpse his banner, in order to purify himself.

[74]Or, if he so wishes, he may make himself a target for armed men who are cognizant of his state. Or, he may throw himself headlong three times into a blazing fire. [75]Or, he may offer a horse sacrifice, a Svarjit sacrifice, a Gosava sacrifice, an Abhijt sacrifice, a Viśvajit sacrifice, a Trivṛt sacrifice, or an Agniṣṭut sacrifice. [76]Or, to rid himself of the Brahmin's murder, he may walk one hundred leagues* reciting one of the Vedas, eating little, and keeping his organs under control. [77]Or, he may present to a Brahmin learned in the Vedas all his possessions, or wealth sufficient to maintain a person, or else a house with furniture. [78]Or, he may walk upstream along the Sarasvatī,* subsisting on sacrificial food. Or, he may recite three times softly one Collection of the Veda, while limiting his food. [79]Or, after getting his hair shaved, he may live in the outskirts of the village, in a cowshed, in a hermitage, or at the foot of a tree, taking pleasure in doing what is beneficial to cows and Brahmins. [80]Or, he may duly give up his life for the sake of a Brahmin or a cow; one who protects a cow or Brahmin is freed from the murder of a Brahmin. [81]Or, he becomes freed from it by fighting at least three times in defense of a Brahmin, by recovering all the property of a Brahmin, or by losing his life for the sake of a Brahmin.

[82]Thus always remaining steadfast in his vow, collected in mind, and chaste, he rids himself of the Brahmin's murder at the end of the twelfth year.*

[83]Or, he is freed from his sin by proclaiming it in a gathering of the gods of earth and the gods of men and participating at the bath concluding a horse sacrifice.* [84]The Brahmin is said to be the root of the Law, and the Kṣatriya its crest; therefore, by broadcasting a sin at a gathering of theirs, he becomes purified. [85]By his very origin, a Brahmin is a deity even for the gods and the authoritative source of knowledge for the world; the Veda clearly is the reason for this. [86]When even three of them who know the Veda declare an expiation for sins, it is sufficient for their purification;* for the speech of the learned is a means of purification.

[87]By resorting to any one of the above procedures with a collected mind, a Brahmin will rid himself of the sin of killing a Brahmin by means of his self-control.

[88]One must perform the same observance for killing a fetus whose sex cannot be identified, a Kṣatriya or a Vaiśya who is engaged in a sacrifice, or a woman soon after her menstrual period;* [89]for bearing false testimony; for assailing an elder; for stealing a deposit; and for killing a woman or a friend.

[90]This purification is enjoined for killing a Brahmin unintentionally; for killing a Brahmin deliberately, there is no prescribed expiation.

Drinking Liquor [91]If a twice-born man in his folly drinks liquor, he should drink boiling-hot liquor; when his body is scalded by it, he will be released from that sin. [92]Or, he may drink boiling-hot cow's urine, water, milk, ghee, or watery cow dung until he dies. [93]Or, he may eat only broken grain or oil-cake once a day during the night for a full year, wearing a garment of hair, keeping his hair matted, and carrying a banner,* in order to remove the guilt of drinking liquor.

[94]Liquor is clearly the filth* of various grains; sin is also called filth. Therefore, Brahmins, Kṣatriyas, and Vaiśyas must not drink liquor. [95]It should be understood that there are three kinds of liquor: one made from molasses, another from ground grain, and a third from honey. Just as drinking one of them is forbidden to Brahmins, so are all.* [96]Intoxicants, meat, liquor, and spirits* are the food of demons and fiends;

they must not be consumed by a Brahmin, who eats the oblations to the gods. [97]When a Brahmin is intoxicated, he may tumble into filth, blabber vedic texts,* or do other improper things. [98]If the *brahman** resident in a man's body is drenched with liquor even once, his Brahmin nature departs from him and he sinks to the level of a Śūdra.

> [99]I have described above the various expiations for drinking liquor. Next, I will explain the expiation for stealing gold.

Stealing Gold [100]A Brahmin who has stolen gold should go up to the king, proclaim his deed, and say: "Lord, punish me!" [101]Taking the pestle, the king himself should strike him once. A thief is purified by being put to death or, if he is a Brahmin, solely by ascetic toil.*

[102]If a twice-born wants to rid himself of the sin of stealing gold by means of ascetic toil, however, he should carry out the observance prescribed for killing a Brahmin, living in the wilderness and dressed in tree bark (6.6 n.).

> [103]A twice-born should eliminate the sin resulting from stealing by means of the above observances. The sin of having sexual intercourse with an elder's wife, on the other hand, he should remove by means of the following observances.

Sex with an Elder's Wife [104]A man who had sex with an elder's wife should proclaim his crime and lie down on a heated iron bed, or embrace a red-hot metal cylinder;* he is purified by death. [105]Or, he may cut off his penis and testicles by himself, hold them in his cupped hands, and walk straight towards the south-west until he falls down dead. [106]Or, he may perform the Prājāpatya penance (11.212) for one year with a collected mind, carrying a bed-post, dressed in tree bark (6.6 n.), wearing a long beard, and living in a desolate forest. [107]Or, he may perform the lunar penance (11.217) for three months, keeping his organs under control and subsisting on sacrificial food or barley gruel, so as to remove the sin of sexual intercourse with an elder's wife.

> [108]Men guilty of a grievous sin causing loss of caste should eliminate their sin by means of the above observances, but men guilty of a secondary sin causing loss of caste should do so by means of the various observances given below.

Penances for Secondary Sins Causing Loss of Caste

Killing a Cow [109]A man guilty of a secondary sin causing loss of caste by killing a cow should drink barley gruel* for a month and live in a cow pen with his hair shaved and wrapped in the skin of that cow. [110]During two months,* he should eat a small amount of food without artificial salt at every fourth mealtime (6.19 n.), bathing with cow's urine, and keeping his organs under control. [111]During the day, he should follow those cows,* remain standing, and inhale their dust; at night, after attending to them and paying them homage, he should remain seated on his haunches. [112]When they stand, he should stand behind them; when they walk, he should also walk behind them; when they sit down, he should likewise sit down, self-controlled and free from rancor.* [113]When a cow is sick, is threatened by dangers from thieves, tigers, and the like, has fallen down, or has got stuck in mud, he should free her with all his strength.* [114]When it is hot, raining, or cold, or when the wind is blowing strong, he must never find shelter for himself without first providing it for the cow to the best of his ability. [115]When a cow is eating from his own or another's house, field, or threshing floor, or when the calf is drinking milk, he must not inform anybody of it.

[116]When a man who has killed a cow follows cows in this manner, in three months he rids himself of the sin resulting from killing a cow. [117]After he has duly completed this observance, furthermore, he should give ten cows along with a bull or, if that is impossible, all his possessions to those who know the Veda.

Other Secondary Sins [118]The very same observance should be performed by twice-born men who commit any secondary sin causing loss of caste, with the exception of a vedic student who has broken his vow of chastity, in order to purify themselves; alternatively, they may perform the lunar penance (11.217).

Student Breaking the Vow of Chastity [119]A vedic student who has broken his vow of chastity should offer at night a one-eyed donkey to Nirṛti at a crossroads, employing the ritual procedure of a cooked oblation.*

[120]After offering the oblations in the fire according to rule, he should finally offer oblations of ghee to Wind, Indra, Teacher, and Fire, reciting the verse: "May the Maruts. . . ." [121]Vedic savants who know the Law declare that when a twice-born votary ejaculates his semen intentionally he breaks his vow. [122]When a votary breaks his vow of chastity, the vedic energy within him enters these four: Wind, Indra, Teacher, and Fire.* [123]When he has committed this sin, he should wear the skin of a donkey and beg food from seven houses, proclaiming his deed. [124]Subsisting on the almsfood obtained from them once a day and bathing three times a day, he is purified in a year.

Penances for the Remaining Categories of Sins

[125]Someone who has committed any of the acts that cause exclusion from caste (11.68) should perform a Sāntapana penance (11.213) if he did it deliberately, and a Prājāpatya penance (11.212) if he did it inadvertently.

[126]For committing acts that cause a person to be of a mixed caste or that make a person unworthy of receiving gifts (11.69–70), the purification is to perform the lunar penance (11.217) for one month, and for those that make a person impure (11.71), the purification is to drink hot barley gruel for three days.

Excursus: Penances for Injury to Living Beings

Homicide [127]One-fourth the penance for the murder of a Brahmin is prescribed by tradition for the murder of a Kṣatriya; one-eighth for the murder of a virtuous* Vaiśya; and one-sixteenth for the murder of a Śūdra.

[128]If a Brahmin kills a Kṣatriya unintentionally, however, he should give one thousand cows and a bull to purify himself.* [129]Or, he may perform during three years

the observance prescribed for killing a Brahmin, keeping himself controlled, wearing matted hair, living far away from the village, and making his home at the foot of a tree. [130]A Brahmin who kills a virtuous Vaiśya should perform the same observance for one year, or give one hundred cows along with a bull. [131]One who kills a Śūdra should perform the same vow completely for six months, or give ten white cows along with a bull to a Brahmin.

Killing Animals [132]For killing a cat, a mongoose, a blue jay, a frog, a dog, a monitor lizard, an owl, or a crow, a man should perform the observance for killing a Śūdra. [133]Alternatively, he may drink milk for three days, or walk a distance of one league (11.76 n.), or bathe in a river, or recite softly the hymn addressed to the waters (8.106 n.).

[134]For killing a snake, a Brahmin should give an iron spade; for killing a castrate,* a load of straw and a Māṣa of lead; [135]for killing a boar, a pot of ghee; for killing a partridge, a Droṇa of sesame seeds; for killing a parrot, a 2-year-old calf; and for killing a Krauñca crane, a 3-year-old calf. [136]For killing a ruddy goose, a Balāka flamingo, a Baka heron, a peacock, a monkey, a Śyena hawk, or a Bhāsa vulture, he should give a cow to a Brahmin. [137]For killing a horse, he should give a garment; for killing an elephant, five black bulls; for killing a goat or a sheep, a draft ox; and for killing a donkey, a 1-year-old calf. [138]For killing wild animals, he should give a milk cow if they are carnivorous, and a heifer if they are non-carnivorous; for killing a camel, one Kṛṣṇala. [139]For killing a licentious woman belong to any of the four classes, he should give a leather bag, a bow, a goat, and a sheep, respectively.+ [140]If a twice-born is unable to expiate the killing of snakes and the rest by giving gifts, to remove the sin he may perform one arduous penance (11.212) for each.

[141]For killing one thousand creatures with bones or a cart-full of boneless creatures, he should perform the observance for killing a Śūdra. [142]For killing creatures with bones, he should give a little something to a Brahmin; when he kills boneless creatures, he is purified by controlling his breath.

Injuring Vegetation [143]For cutting down fruit trees a person should recite softly one hundred Ṛc verses; so also for cutting down shrubs, vines, creepers, or flowering plants.

[144]For killing any kind of creature growing in food stuffs, condiments, fruits, or flowers, the purification is to consume ghee.

[145]For needlessly tearing out cultivated plants or ones that grow spontaneously in the forest, he should follow a cow for one day, subsisting on milk (11.109–15).

> [146]Through these observances a man should remove all sins he has committed deliberately or inadvertently by causing injury. Listen now to the observances relating to eating food that ought not to be eaten.

Excursus: Penances for Eating Forbidden Food

[147]When someone drinks Vāruṇī liquor inadvertently, he is purified only by undergoing vedic initiation. If he drinks it intentionally, no penance is prescribed; its

penance ends in death—that is the settled rule.* [148]If someone drinks water that has stood in a vessel for keeping liquor or an intoxicant (11.96 n.), he should drink milk boiled with Śaṅkhapuṣpī plant for five days. [149]If he touches, gives, or receives according to rule an intoxicant, or drinks water left over by a Śūdra, he should drink water boiled with Kuśa grass for three days. [150]If a Brahmin who has drunk Soma, however, smells the odor coming from a man who has drunk liquor, he is purified by controlling his breath three times while submerged in water and then consuming ghee. [151]Persons of all three twice-born classes ought to undergo re-initiation if they inadvertently consume urine or excrement, or anything that has come into contact with liquor.

[152]Shaving, girdle, staff, begging, and the vows are dispensed with in the rite of re-initiation of twice-born men.

[153]If someone eats the food of individuals whose food is not to be eaten or the leftovers of a woman or a Śūdra, or consumes forbidden meat,* he should drink barley gruel (11.109 n.) for seven days. [154]When a twice-born drinks anything turned sour or pungent decoctions, even though they may be pure,* he remains ritually impure until it has been excreted.*

[155]If a twice-born consumes the urine or excrement of a village pig, a donkey, a camel, a jackal, a monkey, or a crow, he should perform the lunar penance (11.217). [156]He should perform the same observance after eating dried meat, the Bhauma plant, mushrooms (6.14 n.), the meat of an unknown animal (5.17), or meat from a slaughter house.

[157]The hot-arduous penance (11.215) is the purification for eating the meat of carnivorous animals, pigs, camels, cocks, humans, crows, or donkeys.

[158]If a twice-born student who has not performed the rite of return eats food given at a monthly ancestral rite, he should fast for three days and remain in water for one day. [159]If someone observing the student vow eats honey or meat in any way, he should perform the standard arduous penance (11.212) and complete the remainder of his vow.

[160]If someone eats anything that has become impure from the mouth of a cat, crow, rat, dog, or mongoose, or that has been contaminated by hair or insects, he should drink a decoction of the Brahmasuvarcalā plant.

[161]A person who desires to remain pure should never eat unfit food (5.5 n.); he should vomit any such thing that he has eaten inadvertently or purify himself quickly with the various methods of purification.

> [162]I have described above the various rules pertaining to the observances for eating food that ought not to be eaten. Listen now to the rules pertaining to the observances that remove the sin of theft.

Excursus: Penances for Theft

[163]A Brahmin who deliberately steals grain, cooked food, or money from the house of someone belonging to his own caste is purified by performing the arduous penance (11.212) for one year. [164]For stealing men, women, a field, a house, or water from a well or a tank, tradition prescribes the lunar penance (11.217) as purification.

[165]If he steals articles of little value from the house of someone else, to purify himself he should return the stolen goods and perform the Sāntapana penance (11.213).

[166]For stealing food or delicacies, as also a vehicle, a bed, a seat, flowers, roots, or fruits, the purification consists of consuming the five products of the cow.* [167]For stealing grass, wood, trees, dried food, molasses, clothes, skins, or meat, he should abstain from food for three days. [168]For stealing gems, pearls, coral, copper, silver, iron, brass, or stone, he should subsist on broken grains for twelve days. [169]For stealing cotton, silk, wool, a single-hoofed or double-hoofed animal, a bird, perfume, medicinal herbs, or a rope, he should subsist on milk for three days.

> [170]Through these observances, a twice-born should remove a sin incurred by stealing. The sin incurred by having sex with a woman with whom sex is forbidden, on the other hand, he should remove by means of the following observances.

Excursus: Penances for Sexual Offenses

[171]If a man has sexual intercourse with his uterine sisters, the wives of a friend or son, unmarried girls, or lowest-born women, he should perform the observance prescribed for sex with an elder's wife (11.55).

[172]If he has sex with his sister—the daughter of his father's or mother's sister—or the daughter of his mother's uterine brother, he should perform the lunar penance (11.217).* [173]A wise man must not take these three to be his wife. Marriage with them is forbidden because they are blood relatives, and anyone marrying them proceeds downward (6.35 n.).

[174]If someone ejaculates his semen in non-human females, in a man, in a menstruating woman, in any place other than the vagina, or on water,* he should perform the Sāntapana penance (11.213). [175]If a twice-born has sexual intercourse with a man or a woman in an ox-cart, on water (11.174 n.), or during the day, he should bathe with his clothes on.

[176]If a Brahmin has sex with Cāṇḍāla or lowest-born women, or eats food or accepts presents given by them, he falls from his caste if he does it inadvertently and becomes equal to them if he does it intentionally.

[177]The husband should keep an adulterous wife confined in a single room and make her perform the observance* prescribed for a man who has sex with another man's wife. [178]If she commits adultery again when solicited by a man of the same caste, tradition prescribes an arduous penance (11.212) and a lunar penance (11.217) as the means of her purification.+

[179]The sin that a twice-born commits in a single night by having sex with a Śūdra woman he removes in three years by living on almsfood and performing soft recitations every day.

> [180]I have described above the expiation for all four kinds of sinners.* Listen now to the following expiations for those who associate with outcastes.

Association with Outcastes

[181]When someone associates with an outcaste by officiating at sacrifices, by teaching, and by contracting marriages—but not by occupying the same vehicle or seat or by eating together—in one year he himself becomes an outcaste.*

[182]When a man forges links (2.40 n.) with any one of these outcastes, he should perform the same observance prescribed for that man in order to purify himself of his linkage with him.

Excommunication [183]In the evening of an inauspicious day and in the presence of his blood relations, officiating priests, and teachers, the rite of offering water to the outcaste should be performed by the relatives belonging to his ancestry (5.60 n.) together with his relatives by marriage. [184]A slave woman* should overturn a pot filled with water with her foot, as for a dead man;* and they, along with his relatives by marriage, shall observe a period of impurity for a day and a night. [185]They should suspend conversing or sitting together with him, giving him his inheritance, and even ordinary interaction with him. [186]The rights of primogeniture are also suspended in his case, along with the preemptive property owed to the eldest; the preemptive share of the eldest should go to a younger brother of his with the highest qualities.

Re-admission [187]After he has performed the penance, however, they should bathe in a sacred body of water and, along with him, throw into it a brand-new pot filled with water. [188]After he has thrown that pot in the water and entered his own house, he should participate in all the activities of the relatives just as he had done before.

[189]These same rules should be adhered to also in the case of women who become outcastes; but they should be provided with clothes, food, and drink, and permitted to live near the house.

[190]No one should transact any business with uncleansed sinners; and under no circumstances should anyone abhor those who have been cleansed.*

Excursus: Miscellanea on Sin and Penance

[191]One must not live together with people who have killed children, women, or those who come to them for protection, or with people who are ingrates, even if they have been purified in accordance with the Law.

[192]When any twice-born men have not been taught the Sāvitrī verse according to rule (2.38 n.), one should make them undergo three arduous penances and have them initiated according to rule. [193]One should prescribe the same when twice-born men who have followed wrong occupations or neglected the Veda seek to perform a penance.

[194]When Brahmins have acquired wealth through a reprehensible activity, they are purified by giving away that wealth and by engaging in soft recitation and ascetic toil. [195]A man is freed from the sin of accepting gifts from a bad individual by softly reciting the Sāvitrī verse three thousand times with a collected mind and by subsisting on milk for a month while remaining in a cow pen. [196]When that man, emaciated by the fast, returns from the cow pen and remains bowing down, they should ask him: "Friend, do you seek equality?" [197]Saying "Truly" to the Brahmins, he should scatter some grass for the cows. At that place made holy by the cows,* they should perform his re-admission.

[198]If someone officiates at a sacrifice of Vrātyas (2.39), performs the funeral of outsiders, or carries out a rite of sorcery or an Ahīna sacrifice, he is purified by doing an arduous penance (11.212) three times.

[199]When a twice-born has forsaken someone who has come to him for protection or has misused* the Veda, he removes that sin by subsisting on barley for one year.

[200]When a man has been bitten by a dog, a jackal, a donkey, a carnivorous animal of the village, a man, a horse, a camel, or a pig, he is purified by controlling his breath.

[201]Eating at every sixth mealtime (6.19 n.) for one month, reciting a Vedic Collection, offering daily a Śākalā oblation—these are the means of purification for individuals alongside whom it is unfit to eat.

[202]When a Brahmin deliberately gets onto a camel-cart or a donkey-cart, he is purified by bathing naked and controlling his breath. [203]If someone in distress discharges his bodily waste either without water or in water,* he is purified by bathing with his clothes on outside the village and then touching a cow.

[204]For neglecting the daily rites prescribed by the Veda and for breaking the vow of a bath-graduate, the penance is fasting. [205]When someone says "Huṃ"* to a Brahmin or addresses a superior as "you,"* he should bathe, fast the rest of the day, and placate that person by paying him obeisance. [206]If he strikes such a man with even a blade of grass, throttles his neck with a cloth, or defeats him in an argument, he should placate him by prostrating himself on the ground. [207]By wanting to hurt a Brahmin, a man goes to hell—if he threatens him, for one hundred years; if he strikes him, for one thousand years. [208]As many particles of dust the blood of a twice-born lumps together, for so many thousands of years will the man who spilled it live in hell (4.168). [209]For threatening, he should perform an arduous penance (11.212); for striking, a very arduous penance (11.214); and for spilling a Brahmin's blood, both an arduous and a very arduous penance.

[210]For the removal of sins for which no expiation has been specified, one should fix a penance after taking into consideration both the type of sin and the strength of the sinner.

> [211]I will describe to you the means whereby a human being may
> remove sins, means employed by gods, seers, and ancestors.

Types of Generic Penance [212]A twice-born practicing the *Prājāpatya* penance should eat in the morning for three days and in the evening for three days, eat what is received unasked for three days, and abstain from food during the final three days.

[213]Subsisting on cows's urine, cow dung, milk, curd, ghee, and water boiled with Kuśa grass, and fasting during one day*—tradition calls this the *Sāntapana* penance.

[214]A twice-born practicing the *Atikṛcchra* (very arduous) penance should eat as before (11.212) one mouthful a day during the three three-day periods and fast during the final three days.

[215]A Brahmin practicing the *Taptakṛcchra* (hot-arduous) penance should drink hot water, hot milk, hot ghee, and hot air during each three-day period and bathe once with a collected mind.

[216]When a man, controlled and vigilant, abstains from food for twelve days, it is called the *Parāka* penance, which removes all sins.

[217]He should decrease his food by one rice-ball a day during the dark fortnight and increase it likewise during the bright fortnight, bathing three times a day—

tradition calls this *Cāndrāyaṇa* (the lunar penance). [218]This same procedure in its entirety should be followed when a man, with his mind controlled, performs the lunar observance with its middle shaped like a barley corn, beginning it on the first day of the bright fortnight.*

[219]A man practicing the lunar penance of ascetics should eat each day at noon eight rice-balls from the sacrificial oblation, controlling his self. [220]A Brahmin should eat four rice-balls in the morning with a collected mind and four after sunset—tradition calls this the lunar penance of children.

[221]If a man eats thrice eighty rice-balls from the sacrificial oblation in any manner whatsoever during one month with a collected mind, he obtains residence in the same world as the Moon.

[222]This observance was practiced by the Rudras, the Ādityas, the Vasus, and the Maruts, along with the great seers, to free themselves from all evil.

Observances by the Penitent [223]He should offer a burnt oblation every day by himself, reciting the Great Calls; and he should practice abstention from injuring, truthfulness, abstention from anger, and honesty. [224]He should enter water with his clothes three times during the day and three times during the night, and under no circumstance may he speak with women, Śūdras, or outcastes. [225]He must remain standing during the day and seated at night or, if he is unable, lie down on the ground (6.22 n.). He must remain chaste and devoted to his vow, paying homage to teachers, gods, and Brahmins. [226]He should recite softly the Sāvitrī verse and the purificatory texts* every day to the best of his ability, remaining diligent in this way with respect to all observances carried out for the purpose of a penance.

[227]By these observances should twice-born persons cleanse themselves of public sins; they may cleanse themselves of secret sins, however, through ritual formulas and burnt offerings.

Four Means of Expiation [228]A sinner is freed from his sin by declaring it publicly, by being contrite, by performing ascetic toil, and by reciting the Veda; during a time of adversity, also by giving gifts.

[229]To the extent a man on his own publicly acknowledges an infraction of the Law he has committed, to that extent is he freed from that infraction, like a snake from his slough.

[230]The more his mind abhors that evil deed, the more his body is freed from that infraction; [231]for when a man is contrite about a sin he has committed, he is freed from that sin. "I will never do so again"*—by this forswearing he is purified. [232]Having thus contemplated in his mind the consequences his actions have on his afterlife, he should always pursue wholesome activities with his thoughts, speech, and body. [233]If a man commits a reprehensible act, whether it is inadvertent or deliberate, he must not commit it a second time if he wants to be freed from it.

[234]If someone's mind is not at ease with respect to a particular act he has committed, he should practice ascetic toil for it until his mind is assuaged.* [235]All happiness here, whether divine or human, has ascetic toil as its root, as its middle, and as its end—so have wise men who saw the Veda declared. [236]Knowledge is the ascetic

toil for a Brahmin; protection, for a Kṣatriya; trade, for a Vaiśya; and service, for a Śūdra. [237]Solely by ascetic toil do well-disciplined seers, subsisting on fruits, roots, and air, observe the three worlds together with their mobile and immobile creatures. [238]Solely by ascetic toil do medicines, antidotes, spells, and the various divine conditions become effective; for ascetic toil is the means by which they become effective.* [239]What is difficult to cross, what is difficult to obtain, what is difficult to enter, what is difficult to do—all that is accomplished by ascetic toil, for it is difficult to prevail over ascetic toil. [240]Persons guilty of a grievous sin causing loss of caste, as also others who have committed misdeeds, are freed from their sins simply by ascetic toil vigorously carried out. [241]Insects, snakes, moths, animals, birds, and immobile creatures attain heaven by the power of ascetic toil. [242]Whatever sin people commit through their mind, word, or body—with ascetic toil as their only wealth, they quickly burn off all that simply by ascetic toil. [243]The denizens of heaven accept the offerings of a Brahmin purified solely by ascetic toil, and they fulfill his desires. [244]Prajāpati, the Lord, created this Treatise solely by ascetic toil; the seers, likewise, obtained the Vedas by ascetic toil. [245]Thus did the gods proclaim this grandeur of ascetic toil, as they observed the sacred origin of this whole world from ascetic toil.+

[246]Reciting the Veda daily to the best of one's ability, performing the great sacrifices, and forbearance quickly destroy sins, even those rising from grievous acts causing loss of caste. [247]As a fire by its energy burns up in an instant a piece of kindling placed in it, so a man who knows the Veda burns up all sins by the fire of his knowledge.+ [verse 248 of the vulgate has been eliminated in the critical edition]

Further Means of Expiation [249]Controlling the breath sixteen times while reciting the syllable OṂ along with the Calls, when it is performed every day, purifies even the murderer of a learned Brahmin (4.208 n.) within one month.

[250]Even a man who has drunk liquor is purified by reciting softly Kutsa's hymn "Burning away our evil . . . ," the triple verse of Vasiṣṭha "To welcome the Dawn . . . ," the Māhitra hymn, and the Śuddhavatī verses.

[251]A man who has stolen gold, on the other hand, becomes instantly stainless by reciting softly the Asyavāmīya hymn and the Śivasaṃkalpa formulas.

[252]A man who has had sex with an elder's wife is freed from his sin by reciting softly the hymns Haviṣpāntīya, "No anxiety, no danger . . . ," and "This, yes, this is my inclination . . . ," and the Puruṣa hymn.

[253]A man who wants to remove grave or slight sins should recite softly during one year the verse "May we remove . . . ," and the verse "Whatever offense. . . ." [254]If a man has accepted a forbidden gift or has eaten reprehensible food, he is purified in three days by reciting softly the Taratsamandī hymn. [255]A man who has committed many sins is purified by reciting the Somāraudra hymn and the three verses "Aryaman . . ." while bathing in a river. [256]A sinner should recite softly the seven verses "Indra . . ." for half a year; but if someone commits a reprehensible act* in the water, he should subsist for a month on almsfood. [257]A twice-born removes even a grave sin by offering oblations of ghee during one year while reciting the Śākalahomīya formulas or by reciting softly the verse "Adoration. . . ."

[258]A man guilty of a grievous sin causing loss of caste should follow cows with a collected mind; he comes purified by subsisting on almsfood and reciting the Pāva-

mānī verses for one year (11.109–17). [259]Or, if a man, being ritually pure, recites three times a Vedic Collection in the wilderness and cleanses himself by means of three Parāka penances, he is freed from all the sins causing loss of caste. [260]If a man, self-controlled, fasts for three days while bathing three times a day and reciting the Aghamarṣaṇa hymn three times, he is freed from all the sins causing loss of caste. [261]As the horse sacrifice, the king of sacrifices, removes all sins, so the Aghamarṣaṇa hymn removes all sins.

[262]Even if he has slaughtered these three worlds and even if he has eaten food of anyone at all, no sin taints a Brahmin who retains the Ṛg-veda in his memory. [263]If a man recites three times with a collected mind the Collection of the Ṛg-veda, the Yajur-veda, or the Sāma-veda, along with the secret texts (2.140 n.), he is freed from all sins. [264]As a clod dissolves quickly when it falls into a large lake; so all sins become submerged in the triple Veda. [265]The Ṛg verses, the primary Yajus formulas,* and the diverse Sāman chants—these should be known as the triple Veda. A man who knows it is one who knows the Veda. [266]The primary tri-syllabic Veda,* upon which the triple Veda is based, is another secret triple Veda. A man who knows it is one who knows the Veda.+

CHAPTER TWELVE

1"You have described this Law for the four classes in its entirety, O Sinless One! Teach us accurately the ultimate consummation of the fruits of actions."

2Bhṛgu, the son of Manu and the very embodiment of the Law, said to those great seers, "Listen to the determination with respect to engagement in action."

ACTION

The Fruits of Action

3Action produces good and bad results and originates from the mind, speech, and the body. Action produces the human conditions—the highest, the middling, and the lowest.

4One should understand that the action of the embodied self—action that in this world is of three kinds, has three bases, and contains ten characteristics—is set in motion by the mind.*

5Coveting the property of others, reflecting on undesirable things in one's mind, and adhering to false doctrines are the three kinds of mental action. 6Harshness, falsehood, slander of every sort, and idle chatter are the four kinds of verbal action. 7Taking what has not been given, unsanctioned killing, and sex with another's wife are given in tradition as the three kinds of bodily action.

8A man experiences the good and bad results of mental actions in his mind alone; those of verbal actions, in his speech; and those of bodily actions, in his body alone.+ 9On account of faults resulting from bodily actions, a man becomes an immobile creature; on account of faults resulting from verbal actions, he becomes a bird or an animal; and on account of faults resulting from mental actions, he becomes a man of the lowest caste.

10The rod of speech, the rod of mind, and the rod of action—a man in whose intellect these are kept under control is said to be "triple-rodded."*+ 11When a man has laid down these rods with respect to all creatures and brought lust and anger under control, he thereby secures success.

The Inner Selves 12The one who makes this body act is called Kṣetrajña, "the knower of the field"; the one who does the actions, on the other hand, the wise call Bhūtātman, "the elemental self." 13Another inner self innate to all embodied beings bears the name Jīva, "individual self," by whom are experienced all the pleasures and pains in succeeding births.*

14These two—Mahat,* "the Great," and Kṣetrajña, "the knower of the field"—united with the elements, remain pervading the one who abides in creatures both great and small.+ [15]From his body innumerable forms stream forth, which constantly set in motion the creatures both great and small.

The Process of Rebirth [16]When evil men die, another firm body is produced for them from the same five elemental particles,* a body designed to suffer torments. [17]After experiencing there the torments of Yama with that body, they merge into those very elemental particles, each into its corresponding particle.*

[18]After paying for the sins resulting from attachment to sensory objects, sins that lead to misery, he is freed from taint and approaches the same two beings of great power.* [19]Unwearied, these two jointly examine his merits and sins, linked to which one secures happiness or suffering here and in the hereafter.

[20]If he acts righteously for the most part and unrighteously to a small degree, enveloped in those very elements, he enjoys happiness in heaven. [21]If, on the other hand, he acts unrighteously for the most part and righteously to a small degree, abandoned by those elements, he suffers the torments of Yama. [22]After enduring the torments of Yama, Jīva, "the individual self," becomes freed from taint and enters those same five elements, each into its corresponding particle.

[23]Seeing with his own intellect those transitions of this Jīva, "the individual self," resulting from righteous and unrighteous conduct, let him always set his mind on righteous conduct.

The Three Attributes [24]One should understand Goodness, Vigor, and Darkness as the three attributes of the body,* attributes by which Mahat, "the Great," remains pervading all these existences completely.

[25]When one of these attributes thoroughly suffuses the body, it makes the embodied self dominant in that attribute. [26]Goodness is knowledge, tradition tells us; Darkness is ignorance; and Vigor is passion and hatred. These are their pervasive forms that inhere in all beings.

[27]Among these—when someone perceives within himself a condition full of joy, a sort of pure and tranquil light, he should recognize it as Goodness; [28]when it is full of pain and causing anguish to himself, he should understand that it is Vigor, irresistible and constantly drawing embodied beings; [29]when it is full of confusion, with an unclear object, unfathomable by argument, and indiscernible, he should recognize it as Darkness.

> [30]I will explain to you completely the fruits arising from all these
> three attributes—the highest, the middling, and the lowest fruits.

[31]Vedic recitation, ascetic toil, knowledge, purification, the control of the organs, righteous activity, and contemplation of the self—these mark the attribute of Goodness. [32]Delight in undertaking activities, resolve,* taking up improper tasks, and constant indulgence in sensual pleasures—these mark the attribute of Vigor. [33]Greed, sloth, lack of resolve, cruelty, infidelity, deviation from proper conduct, habitual begging, and carelessness—these mark the attribute of Darkness.

[34]These, in brief and in the proper order, should be known as the marks of all these three attributes located in the three times. [35]An act about which a man is ashamed

after he has committed it, while he is committing it, and when he is about to commit it—a learned man should recognize all that as the mark of the attribute of Darkness. 36An act by which a man seeks to win wide fame in the world and is not disappointed when he fails to win it—one should recognize it as the mark of the attribute of Vigor. 37What a man seeks to know with all his heart and is not ashamed to perform, at which his inner being rejoices—that is the mark of the attribute of Goodness.

38Pleasure is said to be the mark of Darkness; Profit, of Vigor; and Law, of Goodness (2.224 n.). Each later one is superior to each preceding.

> 39Which of these attributes leads to which types of cyclical existence—I will briefly state them in due order with respect to this entire world.

40Those who possess Goodness become gods; those who possess Vigor become humans; and those who possess Darkness always become animals—that is the threefold course. 41One should recognize, however, that this triple course based on attributes is itself threefold, namely, lowest, middle, and highest, depending on the specific type of action and knowledge within each.

42Immobile creatures, worms and insects, fish, snakes, creeping animals, farm animals, and jackals—these constitute the lowest course related to Darkness. 43Elephants, horses, Śūdras, despised foreigners, lions, tigers, and boars—these constitute the middle course related to Darkness. 44Cāraṇas, Suparṇas, hypocritical men, fiends, and ghouls—these constitute the highest among the courses related to Darkness.

45Jhallas, Mallas, Naṭas (10.22), men who live by vile occupations,* and people addicted to gambling and drinking—these constitute the first course related to Vigor. 46Kings, Kṣatriyas, royal chaplains, and professional debaters and soldiers—these constitute the middle course related to Vigor. 47Gandharvas, Guhyakas, Yakṣas, divine attendants, and all the Apsarases—these constitute the highest among the courses related to Vigor.

48Hermits, ascetics, Brahmins, divine hosts in celestial chariots, asterisms, and Daityas—these constitute the first course related to Goodness. 49Sacrificers, seers, gods, Vedas, celestial lights, years, ancestors, and Sādhyas—these constitute the second course related to Goodness. 50Brahmā, creators of the universe (1.34–7), Law, Mahat (12.14), and the Unmanifest—the wise call this the highest course related to Goodness.

> 51I have declared above everything coming from the three kinds of action—the entire transmigratory cycle affecting all beings, a threefold cycle which contains a further threefold division.

52Vile and ignorant men attain evil transmigratory paths by their attachment to the senses and by their failure to follow the Law.

> 53Which kind of womb this Jīva, the "individual self," attains in due order within this world through which kind of action—listen to all of that.

Sin and Rebirth [54]Those who commit grievous sins causing loss of caste first go to dreadful hells during large spans of years; upon the expiration of that, they reach the following transmigratory states.

[55]A murderer of a Brahmin enters the wombs of a dog, a pig, a donkey, a camel, a cow, a goat, a sheep, a deer, a bird, a Cāṇḍāla, and a Pulkasa.

[56]A Brahmin who drinks liquor enters the wombs of worms, insects, moths, birds that feed on excrement, and vicious animals.

[57]A Brahmin who steals enters thousands of times the wombs of spiders, snakes, lizards, aquatic animals, and vicious ghouls.

[58]A man who has sex with an elder's wife enters hundred of times the wombs of grasses, shrubs, creepers, carnivorous animals, fanged animals, and creatures that commit cruel deeds.

[59]Vicious individuals become carnivorous animals; those who eat forbidden food become worms;* thieves become cannibals; and those who have sex with lowest-born women become ghosts.

[60]A man who forges links with outcastes, has sex with someone else's wife, or steals what belongs to a Brahmin becomes a Brahmin fiend.

[61]A man who steals gems, pearls, corals, or any of the various precious substances out of greed is born among goldsmiths.* [62]By stealing grain, one becomes a rat; by stealing bronze, a ruddy goose; by stealing water, a Plava coot; by stealing honey, a gnat; by stealing milk, a crow; by stealing sweets, a dog; by stealing ghee, a mongoose; [63]by stealing meat, a vulture; by stealing fat, a Madgu cormorant; by stealing oil, a cockroach; by stealing salt, a cricket; by stealing curd, a Balāka flamingo; [64]by stealing silk, a partridge; by stealing linen, a frog; by stealing cotton cloth, a Krauñca crane; by stealing a cow, a monitor lizard; by stealing molasses, a flying fox; [65]by stealing fine perfumes, a muskrat; by stealing leafy vegetables, a peacock; by stealing various kinds of cooked food, a porcupine; by stealing uncooked food, a hedgehog; [66]by stealing fire, a Baka heron; by stealing household utensils, a mason-wasp; by stealing dyed clothes, a francolin partridge; [67]by stealing a deer or an elephant, a wolf; by stealing a horse, a tiger; by stealing fruits or flowers,* a monkey; by stealing a woman, a bear; by stealing water, a cuckoo; by stealing vehicles, a camel; and by stealing farm animals, a goat. [68]If a man steals anything at all belonging to some one else by force or eats an oblation before the offering has been completed, he inevitably becomes an animal.

[69]Women also, when they steal in the above manner, incur guilt; they become the wives of the very same creatures.

[70]When people belonging to the social classes deviate from their respective occupations outside a time of adversity, they go through evil cyclical existences and end up as servants of the Dasyu* people. [71]When a Brahmin deviates, he will become an Ulkāmukha ghost eating vomit; a Kṣatriya will become a Kaṭapūtana ghost eating filth and corpses; [72]a Vaiśya will become a Maitrākṣajyotika ghost feeding on pus; and a Śūdra who deviates from the Law proper to him will become a Cailāśaka ghost.

[73]The more that people addicted to sensual pleasures indulge in sensual pleasures, the more their proclivity to them grows. [74]By repeatedly engaging in these sinful actions, these men of little understanding undergo torments here in various births—[75]tossing about in dreadful hells such as Tāmisra; the hell Asipatravana and the

like; being tied up and cut up; [76]various kinds of torture; being eaten by crows and owls; being burnt by hot sand-gruel; the unbearable tortures of being boiled in vats;* [77]taking birth constantly in evil wombs full of suffering; being assailed by cold and heat; terrors of various kinds; [78]repeated residence in different wombs; being born agonizingly; being wrapped up in painful ways; doing servile work for others;* [79]being separated from relatives and loved ones; having to live in the company of evil people; earning and losing wealth; winning friends and enemies; [80]old age, against which there is no remedy; being assailed by illnesses; various afflictions; and death itself, which is impossible to overcome.

[81]When a man engages in any act with a certain inner disposition, he reaps its fruits with a body corresponding to that disposition.

> [82]I have declared to you above all the fruits arising from actions. Listen now to these rules of action for a Brahmin, rules that secure the supreme good.

Actions Leading to the Supreme Good

[83]Vedic recitation, ascetic toil, knowledge, controlling the senses, refraining from causing injury, and service of the teacher—these are the highest means of securing the supreme good.

[84]Among all these splendid activities, a particular activity has been declared as the best means for a man here to secure the supreme good. [85]Among all these, tradition holds the knowledge of the self to be the highest; it is, indeed, the foremost of all sciences, for by it one attains immortality.*

[86]One should understand that acts prescribed by the Veda are always a more effective means of securing the highest good both here and in the hereafter than the above six activities. [87]All these activities without exception are included within the scheme of the acts prescribed by the Veda, each in proper order within the rules of a corresponding act.

[88]Acts prescribed by the Veda are of two kinds: advancing,* which procures the enhancement of happiness; and arresting,* which procures the supreme good. [89]An action performed to obtain a desire here or in the hereafter is called an "advancing act," whereas an action performed without desire and prompted by knowledge is said to be an "arresting act." [90]By engaging in advancing acts, a man attains equality with the gods; by engaging in arresting acts, on the other hand, he transcends the five elements.

[91]A man who offers sacrifices within himself attains absolute sovereignty when he sees equally himself in all beings and all beings in himself. [92]Leaving behind even the acts prescribed above, a Brahmin should apply himself vigorously to the knowledge of the self, to inner tranquillity, and to vedic recitation. [93]This, indeed, is the consummation of one's existence, especially for a Brahmin; for only by achieving this does a twice-born accomplish all he has to do, and never otherwise.*

[94]The Veda is the eternal eyesight for ancestors, gods, and humans; for vedic teaching is beyond the powers of logic or cognition (1.3 n.)—that is the settled rule. [95]The scriptures that are outside the Veda, as well as every kind of fallacious doctrine—all these bear no fruit after death, for tradition takes them to be founded on Darkness.

[96]All those different from the Veda that spring up and then flounder—they are false and bear no fruit, because they belong to recent times.*

[97]The four social classes, the three worlds, and the four orders of life, the past, the present and the future—all these are individually established* by the Veda. [98]Sound, touch, visible appearance, taste, and, the fifth, smell, are established by the Veda alone;* their origin is according to attribute and action.* [99]The eternal vedic treatise bears all beings; it is the means of success for these creatures; therefore, I consider it supreme.

[100]A man who knows the vedic treatise is entitled to become the chief of the army, the king, the arbiter of punishment, and the ruler of the whole world. [101]As a fire, when it has picked up strength, burns up even green trees, so a man who knows the Veda burns up his taints resulting from action. [102]A man who knows the true meaning of the vedic treatise, in whatever order of life he may live, becomes fit for becoming Brahman while he is still in this world.

[103]Those who rely on books are better than the ignorant; those who carry them in their memory are better than those who simply rely on books; those who understand are better than those who simply carry them in their memory; and those who resolutely follow them are better than those who only understand.

[104]For a Brahmin, ascetic toil and knowledge are the highest means of securing the supreme good; by ascetic toil he destroys impurity and by knowledge he attains immortality.

[105]Perception, inference, and treatises coming from diverse sources—a man who seeks accuracy with respect to the Law must have a complete understanding of these three. [106]The man who scrutinizes the record of the seers* and the teachings of the Law by means of logical reasoning not inconsistent with the vedic treatise—he alone knows the Law, and no one else.

> [107]This is the totality of activities leading to the supreme good as prescribed. The secret doctrine of this Treatise of Manu will now be taught.

Excursus: Secret Teaching

[108]If it be asked: what happens in cases where specific Laws have not been laid down? What "cultured" Brahmins state is the undisputed Law. [109]Those Brahmins who have studied the Veda together with its supplements in accordance with the Law and are knowledgeable in scripture, perception, and inference,* should be recognized as "cultured."

[110]Alternatively, when a legal assembly with a minimum of ten members, or with a minimum of three members firm in their conduct, determines a point of Law, no one must question that Law. [111]A man who knows the three Vedas, a logician, a hermeneut, an etymologist, a specialist in Law, and three individuals belonging to the first three orders of life—these constitute a legal assembly with a minimum of ten members.* [112]A man who knows the *Ṛgveda*, a man who knows the *Yajurveda*, and a man who knows the *Sāmaveda*—these should be recognized as constituting a legal assembly with a minimum of three members for settling doubts regarding the Law.

[113]When even a single Brahmin who knows the Veda determines something as the Law, it should be recognized as the highest Law, and not something uttered by myriads of ignorant men. [114]Even if thousands of men who fail to follow the observances, who are unacquainted with the Veda, and who merely use their caste to earn a living, come together, they do not constitute a legal assembly. [115]When fools enveloped by Darkness declare something as the Law, though they are ignorant of it—that sin, increased a hundredfold, stalk those who declare it.

> [116]I have explained to you above all the best means of securing the
> supreme good. A Brahmin who does not deviate from them obtains
> the highest state.

CONCLUSION

Excursus: Summation

[117]In this manner, the blessed god, desiring to do what is beneficial for the people, revealed to me in its entirety this highest secret of the Law.

[118]With a collected mind, a man should see in the self everything, both the existent and the non-existent; for when he sees everything in the self, he will not turn his mind to what is contrary to the Law. [119]All the deities are simply the self, the whole world abides within the self; for the self gives rise to engagement in action on the part of these embodied beings.

[120]Let him deposit space within his spaces;* the wind within his motion and touch; the highest fire within his digestive organ and eyes; water within his fluids; earth within his physical form; [121]the moon in his mind; directions in his ears; Viṣṇu in his stride; Hari* in his strength; Fire in his speech; Mitra in his organ of evacuation; and Prajāpati in his organ of procreation.

[122]The ruler of all, more minute than even an atom, resplendent like gold, and to be grasped by the sleeping mind—he should know him as the supreme Person. [123]Some call him Fire, some Manu the Prajāpati, others Indra, still others Breath, and yet others the eternal Brahman. [124]This one, pervading all beings by means of the five forms (12.16), makes them go around like a wheel through birth, growth, and death. [125]When a man thus sees by the self all beings as the self, he becomes equal towards all and reaches Brahman, the highest state.

[126]When a twice-born recites this Treatise of Manu proclaimed by Bhr̥gu, he will always follow the proper conduct and obtain whatever state he desires.

NOTES TO THE TRANSLATION

CHAPTER ONE

1.1 Additional verse before verse 1: "To the Self-existent One, to Brahman of boundless energy, I pay homage, as I set out to promulgate the diverse and eternal Laws proclaimed by Manu." This verse is widespread in both the manuscript tradition and among commentators and introduces the narrator's voice explicitly and in the first person, although he appears implicitly in 1.1, 4, 60; 5.1, 3; and in 12.2, where he introduces the three interlocutors within the treatise: the seers, Manu, and Bhṛgu. Govinda identifies the narrator as a pupil of Bhṛgu, whereas Nārāyaṇa, Rāghavānanda, and Rāmacandra think that it is Bhṛgu himself.

1.2 *precisely and in their proper order:* the expression *yathāvad anupūrvaśaḥ* occupying either *pāda-b* or *pāda-c* in introductory verses is common in Manu: see 2.89; 5.57; 7.36; and the similar one in 8.229.

those born in between: namely, the mixed classes dealt with at 10.8–73.

Two additional verses: "Likewise the origin and destruction of the entire mass of creatures: those born from placentas, eggs, warm moisture, and sprouts; as well as the settled decision regarding all practices and rites with respect to time and appropriateness—please tell all of that completely."

1.3 *ordinance* (vidhāna): probably refers to the "treatise" (*śāstra*) on *dharma* that Svayaṃbhū composed and taught to Manu: see 1.58. Commentators give diverse explanations. Medhātithi, followed by Nārāyaṇa, Kullūka, and Rāghavānanda, takes *vidhāna* to be the Veda and interprets *svayaṃbhuvaḥ* as in apposition to *vidhānasya*, giving the verse a strictly Mīmāṃsic interpretation: the Veda is self-existent, therefore eternal and without an author (*apauruṣeya*). Medhātithi gives "vedic injunction" (*vidhi*) as another possible meaning of *vidhāna*. Govinda glosses simply with *śāstra*. Rāmacandra takes *vidhāna* to mean "creation" and to be in apposition to *asya sarvasya* ("of this whole creation"), which is also the interpretation of some scholars cited by Medhātithi in his comments on 1.11. The latter interpretation is doubtful because the question of the seers concerned not the universe but the *dharmas* of social groups.

beyond the powers of cognition: the expression *aprameya* probably has a technical meaning: the contents of this treatise cannot be known through the normal means of knowledge (*pramāṇa*), principally perception and inference. See the very similar expression at 1.5 and 12.94.

1.4 *in the proper manner:* Bühler, following Medhātithi and Kullūka, takes the adverb *samyak* (in *pāda-a*) as qualifying Manu's reply (in *pāda-c*): "replied in the proper manner." I follow Govinda and Rāmacandra. Within *ślokas* generally the each *pāda* tend to be a syntactic unit; unless the context is compelling, therefore, I follow the *pāda* syntax.

1.5 *There was this world:* the initial words *āsīd idam* clearly indicates the beginning of a story (cf. for example, the story of Nala), here the story of creation; my translation seeks to capture this style. Bühler translates more literally: "This (universe) existed in the shape of Darkness. . . ." Commentators note the anomaly of Manu's describing the process of creation when the question related to *dharma*. The answer, I think, lies in the structure of Manu's text. The account of creation ends, as in the Puruṣasūkta (*ṚV* 10.90), with the creation of the four *varṇas* (1.31). If I am right that 1.32–57 is an interpolation (see Introduction, p. 53), then the Creator's composition of the treatise containing the *varṇadharmas* (1.58) is directly related to his creation of the *varṇas*. For a detailed study of the cosmology presented in the first chapter of the *MDh*, see Hacker 1959, 1961; Lane 1981.

pitch-dark: the expression *tamobhūtam* may also be a reference to the cosmic attribute (*guṇa*) of darkness (*tamas*) within Sāṃkhya philosophy (see 12.24–49). There is, however, a clear resonance with the Nāsadīya hymn (*ṚV* 1.129), which also describes the initial state of the cosmos as "darkness hidden by darkness": *tama āsīt tamasā gūḷham*.

1.6 *beginning with the elements:* I take the compound *mahābhūtādi* as qualifying "this world" (*idam.*). Medhātithi, Rāghavānanda, and Rāmacandra read *mahābhūtādivṛttaujāḥ* as a compound (Bahuvrīhi). The translation would then be: "Then the Self-existent Lord, whose power exerts itself upon the elements and the rest, appeared —the Unmanifest manifesting this world and dispelling the darkness." If we follow Medhātithi's reading *avyaktam* for *avyaktaḥ*, the translation would be: ". . . appeared, manifesting this unmanifest world. . . ."

1.7 *beyond the range . . . grasped:* most mss. and commentators read *atīndriyagrāhyaḥ*, taking *atīndriya* ("what is beyond the senses") as *manas*. The translation would then be: "who can be grasped by the mind." Medhātithi gives a further interpretation based on the compound being adverbial (*avyayībhāva*); the meaning being that he is grasped by going beyond the senses, namely, by yogic knowledge. Govinda accepts *atīndriya* as mind, but takes the compound to mean *atīndriyeṇa manasā grahītum aśakyaḥ*, "unable to be grasped by what is beyond senses, i.e., by the mind." The compound then would be *atīndriyāgrāhyaḥ*.

shone forth (udbabhau): commentators give various explanations: Medhātithi: *udbhūtaḥ śarīragrahaṇaṃ kṛtavān*; alternatively, with the normal meaning of shining, *svayaṃprakāśa āsīt*. Govinda: *śarīraṃ jagrāha*. Nārāyaṇa: *āvirbhūtaḥ*. Kullūka: *mahadādikāryarūpatayā prādur babhūva*. Rāghavānanda: *prādur āsīt*. Nandana: *vyakto babhūva*. Rāmacandra: *utpannaḥ*.

1.8 *it was the waters:* for the creation of the world through the golden egg floating on the primordial waters, see *ŚB* 11.1.6.

1.10 *The waters . . . "Nārāyaṇa"*: the three terms indicate three levels of word formation in Sanskrit. "Nara" is the most simple and means "man." "Nārā" is something related to or proceeding from Nara. Finally, Nārāyaṇa is a patronymic derived from Nara, although here derived from Nara and *ayana*, meaning way, sojourn, or refuge: "the sojourn of Nara."

Additional verse: "Nārāyaṇa is higher than the Unmanifest; and the egg came into being from the Unmanifest. These worlds and the earth with its seven continents are within the egg. " In this verse and in verse 11, "unmanifest" (*avyakta*) probably refers to the primordial stuff (*prakṛti*) from which, according to Sāṃkhya cosmology, the manifest creation was produced.

1.10–1 These two verses appear to be either interpolations or a parenthetical remark linking Brahmā with the cosmic waters and with Nārāyaṇa, an epithet associated with Viṣṇu. The beginning of verse 12, "in that egg" (*tasmin aṇḍe*) connects it syntactically with verse 9, which introduced the golden egg.

1.11 *Brahmā:* the sandhi in *brahmeti* makes is difficult to decipher whether the original is the masculine *brahmā* or the neuter *brahman*. Nārāyaṇa clearly takes it as the masculine, others are unclear. Bühler translates the term as "Brahman."

1.12 *full year:* most commentators take *parivatsaram* this to be a simple year, in accordance with *ŚB* 11.1.6.2. Kullūka, however, takes it to be a year of Brahmā (see 1.68–73), and Rāmacandra, 1000 years.

1.13 *place of the waters:* the reference is probably to the Milky Way, which is regarded also as the bright ocean of heaven in vedic cosmology. See Witzel 1984.

1.16 *these six:* the reference is unclear. Nandana sees here a reference to the list given in the preceding two verses. He lists the six as great (self), ego, mind, subtle elements (*tanmātra*), and the organs of cognition and action. Rāghavānanda and Rāmacandra: mind and the five senses. Medhātithi and Kullūka: ego and the five subtle elements. Govinda: great (self) and the five subtle elements. The five elements rising from the mind are given at 1.75–8, which section, however, probably forms part of a later addition (Introduction, p. 53). The exact meaning of "six" remains unclear, but mind and the five elements are the best candidates because they are again referred to in verse 18.

1.19 *seven males:* the term "male" (*puruṣa*), as all commentators acknowledge, is used metaphorically, possibly echoing the image of the body of Puruṣa in the *ṚV* hymn 10.90. The meaning of "seven," once again, is unclear. It probably refers to the six already mentioned, with the addition of the Creator, particles of whose body combines with those six to create the world (verses 16–7).

1.20 *Of these . . . in the series:* the order of the series is: ether, air, fire, water, and earth. The distinctive quality of each is sound, touch, visibility, taste, and smell, respectively. Ether has only the first; air has the first two (its own and that of ether); fire, the first three; water, the first four; and earth, all five. See 1.75–8.

1.21 *stations:* the meaning of the term *saṃsthā* is unclear. Bühler translates "conditions," again with an unclear meaning. Nārāyaṇa takes it to mean the different levels of creature, that some are birds, others trees, etc. Most other commentators take it as referring to the various occupations of castes, such as making pots in the case of potters. Nandana is alone in taking it to mean physical appearances (*rūpāṇi*), gods having one and humans another. Rāmacandra takes it to mean *maryādā*, that is, the boundaries existing within the three worlds. I detect a contrast between "specific activities" (*pṛthak karmāṇi*) of *pāda-b* and "specific stations" (*pṛthak saṃsthāḥ*), and Govinda may be right in seeing ritual obligations in the first and ordinary worldly or professional activities in the second.

1.22 *The Lord . . . sacrifice:* the syntax of the verse is unclear and commentators offer various interpretations. Medhātithi says that *ca* of *pāda-a* should come after *devānām*, and he connects *prāṇinām* with *karmātmanām*, takes the genitive as having the sense of purpose, and interprets the verse to mean: "And for the sake of living beings devoted to rites, the Lord created the group of gods, the subtle group of Sādhyas, and the eternal sacrifice." The meaning of *karmātmanām* is unclear (see its parallel use at 1.53). Many commentators take this to mean that these gods are in some essential way connected with rites. Govinda, however, thinks that it refers to their being a subsidiary element (*aṅga*) of a rite, a very Mīmāṃsic interpretation. Cf. *ĀpDh* 1.11.3 about gods who were originally humans (*manuṣyaprakṛti*).

1.23 *squeezed out:* the term *dudoha* evokes the image of milking a cow. Each Veda is drawn out from each deity, the Ṛgveda from fire, the Yajurveda from the wind, and the Sāmaveda from the sun. This cosmogonic story is found in the *AB* 25.7.

1.25 *he brought forth . . . these creatures:* these words conclude the creation of the physical universe, and they echo nicely the beginning of the story at 1.8.

1.32 I think this second account of creation (1.32–41) is an interpolation. The original discourse on creation ended at verse 31 with the creation of the four *varṇas*. I think in the original text verse 31 was immediately followed by the section on transmission of the *dharmaśāstra* (1.58–60). See Introduction, p. 53.

1.39 *pseudo-humans:* the term *kiṃnara* refers to mythical animals/humans, sometimes depicted as having the body of a man and the head of a horse. The term is also connected to the older *kiṃpuruṣa*, possibly relating to barbarians in the jungle or "wild men." See Smith 1994: 255–6.

Variant reading: "birds of various kind, lions, tigers, boars, predatory animals."

1.42 *here:* the particle *iha* simply means "here," but in different contexts can mean "here, in this world" or "here, in this treatise." Professor Albrecht Wezler in a personal communication expressed his belief that *iha* often implies a reference to the generally accepted view about something, as for example in 1.79 and 2.143, 149, 166. Commentators usually take the term to mean "here, in this world" or "here, in this book," i.e., the treatise of Manu.

1.49 *inner awareness:* for a detailed analysis of the concept of *antaḥsaṃjña*, see Wezler 1987; Schmithausen 1991. In brief, this term is used by our author to explicitly reject another opinion prevalent at the time and expressed in Purāṇic texts that plants lack both external and internal awareness. See also *GDh* 8.2 where the same expression occurs.

1.51 *disappeared . . . with time:* the reference is to the end of time, when the Creator withdraws everything into himself. Most commentators interpret "striking down time with time" as destroying the time of creation with the time of dissolution. These two times are conceived as the times when the Creator is awake and asleep.

1.56 *When . . . bodily frame:* the subject of this verse, as also that of the preceding one, is unclear. Bühler and commentators take it to be the individual human self. Then, these verses would describe the reemergence of individual humans after their dissolution at the end of time. Commentators and Bühler interpret the final *pāda* differently from me: "then he assumes a (new) corporeal frame." This is quite unnecessary, and the verb *vimuñcati* generally means to give up rather than to assume (Doniger 1991, lxv). I think this clause parallels the conclusion of verse 55; in both instances the individual self emerges from or discharges the bodily frame (*mūrti*) of the Creator into which he had been merged.

1.58 *treatise:* clearly a reference to the primordial form of Manu's own treatise, which was introduced at 1.3; see the note to it.

Marīci: he is the first of the ten seers that Manu procreated, listed at 1.35, Bhṛgu being the ninth in the list. They are viewed here as both his sons and his pupils.

1.61 *six further Manus:* in the Indian cosmological tradition, each Kalpa, which is the largest time span and is considered a day of Brahmā, contains 14 units called Manvantaras ("Manu intervals" or epoch), each presided over by a different Manu. There are 14 such epochs within each Kalpa, or a day of Brahmā. This roughly translates into 12,000 divine years or 4,320,000 human years. Within each Manvantara there are other units called Yuga (Age). The seven Manus listed here are the first seven; the other seven are given diverse names in the Purāṇas. See Kane, 1962–75, v: 686–93. The temporal extents of a Kalpa, Manvantara, and Yuga are given by Kane, 1962–75, i: 68–73, 79–80.

1.63 *secured:* commentators take *āpuḥ* (literally, "obtained") to mean "protected" or "governed." There must be an implicit reference here to the image of a king "taking possession of" newly conquered territory; hence the extended meanings of protecting and governing.

1.64 *Muhūrta:* this is the basic division of a 24-hour day. It is 48 minutes long. Kalā, the Indian minute, therefore, is 1.6 minutes; and a Kāṣṭha approximately 0.05 seconds. In legal and ritual literature, however, the term Muhūrta is frequently used with a more generic meaning and refers to a specific time during the day or the night. Auspicious times for significant activities, such as marriage, are also called Muhūrta.

1.66 *For ancestors . . . sleeping:* the day and night are here inverted, as are most things relating to ancestors, the bright constituting the night and the dark the day. The reason is ritual, because offerings to ancestors are offered during the dark half of the month (waning moon) when the ancestors are awake. See 3.277.

1.70 *For each . . . by one:* Tretā: 3,000 years, with twilights of 300 years each; Dvāpara: 2,000 years, with twilights of 200 years each; Kali: 1,000 years, with twilights of 100 years each. The total for all four Ages comes to 12,000 years.

1.71 *These four . . . of the gods:* Medhātithi and most other commentators interpret this verse differently, taking 12,000 not as the sum total of years within four Ages, but as the number of such four-Age periods that constitutes one Age of the gods. This interpretation is rejected, I think rightly, by Kullūka. My interpretation is also supported by verse 79, where 12,000, mentioned without qualification, must be assumed to be years. The confusion is created by the repetition of *etat* in both half-verses. I think the repetition is purely rhetorical: "This, which has been enumerated . . . ; this 12,000–period is called an Age of the gods."

1.81 *four feet:* various identifications are offered. Medhātithi: the four principle priests of a sacrifice, or the four *varṇas* (so also Nandana), or the four *āśramas*, or the four kinds of speech (*ṚV* 1.164.45). He is clearly unable to make up his mind! Medhātithi, as well as Nārāyaṇa, Kullūka, and Rāghavānanda, also take them to be austerity, knowledge, sacrifice, and gift giving mentioned in 1.86. "Four" is clearly a whole and sacred number, and here may also refer to the four feet of an animal, indicating firm footing and stability.

1.82 *By acquiring:* commentators are sharply divided over the interpretation of the term *āgamāt*. Kullūka is right here in seeing a carryover (*anuvṛtti*) of "through unlawful means" (*adharmeṇa*) from the previous verse. Other commentators are off the mark when they take *āgama* to mean either the Veda or a *śāstra*.

theft, falsehood, and fraud: it is possible that Manu intended to ascribe each of these vices to each succeeding Age: theft to Tretā, falsehood to Dvāpara, and fraud to Kali. This is the interpretation offered by Rāmacandra, but Kullūka explicitly rejects it.

1.83 *by a quarter:* note that in Sanskrit both quarter and foot have the same word *pāda*. So, we have a clear parallel between the loss of a foot (Law) and the loss of a quarter of the life span (humans).

1.85 *progressive shortening . . . Age:* all the commentators, as well as Bühler, interpret the compound *yugahrāsānupūrvaśaḥ* to mean "in keeping with the shortening of the Ages." According to this reading, the different *dharmas* for the Ages are caused by the decrease in their length. I think this is less likely. I prefer to connect *hrāsa* ("shortening") with the human life span; indeed, the same term was used with regard to human life in verse 83. According to my reading, the meaning is: "in keeping with the progressive shortening (of the human life span) in each Age." Alternatively, the "shortening" or decrease may have a broader meaning, including the Ages themselves, the human life spans, as well as the feet of *dharma* (cf. 1.81; this being Rāghavānanda's interpretation), each of which diminishes with each succeeding Age. On verse 85, see Lingat 1973, 184.

1.92 *A man . . . purest part:* the reason for the relative impurity of the lower half is given at 5.132. Govinda appears to take both parts of this verse as the words of the Self-existent One.

1.93 *retains the Veda:* the term *dhāraṇa* means both carrying and retaining in memory. This statement is more powerful than it may first appear, because at a time when the Veda did not exist externally in manuscript form it could exist in the world only within the memory of Brahmins who had learnt it. The Brahmin is thus the receptacle of the Veda in the world.

1.96 *those who subsist by intelligence:* the reference here is to higher animals, such as dogs and jackals, who know to take shelter when it rains and to go after food and water. This contrasts with plants, which are *antaḥsaṃjña;* see 1.49 n.

1.97 *made the resolve:* my interpretation of the expression *kṛtabuddhayaḥ* is supported by Govinda and Kullūka. Govinda refers to *saṃkalpa,* i.e., the firm and publicly stated intention to perform a particular rite. Others take the expression to mean persons who have properly understood the Veda. It may also refer to persons whose minds are cultivated. See also 7.30, where *akṛtabuddhi* refer to someone who is irresolute.

Additional half-verse: "There is no being in this world that is higher than those who know Brahman."

1.99 *a ruler . . . of Laws:* the parallel with the birth of a king is obvious. A king is born in a particular region to protect the treasures (property) of a particular people. A Brahmin, on the other hand, rules over all and the treasure he protects is *dharma* itself.

1.101 *The Brahmin . . . people eat:* if the whole world belongs to the Brahmin *de jure*, then whatever he eats cannot but be his own. So, as Medhātithi points out, even when a Brahmin eats someone else's food as a guest, he is actually eating his own food. A principle such as this is invoked as a justification for stealing or taking forcibly the property of Śūdras, or even of other individuals, in order to perform a sacrifice: see 11.11–15. This ideology appears to be based on the principle that property is intended to be sacrificed. Indeed, the transaction between humans giving to the gods in sacrifice and the gods sending rain to produce crops is embedded in vedic thought. Given that Brahmins are closely connected with the offering of sacrifice, they can claim ownership of all property—at least at the level of ideological rhetoric.

1.103 Additional verse given after verse 103, or 104, or 105 in different manuscripts: "A Brahmin who desires heaven should study this Law Treatise constantly, just as he does the Veda."

1.106 Variant reading: "it procures fame and long life."

Two additional verses: "It bestows wealth, fame, long life, merit, heaven, and liberation; retaining the Law Treatise in the memory is equal to retaining the Vedas." "Simply by retaining the Treatise in the mind, a man will not die childless or endure evils in this world, and he will become the equal of good men."

1.107 *In this . . . social classes:* here we have a clear distinction made between *dharma* ("Law") and *ācāra* ("proper conduct" or "normative practice"). It is clear that much of the material in the legal texts is drawn from *ācāra* rather than vedic precept, in spite of the oft-repeated statement that the Veda is the root of the Law; and 1.110 strongly suggests both that *dharma* proceeds from *ācāra* and that this is distinct from what is prescribed in the Veda: see Lariviere 1997b. For a detail discussion of this topic, see Wezler 1999 (especially pp. 101–13). Commentators and translators have taken the three elements here (Law, good/bad qualities of actions, and proper conduct) as three separate items (A and B and C). I think Wezler is correct in taking the last two (qualities of action and proper conduct) as explicating Law (A: B and C). The central position of *ācāra* is reiterated in the subsequent verses. For a similar statement on the centrality of good conduct, see 4.155–6.

1.108 *to this treatise:* the term *asmin* ("in/to this") is taken by most commentators and translators as referring to proper conduct. Although that is the obvious choice as the antecedent, given the proximity, I think that the word refers back to the treatise of Manu, just as it does in verses 107 (and later in verse 118). See also the repeated use of *idam* ("this") to refer to the treatise in verses 102, 103, 104, and 106. Coming immediately after the word *smārta*, this pronoun implies that Manu is the preeminent *smṛti:* see 2.10.

1.114 *Renunciation* (mokṣa), *Retirement* (saṃnyāsa): the Sanskrit term *mokṣa* literally means liberation. Manu, however, attaches a technical meaning to the term, using it as a synonym of renunciation and the fourth order of life dedicated exclusively to the search after personal liberation. The term *mokṣa* has the same meaning when used in the common compound *mokṣadharma*, which is a section of the *MBh* and a distinct topic in medieval legal digests (*nibandha*). Manu makes a clear distinction between this renunciatory asceticism and the life of a vedic retiree, which he designates as *saṃnyāsa* (see 6.86 n.). This term, which is the common word for renunciation in later literature, is never used by Manu with that meaning. Bühler's "(manner of gaining) final emancipation and (of) renouncing the world," and Doniger's "Freedom, and renunciaton" ignore the technical use of these two terms here and in ch. 6. For a more detailed study, see Olivelle 1981.

1.117–8 *Examination of . . . and guilds:* these three topics are not found at the end of the *MDh*, although aspects of these are dealt with in different parts of the treatise. Their absence raises significant questions about the relationship of the synopsis to the text. The synopsis was clearly written at a later date and inserted into the *MDh*; but the lack of these topics suggests the possibility that the author of the synopsis may have been working with a somewhat different text than the extant version of the *MDh*. Note also that most of the *vyavahārapadas* are not listed in the table of contents.

CHAPTER TWO

2.1 *the Law assented to by the heart:* I have taken *pāda-c* as an independent clause. Others take it as a syntactic unit with the preceding; it is the erudite people who assent to the Law in their heart. Taking it as a separate clause, however, makes the Law something that all people acknowledge in their hearts, paralleling the "what is pleasing to oneself" (*ātmatuṣṭi*) of verse 2.6. See also 4.161, 11.234, and 12.35 for the elaboration of the same theme; what offends one's conscience is against the Law.

2.2 This section on desire (2.2–5) is out of place here. Bühler (1886, lxvii) takes it to be spurious. At the very least this section appears to be parenthetical within the larger discourse on the sources of the Law.

motivated by desire: Thieme (1931, 31), commenting on *VaDh* 1.6, takes the expression *akāmātmā* to be not "someone free from desire" but a person who does not act freely and at his own pleasure but in a controlled manner and in accordance with the norms. This would then be synonymous with *niyatātmā*, "a man who is self-controlled." Thieme also thinks that in this context *kāma* should be taken as part of the *trivarga*, the three aims of humans: *dharma, artha, kāma*—Law, Wealth, and Pleasure. In this passage of Manu, however, *kāma* appears to have the clear meaning of desire.

2.3 *Intention is the root of desire:* most commentators, as also Bühler, take the compound *saṃkalpamūlaḥ* as possessive (Bahuvrīhi). I think this is the right interpretation. This is also the understanding in the version given in the *BhP* 7.50: *saṃkalpāj jāyate kāmaḥ*. The word *mūla*, although it can be masculine, is used throughout by Manu as a neuter noun. If it were a dependent determinative (Tatpuruṣa) compound the reading should have been *saṃkalpamūlam*. Only Nandana, who records the reading *mūlam*, takes it as Tatpuruṣa. Doniger's translation "Desire is the very root of the conception of a definite intention" also takes the compound as Tatpuruṣa. See 4.24, where we have a similar Bahuvrīhi in the feminine: *jñānamūlāṃ kriyāṃ;* and 4.12, where we have both a Bahuvrīhi and a Tatpuruṣa.

2.4 *the work of someone who desired it:* Medhātithi, Govinda, and Kullūka take *tat tat* of *pāda-d* as correlatives of *yad yad* of *pāda-c*. This appears to be the natural way to interpret the syntax, and it is followed by Bühler. The translation would then be: "it is the work of desire." I think, however, that the second *tat* forms a Bahuvrīhi compound with *kāmasya* with the meaning "one who has the desire for it." This eliminates the awkwardness of desire actually doing some work, unless Desire is here personified. This awkwardness makes Bühler give a labored translation: "it is (the result of) the impulse of desire." Supporting my view is the nice parallel of *tatkāmasya* of last *pāda* with *akāmasya* of the first *pāda*. Further, the intervening *kiṃcit*, to which *yad yad* relates, makes the case for taking both *tat tat* as correlatives weaker.

2.5 *in them:* the precise antecedent *teṣu* is unclear. Bühler, following Govinda, Kullūka, Rāghavānanda, and Rāmacandra, takes these to be "prescribed duties." Doniger and Dave, following Medhātithi: "desires"; Nārāyaṇa: "sacrifices"; Nandana: "studying the Vedas, and other such activities." The closest antecedent appears to be the activities listed in verse 3: sacrifices, observances, and restrains.

Two additional verses: "When a man, his mind blinded by desire, behaves improperly with regard to objects of desire, he goes to hell and does not reap their rewards [probably of rites]. Optional rites taught in the Veda and traditional texts and carried out according to rule, therefore, advances prosperity in this world and not its opposite."

2.6 *The root . . . oneself:* the first half of this verse parallels *GDh* 1.1–2 (*vedo dharmamūlam; tadvidāṃ ca smṛtiśīle*) and appears to be a versification of the latter. As Bühler (1886, 30) notes, the distinction that commentators seek between "practice" (*śīla*) and "conduct" (*ācāra*) may be misplaced. The two probably mean more or less the same, the first being taken from *GDh* and the latter from other sources, such as *VaDh* 1.5 (*śiṣṭācāra*). Indeed, at 1.12 only four sources are listed with *sadācāra* and without *śīla*. On the close connection between Manu and the *GDh*, see Introduction, p. 44. For further elaboration of "what is pleasing to oneself," which is not simply one's pleasure but rites that give a sense of satisfaction, see 4.161, 11.234; see also 12.35 for similar ideas regarding one's conscience as a guide for what is right and wrong.

2.7 *for it contains all knowledge* (sarvajñānamayo hi saḥ): most commentators and interpreters take the pronoun *saḥ* as referring to the Veda. I think this is correct. Kullūka and Nandana, however, take it as referring to Manu. The translation would then be: "for he embodies all knowledge."

2.8 *all this:* the referent is unclear. Medhātithi: "all that is to be known" (*sarvaṃ jñeyam*); Nārāyaṇa and Rāghavānanda: "treatise of Manu"; Govinda and Kullūka: "all kinds of treatises" (*sarvaṃ śāstrajātam*); Nandana: "Veda and the other sources of Law"; Rāmacandra: "the entire Law" (*sarvaṃ dharmam*). The word *nikhila* clearly resonates with *vedo 'khilaḥ* of verse 6, which lends support to Nandana's interpretation.

2.10 "*Scripture*": it is significant that Manu felt the need to define *śruti*. Bühler (1886, lxvii) takes this to be a sign that this section is a later addition. See, however, 12.95, where Manu speaks about *vedabāhyāḥ śrutayaḥ* ("scriptures outside the Veda"). All this may be a sign that the term *śruti* had not become a synonym of Veda by the time of Manu. Note that the authors of the early *Dharmasūtras* never use *śruti* within the context of the sources of *dharma*. The first to do so is Vasiṣṭha (*VaDh* 1.4).

These two . . . any matter: most mss. and commentators read *sarvārtheṣv amīmāṃsye*, a reading adopted in the critical edition. But a substantial number of mss., as well as the *Bhaviṣya Purāṇa* (7.55), read *sarvārtheṣu mīmāṃsye*. The translation would then be: "These two should be examined in all matters." This reading is strongly defended by Rāghavānanda and follows the common meaning of *mīmāṃsā* as vedic exegesis. The meaning then is this: the principles of vedic exegesis should be applied to these two sources of the Law in every matter. This is an appealing interpretation, even though the manuscript tradition does not support the reading. Could the negative formulation of the next verse have influenced the reading of this? See 12.106 where the use of logical argumentation (*tarka*) is a significant way to determine the Law. The only other occurrence of *mīmāṃsā* in Manu is at 4.224, and there it is used with a positive meaning.

2.11 Variant reading: "these two roots by relying."

2.13 *authority:* the term *pramāṇa* has epistemological implications. Beyond mere authority, it indicates the means of cognition (see 1.3 n.). There are other meanings of knowing the Law, such as observing the conduct of virtuous people (perception); and even logical argument (inference: see 12.106). Among all these means, *śruti*, which falls under "verbal authority" (*śabda*) in the enumeration of *pramāṇas*, is the highest.

2.14–5 *When there . . . a vedic scripture:* here we have a basic principle of vedic exegesis. When two vedic injunctions contradict each other, both are authoritative; such a contradiction gives rise to an option. An example of such an option is given in verse 15. Some vedic passages prescribe the morning fire offering (*agnihotra*) to be performed just before sunrise, and others after sunrise. One has, therefore, the option to follow either rule. A contradiction, however, gives rise to an option only when the two injunctions are of equal force (see *GDh* 1.4). If one of them is weaker (e.g., a traditional text) and the other stronger (e.g., an explicit vedic text), then the stronger prevails. The expression *samayādhyuṣite* is unclear. Bühler, following Kullūka and Rāghavānanda, translates: "when neither sun nor stars are visible." Medhātithi takes it to mean dawn in general and refers to the opinion of some who take it to mean the time of twilight when the night is over but the sun has not yet risen. Nandana takes it as the time when the sun has partially risen (*uditānudite sūrye*). Rāmacandra cites a long passage from Kātyāyana, who defines *samayādhyuṣita* as the time of the morning when stars are invisible but the sun is not yet seen (*tathā ca prātaḥsamaye naṣṭe nakṣatramaṇḍale / ravir yāvan na dṛśyeta samayādhyuṣitaṃ ca tat //*).

Two additional verses : "Sages see the scriptures and remember the traditional texts. Therefore, authoritative persons have promulgated on earth that both these are authoritative. We see transgressions of the Law and violence by eminent persons; when a foolish man of later times sees that and follows it, he will perish." The last verse follows *GDh* 1.3.

2.16 *A man . . . this treatise:* the implication of this rule is to exclude all women, as well as Śūdras and other lower castes. The significant term here is *mantraiḥ* ("with the recitation of vedic formulas"), because women's *saṃskāras* are performed without the recitation of mantras: see 2.66–7.

2.17–23 This section contains elaborations and further classifications of the original concept of Āryāvarta first encountered within the legal tradition in *BDh* 1.2.9 and *VaDh* 1.8–12, and recorded also by Patañjali (on Pāṇini 2.4.10 and 6.3.109). In these sources the extent of the Āryāvarta corresponds to the "middle region" of Manu (1.21), and this region coincides with the natural range of the black buck. The meaning of *brahma* in Brahmāvarta is unclear. Only two commentators explain the term. Nārāyaṇa: *brahmāvartate 'nuvartate yatra*, which leaves the meaning somewhat in doubt; although it probably means the Veda, which would be my first choice also. Nandana glosses with *dharma*.

2.23 *foreigners:* often translated "barbarians," *mleccha* refers to individuals and groups that do not belong to the mainstream of society represented by the four *varṇas* as envisaged by Brahmanical theologians. They include foreigners, as well as tribal and other groups not forming part of the accepted society. Their speech is different (see 10.45), they tend to live in geographically distinct areas (see 2.23), and sometimes they are coupled with Śūdras (12.43). See Parasher 1991.

2.27 *tying of the Muñja-grass cord:* the reference is to vedic initiation (2.36f), at which the tying of the girdle around the boy's waist is a central ritual element (2.43).

2.28 *body is made brāhmic:* all commentators take this to mean that the body is made fit for union with Brahman, all, except Medhātithi, repeating the same gloss: *brahmaprāptiyogyā* ("fit for attaining Brahman"). That this was not a unanimous view is evidenced by Medhātithi, who gives two opinions of other interpreters. One of these takes *brahma* in this expression to be the Veda. The meaning would then be that the man's body is made fit for learning and reciting the Veda, or a fit receptacle for the Veda (see 1.93 n). There is, I think, much to commend this interpretation. The other interpretations are clearly influenced by Vedāntic thinking. Further, it is difficult to see how, within a Vedāntic view, the *body* can be made fit for attaining Brahman! This passage clearly relates to verse 26 that spoke of consecrating or perfecting (*saṃskāra*) the body and must carry a similar meaning. The term *brāhmīya* does not occur elsewhere in Manu.

2.29 *male child:* the specification relates to the phrase "to the accompaniment of vedic formulas" (*mantravat*). For girls, the same ceremony is performed without such formulas (cf. 2.16 n; 2.66). Commentators also note that the specification "male" also excludes a *napuṃsaka*, children of indeterminate sex, such as hermaphrodites.

fed gold, honey, and ghee: clearly, the baby is too young to feed him any of these things. A small mixture is placed within the mouth. Further, gold is obviously not fed to the child. Either a piece of gold is placed in the mouth or, as some commentators explain, the ghee and honey are touched with gold before being placed in the baby's mouth. Some *Gṛhyasūtras* (*ŚāṅkhGṛ* 1.24.3; *PārGṛ* 1.16.4) state that these are fed with a golden spoon or from a golden vessel, while others include gold dust in the mixture (*ĀśGṛ* 1.15.1).

2.31–3 *For a Brahmin . . . for blessing:* Kullūka gives the following examples for the four classes: *śubhaśarmā, balavarmā, vasubhūti, dīnadāsa*. For girls irrespective of class: *yaśodā, devī, suvadanā, maṅgaladevī, subhadrā*.

2.38 *Sāvitrī:* the Sāvitrī verse is frequently used as a metonym for the rite of initiation, the imparting of this verse constituting a central element of it.

sixteenth year: we must assume on the basis of the statement in verse 36 that all ages are counted from conception rather than from birth.

2.40 *vedic links:* these refer to any type of ritual relationships, such as officiating at an initiation or a sacrifice, teaching, studying, and the like.

2.43 *When Muñja . . . Balvaja grass:* the plural *kartavyāḥ* ("they should be made"), according to the commentators, indicates that many girdles are intended. Thus the three substitutes are meant for the three classes, respectively. According to this interpretation, the statement "When Muñja grass is unavailable" must implicitly mean when any of the standard material for the three classes is unavailable. Nārāyaṇa sees *muñja* as elliptical, the full form being *muñjādi* ("Muñja etc."): *muñjādyalābha ity ādipadaṃ luptaṃ draṣṭavyam.*

One should wrap . . . five knots: the Sanskrit is very terse and elliptical. The major problem in interpretation is the first word *trivṛtā* ("threefold"). Most commentators take it as an adjective qualifying *granthinā* ("with a knot"), supported by the fact that both are in the instrumental. Bühler translates: "a single threefold knot." Jha appears to take it separately: "triplicated"; Doniger also: "triple-ply." The connection with the knots appears to make little sense, because the number of possible knots are clearly given. Bühler is forced to give a convoluted explanation: "seems to mean that each of the strings of the girdle shall first be knotted, and the three knots be afterwards tied together in one." The fact that the cord is made combining three strings (Doniger's triple-ply) is already stated in verse 42. I think that in the second half of verse 43 Manu is making a transition from the girdle's manufacture to the way it is worn; hence the mention of the knots. Within this context, *trivṛtā* probably refers to the number of times the cord is wrapped around the waist before tying the knots. This is precisely the meaning given to it by Nārāyaṇa: *sā ca mauñjī triguṇavalitā trivṛtā kaṭau trir veṣṭanena dharyā*. For this custom of wrapping three times, see *ŚaṅkhGṛ* 2.2.1; *ĀpGṛ* 4.10.11. The commentators are unanimous that the number of knots are not specific to the three classes; because the particle *vā* ("or") is used, they see here a simple option, some noting that one should have the number of knots customary in one's own family.

2.44 *twisted upwards:* most commentators take this to mean that the strands are twisted to the right. The Sanskrit *ūrdhva* may, however, mean also the north. Nandana comments that the person places the strands on his left palm and twists them upward with his right palm. Both, however, may be correct, in that the strands are twisted upwards and towards the right of the person performing the task. Doniger's "put on above (the right shoulder)" is off the mark; the discussion here is about the manufacture rather than the manner of wearing; and the term is *vṛta* and not *dhṛta*.

2.49 *placing . . . at the end:* the set formula for requesting almsfood is: "Madam, give food" (*bhavati bhikṣāṃ dehi;* see *BDh* 1.3.16), which is how a Brahmin would say it. A Kṣatriya would say "Give, Madam, food" (*bhikṣāṃ bhavati dehi*) and a Vaiśya, "Give food, Madam" (*bhikṣāṃ dehi bhavati*). The formula implies that it was the housewife who normally distributed food to students and mendicants.

2.51 *without guile:* commentators and translators connect this syntactically with the presentation of the food to the teacher. The translation would then be: "After collecting as much almsfood as he needs, he should present it to his teacher without guile." Medhātithi says that the student should not cover delicious items with inferior ones when he presents the food to the teacher. I think, however, that the expression refers rather to the manner of collecting food; for example, he should not hide any food that may make the donor think he has less food than he actually has. The major reason for this interpretation is that the expression occurs in the same foot of the verse as the other term qualifying begging, namely, "as much as he needs" (*yāvadartham*). In general, each foot of a verse tends to form a single syntactic unit (see 1.4 n.).

2.52 *truth:* the precise meaning of *ṛtam* is unclear. Medhātithi gives three alternatives: truth, sacrifice, and the fruit of sacrifice, i.e., heaven. Nārāyaṇa gives the first two, and the rest of the commentators take it to mean truth. Govinda, however, equates truth with immortality (*amṛta*). There is a slight possibility that the original reading was *amṛtam*, with the elision of the initial vowel due to sandhi; thus *'mṛtam* may have been changed to *ṛtam*. But this reading is not found in any manuscript.

Addtional verse: "For twice-born persons, scriptures prescribe eating in the morning and in the evening; one should not eat in between. This practice is equal to a fire sacrifice."

2.53 *after sipping* (upaspṛśya): Bühler translates: "after performing an ablution"; Doniger: "after he has washed." Both interpretations are wrong. The commentators uniformly take the term to mean sipping water, and they are correct. Here we are dealing not with washing or bathing but with the ritual sipping of water before and after a meal, as described in verse 60. The same term *upaspṛśet* occurs also in verse 58, where the meaning is clear, and Bühler translates it there correctly as sipping. See 3.208 n.

orifices: they are eyes, ears, nostrils, and mouth. For the procedure, see 2.60.

2.56 *eat between meals:* the meaning is that he should not eat between the two main meals taken in the morning and in the evening (see the verse added after 2.52). Medhātithi agrees with this, but gives another possible meaning: one should not eat again after interrupting a meal by getting up. He also cites the view of some who interpret the term *antarā* to mean that a man should hold the plate in the left hand and eat with the right. According to this interpretation, the provision forbids eating food without holding the plate in the left hand.

sullied with remnants: the word *ucchiṣṭa* is a technical term for the state of impurity resulting from the remnants of food attached to lips and fingers after eating. The same term is used for food that remains after someone has eaten (leftovers), which are also impure because they have come into contact with one's saliva. The extended meaning of the term covers also impurities caused by other bodily functions, such as after voiding urine or excrement. See Olivelle 1998b.

2.58 *part of the palm . . . ancestors:* the area of the palm used to pour water into the mouth during sipping bears the technical name *tīrtha,* literally a ford on a river. As a *tīrtha* on a river is where water comes into contact with the body, so the various parts of the palm are the *tīrthas* through which water enters the mouth and the body.

2.59 *beneath these two:* according to the commentators, this is at the bottom of the thumb and the index finger.

2.63 *When the right . . . cord down:* the sacred cord is worn over the left shoulder and under the right arm for rites connected with gods and on most other occasions (see 8.2 n.). To wear it in this manner, one raises the right hand to pass the cord under it. The cord is worn over the right shoulder and under the left arm (a pattern called *prācīnāvīta* involving the raising of the left arm) at ancestral rites, and over the neck like a garland (a pattern called *nivīta*) in rites involving humans, such as sexual intercourse, sacramentary rites, and going to the toilet. Another mode of wearing it ("suspended or tied below") is given in *BDh* 1.8.10. The commentator Govinda explains this as tying it below the navel when engaged in activities such as applying oil on or massaging the body. See *BDh* 1.8.7–9; *TS* 2.5.11.1; Kane 1962–75, ii. 287–97.

2.65 *shaving ceremony* (keśānta): this rite of passage relates to the first shaving of the beard of a teenage boy. The rite is also known by the name Godāna ("gift of cow"), because it involved giving a cow to the teacher.

2.67 *For females . . . fires:* this verse contradicts the previous one where all the consecratory rites (*saṃskāra*) were supposed to be performed also for women. Similar contradictions abound in Manu (see Introduction, pp. 29–36). On the initiation of women, see Kane 1962–75, ii. 293–95; Schmidt 1987, 25.

Two additional verses: "He should perform these together with her: cooking the vedic oblation, establishing the sacred fires, offering all the sacrifices, and acts such as eating the oblations. Every day the wife should tend the sacred fire, carrying it out in the evening, and offer the daily offering of Bali."

2.70 *dress in light clothing:* commentators give diverse interpretations. Medhātithi: *dhautavāsāḥ,* "washed clothes"; Nārāyaṇa: *svalpavāsāḥ,* "minimal clothing"; Govinda: *asthūlavasanaḥ,* "not heavy clothing," which is given by Medhātithi as an alternate interpretation, the reason offered being that when the pupil is being punished, heavy clothes will prevent him from feeling the pain! Kullūka and Rāghavānanda: *pavitravāsāḥ,* "clean clothes"; Nandana: *anulbaṇavastraḥ,* "not excessive clothing."

2.73 *When he . . . should cease:* for the reading adopted in the critical edition and my interpretation of this verse, see my note to this verse in the critical edition. I take "Teach, Sir" to be uttered by the pupil and "Stop" to be uttered by the teacher. That the first is said by the pupil is supported by *TU* 3.1–6; *GobhGṛ* 2.10.38; Oldenberg 1886–92, I: 67 n. The ambiguity of the Sanskrit verb *adhīhi,* which means "recite," makes it possible to ascribe it to the teacher. Bühler, following the reading of the vulgate, translates: "But to him who is about to begin studying, the teacher, always unwearied, must say, Ho, recite!" For the term *bho,* see 2.124.

2.75 *cleansed . . . grass:* these are blades of grass carried in the hands or twisted around the fingers to form a purificatory ring. The *GDh* (1.48) specifies that the various organs are touched with blades of Darbha grass. Medhātithi, Nārāyaṇa, and Govinda agree with this, whereas Kullūka and Rāghavānanda take this to mean carrying the blades in the hands. The Sanskrit *pavitra* can also refer to various purificatory texts and rites (see 11.226), and Nandana prefers this meaning.

2.76–7 *The phonemes . . . Sāvitrī verse:* these phonemes are the constituent parts of the syllable OṂ, the initial "o" being dissolved into the two simple vowels "a" and "u." The three terms for the three spheres of the cosmos are referred collectively as *vyāhṛti* (call or utterance) and are considered sacred sounds. Each of these triads, as well as each foot of the three-footed Sāvitrī verse, is viewed as the essence squeezed out (the Sanskrit evokes the milking of a cow) from each of the three Vedas, respectively. See 1.23. Variant reading: "milked these from the three Vedas."

2.80 *timely . . . rite:* Medhātithi and Govinda take this as a reference to initiation (see 2.38–40), and other commentators as referring to such daily and obligatory rites as the fire sacrifice and twilight worship. I prefer the latter interpretation, because the context is the recitation of the Sāvitrī rather than its initial imparting at initiation.

2.82 *highest Brahman:* here we have a subtle, and in Sanskrit imperceptible, transition from *brahman* as Veda (in verse 81) to *brahman* as the absolute being or state (in verses 82–4).

2.84 *Offering ghee . . . standing:* the reference is to a twofold division of rites within the vedic exegetical tradition. The term *juhoti* refers specifically to the offering of ghee in the sacred fire (*homa*) carried out while the priest is seated on his haunches. The term *yajati* refers to the offering of other substances in the fire (*yāga*) while the priest remains standing.

The syllable . . . imperishable: here again we have a play on the double meaning of the Sanskrit term *akṣara*, which can mean both a syllable and something imperishable. The *akṣara* par excellence in both senses is the syllable OṂ, which is both a syllable and the absolute Brahman.

2.86 *four types of cooked oblations:* probably four of the five great sacrifices that involve cooked food: offerings to gods, ancestors, beings, and human guests (3.70).

2.87 *Maitra:* most commentators take this term in its usual sense to mean a man who does good to all and harms none; all translators follow this interpretation. Bühler: "he who befriends (all creatures) is declared (to be) a (true) Brāhmaṇa." Rāghavānanda, however, proposes an interesting interpretation: *mitra* (friend and the deity Mitra) is the sun, and *maitra* is a man devoted to the sun, i.e., to the Sāvitrī verse, whose deity is the sun. Thus *maitra* means a man who constantly recites the Sāvitrī, an interpretation fitting the context, which is an eulogy of this verse. Especially in view of the fact that this verse probably was followed immediately by verse 101 (on the possibility that verses 88–100 were interpolations, see Introduction, p. 54), this interpretation of *maitra* fits nicely with the discussion of the twilight worship of the sun in verse 101.

2.96 Variant reading: "Strongly attached as these sense organs are . . ."

2.97 *gifts:* some commentators take the term *tyāgāḥ* to mean renunciation (*saṃnyāsadharmāḥ*). Medhātithi takes it as either gifts or giving up even permissible things, such as honey and meat.

constraints: for the kinds of observances falling under the rubric *niyama*, see 2.175–7, and 4.204 n.

2.99 *foot of a skin:* the simile is a water bag made of an animal skin. If any one of its feet is not properly sealed, water will spill through it, just as one's wisdom will slip away through a single organ that is not properly mastered.

2.101 Variant reading: "he should remain always seated . . ."

2.104 *ritual of daily recitation* (*naityakaṃ vidhim*, literally, "the daily ritual"): the term *naityaka* is used here by Manu, however, with specific reference to the daily vedic recitation. See, for example, its use with this meaning in verses 106; and in verse 105 it qualifies *svādhyāya* ("vedic recitation").

controlled: Medhātithi, Nārāyaṇa, and Govinda gloss *niyataḥ* with *śuciḥ*, "pure." In verse 107, however, we see both these terms used, indicating that they are not used as synonyms by Manu; see also 3.258.

2.105 *Vedic Supplements:* the six such supplementary sciences: pronunciation (*śikṣā*), meter (*chandas*), grammar (*vyākaraṇa*), astronomy (*jyotiṣa*), and ritual (*kalpa*)

2.106 *The daily . . . Vaṣaṭ:* this verse is a very brief allusion to a long passage in the *ŚB* 11.5.6.8 and cited in *ĀpDh* 1.12.3, where this theme is fully developed. A sacrificial session (*sattra*) is a sacrifice where the officiating priests and the patrons are the same individuals and which lasts a long period of time.

2.107 *every single day:* Manu may be using the word *nityam* intentionally, paralleling *naityaka* (see 1.104 n.), which is used to qualify *svādhyāya* ("vedic recitation").

Variant reading: "When a twice-born, after controlling himself, performs . . ."

2.108 *rite of returning home:* the rite of *samāvartana,* which includes a ritual bath, concludes the period of studentship (see 2.245; 3.4). For a description of this rite, see Kane 1962–75, ii: 405–15; Heesterman 1968. This verse appears to signal the transition from the duties of the student to his relationship to his teacher.

2.109 *an honest person:* the term *śuciḥ* could also mean a pure person (Olivelle 1998b). Given that all the terms in this verse refer to internal dispositions or relationships to the teacher, I have opted for honesty.

someone close to him: the term *āptaḥ* indicates a close, often blood, relationship. See 5.101; 11.171.

one who is his own: commentators offer various interpretations of the term *svaḥ*. Medhātithi and Rāmacandra: a son; Medhātithi and Govinda: a boy one has initiated; Nārāyaṇa, Kullūka, Rāghavānanda and Nandana: a relative.

2.110 *idiot:* all the commentators interpret the term *jaḍa* to mean a man who cannot speak (*mūka*).

2.114 Variant reading: "Vedic knowledge said thus to the Brahmin . . ."

2.114–5 *Vedic knowledge . . . treasure:* these two verses appear to be modifications of the two verses in the Triṣṭubh meter in *VaDh* 2.8–9. See also *Nirukta* 2.4.

2.117 *greet first:* most commentators take this to mean that the student should greet the teacher before he greets anyone else. Medhātithi and Govinda, however, interpret "first" (*pūrvam*) to mean that the student should greet the teacher before the teacher greets him.

2.120 *for when an older . . . retrieves them:* this was probably a common proverbial saying. It is cited also by Patañjali on Pāṇini 6.1.84.

2.123 *When greeting . . . simply say "I":* Medhātithi and Govinda explain that this refers to people who do not know Sanskrit and are thus unable to grasp the meaning of an elaborate greeting. In such cases, one simply says "I greet you" (*abhivādaye 'ham*), the word "I" (*aham*) in the verse being an allusion to this form of greeting.

2.124 *bho:* this is an interjection commonly used in addressing someone. It is especially common in greetings between teacher and pupil, both using this particle to address each other. It connotes both respect ("Sir") and endearment ("my dear"). It is viewed as containing the essence of all names, because it can be used in place of any proper name. Govinda gives the full form of such a greeting: *bhadranāmāham asmi bho,* "I am named Bhadra, *bho.*"

2.125 *he should say . . . prolate the previous syllable:* there has been a lot of controversy regarding both the exact reading of this verse and its interpretation. For a detailed explanation, see my note to this verse in the critical edition.

2.131 *teacher's wife* (gurupatnī): I am not certain whether *guru* here refers specifically to the teacher (see Note on the Trans., p. 69). In verse 142 *guru* is defined as the father. In verse 133, however, we have a clear comparison with the mother, and it seems unlikely that Manu would have used this roundabout way to refer to his own mother or stepmother.

2.132 *paternal and maternal relatives:* the distinction between *jñāti* and *sambandhin* (also *bāndhava*) is not always clear. Sometimes the terms refer in general to relatives; but when they are used together the terms appear to have more specific meanings, the former referring to paternal relatives and the latter to maternal relatives. The latter term can also refer to relatives by marriage. See 4.179 n., 5.74, and Note on the Trans., p. 69.

2.137 Addtional verse: "Even a Śūdra who follows the prescribed Law and practices the Law every day ought to be honored always by people of all classes."

2.140 *secret texts:* the term *rahasya* probably refers to the Upaniṣads and perhaps also to the Āraṇyakas.

2.142 *"Elder"* (guru): the term here is clearly applied to one's own father. For other meanings of this term, see Note on the Trans., p. 69.

2.144 Variant reading; "who pierces both his ears . . ."

2.145 *greater:* the Sanskrit term *gaurava,* literally "heaviness" or "gravitas," also refers to the state of being a *guru* ("elder"). At one level then, the meaning is that the mother is a thousand times more a *guru* than the father, who was presented as the *guru* par excellence in verse 142.

2.158 According to an interesting variant reading in the parallel passage in *BhP*, the translation is: "As fruitless as a woman with women," which nicely parallels the next comparison of a cow with cows. This is a significant reference to lesbian relationships in ancient India: see also 8.369–70.

2.160 *reaching the end of the Veda:* commentators offer diverse explanations of the expression *vedāntopagatam*. Most take *vedānta* to mean the Upaniṣads and the entire expression as a reference to the fruit of Upaniṣads, which is final liberation (*mokṣa*). I follow Nandana's interpretation. A teacher is supposed to have studied the entire Veda, that is, gone to its very end. The fruit of such learning is obtained only by a man who purifies and guards his mind. It is possible that both meanings are implied here. Medhātithi takes *anta* to mean *siddha* and explains the expression to mean the fruits of various rites established in the Veda.

2.161 *aberrant language:* all the commentators take *alokyām* to mean speech that prevents one from attaining heaven. I prefer to see *lokya* as something common or usual among people, and its opposite as something aberrant or uncouth. I think the verse refers to the use of foul language.

2.164 *ascetic toil consisting of vedic study:* the meaning of the expression *brahmādhigamikaṃ tapaḥ* is unclear. All the commentators, except Nandana, take it to mean austerities that are prescribed as connected with or conducive to the study of the Veda. Bühler gives a somewhat different interpretation: "cumulatively perform the various austerities and the vows prescribed by the rules (of the Veda)." I follow Nandana in seeing the study of the Veda itself as the ascetic toil of students, as clearly stated in verses 166–7. Being the very first verse of this section, it is natural to see here a reference to the central element of a student's life; the practice of other observances and austerities is dealt with in the very next verse.

2.174 *The very same . . . initiation:* Bühler places "student at the initiation" within parentheses, because the words are missing here. I believe, however, that the phrase *kṛtopanayanasyāsya* ("for one who has been initiated") is carried over into this verse by the common practice of *anuvṛtti*.

2.184 *He should not . . . are available:* this sentence is extremely elliptical, and my translation, just like Bühler's, is explanatory rather than literal. For paternal and maternal relative (*jñātibandhu*), see 2.132 n.; 5.74 n.

2.185 *heinous sinners:* the technical term *abhiśasta* probably refers to public sinners or socially ostracized people. Acts making someone a heinous sinner are given at *ĀpDh* 1.24.6–9 and *VaDh* 23.14.

2.186 *above ground:* the word *vihāyasi* literally means in the sky. Clearly this is an idiomatic expression meaning above ground or on an elevated space. Indeed, a variant recorded in *BhP* and *Lakṣ* reads *gṛhopari* ("on top of the house/roof").

2.188 Two additional verses: "Almsfood shall not be counted as 'other people's cooking' [cf. 3.104], nor does almsfood constitute the acceptance of a gift. Almsfood is equal to drinking Soma; therefore, he should subsist on almsfood. Almsfood that is pure in its origin, that has been sprinkled with water, and that has been offered in the fire—each mouthful that he eats from such almsfood is equal to a sacrifice."

2.193 *right arm uncovered:* the literal meaning of *uddhṛtapāṇiḥ* is that he should have his hand raised. Most commentators rightly take "hand" (*pāṇi*) here as meaning "arm" (*bāhu*). Raising here, as in the context of wearing the sacrificial cord (cf. 2.63 n), means raising the (right) arm when wearing the upper garment or shawl. It goes over the left shoulder and under the right arm, thus leaving the right arm and shoulder uncovered. Incidentally, this is precisely the way Buddhist monks are depicted as wearing their robes when they were in the presence of the Buddha. Uncovering the right shoulder appears to have been a mark of respect (8.2 n.).

cover himself well: the critical edition has adopted the reading *susaṃvṛtaḥ*. Medhātithi interprets this to mean controlling speech, mind, and eyes (*vāṅmanaścakṣubhir niyatātmā*). But this was already stated in the previous verse. He gives the opinion of some that it refers to covering the body with a garment (*vastreṇācchāditaśarīraḥ*); and this interpretation is followed by Rāghavānanda and Kullūka. See 11.109 where the term is used with the same meaning; and 7.102, 104 where we have the extended meaning "cover" in the sense of keeping well guarded ("under wraps"). If we follow the alternate readings *susaṃyataḥ*, the translation is: "keeping himself well controlled"; and *samāhitaḥ*: "self-possessed."

2.195 *standing:* if we take this literally and in conjunction with not sitting or lying down, then the student can never speak with the teacher! Only Medhātithi and Rāghavānanda note this problem. The latter explains that the student should not speak "standing far away." Medhātithi, rightly I think, explains that the student should not speak while standing in one place. This agrees with the statement in verse 196 that when the teacher is standing the student should walk towards him when he wants to speak. Doniger's "standing with his face turned away" does not work because we have a *na* ("not") before each word.

2.200 *Wherever . . . else:* given the context and especially the statement in verse 201 directed at the pupil, those doing the reviling are most likely his fellow students living at the teacher's house, who may occasionally say nasty things about their teacher, rather than evil people out in the world (so Medhātithi).

2.204 *on a cart . . . spread of grass:* all the commentators divide the long Dvandva compound *go'śvoṣṭrayānaprāsādaprastareṣu* into two section: first a Tatpuruṣa section: *go'śvoṣṭrayāna* which combines with the rest as Dvandva. Medhātithi recognizes that this is an odd way to dissolve the compound and explains that it is impossible for two men to ride on the bare back of an ox. He further explains that *yukta* ("yoked") is dropped from the compound, just as we drop it in *dadhighaṭa* (curd pot), when it should be *dadhiyuktaghaṭa* "pot containing curd." If we take each item in the compound separately, then the translation would be: "He may sit by his teacher on an ox, horse, camel, cart, terrace, or a spread of grass." See *ĀpDh* 1.8.12.

2.205 *his own elders* (svān gurūn): this is a wonderful example of the multiple meanings of the term *guru* (see Note on the Trans., p. 69). The term is used five times in the verse, four times as teacher and once as elders, meaning one's own father and other senior relatives.

2.207 *Ārya sons:* in all likelihood "Ārya" here refers to the three twice-born classes. This would exclude any son born to a Śūdra wife of the teacher, something implied here in spite of its condemnation at 3.14–9. On the number of wives permitted to a Brahmin, see 9.149–151. I follow Medhātithi, Nārāyaṇa, Govinda, Kullūka, and Nandana in taking Ārya as qualifying the teacher's sons. Some take Ārya as referring specifically to sons born to Brahmin mothers. The reading preferred by Medhātithi is *guruputre tathācārye*, according to which the translation would be: "Towards distinguished persons, as well as the teacher's son who has taught him. . . ." This is quite out of place, because that eventuality is the subject of verse 208.

2.212 *the attractive and the unattractive:* the literal meaning of *guṇadoṣau* is "good/quality and bad/fault," and many commentators accept a moral meaning. I think Medhātithi is correct in connecting this with sexual attraction: "The 'good' and 'bad' meant here are the pleasures and pains arising from sexual love, also the beauty and ugliness of women." The reference may simply be to boys old enough to be sexually attracted to the young wives of the teacher.

2.220 *for one day . . . recitation:* the recitation is of the Sāvitrī verse. Several commentators specify that when he is asleep at sunrise he should fast that day, and when he is asleep at sunset he should fast that night. They follow *GDh* 23.21: "Someone who is asleep at sunrise should stand during that day, remaining chaste and without eating any food; while someone who is asleep at sunset should stand during that night reciting the Sāvitrī verse." A similar provision is given in *ĀpDh* 2.12.13–4; *BDh* 2.7.16; *VaDh* 20.4–5. Medhātithi, however, disagrees because day (*dinam*) is specified. He sees here an option: a strong person may do it during the night; others can do it during the day.

2.224 *triple set* (trivarga): commonly called *puruṣārtha* (7.100), the three aims or goals of human existence, this classification of the three areas of human enterprise is mentioned by Manu at 7.27, 151; 4.175; 12.38. See also 2.13, 112; 4.92, 176; 6.64; 8.75. For a study, see Malamoud 1982.

2.229 *other rule of conduct:* the meaning of *dharmam anyam* is not altogether clear. Only Medhātithi comments on this, saying that the student should not undertake any religious activity that would hinder his service to his parents and teacher. Examples include going on pilgrimage and fasting. Manu may also have in mind a student becoming an ascetic before getting married, a common theme in Brahmanical literature.

2.230 *three orders of life:* some have taken this as evidence of a primitive structure of three *āśramas*. Within the context of the student, who is already in the first *āśrama*, the three must refer to the remaining three to which he aspires. See Olivelle 1993, 109.

three Vedas: Rāghavānanda further specifies that the father is the Ṛgveda, the mother is the Yajurveda, and the teacher is the Sāmaveda.

2.232 *householder:* it is anomalous to bring in the householder within the section addressed to a student. Govinda says that this simply indicates that these duties are incumbent also on the householder. Medhātithi tries to explain away the problem by saying that it is only as a householder, when his parents are old, that a student needs to look after them. It is more likely that this is an indication that these verses were incorporated here by Manu from a different source and a different context.

2.235 *another rule of conduct:* the Sanskrit has the elliptical *anyam*. This is probably a shorthand for *anyaṃ dharmam* of verse 229, which is also the interpretation of Govinda and Kullūka.

2.237 *When these three are gratified:* the Sanskrit is again elliptical *triṣv eteṣu*. Here also I detect a shorthand for these three being gratified, as we see in verse 228.

2.240 Variant reading; "as well as irreproachable crafts, may be accepted . . ."

2.243–4 *If he wishes . . . Brahman:* these two verses are connected to the section on life-long students at 2.247–9, and it is somewhat of an anomaly for the verses concluding the life of a student (245–6) to intervene. Logically, it would have been better for 243–4 to come immediately before verse 247.

2.246 Variant reading: "a cow, a horse, an umbrella, footwear, a seat, grain, vegetables . . ."

CHAPTER THREE

3.2 *three Vedas:* the Sanskrit *vedān* is in the plural denoting simply that there are more than two. The reference to the three Vedas in the first verse makes it clear, however, that the reference here is to the three Vedas.

without violating his chastity (aviplutabrahmacaryaḥ): the Sanskrit is vague and can refer to any rules or vows associated with studentship. I think, however, that *brahmacarya* here refers specifically to his vow of chastity, which is also the interpretation of Medhātithi and Govinda. See *ĀpDh* 2.21.8 *ata eva brahmacaryavān pravrajati*, "from that very state [i.e., studentship], remaining chaste, he goes forth," where *brahmacarya* has the same meaning within a similar context.

3.3 *When he has . . . a garland:* the first half of this verse is quite obscure and commentators interpret it in widely different ways. Most gloss *pratītam* with *khyātam*, "renowned/famous," and this interpretation if followed by Bühler and Doniger. Medhātithi takes it to mean "inclined to enter the householder's state." I think Nandana is correct in taking it as referring to the student's return home from his teacher's house. The compound *brahmadāya* also is variously explained. Many take it as a Dvandva: the Veda and the inheritance; or as meaning "the inheritance that is the Veda." Nandana thinks that the student takes money from the father to give the teacher his fee. Bühler takes this as referring to the Madhuparka (honey mixture, 3.119 n) that the teacher gives his student upon completion of his studies.

3.5 *lineage:* the term *sagotra* refers to a family line that is connected to a single ancient teacher as a common ancestor. The definition of this relationship is quite vague and often confused in the literature: see Kane 1962–75, ii. 479–501. *Gotra* is connected to another ancient Indian kinship category called *pravara* based on having the same ancestral seer. Each *gotra* may have several *pravaras*. "Connection of gotra and pravara may be stated thus: Gotra is the latest ancestor or one of the latest ancestors of a person by whose name his family has been known for generations; while pravara is constituted by the sages or in some cases the remote ancestor alone" (Kane, 1962–75, ii. 497). Two persons related through the one or the other are not permitted to marry each other.

unrelated to him by marriage: for the reading *amaithunī* and its possible meaning see the note to this verse in the critical edition. The vulgate reading is *maithune*, whose meaning is unclear. Bühler, following most commentators, translates: "is recommended to twice-born men for wedlock and conjugal union." Nandana, who reads *amaithunī*, interprets it to mean a woman who is a virgin (*akṣatayoni*), which is the interpretation also of Doniger.

3.8 *without or with too much bodily hair:* this provision goes against the other which requires a girl to be given in marriage before puberty. "Without hair" (*alomikā*) refers frequently to a pre-pubescent girl who has no pubic hair, often called *nagnikā* (*BDh* 4.1.11; *VaDh* 17.70). On the prohibition of sex with a "girl without hair," see *PārGṛ* 2.7.9 (*ajātalomnīm*). For a long description of the bodily characteristics of a girl, see *ĀpGṛ* 1.3.11–8. For a discussion of the verses dealing with factors that disqualify a woman, see Sandahl 2001.

jaundiced-looking: several commentators take *piṅgalām* as referring to red eyes, an interpretation followed by Bühler. Nandana thinks that the term can refer to either eyes or skin, and Nārāyaṇa takes it as referring to reddish yellow color.

3.9 Additional verse: "He should not marry a woman who is too fat, too lean, too tall, too short, or too old; who is deficient in any limb; and who is fond of quarreling."

3.11 *A wise man . . . in force:* the major disagreement among interpreters centers on the compound *putrikādharmaśaṅkayā*. Nārāyaṇa, Kullūka, and Rāghavānanda divide this compound thus: *putrikā-adharma-śaṅkayā*. Bühler and Doniger follow this division. The translation would then be: "because of the fear (the she is) a 'female-son' or (of committing) a sin." The first fear is generated by the absence of a brother and the second by the absence of the father (she may be related to the prospective husband or born illegitimately). I follow the interpretation of Medhātithi, Govinda, and Nandana, who divide the compound thus: *putrikā-dharma-śaṅkayā*, "because of the fear that the Law of 'female-son' may be in force." In this interpretation, the absence of either a brother or the father may give rise to this fear. The first is obvious. As Medhātithi points out, when the father is absent it is not possible to find out whether the girl has been appointed as *putrikā*. On this institution, see 9.127–140. This custom was very old and discussed at length with Iranian parallels by *Schmidt* 1987. See *VaDh* 17.16 citing *ṚV* 1.124.7; the same interpretation of this *ṚV* verse is given by Yāska, *Nirukta* 3.5.

3.12 *preferable women* (varāḥ): because manuscripts regularly omit the *avagraha*, the reading of *kramaśo varāḥ* is ambiguous; it could also be *kramaśo (a)varāḥ*. Medhātithi, Nārāyaṇa, Govinda, and Kullūka take it as *varāḥ*, with the gloss *śreṣṭhāḥ* ("best"). Rāghavānanda, Nandana, and Rāmacandra read *avarāḥ*, meaning either lower or of lower caste. Because the preferable wives in terms of *varṇa* are given later in the list, I think the reading without *avagraha* is more plausible. See the note to this verse in the critical edition.

3.14 *story:* the reference must be to stories of ancient people, whose behavior may be viewed as providing legitimation for taking a Śūdra wife. For such stories, see 7.41; 10.105–8.

3.16 *by producing . . . through her:* I follow Medhātithi, Govinda, and Nandana in interpreting the rather ambivalent compound *tadapatyatayā*. Literally, it means "by means of the state of his being a man-with-children through her"; in other words, he has children only through the Śūdra wife. This interpretation is supported by the statement in 3.64. Others take it as referring to a son's son; so a man falls if he gets a grandson through a Śūdra wife. This interpretation is given in some interpretive verses of the *Bhaviṣya Purāṇa* cited by Nārāyaṇa. Both the *Bhaviṣya* and Nārāyaṇa also think that these are not the views of the respective seers, but injunctions that apply to people who belong to their lineages (*gotra*). So, for example, a man belonging to the lineage of Atri falls from his caste simply by marrying a Śūdra woman. This is quite implausible.

3.19 *begets himself:* on the theme of a husband begetting himself as his son through his wife, see Olivelle 1993, 41–6.

3.23–6 It is very clear that these four verses contain differing opinions about the legitimacy of the ten types of marriage. These ten were ingrained in the tradition, and Manu could not simply ignore them. Here, I think, Manu gives three views of different authorities. In the normal manner of Brahmanical disputation, the views to be rejected are given first (*pūrvapakṣa*) and Manu's own view is given last in verses 25 and 26; the word *iha*, namely "here in this treatise" (see 1.42 n.), supports my conjecture. Commentators, however, attempt to reconcile these conflicting views.

3.26 *conjointly:* that is, when the two have become lovers first according to the Gāndharva mode, and then the man abducts the willing girl from her father's house.

3.31 *When a girl is given:* all the commentators, except Rāmacandra, divide the compound *kanyāpradānam* as *kanyā* + *āpradānam*, Medhātithi glossing *ānayanam* and the others *svīkāram*. The word *āpradāna* is not noted in any dictionary. The problem is created by the gerund *dattvā*, whose subject, according to normal Sanskrit syntax, should be the same as the subject of the verb or verbal equivalent of the main clause. Here, it is clear that the subject of *dattvā* is the prospective bridegroom. In this context, dividing *kanyāpradānam* as *kanyā* + *pradānam* ("giving away the girl") will not work. The commentators have resorted to reading the word *āpradānam* ("receive") rather than the more common *pradānam* ("giving away'). Either the commentators are correct in recording this uncommon word, which I very much doubt; or, more likely, *kanyāpradāna* is a frozen form that Manu uses for the giving away of the girl after the payment of the bride-price by the groom.

3.32 *based on sexual union:* all the commentators, except Nārāyaṇa, interpret the term *maithunyaḥ* to mean that this sort of marriage is conducive to sexual love. Medhātithi explains: *maithunaprayojano maithunaḥ, tasmai hito maithunyaḥ* (see Pāṇini 5.1.5). Accordingly, Bühler translates: "has sexual intercourse for its purpose." I agree with Thieme (1963, 197) that the meaning here is that the marriage springs from or is founded on their act of sexual intercourse. Thieme points to Pāṇini 4.3.53 explaining the derivative as *tatra bhavaḥ*.

3.33 *"Fiendish" procedure:* on the Indo-European parallels to this form of marriage, especially the Roman abduction, see Watkins 1994a, 425.

3.37 *does good deeds* (sukṛtakṛt): all the commentators interpret this to mean "if (*yadi*) he performs meritorious acts," an interpretation followed by Bühler. It is also possible that such a son was viewed as naturally prone to doing good deeds. Such natural propensities of sons resulting from their parent's marriages are assumed in verses 39–42.

from evil: Medhātithi and Kullūka take the term *enasaḥ* as a reference to the evil state, i.e., hell. Others, followed by Bühler, think that it refers to sins (*pāpa*).

3.40 *beauty, spirit, and virtue:* I take the compound *rūpasattvaguṇa* to contain three separate items (following Kullūka and Rāghavānanda) and interpret *sattva* to mean "spirit" in the sense of energy and intelligence (Rāghavānanda: *bala*). Bühler translates: "Endowed with the qualities of beauty and goodness," which is the interpretation of Medhātithi, Nārāyaṇa, and Nandana.

3.42 *inviting people's reproach:* the exact syntactical relation of the genitive *nṛṇām* is not altogether clear. Govinda and Kullūka, followed by Bühler, connect it with *prajā* ("offspring") of *pāda-b*; this seems to me improbable. Rāmacandra connects it with the implicit *prajā* of *pāda-c*: *ninditā prajā bhavati nṛṇām*, which is also the interpretation of Doniger: "Blameworthy progeny comes to men from blameworthy (marriages)." I think the term is connected to *ninditā* in the sense of a partitive genitive: "blamed among men," that is, they are treated with contempt in the world.

3.45 *during her season:* the "season" for the wife is the days of the month when she is fertile, which were thought to be the days following her menstrual period. During that time a husband was obligated to have sexual intercourse with his wife. *ĀpGṛ* 3.9.1 recommends even days from the fourth day (that is, the day when the period of menstrual impurity ends with the wife's bath) to the sixteenth following the start of the menstrual flow. See also 3.46–8.

moon's change (parvan): the new moon, the eighth day after the new moon, the full moon, and the fourteenth day after the full moon. See 4.128.

3.46 *natural* (svābhāvika): Medhātithi and most other commentators say that an illness may prevent menstruation at the normal time and certain foods, such as ghee, may increase the flow or bring it before its normal time. The time given is not simply the natural but also the standard or the typical.

together with the other four days (caturbhir itaraiḥ sārdham): Bühler, following the interpretation of most commentators, translates: "including four days which differ from the rest;" so also Doniger. This is a laborious rendering of *itara*, which in its numerous occurrence in Manu, always points to a contrast with the previous (see **1**.70, 82, 101; **3**.35, 41, 77, 113,137, 182, 276; **4**.225; 8.379; **9**.102, 107, 156,162, 181, 189, 191, 242; **10**.1, 2, 93; **11**.3; **12**.106). The obvious meaning of *itara* forces us to take these four days as "other" and, therefore, outside the 16 days mentioned in *pāda-b*. Interpreted this way, the period of *ṛtu* lasts for 20 days. This is precisely what Nandana says in his comments on verse 50, namely that the period beginning with the 21st day from the onset of menses is outside *ṛtu*.

It is clear that verses 46–50 are a commentary on the expression *ṛtukālābhigāmī syāt* ("he should have sex with her during her season") of verse 45. The commentary spells out what is meant by *ṛtu* and further demarcates the days when sex is permitted. The term *ṛtu* covers a longer period of time than the period when sex is enjoined; for example, it begins at the onset of menses, establishing a clear beginning to the season. But during the four days of the menstrual period, even though it is technically *ṛtu*, he is not permitted to have sex with his wife.

3.47 *Of these . . . recommended:* this verse is as obscure as the preceding. The commentators and translators take the "first four" to refer to the four days of menstruation. Then we have only 12 days remaining, and excluding the 11th and the 13th, there are 10 nights when sex is permitted. This appears to be the view also expressed in the *YDh* 1.79. I think, however, that this is erroneous. The 16 days, as we saw in the previous note, excluded the days of menstruation. Further, the word *tāsām* ("of these") is in the feminine, agreeing with the 16 nights (*rātryaḥ*, feminine), whereas the other four "days" (*ahobhiḥ*) is neuter. It seems, further, unnecessary to repeat that the four days of menstruation is forbidden, when it was already stated clearly in verse 46. According to my interpretation, the first four must refer to the first four nights after the menstrual period. So, the prohibited nights are the four days of menstruation, the first four days after that, and the 11th and 13th days of the menstrual cycle. For further support of this interpretation, see note to verse 50. For other forbidden days of the month, see 4.128.

3.49 *When the man's . . . takes place:* this statement supports the previous one that one should have sex on even nights. Govinda cites an Āyurvedic text to the effect that the female seed diminishes during even nights and increases during odd nights. For an extended discussion of this topic, see *Carakasaṃhitā, Śarīrasthāna*, 8.

3.50 *Regardless . . . man lives:* all the commentators take this statement literally and have some trouble in explaining it. Govinda goes to the extreme in thinking that this provision even permits a renouncer whose son dies to have sex with his former wife twice during her season without breaking his vow of chastity. Kullūka takes this provision as referring to forest hermits. I think the meaning is more simple. Irrespective of his *āśrama*, even a householder can be a *brahmacārin* if he follows this rule. See similar expressions at 6.66; 12.102.

during the other eight nights: most commentators take these eight nights to be part of the 16 nights of the *ṛtu*, an interpretation followed by Bühler and Doniger. Under this interpretation, as the commentators clearly state, sex is permitted only on two nights, excluding these eight plus the six forbidden nights out of the 16-night season. I think the word *anya* here, just as *itara* in verse 46, contrasts these eight nights to the nights of *ṛtu* mentioned earlier (20, if my interpretation of verse 46 is accepted). Then the rule is very simple. A man who has sex with his wife only to produce offspring and not for lust should be considered a celibate. During the last eight days of the cycle (outside the above 20) the wife is infertile. During the four days of menstruation, she is both infertile and unclean. During the first four days after menstruation and on the 11th and the 13th, he is forbidden to have sex. All this accounts for 18 days. He should have sex outside these 18 days; that is, during the 10 days, which is precisely what is stated in verse 49. This interpretation has the added benefit of accounting for the 28-day menstrual cycle. The only commentator who appears to support my interpretation is Nandana, whose language is, however, somewhat unclear. But he makes this significant remark about the eight days: *ekaviṃśīprabhṛtīnām ṛtor akālatvād aṣṭāsv ity uktam*, "the statement 'during eight' is made because the nights beginning with the 21st is a period outside the season."

3.52 *When relatives . . . course:* relatives, as Medhātithi clearly points out, are the woman's father and the like, and not her in-laws. The context is the prohibition of a bride-price. It is unclear whether *nārīyānāni* is a Tatpuruṣa or a Dvandva compound. Among the commentators, Govinda, Kullūka, Nandana, and Rāmacandra support a Dvandva, whereas Medhātithi, Nārāyaṇa, and Rāghavānanda assume a Tatpuruṣa, as do Bühler and Doniger. I have taken it to be a Dvandva; it appears pleonastic to say the vehicles belong to the women when the entire verse is dealing with the property of women. I follow Govinda and Nandana in taking *nārī* to mean "women," i.e., slave women. For slavery in ancient India, see Bongert 1963. The sentence is clumsy, but I think we are justified in taking the three words of *pāda-c* as separate items illustrating "woman's wealth" (*strīdhana*). For studies on slavery in ancient India, see the bibliography in Silk 1992.

3.53 *At a "Seer's" . . . a sale:* there is a diversity of opinion regarding the exact meaning of this verse. The majority of commentators (Medhātithi, Nārāyaṇa, Govinda, Nandana, Rāmacandra) think that Manu is prohibiting the giving of a cow and a bull to the bride's parents. They recognize that this contradicts the provisions of verse 29. Govinda says that the latter is the view of others (*paramata*), which Manu rejects. Kullūka, on the other hand, disagrees with this interpretation. According to him, what Manu rejects is the designation of *śulka* for this gift of a cow and bull. He recalls that in verse 29 Manu uses the expression *dharmataḥ*, which he interprets to mean *dharmārtham*, "for the sake of the Law." This cow and bull are to be used for ritual expenses. The term *śulka*, on the other hand, refers to gratuities that the parents keep for their own enjoyment. This, according to Kullūka, is what Manu objects to. Rāghavānanda basically agrees with Kullūka, except that he takes the second half of the verse also to be part of what "some say." I think Kullūka is right. Verses 51–4 appear to constitute a single argument against bride-price. Verses 51 and 52 lay down Manu's point of view. In verse 53, I think, we have a possible argument against such a view. The opponent cites the example of the Seer's marriage where a bride-price in the form of a cow and bull is clearly recognized. Manu rejoins, saying that this is untrue. That gift does not constitute a true bride-price (*śulka*). The reason is spelled out in the next verse (54): when the relatives do not keep the bride-price for themselves, then it does not constitute a sale; so it is not really a bride-price. Manu uses the word *śulka* only three times (5.51, 53, 54) and always with a negative connotation.

That the bride-price was a common practice in ancient India is evident even from Manu's own statements elsewhere in his treatise. For example, at 8.204–5 the giving of a girl to her husband is viewed as a sale, and it is indeed listed under the third *vyavahārapada*, sale without ownership (see also 8.224). At 9.93, 97 also the bride-price is presupposed, although at 9.98, 100 he again condemns it. The sale of the girl is explicitly recognized in *MS* 1.10.11, where adultery on the part of the wife is condemned because she is cheating her husband who has bought her. See Thieme 1963, 208.

Two additional verses: "In this connection, those who know the past relate verses sung by Yama. 'Given that even another man should not be sold, how much more one's own offspring. When a human being wants to get money by selling another human being, in the hereafter he will live on that person's urine and excrement.'"

3.56 *Where women are revered:* following Kullūka and Govinda, I take *yatra* ("where") to stand for *yatra kule* ("in which family"), an interpretation supported also by the parallel reading of verse 57 *tat kulam* (see also verse 60). The word *pūjyante* ("are revered") implies—just as in the case of divine *pūjā*—not just a mental attitude but outward expressions of honor, as illustrated in verse 59. See 3.70 n.

3.63 Variant reading: "respectable families fall into disrepute."

3.65 *by officiating . . . vedic knowledge:* Kullūka and Nandana take *pāda-d* as qualifying *kulāni*, an interpretation followed by Bühler and Doniger. Accordingly, the translation would be: "Those families that are bereft of vedic knowledge quickly come to ruin by officiating at sacrifices. . . ." Under this interpretation, as Nandana explicitly states, we would have the absurd conclusion that if a family is *not* bereft of such knowledge, then it will not come to ruin even by engaging in these activities. I think this is mistaken. By engaging in activities spelled out in verses 64 and 65 any family will come to ruin; and then Manu adds a further provision in *pāda-d:*: even without doing the above, a family comes to ruin if it is bereft of vedic knowledge. See the parallel in *pāda-d* of 63, where also an added reason is given for the ruin of families. Variant reading: "respectable families quickly come to ruin."

3.68 *broom:* the term *upaskara* can refer to any type of household utensil; so Medhātithi: *gṛhopayogi bhāṇḍaṃ kuṇḍakaṭāhādi* ("a vessel used in the house such as a bowl or frying pan"). Kullūka agrees. Rāmacandra: "winnowing basket"; Nārāyaṇa and Rāghavānanda: "broom." The only other place where this term occurs is at 12.66, where also the meaning is unspecified. In the current context, however, it may be preferable to take it as referring to a specific household item, such as a broom, rather than to a vague category, because all other items listed are specific. Given that this tool is supposed to cause harm to living beings, broom is a better candidate than the other items suggested.

3.70 *honoring:* especially when it entails hospitality, honoring (*pūjā*) always entails giving of food etc. This connection between *pūjā* and feeding is reflected in the manuscripts, which often give the variant *bhojayet* ("he should feed") for *pūjayet* ("he should honor"): see 3.106, 264. For *pūjā*, see Thieme 1939, 105–23.

3.75 *here* (iha): no commentator explains this word. Bühler and Doniger see it as a reference to the man's current order of life (*āśrama*). I think this is wrong; in Manu, *iha* refers regularly to this world or to this treatise (i.e., Manu). That the term in this verse refers to this world is supported by the use of *idam* ("this") to refer to this world. The meaning is that when he is devoted to these activities in this world, he supports this world containing mobile and immobile beings. For the meaning of the term, see 1.42 n.

3.76 *from food, offspring:* Bühler, I think, has misunderstood this passage, translating: "therefrom the living creatures (derive their subsistence)," although such a meaning may also be implied here, given the context of the very next verse. The thrust of the passage, however, is the chain of causation that brings about children, and the main source of this image, I think, is the doctrine of five fires (*pañcāgnividyā*) found in the Upaniṣads (*BṛU* 6.2.9–16; *ChU* 5.4–10). This verse appears to have combined the view that fire sacrifices reach the sun and bring down rain and the more specific doctrine of the re-birth process entailed in the passage to the sun and back to the earth: the dead person when cremated goes to the sun as smoke, returns to earth as rain, becomes absorbed into plants, and when eaten becomes semen and finally a child.

3.77 Variant reading: "so people in all orders of life."

3.78 *most senior order of life:* translators generally render *jyeṣṭha* as "most excellent" or "best." I think, however, that Manu is here playing with the word *jyeṣṭha*, which is also the term for the oldest brother (see 9.105–10). The eldest is supposed to look after his younger siblings like a father. Manu applies this image to the *āśramas*. The householder supplies food and knowledge to the others; so he is comparable to the oldest brother. See also 1.93 where the Brahmin is called the eldest among the *varṇas*.

3.79 *shouldered*: here again Manu is playing with the word *saṃdhārya*. In the previous verse he uses *dhāryante* with reference to the householder supporting people in other orders. Now, he uses *saṃdhārya* with the double meaning of "undertaking/assuming" and "bearing" the heavy burden of a householder's life. It is the householder who through his five daily sacrifices supports the entire cosmos.

3.83 *at this:* namely, at the daily ancestral offering forming part of the five great sacrifices. At other types of *śrāddhas*, such as the monthly *pārvaṇaśrāddha*, Brahmins are invited to represent the All-gods (3.209). See, Kane 1962–75, iv: 403.

Variant reading: "he should not feed anything to a Brahmin."

3.84 *From the oblation to All-gods:* the description of this rite in the 3.84–92 parallels its description in *ŚāṅkhGṛ* 2.14: see Gopal 1962.

3.90 *being that . . . night:* the *ŚāṅkhGṛ* 2.14.16 specifies that he throw an offering in the evening to those that roam during the night, and in the morning to those that roam during the day.

3.91 *In the back house* (pṛṣṭhavāstuni): Bühler's translation "In the upper story" and Doniger's "In the upper part of the house" are off the mark; so are the dictionaries of B-R and M-W that assign this meaning to the compound citing this verse of Manu. Back of a house is not at the top but the rear (as opposed to the front). The expression must be an euphemism for the lavatory, like the English "out-house." In the context of this rite, *ŚāṅkhGṛ* 2.14.15 has *anugupte deśe*, clearly referring to the "privy." The *GobhGṛ* 1.4.10 uses the term *adhivarcam*, which the commentator Bhaṭṭanārāyaṇa explains *mūtroccāraṇapradeśaḥ* ("place for voiding urine").

Variant reading: "Sarvātmabhūti."

3.92 *evil diseases:* the term *pāparoga*, which recurs frequently in Manu, does not refer simply to a serious sickness. The disease is regarded as the consequence of sins committed in previous lives (see 11.48–53). Evil diseases are generally viewed as skin diseases of various types.

3.94 *to a mendicant student of the Veda:* opinion is divided as to the syntax of this sentence. Medhātithi first takes *bhikṣave* as qualifying *brahmacāriṇe*, which is the interpretation I have followed. He gives an alternate opinion that takes the two words separately.

This is also the view of Nārāyaṇa, Kullūka, and Rāghavānanda, followed by Bühler and Doniger: "to an ascetic and to a student." However, this would require the copulative *ca* ("and") to be placed after *brahmacāriṇe* rather than after *bhikṣām*, as Medhātithi points out: *caśabdaś cāsthāne vṛttānurodhād brahmacāriṇe ceti paṭhitavyam*. Govinda takes *brahmacāriṇe* as qualifying *bhikṣave:* "to a mendicant who is celibate."

3.95 *to a poor man:* for the reading *gāṃ dattvāgor yathāvidhi* of the critical edition, see the note there. The reading found in most editions and followed by all translators is *gāṃ dattvā vidhivad guroḥ*, and according to this, the translation would be: "by giving a cow to his teacher according to rule."

3.96 *garnish:* the term *satkṛtya* can also mean "having honored," which is the interpretation of Medhātithi and Govinda. Then it refers to the Brahmin, who is to be so honored. The expression *satkṛtya vidhipūrvakam* occurs also at 3.99, where both these commentators take it to mean garnishing or an elaborate preparation of food. The past participle *satkṛtam* occurring at 3.264 in a similar context also means garnishing. See also, 3.126; 9.129.

3.97 *equivalent of ashes:* sacrifices are offered in a fire set ablaze. The mouth of a Brahmin is often compared to such a fire, and his fire is ablaze only through vedic knowledge (3.98). Feeding an ignorant Brahmin is like offering a sacrifice in ashes; both are equally futile. See 3.168, 181; *VaDh* 3.10.

3.98 Four additional verses: "When someone gives to an unworthy man and fails to give to a worthy man, he loses both wealth and merit by his failure to discriminate between the worthy and the unworthy. What is given according to rule to a deserving person who has come in the proper way and at the proper time yields the highest reward both in this world and in the next. Twice-born persons acquire wealth lawfully through the proper acceptance of gifts, through conquest, and through trade, in that order. If he desires an imperishable reward, he should give to a virtuous man whatever is most desirable in the world and whatever is most cherished in his house."

3.99 Two additional verses: "A man obtains the same—and even a more excellent—reward by feeding a Brahmin as he would by offering an oblation in the fire according to rule. The reward of the latter is destroyed for the performer through a mistake in the ritual formula or by a wrongly made oblation or fire offering, and that of the former by doing it without a spirit of generosity."

3.102 *He is called . . . is brief:* here we have a phonetic etymology of "guest" (*atithi*) derived from combining "*a*" from *anitya* ("brief") and "*tithi*" from *sthiti* ("stay"). Identical verse at *VaDh* 8.7.

3.103 *A Brahmin . . . sacred fires:* that there is a problem with this verse is evident because the identical verse at *VaDh* 8.8 has a very different second half syntactically separated from the first half and identical with *MDh* 3.105 cd. First, the word *sāṃgatika* is somewhat unclear. Medhātithi thinks it is a gregarious man fond of telling wonderful and hilarious stories. Similar interpretations are given by Govinda, Kullūka, and Rāghavānanda. Clearly, the commentators are unsure of its meaning. I think Bühler is right in following the lead of Nārāyaṇa and taking it to mean someone who visits a house on some business or for some social purpose. I think it refers specifically to a friendly social visit; see *saṃgata* used in the sense of "friendship" at 3.140. There is also much dispute regarding the meaning of the last *pāda*. Medhātithi has the most elaborate explanation: a) when he is away and his wife and fires are at home, then a guest should be honored; b) when he is away accompanied by his wife and fires, then also he must honor a guest, even though he is not at home. I think the meaning is probably more simple: a man described in the first half is not to be regarded as a guest even when he comes to a house that is "a complete house," i.e., with both wife and fires. The implication is that when his wife is away, the husband should not be expected to entertain a guest.

3.104 Additional verse: "When a householder thrives constantly on someone else's food, all his sacrifices, gifts, ascetic toil, and learning will belong to the owner of the food."

3.106 Variant reading: "Feeding a guest."

3.107 *accompanying them as they leave:* the host is expected to accompany the guest from his house some distance as he leaves. Āpastamba (2.9.2–4) is specific: "If a guest has come in a carriage, he should follow him as far as the carriage; others he should follow until they give him leave to return. If a guest forgets to do so, he may turn back at the village boundary."

3.108 *he need not . . . offering:* the assumption is that the guest has arrived after the family members have eaten and the food is over. Fresh food has to be cooked for the guest. Generally, after cooking food one has to perform the Vaiśvadeva and Bali offerings. This provision calls for the omission of these offerings in the event of a second cooking of food.

3.110 *elder:* most take *guru* here to mean "the teacher," whereas Nārāyaṇa takes it to mean "the father." Given that relatives are listed separately, the meaning here favors the teacher. See Note on the Trans., p. 71.

3.111 *fulfilling the conditions of a guest* (atithidharmeṇa): Medhātithi gives three such conditions: that he has exhausted his provisions; that he lives in another village; and that he arrives at mealtime. Nandana adds that he should be an unknown person.

3.113 *with his wife:* commentators note that this does not indicate that she eats at a time different from the husband's, because according to verse 116 the husband and wife eat together after the rest of the household, a practice rejected later at 4.43. Wife is mentioned because guests other than close friends do not eat alongside the wife.

3.114 *right after:* the meaning, according to Medhātithi, is that these should be given their food as soon as the guests have started to eat; that is, they do not have to wait until the guests have completed their meal, unlike other members of the family.

All the NT manuscripts read *agra eva* in place of *anvag eva* adopted in the critical edition. According to that reading, the translation would be: "these he may feed without hesitation even before the guests."

3.119 *a friend:* Bühler, following Medhātithi, Govinda, Kullūka, Rāghavānanda, and Rāmacandra, translates *priya* as "son-in-law." Nārāyaṇa and Nandana take it as referring to a friend.

honey-mixture (madhuparka): this drink presented to an important guest is made by mixing honey into curd, milk, or water. See *ĀpDh* 2.8.5–8.

3.122 *sacrifice to ancestors:* this is a vedic (*śrauta*) sacrifice called Piṇḍapitṛyajña: cf. *ĀśŚr* 2.6–7.

supplementary offering of rice balls: this refers to the monthly ancestral offering (*śrāddha*), which is not a *śrauta* but a *smārta* rite, that is, a rite that is only enjoined in the traditional texts, especially the Gṛhyasūtras, and not the vedic texts.

3.126 *offering proper hospitality* (satkriyā): Medhātithi and Rāmacandra take this as referring to special preparation of food, which agrees with the usage of *satkṛtya*: see 3.96 n.

3.127 *This rite . . . him always:* this verse is very obscure, and I am not sure whether even the commentators have understood it. It may be that the *pretakṛtyā* of *pāda-a* refers to the vedic (*śrauta*) offering for the dead, whereas the "non-vedic (lit., 'worldly') rite" refers to the *smārta* ancestral rite (*śrāddha*): see 3.122 n.

3.130 *search far and wide:* most commentators interpret *dūrād eva parīkṣeta* to mean that one should look into even the remote ancestors of that person, an interpretation followed by Bühler and Doniger. I think this is farfetched. I follow Nārāyaṇa (*dūragrāmastham*) and Burnell in taking *dūrāt* as referring to distance rather than to kinship.

3.134 *Some Brahmins . . . ritual activities:* Medhātithi and Nārāyaṇa take these four kinds of individuals as representing the four orders of life: ascetic, forest hermit, vedic student, and householder, respectively.

3.136–7 *Between a man . . . as superior:* the commentators and translators alike take these two somewhat elliptical verses as referring to a father–son pair. In one case the father is learned and the son ignorant, and in the other the son is learned and the father is ignorant. The conclusion is that the ignorant son whose father is learned is superior to the learned son with an ignorant father. But this would contradict the statement of verses 133 and 142 that one should not invite an ignorant man (here the son) to a rite. According to my interpretation, the verses are speaking about two men who are assumed to be learned. The question is who is better: the one whose father is learned but whose son is ignorant, or the one whose father is ignorant but whose son is learned? Manu comes down in favor of the former.

3.139 *When a friend takes center stage:* the compound *mitrapradhānāni* is not altogether clear. Most commentators take it as referring to striking friendships through extending invitations to ancestral and divine rites. Accordingly, Bühler translates: "chiefly for the sake of (gaining) friends." See, however, 3.18 where *tatpradhānāni* refers to a Śūdra wife's participating at a rite performed by her Brahmin husband. See also 4.243; 12.46.

3.141 *Such a sacrificial . . . same stall:* variants of this interesting verse are found in *ĀpDh* 2.17.8 and *MBh* 13.90.39, both in the Triṣṭubh meter probably indicating an earlier version. In the *ĀpDh*, as well as in some recension of the *MBh*, the reading is *piśācabhikṣā*, "almsfood of ghouls." The simile is also different; instead of a blind cow in the same stall, the point of which is unclear, we have a cow who has lost its calf and is roaming around the corrals (*śālāntare gaur iva naṣṭavatsā*). The meaning appears to be that the cow remains in the corral and does not go out to the pastures. Comparing the sacrificial fee (*dakṣiṇā*) to a cow is common in the vedic literature, principally because the paradigmatic sacrificial fee is a cow.

3.144 *handsome:* Bühler and Doniger, following the commentators, take the term *abhirūpam* to mean someone well qualified. I cannot understand how *abhirūpa* can be taken to mean *vidvat* or *guṇavat*, as the commentators do; and Nārāyaṇa's gloss *uktābhimatarūpaśālinam* is an example of a clever pandit stretching a word beyond recognition. The simple meaning of the term is "handsome," and it is used with precisely this meaning by Manu at 9.88. Indeed, among the qualities of an invitee to an ancestral offering listed by Gautama (*GDh* 15.9–10) are youth and beauty (*rūpa*).

3.149 Additional verse: "Of these, some defile those alongside whom they eat, as others purify those alongside whom they eat. I will now describe those alongside whom it is unfit to eat, the lowest of twice-born who are unfit to be invited to an ancestral rite."

3.150–2 I think that these verses are taken from a source different from that of the long list which follows. The two lists are somewhat repetitive, and *kitava* ("gambler") is actually listed twice (151 and 159), which has prompted some scribes to change it to *kekara* fearing tautology (*punarukti*), as explicitly stated by Nandana. See also those who sacrifice for *pūgas* paralleling *gaṇa* of 163; and *klība* ("impotent") at 150 and 165.

3.150 *impotent:* the term *klība* has been subject to widely different interpretations. It probably did have a range of meanings, and in different contexts may have assumed somewhat different meanings. In general, it refers to males who are in some way sexually dysfunctional or deviate from the cultural constructed notions of masculinity. Such individuals include the impotent, the effeminate, transvestites, hermaphrodites, and the like. This term does not refer to castrated eunuchs; I think the term *ṣaṇḍha* indicates such a person, although there is scholarly disagreement even with regard to this. A verse of Kātyāyana cited in the *Dāyabhāga* (5.8,) gives a definition of *klība:* "If a man's urine does not foam, if his stool sinks in water, if his penis has no erection or sperm, he is called *klība.*"

3.151 *bald-headed:* all commentaries take the term *durvāla* to mean bad skin; so also Bühler. Doniger (reading *durbala*) translates as "weakling." Bad skin or weakling does not fit with the rest of the terms; they all refer to classes of people. "Bald-headed" here may refer to kinds of ascetics, just like "matted hair."

3.154 *neglects his ritual duties:* a wide variety of opinions exist with regard to the meaning of the term *nirākṛtiḥ*, Medhātithi listing no less than five possibilities. Medhātithi, followed by Kullūka, Rāghavānanda, and Rāmacandra, prefers the meaning "a man who neglects the five great sacrifices"; so also Bühler. Nārāyaṇa: "one who neglects his vedic recitation"; and Govinda: "one who repudiates the Vedas and the like." Nandana cites verses from Devala and Kātyāyana, the former taking him to be a man who has learnt and then forgotten the Veda, and the latter taking him to be a man who has set up his sacred fires but then failed to perform the rituals due to laziness. The term also occurs in *GDh* 15.18.

linked to an association: the precise meaning of *gaṇābhyantaraḥ* is quite unclear. Nārāyaṇa: "a village headman," with which Nandana appears to agree. Kullūka and Rāghavānanda think it means someone who has embezzled money from a corporation. The term literally means "one who is within (or intimately connected with) a corporate body." No other legal treatise has this term; the closest parallel I have come across is *GDh* 15.18, where, within a similar list of people unfit to be invited, it lists *gaṇapreṣya* "a servant of a corporation." I think a similar person may be intended here.

3.159 *poison vendor* (rasavikrayin): the term *rasa* may refer to any liquid, such as milk and sugarcane juice, and also to poison, generally also a plant extract. Medhātithi and Nandana opt for poison, whereas others take it to be sugarcane juice, sugar or other sweets, and milk. The context, I think, supports poison.

3.163 *breaches . . . obstructing them:* the meaning, as Medhātithi clearly explains, is that such a person cuts the side of a public water course to divert water to his own field. Obstructing them may have the same purpose or, because the term *rataḥ* is used, may indicate a man who takes perverse delight in obstructing the free flow of water.

3.164 *officiates . . . bodies* (gaṇānāṃ yājakaḥ): Nārāyaṇa and Nandana, rightly I believe, take *gaṇa* to refer to a group of individuals (see verse 154). The meaning here cannot be much different from that of verse 151 (*yājayanti ca ye pūgān*); both refer to someone who officiates at a sacrifice collectively financed by a group. The *GDh* 15.16 has the expression *grāmayājaka* with a very similar meaning. Other commentators take *gaṇa* to refer to a particular class of deities, such as Gaṇapati, an interpretation followed by Bühler and Doniger.

3.171–5 It is likely that these verses, which constitute a commentary on five technical terms used in verses 154–69, are a later interpolation to the text. At the very least, they constitute a parenthetical remark. Their intrusion also breaks the natural continuity between verses 170 and 176–82.

3.173 *Didhiṣūpati:* this and the related term *agredidhiṣūpati* have been subjected to different interpretations. In many texts these two form a pair, and the meaning appears to be a man who marries a woman whose younger sister is already married and a man who marries a woman whose older sister is still unmarried, respectively. See, *ĀpDh* 2.12.22; *GDh* 15.16; *VaDh* 1.18; 20.9–10. Manu gives here a very different meaning to *didhiṣūpati*. I agree with Bühler that Manu takes these two terms as synonyms, because 173 is clearly a commentary on the term *agredidhiṣūpati* of verse 160.

3.184 *expository texts:* explained by the commentators as the Vedic Supplements (2.105 n.).

3.185 *three Nāciketa:* Bodewitz (1985, 8–10, 25) has shown that this term refers not to particular fires but to the building of a special fire-altar bearing the name of Naciketas, the central figure in the *Kaṭha Upaniṣad.*

five sacred fires: the three mentioned at 2.231, as well as the hearth fire (*āvasathya*) and the hall fire (*sabhya*).

3.186 *given a 1,000:* when the number is unspecified, cows, the paradigmatic gift, are understood. Nandana, however, interprets it to mean either feeding a thousand Brahmins or giving 1,000 Suvarṇas (gold coins: 8.135). For numbers in the context of fines, see 8.120 n.

3.189 Additional verse: "Gods, together with the hosts of ancestors, would eat that food, making the Brahmin their mouth; therefore, he should not neglect it."

3.192 *primeval deities* (pūrvadevatāḥ): from the statements in verses 194–9 it is apparent that these "ancestors" are not the immediate forefathers of a person but mythical ancestors who originated at the very beginning of creation, identical with the great seers of the creation account (1.34–37; see also 3.201). Gods themselves are the creation of these seers. In verse 201, however, ancestors are called the sons of seers, but there "ancestors" may be used more restrictively with reference to the specific ancestors of various beings spelled out in verses 196–9.

3.201 Variant reading: "from ancestors, the gods and humans."

3.202 *with a generous spirit* (śraddhayā): the Sanskrit terms *śraddadhāna* and *śraddhā* are often taken as referring to "faith." In the early literature, however, these terms are closely associated with hospitality and generous giving. Greed and envy are given as the opposites of *śraddhā* at *VaDh* 6.8; 8.9. See also *MDh* 4.224–5, where *śraddhā* of the generous usurer is contrasted with the *aśrāddha* of the miserly scholar. For *śraddhā* as generosity, see Jamison 1996, 176–84; Hara 1979, 1992; Köhler 1973.

3.207 Additional verse: "He should offer it diligently at Vyatipātas, at solstices, at solar and lunar eclipses, and at equinoxes." Vyatipāta is an astronomical point when the sun and moon are in opposite courses, the sum of their longitudes being 180°.

3.208 *after they have sipped water:* commentators interpret the compound *upaspṛṣṭodakān* as both sipping water (*ācāntān*) and bathing (*snātān*). Within the context of eating, the verb *upa √spṛś* generally refers to the ritual sipping of water: see 2.53 n.

3.210 *collective consent of those Brahmins:* the expression *anujñāto brāhmaṇaiḥ saha* is quite unusual. The straightforward way to interpret the syntax is to relate *brāhmaṇaiḥ saha* with the verb *kuryāt;* the translation would then be: "with (their) consent, the Brahmin should make an offering in the sacred fire together with those Brahmins." Clearly, this is not the way the rite was performed; therefore, the commentators are forced to read a lot into the word *saha*. Medhātithi comments: *brāhmanair anujñātaḥ kuryād iti sambandhaḥ / saha sarve yugapad anujñāṃ dadyuḥ* ("permitted by the Brahmins, he should make—that is the syntax; 'with', i.e., all should give their permission simultaneously"). In some way, therefore, *saha* should be related to *anujñātaḥ*, in a way similar to *sahodita* ("collectively stated").

3.213 *ancient:* Medhātithi reads the nominative *purātanāḥ*, followed by Mandlik and Jha. All other commentators and the critical edition read the accusative *purātanān*, which gives a better meaning and is the *lectio difficilior*. See 3.192 where ancestors are called *pūrvadevatāḥ*. Medhātithi himself gives the alternative accusative reading, which he evidently prefers. If we follow the nominative reading, the translation should be: "the ancients call these the gods of the ancestral offering."

3.214 *end in the south:* the term *apasavyam* is obscure and is variously interpreted by commentators. See the attempt by ST to change the reading to *prasavyam* ("towards the left"). Medhātithi, followed by Govinda, Kullūka, and Rāghavānanda, takes it as a synonym of *dakṣiṇāsaṃstha*, that is, performing any series of actions so as to terminate towards the south. Nārāyaṇa and Rāmacandra think it means wearing the sacrificial cord over the right shoulder (*prācīnāvīta;* see 2.63 n); this is also Vijñāneśvara's interpretation of the term at *YDh* 1.232. Nandana sees in it a reference to a hand gesture (*hastamudrā*). Kangle regularly translates this term in the *Arthaśāstra* as "leftwise," i.e., anti-clockwise (*AŚ* 1.20.4; 13.2.24; 14.2.38; 14.3.84).

3.216 *those who partake of leavings* (lepabhāgin): these are the three ancestors beyond the third generation, i.e., the great-great-grandfather, and his father and grandfather.

3.220 *If his father . . . Brahmins:* why would the son perform an ancestral offering if his father is alive? The father would normally do this. Here perhaps we have evidence of retirement, when the property is divided during the father's lifetime and the son becomes the head of household and the chief ritual performer. Variant reading: "or he may feed his own father at the ancestral offering."

3.226 Variant reading: "he should first set down on the ground the side dishes."

3.228 *pressing . . . on them:* I follow the interpretation of Nārāyaṇa and Nandana. The word *guṇa* here must mean side dishes (*vyañjana*), which is its meaning in verses 226 and 233. All the commentators interpret the parallel in 233 in this manner, and it is unlikely that the term would have a different meaning here. Medhātithi, Govinda, Kullūka, and Rāghavānanda interpret the phrase in this verse, however, to mean: "proclaiming all their qualities." This is followed by Bühler and Doniger.

3.230 *ghosts:* the term *preta* generally refers to newly deceased persons, but here it probably has an extended meaning of malevolent spirits. Several commentators gloss with *piśāca*, "ghoul."

3.232 *ancillary texts:* the meaning of *khila* is unclear, but the probable reference, according to commentators, is to ancillary texts of the Veda, such as Śrīsūkta, legends, etc. A significant variant reads *purāṇāny akhilāni*, according to which the translation would be: ". . . epic narratives, and all the Purāṇas."

3.234 *goat's wool blanket:* the term *kutapa* is ambiguous and medieval authors assign up to eight meanings to it: midday, vessel of rhinoceros horn, woolen blanket, silver, Darbha grass, sesame seed, cow, and daughter's son. See Kane 1965–75, iv: 376–7.

3.245 *committed suicide:* the term *tyāginām* occurs only once more in Manu, at 5.89 (*ātmanas tyāginām*) referring to suicides. This is the interpretation given here also by Nārāyaṇa and Rāmacandra. Various other interpretations are offered: Medhātithi, Rāghavānanda and an alternate opinion quoted by Kullūka: "those who abandon a teacher and the like"; Nandana: "renouncers" (so also Doniger). Kullūka, as also authors quoted by Medhātithi, join this word with *kulayoṣitām* and interpret: "those who have abandoned women of good family," which is followed by Bühler. See *VaDh* 11.22–4.

3.247 *For a deceased . . . rice ball:* the language of this verse is terse and compact, which has led to both variant readings and variant interpretations. Many mss. and commentators read *āsapiṇḍakriyākarma*. The translation would then be: "Until the rite of Sapiṇḍa (has been performed), at an ancestral offering for a newly deceased twice-born he should feed one person omitting . . ." (so Bühler). Under this interpretation, the particle *ā* would govern the accusative, a feature not encountered elsewhere in Manu, who regularly uses the ablative (2.22, 38, 108, 167, 171, 243, 244; 3.279; 4.137; 5.88; 6.31; 9.89; 10.64; 11.104).

The second half of the verse is also compact, a lot of information being implied. The word *adaivam* (singular) says both that a single Brahmin is fed and that he does not represent the gods (Vaiśvadeva). So, only one Brahmin representing the newly deceased is fed; all others are eliminated. This type of *śrāddha* is technically called *ekoddiṣṭaśrāddha*, an ancestral offering intended for a single person. Such rites are performed until the rite of Sapiṇḍa (or Sapiṇḍana or Sapiṇḍīkaraṇa) is performed, usually on the 12th day after death. This rite makes the newly deceased "share in the rice balls" offered to the three preceding generations of deceased and thus formally constitutes him as an "ancestor" (*pitṛ*). On ancestral rites, see Kane 1962–75, iv: 334–551.

3.248 *above manner:* verse 247 dealing with the newly deceased is a parenthetical comment. Manu now picks up the thread of his argument by saying that after the Sapiṇḍana the ancestral offering is carried out precisely in the manner described before the interruption.

3.251 *Please, stay around:* Bühler, following Medhātithi's explanation of *abhitaḥ*, translates: "Rest either (here or at home)." I think both read too much into this polite invitation to leave. That *abhitaḥ* caused some problems is evident in the variant reading invented: *bho abhiramyatām* ("Sirs, do stay"). In polite discourse one does not ask a guest to simply leave; so we have here the euphemistic "stay," which really mean "go." A similar example is found in my mother tongue, Sinhala. When guests leave they say "we'll come."

3.254 *cow-pen offering:* generally called Goṣṭhīśrāddha, this is one of the twelve types of ancestral offerings listed in medieval sources. Kane (1962–75, iv: 381–2) gives the following description: "The Goṣṭhī-śrāddha is one which is performed when a man becomes enthusiastic owing to talk about śrāddha or when many learned men gather together at a sacred place and, finding it impossible to have separate cooking arrangements for each, pool their resources for collecting śrāddha materials and perform simultaneously śrāddha for the pleasure it affords to themselves and for the gratification of the pitṛs."

offering for prosperity: called Abhyudayaśrāddha, these ancestral offerings are performed on joyous occasions, such as the birth of a son.

3.256 *Darbha . . . stated above:* this verse is quite unclear. The repetition of *pavitra* (lit. "means of purifications") has been interpreted differently. The first one is taken to mean purificatory texts taken from the Veda, as well as purificatory blades of Kuśa grass (3.210). The second poses greater problems, because it is unclear whether it stands alone or is syntactically connected with what follows. Bühler opts for the latter, translating: "and those means of purification, mentioned above." I have followed Medhātithi and Nandana in taking *yac ca pūrvoktam* as a separate category (see the similar expression beginning with *yac ca* in verse 257). The placement of *ca* after *yat* clearly indicates that this is a separate entry. I think we should take one *pavitra* as referring to purificatory Kuśa grass and the other to purificatory texts.

3.257 *food of sages* (munyannāni): the designation for a variety of food items that are in some way uncultivated (see 6.12–21), the most common being *nīvāra*, a kind of wild rice.

meat, food without elaborate preparation: here again we have the expression *māṃsaṃ yac cānupaskṛtam* (see 3.256 n.). Commentators and translators take *anupaskṛtam* as qualifying *māṃsam*, although there is no unanimity about the meaning of the former term. Medhātithi and Rāmacandra: not forbidden; Nārāyaṇa: not prepared with spices (which appears to be Govinda's interpretation also: *anatitīkṣṇam*); Kullūka and Rāghavānanda: not smelly or rotten. See 5.112; 7.98; 10.62 n. Following the pattern of verse 256, however, I think *yac cānupaskṛtam* is a separate category in this list.

3.259 Additional verse: "May we have an abundance of food! May we obtain guests! May there be people who beg from us! May we never have to beg from anyone!"

3.261 *towards the east:* following the vulgate reading *parastāt* ("after") Bühler translates: "Some make the offering of the cakes after (the dinner)." The critical edition has adopted the reading *purastāt* (either "before" or "toward the east"). Clearly this verse gives alternative procedures of performing the rite. It is unclear, however, whether *purastāt* refers to the direction (as I have taken it) or to the temporal sequence ("before"). My interpretation is supported by verse 215 giving the standard procedure, according to which the rice balls are offered toward the south. Here we have an alternate procedure.

3.264 Variant reading: "feed also his maternal relatives."

3.267 Variant reading: "ancestors of men are satisfied for one month."

3.271 *beef, milk* (gavyena payasā): I take each word in this list to represent one item, an interpretation supported by Rāghavānanda and authors cited by Medhātithi. Given that the three preceding verses contain exclusively the meat of various animals and the second half of this verse also deals with meat, it is likely that here also we are dealing with meat, with milk and milk products (which are generally cow's, in any case) acting as substitutes for cow's meat. Most commentators, including Medhātithi, however, take *gavyena* as an adjective qualifying *payasā*. The translation would then be: "by offering cow's milk"; so Bühler and Doniger. This interpretation is probably influenced by the later abhorrence of cow's meat.

3.273 *Magha:* this is the 10th of the 15 constellations (*nakṣatra*). Nandana takes it as referring to the Māgha month, roughly corresponding to January–February. Others take this phrase to refer specifically to the 13th day of the dark half of the month of Bhādra (August–September) within the rainy season, when a particularly important ancestral offering named Mahālayaśrāddha is offered. The legal literature developed intricate rules regarding the dates and times for the performance of ancestral offerings. For details, see Kane 1965–75, iv: 369–77.

3.274 *elephant's eastern shadow:* this day is also called Gajachāyā. As Kane (1965–75, iv: 371 n) has shown, medieval authors interpret this word differently, some even taking it literally: one should perform the offering in the shadow of an elephant (so Rāghavānanda). Most, however, interpret it astronomically: it is the 13th day of Bhādrapada (August–September) when the moon is in the Māgha constellation and the sun in the Hasta constellation. See also Vijñāneśvara and Viśvarūpa on *YDh* 1.218. Medhātithi, Nārāyaṇa, and Rāmacandra take it to mean late afternoon when the shadow of an elephant is cast towards the east.

3.275 Six additional verses: "When a man performs an ancestral offering on the first day of the fortnight, he obtains handsome sons; on the second day, daughters; on the third, horses; on the fourth, small animals; on the fifth, splendid sons; on the sixth, success in gambling; on the seventh, success in agriculture; on the eighth, success in trade; on the ninth, one-hoofed animals; on the tenth, a lot of cloven-hoofed animals; on the eleventh, money and sons excelling in vedic learning; on the twelfth, gold, silver, and money; on the thirteenth, superiority over relatives; and on the fourteenth, bad offspring. All his ancestors who have been killed by the sword in battle are gladdened. A man who performs an ancestral offering on the fifteenth day obtains an abundance of things that his heart loves and those specified for people who perform it on the first days of a fortnight, as well as all his desires."

3.277 *later fortnight, earlier fortnight:* a lunar month begins on the new-moon day. The first or earlier fortnight (*pūrvapakṣa*) is when the moon is waxing, and the later (*aparapakṣa*) is the fortnight of the waning moon.

3.284 Variant reading: "this is the eternal scriptural statement."

CHAPTER FOUR

4.1 *After spending . . . at home:* see parallels at 5.169; 6.1, 33.

4.2 *little or no harm:* Medhātithi interprets *droha* not as injury (*hiṃsā*), because, according to him, not causing injury is already prescribed, but as vexation (*kheda*). The prohibition here, according to Medhātithi, is against begging, which is annoying to the donors. So one should avoid begging altogether or, if that is not possible, beg as little as possible.

4.3 *without fatiguing his body:* according to Medhātithi, this refers to trade and service, two activities that cause fatigue.

4.5 *gleaning and picking:* Medhātithi gives the following distinction between the two. Gleaning (*uñcha*) is gathering up ears of corn that have fallen on the ground when farmers take their harvest to their homes or granaries. Picking (*śila*) is gathering up ears of corn that have fallen to the ground from the plants in the field either before or after the harvest. The major difference is that the former is collected along the road and the latter in the field. See 10.112.

4.7 *to fill a granary . . . jar:* commentators understand these to mean individuals who have grain sufficient for a certain period of time, just like the last two kinds of persons. One who has a granary-full is taken by different commentators to mean a man who has grain sufficient to last three years, one year, or twelve days. One who has a jar-full is a man who has grain sufficient to last one year, six months, or six days.

4.8 *better at winning . . . the Law:* I follow the commentators. Bühler translates: "through his virtue to have conquered the world more completely." Although such a meaning is possible, I think the commentators are right in relating these means of livelihood to the worlds that the individuals will obtain after death.

4.9 *One of these . . . of the Veda:* commentators offer different and contradictory explanations (see Bühler's comment on this verse). I think Govinda is correct in relating these to the six occupations of a Brahmin (see 10.75). Three activities are studying, offering sacrifices, and giving gifts; two are the first two of these; and one is studying, which is here referred to as *brahmasattra* (2.106 n.). Bühler, however, thinks that the latter refers to teaching, which is also the interpretation of commentators.

4.15 *with excessive passion:* the meaning of *prasaṅgena* is unclear. Medhātithi, Govinda, and Kullūka take it as referring to activities that people are attached to, such as singing and music (thus probably connecting this term implicitly with *karmaṇā*). Bühler follows this interpretation. I think Nārāyaṇa and Nandana are right in taking it to mean excessive passion. See the similar use of this term at 2.93; 4.186; 8.368; 9.5; 12.52. This meaning also fits with the repeated use of words derived from *pra* √*sañj* in the next verse.

4.17 *eking out a living:* the term *yāpayan* could also mean "supporting his family," which is the interpretation of most commentators. However, note the Pāli *yāpeti* and the Buddhist Sanskrit *yāpayati* regularly used with regard to eking out a living especially by begging.

4.19 *treatises:* the term *śāstrāṇi* may refer also to the Vedas, which are often referred to simply as the *śāstra*, and this interpretation is supported by the use of the singular in verse 20. Commentators, however, take the term as referring to other treatises, including epics, Purāṇas, Dharmaśāstras, and treatises on logic, grammar, Mīmāṃsā, astrology, and medicine (Medhātithi, Govinda, Nandana, Kullūka); or simply the fourteen fields of knowledge (*vidyāsthānāni*): four Vedas, six Vedāṅgas, Purāṇa, Nyāya, Mīmāṃsā, and Dharmaśāstra. On *śāstra,* see Pollock 1989a.

ancillary texts: Medhātithi takes these to be texts that facilitate the understanding of the Veda, such as etymologies, grammar, and exegesis. Others take the term as referring to a specific class of explanatory texts.

4.20 Additional verse: "After learning thoroughly a book (*śāstra*), however, he should study it repeatedly. He should not disfigure a book or throw it away after studying it."

4.22–4 *Some individuals . . . rooted in knowledge:* the ritual tradition, often under the influence of ascetic ideologies, reinterpreted ritual activities providing many substitutes for actual ritual acts. The offering of food in the breaths (*prāṇāgnihotra*) in the act of eating is one of them. See *ChU* 5.19–24; Bodewitz 1973.

4.26 *at the end of each harvest* (sasyānte): Bühler, following most commentators, translate: "When the old grain has been consumed." This may well be true, given that the old crop may have been consumed by the time the new crop was harvested. However, the parallel with all other terms in this list supports Nārāyaṇa's and Nandana's interpretation that the reference here also is to a calendrical time, that is, the end of the harvest when the new crop is brought in.

Variant reading: "at the beginning of each half-year."

4.31 *after completing the Vedas . . . or vedic vows:* most commentators take *vedavidyāvrata* as three separate categories. The first refer to those who have only learned the Veda by heart; the second to those who have mastered its meaning; and the third to those who have completed the vows associated with vedic study, such as living with the teacher for a certain number of years, even if they have not mastered the Veda.

4.32 *those who do not cook:* namely, vedic students and ascetics. Medhātithi objects to this interpretation, because giving to these have already been enjoined (3.94). He thinks that the reference here is to the poor and common beggars.

4.39 *mound of earth* (mṛd): the meaning is obscure. Most commentators take it as a mound of earth artificially created. It may then refer to some kind of memorial mound. Some mss., as well as Rāmacandra, connect the first two words and read *mṛdaṅgam*, a type of small drum.

4.42 Variant reading: "his wisdom, prosperity, fame, sight, and life-force."

4.44 *nor should a Brahmin:* Bühler takes this verse as a general statement about not looking at women; I think it is continuation of 43 and refers specifically to the wife.

Additional verse: "A wise bath-graduate should not come near and look at another man's wife when she is naked; and he should avoid secret conversations with someone else's wife."

4.46 *onto a mound:* I have taken *cityām* to mean some kind of memorial mound, as in verse 39. Commentators, however, take it as referring specifically to a fire altar (abandoned?) made with bricks.

4.49 *remaining steadfastly attentive:* generally *prayata* means to be or to make oneself pure (so Bühler) and ready for a ritual act. That cannot be its meaning here; there is no purificatory rite before voiding urine or excrement, which are by definition polluting activities. Commentators are hard pressed to find a meaning.

4.52 *When someone . . . perishes:* this verse directly relates to verse 48. The intervening verses, therefore, must be either an interpolation or given parenthetically. Several mss. and Jha actually place this verse immediately after 48.

4.55 *take off his own garland:* Medhātithi comments that one should get someone else to remove it from one's neck. The reason is unclear; it may have been thought to be inauspicious to remove it by oneself.

4.57 *awaken a sleeping superior:* see Jamison's (2000) detailed analysis of this expression derived from *MS* 3.4.5. The two variants in the manuscript tradition—*śreyāṃsam* and *śayānam*—are related to the two words in the vedic precedent: *śreyāṃsaṃ viṣuptam*. According to the variant reading, the translation would be: "awaken sleeping man."

Additional verse: "He may freely go to a sacrifice to pay reverence or to witness it. He should not go from house to house to obtain secrets without a good reason."

4.60 *diseases run rampant:* Kullūka and Rāghavānanda take *bhṛśam* as qualifying *vaset* and meaning "long." Bühler accordingly translates: "nor (stay) long where diseases are endemic." I think Govinda is right in taking it to mean *atyartham* and connecting it with *vyādhibahule*.

4.64 *clap; whistle:* the precise meanings of the terms *āsphoṭayet* and *kṣeḍet* are unclear. The former refers to a noise made through a limb. Commentators give the following possibilities: clapping or striking the floor with the palm, slapping the arms, cracking the finger joints. The latter term refers to a noise made with the mouth. Commentators give the following range: grinding the teeth, growling like a lion, whistling with the fingers in the mouth.

4.69 *never cut his nails or hair:* commentators offer diverse interpretations. Most take it to mean that he should not cut them himself but have them cut by a barber. Some think this forbids the man to cut them before the appropriate time. These interpretations are unsatisfactory; if this was the meaning Manu could have said it more straightforwardly. The odd expression here is not the lack of a causative but the use of the verb √*chid*. The Dharmasūtras regularly use the verb √*vap* for cutting hair (see *ĀpDh* 2.3.6; *BDh* 1.5.7; 2.2.44, etc.; *VaDh* 24.5). At *VaDh* 24.5 √*kṛt* is used for cutting the nails. Manu uses √*kḷp* (4.35; 6.52) with regard to the proper maintenance of hair, nails, and beard. The only other place where *chindyāt* is used is in *ViDh* 71.44: *na dantair nakhalomāni chindyāt*, "He must not break his nails or hair with his teeth." This provision is given by Manu in *pāda-d*. Manu uses this verb regularly for cutting off some part of the body, such as hands, feet, and lips for punishment (8.282, 283; 9.277). I think what is prohibited here is the cutting of hair and nails by means other than the proper tools (nail clippers, scissors). We see that in the very next verse the same verb is used to forbid breaking off grass with one's fingers.

4.72 *wear a garland outdoors:* commentators interpret the expression *bahirmālyam* to mean that he should not wear a garland either over his hair or over his clothes, an interpretation followed by Bühler and Doniger. I think it is wrong. The same expression occurs in *GDh* 9.32 with the addition of perfume: *bahirgandhamālya*. It makes little sense to say that one should not wear perfume over the clothes! The prohibition, I think, concerns wearing these ostentatious adornments in public. See the very similar prohibition at *ĀpDh* 1.32.5. See also *BDh* 2.6.9.

4.83 *refrain from . . . head:* it is unclear whose hair and head are meant. Medhātithi gives two interpretations. According to the first, the injunction is general, including one's own as well as that of others. The second is based on the context, which deals with one's own body; so the prohibition affects only one's own hair and head. Pulling the hair of others and striking their head is, of course, forbidden by other injunctions. The meaning then is that one should not pull one's hair or strike one's head in anger.

4.87 *deviates . . . texts* (ucchāstravartinaḥ): the word *ucchāstra*, as far as I know, occurs only here and in the parallel passage in *YDh* 1.140. The dictionary definitions of the expression in B-R ("ausserhalb der Gesetzücher übertrentend") and M-W ("deviating from or transgressing the lawbooks") are based solely on these passages. The term *ucchāstra* parallels *utkula* ("cast out of the family") and may mean someone who has left the *śāstras*. Or it may parallel *utpatha* or *unmārga* ("bad or wrong road") and may mean a man who follows a wrong *śāśtra*, for example, Jain or Buddhist scriptures.

4.90 Variant reading: "Lohadāraka."

4.92 *time sacred to Brahman:* Medhātithi defines this as the last watch of the night (about three hours), and most other commentators agree. Nārāyaṇa simply identifies it as the dawn (*uṣas*). Govinda (on *BDh* 2.17.22) defines it as the final period (about one hour and twelve minutes) of the last watch of the night, a watch being one-twelfth of a day or a period of three hours. On *muhūrta*, see 1.64 n.

4.96 *Puṣya . . . Māgha:* the meaning of Puṣya in uncertain, some commentators taking it to mean a constellation (*nakṣatra*) and others taking it as the Pauṣa month (December–January). The latter is the time indicated by *PārGṛ* 2.112.1 and *KhGṛ* 3.2.26. Given that the period lasts for four and a half months, I take the specification in the last *pāda* to refer to both alternatives. The first alternative (December–January) is followed when one begins the study in Śrāvaṇa and the second when one begins in Prauṣṭapada. Bühler understands this verse differently: "When the Pushya-day (of the month, Pausha), or the first day of the bright half of Māgha has come, a Brāhmaṇa shall perform in the forenoon the Utsarjana of the Vedas."

4.103 *lightning, thunder, and rain:* commentators note, rightly I think, that the suspension takes place only when these three occur together (see verse 106). During the rainy season, it is likely that one or the other of these may occur every day.

4.105 *noise erupts:* the general interpretation of the commentators is that *nirghāte* refers to some sort of atmospheric noise different from thunder. The same interpretation is given by the commentators of *YDh* 1.145. At *GDh* 16.22, however, Maskarin interprets the term to mean a lightning strike.

4.106 *When lightning . . . during the day:* this and verse 104 appear to be commentaries on verse 103. The term *sajyotiḥ* (see also 5.82 and *GDh* 16.31; *VaDh* 13.37) means that the suspension lasts as long as the sun is visible (i.e., until nightfall) if the event happened during the morning twilight, and as long as the stars are visible (i.e., until daybreak) if the event happened during the evening twilight. The expression "the other event" (*śeṣe*) refers to the third event listed in verse 103, namely, rain. The meaning is that if all three occur together, then, irrespective of whether it happens during the day or the night, the provision of verse 103 applies and the suspension lasts until the same time the following day (*ākālika*).

4.112 *squatting . . . knees:* the term *avasaktikā* refers to the band of cloth tied around the waist and over the knees so as to make it easier for a person to remain in the squatting position. It is unclear why this position is forbidden, but it may have something to do with a similar custom among ascetics. The band used by them is called *yogapaṭṭa*, and, as the name suggests, it was used during yogic practice.

4.115 *seated in a row* (paṅktau): Medhātithi, Nārāyaṇa, and Rāghavānanda connect this word with the crying of dogs etc. The translation would then be: "when a pack of dogs, donkeys, or camels are crying out." The particle *ca* coming after *paṅktau*, however, makes this interpretation unlikely. I have not seen the word *paṅkti* used with regard to animals in the Dharma literature.

4.123 *after reciting the conclusion . . . Āraṇyaka:* my translation follows the obvious syntax of the sentence; but it is supported only by Nandana. Medhātithi, followed by most other commentators, takes the second half-verse as a separate clause with an implicit prohibition against reciting another vedic text. Govinda and others specify that this period of suspension lasts for a day and a night. According to this interpretation, the translation would be: ". . . Sāman chanting; and after reciting the conclusion of a Veda or after reciting an Āraṇyaka (he should not recite any other text for a day and a night)." The meaning of "conclusion of a Veda" (*vedasya antam*) is also unclear. Some take it to mean the Upaniṣads, an interpretation supported by the mention of Āraṇyaka; others take it to mean the end of any vedic text (see also 2.160 n.).

4.125 *Knowing . . . then the Veda:* this verse is quite obscure and has been subject to two widely differing interpretations. Medhātithi and, following him, most other commentators take *trayīniṣkarṣa* as referring to the "essence of the Veda," namely the syllable OṂ, the Calls (*vyāhṛti*), and the Gāyatrī verse. The translation would then be: "Knowing this, learned men recite daily and in due order first the 'essence of the Veda' and thereafter recite the Veda." My problem with this interpretation, which is followed by Bühler and Doniger, is that there is a *non sequitur* from the previous verse, on which this is clearly a commentary. The only way it can be connected to the preceding is by taking the initial recitation of OṂ as in some way breaking the connection with the impure recitation of the Sāmaveda. I think, however, that the term *niṣkarṣa* refers to the "extract," probably the first lines, of each Veda. These are recited first before the actual recitation of the particular Veda of his branch. Nārāyaṇa and Nandana give still another interpretation, taking *niṣkarṣa* to be the "nature" of the three Vedas spelled out in the previous verse. The translation would be: "Knowing this nature of the triple Veda, learned men recite daily and in the proper order the early Veda first and then the later Veda." The meaning is that one first recites the Ṛgveda, then the Yajurveda, and finally Sāmaveda.

4.126 *passes in between:* the meaning is that an animal passes either between the teacher and the pupil, or between a group of reciters, while they are engaged in vedic recitation.

4.127 *These alone . . . purified:* both Bühler and Doniger have missed the point of this verse by misunderstanding the crucial word *nityam*. As the commentators point out, this refers to the suspension of the daily vedic recitation (*svādhyāya*), which is one of the five great sacrifices. At 2.105 we have the statement that "Rules regarding the suspension of vedic recitation have no bearing . . . on daily vedic recitation." Thus all the rules given above apply only to vedic study and recitation that are outside *svādhyāya*. This verse, however, specifies that on these two occasions even *svādhyāya* is to be suspended.

4.129 *with his clothes on:* bathing with one's clothes on (*savāsā*) is prescribed for particular observances and as a purification for various types of offenses (11.174, 123). Here the prohibition pertains to doing it on a regular or daily basis.

4.130 *god:* this must surely refer to the shadow cast by an image of a god.

reddish-brown cow: the term *babhru* here appears to refer to be a cow, although Medhātithi thinks that it may also refer to the Soma plant and others take it as a general term applying to any reddish-brown animal. The term also means a particular kind of mongoose (see *BDh* 1.19.6).

4.138 *eternal Law:* this is the first time that the common expression *dharmaḥ sanātanaḥ* occurs in the Dharma literature. Indeed, it is missing in the Dharmasūtras and in the *ViDh* and the *YDh*. The expression occurs again in 9.64; for similar expressions, see 7.98; 9.325; and 10.7.

4.139 *A lucky thing . . . Lucky:* the first half of this verse is very obscure, with a difficult and possibly elliptical syntax. The only other places in the Dharma literature that the term *bhadra* occurs within a similar context are *GDh* 9.20 and *ĀpDh* 1.31.12. In the former, we have the statement that one should call an unlucky thing lucky (*abhadraṃ bhadram iti*); and the latter states that one should not call a lucky thing lucky but use other terms such as holy and auspicious (*na bhadram bhadram iti brūyāt / puṇyaṃ praśastam ity eva brūyāt*). The parallel of these two texts to our verse is unmistakable. Medhātithi follows the *GDh* and sees an implied negative in the first *bhadra* (it should be *abhadra*) and the second *bhadra* he takes as illustrative of the actual words that should be used, namely *kalyāṇa, maṅgala, siddha*, etc. If we follow his interpretation, the translation should be: "He should call an unlucky thing by a lucky name, or he should just say lucky." Nārāyaṇa, on the other hand, whose interpretation is favored by

Bühler, finds an implied negative *abhadra* in the second clause: "He should call a lucky thing lucky, or he should just call an unlucky thing lucky." What is clear is that the context of this verse is the advice in verse 138 that one should not say something unpleasant even though it may be true. This is basic politeness and underlies several of the rules in the *GDh* 9.19–22 and *ĀpDh* 1.31.11. I think the commentators are right in detecting an implied *abhadra* in this statement; most likely this should be in the second clause. Even without that, however, we can interpret the statement to mean that one should call not only what is good and auspicious but everything, good or bad, by a term denoting auspiciousness. Note also that in verse 138 we have two positives in *pāda-a*, followed by positive-cum-negatives in the next two *pādas*.

4.143 *he should . . . with his palm:* an alternative translation, favored by Bühler and Doniger, would be: "he should always apply water with his palm on his organs, all his limbs, and his navel."

4.145 Additional verse: "Gold, sandal wood, vermilion, the five products of the cow (11.166 n.), concrete bile, panic seed, mustard seed, and honey are said to be auspicious."

4.149 Variant reading: "former birth, recites the Veda again."

4.150 *He should . . . fortnight:* Nandana acutely observes that this verse is a commentary on verse 145 containing the injunction to perform fire offerings (*juhuyāt*). In fact, verses 147–9 comment on the injunction to perform soft recitations (*japet*) of verse 145; after which Manu turns to the fire offerings.

4.153 *He should . . . moon's change:* I have followed the sequence of the *pādas* in the verse. This is also the interpretation of Medhātithi and other commentators. Bühler and Doniger, however, take the days of the moon's change as applicable to all these visits, which I think is mistaken.

4.156 *unlucky marks:* Medhātithi gives the example of a black mark (*tilaka*) on the shoulder that foretells poverty and other such misfortunes.

4.163 Variant reading: "hypocrisy."

4.166 *in evil wombs:* Medhātithi takes the compound *pāpayoniṣu* to be Tatpuruṣa: *pāpānāṃ yoniṣu*. He and other commentators, however, interpret it as referring to the wombs of various animals rather than those of evil men, which is Doniger's interpretation: "in the wombs of evil people." Bühler takes *pāpa* as "sin" and gives a torturous translation: "in the wombs (of such beings where men are born in punishment of their) sins." I take the compound as Karmadhāraya.

4.172 *Like the earth* (gaur iva): Medhātithi and, following him, Govinda and Kullūka see a double simile here, the one based on similarity (*sādharmya*) and the other on dissimilarity (*vaidharmya*). In the former case, the comparison is with a cow; in the latter, it is with the earth (also bearing the epithet cow). Like the earth—and unlike a cow—unrighteous conduct does not bear fruit immediately but only with the passage of time.

4.174 *root:* commentators take "root" to mean home, fields, wealth, family, and progeny. The meaning, obviously, is that his destruction is total and leaves no trace behind.

4.175 *disciples:* all the commentators take *śiṣyān* in its etymological meaning "those who ought to be disciplined," meaning the wife, children, servants, and the like. They cite 8.299 in support. It is clear that Manu is playing with alliteration here: *śiṣyān śiṣyāt*.

4.179 *doctors:* like the English term "doctor," *vaidya* can refer to both a very learned person and a medical doctor, although most commentators opt for the former.

paternal, affinal, and maternal relatives: the commentators make a very clear distinction between the three terms: *jñāti*, "paternal relative"; *saṃbhandhin*, "relative by marriage"; and *bāndhava*, "maternal relative": see also 2.132 n.

4.181 *when he is conquered by them:* the critical edition has adopted the reading *etair jitaḥ*. Bühler, following the reading *etaiḥ jitaiḥ*, translates: "by suppressing (all) such (quarrels)."

4.188 *ignorant man:* most commentators take *avidvān* to mean simply an ignorant man. Nārāyaṇa takes this term in its participial sense with the procedure mentioned in the previous verse as its direct object: "a man not knowing the procedure for accepting gifts."

4.192 Variant reading: "to a Brahmin observing."

4.195 Additional verse: "When a man always raises the flag of righteousness as if it were the flag of gods, but conceals his sins, his is called the 'cat's vow'."

4.196 *cruel:* the term *naikṛtika* can mean both cruel and dishonest, generally meaning a vile person.

4.200 *insignia of a religious profession:* the term *liṅgin* is ambiguous. It refers to a person who bears a distinguishing mark or emblem. Generally, this refers to the emblems of a religious professional, such as a vedic student, a forest hermit, or an ascetic. Medhātithi and Nārāyaṇa, correctly I think, take it with a broad meaning, whereas Govinda and Kullūka restrict it to a vedic student.

4.203 *natural ponds:* literally, ponds "dug by the gods" (*devakhāteṣu*), so as to distinguish them from the reservoirs built by humans and forbidden in verse 201.

4.204 *secondary observances* (niyama), *central virtues* (yama): these two are technical terms denoting the first two steps in the eightfold path of Yoga. It is, however, more likely that the terms here refer to two sets of observances, *yama* being central virtues such as non-injury and *niyama* being outward religious rites such as twilight-worship (so Govinda). *YDh* 3.312–3 gives ten virtues falling under these two categories.

Two verses cited by Medhātithi have been incorporated into the text of Manu by several mss.: "Compassion, forbearance, truthfulness, non-injury, self-control, not desiring, meditation, serenity, sweetness, and honesty are the ten central virtues. Purification, sacrifices, ascetic toil, gift giving, vedic recitation, restraining the sexual organs, observances, fasts, silence, and bathing are the ten secondary observances."

Other mss. give two different verses spelling out the contents of *yama* and *niyama*. "Not injuring, speaking the truth, chastity, honesty, and not stealing—these five are the central virtues and the observances. Not being angry, obedience to the teacher, purification, eating moderately, and vigilance—these five are called the secondary observances."

4.205 *A Brahmin must never partake of food:* here begins Manu's discussion of "unfit food," as well as persons whose food is unfit to be eaten, both of which are technically called *abhojyānna* (4.221): see Olivelle 2002a.

4.207 *someone . . . sick:* Medhātithi gives two possible interpretations. The first takes this to refer to someone who is currently intoxicated etc.; the other takes this as referring to people who are habitually such (*bāhulyena*). Under this interpretation the translation would be: "by someone who is a drunkard, quick tempered, or sickly."

4.208 *murderer of a Brahmin:* the Sanskrit term *bhrūṇahan* has two meanings: a killer of a fetus (abortionist) and a killer of a learned Brahmin. The *VkhGṛ* (1.1), giving the definitions of eight types of Brahmins in terms of their learning, defines a *bhrūṇa* as a Brahmin who has mastered the Veda, set up the ritual fires, and offered a Soma sacrifice. See Kane 1962–75, ii. 131, 148 n., 334; iii. 612 n. 1161. The Dharma literature uses the term with both meanings. At *GDh* 21.9 it means an abortionist, while at *BDh* 1.18.13 it clearly refers to a murderer of a Brahmin. At other places it is impossible to tell which meaning is intended. Indeed, both meanings may be intended in many of these passages; *VaDh* 20.23, in fact, gives both definitions of the term. This term appears also at *MDh* 8.317 and 11.248. See also Saksena 1936; Wezler 1994;

4.210 *a prisoner, a shackled man* (baddhasya nigaḍasya ca): the problem here centers around *nigaḍa*, which is a noun meaning a chain for binding the feet. To get it to mean a person so fettered, commentators have to see it as a substitute for *nigaḍitasya* (Nandana) or *nigaḍabaddhasya* (Nārāyaṇa). Kullūka takes the genitive *nigaḍasya* to function as an instrumental, and Nandana in fact says that the correct reading should be *baddhasya nigaḍena*. Under this interpretation, followed by Bühler, we have a single category here: "someone bound by chains." I think, however, that *nigaḍasya* is the *lectio difficilior*, and the final *ca* supports taking these as two separate entries. Medhātithi interprets *baddha* as referring to a man who is kept under arrest only by a judicial sentence (*vāgmātrāvaruddhaḥ*), and *nigaḍa* as referring to a man actually in shackles. The former, as Rāmacandra says, may refer to someone under house arrest. Given the unlikelihood of such people being able to actually distribute food, the prohibition must refer to food given by the family or household of such a man. Medhātithi also gives the variant *viṣadasya* ("of a poisoner") for *nigaḍasya*.

4.211 *food of a Śūdra, leftovers* (śūdrasyocchiṣṭam eva ca): most commentators take these as separate entries. Rāghavānanda and Govinda, however, connect the two: "the leftovers of a Śūdra." Medhātithi shows unusual inconsistency, interpreting this expression here to mean "leftovers of a Śūdra" but in his comments on it under verse 223 takes the two as separate entries. Given the frequency of genitive nouns with an implied *annam* ("food") in this list, I think it is appropriate to take the two as separate. Also in verse 218 we have the prohibition of eating a Śūdra's food (*śūdrānnam*). All this confusion apparently led some to amend the last *pāda* to read *ucchiṣṭam aguros tathā* ("the leftovers of anyone but the teacher/elder"), a reading recorded by Medhātithi.

4.212 *food given . . . birth* (anirdaśam): some connect this syntactically with *sūtikānnam*, "food of a woman during the first ten days after childbirth." This is quite unlikely. Medhātithi takes *anirdaśam* to refer to the milk of a cow during the first ten days after giving birth (see 5.8). The variant reading *paryāyānnam* (for *paryācāntam*) is interpreted by Vijñāneśvara (on *YDh* 1.168) as food specific to someone else, as when a Śūdra gives food specific to Brahmins and vice versa. But Nandana, who has the alternate reading of this verse, says that it means food obtained on a rotational basis.

Additional verse: "When different honor is paid to Brahmins of equal status or equal honor to Brahmins of unequal status, any gift given on such an occasion should not be accepted; nor should a gift be given in such a manner." I follow Lakṣmīdhara's explanation of this elliptical verse.

4.213 *chief of a town:* the meaning of *nagarin* is not altogether clear. Most commentators take the term to mean a leader or chief of a town; some, however, take it as referring simply to a town dweller. This category is absent in the parallel discussions of food in other Dharma texts, although towns and villages are looked down upon: *ĀpDh* 1.32.21; *GDh* 16.45.

4.217 *food of persons . . . newly deceased person* (anirdaśaṃ ca pretānnam): most commentators take the first word as qualifying the second and see here a single category. Bühler thus translates: "nor food (given by men) whose ten days of impurity on account of a death have not passed." I follow Nārāyaṇa and Rāmacandra in taking the two words as referring to two different categories, even though the placement of *ca* is awkward (possibly due to meter). Further, it is difficult to see how *pretānna* could mean food given by a person impure by reason of a death in his family; its obvious meaning is "food offered to a newly deceased person." The term *anirdaśam*, moreover, occurs in verse 212 with reference to a single category.

4.222 *food of any one of them* (anyatamasyānnam): Medhātithi and Govinda think that, even though this prescription (governed by the genitive) refers directly to food given by unfit individuals (*parigrahaduṣṭa*), nevertheless, because of the context, the penance should be performed by anyone eating food that is unfit for other reasons, such as touch, time, and nature (*kāladuṣṭa, saṃsargaduṣṭa, svabhāvaduṣṭa*). Kullūka, however, rejects this argument and takes the prescription to affect only the first category (*parigrahaduṣṭa*).

Additional verse: "He should not eat during an eclipse of the moon or the sun; but when their eclipse is over, he may eat after bathing. When they set before the end of the eclipse, he may eat after he has seen them the next day."

4.223 *who lacks a spirit of generosity* (aśraddhinaḥ): if we accept the reading of the majority of mss., *aśrāddhinaḥ,* the translation should be: "a Śūdra who neglects his ancestral rites."

4.226 Three additional verses: "Learning, bravery, ascetic toil, virgin, person at whose sacrifice one officiates, pupil, and inheritance—what is acquired through these are the seven kinds of 'white' wealth; gains from these are also of the same type. Usury, agriculture, trade, craft, service, ministration, and a man for whom one has done a favor—what is obtained from these is called 'spotted'. Bribery, gambling, theft, coercion, deception, violence, and fraud—what is acquired through these means is called 'black'." The term "virgin" in the first verse probably refers to bride-price.

4.227 Two additional verses: "When a Brahmin accepts a gift and uses it for wrongful ventures, one should not give him anything, even though he may be a worthy recipient. When a man accepts gifts from everywhere and accumulates them without using them for purposes dictated by Law, one should not honor that thief."

4.228 *from all* (sarvataḥ): the meaning of "all" is unclear. Medhātithi, Nārāyaṇa, Rāmacandra: sins; Nandana: suffering (*duḥkha*); Kullūka: things that lead one to hell (*narakahetu*); Rāghavānanda, Govinda: faults (*doṣa*).

4.232 Variant reading: "one who gives the Veda, the eternal Brahman."

4.234 *that very thing* (tat tat): the commentators correctly point out that "that very thing" refers not to the article given as a gift but the corresponding reward listed in the above verses.

4.236 *lie about a sacrifice:* most commentators simply take this phrase to mean that a person who has performed a sacrifice must not tell a lie. Bühler and Doniger follow their interpretation. The whole point of this verse, however, is that people should not boast about or exaggerate religious activities they have undertaken. I think Rāghavānanda's interpretation is correct; the meaning must be that one should not tell a lie about a sacrifice one has performed, most probably by exaggeration.

4.243 Additional verse: "Neither the Vedas that he has recited nor the treatises that he has studied go where he is going; merit alone follows him."

4.249 Additional verse: "He should avoid even what is given spontaneously by a physician, an ingrate, a surgeon, a usurer, a eunuch, or an unchaste woman."

4.253 *a person . . . himself:* commentators take him to be a Śūdra who has fallen on hard times and has voluntarily entered another man's service. It is unclear whether such a man becomes a slave or merely a servant or worker.

4.257 *debts:* fundamental religious obligations of a Brahmin were presented within Brahmanical theology as "debts" (see Malamoud 1972). The theology of debts arose quite early, and three debts are recorded already in the *TS* 6.3.10.5: "A Brahmin, at his very birth, is born with a triple debt—of studentship to the seers, of sacrifice to the gods, of offspring to the fathers. He is, indeed, free from debt, who has a son, is a sacrificer, and who has lived as a student." The *ŚB* (1.7.2.1–6) adds the debt of hospitality to men, bringing the theology of debts into closer alignment with the five great sacrifices. The obligation to marry, to perform sacrifices, and to beget offspring was used by Brahmanical theologians against the ascetical ideals of anti-ritualism and celibacy (6.35). For a discussion of the debts and their relation to asceticism, see Olivelle 1993, 46–53.

CHAPTER FIVE

5.1 *born from the fire:* although Bhṛgu is said to be a son of Manu (1.34), other accounts of his origin record his birth from the fire. See *AB* 3.34; *Bṛhaddevatā* 6.97–9; *MBh* 1.5.216*.

5.5 *forbidden:* the Dharma literature makes a clear distinction between *abhakṣya*, foods forbidden because of their very nature, and *abhojya*, foods that have become unfit for a variety of reasons: given by an unfit individual, touched by an impure person or animal, contaminated by an impure substance, or gone stale or bad due to time, a topic dealt with at 4.205–25. I translate the former as "forbidden" and the latter as "unfit." On this distinction and the dietary restrictions in Dharma literature, see Olivelle 2002a, 2002b.

5.7 *Kṛsara porridge, Saṃyāva cake:* Kṛsara appears to be a dish made with milk, rice, and sesame seeds. Saṃyāva is a sweet cake made with flour, milk, and ghee.

5.11 *single-hoofed . . . permitted:* there is no text that permits the eating of any single-hoofed animal. It may well be that this exception is made in view of the horse-sacrifice during which horse meat is consumed by the priests. Such an exception, however, would be unique in the Dharma literature (Olivelle 2002b). Another possible interpretation is to take the two terms *anirdiṣṭa* and *ekaśapha* as two separate items, in which case the translation would be: "animals not explicitly mentioned; single-hoofed animals; plovers." See *VaDh* 14.44 where animals not specifically indicated are forbidden.

5.17 *animals with five nails:* this is an ancient and widespread rule forbidding the eating of animals with five nails or claws, with the exception of some. Here seven such exceptions are listed, whereas the standard rule contains only five exceptions. The general formulation of this rule is: "The five five-nailed animals may be eaten" (*pañca pañcanakhāḥ bhakṣyāḥ)* meaning that five-clawed animals other than those enumerated are forbidden. This is an example of the so-called *parisaṃkhyā* injunction, which is a prohibition couched as an injunction. Thus, the intent of the rule is to prohibit five-clawed animals, not to enjoin the eating of the five listed animals. Accordingly, someone may avoid eating *all* five-clawed animals, even those listed, without violating this injunction. The forbidding of animals with five "nails" may indeed be a residue of the proscription of cannibalism, since human beings are among animals with five nails. See *ĀpDh* 1.17.37; *GDh* 17.27; *BDh* 1.12.5; *VaDh* 14.39. For a detailed study, see Jamison 1998.

5.18 *animals with incisors in only one jaw:* literally "those with a single row of teeth," the reference is to animals that have incisor teeth only on the lower jaw; cows, goats, and sheep are examples. These are the paradigmatic farm animals whose meat may be eaten. The opposite of these are animals with incisor teeth on both jaws. Haradatta and Govinda (on *BDh* 1.2.4) give as an example the horse, while Maskarin's (on *GDh* 17.28) example is a man. In the Puruṣa Hymn (*ṚV* 10.90.10) also animals with teeth on both jaws are associated with the horse. Other examples include donkeys and mules, as well as dogs, cats, and most carnivorous animals. See Smith 1994, 244; Olivelle 2002b.

5.23 Variant reading: "For, even at ancient sacrifices and at the Soma offerings."

5.24 *infused with oil:* many commentators interpret this verse to mean the following: "Any non-forbidden food or delicacy may be eaten even if it is stale after mixing it with oil." Medhātithi realizes the syntactical problem of taking *snehasaṃyuktam* as part of the main cause and qualifying *tat*. Nevertheless, he feels forced to accept this indirect meaning, because otherwise, according to him, the separate mention of the sacrificial oblation would become pointless. This interpretation is followed by Bühler, Doniger, and all other commentators, except Nārāyaṇa and Nandana. I follow these two. The clear meaning is that food prepared with oil does not become stale; leftovers of a sacrificial oblation, on the other hand, even if it is not made with oil, is by definition not subject to becoming stale. The parallel passages in *YDh* 1.169 and *ViDh* 51.35 support this interpretation.

5.27 *He may eat . . . at risk:* this verse opens the discussion on eating meat with a broad and general statement giving four occasions for eating meat. The discussion ends with verse 56, which is again a broad statement attempting to reconcile the opposing viewpoints given earlier. These two verses bracket the discussion, which, I think, contains two views. The first (28–30) defends the traditional position regarding meat eating; that is the natural order of creation established by the Creator himself. The second position (31–55) proposes the ethic of vegetarianism and non-injury, strongly condemning killing and eating meat outside very restrictive parameters established by the needs of the vedic sacrifice. Manu does not tell us explicitly his own view. It is, however, the traditional method to give the view of an opponent or the view to be refuted first (*pūrvapakṣa*) and the view of the author himself last (*uttarapakṣa*). If this holds good here, then Manu must have favored the restriction of meat to sacrificial occasions. This is supported by the fact that Manu dispenses with the first view in three verses, whereas he devotes 25 verses to defending the second view.

Commentators explain the term *niyuktaḥ* ("ritually commissioned") as referring to a person who is undertaking a rite such as an ancestral offering and the "honey mixture" (*madhuparka*: 3.119 n.). This is distinguished from sacrificial consecration (*prokṣita*) listed earlier. The latter refers to vedic sacrifices, while the former refers to non-vedic rites. The term *niyukta* is also used at 5.35.

5.28 *created:* the term *akalpayat* appears to have a double meaning here. On the one hand, Prajāpati created the whole world to serve as food for lifebreath, or for living creatures (see 5.39 where *sṛṣṭa* is used). This echoes the creation motif of the Brāhmaṇas and Upaniṣads. On the other hand, the term also has a prescriptive meaning; Prajāpati designated this world as food for lifebreath (see the similar meaning of *akalpayat* at 1.87–8).

5.31 *rule of gods, rule of fiends:* possibly, we have here a double entendre. On the one hand, saying that the rules are divine or fiendish indicates the goodness of the one and the evil of the other. On the other hand, we can take *vidhi* as the manner of acting: thus, gods eat meat only during vedic sacrifices, whereas Rākṣasas are well-known as always relishing blood and meat.

5.36 Variant reading: "Abiding by the eternal Law (*dharma*)."

5.39 *The Self-existent . . . for sacrifice*: this statement refutes the claim made in verse 28 by the defenders of meat eating that Prajāpati created the whole world as food for living beings.

5.44 *well-established . . . creation* (niyatāsmiṃś carācare): Medhātithi and Govinda interpret *niyatā* to mean "without beginning" (*anādi*); the sacrificial killing has existed in the world always. This may be related to the fact that other types of killing, such as those sanctioned by Tantra, are recent customs. The "beginninglessness" of sacrificial killing is related to the timelessness of the Veda itself, which is the basis of *dharma*.

Therefore, ethical norms of *ahiṃsā* that contradict the Veda cannot be part of *dharma*. Bühler, following Kullūka, interprets this verse differently: "Know that the injury to moving creatures and to those destitute of motion, which the Veda has prescribed for certain occasions, is no injury at all." I think this is a misinterpretation of the locative *asmiṃś carācare*; it is syntactically connected to *niyatā* and not to *hiṃsā*. Further, the expression *carācara* normally refers to the whole world as such and not to individual creatures (see 1.57, 63; 3.75; 7.29; 11.237).

5.46 *tie up, kill, or cause pain* (bandhanavadhakleśān): I follow Govinda and Kullūka, who take this as a Dvandva compound of three members. Medhātithi and Rāghavānanda take *bandhanavadha* + *kleśa* as Karmadhāraya: "pains consisting of tying up and killing" (*bandhanavadhā eva kleśāḥ*), which is followed by Bühler and Doniger.

5.47 Variant reading: "on whatever a man fixes his mind."

5.50 *except when the rules prescribe it* (vidhiṃ hitvā): Bühler takes *hitvā* as "disregarding." The meaning then is that he disregards the rule that he should eat meat at a sacrifice and the like. I think this is mistaken. The meaning, as Medhātithi points out, is that he does not eat meat *except* according to the rule. Because of the multiple negatives in this sentence, the comparison inherent in the simile *piśācavat* "like a Piśāca" is also unclear. I think it means that he acts *unlike* a Piśāca, who eats anything and everything (see 5.31).

The fact that this verse caused problems to readers and scribes is evident in variants recorded. Some, including Hemādri and Lakṣmīdhara, take the verse in a negative manner, reading *yas tu bhakṣayate* in *pāda-a*; taking *loke 'priyatām* (with an *avagraha* rendering it negative); and eliminating *na* in *pāda-d: vyādhibhiś caiva pīḍyate*. According to this traditional interpretation, the translation would be: "When a man eats meat disregarding the rules like a goblin, he is hated in the world and becomes afflicted with diseases."

5.53 *reward for their meritorious acts* (puṇyaphalam): I follow Govinda and Kullūka in taking this as a Tatpuruṣa compound. Medhātithi rejects this and takes it as a Dvandva: *puṇyaṃ ca phalaṃ ca puṇyaphalam / samāhāradvandvaḥ / ṣaṣṭīsamāse hy asāmarthyam.*

5.55 *Me he . . . nature of "meat":* the belief that the food a person eats may in turn eat him appears to have been old. Such sentiments are expressed in the vedic literature with reference not only to animals but also to plants and grains: *JB* 1.43; *ŚB* 12.9.1.1. Here Manu gives a phonetic etymology of the Sanskrit term for meat *māṃsa*, the two syllables of which mean "me" (*mām*) and "he" (*sa*). See Smith 1994, 253.

5.58 *Someone who has teethed . . . of hair:* the meaning of "younger" (*anujāte*), literally "born after," is unclear. Medhātithi and most other commentators take it to mean someone younger than a child who has teethed, an interpretation that has led to one scribe (ms. Tj[1]) emending the text to *dantajāte adante ca*. Nandana takes it as referring to a boy who has undergone vedic initiation. Needless to say, all these explanations are unsatisfactory. A possible clue to the meaning may be found in verse 70 where a child who has teethed is juxtaposed with a child whose naming ceremony has been performed. If the naming ceremony is considered some kind of birth, then the unusual term *anujāta* may refer to it (Nandana's view is based on taking the term to mean an initiatory birth). Commentators also point out that the full ten-day period of impurity is observed only when someone who has undergone vedic initiation dies. At the death of a child who has undergone the hair-cutting ceremony, the period is three days (see *YDh* 3.23); for a child who has teethed, one day; and for a baby who has not teethed, purity is restored immediately. Bühler connects *anujāte* with *kṛtacūḍe* and translates: "When (a child) dies that has teethed, or that before teething has received (the sacrament of) the tonsure." This is unlikely because of the *ca* after both *anujāte* and *kṛtacūḍe*. Doniger translates: "When a child dies when he has just got his teeth, or after he has his teeth"; though novel and interesting, I do not see how that meaning can be derived from the Sanskrit.

5.59 *until the collection of bones:* according to the *ViDh* 19.10, this takes place on the fourth day after death.

5.60 *common ancestry:* the Sanskrit term *sapiṇḍa* refers to a group of close relatives, but there is great controversy in the tradition with regard to both its meaning and the extent of the group covered. One interpretation takes *piṇḍa* (lit., "round lump") to mean a bodily particle and *sapiṇḍa* to mean people who through birth have bodily particles in common. Another interpretation takes *piṇḍa* to mean the balls of rice offered to ancestors and *sapiṇḍa* to mean people who are connected through these ancestral offerings. In general, the relationship extends to six generations before and after the father and five generations before and after the mother. See *BDh* 1.11.9; Jolly 1885, 168–74; Kane 1962–75, ii. 452–78.

relationship based on offering libations: the term *samānodaka* refers to a broad and ill-defined group of extended relatives. Some take it as comprehending the seven generations of ancestors beyond the seven comprising "common ancestry": see Vijñāneśvara on *YDh* 2.136.

5.61 This single verse was expanded in some manuscript traditions into two verses, which are found in all editions and translations. According to this reading, the translation would be: "As this period of death-impurity is prescribed for those who belong to the same ancestry, so the same holds true at a birth for those who desire perfect purity. Death-impurity affects all, but birth-impurity affects only the mother and the father. The mother alone is subject to the period of birth-impurity; the father becomes pure by bathing." For a detailed discussion, see the note to this verse in the critical edition and Introduction, pp. 44–46.

After the expanded two verses, some manuscripts give two additional verses: "In both cases, during ten days one does not eat food from that family; further, giving gifts, accepting gifts, sacrifice, and vedic recitation are suspended. When a boy is born, one may freely accept on that day a gift of gold, grain, a cow, a garment, sesame seeds, sugar, and ghee."

5.63 *On the contrary . . . three days:* the meaning of this verse and its connection to the rest of this section are quite unclear. Several commentators take the second half as referring to begetting a child on a woman who is not one's wife or on a remarried woman. I think that this verse should be taken within the context of the differing opinions regarding the impurity affecting a father and mother mentioned in the previous verse. This verse appears to be contradicting the view expressed in the final phrase of the previous verse, namely, that after a birth the father is purified by bathing. The opponent here says that a father is purified by bathing alone only after having sex; when a child is actually born, he has to observe a period of impurity lasting three days. See *VaDh* 4.21, where also the connection of the new-born child to its parents is described as based on semen: *bījanimittatvāt*. This interpretation makes sense of the otherwise incongruous insertion of sexual intercourse within a passage dealing with birth and death. The author may also be alluding to the view on the three births of a man expressed in the *AU* (2.1–3), namely, that the emission of the semen by the man into the woman constitutes his first birth, and the actual birth of the child constitutes the second. If this holds true, then the author of this view is arguing against the earlier view, saying that a bath alone purifies after his first birth (emission of semen: see the added verse after 5.144) but not the second, which is the topic of discussion here. If we follow the reading of the ST (*api* for *abhi-*), the text makes even a stronger connection between the birth impurity and the death impurity given in verse 60: "the impurity resulting *also* from a seminal relationship adheres to him for three days."

5.64 *Those who touch . . . in three:* the Sanskrit for "ten days" is extremely prolix: "one day, one night, and three times three nights." Nandana correctly calls this *uktivaicitryam*, unless, of course, we are misunderstanding this strange calculation. "Those who touch the corpse," I think, refers to those close relatives who actually participate in the funeral, rather than to any person who may happen to touch a corpse, because of the context; this also parallels the statement about the pupil in the very next verse. The expression "those who offer libations" (*udakadāyinaḥ*), as the commentators point out, probably refers to the class of relatives who are required to offer water to the deceased (*samānodaka*): see 5.60 n.

5.65 *those who carry a corpse:* the commentators Govinda, Kullūka, Rāghavānanda, and Nandana take this as a reference to persons of common ancestry (*sapiṇḍa*), whereas Medhātithi, Nārāyaṇa, and Rāmacandra think that the expression simply refers to persons who actually carry a corpse. I prefer the former explanation, because it is superfluous to say that a pupil who carries a corpse is similar to those who carry a corpse!

5.67 Variant reading: "tradition tells us, purity is restored in a single night."

5.68 *lay it down:* the meaning of the verb *nidadhyuḥ* is not altogether clear. Most commentators interpret it to mean "bury"; this is also the understanding of *YDh* 3.1, where this verse is recast as: *ūnadvivarṣaṃ nikhanet*. The image of leaving the body behind like a piece of wood found in the very next verse, however, raises the possibility that, according to Manu, the body was actually left on the ground rather than buried. Customs, of course, may have changed over time. Indeed, Vijñāneśvara, citing this passage (on *YDh* 3.2–3), says that it should not be understood literally; one should bury the child in the wilderness and return without sorrow, just as one would after throwing a stick away.

5.69 *keep the observances:* most commentators, followed by Bühler, interpret the verb *kṣapeta* to mean that one should observe three days of impurity (*āśauca*). The term, however, normally means fasting or undertaking a religious observance (see 4.222). Medhātithi says that the person should remain secluded without participating in regular activities: *udāsyeta śāstracoditaṃ vyāpāraṃ na kuryāt*. Such a meaning is possible: see the use of *kṣapaṇa* as "waiting" in *GDh* 18.15. and as "interruption of study" in *PārGṛ* 2.12.4. The three days of impurity is clearly indicated here, but the term may directly refer to the kinds of observances associated with mourning: see below 5.73, and *ĀpDh* 2.15.5–10; *GDh* 11.24–42.

5.72 *The relations . . . prescribed rule:* the verse is quite obscure and a slightly variant version occurs in *BDh* 1.11.5 with *akṛtavivāhānām* for *asaṃskṛtānām*. It is possible that the verse is taken from a source which may have provided a different context for understanding it. So, for example, the context here or in *BDh* does not permit us to understand what the meaning of "according to prescribed rule" means. Commentators offer different views, mostly guesses. According to the majority, the reference is to a period of three days, which is the same as the period for the relatives given in the first half of the verse and makes no sense. Nandana takes it as referring to the standard 10 days, which is also the view of some authors cited by Medhātithi. Most commentators also take the verse as referring to women who have been betrothed but not given in marriage and understand "relatives" (*bāndhavāḥ*) as her future husband's relatives. I see no reason to take these women as betrothed but unmarried. Although *bāndhava* in its restrictive use does refer to relatives by marriage, it has frequently a wider application (see 2.132 n.). Here the straightforward meaning, I think, is that when an unmarried woman dies, her relatives (maternal and paternal; possibly *sapiṇḍas*) are impure for three days, whereas her siblings (and one must assume also her parents) remain impure for the standard statutory period of 10 days.

siblings: commentators here give diverse interpretations of *sanābhayaḥ* (literally, "those connected by the same navel"): those belonging to the same ancestry (*sapiṇḍa*), paternal relatives, and brothers (sisters?). At verse 84, where the verse recurs, they give different meanings: sons etc. (*putrādi*), those belonging to the same lineage (*sagotra*), and those belonging to the same ancestry (*sapiṇḍa*). Clearly, this term must have the same meaning in both contexts. I think it refers to either the "uterine" (brothers and possibly sisters) or, more likely, to the immediate family, including the parents.

5.73 *For three days:* commentators, as well as Bühler and Doniger, take this as referring specifically to bathing rather than to all the observances mentioned here. The parallel passages in *VaDh* 4.14 and *YDh* 3.16 clearly indicate that all the observances connected with mourning are carried out during three days.

5.74 *kinsmen and relatives:* most commentators take the two terms *saṃbandhi* and *bāndhava* as referring to relatives by common ancestry (*sapiṇḍa*) and by reason of offering libations (*samānodaka*): see 5.60 n. Nārāyaṇa, Nandana, and Rāmacandra, however, take *bāndhava* as referring to paternal relatives. These two terms have wide applications, although in their restrictive usage, the former refers to relatives by marriage and the latter to maternal relatives (see 2.132 n.; 4.179 n.). Elsewhere, however, *sambandhin* refers to maternal relatives (2.132).

5.78 *a child . . . ancestry:* in the expression *bāle deśāntasthe ca pṛthakpiṇḍe ca* the number of persons enumerated is uncertain. Medhātithi takes all three terms to be in apposition: "when a child living in a far away place and belonging to a different ancestry dies." Others see two categories: a child and an adult belonging to a different ancestry. When these die in a distant land, one is purified by bathing. The repetition of *ca* ("and") makes the latter interpretation more probable.

5.81 *vedic scholar living near by:* Medhātithi gives several meanings of *upasaṃpanna*, including someone living with a person and someone endowed with virtues. He also says that dictionaries give this as a synonym of dead (*mṛta*). This verse parallels *GDh* 14.22, which also has *śrotriye copasaṃpanne*. The term cannot mean "dead"; the term *saṃsthite* of verse 80 governs all these phrases (*anuvṛtti*). The term is taken by many commentators as referring to someone living in one's house. Medhātithi also gives the view of some who connect *śrotriya* with *mātula* ("a vedic scholar who is one's maternal uncle"), because the latter is redundant as it is comprehended by the term *bāndhava* ("maternal relatives"). This is quite unlikely; *bāndhava* probably has a wider meaning here, thus making the special mention of the uncle not superfluous.

5.82 *realm:* for a discussion of *viṣaya* as the realms of a king, see Scharfe 1993, 118–9.

someone who is . . . or an elder: this half-verse is very obscure and commentators give contradictory explanations. First, I agree with the commentators that the term *upasaṃpanne* must be understood here from the preceding verse; this is somewhat problematic because two half-verses intervene, but without that term this injunction would require a period of impurity whenever a non-vedic scholar dies, which is absurd. Commentators are also divided about the final *pāda*. Govinda, Kullūka, and Rāghavānanda connect the two words: "an elder (or teacher) who is a vedic savant." Nārāyaṇa and Rāmacandra take the words as separate, while Medhātithi connects *anūcāne* with *aśrotriye*, and take *gurau* separately. Nandana reads *tathāgurau,* thus reading *agurau* ("a vedic savant who is not an elder"). In the parallel at *YDh* 3.24 also, the words *guru* and *anūcāna* are taken as separate entries. I think the testimony of Yājñavalkya, Medhātithi, and Nārāyaṇa is compelling; this verse contains three categories of individuals at whose death the period of impurity lasts for a single day.

5.84 *while performing . . . to impurity:* for the view that ritual and royal (5.93–7) obligations take precedence over the observance of impurity, see *GDh* 14.45–6; *YDh* 3.27–9.

5.85 *Divākīrti:* the meaning of this term (literally "calling *or* declaring during the day") is unclear. Most commentators take it to mean a Caṇḍāla. Rāmacandra is alone in taking it as a barber, a meaning rejected by Medhātithi, who cites *MBh* 12.136.106, where its meaning is clearly a Caṇḍāla (see also *MBh* 12.136.110). The form *divākīrtya* occurs also at *GDh* 16.19 and *VaDh* 13.11. The term may refer to the fact that these individuals were expected to go about only during the day and to announce their presence. Fa-hien during his travels in India (399–414 CE) notes this practice: "When they [Caṇḍālas] enter the gate of a city or a market-place, they strike a piece of wood to make themselves known, so that men know and avoid them, and do not come into contact with them." *A Record of Buddhistic Kingdoms*, tr. J. Legge, reprint of 1886 ed. (New York: Dover, 1965), p. 43.

5.88 *votary:* the term *ādiṣṭī* is a hapax in the ancient Dharma literature, except for the citation of this very verse in *ViDh* 22.87. All commentators take it as a synonym of *brahmacārin* ("vedic student"). See the similar use of *vratin* at 2.188; 5.91,93; 11.121, 224.

Variant reading: "he becomes impure for three days."

5.89 *born through capricious caste mingling:* the meaning of the compound *vṛthāsaṃkarajātānāṃ* is obscure, and commentators offer interpretations mostly based on taking it as constituting two separate categories: *vṛthājātānām* and *saṃkarajātānām.*. The second is generally taken to mean children born through caste intermixture. For the first there is a variety of interpretations. Medhātithi : those who do not honor gods, ancestors, or human (*yo na devān arcayati na pitṝn na manuṣyān iti* = *AB* 7.9); or those who remain outside the orders of life. Nārāyaṇa: effeminate or impotent men (*klība*); Govinda and Kullūka: those who, for the most part, have given up their *dharma;* Rāghavānanda: those who give up the five great sacrifices. The expression evokes the vedic expression *anaddhāpuruṣa* of the *AB* (7.9), who is defined there in exactly the same words as that of Medhātithi. The *anaddhāpuruṣa* probably means a "good-for-nothing fellow." See Olivelle 1993, 50. I have taken *vṛthāsaṃkarajātānām* as referring to a single category and assumed *vṛthā* as meaning "wantonly" or "wrongly." This sort of caste mixture would be different from the *anuloma* ones permitted in 3.12–3. See the similar use of *vṛthāmāṃsa* at 4.213 and 5.34, and *vṛthākṛsarasaṃyāvaṃ* at 5.7.

5.92 *as appropriate:* all the commentators interpret *yathāyogam* to mean that a Vaiśya is carried through the western gate, a Kṣatriya through the northern, and a Brahmin through the eastern. Variant readings: "according to number"; "according to class"; "according to honor."

5.93 *for they . . . with brahman:* commentators, rightly I think, see an implied "respectively" in the second half-verse. The meaning is that the king is seated on Indra's throne; whereas vedic students and those performing sacrificial sessions are united with *brahman*. The meaning of *brahman* is also unclear. Medhātithi, Govinda: attaining the state of Brahman (*brahmatva*); Nārāyaṇa, Kullūka, Rāghavānanda: pure like Brahman; Nandana: having the very nature of *dharma*. Given that the context is a student and a sacrificer, I think it is more likely that *brahman* here refers to the Veda and vedic rites in which these two are immersed. For a discussion of the statutory purity of certain individuals, see Olivelle 1998b. On the king, see also von Stietencron 1997.

5.95 *for anyone the king wants:* the meaning, as most commentators note, is that a person delegated by the king to carry out his duties, such as his chaplain or judge, is also subject to instant purification in order for him to carry out his official functions. This appears to be an extension of the king's own instant purification. The principle articulated here is that rules of impurity and the like are overridden by the requirements of public office and ritual obligations. Note that the term *sadyaḥśaucam* is carried over (*anuvṛtti*) into this verse from the previous one.

5.97 *for it is . . . mortal beings:* the reading of the last *pāda* has caused numerous problems to scribes and commentators, resulting in a large number of variant readings. One way to understand the final compound *lokeśaprabhavāpyayam* is to connect *prabhava* with *śauca*, and *apyaya* with *āśauca*. Thus, gods are viewed as the ones who bring about purification and eliminate impurity.

5.98 *both sacrifice . . . instantly:* all the commentators, as well as Bühler and Doniger, see a sandhi in *tathāśaucam* (*tathā* + *āśaucam*). The meaning they derive is not very different from mine; they take *āśaucam saṃtiṣṭhate* to mean that the period of impurity is completed, i.e., concluded (Medhātithi glosses: *samāptim eti*). I have never seen, however, the expression *sadyaḥ āśaucam*. It is much better to disregard sandhi and see here two separate words *tathā śaucam* (this is how Burnell takes it). Thus we get two positive acts, sacrifice and purification (*yajña, śauca*) that are accomplished by death in battle.

5.99 *After completing the required rite* (kṛtakriyaḥ): Medhātithi says that the rite is bathing, because no other ritual has been prescribed. The completion of the required rite is obligatory on all classes. See also the parallel prescriptions for the four classes within the context of a judicial oath at 8.113.

5.102 Additional verse: "If, out of affection, a person of a lower class touches a person of a higher class who is in a period of impurity—or a person of a higher class similarly touches a person of a lower class—he is purified in accordance with the time of impurity prescribed for the person whom he has touched."

5.104 *When one's . . . heaven:* "one's own people" (*sveṣu*) is taken by most commentators to refer to either relatives or persons of one's own class. The term, however, usually refers to persons belonging to one's own household. The cremation is considered the final sacrifice (*antyeṣṭi*) of the deceased; this is the context of the statement in the last clause regarding the "sacrificial offering."

5.105 *Knowldge . . . time:* "smearing" (*upāñjana*) refers specifically to daubing an area with cow dung (see verses 5.122, 124; and 3.206); "food" refers to special penitential foods, such as milk and roots, or possibly to fasting (*YDh* 3.31 *nirāhāraḥ*); "time" means the passage of the statutory period of impurity discussed earlier. Variant reading: "austerity, fasting, earth."

Additional verse: "When earth, leaves, grass, and wood are touched by a Caṇḍāla, a lowest-born, a dog, or a crow, the rule is that they are made pure by the touch of Soma, sun, fire, and wind."

5.108 *What needs . . . renunciation:* a point worth noting in this proverbial saying is that all the instruments of purification (muddy water, fast current during the rains, menstrual flow, and the ochre garment of a renouncer) are all dirty colored. This verse recurs with some variations in *VaDh* 3.58; *ViDh* 22.91; *YDh* 3.32.

5.111–2 *lapidary:* all the commentators, followed by Bühler and Doniger, take the term *aśmamaya* here as referring to articles made of stone. I think this is mistaken. The two verses, 111 and 112, are related; the first telling us how to clean certain articles when they are stained, and the second when they are unstained. We should expect to find the same or similar articles in the two lists; and we do. Stone implements would be out of place here amidst precious articles. Of the metal objects in 111, gold and unembellished silver are singled out in 112; and I think *abja* and *aśmamaya* of 112 parallels *maṇi* and *aśmamaya* of 111. That the tradition recognized two types of precious stones, the one aquatic (e.g., pearls, corals) and the other stone (e.g., sapphire, ruby, diamond), is clear from what Manu says at 8.100 (where also we find the expression *sarveṣv aśmamayeṣu*). The term *maṇi* is probably a generic term for precious gems; here it means pearls while in 9.329 it is opposed to pearls and must mean stone gems.

unstained: I think the word *nirlepam* qualifies all the articles listed in this verse. Stain, often in concert with smell, refers to staining with impure substances such as urine and excrement: see 4.111; 5.126.

5.115 Variant reading: "All substances."

straining: commentators offer a variety of interpretations of the term *utpavana*. Medhātithi: pouring out a small amount of the polluted liquid, using, according to some, two blades of Kuśa grass (so also Govinda, Kullūka, and Rāghavānanda), or filling the pot containing the polluted liquid with clean liquid of the same kind until the pot overflows (so also Rāmacandra); Nārāyaṇa: straining with a cloth. Variant reading: "by skimming."

Additional verse providing a definition of "solids" in verse 115: "Beds, seats, vehicles, things tied with hair, and clothes are declared to be 'solids'."

5.116 *During . . . by washing:* Bühler, following Kullūka, translates: "At sacrifices the purification of (the Soma cups called) Camasas and Grahas, and of (other) sacrificial vessels (takes place) by rubbing (them) with the hand, and (afterwards) rinsing (them with water)." The syntax of the verse, however, makes this interpretation untenable, and commentators such as Nārāyaṇa and Govinda explain it correctly. Regarding the cleansing of implements during a sacrifice, see the detailed account in *BDh* 1.13.11–32.

5.118 Additional verse (in some manuscripts after 126 or 128): "Clothes that are new or that have been purchased or washed are to be purified by sprinkling water or by burning incense over it, but those that are dirty by washing."

5.122 Verse 123 of the vulgate has been expunged from the critical edition: "Earthenware that has come into contact with liquor, urine, feces, phlegm, pus, or blood cannot be purified by firing it again."

5.124 Additional verse: "Each drop of water when sprinkled purifies an area as large as a cow's hide irrespective of whether the ground has been swept or not, so long as one does not notice any stain on it."

5.125 *shaken:* the meaning of *avadhūta* is not quite certain. Medhātithi: something over which someone has blown with the mouth or shaken a cloth. Nārāyaṇa and Govinda agree with the second view of Medhātithi; Nandana also has a similar meaning but refers to the flapping of a chicken's wings. I think something like this must be intended. Kullūka and Rāghavānanda (followed by Bühler and Doniger): what someone has touched with the foot.

5.127 *Gods . . . as suitable:* for a detailed study of these significant verses on statutory purity that, interestingly, includes ignorance as one reason for the purity of something, see Olivelle 1998b.

5.131 Two additional verses: "Fire is pure; wind that blows outdoors is pure; water in a secluded place is pure; and a road is pure for traveling. Goats and horses are pure at their mouths; cows are pure at their backs; Brahmins are pure at their feet; and women are pure all over."

5.133 *droplets of water:* the meaning of *vipruṣaḥ* is not altogether clear. Medhātithi and Govinda take it as referring to tiny droplets perceptible only to the touch. Nārāyaṇa and Rāmacandra: very tiny drops even when they are impure, or droplets falling on the feet when sipping water (see 5.142); Kullūka, Rāghavānanda: droplets of spit coming from the mouth (see 2.141). Given that the same term *vipruṣaḥ* is used at 5.141 for spit, I think Kullūka's interpretation is correct.

5.135 *marrow:* the inclusion of marrow in this list is anomalous. All others are substances that commonly ooze out of the human body; I cannot imagine marrow oozing out unless someone is seriously wounded. Most commentators ignore the word. Rāghavānanda takes it as the fat in bones (*asthigatasnehaḥ*). Kullūka, following Govinda, comments: *śiromadhye piṇḍitasnehaḥ*. Bühler appears to understand this gloss to mean "(the fatty substance of the) brain." But how would the brain ooze out unless there is a serious head wound? Could *majjan* refer to oily residue on the skin after sweating?

Variant reading: "urine, feces, mucus of the nose, ear-wax, phlegm."

5.136 *on one hand:* within the context the meaning is clear: "one hand" refers to the left hand, with which the person applied the earth and water to the penis and anus. All purifications below the navel are carried out using the left hand. Variant reading: "on the left hand."

5.143 *If a sullied . . . thing down:* a similar provision is given at *GDh* 1.28. In the other parallel passages (*BDh* 1.8.27–31; *VaDh* 3.43) the person is required to lay down the thing he is carrying. The commentators are of little help in understanding this provision. My view is that the context is a meal, and the man is carrying dishes for serving the guests. During this time if one of the diners, who is by definition sullied with remnants of food on his hand, happen to touch the man serving, the latter need not put the dish down (which he carries in his left hand) but simply sip some water.

5.144 *after eating food:* all the commentators interpret this within the context of vomiting. Medhātithi: if after eating one vomits or purges on the same day; Govinda, Kullūka: if immediately after eating one vomits (no mention of purging (Rāghavānanda cites Govinda on this); Nandana: if immediately after eating one vomits or purges. Bühler and Doniger appear to follow Nandana. Medhātithi, however, records the view of some who take the eating of food (*bhuktvā*) to be an independent event. I have preferred to follow the latter interpretation, although it is possible to see a connection between vomiting/purging and eating, especially because the former are past participles (*vānto, viraktaḥ*) and the latter is a gerund (*bhuktvā*). Given the distance between the two (*pāda-a* and *pāda-c*), and because *pādas* generally constitute discreet units, I prefer to take *pāda-c* as containing a distinct provision, just as *pāda-d*.

5.147 *Even in their . . . independently:* this and the following verse have become *cause celebre* in anti-Manu rhetoric, even though these or similar provisions are encountered in numerous other legal texts: *GDh* 18.1–2; *BDh*2.3.44–6; *VaDh* 5.3; *ViDh* 25.13; *YDh* 1.85–6. Similar sentiments are expressed later by Manu (9.2–3). Clearly, Brahmanical law saw women as eternal minors to be guarded and protected by their male relatives. Other and more positive depictions of the role of women and their relationship to males, however, are found in Manu, but are mostly ignored by modern critics (see Introduction, p. 35). The term *svatantra* ("independent") has specifically legal connotations. In Nārada (*NSm* 1.29–30), for example, the term is taken to indicate a person who can undertake actions that are legally binding, such as sales and contracts. He says specifically that a king is independent (*svatantra*) and his subjects non-independent (*asvatantra*); a teacher is independent, and his pupil is not; a head of a household is independent, and the women, children, and servants are not.

5.149 *both families:* that is, her natal family and that of her husband. See 9.5.

5.152 *act of giving away:* this is a significant observation about the centrality of the giving away (alienation; *pradānam*) by the father with respect to the husband's authority over his wife. The term *svāmya*, which I have translated with the broad "lordship," can also mean ownership; this term is regularly used with regard to someone's legal ownership of property (see 8.197–205). A factor that is implicit in this statement regarding "giving away" may be the ancient custom of bride purchase, alluded to at 8.204. If marriage is a sale, then ownership is transferred from the previous owner (father) to the new owner (husband).

5.160 *Just like . . . death:* this and the following verses are clearly directed both against the custom of levirate (*niyoga:* see 9.57–70) and against a woman's own desire to have children, perhaps through re-marriage. The term "good woman" (*sādhvī*) is probably used with a pregnant meaning: a woman who is *always* faithful to her husband (see verse 165).

5.161 Variant reading: "excluded from the next world."

5.163 *a woman who has had a man before:* the technical term *parapūrvā* is often taken as a synonym of *punarbhū* ("a remarried woman"). I think the former term has a broader application than *punarbhū*, although the former comprehends the latter. The term *parapūrvā* probably refers to a woman who has had a sexual relationship with another man under any circumstances. Nārada (*NSm* 12.45–52) makes a sevenfold classification of *parapūrvā*, calling three of them *punarbhū* and four *svairiṇī* ("wanton or unchaste woman").

5.169 *In accordance . . . of his life:* this concluding verse of the section on the householder who is a bath-graduate nicely recapitulates the subject. Note that the last half-verse here is identical with the second half-verse of 4.1, thus bracketing the section with this repetition. See parallels at 6.1, 33.

CHAPTER SIX

Additional verse before verse 1: "Hereafter I shall explain the Law pertaining to the hermit's order of life, as well as the rules regarding the gathering of roots and fruits of the forest and their relinquishment."

6.1 *After living . . . his organs:* see parallels at 4.1; 5.169; 6.33.

6.6 *bark:* the term *cīra*, related to the Buddhist *cīvara*, can refer to both a tattered garment or cloth (so Medhātithi) or a garment manufactured from strips of tree bark or grass (so Nārāyaṇa, Rāmacandra). Govinda, Rāghavānanda, and Kullūka give both possibilities, and Nandana specifies a garment made of Kuśa grass. Other texts refer to *valkala* (*BDh* 1.13.12–3; *YDh* 2.180, 246). Emeneau (1962) has clearly demonstrated that the reference is not to garments made directly from tree bark but to those probably woven out of fibers from the inner bark of certain trees. It would clearly have been difficult to make garments directly out of the other bark of trees.

6.10 *constellation-sacrifice:* a sacrifice, also called Nakṣatreṣṭi, that is offered to the lunar mansions and described in *TB* 3.1.

Turāyaṇa sacrifice: the first of a series of yearly sacrifices performed on the full-moon day of Phālguṇa (February–March) or Caitra (March–April). See *ĀśŚr*, II.14. Variant reading: "Uttarāyaṇa sacrifice."

Dākṣāyaṇa sacrifice: another in the series of yearly sacrifices. This sacrifice is performed both on the Full-moon and the New-moon. For a description, see Eggeling's introduction to ŚB 2.4.4 (p. 374).

6.13 *flowers . . . trees:* Bühler takes *medhyavṛkṣodbhavāni* as a separate item and translates: "flowers, roots, and fruits, the productions of pure trees"; so also Doniger. Of the commentators, only Govinda offers an opinion, and he takes this compound as qualifying *puṣpamūlaphalāni* of *pāda-b*. I agree with this interpretation, both because of the lack of a *ca* after the second compound and because I cannot think of any products of tree other than flowers, roots, and fruits, excepts perhaps leaves and sap. It also parallels nicely *snehāṃś ca phalasaṃbhavān* of *pāda-d*.

6.14 *Bhauma plant, mushrooms* (bhaumāni kavakāni ca): most commentators take the former as qualifying the latter, and following them Bühler translates: "mushrooms growing on the ground." As Medhātithi observes, given that all types of mushrooms are forbidden, it is superfluous to specify ground mushrooms here. Both Medhātithi and Bhāruci, our two oldest commentators, take the two as separate items. The meaning of *bhauma* is uncertain, however. The manuscript of Bhāruci's commentary is torn at this point, but Medhātithi is probably citing Bhāruci when he identifies the plant as *gojihvikā*, which Jha identifies as cabbage. The identical expression occurs also at 11.156, which Medhātithi explains as mushrooms growing on the ground; clearly he has forgotten the (better!) explanation he gave at 6.14.

6.16 Variant reading: "roots and fruits."

6.18 *clean up immediately* (sadyaḥprakṣālikaḥ): the meaning is that the hermit cleans his bowl immediately after eating, leaving nothing for the next time. Such a man does not maintain a store of provisions, but lives from day to day.

6.19 *he may . . . eighth mealtime:* the standard mealtime for a normal human being is twice a day in the morning and in the evening (see 2.56 n.). Eating only at night (i.e., evening) or during the day implies that he skips one meal. Eating every fourth mealtime means that he skips three meals; when one eats every eighth mealtime, one skips three days and eats in the evening of the fourth.

6.21 *wilted on their own:* Bühler, following Kullūka, translates *svayaṃśīrṇaiḥ*: "fallen spontaneously"; so also Doniger. Nārāyaṇa explains: *phalāṅkurādijananaśaktihīnatāṃ prāptaiḥ* ("reached a state where they are unable to produce fruit or sprouts"); Govinda and Rāmacandra agree. I think the latter is the more likely meaning, also because falling cannot apply to roots.

Vaikhānasa doctrine: the term Vaikhānasa is frequently used to refer to forest hermits. The term also refers to the doctrine or treatise of the sage Vikhanas (see *BDh* 2.11.14).

6.22 *spend the day standing and the night seated:*: surprisingly, no commentator or translator has understood the correct meaning of the technical expression *sthānāsanābhyāṃ viharet*. It refers to a religious observance during which the person has to remain standing during the day (without sitting down) and seated during the night (without lying down). The *VaDh* (24.5) clearly specifies that this observance involves standing during the day and sitting at night: *sthānāsanaśīlo 'has tiṣṭhed rātrāv āsīta*. See *ĀpDh* 1.25.10; *GDh* 22.6; *BDh* 2.2.10; 4.7.17. The same expression recurs in Manu at 11.224. For this ascetic/penitential practice, see also 11.111.

6.23 *the five fires:* the hermit sits in the middle of four blazing fires at each cardinal point, with the summer sun scorching overhead as the fifth fire. Note the connection to the five ritual fires: see 3.185 n.

6.24 *inflict punishment:*: beginning at least with Burnell, translators have rendered the term *śocayet* uniformly as "dry up." Although emaciating the body through fasting may also be intended, I think the term has a broader meaning of causing severe pain to the body.

6.25 *depositing the sacred fires in his body:* Brahmanical theology of renunciation presents the abandonment of rites and ritual fires as a process of internalization. The technical expression for the ritual process by which this internalization is accomplished is called "depositing the fires in one's body/self" (*ātmasamāropaṇa*). Its procedure is patterned after the vedic custom of depositing the fires either in the fire-drills or in the body when a sacrificer has to undertake a journey. He brings back his fires either by producing a fire using the drills or by blowing on to an ordinary fire. The *BDh* (2.17.26) gives a simple form of this rite: the ascetic breathes in the smell of each fire, reciting the vedic formula "With that body of yours worthy of sacrifice" (*TB* 2.5.8.8). After this rite the ascetic carries the fires in the form of his breaths.

6.29 Variant reading: "For the purification of his self."

6.30 *pursued:* the term *sevitāḥ* has the meaning of both practicing religious observances and studying scriptural texts. I attempt to capture this double meaning with "pursue."

Brahmins, and householders: several commentators, as well and Bühler and Doniger, take these to be in apposition: i.e., Brahmin householders. The natural way to read the three nouns is to see three separate categories here.

6.33 *After spending . . . during the fourth:* see parallels at 4.1; 5.169; 6.1.

6.35 *proceed downward* (vrajaty adhaḥ): going downward here and in other similar contexts (see 6.37; 7.53; 11.173) probably implies both fall from caste (sociologically, going down the social ladder) and going down to the netherworlds (cosmologically). See the similar expression at 11.153, where it means that the food eaten has gone down, i.e., been excreted.

6.39 *freedom from fear* (abhaya): the meaning is that the ascetic assures all creatures that no harm will come to them from him. This is commonly referred to as the "gift of safety" (*abhayadāna*), and it is also associated with a king after his conquest of a new region (see 7.201). He is supposed to assure the safety of the people living there. Verse 40 picks up this theme of "fear" with reference to the ascetic's afterlife.

6.43 *keep no store* (asaṃcayika): the vulgate reading is *asaṃkusuka*, which has been interpreted to mean "firm of purpose" (Bühler) or "unwavering."

6.44 *A bowl, the foot of a tree:* the Sanskrit *kapāla* here probably means simply a begging bowl (see 6.53), although the term can have the meanings of a skull (so Doniger) and a potsherd (so Bühler). Foot of a tree is presented as the ideal lodging place for an ascetic (6.26).

renouncer: although the term *mukta* means literally "a liberated man," it is used here in the same way as *mokṣa* (see 1.114 n.) to refer to a wandering ascetic. Bühler's "one who has attained liberation" and Doniger's "one who is Freed" are, I think, overly literal. The discussion here is about asceticism and ascetics, not about liberation and liberated individuals.

6.45 *his wages* (niveśa): according to the vulgate reading *nirdeśam*, the translation would be "as a servant his orders."

Three additional verses: "A mendicant should wander about during the eight months of summer and winter; compassionate towards all living being, he should live in one place during the rainy season. He must not travel on a sunless road or step on uninspected ground; and he should always perform his rites using well-strained water. He should utter words that are true, harmless, inoffensive, without deceit, not harsh, compassionate, and not slanderous."

6.46 *purified by his sight:* the meaning is that he should look at the spot where he is about to place his foot, lest he trample to death any living creatures such as ants and worms (see 6.68). This must have been a value and custom common to most ascetic communities; Jain ascetics carry a broom to sweep the ground in front of them lest they step on a tiny insect unintentionally.

6.48 *seven gates:* the meaning was obscure even to the commentators, who give a variety of interpretation, many of them educated guesses. Medhātithi and Govinda relate them to the triple set (2.224 n.) in different pairs: Law-Wealth, Law-Pleasure, Wealth-Pleasure, Pleasure-Wealth, Pleasure-Law, Wealth-Law, and finally the three together. This is truly far-fetched, as is the opinion of some given by Bhāruci, according to whom the seven refer to the seven grammatical cases. Nārāyaṇa: the five senses, mind, and ego. My own view is that they refer to the seven openings of the head: two eyes, two nostrils, two ears, and mouth, which are the major organs of perception and communication. This interpretation is recorded as the view of some by Medhātithi and Bhāruci.

6.49 *Taking delight . . . felicity:* commentators have failed to appreciate the contrast drawn here between being seated and walking (*vicaret*). The first refers to yogic posture and meditation, as Kullūka has rightly pointed out. Walking must refer to the actual act rather than living in this world (*saṃsāra*) as some commentators explain. The life of the ascetic is split between sitting in meditation and walking about, especially to beg for food, which is the very next topic. See the use of *vicaret* again in verse 52.

6.50 *palmistry:* the term *aṅgavidyā* has a broader meaning than palmistry, although this must have been the principal form. It can include the interpretation of other physical characteristics and marks.

6.57 *belongings:* the term *mātrā* has acquired somewhat of a specialized meaning in ascetic vocabulary. It refers to the meager possessions of an ascetic, especially his garment, bowl, water-pot, and staff. Note the interesting juxtaposition of *-mātra* at the end of the compound in *pāda-c* with the meaning "only or merely" and *mātrā* in the sense of the meager articles of an ascetic in *pāda-d*.

6.58 *with a show of reverence:* it is unclear who shows the reverence. Medhātithi thinks that it is the donor; others think it is the ascetic himself who shows reverence to the giver. Bühler appears to follow the latter interpretation, which is the most plausible grammatically. Ascetic literature, however, warn the ascetic to fear honors bestowed on him by ordinary people and to shun such honors as if they were poison, and recommend that he welcome disrespect as if it were ambrosia: see 2.162 with reference to a student.

6.66 *Though decked in finery* (bhūṣita): the vulgate reading is *dūṣita*, following which Bühler translates: "though blemished (by a want of the external marks)," and Doniger "even if he is flawed (in that duty)."

an emblem . . . Law (na liṅgaṃ dharmakāraṇam): literally, "an emblem is not the cause of *dharma*." Bühler takes *dharma* as merit, but that would result in the term being used with two different meanings in the same verse. The meaning, I think, is that wearing an ascetic emblem does not *ipso facto* mean that the man is following the Law. In the very next verse the emblem appears to be compared to a Kataka fruit, which is believed to have the property of making turbid water clear. But the fruit has to be immersed in the water for this to happen. Likewise, an emblem itself will not make an ascetic virtuous; he must live according to the Law of which the emblem is merely an outward sign.

6.70 *Controlling the breath:* the definition of what constitutes a single control of breath is given in a verse cited by commentators and found in *VaDh* 25.13: "When someone recites three times the Gāyatrī verse together with the Calls, the syllable OṂ, and the Śiras formula while controlling his breath, it is called 'control of breath'."

6.73 Variant reading: "Through the practice (*yoga*) of knowledge."

6.75 *that state:* the meaning of *tat padam* is not altogether clear. In all likelihood, the phrase refers to the highest state of the liberated self, namely the state of Brahman (see 6.79, 81, 85).

6.76–7 *Constructed . . . ghosts:* the human body is here compared to a house, a common image in ascetic literature. The ascetic has, of course, abandoned his house, but he still carries his body with him. This imagery invites the reader to regard the house, commonly perceived as offering safety and shelter, as a place of torment and danger. The expression "dwelling place of ghosts" (*bhūtāvāsa*) carries a double meaning; *bhūta* can mean both ghost and element. Indeed, the body is composed of elements, but it is, at another level, the abode of impure and dangerous ghosts. See *Maitrī Upaniṣad*, 3.4.

6.78 *When a tree . . . painful grasp:* I think commentators and translators alike have failed to understand this simile, which, I must admit, has been cast in turbid syntax. All take the tree falling from the bank and the bird leaving the tree as two independent similes. That is very unlikely, given that the first foot concludes with *vṛkṣa* ("tree"), and the second foot begins with it, indicating that the latter picks up the theme of the former. Further, they take *grāha* (which I think means alligator rather than shark) only with the giving up of the body in the second half of the verse. I think the last foot is connected to both the simile and the ascetic giving up the body. The meaning then seems to be that a bird flying off before the fall of the tree escapes the alligator's grasp in the river. Likewise, when an ascetic abandons the body before its natural fall at death (which is here compared to the fall of the tree), he escapes thc grasp of the alligator, probably Yama (6.61). This fits nicely with the theme of the preceding verse, namely, that an ascetic must abandon the body voluntarily. Variant reading: "he escapes from the painful village."

6.80 *by the passion . . . object of passion:* Manu is clearly playing with the double meaning of *bhāva*, which means both the inner disposition of the spirit and external objects, especially those that are the object of passion.

6.83 *those named "Vedānta":* Medhātithi takes *vedāntābhihitam* to mean what has been called Vedānta; thus he should softly recite the Upaniṣads. Others take it to mean what has been stated in the Vedāntas; thus he should softly recite what the Upaniṣads recommend. Nandana and Rāmacandra think that this is OṂ. I prefer Medhātithi's interpretation because *yat* of *pāda-d*, I think, clearly refers back to *brahma* of *pāda-a*.

6.85 *sequence of practices:* some commentators take *kramayogena* as a reference to yogic and other practices enjoined on the ascetic. Others take it as a reference to the obligation to go through the first three *āśramas* or to pay his three debts before he undertakes the life of a wandering ascetic. Bühler accordingly translates: "A twice-born man who becomes an ascetic, after the successive performance of the above-mentioned acts." The verb, however, is *parivrajati* (which means to wander about, and by extension live the ascetic life) rather than *pravrajati* (which refers to the initial departure from home, and thus to the initiation into asceticism).

6.86 *Listen . . . vedic retirees:* this verse signals the passage to a different topic. Throughout his work Manu uses similar verses to signal the transition from one topic to another (see Introduction, p. 7). In the table of contents given in the first chapter, moreover, Manu clearly indicates that he has two separate topics in mind. The sequence of topics at 1.114 (see note to it) is *tāpasyaṃ mokṣaṃ saṃnyāsam eva ca*. The term *saṃnyāsa* signals a topic different from *mokṣa*; nowhere else in this list does Manu use two terms to refer to a single topic. *Saṃnyāsa* refers to the life of Vedasaṃnyāsikas, which is the subject of the last section of chapter six that opens with the above verse. Many commentators, such as Kullūka, consider Vedasaṃnyāsika to be a lower type of renouncer. I think that commentators, such as Govinda and Bhāruci, who take them to be a type of householder are right. Manu's discussion, furthermore, confirms that he considers Vedasaṃnyāsikas to be retired householders who aspire to holiness without resorting to the two types of asceticism that he had described earlier. A similar use of the term with reference to retirement of an aged Brahmin occurs in the *Mānava Śrautasūtra*, 8.25: see Sprockhoff 1987. In what follows, Manu appears to be saying: "I grant that all these four *āśramas* can lead a person to the highest state. Nevertheless, the householder is the best and chief among them, and as such it is unnecessary to leave the household life in old age. I give now this alternative way of leading a holy life in old age in one's own house." Manu reserves the term *saṃnyāsa* for this institution; within this context the term means retirement rather than renunciation.

6.89 Variant reading: "according to the Veda and the *smṛtis*."

6.90 *end up:* most commentators take *saṃsthiti* as a reference to the fact that persons in the other *āśramas* must get their sustenance from the householder, even though this is not strictly true in the case of a forest hermit. The image of the rivers flowing into the ocean, however, evokes another image: that of the rebirth process as described in the *BṛU* 6.2.9–14 and the *ChU* 5.1–9. After death all beings go through the transformations of smoke, rain, and plants, and finally end up as the semen of a householder before taking birth in the womb of his wife.

CHAPTER SEVEN

7.2 *vedic consecration:* all the commentators take *brāhmaṃ saṃskāram* as a reference to vedic initiation. Nandana is the only one who gives the royal consecration (*abhiṣeka*) as one alternative, alongside initiation. As Bühler indicates, the royal consecration is clearly what is intended here, because that is what makes a man a king along with the obligation to protect his subjects.

7.4 *Indra . . . lord of wealth:* these are the eight guardian deities of the cardinal points, beginning with Indra in the east and ending with Kubera, the lord of wealth, in the north.

7.5 *overpowers* (abhibhavati): Medhātithi glosses *durnirīkṣyamukho bhavati* ("he becomes one whose face is difficult to be gazed upon"), which is supported by the comparison with the sun in the very next verse. Kullūka glosses *atiśete* ("surpasses"), which is followed by Bühler, using *tejasā* as an instrumental of comparison. I think Medhātithi is on the right track, but the meaning is probably broader: overpower and overwhelm due to both his majesty and his power.

7.10 *every aspect* (viśvarūpam): the aspects he assumes are indicated in the next verse: benevolence, valor, anger. Commentators also say that he can be a friend one minute and an enemy the next. I also think that, in light of his comparison to the sun in verse 6, that the old meaning of *viśvarūpa* (Bodewitz 1985) as dazzling or brilliant (like gold and the sun) may resonate here also.

7.11 *he, in whose:* I am assuming (contra Bühler) that *yasya* of this verse is the correlative of *saḥ* of verse 10 rather than that of*pāda-d* of this verse. First, the three aspects given in verse 11 seem to be an explication of "all aspects" of verse 10. Second, the presence of the causal *hi* ("for") in *pāda-d* makes it very likely that this *pāda* gives the reason why the king is all that he stated to be in verses 10 and 11. See the very similar construction in 2.7. We see the last *pāda* with a *hi* giving the reason for what was stated in the earlier *pādas* in 8.37, 39, 270, 338, 417; 9.144.

of them all: namely, the eight gods from whose particles he was created.

7.12 *to destroy him quickly* (āśuvināśāya): I follow Medhātithi and Govinda in connecting *āśu* with *vināśāya*. I think the two words form a compound. The fact that the two words are in the same *pāda* also supports the syntactic connection between the two. Others take *āśu* as an adverb modifying the verb: "he quickly makes up his mind" (so Bühler and Doniger).

7.13 *When the king . . . that Law:* the verse is not altogether clear. I think Medhātithi is correct in taking *dharma* here as a royal decree or edict rather than as simply *dharma*, which, as Bhāruci points out, comes not from the king but from the *śāstras*. Medhātithi gives examples of such decrees: "There is a wedding in the minister's house, and all should gather there." Against those in disfavor: "No one should associate with this man."

7.14 *Punishment* (daṇḍa): it appears that Manu begins the discussion of punishment by personifying it. Punishment is the son of the Lord made from Brahman's energy. But by verse 32 he passes on imperceptibly to its common meaning of punishment imposed by the king.

7.15 *accede to being used:* verses 22 and 23 make the meaning of the unusual expression *bhogāya kalpante* clear. Different beings open themselves to being used (literally "enjoyed") by others; one can think of the chain of food and eaters. In a socio-political context, moreover, "being used" may refer specifically to the king's enjoyment of his subjects' wealth through taxes and duties.

7.16 *the place and the time:* that is, when and where the crime was committed.

7.19 *after careful examination* (samīkṣya): the reference is probably to a judicial inquiry. Medhātithi correctly observes that this phrase relates to what was said in verse 16 (*avekṣya tattvataḥ*). The two verses bracket this brief discussion of the proper way to inflict just punishment.

7.21 *lap up* (avalihyāt): this makes sense because the term *havis* refers specifically to ghee that is poured into the sacred fire.

topsy-turvy: commentators *adharottaram* take to mean that the lower castes would usurp the roles and privileges of upper castes.

7.24 *revolt:* I take the term *prakopa* here to mean revolt or tumult among the populace, a meaning common in the *AŚ* (see, e.g., 1.18.1; 1.19.28).

7.25 *administrator:* the term *netā* (literally "leader"; see verse 17) must refer to the king who actually administers punishment. See the use of *pra √nī* with reference to inflicting punishment in verses 19–20, 31, and again in verses 26–7; and we have the simple verb *nī* in verse 30.

7.29 *as well as . . . mid-space:* another translation would be: "as well as sages, gods and those who dwell in mid-space."

7.32 *friends and loved ones* (suhṛtsu snigdheṣu): so Bhāruci, Nārāyaṇa, and Kullūka. However, Medhātithi takes this as a single category: "friends who are dear to him"; that is, where friendship is not based on some ulterior motive as in the case of an ally.

7.35 *The king . . . to them:* this verse concludes the section on the creation of the king to be the protector of the people, a section that began with verse 3. The connection to the latter verse is clearly established by the use here of the word *sṛṣṭaḥ* echoing *asṛjat* of verse 3.

devoted to . . . them (dharme niviṣṭānām): Medhātithi offers another possibility with an elided "a": *dharme (a)niviṣṭānām*. The translation would then be: "people . . . are not devoted to the law specific to them."

7.37 *After getting up in the morning:* note that the entire section on the duties of the king is structured to encompass a single day in the life of the king. Other materials, such as the appointment of officials, organization of the state, and political strategies, are all presented, sometimes quite artificially, within that overall structure. The artificiality of the structure is apparent, because at 7.145 Manu returns to the morning duties of the king, possibly because so much material (108 verses) had intervened. This is followed by the afternoon routine (7.216–22) and the evening (7.223–26). Note that this structure parallels the *AŚ* 1.19.6–25, which recommends that the king develop a routine for the day and the night. He is asked to divide the day and the night into eight parts each and to perform specific tasks during each period. For example, during the first part of the day he reviews matters of defense and revenue; during the second, he looks into the affairs of the citizens; and during the third, he takes his bath and the midday meal. Likewise, during the first part of the night he interviews secret agents. This admonition of the AŚ, perhaps, was the inspiration for the structure that Manu gives to this central section on the duties of a king (*rājadharma*).

7.40 *those residing in the forest:* the reference is probably to the Pāṇḍava brothers of the *MBh*. They recovered their kingdom after the great war. I thank Professor Albrecht Wezler for this insight. Commentators ignore this point and take the term as referring simply to poor persons.

7.41–2 *Vena came . . . rank of a Brahmin:* these are well-known stories from ancient lore. Vena was a king notorious for his evil conduct. He prohibited sacrifice and, consequently, was killed by Brahmin ascetics with their spells. Among the many legends surrounding the figure of King Nahuṣa is one where he wanted to obtain Indra's wife and was therefore cursed to become a snake. Sudās Paijavana (the son of Pijavana) is a king named in the *Ṛgveda*. The famous seers Vasiṣṭha and Viśvāmitra were his priests. Sudās killed Vasiṣṭha's son and, abandoned by Viśvāmitra, comes to ruin. No information appears to be available on Sumukha. Nimi, too impatient to wait for Vasiṣṭha, started a sacrifice on his own and dies under a curse by Vasiṣṭha. Pṛthu is the son of Vena produced posthumously by Brahmins by churning Vena's body. He ruled the earth justly, and for this reason the earth is named Pṛthvī, the wife of Pṛthu. Both Kubera and Viśvāmitra (the son of Gādhi) came to their respective positions because of ascetic toil (*tapas*). Kubera, the guardian of the north, became the lord of wealth, and Viśvāmitra, originally a Kṣatriya, rose to the rank of a Brahmin.

7.43 *From experts . . . enterprises:* this verse lacks a verb and, as Bhāruci and Medhātithi point out, the verb *adhigacchait* ("he should learn") is carried over (*anuvṛtti*) from verse 39. In this case, it is likely that the verses 40–2 are either interpolations or at best a parenthetical comment. Their intervention probably necessitated some scribes and commentators, including Medhātithi, to change *vidyām* to the verb *vidyāt*. This verb is used frequently by Manu but always in the sense of "one should know" (when Bhṛgu is imparting some knowledge: e.g., 2.149; 7.50, 100) or "one should discover" (as when a king should learn the weakness of his enemy: 7.105). It is never used in the sense of learning from a teacher or studying.

7.52 Variant reading: "rampant everywhere, a man should recognize that each preceding vice is more perilous to himself than each subsequent."

7.54 *counselors:* this term *sacivān* occurs only once elsewhere in Manu (7.120), where also it refers to a very high official. The term occurs only once in the *AŚ* (in the verse 1.7.9). Given that Manu deals with *amātyas* (government officials) in a later section (7.60–2), it appears that he uses *saciva* as the equivalent of *mantrin* in the *AŚ* (counselors or the highest kind of ministers). See Scharfe 1993, 125–37. In the *MBh* (15.14.11) Yudhiṣṭhira's four brothers are called his *sacivas*, indicating the high rank of officials bearing that name.

natives of the land: the meaning of *maulān* is unclear. Commentators take it to mean people whose ancestors were in royal service. This is followed by Bühler and Doniger. The term is used in the *AŚ* (2.33.8; 7.8.27; 9.2.1–3, 14; 10.1.7; 12.1.28) always with reference to the first of six classes of troops; and the term is translated by Kangle as "hereditary." Within that context that indeed may be the meaning, even though it may also refer to the fact that these soldiers are native inhabitants of the original territory of the king (*mūla*). The term *maula* is used by Manu in two other places (8.62, 259), both in the context of competent witnesses. The meaning of "hereditary" makes no sense within those contexts. I think that in all three instances *maula* refers to native or original inhabitants of the locality as opposed to newcomers; that is, people with deep roots in the region. In this sense, it may also imply "hereditary," because the ancestors of these people were inhabitant of the region.

well-accomplished: the exact meaning of *labdhalakṣa* is unclear. Skill in the use of weapons is highlighted by commentators; but the term probably means more than this and includes accomplishment in various undertakings, including ministerial posts and past battles.

7.56 *state:* all the commentators, except Nandana, state that *sthāna* consists of the army, treasury, fort, and territory. I have not been able to find this term used technically in the *AŚ*.

pacification of acquisitions (labdhapraśamanāni): this is a topic of the *AŚ* (1.1.15) and dealt with extensively at *AŚ* 13.5.1–24. The pacification of newly won territories is done both through reconciliation and kindness and by means of force. The king is supposed to publicize the vices of the defeated king, contrasting that with his own virtues and piety.

7.57 *about his affairs:* Bühler and Doniger, possibly following Kullūka, connect the word *kāryeṣu* with *pāda-d:* "do what is (most) beneficial for him in his affairs." I think it is syntactically connected to what precedes, because this term concluding that clause as correctly pointed out by Govinda; the king seeks advice about his affairs.

7.60 *officials* (amātyān): this is a generic term used with reference to all high ranking government officials (see Scharfe 1993, 132), especially those below the level of *mantrin* ("counselor"). Revenue collection is, of course, one of the principal duties of such officials. Within the state organization envisaged in the *AŚ*, there was a special official called Samāhartṛ (precisely the same word used here by Manu) who was the revenue collector: see Scharfe 1993, 157–9. Note the parallel between this verse on the appointment of *amātyas* and verse 54 on the appointment of counselors, both verses ending in *suparīkṣitān*.

7.62 *employing . . . his residence:* I have a feeling that there is something wrong with this verse. Bhāruci, for example, says that the brave are chiefs of the armed forces, even though the army is not mentioned here. Also, *pādas a, c,* and *d*, form nice self-contained units; this structure is violated in *pāda-b*, which, as it stands, forms a syntactic unit with *pāda-a*. The initial *teṣām* ("among them") looks suspiciously like a commentarial introduction to this verse, a comment that found its way into the root text (but see 8.4 where the initial *teṣām* has a similar meaning). One candidate for emendation is *dakṣān*, which is found also in verse 61. If we read *daṇḍe* in its place following the ST mss., and replace *teṣām* with *śucīn*, we would have four self-contained *pādas*. The repetition of *śucīn* in *pāda-c* makes this emendation somewhat problematic, but both Bhāruci and Medhātithi take the statement about mines and factories to be an example of *artha*, which they take to mean "activities relating to income and expenditure." See also the parallel passage of *ViDh* (3.16–21), where those employed in mines are called *āpta*. With this type of emendation, the verse would read: "appointing the honest to financial affairs, the brave from illustrious families to the army; the honest to mines and factories; and the timid to the interior of his residence."

7.63 *hint, bearing, or gesture:* the *AŚ* (1.15.7–9) gives only two: *iṅgita* ("hint") and *ākāra* ("bearing"), and defines the former as non-normal movement or gesture (*anyathāvṛttiḥ*), and the latter as "putting on an expression" (*ākṛtigrahaṇam*), explained by commentators as unnatural facial expressions, such as paleness. All three terms clearly refer to the ability of the envoy to interpret properly the signs that may betray the inner thoughts of the rival king.

7.65 *realm:* according to Scharfe (1993, 124) *rāṣṭra* may also have a more restricted meaning, referring to "incorporated states with some degree of autonomy." See also 7.122 n.

7.67 *seducible men* (kṛtyeṣu): most commentators and all translators have missed the technical meaning of *kṛtya* within the vocabulary of political science. Bühler, for example, translates "with respect to the affairs" and produces a forced translation of the verse. In the *AŚ* (see 1.16.24) *kṛtya* means a person in the enemy king's service who is open to being seduced. Nandana correctly detects this meaning: *svarājñā bhedyeṣu parapakṣasthiteṣu puruṣeṣu* ("among men in the service of the enemy who can be induced to break with their king"). See Scharfe 1993, 213–4.

servants (bhṛtyeṣu): the ST mss. read here also *kṛtyeṣu*. The translation would then be: "his plans with the help of seducible men."

7.68 *he should take:* the subject of the verb *ātiṣṭhet* is unclear. Is it the ambassador, whose activities were the focus of the preceding verses, or the king? Bhāruci, Govinda, Rāghavānanda, and Nandana take the subject to be the ambassador; and I would tend to agree. Nārāyana, Kullūka, and Rāmacandra take it to be the king, who finds all this out through his envoy. Medhātithi's commentary on this verse is missing.

7.69 *healthy* (anāvilam): I follow the interpretation of Bhāruci, Govinda, Kullūka, and Rāghavānanda. The meaning, according to these, is that the region is free from both disease and from other harmful things, such as mosquitoes, snakes, vicious animals, and the like. Nārāyaṇa, Nandana, and Rāmacandra take the term to mean a region free from mixed castes.

7.70 *A fortress . . . by a hill:* on the different kinds of fortresses and their relative merits, see *AŚ* 2.3.1–35.

7.74 Variant reading: "a fortress is enjoined."

Additional verse: "Even the top of the Mandara mountain devoid of soldiers is not commended. A fort with soldiers, Manu the son of the Self-existent One has declared, is the best kind of fort."

7.75 *conveyances:* the term *vāhanāni* is difficult to translate because it includes vehicles (carts, carriages, chariots), as well as draft animals, beasts of burden, and riding horses (cavalry).

7.76 *provided with pools and groves:* I follow the interpretation of Medhātithi and Nandana. Others understand this as referring simply to water and trees.

7.78 *domestic rites . . . fires:* the distinction here is between the domestic rites (*smārta*) that are described in the *Gṛhyasūtras*, and the solemn vedic rites (*śrauta*) that require the three vedic fires (2.231).

7.82 Variant reading: "for this is called the inexhaustible treasure of kings deposited with Brahmins."

7.84 Variant reading: "to the teacher, a thousandfold reward."

7.86 Two additional verses: "When an article is given to a worthy recipient at the proper place and time, according to rule, and in a spirit of generosity—that is the accomplishment of the Law. This alone is the highest and the complete Law laid down for a king—he should obtain wealth through victory in battle and donate it to the twice-born."

7.90 *treacherous:* most commentators take *kūṭa* as referring to be a weapon concealed in a wooden exterior.

7.91 *a man standing on the ground:* the implication is that the soldier, in this case the king, is fighting on a chariot or a mount.

7.94 *master:* see Scharfe 1993, 106 for the use of *bhartṛ* with reference to the king. On the loyalty to the king, see Hara 1994–95.

7.97 *preemptive share:* the term *uddhāra* is used also with reference to the extra share reserved for the oldest brother in partitioning ancestral property (see 9.112–7). It appears that in the division of war booty also, the king, as the chief, received a share of the best pieces before the rest was divided among the soldiers, as also the best item from the booty won by individual soldiers in single combat. See also *GDh* 10.22.

vedic scripture: Medhātithi and other commentators cite *AB* 3.21: after his victory over Vṛtra, Indra demanded his preemptive share: *uddhāraṃ ma uddharata*.

Additional verse: "He should distribute the gains among his servants; he alone should not take them all. The king should be satisfied with the mere title and the parasol."

7.99 *The king . . . worthy recipients:* this verse has the hallmarks of a proverbial saying. In the *Pañcatantra* (I, verse 2) there is a very similar statement with regard to a merchant and his ambition to become rich. See the parallel in *AŚ* 1.4.3; Scharfe 1993, 46.

7.101 Variant reading: "he should distribute to deserving people."

7.102 *He should keep . . . readiness:* the phrase *nityaṃ udyatadaṇḍaḥ syāt* is quoted in *AŚ* 1.4.5 and ascribed to "Teachers," making it likely that this is also a proverbial saying.

7.105 *hide his limbs like a tortoise:* a variant of this verse is cited in *AŚ* 1.15.60. The simile may be a comparison of the five *aṅgas* of counsel (*mantra*) to the five *aṅgas* (four feet and head) that the tortoise withdraws into the shell. The five limbs of counsel are given as: means for commencing operations (*karmaṇāṃ ārambhopāyaḥ*); provision of men and material (*puruṣadravyasaṃpad*); distribution of place and time (*deśakālavibhāga*); remedies for setbacks (*vipattipratīkāra*); and success of the undertaking (*kāryasiddhi*).

7.106 *He should ponder . . . like a lion:* Bhāruci has a long comment on these similes: "Just as naturally in order to catch a mass of fish who are safe in their water-fort the 'heron' finds an effective means to take them by employing meditation, after dedicating himself to the task, so the king should not be despondent realizing that if one employs abundant thought on one's affairs even aims very difficult to achieve are attained. Just as the 'hare', because its body is small, is able to double back from even a host of enemies, so even one who has no allies and so cannot withstand when his feudatories are enraged against him and have risen in all quarters, may seal up his fort and fly from it in search of a suitable refuge. Just as a 'wolf' intending to take the cattle, finds out the keeper's negligence and snatches them, so one should not give up one's hope of taking what appears to be the object of careful protection, for the time will come when, like a wolf, he will be able to make his snatch. And just as the 'lion' strikes even large-bodied creatures like the elephant and so on, overcoming them by employing his might and power, so the king should not fear, thinking that the enemy's force is large. For something of large size but weak in spirit is sometimes struck down by a small creature which is large in spirit" (Trans. Derrett). In his commentary on this verse, Medhātithi has plagiarized Bhāruci.

7.107 *strategies beginning with conciliation:* the four strategies are conciliation (*sāman*), gifts (*dāna*), fomenting dissension (*bheda*), and war (*yuddha, vigraha*). See 7.198–200.

Additional verse: "He should not place his trust in an untrustworthy person; nor should he place excessive trust in a trustworthy person. Trust is the source of danger; it cuts him off even by his roots."

7.113 *managing . . . well managed:* I take *saṃgraha* in this context as relating to the management or governance of the king's realm, which is the topic of the very next section. Medhātithi glosses with *rakṣāvidhānam*, which deals with only one aspect of management. Govinda, Kullūka, and Nandana also gloss with *rakṣaṇa*. See *MBh* 12.88.1 where *saṃgraha* is juxtaposed with *gupti*, the latter referring specifically to protection and the former, I think, more generally to good governance that would bring satisfaction to the people.

prospers: on the term *edhate*, see Thieme 1958.

7.116 *troubles:* Govinda and Kullūka take *doṣa* to mean thefts and other such crimes. Nārāyaṇa takes it as referring to agitations among the people and the like (*janavidravādīn*). The term literally means "faults" and can refer to any types of adversities or problems arising within a village.

7.119 *"family":* the term *kula* is interpreted by Medhātithi to mean a segment of a village, known in some regions as *haṭṭa* and in others as *uṣṭa*. Nārāyaṇa cites a saying that a *kula* consists of two *halas*, a *hala* being an area of land that can be plowed by eight or six oxen. The latter view is adopted by Govinda, Kullūka, Rāghavānanda, and Rāmacandra. Nandana thinks it is the share of one cultivator.

7.120 *undertaken by each individually* (pṛthakkāryāṇi): the meaning could also be "activities pertaining to individuals."

7.121 *high stature:* commentators uniformly take *ucchaiḥsthānam* to mean a person coming from an illustrious family or who is in some way eminent. I think that it may well refer to the physical stature or height rather than the social or moral standing of the individual, especially in juxtaposition with his fierce appearance.

7.122 *within their jurisdictions* (rāṣṭreṣu): this is a significant use of the term *rāṣṭra* to refer to an administrative unit within the state (*rājya*): see 7.65 n.

7.124 *people who have business:* commentators generally take *kāryikebhyaḥ* as referring to people who have lawsuits pending. The reference is then to the bribery of judges. The term could also have a wider meaning, including other matters requiring official sanction. In that context, this provision may include bribery and kickbacks.

send them into exile: the term *pravāsanam* can also mean the infliction of capital punishment (see 8.123 n.).

7.125 *He should fix:* for a discussion of the relative wages of the different officials in royal service, see Scharfe 1993, 135.

7.126 *maintenance:* the critical edition has adopted the reading *bhaktakam* in preference to *vetanam* ("wages") found in most editions and mss. For a discussion of this unusual term, see Introduction, p. 36.

7.127 *maintenance* (bhakta): I think this term means more or less the same that *bhaktaka* of the preceding verse and must refer to the expenses of maintaining himself and his employees. I think Nandana has it right when he explains: *karmakārādibhyo deyam* ("what has to be given to the workmen and the like"). Bühler and Doniger take the term literally as meaning "food."

7.130 *share:* on *bhāga* as a technical term for the king's share of any produce, occurring already in the Aśokan inscriptions, see Scharfe 1993, 160, where further literature is given.

7.138 *self-employed:* most commentators take the expression *ātmopajīviṣu* to mean Śūdras employed as manual laborers. This may well be the case; but the expression has a wider application, as seen in its use with regard to wives who earn a living on their own, possibly as prostitutes, at 8.362.

7.139 *He must not . . . to them:* most commentators see an implicit "non-gathering of taxes" in the context of cutting off his own root. That is, by being too lenient with taxation a king cuts his own root, whereas by excessive taxation he cuts off the root of his tax-paying subjects. Bühler follows this interpretation. I think Nandana is correct in seeing excessive greed as the cause of cutting his own root and that of others. "Root" is the wealth produced by the people that supports both the citizens and the king. Excessive taxation cuts this common root.

7.140 *lawsuits:* although the term *kāryam* may have a broader meaning, such as business or affairs (Bühler), I think that here and in the next verse it has the technical meaning of a lawsuit (see 8.8). The mention of "that seat" in verse 141 indicates a judicial proceeding at which a deputized minister is presiding.

7.143 Additional verse: "Fire, flared up by the anguish of the people's oppression, does not turn back until it has burnt up the king's family, wealth, and life."

7.144 *specified rewards* (nirdiṣṭaphala): the reference is to the taxes a king collects, which are considered to be payment for the protection provided by the king.

7.147 *Climbing . . . his counselors:* for a discussion of the place where the king should meet with his counselors, see Sternbach 1972.

7.153 *tying up . . . undertakings* (kāryaśeṣam): the reference is to past activities where some aspects may not have been completely carried out and need further attention. See 7.179.

activities: on the meaning of the term *pracāra*, which has been subject to much misunderstanding, see Scharfe 1993, 195–200. He has demonstrated that the term does not refer to a piece of land or a region but to activities. See 9.219 n.

7.154 *eightfold agenda* (aṣṭavidhaṃ karma): there is no consensus among the commentators as to the identity of these eight. Many cite a verse from Uśanas that lists eight activities of a king: income (*ādāna*), expenditure (*visarga*), dismissal (*praiṣa*, e.g., of bad officials), preventing (*niṣedha*, e.g., wrong activities on the part of officials), propounding the correct meaning (*arthavacana;* others interpret the term to mean resolving difficult points of Law), resolving lawsuits (*vyavahārasya cekṣaṇam*), punishment (*daṇḍa*), and prescribing penances (*śuddhi*). Medhātithi offers two other lists. First: undertaking what has not been done (*akṛtārambha*), carrying out what has been done (*kṛtānuṣṭhāna*), enhancing what has been carried out (*anuṣṭhitaviśeṣaṇa*), reaping the fruit of the activity (*karmasaṃgraha*), conciliation (*sāman*), sowing dissension (*bheda*), bestowing gifts (*dāna*), and using force (*daṇḍa*). This explanation is preferred by Nandana. Second: trade (*vaṇikpatha*), building bridges and dikes (*udakasetubandhana*), building forts (*durgakaraṇa*), keeping them in repair (*kṛtasya tatsaṃskāraniyamaḥ*), trapping elephants (*hastibandhana*), constructing mines (*khanikhanana*), settling uninhabited lands (*śūnyaniveśana*), and clearing forests (*dāruvanacchedana*).

set of five (pañcavargam): most commentators explain this as a reference to the five kinds of spies employed by a king: deceiver (*kāpaṭika*, the meaning of this word being unclear), fallen ascetic (*udāsthita*), householder in distress (*gṛhapati*), trader in distress (*vaideha*), and one wearing the insignia of a hermit (*tāpasavyañjana*). For a discussion of the various types of spies, see Scharfe 1993, 204–39. Nārāyaṇa, Nandana, and Rāmacandra prefer a different set, identical with the five limbs of counsel (7.105 n.).

circle of neighboring kingdoms (maṇḍala): ancient Indian political science envisaged, perhaps somewhat artificially and geometrically, kingdoms as forming circles around any given kingdom. The neighboring kingdoms constitute natural enemies; the kingdoms beyond the immediate neighbors constitute the enemy's enemies, and thus one's own natural allies; the kingdoms beyond these constitute the ally's natural enemies, and therefore one's own enemies; and so on. See Scharfe 1993, 105–17.

Two additional verses: "In the forest he should place forest-dwellers such as ascetics and foresters. He should establish a series of spies who are quick, in order to discover the activities of his enemies. He should uncover those dispatched by his enemy using the same kinds of spies as those deployed by the enemy—whether they are mobile spies or resident spies, secret agents without the outwards marks of secret agents."

7.155 *buffer king:* this is a king whose realm stands between the king and the kingdom he intends to attack.

7.156 *The above constituents . . . twelve:* the constituents (*prakṛtayaḥ*) must be four in order to come up with the total of twelve. Scharfe (1993, 108) appears to take the constituents as the seven listed in *AŚ* 6.1; but it is likely that Manu considers them to be the four encircling kingdoms listed in verse 155. On the "root" of the circle, called "womb" (*maṇḍalayoni*) in the *AŚ*, see Scharfe 1993, 107–8. The "eight others" are identified by the commentators as the eight other kinds of surrounding kingdoms listed by Kāmandaki (*Nītisāra*, 8.16–7). Four in front beyond the enemy: ally (*mitra*), enemy's ally (*arimitra*), ally's ally (*mitramitra*), enemy's ally's ally (*arimitramitra*). Four in the rear: foe at the heel (*pārṣṇigrāha*), rescuer from the rear (*ākranda*), supporter of foe at the heel (*pārṣṇigrāhāsāra*), and supporter of rescuer from the rear (*ākrandāsāra*). For these terms, see 7.207 n.

7.157 *There are also . . . seventy-two:* each of the twelve listed in the previous verse has five constituents, thus bringing the total to 60 (see *AŚ* 6.2.28, which calls these 60 *dravyaprakṛtayaḥ*, "material constituents"). Together with the previous twelve (called *rājaprakṛtayaḥ*, "constituents of kings" in *AŚ* 6.2.28), the total comes to 72.

7.158 Additional verse: "When a neutral and powerful king is located along a long and uncontrolled path that a king desiring conquest and seeking the control of the circle of kings has to take, he is called the buffer king." The verse is somewhat unclear.

7.160 *double stratagem:* the meaning of *dvaidhībhāvam* in Manu is unclear. The explanation given in verse 167 indicates that the strategy consists of separating the army from the king. How this was carried out and the strategy behind it are unclear. Most commentators say that the king divides his army in two, which is also the explanation given in 7.173. I prefer the view of Bhāruci, followed by Medhātithi and Govinda, according to which this strategy calls for pursuing war and peace at the same time. Govinda thinks that he pursues war with one opponent and peace with another. This appears to be the basis for the description of the strategy in the *AŚ* 7.7: the king obtains troops from one neighbor promising him part of his treasury and wages war on another neighbor. The description in verse 167, however, points in another direction. The king pursues peace and diplomacy, while surreptitiously preparing for war. That may be the reason for separating the army (or part of the army) from the king, so he can give the appearance that he is not preparing for war. In verse 167, the meaning may not be that the army stops in one place and the king in another (so Bühler), but that the king remains stationary, while the army is on the march (or vice versa). Here the term *sthiti* may indeed be a synonym of *āsana* (remaining stationary after suspending military operations); the *AŚ* 7.4.2 gives *sthāna* as a synonym of *āsana*. The division of the army into two (7.173) may also envisage such a strategy: one part remaining stationary, giving the impression that war in not imminent, while the other launches a surprise attack.

7.161 *After forging . . . war:* the reading of the critical edition (see note there) is *saṃdhāya ca vigṛhya ca*. Bhāruci gives a very clear and succinct explanation: *saṃdhāyāsanaṃ vigṛhyāsanaṃ saṃdhāya yānaṃ vigṛhya yānaṃ vā kāryaṃ vīkṣya prayuñjīta / tathā dvaidhaṃ saṃśrayam eva ca,* "After forging an alliance, he should suspend operations, and after waging war, he should suspend operations; after forging an alliance, he should march into battle, and after waging war, he should march into battle—he should carefully examine the state of affairs and adopt these tactics. Likewise, the double stratagem or asylum." If we follow the vulgate reading (*saṃdhiṃ vigraham eva ca*), the translation would be: "He should carefully examine the state of affairs and adopt the tactic of suspending operations, marching into battle, forging an alliance, waging war, pursuing a double stratagem, or seeking asylum."

7.162 *to pursue a double stratagem:* the vulgate reads *dvividham* ("of two kinds") for *dvaidham* ("double stratagem"), following which Bühler and Doniger omit double stratagem from the list, giving only five rather than the six strategies. See, however, that in explaining these twofold divisions, the double stratagem is listed in verse 167.

7.163 *two kinds . . . to the future:* this verse has been subject to different interpretations. Bühler (also Doniger) follows Kullūka and takes *tadātvāyatisaṃyuktaḥ* as qualifying *saṃdhiḥ*, and translates: "An alliance which yields present and future advantages, one must know to be of two descriptions." I follow Bhāruci, Nārāyaṇa, and Govinda in taking that clause as referring to the two kinds of alliance. I also think that Bhāruci and Govinda (who is more explicit) are correct in taking the immediate significance (*tadātva*) as relating to an alliance where the allies march together, and the future significance as relating to its opposite. Most take *-karmā* at the end of the compound *samānayānakarmā* as referring to the activity of marching into battle. I think *yānakarma* is a Dvandva and the compound means an alliance where the allies march together (*samānayāna*) and have the same object (*samānakarma*, here *karma* possibly drawing on its grammatical meaning of object). The opposite of this would be allies who march into battle separately to further different objectives. In this case, the alliance has no immediate significance but is undertaken with a long-term strategy in mind.

7.164 *an ally has initiated the offensive* (mitreṇa caivāpakṛte): the critical edition adopts the reading *mitreṇa* accepted by Bhāruci, Govinda, and Nandana, and also noted by Medhātithi. The second kind of war, as Bhāruci clearly points out, is initiated when an ally has attacked one's enemy, who has been rendered vulnerable thereby. The preferred reading of Medhātithi, followed by other commentators and recorded in the majority of the NT mss., is *mitrasya*. Following this reading, Bühler translates: "(that waged to avenge) an injury done to a friend." So also Doniger.

7.168 *Tradition records . . . good people:* the variant readings and the diverse interpretations indicate the difficulties posed especially by the second half of this verse. Medhātithi sees *sādhuṣu* as syntactically connected with *saṃśrayaḥ,* meaning that the king should seek asylum with only virtuous kings; this is implausible. Nandana reads *sādhubhiḥ* and interprets the clause to mean that the second type of asylum is intended to avert future calamities (*bhaviṣadanarthaparihārārtham*). Bhāruci reads the negative *avyapadeśa* and appears to say that even an evil man may seek asylum so as not be singled out as evil among good people (*sādhuṣu*). The term *vyapadeśa* also means fraud or faudulent strategy; the meaning then may be not merely to gain renown among good people but as a fraudulent strategy to be counted as a fine king.

7.170 Variant reading: "then he should wage war."

7.171 *When he believes . . . spirit:* most commentators connect *bhāvena* with *hṛṣṭam.* Bühler translates accordingly: "When he knows his own army to be cheerful in disposition." The principle of keeping a *pāda* as a syntactic unit makes it more likely that *bhāvena* should be connected adverbially with *manyeta*, an interpretation favored by Nārāyaṇa. Govinda (with the gloss *paramārthena*) and Kullūka (with *tattvataḥ*) also probably favor the adverbial meaning.

7.172 *mounted units:* on *vāhana,* see 7.75 n. The reference may be to horses, beasts of burden, vehicles, and the like. But the opposition to *bala*, which here refers to foot soldiers, indicates a division of the army consisting of mounted units (cavalry, elephants, chariots).

7.176 *good war:* commentators explain *suyuddham* by referring to the Kṣatriya martial ethic: in victory one gets to enjoy the kingdom/spoils, and in death one goes to heaven.

7.183 *launch the expedition:* even though the verb *yāyāt* can stand alone (see verse 181), I think the term *yātrām* should be understood here (*anuvṛtti*) from the previous verse, although most commentators have not noticed this. Only Govinda and Rāmacandra mention *yātrām*.

7.185 *three types of roads:* most commentators explain this as dry land (*jāṅgala*), wet land (*anūpa*) and forests (*āṭavika*). Nārāyaṇa prefers villages, wilderness, and hills.

six divisions of his army: most commentators list elephants, horses, chariots, infantry, general, and workmen. Nandana prefers the sixfold division given by Kāmandaki (*Nītisāra* 16.6): hereditary troops, hired troops, troops from guilds, ally's troops, alien troops, and foresters. This same list is given in *AŚ* 9.2.1.

and only then . . . enemy's fort: note that *pāda-d* of this verse is identical with the final *pāda* of verse 181, which opened this section on preparations for a military expedition. This repetition indicates the closure of this small sub-section.

7.187 *staff . . . eagle:* in the staff formation the army is arranged in a line with the field general (*balādhyakṣa*) in the front, the commander in chief (*senāpati*) at the rear, and the king in the middle, with the flanks protected by elephants and horses. This is used when danger is expected from all sides. In the wagon formation, used when there is a threat from the rear, the front is narrow like a needle and the rear is broad. In the boar, used when danger is perceived from the flanks, the front and the rear are narrow and the middle broad. In the crocodile, used when danger is expected from the front and the rear, the front and the rear are broad and the middle is narrow. In the needle, used when an attack is expected from the front, the army is arranged in a thin and long formation. The eagle formation is similar to the boar, except that it has longer wings extending outward on the flanks. For a detailed discussion of these and other military formations, see AŚ 10.5–6.

7.188 *lotus formation:* in this formation the king is placed in the middle for protection, and the various units spread out in semi-circles extending from the center in all directions.

7.189 *post . . . in every direction:* since this is physically impossible, commentators explain that by the commander-in-chief and the general are meant all their subordinates. In other words, these two chief officers are responsible for guarding all the directions.

7.191 *thunderbolt:* in this formation, the army is deployed in three separate units.

7.196 *launch surprise assaults:* the meaning of the verb *samavaskandayet* is not altogether clear. Most commentators appear to indicate something like commando raids. Nandana cites Naighaṇṭakas who take *avaskanda* and *sauptika* as synonyms; the meaning then is attacks on sleeping troops.

7.197 *enemy activity* (tatkṛtam): the precise antecedent of *tat* ("his") is unclear. Medhātithi and Nandana take it to be the enemy king: one should especially keep watch over what the enemy himself may do to foment sedition in one's own ranks or to establish contact with the enemy's allies to his rear. Other commentators take "his" as relating to the seditious people in the enemy ranks.

7.201 *After the victory . . . amnesty:* all these activities refer to what the king must do within the conquered territories. So, the gods and Brahmins are those local to those territories. "Exemptions" (*parihāra*) refer to tax holidays of varying lengths granted to Brahmins and other significant individuals of the conquered lands. Amnesty is the freedom from fear (*abhaya*): see 6.39 n.

7.205 *All activities . . . to the human:* this philosophy is clearly opposed to the "passive" ideology insisting that everything is determined by either fate (*daiva*) or by one's own previous actions (*karma*). See *AŚ* 6.2.6–12, which is a close parallel to this verse. For further discussion of this topic and a somewhat diffferent interpretation of the expression *vidhāne daivamānuṣe*, see Rocher 1977–78.

A few mss. give here fifty additional verses. Their length precludes them from being translated here.

7.206 *alliance with him:* given that this strategy is an alternative to war, the alliance must be with the enemy king.

recognizing . . . rewards: the parallel passage in *AŚ* 7.9.1 reads: *saṃhitaprayāṇe mitrahiraṇyabhūmilābhānām uttarottaro lābhaḥ śreyān*, "When marching off after making an alliance, among the gains—ally, money, land—each subsequent one is better than each preceding." This is exactly the opposite of Manu's view expressed in verse 208. The *AŚ* 7.9.2 says that land is the best because an ally and money can come from it, and money the next, because an ally can come from it.

7.207 *the foe at his heel . . . rear:* these are technical terms for certain kingdoms constituting the circle (see 7.154 n.). "The foe at his heel" (*pārṣṇigrāha*) is the king to his immediate rear, who by definition is an ally of his enemy, whom he is attacking and therefore is located to his front. The enemy can call on the foe at his heel to attack him from the rear. When this happens, the attacking king can call on the king located to the rear of the foe at his heel; this king, being the immediate neighbor of his foe, is his natural ally. He is called "rescuer from the rear" (*ākranda*). This term literally means "cry for help"; evidently, when a rear attack took place, the king could send word (cry for help) to this ally, who would attack the former from his rear. On these terms, see the detailed study by Scharfe 1993, 111–6.

7.209 *agile:* the meaning of *laghu* is unclear. Several commentators take it with a negative connotation, namely weak. Under this interpretation we have to accept an implied *api* ("even"), as Nārāyaṇa and Bühler do. The meaning would then be: "even a weak ally is commended." I think Nandana is correct in taking *laghu* to mean a person who does things quickly (*laghukārī*). Govinda's gloss *dakṣa* ("clever") also probably applies to *laghu*. This positive interpretation is supported by the use of *laghu* at 7.193 with reference to front-line soldiers.

7.211 *generosity* (sthaulalakṣyam): Kullūka cites a verse from a work on synonyms that lists this term with others for generosity. This interpretation is followed by most commentators. Govinda explains the term as "acute perception" (*sūkṣmadarśitvam*): see the use of *lakṣa* at 7.54 n.

7.216 *After conferring . . . in this manner:* these words connect this section on the afternoon routine with the section on the king's morning routine and his conferring with his counselors (7.147). It is to be assumed that the intervening sections on political strategies and war constituted the topics of the king's consultations with his counselors.

7.217 *There he should . . . remove poison:* several interpretations of this verse are offered by commentators. First, Govinda and Kullūka detect an implied *kṛtam* ("made") in the first half-verse. Following them, Bühler translates: "food (which has been prepared) by faithful, incorruptible (servants)." I think this is quite unnecessary; the instrumentals in the first half-verse, as Medhātithi has correctly pointed out, are syntactically connected with *suparīkṣitam* ("thoroughly examined"). The other difficulty in the verse is the syntax of the final instrumentals *mantrair viṣāpahaiḥ*. Nārāyaṇa, Govinda, and Kullūka connect these with *suparīkṣitam*. Bühler, accordingly, translates: "which has been well examined (and hallowed) by sacred texts that destroy poison." Medhātithi explains that the king should recite these mantras over the food. Although this is possible, the simplest way to construct the last *pāda* is to take the instrumentals as indicating the recitation of the mantras while or right before the king eats. This is quite a common use of the instrumental within ritual settings with reference to the sacred texts to be recited while a ritual action is being performed. The expression *ātmabhūtaiḥ,* which I have translated "completely loyal," means literally persons who are (like) one's very self. The expression "knowledgeable about time" (*kālajña*) has been explained as servants who know which course to serve at what time during the meal. Medhātithi explains the term as servants who know what foods and drinks are to be given at what age and under what conditions.

7.218 Variant reading: "with liquids that neutralize poison."

7.224 *escorted by women:* the reference is probably to female guards rather than to servants (so Bühler and Doniger). For a description of the various female guards posted around the king, something already noted by Megasthenes, see Scharfe 1993, 152–3.

CHAPTER EIGHT

8.1 *who are experts in policy* (mantrajñaiḥ): Medhātithi asks what noun this adjective qualifies. He argues that it cannot qualify counselors (*mantrin*), because that would be a tautology, for *mantrins* are by definition (and name) supposed to know *mantra*. He concludes that it must qualify "Brahmins" of the previous *pāda*. This interpretation is followed by Rāmacandra, whereas Nandana thinks it qualifies both the counselors and the Brahmins. My translation leaves this issue as vague as the Sanskrit.

8.2 *raising his right hand* (pāṇim udyamya dakṣiṇam): all commentators take *pāṇi* ("hand") to mean *bāhu* ("arm"), which is reasonable. The reason for raising the right arm, however, in unclear. Medhātithi thinks it is meant to draw attention and to disallow a question. Govinda, Nandana, and Rāghavānanda take it to mean that the king should have his right arm uncovered. Nandana gives the opinion of some who take it to mean that he should be wearing his sacrificial cord (*yajñopavītin;* see 2.63 n.). I think the answer may be in this direction. In ritual contexts (and legal proceedings are quasi-ritual), the right shoulder and arm are always left uncovered. See 2.193 n. for this practice within the context of a vedic student.

8.3 *individually* (pṛthak pṛthak): Kullūka takes the terms to be syntactically connected with *paśyet* ("he should look into") of the previous verse; and this interpretation is followed by Bühler and Doniger: "Daily (deciding) one case after another." I think this is quite unwarranted; Bhāruci, Govinda, and Rāmacandra (and possibly also Medhātithi) are correct in connecting them with *nibaddhāni* ("connected with"). The principle of each *pāda* being in general a syntactic unit argues in favor of this. The meaning is that any lawsuit brought before the court should fall under one or the other of the eighteen grounds for litigation spelled out below. For a detailed explanation of this, see Vijñāneśvara's commentary on *YDh* 2.5–8.

8.6 *sexual crimes against women:* usually the expression *strīsaṃgrahaṇam* refers to adultery. I have given it a broader definition, because under this ground for litigation are included a wide variety of crimes against women, including rape.

8.9 *When the king . . . to do so:* for a more detail account of ancient Indian legal proceedings, see *AŚ* 3.1.

8.11 *officer* (prakṛtaḥ): this is an unusual word. Medhātithi and Nārāyaṇa gloss this with *adhikṛtaḥ*, which is the reading in most mss. and commentaries. The term *prakṛta*, like so many works in this section of Manu, is derived from the *Arthaśāstra* vocabulary. This term occurs twice there with the meaning of officer or minister of the king (AŚ 2.7.10; 2.8.24). The term clearly has the same meaning here. It may well be that *prakṛta* is related to the common term *prakṛti*, which refers to the constituent parts of a kingdom but especially to the ministers (see 7.157). We have a similar usage in the commentary on *KātŚr* 14.3.2. See the use of the verb *prakurvīta* as "appointing" at *MDh* 7.60.

8.12 *pierced by Injustice:* the image here is of Justice that is pierced by a dart, which is Injustice itself, and which the court is obliged to remove. Bhāruci and Medhātithi, however, give a different explanation. Justice is pierced by a dart when a judge decides wrongly and permits a miscarriage of justice to occur in his court. If the other officials of the court let it go unchallenged, then they are themselves wounded by this dart.

8.17 *Justice . . . with the body:* here the meaning of *dharma* shifts imperceptibly from justice to merit. See the more explicit image of relatives who abandon the dead man at 4.238–43.

8.24 *Paying attention . . . social class:* the meaning of the first half-verse is unclear and commentators offer educated guesses. The main problem is the meaning of *arthānarthau* and its relationship to *dharmādharmau*. All take *kevalau* as qualifying only *dharmādharmau*. Govinda gives the most plausible explanation, which is followed by Bühler: "Knowing what is expedient or inexpedient, what is pure justice or injustice." Doniger: "Recognizing both what is profitable and what is not profitable, and what is intrinsically just and unjust." I am not convinced that the commentarial explanations or the translations have grasped the intent of the text. One possible avenue of interpretation is offered by a parallel in the *NSm* (Mā 1.31): *dharmaśāstrārthaśastrābhyām avirodhena mārgataḥ / samīkṣamāṇo nipuṇaṃ vyavahāragatiṃ nayet //* Here the king or judge is required to conduct the judicial proceedings in such a manner that they do not conflict with the provisions of either the Arthaśāstra or the Dharmaśāstra (see also *YDh* 2.21). I think it is likely that in this verse of Manu *artha* and *dharma* stand for Arthaśāstra and Dharmaśāstra, or at least to the provisions of Artha (which may include also local conventions, customs, etc.) and Dharma. In verse 8.41, which comes immediately after the two excursus that may be interpolations, there is again the instruction to examine the Laws of castes, regions, guilds, families, and the like, all of which may fall under *artha*. See *NSm* (Mā 1.24) where *vyavahāra* (recognized standards of behavior) takes precedence over *dharma*. If this interpretation is right, then there is no need to see *kevalau* as qualifying only *dharmādharmau* in opposition to *arthānarthau*. We may connect *ubhau* and *kevalau* together: "only these two," referring to both compounds.

8.27 *no longer a minor:* males reach majority at age 16 and females at 12: see *AŚ* 3.3.1; *NSm* 1.31.

8.30 *Any property . . . without an owner:* all the manuscripts and commentators read *pranaṣṭasvāmikam* as a compound (see note in the critical edition). Accordingly Bühler translates: "Property, the owner of which has disappeared." The use of the term *pranaṣṭa* with reference to the owner is awkward; in the following verses (32, 33, 34) the term is uniformly applied to lost property and not to a lost owner. The parallel in the *GDh* (10.36) clearly shows that the reference is to lost property whose owner is unknown: "If someone finds lost property whose owner is unknown, he should disclose it to the king." Here we have the uncompounded form *pranaṣṭam asvāmikam*, which, I think, is what Manu's verse also read in the original (see Introduction, p. 44 for Manu's dependence on Gautama). It was probably changed to *pranaṣṭasvāmikam*, because the former would make the foot hypermetric with 9 syllables (for hypermeter in Manu, see Introduction, p. 44). It may also be that the original versified form was *pranaṣṭāsvāmikam*, which would have the same meaning as the prose. My translation follows this emendation.

8.37 Additional verse: "When a Brahmin discovers a treasure-trove, he should inform the king quickly. He may enjoy whatever the king gives him. Failure to inform makes him a thief."

8.39 *supreme lord of the earth* (bhūmer adhipatiḥ): for the economic consequences of this conception of kingship, see Scharfe 1993, 240. Note also the parallel with the last *pāda* of verse 37 where the Brahmin is called *sarvasya adhipatiḥ* ("the supreme lord of all").

8.43 *initiate a lawsuit:* Medhātithi interprets this to mean that the king should not instigate others to bring lawsuits against people whom he dislikes or from whom he hopes to obtain fines. It is a common principle of ancient Indian jurisprudence, however, that all lawsuits are initiated by private individuals and not by the state.

nor shall he . . . someone else: Medhātithi records the opinion of some that takes *artha* here to mean money. The meaning then is that he should not take for himself money brought to him except within the parameters of the lawsuit. The clear intent is to avoid bribery of court officials.

8.44 *As a hunter . . . reasoning:* the term *nayati* ("lead") is here used, I think, in an interesting way, deliberately juxtaposing it to *anumāna* ("inference") and echoing its connection to *nyāya* ("logic"). The term *padam* may have a double meaning: the path and the location. With the first meaning, the hunter follows the track of the wounded animal along the trail of blood; and the judge by inferential reasoning proceeds along the path of justice. With the second meaning, the hunter finds the place where the animal has fallen by following the trail of blood; and the judge determines where justice lies by inferential reasoning.

8.45 *appearance:* the meaning of *rūpam* is unclear and commentators offer educated guesses. Medhātithi takes the term to mean the nature (*svabhāva*) of the lawsuit; the judge should see whether it is serious or not (*gurulaghutvam*). Kullūka, Rāghavānanda, and Nandana offer similar explanations, taking *rūpa* as *svarūpa*. I think their interpretation is reasonable, although in a very similar passage of *AŚ* 3.1.15 *rūpa* is used with regard to the appearance of an item subject to a legal transaction (e.g., debt) noted in the document drawn up for the transaction. Bhāruci gives a completely different and somewhat fabulous interpretation of the verse relating it to heaven and celestial beings, an interpretation that Medhātithi ascribes to "others."

8.46 *He should . . . or caste:* commentators offer two interpretations, depending on the syntax of the genitive *deśakulajātīnām*. Bhāruci and Medhātithi connect it with the verb *prakalpayet* and take *aviruddham* independently with the implication that they are not opposed to *śruti* and *smṛti*. The translation would then be: "The practices of virtuous men and righteous twice-born individuals that are not in opposition (to Veda and tradition) the king should establish (as the law) for regions, families, and castes." I have followed the more reasonable interpretation offered by Nārāyaṇa, Kullūka, and Rāghavānanda. This interpretation also fits with what was said in verse 41 with respect to honoring the laws and customs of different regions and groups.

8.47 *facts are established:* for the meaning of *vibhāvitam* in this context, see its use in verse 51.

8.49 *by traditional strategies* (ācaritena): most commentators cite the custom of the creditor fasting at the door of the debtor until he pays up.

8.51 Additional verse: "If the debt owed is admitted, he should be fined 500; but if it is denied, the fine is doubled—that is Manu's decree."

8.52 *document:* on the meaning of the obscure word *deśa*, see Introduction, p. 48.

8.53 *When the plaintiff . . . disavows it:* this statement parallels *AŚ* 3.1.19: *pratijñāya deśaṃ nirdiśety ukte na nirdiśati, hīnadeśam adeśaṃ vā nirdiśati, nirdiṣṭād deśād anyaṃ deśam upasthāpayati, upasthite deśe 'rthavacanaṃ naivam ity apavyayate* / "after promising documentary evidence, when told 'Produce it', does not produce it; or produces a deficient document or something that does not constitute documentary evidence; presents a defective document; when the document is presented, denies a statement whose meaning is transparent, saying 'It is not so'." I think Kangle's rendering of *pratijñāya* as "after making an affirmation" is incorrect. Some of the elements of the *AŚ* passage, I believe, is understood in Manu's verse, which appears to be a very condensed version. Especially the second *pāda* appears to echo the last phrase of the *AŚ*. If this is correct, then the commentators and translators of this verse have misunderstood it. Bühler translates: "who retracts his statements." Clearly *nirdiśya* here must refer to the production of the documents rather than to a previous statement he may have made. The meaning, if we follow the *AŚ*, appears to be that after producing the document the man denies what is clearly stated in it. The term *hīnadeśa* probably refers to a mutilated document; that is, a document in which crucial sections are missing or unreadable. The parallel term *adeśa* is probably a document that is legally inadmissible because of a fatal defect, for example, without the names of the witnesses to the original transaction.

does not realize . . . subsequently: this parallels *AŚ* 3.1.19: *pūrvoktaṃ paścimenārthena nābhisaṃdhatte*, "what is said earlier does not agree with points made later." I think Kangle's rendering of *nābhsaṃdhatte* with "does not corroborate" is not accurate.

8.54 *states his . . . from it:* this parallels *AŚ* 3.1.19: *nibaddhaṃ vādam utsṛjyānyaṃ vādaṃ saṃkrāmati*, "he abandons the dispute set down and passes over to another dispute."

does not acknowledge . . . established: although not an exact parallel, Manu's statement is possibly based on *AŚ* 3.1.19: *sākṣibhir avadhṛtaṃ necchati*, "does not concede a point determined by witnesses."

8.55 *secretly . . . being discussed*: all commentators and translators take *deśe* in this passage to mean a place. Accordingly, Bühler translates: "Or who converses with the witnesses in a place improper for such conversation." The parallel passage in *AŚ* 3.1.19 reads: *asaṃbhāṣye deśe sākṣibhir mithaḥ saṃbhāṣate*, translated by Kangle: "talks secretly with witnesses in a place where no conversation is allowed." This is quite an unusual shift in meaning within this single passage of the *AŚ*, a passage where *deśa* occurs six times, all in the sense of documentary evidence (or witness, according to the other interpretation). We also have the parallel *upasthite deśe* right before *asaṃbhāṣye deśe*. I think here also *deśa* must mean a document. I am also not sure whether *asaṃbhāṣya* can actually refer to a place rather than to a person with whom conversation is forbidden or a thing about which it is forbidden. The term *mithaḥ* occurs at 8.80, 109, 178 with the meaning "together with" or "mutually." Only Nandana and Medhātithi explicitly take the term to mean "secretly." Others either do not comment or take it to mean "together with," i.e., with the witnesses.

objects . . . articulated: the meaning of this phrase is not altogether clear. Most commentators take it to mean that the man does not want to answer a question put to him. Medhātithi, following Bhāruci, thinks that the man buys time by leaving the court on some business rather than answer the question. Bhāruci further thinks that the question is posed not to him but to the witnesses.

retreats (niṣpatet): Bhāruci thinks that the man leaves the court alleging urgent business, thus stopping the proceedings. This interpretation is followed by other commentators and Bühler. Medhātithi, however, takes this to be the same as the backing away from the lawsuit mentioned in verse 54.

8.57 Variant reading: "I have witnesses."

8.58 *If the plaintiff . . . of the Law:* for a discussion of the time limits for the plaintiff and the defendant to file their responses, see *AŚ* 3.1.27–33.

8.61 *should be made to speak:* all the commentators take *vācyam* to be the gerundive of the simple verb √*vac*. Bühler (and Doniger) follows them: "and in what manner those (witnesses) must give true (evidence)." I think the section on the questioning of witnesses (8.79–102) clearly indicates that the issue is not about witnesses speaking the truth but how the court must induce them to speak the truth. In this light, I think we must take *vācyam* as the gerundive of the causative *vācayati;* the confusion is created, unfortunately, because in the case of this verb the gerundive forms of the simple verb and of the causative are the same.

8.66 *a reprehensible person:* most commentators take the term *vaktavyaḥ* to mean a person of bad repute or evil conduct. Bhāruci, on the other hand, thinks it refers to persons with physical disabilities (*aṅgavyasanaḥ*) or people with skin diseases, such as lepers (*kuṣṭyādiḥ*). This interpretation is also mentioned by Medhātithi. See, however, the use of *vaktavyatā* as legal culpability at 8.230.

a single person (ekaḥ): all the commentators take this to mean that one should not call a single witness (so also Bühler; see verse 60). This is implausible, because the term occurs within a long list of individuals who are disqualified from being witnesses because of some disability. The term *ekaḥ* may, within this context, refer to what we would call a "single person," that is, an individual who lives on his own and is not part of a larger household, either his own or of an extended family. Indeed, a single witness is permitted in verse 77, although this is admittedly a proverbial saying.

8.69 *in a case involving bodily harm* (śarīrasyaiva cātyaye): most commentators interpret this to mean physical hurt or death (see this view explicitly stated in verse 72). Nārāyaṇa takes it to mean a case where the death penalty may be imposed. Medhātithi cites an opinion which takes the expression to refer to a situation where without such testimony the case would fail or there would be a mistrial; and the following verse dealing with the absence of regular witnesses, in this view, picks up the same theme. This appears to be the view of Bhāruci also.

8.71 *He should recognize . . . false testimony:* interestingly, all the commentators interpret this verse correctly, but none of the translators. Bühler translates: "But the (judge) should consider the evidence of infants, aged and diseased men, who (are apt to) speak untruly, as untrustworthy, likewise that of men with disordered minds." The issue is not whether what they say is uniformly untrustworthy (then, there is no point in calling them as witnesses), but how the judge can tell when they are giving false testimony.

8.72 *investigate:* the meaning is that the judge should not look into factors that would disqualify a witness (see 8.64–7) in these kinds of cases. Anyone is permitted to testify.

8.76 *not listed as a witness:* the term *anibaddha* probably refers to witnesses not listed in the original plaint and response by the plaintiff and the defendant. In later legal texts, listed witnesses are called *kṛta* ("appointed"), whereas those not on the original list but called later as witnesses are called *akṛta* ("unappointed"). See *NSm* 1.129.

during the trial: Bühler takes *tatra* (lit. "there") as referring back to what the man has seen or heard: "is (afterwards) examined regarding it." So also Doniger and Burnell. The correlative *tatra*, however, must refer back to *yatra* of the dependent clause; and the latter refers to the lawsuit, as acknowledged by the commentators.

8.77 *Even one man . . . and honest:* clearly tradition found this verse somewhat difficult; hence the many variants. A variant reading accepted by Medhātithi and Govinda read: "But one man who is greedy cannot be a witness." Another variant: "But (even) one greedy man may be a witness."

8.78 *anything different . . . no validity:* Bühler, following Kullūka, translates: "(depositions) differing from that, which they make improperly, are worthless for (the purposes of) justice." So also Doniger and Burnell. They connect *dharmārtham* syntactically with *apārthakam*. I follow Medhātithi, Rāghavānanda, and Rāmacandra in connecting *dharmārtham* adverbially with the verb *vibrūyuḥ;* the meaning being that they tell a lie for a higher purpose (so also Derrett and Jha). This point is spelled out in verses 103–4, where also we have perjury committed for the sake of the Law (*dharmataḥ*). Such false statements are made, for example, if the life of the defendant is at stake. For a long list of indicators that point to false testimony, see *NSm* 1.175–8.

8.79 *following manner:* on the speech by the judge to the witnesses, see Rocher 1964.

8.83 *of all social classes* (sarvavarṇeṣu): the locative makes the meaning unclear. It could be "witnesses from among all the social classes" (as I and others have taken it) or "with reference to all the social classes." The last interpretation is offered by Govinda and Kullūka; the meaning then would be that the witness should bear truthful testimony in cases pertaining to people of all social classes.

8.85 *No one sees us:* clearly for exigencies of meter, *iti,* which should come at the end of the quotation, is given in the middle: *paśyatīti naḥ*.

8.87 *In the presence of gods and Brahmins* (devabrāhmaṇasāṃnidhye): commentators and translators take *deva* here to mean images of gods. This may well be the case. But *deva* can also refer to the king (see 7.8; 11.83), and we have an exact parallel in 8.60: *nṛpabrāhmaṇasaṃnidhau*, where the questioning of the witness is done in the presence of the king and Brahmins.

Variant reading: "the judge should ask the twice-born individuals, who have ritually purified themselves, and are clean and facing the north or the east."

8.88 *with a reference to cows, seeds, and gold* (gobījakāñcanaiḥ): Nandana explains, correctly I think, that a Vaiśya is made to touch these substances before testifying; and this is precisely what is stated in verse 113. Alternatively, the judge may have uttered an imprecation about the man's cows etc. Most commentators, however, make *pātakaiḥ* coming at the end of the verse do double duty with regard to both Vaiśyas and Śūdras. According to this interpretation, the judge tells a Vaiśya that by bearing false witness he incurs the same sin as he would by stealing gold, killing or stealing a cow, and the like (see 8.98–100). I think this is rather far-fetched. See also *ViDh* 8.19–23.

but a Śūdra . . . caste: the critical edition has adopted the reading *ebhiḥ* in preference to *sarvaiḥ*. Following the latter reading, Bühler translates: "a Śūdra (threatening him) with (the guilt of) every crime that causes loss of caste." The reading *sarvaiḥ* may have crept into this verse under the influence of the reading of the parallel passage in verse 113. In verse 88, however, *ebhiḥ* is not only supported by better evidence but makes better sense. The long section 89–101 is thus addressed to a Śūdra witness.

8.92 *then you do not . . . Kuru land:* if the witness has no quarrel with Yama, the god of death and the judge of the dead, then there is no need for him to visit the Ganges or the land of the Kurus to expiate his sin.

8.97 *kills:* the term *hanti* is probably used metaphorically here. Medhātithi, Nārāyaṇa, Govinda, Nandana, and Kullūka take it to mean that he sends the relatives to hell. Rāghavānanda: he makes them to be reborn in animal wombs. Medhātithi and Kullūka present another view according to which the man incurs a sin equal to his killing a certain number of his relatives.

8.100 *concerning water:* the reference is unclear. Medhātithi and Kullūka take it as a reference to reservoirs, wells, and the like. Nandana: ponds *(abdhi)*. In discussing the parallel passage in *GDh* 13.18, Watkins (1994b, 725–6) thinks that the reference may be to "the right of way of *aquae ductus*." See the reference to breaking and obstructing water courses at 3.163.

Addtional verse: "(False testimony) concerning honey and ghee is similar to one concerning livestock; that concerning vehicles is similar to one concerning a horse; that concerning silver and clothes, as well as grain and the Veda, is similar to one concerning a cow."

8.101 Bhāruci states that the first eight verses (89–96) are addressed specifically to Śūdras; verse 97 is generic; and the last five verses (98–101) are applicable to all witnesses. Bhāruci must have included the extra verse after verse 100, because without it we have only four verses.

Variant reading: "tell everything forthrightly just as you saw or heard."

8.102 Additional verse: "Those who have turned away from the Laws specific to them, live on the food of others, and yet aspire to the twice-born status—these too he should treat like Śūdras."

8.106 *addressed to water:* these are the three verses (*ṚV* 10.9.1–3): *āpo hi ṣṭhā,* "Waters, you are refreshing." See Appendix III.3.

8.107 *of the total:* the meaning of *sarvataḥ* is unclear. It could be of the total amount under litigation (Bhāruci, Govinda, Nārāyaṇa, Nandana, and Rāmacandra), of the fine that would be owed to the king by the losing party (a view cited by Medhātithi), or of the debt (Kullūka). Medhātithi himself thinks that the word is merely a metrical filler *(ślokapūraṇa)*.

8.109 *oath:* Manu uses the term *śapatha* for both an oath and an ordeal. In later legal texts, such as the *YDh*, *ViDh*, and *NSm*, we find the technical term *divya* for an ordeal. This term must have entered the legal vocabulary somewhat late, because it is not found in any of the Dharmasūtras, in Manu, or in the *AŚ*.

8.110 *Vasiṣṭha:* this is an interesting lapse on the part of the author of our text. He evidently forgot his literary setting: it is Manu speaking through his pupil Bhṛgu. Bringing in a historical episode such as this would not be expected of Manu, the father of Vasiṣṭha himself (see 1.35). We find similar lapses at 8.116 (example of Vatsa) and at 8.140 with a reference to a rule instituted by Vasiṣṭha. The story in this verse probably refers to *ṚV* 7.104.15. Vasiṣṭha was accused of being a fiend who had eaten his own sons. He cleared himself by an oath that if it were true he should die that very day.

8.112 *to protect a Brahmin:* some commentators take *brāhmaṇābhyupapattau* to mean "as a favor for a Brahmin" (so Bühler and Doniger). I follow the obviously correct interpretation of Nandana, Govinda, Kullūka, and Rāmacandra; *abhyupapatti* is used unambiguously as defense in 8.349 and *abhyavapatti* in 10.62.

8.113 *He should make . . . of caste:* see 8.88 n. and, for a discussion of similar legal language in other Indo-European languages, Watkins 1994b, 720. See the parallel prescriptions for the four classes within the context of purification at 5.99.

8.115 *When the blazing . . . strikes him:* the procedures for various ordeals are described in *NSm* 20. In the fire ordeal, eight circles are drawn on the ground. Seven banyan leaves are tied to the palms of the person undergoing the ordeal and a hot iron ball is placed in his hands. He must carry it through the circles and drop the ball at the designated place. If his palms are not burnt, he is declared innocent. In the water ordeal, an arrow is shot from a medium-sized bow. The person undergoing the ordeal must remain submerged in the water until a fast runner brings back the arrow. The third ordeal listed here is actually an oath; if his family does not suffer any mishap soon (during 14 days, according to commentators), he is innocent.

8.116 *Long ago . . . told the truth:* Vatsa was accused by his brother of being the son of a Śūdra woman and thus not a pure Brahmin. Vatsa went through fire to prove his pedigree. See *Pañcaviṃśa Brāhmaṇa* 14.6.6.

8.120 *fined 1,000:* when a simple number is stated, the term Paṇa is understood within the context of fines (see 8.138). A Paṇa was a copper coin widely used in ancient India (8.136). See also 3.186 n.

8.123 *When individuals . . . into exile:* "the three classes" here refer to the three classes below the Brahmin. The major difficulty in interpreting this verse lies in the distinction between *pravāsa* (prescribed for the three lower classes) and *vivāsa* (prescribed for Brahmins). Bühler, Doniger, and Burnell take both to mean "banish"; the difference then being that Brahmins are only banished, whereas the others are both fined and banished. This is the interpretation offered by Nārāyaṇa, Kullūka, and Rāghavānanda. Medhātithi and Govinda take *vivāsa* to mean depriving of clothes, i.e., making him naked. Medhātithi thinks that it may also mean depriving him of his house. I think all these are mistaken. The correct interpretation is offered by Bhāruci and Nandana, both significantly representing the southern tradition. The term *pravāsayet* here has the same meaning as parallel statements in the *AŚ* (1.18.16; 11.1.33, 47; 12.3.4; 12.4.4; 12.5.23; 13.4.29); it refers to execution. The variant reading *pramāpayet* for *pravāsayet* recorded at 9.289 also supports this conclusion. Indeed, Medhātithi (on 8.284) calls this meaning an *Arthaśāstra* usage (*arthaśāstrayā*). Like the modern military-inspired term "liquidate" or the more common "get rid of," *pravāsayet* may have been an euphemism for imposing the death penalty. This meaning of the term is supported by the very next section (8.124–30) that deals with corporal punishment. The only other time that *vivāsa* is used (9.241) it means exile, where also it deals with Brahmins who should be sent into exile without confiscating their property.

8.126 *proclivity:* most commentators take the term *anubandha* to mean repetition (*punaḥpunaḥkaraṇam*), that is, whether the man is a habitual criminal. Bhāruci cites this view, but he contrasts it to his own, which takes the term to mean the reason for the crime: *vayaṃ punar anubandham aparādhakāraṇam ācakṣmahe*. Both these interpretations are also given by Medhātithi. Variant reading: "after he has fully ascertained (the severity of?) the crime." Rocher (1954) has demonstrated that *anubandha* refers to the criminal propensities of the accused individual, that is, the likelihood that he will be a repeat offender in the future because of his past behavior patterns. In my translation that appeared in Oxford World's Classics series (Olivelle 2004) prepared before I had access to Rocher's study, I translated the term as "motive".

8.127 Variant reading: "Punishing those who do not deserve to be punished shatters."

8.130 *If he is unable . . . these four:* it seems strange that when the most severe punishment fails to deter a criminal, he would use all four together, namely that he would use also the weaker punishments. There appears to be something here that we fail to understand, and commentators offer no help.

8.132 This verse is omitted in several southern mss., and not commented by Bhāruci. Medhātithi says that some doubt its authenticity (see note in critical edition). Although I have included it in the critical edition, its authenticity is subject to serious doubt.

Trasareṇu: the term *trasa* means something moving or quivering, and *reṇu* means a speck of dust or pollen. The term refers to the smallest visible particle of matter, often regarded as having the mass of three atoms. For a longer discussion of weights and measures, see *AŚ* 2.19 and the helpful notes of Kangle. For definitions of the weights and measures given in the following verses, see Appendix IV. I have refrained from translating these terms, because they are as much technical terms as our foot, yard, or mile; their common meanings have no bearing on their technical usage.

8.133 *Likṣā, Rājasarṣapa, Gaurasarṣapa:* although these are technical terms for different weights, the terms themselves originally had other meanings. *Likṣā:* literally the egg of a louse, hence a tiny weight. *Rājasarṣapa:* a black mustard seed. *Gaurasarṣapa:* a white mustard seed.

8.134 *Yava, Kṛṣṇala, Māṣa, Suvarṇa:* the literal meaning of Yava is a barley corn, Kṛṣṇala is a small seed of the plant Abrus Precatorius (0.122 or 1.875 grams), and Māṣa is a bean. Suvarṇa literally means gold, but in this context refers to a measure of weight.

8.142 *He may charge . . . classes:* this verse is also found in *VaDh* 2.48. Verses 141 and 142 give somewhat higher rates of interest than the traditional rate of 1.25% per month (or 15% per annum). This figure is given in both *VaDh* 2.51 and *GDh* 12.29. Do these verses of Manu and Vasiṣṭha reflect the later practice of a higher rate of interest, which is considerably more than the traditional one? See also verse 152 where 5% is assumed as the standard rate.

8.143 *nor shall the pledge . . . time has lapsed* (kālasaṃrodhāt): the meaning appears to be that the time for redeeming the loan has passed. This can happen when the interest on the loan equals the amount of the loan (payment then becomes double the original loan). Indian law stipulated that when this happens the interest on the loan stops (see 8.151; this rule is called *dāmdupaṭ* in modern times). Even when this happens a pledge cannot be alienated. Some commentators take this as applying to pledges that are not used, whereas others take it as applying to pledges that are used by the creditors; pledges that are not used may be forfeited, as clearly stated in *YDh* 2.58.

8.145 *Neither . . . a long time:* Medhātithi takes this not as law but friendly advise and gives a very different interpretation, taking *kālātyayam* to mean "long lapse of time" (rather than "forfeiture due to time") and *avahāryau* to mean "liable to appropriation" (rather than "recoverable"). The verse instructs the depositor not to let his pledge or deposit remain too long, for after a long time the man holding the pledge or deposit may think that it is his and appropriate it. This view, also shared by Bhāruci, Govinda, and Nandana, seems improbable, given that verse 149 clearly states the inalienability of pledges and deposits.

8.146 *draft animals:* most commentators take *vahan* as qualifying *aśva;* accordingly, Bühler translates "a riding-horse." I think Medhātithi is correct in taking *vahan* as a separate item; he takes it to mean an ox. This is also the view of Nandana. Lists generally have separate items; rarely do we find adjectives qualifying just one item in a list.

8.148 *within his own locality:* Bhāruci gives two possible meanings of *viṣaya:* within one's sight (*cakṣurviṣaye*) or in one's own country or region. The latter interpretation is followed by Medhātithi and Govinda; and the former by Nārāyaṇa, Kullūka, Rāghavānanda, and Rāmacandra (*jñānaviṣaye* or *darśanaviṣaye*). Nandana, correctly I think, takes it to mean a place where it is possible for the owner to stop his property being used by the other (*nivāraṇayogye deśe*).

8.151 *Interest . . . five times:* "twice the principal" means that the interest should not exceed the amount of the loan, so that the repayment (loan plus interest) is twice the original amount of the loan. Likewise, for grain etc., the interest would be four times the loan; the repayment then being five times. The phrase "when fixed at one time" (*sakṛd āhitā*), according to some, means that the whole of the interest is payable at the end of the loan period; this would then not apply to loans where the interest is paid in installments, for example every month. Medhātithi and Bhāruci take this phrase to mean that the loan is still with the man who originally took out the loan and that it has not been transferred to a third party. Medhātithi also thinks of the possibility that the man may have renewed the loan after it reached double, the new loan including the original loan plus the accrued interest (8.154). Both when the loan is transferred to a third party and when the loan has been renegotiated the interest continues to grow.

8.153 *He must not charge . . . manual labor:* all the commentators take the verse as a syntactic unit with the negative *na* governing the second half of the verse as well. According to this interpretation, the four types of interest given in the second half are also prohibited. All the translators follow this interpretation. Bühler: "Let him not take interest beyond the year, nor such as is unapproved, nor compound interest, periodical interest, stipulated interest, and corporal interest." I think this is mistaken. These four forms of interest are explicitly authorized in *GDh* 12.34–5, a text that Manu follows closely, and also in *NSm* 1.87, a text that follows the *MDh* closely. It is inconceivable to me that Manu would depart from this tradition or that Nārada would have misunderstood Manu in such a fundamental way. Lakṣmīdhara (*Lakṣ* 12.281) cites this verse of Manu immediately before *NSm* 1.87 without noting any contradiction between the two. I think what we have in this verse is broken syntax. The second half-verse is syntactically independent of the first-half. The problem is the correlative *yā* at the end of the second-half, making it a dependent clause. My feeling is that the second half has been taken from a different context and woven into this verse; we have lost the main clause to which this was originally attached.

The cyclical rate is a kind of compound interest calculated, for example, monthly but payable only at the end of the loan period together with the principal (see Lariviere 1989, II. 59). The periodic rate is generally payable each month (*GDh* 12.29). The contractual rate is variable, either above or below the normal rate of interest, depending on the reliability of the person taking the loan. Manual labor is probably connected with indentured labor, the interest on the loan being deducted from the daily wages. On the question of debts in ancient India, see Kane 1962–75, iii. 414–61; Chatterjee 1971.

8.154–5 *When someone . . . as is due:* these two verses probably refer to cyclical interest. When at the end of the loan period the debtor is unable to repay the debt along with the accrued interest, he has the option of paying the accrued interest and renegotiating the contract for the principal. Verse 155 is somewhat obscure; it appears to be a rider on the previous verse and deals with a situation when the debtor is unable even to pay the accrued interest. The intent appears to be that the new debt instrument must include the accrued interest, if the debtor cannot pay off at least part of it at the time of the new loan. That the debtor should at least pay a small amount is the view of several authorities, including Nārada, cited by Medhātithi.

8.156 *When someone . . . place and time:* Medhātithi and, following him, Govinda, Kullūka, and Rāghavānanda, understand *cakravṛddhi* literally as interest accrued on a "wheel," i.e., when a person is traveling. Following this interpretation, Bühler translates: "He who has made a contract to carry good by a wheeled carriage for money and has agreed to a certain place or time, shall not reap that reward, if he does not keep to the place and the time (stipulated)." It seems to me very unlikely that Manu would use this technical term in this verse with a meaning so very different from the one in verse 153. Further, it is quite out of place to talk about payment for carrying goods within a section devoted to interest rates. I follow the reasonable explanation of Nārāyaṇa. Bhāruci also states clearly that according to this rule the creditor cannot enforce the payment of the interest if he fails to show up at the appointed time and place.

8.158 *here* (iha): given that the literary setting of this entire section is the court, it makes sense to take "here" to mean here in this court. Bühler's "in this (world)" does not fit the context: see 1.42.

8.159 *vain gifts:* commentators take *vṛthādānam* to mean money promised to others either frivolously or for illegitimate purposes (to prostitutes, for example). The compound, however, may also be dissolved into *vṛthā-ādānam*, which would refer to loans taken out for illegitimate purposes.

8.160 *The above rule . . . to pay it:* there are three kinds of sureties: a) for appearance, i.e., that the man will appear either at the time stipulated to pay the debt or in court; b) as a guarantor of the debtor's trustworthiness; and c) as a guarantor of payment (see *YDh* 2.53). This rule exempts the heirs of only the first two kinds of sureties from the obligation to repay the debts for which the latter stood as surety.

8.161–2 *When someone . . . his own funds:* these two verses are rather obscure. The question and answer format is also quite unusual for Manu, leading to the possibility that these verses have been taken over from a different source and context. Commentators take *nirādiṣṭadhana* as a surety to whom money had been entrusted by the debtor so that the surety may pay off the debt in the event that the debtor is unable. This, however, makes no sense; why would the debtor take a loan if he has money to put in escrow with the surety sufficient to pay off the debt? The lack of context for this verse makes its interpretation difficult. The term *nirādiṣṭa* appears to be a hapax; it does not occur elsewhere in Manu or in any other Dharma text. The best sense I can make of this verse is that the debtor has given a collateral to the surety as assurance of payment. This collateral may have become part of his wealth that the heirs inherited. In this case, the heirs are bound to repay the debt from their inheritance.

8.164 *contrary to . . . usage:* I follow Medhātithi. Here Manu takes Law (*dharma*) to be based on convention (*vyavahāra*): see 1.107 n. Others see two separate items here: "contrary to Law and/or to settled usage [or, established judicial convention]."

8.166 *If the person . . . estate:* the term *naṣṭa* has been variously explained: dead, gone abroad, absconding, etc. If the loan was used for the benefit of the entire family, then the relative (here probably the brothers or the heirs of the family) must pay the debt even if the family estate has been divided and they are now living separately.

8.167 Variant reading: "must not be questioned by his superior."

8.169 *family:* Medhātithi, Govinda, and Kullūka (followed by Bühler) take *kulam* to mean judges, which, I think, is a forced interpretation of the term. Clearly the verse is a proverbial saying taken from elsewhere.

8.172 *by bringing together the social classes:* the compound *varṇasaṃsargāt* has caused enormous problems for the understanding of the verse. Some have substituted *dharma* for *varṇa* (supported by Burnell); others have inserted the negative particle *varṇāsaṃsargāt*. Commentators give diverse and contradictory explanations. Given that the two other activities are duties performed by the king, I think this also should be something that the king does. On the face of it, *varṇasaṃsarga* means confusion of classes, something the king is sworn to prevent. I think *saṃsarga* here may be used in close to its etymological meaning: combining and bringing together, not in a sexual sense which would cause the intermixing of classes, but in a broader sense. Here we can take it either as supporting the proper functioning of classes within the broader social structure or, more restrictively, as referring to the cohesiveness of each class within itself (which is preferred by Medhātithi).

enhances his power: we have a similar stretching of the meaning here of *saṃjāyate* ("born together"; see the numerous variants of this also); its parallel with *khyāpyate* of the previous verse makes it clear that the meaning is that his strength is not just born but broadcast.

8.181–2 *When a man . . . request it:* the syntax of these two verses is quite confused. That must be one of the reasons for the rearrangement of the verses by several commentators (see note to the edition). Medhātithi is correct, I think, in seeing these two verses as forming a single sentence; he rearranges the verses to give some syntactic coherence by placing verse 182 after the first half of 181, and placing the second half of 181 last. I follow Medhātithi's explanation. The translations of Burnell, Bühler, and Doniger, separate 181 from 182 creating quite a confused meaning.

8.184 *both:* namely, the gold that was deposited by the judge and the original deposit that resulted in the lawsuit.

8.185 *In the event . . . they do not perish:* "both" here refer to sealed and open deposits. The point of the second half of the verse is unclear. We can readily understand the risk the man takes, because if the next-of-kin dies without delivering the deposit, the original depositor has the right to claim it. The last statement "and if there is no mishap, then they do not perish" is so obvious, I cannot understand why it needs to be stated, especially because the second half of the verse is intended to give reasons why the deposit should not be given to a next-of-kin. Stephanie Jamison (personal communication) thinks that this half-verse may be a proverbial saying that has lost some of its punch in this context.

8.188 *That is the rule . . . from it:* the phrase "That is the rule" cannot clearly refer to the previous verse. I think this verse refers back to verse 180, which states that a deposit should be returned in the same state in which it was deposited. An exception is made in the case of sealed deposits, because the man holding the deposit has no way of knowing what the original condition of the deposit was. If this connection between verses 180 and 188 is correct, then the intervening verses (with the possible exception of 187) are either interpolations or given parenthetically.

8.195 *as the delivery, so the recovery:* note that this phrase, occurring also in verse 180, brackets nicely the entire discussion of deposits.

8.196 *open deposit, sealed deposit:* I take the terms *nikṣipta* as a synonym of *nikṣepa*, an open deposit, and *upanihita* as a synonym of *upanidhi*, a sealed deposit (see 8.185). Manu is here recapitulating these two kinds of deposits in this closing verse. Bühler does not recognize the technical nature of the two words and translates: "a deposit or a friendly loan"; so also Doniger.

8.197 *the king should not . . . offer testimony:* the meaning of this half-verse is not altogether clear. Most commentators say that such a man should not be permitted to become a witness in any lawsuit (so Bühler). This seems somewhat of a strange beginning to the section of sale without ownership; we would have expected a statement about what concrete steps should be taken regarding such a person, as indeed stated in the very next verse. Rāghavānanda takes the verse to mean that in a court case on the matter this man should not be allowed to call witnesses in his defense; in other words, the king can issue a summary verdict. This is quite an appealing interpretation. Professor Wezler (personal communication) has suggested another alternative. In any lawsuit filed by the original owner to recover his property from the current owner, the man who sold the article without ownership cannot be permitted to testify; he is after all a thief, though he may not consider himself to be one. Clearly, this verse is a very pithy statement with a whole lot left unsaid.

8.198 *if he did it . . . for theft:* the meaning of *anapasaraḥ* ("has no excuse") is unclear. Many commentators take it to mean that the man has not received it through some means, such as purchase, from a son or relative of the owner. Nārāyaṇa, who reads *anavasaraḥ*, takes it to mean "at an improper place and time," which would add to the seriousness of the crime. For the meanings of *sānvaya* and *niranvaya* (in or outside the presence), see 8.332 n. If the sale was done in the presence of the owner, there can be a presumption of tacit permission; hence the lesser fine. Most commentators erroneously take the two situations as referring to a relative and a non-relative, respectively, an interpretation followed by all the translators.

8.199 Variant reading: "When a purchase or sale is made."

Additional verse: "Someone who engages in a sale without ownership unknowingly should be punished in the above manner; if he does it knowingly, however, he ought to be punished like a thief."

8.201 *through a sale:* Medhātithi, Govinda, and Kullūka take the term *vikrayāt* as referring to the market place (so also Bühler). Rāghavānanda and Nandana take it as referring to the seller. In any case, the meaning is that a purchase made at a public sale is evidence of title.

8.202 *initial seller:* the meaning of the term *mūlam* has been subject to dispute. Govinda and Nandana take it to mean the original value of the article. The meaning then is that if the price cannot be produced in the court because the original seller has disappeared, then the man who purchased it should not be punished. Other commentators, however, take *mūla* to mean the man who sold the article. This interpretation is supported by verses of *BṛSm* (1.12.5–6) that provides the full context, verses cited by Vijñāneśvara on *YDh* 2.170. In either case, the fraudulently sold article is restored to its rightful owner, and the purchaser is left high and dry: *caveat emptor.*

8.205 Three additional verses: "Someone who makes Vaiśyas and other twice-born persons accept forbidden food or drink ought to be punished with the lowest, middle, and the highest fines, respectively. In the case of a Śūdra, the fine is 54 Paṇas; and the king should send those who made them eat it into exile. A person who uses a young cow, an animal belonging to a god, an ox, or a stud bull as a beast of burden should be subject to the lowest fine; if any is killed, the highest fine."

8.206 *If one . . . performed:* it is significant that Manu deals with priestly partnerships as the model (*prakṛti*) for other kinds of commercial partnerships. I think this indicates an older period when priestly speculation centered mostly around priestly matters. In the *NSm* (3.1–11) and *YDh* (2.259–65), commercial partnerships are given first as the model and priestly partnerships later.

8.208 *At a ritual . . . entire fee:* most commentators take this verse as a question to which the answer is provided in verses 209–10; so also Bühler. I see no indication that this is a question, and the following verses do not appear to provide a real answer.

8.210 *Among all the priests . . . to a quarter:* the principal priests are the four mentioned in the previous verse. Next in rank are Maitrāvaruṇa, Pratiprasthātṛ, Brāhmaṇacchaṃsin, and Prastotṛ; then come Acchāvāka, Neṣṭṛ, Agnīdhra, and Pratihartṛ; and finally, Grāvastotṛ, Netṛ, Potṛ, and Subrahmaṇya. According to Medhātithi, assuming the total to be 112, the shares distributed are: 56, 28, 16, and 12. According to others, assuming the total to be 100, the shares distributed are: 48, 24, 16, and 12. See Kane 1962–75, v: 1329–30.

8.212 *gift:* within this ground for litigation, it is apparent that the term *datta*, literally "given," has a technical meaning. It does not refer to what has been given, as the term implies, but to a gift that is pledged but not yet delivered. This pledge appears to have been legally binding so that the potential recipient was able to move a court to enforce payment.

8.219 *When a man . . . from his realm:* the contract dealt with here is not a private one but pertains to a corporate body. When a contract is made with the stipulation that all those who belong to that corporate entity will do something, then each individual is bound by it. Here the corporate entities are a village, a region (group of villages), and a corporation (traders, artisans, sect). See *NSm* 10.1; *YDh* 2.190f. Some interpret the compound *grāmadeśasaṃgha* as a corporation located in a village or region (so Bühler). The term *satyena* is also interpreted by some to mean an oath: see 8.113 where a Brahmin has to swear by the truth.

8.220 *fine him . . . Śatamāna:* some commentators think this passage contains three punishments: four Suvarṇas, six Niṣkas, and one silver Śatamāna.

8.227 *seventh step:* the reference is to the seven steps that the bride and groom take around the sacred fire during the marriage ceremony. The implication in all these verses coming within the context of the cancellation of a sale or purchase is that marriage is precisely such a transaction where the bride is sold by the father and bought by the future husband (see my note on bride-price at 3.53). The reasoning here appears to be that once the seventh step is taken, the transaction is ritually complete and cannot be annulled.

8.234 *yellow bile* (rocanā): this appears to be a yellow pigment prepared with the bile of cows. Yet, Medhātithi takes it to be a powder found in the horns of cows: *gorocanāṃ gavāṃ śṛṅgeṣu cūrṇaṃ bhavati.*

8.237 *one hundred . . . throws:* for these measurements, see App. IV

8.240 *a fenced field:* because of the ambiguous sandhi, the reading could either be *parivṛte* ("fenced") or *(a)parivṛte* ("unfenced"). Bhāruci supports the negative; Medhātithi gives both alternatives; while the other commentators support the positive. The parallel at *GDh* 12.21 (*pathi kṣetre 'nāvṛte*) supports the negative, but the rule there places the blame equally on the herdsman and the farmer. Although generally Manu follows the *GDh*, I think here Manu has deliberately introduced a different rule. He dealt with unfenced fields in verse 238 and introduced fencing in verse 239. And in 241 he refers to "other fields," which can only refer to unfenced fields (it would be odd to refer to fenced fields as "other") in contrast to the fenced ones of verse 240.

8.242 *Manu has . . . herdsman or not:* commentators explain that the bulls meant here are those released at certain festivals or rituals, such as the Vṛṣotsarga. Animals dedicated to gods are temple cattle and the like. It is unclear whether the punishment concerns the animals themselves (beating, impounding) or their owners. Possibly the former, because at least in the case of temple cattle there are no human owners.

8.243 *For an offense . . . of the owner:* the meaning of this verse and its relation to the context that deals with owners and herdsmen are quite unclear. Most commentators take *bhāga* ("share") as the tax that the owner of a field owes to the king; for this meaning of *bhāga*, see 7.130 n. Under this interpretation, the offense must involve the wrongful impounding or injuring of animals that have wandered into his property. Bhāruci, on the other hand, takes this to be a dispute between an owner of a field and his tenant farmers. If the owner damages the crops, then he is fined ten times his share of the crop; whereas, if his servants do the damage unknown to the owner, then the fine is half that amount. This interpretation has the benefit of simplicity, but the problem is that it introduces a different and new topic into the discussion.

8.245 *when landmarks . . . visible:* commentators note that during this month, which is between spring and the rains, the land is parched and the grass is dried up. Hidden landmarks can be seen most clearly during this time of the year.

8.259 *question:* on the word *anuyuñjīta* as a technical term of judicial interrogation, see 8.79.

8.265 *on the basis of utility:* commentators point out that a smaller piece of land may be more productive than a larger parcel. Likewise, a reservoir may be more useful to one village (for example, it has no other water source) than to the other (which may have other sources).

8.268 Two additional verses: "Between a Kṣatriya and a Vaiśya the punishment to be imposed is the same as that between Brahmin and Kṣatriya; the punishment for Kṣatriya or Vaiśya abusing a Śūdra is that for a Brahmin abusing a Kṣatriya or Vaiśya. The punishment imposed on Kṣatriyas, Vaiśyas, and Śūdras is higher or lower just as for a Brahmin, with the exception of verbal reprimand—that is the settled rule."

The first verse is somewhat unclear, but the intent appears to be this. Mutual abuse between Kṣatriyas and Vaiśyas is treated in the same as that that between Brahmins and Kṣatriyas. So, a Kṣatriya abusing a Vaiśya = a Brahmin abusing a Kṣatriya (fine of 50); a Vaiśya abusing a Kṣatriya = a Kṣatriya abusing a Brahmin (fine of 100). The second half of the first verse is very unclear. I think what it states is this. A Kṣatriya abusing a Śūdra = a Brahmin abusing a Kṣatriya (25); a Vaiśya abusing a Śūdra = a Brahmin abusing a Kṣatriya (50). The reading of the last foot is uncertain. Some manuscripts read: "with the exception of monetary fines"; and others: "with the exception of corporal punishment."

8.270 *If a once-born . . . lowest part:* a once-born man is a Śūdra. The implied background of this harsh punishment is the creation myth of the Puruṣasūkta (*ṚV* 10.90), which has become a root metaphor in the Dharma literature. The twice-born here probably refers specifically to Brahmins, who were born from the mouth (speech). When a man born from the feet uses speech to abuse a man born from the mouth, he loses his right to the tongue, the organ of speech.

8.271 *ten fingers:* for the measurement, see App. IV.

8.273 *If a man . . . fined 200:* there are several points that are unclear in this verse. First, does it apply to all or only to Śūdras? Commentators are divided, but I think Bhāruci and Medhātithi are right in taking it as applicable to all. Second, is *śārīram* an adjective qualifying *karma* or is it an independent entry? I think Medhātithi, Rāghavānanda, and Nandana are right in taking the two as independent entries. Others take them as referring to "bodily activities" or to "bodily consecration" such as vedic initiation. I also follow Medhātithi in taking *śārīram* to mean bodily features, especially in the light of what is stated in the very next verse.

8.275 *hurls accusations:* commentators give different meanings of the word *ākṣārayan*. See 8.354–5, where it clearly refers to accusations; here the term possibly refers to accusations relating to crimes or sins.

8.277 *exactly the same punishment:* when a Vaiśya abuses a Śūdra or vice versa, the punishment is the same as for a Brahmin abusing a Kṣatriya or vice versa. See the added verses after 8.268 and the note to it.

Additional verse: "By telling an outcaste 'You're an outcaste!', or a thief 'You're a thief!', a man by his speech becomes as sinful as they; and if his accusation is false, he becomes twice as sinful."

8.283 Variant reading: "by the feet, the nose, the neck."

8.284 *sent into exile* (pravāsyaḥ): this term can also mean imposing the capital punishment (see 8.123 n.). Medhātithi gives this as a possible meaning, following the *Arthaśāstra* usage of the term: *pravāsanam arthaśāstrapravṛttyā māraṇaṃ nirvāsanaṃ vā*.

8.287 *vigor* (prāṇa): the meaning is not altogether clear. Medhātithi glosses with *balam* ("strength"). The vulgate has the easier reading *vraṇa* ("wound"). In any case, a grievous wounding and the shedding of blood are clearly intended.

total fine (sarvadaṇḍam): Bhāruci, Medhātithi, Govinda, and Kullūka explain that if the injured man does not accept the payment for his medical expenses, then that amount should be added to the usual fine and both paid to the king. Nārāyaṇa thinks that this should be done if the perpetrator does not want to pay the medical bills. Nandana says that the perpetrator should either pay for the full recovery or give to the victim also a sum equivalent to the full fine he owes the king. Nandana also mentions the possibility that *sarvadaṇḍam* (*sarvasya daṇḍam*) may mean taking all the man's wealth as a fine, possibly when the man is too poor to shoulder the full medical expenses of his victim. I consider this to be the most natural explanation.

8.295 *In a case . . . vehicle:* Medhātithi and Nandana take the instrumental *paśubhiḥ* and *rathena* as the instruments of killing: "the driver kills living creatures by means of animals or vehicles when his path is obstructed." Others, correctly I think, take the instrumentals as the agents of obstruction. The meaning, I think, is that the driver kills the animals or bumps the vehicle that is obstructing the path.

8.296 *If a human . . . horse:* most commentators take this, correctly I think, as referring to a vehicle accident. Nārāyaṇa and Nandana, however, think that the section on vehicle accidents is over and that this is an independent statement regarding killing humans and animals.

8.299 Variant reading: "a wife, son, slave, servant, or uterine brother."

8.303 *his sacrificial session:* on the *sattra*, see 2.106 n. Here the reign of a king is compared to a sacrificial session of long duration at which the gift of safety to his subjects is considered equal to the sacrificial fee. See also 8.306.

8.309 Variant reading: "fails to provide protection, is predatory, and untrue, one should abandon him."

8.310 Variant reading: "imprisonment, fines, and diverse forms of corporal punishment."

8.314 Variant reading: "A thief, with his hair loose, should run to the king."

8.320 *corporal punishment:* the term *vadha* in the legal literature is used both for corporal punishment, including mutilation and amputation, and for capital punishment. It is often difficult to tell from the context which is meant. In this verse, given the amount stolen, I think corporal punishment is meant. In the next verse, on the other hand, capital punishment is clearly meant, because verse 322 gives lesser forms of corporal punishment.

8.321 *The same goes . . . capital punishment:* I think there is broken syntax in this verse, which may be piecing together *pādas* from different contexts. In *NSm* 19.32, for example, *pāda-a* is placed in a different verse and only a fine is prescribed for stealing articles sold by weight; examples include ghee and other liquids. I have taken *pāda-a* as syntactically connected with the previous verse, and *pāda-b* with the second half of the verse. See Mādhava's citation of this verse that replaces the first half-verse with that from *NSm* 19.34. "more than 100" must refer to weight in the case of gold, etc., and to pieces in the case of clothes, as pointed out by Medhātithi.

8.324 *time and purpose:* the meaning appears to be this. If an article was stolen when it was urgently needed (e.g., stealing a weapon during a time of war), the theft becomes more serious. Likewise, the purpose served by the article may make the theft more severe, such as stealing the medicine of a sick man. See also 9.293 n.

8.325 *in the case . . . of the heel:* this half-verse has been subject to much misunderstanding resulting in several emendations (see the note in the critical edition). One interpretation takes *sthūrikā* (supported by the variant *nāsikā*) as the nose. Following several commentators, Bühler translates: "for piercing (the nostrils of) a barren cow." M-W give "nostrils of a barren cow" as the meaning of *sthūrikā*, while B-R gives the alternative reading *chūrikā* with the meaning "*Kuhschnauze*." I think these interpretations are mistaken; within a section dealing with stealing, there is no reason to introduce the mutilation of animals. Lariviere (1983) and in his translation of *NSm* 19.40 has correctly identified *sthūrā* as the Achilles tendon; and *sthūrikā* cannot be other than a synonym for it. See also Turner 1966, I: 13775 where *sthūra* is related to *thuri* meaning "heel" in the Dardic languages Phalūra and Shina.

8.329 *other similar kinds of food* (anyeṣāṃ caivamādīnām adyānām): Bühler, Burnell, and Doniger follow the alternative: *caivamādīnāṃ madyānām*, and translate: "other things of a similar kind, spirituous liquor."

8.332 *in the presence . . . outside his presence:* this verse is clearly a versification of *AŚ* 3.17.1–2: *sāhasam anvayavat prasabhakarma / niranvaye steyam apavyayane ca /* Kangle translates this passage accurately: "Forcible seizure [or better, violence] is a deed of force in the presence (of the owner). In the absence (of the owner) it is theft, also in case of denial." A similar versification of the first *sūtra* is found in Kātyāyana: *sahasā yat kṛtaṃ karma tat sāhasam udāhṛtam / sānvayas tv apahāro yaḥ prasahya haraṇaṃ ca yat //* "A deed done with violence is called 'violence,' as also a seizure in the presence (of the owner) and a forcible seizure." In all these texts, the aim is to define *sāhasa* "violence." Within this context, it appears that the Arthaśāstra tradition coined the technical terms *anvayavat* and *niranvaya* for thefts and robberies committed in the presence or outside the presence of the owner. The term *sānvaya* used by Manu in 8.198 and 331 appears to be a synonym of *anvayavat* created possibly for metrical exigencies. Although robbery is more serious than theft, yet in 331 theft (in the presence of the owner) is considered the lesser offense, possibly because it may imply an implicit consent, especially if the person taking the article is known to the owner. These two technical terms appear to have fallen into disuse within the Dharma tradition; *NSm* (14.1), for example, which defines *sāhasa* in words reminiscent of Manu and the *AŚ*, does not use these terms. For the meaning of *anvaya*, see Kangle 1965, III: 229. For a discussion of *sāhasa* in the Dharmaśāstras, see Rocher 1976b.

The reason for inserting this verse here is unclear. A definition such as this should have been given in the section on *sāhasa* (8.344), as it is done in both the *AŚ* and the *NSm*. Medhātithi thinks that the following rules deal with robbery rather than theft. It is more likely, however, that Manu inserts this verse to explain *niranvaya* and *sānvaya* that were used in the previous verse. Indeed, we can detect that this verse is a parenthetical statement, because the next verse (333) uses the pronoun *etāni* ("these"), referring back to the articles mentioned in verse 331.

8.333 Variant reading: "the king should impose on him the lowest fine": see 8.138.

8.336 *In a case . . . fixed rule:* this is quite a significant rule. If taken at its face value, it implies that even the king was not above the law! Commentators point out that in the case of the king, the fine should be thrown into water (9.245). Medieval authors evidently found the fining of the king hard to swallow; both Lakṣmīdhara and Devaṇṇabhaṭṭa change the reading from *rājā* to the genitive *rājñāṃ* or *rājñaḥ* (with *janaḥ* of the previous *pāda* understood). The meaning then would be that people connected to the king, such as those mentioned in the previous verse, are subject to this rule.

8.337–8 *With respect . . . good or bad:* the penalty is calculated on the basis of the value of the stolen goods. In general, the principle is that lighter penalties are assessed for people of higher classes. But here a different principle is enunciated, a principle more in keeping with the penances, where the severity of the penance for the same offense increases for those of higher classes. These two verses appear to be versifications of *GDh* 12.15–7. Bühler, following Medhātithi, Govinda, and Kullūka, takes the last clause as applying to all the individuals mentioned. The presence of *hi* ("for"), however, makes it clear that this clause applies specifically to a Brahmin, for he is supposed to know the law. The parallel passage in *GDh* 12.17, on the other hand, makes a more general statement that a learned man should be punished more severely.

8.342 *When someone ties . . . as for theft:* clearly these acts must have been viewed as not real theft, otherwise there is no reason to insist that they should be viewed as theft. The first two acts fit this category well; the reference is probably to untying someone else's cattle so they may get lost, or tying up (i.e., impounding) another's cattle in one's own property, possibly to make use of them. Several commentators take *hartā* to mean "one who steals" with reference to slaves etc. This is implausible, because if it were real theft, then there is no need to insist that they are equivalent to theft. Nārāyaṇa probably has it right when he says that the reference is to someone taking away a slave, horse, or carriage for his own use without authorization.

8.344 *violence:* the distinction between violence as *sāhasa* and physical assault (*daṇḍapāruṣya*, 8.279–301) is not readily apparent from their treatment in Manu. In the *AŚ* (3.17), on the other hand, *sāhasa* is clearly defined as forcible seizure of property, including robbery; whereas physical assault does not involve taking the other's property. The *NSm* (14) includes both simple violent acts and robbery under this heading.

8.345 *someone who is . . . with a rod:* clearly, these three individuals refer to those guilty of offenses under the previous three grounds for litigation.

8.349 *in a conflict over sacrificial fees:* this provision provides an interesting historical note. Conflicts, either between priests or between priests and patrons, over sacrificial fees must have been a common occurrence for it to be noted by Manu; even more interesting is that violence within this context is condoned.

8.352 *execute them* (pravāsayet): for the meaning of this term, see 8.123 n. Commentators uniformly take it to mean banishment; and so do the translators. This is certainly possible, but see verse 359 where the death penalty is imposed on all except Brahmins for adultery. The disfigurement or branding, according to commentators, include cutting off the nose, penis, testicles, and the like. See also 9.248 where almost identical words are used for graphic and diverse modes of execution that drive terror into men.

8.353 *root:* the meaning is unclear. Commentators take it to mean rain that supports life, reasoning that the mixing of castes leads to the cessation of sacrifices, which in turn leads to drought and starvation. See *ŚB* 11.1.6.24, where also the absence of rain is associated with *dharma*.

8.360 *men consecrated for sacrifice* (dīkṣitāḥ): this is the understanding of all commentators and translators. Then this category is somewhat anomalous, because the others deal with individuals who generally visit houses and must come in contact with housewives. It is possible that here *dīkṣita* refers more broadly to holy men of diverse religious sects. See, for example, *MBh* 1.80.25; 15.17.3, 9: *vanavāsāya dīkṣitaḥ; MBh* 1.205.30: *brahmacaryāya dīkṣitaḥ*. Also at *MBh* 13.10.8 and *Rām* 5.3.28 the term appears to include various kinds of holy men rather than strictly persons consecrated to perform a sacrifice.

unless . . . banned (aprativāritāḥ): I follow Medhātithi and Nandana (so also Doniger); the statement about forbidding such conversations in the next verse favors this interpretation. Others take the term to mean "without being hindered," an explanation followed by Bühler.

8.361 Variant reading: "A man should never converse with other people's wives."

8.362 *to wives . . . on their own:* the fact that the compound *nātmopajīviṣu* is masculine has caused some problems to commentators. Many take the compound as referring to the husbands who live off the earnings of their wives. Accordingly, Bühler translates: "This rule does not apply to the wives of actors and singers, nor (of) those who live on (the intrigues of) their own wives." Note the difficulty Bühler has in finding a genitive within the locative construction! I think Nandana is right in taking this as referring to prostitutes; the masculine ending can be justified because it qualifies *dāreṣu*, which is grammatically masculine. The point of the rule appears to be that husbands of such women may use scriptural provisions against adultery to blackmail other men.

8.364 *execution:* I have followed Medhātithi in taking *vadha* to mean the death penalty. Govinda and Kullūka (followed by Bühler) interpret the term as simply corporal punishment, such as the cutting of sexual organs. See 8.320 n.

8.366 *bride-price:* I do not think that this provision forces the man to marry the girl he has violated. It simply means that he should pay reparation to the father in the form of the bride-price that he would have otherwise received at her wedding. See verse 369 where even another woman who violates a virgin has to pay a similar price.

8.367 *two of his fingers:* the cutting of two fingers is prescribed for any deflowering of a virgin short of sexual intercourse. The reason is probably that the violator used his fingers for the sexual act. See verse 370 where a similar punishment is prescribed also for a woman who violates a virgin. The *AŚ* (4.12.3) specifies that the middle and index fingers are to be cut off.

8.369 Variant reading: "pay twice the bride-price."

8.373 *Vrātya woman:* the meaning is unclear. Medhātithi gives several possibilities, including prostitute, wanton woman, unmarried woman, etc. Others take her to be the wife of a Vrātya, that is, a twice-born who has not been initiated at the proper time (2.39).

8.374 *loses everything:* that is, he loses all his property, as well as his life.

8.382 Additional verse: "If a Brahmin has sex with a guarded Kṣatriya or Vaiśya woman, he should not be subject to the urine punishment (8.375), but he should be made to pay the highest fine."

8.385 *lowest-born woman* (antyajastriyam): most commentators identify such women as Cāṇḍālas. Nārāyaṇa specifies washerwomen, leather workers, dancers, basket makers, fisherwomen, and the like.

8.386 *The king . . . world of Indra:* the five crimes referred to here are actually the five grounds for litigation (8.11–5), all involving some degree of violence.

8.390 *living in hermitages* (āśrameṣu): I follow Bhāruci, Medhātithi, and Nandana in taking *āśrama* here as referring to hermitages of ascetics. The context clearly calls for extraordinary individuals engaged in a dispute; otherwise the king would not take such precautions. The *AŚ* (1.19.31–2) also recommends that the king should decide matters relating to ascetics only in the company of his Purohita, because otherwise these ascetics might direct their anger at him. Other commentators take *āśrama* to mean orders of life; and this is followed by Doniger and Bühler, who translates: "If twice-born men dispute among each other concerning the duty of the orders."

8.392 *the one living in front of his house and the one behind* (prātiveśya, ānuveśya): the meaning of these two terms are unclear, although they certainly refer to close neighbors. I follow Medhātithi, who explains the former as *gṛhābhimukhaḥ* and the latter as *pṛṣṭhato vasan*. Bhāruci, however, rejects this explanation and prefers to see the two words as simply referring to close neighbors. Other commentators take the first to be the immediate neighbor and the latter to be the one next to him.

8.395 *honor* (saṃpūjayet): Bühler translates: "treat kindly"; but the term does not mean that.

Many commentators interpret correctly that honoring (*pūjā*) implies giving money and food: see 3.70 n.

8.396 *He must not . . . those clothes:* Bühler, following Kullūka, translates: "he shall not return the clothes (of one person) for those (of another)." But why would one require a rule for that? The point of this verse is to lay down minimum ethical standards on washermen. They are not to tie up a load of clothes within a cloth that has been given for washing (e.g., a large piece of cloth such as a sari or a sheet). This is the interpretation of Medhātithi and Nandana. The meaning of the final phrase is clear: he should not rent out clothes that have been given for washing!

8.397 *A weaver . . . fine of 12:* only Govinda and Rāghavānanda offer an explanation. The weight of the yarn would have increased in the process of making the cloth, with the addition of starch. The fine of twelve is interpreted either as money (Paṇa), or as twelve time the weight of the cloth, or else as a twelfth part of the yarn.

8.399 *royal monopoly:* on the technical term *prakhyāta*, see Wezler 2000: 496–501. This term occurs with a related meaning also in the *AŚ* 9.6.31; 11.1.28, and with a somewhat broader meaning at *AŚ* 5.2.49. For a similar provision see *VaDh* 19.14–6.

8.403 *balances, measures:* I follow Bhāruci and Medhātithi in taking the compound *tulāmānam* as a Dvandva listing two items: balance and measure. Others take it as referring to only weights; so also Bühler.

8.419 *administrative centers* (karmāntān): I follow Medhātithi, Govinda, and Nārāyaṇa. Bühler, following Kullūka, translates: "the completion of his undertakings"; similarly Doniger and Burnell.

CHAPTER NINE

9.1 *when they are together . . . apart:* Manu provides here different rules by which married people should live when they are together and when they are somehow apart, either temporarily, as when the husband is away, or permanently, as when the husband or wife dies. See 9.74f for rules when the husband is missing.

9.4 *reprehensible:* the term *yāpya* is quite unusual. Many mss. have converted this to the easier *vācya*, which is also the reading of the vulgate. For a discussion of the term, see Introduction, p. 36.

9.5 Additional verse: "When the wife is guarded, the offspring becomes guarded; and when the offspring is guarded, one's own self becomes guarded."

9.8 *The husband . . . again in her:* this is a variant of a verse in *AB* 7.13. For a discussion of the son as one's very self born again in the wife, see Olivelle 1993, 41–6. My translation of *jāyātvam* (lit., "state of being a wife") is non-literal; but the abstract noun in Sanskrit does carry a pregnant and multivalent meaning, indicating both the nature of a wife and the etymology of "wife." For a discussion of this usage in Brahmanical literature, especially the Upaniṣads, see my note to *BṛU* 1.2.1 in Olivelle 1998c, 488.

9.11 *household goods:* for a study of the significant term *pāriṇāhya* in early vedic literature, see Jamison 1997. Initially the term referred to the goods that a bride brings with her after her marriage; the term itself probably referred to something tied on a wagon (traveling box). The connection to the wife probably came through the carriage used to covey the new bride to the groom's house.

9.17 *Bed . . . to women:* note the close parallel between this verse and the assigning of the various duties to different classes at 1.87–91. Variant reading: "lust, hatred, dishonesty, malice."

9.18 *Without strength . . . untruth:* I think this may have been viewed by the author as a vedic citation; see the beginning of the very next verse. In *TS* 6.5.8.2 we have a very similar passage: *tasmāt striyo nirindriyā adāyādīr api pāpāt puṃsa upastitaraṃ vadanti* ("Therefore, women are without strength and without inheritance, and they speak more submissively than even a poor man"). For *pāpa* as poor, see Rau 1957, 32–4. See also *BDh* 2.3.46.

9.19 *a sample of these:* for the adopted reading *ākṛtim*, see the note to the critical edition. The alternative reading is *niṣkṛtīḥ/niṣkṛtim*, which is adopted by all previous editions. On the basis of this reading, Bühler translates: "hear (now those texts which refer to) the expiation of their (sins)."

9.20 *Here is an illustration of it:* the text cited is found in *ŚāṅkhGṛ* 3.13. The exact reference of "of it" is unclear. Most take it as a reference to the penance indicated in the previous verse; but we have seen that it is an erroneous reading. Medhātithi and Nandana, correctly I believe, view this as a reference to the true character (*svālakṣaṇya*: 8.19) of women, of which the cited text is illustrative; and this seems to be the view also of Bhāruci.

9.21 *When a woman . . . infidelity:* all the commentators, except Medhātithi and Bhāruci (who are silent on this point), think that the expiation is carried out by the son rather than by the woman who committed the sin.

9.23 *Akṣamālā . . . respect:* Akṣamālā, better known as Arundhatī, was the wife of the sage Vasiṣṭha. Although textual sources give her a high pedigree, the commentators state that she was born in a low caste but attained a high status because of her marriage to Vasiṣṭha. Madanapāla was an ascetic who was barred from celestial worlds because he had failed to father sons. He then became a Śārṅgi bird and mated with the female Śārṅgī, Jaritā. The children born from this union excelled in their knowledge of the Veda (*MBh* 1.220–5).

9.27 Variant readings: "brings them up—with regard to each of these, the wife"; "brings them up—for the sake of joy, the wife."

9.28 *obedient service:* the term *śuśrūṣā* usually refers to the service rendered by a person of lower rank to one of higher rank, especially by a pupil to his teacher. The meaning here is uncertain; some commentators take it as referring to hospitality and others to taking care of the husband's physical needs. The latter is supported by the more explicit statement in 9.86.

9.32 *It is acknowledged . . . of the field:* the critical edition has adopted the reading *kartari;* the vulgate reads *bhartari*, which is tautological and Bühler has to labor hard to find meaning here: "They (all) say that the male issue (of a woman) belongs to the lord, but with respect to the (meaning of the term) lord the revealed texts differ." But, of course, the passage says nothing to resolve any disputes about the meaning of "lord" (husband). The question, rather, centers on what happens when the sire (*kartṛ*) is different from the husband (*bhartṛ*). The first half-verse is rather elliptical: *pāda-a* gives the consensus opinion that a son belongs to the husband; *pāda-b* introduces the dispute, which centers around the man who fathers the son but who is not the husband; and the second half of the verse spells out the two positions in this dispute briefly. Arguments in support of the first position are given in verses 36–40, and arguments for the second position in verses 41–55. It is clear that Manu is here following the classical Indian form of argumentation, presenting first the opinion of the opponent (*pūrvapakṣa*) and then the opinion of the author (*uttarapakṣa*). The traditional enumeration of 12 sons (see 9.166f.), where *gūḍhotpanna, kṣetraja, kānīna*, and *sahoḍha* are all fathered by men other than the husband, indicates that the second opinion was the stronger one within the legal tradition. Derrett cites J.-P. Vernant, *Myth et pensée chez les Grecs* (Paris, 1969), pp. 97f., for Greek sources on this controversy.

9.34 *Sometimes . . . esteemed:* note that Manu uses the term *viśiṣṭa* to refer to the social eminence of the father and the mother in this verse; when both are eminent, you get eminent children. In the very next verse, however, he uses *utkṛṣṭa* to refer to the biological superiority of the seed (father) vis-à-vis the field (mother), from which sociological conclusions, such as to whom the son belongs in reality, are drawn.

9.40 *For one kind . . . sprouts forth:* it appears to me that there is a lacuna here. The argument for the dominance of the seed should have included sociological conclusions from the biological observations given here. See, for example, *VaDh* 6.8–9, where precisely such conclusions are drawn. The suspicion of a lacuna here is strengthened by the beginning of the second argument in verse 41; this verse begins with *tat* ("therefore"), but the statement in it is unrelated to the previous verse, which supported quite the opposite view.

9.41 *knowledge and discrimination:* commentators explain *jñāna* and *vijñāna* in widely different way, indicating educated guesses. Medhātithi: Vedāṅga (vedic supplements) and worldly sciences (logic, fine arts, etc.); Nārāyaṇa and Rāmacandra take them to refer to Dharma and to worldly matters, respectively; Kullūka: Veda and Vedāṅga; Rāghavānanda: *śruti* and *smṛti*; Nandana: worldly knowledge and scriptural/textual (*śāstra*) knowledge.

9.43–4 *When someone shoots . . . owns the arrow:* the examples reinforce the notion that a virgin belongs to the person who first deflowers her, assumed here to be her husband. This is true with a virgin field as with a virgin girl. So, the first king, Pṛthu (after whom is name *pṛthivī*, Earth), who tilled the ground took possession of the entire earth; kings coming after him do not have such a claim. So also a man who first clears the forest has claim to it. The image changes with the hunt, but here too the one who first wounds the unwounded (virgin) animal lays claim to it. The Sanskrit term *kha,* which I have translated "vitals", literally means hole; Bühler translates as "wound." I want to thank Professor Wezler for suggesting that the meaning might be the vital or mortal parts of the animal (*marman*), the parts at which a hunter will shoot an arrow. Shooting another arrow at the wound created by the first arrow does not make much sense. Note also the interesting parallel between arrow, the implied plow, and the penis.

9.45 *Wife, self . . . is the wife:* vedic texts call the wife one half of the husband: *TS* 6.1.8.5; *ŚB* 5.2.1.10; *AĀ* 1.2.5. For a discussion, see Olivelle 1993, 42, and above 9.8 n.

9.52 *agreement:* beyond the agreement that the owners of the field and the seed may reach, the reference here is to leviratic union, where the biological father is officially appointed (*niyoga*) to raise a son for the woman's husband, a topic that immediately follows (8.57–70).

9.54 *When a seed . . . reaps its fruit:* the simile here is of a sower in a neighboring field. If some of the seeds he sows are carried by the wind or by a stream of water (probably in a paddy field) to an adjacent field, the crop that is produced from those seeds belongs to the owner of that field and not to the man who sowed the seeds. Variant reading: "the owner of the seed does not reap its reward."

9.55 *This is the Law . . . buffaloes:* this is a rather strange and unexpected ending to the argument. It elevates a simile, already given in verse 48, to the level of a proposition. See my earlier comments about possible lacunae in this section: 9.40 n.

9.57 *wife of an elder:* it may well be that here the term *guru* (see Note to the Trans., p. 69) refers specifically to the father, because in the absence of the father the eldest brother becomes a surrogate father to his younger siblings (9.108).

9.61 *Some who . . . such women:* commentators cite a proverb: *aputra ekaputraḥ,* "A man who has one son is a sonless man." The reason evidently is the danger that a single son may die before he himself can father a son to continue the line, thus defeating the very purpose of the appointment.

9.64 *Twice-born men . . . eternal Law:* this and the following verse contradict the opinion on levirate just expressed in verses 57–63. This contradiction was already noticed by Bṛhaspati (*BṛSm* 1.25.16), cited by Nandana in his commentary: "after prescribing the levirate, Manu himself forbids it" (*uktvā niyogas manunā niṣiddhaḥ svayam eva tu*). He ascribes this to the shortening of the Yugas and the inability of contemporary men to carry this out in accordance with the rules. I think that here also Manu may be engaging in an argument with an opponent, whose view is given first and then refuted (see 9.32 n.). Manu's own view appears to be that levirate is morally reprehensible in the case of a widow; the only allowance he makes is when the husband dies after the betrothal (8.69–70).

9.69–70 *take* (vindet), *obtaining* (adhigamya): the meaning of these two terms in this context is unclear. All the commentators gloss with words that mean "marry": *vivāhayet, pariṇayet, udvahet* and *vivāhya, udūhya*. My translation leaves the vagueness of the terms intact; clearly this is part of the rite of appointment rather than a true marriage, because the man is allowed to father just one son for his deceased brother.

9.70 *dressed in white:* the social meaning of colors is one area where cultural perceptions may be diametrically opposed. White here may indicate the color of the wedding dress in the west, but in India it is the color of mourning prescribed for the girl who has lost her husband.

9.72 *defiled* (vipraduṣṭa): the meaning is probably that the girl has been deflowered. For other occurrences of this term with the meaning of moral corruption, see 2.97; 11.176.

9.73 Variant reading: "one may annul that gift of the virgin by that evil man."

9.76 *A wife should wait:* Medhātithi astutely observes that the text does not say what she should do after the lapse of the time specified. Manu, indeed, cannot say more because he was against the re-marriage of widows (5.157–62). Medhātithi cites various opinions, including the one which permits her to remarry after that time, which is the interpretation that best suits this context and is explicitly stated in *NSm* 12.97–102. Nandana is the only commentator who agrees with this. Others say that after this time the wife should go in search of her husband, citing *VaDh* 18.76.

9.77 *stop cohabiting with her* (na saṃvaset): Medhātithi observes that *saṃvaset* cannot take the accusative, forgetting that it does take the accusative when it means to have sex with someone. Both Medhātithi and Bhāruci, followed by Nārāyana and Rāmacandra, nevertheless, object to the interpretation that the husband should banish her from the house. Bhāruci, Govinda, Kullūka, Nandana, and Rāghavānanda take *saṃvaset* to mean cohabit.

9.79 *without semen* (abīja): Medhātithi says that both *klība* and *abīja* refer to a *napuṃsaka*, a term that can also mean someone who is not fully a man, such as a hermaphrodite. Others are even less helpful. Clearly, the reference is to some sort of sexual dysfunction different from impotence.

9.80 Variant reading: "When a wife drinks liquor or behaves badly."

9.84 *shows and fairs* (prekṣāsamājau): the meaning of *samāja* is unclear. It probably refers to some sort of fair or public event that attracted crowds, something looked down upon even by the third-century BCE emperor, Aśoka (Rock Edict 1). See Ghosh 1973, 56.

9.86 *husband's physical needs:* these appear to exclude sex, which is separately listed at 9.28. Commentators offer the examples of preparing and serving food.

9.88 *not attained the proper age:* most commentators take *aprāptām* (lit., "not reached") to mean that the girl has not reached the minimum age of eight years. This appears far-fetched to me, because there must be a clear point of arrival when one speaks of "reaching." The probable meaning is that she has not reached puberty (supported by its mention in the very next verse). I think the first half of the verse implies that a suitor has come asking for the girl's hand. Within this context one can understand the second half: one should give the girl to such a suitor even if she is below age.

Several manuscripts place an additional verse after the first half of verse 88, thus creating two verses with a different syntax. I give here the translation of the two with this rearranged order: "When there is a suitor who is eminent, handsome, and of equal status, a wise father should give him the girl fearing the onset of her menstruation. For when a menstruating girl remains, the giver is tainted with sin; one should give the girl to him according to rule, even if she has not attained the proper age."

9.92 *if she takes, it is theft:* variant reading: "if she takes, she is a thief." According to a significant variant given by Bhāruci and Medhātithi, it is the groom who becomes a thief if he accepts these ornaments: "if he takes it, he is a thief."

9.93 *A man who . . . her menses:* Bhāruci thinks that this verse is out of place here and is an interpolation, a view recorded also by Medhātithi.

9.99 *That after promising . . . to another:* several commentators explain, correctly I think, that "promising" here refers to the contract made with the man who gave the bride-price.

9.102 Variant reading: "from being unfaithful and to remain attached to each other."

9.104 *have passed on:* the ambiguity of the term *ūrdhvam*, which literally means "beyond, after," has given rise to different interpretations. That the reference is clearly to the death of the parents is indicated by the last *pāda:* "they are incompetent while those two are alive." Jīmūtivāhana, in his influential *Dāyabhāga* (1.46), says that Manu uses the word "after" rather than "deceased" to indicate that the partition can take place anytime the father's proprietary rights lapse as a result of his becoming an outcaste, abandoning all worldly desires (e.g., becoming an ascetic), or dying.

9.107 *Only that son . . . through lust:* for the vedic theology that posits the son as the source of the father's immortality, see *AB* 7.13; *VaDh* 17.1–5; Olivelle 1993, 41–6.

9.111 *They should . . . meritorious:* clearly, living separately is the preferred option of Manu. The particle *vā*, which generally means simply "or," is here used with the more specific meaning of "or rather," indicating not just an option but the preferred option. On this use of *vā*, see Scharfe 1993, 272–4; P. Kiparsky *Some Theoretical Problems in Pāṇini's Grammar* (Poona: Bhandarkar Oriental Research Institute, 1982). The increase of *dharma* takes place because each brother as the head of a separate household will have to offer separate sacrifices and other rites.

9.120–1 *If a younger . . . the Law:* the issue here is the share of a son born through a leviratic union. Should he, as the heir of the eldest brother, receive the preemptive share reserved for the eldest? The answer given is no; and the argument is that the biological father of the son is the "principal" and not the biological mother, through whom the son's connection to the eldest brother is established. Therefore, the leviratic son (i.e., the nephew) should receive the same share as all brothers. See a similar situation in 9.134 with regard to the "female-son."

9.123 *first-born:* all the commentators, except Nandana, take the compound *pūrvajaḥ* to mean "born to the first (i.e., seniormost) wife" (*pūrvasyāṃ jātaḥ*). This interpretation is followed by Bühler. I think Nandana is correct; the parallel passage in *GDh* 28.14 (note that Manu follows Gautama closely) reads *jyeṣṭha* ("eldest") leaving no ambiguity.

inferior bulls: given the ambiguous sandhi of *(a)pare 'jyeṣṭhavṛṣāḥ*, most commentators omit the *avagraha* and read the positive *jyeṣṭhavṛṣāḥ*. Bühler, accordingly, translates: "the next best bulls," followed by Doniger, a meaning that is hard to extract from the Sanskrit. I think Bhāruci and Medhātithi are correct in seeing an *avagraha* here and reading the negative *ajyeṣṭhavṛṣāḥ*, "inferior bulls."

9.126 *Subrahmaṇyā:* this is the name of a ritual invocation addressed to Indra inviting him to partake of the Soma. See *AB* 6.3.

9.127 *female-son:* the term *putrikā*, which is a feminine construction from *putra* ("son"), has generally been translated as "appointed daughter," an institution that is also found in other Indo-European cultures. This translation is somewhat misleading, because, as Jolly (1885, 147–9) has pointed out, she is not merely the one who produces a son for her father but is actually a "son" in her own right. Many legal texts list her immediately after the natural son and before other kinds of sons (see 8.158–60). See also verse 130 about her right to inherit the paternal estate. Although somewhat awkward, I have opted for "female-son" to highlight the fact that she is truly a son who is female. For an examination of this institution in India and elsewhere, see Schmidt 1980, 30–75. See also *The Law Code of Gortyn* (ed. Ronald F. Willetts. Berlin: de Gruyter, 1967, pp. 23–7 and 45–7), a 5th-century BCE text from Crete, which devotes a substantial section to the "heiress," that is, a daughter who inherits the paternal property in the absence of sons.

Additional verse: "I will give to you in marriage the brotherless girl adorned with finery with the provision that the son she bears will be my son." This is *VaDh* 17.17.

9.128–9 *In ancient times . . . King Soma:* this story of Dakṣa's daughters is told in *MBh* 1.70 (it is unfortunate that van Buitenen translates the technical term *putrikā* here as "puppets"). The term *satkṛtya*, which I have, following Kullūka, translated "after adorning them," can also mean simply "after honoring" (see Bühler and Doniger; it is unclear whether it is the grooms or the girls who are honored). I think the act of embellishing is implied by this term, something one would do to a daughter who is about to get married. See my note 3.96 n.

9.131 *separate property:* the technical term *yautaka* refers to any kind of separate property remaining within the umbrella of common property or carved out of it. See 9.214, where the *yautaka* refers to the separate property of the oldest brother.

9.136 Variant reading: "bears a son of equal status."

9.140 *the second . . . father's father:* Bhāruci and Medhātithi record variants according to which the second rice-ball is offered to his biological father (see 9.132). The reading of the last *pāda* as well as its meaning are uncertain. If we follow one reading, the third rice-ball would be offered to his biological father's father; this interpretation is followed by Bühler. It also appears to be the meaning of the parallel passage in *BDh* 2.3.16. Medhātithi, Nārāyaṇa, Kullūka, Rāghavānanda, and Nandana, however, take the final *pāda* to mean that the third rice-ball is offered to the mother's father's father. This interpretation is based either on the reading *tatpituḥ pituḥ*, where *tat* in the compound is taken as *tasyāḥ* ("her"), or on the reading (adopted in the critical edition) of *tu pituḥ pituḥ*, where *tasyāḥ* ("her") for *pāda-c* is taken as governing this *pāda* also. I have followed this interpretation, even though it would exclude the biological father altogether. I think that *BDh* 2.3.16 also could be interpreted in this way by taking *tasyāḥ* of its *pāda-c* as governing also *pitāmaham* of *pāda-d*. The view expressed here appears to be different from that expressed in verse 132, where rice-balls are offered to both the mother and the biological father.

9.142 *The offering . . . to an end:* the second half-verse is elliptical. The meaning, however, is clear and my translation reproduces the meaning without attempting to be literal.

9.146 *keeps:* the verb *bibhṛyāt* means to keep, in the sense of both carrying away for oneself and keeping safe (taking care of), and it is related to the term for husband (*bhartṛ*). For a study of the connection between the two terms, see Thieme 1963, 466.

9.150 *ornament:* the exact reference is unclear, given that a family would have more than one ornament. Medhātithi gives the example of the father's ring.

one share from the best property: the meaning is unclear. Medhātithi and Kullūka say that the property is divided into shares and the most excellent of these shares is given to the eldest. Nandana takes it to mean that the most excellent items of the property is divided into shares and the best of these given to the eldest.

9.154 *Whether he has . . . no son at all:* several interpretations are offered by Medhātithi. If we take the "proper son" to be a son by a Brahmin wife, then the man may have sons by other wives. In this case also, the son by a Śūdra wife must get only one-tenth of the property. If the man has no son at all, that is, no son from a wife of an upper class, and the son from a Śūdra wife is the only son he has, then too he must give that son only one-tenth of the property. The rest of the property should be divided by the next of kin, following the method for a man who dies without issue.

9.156 *When all the sons . . . equal shares:* this appears clearly to be an alternative (preferable? see 9.111 n.) to the intricate rules spelled out earlier, even though Medhātithi objects strongly to this interpretation.

9.158 *relatives but not heirs* (adāyādabāndhavāḥ): the issue is whether the negative suffix governs only the first member of the compound or both. Nārāyaṇa and Nandana opt for the latter: the last six are neither heirs nor relatives. This appears to be the view of Medhātithi also, although his wording is somewhat unclear (*itare viparītāḥ*, "others are the opposite"). The parallel passage in *GDh* 28.33, however, makes it very clear that these six kinds of sons do share in the lineage (*gotra*) of their father.

9.161 Variant reading: "A man gains the same result."

9.162 *If a natural son . . . not the other:* the verse is obscure. Some commentators assume this situation. A husband who is impotent gets a son through appointment (*niyoga*); after that his impotency is cured and he fathers a natural son. In this case, the natural son inherits the estate of his father, not the son begotten on the wife. Something like this appears to be the intent of the verse, especially in light of what is said in verses 163 and 164. Nārāyaṇa and Nandana take *ekarikthin* as heirs to an undivided estate. They contemplate a situation where one of two brothers dies while the estate is undivided, and the living brother produces a son for the deceased brother by appointment on his widow. The question is whether the latter son can claim more than one share, because he is the leviratic son of the dead brother and the biological son of his uncle. At face value, this is an attractive interpretation; but what is said in the subsequent verses appears to contradict it. See the parallel at 9.191.

9.165 *but the other ten . . . and the estate:* this verse is once again not altogether clear. Many interpretations are offered by commentators. The most probable is the one offered by Bhāruci and Medhātithi: the sons enumerated later inherit the estate in the absence of those enumerated earlier (9.184). This appears to be a version of the so-called obstructed inheritance (*sapratibandha*): Jolly 1885, 176. See *YDh* 2.132.

9.166 *principal son* (prāthamakalpika): following the general view of the commentators, Bühler translates: "the first in rank." Thieme (1963, 477) likewise translates: "der den ersten Rang hat." But why would Manu need to say that he is the first in rank when he is in fact listed first in rank? I think the meaning here is that the natural son is the standard son, the son in the true sense of the term (commentators gloss *mukhya*, which can have a similar meaning), whereas other sons are in some way secondary or substitutes. Indeed, in verse 180 the eleven other sons are in fact called substitutes (*pratinidhi*). See the identical wording with regard to principal and secondary rules at 11.30.

9.175 *marries again* (punar bhūtvā): for an examination of this phrase and the term *punarbhū*, see Thieme 1963, 445–60.

9.176 *the rite of remarriage:* translators and commentators take *paunarbhavena* as qualifying the husband (*bhartrā*). Accordingly, Bühler translates: "she is worthy to again perform with her second (or first deserted) husband the (nuptial) ceremony." Thieme (1963,

445) has shown that *paunarbhavena* refers instead to the special rite of remarriage. The *BDh* 4.1.16 leaves no doubt about this, using the expression *paunarbhavena vidhinā* "following the procedure of a second marriage." On the legal provisions for women to leave their husbands and on the remarriage of women, see Lariviere 1991.

9.179 *a slave woman married to a slave:* the expression *dāsadāsī* has been subject to much misunderstanding. Bühler translates it literally as "female slave of his slave." Rocher (2002) has demonstrated conclusively that *dāsa* and *dāsī*, although literally "slave man" and "slave woman," refer in fact to a Śūdra man and woman, respectively. In other words, *dāsa* here is a synonym for Śudra. In the present context, the Śūdra has fathered a son either by an unmarried Śūdra woman (*dāsī*) or by a Śūdra woman married to some other Śūdra man (i.e., not to the father of her son).

9.182–3 *If among several brothers . . . women who have sons:* variants of these provisions occur also in *VaDh* 17.10–1 and *ViDh* 15.41–2. The connection between the two verses is not altogether clear. The second clearly refers to a polygamous marriage. Wezler (1998) disagrees with Jolly's suggestion that the former may refer to a polyandric marriage of several brothers to a single wife, as exemplified in the marriage of the five Pāṇḍava brothers in the *MBh*. Wezler suggests that when one brother has a son all his other brothers also become "men who have sons," because through that son they are all freed from the debt to their father of bearing a son to continue the line. Likewise, the common wives are relieved of the burden of bearing a son for their common husband. At a linguistic level, moreover, a man can claim "I have a son" when his father gets a grandson, just as a woman can claim "I have a son" when her husband gets a son. Vijñāneśvara (on *YDh* 3.227) cites a verse that he ascribes to Manu, which has a very similar thrust: *bahūnām ekakāryāṇāṃ sarveṣāṃ śastradhāriṇām / yady eko ghāteyet tatra sarve te ghātakāḥ smṛtāḥ //* "If among many men pursuing the same task, all of whom are bearing weapons, one kills, tradition says that all of them are killers."

Variant reading: "If among several wives."

9.186 *To three . . . for a fifth:* the three are father, grandfather, and great grandfather. These are the three to whom the standard monthly ancestral offering (*pārvaṇaśrāddha*) is offered. The person who is obliged to make the offering, that is the son, is the fourth. A fifth individual whether grandson or great great grandfather does not enter into this ritual picture. When the grandson becomes the offerer, his father becomes one of the three and the father's great grandfather falls out of the picture.

9.187 *The closest . . . a pupil:* I have followed the cogent argument of Bühler in his note to this verse with regard to the meaning of *sapiṇḍāt* as referring to the deceased. Here, as in verse 185, the ones mentioned later become heirs only in the absence of the ones mentioned earlier (see 9.165 n.). The term *sakulya* ("belonging to the same family") is defined in *BDh* 1.11.10 as "those who share in separate oblations," that is, distant relations who do not share the rice-balls offered at an ancestral offering. See Kane 1962–75, iii: 746–7.

9.191 *When two . . . of the other:* at issue here is a woman married consecutively to two men who have each fathered a son. The men are dead and their estates are in the hands of their common wife. In this case, each son inherits the estate of his biological father. See the parallel at 9.162 and the note to it.

9.198 *Any property . . . offspring:* the verse is unclear and has been subject to different interpretations. Most commentators interpret it to mean that, when a Brahmin has wives of different classes, the property of a wife of any class goes to the daughter by the Brahmin wife. The phrase "to her offspring" is also ambiguous; it can mean children in general, sons in particular, or, in the view of most commentators, daughters in particular.

9.199 *alienate:* Bühler, Jha, Derrett, and Doniger, following Kullūka and Rāghavānanda (*dhanasaṃcayam*), take *nirhāra* to mean hoarding. Bühler, nevertheless, notes that

Nārāyaṇa and Nandana's explanation as "expenditure" (*vyaya*) is preferable. The latter is probably the interpretation also of Bhāruci, even though Derrett has chosen to translate *nirharet* as "hoards." The term may mean something broader than simply expenditure, however, and may include other types of alienation. Although this term does not occur elsewhere in Manu, it is used in *VaDh* (19.14) with the probable meaning of the exportation of goods from the capital city of a kingdom..

9.201 *lacking manly strength:* commentators uniformly take the term *nirindriyāḥ* to refer to persons lacking a limb or an organ. So, Bühler "deficient in any organ." This condition is generally referred to by the term *vikalendriya*, however, rather than *nirindriya*. Further, persons lacking an organ (though not a limb) were already listed as blind and deaf. The only other place *nirindriya* occurs is at 9.18 (see note to it and the citation from *TS*), where it clearly refers to manly strength, perhaps with a sexual nuance.

9.211 *his share is not lost:* that is, his share has to be reserved for his own heirs; it cannot be divided among themselves by his brothers.

9.212 *Having assembled . . . among themselves:* the verse is ambiguous and commentators offer varying explanations. See also Jīmūtavāhana's *Dāyabhāga* 11.5.32–4 and Rocher's comment there. The antecedent of the pronoun *taṃ* ("it") is unclear. The pronoun cannot refer to the share of the eldest or the youngest mentioned in the previous verse, because that share is not meant to be divided by the brothers. I think that either verse 211 is a parenthetical remark and "it" refers to the joint property mentioned in verse 210; or these verses are taken from diverse sources and do not form part of a single argument. The lost context is largely responsible for the lack of clarity and for the various interpretations offered by the tradition. See Bühler's note to this verse for these interpretations.

9.216 *A son born . . . with them:* the context is a child born to the father after he has partitioned his estate among his sons. That child will inherit the father's portion of the divided estate and any other property the father may have acquired after the partition.

9.219 *A garment . . . from partition:* Vijñāneśvara (on *YDh* 2.118–9) explains that garments, vehicles/mounts, and ornaments that have been used are not subject to partition; they are taken by the person who regularly used them. "Women" probably refers to slaves or servants. Prepared foods are sweets, pickles and the like. Most manuscripts and commentators read *yogakṣemaṃ pracāraṃ ca*. Bühler, following Vijñāneśvara, translates these as "property destined for pious uses or sacrifices, and a pasture-ground." The critical edition has adopted a reading which restores the compound: *yogakṣemapracāram*, which is also the reading of Bhāruci (for more detail, see my note in the critical edition). Scharfe (1993, 195–200), in a close semantic study of the term *pracāra*, has clearly shown that it does not mean land or pasture but activities (see 7.153 n.). One can think of watchmen, fences, and the like. These must be continued undisturbed by the partition.

9.220 *ritual procedure for sons:* Bühler, following Kullūka, translates: "the rules for allotting (shares) to the (several) sons, those begotten on the wife and the rest." I think this makes no sense; why would the natural son (*aurasa*) be left out if Manu wanted to speak about the procedures for partitioning? I think Nārāyaṇa is right in taking this to mean the ritual procedures for establishing these kinds of sons; then we can understand why the natural son is left out, because he is not created by any ritual procedure as in the case of leviratic or adopted sons.

9.221 *The king . . . a kingdom:* interestingly, Manu does not deal with disputes arising from gambling and betting at all. He merely gives a moralistic disquisition about the evils of gambling. See the very different way this section is constructed in *NSm* 17. Bṛhaspati (cited by Mādhava in his *Pārāśāramādhavīya*, 3.393) perceptively says that Manu forbids gambling while others permit it. Variant reading: "vices of rulers that destroy kings."

9.225 *entertainers*: the critical edition has adopted the reading *kerān*. Its meaning is not altogether clear. If we see it as related to the verb *krīḍati*, then a meaning such as a public entertainer (jugglers, magicians, etc.) may be possible. Variant readings include *kelān* (again with an unclear meaning), *krūrān* (vicious persons), and *caurān* (thieves).

9.227 *In a former age:* this may be a reference to the calamities that struck the epic heroes Yudhiṣṭhira and Nala as a result of their addiction to gambling.

9.230 Variant reading omits "those without guardians."

9.231 *inflamed by the heat of money:* the image is of passion for money through bribes.

9.232 *constituents of the realm* (prakṛti): see 9.292 for the six constituents. In the present context, however, the reference may be more specifically to the ministers, as explained by Rāghavānanda and Rāmacandra.

9.233 *adjudicated and a judgment issued* (tīritaṃ cānuśiṣṭam): different interpretations are offered for these two terms. Asahāya (on *NSm Mā* 1.56) takes *tīrita* to mean a unanimous verdict of the court, and *anuśiṣṭa* to be the judgment and punishment ordered by the court. Most commentators of Manu agree with this interpretation. Nandana, however, cites Kātyāyana (495), according to whom *tīrita* is a summary judgment issued by the properly authorized official and *anuśiṣṭa* a judgment based on testimony.

not bring it back again (na tad bhūyo nivartayet): Bühler translates: "and not annul it." That, however, ignores *bhūyas* ("again"). I follow the understanding of most commentators. The meaning appears to be that the king should not retry cases that have already been settled; this may also refer to matters settled by the former administration in newly conquered territories.

9.235 Variant reading: "should be punished individually."

9.240 Variant reading: "not brand all the classes."

9.242 *to be executed* (pravāsanam): the term could also mean exile or banishment. I think the argument here goes something like this. A Brahmin should be given the middle fine of 500 Paṇas (if he does it thoughtlessly?) or sent into exile without the confiscation of property (if done deliberately?). In the case of others, their property is confiscated if done thoughtlessly (and then exile as in the case of the Brahmin?), and they are executed, if they did it deliberately. The contrast between *vivāsa* (exile) and *pravāsa* (execution) is also found in 8.123 (see the note to this). Bhāruci and Medhātithi also interpret *pravāsa* here as *vadha* ("execution"), and the variant *pramāpaṇam* ("killing") in Devaṇṇabhaṭṭa also supports this meaning.

Additional verse: "When a king inflicts punishment in this manner, he gains merit and obtains worlds won by good works—that is Manu's decree."

9.247 Variant reading: "the farmers' crops ripen in the prescribed manner."

9.251 *Carrying out . . . been acquired:* this verse takes us right back to the *rājadharma* section of chapter 7. Manu has clearly embedded his section on legal procedure (*vyavahāra*) squarely within this treatment of the duties of a king, which concludes at verse 9.324.

9.252 *eradication of thorns* (kaṇṭakoddharaṇa): see the parallel *kaṇṭakaśodhana* ("clearing thorns") in verse 253. The word "thorns" here is a technical term for every type of criminal and anti-social person (9.259–60) within the kingdom. Here Manu returns to the theme of the general duties of the king, after the long disquisition on legal procedure that occupied all of chapter 8 and much of chapter 9.

9.257 *bandits of the wild* (āṭavya *or* āṭavika): here terms are used with two different meanings. At a positive level, they refer to tribes inhabiting forest and wild regions. In the *AŚ* such people are used as spies (1.12.23, 13.15), and the king makes alliances with their chiefs (1.18.7) and settle such people in royal forest (2.2.5). The second meaning is negative; such people are viewed as bandits who plunder the country (*AŚ* 2.1.36).

9.258 *fortunetellers* (bhadraprekṣaṇika): the reading adopted by the critical edition is based on the reading of Medhātithi. Most mss. divide this compound: *bhadrāś cekṣaṇikaiḥ*. In either case the meaning is not altogether clear. Bühler, following Kullūka, takes *bhadra* to be "sanctimonious hypocrites" and the second term to be "fortunetellers."

9.260 *non-Āryas wearing Ārya marks:* the reference clearly is to low-caste or tribal people attempting to pass off as Āryas by assuming clothing or other marks normally associated with Āryas, e.g., the sacrificial cord. For a detailed study of the meaning of non-Ārya, see Deshpande 1999.

9.266 *patrolled by . . . mobile agents:* mobile and stationary squads refer to regular police and army units employed in internal security. Mobile agents work for the secret service, which employs besides the mobile agents also agents resident in spy establishments that are stationary. For a study of secret agents, see Scharfe 1993, 204–39.

9.269 *suspicious of the source:* the meaning of the expression *mūlapraṇihita* is unclear. I have taken *mūla* to be the source of their invitation to attend the events listed earlier, that is, former associates of the thieves and the like.

9.271 *implements, or shelter:* commentators and translators alike take the compound *bhāṇḍāvakāśadāḥ* to mean those who "grant them room for concealing their implements" (Bühler). See, however, the parallel expression *śastrāvakāśadān* at 9.278, which is interpreted by most to mean those who provide weapons and shelter. The two compounds must be constructed alike. The parallel passage in *AŚ* 4.11.9 also include giving them shelter (*vāsa*).

9.272 *provinces:* for the meaning of *rāṣṭra* as incorporated states with a fair degree of autonomy, see Scharfe 1993, 124.

9.273 *When a man . . . specific to him:* commentators explain this as referring especially to Brahmins who function as priests or obtain gifts. It could also refer to royal officials who act improperly (see 7.123–4; 9.259).

9.277 *two fingers:* Nārāyaṇa, Kullūka, and Rāghavānanda take the two to be the thumb and the index finger, while Nandana takes them to be the index and middle fingers. See also the cutting of fingers in the case of sexual intimacy at 8.267.

9.278 Variant reading: "the king should execute."

9.279 *clean execution* (śuddhavadha): this is another instance of Manu employing Arthaśāstra terminology. This expression is not found in any other Dharma text. It occurs only in the *AŚ:* 4.9.2; 4.10.16; 4.11.2, 15, 26. At *AŚ* 4.11.1 we have the expression *citro ghātaḥ*, "colorful execution," that is, killing that involves various forms of torture. The very next *sūtra*, 4.11.2, has the expression *śuddhavadha*, which must, therefore, be contrasted with *citravadha*. A neat and clean execution is probably what is meant. Several commentators of Manu interpret the expression to mean decapitation, which is quite probable. At *AŚ* 4.11.26 *śuddhavadha* is contrasted with *kleśadaṇḍa*, "painful punishment," which must mean something close to *citravadha*. See 9.291 n.

9.280 *elephants, horses, or chariots:* in all likelihood, the reference is to those owned by the king. A parallel passage in *AŚ* 4.11.7 explicitly refers to king's elephants, horses, and chariots.

9.282 *Anyone who drops . . . that filth:* for the royal highway (*rājamārga*), see Scharfe 1993, 159; *AŚ* 2.4.1, 4. On the prohibition against throwing rubbish or filth on a royal highway, see *AŚ* 2.36.26–7.

9.286 *For adulterating . . . lowest fine:* I have followed the majority of commentators in taking *bhedane* with *maṇīnām*, "breaking of gems." The syntax, however, is not very clear; the obvious way to take it is with *dravyāṇām* (so Nārāyaṇa). But given the context of business transactions, this seems unlikely.

9.287 *If a man deals . . . middle fine:* as Derrett (trans. of Bhāruci, note on 9.287) observes, this appears to be an arcane rule that has not been well understood. The meaning, as explained by Medhātithi, appears to be that the man barters commodities that should be bartered as equal (e.g., one measure of rice for one measure of sesame seeds; see this principle articulate in 10.94) in an unequal manner either directly or in terms of price. That is, he buys one commodity at one price and sells the other at a different price. Bühler, following Nārāyaṇa and Kullūka, translates: "But the man who behaves dishonestly to honest (customers) or cheats in his prices." This appears improbable.

9.291 *jacks up the price of seed corn* (bījotkraṣṭā): the meaning is unclear. Several commentators explain that the man actually pulls up sprouting seed from the fields in order to sell more corn! Others think that the man gathers up seeds already sown and sells it again (so Bühler). I wonder how this was possible. I follow the clear explanations of Bhāruci and Nārāyaṇa; such price hikes may have been associated with sowing times (Nārāyaṇa: *bījakāle*) when there may be a shortage of seed corn.

executed with mutilation: the term *vikṛta* appears to be a synonym of or a parallel to *citra* and *kleśa* in the *AŚ*, all indicating that the execution of the criminal is preceded by torture and mutilation (see 9.279 n.).

9.293 *the time and the purpose:* Medhātithi explains that stealing agricultural implements is more serious during times of cultivation; likewise medicine when someone is sick and weapons during a time of war. See also 8.324 n.

9.294 Variant reading: "are said to form a kingdom of seven constituents."

9.296 *like a tripod:* all translators take *tridaṇḍa* to mean "a triple staff," that is, three sticks tied together; this is an emblem of certain kinds of ascetics. The commentators are not altogether clear, but Medhātithi at least appears to understand that the simile is based on the three components of the *tridaṇḍa* supporting each other. This is not the case in a triple staff with three sticks tied together. What keeps the three together is not each other but the binding. Manu is cleverly playing with the terms *tridaṇḍa* and *viṣṭabdha,* the latter being an old term for the tripod of a Brahmin. He carried his water pot tied to it, and when the tripod was planted on the ground the pot hung from the middle. When the tripod is thus standing on the ground, each foot supports the others; if you take off one, the entire tripod would fall. This is the point of the simile. For a detailed discussion of *tridaṇḍa* and the tripod in the ascetic history of India, see Olivelle 1986–87, I: 42–52.

9.303 *The king . . . and Earth:* these eight guardian deities of the directions are the gods from whose particles the king was initially created (see 7.4); the only difference is that Earth is here substituted for Kubera. The king must, therefore, imitate the activities of these deities.

9.304–5 *four months, eight months:* the monsoon rains come during the summer season; ideally the rainy season is depicted as lasting four months. Here, Indra, the god of rain, is said to rule over these months. The remaining eight months constitute the dry season when the sun shines and extracts water from the earth.

9.312 *In this and . . . in others:* clearly, this concluding verse is directly connected with verse 293 and what preceded it. The intervening sections had little to do with the eradication of thorns. I suspect that they are an interpolation; so also, in all likelihood, the section on Brahmins that follows (9.313–23).

9.314 *They made the fire . . . wane and wax:* these are well-known legends recorded in the *MBh* concerning great Brahmin sages. Bhṛgu cursed Fire to be an omnivore when he claimed to have the right to take Bhṛgu's wife (*MBh* 1.6; 12.329.43). When the Ocean refused to come when called, Vaḍavāmukha cursed him to become undrinkable and made him salty with his sweat (*MBh* 12.329.48). Because Moon, to whom he had given

27 of his daughters in marriage (see 9.129), favored one and neglected the others, Dakṣa cursed him to wane and wax (*MBh* 9.34.40–67, 12.329.45–6).

9.321 *Kṣatriya from Brahmin:* this doctrine is articulated already in the *BṛU*, 1.4.11, which calls *brahma* (the priestly power) the womb of the *kṣatra* (the ruling power).

CHAPTER TEN

10.5 *in the direct order of class* (ānulomyena): given that the wife belongs to the same class as the husband, this specification makes little sense within the context of this verse. It may well be stated here, in the manner of *sūtra* texts, so as to govern what is stated in the verses that follow (6–10), namely the marriage of higher-class men to lower class wives.

10.8 *girl:* the term *kanyā* (lit., "virgin") may actually be a shorthand for a girl properly given in marriage (*kanyādāna*). The reference then would be to sons born from a legal marriage to these wives and not merely a son born from a liaison: so Govinda and Kullūka, citing *YDh* 1.92. Medhātithi, on the other hand, takes *kanyā* as a mere synecdoche (*upalakṣaṇa*) for any woman. For a detailed study of the development of the mixed-caste systems through intermarriage, see Brinkhaus 1978. For a critical study of mixed castes in the legal texts, see Aktor 1999.

10.13–4 *When there . . . mother's defect:* these two verses say nothing new and are probably interpolations. Indeed, I think that the final word of verse 12, *jāyante varṇasaṃkarāḥ* ("so originate the intermixture of classes"), was meant as a fitting close to the discussion. Also the name Anantara given to a son born from a wife of the next class is different from Sadṛśa ("similar") given in verse 6.

10.16–7 *From a Śūdra . . . a Sūta:* these verses and this entire second discourse on mixed classes is suspect. These verses basically repeat what has been stated in verses 11–2. Further, the term *apasada* is defined here as sons born in the inverse order, whereas earlier in verse 10 it is defined as sons born in the direct order. The last phrase here is elliptical. From a Vaiśya man by Kṣatriya and Brahmin girls are born Māgadha and Vaideha; and from a Kṣatriya man by a Brahmin girl is born a Sūta (see verse 11).

10.21–3 *From a Vrātya . . . Sātvata:* many of these are ethnic and tribal names. This passage appears to be an attempt to account for ethnic groups within the ideology of caste intermixture (see 10.43–5). See a similar attempt in *GDh* 4.21.

10.24 *By adultery . . . classes:* here we begin yet another discourse on mixed classes, a section that is also quite suspect. Note the final *pāda* of this verse: *jāyate varṇasaṃkaraḥ*, which parallels the final *pāda* of the closing verse of the first discourse (10.12).

10.27 *by women of their mother's caste . . . higher castes:* this half verse is very obscure and elliptical. The numerous variant readings testify to the attempts by the tradition to understand it. See Bühler's note and Brinkhaus 1978, 38f for different explanations and interpretations. Note the interesting use of *varṇa* with reference to mixed classes and even outcastes. A similar usage is found at 10.31.

10.28 *As from two . . . excluded men:* once again we have an elliptical verse. The meaning appears to be this. From a woman of two of the three upper classes (that is, from a Brahmin and a Kṣatriya woman), a Brahmin begets a son that is his own self (9.8 n.). The phrase *ānantaryāt svayonyāṃ* is elliptical containing an argument supporting the above claim. The meaning is that even a Kṣatriya woman can be counted as "a woman of his own class" because of her contiguity (see 10.6). The term *bāhya* to indicate an outcaste is quite unusual in the early Dharma vocabulary. In Manu, the term is found only in these sections (10.28, 29, 30, 31, 39, 62). It does not occur in any other Dharma text, except *ViDh* 16.18 (which is merely a citation of *MDh* 10.62), or in the *AŚ*.

10.35 *By Āyogava . . . these three low-borns:* the question here is whether "these" (*ete*) refers to the three mentioned previously in verses 32–4, or the three listed in the very next verse. Bhāruci, Govinda, and Kullūka, and possibly also Medhātithi and Rāghavānanda, opt for the former; this interpretation is followed by Bühler and Doniger. I follow the latter interpretation, favored by Nārāyaṇa and Nandana. If we follow the construction of these verses, we see that the lists contain one kind of woman and several kinds of men (32, 35, 37). The mother of children listed in verses 32–4 is listed at the beginning in verse 32 (*āyogave*). Further, if we do not take verse 35 as relating to verse 36, then we have to supply within the latter verse all the mothers, which is exactly what Bühler (within parenthesis) and Doniger (in a footnote) do, following the commentators who prefer the first option. Variant reading: "By Āyogava women, who wear the clothes of the dead."

10.38 *Sopāka . . . good people:* the term Sopāka may be a Prakṛtic form of the Sanskrit Śvapāka (10.19,51). The meaning of the expression *mūlavyasana* is unclear. Bhāruci, Medhātithi, Govinda, and Kullūka take it as referring to a public executioner. Nārāyaṇa, Nandana, and Rāmacandra (who also gives the other meaning) take it to mean a man who digs for roots. Bühler, following B-R, translates: "who lives by the occupation of his sire," which appears very unlikely. See also the equally difficult expression *mūlakarma* at 11.64 n.

10.40 *activities:* Aktor (1999, 272) appears to take the term *karma* to mean "work," i.e., occupation. That is clearly implicit. See, however, the use of the same term in the sense of "what someone normally does" in verse 46. The activities that reveal a non-Ārya man are listed in verse 58.

10.42 *in each succeeding generation:* the term *yuge* here is interpreted by Medhātithi, Nārāyaṇa, Rāghavānanda, Nandana, and Rāmacandra as referring to the process of rebirth; whereas Kullūka takes it literally as referring to world ages. The former is correct, because in verse 64 the term *yugāt* is used unambiguously as referring to births.

10.43 Variant reading: "by trespassing against Brahmins."

10.44 *Puṇḍrakas . . . Daradas:* these are clearly ethnic names. Coḍas and Draviḍas were ethnic groups of the south (Dravidians). Kāmbojas were a group in what is today northwestern Pakistan; Pahlavas (Parthian) = Persians; Yavana = Greeks; Cīna = Chinese.

10.46 *low-born* (apasada), *delinquent-born* (apadhvaṃsaja): the distinction between these two categories is not altogether clear. In this verse, the low-born appear to indicate mixed-caste individuals born in the proper order of classes (higher man and lower woman). This is also the meaning of the term in verse 10. In verse 17, however, those born in the inverse order (lower man and higher woman) are designated low-born. The delinquent-born here appear to indicate precisely such individuals born in the inverse order.

10.50 *well-recognizable* (vijñātāḥ): the meaning is that these people should wear certain kinds of clothes and other marks that would identify their castes. See the punishment of low-caste men wearing the marks of Āryas at 9.260.

10.51 *Apapātras:* this is a term used frequently in the Dharmasūtras, especially by Āpastamba (1.3.25; 1.16.30; 1.21.6, 17; 2.17.20). Āpastamba juxtaposes it with *abhiśasta* ("heinous sinner") at 1.3.25, with *patita* ("one fallen from caste") at 1.21.6, and with dogs at 1.6.30; 2.17.20. The *BDh* 2.2.13 and *VaDh* 20.16, in a very similar passage, also juxtapose the term with outcastes; and *BDh* 1.21.15 with Śūdras. Āpastamba (1.21.6) appears to identify *apapātra* as people who have committed certain kinds of sins that make a person sordid (*aśucikara*). It appears that this term in its early usage referred to certain individuals excluded from society because of some serious lapse. The term fell into disuse in later Dharma vocabulary; it does not occur in the *YDh*, *ViDh*, or *NSm*; and in Manu also this is the only verse where it occurs. Bühler prefers Medhātithi's interpretation of this word: when an *apapātra* eats food from someone in a vessel, that vessel should be thrown away. See also the mention of broken vessels in verses 52 and 54. Another interpretation is that the food should not be placed in vessels that they hold in their hands but either placed on the ground or held by someone else.

10.57 *without the proper complexion* (varṇāpetam): all the commentators and translators take this compound to mean a man who is without or outside the social classes. This makes little sense, because the question at issue is how to identify a man who looks more or less like an Ārya. I think *varṇa* here means color or complexion. That color of skin and hair was used as an identifier of a Brahmin is evident from the interesting remarks of the grammarian Patañjali (2nd cent., BCE), who describes a Brāhmaṇa as "white in color, of pure conduct, with hair that is yellowish or reddish brown." See also 9.260 n.

10.62 *without artifice:* see 3.257 n. for the other usages of the term *anupaskṛtaḥ* by Manu. It clearly refers to anything that is not overly crafted (in cooking, in embellishment, etc.); and here it means that the man does this with a pure and simple heart, without expectation of any reward.

10.63 Variant reading: "truthfulness, not stealing."

Additional verse after the first half of verse 63 and syntactically connected with it: "ancestral offerings, hospitality, gift giving, honesty, fathering children by their own wives, freedom from envy."

10.65 *so does a Brahmin the rank of a Śūdra:* the meaning is not altogether clear. According to Medhātithi, the offspring of a Brahmin man from a Śūdra woman (i.e., a Pāraśava) will become a pure Śūdra in the seventh generation by marrying Śūdra women.

10.74 *that whose source is the Veda* (brahmayonisthāḥ): the meaning is quite uncertain. Govinda and Kullūka: persons devoted to the contemplation of Brahman. Nārāyaṇa and Rāghavānanda: persons born from a Brahmin father and mother. Bhāruci thinks that it means the same as *svakarmaṇy avasthitāḥ*. Nandana offers, in my mind, the best explanation, taking *brahmayoni* as a Bahuvrīhi compound ("that whose source is the Veda") referring to *dharma* (see 2.25). So the compound refers to a man who is firmly established in the Law.

10.83 *dependence on others* (parādhīnam): commentators point to the dependence on plows and animals. This may, however, refer to the condition of a tenant farmer. If a Brahmin or a Kṣatriya has fallen on hard times, it is unlikely that he has his own farm to cultivate.

10.88 *bees-wax:* the term *madhu* simply means honey, but given that honey (*kṣaudra*) is already mentioned, commentators interpret this to mean *madhūcchiṣṭa* or bees-wax. Although the interpretation is labored, it may be correct; in a parallel passage, the *YDh* 3.37, in fact, lists bees-wax (*madhūcchiṣṭa*) right next to honey.

10.89 Additional verse giving further items: "tin, lead, copper, all kinds of metal articles, tails, skin, bones, fat, tendons, and concrete bile."

10.90 *pure* (śuddhān): most commentators take this to mean unadulterated with other kinds of seeds or refuse. Nandana, however, takes it to mean white sesame seeds, black ones being implicitly prohibited.

10.94 Variant reading: "but never salt for sesame seeds."

10.103 *like fire and water:* water (specifically flowing water in rivers) and fire are viewed as pure by definition. See 9.318 where fire is said to be undefiled by burning a corpse. The *VaDh* 28.1 cites a proverb: "A woman is not polluted by a lover, a Brahmin by vedic rites, water by urine and feces, and fire by the act of burning." Variant reading; "for they are like fire and the sun."

10.105–8 *Ajīgarta . . . hand of a Cāṇḍāla:* the story of Ajīgarta is told in the *AB* 7.13–6, although there the father did not intend to eat the son. The plot must have changed over time. The story of Vāmadeva eating dog's meat is told in the *MBh* 13.94–5. The story of Bharadvāja is told in Sāyaṇa's commentary on *ṚV* 6.45.31. Viśvāmitra's story is the most famous and is told in the *MBh* 12.139.

10.116 *fortitude:* the meaning of the term *dhṛtiḥ* within the context of livelihood is unclear. Commentators take it to mean being content with little; but that is hardly a way to obtain a livelihood.

10.117 *A Brahmin . . . small interest:* this appears to be a versification of *VaDh* 2.40, 43.

10.119 Variant reading: "he must not turn back in battle."

10.122 *when he has the name "Brahmin" attached to him* (jātabrāhmaṇaśabdasya): the meaning appears to be that when a Śūdra serves a Brahmin, that name attaches to him; e.g., "he is a Brahmin's servant." By some extension of the name, he can call himself a Brahmin!

10.124 *They:* the antecedent of *taiḥ* is not certain, but it must refer to Brahmins who employ Śūdras.

10.126 *he is not prohibited . . . the Law* (na dharmāt pratiṣedhanam): commentators explain that Śūdras are not prohibited from doing some acts prescribed by Law, such as bathing, performing the five great sacrifices, and the like.

CHAPTER ELEVEN

11.1–2 *A man seeking:* Manu ended the last chapter saying: "Next, I will explain the splendid rules pertaining to penance." Instead of penance, however, he spends 43 verses on unrelated topics, turning to the subject of penance only in verse 44. I believe that the first 43 verses are interpolations. Bhāruci himself saw the problem. He begins his commentary on Chapter 11 with the objection that after promising to deal with penance we should have expected Manu to begin this chapter with verse 44. Bhāruci's defense of Manu is rather lame.

11.3 *sacrificial arena* (vedi): technically this is the area measured out and consecrated for a vedic sacrifice and containing the three vedic fires. The meaning appears to be that if these individuals come to beg while a sacrifice is taking place, they should be given food and a sacrificial fee, as if they were priests.

11.5 Additional verse: "Aged parents, a virtuous wife, a son, and a pupil, Manu has proclaimed, should be supported even if they have committed a hundred transgressions."

The vulgate gives here the following as verse 6, which is eliminated in the critical edition: "A man should give wealth to Brahmins who know the Veda and live in solitude according to his ability; he will thus attain heaven after death."

11.8 *even though . . . before:* the critical edition (see note there) has adopted the negative form *apītasomapūrvaḥ*. Most commentators accept the positive form, followed by Bühler and Doniger. The translation would then be: "though he may have drunk Soma before." The commentators explain that the prohibition affects only Soma sacrifices undertaken voluntarily and not the very first one, which is prescribed (Medhātithi: *anena prathamayajñasyāvaśyakartavyatāṃ darśayati*). Under the positive interpretation, the final *api* ("even though") does not make much sense. One should have then expected a word such as *cet* ("if"): the Soma sacrifice does not yield fruit *if* someone has drunk Soma before. I think the negative is the original. The rule prohibits *even* a man who has not drunk Soma before from performing a Soma sacrifice if he does not have sufficient resources to maintain his family. *A fortiori*, of course, a man who has already drunk Soma is forbidden to perform it also. My interpretation follows Bhāruci.

11.11–2 *While a righteous . . . complete the sacrifice:* opinion is divided over who actually takes the property from the Vaiśya. Medhātithi, Govinda, and Kullūka, following the syntax, say that it is the sacrificer himself. Nārāyaṇa, Nandana, and Rāmacandra, however, taking a cue from the mention of the king, think that it is the king who should confiscate the property. The term *āharet* (literally, "take") is also ambiguous; it can mean either steal or take (perhaps by force). Medhātithi thinks that there is no restriction as to the method of appropriation: it could be begged, stolen, or taken by force. Kullūka: by theft or force. Govinda: by theft. Verse 17 appears to imply theft. For a justification of such an act, see 1.100–1.

11.15 *a man who is always a taker:* Bhāruci cites an opinion that takes *ādānanitya* as a technical term referring to a money lender.

11.16 *the rule . . . next day* (aśvastanavidhāna): the meaning is that he should take only sufficient food to last just that day. This rule is often associated with certain types of ascetics: see 4.7.

11.19 *both:* that is, the man from whom he takes and the man to whom he gives.

11.21 *such a man:* that is, the man referred in verses 16–7. This reference makes the authenticity of the intervening verses suspect.

11.23 *one-sixth of his merits:* this is viewed as the "tax" the king obtains from him, as from other religious professionals, for providing protection. On the rates of taxation, see 7.127–39; on the king obtaining one-sixth of the merits of his subjects by protecting them, see 8.304–5.

11.24 Variant reading: "Under no circumstances should a man beg money from a Śūdra."

11.27 *turn of the year:* the new year begins on the first day of the bright fortnight of Caitra (March-April).

11.28 Following the NT reading, Bühler translates: "that is the opinion (of the sages)."

11.33 Additional verse: "For, doing that in accordance with the scriptural provisions, he obtains the highest state. That is the most fierce of all weapons; it cannot be averted by enemies."

11.40 Additional verse: "When the food is inadequate, it burns up the realm; when the ritual formulas are inadequate, it burns up the officiating priests; and when the sacrificial fees are inadequate, it burns up the man consecrated for the sacrifice—there is no enemy equal to the sacrifice."

11.41 *killing a hero* (vīrahā): in *GDh* 15.6 and *VaDh* 1.18 a man who extinguishes his sacred fires is called simply "a killer of a hero" (*vīrahā*). The meaning clearly is that by extinguishing the fire he has killed a hero, fire being the hero among the gods. This is spelled out in the *TS* 1.5.2: "Clearly, he is a slayer of the hero of gods who extinguishes the fire." Manu, however, says that extinguishing the fire is *equal to* the killing of a hero. Within this context, the hero may not be the fire itself but some other man. Most commentators take it to be the son.

11.47 *When a twice-born . . . that penance:* this appears to be an introduction verses 48–53, which deal with evil diseases and deformities believed to be caused by either fate or by sins committed in a past life. Such "sins" are different from the sins actually committed that were the subject of verses 45–6.

Additional verse giving a popular etymology of *prāyaścitta,* ("penance"): "*prāyas* is said to be ascetic toil, and *citta* is called the firm decision. Tradition says that *prāyaścitta* consists of ascetic toil and a firm decision." The decision probably refers to the resolution not to commit that sin again.

11.51 *steals speech:* this appears to be an early indictment of plagiarism. It is interpreted as plagiarism by Nārāyaṇa, while Rāghavānanda appears to say that the man actually writes his name as the author of a book authored by someone else. Rāmacandra takes it to mean a man who steals books. Bühler says that Govinda and Kullūka interpret this to mean a man who steals the Veda by eavesdropping on someone reciting it (see 2.116), but the editions of these two commentators do not contain a commentary on this verse.

Additional verse given as 52 in Bühler's translation but omitted in the critical edition: "A man who steals a lamp becomes blind; and a man who extinguishes one becomes one-eyed. By causing injury, a man becomes frequently sick; and by not causing injury, a man becomes free from sickness."

11.53 Variant reading: "as a result of the special property of their past deeds."

11.55 *drinking liquor, stealing:* it appears that drinking liquor becomes a grievous sin only when done by Brahmins: see *GDh* 2.20. Stealing is also a grievous sin when it involves the gold of Brahmins: see 11.57, 100.

11.56 *A lie concerning one's superiority:* that is, falsely claiming a superior status either by birth or with respect to other attributes such as learning and virtue.

11.57 *killing a friend:* the term *vadha* can mean both killing and causing physical harm (see 8.320 n.). As in verse 11.89, I think the seriousness of the crime argues for taking the term as killing.

unfit food or forbidden food: the compound *garhitānādya,* as Nārāyaṇa points out, must refer to the two well-known categories of food that should not be eaten: *abhojya* ("unfit food") and *abhakṣya* ("forbidden food"): see 4.205 f., 5.4 f., 5.5 n., and Olivelle 2002a.

11.62 *breaking the vow* (vratalopanam): Medhātithi and Nārāyaṇa take this to mean the breaking of any vow undertaken. Given the seriousness of the offense, however, I think Govinda, Kullūka, and Rāghavānanda are correct in taking this to be the breaking of the vow of chastity by a vedic student. This is confirmed by its inclusion in the section on penances for these sins (11.119 f.).

11.64 *root-witchcraft:* the meaning of expression *mūlakarma* is quite unclear. The commentators are unanimous in taking it to mean some kind of witchcraft by which another person is brought under one's power (*vaśīkaraṇa*): see 9.290 where the meaning is clearly some form of witchcraft. In the *Kāma Sūtra* (4.1.9) a class of women is designated as *mūlakārikā*, and at 6.2.56 a reference is made to *mūlakarma.* The reference appears to be to some form of magic potion made with roots to win the love of a woman; this is the interpretation of the commentator Yaśodhara. See also *AV* 4.28.6 where *mūlakṛt* ("root-cutter") is in apposition to *kṛtyākṛt* ("witchcraft-maker"). This is also the meaning ascribed to the expression in B-R.

11.66 *acting like a woman* (straiṇyam): all the NT mss. and editions read *steyam* ("stealing").

living a corrupt life; engaging in vices (kauśīlyaṃ vyasanakriyā): all the editions, including Jolly's read *kauśīlavyasya ca kriyā.* Bühler translates this as "practicing (the arts of) dancing and singing."

11.68 *cause exclusion from caste* (jātibhraṃśakaram): it is unclear how exactly this differs from "falling from caste" (*pātaka*). Clearly it is a lesser sin than the latter. The commentators offer no help. It is possible that this sin did not result in the formal excommunication of the sinner (see 11.183–6); it may have resulted merely in social ostracism within the caste.

11.76 *one hundred leagues:* a *yojana* is a distance of approximately 9 miles or 14.5 kilometers. The total distance he walks comes to about 900 miles.

11.78 *walk . . . Sarasvatī:* Nārāyaṇa says that the penitent starts from Prabhāsa and goes up along the river bank to Plakṣasravaṇa.

11.81 Variant reading: "by fighting three times in defense of a Brahmin."

11.82 *Thus . . . twelfth year:* this verse is directly connected with verse 73 and appears to ignore verses 74–81, casting doubt on their authenticity.

11.83 *by proclaiming . . . horse sacrifice:* "gods of earth" are Brahmins, and "gods of men" are kings or, more generally, Kṣatriyas. Medhātithi, Govinda, Kullūka, and Rāghavānanda think that the gathering is for the purpose of a horse sacrifice.

11.86 *for their purification* (teṣāṃ pāvanāya): Nārāyaṇa, Govinda, and Kullūka take "their" as referring to the sinners. The syntax of the verse, however, suggests rather that the antecedent is "sins." This verse appears to be a general statement about the efficacy of penances for various sins determined by an assembly (*pariṣad*) of Brahmins: see 12.108–12.

11.88 *One must . . . menstrual period:* the implicit understanding here is that the fetus is that of a Brahmin (see *GDh* 22.13). The argument is that a fetus without developed sexual organs will turn out to be a male. The *VaDh* 20.24 says that the fetus can be turned into a male through the power of pre-natal rites such as the *puṃsavana* ("quickening a male child"). Aborting such a fetus, therefore, is equivalent to murdering a Brahmin (always assumed to be male, because the murder of a female does not carry the same sanction). A Kṣatriya or a Vaiśya, when they have been consecrated for a sacrifice (*dīkṣita*) is considered a Brahmin at least in some ritual traditions: see *ĀpŚr* (10.11.5–6): *brahmaṇo vā eṣa jāyate yo dīkṣate; tasmād rājanyavaiśyāv api brāhmaṇa ity evāvedayati.* "A man who is consecrated for a sacrifice is indeed born from the Veda. Therefore, even a Kṣatriya or a Vaiśya, it has been taught, is a Brahmin." The *VaDh* 20.34 specifies that he is engaged in performing a Soma sacrifice. A woman soon after her menstruation is called by the technical term *ātreyī,* which is given an interesting etymological spin in *VaDh* 20.35–6. The woman is in her fertile period (3.46–50) and killing her is tantamount to killing a future Brahmin. Here there is the added possibility that the woman is pregnant. For a detailed study of this provision, see Jamison 1991, 213–23; Wezler 1994.

11.93 *banner:* in *BDh* 1.18.18 the banner is specified as *surādhvaja,* literally "liquor banner." Commentators on Manu specify a drinking cup. It may well have been that liquor taverns in ancient India advertised themselves with a special banner. See 9.237.

11.94 *filth:* Manu plays on the word *mala,* which can mean any filthy or putrid substance (here fermentation being equated with putrefaction) and also the filth of sin (see 11.72, 102, 107 for the latter meaning).

11.95 *It should . . . so are all:* the issue here appears to be whether all kinds of liquor are forbidden or only certain kinds. Liquor made from grain was explicitly forbidden in verse 94; this verse extends that prohibition to all three kinds. The *VaDh* 20.19 appears to single out liquor called *surā* as particularly pernicious and prescribes a lighter penance for drinking non-*surā* kinds of liquor (see next note). Commentators are divided about the meaning of *mādhvī*, the third type of liquor. Some take it as derived from honey (a kind of mead), whereas others think that it is made from the flowers of the Madhuka tree (see next note).

11.96 *Intoxicants, liquor, spirits:* there appears to be a distinction made here between liquor (*surā*) and intoxicant (*madya*). The latter has probably a broader meaning, whereas *surā* is more specific and viewed as more pernicious (see 11.95 n.). Kullūka cites a verse from Pulastya that lists eleven types of *madya*, and calls the twelfth, *surā*, the worst kind of intoxicant. Kullūka himself thinks that the three kinds listed in verse 95 are *surā*, whereas the other nine kinds are *madya*. The meaning of "spirit" (*āsava*, literally, pressing or distillation) is unclear; commentators call it a variety of *madya;* given its name, it may refer to some type of wine or distilled liquor.

11.97 *blabber vedic texts* (vaidikam udāharet): most commentators take this to mean that an intoxicated Brahmin may not be able to pronounce vedic texts correctly or may recite them when he is impure. I think Nandana is correct in thinking that an intoxicated Brahmin would recite the Veda in the presence of people who are forbidden to hear it.

11.98 *brahman:* the term is used with a double entendre here. On the one hand, *brahman* is the Veda residing in the Brahmin's memory; on the other hand and closely related to the first meaning, it is his Brahmanical nature (*brāhmaṇya*) that makes him a Brahmin (see 1.93 n.).

11.100–01 *A Brahmin . . . ascetic toil:* there is something amiss in these two verses. The king takes the pestle, which has not been introduced in the first verse. Traditionally, the thief was supposed to take the pestle with him (see 8.315). Then, in the last half verse, the thief is purified by being killed. Given that the thief is a Brahmin, we must assume that the king kills him. But this would go against the general prohibition of the death penalty in the case of Brahmins. Finally, a Brahmin is said to be freed from the sin by ascetic toil alone. The verses are garbled; I assume that sections of these verses have been taken from different sources and condensed here. See the parallel at 8.314–5. For purification of sins through the death of the sinner, see Wezler 1995.

11.104 *metal cylinder:* the meaning of the term *sūrmī* is not altogether clear. It is certainly a cylindrical object made of metal. Most commentators take it to be a metal image of a woman (*strīprakṛti* or *pratimā*). At *ĀpDh* 1.28.15, however, the criminal is said to enter it (*praviśya*), which points to something, such as a column, that is hollow. Only Nandana identifies it as a column (*sthūṇā*). The recent study by Falk (2001) has cast much light on the history of the term *sūrmī*. Falk demonstrates that originally the term referred to a clay cylinder with openings at both ends for casting metal, that is, a primitive furnace. Such a cylinder was about the size of a human being; it could be both embraced and entered. The obsolescence of this kind of metal casting and the subsequent loss of the original meaning may have changed the term's meaning to that of a female figure, especially within the context of this penance for sexual misconduct.

11.109 *barley gruel:* the statement *yavān pibet* means literally "he should drink barley." Medhātithi observes that a secondary meaning must be intended, because it is not possible to drink barley seeds. Some take it to mean drinking barley mixed with water. Others think "barley" is used figuratively to indicate a product made with barley, namely, barley gruel. Medhātithi and most commentators prefer the latter.

11.110 *During two months:* although the connection between this and the preceding verse is not altogether clear, it appears that the two months mentioned here are in addition to the one month mentioned in the previous verse. Thus, the entire penance lasts for three months, as made clear in verse 116.

11.111 *follow those cows:* much is implied here. The vow consists of attending to cows during three months. During the day the man follows the cows into the pasture or the forest; brings them back to the cow-pen in the evening; attends to all their needs; and sits in the cow-pen by their side during the night. For a literary description of this observance, see Kālidāsa's *Raghuvaṃśa* (1.88–95; 2.1–75). On the ascetic practice of standing during the day and remaining seated at night, see 6.22 n.

11.112 *free from rancor* (vītamatsaraḥ): the meaning of *matsara* in this context is unclear. Nārāyaṇa glosses with *krodha* ("anger"), Medhātithi with *lobha* ("greed"), and Kullūka with *anudvignahṛdayaḥ* ("with an unagitated heart"). Medhātithi further explains that the term is merely illustrative; the man should free his mind from faults such as passion.

11.113 Variant reading: "he should free her using every means."

11.119 *cooked oblation:* the procedure for cooked oblations (*pākayajña*) is given at the very beginning of most Gṛhyasūtras: see *ŚāṅkhGṛ* 1.1.

11.120–2 *After offering . . . and Fire:* "Teacher" is an epithet of Bṛhaspati, the teacher of the gods, also identified with the planet Jupiter. See the parallel passage in *GDh* 25.1–2: "So, they ask: "Into how many does a student who has broken his vow of chastity enter?"—"Into the Maruts with his breaths; into Indra with his strength; into Bṛhaspati with the splendor of his vedic learning; and into just the Fire with everything else."

11.127 *virtuous* (vṛttasthe): commentators explain *vṛtta* as the specific duties, especially the proper means of livelihood, of each class. Bühler, following Nārāyaṇa and Kullūka, takes the adjective as qualifying the Śūdra. This is unlikely, both because the term occurs in the same *pāda* as the Vaiśya (*pādas* normally form syntactic units) and because the same expression is used with clear reference to a Vaiśya in verse 130. Medhātithi, Rāghavānanda, and Rāmacandra (possibly also Nandana) take it as qualifying all three classes.

11.128 Variant reading: "he should give one thousand cows and a bull after performing the vow properly."

11.134 *castrate* (ṣaṇḍha): the same provision occurs at *GDh* 22.23. Most commentators gloss with *napuṃsaka* (9.79 n.). The term, however, is often distinguished from *klība* and refers specifically to an eunuch. Medhātithi gives four kinds of *ṣaṇḍha: aretas* (one who is without seed), *vātaretas* (one who has windy seed, 9.79 n.), *apravṛttendriya* (Jha: one without an erection; could it mean one whose sexual organs are not fully developed?), and *ubhayavyañjana* (one with male and female sexual organs). Rāghavānanda gives a different four: *kṛtrima* (artificially castrated), *akṛttima* (natural, i.e., born without the sexual organs), *ubhayavyañjana* (one with male and female sexual organs), and *sadṛśendriya* (one with organs that only resemble?). All the commentators appear to take this provision as referring to humans. Haradatta, commenting on *GDh* 22.23, however, cites an opinion according to which the reference is to castrated animals. Coming, as it does, right in the middle of a list of animals, in this verse the term certainly could refer to a castrated ox.

11.139 Additional verse: "When someone kills unintentionally a woman belonging to one of the three classes in the proper order [i.e., Brahmin, Kṣatriya, or Vaiśya], he should perform the observance for killing a Śūdra irrespective of her class."

11.147 *When someone . . . settled rule:* commentators take Vāruṇī to include liquor made from honey (*mādhvī*) and molasses (*gauḍī*) and to exclude that made from grain: see 11.95 n., 96 n.). Bühler (see his long note to this verse) thinks that the term is another name for *surā*. Most commentators (except Medhātithi, Bhāruci, and Nandana) take the second half of the verse to mean that even if someone drinks liquor intentionally a penance resulting in death should not be prescribed (see Wezler 1995). Bühler's translation follows this interpretation, although in his note he correctly disagrees with it. See the very similar use of *anirdeśya* and *prāṇāntika* in the *GDh* 20.15 and 21.7 (the latter passage ascribing the view to Manu).

11.153 *forbidden meat* (māṃsam abhakṣyaṃ ca): most commentators and all translators take *abhakṣyam* ("forbidden") as qualifying meat. Only Rāghavānanda and, perhaps, Rāmacandra take *abhakṣyam* as a separate category, referring to forbidden foods (see 5.5 n.). The presence of *ca* ("and") after *abhakṣyam* supports the view that we are dealing with two items here. Further, at 5.31 f. Manu condemns the eating of any kind of meat. The parallel phrase in *pāda-a*, on the other hand, supports taking *abhakṣyam* as qualifying *māṃsam;* so also does the listing of forbidden animals in verses 155–6. Under the latter interpretation, the *ca* would join the two phrases with the verbs *bhuktvā* and *jagdhvā*, even though it comes at the end of the phrase rather than after the first word.

11.154 *even though they may be pure* (medhyāni): that is, even though the substances in their natural state may be fit for eating. Commentators explain *medhyāni* as *apratiṣiddhāni* ("not explicitly forbidden"). Nandana reads *amedhyāni*, positing the sandhi *pītvāmedhyāni*. The translation would then be: "When a twice-born drinks anything turned sour, pungent decoctions, or even impure substances. . . ."

until it has been excreted: the *GDh* 23.23and *VaDh* 23.30 use the term *niṣpurīṣībhāva* for the total evacuation of the bowels. According to *GDh* 23.24, this happens in three days, whereas the *VaDh* implies seven days.

11.166 *five products of the cow:* milk, curd, ghee, urine, and dung.

11.172 *If he has sex . . . lunar penance:* the first half-verse is somewhat confusing. The next verse makes it clear that we are dealing with *three* women closely related to a man; if we take *bhaginīm* ("sister") as a separate category, there will be four. The likely explanation is that "sister" here is used with reference to the first cousin, a common practice in India; and this term is qualified by both *paitṛṣvaseyīm* and *mātur svasrīyām*. The next verse further shows that the context is marriage and not just a sexual encounter. These two verses appear to be directed at cross-cousin marriages common in southern India. For the meaning "close relative" for *āpta*, see 2.109; 5.101; 9.290. The difficulty of the term may have been responsible for the variant *tanayām* found in vulgate editions and many mss.

11.174 *If someone . . . on water:* the sandhi of *puruṣa udakyāyām* is ambiguous. It could be the locative *puruṣe* or the nominative *puruṣaḥ*. Only Bhāruci prefers the former; all other commentators (and translators) take it to be a nominative. I have followed Bhāruci, because the context calls for illegitimate individuals and locations. Further, the very next verse also mentions homosexual intercourse. If we follow the others, the translation would be: "If a man ejaculates his semen in non-human females, in a menstruating woman. . . ." Most also take *jale* to mean in water. Bhāruci takes this to mean "on water," that is, in a boat or ship. I think Bhāruci is right; in the very next verse the connection between an ox cart and water clearly indicates that we are dealing with vehicles. Commentators explain that this rule applies only to sex with female animals other than cows, because sex with a cow is considered equal to violating an elder's bed (*gurutalpa*): see *GDh* 22.36.

11.177 *observance:* adultery by a man is counted among the secondary sins causing loss of caste (*upapātaka*) in 11.60. The penance for such sins is given in 11.118: either the lunar penance (11.217) or the cow-vow described in 11.109–17. For adultery as a crime, see 8.332–59.

11.178 Additional verse: "When wives of Brahmins, Kṣatriyas, or Vaiśyas have sex with a Śūdra, they are purified if they do not bear any children, not otherwise."

11.180 *I have . . . four kinds of sinners:* Nandana and Rāmacandra take "four" as referring to the four social classes. Govinda and Kullūka take the four to be the four kinds of sinners listed immediately before: those guilty of killing, eating forbidden food, stealing, and sexual offenses. This, however, excludes the major categories of sins that were dealt with in the early sections of this chapter. If my hypothesis that the previous four sections (11.127–79: which I have called "*Excursus*") are interpolations is right (see Introduction, p. 59–60), then the four sinners refer to the categories mentioned in 11.55–71. The problem is how we come up with four. The grievous and secondary sins causing loss of caste (*mahāpātaka* and *upapātaka*) make two. I think the third is sins that cause exclusion from caste (*jātibhraṃśakara:* 11.68). Three other sins are enumerated in 11.69–71; but I think Manu thinks of these three as a single large category, because when dealing with the penances for them he deals with them together in a single verse (11.126).

11.181 *When someone . . . an outcaste:* the syntax of this verse is not straightforward. Bhāruci, Medhātithi, Kullūka, Rāghavānanda, and Rāmacandra explain that one becomes an outcaste when one associates with an outcaste for one year by using the same vehicle or seat or by eating with him; if he establishes ritual or marriage connections, on the other hand, he falls immediately. This is the view expressed also in *ViDh* 35.3–5. To arrive at this meaning, one would have to syntactically connect *na tu* of *pāda-d* with *pāda-c;* and further ignore the unnatural position of *na tu* at the end of the phrase rather than at the beginning. Scharfe (1993, 44–6) rightly objects to this interpretation. He takes the ablatives in the second half-verse to be connected with *patati* ("he falls"), indicating the activities that he is barred from. Scharfe offers the following translation: "A person having dealings with an outcast within a year loses the right to offer sacrifices [for others], teach the Veda, and enter into marital alliances, but not the right to ride, sit, or eat [with others]." There are, however, several problems with Scharfe's translation. First, when the ablative is used with *patati,* the word in the ablative always indicates the *state from which he falls* rather than some specific activity: *MDh* 10.97 *patati jātitaḥ* ("falls from castes"); *MBh* 13.131.24–5 *patati brahmayonitaḥ* ("falls from the Brahmin birth"). I have found no example in the Dharma literature where *patati* is used with an ablative in the way Scharfe assumes here. Second, Scharfe assumes that it is permissible for people to associate with an outcaste in ordinary social dealings, such as traveling in the same vehicle and sitting and eating together. But such interactions are explicitly forbidden a few verses later at 11.185.

I think Nārāyaṇa, Govinda, and Nandana are correct in reading the verse the way it is written. A man falls within a year if he continues to maintain ritual or matrimonial relations with a fallen man, *but not* if he maintains only casual contact. This interpretation is supported by the context in which this verse is cited in *VaDh* 1.20–2. In *sūtras* 20–1, Vasiṣṭha lists the five *mahāpātakas,* the last of which he describes as: "associating with outcastes either through vedic instruction or through marriage" (*patitasaṃyogaḥ brāhmeṇa vā yaunena vā*). In the next *sūtra* he cites this verse in support of his position. Clearly, the words *yājanādhyāpanād yaunāt* of the verse must relate to and have the same meaning as *brāhmeṇa vā yaunena vā* of the previous *sūtra*. For both Vasiṣṭha and, in his eyes, this proverbial saying, only connections of a serious nature with an outcaste makes a man an outcaste, not ordinary day-to-day contact.

It appears that the author of *ViDh* was responsible for the new interpretation. It may well be, as Scharfe notes, that customs had changed and that serious connections with an outcaste was thought to bring about immediate exclusion from caste. The *ViDh,* which appears to be a commentary on this verse, had the freedom to say exactly what he wanted in his *sūtras*. The commentators of the verse, however, had a more difficult time, because the syntax of the verse clearly did not support such an interpretation.

11.183 Variant reading: "together with his relatives by marriage outside the village."

11.184 *A slave woman:* the term *dāsī* may refer simply to a Śūdra woman: see 9.179 n.

Variant reading: "A slave woman should then (*or* always) overturn a pot filled with water, as for a dead man."

11.190 *No one . . . cleansed:* this verse appears to conclude Manu's discussion of penance. The excursus on miscellaneous matters relating to penance (verses 191–247) appears to be an interpolation. Verse 208 is a repetition of 4.168. Indeed, the very first verse of this excursus (verse 191) appears to be a commentary listing exceptions to the provisions of verse 190.

11.197 *made holy by the cows:* the verse is elliptical. The place is made holy only if the cows actually eat the grass given by the penitent. The acceptance of the grass by the cows is viewed as a sign that the man has freed himself from his sin.

11.199 *misused:* the term *viplāvya* has a very broad meaning. Most commentators take it to mean that the man has divulged the Veda to an inappropriate person. Medhātithi gives several possibilities: reciting the Veda at a time when recitation is forbidden (see 4.101f), interfering with someone who is properly reciting it, and reciting the Veda uninvited for monetary gain.

11.203 *without water or in water:* "without water" means that the man did not have water with him to perform the normal purification after voiding urine or excrement; and "in water" means that he voided it into water.

11.205 *Huṃ, you* (huṃkāra, tvaṃkāra): it appears that "Huṃ" was an exclamation or curse hurled at someone in anger. When addressing a superior one should not use the informal singular *tvam* but an honorific term such as *bhavān* or the plural *yūyam* (*yuṣmad*) much like the *tu*/*vous* of French and other Romance languages.

11.208 Variant reading: "As many particles of dust the blood lumps together on earth."

11.213 *Subsisting . . . one day:* commentators point out two procedures. The man may subsist on the listed substances during one day and fast the next; or he may subsist on one of the six substance for a day during six days and fast on the seventh.

11.217–8 *He should decrease . . . bright fortnight:* the standard lunar penance begins on the full-moon day, when the penitent eats fourteen mouthfuls. He decreases the food by one mouthful a day, fasting completely on the new moon day. The intake of food is similarly increased by one mouthful a day during the fortnight of the waxing moon. Here the month is shaped with the middle narrow (fasting on the new moon) and the two ends are broad (fourteen mouthfuls at the beginning and the end). The alternate procedure with the middle broad and ends lean (like a barley corn) begins on the new-moon day with a total fast; the quantity of food is increased by one mouthful a day during the first fortnight until the full moon, and then decreased during the second fortnight. For a detailed description, see *BDh* 3.8.

11.226 *purificatory texts:* commentators identify these variously as the Aghamarṣaṇa, the Pāvamānī verses, the Puruṣa hymn, the Asyavāmīya, and the like (see App. III.2). Clearly the term referred in general to vedic texts viewed as particularly purifying.

11.231 Variant reading: "He should never do so again."

11.234 *If someone's mind . . . assuaged:* the meaning is somewhat unclear. The commentators, rightly I think, explain that if after someone has performed a penance for a particular sin, he still has a heavy heart, he may continue to perform the same penance until his mind is at ease.

11.238 *Solely by . . . effective:* the term *vidyā* can refer to any type of knowledge or learning; but in this context, I think it must refer to charms or spells that are effective against sicknesses, snakes, and the like. Medhātithi glosses *bhūtaviśeṣādiviṣayā*, which may refer to knowledge of either elements (so Jha) or various ghosts and spirits. The *ChU* (7.1.2) lists *bhūtavidyā* and *sarpavidyā* in a list of sciences. Medhātithi explains "divine conditions" as the yogic powers to become very small and the like. Others take it to mean becoming like the gods or reaching the world of various gods. I think Medhātithi is on the right track; all these items refer to various medicines, spells, and the like employed in ritual settings. The point of the verse is that without *tapas* these means cannot be properly acquired. The term *prasidhyanti* can mean "become effective" (so Nārāyaṇa and Nandana) and "acquired" (other commentators and Bühler). In the very next verse (239) *sādhyam* is used with reference to accomplishment. I think here also the meaning must be that these means become effective, that is, accomplish the objective, only when those who employ them perform the appropriate austerities.

11.245 Additional verse: "Chastity, ascetic toil, burnt offering, eating a little pure food at the proper time, and freedom from passion, hatred, and greed—the Self-existent One has proclaimed these to be ascetic toil."

11.247 The vulgate editions and most manuscripts add here a verse, which is 248 in Bühler's translation: "Thus I have described to you above penances for sins in accordance with the rules. Listen next to the penances for secret sins." This verse is omitted in the critical edition.

11.256 *a reprehensible act* (apraśastam): most commentators take this as referring to voiding urine or excrement in water. Medhātithi, Bhāruci, and Govinda, correctly I think, take it to mean sexual intercourse. This may be carried out in water or on water, i.e., in a boat. See 11.174 n. and 11.175.

11.265 *primary Yajus formulas:* according to Bhāruci, these are the formulas found in the *Yajurveda Saṃhitā* and not those given within the Brāhmaṇas; according to Medhātithi and Govinda, the "chief ones" (*mukhyāni*). The alternate reading, supported by most commentators and mss., is *anyāni:* "Yajus formulas that are different (from the Ṛc)."

11.266 *tri-syllabic Veda:* that is, the syllable OṂ, which consists of the phonemes "a," "u," and "m." But see the different explanation in the additional half-verse below.

Additional verse: "I have described to you above all the set rules with regard to penance. Listen now to the rules of action that secure the supreme good" (cf. 12.82).

Two additional half-verses: "Next, I will describe the highest rules relating to cyclical existence." And: "By taking the Brāhmaṇas and the Kalpas separately, the Veda is called by tradition threefold."

CHAPTER TWELVE

12.4 *One should . . . by the mind:* the genitive *dehinaḥ* has been understood differently by commentators. Govinda and Kullūka, and following them Bühler, take it as an adjective qualifying *tasya,* just like the other genitives in the sentence. The meaning then is that action is "connected to the body." The term *dehin* as meaning "he who possesses a body," i.e., the embodied self, is so ingrained the Sāmkhya philosophical tradition within which Manu operates, that it is unlikely to have a different meaning here; we find the term used with this meaning at 12.13. Further, in the previous verse only one kind of action is connected with *deha,* the other two are connected with speech and mind. The confusion is created by the numerous genitives in the sentence with somewhat different syntactical functions. "Three kinds": highest, middling, and lowest; "three bases": mind, speech, and body (although, Medhātithi inverts these two lists); "ten characteristics" are the three kinds of mental action, the four kinds of verbal action, and the three kinds of bodily action listed in 5–7.

12.8 Additional verse: "A man should abandon the path of ten actions—three kinds performed with the body, four with speech, and three with the mind."

12.10 *The rod of speech . . . triple-rodded:* the critical edition has adopted the reading *niyatāḥ* in place of the vulgate *nihitāḥ*. If we follow the latter, the translation would be: "a man in whose intellect these are firmly fixed." The rods then would have a positive significance. But in the very next verse (12.11), rod is viewed as something that should not be used, giving it a negative meaning; the same negative meaning is apparent in the three verses added in several mss. I think this is correct; rod means the use of mental, verbal, and physical actions to harm other creatures. "Triple-rodded" (*tridaṇḍin*), or triple-staffed, is an allusion to a Brahmanical renouncer who carries a triple-staff or a tripod (see 9.296 n.). If we take the three rods as tied together (restrained) to form the triple-rod (or triple-staff), then we can see how *niyata* (restrained, controlled) makes sense within this simile. This verse also occurs in ascetic literature and is probably borrowed by Manu from such a source. Variant reading: "the rod of mind, and the rod of body."

Two additional verses: "When they are not well guarded, the rod of speech destroys the intelligence; the rod of mind, the highest state; and the rod of action, the three worlds. One should practice silence with respect to the rod of speech, and fasting with respect to the rod of action; but with respect to the rod of mind, the control of breath is enjoined."

Third additional verse.: "A Yogin should carry the bodily triple staff and not the one of bamboo: he should carry according to rule the one consisting of speech, body, and mind."

12.12–3 *The one who . . . succeeding births:* these verses contain several technical terms: *kṣetrajña* refers to the spirit that observes the body and its activities as if they were a field (*kṣetra*); *bhūtātman* is a term that is less clear (see also 5.109), but probably refers to a self made of material elements but which acts as a center of consciousness; *jīva* generally refers to the individual self within the body and identical with *kṣetrajña*. Here Manu appears to be making a distinction between the two.

12.14 *Mahat:* in Sāṃkhya philosophy this term refers to the intellect (*buddhi*).

Additional verse: "The highest Person, however, is another. He is called the Highest Self, the Lord, who, entering the three worlds, bears the Unmanifest."

12.16 *five elemental particles:* earth, water, air, fire, and ether, which constitute the normal earthly body of a human being.

12.17 *After experiencing . . . corresponding particle:* this verse is extremely unclear. Bühler admits that the interpretation of Medhātithi and others, which he follows, assumes that the verse is ungrammatical. Given that verse 18 flows directly from verse 16, it is possible that this verse has been taken from a different source with a different context, making it difficult to understand its original meaning. On the meaning of *vibhāgaśaḥ*, see *bhāgaśaḥ* in verse 22.

12.18 *two beings of great power:* commentators identify these differently: Medhātithi, Rāghavānanda: Great One (*mahat*) and the Knower of the field (*kṣetrajña*); Nārāyaṇa: individual soul (*jīva*) and the Highest Self (*paramātman*); Bhāruci, Govinda, Kullūka: Great One and Highest Self. I favor the first interpretation, because they are mentioned in verse 14.

12.24 *body:* I take *ātman* here to mean body, the same way as it did in verse 12. In the very next verse (25), *deha* ("body") appears to be used as a synonym.

12.32 *resolve* (dhairyam): the sandhi *ārambharucitādhairyam* makes it possible also to read *adhairyam*, and this reading is preferred by all the commentators. Bühler, following this reading, translates: "want of firmness." I have preferred to take *dhairyam* (without sandhi coalescence with the previous word) because resolve and firmness is actually an attribute of vigor. In verse 36, for example, seeking to win fame and not giving way to disappointment are given as characteristics of vigor; and in verses 46 kings, royal chaplains, and soldiers are said to possess the attribute of vigor, and these individuals clearly have resolve and firmness. The virtue of *dhairya* here also contrasts nicely with *adhṛti* (lack of resolve) of Darkness in the very next verse.

12.45 Variant reading: "men who live by the use of arms."

12.59 Variant reading: "those who eat impure food become worms."

12.61 *goldsmiths:* some, including Medhātithi, interpret the term *hemakartṛ* as referring to a particular species of bird.

12.67 Variant reading: "by stealing fruits or roots."

12.70 *Dasyu:* this term can refer to a particular ethnic group (10.32), or barbarians ((10.45), or simply bandits (7.143).

Variant reading; "servants of their enemies."

12.76 Variant reading: "the dreadful tortures of being boiled in vats."

12.78 *being wrapped . . . for others:* Bühler translates: "imprisonment in fetters hard to bear, and the misery of being enslaved by others." I think the second half of this verse deals with childhood, as the first half did with birth; the following two verses likewise deal with various vicissitudes of life and finally with old age, sickness, and death. The wrapping must refer to the swaddling of infants, and servile work to serving the teacher during studentship.

12.84–5 *Among all these . . . immortality:* it could also be that verse 84 is a question to which 85 provides the answer. I think that these two verses may be interpolated, because verse 86 directly flows from 83, and the rest of this section deals with the centrality of the Veda and vedic rites.

12.88 *advancing, arresting:* this is a well-known division of activities enjoined by the Veda. The advancing (*pravṛtta*) acts prolong saṃsāric existence by procuring heaven or better births. These activities include all rituals and moral/immoral acts. The arresting (*nivṛtta*), on the other hand, are intended to suppress the advance of saṃsāric existence and to bring about liberation. These include pursuit of knowledge, meditation, and renunciation. For a study of these two concepts, see Bailey 1985.

12.91–3 *A man who . . . never otherwise:* just like verses 84–5 (see note to them), these also look suspicious. Verse 94 and the rest of this section dealing with the Veda quite naturally connect with verses 88–90 dealing with vedic rites.

12.95–6 *The scriptures . . . to recent times:* the reference here must be to scriptural texts of traditions such as Buddhism and Jainism, which were gaining in popularity and power during the time when the *MDh* was composed. A common variant for "scriptures" (*śrutayaḥ*) of the critical edition is *smṛtayaḥ* ("traditional texts") found in many manuscripts and editions.

12.97 *established:* Bhāruci, Nandana, and Rāghavānanda take the term *prasidhyati* to mean "known from the Veda." This is followed by Bühler. Medhātithi, Govinda, and Kullūka take it to mean receiving the authority from the Veda. See the similar use of *prasidhyati* at 11.238 and my note to it.

12.98 Variant reading; "are born from the Veda alone."

their origin . . . and action: this *pāda* has numerous variants and the reading is uncertain. Medhātithi says that he found a great many variants which he did not cite. Medhātithi take *guṇakarma* as a Karmadhāraya compound, and following this interpretation Bühler translates: "(their) production (is) through the (Vedic rites, which in this respect are) secondary rites." This is a labored interpretation. I think *guṇakarma* is a Dvandva compound. For the various interpretations offered by commentators, see Bühler's note to this verse.

12.106 *record of the seers* (ārṣa): the meaning is not altogether clear. Most commentators take the term to mean the Veda. Nārāyaṇa thinks it refers to the *smṛtis*.

12.109 *knowledgeable in scripture, perception, and inference* (śrutipratyakṣahetavaḥ): Bühler, following Kullūka, translates: "are able to adduce proofs perceptible by the senses from the revealed texts." I think Medhātithi is right in taking this to be a Bahuvrīhi compound, although admittedly somewhat unusual. For Dvandvas used as Bahuvrīhis, see Wackernagel 1957–78, II-1, 280. See verse 105 where these three sources of knowledge are viewed as essential for a man who knows the Law.

12.111 *A man who . . . ten members:* the difference between *hetuka* and *tarkin* is unclear. Commentators take the latter to mean a Mīmāṃsika. The term *nairukta* refers to a specialist in the Nirukta, the science of explaining words that is much more than mere etymology. The first three orders, according to most commentators, are student, householder, and hermit. Some, however, think that they are student, householder, and wandering ascetic, both because a hermit is not allowed to enter a village and because in Gautama (*GDh* 3.2) the hermit is listed last.

12.120 *spaces:* the reference probably is to bodily cavities.

12.121 *Hari:* generally, this is an epithet of Viṣṇu. Given that Viṣṇu is already mentioned, the epithet probably refer to Indra, as pointed out by several commentators. A common variant reads "Hara," i.e., Śiva.

CRITICAL EDITION

Introduction to the Critical Edition

I. Editorial History and the Need for a Critical Edition

The *MDh* was the first Indian legal text to be introduced to the western world through the translation of Sir William Jones in 1794. A few years later, 1813, the first printed edition of the Sanskrit text was published in Calcutta, with a revised edition appearing in 1830. The two early European editions were published by G. C. Haughton in 1825 and by Loiseleur Deslongschamp in 1830. Three major events in Manu scholarship followed each other in quick succession: the publication of the text with eight commentaries by V. N. Mandlik in 1887, Jolly's edition the same year, and Bühler's translation in 1886. The Sanskrit text of the *MDh* has been published in various editions far more frequently than any other legal text. On the whole, Jolly's (1887, v) assessment that most subsequent editions "are on the whole nothing but reprints of the two earliest Calcutta editions" holds good even for those published in more recent times.

All the editions of the *MDh*, except for Jolly's, reproduce the text as found in the manuscripts containing the commentary of Kullūka. I have called this the "vulgate version." Indeed, Jolly (1887, xiv) distinguishes his work from the other editions with the remark that "the fundamental difference between all previous editions on the one hand and the *present text* on the other hand consists of its independence of Kullūka." It was Kullūka's version that has been translated repeatedly: Jones (1794), Burnell (1884), Bühler (1886), and Doniger (1991). The exceptions are the edition and translation by Jha (1920–39), which was based on Medhātithi's commentary, and by Derrett (1975), which was based on Bhāruci's commentary. The belief in the authenticity of Kullūka's text was openly articulated by Burnell (1884, xxix): "There is then no doubt that the *textus receptus*, viz., that of Kullūka Bhaṭṭa, as adopted in India and by European scholars, is very near on the whole to the original text." This is far from the truth. Indeed, one of the great surprises of my editorial work has been to discover how few of the over 50 mss. that I collated actually follow the vulgate in key readings.

Derrett (1975, I: 28) as he edited the commentary of Bhāruci from a single extant manuscript expressed what I think was a collective wish of the scholarly community: "A critical edition of Manu is as much a desideratum as was that of the *Mahābhārata* or the *Rāmāyaṇa*, as Jolly's beginning was only a beginning." My hope is that this edition will fill that desideratum.

II. SOURCES FOR THE CRITICAL EDITION

This critical edition of the *MDh* is based on a systematic search of manuscripts, the collation of 53 manuscripts and of citations by 12 authors, the examination of 38 other manuscripts, and the close reading of 9 commentaries. Although the *MDh* shares numerous verses in common with the *Mahābhārata* and other Dharmaśāstras, I have not used them in constituting the text. I wanted to remain strictly faithful to the manuscript tradition of the *MDh* and to avoid a hybrid edition. The only exception has been the section containing portions of the *MDh* in the *Bhaviṣya Purāṇa*, because I consider the parallel passage in the *Bhaviṣya* to be a citation.

II.1 Description of the Manuscripts

The following are the manuscripts used in the critically constituted text. They are introduced by a siglum. The initial letter in small caps indicate the scripts: B = Bengali; G = Grantha; M = Malayalam; N = Old Nāgarī; S = Śāradā; T = Telugu; W = Newari; no letter is appended when the script is Devanāgarī. The two following letters identify the current location of the manuscript. A final superscript digit is added if there are multiple manuscripts from the same location.

Be¹ Banaras Hindu University. Ms. No. B 1843. *Descriptive Catalogue Samskrit Manuscripts in Gaekwada Library, Bhārat Kalābhavana Library and Samskrit Mahā-Vidyālaya Library, Banaras Hindu University*. Ed. Ramā Śaṅkar Tripāṭhī. 1971, p. 384. Serial number 7/3916.

Paper; Devanāgarī script; 26.7 x 13.2 cms; 155 folios; 10 lines on a page; 29 *akṣaras* on a line; complete. Dated Saṃvat 1850 [= 1793 CE]. Verses are numbered. Carefully written, but with frequent haplography. Occasional marginal comments explaining words. A photocopy was used. Colophon:

संपूर्णः शुभं सं 1850 वैशाखशुदि 7 शुक्रे समाप्तं

BBe² Government Sanskrit College, Benares. Ms. No. 12846. *A Descriptive Catalogue of the Sanskrit Manuscripts Acquired for and Deposited in the Government Sanskrit College Library, Sarasvati Bhavana, Banaras, during the years 1791–1950*. Ed. Kuberanath Shukla. Vol. III. Banaras, 1956, pp. 100–01.

Palm leaf [written with ink]; Bengali script; 15.3 x 3.3 ins. 75 folios; 10 lines on a page; 72 *akṣaras* on a line; complete. Carefully written. A photocopy was used. The colophon occupies two lines but is difficult to decipher.

Be³ Banaras Hindu University. Ms. No. B 1844. *Descriptive Catalogue Samskrit Manuscripts in Gaekwada Library, Bhārat Kalābhavana Library and Samskrit Mahā-Vidyālaya Library, Banaras Hindu University*. Ed. Ramā Śaṅkar Tripāṭhī. Banaras, 1971, p. 384. Serial number 7/3907.

Paper; Devanāgarī script; 38.5 x 20 cms; 70 folios [but folios 1-10, 36, 51 missing]; 10 lines on a page; 40–45 *akṣaras* on a line; incomplete [contains only 2.70 — 8.347]. No date. Some pages damaged and torn; carefully written by several hands. A photocopy was used.

Bo Bombay University Library. Ms. No. 945. *Descriptive Catalogue of the Saṃskṛta and Prākṛta Manuscripts (Bhagvatsinghji Collection & H. M. Bhadkamkar Collection) in the Library of the University of Bombay*, Book I (Vol. I & II: Parts I–III). Ed. G. V. Devasthale. Bombay, 1944, p. 343.

Paper; Devanāgarī script; 8.25 x 4 ins; 152 folios; 9 lines on a page; 33 *akṣaras* on a line; complete [folio 93 missing containing 8.223–42]. Dated Śaka 1672 [= 1750 CE]. Carefully written. A photocopy was used. Colophon:

शके 1672 प्रमोदाब्दे कार्तिकवददशम्यांमिंदौ इदं पुस्तकं समाप्तिमगमत् श्रीराम जय राम जय जय रामार्पणं

BCa Asiatic Society of Bengal. Ms. No. 5218. *A Descriptive Catalogue of Sanskrit Manuscripts in the Government Collection under the care of The Asiatic Society of Bengal.* Ed. Haraprasad Shāstrī. Vol. III: Smṛti Manuscripts. Calcutta, 1925. Serial No. 1852.

Palm leaf [written with ink]; Bengali script; 36.25 x 4.4 cms; 142 folios; 5 lines on a page; 56–61 *akṣaras* on a line; complete [but the Chapter 1 is so torn that I was unable to collate it]. Dated Śaka 1462 [= 1540 CE]. Much damaged. A microfilm was used. Colophon (as given in the catalog):

शुभमस्तु शकाब्दाः 1462 से 937 ।। तिथौ षष्ट्यां शुक्रवारे संपूर्णां चापि पुस्तिका । भुजे ऋतुवेदचन्द्रे शाके मासे च आषाढे ।। विलिखेद्रामचन्द्रेण सदा ग्रन्थावलोकिना । वरेन्द्रे तिष्ठता तेन धर्म्मसं + + + सदा ।। श्रीरस्तु लेखके । श्रीकृष्णचरणेभ्यो नमः । सिद्धिरस्तु क्रियारम्भे वृद्धिरस्तु धनागमे । पुष्टिरस्तु शरीरे मे शान्तिरस्तु सदा गृहे ।।

Ho Panjab University, Hoshiarpur. Acc. No. 799. *Descriptive Catalogue of Manuscripts of the VVBISIS Collection, Panjab University.* Ed. B. R. Sharma. Hoshiarpur, 1975, p. 26. Serial No. 322.

Paper; Devanāgarī script; 23.5 x 11.3 cms; 174 folios; between 9 and 12 lines on a page; 29 *akṣaras* on a line; complete [first folio torn containing 1.1–5]. Dated Saṃvat 1763 [= 1707 CE]. Carefully written; verses are numbered. A photocopy was used. Colophon:

संवत् 1763 अत्र वर्षे शुभमासमहामांगल्यमाघशुक्ला अचर[इ]डा 7 सप्तमीबुधदिने [3 letters unreadable] तद्दिने लिखितमिदं यादवराइ [several letters unreadable] शुभं भूयात् ।। संपूर्णमस्तु

Hy Osmania University, Hyderabad. Acc. No. B 23/7. *A Catalogue of the Sanskrit Manuscripts in the Osmania University Library.* Ed. A. Sharma et al. Hyderabad, 1964, p. 35.

Paper; Devanāgarī script; 20 x 13 cms; 181 folios; 9 lines on a page; 25 *akṣaras* on a line; complete. No date [catalog assigns it to 18th century]. Neatly but somewhat carelessly written, with frequent omissions of vowel signs. A photocopy was used. No colophon.

Jm Sri Ranbir Sanskrit Research Institute, Jammu. Ms. No. 636. *Descriptive Catalogue of Sanskrit Manuscripts in Shri Ranbir Sanskrit Research Institute.*

Ed. M. M. Patkar. Vol. 2. Jammu, 1973, p. 422. Serial nos. 373, 374, 379. Contains a commentary in Hindi.

Paper; Devanāgarī script; 34 x 21 cms; 565 folios; written with a broad pen and having varying numbers of lines on a page and *akṣaras* on a line; complete. No date. Folios containing 8.54–94; 9.14–18; 9.283–85; 10.45–50, 12.66–126 are missing. A photocopy was used. No colophon because the last pages are lost.

Jo[1] Rajasthan Oriental Research Institute, Jodhpur. Ms. No. 8599. *A Catalogue of Sanskrit and Prakrit Manuscripts in the Rajasthan Oriental Research Institute*. Ed. Padmashri Muni Jinavijaya. Part II (A). Jodhpur, 1964, p. 32.

Paper; Devanāgarī script; 28.8 x 15.6 cms; 138 folios; 10 lines on a page; 35 *akṣaras* on a line. Carefully written; verses are numbered. A photocopy was used. Colophon:

समाप्तैषा मनुसंहिता ।।

Jo[2] Maharaja Mansingh Pustak Prakash, Jodhpur. Acc. No. 898. Contains the commentary of Rāghavānanda Sarasvatī.

Paper; Devanāgarī script; 12 x 27 cms; 249 folios; 12–13 lines on a page; 42 *akṣaras* on a line in the section containing the text. Dated Saṃvat 1595 [= 1538 CE]. Carefully written. A photocopy was used. Colophon:

संवत् 1595 वर्षे आश्वनवदि 14 शुक्रे लिखितोयं ग्रंथः । करकृतमपराधं क्षंतुमर्हंतु संतः । श्रीमन्मुरार्यायार्यात्मजश्रीनाथेन लिखितभटोत् [last letters unclear]

wKt[1] National Archives, Kathmandu, Nepal. Ms. No. 4.713.

Paper; Newari script; 121 folios; 29 x 9.5 cms; 9 lines on a page; 35 *akṣaras* on a line; new hand from folio 31b (3.242); frequently "l" for "r" and vice versa; confusion between dental and palatal sibilant (Nepali way of pronouncing?). No date. A microfilm was used. Colophon:

यादृशं पुस्तकं दृष्टं तादृशं लिखितं मया । यदि शुद्धमशुद्धं वा मम दोषो न दीयती ।।

Kt[2] National Archives, Kathmandu, Nepal. Mss. No. 2.59. Contains the commentary of Kullūka.

Paper; Devanāgarī script; 290 folios; 40 x 16.5 cms; 11–14 lines on a page; 55 *akṣaras* on a line; clearly written; complete. No date. First 11 folios contain an *anukramaṇikā* up to the 7th *adhyāya*. A microfilm was used. No colophon.

wKt[3] National Archives, Kathmandu, Nepal. Ms. No. 1.1266.

Palm leaf written with ink; Newari script, with occasional Devanāgarī; 110 folios; 29.5 x 9 cms; 6 lines on a page; 60 *akṣaras* on a line; Incomplete; ends at 12.118. No date. A microfilm was used. Frequent scribal errors, especially metathesis and confusion between dental and palatal sibilants, dental and retroflex nasals; "l" and "r."

NKt[4] National Archives, Katmandu, Nepal. Ms. No. 411.

Palm leaf [written with ink]; Old Nāgarī script; 206 folios; 25 x 5 cms; 5 lines on a page; 45 *akṣaras* on a line; first page [up to 1.4c] missing; complete. Dated

Saṃvat 1239 [= June 10, 1182]; written in Vārānasī. Some lacunae, indicating that the scribe's exemplar was defective. A microfilm was used. Colophon [very faint; this is an approximation]:

अद्य ह श्रीमद्वाराणस्यां महाराजाविरजश्रीजयच्चन्द्रदेवराष्ट्रे ।। संवत् 1239 आषा-ढसुदि 7 बुध ।। उत्थासनिकराउतश्रीसुरहि आत्मार्थे इदं पुस्तिका लिखापि-तमिति ।। मङ्गलं महाश्री: शुभं भवतु लेखकपाठकयोरिति ।।

BKt[5] National Archives, Kathmandu, Nepal. Ms. No. 5.336.

Palm leaf; Bengali script with Newari influence; 36.5 X 5 cms; 130 folios; 5 lines on a page; 65-75 *akṣaras* on a line; complete; frequent marginal additions and corrections; many lacuna indicating that his exemplar was defective; frequently writes "y" for "j"; "n" for "ḍ". A microfilm was used. Closely related to wKt[6]. Colophon:

न सं 388 कार्त्तिक शुदि दशम्यां

wKt[6] National Archives, Kathmandu, Nepal. Ms. No. 1.1283.

Palm leaf; Newari script; 64 folios; 7 lines on a page; 48–50 *akṣaras* on a line. First 6 folios not the *MDh*, which starts at 2.179c [so Chapters 1 and 2 up to 178b are missing]; again 2.187-207 are omitted; incomplete [ends at 8.8]. A microfilm was used. Closely related to wKt[5].

La[1] Panjab University Library, Lahore. Acc. No. 5112. *Catalogue of the Sanskrit Manuscripts in the Panjab University Library*. Vol. 1. Lahore, 1932, p. 97. Cat. No. 466.

Paper; Devanāgarī script; 24 x 10.3 cms; 111 folios; 10 lines on a page; 40 *akṣaras* on a line; complete [folios 5, 14, and 109 missing]; numerous marginal glosses and correction. The catalog and library card attached to the ms. give the date as Saṃvat 1507 [= 1450–51 CE], even though I do not find a date in the ms. itself. The last page, however, is now missing, and it may have contained the colophon with the date. A photocopy was used.

La[2] Panjab University Library, Lahore. *Catalogue of the Sanskrit Manuscripts in the Panjab University Library*. Vol. 1. Lahore, 1932, p. 97. Cat. No. 470.

Paper; Devanāgarī script; 20.3 x 17 cms; 67 folios; 22 lines on a page; 19 *akṣaras* on a line; incomplete [ends at 8.5]. No date. A photocopy was used.

Lo[1] Welcome Institute, MS Indic ß 1192

Paper; Devanāgarī script; 9.5 x 25 cms; 9 lines on a page; 25 *akṣaras* on a line; complete. A microfilm was used. No colophon.

Lo[2] British Library [India Office], Ms. No. IO 2337. *Catalogue of the Sanskrit Manuscripts in the Library of the India Office*. Ed. J. Eggeling. Part I. Vedic Manuscripts. London: 1887, p. 367. Cat. No. 1257.

Paper; Devanāgarī script [Bengali influence]; 257 folios; 25 x 13.1 cms; 10 lines on a page; 30 *akṣaras* on a line; complete. A microfilm was used. No colophon.

Lo[3] British Library [India Office], Ms. No. Burnell 527. *Catalogue of Sanskrit and Prākrit Manuscripts in the Library of the India Office*. Ed. A. B. Keith.

Vol. II. Oxford, 1935, p. 360–61. Cat. No. 5285. Contains the commentary of Rāghavānanda Sarasvatī.

European paper [watermarked Dorling & Gregory, London, 1875]; Devanāgarī script [Ch. 12. in a different hand]; 355 + 20 folios; 124.4 x 8.8 cms; 20 lines on a page; 23 *akṣaras* on a line; complete. Date given in a note on the fly-leaf as A. B. [AD?] 1876 in Tanjore. A microfilm was used. No colophon. This ms. was used by Jolly with the siglum R1. No colophon.

Lo[4] British Library [India Office], Ms. No. IO 1407–10. *Catalogue of the Sanskrit Manuscripts in the Library of the India Office*. Ed. J. Eggeling. Part I. Vedic Manuscripts. London: 1887, p. 367–68. Cat. No. 1264–67. Contains the commentary of Medhātithi.

Paper; Devanāgarī script; 31.3 x 13.2 cms; ms. in four parts with 253 [*adhyāyas* 1–3], 190 [*adhyāyas* 4–7], 186 [*adhyāyas* 8, 10, 11], and 55 [*adhyāya* 9] folios; 10 lines on a page; 45–50 *akṣaras* on a line; incomplete [Ch. 12 is missing]. First three parts dated Saṃvat 1845–46 [= 1789–90 CE], and the last part dated Saṃvat 1865 [= 1809 CE]. This ms. was used by Ganganath Jha in his edition of Medhātithi. A microfilm was used. This ms. was used by Jolly with the siglum M4.

Lo[5] British Library [India Office], Ms. No. Burnell 522–23. *Catalogue of Sanskrit and Prākrit Manuscripts in the Library of the India Office*. Ed. A. B. Keith. Vol. II. Oxford, 1935, p. 359; Cat. No. 5281. Contains the commentary of Medhātithi.

European paper [watermarked Charles & Thomas, London, 1879]; Devanāgarī script; 26.3 x 20.1 cms; ms. is in two parts with 246 and 196 folios; 23 lines on a page; 26 *akṣaras* on a line; incomplete [only chapters 1–8; verses 9.52–58 inserted after 8.58]. According to a note on folio 1, this is a copy of Lo[4]. A microfilm was used.

GMd[1] Adyar Library, Madras. Ms. No. VB 135. *Descriptive Catalogue of Sanskrit Manuscripts*. Ed. E. R. Sreekrishna Sarma. Vol. 13: Viśvabhāratī Collection. Madras, 1976, p. 134. Cat. No. 730E.

Palm leaf; Grantha script; 39.5 x 3.5 cms; 112 folios; 8 lines on a page; 48 *akṣaras* on a line. Complete. Good handwriting with few mistakes [handwriting changes at 3.21; then at 3.282; and goes back to original hand at 4.32]. Very small letters sometimes difficult to read; ms. is broken at the ends and moth eaten; so some letters missing. No date. A photocopy was used. Ms. belonged to one Dharmaśivācārya. Colophon [faint, letters broken and difficult to read; the following is an approximation]:

हरिः ॐ श्रीरघुनन्दनाय नमः हरिः ॐ श्रीमान्धर्मवोर्ग्यो विलसतु लोके सफलयन्साधून् यस्मिन्नन्यदुरापा [two *akṣaras* broken] शंभोः रुजा [several *akṣaras* broken] योगिनां प्रवरो धर्मशिवाचार्य इति क्षितौ विख्यातश्शोभते यस्तु तस्येयं मानवी स्मृतिः हरिः ॐ शुभमस्तु

OMd[2] Adyar Library, Madras. Ms. No. 33A20. *A Catalogue of the Samskrit Manuscripts in the Adyar Library*. Madras, 1926, p. 102.

Palm leaf; Oriya script; 77 folios; approximately 37 x 3.6 cms; 4 lines on a page; 60 *akṣaras* on a line. Incomplete [ends at 4.258, after which are the words *bhṛgusaṃhitāḥ samāptāḥ*. A photocopy was used.

TMd³ Government Oriental Manuscripts Library, Madras. Ms. No. D 2664. *A Descriptive Catalogue of the Sanskrit Manuscripts in the Government Oriental Manuscripts Library, Madras*. Ed. M. Raṅgācārya. Vol. V: Dharma-śāstra. Madras, 1909, p. 1957.

Paper; Telugu script; 31.3 x 20 cms; 122 folios [244 numbered pages]; 20 lines on a page; 19 *akṣaras* on a line; complete. No date [appears modern]. Subject headings are placed at the top of pages; frequent glosses explaining words. A photocopy was used. No colophon.

TMd⁴ Government Oriental Manuscripts Library, Madras. Ms. No. D 2665. *A Descriptive Catalogue of the Sanskrit Manuscripts in the Government Oriental Manuscripts Library, Madras*. Ed. M. Raṅgācārya. Vol. V: Dharma-śāstra. Madras, 1909, p. 1957.

Palm leaf; Telugu script; 42.5 x 3.5 cms; 8 lines on a page; 70 *akṣaras* on a line; complete. No date. This ms. begins on folio 83 of a larger composite ms., the first 82 folios containing another work [= Ms. No. 2616]. Several times the scribe leaves lacunae showing break or illegibility of the scribe's exemplar; shows also his faithfulness to the original, since often the break is just one syllable [cf. 2.108, 111, 178; 3.114, 118, 194, 250, 265; 4.151]. At 1224, the scribe gives 10.109—11191, indicating that his exemplar probably had folios mixed up and not in proper order. A photocopy was used. Much of the colophon is torn. The end of the śloka is legible: *mama doṣo no vidyate* [see under wKt¹].

GMd⁵ Government Oriental Manuscripts Library, Madras. Ms. No. D 2670. *A Descriptive Catalogue of the Sanskrit Manuscripts in the Government Oriental Manuscripts Library, Madras*. Ed. M. Raṅgācārya. Vol. V: Dharma-śāstra. Madras, 1909, p. 1958.

Palm leaf; Grantha script; 42 x 3.5 cms; 133 folios; 7 lines on a page; 60 *akṣaras* on a line; complete. No date. Carefully written by at least two scribes; in good condition. A photocopy was used. Colophon:

हरिः ॐ शुभमस्तु अविघ्नमस्तु श्रीमते रामानुजाय नमः श्रीमते श्रीनिवास-महादेषिकाय नमः

GMy Government Oriental Library, Mysore. Ms. No. 3899. *A Descriptive Catalogue of the Sanskrit Manuscripts in the Government Oriental Library, Mysore*. Ed. H. R. Rangaswami Iyengar and T. T. Srinivasagopalachar. Vol. II: Dharmaśāstra. Mysore, 1944, pp. 97–98. Cat, No. 82.

Palm leaf; Grantha script; 30.6 x 3 cms; 146 folios; 7 lines on a page; 43 *akṣaras* on a line; complete. No date. The ms. is moth-eaten and, especially at the beginning and end, torn; sometimes marginal glosses on words. A photocopy was used. Colophon:

ग्रन्थश्च समाप्तः । मनुस्मृतिसम्पूर्णम् ।। हरिः ॐ शुभमस्तु श्रीरामार्पणमस्तु

NNg Nagpur University Library, Ms. No. 1510. Catalogue of Sanskrit Manuscripts in the Nagpur University Library. Ed. V. W. Karambelkar. Nagpur, 1958, p. 325.

Paper; Old Nāgarī; 22.5 x 12.5 cms; 133 folios [first folio containing 1.1-12 missing]; 11 lines on a page; 36 *akṣaras* on a line; complete. Dated Saṃvat 1560 [= 1503 CE]. Carefully written by one Puruṣottamaka, but with numerous marginal corrections in first and second hand. A photocopy was used. Colophon [partly torn]:

ग्रंथसंख्या 2685 ।। श्रीरस्तु ।। स्वस्ति श्रीसंवत् 1560 वर्षे चैत्रमासे शुक्ल [broken] नक्षत्रे पौर्णमायां तिथौ शनिवारे अद्येह राजपुरवास्तव्यउदीच्य [broken] तीयबंधुलसगोत्रभटनरसिंहसुतपुरुषोत्तमकेन लि [broken] तथा भ्रातृपुत्रपौत्राणां अध्ययनार्थं मनुस्मृतिर्लिखितम् ।। श्रीर [broken] कल्याणमस्तु ।। श्रीविष्णोप्रसादात् सर्वं परिपूर्णतामस्तु ।। श्री ।। ।। श्री ।। भग्नपृष्टकटिग्रीवो बद्धमुष्टीरधोमुखी । कष्टेन लिखितं शास्त्रं यत्नेन परिपालयेत् ।। यादृशं पुस्तके दृष्ट्वा तादृशं लिखितं मया । यदि शुद्धमशुद्धं वा मम दोषो न दीयते ।। श्री ।।

oOr Orissa State Museum, Ms. No. Dh/785. *An Alphabetical Catalogue of Sanskrit Manuscripts in the Collection of the Orissa State Museum*. Ed. N. Mishra. Part I. Bhubaneswar, 1973, p. 179. Cat. No. 1703.

Palm leaf; Oriya script; 157 folios; 4 lines on a page; 65 *akṣaras* on a line; complete. No date. Carelessly written with frequent scribal errors. A microfilm was used. Colophon:

यदि शुद्धमशूद्धं वा मम दोषो न दीयते । [broken] पुस्तकं हरते [broken] । मृताः स्वर्गं न गच्छति पितरं नरकं व्रजेत् ।।

sOx¹ Bodleian Library, Oxford. Ms. No. Sanskrit e. 64. *Catalogue of Sanskrit Manuscripts in the Bodleian Library*. Ed. M. Winternitz and A. B. Keith. Vol. II. Oxford, 1905. Cat. No. 1484.

European paper; Śāradā script; 15 x 22 cms; 128 folios; 23 lines on a page; 21 *akṣaras* on a line; complete. Date 1857 CE; different hand from folio 90a. The manuscript was bought by Bodleian from Eugen Hultzsch in 1887. This is a copy of ms. sPu⁶ [Bhandarkar Oriental Research Institute, Pune. Ms. No. 355 of 1 875-76] and was probably made for Hultzsch. Frequently sOx¹ gives the marginal corrections found in sPu⁶ (see 5.85b). At 8.85 there is a lacuna in sPu⁶ and filled in *sh* incorrectly; this is replicated in sOx¹. The ms. is still useful because it contains several sections that are currently missing or torn in the original sPu⁶; the copy was, therefore, made before the original was damaged. A microfilm was used. Colophon:

संवत् 34 अश्ववाति 7 परतः 10 शनौ ।। संपूर्णं समाप्तम् ।।

Ox² Bodleian Library, Oxford. Ms. No. Sanskrit c. 32. *Catalogue of Sanskrit Manuscripts in the Bodleian Library*. Ed. M. Winternitz and A. B. Keith. Vol. II. Oxford, 1905. Cat. No. 1483.

European paper with watermark; Devanāgarī script; 25.4 x 37 cms; 155 folios; 15 lines on a page; 22 *akṣaras* on a line; complete. Dated November 27, 1789; scribe Lala Mahatab Rai. The copy was made for Sir William Jones and acquired by the

Bodleian in 1833. Contains an interlinear translation by Jones partly into Latin and partly into English. A microfilm was used.

Ox³ Bodleian Library, Oxford. Ms. No. Max Müller memorial c. 33. *A Catalogue of the Manuscripts Purchased for the Administrators of the Max Müller Memorial Fund.* Ed. T. R. Gambier-Parry. Oxford, 1922, p. 55. Contains the commentary of Medhātithi.

Indian paper; Devanāgarī script [with some Bengali influence]; 33.75 x 13.75 cms; 394 folios; 12 lines on a page; 46 *akṣaras* on a line; incomplete; carelessly written; verses of chapters 8 and 9 mixed up, the following being omitted: **8.**1–14, 47–9, 59–61, 133–8, 147–89, 198–364, 384–420; **9.**1–50, 60–137, 164–234, 247c–336; and chapters 10–12. No date but appears not too old. A microfilm was used. No colophon.

ɴPu¹ Bhandarkar Oriental Research Institute, Pune. Ms. No. 237 of 1879–80. *Descriptive Catalogue of Manuscripts in the Government Manuscripts Library Deposited at the Bhandarkar Oriental Research Institute*. Ed. H. D. Sharma. Vol. VII, Part II. Pune, 1996. Cat. No. 981.

Country paper; Old Nāgarī; 28.75 x 12 cms; 141 folios; 9 lines per page; 36 *akṣaras* on a line; complete. Date Saṃvat 1646 [= 1589 CE]. A photocopy was used. Colophon:

अपरं पुस्तकं वीक्ष्य शोधनीयं सदा बुधैः । हीनाधिक्यैः स्वरैर्वर्णैरस्माकं दूषणं न हि ।। संवत् 1646 वर्षे फाल्गुणवदि 11 शनौ अद्ये श्रीशक्रपुरवास्तव्यं उदीच्यग्न्या[ज्ञा]तीयश्रीश्रीराउलसोमनाथसुतविश्वनाथेन लिखितं यस्य पुस्तके विधान् [?] उपाध्याराजुरक्षसुतमहेंद्रपठनाय ।। श्रीरस्तु ।। छ ।। कल्याणमस्तु ।। श्लोकसंख्या 2709

Pu² Bhandarkar Oriental Research Institute. Ms. No. 208 of A/1881–82. *Descriptive Catalogue of Manuscripts in the Government Manuscripts Library Deposited at the Bhandarkar Oriental Research Institute*. Ed. H. D. Sharma. Vol. VII, Part II. Pune, 1996. Cat. No. 982.

Country paper; Devanāgarī script; 28 x 12.5 cms; 110 folios; 10 lines on a page; 38 *akṣaras* on a line; complete. A photocopy was used. Colophon:

मानवं शास्त्रं समाप्तं ।। शुभं भवतु ।।

Pu³ Bhandarkar Oriental Research Institute, Pune. Ms. No. 151 of 1895–1902. *Descriptive Catalogue of Manuscripts in the Government Manuscripts Library Deposited at the Bhandarkar Oriental Research Institute.* Ed. H. D. Sharma. Vol. VII, Part II. Pune, 1996. Cat. No. 985.

Country paper; 26.25 x 11.25 cms; 118 folios; 12 lines on a page; 31 *akṣaras* on a line; complete. Date Saṃvat 1681 [= 1624 CE]. Colophon:

संवत् 1672 श्रावणापरपक्षे त्रयोदश्यां सोमवासरे

Pu⁴ Jayakar Library, University of Poona. Ms. No. 1537. *Descriptive Catalogue of Manuscripts Available in the Jayakar Library, University of Poona*. Ed. S. G. Mahajan. Poona, 1986. Vol. 1. Cat. No. 544.

Paper; Devanāgarī script; 29 x 12.5 cms; 101 folios; 11 lines on a page; 35 *akṣaras* on a line; complete. Appears to follow Pu^2 closely, possibly a copy.

Pu^5 Bhāratīya Itihāsa Saṃśodhana Maṇḍala, Pune. Ms. No. 52/401. *Bhārata-Itihāsa-Saṃśodhana-Maṇḍalastha-Hastalikhitagranthānukramaṇikā*. Ed. H. G. Khare. Pune, 1960, p. 203. Contains the commentary of Govindarāja. Clearly a copy of Pu^7.

Paper; Devanāgarī script [but with many features of the Old Nāgarī]; 28.5 x 13 cms; 10 lines on a page; 41 *akṣaras* on a line; complete. No date. Very carelessly written; from folio 29b written by a different hand; numerous verses omitted. A photocopy was used. Colophon:

इदं पुस्तकं भागवतेत्युपनामकानां अबादैवज्ञानाज्ञेयं ।। श्रीलक्ष्मीनृसिंहार्पणमस्तु ।।

sPu^6 Bhandarkar Oriental Research Institute, Pune. Ms. No. 355 of 1875–76. *A Catalogue of the Collections of Manuscripts Deposited in the Deccan College with an Index*. Ed. S. R. Bhandarkar. Bombay, 1888, p. 93. Contains an anonymous and brief commentary.

Birch Bark; Śāradā script; 106 folios; 22 lines on a page; 27 *akṣaras* on a line; complete [last page lost, ms. ends at 12.120; thus, any colophon that may have existed is lost]. No date. A photocopy was used.

This ms. was used by Jolly in his 1887 edition using the siglum K, and by Bühler in his 1886 translation (see p. cxxxv, note 2). Jolly comments: "The last portion, from XI.218 onwards, has been partly lost." Although there are sections torn, much of the last section can be read. It is unclear whether the last page with any colophon was extant when Jolly examined this ms. Unfortunately, some of Jolly's readings from this ms. listed in his variants are wrong when compared to the original (e.g. 1.66, 80, 92; 5.60, 64, 65, 67; 11.90; Jolly says 2.79 is omitted when it is present); either Jolly or a collator of his has misread the Śāradā.

Pu^7 Bhandarkar Oriental Research Institute, Pune. Ms. No. 239 of 1879–80. *A Catalogue of the Collections of Manuscripts Deposited in the Deccan College with an Index*. Ed. S. R. Bhandarkar. Bombay, 1888, p. 138. Contains the commentary of Govindarāja.

Paper; Devanāgarī script [but with many features of the Old Nāgarī]; 29 x 12.5 cms; 250 folios; 13 lines on a page; 42 *akṣaras* on a line; complete; verses are numbered. No date. A photocopy was used. Colophon:

स्वस्ति श्रीश्रीस्तंभतीर्थे श्रीश्रीगुंरुज्ञातीयज्योतिर्विद्दी । धरणीधरसुतज्योतिर्व्वित्
मांइआसुतज्योतिर्व्वित्

The last page containing the rest of the colophon is lost. The last page of the ms. contains some extraneous material; this page is probably from a different ms., the paper and handwriting do not match the rest of the ms.

Pu^8 Bhāratīya Itihāsa Saṃśodhana Maṇḍala. Ms. No. 46/78. *Bhārata-Itihāsa-Saṃśodhana-Maṇḍalastha-Hastalikhitagranthānukramaṇikā*. Ed. H. G. Khare. Pune, 1960, p. 202.

Paper; Devanāgarī script; 28 x11.5 cms; 71 folios; 14 lines on a page; 60 *akṣaras* on a line; complete. Dated Saṃvat 1810 [= 1754 CE] Clear handwriting; very few corrections. A photocopy was used. Colophon:

श्रीसंवत् 1810 माघमासे कृष्णपक्षे बुधवारे शुभमस्तु ॥

Pu[9] Bhandarkar Oriental Research Institute, Pune. Ms. No. 650 of Viśrāma. *Descriptive Catalogue of Manuscripts in the Government Manuscripts Library Deposited at the Bhandarkar Oriental Research Institute*. Ed. H. D. Sharma. Vol. VII, Part II. Pune, 1996. Cat. No. 9896. Contains the commentary of Govindarāja. Clearly a copy of Pu[7].

Country paper; Devanāgarī script; 25.5 x 11.9 cms; 228 folios [but many folios missing]; 10 lines on a page; 38 *akṣaras* on a line; incomplete [first 13 folios missing; begins at 1.64 and ends at 7.56; folios containing verses 2.178c–194; 2.202–07; 3.02–224 4.107c–5.37 missing]. No date. A photocopy was used. No colophon.

Pu[10] Bhandarkar Oriental Research Institute, Pune. Ms. No. 105 of Viśrāma(i). *Descriptive Catalogue of Manuscripts in the Government Manuscripts Library Deposited at the Bhandarkar Oriental Research Institute.* Ed. H. D. Sharma. Vol. VII, Part II. Pune, 1996. Cat. No. 993. Contains the commentary of Medhātithi.

Country paper; Devanāgarī script; 28.5 x 12.5 cms; 453+8 folios; 12 lines on a page; 40 *akṣaras* on a line; incomplete [contains chapters 1-6 and 10-12]; 8 folios in the beginning contains table of contents. No date. A photocopy was used. Colophon:

समाप्तोयं मेधातिथिग्रन्थः ॥ शुभं भवतु ॥ लेखकयोः शुभं भवतु ॥ शुभं ॥

Tj[1] Sarasvati Mahal Library, Tanjore. Ms. No. B. L. 270. *A Descriptive Catalogue of the Sanskrit Manuscripts in the Tanjore Mahārāja Serfoji's Sarasvatī Mahāl Library, Tanjore.* Ed. Vidyāsāgara P. P. S. Sastri. Vol. XVIII. Sriranjam: Sri Vani Vilas Press, 1934. Cat. No. D 17880.

Paper; Devanāgarī script; 26.5 x 10.4 cms; 225 folios; 7 lines on a page; 30 *akṣaras* on a line; complete; verses are numbered with chapter headings; very clearly and carefully written; chapters 4–6 written in a different hand without chapter headings or verse numbers; Ch. 7 returns to the original scribe with chapter headings and numbers. No date. A photocopy was used. Colophon:

श्रीसांबसदाशिवो रक्षतु ॥ श्रीरस्तु ॥

Tj[2] Sarasvati Mahal Library, Tanjore. Ms. No. B. L. 271. *A Descriptive Catalogue of the Sanskrit Manuscripts in the Tanjore Mahārāja Serfoji's Sarasvatī Mahāl Library, Tanjore*. Ed. Vidyāsāgara P.P.S. Sastri. Vol. XVIII. Sriranjam: Sri Vani Vilas Press, 1934. Cat. No. D 17881.

Paper; Devanāgarī script; 30.7 x 11.5 cms; 83 folios; 11–13 lines on a page; 49 *akṣaras* on a line; complete; verses are numbered; many scribal errors. Date Saṃvat 1858 [= 1801 CE]. A photocopy was used. Colophon:

संवत् 1858 ॥ कार्त्तिककृष्णतृतीयायां धीनहुत्रीपाठीना लेष्य ॥ शुभमस्तु ॥ सिद्धिरस्तु ॥

Tr[1] University of Kerala Oriental Manuscript Library, Trivandrum. Ms. No.

7878. *Alphabetical Index of Sanskrit Manuscripts in the University Manuscripts Library, Trivandrum.* Ed. K. Raghavan Pillai. Trivandrum Sanskrit Series, No. 215. Trivandrum, 1964. Cat. No. 12504.

Paper; Devanāgarī script; approximately 26 x 11 cms; 124 folios; 9 lines of a page; 40 *akṣaras* on a line; incomplete [ms. ends at 12.98, final folios missing]; numerous marginal corrections by a second hand probably using a NT ms [see 9.161, 162, 166, 167, 205, 225, 251, 235, 243, 257]. No date. No colophon. A photocopy was used.

Tr² University of Kerala Oriental Manuscript Library, Trivandrum. Ms. No. 9648. *Alphabetical Index of Sanskrit Manuscripts in the University Manuscripts Library, Trivandrum.* Ed. K. Raghavan Pillai. Trivandrum Sanskrit Series, No. 215. Trivandrum, 1964. Cat. No. 12511. Contains the commentary of Rāmacandra.

Paper; Devanāgarī script; 256 folios; 10 lines on a page; 40 *akṣaras* on a line; complete; subject index at the end of ms. No date. No colophon. A photocopy was used.

mTr³ University of Kerala Oriental Manuscripts Library, Trivandrum. Ms. No. L89A. *Alphabetical Index of Sanskrit Manuscripts in the University Manuscripts Library, Trivandrum.* Ed. K. Raghavan Pillai. Trivandrum Sanskrit Series, No. 215. Trivandrum, 1964. Cat. No. 12502.

Palm leaf; Malayalam script; 90 folios; 10 lines on a page; 52 *akṣaras* on a line; incomplete [ends at 11.162a, although given as complete in the catalog]; neatly and legibly written; verses numbered; written in several different hands; in margins the topics treated in the corresponding verses are given. Date Malayalam era 1057 [= 1882 CE] according to the catalog. No colophon. A microfilm was used.

mTr⁴ University of Kerala Oriental Manuscripts Library, Trivandrum. Ms. No. 14704. *Alphabetical Index of Sanskrit Manuscripts in the University Manuscripts Library, Trivandrum.* Ed. K. Raghavan Pillai. Trivandrum Sanskrit Series, No. 215. Trivandrum, 1964. Cat. No. 12502.

Palm leaf; Malayalam script; 92 folios; 10 lines on a page; 55 *akṣaras* on a line; complete; good condition; neat and legibly written; verses unnumbered; chapters unnumbered; complete. No date. A microfilm was used. Colophon has many verses on a variety of topics and finally ends with:

यादृशं पुस्तके दृष्टं तादृशं लिखितं मया । यदि युक्तमयुक्तं वा मम दोषो न विद्यते ।। मानवं ग्रन्थं ।

mTr⁵ University of Kerala Oriental Manuscripts Library, Trivandrum. Ms. No. L320. *Alphabetical Index of Sanskrit Manuscripts in the University Manuscripts Library, Trivandrum.* Ed. K. Raghavan Pillai. Trivandrum Sanskrit Series, No. 215. Trivandrum, 1964. Cat. No. 12509. Contains the commentary of Bhāruci.

Palm leaf; Malayalam script; incomplete [the ms. begins at 6.9 and, although it contains the last verse 12.126, the final page is lost and the commentary on the last verse is incomplete]. No date.

I have used a color photograph of the original Malayalam ms. Two Devanāgarī copies of the original appear to have been made in Trivandrum, one for Derrett and used in his edition [now deposited in the Library of the School of Oriental and African Studies, London] and the other probably for Dave's edition. I have examined both copies, which often diverge from the original.

mTr⁶ University of Kerala Oriental Manuscripts Library, Trivandrum. Ms. No. 13002. *Alphabetical Index of Sanskrit Manuscripts in the University Manuscripts Library, Trivandrum.* Ed. K. Raghavan Pillai. Trivandrum Sanskrit Series, No. 215. Trivandrum, 1964. Cat. No. 12501.

Palm leaf; Malayalam script; 179 folios; 8 lines on a page; 39 *akṣaras* on a line; complete; carelessly written with numerous scribal errors; worm-eaten and damaged; from verse 5.86 written by a different hand; complete. No date. No Colophon. A microfilm was used. Colophon:

सर्वज्ञाय नमस्तस्मै महत्याकृपया त्विदम् । करोति धर्मशास्त्रं यो मनवे ब्रह्मसूनवे
।। श्रीकृष्णाय नमः श्रीषट्मुखाय नमः श्रीशंकराय नमः शुभमस्तु ।।

Wa Prājña Pāṭhaśālā Maṇḍala, Wai, Ms. No. 2840. *Descriptive Catalogue of Sanskrit Manuscripts*. Ed. Laxmanshastri Joshi. Part I. Wai, 1970, p. 360.

Paper; Devanāgarī script; 29.5 x 12.7 cms; 128 folios; 10 lines on a page; 36 *akṣaras* on a line; complete. No date. A photocopy was used. Colophon:

समाप्तमीदं शास्त्रं लेषकपाठयोः शुभं भूयात्

Other Manuscripts: In the course of preparing this edition, I examined manuscripts other than the ones used in critically constituting the text. To use all the mss. I had obtained would have been unwieldy and unnecessary. Just as taking multiple samples of the same puddle of blood from a crime scene does not provide better evidence, so having more manuscripts of the same genealogical branch does not enhance the edition. My method was then to collate a significant number of mss. fully thus creating a reliable genealogy. Then I collated only the third chapter of all the remaining mss. This gave me reliable clues with regard to the genealogy of each ms. Thereafter, I collated fully only those mss. that I thought held out hope of giving new data. I give below the 37 mss. that were not considered for the critical edition after the collation of chapter three:

Benares: Banaras Hindu University, Ms. No. C 5452. Bengali script with Kullūka's commentary. Follows NT–y (vulgate).

Benares: Banaras Hindu University, Ms. No. B 1844. Devanāgarī script. Follows NT–x.

Benares: Banaras Hindu University, Ms. No. B 4403. Devanāgarī script with Kullūka's commentary. Follows NT–y (vulgate).

Benares: Government Sanskrit College Library, Sarasvati Bhavan, Ms. No. 12881. Bengali script. Follows NT–x.

Benares: Government Sanskrit College Library, Sarasvati Bhavan, Ms. No. 13545. Devanāgarī script. Follows NT–x.

Jammu: Shri Raghunathji Temple, Dharmartha Trust Council. Ms. No. 2578.

Devanāgarī script with Kullūka's commentary. Follows NT–y (vulgate).

Jodhpur: Rajasthan Oriental Research Institute, Ms. No. 23493. Devanāgarī script. Follows NT–x.

Jodhpur: Rajasthan Oriental Research Institute, Ms. No. 3038. Devanāgarī script. Follows NT–x.

Jodhpur: Rajasthan Oriental Research Institute, Ms. No. 36614. Devanāgarī script. Follows NT–x.

Jodhpur: Rajasthan Oriental Research Institute, Ms. No. 4519. Devanāgarī script. Follows NT–x.

Katmandu: National Archives, Ms. No. E 725/1. Newari script. Follows NT–x.

Katmandu: National Archives, Ms. No. 3.575. Newari script. Follows NT–x.

Katmandu: National Archives, Ms. No. 5.2188. Newari script. Follows NT–x.

Katmandu: National Archives, Ms. No. 2.276. Devanāgarī script with Kullūka's commentary. Follows NT–y (vulgate).

Katmandu: National Archives, Ms. No. missing; Reel No. E-1351/5. Devanāgarī script. Follows NT–y (vulgate).

Katmandu: National Archives, Ms. No. 3.10. Devanāgarī script. Follows NT–x.

Katmandu: National Archives, Ms. No. 5.1876. Devanāgarī script. Follows NT–y (vulgate).

Katmandu: National Archives, Ms. No. 5.7757. Devanāgarī script. Follows NT–y (vulgate).

Katmandu: National Archives, Ms. No. 3.178. Devanāgarī script with a Nepali commentary. Follows NT–y (vulgate).

Katmandu: National Archives, Ms. No. missing; Reel No. G 23/3. Devanāgarī script. Follows NT–x.

Katmandu: National Archives, Ms. No. missing; Reel No. E 1430/36. Devanāgarī script. Follows NT–y (vulgate).

Katmandu: National Archives, Ms. No. 2.159. Devanāgarī script, with Nepali commentary. Follows NT–y (vulgate).

Katmandu: National Archives, Ms. No. 5.1514. Devanāgarī script. Follows NT–x.

London: British Library [India Office], Ms. No. OR 2151. Devanāgarī script with Kullūka's commentary. Follows NT–y (vulgate).

London: British Library [India Office], Ms. No. San Ms IO 236. Devanāgarī script with Kullūka's commentary. Follows NT–y (vulgate).

London: British Library [India Office], Ms. No. San Ms. 3235. Devanāgarī script. Follows NT–x.

Madras: Government Oriental Manuscripts Library, Ms. No. 2672. Grantha script. Follows NT–x.

Oxford: Bodleian Library, Chandra Shum Shere, Ms. No. b (87) (1). Bengali script. Follows NT–x.

Oxford: Bodleian Library, Max Müller memorial, d. 45. Devanāgarī script. Follows NT–x.

Oxford: Bodleian Library, Max Müller memorial, d. 46. Devanāgarī script. Follows NT–x.

Oxford: Bodleian Library, Sanskrit d. 134. Devanāgarī script. Follows NT–x.

Paris: Bibliotheque Nationale, Ms. No. 810. Bengali script. Follows NT–x.

Poona: Bhandarkar Oriental Research Institute. Ms. No. 53 of 1883–84. Devanāgarī script. Follows NT–x.

Poona: Bhandarkar Oriental Research Institute. Ms. No. 53 of 1883–84; New No. 430. Devanāgarī script, with Kullūka's commentary. Follows NT–x.

Poona: Bhandarkar Oriental Research Institute. Ms. No. 52 of 1883–84, New No. 3. Devanāgarī script. Follows NT–x.

Trivandrum: University of Kerala Oriental Manuscripts Library, Trivandrum. Ms. No. 22039. Follows ST.

Wai: Prājña Pāṭhaśālā Maṇḍala, Ms. No. 2841. Devanāgarī script. Follows NT–x.

Wai: Prājña Pāṭhaśālā Maṇḍala, Ms. No. 2842. Devanāgarī script. Follows NT–x.

There were some other manuscripts that I tried every possible way to obtain but without success. The most significant among them are four Śāradā manuscripts located in the State Archives in Shrinagar, Kashmir: 1. Ms-No. 2355, Acc. No. 914, Kashmiri paper, 127 folios; 2. Ms-No. 2356, Acc. No. 1594, Kashmiri paper, 93 folios, with Kullūka's commentary; 3. Ms-No. 2357, Acc. No. 1817, Kashmiri paper, 128 folios; 4. Ms-No. 2358, Acc. No. 2169, 317 folios, with Kullūka's commentary. The unsettled situation in Kashmir made it impossible even for highly placed officials to acquire copies of these manuscripts. The ones with Kullūka's commentary are probably modern and not very significant. These mss. are listed in the *Catalogue of the Sanskrit Manuscripts* published in 1989 as a Xerox copy publication by the Research and Publication Depart, Jammu & Kashmir Government, in Shrinagar.[1]

II.2 Commentators

There are nine extant commentaries on *MDh*. They are, in approximately chronological order: Bhāruci, Medhātithi, Govindarāja, Nārāyaṇa, Kullūka, Rāghavānanda, Nandana, Rāmacandra, and Maṇirāma. Many of these authors are older, some by several centuries, than the oldest manuscripts we possess. Their readings, therefore, are invaluable in establishing the critically constituted text.

Some of the commentators, especially Bhāruci, Medhātithi, and Nārāyaṇa, are especially useful, because they note variant readings they found either in manuscripts or in the oral tradition. I have noted these as [pāṭha].

Bhāruci, *Ṛjumitākṣarā*. He is the oldest commentator. Derrett (1975, I: 10) places him 500–600 CE, whereas Kane (1962–75, i: 569) opts for 800–850. The dates are educated guesses, although it is clear that Bhāruci is earlier than

1. I want to thank Ernst Pretz for obtaining this information for me during one of his visits to Shrinagar.

Medhātithi. Only a single incomplete and damaged ms. of the commentary in Malayalam script is extant (see ms. MTr[5]). It was edited and translated on the basis of a faulty Devanāgarī transcript by Derrett (1975). I obtained a color photograph of the original Malayalm ms. through the kindness of Professor Albrecht Wezler.

Medhātithi, *Manubhāṣya.* His is the most celebrated and the longest commentary. Kane (1962–75, i: 583) places him 825–900 CE. Medhātithi gives the most detailed commentary and notes the largest number of variant readings he encountered. The use of this commentary to constitute the critical edition is complicated by the fact that all the mss. we have are derived from a "new edition" prepared by King Madana. He is said to have gathered defective copies from various regions and prepared a hybrid restoration (*jīrṇoddhāra;* cf. Jha 1920–39, I: ix–ix). This edition is clearly defective; several citations from Medhātithi found in later commentaries are missing in it.

Govindarāja, *Manuṭīkā.* Kane (1962–75, i: 663) places him 1000–1100 CE. The commentary is rather brief and was plagiarized by Kullūka. References to him by Jīmūtavāhana and Lakṣmīdhara indicate that he was held in high esteem. If the recent dating of Jīmūtavāhana by Rocher (2002, 24) to the beginning of the 12th century is accepted, then we may have to place Govindarāja in the 11th century.

Nārāyaṇa, *Manvarthavivṛtti.* Also called Sarvajña Nārāyaṇa, little is known about him. Kane (1962–75, i: 1190) places him prior to 1400 CE. Bühler (1886, cxxix) thinks that the order of the authorities listed by Rāghavānanda places Nārāyaṇa after Kullūka. Nārāyaṇa gives numerous variant readings, and his commentary has proved quite useful for the edition.

Kullūka, *Manvarthamuktāvalī.* Kane's (1962–75, i: 756) characterization as "the most famous of all commentaries on Manu," I believe, is not due to its antiquity or excellence but because it has had the good fortune of being printed repeatedly and used by such influential translators as Bühler. The root text attached to Kullūka's commentary has become the "standard" or the vulgate, also because of repeated printings. The commentary of Kullūka would today be considered a plagiary of Govindarāja, even though Kullūka has the temerity to criticize him on numerous occasions. Bühler places him in the 15th century as does Jolly (1887, xii), whereas Kane (1962–75, I: 759) dates him to about 1250 CE. I think Bühler and Jolly are correct in their assessment of Kullūka as a relatively late commentator.

Rāghavānanda, *Manvarthacandrikā.* Little is known about this author. He was an ascetic belonging to the Śaṃkarite Sarasvatī order. He states that he follows the opinions of Medhātithi, Govindarāja, Kullūka, and Nārāyaṇa. Kane (1962–75, i: 1210) says that he must be later than 1350 CE.

Nandana, *Nandinī.* This is a short commentary, and Nandana probably came from the south. He is especially significant, because he generally follows the readings of the Southern Transmission. Bühler's (1886, xxxiii–xxxv) identification of Nandana with Nandapaṇḍita, the author of the commentary on *Viṣṇusmṛti*, is mistaken; Nandapaṇḍita lived in Benares, and Nandana is clearly from the south. He is especially conversant with the *Arthaśāstra* (see his correct interpretation of *pravāsayet* as execution at *MDh* 8.123) and cites Kauṭilya by name in his commentary on *MDh* 7.119. See Derrett 1975, I: 33.

Nothing more than the names are known of the last two commentators, **Rāmacandra** and **Maṇirāma**. They must be rather recent authors. Dave assigns Maṇirāma to between 1630 and 1660 CE.

II.3 Testimonia

The *MDh* begins to be cited from Śabara onward more frequently than any other *Dharmaśāstra*. These citations, for the most part much older than most of the extant mss. and commentaries, constitute another significant body of evidence for constituting the text. In the early days of this project I envisaged these citations to be crucial for decisions regarding original readings. At the end of the project, however, the significance of the citations has diminished; they have been useful mostly as corroborative evidence. The use of these sources is handicapped by the lack of critically edited texts of these works. It appears that frequently the modern editors have simply substituted the vulgate version of Manu they knew for the readings they found in the mss. See, for example, 11.249 where editions of *Vij* and *Dev* reproduce the reading of the vulgate Manu, a reading found in just five mss. I have used 14 major writers spanning about 900 years, from the 5th to the 14th centuries, as well as the citation of long sections of the *MDh* in the *Bhaviṣya Purāṇa* (see Laszlo 1971; Sternbach 1974).

Śabara (5th cent. CE), commentary on the *PMS*.
Śaṃkara (8th cent. CE), commentaries on the *VeS*, *BṛU*, *TU*, and *BhG*.
Kumārila (9th cent. CE), *Tantravārtika* com. on *Śabarabhāṣya*.
Viśvarūpa (9th cent. CE), commentary on the *YDh*.
Vijñāneśvara (12th cent. CE), commentary on the *YDh*.
Aparāditya (13th cent. CE), commentary on the *YDh*.
Jīmūtavāhana (13th cent. CE), *Dāyabhāga*.
Haradatta (13th cent. CE), commentaries on *ĀpDh*, *GDh*.
Lakṣmīdhara (13th cent. CE), *Kṛtyakalpataru*.
Hemādri (13th cent. CE), *Caturvargacintāmaṇi*,
Devaṇṇabhaṭṭa (13th cent. CE), *Smṛticandrikā*.
Mādhava (14th cent. CE), *Parāśaramādhavīya*.

II.4 Editions

Except for Jolly's (1887), all previous editions of *MDh* are based on either selected mss. or on previous editions. Jolly (1887, v) comments that "the numerous Indian editions are on the whole nothing but reprints from the two earliest Calcutta edition, published in 1813 and 1830." Nevertheless, I have used five editions that are commonly used by scholars not so much to use them as evidence for the critical edition but to distinguish its readings from those of previous editions. They are: Mandlik (1886), Jolly (1887), Jha (1920–39), KSS (1970), Dave (1975–84).

The one exception is Jolly's edition (see IV.3). I have given the readings of the mss. used by Jolly as supplementary to the manuscript evidence gathered by me whenever I was not able to identify and make use of the manuscripts he used. These mss. are given within brackets, e.g. [*Jolly* M R]. The following is the list of Jolly's mss: M^1 = India Office, Ms. Nos. 1551–52; M^2 and M^4 = Haug's collection; M^3 = my ms. Lo^4; M^5 = private ms. of Jolly; M^6 = ms. in Royal Library, Berlin; M^7 = private ms. of Jolly; M^8 = a ms. from Deccan College, Pune; M^9 = a ms. from Deccan College, Pune; M = siglum used for reading common to all mss. of Medhātithi; Me = readings attested by the commentary of Medhātithi [these two ways of reference are very confusing]; G or G^1 = ms. from Deccan College, Pune; G^2 = ms. from Deccan College Pune; Go = Govindarāja's commentary; N = ms. with Nārāyana's commentary discovered by Bühler and dated Saṃvat 1544 (= 1497 CE); R^1 = my ms. Lo^3; R^2 = Anquetil's copy now in Bibliothèque Nationale, Paris; R^3 = ms. from Deccan College, Pune; Rā = Rāghavānanda's commentary; Nd^1 (Nd) = a private ms.; Nd^2 = modern ms. of chapters 8 and 9 in Grantha script from Burnell's collection in the India Office; Ndd = Nandana's commentary; Gr = a Grantha ms. of Burnell.

Mandlik notes the mss. in which he found additional verses given in his edition. These mss. are given the following alphabetical sigla, which are noted in the critical apparatus: अ (Asiatic Society, Calcutta, with Kullūka's commentary); क (Ujjain); ख (Ujjain, with Rāmacandra's commentary); ग, घ, ङ, च (Prayāg); छ (Khaṇḍvā, with Medhātithi's commentary); ज, झ (Miraj); ञ (Satara); ट, ठ, ड (Pune); ढ (Ahmadabad); ण (Indore); त (Calcutta, Asiatic Society); द (London); ध (Calcutta printed edition, with Kullūka's commentary); न (Miraj, with Rāghavānanda's commentary); ब (Baroda, with Kullūka's commentary); भ (Jaipur, with Rāghavānanda's commentary); म (Madras, with Nandana's commentary); य, र (Pune); ल (Jaipur), व (Mandlik's own ms., with Nārāyaṇa's commentary); श or क्ष (Āṣṭe).

III. Genealogy of Manuscripts

It is not possible to constitute a text such as the *MDh* purely through the classical editorial methods dependent on isolating independent manuscript traditions. The *MDh* was too widely known to permit the existence of totally isolated and independent traditions. As Jolly (1887, xvi) observes: "The great celebrity of the Code appears to have guarded it against sweeping alterations, so that the text has remained essentially the same nearly in all Commentaries, however widely distant from one another as to the time and locality of their composition." In the process of collation it became apparent that all extant mss. of the *MDh* are at some level hybrid; over time readers and scribes appear to have changed the readings of one traditions according to those of another.[2] It is, therefore, impossible to isolate different

2. Most, if not all, of our mss. have above-line or marginal corrections made by subsequent readers. A good example is Ho at 11.208 where a reader has recorded the variant *mahītalāṭ* and noted *vā pāṭhaḥ*. The best example, however, is Tr^1, which belongs to the ST. A reader who was familliar with the NT has gone through this ms. and corrected the ST readings to NT ones. If these mss. were later copied, then it is likely that the marginal and above-line corrections would have been incorportaed into the copies, creating hybrid mss. Indeed, in the colophon to ms. NPu^1, the scribes explicitly exhorts the reader to consult other mss. and to correct his copy accordingly: *aparaṃ pustakaṃ vīkṣya śodhanīyaṃ sadā budhaiḥ*.

recensions of the text, if we mean by "recension" versions that had a more or less independent life.

Nevertheless, a close reading of the mss. makes it possible to establish clear genealogies. At the broadest level, the mss. divide into two groups: a Southern Transmission [ST] consisting for the most part of southern mss. written in Grantha, Telugu, and Malayalam scripts, and a Northern Transmission [NT] that comprehend most mss. from other parts of India and in northern scripts. The following Stemma Codicum, where Z* represents the hypothetical archetype of all extant mss., presents the genealogical tree of the mss. schematically. Given the large number of mss. used in this edition, it is impractical to identify within the Stemma the mss. falling within each genealogical branch; they will be listed in the following discussion of those branches.

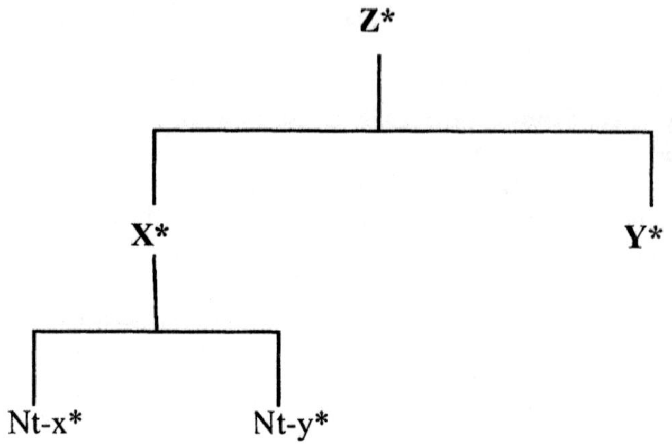

III.1 Southern Transmission

The ST is represented by the following mss.: GMd^1 TMd^3 TMd^4 GMd^5 GMy, Tr^1 MTr^4 MTr^5 MTr^6. Most mss. written in the southern scripts of Grantha, Telugu, and Malayalam appear to fall under ST, although there are exceptions. Tr^1, which is written in Devanāgarī, follows the ST; it is probably a Devanāgarī copy of an original in a southern script. The ms. MTr^3, on the other hand, although written in the Malayalam script, follows NT; it is probably a Malayalam copy of a northern original.

A careful scrutiny of the critical apparatus shows the frequency and consistency with which the mss. of the ST display unique readings. The following are a few examples: 3.44c-d वासोदशा शूद्रया तु वर्णोत्कृष्टस्य वेदने; 3.77a यथा मातरमाश्रित्य; 3.134c स्वाध्याययज्ञनिष्ठाश्च; 3.180a-b अप्रतिष्ठं वार्धुषिके नष्टं देवलके भवेत्; 3.189c वायुभूतास्तु गच्छन्ति; 3.211a अग्निसोमयमानां च; 3.214a प्रसव्यमग्नौ कृत्वा तु; 3.263: सुतं विन्देत्; additional verses after 3.275; omission of 4.44, 46, 47; at 4.70a न मृल्लोष्टानि मृद्नीयात्; 7.129b वत्सवार्योकषट्पदाः; 8.79a साक्षिणस्सर्वान्; 8.82b वारुणैर्नरः; additional verse after 8.100; 8.403b सर्वं पार्थिवलक्षितं; 9.50d

मोघं वृषभचेष्टितं; 9.299c-d गुरुलाघवतो ज्ञात्वा ततः कार्यं समाचरेत्; 10.65d विद्यात्क्षत्रियतां गतं; 11.3d नाकृतान्नं विधीयते; 12.16a पञ्चानामेव; 12.56d ब्राह्मणोसकृत्. A distinctive feature of the ST is the use of *māse* for *māsi* of the NT: cf. 2.34a, 7.138d, 8.245.

In many instances the ST has preserved older and bctter readings. For example, the spurious verse 11.248, which is expunged in the critical edition, is omitted in all the mss of ST. Likewise, the reading मित्रेण at 7.164 recorded in all the ST mss. is superior to मित्रस्य found in all but a handful of NT mss. At 3.39 ST has preserved the older ब्रह्मवर्चसिनः, and at 9.19 the reading आकृतिम्, which is superior to निष्कृतीः of NT. Again at 7.67 the superior reading and the *lectio difficilior* कृत्येपु is found in all ST mss. but in only a few NT ones. At 3.114b only the ST has preserved the older reading अन्वक् attested to by all the older commentators, and at 3.95b the very rare word अगोः.

Nevertheless, the ST has not been insulated from corruption and hybridization; it is, therefore, not possible to follow its readings in all instances. I have already referred to its use of the more common locative *māse* (from *māsa*), whereas most NT mss. have preserved the older and less common *māsi* (from *mās*). The ST has a tendency to "correct" ambiguities, as when it changes पाणि ("hand") to the more appropriate बाहु ("arm") at 4.58, where a man has to raise his arm rather than simply the hand (but see 2.193). At 7.129 also unanimously has corrected the more difficult वार्योकस् reaading to the more common वार्योक with the thematic ending.

A limited number of readings are shared by ST and NT–y [i.e., the vulgate], indicating some historical influence of NT–y on the ST. See, for example, 3.47, 234, 240, 273a.

III.2 Northern Transmission

Most mss. written in northern scripts belong to the NT. These scripts include Bengali, various forms of Nāgarī, Newari, Oriya, and Śāradā. Examination of the readings unique to the ST clearly points also to the distinct transmission of the NT mss. The NT has two branches: NT–x, which is the older and the main branch, and NT–y, which I call the "vulgate," because this is the version represented by most printed editions of the *MDh* and the one accompanying the commentary of Kullūka in most mss.

NT–x (Northern Traditional): This branch of the NT constitutes the largest single group of mss. covering all the northern scripts. It is represented by the following mss.: Be^1 BBe^2 Be^3 Bo BCa Ho WKt^1 WKt^3 NKt^4 BKt^5 WKt^6 La^1 La^2 Lo^1 Lo^2 Lo^3 Lo^4 Lo^5 NNg OOr SOx^1 Ox^2 Ox^3 NPu^1 Pu^2 Pu^3 Pu^4 Pu^5 SPu^6 P^7 Pu^8 Pu^9 Pu^{10} Tj^1 Tr^1 Tr^2 Wa. In the early chapters Jo^2 follows the NT-x, but from about chapter seven it agrees more with NT-y. Given the hybrid nature of most mss., especially of those belonging to the NT, however, several of the above mss. show the influence of NT–y. The examination of the readings unique to NT–y shows the distinctive characteristics of NT–x.

The NT-x is followed by most major commentators: Medhātithi, Govindarāja, and Nārāyaṇa. The exceptions are Kullūka and Maṇirāma, a very late commentator known to us only from the flawed edition of Dave, and possibly Rāghavānanda[3] and Rāmacandra.

The only modern printed edition of the *MDh* that follows the NT–x, as far as I know, is that of Jolly (1887). The root texts contained in Jha's edition of Medhātithi's commentary also by and large follows NT–x, because this is the text found in all the extant mss. of that commentary.

NT–y (Northern Vulgate): Of the mss. used in this edition, the NT–y is represented by the smallest group of mss.: Hy Jm Jo^1 Kt^2 oMd^2 Tj^2 MTr^3. The only ms. in a southern script to follow this tradition, indeed the NT as a whole, is MTr^3. Given its late date, it is likely that the ms. was copied either from a printed copy or a ms. of the vulgate. From about chapter seven, Jo^2 frequently follows the vulgate.

The transmission represented by NT-y is the least faithful and contains the greatest number of corruptions and deviations from what must be presumed to be the old readings based on the evidence of NT–x and ST. Although I cannot be certain of this, it appears probable that this version arose in the late medieval period, possibly under the influence of Kullūka himself or those under the influence of his well-known commentary. The reason for this is that mss. of Kullūka's commentary invariably contains the NT–y as the root text.

In numerous places the NT–y has unique readings different from either the NT–x or the ST. Even more numerous are the instances where the NT–y has readings shared by a few NT–x mss. (clear cases of hybridization) but different from the majority of NT–x mss. The following is a sample: 2.11; transposition of verses 2.225 and 226; 3.77, 81, 85, 88, 163a, 267c, 278c, 283c; 9.147, 169; 10.20, 28; 11.128d.

Maṇirāma follows the NT–y readings most times, although not consistently; he probably commented on a hybrid ms. For example, at 3.77 he records the NT–y reading *vartante*, whereas at 3.81 he has the old reading *śrāddhena*. Kullūka's case is even more difficult. As I have noted, his commentary is nothing more than a plagiarized version of Govindarāja's lesser known commentary. In many places, therefore, the root text presupposed by Kullūka is the NT–x, because that is the text on which Govindarāja commented. Nevertheless, Kullūka frequently departs from that and appears to be commenting on a text close to, if not identical with, the NT–y. This may explain the reason why the NT–y is given as the root text in mss. containing Kullūka's commentary.

The Vulgate and Printed Editions: The presence of Kullūka's commentary may be the reason why the NT–y entered the printed tradition; many early printings of the *MDh*, such as the first (1813) and the second (1830) Calcutta editions (the latter reprinted by Jibananda in 1874), contained Kullūka's commentary as well. It is the northern vulgate that is given also in the edition of Loiseleur Deslongchamps (Paris, 1830). I say "the printed tradition," because it appears that as mss. were copied from each other and thus established genealogies, so the printed versions of the *MDh*

3. Considered by Jolly (1887, xv) to have followed Kullūka rather than the older commentators.

were for the most part nothing but reprints of earlier versions. This is true of editions that most Sanskritists use even today, such as that of Mandlik (1886), the ones printed by the Nirṇaya Sāgar Press (Bombay, 1946 with many reprints), by the Kāśi Sanskrit Series (Varanasi, 1970), and the latest edition with 9 commentaries by Dave (Bombay, 1972–84). It is surprising how few mss. contain some readings adopted by most printed versions: see **2**.11, 96; **3**.78, 85, 88, 163, 253, 283; **8**.172; **11**.111, 120, 245, 249, 252; **12**.10, 28,70, 76, 82, 98, 104. In one instance (7.86) the reading of these editions is not supported by a single manuscript I have used.

IV. Constitution of the Text

All the mss. and commentaries of the *MDh* contain basically the same text. The additional verses found in some can easily be detected. There are no major recensions of the *MDh* giving longer or shorter versions of the text, as, for example, in the case of the two epics. The constitution of the text, therefore, boils down to the editorial judgment as to which of two or three competing readings has great claimer to be accepted as the original.

IV.1 Editorial Principles

I give below some general principles that have guided the constitution of the text and the selection of reading:

1. At the most general level, a reading supported by the ST and NT is adopted in the critical edition. Any variants restricted to a limited range of mss. must have been introduced by a scribe or reader. Clearly the vast majority of the readings in the critical edition fall under this rule.

2. Readings supported by the ST and NT–x are adopted in preference to those supported only by NT–y. The superiority of the former transmissions is clearly established by a close scrutiny of the critical apparatus. They are the ones, moreover, that are recorded in the medieval literature used as external testimonia in this edition. They are also supported by the vast majority of the early commentators.

3. In cases where the ST and the NT have different readings, or where the ST and the NT–y have readings different from NT–x, the determination of the original reading becomes a lot more difficult. It is not possible to formulate a general and rigid principle that can be applied in all these instances. I have analyzed each case separately, taking into account the evidence provided by the commentaries and testimonia, the general sense of the text, and parallel passages within the *MDh*.

4. The most significant editorial principle is that of *lectio difficilior*. It is easier to explain how a more difficult reading is changed to an easier one than the other way round. The difficulties may be of different sorts. Some are orthographic; scribes often fail to comprehend a complex combinations of consonants or a strange looking form created by sandhi. More frequently, however, the difficulty is either in the term, which is unusual or obscure, or in the resultant meaning. Scribes and readers generally tend to change these to easier and more comprehensible forms.

5. In only a handful of instances have I rejected the nearly unanimous readings of the mss. in favor of the reading attested by the commentators. For example, at 3.217d, every genealogical branch of the mss. record *mantravit.* I have opted for *mantravat* that has the support of all but one commentator.

Departing from normal editorial practice, I have articulated my reasons for adopting a particular reading in the endnotes. Whenever I have selected a reading supported by only a minority of mss., such as at 5.61–62 and 8.57, I have explained my reasons fully in an endnote. At 8.57, for example, the old commentaries of Bhāruci and Medhātithi clearly show that the reading should be *iti*, even though it violates grammar. Precisely for this reason, it is also the *lectio difficilior*. I think these notes will be useful to readers as they weigh the options themselves; they can know, rather than guess at, the reasons why I have adopted a particular reading and the kinds of mss., commentarial, and testimonial support it has.

IV.2 Testimonia and Commentaries

At the initial stages of this project I had hoped that the collation of citations of the *MDh* in major medieval legal texts would provide a valuable source for determining correct readings. Most of these texts, after all, are older by several centuries than the extant mss. of the *MDh*. These testimonia, however, have proved much less useful than I had anticipated. A major drawback is the very editions of these texts; they are not critically edited and I can never be sure that the reading given in an edition goes back to the author or has been introduced by the editor. The *MDh* is a well-known text; some editors probably knew much of it by heart. They were thus prone to introduce "correct" (i.e., vulgate) readings in place of what they perceived as corrupt readings of their mss. Thus, for example, I found that the same verse of the *MDh* cited in different places in the same text had different readings. Taken cumulatively, nevertheless, these external testimonia did provide an external check on the readings. It was also a welcome surprise to discover that many of the medieval legal digests regularly followed the readings of the Southern Transmission.

The other non-manuscript evidence I have relied on are the commentaries, especially the older ones of Bhāruci, Medhātithi, Govindarāja, and Nārāyaṇa. I will deal below [IV.3] with Jolly's argument that commentaries alone can supply us with the correct readings of the text. Taken together with the mss., however, the commentaries provided the most significant check on the selection of readings. Several problems, nevertheless, emerged. First, Bhāruci's commentary exists only for chapters 6–12 and in a single mutilated manuscript. Its edition by Derrett depended on a Devanāgarī transcript of the Malayalam original, a transcript which Derrett himself acknowledges to be faulty. I have used a photocopy of the original Malayalam ms. for this edition, but even then I cannot be sure that the readings preserved in this ms. faithfully represent Bhāruci's own readings.

Second, all the mss. of Medhātithi's commentary go back to a reconstruction made under the patronage of the 14th-century king Madana. This reconstruction was based on fragmentary or defective originals. The absence of a verse in the current mss. of Medhātithi, for example, cannot be taken as evidence that it was lacking also in the original commentary. We see many instances where other commentators, such as Govindarāja and Kullūka, refer to the commentary of Medhātithi on a particular verse which is lacking in the extant mss. For example, all the mss. of Medhātithi omit his commentary on 9.182-201; yet Kullūka refers to his comments on these verses showing that his ms. of Medhātithi contained comments on these verses. Likewise, Rāghavānanda refers to a reading of Medhātithi on 7.132, although his commentary on this verse has not survived. Thus, when the commentary on a particular verse is lacking in the mss. or editions, we cannot assume that Medhātithi did not recognize that verse as authentic. It may simply have been lost in the transmission (Bühler 1886, cxxvi).

To complicate matters further, we do not have a reliable critical edition of this commentary; even the one done by Jha is defective. I have found that in many crucial readings the ones given by Jha differ from the ones I find in the original mss. Indeed, sometimes the old versions given in Mandlik's edition are more faithful than Jha's. To give just one example, the editions give Medhātithi's reading at 3.104d as *annādidāyinām*, whereas my ms. Pu^{10} reads *annādyadāyinām*, the reading adopted in the critical edition.

The only editions we have for the other commentaries are the very imperfect one of Mandlik, and the even more flawed one produced recently by Dave.

IV.3 Jolly's Edition

Jolly (1887) raises a fundamental question regarding editorial principles for constituting the *MDh*. Explaining his dependence almost exclusively on mss. containing commentaries and his reluctance to use mss. containing only the text of the *MDh*, Jolly (1887, xi) notes: "It is sufficiently obvious that MSS. of the text alone are of very inferior value generally for deciding questions of verbal criticism in a work of established authority such as the Code of Manu, on which copious Commentaries explaining nearly every word of the text were composed at an early period and carefully handed down to posterity." It is, of course, obvious that all our extant mss. come from periods much later than those of the early commentators, such as Bhāruci, Medhātithi, and Govindarāja. There are, however, problems with the principle articulated by Jolly. First, it is not true that "nearly every word of the text" has been explained by commentators; I estimate that up to 50% of the words are not commented on or at the most simply listed. Given the fact that we do not have a critical edition of a single commentary, it is difficult to know for certain the reading of a term given in the commentary when there is no explanation attached. I have found frequently that readings in my mss. of Medhātithi differ from those given in the editions of Jha and Dave.

Second, it appears that Jolly often takes the reading found in the root text attached to a commentary in the mss. as the reading of that commentator; this is misleading, because frequently the root text in these mss. do not follow the readings presupposed in the commentary. It is clear that scribes inserted readings into the root text from their memory. At 3.114c, for example, Jolly records no variants and takes the reading of the root texts to be that of Medhātithi and Govindarāja. Here he has failed to read the commentary itself, for both clearly record their reading as *anvak* and gives *agre*, the reading in most mss. and adopted by Jolly, as an alternate reading they found in their sources (pāṭha). Likewise, at 3.140a Jolly reads *śrāddhāni* following the root text, which he ascribes to Medhātithi, whereas the commentary itself clearly reads *śrāddhena*. At 3.220c, my ms. Pu[10] containing Medhātithi's commentary reads *śrāddhe*, whereas the commentator himself clearly read *śrāddham*. At 8.314, likewise, the mss. Lo[4] Lo[5] give the reading *dhāvatā*, while Medhātithi's commentary clearly shows that his reading was *dhīmatā*, and at 8.380 they read *vyavasthitam* whereas Medhātithi's explicit gloss shows that his reading was *api sthitam*. Only those readings that can be supported by the explanations given in a commentary, therefore, can be accepted as the readings of that commentator.

My experience in editing this text has been that a large number of mss., including those of the text alone, taken together with the commentarial evidence is the best method to constitute the text.

The text constituted by Jolly was a great advance over the then extant editions. His dependence on just 18 mss. containing commentaries,[4] supplemented by five mss. of the text only, however, makes his editorial decisions not always correct and, even when correct, not supported fully by the evidence. Jolly does not present a Stemma Codicum in his edition. The present edition, I believe, is an improvement on Jolly's version, although not drastically different from it. My discovery of the Southern Transmission, of which Jolly was unaware, has given me an important and independent check on the readings presented in the northern mss.

Jolly also appears not to have read and noted down variants carefully even in the manuscripts he collated. In numerous instances, I find that Jolly does not record important variants found in numerous manuscripts, some found even in the manuscripts he had access to, such as the Śāradā: see, for example, 2.80c, 198b-c, 220; 3.110a, 228c; 5.64a, 64d, 65b, 65c, 67b.

IV.4 Critical Edition and Critical Apparatus

In the post-modern and post-colonial rhetoric, the value and the rationale for critically editing texts have come under scrutiny. Some reject the entire enterprise as a relic of the "indological" past; "indology" itself has become a dirty word associated with colonial collaborators. For me, indology is nothing more and nothing less than the study of India, just as biology is the study of life forms; it does not carry any ideological baggage.[5]

Much of this criticism of critical editions is based, I believe, on ignorance,

4. Nine of these 18 are mss. of Medhātithi, all of which go back to the 14th-century reconstruction and are, therefore, not independent sources.

5. This is not the place to defend indology. Others have done it better and more extensively than I can within the confines of this introduction: see W. Halbfass, "Research and Reflection: Responses to My Respondents," in *Beyond Orientalism: The Work of Wilhelm Halbfass and its Impact on Indian Cross-Cultural Studies*, ed. E. Franco and K. Preisendanz (Amsterdam: Rodopi, 1997), pp. 1–25.

misinformation, and misunderstanding of both the process and the aim of critically constituting ancient texts. It is not true that the editor looks at the different readings before him or her and selects one that he or she thinks is the original. Although it is impossible to remove the subjective altogether and it is true that editing is more an art than a science, yet a good editor abides by accepted principles in selecting readings and constituting the text. What is even more important, unlike the reader of an anthropological construction of native categories, societies, and value systems who has no way of checking whether that is the only construction that can be made from the data, the reader of a critical edition is provided with all the information that the editor himself or herself used and, therefore, can come up with different conclusions. This information concerning the variant readings found in the mss. is provided in perhaps the most important and also the most neglected element of a critical edition: the critical apparatus.

The aim of a critical edition is, no doubt, to establish a text as close to the original written by the author as the extant evidence permits.[6] This is often merely the editorial horizon towards which we march determinedly but which we never reach. After it leaves the hand of the author a text begins a life of its own in the hands of readers, commentators, and copyists. Over this after-life of a text the author has no control; but it is, nevertheless, as much a part of the text as the labors of the author that brought it into being. The richer a text is and the more it becomes part of a culture and society, the richer its after-life will be. And the *MDh* has been a text that has occupied a central position in the culture and intellectual life of India for close to two millennia; it has had a rich after-life. The aim of a critical edition is not merely to reconstruct the original text but also to document its after-life. Just as at an archeological dig the archeologists do not throw aside all the earlier layers to get at the oldest stratum, so the editor does not throw away all the changes and accretions to get at the original text. The story both at the dig and of the text is told not just in the oldest stratum but at every stratum. The documentation about the after-life of the text is found in the critical apparatus, which provides information on all the significant variant readings, additions, and omissions found in mss. and citations and on the readings and the interpretations provided by the various commentators. The critical apparatus provides the textual history of the *MDh*.

Unfortunately, most readers pay scant attention to the information found in the critical apparatus. One reason for this is the very nature of such an apparatus: often the significant variants and interpretations are buried among other less significant ones and simple scribal errors. To remedy this at least partially, I have selected the most important variants and translated them in the notes to my translation. The reader of the translation, thus, will be able to see how the text would read if we follow different versions.

A critical edition, however carefully and painstakingly carried out, is limited by the available data: manuscripts, testimonia, commentaries. Any additions and

6. When there is no identifiable author, as in the case of the epics, then the goal is to reconstruct the oldest version of the text that can be discovered on the basis of extant evidence. See Sukthankar's comments in the introduction to the *Ādiparvan* of the *MBh*, pp. iii, lxxxvi.

emendations carried out between the author's original and the beginning of the extant manuscript tradition are beyond the scope of a critical edition. Thus, it has been called "lower criticism" to distinguish it from "higher criticism," which depends on a close reading of the text and the acumen of the scholar. Higher criticism aims at disclosing different sources and layers within a text, layers that may be older and younger. It is this sort of criticism that discovered the four sources of the Pentateuch: J (JHVH), E (Elohim), P (Priestly), and D (Deuteronomic). A critical edition is not the place to undertake this sort of criticism. I have attempted to identify latter additions to the *MDh* using higher criticism in my general introduction that precedes the translation.

Note on the Critical Edition

Given the inevitable complexity of the critical apparatus to an edition involving over 50 manuscripts, citations from medieval texts, and commentaries, it may be helpful to spell out some of the conventions I have used.

1. The sigla that identify the mss. are given in the Introduction to the Edition II.2: Description of the Manuscripts. The initial letter in small caps indicates the script. A notation within brackets added after a siglum apply only to that ms. The notation [*cor to*] indicates that the original reading of the ms. is the same as that of the critical edition, but that it was subsequently corrected to the variant reading recorded in the critical apparatus. The notation [*but cor*] indicates that the original reading of the ms. is the variant recorded but that it has been subsequently corrected to the reading in the critical edition. Abbreviations: *mc* = marginal correction; *ma* = marginal addition; *fh* = first hand; *sh* = second hand.

2. In citations from medieval texts, the abbreviation *vl* (varia lectio) indicates a variant reading in the mss. recorded by the editors. In the commentaries, the notation [pāṭha] indicates that the reading is given by a commentators as a variant reading he had encountered in his sources.

3. I have added end notes to explain some of the editorial decisions I have made. Such notes are signaled by an asterisk after the verse number in the critical apparatus. The end notes normally refer to a specific pāda. When the note pertains to an additional verse found in some mss. after a particular verse, this is indicated by an "x" after the verse number.

4. In order not to overload the critical apparatus thereby undermining its very purpose, I have omitted obvious scribal errors, especially when these errors are confined to a single ms. I have noted the absence of an *anusvāra* only when the absence affects the syntax; scribes often forget the *anusvāra* dot of the northern scripts. Unintentional omission of *anusvāras* is less common is southern scripts where the *anusvāra* is written after the letter. Scribes also omit the *visarga* frequently, especially when it occurs before a sibilant. This is markedly so in southern mss. I have not noted these variants unless they affect the syntax. Although I have noted *avagrahas* in the edition, they are uniformly omitted in the variants given in the critical apparatus; mss. hardly ever note *avagrahas*.

5. I have recorded the variants found in the mss. used by Jolly in his 1887 edition. These mss. are given within brackets with *Jolly* at the beginning. Thus [*Jolly* Gr] refers to the ms. Gr in Jolly's edition. The sigla of these mss. are given in the Introduction to the Edition II.4: Editions.

6. An asterisk after a word in the edition indicates that the reading is uncertain.

[प्रथमोऽध्यायः]

मनुमेकाग्रमासीनमभिगम्य महर्षयः ।
प्रतिपूज्य यथान्यायमिदं वचनमब्रुवन् ॥१॥
भगवन्सर्ववर्णानां यथावदनुपूर्वशः ।
अन्तरप्रभवाणां च धर्मान्नो वक्तुमर्हसि ॥२॥
त्वमेको ह्यस्य सर्वस्य विधानस्य स्वयंभुवः ।
अचिन्त्यस्याप्रमेयस्य कार्यतत्त्वार्थवित्प्रभो ॥३॥

Initial folios are missing in the following mss: NKt^{4} containing verses 1–4b; NNg containing verses 1–12; Pu^{9} containing verses 1–64. The folios containing the first chapter is so mutilated in BCa that I was not able to collate it.

Before verse 1 the following verse is added in Be^{1} BBe^{2} Bo Ho wKt^{1} wKt^{3} BKt^{5} La^{1} Lo^{1} Lo^{3} oOr sOx^{1} NPu^{1} Pu^{5} sPu^{6} Pu^{7} Pu^{8} Tj^{1} Tr^{2} *Go Nā Rn Rc:*

स्वयंभुवे नमस्कृत्य ब्रह्मणेऽमिततेजसे ।
मनुप्रणीतान्विविधान्धर्मान्वक्ष्यामि शाश्वतान् ॥

a) La^{1} नमस्यामि [*but mc fh*] — d) Ho शाश्वत:

1.* Pāda-b cited by *Viś* 1.2 — a) Pu^{8} °कामाग्रमा° — c) GMd^{5} प्रणिपत्य — d) Be^{1} Bo Jm Pu^{10} Wa °ब्रवीत्; La^{2} °ब्रुवीत्

2.* Pādas b-d lacuna in Ho — c) Ox^{2} अक्षरप्रभ°; oOr °प्रत्यनां

Two additional verses in Be^{1} Ho wKt^{1} wKt^{3} La^{1} Lo^{2} TMd^{3} TMd^{4} GMd^{5} GMy Tr^{2} MTr^{4} MTr^{6}; both commented by *Nd*. The first half-verse of 1 and second half-verse of 2 in sOx^{1} sPu^{6}, and the second verse in oOr:

जरायुजाण्डजानां च तथा संस्वेदजोद्भिदाम् ।
भूतग्रामस्य सर्वस्य उत्पत्तिं प्रलयं तथा ॥१॥
आचाराणां च सर्वेषां कार्याणां च विनिर्णयम् ।
यथाकालं यथायोगं वक्तुमर्हस्यशेषत: ॥२॥

1. a) La^{1} °जातां — b) wKt^{1} wKt^{3} तथा वै स्वेद°; Lo^{2} स्वंस्वेद°; Tr^{2} °जोद्भजां; Ho °द्भिजां; Lo^{2} °द्भिदो:; GMd^{5} adds a further half-verse आश्रमाणां च सर्वेषां यथावदनुपूर्वश: — c) MTr^{4} MTr^{6} [*Jolly Nd*] कृत्स्नस्य — d) Be^{1} Ho प्रभवं प्रलयं तथा; MTr^{4} MTr^{6} ह्युत्पत्तिं; GMd^{5} चोत्पत्तिं; Lo^{2} सोत्पत्तिं; TMd^{3} *om* प्रलयं; *Nd Rc* support उत्पत्तिं

2. a) wKt^{3} आचाराणनुसर्वेषां; La^{1} आचारान्चैव वर्णानां [*but mc*]; Ho Tr^{2} आचारांश्चैव; wKt^{1} आबालानां तु; GMy *om* च — b) Ho wKt^{1} wKt^{3} La^{1} [*mc to*] Tr^{2} कार्याकार्यविनिर्णयं; TMd^{3} तथाकार्यविनिर्णयं — c) wKt^{3} यथाश्रुतं यथा°; sOx^{1} sPu^{6} Tr^{2} [*Jolly Nd*] *Rc* यथाक्रमं यथा°; oOr यथाकामं यथा°; Lo^{2} °कालं च योगं च; La^{1} °कालं यथान्यायं; wKt^{1} wKt^{3} °कालं यथादृष्टं; sOx^{1} यथायोग्यं

3. Omitted in Wa — a) Be^{1} त्वमेको स्वस्य; TMd^{3} ह्यसि; GMy धर्मस्य — b) NPu^{1} स्वयंभुवा — c) Bo अचित्तान्याप्र° — d) Hy कार्यं

स तैः पृष्टस्तथा सम्यगमितौजा महात्मभिः ।
प्रत्युवाचार्च्य तान्सर्वान् महर्षीञ्छ्रूयतामिति ॥४॥
आसीदिदं तमोभूतमप्रज्ञातमलक्षणम् ।
अप्रतर्क्यमविज्ञेयं प्रसुप्तमिव सर्वतः ॥५॥
ततः स्वयंभूर्भगवानव्यक्तो व्यञ्जयन्निदम् ।
महाभूतादि वृत्तौजाः प्रादुरासीत्तमोनुदः ॥६॥
योऽसावतीन्द्रियोऽग्राह्यः* सूक्ष्मोऽव्यक्तः सनातनः ।
सर्वभूतमयोऽचिन्त्यः स एष स्वयमुद्बभौ ॥७॥
सोऽभिध्याय शरीरात्स्वात् सिसृक्षुर्विविधाः प्रजाः ।
अप एव ससर्जादौ तासु वीर्यमवासृजत् ॥८॥
तदण्डमभवद्धैमं सहस्रांशुसमप्रभम् ।
तस्मिञ्जज्ञे स्वयं ब्रह्मा सर्वलोकपितामहः ॥९॥
आपो नारा इति प्रोक्ता आपो वै नरसूनवः ।
ता यदस्यायनं पूर्वं तेन नारायणः स्मृतः ॥१०॥

4. a) Pu^{8} पृष्टा तथा; Lo^{2} GMy Tj^{2} पृष्टस्तदा — b) Lo^{2} °मितोजा; sOx^{1} sPu^{6} °मितौज — c) Pu^{5} Pu^{7} प्रत्युवाचार्चितान्सर्वान्; MTr^{6} *Me* [pāṭha] प्रत्युवाचार्चयित्वा तान्; TMd^{3} TMd^{4} प्रत्युवाचाथ — d) Wa प्रीतात्मा श्रूयतामिति

5. Omitted in oOr. Pādas c-d cited by *Śaṃ* on *VeS* 1.2.19 — a-b) *BhP* 2.9 जगदासीत्पुरा तात तमोभूतमलक्षणम् — b) BKt^{5} [*but mc*] Wa °भूतमज्ञात°; wKt^{1} °मलक्षितं — c) *BhP* 2.9 अविज्ञेयमतर्क्यं च — d) *BhP* 2.9 सर्वशः; NKt^{4} पर्वतः

6.* a-b) *BhP* 2.10 ततः स भगवानीशो ह्यव्यक्तो — b) *Me* appears to prefer the reading अव्यक्तम् as qualifying इदम् — c) *Me* [pāṭha] महाभूतानुवृत्तौजाः; La^{2} GMy *BhP* 2.10 °भूतानि; *Rc* appears to read महाभूतादिः [as adjective of स्वयंभूः]; sOx^{1} sPu^{6} वृत्तौजः — d) *BhP* 2.10 प्रोत्थितस्तमनाशनः

7.* Cited by *Śaṃ* on *BU* 1.4.6 — a) NPu^{1} सोसाव°; Be^{1} BBe^{2} Bo Jm Jo^{1} wKt^{1} Kt^{2} wKt^{3} BKt^{5} La^{2} Lo^{1} Lo^{2} Lo^{4} Lo^{5} GMd^{1} oMd^{2} TMd^{3} TMd^{4} GMd^{5} sOx^{1} NPu^{1} Pu^{2} Pu^{4} Pu^{5} sPu^{6} Pu^{7} Pu^{8} Pu^{10} Tj^{2} Tr^{1} MTr^{4} MTr^{6} *Mandlik Jolly Jha KSS Dave* °तीन्द्रियग्राह्यः [this section torn in GMy] — c) GMy सर्वभूतमनो; NKt^{4} °मयो हंसो; wKt^{3} °चिन्त्या — d) GMd^{5} स एवाग्रे स्वयं बभौ; Bo Ho Hy Jm Jo^{1} Kt^{2} TMd^{3} TMd^{4} GMy NPu^{1} Pu^{5} Pu^{7} Tj^{2} Tr^{1} *Mandlik Jolly KSS* स एव; Pu^{2} स पूर्वं स्वय°; *BhP* 2.11 स्वयमुत्थितः

8. a) MTr^{6} सोतिध्याय; BKt^{5} शरीरस्थाः — b) Hy sOx^{1} sPu^{6} प्रजः — d) BBe^{2} Bo Hy Jo^{1} Lo^{1} Lo^{3} oMd^{2} Tj^{1} MTr^{3} Kt^{2} *Ku Rn* बीजमवा°; La^{2} Tj^{2} वीजमवा°; *Me Go Nā Rc* support वीर्यम्; GMd^{5} °मपसृजत्

9. b) *BhP* 2.15 ज्वालामालाकुलं विभो — c) NKt^{4} La^{1} *BhP* 2.16 यस्मिञ्जज्ञे; BBe^{2} Ho Tj^{2} तस्मिन्यज्ञे — d) TMd^{3} सर्वभूतपितामहः

10.* Omitted in Lo^{3} — a) sOx^{1} नार; NKt^{4} नरो — c) Jo^{2} La^{1} Lo^{1} [*mc*] Ox^{2} GMd^{5} Tj^{1} MTr^{4} Wa अयनं तस्य ताः पूर्वं [La^{1} तत्पूर्वं; Wa ता पूर्वं]; wKt^{1} यदस्य अयनं [*om* ता]

Additional verse in Be^{1} [*ma*] TMd^{4} GMd^{5} sOx^{1} sPu^{6} MTr^{4} MTr^{6}:

यत्तत्कारणमव्यक्तं नित्यं सदसदात्मकम् ।
तद्विसृष्टः स पुरुषो लोके ब्रह्मेति कीर्त्यते ॥११॥
तस्मिन्नण्डे स भगवानुषित्वा परिवत्सरम् ।
स्वयमेवात्मनो ध्यानात् तदण्डमकरोद् द्विधा ॥१२॥
ताभ्यां स शकलाभ्यां तु दिवं भूमिं च निर्ममे ।
मध्ये व्योम दिशश्चाष्टावपां स्थानं च शाश्वतम् ॥१३॥
उद्बबर्हात्मनश्चैव मनः सदसदात्मकम् ।
मनसश्चाप्यहंकारमभिमन्तारमीश्वरम् ॥१४॥
महान्तमेव चात्मानं सर्वाणि त्रिगुणानि च ।
विषयाणां ग्रहीतॄणि शनैः पञ्चेन्द्रियाणि च ॥१५॥

नारायणः परोऽव्यक्तादण्डमव्यक्तसंभवम् ।
अण्डस्यान्तस्त्विमे लोकाः सप्तद्वीपा च मेदिनी ॥

d) sOx[1] sPu[6] सप्तद्विपात्र मेदिनी

A further verse in sOx[1] sPu[6] [very faint and difficult to read]:

सहस्रशीर्षः पुरुषो रुक्मबाहुः स्वतीन्द्रियः ।
ब्रह्मानारायणाख्यस्तु स्रष्ट्वापसलिले तदा ॥

11. Be[1] transposes 11 and 12 — a) BKt[5] यत्ताका°; TMd[3] °रणमव्यंग्यं — a-b) wKt[1] नित्यमानन्दमव्यक्तं सदसत्स सदात्मकं — b) Pu[10] नित्यं सदात्मकं; sOx[1] sPu[6] लोके सद° — c) Pu[10] सद्विसृष्टः; NKt[4] तद्विसिप्टः — d) Ox[2] ब्रह्मैति; Jo[2] Lo[3] Tj[1] गीयते

12. a-b) *BhP* 2.21 एवं स भगवानण्डे तत्त्वमेव निरूप्य वै — c) *BhP* 2.22 ध्यानमास्थाय राजेन्द्र

13.* a) *BhP* 2.22 शकलाभ्यां च राजेन्द्र; sOx[1] sPu[6] ताभ्यामण्डकपालाभ्यां [this is *Me*'s gloss]; TMd[3] तस्यां; Tr[2] *om* स; La[1] च शक°; La[1] Tj[1] सकलाभ्यां; wKt[1] स्वकलाभ्यां; BBe[2] Hy Jm Jo[1] Jo[2] Kt[2] wKt[3] oMd[2] NNg sOx[1] Ox[2] NPu[1] Pu[5] sPu[6] Pu[7] Tj[1] Tj[2] Tr[1] Wa *Mandlik Jolly Jha KSS Dave* शकलाभ्यां च; Lo[3] °भ्यां स — b) Tj[1] स निर्ममे; BKt[5] निर्ममौ — c) *BhP* 2.23 अन्तर्व्योम; Be[1] दिशस्त्वष्टा°; GMy दिशाश्चाष्टा°; Pu[5] Pu[7] दिशश्चाष्टौ अपां; *Me* दिशोऽष्टौ च [unclear whether root or gloss] — d) *BhP* 2.24 °ष्टौ वारुणं स्थानमेव हि; TMd[4] °ष्टावाकारं स्थानं; Lo[1] °ष्टावपस्थानं; MTr[3] तु

14. Omitted in Tr[2] — a-d) *BhP* 2.23 ऊर्ध्वं महान् गतो राजन्समन्ताल्लोकभूतये | महतश्चाप्यहंकारस्तस्माच्च त्रिगुणानि तु ॥ — a) Kt[2] Lo[5] *Jolly* उद्बवर्हा°; Pu[10] उर्द्वदर्हात्म°; Be[1] Bo उद्बर्हात्म°; TMd[4] तद्बबर्हात्म°; Hy उच्छबर्हात्म°; NPu[1] ऊर्ध्ववर्हात्म°; Lo[2] °बर्हात्मिनश्चैव; GMy °नश्चैनं

Additional half-verse in Lo[2] TMd[4]:

इन्द्रियाणां समस्तानां प्रभवं प्रलयं तथा ॥

15. a) TMd[3] वात्मानं — b) Ox[3] विगुणानि; Jo[1] वा; wKt[1] हि — c) *BhP* 2.24 तेषामेव गृहीतानि; Ho wKt[1] Lo[1] Lo[4] [*but cor*] Pu[5] Pu[7] गृहीतॄणि; TMd[4] गृहीत्राणि; Bo NKt[4] NPu[1] ग्रहीत्रीणि; Lo[5] गृहीत्रीणि; TMd[3] दुहित्रीणि — d) NKt[4] वा; *BhP* 2.25 तु

Additional verse in TMd[4] MTr[4] MTr[6]; *ma sh* after 14 in Lo[2]:

वैकारिकं तैजसं च तथा भूतादिमेव च ।
एकमेव त्रिधाभूतमहमित्येव संस्थितम् ॥

b) MTr[4] तथा भूत [*rest of the verse omitted*] — d) TMd[4] °भूतं महानित्येव; Lo[2] TMd[4] सुस्थितं

तेषां त्ववयवान्सूक्ष्मान् षण्णामप्यमितौजसाम् ।
संनिवेश्यात्ममात्रासु सर्वभूतानि निर्ममे ॥१६॥
यन्मूर्त्यवयवाः सूक्ष्मास्तस्येमान्याश्रयन्ति षट् ।
तस्माच्छरीरमित्याहुस्तस्य मूर्तिं मनीषिणः ॥१७॥
तदाविशन्ति भूतानि महान्ति सह कर्मभिः ।
मनश्चावयवैः सूक्ष्मैः सर्वभूतकृदव्ययम् ॥१८॥
तेषामिदं तु सप्तानां पुरुषाणां महौजसाम् ।
सूक्ष्माभ्यो मूर्तिमात्राभ्यः संभवत्यव्ययाद्व्ययम् ॥१९॥
आद्याद्यस्य गुणं त्वेषामवाप्नोति परः परः ।
यो यो यावतिथश्चैषां स स तावद्गुणः स्मृतः ॥२०॥
सर्वेषां तु स नामानि कर्माणि च पृथक्पृथक् ।
वेदशब्देभ्य एवादौ पृथक्संस्थाश्च निर्ममे ॥२१॥
कर्मात्मनां च देवानां सोऽसृजत् प्राणिनां प्रभुः ।
साध्यानां च गणं सूक्ष्मं यज्ञं चैव सनातनम् ॥२२॥

Additional half-verse in Lo^{2} TMd^{4} GMd^{5}:

अविशेषान्विशेषांश्च विषयांश्च पृथग्विधान् ॥

16. a) *BhP* 2.26 तथैवावयवा: सूक्ष्मा:; TMd^{3} TMd^{4} तेषामवय°; MTr^{6} चावय°; Lo^{2} °वान्कृत्स्नान्; TMd^{3} *om* सूक्ष्मान्; Be^{1} sOx^{1} after अवयवान् jump to सूक्ष्मास् in 17a omitting 16b-d and 17a [haplo] — b) Hy षण्णामथामितौ°; Bo षण्णामित्यमितौ°; NKt^{4} व्यक्तामप्यमितौ° — c) Lo^{1} संनिपत्यात्म° [*but mc*]; TMd^{3} TMd^{4} संनिवेशात्म; *Me* [pāṭha preferred by *Me*] °मात्राभि: — d) *BhP* 2.27 [gives here two pādas] भूतानि निर्ममे तात सर्वाणि विधिपूर्वकम्

17. a) Bo °वयवान्; Hy °वयव:; TMd^{4} °वयवां — b) Pu^{10} सूक्ष्माख्यानीमान्याश्र°; Lo^{4} Lo^{5} NNg Ox^{3} Pu^{2} Pu^{4} MTr^{3} *Me Mandlik Jha Dave* °स्तानीमान्या°; GMy °स्तस्मै नित्याश्रयन्ति; *BhP* 2.28 °श्रयाणि — d) La^{1} TMd^{3} मूर्तिर्मनी°; NKt^{4} मूर्तिस्मनी°; Be^{1} Bo मूर्तिमनी°; TMd^{4} मनीषिणो:

18. a-d) *BhP* 2.29 महान्ति तानि भूतानि आविशन्ति ततो विभुम् । कर्मणा सह राजेन्द्र सगुणाश्चापि वै गुणा: — b) oMd^{2} Pu^{10} सर्वकर्मभि: — d) Bo °कृदद्वयं; TMd^{4} °कृदेव च

19. a) Lo^{3} सुप्तानां — c) wKt^{1} °मात्रेभ्य:; NNg °मात्राद्य: [*but mc fh*] — d) Kt^{2} संभवन्त्य°; NKt^{4} साभवत्य°; Hy सभवत्य°; Bo °त्यव्यधाव्ययं; Tj^{1} °त्यव्ययाव्ययं; GMd^{5} °त्यव्ययात्मकं

20.* Before verse 20 TMd^{3} and GMd^{5} insert verse 27 — a) GMd^{5} गुणांस्तेषाम°; wKt^{1} Tr^{2} MTr^{6} तेषाम° — a-b) GMy आद्याद्यस्य गुणानेतानाप्नोति च पर: पर: — b) GMd^{5} परंपरं; wKt^{1} परस्परं — c) Bo TMd^{3} Tj^{1} यावतियश्चैषां — d) GMy स्मृतं; Pu^{10} स्मृता:

21. Cited in *Śaṃ* on *VeS* 1.3.28 — a) Bo सर्वेव तु; Jo^{2} Lo^{3} Tj^{1} स तु; Be^{1} wKt^{1} BKt^{5} NPu^{1} Pu^{5} Pu^{7} च स; Tr^{2} *om* स; BBe^{2} TMd^{3} GMd^{5} मानानि — b) wKt^{1} सर्वाणि; oOr *om* च; Tj^{1} तु — c) TMd^{3} TMd^{4} एवासां — d) [*Jolly* G R] पृथक्संस्थास्तु; TMd^{4} पृथक्संस्थां च

22.* a) *BhP* 2.42 कर्मोद्भवानां देवानां; MTr^{4} कर्मात्मतां; TMd^{4} °त्मनश्च; Be^{1} *om* च; Lo^{2} NPu^{1} तु; sOx^{1} NNg वेदानां; TMd^{3} साध्यानां — b) La^{1} देवानामसृजत्; Bo °सृजन्; *BhP* 2.43 देहिनां; TMd^{3} *om* प्रभु:; La^{2} विभु: — c) *BhP* 2.43 तुषितानां गणं राजन्; Ho *om* च; BBe^{2} Pu^{7} [*but cor*] Tr^{2} गुणं; Tr^{2}

अग्निवायुरविभ्यस्तु त्रयं ब्रह्म सनातनम् ।
दुदोह यज्ञसिद्ध्यर्थमृग्यजुःसामलक्षणम् ॥२३॥
कालं कालविभक्तीश्च नक्षत्राणि ग्रहांस्तथा ।
सरितः सागराञ्छैलान् समानि विषमाणि च ॥२४॥
तपो वाचं रतिं चैव कामं च क्रोधमेव च ।
सृष्टिं ससर्ज चैवेमां स्रष्टुमिच्छन्निमाः प्रजाः ॥२५॥
कर्मणां तु विवेकाय धर्माधर्मौ व्यवेचयत् ।
द्वंद्वैरयोजयच्चेमाः सुखदुःखादिभिः प्रजाः ॥२६॥
अण्व्यो मात्रा विनाशिन्यो दशार्धानां तु याः स्मृताः ।
ताभिः सार्धमिदं सर्वं संभवत्यनुपूर्वशः ॥२७॥
यं तु कर्मणि यस्मिन्स न्ययुङ्क्त प्रथमं प्रभुः ।
स तदेव स्वयं भेजे सृज्यमानः पुनः पुनः ॥२८॥

सूक्ष्म; TMd⁴ सूक्ष्मान् — d) Kt² यज्ञश्चैव

23. GMy omits pādas a-b — a) sOx¹ sPu⁶ अग्निवायुभ्यश्च; Hy Jm Jo¹ Jo² [*mc to*] Kt² NKt⁴ Lo³ oMd² Tj¹ Tj² Tr² MTr³ *Mandlik Jha KSS Dave* °रविभ्यस्तु — a-b) *BhP* 2.43दत्त्वा वीर समानेभ्यो गुह्यं ब्रह्म सनातनं — b) Ho स्वयं ब्रह्म — c) GMy दुर्दोह — d) Be¹ °लक्षणे; GMy °रक्षणं

Additional verses in TMd⁴ GMd⁵:

तेषामर्थानुसारेण ऋषिभिस्तत्त्वदर्षिभिः ।
पशुभिश्चौषधिभिश्च महायज्ञाः प्रवर्तिताः ।
सृष्ट्वैतानपरान्श्रेयस्सोऽसृजत्कार्यसाधकान् ॥

d) TMd⁴ महायज्ञप्र° — e) TMd⁴ स सृष्टवान्वरा° — f) TMd⁴ °साधनं

24. a) TMd⁴ कालः काल°; TMd³ TMd⁴ GMy °विभक्तीं च; Jo² °विभक्तिश्च Tr² °विभक्तांश्च; Ox² °विभक्ताश्च — b) La² Lo⁴ गृहास्तथा — c) Ho सरतः सागरांश्चैलान्; La² सरिता; NPu¹ सागरान् शिलान्

25. a) TMd³ GMd⁵ GMy MTr⁴ MTr⁶ तपश्शोकं रतिं वाचं [MTr⁴ MTr⁶ तपः शौचं]; NKt⁴ तमो; Tr² तपो वलं; Kt² रतिश्चैव — a-b) *BhP* 2.45कामं क्रोधं तथा वाचं रतिं चापि कुरूद्वह — b) GMd⁵ GMy Ox² [*but cor*] MTr⁴ MTr⁶कामं क्रोधमनित्यतां — c) *BhP* 2.46 ससर्ज राजेन्द्र; Hy TMd³ चैवैमां — d) *BhP* 2.46 सिसृक्षुर्विविधाः प्रजाः; TMd³ सृष्टुमिच्छतीमाः

26. Omitted in Wa — a-d) *BhP* 2.46धर्माधर्मौ विवेकाय कर्मणां च तथासृजत् । सुखदुःखादिभिर्द्वंद्वैः प्रजाश्चेमा न्ययोजयत् ॥ — a) BBe² Ho Hy Jm Jo¹ Jo² Kt² NKt⁴ Lo² Lo³ oMd² Ox² NPu¹ Pu² Tj¹ Tj² MTr³ *Mandlik Jha KSS Dave* च; Hy Jo¹ Kt² oMd² oOr NPu¹ MTr³ विवेकार्थं [*Nā* and *Rc* support this reading]; *Me Rc* विवेकाय supported also by the glosses of *Go* and *Ku* विभागाय — b) Kt² wKt³ BKt⁵ व्यवेचयन्; TMd⁴ विवेचयत्; wKt¹ विवेचयन्; Ox² व्यचिन्तयत् — c) Be¹ °योजयश्चैमाः; Lo¹ °योजयंश्चेमाः

27. Cited by *Śaṃ* on *VeS* 4.2.6 — a) Kt² *om* अण्व्यो; La¹ अण्वो; Hy अण्व्यौ; MTr⁴ अन्यो; TMd³ अन्तो; Ho अपृव्यो *cor to* अण्वो; wKt¹ नव्यो; GMy अतिमात्रा; Ox³ मात्र; Hy विनासित्यो — b) Hy दशार्ध्यानां; MTr³दशार्थानां; Ox³ दशार्धान्यां; TMd³ दशधानां; TMd⁴ च याः — c) *BhP* 2.48 ताभिः सर्वमिदं वीर; Be¹ sOx¹ sPu⁶ ताभिर्विश्वमिदं सर्वं; MTr⁶ साकमिदं — d) Be¹ पूर्वशा; wKt³ °पूर्वः

28. a) Jm Tj¹ यत्तु; BKt⁵ यत्र; wKt¹ Lo¹ कर्माणि; Bo यस्मिंत्स; La¹ यस्मिंसु — a-b) *BhP* 2.48

हिंस्राहिंस्रे मृदुक्रूरे धर्माधर्मावृतानृते ।
यद्यस्य सोऽदधात्सर्गे तत्तस्य स्वयमाविशत् ॥२९॥
यथर्तुलिङ्गान्यृतवः स्वयमेवर्तुपर्यये ।
स्वानि स्वान्यभिपद्यन्ते तथा कर्माणि देहिनः ॥३०॥
लोकानां तु विवृद्ध्यर्थं मुखबाहूरुपादतः ।
ब्राह्मणं क्षत्रियं वैश्यं शूद्रं च निरवर्तयत् ॥३१॥
द्विधा कृत्वात्मनो देहमर्धेन पुरुषोऽभवत् ।
अर्धेन नारी तस्यां स विराजमसृजत् प्रभुः ॥३२॥
तपस्तप्त्वासृजद्यं तु स स्वयं पुरुषो विराट् ।
तं मां वित्तास्य सर्वस्य स्रष्टारं द्विजसत्तमाः ॥३३॥
अहं प्रजाः सिसृक्षुस्तु तपस्तप्त्वा सुदुश्चरम् ।
पतीन् प्रजानामसृजं महर्षीनादितो दश ॥३४॥

यत्कृतं तु पुरा कर्म संनियुक्तेन वै नृप — b) Lo^{1} न्ययुङ्क्तं; Kt^{2} न्ययुक्त; wKt^{3} BKt^{5} न्ययुक्तं — c) Tr^{2} भेदे — d) *BhP* 2.49 सृज्यमानं

Additional half-verse in GMd^{5} [partly moth eaten]:

नृभिस्सार्धमिदं सर्वं प्रजापतिरकल्पयेत् ॥

29. a) La^{1} हिंसाहिंस्रे; GMy °हिंस्रैर्मृदु° — b) Lo^{3} NPu^{1} Tr^{2} धर्माधर्मानृता°; *BhP* 2.49 °धर्मे ऋता° — c) *BhP* 2.50 यद्यथास्याभवत्सर्गे; TMd^{3} यदस्य; oOr सोसृजत्सर्गे; BBe^{2} wKt^{3} La^{1} Lo^{4} °दधत्सर्गे; Ox^{3} Pu^{5} Pu^{7} °ददात्सर्गे; TMd^{3} °दधाद्गर्भे; Wa °त्सर्गो; Pu^{10} °त्स्वर्गे — d) Ho GMd^{5} GMy Pu^{5} Tj^{1} Tr^{2} MTr^{4} तत्तत्स स्वयमाविशत् [GMd^{5} स तत्तत्स्वय°]; La^{2} तत्तत्स्वस्व°; MTr^{3} तत्तं स्व°; Hy Jo^{1} Kt^{2} Lo^{4} Pu^{10} MTr^{3} MTr^{4} MTr^{6} °विशेत्; Wa °विशोत्; Jo^{2} NNg °दिशत्; GMy °दिशेत्

30. a) Bo La^{1} यथार्तु°; MTr^{3} यथार्थ°; *BhP* 2.50 यथा च लिङ्गां°; Pu^{10} यद्यत्तु लिङ्गा°; Bo La^{1} Tr^{2} °लिङ्गानृतवः — b) wKt^{1} *Dave* स्वयमेव तु पर्यये; *BhP* 2.50 स्वयमेवानुपर्यये; Pu^{10} °पर्ययैः; wKt^{3} °पर्यते — d) Tj^{1} यथा; TMd^{4} तथाकरणानि; NNg लिङ्गानि

31. a) *BhP* 2.51 लोकस्येह; BKt^{5} *om* तु; Lo^{2} Ox^{2} Pu^{5} Pu^{7} च; La^{2} विवृद्धार्थं — c-d) *BhP* 2.52 ब्रह्मक्षत्रं तथा चोभौ वैश्यशूद्रौ नृपोत्तम — d) MTr^{3} *om* च; La^{1} तु; Tr^{2} निरवर्जयत्

Additional verse in wKt^{3}:

आस्येन ब्राह्मणाः स्रष्टा बाहुभ्यां क्षत्रियः स्मृतः ।
उरुभ्यां तु विशो जाताः शूद्रः पद्भ्यां स्वयंभुवा ॥

32. a) NKt^{4} कृत्यात्मनो; La^{2} कृतात्मनो — b) Tj^{1} Wa भवेत् — c) NPu^{1} आर्धेन; TMd^{3} अर्धे नारी; TMd^{4} GMy *BhP* 2.59 तस्यां तु; oOr sOx^{1} sPu^{6} तस्यां च; MTr^{6} ताभ्यां तु — c-d) wKt^{1} अर्धेन नारीमसृजत्स्वयमेव स्वयंप्रभुः

33. a) GMy °सृजन्यस्तु; MTr^{6} °सृजद्यस्तु; MTr^{4} °सृजद् जन्तुं; TMd^{4} *om* तु — c) La^{1} तन्मात्राः सर्वलोकानां; NKt^{4} *pāda reads* तस्माद्येतस्य; MTr^{6} तदा वित्तास्य; TMd^{3} मातावितास्य; Kt^{2} वित्तस्य; TMd^{4} वित्तस्य यार्तस्य — d) TMd^{4} त्वष्टारं; TMd^{3} द्विजोत्तमाः; TMd^{4} °सत्तम

Additional half-verse after 33b in GMd^{5}:

माता पिता [torn] स्रष्टारं मा द्विजोत्तमाः ।

34. Cited by *Hem* 1.242 — b) BBe^{2} Bo TMd^{3} NPu^{1} सुदुस्तरं; Ox^{2} [*Jolly* Nd] सुदुष्करं; Lo^{1} च

मरीचिमत्र्यङ्गिरसौ पुलस्त्यं पुलहं क्रतुम् ।
प्रचेतसं वसिष्ठं च भृगुं नारदमेव च ॥३५॥
एते मनूंस्तु सप्तान्यानसृजन्भूरितेजसः ।
देवान्देवनिकायांश्च महर्षींश्चामितौजसः ॥३६॥
यक्षरक्षःपिशाचांश्च गन्धर्वाप्सरसोऽसुरान् ।
नागान्सर्पान्सुपर्णांश्च पितॄणां च पृथग्गणान् ॥३७॥
विद्युतोऽशनिमेघांश्च रोहितेन्द्रधनूंषि च ।
उल्का निर्घातकेतूंश्च ज्योतींष्युच्चावचानि च ॥३८॥
किंनरान्वानरान्मत्स्यान् विविधांश्च विहङ्गमान् ।
पशून्मृगान्मनुष्यांश्च व्यालांश्चोभयतोदतः ॥३९॥
कृमिकीटपतंगांश्च यूकामक्षिकमत्कुणम् ।
सर्वं च दंशमशकं स्थावरं च पृथग्विधम् ॥४०॥

पुष्करं — c) MTr^{4} °सृजत् — d) Lo^{2} °दितोदथ; Lo^{1} TMd^{4} दशः; Wa दशो; *BhP* 2.60–62 parallels Manu 1.34–5 but with significant variants.

35. Cited by *Hem* 1.242 — a) Jo^{1} मरीचिमङ्गिरसौ; Jo^{2} मरीचिर°; Lo^{2} OMd^{2} Wa °ङ्गिरसो; NKt^{4} La^{1} TMd^{4} SOx^{1} SPu^{6} NPu^{1} *Hem* °ङ्गिरसं — b) TMd^{4} पुलह; MTr^{6} पुलहः क्रतुः; Tr^{2} क्रतु — c) Tr^{2} प्राचेतसं — d) Be^{1} Hy भृगु

36. Pādas c-d omitted in BBe^{2} — a) *BhP* 2.62 एतांश्चान्यांश्च राजेन्द्र; Lo^{4} Lo^{5} एतान्; Be^{1} BBe^{2} Ho Kt^{2} NKt^{4} Lo^{4} Lo^{5} SOx^{1} Pu^{5} SPu^{6} Pu^{7} Tr^{2} [*Jolly* G M^{4}] मनूंश्च; NPu^{1} मनूश्च; TMd^{3} मनांश्च; Bo मनूषु; Tr^{2} सप्तानसृज° — b) GMy °न्यान्ससृज°; TMd^{3} GMd^{5} MTr^{4} MTr^{6} °न्यान्ससृजुर्भूरि°; *BhP* 2.62 °सृजद्भूरि°; TMd^{3} °सृजुर्हारितेजसः — c) NKt^{4} देवादेव°; TMd^{3} देवदेव°; GMd^{5} °निकाशांश्च — c-d) *BhP* 2.63 अथ देवानृषीन्दैत्यान्सोऽसृजत्कुरुनन्दन — d) Be^{1} महर्षींश्चा°; SOx^{1} SPu^{6} महर्षीनमितौ°; La^{2} °र्षींश्च मिततेजसः; Lo^{2} °मितौजसाः

37. a) NKt^{4} GMy Tj^{1} °रक्षपिशा°; Ox^{3} °रक्षंपिशा° — d) MTr^{4} पितृंश्चैव; Tj^{1} पृथग्गणं; Tr^{2} पृथग्गुणान्. In place of pādas c-d, *BhP* 2.64 gives four pādas: मनुष्याणां पितॄणां च सर्पाणां चैव भारत । नागानां च महाबाहो ससर्ज विविधान् गणान् ॥

38. a) *BhP* 2.65 [does not have pāda-b] क्षणरुचोऽशनिगणान्; Bo after pāda-a adds: गन्धर्वाप्सरसोसुरान् —b) MTr^{6} लोहिते° — c-d) *BhP* 2.65 धूमकेतूंस्तथा चोल्कान्निर्घाताञ्ज्योतिषां गणान्

39. *ma* in Lo^{4} — a) *BhP* 2.66 मनुष्यान्किंनरान्मत्स्यान्; TMd^{3} किंनरांश्च नरान्मत्स्यान्; Lo^{3} Tj^{1} °रान्मछान् — b) *BhP* 2.66 वराहांश्च — c) GMy MTr^{4} सिंहान्व्याघ्रान्वराहांश्च — c-d) *BhP* 2.66 गजानश्वानथ पशून्मृगान्व्यालांश्च भारत — d) Pu^{10} °भयतोदितान्

40. a) NKt^{4} TMd^{3} GMd^{5} Tj^{1} क्रिमि°; Wa कृमी°; Hy *lacuna at* °पतंगांश्च; BKt^{5} Pu^{5} Pu^{7} °पतंगं च — b) Bo Ho Lo^{2} TMd^{4} Ox^{2} Pu^{8} यूकामत्कुणमक्षिकाः [Pu^{8} °क्षिकं; Bo Ho °क्षिकः]; TMd^{3} यूकान्मत्कुणमक्षिकान्; *BhP* 2.67 यूकालिक्षक°; NKt^{4} Lo^{3} GMd^{5} SOx^{1} Tj^{1} Tr^{2} *BhP* 2.67 °मत्कुणान्; MTr^{4} °मंकुणान् — c) La^{2} सर्वे

Additional verse in TMd^{4} GMd^{5} Tr^{2}; given after verse 42 in WKt^{1} La^{1}, and after 44 in WKt^{3}:

यथाकर्म यथाकालं यथाप्रज्ञं यथाश्रुतम् ।

एवमेतैरिदं सर्वं मन्नियोगान्महात्मभिः ।
यथाकर्म तपोयोगात् सृष्टं स्थावरजङ्गमम् ॥४१॥
येषां तु यादृशं कर्म भूतानामिह कीर्तितम् ।
तत्तथा वोऽभिधास्यामि क्रमयोगं च जन्मनि ॥४२॥
पशवश्च मृगाश्चैव व्यालाश्चोभयतोदतः ।
रक्षांसि च पिशाचाश्च मानुषाश्च जरायुजाः ॥४३॥
अण्डजाः पक्षिणः सर्पा नक्रा मत्स्याः सकच्छपाः ।
यानि चैवंप्रकाराणि स्थलजान्यौदकानि च ॥४४॥
स्वेदजं दंशमशकं यूकामक्षिकमत्कुणम् ।
ऊष्मणश्चोपजायन्ते यच्चान्यत्किंचिदीदृशम् ॥४५॥
उद्भिज्जास्तरवः सर्वे बीजकाण्डप्ररोहिणः ।
ओषध्यः फलपाकान्ता बहुपुष्पफलोपगाः ॥४६॥

यथायुगं यथादेशं यथावृत्ति यथाक्रमम् ।।

a) GMd^{5} यथाक्रमं यथा° — b) wKt^{1} wKt^{3} La^{1} GMd^{5} यथोत्पत्तिर्यथाक्रमं [wKt^{1} यथोत्पत्ति] — c) Tr^{2} *om* यथायुगं; wKt^{1} La^{1} यथोद्देशं; wKt^{3} यथोद्वेगं; TMd^{4} यथावेगं; GMd^{5} यावद्दुर्गं — d) Tr^{2} यथोपत्ति यथाक्रमं; TMd^{4} यथाभूतं यथाभवं; GMd^{5} यथाभूतं यथोद्भवं; wKt^{1} wKt^{3} La^{1} सर्वभूतान्यकल्पयत् [wKt^{3} °कल्पयन्]

41. b) TMd^{3} मन्नियोगं मही° — c) wKt^{1} तथाकर्म; Tr^{2} तपोयोगं — d) BKt^{5} सृष्टिं

42. a) Tr^{2} तेषां; Lo^{1} Lo^{3} Lo^{5} GMd^{5} GMy Tj^{1} एषां; TMd^{3} यादृशं कर्तुं — b) Tj^{1} °नामिव; TMd^{3} °मिह वर्तिनां — c) *BhP* 2.69 कथयिष्यामि तत्सर्वं; TMd^{4} तत्र वै वो; wKt^{1} वोविधास्यामि; wKt^{3} वोविवाधास्यामि; GMy °धास्यानि — d) Tr^{2} क्रमंयोगं; GMd^{5} जन्मसु

43. a-d) *BhP* 2.69 गजा व्याला मृगास्तात पशवश्च पृथग्विधाः । पिशाचा मानुषास्तात रक्षांसि च जरायुजाः ।। — a) NNg मृगश्चैव — b) TMd^{3} °श्चोभयभेदतः — c) Lo^{1} TMd^{4} पिशाचांश्च — d) Hy TMd^{3} GMd^{5} GMy NNg MTr^{3} MTr^{4} [*Jolly* M$^{1-2-4-7-8-9}$ Nd] मनुष्याश्च; Tj^{2} [*Jolly* R] मानुष्याश्च; TMd^{4} मनुष्यांश्च; La^{2} मानुषीश्च

44.* a) *BhP* 2.70 द्विजास्तु अण्डजाः सर्पा; TMd^{4} अण्डजान्पक्षिणः सर्पान्; GMy NNg पक्षिणः सर्वे — b) TMd^{4} नक्रान्मत्स्यांश्च कच्छपाः; wKt^{3} GMd^{1} नक्र; Tr^{2} नकृ; Lo^{3} Tj^{1} मच्छाः; Be^{1} Bo Ho Hy Jm Jo^{1} wKt^{1} Kt^{2} wKt^{3} BKt^{5} La^{2} Lo^{2} oMd^{2} GMd^{5} GMy sOx^{1} Ox^{2} Ox^{3} sPu^{6} Pu^{8} Tj^{2} मत्स्याश्च कच्छपाः — c) *BhP* 2.71 एवंविधानि यानीह; TMd^{4} °प्रकारेण — d) oOr स्थावराणि चराणि च; Wa स्थाल्वजा°; NKt^{4} °जान्युदजानि

45.* a) TMd^{3} स्वेदजा; TMd^{3} °मशक — b) *BhP* 2.71 यूकालिक्षकमत्कुणाः; oOr TMd^{4} यूकामत्कुणमक्षिकं; GMy लूतमत्कुणमक्षिकं; TMd^{3} यूनामत्कुणमक्षिकाः; GMd^{5} यूकमाक्षिक°; MTr^{4} °मत्कुणः — c) TMd^{3} GMd^{5} GMy MTr^{4} उष्मणो ये च जायन्ते; Tr^{2} उष्मणश्चोप°; NKt^{4} GMy *BhP* 2.72 ऊष्मणा चोप°; Be^{1} Ho NNg Pu^{5} Pu^{7} Wa *Me Ku* °जायेत; Lo^{2} °जायोत; Pu^{10} °जायन्त — d) oOr यत्किंचिदन्यदीदृशं

46.* a) Bo ईदृशास्तमसः सर्वे; Hy Jm Jo^{1} Kt^{2} wKt^{3} NKt^{4} La^{1} Lo^{5} GMd^{1} oMd^{2} TMd^{3} TMd^{4} GMd^{5} GMy Tr^{1} Tr^{2} MTr^{3} MTr^{4} MTr^{6} *BhP* 2.72 *Nā Rc Mandlik Jha KSS Dave* उद्भिज्जाः स्थावराः; TMd^{4} उद्भिज्जस्थावराः; Hy सर्वं — b) MTr^{4} MTr^{6}वीज°; Ho जीवकाण्ड° — c) Tr^{2} औषध्यः; NKt^{4} ओषधः; TMd^{3} °पाकानां — d) *BhP* 2.73 नानाविधफलोपगाः; TMd^{3} °फलोदकाः; TMd^{4} °फलोद्रमाः

अपुष्पाः फलवन्तो ये ते वनस्पतयः स्मृताः ।
पुष्पिणः फलिनश्चैव वृक्षास्तूभयतः स्मृताः ॥४७॥
गुच्छगुल्मं तु विविधं तथैव तृणजातयः ।
बीजकाण्डरुहाण्येव प्रताना वल्ल्य एव च ॥४८॥
तमसा बहुरूपेण वेष्टिताः कर्महेतुना ।
अन्तःसंज्ञा भवन्त्येते सुखदुःखसमन्विताः ॥४९॥
एतदन्तास्तु गतयो ब्रह्माद्याः समुदाहृताः ।
घोरेऽस्मिन्भूतसंसारे नित्यं सततयायिनि ॥५०॥
एवं सर्वं स सृष्ट्वेदं मां चाचिन्त्यपराक्रमः ।
आत्मन्यन्तर्दधे भूयः कालं कालेन पीडयन् ॥५१॥
यदा स देवो जागर्ति तदेदं चेष्टते जगत् ।
यदा स्वपिति शान्तात्मा तदा सर्वं निमीलति ॥५२॥
तस्मिन् स्वपति तु स्वस्थे कर्मात्मानः शरीरिणः ।

47. Omitted in BKt^{5}; pādas c-d omitted in Ox^{1} sPu^{6} — a) Tr^{2} आपुष्पाः; GMy अपुष्प — b) Kt^{2} *om* ते; wKt^{3} स्मृतः — c) NPu^{1} पुष्पितः; wKt^{1} फलवन्तश्च; Hy फलितश्चैव — d) NKt^{4} °स्तूभयः; Jo^{1} °स्तूभयताः; MTr^{4} °स्तूभयथा; TMd^{3} °स्तूभयधा

48. Cited by *Lakṣ* 14.111 — a) Lo^{3} NNg Tj^{2} गुच्छं; Tr^{2} युच्छां गुल्मां; Be^{1} Bo Ho La^{1} Lo^{1} Lo^{2} Lo^{3} NNg sOx^{1} NPu^{1} sPu^{6} Pu^{8} Pu^{10} Tj^{1} Tr^{2} [*Jolly* M^{4-7-9} Ku Nd] च; Pu^{5} Pu^{7} [*Jolly* G] तु विज्ञेयं — a-b) *Lakṣ* प्रतानाश्चैव वल्यश्च वीरुधः परिकीर्तिताः — c) MTr^{4} MTr^{6} वीज°; Lo^{5} जीवकाण्ड°; GMd^{5} °काण्डो°; TMd^{4} sOx^{1} sPu^{6} °रुहश्चैव; Pu^{5} Pu^{7} °रुहास्त्वेव — c-d) Pu^{8} प्रतानाश्चैव वल्यश्च वीरुधः परिकीर्तिताः — d) Ox^{2} प्रतानाश्चैव वल्लयः; NKt^{4} प्रतता; TMd^{3} प्रतनाचल्य

Additional half-verse in NKt^{4}:

प्रतानाश्चैव वल्यश्च वीरुजः परिकीर्तितः ॥

49. a) wKt^{1} तमसावृतरूपेण; oOr तामसा; TMd^{3} तपसा — b) wKt^{1} BKt^{5} कर्मवायुना — c) wKt^{1} अन्तःसत्वा; Bo भवेत्येते — d) Jo^{2} Lo^{3} Tj^{1} फलपुष्पसमन्विताः

50. a) *BhP* 2.75 एतावत्यस्तु; oOr Pu^{8} °दन्ताश्च — b) *BhP* 2.75 प्रोद्भूताः कुरुनन्दन; TMd^{3} GMd^{5} GMy Pu^{10} MTr^{4} MTr^{6} परिकीर्तिताः — c) *BhP* 2.77 तात संसारे; wKt^{1} BKt^{5} sOx^{1} sPu^{6} °संहारे — d) Bo La^{2} Lo^{1} TMd^{3} GMd^{5} GMy MTr^{4} *Nā* नित्ये; Tj^{2} सन्तत°; Wa °यायिनी; Lo^{2} TMd^{3} °यायनी; Tr^{2} °याजनि

51. a) Lo^{3} Tj^{1} [*Jolly* R] एवं च सवं सृष्ट्वेदं; BBe^{2} एतत्सर्वं; Pu^{5} Pu^{7} सर्वमेवं स; Tj^{1} सृष्ट्वैदं; NKt^{4} सृष्ट्वेदः — b) *BhP* 2.78 राजंल्लोकगुरुं परम्; TMd^{3} मत्या चाचि°; NPu^{1} याचिन्त्य°; GMy Tr^{2} चचिन्त्य°; Tj^{1} चाचित्य°; TMd^{4} °पराक्रमं — c) *BhP* 2.78 तिरोभूतः स भूतात्मा; oMd^{2} भूयं

Additional verse in La^{1}:

प्रजायते स्तमोमात्राः प्रवर्त्तयति संहरन् ।
ककुदं सर्वभूतानां पदेदं गहनीकृतम् ॥

52. b) Bo तदिदं; Kt^{2} Tj^{1} तदेवं; wKt^{1} चेष्टितं — c) Tr^{2} तदा; sOx^{1} sPu^{6} Tr^{2} स्वपति; Hy सुपिति; Lo^{4} स्वपिते — d) NKt^{4} दाता; Tr^{2} निमीलयति; Hy निमीति; oOr sOx^{1} sPu^{6} Pu^{7} [*Jolly* G] प्रलीयते

स्वकर्मभ्यो निवर्तन्ते मनश्च ग्लानिमृच्छति ॥५३॥
युगपत्तु प्रलीयन्ते यदा तस्मिन्महात्मनि ।
तदायं सर्वभूतात्मा सुखं स्वपिति निर्वृतः ॥५४॥
तमोऽयं तु समाश्रित्य चिरं तिष्ठति सेन्द्रियः ।
न च स्वं कुरुते कर्म तदोत्क्रामति मूर्तितः ॥५५॥
यदाणुमात्रिको भूत्वा बीजं स्थास्नु चरिष्णु च ।
समाविशति संसृष्टस्तदा मूर्तिं विमुञ्चति ॥५६॥
एवं स जाग्रत्स्वप्नाभ्यामिदं सर्वं चराचरम् ।
संजीवयति चाजस्रं प्रमापयति चाव्ययः ॥५७॥
इदं शास्त्रं तु कृत्वासौ मामेव स्वयमादितः ।
विधिवद्ग्राहयामास मरीच्यादींस्त्वहं मुनीन् ॥५८॥
एतद्वोऽयं भृगुः शास्त्रं श्रावयिष्यत्यशेषतः ।
एतद्धि मत्तोऽधिजगे सर्वमेषोऽखिलं मुनिः ॥५९॥

53. a) wKt[3] तस्मिंस्तु स्वपति स्वस्थे; Hy सुपति; Be[1] Bo Ho wKt[1] NKt[4] La[2] TMd[3] GMd[5] Pu[10] स्वपिति; *BhP* 2.80 स्वपिति राजेन्द्र; La[1] स्वपिव स्वस्थे; Ox[2] च; NPu[1] स्वस्थे तु; sOx[1] sPu[6] MTr[3] सुस्थे तु; wKt[1] स्वतस्थे [*om* तु]; Hy Kt[2] Jo[2] oMd[2] *Jolly* [who gives no variants] सुस्थे; BKt[5] तस्थे — b) *BhP* 2.80 जन्तवः कर्मबन्धनाः — c) GMy स्वकीयेभ्यो — d) TMd[3] मनश्चाग्ला°; sOx[1] sPu[6] मनग्ला°; Lo[1] ग्लानिमिच्छति

54. a) Lo[1] युगपत्सु; Pu[5] Pu[7] [*Jolly* G] युगपच्च — b) Jo[2] Lo[4] Tj[1] Tr[2] तदा — c) TMd[4] तदा सर्व° — d) *BhP* 2.81 स्वपिति भारत; GMd[5] निवृतः

55. a) La[1] Lo[2] NNg oOr sOx[1] NPu[1] Pu[5] sPu[6] Pu[7] Pu[8] Tr[2] [*Jolly* G] *BhP* 2.82 *Go* तमो यदा समा°; oOr तमो यदि समा°; NKt[4] La[2] समासृत्य — b) Kt[2] तिष्ठन्ति; Pu[10] चेन्द्रियं — c) *BhP* 2.82 न नवं कुरुते; sOx[1] sPu[6] न च संकुरुते

56. Omitted in TMd[3] — a) Lo[4] Lo[5] तदा°; wKt[3] TMd[4] NNg यदानुमा°; *BhP* 2.83 यदाहंमात्रिको; Be[1] °मात्रको; wKt[1] NKt[4] BKt[5] °मातृको — b) MTr[4] MTr[6] वीजं; TMd[4] बीज; Wa स्थानु; Lo[3] NPu[1] स्थाणु; Bo Tj[1] स्थाष्णु; BKt[5] स्थाष्ण; sOx[1] sPu[6] स्थास्नुश्चरि°; Jo[1] *om* चरिष्णु; Be[1] परिष्णु; NKt[4] TMd[4] GMd[5] GMy वा — c) Lo[2] समाविशन्ति; La[2] स आविशति; GMd[5] MTr[6] [*Jolly* Nd] संसृष्टौ तदा; sOx[1] sPu[6] संपृष्टस्तदा — d) TMd[4] °स्तथा मूर्तिर्विमुञ्चते; BKt[5] च मुच्यति; Tj[2] विगृह्णति

57. a) TMd[4] यथा स; TMd[3] सा — b) *BhP* 2.84 सर्वं जगत्प्रभुः; oMd[2] चराचरः; Hy चराचमं — d) wKt[1] प्रमादयति; sOx[1] sPu[6] समापयति; GMd[1] चाव्ययं

58. Cited by *Mādh* 1.106 — a) oMd[2] च; Wa कृत्वासो; TMd[4] कृत्वासा; TMd[3] कृत्वादा — c) Ox[2] विधिवद्दाहया°; TMd[3] विधिवदाहया° — d) GMd[5] मारीच्या°; Lo[1] TMd[4] *Mādh* °च्यादीनहं; Jo[2] °च्यादीन्स्वयं

59. Cited by *Apa* 4 — c) TMd[3] एतद्वायं; Bo भृगुं; Tj[1] भृगु — b) La[1] °यिष्यन्त्यशे° — c) GMd[5] मत्तो जग्रहे; wKt[1] मत्यां जगृह; TMd[3] मत्तोजगत् — d) wKt[3] Lo[2] Lo[4] sOx[1] Ox[2] sPu[6] Tr[2] [*Jolly* M[4] G R Nd] *Rc* सर्वमेवाखिलं; Kt[2] GMy °मेवोखिलं; Bo °मेषाखिलं जगत्

Additional half-verse in TMd[4] GMd[5]:

मनुर्मुनीनेवमुक्त्वा भृगुं ब्रूहीत्युवाच ह ॥

ततस्तथा स तेनोक्तो महर्षिर्मनुना भृगुः ।
तानब्रवीदृषीन्सर्वान् प्रीतात्मा श्रूयतामिति ॥६०॥
स्वायंभुवस्यास्य मनोः षड्वंश्या मनवोऽपरे ।
सृष्टवन्तः प्रजाः स्वाः स्वा महात्मानो महौजसः ॥६१॥
स्वारोचिषश्चौत्तमिश्च तामसो रैवतस्तथा ।
चाक्षुषश्च महातेजा विवस्वत्सुत एव च ॥६२॥
स्वायंभुवाद्याः सप्तैते मनवो भूरितेजसः ।
स्वे स्वेऽन्तरे सर्वमिदमुत्पाद्यापुश्चराचरम् ॥६३॥
निमेषा दश चाष्टौ च काष्ठा त्रिंशत्तु ताः कला ।
त्रिंशत्कलो मुहूर्तः स्यादहोरात्रं तु तावतः ॥६४॥
अहोरात्रे विभजते सूर्यो मानुषदैविके ।
रात्रिः स्वप्नाय भूतानां चेष्टायै कर्मणामहः ॥६५॥

a) TMd^{4} मुनिर्मुनेवमुक्त्का

60. a) La^{2} तेजोक्तो — b) Tr^{2} महर्षीमनुना; NKt^{4} महर्षिमनुना; Lo^{4} महर्षिं मनुना; GMd^{5} महर्षिमानवे; wKt^{1} [*but cor*] °र्मुनिना — c) Bo तामब्र° — d) La^{2} महर्षीन्श्रूयतामिति; Lo^{1} शान्तात्मा

61.* a) *BhP* 2.108 मनोः स्वायंभुवस्येह; sOx^{1} sPu^{6} Pu^{10} Tr^{2} स्वयंभु°; Tr^{2} °भुवोस्यास्य — b) La^{2} षड्वंशा; Be^{1} षड्वंशाः; wKt^{1} षडार्या — c) Tr^{2} *om* स्वाः; GMd^{1} TMd^{4} स्वास्वा — d) Be^{1} NKt^{4} La^{1} [*cor to*] La^{2} Lo^{2} TMd^{4} NNg sOx^{1} Ox^{2} Ox^{3} NPu^{1} Pu^{2} Pu^{4} sPu^{6} Pu^{8} Pu^{10} Tr^{2} Wa *Rn Jolly* महात्मानोमितौजसः; Tj^{1} महोजसः; Ox^{3} महितौजसः; Bo महौयशः

62. a) Lo^{2} स्वारेचि°; MTr^{6} स्वरोमिष°; wKt^{1} Kt^{2} La^{1} La^{2} Lo^{5} sOx^{1} NPu^{1} sPu^{6} °षश्चोत्तमिश्च; NKt^{4} °षश्चोत्तमिच्च; wKt^{3} °षश्चौत्तमीश्च; Lo^{1} Lo^{2} Pu^{2} Pu^{7} °षश्चौत्तमश्च; Bo Jo^{1} GMd^{1} TMd^{3} TMd^{4} GMd^{5} GMy Ox^{3} Tr^{1} MTr^{4} MTr^{6} Wa*Mandlik Jha KSS Dave* °षश्चोत्तमश्च — b) BBe^{2} तमसो; Bo Ox^{3} तामसौ; TMd^{3} GMy MTr^{4} MTr^{6} तापसो; Hy वैवतस्तथा— c) GMd^{1} चक्षुषश्च; Hy Pu^{5} चाक्षषश्च; Be^{1} महातेजाः

63. a) Hy TMd^{3} sOx^{1} sPu^{6} Pu^{10} स्वयंभु°; TMd^{3} °भुवाश्च — a-b) GMy °भुवाद्या मनवस्सप्तैते भूरि° — c) MTr^{6} ये स्वे — d) TMd^{4} °मुत्ततेयुश्चरा°; NKt^{4} °मुत्पाद्य चरा°; Be^{1} NPu^{1} MTr^{3} °द्यायुश्चरा°; Bo Lo^{1} °द्येयुश्चरा°

Additonal half-verse in Lo^{2} TMd^{4} GMd^{5} MTr^{6}:

कालप्रमाणं वक्ष्यामि यथावत्तन्निबोधत ॥

b) GMd^{5} यथावद्धर्मतत्त्वतः; MTr^{6} यथावत्तं निबोधत

64.* Parallel in *BhP* 2.86–8 but in a greatly expanded version. — a) NPu^{1} निमिषा; La^{1} काष्टौ च — b) Tj^{1} काष्ठ; Lo^{3} काष्ट; TMd^{3} त्रिंशत्कलास्स्मृताः; Bo Hy Kt^{2} NKt^{4} BKt^{5} La^{1} La^{2} Lo^{1} Lo^{5} oOr Pu^{2} Pu^{4} Tr^{2} MTr^{3} कलाः; Lo^{3} काला — c) BBe^{2} Jm Jo^{1} Kt^{2} oMd^{2} TMd^{3} TMd^{4} GMy Tj^{1} Tr^{1} MTr^{4}MTr^{6} *Mandlik Jha KSS Dave* त्रिंशत्कला; GMd^{5} त्रिंशःकला; Bo °शत्काले; Lo^{3} °शत्काला; TMd^{4} GMd^{5} MTr^{6} मुहूर्तं; Tr^{1} [*but cor*] मुहूर्त्ता स्युरहो° — d) GMd^{1} GMd^{5} स्यात्तेऽहोरात्रं; MTr^{6} °रात्रं तथैव च; Ho La^{1} Lo^{2} GMd^{1} GMd^{5} GMy sOx^{1} Pu^{2} sPu^{6} Tr^{2} *Nā* [pāṭha] *Rc Jolly* तावता; Ho तावताः

65. a) Kt^{2} °रात्रं; Lo^{3} °रात्रो; Kt^{2} विभजन्ते; La^{2} विभजने — b) GMd^{1} मानुषलौकिके; sOx^{1} sPu^{6} °देवके; Ho °दैवके; NKt^{4} Lo^{3} °देविके; Hy °देविकेः; BKt^{5} °दैवते — c) Tr^{2} स्वप्राव — d) NKt^{4} चेष्टये;

पित्र्ये रात्र्यहनी मासः प्रविभागस्तु पक्षयोः ।
कर्मचेष्टास्वहः कृष्णः शुक्लः स्वप्नाय शर्वरी ॥६६॥
दैवे रात्र्यहनी वर्षं प्रविभागस्तयोः पुनः ।
अहस्तत्रोदगयनं रात्रिः स्याद्दक्षिणायनम् ॥६७॥
ब्राह्मस्य तु क्षपाहस्य यत्प्रमाणं समासतः ।
एकैकशो युगानां च क्रमशस्तन्निबोधत ॥६८॥
चत्वार्याहुः सहस्राणि वर्षाणां तत्कृतं युगम् ।
तस्य तावच्छती संध्या संध्यांशश्च तथाविधः ॥६९॥
इतरेषु ससंध्येषु ससंध्यांशेषु च त्रिषु ।
एकापायेन वर्तन्ते सहस्राणि शतानि च ॥७०॥
यदेतत्परिसंख्यातमादावेव चतुर्युगम् ।
एतद् द्वादशसाहस्रं देवानां युगमुच्यते ॥७१॥
दैविकानां युगानां तु सहस्रं परिसंख्यया ।
ब्राह्ममेकमहर्ज्ञेयं तावती रात्रिरेव च ॥७२॥
तद्वै युगसहस्रान्तं ब्राह्मं पुण्यमहर्विदुः ।

TMd^{3} चेष्टावै

66. a) oOr पैत्रे; TMd^{4} पित्रे; Pu^{9} पित्रो; GMd^{1} पितृ; BKt^{5} TMd^{3} मास; sOx^{1} sPu^{6} मासाः — b) Lo^{4} Pu^{10} Wa °भागश्च — c) Lo^{4} °चेष्टास्त्वहः; Jo^{1} °स्वहाः; Pu^{9} °स्वाहः; Jo^{1} Lo^{3} कृष्णाः — c-d) GMd^{5} शुक्लः कृष्णः — d) Ox^{3} शुक्लं; Pu^{10} शुक्तः; wKt^{1} सर्वरी

67. a) sOx^{1} sPu^{6} दैवी; Wa देव; Lo^{4} Lo^{5} देवे; Pu^{10} रात्र्यहना; BBe^{2} Hy La^{1} वर्षः — b) Jm सविभाग°; TMd^{3} °भागस्तुयोः; GMd^{1} °भागः पुनस्तयोः — d) Ox^{3} रात्रिं; TMd^{3} रात्रिर्या दक्षि°

68.* a) Jo^{1} ब्रह्मस्य; Kt^{2} ब्राह्मण्य; wKt^{3} TMd^{3} ब्राह्मणस्य क्षपा°; Lo^{2} च; TMd^{4} क्षपाहश्च; NPu^{1} Pu^{2} Pu^{5} Pu^{7} क्षिपाहस्य; Bo क्षयाहस्त — b) TMd^{4} GMd^{5} GMy MTr^{4} MTr^{6} प्रमाणं यत्समासतः; Bo यद्यत्प्राणं समासगः; *BhP* 2.92 यत्प्रमाणं महीपते — c) BBe^{2} Hy Jm Jo^{1} Jo^{2} Kt^{2} wKt^{3} BKt^{5} Lo^{1} Lo^{2} Lo^{3} TMd^{3} TMd^{4} GMd^{5} GMy Tj^{1} Tj^{2} Tr^{1} MTr^{3} MTr^{4} [*Jolly* M^{4} R Nd] *BhP* 2.93 *Mandlik Jha KSS Dave* तु — d) Tr^{2} क्रमशश्च तथाविधः [see 69d]; La^{1} °बोधयत्; *BhP* 2.93 °बोध मे

69. b) TMd^{3} वर्षाणां तन्त्रकृष्णायतं युगं; Be^{1} Bo Ho Hy Jm Jo^{1} Kt^{2} La^{2} oMd^{2} Tj^{2} MTr^{3} *Jolly* तु कृतं; Ox^{2} च कृतं — c) Ho Wa *om* संध्या — d) Bo संध्याशश्च; TMd^{4} संध्या तच्च; wKt^{3} संध्यांश्च; Jo^{1} संध्यांशस्त्र; NNg [*but cor fh*] Pu^{10} °विधिः; TMd^{3} °विधि

70. a) La^{1} चसंध्येपु — b) wKt^{1} °ध्यांशःस च; sOx^{1} °शेषु रात्रिषु — c) Tj^{1} एकोपायेन; NKt^{4} एकायेन; GMy एकपायेन — d) oOr *om* च

71. a) wKt^{3} La^{2} यदैत°; Lo^{5} तदेत° — b) TMd^{4} °ख्यातमादानचतु°; TMd^{3} चतुर्युगः — c) TMd^{3} °सहस्रं — d) TMd^{3} वर्षमुच्यते

72. a) Jo^{2} La^{2} Lo^{1} NPu^{1} Tj^{1} MTr^{6} च — b) Tj^{1} Tr^{2} सहस्र; Pu^{9} °संख्येया — c) BKt^{5} ब्रह्ममे°; Lo^{1} ब्राह्मकल्पम°; GMd^{1} °कमहो ज्ञयं; TMd^{3} °कमभिज्ञेयं — d) NPu^{1} तावता; Jo^{1} *KKS* तावतीं; Jm Jo^{1} Kt^{2} La^{1} Lo^{1} NPu^{1} Tj^{1} *KKS* रात्रिमेव; *BhP* 2.99 रात्रिरुच्यते; oOr रात्रिरिष्यते

रात्रिं च तावतीमेव तेऽहोरात्रविदो जनाः ॥७३॥
तस्य सोऽहर्निशस्यान्ते प्रसुप्तः प्रतिबुध्यते ।
प्रतिबुद्धश्च सृजति मनः सदसदात्मकम् ॥७४॥
मनः सृष्टिं विकुरुते चोद्यमानं सिसृक्षया ।
आकाशं जायते तस्मात् तस्य शब्दं गुणं विदुः ॥७५॥
आकाशात्तु विकुर्वाणात् सर्वगन्धवहः शुचिः ।
बलवाञ्जायते वायुः स वै स्पर्शगुणो मतः ॥७६॥
वायोरपि विकुर्वाणाद् विरोचिष्णु तमोनुदम् ।
ज्योतिरुत्पद्यते भास्वत् तद्रूपगुणमुच्यते ॥७७॥
ज्योतिषश्च विकुर्वाणादापो रसगुणात्मिकाः ।
अद्भ्यो गन्धगुणा भूमिरित्येषा सृष्टिरादितः ॥७८॥
यत्प्राग्द्वादशसाहस्रमुदितं दैविकं युगम् ।
तदेकसप्ततिगुणं मन्वन्तरमिहोच्यते ॥७९॥

73. Pādas c-d omitted in Pu^{9} — a) GMy तद्वे; Lo^{2} तद्विः; Pu^{10} तद्वो; NPu^{1} तद्यै; Wa तेद्य; Bo Ho NNg Ox^{3} तद्ये; wKt^{1} sOx^{1} sPu^{6} Tr^{2} *BhP* 2.99 एतद्युग°; BKt^{5} °सहस्राणि — b) wKt^{1} BKt^{5} La^{1} Lo^{2} Ox^{2} ब्राह्मयं; Tr^{2} °हर्विदः — c) Lo^{1} Tj^{1} तु — d) Tr^{2} °रात्रिविदो

74. a) *BhP* 2.100 ततोऽसौ युगपर्यन्ते; GMd^{5} तस्यां; Lo^{4} Lo^{5} साहर्नि° — b) Pu^{5} Pu^{7} Pu^{9} प्रसुप्त — c) oOr *BhP* 2.101 प्रतिबुद्धस्तु; Lo^{2} इतिबुद्धश्च; TMd^{4} प्रतिबन्धश्च — d) oOr सदासदात्मकं

75. a) Pu^{10} मनस्त्वष्ट्रा; oOr च कुरुते — b) Jo^{2} Lo^{1} Lo^{3} Pu^{10} Tj^{1} [*Jolly* M$^{1-2-7-8-9}$] नोद्यमानं; sOx^{1} °मानां — c) Bo आकाशे; GMd^{1} TMd^{3} GMd^{5} आकाशो; *BhP* 2.102 विपुलं जायते — d) wKt^{1} sOx^{1} sPu^{6} शव्द; Tj^{2} शव्दे; TMd^{3} शव्दा

76. a) TMd^{4} आकाशाच्च; *BhP* 2.102 विपुलात्तु — b) BKt^{5} तस्य गन्ध°; TMd^{4} सर्वं गन्धवहं — d) TMd^{3} GMd^{5} GMy MTr^{4} MTr^{6} तस्य स्पर्शगुणं विदुः [TMd^{3} GMd^{5} MTr^{6} स्पर्शं; cf. 75d]; Lo^{1} सर्वस्पर्श°; NNg सर्वैस्पर्श°; TMd^{4} तस्य स्पर्श°; Hy स्पर्शो; Bo °गुणोत्तमः; Tr^{2} तमः

77. Pādas c-d omitted in Wa — b) Hy विरौचिष्णु; Lo^{2} TMd^{3} GMy °चिष्णुस्तमो°; BKt^{5} TMd^{3} GMy Pu^{9} तमोनुदः — c-d) *BhP* 2.104 उत्पद्यते विचित्रांशुस्तस्य रूपगुणं विदुः — c) Hy द्योतिरुत्पद्यते; BKt^{5} तेज उत्पद्यते

78.* Pādas c-d omitted in Pu^{9} — a) BBe^{2} Lo^{1} Lo^{3} Tj^{1} Tr^{2} *Nā Rc* ज्योतिषस्तु; BBe^{2} ज्योतिषं च; TMd^{3} ज्योतिषां च; TMd^{4} GMd^{5} GMy MTr^{4} MTr^{6} ज्योतिषोपि — a-b) *BhP* 2.104 तस्मादपि विकुर्वाणादापो जाताः स्मृता बुधैः; TMd^{4} विकुर्वाणो दोषो — b) GMy °णादपो; BKt^{5} °गुणरसाः स्मृताः; GMd^{5} Pu^{8} °गुणात्मकाः; BBe^{2} Bo wKt^{1} wKt^{3} Lo^{1} oMd^{2} °गुणान्विताः; GMd^{1} TMd^{3} °गुणाश्रयाः; Hy Jm Jo^{1} Jo^{2} NKt^{4} Lo^{2} Lo^{3} Lo^{4} NNg sOx^{1} Ox^{3} NPu^{1} Pu^{5} sPu^{6} Pu^{7} Pu^{10} Tj^{1} Tj^{2} MTr^{3} Wa *Mandlik Jolly Jha KSS Dave* °गुणाः स्मृताः; Pu^{9} °गुणाः [*rest om*] — c) TMd^{3} GMy MTr^{4} MTr^{6} *Nd* गन्धवहा — d) TMd^{3} सृष्टेरादितः

Additional verse in Tr^{2}; commented by *Rc:*

परस्परानुप्रवेशाद्धारयन्ति परस्परम् ।
गुणं पूर्वस्य पूर्वस्य धारयन्त्युत्तरोत्तरम् ॥

79. Folio containing verses 79–100 missing in La^{1} — a) Bo तत्प्रा°; Hy TMd^{3} °सहस्र° —

मन्वन्तराण्यसंख्यानि सर्गः संहार एव च ।
क्रीडन्निवैतत्कुरुते परमेष्ठी पुनः पुनः ॥८०॥
चतुष्पात्सकलो धर्मः सत्यं चैव कृते युगे ।
नाधर्मेणागमः कश्चिन्मनुष्यानुपवर्तते ॥८१॥
इतरेष्वागमाद्धर्मः पादशस्त्ववरोपितः ।
चौरिकानृतमायाभिर्धर्मश्चापैति पादशः ॥८२॥
अरोगाः सर्वसिद्धार्थाश्चतुर्वर्षशतायुषः ।
कृते त्रेतादिषु त्वेषां वयो ह्रसति पादशः ॥८३॥
वेदोक्तमायुर्मर्त्यानामाशिषश्चैव कर्मणाम् ।
फलन्त्यनुयुगं लोके प्रभावश्च शरीरिणाम् ॥८४॥
अन्ये कृतयुगे धर्मास्त्रेतायां द्वापरेऽपरे ।
अन्ये कलियुगे नृणां युगह्रासानुरूपतः ॥८५॥
तपः परं कृतयुगे त्रेतायां ज्ञानमुच्यते ।

b) *BhP* 2.106 °स्रमुक्तं सौमनसं युगम्; NNg °स्रं देवानामुदितं युगं; TMd^{3} °स्रं दैविकं द्वादशं युगं; NKt^{4} देविकं; BKt^{5} दैवकं; TMd^{4} Tj^{1} दैवतं — c) GMy तदेकं; TMd^{3} तदेव; Bo °गुण

80. a) TMd^{3} °राण्यशेषाणि — b) Lo^{4} TMd^{3} NNg Ox^{3} Wa सर्गं; Jm सृष्टिः; NKt^{4} संभार; TMd^{3} Wa संहारमेव — c) TMd^{3} क्रीडन्ति चैतत्कुरुते — d) Lo^{1} पारमेष्ठी; Wa परमेष्ठि; *BhP* 2.112 °मेष्ठी नराधिप

81.* Pādas a-b cited by *Apa* 1012 — b) Lo^{4} Ox^{3} चापि; GMd^{1} कृतं — c) TMd^{4} नाधरस्सागमः; *Nd* [pāṭha] नाधर्मो नागमः; MTr^{3} °र्मेणाधमः; TMd^{3} °गमो नापि मनु°; GMd^{1} कश्च मनु° — d) La^{2} oOr *BhP* 2.113 °न्मनुष्याणां प्रवर्तते; Pu^{10} °न्मनुरूपा हि मानवाः; Hy Kt^{2} MTr^{3} *KKS* °ष्यान्प्रतिवर्तते; oMd^{2} °ष्यान्प्रतिपद्यते; wKt^{1} °ष्यान्न प्रवर्तते; TMd^{4} °ष्यान्प्रवर्तते [copy unclear]

82. Pādas c-d omitted in MTr^{3}; a more extensive version in *BhP* 2.113–5. Cited by *Apa* 1012 — a) TMd^{4} इति तेष्वाग°; TMd^{3} TMd^{4} °गमो धर्मः; GMy गमाद्धर्मं — b) GMy पदश°; Ox^{2} पादत°; Kt^{2} °परोपितः; Tr^{2} °परोहितः; Be^{1} Bo La^{2} °लोपितः; TMd^{4} NKt^{4} °रोहितः — c) Lo^{4} Lo^{5} Ox^{3} चोरि°; TMd^{3} चौर°; Bo चौरिकामृत°; sOx^{1} sPu^{6} चौरिकाशतमाया°; Hy चौरिकानतमाया° — d) wKt^{1} °श्चापेति

83. Omitted in GMy [haplo]. Cited by *Apa* 1012 — a) NNg Tj^{1} आरोगाः; Bo सिद्धसर्वार्थाश्चतु°; GMd^{1} सर्वसिद्धाश्च चतु°; *Apa* °सिद्धार्याश्चतु° — b) Pu^{9} °तुर्वार्ष° — c) TMd^{3} TMd^{4} *BhP* 2.115 कृत; NKt^{4} कृतं; Jm Jo^{1} Kt^{2} oMd^{2} MTr^{3} *Mandlik Jha KSS Dave* ह्येषां; Pu^{2} त्वेवं; Hy द्वैषां; *Ku Go* gloss पुनः supports तु [others do not comment] — d) Hy Jo^{1} Kt^{2} oMd^{2} Tj^{2} MTr^{3} *KSS* त्वेषामायुर्ह्रसति; TMd^{3} त्रयो; Jo^{1} पदशः; NKt^{4} lacuna at पादशः

84. A longer version given in *BhP* 2.116–7 — a) NKt^{4} lacuna at वेदोक्त — b) GMy °मायुशश्चापि — c) GMd^{5} भवन्त्यनु°; MTr^{4} MTr^{6} ह्रसत्यनु°; GMy हसन्त्यनु°; BKt^{5} °युगे; MTr^{3} *om* लोके — d) GMy प्रभावश्चैव कर्मणां [cf. pāda b]; Tr^{2} प्रभावाश्च

85. Cited by *Dev* 1.27 — b) TMd^{3} द्वापरे युगे; Hy द्वापरेपरं — c) Bo Tr^{2} कृतयुगे; Lo^{2} °युगं; La^{2} °युग; sOx^{1} sPu^{6} °युगे धर्मा — d) Tr^{2} युगह्रस्वानु°; GMd^{1} युगप्रायानु°; MTr^{6} युगप्रासानु°; *BhP* 2.118 युगधर्मानु°; NKt^{4} °सानुपूर्वतः; sOx^{1} sPu^{6} °रूपशः

द्वापरे यज्ञमेवाहुर्दानमेकं कलौ युगे ॥८६॥
सर्वस्यास्य तु सर्गस्य गुप्त्यर्थं स महाद्युतिः ।
मुखबाहूरुपज्जानां पृथक्कर्माण्यकल्पयत् ॥८७॥
अध्यापनमध्ययनं यजनं याजनं तथा ।
दानं प्रतिग्रहं चैव ब्राह्मणानामकल्पयत् ॥८८॥
प्रजानां रक्षणं दानमिज्याध्ययनमेव च ।
विषयेष्वप्रसक्तिं च क्षत्रियस्य समादिशत् ॥८९॥
पशूनां रक्षणं दानमिज्याध्ययनमेव च ।
वणिक्पथं कुसीदं च वैश्यस्य कृषिमेव च ॥९०॥
एकमेव तु शूद्रस्य प्रभुः कर्म समादिशत् ।
एतेषामेव वर्णानां शुश्रूषामनसूयया ॥९१॥
ऊर्ध्वं नाभेर्मेध्यतरः पुरुषः परिकीर्तितः ।

86. Cited by *Hem* 3/3.657; *Dev* 1.27 — a) Jm NKt^4 sOx^1 ततः; *Dev* [vl] तपः धर्मः; La^2 तपःकृतं; GMd^1 कृतंयुगे; Hy °युगं — b) Lo^1 यागमुच्यते [*but mc*]; oOr *Dev* ज्ञानमेव च; *Hem* ज्ञानमुत्तमम् — c) Bo oOr sOx^1 sPu^6 *BhP* 2.119 यज्ञमित्याहु°; Tr^2 यज्ञमिवाहु° — d) NKt^4 GMd^1 TMd^3 GMd^5 GMy MTr^4 *Hem* °हुर्दानमेव कलौ

Rc omits verse 86 and comments on the following in its place:

ब्राह्मं कृतयुगं प्रोक्तं त्रेता तु क्षत्रियं युगम् ।
वैश्यो द्वापरमित्याहुः शूद्रः कलियुगः स्मृतः ॥

Additional verse in Pu^1:

कृतेप्यस्थिगताः प्राणास्त्रेतायां मांसमेव च ।
द्वापरे रुधिरे चैव कलावन्ने प्रतिष्ठिताः ॥

87. a) *BhP* 2.120 सर्वस्य राजन्सर्गस्य; TMd^3 सर्वस्य तु ससर्गस्य; GMd^5 NNg NPu^1 सर्वस्यैवास्य सर्गस्य [cf. 93c]; sOx^1 sPu^6 नु सर्गस्य; Tr^2 तु सर्वस्य — b) Lo^1 गुप्त्यर्थं महामतिः; Tj^1 तु महा°; *BhP* 2.120 च महाद्युते — c) GMy *BhP* 2.120 °बाहूरुपादानां — d) Tr^2 पृथक्कर्माण्यशेषतः; Tj^2 पृथक्कर्माकल्प°; Be^1 °कल्पयन्; Wa °कल्पयेत्

88. Omitted in BKt^5 [haplo]. Cited by *Lakṣ* 1.8 — a) Lo^3 GMd^1 Tj^1 Tr^2 °पनं चाध्ययनं; Pu^9 °ध्ययन — b) Ho Pu^9 *om* याजनं — c) NKt^4 La^2 °ग्रहश्चैव — d) Wa °कल्पयेत्

89. Cited by *Lakṣ* 1.8; *Mādh* 1.396 — a) GMd^1 प्रजानां पालनं — a-b) *BhP* 2.122 प्रजानां पालनं राजन्दानमध्ययनं तथा — c) wKt^1 NKt^4 TMd^3 *BhP* 2.122 विषयेषु प्रसक्तिं; NKt^4 °शक्तिं च; Hy Jm Jo^1 oMd^2 GMy MTr^3 *Mandlik Jha KSS Dave* °सक्तिश्च; BBe^2 Kt^2 wKt^3 °शक्तिश्च — d) *BhP* 2.122 तथेज्यां क्षत्रियस्य तु; TMd^3 Tr^2 [*Jolly* Nd] क्षत्रियाणामकल्पयत्; TMd^4 क्षत्रियाणां; BBe^2 Bo Ho Hy Jo^1 wKt^1 Kt^2 BKt^5 Lo^1 Pu^5 Pu^7 Pu^9 Tj^2 MTr^3 Wa [*Jolly* G Ku] *Go Ku Mandlik KSS Dave* समासतः; sOx^1 समादिशेत्; GMd^5 GMy समाविशत्; wKt^3 समाहितः

90. Cited by *Lakṣ* 1.8–9; *Mādh* 1.416 — a) wKt^1 पालनं — c) TMd^3 NPu^1 Tr^2 वाणिक्पथं; GMy वणिक्प्रथं; Hy वणिक्पृथं; Pu^5 Pu^7 Tj^1 कुशीदं — d) Tr^2 कृषिरेव

91. Cited by *Lakṣ* 1.9 — a) GMy एकामेव; TMd^4 एक एव; Tr^2 एवमेव — b) *BhP* 2.124 कर्म लोके प्रकीर्तितम्; NPu^1 समादिशेत्; BKt^5 समादिशन् — d) Bo °षामनुसूयया; wKt^3 °षामनसूयकां; *BhP* 2.124 °षामनुपूर्वशः

तस्मान्मेध्यतमं त्वस्य मुखमुक्तं स्वयंभुवा ॥९२॥
उत्तमाङ्गोद्भवाज्ज्यैष्ठ्याद् ब्रह्मणश्चैव धारणात् ।
सर्वस्यैवास्य सर्गस्य धर्मतो ब्राह्मणः प्रभुः ॥९३॥
तं हि स्वयंभूः स्वादास्यात् तपस्तप्त्वादितोऽसृजत् ।
हव्यकव्याभिवाह्याय सर्वस्यास्य च गुप्तये ॥९४॥
यस्यास्येन सदाश्नन्ति हव्यानि त्रिदिवौकसः ।
कव्यानि चैव पितरः किं भूतमधिकं ततः ॥९५॥
भूतानां प्राणिनः श्रेष्ठाः प्राणिनां बुद्धिजीविनः ।
बुद्धिमत्सु नराः श्रेष्ठा नरेषु ब्राह्मणाः स्मृताः ॥९६॥
ब्राह्मणेषु च विद्वांसो विद्वत्सु कृतबुद्धयः ।
कृतबुद्धिषु कर्तारः कर्तृषु ब्रह्मवादिनः ॥९७॥
उत्पत्तिरेव विप्रस्य मूर्तिर्धर्मस्य शाश्वती ।

92. a-d) *BhP* 2.125 पुरुषस्य सदा श्रेष्ठं नाभेरूर्ध्वं नृपोत्तम । तस्मादपि शुचितरं मुखं तात स्वयंभुवः — c) TMd^{3} GMd^{5} SOx^{1} NPu^{1} SPu^{6} °ध्यतरं; Be^{1} Ho Jo^{2} WKt^{1} NKt^{4} Lo^{2} Lo^{3} Lo^{4} Lo^{5} Ox^{3} Pu^{8} Tj^{1} Tr^{2} [*Jolly* M$^{3-4}$ G] *Rc* तस्य; TMd^{3} GMd^{5} GMy MTr^{4} MTr^{6} [*Jolly* Nd] चास्य — d) Lo^{4} मुखं शुक्लं; Be^{1} Tr^{2} *Rc* स्वयंभुवः; Hy स्वयंभुव

93. a-b) *BhP* 2.126 तस्मान्मुखाद् द्विजो जात इतीयं वैदिकी श्रुतिः — c) TMd^{3} सर्वस्यैवात्मसर्गस्य; NNg MTr^{4} MTr^{6} सर्वस्यास्य तु सर्गस्य; NKt^{4} lacuna at सर्वस्यैवास्य; Wa सर्गास्य; *BhP* 2.126 धर्मस्य — d) GMy सर्वतो

94. a) *BhP* 2.127 स सृष्टो ब्रह्मणा पूर्वं — b) Jo^{1} तपस्तप्तादितो; *BhP* 2.127 तपस्तप्त्वा कुरूद्वह — c) *BhP* 2.127 हव्यानामिव कव्यानां; Pu^{10} कव्यहव्ये विवाह्याय; TMd^{3} हव्यंकव्यातिवाह्याथ; MTr^{6} °कव्यातिवाह्याय; NNg °कव्यातिबाह्याय; GMd^{5} °कव्यादिवाह्याय; GMy °कव्यानिवाह्याय; SOx^{1} SPu^{6} °वाहाय; Bo °वाद्याय — d) *BhP* 2.127 सर्वस्यापि च; TMd^{3} सर्वस्तस्य च; SOx^{1} SPu^{6} Tr^{2} तु

95. a) *BhP* 2.128 अश्नन्ति च मुखेनास्य — b) TMd^{3} तिदिवौ°; Jo^{2} °वोकसः; NNg °वैकसः — c) WKt^{1} कव्यानि पितरश्चैव; TMd^{4} चैवं — d) WKt^{3} भूयमधिकं; NPu^{1} भूतेमधिकं; Lo^{3} गतः; NKt^{4} is torn after this verse until the end of Ch. 1

96. a) Bo श्रेष्ठः — b) GMy प्राणिनः; TMd^{4} बुध्यजीविनः; GMy मतिजीविनः — c) GMy मतिमत्सु; TMd^{3} नरः; GMy नर — d) GMd^{5} नृपु च ब्राह्मणाः; Lo^{3} ब्राह्मणां; TMd^{3} ब्राह्मणास्तथा; Tr^{2} स्मृतः

97.* Pādas c-d torn in NKt^{4}; pāda-d omitted in Ox^{3} — a) Jo^{1} ब्रह्मणेषु; Bo Ho NNg Pu^{10} तु — c) TMd^{3} कृतवेदिषु — d) TMd^{3} ब्राह्म°; BBe^{2} Bo Ho Hy Jm Jo^{1} WKt^{1} Kt^{2} WKt^{3} Lo^{1} Lo^{2} Lo^{3} TMd^{3} GMd^{5} NPu^{1} Pu^{5} Pu^{7} Pu^{8} Pu^{9} Tr^{2} MTr^{6} *Mandlik Jha KSS Dave* ब्रह्मवेदिनः; Tj^{1} ब्रह्मवोदिनः (*but cor*); Pu^{10} ब्रह्मनोदिनः

Additional half-verse in Lo^{2} GMd^{1} TMd^{4} GMd^{5} GMy *Mandlik* [क, ग]:

ब्रह्मविद्भ्यः परं भूतं न किंचिदिह विद्यते ॥

b) GMy न भूतं न भविष्यति; TMd^{4} मुच्यते

Additional verse in *Mandlik* [ट, ड]:

तेषां न पूजनीयोऽन्यस्त्रिषु लोकेषु विद्यते ।
तपोविद्याविशेषेण पूजयन्ति परस्परम् ॥

स हि धर्मार्थमुत्पन्नो ब्रह्मभूयाय कल्पते ॥९८॥
ब्राह्मणो जायमानो हि पृथिव्यामधिजायते ।
ईश्वरः सर्वभूतानां धर्मकोशस्य गुप्तये ॥९९॥
सर्वं स्वं ब्राह्मणस्येदं यत्किंचिज्जगतीगतम् ।
श्रैष्ठ्येनाभिजनेनेदं सर्वं वै ब्राह्मणोऽर्हति ॥१००॥
स्वमेव ब्राह्मणो भुङ्क्ते स्वं वस्ते स्वं ददाति च ।
आनृशंस्याद् ब्राह्मणस्य भुञ्जते हीतरे जनाः ॥१०१॥
तस्य कर्मविवेकार्थं शेषाणां चानुपूर्वशः ।
स्वायंभुवो मनुर्धीमानिदं शास्त्रमकल्पयत् ॥१०२॥
विदुषा ब्राह्मणेनेदमध्येतव्यं प्रयत्नतः ।
शिष्येभ्यश्च प्रवक्तव्यं सम्यङ् नान्येन केनचित् ॥१०३॥
इदं शास्त्रमधीयानो ब्राह्मणः शंसितव्रतः ।

98. Omitted in Pu^{9} — a-d) *BhP* 2.131 जन्म विप्रस्य राजेन्द्र धर्मार्थमिह कथ्यते । उत्पन्नः सर्वसिद्ध्यर्थं याति ब्रह्मसदो नृप — a) Jo^{2} BKt^{5} Lo^{3} sOx^{1} sPu^{6} Tj^{1} Tr^{2} उत्पत्तिरेषा — c) sOx^{1} sPu^{6} °त्पन्ना — d) GMd^{5} ब्रह्मभूताय; BKt^{5} कल्प्यते

99. Cited by *Apa* 281 — a) TMd^{4} ब्रह्मणो; wKt^{1} जायमानोपि; *Apa* जायमानो वै — a-b) *BhP* 2.132 स चापि जायमानस्तु पृथिव्यामिह जायते — b) Jo^{2} Lo^{1} °व्यामभिजायते; Lo^{3} °व्यामार्भजायते — c) *BhP* 2.132 भूतानां प्रभवायैव; Ho सर्वधर्माणां; *Apa* [vl]सर्वभूतस्य — d) Lo^{2} ब्रह्मकोशस्य; MTr^{3} ब्रह्मशोकस्य

100. Cited by *Apa* 282 — a) Be^{1} Bo Ho Kt^{2} La^{2} Lo^{1} TMd^{3} GMd^{5} sOx^{1} sPu^{6} Pu^{5} Pu^{7} Pu^{9} Tj^{1} Tr^{2} *Apa* [vl] सर्वस्वं; *BhP* 2.133 सर्व हि ब्राह्म°; GMy °णस्यैतद् — b) *BhP* 2.133 यत्किंचित्पृथिवीगतम्; Pu^{10} °गतीमतं — c) *BhP* 2.133 जन्मना चोत्तमेनेदं; Be^{1} Jo^{1} wKt^{3} La^{2} Lo^{1} Lo^{3} Lo^{4} Ox^{3} GMy NPu^{1} Pu^{10} *KSS* श्रेष्ठ्येना°; TMd^{4} *Apa* श्रेष्ठेना° — d) oOr ब्राह्मणस्सर्वमर्हति; Be^{1} सर्वं च; Tj^{2} संभवे ब्राह्म°; TMd^{4} ब्रह्मणो°; MTr^{3} ब्राह्ममर्हति

101. a-d) *BhP* 2.134 स्वकीयं ब्राह्मणो भुङ्क्ते विदधाति च सुव्रत । करुणां कुर्वतस्तस्य भुञ्जन्तीहेतरे जनाः — a) TMd^{4} स्वमेवं; NNg स्वयमेव [*but cor fh*] — b) Kt^{2} स्ववस्ते; Ho स्वहस्ते; Pu^{10} नस्ते; BBe^{2} ददानि — c) Hy Lo^{1} Tj^{1} अनृशं°; La^{1} स्वानृशं° [*but mc sh*]; BKt^{5} °शंस्यं — d) Pu^{9} भुञ्जात

102. a) Tr^{1} सर्वकर्म°; BKt^{5} तस्यैव च विवे°; TMd^{4} GMd^{5} GMy धर्मविवे°; wKt^{3} °विवेकाय — b) Hy Jm Jo^{1} Kt^{2} oMd^{2} Tj^{2} MTr^{3} [*Jolly* M$^{1-2-7-8-9}$] *Mandlik KSS* शेषानामनुपूर्वशः; Bo भूतानां — c) sOx^{1} sPu^{6} Pu^{10} स्वयं° — d) Wa °कल्पयेत्

103. Cited by *Vij* 1.3; *Dev* 1.10 — a) oOr विदुषां; Tj^{1} ब्रह्म° — b) Tr^{2} °तव्यमशेपतः; MTr^{6} °तव्यमयत्नतः — c) *Dev* विद्वद्भिश्च; wKt^{3} °भ्यश्च वक्तव्यं; *BhP* 1.71–2 °भ्यश्चैव वक्तव्यं — d) *BhP* 1.71–2 चातुर्वर्णेभ्य एव हि; Tr^{2} सम्यक्ज्ञानेन

Additional verse in La^{1} NPu^{1}; given after 104 in GMd^{1} GMd^{5} MTr^{4}, and after 105 in Tr^{2} MTr^{6}; cited by *Dev* 1.9:

यथैव वेदाध्ययनं धर्मशास्त्रमिदं तथा ।
अध्येतव्यं ब्राह्मणेन नियतं स्वर्गमिच्छता ॥

a) La^{1} यथा हि; Tr^{2} यथा त्रिवेदाध्य° — b) La^{1} सर्वशास्त्रमनुत्तमं — c) La^{1} ब्राह्मणेन तथाध्येयं

मनोवाग्देहजैर्नित्यं कर्मदोषैर्न लिप्यते ॥१०४॥
पुनाति पङ्क्तिं वंश्यांश्च सप्त सप्त परावरान् ।
पृथिवीमपि चैवेमां कृत्स्नामेकोऽपि सोऽर्हति ॥१०५॥
इदं स्वस्त्ययनं श्रेष्ठमिदं बुद्धिविवर्धनम् ।
इदं यशस्यं सततमिदं निःश्रेयसं परम् ॥१०६॥
अस्मिन्धर्मोऽखिलेनोक्तो गुणदोषौ च कर्मणाम् ।
चतुर्णामपि वर्णानामाचारश्चैव शाश्वतः ॥१०७॥

104. Pu[7] *ma.* Cited by *Dev* 1.10 — b) Hy wKt[3] BKt[5] TMd[3] GMd[5] NNg sOx[1] sPu[6] *BhP* 1.75 *Dev* संशित°; Kt[2] सांशित° — c) Tj[1] °जैर्नित्य; GMy °जैर्नित्यैः — d) *BhP* 1.75 [vl] लिम्पते

105. a) TMd[4] पुनाति हि स वंश्यांश्च; GMy Tj[1] पङ्क्ति; GMy वांश्यांश्च; BKt[5] वंश्यश्च — a-b) *BhP* 1.78 स पूज्यः सर्वकालेषु सर्वैर्वर्णैर्नराधिप — c) *BhP* 1.78 पृथिवीं च तथैवेमां — d) TMd[4] कृत्स्नामपि पुनाति च; Jo[2] Tj[1] कृत्स्नामपि च सो; Be[1] °मेकेपि; NPu[1] सोर्हसि

106 c) Lo[5] इयं; BBe[2] Hy Jm Jo[1] wKt[1] Kt[2] La[1] Lo[1] oMd[2] Ox[2] Tj[2] Tr[2] MTr[3] *Rn Mandlik Bühler KSS* यशस्यमायुष्यमिदं — d) Jo[2] La[1] Lo[2] Lo[3] GMd[5] sOx[1] Ox[2] sPu[6] Tj[1] नैश्रेयसं; MTr[6] [*Jolly* R Nd] नैःश्रेयसं; Bo TMd[3] निश्रेयसं; oOr श्रेयस्करं परं

Additional verse in La[1] Lo[2] TMd[4] GMd[5] GMy MTr[4] MTr[6]:

धन्यं यशस्यमायुष्यं पुण्यं स्वर्गापवर्गदम् ।
धारणं धर्मशास्त्रस्य वेदानां धारणं यथा ॥

a) La[1] Lo[2] धनं; GMy सत्यं; TMd[4] वशस्य° — b) La[1] नित्यं; La[1] स्वर्गोप° — c) TMd[4] धारणाद्धर्म°; Lo[2] धाराद्धर्म°; La[1] सर्वशा° — d) Lo[2] वेदात्कारणात्तथा; GMy तथा

Additional verse in Lo[2] GMd[5] MTr[4] MTr[6]; pādas c-d in TMd[4]:

म्रियते नानपत्यश्च नानर्थमिह गच्छति ।
ग्रहणादेव शास्त्रस्य सद्भिः साम्यं च गच्छति ॥

a) MTr[6] यथा नीयते नानपत्यश्च— a-b) GMd[5] श्रियस्तेनानतपत्यश्च नार्थकृच्छ्रमिहच्छति — b) Lo[2] नार्थकृच्छ्रमिहार्हति

Additonal verses in Lo[2]; verses 1–2 given in GMd[5] and verses 1 a-b and 3 a-b in TMd[4]:

अर्हः स्याद्धव्यकव्यानां ब्राह्मणो नात्र संशयः ।
पङ्क्तीनां पावनः श्रेष्ठो ब्रह्मणो वेदपारगः ॥१॥
धर्मशास्त्रस्य चैवास्य पारगः पङ्क्तिपावनः ।
यथैव वेदाध्ययनं धर्मशास्त्रमिदं तथा ॥२॥
पुण्यं पवित्रं परममायुषश्च विवर्धनम् ।
अध्येतव्यं ब्राह्मणेन नियतं स्वर्गमिच्छता ॥३॥
गुरुशुश्रूपयोपेतः स्वाध्यायाध्ययने रतः ।
इदं शास्त्रमधीयीत तपस्वी शंसितव्रतः ॥४॥
इदं पुंसवनं श्रेष्ठमिदं स्वस्त्यपरं महत् ।
नीतिशास्त्रमिदं लोक्यं मोक्षशास्त्रमिदं परम् ॥५॥

1. a) TMd[4] अर्हस्तु हव्य° — a-b) GMd[5] अर्हास्याहव्यकव्यानामस्य शास्त्रस्य धारणात् — c-d) GMd[5] पंक्तीनां पावनाश्रैष्ठ्यात् ब्राह्मणा वेदपारगाः

2. a) GMd[5] चैतस्य — b) GMd[5] पारकाः पंक्तिपावनाः

107. Omitted in Hy — a) wKt[3] तस्मिन्ध°; Lo[2] यस्मिन्ध°; Pu[7] अस्मिन्स्मार्तो [*but cor*]; Kt[2] TMd[4] °न्धर्मे; Tr[2] °खिलोनोक्तो; Lo[3] Tj[1] [*Jolly* R] °खिलः प्रोक्तो — b) GMd[5] गुणदोषेण वर्मणां; TMd[4] °दोषे;

आचारः परमो धर्मः श्रुत्युक्तः स्मार्त एव च ।
तस्मादस्मिन्सदा युक्तो नित्यं स्यादात्मवान्द्विजः ॥१०८॥
आचाराद्विच्युतो विप्रो न वेदफलमश्नुते ।
आचारेण तु संयुक्तः संपूर्णफलभाक्स्मृतः* ॥१०९॥
एवमाचारतो दृष्ट्वा धर्मस्य मुनयो गतिम् ।
सर्वस्य तपसो मूलमाचारं जगृहुः परम् ॥११०॥
जगतश्च समुत्पत्तिं संस्कारविधिमेव च ।
व्रतचर्योपचारं च स्नानस्य च परं विधिम् ॥१११॥
दाराधिगमनं चैव विवाहानां च लक्षणम् ।
महायज्ञविधानं च श्राद्धकल्पं च शाश्वतम् ॥११२॥
वृत्तीनां लक्षणं चैव स्नातकस्य व्रतानि च ।
भक्ष्याभक्ष्यं च शौचं च द्रव्याणां शुद्धिमेव च ॥११३॥
स्त्रीधर्मयोगं तापस्यं मोक्षं संन्यासमेव च ।
राज्ञश्च धर्ममखिलं कार्याणां च विनिर्णयम् ॥११४॥

[*Jolly* R] कर्मिणां — c) GMy सर्वेषामपि — d) oOr BKt^{5} *BhP* 1.80 °चारश्चापि; Tr^{2} शाश्वताः

108. a) Jo^{2} La^{2} Lo^{3} Lo^{4} GMy Tj^{1} Tj^{2} *BhP* 1.81 प्रथमो; GMd^{5} प्रभवो — b) *BhP* 1.81 श्रुत्युक्तश्च नरोत्तम — c) GMy °दस्मिंस्त्रयो; GMd^{5} MTr^{4} °दस्मिंस्त्रये; TMd^{3} °दस्मिंस्त्रया; Lo^{2} °दस्मिंस्त्रयी; MTr^{6} °दस्मिन्सूये; Pu^{8} °न्सता; Bo wKt^{3} La^{1} [*but mc sh*] La^{2} Lo^{4} Lo^{5} Ox^{3} NPu^{1} Pu^{10} Tj^{2} Wa *BhP* 1.81 °न्समायुक्तो

109. Pādas a-b and c-d transposed in oOr — a) Tr^{2} °च्युते — b) Pu^{10} °फलभाग्भवेत् — c) TMd4 °रेण विसंयुक्तः; Lo^{5} *om* तु; La^{1} हि [*but mc sh*]; *BhP* 1.81 च — d) NKt^{4} संपूर्णं फलमश्नुते; La^{1} संपूर्णः; MTr^{6} °फलकं स्मृतं; BBe^{2} Hy Jm Jo^{1} Jo^{2} wKt^{1} Kt^{2} wKt^{3} BKt^{5} La^{1} Lo^{3} oMd^{2} TMd^{3} GMy Ox^{2} Tj^{1} Tj^{2} MTr^{3} [*Jolly*Ku R] *Mandlik KSS* °फलभाग्भवेत्

110. a) Bo एवमाचरतो — b) GMd^{5} गतिः

111. a) *BhP* 1.85 त्रिलोक्यास्तु समुत्पत्तिं [vl पत्तिः] — b) sOx^{1} sPu^{6} संस्कारं; *BhP* 1.85 °विधिमुत्तमम् [vl °विधिरुत्तमः] — c) *BhP* 1.86 व्रतचर्याश्रमाचाराः; Pu^{9} प्रकृतव्रतोपचारं च; wKt^{1} ब्रह्मचर्योप°; MTr^{4} MTr^{6} °चारौ; TMd^{3} °चारांश्च — d) *BhP* 1.86 स्नातकस्य परो विधिः; Tj^{1} स्नातस्य; sOx^{1} sPu^{6} MTr^{4} *Nā* स्नातकस्य परं; Be^{1} स्नातकस्य पपं [sic]; Pu^{10} विधिं परं; Lo^{4} विधिः

112. Pādas b-d *ma fh* in NNg — a) GMy *BhP* 1.87 दारादिग°; Hy Lo^{5} Tj^{2} दाराभिग° — b) GMy विवाहादीनां च; Hy *om* च — c) La^{1} NNg sOx^{1} sPu^{6} Tr^{2} *Rc* पञ्चयज्ञ°; TMd^{3} महायन्त्र°; GMy °विधानां — d) sOx^{1} sPu^{6} श्रद्धा°; *BhP* 1.88 शास्त्र°; TMd^{3} GMd^{5} GMy श्राद्धकर्म; Tj^{2} °कल्पे; Pu^{10} °कालं; Jo^{1} Kt^{2} °कल्पश्च शाश्वतः

113. Pāda-a *ma fh* in NNg — a) sOx^{1} sPu^{6} वृत्तानां; Kt^{2} वृत्तिनां; Hy वृत्तीलक्षणं — c) Tr^{2} भक्ष्याभैक्ष्यं; Kt^{2} भक्षाभक्षं; TMd^{4} *om* शौचं च — d) Pu^{5} द्रव्याशुद्धिमेव; Pu^{7} [*but cor*] Pu^{9} बुद्धिमेव; *BhP* 1.89 [vl] शुद्धिरेव; oOr *om* च

114. a) Kt^{2} °योगे; *BhP* 1.90 [vl] °योगस्तापस्यं — b) GMd^{5} *BhP* 1.90 [vl] मोक्षः संन्यास एव; Lo^{1} संन्यासं मोक्षमेव — c) Be^{1} Kt^{2} TMd^{3} राज्ञां च; *BhP* 1.90 [vl] धर्मो ह्यखिलः; Ox^{3} °माखिलं — d)

साक्षिप्रश्नविधानं च धर्मं स्त्रीपुंसयोरपि ।
विभागधर्मं द्यूतं च कण्टकानां च शोधनम् ॥११५॥
वैश्यशूद्रोपचारं च संकीर्णानां च संभवम् ।
आपद्धर्मं च वर्णानां प्रायश्चित्तविधिं तथा ॥११६॥
संसारगमनं चैव त्रिविधं कर्मसंभवम् ।
निःश्रेयसं कर्मणां च गुणदोषपरीक्षणम् ॥११७॥
देशधर्माञ्जातिधर्मान् कुलधर्मांश्च शाश्वतान् ।
पाषण्डगणधर्मांश्च शास्त्रेऽस्मिन्नुक्तवान्मनुः ॥११८॥
यथेदमुक्तवाञ्छास्त्रं पुरा पृष्टो मनुर्मया ।
तथेदं यूयमप्यद्य मत्सकाशान्निबोधत ॥११९॥

॥ इति मानवे धर्मशास्त्रे भृगुप्रोक्तायां संहितायां प्रथमोऽध्यायः ॥

ʙKt^{5} *om* च; Tr^{2} *BhP* 1.90 [vl] विनिर्णयः

115. Pāda b-d omitted in La^{2}; verses 115 and 116 transposed in Kt^{2}. Cited by *Bh* at 9.2 — a) *BhP* 1.91 संक्षिप्तं संविधानं च — b) *BhP* 1.91 [vl] धर्मः — d) Lo^{1} sOx^{1} sPu^{6} Tr^{2} कण्टकानां विशोधनं

116. Pāda-a omitted in La^{2} — a) ɢMy °चारौ — b) ᴛMd^{4} संभवः — c) ᴍTr^{4} आपद्धर्मांश्च — d) ᴛMd^{3} प्रायश्चित्तं विधिं; oMd^{2} ततः

117. ᴛMd^{4} ends the chapter after 117b — b) Kt^{2} ʙKt^{5} विविधं; wKt^{1} धर्मसंभवं; ᴛMd^{3} कर्मसंग्रहं — c) Lo^{1} निश्रेयसं; La^{1} oOr ᴍTr^{6} *BhP* 1.95 नैःश्रेयसं; ᴛMd^{3} ɢMd^{5} ɢMy ᴍTr^{4} नैश्रेयसं

118. a) Bo Ho Lo^{2} ɢMd^{1} ᴛMd^{3} ɢMd^{5} ɴNg ᴍTr^{4} ᴍTr^{6} *BhP* 1.98 जातिधर्मान्देशधर्मान्; Tr^{2} °ञ्जातिधर्मांश्च — a-b) Pu^{10} देशधर्मान्कुलधर्माञ्जातिधर्मांश्च शाश्वतान् — b) Wa *om* कुलधर्मान्; ᴛMd^{3} °धर्मा सदैव च; Ho *om* च; *BhP* 1.98 °धर्मांश्च वै नृप — c) *BhP* 1.99 वैतानव्रतिकानां च; oOr sOx^{1} sPu^{6} पाषाण्ड° [sPu^{6} *mc sh to* पाषाण्डि°]; Lo^{4} ɴNg Ox^{3} Pu^{10} Wa [*Jolly* M$^{3-4-7-9}$] पाषण्डि°; Bo Jo^{2} wKt^{3} ʙKt^{5} Lo^{1} Ox^{2} Pu^{5} Pu^{7} Pu^{9} पाखण्ड°; [*Jolly* M^{1-2-8}] पाखण्डि°; ʙBe^{2} sOx^{1} sPu^{6} [*but mc sh*] °गुण°; Tj^{2} °धर्मौ च — d) *BhP* 1.99 तथासौ प्रोक्तवान्विभुः; Tj^{1} [*but cor*] °वान्मुनिः; ʙKt^{5} °वान्प्रभुः

119. b) ɢMy मया पृष्टो मनुः पुरा; Jo^{2} मनुर्यथा; ᴛMd^{3} मया मनुः — c) ʙKt^{5} तथैव; ᴛMd^{3} स्वयमप्यद्य; Lo^{1} °प्याद्य; Lo^{4} Lo^{5} °प्यस्य

Colophon: Jo^{1} इति मानवीये प्रथमोध्यायः; Be^{1} Lo^{1} sOx^{1} Ox^{2} sPu^{6} Pu^{8} Tj^{1} Tj^{2} Tr^{2} श्रीमानवे; Lo^{3} Tj^{1} मानवीये; oOr wKt^{3} भृगुप्रोक्ते; Lo^{3} sOx^{1} sPu^{6} Wa °प्रोक्तसंहितायां; Be^{1} ʙKt^{5} Lo^{1} ᴛMd^{3} ɴPu^{1} *om* भृगुप्रोक्तायां संहितायां; wKt^{1} wKt^{3} La^{1} ɢMy oOr *om* संहितायां; Tr^{2} भृगुप्रोक्ते जगदुत्पत्तिर्नाम प्रकरणं प्रथमो; La^{1} सृष्टिर्नाम प्रथमो; wKt^{1} सृष्टिक्रमो नाम प्रथमो; Be^{1} जगदुत्पत्तिः प्रथमो; Wa जगदुत्पत्तिर्नाम प्रथमो; ɴNg जगत्समुत्पत्तिर्नाम प्रथमो; wKt^{1} सृष्टिक्रमा नाम प्रथमो; Pu^{1} समस्तव्यवहारापातनिका नाम प्रथमो; ɴNg Pu^{2} °ध्यायः समाप्तः

[द्वितीयोऽध्यायः]

विद्वद्भिः सेवितः सद्भिर्नित्यमद्वेषरागिभिः ।
हृदयेनाभ्यनुज्ञातो यो धर्मस्तं निबोधत ॥१॥
कामात्मता न प्रशस्ता न चैवेहास्त्यकामता ।
काम्यो हि वेदाधिगमः कर्मयोगश्च वैदिकः ॥२॥
संकल्पमूलः कामो वै यज्ञाः संकल्पसंभवाः ।
व्रतानि यमधर्माश्च सर्वे संकल्पजाः स्मृताः ॥३॥
अकामस्य क्रिया काचिद् दृश्यते नेह कर्हिचित् ।
यद्यद्धि कुरुते किंचित् तत्तत्कामस्य चेष्टितम् ॥४॥
तेषु सम्यग्वर्तमानो गच्छत्यमरलोकताम् ।
यथासंकल्पितांश्चेह सर्वान्कामान्समश्नुते ॥५॥

1. Verses 1–17b missing in Pu^{5}. Cited by *Hem* 2/1.10; *Dev* 1.13; *Mādh* 1.80 — a) Bo विवद्भिः; mTr^{3} सेवितं; La^{2} सेविता; tMd^{3} सिवितं — b) Tr^{2} °द्वेषि°; tMd^{3} °द्वैत° — c) Be^{1} °ज्ञाते — d) bKt^{5} योगधर्मस्तं; tMd^{3} यस्तं धर्मं; Tr^{1} धर्मं तं; Wa निबोधते; Tr^{2} निबोधिता; tMd^{3} gMd^{5} gMy Tr^{1} व्यवस्यत; nKt^{4} व्यवस्यता

2. Pādas c-d omited in Tr^{2}. Verses 2–4 referred to by *Śaṃ* on *BU* 1.4.17: मानवे च सर्वा प्रवृत्तिः कामहेतुक्येवेति — a) La^{1} कामार्थतान्प्रश° [*but mc sh*]; Bo कामात्माता; tMd^{3} कामात्मना; gMy प्रशस्या — b) *BhP* 7.49 न वेहास्याप्यकामता; Tr^{2} °हासकामता; tMd^{3} gMd^{5} gMy Tr^{1} mTr^{4} mTr^{6} °कामतः — c) mTr^{4} वेदोधिगमः — d) La^{1} कर्मवेदश्च [*but mc sh*]; Kt^{2} tMd^{3} °योगं च

3. Omitted in Tr^{2}. Pādas a-b cited by *Śaṃ* on *BhG* 6.4 — a) Tr^{1} °मूल; tMd^{3} *Nd* °मूलं; tMd^{3} कामो ह — a-b) *BhP* 7.50 संकल्पाज्जायते कामो यज्ञाद्यानि च सर्वशः — b) La^{2} °संभवः — c) Lo^{1} व्रतानि नियमाः धर्माः — d) Pu^{9} संकल्पजः

4. Pādas c-d cited by *Śaṃ* on *BU* 4.4.5 and *BhG* 6.4 — a) *BhP* 7.51 कामादृते क्रियाकारी — b) Ho La^{2} gMd^{1} tMd^{3} tMd^{4} gMd^{5} gMy Tr^{1} mTr^{4} कस्यचित्; mTr^{6} केनचित् — c) gMd^{1} *om first* यद्; Wa कुरवे; Be^{1} bBe^{2} Bo oMd^{2} Pu^{8} Wa *Śaṃ* on *BU* and *BhG* कुरुते कर्म [*Śaṃ* on BhG Śrīraṅgam ed. reads कुरुते जन्तुः]; Tr^{1} *BhP* 7.51 कश्चित् — d) bKt^{5} °त्काम्यस्य

5. b) Bo गच्छत्परमलोकतां; tMd^{3} °त्यामरलोकतां; La^{1} °त्यपरलोकतां — c) bKt^{5} यथावत्कल्पि-ताश्चेह; nPu^{1} तथा°; tMd^{4} °कल्पितं चेह; gMd^{5} °तांश्चैह; tMd^{3} tMd^{4} Pu^{10} Wa [*Jolly* $^{1-2-7-8-9}$] °तांश्चैव; Tr^{1} °तांश्चैवं

Additional verses in Lo^{2} gMd^{1} tMd^{4} gMd^{5} gMy Tr^{1} mTr^{4} mTr^{6} *Mandlik* [क, ग] *KSS*; first verse only in La^{1}:

असद्वृत्तस्तु कामेषु कामोपहतचेतनः ।
नरकं समवाप्नोति तत्फलं चैव नाश्नुते ॥१॥
तस्मात् श्रुतिस्मृतिप्रोक्तं यथाविध्युपपादितम् ।

वेदोऽखिलो धर्ममूलं स्मृतिशीले च तद्विदाम् ।
आचारश्चैव साधूनामात्मनस्तुष्टिरेव च ॥६॥
यः कश्चित्कस्यचिद्धर्मो मनुना परिकीर्तितः ।
स सर्वोऽभिहितो वेदे सर्वज्ञानमयो हि सः ॥७॥
सर्वं तु समवेक्ष्येदं निखिलं ज्ञानचक्षुषा ।
श्रुतिप्रामाण्यतो विद्वान् स्वधर्मे निविशेत वै ॥८॥
श्रुतिस्मृत्युदितं धर्ममनुतिष्ठन्हि मानवः ।
इह कीर्तिमवाप्नोति प्रेत्य चानुत्तमं सुखम् ॥९॥
श्रुतिस्तु वेदो विज्ञेयो धर्मशास्त्रं तु वै स्मृतिः ।
ते सर्वार्थेष्वमीमांस्ये ताभ्यां धर्मो हि निर्बभौ ॥१०॥
योऽवमन्येत ते तूभे हेतुशास्त्राश्रयाद् द्विजः ।
स साधुभिर्बहिष्कार्यो नास्तिको वेदनिन्दकः ॥११॥

काम्यं कर्मेह भवति श्रेयसे न विपर्यये ॥२॥

1\. a) La^{1} असवृत्तस्तु; MTr^{4} सद्वृत्तस्तु; GMd^{5} काम्येपु — b) MTr^{4} MTr^{6} °पहते; La^{1} °चेतसः — d) Lo^{2} *Mandlik KSS* तत्फलं न समश्नुते; La^{1} न फलं चैव चाश्नुते; GMd^{1} GMy तत्फलश्चैव

2\. a) TMd^{4} GMd^{5} *KSS* तस्माच्छ्रुति° — c) La^{1} GMd^{1} GMy कर्मैव — d) TMd^{4} च विपर्यये; Lo^{2} GMd^{1} *Mandlik KSS* विपर्ययः

6\. Cited by *Viś* 1.7; *Vij* 1.254; *Apa* 82; *Hem* 2/1.17; *Har*-A 1.1.3; *Dev* 1.5; pādas a-b cited by *Apa* 7 — a) Bo °खिले; TMd^{3} °खिला; GMd^{1} °मूलो — a-b) *BhP* 7.52 निगमो धर्ममूलं स्यात्स्मृतिशीले तथैव च — b) TMd^{3} स्मृतिरेते; La^{1} *Viś* °शीलं; Tj^{1} °शील; Lo^{2} °शीलेव; Bo तद्विदा; sOx^{1} तद्विधां — c) La^{2} आचाराश्चैव; La^{1} आचारस्यैव; *BhP* 7.52 तथाचारश्च साधू° — d) *Apa* °धूनां वेदवित्स्मृतिशीलता [vl शीलव्यता]; La^{1} °ष्टिमेव [*but mc sh*]; *Vij* वा

7\. Cited by *Viś* 1.7; *Hem* 3/1.207, 3/3.476 — c) Be^{1} *Viś* सर्वाभिहितो; oOr सर्वेभिहिते; Tr^{1} सर्वोहितो; wKt^{3} सर्वो विहितो; GMd^{5} सर्वोपहितो वेदैस्सर्व°; GMy वेदो; Wa वेद — d) Bo °मयी; Tr^{2} ह

8\. a) La^{1} सर्वाणि समवे° [*but mc sh*]; sOx^{1} NPu^{1} sPu^{6} च; GMd^{5} हि; *BhP* 7.53 समवेक्षेत; TMd^{3} सहवेक्ष्येदं — b) GMy अखिलं; *BhP* 7.53 निश्चितं; GMd^{5} वेदचक्षुषा — c) Ho स्वप्रामा°; BCa La^{1} GMd^{1} GMy NPu^{1} °प्रमाण्यतो; Tr^{2} °प्रामण्यतो; *BhP* 7.53 °प्राधान्यतो; NKt^{4} वृद्धान् — d) TMd^{4} स्वधर्मं; Lo^{3} Tj^{1} सधर्मे; *BhP* 7.53 निवसेत

9\. Cited by *Hem* 2/1.14 — a) Lo^{4} °स्मृत्युदिते; Pu^{10} सर्वमनुति° — b) Tr^{1} धर्मं ह्यनुति°; wKt^{3} °तिष्ठति मानवः; *BhP* 7.54 °तिष्ठन्सदा नरः; NNg मानवाः — c-d) *BhP* 7.54 प्राप्य चेह परां कीर्तिं याति शक्रसलोकताम् [vl ब्रह्मसलो°] — d) Hy वानुत्तमं; Tj^{2} सुखः

10.* Pāda-d omitted in Ox^{3} — a) *BhP* 7.55 [vl] धर्मो विज्ञेयो — b) wKt^{3} GMy °शास्त्रस्तु; TMd^{3} °शास्त्रमलं स्मृतिः — c) Bo Ho wKt^{1} La^{1} La^{2} Lo^{1} [*but mc sh*] Lo^{2} Lo^{4} TMd^{3} Ox^{2} Tj^{1} Tj^{2} MTr^{4} MTr^{6} *BhP* 7.55 *Rn* सर्वार्थेषु मीमांस्ये; Tr^{1} °मांस्य; sOx^{1} sPu^{6} Tr^{2} °मांसे — d) BKt^{5} निर्ममौ; TMd^{3} निश्चितः

11\. Cited by *Viś* 3.222; *Dev* 1.4; *Mādh* 1.12, 2.424 — a) NKt^{4} Wa °मन्यत; Jm Jo^{1} Kt^{2} MTr^{3} *Mandlik KSS Dave* ते मूले; *BhP* 7.56 ते चोभे; Hy wKt^{1} ते भूते; TMd^{4} तूभे ते; Ox^{2} त उभे; Pu^{9} ते कृभे; Pu^{10} हेतूभे; [*Jolly* N] तदुभयं — b) GMy हेतुशास्त्रान्तराश्रयः; Lo^{1} °शास्त्रश्रयाद्; GMd^{5} °शास्त्राश्रयो नरः; TMd^{4} °शास्त्रचरो नरः; Ox^{3} °श्रयान्; Lo^{2} oOr Pu^{10} MTr^{6} *BhP* 7.56 [vl] *Dev* °श्रयो;

वेदः स्मृतिः सदाचारः स्वस्य च प्रियमात्मनः ।
एतच्चतुर्विधं प्राहुः साक्षाद्धर्मस्य लक्षणम् ॥१२॥
अर्थकामेष्वसक्तानां धर्मज्ञानं विधीयते ।
धर्मं जिज्ञासमानानां प्रमाणं परमं श्रुतिः ।।१३॥
श्रुतिद्वैधं तु यत्र स्यात् तत्र धर्मावुभौ स्मृतौ ।
उभावपि हि तौ धर्मौ सम्यगुक्तौ मनीषिभिः ॥१४॥
उदितेऽनुदिते चैव समयाध्युषिते तथा ।
सर्वथा वर्तते यज्ञ इतीयं वैदिकी श्रुतिः ॥१५॥
निषेकादिश्मशानान्तो मन्त्रैर्यस्योदितो विधिः ।

TMd[3] Tr[1] °श्रयान्त्ररः; Bo oOr NPu[1] द्विजाः — c) GMy °भिर्बहिर्भूतो; NKt[4] °हिष्कार्या — d) Be[1] *mc to* सर्वस्माद् द्विजकर्मणः [cf. 103d]; NKt[4] नास्तिका; oOr वेदनिन्दकाः

12. a) NNg MTr[4] MTr[6] श्रुतिः स्मृतिः; TMd[4] स्मृतिस्तदाचारः; oOr समाचारः — b) BBe[2] सम्यक्च प्रिय°; BKt[5] प्रियमिच्छतां — c) *BhP* 7.57 °तुर्विधं विप्राः; TMd[4] प्राह; Ox[3] वाहुः; Lo[4] चाहुः — d) GMd[5] लक्षणात्; GMd[1] कारणं

13. a) La[1] wKt[1] °कामेषु सक्तानां [La[1] शक्ता°] — a-b) *BhP* 7.58 धर्मज्ञानं भवेद्विप्रा अर्थकामेष्वसज्जताम् — b) Hy Jo[1] धर्मं; Pu[9] धर्माज्ञानं; BBe[2] GMd[1] TMd[3] MTr[4] °ज्ञानां — c) GMy धर्म; Lo[1] जिज्ञास्य° — d) *BhP* 7.58 प्रमाणं नैगमं परम्; [*Jolly* M[1-2-8-9]] प्रामाण्यं; Pu[10] प्रमाण्यं; GMy परमां; TMd[4] परम; GMd[5] प्रथमं

14. Cited by *Dev* 1.15–6 — a) TMd[3] श्रुतिर्वैधं; Wa °द्वैधे — c) TMd[3] Tr[1] MTr[4] MTr[6] उभावभिहितौ धर्मौ; wKt[1] हि ता; BKt[5] धर्म्यौ; TMd[4] धर्मैस्सम्य° — d) wKt[3] सौम्यगुक्तौ; TMd[3] सम्यगुक्तं; Tj[1] सम्यगुप्तौ

15. Cited by *Dev* 2.426; *Mādh* 1.288 — a) TMd[3] उदितानुदिते — b) GMd[5] समयाभ्युदिते; Tr[1] समयाविषिते; TMd[3] समयान्विषिते; Lo[1] समयाध्युते; wKt[1] कामनाध्युषिते — c) MTr[3] सर्वधा — d) NNg वैदकी

Additional verses in La[1] Lo[2] GMd[1] TMd[4] GMd[5] Tr[1] MTr[4] MTr[6] *Mandlik* [क, ग, ट] *KSS*; first verse only in GMy *Mādh* 1.12; the second verse in *Dev* 1.7 [this is a versification of ĀpDh 2.13.7–9]:

श्रुतिं पश्यन्ति मुनयः स्मरन्ति तु तथा स्मृतिम् ।
तस्मात्प्रमाणमुभयं प्रमाणैः प्रथितं भुवि ॥१॥
धर्मव्यतिक्रमो दृष्टो महतां साहसं तथा ।
तदन्वीक्ष्य प्रयुञ्जानः संसीदत्यवरोऽबलः ॥२॥

1. a) La[1] भुजं पश्यन्ति — b) TMd[4] मुनय [lacuna] रंते तु श्रुतिः; GMd[5] *Mādh* च; *KSS* यथास्मृति; La[1] *Mandlik* यथाश्रुतं; GMd[1] GMy स्मृति; MTr[4] MTr[6] स्मृतिः— c) Lo[2] GMd[1] TMd[4] *KSS* तस्मात्प्रमाणं मुनयः — d) GMd[5] प्रामाण्यैः; Lo[2] TMd[4] *Mandlik KSS* प्रमाणं; GMd[5] GMy MTr[4] MTr[6] प्रमितं; Tr[1] प्रणितं; GMd[1] प्रमितिं; *Mādh* प्रापितं; GMy विभुः

2. a) La[1] *Mandlik* धर्मे — b) La[1] Lo[2] TMd[4] *Mandlik KSS* दृष्टः श्रेष्ठानां; Tr[1] साहसस्तथा — c) La[1] इदं वीक्ष्य; Lo[2] GMd[1] Tr[1] प्रयुञ्जानाः — d) Lo[2] *Mandlik KSS* सीदन्त्यवरधर्मजाः [*Mandlik KSS* °पर°]; GMd[1] संसीदन्त्यपरेधर्मजाः; Tr[1] संसीदन्त्यावृता नराः; TMd[4] सीदत्यवरवर्णजाः; *Dev* सीदत्यवरजोऽबलः; MTr[4] MTr[6] °परोबलः

तस्य शास्त्रेऽधिकारोऽस्मिञ्ज्ञेयो नान्यस्य कस्यचित् ॥१६॥
सरस्वतीदृषद्वत्योर्देवनद्योर्यदन्तरम् ।
तं देवनिर्मितं देशं ब्रह्मावर्तं प्रचक्षते ॥१७॥
तस्मिन्देशे य आचारः पारंपर्यक्रमागतः ।
वर्णानां सान्तरालानां स सदाचार उच्यते ॥१८॥
कुरुक्षेत्रं च मत्स्याश्च पञ्चालाः शूरसेनकाः ।
एष ब्रह्मर्षिदेशो वै ब्रह्मावर्तादनन्तरः ॥१९॥
एतद्देशप्रसूतस्य सकाशादग्रजन्मनः ।
स्वं स्वं चरित्रं शिक्षेरन् पृथिव्यां सर्वमानवाः ॥२०॥
हिमवद्विन्ध्ययोर्मध्यं यत्प्राग्विनशनादपि ।
प्रत्यगेव प्रयागाच्च मध्यदेशः प्रकीर्तितः ॥२१॥
आ समुद्रात्तु वै पूर्वादा समुद्रात्तु पश्चिमात् ।

16. Cited by *Śaṃ* on *BU* 4.5.15 [pāda-d also repeated at end of 4.5.15]; *Vij* 1.3; *Apa* 14 *Dev* 1.11 — a) Bo Ho *Apa Dave* निषेकादिः; Ho °नान्ते; *BhP* 7.59 [vl] *Dev* [vl as in ex] °नान्तं; TMd^{4} °नान्त; oOr °नान्तैर्मन्त्रै° — b) Hy °दितौ — c) TMd^{4} शास्त्राधिकारो; Tr^{1} °धिकारे; Wa °धिकारौ; BKt^{5} TMd^{3} °धिकारोस्ति ज्ञेयो — c-d) *BhP* 7.59 अधिकारो भवेत्तस्य वेदेषु च जयेषु च [vl जपेषु] — d) *Vij* कर्हिचित् [vl as in ed]

17. Cited by *Apa* 5; *Hem* 2/1.24; *Lakṣ* 1.46; *Dev* 1.17 — b) Lo^{2} °त्योर्दैव°; *Apa* °त्योर्व्योमनद्यो° — c) Hy Jm NPu^{1} तद्देव°; *BhP* 7.60 तदेव निर्मि° — d) Jm देशमार्यावर्तं; GMy ब्रह्मवर्तं; La^{2} oMd^{2} ब्राह्मावर्तं; Hy ब्रह्मावतै; sOx^{1} sPu^{6} °वर्तं विदुर्बुधाः; NPu^{1} प्रचक्ष्यते

18. *ma* in Tj^{2}. Cited by *Apa* 19; *Lakṣ* 1.46; *Mādh* 1.134 — a) NKt^{4} GMd^{5} NNg Tr^{1} अस्मिन्देशे; Lo^{3} TMd^{3} GMy Tj^{1} Tr^{2} *BhP* 7.61 [vl] *Apa* यस्मिन्देशे; Pu^{9} स; Bo यमाचारः; wKt^{1} Tr^{2} यदाचारः — b) *Apa* पारंपर्यात्समागतः; Be^{1} पारंपर्यं; Tr^{2} पारंपार्य° — c) TMd^{3} धर्माणां — c-d) NPu^{1} वर्णानां स सदाचार उच्यते सर्वदा बुधैः — d) TMd^{3} *Lakṣ* सदाचारः स उच्यते

19. Cited by *Apa* 5; *Lakṣ* 1.46; *Hem* 2/1.25; *Dev* 1.17 — a) Pu^{9} °क्षैत्रं; MTr^{4} °क्षेत्राश्च; Tj^{2} मत्स्यश्च; GMd^{1} मात्स्याश्च — b) Be^{1} BBe^{2} Ho Jo^{2} La^{2} wKt^{1} GMd^{1} oMd^{2} TMd^{3} GMd^{5} sOx^{1} NPu^{1} sPu^{6} Tr^{1} Tr^{2} [*Jolly* Go R Nd] *Dev* पाञ्चालाः; BKt^{5} पञ्चलाः; BBe^{2} सूरसेनकाः; *Hem* सूरसैनिकाः; Jo^{2} NKt^{4} TMd^{3} GMy Tj^{1} Tr^{1} *BhP* 7.62 शूरसेनयः; TMd^{4} GMd^{5} सूरसेनयः; BKt^{5} La^{1} Ox^{3} Pu^{5} Pu^{7} Tr^{2} Wa *Apa* सूरसेनजाः; Lo^{2} Lo^{4} Lo^{5} NNg Ox^{2} Pu^{9} *Dev* [vl] शूरसेनजाः; NPu^{1} सौरसेनजाः — c) Lo^{3} Tj^{1} [*Jolly* R] एवं; wKt^{3} एक; NNg ब्रह्मर्षदेशो; Lo^{2} °देशा; Lo^{3} Tj^{1} [*Jolly* R] °देशोयं — d) Jm आर्यावर्ताद°; NPu^{1} °वर्तादिनन्तरः; Bo Lo^{3} oMd^{2} Ox^{2} *BhP* 7.62 *Dev* °नन्तरं; MTr^{3} °नन्तराः

20. Cited by *Lakṣ* 1.46 — b) GMy °शादग्र्यज° — c) Bo स्वस्वं; Hy स्वस्वे; BKt^{5} चरित्रे; Lo^{1} शिक्ष्येरन्; Pu^{5} Pu^{7} Pu^{9} शिष्येरन्; TMd^{3} TMd^{4} GMd^{5} GMy Tr^{1} MTr^{4} MTr^{6} शिक्षन्ते; *BhP* 7.63 शिक्षन्ति; GMd^{1} रक्षन्ते — d) NKt^{4} सर्वमानसः

21. Cited by *Apa* 5; *Lakṣ* 1.46; *Hem* 2/1.25; *Dev* 1.18 — a) BCa Kt^{2} NKt^{4} Lo^{3} Lo^{4} Lo^{5} TMd^{4} oOr sOx^{1} Ox^{2} Pu^{5} sPu^{6} Pu^{7} Pu^{9} Tj^{1} [*Jolly* G R] *Hem* °योर्मध्ये; Tr^{2} *Nā* °योर्मध्यो; *Me Ku Go* support मध्यं — b) BBe^{2} °नसनादपि — c) Tr^{2} प्रत्यगेवं; Be^{1} प्रयोगाच्च — d) [*Jolly* G] स कीर्तितः

तयोरेवान्तरं गिर्योरार्यावर्तं विदुर्बुधाः ॥२२॥
कृष्णसारस्तु चरति मृगो यत्र स्वभावतः ।
स ज्ञेयो यज्ञियो देशो म्लेच्छदेशस्त्वतः परः ॥२३॥
एतान्द्विजातयो देशान् संश्रयेरन्प्रयत्नतः ।
शूद्रस्तु यस्मिन्कस्मिन्वा निवसेद्वृत्तिकर्शितः ॥२४॥
एषा धर्मस्य वो योनिः समासेन प्रकीर्तिता ।
संभवश्चास्य सर्वस्य वर्णधर्मान्निबोधत ॥२५॥
वैदिकैः कर्मभिः पुण्यैर्निषेकादिर्द्विजन्मनाम् ।
कार्यः शरीरसंस्कारः पावनः प्रेत्य चेह च ॥२६॥
गार्भैर्होमैर्जातकर्मचौडमौञ्जीनिबन्धनैः ।
बैजिकं गार्भिकं चैनो द्विजानामपमृज्यते ॥२७॥

22. Cited by *Apa* 5; *Lakṣ* 1.46; *Hem* 2/1.25; *Dev* 1.18 — a) wKt^1 wKt^3 oMd^2 NNg Tj^2 समुद्राच्च; TMd^4 पूर्वमा — b) BBe^2 Jo^2 wKt^1 NKt^4 Lo^3 Lo^4 oMd^2 oOr Ox^3 Pu^5 Pu^7 Pu^9 Tj^1 Tr^2 Wa [*Jolly* M G R] *Dev Jha Dave* समुद्राच्च; GMy समुद्रास्तु; Tr^1 पश्चिमाः; TMd^4 पश्चिमं — c) sOx^1 sPu^6 °वान्तरे — d) La^2 गिर्योर्ब्रह्मावर्तं; Kt^2 °वर्तो; GMd^1 sOx^1 sPu^6 Tr^2 *Lakṣ* °वर्तं प्रचक्षते; *Apa* °वर्तः प्रकीर्तितः

23. Cited by *Apa* 5; *Lakṣ* 1.46–7; *Hem* 2/1.25; *Dev* 1.18; pādas c-d cited by *Viś* 1.2 — a-b) *BhP* 7.66 अटते यत्र कृष्णा गौर्मृगो नित्यं स्वभावतः; La^1 कृष्णसारो मृगो यत्र चरते वै स्वभावतः — b) Bo मृगा; GMy मृगयो यत्र — c) *Apa* स देशो यज्ञियो ज्ञेयो; Tr^1 सा; Lo^3 य; Lo^5 ज्ञेयौ; GMd^5 GMy MTr^4 याज्ञियो; La^2 Lo^3 Tj^1 [*Jolly* R] *BhP* 7.66 याज्ञिको — d) Be^1 wKt^1 BKt^5 Lo^4 TMd^3 Pu^5 Pu^7 Pu^9 Tj^1 Tr^1 Tr^2 *Rc Hem Dev* °देशस्ततः; GMd^1 GMy *Lakṣ* परं; *Me Go Nā Nd Mr suport* अतः

Additional verse in GMd^5:

चातुर्वर्णस्य संस्थानं यस्मिन्देशे न विद्यते ।
स म्लेच्छदेशो विज्ञेय आर्यावर्तादनन्तरः ॥

24. Cited by *Apa* 6; *Lakṣ* 1.47; *Hem* 2/1.25; *Dev* 1.21 — a-d) *BhP* 7.67 एतान्नित्यं शुभान्देशान्संश्रयीत [vl संश्रयेत] द्विजोत्तमः । यस्मिन्कस्मिंश्च निवसेत्पादजो वृत्तिकर्शितः — a) NPu^1 तान्द्वि°; Lo^4 °जातदेशान् [*but mc*]; NKt^4 देशात्; Bo देवान् — b) Jo^2 देशानाश्रये° — c) BBe^2 [*but cor*] wKt^3 NKt^4 La^1 Lo^4 Lo^5 oOr Ox^3 Pu^5 Pu^7 Pu^9 Wa *Apa Lakṣ Jha Dave* यस्मिंस्तस्मिन्वा; La^2 Lo^2 Lo^3 TMd^3 यस्मिन्कस्मिंश्च; Bo Ho sOx^1 Ox^2 sPu^6 Tj^1 [*Jolly* R Nd] यस्मिन्कस्मिंश्चिन्निव°; Tr^2 यस्मिन्यस्मिंश्चिद् निव° — d) GMy निवसेद्वित्त°; Hy Jm Jo^1 Jo^2 La^1 sOx^1 sPu^6 Pu^8 Tj^2 *Jolly* कर्षितः [see 8.411b note]

25. Cited by *Hem* 2/1.25 — a) oOr *Hem* एष; Lo^1 *mc to* सर्वस्य; Jo^2 *om* वो; wKt^1 TMd^3 GMd^5 GMy Tr^1 वै; sOx^1 sPu^6 यो — a-b) *BhP* 7.68 प्रकीर्तितेयं धर्मस्य बुधैर्योनिर्द्विजोत्तमाः — b) *Hem* समासात्कथितः किल; La^2 समासीन; Bo NNg Tj^2 प्रकीर्तिताः; wKt^3 sOx^1 sPu^6 Tr^1 प्रकीर्तितः — c) GMd^5 GMy संभवस्यास्य; Bo Jo^2 Lo^3 GMy sOx^1 sPu^6 Tj^1 [*Jolly* R] धर्मस्य; all commentators read सर्वस्य — d) *BhP* 7.68 समासात्र तु विस्तरात्; Pu^5 Pu^7 Pu^9 [*Jolly* G] सर्वधर्मान्नि°; NKt^4 Tr^1 °बोधतः

26. Cited by *Dev* 1.36 — b) GMy Tr^1 MTr^4 *BhP* 3.167 *Dev Nā* °षेकाद्यैर्द्विज°; Be^1 wKt^1 NKt^4 BKt^5 La^2 Tr^2 °षेकादिद्विज°

27. Cited by *Vij* 3.253; *Apa* 25; *Dev* 1.36; pādas c-d cited by *Viś* 1.13; cited with pratīka गार्भैर्होमैः by *Śaṃ* on *BU* 3.1.1 [intr.]; expanded version of pādas a-b in *BhP* 3.2.3 — a) Tr^2

स्वाध्यायेन व्रतैर्होमैस्त्रैविद्येनेज्यया सुतैः ।
महायज्ञैश्च यज्ञैश्च ब्राह्मीयं क्रियते तनुः ॥२८॥
प्राङ् नाभिवर्धनात्पुंसो जातकर्म विधीयते ।
मन्त्रवत् प्राशनं चास्य हिरण्यमधुसर्पिषाम् ॥२९॥
नामधेयं दशम्यां तु द्वादश्यां वास्य कारयेत् ।
पुण्ये तिथौ मुहूर्ते वा नक्षत्रे वा गुणान्विते ॥३०॥
मङ्गल्यं ब्राह्मणस्य स्यात् क्षत्रियस्य बलान्वितम् ।
वैश्यस्य धनसंयुक्तं शूद्रस्य तु जुगुप्सितम् ॥३१॥
शर्मवद् ब्राह्मणस्य स्याद्राज्ञो रक्षासमन्वितम् ।
वैश्यस्य पुष्टिसंयुक्तं शूद्रस्य प्रेष्यसंयुतम् ॥३२॥
स्त्रीणां सुखोद्यमक्रूरं विस्पष्टार्थं मनोहरम् ।

गर्भै° ; GMy गार्भ्यै° ; Lo^{5} भगैर्हो° ; Wa °र्होमैज्जति° — b) Be^{1} Bo Ho La^{2} TMd^{3} Ox^{2} Tj^{1} Tr^{1} Tr^{2} °चौल° ; GMd^{5} GMy °चौळ° ; Pu^{5} Pu^{7} [*cor to*] Pu^{9} *Vij Dev* °चूडा° ; Pu^{10} °चूड° ; wKt^{3} °चुडा° ; Tr^{1} °मौञ्जिनि° — c) MTr^{3} MTr^{4} वैजिकं; Kt^{2} वैदिकं; NKt^{4} गार्हिकं; Lo^{5} मार्भिकं; wKt^{3} Pu^{9} चेनो; TMd^{3} ह्येनो; wKt^{1} चैनां; NNg [*but cor fh*] चैव; sOx^{1} चैवो — d) oOr °नामभिमृज्यते; NKt^{4} °नामुपमृज्यते; GMd^{5} °नां परिमृज्यते; *Dev* °नामपमार्जति

28. Pādas c-d omitted in oOr. Pādas c-d cited by *Viś* 1.50; *Mādh* 1.346; pāda-d cited by *Śaṃ* on *BU* 3.1.1 [intr.] — b) Pu^{9} °स्त्रेविद्ये° ; Pu^{10} °स्त्रिविद्ये° ; Bo °स्त्र्यविद्ये° ; wKt^{1} °नेज्ययान्वितैः; GMd^{1} °विद्येन तपश्चरैः; BKt^{5} *BhP* 3.3श्रुतैः — c) Hy Ox^{3} Pu^{8} Tr^{2} Wa *om* यज्ञैश्च — c-d) *BhP* 3.4 महायज्ञैश्च ब्राह्मीयं यज्ञैश्च क्रियते तनुः — d) La^{2} ब्राह्मायं; Tr^{2} ब्राह्म्यायं; Tj^{2} ब्राह्मी च

29. Pādas a-b cited by *Hem* 3/1.326; *Dev* 1.49 — a) *BhP* 3.4 °कर्तनात्पुंसो; GMd^{5} °कृन्तनात्पुंसो; *Dev* °नात्पुंसां — c) wKt^{1} प्रासनं; Bo Ox^{3} वास्य — d) Tj^{1} हिरण्यं; Hy NPu^{1} *BhP* 3.5 [vl] °सर्पिषा; Tr^{2} °सर्पिषात्

30. Cited by *Dev* 1.52; *Mādh* 1.440; pādas a-b cited by *Viś* 1.12 — a) TMd^{3} °धेया; Pu^{5} Pu^{7} Pu^{9} [*Jolly* G] च; NKt^{4} वा — b) *BhP* 3.5 expanded version: केचिदिच्छन्ति पार्थिव । द्वादश्यामपरे राजन्; Bo *Viś* चास्य; Tr^{1} वाथ; Tr^{2} वापि — c) GMy पुण्यौ; Jo^{2} Lo^{3} sOx^{1} sPu^{6} Tj^{1} Tr^{2} Wa [*Jolly* R] पुण्येहनि [*Me Rc* have पुण्येहनि but unclear whether it is simply a gloss; *Nā Ku* read तिथौ]; Be^{1} मुहूर्तं; *BhP* 3.6 च — d) *BhP* 3.6 च

31 Cited by *Apa* 27; *Dev* 1.53-4; *Mādh* 1.441; pādas b-d omitted in NPu^{1} and pāda-d in sOx^{1} sPu^{6} [both haplo] — a) Bo La^{2} oMd^{2} GMd^{5} oOr Pu^{5} Pu^{7} Pu^{9} Pu^{10} Tr^{2} *Apa* [vl as in ed.] माङ्गल्यं; Tr^{2} ब्रह्मस्य; TMd^{3} ब्राह्मणस्स्यात्; Bo °णस्यास्य; La^{1} °णस्योक्तं — a-b) *BhP* 3.8 मङ्गल्यं तात विप्रस्य शिवशर्मेति पार्थिव — b) Wa राज्ञो रक्षासमन्वितं [cf. 3.32b]; Ox^{2} Pu^{8} राज्ञो बलसमन्वितं — c) Ho वैश्यस्य च धनं युक्तं; Tr^{2} पुष्टिसंयुक्तं [cf. 3.32c] — d) BKt^{5} *om* तु; BBe^{2} Jo^{2} Pu^{10} Tj^{1} Wa *BhP* 3.9 च; GMd^{5} त्वजुगुप्सितं; wKt^{1} स्वगाव्दितं [*but cor*]; Lo^{3} जुगुप्सिते

32. Omitted in Be^{1}; pādas a-c omitted in sOx^{1} sPu^{6} and pāda-a NPu^{1}; pādas a-b and c-d transposed in Ca. Cited by *Viś* 1.13; *Dev* 1.54; *Mādh* 1.441 — b) Pu^{10} राक्षा° ; wKt^{1} वर्मसमन्वितं; MTr^{3} °समन्वितान् — c) GMy तुष्टि° ; La^{1} Tr^{2} वृद्धि° ; wKt^{1} गुप्ति° [*but cor*]; BCa धन° — d) Hy wKt^{3} Ox^{2} *Viś Jolly* प्रैष्य° ; wKt^{1} प्रैष°

मङ्गल्यं दीर्घवर्णान्तमाशीर्वादाभिधानवत् ॥३३॥
चतुर्थे मासि कर्तव्यं शिशोर्निष्क्रमणं गृहात् ।
षष्ठेऽन्नप्राशनं मासि यद्वेष्टं मङ्गलं कुले ॥३४॥
चूडाकर्म द्विजातीनां सर्वेषामेव धर्मतः ।
प्रथमेऽब्दे तृतीये वा कर्तव्यं श्रुतिचोदनात् ॥३५॥
गर्भाष्टमेऽब्दे कुर्वीत ब्राह्मणस्योपनायनम् ।
गर्भादेकादशे राज्ञो गर्भात्तु द्वादशे विशः ॥३६॥
ब्रह्मवर्चसकामस्य कार्यं विप्रस्य पञ्चमे ।
राज्ञो बलार्थिनः षष्ठे वैश्यस्येहार्थिनोऽष्टमे ॥३७॥
आ षोडशाद् ब्राह्मणस्य सावित्री नातिवर्तते ।
आ द्वाविंशात् क्षत्रबन्धोरा चतुर्विंशतेर्विशः ॥३८॥
अत ऊर्ध्वं त्रयोऽप्येते यथाकालमसंस्कृताः ।
सावित्रीपतिता व्रात्या भवन्त्यार्यविगर्हिताः ॥३९॥

33. Cited by *Apa* 27; *Dev* 1.55; *Mādh* 1.441 — a) oOr सुखाद्यम° — b) oOr विस्पष्टाद्यं मनोरमं; Tr[2] वैस्पष्टार्थं; Tr[1] सुविस्पष्टं; NNg *BhP* 3.11 °ष्टार्थ — c) GMd[5] oOr Tr[2] *Apa* माङ्गल्यं; wKt[1] TMd[3] मङ्गल्य — d) Ho °धानवित्; TMd[4] °धानकं

34. Pāda-d omitted in Ox[3] and *ma* in Lo[4]. Pādas a-b cited by *Dev* 1.55; *Mādh* 1.442; pādas c-d by *Dev* 1.57 — a) La[1] GMd[4] TMd[3] TMd[4] GMd[5] GMy Pu[10] Tr[1] MTr[4] MTr[6] [*Jolly* M[1-2-3-7-8-9] Me Nd] मासे चतुर्थे; TMd[3] कर्तव्या — b) *BhP* 3.12 तथान्येषां मतं विभो; GMd[1] GMy °ष्क्रामणं — c) GMd[1] GMd[5] GMy Tr[1] MTr[4] MTr[6] मासे; TMd[3] पाने — d) BKt[5] La[1] NPu[1] *BhP* 3.13 यथेष्टं; Ho [*Jolly* G] यच्चेष्टं; Tr[2] मङ्गले; Tr[1] कुलं

Additional verse in La[1]:

आयुःकामस्य यशसा पशूनां पुष्टिमिच्छतः ।
मन्त्रैर्विजयकामस्य अर्थेनार्थाद्यकामिनः ॥

35. Cited by *Hem* 3/3.742; *Dev* 1.58; *Mādh* 1.605 — a) MTr[4] चौड°; GMd[5] GMy चौळ° TMd[4] चौल°; GMd[5] द्विजादीनां; TMd[4] द्विजानां च — b) *BhP* 3.14 सर्वेषामनुपूर्वशः — c) Lo[4] त्रितीये; Ox[3] द्वितीये वा — d) *BhP* 3.14 कर्तव्यं कुरुनन्दन; GMy वेदचोदनात्; NNg Pu[10] Tr[2] °नोदनात्

36. Cited by *Hem* 3/1.112, 3/3.746; *Mādh* 1.446 — a) *Hem* 3/1.112 °ष्टमे वै; MTr[4] MTr[6] °ष्टमे वा कुर्वीत; GMd[5] °ष्टमे प्रकुर्वीत; *Hem* 3/3.746 °ष्टमेषु कुर्वन्ति — b) Lo[2] GMd[1] °णस्यौपनायनं — c) TMd[3] गर्भेकादशने; *BhP* 3.16 राजन् and adds a pāda: क्षत्रियस्य विनिर्दिशेत् — d) *BhP* 3.17 द्वादशेऽब्देऽपि गर्भात् and adds a pāda: वैश्यस्य व्रतमादिशेत्

37. Pādas c-d omitted in Pu[8]. Cited by *Hem* 3/3.748–9; *Dev* 1.68–9; *Mādh* 1.446; pādas a-b cited by *Apa* 31 — a) Pu[10] ब्रह्मचर्यस°; *BhP* 3.16 °कामेन — c-d) *BhP* 3.17 with addtional pādas: बलार्थिना तथा राज्ञः अष्टमे कुरुनन्दन | अर्थकामेन वैश्यस्य अष्टमे कुरुनन्दन || — d) TMd[3] GMd[5] Tr[1] वैश्यस्यार्थार्थिनो; GMy सवैश्यस्यार्थिनो

38. Cited by *Hem* 3/3.751; *Dev* 1.72; *Mādh* 1.446 — c) NKt[4] *BhP* 3.18 द्वाविंशतेः क्षत्र° [*om* आ]

39. Cited by *Mādh* 1.446; pādas c-d cited by *Mādh* 1.544 — a) *BhP* 3.19 अत ऊर्ध्वं तु ये

नैतैरपूतैर्विधिवदापद्यपि हि कर्हिचित् ।
ब्राह्मान् यौनांश्च संबन्धानाचरेद् ब्राह्मणः सह ॥४०॥
कार्ष्णरौरवबास्तानि चर्माणि ब्रह्मचारिणः ।
वसीरन्नानुपूर्वेण शाणक्षौमाविकानि च ॥४१॥
मौञ्जी त्रिवृत्समा श्लक्ष्णा कार्या विप्रस्य मेखला ।
क्षत्रियस्य तु मौर्वी ज्या वैश्यस्य शणतान्तवी ॥४२॥
मुञ्जालाभे तु कर्तव्याः कुशाश्मन्तकबल्वजैः ।
त्रिवृता ग्रन्थिनैकेन त्रिभिः पञ्चभिरेव वा ॥४३॥
कार्पासमुपवीतं स्याद् विप्रस्योर्ध्ववृतं त्रिवृत् ।
शणसूत्रमयं राज्ञो वैश्यस्याविकसूत्रिकम् ॥४४॥

राजन्; Lo^{1} त्रयो एते; TMd^{4} Tj^{2} पतन्त्येते — c) GMd^{5} वृत्या — d) *BhP* 3.19 न ते संस्कारभागिनः [vl व्रात्यस्तोमादृते क्रतोः]; TMd^{3} भवन्त्यार्यावि°

40.* Omitted in Jo^{2} Lo^{3} Tj^{1} [*Jolly* R Nd]. Cited by *Apa* 13, 68; *Dev* 1.73; *Mādh* 1.446 — a) *BhP* 3.20 न चाप्येभिरपूतैस्तु; GMy नेतैरपूर्वैविधि° — b) TMd^{3} GMd^{5} GMy Tr^{1} MTr^{4} MTr^{6} °पद्यपि कदाचन; oOr *om* हि; Tj^{2} *Dev* च — c) Tr^{2} ब्राह्मयान्; Ho ब्रह्मन्; Lo^{4} ब्राह्मन्; Ox^{3} ब्राह्मात्र यौ°; *BhP* 3.20 ब्राह्मयं योनिं च [vl ब्राह्मं यौनं]; Lo^{1} यौनाश्च; Bo यौर्नाश्च; sOx^{1} योनींश्च; GMy योनांश्च; wKt^{1} नारांश्च — d) Jm Jo^{1} Kt^{2} BKt^{5} Pu^{5} Pu^{7} [*cor to*] Pu^{9} Tr^{2} *Dev Mandlik Jha Dave* संबन्धात्राचरेद्; Kt^{2} संबन्धात्र चरेद् [*Jolly* also gives this reading but corrects it in the corrigenda]; La^{1} Lo^{1} Lo^{4} Lo^{5} TMd^{3} TMd^{4} GMd^{5} GMy oOr NPu^{1} Pu^{2} Pu^{8} Pu^{10} Tj^{2} Tr^{1} MTr^{4} MTr^{6} [*Jolly* M] *Nā* [pāṭha] *Mandlik Jha Dave* ब्राह्मणैः सह; NKt^{4} Tr^{2} ब्राह्मणः क्वचित्; NNg Pu^{5} Pu^{7} Pu^{9} सदा

41. Cited by *Apa* 57; *Mādh* 1.446; pādas c-d by *Dev* 1.75 — a) Ho कृष्ण°; Tj^{1} कार्ष्णि°; Bo wKt^{1} °रौरवास्तानि; Tr^{2} °रौरवस्तानि; TMd^{3} °कारवबस्तानि; GMy °बस्तानि; La^{1} °वस्त्राणि; Kt^{2} °वासानि — b) *BhP* 3.21 ब्रह्मचारिविशां नृप; GMy ब्रह्मचारिणां — c) sOx^{1} sPu^{6} वसेरन्ना°; Kt^{2} वसोरन्ना°; Tj^{1} वसीरश्चानु°; Lo^{2} Lo^{3} *BhP* 3.22 वसीरंश्चानु°; NKt^{4} °रन्नानपूर्वाण; Bo Jo^{2} Lo^{2} Lo^{3} Lo^{4} GMd^{1} TMd^{4} GMd^{5} Ox^{2} Ox^{3} NPu^{1} Tj^{1} Tj^{2} Tr^{1} MTr^{4} MTr^{6} Wa *Apa Dev Mādh Mandlik Jha KSS Dave* °पूर्व्येण — d) Kt^{2} °क्षौमादिकानि; MTr^{4} °क्षौमाविकादि

42. Cited by *Viś* 1.29; *Apa* 58; *Dev* 1.79; *Mādh* 1.447 — a) Tr^{2} *Viś* तृवृत्समा; Be^{1} GMy Pu^{9} श्लक्ष्ण — b) GMy कार्यं; wKt^{3} मेखलाः — c) BKt^{5} *om* तु; *BhP* 3.23 च; NPu^{1} Tj^{1} मौञ्जी; Lo^{3} मौर्जी; sOx^{1} sPu^{6} ज्य; Pu^{7} ज्यां — d) sOx^{1} sPu^{6} Tj^{2} [*Jolly Go*] शाण°; *Apa* [vl] षण°; Tj^{1} शर°

43. Cited by *Apa* 58; *Dev* 1.80; *Mādh* 1.447; pāda-c cited by *Kum* 1.3.9 — a) Tr^{2} मुञ्जलाभे; La^{1} TMd^{3} Pu^{10} *Dev* [*Jolly* M$^{1-2-7-8-9}$] मुञ्जाभावे; Be^{1} Bo Ho wKt^{1} NKt^{4} BKt^{5} La^{1} Lo^{4} GMy NNg sOx^{1} Ox^{3} sPu^{6} Pu^{7} Tj^{1} Tj^{2} Tr^{1} Tr^{2} *BhP* 3.24 *Apa Dev* कर्तव्या; TMd^{3} रक्तव्या; *Me* clearly sees a plural here: बहुवचनमुपपन्नतरम्; so also *Go Ku Mr* — b) La^{1} कुशाश्मकाशवल्वजैः; Jo^{1} [*but cor*] Kt^{2} *Jolly* कुशाश्मान्तक° [the vast majority of my mss. have the reading adopted, although Jolly gives no variants]; *Dev* [vl as in ed] कुशाश्मातक°; TMd^{3} °बल्बजैः; sOx^{1} sPu^{6} *Apa* [vl] °बिल्वजैः; Bo °वल्कजैः; Lo^{4} °बिल्वनैः; Lo^{5} °विल्वनैः; Ox^{3} °बल्वनैः — c) Tr^{2} तृवृता; Bo ग्रन्थिरेकेन; Be^{1} ग्रन्थिनेकेन — d) Bo La^{2} Tr^{2} Wa *BhP* 3.24 च

44.* Cited by *Apa* 58; *Dev* 1.80; pādas a-b cited by *Kum* 1.3.9; *Har*-A 1.15.1, and pāda-a by *Viś* 1.29 — a) wKt^{3} *Viś* °मुपलीतं — b) Be^{1} TMd^{3} विप्रस्योर्ध्वं; Tr^{2} तृवृत् — c) Jo^{2} Lo^{3} TMd^{3} [*Jolly* R] *Apa* [vl] शाण°; Pu^{10} शणतन्तुमयं; Tj^{1} °सूत्रवृतं; BKt^{5} °मयो — d) BBe^{2} Bo Ho wKt^{1} La^{2}

ब्राह्मणो बैल्वपालाशौ क्षत्रियो वाटखादिरौ ।
पैलवौदुम्बरौ वैश्यो दण्डानर्हन्ति धर्मतः ॥४५॥
केशान्तिको ब्राह्मणस्य दण्डः कार्यः प्रमाणतः ।
ललाटसंमितो राज्ञः स्यात्तु नासान्तिको विशः ॥४६॥
ऋजवस्ते तु सर्वे स्युरव्रणाः सौम्यदर्शनाः ।
अनुद्वेगकरा नृणां सत्वचोऽनग्निदूषिताः ॥४७॥
प्रतिगृह्येप्सितं दण्डमुपस्थाय च भास्करम् ।
प्रदक्षिणं परीत्याग्निं चरेद्भैक्षं यथाविधि ॥४८॥
भवत्पूर्वं चरेद्भैक्षमुपनीतो द्विजोत्तमः ।
भवन्मध्यं तु राजन्यो वैश्यस्तु भवदुत्तरम् ॥४९॥
मातरं वा स्वसारं वा मातुर्वा भगिनीं निजाम् ।

Lo^{2} Lo^{3} TMd^{3} GMd^{5} GMy sOx^{1} NPu^{1} Pu^{5} sPu^{6} Pu^{7} Pu^{9} Tj^{1} Tr^{1} MTr^{4} [*Jolly* G R Nd] °सूत्रकं; Ox^{2} °सूत्रजं; BCa Hy Jm Jo^{1} La^{1} Lo^{1} Kt^{2} wKt^{3} NKt^{4} oMd^{2} NNg oOr Tj^{2} *BhP* 3.25 *Dev Mr Mandlik Jha KSS Dave* °सौत्रिकं — After verse 44 TMd^{3} GMd^{5} insert 2.63

45. Cited by *Apa* 57; *Dev* 1.77; *Mādh* 1.447 — a) Pu^{9} Tj^{1} ब्राह्मणौ; GMy ब्राह्मणै; La^{1} [*but cor*] NPu^{1} बिल्व; wKt^{1} बेल°; TMd^{3} °पालाशा — b) *BhP* 3.26 वाटखादिरौ क्षत्रियस्तु [hypermetric] and adds तथान्यं वेतसोद्भवम्; GMd^{1} राजा अश्वत्थखादिरौ; GMy क्षत्रियौ; Bo BKt^{5} Lo^{2} TMd^{4} NNg Tr^{1} Tr^{2} *Apa* °वट; Hy वारखा°; TMd^{3} °खादिनौ — c) Be^{1} wKt^{1} wKt^{3} Lo^{2} Lo^{3} oMd^{2} TMd^{3} Ox^{3} Pu^{5} Pu^{7} Pu^{9} Pu^{10} Tj^{1} Tr^{2} Wa पैलवोदु°; Ox^{2} वैनवौदु°; GMd^{5} Tr^{1} *Apa* पैप्पलौदु°; GMy बैप्पलौदु°; Lo^{1} पौलवौदु° *mc to* पिलुवौदु°; NPu^{1} पिप्पजौदु°; GMy Tr^{1} वैश्यौ; sOx^{1} sPu^{6} Tr^{2} वैश्ये; *BhP* 3.27 adds: तथाश्वत्थजमेव हि — d) *BhP* 3.27 दण्डानेतान्महाबाहो and adds: धर्मतोऽर्हन्ति धारितुम्; Lo^{3} दण्डामर्हन्ति; Bo Lo^{3} TMd^{3} Tj^{1} MTr^{4} *Apa* दण्डानर्हति; Lo^{4} धर्मता

46. Cited by *Apa* 57; *Dev* 1.78; *Mādh* 1.448 — a) Lo^{1} Lo^{4} Pu^{10} [*Jolly* Nd] केशान्तको; Lo^{5} Ox^{3} [*Jolly* M] केशान्तगो [*Me* gives this as his first reading; but gives केशान्तको as an alternate; both forms recorded also by *Rn*] — b) MTr^{4} MTr^{6} कार्यो दण्डः; GMd^{1} oOr प्रयत्नतः — c) TMd^{3} °संमिता — d) wKt^{1} NKt^{4} नाशान्तिको; Ox^{3} नासान्तगो; Wa विशेत्; Ox^{3} विदः

47.* Pādas c-d omitted in Pu^{2}. Cited by *Apa* 57; *Mādh* 1.448 — a) Pu^{9} ऋजवास्ते — b) Kt^{2} स्युरव्रणः; Ox^{3} स्युरत्रणाः; TMd^{3} स्युरग्रेणा; BKt^{5} स्युरव्रणाश्च सौम्य°; *BhP* 3.29 स्युर्ब्राह्मणाः सौम्य°; Tj^{1} सर्वदर्शनाः; Be^{1} Ox^{3} °दर्शनः — c) Ho °करां; Tr^{2} °करः — d) GMy सत्वचे; Be^{1} BBe^{2} Bo Ho Hy Jm Jo^{1} wKt^{1} Kt^{2} wKt^{3} NKt^{4} La^{1} La^{2} Lo^{1} Lo^{3} oMd^{2} TMd^{3} GMd^{5} GMy oOr sOx^{1} sPu^{6} Tj^{1} Tj^{2} Tr^{2} MTr^{3} MTr^{4} MTr^{6} *BhP* 3.30 *Mādh NāRc Jolly* सत्वचो नाग्नि°

48. Cited by *Apa* 60; *Dev* 1.108; *Mādh* 1.451; pāda-a cited by *Viś* 1.29 — a) *Apa* परिगृ°; *BhP* 3.30 प्रगृह्य चेप्सितं; Lo^{3} °गृह्यासितं; Tr^{2} °गृह्योत्थितं — b) GMy °स्थायाथ — c) *BhP* 3.31 सम्यग्गुरुं तथा पूज्य — c-d) GMy परीत्याग्निं चरेत् भैक्षं ब्राह्मणस्तु यथाविधि — d) Bo °द्भैक्षां; BCa BKt^{5} oMd^{2} oOr Ox^{2} Pu^{5} Pu^{7} Pu^{10} *BhP* 3.31 °द्भैक्ष्यं; Pu^{9} °द्भैक्ष्य

49. Cited by *Dev* 1.108; *Mādh* 1.453 — a) BCa oMd^{2} oOr Ox^{2} Pu^{10} *BhP* 3.31 °द्भैक्ष्यमु°; Bo °द्भैक्षामु°; sOx^{1} sPu^{6} °द्भक्षमु° — b) Tj^{1} °पनीता; BBe^{2} Tr^{2} °पवीतो — d) Wa वैश्यश्च; GMd^{5} Pu^{8} Tr^{2} *BhP* 3.32 वैश्यस्य; TMd^{4} भवदन्तिकं

भिक्षेत भिक्षां प्रथमं या चैनं न विमानयेत् ॥५०॥
समाहृत्य तु तद्भैक्षं यावदर्थममायया ।
निवेद्य गुरवेऽश्नीयादाचम्य प्राङ्मुखः शुचिः ॥५१॥
आयुष्यं प्राङ्मुखो भुङ्क्ते यशस्यं दक्षिणामुखः ।
श्रियं प्रत्यङ्मुखो भुङ्क्ते ऋतं भुङ्क्त उदङ्मुखः ॥५२॥
उपस्पृश्य द्विजो नित्यमन्नमद्यात्समाहितः ।
भुक्त्वा चोपस्पृशेत्सम्यगद्भिः खानि च संस्पृशेत् ॥५३॥
पूजयेदशनं नित्यमद्याच्चैतदकुत्सयन् ।
दृष्ट्वा हृष्येत् प्रसीदेच्च प्रतिनन्देच्च सर्वशः ॥५४॥

50.* Cited by *Apa* 59 [also *Apa* 60 but there ascribed to the *BhP*]; *Dev* 1.109 — b) TMd⁴ भगिनीं; NKt⁴ निजां adds तथा — c) Ox² Pu⁸ भिक्षेत्प्रथमतो भिक्षां; BCa BKt⁵ Pu¹⁰ भिक्ष्येत; *BhP* 3.33 भैक्षं [vl भैक्ष्यं]; BCa प्रथमं भिक्षां; Tr² *Dev* प्रथमां — d) Ho य; Pu⁵ चैनां; GMy चेनं; TMd⁴ चैवं; Pu⁷ Pu⁹ चैनान्न; GMy नाविमानयेत्; BBe² Bo Ho Hy Jm Jo¹ Kt² La² Lo¹ sOx¹ Ox² Pu⁵ sPu⁶ Pu⁷ Pu⁸ Pu⁹ Tj² Tr² Wa [*Jolly* G Ku] *Dev Mandlik Jolly Jha KSS Dave* नावमानयेत्

51. Cited by *Apa* 61; *Lakṣ* 1.119; *Dev* 1.113; *Mādh* 1.454 — a) Pu¹⁰ समाधृत्य; *Mādh* °हृत्याथ; *BhP* 3.34 °हृत्य ततो भैक्ष्यं; BBe² BCa Hy wKt¹ BKt⁵ oMd² oOr Ox² Pu⁵ Pu⁷ Pu⁹ Pu¹⁰ *Go Ku Rc* तद्भैक्ष्यं; Bo तद्भैक्षां; NKt⁴ सद्भैक्षं; wKt¹ तं भक्षं — b) oMd² oOr *Lakṣ* यावदन्नममायया — d) Be¹ *mc to* प्रयतः शुचिः

52. Cited by *Apa* 61; *Dev* 1.115, 2.599; *Mādh* 1.377 — a) Ox³ आयुख्यं; NKt⁴ प्रायुष्यं; GMy भुङ्क्तो — b) GMy °मुखं — c) TMd³ प्रत्यङ्मुखे; Pu⁸ Tr¹ भुङ्क्त; Lo² भुङ्क्तं — d) NKt⁴ सतं भुङ्क्त; oOr Pu² भुङ्क्ते उद°; BBe² Hy Jm Jo¹ oMd² sOx¹ Ox² sPu⁶ *Mandlik Jha KSS Dave* भुङ्क्ते ह्युदङ्मुखः; GMy उदङ्मुखं; TMd⁴ उदङ्मुखे

Additional verse in GMd¹ TMd⁴ GMd⁵ GMy oOr sOx¹ NPu¹ sPu⁶ Tr¹ Tr² MTr⁴ MTr⁶ *Rc Mandlik* [ख, ट] *KSS*; cited by *Dev* 2.609; *Lakṣ* 3.224:

सायं प्रातर्द्विजातीनामशनं श्रुतिचोदितम् ।
नान्तरा भोजनं कुर्यादग्निहोत्रसमो विधिः ॥

a) MTr⁴ omits pāda-a; GMd⁵ प्रातर्द्विजादीनाम° — b) sOx¹ sPu⁶ स्मृतिचोदितं; Tr² स्मृतिनोदितं; *Lakṣ* देवनिर्मितं — c) sOx¹ sPu⁶ नानुरामेण तं कुर्याद°; Tr² *Rc Mandlik* नान्तरे; GMd¹ *Lakṣ* कार्यमग्नि° — d) Tr¹ °होत्रेसमो

Additional verse in GMd⁵:

उपविश्य शुचौ देशे पात्रमादाय भूतले ।
हविष्यमद्यात्सततं नातिसौहित्यमाचरेत् ॥

53. a) Jo¹ द्विजा; *BhP* 3.36द्विजो राजन् — b) GMd⁵ नित्यं तमद्यात्सुसमाहितः — c) Lo⁴ NNg Tj¹ भुक्ता; La¹ [*but mc*] GMy Ox² °शेन्नित्यमद्भिः; GMd¹ °शेदद्भिस्सम्यक्खानि — d) Ho संस्पृशन्

54. Cited by *Lakṣ* 3.225; pādas a-b cited by *Dev* 1.114 — a) *BhP* 3.37तथान्नं पूजयेन्नित्यम° — b) GMd¹ °द्यादेनमकु°; NKt⁴ TMd³ GMy sOx¹ Ox² sPu⁶ MTr⁴ MTr⁶ [*Jolly* M¹⁻²⁻⁸⁻⁹] °च्चैनमकु°; Tr² °च्चैतमकु°; [*Jolly* Me] °च्चान्नमकु°; GMy °च्चैतन्नकुत्सयेत्; TMd³ Pu⁸ °कुत्सयत् — c) Tr¹ प्रशंसेच्च; oOr प्रसीदेत — c-d) *BhP* 3.37–8 expanded reading: दर्शनात्तस्य हृष्येद्वै प्रसीदेच्चापि भारत । अभिनन्द्य ततोऽश्नीयादित्येवं मनुरब्रवीत् — d) TMd³ प्रतिनन्देत सर्वदा; *Lakṣ* प्रसीदेच्चाप्यभिनन्देच्च; TMd⁴ Pu⁹ सर्वतः; GMd⁵ *Nd* सर्वदा

पूजितं ह्यशनं नित्यं बलमूर्जं च यच्छति ।
अपूजितं तु तद्भुक्तमुभयं नाशयेदिदम् ॥५५॥
नोच्छिष्टं कस्यचिद्दद्यान्नाद्यादेतत्तथान्तरा ।
न चैवात्यशनं कुर्यान्न चोच्छिष्टः क्वचिद्व्रजेत् ॥५६॥
अनारोग्यमनायुष्यमस्वर्ग्यं चातिभोजनम् ।
अपुण्यं लोकविद्विष्टं तस्मात्तत्परिवर्जयेत् ॥५७॥
ब्राह्मेण विप्रस्तीर्थेन नित्यकालमुपस्पृशेत् ।
कायत्रैदशिकाभ्यां वा न पित्र्येण कदाचन ॥५८॥
अङ्गुष्ठमूलस्य तले ब्राह्मं तीर्थं प्रचक्षते ।
कायमङ्गुलिमूलेऽग्रे दैवं पित्र्यं तयोरधः ॥५९॥
त्रिराचामेदपः पूर्वं द्विः प्रमृज्यात्ततो मुखम् ।
खानि चैव स्पृशेदद्भिरात्मानं शिर एव च ॥६०॥

55. Cited by *Dev* 1.114 — a) Bo पुजिनं कृशनं नित्य; Ox^{3} पूजितां; sOx^{1} पूजनं; Pu^{9} पूर्जितं; *BhP* 3.38 त्वशनं — b) Pu^{7} बलमूर्ध्वं [*but cor*]; *BhP* 3.38 [vl] बलमोजश्च; Ho BKt^{5} TMd^{3} TMd^{4} GMd^{5} GMy Pu^{5} Pu^{7} Pu^{9} Tr^{1} MTr^{6} प्रयच्छति; sOx^{1} sPu^{6} Tr^{2} नियच्छति — c) Lo^{3} Tj^{1} च; BKt^{5} Lo^{3} Lo^{4} GMd^{1} TMd^{3} GMd^{5} sOx^{1} Ox^{3} sPu^{6} Tj^{1} Tr^{1} Tr^{2} Wa *Rc Dev* यद्भुक्त°; TMd^{4} यद्युक्त° GMy तन्नित्यमुभयं — d) *Dev* °मुभयं तु हिनस्ति तत्; Pu^{5} Pu^{7} Pu^{9} Pu^{10} °येदिति

56.* Pādas c-d omitted in Pu^{9}. Cited by *Apa* 61; *Lakṣ* 1.123; pādas c-d cited by *Dev* 1.115 — b) TMd^{3} °न्नाद्याच्चैतरतस्तथा; *Apa* °न्नाद्यादेनमथान्तरा; BKt^{5} °न्नाद्यायदेतं तथा°; La^{1} Ox^{3} °न्नाद्यादेनं तथा° [La^{1} *mc to* °द्यादेतदथा°]; Bo Ho wKt^{1} La^{2} Lo^{1} GMd^{5} GMy [*Jolly* R Nd] *BhP* 3.39 °न्नाद्याच्चैतत्तथा°; sOx^{1} sPu^{6} °न्नाद्याच्चैतदथा°; Be^{1} Hy Jo^{1} Jo^{2} Kt^{2} Lo^{3} Pu^{8} Tj^{1} Tj^{2} MTr^{3} Wa *Lakṣ Mandlik Jolly KSS* °न्नाद्याच्चैव तथा°; Tr^{1} MTr^{4} °न्नाद्याच्चैनं तथा°; wKt^{3} °न्नाद्यादन्तं तथा°; BCa NKt^{4} Ox^{2} Pu^{5} Pu^{7} °न्नाद्यादन्नं तथा°; wKt^{1} TMd^{4} °थान्तरं; Lo^{2} °थान्तरो — c) Lo^{3} Tj^{1} नैवात्य°; Lo^{1} चैवात्याशनं; Bo चैवाप्यशनं; Kt^{2} चैवाह्यशनं; Lo^{1} कार्यं न; *Nā* appears to read अनशनं for अत्यशनं — d) TMd^{3} कुर्यान्नोच्छिष्टं कुत्रचिद्व्रजेत्; MTr^{4} MTr^{6} चोच्छिष्टं

57. Cited by *Apa* 156; *Dev* 1.115, 2.614 — a) wKt^{1} अनायुष्यमनारोग्यम° — b) TMd^{3} TMd^{4} GMd^{5} GMy Tr^{1} °स्वर्ग्यमतिभो°; Ho °भोजिनं — c) Tr^{1} अपथ्यं लोक° — d) Tj^{1} तस्य तत्परि°; Ox^{3} °वर्जयत्

58. Cited by *Hem* 3/2.991; *Dev* 2.253 — a) GMy ब्राह्मणेविप्रतीर्थेण; BKt^{5} ब्राह्मणेन; NKt^{4} La^{1} Tr^{2} विप्रती°; Pu^{9} विप्रर्थेन — b) MTr^{4} MTr^{6} द्विजो नित्यमुप°; TMd^{3} sOx^{1} नित्यं; Lo^{1} °कायमुप°; GMy °काल उप° — c) TMd^{3} राजयत्रैदेशिकाभ्यां; Tj^{1} °दिशिकाभ्यां; Ho NKt^{4} La^{2} GMd^{1} TMd^{4} GMd^{5} GMy NNg sOx^{1} sPu^{6} Pu^{10} Tr^{1} °दशकाभ्यां — d) Bo नापित्र्येन; BKt^{5} Lo^{4} TMd^{4} oOr Ox^{3} पित्रेन; Tr^{2} पैत्रेन; NKt^{4} पित्रैन

59. b) Lo^{1} TMd^{3} GMy Tj^{2} Tr^{1} [*Jolly* R] ब्राह्म; wKt^{1} Lo^{3} Tj^{1} ब्रह्म; BBe^{2} Ho ब्राह्मयं; [*Jolly* R] तीर्थे — c) NKt^{4} कग्रम°; wKt^{1} °ङ्गुष्ठमूले; La^{2} oOr °मूलाग्रे — d) Lo^{2} देव्यं; Pu^{5} Pu^{7} दैव; Pu^{9} दैवा; NKt^{4} पैत्र्यं

60. Cited by *Apa* 40; *Hem* 3/2.992 — a) *Hem* त्रिः प्राशयेदपः; wKt^{1} TMd^{4} GMy NPu^{1} Pu^{5} Pu^{7} Pu^{9} *Apa* °चमेदपः; GMd^{1} °चमेत्ततः — b) TMd^{4} द्वि; GMd^{1} द्विर्त्रृज्यात्ततो; *Hem* द्विरुन्मृज्यात्ततो; Tr^{2} प्रमृज्य ततो — c) Ho चैवं; Be^{1} Bo Jo^{2} La^{1} La^{2} Lo^{2} Lo^{3} GMd^{5} Ox^{2} NPu^{1} Pu^{5} Pu^{7} Pu^{9} Tj^{1} MTr^{4} Wa

अनुष्णाभिरफेनाभिरद्भिस्तीर्थेन धर्मवित् ।
शौचेप्सुः सर्वदाचामेदेकान्ते प्रागुदङ्मुखः ॥६१॥
हृद्गाभिः पूयते विप्रः कण्ठगाभिस्तु भूमिपः ।
वैश्योऽद्भिः प्राशिताभिस्तु शूद्रः स्पृष्टाभिरन्ततः ॥६२॥
उद्धृते दक्षिणे पाणावुपवीत्युच्यते द्विजः ।
सव्ये प्राचीनमावीती* निवीती कण्ठसज्जने ॥६३॥
मेखलामजिनं दण्डमुपवीतं कमण्डलुम् ।
अप्सु प्रास्य विनष्टानि गृह्णीतान्यानि मन्त्रवत् ॥६४॥
केशान्तः षोडशे वर्षे ब्राह्मणस्य विधीयते ।
राजन्यबन्धोर्द्वाविंशे वैश्यस्य द्व्यधिके ततः ॥६५॥
अमन्त्रिका तु कार्येयं स्त्रीणामावृदशेषतः ।
संस्कारार्थं शरीरस्य यथाकालं यथाक्रमम् ॥६६॥

Apa Me चोपस्पृशेद° — d) La[2] शिरमेव

61. Cited by *Hem* 3/2.983; cited with *pratīka* अनुष्णाभिः by *Viś* 1.20— a) Pu[10] °फैनाभि° — b) gMd[1] tMd[4] °नाभिरबुद्बुदाभिश्च धर्मवित्; *Hem* °नाभिरदुष्टाभिश्च धर्मतः; gMd[5] धर्मवत् —c) gMd[1] शौचे नित्यमनाचामेदे° — d) nKt[4] °मेदेवान्ते; gMd[1] mTr[4] mTr[6] *Hem* °मेदासीनः प्रागु°; nPu[1] °दङ्मुखाः

62. Omitted in Pu[1]. Cited by *Hem* 3/2.985; *Mādh* 1.221 — a) gMd[1] विप्रश्शुध्यति हृद्गाभिः; nKt[4] हृष्टाभिः; tMd[4] शुध्यते; Tr[2] पूजिते; Ho पूजयेद्विप्रः; mTr[4] विप्रं — b) Be[1] °भिश्च; *Mādh* भूपतिः — c) Pu[10] °द्भिराशिताभिस्तु; Tj[2] °द्भिस्तालुगाभिस्तु; t Md[3] °द्भिस्तालकाभिस्तु; wKt[3] प्रासिता°; Ox[3] प्राशितोद्भिश्च; Lo[1] Lo[4] gMd[1] Tr[2] °ताभिश्च — d) tMd[4] gMd[5] gMy स्पृष्टात्भिरन्ततः [sic]

63.* Placed after 2.45 in tMd[3]. Pādas a-b cited by *Har*-A 1.15.1 and pāda-a by *Viś* 1.29 — a) nNg दक्षिणां — b) oOr *BhP* 3.78 *Har*-A [but vl as in ed] बुधः; gMd[1] gMy mTr[4] mTr[6] बुधैः; gMd[5] जनाः — c) La[1] [*but* न *struck off*] *BhP* 3.78 सव्येन प्राचीनावीती; gMd[1] tMd[3] tMd[4] gMy Tr[1] mTr[4] mTr[6] सव्ये तु प्राचीनावीती; Be[1] bBe[2] Bo Jm Jo[1] Jo[2] Kt[2] wKt[3] Lo[1] Lo[3] Lo[5] oMd[2] Pu[8] Tj[1] Tj[2] [*Jolly* M[3–4]] *Ku Mandlik Jha KSS Dave* सव्ये प्राचीन आवीती; bCa nKt[4] bKt[5] Lo[2] Lo[4] nNg sOx[1] Ox[2] Ox[3] oOr nPu[1] Pu[2] Pu[4] Pu[5] sPu[6] Pu[7] Pu[9] Pu[10] Tr[2] Wa [*Jolly* M[1–2–8–9] G N R] *Jolly* सव्ये प्राचीनमावीती [Pu[10] °नानीती Wa °वीते]; gMd[5] प्राचीनावीतकस्सव्ये; Ho wKt[1] सव्ये प्राचीनावीती [wKt[1] °वीची] — d) nKt[4] *om* निवीती; tMd[3] निवीति; Be[1] sOx[1] sPu[6] निवीते; gMd[5] gMy Tr[1] निवीतं; tMd[4] निवतं; Tr[1] कर्ण°; gMd[5] कर्णसर्जने; Bo °सज्जते; *BhP* 3.78 °संज्ञिते; tMd[4] °लम्बनात्

64. Cited by *Apa* 59; *Dev* 1.85; *Mādh* 1.451 — a) nKt[4] मेखलमजिने — b) nKt[4] कमण्डलुः — c) Lo[3] प्रास्यं; Bo Ho La[1] tMd[3] प्राश्य; *Apa* प्राप्य; tMd[4] प्रास्यद्भिनष्टानि; Lo[4] Tj[1] विनिष्टानि — d) oOr गृह्णीतान्यन्त्रिमन्त्रितः; tMd[4] Wa *Dev* गृहीत्वान्यानि; Be[1] tMd[3] mTr[4] गृहीतान्यानि; bBe[2] wKt[1] nKt[4] Lo[3] tMd[3] gMy Ox[2] [*cor to*] Tj[1] Tj[2] *BhP* 3.79 *Apa* [vl] मन्त्रवित्; Lo[5] *Apa* मन्त्रतः; tMd[4] मन्त्रदः; bCa धर्मवित्; *Me Rn Rc Go* support मन्त्रवत्; cf. similar range of variants at 3.217 and the note to it.

65. Cited by *Apa* 67; *Hem* 3/3.778; *Dev* 1.167; *Mādh* 1.457-8 — a) mTr[4] *BhP* 41 [vl] केशान्तं — b) sPu[6] ब्राह्मस्य विधी°; sOx[1] ब्राह्मस्य तु विधी°; Wa ब्राह्मण — d) tMd[3] द्वाधिके; *BhP* 4.1 त्र्यधिके; Lo[4] ह्यधिके

66. Cited by *Apa* 30; *Dev* 1.60 — a-d) *BhP* 4.2 अमन्त्रका सदा कार्या स्त्रीणां चूडा महीपते संस्कारहेतोः कायस्य यथाकालं विभागशः ॥ — a) gMd[5] अमन्त्रका; bKt[5] अमन्त्रिता; sOx[1] [*but mc*]

वैवाहिको विधिः स्त्रीणां संस्कारो वैदिकः स्मृतः ।
पतिसेवा गुरौ वासो गृहार्थोऽग्निपरिक्रिया ॥६७॥
एष प्रोक्तो द्विजातीनामौपनायनिको विधिः ।
उत्पत्तिव्यञ्जकः पुण्यः कर्मयोगं निबोधत ॥६८॥
उपनीय गुरुः शिष्यं शिक्षयेच्छौचमादितः ।
आचारमग्निकार्यं च संध्योपासनमेव च ॥६९॥
अध्येष्यमाणस्त्वाचान्तो यथाशास्त्रमुदङ्मुखः ।
ब्रह्माञ्जलिकृतोऽध्याप्यो लघुवासा जितेन्द्रियः ॥७०॥
ब्रह्मारम्भेऽवसाने च पादौ ग्राह्यौ गुरोः सदा ।

sPu^6 [*but mc*] Tr^2 कर्तव्या — b) TMd^4 °माहुरशेषतः — c) Kt^2 La^1 Ox^3 Pu^5 Wa *KSS* संस्कारार्थे — d) Ox^3 *om* यथाकालं; Tj^2 °कालं यथाबलं

Additional verse in GMd^5:

प्राजापत्यं पाणितले कनिष्ठा तलयोरधः ।
प्रदेशिन्या सहाङ्गुष्ठे पित्रं स्यात्पितृकर्मणि ॥

67. Cited by *Dev* 1.61; pādas a-b cited by *Viś* 1.15; *Apa* 908 — a) La^2 वैवाहिक; Wa वैवाहिका — b) GMd^1 TMd^4 *Apa Dev* औपनायनिकः स्मृतः [Ng gives this in margin with इति वा पाठः; cf. 2.68b]; *BhP* 4.3 नैगमः स्मृतः — c) *BhP* 4.3 निवसेद्वा गुरोर्वापि; Lo^2 Tr^1 गुरो; GMd^1 गुरौ सेवा; Wa वासौ — d) Lo^5 TMd^3 Ox^3 NPu^1 गृह्यार्थो; wKt^3 Lo^3 Tj^1 गृहार्थे; GMy गृहार्थ; MTr^4 गृह्यते; *BhP* 4.3 गृहे वाग्नि°; Be^1 BKt^5 sOx^1 sPu^6 Tj^1 [*Jolly* N R] °परिष्क्रिया; Bo °परिस्त्रिया; GMd^1 °क्रियः

Additional verses in GMd^1 TMd^4 Tr^1 MTr^4 MTr^6; second verse alone in Tr^2 *Mandlik* [ख] and commented by *Rc*:

सह ब्रह्मोदनं कुर्यात् सहाग्न्याधानमेव च ।
सह यज्ञक्रियाः सर्वा हविषां भक्षणाद्विना ॥१॥
अग्निहोत्रस्य शुश्रूषा सायमुद्वासनमेव च ।
कार्यं पत्न्या प्रतिदिनं बलिकर्म च नैत्यकम् ॥२॥

1. d) Tr^1 हविषो भक्षणं विना; MTr^4 हविष्टां; TMd^4 भोजनाद्विना

2. b) Tr^1 अग्न्युद्वा°; GMd^1 TMd^4 सायोद्वा°; MTr^4 MTr^6 संध्योपासनमेव— c) GMd^1 सायं पत्न्या; MTr^4 MTr^6 कार्यं पुण्यं; Tr^1 कार्यं पत्युः — d) Tr^2 *Mandlik* इति कर्म च वैदिकं; MTr^6 *om* च; Tr^1 च लौकिकं

68. a) *BhP* 4.4 [with added pāda] एष ते कथितो राजन् द्विजातीनां महाबाहो; Tr^1 द्विजन्मनामौ° — b) NKt^4 °मोपनायनको; Bo NPu^1 Tr^2 °नायनको; Kt^2 °नायानिको; wKt^3 विधिं — c) GMy उत्पत्तिं; MTr^4 °व्यञ्जकं; NKt^4 MTr^4 पुण्यं; Kt^2 पुण्य; *BhP* 4.4 परः — d) *BhP* 4.5 [with added pāda] कर्मयोगमिदानीं ते कथयामि महाबल; Wa निबोधते; Ox^3 निबोधतां; NNg निबोधतः

69. Cited by *Viś* 1.15 pāda-a cited by *Vij* 3.259 — b) *BhP* 4.5 प्रथमं शौचमादिशेत्; Ox^3 शिक्षायच्छौच° — c) Hy Tj^2 तु

70. Cited by *Apa* 34; *Lakṣ* 1.244; *Dev* 1.136 — a-d) *BhP* 4.6–7 [with added pādas] अध्यापयेत्तु सच्छिष्यान्सदाचान्त उदङ्मुखः । ब्रह्माञ्जलिकरो नित्यमध्याप्यो विजितेन्द्रियः । लघुवासास्तथैकाग्रः सुमनाः सुप्रतिष्ठितः ॥ — a) Tr^1 अध्येष्यमायास्त्वा°; Lo^3 °माणश्चाचान्तो; Tj^1 °माणश्चाचान्ते; La^2 °चान्ते — b) *Apa* °स्त्रमतन्द्रितः; Tr^2 °ङ्मुखं — c) sOx^1 sPu^6 ब्राह्मा°; *Me* [pāṭha] °लिकृदध्याप्यो — d) Lo^5 लजीवासा; NNg Ox^3 यतेन्द्रियः

संहत्य हस्तावध्येयं स हि ब्रह्माञ्जलिः स्मृतः ॥७१॥
व्यत्यस्तपाणिना कार्यमुपसंग्रहणं गुरोः ।
सव्येन सव्यः स्प्रष्टव्यो दक्षिणेन तु दक्षिणः ॥७२॥
अध्येष्यमाणस्तु गुरुं* नित्यकालमतन्द्रितः ।
अधीष्व भो इति ब्रूयाद्विरामोऽस्त्विति चारमेत् ॥७३॥
ब्रह्मणः प्रणवं कुर्यादादावन्ते च सर्वदा ।
स्रवत्यनोंकृतं पूर्वं परस्ताच्च विशीर्यते ॥७४॥
प्राक्कूलान्पर्युपासीनः पवित्रैश्चैव पावितः ।
प्राणायामैस्त्रिभिः पूतस्तत ओंकारमर्हति ॥७५॥
अकारं चाप्युकारं च मकारं च प्रजापतिः ।
वेदत्रयान्निरवृहद् भूर्भुवः स्वरितीति च ॥७६॥
त्रिभ्य एव तु वेदेभ्यः पादं पादमदूदुहत् ।

71. GMd[1] TMd[4] transpose pādas a-b and c-d. Cited by *Dev* 1.136; *Lakṣ* 1.244; pādas c-d cited by *Apa* 34 — a) Lo[3] Tj[1] °रम्भावसाने; GMd[1] विरामे च — b) Ox[3] गृह्यौ; *BhP* 4.8 पूज्यौ — c) Bo TMd[4] संहृत्य; GMy संगत्य; GMy °ध्येय; TMd[3] °ध्येयस्स — d) Tr[1] संति ब्रह्मा°

72. Omitted in Pu[5] Tj[2]. Cited by *Viś* 1.26; *Apa* 55; *Lakṣ* 1.244; *Har*-A 1.5.22; *Dev* 1.103; *Mādh* 1.300 — a) Kt[2] व्यस्तपा°; NKt[4] ह्यस्तपा°; *Me* [pāṭha] विन्यस्तपा° — b) Lo[2] °ग्रहकं; TMd[3] °ग्रहिणं; NKt[4] GMd[1] सदा — c) Ho wKt[1] BKt[5] TMd[3] GMd[5] Pu[7] Pu[9] Tr[1] *Lakṣ* स्पृष्टव्यो; Be[1] wKt[3] NKt[4] प्रष्टव्यो; Be[3] स्रष्टव्यो — d) Hy Jm Jo[1] Kt[2] *Har*-A *Mādh Mandlik Jha KSS Dave* च

73.* Cited by *Apa* 34; *Lakṣ* 1.244; *Dev* 1.142; *Mādh* 1.136 — a) Tj[2] °माणश्च; Lo[2] °माणं च; only BBe[2] GMd[1] TMd[3] GMd[5] GMy Ox[3] Tr[1] Wa [*Jolly* N Nd] *Nā* read °माणस्तु गुरुं नित्य°; others read °माणं तु गुरुर्नित्य° [*Nā* gives गुरुः as *kvacit pāṭhaḥ*; for my conjectural reading see endnote]; BBe[2] गुरोर्नित्य° — b) TMd[3] यथाकालम°; wKt[3] °तन्द्रियः — c) Be[1] स्वधीष्व; GMd[1] अधीष्ये; *Apa* भोरिति — d) Tr[1] °द्विरमो; Bo *Mādh* वारमेत्; Lo[5] GMd[1] चारमे; Tr[2] चारयेत्; Ho *BhP* 4.10 वारयेत्

74. Cited by *Lakṣ* 1.244; *Dev* 1.136; pāda-c cited by *Viś* 1.15 — a) Lo[4] OMd[2] NPu[1] MTr[4] MTr[6] *BhP* 4.11 [vl] ब्राह्मणः; TMd[4] ब्राह्मण; NKt[4] प्रणवः; Bo Lo[4] Ox[3] प्रवणं; La[2] प्रावरं; TMd[3] कुर्यावादा° — b) Tj[1] °दावन्त्ये; Jo[2] Lo[3] Tj[1] [*Jolly* R] सर्वतः — c) wKt[3] TMd[4] स्रवन्त्य°; TMd[3] च्यवन्त्य°; GMd[1] स्रवत्येनःकृतं; TMd[3] Pu[5] Pu[7] Pu[9] °कृतं ब्रह्म — d) Lo[4] [*but cor*] Pu[5] Pu[7] Pu[9] पुरस्ताच्च; NNg परहस्ताच्च; BBe[2] Hy Jm Jo[1] wKt[1] Kt[2] wKt[3] La[1] [*but cor*] OMd[2] Ox[2] Tj[2] *Dev Mandlik Jha KSS Dave* विशीर्यति; NPu[1] विशीर्यत

75.* Omitted in Pu[5]. Cited by *Lakṣ* 1.244; *Dev* 1.135 — a) Ox[2] प्राक्कूशा°; [*Jolly* M[4]] प्राक्चूला°; *Jolly* [conjecture citing B-R sv and *GDh* 1.50] प्राक्तूला°; NPu[1] प्राञ्जलिः पर्युपा°; Lo[4] Ox[3] °पासीत; GMy °पासीतिन; Kt[2] °सीनान् — b) *Lakṣ* पवित्रैरेव; Ho °त्रैश्चापि; Tr[2] पारितः; Ox[3] पादितः — c) Be[1] °यामस्त्रिभिः; Bo °ग्रामैस्त्रिभिः — d) *BhP* 4.13 पूतस्ततस्त्वोंका°

76. Omitted in Pu[5]. Cited by *Apa* 33; *Dev* 2.377 — a) Kt[2] अकारश्चाप्युकारश्च; NKt[4] आकारं; Lo[2] Ox[3] Pu[7] Pu[9] वाप्यु°; Ho वा — b) Kt[2] मकारश्च — c) TMd[3] *Apa* [vl] °त्रयान्निरबृहद्; [*Jolly* N] °त्रयान्निरवृंहद्; wKt[1] Tr[1] Wa [*Jolly* Nd] *Apa* °त्रयान्निरवहद्; GMy °त्रयान्निवहेद्; Be[1] Bo Ho Hy Jm Jo[1] Jo[2] Kt[2] wKt[3] BKt[5] La[1] La[2] Lo[1] Lo[3] Ox[2] Pu[8] Tj[1] Tj[2] Tr[2] *Mandlik Jha KSS Dave* °त्रयान्निरदुहद्; sOx[1] sPu[6] °त्रयान्निरवहद् *both cor to* °त्रयान्निरदुहद्; *BhP* 4.14 °त्रयात्तु निर्गृह्यः; cf. *VaDh* 55.10

तदित्यृचोऽस्याः सावित्र्याः परमेष्ठी प्रजापतिः ॥७७॥
एतदक्षरमेतां च जपन् व्याहृतिपूर्विकाम् ।
संध्ययोर्वेदविद्विप्रो वेदपुण्येन युज्यते ॥७८॥
सहस्रकृत्वस्त्वभ्यस्य बहिरेतत्त्रिकं द्विजः ।
महतोऽप्येनसो मासात् त्वचेवाहिर्विमुच्यते ॥७९॥
एतयर्चा विसंयुक्तः काले च क्रियया स्वया ।
विप्रक्षत्रियविड्योनिर्गर्हणां याति साधुषु ॥८०॥
ओंकारपूर्विकास्तिस्रो महाव्याहृतयोऽव्ययाः ।
त्रिपदा चैव सावित्री विज्ञेयं ब्रह्मणो मुखम् ॥८१॥
योऽधीतेऽहन्यहन्येतां त्रीणि वर्षाण्यतन्द्रितः ।
स ब्रह्म परमभ्येति वायुभूतः खमूर्तिमान् ॥८२॥
एकाक्षरं परं ब्रह्म प्राणायामः परं तपः ।

77. Omitted in Pu^{5}; pādas a-b and c-d transposed in TMd^{3}. Cited by *Apa* 34; *Har*-A 1.1.10; *Dev* 2.377; *Mādh* 2.52 — a) sOx^{1} sPu^{6} एव च; Wa तु एव; Be^{3} Ho wKt^{3} *Apa* [vl] देवेभ्यः; *Apa* [vl] विप्रेभ्यः; wKt^{1} विप्रस्य — b) wKt^{3} पादमदूदुहन्; Tj^{2} पादमदुहत्; Tr^{2} पादमदूहतः — c) *Apa* [vl] उदित्यृचो°; TMd^{3} तदित्यृचास्याः — d) Pu^{10} Wa °मेष्ठि

78. Cited by *Viś* 1.22; *Apa* 50; *Dev* 2.392–3 — a) Tr^{2} एतदन्तरमेतां; Tj^{1} °मेता; GMd^{5} °मेतं; Be^{3} *Apa* [vl] °मेनां; Bo Lo^{2} Tj^{2} तु — b) Kt^{2} GMd^{5} GMy Pu^{5} Tr^{2} °पूर्वकां; *Apa* °पूर्वकम् — c) Jo^{2} BKt^{5} La^{1} Lo^{3} NPu^{1} Tj^{1} *BhP* 4.16 *Viś Apa* संध्ययोरुभयोर्विप्रो [NPu^{1} उभये]

79. Cited by *Apa* 1220; *Dev* 2.400 — b) Tr^{1} °रेकत्त्रिकं; Jo^{2} °रेकत्रिकं; NPu^{1} द्विजे — c) Lo^{1} महतस्यैनसोप्याशु; NNg महताप्ये°; wKt^{1} BKt^{5} La^{1} [*mc*] मासान् — d) GMy त्वचैवाहिर्वि°; TMd^{4} त्वचैवाहिर्वि°; Tr^{1} त्वचैवाभिर्वि°; BKt^{5} त्वचैर्वर्हिर्वि°; [*Jolly* Be] त्वचो वाहिर्वि°

80.* Pādas a-c omitted in Pu^{9} — a) Ox^{3} एतयर्चाधिसंयुक्तः; NPu^{1} एतयर्चे; Tr^{2} एतयाचा; wKt^{1} Lo^{1} एतदृचा; GMy एतावच्चा; TMd^{4} एतावाचा; Be^{3} एतद्यर्चा [*but mc*]; TMd^{3} यतयर्चा — b) Lo^{2} oOr Tj^{1} कालेन क्रि°; GMd^{1} तु; Lo^{1} क्रियाया; TMd^{3} स्वधा — c) BBe^{2} Bo BCa Hy Jm Jo^{1} Kt^{2} Tj^{2} Tr^{1} MTr^{3} *Mandlik Jolly Jha KSS Dave* ब्रह्मक्षत्रि° — d) Tj^{1} °निर्गृहणीयानि साधुषु; Lo^{3} [*Jolly* R] °निर्गर्हणीयो हि साधुषु; GMd^{5} °निर्गर्हणं; La^{1} Wa °निर्गर्हिणां; MTr^{6} °निर्गर्ह्यतां; GMy MTr^{4} °निर्गृह्यतां; Pu^{7} °निर्गहतां [*but mc*]; TMd^{4} *Nā* [pāṭha] °निर्ग्रहणं; Ho यान्ति; GMd^{5} साधुनि

81. Cited by *Viś* 1.15; *Apa* 33; *Lakṣ* 3.99; *Dev* 1.135, 2.361; pādas a-b cited by *Apa* 1246 — a) Be^{1} विकार°; GMd^{5} °पूर्वका° — b) NNg महाहृतयो — c) Ho wKt^{3} Tj^{1} त्रिपादा; Jo^{2} OMd^{2} TMd^{3} TMd^{4} GMd^{5} Ox^{2} NPu^{1} Pu^{5} Pu^{7} Pu^{8} Pu^{9} Tj^{1} Wa [*Jolly* G R Nd] *Dev* 1.135 [vl], 2.361 *Lakṣ ViDh* 55.15 गायत्री — d) TMd^{4} GMd^{5} Tr^{1} MTr^{4} *BhP* 4.20 *Viś Dev* 1.135 विज्ञेया; Tr^{2} विज्ञेयो; Lo^{4} *Apa* [vl] ब्राह्मणो; wKt^{3} ब्रह्मणोन्मुखं; Ho सुखं

82. Cited by *Dev* 2.378; *Mādh* 1.286 — b) wKt^{3} TMd^{3} [*but cor*] °तन्द्रियः — c) *Bh* [ad 12.90] तद्ब्रह्म; TMd^{4} परमाभ्येति; GMd^{5} Tr^{1} MTr^{6} *Nd Dev Mādh* परमप्येति; *Rc* परमध्येति; Tr^{2} परमात्मेति; TMd^{3} पदमाप्नोति — d) Tj^{1} वायुमूर्तिस्वमूर्तिमान्; TMd^{4} वायुरूपेण मूर्तिमान्; NNg वायुःभूतः; GMd^{1} वायुभूतं; NKt^{4} *Mādh* °भूतश्च मूर्तिमान्; Hy समूर्तिमान्; NPu^{1} Bo *BhP* 4.21 *Dev* स्वमूर्तिमान्

सावित्र्यास्तु परं नास्ति मौनात्सत्यं विशिष्यते ॥८३॥
क्षरन्ति सर्वा वैदिक्यो जुहोतियजतिक्रियाः ।
अक्षरं त्वक्षरं ज्ञेयं ब्रह्म चैव प्रजापतिः ॥८४॥
विधियज्ञाज्जपयज्ञो विशिष्टो दशभिर्गुणैः ।
उपांशुः स्याच्छतगुणः साहस्रो मानसः स्मृतः ॥८५॥
ये पाकयज्ञाश्चत्वारो विधियज्ञसमन्विताः ।
सर्वे ते जपयज्ञस्य कलां नार्हन्ति षोडशीम् ॥८६॥
जप्येनैव तु संसिध्येद् ब्राह्मणो नात्र संशयः ।
कुर्यादन्यन्न वा कुर्यान्मैत्रो ब्राह्मण उच्यते ॥८७॥
इन्द्रियाणां विचरतां विषयेष्वपहारिषु ।
संयमे यत्नमातिष्ठेद् विद्वान्यन्तेव वाजिनाम् ॥८८॥
एकादशेन्द्रियाण्याहुर्यानि पूर्वे मनीषिणः ।

83. a) TMd^{4} °क्षर — b) BBe^{2} Be^{3} Hy Jo^{1} wKt^{1} Kt^{2} wKt^{3} BKt^{5} Lo^{1} Lo^{2} Lo^{3} oMd^{2} Tj^{2} *Ku Rc Mandlik Jolly Jha KSS Dave* प्राणायामाः; TMd^{4} MTr^{4} °याम — c) Lo^{2} सावित्र्यास्त्वपरं; TMd^{3} परं ब्रह्म — d) Pu^{8} विधीष्यते

Additonal verses in La^{1}; first verse in *Dev* 2.369; *Mādh* 1.270; cf. *BDh* 4.1.28:

सव्याहृतिं सप्रणवां गायत्रीं शिरसा सह ।
त्रिः पठेदायतप्राणः प्राणायामः स उच्यते ॥१॥
सावित्री चैव वेदाश्च तुलया तुलिते पुरा ।
एकत्र चतुरो वेदाः समा गायत्रिरेव च ॥२॥

1. a) La^{1} सप्रणवी — c-d) La^{1} omits all after पठेत्

84. Cited by *Lakṣ* 3.99 — a) La^{1} *mc to* नश्यन्ति; Bo GMd^{5} सर्व; GMy सर्वदैवत्यो; Tr^{1} वैदिक्ये; NPu^{1} वैदिको; TMd^{3} वैदित्यो — b) GMy °क्रियः; BBe^{2} Be^{3} °क्रिया — c) Jm Jo^{1} Kt^{2} BKt^{5} *Mandlik KSS* अक्षरं दुष्करं; [*Jolly* Ku R] *Go* अक्षरमक्षयं; Tj^{1} अक्षरं च क्षरं; BBe^{2} GMy MTr^{4} MTr^{6}*Nd* अक्षरं न क्षरं; Lo^{3} अक्षरं च क्षयं; *BhP* 4.23 अवरं त्वक्षरं; TMd^{3} अक्षरं सक्षरं; oMd^{2} Ox^{2} अक्षरं प्रणवं; TMd^{4} ज्ञेया — d) Lo^{2} Lo^{3} GMd^{5} Tj^{1} Tr^{1} MTr^{4} MTr^{6} [*Jolly* N Nd] *BhP* 4.23 ब्रह्मा

85. Pādas a-b cited by *Dev* 2.497 — a) TMd^{3} सर्वयज्ञाज्ज°; Lo^{4} विधियज्ञो जप°; GMd^{5} °ज्जपो-यज्ञो; Ho °यज्ञो हि विशिष्टो — a-b) *BhP* 4.24 विधियज्ञात्सदा राजन् जपयज्ञो विशिष्यते — c) Tj^{1} उपांसु; *BhP* 4.25 स्याल्लक्षगुणः; TMd^{4} °गुणं — d) Be^{1} Bo Ho Jm wKt^{1} wKt^{3} NKt^{4} La^{1} GMd^{1} GMd^{5} GMy sOx^{1} sPu^{6} Pu^{10} Tj^{1} Tr^{1} Tr^{2} MTr^{4} MTr^{6} [*Jolly* M$^{1-2-8-9}$ R] *VaDh* 26.9 सहस्रो; Lo^{4} TMd^{3} TMd^{4} Ox^{3} [*Jolly* R] सहस्रं; TMd^{4} मानसं स्मृतं; TMd^{3} मानसं ततः; Ho मानसो जपः; NPu^{1} स्मृताः

86. b) *BhP* 4.25 विधियज्ञेन चान्विताः; GMy °यज्ञास्समन्विताः — c) TMd^{3} सर्व; Pu^{10} °यज्ञश्च — d) La^{2} कालां; NPu^{1} षोडशं

87. Cited by *Śaṃ* on *VeS* 3.4.38 and on *BU* 1.4.15; *Lakṣ* 3.103; pādas a-b cited by *Dev* 2.497 — a) Tr^{2} जाप्येनैव; La^{2} Tj^{1} जपेनैव; *BhP* 4.26 जपादेव; La^{1} हि [*but mc*]; NKt^{4} Tj^{1} संसिध्ये; Hy संसिद्ध्याद्; TMd^{3} संसिद्धेद्; *Lakṣ* संसिद्धो; NNg संशुध्येद् — b) Ho GMd^{5} ब्रह्मणो; GMd^{5} नास्ति संशयः — c) GMd^{5} कुर्यादन्यन्न कुर्याद्वा; Tj^{1} कुर्यादित्यनवा; Be^{1} Lo^{5} कुर्यादन्यत्र वा — d) TMd^{4} °न्मन्त्रो; Tj^{2} ब्राह्म उच्यते

88. a) Jo^{2} Lo^{3} GMy [*Jolly* R] हि चरतां; TMd^{3} विहरतां; Tj^{1} चरहितां — b) NNg °येष्वनपायिषु — c) TMd^{4} यत्नमुत्तिष्ठेद्; NNg °तिष्ठद् — d) TMd^{3} विद्वान्तेनेव; Tr^{2} वाजिनं

तानि सम्यक् प्रवक्ष्यामि यथावदनुपूर्वशः ॥८९॥
श्रोत्रं त्वक्चक्षुषी जिह्वा नासिका चैव पञ्चमी ।
पायूपस्थं हस्तपादौ वाक्चैव दशमी स्मृता ॥९०॥
बुद्धीन्द्रियाणि पञ्चैषां श्रोत्रादीन्यनुपूर्वशः ।
कर्मेन्द्रियाणि पञ्चैव पाय्वादीनि प्रचक्षते ॥९१॥
एकादशं मनो ज्ञेयं स्वगुणेनोभयात्मकम् ।
यस्मिञ्जिते जितावेतौ भवतः पञ्चकौ गणौ ॥९२॥
इन्द्रियाणां प्रसङ्गेन दोषमृच्छत्यसंशयम् ।
संनियम्य तु तान्येव ततः सिद्धिं नियच्छति ॥९३॥
न जातु कामः कामानामुपभोगेन शाम्यति ।
हविषा कृष्णवर्त्मेव भूय एवाभिवर्धते ॥९४॥
यश्चैतान् प्राप्नुयात्सर्वान् यश्चैतान् केवलांस्त्यजेत् ।
प्रापणात्सर्वकामानां परित्यागो विशिष्यते ॥९५॥
न तथैतानि शक्यन्ते संनियन्तुमसेवया ।
विषयेषु प्रदुष्टानि यथा ज्ञानेन नित्यशः ॥९६॥

89. b) Tj^{1} पूर्व; BKt^{5} TMd^{3} GMd^{5} GMy पूर्वं; Jo^{2} NNg महर्षयः; sOx^{1} sPu^{6} विचक्षणः — c) Jo^{2} Lo^{3} Tj^{1} Wa तानि सर्वाणि वक्ष्यामि

90. *ma sh* in Ox^{2}. Cited by *Apa* 982 — a) TMd^{3} Tj^{1} Tr^{1} श्रोत्र; TMd^{3} त्वक्चक्षुषो — b) Pu^{10} [*Jolly* M$^{1-2-8-9}$] नासिकेति च; Jo^{2} Lo^{4} NNg Ox^{3} [*Jolly* M$^{3-4}$] चेति; BKt^{5} चैति — c) Kt^{2} °पस्थे; Lo^{1} °पस्थ; Lo^{3} °पस्थां; sOx^{1} sPu^{6} *Apa* °पस्थौ; Bo La^{2} करपादौ; NPu^{1} °पादो; Kt^{2} NNg °पादे; Be^{1} BBe^{2} Ho Jm Jo^{1} wKt^{1} NKt^{4} BKt^{5} Lo^{1} Lo^{2} TMd^{4} Ox^{2} Pu^{5} Pu^{7} Pu^{9} [*Jolly* G Ku] *Ku Mandlik Jha KSS Dave* °पादं — d) Be^{3} wKt^{3} NNg oOr स्मृताः; TMd^{3} मता

91. Cited by *Apa* 982 — a) *Apa* ज्ञानेन्द्रियाणि; Jo^{2} Lo^{1} Lo^{2} *Apa* पञ्चैव — b) Lo^{2} श्रोत्रादीननु° — c) Pu^{2} Wa पञ्चैवं; Jm Jo^{1} Kt^{2} oMd^{2} Tj^{2} *Mandlik Jha KSS Dave* पञ्चैषां — d) Ho La^{2} Lo^{5} Hy NPu^{1} पाद्यादीनि; Bo पादादीनि; La^{1} पार्थादीनि; Ox^{3} प्रचक्षेते; BKt^{5} प्रवर्तते

92. Cited by *Apa* 982 — b) La^{2} GMd^{1} °गुणेनाभया°; Bo °भयात्मकां; La^{2} °भयात्मनः — c) BCa तस्मिञ्जिते; TMd^{3} यस्मिञ्जीवे — d) GMd^{1} TMd^{4} पञ्चके; Wa पञ्चको; Lo^{3} GMd^{1} GMd^{5} GMy sOx^{1} [*but cor*] Ox^{3} NPu^{1} sPu^{6} [*but cor*] Tj^{1} Tr^{2} MTr^{4} *Apa* गुणौ

93. b) TMd^{3} रोषमृच्छ°; GMy रोषमिच्छ°; BBe^{2} wKt^{3} Lo^{1} GMy TMd^{4} °संशयः — c) TMd^{3} °यम्य कृतान्येव — d) wKt^{3} सिद्धं; Be^{3} NPu^{1} सिद्धिर्नि°; wKt^{1} Lo^{5} GMd^{1} GMy Tr^{1} MTr^{6} *Jha* निगच्छति

94. a) BBe^{2} कामाः — b) La^{2} °भोगं न शाम्यति; Lo^{2} साम्यति; La^{1} काम्यति [*but mc*] — c) sOx^{1} sPu^{6} हविष्या; Bo °वर्मेव; La^{1} °वर्त्मेण — d) NKt^{4} °वर्हते; La^{1} °वर्धयेत्

95. a) [*Jolly* Nd] यच्चैतान्; Bo यश्चैतत्; MTr^{4} यः कामान्; TMd^{3} प्राप्नुयाच्चैतान् — b) wKt^{1} केवलान्विषयांस्त्यजेत्; NKt^{4} यश्चैनान्; TMd^{4} यश्चैनां; BCa यश्चेमान्; Bo केवलं त्यजेत्; Lo^{4} TMd^{3} sOx^{1} Ox^{3} Pu^{5} sPu^{6} Pu^{7} केवलान्त्यजेत्; Be^{3} केवलास्त्यजेत्; BKt^{5} केवलस्त्यजेत् — c) TMd^{4} प्रोक्षणात्सर्व° — d) La^{2} Lo^{3} Tj^{1} [*Jolly* R] विधीयते; BKt^{5} विनिष्यते

96. Cited by *Lakṣ* 14.97; pādas a-b cited by *Vij* 2.136 — a) Tr^{1} *om* न; Tj^{1} तथैव तानि [*om*

वेदास्त्यागाश्च यज्ञाश्च नियमाश्च तपांसि च ।
न विप्रदुष्टभावस्य सिद्धिं गच्छन्ति कर्हिचित् ॥९७॥
श्रुत्वा स्पृष्ट्वा च दृष्ट्वा च भुक्त्वा घ्रात्वा च यो नरः ।
न हृष्यति ग्लायति वा स विज्ञेयो जितेन्द्रियः ॥९८॥
इन्द्रियाणां तु सर्वेषां यद्येकं क्षरतीन्द्रियम् ।
तेनास्य क्षरति प्रज्ञा दृतेः पादादिवोदकम् ॥९९॥
वशे कृत्वेन्द्रियग्रामं संयम्य च मनस्तथा ।
सर्वान्संसाधयेदर्थानक्षिण्वन्योगतस्तनुम् ॥१००॥
पूर्वां संध्यां जपंस्तिष्ठेत् सावित्रीमार्कदर्शनात् ।
पश्चिमां तु समासीत* सम्यगृक्षविभावनात् ॥१०१॥

न]; TMd[4] तथेतानि; NKt[4] तथैवानि; Tj[1] शक्यन्त; Pu[9] शक्यन्ति; TMd[3] शक्यन्तो — b) TMd[3] संत्रियन्तुम°; NKt[4] *om* सं° — c) BBe[2] Hy Jm Kt[2] oMd[2] *Mandlik Jha KSS Dave* प्रजुष्टानि; Jo[1] प्रविजुष्टानि; Tj[1] प्रहृष्टानि; Be[1] [*but cor*] sOx[1] Ox[2] sPu[6] Tr[1] *Ku* प्रसक्तानि; wKt[1] प्रशक्तानि; Lo[3] [*Jolly* R] प्रदुष्टानि — d) TMd[4] यदा; oOr कामेन

97. a) La[1] वेदांस्त्यागांश्च यज्ञांश्च; TMd[4] वेदस्त्यागश्च; Tj[2] वेदाभ्यासश्च; Hy Jm Jo[1] Kt[2] NKt[4] *Mandlik Jha KSS Dave* वेदास्त्यागश्च; Ox[3] वेदास्त्यागाच्च — b) Jo[2] Lo[3] TMd[3] TMd[4] GMd[5] GMy Tj[1] Tr[1] MTr[4] MTr[6] Wa [*Jolly* R] तपांसि नियमास्तथा [GMd[5] नियमस्तथा; TMd[3] Tj[1] नियमांस्तथा]; Be[3] Hy La[1] नियमांश्च — c) Tj[2] न प्रदुष्टस्य भावस्य — d) TMd[3] गच्छति; GMd[5] कुर्वन्ति; BKt[5] कुत्रचित्; sOx[1] sPu[6] कस्यचित्

98. Cited by *Lakṣ* 14.97 — a) Ox[3] कृत्वा स्पृष्ट्वा; Lo[1] दृष्ट्वा च स्पृष्ट्वा च; BKt[5] NNg *om first* च; Tr[1] *om second* च; Ox[3] *om* दृष्ट्वा च; Lo[4] *ma* दृष्ट्वा च — b) Tj[1] भुक्ता; *Lakṣ* भुक्त्वा दृष्ट्वा — c) wKt[3] हृष्यन्ति; La[1] La[2] न ग्लायति वा; oOr न ग्लायति [*om* वा];; Be[1] ग्लापयति; wKt[3] ग्लायन्ति; TMd[4] नायति; Be[3] च — d) Wa यतेन्द्रियः

99.* Cited by *Dev* 1.122 — a) Be[1] Ho Lo[1] oMd[2] GMd[5] च; Pu[10] तु चरतां — b) NKt[4] यस्यैकं; GMy कर्षती°; BKt[5] रक्षती°; sOx[1] sPu[6] क्षरतेन्द्रियं — c) Be[1] Bo BCa Pu[5] Pu[7] Pu[9] Pu[10] [*Jolly* M G] *Jolly* ततोस्य; *Rn* तेनैव — d) Pu[10] दृतोः; TMd[4] धृतिः; TMd[3] मातैः; La[1] हतेः; Tr[2] पादा इवो°; Jm [*Jolly* Ku] पात्रादिवो°; NNg °वौदकं

100. a) La[1] sOx[1] sPu[6] [*but cor*] Pu[10] Tj[1] Wa [*Jolly* M[1-2-8-9] R] *Rn* वशी; BBe[2] वसे; Tj[1] [*Jolly* R] कृत्येन्द्रि°; wKt[3] La[2] कृतेन्द्रि° — b) Be[1] Be[3] Ho Lo[3] Tj[1] Tr[2] *Rc* सन्नियम्य मनस्तथा; sOx[1] sPu[6] सन्निवेश्य मनस्तथा; TMd[4] सचाय मनसस्तथा; GMy समं कृत्वा मनस्तथा; MTr[4] MTr[6] मनस्तदा; oOr मनः सदा — d) Bo °र्थानक्षिप्त्वान्योगतस्तनुं; MTr[4] °र्थान्योगेनात्मविमोक्षणात्; MTr[6] °र्थानक्षिजयोगेनात्मविमोक्षणात्; Jo[1] °र्थानाक्षिण्व°; Tj[1] °र्थान्दक्षिण्व°; Hy Ox[3] °र्थान्क्षिण्व°; Be[1] °र्थानक्षुण्व°; BKt[5] °र्थानक्षण्व°; wKt[3] °तस्तनून्

101.* Omitted in Pu[1]. Cited by *Hem* 3/3.695; *Dev* 2.398— a) Tj[2] *Hem* पूर्व; Bo संध्यं; GMy जपेत्तिष्ठन्; GMd[5] *Dev* °स्तिष्ठन्; TMd[4] °स्तिष्ठेन् — b) Kt[2] नैशमेनो व्यपोहति [cf. 2.102b]; NPu[1] *om* सावित्रीम् ... [102a] °स्तिष्ठन्; BBe[2] wKt[1] La[1] °त्रीमर्क° — c) Ox[3] पश्चिमो; TMd[4] *om* तु; Be[3] समासीतः *but cor to* समासीनः; *Me Jha Dave* सदासीत; NKt[4] Pu[2] Pu[4] [*Jolly* M[1-2-8-9]] सदासीनः; Be[1] BBe[2] Bo Ho Hy Jm Jo[1] Jo[2] wKt[1] Kt[2] wKt[3] BKt[5] La[2] Lo[1] Lo[2] Lo[3] Lo[4] Lo[5] oMd[2] TMd[3] NNg oOr Ox[2] Ox[3] Pu[7] Pu[8] Pu[9] Tj[1] Tj[2] Tr[2] *BhP* 4.28 *Hem Dev* [*Jolly* M[4] G Ku R Nd] *Rc Mr Mandlik Jolly KSS* समासीनः; Wa समासीनो; Kt[2] समानः; GMy समासीनास्सम्य° — d) wKt[3] सम्यगर्कवि°; Lo[4] Lo[5] Ox[3] *Hem*

पूर्वां संध्यां जपंस्तिष्ठन् नैशमेनो व्यपोहति ।
पश्चिमां तु समासीनो मलं हन्ति दिवा कृतम् ॥१०२॥
न तिष्ठति तु यः पूर्वां नोपास्ते यश्च पश्चिमाम् ।
स शूद्रवद्बहिष्कार्यः सर्वस्माद् द्विजकर्मणः ॥१०३॥
अपां समीपे नियतो नैत्यकं विधिमास्थितः ।
सावित्रीमप्यधीयीत गत्वारण्यं समाहितः ॥१०४॥
वेदोपकरणे चैव स्वाध्याये चैव नैत्यके ।
नानुरोधोऽस्त्यनध्याये होममन्त्रेषु चैव हि ॥१०५॥
नैत्यके नास्त्यनध्यायो ब्रह्मसत्त्रं हि तत्स्मृतम् ।
ब्रह्माहुतिहुतं पुण्यमनध्यायवशट्कृतम् ॥१०६॥
यः स्वाध्यायमधीतेऽब्दं विधिना नियतः शुचिः ।

[*Jolly* M$^{3-4}$] सम्यगर्क्ष° ; GMd^{5} NNg MTr^{6} *Nd Dev* सम्यगार्क्ष°

102. Cited by *Lakṣ* 1.179; *Mādh* 1.281; pādas a-b cited by *Viś* 1.25 — a) *BhP* 4.29 जपंस्तिष्ठन्परां संध्यां; *Mādh* पूर्व्यां; Ho सर्वां संध्यां; GMy जपेत्तिष्ठन्; Be^{1} La^{2} Lo^{4} TMd^{3} Ox^{3} Tj^{1} sOx^{1} sPu^{6} Pu^{7} Tr^{1} MTr^{4} °स्तिष्ठेन् — a-b) *Viś Mādh* °स्तिष्ठेत्सावित्रीमार्कदर्शनात् [cf. 2.101b]; BKt^{5} नैषमेनं — c) *BhP* 4.30 अपरां तु; NKt^{4} सदासीनो — d) *LakṣMādh* °सीनः सम्यगृक्षविभावनात् [cf. 1.101d]; TMd^{4} पालं हन्ति; Pu^{9} दिवाकृतः

103. Omitted in Ox^{3}; *ma* in Lo^{4}. Cited by *Lakṣ* 1.180; *Dev* 2.366 — a) Be^{3} Bo Ho La^{2} Lo^{1} Pu^{5} Pu^{7} Pu^{8} Pu^{10} Tj^{2} *Go Ku Mr* नानुतिष्ठति यः; Lo^{3} NNg Tj^{1} [*Jolly* R] *BhP* 430 *Lakṣ* नोपतिष्ठति यः; GMy MTr^{4} न तु तिष्ठति यः; La^{1} तिष्ठन्ति; TMd^{4} तिष्ठते; Tr^{2} च यः — b) *BhP* 4.30 नोपासते पश्चिमां नृप; La^{1} La^{2} NKt^{4} Lo^{2} TMd^{3} TMd^{4} GMd^{5} GMy oOr Pu^{8} Tr^{1} Tr^{2} MTr^{4} MTr^{6} पूर्वामुपास्ते न तु पश्चिमां [NKt^{4} La^{2} Lo^{2} TMd^{4} Pu^{8} न च]; Bo Lo^{1} Wa यस्तु — c) Tr^{2} स विद्वद्भिर्बहि° ; TMd^{4} °वद्रहिष्कार्यः; wKt^{3} La^{1} °हिष्कार्यं — d) wKt^{3} °कर्मणां

In NKt^{4} the folio containing verses 103–115 is missing.

104. Cited by *Apa* 70; *Dev* 2.504; *Mādh* 1.312 — a) BCa oOr sOx^{1} sPu^{6} प्रयतो [*but* BCa sOx^{1} sPu^{6} *cor*] — b) Tj^{1} नैत्यक; BBe^{2} sPu^{6} नैत्यिकं; GMy नैत्तिकं; BKt^{5} Tr^{2} नैतिकं; *Apa* [vl as in ed] °माश्रितः — c) TMd^{3} गायत्री° ; Tr^{1} सावित्री समधीयीत; *Mādh* °मभ्यधीयीत; Tr^{2} °प्यधार्यत; sOx^{1} sPu^{6} °धीयेत — d) *Apa* [vl as in ex] °रण्ये; GMy समावृतः; Ox^{3} यथाविधि; Lo^{4} समाविधिः [*but cor*]

105. Cited by *Apa* 137; *Hem* 3/3.775; *Dev* 1.148, 164; *Mādh* 1.314 — a) TMd^{3} वेदोपाकरणे; TMd^{4} °करणा; *BhP* 4.32 °रणे राजन्; Ho नैव; Lo^{3} Tj^{1} [*Jolly* R] चापि — b) [*Jolly* R] चापि; Lo^{4} [*but cor*] NNg NPu^{1} Pu^{7} [*but cor*] Pu^{9} *Mādh* नित्यके; BBe^{2} wKt^{1} sOx^{1} [*but cor*] sPu^{6} नैत्यिके; Jo^{2} नेत्यके; Be^{1} Pu^{10} नैत्यको; GMd^{5} GMy नैत्तिके; Tr^{2} नैतिके — c) Bo Wa नानुरोधास्त्यन° ; *Me* [pāṭha] न निरोधोस्त्यन° ; *BhP* 4.33 नात्र दोषोऽस्त्यन° ; Be^{1} °रोधोस्त्वन° ; Lo^{2} °रोधेस्त्वन° ; Lo^{1} °नाध्याये; sOx^{1} sPu^{6} [*but cor*] °नध्यायी; BKt^{5} °नधर्ये; TMd^{4} °नाध्यायैर्होम° — d) TMd^{3} हेम° ; Lo^{3} Tj^{1} वेदमन्त्रेषु; *BhP* 4.33 °मन्त्रेषु वा विभो; Lo^{2} GMy Wa चैव ह; oOr चैव तु

106. Cited by *Apa* 137; *Dev* 2.508; *Mādh* 1.314; pādas a-b cited by *Har*-A 1.12.8 — a) BBe^{2} sOx^{1} sPu^{6} Tr^{2} नैत्यिके; BKt^{5} Lo^{5} नित्यके; GMd^{5} नैत्तिके; GMy °ध्यायं; NNg oOr °ध्याये — b) TMd^{4} GMy NPu^{1} ब्रह्मसूत्रं; *Apa* ब्रह्ममन्त्रं — d) Ox^{2} °ध्यायं; sOx^{1} sPu^{6} Tr^{2} °ध्याये वषट्कृतं; La^{1} °ध्यायवहिःकृतं; Tj^{1} °कृतिं

तस्य नित्यं क्षरत्येष पयो दधि घृतं मधु ॥१०७॥
अग्नीन्धनं भैक्षचर्यामधःशय्यां गुरोर्हितम् ।
आ समावर्तनात्कुर्यात् कृतोपनयनो द्विजः ॥१०८॥
आचार्यपुत्रः शुश्रूषुर्ज्ञानदो धार्मिकः शुचिः ।
आप्तः शक्तोऽर्थदः साधुः स्वोऽध्याप्या दश धर्मतः ॥१०९॥
नापृष्टः कस्यचिद् ब्रूयान्न चान्यायेन पृच्छतः ।
जानन्नपि हि मेधावी जडवल्लोक आचरेत् ॥११०॥
अधर्मेण च यः प्राह यश्चाधर्मेण पृच्छति ।
तयोरन्यतरः प्रैति विद्वेषं वाधिगच्छति ॥१११॥
धर्मार्थौ यत्र न स्यातां शुश्रूषा वापि तद्विधा ।
तत्र विद्या न वप्तव्या शुभं बीजमिवोषरे ॥११२॥
विद्ययैव समं कामं मर्तव्यं ब्रह्मवादिना ।
आपद्यपि हि घोरायां न त्वेनामिरिणे वपेत् ॥११३॥

107. a) *BhP* 4.34 ऋगेकां यस्त्वधीयीत; GMy यत्स्वा° — b) Be^{1} La^{2} Lo^{2} TMd^{4} GMy Tr^{1} MTr^{4} MTr^{6} *BhP* 4.34 नियतो द्विजः; commentators support शुचिः — c) Kt^{2} La^{2} क्षरन्त्येष; Ho TMd^{3} °त्येषः; *BhP* 4.35 °त्येषा; Tr^{1} °त्येनः; GMy °त्येनो — d) GMd^{5} पयो मेदो स्वतर्मधु; *BhP* 4.35 पयो मेध्यं; TMd^{3} [*Jolly* Nd] पयो मेधो; Be^{3} Pu^{9} मधुः

108. Omitted in BKt^{5}. Cited by *Apa* 76; *Mādh* 1.455 — a) *BhP* 4.36 अग्निशुश्रूषणं भैक्षमधः°; GMy अग्न्याधानं; Pu^{10} °चर्या अधः°; *Apa* [vl as in ed] °चर्यमधः° — b) Pu^{10} °शय्या; Pu^{5} Pu^{7} Pu^{9} °शिय्यां; TMd^{3} गुरोर्हितः — c) BBe^{2} Tr^{2} असमा°; TMd^{4} आसतेवर्त°; *Dev* °वर्तनं कुर्यात्

109. Cited by *Viś* 1.28; *Apa* 57; *Dev* 1.140 — a) Pu^{5} Tj^{1} °पुत्र; BKt^{5} °पुत्रं; *BhP* 4.36 °पुत्रशुश्रूषां ज्ञा° — b) TMd^{3} °शुर्ज्ञानतो; Tj^{1} धर्मिकः; Pu^{9} धार्मिका — c) Lo^{5} आप्त; Lo^{2} शुक्तो; *BhP* 4.37 शक्तोऽन्नदः — c-d) GMd^{1} TMd^{3} TMd^{4} GMd^{5} GMy Tr^{1} MTr^{4} MTr^{6} *Viś Apa* शक्तोऽर्थदोऽर्थी स्वः साधु-रध्याप्या दश धर्मतः [*Apa* शक्तार्थदाप्ताः स्वः] — d) Be^{1} Hy wKt^{1} Lo^{1} Lo^{3} Ox^{3} Tj^{1} *BhP* 4.37 स्वाध्याप्या; Kt^{2} BKt^{5} सोध्याप्या; TMd^{3} sOx^{1} sPu^{6} °ध्याप्यो; Ox^{3} देश; NNg धर्मतो दश

110. Cited by *Lakṣ* 1.242 — a) Lo^{1} नोपृष्टः — b) Bo Pu^{5} Pu^{7} *Lakṣ* वान्यायेन — c) Lo^{1} GMd^{5} MTr^{6} च — d) La^{1} जडवन्मौनमाचरेत् [*but mc*]; Tr^{1} जलव°; BKt^{5} जनव°; Be^{3} Ho wKt^{3} Lo^{1} Lo^{2} TMd^{3} TMd^{4} GMd^{5} GMy NNg sOx^{1} sPu^{6} MTr^{4} MTr^{6} Wa [*Jolly* Nd] °वल्लोकमाचरेत्

111. a) Be^{3} La^{1} Lo^{3} GMd^{5} GMy Tj^{1} Tr^{1} MTr^{4} MTr^{6} Wa तु यः — c) BBe^{2} wKt^{1} GMd^{5} °न्यतरं; Be^{1} TMd^{4} GMy प्रेति; sOx^{1} प्रीति [*but cor*] — d) Ho La^{1} La^{2} Lo^{3} Lo^{4} Lo^{5} Tj^{1} [*Jolly* R] चाधि-गच्छति; TMd^{4} Tr^{1} *BhP* 4.39 वा निगच्छति; BCa वा नियच्छति

112. Cited by *Apa* 57; *Har*-A 1.13.10; *Dev* 1.140 — a) Pu^{9} Wa धर्मार्थो; BBe^{2} BCa [*but cor*] Pu^{10} Tr^{2} यस्य; GMy यदि — b) sOx^{1} sPu^{6} Tr^{2} *BhP* 4.39 चापि; *Apa* नापि; GMy वाभि; TMd^{4} तद्विधां; Lo^{2} तद्विषा — c) Be^{1} Pu^{5} Pu^{7} Pu^{9} *BhP* 4.40 *Har*-A न तत्र विद्या वप्तव्या; NNg तस्य; Wa वाप्तव्या; TMd^{3} व्यप्तव्या; NNg oOr Tj^{1} Tr^{2} MTr^{4} [*Jolly* M$^{1-2-8-9}$ R] *Dev* वक्तव्या; *Apa* दातव्या — d) NNg शुद्धं; *Dev* [vl] उप्तं; *Apa* गुप्तं [*vl as in ed*]; MTr^{4} वीजमि°; La^{1} GMd^{5} GMy NNg NPu^{1} Pu^{5} Pu^{7} Pu^{9} Tr^{1} °मिवौषरे; Jo^{2} Lo^{1} °मिवोखरे; Bo °मिवोप्तरे; Lo^{3} °मिवोपरे; TMd^{3} °मिदोपरे

113. Hy transposes 113 and 114. Cited by *Lakṣ* 1.242 — a) Lo^{4} sOx^{1} sPu^{6} विद्यायैव; Ox^{3}

विद्या ब्राह्मणमेत्याह शेवधिष्टेऽस्मि रक्ष माम् ।
असूयकाय मां मा दास्तथा स्यां वीर्यवत्तमा ॥११४॥
यमेव तु शुचिं विद्या नियतं ब्रह्मचारिणम् ।
तस्मै मां ब्रूहि विप्राय निधिपायाप्रमादिने ॥११५॥
ब्रह्म यस्त्वननुज्ञातमधीयानादवाप्नुयात् ।
स ब्रह्मस्तेयसंयुक्तो नरकं प्रतिपद्यते ॥११६॥
लौकिकं वैदिकं वापि तथाध्यात्मिकमेव वा ।
आददीत यतो ज्ञानं तं पूर्वमभिवादयेत् ॥११७॥
सावित्रीमात्रसारोऽपि वरं विप्रः सुयन्त्रितः ।
नायन्त्रितस्त्रिवेदोऽपि सर्वाशी सर्वविक्रयी ॥११८॥

विद्ययेव; Ho विद्ययैव हि समं; Tr^{1} समं कार्यं; TMd^{3} समं ग्राह्य — b) wKt^{1} Lo^{2} Lo^{5} NPu^{1} Tr^{1} कर्तव्यं; Tr^{2} मंतव्यं; TMd^{3} मत्तव्यं; TMd^{4} मन्त्रव्यं; Pu^{5} Pu^{7} Pu^{9} मर्तत्यं — c) Bo ह; La^{1} TMd^{3} GMd^{5} च; Tr^{2} घोरायो; La^{2} कष्टायां — d) TMd^{3} त्वेवमि°; Ho La^{2} Tj^{2} °मिरणे; *BhP* 4.41 °मीरिणे; Tj^{1} °मिरिपे; sOx^{1} sPu^{6} वपन्

114.* Verses 114 and 115 transposed in oMd^{2}. Cited by *Lakṣ* 1.242 — a) La^{2}ब्रह्मण°; GMy ब्रह्माण°; Jo^{2} La^{1} Lo^{3} GMd^{1} TMd^{3} TMd^{4} GMd^{5} GMy sOx^{1} [*but cor*] Ox^{2} NPu^{1} Pu^{2} Pu^{5} sPu^{6} Pu^{7} Pu^{9} Pu^{10} Tj^{1} Tr^{1} Tr^{2} MTr^{4} MTr^{6} [*Jolly* M$^{1-2-8-9}$ G R Nd] *BhP* 4.41 °णमित्याह — b) Be^{1} Bo Ho Jo^{1} wKt^{3} BKt^{5} La^{1} La^{2} Lo^{1} Lo^{2} Lo^{3} Lo^{4} NNg sOx^{1} Ox^{2} Ox^{3} NPu^{1} sPu^{6} Pu^{8} Tj^{1} Tj^{2} Tr^{2} MTr^{4} MTr^{6} Wa [*Jolly* Ku R] *BhP* 4.41 *KSS* शेवधिस्ते; BBe^{2} Hy Kt^{2} La^{1} oMd^{2} oOr सेवधिस्ते; wKt^{1} सेवावश्यास्मि; Bo °धिस्तेस्य रक्ष; BKt^{5} °धिष्टे ह रक्ष; GMy रक्षणे [*om* माम्] — c) *BhP* 4.41 °काय मा प्रदास्तथा; Be^{1} BKt^{5} Lo^{1} TMd^{3} GMd^{5} Tr^{2} *Lakṣ* मा मा; NPu^{1} मां दद्यांस्तथा; Pu^{5} Pu^{7} Pu^{9} दात्तथा; Be^{3} Ox^{3} दातथा — d) wKt^{1} GMy दास्तदा; TMd^{4} स्याद्वीर्य°; Bo °वत्तमां; Be^{1} GMy °वत्तमाः; GMd^{1} °वत्तम; Lo^{4} °यत्तमा; GMd^{5} °वत्तरा

115.* Cited by *Lakṣ* 1.242 — a) Tr^{1} शुचं; TMd^{3} विद्याः; BCa विद्यां; Be^{1} Bo Ho Hy Jm Jo^{1} Jo^{2} wKt^{1} La^{1} La^{2} Lo^{1} oMd^{2} GMd^{5} NNg NPu^{1} Pu^{5} sPu^{6} Pu^{7} [*cor to*] Pu^{9} Pu^{10} Tj^{1} Tr^{2} MTr^{3} MTr^{6} *Rn Nd Rc Mandlik KSS BhP* 4.43 विद्यान्नियतं; GMd^{1} विद्यात् नियतं — b) Jo^{1} oMd^{2} GMd^{5} *KSS* नियतब्रह्म°; Bo °चारिणां — c) Jm देहि — d) Lo^{5} °प्रभाविने

116. Omitted in Pu^{5}. Cited by *Viś* 3.201–2; *Mādh* 1.301 — a) GMy ब्रह्मवज्रन्त्वननु°; wKt^{3} ब्रह्मस्वस्त्वननु°; TMd^{4} °ज्ञाताम° — b) GMy °धीयानृणमाप्नुयात् — c) Tj^{1} ब्रह्मे; TMd^{3} GMd^{5} Tr^{1} °स्तेयकृद्विप्रो — c-d) *BhP* 4.45 स याति नरकं घोरं रौरवं भीमदर्शनम् — d) Be^{1} प्रतिगच्छति

117. Cited by *Apa* 54; *Dev* 1.97; *Mādh* 1.296, 301; *BhP* 4.44–5 transposes 117 a-b and 116 c-d — a) Ox^{3} लौकिकां; TMd^{3} काकिकं; Ho Lo^{5} Tr^{2} चापि — b) Ox^{3} तथाप्याध्यात्मि°; TMd^{3} तथाप्यात्मि°; *BhP* 4.44 [vl] °ध्यात्मकमेव; Be^{3} Jm Jo^{1} Jo^{2} wKt^{1} Kt^{2} Lo^{1} Lo^{3} Ox^{2} Pu^{5} Pu^{7} Pu^{9} Tj^{1} Tr^{2} Wa [*Jolly* G R] *BhP* 4.44 *Mandlik Jolly KSS* च — c) sOx^{1} sPu^{6} आददाति; *Apa* [vl] आदधीत

Additional verse in *Mandlik* [ट] *KSS:*

जन्मप्रभृति यत्किंचिच्चेतसा धर्ममाचरेत् ।
तत्सर्वं विफलं ज्ञेयमेकहस्ताभिवादनात् ।।

118. Omitted in wKt^{3}. Cited by *Hem* 3/1.444; *Dev* 4156 — a) *Dev* गायत्री°; Lo^{3} TMd^{4} GMy sOx^{1} Pu^{5} sPu^{6} Pu^{7} Pu^{9} Tj^{1} [*Jolly* G R] *BhP* 447 सावित्रीसारमात्रो; *Hem* गायत्रीसारमात्रो; NPu^{1} सावित्रीसारमात्रापि — b) GMd^{1} TMd^{3} TMd^{4} GMd^{5} GMy Tr^{1} MTr^{4} MTr^{6} *BhP* 447 वरो; La^{1} विप्रस्व-

शय्यासनेऽध्याचरिते श्रेयसा न समाविशेत् ।
शय्यासनस्थश्चैवैनं प्रत्युत्थायाभिवादयेत् ॥११९॥
ऊर्ध्वं प्राणा ह्युत्क्रामन्ति यूनः स्थविर आयति ।
प्रत्युत्थानाभिवादाभ्यां पुनस्तान्प्रतिपद्यते ॥१२०॥
अभिवादनशीलस्य नित्यं वृद्धोपसेविनः ।
चत्वारि सम्यग्वर्धन्ते* आयुः प्रज्ञा यशो बलम् ॥१२१॥
अभिवादात्परं विप्रो ज्यायांसमभिवादयन् ।
असौ नामाहमस्मीति स्वं नाम परिकीर्तयेत् ॥१२२॥
नामधेयस्य ये केचिदभिवादं न जानते ।
तान्प्राज्ञोऽहमिति ब्रूयात् स्त्रियः सर्वास्तथैव च ॥१२३॥
भोःशब्दं कीर्तयेदन्ते स्वस्य नाम्नोऽभिवादने ।
नाम्नां स्वरूपभावो हि भोभाव ऋषिभिः स्मृतः ॥१२४॥

यंत्रितः; TMd^3 यन्त्रस्सुयन्त्रितः; La^2 GMd^5 सयन्त्रितः — c) Be^3 TMd^3 GMy *Hem Dev* °न्त्रितश्चतुर्वेदी सर्वाशी [Be^3 °तुर्वेदः]; La^1 °न्त्रितत्रयीवेदो सर्वाशी — d) Lo^4 सर्वाशीः

119. a) TMd^3 TMd^4 शय्यासनाध्या°; Tr^2 °चरितो; sOx^1 sPu^6 °चरितः; oMd^2 °चरते — b) BBe^2 नः; Lo^1 Tj^2 समाश्रयेत्; Ho TMd^3 TMd^4 GMd^5 oOr Tr^1 MTr^4 MTr^6 समाचरेत् — c) Lo^2 Ox^3 °नस्थाश्चै°; Be^1 Be^3 NKt^4 BKt^5 °श्चैवेनं — d) TMd^3 GMy Tr^1 MTr^4 MTr^6 °वैनमवरुह्याभि°; Ho °त्थायापिवादयेत्

120. Cited by *Dev* 1.97 — a) TMd^3 प्राणाप्युत्क्रा°; MTr^4 ह्युत्क्रमन्ति — b) sOx^1 sPu^6 यूनं; Pu^8 पुनः; NKt^4 पूज; Kt^2 आयाति; La^2 Lo^1 TMd^4 GMy [*but cor*] oOr sOx^1 sPu^6 MTr^4 MTr^6 *BhP* 449 *Dev Mr* आगते; TMd^3 आगति; *Go* gloss आगच्छति सति may support आगते — c) Lo^3 Tj^1 समुत्था°; Tr^1 अभ्युत्था° — d) wKt^3 पुनस्ता प्रति°; Ho सहितान्प्रति°; TMd^4 °स्तान्परिपद्यते

121.* Cited by *Dev* 1.97 — a) Lo^2 °शीलश्च — b) *Dev* नित्य — c) NKt^4 सम्यग्वर्धन्त; Tr^1 सम्यग्वर्तन्त; BBe^2 BCa Ho wKt^1 wKt^3 BKt^5 Lo^1 Lo^4 Lo^5 Pu^{10} *Me Dave Jha* संप्रवर्धन्ते; Pu^5 Pu^7 Pu^9 संप्रवर्धन्ति; Ox^3 संवर्धन्ते; Jo^2 Lo^3 Tj^1 नित्यं वर्धन्ते; Be^1 Be^3 Bo Hy Jm Jo^1 Kt^2 La^1 GMd^1 oMd^2 TMd^3 NNg oOr sOx^1 Ox^2 NPu^1 sPu^6 Tr^2 MTr^3 *Dev Rc Mandlik KSS* तस्य वर्धन्ते; *Jolly* तस्य वर्धन्त — d) TMd^3 ह्यायुः; Jm Jo^1 Kt^2 oMd^2 MTr^3 *Rn* [pāṭha] *Mandlik KSS* आयुर्विद्या; Lo^4 Lo^5 Ox^3 Pu^{10} *Me Dave Jha* आयुर्धर्मो [Pu^{10} °र्मौ]; MTr^4 प्रज्ञां; TMd^3 यतोबलं

122. Ox^3 omits pāda-d. Cited by *Apa* 52; *Dev* 1.96; *Mādh* 1.296 — a) TMd^3 TMd^4 GMy NNg sOx^1 sPu^6 Tr^1 MTr^4 °वादात्परो; GMd^1 °वादनात्परं; La^1 La^2 °वादयेत्परं; wKt^1 GMy °वादपरं; *BhP* 4.51 °वादपरो — b) Jo^2 BKt^5 Lo^2 Lo^3 Lo^4 Lo^5 GMd^1 TMd^3 GMy NNg sOx^1 Ox^2 Ox^3 Pu^5 sPu^6 Pu^7 Pu^9 Tj^1 Tr^2 MTr^4 MTr^6 *Rc BhP* 451 *Apa* [vl] °वादयेत् — d) Be^1 GMd^1 TMd^3 GMd^5 GMy *BhP* 4.51 *Apa* स्वनाम; NNg स्वयं नाम; MTr^4 MTr^6 °कीर्तयन्

123. Verse 123 placed after 126 in TMd^3 and after 128 in GMd^5; pādas c-d omitted in NKt^4. Cited by *Apa* 54; *Dev* 1.98 — a) Ox^3 *om* ये; Lo^4 *ma* ये — b) Bo wKt^3 La^1 [*but mc*] Hy GMd^1 TMd^3 GMy जायते — c) TMd^4 तान्प्रज्ञो; Bo तान्प्रज्ञाहमिति; TMd^4 NNg ब्रूया — d) TMd^4 सर्वस्त-थैव; *Apa* [vl] सर्वांस्तथैव

124 Omitted in NKt^4; pādas c-d omitted in Be^1. Cited by *Lakṣ* 1.185; pādas a-b cited by *Apa* 52; *Dev* 1.96; *Mādh* 1.296 — a) Ho wKt^1 भोशव्दं; *Apa* कारयेद° — b) *Mādh* स्वस्वनाम्नाभि-

आयुष्मान्भव सौम्येति वाच्यो विप्रोऽभिवादने ।
अकारश्चास्य नाम्नोऽन्ते वाच्यः पूर्वाक्षरः प्लुतः* ॥१२५॥
यो न वेत्त्यभिवादस्य विप्रः प्रत्यभिवादनम् ।
नाभिवाद्यः स विदुषा यथा शूद्रस्तथैव सः ॥१२६॥
ब्राह्मणं कुशलं पृच्छेत् क्षत्रबन्धुमनामयम् ।
वैश्यं क्षेमं समागम्य शूद्रमारोग्यमेव च ॥१२७॥
अवाच्यो दीक्षितो नाम्ना यवीयानपि यो भवेत् ।
भोभवत्पूर्वकं त्वेनमभिभाषेत धर्मवित् ॥१२८॥
परपत्नी तु या स्त्री स्यादसंबद्धा च योनितः ।
तां ब्रूयाद्भवतीत्येवं सुभगे भगिनीति वा ॥१२९॥
मातुलांश्च पितृव्यांश्च श्वशुरानृत्विजो गुरून् ।

वादनम् — c) TMd^3 Tr^1 *BhP* 4.53 नाम्नः; wKt^1 नाम्नी; wKt^3 *Lakṣ* नाम्ना; TMd^4 GMy °भावे; TMd^3 °भादो — d) Lo^3 Tj^1 भोभावो; GMd^1 भोशब्दो; Wa भोःशब्दः; GMy Ox^2 *Nā* भोशब्द; *Nā* [pāṭha] भोभाव; Pu^5 Pu^7 Pu^9 Wa कविभिः; Lo^2 °भिः सह

125.* Pādas a-b omitted in Kt^4. Cited by *Apa* 53; *Har-A* 1.5.17; *Dev* 1.98; *Mādh* 1.297 — a) Hy सोम्येति — b) La^1 GMd^1 TMd^4 विप्रो वाच्योभि° — c) La^1 NNg आकार°; NKt^4 °रश्च स्वनाम्नो; TMd^4 नाम्नान्ते; *Apa* नाम्नोन्तर्वाच्यः — d) TMd^4 वाच्यं; sOx^1 [*but cor*] sPu^6 कार्यः; Ho Lo^3 TMd^3 GMy NNg sOx^1 [*but mc fh*] NPu^1 [*but cor sh*] sPu^6 [*but mc sh*] Pu^{10} Tj^1 MTr^4 [*Jolly* M^4 R] *Nā* [pāṭha] *Nd Jolly* पूर्वाक्षरप्लुतः; NKt^4 सर्वाक्षरप्लुतः; Jo^1 BKt^5 °क्षरः पुनः; all other mss. read पूर्वाक्षरः प्लुतः

126. Cited by *Dev* 1.98; *Mādh* 1.297 — c) Lo^2 °वादः; Bo स विप्राय; Pu^{10} विदुषां — d) Bo NPu^1 Tr^1 शूद्रस्तथैव च

127. Cited by *Dev* 1.100; *Mādh* 1.298 — a) La^2 ब्रह्मणं; Wa पृच्छ — b) Kt^2 क्षेत्र°; Ox^2 क्षत्रवंशमना°; La^2 तत्रभवमना°; Ox^3 °बन्धमना°; GMy °नामयः — c) GMy वैश्यं क्षेमंकरं ब्रूयाच्छूद्र°; Pu^5 Pu^7 Pu^9 समागत्य — d) wKt^3 शूद्रस्यारोग्यमेव च; Ho °मेव तत्; BKt^5 Lo^2 TMd^4 NNg NPu^1 Tr^1 *BhP* 4.58 *Lakṣ* तु; Be^1 वा

In NKt^4 the folio containing the section °गम्य until 140c is missing.

128. a) Be^3 Jo^2 Lo^4 Lo^5 sOx^1 Ox^3 sPu^6 Tj^1 [*Jolly* M$^{3-4}$ R] *BhP* 4.59 न वाच्यो [*but cor in* sOx^1 sPu^6]; TMd^3 नावाच्यो; TMd^4 अवाच्ये; Bo दीक्षिता; Pu^7 नाम्नो [*but cor*] — b) Lo^2 कनीयानपि; Ox^3 यवीयानमपि; Lo^4 यवीयानानपि; Pu^{10} जवानानपि — c) MTr^4 भोगवत्पूर्वकी; GMd^5 °त्पूर्वकां; GMd^5 Tr^1 चैनम°; TMd^3 चैव अभि° — c-d) *BhP* 4.59 °वत्पूर्वकत्वेन इति स्वायंभुवोऽब्रवीत्; TMd^3 चैव नाभिभाषेत

129.* Cited by *Dev* 1.101; *Mādh* 1.298— a) Be^1 BBe^2 Be^3 BKt^5 Lo^4 Lo^5 TMd^3 GMd^5 GMy sOx^1 Ox^3 NPu^1 sPu^6 Pu^{10} Tr^1 MTr^4 MTr^6 [*Jolly* M$^{3-4}$] च; *BhP* 4.60 या राजन् — b) La^2 Tj^1 [*Jolly* Ku R] *Dev* °बन्धा; TMd^4 °बाधा; Tr^2 *BhP* 4.60 तु; Ho स्वयोनितः; wKt^1 योषितः — c) *BhP* 4.60 वक्तव्या भवतीत्येवं; Tj^1 °द्भगिनीत्येवं; Be^1 Tj^1 *Dev* °त्येव — d) BCa Lo^2 शुभगे; Ox^3 *om* वा; Pu^8 व; BBe^2 Hy Jm Jo^1 Jo^2 Kt^2 Lo^1 Lo^3 TMd^3 TMd^4 sOx^1 Pu^2 Pu^4 Pu^5 sPu^6 Pu^7 Pu^9 Tj^1 Tj^2 MTr^3 Wa *Mandlik Jolly Jha KSS Dave* च

असावहमिति ब्रूयात् प्रत्युत्थाय यवीयसः ॥१३०॥
मातृष्वसा मातुलानी श्वश्रूरथ पितृष्वसा ।
संपूज्या गुरुपत्नीवत् समास्ता गुरुभार्यया ॥१३१॥
भ्रातुर्भार्योपसंग्राह्या सवर्णाहन्यहन्यपि ।
विप्रोष्य तूपसंग्राह्या ज्ञातिसंबन्धियोषितः ॥१३२॥
पितुर्भगिन्यां मातुश्च ज्यायस्यां च स्वसर्यपि ।
मातृवद्वृत्तिमातिष्ठेन्माता ताभ्यो गरीयसी ॥१३३॥
दशाब्दाख्यं पौरसख्यं पञ्चाब्दाख्यं कलाभृताम् ।
त्र्यब्दपूर्वं श्रोत्रियाणामल्पेनापि स्वयोनिषु ॥१३४॥
ब्राह्मणं दशवर्षं च शतवर्षं च भूमिपम् ।
पितापुत्रौ विजानीयाद् ब्राह्मणस्तु तयोः पिता ॥१३५॥
वित्तं बन्धुर्वयः कर्म विद्या भवति पञ्चमी ।

130. a) *BhP* 4.61 पितृव्यान्मातुलान्राजन्; Be^{3} मातुलां स्वपितृ° — b) Pu^{5} Pu^{7} स्वसुरा°; Lo^{4} Pu^{9} श्वसुरा° — d) Lo^{1} यवीयसान्; *BhP* 4.61 जघन्यजः

131. a) Ho पितृष्वसा — b) BBe^{2} श्वश्रूरपि — c) TMd^{4} संपूज्य; Tj^{1} Pu^{8} La^{1} °पत्नीव; Be^{1} Lo^{3} TMd^{3} Tr^{2} *BhP* 4.62 °पत्नीच — d) wKt^{3} BKt^{5} Pu^{10} Tj^{1} Tr^{2} समस्ता; TMd^{3} समस्तं; Bo समर्या

132. Cited by *Dev* 1.103; *Mādh*1.300 — a) *BhP* 4.63 ज्येष्ठस्य भ्रातुर्या भार्या; Tj^{1} भ्रातुभा°; TMd^{3} TMd^{4} MTr^{6} *Dev* भ्रातृभा°; Bo °ग्राह्य; Hy °ग्रह्या — b) after this pāda *BhP* 4.63 adds: पूजयन्प्रयतो विप्रो याति विष्णुसदो नृप — c) *BhP* 4.64 प्रवासादेत्य संपूज्या; Be^{3} विप्रोष्य उपसं°; Bo °ग्राह्य; NPu^{1} Pu^{5} Pu^{7} Pu^{9} °ग्राह्याः; TMd^{4} °ग्राह्यं — d) Kt^{2} TMd^{4} GMd^{5} Tj^{1} °संबन्ध°. Between the first and the second half-verse TMd^{4} adds 3.210c-d.

133. Cited by *Viś* 1.34; *Dev* 1.90; *Mādh* 1.304; an expanded version in two verses is given in *BhP* 4.64–6 — a) GMy °गिन्या मातुलश्च — b) BKt^{5} *om* च; La^{1} Tr^{2} तु; Bo स्वसामपि — c) TMd^{3} पितृव°; *Dev* °वद्धक्तिमाति° — d) BKt^{5} Lo^{2} Lo^{3} NNg Ox^{3} [*Jolly* R] *Dev* त्वाभ्यो

134. Omitted in Bo. Cited by *Apa* 53; *Dev* 1.101; *Mādh* 1.299 — a) TMd^{4} °ख्यं रसख्यं च; La^{1} TMd^{3} Tr^{2} °संख्यं; Tr^{1} °सौख्यं; Pu^{8} °सख्यां — b) wKt^{1} wKt^{3} GMd^{5} GMy °भृतं — c) Hy La^{2} Lo^{1} sOx^{1} Ox^{2} Pu^{2} sPu^{6} Pu^{8} Tj^{1} Tj^{2} Tr^{2} *BhP* 4.67 अव्दपूर्वं — d) BBe^{2} Hy Jm Jo^{1} wKt^{1} Kt^{2} wKt^{3} La^{2} Lo^{2} oMd^{2} oOr Ox^{2} Pu^{8} Tj^{2} MTr^{3} [*Jolly* Ku R] *Me Rn Mr BhP* 4.67 *Dev Mandlik Jha KSS Dave* °याणां स्वल्पेनापि; Ho NNg °याणामव्देनापि

135. Cited by *Dev* 1.101 — a) TMd^{4} ब्राह्मणो; GMy ब्राह्मणे; MTr^{4} ब्राह्मणान्; Hy °वर्षे; TMd^{4} °वर्षस्तु; GMy °वर्षश्च; Be^{1} BBe^{2} Ho Hy Jm Jo^{1} Kt^{2} La^{1} Lo^{1} Lo^{4} Lo^{5} NNg sOx^{1} Ox^{3} NPu^{1} Pu^{2} Pu^{4} Pu^{5} sPu^{6} Pu^{7} Pu^{9} Pu^{10} Tj^{2} Tr^{2} *Dev Mandlik Jolly Jha KSS Dave* तु — b) *BhP* 4.68 दशवर्षं; TMd^{4} *om* शतवर्षं च; Hy °वर्षे; GMy °वर्षश्च; Be^{1} BBe^{2} Ho Hy Jm Jo^{1} wKt^{1} Kt^{2} La^{1} Lo^{1} Lo^{4} Lo^{5} NNg sOx^{1} Ox^{3} NPu^{1} Pu^{2} Pu^{4} Pu^{5} sPu^{6} Pu^{7} Pu^{9} Pu^{10} Tj^{2} Tr^{2} MTr^{3} *Dev Mandlik Jolly Jha KSS Dave* तु; GMy भूमिपः — c) La^{1} *cor to* °पुत्रं; Pu^{5} Pu^{9} Wa °पुत्रो; Tj^{1} °पुत्रोर्वि°; Bo °पुत्रौ तु जानीयाद्; GMy °पुत्रस्तु विज्ञेयौ; GMd^{1} TMd^{4} °पुत्रौ तु विज्ञेयौ — d) TMd^{3} TMd^{4} GMy तयोस्तु ब्राह्मणः पिता; Be^{3} ब्राह्मणस्त्वनयोः पिता; La^{2} ब्रह्मणस्तु; BKt^{5} La^{1} [*but cor*] sOx^{1} sPu^{6} पिता तयोः; MTr^{4} MTr^{6} तयोरपि

एतानि मान्यस्थानानि गरीयो यद्यदुत्तरम् ॥१३६॥
पञ्चानां त्रिषु वर्णेषु भूयांसि गुणवन्ति च ।
यत्र स्युः सोऽत्र मानार्हः शूद्रोऽपि दशमीं गतः ॥१३७॥
चक्रिणो दशमीस्थस्य रोगिणो भारिणः स्त्रियाः ।
स्नातकस्य च राज्ञश्च पन्था देयो वरस्य च ॥१३८॥
तेषां तु समवेतानां मान्यौ स्नातकपार्थिवौ ।
राजस्नातकयोरेव स्नातको नृपमानभाक् ॥१३९॥
उपनीय तु यः शिष्यं वेदमध्यापयेद् द्विजः ।
सकल्पं सरहस्यं च तमाचार्यं प्रचक्षते ॥१४०॥
एकदेशं तु वेदस्य वेदाङ्गान्यपि वा पुनः ।

136. Cited by *Apa* 159; *Dev* 1.106; pāda-a cited by *Viś* 1.115 — a) TMd[4] वित्तबन्धुवयः; Kt[2] GMy Tr[1] बन्धुवयः; Jo[1] कर्मा — b) Hy भवतु — c) *Jha Dave* मानस्था°; Tr[2] मानिस्था° — d) TMd[4] यद्यदुत्तरः

137. Cited by *Apa* 159; *Lakṣ* 1.203–4; *Dev* 1.106; pāda-a cited by *Viś* 1.115; pāda-d by *Har*-A 1.133 — a) Kt[2] वर्षेषु; *BhP* 4.71 वर्गेषु — c) Jo[2] Lo[3] sOx[1] [*but cor*] sPu[6] [*but cor*] Tj[1] Tr[2] [*Jolly* R] यत्र स्युः स्यात्स मानार्हः; *BhP* 4.71 यस्य; BKt[5] श्रोत्र; Ox[2] *Apa* सोऽपि — d) *Lakṣ* मानार्हो शूद्रो; Bo शूद्रेपि; La[2] दशमीगतः; Be[1] दशमोगतः; *Me* appears to read दशमीमितः

Additional verse in La[1] GMd[5] GMy Tr[1]:

शूद्रश्चोदितधर्मा च कुरुते धर्ममन्वहम् ।
सर्वैरेव तु वर्णैस्तु पूज्यो भवति नित्यशः ॥

a) La[1] शूद्रश्चेदपि कल्याणं — b) La[1] धर्मसंस्तवे — c) La[1] सर्वस्यैव तु धर्मस्य; GMy सर्वैरेव हि; GMd[5] वर्णैश्च — d) La[1] भवति धर्मतः

138. Cited by *Dev* 1.107 — a) Be[1] दशमस्थस्य — b) sOx[1] sPu[6] Tr[2] भारिणो रोगिणः; La[1] भारिणं; TMd[3] सारिणः; Pu[10] *om* स्त्रियाः; Be[1] BBe[2] Ho La[1] Lo[3] Lo[4] GMy sOx[1] Ox[2] Ox[3] sPu[6] Tj[1] MTr[6] स्त्रियः — c) sOx[1] sPu[6] स्नातकस्य गुरो राज्ञः; GMd[1] MTr[4] *BhP* 4.72 तु राज्ञश्च; La[1] तु राज्ञस्य; MTr[6] राज्ञास्य; Pu[5] Pu[9] राज्ञ पन्था — d) Lo[4] Lo[5] पथा; GMd[6] GMy Tr[1] MTr[4] MTr[6] तु

139. Omitted in Pu[5]. Cited by *Dev* 1.107 — a) *BhP* 4.73 एषां समागमे तात; Lo[1] oOr sOx[1] sPu[6] [*mc sh to*] एषां; Be[3] च — b) BKt[5] Wa मान्यो; *BhP* 4.73 पूज्यौ — c) *BhP* 4.73 आभ्यां समागमे राजन्; sOx[1] sPu[6] राज्ञास्ना°; Tr[1] *Dev* °कयोरेवं; BBe[2] Be[3] Hy Jm Jo[1] Kt[2] oMd[2] oOr Pu[8] Tj[2] MTr[3] *Mandlik Jha KSS Dave* °कयोश्चैव — d) oOr [*but cor*] Pu[7] [*but cor*] Pu[9] नृपमान्भवेत्

Additional verse in La[1]:

वेदशास्त्रकृदाचार्यो वेदावयव[कृ?]द्गुरुः [sic] ।
वेदाङ्गकृदुपाध्यायो यज्ञकर्तार ऋत्विजः ॥

140. Cited by *Kum* 1.3.13; *Viś* 1.33; *Apa* 65; *Dev* 1.90, 5.38; *Mādh* 1.137, 304 — a) La[2] Lo[2] *Apa* उपनीय गुरुः शिष्यं; GMy तु शिष्यं हि — a-b) *BhP* 4.74 अध्यापयेद्यस्तु शिष्यं कृत्वोपनयनं द्विजः — b) TMd[3] °ध्यापयो द्विजः; La[2] °पयेत्त्रयः — c) Bo La[1] Hy TMd[3] संकल्पं; TMd[4] Pu[10] सकलं; *Kum* साङ्गं — c-d) *BhP* 474 gives an expanded verse: सरहस्यं सकल्पं च वेदं भरतसत्तम । तमाचार्यं महाबाहो प्रवदन्ति मनीषिणः — d) Ox[2] प्रयच्छते

योऽध्यापयति वृत्त्यर्थमुपाध्यायः स उच्यते ॥१४१॥
निषेकादीनि कर्माणि यः करोति यथाविधि ।
संभावयति चान्नेन स विप्रो गुरुरुच्यते ॥१४२॥
अग्न्याधेयं पाकयज्ञानग्निष्टोमादिकान्मखान् ।
यः करोति वृतो यस्य स तस्यर्त्विगिहोच्यते ॥१४३॥
य आवृणोत्यवितथं ब्रह्मणा श्रवणावुभौ ।
स माता स पिता ज्ञेयस्तं न द्रुह्येत् कदाचन ॥१४४॥
उपाध्यायाद्दशाचार्य आचार्याणां शतं पिता ।
सहस्रं तु पितुर्माता गौरवेणातिरिच्यते ॥१४५॥
उत्पादकब्रह्मदात्रोर्गरीयान्ब्रह्मदः पिता ।
ब्रह्मजन्म हि विप्रस्य प्रेत्य चेह च शाश्वतम् ॥१४६॥
कामान्माता पिता चैनं यदुत्पादयतो मिथः ।

141. Cited by *Viś* 1.34; *Apa* 65; *Dev* 1.91; *Mādh* 1.304 — a) TMd³ एके; GMy च — b) wKt³ वेदाङ्गामपि; Be¹ Ho Jo² Lo⁴ TMd³ sOx¹ Ox³ sPu⁶ Tj¹ [*Jolly* M³ R] *Dev Mādh* वेदाङ्गान्यथ वा; *Me* and *Apa* comment अपिपुनःशब्दौ पादपूरणार्थौ supporting the edition — d) GMd¹ वृत्त्यर्थं स उपाध्याय उच्यते; NNg *om* स

142. Omitted in Bo. Cited by *Viś* 1.34, 3.222; *Vij* 3.259; *Dev* 1.88; *Mādh* 1.302, 2.259 — a) *BhP* 4.76 कार्याणि— b) *BhP* 4.76 यः करोति नृपोत्तम; Ox³ °विधे — c) *BhP* 4.76 अध्यापयति चान्येन; Ho GMd⁵ संभावति; Ho वानेन; wKt¹ चार्थेन; Lo¹ चान्तेन; TMd³ NNg Ox² चान्येन; *Me* [pāṭha] चैवैनं

143. Omitted in Tj². Cited by *Viś* 1.34; *Apa* 66, 919; *Dev* 5.66 — a) Lo¹ *Dev* °यज्ञमग्नि° — b) Pu¹⁰ °यज्ञानाग्नि°; NKt⁴ °ग्निहोमादि°; NKt⁴ °कान्मषान् — c) BBe² व्रतो; *Viś* वृतो यज्ञे

144. Omitted in Ox³. Cited by *Lakṣ* 1.224; *Dev* 1.93 — a) Ho Lo² यश्चावृ°; Pu¹⁰ यत्रावृ°; Wa आवृणत्य°; TMd³ MTr⁴ [*Jolly* M³⁻⁴] आतृणोत्य°; *Me* [pāṭha] *Nā* [citing śruti] आतृणत्त्य°; GMd⁵ Tr¹ MTr⁶ आतृणत्य°; GMd¹ आतृणत्ति तथ्येन; GMy आदिशति तथ्येन; NNg °वितथ; *Lakṣ* °वितथा — b) Lo¹ पठनश्रवणे उभे; La¹ ब्राह्मणा; GMy ब्राह्मण; TMd³ ब्रह्मण; Pu⁵ Pu⁷ Pu⁹ ब्रह्मण्या; Bo ब्रह्मणान्; *Lakṣ* कर्मणा — c) TMd⁴ सा माता; BKt⁵ समता; TMd³ स च माता पिता — d) Lo¹ द्रुहेत्; MTr⁴ द्रूहेत्; Ox² दुष्येत्; oMd² *BhP* 4.78 कथंचन

145.* Damaged unreadable in MTr⁶. Cited by *Dev* 1.92; *Mādh* 1.304; pādas a-b cited by *Vij* 3.259; pādas c-d by *Viś* 1.34; *Dev* 3.688 — a) La² *BhP* 4.79 उपाध्याया दशा°; BBe² Hy Jm Jo¹ Jo² Kt² wKt³ La² Lo³ Lo⁴ Lo⁵ NNg Ox³ Pu² Pu⁵ Pu⁹ Pu¹⁰ Tj¹ Tj² Wa *Dev Mādh Mandlik Jolly Jha KSS Dave* उपाध्यायान्दशा°; wKt¹ उपाध्यायां दशा°; Bo sOx¹ sPu⁶ Tj¹ Wa °चार्या — b) Ho GMd¹ TMd⁴ MTr⁴ आचार्यात्तु शतं — c) La¹ [*but mc sh to* सहस्रं तु] *BhP* 4.79 सहस्रेण पितुर्माता; Pu⁵ Pu⁷ Pu⁹ च; BKt⁵ पिता माता; Jm Jo¹ Kt² wKt³ oMd² NNg Pu² Pu⁸ MTr⁶ Wa *Dev* 1.92 *Mandlik Jolly Jha KSS Dave* पितृन्माता

146. Cited by *Apa* 67; *Dev* 1.93; *Mādh* 1.305; pādas a-b cited by *Vij* 3.259; *Jmv* 11.4.3 — a) Pu⁵ Pu⁷ Pu⁹ उत्पादकः; TMd⁴ उत्पादकं; La¹ °ब्रह्ममात्रो°; Lo³ °ब्रह्मदाशो°; GMd¹ GMy NPu¹ Tr¹ [*Jolly* N Nd] °ब्रह्मपित्र्यो°; MTr⁴ °ब्रह्मपित्रो°; MTr⁶ °ब्रह्मचित्रो°; NKt⁴ °ब्रह्मदारोगरी° — c) Lo⁴ [*but mc*] Ox³ ब्रह्मकृन्म; Ho Lo³ Tj¹ च — d) Bo चेह हि

संभूतिं तस्य तां विद्याद् यद्योनावभिजायते ॥१४७॥
आचार्यस्त्वस्य यां जातिं विधिवद्वेदपारगः ।
उत्पादयति सावित्र्या सा सत्या साजरामरा ॥१४८॥
अल्पं वा बहु वा यस्य श्रुतस्योपकरोति यः ।
तमपीह गुरुं विद्याच्छ्रुतोपक्रियया तया ॥१४९॥
ब्राह्मस्य जन्मनः कर्ता स्वधर्मस्य च शासिता ।
बालोऽपि विप्रो वृद्धस्य पिता भवति धर्मतः ॥१५०॥
अध्यापयामास पितॄन् शिशुराङ्गिरसः कविः ।
पुत्रका इति होवाच ज्ञानेन परिगृह्य तान् ॥१५१॥
ते तमर्थमपृच्छन्त देवानागतमन्यवः ।
देवाश्चैतान्समेत्योचुर्न्याय्यं वः शिशुरुक्तवान् ॥१५२॥
अज्ञो भवति वै बालः पिता भवति मन्त्रदः ।
अज्ञं हि बालमित्याहुः पितेत्येव च मन्त्रदम् ॥१५३॥

147. a) Lo^{5} चैवं; NKt^{4} चैव — b) Lo^{4} यद्युत्पातयतो; TMd^{3} TMd^{4} GMy Tj^{1} °दयते; Lo^{1} °दयतोर्मिथः — c) wKt^{1} Tj^{1} संभूति; TMd^{4} संभूते; Tr^{2} सस्य; Hy तं — d) Lo^{1} यद्योनोनाभिजायते; GMy Ox^{3} *om* यद्; NPu^{1} तद्यो°; Lo^{2} °नामभिजायते; GMd^{1} °नावजायते; sOx^{1} sPu^{6} °नावपिजायते; [*Jolly* R] °नावधिजायते

148. Cited by *Lakṣ* 1.209-10 — a) BKt^{5} Lo^{5} TMd^{4} GMd^{5} Pu^{10} Tj^{1} Tr^{2} *BhP* 4.82 *Lakṣ* आचारस्तस्य; sOx^{1} sPu^{6} [*but cor*] यो जातिं; Lo^{1} Pu^{10} *BhP* 4.82 तां जातिं — c) La^{1} Lo^{2} sOx^{1} sPu^{6} सावित्र्यां; MTr^{6} सावित्र्यः — d) La^{1} सत्या सा साजरा°

149. Cited by *Apa* 65; *Hem* 3/1.353; *Dev* 1.89, 5.43; *Mādh* 1.303, 2.259; pādas a-c cited by *Vij* 3.259 — a) *Vij* स्वल्पं; Tj^{1} अन्यं वा; Lo^{4} बहु यस्य — b) NKt^{4} श्रुतं तस्योप° — c) wKt^{1} विन्द्या° — d) Lo^{3} °तापक्रियया; Jo^{2} wKt^{1} La^{1} NNg *BhP* 4.91[vl] *Hem* तथा; Lo^{1} यथा; Tr^{2} तदा; Pu^{10} मया

150. Pādas a-b omitted in GMy Pu^{10} — a) Jo^{1} ब्रह्मस्य; BBe^{2} wKt^{3} La^{2} ब्राह्मणस्य — b) GMd^{5} MTr^{4} MTr^{6} स्वकर्मस्य; Lo^{2} Tr^{2} *om* च; BBe^{2} शाशिता; Be^{3} शंशिता; BKt^{5} साशिता; NKt^{4} शात्रिया; MTr^{6} स्वाधीत — c) Lo^{4} *ma* विप्रो; Ox^{3} वृद्धो विप्रस्य; Lo^{3} वृद्धस्यात् — c-d) Tj^{1} बालोपि प्राविवृद्धस्यात्पिता भवति — d) TMd^{3} GMd^{5} GMy Tr^{1} MTr^{4} MTr^{6} भवति मन्त्रदः

151. Cited by *Dev* 1.93 — a-b) Bo La^{2} TMd^{3} NNg *Jolly* पितॄञ्छिशुरा° — c) MTr^{6} पुत्रकाम इहोवाच; Be^{1} La^{1} पुत्रिका; Jo^{1} पुत्राका; TMd^{3} चोवाच; Pu^{8} कोवाच — d) sOx^{1} sPu^{6} ज्ञानेन परितोषितान् [*but both cor*]

152. Cited by *Dev* 1.93 — a) Bo °पृछन्तो; Pu^{5} Pu^{7} Pu^{9} °पृच्छन्तं; Lo^{2} °पृच्छन्ता — b) Tj^{1} देवानांगत°; Lo^{2} देवानामागत°; BKt^{5} NNg °मन्यतः; TMd^{4} °मन्यना — c) Jo^{2} Lo^{3} Tj^{1} देवास्त्वेता°; NKt^{4} MTr^{4} MTr^{6} देवाश्चैना°; Pu^{10} देवान्चैता°; NPu^{1} °तान्सामान्याचु°; Be^{1} °तान्समेतेचु°; Pu^{5} Pu^{7} Pu^{9} °तान्समत्योचु° — d) MTr^{3} °चुर्न्यायं; *BhP* 4.94 °चुरन्याय्यं शिपु° [vl °चुर्न सत्यं शिपु°; °चुर्न्याय्यं वै शिपु°]; Ox^{3} °चुर्न्यायतः शिपु°; Lo^{3} Tj^{1} वो; Be^{3} कः

153. *Lakṣ* 1.210; *Dev* 1.93 — a) Bo अज्ञा; MTr^{3} यज्ञो — b) wKt^{1} Tr^{2} मन्त्रतः; GMd^{1} धर्मतः — c) GMd^{1} अज्ञं बालकमित्याहुः; NNg तु; *Dev* बाल इत्याहुः; *Lakṣ* पुत्रमित्यूचुः — d) *Lakṣ* पितरं मन्त्रदायिनम्; NPu^{1} पितरं त्वेव मन्त्रदं; La^{2} Lo^{2} Tj^{2} पितेत्येवं; Ox^{3} पित्रेत्येव; GMy पितेत्येति; Be^{3} Bo

न हायनैर्न पलितैर्न वित्तेन न बन्धुभिः ।
ऋषयश्चक्रिरे धर्मं योऽनूचानः स नो महान् ॥१५४॥
विप्राणां ज्ञानतो ज्यैष्ठ्यं क्षत्रियाणां तु वीर्यतः ।
वैश्यानां धान्यधनतः शूद्राणामेव जन्मतः ॥१५५॥
न तेन स्थविरो भवति येनास्य पलितं शिरः ।
यो वै युवाप्यधीयानस्तं देवाः स्थविरं विदुः ॥१५६॥
यथा काष्ठमयो हस्ती यथा चर्ममयो मृगः ।
यश्च विप्रोऽनधीयानस्त्रयस्ते नाम बिभ्रति ॥१५७॥
यथा षण्ढोऽफलः स्त्रीषु यथा गौर्गवि चाफला ।
यथा चाज्ञेऽफलं दानं तथा विप्रोऽनृचोऽफलः ॥१५८॥

BCa Hy Jm Jo^{1} Kt^{2} La^{1} La^{2} Lo^{1} Lo^{2} Lo^{4} Lo^{5} oMd^{2} NNg Ox^{2} Ox^{3} Pu^{2} Pu^{8} Tr^{1} Tr^{2} *BhP* 4.95 *Mandlik Jha KSS Dave* तु; TMd^{4} नु; BBe^{2} wKt^{1} oOr हि; BBe^{2} Lo^{4} NNg मन्त्रदः

154. Pādas c-d omitted in Jo^{1}. Cited by *Dev* 1.93 — b) Be^{1} Be^{3} Bo Ho La^{2} Lo^{1} Lo^{2} TMd^{3} TMd^{4} GMd^{5} GMy sOx^{1} Ox^{2} sPu^{6} Tr^{1} MTr^{4} MTr^{6} *Dev* वित्तैर्न च बन्धुभिः; *BhP* मित्रेण; Ox^{3} वित्तेन बन्धु° — c) Wa °क्रिरे पूर्मं; TMd^{3} °क्रिरे मन्त्रं — d) wKt^{3} *om* यो; Bo °नूवाचः; wKt^{3} महात्

155. a) MTr^{3} जानतो; MTr^{4} ज्यैष्ठ्यः; La^{1} Lo^{3} Tr^{2} ज्येष्ठ्यं; Hy La^{2} oOr Tj^{1} MTr^{6} ज्यैष्ठं; Be^{1} Bo Kt^{2} ज्येष्ठं; Wa ज्येष्ठां; Ho TMd^{3} Pu^{5} Pu^{7} Pu^{9} [*Jolly* G Nd] श्रैष्ठ्यं — b) wKt^{3} क्षत्रियां; BCa Jo^{2} BKt^{5} oMd^{2} Tj^{1} [*Jolly* R] च; NNg च तु वीर्यतः — c) Be^{3} धनधान्येन; La^{1} धनतः श्रेष्ठः; GMy धान्यतः श्रेष्ठं — d) TMd^{3} GMd^{5} GMy [*Jolly* Nd] शूद्राणां चैव; La^{1} GMd^{1} Tr^{1} शूद्राणांश्चैव; Ho Lo^{4} NNg Ox^{3} Pu^{5} Pu^{7} Pu^{9} Pu^{10} [*Jolly* MG] *Jolly* शूद्राणां त्वेव; NKt^{4} sOx^{1} sPu^{6} जन्मनः

BhP 4.98–9 gives two verses in place of 155: ब्राह्मणक्षत्रियविशां शूद्राणां च विशां पते । ज्येष्ठं वदन्ति राजेन्द्र संदेहं शृणु वै यथा ।। ज्ञानतो वीर्यतो राजन्धनतो जन्मतस्तथा । शीलतस्तु प्रधाना ये ते प्रधाना मता मम ।।

156.* Omitted in Pu^{9} — a) Jm Jo^{1} Jo^{2} Kt^{2} BKt^{5} Lo^{3} Lo^{4} Lo^{5} oMd^{2} NNg oOr Ox^{3} NPu^{1} Pu^{2} Pu^{3} Pu^{4} Pu^{5} Pu^{7} Pu^{10} Tj^{1} Tr^{2} MTr^{3} Wa [*Jolly* M G R Ku] *Mandlik Jolly Jha KSS Dave* वृद्धो भवति; Be^{1} sOx^{1} sPu^{6} स्थविरो ज्ञेयो; oOr भवते; GMd^{1} Ox^{2} भूयाद्येनास्य — b) TMd^{4} येनाद्यं; NKt^{4} शिरं — c) TMd^{3} Ox^{2} यो वा; Ho युवा त्वधीया°; TMd^{4} °प्यनूदानस्तं — d) NKt^{4} °नस्तं विद्या; La^{2} विभुः

157. a) Ox^{2} चर्ममयो; Bo °मयं — b) Ox^{2} नृणमयो; wKt^{1} काष्ठमयो — c) BCa La^{1} TMd^{3} oOr ब्राह्मणश्चानधीयान°; wKt^{1} Lo^{1} ब्राह्मणस्त्वनधीयान°; Be^{3} यो वै विप्रो; Bo GMd^{5} GMy यथा विप्रो; Lo^{5} Ox^{3} Tr^{1} MTr^{4} MTr^{6} तथा विप्रो — d) GMy °यानस्ततस्ते; BCa La^{1} Lo^{4} [*but cor*] TMd^{3} oOr Ox^{3} Pu^{5} Pu^{7} Pu^{8} Pu^{9} Wa [*Jolly* G M$^{3-4}$] *Jolly BDh* 1.1.10, *VaDh* 3.11, *MBh* 12.37.39 नामधारकाः; GMd^{1} TMd^{4} GMy Pu^{10} [*Jolly* M$^{1-2-8-9}$] नामधारिणः

Additional verse in wKt^{1}:

ग्रामस्थानं यथा शून्यं यथा कूपश्च निर्जलः ।
ब्राह्मणश्चानधीयानस्त्रयस्ते नामधारकाः ।।

158. In MTr^{6} 158c to 159b damaged and unreadable. Cited by *Dev* 1.129; *Mādh* 1.307 — a) *BhP* 4.102 यथा योषाफला स्त्रीषु; Ho षठो; Be^{3} Jo^{2} Pu^{5} Pu^{7} Pu^{9} Pu^{10} Wa खण्ढो; Kt^{2} °वरः स्त्रीषु — b) wKt^{1} गौर्गव्य; NNg चाफलाः; Ho Ox^{2} वाफला; wKt^{1} sOx^{1} sPu^{6} निष्फला; NKt^{4} Tr^{2} निःफला — c) La^{1} यथाज्ञे चाफलं; Ox^{3} चाज्ञैःफलं; Tr^{1} दत्तं — d) Tr^{2} यथा; GMy विप्रोवचो; BKt^{5} विप्रोफलोनृचः; MTr^{3} °नृतो; GMd^{1} TMd^{4} °फलं

अहिंसयैव भूतानां कार्यं श्रेयोऽनुशासनम् ।
वाक्चैव मधुरा श्लक्ष्णा प्रयोज्या धर्ममिच्छता ॥१५९॥
यस्य वाङ्मनसी शुद्धे सम्यग्गुप्ते च सर्वदा ।
स वै सर्वमवाप्नोति वेदान्तोपगतं फलम् ॥१६०॥
नारुंतुदः स्यादार्तोऽपि न परद्रोहकर्मधीः ।
ययास्योद्विजते वाचा नालोक्यां तामुदीरयेत् ॥१६१॥
संमानाद् ब्राह्मणो नित्यमुद्विजेत विषादिव ।
अमृतस्येव चाकाङ्क्षेदवमानस्य सर्वदा ॥१६२॥
सुखं ह्यवमतः शेते सुखं च प्रतिबुध्यते ।
सुखं चरति लोकेऽस्मिन्नवमन्ता विनश्यति ॥१६३॥
अनेन क्रमयोगेन संस्कृतात्मा द्विजः शनैः ।
गुरौ वसन्संचिनुयाद् ब्रह्माधिगमिकं तपः ॥१६४॥
तपोविशेषैर्विविधैर्व्रतैश्च विधिचोदितैः ।
वेदः कृत्स्नोऽधिगन्तव्यः सरहस्यो द्विजन्मना ॥१६५॥

159. a) La^{1} अहिंसैव — b) La^{2} श्रेयानु° ; TMd^{3} °नुपालनं — c) TMd^{3} मधुना; GMd^{1} TMd^{4} MTr^{6} GMy मधुरा सत्या; Wa श्लक्षा — d) La^{2} TMd^{3} TMd^{4} GMy NNg Ox^{2} Tr^{1} *BhP* 4.124 धर्ममीप्सिता; Be^{3} Bo Pu^{8} धर्ममीप्सता; GMd^{1} °मिच्छया; *Nd* gloss अभीप्सता supports ईप्सता; all other commentators support इच्छता

160. a) Ho यस्यास्यरसने शुद्धे; Be^{1} Bo Jo^{2} La^{2} Lo^{1} Lo^{2} GMd^{1} TMd^{3} GMy Ox^{2} NPu^{1} Pu^{8} Tr^{1} वाङ्मनसे — b) *BhP* 4.125 सत्यगुप्ते च भारत; Jo^{2} Tj^{1} यस्य गुप्ते; wKt^{1} सर्वसा — c) oOr स चैव सर्वमाप्नोति; Lo^{1} सैव; GMy धर्ममवा° — d) TMd^{4} वेदान्तेपिगतं; Lo^{4} Ox^{3} वेदाङ्गोपगतं; BBe^{2} wKt^{3} वेदान्ताधिगतं

161. b) BBe^{2} पार° ; Ho °कर्मधी — c) Be^{1} ययास्येद्वि° ; BKt^{5} ययन्योद्वि° ; Tr^{2} यथाश्चोद्वि° ; NPu^{1} यथयास्योद्वि° ; Jo^{2} Lo^{3} TMd^{3} TMd^{4} GMd^{5} GMy Tj^{1} Tr^{1} MTr^{4} MTr^{6} यया चोद्विजते; GMy °द्विजतो लोके; GMd^{1} °द्विजते लोको; *BhP* 4.126 वाचं — d) *BhP* 4.126 वाचा न च तां समुदीरयेत् [vl लोको न तां वाचमुदीरयेत्]; Kt^{2} नालोक्य; Lo^{1} नालोक्या; GMy नालौक्या; NKt^{4} नालोके; TMd^{3} तमुदी°

162. a) GMd^{1} समानाद्; Ox^{3} तन्मानाद्; *BhP* 4.129 अर्हणाद्; GMd^{1} ब्रह्मणो; Ox^{3} ब्राह्मणा; Lo^{4} NNg Ox^{3} Pu^{10} विद्वानुद्वि° — b) wKt^{3} विषादिच; oOr विषादिति — c) Bo BKt^{5} GMd^{1} oMd^{2} Tr^{1} अमृतस्यैव; Lo^{4} Lo^{5} वाकाङ्क्षे° ; Lo^{3} चाकाङ्क्ष्ये° — d) TMd^{3} °क्षेन्मनसस्य च सर्वदा; Tr^{1} °क्षेदसंमानस्य; Ho *BhP* 4.129 °पमानस्य; wKt^{1} सर्वतः; TMd^{4} धर्मतः

163. GMy places 163 after 160b — a) GMd^{5} सुखे; sOx^{1} ह्यवमतेः; sPu^{6} ह्यवमतः [corrected with two dots over last त which sOx^{1} read as ते]; Lo^{2} क्वामृतः; wKt^{3} Lo^{5} श्येते — b) Lo^{2} Lo^{4} Lo^{5} मुखं; wKt^{3} °बुध्येते; Pu^{9} °बुध्यत्; BKt^{5} TMd^{3} °पद्यते — d) NNg °वमन्तो

164. a) *BhP* 4.131 अनेन विधिना राजन् — b) Tr^{2} संस्कृतात्म; TMd^{3} संस्कृतायो; TMd^{4} सद्कृतात्मा — c) Ox^{3} गुरो; oOr गुरु; TMd^{3} गुणा; BKt^{5} गुरोर्वस° ; Lo^{3} Tj^{1} वसन्विचिनुयाद्; TMd^{3} °चिनुते — d) wKt^{1} ब्रह्मादि° ; GMd^{5} MTr^{4} MTr^{6} वेदाधि° ; Tr^{1} °गमितं; TMd^{4} °गतिकं; *BhP* 4.131 °गमिदं; TMd^{3} sOx^{1} sPu^{6} °गमनं

165. Pāda-d omitted in Ox^{3}. Cited by *Apa* 76; *Dev* 1.132; pādas c-d cited by *Śaṃ* on *TU*

वेदमेव सदाभ्यस्येत् तपस्तप्स्यन्द्विजोत्तमः ।
वेदाभ्यासो हि विप्रस्य तपः परमिहोच्यते ॥१६६॥
आ हैव स नखाग्रेभ्यः परमं तप्यते तपः ।
यः स्रग्व्यपि द्विजोऽधीते स्वाध्यायं शक्तितोऽन्वहम् ॥१६७॥
योऽनधीत्य द्विजो वेदमन्यत्र कुरुते श्रमम् ।
स जीवन्नेव शूद्रत्वमाशु गच्छति सान्वयः ॥१६८॥
मातुरग्रेऽधिजननं द्वितीयं मौञ्जिबन्धने ।
तृतीयं यज्ञदीक्षायां द्विजस्य श्रुतिचोदनात् ॥१६९॥
तत्र यद् ब्रह्मजन्मास्य मौञ्जीबन्धनचिह्नितम् ।
तत्रास्य माता सावित्री पिता त्वाचार्य उच्यते ॥१७०॥
वेदप्रदानादाचार्यं पितरं परिचक्षते ।
न ह्यस्मिन्युज्यते कर्म किंचिदा मौञ्जिबन्धनात् ॥१७१॥

1.12 — a) Lo^{4} ततोवि° — b) Be^{3} °धैर्व्रतैस्तु विधिदेशितैः; sOx^{1} sPu^{6} *BhP* 4.132 विविधोदितैः — c) GMd^{5} कृत्स्नाधिग°; NKt^{4} क्रियाधिग°

166. Cited by *Dev* 1.128; *Mādh* 1.307 — a) BCa OMd^{2} *BhP* 4.133 वेदमेवाभ्यसेन्नित्यं; *Mādh* समभ्यसेत्; La^{2} °भ्यसेत्; Ho Lo^{1} Tj^{1} °भ्यासेत्; Tr^{1} °भ्यस्य — b) Lo^{3} Tj^{1} तपस्तप्स्यन्सदा द्विजः; [*Jolly* R] तपस्तप्स्यन्यदि द्विजः; BKt^{5} Lo^{1} sOx^{1} sPu^{6} Tr^{1} *BhP* 4.133 तपस्तप्यन्द्वि°; WKt^{3} तपस्तप्सान्द्वि°; NKt^{4} Tj^{1} तपस्तप्स्य द्वि°; *Mādh* तपस्तप्त्वा द्वि°; TMd^{3} तपस्तर्प्य द्वि° — c) TMd^{4} *Dev* वेदाभ्यासोपि

167. Pu^{10} places 169 before 167. Cited by *Viś* 1.48; *Apa* 69; *Har*-A 1.12.2; *Dev* 1.128 — a) TMd^{4} स हैव स; GMy हेव; sOx^{1} sPu^{6} Tr^{1} *Apa* ह वै — c) La^{1} यः सूक्ष्मोपि हि योधीते; GMy यो यद्यप्यपि द्विजो; Tr^{2} स्रग्वापि; BKt^{5} स्रग्वपि; WKt^{3} स्रग्व्योपि; *BhP* 4.134 सुप्तोपि; Wa स्रग्वी द्विजो — d) BKt^{5} स्वाध्यायोक्तितोन्वहं; WKt^{3} शक्तितोत्वहं

Additional verse in GMd^{5}:

वेदस्वीकरणं पूर्वं विचारोऽभ्यसनं जपः ।
तद्दानं चैव शिष्येभ्यो वेदाभ्यासो हि पञ्चधा ॥

168. Cited by *Dev* 1.129; *Mādh* 1.140 — a) Lo^{3} TMd^{3} GMd^{5} Tr^{1} MTr^{6} *Dev Mādh* वेदानन्यत्र; Tj^{1} वेदोनन्यत्र; Pu^{5} Pu^{7} Pu^{9} वैदमन्यत्र; GMy विद्वानन्यत्र; BKt^{5} नित्यमन्यत्र

169. Cited by *Lakṣ* 1.101 — a) Tr^{1} मातरग्रेथ जननं; GMy तु जननं; *BhP* 4.137 च जननं — b) *BhP* द्वितीयो; Jo^{2} WKt^{3} Lo^{1} GMd^{1} TMd^{3} TMd^{4} GMy sOx^{1} *BhP* °बन्धनं; GMd^{5} *Lakṣ* °बन्धनात्; Be^{1} °बन्धं — c) BKt^{5} *om* तृतीयं; TMd^{4} GMy तृतीया; *BhP* 4.137 तृतीयो; TMd^{4} Ox^{3} °दीक्षाय; TMd^{3} °दीक्षेयं — d) BBe^{2} sOx^{1} sPu^{6} श्रुतिचोदितं [sPu^{6} *cor to* विधि°]; La^{1} GMd^{1} TMd^{3} TMd^{4} GMd^{5} GMy MTr^{4} MTr^{6} विधिचोदितं; OOr विधिचोदितः; Tr^{1} विधिनोच्यते; NKt^{4} *BhP* विविधोदितं; *BhP* [vl] विधिरीरितः; Be^{3} विधिदेशितं; Ho Jo^{2} Tr^{2} विधिनोदनात्; Bo श्रुतिचोचनात्

170. Cited by *Dev* 1.69; *Har*-A 1.1.16; pādas c-d cited by *Viś* 3.222 — a) Lo^{5} Tj^{1} Tr^{2} यत्र; TMd^{4} ब्रह्मजन्मस्या; TMd^{3} ब्रह्मजननं — b) Hy मौञ्जि°; OMd^{2} °चिह्नितः — c) *Har*-A अत्रास्य; WKt^{1} तदास्य; BBe^{2} तत्रास्या; TMd^{3} तत्र माता तु — d) Tj^{1} त्वार्य

In La^{1} folios containing 2.170c to 2.195c are missing.

171. Pādas a-b cited by *Dev* 1.69; pādas c-d by *Dev* 1.66; *Mādh* 1.790 — a) Tr^{2} वेदप्रमाणादा°; Pu^{5} Pu^{7} Pu^{9} °प्रदानाचार्यं; *BhP* 4.139 °प्रदानात्त्वाचार्यं — b) *BhP* 4.139 पितरं मनुरब्रवीत्; BCa

नाभिव्याहारयेद् ब्रह्म स्वधानिनयनादृते ।
शूद्रेण हि समस्तावद् यावद्वेदे न जायते ॥१७२॥
कृतोपनयनस्यास्य व्रतादेशनमिष्यते ।
ब्रह्मणो ग्रहणं चैव क्रमेण विधिपूर्वकम् ॥१७३॥
यद्यस्य विहितं चर्म यत्सूत्रं या च मेखला ।
यो दण्डो यच्च वसनं तत्तदस्य व्रतेष्वपि ॥१७४॥
सेवेतेमांस्तु नियमान् ब्रह्मचारी गुरौ वसन् ।
संनियम्येन्द्रियग्रामं तपोवृद्ध्यर्थमात्मनः ॥१७५॥
नित्यं स्नात्वा शुचिः कुर्याद् देवर्षिपितृतर्पणम् ।
देवताभ्यर्चनं चैव समिदाधानमेव च ॥१७६॥
वर्जयेन्मधु मांसं च गन्धमाल्यं रसान् स्त्रियः ।
शुक्तानि चैव सर्वाणि प्राणिनां चैव हिंसनम् ॥१७७॥

NNg °चक्ष्यते — c) NKt^{4} TMd^{4} NNg sOx^{1} sPu^{6} [*Jolly* Nd] ह्यस्य युज्यते; GMd^{1} TMd^{3} GMd^{5} GMy oOr Tr^{2} *BhP* 4.140 ह्यस्य विद्यते; Be^{1} Tr^{1} MTr^{4} MTr^{6} *Rc* ह्यस्मिन्विद्यते — d) Pu^{10} केचिदा; NPu^{1} °बन्धनं

172. Pādas a-b cited by *Dev* 1.66; *Mādh* 1.790 — a) Hy नातिव्याहारयद्; wKt^{1} NKt^{4} Lo^{1} GMy NNg [*but cor fh*] °व्याहरयेद्; TMd^{3} °हारयेत्तस्य — b) Be^{1} स्वदा°; sOx^{1} sPu^{6} °नियसनादृते; Tr^{2} °निर्वयनादृते — c) BKt^{5} शूद्रेण नियमस्तावद्; *BhP* 4.141 तु समं तावद् — d) Lo^{1} TMd^{3} Wa *BhP* 4.141 यावद्वेदो; NPu^{1} Pu^{5} Pu^{7} Pu^{9} [*Jolly* G] युज्यते; Wa गृह्यते

173. c) Kt^{2} ब्राह्मणो; Be^{1} ब्रह्मणे; Lo^{3} ग्राहणं — d) Pu^{5} Pu^{7} Pu^{9} [*Jolly* G] तथैव विधि°; sOx^{1} sPu^{6} °पूर्ववत्

174. Cited by *Apa* 58; *Lakṣ* 1.236 — a-d) *BhP* 4.142 यत्सूत्रं चापि यच्चर्म या या चास्य च मेखला । वसनं चापि यो दण्डस्तद्वै तस्य व्रतेष्वपि ॥ — a) TMd^{4} यद्यस्य विधिवद्धर्मं; GMd^{1} यद्यत्सुविहितं; Bo NKt^{4} Lo^{3} Lo^{4} Lo^{5} GMy Ox^{3} Tj^{1} Tr^{1} कर्म; Be^{3} Tr^{2} धर्म — b) Tr^{2} यत्पुत्रं; MTr^{6} यच्च; BKt^{5} मेषला — c) *Lakṣ* सवनं — d) Ho Lo^{4} Ox^{3} [*Jolly* M] *Jolly* तत्तत्तस्य; NNg तच्च तस्य; Be^{1} [*mc to*] sOx^{1} sPu^{6} तत्तत्सर्व; Pu^{5} Pu^{7} Pu^{9} [*Jolly* G] तत्तस्यैव; Lo^{1} तत्तु तस्याद्व्रते°

175. Omitted in Pu^{5}. Cited by *Apa* 62; *Dev* 1.122 — a) oOr सेविते°; BCa Tr^{2} °तेमांश्च; BKt^{5} °तेमान्स्वनियमान् — b) Wa गुरो — d) GMy तपोऋद्ध्यर्थ°

176. Omitted in Pu^{5}. Cited by *Apa* 62; *Dev* 1.117; pādas a-b cited by *Viś* 1.22 — a) *Apa* [*vl*] स्नातः; Tr^{2} शुचिं — b) Pu^{8} °तर्पणां — c) Be^{3} °भ्यर्चनश्चैव; *Dev* °भ्यर्चनं कुर्यात् — d) BBe^{2} समिधादानमेव; Ho समिधनयनमेव; NKt^{4} समिदात्मनमेव; Ox^{3} सामदाधानमेव; *Dev* सन्ध्योपासनमेव

177. Omitted in Pu^{5}. Cited by *Lakṣ* 1.229; *Dev* 1.125; *Mādh* 1.456; pādas a-b cited by *Apa* 62 — a) TMd^{3} GMd^{5} Tr^{1} MTr^{4} MTr^{6} *Apa* वर्जयेन्मधुमांसानि; Hy Lo^{4} वर्जयन्मधु; Be^{3} तु [*but cor fh*] — b) *BhP* 4.146 गन्धमाल्यरथान्स्त्रियः; sOx^{1} sPu^{6} गन्धमाल्ये; Be^{1} BBe^{2} Bo Hy Jm Jo^{1} Kt^{2} wKt^{3} Lo^{2} Ox^{2} *Mandlik Jha KSS Dave* गन्धं माल्यं; Be^{3} Lo^{4} Lo^{5} GMd^{1} oMd^{2} TMd^{3} GMd^{5} TMd^{4} GMd^{5} Ox^{3} NPu^{1} Tr^{1} MTr^{4} MTr^{6} [*Jolly* M$^{3-4}$ Nd] *Dev Apa* गन्धमाल्यरसान् [GMd^{5} °रसां]; Pu^{10} [*Jolly* M^{9} R] रसं; GMy स्त्रियं — c) MTr^{4} शुक्तानि वै सर्वाणि; Tj^{1} सुक्तानि; Lo^{1} शुष्कानि; Be^{3} *BhP* 4.146 *Mandlik* शुक्लानि; GMd^{1} उक्तानि; TMd^{3} कुक्तानि; Hy Jm Jo^{1} Kt^{2} Pu^{2} MTr^{3} *Mandlik Jha KSS Dave* यानि सर्वाणि — d) TMd^{3} च विहिंसनं

अभ्यङ्गमञ्जनं चाक्ष्णोरुपानच्छत्रधारणम् ।
कामं क्रोधं च लोभं च नर्तनं गीतवादनम् ॥१७८॥
द्यूतं च जनवादं च परिवादं तथानृतम् ।
स्त्रीणां च प्रेक्षणालम्भमुपघातं परस्य च ॥१७९॥
एकः शयीत सर्वत्र न रेतः स्कन्दयेत् क्वचित् ।
कामाद्धि स्कन्दयन् रेतो हिनस्ति व्रतमात्मनः ॥१८०॥
स्वप्ने सिक्त्वा ब्रह्मचारी द्विजः शुक्रमकामतः ।
स्नात्वार्कमर्चयित्वा त्रिः पुनर्मामित्यृचं जपेत् ॥१८१॥
उदकुम्भं सुमनसो गोशकृन्मृत्तिकां कुशान् ।
आहरेद्यावदर्थानि भैक्षं चाहरहश्चरेत् ॥१८२॥
वेदयज्ञैरहीनानां प्रशस्तानां स्वकर्मसु ।
ब्रह्मचार्याहरेद्भैक्षं गृहेभ्यः प्रयतोऽन्वहम् ॥१८३॥

178. Cited by *Apa* 62; *Dev* 1.125; *Mādh* 1.456 — a) BKt^{5} °मञ्जनां — b) Pu^{8} °पानत्क्षत्र° — c) wKt^{3} BKt^{5} TMd^{3} GMd^{5} Ox^{3} Tj^{1} काम; wKt^{1} क्रोधश्च लोभश्च; TMd^{3} लोहं — c-d) *BhP* 4.147 संकल्पं कामजं क्रोधं लोभं गीतं च वादनम् — d) Lo^{1} गतिवादनं; Be^{1} Lo^{2} *Apa* [vl] °वादिनं; NKt^{4} oOr *Apa* °वादितं; BCa Lo^{4} Lo^{5} Ox^{3} [*Jolly* M$^{3-4}$] °वादने

Folios containing verses 178c to 194 missing in Pu^{9}

179. Pādas a-b and c-d transposed in GMd^{5}. Cited by *Apa* 62; *Dev* 1.125; *Mādh* 1.456 — a) Lo^{1} जनसंवादं परि° — a-b) *BhP* 4.148 नर्तनं च तथा द्यूतं जनवादं तथानृतम्; then adds परिवादं चापि विभो दूरतः परिवर्जयेत्; BKt^{5} oMd^{2} sOx^{1} sPu^{6} परिवादं च जनवादं तथा° — b) Be^{1} La^{2} परवादं; Tj^{1} तथावृतं; Jo^{1} तथामृतं — c) MTr^{4} MTr^{6} स्त्रीणां प्रेक्षणमालम्भमु°; La^{2} Tr^{2} *om* च; Bo प्रेक्षणालापमुप°; *Me Jha Dave* प्रेक्षणालम्भावुप°; Tr^{2} प्रेक्षणामालंभ उप°; wKt^{3} Pu^{10} °रम्भमुप° — d) *BhP* 4.149 °लम्भमुपरोधं; *Apa* [vl] स्मरस्य च; Jo^{2} परस्परं; wKt^{3} तु

180. Pādas a-b omitted in Be^{1} and pādas c-d in Lo^{4}. Cited by *Apa* 62; *Dev* 1.127; pādas a-b cited by *Mādh* 1.456 — a) sOx^{1} sPu^{6} [*cor to*] शयेत — b) Hy *om* स्कन्दये° . . . [180c] कामाद्धि [haplo]; GMd^{1} *om* क्वचित् — c) GMy कामनिष्कन्द्य विस्रोतो; MTr^{3} कामार्थी; BBe^{2} wKt^{6} GMd^{1} TMd^{3} sOx^{1} sPu^{6} MTr^{4} MTr^{6} *Dev* स्कन्दयेद्रेतो; wKt^{1} स्कन्दयद्रेतो — d) GMd^{1} TMd^{4} व्रतमेव हिनस्ति तत्; Be^{3} NKt^{4} Tr^{2} *BhP* 4.150 *Apa* व्रतमेव तु; TMd^{3} GMd^{5} GMy oOr MTr^{4} MTr^{6} व्रतमेव तत्

181. Cited by *Vij* 3.280; *Apa* 1141; *Dev* 1.127; *Mādh* 2.394 — a) *BhP* 4151 सुप्तः क्षरन्ब्रह्मचारी; TMd^{3} स्वप्नि; TMd^{4} हित्वा — b) MTr^{3} MTr^{4} MTr^{6} *Dev* शुक्लम° — c) Tj^{1} स्नात्वात्रम°; Tr^{1} स्नात्वातम°; BBe^{2} *BhP* 4.151 *Mādh* °यित्वा तु; *Dev* °यित्वापि; Be^{1} त्रि — d) Lo^{3} Tr^{1} [*Jolly* R] पुनर्ममैत्यृचं; TMd^{4} Tj^{1} पुनर्मामेत्यृचं; Pu^{10} पुनर्मेतिचं; [*Jolly* M$^{1-2-8-9}$] पुनर्मैति त्र्यृचं; sOx^{1} sPu^{6} पठेत्

182. Pādas c-d omitted in Be^{1}. Cited by *Apa* 59 — a) Jo^{1} उदकं सुम°; Be^{3} °कुम्भः; GMy TMd^{3} TMd^{4} Tr^{1} MTr^{4} MTr^{6} [*Jolly* Nd] °कुम्भान् — b) BBe^{2} wKt^{6} गोसकृ°; Lo^{4} Lo^{5} GMd^{5} Ox^{3} Tr^{1} [*Jolly* M$^{3-4}$] °न्मृत्तिकाः; Jo^{1} Kt^{2} Lo^{2} GMd^{4} *Mandlik Jha KSS Dave* °न्मृत्तिकाकु°; BKt^{5} wKt^{6} MTr^{4} MTr^{6} °न्मृत्तिकान्कु°; Wa °न्मृत्तिकाङ्कु°; Pu^{5} Pu^{7} °न्मृत्कुशांस्तथा; [*Jolly* G] °न्मृत्तिकास्तथा; Tj^{2} °कां कुर्वान्; TMd^{3} °कां तृदान् — c) oOr आचरे°; sOx^{1} sPu^{6} Tr^{2} °वदर्थं तु — d) *BhP* 4.152 भैक्षं चापि हि नित्यशः; Be^{1} Be^{3} Ho BKt^{5} La^{2} Lo^{4} sOx^{1} Ox^{2} Pu^{2} sPu^{6} Pu^{7} Pu^{10} Tr^{2} भैक्ष्यं; Bo भैक्षां; NKt^{4} भैक्षश्चाह°

183. Cited by *Viś* 1.29; *Apa* 59; *Dev* 1.109; *Mādh* 1.453 — a) NKt^{4} °यज्ञे च हीनानां — a-b)

गुरोः कुले न भिक्षेत न ज्ञातिकुलबन्धुषु ।
अलाभे त्वन्यगेहानां पूर्वं पूर्वं विवर्जयेत् ॥१८४॥
सर्वं वापि चरेद्ग्रामं पूर्वोक्तानामसंभवे ।
नियम्य प्रयतो वाचमभिशस्तांस्तु वर्जयेत् ॥१८५॥
दूरादाहृत्य समिधः संनिदध्याद्विहायसि ।
सायं प्रातश्च जुहुयात् ताभिरग्निमतन्द्रितः ॥१८६॥
अकृत्वा भैक्षचरणमसमिध्य च पावकम् ।
अनातुरः सप्तरात्रमवकीर्णिव्रतं चरेत् ॥१८७॥
भैक्षेण वर्तयेन्नित्यं नैकान्नादी भवेद्व्रती ।
भैक्षेण व्रतिनो वृत्तिरुपवाससमा स्मृता ॥१८८॥

BhP 4.153 longer version: स्वकर्मसु रता ये वै तथा वेदेषु ये रताः । यज्ञेषु चापि राजेन्द्र ये च श्रद्धा-समाश्रिताः ॥ — b) *Rc* प्रसक्तानां; NKt^{4} GMy सुकर्मसु; MTr^{4} स्वकर्मणा — c) Be^{1} Bo Ox^{3} ब्रह्मचर्योहरे°; Tr^{2} °चारी हरे°; NKt^{4} GMy °चर्याहरे°; Be^{1} Be^{3} Ho BKt^{5} La^{2} sOx^{1} Ox^{2} Pu^{2} sPu^{6} Pu^{7} Pu^{10} Tj^{2} Tr^{2} *BhP* 4.154 [vl] °हरेद्भैक्ष्यं; Bo °हरेद्भैक्षां — d) wKt^{3} प्रयतोत्वहं

184. Cited by *Apa* 59; pādas a-b cited by *Dev* 1.109— a) Ox^{3} गुरो; Pu^{5} Pu^{7} Wa कुलं; Tr^{2} भिक्षेत् — b) *BhP* 4.154 स्वज्ञाति° — c) GMd^{5} अभावे; Lo^{1} पूर्वगेहानां; *BhP* 4.155 त्वन्यगोत्राणां — d) Hy *om one* पूर्वं; Pu^{10} पूर्वं सर्वं

185. Omitted in sOx^{1} Pu^{6}; *ma* in Lo^{2}. Cited by *Dev* 1.110; pādas a-b cited by *Viś* 1.29; *Apa* 59 — a) NNg सर्वा; wKt^{1} सर्वद्वानिचरे°; La^{3} सर्वे वा विचरे°; BCa Lo^{5} Pu^{5} *BhP* 4.155 चापि; Be^{1} [*mc to*] BBe^{2} Ho NKt^{4} NNg *Viś Dev* वा विचरे°; Lo^{4} Lo^{5} TMd^{3} Ox^{3} चरेद्भैक्षं; Ho चरेत्कामं — b) NNg °संभवान् — c) wKt^{3} नियम; MTr^{6} नियत्य — c-d) *BhP* 4.155 वाचं नियम्य प्रयतस्त्वग्निं शत्रं च वर्जयेत् — d) Bo °मतिशस्तांस्तु°; BBe^{2} wKt^{3} Lo^{4} Ox^{3} *Dev* °शस्तांश्च; oOr Tr^{2} °शस्तं च; Tr^{1} °शस्तान्विवर्जयेत्

186. Pāda-d omitted in NKt^{4} wKt^{6}. Cited by *Lakṣ* 1.183; *Dev* 1.86; *Mādh* 1.451 — a) Tr^{1} *BhP* 4.157 अरादाहृत्य; Ox^{3} दूरादाहत्य; Ho समिधं — b) NKt^{4} स निदध्या°; *BhP* 4.157 *Lakṣ* °ध्याद्गृहो-परि — c) BCa Tr^{2} *BhP* प्रातस्तु — d) Ho जुहुयात्साग्निमग्निमत°; Bo °तन्द्रियः

187. wKt^{6} omits verses 187–207. Cited by *Vij* 3.281; *Dev* 1.111; *Mādh* 2.438 — a) BKt^{5} Ox^{2} Pu^{7} भैक्ष्य° — a-b) *BhP* 4.158 भैक्ष्याचरणमकृत्वा न तमग्निं समिध्य वै [vl भैक्षा°] — b) wKt^{1} °समेध्य; NKt^{4} °समिद्धा; Be^{3} °समृध्य; Lo^{1} °समिध्यैव च; GMy °समिध्य हुताशनं; Pu^{8} पात्रकं — d) NNg °मविकीर्णि°; Ho Lo^{2} GMy °कीर्णव्रतं; Tj^{1} °कीर्णी व्रतं; La^{2} °कीर्णिकृतं

188. Pādas c-d omitted in Be^{3}. Cited by *Dev* 1.111; *Mādh* 1.455 — a) *BhP* 4.163 तस्माद्भैक्षेण वै नित्यं; Be^{1} Ox^{2} Pu^{7} भैक्ष्येण; Bo भक्ष्येण; GMd^{1} *Jha Dave* वर्तयन्नित्यं; Tj^{1} वर्तयो नित्यं — b) wKt^{1} °न्नित्यमेकान्नादी; sOx^{1} sPu^{6} Tj^{1} °न्नादो; GMd^{5} GMy Tr^{1} °न्नाशी — c) BKt^{5} Ox^{2} भैक्ष्येण; Lo^{4} Lo^{5} Pu^{10} व्रतिना; Tj^{1} वृत्तिमुप° — d) TMd^{3} °वाससमाश्रिता; Ho स्मृतः; oOr स्मृताः

Additional verses in Ho wKt^{1} Lo^{2} [*ma*] Ox^{2} NPu^{1} Tr^{2}; also in 7 of *Mandlik's* mss [he thinks these may be original]; *Rc* comments on both; first verse found in TMd^{4} and second verse in Be^{3}:

न भैक्षं परपाकः स्यान्न च भैक्षं प्रतिग्रहः ।
सोमपानसमं भैक्षं तस्माद्भैक्षेण वर्तयेत् ॥१॥
भैक्षस्यागमशुद्धस्य प्रोक्षितस्य हुतस्य च ।

व्रतवद्देवदैवत्ये पित्र्ये कर्मण्यथर्षिवत् ।
काममभ्यर्थितोऽश्नीयाद् व्रतमस्य न लुप्यते ॥१८९॥
ब्राह्मणस्यैव कर्मैतदुपदिष्टं मनीषिभिः ।
राजन्यवैश्ययोस्त्वेव नैतत्कर्म प्रचक्षते ॥१९०॥
चोदितो गुरुणा नित्यमप्रचोदित एव वा ।
कुर्यादध्ययने योगमाचार्यस्य हितेषु च ॥१९१॥
शरीरं चैव वाचं च बुद्धीन्द्रियमनांसि च ।
नियम्य प्राञ्जलिस्तिष्ठेद् वीक्षमाणो गुरोर्मुखम् ॥१९२॥
नित्यमुद्धृतपाणिः स्यात् साध्वाचारः सुसंवृतः।
आस्यतामिति चोक्तः सन्नासीताभिमुखो गुरोः ॥१९३॥

यांस्तस्य ग्रसते ग्रासांस्ते तस्य क्रतुभिः समाः ॥२॥

1. a) Ho Lo² ɴPu¹ Tr² भैक्ष्यं; Tr² परिपाकः; Lo² ᴛMd⁴ °पाकस्तु न — b) Lo² स्यान्नैव; ɴPu¹ स्यान्न भैक्ष्यं च; Ho Lo² Tr² भैक्ष्यं — c) Ho Lo² ɴPu¹ Tr² भैक्ष्यं — d) ᴛMd⁴ तस्माद्भैक्षं प्रशस्यते; Ho Lo² ɴPu¹ Tr² °द्भैक्ष्येण

2. a) Tr² भैक्षस्यान्नशुद्धस्य; Ho Lo² ɴPu¹ Tr² भैक्ष्यस्या°; Be³ भैक्षेणाग° — c) Tr² यां यस्य; Lo² यांश्चास्य; wKt¹ यावतो ग्रसते; Be³ Ox² Tr² ग्रसति

189. Cited by *Viś* 1.31; *Hem* 3/1.424; *Mādh* 1.455; pādas c-d cited by *Dev* 1.116 — a) *BhP* 4.160 दैवत्ये व्रतवद्राजन्; ᴛMd⁴ Wa °दैवदेवत्ये; ɴKt⁴ °दैवदेवत्येवं; Lo² Lo⁴ ɢMd¹ ᴛMd³ Ox³ Pu⁷ Pu¹⁰ *Hem Viś* ° देवत्ये; Bo ° दैवत्यो; Lo¹ ° दैत्येपि — b) Be³ ʙKt⁵ oOr पित्रे; oMd² ɢMy पितृ; *Viś* कर्मण्युपस्थिते — c) Lo¹ °भ्यर्थिता; Tr¹ °भ्युत्थितो; Pu⁵ Pu⁷ °भ्यर्चितो — d) *Hem* व्रतं तस्य; Tj¹ लिप्यते

190.* Pādas c-d cited by *Lakṣ* 1.122 — a-d) *BhP* 4.161: ब्राह्मणस्य महाबाहो कर्म यत्समुदाहृतम् । राजन्यवैश्ययोर्नैतत्पण्डितैः कुरुनन्दन — a) ᴛMd³ ब्राह्मणस्य तु; ᴛMd⁴ कर्मैधमुप° — b) ɢMy °पतिष्ठं; ɴNg °परिष्टं; Ho °दिष्टं स्वयंभुवा — c) Be¹ ʙBe² Bo ʙCa Jm Jo¹ wKt¹ Kt² La² Lo¹ Lo⁴ Lo⁵ oMd² ɢMd⁵ sOx¹ Ox³ ɴPu¹ sPu⁶ Pu⁸ Tj² Tr¹ *Mandlik Jha KSS Dave* °योस्त्वेवं; Be³ Ho wKt³ ᴛMd⁴ ᴍTr⁴ Wa *Lakṣ* °योश्चैव; Tr² °योश्चैवं; ʙKt⁵ °योरेव — c-d) ɴKt⁴ °योस्त्वेतन्नैवं तत्कर्म — d) ʙKt⁵ न तत्कर्म; ʙCa प्रचक्ष्यते; ɴNg प्रवक्ष्यते; ᴍTr⁶ प्रवर्तते; Hy Jm Jo¹ Jo³ Kt² ɢMd¹ oMd² oOr Tj² Tr² ᴍTr³ *Lakṣ Rc Mandlik Jha KSS Dave* विधीयते

191.* Pāda-c torn in ᴍTr⁶. Cited by *Apa* 64; *Lakṣ* 1.215 — a) Be¹ Jo² ʙKt⁵ Lo³ Lo⁴ Lo⁵ Ox³ Pu⁵ Pu⁷ Tj¹ Tr² Wa [*Jolly* M⁴ Me G R] *Me Jolly* नोदितो; Pu² Pu⁴ वादितो; Be³ वेदितो; Kt² प्रचोदितो गुणा; Ho गुरुणादित्यम° — a-b) *BhP* 4.162 चोदितोऽचोदितो वापि गुरुणा नित्यमेव हि; ʙKt⁵ गुरुणा चैव न प्रचोदित — b) Jo² Lo³ Lo⁴ Lo⁵ Ox³ Pu⁵ Pu⁷ Pu¹⁰ Tj¹ Tr² Wa [*Jolly* M¹⁻²⁻⁴⁻⁷⁻⁸⁻⁹ Me G R] *Jolly* °प्रणोदित; Pu² Pu⁴ °प्रवोदित; Be³ °प्रदेशित; Be³ Ox² ɴPu¹ एव च — c) Bo °ध्ययनो; ᴛMd⁴ °ध्ययन; Tj¹ °ध्ययनाद्वेगः आचा°; Lo³ °ध्ययनाद्धेगः आचा°; Hy Jm Jo¹ Kt² Lo² Lo³ oMd² Tr² ᴍTr³ *Nā* [pāṭha] *Mandlik KSS* यत्नमाचा°; ᴛMd³ नित्यमाचा° — d) Lo² °चार्याय; Pu⁸ °चार्यहितेपु; ɢMd¹ हिते तथा; Pu¹⁰ वा

192. Cited by *Apa* 55; *Lakṣ* 1.215 — a) Ho सशरीरं च वाचं च; ᴛMd³ वाचश्च; oOr वालं च — a-b) *BhP* 4.163 बुद्धीन्द्रियाणि मनसा शरीरं वाचमेव हि — c) Hy नियमा; wKt³ नियम; Wa प्राञ्जलीस्ति°; *Apa* प्राङ्मुखस्ति° — d) Be³ Tj¹ Tr¹ [*Jolly* R] ईक्षमाणो; ʙKt⁵ Pu⁵ *Apa* [vl] ईक्ष्यमाणो; Lo⁵ ᴛMd⁴ ईक्षमाणा; Be¹ ईक्षप्राणो

193.* *ma* in Be³ [last part of pāda-d torn]. Cited by *Apa* 56; *Lakṣ* 1.215 — a) ʙKt⁵

हीनान्नवस्त्रवेषः स्यात् सर्वदा गुरुसंनिधौ ।
उत्तिष्ठेत् प्रथमं चास्य चरमं चैव संविशेत् ॥१९४॥
प्रतिश्रवणसंभाषे शयानो न समाचरेत् ।
नासीनो न च भुञ्जानो न तिष्ठन्न पराङ्मुखः ॥१९५॥
आसीनस्य स्थितः कुर्यादभिगच्छंस्तु तिष्ठतः ।
प्रत्युद्गम्य त्वाव्रजतः पश्चाद्धावंस्तु धावतः ॥१९६॥
पराङ्मुखस्याभिमुखो दूरस्थस्यैत्य चान्तिकम् ।
प्रणम्य तु शयानस्य निदेशे चैव तिष्ठतः ॥१९७॥
नीचं शय्यासनं चास्य नित्यं स्याद्गुरुसंनिधौ ।
गुरोश्च चक्षुर्विषये न यथेष्टासनो भवेत् ॥१९८॥

°मुद्धृतःपाणिः; Hy °मुद्धृत्यपाणिः; Ho *Lakṣ* °मुद्यतपाणिः; NPu^1 °मुद्यतदण्डः — b) Pu^5 Pu^7 सर्वदा गुरु-संनिधौ [cf. 194b]; Ox^3 °चारं; Ho Hy Jo^1 Lo^3 NKt^4 sOx^1 NNg NPu^1 sPu^6 Tj^1 Tj^2 MTr^3 Wa [*Jolly* Go N] *Apa Nā Rc Mandlik KSS* सुसंयतः; *BhP* 4.164 तु संयतः; Tr^2 सुसंपुतः; Bo La^2 Lo^2 Ox^2 सुयन्त्रितः; GMd^1 TMd^3 TMd^4 GMd^5 Tr^1 MTr^4 MTr^6 समाहितः — d) NPu^1 °सीनाभि°; TMd^3 °सीनोभि°; Pu^{10} °मुखोः; Be^1 BBe^2 Bo BCa Hy Jm Jo^1 wKt^1 Kt^2 wKt^3 La^2 Lo^1 oMd^2 GMd^5 NNg oOr Ox^2 NPu^1 Pu^8 Tj^2 Tr^2 MTr^3 [*Jolly* Ku N Nd]*BhP* [vl] *Apa Mandlik Jha KSS Dave* °मुखं; Pu^5 Pu^7 *BhP* गुरौ; Pu^2 गुरु

194. Cited by *Apa* 56 — a) BKt^5 हीनान्त°; *Apa* [vl] हीनानुवस्त्र°; GMd^5 °वस्त्रवेष्टः; Lo^1 GMd^1 °वेषवस्त्रः — a-b) *BhP* 4.165 वस्त्रवेषैस्तथान्नैस्तु हीनः स्याद्गुरुसंनिधौ — b) Lo^4 Lo^5 Ox^3 नित्यं स्याद्गुरुसंनिधौ [cf. 2.198b] — c) Jo^1 आतिष्ठेत्; *Apa* [vl] प्रथमे — d) *BhP* 4.165 जघन्यं चापि; Tr^2 नैव; Ho संवसेत्; after pāda-b MTr^4 adds 198 a-b.

195. Cited by *Apa* 56; *Lakṣ* 1.215 — a) Tr^2 प्रतिश्रयण°; TMd^4 प्रक्रमण° — b) TMd^3 GMy शयनो; TMd^4 शयिनो; *BhP* 4.166 तल्पस्थो न; Pu^5 Pu^7 Pu^9 न शयानः समा° — c) *BhP* 4.166 न चासीनो न भुञ्जानो; MTr^6 आसीनो न

196. Cited by *Apa* 56; *Lakṣ* 1.215 — a) Lo^4 Ox^3 *BhP* 4.167 आसीनश्च — b) TMd^4 °दनु-गच्छंस्तु; Be^1 Be^3 BCa La^1 GMd^1 NNg sOx^1 Pu^5 sPu^6 Pu^7 Pu^9 [*Jolly* G] *Apa* [vl] °गच्छंश्च; *Apa* °गच्छेच्च; NKt^4 Lo^4 Lo^5 oOr Ox^2 Ox^3 Tr^1 MTr^4 पृष्ठतः; TMd^3 GMd^5 Pu^5 Pu^7 Pu^9 MTr^6 *Apa* गच्छतः — c) *BhP* 4.167 प्रत्युद्गन्ता तु व्रजतः; GMy °द्गम्यस्त्वव्रजतः; Ho °द्गम्यानुव्रज्यश्च; Tr^2 °द्गम्यानुव्रजतः; Be^1 °द्गम्यातव्रजतः; sOx^1 sPu^6 °द्गमित्वाव्रजतः; Tr^1 त्वद्व्रजतः; Ox^3 चाव्रजतः; Lo^4 चव्रजतः; TMd^3 त्वपानीत — d) Be^3 Pu^5 Pu^7 Pu^9 [*Jolly* G] *BhP* 4.167 °द्धावंश्च; Pu^{10} धावयत्

197. Cited by *Apa* 56; *Lakṣ* 1.215 — a) MTr^4 प्राङ्मुख°; Tr^1 °खेस्याभि°; BKt^5 °खोस्याभिमुखे; Lo^2 °भिमुखं; TMd^3 °भिमुख — b) Jo^2 BKt^5 GMy *Lakṣ* °स्थस्येत्य; TMd^4 °स्थस्येत; sOx^1 sPu^6 °स्थस्यैव; TMd^3 वान्तिकं — c) *BhP* 4.168 नमस्कृत्य शया°; TMd^3 MTr^4 MTr^6 च — d) BKt^5 निर्दिशेश्चेव सर्वतः; *BhP* 4.168 निदेशे तिष्ठेत्सर्वदा; La^1 निदिशे; Lo^4 TMd^4 NNg Ox^3 *Apa* [vl] निर्देशे; oOr निदिशो; GMd^1 GMd^5 Tr^1 *Nd Apa* [vl] विदेशे; MTr^4 MTr^6 निवेशे; Tr^1 वै तु; TMd^4 पृच्छतः

198.* Pādas c-d placed after 194b in MTr^6. Cited by *Apa* 56; *Lakṣ* 1.215; *Dev* 1.120 — a) Bo TMd^4 Pu^5 Pu^7 Tr^1 *Dev* नीच; Ho नावं; Tr^2 राज्यऽसनं; BKt^5 Pu^{10} Wa [*Jolly* M$^{1-2-7-8-9}$] चैव — b) Be^3 Bo Ho Hy Jm Jo^1 Jo^2 Kt^2 La^2 Lo^2 Ox^2 Pu^8 MTr^3 *BhP* 4.169 *Nd Mandlik KSS* सर्वदा गुरु°; Lo^3 Tj^1 Tj^2 सर्वथा गुरु° — c) Hy Jm Jo^1 Kt^2 oMd^2 Tj^2 MTr^3 *Mandlik Jolly Jha KSS Dave* गुरोस्तु; NKt^4 BKt^5 गुरोश्चक्षु°; oOr °र्विनये — d) NPu^1 यथेष्टात्मनो; Tr^2 यथेष्टाशमनो

नोदाहरेदस्य नाम परोक्षमपि केवलम् ।
न चैवास्यानुकुर्वीत गतिभाषितचेष्टितम् ॥१९९॥
गुरोर्यत्र परीवादो निन्दा वापि प्रवर्तते ।
कर्णौ तत्र पिधातव्यौ गन्तव्यं वा ततोऽन्यतः ॥२००॥
परिवादात् खरो भवति श्वा वै भवति निन्दकः ।
परिभोक्ता कृमिर्भवति कीटो भवति मत्सरी ॥२०१॥
दूरस्थो नार्चयेदेनं न क्रुद्धो नान्तिके स्त्रियाः ।
यानासनस्थश्चैवैनमवरुह्याभिवादयेत् ॥२०२॥
प्रतिवातेऽनुवाते च नासीत गुरुणा सह ।
असंश्रवे चैव गुरोर्न किंचिदपि कीर्तयेत् ॥२०३॥

199. Omitted in Ho; pādas c-d placed after 202d in TMd^3. Cited by *Apa* 56; *Lakṣ* 1.215; *Har*-A 1.8.15; *Dev* 1.121 — a) TMd^3 न व्याहरेदस्य; *Har*-A °हरेत्तस्य — a-b) *BhP* 4.170 नामोच्चारणमेवास्य परोक्षमपि सुव्रत — c) Bo न चैवास्य न कुर्वीत; *BhP* 4.170 चैनमनुकुर्वीत — d) GMd^1 गतिचेष्टितभाषितं; OMd^2 प्रतिभाषि°; Lo^5 गमिभाषि°; Bo Lo^1 OOr Pu^8 *Lakṣ* °भाषण°; TMd^4 °भाषेत°; SOx^1 SPu^6 °वेष्टितं; *BhP* °चेष्टितैः

200. Omitted in Tr^2. Cited by *Apa* 56; *Lakṣ* 1.215 — a-b) *BhP* 4171 परीवादस्तथा निन्दा गुरोर्यत्र प्रवर्तते — b) BBe^2 निन्दावादोपि वर्तते; WKt^1 निन्दा यत्र; *Lakṣ* वाभिप्रवर्तते; TMd^3 TMd^4 GMd^5 GMy Tr^1 MTr^4 MTr^6 प्रयुज्यते — c) TMd^3 सनौ; Wa तत्र कर्णौ; *Apa* [vl] तत्रापिधा°; TMd^3 पिधातव्यं; OOr विधातव्यो

201.* Pāda-a omitted in Ox^3 and pādas c-d in GMd^5. Cited by *Lakṣ* 1.216; *Dev* 1.120 — a) Pu^2 भवेत्खरः परीवादात्; Be^3 आचार्यस्य परीवादात्; GMd^5 परिवादी खरः स्यात्तु; Tr^2 परीवादी खरो नूनं; Lo^3 Tj^1 परीवादो सूकरः स्यात् [Lo^3 °वादे]; BBe^2 Be^3 BCa Ho Hy Jm Jo^1 WKt^1 WKt^3 BKt^5 La^1 Lo^4 Lo^5 GMd^1 OMd^2 NNg SOx^1 Ox^2 SPu^6 Pu^8 Tj^2 *Mandlik Jha KSS Dave* परीवादात्; TMd^3 TMd^4 GMd^5 GMy परिवादी; Tr^2 MTr^4 MTr^6 *Nd* परीवादी; Pu^{10} Tj^2 परो; Pu^8 वरो; Be^1 NKt^4 GMd^1 SOx^1 SPu^6 खरो हि स्यात्; NPu^1 Wa खरः स स्यात् [Wa त स्यात्]; Pu^5 Pu^7 Pu^9 [*Jolly* G] खरः स्यात्तु; Ox^2 Tr^2 खरो नूनं; Lo^3 [*Jolly* R] सूकरः स्यात्; TMd^3 खरो न भवति; GMy रासभस्स्यात्; NNg भवेत् — a-b) *BhP* 4.172 परीवादाद्रसभः स्यात्सारमेयस्तु निन्दकः — b) Bo निन्दकं; WKt^3 निन्दितः — c) Wa परीभा कृमिकश्चैव; GMy °भोक्त; GMy कृमीभावं; Be^1 कृमि भवति; Bo कृमी भवति; Lo^3 Lo^4 Lo^5 Ox^3 Tj^1 [*Jolly* R] कृमिश्चैव; NKt^4 SOx^1 Ox^2 SPu^6 कृमिस्तु स्यात्; NNg कृमिस्तस्य

202. Folio containing 202–207 missing in Pu^9; pādas c-d omitted in Ox^3. Cited by *Apa* 56; *Lakṣ* 1.216 — a) Pu^{10} दूरास्थानानर्चयेदेनं; TMd^4 दूरस्थे; GMy नर्चये°; NPu^1 °येदेव — b) Tj^1 नाक्रुद्धो; *Me* [pāṭha] क्रुद्धं; *Go* gloss नाप्येनं प्रत्युपजातक्रोधं supports क्रुद्धं; Tr^1 नान्तरे; MTr^4 नातिके; TMd^3 नातिशे; Bo Ho NKt^4 La^2 Lo^3 Lo^4 Lo^5 GMd^5 NPu^1 स्त्रियः; GMy स्त्रियां; Be^3 Pu^5 Pu^7 स्त्रिया; GMd^1 स्मृतः — c) *BhP* 4.173 यानासनगतो राजन्; TMd^3 °सनसंश्चैनम°; BCa Jo^1 NKt^4 GMy Pu^{10} Wa °श्चैवेनम° — d) Be^3 °मवरुध्याभि°; La^1 °मवतीर्याभि°

203. Pādas a-b omitted in Ox^3. Cited by *Lakṣ* 1.216 — a) *Jha Dave* प्रतिवातानुवाते च; *BhP* 4.1774 प्रतिकूले समाने तु; GMy प्रतिवायेनुवादे च; Ox^3 °नुवातेथ; Be^1 Bo Ho GMd^5 Tj^1 Tr^1 वा — b) TMd^3 न च रासीत; Wa चानासीत; Jo^1 मासीत — c) *BhP* अशृण्वति गुरौ राजन्; NNg असंश्रेवे; Lo^4 Lo^5 असंश्रये; GMd^5 गुरौ न; BBe^2 गुरुर्न — d) NNg कीर्तये

गोऽश्वोष्ट्रयानप्रासादप्रस्तरेषु कटेषु च ।
आसीत गुरुणा सार्धं शिलाफलकनौषु च ॥२०४॥
गुरोर्गुरौ संनिहिते गुरुवद्वृत्तिमाचरेत् ।
न चानिसृष्टो गुरुणा स्वान् गुरूनभिवादयेत् ॥२०५॥
विद्यागुरुष्वेतदेव नित्या वृत्तिः स्वयोनिषु ।
प्रतिषेधत्सु चाधर्माद्धितं चोपदिशत्स्वपि ॥२०६॥
श्रेयःसु गुरुवद्वृत्तिं नित्यमेव समाचरेत् ।
गुरुपुत्रेषु चार्येषु गुरोश्चैव स्वबन्धुषु ॥२०७॥
बालः समानजन्मा वा शिष्यो वा यज्ञकर्मणि ।
अध्यापयन् गुरुसुतो गुरुवन्मानमर्हति ॥२०८॥
उत्सादनं च गात्राणां स्नापनोच्छिष्टभोजने ।
न कुर्याद्गुरुपुत्रस्य पादयोश्चावनेजनम् ॥२०९॥
गुरुवत्प्रतिपूज्याः स्युः सवर्णा गुरुयोषितः ।

204. Cited by *Lakṣ* 1.223; *Dev* 1.120 — a) Ho गोश्वेष्ट्र° ; GMd^{1} NPu^{1} गोष्ट्रोश्वयान° ; GMd^{5} गो-प्ट्राश्वयान° ; Pu^{5} Pu^{7} °याने; Tr^{2} °प्राशा° — a-b) GMy गोष्ट्रोश्वयानासनेषु स्वस्तरेषु — b) Ox^{2} °प्रस्तरे कट-केषु च; MTr^{4} °प्रास्तरेषु; Be^{1} °प्रस्तारेषु; *Nā Ku Nd Rc Mr Mandlik KSS* °स्रस्तरेषु; NKt^{4} Tj^{1} *Rn Lakṣ* °संस्तरेषु; TMd^{3} °स्वस्तरेषु; GMd^{1} GMd^{5} Tr^{1} °स्वास्तरेषु; Ho करेषु च — c) GMd^{5} Tr^{1} MTr^{6} नासीत; Tr^{2} आसीत्; Lo^{3} सार्थं — d) TMd^{4} °कनेषु च

205. Pādas c-d omitted in MTr^{6}. Cited by *Apa* 54; *Mādh* 1.306 — a) Lo^{5} गुरोर्गुरोः; Ox^{3} *om* सं; Lo^{4} *ma* सं; *Apa* [vl] संनिवृत्ते; GMy संनिपते— b) NKt^{4} °चरत् — c) Ho वानिसृष्टो; La^{1} चानुत्सृष्टो; Be^{1} Be^{3} Bo La^{2} Lo^{4} चातिसृष्टो; GMd^{1} Tj^{1} चासृष्टो

206.* *ma* in Lo^{1} — a) Be^{3} Bo Ho BKt^{5} Lo^{1} Lo^{2} Lo^{4} Lo^{5} NNg Ox^{2} Ox^{3} NPu^{1} Pu^{2} Pu^{5} Pu^{7} Pu^{10} Tj^{2} Tr^{1} Wa [*Jolly* M] *Me Go Jha Dave* °ष्वेवमेव; BCa WKt^{3} La^{1} TMd^{3} °ष्वेतदेवं; GMy °ष्वेकमेव; *Rc* °ष्वेषैव; OOr °ष्वेव तदेवं — b) Ho GMy NNg नित्य; TMd^{3} TMd^{4} नित्यं; Ho वृत्तिं; GMy Tj^{1} Tr^{1} वृत्ति — c) Bo °षेधस्तु; La^{1} °धत्स्वेवाधर्मा° ; Ho Pu^{8} वाधर्मा° ; Jm Jo^{1} WKt^{1} Kt^{2} OMd^{2} Pu^{10} Tj^{2} *Mandlik KSS* चाधर्मान्हितं; TMd^{3} GMy चाधर्मं हितं; Ox^{3} चाधर्माहितं; Pu^{2} वाधर्माहितं

207. Omitted in Pu^{5}. Cited by *Lakṣ* 1.225 — a) Be^{1} Ox^{3} श्रेयस्तु; Lo^{2} श्रेयत्सु; WKt^{1} श्रेयःस्वगुरु° ; Pu^{7} °वद्वृत्तं; NNg °वद्विर्त्तिं — c) Jo^{2} Lo^{3} Lo^{4} Lo^{5} Ox^{3} Tj^{1} Tr^{2} [*Jolly* M R] *Me Rc Jha Dave* °पुत्रे तथाचार्ये; La^{1} NPu^{1} Pu^{2} Pu^{7} Wa *Me* [pāṭhā] *Jolly* °पुत्रेष्वथार्येषु; NNg Pu^{10} °पुत्रेष्वथाचार्ये; Ho Hy °पुत्रेष्वाचार्येषु; MTr^{4} चान्येषु— d) Lo^{4} Ox^{3} Lo^{5} Pu^{7} गुरुवद्वृत्तिमाचरेत् [cf. 205b]; Jo^{1} गुरुश्चैव; La^{1} सुबन्धुषु; Bo सबन्धुषु

208. Ho places pādas c-d after 207b — a) Tr^{1} बाल; Bo सबालजन्मा; Lo^{4} °जन्म; TMd^{4} °जन्माता — b) Be^{3} GMd^{5} शिष्टो वा; *BhP* 4.177 विशिष्टो यज्ञ° ; Bo जन्मकर्मणि — c) Ho गुरुसुतं; Tj^{1} गुरुसुतौ

209. Cited by *Mādh* 1.457–8 — a) Lo^{5} GMd^{1} Ox^{3} Pu^{10} Tr^{1} उच्छादनं; La^{1} उद्वर्तनं [*but mc*]; *BhP* 4.178 °दनमथाङ्गानां; Be^{1} Be^{3} NKt^{4} Tr^{1} Tr^{2} तु; Tr^{1} शास्त्राणां — b) *BhP* 4.178 स्थापनोच्छि° ; BCa SOx^{1} Ox^{3} SPu^{6} [*but cor*] °भोजनं — c-d) *BhP* 4.178 पादयोर्नेजनं राजन्गुरुपुत्रेपु वर्जयेत् — d) La^{1} °योश्चावनेजलं; WKt^{6} °योश्चालनेजलं

असवर्णास्तु संपूज्याः प्रत्युत्थानाभिवादनैः ॥२१०॥
अभ्यञ्जनं स्नापनं च गात्रोत्सादनमेव च ।
गुरुपत्न्या न कार्याणि केशानां च प्रसाधनम् ॥२११॥
गुरुपत्नी तु युवतिर्नाभिवाद्येह पादयोः ।
पूर्णविंशतिवर्षेण गुणदोषौ विजानता ॥२१२॥
स्वभाव एष नारीणां नराणामिह दूषणम् ।
अतोऽर्थान्न प्रमाद्यन्ति प्रमदासु विपश्चितः ॥२१३॥
अविद्वांसमलं लोके विद्वांसमपि वा पुनः ।
प्रमदा ह्युत्पथं नेतुं कामक्रोधवशानुगम् ॥२१४॥
मात्रा स्वस्रा दुहित्रा वा न विविक्तासनो भवेत् ।
बलवानिन्द्रियग्रामो विद्वांसमपि कर्षति ॥२१५॥
कामं तु गुरुपत्नीनां युवतीनां युवा भुवि ।
विधिवद्वन्दनं कुर्यादसावहमिति ब्रुवन् ॥२१६॥
विप्रोष्य पादग्रहणमन्वहं चाभिवादनम् ।

210. Cited by *Dev* 1.103; *Mādh* 1.300; pādas a-b cited by *Dev* 1.123 — a) Lo^3 GMd^5 Tj^1 Tr^1 MTr^4 MTr^6 Wa *BhP* 4.179 °पूज्यास्तु; TMd^3 °पूज्यास्तास् — b) TMd^4 *Dev* 1.103 सवर्ण — c) TMd^4 प्रसवर्णास्तु; BKt^5 NPu^1 °वर्णाश्च; GMy संपूज्या; TMd^4 संपूज्य — d) TMd^4 °भिभाषणैः; NPu^1 °भिवादनं; BBe^2 °भिवन्दनैः

211. Cited by *Mādh* 1.301, 457–8 — a) Lo^1 अभ्यञ्जन; GMd^1 च स्नापनं च; *BhP* 4.180 [vl] च स्नापनं गात्रो° — b) Bo गोत्रो°; La^1 [*but mc*] TMd^3 TMd^4 गात्रोद्वर्तन°; Tj^2 गात्रोत्सर्जन°; GMd^5 Pu^5 Pu^7 Tr^1 गात्रोच्छादन°; GMy MTr^6 गात्रोच्छेदन°; Pu^5 तु — c) Lo^5 TMd^4 °पत्न्यां; Lo^3 Pu^5 Tj^1 °पत्न्या-वकार्याणि — d) TMd^3 GMd^5 गात्राणां च; BKt^5 *om* च; La^2 Lo^3 OMd^2 SOx^1 [*cor to*] SPu^6 Tr^2 प्रसादनं

212. Cited by *Dev* 1.104; *Mādh* 1.301 — a) *BhP* 4.181 गरुपत्नीं तु युवतीं; SOx^1 SPu^6 Pu^{10} [*Jolly* M$^{1-2-8-9}$] च; Lo^2 ह; Lo^5 युवतीर्नाभि°; Lo^1 TMd^4 Tr^1 Tr^2 युवती नाभि°; TMd^3 युवतिं नाभि° — b) TMd^4 °भिमध्येत; SOx^1 SPu^6 °वन्द्येह; WKt^1 GMy *BhP* 4.181 [vl] °वाद्येत; *BhP* 4.181 [vl] °वादेत; GMd^1 °वाद्ययाह; WKt^6 पाद्ययोः — c) Lo^1 Tr^1 पूर्णाविंश° — d) La^2 Tj^2 गुरुदोषौ; Bo Lo^4 Ox^3 Wa °दोषो; WKt^3 °दोषैर्विजा°; MTr^3 विजानतः; Be^1 विधानता

213. a) Be^3 BCa [*but cor*] Jo^2 Lo^3 GMd^1 TMd^4 GMd^5 GMy Tj^1 MTr^4 MTr^6 Wa एव; all commentators support एष — b) SOx^1 SPu^6 °णामेव — c) BKt^5 La^1 [*Jolly* M$^{1-2-8-9}$ Nd] अतोर्थं न; NKt^4 WKt^6 अतोर्थन्न; GMy अतोर्थौ न; TMd^4 अथो न च प्रमा°; Jo^1 TMd^4 प्रमाद्यन्ते — d) Hy BKt^5 La^2 Lo^3 प्रमादासु; La^1 प्रमादास्तु; Wa प्रमदास्तु; WKt^6 प्रमदाः स्वविप°; *BhP* 4.182 प्रतिपाद्य विप°; Wa विपश्चिताः; GMd^1 विपश्चिता

214. Cited by *Dev* 1.104 — a) TMd^3 °समिमं लोके — c) Be^1 Be^3 Bo La^1 TMd^4 Pu^7 [*but cor*] Tj^1 प्रमादा; BKt^5 प्रमादां; Ho प्रमादात्

215. a) Tj^2 मात्रा स्वदुहित्रा वा; Wa स्वसा; Lo^4 स्वश्रा — b) Wa विविक्तासमो; Ho विविक्तनो — d) TMd^4 °समुपकर्षति

216. Pāda-b omitted in Ox^3 — a) *BhP* 4.185 राजेन्द्र गुरुपत्नीनां — b) Lo^4 *ma* युवतीनां

गुरुदारेषु कुर्वीत सतां धर्ममनुस्मरन् ॥२१७॥
यथा खनन्खनित्रेण नरो वार्यधिगच्छति ।
तथा गुरुगतां विद्यां शुश्रूषुरधिगच्छति ॥२१८॥
मुण्डो वा जटिलो वा स्यादथवा स्याच्छिखाजटः ।
नैनं ग्रामेऽभिनिम्लोचेत् सूर्यो नाभ्युदियात् क्वचित् ॥२१९॥
तं चेदभ्युदियात्सूर्यः शयानं कामकारतः ।
निम्लोचेद्वाप्यविज्ञानाज्जपन्नुपवसेद्दिनम् ॥२२०॥
सूर्येण ह्यभिनिर्मुक्तः शयानोऽभ्युदितश्च यः ।
प्रायश्चित्तमकुर्वाणो युक्तः स्यान्महतैनसा ॥२२१॥
आचम्य प्रयतो नित्यमुभे संध्ये समाहितः ।
शुचौ देशे जपञ्जप्यमुपासीत यथाविधि ॥२२२॥

217. Omitted in Bo. Cited by *Dev* 1.104 — a) *BhP* 4.186 विप्रोऽस्य; BBe² *Dev* [vl] विप्रस्य; *Dev* विप्रस्तु; GMd⁵ विशेष — b) Tr² चाभिवन्दनं — d) Kt² सतो; oOr *om* धर्मम्; Ox² वृत्तमनुस्मरन्

218. Cited by *Har*-A 1.144; *Dev* 1.139 — a) Tr¹ खनत्कनि° — b) *BhP* 4.187 जलमाप्नोति मानवः; NKt⁴ वार्यविग° wKt⁶ वार्यभिग° — c) Bo wKt⁶ यथा; Be¹ La² Tj¹ Wa [*Jolly* R] *Dev* एवं गुरु° [*Me Go Nd Ku* have एवम् but it is unclear whether it is the root text or simply a gloss]; [*Jolly* R] गुरुतरां — d) NKt⁴ °पुरविगच्छति

219. Cited by *Apa* 64; *Dev* 1.126 — b) TMd³ स्याद् गृहस्थो वा शिखाजठाः; Tr² *om* वा; sOx¹ sPu⁶ °थवा शिखान्वितः; *BhP* 4.188 स्याच्छिखी जटी; La² °खाव्रतः; wKt¹ °खायुतः; Lo² °जटीः — c) Lo¹ नैवं; Lo⁵ TMd⁴ ग्रामो; Tr¹ ग्रामे हि निम्रोचेत्; NKt⁴ GMd¹ TMd³ TMd⁴ sOx¹ sPu⁶ MTr⁴ MTr⁶ [*Jolly* Nd] °भिनिम्रोचेत् — d) *BhP* 4.188 °म्लोचेदर्को; Be³ GMy सूर्ये; BKt⁵ सूर्योभ्युदिया°; Be¹ Kt² TMd⁴ NNg Ox³ Pu⁵ Pu⁷ Tj¹ MTr⁴ Wa *Apa* [vl] नाभ्युदयात्; *Apa* [vl] °भ्युदये; GMd¹ °दियात्तथा

220.* Cited by *Lakṣ* 1.234; *Mādh* 2.447 — a) *Lakṣ* सूर्येण ह्यभिनिर्मुक्तः; Ho यद्युदिति दिवा सूर्यः; Lo⁴ *ma* तं; Pu⁷ [*but cor*] ते चेद°; sOx¹ sPu⁶ न चेद°; Kt² Pu⁹ °भ्युदयात्सूर्यः; TMd⁴ °भ्युदितात्सूर्यः — b) Ho प्रायानं; BBe² Be³ Hy Jm Jo¹ Kt² wKt³ Lo¹ oMd² Tj² MTr³ *Lakṣ Me Mandlik Jolly Jha KSS Dave* कामचारतः — c) NKt⁴ GMd¹ TMd³ TMd⁴ GMy Tr¹ MTr⁴ MTr⁶ *Mādh* निम्रोचे°; La¹ Tr¹ °द्वापि विज्ञाना°; wKt¹ °द्वास्यविज्ञाना°; TMd³ GMd⁵ °द्वाभ्यनुज्ञाना°; BBe² GMy *BhP* 4.189 °प्यभिज्ञाना° — d) Tr² °नाज्जपंस्तूप°; Ho °नाज्जपंस्तु उप°; Lo⁴ °पविशेद्दिनं

Additional verse in La¹:

प्रतिवाते तथादित्ये ब्रह्मचारी शयीत यः ।
रात्रौ तिष्ठेदभुञ्जानो जपन्जप्यमतन्द्रितः ॥

221.* Cited by *Dev* 1.126 — a) MTr⁴ MTr⁶ सूर्येणाभ्यतिनिर्मुक्तः; BKt⁵ wKt⁶ त्वभि°; Pu² ह्यतिनिमुक्तः; [*Jolly* G] °निर्मुक्तः; GMd¹ °निमृक्तः; GMd⁵ GMy *VaDh* 1.18 °निम्रुक्तः; Be¹ BBe² Be³ Bo BCa Ho Hy Jm Jo¹ Jo² wKt¹ Kt² wKt³ NKt⁴ BKt⁵ wKt⁶ La¹ La² Lo¹ Lo² Lo³ Lo⁴ Lo⁵ oMd² oOr sOx¹ Ox² NPu¹ sPu⁶ Pu⁸ Pu⁹ Pu¹⁰ Tj¹ Tj² Tr² Wa [*Jolly* M N Ku R Nd] *Dev Ku Rn Rc Mandlik KSS* °निर्मुक्तः; Ox³ °नियुक्तः — b) Lo² शयाने — d) wKt⁶ Tr¹ °हतेनसा; Lo² GMy Tr² °हदेनसा; Kt² °हतैजसा

222. Pādas a-b omitted in Tr¹. Cited by *Dev* 2.391; *Mādh* 1.280 — a) *BhP* 4.191 उपस्पृश्य महाराज; Pu¹⁰ आचाम्य; GMd¹ आगम्य — c) NKt⁴ जपंजाप्यं उपा° — d) Be³ °मुपासीनो; wKt⁶ Lo⁴ Ox³

यदि स्त्री यद्यवरजः श्रेयः किंचित्समाचरेत् ।
तत्सर्वमाचरेद्युक्तो यत्र वास्य रमेन्मनः ॥२२३॥
धर्मार्थावुच्यते श्रेयः कामार्थौ धर्म एव वा ।
अर्थ एवेह वा श्रेयस्त्रिवर्ग इति तु स्थितिः ॥२२४॥
आचार्यश्च पिता चैव माता भ्राता च पूर्वजः ।
नार्तेनाप्यवमन्तव्या ब्राह्मणेन विशेषतः ॥२२५॥
आचार्यो ब्रह्मणो मूर्तिः पिता मूर्तिः प्रजापतेः ।
माता पृथिव्या मूर्तिस्तु भ्राता स्वो मूर्तिरात्मनः ॥२२६॥
यं मातापितरौ क्लेशं सहेते संभवे नृणाम् ।
न तस्य निष्कृतिः शक्या कर्तुं वर्षशतैरपि ॥२२७॥
तयोर्नित्यं प्रियं कुर्यादाचार्यस्य च सर्वदा ।
तेष्वेव त्रिषु तुष्टेषु तपः सर्वं समाप्यते ॥२२८॥

Pu^{7} यथाविधिः; sOx^{1} sPu^{6} समाहितः [*but both cor*]

223. b) Be^{3} किंचिच्छ्रेयः समाचरेत्; wKt^{3} श्रेयं; Tr^{2} श्रेष्ठः; GMy कश्चित्समा° — d) *BhP* 4.192 यत्र वा रमते मनः; Wa यत्रास्य रमते मनः; Lo^{3} Tj^{1} यत्र वा स्यान्न चात्मनः; Jo^{2} यत्र वा स्यान्निजन्मनः; TMd^{3} यस्य यत्र रमे°; BCa Lo^{4} Lo^{5} GMy sOx^{1} NPu^{1} sPu^{6} Pu^{10} [*Jolly* M] *Jha Dave* चास्य; Be^{1} BBe^{2} Be^{3} Bo NKt^{4} BKt^{5} Lo^{2} Pu^{2} Pu^{5} Pu^{7} Pu^{9} Tr^{2} वास्यारमे°; La^{1} La^{2} Pu^{8} चास्यारमे°; Ox^{2} वास्यारमे° *cor to* चास्यारमे°; BBe^{2} चरेन्मनः

224. Pādas c-d omitted in TMd^{4}. Cited by *Apa* 158 — a) Lo^{3} धर्मार्थमु°; Jo^{1} धर्मार्थामु°; Lo^{4} Ox^{3} धर्मार्थादु°; Be^{3} धर्मार्थानु°; Tj^{1} धर्मामु° — b) Bo Tj^{1} कामार्थो; *BhP* 4.193 धर्ममेव; Be^{3} Ho Jm Jo^{1} Kt^{2} Lo^{1} Lo^{3} Lo^{4} Lo^{5} oMd^{2} Ox^{2} Ox^{3} Tr^{2} MTr^{3} Wa [*Jolly* R] *BhP Mandlik Jha KSS Dave* एव च; TMd^{3} एव ह — c) Bo अर्थ एव ह चाश्रेय°; Pu^{10} अर्थ एव भवेच्छ्रेय°; Lo^{1} अपि वा चेह; Lo^{4} *Apa* श्रेयांस्त्रि° — d) GMd^{1} इति हि; Tr^{1} इव तु स्थितः; oOr *BhP* इति संस्थितिः; Lo^{1} सुस्थितः

225. Omitted in TMd^{4} Ox^{3}; *ma* in Lo^{4}; verses 225 and 226 transposed in Hy Jm Jo^{1} Kt^{2} Tj^{2} MTr^{3} [*Jolly* Ku]. Cited by *Dev* 1.94 — a) wKt^{3} आचार्यस्य; Lo^{1} आचार्यः स्वपिता — a-b) *BhP* 4.194 पिता माता तथा भ्राता आचार्यः कुरुनन्दन — b) La^{2} भ्राता भ्रातानुपूवजः; Be^{3} तु; NKt^{4} पूर्वजाः — c) Tr^{1} नार्थेना°; TMd^{3} °प्यमन्तव्य; GMd^{1} °वमन्तव्याः; sOx^{1} sPu^{6} °वमन्तव्यो — d) Pu^{9} *om* विशेषतः; wKt^{6} विभाषतः

226. Omitted in Ox^{3}; *ma* in Lo^{4}; pādas a-b omitted in TMd^{4} — a) BBe^{2} wKt^{3} NNg sPu^{6} ब्राह्मणो [*but cor in* NNg sPu^{6}] — b) Be^{3} wKt^{3} GMy प्रजापते — c) BCa wKt^{1} wKt^{3} माता मूर्तिः पृथिव्यास्तु; *BhP* 4.195 माताप्यथादितेर्मूर्तिर्भ्राता; NKt^{4} पितृव्या; TMd^{4} पितृव्य; Be^{1} Pu^{5} Pu^{7} Pu^{8} Pu^{9} Pu^{10} [*Jolly* M$^{1-2-8-9}$ G] *Jolly* मूर्तिश्च — d) TMd^{4} भ्राता सा; GMy भ्रातरो मूर्ति°; GMd^{1} Tr^{1} [*Jolly* Nd] स्वा; NPu^{1} स्वान्मूर्ति°; *BhP* 4.195 स्यान्मूर्ति°

227. Cited by *Dev* 1.95 — a) La^{1} Tr^{1} *BhP* 4.196 यन्माता°; GMy °तरौ वापि — b) Ho सहते; Kt^{2} सेहेते; La^{2} सहिते; GMd^{1} संभवा — c) Pu^{10} नेतस्य; sOx^{1} sPu^{6} तस्य नो निष्कृतिः; Ox^{3} तयोर्निःकृतेः; GMd^{5} शत्त्या — d) Be^{3} वक्तुं; Ho Lo^{2} TMd^{4} NNg गन्तुं; BKt^{5} गन्तु; wKt^{3} गर्तुं; NKt^{4} Ox^{2} गतुं

228. Pādas c-d *ma* in wKt^{6}. Cited by *Dev* 1.95— a) Be^{3} तयोर्नित्य — b) TMd^{3} °चार्यस्यैव; NKt^{4} *om* च; Be^{1} Be^{3} La^{2} तु; *BhP* 4.197 च भारत — c) Ho wKt^{6} TMd^{3} GMy Tr^{1} तेपु त्रिषु च [TMd^{3} Tr^{1} तु; GMy हि]; NKt^{4} TMd^{4} NNg Ox^{2} Pu^{8} MTr^{4} MTr^{6} *Nā BhP* तेषु हि; La^{1} oOr तेपु च;

तेषां त्रयाणां शुश्रूषा परमं तप उच्यते ।
न तैरनभ्यनुज्ञातो धर्ममन्यं समाचरेत् ॥२२९॥
त एव हि त्रयो लोकास्त एव त्रय आश्रमाः ।
त एव हि त्रयो वेदास्त एवोक्तास्त्रयोऽग्नयः ॥२३०॥
पिता वै गार्हपत्योऽग्निर्माताग्निर्दक्षिणः स्मृतः ।
गुरुराहवनीयस्तु साग्नित्रेता गरीयसी ॥२३१॥
त्रिष्वप्रमाद्यन्नेतेषु त्रींल्लोकान्विजयेद्गृही ।
दीप्यमानः स्ववपुषा देववद्दिवि मोदते ॥२३२॥
इमं लोकं मातृभक्त्या पितृभक्त्या तु मध्यमम् ।
गुरुशुश्रूषया त्वेव ब्रह्मलोकं समश्नुते ॥२३३॥
सर्वे तस्यादृता धर्मा यस्यैते त्रय आदृताः ।
अनादृतास्तु यस्यैते सर्वास्तस्याफलाः क्रियाः ॥२३४॥

GMd[5] तेषु तु; Bo त्रिषु लोकेषु; La[2] तृप्तेषु — d) Hy *om* सर्वं

229. Cited by *Dev* 1.95 — a) Pu[5] Pu[7] Pu[9] Tj[1] एषां; Tr[2] शुश्रूषां — b) oOr परमस्तप — c) GMy Tr[1] नैतैर°; BBe[2] Hy Jo[1] Jo[2] wKt[1] oMd[2] TMd[4] Tj[2] *Dev* तैरभ्यननुज्ञातो — d) Be[1] धर्ममन्ये

230. Pādas a-b omitted in Ho. Cited by *Dev* 1.95 — a) BCa GMy एव च — c) Be[3] La[2] TMd[3] GMd[5] GMy NNg Ox[2] NPu[1] Pu[5] Pu[7] Pu[8] Pu[9] Tr[1] MTr[6] *BhP* 4.199 एव च; Bo एव तु; La[1] एव व — d) Tr[1] Tr[2] वेदास्त्रयो वोक्तास्त्रयोग्नयः; BBe[2] BKt[5] wKt[6] Lo[5] वेदास्त एव हि त्रयो; wKt[3] °क्तास्त्रयग्नन:

231. Cited by *Dev* 1.95 — a) *BhP* 4.200 माता; sOx[1] sPu[6] गार्हस्पत्यो; Tr[1] *BhP* 4.200 *Dev* °पत्याग्नि° — b) Tr[1] °ग्निर्माता वै दक्षिणा स्मृता; Tr[2] *om* माताग्निर्; La[2] TMd[3] TMd[4] Ox[3] MTr[4] MTr[6] °ग्निर्माता वै दक्षिणः; Lo[4] °ग्निर्माता व दक्षिणः; *BhP* 4.200 °ग्निः पिता वै दक्षिणः; GMy GMd[1] °क्षिणा स्मृता — c) wKt[1] Lo[1] TMd[3] NPu[1] *BhP* 4.200 °हवनीयश्च; Bo Lo[2] Lo[4] Lo[5] GMd[1] TMd[4] Ox[2] Ox[3] Pu[5] Pu[7] Pu[8] Pu[9] *Dev* °हवनीयोग्निः; La[1] °हवनीयाग्निः [*but mc sh*] — d) La[1] GMd[1] Pu[5] Pu[7] Pu[9] Tr[1] MTr[4] MTr[6] साग्निस्त्रेता

232. Pādas c-d omitted in Ox[3] Tj[1] and *ma* in Lo[4] — a) *BhP* 4.201 त्रिषु तुष्टेषु चैतेषु; NKt[4] विष्वप्रमा°; Bo °प्रमाद्ययन्नेते — a-b) GMd[1] त्रिषु तेष्वप्रमादयन्ते लोकान्विजयते गृही — b) GMy *om* त्रीन्; NNg त्रींल्लोकांस्तु जये°; NKt[4] BKt[5] wKt[6] La[2] TMd[4] NPu[1] Pu[10] Tr[1] °कान्हि जये°; Be[1] Be[3] Ho sOx[1] Ox[2] sPu[6] °कान्स जये°; Bo °कान्त्रिजये°; Lo[2] °कान्सोजये°; Tr[2] °कान्संजये°; GMy °कान्विजयते गृही; Pu[5] Pu[7] Pu[9] *BhP* 4.201 °कान्जयते गृही; Ox[3] *om* गृही; Lo[4] *ma* गृही— c) wKt[3] दीप्यमानं; TMd[3] GMd[5] Tr[1] °मानश्च वपुषा; Lo[2] GMy °मानस्तु वपुषा; wKt[6] स्वपुरुषा — d) Lo[3] [*Jolly* R] देववद्दिचरेद्गृही; Jo[2] देववद्विजयेद्गृही; Tr[2] देववत्सह मोदते; wKt[6] मोहितः; TMd[3] रोचते

233. Pādas c-d omitted in Ox[3] and *ma* in Lo[4]. Cited by *Dev* 1.95 — a) *BhP* 4.202 पितृभक्त्या — b) La[2] मध्यमं पितृभक्तितः; Pu[5] Pu[9] *om* and Pu[7] *mc* पितृभक्त्या; *BhP* मातृभक्त्या; Lo[4] Ox[3] *om* तु; Kt[2] मध्यं — c) Pu[5] Pu[7] Pu[9] [*Jolly* G] °श्रूषयाप्येव; Jo[2] wKt[1] BKt[5] wKt[6] Lo[3] TMd[4] Tj[1] Tr[1] [*Jolly* R] *BhP* 4.202 *Dev Mādh* चैव; Ho Hy Jm Jo[1] wKt[3] La[1] oMd[2] TMd[3] oOr Tj[2] MTr[3] MTr[6] *Rc Mandlik Jha KSS Dave* त्वेवं — d) oOr ब्रह्मलोके महीयते; *BhP* 4.202 गच्छेच्छक्रसलोकताम्

234. Cited by *Dev* 1.95; *Mādh* 1.336 — a) wKt[6] सर्वस्य तस्यादृता; BKt[5] सर्वस्य तस्याकृता; Jo[2] Lo[3] Tj[1] तस्याश्रिता; TMd[4] सस्यादृती; *BhP* 4.203 [vl] तेनादृता; MTr[4] तस्मादृते — b) Lo[3] Tj[1] आश्रिताः; Wa आश्रितः — c) Lo[1] अनादृता तु; Ho अदृतायास्तु; Lo[3] Tj[1] Wa अनाश्रितास्तु; Lo[4] Ox[3] यस्यैव; *BhP*

यावत् त्रयस्ते जीवेयुस्तावन्नान्यं समाचरेत् ।
तेष्वेव नित्यं शुश्रूषां कुर्यात् प्रियहिते रतः ॥२३५॥
तेषामनुपरोधेन पारत्र्यं यद्यदाचरेत् ।
तत्तन्निवेदयेत्तेभ्यो मनोवचनकर्मभिः ॥२३६॥
त्रिष्वेतेष्वितिकृत्यं हि पुरुषस्य समाप्यते ।
एष धर्मः परः साक्षादुपधर्मोऽन्य उच्यते ॥२३७॥
श्रद्दधानः शुभां विद्यामाददीतावरादपि ।
अन्त्यादपि परं धर्मं स्त्रीरत्नं दुष्कुलादपि ॥२३८॥
विषादप्यमृतं ग्राह्यं बालादपि सुभाषितम् ।
अमित्रादपि सद्वृत्तममेध्यादपि काञ्चनम् ॥२३९॥
स्त्रियो रत्नान्यथो विद्या धर्मः शौचं सुभाषितम् ।
विविधानि च शिल्पानि समादेयानि सर्वतः ॥२४०॥

4.203 [vl] येनैते — d) Lo^{1} सर्वा तस्या°; Be^{3} wKt^{6} Lo^{1} °फला; Be^{1} Be^{3} Ox^{3} क्रिया

235. Pādas c-d omitted in BKt^{5} wKt^{6} [haplo]. Cited by *Dev* 1.95; *Mādh*1.336 — a) TMd^{3} या च त्रयस्ते; Ox^{3} त्रयस्तु — b) Ho sOx^{1} sPu^{6} *Nā BhP* 4.204 °वन्नान्यत्समा° — c) Ho तेषामेव तु शुश्रूषां; GMd^{1} त्रिष्वेव

236. Pādas a-b omitted in BKt^{5} wKt^{6}. Cited by *Dev* 1.95 — b) Ho La^{2} Lo^{1} TMd^{3} sOx^{1} Ox^{3} NPu^{1} sPu^{6} Pu^{8} Tr^{2} पारतन्त्र्यं यदाचरेत्; GMy पारतन्त्र्यं समाचरेत्; Tj^{2} पारत्रं; TMd^{4} पारस्यं; Pu^{5} Pu^{7} Pu^{9} पारित्र्यं; *BhP* 4.205 पार्थक्यं — c) Tr^{2} तं तं निवे°; GMd^{1} तत्तन्नावे°; Be^{3} °वेदयंस्तेभ्यो; TMd^{3} °वेदयत्तेभ्यो — d) La^{1} GMd^{1} GMy sOx^{1} sPu^{6} Tr^{2} MTr^{4} *Rc* मनोवाक्कायकर्मभिः [gloss of *Go* मनोवाक्कायव्यापारेण appears to support the latter reading]; MTr^{6} मनोवाचानकर्मभिः

237. Pādas c-d cited by *Dev* 1.95 — a) GMd^{1} त्रिष्वेतेष्वमतं कृत्वा; TMd^{3} °तेष्विहकृत्यं — c) TMd^{4} धर्म; TMd^{3} परस्याक्षादुप° — d) Lo^{4} Lo^{5} Ox^{3} इष्यते

238. Pādas c-d omitted in wKt^{1} [haplo]. Cited by *Dev* 1.144 — a) MTr^{6} °धानाः; Ho GMd^{1} शुभं; sOx^{1} sPu^{6} Tr^{2} परां विद्या° — b) GMy °ददीत वरादपि; Tr^{2} °ददीतापरादपि; Ho °ददीताचिरादपि — c) GMd^{1} अन्त्यादपि वरं ग्राह्यं; *Dev* अत्यापदि परं; La^{2} धर्मे

239. Jo^{1} replaces pādas c-d with 240 c-d; pādas c-d omitted in MTr^{6}. Cited by *Dev* 1.144; pāda-d cited by *Viś* 1.195 — b) Pu^{5} Pu^{7} बलादपि; Pu^{9} बलोदपि; La^{2} सुभाषितां; Tr^{1} सुभाषितः — c) GMy अमृतादपि; NKt^{4} अमेत्रादपि

Additional verse in La^{1}:

गुरुर्देवो गुरुर्दाता गुरुः स्वामी गुरुः पिता ।
यस्यैष निश्चितो भावः श्रेयस्तस्य न दूरतः ॥

240.* Omitted in Ox^{3} *Rc* and *ma* in Lo^{4}; pādas a-b omitted in MTr^{6}; pādas c-d placed after 239b in Tr^{2} — a) La^{1} स्त्रीरत्नोन्यथा विद्या; GMd^{1} स्त्रियो वित्तमथो; Lo^{3} Tj^{1} रत्नाद्यथो; TMd^{3} GMd^{5} रत्नं तथा; TMd^{4} रत्नान्यथा; NKt^{4} रत्नान्यथ; *BhP* 4.209 रत्नं नयो विद्या — b) Be^{3} TMd^{3} Tr^{1} MTr^{4} धर्मं; Lo^{4} धर्मशौचे; Pu^{5} Pu^{7} Pu^{9} धर्मशौचं — c) Be^{1} BBe^{2} Bo Jo^{2} wKt^{1} wKt^{3} BKt^{5} wKt^{6} La^{2} Lo^{2} Lo^{3} Lo^{4} Lo^{5} TMd^{4} NPu^{1} Pu^{2} Pu^{5} Pu^{7} Pu^{9} Pu^{10} Tj^{1} Wa [*Jolly* M G N Ku R] *Me Go Nā Rn Jolly* शिल्पानि चाप्यदुष्टानि [Pu^{2} Wa वाप्यदु°; NPu^{1} ह्यप्यदु°; Lo^{2} चाध्यदु°; Lo^{2} Lo^{3} Lo^{4} Lo^{5} चाप्यदृष्टानि]; BCa Ho अदुष्टानि च शिल्पानि [BCa विदुष्टानि]; Be^{3} विविधान्यपि; La^{1} *om* च — d) TMd^{4} समादायानि; Ho

अब्राह्मणादध्ययनमापत्काले विधीयते ।
अनुव्रज्या च शुश्रूषा यावदध्ययनं गुरोः ॥२४१॥
नाब्राह्मणे गुरौ शिष्यो वासमात्यन्तिकं वसेत् ।
ब्राह्मणे चाननूचाने काङ्क्षन् गतिमनुत्तमाम् ॥२४२॥
यदि त्वात्यन्तिकं वासं रोचयेत गुरोः कुले ।
युक्तः परिचरेदेनमा शरीरविमोक्षणात् ॥२४३॥
आ समाप्तेः शरीरस्य यस्तु शुश्रूषते गुरुम् ।
स गच्छत्यञ्जसा विप्रो ब्रह्मणः सद्म शाश्वतम् ॥२४४॥
न पूर्वं गुरवे किंचिदुपकुर्वीत धर्मवित् ।
स्नास्यंस्तु गुरुणाज्ञप्तः शक्त्या गुर्वर्थमाहरेत् ॥२४५॥
क्षेत्रं हिरण्यं गामश्वं छत्रोपानहमन्ततः ।
धान्यं वासांसि शाकं वा गुरवे प्रीतिमाहरेत् ॥२४६॥

प्रमादेयानि; GMy Tr^1 MTr^4 MTr^6 *BhP* सर्वशः

241. Cited by *Dev* 1.143; 2.449; pādas c-d cited by *Apa* 160 — b) GMd^5 GMy °पत्कल्पो; Lo^2 oOr *Go* [pāṭha] *Me* [pāṭha] *Nā* °पत्कल्पे — c) La^1 NKt^4 अनुव्रज्यानुशुश्रूषा; Ox^3 अनुयाज्या; Be^1 BBe^2 Hy BKt^5 wKt^6 TMd^4 NNg Tj^2 तु — d) Tr^2 °ध्यायनं; Kt^2 गुरो

242.* Pādas c-d omitted in GMd^1. Cited by *Apa* 70; *Lakṣ* 1.274; *Dev* 1.168 — a) BKt^5 नाब्रह्मणे; Be^3 Ox^3 नब्राह्मणे; GMd^5 नाब्रह्मणो; Bo Pu^{10} शिष्ये; TMd^4 Wa शिष्या — b) TMd^4 °माद्यन्तिकं; TMd^4 Tj^1 भवेत्; NNg वदेत् — c) Ho Lo^4 Lo^5 TMd^4 NNg sOx^1 Ox^3 NPu^1 Pu^2 Pu^5 sPu^6 Pu^9 Pu^{10} Tj^2 MTr^4 MTr^6 Wa *Jha Dave* वाननूचाने; *Apa* [vl] चानधीयाने — d) Wa गतिमवाप्नुयात्; NKt^4 °नुत्तमं

243. Omitted in GMd^1. Cited by *Apa* 72; *Dev* 1.171; *Mādh* 1.458 — a) Be^1 BBe^2 Wa चात्यन्तिकं; BKt^5 wKt^6 La^2 GMy वात्यन्तिकं; TMd^4 त्वाद्यन्तिको वास्या; TMd^3 °न्तिका; *BhP* 4.212 *Mādh* °न्तिको वासो; Be^3 GMy NPu^1 *Apa* वासो — b) Lo^3 [*Jolly* M$^{1-2-8-9}$ R] रोचयेत्तु; [*Jolly* M$^{3-4}$ G Nd] रोचयेते; TMd^3 रोचयात; *BhP* 4.212 रोचते च; TMd^4 रोचते स्वगुरोः; La^2 रोचयेद्यद्गुरोः; *Mādh* रोचयेतास्य गुरोः — c) Ho TMd^4 युक्तं; NKt^4 सुक्तः; BKt^5 शुक्तः; BKt^5 wKt^6 परिचयेदे°

244. Cited by *Viś* 1.50; *Dev* 1.170; *Mādh* 1.459 — a) *Viś* आ निपाताच्छरीरस्य [cf. 6.31c]; Pu^5 Pu^7 Pu^9 समाप्तैः; Be^3 समाप्तः — c) TMd^4 गच्छन्त्य°; Lo^1 °त्यन्ततां — d) BBe^2 Kt^2 wKt^6 Pu^9 Wa ब्राह्मणः

245. Tj^1 transposes pādas a-b and c-d. Cited by *Dev* 1.179; *Mādh* 1.460-1 — a) GMd^1 स पूर्वं; Be^3 तत्पूर्वं; Lo^4 Lo^5 [*but cor*] Ox^3 गुरवे दद्यादुप° — b) wKt^1 धर्मतः; wKt^3 कर्मवित्; TMd^4 धर्मतत् — c) Lo^4 स्नाप्यं तु; BKt^5 wKt^6 स्नातस्तु; wKt^1 शिष्यस्तु; Lo^2 सास्यत्स्वगुरु°; *BhP* 4.214 स्नानाय गुरु°; MTr^4 MTr^6 °ज्ञप्तं — d) MTr^4 MTr^6 शक्यं; NKt^4 La^2 GMd^1 sOx^1 sPu^6 MTr^4 MTr^6 [*Jolly* Be] °माचरेत्

246. Cited by *Lakṣ* 1.275; *Dev* 1.178; *Mādh* 1.460–1; pādas c-d cited by *Apa* 76 — a) Be^3 BKt^5 wKt^6 हिरण्य; Tr^1 गावाश्व; Ho गामश्च — b) Lo^1 छत्त्रं यानमहंततः; Be^1 Hy Jm Jo^1 Kt^2 La^1 [*but mc*] La^2 oMd^2 Ox^2 Tj^2 MTr^3 *Mādh Mandlik KSS* °पानहमासनं; TMd^3 °पासनमन्ततः; Wa °नहंततः; *BhP* 4.214 °नहमेव च — c) Hy Jm Jo^1 Kt^2 La^1 Tj^2 MTr^3 *Lakṣ Mandlik KSS* धान्यं शाकं च वासांसि; *Apa* शाकं च — d) MTr^4 MTr^6 प्रीतिमान्हरेत्; BCa [*but cor*] wKt^1 NNg *Lakṣ Me Jha Dave* °माहरन्; Hy Jm Jo^1 Jo^2 Kt^2 oMd^2 TMd^4 Tj^2 MTr^3 *Me* [pāṭha] *Mr* °मावहेत्; *Rc Mandlik KSS* °मावहन्; cf. similar variants at 3.82d.

आचार्ये तु खलु प्रेते गुरुपुत्रे गुणान्विते ।
गुरुदारे सपिण्डे वा गुरुवद्वृत्तिमाचरेत् ॥२४७॥
एतेष्वविद्यमानेषु स्थानासनविहारवान् ।
प्रयुञ्जानोऽग्निशुश्रूषां साधयेद्देहमात्मनः ॥२४८॥
एवं चरति यो विप्रो ब्रह्मचर्यमविप्लुतः ।
स गच्छत्युत्तमं स्थानं न चेहाजायते पुनः ॥२४९॥

॥ इति मानवे धर्मशास्त्रे भृगुप्रोक्तायां संहितायां द्वितीयोऽध्यायः ॥

247. Omitted in La^{2}. Cited by *Viś* 1.49; *Dev* 1.167 — a-d) a longer version in *BhP* 4.216 स्वर्गते गां परित्यज्य गुरौ भरतसत्तम । गुणान्विते गुरुसुते गुरुदारेऽथ वा नृप । सपिण्डे वा गुरोश्चापि गुरुवद्वृत्तिमाचरेत् — a) Pu^{5} Pu^{7} [*but cor*] Pu^{9} आचार्यो; TMd^{3} आचार्या; BKt^{5} आर्ये तु; wKt^{1} आचार्येषु खलु; Lo^{3} TMd^{4} sOx^{1} sPu^{6} Tj^{1} MTr^{4} प्रीते— c) Tj^{2} च — d) *Viś* काङ्क्षन् गतिमनुत्तमाम् [cf. 2.242d]; Lo^{4} Lo^{5} NNg Ox^{3} °माहरेत्

248. Cited by *Lakṣ* 1.274; *Dev* 1.167; *Mādh* 1.458 — a) NKt^{4} Lo^{2} GMd^{1} TMd^{3} TMd^{4} GMy Pu^{5} Pu^{7} Pu^{9} Pu^{10} MTr^{4} MTr^{6} [*Jolly* M$^{1-2-8-9}$ G]*Lakṣ Mādh* एषु त्वविद्य° ; Bo एषेत्वविद्य° ; La^{1} एषुष्वविद्य° ; wKt^{1} wKt^{6} एतेषु विद्य° — b) Hy स्नानासन° ; BBe^{2} स्थानाशन° — d) Tr^{1} संश्रयेद्देह° ; NNg °येद्देशमात्मनः; Pu^{10} [*Jolly* M$^{1-2-8-9}$] °हमात्मवान्

249. Cited by *Lakṣ* 1.274 — a) *BhP* 4.218 चरत्येवं हि यो विप्रो; Lo^{3} Tj^{1} यो विद्यो; Tr^{2} विप्रं — b) BKt^{5} wKt^{6} MTr^{4} *Lakṣ* °विप्लुतं; Pu^{10} °निप्लुतः — c-d) *BhP* 4.218 स गत्वा ब्रह्मसदनं ब्रह्मणा सह मोदते — c) BKt^{5} wKt^{6} गच्छत्यमलं स्थानं; Lo^{5} °त्युत्तरं; BBe^{2} Jo^{1} Jo^{2} Kt^{2} wKt^{3} Lo^{5} Tr^{2} MTr^{3} *Me Rc Mandlik Jha KSS Dave* °त्युत्तमस्थानं — d) TMd^{4} गच्छेहाजायते पुनः; GMd^{5} sOx^{1} sPu^{6} Tr^{2} चेह जायते

Colophon: Be^{1} Bo Ho Lo^{1} GMy NNg Tj^{2} इति श्रीमानवे; Lo^{3} Tj^{1} इति श्रीमानवीये; Ho wKt^{3} La^{1} भृगुप्रोक्ते; Be^{3} BKt^{5} wKt^{6} Lo^{3} GMy sOx^{1} sPu^{6} *om* भृगुप्रोक्तायां संहितायां; Hy Lo^{1} भृगुप्रोक्त-संहितायां; Ho wKt^{3} *om* संहितायां; La^{1} धर्मविधिर्नाम द्वितीयो; Ho Lo^{1} ब्रह्मचारिलक्षणो नाम द्वितीयो; Pu^{5} Pu^{7} Pu^{9} ब्रह्मचारिविधानं नाम द्वितीयो; Be^{1} सोपनयनविधिर्नाम द्वितीयो; wKt^{1} ब्रह्मचारिकथनं नाम द्वितीयो; NNg ब्रह्मचारिधर्मो नाम द्वितीयोऽध्यायः समाप्तः

[तृतीयोऽध्यायः]

षट्त्रिंशदाब्दिकं चर्यं गुरौ त्रैवेदिकं व्रतम् ।
तदर्धिकं पादिकं वा ग्रहणान्तिकमेव वा ॥१॥
वेदानधीत्य वेदौ वा वेदं वापि यथाक्रमम् ।
अविप्लुतब्रह्मचर्यो गृहस्थाश्रममावसेत् ॥२॥
तं प्रतीतं स्वधर्मेण ब्रह्मदायहरं पितुः ।
स्रग्विणं तल्प आसीनमर्हयेत् प्रथमं गवा ॥३॥
गुरुणानुमतः स्नात्वा समावृत्तो यथाविधि ।
उद्वहेत द्विजो भार्यां सवर्णां लक्षणान्विताम् ॥४॥
असपिण्डा च या मातुरसगोत्रा च या पितुः ।
सा प्रशस्ता द्विजातीनां दारकर्मण्यमैथुनी* ॥५॥

1. Cited by *Apa* 67; *Hem* 3/3.779; *Har*-A 1.2.16; *Dev* 1.166; *Mādh* 1.457–8; pāda-d cited by *Vij* 1.36 — a) TMd^{4} [*Jolly* M$^{1-2}$] पाट्° ; Ho पड्विंश° ; Ox^{2} °शदादिकं; Hy चर्ये; GMd^{5} चार्यं; wKt^{6} चार्यां; TMd^{3} कार्यं; Tr^{1} सर्वं [*but cor fh*] — b) NKt^{4} Lo^{2} Ox^{3} गुरो; GMy गुरवे वैदिकं; NKt^{4} Tj^{1} Pu^{10} त्रैवैदिकं; Hy oOr त्रेवेदिकं; *Har*-A *Hem Apa* [vl as in ed] त्रैविद्यकं; La^{2} स्मृतं — c) *Hem* तदर्द्धे पादिकं वापि; Tr^{2} तदार्धिकं; Lo^{1} तदर्धकं; sOx^{1} sPu^{6} तदविकं; NKt^{4} तदधिकं; Tr^{2} *om* पादिकं; La^{2} Lo^{1} Tj^{1} पादकं; GMy पातिकं; *Apa* [vl] पाक्षिकं — d) *BhP* 5.1 च

2. Folios containing verses 3.2–224 missing in Pu^{9}. Cited by *Hem* 1.680; pādas a-b cited by *Kum* 2.1.1 [*pratīka* also at *Kum* 2.4.9]; *Viś* 1.36 51; *Vij* 1.36 — a) sOx^{1} वेदादधीत्य; TMd^{3} वेदा अधीत्य; MTr^{3} वेदान्यधीत्य; Lo^{2} Wa वेदो वा; GMy च — b) *BhP* 5.2 वापि नृपोत्तम; Jo^{2} Lo^{3} Tj^{1} [*Jolly* R] यथाविधि — c) Lo^{1} अविप्लुतो; NKt^{4} °चर्या — d) oMd^{2} °मावशेत्; Be^{3} Jm BKt^{5} wKt^{6} La^{1} Lo^{1} Pu^{10} [*Jolly* M$^{1-2-8-9}$] °माविशेत्; La^{2} Lo^{3} Tj^{1} °माचरेत्

3. b) BKt^{5} ब्रह्मदाय स्वयं पितुः; wKt^{6} ब्रह्मदायस्ययं पितुः; GMy ब्रह्मादय°; TMd^{3} °दायं हरं; sOx^{1} sPu^{6} [*but mc sh*] °हरं गुरोः — c) wKt^{6} श्रग्विणं; Tj^{2} स्रग्विण; BBe^{2} Jo^{2} NNg TMd^{3} Tr^{2} तल्पमासीन° — d) BBe^{2} °मर्हयत्; wKt^{6} °मर्हयः; wKt^{1} Wa गवां

4. Cited by *Apa* 76; *Hem* 1.680; *Mādh* 1.462 — a) *BhP* 5.4 *Dev* गुरुणा समनुज्ञातः समा°; Pu^{10} °मत; Lo^{1} °मतः सोपि — b) NNg Pu^{5} Pu^{7} °वृत्तौ; GMd^{5} °वृत्ते; GMd^{1} °वर्तो; BBe^{2} BCa oOr Pu^{7} °विधिः — c) TMd^{4} उद्वहेच्च — d) TMd^{4} सुवर्णां; Tj^{1} सवर्णाल्लक्ष°; Tr^{2} °न्वितं; *Dev* °न्वितात् [typo?]

Additional half-verse in Tr^{2}:

पञ्चमात्सप्तमादूर्ध्वं मातृतः पितृतस्तथा ।

5.* *ma* in Pu^{7}. Cited by *Vij* 1.53; *Apa* 81; *Dev* 1.184, 189; *Mādh* 1.468–9 — a) Be^{1} तु या; Bo ये — b) *Vij* मातुरसपिण्डा [vl as in ed]; sOx^{1} *om* च; Bo ये — c) GMd^{1} TMd^{3} TMd^{4} GMd^{5} GMy Tr^{1} MTr^{4} MTr^{6} सा द्विजानां प्रशस्ता स्त्री; wKt^{3} स; Tj^{2} द्विजाग्र्यां न दार° — d) *Me* [pāṭha] Tr^{1} °कर्मण्यमैथुने; TMd^{3} °कर्मणामैथुनी; Be^{1} BBe^{2} Be^{3} Bo BCa Ho Hy Jm Jo^{1} Jo^{2} wKt^{1} Kt^{2} wKt^{3} NKt^{4} BKt^{5}

महान्त्यपि समृद्धानि गोऽजाविधनधान्यतः ।
स्त्रीसंबन्धे दशैतानि कुलानि परिवर्जयेत् ॥६॥
हीनक्रियं निष्पुरुषं निश्छन्दो रोमशार्शसम् ।
क्षय्यामयाव्यपस्मारिश्वित्रिकुष्ठिकुलानि च ॥७॥
नोद्वहेत्कपिलां कन्यां नाधिकाङ्गीं न रोगिणीम् ।
नालोमिकां नातिलोमां न वाचालां न पिङ्गलाम् ॥८॥
नर्क्षवृक्षनदीनाम्नीं नान्त्यपर्वतनामिकाम् ।
न पक्ष्यहिप्रेष्यनाम्नीं न विभीषणनामिकाम् ॥९॥

wKt[6] La[1] La[2] Lo[1] Lo[2] Lo[3] Lo[4] Lo[5] GMd[1] oMd[2] TMd[4] NNg oOr sOx[1] Ox[2] NPu[1] Pu[2] Pu[3] Pu[4] Pu[5] sPu[6] Pu[7] Pu[8] Pu[10] Tj[1] Tj[2] Tr[2] Wa *Vij Apa Dev Mādh Go Nā Ku Rn Mr Mandlik Jolly KSS* °कर्मणि मैथुने; Ox[3] °कर्माणि मैथुने

6. Cited by *Viś* 1.54; *Apa* 84; *Dev* 1.204; *Mādh* 1.477 — a) Pu[10] [*Jolly* M[1-2-8-9]] समर्थानि — c) Pu[10] स्त्रीणां बन्धे; TMd[4] °संबन्ध; Lo[2] दशेतानि ; Jo[2] NKt[4] Lo[4] TMd[4] GMd[5] Ox[3] Tr[1] MTr[4] MTr[6] Wa *Apa Go Ku* दशेमानि; oOr *om* कुलानि

7. Cited by *Viś* 1.54; *Apa* 84; *Dev* 1.204; *Mādh* 1.477 — a) Tj[1] हीना°; BKt[5] हीनः; Jm °क्रियां; TMd[3] °क्रयं; sOx[1] sPu[6] Pu[10] निपुरुषं; Lo[1] विरूपं च — b) Lo[1] निश्छन्दं; Lo[4] Pu[10] Tr[1] निछन्दो; Lo[2] निच्छेदो; Be[3] wKt[1] La[1] *Lakṣ Apa* [vl as in ed] लोम° ; BBe[2] रोमसार्शसं; Tr[2] रोमशार्सनं; Pu[5] Pu[7] रोमश्मेहर्शसं; BCa Lo[5] रोमशासनं — c) Hy क्षयमंग्र्ययस्मारि° ; Lo[1] TMd[3] *BhP* 5.104 क्षया° ; GMy Pu[10] क्षय्यामय्या° ; Lo[4] °मयाध्ययस्मारि° ; BKt[5] wKt[6] °व्यस्मारि° ; Bo GMy °स्मारी° ; Tr[2] °स्मरी° ; Ho °स्मरि° — d) Bo °श्वित्री° ; Ho °स्वित्रि° ; Lo[2] °श्वत्रि° ; *BhP* 5.104 Pu[10] [*Jolly* M] °श्वित्र° ; MTr[3] °श्वित्रं; Tr[1] °द्वित्रिहीनकुलानि; Bo Tr[2] °कुष्ठी° ; Kt[2] °कुष्टि° ; GMy °कुष्टा° ; GMd[1] sOx[1] sPu[6] °कुलान्यपि

8. Pādas c-d omitted in Ho. Cited by *Apa* 78; *Lakṣ* 2.27; *Dev* 1.200 — a) TMd[4] नोद्वहत्क° — b) MTr[4] MTr[6] कन्यामधिकाङ्गीं; Jm °काङ्गी; GMy °काङ्गां; BKt[5] सरोगिणीं; GMy रोगिणीः — c) La[1] GMy Pu[10] न लोमिकां; Jo[2] NNg Pu[10] Tj[1] Wa *Apa* नातिलोम्नीं; Lo[1] न निर्लोमं; *BhP* 5.100 नातिह्रस्वां — c-d) Tr[1] नालोमिकां न चाचालात्रातिलोमां न पिङ्गलां — d) Jm नावाचाटान्; BBe[2] Jm Jo[1] Jo[2] wKt[1] Kt[2] wKt[3] Lo[2] GMd[1] oMd[2] TMd[4] GMd[5] NNg oOr Ox[2] [*but cor*] MTr[3] *Rn Rc Mr BhP* 5.100 *Apa Dev Mandlik KSS* वाचाटां; Lo[1] वाचाटं; Hy वाचाठां; TMd[3] वाचातां; Pu[2] वाचाडां; sOx[1] sPu[6] वाचाजां; NKt[4] वाचांगं; Bo पिङ्गवान्

9 Pādas b-c omitted in Lo[2]. Cited by *Apa* 78; *Lakṣ* 2.27; *Dev* 1.201— a) NPu[1] नऋक्ष° ; NKt[4] नक्षावृ° ; Lo[1] नवृक्षनदी° ; Lo[2] °नाम्नां; NNg °नार्मि [*but cor*]; Bo °नारीं — b) Be[1] Bo नात्यपर्व° ; Lo[1] चनतुपर्व° ; Tj[2] °नामिनीं — c) wKt[6] Tj[1] पक्षाहि° ; Jm Lo[1] पक्षहि° ; Bo La[1] NPu[1] MTr[3] °प्रेक्ष्यनाम्नीं; *Apa* °पुष्यनाम्नीं; Jm °नाम्नी — d) Lo[2] न भीपणकनामिकां; oOr नातिभीषणनामिकां; Lo[1] Lo[4] Lo[5] Ox[3] Pu[2] Pu[10] Tj[1] न बिभीषण° ; Pu[10] नाविभीषण° ; Be[1] BBe[2] Be[3] Hy Jm Jo[1] wKt[1] Kt[2] wKt[3] oMd[2] Pu[5] Pu[7] Pu[8] Tj[2] MTr[3] [*Jolly* G] *BhP* 5.101 *Dev Mandlik Jha KSS Dave* न च भीषण° ; GMd[5] नापि भीषण°

Additional verse in Be[3] BCa Ho La[1] oOr Ox[2] [but in parentheses *sh*] *Mandlik* [ख, ग, ञ, ल] *KSS:*

नातिस्थूलां नातिकृशां नातिदीर्घां न वामनाम् ।
वयोऽधिकां नाङ्गहीनां न स्तेयकलहप्रियाम् ॥

a) La[1] °स्थूला; La[1] न कृशां — b) La[1] *Mandlik KSS* न दीर्घां; La[1] न च वामनां; *Mandlik KSS* नातिवामनाम् — c) Ho Ox[2] वयोधिकाङ्गहीनां वा; La[1] चाङ्गहीनां — d) Be[3] *Mandlik*

अव्यङ्गाङ्गीं सौम्यनाम्नीं हंसवारणगामिनीम् ।
तनुलोमकेशदशनां मृद्वङ्गीमुद्वहेत् स्त्रियम् ॥१०॥
यस्यास्तु न भवेद्भ्राता न विज्ञायेत वा पिता ।
नोपयच्छेत तां प्राज्ञः पुत्रिकाधर्मशङ्कया ॥११॥
सवर्णाग्रे द्विजातीनां प्रशस्ता दारकर्मणि ।
कामतस्तु प्रवृत्तानामिमाः स्युः क्रमशो वराः ॥१२॥
शूद्रैव भार्या शूद्रस्य सा च स्वा च विशः स्मृते ।
ते च स्वा चैव राज्ञः स्युः ताश्च स्वा चाग्रजन्मनः ॥१३॥
न ब्राह्मणक्षत्रिययोरापद्यपि हि तिष्ठतोः ।
कस्मिंश्चिदपि वृत्तान्ते शूद्रा भार्योपदिश्यते ॥१४॥

KSS न सेवेत्कलह°; Ho Ox^{2} नोद्वहेत्कलह°

Additional verse in TMd^{4}:

एतैर्दोषैश्च संयुक्ता गृह्यन्ते याः कुलाङ्गनाः ।
तांगुलद्वयम [rest illegible]

10.* Cited by *Apa* 78; *Dev* 1.200; *Mādh* 1.462; pādas a-b cited by *Viś* 1.52; pāda-c by *Vij* 1.52 — a) NKt^{4} अव्यंगां सौम्य°; GMy सौक्ष्म्यनाम्नी; Lo^{2} °नाम्नां — b) TMd^{3} हंसिसारसगाभिनीं; *Apa* [vl] नाधिकाङ्गीं न रोगिनीं [cf. 1.8b]; Tr^{2} हंसगामिनीं — c) TMd^{3} तनुरोमशादशनां; GMd^{5} MTr^{4} MTr^{6} [*Jolly* Nd] तनुरोम°; Kt^{2} नतुलोम°; Lo^{4} Lo^{5} Ox^{3} Pu^{10} [*Jolly* M] तन्वोष्ठकेश°; NNg Pu^{5} Pu^{7} [*Jolly* G] *Jolly* °केशदन्तां; Tr^{2} °केशदतीं; *Apa* [vl as in ed.] °केशदशां — d) *Apa* मृद्वङ्गीं चारुभाषिणीं; TMd^{3} °शनामुद्वङ्गीमुद्वहेत्; Pu^{10} मृद्वङ्गामु°; Wa °मुद्वहत्; Pu^{5} Pu^{7} MTr^{3} °मुद्वयेत्; Be^{3} Lo^{5} स्त्रियां

Jm gives the verses in the following order: 10ab, 11cd, 11ab, 10cd.

11. Cited by *Apa* 79; *Lakṣ* 2.27; *Dev* 1.181; *Mādh* 1.474 — a) sOx^{1} sPu^{6} Tr^{2} यस्याश्च; MTr^{3} *om* न — a-b) *BhP* 7.2 सहजो न भवेद्यस्या न च विज्ञायते पिता — b) TMd^{3} अविज्ञा°; La^{1} [*cor to sh*] Lo^{3} Pu^{10} Tj^{1} Tr^{1} Wa [*Jolly* M$^{1-2}$R] *Jha Dave* वै; [*Jolly* M^{8}] वो; *Me* supports वा with gloss वाशब्दश्चेच्छब्दार्थे — c) Be^{3} नोपगच्छेत; Tr^{2} नोपयक्षेत; GMy °येच्छेत — d) Wa °शङ्किता

12.* Cited by *Viś* 1.55; *Vij* 1.56; *Jmv* 92; *Dev* 1.205–6; *Mādh* 1.493; pādas c-d cited by *Apa* 88 — a) GMd^{5} द्विजादीनां — a-b) *BhP* 7.3 ब्राह्मणानां प्रशस्ता स्यात्सवर्णा दारकर्मणि — b) TMd^{3} Tr^{2} दान° — d) GMy Ox^{3} °नामिमां; TMd^{3} °नामिमास्तु; wKt^{6} क्रमतो; Lo^{5} क्रमणे; *BhP* 7.3 *Vij Apa Jmv Dev Mādh Mandlik Jha KSS Dave* क्रमशोऽवराः; Pu^{5} क्रमशोधाः; Bo वरः; Tj^{1} वरा

13.* *ma* in Pu^{7}; pādas c-d omitted in Pu^{10}. Cited by *Apa* 87–8; *Jmv* 9.2; *Lakṣ* 2.38; *Dev* 1.206; *Mādh* 1.494 — a) *Lakṣ* शूद्रस्य भार्या शूद्रैव; NKt^{4} wKt^{6} शूद्रेव — b) *BhP* 7.6 धर्मतो मनुरब्रवीत्; Tr^{2} स्वो च विशां; Tj^{2} विंशः; GMd^{1} विश; BKt^{5} GMd^{1} स्मृतेः; Pu^{5} Pu^{7} Pu^{10} [*Jolly* M^{1-2-8} G] *Jolly* स्मृता; Ho TMd^{4} स्मृताः; *Lakṣ* स्मृतः — c) MTr^{6} ते तु; Hy स्वां; Be^{1} BBe^{2} Be^{3} TMd^{3} oOr La^{1} Pu^{5} Pu^{7} MTr^{4} MTr^{6} *Jmv Lakṣ* राज्ञस्तु; wKt^{3} राज्ञस्य; Hy Jm Jo^{1} wKt^{1} Kt^{2} GMd^{1} oMd^{2} Tj^{2} MTr^{3} *Mandlik Jolly Jha KSS Dave* राज्ञश्च — d) Bo तच्च स्वा; GMy या चाग्र°; NKt^{4} *Apa* चाग्र्य°; Tj^{1} °जन्मनिः

14. Cited by *Apa* 87; *Dev* 1.206; *Mādh* 1.495 — a) Pu^{5} Pu^{7} ब्रह्मण° — b) TMd^{3} ह; Tj^{2} च; sOx^{1} sPu^{6} हि कर्हिचित्; Tr^{2} तिष्ठतः; TMd^{4} तिष्ठति — c) TMd^{3} कस्मिंश्च न हि वृत्तान्ते — d) Bo शूद्रो; wKt^{6} GMd^{5} *Dev* शूद्र; wKt^{6} °दिश्यति; TMd^{3} °दृश्यते

हीनजातिस्त्रियं मोहादुद्वहन्तो द्विजातयः ।
कुलान्येव नयन्त्याशु ससंतानानि शूद्रताम् ॥१५॥
शूद्रावेदी पतत्यत्रेरुतथ्यतनयस्य च ।
शौनकस्य सुतोत्पत्त्या तदपत्यतया भृगोः ॥१६॥
शूद्रां शयनमारोप्य ब्राह्मणो यात्यधोगतिम् ।
जनयित्वा सुतं तस्यां ब्राह्मण्यादेव हीयते ॥१७॥
दैवपित्र्यातिथेयानि तत्प्रधानानि यस्य तु ।
नादन्ति पितृदेवास्तन्न च स्वर्गं स गच्छति ॥१८॥
वृषलीफेनपीतस्य निःश्वासोपहतस्य च ।
तस्यां चैव प्रसूतस्य निष्कृतिर्न विधीयते ॥१९॥
चतुर्णामपि वर्णानां प्रेत्येह च हिताहितान् ।
अष्टाविमान्समासेन स्त्रीविवाहान्निबोधत ॥२०॥

15. Cited by *Apa* 87; *Jmv* 9.9; *Dev* 1.207; *Mādh* 1.495 — a) Be^{1} Bo Hy wKt^{1} nKt^{4} Lo^{2} gMd^{5} sOx^{1} sPu^{6} Pu^{10} Tj^{1} Tr^{2} [*Jolly* M^{1-2-8} R N] *Jmv* [vl]हीनजातिं; bKt^{5} °जातिद्विजं — b) nKt^{4} °द्वहन्त; Pu^{10} °द्वहान्त; tMd^{3} °द्वहन्ते; wKt^{6} °द्विजन्तो — c) mTr^{3} कुल्यानेव; Ho नयत्याशु; Pu^{10} पतन्त्याशु — d) Ho °न्त्याशु सन्तानि; tMd^{3} ससन्तानि; gMd^{1} स्वसन्तानानि; Ho शूद्रतां *mc to* व्रजेत्

16. Cited by *Apa* 88; *Lakṣ* 2.41; *Jmv* 9.9; *Dev* 1.208; *Mādh* 1.495 — a-d) *BhP* 7.9 gives an expanded version: शूद्रामारोप्य शय्यां तु पतितोऽत्रिर्बभूव ह । उतथ्यः पुत्रजननात्पतितत्वमवाप्तवान् ॥ शूद्रस्य पुत्रमासाद्य शौनकः शूद्रतां गतः । भृग्वादयोऽप्येवमेव पतितत्वमवाप्नुयुः ॥ Obviously the author of the *BhP* misunderstood the verse — a) gMy शूद्रवेचन्दिपत्यत्रे°; tMd^{3} शूद्राप्रेतादिपतन्त्यत्रे°; tMd^{4} शूद्रावंशे पतत्यत्र उतथ्य°; wKt^{1} Lo^{1} पतत्यत्र उतथ्य°; gMd^{1} °त्यत्रिरुतथ्य°; wKt^{6} °त्यन्धेरुतथ्य°; Tr^{1} °त्यत्ररुतथ्य° — a-b) tMd^{4} °त्यत्र कुलस्य तनयस्य — b) gMd^{1} tMd^{3} gMd^{5} gMy Tr^{1} °त्रेरुचथ्य°; mTr^{4} °त्रेरुचर्थ्य°; Jo^{1} °त्रेरुपथ्य°; nPu^{1} वा; wKt^{1} तु — c) Jo^{1} शोनकस्य; *Lakṣ* गौतमस्य

17. Cited by *Vij* 3.265; *Apa* 87; *Jmv* 9.9; *Dev* 1.208; *Mādh* 1.495 — a) Hy शूद्राशयन° — b) tMd^{3} यान्त्यधो° — c) Tr^{2} तस्यामपत्यमुत्पाद्य; wKt^{3} सुता; Lo^{5} Pu^{10} तस्या; tMd^{4} तस्य — d) Lo^{3} °ण्यादवहीयते; gMd^{5} नश्यते

18.* Omitted in Pu^{5}. Cited by *Apa* 88 — a) Bo Lo^{3} nPu^{1} Tr^{2} Wa देव°; Tj^{1} वेद°; sOx^{1} sPu^{6} देवेपित्र्येति°; Jm °पैत्र्याति° — b) Tj^{1} न प्रधा°; La^{1} तदधीयानि; wKt^{3} तस्य; Bo यानि तु; La^{1} वै — c) Be^{1} bBe^{2} Be^{3} bCa Hy Jo^{1} Jo^{2} wKt^{1} Kt^{2} wKt^{3} bKt^{5} wKt^{6} [*but cor*] Lo^{1} Lo^{4} [*mc to*] Lo^{5} tMd^{4} nNg oOr sOx^{1} Ox^{2} nPu^{1} sPu^{6} Tj^{2} mTr^{3} mTr^{4} mTr^{6} *Apa Ku Mandlik Jha KSS Dave* नाश्नन्ति; Jm Lo^{3} Tj^{1} नश्यन्ति; mTr^{6} °देवास्तान्न; *Dev* °देवास्तं न; *Me* appears to read तम् — c-d) Tr^{2} पितृत्रिदैवास्तु न; *BhP* 7.12 पितरो देवाः न; *Apa* पितरस्तस्य न; sOx^{1} sPu^{6} °देवांस्तन्न; Pu^{7} [*Jolly* G] °देवाश्च न; Pu^{10} °देवास्तां तच्च; tMd^{4} °देवास्तु स च — d) Ho Lo^{3} *BhP* 7.12 °वास्तत्स न; Bo सर्गं; bKt^{5} wKt^{6} स्वर्गं प्रयच्छति; nKt^{4} Lo^{3} tMd^{4} Tj^{1} *BhP* 7.12 न गच्छति; Bo Pu^{8} च गच्छति

19. Cited by *Har*-A 1.27.11; *Mādh* 1.495 — a) bKt^{5} wKt^{6} वृषलीपतिफेनस्य; Tj^{2} *Me* [pāṭha] °पीतफेनस्य — b) Bo wKt^{1} nKt^{4} Tj^{1} निश्वा° — c) Ho चैवं; *Mādh* प्रसृतस्य; tMd^{3} प्रसक्तस्य — d) Hy निषूतिर्न; wKt^{1} °तिर्नाभिधीयते; Ho °तिर्नैव विद्यते

20. Cited by *Mādh* 1.485; pādas c-d cited by *Jmv* 43.4; *Dev* 1.227 — a) *BhP* 7.14 °मपि विप्रेन्द्राः — b) Hy Jm Jo^{1} Jo^{2} Kt^{2} La^{1} Lo^{3} gMy Pu^{2} Tj^{1} Tj^{2} mTr^{3} Wa [*Jolly* R] *Mādh Mandlik*

ब्राह्मो दैवस्तथैवार्षः प्राजापत्यस्तथासुरः ।
गान्धर्वो राक्षसश्चैव पैशाचश्चाष्टमोऽधमः ॥२१॥
यो यस्य धर्म्यो वर्णस्य गुणदोषौ च यस्य यौ ।
तद्वः सर्वं प्रवक्ष्यामि प्रसवे च गुणागुणान् ॥२२॥
षडानुपूर्व्या विप्रस्य क्षत्रस्य चतुरोऽवरान् ।
विट्शूद्रयोस्तु तानेव विद्याद्धर्म्यानराक्षसान् ॥२३॥
चतुरो ब्राह्मणस्याद्यान् प्रशस्तान्कवयो विदुः ।
राक्षसं क्षत्रियस्यैकमासुरं वैश्यशूद्रयोः ॥२४॥
पञ्चानां तु त्रयो धर्म्या द्वावधर्म्यौ स्मृताविह ।
पैशाचश्चासुरश्चैव न कर्तव्यौ कथंचन ॥२५॥
पृथक्पृथग्वा मिश्रौ वा विवाहौ पूर्वचोदितौ ।

Jha KSS Dave प्रेत्य चेह; NKt^{4} *om* हिता°; *BhP* 7.14 हिताहितं — c-d) *BhP* 7.14 समासतो ब्रवीम्येष विवाहाष्टकमुत्तमम् — c) NPu^{1} Pu^{8} अष्टावेतान्समा°; sOx^{1} sPu^{6} °मान्समासीन; MTr^{3} °मान्समानेन — d) Jm °विवाहं निबोधत

21. Cited by *Dev* 1.227; *Mādh* 1.485; pādas a-b cited by *Jmv* 4.3.4 — a) Tr^{2} ब्रह्मचो; BKt^{5} ब्राह्म; wKt^{6} ब्रह्म; NKt^{4} देव°; TMd^{3} दिव°; Lo^{5} दैवंस्त°; *BhP* 7.15 दैवस्तथा चार्षः; GMy दैवस्तथावार्षः; wKt^{1} दैवस्तथार्षश्च — b) NKt^{4} प्रजा° — c) wKt^{6} NPu^{1} गन्धार्वो — d) TMd^{4} पैशाचाष्टमो मतः; Pu^{7} [*but cor*] Pu^{10} पिशा°; sOx^{1} sPu^{6} [*but cor*] पैशाचाश्चा°; Bo °धमा:

22. a) GMy NNg Pu^{5} Pu^{7} MTr^{4} Wa ये यस्य; Be^{1} Pu^{10} य यस्य; NKt^{4} येस्य [*om* यो]; NKt^{4} Lo^{2} Wa धर्म्या; sOx^{1} Pu^{5} sPu^{6} Pu^{7} Pu^{10} MTr^{4} *BhP* 7.16 धर्मा; Bo BKt^{5} wKt^{6} TMd^{4} धर्मो; GMy धर्मे; Lo^{3} Tj^{1} धर्म्यः प्रसवे; Hy वर्णास्य — b) NKt^{4} °दोषोस्य च; TMd^{4} °दोषस्य यस्य; Tr^{2} °दोषस्व यस्य; NKt^{4} यस्य वे — c) TMd^{3} तद्वस्सम्यक्प्रवक्ष्यामि; Tr^{2} एतत्सम्यक्प्रवक्ष्यामि; *BhP* 7.16 शृणुध्वं तद् द्विजश्रेष्ठाः; Hy तच्च; Bo TMd^{4} तद्वत्सर्वं; Tr^{1} तत्तत्सर्वं; Jo^{2} तद्वः संप्रव° — d) GMd^{5} प्रसवो; TMd^{3} प्रसवेषु गुणा°; Bo TMd^{4} प्रसवेन गुणा°; La^{1} गुणान्गुणान्; *BhP* 7.16 गुणागुणम्

23.* Cited by *Apa* 91; *Lakṣ* 2.72; *Dev* 1.231; *Mādh* 1.487 — a) *BhP* 7.17 [vl] विप्रस्य चतुरः पूर्वान्; Pu^{10} °पूर्वा; GMd^{5} Tr^{1} MTr^{4} °पूर्व्याद्विप्रस्य; *Apa* [vl] °पूर्व्यान्विप्रस्य — b) TMd^{3} क्षत्रियस्य; *Dev* °परान् — c) Bo षट्शूद्र°; La^{1} °शूद्रस्य तु; Tr^{2} °शूद्रस्तु; La^{1} तान्येव; *BhP* 7.17 त्रीनेव — d) TMd^{3} विद्यां धर्मान्न राक्षसान्; Lo^{2} विद्या धर्म्या°; Bo oMd^{2} TMd^{3} Ox^{2} Tr^{2} *BhP* 7.17 °द्धर्मानरा°; Be^{1} BCa Jm wKt^{1} Kt^{2} oOr Pu^{5} Pu^{7} Tj^{1} [*Jolly* M$^{3-4}$ R Nd] *Rc* °द्धर्म्यान्न राक्ष°; wKt^{6} MTr^{4} °द्धर्मान्न राक्ष°; TMd^{4} °द्धर्मं न राक्ष°; MTr^{6} °द्धर्मांस्तु राक्ष°; Lo^{5} °द्धर्म्याचराक्ष°; Be^{3} NNg Pu^{5} Pu^{7} Pu^{10} [*Jolly* M$^{1-2-5-8-9}$ G N] *Nā Jolly Jha* °द्धर्म्यान्न राक्षसम्; NPu^{1} °द्धर्म्यं न राक्षसम्

24. Cited by *Dev* 1.231 — a) NKt^{4} ब्रह्मण° — b) Tr^{2} प्रशस्ता कवयो — c) TMd^{4} राक्षस्यं; Tr^{2} क्षेत्रि°; NPu^{1} °यस्यैव आसुरं; TMd^{3} °यस्यैवमासुरं — d) Tj^{1} °कमसुरं

25.* Cited by *Mādh* 1.488 — a) *BhP* 7.19 क्षत्रियाणां त्रयो; Ho *om* तु; Be^{1} BCa च; Jm Lo^{4} Lo^{5} oMd^{2} sOx^{1} sPu^{6} Pu^{10} धर्मा; Lo^{2} धन्या — b) Wa °धर्म्यो; Bo Jm wKt^{3} Lo^{4} Lo^{5} oMd^{2} sOx^{1} sPu^{6} Pu^{10} °धर्मौ; Tr^{1} °धर्म्यौ तु तौ स्मृतौ; GMy स्मृतावपि; BKt^{5} wKt^{6} स्थिताविह; Lo^{2} हि ताविह — d) Wa कर्तव्यो; Be^{1} BBe^{2} Be^{3} Bo Hy Jm Jo^{1} wKt^{1} Kt^{2} wKt^{3} NKt^{4} BKt^{5} wKt^{6} La^{1} La^{2} Lo^{2} oMd^{2} NNg oOr sOx^{1} Ox^{2} NPu^{1} Pu^{5} sPu^{6} Pu^{7} Pu^{8} Pu^{10} Tj^{2} MTr^{3} *Ku Mandlik Jolly Jha KSS Dave* कदाचन

गान्धर्वो राक्षसश्चैव धर्म्यौ क्षत्रस्य तौ स्मृतौ ॥२६॥
आच्छाद्य चार्हयित्वा च श्रुतशीलवते स्वयम् ।
आहूय दानं कन्याया ब्राह्मो धर्मः प्रकीर्तितः ॥२७॥
यज्ञे तु वितते सम्यगृत्विजे कर्म कुर्वते ।
अलंकृत्य सुतादानं दैवं धर्मं प्रचक्षते ॥२८॥
एकं गोमिथुनं द्वे वा वरादादाय धर्मतः ।
कन्याप्रदानं विधिवदार्षो धर्मः स उच्यते ॥२९॥
सहोभौ चरतां धर्ममिति वाचानुभाष्य तु ।
कन्याप्रदानमभ्यर्च्य प्राजापत्यो विधिः स्मृतः ॥३०॥
ज्ञातिभ्यो द्रविणं दत्त्वा कन्यायै चैव शक्तितः ।
कन्याप्रदानं स्वाच्छन्द्यादासुरो धर्म उच्यते ॥३१॥

26. Pāda-d omitted in BBe^{2} — a) NPu^{1} °थ्विमिश्रौ; BKt^{5} *om second* वा — b) Tr^{2} °नोदितौ — c) Bo Ho Jm गान्धर्वौ; Kt^{2} गान्धर्वा; sOx^{1} Tr^{1} गान्धर्व; oOr गन्धर्वो; BBe^{2} राक्षसश्चैवं — d) wKt^{6} धर्म्यो; TMd^{3} GMd^{5} sOx^{1} MTr^{3} धर्मौ; oMd^{2} धर्मो; TMd^{4} तं स्मृतौ

27.* Omitted in BBe^{2}. Cited by *Apa* 87; *Dev* 1.227 — a) TMd^{4} आच्छाद्याप्यर्चयित्वा; Pu^{2} वार्हयित्वा; BBe^{2} BCa Jm Jo^{1} Jo^{2} wKt^{1} Kt^{2} Lo^{4} Lo^{5} oMd^{2} Ox^{2} [*cor to*] Tj^{2} *Rn Mr Mandlik Jolly Jha KSS Dave* चार्चयित्वा; Hy वार्चयित्वा; Pu^{10} *om* च; Lo^{5} Pu^{7} [*Jolly* G] *BhP* 7.21 तु — b) Jm Jo^{1} Kt^{2} oMd^{2} GMd^{5} NPu^{1} MTr^{4} MTr^{6} *Rc Mandlik KSS* श्रुति°; Pu^{10} श्रुतः; GMy गुणशील°; TMd^{4} °शीलवति; MTr^{3} °शीलयते; Lo^{3} Tj^{1} स्मृतं — d) GMd^{6} ब्राह्मयो; Bo ब्रह्म; Ho NKt^{4} ब्रह्मो; GMd^{5} Pu^{7} Tr^{1} धर्म्यः

28. Pādas a-c omitted in BBe^{2}. Cited by *Hem* 1.684; *Dev* 1.228 — a) GMy यज्ञेपु; Jo^{2} Lo^{3} Pu^{5} Pu^{7} Tj^{1} Wa [*Jolly* G] च; La^{1} वितने; Tr^{2} वितन्ते — a-b) *BhP* 7.22 वितते चापि यज्ञे तु कर्म कुर्वति चर्त्विजि — b) oOr Pu^{5} Pu^{7} *Hem* सम्यक्कर्म कुर्वति ऋत्विजे [oOr कुर्वीत]; La^{1} सम्यक्कर्म कुर्वति चत्विति; Tj^{1} °त्विजो; NNg धर्म — c) TMd^{3} सुतांदानं — d) *BhP* दैवो धर्म उदाहृतः; BBe^{2} *om* दैवं; Ho TMd^{3} Tr^{1} दैव; GMd^{5} दैवो धर्म्यः; BKt^{5} GMy Pu^{7} MTr^{4} MTr^{6} धर्म्यं; Tr^{1} धर्म्य; Bo धर्मां; Ho धर्मे; Pu^{5} धर्म्मे; Be^{3} धर्म्यः प्रकीर्तितः; BCa NNg प्रचक्ष्यते

29. Pādas c-d omitted in Wa. Cited by *Hem* 1.684; *Dev* 1.228; pādas a-b cited by *Viś* 1.59 — a) Jm एकां; TMd^{4} एवं; NKt^{4} गोमिक्षुवं; Tj^{1} द्वेमिथुनं — b) BKt^{5} sOx^{1} वारादा°; TMd^{3} Pu^{5} वरदा°; Lo^{2} चरादा° — c) sOx^{1} sPu^{6} कन्यादानं तु विधि°; Jm °प्रधानं — d) GMy °वत्स आर्षो धर्म उच्यते; *BhP* 7.23 °वदार्षेयो धर्म उच्यते; Bo °वदार्ष; GMd^{1} Tr^{1} धर्म्यः; Be^{1} Ho धर्मः प्रकीर्तितः

After 29 wKt^{1} gives 3.32 and GMy 3.32 a-b up to कन्या°

30. Pādas a-b omitted in Wa. Cited by *Hem* 1.685; *Dev* 1.228 — a) Tr^{2} सहौभौ; oOr सहोभे; NPu^{1} सहितौ; wKt^{6} सहोतौ; Jm Kt^{2} सहनौ; Be^{3} NKt^{4} चरतं — b) NNg वाचाभिभाष्य; wKt^{6} °भाष्यते; TMd^{3} °भष्यत; sOx^{1} sPu^{6} °भाषत *both cor to* °भाष्य च; BBe^{2} Hy Jm Jo^{1} Jo^{2} Kt^{2} La^{1} La^{2} Lo^{3} Tj^{1} Tj^{2} Tr^{2} MTr^{3} [*Jolly* M^{6} R] *Mandlik Jha KSS Dave* च — c) *Hem* कन्यादानं समभ्यर्च्य — d) Jo^{1} La^{1} प्रजापत्यो; *BhP* 7.24 प्राजापत्यविधिः

31. Omitted in Pu^{5}. Cited by *Viś* 1.61; *Dev* 1.229 — a) *Dev* ज्ञातये — b) TMd^{3} GMd^{5} कन्यायै च स्वशक्तितः; TMd^{4} कन्यायैव स्वशक्तितः; Tr^{1} कन्यायास्तु स्वशक्तितः; GMy MTr^{6} कन्यायाश्च स्वशक्तितः; Ox^{3} कन्याये; *BhP* 7.25 कन्यायाश्चैव; GMd^{1} चास्य — c) *Viś* कन्यादानं तु स्वा°; TMd^{3}

इच्छयान्योन्यसंयोगः कन्यायाश्च वरस्य च ।
गान्धर्वः स तु विज्ञेयो मैथुन्यः कामसंभवः ॥३२॥
हत्वा छित्त्वा च भित्त्वा च क्रोशन्तीं रुदतीं गृहात् ।
प्रसह्य कन्याहरणं राक्षसो विधिरुच्यते ॥३३॥
सुप्तां मत्तां प्रमत्तां वा रहो यत्रोपगच्छति ।
स पापिष्ठो विवाहानां पैशाचः प्रथितोऽष्टमः ॥३४॥
अद्भिरेव द्विजाग्र्याणां कन्यादानं प्रशस्यते ।
इतरेषां तु वर्णानामितरेतरकाम्यया ॥३५॥
यो यस्यैषां विवाहानां मनुना कीर्तितो गुणः ।
सर्वं शृणुत तं विप्राः सम्यक्कीर्तयतो मम ॥३६॥
दश पूर्वापरान्वंश्यानात्मानं चैकविंशकम् ।
ब्राह्मीपुत्रः सुकृतकृन्मोचयत्येनसः पितॄन् ॥३७॥

स्वच्छ°; Tr^{2} *BhP* 7.25 °च्छन्दादासुरो

32. Cited by *Viś* 1.61; *Hem* 1.32; *Dev* 1.229 — a) Lo^{2} इच्छाया°; Lo^{3} Tj^{1} MTr^{4} MTr^{6} [*Jolly* R] °संसर्गः — b) Kt^{2} कन्यायां च; GMd^{1} कन्यायास्तु — c) Jo^{2} Lo^{3} Tj^{1} Wa [*Jolly* R] *Hem* स च; NKt^{4} GMd^{1} TMd^{3} GMd^{5} oOr Tr^{1} MTr^{4} MTr^{6} *BhP* 7.26 *Viś* स विधिर्ज्ञेयो — d) GMy sOx^{1} Pu^{5} sPu^{6} Pu^{5} Pu^{7} [*Jolly* M^{1-2-8} G] मैथुनः; Pu^{10} मैथुन; GMy °संभवं

33. Cited by *Viś* 1.61; *Lakṣ* 2.92; *Dev* 1.229 — a) TMd^{3} हित्वा; sOx^{1} sPu^{6} भित्त्वा च छित्त्वा च; NKt^{4} भित्त्वा क्रो°; Tr^{1} हित्वा च क्रो° — b) Hy Lo^{4} Ox^{3} क्रोशन्ती; Lo^{2} क्रोशतीं; Lo^{4} Ox^{3} Pu^{5} रुदती; Bo तुदन्तीं; Lo^{1} सुदतीं; BKt^{5} wKt^{6} गृहे; Wa बलात् — c) GMd^{1} प्रसह्यस्य कन्या°; Bo कन्यावरणं; MTr^{4} MTr^{6} कन्याग्रहणं; sOx^{1} sPu^{6} *Lakṣ* कन्यां हरतो — d) sOx^{1} sPu^{6} विधिराक्षस उच्यते; Tj^{1} राक्षसे

34. Cited by *Viś* 1.61; *Apa* 91; *Lakṣ* 2.94; *Hem* 1.685 — a) sOx^{1} sPu^{6} सुप्तां पत्नीं; Tj^{2} *om* मत्तां; TMd^{3} प्रमत्तां मत्तां; wKt^{6} मत्तांश्च मत्तां वा; *Hem* मत्तां रहश्छद्म; Jm प्रमत्तं; *BhP* 7.28 च — b) Lo^{3} Tj^{1} Wa [*Jolly* R] रहो वा यदि गच्छति [Wa वा यत्र]; *Hem* कृत्वा यत्रोपनीयते; sOx^{1} [*mc to*] sPu^{6} [*mc to*] *Apa* [vl as in ed] यत्रोपयच्छति; GMd^{5} यत्रावगच्छति; Jo^{2} यत्र गच्छति — c) Lo^{3} पापिष्ठे — d) Be^{3} Hy Jm Jo^{1} Kt^{2} Tj^{2} MTr^{3} *KSS* पैशाचश्चाष्टमोधमः [cf. 3.21d]; wKt^{6} पैशाचाः; Tr^{2} पृथितोष्टमः; La^{1} कीर्तितोष्टमः; wKt^{1} oOr sOx^{1} sPu^{6} *BhP* 7.28 *Apa* कथितोऽष्टमः; Pu^{10} *Mandlik Jha Dave* प्रथितोऽधमः; BKt^{5} wKt^{6} कीर्तितोधमः

35. Cited by *Lakṣ* 2.68 — a) *BhP* 7.29 जलपूर्वं द्विजा°; BBe^{2} Hy Jm wKt^{3} BKt^{5} wKt^{6} द्विजाग्राणां; Pu^{5} Pu^{7} [*Jolly* G] द्विजातीनां — b) La^{2} प्रशास्यते; GMy प्रचक्षते; Hy Jm Jo^{1} wKt^{1} Kt^{2} La^{1} Pu^{10} Tj^{2} MTr^{3} [*Jolly* M$^{1-2-3-8-9}$] *Mandlik Jha KSS Dave* विशिष्यते — c) oOr इतरे तु; Ox^{2} च; BKt^{5} wKt^{6} तु धर्म्याणामित° — d) Lo^{3} Tj^{1} [*Jolly* R] °काङ्क्षया

36. Cited by *Hem* 1.683; *Lakṣ* 2.97 — a) Tr^{1} यस्यैषां तु [*om* यो]; GMy यस्यैनां; *Hem* यश्चैषां — b) GMy कीर्तितो मनुना गुणः; TMd^{4} यमुना; *BhP* 7.30 विभूनां कीर्तितो°; Pu^{10} कीर्ततो; TMd^{4} *Lakṣ* कीर्तिता गुणाः; MTr^{6} गुणाः — c) *BhP* 7.30 तं निबोधत वै पिप्राः; Be^{3} Ho सर्वे; MTr^{4} सम्यक्शृणुत; Bo श्रुतव; NKt^{4} श्रुजत; TMd^{3} तद्विप्राः; GMd^{1} GMd^{5} वै विप्राः — d) Hy Jm Jo^{1} Kt^{2} oMd^{2} MTr^{3} *Ku Hem Mandlik KSS* सर्वं कीर्तयतो; Bo [*but cor*] Pu^{2} मया

37. Cited by *Apa* 88; *Hem* 1.683; *Lakṣ* 2.98; *Dev* 1.227 — a) Jm दशापूर्वा परावंश्या°; La^{1} पूर्वापरो वंश्या°; Jm पूर्वापरा वंश्या°; BBe^{2} Ho Hy Jo^{1} wKt^{1} Kt^{2} wKt^{3} BKt^{5} wKt^{6} Lo^{1} Lo^{3} Lo^{4} Lo^{5}

दैवोढाजः सुतश्चैव सप्त सप्त परावरान् ।
आर्षोढाजः सुतस्त्रींस्त्रीन् षट् षट् कायोढजः सुतः ॥३८॥
ब्राह्मादिषु विवाहेषु चतुर्ष्वेवानुपूर्वशः ।
ब्रह्मवर्चसिनः पुत्रा जायन्ते शिष्टसंमताः ॥३९॥
रूपसत्त्वगुणोपेता धनवन्तो यशस्विनः ।
पर्याप्तभोगा धर्मिष्ठा जीवन्ति च शतं समाः ॥४०॥
इतरेषु तु शिष्टेषु नृशंसानृतवादिनः ।
जायन्ते दुर्विवाहेषु ब्रह्मधर्मद्विषः सुताः ॥४१॥

oMd^2 oOr Ox^2 NPu^1 Pu^{10} Tj^1 Tj^2 MTr^3 [*Jolly* M$^{1-4-8-9}$ Ku R] *Hem Lakṣ Mandlik Jha KSS Dave* पूर्वान्परान्वंश्या° ; Be^1 पूर्वान्दशापरात्रात्मानं; wKt^1 GMy °रान्वंशा° ; *Dev* °रान्वर्गाना° — a-b) *BhP* 7.31 expanded version: कुलानि दश पूर्वाणि तथान्यानि दशैव तु । सहितान्यात्मना चैव मोचयत्येनसो ध्रुवम् — b) Jm °नात्मनं; wKt^6 °त्मानश्चैक° ; GMy °त्मनश्चैव विंशकं; Lo^2 चैव विंशकं; Lo^3 TMd^3 Tj^1 MTr^4 *Apa* [vl] °विंशतिं; GMd^1 °विंशकिं; MTr^6 °विंशकीं — c) Be^1 ब्राह्मय° ; Bo °पूर्वः; NPu^1 °पुत्रस्य सुकृतन्मो° ; oOr °पुत्रः कृत° ; NKt^4 सकृत° ; GMy सकृच्चैव मोच° — d) *BhP* 7.31 °कृद्दैवोडाजं सुतं शृणु; Hy Jm Jo^1 GMd^1 GMd^5 Tj^2 Tr^1 Tr^2 MTr^3 *Rc Jolly KSS* °चयेदेनसः; La^2 °चयेत्येनसः; wKt^1 MTr^6 °चयत्येनसा; oMd^2 °चयनेनसः; TMd^3 °चयदेनसः

38.* Cited by *Viś* 1.59; *Hem* 1.683; *Lakṣ* 2.98; *Dev* 1.228 — a) Hy Tr^2 देवो° ; NNg दैवौ° ; Hy Jo^2 wKt^1 BKt^5 wKt^6 Lo^2 oOr Ox^2 [*but cor sh*] Tj^1 Tj^2 [*Jolly* R N] *Dev* °ढजः; GMd^1 TMd^3 TMd^4 GMd^5 GMy Tr^1 [*Jolly* Nd] *Viś* °ढायाः; MTr^4 MTr^6 °ढायः; Be^3 NKt^4 La^1 *BhP* 7.32 [vl] *Lakṣ* °ढजासुतश्चैव [Be^3 °ढाजा]; *BhP* सुतो विप्राः — b) Lo^4 Ox^3 परापरान् [*but mc* Lo^4]; Pu^5 Pu^7 [*Jolly* G] तथावरान्; [*Jolly* Go] तथापरान्— c) Be^1 Bo Hy Jo^2 wKt^1 BKt^5 wKt^6 La^1 Lo^1 Lo^2 Lo^3 oOr sOx^1 Ox^2 [*but cor sh*] NPu^1 sPu^6 Tj^1 Tj^2 [*Jolly* R N] *Dev* °ढजः; NKt^4 *Lakṣ* °ढजा; Be^3 °ढाजा; TMd^3 TMd^4 GMd^5 GMy Tr^1 [*Jolly* Nd] *Viś* °ढायाः; MTr^4 MTr^6 °ढायः; *BhP* °ढजसुतः स्त्रीणां [vl °ढजः] — d) *BhP* पुरुषांस्तारयेद् द्विजः; *Hem* षटकं कायो° ; Ho oMd^2 Pu^{10} *om one* षट्; Lo^4 *ma one* षट्; NKt^4 कामोढजा; Ho *Mr* °ढाजः; Wa °ढजाः; MTr^4 MTr^6 °ढायः; TMd^3 [*Jolly* Nd] °ढाया; Tr^1 °ढया; Be^3 *Lakṣ* °ढजासुतः; NPu^1 Pu^{10} स्मृतः

Additional verse given in margin in Pu^1:

आर्षस्त्रिपुरुषः पुत्रो ब्राह्मण्यो दशपूरुषः ।
दैवेन सदृशः पुत्रः प्राजापत्य इति स्थितिः ॥

39.* Cited by *Apa* 117; *Hem* 1.683; *Dev* 1.230 — a) Be^1 Bo sOx^1 sPu^6 Pu^{10} ब्रह्मा° ; Ho GMd^5 Ox^2 ब्राह्मया° ; wKt^3 विवादेषु — b) Pu^5 Pu^7 चतुर्थेष्वानु° ; Tr^2 चतुर्थेष्वेवानु° ; Ox^3 चतुर्थे वानु° ; GMy चतुर्पोधनपूर्वशः — c) Be^1 BBe^2 Be^3 Bo Ho Hy Jm Jo^1 Jo^2 wKt^1 Kt^2 wKt^3 NKt^4 wKt^6 La^1 La^2 Lo^1 Lo^3 Lo^4 Lo^5 oMd^2 TMd^4 NNg oOr sOx^1 Ox^2 Ox^3 NPu^1 Pu^2 Pu^3 Pu^4 Pu^5 sPu^6 Pu^7 Pu^8 Pu^{10} Tj^1 Tj^2 Tr^2 MTr^4 MTr^6 Wa *Apa Hem Jolly KSS* °वर्चस्विनः; BKt^5 °वर्चिस्विनः; Jm पुत्रः — d) Hy जायन्तो; NPu^1 जायन्ति; MTr^3 °संमतः

40. Cited by *Apa* 117, *Hem* 1.683; *Dev* 1.230 — a) NKt^4 °सत्त्वे° ; TMd^3 °सत्त्वंबलोपेता — b) Pu^5 Pu^7 [*Jolly* G] बलवन्तो — c) *BhP* 7.34 पुत्रवन्तोऽथ धर्मिष्ठा; wKt^6 TMd^4 °भोग; MTr^3 धर्मिष्ठो — d) Tr^2 सतां; Kt^2 सतं; Bo NKt^4 समः; Lo^5 समां

41. Cited by *Apa* 117; *Hem* 1.683; *Dev* 1.230 — a) *BhP* 7.35 इतरेषु निबोधध्वं; Lo^3 TMd^4 oOr [*but cor*] NPu^1 Tj^1 Tr^2 [*Jolly* R] *Hem Apa* °रेषु च शिष्टेषु; wKt^6 °रेष्वतु शिष्टेषु; TMd^3 °रेष्वपिशिष्टेषु; Pu^{10} [*Jolly* M$^{1-2}$] °रेष्वविशिष्टेषु; Be^1 Be^3 Bo La^2 Lo^1 NNg Ox^2 Pu^5 Pu^7 Pu^8 Wa

अनिन्दितैः स्त्रीविवाहैरनिन्द्या भवति प्रजा ।
निन्दितैर्निन्दिता नृणां तस्मान्निन्द्यान्विवर्जयेत् ॥४२॥
पाणिग्रहणसंस्कारः सवर्णासूपदिश्यते ।
असवर्णास्वयं ज्ञेयो विधिरुद्वाहकर्मणि ॥४३॥
शरः क्षत्रियया ग्राह्यः प्रतोदो वैश्यकन्यया ।
वसनस्य दशा ग्राह्या शूद्रयोत्कृष्टवेदने ॥४४॥
ऋतुकालाभिगामी स्यात् स्वदारनिरतः सदा ।
पर्ववर्जं व्रजेच्चैनां तद्व्रतो रतिकाम्यया ॥४५॥
ऋतुः स्वाभाविकः स्त्रीणां रात्रयः षोडश स्मृताः ।
चतुर्भिरितरैः सार्धमहोभिः सद्विगर्हितैः ॥४६॥
तासामाद्याश्चतस्रस्तु निन्दितैकादशी च या ।
त्रयोदशी च शेषाः स्युः प्रशस्ता दश रात्रयः ॥४७॥
युग्मासु पुत्रा जायन्ते स्त्रियोऽयुग्मासु रात्रिषु ।

[*Jolly* M$^{8-9}$G] *Nd Jolly* °रेष्ववशिष्टेषु — b) GMd^{5} नृहिंसानृत°; Jm °सासत्यवादिनः; NKt^{4} °वादितः — d) *Apa* ब्राह्म°

42. Cited by *Apa* 117; *Hem* 1.683— a) La^{1} आनिन्दि°; oOr अहतैः स्त्री° — b) Jm °निन्दा; wKt^{6} जायते प्रजा; Kt^{2} Lo^{1} TMd^{4} NNg Pu^{5} Pu^{7} प्रजाः — c) oMd^{2} निन्दिता निन्दितैर्नृणां; TMd^{4} °न्दितो नृणां; Tr^{2} °न्दितां स्त्रीणां; La^{1} पुंसां — d) Bo °न्निन्द्याद्विव°; wKt^{6} °न्निन्द्यां विव°; TMd^{3} °न्निन्द्यानि विव°; TMd^{4} °न्निन्द्यांस्तु वर्जयेत्

43. Cited by *Mādh* 1.496 — a) Ho sOx^{1} °ग्रहणं; Pu^{5} °ग्रहणां; MTr^{3} °संस्कारेः — a-b) *BhP* 7.37 करग्रहणसंस्काराः सवर्णासु भवन्ति वै — b) Be^{3} BKt^{5} wKt^{6} GMy Ox^{2} [*but cor sh*] MTr^{3} °पदृश्यते — c) Ho अस्ववर्णा°; BKt^{5} wKt^{6} अस्वर्णाःस्वयं; Lo^{1} गेयो — d) Ho Jm विधिरुद्दाह°

44. Cited by *Mādh* 1.496; pādas c-d cited by *Vij* 1.62;*Apa* 92 — a) *BhP* 7.38 बाणः; Bo क्षत्रिया; wKt^{3} Lo^{2} ग्राह्याः; TMd^{3} धार्यः — b) Bo Ho Lo^{3} Lo^{4} Lo^{5} NNg Tj^{1} प्रतोदौ; TMd^{3} प्रतोदे; NKt^{4} प्रतौदो; GMy प्रदोतो; BKt^{5} प्रेतदो; wKt^{6} प्रतदो; NKt^{4} °कान्यया; Jm Wa °कन्यका — c) Pu^{10} वेसनस्य; Bo ग्राह्य — c-d) GMd^{1} TMd^{3} TMd^{4} GMd^{5} GMy Tr^{1} MTr^{4} MTr^{6} *Mādh* वासोदशा शूद्रया तु वर्णोत्कृष्टस्य वेदने [GMy विन्दते] — d) Lo^{2} शूद्रयोकष्ट°; BKt^{5} wKt^{6} °त्कृषिवेदने; Bo °वेदनं

45. Cited by *Hem* 3/3.724; *Dev* 1.41; *Mādh* 1.497; pāda-a cited by *Viś* 1.79; *Apa* 103 — a) Tr^{1} °कालानुगामी — b) MTr^{3} सदार°; NKt^{4} सदाचारनिरतः; GMy °नियतः; *Hem* °निरतः शुचिः — c) GMd^{5} °वर्ज्यं; *Dev* व्रजेदेनां; BKt^{5} wKt^{6} व्रजेत्येनां — d) NKt^{4} तद्वृतो; *Hem* न स्मृतौ रति°

46. Cited by *Dev* 1.38; *Mādh* 1.437-8 — a) Bo Hy Tr^{2} स्वभा°; GMd^{5} स्वाभाविकं — b) Be^{1} wKt^{3} पोडशः; Jm षोडशा; Jm GMd^{5} sOx^{1} स्मृतः; Bo wKt^{3} स्मृता — d) GMy सविगर्हितैः; NKt^{4} सार्द्ध-गर्हितैः; TMd^{3} तद्विगर्हितैः

47.* Cited by *Apa* 104; *Hem* 3/3.727; *Lakṣ* 3.339; *Dev* 1.38; *Mādh* 1.437-8 — a) TMd^{4} *Hem* आसामा°; Be^{1} Ho Tr^{1} °तस्रश्च — b) wKt^{3} निन्दतैका°; TMd^{4} निन्द्या एका°; Ho *Apa Hem Dev* °दशी तथा; oOr Pu^{10} °दशी यथा; sOx^{1} *om* च; Lo^{4} *ma* च; Jo^{2} Lo^{3} Pu^{5} Pu^{7} Tj^{1} Tr^{2} Wa तु — c) BKt^{5} wKt^{6} Lo^{3} sOx^{1} sPu^{6} Tj^{1} Tr^{2} तु; BKt^{5} शेषाश्च; Hy Jm Jo^{1} Kt^{2} NKt^{4} La^{1} GMd^{1} TMd^{3} TMd^{4} GMd^{5} GMy Ox^{2} [*cor to sh*] Tj^{2} MTr^{3} MTr^{4} MTr^{6} *Mandlik Jha KSS Dave* शेषास्तु

तस्माद्युग्मासु पुत्रार्थी संविशेदार्तवे स्त्रियम् ॥४८॥
पुमान्पुंसोऽधिके शुक्रे स्त्री भवत्यधिके स्त्रियाः ।
समेऽपुमान्पुंस्त्रियौ वा क्षीणेऽल्पे च विपर्ययः ॥४९॥
निन्द्यास्वष्टासु चान्यासु स्त्रियो रात्रिषु वर्जयेत् ।
ब्रह्मचार्येव भवति यत्र तत्राश्रमे वसन् ॥५०॥
न कन्यायाः पिता विद्वान् गृह्णीयाच्छुल्कमण्वपि ।
गृह्णन्हि शुल्कं लोभेन स्यान्नरोऽपत्यविक्रयी ॥५१॥
स्त्रीधनानि तु ये मोहादुपजीवन्ति बान्धवाः ।
नारीयानानि वस्त्रं वा ते पापा यान्त्यधोगतिम् ॥५२॥

48. Omitted in Hy. Cited by *Apa* 103; *Dev* 1.37; *Mādh* 1.438 — a) NKt⁴ युग्मास्तु; Jm युग्मांसु — c) GMy पुत्रार्थं — d) NKt⁴ BKt⁵ wKt⁶ Lo² Ox³ संवसेदा°; Tr² °दार्तवं; Tj¹ °दार्तवौ; Kt² °दार्दवे; Ho °दार्तये स्त्रियः; Be³ Lo² Tr² स्त्रियां; sPu⁶ [*but cor*] स्त्रियः

49. Cited by *Dev* 1.40; *Mādh* 1.499; pāda a-b cited by *Vij* 2.117; pāda-a by *Viś* 1.79— a) TMd³ पुमान्पुंसे; Be¹ युग्मात्पुंसो; Lo³ TMd³ TMd⁴ Tj¹ Tr¹ MTr⁴ *Dev Viś* शुक्ले; GMd⁵ शुक्ल्ये; [*Jolly* Gr] शुद्धे — b) GMy भवत्याधिके; oOr भवेदधिके; sOx¹ sPu⁶ भवेदाधिके; Tr² रोजोभ्यधिके; TMd⁴ °त्यतिके; Bo GMd⁵ Pu⁵ Pu⁷ Pu¹⁰ *Dev* स्त्रियः; Lo² TMd³ स्त्रिया — c) *Me* [pāṭha] साम्ये; BBe² Lo⁵ TMd³ oOr NPu¹ °स्त्रियो; BKt⁵ wKt⁶ Lo⁴ Tj² °स्त्रियोर्वा — d) Hy क्षीने चैव विप°; Be³ *om* च; BBe² Ho BKt⁵wKt⁶ तु

Addition verse in GMd⁵ [*Jolly* Gr]:

तस्माच्छुक्लविशुद्ध्यर्थं स्निग्धं वृष्यं च योजयेत् ।
लघ्वाहाराः स्त्रियः कुर्यादेवं स जनयेत्सुतम् ॥

a) [*Jolly* Gr] तस्माच्छुद्ध° — b) [*Jolly* Gr] प्रियं च — c) [*Jolly* Gr] लव्धाहारां स्त्रियं — d) GMd⁵ सञ्जनये°

50.* Pādas c-d omitted in Pu¹⁰. Cited by *Viś* 1.79 — a) oMd² sOx¹ sPu⁶ निन्द्यास्वन्यासु चाष्टासु; wKt¹ नित्यासु यासु चान्यासु; Tr² निन्द्याषष्टासुथान्यासु; NKt⁴ निन्द्यास्वेतासु; TMd³ °ष्टसु; Bo वान्यासु — b) Bo रात्रीषु; Be¹ BBe² Be³ [*cor to*] BCa Hy Jm Jo¹ Jo² wKt¹ Kt² NKt⁴ Lo¹ Lo² Lo⁴ Lo⁵ oMd² TMd³ Ox³ Pu⁸ Tr¹ MTr³ वर्जयन् — d) Tj² कुत्राश्रमे; GMyयत्राश्रमे; Wa वसेत्

Additonal verse in Ho oOr; placed after 3.54 in TMd⁴:

ऋतुकाले तु यो दारान्संनिधौ नोपगच्छति ।
तस्या रजसि तं मासं पितरस्तस्य शेरते ॥

a) Ho °कालेषु; oOr भार्यां संनिधौ — c) TMd⁴ तस्या रेतांसि मासं च — c-d) oOr यदेनो ब्रह्महत्यायाः स तत्प्राप्नोति मानवः

51. Cited by *Lakṣ* 2.88; *Jmv* 4.3.24; *Dev* 1.232 — a)sOx¹ sPu⁶ कन्याया; Pu⁵ Pu⁷ *Dev* कन्यया:; Jo¹ कन्यायः — c) sOx¹ sPu⁶ गृह्णन्ति; Hy Jo¹ Kt² La¹ oMd² TMd³ Pu¹⁰ Tj² [*Jolly* M¹⁻²⁻⁸⁻⁹] *Dev Mandlik Jha KSS Dave* गृह्णञ्छुल्कं हि [La¹ च; TMd³ तु]; Jm गृह्णत शुल्कं हि; Be¹ कुलोभेन; BBe² मोहेन — d) La¹ भवेत्सोऽपत्य°; TMd³ °विक्रयं; GMd⁵ GMy [*Jolly* Gr] insert here 9.98 and 100; Tr¹ inserts 9.98a-b, 100a-b, 98c-d, and 100c-d.

52. a) Pu⁵ Pu⁷ च ये; Lo⁴ *ma* ये; Be³ wKt⁶ La¹ GMy oOr [*but cor fh*] Ox² [*but cor sh*] यो; sOx¹ sPu⁶ Tr² लोभादुप° — b) TMd³ °दुपभुङ्क्ते — c) Lo² sOx¹ sPu⁶ Tr¹ [*Jolly* N Nd] नारीर्यानानि; wKt¹ नारीयान्नानि; GMy नारीयुतानि; oOr यास्त्रीयानानि; TMd³ La¹ वस्त्रां; wKt⁶ वस्त्रानि [*om* वा]; Lo¹ च

आर्षे गोमिथुनं शुल्कं केचिदाहुर्मृषैव तत् ।
अल्पोऽप्येवं महान्वापि विक्रयस्तावदेव सः ॥५३॥
यासां नाददते शुल्कं ज्ञातयो न स विक्रयः ।
अर्हणं तत्कुमारीणामानृशंस्यं च केवलम् ॥५४॥
पितृभिर्भ्रातृभिश्चैताः पतिभिर्देवरैस्तथा ।
पूज्या भूषयितव्याश्च बहु कल्याणमीप्सुभिः ॥५५॥
यत्र नार्यस्तु पूज्यन्ते रमन्ते तत्र देवताः ।
यत्रैतास्तु न पूज्यन्ते सर्वास्तत्राफलाः क्रियाः ॥५६॥
शोचन्ति जामयो यत्र विनश्यत्याशु तत्कुलम् ।
न शोचन्ति तु यत्रैता वर्धते तद्धि सर्वदा ॥५७॥

— d) Pu^{10} °धोगतिः; tMd^{3} °धोमुखं

53.* Cited by *Dev* 1.231 — a) sOx^{1} sPu^{6} आर्षं; Lo^{5} आर्षो— c) wKt^{3} nNg स्वल्पो; Tj^{1} अन्येप्येवं; Jo^{2} अन्योप्येवं; Tr^{2} *Dev* अल्पोपि वा महा° [Tr^{2} अल्पेपि]; Lo^{1} tMd^{3} gMy Ox^{2} *BhP* 7.41 अल्पो वापि महा°; nKt^{4} Wa °प्येव; Be^{3} Lo^{2} [*cor to*] महन्वापि; sOx^{1} महद्वापि — d) Be^{1} Jo^{2} bKt^{5} wKt^{6} La^{2} Lo^{3} Lo^{4} Lo^{5} gMy sOx^{1} Ox^{2} Ox^{3} Pu^{2} Pu^{4} sPu^{6} Pu^{8} Pu^{10} Tj^{1} Tr^{2} Wa [*Jolly* M R] *Me Rc Jha Dave* तावानेव स विक्रयः [bKt^{5} Tr^{2} तावदेव; wKt^{6} तावतैव; wKt^{6} विक्रियः]; nNg as in ed. but *mc* to तावानेव स विक्रयः with the comment इति पाठः; nKt^{4} विक्रयास्ता°; oOr विक्रियस्ता°; tMd^{3} °स्तावतैव

Additional verses in gMd^{1} tMd^{4} gMd^{5} gMy oOr Tr^{1} mTr^{4} mTr^{6} [cf. 9.42]:

अत्र गाथा यमोद्गीताः कीर्तयन्ति पुराविदः ।
यथान्योऽपि न विक्रेयः पुरुषः किं पुनः प्रजाः ॥१॥
यो मनुष्यो मनुष्यं हि विक्रीय धनमिच्छति ।
तस्य मूत्रं पुरीषं च स परत्रोपजीवति ॥२॥

1. a) gMd^{1} oOr mTr^{4} mTr^{6} गाथां यमोद्गीतां; gMy यमोद्गीता; tMd^{4} वायुगीता — c) mTr^{4} *om* न; mTr^{6} विक्रयः — d) mTr^{6} प्रजा

2. a-b) gMd^{1} मनुष्यः [lacuna] शोधनमिच्छति; gMd^{5} मनुष्यस्य विक्रयाद्धन° — b) mTr^{4} विक्रयन्नधिगच्छति; tMd^{4} विक्रीणान्धनमिच्छति — c) gMd^{1} कस्य; tMd^{4} mTr^{4} मूत्रपुरीषं

54. Cited by *Dev* 1.233 — a) mTr^{4} तासां — b) gMd^{5} ज्ञातये; sOx^{1} sPu^{6} ज्ञायते; Pu^{8} ज्ञातयोरसंविक्रयः; nKt^{4} न समविक्रयः — c) tMd^{3} अर्हणस्तत्कुमा°; Pu^{10} [*Jolly* M$^{1-2-8-9}$] तु कुमा° — d) gMy °णामनृशंस्यं; Pu^{5} Pu^{7} °शंसं; Be^{1} oOr Pu^{5} Pu^{7} [*Jolly* G] तु

Additional verse in tMd^{4}: same as added verse after 3.50.

55. Cited by *Dev* 3.570; *Mādh* 1.505 — a) Tr^{2} पितृभिर्मातृभि°; bBe^{2} °भिश्चैता; bKt^{5} wKt^{6} Lo^{1} Lo^{4} Lo^{5} tMd^{3} nPu^{1} °भिश्चैव; Ox^{3} °भिश्चैवं — b) tMd^{3} °श्चैव ताः पतिर्वेवकैस्तथा — c) Tj^{2} पूज्या च भूषितव्या च; gMd^{1} पूज्याः पूजयितव्याश्च; Tr^{1} हर्षयितव्याश्च; sOx^{1} sPu^{6} °तव्या च — d) Tr^{2} बहुकन्यामभीप्सुभिः

56. Cited by *Apa* 107; *Lakṣ* 12.610; *Dev* 3.571; *Mādh* 1.505 — a) bKt^{5} wKt^{6} नार्याश्च; *Apa* नार्यः प्रपूज्यन्ते — b) Pu^{10} *om* रमन्ते; Pu^{5} Pu^{7} [*Jolly* G] रमन्ति; Be^{1} देवता — c) sOx^{1} sPu^{6} यत्रैता न हि पूज्यन्ते; wKt^{3} यत्रैताश्च; *Dev* यत्र तास्तु — d) Pu^{10} सर्वानिफलाः क्रियाः; mTr^{3} सर्वास्तथाफलाः; gMd^{1} gMd^{5} Tr^{1} [*Jolly* Nd] सर्वास्तस्याफलाः; tMd^{3} gMy सर्वास्तस्याःफलाः; gMy प्रजाः

57. Cited by *Lakṣ* 12.610; *Dev* 3.571; *Mādh* 1.506 — a) Pu^{10} शोचयन्ति; Tj^{1} Wa शौचन्ति; Be^{1} bBe^{2} bCa wKt^{1} wKt^{3} nKt^{4} bKt^{5} wKt^{6} Lo^{4} Lo^{5} oOr Ox^{2} Ox^{3} Pu^{8} Pu^{10} Tr^{2} यामयो; sOx^{1} sPu^{6}

जामयो यानि गेहानि शपन्त्यप्रतिपूजिताः ।
तानि कृत्याहतानीव विनश्यन्ति समन्ततः ॥५८॥
तस्मादेताः सदाभ्यर्च्या भूषणाच्छादनाशनैः ।
भूतिकामैर्नरैर्नित्यं सत्कारेषूत्सवेषु च ॥५९॥
संतुष्टो भार्यया भर्ता भर्त्रा भार्या तथैव च ।
यस्मिन्नेतत्कुले नित्यं कल्याणं तत्र वै ध्रुवम् ॥६०॥
यदि हि स्त्री न रोचेत पुमांसं न प्रमोदयेत् ।
अप्रमोदात्पुनः पुंसः प्रजनं न प्रवर्तते ॥६१॥
स्त्रियां तु रोचमानायां सर्वं तद्रोचते कुलम् ।
तस्यां त्वरोचमानायां सर्वमेव न रोचते ॥६२॥
कुविवाहैः क्रियालोपैर्वेदानध्ययनेन च ।

जोमयो; Lo^1 ज्यामयो; *Dev* योपितो — b) Kt^2 विनश्यन्त्याशु; GMd^1 विनश्येत्याशु; BKt^5 wKt^6 तत्फलं — c) Tr^2 न च शोचन्ति यत्रैता; Lo^3 Tj^1 शोचन्त्यत्तु; NKt^4 *om* तु; oOr *ma* तु; BBe^2 wKt^1 La^1 Lo^4 Lo^5 TMd^3 Ox^3 Pu^{10} च; Ho wKt^3 यत्र ता — d) BKt^5 wKt^6 वर्धन्ते; Lo^3 Tj^1 वर्तते; TMd^4 Tr^1 *Dev* तत्र सर्वदा

58. Not commented by *Me;* omitted in Lo^4 Lo^5 Ox^3 Pu^{10}. Cited by *Apa* 107; *Lakṣ* 12.610; *Mādh* 1.506 — a) Be^1 BBe^2 BCa wKt^1 wKt^3 wKt^6 oMd^2 Ox^2 Tr^2 यामयो — b) Tr^2 सापत्याः नतिपूजिताः; sOx^1 sPu^6 पश्यन्त्य°; wKt^6 सपत्न्यः प्रति°; Jm °पतिपूजिता — c) Lo^1 °हतानि च — d) MTr^6 विनश्यति

59.* Not commented by *Me;* omitted in Lo^4 Lo^5 Ox^3 Pu^{10}. Cited by *Lakṣ* 12.610; *Mādh* 1.506 — a) NNg तस्मादेनाः; wKt^3 सदात्यर्च्या; Be^1 wKt^1 BKt^5 wKt^6 Lo^3 GMd^1 TMd^3 GMd^5 GMy sPu^6 Tj^1 MTr^4 MTr^6 [*Jolly* R] समभ्यर्च्या; Be^3 Hy Jm Jo^1 Kt^2 La^1 oMd^2 Tj^2 MTr^3 [*Jolly* Ku] *Ku Mandlik KSS Dave* सदा पूज्या — b) Lo^3 Tj^1 *Mādh* °दनादिभिः — c) BBe^2 °मैर्नरो नित्यं — d) Pu^5 Pu^7 [*Jolly* G] संकरेषू°; wKt^3 सत्कालेषू°; NKt^4 Lo^2 GMd^1 TMd^3 GMd^5 NNg Ox^2 [*but cor sh*] Tr^1 Tr^2 MTr^4 MTr^6 Wa [*Jolly* N Nd] *Nā* सत्कारेणोत्स°; *Nā* gives reading of edition as a pāṭha.

60. Not commented by *Me;* omitted in Lo^4 Lo^5 Ox^3 Pu^{10}. Cited by *Lakṣ* 12.613; *Dev* 3.581; *Mādh* 1.506 — a) Bo संतुष्टा — b) Kt^2 भर्ता भार्या; GMd^5 Tr^2 भार्या भर्त्रा; Bo तथैव सा — c) Jm Jo^1 Kt^2 GMd^1 oMd^2 GMd^5 Tj^2 MTr^3 *Mādh Mandlik Jolly KSS Dave* यस्मिन्नेव कुले — d) GMy कल्याणं भवति ध्रुवं; Bo तत्र ये; oOr तत्रैवं ध्रुवं

61. Not commented by *Me;* omitted in Lo^4 Lo^5 Ox^3 Pu^{10}. Cited by *Lakṣ* 12.613; *Dev* 3.581 — a) GMd^5 यदा; Tr^2 यत्र; Hy Jo^2 Pu^5 Pu^7 ह; Ho रोचेत्तु; Tj^1 रोचेन; Hy रोचत — b) Tr^2 प्रमोदयत्; Wa प्रमोदते; TMd^3 प्ररोचयेत् — c) TMd^3 Wa अप्रमादा° — d) BBe^2 BCa wKt^1 BKt^5 wKt^6 Lo^3 Tj^1 प्रजनो; wKt^3 प्रजना; Hy *om* न; Ho न निवर्तते; wKt^6 न वर्तते; Lo^3 Tj^1 प्रवर्धते

Additional verse in *Mandlik* [त] *KSS Dave;* placed after 3.60b in GMd^1 GMd^5:

यदा भर्ता च भार्या च परस्परवशानुगौ ।
तदा धर्मार्थकामानां त्रयाणामिह संगतिः ॥

d) *Mandlik KSS Dave* °णामपि संगतं

62. Not commented by *Me;* omitted in Lo^4 Lo^5 Ox^3 Pu^5 Pu^{10}; pādas c-d omitted in GMy. Cited by *Lakṣ* 12.613; *Dev* 3.581 — a) Tr^2 हि — c) Ho NKt^4 तस्या; MTr^6 अस्यां; *Dev* तस्यामरोच°; Tr^1 अस्यां चारोच°; Jm तु रोच°; BBe^2 न रोच° — d) oMd^2 सर्वमेवं; Tr^1 सर्वं चैव; Be^1 तु रोचते

कुलान्याशु विनश्यन्ति* ब्राह्मणातिक्रमेण च ॥६३॥
शिल्पेन व्यवहारेण शूद्रापत्यैश्च केवलैः ।
गोभिरश्वैश्च यानैश्च कृष्या राजोपसेवया ॥६४॥
अयाज्ययाजनैश्चैव नास्तिक्येन च कर्मणाम् ।
कुलान्यकुलतां यान्ति यानि हीनानि मन्त्रतः ॥६५॥
मन्त्रतस्तु समृद्धानि कुलान्यल्पधनान्यपि ।
कुलसंख्यां च गच्छन्ति कर्षन्ति च महद्यशः ॥६६॥
वैवाहिकेऽग्नौ कुर्वीत गृह्यं कर्म यथाविधि ।
पञ्चयज्ञविधानं च पक्तिं चान्वाहिकीं गृही ॥६७॥
पञ्च सूना गृहस्थस्य चुल्ली पेषण्युपस्करः ।
कण्डनी चोदकुम्भश्च बध्यते यास्तु वाहयन् ॥६८॥

63.* Not commented by *Me;* omitted in Lo^4 Lo^5 Ox^3 Pu^{10}. Cited by *Dev* 1.232 — a) *Dev* दुर्विवाहैः; GMy कुविवाहे; BKt^5 wKt^6 कुविवाह; Bo स्त्रियालो°; Lo^1 कृपालो° — b) Lo^2 °लोपैर्वेदाध्ययनमेव च — c) Be^1 BBe^2 Bo Ho Hy Jm Jo^1 Jo^2 wKt^3 wKt^5 wKt^6 La^2 Lo^1 Lo^2 Lo^3 oMd^2 Ox^2 Pu^2 Pu^4 Pu^5 Pu^7 Pu^8 Tj^1 Tj^2 *Dev Mandlik Jolly KSS Dave Rn* कुलान्यकुलतां यान्ति — d) *Dev* ब्राह्मण्याति°

64. Not commented by *Me;* omitted in Lo^4 Lo^5 Ox^3 Pu^{10}. Cited by *Dev* 1.208 — a) sOx^1 sPu^6 शिल्पसंव्यवहारैश्च — c) TMd^3 Tr^1 MTr^6 [*Jolly* Gr] गोभिरुष्ट्रैश्च — d) Tr^2 कृष्यै; GMd^5 कृष्ये; Kt^2 BKt^5 कृष्य; Be^1 राज्ञोप°

65.* Not commented by *Me;* omitted in Lo^4 Lo^5 Ox^3 Pu^{10}. Cited by *Lakṣ* 2.333; *Dev* 1.208 — a) sOx^1 sPu^6 °जनैश्च; Pu^5 Pu^7 [*Jolly* G] °जनेनैव; *Lakṣ* °जनं चैव; TMd^3 [*Jolly* Nd] °जनैश्चैतैर्नास्ति° — b) BKt^5 Lo^1 नास्तिकेन; wKt^6 नास्तिकोन; sOx^1 sPu^6 नास्तिक्येनैव; Be^3 wKt^1 NKt^4 Lo^1 TMd^3 GMy NNg Ox^2 NPu^1 Pu^5 Pu^7 Tj^1 कर्मणा; GMd^1 कर्मसु; La^1 धर्मणा — c) Be^1 BBe^2 Ho Hy Jm Jo^1 wKt^1 Kt^2 wKt^3 BKt^5 wKt^6 La^2 Lo^1 oMd^2 sOx^1 NPu^1 Pu^2 Pu^4 Pu^5 sPu^6 Pu^7 Tj^2 MTr^3 *Dev Mandlik Jolly KSS Dave* कुलान्याशु विनश्यन्ति [Pu^5 कुल्या°] — d) BKt^5 wKt^6 यानि मन्त्राणि हीनतः; oOr मन्त्रितः; Bo सर्वतः

66. Not commented by *Me;* omitted in Lo^4 Lo^5 Ox^3 Pu^{10}. Cited by *Viś* 1.54 — a) TMd^3 मन्त्रवन्ती; sOx^1 sPu^6 विशुद्धानि — b) Pu^5 Pu^7 कुल्या°; wKt^3 कुलाल्पध°; wKt^1 wKt^3 wKt^6 TMd^3 Tr^1 °धनानि च — c) wKt^6 कुलं; NNg °संख्यं; GMy °संख्याश्च; wKt^1 यच्छन्ति — d) Bo कर्षती; Lo^1 कुर्वन्ति; Tr^2 चर्षन्ति; *Viś* प्राप्नुवन्ति मह°; Ox^2 [*but cor sh*] कर्षं च सुमह°

67. Omitted in Lo^5 Pu^{10}. Cited by *Hem* 3/2.1329; *Lakṣ* 2.114; *Dev* 2.571 — a) wKt^1 wKt^6 Tr^1 MTr^4 MTr^6 *BhP* 164 वैवाहिकाग्नौ; *Hem* औपासानाग्नौ; oOr प्रकुर्वीत — b) Lo^2 sOx^1 sPu^6 *Lakṣ Dev* गृह्य; Jo^2 La^1 Lo^1 Lo^3 TMd^4 GMd^5 GMy Ox^2 [*but cor sh*] Pu^8 Tj^1 Tr^1 Wa [*Jolly* N] गार्ह्यं; Be^1 गर्ह्यं; Ho गाह्यं; Tr^2 ग्राह्यं; Bo कार्यं कर्म; Jm चर्म; Be^1 तथाविधि; Wa °विधिं — c) *Hem* पञ्चयज्ञान्नपक्तिं च; sOx^1 पञ्चगव्य°; *BhP* 16.4 तु — d) *Hem* यच्चान्यद्गृह्यकृत्यकम्; *BhP* 16.4 पक्तिं कुर्यात्सदा गृही; Jo^2 wKt^1 BKt^5 Lo^2 GMd^1 TMd^3 GMd^5 GMy MTr^4 MTr^6 पंक्तिं; Tj^1 पंक्ति; Lo^3 पांक्तिं; *Lakṣ* पक्तिरन्वा°; La^1 वान्वा°; Tr^1 चान्नाहिकीं; Hy Tj^1 °हिकी; Jm °हकीं; Wa °हिकां; TMd^3 °हिकं; NKt^4 Lo^2 Lo^4 GMd^1 Ox^3 गृहे

68. Cited by *Lakṣ* 3.143 — a) wKt^1 शूना; MTr^3 सूनां — b) *BhP* 16.5 तेन स्वर्गं न गच्छति; Tj^1

तासां क्रमेण सर्वासां निष्कृत्यर्थं महर्षिभिः ।
पञ्च कॢप्ता महायज्ञाः प्रत्यहं गृहमेधिनाम् ॥६९॥
अध्यापनं ब्रह्मयज्ञः पितृयज्ञस्तु तर्पणम् ।
होमो दैवो बलिर्भौतो नृयज्ञोऽतिथिपूजनम् ॥७०॥
पञ्चैतान्यो महायज्ञान्न हापयति शक्तितः ।
स गृहेऽपि वसन्नित्यं सूनादोषैर्न लिप्यते ॥७१॥
देवतातिथिभृत्यानां पितॄणामात्मनश्च यः ।
न निर्वपति पञ्चानामुच्छ्वसन्न स जीवति ॥७२॥
अहुतं च हुतं चैव तथा प्रहुतमेव च ।
ब्राह्म्यं हुतं प्राशितं च पञ्च यज्ञान्प्रचक्षते ॥७३॥

चुल्लि; wKt^{6} चुल्लो; NNg Ox^{3} Pu^{5} Pu^{7} Pu^{10} चुल्ही; Lo^{2} चुल्हि; MTr^{6}पुल्ली; Tr^{1} पेषस्युप°; wKt^{6} पेषभ्युप°; GMd^{5} °ण्यपस्करं ; MTr^{6} °ण्युपस्करं — c) wKt^{1} कन्दनी; Be^{1} [*but cor*] NKt^{4} TMd^{4} GMy sOx^{1} sPu^{6} MTr^{4} MTr^{6} खण्डनी; Tr^{1} खण्डिनी; GMd^{5} खण्डानि; wKt^{6} कण्डली; TMd^{3} खंतिनी; MTr^{3} अण्डनि; Tj^{2} चोपकु°; NKt^{4} चेवकु°; TMd^{3} GMd^{5} Tr^{1} MTr^{4} MTr^{6} चैव कुम्भश्च [MTr^{6} कुंम्भं च; GMd^{5} °कुम्भ्यश्च]; Kt^{2} Tr^{2} °कुम्भं च; sOx^{1} sPu^{6} °कुम्भी च; TMd^{4} °कुम्भस्य — c-d) *BhP* 16.5 कण्डनी पेषणी चुल्ली उदकुम्भः प्रमार्जनी [vl °कुम्भीः] — d) TMd^{3} बाध्यते; GMd^{5} बाध्यन्ते; oOr बधन्ते; GMd^{1} GMy वध्यते; *Lakṣ* वधन्ते; Pu^{10} बध्यन्तेन्यास्तु; Wa योस्तु; Jo^{2} Pu^{5} Pu^{7} तास्तु; wKt^{1} NKt^{4} BKt^{5} wKt^{6} याश्च; Bo Ho Lo^{1} Lo^{4} Ox^{3} यस्तु; MTr^{4} यं तु; NPu^{1} वाहयत्; TMd^{3} वाहयेत्; GMy पाचयन्; TMd^{4} हापयन्

69. Cited by *Lakṣ* 3.143 — a) GMy Tr^{1} MTr^{4} *BhP* 16.6 *Lakṣ* आसां; wKt^{6} पूर्वासां — a-b) GMy सर्वेषामनिष्कृत्यं मह° — b) Ox^{3} निकृ°; sPu^{6} महर्पभिः; sOx^{1} महार्पभिः; TMd^{3} *BhP* 16.6 मनीषिभिः — c) *BhP* 16.6 पञ्चोद्दिष्टा महायज्ञाः; TMd^{4} पञ्चसूना; GMy क्लृप्त; sOx^{1} sPu^{6} क्लिप्ता

70. Cited by *Dev* 2.562–3 — a) TMd^{3} TMd^{4} MTr^{6} अध्यायनं; Tr^{1} अध्ययनं; wKt^{6} महायज्ञः — b) *BhP* 16.7 °यज्ञश्च; TMd^{4} °यज्ञं तु — c) GMy होमो दैवो भूतबलिं; La^{1} होम; Jm हौमौ; sOx^{1} sPu^{6} MTr^{4} MTr^{6} दैवो होमो; Pu^{5} Pu^{7} देवो; Tj^{1} बलिभौतो; TMd^{3} बलिर्भूतो; Pu^{10} बलिर्भौमो; oOr बलिभुजो; BKt^{5} बलिर्भोक्तो; wKt^{6} बलिर्भोक्ता — c-d) *BhP* 16.7 बलिर्भौमस्तथान्योऽतिथिपूजनम् — d) Tr^{1} °तिथिभोजनं

71. a) Lo^{1} पञ्चैतांश्च महा°; Tr^{1} पञ्चैतानि महा° — b) GMy °यज्ञानर्हापयति; Lo^{1} पहायति — c) Bo TMd^{3} स्वगृहेपि; wKt^{6} गृहोपि; Bo oOr sOx^{1} sPu^{6} MTr^{4} MTr^{6} वसेन्नित्यं; GMd^{5} वसन्विप्रस्सूना° — d) Wa सूनोदो°; Pu^{10} शूनादो°

72. Omitted in MTr^{3}. Cited by *Apa* 146; *Dev* 2.595 — a) Lo^{5} दैवातिथि°; TMd^{3} [*Jolly* Nd] °तिथिभूतानां — a-b) *Me* [pāṭha] देवतातिथिभृत्येभ्यः पितृभ्यश्चात्मने तथा — c) BKt^{5} निर्वपन्ति; *Me* [pāṭha] पञ्चभ्यः — d) GMy °मुच्छ्वासन्न; TMd^{4} °मुत्स्वजन्न; *BhP* 16.9 °सन्न च; Bo °सन्निव जीवति; Lo^{1} °सन्नपि जीवति

73. The section 3.73–117 is omitted in [*Jolly* M^{5}]; pādas c-d omitted in Lo^{3} Tj^{1}. Cited by *Apa* 142 — a) Pu^{10} अहुतं प्रहुतं चैव; Bo Ho आहुतं; GMy अहुतश्च; NKt^{4} wKt^{6} वा — b) Ho प्रहुतमेवमेव च; Lo^{4} NNg [*but cor*] Ox^{3} प्राहुत°; Lo^{1} after तथा jumps to verse 74b [haplo] — c) Be^{1} BCa wKt^{3} NKt^{4} wKt^{6} Lo^{2} TMd^{3} GMd^{5} GMy NNg sOx^{1} Ox^{2} Ox^{3} sPu^{6} Pu^{10} Tr^{1} MTr^{4} [*Jolly* M$^{1-2-5-8-9}$ Me N Nd] *Apa* ब्राह्मं; Bo ब्रह्मं; La^{1} ब्राह्मयाहुतं; GMd^{1} ब्रह्मयाहुतं; Hy ब्रह्मयहुतं; Lo^{1} ब्रह्माहुतं — d) Tr^{1} पाञ्चयज्ञा°; GMy पाकयज्ञा°; MTr^{4} यज्ञं प्रशाक्षते; *Apa* यज्ञाः प्रकीर्तिताः

जपोऽहुतो हुतो होमः प्रहुतो भौतिको बलिः ।
ब्राह्म्यं हुतं द्विजाग्र्यार्चा प्राशितं पितृतर्पणम् ॥७४॥
स्वाध्याये नित्ययुक्तः स्याद् दैवे चैवेह कर्मणि ।
दैवे कर्मणि युक्तो हि बिभर्तीदं चराचरम् ॥७५॥
अग्नौ प्रास्ताहुतिः सम्यगादित्यमुपतिष्ठते ।
आदित्याज्जायते वृष्टिर्वृष्टेरन्नं ततः प्रजाः ॥७६॥
यथा वायुं समाश्रित्य सर्वे जीवन्ति जन्तवः ।
तथा गृहस्थमाश्रित्य वर्तन्त इतराश्रमाः ॥७७॥
यस्मात् त्रयोऽप्याश्रमिणो ज्ञानेनान्नेन चान्वहम् ।
गृहस्थैरेव धार्यन्ते तस्माज्ज्येष्ठाश्रमो गृही ॥७८॥

74. Cited by *Apa* 142 — a) wKt[6] तपोहुतो; Ox[3] पतोहुतो; NPu[1] जपो हुतोऽहुतो; Hy *om* होमः; Ho होमो; wKt[6] मोहः — b) Be[1] प्रहृतो; Ox[3] प्राहुतो होतिको; Wa भौमिको; TMd[3] भौतियो — c) Be[1] BCa wKt[3] NKt[4] wKt[6] TMd[3] GMd[5] GMy NNg sOx[1] Ox[2] Pu[5] sPu[6] Pu[10] Tr[1] MTr[4] [*Jolly* M[1–2–5–8–9] Me N Nd] *Apa* ब्राह्मं; Ox[3] ब्राह्मां; Lo[2] ब्रह्मां; GMd[1] ब्राह्मयाहुतं; wKt[6] गतं द्विजा°; GMy द्विजाग्र्याच्र्या; NNg द्विजाग्र्याच्र्य; Be[1] द्विजाग्रार्चा; Kt[2] द्विजाभ्यार्चा; BKt[5] द्विजानर्च्यः; wKt[6] द्विजानर्चाः; TMd[3] द्विजाग्र्याच्च; Tj[1] द्विजोग्र्याणां; Lo[3] द्विजाग्र्याणां

75. Cited by *Lakṣ* 3.148–9 — a) Bo स्वाध्यायो; TMd[3] GMy चैव युक्तः; BKt[5] wKt[6] °युक्तिः — b) Lo[4] Lo[5] Pu[7] *Lakṣ Go* दैवे पित्र्ये च कर्मणि [Lo[4] Lo[5] देवे] — c) Pu[5] Pu[7] *Go* उभयत्रापि युक्तो हि; Wa उभयत्रापि संयुक्तो; Ho Jm Jo[1] Kt[2] Tj[1] Tr[1] MTr[6] *Mandlik Jha KSS Dave* दैवकर्मणि; Bo देवे कर्मणि; Jo[2] Lo[3] Tj[1] Tj[2] संयुक्तो [*om* हि]; BKt[5] wKt[6] युक्तोपि — d) Lo[4] Lo[5] बिभर्तीवं; *Lakṣ* चराचरैः

76. Cited by *Apa* 994 — a) sOx[1] Ox[3] sPu[6] प्राप्ताहुतिः; oOr प्रशस्ताहुतिः; GMy प्रशस्ताहुतिभिस्सम्य°; MTr[4] °हुतः — b) La[1] sOx[1] Ox[3] NPu[1] sPu[6] Pu[10] Wa °तिष्ठति; NKt[4] Lo[2] Lo[5] GMd[1] TMd[4] °गच्छति — d) Lo[2] °ष्टेरेतं ततः

77.* a) GMd[1] TMd[3] TMd[4] GMd[5] GMy Tr[1] MTr[4] MTr[6] [*Jolly* Nd Gr] यथा मातरमाश्रित्य [cf. VaDh 8.16]; NKt[4] तथा; NKt[4] समासृत्य — b) BCa Hy Jm Jo[1] Kt[2] wKt[3] NKt[4] La[1] GMd[1] GMy oOr NPu[1] Tj[2] Tr[2] MTr[3] *Mr Mandlik Bühler KSS* वर्तन्ते सर्वजन्तवः — c) GMd[5] एवं गृह°; wKt[1] गृहस्थानाश्रित्य — c-d) NKt[4] TMd[3] NNg sOx[1] sPu[6] Tr[1] Tr[2] MTr[4] MTr[6] [*Jolly* Nd] वर्तन्ते गृहिणं तद्वदाश्रित्येतर आश्रमाः [Tr[1] गृहिणस्तद्व°] — d) Hy Jm Jo[1] Kt[2] Tj[2] MTr[3] *Ku Mr Mandlik Bühler KSS* वर्तन्ते सर्व आश्रमाः [MTr[3] आश्रमः]; La[1] इतरेश्रमा — GMd[5] next repeats verse 77 giving the vulgate reading [of *Mandlik* etc.]

Additional verse in NPu[1] *Mandlik* [ट]; cf. 6.90:

यथा नदीनदाः सर्वे समुद्रे यान्ति संस्थितिम् ।
एवमाश्रमिणः सर्वे गृहस्थे यान्ति संस्थितिम् ॥

d) NPu[1] संश्रितं

78. Cited by *Lakṣ* 3.209 — a) Ho TMd[4] MTr[4] तस्मात्; GMy यया त्रयो; Tj[1] त्रयोथाश्रमिणो — b) GMd[1] जानेना°; Bo wKt[6] Ox[2] ज्ञानेनानेन; Pu[10] ज्ञानेनान्येन; La[1] ज्ञानेचानेन; Hy ज्ञानेनान्वेन; Jm ज्ञानेनान्नेह; wKt[3] चान्वहः; Ho नित्यशः — c) BBe[2] Hy Jm Jo[1] Kt[2] MTr[3] *Mandlik Bühler Jha KSS Dave* गृहस्थेनैव; BKt[5] गृहस्थेव — d) wKt[1] *Lakṣ* तस्माच्छ्रेष्ठो गृहाश्रमी; Lo[3] Pu[10] Tj[1] [*Jolly* M[1–2–8] R] तस्माच्छ्रेष्ठाश्रमो; *Me Dave Jha* गृहम्; *Me* gives गृही as a pāṭha, saying that if the latter reading is followed then the previous compound is a Bahuvrīhi; if the former is followed it is a Karma-

स संधार्यः प्रयत्नेन स्वर्गमक्षयमिच्छता ।
सुखं चेहेच्छतात्यन्तं योऽधार्यो दुर्बलेन्द्रियैः ॥७९॥
ऋषयः पितरो देवा भूतान्यतिथयस्तथा ।
आशासते कुटुम्बिभ्यस्तेभ्यः कार्यं विजानता ॥८०॥
स्वाध्यायेनार्चयेतर्षीन् होमैर्देवान्यथाविधि ।
पितॄञ्छ्राद्धेन नॄनन्नैर्भूतानि बलिकर्मणा ॥८१॥
दद्यादहरहः श्राद्धमन्नाद्येनोदकेन वा ।
पयोमूलफलैर्वापि पितृभ्यः प्रीतिमाहरन् ॥८२॥
एकमप्याशयेद्विप्रं पित्रर्थे पाञ्चयज्ञिके ।
न चैवात्राशयेत्कंचिद्* वैश्वदेवं प्रति द्विजम् ॥८३॥

dhāraya; गृही is supported by *Go Ku* and *Rc*.

79.* *ma* in Pu^{7} — a) Jo^{2} *om* स; wKt^{6} संधार्याः; nKt^{4} संचार्यः; oMd^{2} सम्बन्धार्यः [*om* स]; sOx^{1} sPu^{6} संधार्योपि यत्नेन; Pu^{5} Pu^{7} संधार्यो गृहस्थेन — b) Lo^{2} स्वर्गमिच्छयामिच्छता; oOr स्वर्गमोक्षयमि°; gMy स्वयं क्षत्रियमि°; Lo^{4} सुखमक्षयमि°; Tj^{1} Tr^{1} °मक्षय्यमि°; Lo^{1} °मिक्षता — c) Ox^{3} °च्छयात्यन्तं; bBe^{2} Be^{3} Bo bCa Ho Hy Jm Jo^{1} Jo^{2} wKt^{1} Kt^{2} wKt^{3} wKt^{6} Lo^{1} Lo^{3} oMd^{2} oOr nPu^{1} Pu^{5} Pu^{7} Tj^{1} Tj^{2} mTr^{3} [*Jolly* G R] *Mandlik Jolly KSS* °च्छता नित्यं — d) Tr^{2} *om* यो; oOr *om* धार्यो; Tj^{1} °धार्यं; nKt^{4} °धार्या; gMy °लेन्द्रियः

80. Cited by *Lakṣ* 3.147–8; *Dev* 2.563 — a) nKt^{4} समयः पितरो; Kt^{2} पितरौ; nKt^{4} देवाद्भूता° — b) Tj^{1} °तिथिय°; nKt^{4} °तिथं यथा — c) bKt^{5} आशासन्ते; wKt^{6} tMd^{3} gMd^{5} Tr^{1} आशंसन्ते; gMy आशंसते; Be^{1} आशास्यते; Jm आशासिते; Ho असासते; gMy कुडु° — d) Tr^{2} *om* तेभ्यः; Be^{3} °स्तेषां; Jm nKt^{4} कार्य

81. Cited by *Jmv* 11.6.17; *Lakṣ* 3.148; *Dev* 2.563 — a) Tr^{2} स्वाध्यायेन ऋषीनर्चेद्; bBe^{2} Kt^{2} wKt^{3} nPu^{1} mTr^{3} *Jmv* °नार्चयेदृषीन्; nNg °नार्चयेनर्षीन्; wKt^{1} °नार्चयेचार्षीन्; Tj^{1} °नार्चयेतेर्षीन् — b) Jm होमैर्देवा°; oOr °विधिः — c) gMd^{5} पितॄञ्छ्राद्धप्रदानेन भूतानि; La^{1} पितृश्राद्धेन तृप्यन्ते भूतानि; Jo^{2} Lo^{3} Tj^{1} पितॄन्श्राद्धेतिथीनन्नैर्भूतानि; bKt^{5} wKt^{6} पितॄञ्छ्राद्धेनार्चयेद्भूतानि; Hy Jm Jo^{1} Kt^{2} oMd^{2} Tj^{2} mTr^{3} *Mandlik Jha KSS Dave* पितॄञ्छ्राद्धैश्च; Lo^{1} पितॄन् श्राद्धैर्नॄन° — d) tMd^{3} °न्नैर्व्रतानि; gMy °न्नैर्भूतानि च कर्मणां

82.* Cited by *Vij* 1.217, *Apa* 145; *Lakṣ* 3.169; *Hem* 3/1.208, 3/2.1564, 3/3.477; *Dev* 2.565 — a) Be^{3} Hy Jm Jo^{1} Kt^{2} wKt^{3} nKt^{4} Lo^{1} Lo^{2} Lo^{4} Lo^{5} gMd^{1} oMd^{2} gMy sOx^{1} [*but mc*] Ox^{2} Pu^{2} Pu^{4} sPu^{6} [*but mc*] Pu^{8} Tj^{2} mTr^{3} Wa [*Jolly* Ku N] *Vij Apa Mandlik KSS* कुर्यादह° which is supported by *Ku Nd* — b) Jm °न्नादेनो°; Lo^{1} gMd^{1} Ox^{2} Tr^{2} *Lakṣ* च — c) Bo पचोमू°; nKt^{4} यथोमू° — d) gMd^{5} पितृभ्यः पितृमान्हरेत्; *Hem* 3/2.1564 तृप्तिमावहन्; wKt^{3} mTr^{6} °माहरेत्; Be^{1} bBe^{2} Bo [*but cor*] Hy Jm Jo^{1} Jo^{2} wKt^{1} Kt^{2} wKt^{3} bKt^{5} wKt^{6} Lo^{3} oMd^{2} tMd^{3} Ox^{2} Pu^{2} Pu^{8} Tj^{1} Tr^{1} Tr^{2} mTr^{3} [*Jolly* R Nd] *Vij Mandlik Jha KSS Dave* °मावहन् which is supported by *Rn Rc*; gMy °मावहेत्; Tj^{2} °माहवन् [cf. the similar variants at 2.246d]

In Hy the folio containing 3.83–97 is missing.

83.* Cited by *Hem* 3/2.1565; *Lakṣ* 3.169; *Dev* 2.564 — a) Tr^{2} एवम°; Jm La^{1} °मप्यशये° — b) Be^{3} bCa Ho Kt^{2} bKt^{5} Lo^{2} Lo^{4} Lo^{5} tMd^{4} nNg Pu^{2} Pu^{4} Pu^{8} Tj^{2} Tr^{2} mTr^{3} *Hem Dev Jha Dave* पित्रर्थं; wKt^{6} पित्रंत्वं; Lo^{4} पञ्च°; bKt^{5} Lo^{5} °याज्ञिके; Lo^{1} gMd^{5} °यज्ञके; tMd^{4} Ox^{3} Pu^{10} °यज्ञिकं; gMy °यज्ञकः; Ox^{2} Pu^{8} Tr^{2} Wa °यज्ञिये; Pu^{5} °यज्ञिनो – c) tMd^{3} नात्रचैवाशये°; Lo^{4} Lo^{5} चैवान्वाशये°; Ho

वैश्वदेवस्य सिद्धस्य गृह्येऽग्नौ विधिपूर्वकम् ।
आभ्यः कुर्याद्देवताभ्यो ब्राह्मणो होममन्वहम् ॥८४॥
अग्नेः सोमस्य चैवादौ तयोश्चैव समस्तयोः ।
विश्वेषां चैव देवानां धन्वन्तरय एव च ॥८५॥
कुह्वै चैवानुमत्यै च प्रजापतय एव च ।
सह द्यावापृथिव्योश्च तथा स्विष्टकृतेऽन्ततः ॥८६॥
एवं सम्यग्घविर्हुत्वा सर्वदिक्षु प्रदक्षिणम् ।
इन्द्रान्तकाप्पतीन्दुभ्यः सानुगेभ्यो बलिं हरेत् ॥८७॥
मरुद्भ्य इति तु द्वारि हरेदप्स्वद्भ्य इत्यपि ।
वनस्पतिभ्य इत्येवं मुसलोलूखले हरेत् ॥८८॥
उच्छीर्षके श्रियै कुर्याद् भद्रकाल्यै तु पादतः ।
ब्रह्मवास्तोष्पतिभ्यां तु वास्तुमध्ये बलिं हरेत् ॥८९॥

GMy °त्रशये°; MTr^{3} °त्रादये°; BBe^{2} Be^{3} BCa [*but cor*] Ho Jm Jo^{1} Jo^{2} wKt^{1} Kt^{2} BKt^{5} wKt^{6} La^{1} La^{2} Lo^{3} Lo^{4} Lo^{5} GMd^{1} TMd^{3} TMd^{4} GMy oOr Ox^{2} Ox^{3} NPu^{1} Pu^{2} Pu^{4} Pu^{10} Tj^{2} Tr^{2} MTr^{4} MTr^{6} *Nd Go* [*Jolly* M R Nd] °शयेत्किंचिद्; Tr^{1} °शयेद्रव्यं — d) GMd^{1} °देवं प्रचक्षते द्विजं; TMd^{3} Ox^{2} Tr^{1} *Dev* द्विजः; TMd^{4} द्विजैः

84. a) TMd^{4} °देवप्रसिद्धस्य; wKt^{6} *ma* सिद्धस्य — b) Ox^{3} MTr^{4} गृहे; Lo^{4} Lo^{5} गृह्यो; wKt^{6} Lo^{1} TMd^{3} GMd^{5} Tr^{2} गृह्याग्नौ; GMy ग्राह्यग्नौ — c) NKt^{4} GMd^{1} अद्भ्यः — d) GMy ब्रह्मणे; Wa होममन्वयं

85. Placed after 87 in Jm. Cited by *Lakṣ* 3.154–5 — a) Be^{1} आग्नेः; Ho सामस्य; Lo^{2} TMd^{3} NPu^{1} चैवादो; MTr^{3} चैवासौ; Tj^{1} दैवादौ — b) Bo तया चैव; Be^{1} समस्नयोः — c) Jm Jo^{1} Kt^{2} La^{1} [*but mc*] Tj^{2} MTr^{3} *Mandlik Jha KSS Dave* विश्वेभ्यश्चैव देवेभ्यो — d) Be^{1} MTr^{4} धान्वतरय; Ox^{3} धन्वन्तरक; Pu^{10} [*Jolly* M^{1-2-8}] एव वा

86. Pādas a-b omitted in MTr^{3} [haplo]; verses 86 and 87 transposed in Jm — a) Lo^{3} Lo^{4} Lo^{5} कुह्वे; oOr कुषौ; wKt^{6} कुत्ये; wKt^{1} पूर्वे चैवा°; Lo^{4} °मत्यैव; Pu^{10} °मन्येव — b) Pu^{5} Pu^{7} प्राजा°; wKt^{3} प्रजापत्य — c) TMd^{4} °पृथिव्याश्च; Jm °पृथिव्यौश्च; oOr °पृथिव्ये च — d) BBe^{2} BKt^{5} wKt^{6} Ox^{2} स्विष्टि°; Tr^{2} श्विकृते; Bo GMd^{1} °कृत; Ho wKt^{1} BKt^{5} wKt^{6} Lo^{1} Lo^{4} TMd^{3} sOx^{1} sPu^{6} [*but cor*] Tr^{2} °कृतेततः; Tj^{1} °कृतंततः; Pu^{5} °कृतेन्तिच; Pu^{7} °कृतेतिच; [*Jolly* G] °कृतेपि च; GMy °कृते तथा

87. a) sOx^{1} sPu^{6} Tr^{2} सम्यग्बहिर्हुत्वा; NKt^{4} Ox^{3} सम्यग्यविर्हुत्वा; TMd^{4} सम्यग्भुविर्हुत्वा; TMd^{3} सम्यग्घविर्भुक्त्वा; wKt^{6} सम्यग्विवर्गत्वा — b) Ho सर्वादिक्षु — d) wKt^{6} Pu^{10} [*Jolly* M^{1-2-8}] स्वानुगेभ्यो; [*Jolly* Be] सान्वेभ्यो

88. Omitted in GMy [haplo] — a) TMd^{3} इति चत्वारि; wKt^{1} च; oOr तद्द्वारि; Bo द्वारी — b) Jm Jo^{1} Kt^{2} oMd^{2} Tj^{2} MTr^{3} [*Jolly* Nd] *Mandlik Jha KSS Dave* क्षिपेद°; Tr^{2} हरेदश्वा इत्यपि; wKt^{1} oMd^{2} °द्भ्य एव च — c) TMd^{3} इत्येव — d) Bo मूसलो°; Tj^{1} मुसला°; Jo^{2} NKt^{4} BKt^{5} wKt^{6} Lo^{4} Ox^{2} Pu^{5} Pu^{7} Tj^{2} Tr^{2} मुशलो°; Ox^{3} मुशले°; oMd^{2} मूषलो°; TMd^{3} oOr °लूखलो; TMd^{4} °लूखलं; Pu^{10} °लूषले; NNg °लूखलेरेव हरेत्

89. Omitted in GMy Pu^{5}. Cited by *Lakṣ* 3.157 — a) MTr^{4} उच्छीर्षकेन्द्रियैर्कुर्याद्; Lo^{1} उच्छेषके; oOr Tj^{1} श्रिये; Bo wKt^{3} GMd^{1} TMd^{3} GMd^{5} sOx^{1} sPu^{6} MTr^{6} दद्याद् — b) Jo^{2} wKt^{1} भद्रपाल्यै; Jm Jo^{1} Kt^{2} Tj^{2} MTr^{3} *Mandlik Jha KSS Dave* च; NNg पादयोः — c) wKt^{6} Tj^{1} ब्रह्मा°; Be^{1} BKt^{5} °वास्तोपति°; wKt^{6} °वास्तोःपति°; sOx^{1} sPu^{6} °वास्तुष्पति°; Lo^{2} °तिभ्यो; Tr^{1} °तीभ्यां; BBe^{2} Lo^{4} sOx^{1} Ox^{2} Ox^{3} sPu^{6} Pu^{10} [*Jolly* M] च

विश्वेभ्यश्चैव देवेभ्यो बलिमाकाश उत्क्षिपेत् ।
दिवाचरेभ्यो भूतेभ्यो नक्तंचारिभ्य एव च ॥९०॥
पृष्ठवास्तुनि कुर्वीत बलिं सर्वान्नभूतये* ।
पितृभ्यो बलिशेषं तु सर्वं दक्षिणतो हरेत् ॥९१॥
शुनां च पतितानां च श्वपचां पापरोगिणाम् ।
वायसानां कृमीणां च शनकैर्निर्वपेद्भुवि ॥९२॥
एवं यः सर्वभूतानि ब्राह्मणो नित्यमर्चति ।
स गच्छति परं स्थानं तेजोमूर्तिः पथर्जुना ॥९३॥
कृत्वैतद्बलिकर्मैवमतिथिं पूर्वमाशयेत् ।
भिक्षां च भिक्षवे दद्याद् विधिवद् ब्रह्मचारिणे ॥९४॥
यत्पुण्यफलमाप्नोति गां दत्त्वागोर्यथाविधि* ।
तत्पुण्यफलमाप्नोति भिक्षां दत्त्वा द्विजो गृही ॥९५॥

90. Omitted in oOr; pādas c-d omitted in MTr^4 Wa — b) Ho °काशे; Be^3 La^1 TMd^3 Tr^2 °काशमुत्क्षिपेत्; TMd^4 °काशमाहरेत् — c) wKt^1 TMd^3 °चरिभ्यो — d) GMy नक्तचारि°; NNg °चरेभ्यश्च एव च

91.* Omitted in oOr MTr^4; pādas a-b omitted in Wa and *ma* in Lo^4 — a) GMy पृथिव्यास्त्वपि कुर्वीत; Be^1 BBe^2 BKt^5 La^2 Lo^2 Lo^3 Lo^4 Lo^5 sOx^1 Ox^2 Pu^5 sPu^6 Pu^7 Pu^8 Tj^1 Tj^2 Tr^2 *Nā Go Rc* पृष्ठे°; Ho पष्टे; NPu^1 इष्टवास्तुनि — b) [*Jolly* M^5] सर्वान्नयते; sOx^1 sPu^6 सर्वान्ननुतये; Be^3 Bo Ho La^1 Lo^1 GMd^1 TMd^3 TMd^4 GMd^5 Ox^2 Pu^8 Tr^1 [*Jolly* N Nd] सर्वानुभूतये; GMy सर्वानुभूतले; NKt^4 सर्वान्न-भूतले; [*Jolly* M$^{1-8}$] सर्वानिभूतये; [*Jolly* M^2] सर्वांनिभूतये; Pu^{10} [*Jolly* M^9] सर्वंनिभूतये; Pu^5 सर्वाभूतये; wKt^3 सर्वान्भूतये; Be^1 BBe^2 Jm Jo^1 Jo^2 wKt^1 Kt^2 wKt^3 Lo^3 Lo^4 [*ma*] Lo^5 oMd^2 Tj^1 Tj^2 Tr^2 MTr^3 [*Jolly* M$^{3-4}$ Ku R] *Nā Ku Rn Nd Mandlik KSS* सर्वात्मभूतये; MTr^6 सर्वात्मनुभूतये— c) Pu^5 Pu^7 [*Jolly* G] च — d) La^1 सर्वे; TMd^3 GMd^5 Ox^2 Pu^5 सर्व

92.* Omitted in Tr^2. Cited by *Vij* 1.103; *Apa* 143; *Dev* 2.584 — b) TMd^3 श्वपचानां च रोगिणां; MTr^6 पापकर्मणां; Lo^4 °रागिणां — c) GMy Pu^{10} Tr^1 *Jha Dave* वयसां च कृमी°; BKt^5 वायसानां च कृमी°; NKt^4 NNg Tj^1 *Apa* क्रिमीणां; Lo^5 श्रमीणां — d) oOr चलजैर्निक्षिपेद्बलिं; Be^1 [*mc to*] Be^3 Bo Jm Jo^2 BKt^5 wKt^6 Lo^1 Lo^3 Lo^4 Lo^5 TMd^4 sOx^1 Ox^3 NPu^1 Pu^2 Pu^5 sPu^6 Pu^7 Pu^{10} Tj^1 [*Jolly* M G R] *Vij Apa Dev Me Go Rc* °कैर्निक्षिपेद्भुवि; Ho wKt^1 *Me* °कैर्निःक्षिपेद्भुवि; TMd^3 inserts here 3.121.

93. Pādas a-b omitted in Pu^{10}. Cited by *Dev* 2.584; pāda-d cited by *Kum* 3.1.13— b) Tj^1 ब्राह्मणा; NKt^4 ब्रह्मणा; TMd^4 °णोन्वहमर्चति; GMy Tr^2 नित्यमर्चयेत् — c) Kt^2 स्वगच्छति; Lo^1 पर — d) BBe^2 Ho wKt^1 NKt^4 BKt^5 La^1 Lo^4 NNg NPu^1 [*Jolly* G Ku] *Ku* °मूर्ति [*Ku* gives मूर्तिः as pāṭha]; Kt^2 °मूर्तिं; Ox^2 Ox^3 Pu^{10} पथार्जुना; oMd^2 पथर्जुणा; Bo sOx^1 sPu^6 पथर्जुन; Be^1 NPu^1 पथार्जुन; sPu^6 यथार्जन *mc to* पथार्जन; wKt^6 TMd^3 पथोर्जुना; Kt^2 पथर्जुनां

94. Pādas c-d cited by *Lakṣ* 3.166; *Dev* 1.112 — a) wKt^1 NPu^1 कृत्वैव बलि° — b) Be^1 Lo^2 °वमतिथि; Jm °वमातिथिं — c) Ox^3 भिक्षं; NNg *om* च; TMd^4 वा; La^1 भिक्षये — d) Wa °चारिणा; GMd^5 °चारिणो

Additional half-verse in GMy:

भिक्षामप्पूर्विकां दत्त्वा गोप्रदानफलं भवेत् ॥

95.* Pāda b-c omitted in Kt^6 My^1 and *ma* in Lo^4; pādas a-b *ma* in Ox^2; pādas b and d

भिक्षामप्युदपात्रं वा सत्कृत्य विधिपूर्वकम् ।
वेदतत्त्वार्थविदुषे ब्राह्मणायोपपादयेत् ॥९६॥
नश्यन्ति हव्यकव्यानि नराणामविजानताम् ।
भस्मीभूतेषु विप्रेषु मोहाद्दत्तानि दातृभिः ॥९७॥
विद्यातपःसमृद्धेषु हुतं विप्रमुखाग्निषु ।
निस्तारयति दुर्गाच्च महतश्चैव किल्बिषात् ॥९८॥

transposed in Jm. Cited by *Lakṣ* 3.167 — a) TMd^{3} यत्पुण्यं समवाप्नोति; Pu^{10} यत्पुण्यं — b) MTr^{4} MTr^{6} गां दत्त्वागौर्यथाविधि; *Me* [pāṭha] गां दत्त्वागुर्यथाविधि; NKt^{4} GMd^{1} GMd^{5} sOx^{1} sPu^{6} गां दत्त्वा तु यथाविधि; Be^{1} BBe^{2} Be^{3} BCa Ho Hy Jm Jo^{1} Jo^{2} wKt^{1} Kt^{2} BKt^{5} wKt^{6} La^{1} La^{2} Lo^{1} Lo^{3} oMd^{2} NNg Ox^{2} NPu^{1} Pu^{2} Pu^{3} Pu^{4} Pu^{5} Pu^{7} Pu^{8} Tj^{1} Tj^{2} Tr^{2} MTr^{3} Wa [*Jolly* G Ku R] *Lakṣ Mandlik Jolly Jha KSS Dave* गां दत्त्वा विधिवद्गुरोः [Jo^{2} Lo^{3} Tj^{1} दत्त्वा गां; Lo^{1} °द्गुरूं]; Bo wKt^{3} Lo^{2} Lo^{4} Lo^{5} oMd^{2} oOr Ox^{3} Pu^{10} [*Jolly* M] गां दत्त्वा विधिवद्गुरौ — d) *Lakṣ* दत्त्वा तु भिक्षवे गृही; TMd^{3} भिक्षां दत्त्वा द्विजातये; Kt^{2} द्विजा; Ox^{3} Pu^{10} द्विजे; BCa द्विजो गुरौ; Lo^{4} Lo^{5} ततो गृही

96. Cited by *Lakṣ* 3.167 — a) GMd^{1} TMd^{3} GMd^{5} sOx^{1} sPu^{6} Tr^{1} भिक्षां वाप्युद°; wKt^{6} °मभ्युद°; wKt^{1} च — b) *Rn* संस्कृत्य; Tr^{2} सत्कृत्वा — c) wKt^{6} °तत्त्वानुविदुषे; Tj^{1} °तत्त्वार्थहविषे

TMd^{4} adds here the additional verses given after 3.98 and after them inserts verse 3.84.

97. Omitted in Ho; verses 97 and 98 transposed in NPu^{1}. Cited by *Lakṣ* 3.167 — a) La^{1} हव्ये — c) BKt^{5} wKt^{6} Lo^{2} TMd^{4} Ox^{3} Pu^{10} Tj^{1} Wa [*Jolly* M^{1-2-8} N] *Me Nā Jha Dave* भस्मभूतेषु; Lo^{4} *ma* विप्रेषु — d) La^{1} मोहदत्तानि; Tr^{2} महादत्तानि; sOx^{1} sPu^{6} [*but cor*] यानि दत्तानि; GMy °त्तानि सर्वशः

98. Pādas a-b omitted in Ho and pādas c-d in Pu^{10}. Cited by *Lakṣ* 3.167; *Dev* 2.598 — a) *Dev* °समिद्धेषु; TMd^{4} °समुद्रेषु — b) Lo^{3} Tj^{1} गतं विप्र° — c) *Dev* तत्तारयति; Be^{1} Be^{3} संतारयति; GMy °रयत; TMd^{4} दुर्गाय; wKt^{6} दुग्रास्थ; BKt^{5} दुर्गाः मह° — d) Ox^{3} किल्बिपान्; Lo^{2} किलिषान्

Additional verses in Be^{3} La^{1} GMy oOr MTr^{4} MTr^{6}; given after 3.99 in GMd^{1} [verse 99 is repeated indicating that in fact these may have come after 98], after 3.96 in TMd^{4} [after which is inserted 7.84], and after 3.100 in GMd^{5}; first three verses cited in *Mandlik* [क, ल] *KSS*; first verse alone in *Apa* 287; *Hem* 1.37:

अनर्हते यद्ददाति न ददाति यदर्हते ।
अर्हानर्हापरिज्ञानाद् धनाद्धर्माच्च हीयते ॥१॥
काले न्यायागतं पात्रे विधिवत्प्रतिपादितम् ।
फलं ददाति परममिह लोके परत्र च ॥२॥
प्रतिग्रहेण शुद्धेन जयेन क्रयविक्रयात् ।
यथाक्रमं द्विजातीनां धनं न्यायादुपागतम् ॥३॥
यद्यदिष्टतमं लोके यच्चास्य दयितं गृहे ।
तत्तद्गुणवते देयं तदेवाक्षयमिच्छता ॥४॥

1. a) Be^{3} यो ददाति — b) GMy तदर्हते; Be^{3} तथार्हते — c-d) *Hem* अर्हानर्हानभिज्ञानात्सोऽपि धर्माच्च हीयते — d) Be^{3} *Mandlik KSS* धनी धर्मान्न हीयते; La^{1} धर्माद्यपरिहीयते; Be^{3} बलाद्धर्माद्यहीयते; GMy धनात्सर्वाच्च; TMd^{4} धनाधर्माश्च

2. a) oOr कालेथवागतं; MTr^{4} पात्रं — c) *Mandlik KSS* ददाति परमं सौख्यमिह; GMy वरं ददाति

3. a-b) Be^{3} प्रतिग्रहेण दण्डेन वाणिज्येन च कर्मणा — b) *Mandlik KSS* शस्त्रेण; GMy जन-

संप्राप्ताय त्वतिथये प्रदद्यादासनोदके ।
अन्नं चैव यथाशक्ति सत्कृत्य विधिपूर्वकम् ॥९९॥
शिलानप्युञ्छतो नित्यं पञ्चाग्नीनपि जुह्वतः ।
सर्वं सुकृतमादत्ते ब्राह्मणोऽनर्चितो वसन् ॥१००॥

येत्क्रय°; TMd[4] °विक्रयैः; MTr[6] °विक्रयां — d) oOr °तीनामेवं न्याया°

4. a) GMy यद्यतिष्टतमं; La[1] यदितिष्टतमं — b) La[1] यद्वास्य; MTr[4]MTr[6] यत् स्याच्च; GMd[1] यच्चान्यदधिकं — c) La[1] तत्र कृतवने — d) La[1] तदेतन्जय्यमिच्छता

Following the above four, five additional verses in TMd[4] [some quite faint and unclear; the 5th verse in unreadable]:

अर्चितं प्रतिगृह्णाति ददात्यर्चितमेव च ।
तयोर्हि सकलो धर्मो विपरीतो विपर्यये ॥१॥
समासमाभ्यां विप्राभ्यां विषमं सममेव च ।
पूजितानर्चयश्चैव न ग्राह्यादियमेव च ॥२॥
पात्रभूतो हि यो विप्रः प्रतिगृह्य प्रतिग्रहम् ।
असत्सु विनियुञ्जीते देयं तस्मै न किंचन ॥३॥
संशयं कुरुते यस्तु प्रतिगृह्य समन्ततः ।
धर्मार्थं नोपयुङ्क्ते च न तं तस्करमर्चयेत् ॥४॥

99. Cited by *Hem* 3/1.433; *Dev* 2.590 — a) Hy सप्राप्ताय; Ho °प्तायातिथियेषु; Be[3] ह्यतिथये; TMd[4] त्वतिथिये; Pu[10] त्वतिषये — b) Tj[1] °दासनेनोदके; Pu[10] °सनोदकं — c) wKt[3] यथायुक्ति; GMy यथाशक्त — d) Pu[10] [*Jolly* M[1-2-8]] *Me Dave Jha* संस्कृत्य; oOr सत्कृत्ये; GMy विधिवत्स्वयं

Additional verse in Ho La[1] GMd[1] TMd[3] GMd[5] GMy oOr Tr[1] MTr[4] MTr[6] [*Jolly* Gr] *Lakṣ* 3.175–6; given after verse 96 in TMd[4] [*Jolly* Gr] and after verse 98 [at the end of the addition] in Be[3]:

अग्निं हुत्वा विधानेन यत्पुण्यफलमाप्यते ।
तेन तुल्यं विशिष्टं वा ब्राह्मणे तर्पिते फलम् ॥

a) Be[3] Ho GMd[1] MTr[4] *Lakṣ* अग्नीन्हुत्वा — b) MTr[6] यत्पुण्यं; Be[3] GMd[1] °लमाप्नुयात्; TMd[4] °लमश्नुते — c) GMd[1] TMd[3] TMd[4] Tr[1] तत्तुल्यं तद्विशिष्टं; La[1] तुल्यं च शिष्टं च; oOr विशिष्टस्य; GMd[5] यथेष्टं वा — d) [*Jolly* Gr] ब्राह्मणस्तर्प्यति; Ho La[1] तर्प्यते; oOr तर्पणे

Additional verse in La[1] GMd[1] TMd[3] TMd[4] GMd[5] GMy oOr Tr[1] MTr[4] MTr[6]; given after verse 96 in TMd[4]:

मन्त्रकर्मविपर्यासाद् दुरिष्टादुर्हुतादपि ।
तत्फलं नश्यते कर्तुरिदं न श्रद्धया कृतम् ॥

b) La[1] °सादृष्ट्यार्थाच हुतादपि; GMd[1] दुरुक्ताद्दुर्हुतादपि; GMd[5] दुरिक्ताद्दुर्हुतादपि; GMy दुरिक्ताद्दुर्गतादपि; TMd[3] दुरिष्टं दुर्हृतादपि — c) La[1] त्रस्यते; oOr MTr[4] भूष्यते — d) GMd[5] कर्तुरिदमश्रद्धया; La[1] च श्रद्धया

After this GMd[1] TMd[3] insert 7.84; GMd[1] inserts the four additional verses given in several mss. after 3.98; and La[1] inserts 3.99.

100. Verses 100 and 101 transposed in Tr[2] — a) Hy Tr[2] शिलामप्यु°; GMy शिलादप्यु°; NPu[1] शलादप्यु°; GMd[5] Tj[2] शिलातप्यु°; Tr[1] सिलानप्यु°; Jm शल्पानप्यु°; TMd[4] °प्युञ्छते — b) Lo[4] Lo[5] दुह्वतः; wKt[1] स्वर्गतः — c) Lo[1] GMd[5] सर्वं; sOx[1] sPu[6] एवं सुकृत° [*but both cor*] — d) oMd[2] Tr[2] नार्चितो; TMd[4] °नर्चिते; TMd[3] GMd[5] Tr[1] °नर्चितोतिथिः; Pu[8] वसत्; wKt[3] BKt[5] wKt[6] Lo[2] व्रजन् — GMd[5] adds here verse 7.84.

तृणानि भूमिरुदकं वाक् चतुर्थी च सूनृता ।
एतान्यपि सतां गेहे नोच्छिद्यन्ते कदाचन ॥१०१॥
एकरात्रं तु निवसन्नतिथिर्ब्राह्मणः स्मृतः ।
अनित्यं हि स्थितो यस्मात् तस्मादतिथिरुच्यते ॥१०२॥
नैकग्रामीणमतिथिं विप्रं सांगतिकं तथा ।
उपस्थितं गृहे विद्याद् भार्या यत्राग्नयोऽपि वा ॥१०३॥
उपासते ये गृहस्थाः परपाकमबुद्धयः ।
तेन ते प्रेत्य पशुतां व्रजन्त्यन्नाद्यदायिनाम् ॥१०४॥
अप्रणोद्योऽतिथिः सायं सूर्योढो गृहमेधिना ।
काले प्राप्तस्त्वकाले वा नास्यानश्नन् गृहे वसेत् ॥१०५॥
न वै स्वयं तदश्नीयादतिथिं यन्न भोजयेत् ।
धन्यं यशस्यमायुष्यं स्वर्ग्यं चातिथिपूजनम्* ॥१०६॥

101. Cited by *Vij* 1.107 — b) Lo^{3} चतुर्थी वाक्च सूनृता; Tj^{1} च चतुर्थी वाक् सूनृता; GMy सुनृता: — c) Tr^{1} एतानि च; TMd^{4} गेहो — d) Lo^{3} Pu^{10} Tj^{1} छिद्यते न कदाचन [Pu^{10} *om* न]; Lo^{5} नोच्छेद्यन्ते; sOx^{1} sPu^{6} नोच्छिष्ठन्ते; Bo नोच्छिद्येत; TMd^{3} नोच्छिद्यात्ते; wKt^{3} °द्यन्ति; Tr^{2} कथंचन

102. Cited by *Apa* 155; *Hem* 3/1.427; *Dev* 2.589; pādas a-b cited by *Mādh* 1.351 — a) GMy °रात्रिं; Tj^{2} च — b) Ox^{3} °ह्मणान्स्मृत: — c) TMd^{4} अनित्यमागतो यस्मात्; GMd^{1} GMd^{5} अनित्या; Kt^{2} ह; GMy य स्थितो; Lo^{2} GMd^{1} GMd^{5} oOr स्थितिर्यस्मात् — d) TMd^{3} तस्मात्सोतिथि°

103. Pādas c-d omitted in wKt^{3}. Cited by *Mādh* 1.353 — a) MTr^{4} एकग्रा°; BKt^{5} °ग्रामिण°; Lo^{5} °ग्रामेण°; TMd^{4} °णमातिथ्ये — b) Tr^{2} विप्र:; wKt^{6} विप्रसंगतिकं; La^{1} °तिकं गृही — c) wKt^{6} गृहं विद्या — d) Bo °ग्रयेपि

104. Cited by *Lakṣ* 3.274; *Hem* 3/1.769 — a) BKt^{5} उपासने; Jm यो; Bo Jo^{2} Lo^{3} TMd^{4} Tj^{1} *Lakṣ* गृहस्था ये; TMd^{3} य गृहस्थाश्च — b) Bo पदपाक°; *Hem* °मशुद्धय: — c) NNg तेनैते; GMd^{1} तेनेह — d) wKt^{1} MTr^{6} व्रजत्य°; oOr °न्त्यर्थादिदायिनां; Hy Jm Jo^{1} Kt^{2} wKt^{6} oMd^{2} Tj^{2} MTr^{3} [*Jolly* Ku] *Ku Mandlik Jha KSS Dave* °न्नादिदायिनां; Ox^{2} °न्नान्नदायिनां *mc to* °न्नादिदायिनां; Lo^{1} TMd^{3} Pu^{2} Tj^{2} °दायिन:; TMd^{4} °दायिनं; Jo^{1} °दायितान्

Additional verse in Be^{3} Ho wKt^{1} wKt^{3} La^{1} oOr Ox^{2} NPu^{1} Pu^{8} Tr^{2} *Rc Mandlik* [अ, ख, ञ, ट, ड, ढ, ल] *KSS Dave* [unnoticed by Jolly]:

परपाकान्नपुष्टस्य सततं गृहमेधिन: ।
इष्टं दत्तं तपोऽधीतं यस्यान्नं तस्य तद्भवेत् ॥

a) Pu^{8} परपाकीयान्न° — c) Tr^{2} इष्टं दत्तमधीतं च; *Mandlik KSS Dave* दत्तमिष्टं तपो — d) La^{1} तस्मात्तस्य तद्भवेत्; wKt^{3} तस्यान्नं

105. Cited by *Apa* 152; *Hem* 3/1.429; *Dev* 2.593–4; *Mādh* 1.351 — a) Tr^{1} अप्रोणोद्यातिथि: सोयं; GMd^{1} Wa अप्राणोद्यो; wKt^{6} स्वप्राणेभ्योतिथि:; oOr सालं — b) Be^{1} Bo सूर्योढा; wKt^{1} BKt^{5} wKt^{6} Tj^{2} सूर्योढे; Be^{3} Hy Lo^{2} Lo^{3} Lo^{5} oOr Ox^{2} Ox^{3} Pu^{5} Pu^{7} Pu^{8} Pu^{10} MTr^{4} [*Jolly* M^{3-4-9} R] *Mādh* °मेधिनां; TMd^{3} °मेधिन: — c) Lo^{4} Lo^{5} प्राप्तकालस्त्वकाले वा; Tr^{2} प्राप्तेस्त्व°; Kt^{2} प्राप्तास्त्व°; TMd^{4} प्राप्तस्याकाले — d) sOx^{1} sPu^{6} *Apa* [vl as in ed] गृही; BBe^{2} Jm Jo^{1} Kt^{2} oMd^{2} TMd^{4} Tj^{1} वसन्; wKt^{6} वशेत्

106.* Omitted in oOr. Cited by *Mādh* 1.356 — a) Ox^{3} *om* न; TMd^{4} GMy Ox^{2} *Mādh* नैव;

आसनावसथौ शय्यामनुव्रज्यामुपासनम् ।
उत्तमेषूत्तमं कुर्याद्धीने हीनं समे समम् ॥१०७॥
वैश्वदेवे तु निर्वृत्ते यद्यन्योऽतिथिराव्रजेत् ।
तस्मै चान्नं यथाशक्ति प्रदद्यान्न बलिं हरेत् ॥१०८॥
न भोजनार्थं स्वे विप्रः कुलगोत्रे निवेदयेत् ।
भोजनार्थं हि ते शंसन् वान्ताशीत्युच्यते बुधैः ॥१०९॥
ब्राह्मणस्य त्वनतिथिर्गृहे राजन्य उच्यते ।
वैश्यशूद्रौ सखा चैव ज्ञातयो गुरुरेव च ॥११०॥
यदि त्वतिथिधर्मेण क्षत्रियो गृहमाव्रजेत् ।
भुक्तवत्सु च विप्रेषु कामं तमपि भोजयेत् ॥१११॥
वैश्यशूद्रावपि प्राप्तौ कुटुम्बेऽतिथिधर्मिणौ ।

GMy तमश्री° — b) Ox[3] यत्र भोज°; GMy पूजयेत् — d) BBe[2] TMd[4] Pu[10] Tr[2] स्वर्गं; Jo[1] MTr[3] *Mandlik Jha KSS Dave* वातिथि°; Be[1] BBe[2] Be[3] Bo Ho Jo[2] WKt[1] NKt[4] La[1] La[2] Lo[1] Lo[2] Lo[3] oMd[2] GMy NNg sOx[1] Ox[2] Ox[3] NPu[1] Pu[5] sPu[6] Pu[7] Pu[8] Pu[10] Tr[2] Wa [*Jolly* M[1–2–8] M G Ku R] *Rc Jolly* °थिभोजनं

107. Omitted in oOr. Cited by *Apa* 156; *Hem* 3/1.435; *Dev* 2.592 — a) WKt[6] शय्यास्वनु° — b) TMd[4] Tr[2] °व्रज्यमु°; Pu[5] Pu[7] °व्रज्यानु°; Jm Pu[8] °व्रज्या उपा°; Jm Jo[1] WKt[3] Tj[1] *Hem Dev* °पासनां — c) Tj[1] °पूत्तमे; Jm °षूत्तमां; GMd[5] विद्याद्धीने — d) TMd[3] कुर्यान्निचे नीचं; Jm GMd[5] °द्धीनं हीने; GMy समं समे; La[1] समासतं

108.* Omitted in oOr. Cited by *Vij* 1.103; *Lakṣ* 3.200 — a) Lo[4] Lo[5] विश्वदेवे; WKt[1] Pu[5] Pu[7] निर्वृत्ते तु; TMd[3] निर्वृते; NKt[4] Lo[4] GMd[5] [*Jolly* M[3–4]] निवृत्ते; Wa निवृत्ति — b) Bo Tr[1] यद्यन्याति°; Ox[3] यद्यन्येति°; TMd[4] °थिरापक्षात्; Hy °व्रजत् —c) Lo[2] GMd[5] Pu[8] *Vij* तस्मा अन्नं; GMd[1] TMd[3] TMd[4] GMy Tr[1] [*Jolly* Nd] *Lakṣ* तस्मादन्नं; Be[1] BBe[2] Be[3] Bo BCa Ho Hy Jm Jo[1] WKt[1] Kt[2] WKt[3] La[2] oMd[2] Ox[3] Pu[10] Tj[2] MTr[3] [*Jolly* M[6–9] Ku] *Mandlik Jolly Jha KSS Dave* तस्याप्यन्नं [Ox[3] °प्यन्यं]; MTr[6] तस्य चान्नं; NNg प्रकृत्यान्नं; [*Jolly* M[1–2–8]] तथाप्यन्नं; NKt[4] वान्नं

109. Omitted in oOr. Cited by *Mādh* 1.358 — a) Be[3] Lo[4] Lo[5] Ox[3] Pu[5] Pu[7] Pu[10] [*Jolly* M G N] *Jolly* °नार्थे; TMd[4] °नार्थस्य विप्रः; WKt[3] स्वयं विप्रः; TMd[3] सद्विप्रः; Tj[1] त विप्रः Lo[3] तं विप्रः; Be[3] विप्रः स्वे — b) Ox[3] °गोत्र; NNg °गोत्रेषु [*but cor*]; Pu[10] विवेदयेत् — c) Ox[3] Pu[10] [*Jolly* M G] *Jolly* °नार्थे; Lo[4] Lo[5] °नार्थो; BCa °नार्थ; La[1] ते सर्वं; TMd[3] शासन्

110.* Omitted in oOr; pādas c-d omitted in Lo[1]. Cited by *Hem* 3/1.428; *Dev* 2.589; *Mādh* 1.354 — a) BCa Hy Jm Jo[1] Kt[2] Lo[2] oMd[2] sOx[1] Ox[2] Ox[3] sPu[6] Pu[10] Tj[2] MTr[3] *Hem Mandlik Jolly Jha KSS Dave* न ब्राह्मणस्य त्वतिथिर्गृहे; Ho ब्राह्मणस्य न त्वतिथि°; Tr[2] ब्राह्मणः सन् त्वतिथिर्गृहे — c) Bo NKt[4] BKt[5] WKt[6] GMd[5] Pu[5] Pu[7] Pu[10] °शूद्रो; sOx[1] sPu[6] [*cor to*] °शूद्र; WKt[6] सखां; Tr[2] सखाश्चैव — d) WKt[1] गुरवोपि च

111. Omitted in oOr. Cited by *Apa* 152; *Hem* 3/1.440; *Dev* 2.594; *Mādh* 1.354 — a) sOx[1] sPu[6] [*mc sh to*] Tr[2] यदा; Bo यद; WKt[6] यदन्वति° — b) Jm GMd[1] °माविशेत् — c) BBe[2] Jo[2] Lo[3] GMy sOx[1] sPu[6] [*Jolly* R] भुक्तवत्स्वपि; Tj[1] °वत्स्वविप्रेषु; Jm Jo[1] Kt[2] MTr[3] *Dev* °वत्सूक्तविप्रेषु; Hy BKt[5] WKt[6] Lo[1] Lo[2] Lo[4] Lo[5] TMd[3] GMd[5] NNg Pu[8] Tr[1] MTr[4] *Apa* तु; Ho त; Ox[3] Pu[10] [*Jolly* M[1–2–8]] स — d) Pu[10] तदपि; Be[1] पूजयेत्

भोजयेत्सह भृत्यैस्तावानृशंस्यं प्रयोजयन् ॥११२॥
इतरानपि सख्यादीन् संप्रीत्या गृहमागतान् ।
प्रकृत्यान्नं यथाशक्ति भोजयेत्सह भार्यया ॥११३॥
सुवासिनीः कुमारीश्च रोगिणो गर्भिणीस्तथा ।
अतिथिभ्योऽन्वगेवैतान् भोजयेदविचारयन् ॥११४॥
अदत्त्वा तु य एतेभ्यः पूर्वं भुङ्क्तेऽविचक्षणः ।
स भुञ्जानो न जानाति श्वगृध्रैर्जग्धिमात्मनः ॥११५॥
भुक्तवत्सु तु* विप्रेषु स्वेषु भृत्येषु चैव हि ।
भुञ्जीयातां ततः पश्चादवशिष्टं तु दंपती ॥११६॥

112. Omitted in oOr. Cited by *Apa* 152; *Dev* 2.595; *Mādh* 1.354 — b) GMy कुडुम्बे; Tj^{2} कुटुम्बो; MTr^{4} कुटुम्व्याति°; TMd^{4} °धर्मिणा — c) Bo GMd^{1} विप्रैस्तावा°; Tj^{2} भृत्यैवानृ°; BKt^{5} भृत्यैश्च सुरानृ°; Pu^{5} Pu^{7} भृत्यैस्तौ आनृ°; wKt^{3} भृत्यैस्तुवानृ°; Ox^{2} Tr^{2} भृत्यैस्तानानृ° — d) TMd^{4} °नृशंसं; Be^{1} Bo Ho Jm wKt^{1} Kt^{2} La^{1} Lo^{4} Lo^{5} GMy NPu^{1} Pu^{5} Pu^{7} MTr^{4} MTr^{6} *Mādh* प्रयोजयेत्; wKt^{6} प्रयोजनं; TMd^{3} GMd^{5} प्रकल्पयेत्; Tr^{1} प्रकल्पयन्; Be^{3} Lo^{1} sOx^{1} च योजयेत् [sOx^{1} *cor to* च यो व्रजेत्]; sPu^{6} च यो व्रजेत्

113. Omitted in oOr. Cited by *Apa* 154; *Mādh* 1.354 — a) La^{1} इतरादपि; GMy इतरावपि; wKt^{6} इहव्रानपि; TMd^{4} संख्यादीन्; Tr^{1} सख्यादि; La^{1} सखादीनां — b) wKt^{6} Pu^{5} संप्रत्या; BKt^{5} संप्रत्य — c) NKt^{4} प्रकृत्यन्नं; *Go* संस्कृत्यान्नं; Kt^{2} oMd^{2} Ox^{2} MTr^{3} *Mādh Nā* सत्कृत्यान्नं; Bo Hy Jm Jo^{1} Tj^{2} सकृत्यान्नं; MTr^{3} यथाकामशक्ति — d) MTr^{3} भोजयेदविचारयन् [cf. 114d]; *Apa* [vl] धर्मया

114.* Omitted in oOr. Cited by *Apa* 147; *Lakṣ* 3.211–2 — a) Be^{1} Be^{3} NKt^{4} BKt^{5} Lo^{2} Pu^{8} [*Jolly* M^{9} Nd] स्ववा°; wKt^{3} स्वंवा°; Ho स्ववाचास्विनी; Bo Jo^{2} BKt^{5} Lo^{4} sOx^{1} Pu^{5} sPu^{6} [*but cor*] Pu^{7} °वासिनी; Jm Jo^{1} Kt^{2} GMd^{1} TMd^{4} GMy Tj^{2} °वासिनीं; Tr^{2} NPu^{1} °वासिन्यः; BBe^{2} Bo BCa Ho wKt^{3} NKt^{4} Lo^{2} Lo^{4} Lo^{5} GMy sOx^{1} sPu^{6} Tr^{1} Tr^{2} MTr^{4} MTr^{6} [*Jolly* M^{3-4-9} Ku Nd] *Nā* कुमारांश्च; BKt^{5} wKt^{6} कुमाराश्च; TMd^{4} कुमारीं च; GMd^{1} Pu^{5} Pu^{7} [*Jolly* G] कुमार्यश्च — a-b) TMd^{3} स्ववासिनी सबालवृद्धान् गर्भिनी रोगिणीस्तथा — b) TMd^{4} GMy रोगिणीं; Ox^{3} Pu^{10} रोगिणी; Jo^{2} GMd^{1} TMd^{4} GMy Tr^{2} गर्भिणीं तथा; Bo Pu^{5} Pu^{7} गर्भिणी तथा; oMd^{2} MTr^{3} *Mandlik Jha KSS Dave* गर्भिणीः स्त्रियः; Hy Jo^{1} Kt^{2} Tj^{2} गर्भिणीस्त्रियः; Jm गर्भिणीः स्त्रिया — c) All NT mss., *Apa* °भ्योग्र एवैतान् [sOx^{1} °ग्र्य; Wa एव तान्; NKt^{4} °भ्योत्वरोवैना; Ho La^{1} °ग्रतश्चैतान्; Ox^{2} °ग्रतस्त्वेतान्] — d) Tr^{2} °विचारयेत्

115. Omitted in oOr — a) TMd^{3} अभुत्का; GMy तु मया तेभ्यः — b) TMd^{4} पूर्ण; Be^{1} भुङ्क्तो; Bo दत्त्वाविच° — c) Tj^{1} स्वभुञ्जानो; Tr^{2} स्वयं भुञ्जानो; Ho न जानश्च

Additional verses in NPu^{1}:

पात्रमुत्सृजेत् ।
उत्सृष्टमन्नमुद्धृत्य ग्रासमेकं भुवि क्षिपेत् ।
आचान्तः साधुसंगेन सद्विद्यापठितेन च ।
पुरावृत्तक्र[क्रि?]याभिश्च शेषाहमतिवाहयेदिति ॥

116.* Cited by *Dev* 2.598; *Mādh* 1.364 — a) Bo Ho wKt^{1} wKt^{3} NKt^{4} La^{1} La^{2} Lo^{1} Lo^{2} Lo^{4} Lo^{5} TMd^{4} GMy NNg Ox^{2} Ox^{3} Pu^{2} Pu^{4} Pu^{8} Tr^{1} MTr^{4} MTr^{6} [*Jolly* M^{3-4-9}] °वत्सु तु; NPu^{1} °वत्सु नु; Be^{1} Be^{3} BCa GMd^{1} TMd^{3} GMd^{5} oOr sOx^{1} Pu^{5} sPu^{6} Pu^{7} Tr^{2} [*Jolly* M^{8} G] *Dev Mādh ViDh* 67.40 *Jolly* °वत्सु च; Hy Jm Jo^{1} Kt^{2} BKt^{5} wKt^{6} oMd^{2} Tj^{2} MTr^{3} *Mandlik KSS Dave* °वत्स्वथ; BBe^{2} Jo^{2} Lo^{3} Tj^{1} Wa [*Jolly* R] °वत्स्वपि; Pu^{10} *om* तु; Tr^{2} MTr^{4} MTr^{6} सर्वेषु — b) *Dev* भृत्येष्वन्येषु

देवानृषीन्मनुष्यांश्च पितॄन् गृह्याश्च देवताः ।
पूजयित्वा ततः पश्चाद् गृहस्थः शेषभुग्भवेत् ॥११७॥
अघं स केवलं भुङ्क्ते यः पचत्यात्मकारणात् ।
यज्ञशिष्टाशनं ह्येतत् सतामन्नं विधीयते ॥११८॥
राजर्त्विक्स्नातकगुरून् प्रियश्वशुरमातुलान् ।
अर्हयेन्मधुपर्केण परिसंवत्सरात्पुनः ॥११९॥
राजा च श्रोत्रियश्चैव यज्ञकर्मण्युपस्थिते ।
मधुपर्केण संपूज्यौ न त्वयज्ञ इति स्थितिः ॥१२०॥
सायं त्वन्नस्य सिद्धस्य पत्न्यमन्त्रं बलिं हरेत् ।
वैश्वदेवं हि नामैतत् सायंप्रातर्विधीयते ॥१२१॥
पितृयज्ञं तु निर्वर्त्य विप्रश्चन्द्रक्षयेऽग्निमान् ।
पिण्डान्वाहार्यकं श्राद्धं कुर्यान्मासानुमासिकम् ॥१२२॥

चैव हि; TMd^{4} तथा भृत्येषु; Jo^{2} Lo^{3} Tj^{1} [*Jolly* R] बन्धुभृत्येषु; Lo^{4} *ma*भृत्येषु; Lo^{1} विप्रेषु; GMy ज्ञातिषु; GMd^{1} सर्वेषु; NKt^{4} Lo^{2} ह — c) GMd^{1} शेषादवशि° — c-d) MTr^{6} ततः शेषं विघसं तु दंपती — d) *Dev* पश्चाद्विघसं तं तु; BKt^{5} wKt^{6} च; GMd^{5} दम्पतीं

117. Omitted in Be^{3}. Cited by *Mādh* 1.203— a) Tr^{2} देवांश्च ऋषीन्मनुष्यां; Kt^{2} wKt^{6} °ष्याश्च; BBe^{2} °ष्यांस्तु — b) TMd^{3} पितृभूतानि देवताः; Tr^{2} स्वपितॄन्; NKt^{4} Tj^{1} गृह्यांश्च; Pu^{10} ग्राह्याश्च; GMd^{5} भृत्यांश्च — c) TMd^{3} [*Jolly* Gr] भोजयित्वा

118. Cited by *Dev* 2.599;*Mādh* 1.203; pādas a-b cited by *Vij* 3.234–42; *Apa* 146, 1050 — a) NKt^{4} अयं; Lo^{3} अचं; Ox^{3} अय; Lo^{5} अद्वं; GMy सुकेवलं — b) Bo wKt^{6} TMd^{4} ये पचन्त्या°; Be^{3} पचेदात्म°; GMy °कारणं — c) TMd^{4} ह्येनं; GMy MTr^{6} ह्येव; Pu^{10} सतां सत्रं

119. a) wKt^{6} राजार्थस्ना°; NPu^{1} °क्स्नातकाचार्य; Be^{1} Bo Ho Hy wKt^{1} wKt^{6} Lo^{2} Lo^{4} NNg sOx^{1} Ox^{2} Ox^{3} Pu^{5} sPu^{6} Pu^{7} Pu^{8} Pu^{10} [*Jolly* G] *Go* °गुरु°; GMd^{1} °गरुः — b) Tr^{1} प्रियः; Pu^{5} Pu^{7} °स्वसुर°; wKt^{6} Lo^{5} Ox^{3} °श्वसुर°; Bo Lo^{2} °मातुलात् — c) Hy Ox^{3} अर्हयन्मधु°; Pu^{10} अर्हन्तो मधु°; wKt^{6} अर्हणमधु° — d) Be^{3} NKt^{4} La^{1} La^{2} Lo^{1} GMy sOx^{1} Ox^{2} NPu^{1} sPu^{6} Tj^{2} Tr^{2} Wa *Rc* प्रतिसं°; Be^{3} La^{1} GMd^{5} sOx^{1} sPu^{6} °वत्सरं पुनः; NNg [*Jolly* M] *Me Rn JhaDave* °वत्सरान्पुनः; La^{2} TMd^{3} Tr^{1} °वत्सरागतान्

120.* a) sOx^{1} sPu^{6} राजाश्च; NKt^{4} राजानः श्रोत्रि° — b) GMd^{1} *Me* [pāṭha] तते यज्ञ उपस्थितौ [GMd^{1} ततो]; TMd^{4} तन्त्रयज्ञे उपस्थिते; Be^{1} Bo Ho Hy Jm Jo^{1} Jo^{2} wKt^{1} Kt^{2} wKt^{3} BKt^{5} wKt^{6} La^{1} La^{2} Lo^{1} Lo^{3} oMd^{2} TMd^{3} GMd^{5} GMy NNg oOr Ox^{2} sPu^{6} [*but cor*] Pu^{8} Tj^{1} Tj^{2} Tr^{1} MTr^{3} MTr^{4} MTr^{6} [*Jolly* Ku R Nd] *Go Nā Ku Rc Mandlik KSS* °पस्थितौ; BBe^{2} °पस्थितेः; Pu^{2} °पस्थितः — c) BBe^{2} Pu^{5} Wa संपूज्यो; GMd^{5} संपूज्या; La^{1} संयोज्यौ — d) TMd^{3} GMy त्वन्यत; wKt^{1} तु यज्ञ; Lo^{1} स्थितौ

121. Omitted in [*Jolly* Nd]. Cited by *Apa* 145 — a) GMd^{5} सायं तस्य सिद्धस्य; BBe^{2} wKt^{1} wKt^{3} TMd^{3} sOx^{1} sPu^{6} *Apa* सायमन्नस्य; Tr^{2} °न्नस्य मन्त्रस्य — b) sOx^{1} sPu^{6} पत्न्यत्रं; Lo^{2} Pu^{5} Pu^{7} Pu^{10} °मन्त्र; GMd^{1} हरेद्वलिं

122. Cited by *Apa* 418; *Lakṣ* 410; *Hem* 3/1.72, 171, 321, 3/2.1064, 3/3.609; *Dev* 433, 83 — a) NNg oOr हि; Pu^{5} Pu^{7} [*Jolly* G] च; wKt^{1} Lo^{2} Lo^{4} sOx^{1} Tj^{1} निर्वृत्य; GMd^{5} निवृत्य; wKt^{6} निवर्त्य — b) Hy Jm Jo^{1} Kt^{2} *Mandlik KSS* °श्चेन्दुक्षये; Ho wKt^{6} °क्षयो — c) *Hem* 3/1.72 कृत्वान्वाहा°; Ox^{3} Pu^{5} °हर्यकं; Kt^{2} °हार्यक — d) wKt^{6} °माषिकं

पितॄणां मासिकं श्राद्धमन्वाहार्यं विदुर्बुधाः ।
तदामिषेण कर्तव्यं प्रशस्तेन प्रयत्नतः ॥१२३॥
तत्र ये भोजनीयाः स्युर्ये च वर्ज्या द्विजोत्तमाः ।
यावन्तश्चैव यैश्चान्नैस्तान्प्रवक्ष्याम्यशेषतः ॥१२४॥
द्वौ दैवे पितृकृत्ये त्रीनेकैकमुभयत्र वा ।
भोजयेत् सुसमृद्धोऽपि न प्रसज्जेत विस्तरे ॥१२५॥
सत्क्रियां देशकालौ च शौचं ब्राह्मणसंपदः ।
पञ्चैतान्विस्तरो हन्ति तस्मान्नेहेत विस्तरम् ॥१२६॥
प्रथिता प्रेतकृत्यैषा पित्र्यं नाम विधुक्षये ।
तस्मिन्युक्तस्यैति नित्यं प्रेतकृत्यैव लौकिकी ॥१२७॥

123.* Cited by *Hem* 3/1.573 — a) NKt^{4} Lo^{2} GMd^{1} TMd^{3} GMd^{5} GMy Pu^{5} Pu^{7} Tr^{1} MTr^{4} MTr^{6} [*Jolly* G Nd] *Go Nd Me* [pāṭha] *Ku* [pāṭha] पिण्डानां; NKt^{4} मासिकः — b) GMy °मन्वहार्यं; Bo विदुर्बुधः — c) Hy Jm Jo^{1} Kt^{2} OMd^{2} Tj^{2} MTr^{3} [*Jolly* Ku] *Ku Mandlik Jha KSS Dave* तच्चामिषेण; Tr^{1} तदामिक्षेण — d) GMd^{1} प्रयत्नेन प्रशस्ततः; Jm Jo^{1} Kt^{2} समंततः

Additional verse in Tr^{2}; commented by *Rc:*

न निर्वपति यः श्राद्धं प्रमीतपितृको द्विजः ।
इन्दुक्षये मासि मासि प्रायश्चित्ती भवेत्तु सः ॥

124. Cited by *Hem* 3/1.377; *Dev* 4.154 — a) Tj^{1} यो — b) SOx^{1} SPu^{6} स्युर्ये विवर्ज्या; Jo^{2} Lo^{3} Tj^{1} स्युर्वर्ज्या ये च द्विजो°; WKt^{1} GMd^{1} OOr द्विजातयः — c) Ox^{3} स्रवन्तश्चैव; GMd^{1} यावन्तयैश्चन्नै°; WKt^{1} यैश्चार्थस्ता°; Pu^{10} यैश्चाद्यैस्ता°; GMd^{5} Ox^{3} *Hem* यैश्चान्यैस्ता°; GMy ये चान्ये तान्प्र° — d) Bo WKt^{1} Lo^{1} Ox^{2} [*cor to*] °न्नैस्तत्प्रव°; Kt^{2} °न्नैस्ता प्रव°

125.* Omitted in Pu^{10}. Cited by *Viś* 1.225; *Hem* 3/1.159, 3/2.1148; *Apa* 430, 463; *Dev* 4.192–3; *Mādh* 1.699 — a) BBe^{2} Hy Jm Jo^{1} Kt^{2} WKt^{6} GMd^{1} GMd^{5} GMy SOx^{1} Pu^{5} Tj^{2} Tr^{1} Tr^{2} MTr^{3} देवे; Hy Jm Jo^{1} Jo^{2} Kt^{2} Lo^{3} OMd^{2} TMd^{3} GMd^{5} GMy NNg Tj^{1} Tj^{2} Tr^{1} MTr^{3} MTr^{4} MTr^{6} [*Jolly* R Nd] *Viś Apa* [vl] *BDh* 2.15.10 *Mādh Mandlik KSS* पितृकार्ये; *Apa* [vl] पित्र्यकार्ये; Be^{3} पितृयज्ञे — b) Ox^{2} क्रमादेकैकमेव च; Tr^{2} त्रीनैकै°; BKt^{5} WKt^{6} Ox^{3} च — c) GMy भोजयेद्धि समृद्धोपि; Be^{1} WKt^{6} स्वसमृ°; GMd^{1} ससमृ° — d) Ho BKt^{5} WKt^{6} La^{1} Lo^{1} Lo^{2} Lo^{4} TMd^{3} GMd^{5} GMy NNg SOx^{1} Ox^{2} NPu^{1} SPu^{6} Tr^{1} Tr^{2} [*Jolly* M Nd] *Viś Apa Hem Dev Rc* प्रसज्येत; Be^{1} Ox^{3} प्रसह्येत; *Me Go Ku Jha Dave* प्रवर्तेत; Wa विस्तरात्; TMd^{4} विस्तरः

126. Cited by *Viś* 1.225; *Apa* 463; *Mādh* 1.699 — a) Lo^{1} Tr^{2} सत्क्रिया; Tj^{1} सत्क्रियाया; GMd^{5} सत्कृतां — b) GMd^{1} चाशौचं; Ho NKt^{4} Lo^{2} La^{1} GMd^{5} NNg MTr^{6} *Viś Apa* °संपदं; NPu^{1} °संपदाः — c) Pu^{10} पञ्चैताग्निप्ररोहंति — d) *Viś* तस्मात्तं परिवर्जयेत्; La^{1} विस्तरान्; Lo^{5} GMd^{5} GMy Pu^{5} Pu^{7} Tr^{1} [*Jolly* G Gr Nd] विस्तरे

127. a) Bo La^{1} SOx^{1} Pu^{5} Pu^{7} प्रेत्य°; WKt^{1} TMd^{4} GMy SPu^{6} Tj^{1} °कृत्येषा; Tr^{1} °कृत्येषां; BBe^{2} Be^{3} °कृत्यैव — b) Lo^{1} पित्र्य; Lo^{2} NNg Pu^{5} Pu^{7} [*Jolly* G] पित्र्यो; WKt^{6} OOr पैत्र्यं; NKt^{4} पित्रा; NKt^{4} Lo^{2} NNg Pu^{5} Pu^{7} Wa [*Jolly* G] *Go Me* [pāṭha] विधिः क्षये; *Me* [pāṭha] तिथिक्षये; MTr^{4} विधीयते — c) TMd^{3} तस्मिन्मुक्तस्य वै नित्यं; Pu^{10} यो तस्मिन्युक्तश्चेन्नित्यं; WKt^{1} यस्मि°; NNg अस्मि°; Ho WKt^{1} Kt^{2} Lo^{2} SOx^{1} Pu^{5} SPu^{6} Pu^{7} Tr^{1} °क्तस्येति; GMd^{1} °क्तस्येह — d) Tr^{2} La^{1} SOx^{1} प्रेत्य°; कृतकृत्येह; Be^{1} BBe^{2} Wa °कृत्येव; Bo BCa Jo^{2} WKt^{1} WKt^{3} BKt^{5} Lo^{1} Lo^{3} Lo^{4} Lo^{5} GMy Tj^{1} Tr^{1} *Nā Nd* °कृत्येह; GMd^{5} °कृत्यैह; GMd^{1} °कृत्येति; Be^{3} °कृत्येन; TMd^{3} °कृत्येभि; WKt^{6} °कृत्या च; Kt^{2} लौकिकं

श्रोत्रियायैव देयानि हव्यकव्यानि दातृभिः ।
अर्हत्तमाय विप्राय तस्मै दत्तं महाफलम् ॥१२८॥
एकैकमपि विद्वांसं दैवे पित्र्ये च भोजयेत् ।
पुष्कलं फलमाप्नोति नामन्त्रज्ञान्बहूनपि ॥१२९॥
दूरादेव परीक्षेत ब्राह्मणं वेदपारगम् ।
तीर्थं तद्धव्यकव्यानां प्रदाने सोऽतिथिः स्मृतः ॥१३०॥
सहस्रं हि सहस्राणामनृचां यत्र भुञ्जते ।
एकस्तान्मन्त्रवित् प्रीतः सर्वानर्हति धर्मतः ॥१३१॥
ज्ञानोत्कृष्टाय देयानि कव्यानि च हवींषि च ।
न हि हस्तावसृग्दिग्धौ रुधिरेणैव शुध्यतः ॥१३२॥
यावतो ग्रसते पिण्डान् हव्यकव्येष्वमन्त्रवित् ।
तावतो ग्रसते प्रेत्य दीप्ताञ्छूलर्ष्ट्ययोगुडान् ॥१३३॥

128. Cited by *Apa* 437; *Hem* 3/1.377; *Mādh* 1.679 — a) Be^{1} दीयानि — c) TMd^{4} अर्हमाया; wKt^{1} °त्तमाया; Bo °त्तमाग्र — d) TMd^{4} GMy महत्फलं; TMd^{3} माहात्फलं; Hy महफलं

129. Omitted in oOr Ox^{3}; pādas c-d *ma* in Pu^{7}. Cited by *Apa* 437; *Mādh* 1.679 — b) Jm देवे; wKt^{6} पैत्रे; BCa पित्रे; NNg भोजयन्; [*Jolly* Nd] पूजयेत्; TMd^{4} याजयेत् — c) NPu^{1} पुष्कजं; sOx^{1} sPu^{6} [*mc sh to*] शाश्वतं — d) TMd^{4} नैवामन्त्र्यान्बहूनपि; Ho मन्त्रज्ञान्वा बहूनपि; Tr^{2} नामन्त्रःकान्बहूनपि; NKt^{4} °हून्यपि

130. Omitted in oOr. Cited by *Apa* 437; *Hem* 3/1.506; pādas a-b cited by *Dev* 4154; *Mādh* 1.356 — a) Ho दूरादेवं; wKt^{1} पूर्वादेव — d) sOx^{1} sPu^{6} [*mc sh to*] प्रधानं; TMd^{4} सातिथिः

131. Cited by *Hem* 3/1.377 — a) BCa साहस्रं; Be^{1} La^{1} TMd^{3} TMd^{4} GMd^{5} GMy sOx^{1} sPu^{6} [*mc sh to*] Tr^{1} MTr^{4} सहस्राणि सह°; *Go* pratīka सहस्राणि; NKt^{4} च — b) GMd^{1} °मानृचां; wKt^{1} Pu^{5} Pu^{7} *Me* [*pāṭhāntara* as nom. plu.] °मनृचा; TMd^{4} °मवृता; GMy °मनुजा; wKt^{3} °नृचामत्र; Bo La^{1} [*but cor*] भुञ्जयेत्; GMy भुज्यते — c) wKt^{6} एकस्तावन्मन्त्र°; TMd^{4} एकस्मान्मन्त्र°; Be^{3} sOx^{1} sPu^{6} [*Jolly* Nd] °विद्विप्रः [sPu^{6} *cor to* °विद्युक्तः]; Tr^{1} °वद्विप्रः; GMd^{5} °वित्प्राज्ञः; [*Jolly* N] *Nā* [possibly] °विद्युक्तः — d) GMd^{1} TMd^{4} सर्वमर्हति; wKt^{3} सर्वानर्हन्ति; MTr^{4} सर्वतः; TMd^{4} मन्त्रवित्

132. Cited by *Hem* 3/1.378 — a) Be^{3} Bo Ho sOx^{1} Ox^{3} NPu^{1} sPu^{6} Pu^{10} [*Jolly* M$^{1-2-8-9}$ Me] *Hem* °त्कृष्टेपु; TMd^{3} oOr °त्कृष्टानि; wKt^{6} °त्सृष्टाय — b) wKt^{6} क्रव्यानि; Lo^{5} oOr कर्तव्यानि हवींपि; Lo^{2} *om first* च — c) GMy न च; Be^{1} हस्तौ असृ°; Tr^{1} °वसंदिग्धौ; Pu^{5} Pu^{7} Wa °सृग्दिग्धो; TMd^{4} °सृग्दग्धौ — d) TMd^{4} रुधिरेण च शुध्यति; Ox^{2} शुध्येते रुधिरेण वै; TMd^{3} याप्येते रुधिरेण वै; GMd^{5} Tr^{1} धाव्येते रुधिरेण वै; MTr^{4} धार्येत रुधिरेणैव; Wa शुध्यते; wKt^{3} सिध्यतः

133.* Cited by *Apa* 449; *Lakṣ* 4.75; *Hem* 3/1.461 — a) Pu^{10} [*Jolly* M^{1-2-8}] यावद्भिः; MTr^{3} ग्रसिते; Be^{1} Be^{3} Bo Ho Hy Jm Jo^{1} Jo^{2} Kt^{2} wKt^{3} La^{2} Lo^{1} Lo^{2} Lo^{3} oMd^{2} NNg oOr Ox^{2} NPu^{1} Pu^{2} Pu^{3} Pu^{4} Pu^{5} Pu^{7} Pu^{8} Tj^{1} Tj^{2} MTr^{3} Wa [*Jolly* G Ku Nd R] *Go Ku Rn Rc Mandlik Jolly Jha KSS Dave* ग्रासान् — b) Jm wKt^{6} sOx^{1} sPu^{6} Pu^{10} °कव्येपु मन्त्र° — c) sOx^{1} sPu^{6} यावतो; GMd^{1} ग्रसतो; *Me* प्रेतो [but gives प्रेत्य as *pāṭhāntara*] — d) BKt^{5} wKt^{6} GMd^{1} TMd^{4} GMy oOr sOx^{1} Ox^{2} sPu^{6} Pu^{8} Tr^{2} दीप्तान्शूलानयोगुडान् [GMy °गुलान्; Ox^{2} °मयान्]; Ho La^{1} NPu^{1} *Rc* दीप्तान्स्थूलानयोगुडान्; *Hem* दीप्तान् ऋष्टीनयोगुडान्; [*Jolly* Nd] दीप्ताञ्छूलान्ह्ययोहुलान्; Tr^{1} दीप्ताञ्छूलान्ह्यपोहुजान्; Lo^{1} दीप्तान्शू-लव्ययोगुडात्; wKt^{1} दीप्तान्पिण्डान्योगुडान्; Hy Jm Jo^{1} Kt^{2} Pu^{2} Pu^{4} MTr^{3} *Mandlik Jha KSS Dave* दीप्त-

ज्ञाननिष्ठा द्विजाः केचित् तपोनिष्ठास्तथापरे ।
तपःस्वाध्यायनिष्ठाश्च कर्मनिष्ठास्तथैव च ॥१३४॥
ज्ञाननिष्ठेषु कव्यानि प्रतिष्ठाप्यानि यत्नतः ।
हव्यानि तु यथान्यायं सर्वेष्वेव चतुर्ष्वपि ॥१३५॥
अश्रोत्रियः पिता यस्य पुत्रः स्याद्वेदपारगः ।
अश्रोत्रियो वा पुत्रः स्यात् पिता स्याद्वेदपारगः ॥१३६॥
ज्यायांसमनयोर्विद्याद् यस्य स्याच्छ्रोत्रियः पिता ।
मन्त्रसंपूजनार्थं तु सत्कारमितरोऽर्हति ॥१३७॥
न श्राद्धे भोजयेन्मित्रं धनैः कार्योऽस्य संग्रहः ।
नारिं न मित्रं यं विद्यात् तं श्राद्धे भोजयेद् द्विजम् ॥१३८॥
यस्य मित्रप्रधानानि श्राद्धानि च हवींषि च ।
तस्य प्रेत्य फलं नास्ति श्राद्धेषु च हविःषु च ॥१३९॥

शूल° ; NKt^4 दीप्तांस्तूल° ; Jo^2 दीप्ताशूल° ; Wa °गुडा; Lo^2 °गुणान्

134. Pādas c-d omitted in MTr^6 and *ma* in Ox^2. Cited by *Hem* 3/1.416; *Lakṣ* 4.59 — a) Lo^2 [*but cor*] Wa °निष्ठो; TMd^3 °निष्ठान्; TMd^4 °निष्ठं; wKt^6 Ox^3 द्विजः; GMy प्रजाः — b) Bo तयोर्निष्ठा° ; Lo^2 °स्तथोपरे; Lo^5 °स्तथैव च — c) GMd^1 TMd^3 TMd^4 GMd^5 GMy Tr^1 MTr^4 *Lakṣ* स्वाध्याययज्ञनिष्ठाश्च; wKt^6 °निष्ठा च — d) Hy Jm Jo^1 Kt^2 NKt^4 oMd^2 oOr sOx^1 Pu^5 sPu^6 Pu^7 Tj^2 MTr^3 [*Jolly* G Ku] *Mandlik Jha KSS Dave* °निष्ठास्तथापरे

135. Cited by *Hem* 3/1.416; *Lakṣ* 4.59 — a) Be^1 Ho Jo^2 Lo^3 sOx^1 Ox^3 sPu^6 Tj^1 Tr^2 ज्ञानोत्कृष्टेषु [cf. 3.132]; NPu^1 ज्ञानोत्कृष्ठेन; wKt^6 ज्ञानिनिष्ठयि — b) Ox^2 प्रतिपाद्यानि; La^1 जन्मतः; TMd^3 सर्वतः — c) *Hem* हव्यकव्यानि देयानि [vl as in ed]; TMd^3 GMd^5 Tr^1 MTr^4 [*Jolly* Nd] वेदार्थवित्सु हव्यानि; oMd^2 कव्यानि; BCa Ho Jo^2 wKt^1 BKt^5 wKt^6 Lo^4 TMd^4 NNg sOx^1 Ox^2 Ox^3 NPu^1 Pu^5 sPu^6 Pu^7 Tj^1 Tr^2 [*Jolly* M G R] *Rc Jolly* च; Tj^2 तथान्यायं; GMd^1 TMd^4 GMy Ox^2 [*but cor sh*] *Lakṣ* यथाश्राद्धं; NNg यथाश्रद्धं — d) La^1 चतुर्थे वानुपूर्वशः; Be^3 Ox^2 चतुर्ष्वेवानुपूर्वशः; Bo Lo^4 Lo^5 TMd^4 Pu^8 *Lakṣ* °न्यायमेतेष्वेव; Lo^2 GMd^1 °न्यायमेतेष्वपि; GMy °न्यायमेतेष्वेषु

136. Pādas a-b omitted in Ho. Cited by *Hem* 3/1.443; *Lakṣ* 4.59; *Mādh* 1.678 —a) Tr^1 *om* अश्रोत्रियः; Be^1 अश्रोत्रिय; *Lakṣ* तस्य — c) GMd^1 *om* वा — c-d) Lo^5 repeats pādas a-b in place of c-d — d) wKt^1 BKt^5 wKt^6 पुत्रः वा वेद°

137. Cited by *Hem* 3/1.443, 461; pādas a-b cited by *Mādh* 1.678 — a) TMd^4 °समुभयोर्वि° ; wKt^6 °योर्विद्या — c) Ox^3 Pu^{10} [*Jolly* M$^{1-2-5-8-9}$] °जनार्थाय; BKt^5 च; Jo^2 Lo^4 Lo^5 [*Jolly* M$^{3-4}$] हि — d) Lo^3 TMd^3 संस्कारमित°

138. Cited by *Apa* 448; *Dev* 4.162 — a) TMd^3 TMd^4 श्राद्धं; BKt^5 भोजयन्मित्रं; Tj^1 °येन्मन्त्रं; TMd^3 °येन्मिश्रं — b) Jm धनः; GMy कार्योथ; TMd^4 कार्यैस्य — c) Tj^1 नारी; Lo^1 तं मित्रं यं; GMd^1 sOx^1 sPu^6 यो विद्यात्; Kt^2 विद्यान् — d) Kt^2 तेन श्राद्धे; Be^1 TMd^4 oOr श्राद्धं

139. Cited by *Hem* 3/1.462; *Dev* 4.162 — b) GMd^5 Ox^2 कव्यानि च हवींषि; Lo^2 Tr^1 *om first* च — c) Ho प्रेत; Jm प्रीति; Be^1 फले — c-d) *Hem* पितृषु दैवयज्ञेषु दाता स्वर्गं न गच्छति — d) Wa श्राद्धे मित्रो द्विजाधमः [cf. 3.140 d]; TMd^4 सस्येषु; Ox^2 कव्येषु; Tr^2 *om first* च; Bo हवींषु; TMd^4 हविंषि; TMd^3 हविंषु; wKt^6 GMy हविःष्वपि

यः संगतानि कुरुते मोहाच्छ्राद्धेन मानवः ।
स स्वर्गाच्च्यवते लोकाच्छ्राद्धमित्रो द्विजाधमः ॥१४०॥
संभोजनी साभिहिता पैशाची दक्षिणा द्विजैः ।
इहैवास्ते तु सा लोके गौरन्धेवैकवेश्मनि ॥१४१॥
यथेरिणे बीजमुप्त्वा न वप्ता लभते फलम् ।
तथानृचे हविर्दत्त्वा न दाता लभते फलम् ॥१४२॥
दातॄन् प्रतिग्रहीतॄंश्च कुरुते फलभागिनः ।
विदुषे दक्षिणा दत्ता विधिवत् प्रेत्य चेह च ॥१४३॥
कामं श्राद्धेऽर्चयेन्मित्रं नाभिरूपमपि त्वरिम् ।
द्विषता हि हविर्भुक्तं भवति प्रेत्य निष्फलम् ॥१४४॥
यत्नेन भोजयेच्छ्राद्धे बह्वृचं वेदपारगम् ।
शाखान्तगमथाध्वर्युं छन्दोगं वा समाप्तिकम् ॥१४५॥

140. Cited by *Hem* 3/1.462 — a) TMd^{4} यो — b) Be^{1} [*but mc*] Ho Jo^{2} La^{1} Lo^{3} sOx^{1} Ox^{2} NPu^{1} Pu^{2} sPu^{6} Tj^{1} Tj^{2} Tr^{2} [*Jolly* R] मोहाच्छ्राद्धेषु; wKt^{6} GMd^{1} GMd^{5} Pu^{5} Pu^{7} Pu^{10} [*Jolly* M G] *Hem Jolly* °च्छ्राद्धानि; BKt^{5} °च्छ्राद्धेनि; TMd^{3} °च्छ्राद्धे नराधमः; *Me Go Ku Rn Rc Mr* support the adopted reading — d) *Hem* °मित्रं; GMd^{5} GMy Tr^{1} MTr^{4} MTr^{6} °मित्रो विनश्यति; TMd^{3} °मित्रोपि नश्यति; Tr^{2} द्विजोधमः; Bo द्विजातयः; Be^{3} BCa [*but cor*] नराधमः

141. Cited by *Hem* 3/1.462 — a) Ho BKt^{5} wKt^{6} Lo^{3} Tj^{1} संभोजिनी; TMd^{4} सुभोजनी; wKt^{3} °जनीभिहिता; Be^{1} Lo^{3} Ox^{3} Pu^{10} Tj^{1} Tr^{2} *Hem* याभिहिता; GMy चाभिहिता — b) Ox^{3} पिशाची; Tj^{2} द्विजः; sOx^{1} sPu^{6} बुधैः — c) Lo^{1} इहैवास्ति; TMd^{4} इहैवस्ते; sOx^{1} sPu^{6} च सा; wKt^{1} न ता— d) *Hem* गौरवे चैकवेश्मनि; Jo^{1} गोर°; wKt^{1} Lo^{3} GMy Tj^{1} °न्धेवेकवे°

142. Pāda c-d omitted in GMd^{1}. Cited by *Hem* 3/1.465 — a) Tr^{1} यथैरिणे; Wa यथेरिणो; Tr^{2} यथारिणो; Ho Ox^{2} यथेरणे; TMd^{4} यथेरेणे; oOr यथोपरे; TMd^{4} बीजमुप्ते; Be^{3} बीजमुप्तं — b) TMd^{3} नोप्ता च लभते; Tr^{2} न समालभते — c) Lo^{3} यथानृचे; Be^{3} wKt^{3} तथानृते; *Hem* हविर्दद्यान्न — d) Bo Lo^{2} Lo^{4} Lo^{5} Ox^{3} Pu^{10} [*Jolly* M] दाता न

143. Pādas a-b omitted in GMd^{1}. Cited by *Lakṣ* 4.57; *Hem* 3/1.378 — a) Ho दातृप्रति°; sOx^{1} Ox^{2} Ox^{3} sPu^{6} Pu^{10} Tr^{1} Tr^{2} °गृहीतॄंश्च; Ho BKt^{5} La^{1} °ग्रहीत्रींश्च; NPu^{1} °ग्रहंतॄंश्च; wKt^{6} °सहितॄंश्च — b) MTr^{3} °भागिना; Kt^{2} °भोगिनः — c) Ox^{2} विदुषो; Be^{1} विद्विषे; GMd^{1} GMd^{5} *Lakṣ* विद्वद्भ्यो; Wa दक्षिणे; Jm Jo^{1} Kt^{2} BKt^{5} wKt^{6} Lo^{5} oOr MTr^{3} MTr^{4} MTr^{6} *Mandlik Jolly Jha KSS Dave* दक्षिणां दत्त्वा; Tr^{2} दक्षिणां दत्तं; Ox^{2} दत्त्वा [*but cor*] — d) Pu^{5} Pu^{7} भवति प्रेत्य; NNg चेह वा

144. Cited by *Apa* 448; *Hem* 3/1.447, 464; *Dev* 4.162; *Mādh* 1.684 — a) TMd^{3} TMd^{4} GMd^{5} GMy MTr^{4} काममभ्यर्चयेन्मित्रं [TMd^{4} °चयन्मित्रं; MTr^{4} °येन्नित्यं]; [*Jolly* Gr] कामं मास्येर्चये° — b) Lo^{1} नार्चाभिरर्चयत्वरिं — c) TMd^{3} GMy Tr^{1} द्विषतापि; wKt^{6} द्विषताचिर्हवि°; Pu^{10} Tj^{1} च; [*Jolly* Gr] हविर्दत्तं — d) Be^{1} Lo^{3} Tj^{1} [*Jolly* R] प्रेत्य चेह च निष्फलं; oOr *om* भवति

145. Cited by *Lakṣ* 4.57; *Hem* 3/1.382 — c) Lo^{1} TMd^{3} Pu^{10} शाखान्तरमथा°; TMd^{4} शाखांपरमथा°; BKt^{5} wKt^{6} °न्तकमथा°; Jo^{1} °गमयथाध्वर्युं; GMd^{1} TMd^{3} GMd^{5} GMy Tr^{1} MTr^{4} MTr^{6} °न्तगं वाप्यध्वर्युं; Lo^{1} °गमथाचार्यं; wKt^{6} °गमथाधर्यं; TMd^{4} °ध्वर्यु; Be^{1} °ध्वर्यं — d) Pu^{10} छन्दोगा; *Hem* छन्दोगंश्च; Hy Jm Jo^{1} Kt^{2} Tj^{2} MTr^{3} *Mandlik Jha KSS Dave* तु; Be^{1} Be^{3} Bo BCa Ho La^{2} Lo^{1} Lo^{2} Lo^{3} GMd^{5} sOx^{1} Ox^{2} NPu^{1} Pu^{2} Pu^{4} sPu^{6} Tj^{1} Tr^{1} Tr^{2} Wa *Nā* [pāṭha] *Rn Nd Rc* [*Jolly* R Nd M^{3}]

एषामन्यतमो यस्य भुञ्जीत श्राद्धमर्चितः ।
पितॄणां तस्य तृप्तिः स्याच्छाश्वती साप्तपौरुषी ॥१४६॥
एष वै प्रथमः कल्पः प्रदाने हव्यकव्ययोः ।
अनुकल्पस्त्वयं ज्ञेयः सदा सद्भिरनुष्ठितः ॥१४७॥
मातामहं मातुलं च स्वस्रीयं श्वशुरं गुरुम् ।
दौहित्रं विट्पतिं बन्धुमृत्विग्याज्यौ च भोजयेत् ॥१४८॥
न ब्राह्मणं परीक्षेत दैवे कर्मणि धर्मवित् ।
पित्र्ये कर्मणि तु प्राप्ते परीक्षेत प्रयत्नतः ॥१४९॥
ये स्तेनाः पतिताः क्लीबा ये च नास्तिकवृत्तयः ।
तान्हव्यकव्ययोर्विप्राननर्हान्मनुरब्रवीत् ॥१५०॥
जटिलं चानधीयानं दुर्वालं कितवं तथा ।
याजयन्ति च ये पूगांस्तांश्च श्राद्धे न भोजयेत् ॥१५१॥

समाप्तिगं; TMd^{4} समन्त्रकं

146. Cited by *Dev* 4.160 — a) GMd^{1} तेषाम°; TMd^{3} येषाम°; Bo °तमा — b) Tr^{1} °मर्चितं; Lo^{3} °मर्जितः — c) MTr^{4} तत्र तृप्तिः; Tr^{1} चैव तृप्तिः — d) TMd^{3} Tr^{1} Tr^{2} सप्त°; Hy °पौरुषि; GMd^{1} °पौरुषं; Jo^{1} °पारुषी; TMd^{4} °पूरुषी

147. Cited by *Vij* 1.220; *Hem* 3/1.441; *Dev* 4.160; pādas c-d cited by *Mādh* 1.683 — a) TMd^{3} एषैव — b) Jm प्रधाने; BKt^{5} Tr^{1} कव्यहव्ययोः — c) WKt^{6} °कल्पस्स्वयं; GMy ज्ञेया; *Vij* प्रोक्तः — d) GMy नित्यं सद्भि°; *Vij* सद्भिरगर्हितः

148. Cited by *Hem* 3/1.447; *Dev* 4.160; *Mādh* 1.683 — a) Be^{1} Jo^{2} Lo^{3} SOx^{1} SPu^{6} Tj^{1} [*Jolly* R] वा — b) Lo^{2} स्वश्रीयं; OOr श्वस्रीय; TMd^{3} [*but cor sh*] स्वश्रियं; BKt^{5} WKt^{6} स्वस्रीश्च; Pu^{10} स्वगुरुं गुरुं; Jo^{2} गुरोः — c) Lo^{1} जामात्रं हि दौहित्रमृत्वि°; TMd^{3} दौहत्रं; Be^{1} विट्पतं; Bo विधतिं; NKt^{4} वेगतिं — d) BKt^{5} WKt^{6} °त्विग्याज्यं; *Hem* °त्विग्याज्यांश्च

149. Cited by *Lakṣ* 4.56; *Hem* 3/1.510 — a) Ho ब्रह्मणं; OOr परीक्ष्येत — b) NKt^{4} Tr^{1} देवे; GMy OOr दैव; GMd^{1} OOr मन्त्रवित्; Be^{3} कर्मवित्; Lo^{4} कर्हिचित् — c) Kt^{2} WKt^{6} पित्रे; OOr पैत्रे; TMd^{4} च कर्मणि प्राप्ते; Tr^{2} च; NPu^{1} *Lakṣ* संप्राप्ते; NNg प्राप्ते तु; *Hem* तु प्राज्ञः; Lo^{3} [*Jolly* R] प्राप्तं — d) TMd^{4} परीक्षेतो; TMd^{3} विशेषतः

Additional verse in GMd^{1} TMd^{4} GMd^{5} NNg OOr Tr^{1} Tr^{2} MTr^{4} MTr^{6}; commented by *Rc:*

तेषामन्ये पङ्क्तिदूष्यास्तथान्ये पङ्क्तिपावनाः ।
अपाङ्क्तेयान्प्रवक्ष्यामि कव्यघ्नांस्तु द्विजाधमान् ॥

a) Tr^{1} एषामन्ये पङ्क्तिदुष्टा°; Tr^{2} यथान्ये पङ्क्तिसंदूष्या°; MTr^{4} MTr^{6} °दूषा° — a-b) OOr तेषामन्यान्पंक्तिदोषांस्तथान्यान्पंक्तिपावनान् — c) OOr अपांक्तेयांश्च वक्ष्यामि; Tr^{2} आपा° — d) Tr^{1} कर्मघ्नांस्तान्द्वि°; GMd^{1} कव्यानर्हान् च द्वि°; Tr^{2} कव्यानर्हद्वि°

150. Cited by *Apa* 447; *Lakṣ* 4.84; *Hem* 3/1.480; *Dev* 4.166; *Mādh* 1.687 — a) BBe^{2} BCa Jm Jo^{1} Kt^{2} NKt^{4} Lo^{2} GMd^{1} OMd^{2} OOr MTr^{3} *Apa Mādh Mandlik Jha KSS Dave* स्तेनपतितक्लीबा; GMy SOx^{1} SPu^{6} क्लीबाः पतिताः स्तेना; MTr^{6} पतित; TMd^{3} पतितां — b) Kt^{2} य; BKt^{5} WKt^{6} ये तु; GMd^{1} नास्तिक्य° — c) OOr तान्कव्यहव्ययो°; WKt^{3} °योर्विद्वान° — d) Pu^{5} Pu^{7} °नर्ह्यान्मनु°

151.* Cited by *Apa* 450; *Lakṣ* 4.84; *Hem* 3/1.480; *Dev* 4.166; *Mādh* 1.687 — a) Tj^{2} जरितं; Lo^{1} SOx^{1} Ox^{3} SPu^{6} Pu^{10} [*Jolly* M$^{1-2-5-8}$ Nd] वानधी°; MTr^{3} °यानो; NKt^{4} Lo^{2} °यानां — b)

चिकित्सका देवलका मांसविक्रयिणस्तथा ।
विपणेन च जीवन्तो वर्ज्याः स्युर्हव्यकव्ययोः ॥१५२॥
प्रेष्यो ग्रामस्य राज्ञश्च कुनखी श्यावदन्तकः ।
प्रतिरोद्धा गुरोश्चैव त्यक्ताग्निर्वार्धुषिस्तथा ॥१५३॥
यक्ष्मी च पशुपालश्च परिवेत्ता निराकृतिः ।
ब्रह्मद्विट् परिवित्तिश्च गणाभ्यन्तर एव च ॥१५४॥
कुशीलवोऽवकीर्णी च वृषलीपतिरेव च ।
पौनर्भवश्च काणश्च यस्य चोपपतिर्गृहे ॥१५५॥

Be[3] Ho NKt[4] La[2] Pu[8] Tr[2] *Hem* दुर्वलं; *Apa* दुर्बालं; GMy दुर्वारं; MTr[4] दुर्वाचं; Be[1] BBe[2] Bo Hy Jm Jo[1] wKt[1] Kt[2] wKt[3] BKt[5] wKt[6] La[1] Lo[1] Lo[2] Lo[3] oMd[2] TMd[4] NNg sOx[1] Ox[2] NPu[1] Pu[2] Pu[3] Pu[4] Pu[5] sPu[6] Pu[7] Pu[10] Tj[1] Tj[2] MTr[3] Wa *Mandlik Jolly Jha KSS Dave* दुर्बलं; GMd[1] बालं च कितवं — c) TMd[4] योजयन्ति; *Dave* याचयन्ति [typo?]; BKt[5] wKt[6] यावन्ति; wKt[3] तु; Lo[4] *ma* ये; TMd[4] यो; sPu[6] पूढां°; wKt[1] Ox[2] [*but cor*] शूद्रां°; Ox[3] Pu[10] Tj[1] पूगां तांश्च; *Mādh* पूर्वान्तांश्च — d) GMy °स्तां श्राद्धे नैव भोजयेत्; TMd[3] °स्तान् श्राद्धे न तु पूजयेत्; Ho °स्ताश्च; Tj[1] °स्तां च; La[1] *Apa* श्राद्धे विवर्जयेत्; Be[3] GMd[5] पूजयेत्

152.* Cited by *Lakṣ* 4.84; *Hem* 3/1.480–1; *Dev* 4.167; *Mādh* 1.687 — a) BBe[2] Be[3] BCa [*but cor*] Ho Hy Jm Jo[1] Jo[2] Kt[2] NKt[4] wKt[6] La[1] Lo[3] Lo[4] Lo[5] oMd[2] TMd[4] GMd[5] GMy NNg oOr sOx[1] Ox[2] Ox[3] NPu[1] Pu[2] Pu[3] Pu[4] Pu[5] sPu[6] Pu[7] Pu[10] Tj[2] Tr[2] MTr[4] MTr[6] Wa *Hem Dev Nā Mādh Mandlik Jolly KKS* चिकित्सकान्देवलकान्मांस°; BKt[5] विचिकित्सान्देवलकान्मांस° — c) NNg विपण्येन; Tj[1] विपुणेन; TMd[4] विपणेरपि; Pu[10] त्वजीवन्तो; Bo wKt[6] Lo[5] जीवन्ति — d) GMd[5] लज्जा स्यु°; *Hem* वर्ज्यास्ते हव्य°

153. Verses 153 and 154 transposed in Ox[2] *Dave*. Cited by *Lakṣ* 4.84; *Hem* 3/1.481; *Dev* 4.167 — a) wKt[6] प्रैष्यो; NNg प्रेष्या; Ox[3] प्रेषो; Be[1] Wa प्रोष्यो; Ho La[1] NPu[1] ग्रामश्च; TMd[4] ग्रामस्स; TMd[3] राज्ञस्यः — b) Be[1] शाव°; NKt[4] Ox[2] [*but cor*] Tr[1] श्यावदन्नपि; Lo[2] श्यावदन्तपि; Tj[1] °दन्तिकः; TMd[3] °दन्तरः — c) Bo प्रतिराद्धा; Jm परिरोद्धा; NNg प्रतिषिद्धा; Tr[2] प्रतिबोद्धा; Lo[1] गुरोश्चैवं; GMy गुरुश्चैव; TMd[3] गुरोस्तैव — d) Jo[2] Tr[2] त्यक्ताग्निवार्धु°; wKt[3] Tj[1] त्यक्तानिवार्धु°; Tj[1] °षीस्तथा; sOx[1] sPu[6] °षीतथा; Lo[1] °षस्तथा

Additional verses in TMd[3] [cf. *VaDh* 2.40]:

समर्घ्यं पण्यमाहृत्य महार्घ्यं यः प्रयच्छति ।
स वै वार्धुषिको नाम स वै वृद्ध्या प्रयोजयेत् ।।
यश्च निन्द्यात्परं जीवन्प्रशंसत्यात्मनो गुणान् ।
स च वार्धुषिको नाम ब्राह्मवादिषु गर्हितः ।।

154. Cited by *Lakṣ* 4.84; *Hem* 3/1.481; *Dev* 4.167; *Mādh* 1.687 — a) oOr यशुश्च पशुपालाश्च; wKt[6] यक्षी; Lo[1] यक्ष्मा; GMy क्षयी; Bo लक्ष्मी; BBe[2] लक्ष्मीश्च; Bo °पालैश्च; TMd[4] °पालं च — c) Kt[2] TMd[3] NPu[1] Pu[10] ब्रह्मविट्; GMy Tr[1] ब्रह्महा; La[1] ब्रह्मविद् पतिवि°; sOx[1] sPu[6] परिवेत्तिश्च; GMy Tj[1] Tr[1] परिवित्तश्च; Pu[5] Pu[7] परिवृत्तिश्च; TMd[3] परिचित्तश्च — d) TMd[3] गुणा°; Tr[1] गौणा°

155. Pādas a-b omitted in BKt[5]. Cited by *Lakṣ* 4.85; *Hem* 3/1.481; *Dev* 4.167; *Mādh* 1.687 — a) GMy कुशीलको वणिक् चैव; GMd[1] कुशीलोवावदग्रकश्च; TMd[3] MTr[3] °वकर्णी; NKt[4] Lo[4] Lo[5] °वकीर्णा; TMd[4] °वकीर्णौ; wKt[6] °वकीर्णश्च — c) Wa योनभवश्च; wKt[6] कालश्च; Pu[10] कारश्च; Ox[3] काणे यस्य — d) Pu[7] Pu[10] यश्च; Jo[1] यस्मै; TMd[4] °पतिर्गृही; oMd[2] °पतिर्गृभे

भृतकाध्यापको यश्च भृतकाध्यापितस्तथा ।
शूद्रशिष्यो गुरुश्चैव वाग्दुष्टः कुण्डगोलकौ ॥१५६।
अकारणे परित्यक्ता मातापित्रोर्गुरोस्तथा ।
ब्राह्मैर्यौनैश्च संबन्धैः संयोगं पतितैर्गतः ॥१५७॥
अगारदाही गरदः कुण्डाशी सोमविक्रयी ।
समुद्रयायी बन्दी च तैलिकः कूटकारकः ॥१५८॥
पित्रा विवदमानश्च कितवो मद्यपस्तथा ।
पापरोग्यभिशस्तश्च दाम्भिको रसविक्रयी ॥१५९॥
धनुःशराणां कर्ता च यश्चाग्रेदिधिषूपतिः ।
मित्रध्रुग्द्यूतवृत्तिश्च पुत्राचार्यस्तथैव च ॥१६०॥
भ्रामरी गण्डमाली च श्वित्र्यथो पिशुनस्तथा ।
उन्मत्तोऽन्धश्च वर्ज्याः स्युर्वेदनिन्दक एव च ॥१६१॥

156. mTr^{3} has the following order: 156a-b, 157c-d, 156c-d, 157a-b. Cited by *Lakṣ* 4.86; *Hem* 3/1.481; *Dev* 4.167; *Mādh* 1.687 — a) gMd^{1} °ध्यापितो; Ho wKt^{1} sOx^{1} sPu^{6} °ध्यापकश्चैव; Lo^{4} Ox^{3} यस्य — b) oOr °ध्यापकस्तथा; wKt^{3} *Lakṣ Hem* [vl as in ed] °ध्यापितश्च यः; gMd^{1} °ध्यापकश्चः [°कश्च यः?] — d) gMy वागुष्टः; tMd^{3} वाग्दुषः; sOx^{1} sPu^{6} वाचाटः; Pu^{10} [*Jolly* M^{1-2-8}] वाग्दुर्वाक्; Lo^{5} गुण्ड°; La^{1} कुलुगो°; Bo °गोळकौ; gMd^{5} °गोलकाः; Tr^{1} °गोलकः; gMy °कोलकौ; Tr^{2} °कोलकै

157. Cited by *Hem* 3/1.481; *Lakṣ* 4.85; *Dev* 4.167; *Mādh* 1.687; pādas a-b cited by *Apa* 447 — a) La^{1} अकारेण; bBe^{2} Be^{3} bCa Jm Jo^{1} Jo^{2} Kt^{2} wKt^{3} bKt^{5} wKt^{6} Lo^{1} Lo^{2} Lo^{4} Lo^{5} oMd^{2} tMd^{4} Pu^{2} Pu^{4} Pu^{5} Pu^{7} *Mādh Mandlik KSS Dave* अकारणपरि°; nKt^{4} आकारणपरि°; Ox^{2} आकारण° *cor to* अकारणपरि°; wKt^{1} *Apa Lakṣ Hem Nā* अकारणात्परि°; Be^{1} अकारेणापरि°; tMd^{3} °त्यक्त; tMd^{4} °त्यागी — b) oOr मात्रा°; nKt^{4} Tr^{1} °पित्रोगु°; Bo nKt^{4} Tj^{1} °त्रोर्गुरुस्तथा; oOr °त्रोगुरूस्तथा; bBe^{2} Lo^{1} °त्रोर्गुरूस्तथा — c) Pu^{5} Pu^{7} ब्राह्मयैर्यौ°; nKt^{4} ब्राह्मायौ°; Be^{1} bCa Ho Lo^{3} Lo^{4} Lo^{5} gMd^{1} Pu^{10} Wa °र्योनैश्च; Lo^{1} gMy °र्यानैश्च; oOr °र्योनिश्च; mTr^{6} °र्यातैश्च; tMd^{4} संबन्धास्संयोगं — d) Bo संयोगपतितोगतः; bKt^{5} wKt^{6} La^{1} संयोगैः; Lo^{4} Lo^{5} Ox^{3} पतितैर्गताः

158. Pādas c-d omitted in bKt^{5} and *ma* in wKt^{6}. Cited by *Lakṣ* 4.85; *Hem* 3/1.481; *Dev* 4.167; *Mādh* 1.687 — a) Be^{1} bBe^{2} Be^{3} Bo Jo^{2} wKt^{1} wKt^{3} nKt^{4} bKt^{5} wKt^{6} La^{1} La^{2} Lo^{4} oMd^{2} sOx^{1} sPu^{6} Tj^{2} Tr^{2} *Jolly* आगार°; Ho tMd^{3} अङ्गार°; tMd^{3} नरदः — c) Tr^{2} शूद्रयाती च बन्दी च; Jo^{1} °यायीं बन्दीं; gMd^{1} mTr^{4} mTr^{6} *Dev* वन्दी — d) Ho gMy Ox^{2} [*but cor*] तैलकः; gMd^{1} तैलिकं; Tj^{1} तौलिकः; nKt^{4} तलिकः; Tr^{1} तैलकृत्; wKt^{6} कूटकालकः; tMd^{3} °कोरकः

159. Omitted in bKt^{5} and *ma* in wKt^{6}. Cited by *Lakṣ* 4.85; *Hem* 3/1.481; *Dev* 4.167; *Mādh* 1.687 — a) tMd^{4} पिता; Jm gMy Wa विवाद°; tMd^{4} विगद°; tMd^{3} विवश° — b) gMd^{1} tMd^{4} sOx^{1} sPu^{6} Pu^{8} Tr^{1} *Dev Lakṣ* केकरो [given as pāṭha in *Me Nā Go Ku Nd*]; Ho केररो; Be^{3} केरके — c) Ox^{2} [*but cor*] °रोगाभि°; tMd^{4} °रोगभि°; Tr^{1} °भिशप्तश्च — d) gMd^{1} धाम्भिको; Tr^{1} डाम्भिको; Pu^{5} Pu^{7} [*Jolly* G] जालिको

160. Cited by *Lakṣ* 4.85–6; *Hem* 3/1.481; *Dev* 4167; *Mādh* 1.688 — a) Bo °शरणं; Tj^{1} °शराणं; nNg °शरणां — b) Bo यच्चाग्रे°; gMy यथाग्रे°; Lo^{3} °दीधिषू°; bBe^{2} Lo^{1} °दिधिपुःपतिः — c) nNg मित्रध्रुम्द्रूत°

161. Pādas c-d omitted in Tr^{1}. Cited by *Apa* 452; *Lakṣ* 4.86; *Hem* 3/1.481; *Dev* 4167;

हस्तिगोऽश्वोष्ट्रदमको नक्षत्रैर्यश्च जीवति ।
पक्षिणां पोषको यश्च युद्धाचार्यस्तथैव च ॥१६२॥
स्रोतसां भेदकश्चैव तेषां चावरणे रतः ।
गृहसंवेशको दूतो वृक्षारोपक एव च ॥१६३॥
श्वक्रीडी श्येनजीवी च कन्यादूषक एव च ।
हिंस्रो वृषलवृत्तिश्च गणानां चैव याजकः ॥१६४॥
आचारहीनः क्लीबश्च नित्यं याचनकस्तथा ।
कृषिजीवी श्लीपदी च सद्भिर्निन्दित एव च ॥१६५॥
औरभ्रिको माहिषिकः परपूर्वापतिस्तथा ।
प्रेतनिर्यातकश्चैव वर्जनीयाः प्रयत्नतः ॥१६६॥

Mādh 1.688 — a) Tr^{2} भ्रामली; gMd^{5} भ्रमरी; Wa भ्रामयी; Lo^{5} °माला — b) oOr श्वित्र्यथोपिस्तथा पुनः; Tr^{2} स्वित्र्यथो; Bo श्वित्राथो; Pu^{5} Pu^{7} श्वित्र्यर्थो; Lo^{5} श्वित्र्ययो; Jo^{2} श्वित्रीयो; Pu^{10} श्वित्र्यार्शो; Lo^{2} श्वित्र्यर्शो; Ox^{3} श्वित्र्यर्शी; mTr^{3} mTr^{4} श्वित्र्यन्धो; Be^{1} bBe^{2} Wa श्वित्री च पिशु° — c) Wa उन्मत्तान्धश्च — c-d) tMd^{4} उन्मत्तो बधिरोन्धश्च वर्ज्यास्युर्वेदनिन्दकः

162. Cited by *Apa* 452; *Lakṣ* 4.86; *Hem* 3/1.481–2; *Dev* 4.167–8; *Mādh* 1.688 — a) Pu^{5} Pu^{7} हस्तिनोश्वो° — b) Pu^{8} °त्रैर्यस्य — c) Ox^{2} [*but cor*] पक्षिणी; Lo^{5} पोषवो; *Hem* [vl] पातको; *Apa* [vl] मोषको; Jo^{2} bKt^{5} wKt^{6} Lo^{1} Lo^{3} nNg oOr sOx^{1} sPu^{6} mTr^{4} mTr^{6} Wa पोषकश्चैव; [*Jolly* R] पोषिकश्चैव; Tj^{1} पोषतुश्चैव; Ho यस्तु — d) wKt^{1} योद्धाचौर्य°; bKt^{5} wKt^{6} शूद्राचार्य°; Tr^{1} वृद्धाचार्य°

163. Cited by *Apa* 452; *Lakṣ* 4.86; *Hem* 3/1.482; *Dev* 4.168; *Mādh* 1.688 — a) wKt^{6} श्रोतसां; Hy Jm Jo^{1} Kt^{2} Tj^{2} mTr^{3} [*Jolly* Nd] *Dev Mandlik Jha KSS Dave* भेदको यश्च; mTr^{4} दिशिकश्चैव; *Nā* [vl] देशिकश्चैव — b) nNg तेषामावरणे; *Rc* तेषां वा आचरणे; Ho तेषां वारणे; *Apa* रताः; wKt^{6} ततः — c) gMd^{5} गृहन्निवेशको; Lo^{3} Tj^{1} °संवेशिको; gMd^{1} tMd^{3} °संनिवेशको; Tj^{2} °संदेशको; *Apa* [vl as in ed] °संबीजको; wKt^{1} °सर्पशको; Ho °वेशको यस्तु; sOx^{1} sPu^{6} द्यूतो; tMd^{3} दूता — d) tMd^{3} gMd^{5} Tr^{1} °रोहक; Lo^{4} Lo^{5} एव वा

164. Omitted in Tr^{1}; following sequence in nNg 164a-b, 165c-d, 166, 164c-d, 165a-b. Cited by *Apa* 452; *Lakṣ* 4.86; *Hem* 3/1.482; *Dev* 4168; *Mādh* 1.688 — a) Ho श्वि°; Tj^{1} श्वः; Ox^{3} °क्रीडि; Lo^{1} °क्रीडो; gMy °कुधी; Tr^{2} °क्रीडाख्येन जीवी; wKt^{6} °क्रीडश्चेनजीवी; Be^{1} °जीवे; Hy °जीवि — b) tMd^{3} °दूषण — c) Hy हिंसो; mTr^{4} हिंस्रश्च; wKt^{1} nKt^{4} Ox^{2} Tr^{2} Wa [*Jolly* N Nd] *Lakṣ Dev Mādh* [given as pāṭha in *Me Go Ku Rn Mr*] वृषलपुत्रश्च; gMd^{1} mTr^{4} mTr^{6} वृषलीपुत्रश्च; Lo^{5} °वृत्तीश्च; gMy °वृत्तश्च — d) Ho oMd^{2} गणानां याजकस्तथा; gMd^{1} gMy गणानांश्चैव; Lo^{2} gMy याजकाः; Ox^{3} पालकः

165. Omitted in Tr^{1}; pādas c-d omitted in Be^{3} [haplo]. Cited by *Apa* 452; *Lakṣ* 4.86; *Hem* 3/1.482; *Dev* 4.168; *Mādh* 1.688 — a) Lo^{4} [*but mc*] क्लीबस्तु — b) tMd^{3} gMd^{5} gMy *Apa* नित्य; Lo^{1} याचनिक°; bCa [*but cor*] wKt^{1} gMd^{1} gMd^{5} याजनक° — c) nNg कृषी°; wKt^{1} श्वपदी; gMd^{1} tMd^{3} gMd^{5} gMy mTr^{4} mTr^{6} [*Jolly* Gr] *Mādh* शिल्पजीवी सद्भि° — d) Be^{1} [*mc to*] Bo Lo^{2} Pu^{10} सद्भिर्नन्दित; gMy सद्भिर्निष्कृत

166. Pādas a-b omitted in Be^{3}. Cited by *Apa* 452; *Lakṣ* 4.86; *Hem* 3/1.482; *Dev* 4.168; *Mādh* 1.688 — a) gMd^{1} gMd^{5} gMy *Dev* औरभ्रको; Tr^{1} औरभृको; nKt^{4} La^{1} Lo^{2} Ox^{3} Pu^{7} अरभ्रिको; nPu^{1} उरभ्रिको; Be^{1} माहिषिक; Tr^{1} *Apa* [vl] *Dev* माहिषकः — b) Be^{1} परिपू°; Tj^{1} °पूर्वापरस्तथा; Lo^{4} [*but mc*] °पतिस्तया — c) Kt^{2} प्रेम°; Lo^{4} Lo^{5} Ox^{3} Pu^{10} [*Jolly* M$^{1-2-4-5-8}$] *Me Jha Dave* °निर्याप-

एतान्विगर्हिताचारानपाङ्क्तेयान्द्विजाधमान् ।
द्विजातिप्रवरो विद्वानुभयत्र विवर्जयेत् ॥१६७॥
ब्राह्मणो ह्यनधीयानस्तृणाग्निरिव शाम्यति ।
तस्मै हव्यं न दातव्यं न हि भस्मनि हूयते ॥१६८॥
अपाङ्क्त्यदाने यो दातुर्भवत्यूर्ध्वं फलोदयः ।
दैवे हविषि पित्र्ये वा तं प्रवक्ष्याम्यशेषतः ॥१६९॥
अव्रतैर्यद् द्विजैर्भुक्तं परिवेत्रादिभिस्तथा ।
अपाङ्क्तेयैर्यदन्यैश्च तद्वै रक्षांसि भुञ्जते ॥१७०॥
दाराग्निहोत्रसंयोगं कुरुते योऽग्रजे स्थिते ।
परिवेत्ता स विज्ञेयः परिवित्तिस्तु पूर्वजः ॥१७१॥
परिवित्तिः परिवेत्ता यया च परिविद्यते ।
सर्वे ते नरकं यान्ति दातृयाजकपञ्चमाः ॥१७२॥

कश्चैव; BBe² GMd¹ *Go Ku Apa Hem* [vl] °निर्हारकश्चैव — d) sOx¹ sPu⁶ *Apa* वर्जनीयः; TMd⁴ वर्जनीयां

167. Cited by *Apa* 453; *Lakṣ* 4.86; *Hem* 3/1.482; *Dev* 4.168; *Mādh* 1.688 — a) *Lakṣ* एते विगर्हिताचारा अपाङ्क्ते°; oOr °गृहीताचारा°; TMd³ °गर्हिताकारा° — b) Be¹ Tr¹ °चारान्नपाङ्क्ते°; GMy °नापाङ्क्ते°; wKt⁶ TMd³ *Lakṣ* °नपाङ्क्तेयाद्वि°; Pu⁸ °नपङ्क्त्याद्वि°; GMy Tr¹ MTr⁴ MTr⁶ *Dev Mādh* °यान्नराधमान्; TMd³ °यान्द्विजातयः; *Lakṣ* °धमाः — c) Ho द्विजात°; La¹ धीमानुभ°; *Apa* विप्रानुभ° [vl as in ed.] — d) Bo °यत्रातिवर्जयेत्; Be³ sOx¹ sPu⁶ *Mādh* °यत्रापि वर्जयेत्

168. Cited by *Lakṣ* 4.74; *Hem* 3/1.465; *Mādh* 1.688 — a) Hy Jm Jo¹ Kt² Lo¹ oMd² Tj² MTr³ *Mr Mandlik KSS* ब्राह्मणस्त्वनधी°; MTr⁴ ब्राह्मणोप्यनधी°; GMy ब्राह्मण्योप्यनधी°; oOr ब्राह्मणे त्वनधी° — c) sOx¹ sPu⁶ तस्मिन्हव्यं न होतव्यं — d) BKt⁵ wKt⁶ TMd⁴ न भस्मनि च हूयते

Additional verse in Be³ La¹: the same as *VaDh* 11.20 and cited by *Me*.

169.* a) TMd³ अपङ्क्त्याद्दानयोर्भव°; NKt⁴ Pu⁵ Pu⁷ *Go Jha Dave* अपङ्क्त्य° [*Me* gloss supports this reading]; Jm Jo¹ wKt¹ Kt² oOr *Nā Mandlik KSS* अपाङ्क्त°; BBe² °दानो; NKt⁴ या; Lo⁵ दातुं भव° — b) Tr² दातुर्भवेदूर्ध्वं; Bo Lo¹ दातुर्भवत्पूर्वं; Lo² दातुर्भवेत्पूर्वं; Tr¹ °त्यूर्ध्व — c) NPu¹ दैवे कर्मणि हवींषि पेत्र्ये वा; Hy दैव; Lo⁴ Lo⁵ TMd³ GMd⁵ GMy NNg Ox³ Pu¹⁰ Tr¹ MTr⁴ MTr⁶ [*Jolly* M G Nd Gr] *Rc Jolly Jha Dave* दैवे कर्मणि; oMd² पैत्र्ये; NKt⁴ BKt⁵ wKt⁶ Tr² पित्रे; Lo² Lo⁴ Lo⁵ TMd³ Ox³ Tr¹ च — d) Bo Jm Jo¹ Kt² [*but cor*] sOx¹ sPu⁶ Pu⁸ Tj² MTr³ *Go Rc Mandlik KSS* तत्प्रव°

170. Cited by *Hem* 3/1.465, 493; *Lakṣ* 4.95 — a) Kt² oOr अव्रतेर्यद्; NKt⁴ अव्रते यद्; BBe² अव्रतैर्ये — b) GMd¹ परिवित्रा°; NNg परिवित्यादि°; Bo Ho wKt⁶ GMy °वेत्तादि°; TMd⁴ °वेतादि°; NKt⁴ °वत्ताभिस्तथा — c) Tr² अपाङ्गयै°; GMy °यैस्तदन्यैश्च — d) Be³ भुञ्जति; *Lakṣ* भोजयेत्; TMd⁴ तेजते

171. Cited by *Vij* 1.223; *Apa* 445, 1050; *Hem* 3/1.371, 3/3.811; *Mādh* 1.690 — a) Pu¹⁰ °होत्रयोगं तु; *Hem* 3/3.811 °संबन्धं — b) Jo² NNg यः कुर्यादग्रजे; *Vij* यः करोत्यग्रजे; Ho योग्रजो; TMd³ योग्रज; Tr² योग्रते; Jo¹ *om* स्थिते— c) TMd³ तु विज्ञेयः — d) Lo² °वित्तिश्च; sOx¹ sPu⁶ °वेत्तिस्तु; GMy Tj¹ Tr¹ Tr² °वित्तस्तु; oMd² °वत्तातु; Ox³ °वेत्ताः तु; *Apa* °वित्तैः स

172.* Cited by *Vij* 1.223 — a) sOx¹ sPu⁶ परिवेत्तिः; NKt⁴ °वित्तिं; Lo¹ °वित्ति; TMd⁴ GMy Tr¹ °वित्तः; Hy Jm Jo¹ TMd⁴ Tj¹ Tj² Tr¹ Wa *Mandlik Jolly Jha Dave* परीवेत्ता; Lo⁵ °वेक्षा; Ho wKt¹ La¹ TMd³ GMd⁵ GMy NNg NPu¹ [*but cor*] Pu² Pu⁵ Pu⁷ Tr¹ Tr² Wa °वेत्ता च — b) Ox³ या च स्त्री

भ्रातुर्मृतस्य भार्यायां योऽनुरज्येत कामतः ।
धर्मेणापि नियुक्तायां स ज्ञेयो दिधिषूपतिः ॥१७३॥
परदारेषु जायेते द्वौ सुतौ कुण्डगोलकौ ।
पत्यौ जीवति कुण्डस्तु मृते भर्तरि गोलकः ॥१७४॥
तौ तु जातौ परक्षेत्रे प्राणिनौ प्रेत्य चेह च ।
दत्तानि हव्यकव्यानि नाशयेते प्रदायिनाम् ॥१७५॥
अपाङ्क्त्यो यावतः पाङ्क्त्यान् भुञ्जानाननुपश्यति ।
तावतां न फलं तत्र दाता प्राप्नोति बालिशः ॥१७६॥

परि°; Tj² °वेद्यते — c) ᴛMd⁴ सर्वे च; ɴNg त्रयस्ते — d) ʙKt⁵ wKt⁶ Lo² Lo³ ɴPu¹ °याचक°; Tj¹ °पातक°; Bo °पञ्चमः

173. ᴛMd³ places 173 after 175; La¹ *ma sh* 173c to 174d. Cited by *Apa* 452; *Hem* 3/1.358 — a) ᴛMd³ भार्यां तु; Tr¹ जायायां — b) Tj¹ °बुरज्जेत; Lo⁴ °नुरन्येत; ʙCa oMd² °नुरज्यत; ᴍTr⁶ कामकः; Pu⁵ Pu⁷ [*Jolly* G] रागतः — c) ɴKt⁴ धर्मणापि; ᴍTr⁴ᴍTr⁶ धर्मेणाभिनि°; wKt³ नियुक्तानां; ɢMd¹ नियुक्तापि; ᴛMd³ नियुक्तो वै — d) ɢMd⁵ ज्ञेयोग्रेदिधिषूपतिः [*om* स]; ᴛMd³ संज्ञेयो; ɴNg विज्ञेयो; Lo¹ दिधिषुःपतिः. According to an opinion cited by *Me,* this verse is spurious.

Additional verse in Be³ ᴛMd⁴:

अभिरूपां धर्मपत्नीमनादृत्यैव यो द्विजः ।
भ्रातुर्भार्यानुरज्येत स चाग्रेदिधिषूपतिः ॥

a) ᴛMd⁴ अतिरूपां — b) Be³ °दृत्यैव योषितः — c-d) Pādas c-d blurred in ᴛMd⁴

174. Cited by *Viś* 1.219–21; *Vij* 1.222; *Apa* 445; *Hem* 3/1.174; *Dev* 4.179 — a) wKt¹ ɢMd¹ ɴNg Pu¹⁰ [*Jolly* M] जायन्ते — b) Hy द्वौ सुकुण्डसुगोलकौ; Lo⁵ गुण्ड°; Tr² °कोलकौ — c) *Apa Dev* जीवे भर्तरि कुण्डस्तु; Wa पत्यो; Lo⁵ गुण्डस्तु; Hy Jm Jo¹ Kt² ᴛMd³ ɢMd⁵ sOx¹ sPu⁶ Tj² ᴍTr³ [*Jolly* R Nd] *Dev Mandlik Jha KSSDave* कुण्डः स्यान्मृते — d) Hy मृतपतिकायां च गोलकः; ʙKt⁶ भर्तृगो°; Tr¹ गोळकः; ᴛMd³ गोलके; Tr² कोलकः

Additional verse in *Mandlik* [ञ] *KSS*; pādas c-d in ɢMd¹ *Dev* 4.183, *Apa* 447:

उत्पन्नयोरधर्मेण हव्यकव्ये च नैत्यके ।
यस्तयोरन्नमश्नाति स कुण्डाशी द्विजः स्मृतः ॥

d) *Dev Apa* [vl] कुण्डाश्युच्यते द्विजः; *Apa* कुण्डाश्युच्यते बुधैः

175.* In place of pādas a-b ɢMd¹ gives pādas c-d of the additional verse above. Cited by *Hem* 3/1.362 — a) Lo³ Tj¹ Wa द्वौ तु; oOr द्वौ जातौ तु; ʙBe² Bo Ho Jo² wKt³ La² Lo² Lo⁴ Lo⁵ ɴNg Ox³ ɴPu¹ Pu² Pu⁴ Pu⁵ Pu⁷ [*Jolly* M G] *Me Go Rn Rc* [pāṭha] ते तु जाताः [La² ये]; Lo² Pu¹⁰ ते नु जाताः; ɴPu¹ तेनजन्मःपर°; ɴKt⁴ ʙKt⁵ wKt⁶ यातौ; sOx¹ sPu⁶ परे; oMd² oOr Tj¹ परिक्षेत्रे; ɴKt⁴ °क्षेत्रं — b) ʙBe² Ho Jo² wKt³ La² Lo² Lo³ Lo⁴ Lo⁵ ᴛMd⁴ ɴNg sOx¹ Ox³ ɴPu¹ Pu² Pu⁵ sPu⁶ Pu⁷ Pu¹⁰ Tj¹ [*Jolly* M G] *Me Rn Go Rc* [pāṭha] प्राणिनः; Be³ Bo ʙKt⁵ wKt⁶ Lo² Pu⁸ ᴛMd³ oOr Tr¹ *Hem* प्राणिनां; wKt¹ मलिनौ; ᴛMd⁴ प्रीत्य; *Hem* चेह वै; Pu⁸ *om* च — c) ɢMd¹ तौ सदा हव्य°; *Hem* नियुक्तौ हव्य° — d) Be³ नाशयन्त्यन्नदायिनां; ɢMy नाशयेत्प्रेतदायिनां; ʙBe² Bo Ho Jo² wKt³ ʙKt⁵ La² Lo² Lo⁴ Lo⁵ ɢMd¹ ɴNg Ox³ ɴPu¹ Pu² Pu⁵ Pu⁷ Pu¹⁰ [*Jolly* M G] *Me Rn Go* नाशयन्ति; Ox² नाशयन्ते; ʙKt⁵ wKt⁶ ननाशन्ति; oOr *Hem* नाशयेतां

176. Cited by *Apa* 454; *Hem* 3/1.498 — a) *Hem* अपाङ्क्त्यां यावतः पङ्क्त्यो; ɴNg Ox³ Pu¹⁰ *Jha Dave* अपङ्क्त्यो; Tr² अपाङ्क्तो; wKt⁶ अपाङ्क्तौ; Lo⁴ अपङ्क्तौ; Lo⁵ अपाङ्क्त्यौ; Tj¹ अपाङ्क्या; Lo³ Lo⁵ ɢMd⁵ ɴNg oOr Pu¹⁰ Tj¹ Tr² *Jha Dave* पङ्क्त्यान्; Bo Lo⁴ पाङ्क्तान् — b) ɴPu¹ संस्पृशेद् ब्राह्मणः

वीक्ष्यान्धो नवतेः काणः षष्टेः श्वित्री शतस्य तु ।
पापरोगी सहस्रस्य दातुर्नाशयते फलम् ॥१७७॥
यावतः संस्पृशेदङ्गैर्ब्राह्मणाञ्छूद्रयाजकः ।
तावतां न भवेद्दातुः फलं दानस्य पौर्तिकम् ॥१७८॥
वेदविच्चापि विप्रोऽस्य लोभात्कृत्वा प्रतिग्रहम् ।
विनाशं व्रजति क्षिप्रमामपात्रमिवाम्भसि ॥१७९॥
सोमविक्रयिणे विष्ठा भिषजे पूयशोणितम् ।
नष्टं देवलके दत्तमप्रतिष्ठं तु वार्धुषौ ॥ १८०॥
यत्तु वाणिजके दत्तं नेह नामुत्र तद्भवेत् ।
भस्मनीव हुतं हव्यं तथा पौनर्भवे द्विजे ॥१८१॥

क्वचित्; Lo^{1} gMd^{1} °नानुपपश्यति; gMy °नानुपदिश्यति — c) nKt^{4} tMd^{3} तावता; Lo^{1} तावतं; sPu^{6} [*but cor*] यावतः; sOx^{1} तावतः; gMy तावतस्तत्फलं; Hy Jm Jo^{1} Jo^{2} Kt^{2} Lo^{3} Lo^{4} Lo^{5} nNg Ox^{3} nPu^{1} Pu^{2} Pu^{10} Tj^{1} Tj^{2} mTr^{3} Wa *Jolly* फलं प्रेत्य; *Hem* फलं तेषां — d) bKt^{5} wKt^{6} gMd^{1} tMd^{3} tMd^{4} gMd^{5} gMy Tr^{1} mTr^{4} mTr^{6} प्रदाताप्नोति; wKt^{6} मानवः

177. Pāda-d omitted in La^{1}. Cited by *Apa* 454; *Hem* 3/1.499; *Dev* 4.187 — a) Bo Ho Ox^{3} Pu^{10} वीक्षान्धो; Lo^{5} वीक्ष्यान्धा; nPu^{1} नवकेः; nKt^{4} नवते कालः — b) wKt^{1} sOx^{1} sPu^{6} [*but cor*] षष्टे; Wa षष्टिः; Tr^{1} षष्ठो; Tr^{2} स्वित्री; gMy श्वत्री; Jm Jo^{2} wKt^{1} bKt^{5} wKt^{6} Lo^{1} Lo^{4} oMd^{2} nNg sOx^{1} Ox^{3} sPu^{6} Pu^{10} Wa [*Jolly* M R] *Dev Jha Dave* च — d) oOr [*but cor fh*] °तुर्नश्येते

178.* *ma* in La^{1}. Cited by *Apa* 454; *Hem* 3/1.498; *Dev* 4.187 — a) sOx^{1} sPu^{6} यावतां; Ox^{2} यावतो; Be^{1} Bo Ho Jo^{2} wKt^{3} bKt^{5} wKt^{6} La^{1} La^{2} Lo^{2} Lo^{4} Lo^{5} nNg sOx^{1} Ox^{3} Pu^{2} Pu^{5} sPu^{6} Pu^{7} Pu^{8} Pu^{10} Tr^{2} Wa [*Jolly* M N] संस्पृशत्यङ्गै°; wKt^{3} संस्पृशेत्यङ्गै°; wKt^{1} bKt^{5} *Dev* °शेदङ्गे ब्राह्म°; wKt^{6} °शेदङ्गं ब्राह्म° — b) nKt^{4} °ङ्गैर्ब्रह्म°; Ho °ङ्गैर्ब्राह्मणः शूद्र°; tMd^{3} °ङ्गैर्ब्राह्मण शूद्र°; tMd^{4} °ङ्गैर्ब्राह्मणं शूद्र°; gMy °ङ्गैर्ब्राह्मणश्शूद्र° — c) Ho gMy तावता; Lo^{1} तावतं; Be^{3} तावतो; oOr भवेद्दान्तः — d) Wa दानस्यापौ°; sOx^{1} sPu^{6} दानसमुद्भवं; Be^{1} nKt^{4} पौतिकं; bKt^{5} wKt^{6} gMd^{5} Ox^{2} Pu^{5} Pu^{7} [*but cor*] पैतृकं; Lo^{4} पौर्विकं; tMd^{4} पार्थिकं; Tr^{2} वार्त्तिकं

179. Pāda-a omitted in La^{1} — a) tMd^{4} अवेदवित्तु विप्रस्तं; Ox^{2} [*but cor*] वेदविद्यापि विप्रो वै; oOr Ox^{3} वेदविद्वापि; Lo^{5} वेदविद्या च; Ho वेदज्ञश्चापि; Jm nKt^{4} विप्रस्य; tMd^{3} विप्रस्तु — b) Be^{1} कृत्वा लोभात्प्रतिग्रहं; wKt^{3} मोहात्कृत्वा — c) oOr नाशं — d) gMy °माम्रपात्रमिवा°

180. sOx^{1} sPu^{6} place 180a-b after 178d. Cited by *Apa* 454; *Lakṣ* 4.95 — a) Pu^{8} साम°; bKt^{5} wKt^{6} मांसवि°; oMd^{2} सोदावि°; sOx^{1} sPu^{6} °क्रयिणो; bBe^{2} °क्रयिण; mTr^{4} विष्टां; Bo विष्वा — b) sOx^{1} sPu^{6} भजते — c-d) Be^{3} nKt^{4} La^{1} gMd^{1} tMd^{3} tMd^{4} gMd^{5} gMy Tr^{1} mTr^{4} mTr^{6} *Apa Lakṣ* अप्रतिष्ठं वार्धुषिके नष्टं देवलके भवेत् [tMd^{4} अप्रतिष्ठा; nKt^{4} °षिकं; tMd^{4} °षिकी; nKt^{4} °लकं] — d) Ho Hy वार्धुषे; nPu^{1} वार्द्धष्ये; wKt^{6} वार्धकौ

Additional verse in gMd^{5}:

वृत्त्यर्थं पूजयेद्यस्तु देवतां लिङ्गमेव च ।
देवान्देवयते यस्तु स वै देवलकः स्मृतः ॥

181. Cited by *Apa* 454 — a) bBe^{2} Jo^{2} wKt^{1} *Jolly* वाणिजिके; Hy tMd^{3} Wa वाणिज्यके; Jm वाणिजकं — c) Tr^{2} भस्मिनीव; Lo^{4} Lo^{5} भस्मनैव; Ox^{3} भस्मना तद्धुतं; Lo^{4} Ox^{3} हुतं द्रव्यं — d) Jm Lo^{5} Ox^{3} Pu^{10} यथा; tMd^{3} तदा; tMd^{4} पौनर्भव; Tr^{1} पौनर्भवी; Pu^{5} Pu^{7} [*Jolly* G] पौनर्भवे भवेत्; nNg द्विजाः

इतरेषु त्वपाङ्क्त्येषु यथोद्दिष्टेष्वसाधुषु ।
मेदोऽसृङ्मांसमज्जास्थि वदन्त्यन्नं मनीषिणः ॥१८२॥
अपाङ्क्त्योपहता पङ्क्तिः पाव्यते यैर्द्विजोत्तमैः ।
तान्निबोधत कार्त्स्न्येन द्विजाग्र्यान्पङ्क्तिपावनान् ॥१८३॥
अग्र्याः सर्वेषु वेदेषु सर्वप्रवचनेषु च ।
श्रोत्रियान्वयजाश्चैव विज्ञेयाः पङ्क्तिपावनाः ॥१८४॥
त्रिणाचिकेतः पञ्चाग्निस्त्रिसुपर्णः षडङ्गवित् ।
ब्रह्मदेयानुसंतानो ज्येष्ठसामग एव च ॥१८५॥
वेदार्थवित्प्रवक्ता च ब्रह्मचारी सहस्रदः ।
शतायुश्चैव विज्ञेया ब्राह्मणाः पङ्क्तिपावनाः ॥१८६॥
पूर्वेद्युरपरेद्युर्वा श्राद्धकर्मण्युपस्थिते ।
निमन्त्रयेत त्र्यवरान् सम्यग्विप्रान्यथोदितान् ॥१८७॥

182. Cited by *Apa* 454 — a) ᴍTr^{4} इतरेष्वल्पपङ्क्त्येषु; oMd^{2} ɴNg Pu^{10} *Me Jha Dave* त्वपङ्क्त्येषु; Lo^{4} Ox^{3} त्वपङ्क्तेषु; ᴛMd^{3} त्वपाङ्क्तेषु; ᴛMd^{4} त्वपपाङ्क्तेषु; Lo^{2} स्वपङ्क्त्येषु — b) ᴛMd^{4} यथादिष्टे°; ɢMy यदिदृष्टे°; Bo Jm wKt^{1} wKt^{6} Lo^{4} Lo^{5} °द्दिष्टेषु साधुषु — c) Lo^{2} मदासृ°; Pu^{5} Pu^{7} °मज्जादि

183. Cited by *Dev* 4.188 — a) ʙBe^{2} ɴKt^{4} ᴛMd^{3} अपाङ्क्तोप°; Lo^{4} ɴNg Pu^{5} Pu^{7} Pu^{10} *Me Dave Jha* अपङ्क्त्योप°; Ox^{3} अपङ्क्त्यापहता; *Dev* अपाङ्क्तेयहता; wKt^{1} °पाहता; La^{1} ᴛMd^{3} ɴPu^{1} °हतां; ʙKt^{5} La^{1} ɴPu^{1} पङ्क्तिं — b) ɴNg पव्यते; Pu^{5} Pu^{7} Wa [*Jolly* G] पूयते; ᴛ Md^{3} पाच्यते; ᴍTr^{4} प्राप्यते; ᴛMd^{4} य द्विजो°; ɢMy *Dev* यैर्द्विजातिभिः — c) Bo ᴛ Md^{4} ɢMy तन्निबो°; wKt^{1} तं निबो°; Tr^{1} ता निबो°; Lo^{5} °बोधेत; ʙCa Ho कार्त्स्नेन; wKt^{1} कार्ष्णेन; Lo^{4} कार्क्येन [*but mc*]; ʙKt^{5} कार्येण; wKt^{6} कार्येषु — d) ʙBe^{2} ʙKt^{5} wKt^{6} ɢMd^{1} Ox^{3} Pu^{10} द्विजाग्रा°; sOx^{1} *om* पङ्क्ति and jumps to end of 184d [haplo]; Kt^{2} °पावनात्; wKt^{3} °पावकान्; Wa °पावनः

184. Cited by *Dev* 4.188 — a) ᴛMd^{3} अग्र्यास्युस्सर्ववेदेषु; ᴛMd^{4} अर्घ्याः; ᴍTr^{6} अश्च्यः; ɢMd^{1} अग्र्यस्सर्वेषु; *Dev* वेदेषु सर्वेषु; Bo wKt^{3} Lo^{4} Lo^{5} देवेषु — b) sPu^{6} सर्व° *mc sh to* पूर्व°; ᴛMd^{4} °प्रस्रवणेषु — c) ᴛMd^{3} श्रोत्रिया ऋत्विजश्चैव; ᴛMd^{4} श्रोत्रियाः कुलजाश्चैव; ɢMy °यजैश्चैव; ʙKt^{5} wKt^{6} °यजाताश्च

185. Cited by *Lakṣ* 4.63; *Dev* 4.188 — a) ʙBe^{2} wKt^{1} ɴKt^{4} ʙKt^{5} wKt^{6} Lo^{2} oOr Ox^{2} ᴍTr^{3} तृणाचि°; ɢMd^{1} °केतस्त्रिमधुस्त्रिसु°; wKt^{1} पाञ्चाग्नि°; ɢMy पञ्चाग्नित्रिसु° — b) ʙBe^{2} ɢMy °षुपर्णः; Lo^{4} Lo^{5} Tr^{2} °पुवर्णः; *Lakṣ* °सौपर्णः; Wa °सुपर्णकः; ʙKt^{5} wKt^{6} °पर्णः सुपर्णवित् — c) ʙBe^{2} Hy Jm Jo^{1} Jo^{2} wKt^{1} Kt^{2} wKt^{3} Lo^{3} oMd^{2} Tj^{1} Tr^{2} ᴍTr^{3} *Ku Rn Nd Rc Mr Mandlik KSS* °देयात्मसंतानो; Pu^{10} °संताना — d) ɢMd^{1} Ox^{3} *Lakṣ* धर्मविज्ज्येष्ठसामगः; ᴛMd^{3} ᴛMd^{4} ɢMd^{5} ɢMy Tr^{1} ᴍTr^{4} [*Jolly* Nd] *Dev* छन्दोगो ज्येष्ठसामगः [ɢMy °सामिकः; ᴛMd^{3} °साविकः]; Pu^{7} जैष्ठ°; Lo^{2} ज्येष्ठं; oOr ज्येष्ठे; ɢMy ɴKt^{4} °सामिक; wKt^{6} °मासग

186. Cited by *Dev* 4.188 — a) ʙKt^{5} देवार्थ°; wKt^{6} वेदानुवित्प्र°; ᴛMd^{3} वेदान्तवित्प्र° — b) Lo^{1} सहस्रदाः — c) Tj^{2} Wa विज्ञेयो — d) Lo^{2} Tj^{2} ब्राह्मणः; ɴKt^{4} Tj^{2} °पावनः

187.* Cited by *Vij* 1.225; *Hem* 3/2.1133, 1146; *Dev* 4.192; *Mādh* 1.697 — a) *Dev* पूर्वेद्युर्वापरे° — b) Pu^{5} Pu^{7} श्राद्धे; wKt^{3} °स्थितः — c) ʙBe^{2} Bo ʙCa wKt^{1} wKt^{3} Lo^{1} ɴNg ɴPu^{1} Pu^{5} Pu^{7} Pu^{8} Pu^{10} [*Jolly* M^{1-2-8} G Nd] *Hem Dev Mādh Jolly Jha Dave* निमन्त्रयीत; Be^{3} निमन्त्रयत *cor to* निमन्त्रयेत; [*Jolly* M$^{3-4-5-9}$ R] either निमन्त्रयेत or निमन्त्रयेत्तु; Lo^{4} Lo^{5} °मन्त्रयेत्तु; Tr^{2} °मन्त्रयेतु;

निमन्त्रितो द्विजः पित्र्ये नियतात्मा भवेत्सदा ।
न च छन्दांस्यधीयीत यस्य श्राद्धं च तद्भवेत् ॥१८८॥
निमन्त्रितान्हि पितर उपतिष्ठन्ति तान्द्विजान् ।
वायुवच्चानुगच्छन्ति तथासीनानुपासते ॥१८९॥
केतितस्तु यथान्यायं हव्यकव्ये द्विजोत्तमः ।
कथंचिदप्यतिक्रामन् पापः सूकरतां व्रजेत् ॥१९०॥
आमन्त्रितस्तु यः श्राद्धे वृशल्या सह मोदते ।
दातुर्यद्दुष्कृतं किंचित् तत्सर्वं प्रतिपद्यते ॥१९१॥
अक्रोधनाः शौचपराः सततं ब्रह्मचारिणः ।
न्यस्तशस्त्रा महाभागाः पितरः पूर्वदेवताः ॥१९२॥

TMd^4 °मन्त्रयात; wKt^6 °मन्त्रयेद्यौ; BKt^5 मन्त्रयेन्; wKt^1 हि वरान् — d) wKt^1 सौम्यान्वि°; [*Jolly* Be] °प्रांस्तथो°; Ho °थोचितान्

188. Omitted in Wa; pādas c-d omitted in sOx^1. Cited by *Apa* 456; *Hem* 3/2.1014 — a) TMd^4 GMd^5 निमन्त्रिणो; TMd^4 द्विजां; wKt^6 द्विजाः — b) Pu^5 Pu^7 [*Jolly* G] संयतात्मा; Lo^3 Tj^1 निवृतात्मा; [*Jolly* R] निवृत्तात्मा; GMy शुचिस्सदा — c) NKt^4 वचस्छन्दां°; Be^1 sPu^6 °धीयेत — d) Bo wKt^1 oOr तस्य; GMy यस्याश्राद्धं; Ox^2 [*but cor*] श्राद्धे; BKt^5 wKt^6 GMy तु; NPu^1 यद्भवेत्

189. a) GMd^1 नियमाश्रितान्हि; Pu^{10} निमन्त्रिता हि; GMy निमन्त्रिते हि; TMd^3 निमन्त्रितान्य — b) Ho उपविष्टन्ति — c) NKt^4 La^1 oOr वायुभूतानु°; Tr^2 वायुभूतानिगच्छ°; GMd^1 TMd^3 TMd^4 GMd^5 GMy Tr^1 MTr^4 MTr^6 वायुभूतास्तु गच्छ° [GMd^1 TMd^4 °भूताश्च]; GMd^5 गच्छन्तस्तथा° — d) Tr^1 तदासी°; sOx^1 Tj^1 sPu^6 [*cor to*] यथासी°; Pu^5 Pu^7 अथासी°; TMd^3 °नुपासिते

Additional verse in GMy; given after 190 in GMd^5 oOr:

ब्राह्मणं तु मुखं कृत्वा देवा पितृगणैः सह ।
तदन्नमुपभुञ्जीरन् तस्मात्तन्न व्यतिक्रमेत् ॥

a) oOr ब्राह्मणस्य मुखे दत्तं; GMd^5 दत्त्वा — c) GMy °मपयुञ्जीरन्; oOr मपजीवन्ति — d) GMy तस्मादन्नं व्यतक्रिमेत्

190. Omitted in GMd^1. Cited by *Apa* 457; *Lakṣ* 4.107; *Hem* 3/2.1002; *Dev* 4.198; *Mādh* 1.701 — a) TMd^3 केततेस्तु; Pu^5 Pu^7 [*cor to*] कतितस्तु; La^1 केर्त्तितस्तु; NNg केचितस्तु; oMd^2 चिकेतस्तु; GMd^5 क्षेमतस्तु; GMy MTr^4 वेदितस्तु; sPu^6 कीर्तितस्तु *mc sh to* निमन्त्रितो; sOx^1 Tr^2 निमन्त्रितो यथा°; Lo^1 निकेतितो यथा°; wKt^1 निकेतिनोन्यथा° — b) *Lakṣ* ब्राह्मणो हव्यकव्ययोः; Jo^2 Lo^4 oOr Ox^3 Tj^1 *Hem Me Jha Dave* हव्ये कव्ये; wKt^3 °कव्यौ; wKt^6 °कव्यो; Lo^1 °कव्य; Wa द्विजोत्तमाः — c) NPu^1 कदाचिद°; Tj^1 °क्रामान्; Lo^1 NNg Ox^3 NPu^1 Pu^5 Pu^7 Pu^{10} °क्रामेत्; wKt^6 °क्राम — d) TMd^3 पापी; Ho Hy Jm Kt^2 oMd^2 NNg Ox^2 Ox^3 Pu^7 Pu^{10} Tj^1 शूकरतां

191. Pādas a-b omitted in GMd^1. Cited by *Apa* 457; *Hem* 3/2.1006; *Dev* 4.200; *Mādh* 1.702 — a) Lo^5 अमन्त्रि°; sOx^1 sPu^6 [*mc sh to*] नामन्त्रि°; Be^1 BBe^2 BCa TMd^4 Ho NKt^4 La^1 Lo^1 TMd^4 GMd^5 GMy oOr NPu^1 Tr^1 MTr^4 *Apa* निमन्त्रि°; Ox^3 आमन्त्रितास्तु; TMd^3 MTr^6 निमन्त्रितास्तु — b) Bo वृशल्याः; Tr^1 वृसळ्या — c) wKt^6 NNg Pu^7 Pu^{10} दातुर्यदुष्कृतं — c-d) *Dev* भवन्ति पितरस्तस्य तन्मासं शुक्लभोजनाः — d) oOr *om* तत्

192. Cited by *Hem* 3/1.61, 3/2.1005 — a) NNg Wa शौचरताः — b) wKt^6 द्रव्यचारिणः; MTr^3 °चारिणा — c) Lo^5 न्यष्ट°; wKt^1 °शस्त्रान्महा°; Lo^1 माहा° — d) NNg sOx^1 sPu^6 श्राद्धदेवताः; wKt^1 °देवता

यस्मादुत्पत्तिरेतेषां सर्वेषामप्यशेषतः ।
ये च यैरुपचर्याः स्युर्नियमैस्तान्निबोधत ॥१९३॥
मनोर्हैरण्यगर्भस्य ये मरीच्यादयः सुताः ।
तेषामृषीणां सर्वेषां पुत्राः पितृगणाः स्मृताः ॥१९४॥
विराट्सुताः सोमसदः साध्यानां पितरः स्मृताः ।
अग्निष्वात्ताश्च देवानां मारीच्या लोकविश्रुताः ॥१९५॥
दैत्यदानवयक्षाणां गन्धर्वोरगरक्षसाम् ।
सुपर्णकिंनराणां च स्मृता बर्हिषदोऽत्रिजाः ॥१९६॥
सोमपा नाम विप्राणां क्षत्रियाणां हविर्भुजः ।
वैश्यानामाज्यपा नाम शूद्राणां तु सुकालिनः ॥१९७॥
सोमपास्तु कवेः पुत्रा हविष्मन्तोऽङ्गिरःसुताः ।
पुलस्त्यस्याज्यपाः पुत्रा वसिष्ठस्य सुकालिनः ॥१९८॥
अनग्निदग्धाग्निदग्धान् काव्यान्बर्हिषदस्तथा ।
अग्निष्वात्तांश्च सौम्यांश्च विप्राणामेव निर्दिशेत् ॥१९९॥

193. a) Be³ °त्तिरित्येषां — b) Wa सर्वेषामशेषतः — c) sPu⁶ [*but mc sh*] यैः परिचर्यन्ते; Ox² [*but cor*] °पचार्याः; TMd⁴ °पचार्य — d) Be¹ °मैस्ता निबो°; Ox³ °मैस्तन्निबो°; Wa °बोधते

194. Cited by *Hem* 3/1.43; *Lakṣ* 4.110 — a) Tr² मनोहैर°; BBe² BKt⁵ wKt⁶ Lo³ Lo⁴ Lo⁵ TMd⁴ GMd⁵ Ox² [*but cor*] *Lakṣ* मनोर्हिर° — b) TMd⁴ *om* ये; Lo¹ मरीचादयः; Lo³ Tj¹ स्मृताः — d) Pu⁵ Pu⁷ [*Jolly* G] सर्वेषामेते पितृगणाः स्मृताः; Jm पुत्रः; GMy सुताः

195. *ma sh* in Be³; pādas a-b and c-d transposed in sOx¹ sPu⁶. Cited by *Hem* 3/1.55 — a) TMd⁴ sOx¹ Tr² विराट्सुतः; BKt⁵ सोमदः; wKt⁶ सोमदाश्च; sOx¹ [*but cor*] sPu⁶ सोमसुतः; GMd¹ TMd³ GMy Tr¹ [*Jolly* M⁸ Nd] सोमसुताः — b) NNg पितरः सुताः; Tr² पितृदेवताः — c) Be¹ BCa wKt¹ NKt⁴ Lo¹ GMd¹ TMd⁴ NNg oOr °त्तास्तु; Lo⁴ Lo⁵ °त्ताख; wKt¹ दिव्यानां; TMd³ दीवानां — d) Bo Hy Jm La¹ TMd³ TMd⁴ GMd⁵ GMy Pu² Pu⁵ Pu⁷ [*cor to*] मरीच्या; Lo¹ Lo⁴ मारीच्य; wKt³ NNg Pu¹⁰ *Me Mandlik Jha KSS Dave* मारीचा; NKt⁴ मारीच; oOr मरीचा

196. Cited by *Hem* 3/1.55 — a) Lo³ Tj¹ देवदानव°; Pu⁵ Pu⁷ °रक्षाणां — b) Tj² गन्धर्वौरग°; Be¹ Ho Lo⁴ sOx¹ Pu⁵ Pu¹⁰ °राक्षसां — c) Lo¹ सुपर्णा°; GMy सुपर्णगुह्यकानां — d) Lo⁴ Lo⁵ चात्रिजा बर्हिषदाः प्रजाः; Lo³ Tj¹ श्रुता; GMd¹ GMd⁵ तथा बर्हि°; GMy सुता बर्हि°; BKt⁵ wKt⁶ स्मृता किं बर्हि°; Bo °षदोत्रिजः; GMd⁵ Tj¹ °षदोत्रजाः; wKt¹ °षदोद्विजाः

197. Omitted in Hy; pādas c-d omitted in Ng. Cited by *Hem* 3/1.55 — b) NKt⁴ हविर्भुजां — c) Lo⁴ [*but mc*] Lo⁵ GMd¹ Ox³ °ज्यपानां च; Tr² नामा — d) Jo² BKt⁵ wKt⁶ Lo⁴ Ox³ Pu⁵ Pu⁷ Wa च; Tj¹ व; TMd⁴ सुकालिनं; TMd³ सुकालिजः; wKt⁶ स्वकालिनः

198. Omitted in GMd¹ TMd⁴ Tj² Wa [haplo]; pādas a-b omitted in Ng. Cited by *Hem* 3/1.55; *Lakṣ* 4.110 — a) Lo² सामपास्तु — b) TMd³ हविष्यन्तुगिरेस्सुताः; Lo² हविष्यन्तो; Jo² बर्हिष्मन्तो; Lo⁵ Tr² °सुतः; wKt¹ °सुता — c) GMd⁵ पुलस्त्याज्यपाः; Tr² Lo² पुलहस्याज्यपाः [Tr² °पा]; Lo⁴ Lo⁵ NNg पुलहस्त्याज्यपाः; NKt⁴ पुलकस्याज्यपाः; *Lakṣ* °पाः नाम — d) NKt⁴ Ox² Pu⁵ Pu⁷ Tr² वशि°; wKt⁶ wKt¹ स्वकालिनः; Be³ Tr² तु कालिनः; TMd³ सुमालिनः

199.* Omitted in Ox³. Cited by *Hem* 3/1.55 — a) Lo⁴ Lo⁵ अनग्निदग्धा अग्निदग्धाः; BKt⁵ wKt⁶

य एते तु गणा मुख्याः पितॄणां परिकीर्तिताः ।
तेषामपीह विज्ञेयं पुत्रपौत्रमनन्तकम् ॥२००॥
ऋषिभ्यः पितरो जाताः पितृभ्यो देवदानवाः ।
देवेभ्यश्च जगत्सर्वं चरं स्थाण्वनुपूर्वशः ॥२०१॥
राजतैर्भाजनैरेषामथ वा रजतान्वितैः ।
वार्यपि श्रद्धया दत्तमक्षयायोपकल्पते ॥२०२॥
देवकार्याद् द्विजातीनां पितृकार्यं विशिष्यते ।
दैवं हि पितृकार्यस्य पूर्वमाप्यायनं स्मृतम् ॥२०३॥
तेषामारक्षभूतं तु पूर्वं दैवं नियोजयेत् ।

Pu⁷ Pu¹⁰ Tr² [*Jolly* G] *Jha Dave* अनग्निदग्धानग्नि° ; ʙBe² Be³ Bo ʙCa Ho Hy Jm Jo¹ Jo² wKt¹ Kt² wKt³ ʙKt⁵ La² Lo¹ Lo³ oMd² ᴛMd³ ɢMy ɴNg oOr Ox² Pu⁸ Tj¹ Tj² Tr¹ ᴍTr⁴ ᴍTr⁶ Wa [*Jolly* Ku N R Nd] *Mandlik KSS* अग्निदग्धानग्नि°; Be¹ अग्निदग्धान्नग्नि° ; La¹ अग्निदग्धाग्नि° ; ɢMd⁵ [defective pāda] अग्निदग्धान् कव्य°; ɴPu¹ °दग्धः; Pu² °दग्धाः — b) ɢMy बह्व्यबर्हिषद्देवतां; Lo¹ Ox² [*but cor*] Tj¹ कव्यान्बर्हि° ; Be³ ɴPu¹ Tr¹ काव्यबर्हि° ; Pu² काव्या बर्हि° ; ɴKt⁴ ʙKt⁵ wKt⁶ Lo⁴ Lo⁵ ɢMd¹ ɢMd⁵ Pu⁵ Pu⁷ ᴍTr⁴ ᴍTr⁶कव्यबर्हि° ; ᴛMd³ यप्यबर्हि° ; Be¹ Bo Pu⁸ Tr² [*Jolly* N] °र्हिषदो बहून्; sPu⁶ °र्हिषदोपि च *cor to* °र्हिषदोपरान्; Jo² Lo³ ɢMd⁵ sOx¹ Tj¹ [*Jolly* R] °र्हिषदोपरान्; ɴKt⁴ Tr¹ ᴍTr⁴ ᴍTr⁶ [*Jolly* Nd] °र्हिषदो वहान्; ᴛMd⁴ °र्हिषदो महान्; wKt³ °र्हिषदायनां;ɢMd¹ °र्हिषदापहान्; ᴛMd³ °र्हिषदोहमान्; ʙBe² ɴNg Wa [*Jolly* Me M¹⁻²⁻⁸] °र्हिषदोत्रिजान्; Pu¹⁰ °र्हिषदोत्रीन् — c) Wa अग्नी° ; Kt² अग्निकांताश्च; Be¹ Bo wKt¹ ᴛMd⁴ ɢMd⁵ °त्ताश्च; Be¹ wKt¹ Kt² wKt⁶ ᴛMd⁴ सौम्याश्च; Bo सौम्यश्च; ɴKt⁴ सोम्यांश्च — d) Lo² विप्रामेव विनिर्दिषेत्; ᴛMd³ दीपानमेव; wKt⁶ विश्वानामेव; ᴛMd³ निर्दिशत्; Lo⁴ निर्धरेत्; Lo⁵ निर्हरेत्

Additional verse in *Mandlik KSS:*

अग्निष्वात्ता हुतैस्तृप्ताः सोमपाः स्तुतिभिस्तथा ।
पिण्डैर्बर्हिषदः प्रीताः प्रेतास्तु द्विजभोजने ॥

200. Cited by *Hem* 3/1.48 — a) Lo⁴ *ma* य; ᴛMd³ गुणा; wKt⁶ मुख्या — b) wKt³ °कीर्तितः — c) ᴍTr⁴ तेषामपि हविर्देयं; Tj¹ तेषामपि हि; wKt¹ °पीहं; Jm °प्येह; Hy °पीह ज्ञेयं — d) Pu⁵ Pu⁷ °त्रमनन्तरं

201. Cited by *Lakṣ* 4.110 — b) Jo¹ Kt² oMd² Wa *Ku Mandlik Jha KSS Dave* देवमानवाः; Jm देवमानवः; ʙKt⁵ wKt⁶ देवतानराः — c) Be³ Hy Jm Jo¹ Kt² wKt³ ɢMd⁵ Tj² Tr² ᴍTr³ *Mandlik KSS Dave* देवेभ्यस्तु— d) sOx¹ sPu⁶ स्थावरं च चरिष्णु च; Tr² चरं चाचरमेव च; ɢMd⁵ ɢMy *Lakṣ* चरः; Tr¹ चरस्थास्त्वनु° ; ɢMy °पूर्वशं; ᴍTr⁴ °पूर्वकं

202. Cited by *Apa* 488; *Hem* 3/1.675 — b) Hy Jm Jo¹ Kt² Tj² ᴍTr³ *Mandlik Jha KSS Dave* °पामथो वा; ɴKt⁴ La¹ ɢMd¹ ᴛMd³ ɢMy Tr¹ *Apa Hem* °पामपि वा; Lo² ᴛMd³ ᴛMd⁴ Ox³ [*Jolly* M⁴⁻⁵⁻⁶⁻⁹] *Apa* राजता°; Lo⁴ राजना° — c) ɢMd¹ युक्तमक्षया° — d) ᴛMd³ दत्तं तमक्षय्योपकल्पते; wKt³ °यायोपपद्यते; sPu⁶ [*but mc sh*] °यायोपतिष्ठते; ʙKt⁵ wKt⁶ ɢMd⁵ °कल्प्यते; wKt¹ Lo¹ °कल्पयेत्

203. Cited by *Hem* 3/1.135; *Dev* 4.281–2 — a) Be³ Bo Hy ɢMd¹ ɢMd⁵ *Hem* दैव° ; wKt³ द्वितीयानां — b) Pu⁵ Pu⁷ [*Jolly* G] प्रशस्यते — c) Pu¹⁰देवं; ᴛMd⁴ पितृकार्येपु — d) ᴛMd³ पूर्वामा° ; La¹ ɢMy sOx¹ sPu⁶ °मप्यायनं; ʙKt⁵ ᴛMd⁴ °मप्ययनं; Tj¹ °माप्यायतं; Lo³ °माप्यियितं; wKt⁶ °मव्ययनं; ᴍTr⁴ °मप्यायिकं मतं; ɴKt⁴ *om* स्मृतम्; Jo¹ श्रुतं

रक्षांसि विप्रलुम्पन्ति* श्राद्धमारक्षवर्जितम् ॥२०४॥
दैवाद्यन्तं तदीहेत पित्राद्यन्तं न तद्भवेत् ।
पित्राद्यन्तं त्वीहमानः क्षिप्रं नश्यति सान्वयः ॥२०५॥
शुचिं देशं विविक्तं च गोमयेनोपलेपयेत् ।
दक्षिणाप्रवणं चैव प्रयत्नेनोपपादयेत् ॥२०६॥
अवकाशेषु चोक्षेषु जलतीरेषु चैव हि ।
विविक्तेषु च तुष्यन्ति दत्तेन पितरः सदा ॥२०७॥
आसनेषूपकॢप्तेषु बर्हिष्मत्सु पृथक्पृथक् ।
उपस्पृष्टोदकान्सम्यग्विप्रांस्तानुपवेशयेत् ॥२०८॥

204.* Cited by *Apa* 476; *Hem* 3/1.136; *Dev* 4.282 — a) wKt^{1} तेषामादौ रक्षभूतं; BKt^{5} Tj^{1} °मरक्ष°; oOr Pu^{10} °मारक्ष्य°; wKt^{6} °मश्रक्ष°; TMd^{3} TMd^{4} NPu^{1} °माक्षरभूतं — b) Jo^{1} Pu^{10} पूर्व; NPu^{1} सर्वं दैवं; NNg *Dev* दैवं पूर्वं; GMd^{1} oMd^{2} Tr^{2} देवं; Jo^{1} नियोजयत्; NKt^{4} नियोजयन्; Pu^{5} Pu^{7} प्रयोजयेत्; *Apa* निवेदयेत् — c) BBe^{2} Hy Jm Jo^{1} wKt^{1} Kt^{2} wKt^{3} NKt^{4} Lo^{1} GMd^{1} oMd^{2} TMd^{3} GMd^{5} GMy oOr MTr^{3} MTr^{4} MTr^{6} [*Jolly* Nd] *Hem* [but vl as in ed] *Mandlik KSS* रक्षांसि हि विलुम्पन्ति [GMy च; oOr ह]; Tr^{1} रक्षांसि तद्विलुम्पन्ति

205. Kt^{2} gives only the *pratīka* दैवाद्यन्तं. Cited by *Apa* 456; *Hem* 3/2.1045, 1156 — a) TMd^{3} दैवमाद्यन्तमीहेत; Hy Tj^{2} Pu^{10} देवा°; wKt^{6} दैवार्थन्तं; *Apa* यदीहेत; *Hem* 3/2.1045 समीहेत — b) Ho पित्राद्यं न च तद्भवेत्; GMy पित्र्यान्तं तत्र तद्भवेत्; Lo^{2} TMd^{3} Ox^{3} पित्र्याद्यन्तं — c) TMd^{4} पित्रा-न्त्यमीहमानस्तु; GMd^{5} NPu^{1} पित्राद्यन्तं तदीहानः; TMd^{3} Ox^{3} पित्र्या°; Ho °न्तमीहमानः; GMy त्वीहदानं — d) Bo Lo^{2} oOr [*but cor*] sOx^{1} sPu^{6} MTr^{4} नश्यन्ति; wKt^{1} नश्यत्यसंशयः; Be^{1} सान्वयाः; GMy सान्वयं; TMd^{3} सोन्वयः; Ox^{3} सात्वतः

206. Cited by *Apa* 471; *Hem* 3/1.160, 3/2.1164; *Dev* 4.142 — a) Ho Lo^{1} Lo^{2} TMd^{4} शुचि; BBe^{2} *om* च; Lo^{4} Lo^{5} Ox^{3} Tj^{2} तु — b) Be^{3} °येनानुलेपयेत् — c) Lo^{4} Lo^{5} Ox^{3} दक्षिणां; wKt^{3} °प्रणवं; Lo^{1} °प्रवरं; Jm चैवं; Lo^{2} चैष

207.* Cited by *Apa* 471; *Hem* 3/1.160; *Lakṣ* 4115 — a) Ox^{2} [*but cor*] Ox^{3} MTr^{4} चोक्तेषु; Pu^{8} चोच्छेषु; Pu^{5} Pu^{7} *Apa* [vl] सोक्षेषु; wKt^{1} सौख्येषु; GMd^{1} शुचिषु — b) Be^{1} BBe^{2} Be^{3} Bo BCa Hy Jm Jo^{1} Jo^{2} wKt^{1} Kt^{2} wKt^{3} La^{2} Lo^{3} oMd^{2} Pu^{3} Pu^{5} Pu^{7} Pu^{10} Tj^{1} Tj^{2} MTr^{3} *Hem Mandlik Jolly KSS* नदीतीरेषु; Kt^{2} चेव; Lo^{4} *om* हि; NKt^{4} Lo^{2} GMd^{1} ह; Lo^{5} च — c) GMd^{1} Pu^{5} Pu^{7} [*Jolly* G] विविक्तेन; Be^{3} विपक्तेषु; sOx^{1} sPu^{6} विविक्तेषु हि च; wKt^{1} तु — c-d) *Lakṣ* दत्तेन तुष्यन्ति — d) Ho दत्तैरिह पितामहाः; BKt^{5} wKt^{6} GMd^{5} GMy NNg Tr^{1} MTr^{4} पितरस्तथा; TMd^{3} पितरस्तदा

Additional verse in Be^{3} GMd^{1} GMd^{5} oOr Ox^{2} Tr^{1} MTr^{4} MTr^{6}:

व्यतीपातेषु दातव्यमयनेषु तथैव च ।
चन्द्रसूर्योपरागेषु विषुवत्सु च यत्नतः ॥

a) GMd^{1} व्यति°; MTr^{4} व्यतीपाकेषु — b) Be^{3} मद्यासु च; GMd^{5} मखासु च — c) oOr सूर्य-चन्द्रोपरागे च — d) GMd^{5} Tr^{1} विषुवेषु यत्नतः; Be^{3} विषुवेष्वष्टकासु च

Prior to the previous verse GMd^{5} adds:

स्थाप्येषु गिरिपृष्ठेषु तीर्थेष्वायतनेषु च ॥
गोष्ठेषु च विविक्तेषु तुष्यन्ति पितरस्तथा ॥

208. Cited by *Mādh* 1.726–7 — a) Be^{1} आसनेषु प्रक्लृप्तेषु; NKt^{4} TMd^{3} GMd^{5} Tr^{1} आसनेषु च कॢप्तेषु; MTr^{4} *Mādh* आसनेषु तु कॢप्तेषु; Be^{3} आसनेषूपविष्टेषु; NNg sOx^{1} sPu^{6} °क्लिप्तेषु — b) GMy बर्हिषत्सु;

उपवेश्य तु तान्विप्रानासनेष्वजुगुप्सितान् ।
गन्धमाल्यैः सुरभिभिरर्चयेद्देवपूर्वकम् ॥२०९॥
तेषामुदकमानीय सपवित्रांस्तिलानपि ।
अग्नौ कुर्यादनुज्ञातो ब्राह्मणो ब्राह्मणैः सह ॥२१०॥
अग्नेः सोमयमाभ्यां च कृत्वाप्यायनमादितः ।
हविर्दानेन विधिवत् पश्चात्संतर्पयेत्पितॄन् ॥२११॥
अग्न्यभावे तु विप्रस्य पाणावेवोपपादयेत् ।
यो ह्यग्निः स द्विजो विप्रैर्मन्त्रदर्शिभिरुच्यते ॥२१२॥
अक्रोधनान् सुप्रसादान् वदन्त्येतान् पुरातनान् ।
लोकस्याप्यायने युक्ताञ्छ्राद्धदेवान् द्विजोत्तमान् ॥२१३॥
अपसव्यमग्नौ कृत्वा सर्वमावृत्परिक्रमम् ।

TMd^{3} बर्हिष्यात्सु; Lo^{1} हविष्मत्सु — c) Tj^{1} उपस्पष्टो°; GMd^{1} Ox^{3} उपसृष्टो°; NKt^{4} OMd^{2} °दकात्स° — d) GMd^{5} NNg °म्यम्द्विजांस्तानुप°; GMd^{1} °म्यम्द्विजान्तानुप°; OMd^{2} °प्रानुपवे°; Ho °स्ताननुवेशयेत्; TMd^{3} °नुपदेशयेत्; Hy °शयत्

209. Cited by *Hem* 3/2.1306; pādas c-d cited by *Apa* 481 — a) GMd^{5} उपवेश्य द्विजान्सर्वानासने°; TMd^{3} उपविश्य; Be^{3} उपविष्ट्यांस्तु; GMy च; MTr^{6} तान्सर्वानासने° — b) Be^{1} Jm GMy *Hem* °सनेषु जुगु°; Ho °सनेषु यथाविधि; Bo °गुप्सतान् — c) Ho °माल्यैश्च सुरभिरर्चये°; GMy ससुरभिरर्चये°; Ox^{3} Tr^{2} सुरभिरर्चये° — d) Be^{3} BCa wKt^{3} Lo^{1} Lo^{3} Lo^{4} Lo^{5} NNg Ox^{3} *Apa Jha Dave* °येद्दैव°; Wa °पूर्विकान्

210. Pādas a-b omitted in GMy. Cited by *Hem* 3/2.1349; pādas c-d cited by *Apa* 489; *Dev* 4.318 — a) GMd^{5} तेषां दत्त्वा तु हस्तेषु — b) TMd^{3} GMd^{5} Tr^{1} MTr^{4} MTr^{6} सपवित्रं तिलोदकं [Tr^{1} °वित्रे]; Bo °वित्रास्तिला°; NNg °स्तिलामपि; sOx^{1} sPu^{6} °स्तिलांस्तथा; NKt^{4} °स्तिलान्यपि — c) Lo^{2} अग्ने — d) Tj^{2} *om* ब्राह्मणो; Tj^{1} ब्राह्मणौ ब्रा°; NKt^{4} TMd^{4} सदा; GMd^{1} तदा

211. Cited by *Hem* 3/2.1353 — a) GMd^{1} TMd^{3} TMd^{4} GMd^{5} GMy Tr^{1} MTr^{4}MTr^{6} अग्निसोमयमानां च; Tj^{1} सोमा°; Lo^{1} GMd^{1} तु — b) GMd^{1} कृत्वाद्ययन°; sOx^{1} sPu^{6} °प्यायिन°; GMy °नमाद्यतः; Lo^{2} °नमायतः — c) GMd^{1} हविर्दाने च — d) NKt^{4} °तर्प्ययेत्पितॄन्

212. Cited by *Hem* 3/2.1337; *Dev* 4.333; *Mādh* 1.739;pādas a-b cited by *Vij* 1.237;*Apa* 491 — a) Be^{3} TMd^{3} °भावेपि — b) *Mādh* पाणौ दद्यात्तु दक्षिणे; OOr Pu^{10} Tr^{2} प्राणा°; Ho पाणाभावोप°; *Dev* °पसाधयेत् — c) Be^{3} सो ह्यग्निः; wKt^{6} द्विजे विश्वैर्म°; NKt^{4} द्विजैर्विप्रो मन्त्र°; TMd^{3} द्विजैर्विप्रैर्मन्त्र°; GMy द्विजो विप्रो मन्त्र° — d) wKt^{3} विप्रैर्मन्त्रविद्भिरुदाहृतः; MTr^{4} विप्रैर्मन्त्रंदर्शि°; NPu^{1} Tj^{1} °दर्शभिरुच्यते

213. Omitted in Lo^{3} Lo^{4} Lo^{5} Ox^{3} Tj^{1} — a) Ho GMd^{1} अक्रोधान्; TMd^{4} Wa अक्रोधनांत्सु°; wKt^{6} °धनानप्रसादान्; TMd^{3} °धनांस्तु प्रसन्नान्; NKt^{4} सुप्रदातान्; GMd^{5} GMy Tr^{1} MTr^{4} सुप्रसन्नान्; Lo^{2} सुप्रसादाच्च; GMd^{1} सुप्रदानां च — b) NKt^{4} वदन्तोतान्; GMd^{1} वदन्त्येताः; Be^{3} NKt^{4} BKt^{5} wKt^{6} GMd^{1} NNg OOr Pu^{10} [*Jolly* M Nd] *Me Go* [possibly] *Jha Dave* पुरातनाः; sOx^{1} पुराकृतान्; TMd^{4} सुरोत्तमान्; Pu^{2} पुरोहितान्; *Me* gives पुरातनान् as pāṭha, saying: द्वितीयान्तो वा पठितव्यः — c) wKt^{3} °प्ययने; Tr^{2} °प्यायनैर्युक्ता° — c-d) GMd^{1} प्यायने पुण्यदेपिद्विजोत्तमान् [sic] — d) Bo BCa wKt^{3} Lo^{2} NPu^{1} MTr^{4} MTr^{6} [*but cor*] *Me Mandlik Jha Dave* युक्ताञ्छ्राद्धे देवान्; Ho °दैवान्; Lo^{2} °देवा; TMd^{3} द्विजोत्तमाः

अपसव्येन हस्तेन निर्वपेदुदकं भुवि ॥२१४॥
त्रींस्तु तस्माद्धविःशेषात् पिण्डान्कृत्वा समाहितः ।
औदकेनैव विधिना निर्वपेद्दक्षिणामुखः ॥२१५॥
न्युप्य पिण्डांस्ततस्तांस्तु प्रयतो विधिपूर्वकम् ।
तेषु दर्भेषु तं हस्तं निमृज्याल्लेपभागिनाम् ॥२१६॥
आचम्योदक्परावृत्य त्रिरायम्य शनैरसून् ।
षड्ऋतूंश्च नमस्कुर्यात् पितॄनेव च मन्त्रवत्* ॥२१७॥
उदकं निनयेच्छेषं शनैः पिण्डान्तिके पुनः ।
अवजिघ्रेच्च तान्पिण्डान् यथान्युप्तान्समाहितः ॥२१८॥

214. Omitted in Lo[4] Lo[5] Ox[3]. Cited by *Lakṣ* 4.207; *Hem* 3/2.1321, 1404; *Dev* 4.326; pādas c-d cited by *Hem* 3/2.1423; *Dev* 4367 — a) GMd[1] TMd[3] TMd[4] GMd[5] GMd[5] GMy Tr[1] MTr[4] MTr[6] प्रसव्यमग्नौ कृत्वा तु; oOr कृत्वापसव्यमग्नौ च; Lo[1] पसव्यं तु अग्नौ — b) Hy Jm Jo[1] NKt[4] La[1] La[2] Tj[2] MTr[3] *Mandlik KSS* सर्वमावृत्य विक्रमं; wKt[1] सव्यमावृत्प°; Tj[1] °मादत्परि°; TMd[3] °मापत्परिश्रमं; Tr[2] °वृत्तपरि°; NPu[1] °वृत्प्रदक्षिणं; *Hem* 3/2.1404 [vl as in ed] °वृत्परिश्रुतम्; GMd[1] MTr[4] °क्रमात् — c) GMy अप्रसव्येन — d) *Lakṣ Hem* शुचि; GMd[1] TMd[3] GMd[5] Tr[1] निवपे°; Be[1] [*cor to*] BKt[5] wKt[6] sOx[1] sPu[6] *Me* [pāṭha] शनैः [*but cor in* sOx[1] sPu[6]]; MTr[4] MTr[6] शुचिः

215. Pādas a-b omitted in sOx[1]. Cited by *Lakṣ* 4.207; *Hem* 3/2.1404, 1427; *Mādh* 1.751 — a) GMy त्रींस्तु धर्मविशेषांश्च; NNg त्रीस्तु; Tr[1] स्त्रींस्तु; Bo Pu[5] Pu[7] °शेपान्; *Lakṣ* °शेपं — b) oOr पिण्डान्दत्वा; sPu[6] [*but cor sh*] Tr[1] विशेपतः; Wa यथाविधि — c) Jm GMy ओदकेनैव; Lo[2] Lo[5] Ox[2] [*but cor*] Ox[3] NPu[1] Pu[5] Pu[7] उदकेनैव — d) TMd[3] GMd[5] Tr[1] निवपे°

216. Cited by *Apa* 507; *Lakṣ* 4.207; *Hem* 3/2.1449; *Dev* 4.372, 375; *Mādh* 1.754 — a) *Hem* पुष्पपिण्डान्पितृभ्यश्च; sOx[1] sPu[6] न्युप; Ho नुप्य; *Apa* [vl] न्यस्य; BKt[5] wKt[6] पिण्डानतस्तांस्तु; *Apa Dev* पिण्डान्पितृभ्यस्तु; NPu[1] पिण्डान्पुरस्तांस्तु; Bo °तस्तास्तु — b) GMy प्रयते; Wa °पूर्विकं — c) wKt[6] गर्भेषु; sOx[1] sPu[6] *Apa* पिण्डेषु; sOx[1] sPu[6] तौ हस्तौ —d) BBe[2] Be[3] Bo BCa Ho wKt[1] La[2] Lo[1] Lo[2] NNg Ox[2] NPu[1] Pu[2] Pu[4] Pu[8] Tj[2] Tr[2] Wa *Apa Lakṣ Jha Dave* निर्मृज्या°; La[1] विमृज्या°; NNg निज्या°; Pu[10] निमृज्याल्लोप°; sPu[6] °भागिनौ *cor to* °भागिना; sOx[1] °भागिना; oOr °भागिनाः; NNg Tj[2] °भाजिनां; TMd[3] °भाजतं

217.* Cited by *Apa* 507; *Hem* 3/2.1451, 1462; *Lakṣ* 4.207; pādas c-d cited by *Hem* 3/2.1462 — a) Wa आचाम्यो°; GMd[1] आपत्यो°; GMy °म्योदङ्परा°; NPu[1] °दकमावृत्य; Pu[5] Pu[7] [*Jolly* G] °रावर्त्य; Ho °रीवृत्य; NKt[4] °रावित्रा — b) BBe[2] [*but cor*] Be[3] Hy Jo[2] [*cor to*] Lo[5] GMd[1] NPu[1] Tj[2] Tr[2] MTr[3] Wa *Lakṣ* त्रिराचम्य; GMy त्रिधाचम्य; TMd[3] निरायम्य — c) Be[1] La[1] GMd[5] NPu[1] *Hem* 3/2.1451 पडप्यृतूत्रमस्कुर्यात् [La[1] °स्कृत्वा]; NKt[4] पडप्टतत्रमस्कुर्यात्; GMd[1] पडावृत्या नमस्कुर्यात्; GMy पडप्सुतं नमस्कुर्यात्; Tr[1] पडप्यन्यं नमस्कुर्यात्; TMd[4] पडद्यामात्रमस्कुर्यात्; *Hem* 3/2.1462 षट्पितृंश्च नमस्कुर्यात्; sOx[1] sPu[6] पड्तूंस्तु; MTr[6] पडप्यृतुं; wKt[1] पड् भूयश्च; TMd[3] नमस्कृत्य — d) Jo[1] पितृनेवं; Lo[2] Lo[4] Lo[5] sPu[6] तु; Be[1] BBe[2] Bo BCa Ho Hy Jm Jo[1] Jo[2] Kt[2] wKt[3] NKt[4] BKt[5] wKt[6] La[1] La[2] Lo[2] Lo[3] Lo[4] [*but mc sh*] Lo[5] oMd[2] TMd[3] TMd[4] GMy NNg oOr sOx[1] Ox[2] Ox[3] NPu[1] Pu[2] Pu[3] Pu[4] Pu[5] sPu[6] Pu[7] Pu[8] Pu[10] Tj[1] Tj[2] Tr[2] MTr[3] MTr[4] MTr[6] Wa [*Jolly* M[8–9] G R] *Apa Hem* 3/2.1462 *Lakṣ Rc Mandlik Bühler* मन्त्रवित्; GMd[1] मन्त्रतः

218. Cited by *Hem* 3/2.1473; pādas a-b cited by *Hem* 3/2.1462; and pādas c-d by *Apa* 508 — a) oMd[2] निनयेद्गुदकं शेपं; NKt[4] TMd[3] GMd[5] उदशेपं तु निनयेच्छनैः [NKt[4] *om* तु]; La[1] उदकशेपं

पिण्डेभ्यस्त्वल्पिकां मात्रां समादायानुपूर्वशः ।
तानेव विप्रानासीनान् विधिवत्पूर्वमाशयेत् ॥२१९॥
ध्रियमाणे तु पितरि पूर्वेषामेव निर्वपेत् ।
विप्रवद्वापि तं श्राद्धं* स्वकं पितरमाशयेत् ॥२२०॥
पिता यस्य तु वृत्तः स्याज्जीवेद्वापि पितामहः ।
पितुः स नाम संकीर्त्य कीर्तयेत् प्रपितामहम् ॥२२१॥
पितामहो वा तच्छ्राद्धं भुञ्जीतेत्यब्रवीन्मनुः ।
कामं वा समनुज्ञातः स्वयमेव समाचरेत् ॥२२२॥
तेषां दत्त्वा तु हस्तेषु सपवित्रं तिलोदकम् ।
तत्पिण्डाग्रं प्रयच्छेत्तु स्वधैषामस्त्विति ब्रुवन् ॥२२३॥
पाणिभ्यां तूपसंगृह्य स्वयमन्नस्य वर्धितम् ।

निनयच्छनैः; GMd^1 TMd^4 GMy च नयेच्छेषं; Tr^2 निर्वपेच्छेषं; wKt^6 निलयेच्छेषं — b) GMd^1 TMd^4 GMy oOr Tr^1 पिण्डान्तिकं; BKt^5 wKt^6 पिण्डान्तके; *Hem* 3/2.1473 पिण्डादिके; TMd^3 खण्डादिकं — c) Tj^1 अविजि°; oOr °जिघ्रेत तान्पि° — c-d) BKt^5 wKt^6 अवजिघ्रेन्यथान्युप्तान्पिण्डांश्च सुसमाहितः — d) GMd^1 यथान्युञ्जान्समा°; GMy यथायुक्तान्समा°; sOx^1 sPu^6 [mc sh to] यथान्युक्तः समा°; Ox^2 [*but cor*] °हितान्

219. Pādas a-c omitted in wKt^3. Cited by *Hem* 3/2.1476 — a) GMd^5 पिण्डेभ्य स्वल्पिकामात्राः; Lo^4 Lo^5 sOx^1 Ox^2 Ox^3 Pu^5 sPu^6 Pu^7 Pu^{10} MTr^4 MTr^6 [*cor to*] *Jolly Jha Dave* पिण्डेभ्यः स्वल्पिकां; GMd^1 °मात्रान्; TMd^3 °मात्रात्; GMy Tr^1 °मात्राः — c) Bo तामेव; *Hem* ता एव; NPu^1 Tr^1 तेनैव; TMd^3 पिण्डानासीनान्; Tr^1 विप्रासमासीनान् — d) TMd^3 °वत्पूर्वं समाश्रयेत्

220.* Omitted in Pu^2; verse 220 placed after 222 in Bo. Cited by *Viś* 1.225; *Dev* 4.16 — a) wKt^1 GMd^1 प्रीयमाणे; TMd^3 म्रियमाणे — b) GMd^1 पूर्वेषामपि — c) *Dev* विप्रवद्धावितं श्राद्धे; GMy विप्रवच्चापि; TMd^4 Tr^1 MTr^4 तच्छ्राद्धं; GMd^5 तच्छ्राद्धे; Be^1 BBe^2 Bo Ho Hy Jm Jo^1 Jo^2 wKt^1 Kt^2 wKt^3 NKt^4 La^1 La^2 Lo^1 Lo^2 Lo^3 oMd^2 GMy NNg oOr sOx^1 Ox^2 [*cor to*] NPu^1 Pu^5 sPu^6 Pu^7 Pu^8 Pu^{10} Tj^1 Tj^2 Tr^2 *Viś Go Rc Mandlik Jolly KSS* श्राद्धे; Wa श्राद्ध — d) Bo GMy स्वयं; TMd^3 नवकं पित°; Jm °माविशेत्; Lo^2 °शयत्

221.* Cited by *Viś* 1.225; *Lakṣ* 4.236; *Dev* 4.16; pādas a-b cited by *Vij* 1.254 — a) TMd^4 पिता तु यस्य वृत्ता; *Vij Nā KSS Mandlik* यस्य निवृत्तः; Tr^1 यस्यातिवृत्तः; BBe^2 यस्य वृत्तः; Kt^2 यस्य नवृत्तः; BKt^5 यस्य वृत्ततुः; Bo यस्य तु जीवः — b) wKt^1 स्याद्दीरेद्वा पिता°; Hy Jm Jo^1 Kt^2 TMd^3 GMd^5 GMy Ox^2 [*cor to*] Pu^8 Tj^2 Tr^1 MTr^3 MTr^4 MTr^6 *Mandlik Jha KSS Dave* °वेच्चापि — c) TMd^3 पितुस्सपत्नान्संकीर्त्य; *Dev* पितुस्तु नाम; Lo^5 GMd^5 GMy Ox^2 [*but cor*] MTr^4 MTr^6 पितुः स्वनाम; Lo^2 नाम कीर्तये; GMd^1 संकीर्त्या — d) TMd^3 प्रपितामहः

222. Cited by *Lakṣ* 4.236; pādas a-b cited by *Dev* 417 — a) TMd^3 पितामहोगतश्राद्धं; NNg °महो वो; Be^1 Ho oOr तच्छ्राद्धे — c) TMd^3 कामं ह; BBe^2 Ho wKt^1 GMd^5 Ox^2 Tr^2 MTr^6 *Lakṣ* तदनुज्ञातः — d) GMd^1 GMd^5 GMy Tr^1 MTr^6 [*Jolly* Gr] °ज्ञातो यद्युक्तं तत्समाचरेत्; sOx^1 sPu^6 तदाचरेत्

223. Tr^1 [*Jolly* Nd] place 223 after 119; pādas c-d omitted in TMd^4. Cited by *Lakṣ* 4.207; *Hem* 3/2.1476 — a) Jo^2 Tj^1 तु दत्त्वा; BCa दत्त्वा स्वहस्तेपु; Lo^4 Ox^3 तु हस्ते तु — c) GMd^1 तत्पिण्डानां प्रवृत्ते तु; TMd^3 GMy तं पिण्डा°; La^1 तत्पिण्डाग्रे; Be^3 Hy Jm Jo^1 Kt^2 BKt^5 wKt^6 Lo^3 GMy NPu^1 Tj^2 MTr^3 [*Jolly* M$^{4-9}$] *Mandlik KSS* प्रयच्छेत; wKt^1 प्रयच्छं तु; Pu^{10} [*Jolly* M^{1-2-8}] प्रसिंचेत्तु; *Rc* appears to read प्रक्षिपेत् glossing it with दद्यात्

विप्रान्तिके पितॄन् ध्यायञ्छनकैरुपनिक्षिपेत् ॥२२४॥
उभयोर्हस्तयोर्मुक्तं यदन्नमुपनीयते ।
तद्विप्रलुम्पन्त्यसुराः सहसा दुष्टचेतसः ॥२२५॥
गुणांश्च सूपशाकाद्यान् पयो दधि घृतं मधु ।
विन्यसेत् प्रयतः सम्यग्भूमावेव समाहितः ॥२२६॥
भक्ष्यं भोज्यं च विविधं मूलानि च फलानि च ।
हृद्यानि चैव मांसानि पानानि सुरभीणि च ॥२२७॥
उपनीय तु तत्सर्वं शनकैः सुसमाहितः ।
परिवेषयेत् प्रयतो गुणान्सर्वान् प्रचोदयन् ॥२२८॥
नास्रमापातयेज्जातु न कुप्येन्नानृतं वदेत् ।
न पादेन स्पृशेदन्नं न चैतदवधूनयेत् ॥२२९॥

224. Omitted in TMd^{4}. Cited by *Apa* 492; *Hem* 3/2.1368; *Dev* 4.339; *Mādh* 1.742 — a) Be^{3} Ho *Apa Hem Dev Mādh* पाणिभ्यामुपसं° ; Be^{1} पाणिभ्यामपसं° ; [*Jolly* Gr] °संवृत्य — b) GMy स्वयमन्यस्य; Lo^{1} वर्धितां; *Dev* बन्धुकम् — c) Ho विप्रान्तके; Lo^{1} पितृ — d) *Dev* ध्यायन्शनैरुपरि निक्षिपेत्; GMd^{1} ध्यायन्यज्ञकैरुप° ; Ho °नकैः निःक्षिपेद्धुवि; Be^{1} Be^{3} sOx^{1} Pu^{5} sPu^{6} Pu^{7} [*Jolly* G] °पसंक्षिपेत्; BBe^{2} wKt^{6} °निःक्षिपेत्

225. Cited by *Apa* 493; *Lakṣ* 4.173; *Hem* 3/2.1368 — a) GMd^{1} GMd^{5} GMy Tr^{1} *Lakṣ* मुक्तं ह्युभाभ्यां हस्ताभ्यां [GMd^{5} मुक्तिं; Tr^{1} पाणिभ्यां]; oMd^{2} °योर्युक्तं — b) Lo^{1} यदन्नं यदि दीयते; Tj^{1} तदन्नमुप° ; Lo^{3} Tj^{1} °पदीयते — c) GMy तद्विलुम्पन्त्यन्धासुराः; *Lakṣ* तद्धि प्रलुम्प° — d) TMd^{3} सहस्र-दप्टचेतसः; GMy तुप्टचेतसः

226.* Cited by *Apa* 493; *Hem* 3/2.1372; *Dev* 4.342 — a) Bo TMd^{4} गुणाश्च; TMd^{3} गुणांस्तु; Ho GMd^{5} गुडांश्च; BKt^{5} wKt^{6} सूपकाराद्यान्; Bo °शाकाद्या — c) NNg विन्यस्येत्; Hy Jm Jo^{1} Kt^{2} La^{1} oOr Tj^{2} MTr^{3} *Mandlik Jha KSS Dave* पूर्वं भूमा°; NKt^{4} GMd^{1} TMd^{3} TMd^{4} GMd^{5} GMy Tr^{1} MTr^{4} MTr^{6} सर्वं भूमा°

227. Cited by *Hem* 3/2.1368; *Dev* 4.342; *Mādh* 1.744 — a) Ho भक्ष्य; Lo^{2} Pu^{10} भक्षं; Kt^{2} भोज्ये; *Hem* च विधिवत् — b) Tr^{2} विविधमन्नानि मूलानि च; [*Jolly* R] पानानि विविधानि च; Pu^{5} Pu^{7} Pu^{9} [*Jolly* G] सुरसानि फलानि च; sPu^{6} [*but mc sh*] फलं मूलं तथैव च — c) BCa मांसानि चैव हृद्यानि — d) Lo^{1} यानानि सुरभानि च; TMd^{4} पाकानि; oMd^{2} पाहानि; Lo^{3} Tj^{1} विविधानि च

228.* Cited by *Hem* 3/2.1368; *Dev* 4.342; *Mādh* 1.744 — a) Bo^{1} wKt^{1} wKt^{3} NKt^{4} La^{1} La^{2} Lo^{1} Lo^{2} Lo^{4} Lo^{5} TMd^{4} Ox^{3} NPu^{1} Pu^{2} Pu^{5} Pu^{7} Pu^{8} Pu^{9} MTr^{4} *Me Go Ku Mr Hem* उपनीय सर्वमेत-च्छनकैः; TMd^{3} पानीयं सवमेतच्च; MTr^{4} उपनीयं; [*Jolly* M^{3}] उपनीतं; GMd^{5} *Dev* च; Lo^{3} तत्सर्वे — a-b) BKt^{5} wKt^{6} उपनीय शनैः सर्वमेतच्च सुसमाहितः — b) Ho Jo^{2} Lo^{3} Tj^{1} °कैस्तु समा° — c) TMd^{4} °वेष-यीत; *Dev Mādh* °वेषयेत्तु; Lo^{1} Lo^{5} TMd^{3} Pu^{5} Pu^{7} Pu^{9} °वेषयेच्च; Be^{1} Jm Jo^{1} wKt^{1} Kt^{2} GMd^{1} oMd^{2} GMy Pu^{2} Pu^{10} Tr^{1} MTr^{4} MTr^{6} *Nd Rc Mandlik Jha KSS Dave* °वेषयेत; Lo^{4} °वेषये [*ma* त]; GMd^{1} प्रयते — d) Ho गुणान्वा प्रचो° ; Be^{3} Bo GMd^{1} sOx^{1} sPu^{6} MTr^{6} प्रचोदयेत्; Lo^{4} Lo^{5} Ox^{3} Pu^{5} Pu^{7} Pu^{9} Tj^{2} प्रणोदयन्; Wa प्रणोदयत्; Hy प्रबोधयन्

229. Pāda-a moth eaten in oOr. Cited by *Hem* 3/2.1029 — a) NKt^{4} GMd^{1} TMd^{3} TMd^{4} GMd^{5} GMy NNg Ox^{3} NPu^{1} Pu^{5} Pu^{7} Pu^{9} Pu^{10} [*Jolly* M$^{1-2-5-8-9}$ Me G] *Jolly* नाश्रुमा° ; Be^{3} La^{1} Pu^{2} Wa नाश्रमा° ; Lo^{4} Lo^{5} न चाश्रं पात° ; BBe^{2} Lo^{1} Lo^{3} oMd^{2} Ox^{2} [*Jolly* R] न चाश्रुं पात° ; Be^{1} Ho Hy

अस्रं गमयति प्रेतान् कोपोऽरीननृतं शुनः ।
पादस्पर्शस्तु रक्षांसि दुष्कृतीनवधूननम् ॥२३०॥
यद्यद्रोचेत विप्रेभ्यस्तत्तद्दद्यादमत्सरः ।
ब्रह्मोद्याश्च कथाः कुर्यात् पितॄणामेतदीप्सितम् ॥२३१॥
स्वाध्यायं श्रावयेत् पित्र्ये धर्मशास्त्राणि चैव हि ।
आख्यानानीतिहासांश्च पुराणानि खिलानि च ॥२३२॥
हर्षयेद् ब्राह्मणांस्तुष्टो भोजयेच्चाशनं शनैः ।
अन्नाद्येनासकृच्चैतान् गुणैश्च परिचोदयेत् ॥२३३॥
व्रतस्थमपि दौहित्रं श्राद्धे यत्नेन भोजयेत् ।
कुतपं चासनं दद्यात् तिलैश्च विकिरेन्महीम् ॥२३४॥

Jo^{2} sOx^{1} sPu^{6} Tj^{1} Tr^{2} न चाश्रु पात° [Be^{1} चासु]; wKt^{1} न चाश्रापात°; Pu^{8} नाश्रु चापात°; Tr^{1} *Hem* °पादये° — b) NPu^{1} कुप्येतानृतं; Be^{1} [*but mc*] La^{1} GMy कुप्येदनृतं; Bo कुप्यन्नानृतं; Jm NKt^{4} कुप्यं नानृतं — c) Be^{3} पद्भ्यां — d) Be^{3} BCa Ho wKt^{1} wKt^{3} Lo^{2} GMd^{1} TMd^{3} sPu^{6} Pu^{7} Pu^{9} चैनमव°; Tj^{1} चैनदव°; Tr^{2} चैवमव°; *Hem* वैतदव°; sOx^{1} sPu^{6} [*mc sh to*] हीनमव°; NKt^{4} चैनं यविधू°

230. Omitted in Pu^{9} — a) Tr^{2} गमयत्यश्रु वै प्रेतान्; GMd^{1} GMd^{5} GMy Tr^{1} MTr^{6} आस्रं; sPu^{6} अस्र; TMd^{3} नास्रं; Pu^{2} असं; Be^{1} La^{1} असुं; BBe^{2} Wa अश्रं; Be^{3} oOr Ox^{3} Pu^{7} अश्रुं; NKt^{4} NNg NPu^{1} Pu^{5} Pu^{10} [*Jolly* M G] *Jolly* अश्रु; NPu^{1} प्रापयति; Bo प्रेता; La^{1} प्रेत्यान्; TMd^{3} प्रीतान्; sOx^{1} प्रीतां — b) sOx^{1} sPu^{6} [*both mc to*] कोपो न च कृतं शुनः; Pu^{5} Pu^{7} Pu^{10} क्रोधो; TMd^{3} कुपो — c) BBe^{2} °स्पर्शश्च; TMd^{3} °स्पर्शं तु; Tr^{2} °स्पर्शे तु; oOr °स्पर्शांस्तु; BKt^{5} wKt^{6} °स्पृष्टस्तु — d) Tj^{1} दुष्कृतीनेव धूतकं; Pu^{5} Pu^{7} दुष्कृतीमव°; sOx^{1} sPu^{6} [*but cor*] दुष्कृतंनव°

231. Placed before 229 in TMd^{3} GMd^{5} [*Jolly* Gr Nd]. Cited by *Hem* 3/2.1027 — b) GMy °भ्यो दद्यात्तत्तदमत्सरः; TMd^{4} °भ्यस्तद्दद्या°; Pu^{10} °भ्यस्तन्न दद्या°; Be^{1} °तत्कुर्यादमत्सरः; TMd^{4} °द्यादवमत्सरः — c) Tr^{1} ब्राह्मो°; Ho sOx^{1} sPu^{6} ब्रह्मोद्यास्तु; Wa *Me* [pāṭha] ब्रह्माद्याश्च; Be^{3} ब्रह्माद्यांश्च; Pu^{5} Pu^{7} Pu^{9} ब्राह्मयाद्याश्च; La^{1} ब्रह्मोद्याः स्वकथाः; Be^{1} Bo कथा; GMd^{1} तथा; sOx^{1} sPu^{6} कुर्वन्; Kt^{2} कार्यात् — d) Lo^{4} °मेनदीप्सितं°; GMy °प्सितः

232. *Apa* 502; *Hem* 3/2.1069; *Dev* 4.351; *Mādh* 1.746 — a) Lo^{4} Ox^{3} स्वाध्यायान्; TMd^{3} स्वयं तु श्राव°; Lo^{4} Ox^{3} पित्रे; *Hem* पैत्र्ये; BKt^{5} wKt^{6} TMd^{4} NPu^{1} Pu^{7} Pu^{9} Tj^{2} Tr^{2} पित्र्यं — b) NKt^{4} Lo^{2} MTr^{4} ह; BKt^{5} wKt^{6} तु — c) TMd^{3} आख्यातानी°; TMd^{4} °नीतिमहानानीश्च — d) Ho wKt^{1} BKt^{5} La^{1} GMd^{1} TMd^{3} TMd^{4} GMy Ox^{2} NPu^{1} Pu^{5} Pu^{7} Pu^{9} Tj^{2} Tr^{1} [*Jolly* G] *Dev Apa* [vl] पुराणान्यखिलानि; Tj^{1} खलानि

233.* Cited by *Hem* 3/2.1026 — a) Tr^{2} हर्पयन्; Hy ब्राह्मणास्तुष्टो; BKt^{5} wKt^{6} ब्राह्मणान्तुष्टो; Ox^{3} °णांस्तुष्टौ — b) Hy Jm Jo^{1} Kt^{2} Lo^{3} oMd^{2} TMd^{3} sOx^{1} Ox^{2} [*mc fh to*] sPu^{6} Pu^{9} Tj^{1} Tj^{2} Tr^{1} Tr^{2} MTr^{3} [*Jolly* R Nd] *Rc Mandlik Bühler Jha KSS Dave* भोजयेच्च शनैः शनैः; MTr^{6} भोजयेद्वा गुणं शनैः; GMy भोजनेच्चा°; NKt^{4} भोजयेच्चाशने; Bo भोजयेच्चाशनैः; wKt^{3} भोजये वाशनं — c) GMy °द्येनसकृ°; BKt^{5} wKt^{6} °द्येनाशयेच्चैतान्; Lo^{3} GMy °कृच्चेतान्; La^{1} Lo^{2} TMd^{3} TMd^{4} NNg NPu^{1} MTr^{6} °कृच्चैनान्; Pu^{5} Pu^{7} Pu^{9} °कृच्चेनान्; Bo °कृच्चैनं — d) GMd^{1} GMy Ox^{3} गुणांश्च; Wa गुणोश्च; BCa Jo^{2} Lo^{3} Tj^{1} [*Jolly* R] °चोदयन्; Be^{1} Pu^{10} °नोदयेत्; NNg °नोदयन्; Pu^{5} Pu^{7} *Go* [*Jolly* G] °बोधयेत्; Ho TMd^{3} GMd^{5} Tr^{1} Tr^{2} °तोषयेत्; Bo °तारयेत्; *Rc* °वेपयेत्

234.* Omitted in Ox^{3}. Cited by *Apa* 475; pādas a-b cited by *Dev* 4.165; *Mādh* 1.685 — a) Lo^{3} व्रतस्थामपि — b) Ox^{2} श्राद्धं — c) TMd^{4} कुतुपं; BBe^{2} GMd^{1} MTr^{3} कुतपश्चा°; NPu^{1} Tr^{2} चाशनं;

त्रीणि श्राद्धे पवित्राणि दौहित्रः कुतपस्तिलाः ।
त्रीणि चात्र प्रशंसन्ति शौचमक्रोधमत्वराम् ॥२३५॥
अत्युष्णं सर्वमन्नं स्याद् भुञ्जीरंश्चैव वाग्यताः ।
न च द्विजातयो ब्रूयुर्दात्रा पृष्टा हविर्गुणान् ॥२३६॥
यावदूष्मा भवत्यन्ने यावदश्नन्ति वाग्यताः ।
तावदश्नन्ति पितरो यावन्नोक्ता हविर्गुणाः ॥२३७॥
यद्वेष्टितशिरा भुङ्क्ते यद्भुङ्क्ते दक्षिणामुखः ।
सोपानत्कश्च यद्भुङ्क्ते तद्वै रक्षांसि भुञ्जते ॥२३८॥

Wa वासनं; Hy Jm wKt^{1} Kt^{2} wKt^{3} gMd^{1} oMd^{2} tMd^{3} tMd^{4} gMd^{5} gMy oOr Pu^{2} Pu^{4} Pu^{8} Tr^{1} mTr^{3} mTr^{4} mTr^{6} [*Jolly* M^{3} Nd Ku] *Ku Mandlik Bühler KSS* चासने; Jo^{1} नासने — d) gMy तिलांश्च; gMd^{1} tMd^{3} gMd^{5} gMy nNg Tr^{1} mTr^{4} mTr^{6} [*Jolly* M^{1-2-8} G Nd] *Apa Jolly* तिलैश्चावकिँ; Be^{3} Pu^{5} Pu^{7} Pu^{9} तिलैश्चाविकि°; tMd^{4} प्रकिरे°; Be^{1} Ho Lo^{5} विकरे°; Tr^{2} विकरे महीं; nPu^{1} विकिरन्महीं

235. Cited by *Apa* 474; *Hem* 3/2.1175 — a) Ho Wa श्राद्धे त्रीणि; Lo^{4} पवित्रापि; Lo^{5} पवित्रोपि — b) Be^{1} bCa Ho wKt^{1} bKt^{5} wKt^{6} Lo^{4} Lo^{5} nNg oOr sOx^{1} Ox^{3} Pu^{5} sPu^{6} Pu^{7} Pu^{9} Pu^{10} Wa *Rc* [pāṭha] दौहित्रं; wKt^{1} Tr^{1} °पस्तिला; Lo^{5} °पस्तिलः — c) gMy त्रीणि श्राद्धे — d) oOr सत्यमक्रो°; Ho °क्रोधनोत्वरं; Jm Lo^{2} Ox^{3} Pu^{5} Pu^{7} Pu^{9} Tj^{2} Tr^{2} Wa °त्वरं; gMd^{1} tMd^{3} gMd^{5} °त्वरा; oOr °त्वर; Lo^{4} Lo^{5} °त्वराः

236.* Cited by *Hem* 3/2.1017; *Lakṣ* 4187; *Dev* 4.355; *Mādh* 1.748; pādas c-d cited by *Apa* 497 — a) wKt^{6} अत्योष्णं; tMd^{3} Tr^{1} Wa *Hem* अभ्युष्णं; gMd^{1} tMd^{3} gMd^{5} sOx^{1} sPu^{6} Tr^{1} °ष्णमन्नं सर्वं — b) tMd^{3} भुञ्जीतश्चैव; Tr^{1} भुञ्जीरन्नेव; wKt^{1} nKt^{4} भुञ्जीरंश्चापि; nPu^{1} भुञ्जीरंस्यापि; La^{1} भुञ्जीतं चापि; Be^{1} bBe^{2} Bo Ho Jm Jo^{2} wKt^{6} La^{2} Lo^{1} Lo^{2} Lo^{3} Ox^{3} Pu^{5} Pu^{7} Pu^{9} Tj^{1} Tj^{2} Wa [*Jolly* G R] *Lakṣ* भुञ्जीरंस्तेपि; Hy Jo^{1} Kt^{2} oMd^{2} mTr^{3} *Mandlik Jha KSS Dave* भुञ्जीरंस्ते च; *Dev Mādh* अश्नीरंश्चैव; wKt^{1} wKt^{6} gMy वाग्यतः; Wa वाग्यतां; Tr^{1} वाग्यता — c) Tj^{1} द्विजातये — d) tMd^{4} Tj^{1} ब्रूयुर्दातृ; Lo^{3} ब्रूयुर्दाति; oOr ब्रूयुर्दात; wKt^{1} ब्रूयुर्गात्रस्पृष्टान्हवि°; Hy Tj^{2} Tr^{2} mTr^{4} *Dev* पृष्टान्हवि°; bKt^{5} wKt^{6} हविर्गुणाः; Be^{3} हवेर्गुणान्; tMd^{3} हरेर्गुणान्; sOx^{1} *om* हविर्गुणान् and jumps to 237d हविर्गुणाः [haplo]

237.* Omitted in La^{1} oOr sOx^{1} Pu^{9} [haplo]. Cited by *Apa* 497; *Lakṣ* 4.187; *Hem* 3/2.1019 — a) Ho *Hem* यावदन्नं भवत्युष्णं; Be^{3} यावदन्नं भवेदुष्णं; Bo Hy Jo^{1} wKt^{1} Kt^{2} wKt^{3} Lo^{1} tMd^{3} tMd^{4} gMd^{5} Ox^{2} Pu^{8} Tj^{2} Tr^{1} mTr^{3} mTr^{4} mTr^{6} Wa *Mandlik KSS* [cf. *VaDh* 11.32; *ViDh* 81.20] यावदुष्णं; oMd^{2} यावदूष्णं; Lo^{5} यावदुष्ण; Be^{1} Jm La^{2} यावदुस्मं; Pu^{7} भवत्येन्ने; Pu^{5} भवत्येभे; Bo Hy Jm Jo^{1} Kt^{2} wKt^{3} La^{2} oMd^{2} tMd^{3} gMd^{5} Ox^{2} Pu^{8} Tj^{2} Tr^{1} mTr^{3} mTr^{4} mTr^{6} Wa *Mandlik Jha KSS* भवत्यन्नं; Be^{1} wKt^{1} Lo^{1} tMd^{4} भवेदन्नं — b) bBe^{2} तावद°; Jm Kt^{2} यावदश्नाति; Wa यावद्भुञ्जति; tMd^{3} यावद्भुञ्जीत; tMd^{3} Wa वाग्यतः — c) nKt^{4} tMd^{3} gMd^{5} Tr^{1} mTr^{4} mTr^{6} तावद्धि पितरोश्नन्ति; bCa Hy Jm Jo^{1} Kt^{2} oMd^{2} Tj^{2} Tr^{2} mTr^{3} *Mandlik Jha KSS Dave* पितरस्तावदश्नन्ति — d) mTr^{3} हविर्गणाः; Be^{3} हवेर्गुणाः; wKt^{3} बहिर्गुणाः

Additional verse in gMd^{5}:

हविर्गुणा न वक्तव्याः पितरो यावदर्पिताः ।
पितृभिस्तर्पितैः पश्चाद्वक्तव्यं शोभनं हविः ॥

238. Kt^{2} transposes 238 and 239. Cited by *Hem* 3/2.1021; *Dev* 1.115 — a) bKt^{5} यो वेष्टित°; Jm ये वेष्टित°; wKt^{6} nPu^{1} यवेष्टित°; tMd^{4} nNg °शिरो; gMd^{1} भुङ्क्तो — b) bKt^{5} wKt^{6} nPu^{1} यो भुङ्क्ते — c) Ho La^{1} °नत्कस्तु; wKt^{6} °नकश्च; bKt^{5} wKt^{6} Lo^{5} tMd^{3} nPu^{1} यो भुङ्क्ते — d) *Dev* रक्षांसि

चण्डालश्च वराहश्च कुक्कुटः श्वा तथैव च ।
रजस्वला च षण्ढश्च नेक्षेरन्नश्नतो द्विजान् ॥२३९॥
होमे प्रदाने भोज्ये च यदेभिरभिवीक्ष्यते ।
दैवे हविषि पित्र्ये वा तद्गच्छत्ययथातथम् ॥२४०॥
घ्राणेन सूकरो हन्ति पक्षवातेन कुक्कुटः ।
श्वा तु दृष्टिनिपातेन स्पर्शेनावरवर्णजः ॥२४१॥
खञ्जो वा यदि वा काणो दातुः प्रेष्योऽपि वा भवेत् ।
हीनातिरिक्तगात्रो वा तमप्यपनयेत्ततः ॥२४२॥
ब्राह्मणं भिक्षुकं वापि भोजनार्थमुपस्थितम् ।
ब्राह्मणैरभ्यनुज्ञातः शक्तितः प्रतिपूजयेत् ॥२४३॥
सार्ववर्णिकमन्नाद्यं संनीयाप्लाव्य वारिणा ।
समुत्सृजेद्भुक्तवतामग्रतो विकिरन्भुवि ॥२४४॥

गच्छति; Ho भुज्यते

239. Cited by *Apa* 472; *Hem* 3/1.516; *Dev* 4.206 — a) Be[1] BBe[2] Bo Ho Jm Jo[1] wKt[1] Kt[2] BKt[5] La[1] Lo[1] Pu[5] Pu[7] Pu[9] MTr[3] *Mandlik Jolly Jha KSS Dave* चाण्डालाश्च — b) Jo[2] Lo[3] Lo[4] TMd[3] TMd[4] Tj[1] Tr[1] [*Jolly* R Gr] *Dev* कुक्कुटश्च तथैव च; GMd[1] कुक्कुट तथैव च; Tr[1] वा — c) Be[1] रजस्वलाश्च; Ox[3] षण्ढाश्च; Kt[2] Pu[5] Pu[7] Pu[9] खण्डश्च; *Dev* खञ्जश्च; TMd[4] मुण्डश्च — d) Be[1] sOx[1] sPu[6] नेक्षीर°; TMd[4] °न्नश्नत

240.* Cited by *Apa* 472; *Hem* 1.108, 3/1.516; *Lakṣ* 4.136; *Dev* 4.206 — a) Lo[2] *Apa* [vl] होम; NKt[4] हेमे प्रभावे; Lo[2] भोज्येन — b) Pu[10] यद्येभिर°; TMd[4] यदेतैरभि°; TMd[3] °भिरवलोकितः; GMd[5] Tr[1] °भिरवलोकितं; Kt[2] TMd[4] MTr[6] °वीक्षते; oMd[2] GMy [*Jolly* Be] *Apa Lakṣ Dev* °वीक्षितं; *Hem* °वीक्ष्यतम् — c) TMd[4] देवे; Tr[1] दैव; Be[3] Hy Jm Jo[1] Kt[2] GMd[1] oMd[2] TMd[3] TMd[4] GMd[5] GMy NNg oOr Tj[2] Tr[1] MTr[3] MTr[4] MTr[6] [*Jolly* Nd]*Dev Mandlik KSS* दैवे कर्मणि; Be[1] Be[3] Ho wKt[1] Lo[5] TMd[3] GMy Ox[3] Tr[2] [*Jolly* M] *Lakṣ* च; Wa व; Lo[1] ना — d) Jo[1] तद्गच्छन्त्य°; wKt[1] NNg Pu[10] *Lakṣ* तद्भवत्य°; Lo[1] *Dev* तद्गच्छति यथा°; Be[1] [*mc to*] BBe[2] Be[3] BCa Jm wKt[1] TMd[4] oOr Pu[2] °यथायथं

241. Cited by *Apa* 472; *Hem* 3/1.517 — a) Lo[2] Pu[9] *om* घ्राणेन; BBe[2] Bo Ho Hy wKt[1] wKt[3] BKt[5] wKt[6] Lo[1] Lo[4] oMd[2] NNg Ox[2] Ox[3] Pu[5] Pu[7] Pu[9] *Jha Dave* शूकरो — b) wKt[1] NNg पक्षि°; Ho wKt[6] TMd[3] oOr Ox[2] [*but cor*] पक्षपातेन; Pu[9] दक्षपातेन; GMy Tr[1] कुक्कुटाः — c) Pu[5] Pu[7] Pu[9] [*Jolly* G] च; Hy °विपातेन — d) Be[1] Tr[1] स्पर्शना°; NNg स्पर्श्येना°; Ox[3] °नापरवार्गिजाः; Lo[4] °नापरवर्जितः; Lo[5] °नापरवर्जिनः; Tr[2] °नावरवर्मजाः

242. Cited by *Apa* 472; *Hem* 3/1.517 — a) wKt[6] Pu[5] Pu[7] षञ्जो; Pu[9] पञ्जो; Hy Jo[2] Lo[3] Tj[1] षण्डो; Tj[2] षण्ढो; Wa काण्यो — b) wKt[6] oMd[2] प्रैष्यो; Pu[5] Pu[7] Pu[9] प्रेक्ष्योपि; GMy प्रेष्येष्वपि; NKt[4] Lo[4] GMd[1] यो भवेत् — c) Bo °रिक्तागोत्रा; Hy wKt[6] °गोत्रो; Ox[3] °मात्रो — d) Lo[1] °पानयेत्ततः; Hy Jm Jo[1] Kt[2] MTr[3] *Mandlik Jha KSS Dave* °नयेत्पुनः

243. Cited by *Apa* 500; *Hem* 3/1.439; *Lakṣ* 4.134; *Mādh* 1.728 — a) Hy ब्राह्मण; Lo[2] *Lakṣ* चापि; GMd[5] वान्यं — b) wKt[6] भोजनान्नमुप°; TMd[4] ब्राह्मणार्थमुप°; *Apa* °मुपागतम्; GMy °स्थितः — c) Lo[1] GMy °णैरप्यनुज्ञातः; BKt[5] wKt[6] °णैरनुज्ञातः; Be[1] °ज्ञातो — d) Pu[5] Pu[7] Pu[9] [*Jolly* G] °ज्ञातो यथाशक्ति प्रपूजयेत्; wKt[1] परिपूजयेत्

244. Cited by *Apa* 504; *Hem* 3/2.1396; *Dev* 4.358; *Mādh* 1.750 — a) Be[1] सर्व°; GMd[5]

असंस्कृतप्रमीतानां त्यागिनां कुलयोषिताम् ।
उच्छिष्टं भागधेयं स्याद् दर्भेषु विकिरश्च यः ॥२४५॥
उच्छेषणं भूमिगतमजिह्मस्याशठस्य च ।
दासवर्गस्य तत्पित्र्ये भागधेयं प्रचक्षते ॥२४६॥
असपिण्डक्रियाकर्म द्विजातेः संस्थितस्य तु ।
अदैवं भोजयेच्छ्राद्धं पिण्डमेकं च निर्वपेत् ॥२४७॥
सहपिण्डक्रियायां तु कृतायामस्य धर्मतः ।
अनयैवावृता कार्यं पिण्डनिर्वपणं सुतैः ॥२४८॥
श्राद्धं भुक्त्वा य उच्छिष्टं वृषलाय प्रयच्छति ।
स मूढो नरकं याति कालसूत्रमवाक्शिराः ॥२४९॥
श्राद्धभुग्वृषलीतल्पं तदहर्योऽधिगच्छति ।
तस्याः पुरीषे तं मासं पितरस्तस्य शेरते ॥२५०॥

°वर्णक° — b) gMd^{1} °द्यमानीयाप्लाव्य; mTr^{4} °द्यमश्नीयाप्लाव्य; Ho Lo^{1} सन्नायाप्लाव्य; tMd^{3} संनिधाप्लाव्य — c) Bo °त्सृजन्भुक्त°; wKt^{1} °भुक्तवरो अग्रतो — d) gMy °ग्रते; Be^{1} Bo Pu^{5} Pu^{7} Pu^{9} Tj^{2} विकरन्भुवि; tMd^{4} विकिरेन्भुवि; Tr^{2} विकरान्भुवि; wKt^{6} वाकिरन्भुवि

245. Cited by *Apa* 504; *Hem* 3/1.150, 3/2.1512; *Mādh* 1.750 — a) Lo^{3} असंस्कृत्य प्रमितानां; Lo^{4} Lo^{5} असंस्कारप्रणीतानां — c) Bo Jo^{2} Kt^{2} tMd^{4} उच्छिष्ट; bBe^{2} भागधेयः — d) tMd^{3} गर्भेषु; gMy दन्तेषु; Be^{1} Bo Lo^{2} nNg Ox^{3} Pu^{5} Pu^{7} Pu^{9} Pu^{10} Tr^{2} विकरश्च; Ho gMd^{5} gMy sOx^{1} sPu^{6} *Apa* [vl] विकिरंश्च; Tr^{1} विकिरेर्चयेत्; Ho tMd^{3} gMd^{5} mTr^{4} °किरश्च यत्

246. Cited by *Apa* 504; *Hem* 3/1.151, 3/2.1511 — a) *Apa* उच्छोषणं; wKt^{6} *Apa* [vl] तच्छेषणं — b) nNg °स्यशठस्य; gMd^{1} °स्याशनस्य; Wa °शठस्तथा; wKt^{3} तु — c) Tr^{2} दासगर्भस्य; Ho दासवस्य च तत्पि°; mTr^{4} यत्पित्र्ये; bBe^{2} Bo wKt^{3} bKt^{5} wKt^{6} Lo^{2} Lo^{4} Ox^{3} तत्पित्रे; Tj^{1} तत्पित्रो; Wa तत्पित्र्यो; *Apa* तत्पित्र्यं — d) Pu^{5} Pu^{7} Pu^{9} भागं मन्वादयो विदुः; bCa wKt^{6} प्रचक्ष्यते; Hy प्रचक्षत

247.* *ma* in Be^{3}. Cited by *Viś* 1.225; *Hem* 3/2.1606 — a) gMy असपिण्डस्य तत्कर्म; tMd^{4} नित्यश्राद्धक्रियाकर्म; Be^{1} bBe^{2} bCa Ho Hy Jm Jo^{1} Jo^{2} wKt^{1} Kt^{2} wKt^{3} bKt^{5} wKt^{6} La^{2} Lo^{1} Lo^{3} Lo^{5} oMd^{2} Ox^{2} Pu^{8} Tj^{1} Tj^{2} mTr^{3} [*Jolly* Ku R] *Nd Rn Mr Mandlik Jha KSS Dave* आसपिण्ड° — b) wKt^{6} gMd^{1} *Hem* °जातैः; Tr^{2} °जातेः स्थितस्य; sOx^{1} sPu^{6} संस्कृतस्य; Be^{1} bBe^{2} Jo^{2} wKt^{1} bKt^{5} wKt^{6} La^{2} Lo^{1} Lo^{3} oMd^{2} tMd^{3} nNg sOx^{1} Pu^{5} sPu^{6} Pu^{7} Pu^{9} Pu^{10} Tj^{1} Tr^{2} Wa [*Jolly* M G R] *Jolly* च — c) gMd^{1} तदैवं; Lo^{2} भोजयेद्विप्रं; Jo^{2} gMy Pu^{7} [*but cor*] °च्छ्राद्धे — d) bCa Ho Hy Jm Jo^{1} wKt^{1} Kt^{2} Lo^{5} tMd^{3} gMy nNg Pu^{5} Pu^{7} Pu^{9} mTr^{3} [*Jolly* G] *Mandlik KSS* तु; *Hem* कारयेत्

248. Omitted in Lo^{4} Lo^{5} Ox^{3}. Cited by *Viś* 1.252 — a) sOx^{1} sPu^{6} Pu^{10} सपिण्डस्य क्रियायां तु — b) tMd^{3} gMy क्रियायामस्य; tMd^{3} धर्मवित्; gMy सर्वतः — c) gMd^{1} tMd^{4} °वावृतं; wKt^{6} gMd^{5} कार्या — d) Pu^{9} mTr^{4} °निर्वापणं; gMd^{1} °निर्वापणे; gMy °निर्वाणकं; tMd^{3} °निर्वाणं; Lo^{2} बुधैः

249. Cited by *Apa* 498; *Lakṣ* 4.192 — a) Be^{1} sOx^{1} sPu^{6} श्राद्धे; Ho श्राद्धभुक्त्वा; tMd^{4} gMy mTr^{3} कृत्वा; gMd^{5} Tr^{1} *Lakṣ* यदुच्छिष्टं; Ho उत्सृष्टं — b) Ho वृषणाय; Kt^{2} वृषलीय; tMd^{3} प्रयच्छते — c) tMd^{3} नवं याति; Bo Lo^{5} nNg Tj^{1} यान्ति — d) Bo Lo^{3} sOx^{1} sPu^{6} [*mc sh to*] Tj^{1} °वाक्शिरः; mTr^{3} °वाक्चिराः; nKt^{4} °वाशिराः; Ox^{3} °वाङ्क्रिराः; Lo^{5} °वास्थिराः; sPu^{6} °वाङ्मुखः

250. c) tMd^{4} पुरीषं; tMd^{4} तन्मांसं; gMy षण्मासं; tMd^{3} षाण्मासं; oMd^{2} मांसं; mTr^{6} मासात्

पृष्ट्वा स्वदितमित्येवं तृप्तानाचामयेत्ततः ।
आचान्तांश्चानुजानीयादभितो रम्यतामिति ॥२५१॥
स्वधास्त्वित्येव तं ब्रूयुर्ब्राह्मणास्तदनन्तरम् ।
स्वधाकारः परा ह्याशीः सर्वेषु पितृकर्मसु ॥२५२॥
ततो भुक्तवतां तेषामन्नशेषं निवेदयेत् ।
यथा ब्रूयुस्तथा कुर्यादनुज्ञातस्तु तैर्द्विजैः ॥२५३॥
पित्र्ये स्वदितमित्येवं वाच्यं गोष्ठे तु सुशृतम् ।
संपन्नमित्यभ्युदये दैवे रोचितमित्यपि ॥२५४॥
अपराह्णस्तथा दर्भा वास्तुसंपादनं तिलाः ।
सृष्टिर्मृष्टिर्द्विजाश्चाग्र्याः श्राद्धकर्मसु संपदः ॥२५५॥

251* Omitted in BKt^5 wKt^6. Cited by *Lakṣ* 4.211 — a) Lo^4 *ma* पृष्ट्वा; wKt^1 wKt^3 Wa स्पृष्ट्वा; La^1 पिष्ट्वा; TMd^3 पृष्ट; NPu^1 दृष्ट्वा; GMd^5 उक्त्वा; GMd^1 पृष्टान्स्वदतमि°; La^1 स्वादितमि°; wKt^1 मुदितमि°; TMd^4 स्वदित इत्येवं; Tr^1 स्वादत इत्येवं; Be^1 Ho GMy °त्येव — b) GMd^1 तप्ताना°; Be^1 Jo^1 TMd^4 Ox^2 [*but cor*] °चमये°; [*Jolly* Gr] °येत्पुनः — c) Pu^5 Pu^7 Pu^9 आचान्तश्चा°; Lo^1 °न्तांस्तानु°; wKt^1 °न्तांश्चात्मजानी°; MTr^4 °न्तांश्चानुमानी°; Lo^3 Tj^1 °न्तांश्चाभिजानी° — d) Jm °यादभ्यतो; [*Jolly* Ku] *Lakṣ* °यादभि भो रम्य°; [*Jolly* R] गम्यतामिति

252. Cited by *Hem* 3/2.1486 — a) wKt^1 स्वधेत्येवचनं ब्रह्म ब्राह्मणा°; MTr^4 MTr^6 स्वधामित्येव; Be^1 Ho wKt^3 NKt^4 BKt^5 wKt^6 Lo^2 Lo^4 Lo^5 TMd^3 Ox^3 Tr^1 [*Jolly* M^{3-4-5} Nd] स्वधा इत्येव; BBe^2 Be^3 Jo^2 Lo^1 Lo^3 Pu^5 Pu^7 Pu^9 Tj^1 [*Jolly* G] स्वधेत्येवं तु तं [BBe^2 Be^3 Jo^2 °त्येव; Pu^5 Pu^7 Pu^9 Lo^1 (*Jolly* G) च]; *Hem* °स्त्विति च तं; TMd^3 GMd^5 GMy sOx^1 Ox^2 [*but cor*] Pu^8 Tr^1 Tr^2 MTr^4 MTr^6 ते ब्रूयु°; wKt^6 तं ब्रह्म ब्राह्मणा°; oOr ते ब्रूयाद्ब्राह्मणा°; *Me Rn Rc Go* appear to omit अस्तु — c) BBe^2 [*mc to*] स्वधाकारापरित्यागी; BKt^5 wKt^6 स्वधा च परमा ह्याशीः; GMd^5 स्वधाकाराभ्याशीः; TMd^3 GMy °कार; MTr^4 परं; TMd^3 पराभ्याशि; Ho Lo^5 चाशीः; GMy ह्याशां; TMd^4 ह्यासीत् — d) TMd^4 पितृकर्मणि

253. Omitted in Ho. Cited by *Apa* 504 — a) TMd^3 शेषामन्न° — b) wKt^1 तेषां शेषमन्नं; Tj^2 °मन्नं शेषं — c) NKt^4 TMd^3 तथा; wKt^6 ब्रह्मस्तथा; Lo^5 वायुस्तथा — d) wKt^1 Lo^3 Tj^1 [*Jolly* R] °ज्ञातश्च; Jm °ज्ञातैस्तु; Hy Jm Jo^1 Kt^2 MTr^3 *Mr Mandlik Jha KSS Dave* °ज्ञातस्ततो द्विजैः; *Lakṣ* °ज्ञातो द्विजोत्तमैः; NKt^4 ते द्विजैः

254.* Cited by *Lakṣ* 4.211 — a) BBe^2 oMd^2 TMd^4 पित्रे; oMd^2 तत्स्वदितमि°; La^1 स्वदितिमि°; wKt^1 मुदितमि°; wKt^6 सुदितमि°; GMd^1 स्वादत इत्येवं; TMd^4 स्वदित इत्येव; Hy Jm Jo^1 Kt^2 GMy MTr^3 *Mandlik Jha Dave* °मित्येव — b) sOx^1 sPu^6 गोष्ठीपु वाच्यं त्वश्रुतं; GMy वाच्यं शेषेषु विशृतं; wKt^1 वाक्यं; Bo Ho wKt^3 BKt^5 wKt^6 Lo^2 Lo^4 Lo^5 Ox^2 Ox^3 NPu^1 Pu^2 Pu^5 Pu^7 Pu^8 Pu^9 Pu^{10} Tr^2 *Go* गोष्ठे वाच्यं तु; Jo^2 wKt^1 NKt^4 La^1 Lo^1 Lo^3 GMd^1 TMd^3 TMd^4 GMd^5 oOr Tj^1 Tr^1 MTr^6 [*Jolly* R Nd] *Rc* गोष्ठेषु; MTr^4 गोष्ठिषु; Be^3 गोष्ठैस्तु; Pu^5 Pu^7 Pu^9 *Go* गोष्ठे इति शृतं [Pu^9 कृतं]; Hy oMd^2 Wa [*Jolly* M^4 G N R Ku Nd] सुश्रुतं; NKt^4 Ox^2 सुश्रितं; Lo^1 सुसृतं; GMd^1 साश्रितान् — c) Lo^1 °भ्युदयं — d) Lo^4 Lo^5 देवे; Lo^3 दैव; Tj^1 दैवारोचितमि°; BBe^2 Be^3 Bo Hy Jm Jo^1 wKt^1 Kt^2 Lo^1 oMd^2 Pu^8 Tj^2 MTr^3 [*Jolly* Ku] *Ku Mr Mandlik Jha KSS Dave* रुचितमि°; NKt^4 La^1 GMd^1 TMd^3 TMd^4 GMd^5 GMy Tr^1 MTr^4 MTr^6 रोचत इत्यपि; wKt^3 वाचितमित्यपि

255. Cited by *Apa* 474; *Lakṣ* 4.127; *Hem* 3/2.1172 — a) TMd^3 अपराह्णास्तथा; GMy अपराह्णे तथा; Ho अपराहस्तथा; *Hem* °ह्णस्तिला; GMd^1 दर्भो — b) BKt^5 wKt^6 GMd^5 वस्तु°; *Lakṣ Hem* °दनं तथा — c) GMd^1 TMd^4 Pu^5 Pu^7 Pu^9 Tr^2 सृष्टिमृष्टिद्वि°; Hy Lo^2 Ox^3 सृष्टिर्मृष्टिद्वि°; Lo^4 सृष्टिर्मुष्टिद्वि°;

दर्भाः पवित्रं पूर्वाह्णो हविष्याणि च सर्वशः ।
पवित्रं यच्च पूर्वोक्तं विज्ञेया हव्यसंपदः ॥२५६॥
मुन्यन्नानि पयः सोमो मांसं यच्चानुपस्कृतम् ।
अक्षारलवणं चैव प्रकृत्या हविरुच्यते ॥२५७॥
विसृज्य ब्राह्मणांस्तांस्तु नियतो वाग्यतः शुचिः ।
दक्षिणां दिशमाकाङ्क्षन् याचेतेमान्वरान्पितॄन् ॥२५८॥
दातारो नोऽभिवर्धन्तां वेदाः संततिरेव च ।
श्रद्धा च नो मा व्यगमद्बहु देयं च नोऽस्त्विति ॥२५९॥
एवं निर्वपणं कृत्वा पिण्डांस्तांस्तदनन्तरम् ।

wKt^{1} सृष्टिर्दृष्टिर्द्वि°; MTr^{4} सृष्टिर्वृष्टिर्द्वि°; Ho TMd^{3} TMd^{4} Pu^{5} Pu^{7} Pu^{9} °र्द्विजाग्र्याश्च; GMd^{1} °र्द्विजाग्रांश्च; GMd^{5} Tr^{1} °र्द्विजाग्र्यार्चा; MTr^{4} °जाश्चाग्र्यान्; oMd^{2} °जाश्चाग्रं — d) wKt^{1} श्राद्धकर्मार्थसंपदः; Tr^{2} श्राद्धं; Be^{3} °कर्मणि

256. Omitted in Be^{3}. Cited by *Hem* 3/2.1173 — a) TMd^{3} पवित्राणि च पूर्वाह्णे [*om* दर्भाः]; [*Jolly* Nd] दर्भ; Jm दर्भ्यः; TMd^{4} पवित्र; wKt^{1} NKt^{4} Lo^{3} GMd^{1} GMy sOx^{1} Pu^{5} Tj^{1} MTr^{4} MTr^{6} पूर्वाह्णे — b) TMd^{3} GMd^{5} Tr^{1} MTr^{6} [*Jolly* Nd Gr] शक्तितः — c) BKt^{5} wKt^{6} विज्ञेयं यच्च; Tr^{2} यश्च — d) NNg यज्ञसंपदः

257. Pādas c-d omitted in Lo^{2}. Cited by *Apa* 500, 551; *Hem* 3/1.541, 573 — a) wKt^{1} अस्विन्नानि; Lo^{5} यमः; Jm वयः; *Apa* 500 सोमं; *Apa* 551 सोमौ — a-b) GMd^{1} मत्स्यान्तानि पयश्चादि सोमं यच्चानुसंस्कृतं [reading unclear] — b) TMd^{4} मासं यस्यानु°; BCa wKt^{1} GMy Tr^{2} यश्चानु°; BKt^{5} wKt^{6} °पस्करं — c) GMd^{1} सक्षार°; GMy टक्षार°; BCa °लवणश्चैव

258.* Pādas c-d omitted in TMd^{4}. Cited by *Hem* 3/2.1483 — a) NKt^{4} BKt^{5} wKt^{6} La^{1} Ox^{3} *Dave Jha* विसर्ज्य; TMd^{4} विसृज्या; Tj^{1} विसृत्य — b) Pu^{10} [*Jolly* M$^{1-2-8-9}$] *Jha Dave* नियतो विधिपूर्वकम्; BCa Jo^{2} wKt^{3} BKt^{5} wKt^{6} La^{2} Lo^{2} Lo^{3} Lo^{4} Lo^{5} Ox^{2} Ox^{3} NPu^{1} Pu^{2} Pu^{4} Pu^{5} Pu^{7} Pu^{8} Pu^{9} Pu^{10} Tj^{1} Wa [*Jolly* M$^{1-2-3-4-5-8-9}$ G N] *Nā Jolly Jha Dave* प्रयतो; Bo त्रियतो — c) NKt^{4} La^{1} GMd^{5} Pu^{5} Pu^{7} Pu^{9} Tj^{1} दिशिमा°; Kt^{2} °काङ्क्ष्यन् — d) Jo^{2} Lo^{3} Tj^{1} °तेमान्पितॄन्वरान्; Ho °मान्वरान्शुचिः; TMd^{3} °मान्वरानपि

259. Omitted in TMd^{4}. Cited by *Hem* 3/2.1483 — a) Jo^{1} दातारं; Pu^{5} Pu^{7} Pu^{9} *om* नो; GMd^{1} वो; Pu^{5} Pu^{7} Pu^{9} MTr^{4} °पिवर्धन्तां; MTr^{6} विवर्धन्तां; TMd^{3} °वर्धतां — b) BBe^{2} Lo^{2} Lo^{4} Lo^{5} वेदः; GMy MTr^{4} वेद; Tj^{2} °रेवं; Jo^{2} Lo^{3} Tj^{1} °रेव नः — c) GMd^{1} च वो; NKt^{4} Lo^{2} sOx^{1} Ox^{3} sPu^{6} [*Jolly* M^{5} G] विगम°; GMd^{1} TMd^{3} GMd^{5} GMy Tr^{1} MTr^{4} व्यपगाद्बहु — d) oOr sOx^{1} sPu^{6} °धेयं; GMd^{1} वो; Jo^{2} Lo^{3} Tj^{1} [*Jolly* R] नोस्तु तत् [Jo^{2} *om* तत्]

Additional verse in Be^{3} Ho Jo^{2} BKt^{5} Lo^{3} oMd^{2} oOr Ox^{2} Pu^{8} Tj^{1} Tr^{2} [*Jolly* R] *Mandlik* [क, ख, ग, ज, झ, ञ, ण] *KSS* [cf. *ViDh* 73.30]:

अन्नं च नो बहु भवेदतिथींश्च लभेमहि ।
याचितारश्च नः सन्तु मा च याचिष्म कंचन ॥

c) Tj^{1} याचता° — d) Ox^{2} Tr^{2} मा स्म; Tj^{1} किंचन

Additional verse in *Mandlik* [ग] *KSS;* given after 249 in oOr:

श्राद्धभुक्पुनरश्नाति तदहर्यो द्विजाधमः ।
प्रयाति शूकरीं योनिं कृमिर्वा नात्र संशयः ॥

गां विप्रमजमग्निं वा प्राशयेदप्सु वा क्षिपेत् ॥२६०॥
पिण्डनिर्वपणं केचित् पुरस्तादेव कुर्वते ।
वयोभिः खादयन्त्यन्ये प्रक्षिपन्त्यनलेऽप्सु वा ॥२६१॥
पतिव्रता धर्मपत्नी पितृपूजनतत्परा ।
मध्यमं तु ततः पिण्डमद्यात्सम्यक्सुतार्थिनी ॥२६२॥
आयुष्मन्तं सुतं सूते यशोमेधासमन्वितम् ।
धनवन्तं प्रजावन्तं धार्मिकं सात्त्विकं तथा ॥२६३॥
प्रक्षाल्य हस्तावाचम्य ज्ञातिप्रायं प्रकल्पयेत् ।
ज्ञातिभ्यः सत्कृतं दत्त्वा बान्धवानपि पूजयेत् ॥२६४॥
उच्छेषणं तु तत्तिष्ठेद् यावद्विप्रा विसर्जिताः ।
ततो गृहबलिं कुर्यादिति धर्मो व्यवस्थितः ॥२६५॥
हविर्यच्चिररात्राय यच्चानन्त्याय कल्पते ।

c) oOr स याति शौवरं

260. Pādas c-d omitted in GMd^1. Cited by *Hem* 3/2.1504 — a) GMd^1 सर्वं; GMd^1 TMd^3 GMd^5 GMy MTr^6 निर्वापणं — b) Kt^2 पिण्डास्तास्तद° — c) Pu^5 Pu^7 Pu^9 गो; Kt^2 विप्रजलमग्निं; Lo^3 °जदाग्निं; TMd^3 °जमश्वं वा — d) NKt^4 La^1 प्रापयेद°; TMd^4 प्रायशेद°; TMd^3 भक्षयेद°; Tr^1 °येद्वाप्सु निक्षिपेत्; Tr^2 च

261.* Cited by *Hem* 3/2.1403; *Lakṣ* 4.223; *Dev* 4.361; *Mādh* 1.752; pādas c-d cited by *Hem* 3/2.1504 — a) BCa एवं निर्वपणं; TMd^3 GMd^5 GMy MTr^4 MTr^6 °निर्वापणं — b) Bo BCa wKt^1 BKt^5 wKt^6 Lo^1 Lo^3 oMd^2 TMd^3 GMd^5 Pu^2 Pu^4 Pu^8 Tj^1 *Rn Jolly Jha KSS Dave* परस्तादेव; TMd^3 GMy °स्तादुपकुर्वते; Pu^{10} कुर्वतो — c) Pu^5 Pu^7 Pu^9 स्वादय°; Ox^3 °यन्त्यन्यं; TMd^3 GMd^5 GMy Tr^1 MTr^4 MTr^6 *Lakṣ* °यन्त्येतान्; NKt^4 GMd^1 °यन्त्येनान् — d) GMd^1 खादयन्त्येनलेप्सु वा; Ho प्रक्षिपत्य°; GMy sOx^1 sPu^6 °पन्त्यनिले; *Hem* °पन्त्यनलेषु वा; Ox^3 च

262. Cited by *Apa* 550; *Hem* 3/2.1506; *Dev* 4.402; *Mādh* 1.759 — b) GMd^1 भर्तृपूजन°; BCa [*but cor*] पितृतर्पण° — d) *Hem* °द्यात्पत्नी सुता°; Wa °तार्थिनः; Tj^2 °तर्प्यनी

263.* Cited by *Apa* 550; *Hem* 3/2.1506; *Lakṣ* 4.223; *Dev* 4.403; *Mādh* 1.759 — a) TMd^4 सुतं पिण्डे; GMd^1 TMd^3 GMd^5 GMy Ox^2 Tr^1 MTr^4 MTr^6 [*Jolly* Nd] *Dev Mādh* सुतं विन्देद्; *Lakṣ* सुतं विद्याद् — b) Bo मेधाप्रज्ञासमन्वितं; GMd^1 °मेधान्वितं परं — d) Hy Jm Jo^1 wKt^1 Kt^2 GMd^5 Pu^{10} Tj^2 MTr^3 *Apa Jolly Mandlik Jha KSS Dave* सात्त्विकं धार्मिकं; *Apa* शुचिं for तथा

264. Omitted in Tj^2; pādas c-d omitted in Pu^9. Cited by *Apa* 512; *Lakṣ* 4.226; *Hem* 3/2.1515 — b) oOr प्रकल्पते; NNg निवेदयेत् — c) Pu^2 Tr^1 MTr^4 सत्कृतिं; Lo^4 NNg Ox^3 Tj^1 Wa संस्कृतं; wKt^6 संकृतं; GMd^5 सत्क्रियां; GMy सत्गतिं; *Apa* शक्तितो दत्त्वा; BBe^2 wKt^1 Pu^2 कृत्वा; Pu^{10} *Apa* [vl] दद्याद् — d) Bo ब्राह्मणानपि; GMy °वानभिपूजयेत्; Be^1 Bo BCa Ho Hy Jm Jo^1 Jo^2 Kt^2 wKt^3 La^2 Lo^1 Lo^3 GMd^1 oMd^2 oOr sOx^1 Ox^2 sPu^6 Tj^1 Tj^2 MTr^3 [*Jolly* Ku R] *Ku Mr Mandlik Jha KSS Dave* भोजयेत्

265. Cited by *Hem* 3/2.1062, 1513, 3/3.606; pādas c-d cited by *Apa* 512 — a) wKt^6 तच्छेषणं; wKt^1 तु उत्तिष्ठेद्; Lo^1 तत्तु तिष्ठेद्; GMd^1 तावत्तिष्ठेद्; TMd^4 ततस्तिष्ठेद् — b) oOr यावद्विप्रान्विसर्जयेत्; La^1 विसर्जिनां; Ho TMd^4 विवर्जिताः — c) Ho देवबलिं; Ox^3 °बलिः — d) BCa धर्मे; NKt^4 धर्मा; GMd^1 TMd^4 धर्म; Tr^2 °स्थितिः

पितृभ्यो विधिवद्दत्तं तत्प्रवक्ष्याम्यशेषतः ॥२६६॥
तिलैर्व्रीहियवैर्माषैरद्भिर्मूलफलेन वा ।
दत्तेन मासं प्रीयन्ते विधिवत्पितरो नृणाम् ॥२६७॥
द्वौ मासौ मत्स्यमांसेन त्रीन्मासान्हारिणेन तु ।
औरभ्रेणाथ चतुरः शाकुनेनेह पञ्च वै ॥२६८॥
षण्मासाञ्छागमांसेन पार्षतेनेह सप्त वै ।
अष्टावैणेयमांसेन रौरवेण नवैव तु ॥२६९॥
दश मासांस्तु तृप्यन्ति वराहमहिषामिषैः ।
शशकूर्मयोस्तु मांसेन मासानेकादशैव तु ॥२७०॥

266. Cited by *Apa* 500; *Hem* 3/1.540; *Dev* 4.252 — a) NKt^{4} TMd^{4} हविर्यश्चिर°; wKt^{6} हविस्तच्चिर°; GMd^{1} GMy *Lakṣ* यद्हविश्चिर°; GMd^{1} GMy MTr^{4} MTr^{6} *Lakṣ* °कालाय — b) BKt^{5} तच्चान°; GMd^{1} GMy यश्चान°; Ox^{3} यथान°; GMy Pu^{5} Pu^{7} Pu^{9} °नान्त्याय; Ho °नन्ताय — c) TMd^{3} पितृभ्यो यद्धविर्दत्तं; wKt^{6} बलिवद्दत्तं

267.* Cited by *Vij* 1.259; *Apa* 500, 552; *Hem* 3/1.541, 586; *Lakṣ* 4.41; *Dev* 4.252; *Mādh* 1.705 — a) GMd^{1} तिलव्रीहि° — b) Ho GMd^{1} NNg *Hem* 3/1.541 च — c) La^{1} sOx^{1} Pu^{5} sPu^{6} Pu^{7} मांसं; Tr^{1} दासं; Wa प्रीयन्ति; Ho प्रीयेते; Tj^{1} प्रियते; Pu^{2} प्रीयंतं; Hy Jm Jo^{1} Kt^{2} Tj^{2} MTr^{3} [*Jolly* Ku] *Vij* [but vl as in ed] *Mandlik Jolly Jha KSS Dave* [cf. YDh 1.257] तृप्यन्ति; oMd^{2} तृप्यन्ते — d) *Apa* पितरो विधिवन्नृणाम्; Lo^{1} विधिना पितरो; TMd^{4} विधिकृत्वेतरो; Tr^{1} °वत्पितरौ; GMd^{1} °वत्वृत्तयो

268.* Omitted in Pu^{9}; pādas c-d *ma* in BKt^{5}. Cited by *Hem* 3/1.586; *Lakṣ* 4.41; *Dev* 4.255; *Mādh* 1.705 — a) Lo^{3} oMd^{2} मात्स्य°; GMy °मांसे वा — b) wKt^{6} त्रिमासा°; Ho wKt^{3} wKt^{6} GMy Tr^{2} °सान्हरिणेन; TMd^{3} °सान्वारिणेन; GMy वा; GMd^{1} च — c) Ho औरभ्रेण चतुर्मासं; GMy औरत्रेण चतुरः; Ox^{3} उरभ्रे°; Bo NKt^{4} La^{1} Lo^{2} NPu^{1} अरभ्रे°; GMd^{1} औरगेणाथ; BCa चतुरश्च — d) GMd^{5} शाकुनेन तु पञ्चकान्; Be^{1} BBe^{2} Be^{3} Ho Hy Jm Jo^{1} wKt^{1} Kt^{2} wKt^{3} BKt^{5} wKt^{6} TMd^{3} TMd^{4} sOx^{1} Pu^{5} sPu^{6} Pu^{7} Tj^{2} Tr^{1} MTr^{3} MTr^{4} MTr^{6} [*Jolly* G Nd] *Mandlik Jha KSS Dave* शाकुनेनाथ; NKt^{4} Lo^{4} Lo^{5} oMd^{2} oOr Ox^{3} [*Jolly* M^{3-4-5}] शाकुनेनैव; Pu^{5} Pu^{7} MTr^{4} MTr^{6} [*Jolly* G] पञ्च च; Be^{3} wKt^{3} NKt^{4} BKt^{5} wKt^{6} La^{2} Lo^{4} Lo^{5} GMd^{1} oMd^{2} TMd^{3} oOr Ox^{3} Pu^{2} Tr^{1} [*Jolly* M^{3-4-5}] *Hem* पञ्च तु; GMy पञ्चसु; TMd^{4} पञ्चमाः

269. Omitted in TMd^{4} Pu^{9}; *ma* in BKt^{5}. Cited by *Hem* 3/1.586; *Dev* 4.255; *Mādh* 1.706 — a) *Dev* छागमांसेन षण्मासान्; GMd^{5} षाण्मा°; La^{1} दत्तेन छाग° — b) wKt^{1} wKt^{3} पार्षतेनह; Be^{1} पार्षतेनाह; Hy Jm Jo^{1} Kt^{2} Tj^{2} MTr^{3} *Mandlik Jha KSS Dave* पार्षतेन च; GMd^{1} NNg Pu^{10} [*Jolly* M^{1-2-8}] *Hem* पार्षतेनाथ; GMy पार्षतेनाय; *Lakṣ, Hem* सप्त तु — c) wKt^{6} Lo^{1} Ox^{3} °वैणस्य मांसेन; Pu^{5} Pu^{7} *Hem* °वैणेन मांसेन; Be^{1} BBe^{2} BCa Hy Jm Jo^{1} wKt^{1} Kt^{2} wKt^{3} NKt^{4} GMd^{1} oMd^{2} oOr sOx^{1} Ox^{3} sPu^{6} Tr^{2} MTr^{3} *Mandlik KSS* °वेणस्य मांसेन — d) Ox^{3} Tj^{2} चैव तु

270.* Omitted in TMd^{4}. Cited by *Hem* 3/1.586; *Dev* 4.255; *Mādh* 1.706 — a) Ho मासास्तु; GMd^{1} TMd^{3} मासं तु; Ox^{2} Tr^{2} मासांश्च; Be^{1} तृप्यन्ते; Wa तृप्यन्तु; sPu^{6} पुष्यन्ति [*but cor*]; TMd^{3} Tr^{1} MTr^{4} MTr^{6} तुष्यन्ति; NKt^{4} सृप्यन्ति — b) Ho TMd^{3} NNg Pu^{10} Tj^{1} Tr^{2} वाराह° — c) TMd^{3} Tr^{1} [*Jolly* Ku Nd] शशकच्छपमांसेन; Be^{1} शशि°; Hy शेष°; Be^{3} °कूर्मयोश्च; Be^{1} BBe^{2} BCa La^{1} NNg sOx^{1} Ox^{3} Pu^{5} sPu^{6} Pu^{7} Pu^{9} MTr^{4} MTr^{6} [*Jolly* M^{3-4-5} G] *Jolly* °कूर्मयोर्मांसेन; Ho GMd^{5} [*Jolly* Gr] °कूर्मस्य मांसेन; Lo^{3} Tj^{1} Tr^{2} [*Jolly* R] °कूर्मकमांसेन — c-d) oOr °कूर्मयोर्मांसयोर्मांसेनैकादशैव — d) Pu^{5} Pu^{7} Pu^{9} मासानि द्वादशैव तु; GMd^{1} मासेनैका°; Be^{1} मासेनेका°; NNg च

संवत्सरं तु गव्येन पयसा पायसेन वा ।
वार्ध्रीणसस्य मांसेन तृप्तिर्द्वादशवार्षिकी ॥२७१॥
कालशाकं महाशल्कः* खड्गलोहामिषं मधु ।
आनन्त्यायैव कल्पन्ते मुन्यन्नानि च सर्वशः ॥२७२॥
यत्किंचिन्मधुना मिश्रं प्रदद्यात्तु त्रयोदशीम् ।
तदप्यक्षयमेव स्याद् वर्षासु च मघासु च ॥२७३॥
अपि नः स कुले भूयाद् यो नो दद्यात् त्रयोदशीम् ।
पायसं मधुसर्पिर्भ्यां प्राक्छाये कुञ्जरस्य च ॥२७४॥

271. Cited by *Hem* 3/1.586; *Lakṣ* 4.41; *Mādh* 1.706;pādas a-b cited by *Viś* 1.255; *Apa* 551; *Dev* 4.255; pādas c-d by *Apa* 552; *Dev* 4.256 — b) Be^{3} BKt^{5} wKt^{6} La^{2} Pu^{5} Pu^{7} Pu^{9} Tj^{2} [*Jolly* G] तु; Bo Ho Hy Jm Jo^{1} wKt^{1} Kt^{2} oMd^{2} TMd^{3} GMd^{5} Pu^{2} Tr^{2} MTr^{3} [*Jolly* Ku] *Vij Mandlik Jha KSS Dave* च — c) GMd^{1} पायसैर्मांसमिश्रैः तृप्ति°; NNg Pu^{5} Pu^{7} *Apa* वाध्रीणसस्य; Jm Pu^{9} वर्ध्रीणसस्य; GMd^{5} GMy Tr^{1} वार्ध्राणसस्य; Pu^{10} वार्ध्राणस्य; TMd^{3} वर्ध्राणकस्य; Lo^{1} वार्ध्रीणंतस्य; Ox^{2} वार्ध्रीणस्य तु; TMd^{4} वादिनस्तस्य; *Jolly* comments: "the term vārdhīṇasasya is spelt in many various ways in the Mss." — d) GMy तृप्तिर्द्विदश°

Additional verse in Ho *Mandlik* [ल, ब] *KSS;* probably taken from *Me*'s com:

त्रिपिबं त्विन्द्रियक्षीणं श्वेतं वृद्धमजापतिम् ।
वार्ध्रीणसं तु तं प्राहुर्याज्ञिकाः पितृकर्मणि ॥

a) Ho त्रिःपिबं त्विन्द्रियं —b) *Mandlik KSS* अजापूर्वानुगामिनम् — c-d) *Mandlik KSS* तं वै वार्ध्रीणसं विद्यात् वृद्धं शुक्लमजापतिम्

272.* Cited by *Hem* 3/1.541, 586; *Dev* 4.257; *Mādh* 1.706 — a) Lo^{2} कील°; TMd^{3} GMy Pu^{8} कालशाक; wKt^{1} TMd^{3} *Dev* महाशल्क; BCa Ho Hy Jm Jo^{1} Kt^{2} La^{2} Lo^{4} oMd^{2} oOr Ox^{3} Pu^{2} Tj^{2} *Mandlik Jha KSS Dave* [*Jolly* M^{4-5-9} Me Ku R] महाशल्काः; BBe^{2} Be^{3} Bo wKt^{3} Lo^{1} Lo^{2} Lo^{3} Lo^{5} sOx^{1} sPu^{6} Tj^{1} महाशल्का; Kt^{2} महाशल्क्यः; BKt^{5} wKt^{6} GMd^{5} Ox^{2} NPu^{1} Pu^{5} Pu^{7} Pu^{8} Pu^{9} Tr^{1} Tr^{2} Wa [*Jolly* G Nd] *Mādh* महाशल्कं; Be^{1} महाशल्कां; La^{1} महाशल्को; GMd^{1} TMd^{4} GMy MTr^{4} MTr^{6} महाशाकं; TMd^{3} महाशाक; NKt^{4} महाशाक्ता — b) Ho GMd^{5} खड्गं; Lo^{4} Ox^{3} Tr^{1} खड्ग°; NNg Pu^{10} पड्ग°; TMd^{3} °लोपामिषं; Lo^{1} °लोहामितं — c) TMd^{4} अनन्त्यायै विकल्पन्ते; sOx^{1} sPu^{6} आनन्त्यायै च कल्पन्ते; Ox^{2} आनन्त्याय प्रकल्पन्ते; Lo^{4} Lo^{5} Tr^{1} आनन्त्यायोपकल्पन्ते; Bo Ho Jm Lo^{1} Tj^{1} Tr^{2} अनन्त्या°; Jm Jo^{2} GMd^{1} oMd^{2} *Mandlik Jha KSS Dave* कल्प्यन्ते — d) Jo^{2} Lo^{3} Tj^{1} °न्नानि विशेषतः; Lo^{1} सर्वतः

273.* Pādas c-d omitted in Wa. Cited by *Apa* 555; *Hem* 3/1.201 — a) Bo Jo^{2} NKt^{4} BKt^{5} wKt^{6} La^{1} La^{2} Lo^{2} Lo^{3} Lo^{4} Lo^{5} TMd^{4} NNg sOx^{1} Ox^{2} Ox^{3} NPu^{1} Pu^{2} sPu^{6} Pu^{8} Pu^{10} Tj^{1} Tr^{2} Wa [*Jolly* M R] *Jolly* ° चिन्मधुसंमिश्रं; Pu^{5} Pu^{7} Pu^{9} [*Jolly* G Ku] *Apa Go Ku* °चिन्मधुसंयुक्तं — b) Ho Lo^{1} GMy प्रदद्याच्च; GMd^{1} Tj^{1} Tr^{1} °दशी; Wa °दशिं — c) Kt^{2} तदपेक्ष्यमेव; Lo^{4} Lo^{5} तदस्याक्षयमेव; TMd^{4} °क्षय्यतामेव — d) TMd^{4} *om first* च; GMd^{5} मखासु

Additional verse in GMd^{5}:

एष्टव्या बहवः पुत्रा यद्येकोऽपि गयां व्रजेत् ।
गौरीं वा वरयेत्कन्यां नीलं वा प्रज्ञमुत्सृजेत् ॥

274.* Omitted in Pu^{5} Pu^{7} Pu^{9}; *ma* in Be^{3} Pu^{8}; pādas a-b omitted in Wa. Cited by *Hem* 3/1.66, 245; *Lakṣ* 4.19; *Dev* 4.24 — a) Tj^{1} स कुसले; Lo^{2} GMd^{1} *Hem* 3/1.66 स्वकुले; BBe^{2} Ho Hy Jm Jo^{1} wKt^{1} Kt^{2} wKt^{3} Lo^{1} TMd^{4} GMd^{5} oOr sOx^{1} sPu^{6} Tj^{2} MTr^{3} MTr^{4} [*Jolly* R] *Hem* 3/1.245 *Rn Mandlik KSS* जायाद्; TMd^{3} Tr^{1} [*Jolly* Nd] जातो — b) BBe^{2} TMd^{3} यो न — c) sOx^{1} पायसः; *Hem*

यद्यद्ददाति विधिवत् सम्यक् श्रद्धासमन्वितः ।
तत्तत्पितॄणां भवति परत्रानन्त्यमक्षयम् ॥२७५॥

3/1.66 मधुसंयुक्तं; BBe^{2} Hy wKt^{6} Lo^{2} TMd^{3} GMy Pu^{10} Tr^{1} °सर्पिभ्यां — d) *Hem* 3/1.66 वर्षासु च मघासु च [cf. 3.273d]; TMd^{3} *Me* [pāṭha] प्राक्छायं; NKt^{4} प्राक्कायें; TMd^{4} प्रच्छाये; MTr^{6} प्राच्छाये; Lo^{2} प्रछाये; Tr^{1} पृछाय; GMd^{1} पच्छाये; Tr^{2} प्राक्षये; wKt^{1} प्राग्दाये; Bo NKt^{4} Lo^{1} Lo^{2} Lo^{4} Lo^{5} GMd^{1} TMd^{3} TMd^{4} GMd^{5} GMy oOr Ox^{2} Ox^{3} Pu^{8} Tr^{1} MTr^{4} तु

Additional half-verse in TMd^{4} [cf. added verse 6 after 3.275]:

पक्ष्यादिषु विनिर्दिष्टा विपुलान्मनसः क्रिया ॥

275.* Cited by *Hem* 3/1.153, 3/2.1031 — a) wKt^{3} *om first* यद् — b) Lo^{2} oOr Tj^{1} श्राद्ध°; Be^{3} Ox^{3} श्राद्धा°; Lo^{2} TMd^{3} GMd^{5} Pu^{5} Pu^{7} Tr^{1} °समन्वितं — c) *Hem* 3/1.153 तत्पितॄणां च भवति; Tr^{2} *om one* तत् — d) Be^{3} Ho Hy Jm Jo^{1} Kt^{2} BKt^{5} wKt^{6} Lo^{3} Lo^{4} Lo^{5} GMd^{1} oMd^{2} TMd^{4} sOx^{1} Ox^{2} sPu^{6} Pu^{10} Tj^{1} Tj^{2} MTr^{3} MTr^{4} Wa*Hem Mandlik Jolly Jha KSS Dave* °त्रानन्तम°; GMd^{1} oMd^{2} TMd^{3} TMd^{4} GMy Pu^{5} Pu^{7} Pu^{9} Tr^{1} MTr^{4} MTr^{6} Wa °न्त्यमव्ययं

Additional verses in GMd^{1} TMd^{4} GMy NPu^{1} Tr^{1} MTr^{4} MTr^{6}; cited by *Hem* 3/1.263–4, 3/3.509–10; *Mādh* 1.661; verse 5 by *Hem* 3/1.214; given after 276 in oOr; after 278 in TMd^{3} GMd^{5}; after 3.277 in [*Jolly* Nd Gr]; and after 3.280 in Be^{3} Ho Ox^{2} Tr^{2} *Mandlik* [क, ख, ण, ढ] *Dave KSS; Rc* comments on verse 6:

कुर्वन्प्रतिपदि श्राद्धं सुरूपान्लभते सुतान् ।
कन्यकास्तु द्वितीयायां तृतीयायां तु वन्दिनः ॥१॥
पशून्क्षुद्रांश्चतुर्थ्यां तु पञ्चम्यां शोभनान्सुतान् ।
षष्ट्यां द्यूतं कृषिं चापि सप्तम्यां लभते नरः ॥२॥
अष्टम्यामपि वाणिज्यं लभते श्राद्धदः सदा ।
स्यान्नवम्यामेकखुरं दशम्यां द्विखुरं बहु ॥३॥
एकादश्यां तथा रूप्यं ब्रह्मवर्चस्विनः सुतान् ।
द्वादश्यां जातरूपं च रजतं रूप्यमेव च ॥४॥
ज्ञातिश्रैष्ठ्यं त्रयोदश्यां चतुर्दश्यां तु कुप्रजाः ।
प्रीयन्ते पितरश्चास्य ये शस्त्रेण रणे हताः ॥५॥
पक्षाद्यादिषु निर्दिष्टान्विपुलान्मनसः प्रियान् ।
श्राद्धदः पञ्चदश्यां तु सर्वान्कामान्समश्नुते ॥६॥

1. a) TMd^{4} कुर्यात्प्र° — b) GMd^{1} NPu^{1} *Hem* सरूपा°; Tr^{1} स्वरूपा°; Ho Ox^{2} Tr^{2} सुरूपां लभते; [*Jolly* Nd] सुरूपांल्लभते; [*Jolly* Gr] °पान्विन्दते; Ho TMd^{4} Ox^{2} Tr^{2} Tr^{1} प्रजां — c) GMy oOr Ox^{2} Tr^{1} कन्यकां तु; TMd^{4} कन्याकां तु; MTr^{6} *Hem Mādh* कन्यकान्तु; TMd^{3} कन्यकांस्तु; GMd^{1} कन्यकास्तु; Ho कन्यायास्तु; GMd^{5} Tr^{2} *Hem* 3/1.263–4 कन्यकाश्च — d) TMd^{3} °यायामवाननं; NPu^{1} *Hem* 3/3.509–10 बन्दिनः; GMy वासनः; TMd^{4} दाविनं

2. a) Ox^{2} पशुक्षु°; NPu^{1} क्षुद्रान्पशून् चतु°; GMd^{5} oOr *Jolly* च — c) MTr^{4} द्यूतिं; GMy दूतं; GMd^{5} दूतान्; TMd^{4} भूतं; GMd^{1} ध्वगं; Be^{3} द्यूतजयन्तित्यं; *Hem* 3/3.509 वापि; *Mādh Jolly* चैव — d) NPu^{1} सप्तम्यामत्रभाग्भवेत्; Be^{3} Ho Ox^{2} Tr^{2} *Mandlik KSS Dave* लभते कृषिं

3. b) TMd^{4} Tr^{1} [*Jolly* Nd] °श्राद्धदो नरः — c) NPu^{1} नवम्यामेकशफं तु; Ho नवम्यामेकशःशफान्; Ox^{2} नवम्यां चैवैकशफान्; *Hem* 3/1.263–4 नवम्यामेवैकखुरं; Be^{3} °मेकशफं — d) TMd^{4} द्विशफं; Ox^{2} Tr^{2} द्विखुरान्बहून्; Ho NPu^{1} द्विशफान्बहून्; oOr विसूखरः बहु; *Hem* 3/1.263–4 द्विखुरं तथा; [*Jolly*] चाखुरं तथा

4. a) NPu^{1} तिथौ रूपं; TMd^{3} GMy द्विधारूप्यं; *Hem* 3/3.510 तथारोग्यं; TMd^{4} तु पारुष्यं; *Hem* 3/1.263–4 रौप्यं; MTr^{4} रूप्यान् — a-b) Be^{3} एकादश्यां सुवर्णं तु रजतं लभते नरः — b) GMd^{1} सुतं — c) Ho GMd^{5} जायते रूपं रज°; GMd^{5} NPu^{1} तु — d) Tr^{1} रौप्यमेव; Ox^{2} NPu^{1}

कृष्णपक्षे दशम्यादौ वर्जयित्वा चतुर्दशीम् ।
श्राद्धे प्रशस्तास्तिथयो यथैता न तथेतराः ॥२७६॥
यथा चैवापरः पक्षः पूर्वपक्षाद्विशिष्यते ।
तथा श्राद्धस्य पूर्वाह्णादपराह्णो विशिष्यते ॥२७७॥
युक्षु कुर्वन्दिनर्क्षेषु सर्वान्कामान्समश्नुते ।
अयुक्षु तु पितॄनर्चन् प्रजां प्राप्नोति पुष्कलाम् ॥२७८॥
प्राचीनावीतिना सम्यगपसव्यमतन्द्रिणा ।
पित्र्यमा निधनात्कार्यं विधिवद्दर्भपाणिना ॥२७९॥

Tr[2] कुप्यमेव; Ho कूप्यमेव; TMd[4] कार्यमेव

5. a) TMd[3] oOr NPu[1] °श्रेष्ठ्यं; GMd[5] Tr[2] °श्रेष्ठं — b) [*Jolly*] °श्यां पुत्रप्रजाः; TMd[3] GMy MTr[4] MTr[6] कुप्रजां; Ho *Hem Mādh* सुप्रजाः; NPu[1] वै प्रजाः; TMd[4] न प्रजाः — c) NPu[1] पितरो ह्यस्य; Be[3] oOr MTr[4] MTr[6] *Hem* 3/1.214, 3/3.492 पितरस्तस्य; GMd[1] *Hem* 3/3.510 पितरश्चात्र— d) Tr[2] *Hem* 3/1.214, 263–4 ये च शस्त्रहता रणे; Tr[1] शस्त्रै रणे; Ox[2] हता रणे

6. Omitted in TMd[4]; pādas a-b omitted in *Jolly Mādh* — a) GMy पक्षन्यासिषु; TMd[3] Ox[2] MTr[4] पक्षत्यादिषु; GMd[5] पक्षन्यादिषु; oOr पक्षत्यादिषु विनिर्दि°; *Hem* 3/1.214 पक्षत्यादिविनिर्दि°; Ho पक्षवत्त्या विनिर्दि° *Hem* 3/3.510 इत्यादींश्च विनिर्दि°; NPu[1] निर्दिष्टा विपु° — a-b) Be[3] शस्त्राग्निविषनष्टानां प्रसस्राव चतुर्दशीं — b) GMd[1] °न्विफलान्मनसः; NPu[1] °न्विफलं मनसः प्रियाः; Ho पुन्यैनिमात्मनः प्रियान् — c) MTr[4] MTr[6] *Hem* 3/1.214 च — d) GMd[5] NPu[1] Tr[1] [*Jolly*] °मानवाप्नुयात्

276. Cited by *Apa* 422; *Dev* 4.20; *Mādh* 1.666 — a) TMd[4] कृष्णप्रतिपदि स्याद्या; TMd[3] GMd[5] GMy Tr[1] दशम्याद्या; GMd[1] MTr[4] दशम्यां वा — b) Hy Tj[2] चतुर्दशी — c) GMd[1] शास्त्रे; Bo प्रशस्तस्तिथयो; Lo[1] Lo[2] TMd[3] GMd[5] Ox[2] Tr[1] प्रशस्ता तिथयो; sOx[1] Ox[3] sPu[6] प्रसिद्धास्तिथयो — d) GMd[1] तथैतराः; TMd[3] तथोत्तराः; TMd[4] तदितराः; oOr तथेतरान्

Additional verse in MTr[6]:

यथैव चापरः पक्षः पूर्वपक्षाद्विशिष्यते ।
तथा श्राद्धस्य पूर्वाह्णादपराह्णो विशिष्यते ॥

277.* Verses 277 and 288 are transposed in Bo Hy Jm Jo[1] wKt[1] Kt[2] wKt[3] BKt[5] wKt[6] La[2] Lo[2] Lo[4] Lo[5] oMd[2] Ox[3] Pu[5] Pu[7] Pu[9] Pu[10] Tj[2] Tr[2] MTr[3] and in all editions. Cited by *Apa* 465; *Hem* 3/3.568; *Dev* 4.81 — a) TMd[3] GMd[5] यथैव चापरः; Hy चैव परः; NNg चैव कृष्णः; TMd[4] वैश्यापरः; Pu[5] Pu[7] Pu[9] °पर; Lo[1] °परो — b) TMd[4] पूर्वात्पक्षा° — c) GMy अथ श्राद्धस्य; *Hem* एवं श्राद्धस्य; Lo[1] तस्माच्छ्राद्धस्य; Wa तथा पितॄणां पूर्वा°

278. Omitted in Lo[5]. Cited by *Lakṣ* 4.27; *Hem* 3/1.266, 3/3.512 — a) Lo[4] *ma* युक्षु; Tr[2] युक्ष; TMd[3] यिक्षु; TMd[4] यत्सु; GMy युयुक्षु; Pu[8] युतु; Ox[3] यञ्जौ; Lo[1] दिक्षु; wKt[1] अक्षु दर्वन्दि°; Pu[2] एवं कुर्वन्दि°; wKt[6] यथा कुर्वन्दि°; La[1] °न्दिनेर्केषु; MTr[6] °न्दिनेर्के तु; Pu[5] Pu[7] Pu[9] °न्दिर्षेषु — c) Lo[1] अयुःक्षु पितॄनभ्यर्च्य; Tr[2] आयुक्षं; Pu[5] Pu[7] अयुक्षुस्तु; NKt[4] अयुक्षुन्तत्पि°; Tr[1] अयुक्षुसु पि°; *Hem* च; Bo Lo[2] GMd[5] Pu[8] Tr[1] पितॄनर्च्य; Hy Jm Jo[1] Kt[2] Tj[2] MTr[3] *Mandlik Jha KSS Dave* पितॄन्सर्वान्; Pu[10] *om* अर्चन् — d) BCa Jo[2] Lo[3] Tj[1] Wa प्रजाः; GMd[5] sOx[1] sPu[6] प्रजामाप्नोति; Lo[3] Tj[1] Wa पुष्कलाः; Ox[3] पुष्कलं; Lo[4] पुष्फलां

279. Omitted in Ho; pādas c-d omitted in TMd[3]. Cited by *Hem* 3/2.1107; *Dev* 4.269; *Mādh* 1.725 — a) *Dev* सर्वमपसव्य° — b) GMy °व्यममन्त्रिणं — c) GMd[1] प्रीत्या समाधिना कुर्याद्; BBe[2] पित्रमा; TMd[4] प्रेत्यना; Tr[1] °नात्कुर्याद्

रात्रौ श्राद्धं न कुर्वीत राक्षसी कीर्तिता हि सा ।
संध्ययोरुभयोश्चैव सूर्ये चैवाचिरोदिते ॥२८०॥
अनेन विधिना श्राद्धं त्रिरब्दस्येह निर्वपेत् ।
हेमन्तग्रीष्मवर्षासु पाञ्चयज्ञिकमन्वहम् ॥२८१॥
न पैतृयज्ञिको होमो लौकिकेऽग्नौ विधीयते ।
न दर्शेन विना श्राद्धमाहिताग्नेर्द्विजन्मनः ॥२८२।
यदेव तर्पयत्यद्भिः पितॄन् स्नात्वा द्विजोत्तमः ।
तेनैव सर्वमाप्नोति पितृयज्ञक्रियाफलम् ॥२८३॥
वसून्वदन्ति तु पितॄन् रुद्रांश्चैव पितामहान् ।
प्रपितामहांस्तथादित्याञ्छ्रुतिरेषा पुरातनी ॥२८४॥

280. Cited by *Hem* 3/1.329 — b) Be^{1} रक्षसी; GMd^{1} राजसी; Ho सा परिकीर्तिता — c) *Hem* °भयोर्वापि; Kt^{2} °भयश्चैव — c-d) TMd^{3} GMy सन्ध्ययोश्चैव सूर्येस्ते तस्मिन्वापि विरोदिते — d) *Hem* सूर्ये चैव तिरोहिते; Jo^{1} सूर्या; Tr^{2} सूर्यश्चैवा°; Hy चैवान्विरोदिते; Ox^{3} चैवाविरोदिते; Lo^{2} चैवाधिचोदिते; oOr चैवचिरोहिते; GMd^{1} °चिरोचते

Additional verses in Ho Ox^{2} Tr^{2} *Mandlik* [क, ख, ण, ढ] *Dave KSS; Rc* comments on verse 6 [these are the same as the addition after 3.275].

Additional verses in TMd^{3} GMy; first verse in GMd^{5}:

संध्यारात्र्योर्न कर्तव्यं श्राद्धं खलु विचक्षणः ।
तयोरपि च कर्तव्यं यदि स्याद्राहुदर्शनम् ॥१॥
राहुदर्शनदत्तं हि श्राद्धमाचन्द्रतारकम् ।
गुणवत्सर्वमात्मीयं पितॄणामुपतिष्ठते ॥२॥

1. a) GMy सन्ध्यायामे न; GMd^{5} सन्ध्यारात्र्यान्न — b) GMd^{5} श्राद्धकाले विचक्षणैः
2. d) GMy °पतिष्ठति

281. Cited by *Viś* 1.266; *Apa* 420 — b) wKt^{3} °ब्दस्यैव; TMd^{3} GMy MTr^{4} *Apa* °ब्दस्येव — d) GMd^{5} GMy *Apa Rc* पञ्च°; GMd^{5} GMy °यज्ञकम°; Be^{3} TMd^{4} Ox^{3} Pu^{10} [*Jolly* M] °याज्ञिकम°; Be^{1} [*but mc*] BKt^{5} wKt^{6} Ox^{2} Pu^{5} Pu^{9} Tj^{1} Wa [*Jolly* R] *Apa* [vl] °यज्ञियम°; Lo^{3} Tr^{2} *Rc* °यज्ञीयम°

282.* Cited by *Viś* 1.266; *Hem* 3/2.1679 — a) wKt^{1} पैत्र°; Be^{3} पैत्रि°; Ho BKt^{5} wKt^{6} Pu^{5} Pu^{7} Pu^{9} पैत्र्य°; TMd^{3} GMy °यज्ञको; Lo^{4} Lo^{5} TMd^{4} Pu^{5} Pu^{7} Pu^{9} Pu^{10} °याज्ञिको; GMd^{1} °यज्ञेको; Be^{1} [*but mc*] BBe^{2} Be^{3} Bo BCa Ho Hy Jm Jo^{1} Jo^{2} wKt^{1} Kt^{2} wKt^{3} NKt^{4} BKt^{5} wKt^{6} La^{1} Lo^{1} Lo^{3} oMd^{2} Ox^{2} Pu^{8} Tj^{2} MTr^{3} Wa [*Jolly* R] *Rc Mr Hem Mandlik Jha KSS Dave* °यज्ञियो; Tr^{2} °यज्ञयो; Tj^{1} °यज्ञिया — b) NKt^{4} oOr Ox^{3} लोकिके; BBe^{2} TMd^{3} लौकिको; Be^{3} GMd^{5} Tr^{2} लौकिकाग्नौ; Jm लौकिकीग्नौ; TMd^{4} लौकिकोग्नि — d) wKt^{1} sOx^{1} °हिताग्निर्द्विज°; GMd^{5} °हिताग्नौ द्विज°

283. Cited by *Viś* 1.266; *Lakṣ* 3.134; *Hem* 3/2.946 — a) Ho La^{1} यदैव; wKt^{1} NNg यदेवं; *Lakṣ* य एवं; Be^{1} यदेतत्तर्प°; TMd^{4} यदेवमर्पय°; Be^{3} GMd^{5} sOx^{1} Pu^{5} sPu^{6} Pu^{7} Pu^{9} तर्पयेदद्भिः — b) Lo^{2} द्विजोत्तम; BKt^{5} wKt^{6} द्विजन्मनः; GMd^{5} *Viś* [*Jolly* G] समाहितः — c) Ox^{3} तेन सर्वमवाप्नोति; wKt^{1} तेनैव समवाप्नोति; Tj^{2} तेनैष; Hy Jm Jo^{1} Kt^{2} Tj^{2} MTr^{3} *Mandlik Jha KSS Dave* कृत्स्नमाप्नोति

284.* Cited by *Apa* 560–1; *Hem* 3/1.64 — a) TMd^{4} वसून्व्रजन्ति पितरो; sOx^{1} sPu^{6} °न्वदेति; wKt^{1} °दन्त्यहि; Tr^{2} *om* तु; Ho Pu^{10} *Apa* हि; wKt^{6} NNg च; *Hem* वै; Jo^{2} तत्पितॄन् — b) Bo TMd^{4} रुद्राश्चैव; NKt^{4} NNg Pu^{10} रुद्रांस्त्वेव; wKt^{1} रुद्रानथ; GMd^{5} Tr^{1} MTr^{6} रुद्रानेव; TMd^{4} °महाः — c) Hy °महास्तथा°; TMd^{3} °महान्यथा°; Jo^{2} Pu^{5} Pu^{7} Pu^{9} [*Jolly* M$^{3-9}$ G] °महांश्चादि°; wKt^{3} *Hem* °महांस्त्वादि°;

विघसाशी भवेन्नित्यं नित्यं चामृतभोजनः ।
विघसं भुक्तशेषं तु यज्ञशेषं तथामृतम् ॥२८५॥
एतद्वोऽभिहितं सर्वं विधानं पाञ्चयज्ञिकम् ।
द्विजातिमुख्यवृत्तीनां विधानं श्रूयतामिति ॥२८६॥

॥ इति मानवे धर्मशास्त्रे भृगुप्रोक्तायां संहितायां तृतीयोऽध्यायः ॥

GMy °महान्स्वयादि°; sOx^{1} sPu^{6} °महानादित्या° — d) Ho °त्यानित्येषा वैदिकी श्रुतिः; wKt^{3} °तिरेवो; Pu^{8} सुरातनी; Be^{1} Be^{3} Bo Hy Jm Jo^{1} Kt^{2} NKt^{4} La^{1} La^{2} Lo^{1} TMd^{3} TMd^{4} GMd^{5} Ox^{2} Tj^{2} Tr^{1} Tr^{2} MTr^{3} MTr^{4} MTr^{6} *Hem Rc Mandlik Jha KSS Dave* [*Jolly* Nd] सनातनी

285. Cited by *Lakṣ* 3.214 — a) Be^{1} Lo^{4} विघासाशी; Tr^{2} विघ्रसेसी; Pu^{5} Pu^{7} Pu^{9} विघसासी; BCa विघषासी; GMy विघसव्याशी; TMd^{3} विशेघं ह भवे°; GMd^{1} *om one* नित्यं — b) Hy Jm Jo^{1} Kt^{2} NKt^{4} Lo^{2} Tj^{2} MTr^{3} *Mandlik Jha KSS Dave* वामृत°; oOr त्वामृत°; MTr^{6} चानृत°; TMd^{3} TMd^{4} GMy sOx^{1} NPu^{1} sPu^{6} °भोजनं — c) Hy Jm Jo^{1} Kt^{2} oMd^{2} Tj^{2} MTr^{3} *Ku Lakṣ Mandlik Jha KSS Dave* विघसो; NKt^{4} विघस; Tr^{2} विघ्रसं; BCa विघ्रषं; NPu^{1} विप्रसां; GMd^{1} भुज्यशेषं; Wa भुक्तंशेषं; Tr^{1} भुक्तशिष्टं; Ho NKt^{4} Lo^{1} Lo^{2} GMy oOr Ox^{2} Pu^{8} Tj^{2} MTr^{4} MTr^{6} [*Jolly* Me N] *Lakṣ* भृत्यशेषं; Be^{1} शेषभुक्तं; oMd^{2} °शेषस्तु; TMd^{4} °शेषश्च; BCa °शेषं च; Bo La^{1} Lo^{1} Lo^{2} Ox^{2} Pu^{5} Pu^{7} Pu^{8} MTr^{4} MTr^{6} [*Jolly* M G] °शेषं स्याद् — d) Be^{3} oMd^{2} °शेषस्तथा°; TMd^{3} GMy °शेषस्त्वथामृतं; Bo Ho wKt^{1} NKt^{4} BKt^{5} wKt^{6} La^{2} Lo^{2} Lo^{4} Lo^{5} NNg sOx^{1} Ox^{3} Pu^{5} sPu^{6} Pu^{7} Pu^{8} Pu^{9} Pu^{10} Wa *Jolly* [*Jolly* M G] °शेषमथामृतं; Tr^{2} °शेषं यथामृतं

286. Cited by *Lakṣ* 2.167 — a) NKt^{4} *Lakṣ* एतद्वो विहितं; *Lakṣ* कृत्स्नं — b) TMd^{3} Ox^{2} Pu^{10} पञ्च°; Lo^{4} GMd^{1} TMd^{4} Ox^{2} Pu^{9} Pu^{10} [*Jolly* MG] °याज्ञिकं; GMy °यज्ञकं; Lo^{3} Tr^{2} Wa °यज्ञियं; NKt^{4} °याज्ञियं — c) GMy °मुख्यावृत्तीनां; Tr^{2} °मुख्यजातीनां; Lo^{2} °वृत्तानां — d) GMd^{1} श्रूयतामिति सर्वशः; *Lakṣ* °तामिह

Colophon: Jo^{2} Lo^{3} इति मानवीये; Be^{1} Lo^{1} Lo^{2} TMd^{3} NNg sOx^{1} Ox^{2} sPu^{6} इति श्रीमानवे; Tj^{1} इति श्रीमानवीये; Jo^{2} wKt^{3} भृगुप्रोक्ते; BKt^{5} wKt^{6} Lo^{1} TMd^{3} GMy sOx^{1} Ox^{2} Pu^{5} sPu^{6} *om* भृगुप्रोक्तायां संहितायां; Jo^{2} oOr wKt^{3} *om* संहितायां; Lo^{2} °प्रोक्तसंहितायां; Ox^{2} sOx^{1} sPu^{6} श्राद्धप्रकरणं नाम तृतीयो; Lo^{1} पञ्चयज्ञश्राद्धविधाने तृतीयो; Pu^{5} श्राद्धेविधिर्नाम तृतीयो; Be^{3} NNg °ध्यायः समाप्तः

[चतुर्थोऽध्यायः]

चतुर्थमायुषो भागमुषित्वाद्यं गुरौ द्विजः ।
द्वितीयमायुषो भागं कृतदारो गृहे वसेत् ॥१॥
अद्रोहेणैव भूतानामल्पद्रोहेण वा पुनः ।
या वृत्तिस्तां समास्थाय विप्रो जीवेदनापदि ॥२॥
यात्रामात्रप्रसिद्ध्यर्थं स्वैः कर्मभिरगर्हितैः ।
अक्लेशेन शरीरस्य कुर्वीत धनसंचयम् ॥३॥
ऋतामृताभ्यां जीवेत्तु मृतेन प्रमृतेन वा ।
सत्यानृताभ्यामपि वा न श्ववृत्त्या कथंचन ॥४॥
ऋतमुञ्छशिलं ज्ञेयममृतं स्यादयाचितम् ।
मृतं तु याचितं भैक्षं प्रमृतं कर्षणं स्मृतम् ॥५॥
सत्यानृतं तु वाणिज्यं तेन चैवापि जीव्यते ।

1. Cited by *Lakṣ* 2.435 — b) Tr^{2} °मुषिताद्यं; Pu^{2} Pu^{4} °मुषित्वा तु; Bo NKt^{4} Lo^{2} GMy गुरो; TMd^{4} गुरु; TMd^{3} Tj^{1} गुरोर्द्विजः; Pu^{7} *cor to* गुरोर्गृहे; BBe^{2} Be^{3} BKt^{5} Lo^{3} Lo^{4} NNg oOr Ox^{2} Ox^{3} Tj^{2} MTr^{4} MTr^{6} द्विजाः — d) Pu^{5} Pu^{7} Pu^{9} कृतदासो; Bo कृतभार्यो; *Lakṣ* कृतेद्वाहो [कृतोद्वाहो?]; Tr^{2} °दारे; Lo^{3} °दारा; NPu^{1} वसेद्गृहे; Pu^{2} वसन्; Lo^{3} TMd^{3} वसत्; wKt^{1} विशेत्

2. Pages containing verses 2–27 missing in oOr. Cited by *Vij* 1.127 — a) Lo^{4} अद्रोहेण च — c) Lo^{1} वृत्तिस्तामनास्थाय; oMd^{2} समाश्रित्य

3. Pādas b-d *ma* in Lo^{4}. Cited by *Dev* 2.448; *Mādh* 1.308 — a) Pu^{3} प्राणापात्र°; Ox^{2} Tr^{2} प्राणयात्रा°; Pu^{4} यात्राप्रसि°; Lo^{1} TMd^{4} GMy °मात्राप्रसि°; Bo °सिद्ध्यर्थां — b) MTr^{4} स्वैः स्वैः कर्मभिराहितैः; Pu^{5} Pu^{7} Pu^{9} [*Jolly* G] कर्मभिः स्वैरगर्हितैः; Lo^{4} Ox^{2} स्वकर्म°; NKt^{4} ते कर्म°; Pu^{2} Pu^{4} °भिरबर्हितैः; TMd^{3} °भिर्विगर्हितैः; wKt^{3} °गर्हितौ; BKt^{5} wKt^{6} °गर्हितः — c) Ho lacuna at अक्लेशेन; Tj^{1} शरीरेण — d) Tr^{2} कुर्वत; NPu^{1} °संचितं

4.* Cited by *Lakṣ* 2.170; *Dev* 2.451; *Mādh* 1.309 — a) Pu^{2} Pu^{4} ज्ञातामृता°; TMd^{4} जरामृता°; wKt^{1} शतामृता°; NKt^{4} सतानृताद्य जी°; BBe^{2} Be^{3} Ho Lo^{1} Lo^{3} GMd^{1} oMd^{2} TMd^{4} GMd^{5} NNg Ox^{2} NPu^{1} Pu^{2} Pu^{4} Pu^{5} Pu^{7} Pu^{9} Tj^{1} Tr^{2} [*Jolly* G R] जीवेत; sOx^{1} sPu^{6} जीवेच्च — b) Pu^{9} *om* प्रमृतेन; Bo प्रभृतेन; sOx^{1} sPu^{6} Tj^{1} च; *Lakṣ* तु — c) Ox^{3} Tr^{2} सत्यामृता°; NKt^{4} °नृतामपि; Ho Pu^{5} Pu^{7} Pu^{9} °भ्यामथ वा; Lo^{3} Tj^{1} [*Jolly* R] °भ्यामपि च — d) BBe^{2} नाश्व°; Lo^{4} नीश्व°; wKt^{6} नानुवृत्त्या; Tr^{2} स्ववृत्या; Be^{1} BBe^{2} Be^{3} BCa Ho Hy Jm Jo^{1} Jo^{2} wKt^{1} Kt^{2} wKt^{3} La^{1} La^{2} Lo^{2} Lo^{3} Ox^{2} Pu^{5} Pu^{7} Pu^{9} Tj^{1} Tj^{2} MTr^{3} Wa *Mandlik Jolly Bühler Jha KSS Dave* कदाचन

5. Cited by *Dev* 2.451; *Mādh* 1.309 — a) La^{1} ऋतुमु°; NKt^{4} सतञ्छसिलं; TMd^{4} °शिला; Tr^{1} °सिलं — a-b) TMd^{3} प्रोक्तममृतं; GMy प्रोक्तः मृतं — b) Tj^{1} स्यादयान्वितं — c) Be^{1} च; *Mādh* याचितं प्रोक्तं; Be^{1} Ho La^{1} Lo^{5} Ox^{2} Pu^{1} Pu^{2} Pu^{4} Pu^{5} Tj^{1} भैक्ष्यं; MTr^{3} भिक्षं; Bo भैक्षा — d) Tr^{2} भैक्षममृतं; Kt^{2} पृमृतं; Bo प्रभृतं; NKt^{4} चार्षणं; Pu^{8} स्मृतां; NPu^{1} मतं

सेवा श्ववृत्तिराख्याता तस्मात्तां परिवर्जयेत् ॥६॥
कुसूलधान्यको वा स्यात् कुम्भीधान्यक एव वा ।
त्र्यहैहिको वापि भवेदश्वस्तनिक एव वा ॥७॥
चतुर्णामपि चैतेषां द्विजानां गृहमेधिनाम् ।
ज्यायान्परः परो ज्ञेयो धर्मतो लोकजित्तमः ॥८॥
षट्कर्मैको भवत्येषां त्रिभिरन्यः प्रवर्तते ।
द्वाभ्यामेकश्चतुर्थस्तु ब्रह्मसत्रेण जीवति ॥९॥
वर्तयंस्तु शिलोञ्छाभ्यामग्निहोत्रपरायणः ।
इष्टीः पार्वायनान्तीयाः केवला निर्वपेत्सदा ॥१०॥
न लोकवृत्तं वर्तेत वृत्तिहेतोः कथंचन ।

6. *ma* in BKt[5]. Cited by *Dev* 2.451; *Mādh* 1.309-10 — a) wKt[6] TMd[3] सत्यामृतं; Lo[4] सत्यानृपं; Tj[2] च; wKt[1] वणिज्यं; Pu[4] वाणिजं; Pu[2] वणिजं — b) Ox[2] तेन चापि प्रजीव्यते; GMy तेन जीवोपजीव्यते; BKt[5] चापदि; Be[1] चैवाप्यजीव्यते; TMd[3] चैवोपजीविते — c) GMd[1] सोवा; GMd[1] °त्तिरप्याख्याता; NKt[4] La[1] TMd[3] GMd[5] GMy NNg sOx[1] Ox[3] sPu[6] °त्तिर्व्याख्याता; Tr[1] °त्तिर्विख्याता

7. Cited by *Vij* 3.28–9; *Apa* 169; pādas a-b cited by *Vij* 1.128 — a) Be[1] BBe[2] Bo Ho Jo[1] Kt[2] wKt[3] wKt[6] Lo[2] Lo[4] oMd[2] NNg Ox[3] NPu[1] Pu[2] Pu[4] Pu[7] Pu[8] Pu[9] Tr[2] *Me* [pāṭha] *Nā Vij* कुशूल°; wKt[1] कुशील°; GMy कुसील°; Pu[5] कुशीलकुलाधान्यको वा°; Pu[4] *om* °को वा स्यात्कुम्भीधान्य° — b) Ox[3] °धानक; Jo[2] wKt[6] Tr[1] एव च — c) La[1] त्र्यहैकको; Pu[3] त्र्यहाहिको; sOx[1] sPu[6] त्र्यहैनिको; TMd[3] GMy त्रियाहिको; Pu[10] त्र्यहैको; NKt[4] Pu[9] त्र्यहेहिको; Tr[2] अहैहिको; MTr[6] [*Jolly* Nd] द्व्यहैहिको; Tr[1] द्व्यहेहिको; TMd[4] त्रिहिकोहिकोपि; Tj[1] त्र्यहिको वापि न भवे°; Ho *om* वापि; NKt[4] चापि — d) Pu[2] Pu[4] °श्वस्थनिक; Be[1] [*but mc*] wKt[1] °स्वस्तनिक; Pu[5] °स्तनक; Pu[2] Pu[3] Pu[4] [*Jolly* M[1–2–5]] एव च

Additional verse in *Mandlik* [ट] *KSS:*

सद्यःप्रक्षालिको वा स्यान्माससंचयिकोऽपि वा ।
षण्मासनिचयो वापि समानिचय एव वा ॥

8. Omitted in Ox[3]. Cited by *Apa* 169 — a) sOx[1] sPu[6] बलानामपि; BKt[5] wKt[6] °मपि वर्णानां; Tr[2] °मपि तेषां हि — b) Pu[7] [*but cor*] Pu[9] गृहे; NKt[4] °मेधिना — c) Ho जायान्परः; Pu[2] ज्ञायात्परः; Be[1] न्यायात्परः; Pu[5] प्यायान्परः Lo[2] ज्यायान्यतः; Be[1] °न्परस्परो; BKt[5] °न्परपरो — d) Be[3] Ox[2] NPu[1] *Apa* [*vl*] लोकवित्तमः

9. Cited by *Vij* 1.128; *Apa* 169; *Dev* 2.452 — a) sPu[6] [*cor to*] यकर्मैको; wKt[1] oMd[2] *Apa* °कर्मको; TMd[4] °कर्मिको; Lo[1] °कर्मैषां; Be[3] wKt[1] भवेदेषां; Ho La[1] Pu[5] Pu[7] Pu[9] Tr[1] *Apa* भवेत्तेषां; Bo Lo[1] भवत्तेषां; TMd[3] GMy °त्येषा — c) wKt[1] द्वयमेक°; Wa द्वाभ्यामन्यश्च°; TMd[3] GMy °मेक चतु°; TMd[3] GMy °तुर्थं तु; Lo[3] NPu[1] [*Jolly* R] °तुर्थश्च; Pu[2] Pu[4] °तुर्भिश्च; Ho °तुर्थब्रह्म° — d) GMd[1] TMd[3] GMy Pu[2] Pu[4] Tr[1] *Dev* °सूत्रेण; BBe[2] [*but cor*] °सौत्रेण; MTr[3] °सत्रेषु; Pu[9] °सत्रे

10.* a) BBe[2] Bo BCa Hy Jm Jo[1] Kt[2] wKt[3] NKt[4] Lo[1] Lo[2] Lo[4] Lo[5] oMd[2] sOx[1] Ox[2] Ox[3] sPu[6] Pu[8] Pu[10] Tj[2] Tr[2] *Mandlik Jolly Jha KSS Dave* वर्तयंश्च; BKt[5] wKt[6] वर्तयन्तु; GMd[1] GMd[5] Tr[1] सिलो° — b) GMd[1] °परायणं — c) Tj[1] इष्टिः; NKt[4] इष्टी; GMy इष्टिं; Pu[5] इष्टाः; TMd[3] यिष्टिः; TMd[4] इति; wKt[6] इष्टीश्च पार्वा°; wKt[1] अष्टौ पार्वा°; Lo[1] Pu[10] पर्वा°; BKt[5] wKt[6] पार्वाणान्तीयाः; Pu[5] Pu[7] [*mc sh to*] पार्वायणांग्रयणांतीतीयाः; Hy पार्वाग्रयणातीयाः; Pu[9] °णान्वीतीयाः; wKt[1] °णास्तीयाः; GMy °णान्तीयां; TMd[3] °णान्त्रीयां [many mss. have the retroflex पार्वायण] — d) TMd[3] केवलां; Tr[2] केवलं; GMy केवलान्निर्व°; Pu[10] °पेत्सवा

अजिह्मामशठां शुद्धां जीवेद्ब्राह्मणजीविकाम् ॥११॥
संतोषं परमास्थाय सुखार्थी संयतो भवेत् ।
संतोषमूलं हि सुखं दुःखमूलं विपर्ययः ॥१२॥
अतोऽन्यतमया वृत्त्या जीवंस्तु स्नातको द्विजः ।
स्वर्ग्यायुष्ययशस्यानि व्रतानीमानि धारयेत् ॥१३॥
वेदोदितं स्वकं कर्म नित्यं कुर्यादतन्द्रितः ।
तद्धि कुर्वन्यथाशक्ति प्राप्नोति परमां गतिम् ॥१४॥
नेहेतार्थान् प्रसङ्गेन न विरुद्धेन कर्मणा ।
न कल्पमानेष्वर्थेषु नार्त्यामपि यतस्ततः ॥१५॥
इन्द्रियार्थेषु सर्वेषु न प्रसज्येत कामतः ।
अतिप्रसक्तिं चैतेषां मनसा संनिवर्तयेत् ॥१६॥
सर्वान्परित्यजेदर्थान् स्वाध्यायस्य विरोधिनः ।

11. a) Ho La[1] GMd[1] TMd[3] GMd[5] GMy Pu[5] Pu[7] Pu[9] Tj[2] [*Jolly* G] °वृत्तिं; Tj[1] °वर्तं; NKt[4] NNg [*but cor fh*] वर्तेते; Pu[10] वर्तत — b) Pu[10] °हितो; BBe[2] कदाचन — c) Ox[3] Pu[10] Tr[1] अजिह्मम°; Lo[4] °शठा; Ox[3] °शठं; Hy °शचां; Lo[4] Lo[5] GMy शुद्धा; Lo[2] युद्धां — d) Lo[1] *mc to* जीवेद्विप्रो हि जीविकां; Hy जीवेद्रा जीविकां; TMd[3] GMy श्रयेद्ब्राह्म°

12. Cited by *Apa* 170; *Dev* 2.459; pādas a-b cited by *Vij* 1.129 — b) *Apa* सुखार्थं; Lo[1] संयमो; sOx[1] sPu[6] सर्वतो; Ho भवत् — c) sOx[1] sPu[6] तु; Pu[10] सुपं — d) Kt[2] °मूल; Be[3] °मूलो; NPu[1] हि विपर्ययः; Hy Pu[5] Pu[7] Pu[9] विपर्यायः; Lo[1] विपर्यः

13. Pāda-d cited by *Vij* 3.219–20 — b) Ho Lo[1] जीवं तु; TMd[4] जीवस्तु; Jm sOx[1] sPu[6] Tr[2] जीवेत्तु; Pu[10] स्नातकोविदः — c) Tr[2] स्वर्गायुष्यप्रदाश्यानि; BBe[2] wKt[1] wKt[6] Jo[1] TMd[4] स्वर्ग्य°; Tj[1] °युष्ट्य°; Tr[1] °युष्यंयशस्यानि; La[1] °मुख्ययशस्यानि — d) BBe[2] व्रतान्येतानि चाचरेत्; BKt[5] wKt[6] व्रतानिमानि

14. Cited by *Apa* 217, *Dev* 2.411; *Mādh* 1.52 — a) Pu[5] Pu[5] [*but cor*] Pu[9] वेदोवितं; Pu[7] Pu[9] स्वक; wKt[6] धर्म — a-b) La[1] स्वकं नित्यं कर्म कुर्याद° — b) wKt[3] °तन्द्रियः; Hy °तन्त्रितः — c) Pu[2] Pu[4] कुर्यान्यथा°; Lo[4] Lo[5] °थायुक्ति; Tj[2] °शक्तिं — d) Tj[2] आप्नोति; MTr[3] गतीं

15. Placed after 12 in [*Jolly* Nd]. Cited by *Hem* 1.59; *Lakṣ* 2.228 — a) TMd[4] नेहीतार्था; Lo[4] *Lakṣ* नेहीतार्थं; GMd[1] नेहीतार्थ; Hy °तार्थानप्र°; GMy प्रसङ्गे — b) TMd[4] [*om* न] विरुद्धेन नृकर्मणा; La[1] [*but cor fh*] विरोधेन; *Lakṣ* निषिद्धेन; TMd[3] विरुद्धेनेह; Pu[4] कर्मणः; Pu[2] कर्मणाः — c) Be[1] Jo[2] wKt[1] La[1] Lo[2] TMd[4] Ox[3] NPu[1] Pu[3] MTr[6] *Lakṣ* न कल्प्य°; TMd[3] GMd[5] GMy Tr[1] नाकल्प°; GMd[1] Pu[2] Pu[4] MTr[4] नाकल्प्य°; Hy Jm Jo[1] Kt[2] oMd[2] Ox[2] Tj[2] MTr[3] *Ku* [but may simply be a gloss] *Mandlik KSS* न विद्यमा°; Lo[1] °माने चार्थेषु — d) Be[1] नार्त्यमपि; Pu[4] नार्त्यानपि; BBe[2] Lo[1] Lo[4] Pu[8] नार्तावपि; wKt[1] नर्तावापि; Tr[2] नान्यादपि; NKt[4] नांत्यादपि; TMd[4] नात्यमपि; sPu[6] [*but cor*] नार्त्यादपि; Tj[1] नत्यामपि; TMd[3] नात्यामपि; Lo[3] नान्यामपि; GMy नानामपि; sPu[6] [*but cor*] समन्ततः

16. Cited by *Apa* 217, pādas a-b cited by *Vij* 3.219–20 — b) Pu[2] Pu[4] न सज्येत; BBe[2] Be[3] Ho Hy Lo[1] [*Jolly* R] प्रसज्जेत; NPu[1] प्रसह्येत; Lo[4] प्रस[*ma* ह्ये]त; sOx[1] कामककः; Tr[2] कर्मतः — c) Kt[2] अतिप्रसञ्चैतेषां; BKt[5] wKt[6] अतः प्रसक्तिं; NKt[4] अविप्रसक्तिं; Lo[4] °प्रासक्तिं; wKt[1] °शक्तिं; Hy °संक्तिं; TMd[3] GMy °सक्तिश्चैतेषां; Tj[1] °सक्तिर्वैतेषां; Ox[3] Pu[10] चैवेषां — d) Ox[2] Ox[3] Pu[10] संनिवेशयेत्

यथातथा यापयंस्तु सा ह्यस्य कृतकृत्यता ॥१७॥
वयसः कर्मणोऽर्थस्य श्रुतस्याभिजनस्य च ।
वेषवाग्बुद्धिसारूप्यमाचरन्विचरेदिह ॥१८॥
बुद्धिवृद्धिकराण्याशु धन्यानि च हितानि च ।
नित्यं शास्त्राण्यवेक्षेत निगमांश्चैव वैदिकान् ॥१९॥
यथा यथा हि पुरुषः शास्त्रं समधिगच्छति ।
तथा तथा विजानाति विज्ञानं चास्य रोचते ॥२०॥
ऋषियज्ञं देवयज्ञं भूतयज्ञं च सर्वदा ।
नृयज्ञं पितृयज्ञं च यथाशक्ति न हापयेत् ॥२१॥
एतानेके महायज्ञान् यज्ञशास्त्रविदो जनाः ।
अनीहमानाः सततमिन्द्रियेष्वेव जुह्वति ॥२२॥
वाच्येके जुह्वति प्राणं प्राणे वाचं च सर्वदा ।

17.* c) Pu[10] यथायापयंस्तु [*om* तथा]; Pu[9] यथातथार्यापयंस्तु; Be[1] ʙBe[2] Be[3] ʙCa Ho Hy Jm Jo[1] Jo[2] Kt[2] La[1] Lo[3] Lo[5] oMd[2] sOx[1] Ox[2] ɴPu[1] Pu[3] Pu[5] sPu[6] [*but cor*] Pu[7] [*mc sh to*] Pu[8] Tr[2] ᴍTr[3] *Rc Jolly KSS* यथातथाध्यापयंस्तु; Lo[4] यथा[*ma* तथाध्याप]यंस्तु; Lo[1] यथातथायाचयिष्णुः सा — d) Ho स; Lo[1] सा ह्यस्या; ʙKt[5] wKt[6] सर्वस्य कृत°; ɴPu[1] साध्यस्याकृत°; Hy *om* कृत°; ɢMy कृतकृत्यतः; Pu[10] कृतकृत्यया

18. a) Wa वयसा; ɢMd[1] ᴛMd[3] Wa कर्मणार्थस्य — b) Pu[4] °र्थस्याभिजनस्य च; Tr[2] सुतस्याभिजनस्य; Be[3] ɢMd[5] वा — c) La[1] देशं वाक्बुद्धि°; Lo[1] विवेकवाक्बुद्धि°; ᴛMd[3] वेषवान्बुद्धि°; Pu[10] वेववाम्बद्धि°; Pu[4] °बुद्धिमान्रूप्य°; Pu[9] °रूपमा° — d) ɢMd[5] °माचारान्वि°; ɢMd[1] ᴛMd[3] °माचारं वि°; Pu[4] *om* °चरेदिह; Kt[2] °चरेदिव

19. Pādas a-b omitted in Pu[4]. Cited by *Dev* 1.132, 2.448 — a) ᴛMd[4] °वृत्तिकरा°; ᴛMd[3] °वर्त्तिकरा°; sOx[1] sPu[6] °वृद्धिकरायाशु; ᴛMd[3] ɢMy ᴍTr[3] °कराण्याहुर्धन्या° — b) ɢMd[1] Ox[3] धन्यानि विहितानि च; ᴛMd[4] धर्माणि च हिताय च; ʙBe[2] Jm sOx[1] sPu[6] धनानि; Tj[1] Tr[1] *Dev* 1.132 धान्यानि; *Dev* 2.448 धर्म्याणि; ᴛMd[3] ɢMy वासानि — c) Lo[4] नित्य; Bo नीतिशास्त्रा°; ʙBe[2] शास्त्राण्यविक्षेत; Lo[5] शास्त्राण्यवक्षेत; sOx[1] sPu[6] शास्त्राणि वीक्षेत; Pu[5] Pu[7] Pu[9] शास्त्राणि वेक्षेत [Pu[5] शास्त्र]; Tj[1] शास्त्राणि वैक्षेत; Tr[2] शास्त्राणि चेक्षेत — d) Bo निगमाश्चैव; oMd[2] °श्चैवं; ɢMy ᴍTr[3] वेदिकान्; wKt[6] दैविकान्

20. a) oMd[2] यथा तथा — c) Kt[2] तथा तथापि जानाति; ᴛMd[4] तथा तथा द्विजातीनां; Pu[4] *om first* तथा — d) Tj[1] वास्य; ᴛMd[4] तस्य; Pu[2] Pu[4] रोचति; Bo चोच्यते

Additional verse in Ho Ox[2] *Mandlik* [ज्ञ] *KSS:*

शास्त्रस्य पारं गत्वा तु भूयो भूयस्तदभ्यसेत् ।
न शास्त्रं शबलं कुर्यान्न चाधीत्य त्यजेत्पुनः ।।

c) *Mandlik KSS* तच्छास्त्रं; Ho शवलं; Ox[2] केवलं — d) Ho कुर्यान्नाधीतं संत्यजेत्पुनः

21. a) La[1] भूत and ɴKt[4] सखि *for* ऋषि; Pu[4] *om* देवजज्ञं; wKt[1] ʙKt[5] wKt[6] Tj[1] वेद and wKt[3] पितृ *for* देव; ᴛMd[3] दैव° — b) sOx[1] sPu[6] भूतयज्ञं तथैव च; La[1] तु — c) ᴛMd[3] नृतयज्ञं; Pu[9] *om* च — d) Bo स *for* न; sPu[6] [*but cor*] °शक्तिर्हापयेत्

22. Cited by *Lakṣ* 3.150 — a) Pu[5] °नेक; Lo[2] °नैके; Pu[9] °नेकि; Be[3] ᴛMd[3] ɢMy महायज्ञा — b) wKt[3] वेदशास्त्र°; Lo[4] यथाशास्त्र° — c) ᴛMd[4] अनीयमा°; ᴛMd[3] अनीहमर्हनस्सत°; ɢMy °मानस्सत° — d) Ho °न्द्रियार्थेषु जुह्वति; ɴKt[4] ɢMd[5] जिह्वति

वाचि प्राणे च पश्यन्तो यज्ञनिर्वृत्तिमक्षयाम् ॥२३॥
ज्ञानेनैवापरे विप्रा यजन्त्येतैर्मखैः सदा ।
ज्ञानमूलां क्रियामेषां पश्यन्तो ज्ञानचक्षुषा ॥२४॥
अग्निहोत्रं च जुहुयादाद्यन्ते द्युनिशोः सदा ।
दर्शेन चार्धमासान्ते पौर्णमासेन चैव हि ॥२५॥
सस्यान्ते नवसस्येष्ट्या तथर्त्वन्ते द्विजोऽध्वरैः ।
पशुना ह्ययनान्ते तु समान्ते सौमिकैर्मखैः ॥२६॥
नानिष्ट्वा नवसस्येष्ट्या पशुना चाग्निमान्द्विजः ।
नवान्नमद्यान्मांसं वा दीर्घमायुर्जिजीविषुः ॥२७॥

23. Pādas c-d omitted in Jm. Cited by *Lakṣ* 3.150–1 — a) GMy वाच्येते; Pu^{2} *om* प्राणं; Wa प्राणे; Lo^{4} Lo^{5} प्राप्यं — b) Pu^{4} *om* प्राणे ... [23c] वाचि [haplo]; Lo^{4} *ma* प्राणे; Be^{1} Lo^{2} Pu^{10} [*Jolly* M] प्राणं; Bo प्राणो — c) Lo^{5} चाधिप्राणे; Bo प्राणो; wKt^{1} प्राणस्य; TMd^{4} प्राणानपश्यन्ते; Lo^{4} च यपूयन्तो; GMy पश्यन्ते; BKt^{5} सस्यन्तो — d) Lo^{4} यक्षनिर्वृत्ति°; NKt^{4} TMd^{3} °निवृत्ति°; Lo^{2} Pu^{2} Pu^{4} °त्तिमुत्तमां; Ho NKt^{4} Lo^{3} Lo^{4} TMd^{4} NNg sOx^{1} Pu^{10} °क्षयं; GMy °क्षमां

24. Omitted in [*Jolly* Nd]; *ma* in Pu^{7}; pādas a-b omitted in Jm Pu^{10}; pādas c-d omitted in Tj^{1} and *ma* in Pu^{7}. Cited by *Lakṣ* 3.151 — a) Lo^{4} ज्ञानिनै°; GMd^{1} Tj^{1} °नैवपरे; Lo^{2} Pu^{2} Pu^{4} °नैत्यपरे [Pu^{4} °परै] — b) Ox^{3} यजन्त एतै°; Bo Lo^{1} Lo^{4} Lo^{5} *Rc Jha Dave* यजन्ते तैर्मखैः [Lo^{4} Lo^{5} यजाते]; *Me* gloss यजन्त इति supports the latter reading; *Ku Mr* support यजन्ति; NKt^{4} BKt^{5} wKt^{6} यजन्ते ते मखैः [BKt^{5} यजन्ति]; Tj^{1} °तैर्मखः; Lo^{2} Pu^{2} Pu^{4} °तैर्महामखैः [*om* सदा] — c) BCa BKt^{5} Lo^{3} sOx^{1} °मूलं; Ho °मूल; *Lakṣ* क्रियां तेषां; La^{1} MTr^{4} क्रियां सर्वां; Bo Ho °मेषा; Lo^{1} GMd^{1} GMd^{5} GMy Tr^{1} °मेतां; Ox^{2} °मेकां — d) sOx^{1} sPu^{6} पश्यन्ति; TMd^{3} GMy पश्यन्ते; Lo^{3} °चक्षुषः

25. Pādas a-b omitted in Tj^{1}. Cited by *Apa* 217; *Lakṣ* 2.120; *Dev* 2.414 — a) Lo^{4} Lo^{5} Ox^{3} Pu^{10} [*Jolly* M] तु — b) Pu^{5} Pu^{7} Pu^{9} [*Jolly* G] °न्तेहर्निशं सदा; GMd^{5} °न्तेहन्निशोस्सदा; wKt^{1} द्युनिशं; Tr^{1} द्यानिशोः; Be^{3} द्विनिशो — c) *Apa* दर्शने; NKt^{4} दर्शनमार्ध°; Pu^{2} Tj^{1} वार्ध°; Tr^{1} चार्थ° — d) Ho TMd^{3} TMd^{4} NNg Pu^{3} MTr^{4} MTr^{6} *Lakṣ* पूर्ण°; Tr^{1} पर्ण°; Lo^{2} Pu^{7} °मासन; Pu^{5} °मासान; Pu^{5} Pu^{7} Pu^{9} चैवहं; NKt^{4} MTr^{4} ह; MTr^{6} च

26.* Cited by *Apa* 217; *Lakṣ* 2.120; *Dev* 2.414 — a) Pu^{5} *om* सस्यान्ते; BBe^{2} शस्यान्ते; Ho सस्यां नव°; Tj^{1} नवस्येष्ट्या; Lo^{2} Pu^{2} Pu^{4} नस्येष्ट्या [Lo^{2} °स्येष्ट्वा]; BKt^{5} Pu^{5} Pu^{7} Pu^{9} नचसस्येष्ट्या; BBe^{2} °शस्येष्ट्या; Tr^{2} °सस्याप्ट्या; Kt^{2} °सस्येष्टा — b) GMd^{1} तथार्त्वन्ते; TMd^{3} यथर्त्वन्ते; Hy तदर्त्वन्ते; Tj^{1} तथात्वंते; La^{1} मासस्यान्ते; Tr^{2} तथातेतेः; Lo^{1} द्विजाध्वरैः; Lo^{2} Pu^{2} Pu^{4} द्विजोत्तमैः; BKt^{5} द्विजोन्तरैः; wKt^{6} द्विजोत्तरैः; *Apa* [vl] द्विजेश्वरैः; Pu^{5} Pu^{9} °ध्वारेः; Lo^{3} °ध्वरे — c) La^{1} TMd^{3} GMd^{1} GMy MTr^{4} MTr^{6} अयनान्ते तु पशुना [MTr^{6} damaged after अयनान्ते]; Lo^{2} पशूनां ह्यर्यनां तु; *Jha Dave* त्वयनान्ते तु; Be^{3} BKt^{5} wKt^{6} sOx^{1} sPu^{6} Tj^{1} Tr^{2} *Apa* ह्ययनस्यान्ते [*om* तु]; TMd^{4} *Lakṣ Dev* त्वयनस्यान्ते [*om* तु]; Be^{1} wKt^{1} La^{2} Lo^{1} Lo^{4} Lo^{5} ह्ययनस्यादौ [*om* तु]; BBe^{2} Hy Jm Jo^{1} wKt^{1} Kt^{2} oMd^{2} Pu^{3} Tj^{2} MTr^{3} [*Jolly* M^{3} N Ku] *Mandlik KSS* त्वयनस्यादौ [*om* तु]; Bo ध्ययनादौ तु; wKt^{3} Pu^{5} Pu^{7} Pu^{9} [*Jolly* G] ह्ययनादौ च; Ho Ox^{2} Pu^{8} ह्ययनादौ तु — d) sOx^{1} sPu^{6} सामान्ते; La^{1} NPu^{1} Tj^{1} *Apa* मासान्ते; Ox^{2} सस्यान्ते; Pu^{2} Pu^{4} सोमान्ते; Lo^{2} सोमान्तो; NKt^{4} तमान्ते; Be^{1} Bo समाप्ते [Be^{1} *mc* वर्षान्ते]; Ho सौमकै°; NKt^{4} सौनिकै°; Lo^{4} सौयिके°; Lo^{5} सौपिके°; TMd^{3} GMy sOx^{1} sPu^{6} [*but cor*] सामिकै°; Jm NNg °कैर्मुखैः

27. Cited by *Lakṣ* 2.120; *Dev* 2.416 — a) Bo नानिष्ट्या; Hy नानिस्या; wKt^{3} नशस्येष्ट्या; Tj^{1} नचसस्येष्ट्या; Kt^{2} नसस्येष्टा; Tr^{1} °सस्यैष्ट्या; BBe^{2} °शस्येष्ट्या; Lo^{5} °सस्येष्ट्वा — b) Pu^{2} Pu^{4} पशुना वा

नवेनानर्चिता ह्यस्य पशुहव्येन चाग्नयः ।
प्राणानेवात्तुमिच्छन्ति नवान्नामिषगर्धिनः ॥२८॥
आसनाशनशय्याभिरद्भिर्मूलफलेन वा ।
नास्य कश्चिद्वसेद्गेहे शक्तितोऽनर्चितोऽतिथिः ॥२९॥
पाषण्डिनो विकर्मस्थान् बैडालव्रतिकाञ्छठान् ।
हैतुकान्बकवृत्तींश्च वाङ्मात्रेणापि नार्चयेत् ॥३०॥
वेदविद्याव्रतस्नाताञ्छ्रोत्रियान् गृहमेधिनः ।
पूजयेद्धव्यकव्येन विपरीतांस्तु वर्जयेत् ॥३१॥
शक्तितोऽपचमानेभ्यो दातव्यं गृहमेधिना ।
संविभागश्च भूतेभ्यः कर्तव्योऽनुपरोधतः ॥३२॥

द्विजोत्तमान्; Lo^2 पशुना न वा द्विजोत्तमाः; Ho NKt^4 La^1 GMd^1 TMd^4 GMd^5 GMy Ox^2 Pu^8 Tj^2 Tr^1 Tr^2 MTr^4 MTr^6 Wa वाग्नि° ; TMd^3 MTr^3 नाग्नि° ; TMd^3 GMy °न्द्विजाः — c) Ox^2 Pu^2 Pu^4 Pu^5 Pu^7 Pu^9 नचान्नम° ; Tj^1 नक्तमद्या° ; wKt^1 नवार्थमद्या° ; NKt^4 नवाजसद्यो मांसं; GMy °न्नमयमांसं; TMd^3 °न्नमधिमांसं; oOr *om* वा; sOx^1 sPu^6 च — d) Be^3 दीर्घ्यमा° ; wKt^6 दीर्घायुश्च जि° ; Be^3 Tj^1 °जीविषुं

28. Pādas c-d omitted in Tr^2. Cited by *Lakṣ* 2.121 — a) *Lakṣ* नवेनान्नेन चानिष्ट्वा; TMd^3 नवेनान्नार्चिताभ्यस्य; Lo^2 Pu^2 Pu^4 नवान्नेनर्चिता [Pu^4 नावा° ; Lo^2 °निर्विता]; Lo^1 नवान्नेनार्चिता; GMy नवेनार्चित्वा; GMd^5 °नानर्चता; Be^1 °र्चिता नस्य; Lo^5 स्वस्य — b) TMd^3 पशुरप्यनवाग्नयः; GMd^5 Ox^2 Tj^1 Tr^1 वाग्नयः — c) Tj^1 प्राणावेवा° ; TMd^3 °नेवार्तुमि° — d) Tj^1 नचान्नयिपगर्विनः; TMd^3 GMy नवान्नाशन° ; Pu^{10} नवाक्रमिष° ; Ho La^1 Lo^5 TMd^3 Ox^3 °गृद्धिनः; oOr °गृध्नः; wKt^6 °गृधितः; TMd^4 °ग्रन्थिनः; NKt^4 °गर्हितः; *Lakṣ* °गर्हिताः; GMd^1 Tr^1 °जघ्निनः; Pu^4 °मर्थिनः; Lo^2 °मथिनः

29. Omitted in Lo^3. Cited by *Hem* 1.677, 3/1.438 — a) BKt^5 NNg आसनासन° ; La^1 oOr आशनाशयनशय्या° ; Tj^1 वसनावनशय्या° — b) MTr^3 °छलेन; Ho च — c) Jm न कस्यचिद्वसे° ; NKt^4 कश्चिद्वसेत्स्नेहे — d) Lo^2 Lo^4 Lo^5 Ox^3 Pu^2 Pu^4 Pu^{10} [*Jolly* M] °द्वसेद्गेहेनर्चितः शक्तितोतिथिः [Pu^{10} °सेद्गृहे; Lo^4 °नार्चितः]; wKt^6 TMd^3 *Hem* 3/1.438 °नार्चितो; NKt^4 °तिथेः

30. Cited by *Vij* 1.130; *Apa* 170; pādas a and d cited by *Viś* 1.129 — a) NKt^4 शषडिदोतिकर्मस्तान्; Be^3 Bo Jo^2 Kt^2 BKt^5 wKt^6 Lo^1 P^3 Tj^1 *Vij* पाखण्डिनो; sOx^1 sPu^6 पाषाण्डिनो; Lo^2 विकर्ण° — b) wKt^6 वैतालप्रतिकान्गणं; Pu^5 Pu^7 Pu^9 बिडाल° ; GMy बिलाल° ; GMd^5 वैलाळ° ; TMd^3 बाळव्रति° ; Tr^1 बैलाळघृतिका° ; Ho Lo^1 *Apa* [vl] °वृत्तिका° ; NKt^4 °प्रीतिकां शठान्; Ho Kt^2 Lo^1 Lo^4 TMd^3 NNg sPu^6 Pu^7 *Apa* °कान्शठान्; Tr^2 °कान्शवान्; TMd^4 °कान्ध्वान् — c) BKt^5 wKt^6 Lo^2 Pu^9 हेतु° ; Be^3 BKt^5 Lo^1 Lo^4 °वृत्तीश्च; GMd^1 °वृत्तांश्च; NKt^4 °वृत्ताश्च; TMd^4 °वृत्तिं च; Bo °वृद्धांश्च — d) Pu^5 नार्चयत्; Bo चार्चयेत्; *Apa* वर्जयेत्

Hy gives the verses in the following order: 30, 32, 33, 31, 34.

31. Cited by *Lakṣ* 4.61; *Hem* 3/1.382 — a) Lo^2 °स्नातश्रोत्रि° — b) GMd^1 GMd^5 MTr^4 MTr^6 [*Jolly* Nd Gr] *Nd Lakṣ* गृहमागतान् — c) Pu^9 पूजायद्ध° ; Pu^4 *om* °कव्येन ... [32b] दात° [haplo]; GMd^1 TMd^3 GMd^5 Tr^1 MTr^4 MTr^6 *Lakṣ* °कव्याभ्यां — d) Hy Jm Jo^1 Kt^2 Tj^2 MTr^3 *Mandlik Jha KSS Dave* °रीतांश्च; sOx^1 sPu^6 °रीतान्विवर्जयेत्

32. Cited by *Lakṣ* 3.208 — a) MTr^6 भक्तितो; GMd^1 शक्तितः पच° ; Tr^2 °पाचमा° ; wKt^1 [*mc to*] TMd^3 GMd^5 GMy oOr MTr^4 MTr^6 याचमानेभ्यो; Lo^1 यवमानेभ्यो; Tj^1 परमान्येभ्यो — b) BKt^5 wKt^6 sOx^1 sPu^6 दातव्यो; GMy °मेधिनः; TMd^4 *Lakṣ* °मेधिनां — c) TMd^3 GMy विभागश्चैव भूतानां; oMd^2 समविभा° ; BBe^2 °भागस्तु; Bo °भाव्यश्च; Lo^1 °भागः स्वभूतेभ्यः; GMd^5 Tr^1 MTr^4 MTr^6 *Lakṣ* भूतानां —

राजतो धनमन्विच्छेत् संसीदन् स्नातकः क्षुधा ।
याज्यान्तेवासिनोर्वापि न त्वन्यत इति स्थितिः ॥३३॥
न सीदेत् स्नातको विप्रः क्षुधा शक्तः कथंचन ।
न जीर्णमलवद्वासा भवेच्च विभवे सति ॥३४॥
क्लृप्तकेशनखश्मश्रुर्दान्तः शुक्लाम्बरः शुचिः ।
स्वाध्याये चैव युक्तः स्यान्नित्यमात्महितेषु च ॥३५॥
वैणवीं धारयेद्यष्टिं सोदकं च कमण्डलुम् ।
यज्ञोपवीतं वेदं च शुभे रौक्मे च कुण्डले ॥३६॥

d) Pu^{10} कर्तव्यौ; MTr^{6} कर्तव्ये; wKt^{3} °पनुरोधतः; Lo^{1} °नपराधतः; Lo^{2} Pu^{2} Pu^{4} °नपसेवतः; TMd^{3} °रोधता

33. Cited by *Dev* 2.457 — a) NPu^{1} राजानो; sOx^{1} sPu^{6} °मन्विच्छ; oOr °मन्विच्छेः; Lo^{2} °मान्वेच्छेत् — b) GMd^{1} ससीदन्; Wa संसादन्; Lo^{2} Pu^{2} Pu^{4} स्नातका द्विजाः; Pu^{5} क्षुधाः — c) wKt^{3} ज्यायान्ते°; Ho GMd^{1} sOx^{1} Tj^{1} °वासिनो वापि — d) Pu^{10} न अन्यत; GMd^{1} त्वान्यत; oOr त्वन्यत्र; NPu^{1} चान्यत; Tr^{2} त्वन्यतरिति

34. Cited by *Dev* 2.457; pādas c-d cited by *Vij* 1.131 — a) GMd^{1} नासीदेत्; Lo^{2} Pu^{2} Pu^{4} संसीदेत् [*om* न]; Tj^{1} सीदत्; Be^{1} सीहेत्; GMd^{1} स्नातकी; Tj^{2} स्नातके; Ho सूतको — b) BKt^{5} wKt^{6} Lo^{4} Ox^{3} *Dev* सक्तः; Ho प्राक्तः; Jo^{2} युक्तः — c) Tj^{1} न च जीर्णमलवद्वासी; Bo जीर्य° ; Lo^{4} जीर्णामल°

35. a) GMd^{1} TMd^{3} TMd^{4} GMd^{5} कृन्तकेश° ; Bo Tj^{1} *Go* कृतकेश° ; Be^{3} कृत्तकेश° ; NNg कृप्त-केश° ; BKt^{5} wKt^{6} नचकेश° [नीच?]; MTr^{3} °केशो; Pu^{10} °श्मश्रुदान्तिः — b) TMd^{3} GMy °श्मश्रुश्शुक्लाम्बर-धरश्शुचिः; Lo^{3} °श्रुर्दान्तिः; Tr^{1} °श्रुर्दन्तः; [*Jolly* Be] शुद्धाम्बरः — c) Hy स्वाध्याय; Be^{1} Ho BKt^{5} wKt^{6} GMd^{5} sOx^{1} Pu^{1} Pu^{2} Pu^{3} Pu^{4} sPu^{6} Pu^{8} [*Jolly* N] नित्ययुक्तः; Tj^{1} युक्तस्य नित्यम° — d) Tr^{1} *om* च

36. Cited by *Viś* 1.132; *Vij* 1.133; *Apa* 176 — a) wKt^{1} TMd^{4} वैणवं; wKt^{6} °द्यष्टिः — b) Pu^{2} Pu^{4} सादकं; Tj^{2} तु; Pu^{5} कमण्डलुः; TMd^{3} कमण्डुलं; Pu^{4} *om* कमण्डलुं . . . [37b] कदाचन — c) Tj^{1} °पवी-तेतं वेदं [*om* च]; wKt^{6} स्वेदं; Tr^{2} वेदांश्च — d) MTr^{4} श्रुतौ युग्म च; Pu^{5} Pu^{7} Pu^{9} रौक्मं; Tj^{1} रौप्ये; TMd^{3} GMd^{5} GMy रुक्मे

Additional verses in [*Jolly* Gr]:

पाने तथैव संयोगान्नित्यं मेध्यः कमण्डलुः ।
ब्राह्मणाः सर्वतो मेध्यास्तेषां चैव कमण्डलुः ॥

Additonal verses in NPu^{1}:

कमण्डलुर्द्विजातीनां शौचार्थं विहितः पुरा ।
ब्रह्मणा मुनिभिश्चैव तस्मात्तं धारयेत्सदा ॥१॥ [BDh 1.7.1]
तेन शौचं ततः पानं संध्योपासनमेव च ।
कुर्यात् शुद्धेन मनसा न चित्तं दूपयेद्बुधः ॥२॥
करे सन्निहितोऽप्यग्निर्विप्राणां दक्षिणे सदा ।
दैवतं परमं तेषां संभवः परिकीर्त्तितः ॥३॥
जलप्रसूतिरग्नेस्तु नापश्च शुचयः स्मृताः ।
तस्माद्युमणिसंयोगात्पर्यग्निकरणं स्मृतम् ॥४॥
जलेऽप्यग्निः करेऽप्यग्निर्ब्राह्मणाप्यग्निसंभवः ।
त्रिभिरग्निभिः संस्प्रष्टः शुद्ध एव कमण्डलुः ॥५॥
स्वस्यैपा विहिता शुद्धिः पारुष्यं वर्जयेत्सदा ।
पितृदेवाग्निकार्याणि तस्मात्तत्परिवर्जयेत् ॥६॥
न चार्द्रपाणिर्भाण्डानि संस्पृशेद्धाज्यमेधसा ।

नेक्षेतोद्यन्तमादित्यं नास्तं यान्तं कदाचन ।
नोपसृष्टं न वारिस्थं न मध्यं नभसो गतम् ॥३७॥
न लङ्घयेद्वत्सतन्त्रीं न प्रधावेच्च वर्षति ।
न चोदके निरीक्षेत स्वं रूपमिति धारणा ॥३८॥
मृदं गां दैवतं विप्रं घृतं मधु चतुष्पथम् ।
प्रदक्षिणानि कुर्वीत प्रज्ञातांश्च वनस्पतीन् ॥३९॥
नोपगच्छेत् प्रमत्तोऽपि स्त्रियमार्तवदर्शने ।
समानशयने चैव न शयीत तया सह ॥४०॥
रजसाभिप्लुतां नारीं नरस्य ह्युपगच्छतः ।
प्रज्ञा तेजो बलं चक्षुरायुश्चैव प्रहीयते ॥४१॥
तां विवर्जयतस्तस्य रजसा समभिप्लुताम् ।

आर्द्रभावे तु संशुद्धे न दोषः स्पृशतः स्मृतः ॥७॥

37. Cited by *Vij* 1.135; *Apa* 180; *Dev* 1.124 — a) sOx^{1} sPu^{6} नेक्षेतादित्यमुद्यन्तं; Pu^{10} निक्षे°; Ho निक्षेतोदितमा° — b) TMd^{3} नास्त; Pu^{10} [*Jolly* M$^{1-2}$]नास्तमेतं; NKt^{4} Lo^{3} GMd^{1} GMd^{5} GMy Tj^{1} Tr^{1} MTr^{4} MTr^{6} *Ku Dave* यन्तं; sOx^{1} Ox^{3} sPu^{6} यातं; [*Jolly* M$^{8-9}$] येतं — c) BBe^{2} नोपग्रस्तं; TMd^{3} sPu^{6} [*but cor*] Tj^{1} Tr^{1} नोपरक्तं; Lo^{3} नोपरक्तुं; GMy नोपरक्षं; TMd^{4} नोपशक्तं; OMd^{2} *om* न; wKt^{1} वारिष्टं — d) Pu^{4} *om* न मध्यं; TMd^{4} न च मध्यं; sOx^{1} Ox^{2} sPu^{6} मध्ये; Kt^{2} *Dev* मध्य; Tj^{1} च नभोगतं

38. * Omitted in Tr^{1}; placed after verse 57 in TMd^{3} GMy. Pādas c-d cited by *Vij* 1.135 — a) Ho °द्वसंतन्त्री; Bo °द्वत्सतरी; wKt^{6} Tj^{1} °द्वत्सतरीं; Tr^{2} °द्वत्सरीं च न; Lo^{4} °तन्त्री; Be^{1} °तन्द्रीं; Pu^{7} °तृन्तीं; Lo^{3} TMd^{4} Pu^{2} Pu^{4} °तन्तीं; Lo^{2} TMd^{3} Ox^{3} Pu^{5} Pu^{9} °तन्ती; GMy °दन्ती — b) Pu^{5} Pu^{7} Pu^{9} प्रधावेच्च न वर्षति; oOr न प्रधानेन कर्षति; NPu^{1} प्रधावेत्तु; NKt^{4} प्रधावन्च; TMd^{3} GMy प्रवासेच्च; Kt^{2} °वेच्च प्रवर्षति; Lo^{3} वर्शातिं; GMd^{5} वर्शन्ति — c) MTr^{4} MTr^{6} न चोदमभिवीक्षेत; BBe^{2} NKt^{4} GMd^{1} TMd^{3} GMd^{5} GMy NNg Pu^{2} Pu^{4} न चोदकेभिवीक्षेत; TMd^{4} न चोदके तु वीक्षेत; Ox^{3} निरीक्षेव; TMd^{4} निक्षेत; oOr तितीक्षेत; Tr^{2} निरीक्षेत् — d) Be^{1} Bo Ho wKt^{1} Lo^{1} Lo^{2} Lo^{3} Lo^{5} TMd^{3} TMd^{4} GMd^{5} GMy NNg oOr NPu^{1} Pu^{5} Pu^{10} Tj^{1} Tr^{2} [*Jolly* M$^{1-2-8-9}$ R] *Me Rn Rc Dave Jha* स्वरूप°; MTr^{4} MTr^{6} रूपमिव; GMy °पमपि; Ho GMy धारणं

39. Cited by *Vij* 1.133; *Apa* 176 — a) Tj^{1} नृगं गां; TMd^{3} GMy मृदंगं; TMd^{4} मृदसं; GMd^{1} मृदंगान्दै°; Lo^{1} मृदङ्गदेवता; wKt^{1} सर्वदा दैवतं; *Vij* देवतं; Pu^{5} दैवतविप्र; Bo विप्रो; GMd^{1} विप्रान्; Kt^{2} विघ्नं — b) BKt^{5} wKt^{6} घृतं क्षौद्रं; Ox^{3} घृतं च मधु; Pu^{5} वृतमधु; Tr^{2} चतुःकथं — c) *Apa* प्रदक्षिणं प्रकुर्वीत — d) TMd^{3} GMd^{5} GMy MTr^{4} MTr^{6} प्रज्ञातं च; TMd^{4} Tr^{1} प्रज्ञातां च; wKt^{1} wKt^{3} प्रख्यातांश्च; GMy Tr^{1} MTr^{4} MTr^{6} वनस्पतिं; TMd^{4} सरस्वतिं

40. Pādas a-b cited by *Hem* 3/3.726 — a) wKt^{3} नैव गच्छेत्; Lo^{4} sOx^{1} sPu^{6} नोपयच्छेत्; Pu^{5} प्रमनोपि; TMd^{4} प्रधृत्तोपि; Wa *om* पि — b) Bo TMd^{3} GMy स्त्रियामा° — c) Pu^{4} °शयनो; MTr^{3} °शयते; sOx^{1} sPu^{6} °शयनश्चैव — d) Ox^{3} *om* न; Pu^{5} Pu^{7} Pu^{9} शयीत न; GMd^{1} sOx^{1} sPu^{6} शयीत कदाचन

41. Cited by *Hem* 3/3.726 — a) Tr^{1} रजस्याभि°; wKt^{1} Ox^{3} Pu^{10} °विप्लुतां — b) Bo Lo^{1} नरस्याभ्युप°; Tj^{2} नरस्याप्युप°; NKt^{4} GMd^{1} TMd^{4} GMy द्विजस्य ह्युप°; TMd^{3} GMd^{5} Tr^{1} MTr^{4} MTr^{6} द्विजस्याभ्युप°; Ho ह्यपगच्छतः — c) Pu^{2} Pu^{4} प्रजातिजो; GMd^{1} TMd^{3} GMy *Hem* यशश्चक्षु° — d) Tj^{1} प्रहीते; sOx^{1} sPu^{6} विहीयते; NPu^{1} महीयते; Be^{1} विनश्यति; Ho Ox^{3} *om* प्रहीयते ... [42d] युश्चैव [haplo]

प्रज्ञा तेजो बलं चक्षुरायुश्चैव प्रवर्धते ॥४२॥
नाश्नीयाद्भार्यया सार्धं नैनामीक्षेत चाश्नतीम् ।
क्षुवतीं जृम्भमाणां वा न चासीनां यथासुखम् ॥४३॥
नाञ्जयन्तीं स्वके नेत्रे न चाभ्यक्तामनावृताम् ।
न पश्येत् प्रसवन्तीं च तेजस्कामो द्विजोत्तमः ॥४४॥
नान्नमद्यादेकवासा न नग्नः स्नानमाचरेत् ।
न मूत्रं पथि कुर्वीत न भस्मनि न गोव्रजे ॥४५॥
न फालकृष्टे न जले न चित्यां न च पर्वते ।
न जीर्णदेवायतने न वल्मीके कदाचन ॥४६॥
न ससत्त्वेषु गर्तेषु न गच्छन्नापि च स्थितः ।

42.* Omitted by *Nd;* pādas a-c omitted in Ho Ox[3]. Cited by *Lakṣ* 3.346; *Hem* 3/3.726 — a) sOx[1] sPu[6] हि वर्जय°; NPu[1] विवर्धय°; Pu[5] Pu[7] Pu[9] विसर्जय°; Pu[2] Pu[4] °वर्जयतस्य रजसा — b) GMd[5] रजसाभिपरिप्लुतां — c) NKt[4] Lo[4] Lo[5] GMd[1] TMd[3] TMd[4] GMd[5] GMy Pu[2] Pu[4] Pu[10] Tr[1] MTr[4] MTr[6] [*Jolly* M Nd] *Lakṣ Hem* प्रज्ञा लक्ष्मी यशश्चक्षु° [Lo[5] लक्ष्मीं; GMd[5] Pu[2] Pu[4] Tr[1] MTr[4] MTr[6] लक्ष्मीर्यश°]; Pu[5] Pu[7] Pu[9] तैजो; sOx[1] sPu[6] बलं चैवायुश्चैव — d) Be[1] BBe[2] BCa Ho Jo[2] Lo[2] Lo[5] GMd[1] GMy Pu[3] Pu[5] Pu[7] Pu[8] Pu[9] Tr[1] MTr[4] MTr[6] [*Jolly* G] विवर्धते; NKt[4] पिवर्धते; *Hem* परिवर्धते; Lo[4] विर्धते; Pu[10] प्रहीयते

43. Omitted by *Nd*. Cited by *Vij* 1.135; *Apa* 180; pādas a-b cited by *Viś* 1.130 — b) GMd[1] TMd[3] GMy oOr Tr[1] MTr[4] MTr[6] नैनां वीक्षेत; Ho Ox[3] Tj[1] चाश्नती — c) TMd[3] TMd[4] Ox[2] Tj[1] *Apa* क्षुवन्तीं; Lo[4] क्षुवतां; wKt[6] Pu[5] Pu[7] Pu[9] क्षुवंती; Jm क्षुपतीं; GMy °माणं; *Lakṣ* वै; Ho Jo[2] La[1] Lo[3] Lo[4] Lo[5] GMd[1] TMd[3] GMd[5] GMy sOx[1] sPu[6] Tr[1] Tr[2] MTr[4] MTr[6] Ox[3] Wa *Vij* च — d) sOx[1] sPu[6] MTr[4] MTr[6] न यथासुखमास्थितां; GMd[5] Tj[1] चासीनं; wKt[6] वाशीनां

44. Omitted by GMd[1] TMd[3] GMy Tr[1] MTr[4] MTr[6] *Nd*. Cited by *Apa* 181 — a) NKt[4] नीजयन्तीं; Jo[1] नाजयन्तीं; Ox[3] नर्जयन्तीं; Be[1] Be[3] Hy BKt[5] wKt[6] °यन्ती; Lo[4] °यन्ति; Kt[2] नेत्रै — b) TMd[4] न चात्यन्तवृतांगनां; NPu[1] चाभ्युक्ता° — c) Lo[3] न स्रवन्तीं च नेक्षेत; Jo[2] Wa प्रसवन्तीं च नेक्षेत [Wa प्रसुवन्तीं]; Tj[1] न पश्येत प्रसवन्ती; Bo *Apa* प्रसुवन्तीं; Be[3] प्रस्रुवन्तीं *and om* च; Tr[2] प्रश्नुवन्तीं; Tj[2] प्रसुवतीं; BKt[5] wKt[6] प्रस्वपन्तीं; Hy प्रसवन्ती; *Apa* वा — d) TMd[4] [*Jolly* Be] श्रेयस्कामो

Additional verse in Be[1] Ho Tj[1] Tr[2] *Mandlik* [क, ख, ण, त] *KSS:*

उपेत्य स्नातको विद्वान्नेक्षेन्नग्नां परस्त्रियम् ।
सरहस्यं च संवादं परस्त्रीषु विवर्जयेत् ॥

a) Tr[2] उपेत; Tj[1] °तको विन्नेक्षे° — b) Ho परिस्त्रियं

45. Omitted in *Nd*; placed after 46 in Bo; pādas a-b omitted in Pu[9]. Pādas c-d cited by *Dev* 2.237; *Apa* 179 — a-b) TMd[4] नान्नमद्यादेकं स्नानं च नग्नस्समाचरेत् — b) wKt[1] sOx[1] नानग्नः; Tr[1] न निशि स्नान° — c) Lo[4] न तत्र पथि — d) Be[1] न च भस्मनि गोव्रजे; TMd[3] GMd[5] oOr MTr[3] गोव्रजेत्

Additonal half-verse in GMd[5]:

न चत्वरे न गर्त्तेषु न गच्छन्नभसि स्थितः ॥

46. Omitted in GMd[1] TMd[3] GMy Pu[2] Pu[4] Tr[1] MTr[4] MTr[6] *Nd;* pādas c-d omitted in Wa. Cited by *Apa* 179; *Dev* 2.237 — a) Tj[2] कालकृष्टे; Ox[3] °कृष्णे — b) Lo[1] न च चित्यां न पर्वते; TMd[4] चिन्त्यां; Lo[2] पर्वति — c) Hy *om* न; Hy BKt[5] wKt[6] NNg °देवतायतने; Bo °यतनं — d) Jo[2] Lo[3] वल्मीके न शाङ्वले

न नदीतीरमासाद्य न च पर्वतमस्तके ॥४७॥
वाय्वग्निविप्रमादित्यमपः पश्यंस्तथैव गाः ।
न कदाचन कुर्वीत विण्मूत्रस्य विसर्जनम् ॥४८॥
तिरस्कृत्योच्चरेत् काष्ठं लोष्टं पत्रं तृणानि वा ।
नियम्य प्रयतो वाचं संवीताङ्गोऽवगुण्ठितः ॥४९॥
मूत्रोच्चारसमुत्सर्गं दिवा कुर्यादुदङ्मुखः ।
दक्षिणाभिमुखो रात्रौ संध्ययोश्च यथा दिवा ॥५०॥
छायायामन्धकारे वा रात्रावहनि वा द्विजः ।
यथासुखमुखः कुर्यात् प्राणाबाधभयेषु च ॥५१॥

47. Omitted in GMd^{1} TMd^{3} GMy Tr^{1} MTr^{4}MTr^{6} *Nd;* pādas a-b omitted in Wa. Cited by *Apa* 179; *Dev* 2.238 — a) TMd^{4} न सत्त्वेषु न गर्तेषु; Be^{3} Pu^{5} Pu^{7} Pu^{9} चसत्त्वेषु — b) NKt^{4} BKt^{5} wKt^{6} Ox^{3} Pu^{10} *Apa* गच्छन्न पथि स्थितः; Be^{3} °न्नापि संस्थितः — c) sOx^{1} sPu^{6} °मास्थाय; Pu^{10} °साद्यं — d) TMd^{4} °मस्तकं

Between pādas a-b and c-d of verse 47 an additonal half-verse in GMd^{5}:

न संध्ययोः प्रवाते च न कर्त्तुन्न [?] न पथि स्थितः ॥

48. *ma* in La^{1}; omitted in *Nd Rc*. Cited by *Dev* 2.238 — a) Bo NPu^{1} Pu^{2} Pu^{4} वाद्यग्नि°; MTr^{3} *Dev* °विप्रानादि° — b) TMd^{4} °मपहास्यस्तथैव; Lo^{1} पश्यन्तथैव; GMd^{1} पयस्तथैव; Be^{1} Jm BKt^{5} wKt^{6} Lo^{3} GMd^{1} TMd^{3} GMd^{5} GMy Pu^{5} Pu^{7} Pu^{9} Tr^{1} Wa [*Jolly* G] °थैव गां; sOx^{1} Pu^{2} Pu^{4} sPu^{6} Tj^{1} Tr^{2} °थैव च; NKt^{4} °थैव वः — c) Ho कदाचित्तु; Be^{1} कदाचिन्न; Be^{3} Lo^{4} Lo^{5} Ox^{3} Pu^{10} [*Jolly* M] कथंचन — d) TMd^{4} विर्सजने

49.* Pādas a-b omitted in oOr. Cited by *Apa* 34; *Lakṣ* 1.148; *Dev* 2.235 — a) Jm Jo^{1} Kt^{2} oMd^{2} MTr^{3} Wa *Mandlik Jha KSS Dave* काष्ठ; Pu^{5} कोष्ठं — b) NKt^{4} *om* लोष्टं; Jo^{1} Kt^{2} La^{3} GMd^{1} oMd^{2} Pu^{10} MTr^{3} *Mandlik Jha KSS Dave* लोष्ट; Be^{1} Ho sOx^{1} Ox^{2} Ox^{3} Pu^{3} Pu^{5} sPu^{6} Pu^{7} Pu^{9} Pu^{8} Tr^{2} *Dev Lakṣ Apa* पत्रं लोष्टं; oMd^{2} *om* पत्रं; Jm Jo^{1} Kt^{2} La^{3} Lo^{2} GMd^{1} oMd^{2} Tj^{1} MTr^{3} *Mandlik Jha KSS Dave* पत्र; GMd^{1} TMd^{3} GMy पर्णं; TMd^{4} तत्र; Bo BCa Ho Jo^{2} wKt^{1} La^{2} Lo^{1} Lo^{3} NNg sOx^{1} Ox^{2} Ox^{3} Pu^{2} Pu^{3} Pu^{4} sPu^{6} Pu^{9} Pu^{10} Tr^{2} *Jolly* तृणानि च; Lo^{2} GMd^{1} *Lakṣ* तृणादि वा; *Jha Dave* तृणादि च; Hy Jm Jo^{1} Kt^{2} La^{2} La^{3} Lo^{5} oMd^{2} Tj^{1} Tj^{2} MTr^{3} *Mandlik KSS* तृणादिना; GMy has only तृ — c) sOx^{1} प्रियतो; wKt^{1} प्रणतो; Tr^{1} यत्नतो; Be^{3} वासं — d) MTr^{3} संगीताङ्गो; NPu^{1} °गुण्ठिनः; GMd^{1} TMd^{3} TMd^{4} GMy Tr^{1} MTr^{3} *Dev* °कुण्ठितः; GMd^{5} °कुण्ठिकः

50.* Omitted in Lo^{4} Lo^{5} Ox^{3} Pu^{10}; pāda-b omitted in Tr^{1}. Cited by *Dev* 2.236; *Mādh* 1.210 — a) Tj^{1} मूत्रोचारणमुत्सर्गं; Pu^{2} मूत्रोद्वार°; TMd^{4} मूत्रोत्सार°; Bo °समुच्छिष्टं; Be^{3} °मुत्सर्गां; wKt^{1} °मुत्सर्गे; GMd^{1} °मुत्सर्गः — c) Pu^{4} *om* दक्षिणाभिमुखो — d) Be^{3} La^{1} GMd^{1} उभे संध्ये यथा दिवा; *Dev* °योस्तु; oOr दिवा यथा; Pu^{3} तथा

51.* *Me* says that some omit this verse: केचिदिदं श्लोकमस्मिनध्याये नाधीयन्ते. Cited by *Viś* 1.133; *Apa* 34; *Dev* 2.236; *Mādh* 1.211 — a) BKt^{5} छायामन्ध°; oOr °न्धकारेण [*om* वा]; Kt^{2} *om* वा; Pu^{2} Pu^{4} च — b) TMd^{3} GMy वा स्मृतः; GMd^{5} NNg *Viś* वा सदा — c) GMy यथासुखं यथा कुर्यात्; TMd^{3} यथासुखं प्रकुर्वीत; BCa *om* यथासुखमुखः; Pu^{10} °सुखंमुखः — d) Be^{1} Be^{3} Bo Ho Jm Jo^{2} wKt^{1} Kt^{2} BKt^{5} wKt^{6} La^{1} La^{2} Lo^{3} Lo^{1} Lo^{2} Lo^{3} Lo^{4} Lo^{5} GMd^{1} oMd^{2} oOr Ox^{2} Ox^{3} NPu^{1} Pu^{8} Tj^{1} Tj^{2} Tr^{1} Tr^{2} Wa *VaDh* 6.13 *Mandlik Jha KSS Dave* प्राणबा°; Pu^{10} प्राप्तबा°; Be^{1} Be^{3} Bo Ho La^{1} La^{2} Lo^{3} TMd^{4} GMd^{5} NPu^{1} Pu^{5} Pu^{7} Pu^{9} Tj^{1} Tj^{2} Tr^{1} Tr^{2} *Mandlik* °बाधा°; Wa °बोध°; Lo^{4} [*Jolly* M] वा

प्रत्यग्निं प्रतिसूर्यं च प्रतिसोमोदकद्विजम् ।
प्रतिगु प्रतिवातं च प्रज्ञा नश्यति मेहतः ॥५२॥
नाग्निं मुखेनोपधमेन्नग्नां नेक्षेत च स्त्रियम् ।
नामेध्यं प्रक्षिपेदग्नौ न च पादौ प्रतापयेत् ॥५३॥
अधस्तान्नोपदध्याच्च न चैनमभिलङ्घयेत् ।
न चैनं पादतः कुर्यान्न प्राणाबाधमाचरेत् ॥५४॥
नाश्नीयात्संधिवेलायां न गच्छेन्नापि संविशेत् ।
न चैव प्रलिखेद्भूमिं नात्मनोऽपहरेत् स्रजम् ॥५५॥
नाप्सु मूत्रं पुरीषं वा ष्ठीवनं वा समुत्सृजेत् ।
अमेध्यलिप्तमन्यद्वा लोहितं वा विषाणि वा ॥५६॥

52.* Omitted in La^{2} Ox^{3} Pu^{2} Pu^{10}; placed after 48 in Lo^{1} Lo^{4} Lo^{5} BKt^{5} wKt^{6} Pu^{4} *Jha* possibly also by *Me*; pādas a-b omitted in Bo — a) Be^{1} BBe^{2} Ho Jm Jo^{1} Kt^{2} wKt^{3} BKt^{5} wKt^{6} La^{1} Lo^{1} Lo^{2} Lo^{4} Lo^{5} GMd^{1} TMd^{3} TMd^{4} GMd^{5} GMy oOr sOx^{1} Ox^{2} NPu^{1} Pu^{5} sPu^{6} Pu^{7} Pu^{8} Pu^{9} Tj^{1} Tj^{2} Tr^{1} Tr^{2} MTr^{4} प्रत्यग्निं; Be^{3} °सूर्यश्च; Lo^{5} oMd^{2} NNg वा — b) TMd^{4} प्रतिवायादकं द्वि°; Ho Lo^{1} TMd^{3} sOx^{1} Pu^{5} Pu^{7} Pu^{8} Pu^{9} Tr^{1} Tr^{2} MTr^{4} MTr^{6} [*Jolly* G N] °सोमोदकं द्वि°; GMy °सोमोकथं द्वि°; GMd^{1} TMd^{4} GMy Pu^{5} Pu^{7} Pu^{9} MTr^{4} MTr^{6} [*Jolly* G N] °द्विजः; TMd^{3} द्विजाः; Lo^{4} °द्विजां; BBe^{2} Hy Jm Jo^{1} Jo^{2} wKt^{1} Kt^{2} wKt^{3} NKt^{4} Lo^{3} oMd^{2} oOr sPu^{6} Tj^{1} *Mandlik KSS Dave* [*Jolly* R] °द्विजान्; wKt^{6} °द्विजे; Ho °ध्वजं — c) Be^{3} प्रतिवातं च संध्यां च; Pu^{4} *om* प्रतिगु; BKt^{5} La^{1} Lo^{1} Lo^{4} Tr^{2} [*Jolly* M$^{1-2-5-8-9}$] प्रतिगुं; Be^{1} BBe^{2} BCa Ho Hy Jm Jo^{1} Jo^{2} wKt^{1} Kt^{2} wKt^{3} Lo^{2} Lo^{3} Lo^{5} GMd^{1} oMd^{2} TMd^{3} TMd^{4} GMd^{5} GMy oOr sOx^{1} NPu^{1} Pu^{8} Tj^{2} Tr^{1} MTr^{3} MTr^{4} MTr^{6} [*Jolly* M^{4} R Nd] *Mandlik KSS Dave* प्रतिगां; sPu^{6} Tj^{1} प्रतिगुरुं [sPu^{6} *cor to* प्रतिगां]; Kt^{2} प्रतियातं; Jo^{2} Wa प्रतिवाचं; NKt^{4} प्रतिसंथं; Lo^{4} GMd^{1} TMd^{4} GMy sPu^{6} [*but cor*] Tr^{1} MTr^{4} [*Jolly* Nd M$^{1-2-8-9}$] प्रतिसंध्यं [given as pāṭha by *Me Nā* and *Ku*, although rejected by *Me*; cf. VaDh 6.11]; TMd^{3} GMd^{5} oOr MTr^{6} प्रतिसंध्यां; oMd^{2} वा — d) BKt^{5} wKt^{6} प्रतिज्ञा

53. Cited by *Vij* 1.137; *Apa* 181 — a) TMd^{3} GMy अग्निं; Pu^{9} मुखेनाप° — b) sOx^{1} sPu^{6} °धमेनग्नां; Pu^{9} °न्नग्नीं; GMd^{1} TMd^{3} GMy वीक्षेत; GMd^{5} नेक्षेत्परस्त्रियं; oOr Pu^{8} स्त्रियां — c) wKt^{6} नमेध्यं; Ox^{3} चामेध्यं; Lo^{1} च क्षिपेद° — d) Lo^{4} नवपादौ; Tj^{1} न चाद्यादौ; wKt^{1} oOr प्रदापयेत्; Jo^{1} प्रदातापयेत्; BBe^{2} प्रमापयेत्; Pu^{10} प्रतीपयेत्

54. Pādas a-b and c-d transposed in MTr^{3}. Cited by *Vij* 1.137; *Apa* 181; *Lakṣ* 2.407 — a) Lo^{2} °न्नेपदध्याच्च; NKt^{4} °दध्यात्तु — b) Lo^{4} Ox^{3} [*Jolly* M] चैवम°; La^{1} Lo^{3} TMd^{3} GMd^{5} GMy oOr Tj^{1} Tr^{1} MTr^{3} MTr^{6} °मतिलङ्घयेत्; Wa °मपिलङ्घयेत्; Bo BKt^{5} wKt^{6} Lo^{2} sOx^{1} Pu^{3} sPu^{6} *Nā* °मवलङ्घयेत् — c) Tj^{1} पदतः; Lo^{2} पादता; *Lakṣ* वादतः — d) Lo^{1} Tj^{1} प्राणबाधमा°; wKt^{1} प्राणवधमा°; Tj^{2} प्राणिबाधमा°; Pu^{5} Pu^{7} Pu^{9} [*Jolly* G] *Vij* [vl as in ed] प्राणिवधमा°; Jo^{2} प्राणिबधमा°; Tr^{2} °बाधं समाचरेत्

55. Pāda-a cited by *Vij* 3.289 — a) Be^{3} °त्संध्यवे°; GMd^{5} Tr^{1} °वेळायां — b) NNg गच्छेन्न च संवि°; TMd^{4} गच्छेत न संवशेत्; TMd^{3} GMy °न्नाभिसंविशेत्; Tr^{1} °न्नोपसंविशेत्; BKt^{5} wKt^{6} संवसेत् — c) NKt^{4} न च प्रतिलि°; Pu^{2} Pu^{4} नैव प्रलि°; Be^{1} oMd^{2} Tj^{1} चैवं; Be^{1} Jo^{2} Lo^{3} TMd^{3} GMd^{5} GMy Tj^{1} Tr^{1} MTr^{4} MTr^{6} [*Jolly* R] विलिखे°; BKt^{5} प्रलिपे°; Be^{3} °खेद्भूमौ — d) Pu^{2} Pu^{4} °द्भूमिमिमान्ममोपहरेत्; NKt^{4} sOx^{1} sPu^{6} नात्मनः प्रहरेत्; BKt^{5} wKt^{6} °पसृजेत्; GMd^{1} हि हरेत्; TMd^{3} GMd^{5} GMy Tr^{1} °भिहरेत्; Pu^{5} Pu^{9} न हरेत्; Ox^{3} Pu^{10} स्रजः; TMd^{3} सृजं; BBe^{2} सूयं; TMd^{4} प्रजां

56. a) wKt^{1} Lo^{4} TMd^{3} TMd^{4} Tr^{1} मूत्र — b) Pu^{4} *om* ष्ठीवनं वा; GMd^{1} TMd^{3} निष्ठिवं वा; GMy

नैकः स्वप्याच्छून्यगृहे न श्रेयांसं प्रबोधयेत् ।
नोदक्ययाभिभाषेत यज्ञं गच्छेन्न चावृतः ॥५७॥
अग्न्यगारे गवां गोष्टे ब्राह्मणानां च संनिधौ ।
स्वाध्याये भोजने चैव दक्षिणं पाणिमुद्धरेत् ॥५८॥
न वारयेद्गां धयन्तीं न चाचक्षीत कस्यचित् ।
न दिवीन्द्रायुधं दृष्ट्वा कस्यचिद्दर्शयेद्बुधः ॥५९॥

तिष्ठवं वा; Tr[2] *om* वा — c) Tr[1] नामेध्य°; Pu[4] अमेधा°; Pu[10] अमेध्या°; GMd[5] °लिप्तमन्नं वा — d) TMd[3] GMy लोहितं विपमाणि वा [TMd[3] विषयाणि]; La[1] लौहितं; Lo[1] Pu[2] Pu[3] Pu[4] Pu[10] [*Jolly* M[1-2-8]] विषाणि च

57.* Cited by *Lakṣ* 2.405; pāda-b cited by *Vij* 1.136 — a) Jo[2] Lo[3] Lo[4] Lo[5] NPu[1] Pu[2] Pu[4] Pu[10] [*Jolly* M R] *Jolly Dave Jha* नैकः शून्यगृहे स्वप्यान्; Wa नैकः शून्ये गृहे स्वप्यान्; TMd[4] नैकश्शूद्रगृहान्स्वप्यं; La[1] नैकः शून्यगृहे सुप्यात्; NNg नैकः शून्यगृहे स्वप्येन्; Ox[3] नैकः शून्यगृहे [broken] न्; TMd[3] नैव; Be[1] oOr sOx[1] Pu[5] Pu[9] स्वप्यात्शून्य°; Tr[2] स्वस्यात्शून्य°; Bo Ho wKt[1] GMd[1] *Vij Mandlik KSS* सुप्याच्छून्य°; Lo[1] सुप्यात्शून्य°; Tj[2] सुप्येच्छून्य°; Hy Jm Jo[1] Kt[2] oMd[2] TMd[3] GMd[5] GMy Tr[1] स्वपेच्छून्य°; BCa MTr[3] स्वपेत्शून्य°; Be[1] BBe[2] Hy Jm Kt[2] wKt[3] oMd[2] sOx[1] Ox[2] Pu[3] sPu[6] Tj[2] MTr[3] MTr[4] *Mandlik KSS* °गेहे — b) BCa Tr[2] *Vij Mandlik KSS* श्रेयांसं न; Be[1] BBe[2] Be[3] Ho Hy Jm Jo[1] wKt[1] Kt[2] wKt[3] NKt[4] La[1] Lo[1] oMd[2] oOr Ox[2] Pu[5] Pu[7] Pu[9] Tj[1] Tj[2] MTr[3] [*Jolly* M[3-4] G] *Rn Nā* [pāṭha] *Rc Lakṣ* शयानं न; Jo[2] BKt[5] wKt[6] Lo[3] Lo[4] Lo[5] GMd[1] TMd[4] NNg sOx[1] NPu[1] Pu[2] Pu[4] sPu[6] Wa [*Jolly* Nd] *YDh* 1.138 न शयानं; Bo न श्रेयांसि — c) Be[3] Bo NKt[4] La[1] oOr sOx[1] sPu[6] नोदक्यामभिभाषेत [La[1] °भिसंभाषेत]; GMy Pu[5] Pu[7] Pu[9] नोदक्याया°; oOr °क्यानिभा°; TMd[4] °क्ययानिभा° — d) TMd[3] GMd[5] GMy Tr[1] MTr[4] MTr[6] न यज्ञमव्रतो व्रजेत्; TMd[4] गच्छं न; Jo[1] °न्नाचावृतः; Ox[3] °न्नरावृतः; Ho Lo[4] Lo[5] वावृतः

Additional verse in GMd[1] TMd[3] TMd[4] GMd[5] Tr[1] MTr[4] MTr[6]; pādas a-b in NPu[1] [cf. GDh 9.53–5]:

नमस्कर्तुं व्रजेत्कामं दिदृक्षुर्यज्ञकर्म वा ।
कुलात्कुलं रहस्यार्थी संचरेन्नानिमित्ततः ॥

a) GMd[5] Tr[1] प्रयोगार्थी व्रजे°; TMd[4] वसेत्कामं — b) TMd[4] च — c) TMd[3] MTr[6] °त्कुलं च धमार्थी; GMd[1] रहस्यमतिसंच° — d) MTr[4] °न्नामनिमित्ततः

Additonal verse in Pu[1]; first verse in Be[3] [after 58] *Mandlik* [ट, ड, ढ] *KSS*:

एकः स्वादु न भुञ्जीत स्वार्थमेको न चिन्तयेत् ।
एको न गच्छेदध्वानं नैकः सुप्तेपु जागृयात् ॥१॥
शय्यासने पादुके च दन्तधावनमेव वा ।
पालाषं वर्जयेन्नित्यं भूतिकामपरो द्विजः ॥२॥

1. a-b) NPu[1] भुञ्जीयादेकः स्वार्थं न — b) Be[3] एक स्वार्थान्न विश्वसे — c) NPu[1] नैको हि गच्छेद°

58. a) Be[3] Ho Jo[1] wKt[1] Kt[2] wKt[3] NKt[4] TMd[3] GMy Lo[1] Lo[4] sOx[1] Ox[3] sPu[6] Pu[9] Tj[1] Tj[2] *Rn Jolly* अग्न्यागारे; oOr अग्न्यकारे — b) sOx[1] sPu[6] Tj[1] देवब्राह्मणसंनिधौ; NKt[4] ब्रह्म°; wKt[6] *om* च; GMd[5] तु; GMd[1] च सञ्चये — c) Pu[5] Pu[7] Pu[9] स्वाध्याय; Pu[5] भाजने; Tr[2] भोजनं — d) wKt[6] Tr[2] दक्षिणां; Pu[2] Pu[4] दक्षिपाणि°; GMd[1] TMd[3] GMy Tr[1] MTr[4] MTr[6] बाहुमु°; Tj[1] °द्धरत्; oOr °द्धरे

59. a) Pu[2] Pu[4] न वारयेद्वयन्तं गां; Lo[3] न गां वारयेद्धयन्तीं; Tr[1] नावार°; La[1] वारयेत गां; BBe[2] Jo[2] oOr °येद्धावयन्तीं गां; GMd[1] धायन्तीं; NKt[4] धवन्तीं; Bo वयन्तीं — b) Lo[1] Lo[4] Pu[2] Tj[1] वाचक्षीत; Bo चावक्षीत; TMd[3] चाचक्षेत — c) BKt[5] wKt[6] न तदिन्द्रा°; Lo[1] *cor to* दिवेन्द्रा°; TMd[3] दिविह्लियुधं; MTr[3]

नाधार्मिके वसेद्ग्रामे न व्याधिबहुले भृशम् ।
नैकः प्रपद्येताध्वानं न चिरं पर्वते वसेत् ॥६०॥
न शूद्रराज्ये निवसेन्नाधार्मिकजनावृते ।
न पाषण्डिजनाक्रान्ते नोपसृष्टेऽन्त्यजैर्नृभिः ॥६१॥
न भुञ्जीतोद्धृतस्नेहं नातिसौहित्यमाचरेत् ।
नातिप्रगे नातिसायं न सायं प्रातराशितः ॥६२॥
न कुर्वीत वृथा चेष्टां न वार्यञ्जलिना पिबेत् ।
नोत्सङ्गे भक्षयेद्भक्ष्यान्न जातु स्यात्कुतूहली ॥६३॥
न नृत्येदथ वा गायेन्न वादित्राणि वादयेत् ।
नास्फोटयेन्न च क्ष्वेडेन्न च रक्तो विरावयेत् ॥६४॥

°न्द्रायुषं — d) BBe^{2} wKt^{3} Lo^{1} oOr दर्शयेत्कस्यचिद्बुधः; GMd^{1} °येत्पुनः; MTr^{4} MTr^{6} °येत्तदा; Jm °येत्ततः

60. Pādas c-d omitted in GMd^{1}; pāda-d omitted in oMd^{2} — a) Bo NKt^{4} Lo^{1} TMd^{4} नाधर्मिके; Be^{1} नाधमिके; Kt^{2} नधार्मिके; BBe^{2} BKt^{5} नाधार्मिको — b) Tj^{1} व्याधिर्बहुलं; GMd^{5} Tr^{1} °बहुळे; GMd^{1} °बहुले तथा; GMd^{5} भृतं — c) Be^{3} Ho TMd^{3} GMy Pu^{5} Pu^{7} Pu^{9} प्रपद्येदध्वानं; wKt^{6} प्रपद्यताध्वानं; MTr^{6} प्रपद्येताटवं; Wa प्रपाद्यधाताध्वानं — d) Tr^{2} वशेत्

61.* *ma sh* in La^{1}; illegible in GMd^{1}; pādas a-c omitted in oMd^{2}; pādas c-d in Lo^{4}. Cited by *Lakṣ* 2.338; *Dev* 1.20 — a) wKt^{6} Pu^{5} °राजे; BKt^{5} विवसे°; wKt^{6} विरमे° — b) wKt^{3} °धार्मिका°; TMd^{4} °धर्मिक°; sOx^{1} sPu^{6} [*cor to*] °जनाकुले — c) Ho wKt^{3} TMd^{3} GMy oOr Tj^{2} MTr^{6} *Lakṣ* पापण्ड°; Be^{1} पापाण्ड°; sOx^{1} sPu^{6} पापाण्डि°; Jo^{2} wKt^{1} BKt^{5} wKt^{6} Lo^{1} Pu^{3} Tj^{1} पाखण्डि°; Wa °ण्डिनोजनाक्राते; BCa Hy Jm Jo^{1} wKt^{1} Kt^{2} NKt^{4} Lo^{1} Lo^{5} TMd^{3} GMy Tj^{2} Tr^{1} [*Jolly* Nd] *Mandlik Jha KSS Dave* °गणाक्रान्ते; Ox^{3} °तनाक्रान्ते; Be^{3} °गणाकीर्णे; Ho Pu^{2} Pu^{4} °जनाकीर्णे; *Dev* °द्विजाक्रान्ते — d) BKt^{5} नोपासृष्टे; Hy नापसृष्टे; Tr^{2} नोसृष्टे; Tj^{1} नोपमृष्टे; wKt^{3} नोपसृते; Ox^{3} Pu^{10} °न्त्यजेन तु; BKt^{5} wKt^{6} °जैर्नृपैः; GMd^{5} Tr^{1} °जैर्नरैः; oOr °जैर्वृतः — GMd^{5} MTr^{4} MTr^{6} insert here verse79 (MTr^{4} MTr^{6} give it also at its proper place).

62. Omitted in TMd^{4}. Pāda-c cited by *Vij* 3.289— a) La^{1} °तोद्धृतं स्नेहं; Bo °तोद्धृतः स्तेनं; Pu^{2} Pu^{4} °तोवृतस्नेहं — b) wKt^{1} °सौहत्य° — c) Pu^{2} Pu^{4} नाविप्ररोभ्यतिसायं; Tj^{1} Tr^{1} नातिप्रसङ्गे; Pu^{5} Pu^{7} Pu^{9} Tj^{2} MTr^{4} [*Jolly* G] नातिप्रातर्नाति°; Lo^{4} नातिसाया — d) Tr^{2} नातिमध्यंदिने स्थिते; Be^{3} नासायं; NKt^{4} नाशायं; Lo^{4} प्रातराशिता; Pu^{2} Pu^{4} प्रातराशिनः

63. Omitted in TMd^{4}. Cited by *Apa* 182 — a) Pu^{2} Pu^{4} वृथावत्यं; Tr^{2} चेष्टं; TMd^{3} GMy चेष्टा — c) Ho नोत्सङ्गेन; Hy नात्सङ्गे; wKt^{1} नोत्सृष्टं; Be^{1} Lo^{1} Ox^{2} sPu^{6} Pu^{9} Tr^{2} [*Jolly* R Nd] *Apa* °द्भक्ष्यं न; BBe^{2} द्भक्ष्यन्न; Ox^{3} *Jolly* °द्भक्षान्न; Bo wKt^{1} oOr sOx^{1} Pu^{5} Pu^{7} Tj^{1} [*Jolly* G] °द्भक्षं न — d) Lo^{1} °त्कुतुहली; GMd^{5} Tr^{2} °त्कुतूहलं

64. Cited by *Apa* 182; *Lakṣ* 2.400 — a) Bo Lo^{4} Lo^{5} oMd^{2} NNg sOx^{1} Ox^{2} Ox^{3} Pu^{2} Pu^{4} sPu^{6} Pu^{10} *Apa Dave Jha* न नृत्येन्नैव गायेच्च न; *Jolly* न नृत्येन्नैव च गायेन्न; TMd^{4} न नृत्येन्नापि गायेच्च न; Jo^{2} न नृत्येच्चैव गायेच्च न; Be^{3} न नृत्येन्न च वा गायेन्न; wKt^{3} न नृत्यन्न च गायेच्च न; Tr^{2} न नत्यन्नेत गावेच्च न; oOr न नृत्येन्न च गायेत न; BBe^{2} न नृत्येन्न गायेन्न — c) TMd^{4} न स्फोट°; Tr^{2} न वास्फोट°; Hy नास्थोट°; Tj^{1} नास्फाडये°; *Lakṣ* न चास्फोटेन्न वा; *Apa* °टयेन्न क्ष्वेडेच्च न; *Apa* [vl] °टयेन्न चाक्ष्वेडेन्न; BKt^{5} *om* च; Ho वा क्ष्येडे°; Be^{3} NPu^{1} क्रीडे°; NKt^{4} क्षेडे°; Tr^{1} क्ष्वेळे° — d) TMd^{4} क्ष्वेडेत्स्वं रक्तं विनवारयेत्; GMd^{5} Tr^{1} MTr^{4} MTr^{6} क्ष्वेडेत्संरक्तोपि न वारयेत् [Tr^{1} धारयेत्; MTr^{6} रावयेत्]; Ho Lo^{2} NPu^{1} *Apa* रक्तं; Pu^{2} रक्तौ; Tj^{1} रक्ते; *Nd* [pāṭha] रक्तोपिरागयेत् [acc. to Jolly °रामयेत्]; *Nd* रक्तोपिरावयेत्; sOx^{1} [*but*

न पादौ धावयेत्कांस्ये कदाचिदपि भाजने ।
न भिन्नभाण्डे भुञ्जीत न भावप्रतिदूषिते ॥६५॥
उपानहौ च वासश्च धृतमन्यैर्न धारयेत् ।
उपवीतमलंकारं स्रजं करकमेव च ॥६६॥
नाविनीतैर्व्रजेद्धुर्यैर्न च क्षुद्व्याधिपीडितैः ।
न भिन्नशृङ्गाक्षिखुरैर्न बालधिविरूपितैः ॥६७॥
विनीतैस्तु व्रजेन्नित्यमाशुगैर्लक्षणान्वितैः ।
वर्णरूपोपसंपन्नैः प्रतोदेनातुदन् भृशम् ॥६८॥
बालातपः प्रेतधूमो वर्ज्यं भिन्नं तथासनम् ।
न छिन्द्यान्नखरोमाणि दन्तैर्नोत्पाटयेन्नखान् ॥६९॥

mc] निवारक्षोनियेत्; sPu^{6} [*but cor*] निवारयेत्; NKt^{4} विरामयेत्; Tj^{1} विरेचयेत्; Lo^{2} विराजयेत्; Lo^{4} [*Jolly* M$^{3-4}$] विवारयेत्; Ox^{3} Pu^{10} [*Jolly* Me M^{4-8-9}] विरोधयेत्; [*Jolly* M^{1}] विरोधयन्; [*Jolly* M$^{2-5}$] विनारोधयेत्; [*Jolly* Gr] निवारयेत्; *ViDh* 71.57 *Apa* विरागयेत्

65. a) Tj^{1} न पापदौ; TMd^{3} नापादौ; Hy Kt^{2} धारये°; Lo^{3} °त्काम्ये; Tr^{1} °त्कास्येत् — b) Kt^{2} Lo^{1} [*but cor*] NPu^{1} MTr^{6} भोजने — c) GMy निभिन्न°; GMd^{5} भिक्षभाण्डे; oOr भिन्नपात्रे — d) BBe^{2} भव°; NNg °दूषितेः; Ox^{2} °दूपके; GMd^{5} °पूजिते

Additional verse in oOr:

एक एव यदा भुङ्क्ते विमले कांस्यभाजने ।
चत्वारि तस्य वर्धन्ते आयुः प्रज्ञा यशो बलम् ॥

66. Pādas a-b and c-d transposed in Jo^{2} Lo^{3} NNg Pu^{2} Wa; pādas c-d omitted in Pu^{4} — a) sOx^{1} sPu^{6} उपानहं; NNg उपानहा; oOr Pu^{4} *om* च; Pu^{2} वा; La^{1} यष्टिश्च; Be^{3} Tj^{1} वस्त्रं च — b) Kt^{2} भृतम°; Tr^{2} भृतमन्न धार°; MTr^{6} वारयेत्; NPu^{1} राधयेत् — d) Lo^{1} करकमेव *mc to* कमण्डलुमेव; Be^{3} NPu^{1} वा

67. Cited by *Apa* 173; *Lakṣ* 2.358 — a) TMd^{4} °तैर्व्रजैर्धु°; wKt^{1} Tj^{1} °जेद्धुर्येन; Pu^{5} Pu^{7} Pu^{9} °जेद्धुर्येर्न; Lo^{1} °जेद्धूर्तैर्न; Tj^{2} °जेद्धुर्तैर्न; NKt^{4} °जेद्र्येन — b) Tr^{1} *Apa* चक्षुर्व्याधि°; Pu^{5} Pu^{7} Pu^{9} चक्षु-व्याधि°; Lo^{5} व्यक्षुद्व्याधि°; NPu^{1} *om* च; Lo^{4} *ma* च; NPu^{1} क्षुधाव्याधि°; *Lakṣ* वालधिविरूपितैः — c) GMy निभिन्न°; Pu^{10} भिन्ना°; Be^{3} भिन्नाक्षिशृङ्गखु°; La^{1} Pu^{2} Pu^{4} °शृङ्गास्थिखु°; Lo^{1} °क्षुरैर्न — d) *Lakṣ* °रैर्न चक्षुर्व्याधिपीडितैः; BBe^{2} Lo^{4} °रैर्न च व्याधिविरूपितैः; Tj^{1} वाहनैर्न विरूपितैः; MTr^{3} *Apa* वाल°; Tr^{2} बल°; Pu^{7} Pu^{9} बार्लध्व°; Pu^{5} बालध्व°; Be^{1} बालधिरू°; Lo^{1} बालपुछैर्विरू°; wKt^{1} wKt^{6} बालाविधिरू°; TMd^{3} बालधिविधिरू°; oOr बालवयाधिरूपातितैः

68. a) Tj^{1} विनातैस्तु; Ho La^{1} Pu^{5} Pu^{7} Pu^{9} विनीतैश्च; Be^{3} Bo व्रजन्नि°; Wa व्रजैर्नि° — b) MTr^{4} MTr^{6} °मशुभैर्ल° — c) BKt^{5} वर्णारूपो°; sPu^{6} *cor to* कर्णरूपो°; oOr °रूपोपपन्नैः; Ho wKt^{1} °रूपोपपन्नैश्च — d) Be^{3} TMd^{3} प्रतोदेन तुदन्; BKt^{5} wKt^{6} Lo^{4} Ox^{3} Pu^{10} *Me Dave Jha* [*Jolly* M] प्रतोदेनाक्षिपन्; *Mr* प्रतोदेनार्दयन्; Tj^{1} भृशतं — here GMd^{5} inserts verse 4.140.

69. Cited by *Apa* 183; *Lakṣ* 2.401–2 — a) MTr^{6} पालातपं; wKt^{1} °तप; Lo^{1} °तपे; Be^{3} Lo^{4} [*cor to*] Lo^{5} TMd^{3} GMd^{5} GMy Tr^{1} *Apa* °तपं; Pu^{4} *om* प्रेत ... [69b] तथासनम्; sOx^{1} प्रेतप्रपो; wKt^{1} wKt^{3} °धूमौ; BBe^{2} Be^{3} Lo^{4} [*cor to*] Lo^{5} TMd^{3} GMd^{5} GMy oOr Tr^{1} MTr^{6} *Apa* °धूमं; Tj^{1} °धूम्रो; Lo^{1} °धूम्रौ — b) NKt^{4} La^{1} Lo^{2} वर्ज्यो; Pu^{2} वर्ज्य; Be^{1} Bo Ho Lo^{4} Tr^{2} वर्जं; wKt^{1} वर्ज्यौ; Tj^{1} वर्त्यं — c) Pu^{2} Pu^{4} Pu^{5} *om* न; Pu^{8} °न्नखेमाणि; Hy °लोमाणि; Jm Jo^{1} Kt^{2} BKt^{5} wKt^{6} La^{1} La^{2} Ox^{3} Pu^{3} Pu^{4} MTr^{3} Wa *Mandlik Jolly KSS* °लोमानि; Lo^{3} °लोमा

न मृल्लोष्टं विमृद्नीयान्न छिन्द्यात्करजैस्तृणम् ।
न कर्म निष्फलं कुर्यान्नायत्यामसुखोदयम् ॥७०॥
लोष्टमर्दी तृणच्छेदी नखखादी च यो नरः ।
स विनाशं व्रजत्याशु सूचकोऽशुचिरेव च ॥७१॥
न विगृह्य कथां कुर्याद्बहिर्माल्यं न धारयेत् ।
गवां च यानं पृष्ठेन सर्वथैव विगर्हितम् ॥७२॥
अद्वारेण च नातीयाद्ग्रामं वा वेश्म वावृतम् ।
रात्रौ च वृक्षमूलानि दूरतः परिवर्जयेत् ॥७३॥
नाक्षैः क्रीडेत्कदाचिच्च स्वयं नोपानहौ हरेत् ।
शयनस्थो न भुञ्जीत न पाणिस्थं न चासने ॥७४॥

Additional half-verse after pāda-b in La^1 Tr^2 *Mandlik* [ख, ग] *KSS:*
श्रीकामो वर्जयेन्नित्यं मृन्मये चैव भोजनम् ।

70.* Pādas c-d omitted in oOr, and pāda-d in MTr^4 [haplo]. Cited by *Apa* 183; *Lakṣ* 2.402 — a) Be^3 मृल्लोष्टान्हि मृद्नी°; GMd^1 TMd^3 TMd^4 GMd^5 GMy Tr^1 MTr^4 MTr^6 [*Jolly* Nd] मृल्लोष्टानि मृद्नीया°; Jo^1 Kt^2 Tr^2 *Mandlik Jha KSS Dave* च मृद्नीया°; *Lakṣ* विगृह्णीया°; Jm च गृह्णीया°; Hy चीमृद्नीया°; Kt^2 *Apa* न मृद्नीया° — b) GMy °रकैस्तृणं; Ho NNg MTr^{4}MTr^6 °स्तृणान् — c) Ho स्वकर्म; wKt^6 कर्मणि फलं; Lo^2 कर्मभिः फलं ; *Lakṣ* निष्फलं कर्म — d) *Lakṣ* कुर्यान्नाय आमसुखोदयम् [typo?]; TMd^3 GMd^5 GMy Tr^1 MTr^6 कुर्यादायत्याम°; Tj^1 कुर्यानापत्याम°; BBe^2 °न्नयत्याम°; Tr^2 °न्नाय-त्यम°; Kt^2 °न्नादत्याम°; wKt^6 °सुखोदरं

71. Omitted in oOr MTr^4. Cited by *Apa* 183, 253; *Lakṣ* 2.402 — a) *Lakṣ* लोष्टभक्षी; Pu^2 Pu^4 लोष्टतर्दो; Pu^8 लोष्टमृद्दि; Jo^1 लोष्टमदी — b) Pu^4 *om* नखखादी च यो; sOx^1 sPu^6 नखखादेच्च; Pu^9 यौ — c) Tj^1 व्रजन्त्याशु — d) Pu^4 *om* °शु सूचको [haplo]; Pu^5 Pu^7 Pu^9 शूचको; Tj^1 शुयुको च शुचि°

72. Omitted in oOr; pāda-a omitted in MTr^4. Pādas c-d cited by *Apa* 173 — a) GMy विग्रह; Hy Jm Jo^1 Kt^2 Pu^3 Tj^2 MTr^3 Wa *KSS* विगर्ह्य; GMd^5 विगर्ह; Jo^2 wKt^6 Lo^3 sOx^1 Ox^2 NPu^1 Pu^2 Pu^3 Pu^4 sPu^6 Pu^8 Tj^1 Wa [*Jolly* R] कथाः; Bo कथं; Hy कथी — b) Tj^1 °र्मालां — c) Pu^3 Pu^8 गवां पृष्ठेन यानं तु; Lo^3 यानं च गवां; Jo^2 यानं गवां च; La^1 *om* च; wKt^1 यामं; Ox^2 पृष्ठेन यानं; sOx^1 sPu^6 पृष्ठे हि; TMd^4 पृष्ठे वा — d) Ox^2 *Apa* सर्वदैव; Ho Jo^2 Lo^3 BKt^5 wKt^6 [*Jolly* R] विवर्जयेत्; Ho *om* विगर्हितं ... [73d] परिवर्जयेत्

73. Pādas c-d *ma sh* in Pu^9. Cited by *Lakṣ* 2.370; pādas a-b cited by *Apa* 184 — a) Lo^4 आद्वारेण; Ox^3 Pu^{10} आहारेण; Tj^2 अद्वारेणैव; Be^3 TMd^4 *om* च; BCa Lo^4 Lo^5 TMd^3 GMd^5 GMy oOr Tr^1 MTr^4 MTr^6 Wa तु; Tj^1 नानीया°; MTr^4 नाश्नीया°; Lo^4 Lo^5 मातीया°; *Lakṣ* जातीयान् ग्रामं — b) TMd^3 °द्रामा; Bo BCa wKt^1 Tj^1 *Lakṣ* चावृतं; *Apa* नावृतं; *Mandlik Jha Dave* वा वृतम् [separated without sandhi of अवृतम्]; Kt^2 वाकृतं; *Me Ku Go* support अवृतं — c) NKt^4 *om* च; TMd^3 GMy Tr^1 MTr^4 MTr^6 तु

74.* Pāda-d omitted in Tr^1 [haplo] — a) Tj^1 नाक्षैः क्रीडयन्न कदाचित्तु; TMd^3 नाक्षः; *Jha Dave* दीव्येत्कदा°; La^1 क्रीडेत कदाचित्; BBe^2 Bo Ho Hy Jm Jo^1 wKt^1 Kt^2 wKt^3 BKt^5 wKt^6 Lo^1 Lo^2 Lo^4 Lo^5 GMd^1 oMd^2 TMd^4 NNg sOx^1 Ox^2 Ox^3 NPu^1 Pu^2 sPu^6 Pu^{10} Tj^2 Tr^2 [*Jolly* M] *Mandlik Jha KSS Dave* °चित्तु — b) Hy नोपाहनौ — c) BBe^2 NKt^4 oOr Tj^2 शयान°; Lo^4 शयनार्थो; Lo^5 शयनर्थो — d) Bo पाणिस्थो; TMd^4 पाणिस्थ; Lo^4 Pu^{10} वासने — Pu^9 repeats here 73c-d.

सर्वं च तिलसंबद्धं नाद्यादस्तमयं प्रति ।
न च नग्नः शयीतेह न चोच्छिष्टः क्वचिद्व्रजेत् ॥७५॥
आर्द्रपादस्तु भुञ्जीत नार्द्रपादस्तु संविशेत् ।
आर्द्रपादस्तु भुञ्जानो दीर्घमायुरवाप्नुयात् ॥७६॥
अचक्षुर्विषयं दुर्गं न प्रपद्येत कर्हिचित् ।
न विण्मूत्रमुदीक्षेत न बाहुभ्यां नदीं तरेत् ॥७७॥
अधितिष्ठेन्न केशांस्तु न भस्मास्थिकपालिकाः ।
न कार्पासास्थि न तुषान् दीर्घमायुर्जिजीविषुः ॥७८॥
न संवसेच्च पतितैर्न चाण्डालैर्न पुल्कसैः ।
न मूर्खैर्नावलिप्तैश्च नान्त्यैर्नान्त्यावसायिभिः ॥७९॥

75.* Omitted in Tr¹ — a) La¹ [*Jolly* N Nd] *ViDh* 68.29 °संबन्धं; GMd⁵ °संमिश्रं — b) NKt⁴ Tj¹ °स्तमनं प्रति; Be¹ BBe² Bo BCa Ho Hy Jm Jo¹ Jo² wKt¹ Kt² wKt³ La¹ Lo¹ Lo³ oMd² Pu⁸ Tj² MTr³ *Mandlik Jha KSS Dave* °स्तमिते रवौ; Be³ °स्तं गते रवौ; Lo⁴ Lo⁵ °स्तमयं रवौ — d) La¹ नोच्छिष्टश्च क्वचिद्व्रजेत्; Bo चोच्छिष्टं; Lo¹ चोच्छिष्ट; Lo⁴ वोच्छिष्टः; NKt⁴ GMd¹ TMd³ TMd⁴ GMd⁵ GMy MTr⁴ [*Jolly* Gr] °ष्टः कथंचन; oOr °ष्टः कदाचन

76. Pādas a-b *ma* in Lo⁴; pāda-a omitted in Tr¹ — a) wKt¹ अर्द्र°; TMd⁴ अर्ध° — b) Be¹ Be³ wKt¹ TMd³ GMd⁵ GMy Tj¹ Tr¹ [*Jolly* Gr] संविशेन्न कदाचन; Ox² Tr² न शयीत कदाचन; GMd¹ संविशेत कदाचन; TMd⁴ नार्ध° — c) TMd⁴ नार्ध°; NNg Pu² Pu⁴ °पादो हि — d) Hy दीर्घंश्चायु°; Be¹ Be³ °मायुमवा°; Lo⁴ Lo⁵ °मायुषमाप्नुयात्

77. Omitted in Pu⁵ — a) Ho दुर्गां; Jm¹ वर्गं — a-b) GMy अचक्षुर्विषयस्यात्रं प्रपद्येतस्य कर्हिचित् — b) Tj¹ प्रपद्येम — c) Lo³ विण्मूत्रे न परीक्षेत; Jo² न विण्मूत्रे परीक्षेत; Ox² Wa न विण्मूत्रे निरीक्षेत — d) Be³ wKt³ बाहुभ्यां न नदीं; wKt⁶ नवाकुर्यान्नदीं; Jo¹ बाहुभ्यामुदीरयेत्; Hy नदी

78. Cited by *Apa* 183 — a) Ox² नाधितिष्ठेन; GMy तदितिष्ठेन; TMd³ GMy *Apa* केशांश्च — b) Ho भस्मनकपालिकान्; Pu⁸ °स्थिनकपा°; La¹ °कपालिनः; NPu¹ °कपालिकां; Lo² Lo⁴ GMd¹ Ox³ °कपालिकः; TMd⁴ °कपालिका; MTr⁶ °कपालिकान् — c) Be¹ Be³ Ho wKt³ wKt⁶ Lo¹ Pu⁸ Tr² कार्पासास्थितुषांगारान् [all except Ho *om* न; Be¹ कर्पा°; Ho न कर्पा°]; Tj¹ कणिपास्थितुषागारान् [*om* न]; NKt⁴ BKt⁵ Lo⁴ NNg Ox³ Pu⁷ Pu¹⁰ *Apa* [vl]कर्पा°; TMd⁴ °सास्थे; TMd³ तुषा; TMd⁴ तुर्षा — d) Lo¹ दीघायुश्च जिजी°; Be¹ °मायुजिजीविषु; Ho °मायुष्यजीविषु

79. Cited by *Apa* 182 — a) Jo² wKt⁶ Lo⁴ Ox³ NPu¹ Pu¹⁰ Tj¹ [*Jolly* M] संवसेत्तु; oOr संवसेत; Lo³ NNg Pu³ Pu⁵ Pu⁷ Pu⁹ [*Jolly* G] संविशेच्च; Ho TMd⁴ [*Jolly* R] संविशेत्तु; Wa *Apa* संविशेत — b) BKt⁵ wKt⁶ Lo³ Lo⁴ TMd⁴ GMd⁵ NNg sOx¹ sPu⁶ Ox³ Tr¹ MTr⁶ *Apa* चण्डा°; TMd³ GMy चण्डालैश्च पुल्कसैः; Kt² पुल्कशैः; Ho wKt¹ wKt⁶ Pu⁵ Pu⁷ Pu⁹ [*Jolly* G M³] पुष्कसैः; BBe² Lo⁴ oOr पुक्कसैः [see 10.18b note] — c) Bo NKt⁴ मूखैं°; Be³ Ho La¹ Pu² Pu⁴ Pu⁵ Pu⁷ मूर्षैं°; Pu⁹ मूर्षे°; wKt³ °र्नविलिप्तै°; Pu² Pu⁴ °र्वाविलिप्तै°; Tr² °र्नकवलिप्तै° — d) GMy नावन्नान्तावसायिभिः°; wKt³ नाह्यैर्ना°; Pu² Pu⁴ नान्त्यैर्नाव्याव°; Be¹ नान्त्यैर्नान्त्यव°; NKt⁴ GMd¹ GMy NNg Tr¹ नान्त्यैर्नान्ताव°

Additional verse in NPu¹ *Mandlik* [ट] *KSS:*

न कृतघ्नैरनुद्युक्तैर्न महापातकान्वितैः ।
न दस्युभिर्नाशुचिभिर्नायत्नैश्च कदाचन ।

d) *Mandlik KSS* °भिर्नामित्रैश्च

न शूद्राय मतिं दद्यान्नोच्छिष्टं न हविष्कृतम् ।
न चास्योपदिशेद्धर्मं न चास्य व्रतमादिशेत् ॥८०॥
यो ह्यस्य धर्ममाचष्टे यश्चैवादिशति व्रतम् ।
सोऽसंवृतं नाम तमः सह तेनैव मज्जति ॥८१॥
न संहताभ्यां पाणिभ्यां कण्डूयेतात्मनः शिरः ।
न स्पृशेच्चैतदुच्छिष्टो न च स्नायाद्विना ततः ॥८२॥
केशग्रहान् प्रहारांश्च शिरस्येतान्विवर्जयेत् ।
शिरःस्नातस्तु तैलेन नाङ्गं किंचिदपि स्पृशेत् ॥८३॥
न राज्ञः प्रतिगृह्णीयादराजन्यप्रसूतितः ।
सूनाचक्रध्वजवतां वेशेनैव च जीवताम् ॥८४॥

80. Pādas c-d omitted by Pu^{2} Pu^{4}. Cited by *Apa* 1090; *Lakṣ* 2.380; pādas a-b cited by *Apa* 187, 220; pādas c-d by *Vij* 3.262 — a) Pu^{4} मतं; Pu^{2} मातं — b) Lo^{4} Lo^{5} °न्नोक्षिप्तं; wKt^{1} नाहवि°; Lo^{4} Lo^{5} बहिष्कृतं; Tj^{1} नविःकृता; TMd^{4} °कृते — c) Tj^{2} न चापदिशे°; La^{1} Lo^{4} Lo^{5} [*Jolly* M^{3-4-5}] वास्यो°; Bo °द्धर्म्यं; *Apa* °द्धर्मान् — d) *Lakṣ* चान्यव्रत°; NPu^{1} व्रतिमा°; BKt^{5} wKt^{6} धर्ममादि°; *Vij* °माचरेत्; Bo °माचिरेत्; wKt^{6} °माविशेत्

Additional half-verse in Be^{3} Lo^{1} *Mandlik* [ञ]:

अन्तरा ब्राह्मणं कृत्वा प्रायश्चित्तं समादिशेत् ।

81. Cited by *Apa* 220; *Lakṣ* 2.380 — a) Pu^{4} *om* आचष्टे यश्चैवादिश°; Tr^{2} योस्य धर्मं समाचष्टे; oOr यो हि धर्मस्यमाचष्टे; La^{1} यो ह्यस्याद्दिशेद्धमं; Lo^{4} योस्य धर्म° — b) La^{1} यश्चास्य व्रतमादिशेत्; Bo MTr^{4} यच्चैवा°; Lo^{3} [*Jolly* R] यस्यैवादिशति; Be^{3} Tr^{1} यश्चैवदिशति; TMd^{3} GMy यश्चैवंदिशति; GMd^{1} यश्चोपदिशति; BKt^{5} °दिश्यति — c) Tj^{2} सहस्रसंवृतं नामं (*om* तमः); oOr सो ह्यसंवृतं; Ho Ox^{3} सोसंव्रतं; Pu^{2} असंवृतं [*om* सो]; Pu^{4} आसंवृतं [*om* सो]; Ox^{2} °वृतं न नरकं; BKt^{5} wKt^{6} ततः — d) La^{1} NNg Pu^{2} Pu^{4} तेनैव सह मज्जति; GMd^{1} सह तेनावगच्छति; Be^{3} Bo wKt^{3} NKt^{4} Lo^{1} Lo^{2} TMd^{3} TMd^{4} MTr^{6} *Lakṣ Apa* गच्छति

82. Cited by *Apa* 183 — a) GMd^{1} हस्ताभ्यां — b) Pu^{5} Pu^{7} Pu^{9} कण्डूतादात्म°; Be^{1} BBe^{2} Be^{3} Ho Hy Jm Jo^{1} La^{1} NKt^{4} Tj^{1} Tj^{2} [*Jolly* Ku] *Mandlik Jha KSS Dave* कण्डूयेदात्म° — c) NKt^{4} स्पृष्टे चैत°; *Apa* °च्चैनदुच्छि° — c-d) TMd^{3} स्पृशेच्चैतद्दृष्टो न सदा स्नाया° — d) NPu^{1} Pu^{2} Pu^{4} स्नायाद्विजानतः [Pu^{4} °द्विजोनतः]; Kt^{2} मतः

83.* Cited by *Apa* 183; *Lakṣ* 3.85; *Hem* 3/2.910 — a) Pu^{2} Pu^{4} कैश°; Be^{1} °ग्रहात्; GMd^{1} GMd^{5} GMy Tr^{1} MTr^{4} °ग्रह; TMd^{3} °ग्रहा; Tj^{1} °त्रहान्; Tj^{2} °ग्रहान्च शिर°; Kt^{2} प्रहाराश्च; Ox^{3} प्रहारश्च; La^{1} प्रकारांश्च; TMd^{3} GMy प्रचारांश्च; Tr^{2} प्रहारांश्चैव — b) Jo^{2} Lo^{3} Wa [*Jolly* R] सदा शिरसि वर्जयेत्; TMd^{3} GMd^{5} GMy sOx^{1} Pu^{5} sPu^{6} Pu^{7} Pu^{9} Tr^{1} *Apa* °स्येतानि वर्जयेत्; BKt^{5} wKt^{6} °तान्प्रवर्जयेत्; BCa [*but cor*] °तान्विसर्जयेत् — c) BCa Hy Jm Jo^{1} Kt^{2} wKt^{3} NKt^{4} La^{2} Lo^{1} Lo^{2} Lo^{4} Lo^{5} TMd^{4} oOr Ox^{2} Ox^{3} Pu^{3} Pu^{8} Tj^{2} MTr^{3} *Apa Mandlik Jolly Jha KSS Dave* °स्नातश्च; sOx^{1} sPu^{6} °स्नातोपि — d) wKt^{6} नाङ्गं; Tj^{1} नामं; sOx^{1} कंचिदपि; oOr कश्चिदपि; Be^{3} Bo BCa Ho Lo^{2} TMd^{3} GMy NNg Ox^{2} NPu^{1} Pu^{8} Tr^{1} Tr^{2} MTr^{4} MTr^{6} *Apa* किंचिदुपस्पृशेत्; NKt^{4} GMd^{5} किंचिदपस्पृशेत्; Ox^{3} किंचित्स्पृशेत्

84. Cited by *Lakṣ* 2.234 — b) Ho TMd^{3} GMy Tj^{1} Tj^{2} °ह्णीयात्र राजन्य°; La^{1} NPu^{1} Tj^{1} °राजन्यः; NKt^{4} °राजन्यात्प्रसू°; NKt^{4} NPu^{1} Tj^{1} °प्रसूतिनः; Lo^{4} Lo^{5} °प्रसूतिमः; Hy °प्रसूतिजः; BKt^{5} wKt^{6} °प्रतिसूतितः; Pu^{4} °प्रपातितः; Pu^{2} °प्रपातिनः — c) BBe^{2} Jo^{1} wKt^{1} BKt^{5} oMd^{2} शूना°; Tr^{2} °चक्री°; GMy °चक्रि°; Lo^{1} °चक्रेण जीवतां; Be^{1} °ध्वजवता — d) sOx^{1} sPu^{6} वेश्येनैव; TMd^{4} वेश्यानैव; TMd^{3} वशोनैव;

दशसूनासमं चक्रं दशचक्रसमो ध्वजः ।
दशध्वजसमा वेश्या दशवेश्यासमो नृपः ॥८५॥
दश सूनासहस्राणि यो वाहयति सौनिकः ।
तेन तुल्यः स्मृतो राजा घोरस्तस्य प्रतिग्रहः ॥८६॥
यो राज्ञः प्रतिगृह्णाति लुब्धस्योच्छास्त्रवर्तिनः ।
स पर्यायेण यातीमान्नरकानेकविंशतिम् ॥८७॥
तामिस्रमन्धतामिस्रं महारौरवरौरवौ ।
नरकं कालसूत्रं च महानरकमेव च ॥८८॥
संजीवनं महावीचिं तपनं संप्रतापनम् ।
संघातं च सकाकोलं कुड्मलं पूतिमृत्तिकम् ॥८९॥

wKt^{3} bKt^{5} wKt^{6} वैश्येनैव; Hy Tj^{2} वैशेनैव; oOr °नैवोपजीवितां; bCa Ho oMd^{2} gMd^{5} Tr^{1} Tr^{2} तु; Lo^{4} व; wKt^{3} Tr^{2} जीवितां; Be^{3} जीवितान्; Be^{1} जीवितं

85.* Omitted in Pu^{8}. Cited by *Lakṣ* 2.234 — a) bBe^{2} Jo^{1} wKt^{1} bKt^{5} wKt^{6} oMd^{2} Tr^{2} °शूना°; Tj^{1} °सूनिसमो चक्री; Ho Lo^{3} tMd^{3} Tr^{1} Tr^{2} °समश्चक्री; gMd^{1} La^{1} °समंश्चक्री; Be^{3} gMd^{5} gMy mTr^{4} mTr^{6} चक्री — b) Be^{3} La^{1} gMd^{5} gMy Tr^{1} Tr^{2} °चक्रीसमो; Ho Tj^{1} mTr^{6} °चक्रिसमो; Lo^{1} °चक्रंसमो; Lo^{3} gMd^{1} tMd^{3} gMd^{5} Tr^{1} mTr^{4} mTr^{6} ध्वजी; gMy ध्वजि — c) tMd^{3} gMd^{5} Tj^{1} Tr^{1} °ध्वजि°; gMy mTr^{6} °ध्वजी°; bCa °समा वेशा; Be^{1} bBe^{2} Hy Jm Jo^{1} Jo^{2} Kt^{2} wKt^{3} Lo^{1} oMd^{2} oOr mTr^{3} *Mandlik Jha KSS Dave* °समो वेशो; nPu^{1} °समो वेश्य; gMd^{5} °समो वेश्या; Pu^{7} mTr^{4} mTr^{6} °समो वेश्यो; Tj^{2} °समो वैशो — d) Wa *om* दशवेश्या [haplo]; Bo mTr^{4} °वेश्यसमो; Be^{1} bCa Jm Jo^{1} Jo^{2} Kt^{2} wKt^{3} Lo^{1} Lo^{5} oMd^{2} Tj^{2} mTr^{3} *Mandlik Jha KSS Dave* °वेशसमो; bBe^{2} °वेशः समो

86. Omitted in gMy. Cited by *Apa* 185; *Lakṣ* 2.234 — a) Jo^{1} wKt^{1} bKt^{5} wKt^{6} oOr शूना°; tMd^{4} सून°; Ho सून्या° — b) oOr वादयति; Kt^{2} bKt^{5} wKt^{6} शौनिकः; Ho oOr शौनकः; Tj^{1} सैनिकः — c) Tj^{1} Tr^{2} तुल्यं; Ho तुल्य; tMd^{3} तुल्यस्ततो; Be^{3} तुल्यो भवेद्राजा; Ho Jo^{2} Tj^{1} समो राजा — d) gMd^{1} tMd^{3} घोरस्तस्मात्प्रति°; nKt^{4} Pu^{10} परिग्रहः

Additional verse in gMd^{5} [*Jolly* Gr]:

ततोऽर्धं राजमहिषी राजामात्यपुरोहितः ।
अर्धेनार्धेन हीनाः स्युः सर्वे ते राजकर्मिणः ॥

b) [*Jolly* Gr] °हितं — d) gMd^{5} °कर्मणि

87. Cited by *Apa* 185; *Lakṣ* 2.234; *Dev* 2.461 — a) Ox^{3} ये; gMd^{1} oOr sOx^{1} sPu^{6} Tj^{1} °गृह्णीयाल्लुब्ध° — b) gMy mTr^{3} °स्योच्छस्रवर्तिनः; Tr^{1} °स्योन्मार्गवर्तिनः; Bo °वर्तितः — c) Tj^{2} *om* स; Bo अपर्या° [*om* स]; Hy पर्यायण; Pu^{9} यांती°; Tj^{2} प्रयाती°; Ho जातीयान्नर°; Tj^{1} संजातान्नर° — d) Be^{1} Ox^{3} °विंशति; Bo tMd^{4} oOr Tj^{1} °विंशतिः; Hy °किंशतिं

88. In place of 88 Jm repeats verse 87. Cited by *Apa* 185; *Lakṣ* 2.234; *Dev* 2.461 — a) bBe^{2} wKt^{1} Kt^{2} wKt^{3} La^{1} Lo^{2} oOr Ox^{3} nPu^{1} Pu^{2} Pu^{3} Pu^{4} Pu^{5} Pu^{7} Tr^{2} तामिश्रम°; bBe^{2} Ho wKt^{1} Kt^{2} wKt^{3} La^{1} Lo^{2} oOr Ox^{3} nPu^{1} Pu^{2} Pu^{3} Pu^{4} Pu^{5} Pu^{7} Tj^{1} Tr^{2} °न्धतामिश्रं — b) Wa महारौरवपातकं; sOx^{1} sPu^{6} °वरौरवे; Tj^{2} °वरौरवं; tMd^{3} °वशारवौ — c) gMy °सूत्रस्या महा° — d) nPu^{1} °नरक एव च

89. Pādas c-d omitted in Wa. Cited by *Apa* 185; *Lakṣ* 2.234; *Dev* 2.461 — a) tMd^{4} Pu^{5} Pu^{9} संजीवन; tMd^{3} gMy Ox^{3} संजीविनं; gMd^{5} संजीविनि; Hy मह°; Ho महावीर्यं; Lo^{3} Ox^{2} Tr^{1} mTr^{3} Wa °वीचीं; tMd^{4} Tj^{1} *Apa* °वीचि; Lo^{4} °वीचं; gMd^{1} °वीचिस्तप° — b) Be^{3} Bo Ho gMd^{1} Pu^{3} Pu^{5} Pu^{7} Pu^{9} Tj^{1} *Apa* तापनं; Lo^{1} तपन्तं; nKt^{4} रूपजं संप्र°; nNg सांप्र°; Wa *om* संप्रतापनं; wKt^{3} संप्रदापनं;

लोहशङ्कुमृजीषं च पन्थानं शाल्मलीं नदीम् ।
असिपत्रवनं चैव लोहचारकमेव* च ॥९०॥
एतद्विदन्तो विद्वांसो ब्राह्मणा ब्रह्मवादिनः ।
न राज्ञः प्रतिगृह्णन्ति प्रेत्य श्रेयोऽभिकाङ्क्षिणः ॥९१॥
ब्राह्मे मुहूर्ते बुध्येत धर्मार्थौ चानुचिन्तयेत् ।
कायक्लेशांश्च तन्मूलान् वेदतत्त्वार्थमेव च ॥९२॥

Ho समतापनं; Pu^{4} *om* °प्रतापनं — c) Be^{1} संहातकं च काकोलं; Be^{3} Jo^{1} Kt^{2} BKt^{5} wKt^{6} La^{1} oMd^{2} Tj^{1} *Mandlik Jha KSS Dave* संहातं; Pu^{7} Pu^{9} सघातं; Pu^{5} सघाजं; Ox^{2} संधातं; Hy समर्थ्यतं; Jm संघातकं सका°; Pu^{2} Pu^{4} °घातं बककाकोलं; Ho °बकाकोलं — d) GMd^{1} कुङ्मालं; wKt^{6} कङ्मलं; Be^{1} कुमलं; wKt^{1} कुडनं; Lo^{3} कुड्डनं; GMd^{5} GMy कुद्दालं; TMd^{3} कुंदालं; Tr^{1} कुंदारं; Hy कुघ्नलं; Pu^{10} दुपङ्मलं; Ho कुम्भं च पूति°; Hy Jo^{1} wKt^{1} Pu^{2} Pu^{3} Pu^{4} प्रतिमूर्त्तिकं; La^{1} NPu^{1} प्रतिमृत्तिकं; Jm प्रतितापनं; sOx^{1} Tr^{2} °मृत्तिकां; Pu^{9} Tj^{2} °मूत्तिकं; TMd^{3} °गर्तकं

90.* Pādas a-b except नदीं omitted in Wa. Cited by *Apa* 185; *Lakṣ* 2.235; *Dev* 2.461 — a) Tr^{2} लोहणं कुमृचीं च; sOx^{1} sPu^{6} लर्हशङ्कु°; *Apa* [vl] °शङ्कं समीचं and °शङ्खु°; TMd^{3} °शङ्खुभृहिसं; Pu^{10} °शङ्कुं बबीसं; La^{1} Pu^{2} Pu^{3} Pu^{4} °मृजीशं; MTr^{4} °मृद्बीजं [*om* च]; Be^{1} Bo Lo^{1} NNg sOx^{1} Ox^{3} Pu^{5} Pu^{7} Pu^{9} [*Jolly* G] °मृचीषं; [*Jolly* Nd] °मृचीसं; *Apa* [*Jolly* M$^{1-2-5-8-9}$] °मृबीसं; Lo^{2} °मृवीशं; Tj^{1} °मृषीपं; BKt^{5} °मृसीषं; wKt^{6} °मृसीवं; Be^{3} °मृजीषंश्च; similar variants in *ViDh* 43.17 — b) sPu^{6} पन्तानं *mc sh to* सन्तानं; sOx^{1} सन्तानं; MTr^{4} संधानं; GMd^{1} TMd^{3} GMd^{5} GMy sOx^{1} sPu^{6} शल्मलीं; NNg शाल्मलिं; wKt^{3} NKt^{4} Lo^{2} Lo^{3} Tr^{2} शाल्मलं,; [*Jolly* R] शल्मलं; *Apa* शाल्मलां [vl शल्मलां]; Be^{3} शाल्मलीन्नदीं; Hy नदिं; Jo^{1} नर्दमी — c) Bo Tr^{2} असीपत्र°; Be^{1} Bo Ho La^{2} Wa *Dev* [vl] °वनं घोरं — d) oMd^{2} लौह°; Be^{1} Bo La^{2} Lo^{1} Ox^{2} Wa *Lakṣ* लोहांगारक°; Tj^{1} लोहचामर°; BKt^{5} लोहचारव°; wKt^{6} लोहवारव°; NKt^{4} TMd^{3} GMd^{5} GMy Tr^{1} MTr^{4} लोहकारक°; BBe^{2} Hy Jm Jo^{1} Jo^{2} Kt^{2} wKt^{3} Lo^{3} oMd^{2} Pu^{8} Tj^{2} MTr^{3} [*Jolly* R] *Dev Mandlik Jha KSS Dave* लोहदारक°; La^{1} oOr लोहधारक°; Ho लोहदारुक°; Ox^{3} Pu^{10} [*Jolly* M$^{1-2-4-5-8-9}$] लोहभारक°; *Dev* [vl] कैतवोदक°

91. Cited by *Apa* 185; *Lakṣ* 2.234; *Dev* 2.461 — a) MTr^{4} MTr^{6} एतन्वि°; GMd^{1} TMd^{3} TMd^{4} GMy Tr^{1} Wa एतद्वदित्वा; GMd^{5} एतान्विदित्वा; sOx^{1} sPu^{6} °द्विन्दति — b) sOx^{1} sPu^{6} ब्राह्मवादिनः; Be^{1} ब्रह्मवेदिनः; La^{1} ब्रह्मदेहिनः — c) Pu^{4} *om* °गृह्णन्ति; wKt^{3} °गृह्णाति

Additional verse in Pu^{1}:

यामित्याः पश्चिमे यामे त्यक्तनिद्रो हरिं स्मरेत् ।
आलोक्य मङ्गलं द्रव्यं कर्मावश्यकमाचरेत् ॥

Additional verses in La^{1} [apparently many mistakes here]:

वेदाक्षराणि यावन्ति नियुज्याद्दर्पकारणात् ।
तावतो ब्रह्महत्याश्च वेदविक्रयमाप्नुयात् ॥
वेदं विक्रयायद्विप्रनृशंसयाप्युपार्जितम् ।
प्रख्यापनं नध्ययनं प्रश्नपूर्वप्रतिग्रहम् ॥
याजनाध्यापने वादे षड्विधं वेदविक्रयी ।
एतानि ब्राह्मणः स्पृष्ट्वा सचेलो जलमाविशेत् ॥

92. Cited by *Apa* 158; *Dev* 2.234 — a) Lo^{4} Ox^{3} ब्राह्मये; *Dev* महूर्त उत्थाय; Ox^{3} प्रबुध्येत [but प्र deleted] — b) Tj^{1} Tr^{2} धर्मार्था; Wa धर्मार्थो; TMd^{4} धर्मार्थांश्चानु°; wKt^{3} GMd^{1} TMd^{3} GMd^{5} Ox^{2} Tr^{1} MTr^{4} MTr^{6} *Dev Apa* धर्मार्थावनु°; wKt^{6} Lo^{4} Lo^{5} वानु°; Lo^{1} Pu^{2} Tr^{1} °चिन्तयन् — c) GMd^{5} काल°; Be^{3} Bo °क्लेशाश्च; [*Jolly* G] °क्लेशं च; Pu^{5} Pu^{7} Pu^{9} °क्लेष च; Pu^{5} Pu^{7} Pu^{9} [*Jolly* G] तन्मूलं — c-d) La^{1} कायक्लेशाश्च तन्मूलार्थनं दत्वार्थमेव च — d) BBe^{2} देवतत्त्वा°; Pu^{4} *om* च; Lo^{1} तु

उत्थायावश्यकं कृत्वा कृतशौचः समाहितः ।
पूर्वां संध्यां जपंस्तिष्ठेत् स्वकाले चापरां चिरम् ॥९३॥
ऋषयो दीर्घसंध्यत्वाद् दीर्घमायुरवाप्नुयुः ।
प्रज्ञां यशश्च कीर्तिं च ब्रह्मवर्चसमेव च ॥९४॥
श्रावण्यां प्रौष्ठपद्यां वाप्युपाकृत्य यथाविधि ।
युक्तश्छन्दांस्यधीयीत मासान्विप्रोऽर्धपञ्चमान् ॥९५॥
पुष्ये तु छन्दसां कुर्याद्बहिरुत्सर्जनं द्विजः ।
माघशुक्लस्य वा प्राप्ते पूर्वाह्णे प्रथमेऽहनि ॥९६॥
यथाशास्त्रं तु कृत्वैवमुत्सर्गं छन्दसां बहिः ।
विरमेत्पक्षिणीं रात्रिं तद्वाप्येकमहर्निशम् ॥९७॥
अत ऊर्ध्वं तु छन्दांसि शुक्लेषु नियतः पठेत् ।
वेदाङ्गानि च सर्वाणि कृष्णपक्षेषु संपठेत् ॥९८॥

93. Omitted in Tj^{2} — a) bBe^{2} °यावैश्यकं — b) Be^{1} कृतशौचं — c) Ho पूर्वां; nKt^{4} सर्वां; Lo^{4} gMd^{5} Ox^{3} Pu^{5} Pu^{7} Pu^{9} जपन्तिष्ठेत्; Bo जपं तिष्ठेत्; gMy जपस्तिष्ठेत् — d) Be^{3} Bo nKt^{4} La^{1} sOx^{1} Ox^{3} nPu^{1} Pu^{5} sPu^{6} Pu^{7} Pu^{10} Tj^{1} Wa *Me* स्वे काले; sOx^{1} sPu^{6} चापरा; oMd^{2} चापरं; Bo Lo^{1} oOr वापरां; nKt^{4} न परां; bBe^{2} च परां; Tr^{1} चिरां

94.* Omitted in Tj^{2} — a) tMd^{4} दीर्घदर्शित्वाद्; nKt^{4} °संध्यात्वाद्; La^{1} °संधित्वाद् — b) nNg sOx^{1} Pu^{5} sPu^{6} Pu^{7} Pu^{9} Tr^{1} [*Jolly* G Nd] *Jolly* °वाप्नुवन्; Wa °वाप्नुवत्; Lo^{2} gMd^{1} tMd^{3} tMd^{4} mTr^{4} mTr^{6} °वाप्नुयात् — c) Kt^{2} tMd^{3} Pu^{5} Pu^{7} Pu^{9} प्रज्ञा; La^{1} प्रजा; nPu^{1} Tj^{1} Wa प्रजां; tMd^{4} यज्ञं यज्ञश्च; tMd^{3} यशस्य; Be^{3} कीर्तिंश्च; La^{1} कीर्तिश्च

95. Cited by *Vij* 1.142; *Apa* 186; *Hem* 3/3.396; *Dev* 1.147; *Mādh* 1.517 — a) Pu^{7} *ma* श्रावण्यां; Pu^{9} *om* प्रौष्ठ; Bo bKt^{5} wKt^{6} gMd^{1} gMd^{5} gMy *Hem* प्रोष्ठ°; Lo^{3} पौर्णमास्यां; Hy °पद्या; Lo^{3} tMd^{3} वा उपा° — b) bBe^{2} °पाकर्म; Be^{3} °पाकृतयथाविधिः; La^{1} °पाकर्म समाचरेत् — c) gMd^{1} उक्तश्छ°; tMd^{3} gMy Tr^{1} युक्तछ°; Be^{1} °श्छान्दां°; nKt^{4} °स्यधीयात; Wa °स्यधीयेत; Tr^{2} °स्यधीयात्; tMd^{3} gMy °स्यधीयानो — d) Ho मासाद्विप्रो; tMd^{4} विप्रो मासार्ध°; gMd^{5} °पञ्चकान्

96. Cited by *Vij* 1.143; *Apa* 186; *Dev* 1.147; *Mādh* 1.520— a) oOr पुष्येषु; sOx^{1} Ox^{2} Pu^{3} sPu^{6} Pu^{8} तिष्ये तु; nKt^{4} च; sOx^{1} sPu^{6} छन्दांसि; Be^{3} कृत्वा बहि° — c) Lo^{1} माघशुक्ले स च प्राप्ते; tMd^{4} gMd^{5} माघे; Lo^{2} Pu^{3} माघस्य शुक्ले वा — d) Pu^{5} पूर्वाह्नो; wKt^{1} पूर्वार्धे; Tr^{2} प्रष्टमेहनि; Lo^{1} प्रथमेहिनिः; Ho प्रथमेह्नि वा

97. Omitted in tMd^{3}. Cited by *Apa* 187; *Hem* 3/3.761; *Dev* 1.154 — a) Be^{1} Jo^{2} Tj^{1} Wa च — b) Wa °मुत्सर्गां; mTr^{6} °मुत्सर्गाच्छन्दसां; Lo^{4} Ox^{3} छान्दसां; *Apa* विधिवद्बहिः; Be^{3} बहि; wKt^{1} हविः; Be^{1} वहः — c) Pu^{2} Pu^{4} °त्पक्षणीं; tMd^{4} °त्पक्षणी; Ox^{3} °त्पक्षिणां; Tj^{1} रात्री — d) Be^{3} tMd^{4} Pu^{8} *Dev Hem* यद्वाप्येकम°; Jm Jo^{1} Kt^{2} oMd^{2} mTr^{3} *Mandlik Jha KSS Dave* तदेवैकम°; gMy nPu^{1} तथा-प्येकम°; oOr Tj^{2} तच्चाप्येकम°; wKt^{6} तत्त्वायैकम°

98. Omitted in sOx^{1} nKt^{4} sPu^{6}; pādas c-d omitted in gMd^{5}. Cited by *Apa* 186; *Dev* 1.148; *Mādh* 1.520 — a) *Apa Mādh* अतः परं तु — a-b) gMd^{1} छन्दांस्यूर्ध्वमतोऽभ्यस्येच्छुक्लेषु नियतो द्विजः — b) gMy शुक्ले तु; Tr^{2} शुके तु; Be^{3} bKt^{5} wKt^{6} नियतं; Tr^{1} पठन् — c) *Mādh* अङ्गानि च रह-स्यञ्च; *Apa* वेदाङ्गानि रहस्यं च; Be^{1} bBe^{2} (*ma*) Be^{3} Bo bCa Jo^{2} wKt^{1} La^{1} gMd^{1} nNg Ox^{3} Pu^{2} Pu^{4} Pu^{5} Pu^{7} Pu^{9} Pu^{10} Tj^{1} Tr^{2} Wa [*Jolly* M^{1-2-9}] *Dev Go Ku* तु— d) tMd^{3} gMy कृष्णेषु नियतः पठेत्;

नाविस्पष्टमधीयीत न शूद्रजनसंनिधौ ।
न निशान्ते परिश्रान्तो ब्रह्माधीत्य पुनः स्वपेत् ॥९९॥
यथोदितेन विधिना नित्यं छन्दस्कृतं पठेत् ।
ब्रह्म छन्दस्कृतं चैव द्विजो युक्तो ह्यनापदि ॥१००॥
इमान्नित्यमनध्यायानधीयानो विवर्जयेत् ।
अध्यापनं च कुर्वाणः शिष्याणां विधिपूर्वकम् ॥१०१॥
कर्णश्रवेऽनिले रात्रौ दिवा पांसुसमूहने ।
एतौ वर्षास्वनध्यायावध्यायज्ञाः प्रचक्षते ॥१०२॥
विद्युत्स्तनितवर्षेषु महोल्कानां च संप्लवे ।
आकालिकमनध्यायमेतेषु मनुरब्रवीत् ॥१०३॥
एतांस्त्वभ्युदितान्विद्याद्यदा प्रादुष्कृताग्निषु ।
तदा विद्यादनध्यायमनृतौ चाभ्रदर्शने ॥१०४॥

Pu^{2} Pu^{4} कृष्णे; BBe^{2} Bo BCa Ho La^{1} Lo^{3} Lo^{5} oOr NPu^{1} Pu^{9} Tr^{2} *Go* °पक्षे तु; Ox^{2} °पक्षे सदा पठेत्; GMd^{1} सञ्चरेत्; *Me Ku Rc* support the plural पक्षेषु

99. Omitted in Pu^{9}; *ma* in Pu^{7}. Cited by *Lakṣ* 1.158; *Dev* 1.137; *Mādh* 1.144 — a) *Lakṣ* नाविस्पृष्टम°; Hy नाविष्टस्पम°; Pu^{2} Pu^{4} नाविसृष्टम°; Tr^{2} नाविशिष्टम° — b) *Lakṣ* शूद्रं — c) NKt^{4} निशान्ते च [*om* न]; Ho Kt^{2} Lo^{4} Ox^{3} परिश्रान्ते; NKt^{4} पुनःश्रान्तो — d) TMd^{4} परिस्वपेत्; Hy सुपेत्

100. b) TMd^{3} नित्य; Pu^{2} Pu^{4} ब्रह्मछन्द°; BKt^{5} छन्दकृतं; TMd^{3} Tr^{1} छन्दस्तुतं; TMd^{4} छन्दस्मृतं; Pu^{8} छन्दःतं — c) Tj^{1} Tr^{2} ब्राह्मं; NNg ब्रह्मा; WKt^{6} छन्दकृतं; Pu^{10} स्कन्दस्कृतं — d) Bo द्विजा; Be^{1} द्विजोद्युक्तो; Tr^{1} द्विजो नित्यो

101. sOx^{1} sPu^{6} transpose pādas a-b and c-d. Cited by *Hem* 3/3.776 — a) Pu^{5} Pu^{7} Pu^{9} °न्नेत्यम°; TMd^{3} °त्यमधीयानोनधीया°; Pu^{5} °मन्यध्याया° — b) Tr^{1} °यान्सोधीयानो; TMd^{4} °धीयान; Tr^{2} विवर्तयेत्; WKt^{1} WKt^{3} विसर्जयेत् — c) TMd^{3} GMy योऽध्यापनं च कुर्वीत; Pu^{4} *om* च ... शिष्याणां वि°; WKt^{1} *om* च; BKt^{5} WKt^{6} sOx^{1} sPu^{6} तु; Pu^{8} न; GMd^{1} कुर्वाणा

102. Pādas a-b cited by *Har*-A 1.11.8 — a) Lo^{1} Pu^{5} Pu^{7} Pu^{9} Tj^{1} Tr^{2} [*Jolly* GN] °श्रावे; NPu^{1} °श्रावो; Lo^{3} °श्रवो; TMd^{4} °श्रव; BKt^{5} WKt^{6} MTr^{3} °स्रवे; Be^{3} °स्रावे — b) BBe^{2} Be^{3} Bo BCa Ho Hy WKt^{1} WKt^{3} NKt^{4} BKt^{5} WKt^{6} La^{1} Lo^{1} Lo^{4} oMd^{2} oOr Ox^{3} NPu^{1} Pu^{2} Pu^{4} Pu^{5} Pu^{7} Pu^{9} पांशु° — c) MTr^{4} MTr^{6} एते; Pu^{10} ऐतो; TMd^{4} एत; Tj^{1} वर्ज्यावनध्या°; NKt^{4} °स्वनाध्या°; Lo^{3} °ध्यायानध्या° — d) Pu^{2} Pu^{4} °ध्यायावध्याप्य न प्रचक्षते; MTr^{4} MTr^{6} °ध्यायावर्ज्याप्राज्ञाः प्रचक्षते; BCa प्रचक्ष्यते

103. Cited by *Hem* 3/3.761; *Dev* 1.149 — a) Tj^{1} °त्स्तनिते; Lo^{3} °त्स्तानित°; Tr^{2} °सर्वेषु; BKt^{5} °पर्षेषु; WKt^{6} °पर्षषु — b) Pu^{10} महोत्कानां; *Hem* महोपानां; Tr^{2} संप्लुवं; BKt^{5} GMd^{1} Tr^{1} संभवे — c) Ho Lo^{1} NNg Pu^{2} Pu^{4} sPu^{6} [*but cor*] Tj^{1} Tr^{1} अकालि°; WKt^{3} °लिकाम°

104. Cited by *Dev* 1.1491 — a) Pu^{2} Pu^{4} तांस्त्व°; Tr^{2} Wa एतांश्चाभ्यु°; TMd^{3} GMy *Dev* एतानभ्यु°; Tj^{1} एतास्त्वनुदि°; Lo^{2} °दिताश्चिद्या°; TMd^{3} °दितान्याश्च यदा; WKt^{1} °तान्विद्या यदा; Be^{3} °तान्विन्द्याद्यदा; Kt^{2} oOr °तान्विद्यान्यदा; GMy *om* विद्याद् — b) TMd^{3} GMd^{5} °द्याद्यथा; Lo^{1} °ष्कृतानेषु — c) Bo Lo^{4} Pu^{7} विन्द्याद°; TMd^{3} GMy MTr^{6} °ध्यायाननृतौ — d) GMd^{5} sOx^{1} sPu^{6} [*but cor*] °नृतं; Kt^{2} Wa °नृतो; GMd^{1} °नृता; WKt^{3} °नितौ; Be^{3} °मृतौ; *Dev* [vl] °पर्तौ [but *Dev's* com. reads अनृतौ]; TMd^{3} GMy °नृतावत्र दर्शने; La^{1} Lo^{4} वाभ्र°; sOx^{1} sPu^{6} [*but cor*] चात्र दर्शने; Pu^{2} Pu^{4} च प्रदर्शने; BKt^{5} WKt^{6} चाप्रदर्शने

निर्घाते भूमिचलने ज्योतिषां चोपसर्जने ।
एतानाकालिकान्विद्यादनध्यायानृतावपि ॥१०५॥
प्रादुष्कृतेष्वग्निषु तु विद्युत्स्तनितनिस्वने ।
सज्योतिः स्यादनध्यायः शेषे रात्रौ यथा दिवा ॥१०६॥
नित्यानध्याय एव स्याद्ग्रामेषु नगरेषु च ।
धर्मनैपुणकामानां पूतिगन्धे च सर्वशः ॥१०७॥
अन्तर्गतशवे ग्रामे वृषलस्य च संनिधौ ।
अनध्यायो रुद्यमाने समवाये जनस्य च ॥१०८॥
उदके मध्यरात्रे च विण्मूत्रस्य विसर्जने ।
उच्छिष्टः श्राद्धभुक् चैव मनसापि न चिन्तयेत् ॥१०९॥
प्रतिगृह्य द्विजो विद्वानेकोद्दिष्टस्य केतनम् ।
त्र्यहं न कीर्तयेद्ब्रह्म राज्ञो राहोश्च सूतके ॥११०॥

105. Cited by *Apa* 188; *Dev* 1.151 — a) Pu^{5} Pu^{7} Pu^{9} Pu^{10} निर्घात; nNg mTr^{3} निर्वाते — b) *Apa* चापसर्जने; tMd^{4} [*but mc*] चोपदर्शने; mTr^{3} चोपवासने — c) Pu^{2} Pu^{3} Pu^{4} sPu^{6} Tj^{1} एतानकालि°; Lo^{3} एतांस्तात्कालि°; nNg एतानिकालि° *cor fh to* एतानकालि°; Lo^{2} °लिकां विद्या°; wKt^{1} Pu^{5} Pu^{7} °न्विन्द्यादन°; tMd^{4} sOx^{1} sPu^{6} °न्विद्याननध्या° — d) wKt^{6} °ध्यायनृता°; wKt^{1} °ध्यायात्र तावपि; Lo^{4} °ध्यायानजावपि

106. Pu^{9} omits the section 4.106–5.37 although the page sequence in the ms. continues. Cited by *Hem* 3/3.763; *Dev* 1.150 — a) Ho bKt^{5} wKt^{6} gMd^{1} च — b) Ho विद्वत्स्तनि°; Be^{1} Be^{3} Bo Ho Hy Jm Jo^{1} La^{1} La^{2} sOx^{1} Pu^{5} sPu^{6} Pu^{7} Pu^{9} Tj^{1} Tr^{2} *Mandlik Jha KSS Dave* °निःस्वने; nKt^{4} °निशवने; mTr^{4} °निःस्वनैः — c) Bo °ध्याये — d) gMd^{1} gMd^{5} Tr^{1} mTr^{6} *Me* [pāṭha] *Nd Ku* [pāṭha] शेषं; Hy Lo^{4} Lo^{5} oOr Ox^{3} Pu^{10} शेष; Tj^{1} वर्षे; Lo^{4} Lo^{5} रात्रो; Jm रात्रा; tMd^{3} gMd^{5} gMy दिवा यथा

107. Cited by *Hem* 3/3.770; *Dev* 1.161 — b) mTr^{3} नरकेषु— c) tMd^{4} धर्मे; Bo Ho Jm Jo^{1} wKt^{1} Kt^{2} Lo^{5} oMd^{2} nNg Ox^{2} Pu^{2} Pu^{3} Pu^{4} Pu^{10} mTr^{3} [*Jolly* M^{3} Ku] *Mandlik Jha KSS Dave* °नैपुण्य°; Pu^{2} Pu^{4} °निपुण्य° — d) Tj^{1} कृतिगन्धे; Tj^{2} प्रतिगन्धे; gMd^{5} oOr *Hem* °गन्धेषु सर्वशः; bKt^{5} wKt^{6} tMd^{4} *Dev Hem* सर्वतः; Hy Jm Jo^{1} Kt^{2} oMd^{2} Tj^{2} Tr^{2} mTr^{3} *Mandlik KSS* सर्वदा

108. Omitted in oOr. Cited by *Dev* 1.162 — a) tMd^{4} अन्तर्गते; Be^{3} wKt^{1} nKt^{4} Lo^{2} Lo^{3} gMd^{1} tMd^{3} gMd^{5} gMy nNg Ox^{2} Pu^{3} Tj^{1} Tr^{1} mTr^{4} mTr^{6} Wa अन्तःशवगते; Lo^{1} °सवे; Hy °शरे; wKt^{6} °शठे — b) Lo^{2} वृषभस्य; Tr^{1} °लस्यापि; Lo^{5} सन्निधा — c) nKt^{4} अनध्याये; Wa अध्यायो; gMy sOx^{1} sPu^{6} रुध्यमाने; Lo^{1} रुह्यमाने; Pu^{8} नुद्यमाने; nKt^{4} पच्यमाने; Lo^{5} अद्यमाने; Lo^{4} अद्यमान — d) Tj^{2} सप्रवाये; Lo^{4} Lo^{5} समवायत्र जन°; La^{1} जनस्यापि; bKt^{5} wKt^{6} Lo^{1} तु

109. Cited by *Hem* 3/3.773; *Dev* 1.163 — a) *Me* [pāṭha] उदये; Be^{3} Ho Lo^{1} चार्धरात्रे; La^{1} nPu^{1} चार्द्धरात्रे; Tj^{1} वार्धरात्रे; Ox^{3} Pu^{10} मित्ररात्रे; bKt^{5} wKt^{6} मध्यमरात्रे च; Tr^{2} *Hem* °रात्रौ; nPu^{1} °रात्रेण च — b) La^{1} विन्मूत्रोत्सर्ग एव च; wKt^{1} sOx^{1} Ox^{3} sPu^{6} [*cor to*] Pu^{10} विण्मूत्रं च विसर्जयेत् [sOx^{1} sPu^{6} (*cor to*) °र्जयन्]; wKt^{3} nKt^{4} Lo^{2} nNg Tr^{1} mTr^{4} mTr^{6} विण्मूत्रे च विसर्जयेत् [Lo^{2} विसर्जयन्]; Tr^{1} °र्जिते; nKt^{4} °येत्; nNg mTr^{4} mTr^{6} °यन्]; *Hem* विण्मूत्रे परिवर्जयेत्; tMd^{4} oOr विण्मूत्रं च वि° [oOr °मूत्र]; bKt^{5} °मूत्रस्य च वि°; wKt^{6} विसर्जजं — c) *Dev* उच्छिष्टश्रा°; Pu^{4} *om* °भुक् … चिन्तयेत् Bo nKt^{4} La^{1} Lo^{2} nNg Ox^{3} nPu^{1} Pu^{2} Pu^{3} °भुक्तैव; tMd^{3} °भुक्त्केव; Tj^{2} °भुगेव; Lo^{3} Wa °भुम्वेद; *Hem* °भुक्तौ च — d) oOr मानसापि

110. Cited by *Vij* 1.146, 190; *Apa* 190; *Hem* 3/3.756; *Dev* 1.153 — a) La^{1} °गृह्यो; Hy द्विजौ;

यावदेकानुदिष्टस्य गन्धो लेपश्च तिष्ठति ।
विप्रस्य विदुषो देहे तावद्ब्रह्म न कीर्तयेत् ॥१११॥
शयानः प्रौढपादश्च कृत्वा चैवावसक्थिकाम् ।
नाधीयीतामिषं जग्ध्वा सूतकान्नाद्यमेव च ॥११२॥
नीहारे वाणशब्दे च संध्ययोरेव चोभयोः ।
अमावास्याचतुर्दश्योः पौर्णमास्यष्टकासु च ॥११३॥
अमावास्या गुरुं हन्ति शिष्यं हन्ति चतुर्दशी ।
ब्रह्माष्टकापौर्णमास्यौ तस्मात्ताः परिवर्जयेत् ॥११४॥
पांसुवर्षे दिशां दाहे गोमायुविरुते तथा ।
श्वखरोष्ट्रे च रुवति पङ्क्तौ च न पठेद् द्विजः ॥११५॥

GMd^5 द्विजे; Bo विन्द्यादेको°; Ho विद्यान्नेको° — b) Pu^3 Pu^8 *Jha Dave* °कोद्दिष्टनिकेतनं; Pu^2 Pu^4 °द्दिष्टं च केतनं [Pu^2 *om* च]; wKt^6 केतनः; Lo^4 Lo^5 [*but cor*] केवलं — c) Pu^2 Pu^4 त्र्यदनव्याहरेद्ब्रह्म; Ox^2 अहत्र कीर्त° — d) *Hem* रहोरन्यत्र सूतके; Ho रोहस्तु

111. Cited by *Apa* 190; *Har*-A 1.10.28; *Hem* 3/3.756 — a) Tr^2 एकोदिष्टस्य यावत्तु; NPu^1 Pu^2 Pu^4 Tj^2 °देकोनुदि°; La^1 °देकान्नदि°; Tj^1 °देवानुदि°; *Hem* °देकोद्दिष्टसन्धौ गन्धो; NKt^4 °नुशिष्टस्य — b) sOx^1 sPu^6 गन्ध; BBe^2 Be^3 Tj^1 लेपो गन्धश्च; Lo^3 लेपो गन्धस्य; GMd^5 Tr^1 MTr^4 [*Jolly* Gr] स्नेहो लेपश्च; GMd^1 स्नेहलेपो च; TMd^4 MTr^6 स्नेहो गन्धश्च; NKt^4 स्नेहानगन्धश्च; Be^1 *mc to* विद्यते; sPu^6 [*but cor*] विशियते — c) Lo^5 विग्रहविदुपो; Lo^4 विग्रहस्य विहयो; TMd^3 GMy प्रविश्य विदुषो; Ho विदुषे; Pu^5 Pu^7 Pu^9 विदुष्टो; MTr^4 MTr^6 गेहे— d) Be^3 तावद्ब्रह्मं; wKt^3 Tr^2 तावद्ब्रह्मण की°

112. Cited by *Vij* 1.151; *Hem* 3/3.772; *Dev* 1.162 — a) Ho शयनिः; Bo Lo^4 Tj^1 प्रोढ° — b) TMd^3 GMd^5 GMy Tr^1 MTr^4 MTr^6 बध्वा; TMd^3 चैहाव°; Ox^3 दैवाव°; MTr^3 चैव न सक्थिकां; Lo^4 Lo^5 सेवावसिक्थिकां; Bo Jo^2 GMy Pu^{10} Tj^1 °सक्थिकं; Be^1 °सक्थिकः; Hy °स्विथकां; TMd^4 सक्थिनं; wKt^1 °शक्थिकां; Ox^3 °शक्थिकं; Lo^3 °सक्थितं; NKt^4 °शक्तितां; TMd^3 °शर्धिकं — c) Lo^4 Lo^5 नाधीयाता°; Ho माधीयता°; Tj^1 नादीता°; Ho दग्ध्वा — d) sOx^1 sPu^6 सूतिका°; Hy सूतकत्वाद्यमेव; BBe^2 सूतकान्नामेव; Lo^4 sPu^6 Tj^1 वा

113. Cited by *Dev* 1.159; pādas a-b cited by *Hem* 3/3.769 — a) Lo^3 नीहार; NPu^1 वाणि°; BBe^2 Bo BCa Jm Jo^2 wKt^1 Kt^2 wKt^3 BKt^5 wKt^6 Lo^1 Lo^3 TMd^3 GMd^5 GMy sOx^1 Ox^2 Pu^2 sPu^6 Pu^{10} *Mandlik Jha KSS Dave* बाण°; Tj^1 वात्र°; MTr^6 पाण°; MTr^4 वाद° — b) GMd^1 TMd^3 TMd^4 GMy MTr^6 *Hem Dev* संध्ययोरुभयोरपि — c) Be^1 sOx^1 अमावस्या°; GMd^1 oOr °चतुर्दश्या — d) BKt^5 NNg पूर्ण°; Lo^3 पूर्णि°; Be^1 wKt^1 Lo^4 TMd^4 GMd^5 oOr Ox^3 Pu^5 Pu^7 Pu^{10} °मास्याष्ट°; BCa BKt^5 wKt^6 °ष्टमीपु च

114. Cited by *Hem* 3/3.755; *Dev* 1.152 — a) GMd^1 ब्रह्माष्टमिपौर्णमासि; Hy TMd^3 अमावाश्या — c) Jo^1 ब्रह्माष्टमा°; Tr^1 *Hem* ब्रह्माष्टमी°; BKt^5 Lo^2 sOx^1 sPu^6 ब्रह्माष्टकाः; Ox^3 ब्रह्माष्टलौ; Pu^{10} ब्रह्माप्त्यकौ; Jo^2 °पूर्णिमास्यौ; Lo^3 °पूर्णमास्यै; BKt^5 wKt^6 NNg °पूर्णमास्यस्; Lo^2 sOx^1 NPu^1 Pu^2 Pu^4 sPu^6 [*cor to*] Tj^1 °मास्यस्; Ho La^1 TMd^4 Ox^3 Pu^{10} °मास्यास्; Tr^2 °मास्या; MTr^6 °मास्यः; NKt^4 °मास्ये; TMd^3 GMy Tr^1 °मासी — d) TMd^4 °वर्जयन्

115. Cited by *Dev* 1.163; pāda-a cited by *Apa* 191 — a) BBe^2 Be^3 BCa Ho wKt^1 Kt^2 NKt^4 BKt^5 wKt^6 Lo^2 Lo^4 oMd^2 oOr NPu^1 Pu^2 Pu^4 Pu^5 Pu^7 Pu^{10} *Jolly* पांशु°; Ox^3 पसु°; NKt^4 °वर्षं; TMd^3 °वर्षे च दिग्दाहे; Tr^1 दिशा — b) TMd^4 गोमायुर्निर्यतेतना; GMd^1 sOx^1 sPu^6 गोमायुर्विरुते; TMd^3 GMy गोमारुविरुते; Be^1 °विरते; wKt^3 °नुदिते; oMd^2 °गुरुते — c) Lo^2 Pu^5 Pu^7 *om* श्व; BKt^5 wKt^6 श्वपरोष्ट्रे

नाधीयीत श्मशानान्ते ग्रामान्ते गोव्रजेऽपि वा ।
वसित्वा मैथुनं वासः श्राद्धिकं प्रतिगृह्य च ॥११६॥
प्राणि वा यदि वाप्राणि यत्किंचिच्छ्राद्धिकं भवेत् ।
तदालभ्याप्यनध्यायः पाण्यास्यो हि द्विजः स्मृतः ॥११७॥
चौरैरुपप्लुते ग्रामे संभ्रमे चाग्निकारिते ।
आकालिकमनध्यायं विद्यात्सर्वाद्भुतेषु च ॥११८॥
उपाकर्मणि चोत्सर्गे त्रिरात्रं क्षपणं स्मृतम् ।
अष्टकासु त्वहोरात्रमृत्वन्तासु च रात्रिषु ॥११९॥
नाधीयीताश्वमारूढो न वृक्षं न च हस्तिनम् ।
न नावं न खरं नोष्ट्रं नेरिणस्थो न यानगः ॥१२०॥

[BKt⁵ *ma* श्व]; TMd³ GMy °ष्ट्रे विरुवति; Bo रुवतीं; Be³ TMd⁴ Ox² Pu⁷ [*mc to*] Tr¹ Tr² रुदति; NPu¹ Tj¹ रुदिति; Pu¹⁰ चवति — d) wKt³ पाङ्क्तौ; NKt⁴ Ox³ पङ्क्तो; Lo³ पङ्क्त्या; oMd² न च; Ox³ *om* च न … द्विजः; BKt⁵ wKt⁶ वसेद्; Ho पठेद्विधः

116. Pu² transposes pādas a-b and c-d. Cited by *Hem* 3/3.771; *Dev* 1.160 — a) GMy नाधीयत; Lo⁴ नाधीयात — b) BCa wKt⁶ *Hem* गोव्रजेऽपि च; Be¹ Jo² La¹ Lo³ oMd² TMd³ TMd⁴ GMd⁵ GMy oOr Pu² Pu⁴ Tr¹ MTr⁴ MTr⁶ Wa [*Jolly* R] गोव्रजे तथा — c) Lo¹ वासित्वा; TMd⁴ वशित्वा — d) Ho श्राद्धकं; oOr प्रतिगृह्यते [*om* च]; Lo⁴ Lo⁵ Pu¹⁰ [*Jolly* M] वा

117. Omitted in Ox³. Cited by *Hem* 3/3.757 — a) Pu¹⁰ Tr¹ प्राणी वा — c) wKt⁶ तदालभ्य पुनर्ध्याय; GMy तथाल°; wKt¹ तदलस्या°; GMd¹ तदारभ्या° — d) *Hem* पाण्यास्याः हि द्विजाः स्मृताः; Ho पण्यासो; Pu⁵ Pu⁷ पाण्यासौ; GMd¹ प्राण्यास्यो; oOr प्राणास्यो; Tr¹ पाण्यास्यर्हि; La¹ पाण्यावाहि; GMd⁵ प्राण्यो-स्यस्य द्विजः; BKt⁵ wKt⁶ *om* हि; MTr⁴ द्विजैः

118. Cited by *Apa* 188; *Hem* 3/3.762; *Dev* 1.150; *Mādh* 1.148 — a) oOr चोरैरुपप्लुतैर्ग्रामै; Lo¹ चौरे प्लुते च ग्रामे च; Lo³ GMd¹ TMd³ GMd⁵ GMy चोरै°; Tj¹ वैरै°; La¹ चौप्लापिप्लुते; BBe² Tr¹ °रुपप्लुत; *Hem* °रुपद्रुते; TMd⁴ NNg °रुपप्लवे; TMd³ °रुपपद्रामे; Ox² Pu³ Pu⁸ देशे — b) GMd¹ विभ्रमे; Hy त्यंभ्रमे; *Hem* संत्रासे; Ho Lo³ Ox³ [*Jolly* M¹⁻²⁻⁹ R] *Mādh* वाग्नि°; oMd² °कारते; wKt¹ °कारिके — c) NPu¹ Tj¹ Tr² अकालिक°; wKt¹ आकामिक°; Lo¹ आकालिकाम° — d) Be³ *Hem* विन्द्या°; MTr⁴ MTr⁶ °त्सर्वाहुतेषु; *Mādh* °त्सर्वाद्भुते तथा

119. Pādas c-d omitted in GMd¹. Cited by *Hem* 3/3.760–1; *Dev* 1.154 — a) Lo¹ Ox³ उपकर्मणि — b) Jm Jo¹ Kt² MTr³ *Mandlik Jha Dave* क्षेपणं; GMy Pu⁵ Pu⁷ [*Jolly* G] क्षिपणं; La¹ जापणं — c) MTr⁶ °रात्रिमृ° — d) Pu² Pu⁴ °रात्रंकृत्वंतासु; BKt⁵ wKt⁶ °मृत्यन्तासु; Be¹ Bo TMd³ GMd⁵ NNg °त्वन्त्यासु; TMd⁴ °त्वन्तौसु; GMy °त्वन्यासु; Ho °त्वन्तासु त्रिरात्रिषु

120. Cited by *Hem* 3/3.772; *Dev* 1.162 — a) GMy oOr नाधीयता°; La¹ नाधीताश्वश्वनारूढो; Ho नाधीताश्वसमारूढो; NKt⁴ °रूढा; BBe² [*but cor*] Hy °रूढौ; Pu⁸ °रूढे — b) Pu² Tj¹ च न; MTr⁶ न य — c) Tj¹ वरं नोष्ट्रं; GMd¹ खरोष्ट्रं च; GMd⁵ खरोष्टौ च; Tr¹ खरोष्टस्थं; wKt⁶ लोष्ट्रं — d) MTr⁶ नैरि°; Ox³ Pu¹⁰ नरि°; wKt⁶ नेवि°; BBe² नेरिणिस्थो; Tj¹ नक्रस्थो; Tr¹ [*but cor fh*] यानतं; GMd¹ यागतः

Additional verse in La¹:

ऋतुस्नातां तु यो भार्यां सन्निधौ नोपगच्छति ।
तदेनो ब्रह्महत्याया एवं प्राप्नोत्यसंशयः ॥
भर्तुश्चाभिनिवेशेन या वृथा स्कन्दते ऋतुम् ।
तां ग्राम[मध्ये विख्याप्य भ्रूणघ्नीं निर्धमेद्गृहात्] ॥

न विवादे न कलहे न सेनायां न संगरे ।
न भुक्तमात्रे नाजीर्णे न वमित्वा न शुक्तके ॥१२१॥
अतिथिं चाननुज्ञाप्य मारुते वाति वा भृशम् ।
रुधिरे च स्रुते गात्राच्छस्त्रेण च परिक्षते ॥१२२॥
सामध्वनावृग्यजुषी नाधीयीत कदाचन ।
वेदस्याधीत्य चाप्यन्तमारण्यकमधीत्य च ॥१२३॥
ऋग्वेदो देवदैवत्यो यजुर्वेदस्तु मानुषः ।
सामवेदः स्मृतः पित्र्यस्तस्मात्तस्याशुचिर्ध्वनिः ॥१२४॥
एतद्विदन्तो विद्वांसस्त्रयीनिष्कर्षमन्वहम् ।
क्रमशः पूर्वमभ्यस्य पश्चाद्वेदमधीयते ॥१२५॥

g) La^1 तां ग्राम and omits rest; the two verses are versions of *BDh* 4.1.18 20.

121. Pādas a-b omitted in mTr^4. Cited by *Hem* 3/3.773; *Dev* 1.163 — a) La^1 *om* न विवादे; Tj^1 नापवादे; wKt^3 Lo^1 Pu^5 Pu^7 [*Jolly* G] विवाहे; La^1 कनहे — b) Be^1 सेनायां न तु संगरे; Be^3 wKt^3 bKt^5 wKt^6 La^1 oOr [*but mc fh*] सेवायां; La^1 *om second* न — c) tMd^3 भुञ्जमात्रे; Lo^2 °मात्रेणाजीर्णे; oOr नजीर्णे; mTr^6 नाकीर्णे — d) wKt^1 न च सिद्धा न शुक्लके; wKt^3 शुक्तये; Be^1 शुल्कके; Be^3 Bo Ho Kt^2 bKt^5 wKt^6 Lo^1 tMd^4 nPu^1 Pu^2 Pu^3 Pu^4 sPu^6 Tj^1 [*Jolly* R] *Dev* सूतके; Jo^1 सूतकै; Lo^3 Ox^2 mTr^3 सुतके; sOx^1 सुतके *mc to* सुक्तकये; Lo^4 Lo^5 Ox^3 [*Jolly* M Me] मुक्तके; Pu^5 Pu^7 सक्तये; [*Jolly* G] सुक्तये

122. Cited by *Hem* 3/3.774; *Dev* 1.164 — a) Tr^1 अतिथिन्नाननु°; wKt^6 Lo^1 Lo^4 Pu^5 Tj^1 वाननु°; gMd^5 mTr^4 mTr^6 नाननु°; Ho चाभ्युनुज्ञाप्य; La^1 चाप्यभ्यनुज्ञाप्य; wKt^3 Pu^{10} चाप्यनुज्ञाप्य; [*Jolly* M] वाप्यनुज्ञाप्य — b) gMd^1 मारुते चातिवाति च; Lo^2 tMd^3 gMd^5 gMy nNg sOx^1 Ox^2 Pu^3 sPu^6 Pu^5 Pu^7 Pu^8 Tr^1 mTr^4 mTr^6 *Hem* मारुते चातिवायति [Lo^2 मरुतो; gMd^5 sOx^1 sPu^6 *Hem* वाति°]; tMd^4 oOr nPu^1 मरुते वातिवादति; Lo^4 यारुगेधापति वामृशं; Lo^1 मरुते; Bo चाति वा; nKt^4 Tr^2 वाति वा यदि; Lo^5 वामृशं — c) gMd^1 रुधिरेण स्रुते गात्रे शस्त्रेण; tMd^3 चास्रुगात्रा शस्त्रेण; bBe^2 Be^3 wKt^3 nKt^4 wKt^6 Lo^4 Lo^5 oOr Ox^3 Pu^5 Pu^7 श्रुते; Tr^1 स्मृते; Be^3 Ho गात्रे शस्त्रेण; nKt^4 Lo^4 Lo^5 गात्र शस्त्रेण; Jm Ox^3 गात्रा शस्त्रेण — c-d) Ox^2 Pu^3 Pu^8 शस्त्रेण च क्षते गात्रे रुधिरे च परिश्रुते; Be^3 गात्रे वस्त्रेण — d) Ox^3 Pu^{10} °च्छास्त्रेण; Lo^4 °च्छस्त्रिण; Lo^5 °च्छस्त्रिणं; Ho Lo^3 °स्त्रेण परिचक्षते; bBe^2 °स्त्रेण परिविक्षते; oOr *om* च; nPu^1 Pu^5 Pu^7 परिक्षिते; Hy परीक्षत; Ox^2 Pu^8 परिक्षुते

123.* Cited by *Dev* 1.160; pādas a-b cited by *Hem* 3/3.768 — a) Tj^1 °ध्वंनामृग्य°; bKt^5 wKt^6 Lo^4 gMd^1 gMd^5 Ox^3 °ध्वनौ ऋग्य°; bKt^5 wKt^6 mTr^4 °ध्वनौ नर्य° [wKt^6 नार्ग्य°]; Lo^2 tMd^3 °ध्वनौ चर्म्य°; Lo^2 nKt^4 °जुषे; Lo^3 जुषां; *Dev* °जूंषि; tMd^3 °जुषा; Tr^1 °जुषान् — b) sOx^1 नाधीयेत; La^1 नाधीयान — c) Tr^1 अधीत्य वेदेस्यैवातमा° [वान्तमा?]; Lo^1 वेदं स्वधीत्य; bKt^5 wKt^6 वेदस्याधीन; gMd^1 वैद्यस्याधीत्य; sOx^1 sPu^6 वैश्यस्याधीत्य; nPu^1 °धीतयोप्यन्तमा°; Jm Jo^1 Kt^2 bKt^5 wKt^6 oMd^2 Tj^2 *Mandlik Jolly Jha KSS Dave* वाप्यन्तमा°; Be^1 bCa Hy wKt^1 gMd^1 tMd^3 tMd^4 gMd^5 gMy nNg oOr mTr^4 mTr^6 चैवान्तमा°; Pu^4 चैपांतमा°; Pu^2 वैश्यापांतमा° [*cor to* वैपांतमा°]; nKt^4 वै चान्तमा°; Lo^4 वाङ्गान्तिमा°; Lo^5 चाङ्गानि आरण्य° — d) tMd^4 nNg °मारण्यमधीत्य

124. Cited by *Dev* 1.160 — a) bKt^5 ऋग्वेदौ; wKt^6 oOr दैवदैव°; Be^3 nKt^4 Lo^2 tMd^3 tMd^4 gMy nNg Ox^3 Pu^5 Pu^7 Pu^{10} Tj^1 Tr^1 Tr^2 °देवत्यो; Lo^1 °दैत्योयं — b) Be^3 Lo^3 Tj^1 Wa °वेंदश्च; oMd^2 मानवः — c) tMd^4 स्मृतं; Pu^5 पैत्र्यस्त°; sOx^1 sPu^6 पैतृः तस्मा°; tMd^3 tMd^4 पित्र्यं तस्मा°

125. a) gMd^1 tMd^3 tMd^4 gMy एतद्विदित्वा; gMd^5 Tr^1 एतं विदित्वा; Tr^2 एतद्विद्वन्त्यो; Bo

पशुमण्डूकमार्जारश्वसर्पनकुलाखुभिः ।
अन्तरागमने विद्यादनध्यायमहर्निशम् ॥१२६॥
द्वावेव वर्जयेन्नित्यमनध्यायौ प्रयत्नतः ।
स्वाध्यायभूमिं चाशुद्धामात्मानं चाशुचिं द्विजः ॥१२७॥
अमावास्यामष्टमीं च पौर्णमासीं चतुर्दशीम् ।
ब्रह्मचारी भवेन्नित्यमप्यृतौ स्नातको द्विजः ॥१२८॥
न स्नानमाचरेद्भुक्त्वा नातुरो न महानिशि ।
न वासोभिः सहाजस्रं नाविज्ञाते जलाशये ॥१२९॥
देवतानां गुरो राज्ञः स्नातकाचार्ययोस्तथा ।
नाक्रामेत्कामतश्छायां बभ्रुणो दीक्षितस्य च ॥१३०॥

एतद्वदन्तो; TMd[3] विद्वांसोत्रयी° — c) Jm Jo[1] Kt[2] MTr[3] *Mandlik Jha KSS Dave* क्रमतः; Pu[4] अमतः; TMd[4] पूर्वाम°; Be[3] सर्वम°; NKt[4] °मभ्यस्तु; Pu[10] °मन्यस्य; Lo[5] °मत्यस्य

126. Omitted in Lo[3]. Cited by *Hem* 3/3.767; *Dev* 1.158 — a) La[1] पशुमार्जारमाण्डूक°; Ho पशुं मण्डूकं मार्जारं; Lo[1] पशुमर्दकमार्जार°; TMd[4] MTr[3] °मार्जाल° — b) NKt[4] °सर्प्य°; GMd[5] Pu[2] Pu[4] Tr[1] MTr[4] *Dev* °नकुलादिभिः; Ho °नाकुलापुभिः; Pu[10] °नकुलासुभिः; TMd[3] GMy MTr[6] [*Jolly* Gr] °नकुलादिषु; GMd[1] °नकुलेषु च — c) wKt[1] Pu[7] *Hem* विन्द्याद°; sOx[1] sPu[6] विद्याम°; GMd[1] कुर्याद° — d) NKt[4] °नध्ययम°; Wa °नध्यायोहर्निशं

127. Pādas b-d omitted in Tr[1]. Cited by *Viś* 1.145; *Apa* 193 — a) TMd[3] oOr वर्जयन्नि°; MTr[3] वर्धयेन्नि° — b) TMd[4] Tj[2] °ध्यायो; Tr[2] °ध्याद्यो — c) Tj[1] वाशुद्धा; wKt[3] चाशुद्धात्मानं — d) TMd[3] चाशुचिर्द्विजः; BBe[2] चाशुद्धिर्द्विजः

128. Omitted in Ho; *ma* in La[1]; pādas a-c omitted in Tr[1]; pādas a-b *ma* in Bo. Cited by *Vij* 1.79; *Apa* 103; *Hem* 3/3.724; *Mādh* 1.498 — a) NPu[1] Pu[2] Pu[4] Pu[5] Pu[7] Tr[2] *Mādh* अमावास्याष्टमीं चैव [Tr[2] *Mādh* °ष्टमी]; Tj[1] अष्टमीं चैवामास्यां [*om* च]; Lo[1] अमावस्या° — b) NNg पूर्ण°; BBe[2] पौर्णिमां चतु°; wKt[1] °माशीं; GMd[1] °मास्यां; Hy Tr[2] चतुर्दशी — d) Tr[1] °त्यमनृतौ; wKt[1] °प्युभौ; GMy °प्येतौ; TMd[3] °प्येता स्नातका

Additional verse in Tr[2] *Mandlik KSS Dave;* commented by *Rc:*

षष्ट्यष्टम्यौ त्वमावास्यामुभयत्र चतुर्दशीम् ।
वर्जयेत्पौर्णमासीं च तैले मांसे भगे क्षुरे ॥

129. Cited by *Apa* 135; *Lakṣ* 3.35; *Hem* 3/2.857 3/3.707 — a) Bo °चरन्भुक्त्वा; Lo[5] Tr[1] °द्भुक्ता; Lo[4] °द्भुक्त — b) Pu[4] *om* °निशि ... [129c] सहा°; oOr नान्तरो; Tr[2] *om* न; wKt[3] TMd[3] नामहा°; Tr[2] मनीनिशि; Ox[3] °निशा; oOr °निशं — c) NNg [*bur cor fh*] NPu[1] वासोपि; TMd[4] वासाभिस्; *Lakṣ* °सोभिर्न चाजस्रं; Ho महाजस्रं — d) Lo[4] Tr[2] नाविज्ञात; Wa नाविज्ञातो; Be[1] MTr[4] न विज्ञाते; TMd[3] न विज्ञातो

130. Cited by *Vij* 1.152; *Apa* 193; *Lakṣ* 2.372; *Mādh* 1.522 — a) TMd[4] sOx[1] sPu[6] गुरौ; *Lakṣ* गुरोर्प्रोज्ञः; Tj[1] राज्ञा; NKt[4] राज्ञो — b) sOx[1] स्नातकश्चार्ययोस्तथा; NKt[4] स्नातकार्ययोस्तथा; *Lakṣ* °चार्यमन्त्रिणां; *Mādh* °योस्तया; oOr °कोस्तथा — c) GMd[1] न क्रमेच्च पदजाश [broken] बभ्रुणो; wKt[1] wKt[6] नाक्रमे°; NKt[4] न क्रमे°; wKt[6] GMd[5] °त्क्रामत°; Tr[1] °मेत्पादतश्छायां; Pu[2] Pu[4] °मतस्थायां; TMd[3] GMy °मतश्चाङ्गं — d) *Lakṣ* कपिलस्य च गोरपि; Pu[5] बभ्रणो; GMy बभ्राणो; Tr[2] बभ्रुणं; Tj[1] बभ्रूर्णो; wKt[1] वटुणो; wKt[6] नकुलस्य च; BKt[5] नक्षनस्य च

Lakṣ 2.372 adds a verse immediately after his citation of 130 clearly ascribing it to

मध्यंदिनेऽर्धरात्रे च श्राद्धं भुक्त्वा च सामिषम् ।
संध्ययोरुभयोश्चैव न सेवेत चतुष्पथम् ॥१३१॥
उद्वर्तनमपस्नानं विण्मूत्रे रक्तमेव च ।
श्लेष्मनिष्ठ्यूतवान्तानि नाधितिष्ठेच्च* कामतः ॥१३२॥
वैरिणं नोपसेवेत सहायं चैव वैरिणः ।
अधार्मिकं तस्करं च परस्यैव च योषितम् ॥१३३॥
न हीदृशमनायुष्यं लोके किंचन विद्यते ।
यादृशं पुरुषस्येह परदारोपसेवनम् ॥१३४॥
क्षत्रियं चैव सर्पं च ब्राह्मणं च बहुश्रुतम् ।
नावमन्येत वै भूष्णुः कृशानपि कदाचन ॥१३५॥
एतत् त्रयं हि पुरुषं निर्दहत्यवमानितम् ।
तस्मादेतत् त्रयं नित्यं नावमन्येत बुद्धिमान् ॥१३६॥

Manu:

स्वां तु नाक्रमयेच्छायां क्लीबेन पतितेन च ।
चाण्डालेन द्विपद्भिश्च नित्यं रोगान्वितेन च ॥

131. Cited by *Apa* 193; *Hem* 3/3.699; *Lakṣ* 2.373 — a) *Apa* मध्यंदिने च रात्रौ च; Tr[1] °रात्रौ च; wKt[3] तु; Be[3] BKt[5] wKt[6] Tj[1] [*Jolly* M[1–2–9]]वा — b) Hy सार्धं; Bo Jm Lo[4] Lo[5] Tr[1] भुक्ता; NNg भुक्त्वैव; Be[3] Tj[1] *Lakṣ* [*Jolly* G] तु; Pu[2] Pu[4] सामिकं — c) MTr[3] °भयोश्चेव — d) BKt[5] NNg वसेत; wKt[6] वेसेत; Tr[2] चतुष्पर्थीं; Pu[2] Pu[4] चतुष्पदं

132.* Pāda-d omitted in Lo[4]. Cited by *Vij* 1.152; *Apa* 183 — a) Be[1] Bo wKt[1] Lo[1] Lo[4] Ox[3] °नमपःस्नानं; Pu[8] °नमधस्नानं; NKt[4] oOr °नमवस्नानं; GMd[1] °नमपिस्नान; Pu[3] °नमलस्नानं; TMd[3] °नमपस्नातं; Lo[2] °स्नाने; *Apa* °स्थानं — b) TMd[3] GMy रेतो निण्मूत्रमेव च; *Apa* भक्तं [vl रक्तं] विण्मूत्रमेव च; Be[3] wKt[1] oMd[2] GMd[5] NNg Tr[1] MTr[4] विण्मूत्रं; Lo[4] Tj[1] विण्मूत्र — c) Pu[10] श्लेष्मानिछातवान्तानि; BBe[2] Ho °निष्ठूत°; Wa °निश्रुत°; NKt[4] °निष्वात°; wKt[6] °निकृत°; Ox[2] °निष्ठीवताताानि — d) Be[1] Ho wKt[3] Lo[4] Lo[5] oOr Ox[3] NPu[1] Pu[10] Tj[1] Tr[2] [*Jolly* M] *Vij* °तिष्ठेत; Be[3] Bo Jo[2] La[1] La[2] Lo[1] Lo[2] Ox[2] Pu[2] Pu[3] Pu[4] Pu[8] °तिष्ठेद्धि; BBe[2] Hy Jm Jo[1] Kt[2] GMd[1] oMd[2] TMd[3] GMy sOx[1] sPu[6] Tj[2] [*Jolly* Nd] *Mandlik Jha KSS Dave* °तिष्ठेत्तु

133. Ho transposes verses 133 and 134; pāda-d *ma* in Lo[4]. Cited by *Apa* 194; *Mādh* 1.522 — a) Lo[4] Pu[5] वैरिणां; TMd[3] नोपसव्येत; Lo[3] नैव सेवेत; Be[3] Tj[1] नोपतिष्ठेत — b) La[1] न सहायाश्च वैरिणिः; Be[3] सहाय्यं; Pu[10] सहावैयं; wKt[3] सहायाश्चैव; Lo[1] Tj[2] *Apa* सहायांश्चैव; BKt[5] wKt[6] वैरिणं; GMd[1] वारिणः; GMy विरिणं — c-d) Be[3] चैव परस्यैव तु — d) Be[1] Ho GMd[5] तु; Tj[2] योषितः

134. a) Bo NNg sPu[6] [*but mc sh*] हीदृस्यम°; Be[1] *mc to* हीदृष्ट्यम°; BKt[5] °नाद्यष्यं — b) BBe[2] wKt[6] La[1] TMd[3] GMy NPu[1] किंचित्र; Be[3] किंचित्तु — d) GMd[1] °दारोभिसेवनं; Hy °पसेवते

135. Cited by *Apa* 194; *Lakṣ* 2.397; *Mādh* 1.522 — a) BKt[5] wKt[6] क्षत्रियं कृष्णसर्पं च; MTr[6] राजानं; wKt[3] Tr[2] क्षत्रियश्चैव; oMd[2] चैव निस्तर्पं; Tr[2] सर्पश्च; Pu[2] Pu[4] विप्रं च; GMd[5] तु — b) oOr Tr[1] ब्रह्मणं — c) Lo[5] नावरन्येत; oMd[2] °न्येत वर्जिष्णुः; Pu[2] ते भूष्णुः; Pu[4] तो भूष्णुः; *Lakṣ* वै दृप्टं — d) Ho कृशामपि

136. Cited by *Apa* 194; *Lakṣ* 2.397 — a) *Apa* पुरुषान् — b) Tj[1] निर्दहत्येवमानितं; Pu[2] Pu[4] निर्दहन्त्यममानितं; BCa GMd[1] निर्दहेदेवमानितं; Jo[2] Lo[3] निर्दहत्यपमानितं; wKt[6] निर्दहत्येवमास्थितं; Wa

नात्मानमवमन्येत पूर्वाभिरसमृद्धिभिः ।
आ मृत्योः श्रियमन्विच्छेन्नैनां मन्येत दुर्लभाम् ॥१३७॥
सत्यं ब्रूयात् प्रियं ब्रूयान्न ब्रूयात्सत्यमप्रियम् ।
प्रियं च नानृतं ब्रूयादेष धर्मः सनातनः ॥१३८॥
भद्रं भद्रमिति ब्रूयाद्भद्रमित्येव वा वदेत् ।
शुष्कवैरं विवादं च न कुर्यात्केनचित्सह ॥१३९॥
नातिकल्यं नातिसायं नातिमध्यंदिने स्थिते ।
नाज्ञातेन समं गच्छेन्नैको न वृषलैः सह ॥१४०॥
हीनाङ्गानतिरिक्ताङ्गान् विद्याहीनान्वयोऽधिकान् ।
रूपद्रविणहीनांश्च जातिहीनांश्च नाक्षिपेत् ॥१४१॥
न स्पृशेत्पाणिनोच्छिष्टो विप्रो गोब्राह्मणानलान् ।
न चापि पश्येदशुचिः स्वस्थो ज्योतिर्गणं दिवि ॥१४२॥

नित्यमहन्त्यवमानितं; BBe^{2} Hy Jm Jo^{1} wKt^{1} Kt^{2} wKt^{3} TMd^{3} GMd^{5} GMy Pu^{3} Tj^{2} Tr^{1} MTr^{3} MTr^{4} MTr^{6} [*Jolly* Nd] *Mandlik Jha KSS Dave* निर्दहेदवमा°; Lo^{4} निर्ददृश्यत्यवमा°; TMd^{4} °मानितः; Ho GMd^{5} °मानिनं — c) GMd^{1} तस्मादेतान्प्रयतेत; TMd^{4} तस्मादेतान्प्रयत्नेन; *Lakṣ* तस्मादेतत्प्रयत्नेन; MTr^{4} MTr^{6} अस्मादे°; Bo La^{1} तस्वादेव त्रयं — d) Lo^{4} °मन्येत च द्विजान्

137. *ma* in Be^{3} Pu^{7}. Cited by *Lakṣ* 2.397; *Mādh* 1.522; pādas a-b cited by *Apa* 194 — a) Pu^{2} Pu^{4} आत्मानं नावमन्येत; Tr^{2} °मन्येत् — b) Tj^{1} Tr^{2} पूर्वापरसमृद्धिभिः; Pu^{10} पूर्वोदिर°; TMd^{4} °सबुद्धिभिः — c) Lo^{4} GMd^{1} Tr^{2} MTr^{4} अमृत्योः; Ho GMd^{5} NNg Pu^{5} Pu^{7} [*Jolly* G Nd] श्रियमाकाङ्क्षे° — d) TMd^{3} *Lakṣ* °न्विच्छेन्नैतां; oOr °न्विच्छेन्नैकां; Be^{1} °न्विच्छेन्नानां; TMd^{4} °न्विच्छेत्तेनां; Jm °न्विच्छेत्तेन; Lo^{4} मन्येतु दुर्लभा; La^{1} मन्येत्सुदुर्लभां; BKt^{5} wKt^{6} Pu^{10} MTr^{4} दुर्लिभं; GMd^{5} दुर्लितां; TMd^{3} दुर्लभात्; Tj^{1} दुर्घगां

138. *ma* in Be^{3}. Cited by *Apa* 163; *Dev* 1.14; pādas a-b cited by *Dev* 3.49 — a) Hy ब्रूयास्त्रियं — a-b) Tj^{2} *om* ब्रूयान्न — c) TMd^{3} GMy चा; Lo^{4} Ox^{3} [*Jolly* M] वा; Be^{3} Tj^{1} तु; Kt^{2} नामृतं

139. Pādas a-b *ma* in Be^{3} — a) GMd^{5} अभद्रं भद्रवत् ब्रूयात्; wKt^{3} ब्रूये भद्र° — b) BKt^{5} wKt^{6} ब्रूयान्नाभद्रं तु कदाचन; oOr °मित्येति वा; Pu^{2} Pu^{4} चावदेत्; Be^{1} Be^{3} Bo Ho GMd^{1} TMd^{3} GMy NNg Tj^{1} Tr^{1} Tr^{2} वादयेत्; Pu^{10} वाग्वदेत्; Lo^{4} वाक्वदेत् — c) GMd^{5} शुष्कं; Lo^{4} शुष्कवरं; TMd^{4} शुषं वैरं; Lo^{5} विवादे; Tr^{2} विवादांश्च — d) TMd^{4} °चित्सदा

140. Omitted in oOr. Cited by *Apa* 173; *Mādh* 1.522 — a) Lo^{2} TMd^{3} TMd^{4} NNg Ox^{3} Pu^{10} Tr^{1} [*Jolly* M^{1-2-9} Me N] *Apa* °काल्यं; Pu^{5} Pu^{7} °कल्य; Be^{1} Lo^{1} Tj^{1} °कल्पं; BCa NKt^{4} Tj^{1} °शायं; Lo^{1} °साद्यं — b) TMd^{4} *Mādh* °मध्यंगते रवौ; Tr^{1} °दिने रवौ; wKt^{1} sOx^{1} °दिने तथा; Lo^{1} °दिने सहः — c) *Apa* नाज्ञातेन च संगच्छे°; MTr^{3} न ज्ञातेन; GMd^{1} सेमं; Lo^{4} गच्छन्नैको — d) BKt^{5} wKt^{6} °न्नैके; TMd^{4} °न्नेको; Tr^{1} वृषळैः; *Mādh* वृषलेः

141.* Cited by *Apa* 194; *Mādh* 1.522 — a) MTr^{4} MTr^{6} °तिमुक्तागान् — b) TMd^{3} °हीनो वयो°; Be^{3} BBe^{2} Bo wKt^{1} NKt^{4} BKt^{5} wKt^{6} La^{2} Lo^{2} Lo^{4} Lo^{5} oOr Ox^{3} NPu^{1} Pu^{3} Pu^{8} Pu^{10} Tj^{1} Wa [*Jolly* M N] *Apa Me Nā Dave Jha* °नान्वयोतिगान्; NNg °नान्वयोगतान् — c) Jm Jo^{1} Kt^{2} MTr^{3} *Nd Mandlik KSS* रूपद्रव्यविहीनांश्च; Tj^{2} रूपद्रविहीनांश्च; TMd^{3} रूप्रद्रहीनांश्च; Lo^{1} °द्रविणो°; Tr^{1} °हीनाश्च — d) Be^{3} Ho Tj^{1} नाक्षिपेन्मानुषान्क्वचित्; Pu^{4} *om* जातिहीनांश्च; oMd^{2} °हानांश्च; Lo^{1} Pu^{4} न क्षिपेत्

142* a) TMd^{3} °त्प्राणिनो°; La^{1} Tr^{1} °च्छिष्टं — b) Lo^{1} sOx^{1} Pu^{5} sPu^{6} Pu^{7} विप्र; GMy °ब्राह्मणो-

स्पृष्ट्वैतानशुचिर्नित्यमद्भिः प्राणानुपस्पृशेत् ।
गात्राणि चैव सर्वाणि नाभिं पाणितलेन तु ॥१४३॥
अनातुरः स्वानि खानि न स्पृशेदनिमित्ततः ।
रोमाणि च रहस्यानि सर्वाण्येव विवर्जयेत् ॥१४४॥
मङ्गलाचारयुक्तः स्यात् प्रयतात्मा जितेन्द्रियः ।
जपेच्च जुहुयाच्चैव नित्यमग्निमतन्द्रितः ॥१४५॥
मङ्गलाचारयुक्तानां नित्यं च प्रयतात्मनाम् ।
जपतां जुह्वतां चैव विनिपातो न विद्यते ॥१४६॥
वेदमेव जपेन्नित्यं यथाकालमतन्द्रितः ।
तं ह्यस्याहुः परं धर्ममुपधर्मोऽन्य उच्यते ॥१४७॥

नलान्; TMd³ °नलात्; Be³ °निलान् — c) Pu⁴ तं चापि; Tj¹ वापि; GMd¹ TMd³ GMy चाभि — d) Be³ Ho Tj¹ °शुचिस्तथा ज्यो°; TMd⁴ स्वस्था; BBe² Hy Jm Jo¹ Kt² Lo⁴ Lo⁵ oMd² Pu³ Pu⁴ Tj² MTr³ *Mandlik KSS Jolly* सुस्थो; sOx¹ sPu⁶ ज्योतिर्गणो; Tj¹ ज्योतिर्गणा; BCa Jm Jo¹ TMd³ TMd⁴ ज्योतिर्गणां; Hy Lo¹ Kt² GMd¹ GMd⁵ GMy Tj² Tr¹ MTr⁴ MTr⁶ [*Jolly* Ku Nd]*Ku Mr Mandlik Jha KSS Dave* ज्योतिर्गणान्दिवि; wKt¹ ज्योतिष्कुलान्दिवि

143. Cited by *Vij* 1.155; *Apa* 231 — a) Tr¹ स्पृष्ट्वाता°; *Vij* स्पृष्टैता°; BBe² wKt⁶ TMd⁴ स्पृष्टेता°; Lo⁵ स्पृष्टायैता°; GMd⁵ दृष्ट्वैता°; Be¹ पृष्ट्वैता°; NNg *Apa* स्पृष्ट्वैतानिशुचि°; Pu⁵ Pu⁷ °तानाशुचि°; Lo⁴ °शुचिनित्य°; TMd³ °शुचिं नित्य° — b) *Apa* [vl] °पास्पृशेत् — c) Lo² मात्राणि; Lo⁴ सर्वापि — d) Pu⁴ *om* नाभिं पाणि; GMd¹ पाणितलेपु च *then adds* तथा; BKt⁵ wKt⁶ oOr च; Ho oMd² वै

144.* a) sPu⁶ *cor to* अनारत; oMd² अनालुब्धः; Tr¹ स्वानखानि; TMd⁴ स्वानदाति; Pu¹⁰ *om* खानि; TMd³ खाति — b) Be¹ स्पृशेनमित्ततः — c) Pu⁸ Tr² *om* च; Lo⁴ चा; wKt⁶ रहस्याणि; GMy शिरस्यानि; Tr² सहस्यानि; *Dave* रहःस्थानि — d) NKt⁴ oMd² सर्वाण्येव च वर्जयेत्; GMd⁵ Tr¹ MTr⁴ MTr⁶ सर्वाण्येतानि वर्जयेत्; sOx¹ sPu⁶ सर्वाणि परिवर्जयेत्; wKt¹ सर्वाणि च; TMd³ सर्वाश्येव; Pu³ नित्यमेव; NPu¹ विसर्जयेत्

145. Cited by *Apa* 229 — a) BKt⁵ wKt⁶ °युक्तस्तु प्रय° — b) Pu³ Pu⁸ नियतात्मा; Wa यतेन्द्रियः — d) oMd² °च्चैवानिशमग्निमतन्द्रितः; NNg Tr² नित्यकालमतन्द्रितः; NKt⁴ BKt⁵ wKt⁶ नित्यजलमतन्द्रितः; Wa नित्यमतन्द्रितः; *Apa* विनिपातो न विद्यते [cf 4.146d]; wKt³ °तन्द्रियः; Ox³ °तिन्द्रितः; Tj¹ °तन्द्रितैः; Hy °तन्त्रितः

Additional verse in TMd³ GMd⁵ Tr¹:

सुवर्णं चन्दनं रक्तं पञ्चगव्यानि रोचनाम् ।
प्रियंगुं सर्पपं क्षौद्रं मङ्गलानि प्रचक्षते ॥

b) TMd³ शोचनां — c) TMd³ प्रियगुं; GMd⁵ प्रियंगु; TMd³ क्षाद्रं

146. Omitted in GMy — a) Pu⁸ °मुक्तानां — b) Be³ Tj¹ नियतात्मनां — c) La¹ जपवान्जुह्वतां; Lo⁴ वैव

147. Pādas a-b omitted in GMy and pādas c-d in TMd⁴. Cited by *Apa* 69, 229; *Lakṣ* 3.94; *Dev* 2.499 — a) BCa Hy Jm Jo¹ Kt² oMd² Tj² MTr³ *Dev Mandlik KSS* वेदमेवाभ्यसेन्नित्यं; NKt⁴ जपन्नित्यं; La¹ सदाभ्यसेद् — b) wKt¹ NKt⁴ sOx¹ sPu⁶ [*mc sh to*] यथाकामम°; BKt⁵ wKt⁶ °तन्द्रियः — c) *Apa* [vl] ते ह्य°; TMd³ न ह्य°; Lo¹ तर्ह्य°; Be³ Ho Jo² Lo³ Tj¹ Wa [*Jolly* R] तमेवाहुः; sOx¹ sPu⁶ Tr² तमस्याहुः; Tr¹ ह्यस्याशुः; Tr² धर्मा उप° — d) Be¹ धर्ममपधर्मो; Lo¹ °धर्मोन उच्यते — Hy repeats this verse with the following changes: a) जपन्नित्यं; c) तमेवाहुः

वेदाभ्यासेन सततं शौचेन तपसैव च ।
अद्रोहेण च भूतानां जातिं स्मरति पौर्विकीम् ॥१४८॥
पौर्विकीं संस्मरञ्जातिं ब्रह्मैवाभ्यसते द्विजः ।
ब्रह्माभ्यासेन चाजस्रमनन्तं सुखमश्नुते ॥१४९॥
सावित्राञ्छान्तिहोमांश्च कुर्यात्पर्वसु नित्यशः ।
पितॄंश्चैवाष्टकास्वर्चेन्नित्यमन्वष्टकासु च ॥१५०॥
दूरादावसथान्मूत्रं दूरात्पादावसेचनम् ।
उच्छिष्टान्नं निषेकं च दूरादेव समाचरेत् ॥१५१॥
मैत्रं प्रसाधनं स्नानं दन्तधावनमञ्जनम् ।
पूर्वाह्ण एव कुर्वीत देवतानां च पूजनम् ॥१५२॥

148. Omitted in tMd^{4}. Cited by *Apa* 229; *Dev* 2.499— b) mTr^{4} mTr^{6} सत्येन तप° ; oOr Tj^{1} तपसेन; Jo^{2} हि — c) wKt^{6} Lo^{4} gMd^{5} Ox^{3} Pu^{2} Pu^{4} Pu^{5} Pu^{7} Pu^{10} Tr^{1} mTr^{4} *Jolly* [*Jolly* M G Nd] अद्रोहेणैव; oOr अद्रोहे चैव — d) Tr^{1} जाति; Lo^{5} स्मरते; Be^{1} wKt^{3} gMd^{5} gMy Tr^{1} पौर्वकीं; Ho पौर्वकां; Kt^{2} पौर्विकिं; mTr^{6} पूर्विकीं; Pu^{5} Pu^{7} [*Jolly* G] पूर्विकां

149.* Pādas a-b omitted in tMd^{4}. Cited by *Apa* 229; *Lakṣ* 3.94; *Dev* 2.500 — a) *Lakṣ* संस्मृत्य पौर्वकीं जातिं; tMd^{3} gMd^{5} gMy Tr^{1} mTr^{4} mTr^{6} संस्मरन्पौर्विकीं जातिं [gMd^{5} Tr^{1} °न्पौर्वकीं]; Be^{1} पौर्वकीं; Pu^{7} पूर्विकां; Pu^{5} [*Jolly* G] पूर्वकां; Tr^{2} स्मरणं जातिं; Bo Lo^{3} संस्मरेज्जातिं — b) Tr^{2} ब्रह्मैव चाभ्यसेत्पुनः; wKt^{6} ब्रह्मैवावभ्यते; Lo^{4} ब्रह्मैवान्यस्यते; Jm wKt^{3} Lo^{4} Lo^{5} gMd^{1} tMd^{3} gMd^{5} gMy sOx^{1} Ox^{2} Ox^{3} sPu^{6} Pu^{8} Pu^{10} Tr^{2} *Mandlik Jha KSS Dave* °भ्यस्यते; Be^{1} nKt^{4} Lo^{2} gMd^{1} Tr^{1} °भ्यस्यति; mTr^{4} mTr^{6} °भ्यसति; Hy °भ्यास्यते; Bo °वाक्ष्यते; bBe^{2} Be^{3} bCa Hy Jm Jo^{1} Jo^{2} wKt^{1} Kt^{2} wKt^{3} bKt^{5} wKt^{6} Lo^{1} Lo^{3} oMd^{2} nNg oOr sOx^{1} nPu^{1} Pu^{5} sPu^{6} Pu^{7} Tj^{1} Tj^{2} Tr^{2} Wa [*Jolly* G R Ku] *Apa Mandlik Jolly KSS* पुनः —c) Pu^{5} Pu^{7} ब्राह्मा° ; Bo °भ्यांसन; Tr^{1} °भासेनमेजस्रम° ; Lo^{4} चाजश्रम° ; *Lakṣ* वाजस्रम° ; sOx^{1} sPu^{6} सततमनन्तं — c-d) *Apa* ब्रह्माभ्यासेन चानन्तमजस्रं फलमश्नुते — d) Wa °स्रं सुखमत्यन्तमश्नुते; Lo^{3} °स्रं सुखमनन्तमश्नुते; Be^{3} bCa Lo^{2} Lo^{4} Ox^{3} nPu^{1} Pu^{8} Pu^{10} Tr^{2} [*Jolly* M N] °स्रमानन्त्यं; oOr °स्रमानन्तं; Ox^{2} °स्रमनन्त्यं; Lo^{1} °स्रमनन्तसुख° ; nNg °स्रमानन्त्यसुख° ; Tj^{1} °स्रमानन्त्यात्सुख° ; Bo °स्रमतत्यसुख°

150. Cited by *Apa* 229 — a) wKt^{1} wKt^{3} सावित्र्या° ; mTr^{6} सावित्र्यं शान्ति° ; tMd^{3} gMd^{5} gMy Tr^{1} *Nd* [*Jolly* Nd N] सावित्र्या शान्ति° ; nKt^{4} सावित्रां शान्ति° ; Tj^{1} सावित्री शान्ति° ; tMd^{4} सावित्रीं शान्ति° ; *Apa* सावित्राञ्जातिहो° ; Ox^{2} °त्रांश्छान्ति° ; Be^{3} °होमाश्च; tMd^{4} °होमश्च — b) Lo^{4} कुयाद्वर्चसु — c) *Apa* अष्टकासु पितॄनर्चेन्नि° ; nKt^{4} °ष्टकास्पर्शेन्नि° ; Tj^{1} °ष्टाकाः सर्वे नित्यम° ; bKt^{5} wKt^{6} Lo^{4} Lo^{5} °स्वर्चन्नि° — d) gMd^{1} *om* नित्यम्

151. wKt^{1} places pādas 153a-b after 151a-b. Cited by *Dev* 2.237; *Mādh* 1.211 — a) Lo^{4} °शथान्मूत्रं; Tj^{1} °सधान्मूत्रं; wKt^{6} °सखान्मूत्रं — b) Jo^{2} Lo^{3} Wa दूरे पादा° ; gMd^{5} gMy nNg Tr^{1} mTr^{4} mTr^{6} °वनेजनं; wKt^{1} °वनेजजं; tMd^{3} °वसीजनं; Ho °वसेवनं — c) Pu^{10} तच्छिष्टान्नं; Lo^{1} उच्छिष्टानां; Jo^{1} Kt^{2} La^{1} Lo^{3} gMy Pu^{5} Pu^{7} Tj^{1} Tr^{1} mTr^{4} Wa *Mandlik Jha KSS Dave* °ष्टान्ननिषेकं; mTr^{6} °ष्टाणनिषेकं; Jm °ष्टं सन्ननिषेकं; *Nā* gloss उच्छिष्टान्नस्य निषेकं त्यागम् assumes a Tatpuruṣa compound — d) Be^{1} विसर्जयेत्

152. Pādas c-d omitted in tMd^{4} — a) tMd^{3} मैत्र; Tj^{1} मूत्रप्रासा° ; Tj^{2} प्रधानं; gMd^{1} स्थानं — b) tMd^{3} gMd^{5} gMd^{1} gMy Tr^{1} स्नानमञ्जनं दन्तधावनं — c) La^{1} पूर्वाह्णमेव; Jo^{1} पूर्वाह्णे कुर्वीत [*om* एव] — d) Ho च पूर्वकं

दैवतान्यभिगच्छेत्तु धार्मिकांश्च द्विजोत्तमान् ।
ईश्वरं चैव रक्षार्थं गुरूनेव च पर्वसु ॥१५३॥
अभिवादयेद्वृद्धांश्च दद्याच्चैवासनं स्वकम् ।
कृताञ्जलिरुपासीत गच्छतः पृष्ठतोऽन्वियात् ॥१५४॥
श्रुतिस्मृत्युदितं सम्यङ् निबद्धं स्वेषु कर्मसु ।
धर्ममूलं निषेवेत सदाचारमतन्द्रितः ॥१५५॥
आचाराल्लभते ह्यायुराचारादीप्सिताः प्रजाः ।
आचाराद्धनमक्षय्यमाचारो हन्त्यलक्षणम् ॥१५६॥
दुराचारो हि पुरुषो लोके भवति निन्दितः ।
दुःखभागी च सततं व्याधितोऽल्पायुरेव च ॥१५७॥
सर्वलक्षणहीनोऽपि यः सदाचारवान्नरः ।
श्रद्दधानोऽनसूयश्च शतं वर्षाणि जीवति ॥१५८॥

153. Not commented by *Me;* omitted in Lo^{4} Lo^{5} Ox^{3} Pu^{10}. Cited by *Apa* 127 — a) Pu^{5} Pu^{7} देवतानि अभिगच्छेद्धार्मि°; wKt^{6} GMd^{1} sOx^{1} sPu^{6} देवतान्यभि°; NPu^{1} देवतानभि°; GMd^{5} दैवज्ञानभि°; wKt^{1} Pu^{2} Pu^{4} *Apa* °धिगच्छेत्तु; TMd^{3} GMy °गच्छेच्च; GMd^{1} oOr NPu^{1} °गच्छेत; TMd^{4} °गच्छेप्यधर्मि° — b) Lo^{1} oMd^{2} GMd^{5} धार्मिकांस्तु; Tr^{2} धार्मिकात्र च — c) Tr^{2} ईश्वरश्चैव; *Apa* [vl] दैव — d) wKt^{6} GMd^{1} च सर्वसु; NPu^{1} च सर्वदा

154. Not commented by *Me Nd;* omitted in Lo^{4} Lo^{5} Ox^{3} Pu^{10}. Cited by *Apa* 229 — a) TMd^{4} अभिवाद्येत्सह वृद्धान्; GMd^{1} अभिवायेत विप्रांश्च; Tr^{2} °वाद्याश्च वृद्धांश्च; Be^{1} NPu^{1} Tr^{1} [*Jolly* Nd] °वादेत वृद्धांश्च; NKt^{4} °वादयेत वृद्धान्; wKt^{6} TMd^{3} NNg °वादयेत वृद्धांश्च; Ho °वादयेत्तु वृद्धांस्तु; Lo^{1} Pu^{5} Pu^{7} [*Jolly* G] °वादयेच्च वृद्धांश्च; Bo Jo^{2} Lo^{2} Lo^{3} sOx^{1} Pu^{3} sPu^{6} Pu^{8} *Apa* [*Jolly* R] °वाद्य च वृद्धांश्च; Wa °वाद्यविद्वृद्धांश्च; Be^{3} sOx^{1} sPu^{6} °द्धांस्तु — b) GMd^{1} दद्यात्स्वकमासनं; Pu^{5} Pu^{7} दत्त्वा चैवा°; Lo^{1} देयाच्चैवा°; Pu^{8} °वासन; TMd^{3} GMy °वासनादिकं — c) NPu^{1} °लिमुपासीत — d) TMd^{3} गच्छन्तं; TMd^{4} गर्हितः; wKt^{3} गच्छतस्पृष्ठतो; wKt^{1} Lo^{3} Tj^{1} Tr^{2} °न्वयात्; GMd^{5} Tr^{1} °न्वगात्

155. Not commented by *Me Rc;* omitted in Lo^{4} Lo^{5} Ox^{3} Pu^{10}; *ma* in Pu^{7}. In GMy the page containing verses 155–164 is missing — a) Tj^{1} स्मृत्यस्मृत्यु°; wKt^{3} °दिकं; wKt^{1} TMd^{3} °दितं कर्म; GMd^{1} Tr^{1} °दितं कुर्वन् — b) Tr^{1} निबद्ध; TMd^{4} निबन्धं — c) TMd^{4} मर्धमूलं — c-d) Lo^{1} सदाचारं निषेवेत धर्ममूलमतन्द्रितः — d) Hy °तन्त्रितः; Lo^{2} °तन्द्रियः

156. Not commented by *Nd;* omitted in NKt^{4} Lo^{4} Lo^{5} Ox^{3} Pu^{10}. Cited by *Apa* 231 — a) GMd^{1} TMd^{4} GMd^{5} °ल्लभ्यते; Wa चायुरा°; Lo^{2} स्वायुरा° — b) Jo^{2} Lo^{3} Pu^{7} Wa [*Jolly* G R] *Jolly* °प्सितां प्रजां — c) wKt^{1} आचाराद्वलम° — d) Bo हन्तलक्ष°; TMd^{4} ह्यन्तुलक्ष°

Additional verse in Tr^{1}:

आचारो हन्त्यकल्याणमाचारात्कुलवान्भवेत् ।
आचारात्पूज्यते लोक आचाराद्यश आप्नुयात् ॥

157. Not commented by *Me Nd;* omitted in NKt^{4} Lo^{4} Lo^{5} Ox^{3} Pu^{10}. Cited by *Apa* 231 — a) Pu^{2} Pu^{4} पुराचारो; Lo^{3} oOr [*Jolly* R] °चारोपि — b) Pu^{3} गर्हितः— d) Pu^{5} व्याधितौ

158. Not commented by *Me Nd Rc;* omitted in NKt^{4} Lo^{4} Lo^{5} Ox^{3} Pu^{10}. Cited by *Apa* 231 — a) Ho सर्वहीनोपि सततं — b) Bo wKt^{6} TMd^{3} GMd^{5} NNg NPu^{1} Pu^{3} Pu^{4} Tj^{1} Tr^{1} MTr^{4} MTr^{6} समुदाचारवान्नरः; TMd^{4} Pu^{5} Pu^{7} *Go* सम्यगाचारवान्नरः; *Apa* सर्वदाचारवान्नरः; GMd^{1} संमताचारवान्नरः; Tr^{2}

यद्यत्परवशं कर्म तत्तद्यत्नेन वर्जयेत् ।
यद्यदात्मवशं तु स्यात् तत्तत्सेवेत यत्नतः ॥१५९॥
सर्वं परवशं दुःखं सर्वमात्मवशं सुखम् ।
एतद्विद्यात्समासेन लक्षणं सुखदुःखयोः ॥१६०॥
यत्कर्म कुर्वतोऽस्य स्यात् परितोषोऽन्तरात्मनः ।
तत्प्रयत्नेन कुर्वीत विपरीतं तु वर्जयेत् ॥१६१॥
आचार्यं च प्रवक्तारं पितरं मातरं गुरुम् ।
न हिंस्याद्ब्राह्मणान् गाश्च सर्वांश्चैव तपस्विनः ॥१६२॥
नास्तिक्यं वेदनिन्दां च देवतानां च कुत्सनम् ।
द्वेषं स्तम्भं च मानं च क्रोधं तैक्ष्ण्यं च वर्जयेत् ॥१६३॥
परस्य दण्डं नोद्यच्छेत् क्रुद्धो नैनं निपातयेत् ।
अन्यत्र पुत्राच्छिष्याद्वा शिष्ट्यर्थं ताडयेत्तु तौ ॥१६४॥

समवाचारवान्नरः [all the above omit यः]; Ox^{2} [*but cor*] Pu^{2} *om* यः; Be^{1} यत्सदा°; sOx^{1} sPu^{6} स सदा°; [*Jolly* R]यः स्यादाचार°; Ox^{2} यः सर्वचार° — c) Tr^{2} °नसूयुश्च; Pu^{5} Pu^{7} °नुसूयश्च — d) GMd^{5} oOr शत; NNg जीवितं

159. Omitted in NKt^{4}. Cited by *Apa* 224 — a) wKt^{3} तद्यत्पर°; wKt^{1} Tr^{2} °त्परतरं; Bo °त्परवरां; GMd^{5} कृत्यं — b) Be^{3} Jo^{2} Tj^{1} तद्यत्नेन विवर्जयेत् — c) oOr °दात्मवशस्तु; Lo^{4} °दात्मवत्तु; Jo^{2} *om* तु — c-d) La^{1} °वशं तस्मात्तत्र सेवेत; TMd^{3} °वशं तस्यां तत्तत्सेवेत — d) *Apa* [vl as in ed] तत्ततद्यत्नेन सेवयेत्; Ho प्रयत्नतः; oMd^{2} नित्यशः;

160. Omitted in Pu^{2} Pu^{4}. Cited by *Apa* 224 — a) Tr^{2} परतरं — b) Bo °मात्मावशं — c) Lo^{1} Pu^{5} Pu^{7} एतद्विद्या समा°; Be^{3} एतद्विद्वान्समा°; TMd^{4} °मासीन — d) GMd^{1} लक्षकं

161. Omitted in Pu^{2} Pu^{4}. Cited by *Apa* 223; *Mādh* 1.523 — a) sOx^{1} कुरुतोस्य; Ho कुर्वतेस्य; Lo^{1} करुतोतेस्वस्य; *Mādh* कुर्वतोऽप्यस्य परि° — b) Lo^{1} परितोषे; Tr^{1} Wa परितोषान्त°; Bo °तोषो तदात्मनः — c) oMd^{2} यत्प्र°; Be^{3} wKt^{1} Tj^{1} Tr^{2} तत्तद्यत्नेन — d) TMd^{4} परतं तु विवर्जयेत्; Ho Tj^{1} विपरीतांस्तु; Be^{1} °रीतं विवर्जयेत्; wKt^{3} oMd^{2} Tr^{2} च

162. Omitted in Pu^{2} Pu^{4}. Cited by *Vij* 2.21; *Apa* 223; *Lakṣ* 2.393–4 — a) Ox^{3} वा; sOx^{1} °क्तार — b) sOx^{1} sPu^{6} *Vij* मातरं पितरं; Tr^{1} मातरं तथा — c) NKt^{4} BKt^{5} *Apa* °ह्मणं गाश्च; MTr^{6} °ह्मणं गान् च; wKt^{3} BKt^{5} wKt^{6} GMd^{1} TMd^{3} TMd^{4} GMd^{5} NNg sOx^{1} Pu^{5} Pu^{7} sPu^{6} Tr^{1} °ह्मणं गां च [sOx^{1} sPu^{6} वा]; [*Jolly* G] °ह्मणगां च; Tj^{1} °ह्मणांस्तांश्च; wKt^{3} Lo^{2} Lo^{4} Lo^{5} oOr Ox^{3} Pu^{10} °णान्गां च; MTr^{4} °ह्मणंश्चैव — d) Be^{3} सर्वाश्चैव

163. Omitted in Pu^{2} Pu^{4}. Cited by *Apa* 229 —a) Lo^{4} sOx^{1} नास्तिक्य; BBe^{2} नास्तिकं; MTr^{3} सास्तिक्यं; TMd^{3} °निन्दा — b) NKt^{4} *om* देवतानां च; Tr^{2} कुत्सवं; Lo^{2} कुत्समं — c) Wa *add at beginning* न हिंस्याद्; Lo^{4} Lo^{5} Tr^{2} द्विषं; TMd^{3} Pu^{3} द्वेप; wKt^{1} द्वेषं दण्डं; TMd^{4} द्विप्ट्या लोभं च मानं; GMd^{5} स्तोभं; BBe^{2} Be^{3} Hy Jm Jo^{1} wKt^{1} Kt^{2} wKt^{3} La^{1} oMd^{2} Ox^{2} NPu^{1} sPu^{6} [*but cor*] Tj^{1} Tr^{2} MTr^{3} MTr^{4} *Nd Mandlik KSS* दम्भं; Tr^{2} *om* मानं च; Lo^{5} यानं च — d) Ho wKt^{1} Kt^{2} NKt^{4} TMd^{4} Lo^{1} Tj^{1} तैक्ष्णं; Lo^{2} तैक्ष्यं; Bo तीक्ष्यं; wKt^{3} तैक्षं; sPu^{6} *om* च; BCa विवर्जयेत्

164. Omitted in Pu^{2} Pu^{4}; pādas a-b omitted in oOr. Cited by *Apa* 231; *Lakṣ* 2.396 — a) Ho परस्प [*mc* रं] दण्डं; wKt^{6} परदण्डं; Be^{1} sOx^{1} दण्ड; La^{1} नोप्रच्छेत्; wKt^{1} नोमृच्छेत्; Ho नोयच्छेत्; sOx^{1} sPu^{6} नोद्यक्षेत्; Hy नोच्छेत्; BBe^{2} येनेच्छेत् — a-b) TMd^{4} परस्सदं नोद्युच्छे क्रुद्धेन न निपातयेत् — b) *Lakṣ*

ब्राह्मणायावगूर्यैव द्विजातिर्वधकाम्यया ।
शतं वर्षाणि तामिस्रे नरके परिवर्तते ॥१६५॥
ताडयित्वा तृणेनापि संरम्भान्मतिपूर्वकम् ।
एकविंशतिमाजातीः पापयोनिषु जायते ॥१६६॥
अयुध्यमानस्योत्पाद्य ब्राह्मणस्यासृगङ्गतः ।
दुःखं सुमहदाप्नोति प्रेत्याप्राज्ञतया नरः ॥१६७॥
शोणितं यावतः पांसून् संगृह्णाति महीतलात् ।
तावतोऽब्दानमुत्रान्यैः शोणितोत्पादकोऽद्यते ॥१६८॥

क्रुद्धौ; Bo TMd^{3} क्रोधो; GMd^{1} नेनं; MTr^{4} त्रैनं; Jm Jo^{1} Kt^{2} oMd^{2} *Mandlik KSS* नैव; Hy sOx^{1} sPu^{6} *Lakṣ* नैवं — c) Lo^{4} अत्यन्त; NKt^{4} *Lakṣ* पुत्रशिष्याद्वा; sOx^{1} sPu^{6} Tj^{1} °ष्यांश्च; Be^{3} Tr^{2} °ष्याच्च; oOr *om* वा — d) Tj^{1} शिक्षयीताद्रयेव्रतौ; *Lakṣ* शिष्ट्यर्थं तत्र पातयेत्; La^{1} शिष्ट्यार्थं; GMy शिष्टार्थं; TMd^{4} शिष्टर्थं; Bo Ho शिष्यार्थं; TMd^{3} NPu^{1} शिक्ष्यार्थं; GMd^{5} Ox^{3} Tr^{1} *Apa* शिक्षार्थं; sOx^{1} sPu^{6} [*cor to*] शिक्यर्थं; NKt^{4} *om* ताडयेत्; wKt^{6} तालयेत्तु; Tr^{1} ताटयेत्; Wa ताडयेदुभौ; sOx^{1} sPu^{6} ताडयेत्सुतौ; Be^{3} ताडयेच्च तौ; TMd^{3} ता:

165. Omitted in Pu^{2} Pu^{4}. Cited by *Apa* 223; *Lakṣ* 2.394 — a) Tj^{1} ब्राह्मणानच गुर्वर्थे; Be^{3} Tr^{2} ब्राह्मणानवगूर्यैव; sOx^{1} sPu^{6} ब्रह्म°; Pu^{8} °गूर्यैवं; NKt^{4} °गूर्यव; wKt^{1} °गूर्येव; Jo^{1} oMd^{2} *Mandlik Jha KSS Dave* °गुर्यैव; BKt^{5} wKt^{6} °गुर्येत; La^{1} °गृह्यैव — b) Be^{1} Bo TMd^{3} GMd^{5} sOx^{1} sPu^{6} द्विजातिवध°; TMd^{4} द्विजातवध°; BBe^{2} °जातिर्धर्मकाम्यया; sOx^{1} °कामया; Kt^{2} °कान्यया; Be^{1} Ho Tr^{1} [*Jolly* Nd] °काङ्क्षया — c) Lo^{4} शत; BBe^{2} Ho wKt^{3} NKt^{4} La^{1} Lo^{4} oOr Ox^{3} NPu^{1} Pu^{3} Tr^{2} तामिश्रे; TMd^{4} Tj^{1} तामिस्रं — d) Bo Ox^{2} Pu^{3} Pu^{8} परिपच्यते; Lo^{2} परियस्यते; Be^{3} Tr^{2} परिपद्यते; oOr परिपतते; BBe^{2} wKt^{3} Tj^{1} प्रतिपद्यते; TMd^{3} GMy च प्रवर्तते

166. Omitted in Pu^{2} Pu^{4}. Cited by *Apa* 223; *Lakṣ* 2.394 — a) NKt^{4} वाडीर्यित्वो; oOr तृणेवापि — b) Tr^{2} सरभा°; BKt^{5} wKt^{6} संभवा°; oOr संभातान्म°; Ho TMd^{3} संरम्भा मति° — c) wKt^{1} °शतीना°; Hy Ox^{3} MTr^{3} °शतमा°; Tj^{1} °शतिं जन्मनि; Tr^{1} °जातिः; *Nd* °जाते: [with gloss आ जननात्]; *Me* and *Go* comments that the particle आ of आजातीः is without significance — *Me:* आकारोऽनर्थकः प्रलम्बत इतिवत्; *Go:* आजातीरित्याङ् पादपूरणः

167. Omitted in Pu^{2} Pu^{4}. Cited by *Apa* 223; *Lakṣ* 2.394 — a) BBe^{2} अयोध्य°; Tr^{1} आयुध्य° — b) BBe^{2} ब्राह्मणस्याङ्गतोसृजं; *Lakṣ* ब्राह्मणस्यानृशंसिनः; wKt^{3} ब्राह्मस्यासृगमतः; Wa ब्राह्मस्यासृ°; Bo °सृगङ्गताः; Pu^{10} °सृगागतः; Kt^{2} TMd^{3} NNg Tj^{1} Tr^{2} °सृगन्ततः — c) Hy दुःख; Pu^{10} दुःखे; TMd^{4} दुःखस्सुम°; Jm wKt^{6} Pu^{10} समहदा° — d) Tj^{1} प्रेत्य प्राज्ञः तथा नरः; GMd^{5} प्रेत्यताप्रज्ञतान्नरः; Pu^{5} Pu^{7} [*cor to*] प्रेत्यप्रा°; Ho प्रत्याप्रा°; GMd^{1} °प्रज्ञतया; NNg °प्राज्ञनया; TMd^{3} ततः

168. Omitted in Pu^{2} Pu^{4} Pu^{5}. Pādas a-b cited by *Apa* 223; *Lakṣ* 2.394 — a) Lo^{4} शोणिते; wKt^{1} *om* यावतः; GMd^{1} TMd^{3} GMd^{5} oOr Tr^{1} MTr^{4} MTr^{6} यावतः शोणितं; GMy यावन्तश्शोणितं; BBe^{2} Be^{3} BCa wKt^{1} Kt^{2} wKt^{3} NKt^{4} wKt^{6} La^{1} Lo^{1} Lo^{4} Ox^{3} oMd^{2} NPu^{1} Pu^{7} *Jolly* पांशून्; TMd^{3} पांस्रं — b) Ho oMd^{2} Tj^{1} °तलान्; Be^{3} °तलं; BBe^{2} TMd^{3} TMd^{4} GMd^{5} GMy oOr Tr^{1} MTr^{4} MTr^{6} °तले — c) Bo °ब्दादमु°; Lo^{3} °न्यानमु°; Be^{3} MTr^{3} *Lakṣ Rc* °ब्दानमुत्राद्यैः; Tr^{2} °ब्दानियुत्राद्यैः; Tj^{1} °ष्टानमुत्राद्यैः; GMd^{1} °नमत्रान्यैः; wKt^{6} °नमुद्रान्यैः; Lo^{4} °त्राह्यैः; Kt^{2} °त्रत्यैः; TMd^{4} °त्रान्ये — c-d) NPu^{1} तावंयन्वसहस्राणि तत्कर्ता नरके वसेत्; oOr तावतोऽब्दान्हि नरके शोणितोत्पादको वसेत्; [*Jolly* Gr] तावतोऽब्दसहस्राणि तत्कर्ता नरके वसेत [cf. 11.203] — d) GMd^{1} शोणितोत्पादनोद्यतैः; Jo^{1} MTr^{3} °त्पातको; NKt^{4} °त्पादवो; Lo^{1} °त्पाद्यको; Wa °त्पादके; Be^{3} °दको वसेत्

न कदाचिद् द्विजे तस्माद् विद्वानवगुरेदपि ।
न ताडयेत्तृणेनापि न गात्रात् स्रावयेदसृक् ॥१६९॥
अधार्मिको नरो यो हि यस्य चाप्यनृतं धनम् ।
हिंसारतिश्च यो नित्यं नेहासौ सुखमेधते ॥१७०॥
न सीदन्नपि धर्मेण मनोऽधर्मे निवेशयेत् ।
अधार्मिकाणां पापानामाशु पश्यन्विपर्ययम् ॥१७१॥
नाधर्मश्चरितो लोके सद्यः फलति गौरिव ।
शनैरावर्तमानस्तु कर्तुर्मूलानि कृन्तति ॥१७२॥
यदि नात्मनि पुत्रेषु न चेत्पुत्रेषु नप्तृषु ।

169. Omitted in Pu^{2} Pu^{4}. Cited by *Apa* 223; *Lakṣ* 2.394 — a) NKt^{4} *Lakṣ* द्विजं; Ho व्रजे — a-b) GMd^{1} TMd^{3} TMd^{4} GMd^{5} GMy Tr^{1} MTr^{4} MTr^{6} न कदाचिद् द्विजो विद्वान्तस्मादवगुरेदपि [GMd^{5} द्विजं; TMd^{4} GMd^{5} विद्वांस्त°; GMd^{1} GMd^{5} Tr^{1} °दपगुरेदपि] — b) Pu^{3} विप्रान्नवगुरेदपि; Pu^{5} Pu^{7} [*cor to*] °वगुणेदपि; Bo °वगुणादपि — d) NKt^{4} नागोत्रान्यावयेद°; Be^{3} Ho wKt^{1} Pu^{5} Pu^{7} गात्राच्छ्रावयेद°

Additional verses in GMd^{5}; verses 1–3 after verse 170 in Tr^{1}:

नक्तंचर्यं दिवास्वप्नमालस्यं पैशुनं मदम् ।
अतियोगमयोगं च श्रेयोर्थी परिवर्जयेत् ॥१॥
धर्ममेव चरेन्नित्यं सद्भिराचरितं सदा ।
न चानुतप्येत पुनर्धर्मं कृत्वा कदाचन ॥२॥
न गोषु च मनुष्येषु नाकाशे न च वर्त्मसु ।
पुरीषं श्रियमाकाङ्क्षन् रेत उत्स्रष्टुमर्हति ॥३॥
यद्यत्समाचरन्विप्रो नात्मनस्तुष्टिमाप्नुयात् ।
अलाघवं च कृत्वापि तत्सर्वं परिवर्जयेत् ॥४॥

1. c) GMd^{5} अनियोग° — d) GMd^{5} श्रेयांस्तु
2. b) Tr^{1} तथा
3. a) Tr^{1} न च गोषु — b) Tr^{1} न काम्येन च पर्वसु — c) GMd^{5} पुरीषश्श्रिय°

170.* Tr^{1} repeats this verse after the addition given above. Omitted in Pu^{2} Pu^{4}. Cited by *Apa* 230 — a) Tr^{2} न धार्मिको; sOx^{1} sPu^{6} जनो यो; Ho द्विजो यो; Tr^{1} योपि [but not in repetion] — b) Jm तस्य; Ox^{2} Tj^{1} वाप्य°; TMd^{4} चान्य°; NPu^{1} चैवानृतं; oOr वागनृतं; NKt^{4} भव्यनृतं; sOx^{1} sPu^{6} [*but cor*] °नृतं भवेत् — c) Hy Jm Jo^{1} Kt^{2} wKt^{3} Lo^{4} Lo^{5} oMd^{2} Tj^{1} Tj^{2} MTr^{3} MTr^{4} *Mandlik Jolly Jha KSS Dave* हिंसारतश्च; [*Jolly* Gr] हिंसावर्ती च; GMd^{1} हिंसाकारी च; TMd^{4} या — d) Pu^{3} नैहासौ; TMd^{4} हेहेसो; Bo ते ह्यसौ; Be^{1} Ho विन्दते सुखं

171. Omitted in Pu^{2} Pu^{4} Wa; not commented by *Mr*; Jm repeats 169 as 171. Cited by *Apa* 230 — a) TMd^{4} न सिद्धं नापि धर्मेण; wKt^{3} oOr सीदन्नपि हि धर्मेण; Ho संसीदन्नपि धर्मेण; Lo^{1} *cor to* °न्नप्यधर्मेण — b) Tj^{1} नरोधर्मे; oOr °धर्मो; wKt^{6} °धर्मेण वेशयेत्; TMd^{4} °धर्मिणि वेशयेत् — c) Be^{3} अधार्मिणां तु पापा°; Tj^{1} अधर्म्याणां तु पापा° — d) Lo^{5} पश्यद्वि°; Jm पत्यन्वि°; Tr^{1} विपश्यन्वि°

172. Omitted in Hy Pu^{2} Pu^{4}. Cited by *Apa* 230 — a) wKt^{1} नधर्म°; sOx^{1} sPu^{6} साधर्म°; Kt^{2} नाधर्मञ्चरितो; TMd^{4} नाधर्म चेरते; GMd^{5} °श्चरतो — b) NKt^{4} सप्रः फलन्ति; TMd^{4} पलित — c) NKt^{4} GMd^{5} *Me Nā Rn Dave Jha* °रावर्त्यमा°; wKt^{3} °रावर्हमा°; BBe^{2} °रावृत्तमानो हि; Ho sOx^{1} [*but both cor*] °मानश्च; wKt^{1} °माना हि — d) TMd^{3} कर्तुमूलानि; wKt^{3} कर्तुम्मूलाति; Ho शनैर्मूलानि; Be^{3} BKt^{6} wKt^{6} Lo^{4} Ox^{3} °मूलान्निकृन्तति; Tj^{1} °मूलंन्निकृंतति

न त्वेव तु कृतोऽधर्मः कर्तुर्भवति निष्फलः ॥१७३॥
अधर्मेणैधते तावत्ततो भद्राणि पश्यति ।
ततः सपत्नाञ्जयति समूलस्तु विनश्यति ॥१७४॥
सत्यधर्मार्यवृत्तेषु शौचे चैवारमेत्सदा ।
शिष्यांश्च शिष्याद्धर्मेण वाग्बाहूदरसंयतः ॥१७५॥
परित्यजेदर्थकामौ यौ स्यातां धर्मवर्जितौ ।
धर्मं चाप्यसुखोदर्कं लोकसंक्रुष्टमेव च ॥१७६॥
न पाणिपादचपलो न नेत्रचपलोऽनृजुः ।
न स्याद्वाक्चपलश्चैव न परद्रोहकर्मधीः ॥१७७॥
येनास्य पितरो याता येन याताः पितामहाः ।
तेन यायात्सतां मार्गं तेन गच्छन्न रिष्यति ॥१७८॥

173. Omitted in Hy Pu² Pu⁴. Cited by *Apa* 230 — a) Ho Tr¹ पौत्रेषु; wKt¹ पुत्रे च — b) GMd⁵ न पौत्रेषु न नप्तृषु; *Apa* [vl as in ed] नो; Bo wKt³ Tj¹ न च पुत्रेषु; Jo² Lo³ न तत्पुत्रेषु; oMd² TMd³ GMy Tj¹ MTr⁴ MTr⁶ *Apa* [vl as in ed] चेत्पौत्रेषु; GMd¹ चेत्पौतृषु; TMd⁴ चेत्पात्रेषु — c) GMd⁵ न चैव; NNg त्वैव; wKt⁶ त्वेधं; BCa oOr त्वेव हि; *Apa* त्वेवं हि; sOx¹ sPu⁶ Tr² कृतं कर्म; Kt² °धर्म्यः — d) Bo BKt⁵ wKt⁶ TMd⁴ sPu⁶ [*but cor*] निष्फलं; NNg निफलं; GMd¹ फलति

174. Omitted in Hy Pu² Pu⁴ — a) Tr¹ °र्मेणेधते; wKt¹ °र्मेणेवते; Tj¹ °र्मेणैवते; Lo¹ °र्मेणैवधत्तेत; Lo² °र्मेणैदतो; GMd¹ यावत्ततो — c) TMd⁴ सपत्नां जयति; Lo⁵ सपुत्राञ्जयति — d) BKt⁵ wKt⁶ ततो मूलान्निकृन्तति; Be³ Lo⁵ Ox² Pu³ समूलश्च; NKt⁴ Lo² Lo³ Ox³ Tr² समूलं च; Jo² समूलंश्च

175. Omitted in GMy Pu² Pu⁴; pādas c-d omitted in GMd¹ — a) Ho सत्यं; Lo³ Lo⁵ Pu⁵ Pu⁷ °धर्मार्थ°; Lo¹ °धर्माप°; TMd⁴ °धर्माद्य° — b) Tj¹ शैवे; Be¹ Be³ BCa Tr¹ Tr² चैव रमे°; GMd⁵ नैव रमे°; Lo¹ चैवारभे°; TMd³ वैवावारेत्सदा; TMd⁴ चोपरमेत्सदा — c) Jo² शिष्येत शिष्यान्धर्मेण; GMd⁵ शिष्यांस्तु; Lo³ शिष्येण शिष्या°; Bo wKt³ TMd⁴ sOx¹ sPu⁶ Pu⁷ Pu¹⁰ Wa शिष्यधर्मेण; Be³ शिष्यान्धर्मेण — d) TMd⁴ GMd⁵ Tr¹ वाक्शिश्नोदर°; TMd³ वाश्शिश्नोदर°; Ho Lo² sOx¹ sPu⁶ Tr² °संयुतः; Pu⁷ °संयमः; Pu¹⁰ °संचयोः

176.* Omitted in GMy Pu² Pu⁴. Cited by *Apa* 159; pāda-a cited by *Viś* 1.114— a) oMd² °कामो — b) Tj¹ *Apa* [vl as in ed] स्यातां धर्मविवर्जितौ [*om* यौ]; Bo NNg यो; Be³ स्यातां यौ — c) La¹ धर्मश्चाप्य°; Jo² धर्ममप्य°; Pu⁵ धर्ममर्थसु°; MTr³ Pu¹⁰ चास्य°; Tj¹ वाप्य° — d) NPu¹ Pu³ लोकसंधुष्ट°; TMd³ TMd⁴ लोकसंसृष्ट°; Be³ TMd³ Ox² NPu¹ [*but mc sh*] Tj¹ लोकसंघुष्ट°; wKt⁶ Pu¹⁰ लोकसंतुष्ट°; Be¹ BBe² BCa Ho Hy Jm Jo¹ Jo² wKt¹ Kt² wKt³ La¹ Lo¹ Lo³ Tj² MTr³ MTr⁶ [*Jolly* Ku N R] *Nā Ku Rn Mr KSS Mandlik* लोकविक्रुष्ट°; GMd⁵ लोके विक्रुष्ट°; Pu⁸ लोकसंद्विष्ट°; oMd² oOr MTr⁴ लोकविद्विष्ट°; Lo⁴ Lo⁵ Pu¹⁰ [*Jolly* M] वा

177. Omitted in GMy Pu² Pu⁴ — a) Bo ना; GMd¹ पादपाणि°; Wa °चपलौ — b) TMd³ नेत्रे; Tr² वेत्र°; wKt¹ °पलोमृदुः; GMd¹ TMd³ GMd⁵ Tr¹ MTr⁴ MTr⁶ °पलो भवेत्; [*Jolly* Gr] °पलस्तथा— d) TMd³ परिद्रोह°; La¹ परत्रोचकर्म°; Tj¹ °द्रोहकर्कधीः

178.* Omitted in GMy Pu² Pu⁴ Tj². Cited by *Kum* 1.3.7; *Viś* 1.7; *Vij* 1.254; *Hem* 3/2.1680; *Dev* 1.9; *Mādh* 1.523 — a) BBe² Ho wKt¹ wKt³ BKt⁵ wKt⁶ La¹ oOr Pu³ Pu⁵ Pu⁷ Tr² जाता — b) Bo wKt¹ wKt³ La¹ oOr जाताः — c) La¹ जायात्सतां; Pu³ °त्सतीं; TMd⁴ °त्सतं; Ho GMd⁵ मार्गे

ऋत्विक्पुरोहिताचार्यैर्मातुलातिथिसंश्रितैः ।
बालवृद्धातुरैर्वैद्यैर्ज्ञातिसंबन्धिबान्धवैः ॥१७९॥
मातापितृभ्यां जामीभिर्भ्रात्रा पुत्रेण भार्यया ।
दुहित्रा दासवर्गेण विवादं न समाचरेत् ॥१८०॥
एतैर्विवादान् संत्यज्य सर्वपापैः प्रमुच्यते ।
एतैर्जितश्च* जयति सर्वांल्लोकानिमान् गृही ॥१८१॥
आचार्यो ब्रह्मलोकेशः प्राजापत्ये पिता प्रभुः ।
अतिथिस्त्विन्द्रलोकेशो देवलोकस्य चर्त्विजः ॥१८२॥
जामयोऽप्सरसां लोके वैश्वदेवस्य बान्धवाः ।
संबन्धिनोऽपां लोकस्य पृथिव्या मातृमातुलौ ॥१८३॥

— d) Lo^5 येन; *Hem* तं न; nPu^1 mTr^6 गच्छंस्तरिष्यति; Pu^8 गच्छन्तरिष्यति; Pu^{10} गच्छंतरिष्यति; Tr^1 गच्छन्न निरिष्यति; Jm गच्छति रिष्यते; Bo Ho Hy Jo^1 Jo^2 Kt^2 wKt^3 La^2 Lo^1 Lo^2 Lo^3 Lo^4 Lo^5 nNg Pu^3 Pu^5 Pu^7 mTr^3 *Nā Ku Mandlik Jolly KSS Dave* रिष्यते; wKt^1 विष्यते; Hy विष्यति; Tj^1 व्यथते; bBe^2 bKt^5 wKt^6 oMd^2 Wa *Kum Vij Hem* दुष्यति

179. Omitted in gMy Pu^2 Pu^4; pādas c-d omitted in tMd^4. Cited by *Lakṣ* 2.352; pādas c-d cited by *Apa* 233 — a) Pu^5 °ताचार्यौ मातु°; wKt^1 °ताचार्ये मातु°; *Lakṣ* °ताचार्यमातु° — b) La^1 Lo^2 °संसृतैः; wKt^3 °संश्रियैः — c) gMd^1 tMd^3 gMd^5 oOr Tr^1 *Lakṣ* वृद्धबालातु°; wKt^1 वनिकवृद्धातु°; Hy °वृद्ध्यातु°; tMd^3 °तुरोवैद्यै°; Tj^1 Tr^1 °तुरैर्वैद्यैर्ज्ञाति°; Lo^1 °तुरकृशैर्ज्ञाति°; La^1 *Lakṣ* °तुरैर्विप्रैर्ज्ञाति°; Tr^2 °तुरैर्वृद्यैर्ज्ञाति°; Bo °तुरैर्वैद्यं ज्ञाति°; nKt^4 °तुरैर्वैद्येज्ञाति° — d) wKt^3 wKt^6 [*but cor*] gMd^5 °संबन्ध°

180. Omitted in tMd^4 gMy Pu^2 Pu^4. Cited by *Apa* 233; *Lakṣ* 2.352 — a) bBe^2 bCa Ho Hy Jo^1 Kt^2 wKt^3 oMd^2 [*Jolly* Ku] यामीभि°; Be^1 जातीभि°; wKt^1 यामीतिभ्रात्रा; Bo जानीतिभ्रात्रा — b) Ho °भिर्माता — c) Pu^{10} दस°; oMd^2 °वर्गेश्च — d) bBe^2 विवादं मनसाचरेत्; Ox^3 विवादे; Pu^{10} समाचरे

181.* Omitted in gMy; pādas a-b omitted in tMd^4. Cited by *Apa* 233; *Lakṣ* 2.353 — a) Tr^2 एतैस्त्यजन्विवादं तु; *Apa* एतांस्त्यजन्विवादांश्च; *Lakṣ* एतैस्त्यजेद्विवादांस्तु; Pu^2 सर्वान्परित्यज्यं च; Pu^4 सर्वान्परित्यज्यसंच; Be^3 bCa bKt^5 wKt^6 La^1 Lo^3 Lo^4 Lo^5 oOr Ox^2 Ox^3 nPu^1 Pu^{10} Wa [*Jolly* M R] एतान्विवा°; Bo एताविवा°; Jm Kt^2 wKt^3 एभिर्विवा° gMd^1 Tr^1 mTr^4 mTr^6 [*Jolly* Nd] °वादं; sPu^6 °वादात्; nNg संमुच्य — b) Lo^4 Lo^5 सद्यः पापैः; Hy °पापा; wKt^3 °पापैर्न लिप्यते; Pu^5 Pu^7 प्रमुच्यति — c) La^1 एतानजित्वा जयति; wKt^3 mTr^3 एभिर्जि°; Tj^1 एतैर्जितस्य; Lo^1 एतैर्जितांस्तु; Jm Tj^2 एभिर्जितश्च; Ho bKt^5 wKt^6 oOr *Lakṣ* एतैर्जितस्तु; Hy Jo^1 Jo^2 Kt^2 Lo^2 Lo^4 Lo^5 tMd^4 nNg sOx^1 nPu^1 Pu^5 sPu^6 Pu^7 Tr^2 *Apa Mandlik Jolly Jha KSS* एतैर्जितैश्च; Be^1 bBe^2 wKt^1 oMd^2 Pu^2 Pu^4 एतैर्जितैस्तु; Pu^{10} एतैर्जितेश्च; Jo^1 एभिर्जितैश्च; [*Jolly* N] *Nā* [pāṭha] एतान्जित्वा — d) bBe^2 bCa wKt^6 oOr Pu^7 Pu^8 सर्वान्लोका°; Ho Lo^4 tMd^3 gMd^5 Ox^3 Pu^2 Pu^4 Pu^{10} mTr^4 सर्वलोका°; Tr^2 सर्वान्कामानिमान्; tMd^4 °मान्गृहे; Tr^1 °माग्रही

182. Omitted in gMy Pu^5; *ma* in Pu^{10}. Cited by *Apa* 234; *Lakṣ* 2.353 — a) nKt^4 आचार्या; Tj^1 अवरोर्ब्रह्म° — b) tMd^4 प्राजापत्यप्रभुः पिता; nKt^4 प्रजापत्ये; Be^1 sOx^1 sPu^6 प्राजापत्यः; wKt^1 gMd^1 Wa पितामहः; *Apa* [vl] विभुः — c) Be^3 Tj^1 अतिथिश्चेन्द्र°; tMd^3 अतिथिश्चद्र° — d) Bo °लोके च ऋत्विजः; Ho [*mc to*] [*Jolly* G] °कस्य ऋत्विजः; bKt^5 °कस्यर्त्विजः; wKt^1 tMd^3 च द्विजः

183.* Omitted in gMy bKt^5; not commented by *Nd Mr;* folio containing verses 183–206 missing in Be^3. Cited by *Apa* 234; *Lakṣ* 2.353 — a) Be^1 जातयो; bBe^2 bCa Ho Jm Jo^1 wKt^1 Kt^2

आकाशेशास्तु विज्ञेया बालवृद्धकृशातुराः ।
भ्राता ज्येष्ठः समः पित्रा भार्या पुत्रः स्वका तनुः ॥१८४॥
छाया स्वा दासवर्गस्तु दुहिता कृपणं परम् ।
तस्मादेतैरधिक्षिप्तः सहेतासंज्वरः सदा ॥१८५॥
प्रतिग्रहसमर्थोऽपि प्रसङ्गं तत्र वर्जयेत् ।
प्रतिग्रहेण ह्यस्याशु ब्राह्मं तेजः प्रशाम्यति ॥१८६॥
न द्रव्याणामविज्ञाय विधिं धर्म्यं प्रतिग्रहे ।
प्राज्ञः प्रतिग्रहं कुर्यादवसीदन्नपि क्षुधा ॥१८७॥
हिरण्यं भूमिमश्वं गामन्नं वासस्तिलान् घृतम् ।
अविद्वान् प्रतिगृह्णानो भस्मीभवति दारुवत् ॥१८८॥

wKt^{3} NKt^{4} oMd^{2} oOr sOx^{1} sPu^{6} [*Jolly* Ku] *Rn* [pāṭha] यामयो; wKt^{6} जामियात्प्सरसां; Bo जामयो-शरसां; Lo^{1} °प्सरसं — b) Bo बान्धवः — c) La^{1} अपां संबन्धिनो लोके; BBe^{2} Ho Hy Jm Jo^{1} Jo^{2} Kt^{2} wKt^{3} Lo^{1} Lo^{3} Pu^{8} Tj^{2} *Mandlik Jolly Jha KSS Dave* °न्धिनो ह्यपां लोके; oMd^{2} °न्धिनस्त्वपां लोके; Tj^{1} °न्धिनो ये लोकस्य; TMd^{3} °न्धिनोपि लोकस्य; *Lakṣ* लोकेपु — d) Be^{1} BBe^{2} Ho Hy Jo^{1} Jo^{2} wKt^{1} Kt^{2} wKt^{3} BKt^{5} wKt^{6} La^{1} Lo^{3} Lo^{4} Lo^{5} oMd^{2} TMd^{4} Pu^{8} Tj^{2} Tr^{1} *Lakṣ Mandlik Jolly KSS* पृथिव्यां; MTr^{4} पितृव्या; Bo °मातुलैः; TMd^{3} °मातुलः

184. Omitted in GMy BKt^{5}; not commented by *Nd Rc*. Cited by *Apa* 234; *Lakṣ* 2.353 — b) wKt^{3} बल°; GMd^{1} TMd^{3} वृद्धबाल°; Tr^{2} °वृद्धातुराकृशाः — c) Pu^{2} Pu^{4} स्ताता ज्ये°; Pu^{5} Pu^{7} ज्येष्ठ; TMd^{4} NPu^{1} Tr^{1} समं; Pu^{10} समा — d) GMd^{1} TMd^{3} GMd^{5} Tr^{1} MTr^{4} MTr^{6} भार्यापुत्रौ; wKt^{1} wKt^{6} Lo^{1} Lo^{3} *Apa* स्विका; Pu^{5} Pu^{7} तनु; sOx^{1} ततः

185. Omitted in GMy; not commented by *Nd*. Cited by *Apa* 234; *Lakṣ* 2.353 — a) MTr^{4} MTr^{6} जाया; GMd^{1} छायो दास°; Ox^{2} Pu^{3} स्वा छाया दास°; Jo^{1} Kt^{2} oMd^{2} Pu^{5} Pu^{7} [*Jolly* Go] *Mandlik Jha KSS Dave* स्वो [supported by *Go Ku*]; Lo^{1} स्या; BBe^{2} Tr^{1} MTr^{6} [*Jolly* Nd] स्व; Jm स्वे; wKt^{1} दायवर्गश्च; oOr भृत्यवर्गश्च; BBe^{2} Ho Hy Jm Jo^{1} wKt^{1} Kt^{2} oMd^{2} TMd^{3} oOr sOx^{1} Pu^{5} sPu^{6} Pu^{7} Tj^{1} [*Jolly* G] *Mandlik Jolly Jha KSS Dave* °वर्गश्च; Bo °वर्गास्युर्दुहिता — b) TMd^{4} दन्ताकृशान्तपं; TMd^{3} दुहितस्यश्च कृपणं; Tj^{1} कृपणा; Ox^{3} नृपणं; Lo^{3} कृपणः परः; Tr^{1} रूपणं परा — c) Pu^{2} Pu^{4} °तैरभिक्षिप्तः; Tr^{2} °तैरक्षितश्च; sOx^{1} °क्षेप्तः; wKt^{1} °क्षिप्तं; *Lakṣ* °क्षिप्तैः; TMd^{4} °क्षिप्रस्सहे° — d) Ox^{3} Tr^{1} सहेतासज्वरः; Pu^{2} Pu^{4} सहेताः संज्वरः; NPu^{1} NKt^{4} सहेताविज्वरः; La^{1} सहेतापज्वरः; Pu^{5} Pu^{7} सहेतैवाज्वरः; BKt^{5} सहेतातसंज्वरः; GMd^{5} सहेतासज्वलः; NNg सहेतामत्सरः; Tj^{1} सहेतापचरः; MTr^{4} सहेतासंचरः; wKt^{6} सहे-तोर्भूतसङ्करः [*om* सदा]; oOr °ज्वरं

186. a) oMd^{2} प्रतिग्रहे; Lo^{3} [*Jolly* R] °समर्थस्तु — b) TMd^{3} GMy न प्रसज्येत प्रतिग्रहे; TMd^{4} प्रसर्गं — c) Tj^{1} ह्यस्यायु; Jo^{2} Lo^{3} GMd^{1} GMd^{5} oOr [*Jolly* R] तस्याशु — d) Be^{1} TMd^{4} Ox^{3} ब्राह्म; BBe^{2} Bo BCa Ho oMd^{2} Pu^{5} Pu^{7} Tj^{1} ब्राह्मयं; MTr^{6} तेजश्च शाम्यति; MTr^{4} तेजश्च नश्यति; GMd^{1} तेजो विनश्यति; TMd^{3} GMd^{5} GMy Tr^{1} प्रणश्यति; oMd^{2} प्रशास्यति; wKt^{1} प्रहीयते

187. Cited by *Lakṣ* 2.248 — a) Lo^{4} Lo^{5} नो; GMd^{5} न ब्राह्मणमविज्ञाय; Tj^{1} °विज्ञेय — b) Ho Lo^{5} GMy विधि; Be^{1} Ho wKt^{3} wKt^{6} GMd^{1} TMd^{3} sOx^{1} sPu^{6} Tj^{1} Tr^{2} धर्मं; Lo^{1} धर्मे; Lo^{3} धर्म; Pu^{2} Pu^{4} द्रव्यं; TMd^{4} धर्म्यः प्रतिग्रहः; MTr^{4} प्रतिग्रहैः — c) GMy प्राज्ञं; Lo^{2} राज्ञः; *Lakṣ* प्रातः — d) Lo^{1} कुर्यादिवसी°; Bo °न्नपि चक्षुषा

188* Cited by *Lakṣ* 2.248; *Hem* 1.60 — a) Lo^{3} GMd^{1} भूमिं गामश्वमन्नं; Pu^{4} *om* अश्वं गाम्; TMd^{3} गा अन्नं — b) Ho गामन्न; Be^{1} गां मन्त्रं; Lo^{1} वांस°; TMd^{4} °स्तिला — c) Hy Jo^{1} Kt^{2} NKt^{4} La^{1}

हिरण्यमायुरन्नं च भूर्गौश्चाप्योषतस्तनुम् ।
अश्वश्चक्षुस्त्वचं वासो घृतं तेजस्तिलाः प्रजाः ॥१८९॥
अतपास्त्वनधीयानः प्रतिग्रहरुचिर्द्विजः ।
अम्भस्यश्मप्लवेनेव सह तेनैव मज्जति ॥१९०॥
तस्मादविद्वान्बिभियाद् यस्मात्तस्मात् प्रतिग्रहात् ।
स्वल्पकेनाप्यविद्वान्हि पङ्के गौरिव सीदति ॥१९१॥
न वार्यपि प्रयच्छेत्तु बैडालव्रतिके द्विजे ।
न बकव्रतिके पापे नावेदविदि धर्मवित् ॥१९२॥
त्रिष्वप्येतेषु दत्तं हि विधिनाप्यर्जितं धनम् ।
दातुर्भवत्यनर्थाय परत्रादातुरेव च ॥१९३॥
यथा प्लवेनौपलेन निमज्जत्युदके तरन् ।

Lo^{4} Lo^{5} oOr Ox^{3} Pu^{4} Pu^{10} Tj^{2} MTr^{3} [*Jolly* M] *Mandlik Jolly Jha KSS Dave* प्रतिगृह्णन्नविद्वांस्तु [oOr Pu^{2} °विद्वान्हि]; Wa प्रतिगृह्णन्नविद्वांस; Jm प्रतिगृह्णन्नविद्वांस्से; Jo^{2} Lo^{3} Pu^{2} [*Jolly* R] प्रतिगृह्णन्हि — d) Ho °भवतु; Lo^{1} °भवति तत्क्षणात्; Lo^{2} दारुवित्

189. Pādas c-d omitted in GMy — a) Lo^{1} °मायुरत्नं च — b) Wa भूर्गोश्चा°; Tj^{1} भूर्गौवाप्यो°; GMy °श्चास्योष°; TMd^{3} °श्चान्योष°; Tr^{1} °श्चास्यौषधीस्तनुं; Pu^{5} Pu^{7} °श्चैवात्मनस्तनुं; Bo °प्योषित°; La^{1} Lo^{5} Ox^{2} sPu^{6} [*but cor*] Wa °प्युषत°; Lo^{4} °प्यूषत°; Kt^{2} °प्योपतु°; Ho TMd^{3} °तस्तनुः; Hy °तस्तनु — d) wKt^{6} °स्तिलां; sPu^{6} [*but cor*] Tj^{1} प्रजां

190. Cited by *Hem* 1.60 —a) Bo Lo^{2} NNg sOx^{1} Ox^{3} Pu^{5} sPu^{6} Pu^{7} Pu^{10} अतपस्त्व°; NPu^{1} आतपास्त्व°; La^{1} Tr^{2} अतपस्वनधी°; NKt^{4} अतपश्चानधी°; Tj^{1} अतयस्यमधी°; Lo^{1} अपाङ्क्तस्त्वनधी° — b) Tr^{1} °रुचिद्विजः — c) Tj^{1} अम्लस्य°; Lo^{5} अमस्य°; Pu^{5} Pu^{7} °स्यामप्लुवे°; wKt^{6} °श्मपल्लवेनैव; Bo BCa Ho La^{1} Lo^{2} Lo^{3} GMd^{1} TMd^{3} TMd^{4} GMd^{5} GMy NPu^{1} Pu^{5} Pu^{7} Pu^{10} Tj^{2} Tr^{1} °वेनैव — d) La^{1} तेनैव सह मज्जति; GMd^{1} तेन मज्जति; Pu^{2} Pu^{4} मोजति

191. Omitted in Ox^{3}; pādas c-d omitted in Pu^{10}; pāda-b in Pu^{10}. Cited by *Hem* 1.60; *Lakṣ* 2.248 — a) Bo यस्माद°; GMd^{5} कस्माद°; Tr^{1} °विद्यान्बिभृयाद्; Tj^{1} °विद्वान्बिभृयाद्; Tr^{2} °विद्वान्विरम्भयाद् — b) Lo^{1} TMd^{3} GMy Tr^{1} MTr^{4} MTr^{6} यस्मात्कस्मात्; *Hem* कस्मात्तस्मात्; Tj^{1} °ग्रहान्; Bo °ग्रहं — c) wKt^{1} TMd^{3} TMd^{4} GMd^{5} GMy Tr^{1} MTr^{4} MTr^{6} अल्पकेना°; MTr^{4} °केनाल्पविद्वान्हि; La^{1} oOr Pu^{2} Pu^{4} °केनापि विद्वान्हि; *Lakṣ* °केनापि गृह्णन्हि; BKt^{5} wKt^{6} Lo^{4} Lo^{5} sOx^{1} sPu^{6} Tr^{2} Wa °विद्वांस्तु; Ho *om* हि — d) Ox^{2} पङ्के सीदति गौरिव; TMd^{3} GMy मज्जति

192. Omitted in Ox^{3}; pādas c-d omitted in GMd^{1}. Cited by *Apa* 285; *Hem* 1.38; *Mādh* 1.174 — a) Pu^{7} Tj^{1} न चार्यपि; Pu^{5} तचार्यपि; BCa wKt^{1} NNg oOr NPu^{1} Pu^{2} Pu^{4} Pu^{5} Pu^{7} Tj^{1} [*Jolly* G] *Hem ViDh* 93.7 प्रयच्छेत; Tr^{2} प्रयच्छात् — b) GMd^{1} बैडालबकव्रकानि ते; GMd^{5} Tr^{1} बैलाळ°; wKt^{6} वैताल°; Tr^{1} °व्रतिको; Lo^{1} °वृत्तिके; Ho Tr^{2} °प्रतिके; Jo^{1} °व्रते; TMd^{4} द्विजेः — c) TMd^{3} GMy बाक°; Lo^{1} बकं; MTr^{3} वक्र°; wKt^{1} Lo^{2} Pu^{3} °व्रतिने; Pu^{5} Pu^{7} °वृत्तिके; Pu^{8} °वृतिके; wKt^{6} Lo^{1} °प्रतिके; Hy Jm Jo^{1} Kt^{2} Tj^{2} MTr^{3} [*Jolly* R] *Mandlik KSS* °व्रतिके विप्रे — d) Tj^{1} नवेद°; BBe^{2} °वेदविधि

193. Pādas c-d omitted in TMd^{4}. Cited by *Apa* 285; *Hem* 1.38; *Mādh* 1.174 — a) Ho त्रिष्वेतेषु च दत्तं हि; Tj^{1} दंभं हि; BKt^{5} wKt^{6} यद्दत्तं [*om* हि] — b) Jo^{2} Lo^{1} Lo^{3} [*Jolly* G R] *Hem* विधिनोपार्जितं; Pu^{5} Pu^{7} विधिनापार्जितं; wKt^{6} विधिनावर्जितं; GMd^{1} TMd^{3} GMy Tr °प्यार्जितं; TMd^{4} °प्याजितं; BKt^{5} वसं *cor to* धनं — d) Ho °दातुमेव; GMd^{1} °दातुरेद्विजे

तथा निमज्जतोऽधस्तादज्ञौ दातृप्रतीच्छकौ ॥१९४॥
धर्मध्वजी सदा लुब्धश्छाद्मिको लोकदम्भिकः ।
बैडालव्रतिको ज्ञेयो हिंस्रः सर्वाभिसंधकः ॥१९५॥
अधोदृष्टिर्नैकृतिकः स्वार्थसाधनतत्परः ।
शठो मिथ्याविनीतश्च बकव्रतचरो द्विजः ॥१९६॥
ये बकव्रतिनो विप्रा ये च मार्जारलिङ्गिनः ।
ते पतन्त्यन्धतामिस्रे तेन पापेन कर्मणा ॥१९७॥
न धर्मस्यापदेशेन पापं कृत्वा व्रतं चरेत् ।

194. Omitted in TMd^{4} Ox^{3}. Cited by *Hem* 1.38 — a) sOx^{1} sPu^{6} यथा प्लुवेप्लुवेनौपलेन; wKt^{6} पुरेनोदकेन; Pu^{10} °नौपलेपेन; Lo^{4} °नौपलेपन; Bo Lo^{1} Lo^{3} GMd^{1} TMd^{3} GMy Pu^{5} Pu^{7} Tj^{2} °नोपलेन; BKt^{5} °नोदलेन; Tj^{1} °नौपलिन; La^{1} °नौदकेन — b) BKt^{5} निमज्जनुदके; wKt^{6} निमर्जत्युदके; Be^{1} Wa °त्युदकं; Pu^{10} °त्युदक; Ho तरान्; Lo^{4} sOx^{1} sPu^{6} तरत् — c) BKt^{5} wKt^{6} sOx^{1} [*but cor*] यथा; Pu^{5} Pu^{7} निमज्जतौ विप्रावज्ञौ; TMd^{3} निमज्जतो यस्मादज्ञौ — c-d) GMd^{1} *Hem* दातृप्रतिग्रहीतारौ तथा द्वौ वै निमज्जतः [*Hem* तथैवाज्ञौ] — d) Tj^{1} °धस्ताज्ञदातप्रतीक्षकौ; Tr^{1} °दज्ञो; Pu^{2} °दग्नौ; Pu^{4} °दग्नौ; TMd^{3} दातुप्र°; Bo MTr^{4} °प्रयच्छकौ; Ho °प्रतिक्षतौ; Pu^{10} °प्रतीबकौ; *Me* [pāṭha] °प्रतीप्सकौ

195.* Omitted in TMd^{4}. Cited by *Vij* 1.130; *Apa* 170; *Hem* 3/1.364 — a) Ox^{3} धर्मि°; Lo^{4} धनेध्वजी; Tr^{1} °ध्वजः सदालुप्तः — b) BCa Lo^{4} °श्छद्मिको; Bo °श्छद्मिनो; GMd^{1} °श्चामिको; Tj^{1} °श्छाद्विको; Be^{1} La^{2} Lo^{1} Lo^{2} TMd^{3} GMd^{5} Tj^{1} Tr^{2} Wa [*Jolly* Nd] *ViDh* 93.8 *Nd Apa* °दाम्भिकः; GMd^{1} GMy °धाम्भिकः; Tr^{1} °डाम्भिकः; BBe^{2} BCa Hy Jm Jo^{1} wKt^{1} Kt^{2} wKt^{3} BKt^{5} wKt^{6} La^{1} Lo^{1} Lo^{3} oMd^{2} oOr sOx^{1} Ox^{2} NPu^{1} Pu^{3} sPu^{6} Pu^{8} Tj^{2} MTr^{3} [*Jolly* N Ku R] *Mandlik Jha KSS Dave* °दम्भकः; Bo NNg °दाम्भकः; Ho °बञ्चकः — c) Lo^{2} Pu^{10} भिडाल°; GMd^{5} Tr^{1} बैलाळ°; wKt^{6} वैताल°; Ho NKt^{4} °प्रतिको; wKt^{3} Lo^{1} *Apa* [vl] °वृत्तिको; Lo^{5} भेयो — d) NKt^{4} हिंसः; Ox^{3} हिंस्रा; wKt^{6} Lo^{4} GMd^{1} TMd^{3} GMy NNg Pu^{2} Pu^{4} Pu^{10} Tr^{1} MTr^{6} [*Jolly* M Nd] सर्वातिसं°; Wa सर्वाधिसं°; NKt^{4} सर्वानिसं°; Ho सर्वाहिःसं°; GMd^{5} सर्वातिबन्धकः; TMd^{3} MTr^{4} *Apa* °संधिकः; wKt^{1} °सन्नकः

Additional verse in Ho BKt^{5} wKt^{6} La^{1} Lo^{4} NPu^{1} Tr^{2}. Cited by *Apa* 170; *Hem* 3/1.364; *Mādh* 1.174 According to *Me* some teachers recited the verse given in the edition, and some the following additional verse. He takes both to be authoritative.

यस्य धर्मध्वजो नित्यं सुरध्वज इवोच्छ्रितः ।
प्रच्छन्नानि च पापानि बैडालं नाम तद्व्रतम् ॥

a) wKt^{6} धर्मे — a-b) *Mādh* यः कारणं पुरस्कृत्य व्रतचर्यां निषेवते — b) La^{1} नित्यमिद्रध्वज; BKt^{5} *Apa* सुराध्वज; BKt^{5} wKt^{6} इवोच्छितः; Ho इवोत्थितः — c) *Mādh* पापं व्रतेन संछाद्य — d) Tr^{2} बैडालानां व्रतं मतं; wKt^{6} वैतालं

196.* Omitted in TMd^{4}. Cited by *Vij* 1.130; *Apa* 170; *Mādh* 1.174; pāda-a cited by *Viś* 1.129 — a) MTr^{3} अर्थो°; Pu^{7} °दृष्टिनै°; TMd^{3} °दृष्टे नै°; Be^{1} Jm Jo^{1} Kt^{2} Lo^{1} sOx^{1} sPu^{6} *Mandlik Jha KSS Dave* °ष्टिर्नैष्कृतिकः; MTr^{6} °कृतिकाः — b) wKt^{6} सुखिसाध° — c) Tr^{2} °नीतस्तु — d) *Vij Apa* बकवृत्तिरुदाहृतः; GMd^{1} [*Jolly* G] वक्रवृत्तिचरो; Lo^{1} Pu^{5} Pu^{7} °वृत्तिचरो; Pu^{3} °व्रत्तिचरो; oOr °व्रतिचरो; NNg °वृत्तचरो; wKt^{3} °वृतचरो; Hy La^{1} Ox^{2} Tr^{2} °व्रतधरो; Ox^{2} Pu^{3} sPu^{6} [*but cor*] Pu^{8} नरः; Lo^{3} महान्

197. Omitted in TMd^{4} — a) Lo^{1} बकप्रतिमा; Pu^{10} बवव्रतिनो; Pu^{5} Pu^{7} [*Jolly* G] °वृत्तिनो; TMd^{3} °वर्तिनो; BKt^{5} wKt^{6} °व्रतिको; GMd^{1} °वृतिका; Ox^{2} Pu^{3} Pu^{8} मूढा ये — b) NNg °लिङ्गनः; wKt^{6} °लिङ्ग-काः; BKt^{5} °लिङ्गकः — c) BBe^{2} तपन्त्य°; Lo^{3} °मामिस्रे; BBe^{2} Ho wKt^{3} NKt^{4} La^{1} Lo^{1} oOr NPu^{1} Pu^{2} Pu^{4} Pu^{5} Pu^{7} Tr^{2} °मिश्रे

व्रतेन पापं प्रच्छाद्य कुर्वन् स्त्रीशूद्रदम्भनम् ॥१९८॥
प्रेत्येह चेदृशा विप्रा गर्ह्यन्ते ब्रह्मवादिभिः ।
छद्मना चरितं तच्च व्रतं रक्षांसि गच्छति ॥१९९॥
अलिङ्गी लिङ्गिवेषेण यो वृत्तिमुपजीवति ।
स लिङ्गिनां हरत्येनस्तिर्यग्योनौ च जायते ॥२००॥
परकीयनिपानेषु न स्नायाद्धि कदाचन ।
निपानकर्तुः स्नात्वा तु दुष्कृतांशेन लिप्यते ॥२०१॥
यानशय्यासनान्यस्य कूपोद्यानगृहाणि च ।
अदत्तान्युपयुञ्जान एनसः स्यात्तुरीयभाक् ॥२०२॥

198. mTr^3 transposes pādas a-b and c-d; omitted in tMd^4. Cited by *Apa* 230, 1229; *Lakṣ* 2.331 — b) Tj^1 कृत्वा पापं समाचरेत् — c) *Lakṣ* सञ्छाद्य — d) wKt^1 °शूद्रदर्शनं *cor to* °शूद्रदंस्तनं; Ho °शूद्रवञ्चनं; *Apa* 1229 °शूद्रलम्भनं

199. Omitted in tMd^4; *ma sh* in nNg. Cited by *Lakṣ* 2.331 — c) Tj^1 प्रेत्येह न च ते विप्रा; Hy प्रतेहे; nNg प्रेत्य चेहेदृशा; gMd^1 चेदृशो; Hy चेदृशी; Lo^1 चदृशा; Lo^5 वेहशा; *Lakṣ* विप्रो — b) Tr^1 गार्ह्यन्ते; bKt^5 wKt^6 *Lakṣ* गर्ह्यते; Bo wKt^3 गृह्यन्ते; Lo^3 ब्राह्म°; Be^1 वेदवादिभिः; wKt^6 ब्रह्मचारिभिः; Ho °वादिन — c) Hy Jm Jo^1 wKt^1 Kt^2 wKt^3 bKt^5 wKt^6 La^2 Lo^1 gMd^1 oMd^2 Tj^1 Tj^2 Tr^2 mTr^3 [*Jolly* M^6 Ku] *ViDh* 93.12 *Mandlik Jha KSS Dave* यच्च; oOr तत्तु; mTr^4 तस्य; *Me Nā Go* support तच्च

200. Omitted in tMd^4. Cited by *Apa* 230 — a) wKt^6 अलिङ्गा; Be^1 Bo bCa Ho wKt^1 wKt^3 nKt^4 Lo^4 gMd^1 tMd^3 gMd^5 nNg sOx^1 Ox^3 Pu^5 sPu^6 Pu^7 *Apa* लिङ्गवेषेण; Tj^1 लिङ्गिवेद्येन — b) Lo^3 वृत्तीनुप°; Pu^{10} वृत्तिमप°; Tr^2 वृत्तीसुपजीवती; Pu^2 Pu^4 sPu^6 [*but cor*] मुपगच्छति — c) Tr^2 सा; Tr^1 हरन्त्ये°; Ho हरित्येनोस्ति° — d) gMd^1 °ग्योन्याञ्च; gMd^5 gMy Tr^1 [*Jolly* Nd] °ग्योन्यां च; bCa °ग्योनिश्च; Ho Lo^1 Ox^3 Pu^{10} Tj^2 [*Jolly* M] °ग्योनिषु जायते; Tr^2 °ग्योनौ प्रजायते; Bo तु; Pu^8 च यायतो

201.* Omitted in tMd^4. Cited by *Apa* 234; *Hem* 3/2.874; *Lakṣ* 3.40–1; *Dev* 2.334 — a) Bo nKt^4 oMd^2 °निपातेषु; Lo^4 Lo^5 °निपातिषु — b) bBe^2 Hy Jm Jo^1 Jo^2 Kt^2 La^1 Lo^3 tMd^3 Tj^2 mTr^3 *Mandlik Jolly KSS Dave* स्नायाच्च; wKt^3 La^2 Wa स्नायात्तु; Pu^5 Pu^7 स्नायाद्वै; Be^1 Ho La^1 Lo^1 स्नायीत; oOr स्नायात; *Lakṣ Hem* स्नायान्नैव कदा°; gMd^1 स्नायाच्चैन कदा° — c) *Hem* स्नायी हि; wKt^1 bKt^5 wKt^6 nNg sOx^1 Pu^2 sPu^6 *Lakṣ* हि; bBe^2 Ho Lo^1 च

Additional verse in gMd^5 sOx^1 Ox^2 Pu^3 sPu^6 Tr^2 [*Jolly* Gr]; placed after 202 in nPu^1 Tj^1 *Mandlik* [क, ख, च, ड, ढ, ल, र] *KSS Dave* [cf. *YDh* 1.159]:

> सप्तोद्धृत्य ततः पिण्डान् कामं स्नायाच्च पञ्च वा ।
> उदपानात्स्वयं गृह्णन् बहिः स्नात्वा न दुष्यति ॥

a) gMd^5 [*Jolly* Gr] उद्धृत्य चतुरः पिण्डान् — b) nPu^1 स्नायात्तु विधिपूर्वकं; Tr^2 [*Jolly* Gr] स्नायीत; *Mandlik KSS Dave* पञ्चधा — c) nPu^1 उदपानः स्वयं ग्रहात; gMd^5 औद°; Tr^2 गृह्य; gMd^5 [*Jolly* Gr] ग्राह्यं; sOx^1 sPu^6 *Mandlik Dave* ग्राहाद्; *KSS* ग्रामाद् — d) gMd^5 Ox^2 nPu^1 Tr^2 स्नानं न; gMd^5 रिष्यते

Additonal verse in Ho:

> उद्धृत्य पञ्चपिण्डांश्च पारक्ये स्नानमाचरेत् ।
> स्नात्वा च तर्पयेद्देवान्पितृंश्चैव विशेषतः ॥

202.* Omitted in tMd^4; pādas c-d omitted in bBe^2. Cited by *Apa* 237 — a) Pu^4 पान°; nKt^4 Tr^2 °शय्याशनान्यस्य; tMd^3 gMy °सनाद्यस्य; Ho °सनमन्यस्य; gMd^1 °सना अस्य; Wa °सनास्य —

नदीषु देवखातेषु तडागेषु सरःसु च ।
स्नानं समाचरेन्नित्यं गर्तप्रस्रवणेषु च ॥२०३॥
यमान्सेवेत सततं न नित्यं नियमान्बुधः ।
यमान्पतत्यकुर्वाणो नियमान्केवलान्भजन् ॥२०४॥

b) TMd³ कूपोद्यानि; Ho रूपोद्ययान°; Tj¹ Tr² छत्रोपानद्रूहाणि — c) Lo⁵ Tr² अदत्तानुप°; Be¹ Ho Hy Jm Jo¹ wKt¹ Kt² La¹ La² Lo² Lo⁵ oMd² NNg oOr sOx¹ Ox² NPu¹ Pu³ Pu⁴ sPu⁶ Tj¹ Tr² MTr³ MTr⁴ *Mandlik KSS Apa* [vl] °पभुञ्जान; Tj¹ °पभुञ्जीत — d) GMd¹ युञ्जानस्तुरीयं हरतेंहसाम्; Tj¹ येनसः; Tr¹ येनस; MTr⁴ MTr⁶ ऐनसोस्य तुरी°; Pu³ स्यात्तदीयभाक्

203. Omitted in TMd⁴ BBe². Cited by *Vij* 1.159; *Apa* 234; *Hem* 3/2.867; *Dev* 2.333 — a) Tr² देवपातेषु; wKt³ GMy °घातेपु — b) *Apa* ह्रदेपु च सरःसु च; Lo³ sOx¹ sPu⁶ तडाकेपु; TMd³ GMd⁵ GMy Tr¹ *Dev* तटाकेपु; wKt¹ सरत्सु — c) TMd³ समाचरन्नित्यं — d) Ho oOr Pu⁵ Pu⁷ °प्रश्रव°; *Apa* °प्रस्रवणादिपु [*om* च]

Additional verse in oOr:

उद्धृत्य सलिलात्पिण्डान्पञ्च सप्त दशापि वा ।
स्नात्वान्ते तर्पयेद्देवान्पितॄंश्चैव विशेषतः ॥

Additional verse in Pu¹:

स्नानमव्दैवतैः कुर्यात्पावनैश्च समार्जनम् ।
मन्त्रैः प्राणांस्त्रिरायम्य सौरैश्चार्कं विलोकयेत् ॥

204. Omitted in TMd⁴ Pu¹⁰. Cited by *Apa* 230 — a) TMd³ धर्मान्से°; GMd¹ GMy Tr² यस्मात्से°; Tj¹ येमान्सेवेन; Tr² यमान्सवैत; Wa यमान्सवेत; wKt⁶ °वेत्सततं — b) GMd⁵ GMy Pu² Pu⁴ *om* न; Lo⁴ TMd³ NNg *ma* न; sOx¹ sPu⁶ नित्यं न; GMd⁵ नित्यं च; Bo Tr¹ नियमाद्बुधः; TMd³ GMy नियमवान्बुधः; GMd¹ नियमान्बुद्धि; Pu² Pu⁴ Tr² नियमान्द्विजः; sOx¹ sPu⁶ [*cor to*] नियमान्भवेत् — c) Lo³ [*Jolly* R] यमानेतानकुर्वाणो; Tr² यस्मात्पतति कुर्वाणो; GMd¹ इमान्पत° — d) wKt¹ Lo³ Tj¹ Tr² Wa [*Jolly* R] °वलान्भजेत्; Lo² °वलान्भजेन्; wKt⁶ °वलान्भज

Two additonal verses in La¹ GMd¹ TMd³ oOr Tr¹ Tr² *Mandlik KSS Dave;* commented by *Rc;* the two verses are transposed in TMd³ Tr¹; they are placed after the next addition in Tr². These two verses appear to be taken from Medhātithi's commentary.

अहिंसा सत्यवचनं ब्रह्मचर्यमकल्कता ।
अस्तेयमिति पञ्चैते यमाश्चैव व्रतानि च ॥१॥
अक्रोधो गुरुशुश्रूषा शौचमाहारलाघवम् ।
अप्रमादश्च नियमाः पञ्चैवोपव्रतानि च ॥२॥

1. b) GMd¹ °चनमक्रौरत्वमकल्कता; La¹ Tr¹ Tr² °कल्यता — c) Tr² अस्तेयमपि — d) oOr *Mandlik KSS Dave* यमाश्चोपव्रतानि च; La¹ यमादौ परिकीर्त्तिताः; GMd¹ यमाश्च

2. a) GMd¹ अक्रोधेन च शुश्रूषा; Tr² आचारगुरु° — a-b) TMd³ पञ्चैते नियमाः प्रोक्ता अप्रमादो व्रतानि च — c) Tr² अप्रसादश्च — d) La¹ पञ्चैते परिकीर्त्तिताः

Two further additional verses in Be¹ wKt¹ BKt⁵ wKt⁶ La¹ Lo² GMd⁵ oOr Ox²; given after 201 in sOx¹ NPu¹ Pu² Pu³ Pu⁴ sPu⁶ Tj¹ Tr² *Mandlik KSS Dave.* Cited by *Apa* 230:

आनृशंस्यं क्षमा सत्यमहिंसा दममस्पृहा ।
ध्यानं प्रसादो माधुर्यमार्जवं च यमा दश ॥१॥
शौचमिज्या तपो दानं स्वाध्यायोपस्थनिग्रहौ ।
व्रतोपवासं मौनं च स्नानं च नियमा दश ॥२॥

1. b) Be¹ sOx¹ sPu⁶ °महिंसा च दयास्पृहा; oOr °महिंसा हितमार्जवं; wKt⁶ *Apa* दम आर्जवं; BKt⁵ La¹ GMd⁵ दममार्जवं; Lo² दानमस्पृहा — c) La¹GMd⁵ प्रीतिं प्रसादो; oOr प्रातः

नाश्रोत्रियतते यज्ञे ग्रामयाजिहुते तथा ।
स्त्रिया क्लीबेन च हुते भुञ्जीत ब्राह्मणः क्वचित् ॥२०५॥
अश्लीकमेतत्साधूनां यत्र जुह्वत्यमी हविः ।
प्रतीपमेतद्देवानां तस्मात्तत्परिवर्जयेत् ॥२०६॥
मत्तक्रुद्धातुराणां च न भुञ्जीत कदाचन ।
केशकीटावपन्नं च पदा स्पृष्टं च कामतः ॥२०७॥
भ्रूणघ्नावेक्षितं चैव संस्पृष्टं चाप्युदक्यया ।
पतत्रिणावलीढं च शुना संस्पृष्टमेव च ॥२०८॥
गवा चान्नमुपघ्रातं घुष्टान्नं च विशेषतः ।
गणान्नं गणिकान्नं च विदुषा च जुगुप्सितम् ॥२०९॥

प्रसादो — d) GMd⁵ माधुर्यं मार्दवं; Tr² *om* यमा दश

2. b-c) omitted in Be¹ Lo² — b) wKt¹ La¹ Ox² Pu² Pu³ Pu⁴ Tj¹ Tr² °निग्रहः; wKt⁶ °निग्रहे; oOr °निग्रहं — c) BKt⁵ wKt⁶ GMd⁵ sOx¹ Pu² Pu⁴ sPu⁶ °पवासौ; oOr Tj¹ Tr² °पवासो

205. Omitted in TMd⁴; pādas c-d *ma* in BKt⁵. Cited by *Vij* 3.289; *Apa* 1174; *Lakṣ* 3.259; *Hem* 3/1.770 — a) MTr⁴ न श्रोत्रि°; Tj¹ नोश्रोत्रियेततो; GMd¹ न श्रोत्रियकुते; Lo¹ °त्रियेतते; BBe² wKt¹ La¹ Lo³ Pu³ [*Jolly* R] °त्रियहुते; wKt³ °त्रियकृते; Pu¹⁰ °तत — b) wKt¹ NKt⁴ wKt⁶ NNg Ox³ Pu¹⁰ Tr¹ *Hem* ग्रामयाज°; Lo² Ox³ ग्रामायाज°; La¹ ग्रामयावि°; NPu¹ Tr² ग्रामयाचि°; MTr⁴ ग्रामयाजु°; Lo⁵ यामयक्ष°; Tj² ग्रामयाजिते; BKt⁵ °याजहुते; Ox² °हते; Tr¹ °भुते; Hy Jm Jo¹ Kt² wKt³ BKt⁵ MTr³ *Mandlik Jha KSS Dave* °कृते; Pu² °हृते; Tj² °तते; TMd³ यथा — c) GMd¹ स्त्रियाः; TMd³ GMy तथा क्ली°; *Nā* [pāṭha] शूद्रेण च — d) Be¹ Hy ब्रह्मणः

206.* Omitted in TMd⁴; *ma* in BKt⁵. Cited by *Apa* 1174; *Lakṣ* 3.259 — a) Tj² श्लीलभेतचिसाधूनां; BBe² NKt⁴ wKt⁶ Lo² Lo³ GMd¹ sOx¹ sPu⁶ Tr¹ [*Jolly* R] अश्रीक°; wKt¹ Kt² wKt³ Lo⁴ Lo⁵ oMd² TMd³ GMd⁵ GMy NNg oOr Ox³ Pu² Pu⁴ Pu¹⁰ Tj¹ Tr² Wa *Apa* [*Jolly* N] *Jha Dave* अश्लील°; La² अश्लेल°; Pu⁵ Pu⁷ अश्लीलकमेत° — b) Be¹ Ho यत्रैते जुह्वते हविः; Lo¹ *ma* हविस्ते यत्र जुह्वति; Be³ तत्र — c) Tr² प्रतीपमेव देवानां; GMd¹ प्रदीप°; BBe² °तद्दारानां; TMd³ °तद्दावानां — d) Ho तस्मात्ताः परि°; Be³ तस्मात्तं परि°; GMd⁵ तत्तस्मात्परि°

207. Pādas a-b omitted in TMd⁴. Cited by *Vij* 3.289; *Apa* 1174; *Hem*3/1.610, 771 — a) GMd¹ मत्तः; wKt¹ [*cor to*] TMd³ °क्रूरातु°; Be³ Lo⁴ Lo⁵ sOx¹ Ox³ Pu⁵ sPu⁶ Pu⁷ Pu¹⁰ Tj¹ Tr² Wa [*Jolly* M] तु — c) Ho केशं; Pu² Pu⁴ MTr⁴ °कीटोपपन्नं; NKt⁴ NNg °कीटापन्नं; Be³ तु — d) wKt³ NKt⁴ La¹ Tr¹ [*Jolly* R] पादस्पृष्टं; NPu¹ स्पष्टं; Pu¹⁰ Tj¹ Tr² [*Jolly* M¹⁻²⁻⁹] तु

208. Cited by *Apa* 1174; *Hem* 3/1.610 — a) *Apa* [vl] भ्रूणहावे°; sOx¹ sPu⁶ °घ्नवेक्षिं; NKt⁴ °घ्नवीक्षितं; Tj¹ °घ्नविक्षितं; Lo⁴ °घ्नास्ववेक्षितं; Lo² °वैक्षतं; NPu¹ °वेक्षिकं; Jo² Lo³ Pu² Pu⁴ °क्षितं यच्च — b) Lo⁴ संसृष्टं; TMd³ संघुष्टं; Tj¹ च उदक्यया — c) BBe² पततृणा°; La¹ Pu¹⁰ एतत्रिणा°; Jm एतत्त्रिणा°; Tj¹ °लीडं — d) wKt⁶ तेनासंस्पृष्टमेव

209. Cited by *Apa* 1174; *Lakṣ* 3.259; *Hem* 3/1.610; pādas c-d cited by *Vij* 3.289 — a) Bo गवां; Lo¹ वान्न°; BCa wKt⁶ La¹ GMd¹ TMd³ GMd⁵ GMy NPu¹ Pu² Pu⁴ Tj² Tr¹ °न्नमवघ्रातं; Be¹ Lo⁴ Ox³ °पाघ्रातं — b) BKt⁵ wKt⁶ विद्युष्टान्नं विशेषतः; Ox² संघुष्टान्नं विशेषतः; Tr¹ घृष्टान्नं; Bo GMd⁵ NPu¹ Tj¹ Tr² दुष्टान्नं; Pu⁴ द्युष्टान्नं; MTr⁴ सूतान्नं;GMd¹ च विवर्जयेत् — c) Ho गणानां; Tr² कणिकान्नं; Pu¹⁰ गणिकान्ने — d) Jo¹ Kt² Lo¹ GMd⁵ GMy Tr¹ Wa [*Jolly* M³ N Nd] *Vij Apa* विदुषां; GMd¹ TMd³

स्तेनगायनयोश्चान्नं तक्ष्णो वार्धुषिकस्य च ।
दीक्षितस्य कदर्यस्य बद्धस्य निगडस्य च ॥२१०॥
अभिशस्तस्य षण्ढस्य पुंश्चल्या दाम्भिकस्य च ।
शुक्तं पर्युषितं चैव शूद्रस्योच्छिष्टमेव च ॥२११॥
चिकित्सकस्य मृगयोः क्रूरस्योच्छिष्टभोजिनः ।
उग्रान्नं सूतिकान्नं च पर्याचान्तमनिर्दशम् ॥२१२॥
अनर्चितं वृथामांसमवीरायाश्च योषितः ।
द्विषदन्नं नगर्यन्नं पतितान्नमवक्षुतम् ॥२१३॥
पिशुनानृतिनोश्चान्नं क्रतुविक्रयकस्य च ।
शैलूषतुन्नवायान्नं कृतघ्नस्यान्नमेव च ॥२१४॥

gMd5 gMy Tr1 यज्जुगुप्सितं

210. Cited by *Vij* 3.289; *Lakṣ* 3.259; *Hem* 3/1.771; pādas a-b cited by *Apa* 1174 — a) Bo nPu1 तेनगा°; Lo1 oMd2 tMd3 tMd4 gMd5 gMy Tj1 Tr1 *Vij* °गायकयो°; wKt1 La1 tMd4 nNg oOr Wa *Apa* °योश्चैव; *Lakṣ* °योश्चैवं; nKt4 °योश्चव — b) Tj1 तक्ष्णी; tMd3 तीक्ष्णो; Be3 Ho wKt1 Kt2 wKt6 gMd5 sOx1 sPu6 Pu7 तक्ष्णोर्वा°; Pu4 तर्कोर्वा°; sOx1 sPu6 [*mc sh to*] °षितस्य — d) sOx1 sPu6 [*cor to*] बद्धस्य च निगस्य च; Tj1 बद्धो निगद एव च; Pu4 *om* बद्धस्य; wKt6 बन्धस्य; Bo वर्धस्य; Ho nKt4 gMd1 Pu3 [*Jolly* Gr] *Nd* [as *sādhuḥ pāṭhaḥ*] निगदेन च; gMd5 Tr1 निगळेन; wKt6 [*Jolly* Nd] निगलस्य; bKt5 निगनस्य; *Me* [pāṭha] विशदस्य

211. Lo4 gives only the *pratīka* अभिशस्तस्य. Cited by *Apa* 1174; *Lakṣ* 3.260; pādas a-b cited by *Viś* 3.257; *Vij* 3.289; *Hem* 3/1.772 — a) Tr2 अभिशस्त; Tj1 अभिशमस्य; Be1 Be3 Hy Kt2 Ox3 Tj1 Tr1 Tr2 षण्डस्य; Ho bKt5 wKt6 Lo1 Pu10 खण्डस्य; mTr4 दंभस्य— b) gMd1 gMy धाम्भि°; bBe2 दम्भि°; Tr1 डाम्भि° — c) Ho Lo1 Lo2 शुष्कं; Tj1 शुक्लं; oOr सूक्तं; tMd4 सुकं — d) *Me* [pāṭha] उष्छिष्टमगुरोस्तथा; nPu1 °च्छिष्टभोजनं; Lo1 तु

212. Cited by *Vij* 3.289; *Apa* 11745; *Lakṣ* 3.260; *Hem* 3/1.772 — a) sOx1 sPu6 विचिकित्सस्य; Ho चिकित्सिकस्य; tMd4 मृगयो — b) bKt5 wKt6 °ष्टवर्तिनः; Be1 wKt3 °भोजनः; wKt1 tMd4 °भोजनं — c) nKt4 gMd1 Tr1 mTr6 *Me* [pāṭha] सूतकान्नं — d) Lo2 पर्यायान्तम°; Be3 wKt1 bKt5 La1 Lo2 gMd1 tMd3 tMd4 gMd5 gMy Ox3 nPu1 Pu10 Tj1 Tr1 *Vij Apa* पर्यायान्नम°; Lo4 [*but cor*] Pu2 Pu4 पर्याचान्नम°; bBe2 Lo4 Lo5 °न्तमहर्निशं; oOr °निर्दशः; Ho bKt5 Lo1 gMy °निर्दिशं; nKt4 °निदृशं

Additional verse in gMd1 gMd5 nPu1 mTr4 mTr6 *Lakṣ* 3.260:

समासमाभ्यां विप्राभ्यां विषमं सममेव च ।
पूजातो दीयमानं तु न ग्राह्यं देयमेव च ॥

a) nPu1 समोनाभ्यां च विप्रा° — b) mTr4 *om* समम्; gMd5 वा — c) *Lakṣ* पूजान्ते; gMd5 पूज्यादौ; nPu1 दीपतस्तंतु; gMd1 नियमानन्तु; *Lakṣ* च

213. Cited by *Vij* 3.289; *Apa* 1175; *Lakṣ* 3.260; *Hem* 3/1.773 — a) Tj1 आनर्चित; tMd3 अनर्चितायान्नवृथा°; gMy अनर्चितान्नवृथा°; Pu8 यथा°; bKt5 wKt6 वृथाचान्नमवीरा° — b) wKt6 °मधीरायाश्च; Tr1 °मवीराश्च; gMy तोषितः — c) nKt4 विषदष्टं; Pu2 Tr1 नगर्यान्नं; Be3 nKt4 gMd1 tMd3 nPu1 Pu4 Pu5 Pu7 Tj1 mTr4 [*Jolly* G] कदर्यान्नं; Hy बमर्यन्नं — d) Pu4 *om* पतितान्नम्; bKt5 wKt6 पतितानामवक्षुतं; gMy पतितान्नवक्षुतं; Tr2 °वक्ष्यतं; Tr1 °विक्षुतं; wKt1 °वीक्षितं; gMd5 °पक्षुतं; Lo5 °चक्षरं; Bo °दक्षुतं

214.* Pādas c-d *ma sh* in Be3; pāda-d omitted in gMd5. Cited by *Vij* 3.289; *Apa* 1175;

कर्मारस्य निषादस्य रङ्गावतरकस्य च ।
सुवर्णकर्तुर्वेणस्य शस्त्रविक्रयिणस्तथा ॥२१५॥
श्ववतां शौण्डिकानां च चैलनिर्णेजकस्य च ।
रजकस्य नृशंसस्य यस्य चोपपतिर्गृहे ॥२१६॥
मृष्यन्ति ये चोपपतिं स्त्रीजितानां च सर्वशः ।
अनिर्दशं च प्रेतान्नमतुष्टिकरमेव च ॥२१७॥
राजान्नं तेज आदत्ते शूद्रान्नं ब्रह्मवर्चसम् ।
आयुः सुवर्णकारान्नं यशश्चर्मावकर्तिनः ॥२१८॥
कारुकान्नं प्रजां हन्ति बलं निर्णेजकस्य च ।

Lakṣ 3.260; *Hem* 3/1.773 — a) NPu^1 °कृतिनो°; Kt^2 °मृतिनो°; GMd^1 TMd^3 GMy Tr^1 MTr^4 MTr^6 °नृतयोश्चात्रं; Jo^2 Lo^3 °नोश्चापि; *Vij* °नोश्चैव; Pu^7 °नोश्चान्नं च — b) Be^1 Be^3 Bo BCa Jo^2 BKt^5 WKt^6 Lo^1 TMd^4 NNg Ox^2 NPu^1 Pu^5 Pu^7 Tj^1 [*Jolly* M$^{1-2}$ G N Nd] *Hem Jolly* °क्रयिकस्य; WKt^3 °क्रययस्य; Pu^2 Pu^4 °क्रेयकस्य; BBe^2 Hy Jm Jo^1 WKt^1 Kt^2 La^1 OMd^2 GMd^5 OOr SOx^1 SPu^6 Tj^2 Tr^2 MTr^3 Wa *Vij Apa Mandlik KSS* °क्रयिणस्तथा — c) NPu^1 शीलू°; Pu^2 Pu^4 शैलु°; Bo शैशूषतंचवा°; Tj^2 °षतन्नुवा°; Be^1 Ho Jo^2 WKt^1 Lo^1 GMd^1 OMd^2 NNg Ox^2 NPu^1 Pu^2 Pu^3 Pu^4 Pu^5 Pu^7 Tj^1 Tr^1 Wa *Vij Apa* °षतन्तुवा°; SOx^1 SPu^6 °षतनुवा°; Lo^3 °षन्तिवा°; Tr^2 °पन्तुवा°; NPu^1 °वीयान्नं; La^1 °वाह्यान्नं; Lo^1 Tj^1 °वायानं; Wa °चायान्नं — d) GMy कृतवनस्याजकस्य च; TMd^3 कृतवान्नस्यकस्य च

215.* OMd^2 transposes 215 and 216; GMd^1 TMd^4 transpose 215 c-d and 216 a-b; pādas a-b *ma sh* in Be^3; pādas a-c omitted in GMd^5. Cited by *Vij* 3.289; *Apa* 1175; *Lakṣ* 3.260; *Hem* 3/1.773–4 — a) Bo कर्मायस्य — b) Lo^5 *om* रङ्गा°; TMd^3 कङ्गाव°; Tr^2 रङ्गारवतार°; BBe^2 Jm Jo^1 WKt^1 Kt^2 La^1 Lo^3 Lo^4 Lo^5 OMd^2 NPu^1 Pu^5 Pu^7 *Manklik Jolly KSS* °तारकस्य; Lo^1 *Vij* °तरणस्य; Pu^2 °तरस्य — c) Tj^1 सुवर्णकेतु°; GMd^1 TMd^3 GMy Pu^5 Pu^7 Tr^1 *Hem Apa* °कर्तुर्वेनस्य; Lo^1 Lo^2 Lo^3 Pu^5 Tj^1 Tr^2 Wa *Nā Rc* °कर्तुर्वेणस्य; Bo °कर्तुर्वर्णस्य; NKt^4 °कर्तुर्वणस्य; Be^3 °कर्तुर्वैद्यस्य; Hy °कर्तुर्वेशात्स्य — d) *Vij* सोमविक्र°; Lo^3 °क्रयिकस्य च

216.* Cited by *Vij* 3.289; *Apa* 1175; *Lakṣ* 3.260; *Hem* 3/1.774 — a) NKt^4 श्ववता; Pu^5 श्वावतां; WKt^6 श्ववशां; GMd^5 NPu^1 Tr^2 *Rc* [gives श्ववतां as pāṭha] श्वपचां; Lo^1 अयस्वतां; *Apa* [vl] स्ववतां; NKt^4 शोण्डि°; WKt^6 सौण्डि°; Bo शौणिका°; WKt^1 शौण्डिकान्नं; Tj^1 मद्यकृतां च; Lo^1 *om* च; WKt^3 तु — b) BBe^2 BCa Hy WKt^1 Kt^2 La^1 GMd^1 OMd^2 TMd^3 TMd^4 GMy OOr Ox^2 Pu^2 Pu^4 Tr^1 Wa [*Jolly* M$^{3-4}$] चेल°; WKt^3 चल°; NPu^1 जल°; WKt^6 तैल°; SOx^1 SPu^6 °निर्णीज°; WKt^3 °निर्णुजनस्य — c) La^1 Jo^1 Jo^2 *Mandlik Jolly KSS* रञ्जकस्य; Lo^1 Lo^3 नृशंशस्य; Tr^1 नृशंस्य — d) Lo^1 OOr नृशंसस्य चोपपत्तिर्गृहेण च; GMy चोपतितर्गृहे; Bo °पतिगृहे; Tj^1 °पतिगृहो

217. Cited by *Vij* 3.289; *Apa* 1175; *Lakṣ* 3.260; *Hem* 3/1.774 — a) Pu^5 Pu^7 मृशन्ते; Be^3 TMd^3 मृशन्ति; Tj^1 मृशंततो; MTr^4 MTr^6 मुह्यन्ति; *Hem* पुष्यन्ति; Pu^7 [*but cor*] चौपपतिं — b) GMy OOr स्त्रीजितान्नं; TMd^4 स्त्रीजातानां; Lo^1 SOx^1 SPu^6 सर्वतः; *Hem* [vl] सत्तमः — c) Lo^1 अनिर्दशानामेतेषाम्; WKt^6 अनिर्दिष्टं; SOx^1 SPu^6 अविर्दशं; BBe^2 अनिर्दशां; Tr^1 अनिर्देशं; Wa अनिर्दर्शं; *Hem* दशाहिकञ्च; WKt^1 °र्दशान्नं प्रेता°; Lo^2 चाप्रतान्नम°; SOx^1 SPu^6 प्रीतान्नम° — d) TMd^3 °न्नमातुष्णीकरमेव

218. Cited by *Lakṣ* 3.270; *Hem* 3/1.782 — a) Be^1 आदन्ति; NNg Pu^5 Pu^7 Wa [*Jolly* G] आहन्ति — c) BKt^5 वायुः — d) Ox^3 यशः कर्मा°; Bo यत्संचर्मा°; BKt^5 WKt^6 Lo^2 Lo^3 *Lakṣ* °श्चर्मविकर्तिनः; Lo^1 °श्चर्मचकर्तिनः; NNg °श्चस्मविकर्तिनः; GMd^5 °पकृन्तिनः; WKt^3 °कत्तिकः; TMd^3 °कृत्तिनः; Tr^1 °कृन्तिनः; WKt^1 °कीर्तिनः

गणान्नं गणिकान्नं च लोकेभ्यः परिकृन्तति ॥२१९॥
पूयं चिकित्सकस्यान्नं पुंश्चल्यास्त्वन्नमिन्द्रियम् ।
विष्ठा वार्धुषिकस्यान्नं शस्त्रविक्रयिणो मलम् ॥२२०॥
य एतेऽन्ये त्वभोज्यान्नाः क्रमशः परिकीर्तिताः ।
तेषां त्वगस्थिरोमाणि वदन्त्यन्नं मनीषिणः ॥२२१॥
भुक्त्वातोऽन्यतमस्यान्नममत्या क्षपणं त्र्यहम् ।
मत्या भुक्त्वा चरेत्कृच्छ्रं रेतोविण्मूत्रमेव च ॥२२२॥

219. Pādas a-b *ma* in Lo⁴; pādas c-d omitted in Pu⁴. Cited by *Hem* 3/1.782 — a) Lo³ दारु°; BKt⁵ Lo¹ Lo⁴ TMd³ TMd⁴ Ox³ Pu⁵ Pu⁷ प्रजा — b) BKt⁵ wKt⁶ तैलनिर्मजकस्य तु; Kt² बल; Pu⁸ मलं; Tj¹ निर्णेजक च; Tr¹ *om* च; Bo BKt⁵ wKt⁶ Lo³ Pu³ Pu⁸ तु — d) Bo लोकेभ्यश्चैव कृन्तति; NNg °कृन्तिति

Additional verse in Pu²; pādas c-d in Pu⁴:

निवृत्ते क्षीणस्य लुब्धस्य दीनस्यैवातुरस्य च ।
शान्त्यर्थमव्ययो भुङ्क्ते बलाभ्यस्योपहन्यते ॥

220. Cited by *Hem* 3/1.782; *Lakṣ* 3.270 — a) Tj¹ यूयं; TMd³ पूय; Pu² Pu⁴ प्रयं; Tr¹ प्रियां; Kt² पूयश्चिकि°; GMy पूयुश्चिकि°; Tr² चिकित्सकान्नं; TMd⁴ चिकित्सकान्नं च — b) Jo² Lo³ Lo⁵ GMd¹ TMd⁴ MTr⁴ °ल्याश्चान्न°; Pu¹⁰ °न्द्रिया — c) GMd¹ वार्ध्युषि°; Tr¹ वार्धषि°; Tr² वार्धुषिकान्नं; TMd⁴ वार्धुषिकान्नं च — d) *Lakṣ* शल्यविक्रयिणां; GMd¹ बलं

221. Cited by *Hem* 3/1.782; *Lakṣ* 3.270 — a) Bo य एषोन्ये; wKt¹ य एतोन्ये; Tr¹ य एतोन्यो; Ox³ य एतेभ्ये; BBe² Lo¹ एतेभ्योन्ये; Be¹ GMd¹ Ox² Tj² MTr³ [*Jolly* R] *Lakṣ Hem* य एभ्योन्ये; Lo⁴ य एतेभ्यो [*ma* न्ये तु]; Lo⁵ एतेभ्योनेह्यभो°; Lo³ य भयभ्यो त्वभो°; BBe² ह्यभोज्या°; NPu¹ चोभोज्या°; TMd⁴ त्वभुञ्जान्नाः; Be¹ स्वभोज्यान्नाः; La¹ °ज्यान्नः; Bo °ज्यानां — b) sOx¹ sPu⁶ क्रमशस्ते प्रकीर्तिताः — c) After °स्थिरोमा Tj¹ jumps to end of 223 pāda-a: न्नं — d) GMd¹ वदन्त्यन्ये मनीषिभिः; Bo वदत्यन्नं

Additional verse after pādas a-b in Pu¹:

दुष्कृतं हि मनुष्याणामन्नमाश्रित्य तिष्ठति ।
यो यस्यान्नं समश्नाति स तस्याश्नाति किल्बिपम् ॥

Additional verse in BCa [but given in parentheses] *Mandlik* [ड, ढ] *KSS Dave:*

अमृतं ब्राह्मणस्यान्नं क्षत्रियान्नं पयः स्मृतम् ।
वैश्यान्नमन्नमित्याहुः शूद्रस्य रुधिरं स्मृतम् ॥

c-d) BCa वैश्यस्य अन्नमेवायं शूद्रान्नं रुधिरं स्मृतं

222. Omitted in Tj¹; pādas b-d omitted in Pu⁸. Cited by *Viś* 1.175, 3.257; *Vij* 3.289; *Apa* 240, 1175; *Mādh* 2.300, 305 — a) Bo Tr¹ भुक्तातो; Tr² भुक्तवान्तो; Ho भुक्तातता; *Mādh* 2.305 भुञ्जानोऽन्य°; Be³ भुक्त्वा चान्य° — b) TMd³ °स्यान्नं मत्या तु त्रियहं क्षिपेत्; TMd⁴ Tr¹ *Viś Mādh* 2.300 °मत्या तु त्र्यहं क्षपेत्; GMd¹ GMd⁵ °मत्या त्र्यहं क्षिपेत् [GMd⁵ त्र्यहः]; *Apa* 240 [vl] °मत्याभक्षणं त्र्यहं; oOr क्षपयेत् त्र्यहं — c) Pu⁵ Pu⁷ मत्यात्वाभुक्त्वा°; Pu² Pu⁴ क्षुत्वावरे°; Bo Ho Lo⁴ Tr¹ भुक्ता चरे°; *Mandlik Jha KSS Dave* भुक्त्वाचरेत् thus reading आचरेत् but *Me* and *Rc* the only ones to comment on this clearly read चरेत्; oOr चरेत्कृत्स्नं — d) Lo⁴ Lo⁵ Pu¹⁰ [*Jolly* M] *Viś* 3.257 °मेव वा

Additional verse in GMd¹ TMd⁴ [after 222b] oOr NPu¹ Tr¹ MTr⁴ MTr⁶ [*Jolly* Gr] given after 223 in Be³ Tj¹ Tr² *Mandlik* [ms. ख] *KSS Dave;* commented by *Rc;* cited by *Dev* 2.619:

चन्द्रसूर्यग्रहे नाद्यादद्यात्स्नात्वा तु मुक्तयोः ।

नाद्याच्छूद्रस्य पक्वान्नं विद्वानश्रद्धिनो* द्विजः ।
आददीताममेवास्मादवृत्तावेकरात्रिकम् ॥२२३॥
श्रोत्रियस्य कदर्यस्य वदान्यस्य च वार्धुषेः ।
मीमांसित्वोभयं देवाः सममन्नमकल्पयन् ॥२२४॥
तान्प्रजापतिराहैत्य मा कृढ्वं विषमं समम् ।
श्रद्धापूतं वदान्यस्य हतमश्रद्धयेतरत् ॥२२५॥
श्रद्धयेष्टं च पूर्तं च नित्यं कुर्यादतन्द्रितः ।
श्रद्धाकृते ह्यक्षये ते भवतः स्वागतैर्धनैः ॥२२६॥

अमुक्तयोरस्तगयोरद्याद्दृष्ट्वापरेऽहनि ॥

b) oOr °त्स्नात्वान्त मुक्तयोः; GMd[5] *Dev* विमुक्तयोः — c) NPu[1] Tr[2] आमुक्तयोस्तंगतयोर°; *Mandlik KSS Dave* °योरगतयोर°; Be[3] °योरस्तमयोर°; [*Jolly* Gr] °योस्तु तयोर° — d) *Dev* °योर्दृष्ट्वा स्नात्वापरे°; GMd[1] °द्याददृष्टापरे°; Be[3] TMd[4] *Mandlik KSS Dave* °द्याच्चैव परे°; [*Jolly* Gr] °द्यादिष्ट्वापरे°

223.* Pādas a-c until आददीतम° omitted in Pu[8]. Cited by *Apa* 244; *Hem* 3/1.785 — b) GMd[5] विधिज्ञोनापदि द्विजः; Lo[1] sOx[1] Pu[5] sPu[6] विद्वान्नश्राद्धिनो; conjectural reading; all mss. except ST and those listed later read °श्राद्धिनो; NPu[1] Pu[2] Pu[4] °श्राद्धिको; Ho °श्राद्धनो; Lo[4] द्विजाः; MTr[4] नरः — c) GMd[1] La[1] Tr[1] MTr[4] MTr[6] आममेवाददीतास्माद°; Lo[4] Ox[3] °ममेव स्याद° — d) TMd[3] °स्मादद्यात्ता-वैकरात्रिकं; Hy Lo[2] Lo[3] GMd[1] GMy oOr Ox[2] Tr[1] *Hem* °वृत्तावैक°; BKt[5] wKt[6] °वृत्तामेक°; Be[3] °वृत्तादेक°; Tj[1] °वृत्ताचैक°; Lo[5] °वृत्तविकरात्रिकं; La[1] °वृत्ताचैकरावितं; Lo[1] °वृत्तन्धरात्रिकं; Tr[2] °रात्रकं

224. Cited in *Hem* 3/1.768; *Lakṣ* 3.271 — b) TMd[3] वदमवदान्यस्य वार्धुषेः; NKt[4] sOx[1] sPu[6] वदन्यस्य; Pu[2] Pu[4] चदान्यस्य; Tr[2] वदान्य च; GMy *om* च; Be[1] Bo Ho वार्धुपे; sOx[1] sPu[6] Tr[2] वार्धुषैः; Tr[1] वार्धुष्यैः; Lo[1] Wa वार्धुषः; Tj[1] वार्धकेः — c) Lo[1] मीमासीनोभयदस्यापि; Tj[1] °सित्त्वोभयोर्देवाः; Wa °त्वाभयं; Tj[2] °त्वोभयोर्देवाः; Be[3] वेदाः — d) Ox[3] समस्तसप्तमकल्पयन्; TMd[3] GMy सममेवम°; GMd[5] °मन्नं प्रकल्पयन्; Bo Lo[1] oMd[2] oOr °कल्पयत्

225. Cited by *Hem* 3/1.768; *Lakṣ* 3.272; pādas c-d cited by *Har*-A 1.19.5 — a) wKt[1] तत्प्रजा°; GMd[1] TMd[3] GMd[5] GMy sOx[1] NPu[1] sPu[6] Tr[1] Tr[2] MTr[4] MTr[6] *Lakṣ* °पतिरित्याह; *Hem* °पतिराह स्म; BBe[2] Bo NKt[4] wKt[6] Lo[3] °राहेत्य; Wa °रहेत्य; Pu[2] Pu[4] °राहैतात्मा — b) Be[1] Jo[1] Lo[3] TMd[3] NPu[1] Pu[8] Tr[2] [*Jolly* M[4] Nd R] *Lakṣ Mandlik KSS* कृध्वं; Kt[2] Lo[5] oMd[2] कृद्धं; Tr[2] कृधं; wKt[1] BKt[5] wKt[6] कृष्टं; Tj[1] कृछ; Lo[4] क्रुद्धं; oMd[2] कृत्यं; Tr[1] कुरुध्वं विषं — c) Lo[4] Tj[1] श्राद्धपूतं; TMd[3] GMy श्रद्धापूर्वं; MTr[3] श्रद्धाभूतं; NKt[4] sOx[1] sPu[6] वदन्यस्य; Tj[1] मथान्यस्य; Lo[5] वदात्यस्य — d) BBe[2] हुतं श्रोतियेतरत्; Lo[5] हतमाश्रद्धयोतरत्; BKt[5] °यैतरत्; wKt[6] °यैवतत्; NPu[1] °येतरं; La[1] °येतरान्; Pu[2] Pu[4] °येतरन्; Ho °येचरेत्

226.* Omitted in Pu[5] Pu[7]. Cited by *Apa* 290; *Hem* 1.86, 2/1.30 — a) Tj[1] श्राद्ध°; Wa °यैष्टं; Tj[1] पूतं; oOr पूर्णं — b) NKt[4] GMd[5] GMy oOr Tr[1] MTr[4] [*Jolly* Gr] *Hem Apa* कुर्यात्प्रयत्नतः; TMd[3] कुर्याद्विचक्षणः *cor to* कुर्यात्प्रयत्नतः — c) Lo[1] °कृते अक्षयापेते; GMy Tj[1] Tr[2] ह्यक्षय — d) GMd[5] स्वार्जि-तैर्धनैः; NPu[1] °तैर्धनं; Wa °तैर्व्रतैः

Additional verses in Wa; the first two also in BKt[5] wKt[6] and the third in Lo[5] [given after 225]. All three verses commented on by *Me*, and the first only by *Rc*:

श्रुतशौर्यतपःकन्यायाज्यशिष्यान्वयागतम् ।
धनं सप्तविधं शुद्धमुदयोऽप्यस्य तद्विधः ॥१॥
कुसीदकृषिवाणिज्यशिल्पसेवानुवृत्तितः ।

दानधर्मं निषेवेत नित्यमैष्टिकपौर्तिकम् ।
परितुष्टेन भावेन पात्रमासाद्य शक्तितः ॥२२७॥
यत्किंचिदपि दातव्यं याचितेनानसूयया ।
उत्पत्स्यते हि तत्पात्रं यत्तारयति सर्वतः ॥२२८॥
वारिदस्तृप्तिमाप्नोति सुखमक्षयमन्नदः ।
तिलप्रदः प्रजामिष्टां दीपदश्चक्षुरुत्तमम् ॥२२९॥
भूमिदो भूमिमाप्नोति दीर्घमायुर्हिरण्यदः ।
गृहदोऽग्र्याणि वेश्मानि रूप्यदो रूपमुत्तमम् ॥२३०॥

कृतोपकारादाप्तं च शबलं समुदाहृतम् ॥२॥
पार्श्विकद्यूतचौर्यार्तिप्रातिरूपकसाहसैः ।
व्याजेनोपार्जितं यच्च तत्कृष्णं समुदाहृतम् ॥३॥

1. a) Wa °सोर्य° — c) wKt^6 सप्तविधं — d) wKt^6 °मुदयो यस्य ते द्विधः; *Me* °मुभयो; Wa °मुदयोथस्य

2. c) BKt^5 wKt^6 °कारादेवाप्तं शवलं

3. a) Lo^5 पार्श्विकं धूरचौर्यानि; *Me* [pāṭha] °द्यूतवैर्या° — b) Lo^5 °साहसः

227. Pādas a-b omitted in Pu^5 Pu^7. Cited by *Apa* 282; *Mādh* 1.165 — a) Lo^1 oMd^2 GMd^5 *Apa Mādh* दानं; sOx^1 sPu^6 °धर्मौं; Tj^1 °धर्मे; GMd^1 °धर्मा; TMd^3 °धर्म; Bo न सेवेत; Tj^1 निषेवेत्य — b) *Mādh* नित्यनैमित्तसंज्ञकं; Ox^3 नित्यनैष्टि°; wKt^3 NNg °मैष्टिकं; oOr Tr^2 °मौष्टिकपौष्टिकं; GMd^5 °पौर्तकं; Ho °पौर्तिकः; TMd^3 Lo^3 *Apa* °पौष्टिकं; wKt^1 GMd^1 Tr^1 °पूर्तिकं; Pu^4 °पूर्त्तिकं — d) TMd^4 मन्त्रमासाद्य; Bo यत्नतः; Pu^4 adds at end स्मृतः

Additional verses in MTr^4 MTr^6 [*Jolly* Gr] *Mandlik* [ट] *KSS Dave;* cited by *Hem* 1.37; verse 1 in GMd^5:

पात्रभूतोऽपि यो विप्रः प्रतिगृह्य प्रतिग्रहम् ।
असत्सु विनियुञ्जीत देयं तस्मै न किंचन ॥१॥
संचयं कुरुते यस्तु प्रतिगृह्य समन्ततः ।
धर्मार्थं नोपयुञ्जीत न तं तस्करमर्चयेत् ॥२॥

1. a) GMd^5 *Mandlik KSS Dave* °भूतोहि — c) [*Jolly* Gr] स नियु° — d) GMd^5 व्ययन्तस्मिन्न किंचन; *Mandlik KSS Dave* तस्मै देयं न; *Hem* तस्य न

2. a) *Hem Jolly* यश्च; MTr^4 वस्तु — c) *Dave* [*Jolly* Gr] धर्मार्थे; *Mandlik KSS Dave* नोपयुङ्क्ते च; *Hem* नोपयुङ्क्ते यो

228. Cited by *Apa* 282, 385 — a) BKt^5 wKt^6 °चिदेव — b) Tr^2 याचितैर्नानसू°; Lo^1 याच्यतेचानसू°; NNg याच्यतेनानसू°; Ho याचितेनाप्यसू°; Be^1 Be^3 wKt^3 La^1 NPu^1 Pu^2 Pu^4 Pu^5 Pu^7 Tj^1 °नानुसूयया; Ox^3 °नानिसूयता; Pu^{10} °नानस्तसूयता; Lo^4 Lo^5 °नातुसूयया; NKt^4 wKt^6 sOx^1 [*cor to*] sPu^6 *Apa* 282 °सूयता; *Apa* 385 °सूयतः; BKt^5 °सूयतो — c) Ox^3 Pu^{10} उत्पत्स्यति; GMd^1 उत्पस्यते; Pu^4 उत्पश्यते; wKt^1 उत्पश्यतो; NPu^1 तत्पश्यते; Tr^2 उत्पद्यते; Tj^1 उत्पयते; Pu^8 *om* हि; Tj^2 च; Ox^3 यत्पात्रं — d) GMd^1 °त्रमुत्तारयति; wKt^1 तत्तारयति; BCa wKt^3 oOr Ox^2 सर्वशः

229. Pādas c-d omitted in Ox^2. Cited by *Vij* 1.210; *Apa* 385; *Hem* 1.152; *Mādh* 1.177 — a) sOx^1 La^1 sPu^6 Pu^8 °दस्तुष्टिमा°; Wa °दस्तुप्तिमा°; TMd^3 °दस्स्मृतिमा° — b) Pu^{10} सुषम°; Be^1 wKt^1 Lo^1 NNg sOx^1 Ox^3 sPu^6 Tr^1 *Apa* [vl] *Jolly* °क्षय्यम° — c) TMd^4 तिलपस्तु— d) Tr^1 दीपतश्च°

230. Pādas a-b omitted in Ox^2; not commented by *Nd.* Cited by *Vij* 1.210; *Apa* 386; *Hem* 1.152; *Mādh* 1.177; pāda-a cited by *Apa* 367 and pādas a-b by *Hem* 3/1.664 — a) La^1 NPu^1 Pu^2

वासोदश्चन्द्रसालोक्यमश्विसालोक्यमश्वदः ।
अनडुहः श्रियं पुष्टां गोदो ब्रध्नस्य विष्टपम् ॥२३१॥
यानशय्याप्रदो भार्यामैश्वर्यमभयप्रदः ।
धान्यदः शाश्वतं सौख्यं ब्रह्मदो ब्रह्मसार्ष्टिताम् ॥२३२॥
सर्वेषामेव दानानां ब्रह्मदानं विशिष्यते ।
वार्यन्नगोमहीवासस्तिलकाञ्चनसर्पिषाम् ॥२३३॥
येन येन तु भावेन यद्यद्दानं प्रयच्छति ।
तत्तत्तेनैव भावेन प्राप्नोति प्रतिपूजितः ॥२३४॥
योऽर्चितं प्रतिगृह्णाति ददात्यर्चितमेव च ।
तावुभौ गच्छतः स्वर्गं नरकं तु विपर्यये ॥२३५॥
न विस्मयेत तपसा वदेदिष्ट्वा च नानृतं ।

Pu^{4} *Hem* भूमिदः सर्वमाप्नोति; *Apa* 386 भूमिदः स्वर्गमाप्नोति — c) Bo Bo Ho NNg *Hem* °ग्राणि; Lo^{1} °प्राणि — d) Bo Lo^{4} Lo^{5} Ox^{3} NPu^{1} Wa रूपदो; Be^{1} रूपदा; GMy दीप्यतो; Pu^{2} Pu^{4} रूप्यमुत्तमं

231. Not commented by *Nd.* Cited by *Apa* 386; *Hem* 1.152 — b) sOx^{1} sPu^{6} °लोक्यं सूर्यसालो°; wKt^{1} Ox^{2} Tj^{1} Tr^{2} °लोक्यमर्कसालो°; BBe^{2} °माश्विसालो°; GMd^{1} NPu^{1} Pu^{2} Pu^{4} °मश्वसालो°; oMd^{2} °श्विकालो°; Bo *Apa* °श्विदः — c) La^{1} अनडुहदः; Pu^{5} Pu^{7} *Mandlik Jha KSS Dave* अनडुहः; Bo GMd^{5} Wa अनडुदः; wKt^{6} अनच्छद्दः; Lo^{1} अनडद्दः; GMy अनडुदद्; TMd^{3} अनदुदः; MTr^{6} अनद्धुडः; GMd^{1} अनडुदस्तु; Lo^{3} अनदुहस्तु; Lo^{4} Ox^{3} अनुडुद्धः; Lo^{2} अनुडुर्दः; Pu^{10} अनुद्धव्दः; Pu^{2} Pu^{4} अव्दा चैव श्रियं; La^{1} श्रियमाप्नोति; Wa प्रजामिष्टां; Tr^{2} दुष्टां; GMd^{5} Tr^{1} MTr^{4} MTr^{6} जुष्टां; TMd^{3} जुष्ट्य; *Mādh* तुष्टां; oOr प्रष्टो — d) Pu^{10} गोब्रध्नस्य; Tr^{2} Wa बध्नस्य; TMd^{3} भृद्नस्य; Bo ब्रह्मस्य; Pu^{5} Pu^{7} विष्टघं; wKt^{3} विष्टयं; wKt^{1} पिष्टयं; Jo^{1} oOr *Mādh* पिष्टपं; Kt^{2} पिष्टप

232. Omitted in Tj^{2}. Cited by *Apa* 386; *Hem* 1.152; *Mādh* 1.177 — a) Pu^{2} Pu^{4} यानशय्यासनो भार्या° — c) TMd^{4} दानतश्शाश्वतं; Wa शाश्वतः; TMd^{3} GMy शाश्वतस्सौख्यं — d) Be^{3} NKt^{4} La^{1} Lo^{5} Ox^{3} Pu^{2} Pu^{4} Pu^{10} Tj^{1} Tr^{2} [*Jolly* M] *Mādh Apa* ब्रह्म शाश्वतं; Lo^{4} ब्रह्म शाश्वतां; GMd^{1} ब्रह्मसंपदं; Pu^{7} ब्रह्मसार्प्टेतां *mc to* ब्रह्मसाम्यतां; BKt^{5} wKt^{6} °सर्षितां

233. Cited by *Dev* 1.145; pādas a-b cited by *Mādh* 1.177 — a) NKt^{4} GMd^{1} GMd^{5} oOr Tr^{1} MTr^{4} MTr^{6} सर्वेषां तु प्रदानानां — b) oOr प्रशस्यते; Be^{3} प्रशिष्यते; Bo विशेषतः — c) GMd^{1} GMd^{5} GMy Tj^{1} वार्यन्नं; GMd^{1} °महीदानतिल°; TMd^{3} °वासतिल°; TMd^{4} °वासातिल° — d) Bo sOx^{1} °सर्पिषा; Tj^{1} °सर्पिषं

234. Cited by *Hem* 1.17 — a) TMd^{3} GMy *Hem* हि; Lo^{3} दानेन — b) NPu^{1} तद्यद्दानं; Pu^{2} यदादानं; Pu^{4} यद्यदानं; Lo^{3} तु यच्छति — c) Pu^{8} तत्तु तेनैव — c-d) Tr^{2} तत्तत्तेनैव प्राप्नोति प्रतिपूजितः स्मृतः; *Hem* तेन तेन हि भावेन तत्प्राप्नोति हि पूजितः — d) Bo पतिपूजितः; NPu^{1} Pu^{4} °पूजितं; TMd^{3} GMy °पूजनं

235.* Omitted in Lo^{3} [*Jolly* R]; pāda-d omitted in Pu^{4}. Cited by *Apa* 290 — a) GMd^{1} योर्चिता; TMd^{3} योर्चित — b) Be^{1} Ho Lo^{1} दद्यादर्चित°; Pu^{10} तदात्यर्चित°; Be^{1} BBe^{2} Bo BCa Jo^{2} wKt^{3} NKt^{4} La^{1} La^{2} Lo^{2} Lo^{4} Lo^{5} oMd^{2} GMd^{5} NNg oOr sOx^{1} Ox^{2} Ox^{3} NPu^{1} Pu^{5} sPu^{6} Pu^{7} Pu^{8} Pu^{10} Tj^{1} Tj^{2} Tr^{1} MTr^{4} MTr^{6} [*Jolly* M] *Dave Jha* °तमेव वा; TMd^{4} °तमेव यः; *Apa* °तमेव तु — c) Ho स्वर्गे — d) sPu^{6} विपरीतं *cor to* नरकं तु; Be^{1} Ho Lo^{1} NNg Tr^{1} *Apa* च; Pu^{5} Pu^{7} [*but cor*] Wa विपर्ययेत्; Pu^{8} विपर्णये; TMd^{4} विपत्यये

नार्तोऽप्यपवदेद्विप्रान्न दत्त्वा परिकीर्तयेत् ॥२३६॥
यज्ञोऽनृतेन क्षरति तपः क्षरति विस्मयात् ।
आयुर्विप्रापवादेन दानं तु परिकीर्तनात् ॥२३७॥
धर्मं शनैः संचिनुयाद् वल्मीकमिव पुत्तिकाः ।
परलोकसहायार्थं सर्वभूतान्यपीडयन् ॥२३८॥
नामुत्र हि सहायार्थं पिता माता च तिष्ठतः ।
न पुत्रदारं न ज्ञातिर्धर्मस्तिष्ठति केवलः ॥२३९॥
एकः प्रजायते जन्तुरेक एव प्रलीयते ।
एकोऽनुभुङ्क्ते सुकृतमेक एव च दुष्कृतम् ॥२४०॥
मृतं शरीरमुत्सृज्य काष्ठलोष्टसमं क्षितौ ।
विमुखा बान्धवा यान्ति धर्मस्तमनुगच्छति ॥२४१॥
तस्माद्धर्मं सहायार्थं नित्यं संचिनुयाच्छनैः ।

236. Omitted in Ho. Cited by *Apa* 230; *Hem* 1.90 — a) BKt^{5} wKt^{6} Lo^{1} sOx^{1} sPu^{6} विस्मयेन; Pu^{10} विस्मवेन; wKt^{1} मनसा — b) Pu^{4} *om* वदेदिष्ट्वा; Bo वदेदिष्ट्या; MTr^{4} वदेदिष्टा; MTr^{6} वदेदिष्टां; Ox^{2} *Apa* वदेदृष्ट्वा; Lo^{1} [*but cor*] वदेदद्याच्च; BKt^{5} wKt^{6} NNg [*Jolly* M^{1-2-9}] *Hem* न चानृतं; Lo^{5} Ox^{3} [*Jolly* M^{3-4-5}] न वानृतं — c) Tj^{1} नानृते च वदेद्विद्वान्न; Tr^{2} नात्तो; Lo^{2} नार्ते; *Hem* नार्तोविप्रवदे°; Bo °प्यवदे°; La^{1} Tr^{2} °देद्विद्वान्न; Wa °देद्विब्धान्न — d) wKt^{3} GMy °द्विप्रानदत्त्वा; wKt^{1} oMd^{2} Tj^{1} °द्विप्रान्दत्त्वा न परि°; oOr *Apa* [vl as in ed] दत्तं

237.* Cited by *Apa* 230; *Hem* 1.90 — a) Pu^{5} Pu^{7} क्षरते — b) oOr विस्मयं — c) *Apa* °प्रावमानेन — d) Jo^{2} Lo^{3} [*Jolly* R] दानं क्षरति कीर्तनात्; Be^{3} BCa Ho Hy Jm Jo^{1} Kt^{2} BKt^{5} wKt^{6} Lo^{2} oMd^{2} oOr sOx^{1} Ox^{2} NPu^{1} Pu^{2} Pu^{5} sPu^{6} Pu^{7} Tj^{1} Tj^{2} Tr^{2} *Mandlik Jolly Jha KSS Dave* च; NNg [*but mc sh*] Wa °कीर्तयेत्

238. Pāda-d omitted in Be^{1} Lo^{3} Tj^{2}. Cited by *Apa* 232 — b) Tj^{1} वलिकिक्रिमिपूर्तिकः; BBe^{2} Lo^{1} वल्मीक इव; BBe^{2} Be^{3} पुत्तिका; Pu^{3} पूत्तिकाः; Kt^{2} NKt^{4} Lo^{1} Lo^{4} पुत्रिकाः; Ho BKt^{5} wKt^{6} पुत्रिका; Pu^{5} Pu^{7} GMd^{5} MTr^{4} [*Jolly* G] वम्रिकाः; *Apa* वप्रिकाः; [*Jolly* N] वल्मिकाः; wKt^{1} GMy NPu^{1} Pu^{2} Pu^{4} Tr^{1} मृत्तिका [wKt^{1} GMy °काः]; Wa बभ्रिकाः; oOr सुतिकं; Ox^{2} पूजितः — c) Tj^{1} °सदायार्थं; Pu^{5} Pu^{7} °यार्थे; Pu^{2} °यार्थं च — d) wKt^{3} °पीडयत्; Bo oOr MTr^{6} °पीडयेत्; TMd^{3} पीडयेन्

239. Pāda-d omitted in Be^{1} Lo^{3} Tj^{2}. Cited by *Apa* 232; *Dev* 2.459 — a) NNg *ma sh* हि; GMd^{1} oOr Pu^{4} च; TMd^{4} य; Lo^{1} Tj^{1} साहा°; Pu^{5} °यार्थे — b) Ho तु; oMd^{2} हि; TMd^{3} न; oOr तिष्ठति — c) Be^{1} Be^{3} Ho TMd^{3} GMd^{5} GMy Pu^{3} Tj^{1} Tr^{2} °दारा न; MTr^{4} MTr^{6} °दारान्न; sOx^{1} sPu^{6} °दारा अज्ञातिधर्म°; wKt^{1} NKt^{4} TMd^{3} TMd^{4} oOr Tj^{1} ज्ञातिधर्म°; Lo^{4} ज्ञातिं धर्म° — d) Ho La^{1} Lo^{3} TMd^{3} TMd^{4} GMy oOr Tr^{2} केवलं; NNg [*but mc fh*] MTr^{3} केवलाः; Jo^{1} केवलैः

240. Cited by *Apa* 232; *Dev* 2.459 — a) Tr^{2} एका; BKt^{5} wKt^{6} Lo^{3} GMd^{1} TMd^{3} GMd^{5} GMy oOr Pu^{3} Pu^{8} Tr^{1} MTr^{4} MTr^{6} *Nā* प्रसूयते; BKt^{5} wKt^{6} यन्तु° — b) Tj^{1} येव; Jo^{2} wKt^{3} Lo^{3} TMd^{3} GMd^{5} GMy NNg NPu^{1} Pu^{5} Pu^{7} Tr^{1} MTr^{4} MTr^{6} [*Jolly* G R] प्रमीयते — c) Pu^{5} Pu^{7} एको भुङ्क्ते तु; Ho Tj^{1} Tr^{2} एकोत्र भुङ्क्ते; Jo^{1} एकेन भुङ्क्ते — d) Bo Tj^{1} Tr^{2} °तमेकश्चाप्नोति दुष्कृतं; Be^{3} °तमेकः प्राप्नोति दुष्कृतं; La^{1} Pu^{5} Pu^{7} Wa तु; wKt^{1} हि; GMy चतुष्कृतं; Pu^{10} *om* दुष्कृतं; La^{1} [*bu mc sh*] यः कृतं

241. Cited by *Apa* 232; *Dev* 2.259–60 — a) NKt^{4} Lo^{1} मृत; *Apa* शरीरं संत्यज्य — b) MTr^{4} °समा — d) Lo^{4} Lo^{5} Ox^{3} Pu^{10} [*Jolly* M] धर्मस्तिष्ठति केवलं [cf. 239d]

धर्मेण हि सहायेन तमस्तरति दुस्तरम् ॥२४२॥
धर्मप्रधानं पुरुषं तपसा हतकिल्बिषम् ।
परलोकं नयत्याशु भास्वन्तं खशरीरिणम् ॥२४३॥
उत्तमैरुत्तमैर्नित्यं संबन्धानाचरेत्सह ।
निनीषुः कुलमुत्कर्षमधमानधमांस्त्यजेत् ॥२४४॥
उत्तमानुत्तमानेव गच्छन् हीनांश्च वर्जयन् ।
ब्राह्मणः श्रेष्ठतामेति प्रत्यवायेन शूद्रताम् ॥२४५॥
दृढकारी मृदुर्दान्तः क्रूराचारैरसंवसन् ।
अहिंस्रो दमदानाभ्यां जयेत्स्वर्गं तथाव्रतः ॥२४६॥

242. Pādas a-b cited by *Hem* 2/1.14; *Dev* 2.459–60; pādas a-b cited by *Apa* 232 — a) GMd^{5} धर्मेण सहितो येन; Kt^{2} TMd^{4} °द्धर्म; Pu^{4} *om* सहायार्थं — b) Bo धर्मं संचि°; Be^{3} Tj^{1} °नुयाद्बुधः — c) wKt^{1} धर्मेणैव सहा° — d) GMd^{1} ततस्तरति

243. a) TMd^{4} Tr^{1} धर्मं; TMd^{4} प्रधान; GMd^{1} °प्रदानं; GMd^{1} पुरुषस्तपसा — b) Bo तपसा किल्मिषेन हि; Be^{3} Tj^{1} तमसा; wKt^{6} तपसं; NKt^{4} BKt^{5} wKt^{6} GMd^{1} TMd^{3} GMd^{5} GMy NNg Tr^{1} MTr^{6} °कल्मषं; Lo^{3} [*Jolly* R] °दुष्कृतं — c) TMd^{3} GMy पतिलोकं; Ox^{2} °लोके; Lo^{4} GMd^{5} Tj^{1} नयन्त्याशु; wKt^{3} तपत्याशु — d) TMd^{4} सन्तं केसरीणं यथा; TMd^{3} भास्वन्तः; Lo^{1} sOx^{1} sPu^{6} स्वशरी°; Tj^{2} सशरी°; GMd^{1} GMd^{5} GMy Tr^{1} MTr^{4} खेशरी°; Lo^{4} खशरीरिणां; Tr^{1} खशरीरिण; TMd^{3} खेशकीलिणं; Tj^{1} खंशरीरिणां; Ox^{3} च शरीरिणां; Pu^{10} श्वशरीरिणां

Additional verse in GMd^{1} TMd^{4} GMd^{5} Tr^{1} MTr^{4} MTr^{6}:

न हि वेदास्त्वधीतास्तु न शास्त्राणि श्रुतान्यपि ।
तत्र गच्छन्ति यत्रासौ धर्म एकोऽनुगच्छति ।

a) MTr^{4} वेदास्स्वधी°; GMd^{5} °धीयाना — c) MTr^{4} omits the pāda; GMd^{1} Tr^{1} गच्छति; GMd^{1} TMd^{4} यत्रास्य; MTr^{4} MTr^{6} तत्रास्य

A further half-verse added in TMd^{4} Tr^{1}:

तस्माद्धर्मं निषेवेत पीडयाप्यात्मनः सदा ।

b) TMd^{4} दयात्यात्मनस्सदा

244. Cited by *Mādh* 1.478 — a) sOx^{1} sPu^{6} उत्तमैः पुरुषैर्नित्यं; Pu^{5} Pu^{7} उत्तमैः सार्धं नित्यं — b) BBe^{2} यः संब°; Tj^{1} सर्वथा नाचरे°; Tr^{2} °रेत्सदा; TMd^{3} GMy °रेत्समं; BKt^{5} wKt^{6} °रेत्सहि; GMd^{5} °रेद्बुधः — c) Tr^{2} निर्णीषु; wKt^{6} निनीक्षुः — d) Tj^{1} °धमास्पमां त्यजेत्; GMd^{1} TMd^{3} GMd^{5} GMy Tr^{1} MTr^{4} MTr^{6} °त्कर्षमवमानवमांस्त्यजेत्

245.* Omitted in Bo; pādas a-b omitted in TMd^{3} GMy. Cited by *Lakṣ* 2.276 — a) La^{1} °त्तमांश्चैव; Jo^{2} Lo^{2} °मान्च — a-b) BBe^{2} Be^{3} Hy Jm Jo^{1} wKt^{1} Kt^{2} wKt^{3} OMd^{2} Tj^{1} Tj^{2} MTr^{3} *Lakṣ Mandlik KSS* उत्तमानुत्तमान्गच्छन्हीनान्हीनांश्च वर्जयन् — b) Be^{1} Be^{3} Ho BKt^{5} wKt^{6} Lo^{1} Lo^{4} Lo^{5} sOx^{1} Ox^{3} sPu^{6} MTr^{4} *Dave Jha* [*Jolly* M] हीनांस्तु; MTr^{6} हीनां वर्ज°; Be^{1} Be^{3} Ho wKt^{1} Kt^{2} BKt^{5} wKt^{6} La^{1} Lo^{1} Lo^{2} Lo^{3} Lo^{4} Lo^{5} GMd^{1} TMd^{4} GMd^{5} NNg sOx^{1} Ox^{3} NPu^{1} Pu^{2} Pu^{3} Pu^{4} Pu^{5} sPu^{6} Pu^{7} Pu^{8} Pu^{10} Tj^{1} Tr^{2} MTr^{6} Wa *Lakṣ* वर्जयेत्; NKt^{4} वर्जयत् — c) TMd^{4} ब्रह्मण्यश्रेष्टता यान्ति — d) NKt^{4} TMd^{4} MTr^{4} MTr^{6} *Lakṣ* प्रत्यवाये तु; Tr^{1} प्रत्यवायेति

246. a) NPu^{1} दृढचारी तुदुर्दंतिः; Bo मृदुर्दान्तं; Be^{1} मृदुर्दीतः — b) Be^{1} °चारैर्न संवसन्; Ho °चारैर्न संवसेत्; OMd^{2} °संवसत्; wKt^{1} °संविसन्; Jo^{2} Pu^{10} °संचरन्; GMd^{5} MTr^{3} °संवदन्; BBe^{2} °संवहन् — c) Lo^{1} Lo^{3} अहिंस्ला; TMd^{3} GMy Tr^{2} अहिंसा; TMd^{3} GMy दीनदानाभ्यां; Tj^{2} दमबानाभ्यां; Lo^{1} दमनाभ्यां च;

एधोदकं मूलफलमन्नमभ्युद्यतं च यत् ।
सर्वतः प्रतिगृह्णीयान्मध्वथाभयदक्षिणाम् ॥२४७॥
आहृताभ्युद्यतां भिक्षां पुरस्तादप्रचोदिताम् ।
मेने प्रजापतिर्ग्राह्यामपि दुष्कृतकर्मणः ॥२४८॥
नाश्नन्ति पितरस्तस्य दश वर्षाणि पञ्च च ।
न च हव्यं वहत्यग्निर्यस्तामभ्यवमन्यते ॥२४९॥

Ox3 मदनाभ्यां — d) Be1 Be3 Bo Tj1 Tr2 व्रजेत्स्वर्गं; BBe2 Lo2 यजेत्स्वर्गं; NKt4 जयं स्वर्गं; Ox2 यथाव्रतः; Lo4 तथावृतः; [*Jolly* N] तथाव्रतेः; GMd1 शुचिव्रतः; GMd5 Tr1 MTr4 MTr6 दृढव्रतः; TMd3 दृढव्रतं; Bo सदाव्रतः; La1 Pu2 Pu4 तथाविधः; sOx1 sPu6 यथाविधि; Be3 Tj1 Tr2 समाहितः; oOr °व्रतैः

Additional verse in Be3 BCa La1 oOr Tj1:

कर्मणा मनसा वाचा यदभीक्ष्णं समाचरेत् ।
तदभ्यासो हरत्येनस्तस्मात्कल्याणमाचरेत् ॥

b) oOr यदभीष्टं; BCa oOr निषेवते — c) BCa La1 सदभ्यासो; Tj1 तदा ध्यानो; Be3 हरत्येनं तस्मा°; Tj1 हरेत्येनं तस्मा°

247. Cited by *Vij* 1.214; *Apa* 406; *Hem* 1.56; *Mādh* 1.190— a) Ox3 एषोदकं; *Rc* गन्धोदकं; Ho °फले अन्न° — b) Tj1 °न्नमद्यधृतं; Be1 La1 Lo2 NPu1 Pu2 Pu4 Pu5 Pu7 Tr1 MTr4 °भ्युदितं; TMd3 °भ्युद्दितं; *Apa* °भ्युद्धृतं — c) La1 सर्वत्र — d) BKt5 wKt6 °गृह्णीयादध्वर्याभय°; Lo1 °गृह्णीयादथाभय°; *Mādh Hem* °यान्मधु चाभय°; wKt1 °यात्सर्वथाभय°; NKt4 Lo2 Lo3 Lo4 Ox3 NPu1 Pu2 Pu3 Pu4 Pu5 Pu7 Pu10 °थोभय°; Tj1 °योभय°; Ho Lo4 °दक्षिणं

248. Cited by *Apa* 407; *Hem* 1.56 — a) wKt1 wKt6 sOx1 sPu6 आहृत्या°; Tr2 अहृता°; Ho आहता°; Lo1 अहता°; La1 आकृता°; [*Jolly* M1–2–9 G Nd] *ViDh* 57.11 आहुता°; Ho La1 NPu1 Pu2 Pu7 [*mc sh to*] GMd1 Tr1 *Hem Apa* आहृतामुद्यतां; NPu1 Pu2 Pu3 Pu4 Pu5 आहुतामद्यता; *Apa* [vls] अहृतामुदितां and अहृतामुह्यतां; TMd3 GMd5 GMy उद्यतामाहृतां; MTr4 MTr6 उद्धतामाहृतां; Lo3 Pu4 Pu10 Tr2 [*Jolly* M2–9] °भ्युदितां — b) Tr2 °देव चोदितां; *Apa* [vl] °दग्रचोदितां; TMd3 GMd5 [*Jolly* Nd] *ApDh* 1.19.14 °प्रवेदितां; wKt1 °चोदितं; GMy °चेदितां; Ho Ox2 Wa °णोदितां — c) Be1 Ho NKt4 GMy ग्राह्यां प्रजापतिर्मेने; MTr4 MTr6 भोज्यां प्रजापतिर्मेने; NPu1 मनुः; GMd1 तेन; GMd1 GMd5 Tr1 [*Jolly* Gr] °पतिर्भोज्यामपि; Ox3 °ह्यमपि — c-d) TMd3 ग्राह्यां प्रजापतिर्मेने अप्यतिदुष्कृतकारिणः — d) GMd1 GMd5 Tr1 MTr4 MTr6 °कारिणः; GMy °कारिणं

Additional verse in Tr1 [after this it adds the first verse given after 249]:

श्रद्धधानस्य भोक्तव्यं चोरस्यापि विशेषतः ।
न त्वेवं बहुयाज्यस्य यश्चोपनयते बहून् ॥

249. Cited by *Apa* 407; *Hem* 1.56; *Dev* 2.463 — a) GMd1 GMd5 Tr1 *Dev* न तस्य पितरोश्नन्ति; TMd3 नाश्नाति — b) *Apa* [vl] वा— c) Pu5 Pu7 Tj1 दहत्य°; NKt4 वहेदग्नि° — d) TMd3 GMy °स्तमभ्यव°; La1 Tj1 °मप्यवमन्यते; GMd5 °मध्यवमन्यते; *Apa* °भ्यवपद्यते

Additional verse in Be3 wKt1 Lo2 GMd1 TMd4 GMd5 oOr Ox2 Pu2 Pu3 Pu4 Tj1 Tr2 MTr4 MTr6 *Mandlik* [11 mss.] *KSS Dave;* given after verse 248 in Tr1; commented by *Rc*. Cited by *Apa* 407, *Lakṣ* 2.245:

चिकित्सककृतघ्नानां शल्यकर्तुश्च वार्द्धुषेः ।
षण्ढस्य कुलटायाश्च उद्यतामपि वर्जयेत् ॥

a-b) GMd1 कृतघ्नानां शल्यकर्तुर्गणिकायाश्च वार्धुषेः — b) TMd4 Tr2 *Mandlik KSS Dave* शिल्प°; Be3 wKt1 *Apa* [vl] शल्यहर्तुश्च; Pu2 Pu4 Tj1 *Lakṣ* शल्यहर्तुस्तु; *Apa* शल्यहन्तुस्तु; Ox2 गर्भहन्तुश्च; Ox2 Pu2 Pu4 वार्द्धुषः; wKt1 वार्धुकेः — c) Ox2 शण्ढस्य; Be3 Tr1 MTr6 *Lakṣ*

शय्यां गृहान् कुशान् गन्धानपः पुष्पं मणीन्दधि ।
धाना मत्स्यान्पयो मांसं शाकं चैव न निर्णुदेत् ॥२५०॥
गुरून् भृत्यांश्चोज्जिहीर्षन्नर्चिष्यन्देवतातिथीन् ।
सर्वतः प्रतिगृह्णीयान्न तु तृप्येत्स्वयं ततः ॥२५१॥
गुरुषु त्वभ्यतीतेषु विना वा तैर्गृहे वसन् ।
आत्मनो वृत्तिमन्विच्छन् गृह्णीयात्साधुतः सदा ॥२५२॥
आर्धिकः कुलमित्रं च गोपालो दासनापितौ ।
एते शूद्रेषु भोज्यान्ना यश्चात्मानं निवेदयेत् ॥२५३॥
यादृशोऽस्य भवेदात्मा यादृशं च चिकीर्षितम् ।

षण्डस्य; Lo[2] GMd[5] oOr षण्ढश्च — d) GMd[1] MTr[4] MTr[6] सूद्यतामपि; Tr[1] प्रोद्यतामपि

Another additional verse in Be[3] Pu[3] Tj[1] Tr[2] *Mandlik* (ल) *Dave KSS;* commented by *Rc:*

न विद्यमानमेव वै प्रतिग्राह्यं विजानता ।
विकल्पाविद्यमाने तु धर्महीनः प्रकीर्तितः ॥

a) Be[3] °नमेवं — c) *Mandlik KSS Dave* विकल्प्या°; Be[3] Tj[1] विकल्पे; Pu[3] विकल्प° — d) Tj[1] प्रकीर्तिताः

250. Cited by *Vij* 1.214; *Apa* 406; *Hem* 1.56; *Dev* 2.463; *Mādh* 1.190 — a) Ho GMd[5] शय्या; MTr[4] शय्यासनं कुशान्; Be[1] Be[3] Ho NKt[4] Lo[2] GMy NNg Pu[5] Pu[7] Tj[1] MTr[6] Wa [*Jolly* R] *Dev* गृहं; wKt[6] गृहात्; wKt[1] GMd[1] *Mādh* कुशान्गृहान्; Wa कुशानान्धानपः; Pu[10] गन्धावपः; Tr[1] गन्धामपः; TMd[4] मन्दानपः — b) Ox[3] *Apa* गन्धानापः; wKt[6] Lo[1] Lo[3] *Hem* गन्धान्पयः; La[1] NPu[1] Tr[1] मणिं दधिं; Be[3] Bo Lo[1] Tj[1] फलं दधि; *Hem* महीं दधि — c) *Mādh Hem Apa* मत्स्यान्धानाः पयो; La[1] Lo[3] GMd[5] sOx[1] Ox[2] Pu[3] sPu[6] Tr[2] [*Jolly* R] *Dev* [vl] धान्यं; GMd[1] धान्यां; TMd[3] TMd[4] धान्या; Ho wKt[1] MTr[4] धानान्; Tr[1] धनान्; Kt[2] मत्स्यादयो — c-d) Pu[5] मांसशाकानि गन्धवन्ति च — d) Tj[1] शावकं; wKt[3] निर्दहेत्; wKt[6] निर्लयेत्; *Hem* निर्लुठेत्

251. Cited by *Hem* 1.56 — a) Lo[1] *cor to* भृत्यंश्चो°; sOx[1] sPu[6] भृत्यानुज्जि°; Tr[2] °श्चोज्जीही°; GMd[1] °श्चोद्धरिपत्र°; TMd[3] GMy °श्चोधिनिर्ष्यन्न°; GMd[5] °श्चोज्जजिर्पुरर्चि° — b) sOx[1] sPu[6] °न्नर्चिप°; NKt[4] °न्नार्चिष्य°; GMd[1] °न्नर्चयेद्देव° — c) sOx[1] sPu[6] सर्वथा; Ho सर्वप्रति°; BKt[5] wKt[6] °गृह्णानो न — d) Ox[2] °यात्रानुतृप्ये°; Pu[5] Pu[7] °यात्तेन तृप्ये°; Tj[1] °यात्तनुमप्येत्स्वयं; wKt[3] wKt[6] TMd[4] °यान्न तृप्येत स्वयं; Jo[2] Lo[3] च; Be[1] तुष्ये°; NPu[1] ततं

252. a) TMd[3] अधिगुरुपु तृप्यति तेषु; GMd[1] गुरूष्वितेषु गेहेषु; wKt[6] गुरुष्वनभ्यतन्तेषु; GMy त्वप्यती°; BKt[5] त्वभ्यतन्तेषु; GMd[5] त्वप्रतीतेषु — b) Tj[1] विना चान्ते गृहे; Ho न विना तैर्गृहे; Lo[3] विना तैर्वा गृहे; Lo[2] वासैर्गृहे; GMy यातैर्गृहे; wKt[6] वा ते गृहे; TMd[4] तैर्गृही; Be[3] Ho GMd[1] GMd[5] Ox[3] वसेत् — c) NKt[4] आत्मानो; GMd[5] आतुरो; Lo[4] Lo[5] oMd[2] Pu[10] [*Jolly* M] वृत्तिमाकाङ्क्षन्; sOx[1] sPu[6] MTr[6] °न्विच्छेद्; Ox[3] वृत्तिं [*rest of verse om*]

253. Cited by *Hem* 3/1.785 — a) Lo[4] Ng Ox[3] Pu[1] Pu[10] Tj[1] Wa [*Jolly* M G N] *Hem ViDh* 57.16 *Jolly* अर्धिकः; wKt[1] wKt[3] आर्धिकं; Pu[2] Pu[4] Pu[7] अर्धिकं; GMd[5] आर्धितः; Tj[1] अर्थिकः; Pu[5] अद्विकं; TMd[3] अधिकः; BKt[5] कार्धिकः; wKt[6] कार्पिकः; GMd[1] तद्धिकः; Ox[2] कालमित्रं; GMy MTr[4] MTr[6] °मित्रश्च; TMd[3] °मित्रंश्च; Be[3] Tj[1] °मित्राणि गो° — b) La[1] दासो गोपालनापितौ; TMd[4] गोपापि; GMy °नापिताः — c) TMd[3] GMy एतेषु; oOr तेषु; BKt[5] wKt[6] शूद्रस्य; TMd[3] GMy भोज्यान्न; TMd[4] भोज्येन्नं — d) GMd[5] यच्चात्मानं; Lo[4] विनिवेदयेत्

यथा चोपचरेदेनं तथात्मानं निवेदयेत् ॥२५४॥
योऽन्यथा सन्तमात्मानमन्यथा सत्सु भाषते ।
स पापकृत्तमो लोके स्तेन आत्मापहारकः ॥२५५॥
वाच्यर्था नियताः सर्वे वाङ्मूला वाग्विनिःसृताः ।
तां तु यः स्तेनयेद्वाचं स सर्वस्तेयकृन्नरः ॥२५६॥
महर्षिपितृदेवानां गत्वानृण्यं यथाविधि ।
पुत्रे सर्वं समासज्य वसेन्माध्यस्थमास्थितः ॥२५७॥
एकाकी चिन्तयेन्नित्यं विविक्ते हितमात्मनः ।
एकाकी चिन्तयानो हि परं श्रेयोऽधिगच्छति ॥२५८॥
एषोदिता गृहस्थस्य वृत्तिर्विप्रस्य शाश्वती ।
स्नातकव्रतकल्पश्च सत्त्ववृद्धिकरः शुभः ॥२५९॥
अनेन विप्रो वृत्तेन वर्तयन्वेदशास्त्रवित् ।

254. Omitted in Lo[1] Pu[8]; *ma* in BKt[5]. Cited by *Hem* 3/1.785 — b) NPu[1] Tj[1] तादृशं; GMd[1] TMd[3] GMy यादृशश्च; Ox[2] यादृशोस्य; Wa *om* च; BKt[5] wKt[6] तु; TMd[3] चिकीर्षितः; wKt[3] चिकीर्षिकं — c) sOx[1] sPu[6] यो यथोपचरे°; Lo[4] Lo[5] यथा परिचरे°; Ho चोपपरे°; TMd[3] GMy चैवाचरे°; wKt[1] चोपवदेदेनं; Ox[3] °चरेदैनं; wKt[6] °चरेदेतत्तथा° — d) TMd[3] GMy तदात्मानं; Pu[10] निवेशयेत्

255. Page containing 4.255–5.2 missing in GMd[5] — b) Ho °न्यथा प्रतिपद्यते; Lo[4] Tr[1] भाषिते — c) Be[1] °कृत्तिमो — d) BKt[5] wKt[6] स्तेनं; Lo[4] स्तैन; oMd[2] oOr तेन; Pu[10] °हारिकः

256. a) Tj[1] वाच्यर्थ — b) TMd[4] वाङ्गलानि विनिस्तुताः; Lo[1] वाङ्गला; wKt[1] वायूना; Pu[7] °निसृताः; Lo[4] Ox[3] Tr[2] °निश्रिताः; Lo[2] °निःसुतः; Lo[3] °निःस्मृताः; Tr[1] °निर्गताः — c) Pu[2] Pu[4] Tr[2] तं तु; Be[3] Jo[1] *Mandlik KSS* तांस्तु; La[1] यस्तु तां स्तेन°; Ho *om* यः; GMd[1] स्तेयये°; Lo[3] ज्ञेनये°; Lo[4] स्तेनयद्वाचं — d) BKt[5] wKt[6] *om* स; Bo BKt[5] सर्वः; Wa सर्वा°; Pu[2] Tj[1] °स्तेन°; BKt[5] wKt[6] °स्तेयकृतं नरः

257.* Cited by *Lakṣ* 2.434 — b) Ox[2] मत्वा°; TMd[3] GMy कृत्वा°; Bo oOr गत्वानृणां; GMd[1] गत्वारण्यं; GMd[1] MTr[6] *Lakṣ* यथाक्रमं — c) TMd[3] GMy पुत्रं; Ho सर्व; Tj[1] सर्वे; Pu[5] Pu[7] [*but cor*] धर्मं; wKt[3] La[1] TMd[4] NNg oOr समासाद्य; Be[1] Ho समासह्य; Ox[3] समासव्य; Bo समासांत्व; BCa समासस्तु — d) Tj[1] वसन्मा°; BBe[2] Jm GMd[1] oOr Tj[1] °न्मध्यस्थमा°; Be[1] Ho TMd[4] GMy Pu[2] Pu[7] Pu[8] MTr[4] *Jha* °न्माध्यस्थ्यमा°; NNg °न्मध्यस्थ्यमा°; Kt[2] °न्मास्थ्यसमाश्रितः; Pu[10] °मास्थिताः; Be[1] BBe[2] Bo BCa Hy Jm Jo[1] Jo[2] Kt[2] wKt[3] BKt[5] wKt[6] La[2] Lo[1] Lo[3] oMd[2] TMd[3] GMy NPu[1] Pu[2] Tj[2] Tr[1] MTr[4] MTr[6] Wa [*Jolly* R Ku] *Ku Mr Mandlik KSS* °माश्रितः; *Go* appears to support आश्रित.

258. Cited by *Lakṣ* 2.434 — b) Ox[3] विविक्तो; TMd[3] GMy विपिने; Lo[4] हितामात्मनः; Pu[4] ततमात्मनः; NKt[4] Wa °त्मने; Lo[4] Lo[5] Ox[3] Pu[10] [*Jolly* M] °त्मनि — c) wKt[6] Pu[2] चिन्तमानो; Tr[2] चिन्तयामा; GMd[1] TMd[3] TMd[4] Tr[1] *Lakṣ* चिन्तयन्विप्रः; MTr[4] MTr[6] चिन्तयेद्विप्रः; NKt[4] °यानोस्तु — d) oMd[2] परंब्रह्महिते रताः; NKt[4] °विगच्छति; BCa Lo[2] हि गच्छति

oMd[2] comes to an end after this verse with the colophon: भृगुसंहिताः समाप्ताः

259. a) wKt[6] पण्यादिता — b) oOr शाश्वतः — c) TMd[3] sOx[1] sPu[6] स्नातको; Lo[1] °कल्पा च; Ho °कल्पस्तु — d) Kt[2] सचवृद्धि°; GMd[1] Pu[2] Tr[1] MTr[3] MTr[4] MTr[6] °वृत्तिकरः; Lo[3] °भृद्धिकरः; Jo[2] °शुद्धिकरः; Lo[1] °करी; Pu[5] Pu[7] °करेः; Lo[1] शुभा; Pu[10] शुतः; Pu[5] Pu[7] परः; oOr स्मृतः

व्यपेतकल्मषो नित्यं ब्रह्मलोके महीयते ॥२६०॥

॥ इति मानवे धर्मशास्त्रे भृगुप्रोक्तायां संहितायां चतर्थोऽध्यायः ॥

260. b) Ho La^{1} GMd^{1} TMd^{3} GMy NPu^{1} Pu^{2} Tr^{1} MTr^{4} MTr^{6} वर्तयेद्वेद° — d) oOr प्राप्नोति परमां गतिं

Colophon: Be^{1} Lo^{1} TMd^{3} NNg इति श्रीमानवे; Tj^{1} इति श्रीमानवीये; Lo^{3} मानवीये; wKt^{3} भृगुप्रोक्ते; Be^{1} wKt^{1} BKt^{5} wKt^{6} sOx^{1} TMd^{3} GMy NNg sPu^{6} *om* भृगुप्रोक्तायां संहितायां; Lo^{3} भृगुप्रोक्त-संहितायां; wKt^{3} GMd^{1} oOr Pu^{8} *om* संहितायां; Be^{1} आचारो नाम चतुर्थो; wKt^{1} गृहस्थधर्मकथनं नाम चतुर्थो; oOr गृहस्थधर्मो नाम चतुर्थो; Lo^{1} गृहस्थधर्मकथने चतुर्थो; NNg स्नातकव्रतानि चतुर्थो; NNg °ध्यायः समाप्तः

[पञ्चमोऽध्यायः]

श्रुत्वैतानृषयो धर्मान् स्नातकस्य यथोदितान् ।
इदमूचुर्महात्मानमनलप्रभवं भृगुम् ॥१॥
एवं यथोक्तं विप्राणां स्वधर्ममनुतिष्ठताम् ।
कथं मृत्युः प्रभवति वेदशास्त्रविदां प्रभो ॥२॥
स तानुवाच धर्मात्मा महर्षीन्मानवो भृगुः ।
श्रूयतां येन दोषेण मृत्युर्विप्राञ्जिघांसति ॥३॥
अनभ्यासेन वेदानामाचारस्य च वर्जनात् ।
आलस्यादन्नदोषाच्च मृत्युर्विप्राञ्जिघांसति ॥४॥
लशुनं गृञ्जनं चैव पलाण्डुं कवकानि च ।
अभक्ष्याणि द्विजातीनाममेध्यप्रभवाणि च ॥५॥
लोहितान्वृक्षनिर्यासान् व्रश्चनप्रभवांस्तथा ।
शेलुं गव्यं च पीयूषं प्रयत्नेन विवर्जयेत् ॥६॥

1. a) Tr^{2} श्रुतैता° ; Lo^{3} श्रुत्वेता° ; GMd^{1} Tj^{1} श्रुत्वा तानृपयो — c) Lo^{1} °चुर्माहा° ; sOx^{1} Pu^{5} sPu^{6} Pu^{7} °चुर्महाभागमनल° — d) Ox^{3} °नमनलं; Pu^{2} °नमुतलप्र° ; Pu^{4} °नमतुलप्र° ; TMd^{4} °नलप्रतिमं; Be^{1} भृगुः; TMd^{3} GMy NNg Pu^{8} गुरुं

2. a) oOr एतं; Lo^{1} Lo^{4} यथोक्त; TMd^{3} विप्राणः — b) Ox^{3} °नुतिष्ठतं; TMd^{3} °नुतिष्ठता; Tr^{2} °नुष्ठितां — c) TMd^{4} मृत्युं — d) Lo^{2} खेदशास्त्र° ; Lo^{1} °शास्त्रवतां; BKt^{5} wKt^{6} °शास्त्रभृतां; Tr^{1} °शास्त्रविदो

3. b) Tj^{1} महर्षिर्मा° ; sOx^{1} °न्मनवो; Jm °न्मानवे — d) Tr^{1} °र्विप्रा जि°

4. Omitted in sOx^{1} Tr^{1}. Cited by *Mādh* 2.8 — a) Pu^{5} अन्यभासेन; Pu^{7} अनाभ्यासेन; *Mādh* अनभ्यासाच्च — b) BBe^{2} Ho GMd^{1} sPu^{6} °रस्य विवर्जनात्; Tr^{2} °रस्य विसर्जनात्; Pu^{5} Pu^{7} [*Jolly* G] तु; oOr GMy वर्जयेत्; NNg Pu^{2} Pu^{4} Wa *Mādh* लङ्घनात् — c) wKt^{6} °न्नदोपाश्च; GMy °न्नशेपाच्च — d) Bo °र्विप्राज्जि° ; TMd^{3} °घासति

5. Cited by *Har*-A 1.17.27 — a) GMy लशुन; Pu^{10} लशुनां; Ho लसुनं; TMd^{3} अशुनं — b) TMd^{3} GMy Tr^{1} पलण्डुं; Be^{1} Lo^{5} MTr^{6} पलाण्डु; NNg [*Jolly* R] *Har*-A पलण्डु; NKt^{4} पलाण्डुः; Tr^{2} कवचानि; TMd^{3} करकानि; TMd^{4} कतकानि; wKt^{6} *om* च — c) Be^{3} wKt^{1} NKt^{4} अभक्षाणि — d) Tr^{2} °मवेध्य° ; Lo^{5} TMd^{3} NNg Tr^{1} °भवानि; Lo^{1} °भवनि; TMd^{4} °भवान्नि; sOx^{1} sPu^{6} °भवानिव; Pu^{10} °भवानपि

6. Cited by *Hem* 3/1.567; *Dev* 4.232; *Mādh* 1.711; pādas a-b cited by *Viś* 1.170; *Vij* 1.171; *Apa* 247 — a) MTr^{6} रोहिता° — b) Tr^{1} वृश्चनप्र° ; Bo व्रश्चनंप्र° ; NPu^{1} व्रशुप्र° ; TMd^{3} व्रच्चन्नप्र° ; TMd^{4} व्रछन्नप्र° ; NKt^{4} ब्रह्मश्चनप्र° ; Pu^{7} व्रेश्चनप्रसवांस्तथा — c) wKt^{3} Lo^{1} Lo^{3} शैलुं; *Hem* शैलु; BKt^{5} wKt^{6} शैलं; TMd^{3} शलुं; Ho NKt^{4} GMd^{5} सेलुं; wKt^{6} पव्यं; BBe^{2} Ho Hy Jm Jo^{1} wKt^{3} BKt^{5} wKt^{6} oOr Ox^{2}

वृथाकृसरसंयावं पायसापूपमेव च ।
अनुपाकृतमांसानि देवान्नानि हवींषि च ॥७॥
अनिर्दशाया गोः क्षीरमौष्ट्रमैकशफं तथा ।
आविकं संधिनीक्षीरं विवत्सायाश्च गोः पयः ॥८॥
आरण्यानां च सर्वेषां मृगाणां माहिषं विना ।
स्त्रीक्षीरं चैव वर्ज्यानि सर्वशुक्तानि चैव हि ॥९॥
दधि भक्ष्यं च शुक्तेषु सर्वं च दधिसंभवम् ।
यानि चैवाभिषूयन्ते पुष्पमूलफलैः शुभैः ॥१०॥
क्रव्यादः शकुनीन् सर्वांस्तथा ग्राममनिवासिनः ।
अनिर्दिष्टांश्चैकशफांष्टिट्टिभं च विवर्जयेत् ॥११॥

Pu^{3} Tj^{2} Tr^{2} Wa *Mandlik Jha KSS Dave* पेयुषं; La^{1} पेयूष्यं; Pu^{10} पायूपं; wKt^{1} पेयूयं; Pu^{2} Pu^{4} पीयूपं; Kt^{2} पेयुषस्र° — d) Lo^{3} च वर्जयेत्

7. Cited by *Hem* 3/1.610 — a) GMd^{5} वृथा तु सरसंयाव; Tr^{1} वृधा°; oOr तथा°; NKt^{4} wKt^{6} La^{1} Lo^{1} NNg oOr Pu^{2} Pu^{4} Pu^{5} Pu^{7} *Hem* °कृशर°; NPu^{1} °कृशार°; BBe^{2} BCa wKt^{3} °कृपर°; Lo^{5} °कृत्सरं; wKt^{1} °हृपव°; *Hem* °संयाव; La^{1} °संयाचै; Ho °यंयावं — b) Be^{1} °पूयमेव; sOx^{1} Pu^{2} Pu^{3} Pu^{4} sPu^{6} °पूपशष्कुली — c) wKt^{1} wKt^{6} °पाहृत°; TMd^{3} TMd^{4} GMy MTr^{4} *Hem* °मांसं च — d) TMd^{3} देवान्नादि; Lo^{1} देवजानि; Hy हविषि

8. Cited by *Vij* 3.289; *Har*-A1.17.23; *Hem* 3/1.567; *Lakṣ* 3.294; *Mādh* 1.712 — a) Ho wKt^{6} GMy अनिर्दिशाया [Ho °याः]; TMd^{3} अनिर्दिया; TMd^{4} अनिर्दशाहं — b) Be^{1} Kt^{2} Tr^{1} °मोष्ट्र°; Ho °मौध्र°; wKt^{3} Pu^{5} Pu^{7} Tr^{1} Tr^{2} *Vij Lakṣ Dave* °मेकशफं; GMy °मेकशफिं; Tj^{1} °मेकशफस्तथा; Pu^{2} Pu^{4} °शफां — d) Tr^{1} विवत्सायां च; Lo^{1} विपन्नायाश्च; Be^{1} TMd^{4} Tj^{1} MTr^{6} गो

Additional verse in *Mandlik* [ण] *KSS Dave:*

क्षीराणि यान्यभक्ष्याणि तद्विकाराशने बुधः ।
सप्तरात्रव्रतं कुर्यात्प्रयत्नेन समाहितः ॥

9. Omitted in TMd^{4}. Cited by *Vij* 3.289; *Har*-A 1.17.23; *Hem* 3/1.567; *Dev* 4.235; *Mādh* 1.712; pādas a-b cited by *Apa* 246 — a) TMd^{3} अरण्यानां; TMd^{3} GMy सर्वासां — b) Tj^{1} मृगाणामामिषं; Be^{3} sOx^{1} sPu^{6} महिषं; Tr^{2} माहिषा; BBe^{2} *Vij Apa Har*-A *Dev* महिषीं; GMd^{1} GMy महिषिं; oOr महिषां; TMd^{3} मदार्षीं; Tr^{1} *Mādh* माहिषीर्विना; GMd^{5} महिषीर्विना; MTr^{4} MTr^{6} महिषैर्विना — c) GMy क्षीरं चैवापवर्जानि [*om* स्त्री]; sOx^{1} sPu^{6} स्त्रीक्षीरमथ; TMd^{3} चैवापवर्ज्यानि; Lo^{1} वर्जानि — d) *Har*-A °शूक्तानि; Be^{1} Bo °शुल्कानि; Lo^{1} °शुष्कानि; Ho °सुक्तानि; Pu^{2} Pu^{4} °युक्तानि; Tj^{1} °भुक्तानि; NKt^{4} Ox^{3} ह

10. Omitted in TMd^{4}. Cited by *Hem* 3/1.616; pādas a-b cited by *Vij* 3.289 — a) Bo Hy wKt^{1} Kt^{2} Tj^{1} भक्षं; Pu^{5} भक्षां; oOr भक्तं; wKt^{3} La^{1} TMd^{3} GMd^{5} GMy Pu^{5} Pu^{7} Tr^{1} [*Jolly* G R] तु; Bo Tj^{1} शुल्केषु; Ho सुक्तेषु; Tr^{1} भुक्तेषु; Pu^{7} [*Jolly* G] शुक्ते तु — c) GMd^{1} चैवानिपू°; BCa wKt^{1} wKt^{3} °भिसूयन्ते; sOx^{1} sPu^{6} [*but cor*] °भिष्ययन्ते; Ox^{3} °भिपूयन्ते — d) Pu^{2} Pu^{4} पुष्पैर्मूल°; TMd^{3} °मूलं

11.* Before verse 11 GMd^{1} places verse 5.24. Cited by *Hem* 3/1.582; *Lakṣ* 3.298; *Dev* 4.246; *Mādh* 1.717 — a) NNg NPu^{1} Pu^{2} Pu^{3} Pu^{4} Pu^{5} Pu^{7} Pu^{8} Tj^{1} Tr^{2} MTr^{4} MTr^{6} *Go* [*Jolly* G] क्रव्याद; Be^{1} BBe^{2} Bo Ho Hy Jm Jo^{1} Jo^{2} wKt^{1} Kt^{2} wKt^{3} La^{2} Lo^{3} Lo^{4} Lo^{5} TMd^{3} TMd^{4} GMy oOr Ox^{2} Pu^{8} Tj^{1} Tj^{2} [*Jolly* Ku R] *Mandlik Jolly KSS* क्रव्यादान्; Lo^{1} क्रव्यादीन्; Tr^{2} शकुनी; Bo Ho BKt^{5} oOr Tj^{1} *KSS* शकुनान्; wKt^{6} कुशलान्; Wa शकुनींस्स°; Be^{3} Ho BKt^{5} wKt^{6} GMd^{1} TMd^{3} GMy

कलविङ्कं प्लवं हंसं चक्राह्वं ग्रामकुक्कुटम् ।
सारसं रज्जुदालं* च दात्यूहं शुकसारिके ॥१२॥
प्रतुदाञ्जालपादांश्च कोयष्टिनखविष्किरान् ।
निमज्जतश्च मत्स्यादान् सौनं वल्लूरमेव च ॥१३॥
बकं चैव बलाकां च काकोलं खञ्जरीटकम् ।
मत्स्यादान्विड्वराहांश्च मत्स्यानेव च सर्वशः ॥१४॥
यो यस्य मांसमश्नाति स तन्मांसाद उच्यते ।
मत्स्यादः सर्वमांसादस्तस्मान्मत्स्यान्विवर्जयेत् ॥१५॥
पाठीनरोहितावाद्यौ नियुक्तौ हव्यकव्ययोः ।
राजीवाः सिंहतुण्डाश्च सशल्काश्चैव सर्वशः ॥१६॥

oOr Tj^1 *Lakṣ* सर्वान्तथा; Lo^2 सर्वास्तथा; Hy *om* सर्वांस् — b) Lo^1 °स्तथा वै ग्राम°; Pu^4 ग्रामस्य वासिनः— c) Be^3 Lo^1 °प्टाश्चैक°; TMd^3 TMd^4 Tj^1 °प्टां चैक°; BCa Ho wKt^6 Lo^1 GMy sOx^1 Pu^5 sPu^6 Pu^7 Pu^8 Tr^1 °शफान्टि°; BBe^2 Be^3 TMd^3 Tj^1 °शफां टि°; TMd^4 °शफं टि°; NKt^4 °सहांष्टि° — d) Bo °शफान्निधिभं; La^1 °ट्टिभिं; *Hem* °ट्टिभांश्च; Be^1 BCa wKt^3 GMd^1 [*Jolly* Nd] °ट्टिभांश्चैव वर्जयेत्; Lo^4 Lo^5 Ox^3 [*Jolly* M] °ट्टिभं परिवर्जयेत्; Be^1 Bo wKt^1 wKt^3 NKt^4 La^1 Lo^1 TMd^3 TMd^4 GMy NPu^1 Tj^1 Tj^2 Tr^1 MTr^6 Wa *Dev* चैव वर्जयेत्

12.* Pāda-d omitted in Be^3. Cited by *Hem* 3/1.583; *Dev* 4.246; *Mādh* 1.717 — a) Lo^1 कालविङ्के; Pu^8 कालविङ्कं; Tr^1 कलविंगं; Be^1 Hy कलविकं; TMd^4 फलंवप्रस्तं — b) Be^3 Bo Jo^1 wKt^1 Kt^2 Tj^1 MTr^3 *Hem* [vl] *Dev Jolly* चक्राङ्गं; wKt^6 चक्राङ्ग; Tj^2 चक्रागं; Hy चक्रां — c) BBe^2 Hy Jm Jo^1 wKt^1 Kt^2 wKt^3 La^1 Lo^2 Lo^3 TMd^3 TMd^4 GMd^5 GMy oOr sOx^1 sPu^6 Tr^1 MTr^4 MTr^6 *Mādh Mandlik Jha KSS Dave* रज्जुवालं; Tr^2 *Hem* रज्जुबाल; wKt^6 रज्जुदानं; Ox^2 राज्जदानं; GMd^1 रज्जुलाभं; Tj^1 रज्जुदावालं [*om* च]; Pu^8 *om* °दालं च — d) Tj^1 दात्यूहः; MTr^4 नत्यूहं; Lo^1 शूक°; NKt^4 GMd^1 TMd^3 TMd^4 GMd^5 GMy °सारिकं; MTr^4 °सारिकां; Be^1 °शारिके; MTr^6 °शारिकं

13. Omitted in Be^3; pādas c-d omitted in Ho. Cited by *Hem* 3/1.583; *Dev* 4.247; *Mādh* 1.717 — a) Ho La^1 प्रत्युदा°; Tj^1 प्रनुदा°; NNg प्रदातु°; Lo^1 प्रणुदा°; Pu^2 Pu^4 प्रमुदा°; TMd^4 प्रमदा°; Tj^1 °दान्क्षाल°; Ox^3 °पदांश्च; TMd^4 °नादांश्च; *Me* comments that some take जालपाद to be a wrong reading. — b) Lo^1 कोयष्टिं; Tj^1 कोपष्टि; Pu^2 Pu^4 °मखवि° — c) wKt^3 निमज्य°; Pu^8 Tr^2 मत्स्यादीन्; Lo^3 मच्छादीन्; Tj^1 मत्स्यादा; Tj^2 मत्स्यान् — d) Lo^1 °न्सौन; La^1 शौनं; BKt^5 सौवं; TMd^3 GMd^5 GMy सौरं; Be^1 वलूर°; Tr^2 वल्मूर°; Tj^1 वल्लर°; wKt^1 वन्दूकमेव

14. Pāda-a omitted in Be^3. Cited by *Hem* 3/1.583; *Dev* 4.247; *Mādh* 1.717 — a) Ho *om* बकं चैव; wKt^6 करं चैव; TMd^3 TMd^4 GMd^5 NNg oOr sOx^1 Ox^3 sPu^6 Tj^1 Tr^1 MTr^4 MTr^6 बलाकं; Be^1 बलाकांश्च; sOx^1 sPu^6 *om* च — b) Pu^2 Pu^4 कालोलं; Tj^1 खजरी°; Be^3 पञ्जरी°; TMd^3 खजिरंटकं; Kt^2 खजटकं — c) sOx^1 Tr^2 मत्स्यादीन्वि°; Ox^3 Pu^{10} [*Jolly* M$^{2\text{-}5\text{-}9}$] °राहांस्तु

15. Cited by *Hem* 3/1.583 — a) NKt^4 यस्य समश्नाति; Pu^{10} मांसे प्राश्नाति — b) wKt^3 NKt^4 तन्मांसद; Ox^3 तन्मांसा — c) Lo^2 मत्स्यादेः; sOx^1 sPu^6 मत्स्यादास्सर्व°; Tr^1 °मांसादेः तस्मा° — d) TMd^4 °न्मात्स्यान्विव°; GMy °न्मांसं विव°; TMd^3 °न्मांसा विव°

16.* Cited by *Vij* 1.177; *Hem* 3/1.577–8; *Dev* 4248; pāda-a cited by *Viś* 1.177 — a) Ho पाटीन°; La^1 पाठीनो°; GMd^5 NNg °तावद्यौ; TMd^4 NPu^1 °तावाद्यो; Pu^2 Pu^4 °तावद्यो; TMd^3 °तावान्या — b) TMd^4 MTr^6 Wa नियुक्तो; TMd^3 नियुक्ता; *Nā* [pāṭha] नियुक्तैर्हव्य° — c) MTr^4 राजीवा; Be^1 BBe^2 BCa Ho Hy Jm Jo^1 wKt^1 Kt^2 wKt^3 NKt^4 BKt^5 wKt^6 La^1 La^2 Lo^1 Lo^2 Lo^3 Lo^4 Lo^5 GMd^1 TMd^4 GMd^5

न भक्षयेदेकचरानज्ञातांश्च मृगद्विजान् ।
भक्ष्येष्वपि समुद्दिष्टान् सर्वान्पञ्चनखांस्तथा ॥१७॥
श्वाविधं शल्यकं गोधां खड्गकूर्मशशांस्तथा ।
भक्ष्यान्पञ्चनखेष्वाहुरनुष्ट्रांश्चैकतोदतः ॥१८॥
छत्राकं विड्वराहं च लशुनं ग्रामकुक्कुटम् ।
पलाण्डुं गृञ्जनं चैव मत्या जग्ध्वा पतेद् द्विजः ॥१९॥
अमत्यैतानि षड् जग्ध्वा कृच्छ्रं सांतपनं चरेत् ।
यतिचान्द्रायणं वापि शेषेषूपवसेदहः ॥२०॥
संवत्सरस्यैकमपि चरेत्कृच्छ्रं द्विजोत्तमः ।
अज्ञातभुक्तशुद्ध्यर्थं ज्ञातस्य तु विशेषतः ॥२१॥

GMy oOr sOx^{1} Ox^{2} Ox^{3} Pu^{2} sPu^{6} Pu^{8} Pu^{10} Tj^{2} Tr^{1} Tr^{2} MTr^{6} *Hem Mandlik Jolly KSS* राजीवान्; Be^{3} Bo Tj^{1} राजीवं; TMd^{3} राजीवां; Be^{1} BBe^{2} Bo BCa Ho Hy Jm Jo^{1} wKt^{1} Kt^{2} wKt^{3} NKt^{4} BKt^{5} wKt^{6} La^{1} La^{2} Lo^{1} Lo^{2} Lo^{3} Lo^{4} Lo^{5} GMd^{1} TMd^{4} GMd^{5} GMy oOr sOx^{1} Ox^{2} Ox^{3} Pu^{2} sPu^{6} Pu^{8} Pu^{10} Tj^{2} Tr^{1} Tr^{2} *Hem Mandlik Jolly KSS* °तुण्डांश्च; Be^{3} Tj^{1} °तुण्डं च — d) Be^{1} BBe^{2} Be^{3} Bo BCa Ho Hy Jm Jo^{1} Kt^{2} wKt^{3} NKt^{4} BKt^{5} wKt^{6} La^{1} La^{2} Lo^{1} Lo^{2} Lo^{3} Lo^{4} Lo^{5} GMd^{1} TMd^{4} GMd^{5} oOr sOx^{1} Ox^{2} Ox^{3} Pu^{2} sPu^{6} Pu^{8} Pu^{10} Tj^{1} Tj^{2} Tr^{1} Tr^{2} MTr^{4} MTr^{6} *Hem Mandlik Jolly KSS* सशल्कांश्चैव; Lo^{2} सकल्कांश्चैव; wKt^{1} सशल्कां चैव; MTr^{6} सशुखांश्चैव; Pu^{5} Pu^{7} [*Jolly* G] सर्वदा

17. Pādas c-d omitted in GMd^{1} — a) Be^{3} भक्षयेद्विड्वराहानज्ञा°; Kt^{2} °दैकच°; Pu^{8} Tj^{1} °देवच°; TMd^{3} °चराः नज्ञा° — b) Lo^{1} °चरान् ज्ञातांश्चैव; Kt^{2} TMd^{4} °ज्ञाताश्च; wKt^{1} Lo^{3} [*Jolly* R] मृगान्द्विजान् — c) Be^{3} Ho NKt^{4} भक्षेष्वपि; Lo^{2} Pu^{3} Pu^{8} °ष्वपि च निर्दिष्टान्; Tj^{1} समुद्दिष्टा; NKt^{4} समुद्दिष्टं; NPu^{1} समादिष्टान् — c-d) GMy न भक्षयेत्पञ्चनखान्वानरादि न भक्षयेत् [TMd^{3} gives this as an addition after pāda-d] — d) TMd^{3} सर्वास्यंचनखान्स्तथा

18. Cited by *Vij* 1.177–8; *Hem* 3/1.578; *Dev* 4.249 — a) GMy श्वाविध; wKt^{6} श्वविधं; TMd^{4} *Hem* श्वाविदं; Tr^{1} श्वाविडं; Jo^{2} Lo^{3} TMd^{3} NPu^{1} Pu^{2} Pu^{4} Pu^{5} Pu^{7} श्वाविकं; Ox^{3} Pu^{10} श्वावित्कं; NKt^{4} श्वार्विव; GMy शल्यकां; Pu^{5} Pu^{7} शल्यिकं; Bo शल्ककां; *Hem* शल्क्यकां; Ho *Vij* [vl as in ed] शल्लकं; Tr^{1} Pu^{5} Pu^{7} MTr^{6} गोधा — b) TMd^{4} Pu^{5} Pu^{7} *Hem* खड्गं; MTr^{3} खड्ग°; La^{1} Ox^{3} पड्ग°; *Hem* कूर्मं; TMd^{3} °शरांस्तथा — c) wKt^{3} Pu^{5} Pu^{7} भक्षान्पञ्च°; sOx^{1} sPu^{6} भक्ष्याः पञ्च°; Be^{3} भक्षा पञ्च°; Pu^{2} Pu^{4} °मखेष्वा°; *Hem* °नखानाहु° — d) Lo^{1} °तोदतान् [*but cor*]

19. Cited by *Viś* 3.224; *Vij* 1.176, 3.229; *Apa* 1046, 1157; *Mādh* 2.317 — a) *Apa* 1046 पलाण्डुं विड्व°; TMd^{3} °राभं; Tj^{1} °राहांश्च — b) Ho Ox^{2} लसुनं; TMd^{3} अशुनं; *Apa* 1046 छत्राकं ग्राम°; *Mādh Apa* 1046 [vl] ग्राम्य° — c) TMd^{3} MTr^{6} *Viś* पलण्डुं; Tr^{1} पलण्डु; *Apa* 1046 लशुनं गृञ्जनं — d) Be^{3} ज्ञात्वा जग्ध्वा; Ho मत्स्यान्जग्ध्वा; Hy जग्धा; MTr^{6} पातेद्; MTr^{3} जपेद्; Ho पतिः द्विजः; Lo^{4} Lo^{5} पने द्विजाः; *Vij* 3.229 पतेन्नरः

20. Cited by *Vij* 3.229,289; *Apa* 1157; *Mādh* 2.317; pādas a-b cited by *Vij* 1.176; and pāda-d by *Vij* 1.175 — a) Bo अमत्यैतामिषं जग्ध्वा; Lo^{1} अमतैतानि; GMd^{5} अमतैतांस्तु; sOx^{1} sPu^{6} °तानि जग्ध्वा तु — b) Pu^{2} Pu^{4} कृत्स्नं — c) MTr^{6} *om* यति; BKt^{5} wKt^{6} अतिचा°; TMd^{3} GMd^{5} GMy MTr^{3} यदिचा°; wKt^{1} Lo^{2} Lo^{3} Tj^{1} चापि; BCa La^{1} चैव — d) Tr^{2} विशेषेपूप°; Ho सर्वेपूप°; MTr^{4} कृच्छ्रेषूप°; Bo °पचनेदहः; TMd^{4} °वसीदहः; Wa °वसेदिह

21. Cited by *Vij* 3.289 — a) Be^{3} Tj^{1} संवत्सरं चैकमपि; Lo^{1} संवत्सरस्य किमपि; TMd^{3} °मपि च चरे° — b) Jo^{2} Lo^{3} कुर्यात्कृच्छ्रं; Tr^{2} °त्तमाः — c) Be^{1} Lo^{4} Lo^{5} अज्ञान°; Tr^{2} °भुङ्क्त°; Ox^{2} °भुक्ती°; oOr

यज्ञार्थं ब्राह्मणैर्वध्याः प्रशस्ता मृगपक्षिणः ।
भृत्यानां चैव वृत्त्यर्थमगस्त्यो ह्याचरत्पुरा ॥२२॥
बभूवुर्हि पुरोडाशा भक्ष्याणां मृगपक्षिणाम् ।
पुराणेष्वृषियज्ञेषु ब्रह्मक्षत्रसवेषु च ॥२३॥
यत्किंचित् स्नेहसंयुक्तं भक्ष्यं भोज्यमगर्हितम् ।
तत्पर्युषितमप्याद्यं हविःशेषं च यद्भवेत् ॥२४॥
चिरस्थितमपि त्वाद्यमस्नेहाक्तं द्विजातिभिः ।
यवगोधूमजं सर्वं पयसश्चैव विक्रियाः ॥२५॥
एतदुक्तं द्विजातीनां भक्ष्याभक्ष्यमशेषतः ।
मांसस्यातः प्रवक्ष्यामि विधिं भक्षणवर्जने ॥२६॥
प्रोक्षितं भक्षयेन्मांसं ब्राह्मणानां च काम्यया ।
यथाविधि नियुक्तस्तु प्राणानामेव चात्यये ॥२७॥

°भूत° — d) Be^{1} BKt^{5} wKt^{6} Lo^{5} ज्ञानस्य; TMd^{4} ज्ञातव्य तु; Lo^{1} च

22. Cited by *Vij* 1.179 — a) [*Jolly* G] भृत्यर्थं; Tj^{1} °र्वध्यां— b) TMd^{3} प्रशस्त; wKt^{1} प्रशक्ता; Lo^{2} Tr^{2} °पक्षिणां — c) TMd^{3} श्रुत्यानां; wKt^{6} वृत्त्यार्थम°; MTr^{6} वद्धयर्थम° — d) TMd^{4} °त्यर्थं मृगस्या ह्या°; Hy °मागस्त्यो; GMd^{1} GMd^{5} Tr^{1} °गस्त्योप्याचर°; MTr^{4} MTr^{6} °गस्त्योभ्याचर°; oOr °गस्त्यो आचारेत्पुरा°; NKt^{4} ह्यभवत्पुरा; wKt^{6} °चरन्पुरा; TMd^{3} TMd^{4} Tr^{1} °चरस्पुरा; NKt^{4} GMd^{1} TMd^{3} TMd^{4} GMd^{5} GMy Tr^{1} MTr^{4} °चरत्तथा; MTr^{6} °चरेत्तथा

23.* a) TMd^{4} पुरोडाशं — b) Be^{3} wKt^{1} wKt^{3} Pu^{5} Tj^{1} भक्षाणां; GMd^{1} भक्षणं; GMd^{5} भक्ष्यां च; Pu^{3} मांसानि मृग°; GMd^{1} °पक्षिणः — c) MTr^{6} पुराणेषु rest omitted; Be^{1} Ho Jm Jo^{1} wKt^{1} Kt^{2} NKt^{4} BKt^{5} wKt^{6} La^{1} La^{2} Lo^{1} Lo^{4} Lo^{5} TMd^{4} oOr NPu^{1} Pu^{2} Tj^{1} Tj^{2} Tr^{2} Wa *Jolly Bühler KSS* पुराणेष्वपि यज्ञेपु — d) MTr^{6} ब्रह्मक्षत्रे सर्वेपु च; Be^{1} Lo^{2} NNg Pu^{5} Pu^{7} °क्षत्रमखेपु; Ho °क्षत्रोत्सवेपु; wKt^{1} °क्षत्रसरेपु; Pu^{10} °क्षत्रविशेपु

24. GMd^{1} places verse 24 after 5.10. Cited by *Hem* 3/1.616; *Lakṣ* 3.292; *Dev* 4226 — b) TMd^{3} भोज्यमन्त्रमगर्हितं; sOx^{1} sPu^{6} Pu^{7} [*Jolly* G] *Dev* भक्ष्य; Pu^{5} भक्ष; wKt^{1} भक्षं; Jm भोज्यं च गर्हितं — c) GMy *om* तत्; Bo TMd^{4} यत्प°; Lo^{2} °मन्त्राद्यं; Pu^{2} Pu^{4} °मप्याज्यं; wKt^{6} °मप्यायुं — d) *Dev* तु; *Lakṣ Hem* च सर्वशः; wKt^{3} Ox^{3} तद्भवेत्

25. Pāda-d omitted in Ox^{3}. Cited by *Hem* 3/1.616; *Dev* 4.227 — a) Lo^{3} चिरा°; Lo^{4} चिरं; Bo चर°; Pu^{2} Pu^{4} जिर°; oOr चाद्यम°; Pu^{2} Pu^{4} त्वाज्यम°; BKt^{5} त्वात्यम°; NKt^{4} त्वाद्यस्ने° — b) Tr^{1} त्वाद्यं स्नेहायुक्तं; GMd^{5} त्वाद्यं स्नेहाक्तं च; MTr^{4} °स्नेहात्तं; Tj^{2} °स्नेहाकं — c) NKt^{4} °गाधूमजं; GMd^{1} °गोधूमकं; TMd^{3} GMy °गोधूमतत्सर्वं; wKt^{1} Pu^{5} सर्व — d) NKt^{4} पायसश्चैव; TMd^{3} GMy पायसं चैव; *Dev* पयसां चैव; NNg पयश्चैव; MTr^{4} °श्चैष्टविक्रियाः; Pu^{5} Pu^{7} [*Jolly* G] विक्रियां; Be^{1} Hy Jm Jo^{1} TMd^{3} GMd^{5} GMy Pu^{2} Tj^{2} Wa *Mandlik KSS* विक्रिया; Be^{3} विकृया; Lo^{5} NKt^{4} NNg विक्रयाः; La^{2} विक्रया; Bo विक्रयः

26. Omitted in Lo^{4} Lo^{5}. Cited by *Lakṣ* 3.311; *Dev* 4.244 — a) Tr^{2} एतद्भुक्तं; Bo एतद्युक्तं — b) Bo भक्ष्याभक्ष्याद् द्विजातयः; Be^{3} NKt^{4} भक्षाभक्षम°; Ho TMd^{4} GMy °भक्ष्यं विशेषतः — c) Tj^{1} *om* प्रवक्ष्यामि; Be^{3} प्रवक्षामि — d) TMd^{4} भक्षणदर्शने; Pu^{4} तत्क्षणवर्जने

27. Cited by *Lakṣ* 3.311; *Hem* 3/1.574; *Dev* 4.245 — a) *Hem* यत्प्रोक्षितं भवेन्मांसं; Pu^{10} MTr^{3} MTr^{4} प्रोषितं; TMd^{3} GMy प्रोक्षणं — b) Tj^{1} ब्राह्मणाः काम्यया यथा; GMd^{1} TMd^{3} GMd^{5} GMy Tr^{1}

प्राणस्यान्नमिदं सर्वं प्रजापतिरकल्पयत् ।
स्थावरं जङ्गमं चैव सर्वं प्राणस्य भोजनम् ॥२८॥
चराणामन्नमचरा दंष्ट्रिणामप्यदंष्ट्रिणः ।
अहस्ताश्च सहस्तानां शूराणां चैव भीरवः ॥२९॥
नात्ता दुष्यत्यदन्नाद्यान् प्राणिनोऽहन्यहन्यपि ।
धात्रैव सृष्टा ह्याद्याश्च प्राणिनोऽत्तार एव च ॥३०॥
यज्ञाय जग्धिर्मांसस्येत्येष दैवो विधिः स्मृतः ।
अतोऽन्यथा प्रवृत्तिस्तु राक्षसो विधिरुच्यते ॥३१॥
क्रीत्वा स्वयं वाप्युत्पाद्य परोपहृतमेव वा ।
देवान्पितृंश्चार्चयित्वा खादन्मांसं न दुष्यति ॥३२॥

mTr4 mTr6 [*Jolly* Gr]*Dev* ब्राह्मणस्य; Jo2 Lo3 तु — c) Tj1 विधिना विनियुक्तस्तु; Be1 wKt1 wKt3 nKt4 Lo1 tMd4 oOr Wa *Hem Dev* नियुक्तश्च — d) Tr2 ब्राह्मणानामेव; Ox2 °मेव नान्यथा

Additonal half-verse in Lo2:

मधुपर्के च श्राद्धे च प्रोक्षणेनापि भक्षयेत् ॥

28.* Pādas c-d omitted in tMd3 and pāda-d in Ox3. Cited by *Lakṣ* 3.312 — a) wKt3 La1 प्राणस्यार्थमिदं; sPu6 *om* सर्वं — b) Pu5 Pu7 °कल्पयन्; gMd5 Tj1 Wa °कल्पयेत् — c) gMy स्थावर; Be1 bBe2 bCa Ho Jo2 wKt1 wKt3 nKt4 bKt5 wKt6 Lo1 Lo3 Lo4 Lo5 tMd4 oOr Ox2 nPu1 Pu2 Pu3 Pu4 Pu5 Pu7 Pu8 Pu10 Wa [*Jolly* M] *Go Ku Lakṣ* जङ्गमं स्थावरं — d) gMy प्रजापतिरकल्पयत्; Be3 gMd1 mTr6 सर्व; tMd4 सेवनं प्रा°; Pu5 Pu7 [*Jolly* G] भोजने; gMd5 शोधनं

29. Cited by *Lakṣ* 3.312 — a) gMd5 चराणामचरं भक्ष्यं; bBe2 चराणामनुचरणां वा; mTr6 चरणा°; Pu10 °मश्नमचरा; Ho gMd1 tMd3 tMd4 °मचरं; mTr4 mTr6 °मचरन्; Tj1 °मवरा; Tr1 °मचिरं — b) Be1 bCa Jo2 bKt5 wKt6 Lo1 Lo2 Ox2 Pu2 Pu3 Pu4 Pu5 Pu7 Pu8 Tr2 Wa [*Jolly* G] °णां चाप्यदंष्टिणः; Lo3 °णां चापि दंष्टिणः; Be3 °दंष्ट्रिणं — d) bKt5 wKt6 च भीरवः; Ho भीरिवः; nPu1 भैरवः

30. Pādas b-c omitted in Pu10. Cited by *Lakṣ* 3.312— a) Tj1 नान्नादुःखत्यदन्नाद्या; Tj2 नात्तां; Pu10 मात्ता; wKt1 नार्त्ता; Lo4 Lo5 tMd3 gMd5 Tr1 नार्तो; Lo1 नैते; Lo1 दुष्यन्त्य°; gMy मृष्यत्य°; tMd3 तृष्यतदन्ना°; tMd4 रुष्यत्तुतन्ना°; bBe2 Lo1 °दन्नद्यान्; tMd3 °दन्नाष्यान् — b) Ox3 Pu5 mTr6 प्राणिनोहन्यपि; Tj2 प्राणिनामहन्य° — c) tMd3 Wa धात्रेव; gMy धात्रा हि; wKt1 सृष्ट्या; bKt5 wKt6 सृष्टाश्चाद्याश्च; tMd4 सृष्टा आद्याश्च; Be3 Bo Tr1 ह्यद्याश्च; La1 ह्यार्थाश्च; gMd1 ह्यन्नाद्याः प्राणि° — d) Lo1 प्राणिनस्तारयेत्वहं; tMd3 °त्ताश्म एव; gMd1 °त्तारणाय च

31. Pādas c-d omitted in Ox3. Cited by *Lakṣ* 3.312; *Hem* 3/1.582 — a) Be1 यज्ञय; Lo1 यज्ञेव; Pu8 यज्ञाजग्धि°; Pu2 Pu4 यज्ञायर्ज्जाश्चमांस°; Bo sOx1 sPu6 जग्धिमांस°; mTr4 mTr6 बुद्धिर्मांस°; Tr2 °र्मांसेत्येष; Be3 °र्मांस्येत्येष; gMd1 oOr °र्मांसस्य एष — b) wKt1 °त्येषो; Tr1 °त्येषो *cor fh* °त्येषा; Bo La1 gMy Tj1 देवो; tMd3 देव; bKt5 wKt6 स्मृतिः — c) Tr1 अथो; gMd5 हतो; oOr °न्यथावृत्तिस्तु; tMd4 प्रवृत्तिश्च; bKt5 wKt6 Tr2 प्रवृत्तस्तु; Lo4 Lo5 प्रवृत्तस्य; *Hem* प्राकृतस्तु

32. Cited by *Lakṣ* 3.312; *Hem* 3/1.592; pādas c-d cited by *Hem* 3/1.581 — a) Bo wKt6 Lo1 tMd4 gMy कृत्वा; Jm क्रीडा; Ho वा स्वयमुत्पाद्य; Be3 wKt1 sOx1 Ox2 sPu6 Pu8 चाप्यु°; Tr2 चाभ्यु° — b) bBe2 bCa [*but mc*] Hy Jm Jo1 Kt2 wKt3 bKt5 wKt6 Lo3 oOr [*Jolly* Ku N] *Nā Mandlik Jha KSS Dave* परोपकृत°; Ho Ox2 परोपहत°; tMd4 परोपहित°; Ho tMd4 nNg Tr2 mTr3 च — c) mTr6 दैवा°; sOx1 sPu6 °तृन्तर्पयित्वा; nNg *Hem* 3/1.581 °तृन्समभ्यर्च्य; Kt2 °श्चार्थयित्वा — d) Jo2 nNg tMd3 gMy sOx1 sPu6 *Hem* 3/1.581 न दोषभाक्; [*Jolly* Gr] दुष्यते; Tr1 दूष्यति

नाद्यादविधिना मांसं विधिज्ञोऽनापदि द्विजः ।
जग्ध्वा ह्यविधिना मांसं प्रेतस्तैरद्यतेऽवशः ॥३३॥
न तादृशं भवत्येनो मृगहन्तुर्धनार्थिनः ।
यादृशं भवति प्रेत्य वृथामांसानि खादतः ॥३४॥
नियुक्तस्तु यथान्यायं यो मांसं नात्ति मानवः ।
स प्रेत्य पशुतां याति संभवानेकविंशतिम् ॥३५॥
असंस्कृतान्पशून्मन्त्रैर्नाद्याद्विप्रः कथंचन ।
मन्त्रैस्तु संस्कृतानद्याच्छाश्वतं विधिमास्थितः ॥३६॥
कुर्याद्घृतपशुं सङ्गे कुर्यात्पिष्टपशुं तथा ।
न त्वेव तु वृथा हन्तुं पशुमिच्छेत्कथंचन ॥३७॥
यावन्ति पशुरोमाणि तावत्कृत्वो ह मारणम् ।
वृथापशुघ्नः प्राप्नोति प्रेत्य जन्मनि जन्मनि ॥३८॥

33.* Pāda b-c omitted in Hy TMd^4, and pādas b-d in Lo^4. Cited by *Lakṣ* 3.319; *Hem* 3/1.582 [ascribed to Viṣṇu] — a) Lo^4 °दाविधिना; Ox^3 °विधिनो; Tr^1 मासं — b) Bo विधिज्ञा° — c) GMd^1 Tr^1 जग्ध्वाप्यविधिना; TMd^3 GMy जग्ध्वान्यविधिना; MTr^4 MTr^{6}अदन्ह्यविधिना; Tr^2 त्वविधिना; *Hem* तु विधिना — d) oOr प्रेत्यस्तैर°; BBe^2 Be^3 Bo BCa Ho Hy Jm Jo^1 Jo^2 La^1 La^2 Lo^5 GMd^1 TMd^4 Ox^2 Pu^2 Pu^8 Tj^1 Tj^2 Tr^2 MTr^6 [*Jolly* R] *Rn Mandlik KSS* प्रेत्य तैर°; *Hem* °द्यते तु सः; TMd^4 °द्यते हि सः; BKt^5 °द्यते च सः; wKt^6 वसः

34. Pādas c-d omitted in Wa. Cited by *Lakṣ* 3.319 — a) Be^1 नात्मादृशं [*but mc*]; La^1 तादृशो; Pu^{10} तादृशे; Pu^{10} °त्यैनौ; Ox^3 °त्येता — b) TMd^4 Pu^2 Pu^4 मृगं; [*Jolly* Nd] मृगहत्या धना°; BKt^5 wKt^6 °न्तुर्वधार्थिनः; TMd^3 °न्तुर्विनार्दिनः; MTr^4 °नार्थिकः — c) Jo^2 सादृशं; Bo यावृत्ति; Lo^1 भवति ह्येन — d) Tr^1 वृधा°; Jo^2 Lo^2 Pu^{10} पादतः

35. Cited by *Vij* 1.179; *Apa* 251; *Hem* 3/1.577; pāda-a cited by *Viś* 1.179 — a) *Vij* यथाविधि नियुक्तस्तु; Lo^1 *cor to* नियुक्तस्य यथा°; Pu^{10} °न्यायो — b) Ho मांसां; wKt^1 मांसान्यत्ति; Pu^{10} मांसमश्नाति; Be^1 Bo नाति; Lo^5 चाति; La^1 [*but mc sh*] GMd^1 TMd^3 TMd^4 GMd^5 GMy Tr^1 MTr^4 MTr^6 नात्ति वै द्विजः; Pu^4 मानसः — c) BCa Ho GMd^1 GMd^5 Tr^1 पशुतामेति; MTr^4 पशुतामेव; TMd^3 पशुतां यान्ति — d) Bo संभवामेक°; Lo^1 oOr Tj^1 °विंशतिः; TMd^4 °विंशति

36. Cited by *Hem* 3/1.580; *Lakṣ* 3.316; pādas a-b cited by *Dev* 4.246 — a) Tj^1 °तान्यान्मन्त्रै° — b) Hy Jm Jo^1 wKt^1 Kt^2 TMd^4 Tj^2 MTr^3 *Dev Mandlik Jha KSS Dave* कदाचन — c) Bo [*but cor*] मन्त्रैश्च; TMd^3 °तानद्याः शा° — d) Pu^5 Pu^7 [*Jolly* G] °नद्यान्नैत्यकं; *Hem* °नद्याद्वैदिकं; Be^3 NKt^4 TMd^3 TMd^4 GMd^5 GMy Tj^1 Tr^1 MTr^4 MTr^6 [*Jolly* Nd] धर्ममास्थितः

37.* Pādas c-d omitted in NKt^4. Cited by *Lakṣ* 3.329 — a) Pu^2 Pu^4 कुर्यान्न घृत°; TMd^4 °पशू; Ho GMd^5 MTr^6 °पशून्; wKt^1 सर्गे; BBe^2 wKt^3 यज्ञे; GMd^5 यागे; Tj^1 सक्तौ — b) Bo कुर्याद्यष्टि°; BBe^2 Ho GMd^5 oOr °पशूंस्तथा — c) Tr^1 त्वैव; Pu^{10} त्वेतं; GMd^1 त्वेव च; sOx^1 sPu^6 त्वेव हि — d) Be^1 BBe^2 BCa Hy Jm Jo^1 wKt^1 Kt^2 wKt^3 BKt^5 wKt^6 La^1 Lo^2 Lo^4 Lo^5 oOr sOx^1 NPu^1 Pu^5 sPu^6 Pu^7 Pu^{10} Tj^2 Tr^2 MTr^3 Wa *Rc Mandlik Jolly Jha KSS Dave* °त्कदाचन

38.* Omitted in NKt^4. Cited by *Lakṣ* 3.329— b) Be^3 Ho wKt^1 Lo^1 Lo^3 Lo^4 GMd^1 TMd^3 TMd^4 GMy Ox^3 Pu^5 Pu^7 Pu^9 Pu^{10} Tj^2 Tr^1 Tr^2 MTr^6 [*Jolly* M G] *Dave* तावत्कृत्वेह; Bo तावत्कृत्वा ह; Ox^2 तावत्कृते ह; GMd^5 तावत्कृत्वैव; Wa हि; wKt^3 मरणं; BKt^5 wKt^6 मानवः — c) TMd^3 GMy तदा

यज्ञार्थं पशवः सृष्टाः स्वयमेव स्वयंभुवा ।
यज्ञोऽस्य भूत्यै सर्वस्य तस्माद्यज्ञे वधोऽवधः ॥३९॥
ओषध्यः पशवो वृक्षास्तिर्यञ्चः पक्षिणस्तथा ।
यज्ञार्थं निधनं प्राप्ताः प्राप्नुवन्त्युच्छ्रितीः पुनः ॥४०॥
मधुपर्के च यज्ञे च पितृदैवतकर्मणि ।
अत्रैव पशवो हिंस्या नान्यत्रेत्यब्रवीन्मनुः ॥४१॥
एष्वर्थेषु पशून्हिंसन्वेदतत्त्वार्थविद् द्विजः ।
आत्मानं च पशूंश्चैव गमयत्युत्तमां गतिम् ॥४२॥
गृहे गुरावरण्ये वा निवसन्नात्मवान्द्विजः ।
नावेदविहितां हिंसामापद्यपि समाचरेत् ॥४३॥
या वेदविहिता हिंसा नियतास्मिंश्चराचरे ।
अहिंसामेव तां विद्याद्वेदाद्धर्मो हि निर्बभौ ॥४४॥

पशु° — c-d) Pu[10] वृथापशुवधं विप्रः प्राप्नोति प्रेत्य जन्मनि — d) GMd[5] सर्वजन्मनि जन्मनि; Lo[1] प्रेते

39. Pādas a-b omitted in NKt[4]. Cited by *Lakṣ* 3.327— a) TMd[4] धात्रा वै पशवः; MTr[4] स्पृष्ट्वा — b) sOx[1] sPu[6] °भुवः — c) La[1] मधुपर्के च यज्ञे च [*but mc fh;* cf. 5.41a]; Jm Jo[1] Kt[2] Lo[1] oOr Tj[1] *Mandlik Dave* यज्ञस्य; BKt[5] wKt[6] यज्ञास्य; Lo[1] ययज्ञस्य; BCa Hy NKt[4] Pu[2] *KSS* यज्ञश्च; TMd[3] TMd[4] GMd[5] GMy यज्ञोहि; GMd[1] यज्ञेहि; MTr[4] MTr[6] यज्ञोपि; Bo यज्ञे च; Tr[1] यज्ञोभिभूत्यै; Pu[2] Pu[4] भूत्वै; BKt[5] भृत्यै; NKt[4] भूतेः; Wa भूत्यै लोक; Pu[10] भूत्यमेव स्यात्; Ho सर्वत्र — d) Jo[1] NKt[4] MTr[6] तस्माद्यज्ञ; NKt[4] वधावधः

40. Cited by *Lakṣ* 3.327 — a) Tr[1] औषध्यः; La[1] अपध्याः; NKt[4] अपध्यः; Pu[2] Pu[4] उषध्यः; GMd[1] अवध्य; Lo[1] *cor to* ओषधिपशवा; Pu[10] वृक्षस्ति° — b) sOx[1] sPu[6] °स्तिर्यञ्चाः; MTr[6] पक्षिणीस्तथा; Be[3] GMd[1] Tj[1] पक्षिणो मृगाः — c) TMd[3] GMy Ox[3] Pu[10] यज्ञार्थे; Lo[4] [*but mc*] ज्ञानार्थं — d) BBe[2] °न्त्यव्रतीः; Jm Jo[1] *KSS* °न्त्युत्सृतीः; Lo[4] Lo[5] Pu[5] °च्छृतीः; Lo[3] °च्छ्रुतीः; wKt[6] °च्छतीः; Pu[2] Pu[4] °छतीः; TMd[3] °च्छ्रितः; Tj[1] °च्छ्रिताः; Lo[1] °छ्रितं; wKt[1] °द्रतीः; Tj[2] °चिश्वतीः; Ox[2] °च्छ्रितां गतीः; GMd[5] °च्छ्रितां गतिं; MTr[4] पुरा; sOx[1] sPu[6] MTr[6] *Lakṣ* पराः

41. Cited by *Apa* 154; *Lakṣ* 3.328 — a) TMd[4] °पर्केपि यज्ञेपि; Ho BKt[5] wKt[6] *Apa Lakṣ* सोमे च — b) Be[1] Be[3] Bo Tj[1] पित्र्ये दैव्ये च कर्मणि [Bo देवे]; Pu[5] Pu[7] Pu[9] दैवे पित्र्ये च कर्मणि; Wa दैवदैवेपितृकर्मणि; Pu[2] Pu[4] पित्र्य°; GMd[1] °दैवत्य°; GMy °देवत° — c) Jm wKt[3] हिंसा; Tr[1] हिंस्युः; GMd[5] वध्या; Kt[2] TMd[4] Pu[7] हिंस्यान्नान्य° — d) sOx[1] sPu[6] Tr[2] नान्यत्र मनुरब्रवीत्; NKt[4] नान्यवेत्यब्र°

42. Omitted in Lo[4] Lo[5] Ox[3] Pu[10] [*Jolly* M]; not commented by *Me*; pādas c-d omitted in La[2]. Cited by *Lakṣ* 3.328 — a) wKt[3] तेष्व°; Tj[1] येष्व°; wKt[1] Tj[1] °न्हिंसन्वे°; GMd[5] °न्हिंस्याद्वे°; TMd[3] GMy °न्हिंस्यान्वे°; Jo[1] °न्हिंसान्वे° — a-b) TMd[4] °न्हिंस्यानद्यात्तत्त्वर्थविद् — b) NKt[4] °सन्वेदे; TMd[4] °सनद्यात्तत्त्वर्थ°; wKt[3] °तत्त्वार्थाद् द्विजः — c) Bo आत्मनश्च; BCa Hy Jm Jo[1] Kt[2] wKt[3] Lo[3] GMd[1] MTr[3] [*Jolly* R Ku Nd] *Ku Mandlik Jha KSS Dave* पशुं चैव [Jo[1] चैवं]; Be[3] NKt[4] पशुश्चैव

43. Omitted in Lo[4] Lo[5] Ox[3] Pu[10] [*Jolly* M]. Cited by *Lakṣ* 3.328 — a) Hy गुहे; TMd[4] गृहे गृहमरण्ये; Ox[2] गिरावरण्ये; Pu[2] Pu[4] गुरवेरण्ये; GMd[1] गृहोवरण्ये; Wa गुरोवरण्ये — b) Ho निवसन्धर्मवित् द्विजः; Tr[2] निवसेन्वात्म°; Wa निवसेन्नात्म°; BKt[5] wKt[6] °त्मनां द्विजः — c) GMd[1] यावेदरहितां; Tr[1] °विहिता; GMy °विदितां — d) Ho °द्यपि हि समा°; GMd[1] °द्यपि च तारयेत्

44. Omitted in Pu[5]. Cited by *Lakṣ* 3.328 — a) TMd[4] यो; Tr[1] °विहितां; Bo °पिहिता — c)

योऽहिंसकानि भूतानि हिनस्त्यात्मसुखेच्छया ।
स जीवंश्च मृतश्चैव न क्वचित्सुखमेधते ॥४५॥
यो बन्धनवधक्लेशान् प्राणिनां न चिकीर्षति ।
स सर्वस्य हितप्रेप्सुः सुखमत्यन्तमश्नुते ॥४६॥
यद्ध्यायति यत्कुरुते रतिं बध्नाति यत्र च ।
तदवाप्नोत्ययत्नेन यो हिनस्ति न किंचन ॥४७॥
नाकृत्वा प्राणिनां हिंसां मांसमुत्पद्यते क्वचित् ।
न च प्राणिवधः स्वर्ग्यस्तस्मान्मांसं विवर्जयेत् ॥४८॥
समुत्पत्तिं च मांसस्य वधबन्धौ च देहिनाम् ।
प्रसमीक्ष्य निवर्तेत सर्वमांसस्य भक्षणात् ॥४९॥
न भक्षयति यो मांसं विधिं हित्वा पिशाचवत् ।
स लोके प्रियतां याति व्याधिभिश्च न पीड्यते ॥५०॥

Tr^{1} विद्या वेदा° — d) TMd^{4} Wa °द्वेदधर्मो; Bo °द्धर्मेव; BKt^{5} *om* हि; wKt^{6} °द्धर्मो निनिर्बभौ

45. Pāda-a omitted in Pu^{5}. Cited by *Viś* 3.265; *Lakṣ* 3.329; *Dev* 4.251 — a) Lo^{1} यो न हिंसति भूतानि; GMd^{1} यो ह्यहिंसानि — b) TMd^{3} हिंसत्यात्म° — c) NNg संजीवंश्च; Be^{3} wKt^{3} GMy जीवश्च; Be^{1} जीवाश्च; TMd^{4} जीवं च; Jm मृतं चैव — d) wKt^{6} °चित्स्वयमेधते; Lo^{4} [*but mc*] °खमेषते; *Lakṣ* °खमश्नुते; Jm °खमोदते

46. Cited by *Lakṣ* 3.329 — a) GMy °वधो°; Tj^{2} °वधं; sOx^{1} sPu^{6} °परिक्लेशान्; Ho NKt^{4} GMd^{1} TMd^{3} TMd^{4} GMd^{5} Ox^{2} Tr^{1} °क्लेशं; Lo^{2} °क्लेशां; BKt^{5} °क्लेशान्न — b) wKt^{3} TMd^{4} च चिकी°; Tj^{2} चिकीर्षीत — c) GMd^{1} Tj^{2} *om* स; GMd^{1} सर्वस्यैव [*om* स]; sOx^{1} Ox^{2} sPu^{6} Tr^{2} हितं; GMd^{1} GMd^{5} [*Jolly* Nd] सुखप्रेप्सुः; TMd^{4} हिते प्रेत्यं — d) Lo^{2} TMd^{3} GMy oOr Pu^{10} [*Jolly* M] °मानन्त्यमश्नुते; Lo^{4} °मान्यन्तमश्नुते; Lo^{5} °मान्यं समश्नुत; MTr^{6} °मत्यशमश्नुते; wKt^{3} °मक्षयमश्नुते; GMd^{5} °मक्षय्यमश्नुते

47. Cited by *Vij* 1.181; *Lakṣ* 3.330 — a) Lo^{3} GMd^{5} sOx^{1} sPu^{6} *Vij* यद्ध्यायते; TMd^{4} यद्ध्यायन्ति — b) Jo^{1} Kt^{2} Ox^{2} sPu^{6} [*but cor*] Tr^{2} MTr^{3} *Ku Mandlik KSS* धृतिं; Pu^{10} इति बध्नाति; Be^{3} Lo^{5} oOr वा; Pu^{2} Pu^{4} ह; La^{1} वै — c) wKt^{1} Lo^{5} MTr^{4} MTr^{6} *Lakṣ* तत्तदाप्नो°; Be^{1} Ox^{2} Tr^{2} तदेवाप्नो°; wKt^{6} तदैवाप्नो°; Bo La^{1} °प्नोति यत्नेन; *Vij* °प्नोत्यविघ्नेन — d) NPu^{1} नो यो निहस्ति किंचन; GMd^{5} यो हिनस्ति कथंचन; Ho कंचन

48. Pādas c-d omitted in GMy. Cited by *Dev* 4.244 — a) Be^{1} Jm Lo^{3} Lo^{4} Ox^{3} Pu^{10} न कृत्वा; GMd^{1} अकृत्वा; NKt^{4} TMd^{3} प्राणिना हिंसा; MTr^{6} हिंसा — b) Pu^{10} *om* मांसम्; Bo NKt^{4} Tr^{2} °मुत्पाद्यते — c) MTr^{6} *om* च; Be^{1} स्वर्ग्यंस्तस्मा°; Bo TMd^{3} स्वर्ग्य तस्मा°; wKt^{6} स्वर्गस्तस्मा° — d) Tj^{1} स्वर्ग्यस्तन्मांसं तु विवर्जयेत्; BCa स्वर्ग्यस्तस्मात्तत्परिवर्जयेत्; NKt^{4} Pu^{2} Pu^{4} °न्मांसं न भक्षयेत्

49. Omitted in GMy. Cited by *Dev* 4.245 — a) TMd^{4} समुत्तत्तिं; Tr^{1} समुत्पत्तिश्च; Lo^{4} हि — b) GMd^{5} वधं बन्धं च; Lo^{1} °बन्धो हि; BBe^{2} *om* च; Ox^{3} Pu^{10} हि — c) Ho निर्वर्तेन; Kt^{2} निवर्त्येत; Lo^{1} निवर्तन्ते — d) Ho सर्वे; MTr^{6} सर्वमांस्य

50.* Cited by *Lakṣ* 3.322; *Hem* 3/1.581 — a) *Lakṣ Hem* यस्तु भक्षयते मांसं; GMd^{1} यो भक्षयति मांसानि; Lo^{1} अभक्षयति; wKt^{1} Tj^{1} भक्ष्ययति; TMd^{4} भक्षयन्ति — c) Tr^{2} *om* स; *Lakṣ Hem* लोकेऽप्रियतां; Lo^{1} क्षीणतां; BBe^{2} Be^{3} Bo Pu^{5} Pu^{7} Pu^{9} Tj^{1} [*Jolly* G] प्रियतामेति; GMd^{1} यान्ति — d) [*Jolly* Nd] व्याधिभिर्नोपपीड्यते; TMd^{3} GMy व्याधिना च निपीड्यते; GMd^{1} *Lakṣ Hem* °भिश्चैव पीड्यते; Lo^{1} Pu^{3} °भिश्च निपीड्यते; Be^{1} MTr^{4} स पीड्यते

अनुमन्ता विशसिता निहन्ता क्रयविक्रयी ।
संस्कर्ता चोपहर्ता च खादकश्चेति घातकाः ॥५१॥
स्वमांसं परमांसेन यो वर्धयितुमिच्छति ।
अनभ्यर्च्य पितृन्देवान्न ततोऽन्योऽस्त्यपुण्यकृत् ॥५२॥
वर्षे वर्षेऽश्वमेधेन यो यजेत शतं समाः ।
मांसानि च न खादेद्यस्तयोः पुण्यफलं समम् ॥५३॥
फलमूलाशनैर्मेध्यैर्मुन्यन्नानां च भोजनैः ।

51. Cited by *Apa* 251; *Har*-A 1.17.39; pāda-a cited by *Viś* 1.179 — a) La^1 Tj^1 विसंशिता; Tr^2 विशस्ता च; [*Jolly* G] विनिहन्ता — b) Tj^1 Tr^2 नहन्ता; TMd^4 नियन्ता; GMd^1 हिंसकः क्रय°; Lo^1 °विक्रयः — c) Tj^1 योपहर्ता; TMd^3 TMd^4 GMy MTr^6 चोपकर्ता — d) Tr^1 घातकश्चेति घातकाः; Ho WKt^3 NKt^4 oOr Ox^2 Tr^2 खादकश्चाष्टघातकाः [oOr खादकाश्चा°]; GMd^1 GMy खातकश्चेति; GMd^5 खादिकश्चेति; Jm Lo^1 TMd^3 GMy sOx^1 Tr^2 घातकः; GMd^1 खातकाः

Additional verses in sOx^1 sPu^6:

अनुमन्ता विशसिता निहन्ता क्रयविक्रयी ।
घातकाः सर्व एवैते संस्कर्ता षष्ठ उच्यते ॥१॥
निदेशेनानुमन्ता च विशस्ता शासनात्तथा ।
हननेन तथा हन्ता धनेन क्रयिकस्तथा ॥२॥
विक्रयी च धनादानात्संस्कर्ता तत्प्रवर्तनात् ।
धनेन चोपभोगेन वधभद्रेण चाप्यथ ॥३॥
त्रिविधस्तु वधो ज्ञेयो भोक्ता तत्रातिरिच्यते ।
घातकाः षट् समाख्याता भोक्ता ततस्तु सप्तमः ॥४॥
तेषां पञ्च सकाशात्तु ह्युपभोक्तातिरिच्यते ।
क्रेतारं व्रजते पादः पादो भोक्तारमृच्छति ॥५॥
खादकं व्रजते पादः पाद ऋच्छत्यतस्तु यः ।
यदि तत्खादको न स्याद्घातको न तथा भवेत् ॥६॥
खादको घातकः क्रेता त्रयस्तुल्या न संशयः॥७॥

52. Cited by *Lakṣ* 3.320 — b) Be^3 Pu^3 Pu^5 Pu^9 Tj^1 वर्धयतु°; Pu^7 वर्धयेतु° *cor to* वर्धयतु°; TMd^3 GMy °मिच्छता — d) GMd^1 °न्देवानपापो सत्यपुण्यकृत्; La^1 °न्देवानतस्तेण्योस्त्य°; Hy Jm Jo^1 Jo^2 Kt^2 Pu^3 Pu^8 Tj^2 MTr^3 [*Jolly* Ku R] *Mandlik Jha KSS Dave* °न्देवांस्ततोन्यो नास्त्यपुण्य°; GMd^5 Tr^1 MTr^4 MTr^6 °न्देवान्न तदन्योस्त्यपुण्य°; TMd^3 ततोन्यस्यपुण्य°; WKt^6 ततो नास्त्यपुण्य°; WKt^3 ततोन्यः कास्त्य-पुण्य°; GMy ततोस्यमपुण्य°; TMd^4 ततोन्यस्यपुण्य°; Be^1 °न्योस्ति पुण्य°; Pu^5 Pu^7 Pu^9 [*Jolly* G] °पापकृत्

53. Omitted in GMy. Cited by *Vij* 1.181 — a) Bo वर्षे च मेधेन — b) La^1 Tr^2 योजयेत; Pu^4 यजेते; Hy यजत; TMd^3 यजन्ते; WKt^6 यजच्छतं; Lo^1 यजेत समाहितः; La^1 सतं; MTr^6 समां — c) Be^1 Wa न खादेद्यश्च मांसानि तयोः; TMd^4 स मांसेन च खादे°; Be^3 Ho Tj^1 न च; La^1 खादेयुस्तयोः; Lo^3 खादेवस्तयोः — d) Be^3 Tj^1 °द्यस्तस्य; BKt^5 पुण्यं; La^1 GMd^5 पुण्यसमं फलं [La^1 पुण्यं]; Ox^3 सतं; Lo^2 स्मृतं

Additional verse in Be^1 oOr *Mandlik* [ञ, ड, ढ] *KSS Dave:*

सदा यजति यज्ञेन सदा दानानि यच्छति ।
स तपस्वी सदा विप्रो यश्च मांसं विवर्जयेत् ॥

a) oOr यदा यजति सत्रेण — b) oOr दानं प्रयच्छति — c-d) oOr सदा तपस्वी भवति मधु-मांसस्य वर्जनात् — d) Be^1 यस्तु

न तत्फलमवाप्नोति यन्मांसपरिवर्जनात् ॥५४॥
मां स भक्षयितामुत्र यस्य मांसमिहाद्म्यहम् ।
एतन्मांसस्य मांसत्वं प्रवदन्ति मनीषिण: ॥५५॥
न मांसभक्षणे दोषो न मद्ये न च मैथुने ।
प्रवृत्तिरेषा भूतानां निवृत्तिस्तु महाफला ॥५६॥
प्रेतशुद्धिं प्रवक्ष्यामि द्रव्यशुद्धिं तथैव च ।
चतुर्णामपि वर्णानां यथावदनुपूर्वश: ॥५७॥
दन्तजातेऽनुजाते च कृतचूडे च संस्थिते ।
अशुद्धा बान्धवा: सर्वे सूतके च तथोच्यते ॥५८॥
दशाहं शावमाशौचं सपिण्डेषु विधीयते ।
अर्वाक्संचयनादस्थ्नां त्र्यहमेकाहमेव वा ॥५९॥
सपिण्डता तु पुरुषे सप्तमे विनिवर्तते ।
समानोदकभावस्तु जन्मनाम्नोरवेदने ॥६०॥

54. Omitted in GMy; pādas c-d omitted in Pu[10] and pāda-d in Pu[8]. Cited by *Dev* 4.245; *Mādh* 1.719 — a) BKt[5] wKt[6] °मूलासनै°; oOr MTr[6] Wa °शनैर्मध्यैर्मु°; Bo TMd[3] °शनैर्मध्ये मुन्य° — b) wKt[3] भोजयेत् — c) GMd[1] न तत्फलं समवाप्नोति; Tr[2] *om* न — d) wKt[1] यन्मांसस्य विवर्जनात्; Tj[1] यन्मांसफलवर्जनात्; wKt[6] TMd[3] NPu[1] यन्मांसं; TMd[3] °परिवर्जयेत्

55. Omitted in Wa; pādas a-b omitted in Pu[10]. Cited by *Har*-A 1.17.39; *Lakṣ* 3.319–20 — a) Pu[4] भिक्षयि°; NPu[1] °यिता यत्र; TMd[3] TMd[4] °यितामन्त्र — b) TMd[4] तस्य; La[1] °हाक्ष्यहं; NPu[1] °हास्म्यहं; Pu[2] Pu[4] °हाश्वहं — d) TMd[3] GMy [*Jolly* Nd] विपश्चित:

56. Cited by *Kum* 1.3.4; *Har*-A 1.17.39; *Dev* 4.245, 246; *Mādh* 1.719; pāda-a cited by *Viś* 1.180 — a) Lo[4] Wa *om* न; Tj[2] दोषा; Jo[1] देषो — b) Bo न यज्ञे — c) BKt[5] wKt[6] MTr[4] °रेषां — d) Tr[1] निवृत्तिमहा°; Bo GMd[1] Pu[10] °फल:; oOr °फला:; TMd[4] °फलं

57. Cited by *Dev* 5.13 — a) Bo Ho प्रेते; Be[3] प्रवक्षामि — b) BKt[5] wKt[6] °शुद्धिस्तथैव; MTr[6] *om* च

58. Cited by *Mādh* 1.570; pāda-c cited by *Vij* 3.1 [intro] — a) Tj[1] दन्तजाते अदंते च; NNg [*but cor fh*] दन्ते; wKt[3] दन्तजाचनुजाते; Be[3] वा — b) NKt[4] कृतन्जदे च संस्थिते; TMd[4] कृतशौचेन संस्थिते; GMd[5] चाकृत°; GMy कृतचौले; Tr[1] कृतचौळे; MTr[6] कृतचोळे — c) Tr[1] अशुद्धो; NKt[4] शुद्धासं-बान्धवा:; MTr[4] बान्धवो: — d) Ho wKt[3] सूतकं; GMd[1] तदुच्यते

59. Cited by *Vij* 3.28–9; *Apa* 893; pādas a-b cited by *Vij* 1.52; *Dev* 5.35 — a) Pu[2] Pu[4] श्राद्धमाशौचं — b) MTr[6] °शौचमसपिण्डेषु; Lo[4] सपिण्ड्येषु; BKt[5] सपिण्डेमं — c) Hy Jo[1] GMd[5] आर्वा°; BBe[2] आरात्सं°; wKt[1] आरासं°; La[1] Pu[8] अर्वासं°; NKt[4] BKt[5] wKt[6] Tr[1] अवासं°; *Apa* आवासं°; Lo[2] अर्च्चासं°; NPu[1] अर्वाकंचय°; MTr[6] अर्धासंचय° — d) TMd[3] त्रैहमे°; Lo[1] त्रयमेका°; Tr[2] °मेकात्वमेव; wKt[1] °मेकाह एव; Be[1] Jm Jo[1] Kt[2] Lo[4] Ox[3] Pu[8] Pu[10] Tr[2] [*Jolly* M] च

60. Cited by *Viś* 1.53; *Apa* 893; *Jmv* 11.1.42; *Lakṣ* 10.66; *Dev* 5.37; *Mādh* 1.590; pādas a-b cited by *Vij* 1.254; *Jmv* 11.6.17; *Dev* 1.181 — a) Tr[2] सपिण्डते; La[1] सपिण्डन — b) Bo सप्तते; TMd[3] संतमे — c) wKt[1] °दकतावं तु; Be[3] Bo wKt[3] TMd[4] oOr Tj[1] *Lakṣ* °भावश्च — d) La[1] जन्मनाद्योर°; TMd[4] °वेदिने

जननेऽप्येवमेव स्यान्मातापित्रोस्तु सूतकम् ।
सूतकं मातुरेव स्यादुपस्पृश्य पिता शुचिः ॥६१॥
निरस्य तु पुमाञ्छुक्रमुपस्पृश्यैव शुध्यति ।

61.* Most mss. and commentators, as well as all editions, read here the two following verses. The single verse of the critical edition is expanded into two by adding two pādas before and two after pāda-a. In order to maintain the traditional numbering, I have omitted verse number 62. I give below the expanded version together with the variants:

यथेदं शावमाशौचं सपिण्डेषु विधीयते ।
जननेऽप्येवमेव स्यान्निपुणां शुद्धिमिच्छताम् ॥६१॥
सर्वेषां शावमाशौचं मातापित्रोस्तु सूतकम् ।
सूतकं मातुरेव स्यादुपस्पृश्य पिता शुचिः ॥६२॥

Pādas a-b of verse 1 are omitted in BKt[5] wKt[6] Lo[4] TMd[3] GMd[1] GMy NNg Ox[3] Pu[5] Pu[7] Pu[9] Tr[1] MTr[4] MTr[6] [*Jolly* Nd] *Me Go Lakṣ* 10.17; *ma* in wKt[6]; added after verse 58 in NPu[1] Tj[1]. First verse cited by *Apa* 896.

61. a) oOr यथैदं; *Apa*दशाहं शाव° — b) NPu[1] विहितं धर्मकास्यया — c) TMd[3] GMy जनने चैवमेव; Bo जननेष्ठेवमेव; TMd[4] जननस्येवमेव; Hy NKt[4] sOx[1] Ox[2] Pu[5] Pu[7] Pu[9] °वेमेवं — d) *Lakṣ* स्याद्विप्रः; La[1] Pu[4] स्यान्निपुण्यां; Be[1] स्यान्निपुण्यं; Tr[2] शुद्धिमेव च; Kt[2] oOr °मिच्छता; La[1] °मिच्छती

62. a) Wa शावशौचं — b) oOr मात्रा°; La[1] sOx[1] Ox[2] sPu[6] Tr[2] °पित्रोश्च wKt[1] Tj[1] सूतके

After the first verse of the expanded version, two additional verses are given in GMd[1] TMd[4] Tr[2] *Lakṣ* 10.23; *Mādh* 1.583; *Apa* 896; both are given after the 2nd verse in GMd[5] MTr[4] MTr[6]. The first additonal verse is given after verse 58 in Be[3] oOr NPu[1] Tj[1] and it is commented by *Nā Rc:*

उभयत्र दशाहानि कुलस्यान्नं न भुज्यते ।
दानं प्रतिग्रहो यज्ञः स्वाध्यायश्च निवर्तते ॥१॥
जाते कुमारे तदहः कामं कुर्यात्प्रतिग्रहम् ।
हिरण्यधान्यगोवासस्तिलानां गुडसर्पिषाम् ॥२॥

1. c) TMd[4] GMd[5] oOr MTr[4] MTr[6] °ग्रहो होमः

2. a-d) TMd[4] कुमारजन्मादिवनमेकं कुर्यात्प्रतिग्रहं | हिरण्यं भूमिगामश्वं वस्त्रशय्यासनादि च — d) GMd[5] MTr[4] MTr[6] *Lakṣ* °स्तिलान्नगुड° GMd[1] °स्तिलान्नशुद्धसर्पि°

TMd[4] adds several verses, the first before verse 1 of the expanded version and the others after 2. The first verse is given after verse 2 of the expanded version also in Be[3] Ho wKt[1] oOr Tj[1] Tr[2] MTr[4] MTr[6] [the latter two transpose pādas a-b and c-d];it is commented by *Rc:*

सत्रधर्मप्रवृत्तस्य दानधर्मफलेषिणः ।
त्रेताधर्मापरोधार्थमारण्यस्यैतदुच्यते ॥१॥
गीयन्ति देवाः पितरस्तत्परं चोध[द]यन्ति च ।
तस्मात्तद्दिवसः पुण्यः पितृवंशविवर्धनः ॥२॥
ततः सर्वं प्रतिगृह्यं कृतान्नं तु न भक्षयेत् ।
भक्षयित्वा तु तस्माद्धि द्विजश्चान्द्रायणं चरेत् ॥३॥
हिरण्यधान्यगोवासस्तिलान्नगुदसर्पिषाम् ॥४॥

1. a) wKt[1] यज्ञधर्म°; Ho दानधर्म°; TMd[4] समधर्म° — c) TMd[4] क्रीडाधर्मानुरोधार्थ°; MTr[4] MTr[6] सत्रधर्मोपरोधा°; wKt[1] एताधर्मापरोधा°; Tr[2] °धर्मोपलक्ष्यार्थ°; Ho °धर्मोपलक्षार्थ°; Be[3] Tj[1] °धर्मानुधर्मार्थ° — d) oOr °स्यैव दृश्यते

बैजिकादभिसंबन्धादनुरुन्ध्यादघं त्र्यहम् ॥६३॥
अह्ना चैकेन रात्र्या च त्रिरात्रैरेव च त्रिभिः ।
शवस्पृशो विशुध्यन्ति त्र्यहात्तूदकदायिनः ॥६४॥
गुरोः प्रेतस्य शिष्यस्तु पितृमेधं समाचरेत् ।
प्रेताहारैः समं तत्र दशरात्रेण शुध्यति ॥६५॥
रात्रिभिर्मासतुल्याभिर्गर्भस्रावे विशुध्यति ।
रजस्युपरते साध्वी स्नानेन स्त्री रजस्वला ॥६६॥
नृणामकृतचूडानामशुद्धिर्नैशिकी स्मृता ।
निर्वृत्तचूडकानां तु त्रिरात्राच्छुद्धिरिष्यते ॥६७॥

63. Cited by *Mādh* 1.606 — a) gMd^5 Tr^1 mTr^4 पुमाञ्छुक्लमु° ; tMd^3 tMd^4 पुमान्शुक्लमु° ; Be^1 पुमान्युक्तमु° ; Lo^4 Lo^5 gMd^1 पिता शुक्रमु° ; Pu^4 *om* शुक्रमुपस्पृश्यैव — b) bKt^5 °क्रमिव स्पृश्यैव; wKt^1 °स्पृश्य च; Lo^2 °स्पृश्येव; gMd^5 Tr^1 °स्पृश्य विशुध्यति — c) La^1 mTr^3 mTr^6 वैजिका° ; gMd^1 वैदिका° ; Be^1 [*but mc*] gMd^1 tMd^3 gMd^5 gMy nNg Tj^1 Tr^1 mTr^4 mTr^6 *Mādh* [vl] °कादपि संबन्धा° ; sOx^1 sPu^6 °कादेव संबन्धा° ; Be^3 °कादघसंबन्धा° ; Tr^2 °कादप्यसंबन्धा° ; Bo °सन्धानाद° — d) Lo^1 Pu^5 Pu^7 °रुन्ध्यादथ; nPu^1 °रुन्ध्यादपि

Folios containing 5.64–140 missing in La^2. An additional verse in tMd^4 is given below after 5.83.

64.* Cited by *Vij* 3.18; *Apa* 883, 893; pādas a-c cited by *Viś* 1.252 — a) nKt^4 La^1 gMd^1 tMd^3 tMd^4 gMd^5 gMy oOr Tr^1 mTr^4 mTr^6 *Nd* रजन्याह्नैव चैकेन [gMy राजन्यह्नैव; nKt^4 राजन्याह्नैव]; Bo अह्नो; Ho अह्नावेकेन; Tj^1 अह्नावेवेकेन; wKt^3 तु — b) tMd^4 न रात्रैरेव न त्रिभिः; Bo त्रिरात्रमेव; bKt^5 wKt^6 त्रिरात्रेणैव च; Pu^{10} *om* त्रिभिः — c) sOx^1 sPu^6 शाव° ; *Viś* प्रेतस्पृशो; tMd^3 °स्पृश्यो — d) tMd^4 त्र्यहं तूदक° ; bBe^2 bCa Hy Jo^1 Jo^2 wKt^6 Lo^3 Lo^4 Lo^5 gMd^1 oOr Tj^2 *Mandlik Jolly Jha KSS Dave* त्र्यादुदक° ; wKt^3 त्रिहादुदक° ; Kt^2 त्र्यहमुदक° ; Tj^1 त्र्यहानुदक°

65.* Cited by *Vij* 3.24; *Apa* 912; *Lakṣ* 10.51; *Dev* 5.38–9; *Mādh* 1.610 — a) *Apa* [vl] गुरुः; Pu^5 Pu^7 Pu^9 [*Jolly* G] शिष्यश्च; Bo *Apa* [vl] शिष्यस्य — b) wKt^6 पितृनेवं; Tj^1 पितृनिवसमाच° ; bBe^2 Bo Ho Hy Jm Jo^1 Jo^2 wKt^1 Kt^2 La^1 Lo^1 Lo^2 Lo^3 Lo^4 Lo^5 Ox^3 Pu^8 Pu^{10} *Apa Dev Mādh Bh* (ad 11.197) *Mandlik Jolly Jha KSS Dave* समाचरन् — c) Be^1 Ho Hy Jm Jo^1 Jo^2 wKt^1 Kt^2 wKt^3 Lo^1 Lo^3 Ox^2 Tr^2 Wa *Lakṣ Mandlik KSS Dave* प्रेतहारैः; Bo प्रेतोहारैः; oOr प्रेतहारं; tMd^4 प्रेताहारं; *Bh* [ad 11.197] व्रताहारैः; Jo^2 wKt^1 [*Jolly* R] समस्तत्र — d) Ox^2 Pu^3 Pu^8 *Vij* दशाहेन विशुध्यति

66. Pādas c-d omitted in gMd^1. Cited by *Vij* 3.20; *Dev* 5.4; pādas c-d cited by *Apa* 104; *Hem* 3/3.726; *Dev* 2.308; *Mādh* 1.504 — a) mTr^6 त्रिभिर्मा° ; wKt^6 °तुल्यानि गर्भ° — b) Pu^5 Pu^7 Pu^9 °भिःगार्भ° ; Ho Hy La^1 oOr Pu^3 Pu^5 Pu^7 Pu^9 °श्रावे — c) Bo Pu^2 Tj^2 mTr^6 °स्यपरते; Ho °स्यपुरते; Ox^3 °रतेः; Tj^1 °रते शुद्धा; *Dev* 5.4 °रते सर्वा — d) *Apa* [vl] स्नायेत; oOr रजस्वलां — After this tMd^3 gMy Tr^2 Tr^1 [*Jolly* Nd] give verse 78.

67.* Omitted in Pu^5 Pu^7 Pu^9 [because *Go* comments on 66-67 together]. Cited by *Vij* 3.23; *Lakṣ* 10.36 — a) mTr^4 °चौडा° ; tMd^3 °चूळा° ; [*Jolly* Nd] *Nd* °चौला° ; gMd^5 gMy mTr^6 °चौळा° ; Lo^4 Lo^5 Ox^3 [*Jolly* M] °मुण्डा° — b) Lo^2 °डानामाशुद्धि° ; bBe^2 Hy Jm Jo^1 wKt^1 Kt^2 wKt^3 La^1 Lo^4 Lo^5 oOr Ox^3 nPu^1 Pu^2 Pu^{10} Tj^2 *Mandlik Jolly Jha KSS Dave* °डानां विशुद्धि° ; gMd^1 °डानामशुचि° ; Bo °डानामबुद्धिं नैशिकी; Be^3 tMd^3 स्मृताः; gMy स्मृतः — c) nKt^4 निर्वृत्ते; Be^1 bBe^2 wKt^3 La^1 Lo^1 tMd^4 nPu^1 Pu^4 निवृत्त° ; Ho निवृत्ति° ; mTr^6 gMy °चौलकानां; tMd^3 gMd^5 Tr^1 °चौळ-

ऊनद्विवार्षिकं प्रेतं निदध्युर्बान्धवा बहिः ।
अलंकृत्य शुचौ भूमावस्थिसंचयनादृते ॥६८॥
नास्य कार्योऽग्निसंस्कारो नापि कार्योदकक्रिया ।
अरण्ये काष्ठवत्त्यक्त्वा क्षपेत* त्र्यहमेव तु ॥६९॥
नात्रिवर्षस्य कर्तव्या बान्धवैरुदकक्रिया ।
जातदन्तस्य वा कुर्युर्नाम्नि वापि कृते सति ॥७०॥
सब्रह्मचारिण्येकाहमतीते क्षपणं स्मृतम् ।
जन्मन्येकोदकानां तु त्रिरात्राच्छुद्धिरिष्यते ॥७१॥

कानां; *Nd* °चौलानां; Lo^4 Lo^5 Ox^3 Pu^{10} [*Jolly* M] *Me* [but unclear whether root or gloss] *Dave Jha* °मुण्डकानां; Bo Lo^4 Pu^{10} च — d) gMd^5 त्रिरात्राच्छुचिरिष्यते; wKt^6 त्रिरात्राद्धुद्धिरिष्यते; Ox^3 त्रिरा-त्रान्शुद्धि°; nNg त्रिरात्रा शुद्धि°

Additional verses in *Mandlik KSS Dave;* first verse also in Ho; third verse added after 72 in La^1 nPu^1 *Mandlik* [ण] *KSS Dave:*

प्राक्संस्कारप्रमीतानां वर्णानामविशेषतः ।
त्रिरात्रात्तु भवेच्छुद्धिः कन्यास्वह्नो विधीयते ॥१॥
आ दन्तजन्मनः सद्य आ चूडान्नैशिकी स्मृता ।
त्रिरात्रमावृता देशाद्दशरात्रमतः परम् ॥२॥ [= *YDh* 3.23]
परपूर्वासु भार्यासु पुत्रेषु प्रकृतेषु च ।
मातामहे त्रिरात्रं तु एकाहं त्वसपिण्डतः ॥३॥

1. a) Ho प्राक्संस्कारात्प्र° — b) Ho °नामनुपूर्वशः — d) Ho °स्वह्ना

3. a) nPu^1 कन्यासु — a-b) *Mandlik KSS Dave* [after 72] परपूर्वासु पुत्रेषु सूतके मृतकेषु च — d) La^1 तु सपिण्डके; *Mandlik KSS Dave* [after 72] तु सपिण्डने; nPu^1 तु सपिण्डदे

68. Cited by *Viś* 3.1; *Vij* 3.1–2; *Apa* 870; *Dev* 5.20 — a) gMd^5 °वार्षिक; wKt^1 °वार्षिकं बालं — b) Pu^2 Pu^4 निर्दध्यु°; Pu^4 °र्बान्धवाहिनः; tMd^4 बहि — c) tMd^3 अलंकृत — d) Pu^2 °चयनाकृते

69.* Pu^9 give only pāda-a as *pratīka*; pādas c-d omitted in Jm Wa [haplo]. Cited by *Viś* 3.1; *Vij* 3.1–2; *Apa* 870, 911; *Dev* 5.20; pādas c-d cited by *Vij* 3.23 — a) wKt^3 कुर्याग्नि°; gMy कार्यो न संस्कारो; mTr^6 °संस्कारे — b) gMd^5 नैव; Be^3 Bo Ho Hy Jm Jo^1 Kt^2 bKt^5 wKt^6 La^1 Lo^4 Lo^5 gMd^1 sOx^1 Ox^3 sPu^6 Pu^{10} Tj^1 mTr^3 mTr^4 mTr^6 *Mandlik Jolly Jha KSS Dave* न च कार्यो°; wKt^3 °क्रियाः — c) Hy La^1 nPu^1 Pu^3 Pu^4 काप्ट°; Bo Ho Lo^3 nNg Tj^1 Tr^1 °वत्त्यक्ता — d) Pu^5 Pu^7 *Apa* क्षिपेत; Be^3 Tj^1 क्षपेत्तु; tMd^4 क्षपे; Jo^2 gMd^1 tMd^3 gMd^5 gMy Tr^1 [*Jolly* Nd R] क्षपयेच्चिह°; [*Jolly* G] क्षपेत्तच्चिह°; Be^1 sOx^1 Ox^2 sPu^6 [*cor to*] Tr^2 *Rc* क्षपेरंस्त्र्यह°; Bo Ho Hy Jo^1 wKt^1 Kt^2 wKt^3 wKt^6 La^1 Lo^1 Lo^4 Lo^5 nNg oOr nPu^1 Pu^2 Pu^3 Pu^4 Pu^8 Tj^2 mTr^3 [*Jolly* M$^{3-4}$ Me^4 Ku N] *Viś Dev Nā Mr Jolly Mandlik KSS* क्षपेयुस्त्र्यह°; mTr^6 क्षपैतुस्त्र्यह°; Lo^3 क्षपुयेस्त्र्यह°; bBe^2 *Vij* क्षिपेयुस्त्र्यह°; wKt^1 wKt^3 nPu^1 Pu^5 Pu^7 *Apa* 911 [*Jolly* G] वा; Be^3 Bo Ho Hy Jo^1 Kt^2 gMd^1 sOx^1 sPu^6 Tj^1 Tj^2 mTr^3 *Jolly* च

70. Pādas a-b omitted in Jm Wa. Cited by *Vij* 3.1–2; *Apa* 871; *Dev* 5.23; *Mādh* 1.606 — b) tMd^3 °क्रियाः — c) tMd^4 जातदन्तस्सदा कुर्यु°; sOx^1 sPu^6 च; Bo Jo^2 gMd^1 tMd^3 tMd^4 gMd^5 gMy nNg mTr^4 mTr^6 *Vij Dev Mādh* कुर्यान्नाम्नि— d) Bo चापि

71. Pādas a-b cited by *Dev* 5.13 and pādas c-d by *Dev* 5.46 — a) Pu^{10} *om* स°; Lo^1 °चारिणैकाहमतीते — b) tMd^4 °मातीते; gMd^1 °मधीते; Tj^1 क्षेपणं; Lo^4 Lo^5 पक्षणं; gMd^1 पक्षिणि स्मृतं — c) tMd^4 जन्मान्ये°; Lo^1 जन्मनैको°; Pu^5 Pu^7 Pu^9 [*Jolly* G] हि — d) Tj^2 °रिष्यति

स्त्रीणामसंस्कृतानां तु त्र्यहाच्छुध्यन्ति बान्धवाः ।
यथोक्तेनैव कल्पेन शुध्यन्ति तु सनाभयः ॥७२॥
अक्षारलवणान्नाः स्युर्निमज्जेयुश्च ते त्र्यहम् ।
मांसाशनं च नाश्नीयुः शयीरंश्च पृथक् क्षितौ ॥७३॥
संनिधावेष वै कल्पः शावाशौचस्य कीर्तितः ।
असंनिधावयं ज्ञेयो विधिः संबन्धिबान्धवैः ॥७४॥
विगतं तु विदेशस्थं शृणुयाद्यो ह्यनिर्दशम् ।
यच्छेषं दशरात्रस्य तावदेवाशुचिर्भवेत् ॥७५॥
अतिक्रान्ते दशाहे तु त्रिरात्रमशुचिर्भवेत् ।
संवत्सरे व्यतीते तु स्पृष्ट्वैवापो विशुध्यति ॥७६॥

72. Cited by *Vij* 3.24; *Apa* 907; *Dev* 5.31; *Mādh* 1.608 — a) Be^{3} स्त्रीणां तु संस्कृतानां तु; Wa gMd^{5} [*but mc*] *om* तु; nNg च — b) tMd^{4} त्र्यहानुध्यन्ति — c) mTr^{4} mTr^{6} *Dev Dave* कालेन; Pu^{7} कालेन *mc to* कल्पेन; Pu^{5} Pu^{9} *add* कालेन *before* कल्पेन — c-d) *Me* [as pāṭha, but rejected by *Me*] अहस्त्वदत्तकन्यासु बालेपु च विशोधनं — d) *Dev* शुध्यन्त्येव; nNg शुध्यन्तु सना°; bKt^{5} wKt^{6} tMd^{4} *Apa* च; oOr तच्छनाभयः

For the added verse in La^{1} nPu^{1} *Mandlik KSS Dave*, see after 5.67.

73. Only pratīka अक्षार in Pu^{4}. Cited by *Vij* 3.16; *Apa* 885 — a) bKt^{5} wKt^{6} अक्षाराल°; Pu^{7} °लवलान्नाः *mc to* °लणादुन्नाः; Pu^{5} °लणादुन्नाः — b) Wa gives 74b instead; [*Jolly* M$^{3-4}$] स्युर्निर्मज्जे°; bKt^{5} wKt^{6} वै त्र्यहं; tMd^{3} gMy Tr^{1} [*Jolly* Nd] *Nd* [pāṭha] तेन्वहं — c) Lo^{3} मांसं न भक्षयेयुः; Lo^{4} Lo^{5} Ox^{3} Pu^{2} Pu^{10} Wa न चाश्नीयुः; Be^{1} न वाश्नीयुः; oOr नाश्नीयात् — d) tMd^{4} शयीरश्च; Pu^{5} Pu^{7} Pu^{9} शयीरन् च; Lo^{1} oOr शयीरं च; nPu^{1} शरीरंश्च; wKt^{6} शरीरं च; Be^{3} Bo Tj^{1} स्वपेयुश्च; nKt^{4} शयीरनपृथक्; Lo^{1} gMd^{1} Tj^{2} पृथक्पृथक्; bBe^{2} यथाक्षिति; nPu^{1} कृतौ; tMd^{4} यतौ

74. In Ho page containing 74 to 82b is missing, and in gMy page containing 74b to 84c; pāda-d omitted in Pu^{5}. Cited by *Dev* 5.46 — a) *Dev* सन्निधावेव यः कल्पः; Lo^{1} क्षितौ च संनिधावेपः; Jo^{2} Lo^{3} संनिधौ चैप; nPu^{1} °धावेक; nNg °धावेप कल्पस्तु; Bo कल्पाः; Tr^{1} कल्पं; gMd^{1} कल्प्यं — b) Pu^{2} Pu^{9} शवशौचस्य; wKt^{6} Tj^{1} शावशौचस्य; gMd^{5} Wa शवाशौचस्य; Lo^{2} nNg शबाशौचस्य; wKt^{1} शावायस्तु; Pu^{5} Pu^{7} Pu^{9} °शौचेस्य; Pu^{7} कीर्तितां *cor to* कीर्तितं; Pu^{5} Pu^{9} कीर्तितं; gMd^{1} कीर्तिता; tMd^{3} कीर्त्यते — c) *Dev* असन्निधाने स ज्ञेयो; nKt^{4} °निधौ ये ज्ञेयो — d) nKt^{4} विधिः सवविधां वचः; Pu^{7} Pu^{9} विधिं; nPu^{1} विधि; bKt^{5} wKt^{6} Pu^{10} संबन्ध°; La^{1} संवन्ध°

75. Pādas a-b lacuna in nKt^{4}. Cited by *Vij* 3.18; *Dev* 5.46 — a) Be^{3} व्यतीतं तु; Pu^{5} Wa विदेशेस्थं; Pu^{4} विदेशस्थां — b) tMd^{3} Tj^{1} ह्यनिर्दिशं; gMd^{5} mTr^{4} mTr^{6} ननिर्दशं; Be^{3} oOr Pu^{5} Pu^{7} Pu^{9} ह्यहर्निशं — c) Pu^{5} Pu^{7} Pu^{9} [*Jolly* G] तच्छेषं; Pu^{5} Pu^{7} Pu^{9} दशरात्रं स्यात्; tMd^{4} दशरात्रस्यात् — d) Lo^{1} Tj^{1} तावदेव शुचि°

Additional verse in *Mandlik* [ण] *KSS Dave:*

मासत्रये त्रिरात्रं स्यात् षण्मासे पक्षिणी तथा ।
अहस्तु नवमादर्वागूर्ध्वं स्नानेन शुध्यति ॥

76. Pādas a-b omitted in gMd^{1} [haplo]. Cited by *Vij* 3.21; *Lakṣ* 10.33; *Dev* 5.50; pādas c-d cited by *Mādh* 1.598 — a) Lo^{2} दशाहेपु; Hy Jm Jo^{1} Kt^{2} nKt^{4} Lo^{2} Tj^{2} mTr^{3} *Mandlik Jha KSS Dave* च — c) Tr^{1} ह्यतीते; mTr^{3} व्यतीतेपु — d) *Dev* सद्य एव विशुध्यति; mTr^{6} स्पृष्ट्वा चापो

निर्दशं ज्ञातिमरणं श्रुत्वा पुत्रस्य जन्म च ।
सवासा जलमाप्लुत्य शुद्धो भवति मानवः ॥७७॥
बाले देशान्तरस्थे च पृथक्पिण्डे च संस्थिते ।
सवासा जलमाप्लुत्य सद्य एव विशुध्यति ॥७८॥
अन्तर्दशाहे स्यातां चेत् पुनर्मरणजन्मनी ।
तावत् स्यादशुचिर्विप्रो यावत्तत् स्यादनिर्दशम् ॥७९॥
त्रिरात्रमाहुराशौचमाचार्ये संस्थिते सति ।
तस्य पुत्रे च पत्न्यां च दिवारात्रमिति स्थितिः ॥८०॥
श्रोत्रिये तूपसंपन्ने त्रिरात्रमशुचिर्भवेत् ।
मातुले पक्षिणीं रात्रिं शिष्यर्त्विग्बान्धवेषु च ॥८१॥
प्रेते राजनि सज्योतिर्यस्य स्याद्विषये स्थितिः ।
अश्रोत्रिये त्वहः कृत्स्नमनूचाने तथा गुरौ ॥८२॥
शुध्येद्विप्रो दशाहेन द्वादशाहेन भूमिपः ।
वैश्यः पञ्चदशाहेन शूद्रो मासेन शुध्यति ॥८३॥

77. Omitted in NKt^4 [haplo]. Cited by *Vij* 3.21; *Apa* 904; *Dev* 5.48; *Mādh* 1.600; pādas a-b cited by *Vij* 3.18 — a) Tr^2 निर्दिशं; Bo जाति° — b) TMd^3 जन्मनि [*om* च]; Tj^1 वा; Tr^2 तु — c) Tj^1 सवासोज्जल°; Pu^5 Pu^7 [*but cor*] °प्लुत्याशुद्धो — d) Be^1 NNg NPu^1 Wa सद्य एव विशुध्यति [cf. 78d]

78. Omitted in NKt^4 GMd^1; placed after verse 5.66 in TMd^3 Tr^1 Tr^2. Cited by *Apa* 905, 909; *Lakṣ* 10.35; *Dev* 5.47; *Mādh* 1.595— a) Be^3 °रस्थे चेत्° — b) TMd^4 पृथक्पिण्डेन संस्थिते; Bo NPu^1 *Dev* तु — c) Be^1 Wa जलमाविश्य — d) Be^1 Wa शुद्धो भवति मानवः [cf. 77d]; oOr एवास्य शुध्यति

79. Cited by *Dev* 5.59; *Mādh* 1.622 — a) Pu^2 Pu^4 °शाहि; Kt^2 स्याताश्चेत्; Lo^4 Lo^5 Ox^3 Pu^{10} [*Jolly* M R] *Dave Jha* चेत्स्यातां — b) Jo^1 La^1 Pu^4 Pu^{10} Tr^1 °जन्मनि; NKt^4 °जन्मनां — d) oOr यावत्पूर्वमनिर्दशं; wKt^3 NPu^1 यावत्तु; BKt^5 wKt^6 Ox^2 Pu^5 Pu^7 यावन्न; NKt^4 यावत्तस्मादनि°; Tr^2 °दनिर्दिशं; NPu^1 °दहर्निशं

80. Pādas c-d omitted in MTr^3. Cited by *Vij* 3.24; *Apa* 912 — a) wKt^6 Lo^3 °त्रमाहमाशौ° — b) wKt^1 °माचार्ये दूरसंस्थिते — c) Tj^1 पुत्रं; Wa पुत्रो — d) Jo^1 °रात्रामिति; oOr °रात्रमितीक्ष्यते; TMd^4 स्थितः

81. Verses 81–82 given in La^1 in the following order: 81cd, 82ab, 81ab, 82cd. Cited by *Vij* 3.24; *Apa* 912; *Dev* 5.13; pādas a-b cited by *Dev* 5.38; *Mādh* 1.610; and pādas c-d by *Dev* 5.42 — a) oOr क्षत्रिये तूपसमुत्पन्ने; TMd^3 श्रोत्रियं; Hy श्रोत्रियोरुप°; Be^1 Lo^2 Lo^5 MTr^6 रूपसंपन्ने; GMd^1 चोपपन्ने च — c) Bo wKt^6 Lo^1 GMd^5 Tr^2 *Dev* 5.13 पक्षिणी; Tr^2 रात्री; Bo रात्रीं; *Dev* 5.13 रात्रिः

82.* Pādas c-d omitted in Ox^3. Pādas a-b cited by *Vij* 3.25; *Apa* 915; *Dev* 5.44; and pādas c-d by *Apa* 913 — a) MTr^6 प्रेत; Tj^1 संज्योति° — b) Pu^5 Pu^7 Pu^9 [*Jolly* G] स्याद्विपयेपु च; Lo^3 °द्विपयो; NKt^4 °द्विपसंस्थितः; Ho Hy Jo^1 wKt^1 Kt^2 La^1 Lo^2 TMd^3 GMd^5 NNg oOr Ox^2 Ox^3 NPu^1 Pu^2 Pu^8 Pu^{10} Tr^1 *Vij Dev Mandlik Jolly Jha KSS Dave* स्थितः; wKt^3 स्थितेः; TMd^4 स्थिताः

83. Cited by *Dev* 5.35; *Mādh* 1.579 — a) Be^3 Kt^2 BKt^5 TMd^3 Pu^4 Pu^5 Pu^7 Pu^9 शुद्धेद्विप्रो; Bo शुद्धाद्विप्रो; Tr^2 शुद्ध्याद्विप्रो; Be^1 °द्विप्रा — b) Pu^2 Pu^4 *om* द्वा°; Lo^4 *ma* द्वादशाहेन; Tr^1 द्वादशाहे

न वर्धयेदघाहानि प्रत्यूहेन्नाग्निषु क्रियाः ।
न च तत्कर्म कुर्वाणः सनाभ्योऽप्यशुचिर्भवेत् ॥८४॥

भूमि° ; Pu[5] Pu[7] Pu[9] [*Jolly* G] क्षत्रियः — c) Pu[4] *om* वैश्यः — d) Jm जीवति

Four additional verses in Be[1] MTr[4] *Mandlik KSS Dave;* verses 1, 2, and 4 in GMd[1] TMd[4] GMd[5] NPu[1] MTr[6]; verses 1 and 3 in Ox[2] Pu[8] Tj[1]; verses 2 and 4 in La[1]; verses 2 and 4 placed after 94 in Pu[2] Pu[4]; verse 1 in Be[3] Ho wKt[1] wKt[3] oOr Pu[3]; verse 1 placed after 84 in BKt[5] wKt[6]; verse 4 placed after 92 in Tr[1] and after 104 in TMd[3]; verse 4 cited in *Apa* 906; *Mādh* 1.587:

क्षत्रविट्शूद्रदायादा ये स्युर्विप्रस्य बान्धवाः ।
तेषामशौचे विप्रस्य दशाहाच्छुद्धिरिष्यते ॥१॥
राजन्यवैश्ययोश्चैवं हीनयोनिषु बन्धुषु ।
स्वमेव शौचं कुर्यातां शुध्यर्थं तु न संशयः ॥२॥
विप्रः शुध्येद्दशाहेन जन्महानौ सयोनिषु ।
षड्भिस्त्रिभिरथैकेन क्षत्रविट्शूद्रयोनिषु ॥३॥
सर्वे तूत्तरवर्णानां शौचं कुर्युरतन्द्रिताः ।
तद्वर्णविधिदृष्टेन स्वं तु शौचं स्वयोनिषु ॥४॥

1. a) NPu[1] °दायादैः; Ox[2] °दायादे — b) Be[1] *Mandlik KSS Dave* °दायादाः स्युश्चेद्विप्रस्य; GMd[5] ये तु विप्रस्य; TMd[4] यस्य विप्रस्य; NPu[1] °प्रस्य केचन — c) Pu[8] तेषामाशौचे; Tj[1] MTr[6] तेषामाशौच; wKt[1] MTr[4] °शौच; wKt[3] °शौचा; TMd[4] °शौचं

2. a) La[1] Pu[2] Pu[4] °वैश्यमप्येवं; GMd[1] GMd[5] MTr[4] MTr[6] °वैश्यावप्येवं; NPu[1] °वैश्यावर्ण च — b) NPu[1] °योनिस्थबन्धुषु — c) NPu[1] स्वकीयोनेव शौचेन; Pu[2] Pu[4] स्वकीयेनैव कुर्यातां; Be[1] *Mandlik KSS Dave* कर्वीत; TMd[4] कुर्वीतां — d) Be[1] *Mandlik KSS Dave* विशुद्ध्यर्थमिति स्थितिः; NPu[1] Pu[2] Pu[4] शुद्ध्यन्ते नात्र संशयः; La[1] विशुद्ध्यर्थं न

3. a) Ox[2] Pu[8] Tj[1] दशाहाच्छुध्यते विप्रो — b) Ox[2] °हानि; Ox[2] Tj[1] स्वयोनिषु

4. a) La[1] GMd[5] सर्वेपूत्तम°; MTr[4] MTr[6] सर्वैरुत्तम°; Tr[1] चोत्तम°; Be[1] *Mandlik KSS Dave* चोत्तमवर्णास्तु — b) GMd[5] Tr[1] *Apa Mādh* °वर्णानामाशौचं कुर्युरादृताः [*Apa* °रादितः]; TMd[3] शौचं तु [...] आदृताः; TMd[4] GMd[5] Tr[1] *Apa* °नामाशौचं; Be[1] कुर्यादत°; GMd[1] MTr[6] °रतन्द्रितः; La[1] °रथादृताः — c) GMd[1] स्ववर्णशुद्धिदृष्टेन; MTr[6] स्ववर्ण°; *Mandlik KSS Dave* तद्वर्णं; La[1] सुवर्णविधि°; Tr[1] °दृष्टेषु — c-d) Pu[2] Pu[4] प्रजानां परिरक्षार्थमासनं वात्र कारणं [cf. 94cd] — d) GMd[1] स्वयोनिषु तथैव च; NPu[1] स्वं च; La[1] स्वर्णशौचं; Tr[1] *Apa* स्वं त्वाशौचं; *Mādh* स्वाशौचन्तु

Two additional verses in La[1] oOr; verse 2 also in Be[3] Pu[3]; verse 1 added after 5.63 in TMd[4]:

एकाहाच्छुध्यते विप्रो योऽग्निवेदसमन्वितः ।
त्र्यहात्केवलवेदज्ञो द्विहीनो दशभिर्दिनैः ॥१॥
दशाहाच्छुध्यते विप्रो जन्महानौ स्वयोनिषु ।
षड्भिस्त्रिभिरथैकेन क्षत्रविट्शूद्रयोनिषु ॥२॥

1. d) La[1] [lacuna] द्विही[*ma* नो] दशभिर्दिनैः; oOr विहीतनपश्यतिर्दिनैः

2. c) La[1] त्रिभिः षड्भिस्तथैकेन

84. Omitted in Tr[1]. Cited by *Apa* 891; *Lakṣ* 10.25; pāda-b cited by *Vij* 3.17 — a) Pu[10] *om* न; Be[1] वर्तये°; Tj[1] वर्जये°; Hy वर्धयद°; Be[3] Ho oOr Ox[2] Tj[1] °येद्दशाहानि; wKt[3] °येदघ्याहानि; NPu[1] °येदथाहानि; Pu[4] °येददाहानि; GMd[5] °येदवाहानि — b) wKt[1] Lo[1] TMd[4] प्रत्यूहेना°; Tj[1] प्रत्यून्ना°; *Lakṣ* °हेन्नाग्निप्रक्रियां; Be[1] Ho sOx[1] NPu[1] sPu[6] क्रियां; BBe[2] wKt[6] Lo[1] TMd[3] TMd[4] Pu[2] Pu[4] MTr[6] क्रिया — c) Pu[4] Pu[5] कुर्वाणाः — d) Pu[2] Pu[4] सनाभ्योस्यशु°; GMd[1] सशौचोप्यशु°

दिवाकीर्तिमुदक्यां च पतितं सूतिकां तथा ।
शवं तत्स्पृष्टिनं चैव स्पृष्ट्वा स्नानेन शुध्यति ॥८५॥
आचम्य प्रयतो नित्यं जपेदशुचिदर्शने ।
सौरान्मन्त्रान्यथोत्साहं पावमानीश्च शक्तितः ॥८६॥
नारं स्पृष्ट्वास्थि सस्नेहं स्नात्वा विप्रो विशुध्यति ।
आचम्यैव तु निःस्नेहं गामालभ्यार्कमीक्ष्य वा ॥८७॥
आदिष्टी नोदकं कुर्यादा व्रतस्य समापनात् ।
समाप्ते तूदकं कृत्वा त्रिरात्रेणैव शुध्यति ॥८८॥
वृथासंकरजातानां प्रव्रज्यासु च तिष्ठताम् ।
आत्मनस्त्यागिनां चैव निवर्तेतोदकक्रिया ॥८९॥
पाषण्डमाश्रितानां च चरन्तीनां च कामतः ।
गर्भभर्तृद्रुहां चैव सुरापीनां च योषिताम् ॥९०॥

85. Omitted in Tr[1]. Cited by *Vij* 3.30; *Apa* 921; *Hem* 3/1.796; *Dev* 2.304; *Mādh* 1.228; pādas a-b cited by *Viś* 3.257 — a) NKt[4] Lo[2] MTr[6] *Viś* °कीर्त्यमु°; GMd[5] °कीर्यमु°; La[1] °कीर्तिपूदक्यां — b) Lo[2] पतितां; *Apa* पतितान्सूतिकां; *Hem* सूतिकां पतितं; Bo oOr सूतिकं; GMd[5] MTr[4] सूतकं; TMd[3] सूचिकं; sOx[1] sPu[6] [*cor to*] सूतिकं शवं — c) wKt[6] शैवं; BKt[5] wKt[6] Lo[1] तत्स्पृप्टनं; NNg तत्स्पर्शिनं — d) GMd[5] GMy Tr[2] स्पृप्टा; TMd[3] स्पृष्ट

86. Cited by *Apa* 1198; *Hem* 3/1.796; pādas a-b cited by *Dev* 2.262 — b) MTr[6] चरे अशुचि° — c) TMd[3] GMy MTr[4] MTr[6] *Hem* सौर्यान्म°; Lo[1] *cor to* स्वैरान्म°; TMd[4] °न्यथोत्साहुः — d) sOx[1] पावमानीयश्च; sPu[6] पावनीयश्च [*but cor*]; Ho पावमानांश्च; GMy पावमानींश्च; TMd[3] पावमानीं च; Jm पावमानी च; Be[3] BKt[5] सक्तितः; Jm GMd[1] Tr[1] सर्वशः

87. Pādas a-b omitted in NKt[4], placed here and before 86a in TMd[3]. Cited by *Vij* 3.30; *Apa* 924; *Hem* 3/1.796; *Dev* 2.314 — a) sOx[1] sPu[6] नरं; Bo तं स्नेहं — b) Ox[2] विप्रः स्नात्वा — c) Be[3] TMd[3] [both times] GMy Pu[2] MTr[6] आचम्येव; wKt[3] हि; BKt[5] Lo[1] La[1] TMd[3] [both times] Ox[3] Pu[3] Tr[1] निस्नेहं — d) Lo[2] GMd[1] TMd[3] [at 87] GMd[5] GMy Pu[2] Pu[3] Pu[4] Pu[8] Tr[1] MTr[4] MTr[6] [*Jolly* Gr] *Vij Lakṣ Hem* गां स्पृष्ट्वा वीक्ष्य वा रविं [TMd[3] स्पृष्ट्वा गां]; TMd[3] [at 86] sOx[1] [*but cor*] स्नात्वा विप्रो विशुध्यति [cf. 87b]; La[1] °भ्यार्कं वीक्ष्य; Be[3] wKt[6] La[1] GMd[1] TMd[4] Ox[2] Tj[1] Tr[2] *Apa* च; Ox[3] ता

88. Cited by *Vij* 3.5; *Apa* 876 — a) Pu[5] Tr[1] अदिप्टी; Lo[1] आदिप्टि; TMd[3] MTr[4] आदिप्टे; NPu[1] आदिप्ठा; GMd[1] आदिशि; TMd[3] GMd[1] GMy दद्यादा — c) Be[3] समाप्ये; wKt[1] समाप्तेस्तूदकं; GMd[5] कुर्यात्; BKt[5] wKt[6] गत्वा — d) TMd[3] GMd[5] GMy Tr[1] MTr[4] MTr[6] *Vij Apa* त्रिरात्रमशुचिर्भवेत् [cf. 76b]; Pu[2] Pu[4] त्रिसप्तत्यैव शुध्यति

89. Cited by *Viś* 1.225; *Apa* 877; *Dev* 5.120 — a) NPu[1] La[1] °शंकर°; TMd[3] GMy Tr[1] °संस्कार°; wKt[6] °सङ्गर°; NNg Tr[2] Wa °जातीनां — b) GMd[1] प्रव्रज्यासेविनां तथा; GMd[5] प्रव्रज्यावसिनान्तथा; NPu[1] प्रव्रज्याशुचितिष्ठतां; NNg प्रवृज्यासु; wKt[3] प्रवृप्टासु; Hy *om* च — c) Ho Pu[5] Pu[7] [*but cor*] आत्मान° — d) TMd[4] समाप्तेतोदकक्रिया; GMd[1] °क्रियाः; Tr[2] °क्रियां. After this, two verses are given in the mss. that contain the commentary of *Go*. These are, in all likelihood, part of the commentary.

90. Cited by *Dev* 5.120 — a) oOr sOx[1] sPu[6] पाषाण्ड°; Be[1] पाषण्ड्य°; Be[3] Bo Ho Jo[2] Kt[2] BKt[5] Lo[1] Pu[3] Pu[8] Tj[1] पाखण्ड°; GMd[1] पाषण्डानाश्रि°; TMd[4] पाषण्ड्यनाश्रि° — b) Tr[2] चरन्तीनामकामतः

आचार्यं स्वमुपाध्यायं पितरं मातरं गुरुम् ।
निर्हृत्य तु व्रती प्रेतान्न व्रतेन वियुज्यते ॥९१॥
दक्षिणेन मृतं शूद्रं पुरद्वारेण निर्हरेत् ।
पश्चिमोत्तरपूर्वैस्तु यथायोगं द्विजन्मनः ॥९२॥
न राज्ञामघदोषोऽस्ति व्रतिनां न च सत्त्रिणाम् ।
ऐन्द्रं स्थानमुपासीना ब्रह्मभूता हि ते सदा ॥९३॥
राज्ञो माहात्मिके स्थाने सद्यः शौचं विधीयते ।
प्रजानां परिरक्षार्थमासनं चात्र कारणम् ॥९४॥
डिम्बाहवहतानां च विद्युता पार्थिवेन च ।
गोब्राह्मणस्य चैवार्थे यस्य चेच्छति पार्थिवः ॥९५॥
सोमाग्न्यर्कानिलेन्द्राणां वित्ताप्पत्योर्यमस्य च ।
अष्टानां लोकपालानां वपुर्धारयते नृपः ॥९६॥

— c) Be^{3} °द्रुहं; Tj^{2} °द्रुहोश्चैव; wKt^{1} °द्रुहानां च — d) Pu^{10} सुरापी च; Bo Ho La^{1} Lo^{4} Lo^{5} Ox^{3} Pu^{2} Pu^{3} Pu^{4} Pu^{5} Pu^{7} Pu^{9} °पीणां; Be^{1} NKt^{4} Tj^{2} °पानां; Be^{1} NKt^{4} Pu^{5} योषितं

91. Cited by *Apa* 884; *Dev* 5.97; *Mādh* 1.633 — c) TMd^{4} निहृत्य; wKt^{3} निहृत; Lo^{5} निर्हत्य; TMd^{3} Tr^{1} निहत्य; GMd^{1} निवृत्त; *Apa* निर्हृत्यापि; BCa च; *Dev* तु ब्रह्मचारी न; TMd^{4} व्रत; Bo Lo^{2} TMd^{4} Ox^{2} प्रेतं न; Lo^{5} GMd^{1} प्ररेता न; TMd^{3} प्रीतान्न — d) Tj^{1} प्रेतान्व्रतेन न; Kt^{2} नियुज्यते; Be^{3} wKt^{1} wKt^{3} Tj^{1} विमुच्यते; GMd^{5} विबुध्यते; wKt^{6} विपद्यते

92. Cited by *Apa* 870; *Dev* 5.93; *Mādh* 1.634 — b) TMd^{3} *Dev* पूर्वद्वारेण — c) Be^{3} Bo GMd^{1} Tj^{1} °पूर्वैश्च; oOr Pu^{2} Pu^{4} *Dev* °पूर्वेषु; *Jha Dave* °पूर्वस्तु; Lo^{1} °पूर्वं तु — d) wKt^{6} तथा°; Ho यथायोग्यं; Jm Pu^{5} Pu^{7} Pu^{9} Tr^{1} [*Jolly* G] यथासंख्यं; TMd^{4} यथान्यायं; *Apa* यथावर्णं [vl °वर्णे]; Ho TMd^{3} GMy oOr Tr^{1} MTr^{4} MTr^{6} द्विजन्मनां; Pu^{2} Pu^{4} द्विजोत्तमः; Jm Ox^{2} Ox^{3} Pu^{8} [*Jolly* M] *Apa* द्विजातयः

93. Cited by *Mādh* 1.616 — a) wKt^{6} राज्ञां न प्रदोषोस्ति; Bo °मद्यदोषो — b) GMd^{1} TMd^{3} TMd^{4} GMy oOr MTr^{6} व्रतिनां सत्त्रिणां तथा; [*Jolly* Gr] व्रतितानां च विद्युता; wKt^{6} मन्त्रिणां न; La^{1} च न — c) BBe^{2} Ho Lo^{1} TMd^{3} GMd^{5} Pu^{4} Pu^{5} Pu^{7} Pu^{9} ऐन्द्र; Tr^{1} इन्द्रात्स्थान°; GMd^{1} पदमुपासीना; Be^{3} Lo^{1} TMd^{4} °पासीनां — d) *Nā* [pāṭha] ब्रह्मपूता

94. Pādas c-d omitted in Pu^{2} Pu^{4}. Cited by *Vij* 3.27; *Mādh* 1.616 — a) TMd^{4} राज्ञां; Be^{1} Bo wKt^{3} Lo^{1} TMd^{3} TMd^{4} NNg oOr sOx^{1} Ox^{3} NPu^{1} Pu^{2} Pu^{3} Pu^{4} sPu^{6} Tr^{1} [*Jolly* M$^{1-2-8-9}$ R] *Vij* महात्मिके; Ho Pu^{5} Pu^{7} [*cor to*] Pu^{9} [*Jolly* G] महात्मके; GMy महात्म्यके; GMd^{5} माहात्मिक; GMd^{1} महोच्चके — b) GMy सद्यस्थाने *cor to* सद्यस्थानं; TMd^{3} सद्यस्थानं — c) wKt^{3} पतिरक्षा° — d) Bo Pu^{3} °क्षार्थं शासनं; oOr नात्र; Be^{1} तत्र; Pu^{3} MTr^{3} चात्रकारणं; Tj^{1} कारिणां

95. Cited by *Apa* 916; *Lakṣ* 10.47; *Mādh* 1.626 — a) Tj^{1} अशस्त्रकलहानां च; *Lakṣ* डिम्बाहवे; Tr^{1} डिम्बावह°; Bo डिम्बाहम° — b) Pu^{3} Wa पार्थिवैर्द्विजैः — c) Lo^{2} oOr °ब्राह्मस्य; oOr दैवार्थे — d) Tj^{1} चेच्छन्ति; GMd^{1} sOx^{1} sPu^{6} पार्थिवाः; TMd^{3} GMy Pu^{2} Pu^{4} *Mādh* भूमिपः

96. a) oOr सोमोग्न्य°; TMd^{3} GMy सोमाग्न्यर्कोनि°; Lo^{3} °र्कानले°; Jo^{2} °लेन्दूनां — b) Be^{1} Bo वित्तापत्यो°; MTr^{6} वित्तपत्यो°; TMd^{4} वित्तपत्यु°; Lo^{2} वित्तप्यन्यो°; Tr^{1} वित्ताप्यत्यो°; wKt^{6} पिताप्पत्यो°; wKt^{1} वित्तपस्य यमस्य; Tj^{1} वित्तापस्य यमस्य; NPu^{1} वित्तपानां यमस्य; Pu^{2} Pu^{4} धनदापयोयमस्य — d) oOr मात्राभिर्निर्मितो नृपः; MTr^{6} वपुर्धारयेते; sOx^{1} sPu^{6} मूर्तिं धारयते

लोकेशाधिष्ठितो राजा नास्याशौचं विधीयते ।
शौचाशौचं हि मर्त्यानां लोकेशप्रभवाप्ययम् ॥९७॥
उद्यतैराहवे शस्त्रैः क्षत्रधर्महतस्य च ।
सद्यः संतिष्ठते यज्ञस्तथा शौचमिति स्थितिः ॥९८॥
विप्रः शुध्यत्यपः स्पृष्ट्वा क्षत्रियो वाहनायुधम् ।
वैश्यः प्रतोदं रश्मीन्वा यष्टिं शूद्रः कृतक्रियः ॥९९॥
एतद्वोऽभिहितं शौचं सपिण्डेषु द्विजोत्तमाः ।
असपिण्डेषु सर्वेषु प्रेतशुद्धिं निबोधत ॥१००॥
असपिण्डं द्विजं प्रेतं विप्रो निर्हृत्य बन्धुवत् ।
विशुध्यति त्रिरात्रेण मातुराप्तांश्च बान्धवान् ॥१०१॥
यद्यन्नमत्ति तेषां तु दशाहेनैव शुध्यति ।
अनदन्नन्नमह्नैव न चेत्तस्मिन् गृहे वसेत् ॥१०२॥

97. a) Ho TMd^{4} OOr लोकेशो°; TMd^{4} °धिष्ठितां राज्ञा — b) TMd^{4} नस्या°; BKt^{5} Lo^{1} GMd^{1} MTr^{6} नास्य शौचं — c) TMd^{4} शौचाशौचे; sOx^{1} sPu^{6} Tj^{1} च; NNg हि लोकानां — d) La^{1} Pu^{10} लोकेशं; wKt^{3} Lo^{4} Lo^{5} Ox^{3} Pu^{10} [*Jolly* M] °वाप्ययौ; La^{1} °वाप्यहं; Be^{1} Pu^{5} Pu^{7} Pu^{9} [*Jolly* G] *Rn* °वात्ययं; NPu^{1} °वाह्ययं; Be^{3} Bo BKt^{5} Lo^{2} TMd^{3} NNg Pu^{2} Pu^{3} Pu^{4} Tj^{1} Tr^{1} MTr^{4} MTr^{6} [*Jolly* N Nd] °वोह्ययं; TMd^{4} GMy sOx^{1} sPu^{6} Tr^{2} °वोप्ययं; *Nā* [pāṭha] °वोप्ययः; Tj^{2} °वोस्ययं; Ho °वोद्वयं; Ox^{2} °वोत्ययं; OOr °वोक्षयः

98. Omitted in Ox^{3}. Cited by *Vij* 3.21; *Apa* 916 — a) Pu^{2} Pu^{4} उद्यतेरा°; Lo^{2} MTr^{6} °राहवै; wKt^{3} °राहते; TMd^{3} °राहवैश्शस्त्रैः; Lo^{5} MTr^{3} शास्त्रैः — b) TMd^{4} हन्यमानस्य धर्मतः; Lo^{2} °मृतस्य; La^{1} GMd^{1} तु — c) Be^{1} सद्या; TMd^{4} संतिष्ठतौ; GMd^{1} यज्ञैस्तथा; Lo^{1} यज्ञे तथा; sOx^{1} sPu^{6} राज्ञस्तथा [*but both cor*] — d) NPu^{1} Wa यज्ञो नास्य शौचमिति [NPu^{1} यज्ञे]; TMd^{3} TMd^{4} GMd^{5} GMy MTr^{4} MTr^{6} शौचमपि; Pu^{2} यज्ञमिति; GMd^{1} TMd^{3} TMd^{4} GMd^{5} GMy Tr^{1} MTr^{4} MTr^{6} स्मृतं

99. Cited by *Vij* 3.28–9; *Lakṣ* 10.106 — a) TMd^{4} *Lakṣ* शुध्येदपः — c) BBe^{2} प्रतोदो; TMd^{3} प्रतोद; sOx^{1} sPu^{6} [*mc sh to*] प्रचोदं; Tr^{2} प्रदोदं; Pu^{9} प्रयोदं; Be^{3} Bo sOx^{1} sPu^{6} Tj^{1} *Lakṣ* रश्मींश्च; wKt^{1} रश्मिन्वा; Be^{1} Lo^{5} Pu^{5} Pu^{7} Pu^{9} Pu^{10} Tr^{1} Tr^{2} Wa [*Jolly* M G] रश्मिं वा; Pu^{2} Pu^{4} रश्मि वा; TMd^{3} GMd^{5} GMy रज्जुं वा — d) Tj^{1} दण्डं; NPu^{1} Pu^{2} Pu^{4} °क्रियाः

100. Pādas c-d omitted in Bo Pu^{4} — a) TMd^{4} येतद्वो; Tr^{1} °भिहतं; GMd^{1} OOr NPu^{1} Tr^{2} °विहितं; Tj^{1} °पहितं; Bo [*but cor*] °हितं सर्वं शौचं; TMd^{3} GMy Pu^{4} MTr^{4} MTr^{6} °हितं सर्वं; Pu^{2} °हितं सर्वां — b) GMy सपिण्डेषान्द्वि°; Lo^{5} TMd^{3} द्विजोत्तमः — c) GMd^{1} असपिण्डेष्वसर्वेपु — d) TMd^{4} प्रेतकां च निबो°; Tj^{1} Tr^{1} °शुद्धिर्निबो°; GMy °शुद्धिनिबोधता; wKt^{3} निबोधितः

101. Cited by *Vij* 3.14; *Apa* 883, 913; *Dev* 5.95; *Mādh* 1.631 — a) TMd^{3} असपिण्ड; *Apa* 883 नासपिण्डं; MTr^{6} द्विजः — b) NNg द्विजो; BBe^{2} Bo Ho Lo^{5} निर्हत्य; Lo^{1} निर्हर्त्य — c) OOr विशुध्यन्ति — d) wKt^{6} °राप्तश्च; GMd^{1} बान्धवाः

102. Verses 102 and 103 transposed in GMd^{1}. Cited by *Vij* 3.14; *Apa* 883; *Dev* 5.95; *Mādh* 1.632 — a) Lo^{1} NNg यदन्न° — a-b) TMd^{3} TMd^{4} GMd^{5} GMy Tr^{1} MTr^{4} MTr^{6} *DevMādh* तेषां यः स दशाहेन शुध्यति [*Dev* हि स] — b) GMd^{1} sOx^{1} sPu^{6} दशाहेन विशुध्यति; Pu^{2} Pu^{4} दशरात्रेण शुध्यति — c) Wa अनदन्त्वन्नम°; GMd^{5} GMy °मह्नेव — c-d) GMd^{1} शुभमन्नमदन्नेव तस्मिन्नेव गृहे वसेत् — d) BKt^{5} wKt^{6} तस्मिन्नापि गृहे वसन् [wKt^{6} वसेन्]; NPu^{1} Pu^{5} Pu^{7} Pu^{9} तस्मिन्नेव गृहे वसेत्; NKt^{4} तस्मिन्न

अनुगम्येच्छया प्रेतं ज्ञातिमज्ञातिमेव वा ।
स्नात्वा सचैलः स्पृष्ट्वाग्निं घृतं प्राश्य विशुध्यति ॥१०३॥
न विप्रं स्वेषु तिष्ठत्सु मृतं शूद्रेण नाययेत् ।
अस्वर्ग्या ह्याहुतिः सा स्याच्छूद्रसंस्पर्शदूषिता ॥१०४॥
ज्ञानं तपोऽग्निराहारो मृन्मनो वार्युपाञ्जनम् ।
वायुः कर्मार्ककालौ च शुद्धेः कर्तृणि देहिनाम् ॥१०५॥
सर्वेषामेव शौचानामर्थशौचं परं स्मृतम् ।

च गृहे वसेत्; TMd[4] तस्मिन्न गृहे वसेत्; Lo[1] न य तस्मिन्; TMd[3] GMy Tr[1] MTr[4] MTr[6] न च तस्मिन्

Additional verse in Be[3] BCa Ho GMd[1] GMd[4] GMd[5] Pu[3] Tj[1] MTr[4] MTr[6] [*Jolly* Gr]; given after 104 in La[1] TMd[4]:

अवरश्चेद्वरं वर्णमवरं वा वरो यदि ।
आशौचे संस्पृशेत्स्नेहात् तस्य शौचेन शुध्यति ॥

a) GMd[5] अवरश्चेत्परो वर्णम° ; TMd[4] MTr[4] MTr[6] अपरश्चे° — a-b) [*Jolly* Gr] अपरं चेत्परो वर्णो अपरे वा परो यदि — b) GMd[1] वर्णं वरं वावरदो यदि; MTr[4] MTr[6] °मपरं वा परो; TMd[4] च; Be[3] चावरं यदि; GMd[5] परो यदि — c) La[1] TMd[4] संस्पृशन्तु शवं मोहात् [TMd[4] संस्पृशेत्तु]; Ho Tj[1] अशौचे; Be[3] न शौच; Pu[3] अशौचं स स्पृशे° ; GMd[5] आशौचेपु स्पृशे° ; GMd[1] संस्पृशेत्स्नेहात्; MTr[6] संस्पृशन्स्नेहात्; Ho Tj[1] संविशेत्स्नेहात्; Be[3] संवसेत्स्नेहात्; BCa संस्पृशेन्मोहात् — d) Be[3] GMd[5] तस्याशौचेन

103. Cited by *Vij* 3.26; *Apa* 918; *Lakṣ*10.56 — b) Tr[2] ज्ञातिज्ञातिमेव; Be[1] Bo Jm Jo[1] Kt[2] Lo[1] Lo[4] Lo[5] TMd[3] Ox[3] NPu[1] Pu[3] Pu[8] Pu[10] Tj[1] Tr[2] [*Jolly* M Nd] *Vij Mandlik Jha KSS Dave* च — c) Jm *om* स्नात्वा; Be[1] BBe[2] Ho Jo[2] NKt[4] TMd[3] sOx[1] Ox[2] Pu[2] Pu[4] Pu[5] sPu[6] Pu[7] Pu[9] Tj[1] Tr[2] *Me Lakṣ Apa Dave Jha* सचैलं; BCa Jo[1] wKt[1] Kt[2] oOr MTr[6] सचेलः; wKt[3] BKt[5] wKt[6] GMd[1] TMd[4] GMd[5] GMy Tr[1] सचेलं; Ox[3] स्पृष्टाग्निं— d) wKt[1] Tj[1] Tr[2] प्रास्य; Ox[2] प्राश्य ततः शुचिः

104. Cited by *Vij* 3.1–2; *Apa* 870;*Dev* 5.97; *Mādh* 1.634 — a) Ox[3] NPu[1] विप्र; Lo[4] Lo[5] विप्रः — b) La[1] Lo[1] Tj[1] नापयेत्; wKt[1] नानयेत्; Be[3] Bo Ho Lo[2] TMd[3] TMd[4] GMd[5] GMy Ox[2] Pu[3] Pu[8] Tj[2] Tr[1] Tr[2] *Vij Mādh* हारयेत्; oOr *Dev* वाहयेत्; Hy भाजयेत्; MTr[4] MTr[6] निर्हरेत् — c) sOx[1] sPu[6] अस्वर्ग्या गर्हिता सा — d) TMd[3] Pu[2] Pu[4] °च्छूद्रः; Be[3] Bo °संपर्कदूषितः; *Vij* °संपर्कदूषिता; wKt[6] °संपर्कभूरिता; La[1] TMd[4] °दूषिताः; Wa °दूष्यता; Tr[2] °गर्हिता

Additional verse in La[1]:

यस्तु प्रेतगतं शूद्रं ब्राह्मणो ज्ञानदुर्बलः ।
अनुगच्छेन्नीयमानं त्रिभिः कृच्छ्रैर्विशुध्यति ॥

105. Pādas c-d omitted in NKt[4]. Cited by *Hem* 3/1.792; *Bh* ad 11.235— a) Be[3] wKt[1] TMd[3] GMy तपो निराहारो; MTr[3] °ग्निराचारो; Bo °हारौ — b) Bo BKt[5] wKt[6] TMd[4] GMd[5] Pu[10] Tr[2] *Hem* मृण्मयो; TMd[3] मृण्मयोर्वार्यु° ; Hy वाप्युपा° ; wKt[1] La[1] Tr[1] वार्यपाञ्जनं; Pu[2] Pu[4] वार्युपार्जनं; BBe[2] वार्युपासनं — c) wKt[1] कर्मार्ककाशौचं शुद्धेः; GMy °कौलौ — d) *Hem* शुद्धि; TMd[3] शुद्धिकर्ता हि; Tj[1] शुद्ध्येत्कर्तृणि; Pu[2] Pu[3] Pu[4] कर्तृणि; Lo[1] कर्तृहि; BBe[2] GMy कर्मणि

Additional verse in Be[1] Be[3] Ho Tj[1]:

मृत्पर्णतृणकाष्ठानां चण्डालान्त्यश्ववायसैः ।
स्पर्शने विहितं शौचं सोमसूर्याग्निमारुतैः ॥

b) Ho चाण्डा° — c) Be[1] स्पर्शेन — d) Be[3] Tj[1] °सूर्यांशुमारुतैः

योऽर्थे शुचिर्हि स शुचिर्न मृद्वारिशुचिः शुचिः ॥१०६॥
क्षान्त्या शुध्यन्ति विद्वांसो दानेनाकार्यकारिणः ।
प्रच्छन्नपापा जप्येन तपसा वेदवित्तमाः ॥१०७॥
मृत्तोयैः शुध्यते शोध्यं नदी वेगेन शुध्यति ।
रजसा स्त्री मनोदुष्टा संन्यासेन द्विजोत्तमाः ॥१०८॥
अद्भिर्गात्राणि शुध्यन्ति मनः सत्येन शुध्यति ।
विद्यातपोभ्यां भूतात्मा बुद्धिर्ज्ञानेन शुध्यति ॥१०९॥
एष शौचस्य वः प्रोक्तः शारीरस्य विनिर्णयः ।
नानाविधानां द्रव्याणां शुद्धेः शृणुत निर्णयम् ॥११०॥
तैजसानां मणीनां च सर्वस्याश्ममयस्य च ।
भस्मनाद्भिर्मृदा चैव शुद्धिरुक्ता मनीषिभिः ॥१११॥
निर्लेपं काञ्चनं भाण्डमद्भिरेव विशुध्यति ।
अब्जमश्ममयं चैव राजतं चानुपस्कृतम् ॥११२॥

106. Omitted in Pu^{9}. Cited by *Hem* 3/1.792; *Lakṣ* 10.114 — a) *Lakṣ* सर्वेषामपि; sOx^{1} sPu^{6} [*Jolly* Nd] वर्णानामर्थ° — b) Lo^{4} [*cor to*] Lo^{5} °मन्त्रशौचं; MTr^{6} °शौच; MTr^{4} °शौचः; wKt^{1} स्मृतं परं; MTr^{4} MTr^{6} स्मृतः — c) TMd^{4} योर्थ; Lo^{4} योन्ने; Lo^{5} योन्ये; GMy योर्थैश्शुचि°; Bo NNg योर्थे हि शुचिः स; Be^{3} Jo^{2} Lo^{3} sOx^{1} sPu^{6} Tj^{1} योर्थे शुचिः स हि [Tj^{1} योर्थः]; Hy शुचिः स ह; oOr शुचिः स तु; Ho *om* हि; Tr^{2} *om* स — d) GMd^{1} न च मृद्वारिभिः शुचिः; GMy न मृद्वार्यशुचेश्शुचिः; Pu^{2} *om last* शुचिः

107. Omitted in Pu^{9}. Cited by *Hem* 3/1.792 — a) wKt^{1} क्षान्ताः — c) MTr^{4} °पापं; Bo °पापाज्जप्येन; Pu^{10} जाप्येन — d) NPu^{1} La^{1} देववि°; Tr^{2} °वित्तमः

108.* Omitted in Pu^{9}; pādas c-d omitted in Be^{3} GMd^{1} [haplo]. Cited by *Hem* 3/1.792; *Lakṣ* 10.114; *Mādh* 1.533, 2.116; pāda-a cited by *Viś* 1.195, and pāda-c by *Apa* 98 — a) *Lakṣ Hem* शोध्यं शुध्यति मृत्तयैर्नदी; Ho शुध्यति; NKt^{4} Tj^{1} MTr^{4} MTr^{6} *Viś* शोध्यते — b) BKt^{5} wKt^{6} नदी तोयेन; Lo^{1} sOx^{1} sPu^{6} शोध्यते — d) Bo Hy Jm Jo^{1} Kt^{2} wKt^{3} NKt^{4} Lo^{1} Lo^{4} Lo^{5} TMd^{4} GMd^{5} GMy Ox^{2} Tr^{1} Tr^{2} MTr^{3} *Lakṣ Hem Mādh Mandlik Jolly KSS* द्विजोत्तमः

109. Omitted in GMd^{1} Pu^{9}; pādas a-b omitted in Be^{3}. Cited by *Hem* 3/1.792; *Bh* (ad 11.235) — a) Be^{1} अद्भिः शुध्यन्ति गात्राणि; NPu^{1} अद्भिर्मन्त्राणि; Pu^{5} Pu^{7} शुध्यन्ते — b) Tr^{1} सत्वेन; GMy सत्येत्वशु°; wKt^{3} शुध्यंति — c) NNg भूतात्म; GMd^{5} भूतानि — d) Ox^{3} बुद्धिज्ञानेन; Tj^{1} बुद्धिर्ज्ञानात्

110. Omitted in TMd^{4}; not commented by *Nd;* pādas a-b and c-d transposed in Lo^{4} Lo^{5} Ox^{3}. Cited by *Hem* 3/1.805 — a) TMd^{3} एषा; Tr^{1} एषां; NKt^{4} एतः; Be^{3} BCa Pu^{3} Pu^{8} Tr^{2} शौचविधिः प्रोक्तः; NKt^{4} GMd^{1} यः — b) Be^{3} Hy wKt^{1} BKt^{5} wKt^{6} Lo^{3} Lo^{4} Lo^{5} oMd^{2} TMd^{3} GMd^{5} GMy Ox^{2} Ox^{3} Pu^{8} Pu^{10} Tj^{1} MTr^{3} MTr^{4} शरीरस्य; NKt^{4} विनिर्णेयः; TMd^{3} विनिर्णयं; [*Jolly* Gr] विनिर्दिशेत् — d) Tj^{1} शुद्धः; TMd^{3} शुद्धि; Bo शुद्धेऽशृणुत; Jm शृण्वत; Hy Pu^{2} Pu^{3} Pu^{4} Pu^{5} Pu^{7} Pu^{9} निर्णयः; Tj^{1} निर्णय

111. Omitted in TMd^{4}. Cited by *Vij* 182–3; *Apa* 255; *Hem* 3/1.805; *Mādh* 2.134 — a) Pu^{4} Pu^{10} Tr^{1} तेजसानां; NKt^{4} तैजसाजां — b) TMd^{3} GMy कांस्यस्याश्ममयस्य च — c) TMd^{3} भस्मना च मृदा — d) Bo शुद्धेरुक्ता; wKt^{6} मणीषिभिः; GMd^{5} मजर्षिभिः

112. Pādas a-b omitted in TMd^{4}. Cited by *Viś* 1.181; *Vij* 1.182–3; *Apa* 254; *Hem* 3/1.805; *Mādh* 2.134 — a) NKt^{4} निर्लपे; Pu^{2} Pu^{4} निर्लेपनं — c) TMd^{3} Pu^{8} अजम°; NKt^{4} प्रकुमश्म°; Be^{3} आब्ज-

अग्रेश्चापां च संयोगाद्धेम रूप्यं च निर्बभौ ।
तस्मात्तयोः स्वयोन्यैव निर्णेको गुणवत्तरः ॥११३॥
ताम्रायःकांस्यरैत्यानां त्रपुणः सीसकस्य च ।
शौचं यथार्हं कर्तव्यं क्षाराम्लोदकवारिभिः ॥११४॥
द्रवाणां चैव सर्वेषां शुद्धिरुत्पवनं स्मृतम् ।
प्रोक्षणं संहतानां च दारवाणां च तक्षणम् ॥११५॥
मार्जनं यज्ञपात्राणां पाणिना यज्ञकर्मणि ।
चमसानां ग्रहाणां च शुद्धिः प्रक्षालनेन तु ॥११६॥

मार्णमयं; sOx^1 sPu^6 वापि — d) GMd^1 TMd^4 रजतं; Ho BKt^5 wKt^6 वानुप°; TMd^3 चाप्यनुस्कृतं; Tr^1 °पस्करं

113.* Cited by *Hem* 3/1.805; *Lakṣ* 10.133 — a) La Lo^4 Lo^5 GMd ^{1} GMd^5 Ox^3 अग्रेश्चापांश्च; Be^1 BBe^2 BCa wKt^1 Lo^1 TMd^3 GMy NNg oOr [*Jolly* Nd] अग्नेरपां च; Be^1 GMy अग्नेरपांश्च; Be^3 Bo Ho Hy Jm Jo^1 Jo^2 Kt^2 wKt^3 BKt^5 wKt^6 Lo^2 Lo^3 TMd^4 Ox^2 Pu^2 Pu^5 Pu^7 Pu^8 Pu^9 Tj^1 Tj^2 Tr^2 *Lakṣ Nā Mandlik Jolly Jha KSS Dave* अपामग्नेश्च — b) wKt^3 NKt^4 GMd^1 TMd^4 GMd ^{5} Pu^2 Tr^1 MTr^4 MTr^6 Wa °गाद्धेमं; BCa Hy Jm Jo^1 Jo^2 Kt^2 La^1 Lo^3 oOr sOx^1 Ox^2 sPu^6 Tj^2 Tr^2 MTr^3 *Rc Mandlik Jha KSS* °गाद्धैमं; BCa Hy Jm Jo^1 Kt^2 sOx^1 Ox^2 sPu^6 Tj^2 Tr^2 MTr^3 *Rc Mandlik Jha KSS* रौप्यं; Be^1 oOr Wa रोप्यं; NKt^4 La^1 oOr संबभौ — c) Bo तस्मात्तयोस्तयोर्नैव; Lo^2 स्वयोनेव; *Me* [pāṭha] सयोन्यैव; TMd^3 स्वयोश्चैव — d) NKt^4 TMd^3 GMy निर्लेपो; NKt^4 गुणवत्ततः; TMd^3 GMd^5 GMy Tr^1 MTr^4 MTr^6 [*Jolly* Gr Nd] बलवत्तरः

114. Cited by *Vij* 1.190; *Hem* 3/1.805; pāda-c cited by *Viś* 1.195 — a) BKt^5 तम्रायः°; sOx^1 sPu^6 °कांस्यलोहानां; Tr^2 °रैप्यानां; TMd^3 TMd^4 GMd^5 Tr^1 MTr^4 MTr^6 [*Jolly* Nd] °रूप्याणां; GMy [*Jolly* Gr] रूपाणां; Bo NKt^4 Lo^5 GMd^1 NPu^1 Pu^3 Pu^4 Pu^{10} [*Jolly* M$^{1-2-5-8-9}$] *Hem* °रौप्याणां — b) Tr^1 त्रपुंसीसकयोरपि; wKt^6 त्रपुनः; Lo^1 त्रपुषः; Bo त्रपुत्रा; wKt^3 शीशकस्य; La^1 शीसकस्य; Be^3 सिसीकस्य; Pu^2 Pu^4 सीकस्य; Hy सीत्यकस्य; [*Jolly* G] वा — c) Pu^{10} यथार्हः; Bo NKt^4 यथार्थं; *Viś* कार्यं — d) TMd^4 °दकवह्निभिः

115. Pādas c-d omitted in wKt^1. Cited by *Hem* 3/1.805; pādas a-b cited by *Vij* 1.190— a) Ho wKt^1 NKt^4 Lo^5 GMd^1 TMd^3 TMd^4 GMd ^{5} GMy sOx^1 Pu^2 Pu^4 sPu^6 MTr^4 MTr^6 द्रव्याणां; Bo सर्वाणां — b) GMy शुद्धिस्तूत्पवनं; Ho शुद्धिस्तु प्लावनं; BBe^2 °रुत्पावनं; TMd^3 °रुत्पदनं; Be^1 Be^3 wKt^1 wKt^3 NNg sOx^1 NPu^1 Pu^2 Pu^4 Pu^5 sPu^6 Pu^7 Pu^9 Tr^2 [*Jolly* G] *Rc Mr Go* °रुत्प्लवनं; Jo^1 Kt^2 °राप्लावनं; Pu^{10} °रुत्काचनं — c) NKt^4 संहितानां; TMd^3 साहितानां; Lo^2 GMd ^{1} GMd^5 Pu^3 Pu^8 Tr^1 MTr^4 MTr^6 तु— c-d) NPu^1 प्रोक्षणं चैव सर्वेषां संहतानां च तक्षणं — d) Pu^2 Pu^4 दारकाणां; TMd^3 तारकाणां; TMd^4 दारूणां चैव; Tr^1 MTr^4 MTr^6 तु; Pu ^{5} Pu ^{7} Pu ^{9} तक्षणां; Bo La^1 GMy Tr^1 तत्क्षणं

Additional verse in GMd^1 TMd^3 Tr^1 [this is cited by *Nd* and ascribed to Aṅgiras]:

शयनासनयानानि रोमबद्धानि यानि च ।
वस्त्राणि तानि सर्वाणि संहतानि प्रचक्षते ॥

a) TMd^3 रोमबंधानि

TMd^3 places verse 121 here.

116. Omitted in wKt^1. Cited by *Hem* 3/1.805; *Mādh* 2.114 — a) La मार्जानं; TMd^4 °पत्राणां — b) wKt^6 यस्यकर्मणि; NKt^4 °कर्मभि — c) Tj ^{1} चमसानां च सर्वेषां; Ox^3 ग्रहणां; Pu^2 Pu^4 गृहाणां; Lo^1 sOx^1 sPu ^{6} तु — d) GMy शुद्धिं; Tr^1 प्रक्षालणानि; oOr प्रक्षालणे ततः; Be^3 Bo Ho Jo^2 La^1 Lo^3 TMd^4 Tj^1 Tj^2 Tr^1 [*Jolly* R] च; sOx^1 sPu^6 वै

चरूणां स्रुक्स्रुवाणां च शुद्धिरुष्णेन वारिणा ।
स्फ्यशूर्पशकटानां च मुसलोलूखलस्य च ॥११७॥
अद्भिस्तु प्रोक्षणं शौचं बहूनां धान्यवाससाम् ।
प्रक्षालनेन त्वल्पानामद्भिः शौचं विधीयते ॥११८॥
चैलवच्चर्मणां शुद्धिर्वैदलानां तथैव च ।
शाकमूलफलानां च धान्यवच्छुद्धिरिष्यते ॥११९॥
कौशेयाविकयोरूषैः कुतपानामरिष्टकैः ।
श्रीफलैरंशुपट्टानां क्षौमाणां गौरसर्षपैः ॥१२०॥
क्षौमवच्छङ्खशृङ्गाणामस्थिदन्तमयस्य च ।
शुद्धिर्विजानता कार्या गोमूत्रेणोदकेन वा ॥१२१॥

Additional verse in [*Jolly* Gr]; placed after pāda-b in GMd[5]:

कमण्डलूनां च तथा विप्राणां ब्रह्मचारिणाम् ।
हुतेऽग्नौ ब्राह्मणस्यापि तत्त्वतः श्रूयते श्रुतिः ।।

c) GMd[5] हस्तेग्नि ब्राह्मणस्येति

117. Cited by *Hem* 3/1.806; *Mādh* 2.114 — a) Ho चरुणांस्तु श्रुवाणां च; Bo चरुणा च; TMd[3] वणां स्रुक्स्रु°; wKt[1] NKt[4] La[1] oOr Ox[3] श्रुक्श्रु°; Ox[2] स्रुक्स्रुवादीनां शुद्धि°; Tr[2] तु — b) Pu[3] शुद्धिस्तप्तेन — c) Pu[5] Pu[7] Pu[9] स्फासूर्प; Tr[2] स्फ्याशुर्य°; GMd[1] MTr[4] स्फ्यसूर्य°; sOx[1] sPu[6] स्फ्यस्थर्प°; NPu[1] स्युःशूर्प°; Pu[3] स्युसूर्प°; Ho स्यात्सूर्य°; wKt[6] स्वसूर्प°; BKt[5] La[1] Lo[1] oOr °सूर्प°; BKt[5] wKt[6] °सकटानां; Pu[2] Pu[4] °शकलानां; Tr[1] °कटकानां — d) BKt[5] मूसलोमूषलस्य वा; Ho La[1] oOr Ox[3] NPu[1] Pu[3] Pu[5] Pu[7] Pu[8] Pu[9] Wa मुश°; BCa wKt[1] wKt[6] मुष°; Pu[5] Pu[7] Pu[9] °लूषलस्य; NNg दूषलस्य; wKt[6] °दूषणस्य वा

118.* Cited by *Vij* 1.184; *Hem* 3/1.806; *Mādh* 2.136 — a) Pu[5] Pu[7] Pu[9] अद्भिस्तत्प्रोक्षणं; Lo[3] प्रोक्षणे; oOr प्रोक्षणं किंचिद् — c) *Hem* प्राक्षा°; Lo[1] Pu[10] तल्पाना°; GMy Ox[2] Pu[2] Pu[4] स्वल्पाना° — d) GMd[1] *Hem* °मद्भिरेव विधीयते; Lo[3] विशिष्यते

*Additional verse in Be[3] Bo Tj[1] *Mandlik* [ज, झ] *KSS;* added after 126 in GMd[1] TMd[4], and after 128b in MTr[4] MTr[6]:

अहतक्रीतसिक्तानां वाससां शुद्धिरिष्यते ।
पर्युक्षणाद्धूपनाच्च मलिनानां तु धावनात् ।।

a) Tj[1] अर्धं कृतं तु शौचानां; Be[3] अर्हकृतशौचानां तु; *Mandlik KSS* त्र्यहकृतशौचानां तु; MTr[4] MTr[6] °शिक्तं वा; TMd[4] °निक्तानां — b) Be[3] वायसां; Bo *Mandlik KSS* वायसी — c) Bo Tj[1] *Mandlik KSS* °पनाद्वा; TMd[4] °पनं च — d) Be[3] Tj[1] मलिनां चैव धावनात्; *Mandlik KSS* मलिनामतिधावनात्; Bo मलिनां दन्तधावनात्; TMd[4] मलीनां च पावनात्

119. Cited by *Hem* 3/1.806; *Mādh* 2.139 — a) BCa Jo[1] BKt[5] GMd[1] TMd[4] GMy NPu[1] Pu[2] MTr[6] Wa [*Jolly* Nd] *Hem* चेल°; oOr तेनेव चर्मणां — b) GMd[5] Tr[1] °बैंदलानां; Bo Lo[3] °वेंदलानां; Be[1] GMd[1] NNg Pu[2] Pu[4] °विंदलानां; wKt[6] °र्वदनानां; wKt[1] °र्वैकुलांच — c) NKt[4] Lo[4] Lo[5] GMd[1] Pu[10] *Dave Jha* तु — d) La[1] °वच्छौचमिष्यते; GMd[1] °वच्छुचिरिष्यते; *Hem* °द्धिरिष्टकैः

120. Cited by *Hem* 3/1.806; *Mādh* 2.138 — a) Tj[1] काशेयाविकयोः शोषैः; Lo[5] Tr[2] कोशेयावि°; TMd[3] काश्मेयोवि°; Lo[1] °योरुष्यैः; *Mādh* °योर्मापैः — b) Tr[2] कुतकानां°; Tj[1] °मारिष्टकैः — c) Jo[1] °भट्टानां; wKt[1] °पत्रानां; Bo Ho Pu[2] Pu[4] °पादानां — d) wKt[1] श्वेतसर्षपैः

121. Placed after 115 in TMd[3]. Cited by *Apa* 260; *Hem* 3/1.806; *Mādh* 2.138 — a) GMy °वच्छागशृ°; Be[3] Tj[1] °वच्छृङ्गशङ्खानाम° — b) NKt[4] तु — c) Lo[4] °र्विजनता; wKt[6] °र्विजयिता — d) Be[3]

प्रोक्षणात्तृणकाष्ठानि पलालं च विशुध्यति ।
मार्जनोपाञ्जनैर्वेश्म पुनःपाकेन मृन्मयम् ॥१२२॥
संमार्जनेनाञ्जनेन सेकेनोल्लेखनेन च ।
गवां च परिवासेन भूमिः शुध्यति पञ्चभिः ॥१२४॥
पक्षिजग्धं गवा घ्रातमवधूतमवक्षुतम् ।
दूषितं केशकीटैश्च मृत्प्रक्षेपेण शुध्यति ॥१२५॥

Ho NKt[4] Pu[2] Pu[3] Pu[8] Tj[1] *Apa* च

122.* Cited by *Hem* 3/1.806 — a) Tj[1] प्रोक्षणं तृण°; Ho NPu[1] Tj[1] *Hem* °काष्ठानां; Be[1] BBe[2] Bo Hy Jm Jo[1] Jo[2] Kt[2] BKt[5] wKt[6] Lo[2] Lo[3] Lo[4] Lo[5] NNg Ox[3] Pu[2] Pu[5] Pu[7] Pu[8] Pu[9] Pu[10] Tj[2] Tr[2] Wa *Mandlik Jolly Jha KSS Dave* °काष्ठं च — b) Bo पालाशं; TMd[3] पलाकं; oOr फलानां; BBe[2] Be[3] Bo Hy Jm Jo[1] Jo[2] Kt[2] wKt[3] Lo[1] Lo[3] Lo[4] Lo[5] oOr sOx[1] Ox[2] Ox[3] Pu[2] Pu[5] sPu[6] Pu[7] Pu[8] Pu[9] Pu[10] Tj[1] Tj[2] *Mandlik Jolly Jha KSS Dave* चैव शुध्यति — c) NPu[1] °नोलेखनै°; Pu[5] Pu[7] Pu[9] [*Jolly* G] °नोल्लेषणै°; GMd[1] °नोल्लेपनै°; Be[1] TMd[3] oOr Tj[1] °नोपार्जनै° — d) Ho °पाके महीमयं; Be[1] wKt[1] Kt[2] wKt[3] wKt[6] TMd[3] sOx[1] sPu[6] Tr[1] मृण्मयं; GMd[5] °मयः

*This spurious verse is found in all but the following mss.: NKt[4] BKt[5] wKt[6] [*but ma*] Lo[4] Lo[5] GMd[1] TMd[3] GMd[5] GMy NNg Ox[3] Pu[10] Tr[1] MTr[4] MTr[6] Wa [*Jolly* Nd], and given in editions [except *Jha*] as verse 123 [see endnote] and cited by *Vij* 1.187; *Apa* 263. Placed after verse 126 in Bo, which omits pādas c-d. I have eliminated the number 123 from the edition to maintain the traditional numbering of the verses:

मद्यैर्मूत्रपुरीषैर्वा ष्ठीवनैः पूयशोणितैः ।
संस्पृष्टं नैव शुध्येत पुनःपाकेन मृन्मयम् ॥

a) TMd[4] मेद्यै°; La[1] Lo[1] oOr *Vij* [vl] मद्यमूत्र°; Hy Jm Jo[1] Kt[2] Lo[2] Lo[3] GMd[1] sOx[1] sPu[6] Pu[8] Tj[1] Tj[2] Tr[2] MTr[3] *Mandlik KSS Dave* मद्यैर्मूत्रैः पुरी°; oOr *Vij* °पुरीषैश्च [vl as in ed] — b) *Vij Apa* श्लेष्मपूयाश्रुशोणितैः; oOr पूयश्लेष्माश्रुशोणितैः; TMd[4] °शोणितं — c) Tj[1] संस्पृष्टो; *Apa* शुधयेत्तु — d) Jo[2] Lo[3] oOr पुनःपाकान्महीमयं; Tj[1] °पाकेन शुध्यति; Be[1] Ho wKt[1] Kt[2] wKt[3] TMd[4] sOx[1] sPu[6] मृण्मयं

124. Omitted in BKt[5] Ox[3]; *ma* in wKt[6]. Cited by *Lakṣ* 10.152; *Hem* 3/1.821; *Mādh* 2.147 — a) Bo Hy Jm Jo[1] Kt[2] Lo[2] oOr sOx[1] Ox[2] sPu[6] Pu[8] Tr[2] MTr[3] *Mādh Mandlik Jha KSS Dave* संमार्जनोपाञ्जनेन; Ho मार्जनोपाञ्जनेयेन; TMd[4] मार्जनेन च [for the pāda]; NPu[1] संमार्जनेन दाहेन; wKt[1] संमार्जनाञ्जनेन — b) GMy सेचनोल्ले°; Be[3] La[1] oOr वा — d) Ho शुध्यन्ति; sOx[1] Ox[2] sPu[6] [*cor to*] Tr[2] *Lakṣ Hem Mādh* पञ्चधा; Tj[2] पञ्च

Additional verse in GMd[1] TMd[4] MTr[4] MTr[6]; added after verse 122b in GMd[5]; cited by *Hem* 3/1.823 [cf. *BDh* 1.10.1]:

गोचर्ममात्रमब्बिन्दुर्गोः शोधयति पातितः ।
समूढमसमूढं वा यत्र लेपो न दृश्यते ॥

b) *Hem* °न्दुर्गाः; TMd[4] °न्दुर्भूमेः शुध्यति; MTr[4] MTr[6] पातितं — c) GMd[1] समृद्धमसमृद्धं वा; MTr[4] *om* वा — d) GMd[1] लोपे; MTr[4] लेपे; TMd[4] वेदो न

125. Pādas c-d omitted in Ho. Cited by *Mādh* 2.105 — b) Ox[3] °वभूतमव°; NKt[4] °तमनक्षतं; oOr *om* अवक्षुतं; Pu[2] Pu[4] °वक्षूतं; La[1] °वक्षुतो; NPu[1] °वक्षुधं; Tr[2] °वच्छुतं; wKt[1] °वक्षितं; wKt[3] °वक्षयं; GMd[1] °वक्षथं; *Hem* °वक्षतुं — c) Be[1] कीटकेशैश्च; BBe[2] केशकीटाभ्यां — d) GMd[1] TMd[3] *Mādh* मृत्क्षेपेण विशुध्यति; Lo[1] मृदुक्षेपेण; Pu[2] Pu[4] मृत्प्रेक्षेण

यावन्नापैत्यमेध्याक्तात् गन्धो लेपश्च तत्कृतः ।
तावन्मृद्वारि चादेयं सर्वासु द्रव्यशुद्धिषु ॥१२६॥
त्रीणि देवाः पवित्राणि ब्राह्मणानामकल्पयन् ।
अदृष्टमद्भिर्निर्णिक्तं यच्च वाचा प्रशस्यते ॥१२७॥
आपः शुद्धा भूमिगता वैतृष्ण्यं यासु गोर्भवेत् ।
अव्याप्ताश्चेदमेध्येन गन्धवर्णरसान्विताः ॥१२८॥
नित्यं शुद्धः कारुहस्तः पण्यं यच्च प्रसारितम् ।
ब्रह्मचारिगतं भैक्ष्यं नित्यं मेध्यमिति स्थितिः ॥१२९॥
नित्यमास्यं शुचि स्त्रीणां शकुनिः फलपातने ।
प्रस्रवे च शुचिर्वत्सः श्वा मृगग्रहणे शुचिः ॥१३०॥
श्वभिर्हतस्य यन्मांसं शुचि तन्मनुरब्रवीत् ।
क्रव्याद्भिश्च हतस्यान्यैश्चण्डालाद्यैश्च दस्युभिः ॥१३१॥

126. Cited by *Viś* 1.190; *Vij* 1.185; *Apa* 36;*Hem* 3/1.818; *Dev* 2.247; *Mādh* 2.148— a) NKt^{4} Lo^{1} [*cor to*] यावन्नापेत्य°; NPu^{1} यावन्नोपैत्य°; GMd^{1} यावन्नोपैति मे°; Tr^{1} °ध्याक्तान्; wKt^{1} TMd^{3} GMy MTr^{6} °ध्याक्ता; Pu^{5} Pu^{7} Pu^{9} °ध्याक्त; Lo^{1} °ध्याक्तं; TMd^{4} sOx^{1} sPu^{6} [*but cor*] *Hem Apa Mādh* °ध्याक्तो — b) Lo^{1} GMd^{1} sOx^{1} Pu^{5} sPu^{6} Pu^{7} Pu^{9} गन्धलेपश्च; Jo^{1} गन्धालेपश्च; BCa लेपो गन्धश्च; wKt^{1} तत्कृतं; TMd^{3} सत्कृतः; Pu^{5} तक्षतः — c) *Hem Mādh* °द्वारि देयं स्यात्; TMd^{3} GMd^{5} oOr sOx^{1} NPu^{1} Pu^{5} sPu^{6} Pu^{8} Tj^{1} Tr^{1} [*Jolly* R M$^{8-9}$] वादेयं; Ox^{2} चादेयं स्यात्; for added verse in GMd^{1} TMd^{4} MTr^{4} MTr^{6}, see addition after verse 118.

127. Cited by *Hem* 3/1.818; *Mādh* 2.149 — b) Be^{1} ब्रह्म°; wKt^{3} NKt^{4} °कल्पयत्; Bo oOr [*but cor*] °कल्पयेत् — c) TMd^{3} °द्भिर्निनिक्तं; BKt^{5} wKt^{6} °द्भिर्निक्तं यद्यच्च — d) MTr^{4} पञ्च वाचा; Ho प्रशस्यति; MTr^{6} प्रशिष्यते; Tj^{1} प्रशस्यसे

128. Cited by *Apa* 272; *Har*-A 1.15.2; *Lakṣ* 10.157; *Hem* 3/1.618; *Mādh* 2.119 — a) Ho शुद्धिभूमि° — b) *Lakṣ Hem* वितृष्णा यत्र गौर्भवेत्; wKt^{1} GMy sOx^{1} sPu^{6} वैतृष्णं; Tj^{1} वैतृष्णी; Wa वितृष्ण्यं; TMd^{4} वितृष्णं; BKt^{5} wKt^{6} NNg oOr Pu^{3} यत्र गो°; TMd^{3} या गाः भवेत्; Tj^{1} गौर्भवेत् — c) TMd^{3} आव्याप्ता चैवमध्येन; La^{1} अव्याप्तश्चे°; Tj^{2} अव्यक्ताश्चे° — d) GMy गन्धं

129. Cited by *Hem* 3/1.838; *Mādh* 2.145; pādas c-d cited by *Apa* 263 — a) Hy Tj^{1} नित्य; Lo^{4} [*but cor*] शुद्धिः; GMy शुचिकालहस्तः; TMd^{4} °हस्ता — b) Tj^{2} पाण्यं; Jo^{1} Tj^{1} *Dave* पण्ये; Pu^{2} Pu^{4} Tr^{2} पुण्यं; TMd^{4} प्रण्यं; MTr^{6} प्रसारिताः; TMd^{3} प्रसादितं — c) Ho °चारि भवेद्भैक्ष्यं; BKt^{5} °गता; wKt^{6} °गत; Kt^{2} Lo^{1} GMd^{1} TMd^{3} TMd^{4} GMd^{5} GMy NNg Pu^{4} Tr^{1} *Apa Rc Jolly* भैक्षं — d) *Hem* नित्य; Lo^{2} GMd^{5} NNg Pu^{3} Pu^{8} Tr^{1} MTr^{4} MTr^{6} *Hem* शुद्धमिति

130. *ma* in Bo. Cited by *Hem* 3/1.835 — a) BBe^{2} Be^{3} Bo La^{1} sOx^{1} Pu^{2} Pu^{4} sPu^{6} शुचिः; Ox^{3} क्षीणां — b) MTr^{4} MTr^{6} शकुनिश्च पलातने; Tj^{1} शकुनी; TMd^{3} शकुनेः; wKt^{3} °पाटने; GMd^{1} GMd^{5} Tr^{1} °शातने; Hy °यूजने — c) Be^{1} NPu^{1} प्रस्रावे; Lo^{2} oOr Ox^{3} Tr^{2} प्रश्रवे; GMy MTr^{4} MTr^{6} प्रत्स्नवे तु; Bo प्रस्रवेच्च; La^{1} NNg प्रस्रवने शु°; Tr^{1} प्रस्रावने शु°; Pu^{10} प्रश्रवैव शु°; GMd^{5} प्रस्तावने शु°; TMd^{3} TMd^{4} तु — d) TMd^{3} श्व; NPu^{1} °ग्रहणेऽशुचिः; Pu^{4} शुचि; oOr शुचिं

131. Cited by *Hem* 3/1.836; *Mādh* 2.146 — a) MTr^{6} भक्षभिर्ह°; La^{1} °र्हतश्च — b) Lo^{2} शुचिं; GMd^{1} शुद्धं; Hy La^{1} GMd^{5} oOr sOx^{1} Pu^{2} sPu^{6} शुचिस्तन्म°; Tr^{1} GMd^{1} तं मनु° — c) Ho क्रव्यादिभिश्च; TMd^{4} क्रव्यादैश्च; Pu^{5} Pu^{7} Pu^{9} क्रव्याद्भिहतश्चान्यै°; BCa TMd^{3} Ox^{3} Pu^{2} Pu^{4} Tr^{2} हतश्चान्यै°; BBe^{2} हतै-

ऊर्ध्वं नाभेर्यानि खानि तानि मेध्यानि सर्वशः ।
यान्यधस्तान्यमेध्यानि देहाच्चैव मलाश्च्युताः ॥१३२॥
मक्षिका विप्रुषश्छाया गौरश्वः सूर्यरश्मयः ।
रजो भूर्वायुरग्निश्च स्पर्शे मेध्यानि निर्दिशेत् ॥१३३॥
विण्मूत्रोत्सर्गशुद्ध्यर्थं मृद्वार्यादेयमर्थवत् ।
दैहिकानां मलानां च शुद्धिषु द्वादशस्वपि ॥१३४॥
वसा शुक्रमसृङ्मज्जा मूत्रविट्कर्णविण्नखाः ।
श्लेष्माश्रु दूषिका स्वेदो द्वादशैते नृणां मलाः ॥१३५॥

श्वान्यै°; Be[3] Tj[1] हतस्यान्त्यै°; NPu[1] हता ये तु चण्डा° — d) BBe[2] Bo Ho Lo[1] Ox[2] Pu[5] Pu[7] Pu[9] Tj[1] °श्वाण्डाला°; Jo[2] Lo[3] [*Jolly* R] °श्वाण्डालैश्चैव; Be[3] Tj[1] जन्तुभिः; TMd[3] दंष्ट्रिभि

Additional verse in Ho WKt[1] WKt[3] OOr *Mandlik* [ख, ट, ण, त] *KSS Dave:*

शुचिरग्निः शुचिर्वायुर्यः प्रवृत्तो बहिश्चरः ।
जलं शुचि विविक्तस्थं पन्था संचरणे शुचिः ॥

b) *Mandlik KSS Dave* °र्वायुः प्रवृत्तो हि बहि°; Ho °युर्यः वृत्तोस्मि बहि°; WKt[1] हि बहि° — d) OOr निःसरणे

Additional verse in La[1] TMd[4] OOr; placed after 142 in *Mandlik* [ट] *KSS Dave;* pādas a and c transposed in La[1] OOr:

अजाश्वं मुखतो मेध्यं गावो मेध्यास्तु पृष्ठतः ।
ब्राह्मणाः पादतो मेध्या स्त्रियो मेध्यास्तु सर्वतः ॥

a) La[1] OOr अजाश्वौ मुखतो मेध्यौ — b) *Mandlik KSS Dave* मेध्याश्च — d) *Mandlik KSS Dave* मेध्याश्च

Additonal verse in La[1]; placed after 133 in OOr NPu[1], and after 142 in *Mandlik* [ट] *KSS Dave:*

गौरमेध्या मुखे प्रोक्ता अजो मेध्यः प्रकीर्तितः ।
गोः पुरीषं च मूत्रं च मेध्यमित्यब्रवीन्मनुः ॥

a) OOr गौरमेध्यास्तु मुखतः — b) *Mandlik KSS Dave* अजामेध्या ततः स्मृता; NPu[1] अजोस्पर्शो; La[1] प्रकल्पितः — c) NPu[1] गोपुरी°

132. Cited by *Hem* 3/1.842; *Dev* 2.250; *Mādh* 2.148 — b) La[1] Lo[4] Lo[5] TMd[4] NNg Ox[3] Pu[10] सर्वतः; BKt[5] WKt[6] नित्यशः; OOr सर्ववा — c) BBe[2] WKt[3] NKt[4] La[1] TMd[3] GMd[5] GMy OOr SOx[1] SPu[6] Tr[1] MTr[4] MTr[6] *Mādh* यान्यधस्तादमेध्यानि; TMd[4] °धस्तानमे° — d) OOr देहेश्चैव मलाः स्मृताः; TMd[4] देहाच्चैते; Bo देवाच्यैव; Lo[5] देवाश्चैव; La[1] NPu[1] Tr[1] मलाच्युताः; TMd[3] मलाछ्युताः; Hy मलागताः; Ox[2] मलान्विताः; BBe[2] Be[3] Bo NNg Tj[1] च्युता मलाः

133. Cited by *Hem* 3/1.838 — a) La[1] माक्षिका; Ho °पश्छागौ — b) GMy गोरश्वः; Tj[1] गौरवः; TMd[3] गौरपः; TMd[4] गौरग्निः — c) NKt[4] राज्ञो — d) TMd[3] सर्गमेध्यानि; Be[1] निर्दशेत्; GMd[1] OOr सर्वशः; GMy सर्वशः *cor to* सर्वदा; TMd[3] GMd[5] Tr[1] MTr[4] MTr[6] [*Jolly* G] *Hem* सर्वदा; BKt[5] WKt[6] नित्यशः

134. Pādas c-d omitted in Lo[3] GMy. Cited by *Apa* 271; *Hem* 3/1.794; *Dev* 2.250; *Mādh* 2.148 — a) TMd[4] °सिद्ध्यर्थं — b) Tr[2] मृद्वारि देय°; GMd[1] Tj[1] °मर्थवित् — c) Bo TMd[4] NPu[1] Pu[2] Pu[4] देहिकानां; WKt[6] तदैहिका; OOr मेखलानां च; GMd[5] Tr[1] तु — d) Tj[1] शुद्धिः शुद्धादशस्वपि; Ho शुद्धिस्तु; Bo शुद्धित

135. Omitted in Pu[5]; placed after 131 in Tr[2]; pādas a-b omitted in Lo[3]. Cited by *Apa* 271; *Hem* 3/1.794; *Lakṣ* 10.120; *Dev* 2.250 — a) La[1] वशा; TMd[3] TMd[4] GMd[5] Tr[1] शुक्रम°; GMy °सृङ्नेदो

एका लिङ्गे गुदे तिस्रस्तथैकत्र करे दश ।
उभयोः सप्त दातव्या मृदः शुद्धिमभीप्सता ॥१३६॥
एतच्छौचं गृहस्थानां द्विगुणं ब्रह्मचारिणाम् ।
त्रिगुणं स्याद्वनस्थानां यतीनां च चतुर्गुणम् ॥१३७॥
कृत्वा मूत्रं पुरीषं च खान्याचान्त उपस्पृशेत् ।
वेदमध्येष्यमाणश्च अन्नमश्नंश्च सर्वदा ॥१३८॥

— b) Jo[1] Kt[2] *Dev Mandlik Bühler Jha KSS Dave* मूत्रविड्घ्राणकर्णविट्; Jm विण्मूत्रघ्राणकर्णविट्; BBe[2] मूत्रविण्नखाः [for whole pāda]; Be[1] Ho wKt[1] NKt[4] BKt[5] wKt[6] Lo[5] TMd[4] NNg sOx[1] Ox[3] Pu[3] sPu[6] [*Jolly* M]*Apa* मूत्रं; Tr[2] रेतोविट्कर्ण°; Jo[2] °विण्मलाः — c) Pu[2] Pu[4] श्लैष्माश्रु; *Apa* श्लेमासु; GMy दूषिता; GMd[5] Tr[1] MTr[4] MTr[6] पूयिका;GMd[1] पूयका रेतो; Lo[3] स्वेदा; TMd[4] स्वेदं — d) La[1] मलो नृणां; Tr[1] मला नृणां; Be[1] मलाः स्मृताः; NKt[4] मलः

Additional verse in La[1] TMd[4] GMd[5] MTr[4] MTr[6]:

हस्तान्तरिततोयेन कार्यं पादावनेजनम् ।
मृत्पूर्वकं यथादोषमशुचिः क्षालनानि च ॥

a) La[1] हस्तोद्धरित° — b) La[1] कुर्यात्पावने जलं— c) TMd[4] मृत्वार्यं तु यथा° — d) GMd[5] °दोषमशुचिक्षाळनाय च; La[1] °दोषमतिप्रक्षालनानि च

Additonal verse in Be[1] [cited by *Me* and *Ku* at 134]:

आददीत मृदोऽपश्च षट्सु पूर्वेषु शुद्धये ।
उत्तरेषु च षट्स्वद्भिः केवलाभिर्विशुध्यति ॥

136. Omitted in Hy Kt[2]. Cited by *Apa* 36; *Dev* 2.244; *Mādh* 1.215; pādas a-b cited by *Viś* 1.17 — a) sOx[1] sPu[6] एकां; TMd[4] लिङ्ग; wKt[3] गुडे; Tj[1] करे— b) Tj[1] उभयोर्मृद्द्वयं स्मृतं; Be[1] BBe[2] Ho BKt[5] wKt[6] Lo[5] sOx[1] Ox[2] sPu[6] Tr[2] *Apa* °स्तथा वामकरे; Pu[3] °स्तथैवैककरे; Lo[3] GMd[1] TMd[4] GMd[5] GMy Tr[1] MTr[4] MTr[6] [*Jolly* Ku Rd R] *Dev* °स्तथैकस्मिन्करे [TMd[4] °न्कुले]; TMd[3] °स्तदैकस्मिन्करे — c-d) Tj[1] पञ्चापाने दशैकस्मिन्नुभयोः सप्तमृत्तिकाः — d) sPu[6] मृदाः; TMd[3] मृदु; MTr[3] मृतः; wKt[1] शौचम°; *Mādh* [vl] शुद्धिमवाप्नुयात्; BBe[2] Be[3] BKt[5] wKt[6] Lo[4] GMd[1] TMd[3] NNg Ox[3] Tr[1] Wa *Apa* °भीप्सिता; sOx[1] sPu[6] °भीप्सितां; Pu[8] Tr[2] °भीप्सत; Pu[4] °भीप्सतः; Jo[2] °भीप्सुभिः

Additional verse in oOr [the text is unclear]:

पण्यं पण्यं क्रमेणैषां शुद्धिरुक्ता मनीषिभिः ।
मृद्वारिशुद्धिः सर्वेषामुत्तरेणु वारिणा ॥

137.* Cited by *Vij* 3.250; *Apa* 36; *Lakṣ* 1.157; *Dev* 2.246; *Mādh* 1.215 — a) TMd[3] GMy *Dev* गृहस्थस्य — b) TMd[3] GMy *Mādh* °चारिणः; Pu[7] Pu[9] °चारिणं — c) Tr[2] त्रिगुणं वानप्रस्थानां; *Mādh* वानप्रस्थस्य त्रिगुणं; La[1] त्रिगुणस्तु वन°; TMd[3] GMd[5] GMy La[1] oOr sOx[1] sPu[6] Tr[1] *Lakṣ* त्रिगुणं तु वन°; GMy स्याद्वनस्थस्य — d) BBe[2] Hy Jm Jo[1] Jo[2] wKt[1] Kt[2] NKt[4] [*cor to fh*] BKt[5] wKt[6] Lo[3] GMd[1] GMd[5] GMy NNg Ox[2] Pu[8] Tj[2] Tr[1] *Lakṣ Mādh Mandlik Jolly Jha KSS Dave* तु; Lo[1] स्याच्चतु°

138.* Pādas c-d omitted in TMd[4]. Cited by *Hem* 3/2.957; *Dev* 2.260; *Mādh* 1.223 — a) Be[1] BBe[2] Ho BKt[5] wKt[6] Lo[4] TMd[4] GMy oOr Ox[3] Pu[5] Pu[7] Pu[9] [*Jolly* G] मूत्र; Lo[4] Lo[5] Tr[2] पुरीषे; Be[3] [*but cor*] Hy Jm Jo[1] Kt[2] TMd[3] TMd[4] GMy Ox[3] Pu[8] Tj[2] MTr[3] MTr[4] MTr[6] *Nā Dev Mādh Mandlik Jolly Jha KSS Dave* वा; Ho Jo[2] Tr[2] तु; *Me Rc* support च — b) NKt[4] नखान्या°; *Mādh* पाण्याचा°; TMd[3] GMy Tj[1] °चान्तमुप°; Hy °स्पृशत् — c) Bo °मणांश्च; Be[3] Pu[2] Pu[4] Tj[1] °माणस्तु — c-d) GMd[5] *Mādh* पीत्वापोध्येष्यमाणश्च वेदानश्नंश्च सर्वदा [*Mādh* वेदमग्निं च]— d) Be[1] Bo Jo[2] wKt[1] wKt[3] NKt[4] BKt[5] wKt[6] Lo[1] Lo[2] Lo[3] GMd[1] NNg sOx[1] Ox[2] Pu[3] Pu[5] sPu[6] Pu[7] Pu[8] Pu[9] Tr[1] Tr[2] Wa *Hem* °णश्चाप्यन्नम°; Be[3] Pu[2] Pu[4] Tj[1] °णस्तु अन्नम°; BBe[2] °णश्चानन्नम°; Ho °णश्च ह्यन्नम°; Tr[2] सर्वशः;

त्रिराचामेदपः पूर्वं द्विः प्रमृज्यात्ततो मुखम् ।
शारीरं शौचमिच्छन्हि स्त्रीशूद्रं तु सकृत्सकृत् ॥१३९॥
शूद्राणां मासिकं कार्यं वपनं न्यायवर्तिनाम् ।
वैश्यवच्छौचकल्पश्च द्विजोच्छिष्टं च भोजनम् ॥१४०॥
नोच्छिष्टं कुर्वते मुख्या विप्रुषोऽङ्गं न यन्ति याः ।
न श्मश्रूणि गतान्यास्यं न दन्तान्तरधिष्ठितम् ॥१४१॥
स्पृशन्ति बिन्दवः पादौ य आचामयतः परान् ।

for a similar hiatus see 5.145c-d

Additional verse in Be^{3} [cf. 2.60]:

खानि चैव स्पृशेदद्भिरात्मानं शिर एव च ।
ब्राह्मणक्षत्रियविशां सर्वदैव मनीषिणः ॥

139.* Pādas c-d omitted in Pu^{2} — a) GMd^{1} TMd^{3} TMd^{4} GMd^{5} GMy Tr^{1} त्रिराचामन्पिबेद्वारि [TMd^{4} °चान्तान्पि°]; Be^{1} पूर्वे — b) Ox^{3} विप्रमृ°; NKt^{4} द्विः प्रथमं ततो; MTr^{4} °ज्यात्तथा — c) Tr^{1} शारीर; La^{1} GMd^{1} शरीरं; MTr^{4} °मिच्छंस्तु; wKt^{1} wKt^{6} Lo^{3} GMy °मिच्छन्ति; Be^{1} Lo^{4} Lo^{5} GMd^{1} Wa °मन्विच्छन् — d) Be^{1} Pu^{5} Pu^{7} Pu^{9} Wa [*Jolly* G N] °शूद्रं च; BBe^{2} Be^{3} BCa Hy Jo^{1} Kt^{2} wKt^{3} La^{1} Lo^{4} Lo^{5} Pu^{8} Tj^{2} Tr^{2} MTr^{4} *Mr Mandlik Jha KSS Dave* °शूद्रस्तु; Bo Jm Jo^{2} BKt^{5} wKt^{6} Lo^{1} Lo^{3} NPu^{1} °शूद्रश्च; GMd^{5} Tj^{1} Tr^{1} MTr^{6} °शूद्रौ तु; Ho sOx^{1} sPu^{6} Tj^{1} °शूद्रौ च; TMd^{3} GMy [*Jolly* Nd] °शूद्रोपि; TMd^{4} °शूद्रा हि; wKt^{1} °शूद्रस्य; TMd^{3} सकृत्स्पृशेत्

140. Cited by *Apa* 906; *Lakṣ* 2.269 — a) Pu^{2} Pu^{4} सर्वदा कार्यं; wKt^{3} कार्यः; Lo^{5} *Apa* कार्य — b) MTr^{6} वपने; BKt^{5} wKt^{6} पवनं; Tj^{1} पापवर्तिनां — c) TMd^{3} °कल्पैश्च; BBe^{2} Be^{3} Bo BKt^{5} wKt^{6} Lo^{1} Lo^{2} oOr sOx^{1} sPu^{6} Tj^{1} Tr^{2} °कल्पस्तु; Be^{1} Pu^{2} Pu^{4} Wa °कल्पः स्याद् — c-d) Ox^{2} Pu^{3} Pu^{8} भोजनं च द्विजोच्छिष्टं शौचकल्पश्च वैश्यवत् — d) BKt^{5} wKt^{6} °च्छिष्टस्य भोजनं; Be^{1} Be^{3} Bo BCa La^{1} Lo^{1} TMd^{3} GMy Pu^{2} Pu^{4} Tj^{1} Tj^{2} Tr^{2} Wa *Lakṣ* तु; Ox^{3} न भोजनं

141. Cited by *Lakṣ* 1.141; *Hem* 3/2.972 — a) MTr^{6} कुर्वतो; TMd^{3} कुरुते; GMd^{5} Pu^{10} मुख्य — b) Tj^{1} विप्रुषेण न; Be^{1} BBe^{2} Ho Jm Jo^{1} Jo^{2} La^{1} wKt^{1} Kt^{2} wKt^{3} BKt^{5} wKt^{6} Lo^{1} Lo^{3} Lo^{4} Lo^{5} TMd^{3} oOr Ox^{2} Pu^{8} MTr^{3} *Mandlik KSS* °षोङ्गे; oOr °षोङ्गो; Tj^{2} °षोङ्ग; GMd^{1} °ङ्गान्न; Lo^{1} TMd^{3} GMd^{5} GMy MTr^{4} MTr^{6} *Hem* न यान्ति; BBe^{2} BCa Ho Hy Jm Jo^{1} Jo^{2} wKt^{1} Kt^{2} wKt^{3} Lo^{3} Lo^{4} Lo^{5} Ox^{2} Pu^{8} Tj^{2} MTr^{3} [*Jolly* Ku R] *Mandlik Dave KSS* पतन्ति [*om* न]; Ox^{3} तपन्ति [*om* न]; TMd^{4} यां; Pu^{2} Pu^{4} ते — d) MTr^{4} MTr^{6} °रनिष्ठितं; GMd^{1} GMd^{5} GMy Tr^{1} °रविष्ठितं; TMd^{3} °रविष्टेतं; TMd^{4} °रविधिस्मृतं; La^{1} °रधिचेष्टितं

Additional verse in GMd^{1} GMy Tr^{1} MTr^{4} MTr^{6} [*Jolly* Gr]; placed after 142 in La^{1} *Mandlik* [क] *KSS Dave*; placed after 143 in TMd^{4} GMd^{5} oOr; pādas a-b in TMd^{3}. Cited by *Hem* 3/2.975; *Dev* 2.267; *Mādh* 1.226 [cf. *VaDh* 3.41]:

दन्तवद्दन्तलग्नेषु जिह्वास्पर्शे तथा शुचिः ।
परिच्युतेषु च स्थानान्निगिरन्नेव तच्छुचिः ॥

b) TMd^{3} शुचिस्थानाच्युतेषु च; MTr^{4} जिह्वस्पर्शे; GMd^{1} °स्पर्शो; GMd^{5} Tr^{1} °स्पर्शेथवा शुचिः; La^{1} GMd^{1} oOr °स्पर्शेशुचिर्न तु; MTr^{4} MTr^{6} °स्पर्शे शुचीनि तु; *Mādh* °स्पर्शकृते न तु; *Mandlik KSS Dave* °स्पर्शेषु चेन्न तु; *Hem* °स्पर्शे शुचिर्भवेत् — c) *Dev Mandlik* °च्युतेषु तत्स्था°; GMd^{5} °च्युतेषु वा स्था°; Tr^{1} °च्युतेषु स्वस्था°; TMd^{3} *Hem* °च्युतेष्ववस्था°; oOr °च्युतेथ वा स्था°

भौमिकैस्ते समा ज्ञेया न तैरप्रयतो भवेत् ॥१४२॥
उच्छिष्टेन तु संस्पृष्टो द्रव्यहस्तः कथंचन ।
अनिधायैव तद्द्रव्यमाचान्तः शुचितामियात् ॥१४३॥
वान्तो विरिक्तः स्नात्वा तु घृतप्राशनमाचरेत् ।
आचामेदेव भुक्त्वान्नं स्नानं मैथुनिनः स्मृतम् ॥१४४॥
सुप्त्वा क्षुत्वा च भुक्त्वा च निष्ठीव्योक्त्वानृतं वचः ।
पीत्वापोऽध्येष्यमाणश्च आचामेत् प्रयतोऽपि सन् ॥१४५॥
एष शौचविधिः कृत्स्नो द्रव्यशुद्धिस्तथैव च ।
उक्तो वः सर्ववर्णानां स्त्रीणां धर्मं निबोधत ॥१४६॥

142. Omitted in Ox³. Cited by *Apa* 276; *Hem* 3/2.972; *Dev* 2.266; *Mādh* 1.228— a) wKt¹ पादं — b) Be¹ Lo¹ये आचा° ; MTr⁶यत्र आचा° ; TMd⁴ Pu² Pu⁴ आचमं° ; GMy °मयतस्वकौ; Pu² Pu⁴ परात्; TMd⁴ परे; Ox² करान् — c) TMd⁴ Pu⁸ भौमिगैस्ते; NPu¹ Pu² Pu⁴ भूमिकैस्ते; Ho GMd¹ TMd³ GMd⁵ Tr¹ MTr⁶ भूमिगैस्ते; MTr⁴ भूमिजैस्ते; Lo¹ Pu⁸ °कैस्तै; *Dev* °कैस्तैस्समा — d) Tr¹ *Dev* नैतैर°

143. Omitted in NNg. Cited by *Hem* 3/2.964; *Apa* 264; *Dev* 2.274 — a) sOx¹ sPu⁶ उच्छिष्टेनैव; wKt¹ Lo¹ Wa च; BKt⁵ wKt⁶ संस्पृष्टौ — b) wKt¹ °हस्तं — c) GMd¹ TMd⁴ भूमौ निधाय तद्द्रव्य°

144. Cited by *Vij* 3.30; *Apa* 922, 926; *Hem* 3/1.796; *Mādh* 2.364 — a) GMy वान्ते; MTr⁴ चान्तो; TMd³ दान्तो; La¹ TMd³ Pu⁴ Pu⁵ Pu⁷ Pu⁹ Tj¹ Tr² *Apa* 922 [vl] विरक्तः; Jo² Lo³ *Apa* 922 च — b) wKt³ Lo¹ घृतं प्राश्य विशुध्यति; NKt⁴ °नमारभेत् — c) Be¹ Be³ wKt¹ wKt³ आचमे° ; Bo Lo⁵ Tr¹ भुक्तात्रं; Tj¹ भुक्त्यत्रं — d) Be¹ Tj¹ स्नान; GMd⁵ Tr² मैथुनिनं; Tj¹ मैथुनिनि; TMd³ स्मृतः

Additional verse in Be¹ Pu² Pu⁴ *Mandlik KSS Dave;* pādas a-b and c-d transposed in Pu² Pu⁴:

अनृतौ तु मृदा शौचं कार्यं मूत्रपुरीषवत् ।
ऋतौ तु गर्भशङ्कित्वात्स्नानं मैथुनिनः स्मृतम् ॥

a) Pu² Pu⁴ अन्यत्र तु

145.* Placed after 138b in TMd⁴. Cited by *Vij* 1.196, 3.279; *Apa* 1139; *Hem* 3/2.957–8, 966; *Mādh* 1.224, 2.423 — a) Be¹ BBe² GMd¹ sOx¹ sPu⁶ *Vij* 3.279 *Apa* सुप्त्वा भुक्त्वा च क्षुत्वा च; La¹ स्नात्वा भुक्त्वा च सुप्त्वा च; TMd⁴ भुक्त्वा क्षुत्वा च सुप्त्वा च; Ox³ स्नात्वा क्षुत्वा; GMd⁵ सुप्त्वा च क्षुत्वा च; NPu¹ Tr² क्षुप्त्वा; wKt⁶ oOr क्षिप्त्वा; BKt⁵ क्षित्वा; Ho Tj¹ Tr¹ भुक्ता; BBe² GMd¹ BBe² Ho GMd¹ *om last* च — b) Jo² Lo³ TMd³ GMy Tr¹ MTr⁴ MTr⁶ *Vij* 1.196 ष्ठीवित्वोक्त्वा°; Be¹ BBe² Ho Hy Jm Jo¹ Jo² wKt¹ Kt² wKt³ BKt⁵ wKt⁶ Lo² Lo³ Lo⁴ Lo⁵ oOr sOx¹ Ox² Ox³ Pu⁵ Pu⁷ sPu⁶ Pu⁹ Pu¹⁰ Tj² MTr³ Wa *Vij* 3.279 *ApaHem Mādh* 2.423 *Mr Mandlik Jolly Jha KSS Dave* °क्त्वानृतानि च; Pu⁵ Pu⁷ Pu⁹ [*Jolly* G] °क्त्वानृतानि तु — c) Lo¹ sOx¹ sPu⁶ पीत्वायो; Pu¹⁰ पीत्वा वाध्ये° — c-d) GMd¹ रथ्या श्मशानमाक्रम्याचान्तः पुनराचमेत् — d) Be¹ Bo Ho BKt⁵ wKt⁶ Lo¹ Lo² NNg sOx¹ Ox² NPu¹ Pu² Pu⁴ Pu⁵ sPu⁶ Pu⁷ Pu⁸ Pu⁹ Wa °णश्चाप्याचा° ; Tr¹ त्वाचा° ; GMd⁵ ह्याचा° ; wKt¹ आचमे°

Two additional verses in oOr; first is indeciferable; the second also is unclear:

अजीर्णेत्युदिते वान्ते शुश्रुकर्मणि मैथुने ।
दुःस्वप्नासज्जनस्पर्शे स्नानमात्रं विधीयते ॥

146.* a) Pu² Pu⁴ एषां; BKt⁵ wKt⁶ °विधः — b) GMd¹ द्रव्यशौचविधिस्तथा — c) Hy उक्ता; NKt⁴ उक्तो वै; Bo यः — d) La² स्त्रीधर्मान्निबो° ; wKt³ Lo⁴ GMd¹ धर्मन्निबो° ; TMd⁴ धर्म निबो° ; Be¹ BCa Ho

बालया वा युवत्या वा वृद्धया वापि योषिता ।
न स्वातन्त्र्येण कर्तव्यं किंचित्कार्यं गृहेष्वपि ॥१४७॥
बाल्ये पितुर्वशे तिष्ठेत् पाणिग्राहस्य यौवने ।
पुत्राणां भर्तरि प्रेते न भजेत स्वतन्त्रताम् ॥१४८॥
पित्रा भर्त्रा सुतैर्वापि नेच्छेद्विरहमात्मनः ।
एषां हि विरहेण स्त्री गर्ह्ये कुर्यादुभे कुले ॥१४९॥
सदा प्रहृष्टया भाव्यं गृहकार्ये च दक्षया ।
सुसंस्कृतोपस्करया व्यये चामुक्तहस्तया ॥१५०॥
यस्मै दद्यात्पिता त्वेनां भ्राता वानुमते पितुः ।
तं शुश्रूषेत जीवन्तं संस्थितं च न लङ्घयेत् ॥१५१॥
मङ्गलार्थं स्वस्त्ययनं यज्ञश्चासां प्रजापतेः ।

Hy Jm Jo^{1} Kt^{2} Lo^{1} Lo^{5} sOx^{1} Pu^{5} sPu^{6} Pu^{7} Pu^{9} Tj^{2} MTr^{3} Wa *Mandlik Jha KSS Dave* धर्मान्निबो°; TMd^{3} वर्णा निबो°

147. Cited by *Lakṣ* 12.619; *Dev* 3.584; *Mādh* 2.31— a) wKt^{3} बालया बालवत्या वा; Be^{1} oOr Tj^{1} Tr^{2} बालाया — b) Be^{1} Lo^{4} Lo^{5} Tj^{1} वृद्धाया; TMd^{3} वृद्धायां; Ox^{3} वृद्धावा वापि; NNg वृद्धयाथापि; Ho वृद्धयापि योषि° — c) Pu^{5} Pu^{7} Pu^{9} [*Jolly* G] स्वातन्त्र्येण न कर्तव्यं; GMd^{1} MTr^{6} स्वतन्त्र्येण; Be^{1} [*but mc*] Be^{3} wKt^{1} Lo^{4} Lo^{5} TMd^{3} GMd^{5} Ox^{3} Pu^{2} Pu^{4} Tj^{1} °तन्त्रेण; GMy °तन्त्र्येक — d) *Me* [cited at 8.163] कार्यं किंचिदिति स्थितिः; NKt^{4} GMd^{1} TMd^{3} GMd^{5} GMy Tr^{1} MTr^{6} *Dev* कार्यं किंचिद् गृहे°; Be^{3} MTr^{4} MTr^{6} गृहेण्वपि

148. Omitted in Ox^{3} Pu^{10}. Cited by *Lakṣ* 12.619; *Dev* 3.584; *Mādh* 2.286 — a) Lo^{1} Pu^{2} Pu^{4} बाले; Jm बालेर्पितु°; Be^{3} बालो पितुर्गृहे; TMd^{3} oOr पितृवशे; La^{1} पितुर्वंशे — b) TMd^{3} प्राणि°; wKt^{6} यौधने — c) *Dev* पुत्रस्य; Ho भर्तृपरेते; wKt^{3} प्रेत्य — c-d) *Mādh* पुत्रस्य स्थाविरे भावे न स्त्री स्वातन्त्र्य-मर्हति [cf. 9.3] — d) Pu^{3} भजेत्तु; Bo भजन्त; Ho भजते स्त्री स्व°; Be^{1} BBe^{2} BCa Hy Jm Jo^{1} Jo^{2} wKt^{1} Kt^{2} wKt^{3} La^{2} Lo^{1} Lo^{3} Lo^{4} Lo^{5} Pu^{8} Tj^{2} MTr^{3} Wa *Mandlik Jolly Jha KSS Dave* भजेत्स्त्री स्व°; La^{1} भवत्स्त्री स्व°; *Lakṣ* भजेत्सा स्व°

149. Omitted in Ox^{3} Pu^{10}. Cited by *Lakṣ* 12.619; *Dev* 3.585; *Mādh* 2.31 — a) Lo^{2} पिता; Bo भर्ता; Lo^{1} [*cor to*] TMd^{3} भ्रात्रा; GMd^{1} GMy Pu^{2} Pu^{4} भ्राता; Tr^{1} भार्या; Ox^{2} सुतेनापि — c) GMd^{1} एतैर्विरहितायां स्त्री; TMd^{4} एतैर्विरहिता स्त्री हि; wKt^{6} एषां स्त्रीविरहेण स्त्री; Be^{1} एष; Lo^{2} एषा; Tj^{2} एवं; BBe^{2} Lo^{1} एतेषां विर°; Pu^{5} Pu^{7} Pu^{9} [*Jolly* G] च; wKt^{1} [*Jolly* R] तु — d) TMd^{3} Tj^{1} गर्हे; Pu^{2} Pu^{4} गर्हो; Tj^{2} गूह्ये; Tr^{1} गृह्ये

150.* Cited by *Lakṣ* 12.620 — a) wKt^{3} प्रहृत्यया; Hy प्रहृष्टेया; wKt^{1} प्रकृष्टया भाव्ये; Pu^{4} भाव्यां; Hy भव्यं; TMd^{4} भार्या; MTr^{4} कार्यं — b) Pu^{10} °कार्यो; Lo^{1} °कार्येपि; Hy Jm Jo^{1} Jo^{2} wKt^{1} Kt^{2} Lo^{1} Lo^{2} Lo^{3} TMd^{3} GMd^{5} Ox^{3} Pu^{3} Tj^{2} MTr^{3} MTr^{4} *Mandlik Jolly KSS* °कार्येषु; Tr^{2} °कर्मसु — c) Pu^{8} स्वसंस्कृ°; BBe^{2} °पस्काराया; wKt^{1} °पसरया — d) Ho Tj^{1} वामुक्त°

151. Cited by *Lakṣ* 12.628; *Dev* 1.223, 3.589 — a) wKt^{1} wKt^{3} तस्मै; *Dev* °त्पिताप्येनां; NPu^{1} चैनां — b) oOr भ्रात्रा; oOr NPu^{1} Pu^{5} Pu^{7} Pu^{9} चानुमते; *Dev* चानुमतौ; Lo^{5} चानुमतः; TMd^{4} नानुमते; BBe^{2} °मतेः — c) wKt^{1} शुश्रूषयेत [*om* तं]; Tr^{2} शुश्रूषते; Ho शुश्रूयेत; NKt^{4} शुश्रूयति; TMd^{3} शिश्रूषतं; Jo^{2} Lo^{3} शुश्रूषेच्च; Bo शुश्रूपेन्न; oOr जीवतं; MTr^{6} जीवन्तः; Wa जीवेतं — d) *Dev* दुस्स्थितं; Tr^{2} संस्थं; *Dev* [vl] स्वर्यातं; Be^{1} Bo Jo^{2} sOx^{1} Pu^{5} sPu^{6} Pu^{7} Pu^{9} Tr^{2} [*Jolly* G] न च

प्रयुज्यते विवाहेषु प्रदानं स्वाम्यकारकम् ॥१५२॥
अनृतावृतुकाले च मन्त्रसंस्कारकृत्पतिः ।
सुखस्य नित्यं दातेह परलोके च योषितः ॥१५३॥
विशीलः कामवृत्तो वा गुणैर्वा परिवर्जितः ।
उपचर्यः स्त्रिया साध्व्या सततं देववत्पतिः ॥१५४॥
नास्ति स्त्रीणां पृथग्यज्ञो न व्रतं नाप्युपोषणम् ।
पतिं शुश्रूषते येन तेन स्वर्गे महीयते ॥१५५॥

152.* Omitted in Bo — b) Tj^1 कन्यायां प्रधिकेतया; Lo^4 Lo^5 Ox^3 Tr^2 [*Jolly* M] यज्ञस्त्वासां; wKt^1 sOx^1 °श्चासौ; Be^3 wKt^1 NNg प्रजापते; TMd^3 sOx^1 Pu^2 Pu^4 sPu^6 प्रजापतिः [*but cor in* sOx^1 sPu^6]; Jm TMd^4 GMy NPu^1 प्रजायते; GMd^5 प्रचक्षते — c) BBe^2 विवाहे तु — d) oOr प्रजानां; NKt^4 व्रतानां; Be^1 NKt^4 Lo^4 Lo^5 GMd^1 TMd^3 TMd^4 GMy NNg Ox^3 NPu^1 Pu^2 Pu^4 Pu^{10} Tr^1 MTr^4 MTr^6 [*Jolly* M Nd] स्वामि°; BKt^5 wKt^6 काम्य°; Be^1 BBe^2 BCa Hy Jm Jo^1 Kt^2 wKt^3 Pu^5 Pu^7 Pu^9 MTr^3 Wa *Rn Mr Mandlik Jha KSS Dave* °कारणं

153. Not commented by *Rc*. Cited by *Lakṣ* 12.627; *Dev* 3.590 — a) Lo^1 अनृतानृतु°; Lo^1 °तावृतकाले; Pu^{10} °तावनुकाले; wKt^6 °कालेन; BKt^5 *om* च; Tr^1 lacuna for च; Be^3 Bo wKt^1 Lo^4 Lo^5 TMd^4 Ox^3 Pu^5 Pu^7 Pu^9 Pu^{10} Tj^1 [*Jolly* G] *Lakṣ* तु; GMd^5 वा — b) Ho °संस्कार इत्यपि — c) *Dev* सुखं नित्यं ददातीह; wKt^1 दुःखस्य; Tj^1 सुखस्यानित्य; Tr^2 दाताह; NPu^1 दानेह — d) MTr^6 परे; sOx^1 sPu^6 °लोकेपु; Be^1 Lo^1 TMd^3 GMy GMd^5 MTr^6 योषितां; Tr^2 योषिता; wKt^1 योषितं

154. Omitted in TMd^3 Tr^1; after विशीलः the rest omitted in GMy. Cited by *Viś* 1.76, 2.290; *Vij* 2.290; *Lakṣ* 12.627; *Dev* 3.590 — a) Tj^1 विशालः; La^1 *Vij* दुःशीलः; sOx^1 sPu^6 दुश्शीलः [*but both cor*]; Ho wKt^3 कालवृत्तो— b) wKt^1 गुणैर्वापि विवर्जितः — c) GMd^1 TMd^4 MTr^6 साध्व्या स्त्रियोपचर्यः स्यात्; MTr^4 [*Jolly* Gr] पूजनीयः स्त्रिया सम्यक्; Bo Lo^5 Pu^{10} *Jha* उपचार्यः; oOr उपचर्या; *Vij* परिचार्यः; Lo^5 स्त्रियो; Be^1 Wa साध्या; Bo Ho [*cor to*] Lo^5 साध्वी — d) Pu^{10} दैव°; Ox^2 देवकृत्पतिः

Additonal verse in GMd^1 NPu^1 Tr^2 MTr^4 *Mandlik* [क, ख, ण] *KSS Dave*. Cited by *Apa* 109; *Lakṣ* 12.629:

दानात्प्रभृति या तु स्याद्यावदायुः पतिव्रता ।
भर्तृलोकं न त्यजति यथैवारुन्धती तथा ।।

a) *Mandlik KSS Dave* दानप्रभृति; Tr^2 दानप्रमित — c) NPu^1 *Apa* सा भर्तृलोकमाप्नोति

Additional verse in La^1; added after 155 in oOr:

तुषारे हिमदग्धे वा शीर्णपत्रेण पद्मिनी ।
भस्मी भवति सा नारी यस्या भर्त्ता न तुष्यति ।।

155.* Cited by *Viś* 1.84; *Apa* 102; *Lakṣ* 12627; *Dev* 3.590; pādas a-b cited by *Hem* 3/3.176 — a) Lo^1 न स्त्रीणां च पृथ°; Hy स्त्रीणा; GMd^1 स्त्रियां; TMd^4 स्त्रीया; Tj^2 स्त्री; [*Jolly* G] पृथग्धर्मो — b) TMd^4 नाव्रतं; wKt^3 व्रतै; Be^1 Bo BCa Ho Hy Jm Jo^1 Jo^2 Kt^2 wKt^3 NKt^4 BKt^5 wKt^6 La^1 Lo^2 Lo^4 Lo^5 GMd^1 NNg oOr Ox^3 sPu^6 [*but cor sh*] Pu^{10} Tj^2 MTr^3 Wa [*Jolly* M] *Viś Apa Me Rn Jha* °पोषितं; BBe^2 °पासितं — c) Pu^2 Pu^3 शुश्रूषते पतिं येन; TMd^4 शुश्रूषते यद्भर्तारं; TMd^3 पतिशुश्रूषनं येन; Bo Hy *Dev* शुश्रूयते; Ho शुश्रूषयेद्येन; Be^1 NKt^4 wKt^6 Lo^2 Lo^4 Lo^5 TMd^3 GMd^1 GMd^5 GMy NNg Ox^3 Pu^{10} Tr^1 MTr^4 MTr^6 *Apa* °षते यत्तु; BKt^5 °षते यत्र; wKt^3 यस्मात्तेन — d) Lo^1 स्वर्गं

Additional verse in Ho wKt^1 sOx^1 Pu^2 Pu^4 sPu^6 Tj^1 Tr^2 *Mandlik* [क, ख, ण] *KSS Dave;* added after 154 in La^1; pādas c-d in TMd^4:

पाणिग्राहस्य साध्वी स्त्री जीवतो वा मृतस्य वा ।
पतिलोकमभीप्सन्ती नाचरेत्किंचिदप्रियम् ॥१५६॥
कामं तु क्षपयेद्देहं पुष्पमूलफलैः शुभैः ।
न तु नामापि गृह्णीयात् पत्यौ प्रेते परस्य तु ॥१५७॥
आसीता मरणात् क्षान्ता नियता ब्रह्मचारिणी ।
यो धर्म एकपत्नीनां काङ्क्षन्ती तमनुत्तमम् ॥१५८॥
अनेकानि सहस्राणि कुमारब्रह्मचारिणाम् ।
दिवं गतानि विप्राणामकृत्वा कुलसंततिम् ॥१५९॥

पत्यौ जीवति या तु स्त्री उपवासं व्रतं चरेत् ।
आयुः सा हरते भर्तुर्नरकं चैव गच्छति ॥

a) Tj[1] जीवतु; La[1] wKt[1] Ho या नारी — a-b) sOx[1] sPu[6] या स्त्री स्यादुपोष्य व्रतचारिणी — b) Ho उपोष्य व्रतमाचरेत्; La[1] उपोष्य व्रतचारिणी; wKt[1] Pu[2] Pu[4] उपवासव्रतं — c) TMd[4] sOx[1] sPu[6] *Mandlik KSS Dave* आयुष्यं हरते; Tr[2] संहरते; wKt[1] पत्युर्न° — d) Ho La[1] TMd[4] सा नारी नरकं व्रजेत् [La[1] नरके]

Additional verses in GMd[5] Tr[1]; verses 2–3 given after verse 154 in TMd[4]:

अशीलः कामवृत्तो वा गुणैर्वापि विवर्जितः ।
साध्व्या स्त्रियोपचर्यः स्यात्सततं देववत्पतिः ॥१॥ [cf. 5.154]
दानात्प्रभृति या नारी कर्मणा मनसा गिरा ।
पतिव्रता भवेन्नित्यं यावदायुः समाहिता ॥२॥
प्रार्थिता सज्जनस्त्रीभिः स्वर्गतिनित्यपूजिता ।
सा भर्तृलोकमाप्नोति यथैवारुन्धती तथा ॥३॥

1. a) GMd[5] कामकारो — b) GMd[5] गुणैर्वा परिवर्जितः — c) GMd[5] नास्तिकोप्युपचर्यः
2. a) TMd[4] दानप्रभृति; Tr[1] °भृति नारी तु
3. a) Tr[1] प्रास्थिता स्वर्जन° — c) Tr[1] सा हि त्रिलोकानाप्नोति

156. Cited by *Lakṣ* 12.628 — a) TMd[4] OOr [*but cor*] प्राणि°; Be[1] Bo Jo[1] TMd[3] Tj[1] Tr[2] °ग्रहस्य; Wa साध्वी सा — b) Pu[5] Pu[7] Pu[9] Tr[1] जीवन्तो; Hy TMd[3] जीवितो; Bo पीवतो; La[1] sOx[1] sPu[6] Tr[2] जीवतोथ; NPu[1] जीवतोस्य; BCa Ox[2] जीवतोपि; Be[1] Bo wKt[3] La[1] sOx[1] Ox[2] NPu[1] Pu[3] sPu[6] मृतस्य च — c) TMd[3] परलोक°; Wa पतिमभी°; Lo[3] Jo[2] °लोकानभी°; Lo[2] °मनीप्सन्ती; TMd[4] °मधिष्यन्ति; Tr[2] °प्सन्ते — d) BKt[5] wKt[6] Tr[2] न चरे°; Pu[2] Pu[4] माचरे°

157. Cited by *Vij* 2.127, 290; *Lakṣ* 12.636 — a) TMd[3] °येद्देहः — b) Jo[1] °मूलैः फलैः — c) wKt[1] न चान्नमपि; Be[1] BBe[2] Bo [*but cor*] BCa wKt[3] NKt[4] La[1] GMd[1] TMd[3] TMd[4] GMd[5] GMy Tr[1] MTr[4] MTr[6] Wa न च; La[1] Tr[1] MTr[6] नामाभि; TMd[3] sOx[1] sPu[6] नामानि — d) Ho यतस्य तु; wKt[3] OOr च

158. Pādas a-b omitted in GMy and pādas c-d in Tj[2] [haplo]. Cited by *Vij* 2.127; *Lakṣ* 12.636 — a) TMd[4] सासीता; NPu[1] आसीना; sOx[1] sPu[6] मरणं; wKt[3] क्षान्त्या; TMd[3] TMd[4] कान्ता — b) Tr[2] नियती; Pu[2] Pu[4] नियतः; La[1] नित्यं वा ब्रह्म°; Tj[2] °चारिणां — c) NKt[4] धर्म्य — d) Lo[1] Tj[1] काङ्क्षती; Be[1] व्रतमुत्तमं; BKt[5] wKt[6] धर्ममुत्तमं

159. Pādas a-b omitted in Tj[2]. Cited by *Vij* 2.127; *Lakṣ* 12.636; *Dev* 3.595; *Mādh* 2.45 — a) Wa बहूनीह; Lo[2] Ox[2] बहूनि हि; Pu[8] बहूनह; TMd[4] बहूनि च — b) Bo कुमारी°; BCa wKt[3] NKt[4] Lo[2] TMd[3] GMd[5] GMy NNg Ox[2] Pu[5] Pu[7] Pu[8] Pu[9] Tr[1] Tr[2] [*Jolly* G Gr] *Vij Nā Rc* कौमार°; TMd[4] कौमारं; wKt[1] °चारिणः; Tr[2] °चारिणाः; MTr[6] °चारिणं; TMd[3] °चारिणी; Bo °चारिणीं — c) TMd[3] गतानां

मृते भर्तरि साध्वी स्त्री ब्रह्मचर्ये व्यवस्थिता ।
स्वर्गं गच्छत्यपुत्रापि यथा ते ब्रह्मचारिणः ॥१६०॥
अपत्यलोभाद्या तु स्त्री भर्तारमतिवर्तते ।
सेह निन्दामवाप्नोति पतिलोकाच्च हीयते ॥१६१॥
नान्योत्पन्ना प्रजास्तीह न चाप्यन्यपरिग्रहे ।
न द्वितीयश्च साध्वीनां क्वचिद्भर्तोपदिश्यते ॥१६२॥
पतिं हित्वावकृष्टं स्वमुत्कृष्टं या निषेवते ।
निन्द्यैव लोके भवति परपूर्वेति चोच्यते ॥१६३॥
व्यभिचारात्तु भर्तुः स्त्री लोके प्राप्नोति निन्द्यताम् ।
सृगालयोनिं चाप्नोति पापरोगैश्च पीड्यते ॥१६४॥

— d) GMd¹ °मकृत्वा च कुल°; Ho °संततिः; Wa °संहतिं

160. Cited by *Vij* 2.127; *Lakṣ* 12636; *Dev* 1.225, 3.595 — b) TMd⁴ MTr⁴ MTr⁶ ब्रह्मचर्यव्रते स्थिता; Lo¹ ब्रह्मचर्य; TMd³ विवस्थिता — c) La¹ गच्छेदपु°; TMd³ गच्छेत्यपु°; GMd¹ °त्यपुत्रा वै; NPu¹ °त्यपुत्राणि; wKt¹ °त्यमुत्रापि — d) GMd¹ यथा ये; Ox³ यथा तं; TMd³ GMy यथैते; TMd⁴ यदापि; *Dev* यथावद्ब्रह्म°

161.* Cited by *Vij* 2.127; *Lakṣ* 12.636; *Dev* 3.596; *Mādh* 2.30 — a) T Md⁴ आपद्यपि हि या नारी; TMd³ GMy °लोभाज्जातु स्त्री; Tr¹ °भाद्या स्त्री तु — b) Tr² °तिवर्जते; Tj¹ °भिवर्तते; GMy *Mādh* °तिलङ्घते; Lo² °निवर्तते; TMd³ °तिलङ्घयेत् — c) Lo³ सैह; Tr² स्नेह; TMd⁴ Wa सह — d) wKt⁶ परलोक्यव्यहीयते; BBe² Jm wKt³ Lo⁴ Lo⁵ TMd⁴ Ox³ Pu¹⁰ MTr⁴ [*Jolly* M]*Ku Jha Dave* परलोकाच्च; oOr पतत्येके च

162. Cited by *Lakṣ* 12.636; pādas c-d cited by *Viś* 1.66; *Vij* 2.51— a) GMy अन्योत्पन्ना; TMd³ GMd⁵ Tr¹ °त्पन्न; Lo⁵ Tr¹ प्रजा स्त्रीह; La¹ TMd⁴ Pu⁸ [*Jolly* Gr] प्रजा स्त्रीणां — b) MTr⁴ न चाप्यस्य°; BCa La¹ नाप्यन्य°; GMd¹ TMd⁴ Ox³ NPu¹ Pu² Pu³ Pu⁵ Pu⁷ Pu⁹ Wa *Rn Dave Jha* न चान्यस्य परि°; Lo³ oOr न चाप्यन्यस्य परि°; NKt⁴ sOx¹ sPu⁶ न चाप्यन्यत्परि°; Ho न वान्यस्य परि°; Jo² wKt¹ wKt³ Lo² TMd³ GMd⁵ GMy Tr¹ नाप्यन्यस्य परि°; Ho Lo⁴ Lo⁵ GMy Tr¹ Tr² °ग्रहः; wKt³ Ox² °ग्रहेत् — c) TMd³ नाद्वितीयस्तु; Tj¹ न हि ताभ्यश्च; Be¹ Bo GMd⁵ GMy Wa द्वितीयस्तु; Pu¹⁰ द्वितीयस्य — d) Jo² Lo¹ कश्चिद्भ°; GMy °द्भर्तापदिश्यते; Lo² °द्भर्त्रेपिदिश्यते; wKt¹ °दिश्यति

163.* Pādas a-b omitted in Bo. Cited by *Lakṣ* 12.645; *Mādh* 2.30 — a) Jo¹ हत्वा°; BBe² Be³ Ho Hy Jm Jo¹ Kt² BKt⁵ La² Lo¹ Lo² Lo³ Lo⁴ GMd¹ GMd⁵ Ox² GMy Pu⁸ Tj¹ Tr¹ MTr⁴ MTr⁶ हित्वापकृष्टं; Jo² wKt¹ wKt³ *Lakṣ* हित्वा निकृष्टं; TMd⁴ हित्वाचकृष्टं; Lo⁵ हित्वाप्रकृष्टं; Hy TMd³ °कृष्टं; wKt³ त्वमु°; Ox² *om* स्वम् — a-b) BKt⁵ wKt⁶ °कृष्टं या समुत्कृष्टं निषेवते [wKt⁶ *om* या] — b) wKt³ स्वं प्रकृष्टं; NNg *om* या; wKt³ GMd¹ TMd⁴ GMd⁵ GMy Tr¹ [*Jolly* Gr] *Mādh* योपसेवते; TMd³ योनसेवते; MTr⁴ MTr⁶ या च सेवते; Ox³ निषेविते — c) Be¹ La¹ निन्द्यैव भवति लोके; Hy Jm Jo¹ Kt² wKt³ Lo¹ Ox² Tj² MTr³ [*Jolly* G Ku]*Mandlik Jolly Jha KSS Dave* निंद्यैव सा भवेल्लोके [wKt³ सा निन्द्यैव]; Lo¹ निन्दैव; Pu⁵ Pu⁷ Pu⁹ [*Jolly* G] निन्द्येह — d) wKt³ °पूर्वैव; Tr¹ °पूर्वेव

164.* [= 9.30] Verses 164 and 165 transposed in oOr. Not commented by *Nd.* Cited by *Mādh* 2.30 — a) NNg व्यभीचा°; Kt² °चारास्तु; Tr¹ [*but cor fh*] °चाराच्च; TMd⁴ °चारैस्तु; Lo⁴ Lo⁵ Ox³ °चारे तु; Pu¹⁰ °चरेत्तु; wKt¹ °चारादुपभर्तुः; Bo *om* भर्तुः — b) Pu² Pu⁴ लोकात्प्रा°; Lo¹ प्राप्नोत्यनिन्द्यतां; Ox³ नन्द्यतां; Pu² Pu⁴ निन्दितान्; Hy निन्वतां — c) Ox² शृगालगतिमाप्नोति; BBe² Be³ Bo BCa Ho Hy Jm Jo¹ Jo² wKt¹ Kt² wKt³ NKt⁴ BKt⁵ wKt⁶ La¹ La² Lo¹ Lo² Lo³ Lo⁴ Lo⁵ NNg oOr

पतिं या नाभिचरति मनोवाग्देहसंयता ।
सा भर्तृलोकानाप्नोति सद्भिः साध्वीति चोच्यते ॥१६५॥
अनेन नारी वृत्तेन मनोवाग्देहसंयता ।
इहाग्र्यां कीर्तिमाप्नोति पतिलोकं परत्र च ॥१६६॥
एवंवृत्तां सवर्णां स्त्रीं द्विजातिः पूर्वमारिणीम् ।
दाहयेदग्निहोत्रेण यज्ञपात्रैश्च धर्मवित् ॥१६७॥
भार्यायै पूर्वमारिण्यै दत्त्वाग्नीनन्त्यकर्मणि ।
पुनर्दारक्रियां कुर्यात् पुनराधानमेव च ॥१६८॥
अनेन विधिना नित्यं पञ्च यज्ञान्न हापयेत् ।
द्वितीयमायुषो भागं कृतदारो गृहे वसेत् ॥१६९॥

Ox^{2} Ox^{3} NPu^{1} Pu^{2} Pu^{4} Pu^{8} Pu^{10} Tj^{2} Tr^{2} Wa शृगाल° ; GMy °योनिश्चाप्नोति; Lo^{4} °योनिमाप्नोति; Ho Ox^{3} Wa वाप्नोति; BBe^{2} Bo Hy Jm Jo^{1} wKt^{1} Kt^{2} La^{1} Lo^{1} Lo^{2} Lo^{5} TMd^{4} GMd^{5} NNg sOx^{1} NPu^{1} Pu^{5} sPu^{6} Pu^{7} Pu^{9} Tj^{2} Tr^{2} MTr^{3} *Go* [*Jolly* M$^{5-9}$] *Go Mandlik Jha KSS Dave* प्राप्नोति — d) TMd^{3} पापयोनिं च गच्छति [*mc* पीड्यते]; Ox^{3} °रोगो च; Jo^{2} °रोगैः प्रपीड्यते

165. [= 9.29] Omitted in Lo^{4} Lo^{5} Ox^{3} Pu^{10} [*Jolly* M]; not commented by *Nd Rc;* pādas c-d omitted in Lo^{2} TMd^{3}, and pāda-d by Wa. Cited by *Lakṣ* 12.629 — a) NKt^{4} GMd^{1} TMd^{3} TMd^{4} GMd^{5} GMy NNg Tj^{1} Tr^{1} MTr^{4} MTr^{6} नातिचरति; Be^{3} नाविचरति — b) Be^{1} Ho BKt^{5} wKt^{6} sOx^{1} Pu^{5} sPu^{6} Pu^{7} Pu^{9} Tr^{2} [*Jolly* G] मनोवाक्काय° ; NNg oOr Pu^{2} Pu^{4} Pu^{5} Pu^{7} Pu^{9} Tr^{2} MTr^{3} °संयुता; Be^{1} Ho °कर्मभिः — c) Bo La^{2} GMd^{1} भर्तृलोकमवाप्नोति [GMd^{1} °लोकानवा° ; *om* सा]; Pu^{8} इहाग्र्यां कीर्तिमाप्नोति [cf. 166c]; [*Jolly* N] सा पतिलोकमाप्नोति; Be^{1} Bo Hy Jm Jo^{1} wKt^{1} Kt^{2} wKt^{6} Lo^{1} TMd^{4} oOr Ox^{2} NPu^{1} Pu^{5} Pu^{7} Pu^{9} Tj^{2} Wa [*Jolly* G R] *Mandlik Jolly Jha KSS Dave* °लोकमाप्नोति [cf. 9.29] — d) Tr^{2} साध्वी प्रचोच्यते; Be^{1} गद्यते

166.* Omitted in Lo^{4} Lo^{5} Ox^{3} Pu^{10} [*Jolly* M]; not commented by *Nd;* pādas a-b omitted in TMd^{3} TMd^{4}, and pādas a-c in Wa. Cited by *Lakṣ* 12.629; *Dev* 3.591 — b) Ho मनोवाक्काय-कर्मभिः; Tj^{2} *om* देह; Pu^{5} Pu^{7} Pu^{9} Tr^{2} MTr^{3} °संयुता — c) *Lakṣ* इह कीर्तिमवाप्नोति; wKt^{6} इह श्रीकीर्ति-मवाप्नोति; MTr^{6} इहम्य; Ho इहाग्रां; Pu^{5} Pu^{7} Pu^{9} इहाद्यां — d) Tj^{1} *KSS* पतिलोके; TMd^{4} oOr Pu^{2} पर-लोकं

167.* Not commented by *Nd.* Cited by *Viś* 1.87; *Dev* 2.437 — a) Bo Ho °वृत्तान्तवर्णां; NPu^{1} सवर्णा; Ox^{3} सवर्णं; Lo^{3} सवर्णां च; Be^{3} Jo^{1} Lo^{1} Lo^{5} NPu^{1} Pu^{3} स्त्री; Jm स्त्रीः — b) wKt^{1} द्विजाती; Jo^{1} द्विजातीः; wKt^{3} TMd^{3} द्विजातिं; Ho Ox^{3} द्विजाति; GMd^{1} °मारणीं — c) TMd^{4} रोहयेदग्नि° — d) NPu^{1} °मन्त्रैश्च; Pu^{2} Pu^{4} °पात्रेण धर्म° ; NKt^{4} धर्मवत्

168. Not commented by *Nd.* Pādas a-c cited by *Apa* 77 — a) Pu^{10} भार्या वै; Be^{3} धर्मारिण्यै; Pu^{7} °मारण्यै; Pu^{5} Pu^{9} °मारण्ये —b) Lo^{5} °नन्तकर्मणि — c) oOr पुनर्दाह° ; Lo^{3} °क्रियां यां च पुनराधा°

169. Cited by *Lakṣ* 2.435 — a) Be^{1} नित्यः — b) GMd^{1} पञ्चयज्ञपरो भवेत्; Tj^{1} पाचयज्ञान्न; wKt^{1} Ox^{3} यज्ञं न; Wa *om* न; Jo^{2} Pu^{5} Pu^{7} Pu^{9} Tr^{1} [*Jolly* G] हापयन् — c) TMd^{4} °मायुषा — d) Lo^{2} GMd^{1} TMd^{3} GMy Ox^{2} Ox^{3} Pu^{3} Pu^{8} Pu^{10} Tr^{1} Tr^{2} MTr^{4} MTr^{6} *Lakṣ* गृहेषु ब्राह्मणो वसेत् [NKt^{4} गृहे वै; Ox^{2} गृहे]; [*Jolly* Gr] गृहेषु ब्राह्मणो वनं [sic] [*Nā* gloss ब्राह्मण इति प्राधान्यादुक्तम् supports variant reading]; wKt^{6} हृतदारो; Be^{3} कृतभागो; oOr वसन्

॥ इति मानवे धर्मशास्त्रे भृगुप्रोक्तायां संहितायां पञ्चमोऽध्यायः ॥

Colophon: Be[1] BKt[5] wKt[6] Lo[1] GMd[1] TMd[4] NNg Tr[1] इति श्रीमानवे; Lo[3] मानवीये; wKt[3] भृगुप्रोक्ते; Be[3] BKt[5] wKt[6] Lo[1] GMy sOx[1] sPu[6] MTr[6] *om* भृगुप्रोक्तायां संहितायां; wKt[3] Pu[8] *om* संहितायां; BBe[2] शौचविधिर्नाम पञ्चमो; Ox[2] शुद्धिप्रकरणं नाम पञ्चमो; NNg गृहस्थधर्मो नाम पञ्चमो; oOr शुद्धिर्नाम पञ्चमो; Be[1] अभक्ष्यशौचाध्यायः पञ्चमः; Kt[2] Lo[1] शौचविधिः पञ्चमो; Bo भक्षाभक्ष्यशौचाध्यायः

[षष्ठोऽध्यायः]

एवं गृहाश्रमे स्थित्वा विधिवत् स्नातको द्विजः ।
वने वसेत्तु नियतो यथावद्विजितेन्द्रियः ॥१॥
गृहस्थस्तु यदा पश्येद्वलीपलितमात्मनः ।
अपत्यस्यैव चापत्यं तदारण्यं समाश्रयेत् ॥२॥
संत्यज्य ग्राम्यमाहारं सर्वं चैव परिच्छदम् ।
पुत्रेषु भार्यां निक्षिप्य वनं गच्छेत्सहैव वा ॥३॥
अग्निहोत्रं समादाय गृह्यं चाग्निपरिच्छदम् ।
ग्रामादरण्यं निःसृत्य निवसेन्नियतेन्द्रियः ॥४॥
मुन्यन्नैर्विविधैर्मेध्यैः शाकमूलफलेन वा ।

Additional verse at the beginning in TMd^{4} [reading not very clear]:

यो दहेदग्निहोत्रेण स्वेन भार्यां कथंचन ।
सस्त्री सम्पद्यते तस्य भार्या चास्य श्रीमान्भवेत् ॥

Additional verse in wKt^{1} wKt^{3} GMd^{1} TMd^{4} GMd^{5} oOr Tr^{1} Tr^{2} MTr^{4} MTr^{6}:

अतः परं प्रवक्ष्यामि धर्मं वैखानसाश्रमम् ।
वन्यमूलफलानां च विधिं ग्रहणमोक्षणे ॥

a) wKt^{3} अथापरं — b) Tr^{1} धर्म्यं; wKt^{1} wKt^{3} वैखानसं स्वयं; oOr °साश्रयं — d) GMd^{5} विधिं च ग्रहमोक्षणे; oOr °भक्षणे

1. c) Ho wKt^{1} Lo^{4} Lo^{5} TMd^{3} Ox^{3} Pu^{3} वसेत; wKt^{3} वसेच्च; oOr वसेत्स; MTr^{6} वसेनियतो; Be^{1} वसेत्सुनियतो; Bo वसेत्सुनिपातो

2. Cited by *Vij* 3.45; *Mādh* 1.525 — b) Pu^{2} Pu^{4} °लीपलितुमा° Lo^{3} °लीपक्तिमा°; Ho wKt^{6} °लीपतितमा°; BKt^{5} °लीपतीतमा° — c) TMd^{4} अपत्यस्य च चापत्यं; Jm Pu^{9} अपत्यस्येव; *Vij* वापत्यं — d) oOr पश्येद्विधिवत्स्नातको द्विजः [6.1b]; TMd^{4} तथारण्यं; Ho GMy समाचरेत्; Pu^{3} समाचयेत्

3. Omitted in Ho Tj^{2}; pādas c-d omitted in Tj^{1}. Cited by *Mādh* 1.525; pādas a-b cited by *Vij* 3.46 — a) TMd^{4} संत्यजेद्ग्राम्यमाहारं; Jm BKt^{5} wKt^{6} Lo^{1} GMd^{5} sOx^{1} sPu^{6} Pu^{10} ग्राममा° — b) Tj^{1} सर्वे; Lo^{1} सर्व; oOr गृहं चैव; Ho परिच्छिदं — c) TMd^{3} Pu^{5} Pu^{7} Pu^{9} भार्या; Lo^{3} भार्यो; La^{1} भर्यान्निक्षिप्य; Be^{1} दारान्निक्षिप्य; BKt^{5} wKt^{6} निःक्षिप्य; TMd^{4} निक्षेप्य — d) Be^{1} Lo^{1} Lo^{2} sOx^{1} sPu^{6} Tr^{2} वने; Pu^{2} Pu^{4} °त्सदैव; Ox^{3} Pu^{10} च; Be^{1} सा

4.* Pādas a-b omitted in Tj^{1}. Cited by *Lakṣ* 14.13 — a) sOx^{1} समाधाय; TMd^{3} [*Jolly* Nd] समानीय; wKt^{6} समाज्ञाय — b) GMd^{1} Tr^{1} ग्राह्यं; BBe^{2} [*Jolly* Gr] गृहं; TMd^{4} गुह्यं; Tr^{1} MTr^{4} MTr^{6} चार्थपरि°; [*Jolly* Gr] चाथ परि°; TMd^{4} चार्दपरि°; wKt^{1} BKt^{5} wKt^{6} चैव परि° — c) Kt^{2} NPu^{1} Tr^{2} निसृत्य; Be^{1} निश्रित्य; Be^{3} Bo La^{2} Tj^{1} निर्गत्य; GMd^{1} TMd^{3} TMd^{4} GMd^{5} GMy Tr^{1} MTr^{4} MTr^{6} *Lakṣ* निष्क्रम्य; Lo^{4} Lo^{5} Ox^{3} Pu^{10} [*Jolly* M Nd] निःक्रम्य; NNg निक्रम्य — d) Jo^{2} निवसेद्विजितेन्द्रियः; Pu^{5} Pu^{7} Pu^{9} निवासन्निय°

एतानेव महायज्ञान् निर्वपेद्विधिपूर्वकम् ॥५॥
वसीत चर्म चीरं वा सायं स्नायात् प्रगे तथा ।
जटाश्च बिभृयान्नित्यं श्मश्रुलोमनखानि च ॥६॥
यद्भक्षः स्यात्ततो दद्याद्बलिं भिक्षां च शक्तितः ।
अम्मूलफलभिक्षाभिरर्चयेदाश्रमागतान् ॥७॥
स्वाध्याये नित्ययुक्तः स्याद् दान्तो मैत्रः समाहितः ।
दाता नित्यमनादाता सर्वभूतानुकम्पकः ॥८॥
वैतानिकं च जुहुयादग्निहोत्रं यथाविधि ।
दर्शमस्कन्दयन्पर्व पौर्णमासं च योगतः ॥९॥
ऋक्षेष्ट्याग्रयणं चैव चातुर्मास्यानि चाहरेत् ।
तुरायणं च क्रमशो दक्षस्यायनमेव च ॥१०॥

5. Cited by *Apa* 941; *Mādh* 1.526 — a) Jm wKt^{1} उत्पन्नैर्वि° — b) Pu^{2} Pu^{4} शाकमूलेन वा; BKt^{5} wKt^{6} Pu^{10} च — c) Jo^{1} Tr^{2} एतान्येव; *Mādh* एतैरेव; Tr^{2} महायज्ञो — d) Ho निवपे°

wKt^{1} wKt^{3} place here the additional verses given after 6.45.

6. Omitted in Pu^{5}. Cited by *Apa* 941; pādas c-d cited by *Vij* 3.46 — a) Tr^{2} वशीत; Pu^{10} चीरे; Be^{1} sOx^{1} sPu^{6} च — b) Pu^{7} [*Jolly* G] मार्गं वा वार्क्षमेव वा; Pu^{9} मार्गं [then lacuna]; TMd^{4} स्नायात्सायं प्रगे; Lo^{1} *ma* सायं; TMd^{3} प्रजे — c) BBe^{2} जटांश्च; wKt^{6} जटा च; Pu^{4} जयश्च; Lo^{2} जराश्च — d) wKt^{3} °रोम°; Be^{1} Bo La^{2} Pu^{7} Pu^{9} Wa [*Jolly* M$^{1-2-5-8-9}$ G] *Vij Jolly* °नखांस्तथा; Ox^{3} °नखादि च

7.* Cited by *Vij* 3.46; *Apa* 941 — a) Pu^{9} ms. torn at pāda-a; Be^{1} Lo^{1} Lo^{2} sOx^{1} sPu^{6} Tr^{2} Wa यद्भक्ष्यः; BBe^{2} Hy Jm Jo^{1} Kt^{2} wKt^{3} La^{1} [*cor to*] Lo^{3} GMd^{1} TMd^{4} oOr Ox^{2} Pu^{8} Tj^{2} *Vij Rn Rc Mandlik Jolly KSS* यद्भक्ष्यं ; Be^{3} Bo Jo^{2} La^{2} wKt^{1} BKt^{5} wKt^{6} La^{1} Ox^{3} Tj^{1} यद्भक्षं; TMd^{4} यद्भैक्ष्यं; GMd^{5} यद्भैक्ष्य; Tj^{2} यद्भिक्ष्यं — b) TMd^{4} भिक्षांश्च— c) wKt^{3} अन्नमूलफलंभक्ष्यात्त्वर्चये° ; BBe^{2} अन्नमूल° ; Be^{3} अप्मूल° ; Pu^{5} Pu^{7} Pu^{9} अपमूल° ; La^{1} आमूल° ; Bo NKt^{4} wKt^{6} Ox^{3} अमूल° ; Tj^{1} अमूलं; Lo^{1} कन्दमूल° ; Pu^{4} अम्मूलभिक्षाभिर° — d) Hy °रर्चयदा° ; TMd^{3} °श्रमेगतान्; Lo^{4} Lo^{5} GMd^{1} GMd^{5} Ox^{3} Pu^{10} [*Jolly* M^{4}] °गतं

8. a) Pu^{5} Pu^{7} Pu^{9} Wa [*Jolly* G] स्वाध्यायशीलो नित्यं स्याद्; GMd^{1} Tr^{1} स्वाध्यायेन नियुक्त स्याद्; Be^{1} TMd^{4} स्वध्याय; Bo नित्यमुक्तः — b) Bo मित्रः — c) Pu^{5} Pu^{7} [*Jolly* G] त्यक्तद्वंद्वानिशं दाता [*Jolly* G °द्वंद्वोनिशं]; Be^{3} ददाति नित्यं न दाता; Bo दान्ता; NKt^{4} तदा; Pu^{2} Pu^{4} नित्यमदाता च; Tj^{1} °नादाती; Ox^{3} °नादातः; Pu^{10} °नादिता — d) wKt^{6} GMd^{1} Pu^{7} Pu^{9} °कम्पनः; Pu^{5} °कम्पतः

9. Placed before verse 6 in Jm; pādas b-d torn in MTr^{5}. Cited by *Vij* 3.45; *Apa* 941; *Mādh* 1.526 — a) wKt^{3} वैतालिकं; Pu^{10} वितानिकं; *Apa* [vl] वैताग्निकं; Lo^{1} तु — c) Be^{1} sOx^{1} sPu^{6} Tj^{2} दार्शम° ; Be^{3} Ho दशम° ; NKt^{4} दाशाम° ; *Apa* दशाम° ; Tj^{1} °मास्कन्द° ; Pu^{5} Pu^{7} Pu^{9} °स्कन्धय° ; wKt^{1} °क्षन्दय° ; GMd^{1} Tr^{1} °न्पर्वं; Ox^{3} °न्पवं; Be^{1} °न्कर्म; TMd^{4} °न्पूर्ण; oOr *Apa* [vl as in ed] °न्पूर्वं — d) NPu^{1} *Apa* पूर्ण° ; TMd^{3} GMd^{5} °मास्यां; Bo °मासा; Tr^{1} °मासीं; *Mādh* °मासं प्रयोगतः; TMd^{4} *Vij Apa* शक्तितः

10.* Omitted in Ox^{3}; pādas c-d torn in MTr^{5}. Cited by *Apa* 941; *Lakṣ* 14.17; *Mādh* 1.526 — a) GMd^{1} ऋक्षेष्ट्याग्रयणेष्या च; GMd^{5} ऋक्ष्येट्या° ; Tj^{1} ऋष्येष्ट्या° ; Be^{1} Lo^{5} sOx^{1} sPu^{6} Pu^{10} [*Jolly* M] *Me Dave Jha* दर्शेष्ट्या° ; Jo^{1} Kt^{2} °ग्रायणं; TMd^{4} GMd^{5} Tr^{2} MTr^{4} MTr^{6} °ग्रयणे; TMd^{3} °ग्रहणं; Tr^{1} °ग्रयणैश्चैव; NPu^{1} °यणं कुर्यात् — a-b) Pu^{5} Pu^{7} Pu^{9} *Go* [*Jolly* G] नक्षत्रेष्टिं तथा दर्शपौर्णमासानि चाहरेत्

वासन्तशारदैर्मेध्यैर्मुन्यन्नैः स्वयमाहृतैः ।
पुरोडाशांश्चरूंश्चैव विधिवन्निर्वपेत्पृथक् ॥११॥
देवताभ्यश्च तद्धुत्वा वन्यं मेध्यतरं हविः ।
शेषमात्मनि युञ्जीत लवणं च स्वयंकृतम् ॥१२॥
स्थलजौदकशाकानि पुष्पमूलफलानि च ।
मेध्यवृक्षोद्भवान्यद्यात् स्नेहांश्च फलसंभवान् ॥१३॥
वर्जयेन्मधुमांसानि भौमानि कवकानि च ।
भूस्तृणं शिग्रुकं चैव श्लेष्मातकफलानि च ॥१४॥
त्यजेदाश्वयुजे मासि मुन्यन्नं पूर्वसंचितम् ।
जीर्णानि चैव वासांसि शाकमूलफलानि च ॥१५॥

— b) Ho Ox[2] वाहरेत्; Pu[3] वाहयेत्; GMd[1] वाचरेत् — c) Be[3] त्वरायणं; BBe[2] BCa Hy Jm Jo[1] wKt[1] Kt[2] wKt[3] BKt[5] wKt[6] La[1] Lo[1] (*mc to*) sOx[1] NPu[1] Pu[2] Pu[4] Pu[5] sPu[6] Pu[7] Pu[9] Tj[1] Tr[1] Tr[2] MTr[3] [*Jolly* G Ku] *Rc Mr Go Apa Lakṣ Mādh* उत्तरायणं च [sOx[1] sPu[6] *om* च]; GMd[1] त्रौरायणं च; Ox[2] तुरीयणं च; [*Jolly* Gr] नारायणं च; TMd[3] °यणं चन्द्रमसो; Be[3] Tj[1] *Apa* तु — d) Jo[1] Kt[2] MTr[3] *Mandlik Jha Dave* दाक्षस्यायन°; Be[1] दक्षस्याध्यन°; Ho Pu[2] Pu[4] Pu[5] Pu[7] Pu[9] दक्षणायन°; BBe[2] BCa Ox[2] NPu[1] [*Jolly* G] *Go* दक्षिणायन°; La[1] दक्षिणस्यायन°; Pu[3] दत्तस्यायन°

11. Pāda-c torn in MTr[5]. Cited by *Vij* 3.46; *Apa* 941; *Lakṣ* 14.17; *Mādh* 1.527 — a) TMd[4] GMy वासन्तैश्शार°; Tr[1] *Mādh* वासन्तैः शार°; TMd[3] वासन्तैहरधर्मे°; oOr °दैर्मध्यैर्मु° — b) wKt[1] °ध्यैरुत्पन्नैः; Tj[1] °ध्यैः सत्पन्नैः; Tr[2] चैवमाहृतैः; wKt[3] सुसमाहृतैः; Bo Ho °हतैः — c) Bo °डाशश्च°; Ox[3] °डाशाश्च°; GMy °डाशं च चरूं चैव; TMd[3] °डाशं चरुं चैव; wKt[1] oOr °श्चरुं चैव; Be[3] wKt[6] Ox[3] Pu[2] Pu[4] °श्चरूश्चैव — d) GMd[1] निर्वपेद्विधिवत्पृथक्; Be[1] Bo TMd[3] GMy Wa *Mādh* निर्वपेद्विधिपूर्वकं; Tr[2] *Apa Lakṣ* निर्वपेत्तु पृथक्पृथक् [*Apa* निर्वपेच्च]; TMd[4] निर्वपेत्पृथगात्मवान्

12.* Pādas a-b torn in MTr[5]; pāda-a torn in Pu[9]. Cited by *Vij* 3.46; *Apa* 941; *Lakṣ* 14.18 — a) BBe[2] Be[3] Ho Hy Jm Jo[1] Kt[2] wKt[3] BKt[5] wKt[6] Lo[1] Lo[2] Lo[4] Lo[5] TMd[4] oOr sOx[1] Ox[2] Ox[3] NPu[1] Pu[2] Pu[3] Pu[4] sPu[6] Pu[8] Pu[10] Tj[1] MTr[3] [*Jolly* M[4]] *Apa Mandlik Jha KSS Dave* °भ्यस्तु; Kt[2] तच्छुत्वा; La[1] *Apa* तच्छ्रुत्वा; *Lakṣ* तद्दत्वा — b) TMd[4] तद्धुत्वा अन्यं; Tj[1] Tr[2] मन्यं; wKt[6] oOr मध्यतरं; Be[1] Be[3] Bo Ho Pu[3] Tj[1] मेध्यतमं — c) *Lakṣ* शेषं समुपभुञ्जीत; MTr[5] शेषं समुपयुञ्जीत; Be[1] Ho TMd[4] Pu[2] Pu[4] Pu[8] Tr[2] भुञ्जीत — d) NKt[4] वा; Bo °कृतां; La[1] °हृतं; TMd[3] °वृतं

13. Pādas b-d omitted in Ox[3]; parts of pādas a-c torn in MTr[5]. Cited by *Apa* 942; *Lakṣ* 14.18; pādas c-d cited by *Vij* 3.49 — a) Ox[2] स्थलौदकानि शाकानि; GMd[1] स्थलजौदकानि शाकानि; Pu[2] Pu[4] स्थलोदजातिशाकानि; *Apa* स्थूलोदकजशाकानि; BBe[2] Bo wKt[1] wKt[6] GMy oOr Pu[5] Pu[7] Pu[9] Tj[1] Tr[1] Tr[2] Wa स्थलजोद° — c) Lo[3] स्नेहवृक्षो°; BKt[5] Tr[2] *Vij* °द्भवानद्यात्; MTr[6] °द्भवान्यात्; Bo °द्भवेनद्यात्; TMd[4] GMd[5] GMy Tr[1] °द्भवानन्यान्; TMd[3] °द्भवान्वन्यान्; *Apa Lakṣ* °द्भवान्यन्यान्; Tj[1] °द्भवांश्चैव — d) TMd[3] स्नेहं च; TMd[4] सहांश्च; TMd[3] °संभवं

14. Pādas c-d omitted in wKt[1] and pāda-a in Ox[3]; pādas a-b *ma sh* in Pu[10]. Cited by *Apa* 942; *Lakṣ* 14.18 — a) Hy वर्जयन्मधु°; BBe[2] Be[3] Hy Jm Jo[1] Kt[2] wKt[3] BKt[5] wKt[6] Lo[2] Ox[2] [*cor to*] Tj[1] Tj[2] MTr[3] *Mandlik Jha KSS Dave* °मांसं च — b) GMy भामानि; TMd[3] कफलानि; TMd[4] कतकानि; oOr कनकस्य च — c) Kt[2] भूस्तृणां; Be[1] GMy NNg Tj[1] भूतृणं; Lo[1] भूस्तीर्णं; La[1] सिग्रुकं; Lo[3] श्रिग्रुगं; NNg शग्रुकं; Pu[2] Pu[4] शल्गुलं; Pu[10] शृगुकं; Tj[1] शिलकं; *Lakṣ* सिद्धिकं — d) Be[1] Kt[2] wKt[3] [*Jolly* M[1-2-5-8-9] G] श्लेष्मान्तक°; Pu[5] Pu[7] श्लेष्यान्तक°; GMy श्लोप्मातक°; Pu[10] °भवानि च

15. Pāda-d torn in MTr[5]. Cited by *Apa* 942; *Mādh* 1.527 — a) Lo[1] त्यजेदाश्वमुपासीत; oOr

न फालकृष्टमश्नीयादुत्सृष्टमपि केनचित् ।
न ग्रामजातान्यार्तोऽपि पुष्पाणि च फलानि च ॥१६॥
अग्निपक्वाशनो वा स्यात् कालपक्वभुगेव वा ।
अश्मकुट्टो भवेद्वापि दन्तोलूखलिकोऽपि वा ॥१७॥
सद्यःप्रक्षालको वा स्यान् माससंचयिकोऽपि वा ।
षण्मासनिचयो वा स्यात् समानिचय एव वा ॥१८॥
नक्तं वान्नं समश्नीयाद् दिवा वाहृत्य शक्तितः ।
चतुर्थकालिको वा स्यात् स्याद्वाप्यष्टमकालिकः ॥१९॥
चान्द्रायणविधानैर्वा शुक्ले कृष्णे च वर्तयेत् ।
पक्षान्तयोर्वाप्यश्नीयाद् यवागुं क्वथितां सकृत् ॥२०॥

°श्वयुज; NKt^{4} TMd^{3} TMd^{4} GMd^{5} GMy Tr^{1} MTr^{4} MTr^{5} MTr^{6} *Mādh* मासे — b) wKt^{1} मूलान्नं; wKt^{6} पर्व°; Tj^{1} सर्व° — c) La^{1} MTr^{4} चैव मांसानि

16.* Omitted in Tj^{1} [haplo]; pāda-d torn in Pu^{9} MTr^{5}. Cited by *Apa* 942; *Lakṣ* 14.18 — a) BKt^{5} wKt^{6} फालकृष्टं च नाश्नियादु°; Hy GMd^{1} फालाकृ°; Ox^{3} MTr^{6} फलाकृ°; TMd^{3} पालकृ°; Pu^{4} कालकृ°; Wa °कृष्टान्यश्नी°; Be^{1} °श्नीयामु° — b) Pu^{5} Pu^{7} Pu^{9} [*Jolly* G] °दुच्छिष्टमपि — c) *Lakṣ* न यातयामान्यार्तो; TMd^{3} °जातनार्तो; TMd^{4} °जातान्यत्यापि — d) La^{1} पुष्पमूलफलानि च; Be^{3} Bo BCa Hy Jm Jo^{1} Jo^{2} wKt^{1} Kt^{2} wKt^{3} La^{2} Lo^{1} Lo^{3} NNg sOx^{1} [*but mc*] Ox^{2} Pu^{3} sPu^{6} [*but mc*] Pu^{8} Tj^{2} Tr^{1} MTr^{3} [*Jolly* Ku R] *Apa Mandlik KSS Dave* मूलानि च फलानि च; Pu^{5} *om* फलानि च

17.* Pādas a-b in Pu^{9} lacuna; pādas c-d torn in MTr^{5}. Cited by *Apa* 942; *Lakṣ* 14.24; pādas a-b cited by *Vij* 3.49 — b) wKt^{1} कालपक्वाशनोपिवा; NKt^{4} अर्कपक्व°; NPu^{1} फलपक्व°; Lo^{5} TMd^{3} Pu^{10} च — c) BCa Pu^{5} Pu^{7} अश्मकुदो; Lo^{2} अश्मकुद्ये; BCa oOr NPu^{1} भवेद्वाथ — d) BBe^{2} Ho °खलको; TMd^{3} °खलेपि वा; Be^{1} Be^{3} Jo^{2} wKt^{3} NKt^{4} BKt^{5} wKt^{6} La^{1} Lo^{1} Lo^{2} Lo^{3} Lo^{4} Lo^{5} NNg sOx^{1} Ox^{3} NPu^{1} Pu^{5} sPu^{6} Pu^{7} Pu^{9} Pu^{10} Tj^{1} Tr^{2} Wa [*Jolly* M G R] *Apa Jolly* °खलिकस्तथा; TMd^{4} च

18. Pāda-d omitted in Tj^{2} [haplo]; pādas c-d torn in Pu^{9} MTr^{5}. Cited by *Apa* 942; *Lakṣ* 14.24; *Mādh* 1.527 — a) oOr सदा प्रक्षालितो; BBe^{2} BKt^{5} wKt^{6} wKt^{6} Lo^{3} Pu^{2} Pu^{4} °प्रक्षालिको; Lo^{1} °प्रक्षाल्यको; GMd^{5} Tr^{1} °प्रक्षाळको; TMd^{3} °प्रक्षालितो; Be^{1} °प्रक्षप्रको; TMd^{4} °पक्षानितो — b) MTr^{4} MTr^{5} MTr^{6} मांस°; Ho Pu^{7} Pu^{9} Tr^{2} *Apa* °संचयको; Pu^{10} °संचैयिको — c) GMd^{5} Tj^{1} षाण्मास°; Hy °सानिचयो; wKt^{1} *Apa* °ससंचयो; GMd^{1} TMd^{3} TMd^{4} GMy NNg Pu^{5} Pu^{7} वापि

19.* Pādas a-c omitted in Tj^{2}; lacuna at pāda-d in TMd^{4}; pādas b-d torn in MTr^{5}. Cited by *Vij* 3.50; *Apa* 943; *Lakṣ* 14.24 — a) Jo^{1} रक्तं; Pu^{5} Pu^{7} Pu^{9} उक्तं; Kt^{2} नक्तश्चान्नं; Be^{1} Bo Ho Jm Jo^{1} Jo^{2} Kt^{2} wKt^{3} wKt^{6} La^{1} La^{2} Lo^{1} Lo^{2} Lo^{3} Lo^{5} oOr sOx^{1} Ox^{3} Pu^{2} Pu^{5} sPu^{6} Pu^{7} Pu^{8} Pu^{9} Tr^{2} Wa [*Jolly* G R] *Mandlik Jha KSS Dave* चान्नं; wKt^{1} चार्थं; *Apa* यावं [vl यावः] — b) Tr^{2} दिवाहृत्य तु शक्तितः; oOr दिवाहृत्य; Be^{1} Bo BCa wKt^{1} Pu^{10} चाहृत्य; Lo^{5} चाहुत्य; Ho वाहत्य — c) Ho Tr^{2} चतुर्थि°; TMd^{3} चतुर्थमाचिकं; TMd^{4} *om* स्यात् — d) GMd^{1} TMd^{3} GMd^{5} GMy स्याद्वा षष्टाष्टमाशनः; *Lakṣ* स्याद्वा षष्टाष्टमासतः; wKt^{3} अथचाप्यष्टकालिकः; Be^{3} *Vij* यद्वाप्य°; Be^{1} Bo अथवाष्ट°; Tr^{2} °कालकः

20. Pādas a-c torn in MTr^{5} and pāda-b in Pu^{9}. Cited by *Lakṣ* 14.24 — a) TMd^{3} चन्द्रा°; wKt^{6} °यणविनैर्वापि; Tj^{2} °विधानैश्च — b) Hy Jo^{1} Kt^{2} TMd^{3} Tj^{1} *Mandlik Jha Dave KSS* शुक्लकृष्णे; GMd^{1} शुद्धकृष्णे; Pu^{5} Pu^{7} वर्धयेत्; GMd^{1} वर्जयेत् — d) MTr^{6} यवाङ्गं; wKt^{6} यवाग्निं; TMd^{4} यवोगान्क्वाथितां; MTr^{6} क्वथितं; Be^{3} क्वथिकां; Hy क्वतिकां; wKt^{1} कथितं; TMd^{3} त्वथितां; Tj^{1} क्वथितान्सकृत्; Bo [*but cor*] BKt^{5} wKt^{6} Tj^{1} क्वथितां क्वचित्

पुष्पमूलफलैर्वापि केवलैर्वर्तयेत्सदा ।
कालपक्वैः स्वयंशीर्णैर्वैखानसमते स्थितः ॥२१॥
भूमौ विपरिवर्तेत तिष्ठेद्वा प्रपदैर्दिनम् ।
स्थानासनाभ्यां विहरेत् सवनेषूपयन्नपः ॥२२॥
ग्रीष्मे पञ्चतपास्तु स्याद् वर्षास्वभ्रावकाशिकः ।
आर्द्रवासास्तु हेमन्ते क्रमशो वर्धयंस्तपः ॥२३॥
उपस्पृशंस्त्रिषवणं पितॄन्देवांश्च तर्पयेत् ।
तपश्चरंश्चोग्रतरं शोषयेद्देहमात्मनः ॥२४॥
अग्नींश्चात्मनि वैतानान् समारोप्य यथाविधि ।
अनग्निरनिकेतः स्यान् मुनिर्मूलफलाशनः ॥२५॥

Additional verse in *Mandlik* [ट] *KSS Dave:*

यतः पत्रं समादद्यान्न ततः पुष्पमाहरेत् ।
यतः पुष्पं समादद्यान्न ततः फलमाहरेत् ॥

21. Omitted in Jm; torn in mTr^5; pāda-c lacuna in tMd^4. Pādas a-b cited by *Lakṣ* 14.24 — a) Ho wKt^3 Tj^1 °मूलैः फलैर्वापि — b) Lo^2 वर्तयेत्केवलैः सदा; Pu^{10} °वर्तयेः सदा — c) *Lakṣ* स्वाभाविकैः स्वयं°; oOr *om* स्वयं; wKt^1 °शीर्णवैखा°; wKt^6 oOr °शीर्णे वैखा° — d) Kt^2 °वैश्वासन°; tMd^3 °वैघानस°; Be^3 bKt^5 wKt^6 La^1 nPu^1 Pu^2 Pu^4 Pu^5 Pu^7 Pu^9 °वैषानस° [wKt^6 La^1 °णस°]; Pu^{10} °वैश्वानस°; oOr °वैखानसंस्थितेः; Lo^2 °मतो; Pu^{10} स्थिताः; Tr^2 स्थितिः

Additional verse in La^1 oOr [cf. addition after 6.20]:

आददीत यतः पत्रं नाददीत ततः फलम् ।
आहरेत्तु यतः पत्रं ततः पुष्पाणि नाहरेत् ॥

a-b) La^1 यतः पवनददती भवतः — c) La^1 आहरते — La^1 चाहरेत्

22. Cited by *Apa* 943; *Lakṣ* 14.24; pādas a-b cited by *Vij* 3.51 — a) Pu^{10} भूमौ परि°; tMd^3 वा परि°; wKt^1 °वर्तन्ते — b) Lo^5 तिष्ठेद्वामपदै° — c) nKt^4 gMd^1 tMd^3 tMd^4 gMy *Apa* स्थानासनैर्वा विहरेत्; oOr स्थानाशनैर्वा विहरेत् — d) Lo^1 सवनेषु प्रयन्नतः; Tr^1 वनेषूपवनेपि च; Lo^2 सवनेषूदकं स्पृशेत्; bKt^5 wKt^6 समयेषूप°; Tj^1 °षूपपन्नयः; sOx^1 sPu^6 °पयन्पयः; Jm °पयन्ततः; tMd^3 °पयनहः

23. Cited by *Lakṣ* 14.24 — a) bBe^2 ग्रीष्म; Lo^2 ग्रीष्मं; tMd^4 पञ्चातपस्तु; sOx^1 sPu^6 Tr^2 °तपस्तु; Be^3 °तपाश्च; Tj^1 °तपश्च; gMd^1 °तपस्यात्तु वर्षा° — b) gMd^1 °स्वाकाशगोयदा; tMd^4 °स्वाभोविकोषिकः; Be^1 Be^3 Bo Ho bKt^5 wKt^6 Lo^4 Lo^5 gMd^5 nNg Ox^3 Pu^5 Pu^7 Pu^9 Pu^{10} Tr^1 Tr^2 Wa [*Jolly* M] °काशकः; gMy [*Jolly* Nd] °काशगः; Pu^2 Pu^4 °कासिकः; tMd^3 °काशनः — c) bKt^5 wKt^6 आर्द्रा°; Wa आद्र°; tMd^4 अर्त° — d) bKt^5 wKt^6 Pu^5 sPu^6 Pu^7 *Lakṣ* वर्धयन्तपः; tMd^3 gMy Tj^1 वर्धयेत्तपः

24. Pāda-b torn in Pu^9. Cited by *Apa* 944; *Lakṣ* 14.24; pāda c-d cited by *Vij* 3.52 — a) sOx^1 sPu^6 उपस्पृश्यंस्त्रि°; Pu^5 Pu^7 Pu^9 उपस्पृशन् त्रि°; Tr^2 उपस्पृशोत्रि°; Be^3 wKt^1 nPu^1 Tj^1 *Apa Lakṣ* उपस्पृशेत्रि°; bKt^5 wKt^6 उपस्पृशस्त्रि°; Pu^2 Pu^4 उपस्पर्शस्त्रि°; oOr उपस्पृश्य त्रि° — b) wKt^1 gMd^1 tMd^3 gMy Pu^5 Pu^7 mTr^6 पितृदेवांश्च; Be^1 Be^3 Bo Wa °न्देवांस्तु; Tj^1 °न्देवास्तु; bBe^2 bCa Ho bKt^5 wKt^6 Lo^3 Lo^4 Lo^5 gMd^5 nNg Pu^{10} mTr^4 mTr^6 [*Jolly* M$^{1-2-3-8-9}$] तर्पयन्; La^1 Ox^3 Wa तर्पयत् — c) bKt^5 wKt^6 °श्चोग्रचरं; Pu^2 Pu^4 °श्चोपतरं — d) Hy शोषयद्देह°; gMd^1 शोषयो देह°

25.* Cited by *Vij* 3.54; *Apa* 944; *Mādh* 1.529 — a) wKt^1 nKt^4 oOr sOx^1 Pu^2 Pu^3 Pu^4 sPu^6 Pu^8 Tr^1 *Apa* अग्नींस्त्वात्मनि; Be^3 Ho gMd^5 Tj^1 अग्नीन्स्वात्मनि; nPu^1 अग्नीन्वात्मनि; Jm Jo^1 Kt^2 gMd^1

अप्रयत्नः सुखार्थेषु ब्रह्मचारी धराशयः ।
शरणेष्वममश्चैव वृक्षमूलनिकेतनः ॥२६॥
तापसेष्वेव विप्रेषु यात्रिकं भैक्षमाचरेत् ।
गृहमेधिषु चान्येषु द्विजेषु वनवासिषु ॥२७॥
ग्रामादाहृत्य वाश्नीयादष्टौ ग्रासान्वने वसन् ।
प्रतिगृह्य पुटेनैव पाणिना शकलेन वा ॥२८॥
एताश्चान्याश्च सेवेत दीक्षा विप्रो वने वसन् ।
विविधाश्चौपनिषदीरात्मसंसिद्धये श्रुतीः ॥२९॥
ऋषिभिर्ब्राह्मणैश्चैव गृहस्थैरेव सेविताः ।
विद्यातपोविवृद्ध्यर्थं शरीरस्य च शुद्धये ॥३०॥

TMd[3] TMd[4] GMy Tj[2] MTr[3] MTr[4] MTr[6] *Mandlik Jha KSS Dave*अग्नीनात्मनि; oOr अग्निं स्वात्मनि; Lo[1] अग्निं चात्मनि; wKt[3] वैतालान्; BKt[5] चैतानात् — b) Tr[2] सुसंरोप्य; Lo[1] °रोप्य च यथा° — c) wKt[3] निरग्निर°; BKt[5] wKt[6] °निकेतं — c-d) Ho °निकेतश्च तस्यान्मूलनि° — d) Tr[1] मुनिं मूल°; Be[3] Bo BKt[5] wKt[6] °फलाशिनः

26. Cited by *Mādh* 1.529 transposing pādas a-b and c-d — a) GMd[1] Pu[2] Pu[3] अप्रमत्तः; TMd[3] सुखार्थेन — b) Bo °चारि; Jo[1] Lo[1] दराश्रयः; Lo[2] Ox[3] वराशयः; Pu[10] वनाशयः — c) wKt[6] शरणेपु-रसश्चैव; NNg शरण्येप्वमम°; wKt[1] शरणे निर्मम°; GMd[1] शरीरेप्वमम°; Pu[2] Pu[4] °मतश्चैव; Lo[5] NPu[1] °सम-श्चैव; Tj[2] °वमश्चैव; BKt[5] °वसश्चैव — d) Pu[8] मूलवृक्षे निके°

27.* Cited by *Apa* 945; pādas c-d cited by *Mādh* 1.529 — a) GMd[1] तापसेप्वपि; BBe[2] तापसस्येव; *Apa*तापसेपु च — b) Ho पात्रिकं; Tr[1] यात्रार्थं; Jo[2] भैक्ष्यमा°; Ho Kt[2] La[1] Ox[2] NPu[1] Pu[5] Pu[7] Pu[9] भक्ष्यमा°; oOr भैक्ष्यकं हरेत्; Be[1] BBe[2] Be[3] Bo BCa Ho Hy Jm Jo[1] Jo[2] Kt[2] wKt[3] NKt[4] BKt[5] wKt[6] La[2] Lo[1] Lo[2] Lo[4] Lo[5] TMd[4] Ox[2] Ox[3] NPu[1] Pu[2] Pu[5] Pu[7] Pu[8] Pu[9] Pu[10] Tr[2] MTr[3] Wa *Mandlik Jolly Jha KSS Dave* °माहरेत् — c) Bo °मेधेपु; oOr *om* चान्येपु ; wKt[1] चान्यासु; Jo[2] Lo[3] TMd[3] Ox[3] NPu[1] *Apa* वान्येपु — d) Tr[1] द्विजेष्ववनवासिपु

28. Cited by *Mādh* 1.529 — a) wKt[3] ग्रामादावाह्यमश्नीया°; Ho °हत्य; Lo[1] °हृत्यमश्नीया°; Be[1] BCa [*but cor*] Ho wKt[1] TMd[4] Pu[2] Pu[4] Tj[1] Tr[2] चाश्नीया°; MTr[3] नाश्नीया° — b) wKt[3] Ox[3] ग्रामान्वने; Pu[3] Tr[2] वसेत्; GMd[1] चरेत् — c) wKt[1] प्रगृह्य संपुटेनैव; TMd[4] प्रगृह्य पदेनैव; Tr[1] परिगृह्य; TMd[3] पुटेनैक; Pu[2] Pu[4] पुरेनैव; GMd[5] पर्वतेनैव — d) Pu[5] Pu[7] [*but cor*] Pu[9] शाकलेन; BBe[2] wKt[1] La[1] Pu[3] Tr[2] सकलेन; GMd[1] कलशेन; Pu[2] Pu[4] कलेन

29.* Cited by *Apa* 943; pādas a-b cited by *Mādh* 1.529 and pādas c-d by *Vij* 3.51 — a) La[1] Pu[2] Pu[4] Pu[5] Pu[7] Pu[9] Tj[1] MTr[4] एतांश्चान्यांश्च; TMd[4] एतेनान्याश्च; NKt[4] GMd[1] °न्यांश्च; Tr[2] सेवेत्; Wa सेवत; Pu[10] सेवेतु; GMy कारेत — b) wKt[6] oOr Tj[1] दीक्षां; TMd[3] दीक्षान्विप्रो — c) Be[1] BBe[2] Bo Ho wKt[1] GMd[1] GMd[5] NPu[1] Pu[5] Pu[7] Pu[9] Tr[2] °श्चोपनिप°; TMd[3] °निपदि आत्म°; Lo[1] °निपदो आत्म°; *Apa* °निपद आत्म° — d) Be[1] Jo[2] La[1] [*cor to fh*] BCa BKt[5] wKt[6] TMd[3] GMd[5] GMy sOx[1] Ox[2] Pu[5] sPu[6] Pu[7] Pu[9] Tr[1] Tr[2] MTr[4] MTr[6] [*Jolly* M[1–9] G Nd] *Rn* °त्मसंशुद्धये; oOr °त्मसंशुद्धिने; Be[1] °त्मशु-द्धये; MTr[4] श्रुतीं; Be[3] Lo[4] Lo[5] श्रुती; Tr[1] द्विजः

30. Pāda-b torn in Pu[9]. Cited by *Apa* 943; *Lakṣ* 14.28 — a) *Lakṣ* ऋषिभिर्वृत्तयस्त्वेता; TMd[4] ऋषिभिर्वृत्तयोन्विता; Tr[1] मुनिभि°; Be[1] Bo °ह्मणैर्वापि; BBe[2] °ह्मणश्चैव; Lo[2] °णश्चेव — b) Be[1] Bo *Apa* गृहस्थैश्चोपसेविताः; BBe[2] गृहस्थैरिव सेवते; Be[3] Ho Lo[1] oOr Ox[2] Tj[1] गृहस्थैश्चैव; Pu[5] Pu[7] [*but cor*] °रेवासेविताः; BKt[5] wKt[6] MTr[6] सेवितः; Tj[1] सेविना — c) wKt[3] विद्यातरोवि°; Pu[2] °वृद्ध्यर्थे — d) GMy

अपराजितां वास्थाय व्रजेद्दिशमजिह्मगः ।
आ निपाताच्छरीरस्य युक्तो वार्यनिलाशनः ॥३१॥
आसां महर्षिचर्याणां त्यक्त्वान्यतमया तनुम् ।
वीतशोकभयो विप्रो ब्रह्मलोके महीयते ॥३२॥
वनेषु तु विहृत्यैवं तृतीयं भागमायुषः ।
चतुर्थमायुषो भागं त्यक्त्वा सङ्गान्परिव्रजेत् ॥३३॥
आश्रमादाश्रमं गत्वा हुतहोमो जितेन्द्रियः ।
भिक्षाबलिपरिश्रान्तः प्रव्रजन्प्रेत्य वर्धते ॥३४॥
ऋणानि त्रीण्यपाकृत्य मनो मोक्षे निवेशयेत् ।
अनपाकृत्य मोक्षं तु सेवमानो व्रजत्यधः ॥३५॥
अधीत्य विधिवद्वेदान् पुत्रांश्चोत्पाद्य धर्मतः ।
इष्ट्वा च शक्तितो यज्ञैर्मनो मोक्षे निवेशयेत् ॥३६॥

शारीरस्य; Pu^{4} शरीरेस्य; Ho GMd^{1} GMd^{5} Tr^{1} °रस्य विशुद्धये; BKt^{5} wKt^{6} Pu^{2} Pu^{4} [*Jolly* Gr] सिद्धये

31. Cited by *Apa* 536, 945; *Hem* 3/2.1660; *Lakṣ* 14.28; pādas a-b cited by *Vij* 3.55 — a) TMd^{4} पराजितां वाप्यास्थाय; GMd^{1} अपरातामवस्थाय; BBe^{2} °जिता आस्थाय; TMd^{3} °जितायावास्थायां; sOx^{1} sPu^{6} *Apa* °जितामास्थाय; Tr^{2} °जितांश्चस्थाय; Lo^{1} Lo^{2} Pu^{4} Tj^{1} *Apa Lakṣ* चास्थाय; Lo^{3} Tr^{1} वाप्यास्थाय — b) Tj^{2} व्रजेद्देश°; *Vij* गच्छेद्दिश°; NPu^{1} Tj^{1} °ह्मगाः — c) Ho NPu^{1} अनिपा°; wKt^{6} अभितापाच्छरी° — d) *Hem* ब्रह्मलोके महीयते [cf. 32d]; *Lakṣ* मुक्तो; Ho °नलाशनः; BKt^{5} °निलासनः

32. Cited by *Vij* 3.55; *Apa* 945; *Hem* 3/2.1661; *Mādh* 1.529-30 — a) *Hem* स्थित्वा महर्षि°; Ox^{2} ब्रह्मर्षि°; sOx^{1} sPu^{6} महर्षिवृत्तीनां; Ho °चर्यां च — b) *Hem* त्यक्त्वा पापमयीं तनुं; Bo Tr^{1} त्यक्तान्य°; oOr तनुः; Pu^{7} तनु — c) wKt^{3} वीरशो°; BKt^{5} wKt^{6} *Hem* °शोकमयो; Tr^{1} °शोकतया — d) *Hem* ब्रह्मभूयाय कल्पते

33. Cited by *Lakṣ* 14.30; *Mādh* 1.530 — a) NPu^{1} वनेष्वथ; oOr वनेष्वन्त; BCa Ho Jo^{1} wKt^{1} wKt^{3} Tj^{2} *Mandlik Jha KSS Dave* च; Tr^{2} वनेषु संविहृ°; GMy oOr MTr^{6} विहृत्यैव; T Md^{3} निर्हृत्यैव; Bo Pu^{10} विहत्यैनं — c) TMd^{3} GMy तुरीयमा°; Pu^{2} Pu^{4} भाम्यं; Pu^{5} Pu^{7} Pu^{9} भागस्त्यक्त्वा — d) Pu^{5} Pu^{7} Pu^{9} [*Jolly* G] त्यक्तसङ्गा°; Tr^{1} त्यक्तास्वांगा°; TMd^{4} त्यक्त्वांगां च परि°; GMd^{1} NNg सङ्गं परि°; oOr भागान्परि°; Be^{1} BCa BKt^{5} wKt^{6} TMd^{3} GMd^{5} sOx^{1} sPu^{6} °रित्यजेत्

34. Omitted in Pu^{8}; pāda-d torn in Pu^{9} — a) GMd^{5} कृत्वा; sOx^{1} Ox^{2} Pu^{2} Pu^{4} sPu^{6} Tj^{1} Tr^{2} गच्छेद्धुतहोमो — b) Lo^{5} हुतहोमे; wKt^{3} हुतमोहो; TMd^{3} हन्तहेमो; Ox^{3} यतेन्द्रियः — c) Lo^{1} भिक्षाबल°; NKt^{4} °परिभ्रान्तः — d) Pu^{5} Pu^{7} प्रव्रष्वामभिवर्धते; oOr प्रव्रजन्प्रैत्य; NKt^{4} BKt^{5} Lo^{1} GMd^{1} Tj^{1} Wa प्रव्रजेत्प्रेत्य; Tj^{2} प्रव्रजेन्प्रेत्य; Pu^{10} वर्धेतो

35. Pādas c-d omitted in TMd^{4} MTr^{5}; pāda-b torn in Pu^{9}. Cited by *Vij* 3.56-7; *Hem* 3/3.808; *Mādh* 1.532 — a) wKt^{3} °पाहृत्य — b) Lo^{2} Lo^{5} Tj^{1} मोक्षो; TMd^{3} मक्षनिवेशयन्; Pu^{5} Pu^{7} [*Jolly* G] नियोजयेत् — c) NNg अनिपा°; wKt^{1} wKt^{3} °पाहृत्य; NKt^{4} °पाशत्य; Be^{3} Pu^{5} Pu^{7} Pu^{9} Tj^{1} च — c-d) Lo^{1} ऋणानि ह्यनपाकृत्य मोक्षमिच्छन्व्रजत्यधः — d) oOr मोच्यमानो; sOx^{1} sPu^{6} *both mc to* पतत्यधः; NPu^{1} व्रजत्यथ

36. Omitted in TMd^{4} Tr^{2} MTr^{5}; verses 36 and 37 transposed in Lo^{3}; in pādas c-d after इष्ट्वा Tj^{2} jumps to 37 c-d omitting all in between. Cited by *Mādh* 1.532 — a) Lo^{5} अधीत; TMd^{3} विविधान्वेदान् — b) Lo^{4} Lo^{5} GMd^{5} Ox^{3} *Mādh* पुत्रानुत्पाद्य — c) TMd^{3} अनिष्ट्वा चैव ततो यज्ञैर्मनो; Be^{1}

अनधीत्य द्विजो वेदाननुत्पाद्य तथात्मजान् ।
अनिष्ट्वा चैव यज्ञैश्च मोक्षमिच्छन्व्रजत्यधः ॥३७॥
प्राजापत्यां निरुप्येष्टिं सर्ववेदसदक्षिणां ।
आत्मन्यग्नीन्समारोप्य ब्राह्मणः प्रव्रजेद्गृहात् ॥३८॥
यो दत्त्वा सर्वभूतेभ्यः प्रव्रजत्यभयं गृहात् ।
तस्य तेजोमया लोका भवन्ति ब्रह्मवादिनः ॥३९॥
यस्मादण्वपि भूतानां द्विजान्नोत्पद्यते भयम् ।
तस्य देहाद्विमुक्तस्य भयं नास्ति कुतश्चन ॥४०॥
अगारादभिनिष्क्रान्तः पवित्रोपचितो मुनिः ।
समुपोढेषु कामेषु निरपेक्षः परिव्रजेत् ॥४१॥
एक एव चरेन्नित्यं सिद्ध्यर्थमसहायवान् ।
सिद्धिमेकस्य संपश्यन्न जहाति न हीयते ॥४२॥

Jm दृष्ट्वा; NKt^{4} अक्ष्वा; BCa Pu^{2} Pu^{4} तु; Bo शक्तिता — d) NKt^{4} मोक्षो; Ho न्यवेशयेत्; Bo निवेदयेत्

37.* Not commented by *Nd*; pādas a-b omitted in wKt^{6} Tj^{2}. Cited by *Lakṣ* 1430; *Mādh* 1.532 — a) NKt^{4} अनवात्य; GMd^{1} TMd^{3} TMd^{4} *Mādh* गुरोर्वेदा°; GMy शुरौ वेदा°; Be BKt^{5} Lo^{4} Lo^{5} Ox^{3} NPu^{1} Pu^{7} Pu^{9} Pu^{10} [*Jolly* M^{2-4-5}] *Lakṣ* वेदमनु°; Lo^{2} वेदामनु° — b) Ho वेदानुत्पाद्य च तथा°; Be^{1} Wa °त्पाद्य प्रजामपि; Be^{3} Bo BKt^{5} Lo^{2} Lo^{4} Lo^{5} GMd^{1} Ox^{3} Pu^{10} [*Jolly* M^{2-4-5}] *Jolly Jha Dave* तथा प्रजां; Tj^{1} [*Jolly* M^{9}] तथा प्रजाः; BBe^{2} Hy Jm Jo^{1} Jo^{2} wKt^{1} Kt^{2} wKt^{3} La^{1} Lo^{3} Ox^{2} NPu^{1} Pu^{2} Pu^{4} MTr^{3} *Mandlik KSS* तथा सुतान्; Pu ^{5} Pu^{7} Pu^{9} *Go* [*Jolly* G] यथा सुतं — c) BCa अनिष्ट्वा विधिवद्यज्ञैर्मोक्ष°; Be^{1} Lo^{5} GMy अनिष्टा; Bo अनिष्ट्या; Pu^{2} Pu^{4} च यज्ञैश्च; Be^{3} Jo^{2} NKt^{4} La^{1} Lo^{1} Lo^{2} Lo^{3} TMd^{4} GMd^{5} Tj^{1} Tr^{1} MTr^{4} MTr^{6} यज्ञैस्तु

38. Cited by *Śaṃ* on *BU* 4.5.15; *Mādh* 1.536; pādas c-d cited by *Vij* 3.56–7 — a) Ox^{3} प्रजापत्यां; BKt^{5} wKt^{6} प्राजापत्यं; La^{1} Tr^{1} °पत्यान्निरु°; Bo निरूप्येष्टिं — b) Bo NKt^{4} Lo^{4} GMy NPu^{1} Pu^{3} Tj^{1} Tr^{2} Wa सार्व°; Hy wKt^{6} Lo^{4} °दक्षिणं — c) wKt^{1} Lo^{1} °न्यग्निं समा° — d) Tr^{1} प्रव्रजेन्गृहात्; wKt^{6} sOx^{1} sPu^{6} प्रव्रजेद्गृहान्

39. Omitted in sOx^{1} sPu^{6} — a) Bo सर्वपापेभ्यः — b) Pu^{10} प्रव्रज्यत्त्वभयं; Hy व्रजत्यभयं; Ho °भयं महत्; Tr^{1} गृहान् — c) Pu^{5} Pu^{7} Pu^{9} तस्य ते तैजसा लोका; TMd^{3} °मयो; NKt^{4} °महा — d) Bo भवति; wKt^{3} वदन्ति; La^{1} ब्रह्मवेदिनः

40. a) sOx^{1} sPu^{6} तस्माद°; Lo^{1} यस्मादपि च; Lo^{5} यस्मादेवापि; TMd^{3} यस्मादर्व्रोपि; TMd^{4} यस्मा-त्तुर्वोपि — b) Tr^{1} भयं नोत्पद्यते क्वचित् — c) GMd^{5} देहान्विमु°; TMd^{3} GMy देहविमु°; La^{1} °मुक्तस्तु

41. a) Be^{1} BBe^{2} Be^{3} BCa Ho Ho Hy Jm Jo^{1} wKt^{1} Kt^{2} wKt^{3} BKt^{5} wKt^{6} La^{1} La^{2} Lo^{1} oOr sOx^{1} Ox^{2} sPu^{6} Pu^{8} Pu^{10} Tj^{1} Tj^{2} Tr^{2} *Mandlik Jolly Jha* आगारा°; BKt^{5} wKt^{6} °पिनिष्क्रान्तः — b) Bo La^{1} Pu^{3} Pu^{4} पवित्रोपवितो; GMd^{1} पवित्रैः पाचितो; TMd^{4} सपवित्रोचितो — c) Ho Pu^{2} Pu^{4} समपोढेषु; TMd^{3} समुपोषेषु; TMd^{4} समुपोष्टेषु; Tj^{1} समुपोह्लेषु; Bo समुपोटेषु; La^{1} समुत्पाटेषु; wKt^{6} समुत्पाढेषु; wKt^{1} समुत्पाद्येषु; wKt^{6} कामिषु; Tj^{1} कर्मेषु — d) Lo^{2} परिव्रजन्

42. Omitted in GMd^{5}. Cited by *Apa* 953; *Lakṣ* 14.43; *Mādh* 1.553 — a) wKt^{3} एक एक; NPu^{1} चरन्नित्यं; Lo^{2} Pu^{10} Tj^{1} Wa चरेद्धर्मं; wKt^{6} चरेद्भैक्ष्यं — b) Pu^{5} Pu^{7} Pu^{9} [*Jolly* G] सिद्ध्यर्थः स सहायवान्; Pu^{2} Pu^{4} °पहायवान्; TMd^{4} Tr^{1} MTr^{4} MTr^{6} °सहायकः; GMd^{1} °सहायतः — c) Be^{1} Lo^{1} Pu^{5} Pu^{7} Pu^{9} सिद्धमेकस्य; GMy सिद्धिकेतस्य; MTr^{5} °कस्य पश्य न; Pu^{5} Pu^{7} Pu^{9} संपश्येन्न; TMd^{3} Tj^{1} संपश्य

अनग्निरनिकेतः स्याद् ग्राममन्नार्थमाश्रयेत् ।
उपेक्षकोऽसंचयिको मुनिर्भावसमाहितः ॥४३॥
कपालं वृक्षमूलानि कुचेलमसहायता ।
समता चैव सर्वस्मिन्नेतन्मुक्तस्य लक्षणम् ॥४४॥
नाभिनन्देत मरणं नाभिनन्देत जीवितम् ।
कालमेव प्रतीक्षेत निर्वेशं भृतको यथा ॥४५॥

न; MTr^{4} पश्यद्भिर्न; Tr^{1} पश्यन्हि न — d) TMd^{4} जहाति निजीयते — After 42 TMd^{3} GMy insert 12.10–1.

43.* Pādas a-b omitted in GMd^{5}. Cited by *Apa* 953; *Lakṣ* 14.43 — b) Tr^{1} ग्रामं भिक्षार्थम° — c) Pu^{5} Pu^{7} Pu^{9} अपेक्षको; *Jha* °सांचयिको; Ho NPu^{1} °संचयको; wKt^{3} °शंचयिको *mc to* °शंकशुका; BKt^{5} wKt^{6} °संचयितो; wKt^{1} Kt^{2} sPu^{6} [*mc to*] MTr^{3} *KSS Dave* °संकुसुको; Kt^{2} Jm Jo^{1} *Mandlik* °शंकुसुको; BCa Hy wKt^{1} Lo^{3} Lo^{5} [*Jolly* R] °शंकसुको; Be^{3} Bo °संकुशुको; BBe^{2} °संकुशको; Lo^{4} Pu^{10} *Jolly Bühler* °संकसुको; La^{2} °शंकशुको; Jo^{2} °शंकशूको; Tj^{2} °संचसुरको; Pu^{5} Pu^{7} Pu^{9} [*Jolly* G] °संकुतको; NNg संस्थिरबुद्धिः [सं deleted] — d) Tj^{1} मुनिर्भावः; GMd^{1} GMy Pu^{9} मुनिभाव°; TMd^{3} मुनिर्भाष°; Lo^{2} मुनिर्भोग°; wKt^{1} अग्निर्भाव°; Be^{1} Lo^{1} Lo^{3} GMd^{1} TMd^{3} TMd^{4} GMd^{5} GMy sOx^{1} Ox^{2} Pu^{3} sPu^{6} Tr^{1} Tr^{2} MTr^{4} MTr^{5} MTr^{6} Wa *Apa Lakṣ* °समन्वितः

44. *ma in* Lo^{4}. Cited by *Apa* 953; *Lakṣ* 14.43; *Mādh* 1.564 — a) sOx^{1} sPu^{6} *Lakṣ* कपाल; La^{1} कापालं — b) GMy न कुचेलमहायता; Be^{1} Be^{3} Bo BKt^{5} Lo^{1} Lo^{2} Lo^{4} Lo^{5} NNg Ox^{3} NPu^{1} Pu^{5} Pu^{7} Pu^{8} Pu^{9} Pu^{10} Tj^{1} Tr^{2} Wa *Apa Jha Dave* कुचैल°; TMd^{4} °सहायतां; Lo^{2} °सहायतः; TMd^{3} °सहायत; Ho Pu^{8} °सहायिता; Pu^{5} Pu^{7} Pu^{9} °सहायवान् — c) *Lakṣ* समतामेव — d) MTr^{4} MTr^{6} °न्नेते मुक्तस्य

45.* Pāda-a omitted in Pu^{9}. Cited by *Apa* 953; *Lakṣ* 14.43; *Mādh* 1.564 — a) wKt^{1} अभिन°; Tj^{1} °नन्देतु; Lo^{2} Pu^{2} Pu^{4} °नन्देत्तु; La^{1} °नन्देच्च; GMd^{5} oOr °निन्देत; Pu^{5} Pu^{7} °वन्देत — b) Pu^{2} °नन्देत्तु; GMd^{5} oOr °निन्देत; TMd^{4} °नन्दित; La^{1} Tj^{1} °नन्देच्च; Pu^{5} Pu^{7} Pu^{9} °वन्देत; GMy Wa जीवतं; BBe^{2} जीवतां; BCa Lo^{1} TMd^{4} GMd^{5} जीवनं — c) TMd^{4} इदंकामेव; GMd^{1} परीक्षेत; sOx^{1} sPu^{6} समीक्षेत — d) BBe^{2} Be^{3} Jm Jo^{1} wKt^{1} Kt^{2} wKt^{3} BKt^{5} wKt^{6} La^{1} Lo^{1} TMd^{3} NNg oOr Ox^{2} NPu^{1} Pu^{3} Pu^{5} sPu^{6} [*but cor*] Pu^{7} Pu^{8} Pu^{9} MTr^{3} [*Jolly* G Ku] *Ku NdNā Mandlik KSS Dave* निर्देशं; Be^{1} Bo BCa Hy Jo^{2} wKt^{3} NKt^{4} Lo^{3} Tj^{2} Tr^{2} Wa [*Jolly* N] निदेशं; Tj^{1} निर्देशो; Lo^{2} Pu^{2} Pu^{4} भृतका; Hy भृतके; TMd^{3} GMd^{5} भृशको; Lo^{5} Tr^{2} मृतको; Jm व्रतको

Additional verses in Be^{1} Be^{3} Ho NKt^{4} oOr Tj^{1} Tr^{2} *Mandlik* [क, ख, ग, ट, ठ, ड, ण, त, ल, य] *KSS Dave;* given after 6.46 in wKt^{6} and after 6.5 in wKt^{1} wKt^{3}; first two verses after 6.45 and the last verse after 6.48 in sOx^{1} sPu^{6}; first two verses in *Mandlik* [र]; first verse alone given in Tr^{1} *Mandlik* [त] and cited by *Apa*; first verse given after 6.68 in TMd^{4} GMd^{5} MTr^{4} MTr^{6}, after 652 in La^{1}, and after 6.69 in [*Jolly* Gr]; pādas a-b of first verse cited by *Lakṣ* 14.44. All three verses commented by *Rc;* first verse alone by *Rn:*

ग्रैष्महैमन्तिकान्मासानष्टौ भिक्षुर्विचक्रमेत् ।
दयार्थं सर्वभूतानां वर्षास्वेकत्र संवसेत् ।।१।।
नासूर्यं हि व्रजेन्मार्गं नादृष्टां भूमिमाक्रमेत् ।
परिपूताभिरद्भिस्तु कार्यं कुर्वीत नित्यशः ।।२।।
सत्यां वाचमहिंस्रां च वदेदनपकारिणीम् ।
कल्कापेतामपरुषामनृशंसामपैशुनाम् ।।३।।

1. a) Be^{3} Ho sOx^{1} sPu^{6} Tj^{1} *Mandlik KSS Dave* ग्रैष्मान्हैम°; Tr^{2} ग्रैष्मान्हेम°; GMd^{5} Tr^{1}

दृष्टिपूतं न्यसेत्पादं वस्त्रपूतं जलं पिबेत् ।
सत्यपूतां वदेद्वाचं मनःपूतं समाचरेत् ॥४६॥
अतिवादांस्तितिक्षेत नावमन्येत कंचन ।
न चेमं देहमाश्रित्य वैरं कुर्वीत केनचित् ॥४७॥
क्रुध्यन्तं न प्रतिक्रुध्येदाक्रुष्टः कुशलं वदेत् ।
सप्तद्वारावकीर्णां च न वाचमनृतां वदेत् ॥४८॥
अध्यात्मरतिरासीनो निरपेक्षो निरामिषः ।
आत्मनैव सहायेन सुखार्थी विचरेदिह ॥४९॥
न चोत्पातनिमित्ताभ्यां न नक्षत्राङ्गविद्यया ।

गैष्मे हैम°; Be¹ La¹ ग्रीष्महैम°; NKt⁴ ग्रीष्मे हैम°; wKt⁶ ग्रीष्मे हेम°; Tj¹ *om* मासान् — b) oOr भिक्षुः परिक्रमेत्; Be¹ भिक्षुः परिभ्रमेत्; sOx¹ sPu⁶ भिक्षविदं ग्रसेत्; TMd⁴ GMd⁵ Tr¹ MTr⁴ MTr⁶ [*Jolly* Gr] *Apa Lakṣ* प्रायेण पर्यटेत् [*Jolly* Gr प्राणेन] — c) Be¹ दयालुः सर्वजीवेषु; GMd⁵ दयार्थो; Tr¹ हितार्थं; TMd⁴ MTr⁴ यदर्थं; La¹ यद्वयासर्व°; TMd⁴ MTr⁴ MTr⁶ सर्वजन्तूनां — d) wKt¹ wKt³ एकत्र चतुरो वसेत्; oOr चतुर्ष्वेव तु यं वसेत्; GMd⁵ वर्षरात्रेषु; NKt⁴ °कत्रमावसेत्; Be³ Tj¹ Tr² संविशेत्; La¹ वावसेत्

2. a) wKt⁶ वास्तयं हि समं मार्गं; wKt¹ wKt³ नातुर्यं; NKt⁴ वासूर्यं NKt⁴ समेन्मार्गं; wKt¹ wKt³ व्रजेन्मासं — b) wKt¹ नदृष्टां; Be¹ Tr² *Mandlik* [ड] नाज्ञातां; wKt⁶ °माक्रमान्; Be¹ °माश्रयेत् — c) wKt⁶ परिपूतांसि च छिद्र; Be¹ Ho *Mandlik KSS Dave* परिभूता°; Be³ NKt⁴ Tj¹ °द्भिश्च — d) Be¹ त्रिसंध्यं स्नानमाचरेत्

3. a) wKt¹ NKt⁴ °हिंसां; wKt⁶ °हिंसा — b) wKt⁶ वादवादनकरिणी; Tj¹ °नपवादिनीं; NKt⁴ °कारिणी — c) Be¹ wKt¹ wKt³ NKt⁴ wKt⁶ कल्कोपे°; Tr² कल्कान्विता°; Tj¹ कल्कपीता°; Ho °मपुरुषा°; Be¹ NKt⁴ °मकलुषा° — d) Tr² °पैशुनीं

46. Cited by *Apa* 953; *Lakṣ* 14.43; *Mādh* 1.564 — a) Lo² Lo⁴ Lo⁵ Ox³ Pu² Pu⁴ Pu¹⁰ पदं न्यस्येद्वस्त्र°; TMd⁴ पादं न्यसेद्वस्त्र°; NPu¹ °त्पादौ — b) Hy °पूतजले; Ho पिबेज्जलं — c) MTr⁵ मनःपूतां; Ho BKt⁵ wKt⁶ °पूतं; Be¹ Lo² NNg Pu² Tj¹ Wa वदेद्वाक्यं; BKt⁵ wKt⁶ वदेद्वादं; GMd¹ TMd³ GMd⁵ *Apa Lakṣ* वदेद्वाणीं — d) MTr⁵ सत्यपूतं; GMd⁵ °पूतां

47. Lo² transposes pādas a-b and c-d. Cited by *Apa* 953; *Lakṣ* 14.43; *Mādh* 1.564 — a) wKt⁶ अतिवादात्तितिक्षेत; wKt¹ La¹ Ox³ अभिवा°; GMd¹ नातिवा° — b) La¹ °मन्येत्कथंचन; Pu¹⁰ कांचन; GMy Tr² किंचन — c) Pu⁸ चैमं; Lo¹ चेदं; Bo Ho Jo² La¹ Lo³ TMd³ GMy oOr Tj¹ Tr¹ Tr² MTr⁴ MTr⁶ *Lakṣ* चैनं; TMd⁴ चैव; NKt⁴ °मासृत्य — d) oOr कस्यचित्

48. Pādas c-d omitted in TMd⁴. Cited by *Apa* 954; *Lakṣ* 14.43; *Mādh* 1.564 — a) *Apa* न क्रुध्यन्तं प्रतिक्रुध्ये°; Lo⁴ Lo⁵ NNg Ox³ क्रुध्यन्तं प्रति न क्रुध्ये°; MTr³ क्रुद्धन्तं; Ho wKt³ oOr *om* न; Ho प्रतिक्रुध्येत आक्रु° — b) NNg °क्रुध्ये [*mc sh* त्] पदाकृष्टः; TMd³ °दाकृष्टं; Pu⁸ Tr² °दाकुष्टः; wKt⁶ कुशले; Tj¹ व्रजेत्; Ox³ भवेत् — c) BBe² Ho BKt⁵ Ox³ Tj¹ *Apa* [vl] °कीर्णं; TMd³ GMy Tr¹ °तीर्णां; Lo¹ तु — d) *Apa* न वाचं समुदीरयेत्; Be¹ NNg Tr¹ MTr⁴ Wa °नृतं; Ho °मृतां; TMd³ °कृतां; oOr *om* वदेत्

49. Cited by *Apa* 954; *Lakṣ* 14.43–4; *Mādh* 1.564 — a) BKt⁵ आध्यात्म°; GMd¹ Tj¹ अध्यात्ममतिरा°; NKt⁴ °राशानो; Lo⁴ Lo⁵ NNg Ox³ Pu¹⁰ *Apa* °रासीत; TMd³ °रस्तेनो — b) Tr¹ निरामेपः; *Apa* निरेषणः; Bo [*but cor*] निरायुपः; Ho Lo¹ निराशिपः; sOx¹ sPu⁶ निराश्रयः; Be¹ *mc to* निरैश्रियः — d) Tj¹ सुखार्थ

नानुशासनवादाभ्यां भिक्षां लिप्सेत कर्हिचित् ॥५०॥
न तापसैर्ब्राह्मणैर्वा वयोभिरपि वा श्वभिः ।
आकीर्णं भिक्षुकैर्वान्यैरगारमुपसंव्रजेत् ॥५१॥
कॢप्तकेशनखश्मश्रुः पात्री दण्डी कुसुम्भवान् ।
विचरेन्नियतो नित्यं सर्वभूतान्यपीडयन् ॥५२॥
अतैजसानि पात्राणि तस्य स्युर्निर्व्रणानि च ।
तेषामद्भिः स्मृतं शौचं चमसानामिवाध्वरे ॥५३॥
अलाबुं दारुपात्रं च मृन्मयं वैदलं तथा ।
एतानि यतिपात्राणि मनुः स्वायंभुवोऽब्रवीत् ॥५४॥
एककालं चरेद्भैक्षं न प्रसज्जेत विस्तरे ।
भैक्षे प्रसक्तो हि यतिर्विषयेष्वपि सज्जति ॥५५॥

50. Cited by *Vij* 3.59; *Apa* 963 — a) MTr^{4} °निमित्तः स्यात्र — b) BKt^{5} wKt^{6} नक्षत्राङ्गमविद्यया [*om* न]; TMd^{3} नक्षत्रांशवि° — c) BKt^{5} wKt^{6} GMy °विद्याभ्यां — d) TMd^{3} भिक्षा लङ्घेत; Pu^{8} Tj^{1} लिप्स्येत; NKt^{4} लिप्सेह; MTr^{4} MTr^{6} भिक्षेत

51. Cited by *Vij* 3.59; *Mādh* 1.561 — a) Lo^{2} स ताप°; sOx^{1} sPu^{6} तामसै° — b) Lo^{1} GMd^{1} sOx^{1} sPu^{6} Pu^{5} Pu^{7} Pu^{9} Tj^{1} *Mādh* °भिरथ वा; BKt^{5} वा पतिः; Ox^{3} Pu^{10} वादिभिः — c) Be^{1} आकीर्णा; Pu^{5} Pu^{7} Pu^{9} आकीर्णे; Bo आकीर्ण; Ho आकीर्णः; sOx^{1} sPu^{6} Tr^{2} MTr^{6} °कैश्चान्यै°; Jo^{2} Lo^{3} *Vij* °कैरन्यै°; Be^{3} °कैर्नान्यै°; TMd^{4} °कैरत्रै° — d) Lo^{1} °रगारं तु सुसंव्रजेत्; Be^{1} BBe^{2} Be^{3} Ho Jm Jo^{1} wKt^{1} Kt^{2} NKt^{4} La^{1} La^{2} sOx^{1} NPu^{1} Pu^{2} Pu^{4} sPu^{6} Tj^{1} Tj^{2} Tr^{2} *Mandlik Jolly Jha* °रागार°; BKt^{5} wKt^{6} °रङ्गार°; Be^{3} La^{1} TMd^{4} GMd^{5} Pu^{5} sPu^{6} [*but cor*] Pu^{7} Pu^{9} Tr^{1} MTr^{5} [*Jolly* G] °संविशेत्

52. Cited by *Apa* 954; *Lakṣ* 14.44; *Mādh* 1.564 — a) *Apa* [vl] *Mādh* कृत्तकेश° Ho TMd^{3} GMd^{5} Tj^{1} कृन्तकेश°; TMd^{4} कृतकेश°; NKt^{4} NNg Tr^{2} Wa *Nā* नीचकेश° — b) Ox^{3} पत्री; *Lakṣ* दण्डी पात्री; wKt^{1} कुण्डी; Tr^{2} कुशुंभवान्; La^{1} कुसुम्भका; *Apa* कुसम्भवं; *Apa* [vl] कुसम्भवान्; [*Jolly* Gr] कुटुम्बवान्; TMd^{4} तु संभवान् — c) Lo^{2} TMd^{3} विचरन्नि°; Kt^{2} °रेन्नियमो; MTr^{3} °रेन्नयतो — d) GMd^{1} °भूतानि पीडयन्; MTr^{4} °न्यपीडयेत्; oOr °न्यपीडयत्

53. Cited by *Vij* 3.60; *Apa* 964; *Mādh* 1.562 — b) Be^{3} wKt^{1} wKt^{3} sOx^{1} sPu^{6} स्युरव्रणानि — c) GMd^{5} तेषामद्भिर्मदा शौचं; NPu^{1} कृतं शौचं — d) BKt^{5} °मिवाधरे

54. Cited by *Mādh* 1.562 — a) Pu^{5} Pu^{7} Pu^{9} अलाबुं वा दारुपात्रं [*om* च]; Ho BKt^{5} wKt^{6} GMd^{1} TMd^{3} sOx^{1} Ox^{3} sPu^{6} Tr^{1} Wa अलाबु; TMd^{4} अलाबं; Pu^{2} Pu^{4} वारुपात्रं; Bo Ho GMd^{5} Pu^{3} Pu^{8} °पात्राणि [*om* च]; Be^{3} GMd^{1} TMd^{3} Tr^{1} Tr^{2} MTr^{6} वा — b) TMd^{3} वैष्णवं मृन्मयं तथा; Be^{1} Jo^{1} Lo^{1} GMd^{5} sOx^{1} sPu^{6} Tr^{1} मृण्मयं; Tr^{1} बैदलं; NKt^{4} वेदलं; Lo^{1} विदलं; BKt^{5} wKt^{6} वैतलं; Be^{3} wKt^{1} oOr NPu^{1} Pu^{2} Pu^{3} Pu^{4} MTr^{4} MTr^{6} वैणवं; GMd^{1} वैनिकं; Lo^{2} वैणं — c) Pu^{8} तानि; NKt^{4} Tr^{1} MTr^{5} चत्वारि यति°; wKt^{6} तिलपात्राणि

55. Cited by *Vij* 3.59; *Apa* 963; *Lakṣ* 14.57; *Mādh* 1.558 — a) Ho एककामं; Be^{1} BCa Ho Kt^{2} La^{1} Lo^{5} oOr Ox^{2} °द्भैक्ष्यं; *Vij* °द्भिक्षां; Pu^{5} Pu^{7} Pu^{9} °द्भिक्षं; Lo^{3} °द्भैक्षी — b) Be^{1} *Vij* प्रसज्जेत्र तु विस्तरे; Pu^{5} Pu^{7} Pu^{9} प्रसह्यै न तु विस्तरे; BKt^{5} wKt^{6} Lo^{4} Lo^{5} Ox^{3} NPu^{1} Pu^{10} प्रसज्येत न विस्तरे [wKt^{6} प्रसज्जेत]; wKt^{1} प्रसज्येन्न च विस्तरे; wKt^{3} प्रसज्यस्तु न विस्तरे; TMd^{4} न प्रसज्येत्कथंचन; Bo GMd^{1} TMd^{3} GMd^{5} GMy NNg sOx^{1} Pu^{3} sPu^{6} Tr^{1} Tr^{2} [*Jolly* M] *Apa* प्रसज्येत; Pu^{2} Pu^{4} प्रव्रज्येत; La^{1} प्रसद्येत; Tj^{1} प्रसृज्येत; NPu^{1} प्रसंजेत; Lo^{2} विस्तरात्; Tr^{2} विस्तरं — c) Lo^{1} TMd^{4} प्रसक्तो हि यतिर्भैक्षे; Be^{3} Ho La^{1}

विधूमे सन्नमुसले व्यङ्गारे भुक्तवज्जने ।
वृत्ते शरावसंपाते भिक्षां नित्यं यतिश्चरेत् ॥५६॥
अलाभे न विषादी स्याल्लाभश्चैनं न हर्षयेत् ।
प्राणयात्रिकमात्रः स्यान्मात्रासङ्गाद्विनिर्गतः ॥५७॥
अभिपूजितलाभांस्तु जुगुप्सेतैव सर्वशः ।
अभिपूजितलाभैस्तु यतिर्मुक्तोऽपि बध्यते ॥५८॥
अल्पान्नाभ्यवहारेण रहःस्थानासनेन च ।
ह्रियमाणानि विषयैरिन्द्रियाणि निवर्तयेत् ॥५९॥
इन्द्रियाणां निरोधेन रागद्वेषक्षयेण च ।

NPu^{1} भैक्ष्ये; TMd^{3} GMd^{5} GMy Ox^{3} Pu^{10} Tr^{1} MTr^{4} MTr^{6} *Apa Dave* भैक्ष; Pu^{5} Pu^{7} Pu^{9} भैक्ष्य; Lo^{5} भक्षे; wKt^{1} NKt^{4} La^{1} प्रशक्तो — d) Be^{3} wKt^{1} wKt^{3} Lo^{4} Lo^{5} NNg Ox^{3} Pu^{10} यतिः प्रसज्जेद्विषयेष्वपि [wKt^{3} प्रसह्यद्वि°]; TMd^{4} *Lakṣ* °येष्वभिसज्जति; GMd^{5} °येष्वतिसज्जति; Jo^{2} Lo^{2} Pu^{2} सज्जते; *Apa* मज्जति

56. Cited by *Vij* 3.59; *Mādh* 1.558 — a) TMd^{4} विधूम; Tr^{2} शन्न° ; NNg न्यस्तमुसले; Ho wKt^{1} wKt^{3} NKt^{4} BKt^{5} wKt^{6} La^{1} NPu^{1} Pu^{3} Pu^{5} Pu^{7} Pu^{8} Pu^{9} Tr^{2} °मुशले; BBe^{2} BCa Tj^{2} °मुषले; TMd^{3} °मुपले — b) Ox^{3} भक्त° ; Bo °वज्जनैः; GMd^{1} GMy °वज्जिने; Be^{1} BCa La^{1} oOr sOx^{1} Tr^{1} °वर्जने; wKt^{1} TMd^{4} GMd^{5} °वर्जिते; TMd^{3} °वर्जते — c) Pu^{9} दत्ते; BKt^{5} wKt^{6} Ox^{3} Pu^{10} Tr^{2} सराव° ; BBe^{2} रासव° ; Ox^{3} °संपातो; MTr^{4} °संपन्ने — d) *Vij* नित्यं भिक्षां; TMd^{4} पन्नभिक्षां यति°

57.* Omitted in Lo^{3}. Cited by *Apa* 963; *Mādh* 1.558 — a) Pu^{10} सलाभे; Pu^{5} Pu^{7} Pu^{9} [*Jolly* G] न रागी न विषादी — b) sOx^{1} sPu^{6} स्याल्लाभाश्चैनं; Lo^{2} स्याल्लाभश्चैतत्; Lo^{1} स्याल्लाभश्चैवं; Be^{3} Tj^{1} स्याल्लाभश्चैन्नैव; wKt^{3} स्याल्लाभेश्चै [*rest om*]; Ox^{3} स्याल्लाभे चैनं; Be^{2} BCa Hy Jm Jo^{1} wKt^{1} Kt^{2} BKt^{5} wKt^{6} La^{2} GMd^{1} TMd^{4} GMd^{5} GMy Ox^{2} Pu^{3} Pu^{8} Pu^{10} Tj^{2} Tr^{2} MTr^{3} MTr^{6} [*Jolly* G Nd Ku] *Mandlik Bühler Jha KSS Dave* स्याल्लाभे चैव; Ho NNg स्याल्लाभे चैवं; TMd^{3} स्याल्लाभं चैव; Lo^{2} स्याल्लाभाश्चैतन्न; Tr^{1} MTr^{4} स्याल्लाभे नैव च; GMd^{1} हर्षति; TMd^{3} हार्धयेत् — c) TMd^{3} प्राणमात्रैकयात्र स्या°; Be^{1} °यात्रिकमन्त्रः स्या°; NKt^{4} sOx^{1} sPu^{6} Tr^{2} °यात्रिक एव स्या° — d) GMd^{1} स्यान्मात्रामात्रविनिर्गतः; Tj^{1} स्यात्कमण्डल्वादिनिर्गतः; Lo^{2} °सङ्गविनिर्गतः; Jo^{2} TMd^{4} °सङ्गविवर्जितः; TMd^{3} GMd^{5} GMy °निसृतः; Tr^{1} MTr^{4} MTr^{6} निःसृतः

58. Omitted in Lo^{3}; verses 58 and 59 transposed in Ho. Cited by *Apa* 963 — a) Pu^{5} Pu^{7} Pu^{9} *Go* अतिपूजितलाभात्तु; [*Jolly* M$^{1-2-4-5}$ Nd] °लाभैस्तु; Lo^{1} °लाभस्तु; BBe^{2} GMd^{1} TMd^{3} GMd^{5} GMy oOr sOx^{1} sPu^{6} Tr^{1} MTr^{4} MTr^{6} *Apa* °लाभांश्च — b) Pu^{5} Pu^{7} Pu^{9} *Go* [*Jolly* G] भिक्षां यत्नेन वर्जयेत्; Be^{3} wKt^{3} GMd^{5} Tr^{2} जुगुप्सेच्चैव; TMd^{4} जुगुप्येश्चैव; wKt^{1} जुगुप्सेत च; Ho जुगुप्सेन्नेव; Be^{1} La^{1} Wa सर्वतः; sOx^{1} sPu^{6} Tr^{2} सर्वदा — c) wKt^{3} Pu^{5} Pu^{7} Pu^{9} अतिपूजित° ; Ox^{2} °लाभेस्तु; wKt^{1} TMd^{4} °लाभोस्तु; Lo^{1} °लाभस्तु; *Apa* °लाभात्तु; BBe^{2} Hy Jm Jo^{1} Kt^{2} Pu^{3} Tj^{2} MTr^{3} *Mandlik Jolly Jha KSS Dave* °लाभैश्च; GMd^{1} °लाभैर्हि — d) GMd^{1} यतिर्युक्तो निबध्यते; NKt^{4} Tr^{1} मुनिर्मुक्तो; Lo^{4} Lo^{5} Ox^{3} Pu^{10} यदि मुक्तो; Tj^{1} °क्तोविबध्यते; Be^{3} बाध्यते; Tr^{1} भिध्यते

59. Omitted in Lo^{3} Pu^{5}; pādas c-d omitted in Ho Tr^{2}. Cited by *Apa* 954; *Mādh* 1.564 — a) oOr अल्पलाभावहारेण; Tr^{2} अल्पान्नाध्यव° ; GMd^{1} अल्पान्नव्यवहा° ; BBe^{2} अल्पाद्वाभ्यव° ; TMd^{4} अल्पेनाभ्यव° ; Pu^{10} अत्यस्तोभ्यव° ; GMy °भ्यविहारेण — b) TMd^{4} देहस्था° ; Bo हरस्था° ; Tr^{2} °स्थानाशनेन; Ho °स्नानासनेन; *Apa* वा — c) wKt^{1} Tj^{1} [*but cor*] क्रियमा° ; GMd^{5} हृष्यमा° ; TMd^{3} प्रायामाणानि; Tr^{1} ह्रीयमाणो न विष° ; Lo^{4} Lo^{5} °माणाभिविष° ; GMy हृदयैरि° — d) TMd^{4} निवर्तते; Tr^{1} न वर्तयेत्; Lo^{1} न्यवर्तयन्; Bo wKt^{1} विवर्तयेत्; wKt^{3} निवर्हयेत्

अहिंसया च भूतानाममृतत्वाय कल्पते ॥६०॥
अवेक्षेत गतीर्नॄणां कर्मदोषसमुद्भवाः ।
निरये चैव पतनं यातनाश्च यमक्षये ॥६१॥
विप्रयोगं प्रियैश्चैव संप्रयोगं तथाप्रियैः ।
जरया चाभिभवनं व्याधिभिश्चोपपीडनम् ॥६२॥
देहादुत्क्रमणं चास्मात् पुनर्गर्भे च संभवम् ।
योनिकोटिसहस्रेषु सृतीश्चास्यान्तरात्मनः ॥६३॥
अधर्मप्रभवं चैव दुःखयोगं शरीरिणाम् ।
धर्मार्थप्रभवं चैव सुखसंयोगमक्षयम् ॥६४॥
सूक्ष्मतां चान्ववेक्षेत योगेन परमात्मनः ।
देहेषु चैवोपपत्तिमुत्तमेष्वधमेषु च ॥६५॥

60. Omitted in Lo^{3}; pādas a-b omitted in Tr^{2}. Cited by *Apa* 954; *Mādh* 1.564 — b) Kt^{2} रागदोष° — c) Bo TMd^{3} Tr^{1} अहिंसाया; MTr^{4} अहिंसयैव; Jo^{2} अहिंससैव; wKt^{1} अहिंसैव हि; GMd^{1} अहिंसा चैव; Jo^{1} पूताना° — d) NKt^{4} कल्प्यते; La^{1} कल्पयेत्

61. Omitted in Lo^{3}; in Tj^{1} the sequence is 61c, 62d, 63a-b, 61d, 62a-b, 62c. Cited by *Apa* 968 — a) sOx^{1} sPu^{6} अवेक्षते; TMd^{3} अवेक्ष्येत; Ho अवेक्ष्यापगती°; sOx^{1} sPu^{6} गतेर्नॄणां; NKt^{4} गती नृणां; La^{1} Tr^{1} गतिर्नॄणां; GMd^{1} TMd^{4} GMd^{5} GMy Pu^{2} MTr^{4} MTr^{6} गतिं नृणां; Lo^{5} TMd^{3} गति नृणां — b) BBe^{2} Be^{3} NNg °मुद्भवा; Jo^{1} °मुद्भवः; GMd^{1} GMd^{5} GMy Tr^{1} MTr^{4} MTr^{6} °मुद्भवां; TMd^{3} °मुद्भवात् — c) NKt^{4} sOx^{1} Ox^{2} Pu^{5} sPu^{6} Pu^{7} Pu^{9} Tr^{2} [*Jolly* G] पतनं चैव; TMd^{4} तपनं चैव — d) Pu^{8} यातनाश्चैवमक्षये; BKt^{5} wKt^{6} जातनाश्च; wKt^{1} यातना च; TMd^{3} GMy Tr^{1} यातनां च

62.* Omitted in Pu^{8} Wa; pādas a-b up to संप्रयोगं omitted in Tj^{2}. Cited by *Apa* 968 — a) TMd^{4} Tr^{1} प्रियश्चैव — b) Be^{1} BBe^{2} Be^{3} BCa Ho Hy Jm Jo^{1} wKt^{1} Kt^{2} BKt^{5} wKt^{6} Lo^{1} Lo^{4} Lo^{5} sOx^{1} Ox^{3} Pu^{5} sPu^{6} Pu^{7} Pu^{9} Pu^{10} Tr^{2} *Mandlik Jolly Jha KSS Dave* संयोगं च तथा°; TMd^{4} तथा स्त्रियं — c) TMd^{3} जराया; Bo जरसा; GMd^{1} oOr रजसा; Lo^{1} जरयाश्चाभि°; Tj^{1} वाभि°; Pu^{7} Pu^{9} चाभिवननं; Pu^{5} चाभिवनं; NPu^{1} चाप्यभिभवं — d) NNg Tj^{1} Tr^{1} MTr^{5} °भिश्चैव पीडनं; TMd^{3} GMy °भिश्च निपीडनं; wKt^{6} °भिश्चोपजीवनं; TMd^{4} MTr^{3} °पीडितं; Jo^{1} °पिडयन्

63. Cited by *Apa* 968 — a) TMd^{3} देहाद्युत्क्र°; [*Jolly* M] वास्मात्; oOr तस्मात्; sOx^{1} sPu^{6} चात्मा — b) wKt^{3} GMd^{1} पुनर्गर्भे समुद्भवं [GMd^{1} °नर्गर्भं]; GMy पुनर्दर्भे; TMd^{3} GMd^{5} पुनर्देहे; Jo^{2} La^{1} पुनर्गर्भेषु सं°; *Apa* संभवः — c) Wa °सहस्रैस्तु; Lo^{5} °समस्तेषु — d) TMd^{4} प्रसूतीश्चान्तरात्मनः; GMy Tr^{1} सृतिं चा°; TMd^{3} सृति चा°; MTr^{6} धृतिश्चा°; Hy La^{1} सूतिश्चा°; Tr^{2} नृतीश्चा°; Lo^{2} सृतीयाश्चान्त°; Tr^{1} सृतीश्चैवान्त°

64. Omitted in TMd^{3} GMy [*Jolly* Nd]; pādas b-c omitted in TMd^{4}. Cited by *Apa* 968 — a) BKt^{5} wKt^{6} अधर्मः; Lo^{2} अधर्मे; wKt^{1} sOx^{1} sPu^{6} °प्रभवश्चैव; sOx^{1} °प्रभवंश्चैव; Tj^{1} चैवं — b) Lo^{4} Lo^{5} शरीरिणं — c) BKt^{5} wKt^{6} धर्मार्थः; BCa GMd^{1} °प्रभवश्चैव; Tj^{1} चैवं — d) NPu^{1} सुखयोगमथाक्षयं; Kt^{2} GMd^{5} Tj^{1} सुखं; BKt^{5} °गमन्तमं; BKt^{5} wKt^{6} °गमुत्तमं

65. Omitted in TMd^{3} GMy [*Jolly* Nd] *Nd*. Cited by *Apa* 968 — a) wKt^{1} सूक्ष्मता; Ho वान्व°; GMd^{5} चाप्यवे° — c) Lo^{1} चोपसम्पत्ति°; NPu^{1} चैवापपत्ति°; BBe^{2} BCa Ho Hy Jm Jo^{1} Jo^{2} Kt^{2} Lo^{3} sOx^{1} Ox^{2} Pu^{3} sPu^{6} [*cor to sh*] Tj^{2} Tr^{2} MTr^{3} [*Jolly* R Ku] *Mandlik KSS* च समुत्पत्ति°; Lo^{4} Lo^{5} चैवमुत्पत्ति°; Pu^{10} °पत्तिरुत्तमे°

भूषितोऽपि चरेद्धर्मं यत्र तत्राश्रमे वसन् ।
समः सर्वेषु भूतेषु न लिङ्गं धर्मकारणम् ॥६६॥
फलं कतकवृक्षस्य यद्यप्यम्बुप्रसादकम् ।
न नामग्रहणादेव तस्य वारि प्रसीदति ॥६७॥
संरक्षणार्थं जन्तूनां रात्रावहनि वा सदा ।
शरीरस्यात्यये चैव समीक्ष्य वसुधां चरेत् ॥६८॥
अह्ना रात्र्या च याञ्जन्तून् हिनस्त्यज्ञानतो यतिः ।
तेषां स्नात्वा विशुद्ध्यर्थं प्राणायामान् षडाचरेत् ॥६९॥
प्राणायामा ब्राह्मणस्य त्रयोऽपि विधिवत्कृताः ।
व्याहृतिप्रणवैर्युक्ता विज्ञेयं परमं तपः ॥७०॥

66.* Not commented by *Nd.* Cited by *Vij* 3.65; *Apa* 971— a) *Apa* भूमितो; BBe^{2} Hy Jm Jo^{1} Jo^{2} Kt^{2} Lo^{3} Pu^{3} MTr^{3} MTr^{5} [*Jolly* Ku R Nd] *Vij Ku Rn Mr Mandlik KSS*दूषितो; TMd^{3} GMd^{5} GMy Tr^{1} MTr^{4}MTr^{6} हृपितो; Tr^{2} गृहस्थो; Lo^{4} Lo^{5} Ox^{3} Tr^{1} भूषितो विचरे° — b) TMd^{3} GMy Tr^{1} यत्राश्रमे; TMd^{4} प्रत्राश्रमे; Tr^{2} वसेत्; Be^{1} Bo Ho Hy Jm Jo^{1} Kt^{2} NKt^{4} BKt^{5} wKt^{6} La^{1} [*but cor*] La^{2} Lo^{4} Lo^{5} GMd^{1} TMd^{4} NNg Ox^{3} NPu^{1} Pu^{2} Pu^{4} Pu^{8} Pu^{10} Tj^{2} MTr^{3} MTr^{5} Wa [*Jolly* M^{3-4-5}] *Mandlik Jolly Jha KSS Dave* रतः; wKt^{3} ततः; BCa Lo^{1} स्थितः — c) Ox^{3} MTr^{6} *om* भूतेषु — d) Tr^{2} *om*न; Be^{3} नालिङ्गं

67. a) TMd^{3} कटक°; NNg कनक°; GMd^{1} कैतक°; wKt^{1} कतार° — b) wKt^{1} यद्यपि तत्प्रसादकं; sOx^{1} sPu^{6} यद्यम्बु°; wKt^{6} °प्यतप्रसादकं; Lo^{1} °प्रसादनं; BCa La^{1} °प्रसाधकं; TMd^{3} °प्रसाधनं; oOr °प्रधापकं — c) Lo^{5} TMd^{3} नानाम° — d) TMd^{4} तस्या

68. Pādas c-d omitted in GMd^{1}. Cited by *Apa* 954; *Lakṣ* 14.43; *Mādh* 1.564 — a) wKt^{6} संरक्षार्थं च; Be^{3} *Mādh* भूतानां — b) Pu^{5} Pu^{7} Pu^{9} जन्तूनामहन्यहनि वा; GMd^{1} वर्षास्वेकत्र संविशेत्; Jo^{2} °हनि सर्वदा; Be^{1} Be^{3} La^{1} oOr sOx^{1} sPu^{6} [*cor to*] Tr^{2} Wa *Rc* [pāṭha] वा द्विजः — c) Tj^{1} °स्याप्यये; Pu^{2} Pu^{4} °स्याव्यये; wKt^{6} °स्यव्यये; Bo °त्ययैश्चैव; Be^{3} Jo^{2} NKt^{4} TMd^{3} GMy Pu^{5} Pu^{7} Pu^{9} Tr^{1} Tr^{2} MTr^{6} [*Jolly* G] °त्ययेपीह; sOx^{1} sPu^{6} °त्ययेप्येह; Pu^{3} °त्ययेपिव; Tj^{1} °त्यये तस्य; Lo^{2} TMd^{4} Wa °त्ययेप्यस्य; Tj^{2} °त्ययेपीत्व — d) Bo सभैक्ष्य; Tj^{1} च सुधां — Added verse in TMd^{4} MTr^{4} MTr^{6}: see under 6.45.

69. Omitted in Tr^{2}; not commented by *Rc* — a) Be^{1} NNg अह्नि रात्रौ; TMd^{3} अह्नो रात्रं; Bo wKt^{3} रात्रा; TMd^{4} रात्रं; NNg रात्र्यां; TMd^{3} TMd^{4} यो जन्तून्; Jm यो जन्तु; Lo^{5} यज्जन्तून् — b) Bo NKt^{4} हिनस्ति ज्ञानतो; GMy यतिं; BKt^{5} wKt^{6} यदि; Lo^{5} यतः — c) Be^{1} Lo^{1} स्नात्वा तेषां; Tr^{1} MTr^{4} MTr^{6} ज्ञात्वा; MTr^{5}स्नायाविशु°; TMd^{3} °द्ध्यर्धं — d) Tj^{1} °यामं; TMd^{4} °याममथाचरेत्; NKt^{4} सदाचरेत्; GMd^{1} MTr^{4} MTr^{6} समाचरेत्; Pu^{2} यथाचरेत् — Added verse in [*Jolly* Gr]: see under 6.45.

70. Pādas c-d omitted in GMd^{5}; not commented by *Rc*. Cited by *Dev* 2.368 — a) wKt^{6} °याम; MTr^{3} °यामान्ब्रा° — b) Kt^{2} wKt^{6} sOx^{1} °वत्कृतः — c) BBe^{2} Lo^{1} व्याहृतिः प्रण°; Kt^{2} व्याहृतिर्प्रण°; TMd^{4} व्याहृतैः प्रण°; TMd^{3} °वैर्युक्तो; Bo °वैर्युक्तं; MTr^{3} °वैरुक्ता — d) NKt^{4} GMd^{1} TMd^{3} GMy Tr^{1} MTr^{4} MTr^{6} विज्ञेयाः; TMd^{4} विज्ञेयः; NNg प्रणवं तपः

Additional verse in GMd^{1} TMd^{3} Tr^{1}; this is cited in *Nd*'s commentary [= *VaDh* 25.13]

सव्याहृतिकां सप्रणवां गायत्रीं शिरसा सह ।
त्रिः पठेदायतप्राणः प्राणायामः स उच्यते ॥

a) TMd^{3} सव्याहृतिं विप्रणवां — c) TMd^{3} पठेदायतः प्राणः

दह्यन्ते ध्मायमानानां धातूनां हि यथा मलाः ।
तथेन्द्रियाणां दह्यन्ते दोषाः प्राणस्य निग्रहात् ॥७१॥
प्राणायामैर्दहेद्दोषान् धारणाभिश्च किल्बिषम् ।
प्रत्याहारेण संसर्गान् ध्यानेनानीश्वरान् गुणान् ॥७२॥
उच्चावचेषु भूतेषु दुर्ज्ञेयामकृतात्मभिः ।
ध्यानयोगेन संपश्येद्गतिमस्यान्तरात्मनः ॥७३॥
सम्यग्दर्शनसंपन्नः कर्मभिर्न निबध्यते ।
दर्शनेन विहीनस्तु संसारं प्रतिपद्यते ॥७४॥
अहिंसयेन्द्रियासङ्गैर्वैदिकैश्चैव कर्मभिः ।
तपसश्चरणैश्चोग्रैः साधयन्तीह तत्पदम् ॥७५॥
अस्थिस्थूणं स्नायुबद्धं मांसशोणितलेपनम् ।
चर्मावनद्धं दुर्गन्धि पूर्णं मूत्रपुरीषयोः ॥७६॥

71. Omitted in GMd^5. Cited by *Vij* 3.62; *Lakṣ* 14.63; *Dev* 2.368 — a) Bo मह्यन्ते; Be^1 WKt^3 Lo^5 Pu^2 Tj^1 *Lakṣ* ध्याय°; Bo TMd^3 धाय°; WKt^1 °मानायां — b) Pu^2 Pu^4 यथानलाः; GMy मला यथा; TMd^3 मलं यथा — c) Bo Lo^1 [*but cor*] यथेन्द्रि°; TMd^4 तदिन्द्रि°; WKt^6 °न्द्रियाश्च; Pu^{10} दाह्यन्ते; Bo दह्यन्तो — d) *Vij* दोषः; TMd^4 दोषा; Ox^2 निर्ग्रहात्; TMd^4 Pu^{10} विग्रहात्

Additional verse in La^1:

शव्दः स्पर्शं च रूपं च रसो गन्धश्च पञ्चमः ।
अशरीरं शरीरेषु निरीतिश्च निरिन्द्रियः ॥

72. Pādas a-b omitted in GMd^5; in MTr^6 the scribe jumps from प्रत्याहेरेण to संपन्नः (74a) — a) Lo^1 *cor to* °मैर्दह्ये°; Hy °मैर्दहेर्दोषान्; GMd^1 °मैर्देहदोषान्; Pu^2 Pu^4 °मैर्दग्धदोषान् — b) Bo Ho Pu^8 °णाभिस्तु; Pu^8 किल्बिषां; Be^3 किल्बिखं; TMd^4 SOx^1 SPu^6 Tr^1 Tr^2 MTr^4 किल्बिषान्; NKt^4 किल्बिषात्; Jo^2 कल्मषं; TMd^3 कल्चषान् — c) Tr^1 संसर्गं; GMd^1 संसर्ग; GMd^5 सत्सङ्गान् — d) Lo^1 °नानिश्वरान्; GMd^1 GMd^5 GMy Tr^1 MTr^4 Wa *Nā Nd* °नानैश्वरान्; WKt^6 गुरून्

73. Pādas a-c omitted in Pu^9. Pādas a-b cited by *Apa* 968 — a) GMy उच्चावतेषु — b) Be^1 दुर्ज्ञेयम°; GMd^5 दुर्ज्ञेयान°; GMd^1 *Apa* दुर्ज्ञानम°; MTr^5 दुर्ज्ञानाम°; Ox^3 Pu^{10} दुर्ज्ञाताम°; NKt^4 दुर्जनाम°; Pu^5 Pu^7 दुर्जातानकृ°; Tr^2 °मसदात्मभिः — c) NKt^4 GMd^1 TMd^3 GMd^5 GMy Tr^1 MTr^4 MTr^5 *Bh Nd* ज्ञानयोगेन; GMd^1 संपश्यन्गति°; SOx^1 SPu^6 संपश्ये गति°

74. a) WKt^6 सस्यस्पर्शनसंपन्नः — b) TMd^4 न निबध्येत कर्मभिः; Bo Jo^2 Lo^3 स बध्यते — c) TMd^4 दर्शनेपि; MTr^4 MTr^6 च हीनस्तु — d) MTr^6 संस्कारं;Tr^2 प्रतिवद्यते

75. Cited by *Apa* 960 — a) MTr^4 MTr^6 अहिंसाचेन्द्रि°; WKt^6 °यासगैर्वै°; OOr °याग्रामैर्वै°; — b) Ho Lo^2 °ङ्गैर्वेदकै° — c) BBe^2 [*but cor*] तपसैश्चर°; GMd^1 °णैश्चान्यः — d) BBe^2 साधन्तीह; GMd^1 °यन्ति हि; Bo TMd^3 Wa °यन्ति ह; GMy तत्पराः; Tr^1 तत्परा; GMd^1 TMd^3 GMd^5 Pu^2 MTr^4 MTr^5 MTr^6 [*Jolly* N Nd] *Apa* तत्परं; Bühler says that *Nā* and *Nd* read तत्परं but I do not see this.

76.* a) NNg [*but cor fh*] Pu^2 Pu^4 °स्थूणां; MTr^5 [not *Der*] °स्थूण; WKt^6 GMy °स्थूलं; TMd^3 MTr^5 MTr^6 स्नायुबन्धं; BBe^2 Be^3 Bo Ho Hy Jm Jo^1 La^2 NPu^1 Pu^2 Pu^8 Pu^{10} Tj^2 MTr^3 Wa *Mandlik Jolly Jha KSS Dave* स्नायुयुतं; La^1 स्नायुयुक्तं; Tj^1 स्नानयुतं — b) GMd^1 मांसं; GMy °णितफेनलं; TMd^3 °णितफेनिलं; GMd^5 °लेपितं — c) Tr^1 °नद्ध; Be^1 WKt^3 दुर्गन्धिं; GMd^1 TMd^3 TMd^4 GMy SOx^1 SPu^6 MTr^4 MTr^5 MTr^6 [*Jolly* Nd] दुर्गन्धं

जराशोकसमाविष्टं रोगायतनमातुरम् ।
रजस्वलमनित्यं च भूतावासमिमं त्यजेत् ॥७७॥
नदीकूलं यथा वृक्षो वृक्षं वा शकुनिर्यथा ।
तथा त्यजन्निमं देहं कृच्छ्राद्ग्राहाद्विमुच्यते ॥७८॥
प्रियेषु स्वेषु सुकृतमप्रियेषु च दुष्कृतम् ।
विसृज्य ध्यानयोगेन ब्रह्माभ्येति सनातनम् ॥७९॥
यदा भावेन भवति सर्वभावेषु निःस्पृहः ।
तदा सुखमवाप्नोति प्रेत्य चेह च शाश्वतम् ॥८०॥
अनेन विधिना सर्वांस्त्यक्त्वा सङ्गाञ्छनैः शनैः ।
सर्वद्वंद्वविनिर्मुक्तो ब्रह्मण्येवावतिष्ठते ॥८१॥
ध्यानिकं सर्वमेवैतद् यदेतदभिशब्दितम् ।
न ह्यनध्यात्मवित्कश्चित् क्रियाफलमुपाश्नुते ॥८२॥
अधियज्ञं ब्रह्म जपेदाधिदैविकमेव च ।
आध्यात्मिकं च सततं वेदान्ताभिहितं च यत् ॥८३॥

77. a) TMd^{3} °मादिष्टं — c) Bo Ho Lo^{3} Pu^{4} रजस्वलाम° — d) La^{1} °वासामिमं; Be^{1} MTr^{5} Wa °वासमिदं

78. Cited by *Lakṣ* 10.258 — a) Ox^{3} *om* वृक्षो; Lo^{2} वृक्षौ — d) Bo Ho कृच्छ्रग्राहा°; MTr^{4} कृच्छ्राद्ग्रामा°; NKt^{4} GMd^{1} TMd^{3} GMy oOr Tr^{1} MTr^{4} MTr^{6} कृच्छ्रग्रामा°; Pu^{5} Pu^{7} Pu^{9} कृत्स्नग्राहा°; wKt^{1} दुःखग्राहा°; Be^{3} Tr^{2} दुःखंग्राहा°; GMd^{5} MTr^{5} दुःखग्रामा°; wKt^{3} *Lakṣ* °हात्प्रमुच्यते

79. a) Jo^{1} विप्रियेषु; Lo^{5} Ox^{3} सुकृताम°; Tr^{2} स्वकृतम°; TMd^{3} संकृत्यम° — b) NNg °कृतं विप्रियेषु च; wKt^{1} Tr^{1} तु — c) Tr^{1} विसृजं; Ox^{3} Pu^{10} [*Jolly* M] विमृष्य; NKt^{4} ज्ञानयोगेन — d) TMd^{4} परं ब्रह्माभिगच्छति; TMd^{3} GMd^{5} GMy Tr^{1} MTr^{6} ब्रह्माप्येति; Be^{1} °भ्येति परं पदं

80. a) Pu^{3} Pu^{4} सदा; La^{1} TMd^{4} यथा; TMd^{3} यधा — b) Tr^{2} °भागेषु; Pu^{2} Pu^{4} °लाभेषु; Pu^{3} Pu^{8} °भूतेषु; TMd^{4} °भावेन; TMd^{3} निस्पृहा — c) TMd^{4} तथा; TMd^{3} तधा — d) TMd^{3} GMy प्रेत्य चानुत्तमं सुखं; Pu^{5} *om* च; BKt^{5} wKt^{6} शाश्वतः

81. a-b) Lo^{2} Tj^{1} विधिना त्यक्त्वा सर्वान्सङ्गा° [Tj^{1} सर्वसङ्गा°]; Be TMd^{4} सर्वान्सङ्गान्त्यक्त्वा शनैः शनैः; GMd^{5} सङ्गांस्त्यक्त्वा सर्वाञ्छनैः शनैः — c) Be^{1} सर्वदुःखवि°; Bo Ho Jo^{2} wKt^{6} Lo^{1} Lo^{3} Lo^{4} Lo^{5} GMd^{1} GMd^{5} NNg oOr Ox^{3} Pu^{2} Pu^{4} Pu^{10} Tj^{2} Tr^{1} MTr^{4} MTr^{5} MTr^{6} [*Jolly* M] °द्वंद्वैर्वि°; NKt^{4} °द्वंद्वेवि°; TMd^{3} °द्वंद्वैर्विप्रयुक्तो; MTr^{4} MTr^{5} °विप्रमुक्तो; Tr^{1} °विमुक्तस्तु — d) Be^{3} NKt^{4} °तिष्ठति

82. Omitted in Tr^{2}; *mc* in BKt^{5} — a) GMd^{1} TMd^{3} TMd^{4} GMd^{5} GMy Tr^{1} MTr^{4} MTr^{6} आध्यात्मिकं सर्वमेतद् [MTr^{6} अध्यानिकं]; sOx^{1} sPu^{6} ध्यानकं; NKt^{4} ध्यानिके — b) TMd^{4} यदेतमनुशव्दितं; Tj^{1} यदैतद°; TMd^{3} यधैतद°; GMy यथैतमभि° — c) GMd^{1} ह्यनाध्या°; GMd^{1} GMy NPu^{1} °वित्किंचित्; Pu^{2} °वित्काचित्; TMd^{3} °वित्कंचित् — d) Ho °मुपासते

83. Pādas a-b *mc* in BKt^{5} — a) Lo^{3} आधियज्ञं; MTr^{4} अभियज्ञं; TMd^{3} °यज्ञ — b) Be^{1} GMd^{1} GMd^{5} GMy °दधिदैवक°; Pu^{2} °देविक°; GMd^{5} NNg Pu^{2} Pu^{4} वा — c) BBe^{2} Bo Ho Jo^{1} Kt^{2} wKt^{6} Lo^{3} Lo^{4} Lo^{5} TMd^{3} GMd^{5} GMy Ox^{3} Pu^{2} Pu^{5} Pu^{7} Pu^{9} Tj^{1} [*Jolly* M R] अध्या°; Ho °त्मकं — d) Bo वेदान्तोपगतं; Ho °हतं; Kt^{2} °हितश्च

इदं शरणमज्ञानामिदमेव विजानताम् ।
इदमन्विच्छतां स्वर्गमिदमानन्त्यमिच्छताम् ॥८४॥
अनेन क्रमयोगेन परिव्रजति यो द्विजः ।
स विधूयेह पाप्मानं परं ब्रह्माधिगच्छति ॥८५॥
एष धर्मोऽनुशिष्टो वो यतीनां नियतात्मनाम् ।
वेदसंन्यासिकानां तु कर्मयोगं निबोधत ॥८६॥
ब्रह्मचारी गृहस्थश्च वानप्रस्थो यतिस्तथा ।
एते गृहस्थप्रभवाश्चत्वारः पृथगाश्रमाः ॥८७॥
सर्वेऽपि क्रमशस्त्वेते यथाशास्त्रं निषेविताः ।
यथोक्तकारिणं विप्रं नयन्ति परमां गतिम् ॥८८॥
सर्वेषामपि चैतेषां वेदश्रुतिविधानतः ।
गृहस्थ उच्यते श्रेष्ठः स त्रीनेतान्बिभर्ति हि ॥८९॥
यथा नदीनदाः सर्वे सागरे यान्ति संस्थितिम् ।
तथैवाश्रमिणः सर्वे गृहस्थे यान्ति संस्थितिम् ॥९०॥

84. Pādas c-d omitted in Tr^1 — a) wKt^6 शरण्याम° ; oOr शरीरम° ; Tj^1 °ज्ञानमिद° ; TMd^4 °ज्ञानादिद° — b) Ho विजानता; TMd^3 विजानताः — c) TMd^3 °न्विच्छता; wKt^3 wKt^6 स्वर्ग्यमि° — d) Pu^{10} °मानंदमिच्छ° ; GMd^5 °मारण्यमिच्छ° ; TMd^3 °च्छतान्

85. a) Tr^1 कर्मयोगेन — b) BKt^5 wKt^6 परित्यजति; TMd^3 द्विजाः; Pu^8 नरः — c) GMd^1 विधूयैव; Pu^{10} विभूवेह; TMd^4 विधूयेहमात्मानं; Ho TMd^3 पापानि — d) GMd^1 स्वर्गं ब्रह्मा° ; GMd^5 GMy Tr^1 MTr^4 MTr^6 श्रेयोधि° ; TMd^3 श्रेयाधि° ; NNg °गच्छतां

86. Omitted in GMy. Cited by *Lakṣ* 14.64 — a) NKt^4 धर्मानुशिष्टो; wKt^6 धर्मार्थशिष्टो; Lo^1 धर्मो विशिष्टो; Tr^1 °नुशिष्टा; MTr^4 °निशिष्टो; Tr^2 °नुसृष्टो; Be^1 NKt^4 TMd^3 वा; HoGMd^1 TMd^4 GMd^5 Tr^1 MTr^4 *Lakṣ* वै— c) Pu^{10} वैद° ; Be^1 Bo Jo^2 Lo^2 Lo^3 TMd^3 Pu^2 Pu^4 Wa च — d) BBe^2 TMd^4 [*but cor fh*] धर्मयोगं; Be^1 Be^3 Pu^5 Pu^7 Pu^9 निबोधतः; wKt^3 निबोधित

87. Cited by *Lakṣ* 14.64; *Dev* 1. 173; *Mādh* 1.436 — a) wKt^1 wKt^3 गृहस्थस्तु; Ho गृहस्थो वा; NKt^4 TMd^3 oOr गृहस्थस्य; Hy गृहस्थवान° — b) TMd^3 °प्रस्था; oOr °प्रस्थोथ वा यतिः; MTr^5 °प्रस्थोथ भिक्षुकः — d) Tj^1 प्रथमाश्रमाः

88. In MTr^6 after यथा in pāda-b scribe jumps to वृत्तो at 7.1c [haplo]; Cited by *Lakṣ* 14.65; *Dev* 1.173 — a) sOx^1 sPu^6 सर्वे च; Tr^1 सर्वे विक्रम° ; Be^1 NKt^4 NPu^1 Pu^2 Wa क्रमशश्चैते; Lo^2 Pu^4 क्रमशश्चैव — b) sOx^1 sPu^6 °शास्त्रे; BKt^5 wKt^6 °शास्त्रनिषेदिताः; Tj^1 *Lakṣ* °शास्त्रमनुष्ठिताः; Wa निषेवते — c) Ox^3 न यथो° ; BKt^5 wKt^6 °कारणं; Ho °चारिणं; [*Jolly* Gr] °कारिणं प्राज्ञं; GMd^1 °कारिणो विप्रान् — d) Ho GMy नयान्ति; Bo नयति; TMd^4 नयाति; Lo^2 परमं

89. Pādas c-d omitted in Ox^3. Cited by *Lakṣ* 14.65 — a) MTr^5 सर्वेषामपि तु त्वेषां; GMd^1 NNg सर्वेषामेव — b) Be^1 Be^3 Bo Ho Hy Jm Jo^1 Jo^2 [*cor to*] wKt^1 Kt^2 Lo^1 Lo^3 Tj^2 MTr^3 [*Jolly* R] *Mandlik KSS* वेदस्मृति° — c) Bo श्रेष्ठं — d) Be^1 °भर्ति यः

90. Placed before 6.88 in BBe^2; pādas c-d omitted in Ho BKt^5 wKt^6 TMd^3 TMd^4 Ox^3 Pu^{10} [haplo]. Cited by *Lakṣ* 14.65; *Dev* 1.175 — b) TMd^4 Tj^1 सागरं; NNg समुद्रे; TMd^3 GMd^5 Ox^3 संस्थितं; TMd^4 सुस्थितं — c) Be^3 La^1 NNg Tr^2 एवमाश्रमिणः — d) Tr^1 गृहस्थो; Bo यन्ति; GMd^5 संस्थितं

चतुर्भिरपि चैवैतैर्नित्यमाश्रमिभिर्द्विजैः ।
दशलक्षणको धर्मः सेवितव्यः प्रयत्नतः ॥९१॥
धृतिः क्षमा दमोऽस्तेयं शौचमिन्द्रियनिग्रहः ।
धीर्विद्या सत्यमक्रोधो दशकं धर्मलक्षणम् ॥९२॥
दश लक्षणानि धर्मस्य ये विप्राः समधीयते ।
अधीत्य चानुवर्तन्ते ते यान्ति परमां गतिम् ॥९३॥
दशलक्षणकं धर्ममनुतिष्ठन्समाहितः ।
वेदान्तान्विधिवच्छ्रुत्वा संन्यसेदनृणो द्विजः ॥९४॥
संन्यस्य सर्वकर्माणि कर्मदोषानपानुदन् ।
नियतो वेदमभ्यस्यन् पुत्रैश्वर्ये सुखं वसेत् ॥९५॥

91. Cited by *Lakṣ* 14.65 — a) sOx^{1} Ox^{2} Pu^{3} sPu^{6} Pu^{8} Tj^{1} चतुर्भिरेव चाप्येतैर्नि°; GMd^{5} चतुर्भिरेव तैरपि तु नि°; NPu^{1} Pu^{5} Pu^{7} Pu^{9} चतुर्भिरेवमप्येतैर्नि°; Be^{3} चतुर्भिरपि हि त्वेतैर्नि°; GMd^{1} चतुर्भिरेतैरपि तु नि°; Jo^{2} Lo^{3} Lo^{4} Pu^{10} *Lakṣ* चाप्येतैर्नि°; Bo Ox^{3} वाप्येतैर्नि°; Lo^{2} Pu^{2} Pu^{4} च त्वेतैर्नि°; NNg चैतैस्तु नि°; Tr^{2} तैरेतैर्नि°; Be^{1} Wa न त्वेतैर्नि°; MTr^{5} तूपेतैर्नि°; Lo^{1} चैवैते नि°; TMd^{3} तत्वेतैः नि°; Tr^{1} हि तैः नि°; MTr^{4} कृत्वैतैर्नि° — b) GMd^{5} °श्रमविद्द्विजैः — c) Be^{3} Jo Lo^{4} Lo^{5} NNg Ox^{3} Pu^{2} Pu^{4} Pu^{5} Pu^{7} Pu^{8} Pu^{9} Pu^{10} [*Jolly* G] °लक्षणिको; Lo^{2} °लाक्षणिको; MTr^{5} °लक्षणतो

92.* Cited by *Apa* 972; *Lakṣ* 14.65; *Dev* 1.13 — a) GMd^{1} प्रीतिर्दान्तिर्दमस्तेयं; Ox^{3} वृत्तिः; Pu^{10} वृत्ति; wKt^{1} मदो; NPu^{1} दयास्तेयं; Be^{1} °स्तेयः — b) Bo शौर्यमिन्द्रि°; *Bh* °न्द्रियसंयमः [MTr^{5} is torn here] — c) Be^{3} Ho La^{1} La^{2} TMd^{3} TMd^{4} GMd^{5} GMy NPu^{1} Pu^{2} Pu^{3} Pu^{8} Tr^{2} [*Jolly* N Nd] *Nā Nd Rc Dev* ह्लीर्विद्या; Tr^{1} ह्लीविद्या; Ox^{3} Pu^{10} शौचमक्रोधो — d) Ox^{3} दशको; Pu^{10} दशिको; TMd^{4} दशमं

93.* Omitted in Pu^{8} Tr^{1}; verses 93 and 94 transposed in Lo^{5} Wa. Cited by *Apa* 973; *Lakṣ* 14.65 — a) Bo Jo^{2} La^{1} La^{2} Lo^{1} Lo^{3} Lo^{4} Lo^{5} TMd^{3} Ox^{3} Pu^{10} Wa [*Jolly* M$^{4-5}$ R] *Apa Jolly* दशलक्षणकं धर्मं [Pu^{10} °णकिं]; Lo^{2} GMy Pu^{2} Pu^{4} [*Jolly* M$^{1-2-8-9}$ G Nd] दशलक्षणिकं धर्मं [Lo^{2} Pu^{2} Pu^{4} °लाक्षणिकं]; Be^{1} Be^{3} sOx^{1} sPu^{6} दश चिह्नानि धर्मस्य; Tr^{2} दशलक्षणात्तु धर्मस्य; NKt^{4} Ox^{2} दशलक्षणधर्मस्य — b) TMd^{4} ये पठन्ति द्विजातयः; *Apa* येऽधीयेरन्द्विजातयः; Jm TMd^{3} यो विप्राः; GMd^{1} यो विप्रः; Ox^{2} विप्रः — c) Ox^{3} अतीत्य — d) TMd^{3} परमं

94.* Omitted in BKt^{5}; *ma* in wKt^{6}. Cited by *Lakṣ* 14.65 — a) GMd^{1} दशलक्षणधर्मिममनुति°; Pu^{5} Pu^{7} Pu^{9} Tr^{1} °लक्षणिकं; Lo^{2} Pu^{2} Pu^{4} °लाक्षणिकं; Pu^{10} °लक्षणकिं; NKt^{4} °लक्षणधर्म° — b) BCa [*but cor*] Lo^{2} GMd^{5} GMy oOr Ox^{2} NPu^{1} Pu^{2} Tr^{1} MTr^{4} °तिष्ठन्हि मानवः; TMd^{3} °तिष्ठन्ति मानवः — c) GMd^{1} वेदांश्च विधि°; Hy Jm Jo^{1} wKt^{1} Kt^{2} wKt^{3} La^{1} Lo^{3} TMd^{3} GMy sOx^{1} sPu^{6} Tj^{2} Tr^{2} MTr^{3} *Mandlik Jolly Jha KSS Dave* वेदान्तं विधि°; NKt^{4} °न्विविधान्श्रुत्वा; Lo^{4} Lo^{5} Ox^{3} [*Jolly* M^{4}] °धिवत्सेव्य — d) NNg संन्यस्येद°

Additional verse in TMd^{3}:

काम्यानां कर्मणां न्यासं संन्यासं कवयो विदुः ।
नियतो वेदमभ्यस्यन्पुत्रैश्वर्ये सुखं वसेत् ॥ [= 95 c-d]

95.* Omitted in BKt^{5} Pu^{9}; *ma* in wKt^{6}; pādas b-d omitted in Be^{3} and pādas c-d in Tr^{2}. Cited by *Lakṣ* 14.65 — a) Be^{1} संन्यसेत्सर्व°; Tr^{2} सर्वा° — b) Be^{1} वेदं तु न परित्यजेत्; GMd^{1} TMd^{4} नियतो वेदमामनन्; TMd^{3} GMy सर्वदोषा°; Pu^{10} °पानुपानुदन्; Pu^{5} Pu^{7} Pu^{8} Pu^{9} °पानुदत्; Lo^{2} Lo^{4} Lo^{5} NPu^{1} Pu^{2} Pu^{4} °पानुदेत्; Ox^{3} °पानुदेन्; Tr^{2} °पानह — c) GMd^{1} TMd^{4} अपानुदन्कर्मदोषान्; Be^{1} BBe^{2} Bo BCa Ho Hy Jm Jo^{1} wKt^{1} Kt^{2} wKt^{3} NKt^{4} La^{1} La^{2} Lo^{1} Lo^{4} Lo^{5} TMd^{3} GMy NNg Ox^{2} Ox^{3} NPu^{1}

एवं संन्यस्य कर्माणि स्वकार्यपरमोऽस्पृहः ।
संन्यासेनापहत्यैनः प्राप्नोति परमां गतिम् ॥९६॥
एष वोऽभिहितो धर्मो ब्राह्मणस्य चतुर्विधः ।
पुण्योऽक्षयफलः प्रेत्य राज्ञां धर्मं निबोधत ॥९७॥

॥ इति मानवे धर्मशास्त्रे भृगुप्रोक्तायां संहितायां षष्ठोऽध्यायः ॥

Pu^{2} Pu^{10} Tj^{1} MTr^{5} Wa [*Jolly* M Ku] *Rc Mr Mandlik Jha KSS Dave* वेदमभ्यस्य — d) Be^{1} °श्वर्यः; Bo °श्वर्यैः; Tj^{1} °श्वर्यं; TMd^{3} °श्वर्य; Ox^{3} °श्वर्गे

Additional verse in TMd^{4} oOr MTr^{4} [*Jolly* Gr]*Mandlik* [क] *KSS;* placed after verse 94 in GMd^{5} [= *VaDh* 10.4]:

संन्यसेत्सर्वकर्माणि वेदमेकं न संन्यसेत् ।
वेदसंन्यसनाच्छूद्रस्तस्माद्वेदं न संन्यसेत् ॥

a) [*Jolly* Gr] संन्यस्य सर्व° — b) TMd^{4} वेदं तु सततं पठेत् — This verse in *Mandlik* [ञ ड] reads: संन्यसेत्सर्वकर्माणि वेदं तु न परित्यजेत् । परित्यागाद्धि वेदस्य शूद्रतामनुगच्छति ॥

Additional verse in GMd^{1} GMd^{5} MTr^{4}:

उच्छ्वासमात्रमपि चेदन्तकाले समो भवेत् ।
निमेषमात्रमपि वा प्राप्नोति परमां गतिम् ॥

96. Omitted in BKt^{5} Tr^{2}; *ma* in wKt^{6}; pāda-a omitted in Be^{3}. Cited by *Lakṣ* 14.65 — a) NNg एवं कर्माणि संन्यस्य; TMd^{4} संन्यस्य सर्वकर्माणि — b) TMd^{4} स्वकार्यं; BBe^{2} स्वकर्म°; NKt^{4} °रमो-स्मृतः; TMd^{3} °स्पृहं — c) Tr^{1} संन्यासेनोप°; Bo Ho °हत्येन; Ox^{3} °हत्येना; TMd^{3} °हत्येनाः; NKt^{4} GMd^{1} Ox^{2} Pu^{5} Pu^{7} Pu^{9} Pu^{10} °हत्येनः — d) Tj^{1} *om* प्राप्नोति

97. Omitted in MTr^{5}. Pādas a-b cited by *Vij* 3.56–7; *Dev* 1.176 — a) wKt^{1} wKt^{3} NKt^{4} Ox^{3} वो विहितो; Lo^{4} Lo^{5} को विहितो; Pu^{10} °भिहिता — c) Lo^{2} Pu^{2} Pu^{4} पुण्यं फलक्षयः प्रेत्य; Wa °क्षयः फलः; Lo^{3} °क्षयकरः; Ho Ox^{3} Pu^{10} °फलं — d) BBe^{2} Be^{3} Bo Ho wKt^{1} La^{1} Lo^{1} GMd^{5} GMy NNg oOr Pu^{3} Tr^{1} Tr^{2} राज्ञो; wKt^{3} GMd^{1} TMd^{3} राज्ञा; [*Jolly* M$^{8-9}$]राज; GMd^{1} oOr [*Jolly* Nd]धर्मा; Lo^{3} धर्मां; TMd^{3} धर्म; Be^{1} BBe^{2} wKt^{1} wKt^{3} La^{1} Lo^{4} GMd^{5} Ox^{3} Tr^{1} Wa [*Jolly* M$^{4-5}$ R] *Jolly* धर्मान्निबो°; TMd^{3} निबोध्यत; BKt^{5} wKt^{6} निशामय

Colophon: Be^{1} Lo^{1} Lo^{3} TMd^{3} NNg sOx^{1} sPu^{6} Tr^{1} इति श्रीमानवे; Be^{3} wKt^{3} भृगुप्रोक्ते; BKt^{5} wKt^{6} Lo^{1} Lo^{2} TMd^{3} GMy NNg sOx^{1} sPu^{6} *om* भृगुप्रोक्तायां संहितायां; Lo^{3} भृगुप्रोक्तसंहितायां; Be^{3} wKt^{3} GMd^{5} *om* संहितायां; Be^{1} °प्रोक्तसंहितायां संन्यासाध्यायः शष्ठः; BBe^{2} यतिधर्मो नाम षष्ठो; Lo^{1} वर्णाश्रम-धर्मो नाम षष्ठो; oOr वानप्रस्थो नाम षष्ठो; NNg यतिधर्मः षष्ठो; NNg °ध्यायः समाप्तः

[सप्तमोऽध्यायः]

राजधर्मान्प्रवक्ष्यामि यथावृत्तो भवेन्नृपः ।
संभवश्च यथा तस्य सिद्धिश्च परमा यथा ॥१॥
ब्राह्मं प्राप्तेन संस्कारं क्षत्रियेण यथाविधि ।
सर्वस्यास्य यथान्यायं कर्तव्यं परिरक्षणम् ॥२॥
अराजके हि लोकेऽस्मिन् सर्वतो विद्रुते भयात् ।
रक्षार्थमस्य सर्वस्य राजानमसृजत् प्रभुः ॥३॥
इन्द्रानिलयमार्काणामग्नेश्च वरुणस्य च ।
चन्द्रवित्तेशयोश्चैव मात्रा निर्हृत्य शाश्वतीः ॥४॥
यस्मादेषां सुरेन्द्राणां मात्राभ्यो निर्मितो नृपः ।
तस्मादभिभवत्येष सर्वभूतानि तेजसा ॥५॥
तपत्यादित्यवच्चैव चक्षूंषि च मनांसि च ।
न चैनं भुवि शक्नोति कश्चिदप्यभिवीक्षितुम् ॥६॥

1. Cited by *Vij* 1.368— a) Be^{3} TMd^{4} oOr °धर्मं प्रव°; wKt^{1} wKt^{3} °वक्षामि — b) Pu^{8} °वृत्तौ; TMd^{4} °वृत्ति; Lo^{5} °वृक्षो; Be^{1} [*but mc*] भवेद्विजः; GMd^{1} भवेन्नरः — c) La^{1} संभवस्तु; BKt^{5} wKt^{6} GMy संभवस्य; wKt^{1} तथा — d) GMy NPu^{1} तथा

2. a) Bo BCa Ox^{2} ब्राह्मयं; TMd^{3} ब्राह्मयां; Kt^{2} Pu^{8} ब्राह्मे; Pu^{5} Pu^{7} Pu^{9} प्राप्ते च; Tj^{2} प्राप्नोति — c) sOx^{1} sPu^{6} [*but cor*] धर्मस्यास्य

3. Pādas a-b torn in Pu^{9}. Cited by *Lakṣ* 11.2; *Mādh* 1.391, 3.5 — a) Ho अराजिके; Tj^{1} आराजके; Jo^{1} *om* हि — b) GMd^{1} विद्रुतस्सर्वतो भवेत्; *Lakṣ* सर्वतोभिद्रुते; wKt^{1} NKt^{4} La^{1} Lo^{2} oOr Ox^{3} Pu^{5} Pu^{7} Tr^{2} विद्रुतो; BKt^{5} wKt^{6} विद्यते; TMd^{3} GMy विहितो; TMd^{4} विद्रुताभयेत् — c) Ox^{3} चक्षुर्धर्मस्य सर्वस्य — d) La^{1} °सृजतः प्रभुः

4. Not commented by *Rc*. Cited by *Mādh* 3.5 — a) Tr^{1} इन्द्रनील°; *Mādh* चन्द्रानिल°; La^{1} अग्निवायुयमार्का°; Ho °मार्कायाम° — c) *Mādh* इन्द्रवित्ते° — d) Ox^{2} मात्रां; Tr^{1} मात्रान्निर्हृत्य; GMd^{5} निर्वर्त्य; wKt^{1} Pu^{8} निर्हत्य; Ho निहन्त्य; Bo निर्हय; Pu^{5} Pu^{7} निष्कृष्य; *Mādh* आहृत्य; Be^{3} Ho Pu^{5} Pu^{7} Pu^{9} Tj^{1} शाश्वती; Ox^{2} Tr^{1} शाश्वतीं; TMd^{3} शाश्वतिः; TMd^{4} शाश्वतिं

5. Cited by *Mādh* 3.5 — a) *Mādh* यस्मादेव; TMd^{3} GMd^{5} यस्मादेपा; wKt^{3} यदादेषां — b) Jo^{2} Lo^{3} Tj^{1} मात्रातो; MTr^{4} MTr^{6} मात्राभिर्निर्मितो; Wa निर्मिता; Lo^{1} निर्मितः प्रभुः; NKt^{4} नृतः — c) oOr यस्माद°; TMd^{3} °भवत्येपा

6.* Cited by *Lakṣ* 11.2; *Mādh* 3.5 — a) wKt^{6} Ox^{2} तपन्त्या°; wKt^{3} पतत्या°; Lo^{1} तपाश्चादित्य°; BBe^{2} BCa Jo^{1} Jo^{2} Kt^{2} La^{1} Lo^{2} Lo^{3} Lo^{4} Lo^{5} NNg Ox^{3} NPu^{1} Pu^{2} Pu^{5} Pu^{7} Pu^{9} Tj^{1} Tj^{2} *Mandlik Jolly Jha KSS Dave* °वच्चैष; Wa °वच्चैषां; GMd^{5} °वल्लोके — c) wKt^{3} GMd^{5} *Lakṣ* चैवं; Pu^{3} चैव; NKt^{4} चैनं तु विशक्नोति — d) Be^{1} न कश्चिदभि°; MTr^{6} कश्चिदस्याभि°; BBe^{2} TMd^{4} °वीक्षितं

सोऽग्निर्भवति वायुश्च सोऽर्कः सोमः स धर्मराट् ।
स कुबेरः स वरुणः स महेन्द्रः प्रभावतः ॥७॥
बालोऽपि नावमन्तव्यो मनुष्य इति भूमिपः ।
महती देवता ह्येषा नररूपेण तिष्ठति ॥८॥
एकमेव दहत्यग्निर्नरं दुरुपसर्पिणम् ।
कुलं दहति राजाग्निः सपशुद्रव्यसंचयम् ॥९॥
कार्यं सोऽवेक्ष्य शक्तिं च देशकालौ च तत्त्वतः ।
कुरुते धर्मसिद्ध्यर्थं विश्वरूपं पुनः पुनः ॥१०॥
यस्य प्रसादे पद्मा श्रीर्विजयश्च पराक्रमे ।
मृत्युश्च वसति क्रोधे सर्वतेजोमयो हि सः ॥११॥
तं यस्तु द्वेष्टि संमोहात् स विनश्यत्यसंशयम् ।
तस्य ह्याशु विनाशाय राजा प्रकुरुते मनः ॥१२॥
तस्माद्धर्मं यमिष्टेषु संव्यवस्येन्नराधिपः ।
अनिष्टं चाप्यनिष्टेषु तं धर्मं न विचालयेत् ॥१३॥

7. Omitted in Pu^{9}; not commented by *Rc*. Cited by *Lakṣ* 112; *Mādh* 3.5 — a) *Lakṣ* °ग्निर्भवतु; NKt^{4} वायुः स — b) Jo^{2} Lo^{3} Tj^{1} सोमः सोर्कः स धर्मराट्; Lo^{5} सोमं; La^{1} TMd^{3} GMy sOx^{1} sPu^{6} सोमश्च — c) sOx^{1} *om first* स — d) [*Jolly* M^{8}] स चेन्द्रः स्वप्रभावतः; TMd^{4} प्रतापवान्

8. Not commented by *Rc*. Cited by *Mādh* 3.5 — a) GMy °मन्तव्या — b) Bo मानुष्य; TMd^{3} GMy MTr^{4} MTr^{6} भूपतिः — c) Ho महतीं देवतां; Jo^{1} दैवता; sOx^{1} sPu^{6} ह्येष; Ho Ox^{3} ह्येषां — d) Ho नरूपेण च तिष्ठति; Tr^{1} नृपरूपेण

9. Cited by *Mādh* 3.5 — a) Be^{3} wKt^{3} NKt^{4} एक एव — b) Lo^{2} Pu^{2} Pu^{4} °ग्निर्वरं; TMd^{3} °ग्निर्गरं; GMd^{1} स्वमुपसर्पिणं; TMd^{3} [*but cor*] °सर्पितं; Tr^{1} °सर्पणं — c) TMd^{3} कुलान्दहति राजापि; TMd^{4} राजाग्निं — d) Lo^{2} °संचये; Ho °संचितं; Wa °संग्रहं

10. Cited by *Lakṣ* 11.5; *Mādh* 3.5 — a) Lo^{1} सोवीक्ष्य; TMd^{4} स वीक्ष्य; NKt^{4} सोपेक्ष्य; Be^{3} Ho La^{2} Lo^{4} Lo^{5} NNg sOx^{1} Ox^{3} sPu^{6} Pu^{8} [*Jolly* M R] *Lakṣ Jolly* चावेक्ष्य; NNg चान्वेक्ष्य; BKt^{5} wKt^{6} शक्तिश्च — b) TMd^{4} °कालं; Be^{3} TMd^{3} TMd^{4} GMy NPu^{1} शक्तितः — c) Lo^{2} Pu^{2} Pu^{4} Pu^{5} [*but cor*] Pu^{7} [*but mc*] कर्मसिद्ध्यर्थं — d) Pu^{5} Pu^{7} [*mc to*] धर्मरूपं

11. a) sOx^{1} sPu^{6} places ॐ at the beginning; Be^{1} Ho NKt^{4} Lo^{2} GMd^{1} TMd^{3} TMd^{4} GMd^{5} GMy NNg Pu^{2} Pu^{4} Tr^{1} MTr^{5} MTr^{6} *Nd* तस्य; wKt^{6} Lo^{5} TMd^{3} श्रीवि°; TMd^{4} स्त्रीर्वि° — b) Tj^{1} श्रीर्विनयश्च; Pu^{4} °क्रमो; Lo^{2} °क्रमौ; Wa °क्रम — c) Jo^{2} wKt^{1} मृत्युर्वसति क्रोधे च; wKt^{6} मन्युश्च; TMd^{4} मृत्युश्चावसति; Tj^{1} [*Jolly* R] मृत्युः संवसति; Bo GMd^{1} क्रोधो — d) BBe^{2} *om* हि; NKt^{4} हितः

12. Cited by *Lakṣ* 11.5 — a) Bo wKt^{3} GMd^{1} TMd^{4} GMd^{5} Tr^{1} MTr^{4} MTr^{6} यस्तु तं; TMd^{3} द्वेष्यते मोहात्; Bo TMd^{4} तं मोहात्; GMd^{5} तन्मोहात्; GMy ते मोहात् — b) Lo^{1} विनशत्य°; wKt^{3} TMd^{3} TMd^{4} GMd^{5} GMy °संशयः — c) Be^{1} न ह्यस्याशुविनाशाय; *Lakṣ* तस्मात्त्वाशु°; Be^{3} त्वाशु° — d) Lo^{1} स राजा कुरुते

13.* Pādas c-d *ma* in BKt^{5} — a) Be^{1} तस्मादिप्टेपु यं धर्मं; GMd^{1} तस्माद्धर्मा; GMd^{5} तस्माद्धर्म्यं; MTr^{5} तस्मात्सर्वं — b) MTr^{5} व्यवस्येति नराधिपः; Pu^{5} Pu^{7} Pu^{9} वर्तयेत्तं नराधिपः; Be^{1} Bo Ho Jo^{1} Kt^{2} NKt^{4} BKt^{5} wKt^{6} La^{2} Lo^{4} Lo^{5} GMd^{1} oOr Ox^{3} Tr^{2} *Mandlik Jha KSS Dave* स व्यवस्ये°; Jm संव्य-

तस्यार्थे सर्वभूतानां गोप्तारं धर्ममात्मजम् ।
ब्रह्मतेजोमयं दण्डमसृजत्पूर्वमीश्वरः ॥१४॥
तस्य सर्वाणि भूतानि स्थावराणि चराणि च ।
भयाद्भोगाय कल्पन्ते स्वधर्मान्न चलन्ति च ॥१५॥
तं देशकालौ शक्तिं च विद्यां चावेक्ष्य तत्त्वतः ।
यथार्हतः संप्रणयेन्नरेष्वन्यायवर्तिषु ॥१६॥
स राजा पुरुषो दण्डः स नेता शासिता च सः ।
चतुर्णामाश्रमाणां च धर्मस्य प्रतिभूः स्मृतः ॥१७॥
दण्डः शास्ति प्रजाः सर्वा दण्ड एवाभिरक्षति ।
दण्डः सुप्तेषु जागर्ति दण्डं धर्मं विदुर्बुधाः ॥१८॥
समीक्ष्य स धृतः सम्यक् सर्वा रञ्जयति प्रजाः ।
असमीक्ष्य प्रणीतस्तु विनाशयति सर्वतः ॥१९॥
यदि न प्रणयेद्राजा दण्डं दण्ड्येष्वतन्द्रितः ।

वसे°; TMd^{4} सेव्यवस्ये°; TMd^{3} संव्यवस्ते नरा°; BBe^{2} संव्यवसेन्नरा° — c) GMd^{5} अनिष्टां; Be^{3} Ho sOx^{1} Ox^{3} Pu^{3} sPu^{6} वाप्य° — d) TMd^{4} MTr^{5} तद्धर्मं; wKt^{3} BKt^{5} wKt^{6} La^{1} GMd^{1} TMd^{3} TMd^{4} GMy sPu^{6} Tr^{2} MTr^{5} विचारयेत्

14. *ma* in BKt^{5}. Cited by *Lakṣ* 12.794 — a) Lo^{2} तस्यार्थं; Wa तस्यार्थ; sOx^{1} sPu^{6} तपार्थे; Be^{1} Be^{3} Bo NKt^{4} BKt^{5} La^{2} Lo^{1} Lo^{4} Lo^{5} NNg Ox^{2} Ox^{3} NPu^{1} Pu^{2} Pu^{3} Pu^{4} Pu^{5} Pu^{7} Pu^{8} [*Jolly* M G] *Lakṣ Jolly Jha* तदर्थं; wKt^{6} तदनं — b) Lo^{2} मोक्षारं; Lo^{2} GMd^{1} TMd^{4} GMd^{5} Tr^{1} MTr^{4} MTr^{6} °मात्मनः — c) wKt^{1} ब्रह्मा°; wKt^{3} सर्वतेजो°; wKt^{1} कण्डमसृ°; TMd^{3} GMy धर्ममसृ° — d) MTr^{3} °सृजन्पू°; Pu^{5} Pu^{7} Pu^{9} °जत्सर्वमीश्वरः; Be^{3} NNg °मीश्वरं

15. Omitted in oOr. Cited by *Lakṣ* 12.794 — a) NNg यस्य; TMd^{4} MTr^{6} भूतानि सर्वाणि — b) GMd^{5} चराणि स्थावराणि; Pu^{8} *om* चराणि; Wa चराण्यपि — c) Ho °द्रोपाय — d) Tr^{1} स्वधर्मं न; NKt^{4} चलति; Bo बलन्ति; Jo^{2} हि; Lo^{4} Lo^{5} Ox^{3} [*Jolly* M] ते

16. Cited by *Lakṣ* 11.6 — a) wKt^{3} GMd^{1} तद्देश°; Ox^{3} °कालं; Jm शक्तिश्च — b) Ox^{3} विद्यां चैव स्वधर्मतः; Kt^{2} Lo^{5} sOx^{1} sPu^{6} विद्या; Bo विधां चावेश्य; TMd^{4} चावीक्ष्य; GMd^{1} TMd^{4} NNg *Lakṣ* शक्तितः; [*Jolly* G] धर्मतः — c) wKt^{3} यथार्हं प्रहयेद्दण्डं नरे°; BBe^{2} यथार्हं प्रणयेद्दण्डान्नरे°; Lo^{5} तथा°; TMd^{3} Pu^{5} यथार्हितः; Tr^{1} यथाहतः — d) BBe^{2} Ho °रेषु न्याय°; MTr^{5} °वृत्तिषु

17. Cited by *Lakṣ* 12.794 — a) Ho BKt^{5} TMd^{3} TMd^{4} GMy NPu^{1} Tr^{1} राजपुरुषो; GMy दण्डश्च स — b) MTr^{4} समेता शासिता;Pu^{2} Pu^{4} तु सः — c) GMd^{1} चतुर्णामपि वर्णानां; NNg चतुर्णां वर्णानां च — d) Lo^{2} प्रतिभूश्च सः; Lo^{5} स्मृताः; *Lakṣ* कृतः

18. Cited by *Lakṣ* 12.794 — a) TMd^{4} दण्डा — b) Be^{1} एकाभि°; TMd^{3} एव हि रक्षति; TMd^{4} °रक्षणि — c) Pu^{8} लुप्तेषु — d) Wa दण्डे; Be^{1} wKt^{3} TMd^{3} दण्ड; TMd^{4} धर्मदण्डं; TMd^{3} धर्म; wKt^{1} धर्म्यं; Bo विदुर्बुधः

19. Cited by *Lakṣ* 12.795 — a) TMd^{4} समीक्ष्य सर्वतः सम्यक्; Be^{1} Pu^{3} स समीक्ष्य धृतः; Be^{3} संधृतः; TMd^{3} GMd^{5} Ox^{3} MTr^{6} [*Jolly* M$^{4-5}$ Nd] *Lakṣ* सुधृतः; [*Jolly* M^{9}] संवृत्तः; Lo^{2} कृतः; Bo धनः — b) TMd^{3} सर्वान्; Be^{1} स च रञ्ज°; oOr राजा रञ्ज°; TMd^{4} रजयति; wKt^{6} रक्षयति — c) GMy Ox^{3} असमीक्ष्याप्रणी° — d) wKt^{3} Tr^{2} सर्वशः; Ho सर्वथा

शूले मत्स्यानिवापक्ष्यन् दुर्बलान्बलवत्तराः ॥२०॥
अद्यात्काकः पुरोडाशं श्वावलिह्याद्धविस्तथा ।
स्वाम्यं च न स्यात्कस्मिंश्चित् प्रवर्तेताधरोत्तरम् ॥२१॥
सर्वो दण्डजितो लोको दुर्लभो हि शुचिर्नरः ।
दण्डस्य हि भयात्सर्वं जगद्भोगाय कल्पते ॥२२॥
देवदानवगन्धर्वा रक्षांसि पतगोरगाः ।
तेऽपि भोगाय कल्पन्ते दण्डेनैव निपीडिताः ॥२३॥
दुष्येयुः सर्ववर्णाश्च भिद्येरन्सर्वसेतवः ।
सर्वलोकप्रकोपश्च भवेद्दण्डस्य विभ्रमात् ॥२४॥
यत्र श्यामो लोहिताक्षो दण्डश्चरति पापहा ।
प्रजास्तत्र न मुह्यन्ति नेता चेत्साधु पश्यति ॥२५॥
तस्याहुः संप्रणेतारं राजानं सत्यवादिनम् ।
समीक्ष्य कारिणं प्राज्ञं धर्मकामार्थकोविदम् ॥२६॥
तं राजा प्रणयन् सम्यक् त्रिवर्गेणाभिवर्धते ।

20. Cited by *Lakṣ* 12.795 — a) Hy प्रणवे°; Wa प्रणीये° — b) Hy दण्ड; GMd^{1} दण्ड्यादण्ड्ये°; wKt^{6} दण्डान्दण्ड्ये°; Ho Lo^{5} TMd^{3} दण्डेष्व°; Tr^{2} °तन्द्रियः — c) *Ku* [pāṭha] जले मत्स्यानिवाहिंस्युः; Be^{3} जले; Pu^{5} Pu^{7} Pu^{9} °निवापेक्ष्यन्; NNg °निवापक्ष्या; Be^{1} Lo^{5} °निवापश्यन्; Ox^{3} °निवापक्वान्; TMd^{3} MTr^{4} MTr^{6} °निवाधक्ष्यन्; Tr^{1} °निवाधक्ष्य; GMd^{5} °निवाकुष्यन्; TMd^{4} °निवाभिन्द्यान्; MTr^{5} [*mc to*] °निवाभक्ष्यन्; La^{1} °निवाभिन्यु — c-d) GMd^{1} दुर्बलान्बलिनश्शूलैर्भिन्द्यान्मत्स्यानिवाहयः — d) Jo^{2} दुर्बलं बल°; Bo Tr^{2} MTr^{6} °वत्तरः; wKt^{1} °वत्तरान्; Lo^{2} °वत्तरां; Tj^{2} °वत्तमाः

21. Not commented by *Nd.* Cited by *Lakṣ* 12.795 — a) Bo अद्यात्काङ्क्षः; TMd^{3} °डाशः; Lo^{5} °डाश — a-b) sOx^{1} sPu^{6} पुरोडाशांश्श्वालि° — b) *Jolly* श्वा च लिह्या°; TMd^{4} °लेह्या°; La^{1} °लिष्टा°; wKt^{1} °ह्याद्बलिं तथा — c) wKt^{1} स्वाम्यं न कस्मात्कस्मिंश्चित्; Ho GMd^{1} साम्यं; TMd^{3} स्यात्कस्याश्चित्; Bo स्यात्कस्मिंश्च — d) Be^{3} वर्तेतामधरोत्तरं; Ox^{3} प्रवृत्तेता°; wKt^{6} प्रकर्तेता°; Pu^{8} °रोत्तरां

22. Not commented by *Rc* — a) TMd^{3} सर्वे; Hy दण्डितो; BBe^{2} NKt^{4} Lo^{4} Lo^{5} Ox^{3} Tj^{1} MTr^{6} लोके — b) Be^{1} दुर्बलो; Wa दुर्भगो; NKt^{4} शुचिः क्वचित् — c) Pu^{5} °त्सर्वे; NKt^{4} °त्सर्व

23. a) BCa TMd^{3} GMy °गन्धर्व — a-b) Pu^{5} Pu^{7} [*Jolly* G] देवदानवरक्षांसि गन्धर्वाः पतगोरगाः — b) Lo^{1} Pu^{3} Pu^{8} यक्षराक्षसपन्नगाः; Bo TMd^{3} Tj^{1} यक्षांसि; wKt^{1} वतगो°; Lo^{5} पितरोरगाः; Lo^{4} Ox^{3} पतरोरगाः — c) GMd^{1} ते च; Pu^{3} कल्प्यन्ते — d) Ox^{3} Tj^{1} निपीडितः; MTr^{6} हि पीडिताः

24. a) TMd^{3} दूष्येयुः; GMd^{1} द्विष्येयुः; Ho La^{1} दुःखेयुः — b) Tj^{1} भिक्ष्येर°; Lo^{1} °केतवः; TMd^{4} °सेवकाः — c) Wa °लोके; BBe^{2} °लोकं; Bo °लोकोपकोपश्च — d) TMd^{4} विभ्रमान्; Tr^{1} विप्लुवात्

25. Cited by *Lakṣ* 12.794 — a) Ho oOr स्यामो; wKt^{6} स्यात्मा; Tr^{2} लौहि° — c) MTr^{5} मुह्यन्ते; wKt^{1} द्रुह्यन्ति; MTr^{4} पश्यन्ति — d) GMd^{5} राजा चेत्साधु

26. Cited by *Lakṣ* 12.794 — a) GMd^{1} तत्राहुः; Pu^{5} Pu^{7} Pu^{9} तस्याह्नः; GMd^{5} तस्यास्य; wKt^{1} तस्मात्तु; sOx^{1} sPu^{6} संप्रणीतारं — c) Be^{3} Lo^{4} Lo^{5} TMd^{3} समीक्ष; Tr^{1} परीक्ष्य; Pu^{4} Pu^{5} कारिणां; TMd^{3} कारिण; BBe^{2} La^{1} TMd^{4} कारणं; Pu^{7} [*but mc*] श्राद्धं — d) Tr^{1} धर्मार्थकोविदं; TMd^{3} NPu^{1} धर्मकर्मार्थ°; TMd^{4} °कोविदः

कामात्मा विषमः क्षुद्रो दण्डेनैव निहन्यते ॥२७॥
दण्डो हि सुमहत्तेजो दुर्धरश्चाकृतात्मभिः ।
धर्माद्विचलितं हन्ति नृपमेव सबान्धवम् ॥२८॥
ततो दुर्गं च राष्ट्रं च लोकं च सचराचरम् ।
अन्तरिक्षगतांश्चैव मुनीन्देवांश्च पीडयेत् ॥२९॥
सोऽसहायेन मूढेन लुब्धेनाकृतबुद्धिना ।
न शक्यो न्यायतो नेतुं सक्तेन विषयेषु च ॥३०॥
शुचिना सत्यसंधेन यथाशास्त्रानुसारिणा ।
दण्डः प्रणयितुं शक्यः सुसहायेन धीमता ॥३१॥
स्वराष्ट्रे न्यायवृत्तिः स्याद् भृशदण्डश्च शत्रुषु ।
सुहृत्स्वजिह्मः स्निग्धेषु ब्राह्मणेषु क्षमान्वितः ॥३२॥
एवंवृत्तस्य नृपतेः शिलोञ्छेनापि जीवतः ।
विस्तीर्यते यशो लोके तैलबिन्दुरिवाम्भसि ॥३३॥

27. Cited by *Lakṣ* 12.795 — a) Be^1 प्राणयत्; Jo^2 Lo^1 TMd^3 GMy प्रणयेत् — b) Pu^5 Pu^7 त्रिवर्गेण निवर्तते; GMd^1 त्रिवर्म्येणा°; NPu^1 °णापि वर्धते; TMd^3 °वर्धति; Lo^5 °वर्तते — c) TMd^4 कामात्म; Lo^4 Lo^5 Ox^3 [*Jolly* M]कमान्धो; MTr^3 विषयः; TMd^4 क्षुद्र; NNg Pu^2 Pu^4 क्रुद्धो — d) Pu^2 Pu^4 दण्डेनैवं; MTr^6 नहन्यते; Be^1 Ho NNg विहन्यते; La^1 TMd^3 GMy हि हन्यते; sOx^1 Ox^2 sPu^6 Tr^2 निपात्यते

28. Omitted in Pu^5. Cited by *Lakṣ* 12.795 — a) TMd^3 दण्डे; *Lakṣ* सुमहातेजो; GMd^1 °हत्तेजा; TMd^4 °हत्ताजो — b) GMd^1 दुर्धरोश्चा°; MTr^4 दुर्धराश्चा°; TMd^4 दुर्धर्शश्चा°; MTr^6 दुर्धरान्चा°; Bo GMd^1 °रश्चकृता° — c) MTr^5 MTr^6 धर्माद्धि चलितं; wKt^1 wKt^3 °चरितं; Lo^4 Lo^5 oOr Ox^3 [*Jolly* M^4] °चलितो; Hy °बलितं; sOx^1 sPu^6 °चलितं हवि — d) GMd^1 नृणमेव

29. Cited by *Lakṣ* 12.795 — a) GMd^1 अतो — b) BKt^5 लोकः सचरा°; wKt^6 *ma* च — c) BKt^5 अन्तकाक्षग°; Ox^3 °गताश्चैव; TMd^4 Tj^2 °चरांश्चैव — d) Be^1 Tj^2 मुनींश्चैव प्रपीडयेत्; *Lakṣ* यतीन्दे°; Lo^5 °न्देवानपीडयेत्; Pu^5 Pu^7 Pu^9 पीडयन्; TMd^3 दण्डयेत्; oOr पूजयेत्

30. Cited by *Lakṣ* 12.794 — a) NKt^4 सासहा°; *Lakṣ* असहा° [*om* सो]; Pu^2 Pu^4 Pu^5 Pu^7 Pu^9 *Ku Go* मूर्खेन — b) Be^3 लुब्धेनानृतवादिना; GMy °नकृत°; Be^1 °नाहतबुद्धिना; Pu^2 Pu^4 °बुद्धिमान्; BKt^5 °बुद्धिमाना — c) Pu^2 Pu^4 अशक्यो; TMd^4 शक्यं; GMd^5 शक्ये; GMy न्यायत; BKt^5 नायतो; wKt^6 नामतो; Be^3 न्यायतोन्नेतुं; Kt^2 जेतुं — d) *Lakṣ* नेतुमृक्थेषु विषयेषु च; BBe^2 wKt^1 BKt^5 शक्तेन; TMd^3 शक्योन

31.* Not commented by *Nd*. Cited by *Lakṣ* 12.794 — b) TMd^3 °सारिणी — c) Be^1 Be^3 Bo Ho Hy Jm Jo^1 Kt^2 NKt^4 BKt^5 wKt^6 La^2 Lo^1 Lo^2 Ox^2 Pu^2 Pu^3 Pu^4 Pu^5 Pu^7 Pu^8 Pu^9 Tj^2 MTr^3 Wa [*Jolly* G] प्रणेतुं शक्यते दण्डः [NKt^4 प्रणतुं; Bo दण्डं]; Ho प्रणियतुं; TMd^3 TMd^4 GMd^5 GMy Tr^1 MTr^4 MTr^6 [*Jolly* Nd] प्रणेतुं शक्यस्तु [TMd^4 प्रणेतु]; GMd^1 प्रणेतुं शक्तस्स्यात्; Ox^3 शक्यं; [*Jolly* M R] *Jolly* शक्तः — d) Lo^2 ससहा°

32.* Not commented by *Nd*. Cited by *Lakṣ* 11.21 — a) TMd^4 सराष्ट्रे; BBe^2 Be^3 Bo BCa Ho Hy Jm Jo^1 Jo^2 wKt^1 Kt^2 NKt^4 BKt^5 wKt^6 La^1 La^2 Lo^1 Lo^2 Lo^3 oOr sOx^1 Ox^2 NPu^1 sPu^6 Pu^8 Tj^1 Tj^2 Tr^2 MTr^5 MTr^6 *Mandlik Dave Jha KSS* [*Jolly* R] °वृत्तः — b) BCa TMd^3 GMy स्यादुग्रदण्डश्च; Be^3 wKt^1 wKt^3 La^1 Lo^1 TMd^4 Ox^3 NPu^1 Pu^3 Pu^8 भृशं; GMd^5 Tr^1 धृतदण्डश्च; Be^3 TMd^3 TMd^4 GMy °दण्डस्तु — c) La^1 सुकृत्स्वजिह्मः — d) TMd^4 क्षमान्विताः

33. Omitted in Bo — a) BBe^2 नृपतिः — b) GMd^1 MTr^5 सिलो°; TMd^3 GMy [*Jolly* Nd]

अतस्तु विपरीतस्य नृपतेरजितात्मनः ।
संक्षिप्यते यशो लोके घृतबिन्दुरिवाम्भसि ॥३४॥
स्वे स्वे धर्मे निविष्टानां सर्वेषामनुपूर्वशः ।
वर्णानामाश्रमाणां च राजा सृष्टोऽभिरक्षिता ॥३५॥
तेन यद्यत्सभृत्येन कर्तव्यं रक्षता प्रजाः ।
तत्तद्वोऽहं प्रवक्ष्यामि यथावदनुपूर्वशः ॥३६॥
ब्राह्मणान्पर्युपासीत प्रातरुत्थाय पार्थिवः ।
त्रैविद्यवृद्धान्विदुषस्तिष्ठेत्तेषां च शासने ॥३७॥
वृद्धांश्च नित्यं सेवेत विप्रान्वेदविदः शुचीन् ।
वृद्धसेवी हि सततं रक्षोभिरपि पूज्यते ॥३८॥
तेभ्योऽधिगच्छेद्विनयं विनीतात्मापि नित्यशः ।
विनीतात्मा हि नृपतिर्न विनश्यति कर्हिचित् ॥३९॥
बहवोऽविनयान्नष्टा राजानः सपरिच्छदाः ।
वनस्थाश्चैव राज्यानि विनयात्प्रतिपेदिरे ॥४०॥

शिलोञ्छादपि; GMd[5] शिलोञ्छेन तु; Pu[2] Pu[4] शिलोञ्छेनेव; Kt[2] wKt[3] BKt[5] wKt[6] GMy Tj[1] Wa जीवितः — c) Ox[3] यथो लोके — d) Lo[1] °बिन्दुमिवा°

34. Omitted in BKt[5] wKt[6] sOx[1]; not commented by Nd. — a) TMd[4] अन्तस्तु — b) GMd[1] नृपस्योच्छास्त्रवर्तिनः — c) NPu[1] संलिप्यते; TMd[3] विस्तीर्यते — d) Lo[1] °बिन्दुमिवा°; NNg Wa °रिवोदके

35. Not commented by Rc. Cited by *Lakṣ* 11.156 — a) [*Jolly* M[4–5]] स्वेषु धर्मेषु निष्ठानां; Lo[2] स्वस्वे; Be[3] TMd[4] धर्म; *Me* [pāṭha] धर्मेऽनिविष्टानां; Bo निवृष्टानां; Ox[3] निष्टानां — b) Pu[2] Pu[4] °मानुपूर्वशः — c) oOr तुल्यानामाश्र° — d) BKt[5] wKt[6] राजा भवति रक्षिता; Be[1] Bo Ho Jo[2] wKt[1] wKt[3] Lo[1] Lo[3] TMd[3] Pu[3] Pu[8] Tj[1] *Lakṣ* हि रक्षिता; Pu[2] Pu[4] °रक्षतः; Jo[1] °रक्षितौ

36. Cited by *Lakṣ* 11.156 — a) TMd[3] GMy यद्यत्प्रभृ°; BBe[2] यद्यत्स्वभृ° — b) TMd[3] कर्तव्यो; Kt[2] BKt[5] रक्षताः; wKt[6] La[1] oOr रक्षिताः; Pu[8] रक्षिता; TMd[4] रक्षते; GMd[5] प्रजा — c) Ho Pu[5] Pu[7] Pu[9] [*Jolly* G] तद्वोहं संप्रवक्ष्यामि [Ho तत्तेहं]; Pu[2] Pu[4] तत्ततोहं; TMd[4] Tr[2] तत्तद्वाहं; Be[3] wKt[1] La[1] NPu[1] प्रवक्षामि

37. Omitted in Ox[3]; lacuna at pādas c-d in NKt[4]. Cited by *Lakṣ* 11.156 — a) GMd[5] °णान्समुपा°; wKt[1] °पासीषु — a-b) GMd[1] ब्राह्मणान्प्रातरुत्थाय पर्युपासीत पार्थिवः — b) GMy पार्थिवा; MTr[3] प्रार्थिनः — c) TMd[3] त्रैविद्यविधा पुरुषस्तिष्ठे°; sOx[1] sPu[6] त्रैवेद्य°; Pu[2] Pu[4] त्रिविद्य°; Be[1] °दुषास्तिष्ठे°; La[1] °दुषांस्तिष्ठे° — d) BCa Jo[2] Lo[3] Tj[1] °दुषस्तेषां तिष्ठेच्च शासने; Ho °स्तिष्ठंस्तेषां; Be[1] wKt[1] °स्तिष्ठेद्येषां; TMd[3] GMd[5] GMy °स्तिष्ठेदेषां; La[1] Pu[3] Pu[8] तु

38. Cited by *Lakṣ* 11.156 — a) Wa *om* नित्यं — b) oOr शुचिः — c) Be[1] BKt[5] wKt[6] NNg Tj[1] Tr[1] Wa च — d) Lo[2] GMd[1] TMd[3] GMd[5] oOr Ox[2] Tj[1] Tr[1] MTr[4] MTr[6] Wa °भिरभिपूज्यते

39. Pāda-b omitted in Pu[5] [haplo]. Cited by *Lakṣ* 11.156 — a) TMd[3] GMy तेभ्योभिगच्छे°; La[1] Ox[2] तेभ्योपि गच्छे°; Bo तेभ्यो हि गच्छे°; sOx[1] sPu[6] तेभ्यो गच्छे° — b) NKt[4] विनीतस्वहि; GMd[1] TMd[3] TMd[4] GMd[5] GMy NNg MTr[6] °तात्मा हि; Jm °तात्माभि — c) BBe[2] oOr °तात्मापि; Bo नृपतीर्न — d) Bo विनश्यन्ति; Ho विनश्येत; GMy कस्यचित्

40. Pāda-d omitted in Be[3]. Cited by *Lakṣ* 11.156-7 [with pādas a-b and c-d transposed]

वेनो विनष्टोऽविनयान्नहुषश्चैव पार्थिवः ।
सुदाः पैजवनश्चैव सुमुखो निमिरेव च ॥४१॥
पृथुस्तु विनयाद्राज्यं प्राप्तवान्मनुरेव च ।
कुबेरश्च धनैश्वर्यं ब्राह्मण्यं चैव गाधिजः ॥४२॥
त्रैविद्येभ्यस्त्रयीं विद्यां दण्डनीतिं च शाश्वतीम् ।
आन्वीक्षिकीं चात्मविद्यां वार्तारम्भांश्च लोकतः ॥४३॥
इन्द्रियाणां जये योगं समातिष्ठेद्दिवानिशम् ।
जितेन्द्रियो हि शक्नोति वशे स्थापयितुं प्रजाः ॥४४॥
दश कामसमुत्थानि तथाष्टौ क्रोधजाति च ।
व्यसनानि दुरन्तानि प्रयत्नेन विवर्जयेत् ॥४५॥

— a) GMd^{5} बहुपो; wKt^{3} TMd^{3} GMy °विनयानष्टा — b) BKt^{5} wKt^{6} Lo^{4} Lo^{5} NNg Ox^{3} [*Jolly* M] *Me* सपरिग्रहाः; MTr^{5} सुपरिग्रहाः; Bo TMd^{4} GMd^{5} NPu^{1} °रिच्छदः; Be^{3} °रिच्छदा — c) BCa Jm Jo^{1} Kt^{2} wKt^{3} MTr^{3} [*Jolly* G Ku] *Lakṣ Me Mandlik Jha KSS Dave* वनस्था अपि; Pu^{5} Pu^{7} वनस्था अपि च; Lo^{4} Lo^{5} Ox^{3} राष्ट्राणि

41. Verses 41 and 42 transposed in TMd^{3} GMy; pāda-a omitted in Be^{3}. Cited by *Lakṣ* 11.157 — a) Ho wKt^{1} wKt^{3} NKt^{4} BKt^{5} wKt^{6} La^{1} Tr^{2} [*Jolly* Ku] वेणो; TMd^{3} वेनो नष्टो; Be^{3} वेनुर्विनष्टो; Kt^{2} विनष्टी — b) BKt^{5} Pu^{3} Pu^{5} Pu^{7} °न्नघुप°; Pu^{2} °न्नधुप°; Wa °न्नदुप°; Pu^{4} °न्नध्यपाश्चैव; Lo^{2} GMd^{1} °पश्चापि — c) Be^{1} BBe^{2} Ho Jm Jo^{1} Kt^{2} BKt^{5} wKt^{6} Lo^{1} Lo^{4} Lo^{5} TMd^{4} Pu^{2} Pu^{4} MTr^{3} सुदा; sOx^{1} sPu^{6} MTr^{6} सुधः; Tr^{2} MTr^{4} सुंदः; GMy सुन्दो; TMd^{3} सुंदो; GMd^{5} सूतप्रजव°; Lo^{4} पौजवन°; Be^{1} Pu^{8} पैयवन°; GMd^{1} वैजवन°; MTr^{4} MTr^{6} पञ्चजन°; BBe^{2} wKt^{1} BKt^{5} wKt^{6} सोजवन°; Lo^{5} सौजवन°; Ho Jm Jo^{1} Kt^{2} MTr^{3} सोयवन°; TMd^{4} सापैवज°; NKt^{4} साजवन° — d) TMd^{4} सुमुखा; BBe^{2} सुमखो; wKt^{1} स्वमुखो *cor to* सुमुग्धो; BKt^{5} wKt^{6} सुमुषो; NKt^{4} Pu^{3} सुपुखो

42. Omitted in Ox^{3}. Cited by *Lakṣ* 11.157 — a) Be^{1} Ho wKt^{1} NKt^{4} Tj^{2} पृथुश्च; Lo^{4} एभिस्तु; TMd^{4} विनयाराज्यं; Be^{1} °द्राजं; Lo^{4} °द्राष्ट्रं — b) TMd^{4} GMd^{5} विनयान्मुनिरेव; GMd^{1} °वान्निमिरेव; Tj^{1} °वान्मुनिरेव — c) TMd^{4} कुबेरस्तु — d) Lo^{1} MTr^{6} ब्रह्मण्यं; wKt^{6} oOr ब्राह्मणं; Kt^{2} ब्राह्मण्यश्चैव; Tr^{2} ब्राह्मणांश्चैव; MTr^{3} चेव; Be^{1} गाधिनः; Pu^{4} गाद्विजः

43. Omitted in Tj^{2}. Cited by *Vij* 1.311; *Lakṣ* 11.157 — a) TMd^{4} त्रैवेदेभ्य°; Be^{1} Bo wKt^{6} Lo^{4} Ox^{3} Tj^{1} °भ्यस्त्रयी; Tr^{2} °भ्यस्त्रैयीं; BBe^{2} Bo NKt^{4} Ox^{3} विद्या; Kt^{2} विद्यान्; wKt^{1} Kt^{2} wKt^{3} Tr^{1} MTr^{4} MTr^{6} *Jha* विद्याद्दण्ड° — b) wKt^{1} La^{1} °नीतिश्च; sOx^{1} sPu^{6} *Vij* [vl] च तद्विदः; Tr^{2} च तद्विजः; Ho च तत्त्वतः; NKt^{4} च सांप्रतं; Lo^{4} Lo^{5} च शास्त्रतः; Tr^{1} शाश्वती — c) NKt^{4} आसीक्षितां भायविद्यां; Bo Lo^{5} Tj^{1} अन्वी°; Lo^{4} अन्वि°; TMd^{3} अन्विक्षिकिं; GMy °क्षिकं; BKt^{5} wKt^{6} °क्षकीं; *Vij* चात्मविद्भ्यो — d) Lo^{1} Lo^{5} oOr °रम्भाश्च; Tr^{2} °लम्भांश्च; Kt^{2} °रम्भां च; MTr^{6} °रम्भंश्च; TMd^{3} TMd^{4} GMd^{5} GMy Tr^{1} °रम्भं च; Lo^{3} °रम्भांस्तु; Tj^{1} °रम्भास्तु; *Lakṣ* सर्वतः

44. Omitted in Pu^{9}. Cited by *Lakṣ* 11.143 — a) GMd^{1} जयो; Lo^{2} चये — b) BKt^{5} योगमनुतिष्ठे°; GMd^{5} योगमधितिष्ठे°; GMd^{1} TMd^{3} TMd^{4} GMy योगमातिष्ठेच्च दिवा°; wKt^{1} °तिष्ठेच्च दिवा° — c) NKt^{4} Lo^{4} Lo^{5} GMd^{5} Ox^{3} MTr^{4} MTr^{5} MTr^{6} [*Jolly* M] जितेन्द्रियस्तु; TMd^{3} TMd^{4} GMy [*Jolly* Nd] *Lakṣ* जितेन्द्रियश्च; wKt^{3} *om* हि

45. Omitted in Pu^{9}. Pādas a-b cited by *Mādh* 1.413; *Lakṣ* 11.143 — b) TMd^{4} यथाष्टा; Lo^{4} Lo^{5} Ox^{3} [*Jolly* M] तु — d) NKt^{4} प्रयतोक्तविपर्ययेत्; Be^{3} BKt^{5} wKt^{6} यत्नतः परिवर्जयेत्

कामजेषु प्रसक्तो हि व्यसनेषु महीपतिः ।
वियुज्यतेऽर्थधर्माभ्यां क्रोधजेष्वात्मनैव तु ॥४६॥
मृगयाक्षा दिवास्वप्नः परिवादः स्त्रियो मदः ।
तौर्यत्रिकं वृथाट्या च कामजो दशको गणः ॥४७॥
पैशुन्यं साहसं द्रोह ईर्ष्यासूयार्थदूषणम् ।
वाग्दण्डजं च पारुष्यं क्रोधजोऽपि गणोऽष्टकः ॥४८॥
द्वयोरप्येतयोर्मूलं यं सर्वे कवयो विदुः ।
तं यत्नेन जयेल्लोभं तज्जौ ह्येतावुभौ गणौ ॥४९॥
पानमक्षाः स्त्रियश्चैव मृगया च यथाक्रमम् ।
एतत्कष्टतमं विद्याच्चतुष्कं कामजे गणे ॥५०॥

46. Pādas c-d cited by *Lakṣ* 11.143; *Mādh* 1.413; folio containing verses 46b to 72 missing in Be^{3} — a) Ho कामार्थेषु; GMy कामजो हि प्र°; Be^{1} Pu^{8} प्रसक्ता; BBe^{2} Kt^{2} Ox^{3} Pu^{2} Pu^{4} प्रशक्तो; Jo^{2} NKt^{4} La^{1} Lo^{3} NNg Tj^{1} MTr^{5} प्रसक्तस्तु — c) MTr^{6} वियुज्येते; BBe^{2} नियुज्यते; BKt^{5} wKt^{6} विभज्यते; La^{1} विमुह्यते; Bo वियुज्यत्यर्थ°; NNg Ox^{2} MTr^{4} °र्थकामाभ्यां; TMd^{3} GMy °धर्मेभ्यः — d) Ox^{3} क्रोधज्येष्वा°; wKt^{6} क्रोधेष्वा°; GMd^{1} क्रोधनेष्वा°; Pu^{5} Pu^{7} Pu^{9} क्रोधजेना°; *Lakṣ* क्रोधजे स्वात्मनैव; GMd^{1} हि

47. Omitted in Ox^{3}. Cited by *Vij* 1.311; *Lakṣ* 11.143–4; *Mādh* 1.413 — a) MTr^{4} मृगयोक्षा; BBe^{2} Lo^{1} Lo^{4} Lo^{5} GMd^{1} Tr^{1} Wa [*Jolly* M^{4}] *Vij Mādh Mandlik Jha KSS Dave* मृगयाक्षो; BCa BKt^{5} wKt^{6} मृगयाक्ष; La^{1} मृगयाक्ष *cor sh to* मृगयाक्षो; TMd^{4} मृगयात्रा; NPu^{1} मृगयानां; wKt^{1} मृगया च; Kt^{2} मृगया [lacuna]; Bo Ho Lo^{1} NPu^{1} Pu^{5} Pu^{7} Pu^{8} Pu^{9} दिवास्वापः; NKt^{4} दिवासतः; NNg °स्वप्नं; MTr^{5} °स्वप्ना — b) GMd^{1} °वाद; NKt^{4} स्त्रिया; GMd^{1} दमः — c) TMd^{4} तौर्यत्रिकोणवृद्ध्या च; Be^{1} NNg NPu^{1} Pu^{2} Pu^{4} Pu^{5} Pu^{7} Pu^{9} तूर्य°; Wa तुर्य°; TMd^{3} दौर्य°; NKt^{4} तोर्यविको; Lo^{2} GMd^{5} NNg Pu^{2} Pu^{4} Pu^{5} Pu^{7} Pu^{9} MTr^{5} *Bh* °त्रिको; Be^{1} वृथाग्र्या; NKt^{4} वृथाग्रात; Lo^{1} Tr^{1} वृथाध्वा; BKt^{5} वृथाद्या; TMd^{3} त्रिदाट्या; MTr^{4} वृथापादः काम° — d) Be^{1} कामजा; Bo कामजे; Tj^{1} कामतो; NKt^{4} कायमजो; TMd^{4} दशका; Be^{1} wKt^{1} wKt^{3} Lo^{1} TMd^{3} GMd^{1} GMy sOx^{1} Ox^{2} sPu^{6} Tr^{1} *Lakṣ* गुणः; GMd^{5} गुणाः; NKt^{4} अल्पः

48. Cited by *Vij* 1.311; *Lakṣ* 11.144; *Mādh* 1.413 — a) Ox^{3} Pu^{2} MTr^{5} पैशुनं; NKt^{4} पेशुना; NNg पिशुनं; Pu^{8} पैशुमं; wKt^{3} NKt^{4} Lo^{3} TMd^{3} GMd^{1} TMd^{4} GMy oOr Tj^{1} Tr^{1} MTr^{4} MTr^{6} द्रोहमीर्ष्या° — b) NKt^{4} pāda reads: सूर्यार्थदूषणं; Tj^{2} ईर्षा°; Hy °सूयार्थे; wKt^{6} °सूयानुदूषणं — c) TMd^{4} वाग्दण्डजे च पारुष्ये; Pu^{5} Pu^{7} [*Jolly* G] वाग्दण्डजनपारुष्यं; GMd^{1} वाग्दण्डनं च; wKt^{3} वाग्दण्डं च; Tr^{1} MTr^{4} MTr^{6} वाग्दण्डयोश्च; BBe^{2} Tr^{2} वाग्दण्डश्चैव; Ho TMd^{3} GMy वाग्दण्डं चैव — d) TMd^{4} गणा; GMd^{1} Tr^{1} गुणो; GMy गुणा; NKt^{4} गणोन्वकः; Be^{1} °ष्टमः; wKt^{3} °ष्टः

49. Cited by *Lakṣ* 11.144; *Mādh* 1.413 — a) Jm द्वयोरपि तयो°; wKt^{1} °प्येनयो°; Pu^{2} °प्यनयो° — b) Tj^{1} यः; *Lakṣ* यं पूर्वे; wKt^{1} सर्वं — c) wKt^{3} तं प्रयत्नेन; wKt^{3} जयेल्लोकं — d) TMd^{3} TMd^{4} GMd^{5} GMy NNg Tr^{1} MTr^{4} MTr^{5} MTr^{6} [*Jolly* Nd] *Mādh* तज्जौ ह्येतौ गणावुभौ [TMd^{3} GMy Tr^{1} गुणावुभौ]; wKt^{3} तज्जौ तावुभौ समौ; Be^{1} BBe^{2} Ho Hy Jm Jo^{1} Kt^{2} BKt^{5} wKt^{6} Lo^{4} Lo^{5} Ox^{3} NPu^{1} Pu^{2} Pu^{3} Pu^{4} Pu^{5} Pu^{7} Pu^{8} Pu^{9} Tj^{2} MTr^{3} Wa *Lakṣ Mandlik Jolly Jha KSS Dave* तज्जावेता°; BBe^{2} Bo Lo^{4} Lo^{5} GMd^{1} Ox^{2} Ox^{3} Pu^{5} Pu^{7} Pu^{9} [*Jolly* R] गुणौ; wKt^{3} समौ

50. Cited by *Vij* 1.311; *Lakṣ* 11.144; *Mādh* 1.413 — a) TMd^{4} °मक्षो; Lo^{4} Lo^{5} °मक्ष; Lo^{1} °मक्षस्त्रि° — b) Pu^{5} Pu^{7} मृगयाश्च; GMd^{5} °क्रमः — c) GMd^{1} एतं कष्ट°; Tj^{1} एतत्कृष्णतरं; Jo^{2} Lo^{3} GMd^{5} NNg oOr MTr^{4} MTr^{6} *Lakṣ* °ष्टतरं — d) GMy °च्चतुष्टं; TMd^{3} कामजी; BKt^{5} कामजं; Bo Lo^{3} GMd^{1} TMd^{3} TMd^{4} GMd^{5} GMy oOr Ox^{2} Tj^{1} Tr^{1} गुणे

दण्डस्य पातनं चैव वाक्पारुष्यार्थदूषणे ।
क्रोधजेऽपि गणे विद्यात् कष्टमेतत् त्रिकं सदा ॥५१॥
सप्तकस्यास्य वर्गस्य सर्वत्रैवानुषङ्गिणः ।
पूर्वं पूर्वं गुरुतरं विद्याद् व्यसनमात्मवान् ॥५२॥
व्यसनस्य च मृत्योश्च व्यसनं कष्टमुच्यते ।
व्यसन्यधोऽधो व्रजति स्वर्यात्यव्यसनी मृतः ॥५३॥
मौलाञ्छास्त्रविदः शूराँल्लब्धलक्षान् कुलोद्गतान् ।
सचिवान्सप्त चाष्टौ वा प्रकुर्वीत परीक्षितान् ॥५४॥
अपि यत्सुकरं कर्म तदप्येकेन दुष्करम् ।
विशेषतोऽसहायेन किमु राज्यं महोदयम् ॥५५॥
तैः सार्धं चिन्तयेन्नित्यं सामान्यं संधिविग्रहम् ।
स्थानं समुदयं गुप्तिं लब्धप्रशमनानि च ॥५६॥
तेषां स्वं स्वमभिप्रायमुपलभ्य पृथक्पृथक् ।
समस्तानां च कार्येषु विदध्याद्धितमात्मनः ॥५७॥

51. Cited by *Vij* 1.311; *Lakṣ* 11.144; *Mādh* 1.413–4 — a) TMd^4 GMy Ox^2 Wa पतनं; Tr^1 पादनं; Tr^2 पातनश्चैव — b) BKt^5 WKt^6 TMd^4 वाक्पारुष्या च दूषणे [TMd^4 °रुष्याश्च]; OOr NPu^1 Pu^3 Tr^2 °दूषणं — c) TMd^4 क्रोधजो; Ox^3 क्रोधने; GMd^1 क्रोधजे तु; GMd^5 क्रोधजे हि; GMd^1 TMd^4 GMd^5 Ox^2 Pu^5 Pu^7 Tr^1 गुणे; Pu^7 विन्द्यात् — d) Bo TMd^4 GMd^5 कष्टमेकत्रिकं; BKt^5 WKt^6 त्रयं सदा; TMd^3 sOx^1 sPu^6 तथा; GMd^1 गुणं

52. Cited by *Lakṣ* 11.144 — a) Ox^2 सर्वस्य — b) GMd^1 °पङ्गकः — c) TMd^4 पूर्वः पूर्वं — d) GMd^5 विद्याद्विद्वांसमात्मवान्; Bo विद्या; NKt^4 BKt^5 WKt^6 Lo^4 Lo^5 TMd^3 GMy NNg sOx^1 Ox^2 Ox^3 NPu^1 sPu^6 Tr^2 MTr^4 MTr^6 [*Jolly* M$^{4-5}$ Nd] °मात्मनः

53. Cited by *Mādh* 1.414; *Lakṣ* 11.144 — a) TMd^3 व्यसनश्चैव; OOr तु — c) GMd^1 GMy MTr^5 MTr^6 *Mādh* °न्यधो हि व्रजति; TMd^3 °न्यधो यो हि व्रजति — d) Lo^5 स्वर्याप्तव्यसने; NKt^4 °व्यसनो; GMd^1 Pu^8 Tr^1 नृपः — Wa adds here 7.32 a-b.

54.* Cited by *Vij* 1.312; *Mādh* 1.405 — a) WKt^1 [*cor to*] मौना°; TMd^3 मौलाशास्त्र° — b) NPu^1 °व्धेल°; Be^1 NNg °लक्ष्यान्; Be^1 Bo Ho WKt^3 NKt^4 La^1 Lo^1 Lo^2 Lo^3 GMd^5 sOx^1 Ox^2 Pu^2 Pu^3 Pu^4 sPu^6 Pu^8 Tj^1 Tj^2 Tr^2 MTr^4 MTr^6 *Vij Mandlik KSS* कुलोद्भवान् — c) TMd^3 GMy मन्त्रिणस्सप्त वा पञ्च; Pu^8 सचिवा सप्त; TMd^4 षड्विर्वा सप्त; Ho Lo^4 NNg Tr^1 MTr^4 MTr^5 MTr^6 [*Jolly* M$^{2-4-5-9}$ Nd] वाष्टौ; TMd^4 वाष्टा; GMd^1 Tr^2 च — d) BCa Jo^2 WKt^1 WKt^3 Lo^3 Tj^1 *Vij* कुर्वीत सुपरी°; [*Jolly* M^8] कुर्वीत च परी°; TMd^3 GMy [*Jolly* Nd] परीक्षकान्

55. Cited by *Viś* 1.307 — a) Bo यत्सुवरं — b) BKt^5 °प्यैकेन; Tr^1 °प्येतेन; Lo^1 दुष्कृतं — d) Jm Jo^1 Kt^2 NPu^1 Pu^3 Pu^4 MTr^3 *Mandlik KSS* किं तु; WKt^3 *Dave Jha* किं नु; GMd^1 किन्त्र; Hy Tj^2 किं च; Bo Ox^3 राज्यां; Bo सहोदयं

56. Omitted in TMd^3 GMy. Cited by *Lakṣ* 11.106; *Mādh* 1.405–6 — a) Bo तौ श्राद्धं; TMd^4 तैस्सर्वैश्चिन्त°; Hy चिन्तयन्नित्यं — b) *Mādh* सामादीन्संधिविग्रहान् [vl as in ed.]; Lo^1 सामन्यं; MTr^4 सामात्यं — c) Hy Lo^4 Lo^5 गुप्तिः; Tr^1 MTr^3 गुप्तं — d) MTr^3 लव्धं; Tr^2 वा

57. Verses 57 and 58 transposed in TMd^3. Cited by *Lakṣ* 11.23, 105; *Mādh* 1.406 — a) Bo Lo^5 Ox^3 Tj^1 Tr^1 *Lakṣ* 11.105 स्वस्वम° — c) Ho समर्थानां; BKt^5 *om* च; NKt^4 La^1 स्वकार्येषु — d)

सर्वेषां तु विशिष्टेन ब्राह्मणेन विपश्चिता ।
मन्त्रयेत परं मन्त्रं राजा षाड्गुण्यसंयुतम् ॥५८॥
नित्यं तस्मिन्समाश्वस्तः सर्वकार्याणि निक्षिपेत् ।
तेन सार्धं विनिश्चित्य ततः कर्म समारभेत् ॥५९॥
अन्यानपि प्रकुर्वीत शुचीन् प्राज्ञानवस्थितान् ।
सम्यगर्थसमाहर्तॄनमात्यान् सुपरीक्षितान् ॥६०॥
निर्वर्तेतास्य यावद्भिरितिकर्तव्यता नृभिः ।
तावतोऽतन्द्रितान्दक्षान् प्रकुर्वीत विचक्षणान् ॥६१॥
तेषामर्थे नियुञ्जीत शूरान्दक्षान्कुलोद्गतान् ।
शुचीनाकरकर्मान्ते भीरूनन्तर्निवेशने ॥६२॥

TMd^{3} विदधेद्धि°; Pu^{8} विदध्याहित°; Lo^{2} Ox^{3} Pu^{2} Pu^{4} Pu^{5} Pu^{7} Wa [*Jolly* G] *Lakṣ Me Go* °मात्मने; NKt^{4} °मात्मनि

58.* Omitted in GMy. Cited by *Lakṣ* 11.23; *Mādh* 1.406 — a) wKt^{3} च; Ox^{3} विशिष्टानां; *Lakṣ* विशेषेण — b) oOr विपश्चितः; TMd^{4} विजानता — c) BBe^{2} BCa Bo Ho Hy Jm Jo^{1} Jo^{2} wKt^{1} Kt^{2} La^{2} Lo^{3} TMd^{3} oOr sOx^{1} Ox^{2} sPu^{6} Pu^{8} Tj^{1} Tj^{2} Tr^{1} Tr^{2} MTr^{4} MTr^{6} *Mandlik Jolly Jha KSS Dave* मन्त्रयेत्परमं मन्त्रं [Hy मन्त्रयत्प°]; wKt^{3} Lo^{1} मन्त्रयीत — d) TMd^{4} षड्गुण्य°; Bo षड्गुण°; wKt^{1} साकुल्य-संयुतं; Lo^{1} TMd^{3} °संयुतः; GMd^{1} °संयतं

59. Pādas c-d omitted in Pu^{4}. Cited by *Lakṣ* 11.23, 105; *Mādh* 1.406 — a) Tr^{2} नित्यम-स्मिन्स°; Lo^{2} Pu^{5} Pu^{7} Tr^{2} °मास्वस्तः; wKt^{6} °माश्वस्थः; *Lakṣ* 11.105 °माश्वासः — b) Ho Jm Jo^{1} Kt^{2} wKt^{3} Lo^{1} Tj^{2} *Lakṣ Mādh KSS* निःक्षिपेत्; wKt^{6} निक्षपेत् — c) Tr^{1} तेन कार्यं; Lo^{2} विनिक्षित्य — d) GMd^{5} तत्तत्कर्म; *Lakṣ* कार्यं; Be^{1} BBe^{2} wKt^{1} wKt^{3} BKt^{5} wKt^{6} Lo^{1} Lo^{2} Lo^{4} Lo^{5} TMd^{4} GMd^{5} sOx^{1} Ox^{2} Ox^{3} NPu^{1} Pu^{2} Pu^{3} sPu^{6} Pu^{8} Tr^{2} MTr^{5} Wa [*Jolly* M$^{1-2-4-5}$] *Me* समाचरेत्; Ho समाचरत्

60. Pādas c-d omitted in MTr^{6} — a) Pu^{8} अन्यान्यपि; wKt^{1} MTr^{6} Wa च कुर्वीत — b) Bo Ho BKt^{5} TMd^{3} oOr प्रज्ञान°; NKt^{4} प्रज्ञाम°; MTr^{4} *Nā* [pāṭha] प्राज्ञान्कुलोद्गतान्; Bo °वास्थितान् — c) GMd^{1} TMd^{4} GMd^{5} Tr^{1} MTr^{4} आप्तानर्थसमा°; Kt^{2} °गर्थं; GMy °गर्थं समुधृतान°; TMd^{3} °गर्थं समुद्धुतान°; Tr^{2} °गर्थसमारुह्यन°; TMd^{4} °हर्तुममात्यान् — d) wKt^{1} °मात्यानुपवीक्षितान्; TMd^{4} सपरीक्षितां; Bo °परिक्षिपेत्

61. Omitted in GMy MTr^{6}; pāda-d omitted in Ox^{3}. Cited by *Viś* 1.307 — a) BBe^{2} BKt^{5} wKt^{6} Lo^{1} Lo^{5} TMd^{4} oOr sOx^{1} sPu^{6} [*Jolly* M] *Rn Go Dave* निवर्ते°; Tr^{1} निर्वर्त्येतास्य; Ox^{3} निवर्त्येतास्य; GMd^{1} निवर्त्यतेस्य; Tr^{2} निर्वर्तास्य; Jm तावद्धि° — c) TMd^{4} तावतोमुत्रिणो दक्षान्; NPu^{1} तावतोतन्द्रिया°; wKt^{1} तावतोहन्तिता°; Pu^{2} तावतोतिदृता°; Pu^{4} तावतोतिहृता°; Ox^{2} °तन्द्रिणो दक्षान् — d) BCa [*but cor*] Ho परीक्षितान्

62.* Cited by *Apa* 581 — a) GMd^{1} TMd^{4} तेषां त्वर्थे; Bo तेषामर्था; Pu^{3} तेषामर्ध्ये; Lo^{1} Tj^{2} तेषां मध्ये; GMd^{5} Tr^{1} MTr^{6} तेषां दण्डे; GMd^{5} नियुञ्जेत; BBe^{2} वियुञ्जीत — b) wKt^{6} शूलान्द°; TMd^{3} GMy शुचीन्द°; Pu^{2} शूद्रान्द°; oOr शूरान्रक्षान्कु°; TMd^{4} MTr^{4} शूरान्दण्डे कुलो°; GMd^{5} Tr^{1} MTr^{6} शूरानर्थे कुलो°; GMd^{1} क्रूरान्दण्डे कुलो°; Ho Jo^{2} Lo^{2} sOx^{1} Ox^{2} Pu^{2} Pu^{3} Pu^{4} sPu^{6} Pu^{8} Tj^{2} Tr^{2} *Rc* °लोद्भवान्; *KSS* °लागतान् [cf. 7.54 note] — c) TMd^{3} शूरानाक°; Ho TMd^{3} TMd^{4} NPu^{1} °नाकार°; GMd^{1} °नाचार° — d) TMd^{3} भीरूनन्ते निवेशयेत्; Tr^{1} भीरूनन्ते निवेशने; *Apa* °न्तरवेश्मनि; *Apa* [vl] °न्ततः स्ववेश्मनि; GMd^{5} GMy wKt^{6} °वेशयेत्; BKt^{5} °वेशयात्

Additional verse in Be^{1} Tr^{2}:

समाहर्तॄन्प्रकुर्वीत धर्मशास्त्रार्थनिश्चयान् ।

दूतं चैव प्रकुर्वीत सर्वशास्त्रविशारदम् ।
इङ्गिताकारचेष्टज्ञं शुचिं दक्षं कुलोद्गतम् ॥६३॥
अनुरक्तः शुचिर्दक्षः स्मृतिमान्देशकालवित् ।
वपुष्मान्वीतभीर्वाग्मी दूतो राज्ञः प्रशस्यते ॥६४॥
अमात्ये दण्ड आयत्तो दण्डे वैनयिकी क्रिया ।
नृपतौ कोषराष्ट्रे तु दूते संधिविपर्ययौ ॥६५॥
दूत एव हि संधत्ते भिनत्त्येव च संहतान् ।
दूतस्तत्कुरुते कर्म भिद्यन्ते येन मानवाः ॥६६॥

कुलीनान्वित्तसंपन्नान् समर्थान्कोशवृद्धये ॥

a) Be^1 आयव्ययज्ञान्कुर्वीत — b) Be^1 °र्थकोविदान् — d) Be^1 °न्कोशगुप्तये

63. Omitted in Pu^5 — b) Be^1 Wa °शास्त्रार्थकोविदं; BBe^2 °शारदः — c) GMd^1 इङ्गिताचार°; La^1 oOr °कारतत्त्वज्ञं; wKt^6 Pu^8 °चेष्टाज्ञं — d) wKt^3 शुचि; Lo^1 दक्ष; Tr^2 देशं; BBe^2 wKt^3 GMd^5 sOx^1 Ox^2 sPu^6 Pu^8 Tj^2 Tr^2 कुलोद्भवं [cf. 7.54 note]

64. Omitted in Lo^3 Ox^3; *ma* in Lo^4 — a) TMd^3 अनिरक्तः — c) TMd^4 वपुषान्वी°; wKt^3 Lo^5 sOx^1 °न्वीतभी वाग्मी; Tj^1 °भीर्वाग्मि; TMd^3 °भीर्वंशी

Additional verses in *Mandlik* [क] *KSS Dave:*

संधिविग्रहकालज्ञान् समर्थानायतिक्षमान् ।
परैरहार्यान् शुद्धांश्च धर्मतः कामोऽर्थतः ॥
समाहर्तुं [हर्तॄन्?] प्रकुर्वीत सर्वशास्त्रविपश्चितः ।
कुलीनान्वृत्तिसंपन्नान् निपुणान्कोशवृद्धये ॥
आयव्ययस्य कुशलान् गणितज्ञानलोलुपान् ।
नियोजयेद्धर्मनिष्ठान् सम्यक्कार्यार्थचिन्तकान् ॥
कर्मणि चातिकुशलान् लिपिज्ञानायतिक्षमान् ।
सर्वविश्वासिनः सत्यान् सर्वकार्येषु निश्चितान् ॥
अकृताशांस्तथा भर्तुः कालज्ञांश्च प्रसङ्गिनः ।
कार्यकामोपधाशुद्धा बाह्याभ्यन्तरचारिणः ।
कुर्यादासन्नकार्येषु गृहसंरक्षणेषु च ॥

65. Cited by *Lakṣ* 11.33 — a) Hy wKt^1 Lo^1 GMy आमात्ये; Ox^3 अमात्यो; Wa अमात्यं; Wa आयत्ता; Tj^1 आयतो — b) Tr^2 दण्ड; Jm दण्डी; TMd^3 TMd^4 GMd^5 दण्डो; Lo^1 वैनयकी; Bo वैनायकी; Wa वैनकी — c) TMd^4 Tr^2 नृपते; Bo °राष्ट्रौ; Tr^2 °राष्ट्रेषु; Be^1 Bo BCa Hy Jm Jo^1 Kt^2 BKt^5 wKt^6 GMd^1 NPu^1 Pu^5 Pu^7 Tj^2 MTr^3 MTr^4 MTr^6 [*Jolly* G] *Mandlik Jha KSS Dave* च — d) Bo दूरे; Be^1 °पर्यया

66. a) Be^1 BBe^2 Ho wKt^1 TMd^4 Pu^2 Pu^4 [*Jolly* M$^{8-9}$] च; oOr तु — b) GMd^1 संभिनत्ति हि संयतान्; TMd^3 GMy संभिनत्त्येव संहितान्; GMd^5 MTr^6 संभिनत्ति च; TMd^4 न भिनत्ति च; Bo BKt^5 wKt^6 Lo^1 Pu^8 Tr^1 Tr^2 Wa हि; [*Jolly* M^5 R] तु; Bo संयतान्; NKt^4 Ox^2 NPu^1 संहितान्; GMd^5 संगतान् — c) Be^1 BCa Ho La^1 Lo^1 Lo^4 Lo^5 Ox^3 दूतस्तु कु° — d) MTr^4 MTr^6 भिद्यन्ति; oOr sOx^1 sPu^6 [*Jolly* Nd] भिद्यते; Lo^3 येन भिद्यन्ते; GMd^5 येन भिद्यन्ति; Jo^2 La^1 GMd^1 TMd^3 TMd^4 GMy Tr^1 Tj^1 येन भिद्येत; BCa येन भिद्यते; MTr^6 *om* येन; Kt^2 मानवा; TMd^3 TMd^4 GMd^5 GMy [*Jolly* Nd] मानवः; oOr मानवं; Tr^1 मानव; Be^1 NKt^4 NNg Pu^5 Pu^7 Tr^2 MTr^4 Wa [*Jolly* G Ku] बान्धवाः; MTr^5 दानवाः; Ho Jm Jo^2 wKt^3 Lo^2 Lo^5 [*cor to*] Tj^1 [*Jolly* R] वानवा; BCa BBe^2 BKt^5 wKt^6 वानरा; Jo^1 चानवाः; Pu^2 Pu^4 संहताः

स विद्यादस्य कृत्येषु निगूढेङ्गितचेष्टितैः ।
आकारमिङ्गितं चेष्टां भृत्येषु च चिकीर्षितम् ॥६७॥
बुद्ध्वा च सर्वं तत्त्वेन परराजचिकीर्षितम् ।
तथा प्रयत्नमातिष्ठेद्यथात्मानं न पीडयेत् ॥६८॥
जाङ्गलं सस्यसंपन्नमार्यप्रायमनाविलम् ।
रम्यमानतसामन्तं स्वाजीव्यं देशमावसेत् ॥६९॥
धन्वदुर्गं महीदुर्गमब्दुर्गं वार्क्षमेव च ।
नृदुर्गं गिरिदुर्गं च समाश्रित्य वसेत्पुरम् ॥७०॥
सर्वेण तु प्रयत्नेन गिरिदुर्गं समाश्रयेत् ।
एषां हि बाहुगुण्येन गिरिदुर्गं विशिष्यते ॥७१॥
त्रीण्याद्यान्याश्रितास्त्वेषां मृगगर्ताश्रयाप्चराः ।

67.* a) NKt^{4} संविद्या°; Pu^{3} विंद्या°; Pu^{5} Pu^{7} °द्यादपकृत्येषु; wKt^{3} कृत्तेषु; Bo कृष्टेषु; Tr^{2} Pu^{3} कृत्यं च — b) Tr^{2} °चेष्टितं — c) Lo^{1} अकार°; Tr^{2} आकारीमङ्गितां; Kt^{2} °ङ्गितश्चेष्टां;Lo^{5} चेष्टा; NKt^{4} चेष्टं — d) MTr^{5} कृत्येषु च राजशत्रुषु; Be^{1} NKt^{4} GMd^{1} TMd^{3} TMd^{4} GMd^{5} GMy NPu^{1} Pu^{3} Tr^{1} Tr^{2} MTr^{4} MTr^{6} *Nd Nā Rc* कृत्येषु; BKt^{5} वन्येषु; wKt^{6} हृत्येषु; GMd^{5} तु; GMd^{1} विचिकी°; wKt^{1} चिकित्सितं

68. Pādas a-b omitted in in TMd^{3} GMy Pu^{4} [haplo] — a) wKt^{1} Pu^{3} बुद्ध्या; Lo^{2} बुद्ध्वा सर्वं च; Bo wKt^{1} wKt^{6} Lo^{1} oOr सर्व; MTr^{3}तल्पेन; NNg Pu^{5} Pu^{7} [*Jolly* G] यत्नेन — b) Ho परराजी° — c) Ox^{3} यथा; TMd^{4} प्रयतमा°; Tr^{2} प्रयतुमा°; BBe^{2} प्रयत्नेनाति° — d) oOr °ष्ठेत्तथा°; GMd^{1} °थास्वार्थं; GMd^{5} °थास्वार्थान्; Tr^{1} °थास्वार्थौ; TMd^{4} °थान्वार्थे; Ho निपीडयेत्

69. a) Ox^{3} जाङ्गलां; *Jha Dave* सत्यसंपन्न°; Bo Lo^{1} Pu^{3} Pu^{8} °संपूर्णमा° — b) Tr^{1} °मायुःप्रायमनाविषं; sOx^{1} sPu^{6} °नाबिलं; GMy NNg Pu^{2} Pu^{4} Pu^{5} Pu^{7} *Go* [*Jolly* G] °नाकुलं; Jo^{1} °नाखिलं; wKt^{6} °लाविलं — c) Ox^{3} मन्यमा°; Lo^{1} [*cor to*] °मायाससामन्तं; Tr^{1} °मायतमानत्तं; TMd^{3} GMy oOr °सामन्त; BBe^{2} °सीमन्तं — d) Ox^{2} °मन्तमाजीव्यं; TMd^{3} स्वाजीव्य; Bo Kt^{2} NKt^{4} BKt^{5} स्वजीव्यं; wKt^{1} NNg Pu^{5} Pu^{7} स्वाजीवं; wKt^{6} सुजीव्यं; MTr^{4} स्वादीव्यं; NKt^{4} Lo^{2} oOr °मावशेत्; Ho wKt^{6} La^{1} sOx^{1} Ox^{2} Pu^{3} sPu^{6} Tr^{2} [*Jolly* R] °माविशेत्; NPu^{1} °माश्रयेत्; Lo^{5} °माचरेत्; Bo °मावयत्

70.* Cited by *Viś* 1.317; *Vij* 1.321;*Mādh* 1.406 — a) Lo^{1} धान्य°; TMd^{4} धन°; Hy Jo^{1} Kt^{2} La^{1} Lo^{4} Lo^{5} Ox^{2} Tj^{2} Tr^{2} MTr^{3} Wa [*Jolly* M^{4}] धनुर्दुर्गं; GMd^{5} जलदुर्गं; MTr^{4} सत्वदुर्गं; TMd^{3} °दुर्ग; Ox^{3} महा° — b) NKt^{4} *om* अव्दुर्गं; Pu^{5} Pu^{7} °मपदुर्गं; Wa °व्दुर्गां; MTr^{5} °व्दुर्गः; Ho वार्क्ष्यमेव; NKt^{4} वार्क्रमेव; BBe^{2} Hy Jm Jo^{1} wKt^{1} Kt^{2} BKt^{5} wKt^{6} Lo^{2} Lo^{3} Lo^{4} Lo^{5} GMd^{1} TMd^{4} NNg oOr sOx^{1} Ox^{3} sPu^{6} Pu^{8} Tj^{1} Tj^{2} MTr^{5} *Vij Mādh Mandlik Jolly Jha KSS Dave* वा — c) Tr^{2} Wa नृदुर्गां; Bo गुरुदुर्गं; BBe^{2} Hy Jm Jo^{1} wKt^{1} Kt^{2} wKt^{3} La^{1} Lo^{2} Lo^{4} Lo^{5} GMd^{1} TMd^{4} GMd^{5} oOr Ox^{3} NPu^{1} Pu^{8} Tj^{2} MTr^{5} *Mandlik Jolly Jha KSS Dave* वा — d) *Mādh* समावृत्य; NKt^{4} समासृत्यावसे°; BKt^{5} Lo^{2} Ox^{3} Pu^{2} Pu^{3} Pu^{4} Pu^{5} Pu^{7} MTr^{5} °श्रित्यावसे°; Pu^{8} वसेत्पुरां; wKt^{1} वसेत्पुरीं; Be^{1} GMd^{5} NNg पुरं वसेत्

71. Cited by *Viś* 1.317; *Lakṣ* 11.41; pādas a-b cited by *Mādh* 1.406 — a) GMd^{1} TMd^{4} GMd^{5} MTr^{4} MTr^{6} सर्वेणापि; Pu^{5} Pu^{7} [*Jolly* G] प्रकारेण — b) Tr^{2} Wa °दुर्गां — c) Ho एषां बाहुल्यगुण्येन; GMd^{1} TMd^{4} MTr^{6} *Lakṣ* बाहुगुण्येन एषां हि [MTr^{6} *Lakṣ* तेषां; TMd^{4} तु]; NKt^{4} BKt^{5} wKt^{6} तेषां; Lo^{1} एषो; wKt^{1} Pu^{5} Pu^{7} एवं; *Viś* एतेषां बाहु°; BCa Jo^{2} La^{1} Lo^{3} GMd^{5} Tj^{1} तु; TMd^{3} बहु°; NKt^{4} गुणबाहुल्याद् — d) Tr^{2} Wa °दुर्गां; Lo^{1} °दुर्गो; NKt^{4} TMd^{3} [*but cor fh*] oOr Pu^{2} Pu^{5} Pu^{7} [*Jolly* G] *Viś* प्रशास्यते

त्रीण्युत्तराणि क्रमशः प्लवंगमनरामराः ॥७२॥
यथा दुर्गाश्रितानेतान्नोपहिंसन्ति शत्रवः ।
तथारयो न हिंसन्ति नृपं दुर्गसमाश्रितम् ॥७३॥
एकः शतं योधयति प्राकारस्थो धनुर्धरः ।
शतं दशसहस्राणि तस्माद्दुर्गं विशिष्यते ॥७४॥
तत्स्यादायुधसंपन्नं धनधान्येन वाहनैः ।
ब्राह्मणैः शिल्पिभिर्यन्त्रैर्यवसेनोदकेन च ॥७५॥
तस्य मध्ये सुपर्याप्तं कारयेद्गृहमात्मनः ।
गुप्तं सर्वर्तुकं शुभ्रं जलवृक्षसमन्वितम् ॥७६॥
तदध्यास्योद्वहेद्भार्यां सवर्णां लक्षणान्विताम् ।
कुले महति संभूतां हृद्यां रूपगुणान्विताम् ॥७७॥

72. a) bKt^{5} wKt^{6} त्रीन्याद्याश्रि° ; tMd^{4} °द्यानाश्रि° ; wKt^{1} °श्रितं तेषां; Be^{1} Bo Ho nKt^{4} La^{1} Lo^{1} Lo^{2} Lo^{4} Lo^{5} gMd^{1} tMd^{3} tMd^{4} nNg Ox^{3} °श्रितास्तेषां — b) Tr^{1} मृगभर्ताश्रयापरा: [visarga deleted sh]; Be^{1} wKt^{6} gMd^{1} nNg Ox^{3} nPu^{1} Pu^{5} Pu^{7} मृगगर्ताश्रयाः पुराः; Ho मृगंगर्ताश्रयाः पुरः; gMd^{5} मृगहर्तासमाश्रयः; Jo^{1} mTr^{3} °श्रयाप्सराः; tMd^{3} °श्रयाप्त्सराः; Ox^{2} °श्रयाप्सषाः; nKt^{4} °श्रयाप्ध्वराः; sOx^{1} sPu^{6} °श्रयार्धषाः; Lo^{3} Tj^{1} °श्रयापराः; Lo^{1} Lo^{2} °श्रयाश्वराः; Lo^{5} °श्रयांचराः — d) Pu^{5} Pu^{7} प्लवंगमनिरामयः; Ho प्लवंगरमरानराः; Kt^{2} °नरोमराः; gMy °नरावराः; gMd^{1} °नराः पराः; wKt^{1} °नराः सताः

73. Pādas b-c omitted in Jo^{1} — a) Bo wKt^{1} दुर्गाश्रयाने° — a-b) Lo^{1} यथा दुर्गश्रितान्नोपहिंसन्ति शत्रवश्च ते — b) oOr °न्नापहिंसन्ति — c) wKt^{1} यथारयो; wKt^{6} तथात्रयो; gMd^{5} हिंस्यति; tMd^{4} शंसन्ति — d) Lo^{1} tMd^{4} gMd^{5} gMy nNg mTr^{5} नृप; tMd^{3} नृपः; oOr नित्यं दुर्ग° ; nKt^{4} tMd^{3} gMy Tj^{1} दुर्गं; Tr^{1} mTr^{5} °समाश्रयं; Lo^{1} °श्रिताः

74.* Cited by *Lakṣ* 11.41 — a) tMd^{3} *om* एकः; tMd^{4} एकं; nKt^{4} धारयति — c) *Lakṣ* शतं शतसहस्राणि; tMd^{3} शतदश° — d) Lo^{4} Lo^{5} Ox^{3} [*Jolly* M]तस्माद्दुर्गाणि कारयेत्; Be^{1} bCa Hy Jo^{1} Kt^{2} nKt^{4} bKt^{5} wKt^{6} Lo^{1} Lo^{2} nNg Pu^{2} Pu^{4} Pu^{5} Pu^{7} Pu^{8} Tj^{2} mTr^{5} *Mandlik Jolly Jha KSS Dave* विधीयते; bBe^{2} प्रशस्यते

Additional verse in Be^{3} nPu^{1} Pu^{3} *Mandlik* [ख, ठ] *KSS Dave:*

मन्दरस्यापि शिखरं निर्मनुष्यं न शस्यते ।
मनुष्यदुर्गं दुर्गाणां मनुः स्वायंभुवोऽब्रवीत् ॥

b) Be^{3} निर्मानुष्यं; nPu^{1} Pu^{3} शिष्यते

75. Pādas c-d *ma sh* in Be^{3}. Cited by *Mādh* 1.407 — a) Bo Ho wKt^{1} Lo^{5} gMd^{1} tMd^{3} gMy oOr sOx^{1} Pu^{5} sPu^{6} Pu^{7} तस्मादायुध° ; Wa °दायुधं; Bo °संपन्न — b) bBe^{2} Pu^{5} धनं; Be^{3} Lo^{1} °धान्यैश्च — c) mTr^{3} °भिर्यज्ञैर्यव° ; tMd^{4} °भिर्मन्त्रैर्यव° — d) Be^{3} °न्त्रैर्यवसैरुदकेन्धनैः; Bo Ho Lo^{1} gMd^{5} sOx^{1} Pu^{3} sPu^{6} Pu^{8} Tr^{2} *Mādh* °दकेन्धनैः; gMd^{1} °दकंधनैः; bKt^{5} wKt^{6} °दकैर्धनैः; wKt^{3} वा; oOr [*but cor fh*] वै

76. Cited by *Mādh* 1.407 — a) Lo^{5} यस्य; wKt^{1} La^{1} oOr मध्येषु पर्याप्तं; Bo *Mādh* मध्ये तु पर्याप्तं; tMd^{3} gMy स्वपर्याप्तं; Wa सुपर्याप्तुं; Hy स्वपयाप्तं — b) tMd^{4} चकाराद्गृह° ; wKt^{6} °हमानवः — c) gMd^{5} गुप्त; Ox^{3} तप्तं; tMd^{3} gMd^{5} gMy Tr^{1} mTr^{6} [*Jolly* Nd] *Me*[pāṭha] सर्वर्तुगं; wKt^{1} सर्वत्रिकं; oOr शुभ्र; nKt^{4} शुभं; Pu^{5} Pu^{7} *Mādh* शुद्धं; wKt^{1} शुत्रं — d) Tr^{2} °समुद्भवं

77. a) bBe^{2} तदाध्या° ; Be^{3} °हेत्कन्यां — b) Tr^{2} त्रैसवर्णां; tMd^{4} सुवर्णां; wKt^{6} सुपर्णां; bKt^{5} wKt^{6}

पुरोहितं च कुर्वीत वृणुयादेव चर्त्विजः ।
तेऽस्य गृह्याणि कर्माणि कुर्युर्वैतानिकानि च ॥७८॥
यजेत राजा क्रतुभिर्विविधैराप्तदक्षिणैः ।
धर्मार्थं चैव विप्रेभ्यो दद्याद्भोगान्धनानि च ॥७९॥
सांवत्सरिकमाप्तैश्च राष्ट्रादाहारयेद्बलिम् ।
स्याच्चाम्नायपरो लोके वर्तेत पितृवन्नृषु ॥८०॥
अध्यक्षान्विविधान्कुर्यात् तत्र तत्र विपश्चितः ।
तेऽस्य सर्वाण्यवेक्षेरन् नृणां कार्याणि कुर्वताम् ॥८१॥
आवृत्तानां गुरुकुलाद् विप्राणां पूजको भवेत् ।
नृपाणामक्षयो ह्येष निधिर्ब्राह्मो विधीयते ॥८२॥
न तं स्तेना न चामित्रा हरन्ति न च नश्यति ।
तस्माद्राज्ञा निधातव्यो ब्राह्मणेष्वक्षयो निधिः ॥८३॥

Lo[5] Ox[3] °न्वितं — c) GMd[1] तां संकुले तु संभूतां; Bo समुद्भूतां — d) TMd[3] GMy हृद्य; TMd[4] sOx[1] sPu[6] रूपसमन्वितां

78. Placed before 7.76 in TMd[3] GMy — a) Pu[5] *om* च — b) Tj[1] श्रुणुया°; TMd[4] °यादिव; NNg चर्त्विजाः; Jo[1] Kt[2] [*Jolly* Ku] वर्त्विजं — c) Be[1] Be[3] Bo Lo[2] TMd[4] NNg oOr Ox[3] Pu[5] Pu[7] Tr[2] MTr[6] Wa [*Jolly* M[8] G] तस्य; wKt[3] तेजस्य; TMd[3] TMd[4] GMy गृह्याणि कार्याणि; Wa गृह्याणि सर्वाणि; Bo कृत्याणि कर्माणि; GMd[1] GMd[5] कर्माणि गृह्याणि; Ho कार्याणि गृह्याणि; Tr[1] कार्याणि गार्ह्याणि — d) TMd[4] कुर्याद्वैता°; oOr वा

79. a) TMd[3] Tj[1] राज; Tr[2] कृतु° — b) Be[1] Wa °धैर्भूरिदक्षिणैः; wKt[6] °धैरात्मदक्षिणैः; Be[3] °धैरात्तदक्षिणैः — c) Bo धर्म्यार्थं; TMd[3] GMd[5] GMy MTr[4] यज्ञार्थं — d) GMd[1] दद्यां भोम्यं धनानि; Pu[5] Pu[7] °द्भौजान्ध°; Lo[1] Ox[2] Pu[3] Pu[8] °गान्वसूनि च

80. Cited by *Lakṣ* 11.32 — a) TMd[3] संवत्स°; Lo[2] Pu[5] °माप्तेश्च; wKt[1] °माप्तश्च; TMd[4] °मानैश्च — b) Be[3] स्वराष्ट्रादाहरेद्बलिं; Jo[2] Tj[1] राष्ट्रायाहरये°; BBe[2] °दाहरये°; GMd[5] NNg MTr[4] MTr[6] °हारयेत्करं — c) Bo स्याद्वाम्ना°; Jo[2] Lo[3] GMd[5] Tj[1] स्यादाम्ना°; *Lakṣ* स्यादाश्रय°; TMd[4] स्याच्च न्यायपरो; La[1] GMd[1] NPu[1] Pu[2] Pu[3] लोको — d) sOx[1] sPu[6] वर्तते; TMd[3] पितवन्नृषु; TMd[4] पितृवन्नृपः; sOx[1] पितृवन्नृप; wKt[1] पितृवन्धुषु; wKt[6] पितृबन्धुषु; Tj[1] पितृवान्दषु

81. Cited by *Apa* 581; *Lakṣ* 11.32 — a) wKt[1] अध्याक्षा°; Be[3] अध्यक्षा विवि° — a-b) *Apa* [vl] अध्यक्षान्विविधान्शुद्धान्कुर्यात्तत्र विपश्चितः — c) Be[3] TMd[3] TMd[4] oOr Ox[3] Pu[5] sPu[6] [*but cor*] Pu[7] Tr[2] MTr[6] तस्य; *Apa* [vl] तस्तु; wKt[3] ते सर्वा°; Pu[5] Pu[7] कार्याण्यवे°; GMd[5] GMy कर्माण्यवे°; Bo °वेक्ष्येरन्; sOx[1] *Lakṣ* °वीक्षेरन्; Tr[2] °वक्ष्यरन्; wKt[1] TMd[4] °वेक्षेत — d) GMd[1] oOr कर्माणि

82. Cited by *Jmv* 9.20; *Lakṣ* 11.167 — a) NKt[4] BKt[5] wKt[6] La[1] TMd[3] Tj[1] अवृत्तानां; Tr[1] आवृतानां; NNg [*but cor fh*] आवृतानि; Ox[3] कुरुकुलाद्; Be[1] Pu[2] Pu[4] °कुलान्; BKt[5] wKt[6] °कुला; Tr[2] °कुल — c) Ox[3] °मक्षये — d) BKt[5] wKt[6] TMd[3] TMd[4] GMd[5] निधिब्राह्मो; GMd[1] MTr[4] MTr[6] Wa *Jmv* विधिर्ब्राह्मो; Tj[1] निधिर्ग्राह्यो; TMd[3] °ब्राह्मे; TMd[4] °ब्राह्म; Be[3] Jm Tj[2] MTr[3] [*Jolly* M[8–9]] *Mandlik Dave Jha KSS* °ब्राह्मोभिधीयते; Hy लिधीयते; MTr[4] निधीयते

83. Pādas c-d omitted in Ox[3] and pāda-d in MTr[6] [haplo]. Cited by *Lakṣ* 11.167 — a) BKt[5] wKt[6] TMd[4] Tr[1] न च स्तेना; Ox[2] नैनं स्तेना; Bo न वा विप्रो न; Ox[3] चारित्रा — b) Bo oOr हरति; Tr[2] च न; Ho Pu[2] Pu[4] न विनश्यति; wKt[1] La[1] TMd[3] GMd[5] oOr NPu[1] पश्यति — c) Tr[1] तस्माद्राज्ञो;

न स्कन्दते न व्यथते न विनश्यति कर्हिचित् ।
वरिष्ठमग्निहोत्रेभ्यो ब्राह्मणस्य मुखे हुतम् ॥८४॥
सममब्राह्मणे दानं द्विगुणं ब्राह्मणब्रुवे ।
सहस्रगुणं प्राधीते* अनन्तं वेदपारगे ॥८५॥
पात्रस्य हि विशेषेण श्रद्दधानतयैव च ।
अल्पं वा बहु वा प्रेत्य दानस्यावाप्यते फलम् ॥८६॥
समोत्तमाधमै राजा त्वाहूतः पालयन् प्रजाः ।
न निवर्तेत संग्रामात् क्षात्रं धर्ममनुस्मरन् ॥८७॥

Lo^1 TMd^4 sOx^1 NPu^1 sPu^6 तस्माद्राजा; wKt^6 तस्मात्प्राज्ञो; Pu^2 Pu^4 तस्मात्प्रज्ञा; Ho wKt^1 wKt^3 wKt^6 Pu^5 Pu^7 *Lakṣ* विधातव्यो — d) Ho ब्राह्मणेप्यक्षयो; Lo^4 Lo^5 [*Jolly* M^4] ब्राह्मणे ह्यक्षयो; TMd^3 GMy [*Jolly* Nd] °प्यचलो; Bo Lo^1 विधिः

84. Omitted in Ox^3; pādas a-c omitted in MTr^6. Cited by *Lakṣ* 11167 — a) Be ^{1} Lo^2 NNg NPu^1 [*Jolly* M^{5-8-9}] स्कन्दति; Pu^5 Pu^7 स्कन्दयेन्न; wKt^6 व्यथतो; Be^1 व्यवते; wKt^1 व्ययते; Lo^2 Lo^4 Lo^5 Wa [*Jolly* M$^{4-5}$ N] *MeNā Dave Jha* च्यवते — b) BBe^2 wKt^3 Lo^2 MTr^5 न च नश्यति; La^1 न च पश्यति — c) TMd^3 परिष्ठ°; TMd^4 वरिष्ठेम°; *Lakṣ* °होत्राद्धि — d) Pu^2 Pu^4 ब्राह्मणेस्य; Wa मुख; wKt^6 मुखोद्गतं

85.* Cited by *Apa* 286; pāda-a cited by *Viś* 1.311 — a) TMd^3 सचुतु ब्राह्मणे — b) Ho GMd^5 Tr^1 ब्राह्मणं; Lo^3 ब्राह्मणे; Be^3 °ब्रुवो — c) Be^1 BBe^2 Bo BCa Ho Hy Jm Jo^1 Jo^2 wKt^1 Kt^2 wKt^3 BKt^5 wKt^6 Lo^3 Lo^4 Lo^5 Ox^3 NPu^1 Pu^3 Pu^8 Tj^1 Tj^2 MTr^3 [*Jolly* M] *Mandlik Jha KSS Dave* प्राधीते शतसाहस्रम् [Bo प्रभाते; BBe^2 wKt^3 अधीते; Lo^4 Lo^5 Ox^3 [*Jolly* M] *Jha Dave*आचार्ये]; GMd^1 GMd^5 MTr^4 MTr^6 सहस्रं श्रोत्रिये तु स्याद् [GMd^1 *om* तु]; TMd^3 GMy Tr^1 [*Jolly* Nd] सहस्रं श्रोत्रिये दानम्; Be^3 NKt^4 La^1 Lo^1 Lo^2 TMd^4 NNg oOr sOx^1 Ox^2 Pu^2 Pu^4 Pu^5 sPu^6 Pu^7 Tr^2 MTr^5 Wa [*Jolly* G N] *Apa Ku* [pāṭha] *Jolly* सहस्रगुणमाचार्ये — d) TMd^4 MTr^5 त्वनन्तं; BKt^5 अन्तं

86.* Cited by *Apa* 303; *Hem* 1.27 — a) BCa GMd^1 MTr^6 तु; TMd^4 वा; oOr GMd^5 *Apa* च — b) Be^1 Be^3 Bo Ho Jm BKt^5 wKt^6 La^2 TMd^3 GMy NNg oOr Ox^3 NPu^1 Pu^2 Pu^3 Pu^4 Pu^5 Pu^7 Pu^8 Tj^1 Tr^2 श्रद्दधानं तथैव च [Jm La^2 Ox^3 NPu^1 Pu^8 Tj^1 °धान°; NNg Tr^2 °धानः; Be^3 wKt^6 TMd^3 GMy oOr °धानस्त°]; *Apa* °धानतयापि च; GMd^5 तु — c) TMd^3 GMy MTr^4 MTr^6 अल्पे दत्ते बहुगुणं [TMd^3 अल्प]; Lo^1 प्रेते — d) *Mandlik Jha KSS Dave* दानस्य फलमश्नुते; GMd^1 TMd^4 दानस्य स्याद्यदा फलं; MTr^4 *Hem* दानस्य प्राप्यते

Additional verse in Be^1 Hy Lo^4 Lo^5 Ox^3 Tj^1 *Mandlik* [थ] *Jolly Jha KSS Dave;* commented on by *Me Rn:*

देशे काले विधानेन द्रव्यं श्रद्धासमन्वितम् ।
प्रात्रे प्रदीयते यत्तु तद्धर्मस्य प्रसाधनम् ॥

a) Hy Tj^1 देशकाल; Ox^3 काल — d) Be^1 प्रसादनं

Additonal verse in BCa Ho NPu^1 Tr^2 *Mandlik* [ख, ट, त] *KSS Dave:*

एष एव परो धर्मः कृत्स्नो राज्ञ उदाहृतः ।
जित्वा धनानि संग्रामाद् द्विजेभ्यः प्रतिपादयेत् ॥

a) Tr^2 परं — b) Tr^2 राज्ञो; NPu^1 राज्ञामुदा° — c) NPu^1 संग्रामे

87. Pādas c-d omitted in Wa. Cited by *Lakṣ* 11.131 — a) TMd^4 °त्तमोधमै; NPu^1 °धमैः सांख्य — a-b) BKt ^{5} wKt^6 समोत्तराधमैः संख्य आहूतो नृपतिः परैः [BKt^5 संध्य]; Be^3 राज्ञामाहूतः; sOx ^{1} sPu^6 राजादाहूतः — b) GMd^1 GMd^5 *Lakṣ* त्वाहूतः समरे परैः; NPu^1 आहूतो नृपतिः परैः; NKt^4 Tr^2 वाहूतः; BBe^2

संग्रामेष्वनिवर्तित्वं प्रजानां चैव पालनम् ।
शुश्रूषा ब्राह्मणानां च राज्ञां श्रेयस्करं परम् ॥८८॥
आहवेषु मिथोऽन्योन्यं जिघांसन्तो महीक्षितः ।
युध्यमानाः परं शक्त्या स्वर्गं यान्त्यपराङ्मुखाः ॥८९॥
न कूटैरायुधैर्हन्याद् युध्यमानो रणे रिपून् ।
न कर्णिभिर्नापि दिग्धैर्नाग्निज्वलिततेजनैः ॥९०॥
न च हन्यात्स्थलारूढं न क्लीबं न कृताञ्जलिम् ।
न मुक्तकेशं नासीनं न तवास्मीति वादिनम् ॥९१॥
न सुप्तं न विसन्नाहं न नग्नं न निरायुधम् ।
नायुध्यमानं पश्यन्तं न परेण समागतम् ॥९२॥
नायुधव्यसनप्राप्तं नार्तं नातिपरिक्षतम् ।
न भीतं न परावृत्तं सतां धर्ममनुस्मरन् ॥९३॥

Ho चाहूतः; Lo^2 प्राहुतः; Bo त्वाहूत्य; gMy त्वापूतः; tMd^3 त्वावृतः; wKt^1 चाश्नतः; Be^3 प्रजा — c) Tr^2 नानिव°; Ox^3 नातिव°; Pu^2 Pu^4 निवृत्तेव; Bo संग्रामान्; wKt^1 संग्रामे; nKt^4 Lo^5 tMd^3 संग्रामा — d) Lo^2 Lo^4 tMd^3 gMd^1 gMy Pu^8 Tr^1 mTr^5 क्षात्र; bBe^2 Pu^5 क्षत्रं; Ox^3 *om* धर्मम्

88. Omitted in Wa. Cited by *Lakṣ* 11.154; *Mādh* 1.413 — a) gMy °निवर्तित्व; tMd^3 °निवर्तत्वं; gMd^1 *Bh* [ad 89] °निवृत्तत्वं; nNg °निवृत्तिश्च; Pu^3 mTr^4 °नुवर्तित्वं — b) gMd^5 Pu^5 Pu^7 [*Jolly* G] *Lakṣ* प्रजानां परिपालनं; bKt^5 प्रजानामेव; Pu^2 Pu^4 पालयन्; tMd^4 रक्षणः — c) gMd^1 tMd^3 tMd^4 gMd^5 gMy Tr^1 *Lakṣ* ब्राह्मणानां च शुश्रूषा [gMy शुश्रूषां] — d) *Lakṣ* राज्ञो निःश्रेयसं परं; tMd^4 राज्ञा; Be^3 राज्ञः; tMd^3 gMy राज्ञ

89. a) Tj^1 आवहेषु; tMd^3 gMy वदोन्योन्यं; tMd^4 gMd^5 Tr^1 यदन्योन्यं; Pu^5 Pu^7 °न्योन्यां — b) tMd^4 °सन्ता; Be^1 Wa महीभुजः; La^1 Tr^2 °क्षिताः; tMd^3 tMd^4 °क्षतः — c) tMd^3 gMy वध्यमानाः परैश्शक्त्या; Ho युद्धानां; Pu^2 Pu^4 °मानो; Tr^2 शक्ताः; gMd^5 त्यक्त्वा — d) Bo यात्य°; wKt^3 यान्त्याप°; nNg °पराङ्मुखा; Wa °पराङ्मुखं

90. Omitted in Lo^3 — a) Pu^2 Pu^4 अकूटै°; Pu^5 कूलै° — b) gMy युद्धमानो; Pu^5 Pu^7 °माना; Lo^5 Tj^1 °माने; bBe^2 Be^3 bKt^5 wKt^6 °मानान्; Wa रणा — c) tMd^3 नाकर्णि°; Tr^2 कीर्णीभि°; Pu^5 Pu^7 कर्णिकैर्नापि; Tr^1 °भिर्नाभिदिग्धै°; Be^3 mTr^6 °भिर्नातिदिग्धै°; tMd^3 °र्नावदिग्धै°; gMy °र्नावतिथै°; Be^1 wKt^1 bKt^5 wKt^6 दग्धै° — d) Hy °तेजलैः; gMd^5 °तेजकैः

91. Cited by *Lakṣ* 11.132 — a) gMd^1 tMd^4 gMd^5 न हन्यात्स्थलमारूढं; Lo^3 Tj^1 चाहन्या°; nPu^1 हन्याच्छिला°; mTr^3 °रूढान् — b) Bo च कृता°; Pu^5 Pu^7 [*Jolly* G] पुटाञ्जलिं; wKt^3 °ञ्जलिः — c) mTr^3 नामुक्त°; Be^1 Lo^3 Pu^5 Pu^7 Tj^1 Wa [*Jolly* G R] *Lakṣ* °केशमासीनं; Hy चासीनं

92. sOx^1 omits न निरा° to नग्नं [93b] — a) tMd^3 gMy नाविशन्नाहं — b) Lo^5 Ox^3 *Me* [pāṭha] भग्नं — c) wKt^3 अयुध्य° — d) mTr^6 चरेण; gMd^1 समावृतं

93. Pādas c-d omitted in Tr^2 — a) Be^1 नायुद्ध°; bBe^2 Bo नायुध्य°; Ho Lo^1 tMd^4 नायुधं; Ho Pu^3 °व्यसने; Be^3 Lo^5 gMd^1 tMd^3 tMd^4 gMd^5 gMy nNg Pu^2 Pu^4 Pu^5 Pu^7 Tj^1 °व्यसनं; Lo^2 °न्यसनं — b) Pu^5 Pu^7 °प्राप्तमार्तं; tMd^4 नार्थं; tMd^3 tMd^4 नापि परीक्षितं; Ho wKt^1 bKt^5 wKt^6 Lo^1 Ox^3 Pu^2 Pu^4 Pu^5 Pu^7 mTr^5 °परिक्षितं; Tr^1 °परीक्षितं — c) Bo न नितं; Jo^1 नरावृत्तं — d) nNg *ma sh* सतां; tMd^4 नितां; sOx^1 sPu^6 वृत्तमनुस्मरन्

यस्तु भीतः परावृत्तः संग्रामे हन्यते परैः ।
भर्तुर्यद्दुष्कृतं किंचित् तत्सर्वं प्रतिपद्यते ॥९४॥
यच्चास्य सुकृतं किंचिदमुत्रार्थमुपार्जितम् ।
भर्ता तत्सर्वमादत्ते परावृत्तहतस्य तु ॥९५॥
रथाश्वं हस्तिनं छत्रं धनं धान्यं पशून् स्त्रियः ।
सर्वद्रव्याणि कुप्यं च यो यज्जयति तस्य तत् ॥९६॥
राज्ञे च दद्युरुद्धारमित्येषा वैदिकी श्रुतिः ।
राज्ञा च सर्वयोधेभ्यो दातव्यमपृथग्जितम् ॥९७॥
एषोऽनुपस्कृतः प्रोक्तो योधधर्मः सनातनः ।
अस्माद्धर्मान्न च्यवेत क्षत्रियो घ्नन् रणे रिपून् ॥९८॥

94. Cited by *Lakṣ* 11.135 — a) GMd¹ यस्त्वतीतः; Be³ परावृतः — b) TMd³ नाग्रामे; Lo¹ परे — c) Bo Ho Lo¹ Pu³ Pu⁸ यत्किंचिद्दुष्कृतं भर्तुस्; TMd³ GMd⁵ हन्तुर्यद्दु°; Tr¹ मर्तुर्यद्दु°; wKt¹ भर्तुर्यत्तु कृतं — d) *Lakṣ* सर्वं तत्प्रति°; TMd⁴ °पद्यति

95. Cited by *Lakṣ* 11.135 — a) NPu¹ यश्चास्य; NKt⁴ यथास्य; *Lakṣ* यदस्य; oOr दुष्कृतं — b) wKt¹ किंचिदसुत्वार्थमु° — c) Ho भर्ता च तत्समादत्ते; GMd⁵ मर्ता; TMd³ Tr¹ हन्ता; Tr² तत्सुसमादत्ते; Ho तत्समादत्ते; BBe² तत्सर्वमाप्नोति; TMd³ sOx¹ sPu⁶ °माधत्ते — d) TMd³ GMd¹ GMy परावृत्य हतस्य; Bo परावृत्तमहस्य; Be¹ BBe² Bo Ho Jm wKt¹ BKt⁵ wKt⁶ Lo¹ Lo⁴ oOr Ox³ NPu¹ Pu⁵ Pu⁷ Pu⁸ Tr¹ Tr² Wa [*Jolly* M G] *Jolly* च

96. a) TMd³ GMd⁵ GMy रथाश्व; TMd⁴ तथास्य हस्तिनं; Be³ Lo¹ क्षत्रं; MTr³चक्रं — b) Pu⁵ *om* धनं; Kt² wKt³ NKt⁴ GMd¹ TMd³ TMd⁴ GMy NNg sOx¹ sPu⁶ Tr¹ MTr⁵ धन; TMd³ TMd⁴ GMy धान्य; Be³ Pu⁵ Pu⁷ MTr⁵ पशुं; NKt⁴ TMd⁴ पशुस्त्रियः; Pu⁸ स्त्रियाः; Tr¹ स्त्रियं — c) TMd³ GMy °द्रव्यं च; TMd⁴ कूप्यं; MTr⁴ MTr⁶ रूप्यं;Be³ कुप्यश्च; GMd¹ कुप्यन्ति यो — d) TMd³ GMd⁵ ये; Be¹ Ho TMd⁴ Tr¹ MTr⁴ MTr⁵ यो यं जयति; Lo³ Tj¹ यो जयेत हि तस्य

97.* a) GMd¹ TMd⁴ Tr¹ राज्ञे तु; Be³ BCa Hy Jm Jo¹ Jo² Kt² La¹ Lo² Lo³ Pu³ Pu⁸ Tj¹ Tj² MTr³ *Mandlik Jolly Jha KSS Dave* राज्ञश्च; Bo Ho BKt⁵ NKt⁶ Lo¹ Lo⁴ TMd³ GMy sOx¹ Ox² Ox³ sPu⁶ Pu⁸ TTr⁵ [*Jolly* M] राज्ञस्तु;NKt⁴ राज्ञे दद्यु°; Wa राज्ञेस्ते; Be¹ राज्ञस्ते; *Nā Rc* support राज्ञः; Tr² राज्ञःस्युदद्यु°; TMd³ MTr⁵ दद्यादुद्धा° — b) TMd³ °त्येषां; oOr स्मृतिः; Tr² शुचिः — c) Pu² Pu⁴ राजा; Tr² राज्ञाः सर्व°; TMd⁴ oOr Tr¹ तु; TMd³ GMy Tj¹ सर्वं; MTr⁵ [not *Der*] °यौधेभ्यो; sOx¹ sPu⁶ °योधिभ्यो; Bo °योधाभ्यो; NPu¹ °युद्धेभ्यो — d) Be¹ GMd¹ दातव्यं पृथ°; BBe² TMd⁴ °पृथग्जितः; MTr⁵ [*but mc*] °पृथग्हितं; GMd¹ °पृथक्सिधतं

Additonal verse in Be³ Ho *Mandlik* [ख] *KSS*; pādas a-b in Tr²:

भृत्येभ्यो विभजेदर्थान्नैकः सर्वहरो भवेत् ।
नाममात्रेण तुष्येत छत्रेण च महीपतिः ॥

c) Ho तुष्येत्तु

98. Pādas a-b omitted in Tr² — a) TMd³ TMd⁴ एषा°; Be¹ °पस्कृता; Be³ °पकृतः; GMd¹ °पाकृतः; TMd⁴ °पस्करः; NKt⁴ °पद्भूतः; BCa °पस्कृतः कृत्स्नो — b) GMy प्रोक्तस्पुरधर्मः; TMd³ प्रोक्त-स्पौरधर्मः; Tr¹ MTr⁵यौधधर्मः; GMd⁵ MTr⁴ MTr⁶ युद्धधर्मः; Ox³ योयं धर्मः; BBe² NNg योधर्मः; Lo⁴ यो[*ma* ध]धर्मः; GMd¹ राजधर्मः; Be¹ [*but mc*] °धर्मा; TMd⁴ °धर्मं सनातनं; BCa प्रकीर्तितः — c) TMd⁴ धर्मात्र विच्युतस्तस्मात्; BBe² Bo Pu⁵ Pu⁷ Tr² Wa तस्मा°; Jm BKt⁵ wKt⁶ Ox³ MTr⁶ च्यवते; Ho च्यवेत्; Be¹ NKt⁴ व्यवेत; GMd¹ व्यवतेत्; BBe² मुच्येत — d) GMd¹ क्षेत्रियो; Pu³ घ्नन् रिपून् रणे; Wa रणो; TMd³

अलब्धं चैव लिप्सेत लब्धं रक्षेत् प्रयत्नतः ।
रक्षितं वर्धयेच्चैव वृद्धं पात्रेषु निक्षिपेत् ॥९९॥
एतच्चतुर्विधं विद्यात् पुरुषार्थप्रयोजनम् ।
अस्य नित्यमनुष्ठानं सम्यक् कुर्यादतन्द्रितः ॥१००॥
अलब्धमिच्छेद्दण्डेन लब्धं रक्षेदवेक्षया ।
रक्षितं वर्धयेद्वृद्ध्या वृद्धं दानेन निक्षिपेत् ॥१०१॥
नित्यमुद्यतदण्डः स्यान्नित्यं विवृतपौरुषः ।
नित्यं संवृतसंवार्यो नित्यं छिद्रानुसार्यरेः ॥१०२॥
नित्यमुद्यतदण्डस्य कृत्स्नमुद्विजते जगत् ।
तस्मात्सर्वाणि भूतानि दण्डेनैव प्रसाधयेत् ॥१०३॥
अमाययैव वर्तेत न कथंचन मायया ।
बुध्येतारिप्रयुक्तां च मायां नित्यं सुसंवृतः ॥१०४॥

comments: अनुपस्कृतः अकृतप्रयत्नः

99. Cited by *Mādh* 1.413 — a) Lo^1 लव्धं चैव तु लिप्सेत; Pu^8 अलव्धमीहेद्धर्मेण; GMd^5 लिप्स्येत; TMd^3 रक्षेत — b) Lo^1 लव्धं चैव प्रयत्नतः; Be^1 BBe^2 Be^3 wKt^3 NKt^4 BKt^5 wKt^6 Lo^3 Lo^4 TMd^4 NNg Ox^3 Pu^4 Tj^1 Tr^2 MTr^5 [*Jolly* M R] *Mādh* रक्षेच्च यत्नतः; Ho oOr Pu^5 Pu^7 [*Jolly* G] रक्षेत यत्नतः; sOx^1 sPu^6 यत्नेन रक्षयेत्; TMd^3 GMy [*Jolly* Nd] रक्षेदपेक्षया; *Pañcatantra* I.2 रक्षेदवेक्षया [cf. 7.101] — c) Be^1 Ho Jo^2 Lo^3 Tj^1 वर्धयेन्नित्यं; Pu^2 Pu^4 Wa वर्धयेन्नित्या; Pu^3 वर्धये वृद्धया; NKt^4 sOx^1 sPu^6 MTr^5 °येच्चैनं — d) TMd^4 वृद्ध; GMd^5 वृद्धिं; Pu^3 दानेन निक्षिपेत्; BBe^2 Ho BKt^5 wKt^6 निःक्षिपेत्; Be^1 विन्यसेत्

100. Verses 100 and 101 transposed in NKt^4; pāda-d omitted in GMy — a) TMd^3 विद्या — b) TMd^3 GMy पुरुपार्थं — c) BKt^5 wKt^6 तस्य — d) TMd^3 धर्म्यं कुर्या°

101.* Omitted in GMy Pu^2 Pu^3 Pu^4 — a) GMd^1 लव्धमि° — b) BBe^2 La^1 GMd^1 GMd^5 Pu^8 Tr^1 °दपेक्षया — c) Ox^2 वर्धयेद्वृद्ध्यां; *KSS* वर्धयेद्बुद्ध्या; GMd^5 योजयेद्वृद्ध्या; Be^1 Wa वर्धयेद्युत्त्या; GMd^1 वर्धयेच्छत्त्या; Tr^1 रक्षयेद्वृद्ध्या ; Tj^2 MTr^4 MTr^6 वर्धयेद्द्रव्यं; Lo^2 वर्धयेच्चैव — d) Lo^1 Lo^2 TMd^3 GMd^5 Tr^1 MTr^4 MTr^6 दानेन योजयेत्; Lo^2 Lo^4 Lo^5 Ox^3 NPu^1 Pu^5 Pu^7 MTr^5 [*Jolly* M^{4-5-9} G Nd] *Mandlik Jolly Jha KSS Dave* पात्रेपु निक्षिपेत्; Be^1 Wa पात्रेपु विन्यसेत्; sOx^1 Ox^2 sPu^6 Tr^2 पात्रे निवेदयेत्; BBe^2 BKt^5 wKt^6 निःक्षिपेत्

102. Omitted in TMd^4; *ma sh* in Be^3; verses 102 and 103 transposed in Wa; pādas c-d omitted in Lo^2. Cited by *Lakṣ* 11.151 — a) GMd^5 °मुद्धृतदण्डः; Lo^1 °मुद्यम्य दण्डः — b) Ho स्यान्नित्यविवृत°; *Lakṣ* स्यान्नित्यमुद्धृत°; La^1 oOr Pu^2 विधृत°; Ox^2 बिभृत°; Lo^1 TMd^3 GMy °पौरुपं — c) Be^3 संभृत°; wKt^1 संयुत°; Be^1 Be^3 Ho BKt^5 wKt^6 Lo^5 Ox^3 °संचार्यो; GMd^1 TMd^3 GMd^5 GMy sOx^1 sPu^6 Tr^1 MTr^5 [*Jolly* Nd] °संचारो; wKt^3 oOr NPu^1 Pu^5 Pu^7 [*Jolly* G] °संधार्यो; NNg °संधार्य; Pu^3 °संदार्यो; Kt^2 °सर्वार्यो — d) Tr^1 नित्य; Ho छिद्रापसा°; BKt^5 wKt^6 छिद्रविसा°; Jo^1 °सार्यरैः; wKt^1 °सार्यतेः

103. Pādas a-b omitted in Lo^2. Cited by *Lakṣ* 11.151 — a) sOx^1 sPu^6 °मुद्धत°; GMd^5 *Lakṣ* °मुद्धृत° — b) Be^1 NNg कृच्छ्रमु°; GMd^5 नित्यमुद्वि°; GMy °मुद्वेजते; wKt^1 जयात् — d) GMd^1 TMd^3 TMd^4 GMd^5 GMy Tr^1 MTr^4 MTr^6 दण्डेनैव वशं नयेत्; Wa दण्डमेव

104. Cited by *Lakṣ* 11.151–2; *Mādh* 1.413 — b) La^1 मायया न कथंचन — c) Tj^1 युध्येता°;

नास्य छिद्रं परो विद्याद् विद्याच्छिद्रं परस्य तु ।
गूहेत्कूर्म इवाङ्गानि रक्षेद्विवरमात्मनः ॥१०५॥
बकवच्चिन्तयेदर्थाञ्छशवच्च विनिष्पतेत् ।
वृकवच्चावलुम्पेत सिंहवच्च पराक्रमेत् ॥१०६॥
एवं विजयमानस्य येऽस्य स्युः परिपन्थिनः ।
तानानयेद्वशं सर्वान् सामादिभिरुपक्रमैः ॥१०७॥
यदि ते तु न तिष्ठेयुरुपायैः प्रथमैस्त्रिभिः ।
दण्डेनैव प्रसह्यैताञ्छनकैर्वशमानयेत् ॥१०८॥

TMd^{4} बुध्येतानिप्र°; wKt^{1} बुध्येत विप्रयुक्तां; Jm °युक्ते; Tr^{2} °युक्तं; Kt^{2} °युक्ताश्च; Ox^{3} °युक्तांश्च; *Mādh* °युक्तान्तु; Jo^{2} Lo^{3} Tj^{1} वा; TMd^{3} TMd^{4} GMd^{5} GMy MTr^{5} तु — d) TMd^{4} माया; Lo^{3} सायं; sOx^{1} Ox^{2} Pu^{5} sPu^{6} Pu^{7} Tr^{2} नित्यं मायां; Lo^{4} Lo^{5} Ox^{3} [*Jolly* M] नित्यमतन्द्रितः; Jo^{1} Kt^{2} MTr^{3} *Mandlik KSS* स्वसंवृतः; Jo^{2} °वृतां; Lo^{2} °वृत्ता

105. Cited by *Lakṣ* 11.152 — a) Lo^{3} परा; wKt^{1} पुरो; Tr^{2} *om* विद्याद्; La^{1} Pu^{7} विन्द्याद्; TMd^{4} विद्या — b) *Lakṣ* छिन्द्याच्छिद्रं; Be^{1} La^{1} विन्द्याच्छिद्रं; Kt^{2} Lo^{1} TMd^{4} द्विद्याछिद्रं; Be^{3} Lo^{1} Lo^{2} Lo^{4} Lo^{5} GMy Ox^{3} [*Jolly* M Nd] *Dave Jha* च — c) TMd^{4} गुह्यात्कूर्म; La^{1} ग्रहेत्कूर्म; Pu^{2} Pu^{4} गूहयेत्कूर्म; Jm गृहेत्कूर्म; Ho NNg गूहेत्कर्म; GMd^{1} °त्कूर्मवदङ्गानि — d) Wa रक्षद्वि°; BBe^{2} रक्षेद्विवसमा°; Ox^{3} रक्षेद्विवरणमा°; Lo^{4} Lo^{5} रक्षेद्रविणमा°

Additional verse in BCa La^{1} Tr^{2} *Mandlik* [ख] *KSS:*

न विश्वसेदविश्वस्ते विश्वस्ते नातिविश्वसेत् ।
विश्वासाद्भयमुत्पन्नं मूलादपि निकृन्तति ॥

b) Tr^{2} नापि विश्वसेत् — d) BCa मूलादेव

Additional verses in La^{1}:

विश्वासयिता च – – सांत्वयित्वा च हेतुना ।
ततस्तं प्रहरेत्काले किंचित्प्रचलिते मते ॥१॥
आत्मना भिद्यते यस्तु सचिवाच्च निराकृतान् ।
दूराच्च लिप्यते स्त्रीभिस्तस्य नास्ति प्रतिक्रिया ॥२॥

106.* Cited by *Lakṣ* 11.152 — a) GMy बगव°; TMd^{4} जनव° — b) Be^{1} BBe^{2} Be^{3} BCa Ho Hy Jm Jo^{1} Jo^{2} wKt^{1} Kt^{2} wKt^{3} NKt^{4} La^{1} Lo^{1} Lo^{2} Lo^{3} GMd^{5} NNg oOr sOx^{1} Ox^{2} NPu^{1} sPu^{6} Pu^{8} Tj^{1} Tj^{2} Tr^{1} Tr^{2} MTr^{3} Wa *Mandlik Jha KSS Dave* सिंहवच्च पराक्रमेत् [oOr पराक्रमे]; Be^{3} सिंहवत्स्वपराक्रमे; Bo La^{2} BKt^{5} wKt^{6} पराक्रमेच्च सिंहवत् — c) wKt^{6} *Lakṣ* °च्चानुलु°; Be^{3} °च्चाप्यलुप्येत; NKt^{4} TMd^{4} MTr^{6} °लुम्पेत्तु — d) Lo^{4} Lo^{5} Ox^{3} Pu^{2} Pu^{4} [*Jolly* M] पराक्रमेत सिंहवत् [Lo^{4} °क्रमेत्सिं°]; Be^{1} BBe^{2} Be^{3} BCa Ho Hy Jm Jo^{1} Jo^{2} wKt^{1} Kt^{2} wKt^{3} NKt^{4} La^{1} La^{2} Lo^{1} Lo^{2} Lo^{3} GMd^{5} NNg sOx^{1} Ox^{2} NPu^{1} sPu^{6} Pu^{8} Tj^{1} Tj^{2} Tr^{1} Tr^{2} MTr^{3} Wa *Mandlik Jha KSS Dave* शशवच्च विनिष्पतेत् [wKt^{3} विनिष्यते; Lo^{3} Tj^{1} विनिक्षिपेत्; La^{2} विनिःक्षिपेत्]; TMd^{4} सिंहवत्स

107. Omitted in NKt^{4}. Cited by *Lakṣ* 11.126 — b) GMd^{1} TMd^{3} GMy Tr^{1} यस्य; NNg येस्युः परि° — c) Bo Ho Lo^{1} sOx^{1} Ox^{3} Pu^{3} sPu^{6} Pu^{8} [*Jolly* M$^{4-5}$] °येद्वशे; Tr^{2} °येद्वसेत्सर्वान्; wKt^{3} °येद्वशं कुर्यान् — d) Ox^{3} समादि°; Lo^{1} Tj^{1} °भिरुपाक्रमैः

108. Omitted in NKt^{4}. Cited by *Lakṣ* 11.126 — a) Be^{1} Wa ते नोपतिष्ठे°; wKt^{1} ते नानुतिष्ठे° — a-b) [*Jolly* M^{9}] यदि ते तु न तिष्ठन्ते समाद्यैः प्रथ° — b) wKt^{3} प्रथमस्त्रिभिः — c) GMd^{1} TMd^{3} TMd^{4} GMd^{5} GMy MTr^{4} MTr^{6} *Nd* दण्डेनापि; MTr^{5} दण्डेन तु; Tr^{1} दण्डेन च; Be^{3} प्रसज्येतां शन°; oOr प्रसक्तानां शन°; Pu^{5} Pu^{7} °सह्यैनाञ्छन°; *Lakṣ* °सह्यैनं शन°; TMd^{3} °सह्येतां शन°; TMd^{4} °सह्यैनां शन°

सामादीनामुपायानां चतुर्णामपि पण्डिताः ।
सामदण्डौ प्रशंसन्ति नित्यं राष्ट्राभिवृद्धये ॥१०९॥
यथोद्धरति निर्दाता कक्षं धान्यं च रक्षति ।
तथा रक्षेन्नृपो राष्ट्रं हन्याच्च परिपन्थिनः ॥११०॥
मोहाद्राजा स्वराष्ट्रं यः कर्षयत्यनवेक्षया ।
सोऽचिराद् भ्रश्यते राज्याज्जीविताच्च सबान्धवः ॥१११॥
शरीरकर्षणात् प्राणाः क्षीयन्ते प्राणिनां यथा ।
तथा राज्ञामपि प्राणाः क्षीयन्ते राष्ट्रकर्षणात् ॥११२॥
राष्ट्रस्य संग्रहे नित्यं विधानमिदमाचरेत् ।
सुसंगृहीतराष्ट्रो हि पार्थिवः सुखमेधते ॥११३॥
द्वयोस्त्रयाणां पञ्चानां मध्ये गुल्ममधिष्ठितम् ।
तथा ग्रामशतानां च कुर्याद्राष्ट्रस्य गुप्तये* ॥११४॥
ग्रामस्याधिपतिं कुर्याद्दशग्रामपतिं तथा ।
विंशतीशं शतेशं च सहस्रपतिमेव च ॥११५॥

109. Cited by *Lakṣ* 11.126 — a) NKt^{4} wKt^{6} समा°; TMd^{4} सामाजनामु° — b) Ox^{3} पण्डितः; wKt^{1} पाण्डवाः — c) Bo Ho सम°; wKt^{3} सामा°; GMd^{5} प्रशस्यन्ति — d) TMd^{4} क्षेत्रं राजाभि°; MTr^{4} MTr^{6} *Lakṣ* राज्याभि°; Be^{3} Bo Ho Lo^{1} Pu^{3} राष्ट्रविवृद्धये [Lo^{1} राष्ट्रं]; Be^{1} °भिवर्धये

110. a) GMd^{1} TMd^{4} GMd^{5} Tr^{1} MTr^{4} MTr^{5} MTr^{6} यथा हन्ति तु निर्दाता [TMd^{4} हरति; GMd^{5} Tr^{1} MTr^{5} च]; TMd^{3} यथा हन्त्यवनेर्दाता; NKt^{4} यथाहनिवनिर्वप्ता; wKt^{1} यथोत्वरति; Be^{1} निर्हाता; Ox^{3} *lacuna at* निर्दाता — b) Be^{1} Lo^{1} कक्ष्यं; Tr^{1} कक्ष; TMd^{3} राक्षं — c) Bo तथा राष्ट्रं नृपो राज्यं; Pu^{5} Pu^{7} [*Jolly* G] तथा रक्षन्हि राष्ट्रांश्च; Be^{3} रक्षेत्तथा नृपो राष्ट्रं; Jo^{1} रक्षो नृपो; La^{1} BKt^{5} oOr MTr^{4} MTr^{6} राज्यं — d) Bo हन्याच्चापरि°; BBe^{2} Tr^{1} °पन्थिनं

111. *ma fh* Wa. Cited by *Lakṣ* 11.83; *Mādh* 1.409 — a) wKt^{6} सुराष्ट्रं; Wa स्वयं राष्ट्रं यः; GMd^{5} स्वकं राष्ट्रं यः; BKt^{5} wKt^{6} °राष्ट्रं च — b) MTr^{5} कर्शयत्य°; oOr कर्षत्य°; BKt^{5} wKt^{6} GMd^{5} Pu^{5} Pu^{7} MTr^{5} [*Jolly* G] °नपेक्षया — c) BKt^{5} wKt^{6} Lo^{4} Lo^{5} NNg Ox^{3} स भ्रश्यत्यचिराद्राज्या°; TMd^{4} oOr Pu^{5} Pu^{7} भ्रस्यते; GMd^{1} भ्रश्यति; Be^{1} ग्रस्यते; wKt^{3} नश्यते; Hy धूष्यते; Tr^{1} बृश्यते; MTr^{5} राष्ट्राज्जी°; GMd^{1} MTr^{6} *Lakṣ* स्वाम्याज्जी° — d) Tj^{1} सबान्धवाः; TMd^{4} न संशयः

112. Not commented by *Rc, Nd.* Cited by *Mādh* 1.409 — b) oOr क्षीयते; Jo^{1} प्राणिनं — c) NPu^{1} राज्ञामपि तथा प्राणाः — d) oOr क्षीयते; TMd^{3} क्षयन्ते; NPu^{1} Pu^{2} °कर्पणा; Pu^{4} °कर्मणा

113. a) Be^{1} कर्शने नित्यं; Lo^{1} नित्य — b) GMd^{5} विधानं च समाचरेत्; GMd^{1} विधेयमि°; Lo^{2} निधानमि° — c) Hy wKt^{6} स्वयंगृहीत°; Lo^{1} Tr^{2} °ग्रहीत°; wKt^{1} °गृहीतो; Ox^{3} °राष्ट्रोपि — d) Ho नृपतिः सुख°

114.* Cited by *Lakṣ* 11.79 — a) wKt^{6} पक्षाणां — b) *Lakṣ* °मवस्थितं — d) GMd^{5} °ष्ट्राभिवृद्धये; Bo NNg [*but cor fh*] संग्रहे; all mss. have the reading संग्रहं except the following, which have the reading adopted: GMd^{1} TMd^{4} MTr^{4} MTr^{5} MTr^{6} *Nd Laks.*

115. Cited by *Lakṣ* 11.79 — b) wKt^{3} TMd^{3} °ग्रामाधिपतिं; GMd^{5} *Lakṣ* °ग्रामाधिपं; wKt^{1} °पति-स्तथा — c) TMd^{3} विंशतेशं; GMy विंशतेश; Tr^{2} विंशतीनां शतेशं; sOx^{1} sPu^{6} शतीशं च

ग्रामदोषान्समुत्पन्नान् ग्रामिकः शनकैः स्वयम् ।
शंसेद्ग्रामदशेशाय दशेशो विंशतीशिने ॥११६॥
विंशतीशस्तु तत्सर्वं शतेशाय निवेदयेत् ।
शंसेद्ग्रामशतेशस्तु सहस्रपतये स्वयम् ॥११७॥
यानि राजप्रदेयानि प्रत्यहं ग्रामवासिभिः ।
अन्नपानेन्धनादीनि ग्रामिकस्तान्यवाप्नुयात् ॥११८॥
दशी कुलं तु भुञ्जीत विंशी पञ्च कुलानि च ।
ग्रामं ग्रामशताध्यक्षः सहस्राधिपतिः पुरम् ॥११९॥
तेषां ग्राम्याणि कार्याणि पृथक्कार्याणि चैव हि ।
राज्ञोऽन्यः सचिवः स्निग्धस्तानि पश्येदतन्द्रितः ॥१२०॥
नगरे नगरे चैकं कुर्यात् सर्वार्थचिन्तकम् ।
उच्चैःस्थानं घोररूपं नक्षत्राणामिव ग्रहम् ॥१२१॥
स ताननुपरिक्रामेत् सर्वानेव सदा स्वयम् ।
तेषां वृत्तं परिणयेत् सम्यग्राष्ट्रेषु तच्चरैः ॥१२२॥

116. Pādas c-d omitted in Lo^{2} — a) BBe^{2} Be^{3} Ho Hy Jm NKt^{4} oOr Pu^{2} Pu^{4} Tj^{1} Tj^{2} MTr^{5} Wa *Ku Go Jolly* ग्रामे; wKt^{3} Ox^{3} °दोपात्स°; Pu^{2} Pu^{4} °त्पन्नात् — b) MTr^{5} ग्रामिणः; Lo^{3} शनके; Ho शनकैस्त्वयं — c) Be^{3} wKt^{6} संशेद्ग्राम°; wKt^{3} शंसेद्ग्रामं — d) Tj^{1} दशेशे; Jm Jo^{1} Kt^{2} विंशतीशिनं; GMd^{1} oOr विंशतीशके; GMy विंशतिशिते

117. Pādas a-b omitted in Lo^{2} — a) wKt^{6} Wa विंशतिश°; Ho Pu^{5} Pu^{7} MTr^{3} °तीशश्च — b) oOr शतेशेपि; NNg निवेदयन्; Jo^{1} BKt^{5} wKt^{6} निवेशयेत् — c) BKt^{5} wKt^{6} संशेद्ग्रा°; Be^{1} शंसेद्ग्रामे; Be^{1} Ho Wa °शतेशश्च — d) Tr^{2} सहपतये; Lo^{3} Tj^{1} सहस्राधिपते; Pu^{8} °पतये तथा

118. a) TMd^{4} तानि; TMd^{3} GMy यदि; Ox^{2} राज्य°; NNg TMd^{3} GMy राज्ञे; BBe^{2} MTr^{5} राज्ञः; Lo^{1} प्रदेयाय — c) Pu^{5} Pu^{7} अन्नं; wKt^{1} °पानेषुनादीनि — d) BKt^{5} ग्रामिणस्तान्निवेशयेत्; wKt^{6} ग्रामेशस्तान्निवेशयेत्; Ox^{3} ग्रामैक°; Pu^{5} Pu^{7} ग्रामिकस्वाम्यवा°; La^{1} Lo^{1} °कस्तानवा°

119. a) Bo TMd^{4} दशि; Ho दास; Bo कूलं; Lo^{1} कुले; Be^{1} NKt^{4} Lo^{2} MTr^{4} Wa च — b) sOx^{1} sPu^{6} विंशे; TMd^{4} विंशतिं च कुलानि; Pu^{8} दश कुलानि; Be^{3} Bo Ho BKt^{5} wKt^{6} Lo^{4} Lo^{5} TMd^{3} GMy NNg Ox^{2} Ox^{3} Pu^{8} Tr^{1} Tr^{2} MTr^{5} MTr^{6} [*Jolly* M Nd] तु — c) Ho GMd^{1} ग्रामग्राम°; wKt^{1} °शताधीशः; Tj^{2} °ध्यक्षाः — d) GMd^{1} TMd^{3} GMy परं

120. a) Ho NNg Tj^{2} ग्रामाणि — b) Be^{1} Wa पृथक्कर्माणि; Lo^{4} Lo^{5} Ox^{3} [*Jolly* M] प्रतिपन्नानि; wKt^{1} यानि च; NKt^{4} MTr^{4} MTr^{5} MTr^{6} ह — c) Bo राज्यो; Lo^{1} राजो; Be^{1} स्निग्धास्तानि; TMd^{3} GMy शुद्धस्तानि — d) Hy Tj^{2} °तन्त्रितः

121. Cited by *Lakṣ* 11.80 — a) oOr Tr^{1} *Lakṣ* चैव; Be^{3} TMd^{4} चैवं — b) Lo^{1} सर्वाग्रचि°; BBe^{2} सर्वात्मचि°; BKt^{5} wKt^{6} कार्यानुचिन्तकं [BKt^{5} कर्यान्य°]; Tr^{2} °साधकं — c) Ho गौररूपं; TMd^{3} साररूपं — d) Lo^{1} ग्रहः

122. Cited by *Lakṣ* 11.80 — a) Ho शतानुपरिक्रामेतु [*om* स]; Tr^{2} सा; Bo तामनु°; Tj^{2} तानुपरिसंक्रामेत्; GMd^{5} °परिग्राहेत्; Jm °क्रमे; Pu^{8} °क्रामान् — b) *Lakṣ* सर्वानायुक्तकान्स्वयं; GMd^{5} तदा — c) TMd^{3} GMy तेषां परिश्रयेच्चारैः; *Lakṣ* वृत्ते; La^{1} NPu^{1} Tr^{1} वृत्तिं; Lo^{2} दत्तं; BKt^{5} wKt^{6} वृत्तस्य विनयेत्; GMd^{5} परिचरेत्; NPu^{1} परिपालयेत्; Be^{1} Pu^{2} Pu^{4} परिज्ञाय — d) Be^{1} Lo^{4} Lo^{5} Ox^{3} [*Jolly* M^{4}] सम्यग्रूप-

राज्ञो हि रक्षाधिकृताः परस्वादायिनः शठाः ।
भृत्या भवन्ति प्रायेण तेभ्यो रक्षेदिमाः प्रजाः ॥१२३॥
ये कार्यिकेभ्योऽर्थमेव गृह्णीयुः पापचेतसः ।
तेषां सर्वस्वमादाय राजा कुर्यात् प्रवासनम् ॥१२४॥
राजकर्मसु युक्तानां स्त्रीणां प्रेष्यजनस्य च ।
प्रत्यहं कल्पयेद्वृत्तिं स्थानकर्मानुरूपतः ॥१२५॥
पणो देयोऽवकृष्टस्य षडुत्कृष्टस्य भक्तकम् ।
षाण्मासिकस्तथाच्छादो धान्यद्रोणश्च मासिकः ॥१२६॥
क्रयविक्रयमध्वानं भक्तं च सपरिव्ययम् ।
योगक्षेमं च संप्रेक्ष्य वणिजो दापयेत्करान् ॥१२७॥

तया चरैः [Be[1] Ox[3] °तयापि च]; BKt[5] wKt[6] समयाप्टेपु; GMd[5] ग्रामे राष्ट्रेषु; BCa wKt[1] Pu[2] Pu[4] सम्यग्रा-मेषु; Tr[1] तच्चिरैः; TMd[3] तच्छनैः

123. Cited by *Lakṣ* 12.568 — a) Pu[5] Pu[7] राज्ञोस्तु; Ox[2] राष्ट्रे हि; *Lakṣ* राष्ट्रेषु रक्षा°; Tr[2] राष्ट्रे रक्षा°; GMd[1] राष्ट्राधि°; TMd[3] °कृता; Lo[3] °कृतः; GMy °कृत; Bo °कृतिः; Be[1] °कृतान् — b) NPu[1] °दायिकाः; Ox[3] सठाः; Lo[3] शठः — c) Bo भवति — d) Pu[2] Pu[4] दक्षेदिमाः; Tj[1] रक्षेदिनाः; GMd[1] TMd[4] MTr[4] MTr[6] राक्षेत्सदा

124. a) BKt[5] wKt[6] [*but mc*] ये च कार्येभ्योप्येवं; Lo[3] एकार्थिभ्यो; Tr[1] MTr[5] कार्यकेभ्यो; wKt[1] कायिकेभ्यो; sOx[1] sPu[6] कार्षिकेभ्यो; TMd[3] कार्योभ्यर्थमेवं; BCa Tr[2] कार्यिभ्योर्थमेवं हि; Be[1] Bo Ho wKt[1] La[1] Lo[4] GMy Ox[3] Pu[2] Pu[3] Pu[4] Tr[1] MTr[6] Wa °र्थमेवं; NPu[1] °र्थं विगृह्णी°; Hy °र्थमेवैकं — a-b) GMd[1] TMd[4] oOr कार्येभ्योर्थमुपादाय ये कुर्युः कार्यमन्यथा [oOr कार्यिभ्यो; GMd[1] कार्यस्यार्थ°] — d) Lo[2] कुर्याच्चैव प्रवासनं; Tj[1] प्रवासिनं; GMd[5] प्रवासिनः

125. a) Jo[1] La[1] GMd[1] GMd[5] Tr[2] राजा; Pu[8] °कर्मणि — c) GMd[1] MTr[4] MTr[6] अन्वहं; NKt[4] कल्पयेहृष्टिं; MTr[3] °येद्वृत्तं — d) GMd[1] तेषां कालानुसारतः; Bo Jo[1] La[1] GMd[5] NPu[1] Pu[3] Tr[2] स्थानं; wKt[6] स्यात्तु कर्मा°; wKt[3] °नुरूप्यते; Ho °नुसारतः

126.* Cited by *Lakṣ* 11.82 — a) *Lakṣ* पणा देया; Bo Ho wKt[1] wKt[3] GMd[1] Tj[2] °पकृष्टस्य; Be[1][*mc to*] BKt[5] wKt[6] GMy NNg Pu[2] Pu[4] MTr[4] MTr[6] Wa °वकृष्टाय; Be[3] Tr[1] °पकृष्टाय; TMd[3] प्रकृष्टाय; TMd[4] निकृष्टस्य — b) Tr[1] वषड्डुत्कृष्टया भक्तं; Lo[3] Tj[1] षड्भुक्तस्यास्य चोदनं; *Lakṣ* षट् तूत्कृ°; Be[1] Be[3] BKt[5] TMd[3] GMy NNg Pu[2] Pu[4] षडुत्कृष्टाय; wKt[1] °ष्टस्य च; TMd[3] oOr भुक्तकं; GMd[1] TMd[4] भक्तकः; BBe[2] Bo BCa Ho Hy Jm Jo[1] Jo[2] wKt[1] Kt[2] wKt[3] BKt[5] wKt[6] La[1] La[2] Lo[1] Lo[4] Lo[5] NNg sOx[1] Ox[2] NPu[1] Pu[3] sPu[6] Pu[8] Tj[2] Tr[2] MTr[3] *Mandlik Jolly Jha KSS Dave* वेतनं; Be[1] Ox[3] चेतनं — c) Hy NKt[4] BKt[5] wKt[6] TMd[4] Ox[3] Tj[2] Tr[1] MTr[5] पण्मा°; GMd[1] °सिकास्त°; Lo[3] Tj[1] °सिकंस्त°; TMd[4] Pu[5] Pu[7] °सिकं तथा°; Hy °थाच्छान्दो;Pu[2] Pu[4] °थापादो — d) TMd[4] धान्यं द्रोणस्य मासिकं; MTr[5] धान्यं द्रोणश्च; Lo[5] °द्रोणाश्च; Hy Jm Jo[1] Kt[2] Lo[1] Tj[2] MTr[3] *Mandlik Jha KSS Dave* °द्रोणस्तु; TMd[3] GMd[5] GMy Tr[1] °द्रोणं च मासिकं

127. Cited by *Mādh* 1.404 — a) Pu[8] क्रयं; Jm क्रियविक्रिय°; Be[1] °ध्वान; wKt[1] °ध्मानं; Lo[1] °च्छानां — b) Jm wKt[1] La[1] Lo[3] Tj[1] भुक्तं; sOx[1] sPu[6] चायपरि°; GMy च परितोव्ययं; TMd[3] च परितोह्ययं; Lo[1] सपरिक्षयं; Be[3] GMd[1] Ox[2] सपरिच्छदं; GMd[5] सपरिच्छदः — c) Lo[1] oOr *Mādh* योगं; Hy Tr[2] *om* च; wKt[1] संप्रेष्य — d) GMd[1] TMd[4] MTr[4] MTr[6] वणिग्भ्यो हारयेत्करान्; wKt[6] बलिं यो दाप°; wKt[3] °त्करात्; NKt[4] °त्कवन्

यथा फलेन युज्येत राजा कर्ता च कर्मणाम् ।
तथावेक्ष्य नृपो राष्ट्रे कल्पयेत्सततं करान् ॥१२८॥
यथाल्पाल्पमदन्त्याद्यं वार्योकोवत्सषट्पदाः ।
तथाल्पाल्पो ग्रहीतव्यो राष्ट्राद्राज्ञाब्दिकः करः ॥१२९॥
पञ्चाशद्भाग आदेयो राज्ञा पशुहिरण्ययोः ।
धान्यानामष्टमो भागः षष्ठो द्वादश एव वा ॥१३०॥
आददीताथ षड्भागं द्रुमांसमधुसर्पिषाम् ।
गन्धौषधिरसानां च पुष्पमूलफलस्य च ॥१३१॥
पत्रशाकतृणानां च चर्मणां वैदलस्य च ।
मृन्मयानां च भाण्डानां सर्वस्याश्ममयस्य च ॥१३२॥
म्रियमाणोऽप्याददीत न राजा श्रोत्रियात्करम् ।

128. Verses 128 and 129 transposed in BKt[5] wKt[6] Lo[4] Lo[5] Ox[3]; not commented by *Rc;* pādas c-d omitted in Pu[5]. Cited by *Lakṣ* 11.88; *Mādh* 1.404 — a) TMd[3] यथा परे भुञ्जीत; Ox[2] कालेन; GMy भुञ्जीत — b) TMd[3] राज; Jo[1] कर्मणात्; Tr[2] कर्मणि; wKt[6] Tr[1] कर्मिणां — c) Be[3] Kt[2] तथापेक्ष्य; NKt[4] Lo[4] Lo[5] Ox[3] *Lakṣ* तथा वीक्ष्य; BKt[5] wKt[6] La[1] Tj[1] राष्ट्रं; Be[3] राज्ये — d) TMd[4] कल्पयेत तं करान्; TMd[3] कल्पयेत्पतिं करान्; GMd[1] वर्तये°; Ho कल्पेत सततं

129. Omitted in Pu[5]. Cited by *Mādh* 1.404 — a) TMd[3] GMy यथाकल्पमद°; TMd[4] °दन्त्याद्य; TMd[3] °दत्याद्यं — b) wKt[1] वार्योतकारषट्पदाः; La[1] GMd[1] TMd[3] TMd[4] GMd[5] GMy oOr Ox[2] Tr[1] MTr[4] MTr[5] MTr[6]वत्सवार्योकषट्पदाः; Bo वायोको°; Ox[3] वार्योके°; wKt[3] वार्योक°; Lo[3] Tj[1] वार्योका°; NNg जलौको°; Pu[2] Pu[4] वर्षौको°; Hy °पदः — c) Lo[5] यथा°; Be[1] Ho La[1] Pu[2] Pu[4] Pu[7] MTr[5] तथाल्पोल्पो; Be[1] Be[3] Bo wKt[1] TMd[3] oOr Pu[7] Tj[1] Tr[1] MTr[5]गृहीतव्यो; w Kt[3] गृहीतव्या — d) TMd[4] राष्ट्रे राज्ञा°; Pu[7] राज्ञा राष्ट्राब्दिकः; wKt[6] Tj[1] °द्रजाब्दिकः; TMd[4] °ज्ञाभिहितः; Ho Lo[3] Pu[7] परः; Lo[2] परं; Tj[1] पुरः

130. Not commented by *Rc* — a) Tr[2] °शद्भागं; NNg [*but cor fh*] आदेशो; wKt[1] आकृष्टो — b) Ho राजा — c) BBe[2] Pu[5] Pu[7] भागो; Hy भगः; Ox[3] भागा — d) Kt[2] एवकः; Be[1] Bo wKt[6] sOx[1] Ox[3] Pu[5] sPu[6] Pu[7] Wa [*Jolly* M[4–5] G] च

131. Not commented by *Nd*; pāda-d omitted in Pu[5]. Cited by *Lakṣ* 11.88 — a) *Lakṣ* आदद्याच्चाथ; wKt[1] La[1] °दीतार्थ; GMy °दीताच; TMd[3] °धीताच; Ox[3] °दातोथ; wKt[1] °भागः; TMd[3] °भाग — b) MTr[5] द्रुमाणामथ सर्पिषां; GMd[1] मधुमांसं च सर्पिषां; Be[1] Lo[1] GMd[5] Ox[3] Pu[2] Pu[4] Wa द्रुमाणां मधु°; MTr[4] द्रुवाणां मधु°; Tj[2] द्रुमामधु°; Lo[3] °सर्पिषं — c) Jo[2] GMd[5] Pu[5] Pu[7] गन्धोषधि°; Lo[2] गन्धोबधि°; [*Jolly* M[8]] गन्धासवरसानां; Bo °पधी° — c-d) BKt[5] wKt[6] °षधिफलानां च पष्पमूलरसस्य च — d) sOx[1] sPu[6] तु

132. Pādas a-c omitted in Pu[5]. Cited by *Lakṣ* 11.88 — a) TMd[3] तत्र शाक°; Be[3] °शाकमृणालानां [*om* च]; *Rn* comments: द्रुमाणमिति [in place of तृणानां] पाठो मेधातिथेः; *Me*'s com. on this verse has not survived — b) TMd[4] काष्ठानां च नरस्य च; La[1] *Lakṣ* कर्मणां; NNg पात्राणां; BBe[2] वेदलस्य; TMd[3] बैदळस्य; Tr[1] बैदलस्य; Be[1] Be[3] NKt[4] Lo[2] GMd[1] Pu[2] Pu[4] Pu[7] Tr[2] MTr[4] MTr[5]MTr[6] [*Jolly* G] *Lakṣ* वैणवस्य; Tj[1] दैवलस्य; wKt[3] चदलस्य; Tr[2] तु; Ox[3]वा — c) TMd[4] मृन्मयानां च चार्यानां; Ho Kt[2] wKt[3] wKt[6] Lo[1] TMd[3] sOx[1] sPu[6] Tj[1] Tr[1] मृण्म°; Lo[4] *om* च; Wa पात्राणां — d) TMd[4] °स्यात्ममयस्य; Tr[2] °स्यात्रमयस्य

न च क्षुधास्य संसीदेच्छ्रोत्रियो विषये वसन् ॥१३३॥
यस्य राज्ञस्तु विषये श्रोत्रियः सीदति क्षुधा ।
तस्यापि तत्क्षुधा राष्ट्रमचिरादेव सीदति ॥१३४॥
श्रुतवृत्ते विदित्वास्य वृत्तिं धर्म्यां प्रकल्पयेत् ।
संरक्षेत्सर्वतश्चैनं पिता पुत्रमिवौरसम् ॥१३५॥
संरक्ष्यमाणो राज्ञा यं कुरुते धर्ममन्वहम् ।
तेनायुर्वर्धते राज्ञो द्रविणं राष्ट्रमेव च ॥१३६॥
यत्किंचिदपि वर्षस्य दापयेत्करसंज्ञितम् ।
व्यवहारेण जीवन्तं राष्ट्रे राजा पृथग्जनम् ॥१३७॥
कारुकाञ्छिल्पिनश्चैव शूद्रांश्चात्मोपजीविनः ।
एकैकं कारयेत्कर्म मासि मासि महीपतिः ॥१३८॥
नोच्छिन्द्यादात्मनो मूलं परेषां चातितृष्णया ।

133. Omitted in Pu^{4}; not commented by *Rc Nd;* after म्रियमाणो Ox^{3} omits up to संरक्ष्यमाणो of verse 136a [haplo]. Cited by *Mādh* 1.408 — a) Hy श्रिय°; Wa °ददीते; TMd^{3} °दधीत — b) TMd^{4} राजा न; Be^{3} °यात्करान्; TMd^{3} °यान् करान् — c) Pu^{5} Pu^{7} [*Jolly* G] न च गच्छेद्विषादं च श्रो°; TMd^{4} संसिद्धश्रो°; GMd^{1} संसीदे श्रो° — d) Bo Tr^{1} विषयो

134.* Omitted in Ox^{3}; not commented by *Nd Rc;* pādas a-b omitted in GMd^{5}. Cited by *Vij* 3.44; *Lakṣ* 11.171; *Mādh* 1.408 — a) Tr^{2} राज्ञश्च; Bo GMy राज्ञस्य — b) TMd^{3} श्रोत्रियाः; *Lakṣ* ब्राह्मणः; Wa सीदते; TMd^{3} सीधति — c) TMd^{4} तं क्षुधा; sOx^{1} sPu^{6} च क्षुधा; MTr^{4} MTr^{6} तत्क्षुधी — c-d) Pu^{5} Pu^{7} [*Jolly* G] *Vij* तस्य सीदति तद्राष्ट्रं दुर्भिक्षव्याधिपीडितं [cf. 8.22] — d) BBe^{2} Bo Hy Jm Jo^{1} Kt^{2} BKt^{5} wKt^{6} La^{2} Lo^{1} TMd^{4} sOx^{1} Ox^{2} NPu^{1} sPu^{6} Pu^{8} Tj^{2} Tr^{2} MTr^{3} *Lakṣ Mandlik Jolly Jha KSS Dave* °चिरेणैव; Lo^{4} Lo^{5} °चिरेणावसीदति; GMd^{5} नश्यति

135. Omitted in Ox^{3}; not commented by *Nd Rc.* Cited by *Lakṣ* 11.171; *Mādh* 1.408 — a) wKt^{1} श्रुति°; Hy श्रुते; Lo^{1} Pu^{3} Pu^{8} श्रुतशीले; TMd^{3} GMy °वृत्तो — b) *Lakṣ* वृत्तिधर्मं; BKt^{5} wKt^{6} धर्म्यां वृत्तिं; Tj^{1} धाम्यां; Lo^{5} GMy धर्म्या; Tj^{2} धर्म्य; Ho wKt^{1} wKt^{3} MTr^{3} धर्मां; oOr धर्मान्; TMd^{4} धर्मे; Pu^{5} Pu^{7} [*Jolly* G] च कल्पयेत्; NKt^{4} विकल्पयेत्; TMd^{3} तकल्पयेत्; Tr^{2} प्रकारयेत् — c) Pu^{5} Pu^{7} [*Jolly* G] भयेभ्यश्च तथा रक्षेत्; TMd^{4} Wa रक्षयेत्स°; Lo^{2} °तश्चेनं; Lo^{4} Lo^{5} [*Jolly* M] °तस्त्वेनं; NKt^{4} °तश्चैवं; Be^{1} Pu^{2} Pu^{4} °तश्चास्य

136. Not commented by *Nd* — a) Bo Lo^{1} स रक्ष्य°; Be^{1} Bo wKt^{3} BKt^{5} wKt^{6} Lo^{1} NNg sOx^{1} NPu^{1} Pu^{3} sPu^{6} संरक्षमाणो; wKt^{1} संलक्षमाणो; Be^{1} Pu^{2} Pu^{4} राज्ञोयं; wKt^{3} राज्ञयं; TMd^{3} GMd^{5} यः; GMy याः — c) Ox^{3} तेन तद्वर्धते; Jm राज्ञा; MTr^{6} राज्ञे — d) Pu^{5} Pu^{7} राष्ट्रं द्रविणमेव च; wKt^{1} राष्ट्रमन्वहं

137. a) GMd^{1} वर्षस्यात् — b) TMd^{3} GMy दापयत्क°; Be^{1} °येत्कार°; NNg °संज्ञतं; Ho °संज्ञिकं — d) Pu^{3} Pu^{8} राज्ये राजा; Hy Jm Jo^{1} Jo^{2} Kt^{2} Lo^{3} Tj^{1} Tj^{2} MTr^{3} *Mandlik Jolly Jha KSS Dave* राजा राष्ट्रे; wKt^{6} राज्ञा; NPu^{1} पृथग्जितं

138. The sequence in Lo^{3} Tj^{1} is: 138, 140cd, 139cd, 140ab, 139ab, 141 — a) Pu^{3} कारुकं शिल्पि°; Hy कारुकी शिल्पि°; MTr^{5} कारुजाञ्छिल्पि°; GMd^{5} कारुणां शिल्पि° — b) sOx^{1} sPu^{6} शूद्राश्चा°; TMd^{3} GMy शूलांचा°; Be^{1} °श्चान्योप°; [*Jolly* M^{8}] °श्चाल्पोप°; oOr °श्चैवोप°; wKt^{1} °श्चार्थोप°; GMy °जीवनः; wKt^{3} °जीवितः — c) GMd^{1} एकेकं; Lo^{1} हारये° — d) Be^{3} Lo^{2} GMd^{1} TMd^{3} TMd^{4} GMd^{5} GMy oOr Tr^{1} MTr^{4} MTr^{5} MTr^{6} मासे मासे

उच्छिन्दन्ह्यात्मनो मूलमात्मानं तांश्च पीडयेत् ॥१३९॥
तीक्ष्णश्चैव मृदुश्च स्यात् कार्यं वीक्ष्य महीपतिः ।
तीक्ष्णश्चैव मृदुश्चैव राजा भवति संमतः ॥१४०॥
अमात्यमुख्यं धर्मज्ञं प्राज्ञं दान्तं कुलोद्गतम् ।
स्थापयेदासने तस्मिन् खिन्नः कार्येक्षणे नृणाम् ॥१४१॥
एवं सर्वं विधायेदमितिकर्तव्यमात्मनः ।
युक्तश्चैवाप्रमत्तश्च परिरक्षेदिमाः प्रजाः ॥१४२॥
विक्रोशन्त्यो यस्य राष्ट्राद्ध्रियन्ते दस्युभिः प्रजाः ।
संपश्यतः सभृत्यस्य मृतः स न स जीवति ॥१४३॥
क्षत्रियस्य परो धर्मः प्रजानामेव पालनम् ।

139. Omitted in Tr^1. Cited by *Lakṣ* 11.93 — a) sOx^1 sPu^6 नोच्छिद्या° — b) TMd^3 GMy परेषामपि तृष्णया; Wa परे चाति°; Be^1 Tj^1 वाति°; MTr^4 MTr^6 चापि तृष्णया; BKt^5 चानिकप्यवा; wKt^6 चानिरूप्यवा — c) MTr^6 उच्छिन्द्यन्ह्या°; TMd^3 उच्छिन्द्याह्या°; Ox^2 Wa उच्छिद्य ह्या°; GMy उच्छिन्द्यात्मनो; Lo^4 Lo^5 Ox^3 NPu^1 Pu^2 Pu^4 *Lakṣ* उच्छिन्दन्नात्मनो; Jo^2 उच्छिन्दादात्मनो; NKt^4 उच्छिन्दत्यात्मनो — d) Lo^1 °त्मनश्च निपीडयेत्; wKt^3 TMd^3 NNg Tj^1 ताश्च; TMd^4 सिद्धयेत्

140. Pādas a-b omitted in NKt^4 La^1 sOx^1 Tr^1 [haplo] and *ma* in Be^3. Cited by *Lakṣ* 11.152— a) Pu^5 Pu^7 [*Jolly* G] न तीक्ष्णो न मृदुश्च; BKt^5 wKt^6 मृदुस्तु; Lo^2 मृदुर्वा; Bo oOr मृदुश्चैव [*om* स्यात्] — b) oOr कार्यं चैव; BCa Lo^2 प्रेक्ष्य; Pu^2 Pu^4 दृष्ट्वा; Be^1 दृष्ट्या — c) NPu^1 मृदुश्चैव भवेत्तीक्ष्णो — d) Pu^5 Pu^7 [*but cor*] भवन्ति; TMd^3 GMy Tr^1 [*Jolly* Gr] भवति धर्मतः; GMd^1 सर्वतः

141. a) wKt^1 अमात्यं; Lo^1 आमात्य°; Pu^5 Pu^7 °मुख्य; NKt^4 °मुखा; Pu^2 Pu^4 °मुख — b) GMy प्राज्ञ; TMd^4 प्रजादन्तं; Lo^4 Lo^5 Ox^3 [*Jolly* M$^{4-5}$] शान्तं दान्तं; Bo दानं; Lo^1 दातृकुलो°; Pu^2 Pu^4 कुलोद्गतां; wKt^1 wKt^3 GMd^5 oOr Pu^5 Pu^7 Tr^2 [*Jolly* M G Nd]*Jolly* कुलोद्भवं [cf. 7.54 note] — c) Tr^1 MTr^6 स्वस्मिन् — d) GMy खिन्नं; TMd^3 चिन्नं; Lo^2 कार्योक्षणे; TMd^4 कार्यक्षणे; Tj^2 कार्येखिले; NKt^4 नृणं; MTr^5 नृपः

142. Cited by *Mādh* 1.414 — a) Wa विधायैवमि°; Be^3 विधातव्यमिति° — c) Lo^1 TMd^4 GMy °श्चैवप्रम°; Pu^8 °मत्तस्य — d) Wa °दिमां प्रजां

143.* Pādas a-b omitted in BBe^2 [haplo], and pādas c-d in NKt^4. Cited by *Lakṣ* 12.511 — a) wKt^1 MTr^5 विक्रोशन्तो; TMd^3 TMd^4 °शन्ते; BKt^5 wKt^6 °शन्त्य; Bo °शत्त्यो — a-b) TMd^4 Ox^3 MTr^4 MTr^6 राष्ट्रे ह्रियन्ते; TMd^3 राष्ट्रं ध्रियन्ते; GMd^1 राष्ट्रे व्रजन्ते; GMd^5 राष्ट्रे व्ययन्ते — b) TMd^4 राष्ट्राद्ध्रियते; Lo^5 राष्ट्राद्ध्रीयन्ते; Tr^1 राष्ट्राद्धीयन्ते; Be^3 BKt^5 wKt^6 NNg राष्ट्राद् हृयन्ते; NKt^4 राष्ट्राद् ह्रियते; Wa राष्ट्राद्द्रयन्ते — c) Bo संपृच्छन्तः; Pu^8 संभृत्यस्य; *Lakṣ* सभृत्यश्च; wKt^1 सदुतस्य — d) TMd^3 GMd^5 GMy Tr^1 MTr^4 MTr^6 स मृतः स न जीवति; Wa मृत एव स जीवति; Pu^5 Pu^7 [*Jolly* G] मृतस्तु न जीवति; NPu^1 मृतश्च न स; GMd^1 NNg मृतस्तु न स; oOr Ox^2 मृतः सन्न स; Lo^1 मृतः सन्न तु; BBe^2 मृतस्य न स; Be^1 Ho TMd^4 Pu^8 *Lakṣ* स च न जी°; Be^3 Lo^4 Lo^5 sOx^1 Pu^2 Pu^4 sPu^6 स न च जी°; Tr^2 स तु न जी°; [*Jolly* Nd] स स न जी°; Hy Jm Jo^1 Kt^2 wKt^3 BKt^5 wKt^6 Pu^3 Tj^2 MTr^3 [*Jolly* R] *Ku Go Mandlik Jha KSS Dave* स न तु जी°

Additional verse in wKt^1 Pu^3:

प्रजापीडनसंतापात्समुद्भूतो हुताशनः ।
राज्ञः श्रियं कुलं प्राणान्नाहत्वा विनिवर्तते ॥

b) Pu^3 हृताशनः— c) wKt^1 कुलं श्रियं — d) Pu^3 °न्नादग्ध्वा

निर्दिष्टफलभोक्ता हि राजा धर्मेण युज्यते ॥१४४॥
उत्थाय पश्चिमे यामे कृतशौचः समाहितः ।
हुत्वाग्निं ब्राह्मणांश्चार्च्य प्रविशेत्स शुभां सभाम् ॥१४५॥
तत्र स्थितः प्रजाः सर्वाः प्रतिनन्द्य विसर्जयेत् ।
विसृज्य च प्रजाः सर्वा मन्त्रयेत्सह मन्त्रिभिः ॥१४६॥
गिरिपृष्ठं समारुह्य प्रासादं वा रहोगतः ।
अरण्ये निःशलाके वा मन्त्रयेताविभावितः ॥१४७॥
यस्य मन्त्रं न जानन्ति समागम्य पृथग्जनाः ।
स कृत्स्नां पृथिवीं भुङ्क्ते कोशहीनोऽपि पार्थिवः ॥१४८॥
जडमूकान्धबधिरांस्तैर्यग्योनान्वयोऽधिकान् ।

144. Omitted in NKt^4. Cited by *Dev* 2.450 — a) Lo^5 TMd^3 धर्मं — b) *Dev* प्रजानां परिपालनं; Ho TMd^4 रक्षणं — c) Bo निदृष्ट°; Pu^5 Pu^7 निर्विष्ट°; Pu^3 निर्दिष्टाः; Be^1 °भोगा हि; MTr^4 MTr^6 °भोक्तापि — d) GMy राजधर्मेण

145.* Pādas a-b omitted in NKt^4 and pādas c-d in TMd^4; not commented by *Rc*. Cited by *Lakṣ* 11.101; *Dev* 3.43 — b) Lo^5 Tj^1 कृतः — c) Be^1 oOr sOx^1 NPu^1 Pu^2 Pu^4 sPu^6 Tr^2 MTr^5 हुत्वाग्नीन्ब्राह्म° [Be^1 न्ब्रह्म°]; La^2 हुत्वाग्निर्ब्राह्म°; BBe^2 Be^3 Bo BCa Hy Jm Jo^1 Kt^2 Lo^2 Lo^4 Ox^3 Pu^3 Pu^5 Pu^7 Pu^8 Tj^2 MTr^3 [*Jolly* M G] *Mandlik Jolly Jha KSS Dave* हुताग्निर्ब्राह्म°; NKt^4 wKt^6 Lo^5 हुताग्निब्राह्म°; wKt^1 La^1 Ox^2 हुताग्नीन्ब्राह्म°; Lo^1 कृताग्निर्ब्राह्म° [*Go, Ku* appear to support this reading]; *Dev* [vl] भक्तात्रं ब्राह्म°; Be^1 BCa wKt^1 NKt^4 BKt^5 wKt^6 Lo^1 Lo^4 GMd^5 NNg oOr Ox^2 Ox^3 NPu^1 Pu^2 Pu^3 Pu^4 Pu^5 Pu^7 MTr^5 Wa [*Jolly* M G] *Dev Jolly* °ह्मणानर्च्य; Be^3 Jo^2 wKt^3 Lo^2 Lo^3 Tj^1 °ह्मणानार्च्य; La^1 °ह्मणान्भ्यर्च्य [sic]; Bo °श्चार्च्यः — d) Jo^2 Lo^3 Tj^1 प्रविशेच्च; Lo^1 TMd^3 GMy Ox^3 Tr^1 MTr^5 प्रविशेत्तु; *Dev* प्रविशेद्वै; BCa Lo^4 Lo^5 GMd^5 [*Jolly* M^4] प्रविशेत; Jo^1 Lo^2 Tr^2 प्रविशेत्सुशुभां; Be^3 Ho Jo^2 wKt^1 Lo^3 GMd^1 TMd^3 GMd^5 GMy oOr Tj^1 MTr^5 MTr^6 *Mādh* सभां शुभां; Lo^1 शुभां प्रजां

146.* Omitted in TMd^4; not commented by *Rc*; pādas b and d transposed in Jm. Cited by *Mādh* 1.410; pādas a-b cited by *Lakṣ* 11.101; *Dev* 3.61 — a) *Lakṣ* तत्रास्थिताः; oOr तदा स्थितः; Be^1 Ho GMd^1 Ox^3 MTr^4 MTr^5 MTr^6 [*Jolly* M^4 Nd] स्थिताः — b) NKt^4 सर्वा अभिनन्द्य — c) Bo NKt^4 wKt^6 Ox^2 Pu^8 MTr^3 विसर्ज्य; TMd^3 सर्वान् — d) Be^1 Be^3 wKt^1 La^1 Lo^2 Lo^4 Lo^5 oOr Ox^3 Pu^2 Pu^4 मन्त्रयेन्मन्त्रिभिः सह [Pu^2 Pu^4 मन्त्रयन्म°]

147. Pādas a-b omitted in TMd^4. Cited by *Lakṣ* 11.102; *Mādh* 1.410 — a) sOx^1 sPu^6 गिरिशृङ्गं; Tr^2 °पृष्ठे; BBe^2 °पृष्ठः; Ox^3 [*Jolly* M^{5-8-9}] °पृष्ठमुपारुह्य; MTr^4 समागम्य; Pu^2 Pu^4 °रुह्यं — b) NPu^1 च; Be^3 Ho Jo^2 wKt^1 Lo^3 MTr^4 [*Jolly* R] °गतं — c) Wa अरण्य; Pu^2 °शिलाके; NNg °शलाको; TMd^4 च — d) Be^3 मन्त्रयेन्मन्त्रिभिः सह [cf. 7.146d]; BBe^2 मन्त्रयेताभिभा°; BCa मन्त्रयेतविभा°; Tr^2 मन्त्रयेतुविभा°; La^1 मन्त्रयीताविभा°; TMd^4 मन्त्रयेतात्मभा°; Hy Jm Jo^1 Kt^2 wKt^3 Lo^3 Lo^4 Lo^5 NNg oOr Ox^2 Ox^3 MTr^3 *Mandlik Jolly Jha KSS Dave* मन्त्रयेदविभा°; Pu^5 Pu^7 *Lakṣ* मन्त्रयेद्वाविभा°; wKt^6 °भावतः

148. Cited by *Lakṣ* 11.102 — a) Ho तस्य; Bo BKt^5 wKt^6 जानाति — a-b) GMd^5 यस्य मन्त्रं समागम्य न जानन्ति पृथग्जनाः — b) Be^1 NKt^4 Lo^1 NPu^1 Pu^2 Pu^4 Pu^5 Pu^7 समागत्य; TMd^3 समागत; Bo पृथग्जनः — c) TMd^4 ते कृत्स्नां; La^1 कृत्स्नां मेदिनीं; TMd^4 कृत्स्नां वसुधां — d) MTr^3 कोशलीनो; NKt^4 श्वासहीनो; Wa °हीनापि; GMy °हीनोप्यपार्थिवः; TMd^3 °हीनोह्यपार्थिवः

स्त्रीम्लेच्छव्याधितव्यङ्गान् मन्त्रकालेऽपसारयेत् ॥१४९॥
भिन्दन्त्यवमता मन्त्रं तैर्यग्योनास्तथैव च ।
स्त्रियश्चैव विशेषेण तस्मात्तत्रादृतो भवेत् ॥१५०॥
मध्यंदिनेऽर्धरात्रे वा विश्रान्तो विगतक्लमः ।
चिन्तयेद्धर्मकामार्थान् सार्धं तैरेक एव वा ॥१५१॥
परस्परविरुद्धानां तेषां च समुपार्जनम् ।
कन्यानां संप्रदानं च कुमाराणां च रक्षणम् ॥१५२॥
दूतसंप्रेषणं चैव कार्यशेषं तथैव च ।

149.* Cited by *Lakṣ* 11.103 — a) TMd⁴ GMd⁵ MTr⁶ जडान्धबधिरान्मूकांस्तै° ; BKt⁵ जन° ; wKt⁶ जल° ; BCa Ho NKt⁴ La¹ Lo¹ TMd³ oOr Pu³ Tr¹ MTr⁵ जडान्धमूक° ; GMd¹ जडान्धमूर्ख° — b) Be¹ Be³ Jo¹ Kt² TMd³ GMy Pu² Pu⁴ Pu⁵ Pu⁷ Tj¹ MTr³ *Jolly* °रांस्तिर्यग्यो° ; Lo⁴ Ox² Tr² °ग्यौनान्व° ; wKt³ Pu³ MTr³ °ग्योनीन्व° ; BKt⁵ wKt⁶ GMd⁵ GMy Ox³ Pu⁴ Wa °ग्योन्यान्व° ; Be¹ BBe² Bo BCa [*but mc*] Ho Jm Jo¹ wKt¹ Kt² wKt³ La¹ La² Lo² Lo⁴ Lo⁵ NNg oOr sOx¹ Ox³ NPu¹ Pu² Pu⁴ Pu⁵ sPu⁶ Pu⁷ Pu⁸ MTr⁵ Wa [*Jolly* M G] *Mandlik Jolly Jha KSS Dave* °न्वयोतिगान्; GMd¹ °न्वयोगतान् — c) NKt⁴ BKt⁵ wKt⁶ Tr² स्त्रीक्लीबव्याधि° ; TMd⁴ GMd⁵ °व्याधितान्व्य° ; GMd¹ °व्याधितोव्य° ; sOx¹ sPu⁶ °व्यङ्गा; Tr¹ °व्यग्रा — d) MTr⁵ मन्त्रे तु प्रतिषेधयेत्; Pu⁵ °कालेपसरयेत्; sOx¹ sPu⁶ °काले प्रसारयेत्; MTr⁴ MTr⁶ °काले प्रसाधयेत्; wKt³ wKt⁶ Tr² °काले प्रषेधयेत्; Ox³ °काले प्रशोधयेत्; Be³ °काले प्ररोधयेत्; Pu³ °कालेपरोधयेत्; Bo BCa [*but cor*] Lo¹ Lo⁴ Lo⁵ GMd¹ TMd³ GMy NNg Ox² Pu⁷ Pu⁸ *Lakṣ* °कालेपसेधयेत्; Tr¹ °कालेवसेधयेत्; BBe² NKt⁴ °कालेपसेवयेत्; Be¹ Pu² Pu⁴ °काले निषेधयेत्; TMd⁴ °काले न सेवयेत्; NPu¹ Wa °काले प्रवासयेत्; BKt⁵ °काले प्रधिधयेत्;Ho [*cor to*] °कालेपि सारयेत्; *Me* gives विशोधयेत् and अपशोधयेत् unclear which is root; *Go Nd Ku Rn Rc Mr* support edition.

150. Cited by *Lakṣ* 11.103 — a) GMd¹ *Lakṣ* निन्दन्त्य° ; Hy निबन्त्य° ; Bo भन्दन्त्य° ; wKt¹ भिन्द्यव° ; TMd⁴ भिन्दन्तेवहते; TMd³ भिन्दन्त्येवंकृतो; GMy भिन्दन्त्यवंकृतो; Tr¹ °वमतो; GMd⁵ °वगता; NNg °वमता नित्यं; BKt⁵ wKt⁶ मन्त्रान् — b) Jo¹ Lo² Lo⁴ TMd³ GMy Pu⁵ Pu⁷ तिर्यग्यो° ; Tr¹ °ग्योनस्त° ; Tr² °ग्यौनास्त° ; BKt⁵ wKt⁶ TMd³ GMd⁵ GMy °ग्योन्यास्त° ; MTr⁶ °ग्योन्यस्त° ; Lo⁴ Lo⁵ °ग्योनांस्त° ; wKt¹ °ग्योना तथैव; Be³ हि — d) TMd³ GMy तस्मात्रावमतो भवेत्; TMd⁴ तस्मात्तानिदृतो; Ox³ तस्मात्तत्वादृतो; Be³ तस्मात्तद्रहितो; GMd¹ GMd⁵ Tr¹ MTr⁴ तस्मात्तास्वादृतो; Pu⁵ °दृता; Be¹ NPu¹ Pu² Pu⁴ MTr⁶ °वृतो; Hy भवत्

151. Cited in *Lakṣ* 11.106; *Mādh* 1.410 — a) Tr² मध्ये दिने; wKt¹ °दिने दुरापे वा; *Lakṣ* °दिने च रात्रौ च; GMd⁵ NPu¹ °रात्रौ; wKt³ °रात्रो; TMd⁴ °रात्रिर्वा; NKt⁴ wKt⁶ TMd³ GMd⁵ GMy MTr⁴ च — b) Lo² विश्रान्तौ; NKt⁴ विद्यान्तो; Tr² विगतो; wKt¹ Tj¹ विगतः; wKt¹ Lo⁴ TMd⁴ Ox³ विगतक्रमः — c) Tr² °द्धर्ममर्थान्; TMd⁴ °कामार्थं — d) GMd¹ oOr साद्धयं तैरेक; Pu² Pu³ Pu⁴ Tr² एव च; Be³ एव तु

152. Pādas c-d cited by *Lakṣ* 11.106; *Mādh* 1.410 — a) Lo⁵ परस्परः; Be³ परस्परं; Pu⁵ Pu⁷ परस्पराविं° ; Bo °विशुद्धानां — b) GMd¹ तु; TMd⁴ चैवमुपार्जनं; wKt⁶ °पार्जितं; NNg °पार्जिनं; Tr¹ °पार्जवं; GMd⁵ °पाश्रतः — c) GMd⁵ कन्यायः; Tj¹ कल्पानां; MTr³ अन्यानां; Pu⁴ कन्यकानां प्रदानं; wKt¹ कल्याणमनुदानं; TMd⁴ सुप्रदानं; wKt³ °दानां; GMy °दारं — d) NNg रक्षिणं; TMd⁴ लक्षणं

Additional verses in Lo¹:

आदाने च विसर्गे च तथा प्रैषनिषेधयोः ।
पञ्चमो चानुवचने व्यवहारस्य चेक्षणे ॥
दण्डशुद्धो समायोक्तस्तेनाष्टगतिको नृपः ।
कष्टं चाष्टविधं कर्म पञ्चवर्गं च तत्त्वतः ॥

अन्तःपुरप्रचारं च प्रणिधीनां च चेष्टितम् ॥१५३॥
कृत्स्नं चाष्टविधं कर्म पञ्चवर्गं च तत्त्वतः ।
अनुरागापरागौ च प्रचारं मण्डलस्य च ॥१५४॥
मध्यमस्य प्रचारं च विजिगीषोश्च चेष्टितम् ।
उदासीनप्रचारं च शत्रोश्चैव प्रयत्नतः ॥१५५॥
एताः प्रकृतयो मूलं मण्डलस्य समासतः ।
अष्टौ चान्याः समाख्याता द्वादशैव तु ताः स्मृताः ॥१५६॥
अमात्यराष्ट्रदुर्गार्थदण्डाख्याः पञ्च चापराः ।
प्रत्येकं कथिता ह्येताः संक्षेपेण द्विसप्ततिः ॥१५७॥

153. Omitted in Lo[1]. Cited by *Lakṣ* 11.106; *Mādh* 1.410 — a) *Mādh* दूतस्य प्रेषणं; NKt[4] दूतानां प्रेषणं; MTr[4] आत्मसंप्रेक्षणं; GMy °संप्रेक्षणं; NPu[1] °संरक्षणं — b) NKt[4] कार्यश्रेष्ठं; GMd[1] कार्यश्शेषं; Tr[1] कार्यंशेषं; Lo[5] कार्येशेषं — c) Tj[1] अन्तःपुरं; GMy अन्तःपुरः; *Mādh* °प्रजानाञ्च — d) GMd[1] प्रणधीनां; Ox[3] प्रणिधानं; Tr[2] प्रणवीणां; NKt[4] *om* च; Bo sPu[6] [*but cor*] वेष्टितं

154. *ma* in BKt[5]. Cited by *Lakṣ* 11.107; *Mādh* 1.411 — a) TMd[3] कृत्यं; GMd[5] कृच्छ्रं; Bo वाष्ट°; Be[1] °विधे; wKt[1] धर्मं; wKt[6] धर्म — b) Lo[5] पञ्चवर्गां; *Lakṣ* यत्नतः — d) Tr[2] प्रकारं; wKt[3] प्रचालं; Pu[5] Pu[7] [*Jolly* G] तु

Additional verses in GMd[1] TMd[3] TMd[4] GMd[5] GMy Tr[1] MTr[4] MTr[6] [*Jolly* Nd Gr] *Mandlik KSS Dave*; commented by *Nd;* given as citation (probably from *AŚ* 1.12.23–4) in *Bh*, from which it probably entered the ST ms. tradition:

वने वनचराः कार्याः श्रमणाटविकादयः ।
परप्रवृत्तिज्ञानार्थं शीघ्राश्चारपरंपराः ॥१॥
परस्य चैते बोद्धव्यास्तादृशैरेव तादृशाः ।
चारसंचारिणः संस्था गूढाश्चागूढसंज्ञिताः ॥२॥

1. a) TMd[3] TMd[4] कुर्या — b) [*Jolly* Nd Gr] ग्रामे ग्रामणिकादयः — c) TMd[3] परः; TMd[4] अथप्रवृ°; *Bh AŚ* °ज्ञानार्थाः — d) MTr[4] MTr[6] शीघ्रं चार°; TMd[4] *Mandlik KSS Dave* शीघ्राचार°; MTr[6] °परंपरां

2. a) TMd[4] बोद्धव्यां तादृ° — b) TMd[4] तादृशां — c) Tr[1] चारः; TMd[4] °संचारिणोस्वस्था — d) MTr[4] भूताश्वाग्दुढसंज्ञिताः; TMd[4] गवाश्वागमनं स्थिताः; TMd[3] [*Jolly* Nd Gr] गूढाश्चगूढ°; *Mandlik KSS Dave* शठाश्चागूढ°

155. Pādas a-b *ma* in BKt[5]. Cited by *Lakṣ* 11.107 — a) Bo Lo[3] Tj[1] प्रकारं — b) Pu[5] Pu[7] विजिगीषोस्य च; Bo Ox[3] NPu[1] वेष्टितं — c) TMd[3] उदासीनं च चारस्य; MTr[4] MTr[6] उदासीनस्य चाचारं; GMd[1] उदासीनस्याचारं च; GMd[5] GMy Tr[1] MTr[5] उदासीनस्य चारं च — d) Pu[2] Pu[4] शत्तोश्चैव; Ho Lo[4] Lo[5] Ox[3] [*Jolly* M] विशेषतः

156. Cited by *Lakṣ* 11.107 — a) GMd[1] येषां प्रकृ°; Be[1] °तयोर्मूलं; Kt[2] °तयोः मूलं — c) Ox[3] वान्या; Pu[5] Pu[7] °ख्यातो — d) Ox[3] द्विदशैव; wKt[1] °दशैवं; TMd[4] °दशश्चैव ताः; Tr[1] तत्स्मृताः; wKt[1] स्मृतः

157. Omitted in GMy Ox[3]; *ma* in Lo[4]. Cited by *Lakṣ* 11.107 — a) MTr[5] *Bh* अमात्यपुरराष्ट्रार्थ°; BCa Ho La[1] अमात्यदुर्गराष्ट्रार्थ°; wKt[1] अमात्यस्वर्गराष्ट्राच्च दण्डा°; oOr अमादुर्गं च राष्ट्रं च दण्डा°; Lo[1] Pu[5] Tr[2] आमात्य°; BBe[2] अमात्या°; Lo[1] NPu[1] Pu[2] Pu[5] Pu[7] Tr[1] °दुर्गार्थं; Tr[2] °दुर्गोर्थ°; GMd[1] °दुर्गश्च दण्डा° — b) wKt[1] °दण्डाख्या; oOr दण्डान्यः; Tr[1] °दण्डाद्याः; GMd[5] °दण्डार्थाः — c) Hy *om* ह्येताः; Pu[5] Pu[7] ह्येते; Ho GMd[1] ह्येषां; TMd[4] ह्येषा

अनन्तरमरिं विद्यादरिसेविनमेव च ।
अरेरनन्तरं मित्रमुदासीनं तयोः परम् ॥१५८॥
तान्सर्वानभिसंदध्यात् सामादिभिरुपक्रमैः ।
व्यस्तैश्चैव समस्तैश्च पौरुषेण नयेन च ॥१५९॥
संधिं च विग्रहं चैव यानमासनमेव च ।
द्वैधीभावं संश्रयं च षड्गुणांश्चिन्तयेत्सदा ॥१६०॥
आसनं चैव यानं च संधाय च विगृह्य च ।
कार्यं वीक्ष्य प्रयुञ्जीत द्वैधं संश्रयमेव च ॥१६१॥
संधिं तु द्विविधं विद्याद् राजा विग्रहमेव च ।
उभे यानासने चैव द्वैधं संश्रयमेव च ॥१६२॥

158. Cited by *Lakṣ* 11.107; *Mādh* 1.411 — a) Be[1] Be[3] Bo La[1] sOx[1] NPu[1] sPu[6] विन्द्या° — b) GMy °सेविन एव; wKt[1] BKt[5] wKt[6] sOx[1] Tr[2] °सेवनमेव; sPu[6] °सेवनिमेव *cor to* °सेवनमेव; Be[1] wKt[3] NNg Pu[5] Pu[7] Tr[1] MTr[6] °सेवितमेव — c) wKt[1] अनन्तरमरेर्मित्रमु°; Tr[2] अनेनान्तरं; Bo °नन्तरे मित्रे उदा° — d) TMd[4] मित्रामित्रं तथा परं; Ho °मुदानं [*ma* च]; Lo[1] Ox[2] Pu[3] Pu[8] Tr[2] °सीनमतः परं; GMy तथा तयोः; Ox[3] परः

Additional verse in TMd[3] TMd[4] GMd[5] GMy Tr[1] [*Jolly* Nd Gr] *Mandlik*[ट] *KSS;* cited in *Lakṣ* 11.107:

विकृष्टेऽध्वन्यनायत्त उदासीनो बलान्वितः ।
विजिगीषुर्मण्डलार्थो यस्मिञ्ज्ञेयः स मध्यमः ॥

a) *Mandlik* विप्रकृष्टेऽध्वनीयत्र; *KSS* विप्रकृष्टेऽध्वनो यत्र; [*Jolly* Nd Gr] विकृष्टेध्वन्यनानार्त; TMd[4] प्रकृष्टेपत्यनायत्त; GMy सन्निकृष्टेध्वन्ययत्तु; TMd[3] सन्निकृष्टेध्वन्ययत्रः; *Lakṣ* °ध्वन्यनायत्तमुदा° — b) Tr[1] °न्विता — c) [*Jolly* NNg Gr] विजिगीषुमण्डलार्थी; TMd[4] *Mandlik KSS Lakṣ* सखिलो मण्डलार्थस्तु [TMd[4] अखिलो]; TMd[3] GMy विजिगीषोर्म°

159. Cited by *Mādh* 1.411 — a) GMd[1] TMd[3] GMd[5] GMy NPu[1] Pu[5] Pu[7] Tr[1] MTr[4] MTr[6] Wa °नतिसंदध्यात् [for the reading adopted, see 7.180a]; Pu[3] °नपिसंदध्यात् — b) Ho TMd[3] Tr[2] समादि°; Lo[1] °रुपाक्रमैः — c) TMd[3] GMy व्यस्तैर्वाथ; GMy समस्तैर्वा — d) NKt[4] जयेन; Jo[2] Pu[7] [*Jolly* G] वा

160. Not commented by *Nd;* pādas a-b *ma* in BKt[5]; pādas c-d omitted in GMd[5] Tr[2]. Cited by *Lakṣ* 11.111; *Mādh* 1.411 — a) BKt[5] wKt[6] MTr[6] संधिश्च; BKt[5] wKt[6] Pu[2] Pu[4] विग्रहश्चैव — b) Lo[5] Be[1] °मात्मानमेव — c) Pu[4] Pu[5] Pu[7] द्वेधी°; Be[3] संश्रयश्च; sOx[1] sPu[6] *om* च; Lo[5] वा — d) Be[3] Pu[5] Pu[7] Tj[1] [*Jolly* G R] षाड्गुण्यं चिन्त°; Be[1] Ho TMd[3] TMd[4] oOr षड्गुणान्चिन्त°; GMd[1] GMy षड्गुणां चिन्त°; NPu[1] °न्तयन्सदा

161.* Omitted in GMd[5]; not commented by *Nd;* pādas a-b omitted in Tr[2] and pādas c-d in Bo. Cited by *Lakṣ* 11.111; *Mādh* 1.411 — a) Pu[5] *om* चैव यानं; GMd[1] चापि — b) BBe[2] Be[3] BCa Ho Hy Jm Jo[1] Jo[2] wKt[1] Kt[2] wKt[3] BKt[5] wKt[6] Lo[1] Lo[3] sOx[1] Ox[2] NPu[1] Pu[3] sPu[6] Pu[8] Tj[1] Tj[2] MTr[3] Wa [*Jolly* R M[8]] *Nā Ku Rc Mandlik Jha KSS Dave* संधिं विग्रहमेव च [Be[3] Hy wKt[3] NPu[1] Tj[1] संधि]; TMd[4] संग्रामं च गृहस्य च — d) Pu[3] Wa द्वैधीसंश्र°

162. Omitted in Be[1] Lo[4] Lo[5] GMd[5] sOx[1] Ox[3]; not commented by *Me* and *Nā;* pādas a-b omitted in Bo and pādas c-d in Pu[4]. Cited by *Lakṣ* 11.111 — a) Tr[2] संधिवद्विविधं; Ho wKt[1] BKt[5] wKt[6] TMd[3] GMy NPu[1] Pu[2] Pu[4] sPu[6] [*Jolly* Nd] च; MTr[6] तु वीविधं; wKt[1] विग्रहं विद्याद्; La[1] Tj[1] विन्ध्याद्; TMd[4] NNg Pu[5] Pu[7] कुर्याद् — b) BKt[5] wKt[6] Wa द्विविधं विग्रहं तथा; GMd[1] Tr[2] राज — c)

समानयानकर्मा च विपरीतस्तथैव च ।
तदात्वायतिसंयुक्तः संधिर्ज्ञेयो द्विलक्षणः ॥१६३॥
स्वयंकृतश्च कार्यार्थमकाले काल एव वा ।
मित्रेण चैवापकृते द्विविधो विग्रहः स्मृतः ॥१६४॥
एकाकिनश्चात्ययिके कार्ये प्राप्ते यदृच्छया ।
संहतस्य च मित्रेण द्विविधं यानमुच्यते ॥१६५॥
क्षीणस्य चैव क्रमशो दैवात्पूर्वकृतेन वा ।
मित्रस्य चानुरोधेन द्विविधं स्मृतमासनम् ॥१६६॥
बलस्य स्वामिनश्चैव स्थितिः कार्यस्य सिद्धये ।
द्विविधं कीर्त्यते द्वैधं षाड्गुण्यगुणवेदिभिः ॥१६७॥

TMd^{3} GMy उभयोरासने — d) Ho Hy Jm Jo^{1} Kt^{2} MTr^{3} [*Jolly* R] *Mandlik KSS Jha Dave* द्विविधः संश्रयः स्मृतः; BKt^{5} wKt^{6} तथा संश्रयमेव च [BKt^{5} वा]; TMd^{3} GMy वा

163.* Pādas a-b omitted in GMd^{5}. Cited by *Viś* 1.343; *Lakṣ* 11.111 — a) Ox^{3} समान्यनकर्मा; Tr^{2} *om* च; *Viś* वा — c) GMd^{1} तथात्वायति° ; TMd^{4} तथात्वोयति° ; BBe^{2} तदात्ममति° ; wKt^{3} नादत्वा-यति° ; NPu^{1} Pu^{2} °त्वायाति° ; Bo °त्वावति° ; GMy °त्वायदि° ; TMd^{3} °युक्ता — d) Lo^{1} संधिर्ज्ञेया; TMd^{3} GMy Pu^{5} Pu^{7} संधिज्ञेयो; TMd^{4} स विज्ञेयो; Be^{3} [*but mc sh*] TMd^{3} Tr^{2} विलक्षणः; oOr हि रक्षणः

164.* Pādas c-d omitted in TMd^{3} GMy. Cited by *Lakṣ* 11.111–2 — a) Pu^{5} Pu^{7} स्वयंकृतः परकृतश्चाकाले; GMd^{1} तथा स्वायं° ; TMd^{4} NPu^{1} °कृतस्य; Lo^{4} Lo^{5} °कृतस्तु; *Lakṣ* °कृतं च; Ox^{3} °कृतस्त्वकार्या° ; BKt^{5} यथार्थमकाले; Ho कार्यार्थे अकाले — b) Bo Kt^{2} °मकाल; Tj^{1} °मकालो; wKt^{3} Lo^{1} Tr^{2} कालमेव; Be^{3} *om* वा; Bo wKt^{1} Lo^{1} GMd^{1} TMd^{3} TMd^{4} GMy oOr sOx^{1} Ox^{2} Ox^{3} Pu^{5} sPu^{6} Pu^{7} Tr^{1} Tr^{2} MTr^{4} MTr^{6} [*Jolly* M Nd] च — c) *Lakṣ* मित्रं चैवाप्यपकृते; BBe^{2} Be^{3} Bo BCa Ho Hy Jm Jo^{2} wKt^{1} Kt^{2} wKt^{3} BKt^{5} wKt^{6} La^{1} [*cor to sh*] La^{2} Lo^{1} Lo^{3} Lo^{4} Lo^{5} NNg sOx^{1} Ox^{2} Ox^{3} NPu^{1} Pu^{3} sPu^{6} Pu^{8} Tj^{1} Tj^{2} Tr^{2} MTr^{3} Wa *Mandlik Jolly Jha KSS Dave* मित्रस्य; Jo^{1} मित्रस्यैवाप° ; Ho Pu^{5} Pu^{7} [*Jolly* G] चैवोपकृते; NKt^{4} चैवाकृते; Bo Lo^{5} Ox^{3} चैवाप्रकृते; Lo^{1} चैवापकृतेर्द्वि° ; MTr^{6} °कृतो — d) BBe^{2} GMd^{5} विविधो; TMd^{4} विग्रहस्मृतं

165. Lacuna in NKt^{4} after संहतस्य of pāda-c until 166c. Cited by *Lakṣ* 11.112 — a) NPu^{1} °श्चाभ्यधिके; Wa °त्ययिको — b) NKt^{4} काये ; *Lakṣ* काले; Lo^{2} प्राप्ते कार्ये; wKt^{3} यदिच्छया; BKt^{5} wKt^{6} *Lakṣ* यथेच्छया — c) TMd^{3} GMd^{5} Tj^{1} MTr^{4} MTr^{6} संगतस्य; TMd^{4} संहतश्च; GMd^{5} तु; Tr^{2} मन्त्रेण — d) Jo^{2} यानमिष्यते; Tr^{2} यानमेव च

166. Omitted in GMy; *ma* in BKt^{5}. Cited by *Lakṣ* 11.112 — a) TMd^{3} क्षाणस्य; TMd^{4} यानक्रमशो; NPu^{1} विषक्रमशो — b) Ho oOr देवा° ; TMd^{3} °त्पूर्वंकृतेन; sOx^{1} sPu^{6} Tr^{2} च — c) Lo^{3} Tj^{1} मित्रस्यैवानु° ; BBe^{2} मित्रस्यानु° ; Ho वानुरो° — d) wKt^{6} स्मृतमात्मनं; BBe^{2} GMd^{1} sOx^{1} Tj^{1} स्मृतमानसं; Ho स्थितमासनं; TMd^{3} स्मृतिशासनं; wKt^{1} चासनं स्मृतं; Be^{1} यानमुच्यते; Tr^{2} °सनः

167.* Omitted in Tr^{2}; pādas a-b *ma* in BKt^{5}. Cited by *Lakṣ* 11.112 — a) TMd^{4} NNg [*but cor fh*] बालश्च; wKt^{6} °नश्चैवं — b) wKt^{6} इतिकार्यानुसिद्धये; GMd^{1} स्थित; Be^{1} BBe^{2} Be^{3} BCa Hy Jm Jo^{1} Jo^{2} Kt^{2} wKt^{3} Lo^{3} NNg Ox^{2} Ox^{3} NPu^{1} Pu^{2} Pu^{3} Pu^{4} Pu^{8} Tj^{1} Tj^{2} MTr^{3} Wa *Mandlik Jolly Jha KSS Dave Go Ku Rn Mr* कार्यार्थसिद्धये; Pu^{5} Pu^{7} सर्वार्थसिद्धये; wKt^{1} BKt^{5} wKt^{6} कार्यानुसिद्धये; BKt^{5} कार्यावसिद्धये — c) wKt^{6} विविधं; Be^{1} Wa कथ्यते; BKt^{5} कीर्तितं; GMd^{5} कीर्तयेद् — d) Ho La^{1} षड्गुण्य° ; Bo षड्गुण्यं; Pu^{5} षाड्गुण्ये; wKt^{1} Lo^{4} [*ma*] Lo^{5} GMd^{1} TMd^{3} GMy oOr षाड्गुण्यं; Be^{1} Tr^{1} °वादिभिः; wKt^{3} Lo^{1} °भेदिभिः; Pu^{2} Pu^{4} °वेदिनः

अर्थसंपादनार्थं च पीड्यमानस्य शत्रुभिः ।
साधुषु व्यपदेशश्च* द्विविधः संश्रयः स्मृतः ॥१६८॥
यदावगच्छेदायत्यामाधिक्यं ध्रुवमात्मनः ।
तदात्वे चाल्पिकां पीडां तदा संधिं समाश्रयेत् ॥१६९॥
यदा प्रहृष्टा मन्येत सर्वास्तु प्रकृतीर्भृशम् ।
अत्युच्छ्रितं तथात्मानं तदा मन्येत विग्रहम् ॥१७०॥
यदा मन्येत भावेन हृष्टं पुष्टं बलं स्वकम् ।
परस्य विपरीतं च तदा यायाद्रिपुं प्रति ॥१७१॥
यदा तु स्यात्परिक्षीणो वाहनेन बलेन च ।
तदासीत प्रयत्नेन शनकैः सान्त्वयन्नरिम् ॥१७२॥

168.* Cited by *Lakṣ* 11.112 — a) ᴛMd³ Pu⁵ अर्थसंपा°; wKt⁶ अनुसंपा°; ɢMd⁵ °संपादनं चैव; ɢMd¹ °संपीडनायां च; La¹ °नार्थश्च; Ox³ °नार्थ अपीड्य°; ᴛMd³ ɢMy तु; ʙCa oOr वा — b) ɢMd⁵ oOr पीड्यमानश्च; ᴍTr⁵ पच्यमानस्य — c) ɢMd¹ ᴛMd³ ᴛMd⁴ ɢMd⁵ ɢMy Tr¹ *Nd* साधुभिर्व्यप°; ᴍTr⁵ *Bh* साधुष्वव्यप°; La¹ °देशस्तु; wKt⁶ °देशाच्च ɴPu¹ °देशेन; ʙBe² Bo ʙCa Hy Jm Jo¹ Jo² wKt¹ Kt² Lo¹ Lo² Lo³ Lo⁴ Lo⁵ ɴNg sOx¹ Ox² Ox³ Pu² Pu³ Pu⁴ Pu⁵ sPu⁶ Pu⁷ Pu⁸ Tj¹ Tj² Tr¹ Tr² ᴍTr³ ᴍTr⁴ Wa *Mandlik Jolly KSS Dave* °देशार्थं; Be¹ °देशार्थे; ᴍTr⁶ °देशार्थो; ɢMd¹ °देशोर्थो [but unclear and cor] — d) Jo¹ विविधः; Lo⁵ sOx¹ sPu⁶ संशयः; ɴKt⁴ संचयः; ʙKt⁵ संश्रयो मतः; wKt⁶ संशयो मतः

169. Pādas c-d omitted in Pu⁴. Cited by *Lakṣ* 11.112 — a) ᴍTr⁵ यदाधिगच्छे°; Lo² यदा च गच्छे°; Pu⁵ Pu⁷ यदा न गच्छे°; Ho °दायात्यामा°; wKt⁶ Ox³ °दायत्यमा°; wKt³ Lo² °दागत्यामा° — b) ᴛMd⁴ °धिक्य; ɴPu¹ °धिकं — c) ɢMd⁵ यदा त्वेकात्मिकां पीडां; Pu⁵ Pu⁷ तादात्वे; ᴍTr⁴ यदात्वे; ɢMd¹ यदात्व; wKt¹ तदा तु; Ho [*but mc*] Jo² Tr² चाल्पिकीं; ᴛMd³ ɢMy ɴPu¹ Pu⁸ वाल्पिकां; ᴍTr⁶ चाल्पकां; wKt¹ Pu⁵ Pu⁷ चात्मिकां; ᴍTr⁴ वात्मिकं; *Lakṣ* वाधिकां — d) Be³ Tj² समाश्रये; wKt³ ʙKt⁵ wKt⁶ समाचरेत्

170.* Cited by *Lakṣ* 11.112 — a) ᴛMd⁴ यथा; Wa यदात्र हृष्टा; Ho ᴛMd⁴ प्रहृष्टां; Tj¹ प्रहृष्ट; Hy Jo¹ wKt¹ Kt² wKt⁶ Pu³ Pu⁴ *Lakṣ* प्रकृष्टा — b) Pu² ᴍTr³ सर्वासु; Lo⁴ Lo⁵ Ox³ सर्वाश्च; Lo⁵ ᴛMd³ प्रकृतिर्भृशं; ɢMy प्रकृतीं भृशं; oOr प्रकृते भृशं; ɴKt⁴ प्रकृतो भृशं; Ho °तीर्भृतं; wKt⁶ °तीर्दश — c) ɢMy अत्युच्छृतं; Lo¹ अत्यच्छ्रितं; ᴛMd⁴ Tr¹ अभ्युच्छ्रितं; ᴛMd³ अभ्युच्छ्रित; ᴍTr⁵ अभ्युच्चितं; wKt⁶ इत्युच्छ्रितं; ᴛMd⁴ अत्यर्चितं; Ho प्रत्युष्ठितं; ɢMd⁵ अभ्युत्थानः; ʙKt⁵ wKt⁶ Lo¹ ᴛMd³ ᴛMd⁴ ɢMy sOx¹ sPu⁶ Pu⁸ Tj¹ ᴍTr⁴ ᴍTr⁵ [*Jolly* R] तदात्मानं; ɢMd¹ ɢMd⁵ यदात्मानं — d) ᴛMd³ Pu³ तथा; Be¹ ʙBe² Be³ Ho Hy Jm Jo¹ Jo² wKt¹ Kt² wKt³ La¹ Lo¹ Lo³ ɴNg Ox² ɴPu¹ Pu³ Pu⁸ Tj¹ Tj² ᴍTr³ Wa *Mandlik Jolly Jha KSS Dave* कुर्वीत विग्रहं

171. Omitted in ɴKt⁴; not commented by *Nd.* Cited by *Lakṣ* 11.112 — a) ᴛMd⁴ यथा; ʙKt⁵ wKt⁶ मन्ये च — b) Tr¹ हृष्ट; Lo⁴ Lo⁵ Ox³ हृष्टपुष्ट; Be¹ ʙCa Jo² Lo² Lo³ ᴛMd³ ᴛMd⁴ ɢMd⁵ ɢMy Pu⁵ Pu⁷ Tj¹ Tr¹ ᴍTr⁵ ᴍTr⁶ [*Jolly* G R] स्वकं बलं; wKt¹ स्वयं — c) ɢMy व्यपरीतं; Tr² *om* च; Jo² wKt¹ Lo³ Lo⁴ Lo⁵ Pu⁵ Pu⁷ Tj¹ तु; ʙCa वा — d) ɢMy यायात्रपुं; Bo यायारिपुं; ᴛMd³ यथाद्रिपुं; Lo⁵ ɴNg प्रायाद्रिपुं; Ox³ जायाद्रिपुं; ɴNg Pu³ Tr² यायाद्रिपून्; Be³ La¹ Lo² यायादरिं

172.* Omitted in ɴKt⁴; not commented by *Nd;* pādas c-d omitted in Lo²; verses 172 and 173 transposed in Bo. Cited by *Lakṣ* 11.112— a) ᴛMd⁴ यथा; Wa °त्परीक्षीणो; Ox³ °क्षीणे — b) Ox³ सवाहनबलेन; Tr¹ फलेन च; ʙBe² wKt¹ ɢMd⁵ वा — c) ɢMy तदासीद; ɢMd⁵ Tr¹ तदासीनः — d) ᴛMd³ ɢMy शातयन्नरिं; Be¹ ʙBe² Be³ Ho Hy Jm Jo¹ wKt¹ Kt² wKt³ ʙKt⁵ wKt⁶ La¹ Lo¹ Lo⁴ Lo⁵

मन्येतारिं यदा राजा सर्वथा बलवत्तरम् ।
तदा द्विधा बलं कृत्वा साधयेत्कार्यमात्मनः ॥१७३॥
यदा परबलानां तु गमनीयतमो भवेत् ।
तदा तु संश्रयेत् क्षिप्रं धार्मिकं बलिनं नृपम् ॥१७४॥
निग्रहं प्रकृतीनां च कुर्याद्योऽरिबलस्य च ।
उपसेवेत तं नित्यं सर्वयत्नैर्गुरुं यथा ॥१७५॥
यदि तत्रापि संपश्येद् दोषं संश्रयकारितम् ।
सुयुद्धमेव तत्रापि निर्वितर्कः समाचरेत् ॥१७६॥
सर्वोपायैस्तथा कुर्यान्नीतिज्ञः पृथिवीपतिः ।
यथास्याभ्यधिका न स्युर्मित्रोदासीनशत्रवः ॥१७७॥
आयतिं सर्वकार्याणां तदात्वं च विचारयेत् ।
अतीतानां च सर्वेषां गुणदोषौ च तत्त्वतः ॥१७८॥

Ox^{3} Pu^{3} Pu^{5} Pu^{7} Pu^{8} Tj^{1} Tj^{2} MTr^{3} Wa [*Jolly* M$^{4-5}$ Ku] *Mandlik Jha KSS Dave* °यन्नरीन्; Lo^{3} GMy °यन्नरं; GMd^{5} Tr^{1} MTr^{4} °यन्रिपुं; Bo La^{2} sOx^{1} Ox^{2} sPu^{6} Tr^{2} *Rc* °यन्रिपून्

173. Pādas a-b omitted in Lo^{2}. Cited by *Lakṣ* 11.112–3 — a) Pu^{5} Pu^{7} मुच्येतारिं; Tr^{2} तदा; GMd^{5} GMy Tr^{1} यथा; TMd^{4} राज्ञस् — b) TMd^{4} GMy Pu^{5} Pu^{7} [*Jolly* G] सर्वदा; GMd^{1} सर्वार्थबल° — c) TMd^{3} तथा; Be^{1} Bo sOx^{1} sPu^{6} Tr^{2} बलं द्विधा

174. Cited by *Lakṣ* 11.113 — a) Kt^{2} यदो; Tr^{2} यदा अपर°; wKt^{1} परं; MTr^{4} परबलैर्हन्तुं; NKt^{4} °बलाथ गम°; Lo^{3} Pu^{2} Pu^{4} Tj^{1} च — b) sOx^{1} sPu^{6} गमनायसमो; TMd^{3} Tr^{1} °नीयतरो; oOr °नीयपरो; Kt^{2} °नीयततो — c) MTr^{4} तदानुसं°; Be^{3} NKt^{4} TMd^{3} TMd^{4} Pu^{5} संश्रये; Lo^{5} Tr^{2} संशयेत्; NNg संश्रियेत्; Be^{1} संश्रयो — d) *Lakṣ* बलिनं रिपुं

175. Cited by *Viś* 1.343; *Lakṣ* 11.113 — a) TMd^{3} GMy निग्रह; BKt^{5} नीग्रहं; sOx^{1} sPu^{6} Wa विग्रहं; Pu^{5} Pu^{7} नित्यं ग्रहं; TMd^{3} प्रगृहीतानां च; BBe^{2} Bo Ho Jo^{2} wKt^{1} wKt^{3} NKt^{4} BKt^{5} wKt^{6} Lo^{1} Lo^{2} GMd^{1} TMd^{4} NNg oOr sOx^{1} Pu^{5} sPu^{6} Pu^{7} Pu^{8} Tr^{1} Tr^{2} MTr^{4} MTr^{6} [*Jolly* G]तु — b) MTr^{4} कुर्याद्रिपुबलस्य; Tj^{1} °द्योरिर्बलस्य; TMd^{4} Ox^{3} °द्योनिबलस्य; *Lakṣ* °द्योनिर्बलस्य; Jo^{2} wKt^{1} wKt^{3} Ox^{2} Pu^{5} Pu^{7} [*Jolly* G] तु — c) Lo^{4} Lo^{5} Ox^{3} [*Jolly* M$^{4-5}$] उपसेवेत सततं — d) Ox^{3} मनुर्यत्नै°; Ho सर्वोपायैर्गुरुं; Lo^{2} तथा

176.* Pādas a-b omitted in Pu^{5}; lacuna at pāda-a in NKt^{4}. Cited by *Lakṣ* 11.113 — a) wKt^{1} यदा तदापि; Pu^{8} स्वम्पश्येद् — b) GMd^{5} दोषो संशयकारितः; Be^{1} रोषं; sOx^{1} sPu^{6} [*cor to*] Tr^{2} संशय°; wKt^{3} Wa *Lakṣ* °कारिणं; TMd^{3} GMy °कारिभिः — c) NKt^{4} युयुक्तमेव चत्रापि; Ho Jm sOx^{1} Pu^{5} Pu^{7} sPu^{6} [*Jolly* G] *Jolly* स युद्धमेव; GMd^{5} संयुद्धमेव; Wa सियुद्धमेव — d) GMd^{1} TMd^{3} Tr^{2} निर्वितर्कं; GMy निर्वितर्क [rest broken]; Lo^{4} Lo^{5} निर्वितङ्कः; Be^{1} Jo^{2} wKt^{6} Lo^{2} Pu^{2} Pu^{4} Pu^{5} Pu^{7} Wa *Go* [*Jolly* G] निर्विकल्पः; Hy Jm Jo^{1} Kt^{2} BKt^{5} La^{1} Lo^{1} NNg Ox^{2} Ox^{3} NPu^{1} Pu^{3} Pu^{8} MTr^{3} [*Jolly* M^{5-8-9}] *Mandlik Jha KSS Dave* निर्विशङ्कः; Be^{3} निर्विशङ्कं; Jo^{2} निर्विशङ्कयः; BKt^{5} निर्विकङ्शः

177. Pāda-d omitted in Ox^{3}. Cited by *Lakṣ* 11.113 — a) GMd^{5} °पायैर्यथा; TMd^{4} °पायैस्सदा — b) wKt^{6} °तिज्ञश्च समीपतिः; BKt^{5} °तिज्ञः समीपतिः — c) GMd^{1} TMd^{3} GMy Tr^{1} MTr^{4}MTr^{6} *Nd* यथा-स्मादधिका; GMd^{5} यथात्मनोधिका; *Lakṣ* यथा स्यादधिका; Pu^{5} Pu^{7} °धिकां

178. Pādas a-b omitted in Ox^{3}. Lacuna in NKt^{4} for all after आयतिं. Cited by *Lakṣ* 11.113 — a) TMd^{3} आयतीं सर्वदा कार्या; TMd^{4} आयतिं [lacuna] सर्वाणां; Ho आयति; Be^{1} आयतीः; Tr^{2}

आयत्यां गुणदोषज्ञस्तदात्वे क्षिप्रनिश्चयः ।
अतीते कार्यशेषज्ञः शत्रुभिर्नाभिभूयते ॥१७९॥
यथैनं नाभिसंदध्युर्मित्रोदासीनशत्रवः ।
तथा सर्वं संविदध्यादेष सामासिको नयः ॥१८०॥
यदा तु यानमातिष्ठेदरिराष्ट्रं प्रति प्रभुः ।
तदानेन विधानेन यायादरिपुरं शनैः ॥१८१॥
मार्गशीर्षे शुभे मासि यायाद्यात्रां महीपतिः ।
फाल्गुनं वाथ चैत्रं वा मासौ प्रति यथाबलम् ॥१८२॥
अन्येष्वपि तु कालेषु यदा पश्येद् ध्रुवं जयम् ।
तदा यायाद्विगृह्यैव व्यसने चोत्थिते रिपोः ॥१८३॥

आयतिः; Lo^{1} आयान्ति; Be^{3} NNg [*but cor fh*] °कार्याणि; Ho °कार्यां तत्तदा° — b) Be^{1} wKt^{3} तथात्वं; wKt^{1} तदर्थं — c) GMd^{5} आयातीनां; MTr^{4} MTr^{6} आयतीनां— d) Tj^{2} °दोषो; TMd^{4} °दोष; NKt^{4} °दोषौ भवत्त्वतः; Jo^{2} च विचारयेत्

179. Cited by *Lakṣ* 11.113 — a) Ox^{3} आयत्या; Lo^{1} °दोषज्ञे तदा°; Pu^{2} Pu^{4} °दोषश्च तदा° — b) TMd^{4} °ज्ञस्तथात्विप्रनिश्चयः; GMd^{1} °ज्ञस्तथात्वे; Tj^{1} °ज्ञस्तथात्त्वे; wKt^{1} °ज्ञस्तथात्व; Tr^{2} °ज्ञस्तदा क्षि°; Ho छिन्ननिश्चयः — c) MTr^{5} अतीत; TMd^{4} अदीते; Tr^{1} °शेषज्ञाः; GMd^{1} TMd^{3} °दोषज्ञः — d) Tr^{2} °भूतये

180. Omitted in Ox^{3}; lacuna in NKt^{4}; *ma* in Lo^{4}. Cited by *Lakṣ* 11.113; pādas a-b cited by *Viś* 1.348 [intro] — a) Pu^{2} Pu^{4} तथैनं; MTr^{6} यथैतं; GMd^{5} यदैनं; Lo^{1} अथैवं; Pu^{3} Pu^{8} यथैतान्नाभि°; Lo^{2} GMd^{1} Pu^{3} *Viś* नातिसं° — c) Jo^{2} Lo^{3} Tj^{1} [*Jolly* R] तथा प्रयत्नमातिष्ठेदेष; wKt^{6} GMy यथा; GMd^{5} MTr^{4} तदा; TMd^{4} यदा; Ho sOx^{1} Ox^{2} sPu^{6} यत्नं संवि°; GMd^{1} सर्वे समाविद्यादेष; TMd^{3} GMy संनिदध्यादेष — d) Tr^{2} °दध्यादेवं समासिको; wKt^{1} सामान्सिको; MTr^{3} सामाजिको; GMy सामादिको; TMd^{3} सामादिरो; Ox^{2} विधिः; Wa विधीः

181. Omitted in TMd^{3} GMy; lacuna for pādas b-c in NKt^{4}. Cited by *Mādh* 1.400 — a) TMd^{4} यथा — b) TMd^{4} °ष्ठेत्परराष्ट्रं; Jo^{2} Tj^{1} °दरिराज्यं; Bo प्रभुं — c) Lo^{3} Tj^{1} तथानेन — d) Lo^{1} यायाद्रिपुपुरं; Pu^{8} यायादरिवरं; oOr sPu^{6} °पुरं प्रति [*but both cor*]

Additional verses in TMd^{4}:

मर्यादां च विलुम्पेत मानं राजकुलस्य च ।
क्षत्रियेण समर्थेन सद्वृत्तमनुतिष्ठता ॥
स्वं राष्ट्रं परराष्ट्रं च रक्षतव्यं स्वराष्ट्रवत् ।
रक्ष्यत्वं हि प्रजाधर्मः क्षत्रधर्मस्तु रक्षणम् ॥

182. Cited by *Lakṣ* 11.115; *Mādh* 1.400–1 — a) Tr^{2} °शीर्ष; TMd^{4} °शीर्षं; MTr^{5} शुभ; GMd^{5} पुरे मासे; Be^{3} Lo^{4} Lo^{5} TMd^{3} TMd^{4} GMd^{5} GMy oOr Ox^{3} Pu^{3} Tr^{1} MTr^{4} MTr^{5} MTr^{6} *Lakṣ* मासे — b) wKt^{1} TMd^{3} GMy यायाद्यात्रा; Tj^{2} यायाद्यानं; Lo^{1} यायाद्रात्रौ — c) Pu^{3} फाल्गुने वा तथा चैत्रे; Be^{1} wKt^{1} wKt^{3} Lo^{5} sOx^{1} sPu^{6} फाल्गुणं; Hy फल्गुणं; Tr^{2} फाल्गुलं; Be^{1} Bo NKt^{4} La^{1} Lo^{4} Lo^{5} TMd^{3} GMy oOr Ox^{3} Tr^{1} MTr^{4} MTr^{5} MTr^{6} [*Jolly* M Nd] वापि; TMd^{4} sOx^{1} sPu^{6} Tr^{2} चापि; Pu^{8} वाथ वा चैत्रं — d) Be^{1} BCa Ho Jo^{2} NKt^{4} Lo^{1} Pu^{2} Pu^{3} Pu^{4} Pu^{5} Pu^{7} Wa मासं; NPu^{1} बलाबलं

183. Omitted in Ox^{3}. Cited by *Lakṣ* 11.115; *Mādh* 1.401 — a) GMd^{5} *Mādh* अन्येष्व-प्यृतुकालेषु; Ho Lo^{1} oOr Pu^{5} Pu^{7} [*Jolly* G] च; NKt^{4} हि; BKt^{5} wKt^{6} कार्येषु; MTr^{5} काले तु; Ho wKt^{1} मासेषु — b) Jm MTr^{4} यथा; TMd^{3} GMy यमा; Lo^{1} यदा यस्य ध्रुवं; oOr मन्येद्; Be^{3} ध्रुवं क्षयं — c) Pu^{5} Pu^{7} तत्र; Ho La^{1} जायाद्वि°; BBe^{2} Lo^{1} यायान्निगृ°; NPu^{1} Tj^{2} °ह्यैवं; GMd^{5} °ह्यैप — d) TMd^{3} Pu^{5} वसने;

कृत्वा विधानं मूले तु यात्रिकं च यथाविधि ।
उपगृह्यास्पदं चैव चारान् सम्यग्विधाय च ॥१८४॥
संशोध्य त्रिविधं मार्गं षड्विधं च बलं स्वकम् ।
सांपरायिककल्पेन यायादरिपुरं शनैः ॥१८५॥
शत्रुसेविनि मित्रे च गूढे युक्ततरो भवेत् ।
गतप्रत्यागते चैव स हि कष्टतरो रिपुः ॥१८६॥
दण्डव्यूहेन तन्मार्गं यायात्तु शकटेन वा ।
वराहमकराभ्यां वा सूच्या वा गरुडेन वा ॥१८७॥
यतश्च भयमाशङ्केत् ततो विस्तारयेद्बलम् ।
पद्मेन चैव व्यूहेन निविशेत सदा स्वयम् ॥१८८॥

wKt^3 चोत्थितो; *Lakṣ* वोत्थिते; Tr^2 चोच्छ्रितो; Pu^2 Pu^3 Pu^4 चोछिते; tMd^3 छोदिते; tMd^3 Pu^5 Pu^7 [*Jolly* G] रिपौ; nKt^4 रिष्यः; gMy परे

184. Cited by *Mādh* 1.401 — a) Ox^3 mTr^5 विधान; tMd^3 gMy मूलेन; nNg Pu^2 Pu^4 Pu^5 Pu^7 च — b) Ox^2 यात्रिकं प्रतिगृह्य च; Ho यात्रिकां; tMd^4 यात्रिका; nKt^4 याद्रिकं; bCa nNg nPu^1 तु — c) gMd^5 उपग्राह्या° — d) Bo wKt^3 sOx^1 Pu^3 चरान्; gMd^5 mTr^4 mTr^5 mTr^6 चारं; nKt^4 nPu^1 चरं; Be^1 वारान्; Tr^1 वरं; tMd^3 gMy सारं; Ox^3 वाचा; tMd^4 चारं चैव विधाय; oOr सम्यग्विधीयते; tMd^3 Ho तु

185. Omitted in Ox^3. Cited by *Lakṣ* 11.122; *Mādh* 1.401 — a) Be^3 Ho Lo^1 संशोध्यं; nKt^4 gMd^5 विविधं — b) Be^3 स्वबलं; Be^1 bCa La^1 Lo^1 gMd^5 oOr Pu^2 Pu^3 Pu^4 Pu^8 Tr^2 mTr^5 Wa च स्वकं बलं — c) Ho °परायक°; nKt^4 °परायिकल्पेन; [*Jolly* M^8] °यिकमार्गेण — d) gMd^5 यायाद्रिपुबलं प्रति; tMd^4 mTr^4 mTr^6 यायात्परपुरं; nKt^4 Pu^3 Pu^8 °पुरं नृपः; La^1 Lo^4 Lo^5 gMd^1 tMd^4 oOr sPu^6 [*but cor*] Tr^1 mTr^4 mTr^6 [*Jolly* M] *Lakṣ* °पुरं प्रति

186. Pāda-d omitted in gMy [haplo] — a) tMd^4 Tj^1 °सेविन; Pu^2 Pu^4 °सेतिनि; bBe^2 मैत्रे — a-b) Lo^4 Lo^5 Ox^3 °सेविनि गूढे च मित्रे — b) Be^1 gMy Tj^1 गूढो; gMd^1 गूढा; tMd^4 गूढ; tMd^3 गुढे; nPu^1 गृहे; gMd^5 गूढैर्युक्त°; Tr^2 °तरौ; nKt^4 °तरा — c) nPu^1 गते प्रत्या°; Be^1 °त्यागतो; Lo^2 °त्यागमे; Tr^2 °त्यानते — d) Be^1 Ho Jo^2 Lo^1 Pu^2 Pu^4 Pu^5 Pu^7 Wa *Ku Go* तौ हि; Pu^8 तै हि; [*Jolly* G] तन्निकष्ट°; oOr महत्कष्ट°; Be^1 Jo^2 Lo^1 Pu^2 Pu^4 Wa [*Jolly* G] *Ku Go* °तरौ; Ox^3 Tr^1 °तमो; Be^1 Jo^2 Pu^5 Pu^7 *Go Ku* [*Jolly* G] रिपू; Pu^2 Pu^4 रिपूः; Ho Lo^1 tMd^4 Wa रिपून्

187. Omitted in gMy. Cited by *Mādh* 1.401 — a) Be^3 mTr^5 तं मार्गं — b) La^1 Pu^8 Tj^1 यायातु; bKt^5 यायाद्वे; bKt^5 wKt^6 Tr^2 सकटेन; wKt^1 nPu^1 च — c) Bo nNg oOr [*bur cor fh*] sOx^1 sPu^6 Tr^2 वाराह°; gMd^1 tMd^4 gMd^5 mTr^5 °गरुडाभ्यां; Lo^4 Lo^5 Ox^3 °शकटाभ्यां; Pu^5 Pu^7 Tr^2 च — d) gMd^5 mTr^5 सूच्यां; Ho शूच्या; bBe^2 शुच्या; Ox^3 शूया; Lo^3 sOx^1 sPu^6 [*mc to*] Tj^1 गारुडेन; gMd^1 tMd^4 gMd^5 mTr^5 मकरेण; Be^1 Ox^3 च

188. Omitted up to चैव of pāda-c in gMy; pādas b-d omitted in La^1 [haplo]. Cited by *Lakṣ* 11.124; *Mādh* 1.402 — a) gMd^1 tMd^4 gMd^5 Tr^1 mTr^4 mTr^6 यतो भवेद्भयाशङ्का [tMd^4 भयाद्भ°]; nNg Ox^3 [*Jolly* M] आशङ्केत भयं यस्मात् [Ox^{3}आशङ्केतु]; *Lakṣ* यतः शङ्केत स भयं; tMd^3 [*Jolly* Nd]यतो हि; Bo bCa Lo^1 sOx^1 Ox^2 sPu^6 Tr^2 यतस्तु; wKt^1 wKt^3 ततश्च; nKt^4 °माशङ्कां; wKt^1 °माशोकं — b) Ox^3 °रये हतं — c) Pu^2 Pu^3 Pu^4 Pu^5 Pu^7 Pu^8 पाद्मेन; Ox^3 पद्येन; sPu^6 [*but mc*] यत्नेन; Bo पाप्नेन; wKt^3 पद्मे च चैव; Lo^1 पाद्मेनैव च — d) tMd^4 न विशेत्ततथा स्वयं; Tr^2 विनिवेशेतरं स्वयं; tMd^3 निवेशेत; wKt^1 Tj^1 निवसेत; oOr विनशति; Wa विनिविशेत सदा; Ho wKt^1 tMd^3 gMd^5 sOx^1 Ox^3 sPu^6 Tr^1 Wa *Lakṣ Mādh* तदा

सेनापतिबलाध्यक्षौ सर्वदिक्षु निवेशयेत् ।
यतश्च भयमाशङ्केत् प्राचीं तां कल्पयेद्दिशम् ॥१८९॥
गुल्मांश्च स्थापयेदाप्तान् कृतसंज्ञान् समन्ततः ।
स्थाने युद्धे च कुशलानभीरूनविकारिणः ॥१९०॥
संहतान्योधयेदल्पान् कामं विस्तारयेद्बहून् ।
सूच्या वज्रेण चैवैतान् व्यूहेन व्यूह्य योधयेत् ॥१९१॥
स्यन्दनाश्वैः समे युध्येदनूपे नौद्विपैस्तथा ।
वृक्षगुल्मावृते चापैरसिचर्मायुधैः स्थले ॥१९२॥
कौरुक्षेत्रांश्च मत्स्यांश्च पाञ्चालाञ्छूरसेनजान् ।
दीर्घाँल्लघूंश्चैव नरानग्रानीकेषु योधयेत् ॥१९३॥

189. Pādas a-c omitted in La[1]. Cited by *Lakṣ* 11.124; *Mādh* 1.402 — a) *Mādh* सेनापतीन्बलाध्यक्षान्; Wa °बलोध्य°; NKt[4] wKt[6] Ox[3] Pu[2] Pu[4] Pu[5] Pu[7] Wa °ध्यक्षो; GMd[1] TMd[3] GMy °ध्यक्षान्; *Bh* बलाध्यक्षपुरुषाः appears to support the plural, but *Me* clearly points to the dual. — b) GMd[1] सर्वान्दिक्षु; BKt[5] निविशयेत् — c) TMd[4] GMd[5] MTr[4] MTr[6] यतश्च स्याद्भयाशङ्का; Tr[1] यतो भवेद्भयाशङ्का; NNg sOx[1] sPu[6] Tr[2] आशङ्केत भयं यस्मात्; *Lakṣ* भयं यतो वा शङ्केत; Lo[4] Lo[5] Ox[3] [*Jolly* M] आशङ्केत यतो नीतिं [Lo[4] Lo[5] नित्यं]; Jo[2] Lo[3] Tj[1] यतस्तु; Be[3] ततश्च; TMd[3] यदत्र; NKt[4] भवमा°; Lo[1] बलमा°; Ho wKt[6] °शङ्के; wKt[3] °शङ्क; NKt[4] °शङ्क्यं — d) wKt[6] प्रचीं तामुपकल्पयेत्; BKt[5] प्राचीं तां मम कल्पयेत्; BBe[2] प्राचीस्तां; GMd[1] TMd[3] GMd[5] GMy Pu[5] Pu[7] MTr[6] *Lakṣ Mādh* तां प्राचीं कल्प°; MTr[5] प्राचीनां कल्प°; Be[1] प्राचीं प्रकल्प°; Lo[2] प्राचीं नाकल्प°; Bo °येद्दिशां

190. Omitted in Pu[5]. Cited by *Lakṣ* 11.124; *Mādh* 1.402 — a) TMd[4] Ox[3] गुल्माश्च; TMd[3] गुल्मश्च; Kt[2] गुप्तांश्च; Be[1] °येदीप्तान्; La[1] °येदात्मान्; wKt[1] °येदास्तान् — b) *Lakṣ* शतसंख्यांस्ततस्ततः; Lo[5] °संज्ञास्समन्ततः — a-b) Lo[4] °दाप्तादकृतसंज्ञात् — c) NKt[4] स्थानं; wKt[1] दुर्गे च — d) Bo कुशलान्नभीरुर्नविकारिणः; *Lakṣ* °लानभीतानधिकारिणः; MTr[4] °नविकारिणे; MTr[5] °नविचारणः; Be[1] Be[3] Lo[2] sOx[1] Pu[2] Pu[4] sPu[6] °नधिकारिणः

191. Pādas a-b omitted in Pu[5]. Cited by *Mādh* 1.402 — a) TMd[4] संघाता° — b) Lo[2] विसारये°; TMd[4] °येद्रिपून् — c) Ho wKt[1] Pu[5] Pu[7] शूच्या; BBe[2] Ox[2] शुच्या; Bo सूचा; Ho La[1] चक्रेण; BKt[5] wKt[6] व्यूहेन; Kt[2] GMd[1] Pu[7] Wa चैवेतान्; BCa BKt[5] wKt[6] Tr[1] MTr[6] चैवैनान्; TMd[4] चैवेनान्; Jo[2] Lo[3] Tj[1] चैवेमान् — d) Pu[2] Pu[4] Pu[5] Pu[7] Tj[2] व्यूह्य व्यूहेन; Hy *om* व्यूह्य; TMd[3] TMd[4] oOr Ox[3] व्यूह

192. Cited by *Lakṣ* 11.130; *Mādh* 1.402 — a) TMd[4] GMd[5] Ox[3] Tr[1] *Lakṣ* युध्येत स्यन्दनाश्वेन [Tr[1] युद्धेन; GMd[5] °श्वैश्च; TMd[4] °श्वैव]; Ho स्यन्दनस्थैः; GMd[1] °नाश्व; Bo समा; wKt[1] स्याम; Pu[5] Pu[7] युधेदनू°; Lo[1] युद्धे अनू°; NKt[4] योध्यमनू°; wKt[6] युधमनू°; — b) TMd[3] GMy अनूपेन्चैवनोद्विपंः; GMd[5] नृपेण सह न द्विपैः; *Lakṣ* समे भूपोन्नतद्विपैः; Tr[1] समेनूपे च नौद्विपैः; TMd[4] समनोपि तु सर्वषैः; Ox[3] °ध्येद्यानैः पत्तिद्विपै°; MTr[4] °ध्येद्वनेनूपे द्विपै°; Be[1] °ध्येररूपोनोद्विपै°; Jo[2] नौद्विपादिभिः — c) TMd[3] GMy वृक्षेगुल्मेवृते; GMd[1] °गुल्मायुधे; TMd[4] °गुल्मतृणैश्चापै° — d) TMd[4] °रपिधर्मायुधैः; Tr[1] °युधे; oOr °युध; sOx[1] sPu[6] Tr[2] °युधैस्तथा; Bo °युधैर्यथा; MTr[5] °युधैर्बलैः; GMd[5] स्थलैः

193. Cited by *Lakṣ* 11.130; *Mādh* 1.402 — a) BBe[2] oOr Pu[2] Pu[4] Tj[2] कौर°; Bo Jm Jo[1] Kt[2] wKt[6] Lo[4] Lo[5] TMd[3] GMy Ox[2] Ox[3] Tj[1] MTr[3] [*Jolly* M[4]] *Mandlik KSS Dave* कुरु°; TMd[4] कारु°; GMd[1] TMd[3] GMd[5] sOx[1] Pu[2] Pu[4] sPu[6] Tr[1] मात्स्यांश्च; NNg Ox[3] मत्स्याश्च — b) Be[1] BBe[2] Bo Hy Jm Jo[1] Jo[2] wKt[1] K[2] BKt[5] wKt[6] Lo[2] Lo[4] Lo[5] TMd[4] Ox[2] MTr[3] [*Jolly* M[4-8-9]] *Mandlik Jha KSS Dave* पञ्चाला°; Ox[3] पञ्चालासूरसेनजा; Pu[2] Pu[4] °न्सौर° — c) Lo[4] °घूंश्च; Hy °घूंश्चैवेतरानग्रा°; TMd[3] GMy

प्रहर्षयेद्बलं व्यूह्य तांश्च सम्यक्परीक्षयेत् ।
चेष्टाश्चैव विजानीयादरीन्योधयतामपि ॥१९४॥
उपरुध्यारिमासीत राष्ट्रं चास्योपपीडयेत् ।
दूषयेच्चास्य सततं यवसान्नोदकेन्धनम् ॥१९५॥
भिन्द्याच्चैव तडागानि प्राकारपरिखास्तथा ।
समवस्कन्दयेच्चैनं रात्रौ वित्रासयेत्तथा ॥१९६॥
उपजप्यानुपजपेद् बुध्येतैव च तत्कृतम् ।
युक्ते च दैवे युध्येत जयप्रेप्सुरपेतभीः ॥१९७॥
साम्ना दानेन भेदेन समस्तैरथवा पृथक् ।
विजेतुं प्रयतेतारीन् न युद्धेन कदाचन ॥१९८॥

वीरानग्रा° — d) wKt[1] नरानयाणीकेपु; Lo[3] Tj[1] नरानल्पानीकेपु; GMd[5] MTr[4] MTr[6] नराननीकाग्रेपु; Lo[1] नरानग्रामीणां; *Lakṣ* नरानुग्रानीकेपु; NPu[1] नराननीचेपु च योध°; Pu[5] Pu[7] योजधयेत्; Tr[2] योधरेत्; wKt[6] नियोधयेत्; Be[1] Jm Jo[1] La[1] Lo[4] Lo[5] TMd[3] GMd[5] GMy NNg Ox[3] MTr[4] MTr[6] Wa *Go Nd Ku Mandlik Jha KSS Dave* योजयेत्; NKt[4] गोवयेत्

194. Omitted in Pu[5]. Cited by *Lakṣ* 11.130; *Mādh* 1.402 — a) TMd[4] प्रकृष्टायेन्बलव्यूहं; MTr[5] प्रकर्षये°; Ox[3] MTr[5] व्यूहं; Bo व्यूहान्; Lo[5] व्यूहा; Lo[1] व्यूह्येत् — b) Lo[4] Lo[5] TMd[4] Ox[3] MTr[4] MTr[6] [*Jolly* M] *Lakṣ* भृशं तांश्च परीक्षयेत् [*Lakṣ* भृशात्तांश्च]; *Jha* भृशं परी° [*Me* reads भृशं]; Be[3] Jo[2] Lo[3] Tj[1] [*Jolly* R] सर्वान्परी°; Be[1] °क्प्रहर्षयेत् — c) Bo Ho La[1] Lo[4] Lo[5] GMy sOx[1] Ox[3] Pu[2] Pu[4] Pu[7] MTr[5] *Me Go Rc* चेष्टां चैव; Be[3] चेष्टांश्चैव; BKt[5] wKt[6] Lo[1] TMd[4] चेष्टा चैव; TMd[3] चेष्टान्चैव; *Bh Ku Rn* support चेष्टाः — d) Lo[2] Pu[2] Pu[4] Pu[7] °यादरीणां युध्यतामिति; TMd[4] °यादरेण युध्यतामपि; *Lakṣ* °यादराद्योध°; La[1] °यतामिति

195. Not commented by *Nd;* pādas c-d omitted in Ho. Cited by *Vij* 1.343; *Lakṣ* 11.125; *Mādh* 1.402 — a) wKt[1] उपरन्ध्याविमानासीद्; Be[3] La[1] Ox[3] Pu[2] Pu[3] Pu[4] Pu[5] Pu[7] उपरुंध्या°; BKt[5] wKt[6] °मासीन; GMd[5] °मासीनं; Tr[2] °मासीत्; Ox[3] °मासांत — b) sOx[1] sPu[6] *Lakṣ* वास्योप°; TMd[4] चैश्चपीडयेत् — c) sOx[1] sPu[6] दूषयच्चास्य — d) TMd[4] यवसांमेधकंधनं; Be[1] Lo[2] Lo[5] °न्नोदकं धनं

196. Cited by *Lakṣ* 11.125; *Mādh* 1.402 — a) Ho Pu[5] Tr[2] भिद्याच्चैव; TMd[3] GMy भिन्द्याश्चैव; GMd[5] भिन्द्यां चैव; oOr भिन्द्यादेव; sOx[1] sPu[6] °च्चैतत्तडाकानि; Lo[3] तडाकानि; GMd[1] TMd[3] GMd[5] GMy Tj[1] Tr[1] MTr[5] तटाकानि; BKt[5] तनागानि; wKt[6] तलागानि — b) BBe[2] TMd[4] प्रकार°; GMd[5] प्रासाद°; wKt[1] प्राकारान्परि°; Ho Hy प्राकारं परि°; Tr[2] °परिखांस्तथा; Be[3] Lo[3] TMd[4] NPu[1] Tj[1] Tr[1] °परिघास्तथा; TMd[3] GMy °परिघांस्तथा; Ho Kt[2] Wa °परिषास्तथा; Lo[2] °परिषाखास्तथा; La[1] °परिषां तथा — c) Lo[2] समयस्क°; Jo[1] समस्क° — d) NPu[1] विश्वासयेत्तथा; Lo[1] GMd[5] Pu[5] Pu[7] Tr[2] [*Jolly* G] वित्रासयेद्बलं; TMd[3] GMy वित्रासयीत च; MTr[5] MTr[6] वित्रासयेत च; GMd[1] वित्रासणवच; Jo[1] °येत्तदा; *Mādh* °येदपि; TMd[4] °येत्ततः

197. Cited by *Lakṣ* 11.125–6; *Mādh* 1.402 — a) *Lakṣ* उपरुध्यानुजपेद्; Pu[8] यथाशक्ति निगृह्णीयाद्; wKt[1] °प्यानुपजप्य च; Ox[3] °प्यानुपजपेत; Lo[1] °प्यानुपजपेत्त; TMd[3] °प्यानुपजपे — b) TMd[4] बुध्येवचन तत्कृतं; Ox[3] बुध्यैतेषां च तं कृतं; BKt[5] GMd[5] Tr[2] *Mādh* बुध्येच्चैव; wKt[1] TMd[3] NPu[1] Pu[3] बुध्येचैव; Bo बुध्येचव; *Lakṣ* युध्येतैव; wKt[6] BKt[5] *Mādh* हि; NKt[4] यत्कृतं — c) NNg युक्तेथ; wKt[3] युक्तेपु; Be[1] यत्तैव; Pu[3] Pu[8] युक्ते दैवे तु; Tr[1] देवे युक्ते तु; Lo[3] Tj[1] युक्ते दैवे च; Ho Tr[2] देवे; Lo[1] युद्धेच्च; GMy बुध्येत; Be[3] युद्धे चैव — d) TMd[3] GMy फलप्रेप्सु°

198. *ma* in Lo[4]. Cited by *Lakṣ* 11.129; *Mādh* 1.403 — a) Pu[5] Pu[7] दण्डेन भेदेन; Be[3] Jo[2] Lo[3]

अनित्यो विजयो यस्माद् दृश्यते युध्यमानयोः ।
पराजयश्च संग्रामे तस्माद्युद्धं विवर्जयेत् ॥१९९॥
त्रयाणामप्युपायानां पूर्वोक्तानां परिक्षये ।
तथा युध्येत संयत्तो विजयेत रिपून्यथा ॥२००॥
जित्वा संपूजयेद्देवान् ब्राह्मणांश्चैव धार्मिकान् ।
प्रदद्यात्परिहारांश्च ख्यापयेदभयानि च ॥२०१॥
सर्वेषां तु विदित्वैषां समासेन चिकीर्षितम् ।
स्थापयेत्तत्र तद्वंश्यं कुर्याच्च समयक्रियाम् ॥२०२॥
प्रमाणानि च कुर्वीत तेषां धर्मान्यथोदितान् ।
रत्नैश्च पूजयेदेनं प्रधानपुरुषैः सह ॥२०३॥
आदानमप्रियकरं दानं च प्रियकारकम् ।
अभीप्सितानामर्थानां कालयुक्तं प्रशस्यते ॥२०४॥

TMd[4] GMd[5] Ox[3] Tj[1] MTr[6] *Lakṣ* भेदेन दानेन; [*Jolly* M[8] G] भेदेन दण्डेन — b) NKt[4] TMd[4] °स्तैरपि वा; GMd[1] GMd[5] NNg Tr[1] MTr[5] MTr[6] *Lakṣ* °स्तैरुत वा — c) TMd[4] विजेतु; BBe[2] प्रजेतुं; TMd[4] प्रजवेतारिं; Lo[3] GMd[1] TMd[3] GMd[5] GMy Ox[3] Pu[5] Pu[7] *Jha* °तेतारिं; *Nd* supports singular; others silent — c-d) [*Jolly* M[8]) वियुक्तं प्रयतेतारिं विजेतुं सहसा न तं — d) Bo Ho Lo[2] TMd[4] sOx[1] Ox[3] NPu[1] Pu[4] Pu[5] sPu[6] Pu[7] MTr[4] युद्धेत; TMd[3] GMd[5] MTr[5] MTr[6] युध्येत; Tr[2] युद्धेच्च; Lo[1] युद्धेन्न; La[1] GMd[1] NNg Pu[2] युध्येन

199. Omitted in TMd[3] GMy. Cited by *Mādh* 1.403 — a) wKt[3] अनित्ये; Ox[3] अनन्यो — c) wKt[3] °जयस्तु; Ox[3] °जयस्व — d) TMd[4] यस्मा°; Lo[2] विसर्जयेत्

200.* Omitted in TMd[3] GMy Ox[3]. Cited by *Lakṣ* 11.129; *Mādh* 1.403 — b) TMd[4] GMd[5] सामादीनां परि°; Be[1] Be[3] Hy Jm Jo[1] Kt[2] Ox[2] NPu[1] Pu[2] Pu[4] Tj[2] Tr[1] MTr[3] MTr[4] MTr[5] MTr[6] *Mandlik Jha KSS Dave* °क्तानामसंभवे — c) Pu[5] Pu[7] ततो; Pu[8] तस्माद्युध्येत; Bo युद्धेत; MTr[6] संयक्तो; Ox[2] संयंतो; La[1] [*but cor*] संयुत्तो; BBe[2] Be[3] Lo[4] Lo[5] TMd[4] GMd[5] oOr Tr[1] [*Jolly* M] संयुक्तो; wKt[6] संयत्रो; Jm Jo[1] Kt[2] BKt[5] wKt[6] Lo[2] NPu[1] Pu[2] Pu[4] Tj[2] MTr[3] *Mandlik Jha KSS Dave* संपन्नो — d) NKt[4] विजयेच्च; oOr °येतरिपुंगवान्; La[1] Pu[2] Pu[4] रिपुं यथा; Ho Pu[5] Pu[7] यथा रिपून्; wKt[3] तथा रिपून्

201. Omitted in TMd[3] GMy; pādas b-d omitted in GMd[5]. Cited by *Mādh* 1.403 — a) Lo[4] Lo[5] जित्वारीन्पूजये° — c) Pu[2] Pu[4] प्रहद्या°; TMd[4] °द्यात्प्रतिहारांश्च; Be[3] BKt[5] Pu[5] °हाराश्च — d) wKt[1] La[1] क्षापये°

202. Omitted in TMd[3] GMd[5] GMy. Cited by *Mādh* 1.403 — a) [*Jolly* M[8]] सर्वेण तु; oOr Pu[2] Pu[5] Pu[7] Tr[2] [*Jolly* G] च — b) BBe[2] समासे च — c) Ho wKt[3] Tj[1] तद्वश्यं; BBe[2] तं वंश्यं; Lo[4] Lo[5] तद्वंश्या [*both ma* न्] — d) oOr कुर्यात्समय°; BBe[2] समयं; Bo समयि°; Wa समव°; [*Jolly* Nd] समधि°; Tr[2] °क्रियं; TMd[4] °क्रया

203. Omitted in TMd[3] GMy; pādas a-c omitted in GMd[5]. Pādas a-b cited by *Mādh* 1.403 — a) NKt[4] प्रमाणांश्च; BKt[5] तु — b) wKt[3] NKt[4] MTr[3] धर्म्या°; Tr[1] धर्माद्यथो°; Ox[3] कर्मान्यथो°; [*Jolly* Nd] धर्मान्नियोजयेत्; MTr[5] °न्यथोचितान् — c) Pu[4] रनैश्च; TMd[4] Tr[1] MTr[4] MTr[5] MTr[6] °येदेनान्; NKt[4] °येदेवं — d) Tj[1] प्रधानं; wKt[3] °पुरुषंः समं

204. Omitted in TMd[3] GMy — a) NKt[4] La[1] Pu[5] MTr[4] अदान° — b) Pu[4] तु; Tr[1] प्रियकरं परं — c) Lo[1] अभीप्सता°; Be[3] अधीष्टिता°; wKt[6] Pu[5] Pu[7] °तानां द्रव्याणां; oOr °तानां वाप्नोति — d) Be[3] Ho

सर्वं कर्मेदमायत्तं विधाने दैवमानुषे ।
तयोर्दैवमचिन्त्यं तु मानुषे विद्यते क्रिया ॥२०५॥
सह वापि व्रजेद्युक्तः संधिं कृत्वा प्रयत्नतः ।
मित्रं हिरण्यं भूमिं वा संपश्यंस्त्रिविधं फलम् ॥२०६॥
पार्ष्णिग्राहं च संप्रेक्ष्य तथाक्रन्दं च मण्डले ।
मित्रादथाप्यमित्राद्वा यात्राफलमवाप्नुयात् ॥२०७॥
हिरण्यभूमिसंप्राप्त्या पार्थिवो न तथैधते ।
यथा मित्रं ध्रुवं लब्ध्वा कृशमप्यायतिक्षमम् ॥२०८॥
धर्मज्ञं च कृतज्ञं च तुष्टप्रकृतिमेव च ।
अनुरक्तं स्थिरारम्भं लघु मित्रं प्रशस्यते ॥२०९॥

Jo[1] La[1] Lo[1] Lo[3] Lo[4] Lo[5] Pu[8] Tj[1] Tj[2] MTr[3] MTr[5] *Me Go Nā Ku Rn Mr Mandlik Jolly KSS Dave* काले; wKt[1] कालं युक्तां; wKt[6] कालमुक्तं

205. Omitted in TMd[3] GMy. Cited by *Lakṣ* 11.139 — a) wKt[6] Lo[1] Ox[3] Pu[5] Pu[7] सर्व; Lo[4] Ox[3] कर्मेदमोयत्तं; Be[1] °दमापत्रं; Tj[1] °दमायातं; Lo[1] °दमायन्तं; GMd[1] °दमात्तंवा; TMd[4] °दमायत्तु; oOr °दमादाय — b) Tj[1] विधानै; BKt[5] विधानौ; TMd[4] विधाये; Ox[3] विधिना; wKt[6] विषानौ; wKt[6] Lo[1] देव°; wKt[3] Lo[2] नैव मानुषे; Lo[3] Tj[1] Tr[2] °मानुषं; Ho Wa °पौरुषे — c) wKt[3] BKt[5] Lo[1] Lo[2] TMd[4] MTr[6] तयोर्देव°; *Lakṣ* तत्र दैव°; BBe[2] °चिन्तं; Ho NNg Pu[5] Pu[7] *Lakṣ* च — d) Ox Tr[2] पुरुषे; Ox[2] पुरूषे; oOr पौरुषे; NNg क्रिया:

Fifty additional verses are given here in some mss. Because of their length, they are given as an appendix at the end of this chapter.

206. Omitted in Lo[4] Lo[5] Ox[3]; not commented by *Me*. Cited by *Lakṣ* 11.142 — a) Tr[1] सहसापि; NKt[4] व्रजेद्युक्तं — b) oOr तु यत्नतः — c) GMy मित्रा; sOx[1] sPu[6] Tr[2] भूमिं हिरण्यं; Ox[2] *om* भूमिं; BCa Lo[2] Pu[7] [*Jolly* G] च — d) BBe[2] Be[3] संपश्यन्त्रिविधं; Ho संपशात्त्रिविधं; Lo[3] Tj[1] संपश्येत्त्रिविधं; Tr[1] संपश्यन्विविधं; Hy संपश्यंस्विविधं; Be[3] NKt[4] बलं

207. Omitted in Lo[4] Lo[5] Ox[3]; not commented by *Me;* pādas c-d omitted in Tr[2]. Cited by *Lakṣ* 11.142 — a) Pu[2] Pu[4] Tr[2] पाणिग्राहं; TMd[4] °ग्रहे; Lo[1] Ox[2] °ग्राहांश्च; TMd[3] °ग्रहांश्च; La[1] Pu[2] संप्रेष्य — b) TMd[3] तथाकृधं; TMd[3] GMy मण्डलं — c) TMd[4] Ox[2] Pu[3] Tj[1] मित्रात्तथाप्यमित्राद्वा; TMd[3] GMy मित्रादवाप्यमित्राद्वा°; sOx[1] sPu[6] मित्रादप्यथ वामित्राद्; Bo मित्राद्यथाप्यमि°; Lo[2] मित्रादथोप्यमि°

208. Omitted in Lo[4] Lo[5] Ox[3]; not commented by *Me;* pādas c-d omitted in Tr[2] and placed after 209 in Bo — a) Ho BKt[5] wKt[6] Pu[3] भूमिं हिरण्यं संप्राप्य; La[1] sOx[1] sPu[6] Pu[8] हिरण्यं; Ox[2] भूमिहिरण्य°; Lo[1] sOx[1] sPu[6] MTr[4] °भूमिं; Tr[1] °भूमी संप्राप्य; La[1] NKt[4] TMd[3] GMd[5] GMy Pu[5] Pu[7] Pu[8] *Rc* °भूमिं संप्राप्य; Lo[1] sOx[1] sPu[6] °संप्राप्ता; GMd[1] TMd[4] MTr[5] °संप्राप्य — b) TMd[4] वर्धते न तथा नृपः; sOx[1] sPu[6] पार्थिवा; TMd[3] GMy पार्थिवे; Be[3] नैधते तथा; Pu[5] Pu[7] Tr[1] तथेधते; Lo[2] तथैवते; Tj[1] तयैधते; BBe[2] Bo wKt[3] तथैव च — c) TMd[4] यथा मित्रं तथा लव्ध्वा; Tr[1] मित्र — d) BBe[2] कृतम°; TMd[3] °तिक्षयं; TMd[4] °तिक्षध

209. Omitted in Lo[4] Lo[5] Ox[3]; not commented by *Me;* pādas c-d *ma* in BKt[5] — a) Kt[2] धर्मज्ञश्च कृतज्ञश्च — b) oOr तुष्टप्रीतिकरं तथा; Lo[1] तुष्टं प्रवृतमेव च; MTr[5] हृष्टप्रकृ°; NKt[4] °कृतमेव; BBe[2] Wa °कृतिकं तथा; Hy wKt[3] Lo[2] TMd[4] Tj[2] MTr[4] MTr[6] °कृतिं चैव यत् [MTr[6] °कृतिर्चैव]; NNg तु — c) Lo[1] स्थितारम्भं; wKt[1] स्थिरालम्भं; NKt[4] स्थिसंदेहं [sic] — d) GMd[5] प्रचक्षते

प्राज्ञं कुलीनं शूरं च दक्षं दातारमेव च ।
कृतज्ञं धृतिमन्तं च कष्टमाहुररिं बुधाः ॥२१०॥
आर्यता पुरुषज्ञानं शौर्यं करुणवेदिता ।
स्थौललक्ष्यं च सततमुदासीनगुणोदयः ॥२११॥
क्षेम्यां सस्यप्रदां नित्यं पशुवृद्धिकरीमपि ।
परित्यजेन्नृपो भूमिमात्मार्थमविचारयन् ॥२१२॥
आपदर्थं धनं रक्षेद् दारान् रक्षेद्धनैरपि ।
आत्मानं सततं रक्षेद् दारैरपि धनैरपि ॥२१३॥
सह सर्वाः समुत्पन्नाः प्रसमीक्ष्यापदो भृशम् ।
संयुक्तांश्च वियुक्तांश्च सर्वोपायान्सृजेद्बुधः ॥२१४॥

210. Omitted in Lo^4 Lo^5 Ox^3; not commented by *Me;* pādas a-b *ma* in BKt^5. Cited by *Lakṣ* 11.107 — a) Jo^1 राज्ञं; TMd^3 GMy शूरं कुलीनं च; Bo wKt^1 wKt^3 शूलं — a-b) GMd^1 प्राज्ञं दक्षं कुलीनं च शूरं दातारमेव च; *Lakṣ* प्राज्ञं कुलीनं दातारं शूरं दक्षं तथैव च — b) TMd^3 GMy दान्तं दाता° — c) GMd^1 कृतिज्ञं मतिमन्तं; wKt^1 कृतिमन्तं; Pu^5 Pu^7 वृत्तवन्तं; BKt^5 wKt^6 धृतमित्रं; *Lakṣ* शक्तिमन्तं — d) Jm कृष्टमा° ; TMd^4 कृतमा° ; Ho °हुरिमं; Bo बुधः; TMd^3 GMy पुरा

211. Omitted in Lo^4 Lo^5 Ox^3. Cited by *Lakṣ* 11.108 — a) NKt^4 Lo^1 आर्यतां; Lo^1 पुरुषं; Hy पुरुषाज्ञानं — b) La^1 Pu^5 Pu^7 सौर्यं; Be^1 [*Jolly* R] कारुण्य° ; Lo^3 Wa करुण्य° ; wKt^3 Pu^5 Pu^7 करण° ; GMd^1 Pu^4 करुणमेव वा; Lo^1 ° वेदितां; wKt^1 °चोदिता; BBe^2 °मेदिता — c) Tr^2 स्थौल्य° ; Lo^2 स्थोल° ; Jo^1 स्थोले° ; BKt^5 wKt^6 Lo^1 NNg NPu^1 Pu^2 Pu^4 Pu^5 Pu^7 *Rn Go Lakṣ* स्थूल° ; Be^1 Be^3 Bo Ho wKt^1 NKt^4 BKt^5 wKt^6 La^1 NNg NPu^1 Pu^2 Pu^3 Pu^4 Pu^5 Tj^1 Tj^2 °लक्षं; TMd^3 GMy °लाक्षं; *Lakṣ* °लक्षश्च; Ho तु; TMd^4 च विदितमु° — d) wKt^6 सततं तदासीन° ; Tr^1 °दासीनं; Be^1 TMd^3 TMd^4 GMd^5 GMy Tr^1 Wa °णोदयं; sOx^1 sPu^6 Tr^2 °णोदये

212. Verses 212 and 213 transposed in Lo^4 Lo^5 Ox^3; pādas c-d omitted in Pu^5 Lo^4. Cited by *Lakṣ* 11.142 — a) TMd^4 GMd^5 क्षेम्या; Jm Lo^1 Ox^2 क्षेमां; Ox^3 क्षेमा; TMd^3 क्षेमं; wKt^6 क्षमी; Tr^2 रभ्यां; GMd^1 GMy Tr^1 MTr^4 सस्यवतीं; MTr^6 सस्यप्रतीं; TMd^3 सस्यपती; Be^1 Bo wKt^6 wKt^3 TMd^4 GMd^5 Ox^3 °प्रदा; Kt^2 °प्रदं; Ho °पदां — b) Hy °करिमपि; Pu^7 °करामपि — d) wKt^3 °त्मानमवि° ; wKt^1 °मपिचा° ; GMy °मपि रोचयेत्; TMd^3 °मविरोचयेत्; Lo^5 Pu^2 Pu^4 Pu^7 [*Jolly* G] °मवधारयन्; Ox^3 °मपधारयन्; wKt^6 °चारयेत्

213.* Pādas c-d omitted in Lo^3 Tj^1. Cited by *Lakṣ* 11.142–3 — a) BBe^2 Ho Hy La^1 Lo^1 Lo^2 Lo^4 Lo^5 oOr Ox^3 NPu^1 Pu^3 Tr^2 [*Jolly* M] *Me Go Jha Dave* आपदर्थे; wKt^3 आपदर्थ; Lo^2 रक्ष्येद्; NKt^4 BKt^5 GMd^1 TMd^4 MTr^5 Wa रक्ष्यं — b) NKt^4 BKt^5 Lo^3 GMd^1 TMd^4 GMd^5 [*but cor*] Tj^1 Tr^1 MTr^5 MTr^6 Wa *Me* दारा रक्ष्या धनैरपि; wKt^6 दाररक्ष्यं धनैरपि; Lo^2 दारां; Lo^2 रक्ष्याद्ध° — c) Be^1 NKt^4 Lo^2 GMd^1 MTr^4 MTr^5 MTr^6 Wa *Lakṣ* आत्मा तु सर्वतो रक्ष्यो [GMd^1 MTr^4 सर्वधा; MTr^6 सर्वदा; TMd^4 MTr^5 सततं; GMd^5 रक्ष्यं *cor to* रक्ष्यो]; TMd^4 आत्मानं सततं रक्ष्यं; TMd^3 GMy [*Jolly* Nd] आत्मा तु तथा रक्षेद्; GMd^5 सर्वधा; Pu^5 Pu^7 Tr^1 [*Jolly* G] सर्वदा; BKt^5 wKt^6 La^1 Lo^1 Lo^4 Lo^5 sOx^1 Ox^2 Ox^3 sPu^6 Tr^2 [*Jolly* M^9] सर्वतो

214. Omitted in Pu^5. Cited by *Lakṣ* 11.143 — a) MTr^5 स हि सर्वाः; Bo सार्वाः; TMd^3 GMy सर्व; Lo^5 सर्वां; Tr^1 सर्वात्समु° — b) wKt^3 °क्ष्याप्रदो; TMd^4 °क्ष्यपरा — c) TMd^3 संयुक्तां च वियुक्तां च; Lo^4 Lo^5 संयुक्तान्विप्रयुक्तांश्च; Lo^1 संप्रयु° ; TMd^4 Tr^1 संयुक्ताश्च; BKt^5 संयुक्तां वियु° ; Ox^3 *om* वियुक्तांश्च;

उपेतारमुपेयं च सर्वोपायांश्च कृत्स्नशः ।
एतत्त्रयं समाश्रित्य प्रयतेतात्मसिद्धये ॥२१५॥
एवं सर्वमिदं राजा सह संमन्त्र्य मन्त्रिभिः ।
व्यायम्याप्लुत्य मध्याह्ने भोक्तुमन्तःपुरं व्रजेत् ॥२१६॥
तत्रात्मभूतैः कालज्ञैरहार्यैः परिचारकैः ।
सुपरीक्षितमन्नाद्यमद्यान्मन्त्रैर्विषापहैः ॥२१७॥
विषघ्नैरगदैश्चास्य सर्वद्रव्याणि नेजयेत् ।
विषघ्नानि च रत्नानि नियतो धारयेत्सदा ॥२१८॥
परीक्षिताः स्त्रियश्चैनं व्यजनोदकधूपनैः ।
वेषाभरणसंशुद्धाः स्पृशेयुः सुसमाहिताः ॥२१९॥
एवं प्रयत्नं कुर्वीत यानशय्यासनाशने ।

TMd^4 वियुक्ताश्च; wKt^6 विमुक्तांश्च — d) wKt^1 °पायं सृजे°; NKt^4 °पायांस्त्यजेद्बुधः; *Lakṣ* °पायान् जयेद्बुधः; Ho °जेत्प्रभुः

215.* Omitted in Pu^5. Cited by *Lakṣ* 11.143; *Mādh* 1.411 — a) Pu^2 Pu^4 Tr^2 °मुपेयां; oOr °मुपेतं — b) TMd^3 °पायाश्च; GMd^5 NPu^1 सर्वशः — c) Be^1 एतेषां त्रयमाश्रित्य; Lo^3 Tj^1 एवं त्रयं; Tr^2 समाशृत्य; NKt^4 Ox^3 समासृत्य — d) BBe^2 Bo Hy Jm Jo^1 Jo^2 wKt^1 Kt^2 wKt^3 Lo^3 Lo^4 Lo^5 TMd^4 Tj^1 MTr^3 *Mādh Mandlik Jolly Jha KSS Dave* प्रयतेतार्थसिद्धये; *Me* [pāṭha] साधयेत्कार्यमात्मनः

216.* Omitted in oOr. Cited by *Lakṣ* 11.157 — a) TMd^3 GMy सर्वानिमान् राजा — b) GMd^5 NNg MTr^6 संमन्त्र्य सह; TMd^4 संमन्त्र — c) Kt^2 Ox^3 Pu^5 Pu^7 Wa *Jolly* व्यायाम्या°; GMd^5 नियम्या°; TMd^4 व्यायमाहत्य; Lo^1 NPu^1 Pu^4 °म्याप्लुत; Tj^1 °म्याप्लुत्य — d) Tr^2 °पुरो; BKt^5 wKt^6 °पुरे; Pu^5 Pu^7 वसेत्; Be^1 Bo Hy Jm Jo^1 Jo^2 wKt^1 Kt^2 wKt^3 BKt^5 wKt^6 La^2 Lo^2 Lo^3 Lo^1 sOx^1 Ox^2 Pu^2 sPu^6 Pu^8 Tj^1 Tr^2 MTr^3 Wa *Go Ku Rn Mandlik Jolly Jha KSS Dave* विशेत्

217. Omitted in oOr. Cited by *Lakṣ* 11.157 — a) GMd^1 तत्रभूतैश्च काल°; Ox^3 °भूते — b) BBe^2 NKt^4 La^1 Lo^1 °ज्ञैराहार्यैः; Ox^2 °ज्ञैराचार्यैः; Ho *Nā* [who gives अहार्यैः as pāṭhāntara] °ज्ञैरभेद्यैः; TMd^4 °ज्ञैरहन्ये; GMd^1 °ज्ञैरार्यैश्च परि°; Ho Tr^2 °चारिकैः; wKt^3 °हारकैः — c) TMd^3 GMy व्यपरीक्षि°; BKt^5 °परीक्षत°; NPu^1 Pu^4 °क्षितमन्वाद्यम° — d) GMd^5 °न्नाद्यं मन्त्रैरेव विषापहैः

218.* Omitted in oOr. Cited by *Lakṣ* 11.1158 — a) wKt^1 विषं चैव गदे चास्य; Lo^4 Lo^5 GMd^1 TMd^3 TMd^4 GMd^5 GMy Ox^3 Tr^1 MTr^4 MTr^5 MTr^6 [*Jolly* M Nd] *Lakṣ Dave Jha* °घ्नैरुदकै°; Lo^1 Ox^3 Pu^3 Pu^8 °श्चापि; TMd^3 GMy MTr^4 MTr^6 °श्चैव; BKt^5 wKt^6 °श्चान्यैः; NPu^1 °श्चाद्यात् *cor to* °श्चाद्य — b) BKt^5 wKt^6 °द्रव्यान्नेजयेत्; Pu^2 Pu^4 Pu^5 Pu^7 Wa तेजयेत्; Be^1 BBe^2 Be^3 Bo BCa Ho Hy Jm Jo^1 NKt^4 La^2 Lo^1 Lo^5 TMd^4 sOx^1 sPu^6 Pu^8 Tj^2 Tr^1 Tr^2 MTr^3 [*Jolly* Ku] *Ku Mandlik KSS* योजयेत्; NPu^1 भोजयेत्; Jo^2 La^1 Lo^3 Tj^1 [*Jolly* R] *Rn Jha Dave* शोधयेत् — c) BBe^2 *om* च — d) Ox^3 नियते; Pu^5 Pu^7 [*Jolly* G] प्रयतो; Pu^2 Pu^4 प्रधतो

219. Omitted in oOr. Cited by *Lakṣ* 11.1158 — a) Ox^3 परीक्षितादियश्चैव; Bo BKt^5 La^1 Lo^4 Lo^5 TMd^4 NPu^1 Pu^2 Pu^3 Pu^4 Pu^8 [*Jolly* M] स्त्रियश्चैव; Ox^2 स्त्रियश्चैवं — b) BBe^2 व्यञ्जनो°; Ox^3 विजनो°; wKt^3 Lo^4 Lo^5 Ox^3 °धूपकैः — c) Pu^5 Tr^2 विषाभर°; Hy °भरणासंशुद्धाः; TMd^3 GMd^5 GMy °भरणशुद्धाश्च; Tr^1 °भरणयुक्ताश्च; Lo^2 Lo^4 Lo^5 GMd^1 Ox^3 MTr^4 MTr^5 MTr^6 [*Jolly* M] *Me Lakṣ* °संयुक्ताः — d) BBe^2 Lo^4 Lo^5 GMd^1 TMd^4 Ox^3 [*Jolly* M] *Lakṣ* संस्पृशेयुः समाहिताः; Tj^1 स्पृशतुः; GMd^5 [*but cor*] Tj^1 °हितः

स्नाने प्रसाधने चैव सर्वालंकारकेषु च ॥२२०॥
भुक्तवान्विहरेच्चैव स्त्रीभिरन्तःपुरे सह ।
विहृत्य च यथाकालं पुनः कार्याणि चिन्तयेत् ॥२२१॥
अलंकृतश्च संपश्येदायुधीयं पुनर्जनम् ।
वाहनानि च सर्वाणि शस्त्राण्याभरणानि च ॥२२२॥
संध्यां चोपास्य शृणुयादन्तर्वेश्मनि शस्त्रभृत् ।
रहस्याख्यायिनां चैव प्रणिधीनां च चेष्टितम् ॥२२३॥
गत्वा कक्षान्तरं त्वन्यत् समनुज्ञाप्य तं जनम् ।
प्रविशेद्भोजनार्थं च स्त्रीवृतोऽन्तःपुरं पुनः ॥२२४॥
तत्र भुक्त्वा पुनः किंचित् तूर्यघोषैः प्रहर्षितः ।

220. Omitted in oOr. Cited by *Lakṣ* 11.1158 — a) bBe^{2} wKt^{1} nPu^{1} यत्नं प्रकुर्वीत; Lo^{4} [*ma* प्र]कुर्वीत — b) Pu^{5} Pu^{7} °सनेशने; bCa wKt^{3} tMd^{3} gMy °शनासने; Lo^{2} °सनाशनैः; mTr^{5} °शनासनैः; mTr^{4} °सनासशनैः; Lo^{4} Lo^{5} Ox^{3} [*Jolly* M] °सनादिषु; Jo^{2} nPu^{1} Tj^{1} Tr^{1} [*Jolly* R Gr] °सनेषु च; bBe^{2} °शनेषु च — c) gMd^{1} Wa स्थाने; bBe^{2} sOx^{1} sPu^{6} प्रसादने; tMd^{4} प्रासादने; Lo^{3} Tj^{1} °धने भोज्ये; Pu^{5} Pu^{7} चैवं — d) mTr^{5} स चालंकारिके[torn]; bBe^{2} Be^{3} bCa Hy nNg sOx^{1} Pu^{2} Pu^{3} Pu^{4} sPu^{6} Pu^{8} Tj^{1} Tr^{2} °लंकारिकेषु; gMd^{5} °लंकरणेषु; gMd^{1} °लंकारणेषु; *Lakṣ* °लंकारादिषु; wKt^{1} °लंकालकारिषु च; tMd^{3} gMy °लंकार एव च; Ho °केष्वपि

221. Omitted in Ox^{3} oOr. Cited by *Vij* 1.329;*Lakṣ* 11.161 — a) mTr^{5} °हरेच्चैवं; Be^{3} °हरेच्चैनं — b) nKt^{4} स्त्रीभिः रत्नः पुरैः सह; Ho °पुरं; nKt^{4} Lo^{1} Lo^{2} Lo^{5} tMd^{3} tMd^{4} gMd^{5} gMy °पुरैः — c) Ho Pu^{5} Pu^{7} विहत्य; Hy Jm Jo^{1} Kt^{2} wKt^{3} Ox^{3} nPu^{1} Tj^{2} mTr^{3} *Vij Mandlik Jolly Jha KSS Dave* तु; *Lakṣ* तथा°; Ho यथाकामं; Be^{3} यथाकर्म — d) tMd^{3} कर्माणि; Tr^{2} कार्याणि चैव हि; Wa कारयेत्

222. Omitted in Ox^{3} oOr; *ma* in Lo^{4}. Cited by *Lakṣ* 11161 — a) tMd^{3} gMd^{5} Tr^{1} °कृतं च; *Lakṣ* °कृतस्तथा पश्ये°; Be^{3} °कृतः स्वसंपश्ये° — b) gMy °श्येत्तदाधीयं; wKt^{3} °युधीनं; tMd^{4} °युधीर्यं; Bo पुनर्जना; Jo^{2} La^{1} Lo^{3} tMd^{3} gMd^{5} gMy Tr^{1} mTr^{4} mTr^{6} पृथग्जनं— c-d) tMd^{4} च शस्त्राणि सर्वाण्याभर° — d) Ho शास्त्रा°; gMd^{5} *Lakṣ* वस्त्रा°; gMd^{1} gMd^{5} °वरणानि

223. Omitted in oOr; pādas c-d omitted in Ox^{3}. Cited by *Vij* 1.330;*Lakṣ* 11.162 — a) *Lakṣ* संध्यामुपास्य; tMd^{3} gMy संध्यां कृत्वाथ — b) Lo^{4} Lo^{5} Ox^{3} °वेंश्म सुसंभृतः; Pu^{2} Pu^{4} शस्त्रकृत् — c) tMd^{4} प्रहस्याख्यायिकां; wKt^{6} °ख्यायिनं; sOx^{1} sPu^{6} °ख्यायनं; tMd^{3} °ख्यायिकं; La^{1} gMy °ख्यायि-कांश्चैव; Hy चैवं — d) Kt^{2} gMd^{1} Tr^{2} प्रणधीनां; wKt^{3} प्रणिधीतं; wKt^{3} वेष्टितं

224. Omitted in oOr; not commented by *Nd;* pādas a-b omitted in mTr^{3}. Cited by *Vij* 1.330; *Lakṣ* 11.162 — a) gMd^{1} वसेत्कक्षा°; Tr^{2} कक्षान्तरे; Bo कक्षोत्तरं; tMd^{3} tMd^{4} gMy रक्षान्तरं; Lo^{5} *om* त्वन्यत्; Bo Ho Jo^{2} La^{2} Lo^{1} Lo^{3} tMd^{4} Pu^{3} Pu^{8} Tj^{1} Tr^{1} चान्यत्; Be^{3} वान्यत्; Tr^{2} त्वन्यं; sOx^{1} sPu^{6} चान्यं; tMd^{3} gMd^{5} gMy mTr^{6} सम्यक्; gMd^{1} चैव — b) gMd^{1} tMd^{3} tMd^{4} gMd^{5} gMy Tr^{1} mTr^{4} mTr^{6} °ज्ञाय; Ox^{3} °प्राप्य; La^{1} °ज्ञाय च तं; Tr^{1} तज्जनं; Lo^{5} जलं — c) wKt^{6} °जनानां च; bKt^{5} Ox^{3} °जनां च; Lo^{4} Lo^{5} gMd^{1} Tr^{1} mTr^{4} °जनायैव; tMd^{4} °जनायैत; Pu^{2} Pu^{4} °जनार्थाय; Be^{1} Be^{3} Bo Ho Jo^{2} wKt^{1} wKt^{3} nKt^{4} La^{1} Lo^{1} tMd^{3} gMd^{5} gMy sOx^{1} Ox^{2} Pu^{3} Pu^{5} sPu^{6} Pu^{7} Pu^{8} Tj^{1} Tj^{2} Wa [*Jolly* R] *Lakṣ* तु; Tr^{2} हि — d) Wa स्त्रीवृतान्तःपुरं; Be^{3} bCa wKt^{1} La^{1} Lo^{4} Lo^{5} tMd^{3} tMd^{4} gMd^{5} gMy sOx^{1} Ox^{3} sPu^{6} Tr^{2} [*Jolly* R] *Vij* स्त्रीभिरन्तःपुरं; bKt^{5} wKt^{6} La^{1} °पुरे; Jo^{2} Lo^{3} Tj^{1} °पुरं ततः; *Vij* °पुरं सह

संविशेच्च यथाकालमुत्तिष्ठेच्च गतक्लमः ॥२२५॥
एतद्वृत्तं समातिष्ठेदरोगः पृथिवीपतिः ।
अस्वस्थः सर्वमेतत्तु भृत्येषु विनियोजयेत् ॥२२६॥

॥ इति मानवे धर्मशास्त्रे भृगुप्रोक्तायां संहितायां सप्तमोऽध्यायः ॥

225. Omitted in oOr; not commented by *Nd.* Cited by *Lakṣ* 11.162 — a) wKt^3 ततः; Ho भुक्ता; Lo^4 भुक्त; TMd^3 Tr^1 गत्वा — b) TMd^3 GMy °तौर्य°; Hy °घौषैः; TMd^4 °घोष; Lo^4 Lo^5 Ox^3 Pu^5 Pu^7 प्रहर्षिभिः — c) Hy Jm Jo^1 Kt^2 wKt^3 BKt^5 Lo^5 TMd^4 Tj^2 MTr^3 *Mandlik Jolly Jha KSS Dave* संविशेत्तु; wKt^6 Lo^3 संविशेत; NKt^4 संविशेत्स; Tj^1 संविशेन; Ox^3 प्रविशेत्तु; Ox^3 *om* and Lo^4 *ma* यथाकालं — d) Ox^3 °कालं तिष्ठेद्विगतः क्लमः; Lo^3 Tj^1 °कालं समुत्तिष्ठेद्गतक्लमः; Lo^4 Lo^5 TMd^3 GMd^5 GMy Tr^1 MTr^4 [*Jolly* M Nd] °त्तिष्ठेद्विगतक्लमः; Pu^5 Pu^7 °त्तिष्ठेद्विगतज्वरः;Lo^2 °ष्ठेद्धि; BKt^5 गतः; BBe^2 wKt^1 NPu^1 °क्रमः

226.* Omitted in Lo^4; not commented by *Nd.* Cited by *Vij* 1.331; *Lakṣ* 11.162 — a) Be^1 BBe^2 Bo Ho Hy Jm Jo^1 Jo^2 wKt^1 Kt^2 wKt^3 BKt^5 wKt^6 La^2 Lo^1 Lo^3 Lo^5 NNg sOx^1 Ox^2 Ox^3 NPu^1 Pu^3 Pu^5 sPu^6 Pu^7 Pu^8 Tj^1 Tj^2 Tr^2 MTr^3 Wa *Mandlik Jolly Jha KSS Dave* एतद्विधानमातिष्ठेद°; Ox^3 उत्तिष्ठेत समे देशे — b) TMd^4 °रोगं — c) BKt^5 अस्वस्थं; Be^3 असुस्थः; Hy असूस्थः; wKt^6 असुस्थं; Kt^2 La^1 Lo^2 TMd^3 oOr Pu^3 Pu^4 अश्वस्थः; Ox^3 सुस्वस्थः; Lo^5 GMd Ox^3 Tr^1 MTr^4 MTr^6 [*Jolly* M] सर्वमेवेदं; Be^1 Bo Ho Lo^1 TMd^3 GMd^5 GMy Pu^3 Pu^8 Wa [*Jolly* Nd] सर्वमेवैतद् — c-d) *Lakṣ Vij* सर्वमेवैतन्मन्त्रिमुख्ये निवेशयेत् — d) Be^1 Be^3 Bo Jo^2 NKt^4 Lo^3 TMd^3 TMd^4 GMy NNg Pu^3 Pu^8 Tj^1 MTr^5 Wa विनिवेशयेत्

Colophon: Be^1 Lo^1 Lo^3 TMd^3 NNg sOx^1 sPu^6 इति श्रीमानवे; Be^3 wKt^3 भृगुप्रोक्ते; Be^1 BKt^5 wKt^6 Lo^2 GMd^1 GMd^5 sOx^1 TMd^3 MTr^6 *om* भृगुप्रोक्तायां संहितायां; Lo^1 Lo^3 भृगुप्रोक्तसंहितायां; Be^3 wKt^3 *om* संहितायां; Be^1 NNg राजधर्मः सप्तमो, BBe^2 wKt^1 Kt^2 Lo^3 oOr Tj^1 राजधर्मो नाम सप्तमो, Lo^1 राजधर्माणि सप्तमो

Appendix

The following additional verses are given after verse 205 in GMd[1] MTr[4]MTr[6]; verses 2, 5, 6 given in Lo[4]; verse 2 in Lo[5]; verse 7 in wKt[1]; verses 1, 7, 9, 10 cited by *Lakṣ* 11.140; verses 2, 5, 6 are cited in *Me's* commentary on verse 205:

दैवमानुषसंपन्ना यात्रा सर्वार्थसाधका ।
तस्यामतिशये दैवं वर्तते पौरुषं समम् ॥१॥

b) MTr[4] MTr[6] °साधिका

दैवेन विधिना युक्तं मानुषं यत्प्रवर्तते ।
परिक्लेशेन महता तदर्थस्य प्रसाधनम् ॥२॥

a) Lo[4] Lo[5] दैवे विधानयुक्तस्य — b) GMd[1] यः प्रव° — d) MTr[4] MTr[6]प्रधानकं; Lo[4] Lo[5] *Me* समाधकं

पुरुषार्थस्तु दैवेन संयुक्तो यः प्रवर्तते ।
अक्लेशेन स सर्वेषामत्रार्थानां प्रसाधकः ॥३॥

c) MTr[4] MTr[6] अक्लेशेनैव

किंचिदुप्तमपि क्षेत्रं युक्तं पुरुषकर्मणा ।
दैवहीनाय न फलं कस्मैचित्संप्रयच्छति ॥४॥

a-b) GMd[1] °प्तमिवाक्षेत्रमशुक्तं —c) MTr[6] दैवे

संयुक्तस्यापि दैवेन नाकृष्टं बीजवर्जितम् ।
विना पुरुषकारेण फलं क्षेत्रं प्रयच्छति ॥५॥

a) Lo[4] °क्तस्य वा — b) Lo[4] कृष्टवीरणवर्जितं; *Me* पुरुषकारेण वर्जितं; MTr[4] दैवेनाकृष्टं

चन्द्रार्काद्या ग्रहा वायुरग्निरापस्तथैव च ।
इह दैवेन साध्यन्ते पौरुषेण च यत्नतः ॥६॥

a) Lo[4] चन्द्रासूर्यग्रहा — c) GMd[1] शुभदैवेन

केचित्पुरुषकारेण केचिद्दैवेन कर्मणा ।
उभाभ्यां केचिदिच्छन्ति फलं कुशलबुद्धयः ॥७॥

c) GMd[1] इह यं केचि° — d) GMd[1] कुशलं वृद्धयः

नारीपुरुषवद्योगो दैवमानुषयोर्यदा ।
तदा तद्गर्भवत्सिद्धिः कर्मणां सफला भवेत् ॥८॥

b) MTr[4] नारीमनुष्य° — c-d) GMd[1] °वद्विधिकर्मणा सफलो

न हि दैवमुदासीनं कदाचिदपि मानवम् ।
अर्थानर्थफलेनेह संयुनक्त्यवशः क्वचित् ॥९॥

a) GMd[1] °मुपासीनं —b) MTr[6] मानवः — c) GMd[1] अनर्थानां फलेनेह — d) MTr[4] MTr[6] °वशं

काकतालीयवद्दैवाद् दृष्ट्वापि निधिमग्रतः ।
न पुरुषादृते तेन निधिना युज्यते पुमान् ॥१०॥

a) MTr[6] °तालय°; MTr[4] °वदैवं; MTr[6] °वदेवं — b) GMd[1] दृष्टापि सन्निधि° — d) MTr[4] MTr[6] विधिना

दैवेन हि नरे किंचित् क्वचित्समुपपादितम् ।
प्रतिकर्तुं न तच्छक्यं दैवहीनेन तेन तु ॥११॥

c) MTr[4] MTr[6] प्रतिकर्तृत्र— d) GMd[1] तेन तत्

न नाशः कर्मणां कश्चिदनृतं च न विद्यते ।
तस्मादेवोपचारोऽयमात्मन्येव विधीयते ॥१२॥

a) GMd[1] कर्मणः किंचि° — b) MTr[6] °दकृतं च न; GMd[1] °दकृत न विद्यते —d) MTr[6] विद्यते

तस्मात्प्राकारयन्त्रादिपराक्रान्तं च पौरुषम् ।
तस्मादुद्योग एवात्र सम्यगर्थप्रसाधकः ॥१३॥

b) MTr[4] MTr[6] °क्रान्तश्च — d) GMd[1] °साधकं

उत्साहवन्तमश्रान्तं व्यसनैः परिवर्जितम् ।
पुरुषं नयसंपन्नं दैवमप्युपतिष्ठति ॥१४॥

c) GMd[1] पुरुषन्तं संपन्नं — d) GMd[1] °तिष्ठते

निष्प्रयोजनमेवेह दैवं सापेक्षमिष्यते ।
आत्मसंस्थं स्वतन्त्रं च पुरुषं सर्वकार्यकृत् ॥१५॥

b) GMd[1] दैव; MTr[6] °मिक्ष्यते

कस्यानिष्टं सुखं लोके दुःखं को वाभिनन्दति ।
कृपणः पुरुषो दैवादुभयं प्रतिपद्यते ॥१६॥

a) GMd[1] कस्यातिषं — b) GMd[1] वा हि नन्दति — c) GMd[1] कृपणं पौरुषं दैवमु°

गर्भस्थं चैव पुष्णाति जातं संवर्धयत्यपि ।
संयुनक्ति च कालेन दैवमेव हि देहिनाम् ॥१७॥

a) MTr[4] गर्भस्थस्यैव; GMd[1] प्रश्नानि

स्थाने नियुङ्क्ते पुरुषं शुभे वा यदि वाशुभे ।
यत्र दैवं स रमते तत्र दैवप्रचोदितः ॥१८॥

a) GMd[1] नियुक्तं — b) GMd[1] शुभं वा — d) GMd[1] दैवः प्रमोदितः

दैवोपनीतमर्थं हि पुरुषः प्रतिपद्यते ।
तस्य वृद्धिः क्षयो वापि दैवादेवोपजायते ॥१९॥

c) MTr[4] वृद्धि

प्रारब्धं कर्म यत्नेन पुरुषेणोपपादितम् ।
निष्फलं विमुखे दैवे दृष्टार्थमपि यद्भवेत् ॥२०॥

a) MTr[4] MTr[6] प्रारम्भं — c) GMd[1] विमुक्ते

सर्वथाभ्युद्यतं दैवं वध्यमेव जिघांसति ।
शस्त्राग्निविषदुर्गेभ्यो रक्षतव्यं च रक्षति ॥२१॥

a) MTr[4] °भ्युदितं — c) MTr[4] MTr[6] शस्त्रादिगिरिदुर्गेभ्यो; GMd[1] °विषदुश्शोभ्यो

दैवं नरस्य कुरुते यदा बुद्धिविपर्ययम् ।
तदासौ विनयश्लाघी करोत्यात्मविनाशनम् ॥२२॥

c) GMd[1] तदा सो

मन्त्रमङ्गलकर्माणि पवित्राण्यौषधानि च ।
विषमन्त्रप्रयोगाश्च शस्त्राण्यावरणानि च ॥२३॥
अस्त्राणि चैव दिव्यानि वाहनान्यर्जितानि च ।
सर्वोपायैः प्रयुक्तानि नीतिशास्त्राणि चैव हि ॥२४॥

b) MTr[4] °नान्यूर्जितानि — d) MTr[4] MTr[6] ह

सौभाग्यकानि सर्वाणि तथा विद्वेषणानि च ।
पुण्यानि च समस्तानि शिल्पजातानि यानि च ॥२५॥

b) MTr[4] MTr[6] तथापि द्वेष° — c) MTr[4] पण्यानि

यच्चाभिचारिकं किंचिद्दीपप्रहरणानि च ।
देशकालप्रयुक्तानि यद्यपि स्युः प्रयत्नतः ।
सर्वाणि दैवहीनस्य तरन्ति न पराक्रमे ॥२६॥

a-b) GMd[1] यश्चापि चरितं किंचित्त --- त्या च प्रभवणानि च

तस्माद्दैवं पुरस्कार्यं नरेण शुभमिच्छता ।
दैवेन हि समायुक्तो ज्वलत्यग्निरिवाध्वरे ॥२७॥
हीनसत्त्वगुणोऽपीह पुरुषो निरुपक्रमः ।

तरत्यर्णवमश्रान्तः पर्वतान्योधयत्यपि ॥२८॥

a) GMd[1] °सत्त्वशुणः खिन्नः — d) GMd[1] °धयन्त्यपि

अबलोऽप्यनुपायेन युक्तो दैवेन कर्मणा ।
वज्रमप्यस्युतृणतां दैवहीनस्य गच्छति ॥२९॥

Pādas c-d of 29 omitted in MTr[4] MTr[6]

पुरुषार्थमतिक्रम्य दैवं युङ्क्ते स्वकर्मणा ।
न तु दैवमतिक्रम्य पुरुषार्थः प्रवर्तते ॥३०॥

Pādas a-b 30 omitted in MTr[4] MTr[6] — d) MTr[4] MTr[6] पुरुषार्थे

संस्कारं कर्मणां केचिद्दैवमाहुश्च पण्डताः ।
निष्क्रयं चानभिज्ञं च येन कर्माप्यनीश्वरम् ॥३१॥

a) GMd[1] कर्मणा — b) MTr[4]MTr[6] °माह च पण्डितः — c) MTr[6] चानभिगम्य (om च); MTr[4] *om* °नभिज्ञं च — d) MTr[4] MTr[6] °नीश्वरं; GMd[1] °नीवरं

देवतिर्यङ्मनुष्यानां बुद्धिसंस्कारकर्मसु ।
दैवं तिष्ठत्यप्रमत्तं कारणं सुखदुःखयोः ॥३२।

b) MTr[6] सिद्धिसंस्कार°

संयुनक्ति च भूतानि सर्वस्थानगतान्यपि ।
दैवं स्वकर्मणा नित्यमदृष्टमृतुकालवत् ॥३३॥
न खल्वचेतनं कर्म कर्तारमभिमन्यते ।
न चाज्ञः पुरुषः कर्म ममेदमिदति बुध्यते ॥३४॥
न खल्वेतत्स्वतन्त्रस्य सर्वज्ञस्य कदाचन ।
प्रभोरनधिदैवस्य वैक्लव्यमुपजायते ॥३५॥
एक एव यथा सूर्यः सर्वलोकप्रकाशकः ।
तथैव सर्वसंस्कारः कारणं दैवमुच्यते ॥३६॥

a) GMd[1] पुंसवनतथा सूर्यं

दैवमेव परं भूतं सर्वं दैवे प्रतिष्ठितम् ।
दैवमेव नृणां कर्म करोतीह शुभाशुभम् ॥३७॥

d) GMd[1] करोति ह

यथा वनस्पतीनां हि पुष्पानि च फलानि च ।
कालः सृजति सृष्टं च फलत्येषामचक्षुषाम् ॥३८॥

c) MTr[4] कालं सृजति असृष्टं च

तथैव सर्वभूतानां कर्माण्युच्चावचान्यपि ।
दैवमेकं प्रभुत्वेन निर्वर्त्य पचति स्वयम् ॥३९॥

a) MTr[6] तथापि — d) GMd[1] lacuna for पचति

सर्वात्मकं सर्वगतं सर्वभूतपरायणम् ।
सर्वतत्त्वविभागज्ञमसंस्पृष्टपरावरम् ॥४०॥

d) MTr[4] MTr[6] °संसृष्टभवाभवं

यथा हि सत्ता भूतेषु सर्वेष्वव्यभिचारिणी ।
व्यूहसंकरनिर्मुक्ताः त्रिषु लोकेषु वर्तते ॥४१॥

a) MTr[4] °सत्ता; MTr[6] °सत्तात्तेषु — a-b) GMd[1] भावं यथा हि सत्ताहुस्सर्वेष्वभिचारिणी — c-d) GMd[1] व्यूहसंस्कारनि...तान्यन्धकारेषु वर्तते

तथैव दैवं देवत्वमकार्यत्वमसङ्गता ।
प्रभुत्वं च विभुत्वं च सर्वज्ञत्वं च वर्तते ॥४२॥

b) GMd[1] °कार्यर्थसङ्गता; MTr[4] °सङ्गत्वं; MTr[6] °सङ्गतं

यथा हि कार्ये कार्यत्वं कारणत्वं च कारणे ।
भावाभावौ तथा दैवे वर्तते प्रत्ययात्मकौ ॥४३॥

a) MTr[4] MTr[6] यथैव— d) MTr[4] प्रत्येते प्रत्य° ; MTr[6] प्रत्येके प्रत्य°

क्रियाभिर्व्यञ्जते कर्म कर्म द्रव्येष्वसंशयः ।
दैवमेतस्य लोकस्य स्थितिप्रलयसृष्टिभिः ॥४४।

a-b) MTr[4] MTr[6] °भिर्व्यज्यते; MTr[6] लोक; GMd[1] कालः; MTr[4] लोकर्म; ed. कर्म *ex conj*. — b) GMd[1] °संश्रयः

निर्निमित्तं सदा दैवं भूतानामपि वर्तते ।
आत्मसंस्थः स्वतन्त्रश्च निग्रहानुग्रहेश्वरः ॥४५॥

b) MTr[4] MTr[6] °नामधिवर्तते — c) GMd[1] °संस्थं स्वतन्त्रं च — d) GMd[1] °हेश्वरं

अचेतनेषु भूतेषु निःसंज्ञेषु तथैव च ।
यत्क्रियासंज्ञकं किंचित् तद्दैवमिति निर्दिशेत् ॥४६॥
अनीशान्यनभिज्ञानि सुखदुःखमयानि च ।
जायन्ते सर्वभूतानि म्रियन्ते चापि कर्मणा ॥४७॥

d) GMd[1] क्रियन्ते

सर्वलोकमचिन्त्यं हि दैवं कर्म न संशयः ।
अनिमित्तान्निमित्ताद्वा दैविकं फलमिष्यते ॥४८॥

a) GMd[1] च — c) GMd[1] अनिमित्तनिमित्तं च

कृणति दैवं प्रत्यक्षं शिरः पुंसो न कस्यचित् ।
संयुनक्त्यवशं बुद्ध्या ययास्योत्कृत्यते शिरः ॥४९॥

a) GMd[1] कृणन्ति — c-d) GMd[1] संयुनक्ति न बुध्वाथ या ते स्यात्कृत्यके शिरः

एवं दैवकृतं सर्वं बुद्ध्या निश्चित्य पण्डितः ।
दैवमेव प्रपद्येत सर्वकालमतन्द्रितः ॥५०

a) GMd[1] दैवे — d) GMd[1] यथाकालम°

[अष्टमोऽध्यायः]

व्यवहारान्दिदृक्षुस्तु ब्राह्मणैः सह पार्थिवः ।
मन्त्रज्ञैर्मन्त्रिभिश्चैव विनीतः प्रविशेत्सभाम् ॥१॥
तत्रासीनः स्थितो वापि पाणिमुद्यम्य दक्षिणम् ।
विनीतवेषाभरणः पश्येत्कार्याणि कार्यिणाम् ॥२॥
प्रत्यहं देशदृष्टैश्च शास्त्रदृष्टैश्च हेतुभिः ।
अष्टादशसु मार्गेषु निबद्धानि पृथक्पृथक् ॥३॥
तेषामाद्यमृणादानं निक्षेपोऽस्वामिविक्रयः ।
संभूय च समुत्थानं दत्तस्यानपकर्म च ॥४॥
वेतनस्यैव चादानं संविदश्च व्यतिक्रमः ।
क्रयविक्रयानुशयो विवादः स्वामिपालयोः ॥५॥
सीमाविवादधर्मश्च पारुष्ये दण्डवाचिके ।

1. Omitted in Lo^4 Lo^5 Ox^3. Cited by *Apa* 600; *Lakṣ* 12.7; *Dev* 3.31, 43; *Mādh* 3.18 — a) Lo^1 °हारादिद्दृ°; GMd^1 *Dev* °हारदिद्दृ°; BKt^5 wKt^6 oOr °हारं दिद्दृ°; Pu^5 Pu^7 °हारान्नृपः पश्येद् — b) Pu^2 Pu^4 ब्राह्मणः; *Apa* पार्थिव — c) wKt^3 °र्मन्त्रभिश्चैव; Bo °र्मन्त्रभृच्चैव; *Lakṣ* °र्मन्त्रिभिस्सार्धं

2. Omitted in Lo^4 Lo^5 Ox^3. Cited by *Apa* 600; *Lakṣ* 12.7; *Dev* 3.52; *Mādh* 3.18 — a) wKt^3 Pu^5 Pu^7 तत्रासीनं; GMd^1 तत्रासन; NKt^4 तेवासीनः; Lo^1 स्थितोदायी — b) Ho पाणिपाद्यम्य; BKt^5 °मुद्दम्य — c) MTr^4 °पाधरणः — d) Bo TMd^4 कारिणां; GMd^1 कारिणः; GMd^5 कर्मिणां; GMy कार्यतां; Tr^2 कारणं

3. Omitted in Lo^4 Lo^4 Ox^3. Cited by *Lakṣ* 12.7; *Dev* 3.57; *Mādh* 3.18 — a) Hy प्रत्यहे; Pu^7 देशदृष्ट्यैश्च; Pu^5 देशदृष्यैश्च; GMd^1 वेददृष्टैश्च — b) Ho देहदृष्टैश्च — d) *Dev* निबन्धानि; *Mādh* व्यवहारान्पृथ°

Additional verse in oOr:

हिंसां यः कुरुते कश्चिद्देयं वा न प्रयच्छति ।
स्थाने ते द्वे वादस्य भिन्नष्टा दशधा पुनः ॥ [unclear]

4. Omitted in Lo^4 Lo^5 Ox^3. Cited by *Vij* 2.5; *Apa* 596; pāda-a cited by *Viś* 2.1 — a) Pu^8 °मृगादानं; wKt^1 °दान — b) GMd^1 TMd^4 निक्षेप; BKt^5 निःक्षेपो; Kt^2 निक्ष्येपो; Bo निक्षिपो; TMd^3 निक्षिप्यो; wKt^6 निःक्षिपो — c) GMd^1 सम्भूतयस्समु°; TMd^4 समुत्थान — d) wKt^6 दत्तस्यालयकर्मसु; Ho दत्तस्यान्नपकर्म च; TMd^3 तत्तस्यानवकर्म च; Tr^2 तस्यानपकर्म च; BKt^5 °पकर्मस्य [*om* च]

5. Omitted in Lo^4 Lo^5 Ox^3. Cited in *Vij* 2.5; *Apa* 596 — a) Lo^2 चेतन°; Pu^2 Pu^4 तेनतस्यैव; GMd^1 °नस्य च चादानं; Wa °नस्य तथादानं; Tr^2 °नस्यैवमादानं; wKt^1 नस्यैव दानं [*ma* च]; oOr वादानं — b) Jo^1 संविदंश्च; Bo °दश्चाप्यतिक्रमः — c) GMd^1 °विक्रयावनशयो; GMd^5 °विक्रयाद्यनुशयो; Tr^1 °नुशयौ; NPu^1 °नुशयोर्विवा°; Lo^1 Pu^3 Pu^5 Pu^7 °नुशययोर्विवा° — d) GMd^1 विवाद; GMd^1 °पाल्ययोः

स्तेयं च साहसं चैव स्त्रीसंग्रहणमेव च ॥६॥
स्त्रीपुंधर्मो विभागश्च द्यूतमाह्वय एव च ।
पदान्यष्टादशैतानि व्यवहारस्थिताविह ॥७॥
एषु स्थानेषु भूयिष्ठं विवादं चरतां नृणाम् ।
धर्मं शाश्वतमाश्रित्य कुर्यात्कार्यविनिर्णयम् ॥८॥
यदा स्वयं न कुर्यात्तु नृपतिः कार्यदर्शनम् ।
तदा नियुञ्ज्याद्विद्वांसं ब्राह्मणं कार्यदर्शने ॥९॥
सोऽस्य कार्याणि संपश्येत् सभ्यैरेव त्रिभिर्वृतः ।
सभामेव प्रविश्याग्र्यामासीनः स्थित एव वा ॥१०॥
यस्मिन्देशे निषीदन्ति विप्रा वेदविदस्त्रयः ।
राज्ञश्च प्रकृतो विद्वान् ब्रह्मणस्तां सभां विदुः ॥११॥

6. Omitted in Lo^{4} Lo^{5} Ox^{3}. Cited by *Vij* 2.5; *Apa* 596; pādas c-d cited by *Dev* 3.15— a) *Apa* [vl]सीमाविवादश्च तथा; w Kt^{3} sOx^{1} sPu^{6} °धर्माश्च — b) Pu^{2} Pu^{4} पारुषे; wKt^{1} पारुषो; NKt^{4} पानषो; Ho [*cor to*] TMd^{3} Pu^{5} Pu^{7} *Apa* [vl] °वाचके; Pu^{2} Pu^{4} °बाधिके — c) Be^{3} Kt^{2} स्तेयश्च — d) BKt^{5} wKt^{6} Tj^{1} °संग्रहमेव

7. Omitted in Lo^{4} Lo^{5} Ox^{3}. Cited by *Vij* 2.5; *Apa* 596 — a) Pu^{8} स्त्रीषु धर्मो; Tr^{2} रिपुधर्मो; wKt^{3} °धर्मा; GMd^{1} *Apa* °धर्म; MTr^{6} विभागं च; La^{1} विवादश्च — b) wKt^{1} द्यूतमार्गयमेव; Hy °माद्र्य एव; wKt^{3} wKt^{6} Jo^{2} NNg sOx^{1} sPu^{6} Tr^{2} Wa [*Jolly* M G] °ह्वयमेव; Bo °ह्वायमेव; Be^{3} GMd^{1} TMd^{3} TMd^{4} GMd^{5} GMy NPu^{1} Pu^{2} Pu^{3} Pu^{4} MTr^{4} MTr^{5} MTr^{6} [*Jolly* R Nd]*Nd Apa* ह्वानमेव; MTr^{4} °ह्वनमेव; La^{1} °ह्वान एव; Pu^{8} °हयमेव; Tj^{1} °ह्वान एव; *Nā* [pāṭha] °हव एव — c) TMd^{3} वदान्य°; Tr^{2} पदानष्टा°; wKt^{6} °ष्टौदशै° — d) Lo^{1} व्यवहारः; TMd^{4} व्यवहारे; Be^{1} °स्थितानि च

8. Omitted in Lo^{4} Lo^{5} TMd^{3} GMy Ox^{3} [*Jolly* Nd]. Cited by *Apa* 596; *Lakṣ* 12.43; *Dev* 3.30 — a) wKt^{3} एष; Lo^{3} TMd^{4} Tj^{1} *Dev* येपु; GMd^{1} शेष; wKt^{1} भूयिष्ठ; Wa भूमिष्ठं — b) Kt^{2} विवादश्चरतां; Bo चरतं; Tj^{1} चरता; NPu^{1} Pu^{5} Pu^{7} [*Jolly* G] वदतां; MTr^{4} विवितं — c) *Lakṣ* धर्मशास्त्रं समाश्रित्य; NKt^{4} °मासृत्य — d) *Dev* कुर्युस्तेषां विनि°; *Apa* कुर्यात्कार्ये विनि°; *Apa* [vl] कुर्यात्कर्मविनि°; BCa wKt^{3} °विनिश्चयं

9. Omitted in Lo^{4} Lo^{5} Ox^{3}. Cited by *Dev* 3.36; *Mādh* 3.21 — a) BCa कुर्याच्च — b) Be^{1} BKt^{5} नृपति; GMd^{5} कार्यशासनं — c) TMd^{3} GMy तथा; Bo Hy Lo^{1} Tj^{1} नियुज्या°; NNg विन्युञ्ज्या°; BKt^{5} नियोज्यो विद्वान्स्याद् — d) BKt^{5} ब्राह्मणः; GMd^{5} नृपतिं कार्य°; wKt^{1} °दर्शिणं

Additional verse in Ox^{2}:

अष्टादशपदाभिज्ञं प्राड्विवाकेति संज्ञितम् ।
आन्वीक्षिक्यां च कुशलं श्रुतिस्मृतिपरायणम् ॥

10. Omitted in Lo^{4} Lo^{5} Ox^{3}. Cited by *Dev* 3.37; *Mādh* 3.21— a) Tr^{2} सोयं; Ho sOx^{1} sPu^{6} कार्याणि पश्येत; Ox^{2} Tr^{2} कार्याणि पश्येत्; Bo सापश्येत् — b) BKt^{5} सभ्यैरेवं; Pu^{8} स्वल्पैरेव; GMd^{1} सभ्यैरेभिस्त्रि°; Ox^{2} तृभिर्वृतः; Pu^{2} Pu^{4} नृभिर्वृतः — c) Pu^{2} Pu^{4} Pu^{5} Pu^{7} [*Jolly* G] सभामेवोपवि°; Bo प्रविष्टा°; GMd^{1} प्रविश्यान्यामा° — d) La^{1} TMd^{4} स्थितमेव; Be^{1} Pu^{2} Tj^{1} एव च

11.* Omitted in Lo^{4} Lo^{5} Ox^{3}. Cited by *Dev* 3.46; *Lakṣ* 12.27; pādas a-b cited by *Vij* 2.2 — a) oOr यस्मिन्वशे; Bo निषेदन्ति; TMd^{3} निषादन्ति; TMd^{4} निवेदन्ति — c) TMd^{3} GMd^{5} GMy राज्ञस्तु; Bo GMd^{1} राज्ञा च; Tr^{2} राज्ञं प्रकृतौ; Be^{1} Be^{3} Hy Jm Jo^{1} Jo^{2} Kt^{2} wKt^{3} Tj^{2} MTr^{3} [*Jolly* Ku] *Ku Rn*

धर्मो विद्धस्त्वधर्मेण सभां यत्रोपतिष्ठते ।
शल्यं चास्य न कृन्तन्ति विद्धास्तत्र सभासदः ॥१२॥
सभा वा न प्रवेष्टव्या वक्तव्यं वा समञ्जसम् ।
अब्रुवन्विब्रुवन्वापि नरो भवति किल्बिषी ॥१३॥
यत्र धर्मो ह्यधर्मेण सत्यं यत्रानृतेन च ।
हन्यते प्रेक्षमाणानां हतास्तत्र सभासदः ॥१४॥
धर्म एव हतो हन्ति धर्मो रक्षति रक्षितः ।
तस्माद्धर्मो न हन्तव्यो मा नो धर्मो हतो वधीत् ॥१५॥
वृषो हि भगवान्धर्मस्तस्य यः कुरुते त्वलम् ।
वृषलं तं विदुर्देवास्तस्माद्धर्मं न लोपयेत् ॥१६॥
एक एव सुहृद्धर्मो निधनेऽप्यनुयाति यः ।
शरीरेण समं नाशं सर्वमन्यद्धि गच्छति ॥१७॥

Go Mandlik Jha Dave KSS राज्ञश्चाधिकृतो; Lo¹ Lo³ Tj¹ राज्ञा चाधिकृतो; wKt¹ राज्ञस्त्वधिकृतो; BKt⁵ GMd⁵ प्राकृतो; GMy प्रकृतौ; Pu² Pu⁴ प्रकृते; NKt⁴ प्रयतो — d) Bo Lo² GMd⁵ *Bh* [as pāṭha, but rejected] ब्राह्मणस्तां;Ox² ब्राह्मणास्तां; TMd³ GMy ब्रह्मणस्तान्; TMd³ Tr² सभा

12. Omitted in Lo⁴ Lo⁵ Ox³. Cited by *Dev* 3.48 — a) Pu⁸ Tr² धर्मे; Bo Pu⁸ विद्धो ह्यध°; Be³ विध्यस्त्वध°; TMd³ MTr⁶ विध्वस्त्वध° — b) Wa सभायां यत्र तिष्ठति; wKt³ Tr² सभा; Wa सभ्यां; GMd¹ हवं; Be¹ Be³ wKt¹; NKt⁴ Lo² GMd⁵ oOr NNg Pu² Pu⁸ Tr¹ *Dev* °तिष्ठति — c) Kt² शल्यश्चास्य; TMd³ कुलं चास्य; Be¹ Lo² वास्य; NNg *cor sh to* नास्य; NKt⁴ NPu¹ Pu² Pu³ Pu⁴ Pu⁵ Pu⁷ निकृन्तन्ति; BBe² Be³ BKt⁵ GMd¹ TMd³ GMy NNg निकृन्तन्ति; Hy कृन्तन् — d) NPu¹ विद्धां तत्र; Be¹ Lo³ विद्धांस्तत्र; La¹ Pu⁴ Tj¹ विद्वांस्तत्र; NNg विद्वास्तत्र; GMd¹ वृद्धास्तत्र; *Dev* हतास्तत्र; GMd⁵ हन्तारस्तत्र; Tj² सभासह

13.* Omitted in Lo⁴ Lo⁵ Ox³. Cited by *Vij* 2.2;*Apa* 604; *Lakṣ* 12.35; *Dev* 3.34, 49; pādas c-d cited by *Vij* 2.83 — a) Be¹ BBe² Be³ BCa Hy Jm Jo¹ wKt¹ Kt² wKt³ BKt⁵ TMd⁴ Pu³ MTr³ [*Jolly* Ku] *Mandlik KSS Dave* सभां वा न प्रवेष्टव्यं [Hy TMd⁴ सभा; TMd⁴ च]; Ox² *Lakṣ* सभायां न प्रवेष्टव्यं; wKt¹ सभां वा न *then ma* प्रवेष्टं तु; GMd¹ च न — b) Hy वक्तव्य; wKt³ समंजनं; TMd⁴ सभासदं — c) Lo² *om* विब्रुवन्

14. Omitted in Lo⁴ Lo⁵ Ox³. Cited by *Dev* 3.48 — a)GMy sOx¹ sPu⁶ धर्मस्त्वधर्मेण; wKt³ ह्यकर्मेण — b) Pu³ यच्चानृतेन; Pu⁴ यत्रानृतेन; *Dev* चैवानृतेन वा; Jo² Pu⁵ Pu⁷ [*Jolly* G] तु ; Be³ वा — c) wKt¹ Kt² BKt⁵ sOx¹ NPu¹ Pu⁵ sPu⁶ Pu⁷ प्रेक्ष्य°; NKt⁴ प्रेष्य°; Bo पक्ष°

15. Cited by *Hem* 2/1.15; *Dev* 3.48 — a)wKt¹ धर्म एवं स हि हतो धर्मो; TMd⁴ एवं — b) NKt⁴ धर्मा; MTr⁶ रक्षतः — d) [*Jolly* Nd] मा वो; NNg Lo² मनो; TMd³ GMy मन्यो; Pu⁸ माने; Ox² यतो; Jo¹ हतोऽवधीत्; Be³ वधीः; Tr² वधात्

16.* Cited by *Apa* 447; *Lakṣ* 12.37; *Hem* 2/1.14; *Dev* 3.48, 4.184 — a) Bo भगवन्ध°; BKt⁵ *om* धर्मस् — b) Lo¹ वः कुरुते; *Dev* 4.184 कुरुतेत्ययं [typo?]; TMd⁴ कुरुतेफलं; Bo कुरुतेन्वलं; Be¹ BBe² Hy Jm Jo¹ Jo² wKt¹ Kt² wKt³ La¹ Lo¹ Lo³ sOx¹ Pu³ sPu⁶ Pu⁸ Tj¹ MTr³ [*Jolly* Ku] ह्यलं; Tr¹ *ma* ह्यलं; GMd¹ TMd³ GMy MTr⁴ [*Jolly* Nd] लयं; NPu¹ लवं; GMd⁵ वधं — c) BKt⁵ वृषलस्तं; GMd¹ वृषलं हि — d) *Apa* विदुर्देवाः सर्वधमबहिष्कृतं; Pu⁵ *om* न लोपयेत्; wKt¹ निलोपयेत्; BKt⁵ लोपये; Tr² लङ्घयेत्

17. Cited by *Lakṣ* 12.37 — a) Lo¹ GMd¹ Tr² एष एव; TMd³ एक्ष एव — b) Lo⁵ TMd³ Tr¹

पादोऽधर्मस्य कर्तारं पादः साक्षिणमृच्छति ।
पादः सभासदः सर्वान् पादो राजानमृच्छति ॥१८॥
राजा भवत्यनेनास्तु मुच्यन्ते च सभासदः ।
एनो गच्छति कर्तारं निन्दार्हो यत्र निन्द्यते ॥१९॥
जातिमात्रोपजीवी वा कामं स्याद्ब्राह्मणब्रुवः ।
धर्मप्रवक्ता नृपतेर्न तु शूद्रः कथंचन ॥२०॥
यस्य शूद्रस्तु कुरुते राज्ञो धर्मविवेचनम् ।
तस्य सीदति तद्राष्ट्रं पङ्के गौरिव पश्यतः ॥२१॥
यद्राष्ट्रं शूद्रभूयिष्ठं नास्तिकाक्रान्तमद्विजम् ।
विनश्यत्याशु तत्कृत्स्नं दुर्भिक्षव्याधिपीडितम् ॥२२॥
धर्मासनमधिष्ठाय संवीताङ्गः समाहितः ।
प्रणम्य लोकपालेभ्यः कार्यदर्शनमारभेत् ॥२३॥
अर्थानर्थावुभौ बुद्ध्वा धर्माधर्मौ च केवलौ ।

निधाने; Be[3] Wa मरणे; NNg निधनेष्वनु° ; TMd[3] GMy °याति यत्; MTr[4] नः — d) GMd[1] TMd[4] oOr Tr[2] *Lakṣ* सर्वमन्यत्तु; La[1] सर्वमन्यत्र; MTr[6] °न्यद्विगच्छति

18. Omitted in oOr; pādas a-b omitted in Pu[5]. Cited by *Vij* 2.305; *Apa* 866; *Mādh* 3.15 — a) *Vij* पादो गच्छति कर्तारं; Bo Lo[1] पदो — b) GMd[1] Tr[1] MTr[4] MTr[6] *Mādh* पादो गच्छति सक्षिणं [*Mādh* साक्षिणः]; Pu[2] Pu[4] निन्दार्हो यत्र निन्द्यते [cf. 19d]; wKt[3] पाद; Tr[2] °मृक्षति; BBe[2] Ho °मिच्छति — c) Pu[2] Pu[4] जातिमात्रोसदः सर्वान्; Tr[2] सर्वा; NKt[4] सर्वे — d) Ho पापो; Tr[2] °मृक्षति; Tj[2] MTr[6] °मिच्छति

19. Cited by *Apa* 604; *Lakṣ* 12.35; *Dev* 3.49; *Mādh* 3.26 — a) GMd[1] अराजा; NKt[4] राज्ञा च भव° ; GMy °नेनस्तु — b) TMd[4] sOx[1] sPu[6] मुच्यते; *Dev* हि; *Lakṣ* तु; NKt[4] महासदः — c) wKt[1] एषो; TMd[3] हर्तारः — d) TMd[3] निन्दार्हे; GMd[5] निन्दार्हा; *Apa* यदि; NKt[4] निन्दिते; Lo[1] निन्दको

20. Cited by *Apa* 601; *Dev* 3.38; *Mādh* 3.22 — a) Ho GMd[1] TMd[3] जात° ; BKt[5] *om* वा; BCa च — b) wKt[3] कामं वा ब्राह्मणंब्रुवः; *Apa* वरं स्या°; BBe[2] °ह्मणोब्रुवः; Be[3] Ox[3] स्याद्ब्रह्मण° ; oOr °ह्मणब्रुवे — c) *Dev* धर्मवक्ता तु नृप° ; Bo TMd[3] नृपते न; TMd[4] नृपतिर्न — d) Ox[3] °तेर्ननु शूद्रः; Ox[2] °तेर्नन शूद्रः; Tr[1] TMd[3] GMd[5] oOr *Apa om* तु

21. Cited by *Apa* 601; *Lakṣ* 12.29; *Dev* 3.37; *Mādh* 3.22 — a) TMd[4] यस्तु; wKt[1] यत्र; Bo शूद्रस्य; Be[3] TMd[3] GMy *Apa Lakṣ Dev* राज्ञस्तु; GMd[1] Tr[1] MTr[4] MTr[6] शूद्रः प्रकुरुते — b) Be[3] TMd[3] GMy *Apa Lakṣ Dev* शूद्रो धर्म° ; TMd[3] °विचेतनं — c) *Dev* अस्य; oOr सीदति राष्ट्रं च — d) Wa पश्यतिः; Bo पश्यति; La[1] सीदति

22. a) Lo[3] Lo[4] Lo[5] Ox[3] Tj[1] Tj[2] यद्राज्यं; TMd[4] °भूमिष्ठं — b) wKt[1] नास्तिकक्रान्तियद् द्विजं *cor to* नास्तिकः क्रान्तयद् द्विजं; Bo नासिका° ; TMd[3] TMd[4] °द्विजः — c) TMd[3] GMy Wa [*Jolly* Nd] तत्सर्वं; La[1] तद्राष्ट्रं — d) sOx[1] sPu[6] दुर्भिक्ष्य° ; BCa Lo[1] TMd[4] दुर्भिक्षं; GMy °क्षभयपीडितं; Pu[8] °पीडितां; Bo Tr[2] °पीडनं

23. Cited by *Lakṣ* 12.7; *Dev* 3.70; *Mādh* 3.41 — a) TMd[4] °सनं त्वधिष्ठाय — b) Tr[2] संप्रीताङ्गः; GMy संसताङ्गः; TMd[3] संहिताङ्गः — d) wKt[3] Tr[2] °मालभेत्; NKt[4] BKt[5] Lo[1] Lo[2] Ox[3] NPu[1] Pu[3] Pu[5] Pu[7] Pu[8] Wa *Go* [*Jolly* G] °माचरेत्

वर्णक्रमेण सर्वाणि पश्येत्कार्याणि कार्यिणाम् ॥२४॥
बाह्यैर्विभावयेल्लिङ्गैर्भावमन्तर्गतं नृणाम् ।
स्वरवर्णेङ्गिताकारैश्चक्षुषा चेष्टितेन च ॥२५॥
आकारैरिङ्गितैर्गत्या चेष्टया भाषितेन च ।
नेत्रवक्त्रविकारैश्च गृह्यतेऽन्तर्गतं मनः ॥२६॥
बालदायादिकं रिक्थं तावद्राजानुपालयेत् ।
यावत्स स्यात्समावृत्तो यावद्वातीतशैशवः ॥२७॥
वशापुत्रासु चैवं स्याद्रक्षणं निष्कुलासु च ।
पतिव्रतासु च स्त्रीषु विधवास्वातुरासु च ॥२८॥
जीवन्तीनां तु तासां ये तद्धरेयुः स्वबान्धवाः ।
ताञ्छिष्याच्चौरदण्डेन धार्मिकः पृथिवीपतिः ॥२९॥

24. Omitted in BKt^{5}. Cited by *Apa* 611; *Dev* 3.80; *Mādh* 3.46 — a) Tr^{2} MTr^{6} °नर्थानुभौ; TMd^{3} °नर्था उभौ; Jm *Apa* बुद्ध्या — b) TMd^{3} °धर्मा च; MTr^{4} केवलं — c) TMd^{4} वर्णक्रमाणि — c-d) sOx^{1} sPu^{6} वर्णक्रमेण कार्याणि पश्येत्सर्वाणि कार्यिणां — d) GMd^{1} TMd^{4} कारिणां; Tr^{2} कारिणं; TMd^{3} कार्यणां; Bo कर्मिणां; GMd^{5} कर्मणां; GMy कार्यतां

25. Pādas a-b omitted in BKt^{5}. Cited by *Apa* 620; *Lakṣ* 12.77; *Dev* 3.56, 72; *Mādh* 3.30 — a) *Lakṣ Mādh* वाक्यैर्विभा° — c) Pu^{5} Pu^{7} [*Jolly* G] मुखवर्णे° — d) Hy Wa °क्षुषो; *Mādh* °क्षुषोश्चेष्टि°; TMd^{3} चेक्षितेन; *Dev* 3.72 भाषितेन; Lo^{5} *Mādh* वा

26. Pādas a-b omitted in NKt^{4} BKt^{5}. Cited by *Apa* 620; *Lakṣ* 12.77; *Dev* 3.112; *Mādh* 3.43 — a) Tj^{2} *Apa* आकारेणेङ्गि°; TMd^{4} °ङ्गितागत्या — b) TMd^{4} शेषया; Bo Jo^{2} La^{1} Lo^{1} Lo^{4} Lo^{5} GMd^{5} Ox^{3} NPu^{1} Pu^{3} Pu^{5} Pu^{7} Tr^{2} भाषणेन; wKt^{1} TMd^{3} GMy MTr^{3} भावितेन — c) Pu^{2} Pu^{4} नेत्रचक्र°; TMd^{4} नेत्रभक्त्र° La^{1} TMd^{4} *Lakṣ* °विकारेण — d) TMd^{3} गृह्यन्ते; Pu^{5} Pu^{7} [*Jolly* G] ज्ञायते; Tr^{2} ज्ञायेत; La^{1} *Lakṣ* लक्ष्यते; NNg लक्ष्यन्ते; Pu^{2} Pu^{4} लभ्यते; TMd^{3} °न्तर्गते

27. Pādas c-d omitted in MTr^{5}, and *ma* in Lo^{1}. Cited by *Lakṣ* 12.752; *Dev* 3.310 — a) BKt^{5} बाला°; NKt^{4} Lo^{2} GMd^{1} TMd^{3} GMy MTr^{5} *Dev* °दायादकं; wKt^{3} °दायादादिकं; *Lakṣ* °दायागतं; Be^{3} BCa Ox^{2} °दिकमृक्थं; Ho °दिकमित्थं; NKt^{4} °दिकं रिपूं — b) *Lakṣ* तावद्राजा तु पालयेत् — c) sOx^{1} sPu^{6} यावद्वा; TMd^{3} GMy *Dev* यावत्स्यात्स समा°; TMd^{3} °मावर्तो — d) Hy Jo^{1} *Mandlik KSS Dave* [*Jolly* Ku Nd] यावच्चातित°; TMd^{3} यावच्चाचित°; GMd^{1} °शैशवं

28. Omitted in Jm; pādas c-d omitted in GMd^{1}; pādas a-b *ma* in Lo^{1}. Cited by *Lakṣ* 12.685; *Dev* 3.310 — a) Bo वशाः; NKt^{4} वंसा°; TMd^{3} वसा°; Tr^{2} वस्य°; NPu^{1} दशा°; NNg sOx^{1} Pu^{2} Pu^{4} sPu^{6} [*Jolly* G] वन्ध्या°; Pu^{5} Pu^{7} वन्धा°; Pu^{2} Pu^{4} चैव — b) Ho निकुलासु; TMd^{3} निष्कुलानि — c) wKt^{1} तथापतिषु च — d) BBe^{2} °तुरेषु च

Additional verse in *Mandlik KSS Dave*, which is the same as 11.189.

29. Cited by *Vij* 2.147; *Apa* 752; *Lakṣ* 12.685; *Dev* 3.311, 659 — a) Be^{1} जीवतीनां; Bo जीवत्तुनां; BKt^{5} oOr च; GMd^{5} तासां वै — a-b) Pu^{5} Pu^{7} जीवन्तीनां च तासां वै ये हरेयुश्च बान्धवाः — b) Ho sOx^{1} Ox^{2} sPu^{6} Tr^{2} हरेयुर्बान्धवा धनं [Tr^{2} धरां]; Wa हरेयुस्तच्च बान्धवाः; wKt^{3} उद्धरेयुः; Lo^{5} स्वबान्धवः; GMd^{1} सबान्धवाः — c) wKt^{1} तांश्छिष्या°; GMd^{1} Tr^{2} ताञ्छिष्येच्चौर°; Ho ताञ्शिष्यान्चौर°; TMd^{3} ताञ्छिष्यान्चौर°; Pu^{5} Pu^{7} तान् छिंद्याच्चौर°; NPu^{1} तान्दंत्यान्चौर°; Bo Jo^{2} Lo^{3} GMd^{1} TMd^{3} GMd^{5} GMy Tj^{1} Tj^{2} Tr^{1} MTr^{5} MTr^{6} *Dev* °ष्याच्चोर°; MTr^{4} °ष्यान्घोर° — d) TMd^{4} °पतिं

प्रनष्टस्वामिकं रिक्थं राजा त्र्यब्दं निधापयेत् ।
अर्वाक् त्र्यब्दाद्धरेत्स्वामी परेण नृपतिर्हरेत् ॥३०॥
ममेदमिति यो ब्रूयात् सोऽनुयुक्तो यथाविधि ।
संवाद्य रूपसंख्यादीन् स्वामी तद् द्रव्यमर्हति ॥३१॥
अवेदयन् प्रनष्टस्य देशं कालं च तत्त्वतः ।
वर्णं रूपं प्रमाणं च तत्समं दण्डमर्हति ॥३२॥
आददीताथ षड्भागं प्रनष्टाधिगतान्नृपः ।
दशमं द्वादशं वापि सतां धर्ममनुस्मरन् ॥३३॥
प्रनष्टाधिगतं द्रव्यं तिष्ठेद्युक्तैरधिष्ठितम् ।
यांस्तत्र चौरान् गृह्णीयात् तान् राजेभेन घातयेत् ॥३४॥
ममायमिति यो ब्रूयान्निधिं सत्येन मानवः ।
तस्याददीत षड्भागं राजा द्वादशमेव वा ॥३५॥

30.* Cited by *Vij* 2.33, 173; *Apa* 778; *Dev* 3.311–2 — a) Lo^{5} प्रणष्ट°; Bo प्रणष्टः; Tj^{2} प्रसाष्ट°; Pu^{5} प्रणष्टास्वा°; Pu^{2} Pu^{4} °स्वामिन; bCa Ox^{2} °मिकमृक्थं; Ho Lo^{2} gMd^{1} nNg Pu^{2} Pu^{4} sOx^{1} sPu^{6} mTr^{5} *Vij* 2.173 *Apa* द्रव्यं — b) Be^{1} निधारयेत् — c) wKt^{1} त्र्यव्दान्तरे स्वामी — d) Ho sOx^{1} sPu^{6} हरेत परतो नृपः; Tr^{2} धरेच्च परतो नृपः; bKt^{5} nPu^{1} Wa *Vij Apa* परतो

31.* Omitted in Pu^{5}. Cited by *Dev* 3.311 — a) nKt^{4} वो — b) wKt^{1} नानुयुक्तो; Be^{1} bBe^{2} Bo Hy Jm Jo^{1} Jo^{2} Kt^{2} wKt^{3} bKt^{5} La^{1} [*cor to sh*] Lo^{1} Lo^{2} Lo^{3} nNg Ox^{2} Ox^{3} nPu^{1} Pu^{2} Pu^{3} Pu^{4} Pu^{8} Tj^{1} Tj^{2} mTr^{3} Wa *Dev Mandlik Jolly Jha KSS Dave* सोनुयोज्यो; Lo^{4} सोनुयोज्यो *cor to* स नियोज्यो; Be^{3} सोनुयुज्यो; Ho Lo^{5} sOx^{1} Ox^{2} sPu^{6} Tr^{2} सो नियोज्यो; Lo^{4} सनुयोज्यो; Pu^{7} छोनुरक्तो *but mc to* सोनुयोज्यो — c) Ho La^{1} sOx^{1} sPu^{6} संपाद्य; gMy [*Jolly* Nd] संवेद्य; tMd^{3} संवेद; gMd^{1} mTr^{5} °संख्यादि — d) tMd^{3} स्वामिनं द्रव्यम°; Lo^{4} Lo^{5} *om* तद्

32.* Omitted in bKt^{5}. Cited by *Lakṣ* 12.555; *Dev* 3.312 — a) Tr^{2} अवेदयन्प्रणस्य; Be^{1} nKt^{4} nNg nPu^{1} Pu^{2} Pu^{4} *Lakṣ* अवेदयंस्तु नष्टस्य [Be^{1} °यांस्तु]; wKt^{1} अवेदयात्मायस्य; bBe^{2} Be^{3} Bo bCa Hy Jm Jo^{1} Jo^{2} Kt^{2} wKt^{3} La^{1} [*but cor*] Lo^{1} Lo^{3} Lo^{4} Lo^{5} Ox^{3} Pu^{5} Pu^{7} Pu^{8} Tj^{1} Tj^{2} mTr^{3} mTr^{5} *Dev Mandlik Jolly Jha KSS Dave* अवेदयानो नष्टस्य — b) gMd^{1} देश; Bo Ho Jo^{2} wKt^{1} La^{1} Lo^{3} tMd^{3} gMd^{5} gMy sOx^{1} Ox^{2} Pu^{3} sPu^{6} Pu^{8} Tj^{1} Tr^{1} Tr^{2} [*Jolly* R] *Go Ku Rc* देशकालौ; gMd^{5} तु — c) Bo wKt^{3} sOx^{1} nPu^{1} Tr^{2} वर्ण; Pu^{5} Pu^{7} [*Jolly* G] वर्णरूप — d) Pu^{5} Pu^{7} तत्समां

33. Ox^{3} [*Jolly* M] transpose 33 and 34; pādas c-d omitted in Pu^{4}. Cited by *Vij* 2.33, 173; *Apa* 778; *Lakṣ* 12.555; *Dev* 3.313 — a) wKt^{1} °दीतार्थ; Tr^{2} पष्टाङ्गं — b) oOr प्रतिष्ठाधि°; Tj^{1} Tr^{2} °गता नृपः; Lo^{1} tMd^{3} gMy Pu^{4} °गतं नृपः — d) gMd^{1} mTr^{5} भागं धर्म°; Be^{3} °नुस्मरेत्

34. Omitted in Lo^{4} Lo^{5}; pādas c-d omitted in bKt^{5}. Cited by *Lakṣ* 12.555; *Dev* 3.311; pādas c-d cited by *Apa* 841 — a) mTr^{6} °धिकृतं — b) Pu^{2} Pu^{4} तिष्ठेत्शक्तैर°; gMd^{1} °रनुष्ठितं — c) *Dev* ये तत्र चोरा गृह्णीयुः; Lo^{1} यस्तत्र; Lo^{3} gMd^{1} tMd^{3} gMd^{5} gMy nNg Tr^{1} mTr^{4} mTr^{5} mTr^{6} चोरान्; nKt^{4} चोरा; Lo^{2} चोरां; Lo^{1} चौरो; mTr^{4} mTr^{6} *Apa* गृह्णीयुस् — d) *Apa* तान्विताड्य विडम्ब्य च; Pu^{2} Pu^{4} तान्राजेन निपातयेत्; gMd^{1} तान्राजा तेन पातयेत्; tMd^{4} तान्द्राजेशेन पूरयेत्; Lo^{1} *deletes* तान्; mTr^{5} राजाभेन; gMd^{5} राज्ञेतेन; Ho gMd^{1} राजा तेन; Be^{3} Lo^{1} राजा दण्डेन; gMd^{1} पातयेत्; bBe^{2} यातयेत्

35.* Cited by *Vij* 2.34–5; *Apa* 641; *Lakṣ* 12.791; *Dev* 3.313 — a) sOx^{1} sPu^{6} Tr^{2} ममेदमिति — b) Be^{1} wKt^{3} Lo^{5} °न्निधि; bBe^{2} gMd^{5} °न्नित्यं; nKt^{4} gMd^{1} *Lakṣ* सत्येन हेतुतः; tMd^{3} tMd^{4} gMd^{5}

अनृतं तु वदन्दण्ड्यः स्ववित्तस्यांशमष्टमम् ।
तस्यैव वा निधानस्य संख्ययाल्पीयसीं कलाम् ॥३६॥
विद्वांस्तु ब्राह्मणो दृष्ट्वा पूर्वोपनिहितं निधिम् ।
अशेषतोऽप्याददीत सर्वस्याधिपतिर्हि सः ॥३७॥
यं तु पश्येन्निधिं राजा पुराणं निहितं क्षितौ ।
तस्माद् द्विजेभ्यो दत्त्वार्धमर्धं कोशे प्रवेशयेत् ॥३८॥
निधीनां हि पुराणानां धातूनामेव च क्षितौ ।
अर्धभाग्रक्षणाद्राजा भूमेरधिपतिर्हि सः ॥३९॥
दातव्यं सर्ववर्णेभ्यो राज्ञा चौरैर्हृतं धनम् ।
राजा तदुपयुञ्जानश्चौरस्याप्नोति किल्बिषम् ॥४०॥
जातिजानपदान्धर्मान् श्रेणीधर्मांश्च धर्मवित् ।

GMy Tr^{1} [*but mc sh*] MTr^{4} MTr^{6} [*Jolly* Nd Gr] सत्येन हेतुना; Tr^{1} *ma* मानवः — c) sOx^{1} sPu^{6} तस्याददीताथ षड्भागं; Bo सद्भागं — d) Lo^{3} *om* द्वा; Be^{1} Lo^{3} Tr^{2} *Lakṣ* च

36. Omitted in Pu^{5}. Cited by *Lakṣ* 12.791; *Dev* 3.313; pādas a-b cited by *Apa* 641 — a) GMd^{1} वदन्दण्ड्यं; wKt^{1} वदन्ह्यन्यः — b) Pu^{2} *Dev* स वित्त°; Tr^{1} °मष्टकं — c) TMd^{4} तस्य दानं च दानस्य; Ho Pu^{7} च; Ox^{2} चा; MTr^{6}विधनस्य — d) Be^{1} Ho Jo^{1} Tj^{1} MTr^{5} Wa [*Jolly* M$^{8-9}$ G Ku R] संख्याया°; Tj^{1} °ल्पीयसी

37. Cited by *Apa* 640; *Dev* 3.314 — a) GMd^{1} विद्वांसं ब्राह्मणो ह्यद्य; BKt^{5} विद्वानस्य ब्रह्मणो; Ox^{3} द्रष्टा; oOr लव्ध्वा — b) *Apa* [vl] पूर्वोपिनि°; MTr^{3} विधिं; [*Jolly* M$^{1-3-5-8-9}$] धनं — c) Tj^{1} °थाददीत; TMd^{3} °प्यादधीत; Pu^{2} Pu^{4} Wa ह्याददीत; MTr^{6} °भ्याददीत

Additional verse in Pu^{2} Pu^{3} Pu^{4} *Mandlik* [ञ, ट, ठ, ड] *Dave KSS*:

ब्राह्मणस्तु निधिं लव्ध्वा क्षिप्रं राज्ञे निवेदयेत् ।
तेन दत्तं तु भुञ्जीत स्तेनः स्यादनिवेदयन् ॥

d) Pu^{2} °निवेदयेत्

38. Omitted in GMd^{5}. Cited by *Apa* 640; *Lakṣ* 12.793; *Dev* 3.315 — a) Ho Lo^{4} Lo^{5} यत्तु; Be^{3} Lo^{3} MTr^{4} MTr^{6} यस्तु; *Apa* यत्र; *Dev* तत्र; Wa यं संपश्ये°; Hy *om* तु; Be^{3} NKt^{4} पश्यं निधिं — b) MTr^{5} पुराणनिहितं; GMy कारणं निहितं; TMd^{4} नहितं; GMd^{1} निहितं निधिं — c) La^{1} तस्यार्धम° — d) wKt^{3} कोशो; Lo^{2} काशे; wKt^{1} Lo^{1} Tr^{1} MTr^{5} Wa *Apa Lakṣ Dev* निवेशयेत्; wKt^{3} Tj^{1} निवेदयेत्; Lo^{3} प्रवेदयेत्; Jo^{2} नियोजयेत्; GMd^{1} TMd^{3} GMy sOx^{1} sPu^{6} [*Jolly* Nd] *Apa* [vl] विनिक्षिपेत्

39. Omitted in GMd^{5}. Cited by *Lakṣ* 12.793; *Dev* 3.314 — a) Ho निधिना; BKt^{5} *om* हि; Bo Hy Jm Jo^{1} Jo^{2} Kt^{2} Lo^{2} Lo^{4} GMd^{1} oOr Ox^{2} Pu^{3} Pu^{5} Pu^{7} Pu^{8} Tj^{2} MTr^{3} MTr^{4} MTr^{6} [*Jolly* G Nd] तु; Pu^{2} Pu^{4} च — b) *Lakṣ* धातूनामाकरस्य च; oOr °मेव दीक्षितौ — c) GMd^{1} TMd^{4} Tr^{1} MTr^{4} MTr^{5} MTr^{6} रक्षणादर्धभाग्राजा; *Lakṣ* रक्षणाद्धर्मभाग्राजा; Pu^{2} Pu^{4} अर्धं तद्रक्ष° — d) GMd^{1} °पतिर्निधिं

40. Cited by *Vij* 2.36; *Apa* 641 — b) TMd^{4} राज्ञे; GMd^{5} राज्ञां; Bo BCa wKt^{3} GMy sOx^{1} Pu^{2} sPu^{6} राजा; TMd^{3} GMd^{5} GMy Tr^{1} MTr^{5} MTr^{6} चोरै°; GMd^{1} चारै°; NKt^{4} Pu^{2} Pu^{4} *Apa* चौरहृतं; Lo^{3} Tj^{1} चोरहृतं; La^{1} Lo^{4} Lo^{5} sOx^{1} Ox^{3} NPu^{1} sPu^{6} [*Jolly* M^{4}] *Me* [pāṭha] चौराहृतं; Lo^{2} *Bh* [pāṭha] चोराहृतं; Bo BBe^{2} Ho चौरैर्हतं; Be^{3} TMd^{4} चौरैर्हितं; wKt^{1} चौरैर्हित — c) Tj^{1} राजा तु तदु°; Lo^{5} तदपयु°; wKt^{1} तदपजञ्जान°; Lo^{2} Lo^{3} Pu^{5} Pu^{7} Pu^{8} °पभुञ्जान°; Kt^{2} °युञ्जानञ्चौ° — d) Lo^{3} GMd^{1} GMd^{5} NNg Tj^{1} Tr^{1} °नश्चोर°; TMd^{3} GMy °नश्चोरश्चाप्नोति

समीक्ष्य कुलधर्मांश्च स्वधर्मं प्रतिपादयेत् ॥४१॥
स्वानि कर्माणि कुर्वाणा दूरे सन्तोऽपि मानवाः ।
प्रिया भवन्ति लोकस्य स्वे स्वे कर्मण्यवस्थिताः ॥४२॥
नोत्पादयेत्स्वयं कार्यं राजा नाप्यस्य पूरुषः ।
न च प्रापितमन्येन ग्रसेतार्थं कथंचन ॥४३॥
यथा नयत्यसृक्पातैर्मृगस्य मृगयुः पदम् ।
नयेत्तथानुमानेन धर्मस्य नृपतिः पदम् ॥४४॥
सत्यमर्थं च संपश्येदात्मानमथ साक्षिणः ।
देशं कालं च रूपं च व्यवहारविधौ स्थितः ॥४५॥
सद्भिराचरितं यत् स्याद् धार्मिकैश्च द्विजातिभिः ।
तद्देशकुलजातीनामविरुद्धं प्रकल्पयेत् ॥४६॥
अधमर्णार्थसिद्ध्यर्थमुत्तमर्णेन चोदितः ।

41. Cited by *Dev* 3.65; *Mādh* 3.36 — a) Jo² Pu⁵ Pu⁷ [*Jolly* G] जातिधर्मान्जानपदान्; Lo⁵ sOx¹ sPu⁶ ज्ञातिजान° — b) Ho wKt³ sOx¹ sPu⁶ श्रीणी°; Tr² °धमस्य धर्मवित्; GMd¹ TMd⁴ °धमांश्च तत्त्वतः; TMd³ GMd⁵ GMy Tr¹ MTr⁴ MTr⁶ [*Jolly* Nd] *Dev Mādh* °धमांश्च शाश्वतान् — d) BBe² Be³ Bo wKt¹ Lo¹ स्वधर्मान्प्रति°; *Dev* स्वे वर्गे प्रति°; *Mādh* स्वे वर्णे प्रति°; GMy प्रतिदापयेत्; Pu⁸ प्रतिपातयेत्; Be¹ wKt¹ oOr प्रतिपालयेत्; Jo² Lo³ GMd¹ GMd⁵ NPu¹ Tj¹ Tr¹ *Rn* [*Jolly* R] परिपालयेत्

42. Omitted in Be¹ — a) Hy स्वामि; BKt⁵ धर्माणि; Lo² TMd⁴ कुर्वाणो — b) NKt⁴ सान्तापि — c) Bo भवति; Tj¹ लोकेस्य; TMd³ GMd⁵ GMy MTr⁶ [*Jolly* Nd]लोकेस्मिन् — d) GMd¹ TMd³ TMd⁴ GMd⁵ GMy Tr¹ MTr⁴ MTr⁶ [*Jolly* Nd] *Nā* स्वे स्वे धर्मे व्यवस्थिताः [TMd⁴ GMy धर्म]

43. Cited by *Vij* 2.5; *Apa* 605; *Dev* 3.61 — a) GMd⁵ नोत्पातये°; Tr² °येत्सकं; oOr कर्म — b) Pu⁵ Pu⁷ [*Jolly* G] राजा नान्यस्य कस्यचित्; GMd¹ TMd³ GMy राजाप्यस्य न पूरुषः [GMd¹ च पू°]; oOr राजा नापदि; Ho Ox² sPu⁶ [*but cor*] Tr² वाप्यस्य; NPu¹ पौरुषः — c) Lo² Pu⁴ न वा; NKt⁴ TMd⁴ Tj¹ Tr² MTr⁵ *Dev* न चाप्रापि° — d) Be¹ BBe² Be³ BCa Hy Jo¹ Jo² Kt² NKt⁴ Lo³ GMd⁵ GMy oOr Tj¹ Tj² Tr¹ MTr³ MTr⁴ MTr⁵ MTr⁶ [*Jolly* Ku R Nd] *Bh Nā Rn Nd Rc Mr Mandlik KSS Dave* ग्रसेदर्थं; TMd⁴ ग्रसीतार्थं; TMd³ ग्रसेदर्दं; Pu² Pu⁴ ग्रसेवार्थं; Pu⁵ प्रासभर्थं; Tj² *om* कथं

44. Lo³ Tj¹ transpose pādas a-b and c-d. Cited by *Dev* 3.56; *Mādh* 3.30 — b) wKt³ पदा; Pu⁴ परं — c) GMd¹ TMd⁴ तथानुमानेन नयेद् [TMd⁴ तदानु°]; La¹ °त्तथार्थमानेन — d) TMd³ नृपतेः; Lo³ Tj¹ पदे

45.* Pādas b-d omitted in Ox³. Cited by *Lakṣ* 12.15 — a) *Bh* [pāṭha] सत्यमर्थेपु संपश्येद्; TMd³ *Lakṣ* सत्यं धर्मं; Ho La¹ Lo¹ sOx¹ sPu⁶ Tr² तु — b) Wa °नमप्यसाक्षिणं; La¹ Lo² Lo⁴ Lo⁵ NNg oOr Pu² Pu⁴ Pu⁵ MTr⁴ MTr⁵ MTr⁶ [*Jolly* M G] *Bh Me Jolly Jha Dave* साक्षिणं; BKt⁵ साक्षिणां; wKt¹ काङ्क्षिणः — c) La¹ देशं च व्यवहारं च; Tr² देश; Hy Jm Jo¹ Kt² La¹ MTr³ *Mandlik Jha KSS Dave* रूपं च कालं च; BKt⁵ कालं च रूपस्य; Be³ रूपं वा — d) MTr⁶ °विधे; GMd¹ GMd⁵ स्थितिः; Hy *Lakṣ* स्थितं

46. Omitted in Ox³. Cited by *Dev* 1.25 — a) TMd³ Lo⁴ य स्याद्; NNg यस्माद्; *Dev* यच्च; Ox² पश्येद् — b) Lo⁴ Lo⁵ धार्मिकश्चेद्; TMd³ धार्मिकाश्च; Pu⁸ द्विजादिभिः; MTr⁵ द्विजोत्तमैः — c) MTr⁶ तं देश°; BKt⁵ तद्देशकाल°; Ho °जातानाम°; Jo² °जातीयम° — d) Pu⁵ Pu⁷ [*Jolly* G] °नामनुरूपं; Ho विकल्पयेत् — After this verse Lo⁴ inserts verses 9.235–46, and Lo⁵ verses 9.235–47b

दापयेद्धनिकस्यार्थमधमर्णाद्विभावितम् ॥४७॥
यैर्यैरुपायैरर्थं स्वं प्राप्नुयादुत्तमर्णिकः ।
तैस्तैरुपायैः संगृह्य दापयेदधमर्णिकम् ॥४८॥
धर्मेण व्यवहारेण छलेनाचरितेन च ।
प्रयुक्तं साधयेदर्थं पञ्चमेन बलेन च ॥४९॥
यः स्वयं साधयेदर्थमुत्तमर्णोऽधमर्णिकात् ।
न स राज्ञाभियोक्तव्यः स्वकं संसाधयन्धनम् ॥५०॥
अर्थेऽपव्ययमानं तु करणेन विभावितम् ।
दापयेद्धनिकस्यार्थं दण्डलेशं च शक्तितः ॥५१॥

47. Omitted in Lo^{4} Lo^{5} Ox^{3}; pāda-d *ma sh* in Tr^{1}. Cited by *Lakṣ* 12.331 — a) Be^{1} Ho Tj^{1} अधर्मणार्थ°; Bo अर्धमणार्थ°; GMd^{1} अधर्मस्यार्थ°; TMd^{3} अधवर्णर्थ° — b) wKt^{1} °त्तमन्तेन; TMd^{3} °त्तकर्णेन; TMd^{4} °त्तमर्णी तु; sOx^{1} sPu^{6} चोदिताः; Pu^{7} Pu^{5} Tr^{2} Wa [*Jolly* G] *Mr* नोदितः; Be^{1} मोदितः — c) Pu^{2} Pu^{4} पादयेद्ध° — c-d) GMd^{5} °येद्धार्मिकस्यार्थमुत्तमर्णविभावितं — d) GMd^{1} MTr^{5} °धमर्णविभा°; TMd^{4} Pu^{5} °धमर्णाविभा°; Pu^{7} °धमर्णां विभा°; TMd^{3} GMy NNg oOr MTr^{4} MTr^{6} *Nā Go Ku* °धमर्णं विभा°; wKt^{3} °भाषितं. *Bh* gives both readings: दापयेदधमर्णादधमर्णं वा; *Me* supports the ablative; for the accusative, see the similar expression at 8.48d.

48. Omitted in Lo^{4} Lo^{5} Ox^{3}. Cited by *Lakṣ* 12.324 — a) BKt^{5} °यैरर्थः; oOr °पायैः स्वमर्थं; Pu^{5} Pu^{7} °यैरर्थं च; TMd^{4} °यैरर्थस्य — b) Jo^{2} °यादधमर्णिकः; Lo^{1} TMd^{3} Pu^{5} Pu^{7} Wa *Dev* °मर्णकः; Tj^{1} °मिर्णिकः — c) Tr^{2} °पायैस्तं गृह्य — d) GMd^{1} दापयेत्साधयन्धनं [cf. 50d]; TMd^{3} GMd^{5} GMy Tr^{1} MTr^{5} *Nd Lakṣ* साधयेद°; Jo^{1} पादयेद°; Jo^{2} Tj^{1} °येदाधम°; Lo^{1} TMd^{4} Pu^{5} Pu^{7} Tj^{2} °मर्णकं; wKt^{1} sOx^{1} sPu^{6} °मर्णिकां; BBe^{2} °मर्णिकात्

49. Omitted in Lo^{4} Lo^{5} Ox^{3} Pu^{4}; pāda-d omitted in GMd^{5}. Cited by *Vij* 2.40; *Apa* 645; *Lakṣ* 12.324; *Dev* 3.387; *Mādh* 3.191 — a) *Apa* [vl] धर्म्येण — b) T Md^{4} GMy Pu^{2} Tr^{2} *Apa* [vl] छलेन चरि°; *Dev* छद्मनाचरि°; Be^{1} बलेनाचरि°; MTr^{3} फलेनाचरि°; wKt^{3} Lo^{1} TMd^{3} GMy Wa [*Jolly* R Nd] वा; GMd^{1} चा — c) TMd^{4} प्रयुक्तस्साध°; oOr साधयेदेव; GMd^{1} TMd^{4} *om* साधयेदर्थं ... [50a] स्वयं [haplo] — d) Jo^{2} wKt^{3} NKt^{4} La^{1} Lo^{1} Lo^{3} NPu^{1} Pu^{2} Pu^{5} Pu^{7} [*Jolly* G] वा

50. Pādas a-b [up to °त्तमर्णो] omitted in Pu^{4}, and pāda-a in GMd^{5}. Cited by *Lakṣ* 12.329; *Dev* 3.386 — a) Pu^{5} Pu^{7} स्वयं यः; NPu^{1} *Dev* स्वकं; Ho स्वापं; NKt^{4} त्वकं; Ho sOx^{1} sPu^{6} Tr^{2} °येदर्थानुत्त° — b) Jm °त्तमर्णाधम°; Ho TMd^{3} Pu^{7} Wa °मर्णकात्; NKt^{4} sOx^{1} sPu^{6} °मर्णिकान्; Pu^{5} °मर्णकान्; MTr^{4} °मर्णिकं — c) *Dev* [in two mss of *Lakṣ*] स राज्ञा नाभियोक्तव्यः; BBe^{2} न च; BKt^{5} स च; Lo^{4} sOx^{1} sPu^{6} राजाभि°; Wa राज्ञोभि°; Bo °योक्तव्या; TMd^{3} MTr^{6} °योक्तव्यो; GMd^{5} °योक्तव्यं — d) GMd^{1} स्वकं स्वदधमर्णकं; BKt^{5} Pu^{5} Pu^{7} MTr^{4} स्वयं; Pu^{5} Pu^{7} तत्साध°; wKt^{1} स्वंसाधयन्धनं; Lo^{1} *cor to* संसाधाये धनं; Be^{3} wKt^{3} NKt^{4} La^{1} TMd^{3} GMd^{5} GMy oOr Tr^{1} संसाधयेद्धनं; MTr^{4} संसाधयेन्धनं; Ho °यन्धमं; TMd^{4} °यन्दमं; Ox^{3} °यन्वनं

51.* Cited by *Lakṣ* 12.264; *Dev* 3.287; *Mādh* 3.153 — a) Jo^{2} NNg Pu^{2} Pu^{4} Pu^{5} Pu^{7} [*Jolly* G] अर्थे विवदमानं तु; T Md^{4} अर्थपव्यवहारं तु; sOx^{1} sPu^{6} अर्थे न धारयामीति; wKt^{1} NKt^{4} अर्थे न व्ययमानं तु; oOr अर्थेपि व्यययातं तु; Lo^{4} Lo^{5} अर्थो; NPu^{1} अर्थेपि व्यय°; MTr^{4} अर्थे च व्यय°; Lo^{1} GMd^{1} अर्थे तु व्यय°; Lo^{1} अर्थं तु व्यय° — b) TMd^{3} TMd^{4} GMd^{5} GMy NPu^{1} [*Jolly* M$^{1-3-5-8-9}$ Me N Nd] *Dev Jolly* कारणेन; Ox^{2} करुणेन; Bo wKt^{3} विभाषितं; Pu^{5} Pu^{7} विभावयेत्; TMd^{4} विचारितं — d) GMd^{1} °स्यार्थमृणलेशं; Ho स्वशक्तितः

अपह्नवेऽधमर्णस्य देहीत्युक्तस्य संसदि ।
अभियोक्ता दिशेद्देशं करणं वान्यदुद्दिशेत् ॥५२॥
अदेशं यश्च दिशति निर्दिश्यापह्नुते च यः ।
यश्चाधरोत्तरानर्थान् विगीतान्नावबुध्यते ॥५३॥
अपदिश्यापदेश्यं च पुनर्यस्त्वपधावति ।
सम्यक्प्रणिहितं चार्थं पृष्टः सन्नाभिनन्दति ॥५४॥

Additional verse in Be³ Ho NKt⁴ Lo² Pu² Pu⁴ Wa [= 8.139]:

ऋणे देये प्रतिज्ञाते पञ्चकं शतमर्हति ।
अपह्नवे तु द्विगुणं तन्मनोरनुशासनम् ॥

a) Lo² ऋणो; NKt⁴ देशेयतिक्रान्ते — c) Lo² अपह्नयते द्वि°; Pu² Pu⁴ तदि्द्वगुणं — c-d) NKt⁴ तापहवे द्विगुण मनोरनुशाशनं

A further additional verse in BCa *Mandlik* [क, ट, ठ, ड] *KSS Dave;* placed after 52 in La¹ [this is taken from *Me* who cites this verse with तथाहुः]:

यत्र न स्यात्कृतं पत्रं करणं च न विद्यते ।
न चोपलम्भः पूर्वोक्तस्तत्र दैवी क्रिया भवेत् ॥

a) La¹ अत्र; *Mandlik KSS Dave* तत्स्या°; La¹ *Mandlik KSS Dave* °त्कृतं यत्र — b) *Me* साक्षी चैव न — c) La¹ *Mandlik KSS Dave* °लम्भ — d) *Me* पूर्वोक्तो दैवी तत्र; BCa क्रिया श्रुता

52.* Cited by *Lakṣ* 12.88 — a) Kt² TMd³ आपह्न°; BKt⁵ अपह्नअधम°; Ho Tj¹ °धर्मणस्य; Kt² °धर्मण्यस्य; TMd⁴ °धमर्णस्या — b) wKt¹ महीत्यु°; Bo देहीयुक्तस्य — c) Be¹ अभियुक्त; *Me* [pāṭha] अभियुक्तो; BBe² *om* °योक्ता; Be¹ BBe² Be³ BCa Ho Hy Jm Jo¹ Jo² wKt¹ Kt² BKt⁵ Lo¹ Lo³ oOr sOx¹ Ox² sPu⁶ Pu⁸ Tj¹ Tj² Tr¹ [*cor to sh*] Tr² MTr³ [*Jolly* Ku] *Lakṣ Ku Rn Rc Mr Mandlik KSS* दिशेद्देश्यं; GMd⁵ दिशेत्कालं — d) BBe² NKt⁴ TMd³ GMy Pu² Pu⁴ MTr⁴ MTr⁵ [*but mc*] [*Jolly* M¹⁻³⁻⁸⁻⁹ N Nd] *Jolly Jha Dave* कारणं; TMd⁴ करं; Ox² °रणं समुद्दिशेत्; Be¹ Bo BCa Lo³ GMd⁵ sOx¹ sPu⁶ Tj¹ Tr¹ Wa *Rc* [*Jolly* R K] चान्यदुद्दि°; Ho TMd³ GMy चान्यमुद्दि°; Be³ wKt³ GMd¹ oOr वान्यमुद्दि°; Lo⁴ चास्यमुद्दि°; Lo⁵ चासुमुद्दि°; TMd⁴ चान्यदुद्विजेत्; Lo² NNg Ox³ Pu⁵ Pu⁷ [*Jolly* M¹⁻³⁻⁸⁻⁹ G N Nd] *Me* [pāṭha] *Bh Jolly Der* वा समुद्दिशेत्; [*Jolly* M⁴⁻⁵] च स्वमुद्दिशेत्; Pu² Pu⁴ MTr⁴ MTr⁶ चास्य निर्दिशेत्

53. Omitted in GMd¹ TMd⁴ Ox³; verses 53 and 54 transposed in Lo⁴ Lo⁵; folios containing 8.53–94 missing in Jm. Cited by *Lakṣ* 12.80; *Dev* 3.108 — a) Lo⁴ Lo⁵ Pu² Pu⁷ आदेशं; Pu⁵ अदिशं; Be¹ BBe² Be³ Bo BCa Ho Hy Jo¹ Jo² wKt¹ Kt² wKt³ BKt⁵ Lo¹ Lo³ Ox² Ox³ Pu⁸ Tj¹ Tj² Tr¹ [*cor to sh*] Tr² MTr³ Wa [*Jolly* R] *Ku Rn Rc Mr Dev Mandlik KSS* अदेश्यं; Bo आदेश्यं; wKt¹ *Nd* अदेयं; Lo³ Tr² यच्च; Lo¹ यस्तु; Pu² Pu⁴ यस्य; Kt² पञ्च — b) NPu¹ Pu² Pu⁴ निर्देश्या°; Pu⁵ Pu⁷ [*Jolly* G] °पह्नवीति च; Bo °पह्नुवे च; Lo³ BKt⁵ °पह्नवे च; Tj¹ °पह्नवेच्च; TMd³ °पह्नुतेश्च; Lo⁵ °पहुते च; Ho °पहते च — c) GMd⁵ यच्चाध°; sOx¹ sPu⁶ पश्चाधरो°; wKt¹ यश्चाधमोत्तमान°; Ho °त्तरामर्थान्; Bo °त्तरानर्थं — d) wKt¹ विगीतात्मा च बुध्यते; NNg विगीतात्र च बुध्यते; Pu⁸ MTr⁴ MTr⁶ विनीता°; *Dev* विहीना°; GMy अभीता°; TMd³ विगतत्राव°

54. Omitted in GMd¹ TMd⁴. Cite by *Lakṣ* 12.80; *Dev* 3.108 — a) Hy आपदि°; BKt⁵ अदिश्याप°; Wa अपदेश्योप°; Bo Lo⁴ Lo⁵ TMd³ Pu⁷ *Dev* °श्यापदेशं; *Lakṣ* °श्योपदेशं; BKt⁵ तु — b) BBe² °स्त्वपवाधते; Be¹ BCa La¹ Lo³ oOr Ox² NPu¹ Pu² Pu⁴ Pu⁵ Pu⁷ Pu⁸ Tj¹ Tr¹ Tr² Wa [*Jolly* M¹⁻⁵⁻⁸⁻⁹ G R] °स्त्ववधावति; BKt⁵ °स्त्ववधारयेत्; Bo °स्त्वयधावति; NKt⁴ GMd⁵ °स्त्वभिधावति; Lo¹ °स्त्वनेधावति; TMd³ °स्तुपधावति; sOx¹ sPu⁶ °स्त्वेव धावति; MTr⁴ MTr⁶ °स्तेन धावति; Be³ °स्त्ववधायवै — c)

असंभाष्ये साक्षिभिश्च देशे संभाषते मिथः ।
निरुच्यमानं प्रश्नं च नेच्छेद्यश्चापि निष्पतेत् ॥५५॥
ब्रूहीत्युक्तश्च न ब्रूयादुक्तं च न विभावयेत् ।
न च पूर्वापरं विद्यात् तस्मादर्थात् स हीयते ॥५६॥
ज्ञातारः सन्ति मेत्युक्त्वा दिशेत्युक्तो दिशेन्न यः ।
धर्मस्थः कारणैरेतैर्हीनं तमिति निर्दिशेत् ॥५७॥
अभियोक्ता न चेद् ब्रूयाद् वध्यो दण्ड्यश्च धर्मतः ।
न चेत् त्रिपक्षात् प्रब्रूयाद् धर्मं प्रति पराजितः ॥५८॥
यो यावन्निह्नुवीतार्थं मिथ्या यावति वा वदेत् ।
तौ नृपेण ह्यधर्मज्ञौ दाप्यौ तद्द्विगुणं दमम् ॥५९॥

Dev सम्यक्प्राणि° ; bBe^{2} °णिहितानर्थान्; Tj^{1} वार्थं — d) bKt^{5} Lo^{4} Lo^{5} °भिनिन्दति

55. Omitted in gMd^{1} — a) oOr संभाष्ये; wKt^{1} अस्यस्ताये *mc to* अदन्ताये; La^{1} °भाष्यो; Tr^{2} °भाष्यं; tMd^{3} mTr^{5} *Nd* °भाव्ये; gMy °भाव्य; Lo^{1} °भावे; Ho °भाष्ये च साक्षिश्च; bBe^{2} साक्षिभिस्तु — b) bKt^{5} देश्ये; La^{1} देशं; Pu^{5} Pu^{7} [*Jolly* G] संभाषितेन च; Ho संभाषतेभियः; Be^{1} bBe^{2} sOx^{1} Ox^{2} nPu^{1} sPu^{6} Tr^{1} Wa °भाषिते; tMd^{3} gMy °भाविते — c) nKt^{4} विरुप्यमाणं; oOr Pu^{2} Pu^{4} निरुध्यमानं; Tr^{1} निरूध्यमानं; tMd^{3} °मान — d) nNg Pu^{5} Pu^{7} [*Jolly* G] नेक्षेद्यश्चापि; tMd^{3} °श्चाति; Lo^{5} Tr^{2} निष्पते; Tj^{1} निष्यते; tMd^{4} निष्पतत्

56. a) wKt^{1} अभियोक्ता न चेद्ब्रूयादुक्तं [cf. 58a]; mTr^{4} ब्रूहीत्युक्तो न चेद्ब्रूया° ; mTr^{6} ब्रूहीत्युक्तं च न ब्रूया° ; tMd^{4} ब्रूयात्युक्तश्च; Kt^{2} °क्तञ्च; wKt^{3} °क्तंश्च; Be^{3} °क्तस्तु; Lo^{1} नो; Hy श्रूयादुक्तं — b) nKt^{4} न च; tMd^{4} चैव विभा° ; sOx^{1} sPu^{6} च निविभा° ; wKt^{1} च नाविभा° ; Lo^{4} विभाषयेत्; Tr^{1} विवाहयेत् — c) mTr^{4} gMd^{5} पूर्वापरान्; Ho La^{1} विन्द्यात् — d) bBe^{2} °दर्थान्; Tr^{2} °दर्थाश्च; Tj^{1} °दर्थान्महीयते; Ho gMd^{5} °दर्थात्समीहते; gMd^{1} °दर्थात्प्रहीयते; Pu^{8} °दर्थात्सहीयतो

57* Cited by *Lakṣ* 12.80; *Dev* 3.108; pāda-a cited by *Kum* 1.3.24— a) gMd^{1} tMd^{3} gMd^{5} gMy Tr^{1} [*Jolly* M$^{1-3-8-9}$ Nd] *Dev Lakṣ NSm* [Mā] 1.52 [com; Jolly 1.61] सन्ति ज्ञातार इत्युक्त्वा [Tr^{1} ज्ञातारमित्यु° ; gMd^{5} इत्युक्ते]; Bo ज्ञातारं; Pu^{5} Pu^{7} ज्ञानायः; Be^{1} bBe^{2} Hy Jo^{1} Jo^{2} wKt^{1} Kt^{2} Lo^{3} Tj^{1} Tj^{2} mTr^{3} [*Jolly* Ku R] *Go Ku Rn Mr Mandlik KSS* साक्षिणः सन्ति; Bo Ho Lo^{1} Lo^{4} Lo^{5} Ox^{3} Tj^{1} मेत्युक्ता; Lo^{2} Ox^{2} चेत्युक्त्वा; tMd^{4} हीत्युक्त्वा — b) Lo^{5} gMd^{5} दिशेत्युक्ते; gMd^{1} दिशेन्न वा; Tj^{2} दिशेत्तु यः; bKt^{5} दिशेत्ततः — c) gMd^{1} tMd^{3} gMd^{5} gMy Tr^{1} [*but cor sh*] [*Jolly* Nd]धर्मस्थो हेतुनानेन हीनं; tMd^{4} धर्मस्थं; Bo धर्मार्थः; Lo^{1} धर्मस्य; Be^{1} Tj^{1} करणै° ; Bo कारिणै° — d) *Dev* °तैर्हीनोऽसाविति; Be^{1} bBe^{2} Be^{3} Bo bCa Ho Hy Jo^{1} Jo^{2} wKt^{1} Kt^{2} wKt^{3} nKt^{4} La^{1} Lo^{1} Lo^{3} Lo^{4} Lo^{5} tMd^{3} tMd^{4} gMd^{5} gMy nNg oOr sOx^{1} Ox^{2} Ox^{3} sPu^{6} Pu^{8} Tj^{1} Tj^{2} Tr^{1} [*Jolly* R Nd] *Rc Mandlik KSS* तमपि

58.* Omitted in [*Jolly* M$^{1-3}$]; pāda-a lacuna in tMd^{4}. Cited by *Lakṣ* 12.80 — a) Bo अभिनोक्ता; wKt^{3} अभिव्यक्ता; nPu^{1} अभियुक्तो; *Lakṣ* अभियोगे — b) bKt^{5} ब्रूयादध्यो; Be^{3} wKt^{1} Lo^{1} Lo^{4} Ox^{3} Pu^{3} mTr^{3} mTr^{4} *Mandlik* बध्यो; mTr^{5} बद्ध्यो; tMd^{3} Tr^{2} mTr^{6} वन्ध्यो; *Jha* बन्ध्यो; nPu^{1} दण्डश्च; La^{1} धर्मश्च दण्डतः; oOr धर्मवित् — c) Pu^{2} Pu^{4} न चेत्तत्प्रक्रियां ब्रूयाद्; tMd^{3} त्रिपक्षो; tMd^{4} त्रिपक्षान्; gMd^{5} तु पक्षात्; mTr^{6} विपक्षात्; Lo^{3} त्रिपक्षाच्च ब्रूयाद् — d) tMd^{3} gMy धर्म्यं; wKt^{1} धर्मः; gMd^{1} पराजितं; Ox^{3} पराजयः — After this verse Ox^{3} inserts 9.51–9; Lo^{4} Lo^{5} insert 9.52–9.

59. Omitted in Lo^{4} Lo^{5} Ox^{3} [*Jolly* M^{1-3-4}]. Cited by *Lakṣ* 12264; *Dev* 3.286; *Mādh* 3.152 — a) tMd^{3} यो योपह्नुवीतार्थं; gMy यो योपह्नुहीतार्थमो मिथ्या; bKt^{5} *om* यो; bKt^{5} यावन्नह्नुवी° ; *Dev Mādh* यावन्निह्नवी° ; nNg यावन्तं ह्नुवीतार्थं; Lo^{2} यावन्तं ब्रुवीतार्थं; gMd यावदर्थं तद्ब्रूयाद्; wKt^{1} यावन्ति

पृष्टोऽपव्ययमानस्तु कृतावस्थो धनैषिणा ।
त्र्यवरैः साक्षिभिर्भाव्यो नृपब्राह्मणसंनिधौ ॥६०॥
यादृशा धनिभिः कार्या व्यवहारेषु साक्षिणः ।
तादृशान्संप्रवक्ष्यामि यथा वाच्यमृतं च तैः ॥६१॥
गृहिणः पुत्रिणो मौलाः क्षत्रविट्शूद्रयोनयः ।
अर्थ्युक्ताः साक्ष्यमर्हन्ति न ये केचिदनापदि ॥६२॥
आप्ताः सर्वेषु वर्णेषु कार्याः कार्येषु साक्षिणः ।
सर्वधर्मविदोऽलुब्धा विपरीतांस्तु वर्जयेत् ॥६३॥
नार्थसंबन्धिनो नाप्ता न सहाया न वैरिणः ।
न दृष्टदोषाः कर्तव्या न व्याध्यार्ता न दूषिताः ॥६४॥

ब्रवीतार्थं; [*Jolly* M^{8}] यावन्न ब्रवीतार्थं — b) Ho मिथ्या या च विवादयेत्; *Mādh* मिथ्या वा ह्यभिवादयेत्; Pu^{8} मिथ्या यो वा वेदयेत्; TMd^{4} निन्द्या; Tj^{1} यावेति; Pu^{2} Pu^{4} यमिति; TMd^{3} GMy वा यावति; GMd^{5} वा यदि वा वदेत्; Be^{3} Tj^{2} यावति वादयेत्; Be^{1} Pu^{3} यावन्निवेदयेत्; *Dev* यावति वारयेत्; Pu^{5} Pu^{7} वा पुनः — c) TMd^{3} ता नृपेण ह्यधर्मज्ञा; Be^{3} नृपेण तावधर्मज्ञौ; MTr^{4} MTr^{6} नृपेणाप्यधर्मज्ञौ; TMd^{4} त्वधर्मज्ञौ; Kt^{2} Lo^{2} ह्यधर्मज्ञो — d) TMd^{4} दण्ड्यौ; GMd^{1} दण्ड्यं; TMd^{3} दाप्तौ तौ द्वि°; TMd^{4} sOx^{1} sPu^{6} धनं तद्द्वि°; NPu^{1} दिनं तद्द्वि°

60. Omitted in Lo^{4} Lo^{5} Ox^{3} [*Jolly* M^{1-3-4}]; pādas c-d *ma* in Tr^{1}; pāda-b omitted in sOx^{1}. Cited by *Lakṣ* 12.102; pādas c-d cited by *Dev* 3.174 — a) Tr^{2} पृष्टेपव्यथमास्तु; oOr पृष्टोप्यव्ययमानस्तु; wKt^{1} पृष्टोव्ययमानं तु; GMd^{1} दृष्टो; Tj^{1} पृष्टोथव्यय°; Lo^{1} Pu^{2} MTr^{4} पृष्टोप्यव्यय°; Kt^{2} °मानं तु — b) GMd^{1} कृतवास्थो; Be^{3} Tj^{1} कृतावस्थौ; BKt^{5} कृतावस्थ; wKt^{3} कृतावष्ठो; Ho कृतावज्ञो; Be^{1} TMd^{3} GMd^{5} GMy धनेषिणा; *Lakṣ* धनैषिणां; Pu^{2} Pu^{4} धनीषिणा; Ho धनैषिणः — c) Pu^{5} Pu^{7} त्रिवरैः; Lo^{1} आवरैः; BKt^{5} अधरः साक्षि°; Tr^{2} °भिर्भव्यो; GMd^{1} °भिर्भाव्यैः; NNg Pu^{5} Pu^{7} °भिर्वाच्यो — d) Tj^{1} नृपं

61. Omitted in Lo^{4} Lo^{5} Ox^{3} [*Jolly* M^{1-3-4}]; *ma* in Tr^{1}. Cited by *Lakṣ* 12.104 — a) *Lakṣ* यादृशा अर्थिभिः; Bo कार्यो — b) NNg °हारेण तु साक्षिणः — c) Tr^{2} यादृशा°; BKt^{5} °शान्प्रवक्षामि — d) BKt^{5} Tr^{2} वाचमृतं; GMd^{5} वाच्यं धनं; BKt^{5} च तौ

62. Omitted in Pu^{5} [*Jolly* M$^{1-3}$]. Cited by *Apa* 665 — a) wKt^{1} गृहीणः; Ho गृणिणः; GMd^{5} पुत्रिणो ये तु; BKt^{5} मौल्यः; GMd^{1} मूलाः — c) La^{1} अर्थयुक्ताः; NKt^{4} अर्थ्यात्काः; *Apa* अर्थज्ञाः; BBe^{2} sOx^{1} sPu^{6} MTr^{5} अत्युक्ताः; GMd^{1} अर्ध्युक्ता; NPu^{1} Pu^{8} अप्युक्ताः; *Lakṣ* इत्युक्तः; oOr अव्यक्तः; Bo Lo^{5} साक्षम°; BBe^{2} La^{1} oOr साक्षिम°; Be^{3} साक्षमिच्छन्ति; Hy °मर्हति

63. Omitted in [*Jolly* M$^{1-3}$]. Cited by *Lakṣ* 12.104; *Dev* 3.177 — a) NPu^{1} आप्ता वर्णेषु सर्वेषु; TMd^{3} GMy अभूतास्सर्ववर्णेषु; Lo^{1} *Lakṣ* प्राप्ताः — b) Be^{1} Be^{3} wKt^{1} Lo^{1} Lo^{5} oOr कार्याकार्येषु; TMd^{3} GMd^{5} GMy [*Jolly* Nd] कार्याः साक्ष्येषु; Pu^{2} सर्वेषु — c) Tj^{2} सर्वे; Be^{3} La^{1} सर्ववर्ण°; BKt^{5} सर्ववर्त°; La^{1} Tr^{2} °लुब्धान् — d) Be^{3} विपरीतान्विवर्जयेत्; Bo विपरीतास्तु; BCa wKt^{3} TMd^{4} GMd^{5} sOx^{1} NPu^{1} sPu^{6} विपरीतांश्च; TMd^{3} विपरीताश्च

64. Omitted in [*Jolly* M$^{1-3}$]. Cited by *Dev* 3.177; *Mādh* 3.66; pāda-a cited by *Vij* 2.80 — a) Be^{1} नार्थं; BKt^{5} नार्थे; Tj^{1} Tr^{2} नार्थि°; sOx^{1} sPu^{6} MTr^{5} नार्था°; TMd^{4} नार्ता°; GMd^{5} नात्म°; Pu^{2} नात्र°; Lo^{4} Lo^{5} नाप्ताः; Tr^{2} नापाः; GMy नोता; TMd^{3} नेता — b) Pu^{2} Pu^{4} सहाया नैव वैरिणः; Lo^{1} न साहाया; TMd^{3} GMd^{5} न सहाय; Tj^{1} सहायेन वैरिणः — c) GMd^{1} दृष्टदोषा न कर्तव्यो; wKt^{3} पृष्टदोषाः — d) GMy *lacuna at* न व्याध्यार्ता; BBe^{2} व्याधार्था; BCa नध्यार्ता; wKt^{1} वक्तव्यार्ता; Bo GMd^{1} दूषितः

न साक्षी नृपतिः कार्यो न कारुककुशीलवौ ।
न श्रोत्रियो न लिङ्गस्थो न सङ्गेभ्यो विनिर्गतः ॥६५॥
नाध्यधीनो न वक्तव्यो न दस्युर्न विकर्मकृत् ।
न वृद्धो न शिशुर्नैको नान्त्यो न विकलेन्द्रियः ॥६६॥
नार्तो न मत्तो नोन्मत्तो न क्षुत्तृष्णोपपीडितः ।
न श्रमार्तो न कामार्तो न क्रुद्धो नापि तस्करः ॥६७॥
स्त्रीणां साक्ष्यं स्त्रियः कुर्युर्द्विजानां सदृशा द्विजाः ।
शूद्राश्च सन्तः शूद्राणामन्त्यानामन्त्ययोनयः ॥६८॥
अनुभावी तु यः कश्चित् कुर्यात्साक्ष्यं विवादिनाम् ।
अन्तर्वेश्मन्यरण्ये वा शरीरस्यैव चात्यये ॥६९॥
स्त्रियाप्यसंभवे कार्यं बालेन स्थविरेण वा ।
शिष्येण बन्धुना वापि दासेन भृतकेन वा ॥७०॥

65. Omitted in [*Jolly* M[1–3]]. Cited by *Lakṣ* 12.111; *Dev* 3.177; *Mādh* 3.66 — a) wKt[1] नासाक्षी; TMd[3] साक्षः; Be[3] साक्षं — b) Tr[1] न च कारुकुशीलवौ; TMd[3] Tj[1] कारक°; Be[3] °कुसीलवौ; Ho °कुशीलकौ — c) Hy नाश्रोत्रियो; TMd[4] लिङ्गस्थे; Pu[5] Pu[7] [*Jolly* G] गृहस्थो — d) Pu[5] Pu[7] [*Jolly* G] न च सङ्गविवर्जितः; Ox[2] न संभोगविनिर्गतः; Pu[2] Pu[4] विनिर्गतिः; *Lakṣ* निवर्तकः

66. Omitted in [*Jolly* M[1–3]]. Cited by *Dev* 3.177; *Mādh* 3.66 — a) oOr अध्यधीनो; TMd[4] Pu[5] Pu[7] नात्यधीनो; Wa नाभ्यधीनो; GMy नाध्यधीको; TMd[3] नाध्ययिनो; NPu[1] नाव्यधीतो; GMd[5] न व्याधितो; TMd[4] वक्तव्या; Kt[2] व्यक्तव्यो — b) GMd[1] न दस्युन्नापि कर्मकृत्; Pu[8] विकर्मवित् — c) wKt[1] नावृद्धो; NNg विद्धो; wKt[1] Lo[3] Tj[1] नाशिशु°; TMd[3] शुशु° — d) TMd[3] नार्षो न

67. Omitted in [*Jolly* M[1–3]]. Cited by *Dev* 3.177; *Mādh* 3.66 — a) Lo[2] नात्तो — b) Tr[1] °क्षुत्तृष्णावपीडितः — c) TMd[4] नाश्रमार्तो; GMy श्रमार्ते; Tr[2] *om* न कामार्तो; Lo[1] कर्मार्तो — d) wKt[3] न च तस्करः

68. Omitted in NNg [*Jolly* M[1–3]]. Cited by *Apa* 665; pāda-a cited by *Vij* 2.69 — a) GMd[1] स्त्रियं कुर्यु°; GMy कुर्यान्द्वि°; TMd[3] कुर्या द्वि° — b) TMd[4] सदृशं; GMd[5] शास्त्रिणां द्विजाः; Bo Lo[5] द्विजः; TMd[3] द्विजां — c) Wa शूद्राः सन्तश्च शूद्राणाम°; Bo सन्ताः; MTr[4] सन्त; GMd[1] सन्ति — d) Tj[2] *om* अन्तयानाम्; GMy Pu[2] Pu[4] °न्त्यानामन्त्यजातयः; TMd[3] °न्त्यजामन्त्यजातयः; Bo °नामन्ययोनयः

69.* Omitted in [*Jolly* M[1–3]]; pādas c-d *ma* in Lo[4]. Cited by *Apa* 671; *Lakṣ* 12.117; *Dev* 3.181 — a) TMd[4] °भावि; Be[3] °भावीति; BCa °भावी च; Tr[1] °भाव्यपि यः — a-b) Pu[5] Pu[7] कुर्यात्कश्चित्साक्ष्यं — b) Be[3] °त्साक्षं; Lo[5] °त्साक्षिं; GMd[5] °त्साक्षीं; TMd[4] sOx[1] NPu[1] sPu[6] Tr[2] विवादिनं; wKt[1] विवादिना; GMd[1] विवादिनोः; BKt[5] विवादितं — c) TMd[3] °रण्यो — d) wKt[3] शरीरश्चैव; wKt[1] परीस्यैव; Be[3] Bo Ho Hy Jo[1] Kt[2] BKt[5] Lo[1] NNg Ox[3] NPu[1] Pu[2] Pu[3] Pu[4] Pu[5] Pu[7] Pu[8] Tj[2] Tr[2] MTr[3] Wa [*Jolly* M[5–8] G] *Apa Lakṣ Dev Me Rc Mr Mandlik Jolly Jha KSS Dave* शरीरस्यापि; *Apa Dev* वात्यये; BKt[5] चातये

70. Omitted in [*Jolly* M[1–3]]. Cited by *Apa* 671; *Lakṣ* 12.117; *Dev* 3.181; *Mādh* 3.70 — a) MTr[5] *Apa* स्त्रियोप्य°; La[1] स्त्रियायासंभवे; *Lakṣ* स्त्रिया वासंभवे; TMd[4] कार्या — b) TMd[3] GMy च — c) Tr[2] शिष्येण न बन्धुनापि; Ox[2] बन्धुना कार्यं — c-d) *Mādh* शिष्येण वापि दासेन बन्धुना भृतकेन वा — d) Tr[2] न चैव भृतकेन वा; TMd[4] दासीन; NNg बालेन; Be[1] Pu[3] [*Jolly* M[5–8–9] Nd] च

बालवृद्धातुराणां तु साक्ष्येषु वदतां मृषा ।
जानीयादस्थिरां वाचमुत्सिक्तमनसां तथा ॥७१॥
साहसेषु च सर्वेषु स्तेयसंग्रहणेषु च ।
वाग्दण्डयोश्च पारुष्ये न परीक्षेत साक्षिणः ॥७२॥
बहुत्वं परिगृह्णीयात् साक्षिद्वैधे नराधिपः ।
समेषु तु गुणोत्कृष्टान् गुणिद्वैधे द्विजोत्तमान् ॥७३॥
समक्षदर्शनात्साक्ष्यं श्रवणाच्चैव सिध्यति ।
तत्र सत्यं ब्रुवन्साक्षी धर्मार्थाभ्यां न हीयते ॥७४॥
साक्षी दृष्टश्रुतादन्यद् विब्रुवन्नार्यसंसदि ।
अवाङ् नरकमेवैति प्रेत्य स्वर्गाच्च हीयते ॥७५॥
यत्रानिबद्धोऽपीक्षेत शृणुयाद्वापि किंचन ।
पृष्टस्तत्रापि तद्ब्रूयाद् यथादृष्टं यथाश्रुतम् ॥७६॥

71. Omitted in [*Jolly* M$^{1-3}$]. Cited by *Lakṣ* 12.117; *Dev* 3.196 — a) Be^{1} BBe^{2} Be^{3} Bo BCa Hy Jo^{1} Jo^{2} wKt^{1} Kt^{2} NKt^{4} Lo^{2} Lo^{3} NNg Ox^{2} Pu^{2} Pu^{3} Pu^{4} Pu^{8} Tj^{1} Tj^{2} Tr^{2} MTr^{3} MTr^{4} MTr^{5} MTr^{6} [*Jolly* R] *Mandlik Jha KSS Dave* च — b) Tr^{1} साक्ष्ये विवदतां नृणां; Be^{3} Kt^{2} साक्षेषु; GMd^{1} oOr MTr^{4} MTr^{6} साक्ष्ये तु; La^{1} Ox^{2} साक्ष्ये प्रवदतां; TMd^{4} GMd^{5} वदतानृतं; GMd^{1} TMd^{3} GMy MTr^{6} वदतामृतं; MTr^{4} वदतां नृणां — c) Tr^{2} °यादास्थिरां; MTr^{5} °यादस्थिरं; Lo^{1} TMd^{3} वाचामु° — d) TMd^{3} °मुसक्तामनघां; Bo °मनसा; BKt^{5} °मानसां; Lo^{3} Tj^{1} °मनसस्तथा

72. Omitted in [*Jolly* M$^{1-3}$]. Cited by *Lakṣ* 12.117; *Dev* 3.183— a) BBe^{2} Be^{3} Bo Ho BKt^{5} Lo^{1} Lo^{2} Lo^{4} Lo^{5} oOr sOx^{1} Ox^{3} NPu^{1} Pu^{3} Pu^{5} sPu^{6} Pu^{7} Tr^{2} [*Jolly* M G] *Dev Jolly* तु — b) Pu^{8} च *for* स्तेय°; sOx^{1} sPu^{6} स्तेयेषु संग्र°; Lo^{1} °सद्गह°; BKt^{5} *lacuna at* च — c) BBe^{2} Pu^{5} Pu^{7} °योस्तु; Lo^{2} पारुष्यं; TMd^{4} पारुष्य — d) NNg *ma sh* न; Ho Pu^{5} Pu^{7} परीक्ष्येत; Bo परिक्षेत; sOx^{1} [*but cor*] sPu^{6} परीक्षीत; TMd^{4} Wa परीक्षित; Lo^{3} NPu^{1} Tj^{1} Tr^{1} MTr^{6} साक्षिणं

73. Omitted in [*Jolly* M$^{1-3}$]. Cited by *Apa* 677; *Dev* 3.211; *Mādh* 3.83 — a) *Mādh* न हि तं परि°; NPu^{1} Pu^{2} MTr^{5} प्रतिगृ° — b) TMd^{3} साक्ष°; GMd^{1} साक्षा°; Lo^{5} सातिद्वैधे; Tr^{2} °द्वैधं; Bo °द्वैधो — c) GMy स्थलेषु; GMd^{5} Tj^{1} च; Kt^{2} गुणोत्कृष्टाद्; Lo^{5} गुणोत्सृष्टान् — d) BKt^{5} Pu^{5} Pu^{7} Tj^{1} Wa गुण°; Pu^{2} Pu^{4} गुल°; Bo गुणोद्वैधो; GMd^{1} TMd^{3} GMd^{5} GMy Tr^{1} MTr^{4} MTr^{5} MTr^{6} गुणसाम्ये; wKt^{3} द्विजोत्तमात्; Pu^{3} गुणोत्तमान्

74. Omitted in [*Jolly* M$^{1-3}$]. Cited by *Dev* 3.198; pādas a-b cited by *Lakṣ* 12.137; *Vij* 2.38 [intro.] — a) Hy Kt^{2} Lo^{1} Lo^{4} Lo^{5} sOx^{1} sPu^{6} समक्ष्य°; GMy समक्षि°; Pu^{2} Pu^{4} समीक्ष°; GMd^{1} समीक्ष्य; Be^{3} Bo NKt^{4} °नात्साक्षं; BCa BKt^{5} La^{1} °नात्साक्षी — b) GMy °णाच्चेव; GMd^{5} MTr^{6} °णाच्चापि; Hy °णाश्चैव — c) Pu^{5} Pu^{7} तत्र साक्ष्यं तु यत्साक्षी; Tr^{2} तत्र साक्षं; Bo तत्र सत्तं; wKt^{1} ब्रुवत्साक्षी — d) Pu^{2} Pu^{4} विहीयते; BKt^{5} न गृहीयते

75. Omitted in Pu^{5} [*Jolly* M$^{1-3}$]. Cited by *Lakṣ* 12.145; *Dev* 3.200 — a) TMd^{3} साक्ष; Tr^{1} [*but cor fh*] साक्षि; NKt^{4} Tr^{2} *om* अन्यद्; Bo [*but cor*] °तादन्यो — c) Tj^{1} आवाङ्; Wa अर्वाङ्; TMd^{3} GMy वासं नर°; BBe^{2} BCa Ho Hy Jo^{1} Jo^{2} wKt^{1} Kt^{2} wKt^{3} La^{1} Lo^{1} Lo^{3} NNg Tj^{1} Tj^{2} MTr^{3} MTr^{4} MTr^{6} [*Jolly* R] *Rn Mandlik Jha KSS Dave* नरकमभ्येति; Tr^{1} °कमन्वेति; *Jolly* °कमवैति; *Lakṣ* °कमाप्नोति — d) Bo सर्गाच्च; BKt^{5} स्वर्गाः गृहीयते

76. Omitted in [*Jolly* M$^{1-3}$]. Cited by *Lakṣ* 12.101 — a) Ho °निबन्धो; MTr^{5} °निर्बन्धो; TMd^{4}

एकोऽलुब्धस्तु साक्षी स्याद् बह्व्यः शुच्योऽपि न स्त्रियः ।
स्त्रीबुद्धेरस्थिरत्वात्तु दोषैश्चान्येऽपि ये वृताः ॥७७॥
स्वभावेनैव यद्ब्रूयुस्तद्ग्राह्यं व्यावहारिकम् ।
अतो यदन्यद्विब्रूयुर्धर्मार्थं तदपार्थकम् ॥७८॥
सभान्तः साक्षिणः प्राप्तानर्थिप्रत्यर्थिसंनिधौ ।
प्राड्विवाकोऽनुयुञ्जीत विधिनानेन सान्त्वयन् ॥७९॥
यद् द्वयोरनयोर्वित्थ कार्येऽस्मिंश्चेष्टितं मिथः ।
तद् ब्रूत सर्वं सत्येन युष्माकं ह्यत्र साक्षिता ॥८०॥

°निबद्धे; Be^{1} BBe^{2} Be^{3} Bo Ho Jo^{2} NKt^{4} Lo^{1} Lo^{4} Lo^{5} sOx^{1} NPu^{1} Pu^{2} Pu^{3} sPu^{6} Tj^{1} Tr^{1} MTr^{5} *Lakṣ* °बद्धो वीक्षेत; NNg °बद्धो वीक्ष्येत; Pu^{5} Pu^{7} °बद्धोपेक्षेत — b) BKt^{5} °याच्चापि; wKt^{1} TMd^{3} GMy कंचन — c) Lo^{1} दृष्टस्तत्रापि; NPu^{1} Pu^{2} Pu^{4} दृष्टस्तथापि; BBe^{2} wKt^{3} GMd^{1} MTr^{5} यद्ब्रूयाद्; MTr^{4} MTr^{6} तं ब्रूयाद्; Lo^{1} TMd^{3} न ब्रूयाद्; Pu^{8} त ब्रूयाद्; Tr^{2} तद्ब्रयाद्

77.* Omitted in [*Jolly* M$^{1-3}$]. Cited by *Lakṣ* 12.118 — a) NKt^{4} Lo^{2} GMd^{1} GMd^{5} NNg NPu^{1} Pu^{5} Pu^{7} Tr^{1} MTr^{4} MTr^{5}MTr^{6} [*Jolly* M$^{8-9}$ G Nd] *Me Go Ku* [pāṭha] *Rn* [pāṭha] *Jha* एको लुब्धस्त्वसाक्षी स्याद्; TMd^{3} TMd^{4} GMy एको लब्धस्स साक्षी स्याद्; sOx^{1} Pu^{3} sPu^{6} Pu^{8} Tr^{2} एकोप्यलुब्धः साक्षी स्याद्; Be^{3} एको ह्यलुब्धः साक्षी स्याद्; La^{1} एको अलुबद्धस्तु साक्षी [*om* स्याद्]; Bo एकोऽपि लुब्धः साक्षी स्याद्; MTr^{6} °लुब्धश्च; TMd^{4} °लुब्धाश्च — b) GMd^{1} बह्व्यश्शुद्धा अपि स्त्रियः; Tr^{2} बह्व्या; Tj^{1} बाह्व्यः; Lo^{1} वाक्यः; NKt^{4} TMd^{3} GMd^{5} GMy NNg Pu^{2} Pu^{4} Pu^{5} Pu^{7} MTr^{4}MTr^{6} [*Jolly* Nd] च स्त्रियः — c) TMd^{4} °बुद्धिर° ; BBe^{2} Be^{3} Jo^{2} wKt^{1} wKt^{3} La^{1} Lo^{1} Lo^{3} Lo^{4} Lo^{5} GMd^{1} TMd^{3} GMd^{5} GMy Ox^{3} NPu^{1} Pu^{5} Pu^{7} Tj^{1} Tr^{1} MTr^{4}MTr^{6} Wa °स्थिरत्वाच्च; Pu^{2} Pu^{4} °स्थिरत्वाद्य — d) oOr [*but cor*] दोषैश्चान्येपि दोषकृत्; TMd^{3} GMy NPu^{1} Pu^{2} Pu^{4} दोषैरन्ये; GMd^{5} दोषैश्चार्येपि; wKt^{3} दोषैरन्येच्च ये; wKt^{1} ये श्रुताः; Pu^{2} Pu^{4} ये दनाः

78. Omitted in [*Jolly* M$^{1-3}$]. Cited by *Mādh* 3.80 — a) TMd^{4} यद्ब्रूयात्तद्ग्राह्यं — b) BBe^{2} Bo wKt^{3} TMd^{3} TMd^{4} GMd^{5} GMy Tr^{2} MTr^{4} व्यवहा° — c) GMd^{5} अतोन्यथा तु विब्रू° ; *Mādh* यदन्यद्ब्रूयुस्ते धर्मार्थं; TMd^{3} °द्विब्रूयाद्धर्मार्थं — d) Lo^{4} Lo^{5} °र्धर्मार्थवदपार्थकं; Bo Lo^{1} °मार्थे; Be^{1} °मार्थस्तद° ; La^{1} यदपा° ; NNg °पार्थिकं; Be^{1} °पार्यकं; Pu^{5} Pu^{7} °पार्थिवं; BKt^{5} °पावकं

79. Omitted in [*Jolly* M$^{1-3}$]; pādas c-d omitted in Pu^{5}. Cited by *Vij* 2.73; *Lakṣ* 12.124; *Dev* 3.198; *Mādh* 3.75 — a) Md^{4} सभान्ते; Tr^{2} संभातः; wKt^{1} स्तान्तः; GMd^{1} TMd^{3} TMd^{4} GMd^{5} GMy Tr^{1} MTr^{4}MTr^{5} MTr^{6} [*Jolly* M^{8}] *Vij Lakṣ Dev Mādh* साक्षिणः सर्वानर्थि° ; Pu^{2} Pu^{4} प्राप्तो अर्थि° — b) wKt^{1} °नर्थप्रत्य° ; Pu^{5} *om* संनिधौ; Hy °संनिद्यो — c) Hy प्राड्विवाका; Lo^{5} प्राड्विवाक्ये; Pu^{2} Pu^{4} प्राड्विवाहो; wKt^{1} GMd^{1} Pu^{2} Pu^{4} Pu^{7} MTr^{5} प्राग्विवाको; Ho प्राक्विवाको; Kt^{2} प्राङ्गविवाको; wKt^{3} प्रद्युवाका; *Mādh* °वाकः प्रयुञ्जीत; NKt^{4} °नुभुञ्जीत; BKt^{5} Pu^{2} Pu^{4} न युञ्जीत; Be^{3} BCa Lo^{1} Pi^{1} Pu^{3} Tr^{1} *Vij* नियुञ्जीत — d) Tr^{2} विधिनायेन; La^{1} विधिनान्येन; Ho सान्तयन्; TMd^{3} GMy सञ्चयन्

80.* Omitted in Lo^{5} Pu^{5} [*Jolly* M$^{1-3}$]; *ma* in Lo^{4}. Cited by *Lakṣ* 12.124; *Mādh* 3.75 — a) wKt^{1} यत्तु यौवनयोर्वेणु; TMd^{3} यं; BBe^{2} यन्तयोरनयो° ; Pu^{2} द्वयोरन्ययो° ; Bo TMd^{3} Pu^{3} Tj^{2} °योर्वित्त; GMd^{1} MTr^{5} MTr^{6} °योर्वित्तं; MTr^{4} °योर्वित्तः; TMd^{4} °योर्वेत्तं; GMd^{5} Tr^{1} [*but mc*] °योर्वृत्तं; BBe^{2} Jo^{1} wKt^{1} Kt^{2} BKt^{5} Lo^{2} Lo^{3} NNg Ox^{2} Ox^{3} Tr^{2} MTr^{3} [*Jolly* N] *Rn Nd Lakṣ Mādh Mandlik Jha KSS Dave* °योर्वेत्थ; Ho NPu^{1} °योर्वैत्थ; Hy sOx^{1} sPu^{6} °योर्वेत्य; oOr °योर्वत्थ; Lo^{4} Pu^{7} °योरित्थं; Wa °योर्वेण; Be^{3} *Lakṣ* (vl) °योरर्थे; Pu^{2} Pu^{4} °योरिच्छां; Lo^{1} °योरिक्षं — b) NNg कार्यो; NKt^{4} मिषः — c) TMd^{3} तं ब्रूत; Pu^{3} Pu^{4} तद्ब्रतं; Hy *om* सर्वं; Kt^{2} NKt^{4} सर्व; Lo^{1} सत्यं सत्येन — d) GMy Pu^{7} युष्माकमत्र; BKt^{5} चात्र;

सत्यं साक्ष्ये ब्रुवन्साक्षी लोकान् प्राप्नोति पुष्कलान् ।
इह चानुत्तमां कीर्तिं वागेषा ब्रह्मपूजिता ॥८१॥
साक्ष्येऽनृतं वदन्पाशैर्बध्यते वारुणैर्भृशम् ।
विवशः शतमाजातीस्तस्मात्साक्ष्ये वदेदृतम् ॥८२॥
सत्येन पूयते साक्षी धर्मः सत्येन वर्धते ।

Be[1] Bo TMd[3] GMd[5] Tj[2] [*Jolly* Nd] यत्र; MTr[4] साक्षिताः; Pu[7] साक्षितो; NNg NPu[1] साक्षिणः; MTr[6] साक्षिकाः

81.* Omitted in Lo[3] [*Jolly* M[1–3]]. Cited by *Lakṣ* 12.124; *Dev* 3.198; *Mādh* 3.76 — a) Pu[2] Pu[4] Pu[5] Pu[7] सत्यं साक्षी ब्रुवन्साक्ष्ये; *Mādh* ऋतं सत्यं ब्रुवन्साक्षी — b) BKt[5] NNg NPu[1] Pu[2] Pu[4] Pu[5] Pu[7] Wa [*Jolly* Me M[8–9] G] *Jolly* लोकान्प्राप्नोत्यनुत्तमान्; Be[1] BBe[2] Bo BCa Ho Hy Jo[1] Jo[2] [*but cor*] wKt[1] Kt[2] wKt[3] NKt[4] La[1] Lo[1] Lo[2] sOx[1] Ox[2] sPu[6] Tj[1] Tj[2] Tr[1] MTr[3] MTr[4] MTr[5] MTr[6] [*Jolly* Ku N Nd] *Dev Rn Ku Mandlik KSS* लोकानाप्नोति पुष्कलान्; Pu[3] Pu[8] Tr[2] लोकानाप्नोत्यनुत्तमान्; Lo[4] Lo[5] Ox[3] [*Jolly* M[4–5]] *Me* लोकान्प्राप्नोत्यनिन्दितान्; *Dave Jha* लोकानाप्नोत्यनिन्दितान् — c) NPu[1] इदं; Pu[5] Pu[7] [*Jolly* G] चाप्युत्तमां; Lo[1] NNg कीर्ति — d) Be[3] प्रेत्य ब्रह्मपूजिते; GMy वागेष; MTr[5] वाग्ह्येष; TMd[3] वागेर्ष; NNg MTr[5] °पूजिताः; Hy °पूजितां

Additonal verse in *Mandlik* [क] *KSS:*

विक्रयाद्यो धनं किंचिद् गृह्णीयात्कुलसंनिधौ ।
क्रमेण स विशुद्धं हि न्यायतो लभते धनम् ॥

82. Omitted in Lo[3] [*Jolly* M[1–3]]. Cited by *Lakṣ* 12.124; *Dev* 3.199 — a) Be[3] साक्षे; Tr[2] °नृत्यं — a-b) Be[3] NPu[1] Pu[2] Pu[4] Pu[5] Pu[7] *Lakṣ* वदन्साक्षी पाशैर्बध्येत वारुणैः [Pu[5] Pu[7] °र्बाध्यते; Pu[2] Pu[4] दारुणैः] — b) Wa °र्बध्येते; Tr[2] °र्बध्यत; wKt[1] धारणैर्भृशं; Lo[4] Lo[5] दारुणैर्भृशं; NKt[4] GMd[1] TMd[3] TMd[4] GMy Tr[1] [*but cor*] MTr[4] MTr[5] MTr[6] *Dev* वारुणैर्नरः — c) Pu[2] Pu[4] विविशः शममानीत तस्मा°; TMd[4] विवशं; Tr[2] विवेशः सतमा°; BBe[2] °जातास्तस्मा°; Lo[5] GMd[1] TMd[3] °जाती तस्मा°; BCa °जातीः तस्मा°; GMy °जाति तस्मा° — d) Be[3] Hy Jo[2] wKt[1] GMd[1] GMd[5] NPu[1] Tj[2] Tr[2] *Dev* °त्साक्षी; Jo[1] Kt[2] wKt[3] MTr[3] *Mandlik Jha KSS Dave* °त्साक्ष्यं; GMy MTr[4] वदेनृतं; GMd[1] वदेनृतः; Pu[8] वदेदतं

Additional verses in TMd[4] GMd[5] Tr[1] MTr[4] MTr[6] [*Jolly* Gr] *Mandlik* [ञ, ट, ड] *KSS Dave;* second verse given after 8.101 in BCa La[1]. Both verses cited by *Mādh* 3.76; first verse cited by *Dev* 3.198; second verse parallels *NSm* 1.206:

ब्राह्मणो वा मनुष्याणामादित्यस्तेजसामिव ।
शिरो वा सर्वगात्राणां धर्मणां सत्यमुत्तमम् ॥१॥
नास्ति सत्यात्परो धर्मो नानृतात्पातकं परम् ।
स्थितिश्च लोके धर्मश्च तस्मात्सत्यं विशिष्यते ॥२॥

1. b) [*Jolly* Gr] °ष्याणां चादित्य°; *Mandlik KSS Dave* °जसां दिवि; GMd[5] °जसा दिवि; TMd[4] °जसामप — c) GMd[5] शिखा वा — d) GMd[5] धर्माणां

2. c) *Mādh Mandlik KSS Dave* साक्षिधर्मे विशेषेण; Tr[1] [*Jolly* Gr] लोकधर्मश्च; TMd[4] GMd[5] धर्मस्य— d) BCa La[1] तस्मात्सत्यं न लोपयेत्; *Mādh* सत्यमेव वदेत्ततः

Additional verse in GMd[1] TMd[4] Tr[1] MTr[4] MTr[6] [*Jolly* Gr] *Mandlik* [ट] *KSS Dave:*

एकमेवाद्वितीयं तद्यं मर्त्यो नावबुध्यते ।
सत्यं स्वर्गस्य संयानं पारावारस्य नौरिव ॥

a-b) omitted in Tr[1] [*Jolly* Gr]; TMd[4] एकमेव द्वितीये तु तन्मत्वै नावबुध्यते; *Mandlik KSS Dave* °तीयं तु प्रब्रुवन्नावबुध्यते — c) TMd[4] स्वर्गस्य यानं; GMd[1] संज्ञानं; Tr[1] [*Jolly* Gr] सोपानं — d) TMd[4] °रस्य कारव

तस्मात्सत्यं हि वक्तव्यं सर्ववर्णेषु साक्षिभिः ॥८३॥
आत्मैव ह्यात्मनः साक्षी गतिरात्मा तथात्मनः ।
मावमंस्थाः स्वमात्मानं नृणां साक्षिणमुत्तमम् ॥८४॥
मन्यन्ते वै पापकृतो न कश्चित्पश्यतीति नः ।
तांश्च देवाः प्रपश्यन्ति स्वश्चैवान्तरपूरुषः ॥८५॥
द्यौर्भूमिरापो हृदयं चन्द्रार्काग्नियमानिलाः ।
रात्रिः संध्ये च धर्मश्च वृत्तज्ञाः सर्वदेहिनाम् ॥८६॥
देवब्राह्मणसांनिध्ये साक्ष्यं पृच्छेदृतं द्विजान् ।
उदङ्मुखान्प्राङ्मुखान्वा पूर्वाह्णे वै शुचिः शुचीन् ॥८७॥
ब्रूहीति ब्राह्मणं पृच्छेत् सत्यं ब्रूहीति पार्थिवम् ।
गोबीजकाञ्चनैर्वैश्यं शूद्रमेभिस्तु पातकैः ॥८८॥

83. Omitted in [*Jolly* M$^{1-3}$]. Cited by *Lakṣ* 12.124; *Dev* 3.198; *Mādh* 3.76 — a) Pu^{5} Pu^{7} प्रयते — b) NKt^{4} सत्येन वर्धते धर्मः; TMd^{4} आत्मा सत्येन — c) TMd^{4} तस्मात्सत्येन वक्तव्यं; GMd^{5} °त्सत्यो; Pu^{8} Tr^{2} तु; Be^{3} विवक्तव्यं; sOx^{1} sPu^{6} कर्तव्यं — d) Lo^{4} Lo^{5} [*Jolly* M$^{4-5}$] सर्वधर्मेषु

84. Omitted in Hy [*Jolly* M$^{1-3}$]. Cited by *Lakṣ* 12.124; *Dev* 3.199 — a) GMd^{5} चात्मनः; NPu^{1} स्वात्मनः — b) NNg गतिरात्मैव चात्मनः; TMd^{3} तदात्मनः — c) *Lakṣ* मावसंस्थाः; TMd^{3} नावमंस्थाः; Bo मावरंस्थाः; Tr^{2} स्वात्मानं; BBe^{2} Bo समात्मानं; *Dev* त्वमात्मानं — d) *Lakṣ* साक्षित्वमुत्तमं; GMd^{5} साक्ष्येषु साक्षिणं

85.* Omitted in [*Jolly* M$^{1-3}$]. Cited by *Lakṣ* 12.124; *Dev* 3.199 — a) GMd^{1} TMd^{3} मन्यन्तो; Pu^{5} Pu^{7} मन्यन्तेमी पाप°; Ox^{3} वे; GMy वायकृतो; BBe^{2} Lo^{1} °कृता — b) GMy किंचि°; TMd^{3} कंचि°; Lo^{3} Tj^{1} °श्यतीह; Tj^{1} न — c) Be^{3} BCa Ho Hy Jo^{1} Jo^{2} wKt^{1} Kt^{2} BKt^{5} Lo^{1} Lo^{3} Lo^{4} Lo^{5} sOx^{1} Ox^{2} Ox^{3} NPu^{1} Pu^{2} Pu^{4} sPu^{6} Pu^{8} Tj^{1} Tj^{2} Tr^{2} MTr^{3} *Mandlik Jolly Jha KSS Dave* तांस्तु; wKt^{1} संपश्यन्ति — d) sPu^{6} [lacuna] पूरुषः *lacuna filled mc sh to* स्वश्चैवायय°; sOx^{1} स्वश्चैवाययपूरुषः; Be^{1} Be^{3} Bo Jo^{1} Jo^{2} Kt^{2} Lo^{4} [*but cor*] Lo^{5} MTr^{3} *Me Go Ku Mandlik Jha KSS Dave* स्वस्यैवान्तर°; GMd^{1} स्वयैवान्तर°; *Dev* यस्यैवान्तर°; Tr^{2} स्वं चैवान्तर°; [*Jolly* M$^{8-9}$] स्वयं चान्तर°

86. Omitted in [*Jolly* M$^{1-3}$]. Cited by *Lakṣ* 12.124; *Dev* 3.200 — a) sOx^{1} sPu^{6} रुदयं; Kt^{2} हृदयश्चन्द्रा° — b) wKt^{1} चन्द्रार्काचनिलानलौ; GMy चन्द्रार्कानियमानि वा — c) La^{1} संध्ये रात्र्यहनी धर्मो वृ°; *Dev* संध्या; MTr^{6} संध्याश्च; TMd^{4} धर्मैश्च — d) TMd^{3} वृत्तज्ञाश्चैव देहिनां; Lo^{1} Lo^{2} वृत्ताज्ञाः; Ho वृत्तज्ञात्सर्व°

87. Omitted in [*Jolly* M$^{1-3}$]. Cited by *Vij* 2.73 [but ascribed to Kātyāyana]; *Apa* 673; *Lakṣ* 12.124; *Dev* 3.203; *Mādh* 3.78 — a) Tr^{2} सर्वब्राह्म°; wKt^{1} °निध्यं — b) Ho Jo^{1} sOx^{1} sPu^{6} साक्ष्ये; Lo^{1} पृच्छत वै द्विजान्; GMd^{1} पृच्छेत तद् द्विजान्; Be^{3} पृच्छेदतन्द्रितान्; *Apa* द्विजः — c) MTr^{4} MTr^{6} उदङ्मुखः प्राङ्मुखो वा; Tr^{2} *om* प्राङ्मुखान्; NPu^{1} उदङ्मुखाः प्रा° — d) GMd^{1} TMd^{3} TMd^{4} GMy Tr^{1} पूर्वाह्णे प्रयतः शुचीन् [GMd^{1} प्रयतान्शुचीन्]; GMd^{5} पूर्वा वै हि शुचिश्शुचीन्; *Mādh* सर्वानेवोपवेशयेत्; Jo^{2} Lo^{3} Tj^{1} MTr^{4} MTr^{6} Wa तु शुचिः; *Lakṣ Apa* वा शुचिः; Wa रुचिः; oOr शुचीन्शुचीन्

88.* Omitted in [*Jolly* M$^{1-3}$]. Cited by *Apa* 674 — a) La^{1} ब्राह्मणः; GMd^{1} TMd^{4} Tr^{1} *Apa* ब्राह्मणं ब्रूयात् — b) wKt^{1} पार्थिवः; *Apa* भूमिपं; Be^{1} क्षत्रियं — c) Pu^{2} Pu^{4} गौबीज°; Lo^{1} °काञ्चनं वैश्यं; La^{1} °काञ्चने वैश्यं — d) Pu^{5} Pu^{7} शूद्रमद्भिस्तु; [*Jolly* N] *Nā* शूद्रमेतैस्तु; TMd^{3} शूद्रमेतस्तु; Be^{1} BBe^{2} Bo BCa Ho Hy Jo^{1} Jo^{2} wKt^{1} Kt^{2} wKt^{3} La^{1} Lo^{1} Lo^{3} Lo^{4} Lo^{5} sOx^{1} Ox^{3} NPu^{1} Pu^{3} sPu^{6} Pu^{8} Tj^{1} Tj^{2}

ब्रह्मघ्नो ये स्मृता लोका ये च स्त्रीबालघातिनः ।
मित्रद्रुहः कृतघ्नस्य ते ते स्युर्ब्रुवतो मृषा ॥८९॥
जन्मप्रभृति यत्किंचित् पुण्यं भद्र त्वया कृतम् ।
तत्ते सर्वं शुनो गच्छेद् यदि ब्रूयास्त्वमन्यथा ॥९०॥
एकोऽहमस्मीत्यात्मानं यत्त्वं कल्याण मन्यसे ।
नित्यं स्थितस्ते हृद्येष पुण्यपापेक्षिता मुनिः ॥९१॥
यमो वैवस्वतो देवो यस्तवैष हृदि स्थितः ।
तेन चेदविवादस्ते मा गङ्गां मा कुरून् गमः ॥९२॥
नग्नो मुण्डः कपाली च भिक्षार्थी क्षुत्पिपासितः ।
अन्धः शत्रुगृहं गच्छेद् यः साक्ष्यमनृतं वदेत् ॥९३॥

Tr[2] MTr[3] MTr[4] MTr[6] [*Jolly* M[4–5] R] शूद्रं सर्वैस्तु; Tr[2] शूद्रं सर्वैश्च

89. Omitted in [*Jolly* M[1–3]]; not commented by *Nā*. Cited by *Apa* 674; *Dev* 3.204; *Mādh* 3.78 — a) Tr[2] ब्रह्मघ्नानां च ये लोका; T Md[4] ब्रह्मघ्नस्य च ये लोका; Pu[5] Pu[7] *Go* [*Jolly* G] ब्रह्मघ्नानां स्मृता लोका [*Me* supports plural whereas *Ku Rn Nd Mr* support singular]; Lo[1] GMd[1] GMd[5] sOx[1] sPu[6] MTr[6] ब्रह्मघ्ना; *Apa* ब्रह्मघ्नां; Lo[3] Tj[1] ब्रह्मघ्ने; wKt[1] श्रुता; wKt[1] GMd[1] MTr[4] लोके — b) Pu[5] Pu[7] Tr[2] *Apa Go Jolly* °घातिनां; MTr[6] °घातिकः; Lo[4] [*but cor*] °घातिकाः; wKt[1] °पातिनः — c) TMd[3] मित्रद्रोह; Lo[1] मित्रद्रुघ्ना; Tr[2] कृतघ्नानां; BBe[2] Lo[1] MTr[4] MTr[6] कृतघ्नश्च — d) sOx[1] sPu[6] ते त्वासां वदतो मृषा; Tr[2] स्युर्ब्रुवता; BKt[5] Tj[1] स्युर्ब्रुवते; Jo[1] स्युर्ब्रुवतौ; BCa Ho La[1] GMy oOr *Apa* स्युर्वदतो; wKt[1] स्युर्वदते; *Mādh* स्युर्ब्रुवतः तव

90. Omitted in [*Jolly* M[1–3]]; not commented by *Rc*. Cited by *Apa* 674; *Dev* 3.204; *Mādh* 3.78 — a) NNg जन्मप्रकृति; Pu[8] जन्मप्रति — b) Be[3] Bo Tj[1] [*Jolly* R M] *Apa* [vl as in ed] भद्रं; TMd[3] [*but cor sh*] GMy [*Jolly* Nd] भद्रं च यत्कृतं; Be[3] Lo[1] कृतं त्वया — c) Be[1] यत्ते; wKt[1] तत्तत्सर्वं; La[1] तत्सर्वं ते; GMd[1] तत्सर्वमाशुनो; Be[3] Tr[2] शुने; Lo[2] सुनो; Ho गच्छद् — d) Pu[5] Pu[7] ब्रूयात्त्वम°; Be[3] TMd[4] ब्रूया त्वम°

91. Omitted in [*Jolly* M[1–3]]. Cited by *Apa* 674; *Dev* 3.204 — b) GMd[5] lacuna at यत्त्वं; TMd[4] यत्वा; BBe[2] Hy Tj[1] Tr[2] यत्वं; Be[3] Bo wKt[1] NKt[4] BKt[5] Lo[4] Lo[5] TMd[3] GMy Ox[2] Pu[8] Tj[2] Tr[1] MTr[4] MTr[6] Wa [*Jolly* M Nd] *Dev Nd Go Jha Dave* यस्त्वं; Kt[2] य त्वं; *Apa* यदि कल्याण; oOr कल्याणमिच्छसे — c) Lo[1] स्थितं ते; *Apa* स्थितः स; TMd[4] स्थितस्य; *Apa* [vl] स्थितः सुहृद्देश; Lo[1] हृद्येषः; Ox[2] हृद्येषा; MTr[5] हृद्येषु; TMd[3] GMy sOx[1] sPu[6] Tr[2] हृदये पुण्य° — d) Pu[5] Pu[7] पापपुण्येक्षिता; Tr[2] °पापेक्षका; Pu[3] Pu[8] °पापेक्षको; GMd[1] °पापेषता; Be[3] °पापेस्थितो; GMd[5] °पापेकृतो; MTr[3] मुनेः; *Apa* पुनः

92. Omitted in [*Jolly* M[1–3]]. Cited by *Apa* 674; *Dev* 3.204 — b) *Apa* देवस्तवैष हृदये स्थितः; oOr देवस्तवैष हृदि संस्थितः; wKt[3] यस्तवैव; Lo[2] यस्तु चैष — c) Tj[1] तेन वेदविवादस्ते — d) wKt[1] मा गङ्गामातृकसमः; Lo[1] TMd[3] TMd[4] Tj[1] गङ्गा; GMd[1] गङ्गां वा; oOr पापं वा; MTr[4] गुरून्; Hy कुरूनमः; MTr[3] गतः; GMd[1] गमे; Lo[4] Lo[5] Pu[5] Pu[7] Wa [*Jolly* M[4–5–9] G] *Jolly* व्रज; Ox[3] व्रजः

93.* Omitted in [*Jolly* M[1–3]]. Cited by *Apa* 674; *Dev* 3.204 — a) Tr[2] मुण्डो; Pu[7] मुण्डं; Pu[5] मुंकं; Pu[8] कपालो च; Pu[5] Pu[7] कपालंन; GMy कपोलेभिः; BBe[2] BCa Hy Jo[1] Jo[2] wKt[1] Kt[2] wKt[3] NKt[4] Lo[1] Lo[2] Lo[3] GMd[1] TMd[3] NNg oOr sOx[1] Ox[2] sPu[6] Tj[1] Tj[2] MTr[5] Wa *Apa Dev Nā Mandlik Jolly KSS* कपालेन; Wa कपोलेन; La[1] कपालीन [ली *changed sh to* ले] — b) Ho Tj[1] क्षुत्पिपासतः; TMd[4] क्षुत्पिपासकः — c) TMd[4] असिपत्रं वनं गच्छेद्; MTr[5] दीनश्शत्रु°; GMd[1] बद्धश्शत्रु°; BBe[2] Bo BCa Hy Jo[1]

अवाक्शिरास्तमस्यन्धे किल्बिषी नरकं पतेत् ।
यः प्रश्नं वितथं ब्रूयात् पृष्टः सन् धर्मनिश्चये ॥९४॥
अन्धो मत्स्यानिवाश्नाति स नरः कण्टकैः सह ।
यो भाषतेऽर्थवैकल्यमप्रत्यक्षं सभां गतः ॥९५॥
यस्य विद्वान्हि वदतः क्षेत्रज्ञो नाभिशङ्कते ।
तस्मान्न देवाः श्रेयांसं लोकेऽन्यं पुरुषं विदुः ॥९६॥
यावतो बान्धवान्यस्मिन् हन्ति साक्ष्येऽनृतं वदन् ।
तावतः संख्यया तस्मिन् शृणु सौम्यानुपूर्वशः ॥९७॥

wKt^{1} Kt^{2} wKt^{3} Lo^{1} Lo^{3} oOr mTr^{3} [*Jolly* Ku R] *Ku Mandlik Jha KSS Dave* शत्रुकुलं; bKt^{5} *om* °गृहं — d) mTr^{4} साक्ष्याम°; bKt^{5} साक्षम°; Lo^{5} साक्षमानृतं; wKt^{3} साक्ष्यममृतं

94. Omitted in [*Jolly* M$^{1-3}$]; not commented by *Rc*. Cited by *Apa* 674; *Dev* 3.204 — a) Be^{1} nPu^{1} Pu^{2} Pu^{4} *Apa* अर्वाक्शिरा°; Hy अवाक्थिरा°; nKt^{4} अवांगिरा°; Lo^{1} अवाम्छिरा°; nNg अवाच्छि-रा°; wKt^{1} आरास्थिरा°; tMd^{3} gMy अवाक्शिरस्त°; tMd^{4} °स्तमस्यन्ध; Ox^{3} °स्तमस्यन्ध्ये; Kt^{2} °स्तमस्यध्ये — b) tMd^{3} किल्बिषो; tMd^{4} किल्बिषं; Pu^{5} Pu^{7} किल्मिखी; Jo^{2} gMd^{1} tMd^{3} tMd^{4} gMy Pu^{8} mTr^{4} mTr^{6} [*Jolly* G] *Go Rn* नरके; Pu^{5} Pu^{7} [*Jolly* G] नरके वसेत्; Pu^{2} Pu^{4} पवेत्; Ho Hy Jo^{1} wKt^{1} Kt^{2} Lo^{1} nNg Tj^{2} mTr^{3} [*Jolly* Ku] *Dev Mandlik Jha KSS Dave* व्रजेत् — c) mTr^{6} यं; *Dev* यत्प्रश्नं — d) wKt^{3} Tr^{1} [*but mc sh*] Tr^{2} स धर्म°; nKt^{4} स अधर्म°; Be^{3} °निर्णये

95. Omitted in [*Jolly* M$^{1-3}$]. Cited by *Dev* 3.205 — a) wKt^{1} अर्थो; Be^{1} tMd^{4} °श्नन्ति — b) Be^{1} Be^{3} Ho Jo^{2} wKt^{1} nKt^{4} Lo^{2} Lo^{3} gMd^{5} nNg oOr Ox^{2} Ox^{3} nPu^{1} Pu^{2} Pu^{3} Pu^{4} Pu^{5} Pu^{7} Pu^{8} Tj^{1} Tr^{2} mTr^{5} Wa [*Jolly* M^{8} R G Nd] कण्टकैः स नरः सह; Bo स नरे ससकण्टकैः; gMy हृदिस्थैः कण्टकैः सह; tMd^{4} स नरस्समाकं परैः; bCa gMd^{1} Tr^{1} mTr^{4} mTr^{6} सह कण्टकैः — c) sOx^{1} sPu^{6} *lacuna until* °त्यक्षं; tMd^{4} भाषेदर्थ°; Pu^{5} Pu^{7} भपतेर्थं; wKt^{3} भाषतेथ; bKt^{5} भाषते तु वैक°; wKt^{1} भाषते स्ववैकल्या-दप्रत्य°; Bo °वैकल्पम°; Lo^{1} °कैवल्यम°; gMd^{1} °वैकल्प्यात्प्रत्य° — c-d) gMd^{5} यो भाषतेर्थं वैखल्यं प्रत्य-क्षं सह संगतः — d) Ho °प्रत्यक्ष; bKt^{5} tMd^{3} tMd^{4} gMy sOx^{1} sPu^{6} सभागतः; Bo समागतः

96. Omitted in [*Jolly* M$^{1-3}$]. Cited by *Apa* 674; *Dev* 3.198, 205 — a) Pu^{2} Pu^{4} यश्च; gMd^{1} mTr^{4} mTr^{6} विद्वान्विवदतः — b) Pu^{2} Pu^{4} क्षेत्राज्ञो; bBe^{2} क्षत्रज्ञो; gMd^{1} नाभिङ्कितेे; Ho bKt^{5} gMd^{5} nNg Tr^{1} Tr^{2} mTr^{4} mTr^{6} Wa *Me Rc Jha Dave* नातिशङ्कते; La^{1} tMd^{4} gMy नातिशङ्किते; tMd^{3} sOx^{1} sPu^{6} न विशङ्कते; Bo न विशंसते; oOr निर्विशङ्कते; Kt^{2} °शङ्कटे — c) *Mandlik Jha Dave* तस्मिन्न; Bo देयाः; gMd^{1} देया; nNg श्रेयांसि; tMd^{4} श्रेयस्तं — d) oOr लोकोन्यं; gMd^{1} लोकोयं; *Dev* लोकेस्मिन्; bBe^{2} लोकेपु; tMd^{4} लोके च

97. Omitted in Ox^{3} [*Jolly* M$^{1-3}$]; pādas a-d and 98a omitted in wKt^{1} [haplo]. Cited by *Apa* 674; *Dev* 3.205; *Mādh* 3.78–9 — a) Be^{1} Bo gMd^{1} Pu^{2} Pu^{4} Pu^{7} यावन्तो; Be^{1} tMd^{4} mTr^{5} बान्धवा यस्मिन्; *Mādh* बान्धवास्तेऽस्मिन्; tMd^{4} °वान्ध्यस्मिन् — a-b) Jo^{2} mTr^{6} बान्धवान्हन्ति यस्मिन्साक्ष्ये — b) Tr^{2} हन्ति सोनृतं; Lo^{4} साक्षे; gMd^{1} tMd^{3} gMy Tr^{1} *Apa* साक्ष्यनृतं; bKt^{5} gMd^{1} tMd^{4} sOx^{1} sPu^{6} Pu^{8} Tr^{2} वदेत्; Kt^{2} वद — c) Bo तावन्तः संप्रवक्ष्यामि; oOr sOx^{1} sPu^{6} तावता; nPu^{1} संक्ष्यया; gMd^{1} संशयास्तस्मिन्; tMd^{3} तस्मै; Be^{3} ह्यस्मिन्; Be^{1} Tr^{1} *Jolly* तस्मिञ्छृणु — d) tMd^{4} अनुक्राम्यानुपूर्वशः; Tj^{2} *Apa* सोम्यानु°; gMd^{5} संख्यानु°; tMd^{3} gMy सर्वानु°; Tr^{2} °नुकीर्यशः

Additional verse in Pu^{2} Pu^{4} *Mandlik* [ठ] *KSS*:

एवं संबन्धनात्तस्मान् मुच्यते नियतावृतः ।
पशून् गोऽश्वपुरुषाणां हिरण्यं भूर्यथाक्रमम् ॥

a) Pu^{2} Pu^{4} °नात्तत्स्यान् — d) Pu^{2} हिरण्यां; Pu^{4} हिरण्या

पञ्च पश्वनृते हन्ति दश हन्ति गवानृते ।
शतमश्वानृते हन्ति सहस्रं पुरुषानृते ॥९८॥
हन्ति जातानजातांश्च हिरण्यार्थेऽनृतं वदन् ।
सर्वं भूम्यनृते हन्ति मा स्म भूम्यनृतं वदीः ॥९९॥
अप्सु भूमिवदित्याहुः स्त्रीणां भोगे च मैथुने ।
अब्जेषु चैव रत्नेषु सर्वेष्वश्ममयेषु च ॥१००॥
एतान्दोषानवेक्ष्य त्वं सर्वाननृतभाषणे ।
यथाश्रुतं यथादृष्टं सत्यमेवाञ्जसा वद ॥१०१॥

98. Omitted in [*Jolly* M[1–3]]; pāda-a omitted in wKt[1] and pāda-d in TMd[4] Wa [haplo]. Cited by *Apa* 674; *Dev* 1.220, 3.205; *Mādh* 3.79; pāda-a cited by *Apa*680 — a) BBe[2] पञ्चपः-शृणुते; Kt[2] पश्वमृते — b) BKt[5] pāda reads: दहन्ति वानृते; TMd[4] ददाहन्ति; Tr[2] दश पञ्च गवा° — c) Lo[1] शतमाश्वा°; Bo दशमश्वा°

99. Omitted in [*Jolly* M[1–3]]; pādas a-c omitted in TMd[4] Wa, and pāda-d in Lo[2]; verse 99 placed after the addition following verse 100 in TMd[3] GMy [*Jolly* Nd]. Cited by *Apa* 674; *Dev* 3.205; *Mādh* 3.79 — a) NNg Pu[2] Pu[4] Pu[5] Pu[7] जातानुजातांश्च; Bo Kt[2] Lo[1] GMd[1] °नजाताश्च — b) Be[3] Pu[8] °नृते; wKt[1] La[1] GMd[1] NNg वदेत् — c) Lo[1] सर्वं; Ho wKt[3] Lo[1] Lo[5] TMd[3] GMy oOr Tr[2] °नृतं — d) Pu[2] Pu[4] Pu[5] Pu[7] मा त्वं; TMd[3] Tj[1] मात्म; wKt[1] *om* स्म; Bo स्मा; GMd[1] भूम्यानृतं; NKt[4] Tr[2] वद; Ox[3] *Mādh* वदः; wKt[1] वदीत् *cor to* वदी; Be[3] Ho वदी; GMd[1] TMd[3] TMd[4] GMy NNg *Apa* वदेत्; Tr[1] [*but cor fh*] *Apa* [vl] वदेः; GMd[5] वदन्

100.* Omitted in Lo[2] [*Jolly* M[1–3]]. Cited by *Dev* 3.205; *Mādh* 3.79 — a) *Mādh* यच्च भूमि° — b) Wa भोगेष; Be[3] भोगेन — c) Pu[8] MTr[3] अजेषु; GMd[5] GMy तज्जेषु; *Mādh* अन्येषु; GMd[1] सर्वेषु; TMd[3] GMy चैषु — d) Bo °ष्वन्यमयेषु; Pu[8] °ष्वनममयेषु; TMd[4] °ष्वश्रमयेषु

*Additional verse in BCa GMd[1] TMd[3] GMy oOr MTr[4] MTr[5] MTr[6] [*Jolly* Nd] added after 99 in TMd[4] Tr[1]; added after both 99 and 100 in *Mandlik KSS Dave* [parallel in *GDh* 13.20–22; see endnote]; cited by *Lakṣ* 12.133:

पशुवत्क्षौद्रघृतयोर्यानेषु च तथाश्ववत् ।
गोवद्रजतवस्त्रेषु धान्ये ब्रह्मणि चैव हि ॥

a) Tr[1] °वत्क्षीरघृत° — b) TMd[4] GMy Tr[1] °योर्यच्चान्यत्पशुसंभवं — c) Tr[1] गोवद्वसुहिरण्येषु; TMd[4] GMy गोवद्वस्त्रहिरण्येषु; MTr[4] गोवद्रजते; oOr °वस्त्रादौ — d) *Mandlik KSS Dave* धान्ये ब्राह्मणवद्विधिः; TMd[4] GMy Tr[1] धान्यपुष्पफलेषु च [this reading also after 99 in *Mandlik KSS Dave*]

Additional half-verse in GMy [*Jolly* Nd]; added after 99 in TMd[4] Tr[1] *Mandlik KSS Dave:*

अश्ववत्सर्वयानेषु खरोष्ट्राश्वतरादिषु ॥

Additional verse in TMd[3] GMy [*Jolly* Nd] [all place verse 99 after this verse]:

न कृप्यति तु यस्यैव पुरुषस्य दुरात्मनः ।
तस्य पुत्रान्पशून्हन्ति दश पूर्वापरान्वरान् ॥

a) [Jolly Nd] न तु तुष्यन्ति यस्यैव — c-d) [Jolly Nd] तस्य पुत्रांश्च गृह्णन्ति सप्त सप्त परावरान्

101.* Omitted in [*Jolly* M[1–3]]. Cited by *Apa* 674; *Dev* 3.205; *Mādh* 3.79 — a) TMd[3] एतान्सर्वान्निवेक्ष्यैव; Lo[4] एतद्दोषा°; MTr[5] *Mādh* एवं दोषा°; GMd[1] TMd[4] GMd[5] GMy NNg Tr[1] [*but cor*] MTr[4] MTr[6] [*Jolly* Nd] एतान्सर्वानवे°; wKt[1] °वेक्षेतत्वं; GMd[1] °वेक्ष्य स्व; GMy [*Jolly* Nd] °वेक्ष्यैव — b) GMd[1] TMd[3] TMd[4] GMd[5] GMy NNg Tr[1] [*but cor*] MTr[4] MTr[6] [*Jolly* Nd] दोषाननृत°; Be[1] °नृतसा-क्षिणः; *Apa* °नृतवादिनः; Ho °भाषसे; Wa °भाषिणः — c) BKt[5] तथाश्रुतं; TMd[3] यदाश्रुतं — d) Be[1] BBe[2]

गोरक्षकान् वाणिजकांस्तथा कारुकुशीलवान् ।
प्रेष्यान्वार्धुषिकांश्चैव विप्राञ्छूद्रवदाचरेत् ॥१०२॥
तद्वदन् धर्मतोऽर्थेषु जानन्नप्यन्यथा नरः ।
न स्वर्गाच्च्यवते लोकाद् दैवीं वाचं वदन्ति ताम् ॥१०३॥
शूद्रविट्क्षत्रविप्राणां यत्रर्तोक्तौ भवेद्वधः ।
तत्र वक्तव्यमनृतं तद्धि सत्याद्विशिष्यते ॥१०४॥

Be^{3} Hy Jm Jo^{1} Jo^{2} wKt^{1} Kt^{2} NKt^{4} Lo^{1} Lo^{2} Lo^{3} NNg oOr Ox^{2} Ox^{3} NPu^{1} Pu^{2} Pu^{4} Pu^{5} Pu^{7} Tj^{1} Tj^{2} MTr^{3} *Go Ku Mādh Mandlik Jolly Jha KSS Dave* सर्वमेवाञ्जसा; TMd^{3} GMy वदेत्

Additional verse in BCa La^{1} [same as verse 2 after 8.82].

102. Omitted in [*Jolly* M$^{1-3}$]. Cited by *Apa* 674; *Lakṣ* 12.135; *Hem* 3/1.359; *Dev* 3.205 — a) Hy गोरक्षिकान्; BBe^{2} Jo^{1} Jo^{2} wKt^{1} Kt^{2} *Lakṣ Hem Mandlik KSS* वाणिजिकांस्तथा; Ho wKt^{3} BKt^{5} Lo^{3} GMd^{1} TMd^{4} Ox^{2} Tj^{1} Tr^{2} °जकान्तथा — b) Lo^{2} कानुकुशी° ; Be^{3} TMd^{3} °कुसीलवान्; TMd^{4} °कुशी-लवाः — c) Ho प्रेख्यानुवार्धकांश्चैव; Be^{1} Bo Hy Jo^{1} BKt^{5} La^{1} Pu^{8} Tj^{2} Tr^{2} *Hem Jolly* प्रैष्या° ; La^{1} प्रैक्ष्या° — c-d) *Hem* विप्रान्प्रैष्यान्हीनवर्णैः राजन् शूद्रवदाचरेत् [*but vl as in ed*] — d) wKt^{1} sOx^{1} sPu^{6} विप्रांश्छू-द्र° ; Bo °चरत्; NNg °चरते

Additional verse in GMd^{1} NPu^{1} Tr^{1} MTr^{4} MTr^{6} *Mandlik* [ड, ट] *KSS Dave;* given after verse 106 in TMd^{4} and after added verse 1 below in La^{1}; cited by *Lakṣ* 12.135; *Hem* 1.35; 3/1.360; *Dev* 3.206:

ये व्यपेताः स्वकर्मभ्यः परपिण्डोपजीविनः ।
द्विजत्वमभिकाङ्क्षन्ति तांश्च शूद्रवदाचरेत् ॥

a) GMd^{1} येप्यपेताः; NPu^{1} योथपेताः; La^{1} *Mandlik KSS Dave* ये व्यतीताः; MTr^{4} येपेताः; MTr^{6} *Mandlik* [ट] येप्यपेताः; Tr^{1} ते ह्यपेताः; TMd^{4} यत्सरिता; GMd^{1} *Mandlik* [ड] स्वधर्मभ्यः — b) NPu^{1} *Mandlik* [ट] परकर्मोप° ; La^{1} °पिण्डानुजीविनः; TMd^{4} °जीवनः — c) La^{1} विजित्व-मतिकांक्षन्ति; NPu^{1} *Mandlik* [ट] द्विजा धर्मं विजानन्तस्; Tr^{1} °काङ्क्षन्तस् — d) La^{1} तांस्तु; *Mand* [ड] शूद्रानिवाचरेत्

Additional verses in La^{1} [cf. *NSm* 1.192–3]; verse 2 in Ca:

वरं कूपशताद्वापी वरं वापीशतात्क्रतुः ।
वरं क्रतुशतात्पुत्रः सत्यं पुत्रशताद्वरम् ॥१॥
अश्वमेधसहस्रं तु सत्यं च तुलयावृतम् ।
अश्वमेधसहस्राद्धि सत्यमेवातिरिच्यते ॥२॥

2. a) BCa च — d) BCa सत्यमेव विशिष्यते

103. Omitted in [*Jolly* M$^{1-3}$]; *ma* in Tr^{1}; verses 103 and 104 transposed TMd^{3} GMy [*Jolly* Nd]. Cited by *Lakṣ* 12.146 — a) Pu^{5} Pu^{7} तद्विदेन् ; Be^{3} धर्मतो ह्येष — b) wKt^{3} न जानन्न° ; TMd^{3} GMy °प्यथवा नरः — c) Pu^{2} Pu^{4} स्वर्म्या° ; NPu^{1} स्वर्गात्पतते — d) sOx^{1} sPu^{6} धर्म्यां वाचमुदीरयन्; wKt^{3} Pu^{5} Pu^{7} दैवी; Lo^{3} GMd^{1} TMd^{3} GMd^{5} GMy NNg Tj^{1} *Nd* देवीं; TMd^{4} दैविता वाचं; Ho धर्मां वाचं; Tr^{2} तं; TMd^{4} ताः; Pu^{5} Pu^{7} [*Jolly* G] ते

104. Omitted in [*Jolly* M$^{1-3}$]. Cited by *Apa* 682; *Lakṣ* 12.146; *Dev* 3.207; *Mādh* 3.80 — a) BKt^{5} Pu^{3} Tr^{2} क्षत्रविट्शूद्रविप्राणां; TMd^{3} GMy °क्षत्रियवि° — b) [*Jolly* Nd] उक्तर्ते चेद्वधो भवेत्; NNg यत्रार्तोक्तौ; Lo^{4} Lo^{5} oOr यत्रर्तोक्ते; Tr^{1} यत्र [*ma sh* र्तोक्तौ]; La^{1} GMd^{1} TMd^{4} Ox^{3} यत्रोक्तेर्थे; Wa यत्रोक्त-र्थे; MTr^{4} MTr^{6} यत्रोक्त्कार्थं; BBe^{2} योक्तेर्ते; wKt^{3} यत्र तूक्तौ; Kt^{2} यत्रत्तोक्तौ; NKt^{4} यत्रतोक्तौ; Tj^{1} यत्रतोक्तो; NPu^{1} Pu^{2} Pu^{4} यथोक्तेन; *Apa* यत्र चोक्तो; Be^{1} यत्रोक्तौ च; Pu^{5} यत्रोक्ते चैव; Pu^{7} यत्तोक्ते *cor to* यत्रोक्ते चैव; Ho sOx^{1} sPu^{6} *Dev* यत्रोक्ते तु; Be^{3} यत्रोक्तेषु; Ox^{2} यत्रोक्तौ तु; *Mādh* यथोक्तौ तु; *Nd* (pāṭha)

वाग्दैवत्यैश्च चरुभिर्यजेरंस्ते सरस्वतीम् ।
अनृतस्यैनसस्तस्य कुर्वाणा निष्कृतिं पराम् ॥१०५॥
कूष्माण्डैर्वापि जुहुयाद् घृतमग्नौ यथाविधि ।
उदित्यृचा वा वारुण्या तृचेनाब्दैवतेन वा ॥१०६॥
त्रिपक्षादब्रुवन्साक्ष्यमृणादिषु नरोऽगदः ।
तदृणं प्राप्नुयात्सर्वं दशबन्धं च सर्वतः ॥१०७॥
यस्य दृश्येत सप्ताहादुक्तवाक्यस्य साक्षिणः ।
रोगोऽग्निर्ज्ञातिमरणमृणं दाप्यो दमं च सः ॥१०८॥

यत्रोत्क्रार्तं ; GMd^{5} यत्रोक्तेश्चेद्; TMd^{3} मुक्तोर्भे चेद्भवे° ; GMd^{1} भवेद्धतः; TMd^{3} GMd^{5} MTr^{4} MTr^{6} वधो भवेत् — c) TMd^{4} यत्र; Pu^{2} Pu^{4} °नृत्यं— d) *Mādh* तद्विशिष्याद्विशिष्यते; GMd^{1} TMd^{3} GMy MTr^{5} [*Jolly* Nd] तद्धि तत्र विशि° ; GMd^{5} तत्र तद्धि विशि°

105. Omitted in [*Jolly* M$^{1-3}$]. Cited by *Apa* 682; *Lakṣ* 12.147; *Dev* 3.207; *Mādh* 2.390 — a) Ho Hy BKt^{5} NKt^{4} Lo^{2} Lo^{3} GMd^{5} Ox^{3} Tj^{1} Wa *Apa* वाग्देव° ; TMd^{3} GMy पादैव° ; GMd^{1} वाग्देवतां तु; Be^{3} Hy SOx^{1} NPu^{1} Pu^{2} Pu^{3} Pu^{4} Pu^{5} SPu^{6} Pu^{7} Tr^{2} *Apa* °वतैश्च; BBe^{2} BCa WKt^{3} La^{1} Lo^{4} Lo^{5} Tr^{1} MTr^{4} MTr^{5} MTr^{6} [*Jolly* M] *Dev* °वत्यैस्तु; Bo Lo^{1} चतुर्भि° ; Be^{3} चतुभि° — b) Pu^{5} Pu^{7} [*Jolly* G] °भिर्याजेयुस्ते; Tr^{2} °भिर्यजंतस्ते; BKt^{5} °भिर्जयेरंस्ते; GMd^{1} °भिर्यजेतारं सर° ; NKt^{4} °जेरंस्तु; TMd^{4} °जेरंश्च; Be^{3} Bo Hy BKt^{5} सरस्वती — c) GMd^{1} अनृतस्यैवसंस्तस्य; TMd^{3} GMy अतस्तस्यैनसस्तस्य; Ox^{3} प्रमृतस्यैव सप्तस्य; BBe^{2} °तस्येनस° ; *Dev Mādh* °स्यैनसस्तत्र — d) TMd^{3} स कुर्वन्निष्कृतिं परां; GMy कुर्वन्निष्कृतिमपरां; Pu^{2} Pu^{5} Pu^{7} कुर्वाणो; TMd^{4} कुर्वाणं; Wa कुर्वाण; Bo निष्कृतिः; GMd^{1} निष्कृतां; Be^{3} निकृतिं; GMy Bo Pu^{5} Pu^{7} परं

106.* Omitted in [*Jolly* M$^{1-3}$]. Cited by *Apa* 682; *Lakṣ* 12.147; *Dev* 3.207; *Mādh* 2.390 — a) OOr कूष्माण्डकैर्वा जुहुयाद्; Pu^{5} Pu^{7} [*Jolly* G] कूष्माण्डैर्जुहुयान्मन्त्रैर्घृत° ; TMd^{4} कूष्माण्डं वापि; Ho Jo^{2} Lo^{3} SOx^{1} SPu^{6} Tj^{1} °ण्डैश्चापि; Tj^{2} °ण्डैर्वाति; *Dev* °ण्डैर्वाथ; TMd^{3} GMy जुहुयुः — c) Pu^{5} Pu^{7} [*Jolly* G] उदुत्तमेति वारुण्या; Be^{3} उदितृचा; Jo^{2} WKt^{1} WKt^{3} Lo^{3} Tj^{1} तदित्यृचा; TMd^{4} यदित्यृचा; Hy NKt^{4} BKt^{5} TMd^{3} *om* वा; La^{1} *Lakṣ* च; Ho चा; TMd^{4} ना; Ho वारुण्य; Ox^{3} वारुण्ये; Bo चरुण्या — d) NPu^{1} वारुण्यानृते चाब्दै° ; Bo Ho WKt^{1} त्यृचे° ; Lo^{4} *Apa Jolly Dave* त्र्यृचे° ; TMd^{3} GMd^{5} GMy त्रिचे° ; MTr^{3} त्वचे° ; Be^{1} Lo^{1} GMd^{1} SOx^{1} SPu^{6} ऋचेना° ; La^{1} हवेना° ; Ho WKt^{1} Lo^{2} GMd^{1} Tj^{1} MTr^{6} *Dev* °ब्देवतेन; Be^{1} Pu^{3} च; Pu^{2} Pu^{4} तु; NPu^{1} वः; Lo^{5} वाक्

107. Omitted in [*Jolly* M$^{1-3}$]; *ma* in Lo^{1}. Cited by *Vij* 2.76; *Apa* 677; *Lakṣ* 12.143; *Dev* 3.213 — a) Bo Tj^{1} त्रिपक्ष्यादब्रु° ; Be^{3} WKt^{1} NKt^{4} TMd^{4} GMd^{5} NNg Tr^{1} त्रिपक्षात्त्वब्रु° ; TMd^{3} GMy त्रिपक्षात्तुब्रु° ; MTr^{4} MTr^{6} त्रिपक्षात्प्रब्रु° ; Pu^{5} Pu^{7} त्रिपक्षाद्विब्रु° ; Ox^{3} त्रिपक्षीत्यब्रु° — b) Pu^{2} Pu^{4} नरोगदं; NKt^{4} GMd^{5} MTr^{4} MTr^{6} नरोगतः; GMd^{1} नरागतः; TMd^{3} GMy [*Jolly* Nd] गतो नरः — d) Lo^{2} °बन्धे; Kt^{2} °बन्धश्च; Ox^{3} *om* च; Lo^{4} *ma* च; Bo Ho TMd^{3} GMy SOx^{1} Ox^{2} SPu^{6} MTr^{4} *Vij Apa* सर्वशः; NKt^{4} GMd^{1} MTr^{5} Wa तत्त्वतः; [*Jolly* M^{8}] सर्वदा

108. Omitted in [*Jolly* M$^{1-3}$]. Cited by *Vij* 2.80; *Dev* 3.219; *Mādh* 3.82— a) GMy दृश्येते [*cor to* दृश्यते] यस्य उक्ताहा° ; GMd^{5} दृश्यते यत्र; TMd^{4} यस्य ते तत्र सप्ता° ; La^{1} दृश्येह; Bo दस्येन; Be^{3} पश्येत; *Mādh* पश्येत्तु; SOx^{1} SPu^{6} समाहा° ; Ho सप्तादुक्त° — a-b) TMd^{3} दृश्यते ते यस्य उक्ताः उत्तरं वास्य साक्षिणः — b) GMy °हादुत्तरंवास्य; Pu^{5} Pu^{7} [*Jolly* G] °क्तसाक्ष्यस्य — c) Be^{3} GMd^{1} Ox^{3} Pu^{7} रोगोग्निज्ञाति° ; Tj^{1} रोगोग्निर्जाति° ; GMd^{5} रोगोग्निजाति° ; TMd^{4} रोगाग्निराजाति° ; GMy रोगोनिज्ञाति° ; TMd^{3} रोगोनज्ञाति° ; *Mādh* रोगार्त्तिज्ञाति° ; Pu^{2} Pu^{4} रोगातिज्ञाति° ; Ox^{3} रोगोग्निर्जोति° — c-d) GMd^{1} °मरणा दाप्यो दण्डं दमश्च सः — d) TMd^{4} GMd^{5} MTr^{5} °मरणं दाप्यो दममृणं च सः; Ox^{3} दाप्यौ

असाक्षिकेषु त्वर्थेषु मिथो विवदमानयोः ।
अविन्दंस्तत्त्वतः सत्यं शपथेनापि लम्भयेत् ॥१०९॥
महर्षिभिश्च देवैश्च कार्यार्थं शपथाः कृताः ।
वसिष्ठश्चापि शपथं शेपे पैजवने नृपे ॥११०॥
न वृथा शपथं कुर्यात् स्वल्पेऽप्यर्थे नरो बुधः ।
वृथा हि शपथं कुर्वन् प्रेत्य चेह च नश्यति ॥१११॥
कामिनीषु विवाहेषु गवां भक्ष्ये तथेन्धने ।
ब्राह्मणाभ्युपपत्तौ च शपथे नास्ति पातकम् ॥११२॥
सत्येन शापयेद्विप्रं क्षत्रियं वाहनायुधैः ।
गोबीजकाञ्चनैर्वैश्यं शूद्रं सर्वैस्तु पातकैः ॥११३॥
अग्निं वा हारयेदेनमप्सु चैनं निमज्जयेत् ।
पुत्रदारस्य वाप्येनं शिरांसि स्पर्शयेत्पृथक् ॥११४॥

109. Omitted in [*Jolly* M$^{1-3}$]; verses 109 and 110 transposed in Lo^3 Tj^1. Cited by *Apa* 694 — a) Pu^2 Pu^4 °केषु धर्मेषु; BBe^2 °केष्वर्थेषु; TMd^4 °केषु सर्वेषु; GMd^1 चार्थेषु — c) Be^3 TMd^3 Tr^2 अविदंस्तत्त्वतः; *Apa* विवदंस्तत्त्वतः; *Me* [pāṭha] न विन्दन्तत्त्वतः — d) Bo Pu^3 शपथेनोपलम्भयेत्; SPu^6 [*but mc fh*] लङ्घयेत्; Wa लङ्घयोः; GMd^5 भावयेत्; TMd^3 GMy सम्भवेत्

110. Omitted in [*Jolly* M$^{1-3}$]; pādas c-d [after वसिष्ठश्चापि] omitted in Pu^5 — a) TMd^4 दैवैश्च — b) NPu^1 कार्याथः; TMd^4 GMy शपथः; Hy TMd^3 शपथा; Kt^2 कृता; Hy TMd^4 कृतः — c) Kt^2 वाशिष्ठ°; Tj^1 वसिष्ठस्यापि; Lo^3 वसिष्ठो वापि; NPu^1 शपथान् — d) GMd^1 शपे; Pu^8 शैप; TMd^4 शेष; Jo^2 Pu^2 Pu^4 Pu^7 [*Jolly* G] चक्रे; Wa भेजे; Jm Kt^2 MTr^3 पैयवने; GMd^5 पैजनके; WKt^3 SPu^6 वैजवने; Jo^2 बैजवने; Be^3 GMd^1 वैजयने; Jo^1 Ox^2 वैयवने; SOx^1 SPu^6 [*mc sh to*] वैश्रवणे; Tj^1 नृपैः; Ox^3 नृपै; TMd^4 नृप

111. Omitted in [*Jolly* M$^{1-3}$]. Cited by *Lakṣ* 12.259 — a) Ox^3 *om* कुर्यात् — b) La^1 GMd^1 TMd^3 TMd^4 GMd^5 Pu^2 Tr^1 MTr^4 MTr^5 MTr^6 Wa [*Jolly* M Nd] कर्यादल्पे; GMy कुर्यादर्थे; Ox^3 स्वल्पो; Tj^1 °प्यर्थो; Ho SOx^1 SPu^6 °प्यर्थे कथंचन; Pu^5 Pu^7 °प्यर्थेन वै बुधः; GMd^1 °प्यर्थेन कोविदः; Tj^2 बुधो नरः — c) GMd^5 अथापि शपथं; GMd^1 Tr^1 [*but mc sh*] कृत्वा — d) WKt^3 चेह न; WKt^3 oOr पश्यति; here Wa inserts verses 156–9

112. Omitted in [*Jolly* M$^{1-3}$]. Cited by *Lakṣ* 12.259 — a) TMd^3 GMy विवादेषु — b) WKt^1 गवास्तुक्षे; TMd^3 गवामर्थे; Lo^5 SOx^1 SPu^6 Tr^1 [*but cor*] भक्षे; Be^1 Ho Lo^2 NNg NPu^1 Pu^2 Pu^4 Pu^5 Pu^7 MTr^4 MTr^5 MTr^6 Wa [*Jolly* G Nd] *Bh* भक्ते; TMd^4 *Lakṣ* भुक्ते; GMd^5 भोक्ते; Lo^3 Ox^3 तथैन्धने; La^1 तथेन्धनं; TMd^4 पथिंधने — c) TMd^4 ब्राह्मणेभ्योपपत्तौ; Pu^5 Pu^7 [*Jolly* G] ब्राह्मणस्य विपत्तौ; NPu^1 ब्राह्मणार्थे विपत्तौ; NNg TMd^3 Pu^2 Pu^4 Tr^1 MTr^5 Wa °भ्यवपत्तौ — d) Be^3 SOx^1 SPu^6 शपथैर्नास्ति

113. Omitted in [*Jolly* M$^{1-3}$]. Cited by *Vij* 2.73; *Dev* 3.234; *Mādh* 3.78; pāda-d cited by *Vij* 2.75,113 — a) Ox^2 शपये° — d) Bo शूद्रः; Lo^5 शूद्रे; Ox^3 शूद्रैः; Be^3 Wa शूद्रमेभिस्तु; WKt^1 सर्वं तु; WKt^3 पातकं [*Rn* gloss एतानि पातकानि supports एतैः cf. 8.88 and the note to it]

114.* Omitted in Ox^3 [*Jolly* M$^{1-3}$]; pādas c-d *ma* in Lo^4; pādas a-b and c-d transposed in TMd^3 GMy. Cited in *Apa* 694; *Lakṣ* 12.256 — a) GMd^5 अग्नौ; BCa SOx^1 SPu^6 चाहार°; NKt^4 Pu^7 Tj^1 वाहर°; La^1 त्वाहार°; Lo^1 वावाहतेदे°; GMd^1 TMd^4 °रयेत्शूद्रमप्सु — b) NNg Tr^1 [*Jolly* M G R] *Apa* वैनं; [*Jolly* M] *Jolly* चैव; MTr^4 MTr^6 चेह; La^1 निवेशयेत् — c) GMd^1 पुत्रदारैरथाप्येनं; Lo^1 पुत्रदारस्वपाय्येनं; TMd^3 पुत्रदानस्य; Bo Ho Jo^2 BKt^5 La^1 Tj^1 *Lakṣ* चाप्येनं; Pu^5 Pu^7 [*Jolly* G] वाप्येवं; MTr^4

यमिद्धो न दहत्यग्निरापो नोन्मज्जयन्ति च ।
न चार्तिमृच्छति क्षिप्रं स ज्ञेयः शपथे शुचिः ॥११५॥
वत्सस्य ह्यभिशस्तस्य पुरा भ्रात्रा यवीयसा ।
नाग्निर्ददाह रोमापि सत्येन जगतः स्पशः ॥११६॥
यस्मिन्यस्मिन्विवादे तु कौटसाक्ष्यं कृतं भवेत् ।
तत्तत्कार्यं निवर्तेत कृतं चाप्यकृतं भवेत् ॥११७॥
लोभान्मोहाद्भयान्मैत्रात् कामात्क्रोधात्तथैव च ।
अज्ञानाद्बालभावाच्च साक्ष्यं वितथमुच्यते ॥११८॥
एषामन्यतमे स्थाने यः साक्ष्यमनृतं वदेत् ।
तस्य दण्डविशेषांस्तु प्रवक्ष्याम्यनुपूर्वशः ॥११९॥

वाप्यङ्गं — d) Tr^{2} *Apa* शिरसि; Tj^{1} स्पर्शयत्पृथक्; *Apa* स्पर्शयेद्दृढं

115. Omitted in Lo^{5} Ox^{3} [*Jolly* M$^{1-3}$]; *ma* in Lo^{4}. Cited in *Lakṣ* 12.259; pādas c-d cited by *Vij* 2.113; *Dev* 3.274 — a) nKt^{4} तमिद्धो; Bo La^{1} समिद्धो; tMd^{4} यमिन्दो; gMd^{1} यदिभो न — b) wKt^{3} °ज्जयन्त्यपि; Wa °ज्जयन्ति यं; Lo^{1} हि — c) Hy चर्तिमृ°; Tr^{1} वार्तिमृ°; gMd^{5} चार्तमृ°; Be^{1} Ho wKt^{1} bKt^{5} Lo^{2} Pu^{8} °मिच्छति — d) bKt^{5} संज्ञेयः; Lo^{2} साज्ञयः; Tj^{1} शुचि

116. Omitted in Pu^{5} [*Jolly* M$^{1-3}$] — a) Be^{3} Tr^{2} वात्सस्य; bBe^{2} वत्स्यस्य; La^{1} वंशस्य; tMd^{3} gMy वत्सस्यैवाभिश°; Ho ह्यपिश°; Be^{3} ह्यविश°; wKt^{1} sOx^{1} sPu^{6} °शप्तस्य — b) Bo पुना; gMd^{5} पित्रा; Ho tMd^{4} Pu^{4} पुत्रा; nPu^{1} Tr^{2} पुत्र; bKt^{5} tMd^{3} भ्राता; nPu^{1} भृत्या; Be^{3} यवीयसः — c) Hy नानग्नि°; mTr^{3} °ग्निर्दात्राह; wKt^{3} °ग्निर्दहाह; oOr mTr^{6} °ग्निर्दहति; Pu^{7} [*Jolly* G] लोमापि; bBe^{2} Bo [*but cor*] wKt^{1} nKt^{4} La^{1} oOr Pu^{2} Pu^{8} रोमाणि — c-d) sOx^{1} sPu^{6} नाग्नि [lacuna] सप्तेन जगतः — d) bKt^{5} होमार्थं जगतां पतिः; Pu^{7} [*Jolly* G] सत्येन शपतः कृतः; tMd^{4} mTr^{4} mTr^{6} जगति; sOx^{1} sPu^{6} जगतां; Pu^{2} Pu^{4} भजतः स्पृहः; Wa स गतः स्पृहः; gMd^{5} दहनस्पृशः; Be^{1} bBe^{2} Kt^{2} Lo^{1} Lo^{4} tMd^{4} nNg nPu^{1} mTr^{6} [*Jolly* M Nd] *Dave* स्पृशः; tMd^{3} gMy स्पृशा; La^{1} Ox^{2} स्पृशन्; Pu^{8} प्रभुः; Be^{3} sOx^{1} sPu^{6} पतिः

117. Omitted in Lo^{4} Lo^{5} Ox^{3} [*Jolly* M$^{1-3}$]; pādas c-d omitted in bBe^{2}. Cited by *Vij* 2.77; *Dev* 3.217–8 — a) tMd^{3} gMd^{5} gMy [*Jolly* Nd] यस्मिन्यस्मिन्कृते कार्ये; bBe^{2} wKt^{1} Lo^{3} gMd^{1} nPu^{1} Pu^{2} Pu^{4} Pu^{5} Pu^{7} mTr^{4} mTr^{6} °न्विवादेषु — b) bCa यः साक्ष्यं कूटकृतं भवेत्; Be^{1} Jo^{2} nPu^{1} [*Jolly* G Nd] कूट°; Pu^{2} Pu^{4} कूटकेसाकृतं; wKt^{1} °साक्ष्य; La^{1} mTr^{5} °साक्षी; Be^{3} °साक्षनृतं वदेत्; mTr^{5} कृतो; tMd^{4} नृतं भवेत् — c) tMd^{3} Tj^{1} *om one* तत्; Pu^{5} Pu^{7} तत्र कार्यं; mTr^{4} mTr^{6} तत्तत्सर्वं; La^{1} तत्कार्यं च निव° — d) sOx^{1} sPu^{6} कृ [lacuna] वी [lacuna] कृतं; Bo कृतां; La^{1} tMd^{4} Wa कृतमप्यकृतं; wKt^{1} कृतमस्यकृतं; wKt^{3} कृतमप्यमृतं; Ho Lo^{1} Pu^{2} Pu^{4} Tj^{1} Tr^{2} [*Jolly* R] वाप्यकृतं; mTr^{5} *Bh* चाप्यनृतं; Jo^{1} वदेत्

118. Omitted in Lo^{5} Ox^{3} [*Jolly* M$^{1-3}$]; *ma* in Lo^{4}. Cited by *Apa* 680; *Lakṣ* 12.141; *Dev* 3.215; *Mādh* 3.81 — a) wKt^{1} °हाद्भयाद्वापि; Be^{1} Bo Ho nKt^{4} Lo^{2} tMd^{4} Ox^{2} nPu^{1} Pu^{2} Pu^{4} Tr^{1} Tr^{2} °यान्मैत्र्यात्; wKt^{3} °यान्मित्रात्; tMd^{3} nNg °यान्मत्र्या — b) wKt^{1} *om* कामात्; Be^{3} कामक्रो° — c) gMy अज्ञानाद्बल°; Lo^{3} Tj^{1} °भावाद्बा — d) Pu^{2} Pu^{4} सावितातथमुच्यते

119. Omitted in Lo^{4} Lo^{5} Ox^{3} [*Jolly* M$^{1-3}$]. Cited by *Lakṣ* 12.141; *Dev* 3.215; *Mādh* 3.82 — a) tMd^{4} *Dev* तेषाम°; gMd^{1} *Lakṣ* °न्यतमः; Pu^{8} Tr^{1} °न्यतम; *Mādh* °न्यतमत्वेन यः — b) Ho ये; Lo^{1} यत्; Be^{3} साक्षमनृतं; Ho साक्ष्यममृतं; wKt^{3} साक्ष्यं वितथं; wKt^{3} tMd^{3} भवेत् — c) [*Jolly* N] तेषां; wKt^{1} तस्य वै दण्ड°; gMd^{1} दण्डोविशेषोस्तु; tMd^{3} sOx^{1} sPu^{6} °विशेषास्तु; La^{1} °विशेषां तु; [*Jolly* M] °विशेषांश्च; gMd^{5} °विधानं तु

लोभात्सहस्रं दण्ड्यस्तु मोहात्पूर्वं तु साहसम् ।
भयाद् द्वौ मध्यमौ दण्डौ मैत्रात्पूर्वं चतुर्गुणम् ॥१२०॥
कामाद्दशगुणं पूर्वं क्रोधात्तु त्रिगुणं परम् ।
अज्ञानाद् द्वे शते पूर्णे बालिश्याच्छतमेव तु ॥१२१॥
एतानाहुः कौटसाक्ष्ये प्रोक्तान्दण्डान्मनीषिभिः ।
धर्मस्याव्यभिचारार्थमधर्मनियमाय च ॥१२२॥
कौटसाक्ष्यं तु कुर्वाणांस्त्रीन्वर्णान्धार्मिको नृपः ।
प्रवासयेद्दण्डयित्वा ब्राह्मणं तु विवासयेत् ॥१२३॥
दश स्थानानि दण्डस्य मनुः स्वायंभुवोऽब्रवीत् ।
त्रिषु वर्णेषु तानि स्युरक्षतो ब्राह्मणो व्रजेत् ॥१२४॥

120. Omitted in Lo^4 Lo^5 Ox^3 MTr^5 [*Jolly* M$^{1-3}$]. Cited by *Vij* 2.81; *Apa* 680; *Lakṣ* 12.141; *Dev* 3.215; *Mādh* 3.82 — a) Tr^1 लोभाद्दण्ड्या: सहस्रं तु; Tj^1 Tj^2 °त्सहस्र; TMd^4 [*Jolly* Nd *sh*] दण्डस्तु; [*Jolly* Nd *fh*] दण्डस्स; GMy दण्ड्यं तु; TMd^3 दण्डं तु; Jo^2 Lo^3 Pu^7 Tj^1 दण्ड्यश्च; [*Jolly* R] दण्डश्च; Be^1 wKt^3 Lo^2 GMd^1 oOr Ox^2 MTr^4 MTr^6 *Vij Apa* दण्ड्य: स्यान्मोहा° — b) La^1 °त्पूर्वस्तु — c) GMd^1 भयाद्वा मध्यमो; *Dev* भयाद्वै मध्यमो; *Apa* भयादौ मध्यमो; GMd^5 NNg Wa मध्यमो; Be^1 Be^3 Bo BCa wKt^1 wKt^3 GMy sOx^1 NPu^1 Pu^3 sPu^6 Tj^1 दण्ड्यौ; NNg दण्ड्यो; GMd^1 GMd^5 Wa *Dev Apa* दण्डो — d) Be^1 Ho NKt^4 Lo^2 GMd^1 TMd^4 GMy Ox^2 Pu^3 Pu^7 Tr^1 Tr^2 *Vij* मैत्र्या°; wKt^3 मित्रा°; wKt^3 *Lakṣ* °त्पूर्व; La^1 °त्पूर्वश्चतु°; BBe^2 चतुष्टयं; wKt^1 [*but mc*] च तद्गुणं

121. Omitted in Lo^4 Lo^5 Ox^3 [*Jolly* M$^{1-3}$]; pādas a-b omitted in MTr^5. Cited by *Vij* 2.81; *Apa* 680; *Lakṣ* 12.141; *Dev* 3.215; *Mādh* 3.82 — a) Kt^2 पूर्व; Be^3 पूर्णं; BCa La^1 *Lakṣ* प्रोक्तं — b) GMd^5 क्रोधाद्दशगुणं — c) GMd^1 अज्ञाने; sOx^1 sPu^6 द्वै; Pu^5 द्वि; Tj^2 द्व; Pu^5 पूर्णो— d) TMd^4 बालिशात् शतकं त्रय:; GMd^5 GMy बालिशाच्छत°; wKt^1 Pu^2 Pu^4 बालस्याच्छत°; Pu^5 Pu^7 बालिसात् शत°; NKt^4 बालिसाशत°; BBe^2 Bo Ho Jo^2 wKt^3 Lo^3 GMd^1 NNg sOx^1 Ox^2 NPu^1 Pu^2 Pu^3 Pu^4 sPu^6 Pu^8 Tj^1 Tr^2 *Apa Go* °तमेव च; Be^3 °तमुच्यते

122. Omitted in [*Jolly* M$^{1-3}$]. Cited by *Lakṣ* 12.141; pādas a-b cited by *Dev* 3.51, 215; *Mādh* 3.82 — a) Be^3 एतामाहु:; Ox^3 एवानाहु:; TMd^4 एतानाहं; Bo TMd^3 GMd^5 Pu^2 Pu^4 Pu^5 Pu^7 [*Jolly* M^9 G Nd] कूट°; Lo^2 कोट° — b) sOx^1 sPu^6 प्रोक्ता दण्डा मनी°; *Lakṣ* प्रोक्तो दण्डो मनी°; NKt^4 प्रोक्ता वेदान्मनी°; Pu^2 Pu^4 °न्दण्ड्या°; Be^3 BCa [*but cor*] wKt^3 NKt^4 La^1 Lo^3 GMd^1 GMd^5 oOr NPu^1 Tj^1 MTr^4 MTr^6 Wa *Dev* °न्मनीषिण:; TMd^3 °न्महीषिभि: — c) Ho TMd^3 GMy Tr^2 धर्मस्यव्यभि°; wKt^1 °चाराद्यम°; Bo °चारस्यम° — d) wKt^1 °धर्माणियमाय; GMd^1 GMd^5 °नियनाय; TMd^3 TMd^4 GMy Tr^1 [*Jolly* Nd] °निधनाय; Tj^1 °नियमानि

123. Omitted in [*Jolly* M$^{1-3}$]. Cited by *Vij* 2.81; *Apa* 680; *Lakṣ* 12.142; *Mādh* 3.82 — a) Bo NPu^1 Pu^5 Pu^7 [*Jolly* M$^{8-9}$ Nd G] *Lakṣ Mādh* कूट°; Kt^2 कौठ°; wKt^1 च; Be^3 TMd^3 कुर्वाणास्त्री°; TMd^4 कुर्वाणं त्री°; Ox^3 कुर्वीत त्री° — b) *Apa* [*vl as in ed*] °र्णान्पालको; Lo^1 °र्णान्ब्राह्मणो — c) TMd^3 GMy प्रसादये° — d) Bo ब्रह्मणं; BBe^2 MTr^4 MTr^6 [*Jolly* Nd] *Lakṣ* ब्राह्मणांस्तु; Be^1 ब्राह्मणंस्तु; wKt^3 ब्राह्मणान्तु

124.* Omitted in [*Jolly* M$^{1-3}$]. Cited by *Vij* 2.26; *Dev* 3.290–1; *Mādh* 1.399; pādas a-b cited by *Mādh* 3.155 — a) GMd^1 TMd^4 दण्ड्यस्य — b) NNg °ब्रवीन् — c) Be^1 BBe^2 Be^3 BCa Hy Jm Jo^1 Jo^2 wKt^1 Kt^2 wKt^3 NKt^4 BKt^5 Lo^1 Lo^3 Lo^4 Lo^5 NNg Ox^3 NPu^1 Pu^2 Pu^4 Tj^1 Tj^2 MTr^3 Wa *Vij Mandlik Jolly Jha KSS Dave* यानि; Lo^1 यानि तु अक्षतो — d) Pu^5 Pu^7 [*cor to*] स्युरक्षते; NKt^4

उपस्थमुदरं जिह्वा हस्तौ पादौ च पञ्चमम् ।
चक्षुर्नासा च कर्णौ च धनं देहस्तथैव च ॥१२५॥
अनुबन्धं परिज्ञाय देशकालौ च तत्त्वतः ।
सारापराधौ चालोक्य दण्डं दण्ड्येषु पातयेत् ॥१२६॥
अधर्मदण्डनं लोके यशोघ्नं कीर्तिनाशनम् ।
अस्वर्ग्यं च परत्रापि तस्मात्तत्परिवर्जयेत् ॥१२७॥
अदण्ड्यान्दण्डयन् राजा दण्ड्यांश्चैवाप्यदण्डयन् ।
अयशो महदाप्नोति नरकं चैव गच्छति ॥१२८॥
वाग्दण्डं प्रथमं कुर्याद्धिग्दण्डं तदनन्तरम् ।
तृतीयं धनदण्डं तु वधदण्डमतः परम् ॥१२९॥
वधेनापि यदा त्वेतान् निग्रहीतुं न शक्नुयात् ।
तदैषु सर्वमप्येतत् प्रयुञ्जीत चतुष्टयम् ॥१३०॥

Lo^{1} स्युरक्षितो; GMy ब्रह्मणो; TMd^{4} Tj^{1} ब्राह्मणा

125. Omitted in [*Jolly* M$^{1-3}$]. Cited by *Lakṣ* 12.782; *Dev* 3.290; *Mādh* 1.399, 3.156 — a) *Dev* उपस्थ उदरं; Hy °मुदारं; wKt^{1} °मुपरं; TMd^{4} °मुदकं; Tj^{1} जुह्वा; TMd^{4} जिह्वंति — b) NPu^{1} हस्त; Tj^{2} पदो; GMd^{1} पञ्चमः; BKt^{5} पञ्चमौ; Lo^{5} Ox^{3} पञ्चमी — c) BBe^{2} wKt^{1} Pu^{2} Pu^{4} °र्नाशा; Hy °र्नास; *Mādh* 1.399 °र्नासे; TMd^{3} MTr^{6} °र्नासौ; oOr °र्नासिककर्णौ; NKt^{4} कर्णं; TMd^{3} कर्णा — d) *Mādh* 3.156 नरदेहस्तथैव; TMd^{4} देहंस्तथैव; GMd^{1} देहं तथैव; GMy देह तथैव

126. Omitted in [*Jolly* M$^{1-3}$]. Cited by *Dev* 3.297; *Mādh* 1.398— a) GMd^{1} TMd^{3} GMd^{5} GMy MTr^{4} MTr^{6} [*Jolly* Gr] *Nd* *NSm* 19.45 अपराधं; Tr^{1} अ[*ma* नुबन्]धं; TMd^{4} अपरोधं [*Bh* reads here अनुबन्ध but in a reference at 8.285 reads अपराध]; Wa °बन्धे; Jm wKt^{3} च विज्ञाय; *Mādh* परीक्ष्याथ — c) GMd^{1} TMd^{3} TMd^{4} GMd^{5} GMy [*Jolly* Nd] *Nd* सारासारं तथालोक्य [Nd °सारौ; GMd^{5} °लोकं]; Tr^{1} सारासारं तथालोक्य *mc sh* सारापराधौ विज्ञाय; MTr^{6} सारानुबन्धा वापराधौ चालोक्य; oOr सपराधौ समालोक्य; *NSm* 19.45 सारानुबन्धावालोक्य; BBe^{2} °राधो; *Mādh* °राधमथालोच्य; BCa sOx^{1} sPu^{6} *Dev* °राधावालोच्य; Pu^{2} °राधावालोक्य; Ox^{2} Ox^{3} वालोक्य; Ho wKt^{3} MTr^{5} चालोच्य; NNg चावेक्ष्य; Jo^{2} Lo^{3} Tj^{1} [*Jolly* R] विज्ञाय — d) Wa *om* दण्डं; Ox^{3}दण्डे; TMd^{3} दण्ड्यं दण्ड्येषु; TMd^{4} दण्ड्य दण्ड्येषु; BBe^{2} Be^{3} Bo TMd^{4} दण्डेषु; La^{1} [*but mc sh*] स्वेतेषु; GMd^{5} दापयेत्

127. Omitted in [*Jolly* M$^{1-3}$] — a) GMd^{1} अधम°; Ox^{3} धर्मदण्डनं; TMd^{3} TMd^{4} GMd^{5} GMy MTr^{4} MTr^{6} [*Jolly* Nd] अदण्ड्यदण्डनं; Tr^{1} अ[*ma* धर्म]दण्डनं — c) TMd^{4} अस्वर्म्यं च स तत्र स्यात्; BBe^{2} अस्वर्गं; Lo^{3} चापरत्रापि; [*Jolly* M] स्यात्परत्रापि; Ox^{3} परत्राणि— d) Ox^{3} तस्मात्परिचर्ययः; TMd^{3} MTr^{4} तस्मात्तं परि°; wKt^{3} तस्मात्परिविवर्ज°; Be^{3} °वर्तयेत्

128. Omitted in MTr^{5} [*Jolly* M$^{1-3}$]. Cited by *Vij* 2.1;*Lakṣ* 12.796; *Dev* 3.33; *Mādh* 1.391, 3.25 — a) Bo अदण्डान्द°; *Lakṣ* अदण्ड्यं दण्ड°; La^{1} Lo^{1} °न्दण्डयेद् — b) Pu^{5} Pu^{7} दण्ड्यान्वाप्य°; *Lakṣ* दण्ड्यं चैवाप्य° — d) Tr^{2} नरके; Kt^{2} नरकश्चैव; GMd^{1} नरकांश्चैव; TMd^{3} चाधिगच्छति; Pu^{2} वाधिगच्छति

129. Omitted in [*Jolly* M$^{1-3}$]. Cited by *Vij* 1.367, 2.26; *Lakṣ* 12.781; *Dev* 3.295; *Mādh* 3.156 — a) Pu^{5} Pu^{7} वाग्दण्डः; Tj^{1} वाग्दण्ड; Tr^{1} [*but mc sh*] कुर्युर्धि° — a-b) *Vij* धिग्दण्डं प्रथमं कुर्याद्वाग्दण्डं — c) Be^{3} BCa GMd^{1} NNg Pu^{2} Pu^{5} Pu^{7} [*Jolly* G] च — c-d) Lo^{3} Tj^{1} वधदण्डं तु धनदण्डमतः — d) La^{1} वधं; Tr^{1} °दण्डस्त्वतः; TMd^{4} °दण्डस्ततः; GMd^{5} MTr^{6} °दण्डं ततः

130. Omitted in TMd^{3} GMy [*Jolly* M$^{1-3}$]; pādas c-d omitted in Pu^{5}. Cited by *Lakṣ* 12.781;

लोकसंव्यवहारार्थं याः संज्ञाः प्रथिता भुवि ।
ताम्ररूप्यसुवर्णानां ताः प्रवक्ष्याम्यशेषतः ॥१३१॥
जालान्तरगते भानौ यत्सूक्ष्मं दृश्यते रजः ।
प्रथमं तत्प्रमाणानां त्रसरेणुं प्रचक्षते ॥१३२॥*
त्रसरेणवोऽष्टौ विज्ञेया लिक्षैका परिमाणतः ।
ता राजसर्षपस्तिस्रस्ते त्रयो गौरसर्षपः ॥१३३॥
सर्षपाः षड्यवो मध्यस्त्रियवं त्वेव कृष्णलम् ।
पञ्चकृष्णलको माषस्ते सुवर्णस्तु षोडश ॥१३४॥

Dev 3.295 — a) GMd^1 वधेनापि रतानां तु; Bo वेधेनापि; BKt^5 Lo^4 TMd^4 यथा; Kt^2 यत्त्वेतान्; Ox^3 यथाश्येनान्; Be^1 wKt^3 NKt^4 Lo^4 Lo^5 MTr^6 त्वेनान्; BKt^5 त्वेतन्; *Lakṣ* त्वेनं — b) Be^1 Be^3 wKt^1 NKt^4 Lo^4 Tr^2 निगृहीतुं; sOx^1 sPu^6 निग्रहातुं; La^1 MTr^4 MTr^6 निगृह्णीतुं; Tr^1 निगृहीतं; TMd^4 निग्रहीतं; Ho sOx^1 sPu^6 °हीतुमशक्नुयात् — c) Be^1 BBe^2 Bo NKt^4 La^1 Lo^2 GMd^1 TMd^4 NNg oOr NPu^1 Pu^4 Tr^1 MTr^5 MTr^6 तदेपु; Lo^1 तदैषां; Be^3 तदेषां; GMd^5 तदेतत्; Pu^7 [*Jolly* G] तदैव; TMd^4 सर्वमप्येतं; Lo^1 सर्वमेवैतत् — d) NNg नियुञ्जीत

131. Omitted in Pu^5 [*Jolly* M$^{1-3}$]. Cited by *Lakṣ* 12.807; *Hem* 1.115, 2/1.53; *Dev* 3.229; *Mādh* 3.115 — a) TMd^4 लोकस्य व्यवहा°; Pu^2 Pu^4 °रार्थे— b) Pu^7 या संज्ञा; TMd^4 *Mādh* या संख्या; Jo^2 कथिता — c) wKt^3 Jo^2 La^1 TMd^4 Ox^2 Tj^1 Wa *Lakṣ* °रौप्य°; sOx^1 sPu^6 °रूप° — d) Lo^4 Lo^5 Ox^3 Pu^2 Pu^4 तान्प्रव°; Bo प्रवक्ष्याप्यशे°; Be^3 प्रवक्षामि शेषतः

132.* Omitted in GMd^1 GMd^5 MTr^4 MTr^5 MTr^6 [*Jolly* M$^{1-3}$] *Bh.* Cited by *Lakṣ* 12.807; *Hem* 1.115, 2/1.53; *Mādh* 3.115 — a) Ho जला°; Tj^1 नाभौ; Wa भावेनौ — b) Kt^2 यत्सूक्ष्म्यं; Pu^5 Pu^7 यच्छूक्ष्मं; wKt^3 दृश्यते सह — c) Ox^3 प्रथमे; TMd^3 GMy *Hem* परमं — d) La^1 भ्रसरेणुं; Lo^1 Lo^3 TMd^4 Pu^5 Pu^7 Tj^1 Tr^2 Wa *Hem* 1.115 त्रसरेणुः; Lo^1 Lo^4 Lo^5 प्रचक्ष्यते; Hy प्रचक्षेते; NNg प्रवक्ष्यते; La^1 प्रकीर्तितः; Lo^3 Tj^1 स उच्यते— Ox^3 inserts here 9.137–63

133.* Omitted in Lo^4 Lo^5 Ox^3 [*Jolly* M$^{1-3}$]. Cited by *Lakṣ* 12.807; *Hem* 1.115, 2/1.53; *Dev* 3.229; *Mādh* 3.115 — a) TMd^3 GMy [*Jolly* Nd] *Hem* 1.115 त्रसरेण्वष्टकं ज्ञेयं [TMd^3 *Hem* 1.115 ज्ञेया; (*Jolly* Nd) ज्ञेयो]; La^1 भ्रस°; Jo^1 त्रसरेणवौ; *Dave* सरेणवो; TMd^4 त्रसरेण्वष्टौ; GMd^5 त्रसरेणाष्टौ; NKt^4 BKt^5 Wa °ष्टौ ज्ञेया; Pu^2 Pu^4 विज्ञेयौ —a-b) *Hem* 2/1.53 त्रसरेण्वष्टकं लिक्षा ज्ञेयैका परिमाणतः — b) Tr^2 लिक्षैको; GMd^5 लिक्षेका; Be^3 लिक्ष्यैका; NKt^4 लिक्षोका; Lo^1 लिक्षिका; GMd^1 लिक्षःका; BKt^5 लिसंश्यैका; wKt^3 Pu^5 Pu^7 MTr^4 MTr^6 लिख्यैका; Hy लिख्यका; Tj^2 सिक्षैका; NPu^1 °कानुप्रमाणतः; sOx^1 sPu^6 परमाणतः; GMd^5 परिणामतः; *Hem* 1.115 परमाणुतः; Ho °माणता — c) TMd^4 स राज°; MTr^6 सा राज°; BKt^5 [*but cor*] La^1 TMd^3 GMd^5 GMy NPu^1 Pu^2 Pu^4 sPu^6 °सर्षपास्ति° — d) Be^3 Bo TMd^3 TMd^4 GMy °स्तिस्रस्त्रयस्ते गौर°; *Lakṣ* °स्तिस्रस्ते तु द्वे गौर°; GMd^1 ज्ञेयो गौर°; Be^3 La^1 TMd^3 GMd^5 GMy °सर्षपाः

134.* Omitted in Lo^4 Lo^5 Ox^3 [*Jolly* M$^{1-3}$]; pādas c-d omitted in GMd^1. Cited by *Lakṣ* 12.808; *Hem* 1.115, 2/1.54; *Dev* 3.229; *Mādh* 3.116 — a) TMd^4 सर्षपाष्टौ यदा मध्यं त्रि°; wKt^1 *om* सर्षपाः; Kt^2 सर्षपः; NPu^1 सर्षपान्; *Hem* 2/1.54 षट् योमध्यः त्रि°; Be^1 NKt^4 Tj^2 मध्यास्त्रि° — b) TMd^3 GMy °स्त्रियवास्ते तु कृष्णलाः; Be^1 °स्त्रियवैस्त्वेव; NNg Wa कृष्णलः; GMd^5 NPu^1 Pu^2 Pu^4 Pu^5 Pu^7 Tr^1 [*but cor to* चैक] MTr^6 Wa चैव; BBe^2 Be^3 Bo Hy Jm Jo^1 Jo^2 wKt^1 Kt^2 wKt^3 BKt^5 Lo^1 Lo^2 Lo^3 TMd^4 oOr Ox^2 Tj^1 Tj^2 Tr^2 MTr^3 *Rn Rc Lakṣ Hem Dev Mādh Mandlik Jha KSS Dave* त्वेककृष्णलं; *Hem* 1.115 त्वेककृष्णतः; GMd^1 त्वेव केवलं — c) Be^1 NKt^4 Lo^2 NPu^1 Pu^5 Pu^7 MTr^5 MTr^6 Wa [*Jolly* M G] *Me Dave Jha* °लिको [but *Me* notes: पञ्चकृष्णलक इति पाठे कबन्तो बहुव्रीहिः];

पलं सुवर्णाश्चत्वारः पलानि धरणं दश ।
द्वे कृष्णले समधृते विज्ञेयो रूप्यमाषकः ॥१३५॥
ते षोडश स्याद्धरणं पुराणश्चैव राजतः ।
कार्षापणस्तु विज्ञेयस्ताम्रिकः कार्षिकः पणः ॥१३६॥
धरणानि दश ज्ञेयः शतमानस्तु राजतः ।
चतुःसुवर्णको निष्को विज्ञेयस्तु प्रमाणतः ॥१३७॥
पणानां द्वे शते सार्धे प्रथमः साहसः स्मृतः ।
मध्यमः पञ्च विज्ञेयः सहस्रं त्वेव चोत्तमः ॥१३८॥
ऋणे देये प्रतिज्ञाते पञ्चकं शतमर्हति ।
अपह्नवे तद्द्विगुणं तन्मनोरनुशासनम् ॥१३९॥

Pu^{2} Pu^{4} °लिका; MTr^{3} °लतो; Be^{1} माषास्ते; wKt^{1} मासस्ते; TMd^{4} मात्रस्ते — d) Pu^{2} Pu^{4} माषस्तैः; TMd^{4} sOx^{1} sPu^{6} सुवर्णास्तु; *Lakṣ* सुवर्णं तु; Bo GMd^{5} सुवर्णस्य; Be^{3} NNg षोडशः

135. Omitted in Lo^{4} Lo^{5} GMd^{1} Ox^{3} [*Jolly* M$^{1-3}$]. Cited by *Lakṣ* 12.808; *Hem* 1.115, 2/1.54; *Dev* 3.230; *Mādh* 3.116 — a) Ho फलं; La^{1} पलः; wKt^{1} परं; Lo^{1} Lo^{3} TMd^{4} GMd^{5} Tj^{1} सुवर्णश्च° — b) Jo^{1} पेलानि; GMd^{5} फलानि; TMd^{3} GMy पलानां चरणं; TMd^{4} दरणं; Be^{3} wKt^{1} TMd^{4} दशः — c) Pu^{5} Pu^{7} समं धृत्वा; NNg [*but mc sh*] समध्यते — d) Ho Hy Jm Jo^{1} Kt^{2} BKt^{5} sOx^{1} Ox^{2} NPu^{1} Pu^{3} sPu^{6} MTr^{3} *Mandlik KSS* रौप्य°; Bo TMd^{4} रूप°; sOx^{1} sPu^{6} °माषकाः; BBe^{2} °माषकं; MTr^{3} °मापतः

136. Omitted in Lo^{4} Lo^{5} Ox^{3} [*Jolly* M$^{1-3}$]; pādas c-d omitted in MTr^{3}. Cited by *Vij* 1.364–5; *Lakṣ* 12.808; *Hem* 1.115, 2/1.54; *Dev* 3.230; *Mādh* 3.116 — a) Lo^{1} षोडशः — b) TMd^{3} TMd^{4} GMy MTr^{6} *Dev* पुराणं चैव; TMd^{3} GMd^{5} GMy *Dev* राजतं — c) Tj^{1} कार्षप°; Jo^{1} °पणं तु; Kt^{2} °पणन्तु; GMd^{1} oOr विज्ञेयास्ता° — d) TMd^{3} GMy Wa विज्ञेयः कार्क्षिकस्ताम्रिकः पणः; *Lakṣ* °यस्तास्तिस्रः; Bo °म्रिकाः; sOx^{1} sPu^{6} °म्रिका; Bo sOx^{1} Pu^{4} sPu^{6} कर्षिकः; TMd^{4} Tj^{1} कार्षिकं; GMd^{1} कार्षिका; La^{1} कर्षणः; TMd^{4} पणं

137. Omitted in Ho Lo^{4} Lo^{5} Ox^{3}. Cited by *Lakṣ* 12.808; *Hem* 1.115, 2/1.54; *Dev* 3.230; *Mādh* 3.116 — a) sOx^{1} sPu^{6} दरणानि; Lo^{1} धारणानि; TMd^{4} दशे; BKt^{5} GMd^{5} ज्ञेयं — b) oOr ज्ञेयो द्रुतमानं तु; BKt^{5} शतमायन्तु; BBe^{2} Be^{3} wKt^{1} TMd^{3} GMd^{5} *Lakṣ* शतमानं तु; wKt^{1} BKt^{5} राजतं — c) Be^{3} GMd^{1} TMd^{3} TMd^{4} GMy Pu^{8} Tr^{1} MTr^{4} MTr^{6} [*Jolly* M] *Lakṣ* °सुवर्णिको; Be^{1} BBe^{2} Bo BCa Hy Jm Jo^{1} Jo^{2} wKt^{1} Kt^{2} wKt^{3} NKt^{4} BKt^{5} La^{1} Lo^{3} sOx^{1} Ox^{2} Pu^{2} Pu^{4} sPu^{6} Tj^{1} Tj^{2} Tr^{2} MTr^{3} MTr^{5} [*Jolly* R] *Rn Mr Hem Mādh Mandlik Jha KSS Dave* °सौवर्णिको — d) TMd^{4} प्रमाणकः

138. Omitted in Lo^{4} Lo^{5} Ox^{3}. Cited by *Vij* 1.366; *Apa* 592; *Lakṣ* 12.807; *Dev* 3.299 — a) Hy पणनां; oOr Pu^{2} Pu^{4} पलानां; Kt^{2} वणानां; BKt^{5} TMd^{4} सार्धं; Ho स्यार्धे; Hy साधे — b) TMd^{4} प्रथमं; Hy स्मृताः — c) TMd^{4} मध्यमं; Tr^{2} पञ्चमः; GMd^{5} विज्ञेयं — d) NPu^{1} Pu^{2} Pu^{4} सहस्रं चोत्तमः स्मृतः; wKt^{1} साहसं; GMd^{5} Ox^{2} Tr^{1} Wa *Vij Dev* चैव; *Apa* द्वेव; TMd^{3} GMy [*Jolly* Nd] त्वेकमुत्तमं; BCa त्वेकमुत्तमः; oOr त्वेव सत्तमः; Ho Jo^{2} La^{1} Lo^{3} GMd^{5} sOx^{1} sPu^{6} Tj^{1} Tj^{2} Tr^{1} तूत्तमः; TMd^{4} तूत्तमं; GMd^{1} तत्तमः

139.* Omitted by *Nā*. Cited by *Lakṣ* 12.333 — a) Lo^{1} ऋणो; GMd^{5} NPu^{1} ऋण; GMd^{1} रणे; TMd^{3} TMd^{4} देय; TMd^{4} देयि; Hy देशे; TMd^{4} प्रतिज्ञाति; Tr^{2} प्रतिज्ञेये — b) BKt^{5} La^{1} पञ्चमं; wKt^{1} सतम°; oOr दशम°; TMd^{4} शत्रुम° — c) wKt^{3} Lo^{2} NNg NPu^{1} Pu^{5} Pu^{7} MTr^{4} MTr^{6} [*Jolly* M G Nd] *Jolly* तु द्विगुणं

वसिष्ठविहितां वृद्धिं सृजेद्वित्तविवर्धिनीम् ।
अशीतिभागं गृह्णीयान्मासाद्वार्धुषिकः शते ॥१४०॥
द्विकं शतं वा गृह्णीयात् सतां धर्ममनुस्मरन् ।
द्विकं शतं हि गृह्णानो न भवत्यर्थकिल्बिषी ॥१४१॥
द्विकं त्रिकं चतुष्कं च पञ्चकं च शतं समम् ।
मासस्य वृद्धिं गृह्णीयाद् वर्णानामनुपूर्वशः ॥१४२॥
न त्वेवाधौ सोपकारे कौसीदीं वृद्धिमाप्नुयात् ।
न चाधेः कालसंरोधान्निसर्गोऽस्ति न विक्रयः ॥१४३॥
न भोक्तव्यो बलादाधिर्भुञ्जानो वृद्धिमुत्सृजेत् ।
मूल्येन तोषयेच्चैनमाधिस्तेनोऽन्यथा भवेत् ॥१४४॥
आधिश्चोपनिधिश्चोभौ न कालात्ययमर्हतः ।
अवहार्यौ भवेतां तौ दीर्घकालमवस्थितौ ॥१४५॥

140. Pādas a-b omitted in GMd[1]. Cited by *Lakṣ* 12.279; pādas c-d cited by *Dev* 3.361; *Mādh* 3.167 — a) Ho Kt[2] वशिष्ठ°; Pu[3] विशिष्ठ°; GMy Tj[1] °विहितं — b) Jm त्यजेद्वि°; Ho Hy °वर्धिनी; La[1] Lo[4] Lo[5] TMd[4] NNg NPu[1] MTr[6] °वर्धनीं; WKt[3] NKt[4] Ox[3] Tr[1] °वर्धनी — d) Bo °यान्मासान्वा°; WKt[3] °यान्मासावा°; Jo[1] °यान्मासोवा°; Be[3] *Mādh* °यान्मासि वार्धु°; BKt[5] °द्वार्धुषिः शते; Jo[1] शतं; Lo[4] Lo[5] शत; GMy MTr[4] MTr[6] शतैः; TMd[3] शनैः

141. Cited by *Lakṣ* 2.218, 12.280; *Mādh* 3.167 — a) SOx[1] SPu[6] द्वकं; Bo द्वेकं; *Lakṣ* 2.218 शतं प्रगृह्णीयात्; MTr[4] MTr[5] MTr[6] गृह्णीत; GMd[1] TMd[3] TMd[4] GMy Tr[1] Wa [*Jolly* Nd Gr] कुर्वीत — b) TMd[4] शतां धनमनु° — c) BKt[5] *om* हि; TMd[3] ह; BCa Ho SOx[1] SPu[6] तु; GMd[5] OOr Tr[1] वा; Kt[2] Lo[5] गृह्णीनो; Tj[1] गृह्णाने; MTr[5] गृह्णतो

142. Cited by *Lakṣ* 12.280; *Dev* 3.361; *Mādh* 3.167 — a) Ox[3] तृकं; TMd[3] शतुष्कं; TMd[4] वा — b) Ox[2] पञ्चमं; OOr *om* च; Be[3] तु; *Bh* [pāṭha] समां; SOx[1] SPu[6] मतं; GMd[1] स्मृतं — c) Tj[1] न्यायस्य; GMd[1] मासं सवृद्धिं; TMd[4] वृद्धिमादद्याद् — d) Tr[2] वणिनामनु°; GMd[1] TMd[4] °मानुपूर्वशः; Pu[2] Pu[4] °मनुस्मरन्

143. Pādas a-b cited by *Apa* 659; *Dev* 3.325; pādas c-d cited by *Vij* 2.58; *Lakṣ* 2.219, 12.298; *Dev* 3.332 — a) TMd[3] स त्वे°; [*Jolly* M[8–9]] चैवाधौ; BKt[5] सोपकारौ; Lo[3] सौपकारे — b) Lo[4] Lo[5] कौसीदी; Bo OOr कौशिदीं; Tr[1] [*but cor sh*] कौसीदिं; Pu[5] Pu[7] कौसदी; WKt[1] कौशीदीं; TMd[4] कौसीद्धीं; GMd[1] कौशीतीं; TMd[3] कुसीदिं; Tj[2] वृषिमा°; TMd[4] °मवाप्नुयात् — c) GMd[5] चाधैः; GMd[1] चाधे; Pu[2] Pu[4] चाधः; NPu[1] चाधिः; TMd[4] चादेः; Be[1] Ox[2] *Lakṣ* 2.219 वाधेः; Lo[5] SOx[1] SPu[6] बाधेः; Bo चान्धेः; Hy कालसंबोधा°; WKt[1] BKt[5] TMd[3] TMd[4] °रोधानिसर्गो; WKt[3] °रोधो द्विसर्गो — d) Jo[2] °रोधाद्धि सर्गो; MTr[4] MTr[6] हि विक्रयः; Bo NKt[4] विक्रमः; GMd[5] निष्क्रयः; TMd[3] निष्क्रियः

144. Omitted in Ox[3]. Cited by *Mādh* 3.178–9; pādas a-b cited by *Vij* 2.58; *Dev* 3.324; pādas c-d cited by *Dev* 3.328 — a) BBe[2] Be[3] WKt[1] WKt[3] Lo[5] TMd[3] TMd[4] GMy °दाधिभुञ्जानो; NPu[1] Pu[2] °दाधिं भुञ्जानो; Bo °दान्धौ भुञ्जानो — b) OOr °धिर्भुञ्जाने; TMd[4] वृत्तिमु°; Be[3] °मुत्सृजन् — c) Be[1] [*but mc*] Be[3] SOx[1] SPu[6] मूलेन; GMd[5] Pu[2] Pu[4] Pu[5] Pu[7] [*Jolly* G] *Dev Mādh* तोषयेदेनमा°; Lo[2] तोषयेद्धैनमा°; NPu[1] MTr[6] तोषयेद्वैनमा°; MTr[5] दोषयेद्वैनमा°; WKt[3] तोषयेच्चैवमा°; NKt[4] तोषयेद्धैवमा; TMd[3] कल्पयेद्वैनमा°; GMy कल्पयेच्चैनमा°; SOx[1] SPu[6] नाशयेच्चैनमा° — d) TMd[3] °माधिनोन्यथा; TMd[4] °मातिध्येनोन्यथा; GMd[5] °धिस्तेनान्यथा; GMd[1] °न्यथो

145. Omitted in Ox[3] — a) SOx[1] SPu[6] प्रीत्यार्पितं निधिश्चोभौ — b) TMd[4] कला°; Pu[5] Pu[7]

संप्रीत्या भुज्यमानानि न नश्यन्ति कदाचन ।
धेनुरुष्ट्रो वहन्नश्वो यश्च दम्यः प्रयुज्यते ॥१४६॥
यत्किंचिद्दशवर्षाणि संनिधौ प्रेक्षते धनी ।
भुज्यमानं परैस्तूष्णीं न स तल्लब्धुमर्हति ॥१४७॥
अजडश्चेदपोगण्डो विषये चास्य भुज्यते ।
भग्नं तद्व्यवहारेण भोक्ता तद्धनमर्हति ॥१४८॥
आधिः सीमा बालधनं निक्षेपोपनिधिस्त्रियः ।
राजस्वं श्रोत्रियस्वं च न भोगेन प्रणश्यति* ॥१४९॥
यः स्वामिनाननुज्ञातमाधिं भुङ्क्तेऽविचक्षणः ।
तेनार्धवृद्धिर्मोक्तव्या तस्य भोगस्य निष्कृतिः ॥१५०॥

कालाव्यमम°; wKt[1] Lo[1] °मर्हति; tMd[4] °मर्हतां; wKt[3] °मर्थतः — c) mTr[3] अवहर्यौ; gMd[1] Ox[2] Tr[1] अपहार्यौ; Lo[2] अपहार्यो; nPu[1] अवगार्यौ — d) gMy °कालाववस्थितौ; tMd[3] °कालावस्थितौ; nPu[1] °कालव्यवस्थितौ; Pu[2] Pu[4] °कालं व्यवस्थितौ

146. Cited by *Dev* 3.157, *Mādh* 3.109–10 — a) tMd[4] संप्रीत्य; tMd[3] mTr[6] संप्रत्या — b) Pu[5] Pu[7] नश्यन्ति न; Kt[2] sOx[1] sPu[6] [*but mc sh*] पश्यन्ति — c) gMd[5] धेनुरश्वो वहनुष्ट्रो; mTr[5] धेनुश्चोष्ट्रो; gMd[1] Ox[2] वाहनाश्वो; *Mādh* वहद्वृद्धो — d) Ox[2] यश्चादम्यः; Pu[2] Pu[4] यः स्विद्दम्यः; wKt[3] nKt[4] दन्यः; bBe[2] यम्यः; gMd[5] दासीन्प्रयुज्यते; *Mādh* प्रभुज्यते; gMd[1] प्रयुज्यतत् — In Lo[3] Tj[1] the sequence is: 146, 148cd, 147, 148ab.

147. *ma* in Ho; in Ox[3] the sections 8.147–89 and 198–364 are omitted — a) tMd[4] तत्किं° — b) Hy Pu[2] Pu[3] Pu[4] mTr[5] प्रेक्ष्यते; tMd[3] धनि; Lo[5] वनी — c) bCa gMd[1] भुज्यमानः; tMd[4] भुज्यमाने; mTr[6] भज्यमानं; Tr[2] °स्तूर्णं — d) wKt[3] *om* स; nKt[4] Tr[2] तल्लब्धम°

148. Pādas a-b *ma* in Ho; pāda-a omitted in mTr[5]. Cited by *Vij* 2.24; *Apa* 632; *Dev* 3.156 — a) gMd[1] अजखुश्चे°; bKt[5] अजनश्चे°; Lo[2] °श्चैवपोगण्डो; Hy Jo[2] Pu[3] Pu[5] mTr[3] *Vij Apa Dev* °पौगण्डो; wKt[3] °पेगण्डो; oOr °पाषण्डो — b) nPu[1] विषयो; Lo[1] *Vij* विषयश्चास्य; Ho sOx[1] nPu[1] sPu[6] वास्य; Pu[5] Pu[7] चात्य; gMy चास्म; gMd[5] चोपभुज्यते; Lo[1] gMd[1] भुञ्जते — c) Pu[2] Pu[4] भुक्तं तद्व्य° — d) wKt[1] भोक्तुं तं धनम°; bBe[2] Hy Jm Jo[1] Kt[2] Lo[3] Tj[2] mTr[3] [*Jolly* Ku R] *Mr Mandlik KSS* तद्द्रव्यम°. After 148 Lo[4] Lo[5] place verses 365–90.

149.* Cited by *Lakṣ* 12.190; *Dev* 3.158; *Mādh* 3.109 — a) sOx[1] sPu[6] आधस्सीमा; bKt[5] बालं; nKt[4] बल°; Tr[2] बालि°; gMd[1] बाधनं च — b) bKt[5] निःक्षेपो°; Bo विक्षितोप°; Jo[2] [*Jolly* Ku R Nd] *NSm* 1.73 *Lakṣ Jha* °निधी स्त्रियः; Be[3] Hy Jm Jo[1] sOx[1] sPu[6] Pu[8] Tj[2] *VaDh* 16.18 *Mandlik KSS Dave* °निधिः स्त्रियः — c) Be[1] Be[3] Bo Ho bKt[5] Lo[1] Lo[2] oOr Ox[2] nPu[1] Pu[2] Pu[3] Pu[4] Pu[5] Pu[7] Pu[8] Tr[2] [*Jolly* M G] *Dev Me VaDh* 16.18 *NSm* 1.73 *Jolly* श्रोत्रियद्रव्यं [*om* च]; sOx[1] sPu[6] श्रोत्रियेद्रव्यं; tMd[3] gMy [*Jolly* Nd] ब्राह्मणस्वं — d) nNg Ox[2] Pu[8] *Dev Mādh* नोपभोगेन नश्यति; Wa नोपभोगात्प्रनश्यति; Be[1] Lo[2] oOr nPu[1] Pu[2] Pu[4] Pu[5] Pu[7] [*Jolly* M G R] *NSm* 1.73 *Jolly* नोपभोगेन जीर्यते; Be[3] Bo Jo[2] bKt[5] Lo[3] Pu[3] Pu[8] Tj[1] Tr[2] नोपभोगेन जीर्यति; bCa नोपभोगेन प्रनश्यति; Lo[4] विनश्यति; gMd[1] प्रणश्यतः

150. Cited by *Apa* 659; *Dev* 3.324; *Mādh* 3.179 — a) gMd[1] स्वामिनोननु°; Bo स्वामिनमननु°; Pu[5] Pu[7] Tj[1] °ज्ञात आधिं; Lo[3] °ज्ञातः आधिं — b) bBe[2] °माधि; Ho भुक्ते; Hy भुङ्क्त; tMd[4] °चक्षणं — c) tMd[3] gMy तेनोक्तवृद्धि°; *Apa* [vl] तेनाधिवृद्धि°; mTr[3] तेनार्थवृत्ति°; Kt[2] °वृद्धिमोक्त°; Kt[2] La[1] Lo[1] Lo[3] gMd[1] sOx[1] [*cor to*] Pu[4] Tr[2] *Apa Dave* °द्धिर्भोक्तव्या; Bo °द्धिर्भोक्तव्यो — d) gMd[1] नास्य भोक्तस्य

कुसीदवृद्धिर्द्वैगुण्यं नात्येति सकृदाहिता ।
धान्ये शदे लवे वाह्ये नातिक्रामति पञ्चताम् ॥१५१॥
कृतानुसारादधिका व्यतिरिक्ता न सिध्यति ।
कुसीदपथमाहुस्तं पञ्चकं शतमर्हति ॥१५२॥
नातिसांवत्सरीं वृद्धिं न चादृष्टां पुनर्हरेत्* ।
चक्रवृद्धिः कालवृद्धिः कारिता कायिका च या ॥१५३॥
ऋणं दातुमशक्तो यः कर्तुमिच्छेत्पुनः क्रियाम् ।
स दत्त्वा निर्जितां वृद्धिं करणं परिवर्तयेत् ॥१५४॥

निष्क्रयः; Tr² तस्या; sOx¹ sPu⁶ भागस्य; wKt¹ निःक्रियः; oOr mTr⁵ निष्क्रयः; nKt⁴ निःक्रयः; tMd³ निष्कृतः; La¹ निग्रहः

151.* Lo⁴ Lo⁵ omit verses 151–88. Cited by *Vij* 2.39; *Apa* 643–4; *Lakṣ* 12.288; *Dev* 3.374; *Mādh* 3.171-2 — a) bCa wKt¹ कुशीद°; Tj² कुश्चीद°; Tj² °वृद्धिर्द्विगुण्यं; nNg °वृद्धिर्द्वेगुण्यं; La¹ gMd¹ °वृद्धिर्वैगुण्यं — b) Be³ La¹ *Apa* [vl] नाभ्येति; Hyनोभ्येति; t Md⁴ नात्रेति; nPu¹ सकृदाहितात्; gMd¹ सुकृताहिता; wKt¹ Ox² सकृदाहता; Be¹ bBe² Be³ Bo Hy Jm Jo¹ Jo² wKt¹ Kt² wKt³ Lo¹ Lo³ nNg oOr sOx¹ Pu² Pu³ Pu⁴ Pu⁵ sPu⁶ Pu⁷ Pu⁸ Tj¹ Tj² mTr³ *Rn Nd Rc Go Mandlik Jolly KSS* सकृदाहृता; bCa tMd⁴ सकृदाहृताः; La¹ सकृताकृतौ — c) tMd⁴ निद्धान्ये दश चैवार्ह्यं; La¹ धान्ये नवे सदे वाह्ये; mTr⁴धान्यं दशबलं वाह्ये; Be¹ Ho Hy Jm Jo¹ wKt¹ Kt² wKt³ nKt⁴ Lo¹ Lo² Lo³ oOr sOx¹ Ox² nPu¹ Pu² sPu⁶ Tj¹ Tr² Wa [*Jolly* Ku N R] *Mandlik Jha KSS Dave* सदे; gMy शते; bKt⁵ लवे सदे; Tr² लवि; tMd³ यवे; Be¹ nNg *Apa* बाह्ये — d) Pu⁵ Pu⁷ नातिक्रामेत; nKt⁴ oOr Tj¹ Tr² mTr³ नातिक्रमति

152. Cited by *Lakṣ* 12.286; *Dev* 3.364; pādas a-b cited by *Dev* 3.368 — a) tMd³ °धिकाद्व्यतिरिक्ता — b) tMd³ °रिक्तानुसिध्यति — c) Tj² कुषीद°; oOr कुसीदमिदमाहु°; Bo Lo³ gMd⁵ gMy Pu² Pu⁴ °पदमाहु°; gMd¹ °फलमाहु°; tMd³ °मधमाहु°; gMy °हुस्तत्पञ्चकं — d) bKt⁵ पञ्चमं; Tj¹ °मर्हसि

153.* Pādas a-b omitted in nKt⁴ [haplo]. Cited by *Lakṣ* 12.281; *Dev* 3.367 — a) mTr⁵ °संवत्सरिः; Wa °वत्सरिं — b) Tr² नाभिष्टां; bCa nKt⁴ La¹ gMd⁵ mTr⁶ न चादिष्टां; Pu⁸ तं चादिष्टां; tMd⁴ न च दृष्टां; gMd¹ न च नष्टां; Be¹ Be³ Bo wKt¹ wKt⁵ Lo¹ Lo² nNg sOx¹ Ox² nPu¹ Pu² Pu³ Pu⁴ Pu⁵ sPu⁶ Pu⁷ Pu⁸ [*Jolly* M G N] *DevMe Go Nā Jolly Jha Dave* विनिर्हरेत्; La¹ नर्हरेत् — c) *Dev* चक्रवृद्धिं कालवृद्धिं; tMd⁴ करोवृद्धिः — d) Jo² wKt¹ Lo³ Tj¹ कायिका कारिका; Tj² कायिका कारिता; Pu⁵ Pu⁷ कालिका कारिता; tMd⁴ कारिका कायिका; mTr⁶कायकारिका; wKt³ कायिता च; Bo कामिता च; bBe² कारिका च; Lo² कालिका च; gMd⁵ कालका च; nNg कार्यिका च; tMd⁴ च यं; La¹ nPu¹ Tr² यया; [*Jolly* M] न वा

Additonal verse in tMd³ gMy (= *BṛSm* 10.10):

कायिका कर्मसंशोध्या मासग्राह्या च कालिका ।
वृद्धेर्वृद्धिश्च चक्रवृद्धिः कारिता ऋणिना कृता ॥

a) gMy adds at beginning: अत्र बृहस्पतिः — b) tMd³ कारिका

154.* Omitted in nKt⁴. Cited by *Lakṣ* 12.328; *Dev* 3.378; *Mādh* 3.193 — a) Be³ दातुं प्रवृत्तो; wKt³ °मशक्यो; Pu² °मत्रोक्तो; Pu⁴ °मत्रक्रे — b) tMd⁴ °मिच्छत्पुनः; Lo¹ °मिच्छेत्परः; Be³ °मिच्छेत्पुनः पुनः; Tr² क्रियं — c) Tr² निजितां; tMd⁴ निर्णितां; Bo वृद्धि — d) Ho [*cor to*] tMd³ gMy [*Jolly* M Nd] *Bh Jolly* कारणं; gMd⁵ Pu² Pu⁴ Tr² mTr⁴ परिवर्जयेत्; Lo¹ परिवर्धयेत्; bKt⁵ परिवर्तते

अदर्शयित्वा तत्रैव हिरण्यं परिवर्तयेत् ।
यावती संभवेद्वृद्धिस्तावतीं दातुमर्हति ॥१५५॥
चक्रवृद्धिं समारूढो देशकालव्यवस्थितः ।
अतिक्रामन्देशकालौ न तत्फलमवाप्नुयात् ॥१५६॥
समुद्रयानकुशला देशकालार्थदर्शिनः ।
स्थापयन्ति तु यां वृद्धिं सा तत्राधिगमं प्रति ॥१५७॥
यो यस्य प्रतिभूस्तिष्ठेद्दर्शनायेह मानवः ।
अदर्शयन्स तं तस्य प्रयच्छेत्स्वधनादृणम् ॥१५८॥
प्रातिभाव्यं वृथादानमाक्षिकं सौरिकं च यत् ।
दण्डशुल्कावशेषं च न पुत्रो दातुमर्हति ॥१५९॥
दर्शनप्रातिभाव्ये तु विधिः स्यात्पूर्वचोदितः ।
दानप्रतिभुवि प्रेते दायादानपि दापयेत् ॥१६०॥

155. Omitted in NKt^{4}; pādas a-b omitted in GMd^{1}. Cited by *Lakṣ* 12.328; *Dev* 3.378 — a) Hy *om* अदर्शयित्वा; GMd^{5} तत्रैनं — b) Pu^{5} Pu^{7} Tj^{1} Tr^{2} परिवर्जयेत् — c) Ho यावतीं; TMd^{3} साभवे°; Bo संभवद्वृ°; GMd^{1} संभवेवृ°; GMy °वेद्वृद्धिं तावतीं; BKt^{5} °वेद्वृद्धि तावतीं — d) BKt^{5} TMd^{4} °स्तावती; Bo °वतीं परिवर्तयेत्

156. Cited by *Lakṣ* 12.328; *Dev* 3.370 — a) NKt^{4} °वृद्धिः; Be^{3} BKt^{5} Lo^{1} TMd^{4} °वृद्धि — b) Lo^{1} TMd^{3} देशकालौ — c) wKt^{3} अभिक्राम°; Tj^{1} °क्रामान्देश°; Lo^{1} °क्रामं देश°; Tr^{2} °कामं देश°; Hy °क्रमन्देश°; Be^{3} °क्रमे देश°; Be^{3} BKt^{5} °कालो — d) Ox^{2} Pu^{3} Pu^{8} Tr^{2} तद्धनमवा°

157. Cited by *Lakṣ* 12.283; *Dev* 3.471 — a) TMd^{3} TMd^{4} °याने; TMd^{4} °यानकोशादि; Wa °कुशलो; MTr^{6} °कुशलान् — b) TMd^{3} °दर्शनं — c) Wa स्थापयन्ते; Tr^{2} स्थापयन्तु; GMd^{1} स्वापवन्ति; La^{1} Lo^{1} च; TMd^{3} तु या; Jm NKt^{4} BKt^{5} GMd^{1} MTr^{4} तु तां; TMd^{4} तु वां; oOr तया वृद्धिं — c-d) *Dev* नियच्छेयुः भृतिं यां तु सा स्यात्प्रागकृता यदि — d) oOr sOx^{1} स; NPu^{1} तथाधिगमं

158.* Cited by *Dev* 3.348; *Mādh* 3.185 — a) Pu^{4} ये; Be^{3} यो यत्र; GMd^{1} यो यस्य च प्रभुस्ति°; TMd^{4} Tj^{1} प्रतिभू तिष्ठे° — b) wKt^{3} °नाय ह; TMd^{4} °नाय हि; wKt^{1} Tj^{1} °नायेन; sOx^{1} मानवाः [*but cor*] — c) GMd^{1} अदर्शयंस्तु तत्तस्य; BBe^{2} wKt^{1} Lo^{1} अदर्शयन्शतं तस्य; GMd^{5} नादर्शयत्स; Tr^{2} ते तस्य; *Mādh* तं तत्र; TMd^{3} तस्तस्य; TMd^{4} ततस्य — d) Be^{3} Wa यच्छेत स्व°; Be^{1} BBe^{2} Bo Ho wKt^{3} NKt^{4} BKt^{5} La^{1} NNg oOr sOx^{1} Ox^{2} NPu^{1} Pu^{2} Pu^{3} Pu^{4} Pu^{5} sPu^{6} Pu^{7} Tr^{2} [*Jolly* M G Ku] *Me Go Ku Jolly Jha Dave* यतेत स्व°; BCa Lo^{1} Pu^{8} प्रयच्छेत धना°

159. Cited by *Lakṣ* 12.315; *Dev* 3.397; *Mādh* 3.198 — a) Bo प्रतिभव्यं; Ho BKt^{5} प्रतिभाव्यं; BCa प्रतिभाव्य; BBe^{2} तथादान°; NKt^{4} °दातुमाक्षिकं; Kt^{2} °दान आक्षिकं — b) Be^{3} wKt^{1} Kt^{2} Pu^{2} Pu^{3} Pu^{4} °दानं साक्षिकं; Be^{1} GMd^{1} °दानं माक्षिकं; TMd^{4} [lacuna] माक्षिकं च यत्; BKt^{5} °दानमाक्षिप्तं; *Mādh* च तत् — c) Hy दण्ड्य°; Ox^{2} दण्डशेषावशुल्कं; GMy °ल्कावशीर्षं; TMd^{3} °ल्काविशेषं; [*Jolly* Nd] *Lakṣ Dev VaDh* 16.31 °ल्कावशिष्टं — d) Wa तु पुत्रो; TMd^{4} पुत्रा

160. Pāda-d omitted in GMd^{5} [haplo]. Cited by *Lakṣ* 12.315; pādas a-b cited by *Dev* 3.397; pādas c-d cited by *Lakṣ* 12.305; *Dev* 3.355 — a) TMd^{4} दर्शनः; Tr^{2} दर्शनाप्रति°; Bo La^{1} Lo^{2} Lo^{3} TMd^{4} sOx^{1} sPu^{6} Tj^{1} Tj^{2} °प्रतिभाव्ये; wKt^{3} Lo^{1} °भावे; Pu^{5} Pu^{7} °भाव्यो; TMd^{3} GMy °भाव्यं — b) *Lakṣ* विधिः पूवप्रचोदितः; TMd^{3} °चोदितं; NNg Pu^{5} Pu^{7} Tr^{2} °नोदितः; Hy °तोदितः; La^{1} Pu^{2} Pu^{4} °दर्शितः — c) Lo^{1} [*but cor*] Pu^{2} Pu^{4} °भुवे — d) sOx^{1} °दानपि च दापयेत्

अदातरि पुनर्दाता विज्ञातप्रकृतावृणम् ।
पश्चात्प्रतिभुवि प्रेते परीप्सेत्केन हेतुना ॥१६१॥
निरादिष्टधनश्चेत्तु प्रतिभूः स्यादलंधनः ।
स्वधनादेव तद्दद्यान्निरादिष्ट इति स्थितिः ॥१६२॥
मत्तोन्मत्तार्ताध्यधीनैर्बालेन स्थविरेण वा ।
असंबद्धकृतश्चैव व्यवहारो न सिध्यति ॥१६३॥
सत्या न भाषा भवति यद्यपि स्यात् प्रतिष्ठिता ।
बहिश्चेद्भाष्यते धर्मान्नियताद्व्यावहारिकात् ॥१६४॥
योगाधमनविक्रीतं योगदानप्रतिग्रहम् ।
यत्र वाप्युपधिं पश्येत् तत्सर्वं विनिवर्तयेत् ॥१६५॥
ग्रहीता यदि नष्टः स्यात् कुटुम्बे च कृतो व्ययः ।

161. Omitted in wKt^{1}; pādas a-c omitted in GMd^{5}. Cited by *Dev* 3.353 — a) Bo BKt^{5} Lo^{3} आदातरि; Tr^{2} पुनर्दत्त — b) oOr विज्ञातप्रकृतादृणं; Tr^{2} विज्ञातः प्रकृतादृणं; Lo^{1} विज्ञातं प्रकृतमृणं; TMd^{3} TMd^{4} GMy विज्ञाताप्रतिकृतावृणं; Be^{3} विज्ञान°; MTr^{5} निधिज्ञाताप्रकृ°; BKt^{5} °प्राकृतावृणं — c) Jo^{2} °त्प्रातभुवि; MTr^{5} °भुव — d) BKt^{5} परीप्स्ये°; MTr^{3} परीप्सेत्तेन; Lo^{1} परीक्षेत्केन; Bo °प्सेत्केन हेन च

162. Omitted in wKt^{1}. Cited by *Lakṣ* 12.306; *Dev* 3.353 — a) Lo^{1} निरादिवृधनश्चेत्तु; TMd^{4} निरादिष्टं धनं चेत्तु; GMd^{1} निरादिश्वधनश्चेत्तु; Pu^{3} निरादृष्ट°; Kt^{2} °धनञ्चेत्तुः; Jo^{2} Lo^{3} Tj^{1} °धनश्चेह — b) MTr^{6} [*Jolly* Nd] स्यादलक्षितः; Bo °धनाः; La^{1} GMd^{1} TMd^{3} TMd^{4} GMd^{5} GMy Pu^{3} MTr^{4} °धनं — c) La^{1} TMd^{3} तं दद्यान्नि° — d) Ho °दिष्ट प्रतिस्थितिः; Lo^{1} TMd^{4} स्थितः

163. Omitted in Pu^{5}. Cited by *Dev* 3.301; *Mādh* 3.162 — a) GMd^{1} मत्तोन्मत्तान्धबधिरैर्बालेन; NPu^{1} मत्तोन्मत्तैर्व्याधितैर्वा बालेन; TMd^{4} मदोन्मत्तव्याधितापैर्बालेन; MTr^{4} MTr^{6} मत्तोन्मत्तानित्यरोगी बालेन; GMd^{5} °त्तार्तव्यधी°; *Dev* °त्तार्तद्यधीनैः बालेन; *Mādh* °त्तार्त्तव्यसनिबालेन; Be^{1} Bo Lo^{1} sOx^{1} Pu^{3} sPu^{6} Pu^{8} Tj^{2} Wa °त्तव्याधितार्तैर्बालेन [Lo^{1} sPu^{6} °धिनार्तैर्बालेन; Wa °धिनार्ते बालेन]; Be^{3} °त्ताद्याध्यधीनैर्बालेन; Tr^{2} °त्तार्तव्याधिनैः बालेन; BBe^{2} °त्ताध्यधीनैर्बालेन; Pu^{2} Pu^{4} °त्तविधेनेव बालेन; wKt^{1} °त्ताध्यधीनैर्वा बालेन — a-b) NKt^{4} मत्तोन्मत्तार्तव्यसनीबालभीतप्रयोजितः; GMy मत्तोन्मत्ता [lacuna] स्थविरेण वा; TMd^{3} मत्तोन्मन्तागन्तुर्भिर्वालेशस्थविरेण वा — b) Wa °धीनैर्बल्येन; Ho NPu^{1} Tj^{1} च — c) La^{1} Lo^{1} TMd^{3} sOx^{1} sPu^{6} Tr^{1} MTr^{3} असंबन्ध°; Kt^{2} °कृतञ्चैव

164. Cited by *Lakṣ* 12.270; *Dev* 3.90 — a) *Dev* सभ्या भाषा न भवति; GMd^{1} सात्या; wKt^{3} सत्त्वा; TMd^{3} सत्या व; Pu^{5} Pu^{7} [*Jolly* G] भाषा न सत्या; GMy भाष्या; MTr^{6} भवती — b) Pu^{5} प्रतिष्ठितः; Be^{3} प्रतिष्ठितं — c) TMd^{4} बलं चेद्भा°; Be^{3} Ox^{2} Tr^{2} °द्भाषते; MTr^{6} °द्भासते; Bo °द्भाषयेद्धर्मा°; TMd^{4} °द्भाष्यति धर्मं निय°; Tr^{1} धर्म्यान्नि° — d) Be^{3} TMd^{3} GMy °यतान्व्या°; Tr^{1} MTr^{4} MTr^{6} *Nd* °यमाद्व्या°; Be^{3} GMy °हारिकान्

165. Cited by *Vij* 2.176; *Lakṣ* 12.271; *Dev* 3.305 454; *Mādh* 3.162, 229–30 — a) MTr^{4} MTr^{6} योगासनमविक्रीतं; GMd^{1} योगाधनं च विक्रीतं; TMd^{4} योगादमन°; Lo^{1} योगाधयन°; Pu^{2} Pu^{4} योगाध्यापन°; Hy योगाभमन°; NPu^{1} योगार्द्धयन°; Wa योगाधमेन°; GMd^{5} °विक्रीत; Ho °चिक्रीत — a-b) GMy नियमात्समयात् [lacuna] दानप्रतिग्रहः — b) GMd^{1} TMd^{3} TMd^{4} GMd^{5} योगादान° — c) *Vij* यस्य; Bo BKt^{5} Lo^{2} GMd^{1} Pu^{3} Pu^{5} Pu^{7} Tr^{1} MTr^{4} [*Jolly* M G] *Vij* चाप्युपधिं; GMd^{1} वाप्यवधिं; La^{1} वाप्यपधिं; wKt^{1} वाप्यपरं; TMd^{4} पश्ये; TMd^{3} पश्य — d) BKt^{5} GMd^{1} Pu^{8} विनिवर्तते

दातव्यं बान्धवैस्तत्स्यात् प्रविभक्तैरपि स्वतः ॥१६६॥
कुटुम्बार्थेऽध्यधीनोऽपि व्यवहारं यमाचरेत् ।
स्वदेशे वा विदेशे वा तं ज्यायान्न विचालयेत् ॥१६७॥
बलाद्दत्तं बलाद्भुक्तं बलाद्यच्चापि लेखितम् ।
सर्वान्बलकृतानर्थानकृतान्मनुरब्रवीत् ॥१६८॥
त्रयः परार्थे क्लिश्यन्ति साक्षिणः प्रतिभूः कुलम् ।
चत्वारस्तूपचीयन्ते विप्र आढ्यो वणिङ्‌ नृपः ॥१६९॥
अनादेयं नाददीत परिक्षीणोऽपि पार्थिवः ।
न चादेयं समृद्धोऽपि सूक्ष्ममप्यर्थमुत्सृजेत् ॥१७०॥
अनादेयस्य चादानादादेयस्य च वर्जनात् ।
दौर्बल्यं ख्याप्यते राज्ञः स प्रेत्येह च नश्यति ॥१७१॥

166.* Pādas a-b omitted in Ca. Cited by *Apa* 647; *Lakṣ* 12.313; *Dev* 3.411 — a) Bo ग्रहीत; Hy Jm La[1] Lo[3] TMd[3] Pu[5] Pu[7] MTr[6] गृहीता; sOx[1] sPu[6] Tr[2] गृहीतः; Lo[1] गृहीतं; Lo[1] यदि निर्दिष्टं स्यात्; Tr[2] नष्टं — b) TMd[3] GMy कुटुम्बार्थे तथा परैः; *Apa* [vl] कुटुम्बी; BBe[2] BCa Hy Jm Jo[1] Jo[2] wKt[1] Kt[2] wKt[3] Lo[2] GMd[5] Ox[2] Tj[2] MTr[3] [*Jolly* Ku R Nd] *Nā Rn Rc Dave Mandlik KSS* कुटुम्बार्थे कृतो; La[1] कुटुम्बं चेकृतो; Lo[1] *om* च; Bo तु; BBe[2] Hy *Apa* कृत — c) Be[3] GMd[1] TMd[3] GMy बान्धवैस्तस्य; *Apa* बान्धवैस्तस्मात्; BKt[5] बान्धवैस्तस्याप्रवि° — d) Jo[2] प्रविभक्तधनैरपि; *Apa* प्रविभक्तधनैः स्वतः; Tr[2] °त्स्यान्न विभक्तैरपि; oOr °त्स्यादविभक्तैरपि; NPu[1] प्रतिभक्तैरपि; NNg °भक्तिरपि; *Dev* स्मृतः; *Apa* [vl] सुतः; wKt[1] सुतैः

167. Pāda-d omitted in Pu[5]. Cited by *Lakṣ* 12.314; *Dev* 3.308, 410; *Mādh* 3.164 — a) Tj[1] °म्बार्थो; GMy °धधीनो; *Mādh* °प्यधीनो; wKt[1] GMd[1] NPu[1] °व्यधीनो; MTr[4] MTr[6] ह्यधीनो; GMd[5] नधीनो; *Dev* त्वधीनो; Pu[5] Pu[7] [*Jolly* G] °त्यधीनो वा — b) Pu[5] Pu[7] °हारमाचरन्; wKt[3] La[1] TMd[3] TMd[4] NPu[1] Pu[2] Pu[5] Pu[7] Tr[2] MTr[4] MTr[6] [*Jolly* Gr] *Dev Mādh* समाचरेत्; [*Jolly* G] समाचरन् — c) NPu[1] वापि देशे; GMd[1] वाप्यदेशे; TMd[4] विदिशे — d) Pu[7] [*Jolly* G] तमायान्तं विलम्बयेत्; GMd[1] GMd[5] GMy तज्ज्यायान्न; *Dev* तन्न्यायान्न; TMd[4] ज्यायां न; Bo ज्यायान्त; *Lakṣ* विद्वान्न; BBe[2] Be[3] wKt[1] NKt[4] La[1] GMd[1] TMd[3] TMd[4] GMy NPu[1] Tr[1] [*but mc fh*] MTr[4] MTr[5] MTr[6] [*Jolly* Nd] *Nd Rc Bh* विचारयेत्; GMd[5] विपालयेत्

168. Omitted in Pu[5]; pādas c-d omitted in Pu[2] Pu[4]. Cited by *Lakṣ* 12.271 — b) [*Jolly* M] बलाद्यदपि; TMd[4] बलाद्यश्चापि — c) TMd[4] सर्वानलंकृ°; GMd[1] °न्बलात्कृता° — c-d) La[1] सर्वान्बलकृतार्थानकृतार्थान्मनुरब्रवीत् — d) wKt[1] BKt[5] [*Jolly* M] °नर्थान्निवर्त्यान्मनु°

169. a) TMd[3] त्रयोपरार्थे; Bo यत्रापरार्थे; Lo[1] TMd[3] NNg Pu[5] Pu[7] Tr[1] Wa [*Jolly* G] क्लिश्यन्ते; Tr[2] श्लिश्यन्ति — c) TMd[3] चत्वारं तूप°; BCa NKt[4] Jo[2] Lo[3] oOr Pu[2] Pu[4] Tj[1] Wa °रश्चोपचीयन्ते; Be[3] °रस्त्वपचीयन्ते — d) Pu[5] Pu[7] [*Jolly* G] विप्रश्चाढ्यो; Tr[2] आख्यो; Ho आद्यो; Hy अद्यो; Lo[1] आप्तो; TMd[3] वणिक्प्रदः; TMd[4] MTr[5] नृपो वणिक्

170. Omitted in Lo[3]. Cited by *Lakṣ* 11.93 — a) Tr[2] अनादेयस्य यादतीत; Be[1] अनादीयं; BBe[2] अनादेशं; TMd[3] नवादेयं; sOx[1] sPu[6] अनादीयान्नाद°; TMd[4] नादधीत — b) GMy परिक्षीणापि — c) Bo तवादेयं; Pu[3] वादेयं; MTr[6] च देयं

171. Cited by *Lakṣ* 11.94 — a) NPu[1] वादाना°; Lo[1] चादाता आदेयस्य — b) sOx[1] sPu[6] °नाद्देयस्य च विवर्जनात्; Bo [*mc to*] wKt[1] NPu[1] Tr[1] °यस्य विवर्जनात्; Ox[2] °यस्य विसर्जनात्; MTr[5] *om* च; TMd[3]

स्वादानाद्वर्णसंसर्गाद् दुर्बलानां च रक्षणात् ।
बलं संजायते राज्ञः स प्रेत्येह च वर्धते ॥१७२॥
तस्माद्यम इव स्वामी स्वयं हित्वा प्रियाप्रिये ।
वर्तेत याम्यया वृत्त्या जितक्रोधो जितेन्द्रियः ॥१७३॥
यस्त्वधर्मेण कार्याणि मोहात्कुर्यान्नराधिपः ।
अचिरात्तं दुरात्मानं वशे कुर्वन्ति शत्रवः ॥१७४॥
कामक्रोधौ तु संयम्य योऽर्थान्धर्मेण पश्यति ।
प्रजास्तमनुवर्तन्ते समुद्रमिव सिन्धवः ॥१७५॥
यः साधयन्तं छन्देन वेदयेद्धनिकं नृपे ।
स राज्ञा तच्चतुर्भागं दाप्यस्तस्य च तद्धनम् ॥१७६॥

वर्जयेत् — c) MTr^{6} ख्यायते; Be^{3} Ho La^{1} ख्यापते; GMd^{1} न्यायते; TMd^{3} TMd^{4} GMd^{5} जायते; TMd^{4} राज्ञां — d) La^{1} Tr^{1} प्रेत्य चेह च नश्यति; *Lakṣ* प्रेत्येह विनश्यति; Lo^{2} Pu^{4} न पश्यति

172. Omitted in GMd^{1}. Cited by *Lakṣ* 11.94 — a) Be^{1} Be^{3} स्वदाना°; Tr^{2} स्यादाना°; TMd^{4} सादाना°; BBe^{2} Jo^{2} Pu^{8} Tj^{1} *Nā Rn Mr* आदाना°; La^{1} अदाना°; Be^{3} Ho Hy Jo^{2} Lo^{3} NPu^{1} Pu^{2} Pu^{4} sOx^{1} Ox^{2} sPu^{6} Tj^{1} [*Jolly* M] *Rn* °नाद्धर्मसंसर्गाद्; *Nd* °नाद्वर्णसंश्लेषाद्; *Bh Me* [pāṭha] °नाद्वर्णासंसर्गाद्; wKt^{1} °नाद्वर्णसंज्ञा — b) Jm Jo^{1} Kt^{2} Lo^{3} *Mandlik Jha KSS Dave* °सर्गात्त्वबलानां; wKt^{1} °सर्गात्तु दुर्बलानां; BCa दुर्बलस्य; Bo wKt^{3} लक्षणात्; TMd^{4} रक्षणे — c) Be^{1} Lo^{1} Pu^{5} Pu^{7} बलवान्व्याप्यते राजा; Lo^{2} बलवान्व्याथते राजा; wKt^{1} Pu^{2} Pu^{4} संज्ञायते; Wa संवर्धते — d) Tr^{1} प्रेत्य चेह च वर्धते; La^{1} प्रेत्येचेह च वर्धते; Wa प्रेत्य चेह च नश्यति; TMd^{4} वर्धयेत्; Bo बद्धते

173. a) sOx^{1} sPu^{6} तस्माद्यम [lacuna] च स्वामी; La^{1} इति; TMd^{3} स्वामि — b) TMd^{4} स्वयहेत्वा; Be^{1} Bo हत्वा; La^{1} हृत्वा; Tr^{2} प्रियाप्रियो; Ho प्रियेप्रिये; TMd^{3} प्रियाप्रिया — c) TMd^{3} वर्तते; Tr^{2} याम्याया; TMd^{4} याम्ययो

174. Pādas c-d omitted in Pu^{5}. Cited by *Lakṣ* 12.17 — a) TMd^{4} NPu^{1} यस्तु धर्मेण; Pu^{2} Pu^{4} स्वस्त्वधर्मेण; La^{1} यत्स्वधर्मेण; Lo^{1} यस्य धर्मेण; Wa यश्चाधर्मेण; MTr^{5} यं च धर्मं च— b) Be^{3} Ho Jo^{2} BKt^{5} Lo^{1} Lo^{3} sOx^{1} NPu^{1} Pu^{2} Pu^{4} Pu^{5} sPu^{6} Pu^{7} Tj^{1} [*Jolly* M G R] *Jolly* कुर्यान्मोहान्नराधिपः; Be^{1} Bo Pu^{3} Pu^{8} Tr^{2} कुर्यान्मोहान्महीपतिः — c) BBe^{2} GMd^{5} दुराचारं — d) Pu^{7} [*Jolly* G] वश्यं; oOr वशा; Be^{1} La^{1} Lo^{3} Tj^{1} वशी; GMd^{5} वशं; Jo^{1} Tr^{1} वंशे; TMd^{3} दशे; BKt^{5} वशेत्कुर्वन्ति; *Lakṣ* जन्तवः

175. Cited by *Lakṣ* 12.11; *Dev* 3.289— a) Be^{3} Ho Jo^{2} BKt^{5} La^{1} Lo^{1} Lo^{3} GMd^{1} TMd^{3} GMy sOx^{1} Pu^{5} sPu^{6} Pu^{7} Tj^{1} [*Jolly* G] च — b) TMd^{3} GMy Tr^{1} *Dev* योर्थं धर्मेण; TMd^{4} Wa योर्थधर्मेण; *Lakṣ* यथा धर्मेण — c) NKt^{4} °नुवर्तेते — d) TMd^{3} समुद्र इव

176. Cited by *Lakṣ* 12.330; *Dev* 3.286; *Mādh* 3.152 — a) TMd^{4} यः सार्धयन्तं न छन्देन; Pu^{5} Tj^{1} *om* यः; BKt^{5} साधयन्छन्देन; GMd^{5} साधयन्तश्छन्देन; *Mādh* सोधयन्स्वच्छन्देन; wKt^{3} छन्देव; Jo^{2} Lo^{3} छेदेन — a-b) *Bh* [pāṭha] योऽसाध्यं मन्यमानस्तु वेदयेद्धनिकं नरः — b) La^{1} स्वेदयेद्धनिकवन्नृपे; GMy वदये°; Hy TMd^{3} वेदयद्धनिकं; MTr^{5} वेदयन्धनिकं; wKt^{1} Lo^{3} नृप; Pu^{8} नृपो; TMd^{4} नृपं — c) Tr^{1} स तु राज्ञा चतु°; TMd^{4} सर्वाज्ञश्च चतु°; Be^{1} राजा; BKt^{5} GMd^{1} राज्ञास्तच्चतु°; Hy Jo^{2} BKt^{5} Lo^{1} Lo^{3} GMd^{1} sOx^{1} Ox^{2} sPu^{6} Tj^{1} [*Jolly* R] राज्ञा तु चतु°; GMd^{5} NPu^{1} MTr^{6} राज्ञश्च चतु°; oOr राज्ञस्तु चतु°; Be^{3} राज्ञा च चतु°; GMy राज्ञस्स चतु°; TMd^{3} राज्ञस्स्य चतु°; Hy राजा तु चतु°; La^{1} राजं तु चतु°; Bo NKt^{4} NNg Pu^{2} Pu^{3} Pu^{4} Pu^{5} Tj^{2} Tr^{2} Wa [*Jolly* G] *Bh* [pāṭha] *Dev Mādh* राज्ञर्णचतु°; Lo^{2} राज्ञार्णं चतु° — d) Lo^{1} दाप्यतस्तस्य तद्धनं; GMd^{1} दास्यस्तस्य; Jo^{2} Lo^{3} Tj^{1} Tr^{1} दाप्यं तस्य; Pu^{5} Pu^{7} दाप्यर्थं तस्य; Tr^{2} दाप्यस्तस्यैव च; Pu^{5} Pu^{7} *om* च

कर्मणापि समं कुर्याद् धनिकायाधमर्णिकः ।
समोऽवकृष्टजातिश्च दद्याच्छ्रेयांस्तु तच्छनैः ॥१७७॥
अनेन विधिना राजा मिथो विवदतां नृणाम् ।
साक्षिप्रत्ययसिद्धानि कार्याणि समतां नयेत् ॥१७८॥
कुलजे वृत्तसंपन्ने धर्मज्ञे सत्यवादिनि ।
महापक्षे धनिन्यार्ये निक्षेपं निक्षिपेद्बुधः ॥१७९॥
यो यथा निक्षिपेद्धस्ते यमर्थं यस्य मानवः ।
स तथैव ग्रहीतव्यो यथा दायस्तथा ग्रहः ॥१८०॥
यो निक्षेपं याच्यमानो निक्षेप्तुर्न प्रयच्छति ।
स याच्यः प्राड्विवाकेन तन्निक्षेप्तुरसंनिधौ ॥१८१॥
साक्ष्यभावे प्रणिधिभिर्वयोरूपसमन्वितैः ।
अपदेशैश्च संन्यस्य हिरण्यं तस्य तत्त्वतः ॥१८२॥

177. Omitted in Wa. Cited by *Vij* 2.43; *Apa*647; *Lakṣ* 12.326 — a) Tj^{1} कर्मण्यापि; Lo^{3} कर्मण्येपि; TMd^{4} मनः कुर्याद् — b) Tr^{2} धनिकायचमर्णिकः; Lo^{1} Lo^{2} Tr^{1} *Lakṣ Apa* धनिकस्याधम°; Tj^{2} धनिको वाधम°; *Vij* धनिकेनाधम°; La^{1} वणिकम्याधम°; TMd^{4} °मर्णिकं — c) Be^{3} समाव°; WKt^{1} WKt^{3} Lo^{2} Tr^{1} MTr^{5} *Vij* °पकृष्ट°; *Apa* [vl] °वोत्कृष्ट°; Hy Jm Jo^{1} Jo^{2} WKt^{1} Kt^{2} BKt^{5} Lo^{3} Pu^{4} Tj^{1} Tj^{2} MTr^{3} [*Jolly* R] *Mandlik Jha KSS Dave* °जातिस्तु; Ox^{2} °जातिश्चेद्दद्या° — d) Be^{1} श्रेयान्दद्यात्तु; Pu^{5} Pu^{7} [*Jolly* G] °यांश्च; GMd^{1} तद्धनैः; Ho तच्छमैः

178. Pādas b-d omitted in Pu^{5}. Cited by *Lakṣ* 12.769 — a) NNg राज्ञा — b) Kt^{2} मिथ्यो; BBe^{2} NPu^{1} Pu^{2} Pu^{4} *Lakṣ* मिथ्या; Kt^{2} Tj^{1} विवदता; Bo विचरता; Be^{1} Be^{3} NKt^{4} BKt^{5} Lo^{1} Lo^{2} GMd^{1} TMd^{3} TMd^{4} GMd^{5} GMy OOr Ox^{2} Pu^{2} Pu^{4} Pu^{7} Tr^{1} MTr^{6} *Go* [*Jolly* G Nd] विवदमानयोः [*om* नृणां] — c) GMy °विद्धानि — d) Ho शमतां; Bo समती; GMy समदां

179. Cited by *Lakṣ* 12.339; *Dev* 3.415; *Mādh* 3.204 — a) Ho कुलेजे; Tr^{2} वृत्ति°; Be^{1} वित्त°; Lo^{1} सत्यसंपन्ने; WKt^{1} वित्तसंबन्धे — b) GMy the pāda reads: [lacuna] धर्मवानिति; MTr^{6} °वादिनी — c) TMd^{3} GMy महापदि; Tr^{2} धनिन्यर्थे; Be^{1} Pu^{5} Pu^{7} धनिन्यार्थे; TMd^{3} धनिन्याये; Tr^{1} धनिन्याय्ये; Hy धनिनार्ये; *Dev* धनिन्याप्ते; NNg धनिन्यार्यो; Pu^{2} Pu^{4} च नित्यार्थे — d) NKt^{4} *om* निक्षेपं; BKt^{5} निःक्षेपं निःक्षिपे°

180. Cited by *Lakṣ* 12.341; *Dev* 3.422; *Mādh* 3.205 — a) TMd^{3} ये; Bo निक्षयेद्धस्ते; Jo^{1} निक्षिपद्धस्ते; *Lakṣ* निक्षिपेद्वस्तु; WKt^{1} निक्षेप्युस्ते — b) GMy यमर्थ; TMd^{3} यदर्थं; SOx^{1} SPu^{6} धर्मार्थं; GMd^{1} यस्स मानवः — c) BCa Bo Ho Jm WKt^{1} WKt^{3} NKt^{4} Lo^{3} TMd^{3} SOx^{1} Pu^{2} Pu^{4} Pu^{5} SPu^{6} Pu^{7} Tj^{1} Tr^{1} Tr^{2} गृहीतव्यो; Hy Lo^{1} गृहीतव्यौ; MTr^{6} °तव्ये — d) GMy दायं तथा; Lo^{2} TMd^{3} TMd^{4} Ox^{2} Pu^{5} Pu^{7} [*Jolly* G Nd] दानं तथा; MTr^{6} देयस्तथा; GMy OOrग्रहं; TMd^{3} गृहं; Tr^{1} गृहः

181.* For the varying sequences of verses 181–199 see endnote. Cited by *Apa* 664; *Lakṣ* 12.346 — a) NKt^{4} निक्षेपो; BKt^{5} निःक्षेपं; GMd^{5} याच्यमाने; *Apa* याच्यमानं — b) BKt^{5} निःक्षेप्तुर्न; Be^{1} BBe^{2} निक्षिप्तुर्न; TMd^{4} निक्षेपं न; *Apa* निक्षेप्त्रे न; Pu^{4} निक्षेतुं न — c) GMd^{5} Tr^{2} MTr^{4} MTr^{6} *Apa* [vl] वाच्यः; Pu^{5} Pu^{7} MTr^{5} प्राग्विवा°; Tr^{2} प्राज्विवा°; BBe^{2} Ho प्राड्विपाकेन — d) La^{1} NPu^{1} Pu^{2} Pu^{4} तं निक्षे°; Lo^{3} °संनिधा

182. Omitted in BKt^{5}; placed after 184 in Be^{1} Be^{3} Bo BCa NKt^{4} La^{1} Lo^{2} GMd^{5} NNg OOr SOx^{1} Ox^{2} SPu^{6} Pu^{8} Tr^{2} MTr^{5} *Go* [in the pratīkas], and after 183 in Wa. Cited by *Lakṣ* 12.346 — a) Jo^{2} Tr^{2} प्रनधि°; GMd^{1} TMd^{3} GMd^{5} GMy MTr^{5} प्रतिनिधिं वयो°; La^{1} प्रतिनिधिर्द्वयोरू° — b) Lo^{2}

स यदि प्रतिपद्येत यथान्यस्तं यथाकृतम् ।
न तत्र विद्यते किंचिद् यत्परैरभियुज्यते ॥१८३॥
तेषां न दद्याद्यदि तु तद्धिरण्यं यथाविधि ।
उभौ निगृह्य दाप्यः स्यादिति धर्मस्य धारणा ॥१८४॥
निक्षेपोपनिधी नित्यं न देयौ प्रत्यनन्तरे ।
नश्यतो विनिपाते तावनिपाते त्वनाशिनौ ॥१८५॥
स्वयमेव तु यो दद्यान्मृतस्य प्रत्यनन्तरे ।
न स राज्ञाभियोक्तव्यो न निक्षेप्तुश्च बन्धुभिः ॥१८६॥

GMd^1 TMd^3 GMd^5 GMy MTr^4 MTr^5 MTr^6 °समन्वितं; TMd^4 °समन्वितः — c) GMd^5 व्यपदे°; Be^1 Be^3 Lo^1 NPu^1 Pu^2 Pu^4 °देशैस्तु; BBe^2 °देशश्च; GMd^1 °देशे स; TMd^4 °देश्येत्य; Pu^5 Pu^7 °देशैः स्वयं न्यस्य; Wa °देशैः संन्यस्य; [*Jolly* Nd] सत्यस्य; Be^3 यद्यस्य; Be^1 NPu^1 Pu^2 Pu^4 संन्यसेद्धिरण्यं — d) Bo BCa Jo^2 WKt^1 WKt^3 La^1 Lo^1 Lo^3 SOx^1 Ox^2 Pu^3 Pu^5 SPu^6 Pu^7 Pu^8 Tj^1 Tr^2 Wa [*Jolly* G] *Rn* तेषु; BBe^2 Ho Lo^2 GMd^1 TMd^4 Tr^1 MTr^6 तत्र; *Lakṣ* सारतः

183. Omitted in Pu^5 Pu^7. Cited by *Apa* 664; *Lakṣ* 12.347 — a) TMd^4 प्रतिपद्यातं; GMd^1 प्रतिनन्द्यात्तं; TMd^3 GMd^5 GMy [*Jolly* Nd Gr]प्रतिदद्यात्तु; Tr^1 प्रतिदद्येत — a-b) MTr^4 MTr^6 स यदि प्रतिभूर्दद्यादन्यथा तं यथाकृतं — b) GMd^5 यथान्यस्तस्तथाकृतं; TMd^4 यथान्यस्तु; Lo^1 यथाहृतं; GMd^1 यथा-श्रुतं; *Apa* यथाक्रमं; *Apa* [vl] तथाहतं — c) La^1 विद्यात्किंचिद् — d) *Apa* [vl] यत्परैरतियुज्यते; SOx^1 SPu^6 यत्परैरपि युज्यते; GMd^5 Tr^1 यत्परेणाभियुज्यते; TMd^3 GMy यत्परेणाभिपूज्यते; GMd^1 यत्परेण वियुज्यते; MTr^4 MTr^6 यत्परेणापि भुज्यते; Be^3 परैर्यदभिभूयते

184. Omitted in TMd^3 Pu^5 Pu^7. Cited by *Apa* 664; *Lakṣ* 12.347; *Dev* 3.423; *Mādh* 3.209 — a) GMd^5 MTr^4 MTr^6 न दद्यात्तस्य यदि तु; Tr^1 *ma* तेषां; *Mādh* येषां; Be^3 तेषां च —a-b) GMd^1 न दद्यात्तस्य यद्दातु तद्धिरण्यं यथाविधि; OOr तेषां न दद्यादथ चेद्धिरण्यं तु यथाविधि — b) BKt^5 यथानिधि — c) BKt^5 Lo^2 Wa [*Jolly* M N] *Nā Jolly* संनिगृह्योभयं दाप्य इति; *Dave Jha* स निगृह्योभयं दाप्य इति; GMd^1 उभयं निगृह्य; NKt^4 उभयं गृह्य; GMd^5 भयं निगृह्य; *Dev Lakṣ* द्वयं निगृह्य; *Apa* स्वयं निगृह्य; *Mādh* इत्थं निगृह्य; TMd^4 द्वयं संगृह्य; Be^1 Be^3 Ho La^1 SOx^1 Ox^2 NPu^1 SPu^6 [*Jolly* Nd] उपसंगृह्य; BCa संगृह्य; WKt^1 गृह *mc* संगृह्य; *Dev* दाप्यं; MTr^4 MTr^6 याप्यः; Lo^1 दातव्यः — d) Lo^1 स्याद्धर्मस्य च धारणा; Tr^1 धारिणा; TMd^4 दारुणः

185. Pādas c-d *ma sh* in Be^3. Cited by *Lakṣ* 12.342 — a) Tr^2 निक्षेप्यो निधिर्नित्यं; Lo^1 GMd^5 °निधिं; Bo °निधिर्नित्यं; Pu^2 Pu^4 °निधीन्नित्यं — b) Be^1 BBe^2 TMd^3 NPu^1 देयो; TMd^4 दिया; Bo प्रत्यनुत्तरे; Pu^4 °नन्तरो; Lo^3 Tj^1 °नन्तरं — c) Pu^2 Pu^4 Pu^5 Pu^7 MTr^4 MTr^5 MTr^6 नश्येतां; NPu^1 नश्येता; TMd^3 OOr नश्यते; TMd^4 नश्यति; WKt^3 नयष्ट; La^1 नश्यतोपिनिपाते — c-d) MTr^4 MTr^6 °पाते च अनिपाते; GMd^1 °पाते न विनिपाते; Be^3 °पाते न त्वनिपाते; TMd^3 °पाते तौ विनिपाते; Pu^5 Pu^7 °पाते वा विनिपाते; Wa *om* तावनिपाते — d) SOx^1 SPu^6 °निपा [lacuna] तैनाशिनौ; Tr^2 °निपात्ये; WKt^1 °निपाता; WKt^3 °पातेन त्वना°; TMd^4 त्वनाशनौ; Tj^1 त्वनाशितौ; Pu^5 Pu^7 त्वनासितौ; GMd^5 तु नाशनं; Pu^4 च नाशिनौ; TMd^3 च साशनौ

186. Pādas a-b *ma sh* in Be^3. Cited by *Lakṣ* 12.342; *Dev* 3.424 — a) Bo स्वयमेवं; BKt^5 यैर्दद्या° — b) Tr^2 प्रत्यन्वतरे; Lo^1 °नन्तरं — c) GMd^1 TMd^3 TMd^4 GMy MTr^4 MTr^6 स राज्ञा नाभियोक्तव्यो [MTr^4 राज्ञाभियों°; MTr^6 न नियों°]; Lo^1 न च; Wa राज्ञोभि°; Tr^1 राज्ञा [*ma sh* भि] योक्तव्यो; Hy Jm Jo^1 Kt^2 Ox^2 MTr^3 *Mandlik KSS* राज्ञा नियोक्तव्यो — d) TMd^4 स क्षिपेद्यच्च बन्धुभिः; Be^1 न निक्षेप्तुर्न बन्धुभिः; TMd^3 विनिक्षिप्तुश्च; BKt^5 निःक्षेप्तुश्च; BBe^2 Be^3 Bo BCa Ho WKt^1 WKt^3 NKt^4 La^1 Lo^1 Lo^3 NNg SOx^1 Pu^2 Pu^3 Pu^4 SPu^6 Pu^8 Tj^1 निक्षेप्तुः स्वबन्धुभिः

अच्छलेनैव चान्विच्छेत् तमर्थं प्रीतिपूर्वकम् ।
विचार्य तस्य वा वृत्तं साम्नैव परिसाधयेत् ॥१८७॥
निक्षेपेष्वेष सर्वेषु विधिः स्यात्परिसाधने ।
समुद्रे नाप्नुयात्किंचिद्यदि तस्मान्न संहरेत् ॥१८८॥
चौरैर्हृतं जलेनोढमग्निना दग्धमेव च ।
न दद्याद्यदि तस्मात्स न संहरति किंचन ॥१८९॥
निक्षेपस्यापहर्तारमनिक्षेप्तारमेव च ।
सर्वैरुपायैरन्विच्छेच्छपथैश्चैव वैदिकैः ॥१९०॥
यो निक्षेपं नार्पयति यश्चानिक्षिप्य याचते ।
तावुभौ चौरवच्छास्यौ दाप्यौ वा तत्समं दमम् ॥१९१॥
निक्षेपस्यापहर्तारं तत्समं दापयेद्दमम् ।

187. Not commented by *Me*. Cited by *Lakṣ* 12.346; *Dev* 3.424 — a) TMd^{4} अच्छनेचैव; La^{1} अछलेचैव; Tr^{2} अच्छलेनैवान्वि°; GMd^{1} °लेनेव तान्विच्छेत्; La^{1} GMd^{5} Pu^{2} Pu^{4} वान्विच्छेत्; Be^{1} चान्निच्छेत् — b) TMd^{4} प्रतिपूर्वकं — c) Pu^{2} Pu^{4} वा दत्तं; Pu^{5} Pu^{7} वा देयं; Be^{1} वृतं; TMd^{3} वृत्तो — d) GMd^{1} Tj^{1} साम्नेव; sOx^{1} sPu^{6} परिसाधयन्; Pu^{7} परितोषयन्; Pu^{5} परिषयन्; Lo^{2} परिभावयेत्; *Lakṣ* परिशोधयेत्

188.* Omitted in MTr^{5}; pādas c-d omitted in TMd^{4}; 188a-b placed after 187a-b in Be^{1}. Cited by *Lakṣ* 12.341; *Dev* 3.418; pādas c-d cited by *Mādh* 3.206 — a) TMd^{3} निक्षेपेस्वधनसर्वेषु; La^{1} निक्षेपे स्वेषु सर्वेषु; Jo^{2} wKt^{1} NKt^{4} GMd^{5} Ox^{2} sOx^{1} sPu^{6} [*Jolly* M R^{3}] निक्षेपेष्वेव; Be^{1} NPu^{1} Wa निक्षेपेषु च; BBe^{2} Be^{3} Bo Ho Hy Jm Jo^{1} Kt^{2} BKt^{5} La^{1} Lo^{1} Lo^{2} Lo^{3} GMd^{1} GMy oOr Pu^{5} Pu^{7} Pu^{8} Tj^{1} Tj^{2} Tr^{1} Tr^{2} MTr^{4} MTr^{6} [*Jolly* R Nd] *Mandlik Jha KSS Dave* निक्षेपेष्वेषु; BKt^{5} निःक्षिपेष्वेषु; Pu^{2} Pu^{4} निक्षेप्य श्वेषु — b) Tr^{2} विधिं; GMd^{1} निधिः; wKt^{3} बुधिः; Ho sOx^{1} sPu^{6} स्यात्प्रतिसाधने — c) MTr^{4} सपुत्रे; *Dev* समुद्रान्नाप्नुया°; BBe^{2} वाप्नुया°; BKt^{5} प्राप्नुया°

189.* Omitted in TMd^{4}; pādas c-d omitted in Be^{3} Pu^{2} Pu^{4}. Cited by *Apa* 663; *Lakṣ* 12.342; *Dev* 3.418; *Mādh* 3.206 — a) Lo^{3} GMd^{1} TMd^{3} GMd^{5} GMy Tr^{1} MTr^{6} *Dev* चोरै°; Tj^{1} चोरहृतं; Be^{3} जलेनौढ°; La^{1} जले नष्टम° — b) wKt^{1} दग्ध एव; Ho Hy Jm Jo^{1} wKt^{1} Kt^{2} wKt^{3} Lo^{2} oOr sOx^{1} Ox^{2} sPu^{6} Pu^{8} Tj^{2} MTr^{3} *Mandlik Jolly Jha KSS Dave* वा — c) GMd^{1} न दद्यादितरस्तस्मात् [*om* स]; MTr^{4} MTr^{5} MTr^{6} तस्मात्तु; Lo^{3} NPu^{1} Tj^{1} तस्माच्च; Wa तच्च स — c-d) TMd^{3} तस्मान्न संहरेत; GMd^{5} सर्वस्मात्स न संहर किंचन — d) BKt^{5} न च संहरि किंचन

190. Omitted in TMd^{3}; pādas a-b omitted in Be^{3} Pu^{2} Pu^{4}. Cited by *Dev* 3.423; *Mādh* 3.208 — a) Ox^{3} °हन्तारम° — b) Tr^{2} °विक्षेप्तार°; BBe^{2} °निक्षिप्तार°; Hy °निक्षप्तार° — c) Be^{1} °यैरनिच्छे° — d) Ho sOx^{1} Ox^{2} sPu^{6} °पथैरपि; Lo^{2} °पथैरेव; GMd^{1} °पथैश्चापि; TMd^{4} °पथे चैव; GMd^{5} वेदिकैः; NPu^{1} निंदिकैः

191. Omitted in TMd^{3}. Cited by *Apa* 191; *Lakṣ* 12.345; *Dev* 3.423 — a) Be^{1} ये; Pu^{5} Pu^{7} [*Jolly* G] निक्षेपं यो; BKt^{5} निःक्षेपं; Hy निक्षपं; wKt^{1} Lo^{1} नापयति; Wa नार्प्यति; oOr नार्चयति — b) BBe^{2} wKt^{1} यच्चानि°; [*Jolly* M] तथानि°; BKt^{5} °निःक्षिप्य; Bo MTr^{4} MTr^{6} °निक्षेप्य; Be^{1} याचने — c) Bo Pu^{3} Tr^{2} तावेतौ; Lo^{4} Lo^{5} Ox^{3} उभौ तौ; Lo^{3} GMd^{1} GMd^{5} GMy Tj^{1} MTr^{6} *Lakṣ* चोर°; Lo^{3} Pu^{8} Wa °वच्छास्यो; GMd^{1} °वच्छाप्यौ; [*Jolly* M Nd] °वच्छिष्यौ; NKt^{4} °वच्छिष्यो; MTr^{6} °वच्छिष्य; Be^{1} °वच्छिस्व्यौ; Lo^{2} °वच्छिप्यौ; Tr^{2} °वत्स्थाप्यौ; GMd^{5} °वद्दण्ड्यौ — d) *Apa* दाप्यौ दण्डं च तत्समं; GMd^{1} दाप्यो; MTr^{6} दाप्या; Jo^{1} ताप्यौ; *Lakṣ* दाप्यौ तौ तत्समं; *Dev* प्रदाप्यौ तत्समं; BKt^{5} दाप्यौ तावत्समं

तथोपनिधिहर्तारमविशेषेण पार्थिवः ॥१९२॥
उपधाभिस्तु यः कश्चित् परद्रव्यं हरेन्नरः ।
ससहायः स हन्तव्यः प्रकाशं विविधैर्वधैः ॥१९३॥
निक्षेपो यः कृतो येन यावांश्च कुलसंनिधौ ।
तावानेव स विज्ञेयो विब्रुवन्दण्डमर्हति ॥१९४॥
मिथो दायः कृतो येन गृहीतो मिथ एव वा ।
मिथ एव प्रदातव्यो यथा दायस्तथा ग्रहः ॥१९५॥
निक्षिप्तस्य धनस्यैवं प्रीत्योपनिहितस्य च ।
राजा विनिर्णयं कुर्यादक्षिण्वन् न्यासधारिणम् ॥१९६॥
विक्रीणीते परस्य स्वं योऽस्वामी स्वाम्यसंमतः ।
न तं नयेत साक्ष्यं तु स्तेनमस्तेनमानिनम् ॥१९७॥

192. Pādas a-b omitted in TMd^{4}; pāda-c *ma* in Tr^{1}. Cited by *Lakṣ* 12.345; *Dev* 3.421; *Mādh* 3.208 — a) BKt^{5} निःक्षेप°; BBe^{2} निक्षेपहर्तारं; WKt^{3} °पस्यापसर्तारं; Jo^{1} °पस्याहारं — b) Ox^{2} दापयेत्तत्समं दमं; Pu^{2} Pu^{4} दाप्ययेद्दमं; Pu^{5} Pu^{7} दण्डयेद्दमं; Be^{1} Be^{3} °येद्धनं — c) GMd^{1} TMd^{3} TMd^{4} GMy MTr^{4} MTr^{6} [*Jolly* Nd] हर्तारं चाप्युपनिधेरविशे° [GMd^{1} हर्तारश्चाप्यु°; TMd^{4} हर्तारमप्यु°]; Wa तथापनिधि° — d) Lo^{4} Lo^{5} *Dev Mādh* °हर्तारं विशेषेणैव पार्थिवः [Lo^{4} Lo^{5} विशेषेण तु]

193. Cited by *Lakṣ* 12.345 — a) GMd^{5} MTr^{4} MTr^{6} उपाधिभिस्तु; GMd^{1} उपधानस्तु; Tr^{2} उपधातस्तु; BBe^{2} Hy Jm Jo^{1} Jo^{2} Kt^{2} BKt^{5} Lo^{2} Tj^{2} MTr^{3} *Mandlik Jha KSS Dave* उपधाभिश्च; Be^{1} उपाधिभिश्च; BKt^{5} *om* यः; TMd^{3} GMd^{5} GMy Pu^{2} Pu^{4} Pu^{5} Pu^{7} MTr^{6} [*Jolly* G]यत्किंचित्; Tr^{1} *ma sh* कश्चित् — b) TMd^{4} हरं नरः — c) TMd^{4} ससहायां; BKt^{5} ससहायस्तु; Ho सन्तव्यः स; Lo^{1} सप्तायः स; GMd^{1} सहसा तु स — d) Bo प्रकाश; Lo^{3} Tj^{1} विविधं वधैः; sOx^{1} sPu^{6} विविधैर्बलैः; Lo^{1} विविधैर्बुधैः; TMd^{3} विविधैर्धनैः; Pu^{7} विबुधैर्बुधैः; La^{1} विधिवद्बुधैः

194. Cited by *Apa* 664; *Lakṣ* 12.346; *Dev* 3.422; *Mādh* 3.208 — a) *Mādh* निक्षेपो ह्यनिवेद्यो यः; GMd^{5} यं; *Apa* यत्कृतो; TMd^{3} कृता; La^{1} हृतो — b) *Apa* यावान्वा; BKt^{5} यावां कुल°; *Mādh* धनवान्कुल° — c) TMd^{3} Tj^{1} तावान्नेव; Be^{3} तावतैव; Lo^{1} सतिज्ञेयो

195. Cited by *Lakṣ* 12.341 — a) Ox^{3} मिथ्यो; WKt^{1} Lo^{1} दाय; GMd^{1} दायाः — b) TMd^{4} गृह्णीता; Pu^{2} Pu^{4} गृहीता; BBe^{2} मृत एव; La^{1} GMd^{1} Ox^{2} NPu^{1} Tr^{1} च — c) Tr^{1} [*ma sh* प्र] दातव्यो; La^{1} GMd^{1} MTr^{4} MTr^{6} स दातव्यो— d) TMd^{3} तथा; oOr यदा

196. Cited by *Lakṣ* 12.347; *Dev* 3.423; *Mādh* 3.209— a) TMd^{4} निक्षिप्तस्यैव तस्यै प्रीत्यो°; BKt^{5} निक्षिप्तस्यै; GMd^{1} निक्षिप्तसु; Tj^{1} निक्षिप्तस्यैव; NPu^{1} °प्तस्य च तस्यैवं; Be^{3} Bo Lo^{5} धनस्यैव — b) BBe^{2} प्रीतोप°; Lo^{1} प्रीत्याप्यनिहतस्य; oOr प्रीत्या यो निहितस्य; sOx^{1} sPu^{6} °निहतस्य; Be^{1} BKt^{5} वा — c) BBe^{2} BCa WKt^{1} WKt^{3} NKt^{4} La^{1} GMd^{1} TMd^{3} TMd^{4} GMd^{5} GMy Tr^{1} MTr^{4} MTr^{5} MTr^{6} कुर्याद्विनिर्णयं राजा; Pu^{2} Pu^{4} राज्ञा — c-d) *Mādh* कुर्याद्विनिर्णयं राजाऽप्रक्षिष्वन् — d) TMd^{4} कुर्यात्साक्षिनन्यासधारिणा; GMd^{1} MTr^{4} MTr^{6} कुर्यात्साक्षिसंन्यासधारिणां [GMd^{1} °धारिणः]; GMd^{5} कुर्यान्न्यासधारणमक्षिणन्; TMd^{3} GMy कुर्यान्न्यासधारिणमक्षयं; Tr^{1} कुर्यान्न्यासधारिणमाक्षणात्; Be^{3} कुर्याद्दक्षिण्यं न्यासधारिणां; WKt^{3} कुर्याद्भ्यक्षिण्वन्; Lo^{1} कुर्यादाक्षिण्यान्; WKt^{1} न्यायधारिणा; Be^{1} °धारणाः; sOx^{1} sPu^{6} Tj^{1} Tr^{2} °धारणं; La^{1} °हारिणं; Lo^{4} Lo^{5} [*but cor sh*] °वारिणं

197. Cited by *Lakṣ* 12.351; *Dev* 3.498— a) Hy विक्रीणिते; Wa विक्रिणीते; WKt^{1} परस्यै [*mc* वं] — a-b) Pu^{5} Pu^{7} Tj^{1} परस्वं यो अस्वामी — b) GMd^{1} यस्वामी; oOr यः स्वामी; TMd^{3} GMy यो वार्थं

अवहार्यो भवेच्चैष सान्वयः षट्शतं दमम् ।
निरन्वयोऽनपसरः प्राप्तः स्याच्चौरकिल्बिषम् ॥१९८॥
अस्वामिना कृतो यस्तु दायो विक्रय एव वा ।
अकृतः स तु विज्ञेयो व्यवहारे यथा स्थितिः ॥१९९॥
संभोगो यत्र दृश्येत न दृश्येतागमः क्वचित् ।
आगमः कारणं तत्र न संभोग इति स्थितिः ॥२००॥

स्वाम्य°; wKt[3] Pu[4] Tj[1] स्वामिसम्मतः — c) Pu[2] न तत्साक्षं तु यत्सर्वं; GMd[1] न सन्नयेत; Lo[1] ते नयेन; Tr[2] नयत; NNg नयेतु; Be[3] नयेन; Be[3] GMd[1] साक्ष्ये; oOr साक्ष्ये तं; Jo[2] NPu[1] Pu[5] Pu[7] साक्षित्वं स्तेन° — d) Lo[3] Tj[1] स्तेयमस्तेयमानितं; Be[3] स्तेनमस्तेयमानिनं; TMd[4] स्तेयं तु स्तेयमानिनं; Pu[2] स्तेनमातृतमानितं; GMd[1] °मानिलं

198. Cited by *Lakṣ* 12.352 — a) GMd[1] TMd[3] TMd[4] GMd[5] GMy Tr[1] MTr[4]MTr[6] [*Jolly* Nd] अवहार्यस्स तु भवेत् [GMd[1] GMy अपहा°]; Jo[1] °हार्यौ; MTr[5] भवेदेष; BCa Jm Jo[1] Kt[2] sOx[1] sPu[6] MTr[3] *Mandlik Jha KSS Dave* भवेच्चैव; La[1] हरेच्चैष — b) Be[1] सान्वया; BBe[2] सान्वयं; GMd[1] दमः — c) GMy निरन्वयस्सावसुरः; TMd[3] निरन्वयस्सापसरः; Lo[2] निरन्वायानपसरः; Be[3] La[1] sOx[1] sPu[6] Tr[2] Wa *Nā Nd Rc* °न्वयोनवसरः; GMd[1] °न्वयोनिरसरः; GMd[5] °न्वयोनपरसीः; Ox[2] °न्वयो नवशतं — d) *Lakṣ* [vl] प्राप्नुयात् चौरकिल्बिषं; NKt[4] Lo[2] Lo[3] GMd[1] GMd[5] NNg Tj[1] Tj[2] Tr[1] MTr[5] MTr[6]स्याच्चोर°; wKt[3] स्याच्चैव किल्बिषं; GMd[1] °किल्बषी; NNg °किल्बिषीं

199.* GMy Tr[1] place 199–200 after 202. Cited by *Lakṣ* 12.352 — a) TMd[3] अस्वामिनो; Lo[1] स्वामिना तु कृतो; wKt[1] हृतो; Be[3] Tj[2] Wa क्रयो; BKt[5] NPu[1] यश्च — b) BBe[2] Bo Ho wKt[3] NKt[4] BKt[5] TMd[3] GMy La[1] Lo[1] oOr sOx[1] sPu[6] Tj[1] Tr[2] MTr[4] MTr[6] [*Jolly* R Nd] *Bh Rn Nd Mandlik* [ज, झ, ञ, ढ] क्रयो विक्रय [*Bh's* gloss क्रयविक्रयौ probably supports this reading]; Pu[2] Pu[4] कुर्यो विक्रय; GMd[5] कुलविक्रय; *Me Go Ku* support दायो; NPu[1] Pu[2] Pu[4] एव च — c) TMd[3] अकृतं; Pu[2] आकृतः; Pu[4] आकुतः; La[1] अक्रीतः; GMd[5] अकृतस्तु स — d) Tj[1] व्यवहारो; GMy व्यावहारो; Lo[1] Lo[2] NNg Ox[2] NPu[1] Pu[2] Pu[4] Pu[5] Pu[7] [*Jolly* G] व्यवहार इति स्थितिः [Pu[2] °हारौ; Pu[4] °हारै]; oOr यतः; Bo स्थितं

*Additional verse in Be[1] Be[3] Bo BCa Ho NKt[4] Lo[2] TMd[4] Ox[2] Tr[1] Tr[2] Wa [*Jolly* Nd N Gr] *Nā Nd Rc Mandlik* [क, ख, ग, च, ण, ज, झ, ञ, ट, ठ, ड, र, ल] *Dave KSS;* placed after 198 in La[1] oOr NPu[1] Pu[2] Pu[3] Pu[4] GMd[1] TMd[3] GMy MTr[4] MTr[6]; cited by *Lakṣ* 12.352:

अनेन विधिना शास्यः कुर्वन्नस्वामिविक्रयम् ।
अज्ञानाज्ज्ञानपूर्वं तु चौरवद्दधमर्हति ॥

a) Pu[2] Pu[4] विधिनोसोस्य; NKt[4] NPu[1] विधिना राजा; TMd[4] शास्यं; Be[1] Bo Lo[2] TMd[3] Pu[3] शास्य; La[1] शास्युः; Tr[2] *Madlik* शास्ता; TMd[3] [*Jolly* Nd N Gr] शिष्यः; GMy शिष्यं; GMd[1] चास्य; Be[3] स्वामी — b) GMd[1] कुर्वीत स्वामिविक्रयः; Tr[2] °विक्रियं — c) GMd[1] अज्ञानज्ञान° — d) Ho Lo[2] Ox[2] Tr[1] [*Jolly* Nd N Gr] *Mandlik* चोरवद्दण्डमर्हति; La[1] चोरवद्धनमर्हति; TMd[4] चोरविधिमर्हति; GMd[1] TMd[3] GMy Tr[1] MTr[6] चोर°; Bo वैर°

200. Cited by *Apa* 635 — a) TMd[4] NNg संभोगा; Pu[5] Pu[7] संभोगे; Wa संभागो; wKt[1] Lo[2] Ox[2] Pu[5] Tr[2] Wa यत्र दृश्यते; Be[1] BBe[2] Ho Hy Jm Jo[1] Jo[2] Kt[2] La[1] Lo[1] Lo[3] sOx[1] sPu[6] Tj[1] Tj[2] MTr[3] [*Jolly* R] *Mandlik Jha KSS Dave* दृश्यते यत्र — c) wKt[1] Lo[4] Lo[5] करणं; oOr यत्र — d) Lo[2] न भोग इति संस्थितिः; Ho स्थितः

Additional verse in BCa La[1]:

आगमेन विशुद्धेन भोगो याति प्रमाणताम् ।
अविशुद्धागमो भोगः प्रामाण्यं नैव गच्छति ॥

विक्रयाद्यो धनं किंचिद् गृह्णीयात् कुलसंनिधौ ।
क्रयेण स विशुद्धं हि न्यायतो लभते धनम् ॥२०१॥
अथ मूलमनाहार्यं प्रकाशक्रयशोधितम् ।
अदण्ड्यो मुच्यते राज्ञा नाष्टिको लभते धनम् ॥२०२॥
नान्यदन्येन संसृष्टं रूपं विक्रयमर्हति ।
न सावद्यं न च न्यूनं न दूरे न तिरोहितम् ॥२०३॥
अन्यां चेद्दर्शयित्वान्या वोढुः कन्या प्रदीयते ।
उभे ते एकशुल्केन वहेदित्यब्रवीन्मनुः ॥२०४॥
नोन्मत्ताया न कुष्ठिन्या न च या स्पृष्टमैथुना ।
पूर्वं दोषानभिख्याप्य प्रदाता दण्डमर्हति ॥२०५॥

201. Cited by *Lakṣ* 12.352; *Dev* 3.505 — a) Pu^{5} Pu^{7} *Go* विक्रेयाद्यो; BKt^{5} विक्रियादो; oOr विक्रीयाद्यो; wKt^{1} विक्रयार्थे — b) Pu^{5} Pu^{7} [*Jolly* G] गृहीत्वा; Lo^{3} Tj^{1} विक्रीयात्; TMd^{4} तुल° — c) BKt^{5} GMd^{5} [*Jolly* G M^{8}] क्रमेण; Pu^{2} Pu^{4} MTr^{5} *Lakṣ* विशुद्धस्तु; TMd^{3} TMd^{4} GMy विशुध्येत; GMd^{1} GMd^{5} MTr^{4} MTr^{6} विशुद्धेन; the reading adopted is supported by *Me Go Nā Ku Rn Rc Mr.*

202. * Omitted in Be^{1} GMd^{5} [haplo]; 202 and 203 transposed in Lo^{1}. Cited by *Apa* 776; *Lakṣ* 12.352; *Dev* 3.504; *Mādh* 3.215 — a)oOr NPu^{1} अर्थ; GMd^{1} TMd^{3} TMd^{4} GMy MTr^{5} MTr^{6} [*Jolly* Nd] मूल्यम°; NNg मूल्याम°; oOr मूल्याना°; BKt^{5} *om* अनाहार्यं; Lo^{1} °हार्य — b) BKt^{5} प्रकाशः; Hy Jm Jo^{1} wKt^{1} Kt^{2} Tj^{2} MTr^{3} *Mandlik Jha KSS Dave* °शोधितः — c) BKt^{5} Lo^{2} TMd^{4} Pu^{4} *Apa* अदण्डो; TMd^{4} यद्यते राजा; TMd^{3} राज्ञां — d) BBe^{2} wKt^{1} Hy BKt^{5} La^{1} GMd^{1} Pu^{2} Pu^{4} MTr^{4} *Apa* नास्तिको; TMd^{4} नास्तिकं; Tr^{2} नातिष्टिको; TMd^{3} राष्ट्रेको; Lo^{2} नाधिको; GMd^{1} TMd^{3} GMy [*Jolly* Nd] लभते च तत् [TMd^{3} GMy पहते]

203.* Cited by *Lakṣ* 12.437; *Dev* 3.520; *Mādh* 3.262 — a) MTr^{4} अन्यद°; oOr नान्यदन्त्येन; wKt^{1} नान्यदण्डेन; Ho Tj^{1} Tr^{2} संस्पृष्टं; Hy Jm Jo^{1} wKt^{1} Kt^{2} MTr^{3} *Nā Mr Dev Mandlik Jolly Jha KSS Dave* संसृष्टरूपं — b) wKt^{3} La^{1} GMd^{5} रूप; GMd^{5} विक्रम° — c) Hy नासारं; GMd^{1} [*om* न] चापद्यं; TMd^{3} चावस्यं; Jm Jo^{1} wKt^{1} Kt^{2} MTr^{3} [*Jolly* Ku Nd] *Mandlik KSS* चासारं [supported by *Ku Mr*]; NKt^{4} न वा न्यूनं; sOx^{1} sPu^{6} *lacuna at* न्यूनं; GMy चान्यूनं — d) Lo^{4} Lo^{5} न हरेत तिरोहितं; Pu^{5} Pu^{7} न च दूरेण; TMd^{3} GMd^{5} GMy *Dev* दूरं; *Mandlik KSS* दूरेण; Bo दूरे च

204. a) sOx^{1} NPu^{1} अन्या; Pu^{2} Pu^{4} अन्यं; Tj^{2} अन्यो; La^{1} अन्यश्चे°; Pu^{8} Tr^{2} च दर्श°; wKt^{1} चेद्रूणयित्वान्यो; Lo^{1} GMd^{5} Pu^{3} Pu^{5} Pu^{7} MTr^{6} °यित्वान्यां; TMd^{3} GMy °यित्वान्यं; Bo °यित्वान्यान्; BBe^{2} [*but cor*] Wa °यित्वान्यो — b) TMd^{3} कन्या वोढुं प्रतीयते; Jo^{2} TMd^{4} Tr^{1} MTr^{6} कन्या वोढुः; GMy कन्यां वोढुः; Bo वाढुः; BKt^{5} वूढुः; Lo^{3} वेदुः; GMd^{1} GMd^{5} कन्यां — c) TMd^{4} उभे एते कुशुल्केन; TMd^{3} उभौ; Wa उभयो एक°; *Mandlik KSS* त एक°; Be^{3} La^{1} Pu^{3} ह्येक°; Pu^{8} त्वेक°; GMd^{5} एवशुल्केन; oOr °शुष्केन — d) La^{1} °शुल्केनोद्वहेदि°

205. a) BBe^{2} sOx^{1} sPu^{6} Wa नोन्मत्तया; GMd^{5} नोन्मत्ताय; La^{1} Pu^{5} MTr^{6} नोन्मत्तायां; Lo^{3} TMd^{3} Tj^{1} नु; La^{1} MTr^{6} कुष्ठिन्यां — b) Pu^{5} Pu^{7} न या संस्पृष्टमैथुना; Be^{1} Be^{3} [*Jolly* G] न च संस्पृष्टमैथुना; Lo^{4} Lo^{5} न चैव; La^{1} चायां; Tr^{2} स्पृश्य° — c) BBe^{2} Bo Ho wKt^{1} La^{1} Lo^{1} GMd^{5} sOx^{1} Pu^{3} sPu^{6} पूर्व; Tj^{1} दोषावनस्थाप्य; sOx^{1} sPu^{6} °नतिख्याप्य; La^{1} °ननाख्याप्य; wKt^{1} °नभिक्षाप्य; Be^{1} °नभिक्ष्याप्य; Ho °नभिव्याप्य; Lo^{4} Tr^{2} °नविख्याप्य; Jo^{2} °नवख्याप्य; Pu^{5} Pu^{7} °नन्निष्याप्य

Additional verses in GMd^{1} TMd^{4} MTr^{4} MTr^{6}; first two cited by *Apa* 821; *Lakṣ* 12.564; third verse cited by *Apa* 818; *Mādh* 3.291:

ऋत्विग्यदि वृतो यज्ञे स्वकर्म परिहापयेत् ।
तस्य कर्मानुरूपेण देयोंऽशः सहकर्तृभिः ॥२०६॥
दक्षिणासु च दत्तासु स्वकर्म परिहापयन् ।
कृत्स्नमेव लभेतांशमन्येनैव च कारयेत् ॥२०७॥
यस्मिन्कर्मणि यास्तु स्युरुक्ताः प्रत्यङ्गदक्षिणाः ।
स एव ता आददीत भजेरन् सर्व एव वा ॥२०८॥
रथं हरेत चाध्वर्युर्ब्रह्माधाने च वाजिनम् ।
होता वापि हरेदश्वमुद्गाता चाप्यनः क्रये ॥२०९॥

अभक्ष्यमथ वापेयं वैश्यादीन् ग्राहयन्द्विजान् ।
जघन्यमध्यमोत्कृष्टान् दण्डानर्हो यथाक्रमम् ।।१।।
पणाः शूद्रे भवेद्दण्डं चतुष्पञ्चाशदेव तु ।
ग्रसितारः स्वयं कार्या राज्ञा निर्विषयास्तु ते ।।२।।
गोकुमारीं देवपशुमुक्षाणमृषभं तथा ।
वाहयन्साहसं पूर्वं प्राप्नुयादुत्तमं वधे ।।३।।

1. a) *Lakṣ* चापेयं — b) TMd[4] वैश्यादि; MTr[4] ग्रासय°; *Lakṣ* नाशय°; *Apa* भक्षय° — c) *Apa* °त्कृष्टदण्डा° — d) *Lakṣ Apa* दण्डानर्हेद्यथा°

2. a) TMd[4] °द्दण्डः; MTr[4] MTr[6] *Apa* °द्दण्डश्चतु° — c) MTr[6] ग्रसीतारः; GMd[1] TMd[4] ग्रहीतारं; GMd[1] स्वकं — d) GMd[1] TMd[4] निर्विषये स्थिते

3. a-b) *Apa Mādh* गोकुमारीर्देवपशूनुक्षाणं वृषभं तथा

206. Pādas c-d [after तस्य] omitted in wKt[1]. Cited by *Apa* 836; *Lakṣ* 12.364; *Dev* 3.438; *Mādh* 3.222 — a) BBe[2] व्रतो; GMd[1] वृते; Pu[2] Pu[4] मृतो — b) La[1] GMd[1] sOx[1] sPu[6] [*cor to*] Tr[2] परिहारयेत्; GMd[5] *Dev* परिभावयेत् — c) NKt[4] BKt[5] NNg MTr[6] °नुरूप्येण; Bo Pu[2] Pu[4] °नुसारेण — d) GMd[1] स देयो सह°; Jo[2] देयांशः; Tr[2] देवोंशः; Pu[2] Pu[4] सहकर्मभिः

207. Omitted in Lo[4] Lo[5]; pādas c-d omitted in Pu[5] wKt[1], and placed after 206b in Wa. Cited by *Apa* 837; *Lakṣ* 12.364; *Mādh* 3.222 — a) *Mādh* दक्षिणासु प्रदत्तासु; Be[1] Bo NKt[4] BKt[5] GMd[1] NNg sOx[1] Ox[2] Pu[3] sPu[6] Pu[8] Tr[1] MTr[4] MTr[5] MTr[6] Wa [*Jolly* M]तु — b) NKt[4] NNg स्वं कर्म; Be[3] [*but cor*] Jo[1] wKt[3] TMd[3] GMd[5] GMy sOx[1] Ox[2] NPu[1] Pu[2] Pu[4] sPu[6] Pu[7] Pu[8] Tr[1] MTr[4] MTr[6] *Apa Lakṣ* °हापयेत्; GMd[1] Tr[2] °हारयेत्; *Dev* °भावयेत्; *Ku Nd Go* support the present participle — d) Tr[1] °तांशं कर्मान्येनैव कारयेत्; GMd[5] *om* च; Ho NNg Tj[1] [*Jolly* M R]तु

208. Cited by *Apa* 837; *Lakṣ* 12.364; *Dev* 3.437— a) Wa तस्मि°; *Apa Lakṣ Dev* यस्य कर्मणि; La[1] Tr[2] °न्कर्माणि; GMy यस्तु — b) Lo[1] स्युरुक्ता; Be[1] Be[3] °दक्षिणा; Hy GMy NNg °दक्षिणः — c) Ho sOx[1] sPu[6] एव कर्माददीत; Bo तान्याददीत — d) Ox[2] एव च

209. Cited by *Apa* 837; *Lakṣ* 12.364; *Dev* 3.437, *Mādh* 3.221 — a) Bo रथे; MTr[6] रसं; wKt[1] हरेरथाध्व°; BBe[2] BCa Ho La[1] Lo[1] NPu[1] MTr[5] MTr[6] *Apa* हरेदथाध्व°; wKt[3] Lo[2] Lo[4] Lo[5] हरेत्तथाध्व°; GMd[1] हरेद्यथाध्व°; Lo[3] GMd[5] Tj[1] Tr[1] Tr[2] वाध्व° — b) NKt[4] Lo[1] °ब्राह्मा°; TMd[3] °ब्रह्मादाने; GMy °ब्रहमाने — c) *Dev* होता निविद्धरं चाश्वमु°; TMd[4] होतापि निर्हरेद°; TMd[3] GMy होतापि च हरेद°; BBe[2] Bo BCa Hy wKt[1] wKt[3] Lo[4] Lo[5] GMd[1] GMd[5] NNg sOx[1] Pu[3] sPu[6] Tr[2] MTr[4] MTr[5] MTr[6] *Apa* चापि; *Me* supports वा; *Go Ku* support च — d) Be[1] Ho NNg Tj[1] °मुद्गता; La[1] Pu[2] Pu[4] °मुद्गातो; Lo[2] Tj[1] वाप्यनः; BKt[5] चाप्यतः; TMd[4] चानविक्रये; TMd[3] चाप्यनद्रये; GMy क्रयेत्; Hy क्रयो; Be[1] Lo[3] Ox[2] Tj[1] [*Jolly* Nd] क्रतौ; BCa [*but cor*] क्रतो; La[1] कृतौ; sOx[1] sPu[6] कृतो

सर्वेषामर्धिनो मुख्यास्तदर्धेनार्धिनोऽपरे ।
तृतीयिनस्तृतीयांशाश्चतुर्थांशास्तु पादिनः ॥२१०॥
संभूय स्वानि कर्माणि कुर्वद्भिरिह मानवैः ।
अनेन विधियोगेन कर्तव्यांशप्रकल्पना ॥२११॥
धर्मार्थं येन दत्तं स्यात् कस्मैचिद्याचते धनम् ।
पश्चाच्च न तथा तत्स्यान्न देयं तस्य तद्भवेत् ॥२१२॥
यदि संसाधयेत्तत्तु दर्पाल्लोभेन वा पुनः ।
राज्ञा दाप्यः सुवर्णं स्यात्तस्य स्तेयस्य निष्कृतिः ॥२१३॥
दत्तस्यैषोदिता धर्म्या यथावदनपक्रिया ।
अत ऊर्ध्वं प्रवक्ष्यामि वेतनस्यानपक्रियाम् ॥२१४॥

210. Cited by *Vij* 2.265; *Apa* 837; *Lakṣ* 12.364; *Dev* 3.437; *Mādh*3.222 — a) Lo^{4} Lo^{5} MTr^{3} °मर्थिनो; Tj^{1} °मृद्धिनो; wKt^{1} °मृत्विजो — b) Be^{1} °स्तदर्थेना°; Ox^{2} °नोर्धिनो; NNg NPu^{1} °नार्धिनः परे; Pu^{2} Pu^{4} °नार्धितः परे; TMd^{4} °नार्धिनो हरेत्; *Apa* °नार्धिनोऽर्धिनः — c) TMd^{4} तृतीयांस्युस्तृतीयांशश्चतु°; TMd^{3} तृतियांनस्त्रितियांशं चतु°; Bo तृतीयान°; Ox^{2} तृतीयीन°; Be^{1} Be^{3} Jo^{2} wKt^{1} La^{1} Lo^{1} Lo^{3} NPu^{1} Tj^{1} Tr^{2} Wa तृतीयेन तृती°; Pu^{2} Pu^{4} तृतीयेनस्तृती°; GMd^{5} तृतीयानस्तृती°; MTr^{6} तृतीयनस्तृती°; Pu^{5} Pu^{7} °यांशश्चतु°; NNg °यांशाच्चतु° — d) Hy Jm Jo^{1} Jo^{2} Kt^{2} BKt^{5} Pu^{5} Pu^{7} Tj^{2} MTr^{3} [*Jolly* G N Nd] *Vij Apa Mandlik Jolly Jha KSS Dave* °तुर्थांशाश्च; BBe^{2} °तुर्थाश्चैकपादिनः; Tr^{2} सादिनः; MTr^{4} MTr^{6} खादिनः; TMd^{4} वाजिनं

211. Cited by *Lakṣ* 12.365; *Dev* 3.436; *Mādh* 3.221 — a) Hy स्वामि — b) BKt^{5} °द्भिरपि वा नरैः — c) Lo^{1} विधयोगेन; NKt^{4} विधिनियोगेन; Pu^{2} Pu^{4} विधिना योगे; MTr^{6} विधिना योगेन; wKt^{1} wKt^{3} Tj^{1} [*Jolly* R] *Dev* कर्मयोगेन; Be^{3} La^{1} Tr^{1} [*mc sh to*] *Lakṣ* क्रमयोगेन — d) Lo^{4} Lo^{5} Pu^{2} Pu^{4} Pu^{5} Pu^{7} कर्तव्यासंप्रकल्पना; wKt^{3} कर्तव्यंशक्रकल्पना; *Mādh* कर्तव्यांशम्प्रकल्पयेत्; MTr^{6} °व्यांशकल्पना; Kt^{2} MTr^{5} °कल्पनाः

212. Pādas a-b omitted in Lo^{4} Lo^{5}. Cited by *Apa* 782; *Lakṣ* 12.380; *Dev* 3.453 — a-b) BKt^{5} [*Jolly* M] *Apa* कस्मैचिद्याचमानाय दत्तं धर्माय यद्भवेत् [BKt^{5} तद्भवेत्] — b) TMd^{4} कस्माद्वै याचयद्धनं; NKt^{4} तस्मै°; Bo कस्मिंश्चिद्याचते — c) Lo^{1} NPu^{1} पश्चात्तु; Pu^{2} Pu^{4} पश्चात्ते; *Dev* पश्चाच्चेन्न; La^{1} पश्चान्न तथा; Pu^{3} BKt^{5} तथा तु स्यान्न; *Apa* तथा तस्मान्न; Bo तथा तस्या न — d) GMd^{1} TMd^{3} TMd^{4} GMy [*Jolly* Nd] तत्स्यात्तस्मै देयं न तेन तत्; Tr^{1} तत्स्यात् देयं तस्मै न तद्भवेत्; *Dev* तत्स्यादादेयं तेन तद्भवेत्; MTr^{4} तत्स्यात्तस्मै तं तस्य तद्भवेत्; Bo देया; *Lakṣ* तेन तद्भवेत्; BKt^{5} *om* तद्

213. Cited by *Apa* 782; *Lakṣ* 12.380; *Dev* 3.453 — a) GMd^{1} भवेत्तं साधयेत्तत्तु; TMd^{4} संसेध°; Be^{3} La^{1} TMd^{3} TMd^{4} NNg NPu^{1} °येत्तं तु; Pu^{2} Pu^{4} °येत्तत्र; Be^{1} °येत्तन्तु; Bo °येत्तन्तुं; Pu^{5} Pu^{7} °येत्तच्च — b) Pu^{2} Pu^{4} दत्त्वा लोभेन; TMd^{4} दर्पाल्लाभेथ वा; La^{1} TMd^{3} GMd^{5} GMy NNg [*Jolly* Nd] °भेन मानवः — c) Jo^{2} GMd^{1} GMy दाप्यं; TMd^{3} दास्यं; NNg सुवर्णं दाप्यः; Lo^{1} Pu^{7} Tr^{1} [*cor sh to*] सुवर्णः; wKt^{1} सुवर्णं तु तस्य — d) BCa स्यात्तस्यां; TMd^{4} स्तेयास्य; Hy Tr^{2} MTr^{4} MTr^{6} स्तेनस्य; Tr^{2} निकृतिः; BBe^{2} wKt^{1} Lo^{2} Pu^{5} Pu^{7} [*Jolly* G] निष्कृतिं

214. Cited by *Dev* 3.470; pādas a-b cited by *Dev*3.454 — a) La^{1} Pu^{5} Pu^{7} Tj^{1} [*Jolly* G] दत्तस्यैवोदिता; Lo^{1} दत्तस्येवोदिता; La^{1} NPu^{1} Wa °षोदितो; wKt^{1} NKt^{4} धर्मा; La^{1} TMd^{4} NPu^{1} धर्मो — b) La^{1} यथावदनुपूर्वशः; GMy तथा°; Lo^{1} °नवक्रियो; GMd^{1} °नविक्रिया; MTr^{4} °नसक्रिया; Jm TMd^{3} TMd^{4} °नुपक्रिया — c) BBe^{2} NKt^{4} La^{1} Lo^{2} GMd^{1} TMd^{3} TMd^{4} GMy Ox^{2} NPu^{1} Tr^{1} MTr^{4} MTr^{5} MTr^{6} *Dev* अतः परं; GMd^{5} अतः प्रवक्ष्यामि [*om* ऊर्ध्वं] — d) Tj^{1} वैतन°; BKt^{5} Lo^{5} चेतन°; Lo^{2} °नस्यनपक्रियां;

भृतोऽनार्तो न कुर्याद्यो दर्पात्कर्म यथोदितम् ।
स दण्ड्यः कृष्णलान्यष्टौ न देयं चास्य वेतनम् ॥२१५॥
आर्तस्तु कुर्यात् स्वस्थः सन् यथाभाषितमादितः ।
सुदीर्घस्यापि कालस्य तल्लभेतैव वेतनम् ॥२१६॥
यथोक्तमार्तः स्वस्थो वा यस्तत्कर्म न कारयेत् ।
न तस्य वेतनं देयमल्पोनस्यापि कर्मणः ॥२१७॥
एष धर्मोऽखिलेनोक्तो वेतनादानकर्मणः ।
अत ऊर्ध्वं प्रवक्ष्यामि धर्मं समयभेदिनाम् ॥२१८॥
यो ग्रामदेशसंघानां कृत्वा सत्येन संविदम् ।
विसंवदेन्नरो लोभात् तं राष्ट्राद्विप्रवासयेत् ॥२१९॥
निगृह्य दापयेच्चैनं समयव्यभिचारिणम् ।
चतुःसुवर्णान्षण्णिष्कांञ्छतमानं च राजतम् ॥२२०॥

GMd[1] °नस्यनविक्रियां; GMy Tr[2] °क्रिया

215. Cited by *Vij* 2.198; *Apa* 797; *Lakṣ* 12.404; *Dev* 3.473; *Mādh* 3.215 — a) *Apa* भृत्यो; *Vij* भर्त्यो; GMy मृतो; BKt[5] भृतोर्तो; *Jolly* भृतो नार्तो; all com. support अनार्तः — b) WKt[3] NKt[4] दर्प्या°; NPu[1] दर्पाद्धर्म; *Vij* यथोचितं— c) Bo दण्ड्या; GMd[5] Pu[5] Pu[7] Tr[2] [*Jolly* G] *Dev* कृष्णलानष्टौ — d) [*Jolly* G] च देयं; BCa Ho Jo[2] BKt[5] Lo[2] Lo[3] OOr SOx[1] SPu[6] Pu[8] Tj[1] Tr[2] *Vij* तस्य; *Apa* तच्च; Pu[4] Pu[5] Pu[7] [*Jolly* G] चैव; WKt[3] वेदनं; Jo[2] Lo[3] Tj[1] वर्तनं; Hy तेवनं; Lo[2] Lo[5] चेतनं

216. Cited by *Vij* 2.198; *Apa* 797; *Lakṣ* 12.404; *Dev* 3.474; *Mādh* 3.234–5 — a) Bo आर्तस्य; La[1] आर्यस्तु; Be[3] कुर्यात्तु स्वस्थो यथा°; Hy सुस्थः — b) TMd[4] °भाषितं दूषितः; *Apa* [vl] °भाषितमात्मनः — c) MTr[4] MTr[6] सुदीर्घेनापि कालेन; Tr[2] सुदीर्घस्य तस्य कालस्य; Hy Jm Jo[1] La[1] Lo[1] GMd[5] NPu[1] Pu[2] Pu[4] [*Jolly* Ku] *Vij Mandlik Jha KSS Dave* सदीर्घ°; Bc[3] सुदीर्घस्यैव; *Me*'s gloss बहुनापि कालेन appears to support the instrumental. — d) Pu[4] तल्लभेतेव; GMd[5] तल्लभेदेव; NKt[4] तल्लभेनैव; *Vij* स्वं लभेतैव; *Apa* स लभेतैव; Bo वेदनं; NKt[4] Lo[2] चेतनं

217. Omitted in Lo[4] Lo[5]. Cited by *Vij* 2.198; *Apa* 797; *Lakṣ* 12.404; *Dev* 3.474; *Mādh* 3.233 — a) BBe[2] Hy Jo[1] WKt[1] Kt[2] MTr[3] *Ku Mr Mandlik Jha KSS Dave* सुस्थो — b) Bo Lo[3] Tj[1] MTr[6] यत्तत्कर्म; WKt[3] Tr[2] यस्तु कर्म; Ho SOx[1] SPu[6] यः स्वकर्म; *Apa* [vl] न चाचरेत् — c) Ox[2] न चास्य; GMd[1] तत्ते तस्य चेतनं — d) Lo[1] SOx[1] Pu[3] SPu[6] °मल्पकस्यापि; Tj[2] °मल्पं कस्यापि; Bo °मल्पेकस्यापि; Be[3] La[1] GMd[5] °मल्पेनस्यापि; GMd[1] °मरोनस्यापि; Ho °मलोकस्यापि; Ox[2] °मल्पमास्यापि; Pu[5] Pu[7] [*Jolly* G] °मल्पेनाप्यस्य; BKt[5] °मल्पेनापेस्य; GMd[1] कर्मणा; Pu[2] कर्मणि; Tr[1] [*but cor*] कर्मिणः

218. Pādas a-b omitted in Ho TMd[4] and *ma sh* in Tr[1] [haplo] — a) GMd[5] एषां खिलेनाभिहता; Pu[5] Pu[7] एवं; Pu[8] °नोक्ततौ — b) GMd[5] वेतनस्यानपक्रिया; MTr[6] वेतनाद्यानि कर्मणः; Lo[2] चेतना°; Pu[7] [*but cor*] °कर्मणा — c) La[1] अतः परं; Lo[4] प्रवक्षामि — d) TMd[3] धर्मस्समय°; MTr[6] सभय°; Be[1] समभिचारिणां; Bo समधिवेदिनां; GMy °भेदिनं; BKt[5] La[1] Pu[3] °वेदिनां

219. Omitted in Be[1]. Cited by *Vij* 2.187; *Apa* 793; *Lakṣ* 12.424; *Dev* 3.530; *Mādh* 3.253 — a) GMd[5] ग्रामदेय°; WKt[1] °संहानां; *Dev* °संघेषु — b) BBe[2] सत्ये; NNg धर्मेण; SOx[1] SPu[6] सत्येन विन्दति — c) TMd[4] °वदन्नरो; BCa मोहात् — d) NPu[1] तद्राष्ट्रा°; TMd[4] तं स राष्ट्रा°; Tr[1] [*but mc sh*] राष्ट्रं विप्र°; Hy MTr[6] °वासयत्

220. Pādas a-b omitted in Be[1]; pādas c-d omitted in GMd[1] and *ma sh* in Tr[1]. Cited by *Vij*

एवं दण्डविधिं कुर्याद्धार्मिकः पृथिवीपतिः ।
ग्रामजातिसमूहेषु समयव्यभिचारिणाम् ॥२२१॥
क्रीत्वा विक्रीय वा किंचिद्यस्येहानुशयो भवेत् ।
सोऽन्तर्दशाहात्तद्द्रव्यं दद्याच्चैवाददीत च ॥२२२॥
परेण तु दशाहस्य न दद्यान्नापि दापयेत् ।
आददानो ददच्चैव राज्ञा दण्ड्यः शतानि षट् ॥२२३॥
यस्तु दोषवतीं कन्यामनाख्याय प्रयच्छति ।
तस्य कुर्यान्नृपो दण्डं स्वयं षण्णवतिं पणान् ॥२२४॥

2.187; *Apa* 793; *Lakṣ* 12.424; *Dev*3.531; *Mādh* 3.253 — a) Lo^{4} TMd^{3} निगृह्या; Be^{3} MTr^{4} MTr^{6} *Apa* [vl] विगृह्य; BKt^{5} सगृह्य; *Mādh* निकृत्य; oOr *Dev Mādh Vij* दापयेदेनं; MTr^{6} *Bh* [pāṭha] दापयेद्वैनं; Be^{3} °येच्चैनां — b) Hy समये; Pu^{2} सममत्यभि°; TMd^{4} Pu^{4} सममव्यभि°; Be^{3} wKt^{1} °चारिणां — c) *Mādh* चतुःसुवर्णकं निष्कं शत°; *Vij* °सुवर्णं षण्णि°; TMd^{3} °सुवर्णषण्णि°; TMd^{4} °सुवर्णाषण्णि°; *Dev* °सुवर्णं षण्णिष्कं शत°; GMd^{5} °सुवर्णान्त्रिष्कान्वा शत°; BBe^{2} °वर्णान्सशुल्कान्शत° — d) wKt^{1} °मानस्तु; Be^{1} BBe^{2} Bo wKt^{3} La^{1} NNg Pu^{8} तु; Tr^{2} राजतः; Pu^{2} Pu^{4} राजनं; Bo सज्जतं

221. Omitted in GMd^{1} and *ma sh* in Tr^{1}. Cited by *Lakṣ* 12.424; *Mādh* 3.253 — a) BCa Jo^{2} wKt^{1} Lo^{2} Tj^{1} Tr^{1} [*Jolly* Ku R Nd] *Rn* एतं; Jo^{1} Jo^{2} La^{1} एत; Jm Kt^{2} Lo^{3} Pu^{2} Pu^{4} MTr^{3} MTr^{5} *Ku Mr Mandlik Jha KSS Dave* एतद्धण्ड°; TMd^{3} एकदण्ड°; TMd^{4} °विधं — c) Bo °जातिः; oOr °जातिविवाहेषु; NPu^{1} °समूहे तु — d) Bo Kt^{2} wKt^{3} Lo^{2} GMy NNg Pu^{8} MTr^{6} °चारिणं; TMd^{4} °चारिणः

222* Pādas c-d [up to 228b] omitted in Lo^{2} [haplo]. Cited by *Vij* 2.177; *Apa* 831; *Lakṣ* 12.430; *Dev*3.512; *Mādh* 3.257; pādas a-b cited by *Vij* 2.254 — a) Bo HoNNg कृत्वा; Lo^{1} कृत्य विक्रीय; GMd^{5} विक्रय; NPu^{1} विक्रीत; GMd^{1} विक्रयवान्किंचि°; Pu^{2} Pu^{4} चा; TMd^{3} वा छिद्य यस्ये° — c) Bo यो; *Bh* सोऽयं दशा°; Lo^{1} °शाहं तद्द्रव्यं; La^{1} *Apa* °शाहे तद्द्रव्यं; GMd^{1} °शाहात्तत्सर्वं; TMd^{4} GMd^{5} GMy MTr^{4} MTr^{6} *Bh* [in root text, but he rejects it] °शाहात्तत्साम्रा; BCa °शाहाद्द्रष्टव्यं — d) BBe^{2} Bo Ho Hy Jo^{2} wKt^{1} wKt^{3} Lo^{3} sOx^{1} Pu^{2} Pu^{4} sPu^{6} [*cor to*] Tj^{1} Tj^{2} Tr^{2} [*Jolly* R] *Dave Mandlik Jha KSS* वा

223. Omitted in Lo^{2}; verses 223 and 224 transposed in Bo; folio containing 223d–242c missing in Bo. Cited by *Vij* 2.258; *Apa* 831; *Lakṣ* 12.430; *Dev* 3.512 — a) TMd^{3} अपरेण दशा°; GMd^{5} NNg दशाहस्या — b) NKt^{4} TMd^{3} GMd^{5} GMy [*Jolly* Nd] न दद्यान्नाददीत च [GMy नादद्या°; NKt^{4} वा]; oOr नैव दद्यान्न दापयेत्; Ho NNg sOx^{1} sPu^{6} नादद्या°; Be^{3} *Lakṣ* दद्यान्नैव; *Apa* दद्यान्न च — c) Bo GMd^{5} आददाने; BKt^{5} अददानो; Be^{1} Tj^{2} ददश्चैव; TMd^{3} ददंश्चैव; Lo^{1} ददेच्चैव — d) wKt^{3} राज्ञः; Tj^{1} राज्ञां; GMd^{1} दण्ड्यौ राज्ञौ; TMd^{4} पण्या राज्ञा; Lo^{4} Lo^{5} [*Jolly* M] दण्ड्यौ; Tr^{2} दण्डः; Lo^{1} दण्डं; MTr^{5} *Apa* दाप्यः

Additional verses in *Mandlik* [ण, ञ; first verse only in ड] *KSS Dave:*

स्याच्चतुर्विंशतिपणो दण्डस्तस्य व्यतिक्रमे ।
पणस्य दशमे भागे दाप्यः स्याददतिपातिनि ।।१।।
क्रीत्वा विक्रीय वा पण्यमगृह्णन्न ददतस्तथा ।
पणा द्वादश दाप्यश्च मनुष्याणां च वत्सरान् ।।२।।
पणा द्वादश दाप्यः स्यात्प्रतिबोधे न चेद्भवेत् ।
पशूनामप्यनाख्याने त्रिपदादर्पणं भवेत् ।।३।।

224. Omitted in Lo^{2}; order of verses in Pu^{8}: 224a, 225b, 226, 225c-d, 227 (224b, 225a omitted) — a) Pu^{2} Pu^{4} स्वयं दोश°; Jo^{1} wKt^{3} Lo^{4} °वती — b) wKt^{3} °मन्याख्याय; TMd^{4} °मसंख्याय — c) TMd^{3} °न्नृपा; Be^{3} दण्डः — d) Pu^{2} Pu^{4} Pu^{7} षण्णवतिः; Tr^{1} [*but cor*] षण्णवतीं; GMd^{5} °वतीन्पणान्;

अकन्येति तु यः कन्यां ब्रूयाद् द्वेषेण मानवः ।
स शतं प्राप्नुयाद्दण्डं तस्या दोषमदर्शयन् ॥२२५॥
पाणिग्रहणिका मन्त्राः कन्यास्वेव प्रतिष्ठिताः ।
नाकन्यासु क्वचिन्नृणां लुप्तधर्मक्रिया हि ताः ॥२२६॥
पाणिग्रहणिका मन्त्रा नियतं दारलक्षणम् ।
तेषां निष्ठा तु विज्ञेया विद्वद्भिः सप्तमे पदे ॥२२७॥
यस्मिन्यस्मिन्कृते कार्ये यस्येहानुशयो भवेत् ।
तमनेन विधानेन धर्म्ये पथि निवेशयेत् ॥२२८॥
पशुषु स्वामिनां चैव पालानां च व्यतिक्रमे ।
विवादं संप्रवक्ष्यामि यथावद्धर्मतत्त्वतः ॥२२९॥
दिवा वक्तव्यता पाले रात्रौ स्वामिनि तद्गृहे ।
योगक्षेमेऽन्यथा चेत्तु पालो वक्तव्यतामियात् ॥२३०॥

Be3 पणात्; Jo1 पणां; Tr2 परान्; Lo1 वसन्

225. Omitted in Lo2 Pu5 — a) Pu2 Pu4 अकन्यैव तु; mTr4 अकन्याकं तु; mTr6 अकन्यकान्तु; Be3 Lo1 Lo4 Lo5 [*Jolly* M4–5] च — a-b) gMd1 यः कन्यां समनुब्रूयात् यस्तु द्वेषेण मानवः; gMd5 अकन्येति तु यो ब्रूयात् कन्यादेपेण मानवः — b) Kt2 sOx1 sPu6 दोषेण; La1 Pu2 वेषेण — d) Tr2 स्वयं षण्णवतिं परान् [cf. 224d]; Be3 tMd3 Pu2 Pu4 तस्य; wKt3 तस्माद्दोष°; Lo5 tMd4 °दर्शयेत्

226. Omitted in Be1 Lo2 sOx1 sPu6; pādas c-d omitted in gMd5 — a) oOr °ग्राहणिका; Tr2 °ग्राहिणिका — b) Be3 कन्याश्चैव; Jo1 प्रतिष्ठितः — c) mTr4 न कन्यासु; Tr1 क्रिया नृणां — d) Pu2 Pu4 लुप्तकर्म°; tMd4 लुव्धधर्म°; wKt1 नप्तधर्म° *mc to* नष्टधर्म; Lo4 Lo5 गुप्तधर्म°; Be3 Pu5 ता; Wa सा

227. Omitted in Lo2 Lo4 Lo5 gMd5 Pu5; verse 227 placed after 234 in gMy. Cited by *Dev* 1.222; *Mādh* 1.492 — a) *Dev* [vl] पाणिग्रहणमन्त्रस्तु; tMd4 *Mādh* पाणिग्रहणमन्त्रैस्तु; gMd1 °ग्रहणिकं; Jo2 Tr2 mTr6 °ग्राहिणिका; tMd3 मन्त्र; Lo3 मन्त्रान् — b) sOx1 नियतां; tMd3 नियता; Jo1 दारु°; tMd3 gMy °लक्षणे; wKt3 °रक्षणं — c) wKt3 निष्ठां तु; mTr3 निष्ठा न; wKt3 विज्ञेयाद्विद्व° — c-d) tMd4 तु विद्वद्भिर्विज्ञेया — d) Wa नियतं सप्तमे; gMd1 *om* पदे

228.* Omitted in Lo4 Lo5 tMd3 gMy [*Jolly* Nd]; not commented by *Nd;* pādas a-b omitted in Lo2, pādas b-d in nPu1, and pādas c-d in Pu5. Cited by *Lakṣ* 12.430; *Dev* 3.513 — a) Lo1 अस्मिनस्मिन्कृते; Pu2 Pu4 *om first* यस्मिन् — d) Pu2 Pu4 धर्मोपविनिवेशयेत्; bBe2 Be3 Ho Kt2 wKt3 Lo1 Lo3 tMd4 gMd5 oOr sOx1 Ox2 sPu6 Tj1 Tr2 mTr5 *KSS* धर्मे; La1 gMd1 धर्म्मे; Hy निवेशयत्; gMd1 निवेदयेत्; Wa नियोजयेत्

229. Pādas a-c omitted in nPu1. Cited by *Lakṣ* 12.413; *Dev* 3.482; *Mādh* 3.263 — a) wKt1 पशुस्वस्वामिनां; Tr2 स्वामिनं — b) nNg पलानां; tMd3 mTr6 पालनां; bKt5 पाणीनां; gMd1 बालानां; gMd1 tMd4 *Lakṣ* च यथाविधि — c) Pu2 विवादः; oOr विवाहं — d) Pu5 Pu7 यथावद्धर्ममादितः

230. Cited by *Apa* 772; *Lakṣ* 12.415 — a) gMy वक्तव्यतां; Tj1 व्यक्तव्यत्ता; Tr2 वक्तव्यया; Lo3 वक्तवता; gMd1 कर्तव्यता; sOx1 sPu6 [*cor to*] चक्रव्यता; Pu2 Pu4 पालै; tMd3 पाति; Tr2 ताले; tMd4 तारे — b) tMd4 रात्रे; Jo1 स्वामिन; gMy स्वामि; Be1 तद्गृहे — c) La1 योगक्षेमो तथान्यथा चेत्तु; Jo1 Tr2 योगे; Be1 Lo1 °क्षेमौ; bBe2 Be3 Jo2 Lo3 gMd1 tMd3 gMd5 gMy nNg oOr nPu1 Tj1 Wa *Apa* °क्षेमो; tMd4 Pu2 °क्षेमा; mTr6 °क्षेमो यथा; Pu5 Pu7 °क्षेमोथवा चेत्तु; Jo2 Lo3 Tj1 Tr1 चेत्स्यात्; bKt5 यत्तु; gMd5 तत्तु; Be1 वत्तु; wKt1 *om* तु — d) Pu2 पालो न कथ्यतामियात्; wKt3 पाले

गोपः क्षीरभृतो यस्तु स दुह्याद्दशतो वराम् ।
गोस्वाम्यनुमते भृत्यः सा स्यात्पालेऽभृते भृतिः ॥२३१॥
नष्टं विनष्टं कृमिभिः श्वहतं विषमे मृतम् ।
हीनं पुरुषकारेण प्रदद्यात्पाल एव तु ॥२३२॥
विघुष्य तु हृतं चौरैर्न पालो दातुमर्हति ।
यदि देशे च काले च स्वामिनः स्वस्य शंसति ॥२३३॥
कर्णौ चर्म च वालांश्च बस्तिस्नायूनि रोचनाम् ।
पशुषु स्वामिनां* दद्यान् मृतेष्वङ्कांश्च दर्शयेत् ॥२३४॥

231. Placed after 244 in TMd^{3} GMy [*Jolly* Nd] and after 236 in BKt^{5} [*Jolly* M]. Cited by *Apa* 772; *Lakṣ* 12.413; *Dev* 3.483; *Mādh* 3.263 — a) Be^{3} गोपा; wKt^{3} गोप; MTr^{6} गावः; *Mādh* गवां; wKt^{1} यं तु — b) Wa सुदुह्या°; La^{1} संदुष्टा दशतो; Pu^{2} Pu^{4} सद्बुध्या दशतो; MTr^{5} दुहेद्दशतो; Ho दुह्यान्दशतो; Be^{3} दह्याद्दशतो; wKt^{1} दह्याकुशतो चवां; Ho Ox^{2} sPu^{6} Wa वरान्; TMd^{3} GMy Tj^{1} वरं; TMd^{4} वराः; Be^{3} परां; Pu^{2} Pu^{4} वशं — c) Be^{1} गोस्वामिनुमते; BKt^{5} गोस्वामिन्यनुमते; TMd^{3} गोस्वाम्यस्वमतो; GMd^{1} यो धर्मेनुमतं; NPu^{1} °नुभृते; GMy *Mādh Apa* [vl as in ed.] °नुमतो; MTr^{5} °मतां; MTr^{6} °मता; Lo^{2} °मतेभ्यः सा; Pu^{2} Pu^{4} भृत्याः — d) NKt^{4} सास्य स्यात्पालने भृतिः; TMd^{3} सा स्यात्पातिभृतोपतिः; Be^{1} GMd^{1} स; Be^{3} सो; Pu^{5} Pu^{7} स्यात्पाल; Hy स्यात्पालो; BCa [*but cor*] स्याद्गोप; Pu^{2} Pu^{4} *Apa* [vl] °भृतिभृतिः; Lo^{1} NNg °भृते भृति; GMd^{1} °भृते भृदि

232. Cited by *Vij* 2.164; *Apa* 773; *Lakṣ* 12.416; *Dev* 3.485; *Mādh* 3.264 — a) *Vij* नष्टं जग्धं च कृमिभिः; Lo^{3} नष्टां; NNg विनिष्टं; *Lakṣ* विजग्धं; Be^{1} NKt^{4} TMd^{3} NNg Tj^{1} Tr^{1} Tr^{2} क्रिमिभिः; BBe^{2} क्रमिभिः; *Apa* [vl] कृषिभिः — b) BKt^{5} कृमिभिवहतं; wKt^{3} oOr Tr^{2} स्वहतं; Lo^{4} Pu^{2} Pu^{4} स्वाहतं; NPu^{1} श्वहनं; Pu^{5} Pu^{7} स्वहस्तं; sOx^{1} sPu^{6} विषमं; wKt^{1} विषये; Lo^{3} Tj^{1} स्थितं; MTr^{4} हतं; MTr^{6} स्मृतं — c) NKt^{4} हीन — d) *Lakṣ* प्रदद्याद्गोप; GMd^{5} °द्यात्पालनाय तु; TMd^{4} येव तु; Jo^{2} Lo^{3} Tj^{1} एव च; GMd^{1} *Apa* एव तत्

233. Cited by *Vij* 2.164; *Apa* 772; *Dev* 3.484; *Mādh* 3.264 — a) oOr Tr^{2} विघुष्यं; Lo^{2} विघुष्यु; TMd^{3} निघुष्य; Jm विधुष्य; *Mādh* विशिष्य; *Vij* विक्रम्य; MTr^{6} विहृष्य; wKt^{1} La^{1} विघ्नस्य; Ho विघुष्यतहृतं; Tj^{1} विघुष्यतिहृतं; Lo^{3} विघुष्यातिहृतं; NKt^{4} विघुष्यतोहृतं; BKt^{5} विघुष्यनिकृतं; Pu^{2} Pu^{4} विद्युदनुहृतं; Pu^{5} Pu^{7} च हृतं; GMd^{5} हृते; Hy कृतं; Kt^{2} हृतश्चौ°; MTr^{5} हृतश्चोरैर्न; Lo^{2} Lo^{3} TMd^{4} GMd^{5} GMy MTr^{6} *Dev* चोरैर्न — b) Lo^{4} Lo^{5} [*Jolly* M] *Apa* चौरैर्न पालस्तत्र किल्बिषी; Jm धातुम° — c) Pu^{5} Pu^{7} देशे तु काले तु; Ho *om second* च — d) GMd^{1} स्वामिना; TMd^{4} oOr स्वामिनस्तस्य

234.* Omitted in Lo^{5} Wa; pādas a-b *ma sh* in Tr^{1}. Cited by *Lakṣ* 12.418; *Dev* 3.487; *Mādh* 3.265 — a) GMd^{1} TMd^{3} GMd^{5} Tr^{1} MTr^{6} चर्मकर्णावस्थिवालान्; TMd^{4} चर्मचर्मवसेवालम्; GMy [*Jolly* Nd] चर्मकर्णौ सक्थिवालौ; oOr MTr^{5} कर्णौ च चर्मवालांश्च; Hy *om* चर्म; Be^{1} Lo^{2} बालांश्च; Hy Kt^{2} NPu^{1} वालाश्च; Tr^{1} वालं च; Pu^{2} Pu^{4} Pu^{5} Pu^{7} लोमांश्च — b) GMd^{1} अस्थिस्नायूनि रोचतां; TMd^{4} अस्थिस्नायानिरोचनात्; TMd^{3} अस्थिस्नायेनिरोचने; *Mādh* वस्त्यस्थिस्नायुरोचनं; GMd^{5} अस्तिस्नायु च रोचनं; Be^{3} Hy Jm Jo^{1} wKt^{1} Kt^{2} Lo^{1} Lo^{3} oOr sOx^{1} sPu^{6} Pu^{8} Tj^{1} Tj^{2} *Lakṣ Dev Mandlik Jha KSS Dave* बस्तिं स्नायुं च रोचनां [wKt^{1} Lo^{4} वस्ति°; Be^{3} वास्थि]; Be^{1} Jo^{2} NNg NPu^{1} वस्ति°; MTr^{6} अस्ति°; Tr^{2} °स्नायुनिरोधनां — c) Be^{1} Be^{3} Ho wKt^{1} NKt^{4} BKt^{5} La^{1} Lo^{1} Lo^{2} Lo^{4} GMd^{1} TMd^{3} GMd^{5} GMy NNg oOr sOx^{1} Ox^{2} NPu^{1} Pu^{2} Pu^{3} Pu^{4} Pu^{5} sPu^{6} Pu^{7} Pu^{8} Tr^{1} Tr^{2} MTr^{4} MTr^{5} MTr^{6} *Mādh* पशुस्वामिषु दद्यात्तु [BKt^{5} दद्यान् *om* तु; TMd^{3} GMy तद्दद्यान्]; *Lakṣ* पशुस्वामिनि दद्यात्तु; TMd^{4} पशुं तु स्वामिषु दद्यान्; Jo^{2} पशूणां स्वामिने; Lo^{3} Tj^{1} स्वामिने — d) Be^{1} मृतेष्वङ्गान्यदर्शयेत्; *Mādh* मृतेष्वङ्गाभिदर्शनं; Lo^{4} मृतेष्वङ्कं च; *Lakṣ* मृतेष्वङ्कादि; Lo^{2} मृतेष्वेकांश्च; Pu^{2} Pu^{4} मृतेष्वेकाश्च; TMd^{4} मृते ह्येतांश्च; BBe^{2} Be^{3} BCa Ho Hy

अजाविके तु संरुद्धे वृकैः पाले त्वनायति ।
यां प्रसह्य वृको हन्यात् पाले तत्किल्बिषं भवेत् ॥२३५॥
तासां चेदवरुद्धानां चरन्तीनां मिथो वने ।
यामुत्प्लुत्य वृको हन्यान्न पालस्तत्र किल्बिषी ॥२३६॥
धनुःशतं परीहारो ग्रामस्य स्यात्समन्ततः ।
शम्यापातास्त्रयो वापि त्रिगुणो नगरस्य तु ॥२३७॥
तत्रापरिवृतं धान्यं विहिंस्युः पशवो यदि ।
न तत्र प्रणयेद्दण्डं नृपतिः पशुरक्षिणाम् ॥२३८॥
वृतिं तत्र प्रकुर्वीत यामुष्ट्रो नावलोकयेत् ।
छिद्रं च वारयेत्सर्वं श्वसूकरमुखानुगम् ॥२३९॥

Jm Jo^1 Jo^2 wKt^1 Kt^2 wKt^3 La^1 Lo^1 Lo^3 GMd^1 TMd^3 GMd^5 GMy oOr Ox^2 Pu^8 Tj^1 Tj^2 Tr^1 MTr^3 MTr^4 MTr^6 [*Jolly* R Nd]*Dev Rn Nd Mandlik KSS* मृतेष्वङ्गानि; sOx^1 sPu^6 मृगेष्वङ्गानि; Pu^3 Tr^2 मृते अङ्गानि; BKt^5 मृतेष्वङ्गां च; *Nā* appears to read शृङ्गानि दर्शयेत् but gives मृतेष्वङ्गानि as pāṭha; Lo^3 TMd^3 GMd^5 GMy Tj^1 MTr^4 दर्शयन्; MTr^6 Hy दर्शयत् — After this verse GMy inserts 227.

235. Omitted in Lo^5; pādas a-b omitted in GMy and pāda-d in Lo^1 [haplo]; placed after verse 237 in Be^1. Cited by *Apa* 773; *Dev* 3.486; *Mādh* 3.265 — a) Pu^2 Pu^4 Tr^2 अजाविकेषु संरुद्धे — b) Be^1 *adds* वृद्धे *before* वृकैः; TMd^4 वृक्षैः; MTr^6 वृत्तैः पले; MTr^4 व्रजे पाले; wKt^3 पालैः; Lo^1 पालै-स्त्वना°; TMd^4 पालेस्त्वना°; BKt^5 Lo^1 Pu^5 Pu^7 [*Jolly* G] त्वनापदि; La^1 त्वनादपि; TMd^3 त्वनाम्यति; *Apa* [vl] तुनायति — c) TMd^4 Pu^2 Pu^4 या; NPu^1 यान्प्र°; *Apa* यत्प्र°; TMd^4 हन्या — d) Lo^1 न पालस्तत्र किल्बिषी; TMd^3 पातिपु किल्बिषो; Lo^4 Wa तत्पाले किल्बिषं; Tr^2 पातालः तत्किल्बिषं

236. Omitted in Lo^5; pādas a-c omitted Lo^1; following sequence in Be^1: 237a-b, 236, 237c-d. Cited by *Apa* 773; *Dev* 3.486; *Mādh* 3.265 — a) TMd^4 तासामनुपरुद्धानां;Ox^2 आसां; BKt^5 मासां; TMd^3 तागां; Pu^3 Pu^8 Tr^2 चैवावरुद्धानां; MTr^4 त्वनवरुद्धानां; NKt^4 चेदनिरुद्धानां; TMd^3 चेदवरन्दानां; BBe^2 BCa Ho Pu^2 Pu^4 Pu^5 sPu^6 [*but cor*] Pu^7 MTr^6 [*Jolly* M G]*Jolly* चेदविरुद्धानां — b) TMd^4 *om* वने — c) Ho wKt^1 BKt^5 La^1 Lo^4 GMd^5 NNg Pu^5 Pu^7 Tj^1 Tr^1 [*Jolly* M G R] *Go NSm* 6.17 *Jolly Dev* यामुत्पत्य; oOr*Apa* यामुपेत्य; Be^3 यामुन्मथ्य; Kt^2 कृको — d) Be^3 हन्यात्प्रपाल°; GMy पालस्त्वत्र

237. Pādas a-b placed after verse 235 in Be^1. Cited by *Apa* 774; *Lakṣ* 12462 — a) Ho शनुः°; NKt^4 चतुः°; TMd^3 GMy *Apa* °शत; GMy परीवार्यो; [*Jolly* Nd] परीवारो; GMd^5 परिवारो; TMd^3 परीपाको; Tr^2 परीनाहो; [*Jolly* N Gr] *YDh* 2.167परीणाहो; Lo^1 Pu^8 परीहाणो; Wa परीणामां — b) NKt^4 ग्रामस्यास्य समन्ततः; TMd^3 ग्रामसमन्ततः; La^1 Pu^2 Pu^4 ग्रामस्या; Lo^3 ग्रामेऽस्य; Tr^2 ग्रामस्यात्सम° — c) Be^1 Tj^2 शम्याः°; BKt^5 सम्या°; BBe^2 wKt^1 शस्या°; GMd^1 TMd^3 MTr^6 शम्याप्रासा°; sOx^1 sPu^6 [*cor to*] शष्पायाता°; Tr^2 षस्तिपाता°; La^1 शय्याघाता°; Be^3 °पातांस्त्रयो; Lo^1 Tj^1 °पातस्त्रयो; NKt^4 °पातास्तुयो; GMd^5 °स्त्रयोपि स्युस्त्रिगु° — d) Be^1 TMd^3 GMd^5 GMy Tr^1 त्रिगुणं; Tr^2 त्रिगुणा; MTr^6 त्रिगुणान्; Be^1 नररास्य; Tj^2 नरारस्य; Pu^2 Pu^4 नरकस्य; La^1 Pu^2 Pu^4 च

238. Cited by *Vij* 2.162; *Lakṣ* 12.462; *Dev* 3.491; *Mādh* 3.266 — a) wKt^1 अत्रापरि°; Pu^5 Pu^7 °परिहृतं; Pu^2 Pu^4 °परिधृतं; Tr^2 °परिमितं; La^1 नान्यं — b) GMy धान्यमहिंस्युः; Be^3 Pu^5 Pu^7 विहंस्युः; La^1 निहिंस्युः; TMd^3 न हिंस्युः; *Mādh* प्रहिंस्युः; Pu^3 विहिंश्रुः; TMd^4 जातंस्युः; Lo^1 विहत्य — c) wKt^3 प्रणवे° — d) MTr^4 MTr^6 परिरक्षिणां; Wa °रक्षिणं; Be^1 GMd^1 GMy °रक्षणं; Pu^5 Pu^7 °रक्षणां; Be^3 °रक्षणात्; GMd^5 °रक्षकं

239. Cited by *Vij* 2.162 — a) Be^3 La^1 Lo^1 Pu^2 Pu^3 Pu^4 Pu^5 Pu^7 वृत्तिं; Tr^2 वृत्तिः; BBe^2

पथि क्षेत्रे परिवृते* ग्रामान्तीयेऽथ वा पुनः ।
सपालः शतदण्डार्हो विपालान्वारयेत्पशून् ॥२४०॥
क्षेत्रेष्वन्येषु तु पशुः सपादं पणमर्हति ।
सर्वत्र तु शदो देयः क्षेत्रिकस्येति धारणा ॥२४१॥
अनिर्दशाहां गां सूतां वृषान्देवपशूंस्तथा ।
सपालान्वा विपालान्वा न दण्ड्यान्मनुरब्रवीत् ॥२४२॥
क्षेत्रिकस्यात्यये दण्डो भागाद्दशगुणो भवेत् ।
ततोऽर्धदण्डो भृत्यानामज्ञानात् क्षेत्रिकस्य तु ॥२४३॥

वृतिस्तत्र; Lo[1] Lo[5] GMd[1] NPu[1] Pu[7] Pu[8] Tr[2] Be[3] MTr[6] तत्र तु कुर्वीत; Be[1] BCa Ho wKt[3] TMd[4] GMd[5] oOr sOx[1] Pu[2] Pu[4] sPu[6] *Vij* तु तत्र कुर्वीत [*Vij* च तत्र; wKt[3] तु तत]; BKt[5] त्वेकुर्वीत; Tr[1] [*ma* प्र]कुर्वीत; NKt[4] सुकुर्वीत — b) TMd[4] योमुषा; Be[1] नावलोकयन्; Hy Jm Jo[1] Jo[2] Kt[2] BKt[5] Pu[3] Tj[2] MTr[3] *Ku Rc Mandlik Jha KSS Dave* न विलोकयेत् — c) wKt[3] छिन्द्रं; NKt[4] Lo[2] NPu[1] Pu[3] Tr[2] वावारये°; Lo[5] TMd[3] Pu[7] Tj[2] MTr[5] Wa [*Jolly* M Nd] चावारये°; wKt[1] चारावये°; NNg चावरये°; Pu[2] वाचये°; TMd[4] कारये°; Be[3] धारये°; *Dev* पूरये°; Pu[4] वाये°; Hy °येत्सर्व — d) Tr[2] स्वशूकर°; BBe[2] Be[3] BCa Ho Hy Kt[2] wKt[3] Lo[4] Lo[5] NNg NPu[1] Pu[2] Pu[4] Pu[5] Pu[7] Pu[8] °शूकर°; Pu[8] °करखानुगं; BBe[2] °मखानुगं; Pu[5] Pu[7] °नुजं

240.* Cited by *Apa* 771; *Lakṣ* 12.463; *Dev* 3.490; *Mādh* 3.266 — a) wKt[1] पथे; Lo[1] Wa पक्षि; Ho Pu[2] Pu[4] परिवृत्ते; GMd[1] TMd[4] परिक्षेत्रे; oOr अन्यक्षेत्रे — b) oOr [*but mc sh*] ग्राममतिकये पुनः; Pu[8] ग्रामन्तीये; Be[1] ग्रामान्ताये; Be[3] ग्रामात्तीर्थे; TMd[4] गवांतीद्ये; *Apa* ग्रामान्तेयोथ; GMy ग्रामान्ते वाथ वा; Wa ग्रामान्तीयेषुथवा — c) Tr[2] सपालं; Lo[2] सबालः; Tj[2] शतं; TMd[3] शरदण्डार्हाः; NPu[1] स तु दण्डार्हो — d) [*Jolly* M] विपालाद्वार°; GMd[5] GMy Pu[5] Pu[7] MTr[4] MTr[5] MTr[6] [*Jolly* Nd] *Apa Dev* विपालं वार°; TMd[3] येपालं वार°; GMd[1] न पालं वार°; sPu[6] [*but cor*] विपालांश्चार°; Ho Jm विपालान्चार°; TMd[4] विपालं चार°; Tr[1] विपाला [*ma sh* न्धारयेत्पशून्]; wKt[3] °लान्वालये°; GMy °लान्वरये°; NKt[4] °लान्कारये°; Lo[2] °लान्धारये°; Ox[2] °लान्पालये°; TMd[3] GMd[5] GMy MTr[4] MTr[5] [*Jolly* Nd] *Dev* °येत्पशुं

241. Cited by *Apa* 769; *Dev* 3.489–90; pādas a-b cited by *Lakṣ* 12.464 — a) GMd[1] Tr[1] च — b) GMd[1] संपादं; Lo[2] सपाणं; TMd[3] सपापं; TMd[4] पशुमर्हति; *Lakṣ Apa* दण्डमर्हति — c) Be[3] सर्वत्रानुशयो देयः; oOr सर्वस्य; La[1] सर्वं न तु; Ho ससर्वं तु; Tj[2] स शदो; NNg त्वशितं देयं; [*Jolly* G] त्वसितं देयं; Pu[5] Pu[7] च सितं देयं; Lo[1] तु सैव दोषः; Be[1] BBe[2] Jm Jo[1] Jo[2] wKt[1] Kt[2] wKt[3] NKt[4] BKt[5] La[1] Lo[2] Lo[3] Lo[4] Lo[5] oOr Ox[2] Pu[2] Tj[1] Tr[1] Wa *Mandlik Jha KSS Dave* सदो; TMd[3] GMy MTr[4] MTr[6] शतो; GMd[1] दशो; Ho Hy सदा; Lo[2] सतो; TMd[4] शतं देयं — d) TMd[4] क्षेत्रिकस्य तु वारणा; Pu[8] क्षेत्रकस्येति; BBe[2] क्षेत्रियस्येति; La[1] क्षत्रियस्येति; BKt[5] Lo[4] Lo[5] TMd[3] GMd[5] GMy Tr[1] MTr[4] MTr[6] *Dev Apa* क्षेत्रिकायेति; Kt[2] धारणात्; *Apa* [vl] धारणाः; Jo[1] धारिणा

242. Cited by *Apa* 771; *Lakṣ* 12.468; *Dev* 3.496; *Mādh* 3.268 — a) Tr[1] [*but cor*] अनिर्दिशाहां; sOx[1] sPu[6] °शाहा; La[1] Lo[4] Lo[5] TMd[3] °शाहं; Be[3] Ho °शाहाद्रां — b) TMd[3] GMd[5] GMy वृषं देव°; Jo[1] NNg [*but mc sh*] वृषादेव°; Pu[5] Pu[7] घृषां देव°; Kt[2] Pu[4] °पशुस्तथा; GMy °पशुं तथा; TMd[3] °पशुं यथा; TMd[4] °पशूनपि — c) *Dev* अपालान्वा सपालान्वा; *Apa* अपालान्वा विपालान्वा; NKt[4] सपालास्वा विपालास्वा; Be[3] Pu[3] Pu[8] Tr[2] MTr[5] सपालान्वाप्यपालान्वा; Lo[3] Tj[1] सपालांश्च; TMd[4] सहपालान्विपा° — d) GMy Tj[2] न दण्ड्या मनु°; Tr[2] न दण्डान्मनु°; Wa *Apa* अदण्ड्यान्मनु°

243. Cited by *Lakṣ* 12.532 — a) Lo[1] GMd[5] क्षेत्रक°; Hy Jo[1] Kt[2] Lo[3] TMd[4] Ox[2] MTr[6] *Mandlik KSS* क्षेत्रियस्या°; NKt[4] °कस्याभये; wKt[1] La[1] GMd[1] °त्ययो; TMd[4] sOx[1] Ox[2] sPu[6] दण्ड्यो; Lo[1] दण्डे — b) Be[1] GMd[1] भागादश°; Bo भागां दश°; GMd[5] Pu[4] Tr[1] [*but cor*] भोगाद्दश°; oOr सेशाद्दश°; TMd[4]

एतद्विधानमातिष्ठेद्धार्मिकः पृथिवीपतिः ।
स्वामिनां च पशूनां च पालानां च व्यतिक्रमे ॥२४४॥
सीमां प्रति समुत्पन्ने विवादे ग्रामयोर्द्वयोः ।
ज्येष्ठे मासि नयेत्सीमां सुप्रकाशेषु सेतुषु ॥२४५॥
सीमावृक्षांस्तु कुर्वीत न्यग्रोधाश्वत्थकिंशुकान् ।
शाल्मलीसालतालांश्च क्षीरिणश्चैव पादपान् ॥२४६॥
गुल्मान्वेणूंश्च विविधान् शमीवल्लीस्थलानि च ।
शरान्कुब्जकगुल्मांश्च तथा सीमा न नश्यति ॥२४७॥
तडागान्युदपानानि वाप्यः प्रस्रवणानि च ।

वभिागादगुणो — c) Be^{1} NNg Wa अतोर्ध°; sOx^{1} sPu^{6} तदोर्ध°; Lo^{1} ततोर्ध — d) GMd^{1} °ज्ञानां; Be^{3} °ज्ञाना; La^{1} °ज्ञान; Pu^{4} क्षेत्रकस्य; Jm Jo^{1} Kt^{2} क्षेत्रियस्य; TMd^{3} MTr^{6} क्षत्रियस्य; Lo^{4} Lo^{5} च

244. Cited by *Lakṣ* 12.418; *Dev* 3.497 — a) TMd^{3} GMd^{5} GMy एतद्दण्डविधिं कुर्याद्धार्मिकः [GMd^{5} एवं दण्ड°]; TMd^{4} तद्विधान° — c) TMd^{3} स्वामिना; Jm स्वामिनश्च; wKt^{1} स्वामिकानां पशूनां — d) GMd^{1} पालनं; wKt^{1} पादानां; TMd^{4} °क्रमेः; TMd^{3} GMy °क्रमात्; TMd^{3} GMy inserts here verse 8.231.

245.* Cited by *Apa* 758; *Lakṣ* 12.439; *Dev* 3.544; *Mādh* 3.276 — a) TMd^{4} Tr^{1} [*but cor sh*] सीमादेप्रति संभूते; La^{1} सीमान्प्रति; Be^{3} समापन्ने — b) NNg ग्रामयोर्द्विजः — c) BBe^{2} Jm Jo^{1} *Mādh Jolly* ज्यैष्ठे; Be^{1} ज्यैष्टे; GMd^{1} TMd^{4} GMd^{5} GMy NPu^{1} Pu^{5} Pu^{7} MTr^{5} *Dev* ज्येष्ठ; TMd^{3} जेष्ठ; La^{1} GMd^{1} TMd^{3} TMd^{4} GMd^{5} GMy sOx^{1} NPu^{1} Pu^{5} sPu^{6} Pu^{7} Tr^{1} [*but cor sh*] MTr^{4} MTr^{5} MTr^{6} Wa *Mādh* मासे; GMd^{1} *Lakṣ* नयेदेनां; *Apa* नयेदेतां; TMd^{4} नयेदेतान् — d) Lo^{5} NPu^{1} Pu^{2} Pu^{4} Pu^{8} Tr^{2} *Mādh* सप्रकाशेषु; Bo NKt^{4} BKt^{5} Lo^{1} Lo^{2} NNg Pu^{3} Pu^{7} Wa संप्रकाशेषु; Be^{1} Pu^{5} संप्रकाशिषु; BBe^{2} Jo^{2} Lo^{3} Tj^{1} स्वप्रकाशेषु; GMy ह्यप्रकाशेषु; Lo^{4} Lo^{5} [*Jolly* M$^{4-5}$] हेतुषु; TMd^{4} सेवितं

246. Pādas c-d omitted in Be^{1}. Cited by *Vij* 2.150-1; *Lakṣ* 12.439; *Dev* 3.535; *Mādh* 3.270 — a) Be^{1} वृक्षांसीमास्तु; NKt^{4} °वृक्षासु; Be^{3} Hy Jo^{1} wKt^{1} Kt^{2} La^{1} Lo^{2} TMd^{3} GMy Pu^{5} Pu^{7} MTr^{3} *Vij Lakṣ* [*Jolly* G Nd] °वृक्षांश्च; Tj^{2} °वृक्षां कुर्वीत; *Lakṣ* कुर्वीरन् — b) wKt^{1} न्यग्रोधा *mc to* प्रक्षका; NNg न्यग्रोधोश्व°; Tr^{2} °किंशुकाः — c) MTr^{5} शाल्मलीं पालकालांश्च; GMy शल्मली°; Ox^{2} शाल्मलीःसाल°; Lo^{5} NPu^{1} Wa शाल्मलीःशाल°; Hy Jo^{1} Jo^{2} Kt^{2} Lo^{2} Lo^{3} Tj^{2} Tr^{1} MTr^{3} MTr^{4} *Dev Mandlik Jha KSS Dave* शाल्मलीन्साल°; BCa wKt^{1} BKt^{5} NNg NPu^{1} शाल्मलीन्शाल°; GMd^{1} GMd^{5} *Dev* शल्मलीन्साल°; GMy शाल्मलीशालांश्च; La^{1} Lo^{4} Pu^{2} Pu^{3} Pu^{4} °शाल°; *Mādh* °शालवृक्षांश्च; TMd^{4} °शारसालांश्च; Jm Pu^{8} °तालांस्तु; MTr^{6} °तालींश्च — d) Kt^{2} क्षीरण°; Hy °णश्चेव

247.* Pādas a-b omitted in Be^{1}. Cited by *Vij* 2.150-1; *Lakṣ* 12.439-40 — a) Tr^{1} गुलमांश्च वेणून्विविधान्; TMd^{3} °न्वेतान्श्च — b) BBe^{2} समी°; GMd^{1} शमीर्वल्ली°; Pu^{7} Wa शमीर्वल्लीः; Lo^{1} शमीमल्ली°; GMy शमीपल्व°; Lo^{5} कुशवल्ली° — c) GMd^{1} TMd^{3} शरान्कुर्यात् गुल्मांश्च; NKt^{4} कुशानक्रव्यहगुलमांश्च; wKt^{3} शला°; TMd^{4} शरं कुब्ज°; Tr^{2} शरान्कुज्यक°; TMd^{4} GMy MTr^{4} MTr^{6} शरान्कुल्यक°; Kt^{2} शरान्शुब्जक°; Lo^{2} शरान्कुप्यक°; BCa शरान्दब्जक°; NNg °ब्जकवृक्षांश्च — d) wKt^{3} Lo^{4} GMd^{5} NPu^{1} Pu^{2} Pu^{4} यथा; TMd^{4} सेमा; Ho La^{1} सीमात्र; Ho La^{1} Lo^{1} GMd^{5} पश्यति

The order of verses in *Me* appears to be: 247, 250, 249, 248; Jolly says that the order in *Me* is 247ab, 250cd, 249ab, 247cd, 248 [with 249cd and 250ab missing]; the order in Lo^{4} is 247ab, 250cd, 249ab, 250ab, 248. The commentary, however, contains explanations of 250ab. There is no commentary on 249cd.

सीमासंधिषु कार्याणि देवतायतनानि च ॥२४८॥
उपच्छन्नानि चान्यानि सीमालिङ्गानि कारयेत् ।
सीमाज्ञाने नृणां वीक्ष्य नित्यं लोके विपर्ययम् ॥२४९॥
अश्मनोऽस्थीनि गोवालांस्तुषान्भस्म कपालिकाः ।
करीषमिष्टकाङ्गारांश्छर्करा वालुकास्तथा ॥२५०॥
यानि चैवंप्रकाराणि कालाद्भूमिर्न भक्षयेत् ।
तानि संधिषु सीमायामप्रकाशानि कारयेत् ॥२५१॥
एतैर्लिङ्गैर्नयेत्सीमां राजा विवदमानयोः ।
पूर्वभुक्त्या च सततमुदकस्यागमेन च ॥२५२॥

248. Cited by *Vij* 2.150–1; *Lakṣ* 12.440 — a) NKt^{4} Lo^{2} Lo^{3} sOx^{1} MTr^{6} तडाका°; GMd^{5} Tj^{1} Tr^{1} [*but cor sh*] MTr^{5} तटाका°; TMd^{4} ताटका°; TMd^{3} GMy तटाकानुद°; La^{1} °न्युपपानानि; TMd^{3} °दपानां वा — b) La^{1} वापी; Be^{3} वापीं; MTr^{5} वापीः; TMd^{3} वापि; *Lakṣ* सरित्प्रस्र°; Pu^{4} वाप्यश्च श्रवणानि; BBe^{2} Bo^{2} Ho wKt^{3} La^{1} oOr Pu^{2} Pu^{5} Pu^{7} Tr^{2} प्रश्रवणानि; Pu^{8} *om* प्र — c) TMd^{4} सीम°; Tj^{1} सीमां; Pu^{2} Pu^{4} समा°; Pu^{3} Pu^{4} °संधीषु

249. Omitted in Lo^{4}; pādas a-b placed before 248 and pādas c-d omitted in BKt^{5}. Cited by *Vij* 2.150-1; *Lakṣ* 12.440; *Dev* 3.535 — a) Pu^{5} Pu^{7} उपछिन्नानि; TMd^{3} *om* चान्यानि; NKt^{4} कार्याणि — b) TMd^{4} सीम° — c) TMd^{3} सीम°; NKt^{4} °ज्ञानि; wKt^{1} नृणामीक्ष्य; wKt^{3} वीक्ष्यः — d) Pu^{2} नित्यं सीमाविपर्ययं; BBe^{2} Be^{3} Bo BCa wKt^{1} wKt^{3} La^{1} Lo^{2} GMd^{1} NNg NPu^{1} Tj^{1} Tj^{2} Tr^{1} MTr^{4} MTr^{6} Wa *Lakṣ Dev* लोके नित्यं; TMd^{4} GMd^{5} लोक; GMd^{1} विपर्ययात्; Pu^{8} विपर्ययां

Additonal verse in La^{1} oOr [cf. added verse after 8.265]:

ध्वजिनी पद्मिनी चैव एधान्यहर्यवर्जिता ।
राजशासननीता च सीमापञ्चविधाः स्मृताः ॥

b) La^{1} एधान्यहविपर्यवर्जिता *cor to* एधान्यहर्यवर्जिता; oOr नैधान्यभयवर्जिता (unclear)

250. Omitted in BKt^{5} Lo^{4}; pādas c-d omitted in Pu^{5}. Cited by *Vij* 2.150-1; *Lakṣ* 12.440 — a) La^{1} NNg गोवालास्तु°; Pu^{7} गोवालस्तु°; Ho GMd^{5} गोवालान्तु°; TMd^{3} गोवालांतु°; wKt^{3} NKt^{4} गोपालांस्तु°; GMd^{1} गोपालान्तु° — b) Wa *Lakṣ* °लांस्तथा भस्म; Jo^{2} Pu^{2} Pu^{4} °लांस्तुपभस्म; Be^{3} °लांस्तुषं भस्म; Pu^{8} °लांस्तुषान्नस्म; Be^{1} GMd^{1} TMd^{3} GMy MTr^{4} MTr^{6} कपालिकान्; TMd^{4} कपालकान् — c) Pu^{3} कारीष°; Tr^{2} कारिष°; Pu^{2} Pu^{4} कारीष्ट°; NKt^{4} oOr Pu^{7} °काङ्गाराः शर्करा; TMd^{3} GMd^{5} NNg °काङ्गार-न्शर्करा; Be^{3} Lo^{5} *Vij* °काङ्गारशर्करा — d) GMd^{1} °रान्शङ्कुंश्चकरवालुकान्; NKt^{4} Lo^{3} Tj^{1} वालुकांस्तथा; La^{1} Lo^{5} GMd^{5} GMy MTr^{4} वालुकां च ह [La^{1} MTr^{4} °कांश्च; Lo^{5} GMd^{5} °काश्च]; TMd^{3} वालुका च सा; Wa वालुकाश्च हि; MTr^{6} वालुकस्य ह

251. Omitted in Pu^{5} Wa. Cited by *Vij* 2.150-1; *Lakṣ* 12.441; *Dev* 3.535 — a) Be^{1} Hy Jo^{1} Lo^{1} GMd^{1} Tr^{2} चैव प्रका°; wKt^{3} चैनंप्रका° — b) GMy कालान्भूमि°; Tr^{2} कालं भूमि°; GMd^{1} कालभूमि°; Be^{1} NKt^{4} °द्भूमिं न; Pu^{2} Pu^{4} भक्षते — c) TMd^{4} संधिष्वेतानि वैर्सीम्नावप्रका°; Be^{1} नातिसंधिषु — c-d) Be^{1} सीमाया सप्र°; NPu^{1} सीमाया स्वप्र°; Tr^{2} सीमायाप्र°; Be^{3} सीमाया अप्र°; Lo^{4} Lo^{5} सीमायाः अप्र°; GMd^{1} सीमानामप्र°; NKt^{4} सीमायाः सप्रकाराणि — d) MTr^{6} °यामवकाशानि; TMd^{3} GMd^{5} GMy Tr^{1} °प्रकाशं निधापयेत्; TMd^{4} °प्रकारं च धापयेत्; GMd^{1} MTr^{4} MTr^{5} MTr^{6} धापयेत्

252. Pādas a-b cited by *Vij* 2.150–1; *Lakṣ* 12.441; *Dev* 3.537; *Mādh* 3.271 — a) TMd^{3} येकैर्लि° — a-b) TMd^{4} लिङ्गैर्नयन्तस्सीमानमेभिर्विवदता नृपः — b) GMy विविद°; Hy विवेद°; *Lakṣ* विवदतां नृणां — c) Be^{1} wKt^{1} MTr^{6} °भत्त्या; Be^{3} Ho wKt^{3} NKt^{4} Pu^{2} Pu^{4} Pu^{5} °भुक्ता; Ho NKt^{4} BKt^{5}

यदि संशय एव स्याल्लिङ्गानामपि दर्शने ।
साक्षिप्रत्यय एव स्यात् सीमावादविनिर्णयः ॥२५३॥
ग्रामेयककुलानां तु समक्षं सीम्नि साक्षिणः ।
प्रष्टव्याः सीमलिङ्गानि तयोश्चैव विवादिनोः ॥२५४॥
ते पृष्टास्तु यथा ब्रूयुः समस्ताः सीम्नि निश्चयम् ।
निबध्नीयात्तथा सीमां सर्वांस्तांश्चैव नामतः ॥२५५॥
शिरोभिस्ते गृहीत्वोर्वीं स्रग्विणो रक्तवाससः ।
सुकृतैः शापिताः स्वैः स्वैर्नयेयुस्ते समञ्जसम् ॥२५६॥
यथोक्तेन नयन्तस्ते पूयन्ते सत्यसाक्षिणः ।

Lo[1] sOx[1] Pu[5] sPu[6] Pu[7] तु — d) BCa TMd[3] GMy °दकागमनेन च; GMd[1] °दकस्यानमेव च; NNg तु

253. Cited by *Lakṣ* 12.441; *Mādh* 3.271; pādas c-d cited by *Vij* 2.152 — a) TMd[3] शंसय; Tr[2] एवं; GMy एवा — b) TMd[3] स्याल्लिङ्गानां तु विदर्शने; Be[3] Ho Lo[1] दर्शनं — c) Pu[4] Tr[2] साक्षी; Tr[2] एवं; BKt[5] GMy एवा — d) GMd[1] TMd[4] Tr[1] [*but cor sh*] MTr[4] MTr[6] *Lakṣ* विवादे सीमनिश्चयः [GMd[1] सीम्नि; TMd[4] सीम्न]; GMd[5] विवादे सीमनिर्णये; Be[3] Lo[1] Lo[4] Lo[5] oOr Tj[1] MTr[5] Wa सीमावादे; Lo[3] सीमावेद°; Be[1] TMd[3] sOx[1] Ox[2] sPu[6] [*Jolly* Nd] *Vij* °विनिर्णये; Be[3] विनिर्णयेत्; GMy °विनिर्णयं; Bo wKt[1] NKt[4] BKt[5] Lo[1] Lo[2] Lo[4] Lo[5] NNg Pu[4] Pu[8] [*Jolly* M] *Me Ku Dave Jha* °विनिश्चयः; La[1] NPu[1] Pu[2] Pu[4] Tr[2] *Dev* °विनिश्चये

254. Cited by *Vij* 2.152; *Apa* 759; *Lakṣ* 12.442; *Dev* 3.541; *Mādh* 3.273 — a) BCa Jm Jo[1] wKt[1] Kt[2] La[1] Tj[2] MTr[3] [*Jolly* Ku] *Apa Nd Mr Mandlik KSS* ग्रामीयक°; Hy ग्रामीयेक°; Be[1] ग्रामीणीयकुलानां; Tr[2] ग्रामेएककलानां; oOr ग्रामएककुलानां; Pu[2] Pu[4] Wa ग्रामेयकुलानां; Jm Jo[1] Jo[2] Kt[2] wKt[3] Lo[3] Lo[4] Ox[2] Tj[1] MTr[3] *Me Mandlik Jolly Jha KSS Dave* च — b) Bo [*but cor*] समग्रं; Be[3] Ho La[1] Lo[3] GMd[1] TMd[4] GMd[5] sOx[1] Ox[2] sPu[6] Tj[1] Tr[1] MTr[4] MTr[5] Wa *Apa Lakṣ Dev Mādh* सीम; MTr[6] सीमा; Jo[1] सीम्ने; GMy कूटसाक्षिणः; TMd[3] कूटिसाक्षिण — d) Lo[3] Tr[1] द्वयोश्चैव; *Mādh* तथैव च विवा°; Lo[1] विवादिनः; BKt[5] विवादतोः; TMd[3] विवादयोः; Tr[1] [*but cor*] विवदमानयो; Pu[5] Pu[7] [*Jolly* G] विधानतः

255. Pādas c-d *ma* in Tr[1]. Cited by *Vij* 2.15; *Apa* 760; *Lakṣ* 12.442; *Mādh* 3.273 — a) oOr ततः पृष्टा यथा; Lo[5] ते तिष्ठस्तु यथा; Tr[1] पृष्टाश्च; NKt[4] पृष्टासु; Tr[2] पृष्ठ्वास्तु — b) TMd[3] GMd[5] GMy सीमासेतुपु लक्षणं; *Mādh* सीमासन्धिषु लक्षणं [cf. 8.261d]; oOr सामन्तः सीमनिर्णयं; La[1] समस्तां; Tr[2] *Apa* सामन्ता; Ho wKt[1] La[1] Lo[3] TMd[4] sOx[1] Ox[2] sPu[6] Tj[1] *Apa* सीम; GMd[1] MTr[6] निश्चयः; Pu[5] Pu[7] *Go* निश्चितं; BBe[2] Be[3] Lo[3] Tj[1] *Vij Apa* निर्णयं — c) GMd[1] TMd[3] TMd[4] GMd[5] GMy Tr[1] [*but cor sh*] MTr[4] MTr[6] *Apa Lakṣ* तथा तांश्च निबध्नीयात् [TMd[3] GMd[5] GMy तच्च; TMd[4] Tr[1] *Lakṣ* तं च]; Tr[2] °याद्यथा; Lo[5] सीमाः — d) *Apa* समस्तां तांश्च साक्षिणः; Lo[5] TMd[3] सर्वास्ताश्चैव; Pu[5] Pu[7] *Lakṣ* समस्तांश्चैव; GMd[1] मानतः

256. Cited by *Vij* 2.152; *Apa* 762; *Lakṣ* 12.445; *Dev* 3.542; *Mādh* 3.274 — a) *Dev* शिरोभिः स्वैः गृही°; Ho गृहीत्वोर्वी; GMd[1] TMd[4] गृहीतोर्वीं; Be[1] गृहीत्वाउर्वीं; NKt[4] गृहीत्वोर्व्यां; Jo[1] गृहीत्वोर्वां; Pu[5] Pu[7] गृहीत्वोर्पी; Hy गृहीश्वोर्वी; *Dave* गृहीत्वा वा — b) Lo[1] Lo[5] स्रग्विणौ; Lo[3] रिक्त° — c) Jm *Apa* स्वकृतै; Pu[2] Pu[4] सुकृतिः; BBe[2] wKt[1] शापिता; Tr[2] शापितः; La[1] शापितैः; Tj[1] स्वापिता — c-d) GMd[1] TMd[3] TMd[4] GMd[5] GMy MTr[4] MTr[6] नयेयुरञ्जसा सेतुं सुकृतैः शापिताः पृथक् [TMd[3] सुकृताः; TMd[4] प्रापिता] — d) La[1] स्वैर्नयेद्यस्तं; Be[1] BBe[2] Bo Ho Hy Jo[2] wKt[1] wKt[3] NKt[4] BKt[5] Lo[1] Lo[2] Lo[3] Lo[4] Lo[5] NNg oOr sOx[1] sPu[6] Tj[1] *Ku* °येयुस्तां; Wa °येयुस्ता; BCa *Dev* °येयुस्तान्; Ho समञ्जसां

विपरीतं नयन्तस्तु दाप्याः स्युर्द्विशतं दमम् ॥२५७॥
साक्ष्यभावे तु चत्वारो ग्रामाः सामन्तवासिनः* ।
सीमाविनिर्णयं कुर्युः प्रयता राजसंनिधौ ॥२५८॥
सामन्तानामभावे तु मौलानां सीमसाक्षिणाम् ।
इमानप्यनुयुञ्जीत पुरुषान्वनगोचरान् ॥२५९॥
व्याधाञ्छाकुनिकान् गोपान् कैवर्तान् मूलखानकान् ।
व्यालग्राहानुञ्छवृत्तीनन्यांश्च वनगोचरान् ॥२६०॥
ते पृष्टास्तु यथा ब्रूयुः सीमासंधिषु लक्षणम् ।
तत्तथा स्थापयेद्राजा धर्मेण ग्रामयोर्द्वयोः ॥२६१॥
क्षेत्रकूपतडागानामारामस्य गृहस्य च ।
सामन्तप्रत्ययो ज्ञेयः सीमासेतुविनिर्णयः ॥२६२॥

257. After यथोक्तेन rest omitted in NKt[4]. Cited by *Vij* 2.153; *Lakṣ* 12.446; *Dev* 3.548 — a) oOr नयतस्ते; Be[1] नयन्तस्मै; Be[3] नयन्तस्तु — b) oOr पूयते; GMd[5] oOr सत्यसाक्षिणं; Hy सप्तसाक्षिणः — c) Be[3] NNg MTr[5] नयन्तस्ते; oOr नयतस्तु — d) Wa हाप्याः; Lo[1] GMy *Dev* दाप्यास्तु द्वि°; MTr[6] दाप्यास्याद् द्वि°; Lo[2] TMd[3] स्युर्द्विगुणं

258.* Pādas a-c up to कुर्युः omitted in NKt[4]. Cited by *Vij* 2.152; *Apa* 760; *Dev* 3.537; *Mādh* 3.271 — a) Jm NNg साक्षिभावे; Hy °भावं; wKt[3] °भावेपि; La[1] *om* तु; Ho sOx[1] sPu[6] Wa च — b) MTr[3] सामन्ता ग्रामवासिनः; BKt[5] Lo[1] Lo[3] GMd[5] Pu[5] Pu[7] Tj[1] [*Jolly* G R] *Vij Go Mr Der* ग्राम्याः; Lo[4] Lo[5] GMd[1] TMd[3] TMd[4] GMy Ox[2] NPu[1] Pu[2] Wa [*Jolly* Nd M] *Dev Jolly Jha Dave* ग्राम°; Tr[2] ग्रामी; Bo ग्रासाः; Bo [*Jolly* Nd R] सामान्त°; BBe[2] Be[3] Ho wKt[3] BKt[5] La[1] Lo[1] Lo[2] Lo[4] Lo[5] NNg oOr sOx[1] NPu[1] Pu[2] Pu[3] Pu[5] sPu[6] Pu[7] Pu[8] Tr[2] MTr[4] Wa [*Jolly* G M N] *Go Nā Vij Apa Dev Mādh Jolly Jha Dave* सीमान्त°; Ox[2] Tr[2] MTr[6] सीमन्त°; Bo सामात्त° — c) TMd[3] TMd[4] GMd[5] Tr[1] MTr[4] MTr[5] MTr[6] सीम्नो विनि°; GMd[1] GMy सीम्ना विनि°; wKt[1] °प्रनिर्णयं; Be[1] wKt[3] Lo[2] TMd[3] GMy NNg NPu[1] Pu[2] Pu[5] Pu[7] Tr[2] °विनिश्चयं [*Me* gloss निश्चयं supports this]; Pu[4] °विश्चितं — d) TMd[3] प्रयतो; Lo[4] Lo[5] प्रष्टव्या

259. Pādas c-d omitted in Be[1]. Cited by *Lakṣ* 12.444; *Dev* 3.540; *Mādh* 3.272 — a) BBe[2] La[1] Ox[2] Pu[2] Pu[4] Wa सीमान्ता° — b) Ho मालानां; Hy Jm Jo[1] Jo[2] Kt[2] La[1] Pu[2] Pu[3] Pu[8] Tj[2] Tr[2] MTr[3] [*Jolly* G R] *Rc Mandlik Jha KSS Dave* सीम्निसाक्षि°; TMd[3] TMd[4] °साक्षिणः — c) Pu[5] Pu[7] [*Jolly* G] इतरानपि युञ्जीत; BKt[5] sOx[1] sPu[6] हीनानप्य°; Ho °प्यन्वयुञ्जीत; MTr[4] MTr[6] °प्युपयुञ्जीत

260. Omitted in Be[1] BKt[5] Pu[8]; pādas a-c omitted in MTr[6]. Cited by *Vij* 2.150–1; *Lakṣ* 12.444; *Dev* 3.540; *Mādh* 3.260 — a) TMd[3] गोष्ठान्; Tr[2] योषान्; TMd[4] दोषां — b) TMd[4] *cor to* कैवर्तानुधखासखान्; GMy वैकतान्; TMd[3] नैकतान्; NKt[4] Lo[5] GMy oOr *Vij* मूलखातकान्; Tr[1] [*but cor sh*] मूलघातकान्; TMd[3] मूलखातिकन्; GMd[5] मूलकानपि — d) BBe[2] Hy Jm Jo[1] Kt[2] Tj[2] MTr[3] [*Jolly* R] *Rn Mandlik Jha Dave KSS* वनचारिणः; Be[3] La[1] Lo[4] Lo[5] [*Jolly* M] शतशस्तथा

261. Pādas a-b omitted in Be[1]. Cited by *Lakṣ* 12.445; *Dev* 3.541 — a) BBe[2] Be[3] पृष्टाश्च; Tr[2] पृष्वास्तु; TMd[4] पृष्ट्यास्तु — b) TMd[4] लक्षणः — c) TMd[4] तथा संस्थापयेद्राजा; La[1] तं तथा; Jm न तथा; Lo[1] TMd[3] तत्तदा — d) NKt[4] यामयोर्द्वयोः

262. Cited by *Lakṣ* 12.452 — a) Hy क्षत्र°; GMy क्षेत्रकूट°; Lo[3] °तडाकाना°; GMd[1] TMd[3] TMd[4] GMd[5] GMy Tj[1] Tr[1] MTr[4] MTr[5] °तटाकाना°; MTr[6] °तदाकाना° — b) Pu[2] Pu[4] Tr[2] ग्रहस्य — c)

सामन्ताश्चेन्मृषा ब्रूयुः सेतौ विवदतां नृणाम् ।
सर्वे पृथक्पृथग्दण्ड्या राज्ञा मध्यमसाहसम् ॥२६३॥
गृहं तडागमारामं क्षेत्रं वा भीषया हरन् ।
शतानि पञ्च दण्ड्यः स्यादज्ञानाद् द्विशतो दमः ॥२६४॥
सीमायामविषह्यायां स्वयं राजैव धर्मवित् ॥
प्रदिशेद्भूमिमेतेषामुपकारादिति स्थितिः ॥२६५॥
एषोऽखिलेनाभिहितो धर्मः सीमाविनिर्णये ।
अत ऊर्ध्वं प्रवक्ष्यामि वाक्पारुष्यविनिर्णयम् ॥२६६॥
शतं ब्राह्मणमाक्रुश्य क्षत्रियो दण्डमर्हति ।
वैश्योऽध्यर्धशतं द्वे वा शूद्रस्तु वधमर्हति ॥२६७॥

La[1] mTr[6]सामन्त:; Pu[8] सामन्ते; tMd[3] सामात°; bBe[2] oOr Pu[2] Pu[4] सीमान्त°; nNg °प्रत्ययोर्ज्ञेय: — d) gMd[1] समास्ते सेतुनिर्णय:; tMd[3] gMy सीमासेतुपु निर्णयं [tMd[3] °सेतेपु]; tMd[4] सीम°; *Lakṣ* सीमासन्धि°; Pu[2] °सेतुर्विनि°; Be[1] La[1] sOx[1] Ox[2] sPu[6] Wa °विनिर्णये; Bo Lo[1] nNg nPu[1] Pu[3] Pu[8] Tr[2] [*Jolly* M] °विनिश्चय:; bKt[5] Lo[4] Lo[5] Pu[2] Pu[4] °विनिश्चये

263. Cited by *Lakṣ* 12.446 — a) Bo सामाता°; Pu[2] Pu[4] Wa सीमन्ता°; Tr[2] °श्चेन्यथा; Bo °श्चेन्मृषे; Lo[2] °श्चेन्मृगा; Lo[1] °श्चेन्नृपा — b) gMy सेतो; Pu[5] Pu[7] संतो; tMd[3] सेतोर्विव°; Pu[2] Pu[4] ततो विव°; tMd[3] विवदता; tMd[4] विविदतां; gMd[1] निवसतान्नृणां — c) Pu[3] *Lakṣ* सर्वे ते च पृथग्दण्ड्या; bBe[2] सर्वेपि हि पृथग्दण्ड; Lo[3] सर्व — d) bBe[2] न राज्ञा मध्यसाहसं; tMd[4] oOr Pu[2] राजा; Pu[2] मध्यमं

264. Cited by *Vij* 2.155; *Apa* 766;*Lakṣ* 12.456; *Dev* 3.554 — a) Be[1] nKt[4] Lo[2] Lo[3] mTr[6] *Apa* तडाक°; gMd[1] tMd[3] tMd[4] gMd[5] gMy Tr[1] mTr[4] mTr[5] *Dev* तटाक°; nPu[1] तडागानारामं; Pu[2] Pu[4] °माराम° — b) Pu[2] Pu[4] चाभीक्ष्णया; Pu[3] Pu[8] Tr[2] चाप्यन्यथा वदन्; nKt[4] हीयया; gMd[1] विषयान्हरन्; Lo[1] हरत्; tMd[3] gMy हरेत् — c) Be[1] पञ्च दातव्यो; Pu[2] Pu[4] Tr[2] दण्ड:; tMd[4] दण्डं; gMd[1] दण्ड्यायं and jumps to 266d; gMd[5] दण्ड्यास्स्युरज्ञा° — d) Be[1] स्याद् द्विशतोज्ञानता दम:; bKt[5] स्याद्रक्षणाद्; wKt[1] °ज्ञानां त्रिशतो; Pu[5] Pu[7] °ज्ञानात्प्रथमो; Ho द्विशतै; tMd[3] gMy द्विगुणं; tMd[4] gMd[5] Tr[1] mTr[4] mTr[6] द्विशतं दमं

265. Omitted in gMd[1]. Cited by *Vij* 2.153;*Apa* 764; *Lakṣ* 12.450; *Dev* 3.544; *Mādh* 3.275 — a) tMd[4] सीमानाम°; Tr[2] °विषह्यायं; Bo Kt[2] °विषह्याया; wKt[1] wKt[3] °विसह्यायां; Lo[1] °विषण्णायां; La[1] °विस्पष्टायां; bBe[2] °विशिष्टायां; Hy °विशक्यायां; Be[3] °भिषष्ट्यायां — b) wKt[1] La[1] tMd[4] gMd[5] Wa राजेव; Be[3] Bo राज्ञैव; tMd[3] राजेन — c) mTr[4] mTr[6] *Apa* प्रविशे°; Tj[2] प्रहिशे°; tMd[3] प्रवेशे भूमि°; La[1] प्रविवेशद्भूमि°; Lo[1] *cor to* °द्भूमिमेषामुप°; Ho nKt[4] bKt[5] Lo[2] Lo[4] Lo[5] nNg nPu[1] Pu[5] Pu[7] *Dev* *Apa* °मेकेषामुप° — d) tMd[3] gMy °पाकारादिति; nNg °पकारादिभि: स्थिति:; tMd[3] स्मृति:

Additional verse in *Mandlik* [ट, ठ] *KSS Dave* [cf. added verse after 8.249]:

ध्वजिनी मत्सिनी चैव निधानी भयवर्जिता ।
राजशासननीता च सीमा पञ्चविधा स्मृता ॥

266. Pādas a-c omitted in gMd[1] and pādas c-d in tMd[3] — a) La[1] °खिलोनाभिहितो; gMy °खिलोवभिहितो; tMd[3] °भितेनाभिहितो; Lo[1] °खिलेनाविहितो — b) Be[1] wKt[3] Lo[2] धर्म्य:; Tr[1] विधि *mc sh* धर्म्य:; tMd[3] gMy दण्डस्सीमा°; tMd[4] सीम्नि; Be[1] bBe[2] Ho Jo[2] wKt[1] nKt[4] Lo[2] Lo[3] Lo[4] Lo[5] oOr Ox[2] nPu[1] Pu[3] Pu[8] Tj[1] Tr[2] Wa *Rc Go* °विनिर्णय:; tMd[3] °विनिर्णयं; Bo °विनिश्चय: — d) nKt[4] mTr[5] वाक्पारुष्यस्य निर्णयं; tMd[4] वाक्पारुष्ये च निर्णयं; Pu[2] Pu[4] वाक्पारूष्य°; Tr[2] वाक्पारुष्ये; Pu[5] Pu[7] °निर्णय:

267. Omitted in Be[1]. Cited by *Vij* 2.207; *Apa* 808; *Mādh* 3.296 — a) Tr[2] °माक्रुष्य; tMd[3]

पञ्चाशद्ब्राह्मणो दण्ड्यः क्षत्रियस्याभिशंसने ।
वैश्ये स्यादर्धपञ्चाशच्छूद्रे द्वादशको दमः ॥२६८॥
समवर्णे द्विजातीनां द्वादशैव व्यतिक्रमे ।
वादेष्ववचनीयेषु तदेव द्विगुणं भवेत् ॥२६९॥
एकजातिर्द्विजातींस्तु वाचा दारुणया क्षिपन् ।
जिह्वायाः प्राप्नुयाच्छेदं जघन्यप्रभवो हि सः ॥२७०॥
नामजातिग्रहं त्वेषामभिद्रोहेण कुर्वतः ।
निखेयोऽयोमयः शङ्कुर्ज्वलन्नास्ये दशाङ्गुलः ॥२७१॥

°माकृष्य; wKt^{1} °मात्रस्य; gMy °मात्रंश्य — b) gMy oOr क्षत्रिये — c) Be^{3} वैश्यो ह्यर्ध°; Jm Jo^{1} Kt^{2} Lo^{2} [*Jolly* M^{3}] *Rc Mandlik Jha KSS Dave* वैश्योप्यर्ध°; [*Jolly* M$^{8-9}$] वैश्यो वर्ध.°; Lo^{4} Lo^{5} oOr [*Jolly* Me M$^{4-5}$] वैश्य: सार्धशतं [oOr वैश्ये]; *Mādh* °शतं देयं — d) wKt^{3} शूद्रं तु; bBe^{2} धर्ममर्हति

268. Cited by *Lakṣ* 12.478; *Mādh* 3.296 — a) wKt^{1} Lo^{4} Lo^{5} nNg oOr nPu^{1} Pu^{2} Pu^{4} *Lakṣ* विप्र: पञ्चशतं दण्ड्य: [Lo^{4} Lo^{5} nNg पञ्चाशतं]; bKt^{5} विप्रस्तु पञ्चाशद्दण्ड्य:; tMd^{3} °ह्मणं; gMd^{1} दण्ड्या; bBe^{2} दण्ड: — b) mTr^{3} °स्याशंसते; Be^{3} bKt^{5} °भिसंशने; *Dave* °भिमर्शने — c) nNg Pu^{5} Pu^{7} वैस्य:; Bo bKt^{5} tMd^{3} gMy mTr^{6} वैश्य; Tj^{1} वैश्यो; Jo^{1} वैश्यै; gMd^{1} tMd^{4} वैश्यस्य त्वर्ध°; nKt^{4} वैश्यस्य चार्ध°; *Lakṣ* वैश्यस्य वार्ध° — d) Tj^{1} °शत्शूद्र; gMd^{1} °च्छूद्रो; gMy °च्छूद्रा; Wa द्वादशके; gMd^{5} द्वाविंशको; gMd^{1} मद:; oOr mTr^{4} mTr^{6} मत:

Additional verses in Be^{3} gMd^{1} tMd^{4} mTr^{4} mTr^{6}; added after 269 in La^{1} nPu^{1} Pu^{2} Pu^{4} *Mandlik* [ट, ठ, य] *KSS Dave:*

विप्रक्षत्रियवत्कार्यो दण्डो राजन्यवैश्ययो: ।
वैश्यक्षत्रिययो: शूद्रे विप्रे य: क्षत्रवैश्ययो: ।।१।।
समुत्कर्षापकर्षाभ्यां विप्रवद्दण्डकल्पना ।
राजन्यवैश्यशूद्राणामृते वाच्यादिति स्थिति: ।।२।।

1. Pādas c-d omitted in mTr^{6} — a) Be^{3} La^{1} विप्रे — b) La^{1} दण्ड्यो; tMd^{4} द्वन्द्वो — c) La^{1} राजन्यवैश्ययो: शूद्रे; Pu^{2} Pu^{4} वैश्य: — d) tMd^{4} विज्ञेय: क्षत्र°; Be^{3} दण्डो वा क्षत्र°; nPu^{1} Pu^{2} Pu^{4} *Mandlik Dave KSS* क्षत्रशूद्रयो:

2. a) Pu^{2} Pu^{4} समुत्कर्षोप°; gMd^{1} °पाकर्शा स्यात् विप्र°; *Mandlik Dave KSS* °पकर्शास्तु विप्र° — c-d) Be^{3} nPu^{1} Pu^{2} Pu^{4} *Mandlik KSS Dave* °शूद्राणां धनवर्जमिति; La^{1} °शूद्राणां वधवर्जमिति — d) tMd^{4} वास्यादिति

269. Cited by *Lakṣ* 12.476; *Dev* 3.758 — a) *Lakṣ* सवर्णे हि द्वि°; gMy °वर्ण; *Dev* °वर्णे तु सर्वेषां; tMd^{4} द्विजानां; mTr^{6} तु जातीनां — b) tMd^{4} द्वादशेव; gMd^{5} द्वादशैवं — c) wKt^{1} विवादेषु च नीचेषु; gMd^{1} पादेषु वचनीयेषु; Wa वाक्येष्ववच°; Pu^{3} °वदनीयेषु — d) tMd^{4} तदिव; Lo^{2} तादव; tMd^{3} तथैव; Pu^{5} Pu^{7} द्विगुणो

270. Cited by *Apa* 809; *Mādh* 3.297 — a) tMd^{4} [pāda reads] एकजात्वे तु; oOr *Apa* [vl] एका°; gMd^{5} हीनजाति°; nKt^{4} bKt^{5} tMd^{3} एकजातिद्वि°; Be^{1} wKt^{1} एकजातिं द्वि°; mTr^{4} हीनजातिं द्वि°; Ho Kt^{2} °जातीस्तु; Lo^{1} Pu^{3} °जातिस्तु; Be^{1} nKt^{4} bKt^{5} tMd^{3} gMy nNg sOx^{1} nPu^{1} Pu^{2} Pu^{4} sPu^{6} Tr^{1} mTr^{4} mTr^{5} [*Jolly* M$^{8-9}$ Nd] *Apa* °जातिं तु; [*Jolly* M$^{3-5}$] °जातं तु; La^{1} Pu^{5} Pu^{7} [*Jolly* G] °जातिं च; *Apa* [vl] °जात्यं तु; Be^{3} °जातींश्च; wKt^{1} °जातीश्च; Ox^{2} °जातीनां; *Me Go Ku Rc* support the plural — b) La^{1} दारुण्यया; gMd^{1} चारुणया; tMd^{3} दारुणक्षिपन्; *Apa* क्षिपेत् — c) Lo^{1} जिह्वाया; nKt^{4} oOr जिह्वायां; nNg जिह्वया; bKt^{5} °च्छेद — d) oOr जघनेप्रभवो; La^{1} °प्रभवा

271.* Pādas c-d omitted in mTr^{6} [haplo]. Cited by *Apa* 809; *Mādh* 3.297 — a) Lo^{3} Tr^{2}

धर्मोपदेशं दर्पेण विप्राणामस्य कुर्वतः ।
तप्तमासेचयेत्तैलं वक्त्रे श्रोत्रे च पार्थिवः ॥२७२॥
श्रुतं देशं च जातिं च कर्म शारीरमेव च ।
वितथेन ब्रुवन्दर्पाद् दाप्यः स्याद् द्विशतं दमम् ॥२७३॥
काणं वाप्यथ वा खञ्जमन्यं वापि तथाविधम् ।
तथ्येनापि ब्रुवन्दाप्यो दण्डं कार्षापणावरम् ॥२७४॥
मातरं पितरं जायां भ्रातरं तनयं गुरुम् ।
आक्षारयञ्छतं दाप्यः पन्थानं चाददद्गुरोः ॥२७५॥
ब्राह्मणक्षत्रियाभ्यां तु दण्डः कार्यो विजानता ।
ब्राह्मणे साहसः पूर्वः क्षत्रिये त्वेव मध्यमः ॥२७६॥

°गृहं; *Apa* °ग्रहांस्तेषाम°; GMd[1] °ग्रहान्तेषाम°; GMy त्वैषाम°; Be[3] TMd[3] GMd[5] Tr[1] चैषाम°; MTr[5] चैवाम°; Jm Jo[2] wKt[1] NKt[4] Lo[1] Tj[1] *NSm* 15–16.23 तेषाम° — b) Hy Jo[2] Lo[3] Tj[1] Tj[2] °मतिद्रोहेण; La[1] Lo[1] °मद्धिरोहेण; Be[3] Lo[4] Lo[5] कुर्वतां — c) GMy निखायो; Lo[1] निषेयो; BBe[2] Be[3] Hy Jm Jo[1] wKt[1] La[1] Lo[4] Lo[5] Ox[2] Tj[2] MTr[3] Wa *Mandlik Jha KSS Dave* निक्षेप्यो; Kt[2] निःक्षेप्यो; Be[1] BCa निक्षिप्यो; BKt[5] निधेयो; wKt[3] निधेयोः; NPu[1] Pu[2] Pu[4] नियोज्यो; sOx[1] sPu[6] निश्चयो; oOr Tr[2] शङ्कुज्वल°; wKt[3] Pu[7] शङ्कुज्वल° — c-d) TMd[3] नियोयोवंयश्शङ्कुर्जन्नास्ये दशाङ्गुलः — d) BBe[2] wKt[1] °र्ज्वलदास्ये; TMd[3] GMy दशाङ्गुलं

272. Verses 272 and 273 transposed in Kt[2]; pādas a-b omitted in MTr[6]. Cited by *Apa* 809 — a) GMd[5] धर्मोपदेशरूपेण; NKt[4] Pu[2] Pu[4] धर्मोप°; TMd[3] पर्पेण — b) oOr द्विजानामस्य — c) Lo[1] तप्तायसेच वै तैलं; Be[1] Wa °मासिञ्चये°; wKt[3] °मासनये°; GMy °मास्येचये°; La[1] TMd[3] NPu[1] °मासेचयत्तैलं; TMd[4] °माधिवयत्तैलं; Pu[5] °येत्तिलं — d) Lo[2] चक्रे श्रोत्रे; Ox[2] श्रौत्रे; Be[1] श्रोत्रेण पार्थिवः

273. Cited by *Lakṣ* 12.481 — a) Lo[1] श्रुत; Be[1] Ho NNg Pu[5] Pu[7] श्रुतिं; NPu[1] श्रुति; TMd[3] शृतं; TMd[4] GMd[5] च कालं च; wKt[1] जातिं *add* चक्षं — c) Pu[5] Pu[7] वितथैतद्वदन्दर्पाद्; Pu[2] Pu[4] विथतेन; Bo विपथेन; GMy वितथोन; NKt[4] La[1] Pu[2] Pu[4] ब्रुवन्दर्प्याद्; GMd[1] भवन्दर्पाद्; wKt[1] श्रवं दर्पाद्; TMd[4] ब्रवन्दर्पः; Bo ब्रुवन्नर्था — d) TMd[3] द्विगुणं

274. Omitted in GMy BKt[5] oOr; pādas c-d omitted in BKt[5]. Cited by *Vij* 2.204; *Apa* 806; *Lakṣ* 12.475; *Mādh* 3.295 — a) TMd[4] कुणं; Be[1] Tr[2] चाप्यथ; TMd[4] *Apa* वा यदि वा; MTr[3] कञ्जम°; Tr[2] खण्डम° — a-b) Lo[1] वा कुब्जं खटजं वापि — b) Lo[3] Tj[1] °मन्यद्वापि; sOx[1] sPu[6] °मन्धं वापि; Ho Ox[2] °मधं वापि; Ho Tr[2] चापि; TMd[4] तथाविधिः; NNg तथाधनं — c) Lo[2] तथ्येनापि च [*om* ब्रुवन्दाप्यो]; NPu[1] तथोनापि; GMd[1] तथ्येन विब्रुव°; TMd[3] तथ्येनाब्रुव°; GMy ब्रुवा दाप्यो; La[1] ब्रुवन्दर्प्पा — d) *Mādh* दण्डः; Bo NKt[4] TMd[3] दण्ड; Be[1] दण्ड्यं; La[1] दण्ड्यः; GMd[1] TMd[4] Tr[1] MTr[4] MTr[6] दमं; Be[1] TMd[3] Wa कार्षापणं परं; GMy *Apa* कार्षापणं वरं; GMd[1] °पणापरं; wKt[3] °पणाचलं; Tj[1] °पणोवरं; TMd[4] °पणं फणं

275. Omitted in oOr; pādas a-b omitted in BKt[5]. Cited by *Vij* 2.204; *Apa* 853; *Lakṣ* 12.477; *Mādh* 3.295 — b) *Mādh Vij* श्वशुरं गुरुं; TMd[4] गुरून् — c) GMd[1] आक्षारं शयकं दाप्यं; Bo NKt[4] La[1] अक्षार°; BKt[5] आक्षारन्छदन्; Hy आक्षारितश्शतं; wKt[1] आख्यावयन्शतं; BBe[2] आख्यारयन्शतं; Pu[2] Pu[4] आख्यायियन्शतं; NPu[1] अछारयं शतं; Lo[2] दण्ड्यः; TMd[4] दास्या — d) Lo[2] चददद्गुरोः; *Lakṣ* वाददद्गुरोः; Pu[7] वाददन्गुरोः; Ho TMd[3] चाददन्गुरोः; Lo[1] चादरेद्गुरोः; La[1] चाप्यदद्गुरोः; Jo[1] °द्गुरौ

276. Omitted in oOr. Cited by *Lakṣ* 12.482 — a) Be[3] विप्रक्षत्रिययोस्त्वेष; La[1] GMd[1] GMy ब्राह्मणः; La[1] °क्षत्रिययोस्तु; TMd[4] MTr[6] °क्षत्रियाणां तु; Lo[2] °क्षत्रियाभ्यो तु; BBe[2] °क्षत्रियाभ्यस्तु; sOx[1] वा; wKt[3] Pu[5] Pu[7] Pu[8] Tr[2] [*Jolly* G] च — b) Ho दण्डं; MTr[5] दण्डौ कार्यौ; Kt[2] विजानतां; Pu[8]

विट्शूद्रयोरेवमेव स्वजातिं प्रति तत्त्वतः ।
छेदवर्जं प्रणयनं दण्डस्येति विनिश्चयः ॥२७७॥
एष दण्डविधिः प्रोक्तो वाक्पारुष्यस्य तत्त्वतः ।
अत ऊर्ध्वं प्रवक्ष्यामि दण्डपारुष्यनिर्णयम् ॥२७८॥
येन केनचिदङ्गेन हिंस्याच्चेच्छ्रेष्ठमन्त्यजः ।
छेत्तव्यं तत्तदेवास्य तन्मनोरनुशासनम् ॥२७९॥
पाणिमुद्यम्य दण्डं वा पाणिच्छेदनमर्हति ।
पादेन प्रहरन्कोपात् पादच्छेदनमर्हति ॥२८०॥
सहासनमभिप्रेप्सुरुत्कृष्टस्यावकृष्टजः ।
कट्यां कृताङ्को निर्वास्यः स्फिचं वास्यावकर्तयेत् ॥२८१॥

विजानाता; Bo द्विजानतः — c) Bo ब्राह्मणः; BKt^{5} ब्राह्मणं; Be^{1} साहस; BKt^{5} La^{1} TMd^{4} GMd^{5} GMy साहसं; GMy पूर्वा; BKt^{5} TMd^{4} GMd^{5} La^{1} पूर्वं; Pu^{3} पूर्व; NKt^{4} सर्वं — d) Be^{3} La^{1} GMd^{1} TMd^{3} TMd^{4} GMd^{5} GMy Tr^{1} MTr^{4} MTr^{6} क्षत्रिये मध्यमः स्मृतः [TMd^{4} क्षत्रियो; La^{1} TMd^{4} GMd^{5} मध्यमं स्मृतं]; Wa क्षत्रियो; Ho NKt^{4} sOx^{1} Ox^{2} sPu^{6} चैव; WKt^{1} द्वे च मध्यमः; Lo^{4} Lo^{5} एष मध्यमः; NNg [*but cor fh*] मध्यमाः

277. Omitted in oOr; pādas c-d omitted in Be^{1} [haplo]. Cited by *Lakṣ* 12.482; pādas a-b cited by *Vij* 2.207 — a) Tj^{2} °योरेष एव; BBe^{2} °योरेवमेवं; Be^{3} NKt^{4} Jo^{2} Lo^{3} Tj^{1} MTr^{4} MTr^{6} °योस्त्वेवमेव; Pu^{2} Pu^{4} °योस्त्वेव स्व° — b) TMd^{4} स्वजाति; TMd^{3} स्वजातीं; GMy [*Jolly* Nd] सजातिं; GMd^{1} द्विजातिं — c) GMd^{1} °वर्ज्यं; GMd^{5} °वर्ज — d) Bo GMd^{5} NPu^{1} दण्डश्चेति; Be^{3} Ho WKt^{1} BKt^{5} Lo^{1} Lo^{3} TMd^{3} TMd^{4} sOx^{1} Ox^{2} sPu^{6} Tj^{1} विनिर्णयः

Additional verse in Tr^{2} *Mandlik* [ख, ण] *Dave KSS;* placed after 288 in La^{1}; commented by *Nā Rc;* cited by *Har*-A 1.19.15 [= *VaDh* 20.30]:

पतितं पतितेत्युक्त्वा चौरं चौरेति वा पुनः ।
वचनात्तुल्यदोषः स्यान्मिथ्या द्विर्दोषतां व्रजेत् ॥

b) *Har*-A चोरं चोरेति — c) La^{1} वचनात्तस्य दोषः — d) La^{1} तद्दोषतां; *Har*-A द्विर्दोषभाग्भवेत्

278. Omitted in oOr; pādas a-b omitted in Be^{1}. Cited by *Dev* 3.761— a) NKt^{4} एषोखिलेनाभिहितो; TMd^{3} °विधिं; Ho sOx^{1} sPu^{6} °विधिः कृत्स्नो; TMd^{3} TMd^{4} प्रोक्ता — b) GMd^{1} °रुष्येषु; GMd^{5} °रुष्ये च; TMd^{3} TMd^{4} GMy Pu^{5} Pu^{7} °रुष्यतत्त्वतः — c) Jo^{2} Lo^{3} Tj^{1} अतः परं — d) WKt^{1} दण्डपाकस्य निर्णयं; Bo वाक्पारुष्य°; Tj^{1} [*cor to*] TMd^{4} निर्णयः

279.* Omitted in oOr. Cited by *Vij* 2.215; *Apa* 813; *Lakṣ* 12.491; *Dev* 3.763; *Mādh* 3.288 — a) Tr^{1} MTr^{4} MTr^{6} येन येन यथाङ्गेन [MTr^{4} तथा°] — b) BBe^{2} La^{1} GMd^{1} TMd^{3} TMd^{4} GMd^{5} GMy Tr^{1} MTr^{4} MTr^{5} MTr^{6} [*Jolly* Nd] *Vij Apa Lakṣ Dev Mādh Nd* हिंस्याच्छ्रेयांसमन्त्यजः; Wa हिंस्याच्चेच्छ्रेयसमन्त्यजः; TMd^{4} °मन्त्यजं —c) MTr^{6} तत्तदेव स्यात् — d) TMd^{4} यन्मनो°; WKt^{1} जन्मनो°

280. Omitted in Lo^{4} Lo^{5} oOr; pādas c-d omitted in GMd^{1} TMd^{3} TMd^{4} [haplo]. Cited by *Apa* 814; *Lakṣ* 12.491; *Dev* 3.764; pādas a-b cited by *Vij* 2.215; *Mādh* 3.288 — a) Bo °मुद्यस्य; TMd^{4} दण्डो; Lo^{2} हस्तं वा; WKt^{3} *om* वा; Bo च — c) Ho BKt^{5} GMy *Lakṣ* प्रहरेत्कोपात्; Tj^{1} प्रहरेन्कोपात्; Be^{1} प्रहरन्नेको — d) BKt^{5} NNg पादच्छेदमवाप्नुयात्

281.* Omitted in GMy oOr. Cited by *Apa* 814; *Lakṣ* 12.491; *Mādh* 3.289 — a) Jo^{2} सहासनपरिप्रेप्सु°; Lo^{3} °सनं परिप्रेप्सु° — b) WKt^{3} °स्यावकृष्टकः; Be^{3} Hy Jm Jo^{1} WKt^{1} Kt^{2} Lo^{2} GMd^{1} GMd^{5} Tj^{2} Tr^{1} MTr^{3} MTr^{4} MTr^{6} [*Jolly* Nd] *Lakṣ Mādh Mandlik Jha KSS Dave* °स्यापकृष्टजः; MTr^{5}

अवनिष्ठीवतो दर्पाद् द्वावोष्ठौ छेदयेन्नृपः ।
अवमूत्रयतो मेढ्रमवशर्धयतो गुदम् ॥२८२॥
केशेषु गृह्णतो हस्तौ छेदयेदविचारयन् ।
पादयोर्दाढिकायां च ग्रीवायां वृषणेषु च ॥२८३॥
त्वग्भेदकः शतं दण्ड्यो लोहितस्य च दर्शकः ।
मांसभेत्ता तु षण्निष्कान् प्रवास्यस्त्वस्थिभेदकः ॥२८४॥
वनस्पतीनां सर्वेषामुपभोगो यथा यथा ।
तथा तथा दमः कार्यो हिंसायामिति धारणा ॥२८५॥

°स्यापिकृष्टजः; Wa °स्यादकृष्टजः; TMd3 °कृष्टदः — c) wKt3 कट्या; Be1 कटां; TMd3 कव्यां; Ho sOx1 sPu6 कृताको; Pu2 Pu4 कृताङ्गो; Lo1 कृतोन्त; sOx1 sPu6 भि [lacuna] स्य *for* निर्वास्यः — d) *Apa* स्फिजौ वाप्यस्य कर्तयेत्; Be3 स्फिचमेवास्य कर्तयेत्; NKt4 स्फमेकं वास्य कर्तयेत्; TMd4 स्वमेकं वास्य कृन्तयेत्; Be1 Bo Ho Jo2 Lo1 Lo3 GMd1 GMd5 sOx1 NPu1 Pu2 Pu4 Pu5 sPu6 Pu7 Tj1 Tr1 Tr2 MTr3 *Go* स्फिजं; MTr6 स्फीजं; NNg स्पिजौ; Hy स्फिषं; BBe2 स्फितं; Tj2 स्फिद्रं; wKt1 स्थितं; TMd3 स्वैरं वास्या°; Bo चास्या°; Pu2 Pu4 चान्याव°; Pu5 Pu7 वाचास्यकर्त°; GMd1 वास्यापकृन्तयेत्; Lo4 Lo5 *Lakṣ* वास्य प्रकर्तत्येत्; Tj1 वास्य विकर्तयेत्; GMd5 Tr1 *Mādh* वास्य निकृन्तयेत्; MTr6 वास्य हि कृन्तयेत्; TMd3 वाप्यस्य कृन्तयेत्; Wa चास्यानकर्तयेत्; Ho वास्याच्च कीर्तयेत्; Lo3 वास्य विवर्तयेत्; Jo2 वास्य विवर्जयेत्; Jo1 °कर्तयत्; BBe2 °कीर्तयेत्

282. Omitted in oOr. Cited by *Vij* 2.215; *Apa* 814; *Lakṣ* 12.491; *Dev* 3.764; *Mādh* 3.288–9 — a) GMy हेतोः प्रहरताद्दपाद्; Kt2 °ष्ठीव्रतो; TMd4 °ष्ठीतरो; NKt4 दर्प्याद् — b) Lo2 द्वावोष्ठो — c) GMy अपमूत्र°; BCa wKt3 BKt5 Lo2 Lo4 Lo5 Pu3 Pu5 Pu7 Pu8 Tr2 [*Jolly* M G] *Jolly NSm* 15–16.27 °मूत्रयतः शिश्नम°; Be1 मेद्रेव°; TMd3 मेढ्राव°; NKt4 मेढमव° — d) *Mādh* मेढ्रं पुरीषकरणे गुदं; Be3 °वसर्धयतो; GMd1 °वविष्ठयतो; TMd3 GMy MTr6 °वछर्दयतो; TMd4 °वथर्दयतो; Ox2 °वपर्दयतो; Be1 °वमर्ध्यतो गुरुं; Tr2 °यते; Lo1 °यता; wKt1 wKt3 गुडं

283. Cited by *Apa* 814; *Lakṣ* 12.491; *Dev* 3.764; *Mādh* 3.289 — a) Wa गृह्णीतो; Tr1 [*but cor sh*] ग्राहतो; NPu1 गृह्णतौ; La1 गृह्णते; TMd4 Pu7 [*Jolly* G] हस्तं — b) BKt5 छेदयेच्च विचा°; Pu2 °येदतिचारयन्; Tr2 °येदभिधारयन्; wKt3 °चारयत् — c) GMd1 पातयेत् दाढि°; La1 Pu2 Pu4 °योर्दाटिकायां; wKt3 °योर्घटिकायां; TMd3 TMd4 GMd5 GMy Tr1 [*but cor sh*] MTr4 MTr5 MTr6 [*Jolly* Nd] °योर्नासिकायां; Be3 wKt3 La1 Lo1 Lo3 Pu5 Pu7 [*Jolly* M8–9] *Apa* तु; wKt1 oOr Tj1 वा — d) Ho वृषणेन च; GMd1 TMd3 GMd5 Tr1 MTr4 MTr5 MTr6 वृषणे तथा [GMd5 ततः]; GMy वृषणोथ वा; Jo1 *om* च; Be3 wKt1 BKt5 sOx1 Pu3 sPu6 वा; *Apa* [*Jolly* G] तु

284. Omitted in Tr2. Cited by *Vij* 2.218; *Apa* 815; *Lakṣ* 12.488; *Dev* 3.761; *Mādh* 3.287 — a) GMd1 तत्भदे शतकं दण्ड्यो; oOr त्वग्भेदकं; Bo त्वग्भेदतः; TMd4 त्वग्भेदंत्य; GMy दण्ड्य; TMd4 दण्ड्या — b) Tj1 दार्शकः; TMd4 दर्शने — c) *Mādh* मांसच्छेदे शतं निष्कान्; GMd1 TMd3 TMd4 GMy MTr4 MTr5 MTr6 [*Jolly* Nd] मांसभेदी; Tr1 मांसभेदी *mc sh to* मांसछेत्ता; Lo3 Tj1 मांसछेत्ता; BKt5 Pu5 Pu7 [*Jolly* M4–5 G] *Vij Jolly* च; wKt1 La1 सन्निष्कान्; Lo1 पणिकात्; BBe2 सनिष्काणः; TMd3 षण्मासान् — d) sOx1 sPu6 प्रदाप्य°; TMd3 प्रदास्य°; BBe2 प्रवास्यादस्थि°; Ho Pu5 Pu7 °स्यस्त्वास्थि°; TMd4 °स्यस्त्वस्ति°; GMd1 °स्यस्त्वचिभे°; TMd4 Tr1 MTr4 MTr5 MTr6 °भेदकृत्

285. Cited by *Apa* 819; *Lakṣ* 12.503; *Dev* 3.767; *Mādh* 3.292 — b) Be1 sOx1 sPu6 MTr6 °भोगे; NKt4 °भोगा; Jo1 Kt2 *Mandlik KSS* °भोगं; NPu1 Pu5 Pu7 यथा तथा — c) GMd1 मदः; TMd3 गमं; NKt4 कार्या — d) TMd4 हिंसामिति च कारणा; GMd5 °यामथ; BBe2 धारणाः; MTr6 धारणं

मनुष्याणां पशूनां च दुःखाय प्रहृते सति ।
यथा यथा महद्दुःखं दण्डं कुर्यात्तथा तथा ॥२८६॥
अङ्गावपीडनायां च प्राणशोणितयोस्तथा ।
समुत्थानव्ययं दाप्यः सर्वदण्डमथापि वा ॥२८७॥
द्रव्याणि हिंस्याद्यो यस्य ज्ञानतोऽज्ञानतोऽपि वा ।
स तस्योत्पादयेत्तुष्टिं राज्ञो दद्याच्च तत्समम् ॥२८८॥
चर्मचार्मिकभाण्डेषु काष्ठलोष्टमयेषु च ।
मूल्यात्पञ्चगुणो दण्डः पुष्पमूलफलेषु च ॥२८९॥
यानस्य चैव यातुश्च यानस्वामिन एव च ।
दशातिवर्तनान्याहुः शेषे दण्डो विधीयते ॥२९०॥
छिन्ननास्ये भग्नयुगे तिर्यक्प्रतिमुखागते ।

286. Cited by *Lakṣ* 12.489; *Dev* 3.763 — a) NKt^{4} मानुष्याणां — b) Jo^{1} दुःखाय हृते; Bo Ho प्रहते; Be^{1} BBe^{2} wKt^{1} La^{1} प्रकृते; GMd^{1} सदा — c) Pu^{7} [*Jolly* G] भवेद्दुःखं — d) Pu^{5} Pu^{7} दण्डः; MTr^{6} दण्ड्यं; TMd^{3} खण्डं

287.* Cited by *Lakṣ* 12.493 — a) Hy Lo^{1} Lo^{2} अङ्गानां पीड°; GMy अङ्गावयपीडानां [*om* च]; Be^{1} Pu^{5} °पीडतानां; NKt^{4} Lo^{4} Lo^{5} GMd^{1} TMd^{4} oOr Ox^{2} Pu^{5} Pu^{7} Tr^{2} Wa [*Jolly* M G] *Me Jolly* °पीडनानां; BKt^{5} La^{1} NNg NPu^{1} Pu^{2} Pu^{4} °पीडकानां; Be^{3} °पीडिकानां; Lo^{2} Pu^{3} °पीडनं चैव; NNg NPu^{1} तु — b) GMd^{1} प्राणि°; Jm Jo^{1} Kt^{2} BKt^{5} La^{1} TMd^{4} Ox^{2} MTr^{3} MTr^{4} MTr^{6} *Nā Ku Nd Mandlik KSS* [*Jolly* Ku N] व्रणशोणि°; Tr^{2} पुराशोणि° — c) TMd^{4} समर्थानत्ययं दाप्ये; GMd^{5} समुदायस्य संदाप्यः; TMd^{3} समुत्थाने स्वयं वाप्यः; Be^{1} समुत्थायव्ययं; GMy समुत्थानेद्वयं; Ox^{2} समुत्थानेप्ययं; wKt^{1} Tr^{2} °व्ययो; GMd^{1} oOr NPu^{1} दाप्यं — d) Pu^{2} Pu^{3} सर्वं; Pu^{5} Pu^{7} शतं दण्डम°; wKt^{3} °दण्डं तथापि

288.* Pādas a-b omitted in NKt^{4}. Cited by *Vij* 3.263–4; *Apa* 820, 1094; *Lakṣ* 12.558 — a) *Vij* यो यस्य हिंस्याद् द्रव्याणि; *Apa* 1094 हिंस्याद् द्रव्यानि यो यस्य; Pu^{5} Pu^{7} [*Jolly* G] द्रव्यादि; GMd^{5} सर्वाणि; TMd^{3} TMd^{4} हिंसाद्यो; TMd^{4} यस्या — b) wKt^{3} ज्ञानवोपि — c) Ox^{2} तस्य दापयेत्तु°; Bo °येत्पुष्टिं — d) Be^{1} Bo Ho Lo^{2} Lo^{4} Lo^{5} GMd^{5} GMy NNg oOr sOx^{1} Ox^{2} Pu^{5} sPu^{6} Pu^{7} Pu^{8} Tr^{2} MTr^{5} [*Jolly* M G] *Vij Apa Me Go Nd Mandlik Jolly Jha KSS Dave* राज्ञे; wKt^{3} *Lakṣ* राज्ञा; Jm राज्ञी; Be^{1} BBe^{2} दत्त्वा च; *Lakṣ* दण्ड्यश्च; Hy तत्समे

289. Pādas c-d omitted in BKt^{5}. Cited by *Apa* 820; *Lakṣ* 12.559 — a) wKt^{1} चार्मिकाश्मिक-भाण्डेषु; Jo^{1} °भाङ्गेषु; TMd^{4} °भाण्डानां — b) TMd^{3} कापलोष्ट°; BCa °लोहमयेषु; TMd^{4} °मयस्य; GMd^{1} वा — c) Kt^{2} Pu^{5} Pu^{7} मूलात्प°; sOx^{1} sPu^{6} दण्ड; Be^{3} La^{1} Lo^{1} GMd^{1} TMd^{3} GMd^{5} MTr^{6} दण्ड्यः; GMy दण्ड्य — d) Tj^{2} वा

Additional verse in La^{1} [cf. added verse 3 after 8.205]:

गोकुमारीं देवपशूनुक्षाणं वृषभं तथा ।
वाहयन्साहसं पूर्वमाप्नुयादुत्तमं वधे ॥

290. Cited by *Lakṣ* 12.501 — a) BBe^{2} Bo Ho La^{1} sOx^{1} Ox^{2} sPu^{6} यानस्यैव तु यातुश्च; TMd^{3} यानश्च चैव यातश्च; Lo^{2} चेव जन्तुश्च; Pu^{5} Pu^{7} *Lakṣ* यन्तुश्च; [*Jolly* G] गन्तुश्च — b) GMd^{5} oOr sOx^{1} sPu^{6} एव वा — c) Bo NKt^{4} Pu^{2} Pu^{4} Pu^{7} दशानि°; sOx^{1} sPu^{6} दृशाति°; MTr^{6} °वर्तनाद्याहुः; wKt^{1} °वर्त-मान्याहुः; TMd^{4} °वत्सनान्याहुः — d) TMd^{4} शेषो; TMd^{3} Tr^{2} शेष; Pu^{3} दण्डे; oOr दण्डान्विधीयते; Tj^{2} दण्डो-भिधीयते

अक्षभङ्गे च यानस्य चक्रभङ्गे तथैव च ॥२९१॥
छेदने चैव यन्त्राणां योक्त्ररश्म्योस्तथैव च ।
आक्रन्दे चाप्यपेहीति न दण्डं मनुरब्रवीत् ॥२९२॥
यत्रापवर्तते युग्यं वैगुण्यात् प्राजकस्य तु ।
तत्र स्वामी भवेद्दण्ड्यो हिंसायां द्विशतं दमम् ॥२९३॥
प्राजकश्चेद्भवेदाप्तः प्राजको दण्डमर्हति ।
युग्यस्थाः प्राजकेऽनाप्ते सर्वे दण्ड्याः शतं शतम् ॥२९४॥
स चेत्तु पथि संरुद्धः पशुभिर्वा रथेन वा ।
प्रमापयेत् प्राणभृतस्तत्र दण्डोऽविचारितः* ॥२९५॥

291. Cited by *Vij* 2.299; *Apa* 863; *Lakṣ* 12.501; *Dev* 3.766; *Mādh* 3.290 — a) *Dev Mādh* छिन्ने नस्ये युगे भग्ने [*Mādh* नष्टे]; gMy छिन्नानास्ये; Lo^{5} छिन्नानस्य; Pu^{8} *Vij Apa* छिन्ननस्ये; nNg छिन्नस्ये; Tr^{2} °नाशे; bBe^{2} °नाश्ये; Be^{1} भगयुगे; wKt^{1} *Lakṣ* भिन्नयुगे; Lo^{3} Tj^{1} भग्नमुखे; La^{1} °युते — b) Tr^{2} तिर्यक्पाति°; bKt^{5} तिर्यञ्चतिमुखा°; nPu^{1} °मुख्यागते; Pu^{3} Pu^{8} °गमे — c) *Apa* अक्षाभावे; Tr^{2} *Apa* [vl] °भागे; Be^{1} °भङ्गेव; Pu^{2} °भङ्गेन; tMd^{3} °भङ्गस्य — d) *Apa* चक्राभावे [vl चक्रभागे]

292. Omitted in Lo^{4} Pu^{5} Pu^{7}; pādas a-b omitted in Be^{1} Lo^{5} and *ma sh* in Be^{3} [haplo]. Cited by *Vij* 2.299; *Apa* 863; *Lakṣ* 12.501; *Dev* 3.766; *Mādh* 3.290 — a) gMd^{5} gMy mTr^{4} mTr^{6} *Mādh* भेदने; Lo^{2} छेदनो चेव; oOr नैव — b) *Vij Apa* योक्तृ°; Bo °रश्म्यौ तथैव; bKt^{5} °रश्म्यो तथैव; *Dev* °रश्मेस्तथैव — c) tMd^{4} आक्रन्द; Pu^{8} आकन्दे; tMd^{3} आक्रोशो; Be^{1} आक्रन्देच्चाप्य°; Be^{1} Be^{3} Ho Hy Jm Jo^{1} Jo^{2} wKt^{1} Kt^{2} wKt^{3} bKt^{5} Lo^{2} Lo^{3} oOr sOx^{1} Ox^{2} Pu^{2} sPu^{6} Pu^{8} Tj^{1} Tr^{1} [*but cor*] *Apa* [*cor in brackets*] *Dev Mādh Mandlik Jha KSS Dave* चाप्यपैहीति; gMy वाप्यपेहीति; tMd^{3} चाप्यपेहेति; tMd^{4} चाप्यगेहेति; Lo^{1} चाप्यएहीति; Tr^{2} चाप्यवैहीति; *Vij* सत्यपैहीति — d) Ho Lo^{1} Pu^{3} Pu^{8} Tr^{2} दण्ड्यो; gMy दण्ड्या; La^{1} दण्ड्यं; Be^{3} tMd^{3} Ox^{2} mTr^{4} mTr^{5} mTr^{6} दण्ड्यान्; oOr दण्डान्; wKt^{1} दण्डनं

293. Cited by *Apa* 863; *Lakṣ* 12.502; *Dev* 3.766 — a) tMd^{4} यत्रोपवर्तते; Ho यत्रापंवर्तते; bKt^{5} यत्रायंवर्तते; oOr यत्राप्रवर्तते; gMy यत्रावर्ज्यते; wKt^{3} यदा प्रवर्तते; Tr^{2} °पवर्गते; sOx^{1} sPu^{6} *Apa* [vl] °प्रवर्तते; tMd^{3} °पवर्जते; bKt^{5} युग्यो; Be^{3} Bo Ho Kt^{2} sOx^{1} sPu^{6} mTr^{3} युग्मं — b) Lo^{2} gMy व्राजकस्य; gMd^{1} व्योजकस्य; Be^{1} bCa wKt^{1} La^{1} nNg Wa च — c) mTr^{4} °द्दण्डो; tMd^{4} °द्दण्ड्या — d) mTr^{4} mTr^{6} हिंसायामिति धारणा; Tr^{2} हिंस्यायां द्विशती; bKt^{5} Lo^{4} Lo^{5} gMd^{1} nNg oOr nPu^{1} Pu^{2} Pu^{8} Tr^{1} [*but cor*] [*Jolly* M Nd] *Lakṣ* द्विशतो; gMy दशता; Jo^{2} bKt^{5} Lo^{3} Lo^{4} Lo^{5} gMd^{1} tMd^{3} gMy nNg oOr Tj^{1} nPu^{1} Pu^{3} [*Jolly* M Nd] *Lakṣ* दमः

294. Cited by *Apa* 863; *Lakṣ* 12.502; pādas a-b cited by *Vij* 2.300; *Dev* 3.766; *Mādh* 3.290 — a) Lo^{2} sOx^{1} sPu^{6} [*cor to*] व्राजक°; wKt^{1} nKt^{4} *Lakṣ* प्राजकश्च भवे°; gMd^{5} gMy °वेदाप्ता; Tr^{1} °वेदाप्तो — c) tMd^{3} युग्यस्थो; wKt^{3} युगेस्थानः; gMd^{1} अयुग्यस्था; tMd^{3} gMy Pu^{2} Pu^{4} प्राजको; Lo^{2} व्राजके; gMd^{5} gMy Tr^{1} [*but cor*] Wa °नाप्तो; nPu^{1} Pu^{2} Pu^{4} mTr^{6} °नाप्ताः; tMd^{3} °नाप्तः; tMd^{4} °नाप्ति — d) mTr^{6} सर्व; Pu^{8} शतं शतां; tMd^{3} शतं दमं

295.* Cited by *Apa* 863; *Lakṣ* 12.502 — a) Tr^{2} सर्वे तु; gMd^{1} *Apa* प्रतिसंरुद्धः; tMd^{3} gMy mTr^{4} mTr^{6} संक्रुद्धः — b) Lo^{3} Tj^{1} पथिभिर्वा; Lo^{3} रयेन; tMd^{3} तथेन; Bo पथेन; Be^{1} रथेन च — c) bKt^{5} प्रामा°; tMd^{3} प्रमादयेत्; La^{1} प्राणि°; tMd^{4} °भृतेस्तत्र; Lo^{4} °भृतं तत्र; Be^{1} °भूतस्तत्र — d) *Lakṣ* °भृतस्तस्य; gMd^{1} mTr^{6} दण्ड्यो; Lo^{5} दण्डे; sOx^{1} sPu^{6} [*but mc sh*] विवर्जितः; bBe^{2} Lo^{1} tMd^{4} mTr^{6} Wa *Apa* °विचारतः; *Jolly* विचारितः [*without avagraha*]

मनुष्यमारणे क्षिप्रं चौरवत्किल्बिषं भवेत् ।
प्राणभृत्सु महत्स्वर्धं गोगजोष्ट्रहयादिषु ॥२९६॥
क्षुद्रकाणां पशूनां तु हिंसायां द्विशतो दमः ।
पञ्चाशत्तु भवेद्दण्डः शुभेषु मृगपक्षिषु ॥२९७॥
गर्दभाजाविकानां तु दण्डः स्यात्पञ्चमाषिकः ।
माषिकस्तु भवेद्दण्डः श्वसूकरनिपातने ॥२९८॥
भार्या पुत्रश्च दासश्च शिष्यो भ्राता च सोदरः ।
प्राप्तापराधास्ताड्याः स्यू रज्ज्वा वेणुदलेन वा ॥२९९॥
पृष्ठतस्तु शरीरस्य नोत्तमाङ्गे कथंचन ।
अतोऽन्यथा तु प्रहरन् प्राप्तः स्याच्चौरकिल्बिषम् ॥३००॥
एषोऽखिलेनाभिहितो दण्डपारुष्यनिर्णयः ।

296. Cited by *Vij* 2.300; *Apa* 863; *Lakṣ* 12.502; *Mādh* 3.291 — a) Lo³ Tj¹ °मरणे; Wa °मारणा; NPu¹ Pu² °मारणात्; Jo¹ Kt² wKt³ क्षिप्तं; sOx¹ sPu⁶ विप्रं — b) NKt⁴ Lo² Lo³ GMd⁵ GMy Tj¹ Tr¹ MTr⁵MTr⁶ चोर°; Be¹ BBe² wKt¹ wKt³ GMy NPu¹ *Vij* °त्किल्बिषी — c) TMd³ पाण°; *Apa* [vl] °भृत्स्वमह°; sOx¹ sPu⁶ महत्स्वर्धे; *Mādh* महत्पूर्वं; Lo³ महत्स्वर्गं — d) Jo² [*but mc*] Lo³ Tj¹ गजाश्वोष्ट्र-गवादिषु [Lo³ °गवादिभिः]; Pu² Pu⁴ योगजो°; TMd³ GMy °हयेषु च

297. Omitted in Pu⁵ NNg; pāda-d omitted in Lo¹ [haplo]. Cited by *Vij* 2.300; *Apa* 864; *Lakṣ* 12.502; *Mādh* 3.291 — a) Hy क्षुद्रकारणां; TMd⁴ क्षुद्रक्षौणां; Be¹ शूद्रकाणां; *Vij* क्षुद्राणां च पशू°; Be³ BCa wKt¹ wKt³ BKt⁵ La¹ Lo¹ GMd¹ TMd³ GMy oOr Pu⁸ Tr² MTr⁴ *Lakṣ* च — b) oOr *om* हिंसायां; TMd⁴ हिंसानां; *Mādh* हिंसतो दशतो; TMd³ TMd⁴ GMy द्विशतं; Pu⁴ द्विगुणो; TMd⁴ दमं — c) BKt⁵ पञ्चशत्तु; BBe² BKt⁵ oOr भवेद्दण्ड्यः

298. Pādas a-c omitted in Lo¹. Cited by *Vij* 2.300; *Apa* 864; *Lakṣ* 12.502; *Mādh* 3.291 — a) Tj¹ °जाविनां; BCa Jo² BKt⁵ TMd³ GMy oOr Pu⁸ Tj¹ Tr² च — b) GMd¹ दण्डस्य पञ्चमाविकं; Lo⁵ *Jha Dave* स्यात्पाञ्च°; Jm Lo¹ GMd⁵ MTr³ *Apa Mādh* °माषकः; BBe² Bo BCa La¹ oOr °मासिकः — c) Hy Kt² NPu¹ Pu² Pu⁴ Tj¹ Tj² MTr³ [*Jolly* R] *Vij Apa Mādh* माषकस्तु; Be³ माषिकं तु; BBe² Bo oOr [*Jolly* Nd] मासिकस्तु; BCa मासकस्तु; GMy माणिकस्तु; BBe² oOr °द्दण्ड्यः; wKt³ °द्दण्डं — d) GMy सूकराणां निपातने; GMd¹ श्वासूकरपातने; BBe² Bo BCa Ho Hy BKt⁵ La¹ Lo¹ Lo² Lo⁴ Lo⁵ NNg NPu¹ Pu² Pu⁵ Pu⁷ श्वशूकर°; wKt¹ विट्सूकर°; NKt⁴ °पातिने

299. Cited by *Apa* 610, 815; *Lakṣ* 12.494 — a) Pu⁵ Pu⁷ [*Jolly* G] भर्या शिष्यश्च; Bo पुत्रश्च दाराश्च — b) Jo¹ *Dev Mandlik Jha KSS Dave* प्रेष्यो; BKt⁵ नेष्यो; Kt² प्रिष्यो; Pu⁵ Pu⁷ [*Jolly* G] पुत्रो; La¹ TMd³ TMd⁴ GMy oOr *Apa* भ्राता सहोदरः; *Me* gives pāṭha: भ्राता तथानुजः and comments: सोदरस्थाने कनीयान्पठितव्यः — c) oOr सप्तापरा°; Ho sOx¹ sPu⁶ °पराधास्ताड्यास्तु; Pu⁵ Pu⁷ °पराधां ताड्यास्तु; Tr¹ *mc sh to* °राधाः दण्ड्यास्यू; Lo¹ °राधास्ते दण्ड्या रज्ज्वा; TMd³ *om* स्यू — d) GMd¹ रज्ज्वापितलेन; GMd⁵ Tr¹ °दळेन; Pu⁵ Pu⁷ च

300. Cited by *Apa* 610, 815; *Lakṣ* 12.494; *Dev* 1.142; pādas a-b cited by *Vij* 1.155 and pāda-b by *Vij* 2.32 — b) GMd⁵ नोत्तमाङ्गं; Be¹ °माङ्गेन वक्ष्यसि; BBe² Be³ wKt¹ wKt³ GMd¹ NNg oOr NPu¹ Pu² Pu⁴ Wa *Apa* कदाचन — c) sOx¹ sPu⁶ अन्यथा [*om* अथो]; oOr अन्योन्यथा; TMd⁴ अर्थोन्यथा; Lo³ Tj¹ हि; MTr⁴ प्रहरेत्; TMd⁴ पारगो — d) NPu¹ पापयुक्तो भवेन्नरः; Be³ प्राप्नुयाच्चौर°; NKt⁴ Lo³ GMd¹ GMd⁵ GMy Tj¹ Tr¹ MTr⁵ *Bh Dev* स्याच्चोर°; Be¹ °किल्बिषी; Hy °किल्बिष

स्तेनस्यातः प्रवक्ष्यामि विधिं दण्डविनिर्णये ॥३०१॥
परमं यत्नमातिष्ठेत् स्तेनानां निग्रहे नृपः ।
स्तेनानां निग्रहादस्य यशो राष्ट्रं च वर्धते ॥३०२॥
अभयस्य हि यो दाता स पूज्यः सततं नृपः ।
सत्त्रं हि वर्धते तस्य सदैवाभयदक्षिणम् ॥३०३॥
सर्वतो धर्मषड्भागो राज्ञो भवति रक्षतः ।
अधर्मादपि षड्भागो भवत्यस्य ह्यरक्षतः ॥३०४॥
यदधीते यद्यजते यद्ददाति यदर्चति ।
तस्य षड्भागभाग्राजा सम्यग्भवति रक्षणात् ॥३०५॥
रक्षन्धर्मेण भूतानि राजा वध्यांश्च घातयन् ।
यजतेऽहरहर्यज्ञैः सहस्रशतदक्षिणैः ॥३०६॥

301. Cited by *Lakṣ* 12.505 — a) TMd^{4} एषानिले°; Pu^{2} Pu^{4} एताखिले°; Bo एषोपिले°; Be^{1} °खिलोनाभिहतो; MTr^{3} °हिते — b) wKt^{1} GMd^{1} दण्डः; Pu^{2} Pu^{4} °निर्णये — c) GMd^{5} Tr^{1} *Lakṣ* स्तेनस्याथ; Jo^{2} Tj^{1} स्तेयस्याथ; La^{1} स्तेनस्य तु; GMd^{1} परिवक्ष्ये — d) NKt^{4} विविधं दण्डनिर्णयं; Be^{1} GMd^{1} GMd^{5} विधिवद्दण्डनिर्णयं; Pu^{5} Pu^{7} [*Jolly* G] त्रिविधं दण्डनिर्णयं; Lo^{5} GMy विधि; BCa La^{1} TMd^{3} GMy Ox^{2} NPu^{1} MTr^{4} MTr^{6} Wa °विनिर्णयं

Here TMd^{3} GMy Tr^{1} insert 8.332; TMd^{3} omits it at its proper place while GMy Tr^{1} give it in both places.

302. Pādas b-d omitted in GMd^{1}. Cited by *Lakṣ* 12.511 — a) GMd^{1} सततं यत्न° — b) Pu^{2} स्तेयानां; Tr^{2} स्नानानां; BBe^{2} निगृहे; wKt^{3} विग्रहे; Pu^{4} नृपेः; oOr नृपं — c) Jo^{2} NNg Pu^{5} Pu^{7} [*Jolly* G] निग्रहाच्चास्य; Hy NPu^{1} Pu^{2} Pu^{4} Tj^{2} निग्रहाद्यस्य; Lo^{3} Tj^{1} निग्रहात्तस्य; Ho निग्रहे ह्यस्य; Bo निग्रहो यस्य; TMd^{4} निग्रहेणास्य; wKt^{3} विग्रहादस्य; BKt^{5} निग्रहस्य यशो — d) La^{1} राज्यं; TMd^{3} TMd^{4} राष्ट्रस्य वर्धते; Lo^{4} Lo^{5} *Lakṣ* राष्ट्रं विवर्धते; Be^{3} राष्ट्रं प्रवर्धते; Wa वर्धयेत्

303. Pāda-a omitted in GMd^{1}. Cited by *Lakṣ* 12.511 — a) TMd^{4} अभयस्येति यो; Tj^{2} च यो; BCa oOr तु यो; Bo हि वो — b) GMy sOx^{1} sPu^{6} संपूज्यः; GMd^{5} प्रपूज्यः — c) La^{1} शत्रं; Be^{3} NPu^{1} छत्रं; wKt^{3} oOr सतं; BBe^{2} BCa wKt^{1} Pu^{5} Pu^{7} विवर्धते; Be^{1} GMd^{1} GMd^{5} GMy MTr^{4} MTr^{5} MTr^{6} वर्तते; TMd^{4} वर्धतेप्यस्य — d) TMd^{4} सदैव च रक्षणं; Wa सदेवा°; GMd^{1} सदैवहय°; wKt^{3} °वाभक्षदक्षिणं; NKt^{4} BKt^{5} °दक्षिणां; Hy °दक्षणा

304. Pādas c-d omitted in wKt^{1} [haplo]. Cited by *Lakṣ* 11.86; *Mādh* 1.397 — a) TMd^{4} °षड्भागा; Bo °षड्भावा — b) TMd^{4} राज्यो; Be^{1} BCa GMd^{5} Pu^{5} Pu^{7} रक्षितः; Pu^{3} रक्षितुः; wKt^{3} Pu^{2} Pu^{4} रक्षकः; Jo^{2} La^{1} Lo^{3} Tj^{1} *Lakṣ* राक्षणात् — c) NNg अधर्मादस्य — d) TMd^{3} भवेत्तस्यैव रक्षतः; GMy भवत्यस्याप्यरक्षतः; *Mādh* भवत्येव; Lo^{2} Pu^{7} ह्यरक्षितः; Pu^{3} ह्यरक्षितुः; Pu^{8} ह्यरक्षतुः; wKt^{3} ह्यरक्षकः

305. a) wKt^{1} यदधीतेषु यजते; Lo^{2} यद्यधीते; Lo^{1} Lo^{4} Lo^{5} यद्यजति; GMd^{1} यद्यजीते; oOr यद्ददते; Tr^{2} य भजते; BKt^{5} यद्यतते — b) BKt^{5} यद्ददाति जुहोति यत्; Tj^{1} यदर्चयति; oOr यदर्चितं; wKt^{1} यदर्हति; Bo यदर्यति — c) NKt^{4} कस्य; Bo ते च षड्°; sOx^{1} sPu^{6} *om* षड् — d) NPu^{1} रक्षतः; Lo^{4} Lo^{5} [*Jolly* M] पालनात्

306. Cited by *Mādh* 1.397 — a) Bo रक्षन्भूतानि धर्मेण; Jo^{1} Wa रक्षध°; BKt^{5} क्षरन्ध° — b) TMd^{4} GMy राज; Hy वन्ध्यांश्च; Be^{3} Bo wKt^{1} wKt^{3} BKt^{5} Lo^{4} [*but cor*] GMd^{1} GMd^{5} MTr^{4} MTr^{6} Wa

योऽरक्षन्बलिमादत्ते करं शुल्कं च पार्थिवः ।
प्रतिभोगं च दण्डं च स सद्यो नरकं व्रजेत् ॥३०७॥
अरक्षितारं राजानं बलिषड्भागहारिणम् ।
तमाहुः सर्वलोकस्य समग्रमलहारकम् ॥३०८॥
अनवेक्षितमर्यादं नास्तिकं विप्रलुम्पकम् ।
अरक्षितारमत्तारं नृपं विद्यादधोगतिम् ॥३०९॥
अधार्मिकं त्रिभिर्न्यायैर्निगृह्णीयात् प्रयत्नतः ।
निरोधनेन बन्धेन विविधेन वधेन च ॥३१०॥
निग्रहेण च पापानां साधूनां संग्रहेण च ।
द्विजातय इवेज्याभिः पूयन्ते सततं नृपाः ॥३११॥

घातयेत्; Be^{1} घातकान् — c) Ox^{2} यजताहर°; Jo^{2} Lo^{3} Tj^{1} Wa यजत्यहर°; Be^{1} यजति अहर°; Ho sOx^{1} sPu^{6} यजेताहर° — d) oOr सुमहद [lacuna] रदक्षिणैः; TMd^{4} °दक्षिणां

307. Cited by *Mādh* 1.397 — a) NPu^{1} योरक्षित्वमादत्ते — b) Pu^{5} Pu^{7} [*but cor*] शुल्के; Bo Lo^{1} Tj^{1} शुक्लं; Be^{3} शुल्कश्च; GMy शुल्कस्य पा°; Pu^{5} Pu^{7} पार्थिवं — c) Jm Jo^{1} Kt^{2} Lo^{4} Lo^{5} GMd^{1} Pu^{2} Pu^{4} MTr^{3} [*Jolly* M$^{4-5}$ Ku] *Me Ku Mandlik Jha KSS Dave* प्रतिभागं; GMd^{5} GMy Tr^{1} [*but cor*] MTr^{4} MTr^{5} MTr^{6} [*Jolly* Nd] *Nd Rc Rn* प्रीतिभोगं; TMd^{3} प्रीतिभागं; *Mādh* प्रीतिं भोगं; TMd^{4} प्रीतिचोरं; Pu^{5} Pu^{7} *Go* [*Jolly* G] भूतिभोगं; [*Jolly* M^{9}] सूतिभागं — d) Be^{3} सद्यः स

308. Pādas c-d omitted in Lo^{3} — a) BKt^{5} Lo^{4} Lo^{5} Wa [*Jolly* M N] *Me Nā* [but gives the accepted reading as pāṭha] *Dave Jha* अरक्षितारमत्तारं; Be^{3} अरक्षितारं लोकानां — b) Be^{3} °बलहारकं; MTr^{6} °हारिणः — c) Pu^{2} तदाहुः; GMy तमस्तु; Pu^{5} Pu^{7} °लोकानां — d) Be^{1} समग्रं; MTr^{4} समग्रबल°; Pu^{5} Pu^{7} समस्तमबल°; GMd^{1} समग्रबलि°; Jo^{2} GMd^{1} TMd^{3} TMd^{4} GMd^{5} Pu^{5} Pu^{7} Tj^{1} Tr^{1} [*Jolly* G] °हारिणं

309. a) BBe^{2} Hy Jm Jo^{1} Kt^{2} Lo^{2} oOr Pu^{5} Pu^{7} Pu^{8} Tj^{2} Tr^{2} MTr^{3} MTr^{4} MTr^{5} MTr^{6} [*Jolly* M^{4} G Ku Rā] *Rn Go Mandlik KSS* अनपेक्षित°; Bo वृ [lacuna] प्रेक्षित°; Pu^{2} Pu^{4} °मायादं — b) TMd^{4} नास्तेकं; Be^{1} विप्रलुंतकं; Kt^{2} विपुलम्यकं; wKt^{1} विप्रलुम्भकः; Jo^{2} विप्रलुम्पनं; Be^{3} NKt^{4} Lo^{2} GMd^{1} TMd^{3} GMy oOr Pu^{2} Pu^{4} Tr^{1} [*but cor*] MTr^{4} MTr^{5} MTr^{6} [*Jolly* Nd] विप्रलोपकं; Pu^{7} वित्तलोपको *cor to* वित्तलोपकं; Pu^{5} वित्तलोपके — c) TMd^{3} अनक्षतारमुत्तारं; Be^{1} Be^{3} Bo °तारमन्तारं; MTr^{4} MTr^{6} °तारं हन्तारं; GMd^{5} °तारमात्तानां — d) GMd^{1} TMd^{3} TMd^{4} GMy MTr^{4} MTr^{6} [*Jolly* Nd] *Me* [pāṭha] असत्यं च नृपं त्यजेत् [GMd^{1} असत्त्वं]; Pu^{5} Pu^{7} [*Jolly* G] गच्छेदधो°; NKt^{4} दद्यादधो°; La^{1} Pu^{2} विंदादधो°; Be^{3} Lo^{4} Lo^{5} °धोगतं; Bo °धोगिति; BKt^{5} °धोहतं

310. Cited by *Lakṣ* 12.782 — a) sOx^{1} sPu^{6} अधार्मिकैस्त्रि°; GMy अधार्मिकास्त्रि°; TMd^{3} GMd^{5} Tr^{1} MTr^{4} MTr^{6} अधार्मिकांस्त्रि° — b) *Lakṣ* °गृह्णीत; GMd^{5} °गृह्णीयादतन्द्रितः — c) BCa NNg MTr^{5} निरोधेन निबन्धेन; Ho sOx^{1} sPu^{6} रोधनेन च बन्धेन; oOr निरोधेन च बन्धेन; Pu^{5} Pu^{7} [*cor to*] निरोधने च बन्धेन; TMd^{3} GMd^{5} GMy Tr^{1} [*Jolly* Nd] दण्डेन — d) Lo^{1} वधेन विविधेन च; BBe^{2} धनेन च; TMd^{3} TMd^{4} GMd^{5} GMy भयेन च; Tr^{2} वनेन च; Be^{1} La^{1} Pu^{5} Pu^{7} [*Jolly* G] वा; [*Jolly* M^{9}] तु

311.* a) Ho विग्रहेण; GMd^{5} Tr^{1} निग्रहेणापि; Bo Hy Jm Jo^{1} Kt^{2} wKt^{3} NKt^{4} Lo^{2} Pu^{7} MTr^{3} MTr^{6} MTr^{6} *Mandlik Jolly Jha KSS Dave* हि — b) GMd^{1} सतां चानुग्रहेण च; oOr *om* साधूनां; Tr^{2} निग्रहेण; GMd^{5} MTr^{6} प्रग्रहेण; TMd^{3} GMy Pu^{3} रक्षणेन; NKt^{4} Pu^{4} संग्रहणेन च; Be^{3} वा — c) La^{1} इवेक्ष्याभिः — d) TMd^{3} TMd^{4} MTr^{4} oOr पूयते; sOx^{1} sPu^{6} पूज्यन्ते; NKt^{4} स्वयन्ते; wKt^{3} Pu^{5} नृप; TMd^{3} GMy NNg MTr^{4} नृपः

क्षन्तव्यं प्रभुणा नित्यं क्षिपतां कार्यिणां नृणाम् ।
बालवृद्धातुराणां च कुर्वता हितमात्मनः ॥३१२॥
यत्क्षिप्तो मर्षयत्यार्तैस्तेन स्वर्गे महीयते ।
यत्त्वैश्वर्यान्न क्षमते नरकं तेन गच्छति ॥३१३॥
राजा स्तेनेन गन्तव्यो मुक्तकेशेन धीमता ।
आचक्षाणेन तत्स्तेयमेवंकर्मास्मि शाधि माम् ॥३१४॥
स्कन्धेनादाय मुसलं लगुडं वापि खादिरम् ।
शक्तिं चोभयतस्तीक्ष्णामायसं दण्डमेव वा ॥३१५॥
शासनाद्वा विमोक्षाद्वा स्तेनः स्तेयाद्विमुच्यते ।
अशासित्वा तु तं राजा स्तेनस्याप्नोति किल्बिषम् ॥३१६॥

312. Folios containing verses 312–28 missing in the microfilm of mTr^6. Cited by *Lakṣ* 12.47; *Dev* 3.66 — b) tMd^3 क्षिपता; nKt^4 क्षिपातां; sOx^1 sPu^6 क्षिपितां; nPu^1 Pu^2 Pu^4 क्षपतां; tMd^4 क्षिप्तानां; gMd^5 कार्यणां; tMd^4 कारिणां; tMd^3 कारिणा; gMy कारणां; nKt^4 कार्षिणां; Lo^1 कार्पण्यां — c) Bo °तुरास्यं; Lo^4 Lo^5 *Lakṣ* तु — d) Be^1 Be^3 La^1 Lo^1 tMd^3 gMd^5 gMy oOr sOx^1 Pu^2 Pu^4 Pu^5 sPu^6 Pu^7 Tj^2 Tr^2 mTr^4 Wa [*Jolly* M G Nd R] *Rn Go* कुर्वतां; Ho गर्वतां; nNg °मात्मन; Lo^2 gMd^1 Pu^5 Pu^7 °मात्मने; Pu^4 °मात्मना

313.* Pādas c-d *ma sh* in Tr^1. Cited by *Dev* 3.66 — a) Be^1 bBe^2 Bo Ho Hy Jm Jo^1 Jo^2 wKt^1 Kt^2 wKt^3 Lo^1 Lo^2 Lo^3 Lo^4 Lo^5 gMd^1 oOr Ox^2 sPu^6 [*mc to*] Pu^8 Tj^1 Tj^2 Tr^2 mTr^3 Wa [*Jolly* R Ku M^4] *Ku Mandlik Jha KSS Dave* यः क्षिप्तो; sOx^1 यं क्षिप्तो; Pu^2 Pu^4 यत्क्षिप्तैर्मर्ष°; mTr^4 हर्षय°; tMd^4 मर्षयत्यैतैस्तेन; gMd^5 मर्षयत्याशु तेन — b) tMd^4 सर्गे — c) oOr [*Jolly* M$^{5-9}$ G Me] *Jolly* यच्चैश्व°; Be^1 bBe^2 Be^3 Bo Ho Hy Jm Jo^1 Kt^2 wKt^3 nKt^4 Lo^1 Lo^2 Lo^4 Lo^5 gMy sOx^1 Ox^2 sPu^6 Pu^8 Tj^1 Tj^2 Tr^2 mTr^3 Wa [*Jolly* M^4 Nd Ku] *Mandlik Jha KSS Dave* यस्त्वैश्व°; Jo^2 wKt^1 bKt^5 Lo^3 gMd^1 oOr Tr^1 [*ma sh*] [*Jolly* R] यश्चैश्व°; tMd^3 यस्वैर्यान क्षमते; La^1 °श्वर्यानुक्षमते — d) gMy चैव गच्छति; tMd^3 सोधिगच्छति

314.* *ma* in Tr^1. Cited by *Viś* 3.252; pādas a-b cited by *Apa* 1078 — a) Tr^2 राज्ञस्तेनेन — b) nPu^1 धीवता; Be^1 bBe^2 Be^3 Bo bCa Ho Hy Jm Jo^1 Jo^2 wKt^1 Kt^2 wKt^3 La^1 Lo^4 Lo^5 sOx^1 Ox^2 Pu^3 Pu^5 sPu^6 Pu^7 Pu^8 Tj^1 Tj^2 Tr^1 [*ma sh*] Tr^2 mTr^3 Wa [*Jolly* M^4 G N R Ku] *Apa Me* [pāṭha] *Bh* [pāṭha] *Go Nā Ku Mr Mandlik Bühler Jolly KSS Doniger* धावता — c) Be^1 wKt^3 tMd^4 Pu^8 आचक्षणेन; gMd^5 आचक्षमाणेन; HosOx^1 sPu^6 च स्तेय°; La^1 तु स्तेय°; nKt^4 तस्तेय°; Pu^2 Pu^4 तत्कर्ममे°; *Viś* तत्पापमे° — c-d) gMd^5 तत्स्तेयकर्मास्मि — d) Ox^2 °कर्तास्मि; Kt^2 °कर्माणि; Pu^5 Pu^7 °कर्माधिशासि; Lo^2 साधि; *Viś* शास्तु; Hy tMd^4 मा

315. Cited by *Viś* 3.252; *Vij* 3.257; *Apa* 1078 — a) gMd^5 स्कन्धे चादाय; bBe^2 Be^3 Ho wKt^1 nKt^4 Lo^1 Lo^2 Pu^5 Pu^7 Tj^2 *Dave Jha* मुशलं; bCa Hy bKt^5 oOr मुषलं; La^1 मुखलं; wKt^3 मूखलं; Tr^2 शुशलं — b) Tr^2 Wa लकुडं; Bo nKt^4 Lo^2 Pu^3 *Vij Der* लकुटं; Tr^1 लकुटुं; Pu^2 Pu^4 लकुतं; Pu^8 लकुटेनापि; Bo Ho Ox^2 चापि; [*Jolly* M] वाथ— c) *Apa* अभ्रिं; *Vij* असिं; La^1 शक्तितोभय°; bCa Jo^2 wKt^1 Lo^2 gMd^5 nPu^1 Pu^2 Pu^4 Pu^5 Pu^7 Tj^1 mTr^4 mTr^5 *Viś Apa* वोभय°; tMd^3 °भयतः हीर्ष्णामा°; Be^1 gMy *Vij Apa* °स्तीक्ष्णमा° — d) La^1 Lo^1 Ox^2 Pu^7 Pu^8 च

Additional verse in bCa wKt^3 La^1 oOr *Mandlik* [क] *Dave KSS*, which is identical with 11.101.

316. Cited by *Viś* 3.252; *Apa* 1078 — a) bBe^2 शासनाद्वाधिमोक्षाद्वा; bKt^5 *Apa* शासनाद्वापि

अन्नादे भ्रूणहा मार्ष्टि पत्यौ भार्यापचारिणी ।
गुरौ शिष्यश्च याज्यश्च स्तेनो राजनि किल्बिषम् ॥३१७॥
राजभिर्धृतदण्डास्तु कृत्वा पापानि मानवाः ।
निर्मलाः स्वर्गमायान्ति सन्तः सुकृतिनो यथा ॥३१८॥
यस्तु रज्जुं घटं कूपाद्धरेद्भिन्द्याच्च यः प्रपाम् ।
स दण्डं प्राप्नुयान्माषं तच्च तस्मिन्समाहरेत् ॥३१९॥
धान्यं दशभ्यः कुम्भेभ्यो हरतोऽभ्यधिकं वधः ।
शेषेऽप्येकादशगुणं दाप्यस्तस्य च तद्धनम् ॥३२०॥
तथा धरिममेयानां शतादभ्यधिके वधः ।
सुवर्णरजतादीनामुत्तमानां च वाससाम् ॥३२१॥

मोक्षाद्वा — b) TMd4 स्तेना; Pu5 Pu7 तेन स्तेया°; Lo3 TMd4 Tj1 स्तेनाद्वि°; Tj1 °मोच्यते — c) La1 GMd1 TMd3 TMd4 GMd5 GMy Tr1 [*but mc sh*] MTr4 *Nd* अशासनात्तस्य राजा; Be3 Lo3 Tj1 अशासयित्वा तं राजा; oOr आशासित्वा; Hoअसासित्वा; Pu5 Pu7 प्रशाधित्वा; wKt1 असासपित्वा तं; Lo1 च तं; Pu8 *om* तं — d) *Apa* चौरस्याप्नोति; Pu8 किल्बिषां

317. Omitted in Lo4 Lo5. Cited by *Hem* 3/1.781; *pratīka* by *Śaṃ* on *BU* 1.5.2 — a) Lo1 अनादे; TMd3 Pu7 अन्नादेर्भ्रूण°; NNg भ्रूणहो; TMd4 मार्प्टे; TMd3 हार्ष्टि — b) GMd1 त्यौ भार्या परिचारिणी; GMy पतौ; Jo2 Wa जायाप°; Be1 जायाभिचारिणी; BBe2 oOr °पहारिणी — c) Lo2 गुरो; TMd3 सखा शिष्यश्च; TMd3 Pu8 शिष्यस्य याज्यस्य; Lo2 GMd1 याज्यश्च शिष्यश्च; Tj1 शिष्यश्च जायाश्च; *Hem* याज्याश्च; Pu7 [*but mc*] याज्यस्य — d) BKt5 राजकिल्बिषं

318. Cited by *Vij* 3.259 — a) [*Jolly* M3–4–5] राजनिर्धृत°; Kt2 राजनिर्धूत°; MTr3 राजानिद्धुत°; Be1 TMd3 GMy MTr3 Wa [*Jolly* Nd] *Go Mandlik KSS* राजभिः कृत°; Be1 °दण्डस्तु; BBe2 GMd1 Pu3 Pu5 Pu7 Pu8 Tr2 °दण्डाश्च — b) NNg मानवा; sOx1 sPu6 मानवः; Be3 मानुषाः; Lo1 मायया: — c) BBe2 निर्मलं; Bo सर्गमा° — d) oOr सतः; wKt1 सर्वसुकृतिनो; GMy सुकृतनो

319. Cited by *Apa* 848 — a) Hy यंस्तु; wKt1 *om* यस्तु रज्जुं; Be3 Hy NKt4 Lo5 TMd3 रज्जु; sOx1 sPu6 कूपान्हरे°; BBe2 कूपात्हरे°; wKt1 कूपादुरे°; NKt4 कूपाद्रक्षे° — b) GMd5 MTr5 °द्भिद्याच्च; Be3 °द्भिंद्याद्यः प्रपात्; Tj1 प्रापां — c) *Apa* दण्डं स; BBe2 La1 oOr °यान्मासं — d) wKt1 *om* तच्च; TMd3 तं च; TMd4 तस्य तस्मि°; Be3 तस्मै समा°; wKt3 °न्समाचरेत्; GMd1 TMd3 TMd4 GMd5 GMy Tr1 MTr4 °न्समुद्धरेत्; Ox2 °न्सदाहरेत्

320. Pādas a-b omitted in Pu5, and pādas c-d in sOx1 [haplo], and pāda-d in GMd5 BKt5 [haplo]. Cited by *Vij* 2.275; *Apa* 846; *Lakṣ* 12.532; *Dev* 3.739; *Mādh* 3.303 — a) TMd3 GMy कुम्भिभ्यो; wKt1 कुस्तेभ्यो — b) TMd4 हरत्यध्यधिके; Jo2 La1 NPu1 Pu2 Pu4 हरतोप्यधिकं; Tr1 °भ्यधिके *cor fh to* ह्यधिकं; TMd3 °भ्येतिके; *Lakṣ* ह्यधिको; NKt4 Lo2 GMy Pu7 [*Jolly* G Nd] °धिके; Lo4 °धिके *cor to* धिक; La1 sOx1 Ox2 sPu6 °धिको; GMd5 दमः; oOr दिश — c) Be1 Pu5 Pu7 Tr2 [*Jolly* M5–9] *Vij* शेषेष्वेका°; NKt4 BKt5 Lo4 Lo5 NNg Tj2 [*Jolly* M4] शेषे त्वेका°; Lo1 शेषे एका°; TMd3 शेषत्येकंदश°; GMy °गुणान् — d) TMd4 मूल्याद्दण्डं प्रकल्पयेत् [cf. 8.322d]; TMd3 दाप्यो राज्ञा च न सारतः; GMd1 Tr1 [*but mc sh*] दाप्यो राज्ञा स्वसारतः; MTr4 दाप्यो राज्ञा च; wKt1 तद्धलं; Pu3 तद्दमं

321. Omitted in Jo2 BKt5 GMd5; pādas a-b omitted in sOx1. Cited by *Vij* 2.275; *Apa* 847; *Lakṣ* 12.533; *Mādh* 3.303; pādas c-d cited by *Dev* 3.739; *Vij* transposes pādas a-b and c-d and gives रत्नानां as pādas c-d — a) Pu2 Pu4 तया; *NSm* 19.32 तुला; Pu5 Pu7 TMd4 धरणमे°; NPu1 परिममे°; Pu2 Pu4 परममे°; TMd3 दण्डममे°; Lo1 धरमपापानां — a-b) *Vij Mādh NSm* 19.34 रत्नानां चैव

पञ्चाशतस्त्वभ्यधिके हस्तच्छेदनमिष्यते ।
शेषेऽप्येकादशगुणं मूल्याद्दण्डं प्रकल्पयेत् ॥३२२॥
पुरुषाणां कुलीनानां नारीणां च विशेषतः ।
मुख्यानां चैव रत्नानां हरणे वधमर्हति ॥३२३॥
महापशूनां हरणे शस्त्राणामौषधस्य च ।
कालमासाद्य कार्यं च राजा दण्डं प्रकल्पयेत् ॥३२४॥
गोषु ब्राह्मणसंस्थासु स्थूरिकायाश्च भेदनं* ।
पशूनां हरणे चैव सद्यः कार्योऽर्धपादिकः ॥३२५॥
सूत्रकार्पासकिण्वानां गोमयस्य गुडस्य च ।
दध्नः क्षीरस्य तक्रस्य पानीयस्य तृणस्य च ॥३२६॥

सर्वेषां शतादप्यधिकं वधः — b) Tj² Tr² °भ्यधिकं; La¹ Pu⁵ Pu⁷ °प्यधिके; Ox² °प्यधिको — c) GMy NNg °राजतादी° — d) Pu⁵ Pu⁷ [*Jolly* G] °दीनां महार्घाणां च; Ho वाससं

322.* Pādas a-c omitted in Jo² BKt⁵ GMd⁵. Cited by *Vij* 2.275; *Apa*847; *Lakṣ* 12.533; *Dev* 3.739;pādas a-b cited by *Mādh* 3.303 — a) Ho °शतस्त्वधिकेन; Bo °शतस्त्वधिके; TMd³ °शतस्त्वभ्यधिकेन — b) Pu⁸ °नमैष्यते; Be³ °नमिच्छति; Lo⁴ Lo⁵ NNg [*Jolly* M Gr] °नमुच्यते — c) Bo Hy Jm Jo¹ Kt² Lo² Lo⁴ Lo⁵ Pu⁵ Pu⁷ Tj² MTr³ *Apa Mandlik Jolly Jha KSS Dave* शेषेत्वेका° ; Be¹ Be³ NNg NPu¹ Pu³ Tr² Wa [*Jolly* M⁵⁻⁹] *VijDev* शेषेष्वेका° ; [*Jolly* G] शेषेचैका° — d) TMd⁴ दाप्यो राज्ञा स्वसारतः; TMd³ मूला°

323. Omitted in Ca. Cited by *Vij* 2.275; *Apa*847; *Lakṣ* 12.528; *Mādh* 3.303; pādas c-d cited by *Lakṣ* 12.534 — b) GMy नारानां; Be¹ नारीणामविशे° ; *Vij* वा — c) *Mādh* रत्नानां चैव मुख्यानां; *Vij* रत्नानां चैव सर्वेषां; sPu⁶ च रत्नानां; wKt¹ यत्नानां — d) GMd¹ TMd³ हरेण

324.* Omitted in Ca; pādas c-d omitted in Be¹. Cited by *Apa* 847;*Lakṣ* 12.530 — a) TMd³ GMy ग्रहणे — b) TMd⁴ शस्त्राणां च वधश्च सः; La¹ sOx¹ sPu⁶ शास्त्रा° ; wKt¹ °मोषधस्य — c) wKt³ La¹ कालमासाद्य कालं च — d) Be³ Hy Jm Jo¹ Kt² BKt⁵ Lo¹ Lo² Lo³ Lo⁴ Lo⁵ NNg NPu¹ Pu² Pu³ Pu⁴ Pu⁸ Tj¹ Tj² Tr² *Bh Nd* दण्डं राजा प्रकल्पयेत् [sOx¹ sPu⁶ राज्ञा; GMy दण्ड्यं]

325.* Omitted in Be¹. Cited by *Lakṣ* 12.530 — a) Hy ब्रह्मण° — b) Tj¹ स्यूरिकायाश्च; TMd⁴ स्थुलितायाश्च; NNg स्छुरिकार्यश्च; GMd⁵ सूरिकायाश्च; Pu⁴ स्थरिलकायाश्च; Lo⁴ Lo⁵ Tr² [*Jolly* M³⁻⁴⁻⁵] स्फुरिकायाश्च; Be³ सूतिकायाश्च; Hy छूरिकायाश्च; BCa Tr¹ [*but cor*] *Lakṣ KSS* छुरिकायाश्च; Kt² *Mandlik* छूरिकायाञ्च; Jo¹ छुरिकायांश्च; TMd³ छुरिकायास्तु; Ho Pu⁸ *Go* [*Jolly* G] नासिकायाश्च; Pu⁵ Pu⁷ नासकायाश्च; Bo Lo¹ नासिकायास्तु; *Me Dave Jha* खरिकायाश्च; wKt¹ त्वविकाश्च; *Rc* reads प्रच्छुरिकायाः; reading adopted, भेदनं, *ex conjectura*; all mss. (except Wa) and all commentators read the locative भेदने; NNg भेदिने; TMd⁴ खेदने; *Bh* [pāṭha] वाहने — c) Tj² महापशूनां हरणे सद्यः [cf. 8.224a]; *Lakṣ* चैव हरणे; TMd³ हरणं — d) Be³ Pu³ Pu⁸ Tr² दमः कार्यो; TMd³ कार्या; Jo² Lo¹ Pu⁵ Pu⁷ °र्धपादकः; Pu⁸ °र्धपादिकं; TMd⁴ °र्धहारिकः; Bo °भिपादकः; Pu² Pu⁴ द्विपादिकः; NKt⁴ °दिपादिवाः

326. Pādas a-b omitted in Be¹ Lo⁴ Lo⁵ and pādas c-d in Pu⁸. Cited by *Apa* 847; *Lakṣ* 12.535; *Mādh* 3.303-4 — a) Ho wKt³ La¹ NNg NPu¹ Pu² Pu⁴ Pu⁵ Pu⁷ °कर्पास° ; Bo BKt⁵ °कण्वानां; *Apa* [vl] °किण्ठानां; Lo¹ °कीराणां; Be³ °वित्तानां — b) TMd³ GMy [*Jolly* Nd] °ण्वानामायसस्य गुडस्य; wKt³ गुदस्य; MTr⁵ गुळस्य; BBe² गुचस्य — c) BBe² दधि; TMd⁴ कुरस्य; TMd³ क्षीरक्षितक्रस्य; NNg तत्रस्य — d) TMd⁴ हरस्य च; NKt⁴ वा

वेणुवैदलभाण्डानां लवणानां तथैव च ।
मृन्मयानां च हरणे मृदो भस्मन एव च ॥३२७॥
मत्स्यानां पक्षिणां चैव तैलस्य च घृतस्य च ।
मांसस्य मधुनश्चैव यच्चान्यत्पशुसंभवम् ॥३२८॥
अन्येषां चैवमादीनामद्यानामोदनस्य च ।
पक्वान्नानां च सर्वेषां तन्मूल्याद् द्विगुणो दमः ॥३२९॥
पुष्पेषु हरिते धान्ये गुल्मवल्लीनगेषु च ।
अल्पेष्वपरिपूतेषु दण्डः स्यात्पञ्चकृष्णलः ॥३३०॥
परिपूतेषु धान्येषु शाकमूलफलेषु च ।
निरन्वये शतं दण्डः सान्वयेऽर्धशतं दमः ॥३३१॥
स्यात्साहसं त्वन्वयवत् प्रसभं कर्म यत्कृतम् ।
निरन्वयं भवेत्स्तेयं कृत्वापव्ययते च यत् ॥३३२॥

327. Omitted in Be^{3} Lo^{4} Lo^{5} Pu^{8}. Cited by *Apa* 847; *Lakṣ* 12.535; *Mādh* 3.304 — a) TMd^{4} वेणुभाण्डलकांधाना; La^{1} GMd^{1} MTr^{4} MTr^{5} *Apa Mādh* वेणुवैणव°; Pu^{2} Pu^{4} वेणुवैडल° — b) La^{1} सर्वस्याश्ममयस्य च; NKt^{4} *om* लवणानां — c) Ho Jm TMd^{3} TMd^{4} GMd^{5} GMy sOx^{1} sPu^{6} Tj^{1} Tj^{2} Tr^{1} *Jha Dave* मृण्म°; BBe^{2} च भाण्डानां — d) La^{1} मृदा; GMd^{1} दाम्नो भस्मन

328. Omitted in Lo^{4} Lo^{5} GMd^{5}; pādas a-b omitted in Be^{3} and pādas c-d in GMd^{1}. Cited by *Apa* 847; *Lakṣ* 12.535; *Mādh* 3.304 — a) *Mādh* अजानां पक्षि°; NKt^{4} सस्यानां सतृणां; TMd^{3} दक्षिणां — b) Kt^{2} वैलस्य; Bo मृतस्य; TMd^{4} गुडस्य — c) TMd^{3} GMy NNg मांसश्च — d) Pu^{2} Pu^{4} यत्त्वन्यत्पशु°; TMd^{3} यदन्यत्पशु°; Be^{3} यश्चान्यत्पशु°; wKt^{3} यच्चान्यपशु°

329.* Folios containing verses 329–45 badly microfilmed and only parts are visible in MTr^{6}. Omitted in Lo^{4} Lo^{5} GMd^{1}; pādas a-b omitted in GMd^{5}. Cited by *Lakṣ* 12.535; *Mādh* 3.304 — b) La^{1} GMd^{4} oOr Tr^{2} Wa °दीनामाद्यानामो°; Be^{1} BBe^{2} Bo Hy Jo^{2} wKt^{1} wKt^{3} Lo^{1} Lo^{2} Lo^{3} NNg [*but cor fh*] Ox^{2} Pu^{8} Tj^{1} Tj^{2} Tr^{1} *Lakṣ Mādh Jolly KSS* °दीनां मद्यानामो°; NKt^{4} °दीनां यद्यानामो°; Pu^{7} °दीनां मद्यौनामो°; sPu^{6} °दीनां माषाकामो° *cor to* माषाणामो°; sOx^{1} °दीनां माषाणामो°; Ox^{2} °दीनां संघानामौ°; TMd^{3} °दीनां मत्स्यानामो°; MTr^{4} °दीनां क्षुद्राणामो°; Be^{3} °द्यानां मोदकस्य; wKt^{3} °मोदकस्य; La^{1} °मौषधस्य — c) GMy पाकान्नानां; TMd^{3} पाकानांगां च — d) TMd^{3} GMy द्विगुणो दम उच्यते [TMd^{3} द्विगुणा]; Pu^{5} Pu^{7} तन्मूलाद्; GMd^{5} द्विगुणं

330. *ma* in Ho; pādas a-b omitted in GMd^{1}; pādas c-d omitted in Pu^{8}. Cited by *Lakṣ* 12.534 — a) TMd^{4} पुष्पे हरतते धान्ये; sOx^{1} sPu^{6} हरते; BKt^{5} हरितो; Lo^{2} हरितौ— b) TMd^{3} °वल्लि°; GMd^{5} °वारनगेषु; Pu^{2} Pu^{4} °वल्लीनागपुचच; sOx^{1} sPu^{6} °वल्लीलतासु च; NNg *om* च — c) Lo^{2} स्वल्पेष्व°; BBe^{2} Hy Jo^{1} Jo^{2} wKt^{1} Kt^{2} wKt^{3} Lo^{3} Ox^{2} Pu^{2} Pu^{4} Tj^{1} Tj^{2} [*Jolly* Ku R] *Ku Mr Mandlik Jha KSS Dave* अन्येष्व°; Jm La^{1} oOr NPu^{1} अन्येषु परि°; Be^{3} Pu^{2} Pu^{4} °भूतेषु; La^{1} °पूर्त्तेषु — d) GMd^{5} स्यात्कृष्णलः; La^{1} sOx^{1} sPu^{6} °कृष्णलाः; GMy oOr °कृष्णलं

331. Pādas a-b omitted in Pu^{8} — a) Be^{1} परिपूज्येषु; La^{1} Pu^{3} °पूर्त्तेषु — b) GMd^{1} *om* च — c) Jo^{1} निरन्वयं; TMd^{3} GMd^{5} निरन्वयश्शतं; Be^{1} Jo^{2} NKt^{4} La^{1} Lo^{1} Lo^{3} GMy sOx^{1} Pu^{2} Pu^{4} sPu^{6} Tj^{1} Tr^{1} Wa [*Jolly* M R] *Ku* दण्ड्यः; Lo^{4} Lo^{5} दण्ड्याः; oOr दण्डं; Ho GMd^{1} दण्ड्यं — d) GMd^{5} सान्वयश्शतकं दमं; TMd^{3} सान्वयषर्धतं दमं; Tr^{1} °र्धद्विशतं [द्वि deleted]; Be^{3} Tr^{2} द्विशतं दमः; Lo^{5} द्वशतं दमः

332. Omitted in Lo^{4} Lo^{5}; from pāda-b until 8.359 omitted in Pu^{5}; placed after 8.301 in

यस्त्वेतान्युपक्लृप्तानि द्रव्याणि स्तेनयेन्नरः ।
तं शतं* दण्डयेद्राजा यश्चाग्निं चोरयेद्गृहात् ॥३३३॥
येन येन यथाङ्गेन स्तेनो नृषु विचेष्टते ।
तत्तदेव हरेत्तस्य प्रत्यादेशाय पार्थिवः ॥३३४॥
पिताचार्यः सुहृन्माता भार्या पुत्रः पुरोहितः ।
नादण्ड्यो नाम राज्ञोऽस्ति यः स्वधर्मे न तिष्ठति ॥३३५॥
कार्षापणं भवेद्दण्ड्यो यत्रान्यः प्राकृतो जनः ।
तत्र राजा भवेद्दण्ड्यः सहस्रमिति धारणा ॥३३६॥
अष्टापाद्यं तु शूद्रस्य स्तेये भवति किल्बिषम् ।
षोडशैव तु वैश्यस्य द्वात्रिंशत् क्षत्रियस्य तु ॥३३७॥

TMd^{3}; pādas c-d *ma sh* in Tr^{1}; pādas a-b and c-d transposed in NNg; verses 332 and 333 transposed in BKt^{5} Wa [*Jolly* M N]. Cited by *Vij* 2.266 [intr]; *Lakṣ* 12.505; *Mādh* 3.298; pādas a-b cited by *Lakṣ* 12.557 — a) TMd^{3} तत्साहसं; Pu^{2} °हसकं; La^{1} °हसमन्वयवत्; Pu^{2} Pu^{4} त्वन्वयकं; Be^{1} त्वनयवत्; Kt^{2} Wa त्वन्ययवत् — b) sOx^{1} sPu^{6} [*cor to*] समक्षं कर्म; BKt^{5} तत्कृतं; oOr सकृतं — c) BCa La^{1} Tr^{2} निरन्वये; Tj^{2} भवोस्तेयं; Tr^{2} °त्स्तेयः; La^{1} °त्स्तेय — d) *Vij* कृत्वापह्नूयते च यत्; GMd^{5} कृत्वापव्ययमेव यत्; Bo कृत्वातेपव्ययं च यत्; GMd^{1} कृत्वोप°; Jm Jo^{1} Kt^{2} MTr^{3} *Mandlik Jha KSS Dave* हृत्वाप°; wKt^{1} कृत्वापयते; Tr^{2} कृत्वाव्ययते तु; *Mādh* °व्ययते यदि; Ox^{2} NPu^{1} Pu^{3} Pu^{8} तु; BKt^{5} च यं; wKt^{5} च यः; La^{1} च सः

333.* Cited by *Apa* 848; *Lakṣ* 12.536 — a) Be^{1} Pu^{7} Wa [*Jolly* G] यश्चैतान्युप°; *Apa* यज्ञार्थान्युप°; NKt^{4} °न्यवक्लृप्तानि; La^{1} Pu^{4} °क्लिप्तानि; wKt^{1} °तृप्तानि; GMd^{5} °युक्तानि — b) TMd^{3} स्तेनयन्नरः — c) MTr^{4} *om* तं; BBe^{2} Be^{3} Bo BCa Ho Jm Jo^{1} Jo^{2} wKt^{1} Kt^{2} wKt^{3} NKt^{4} Lo^{1} Lo^{2} Lo^{3} NNg oOr sOx^{1} Ox^{2} NPu^{1} Pu^{3} sPu^{6} Pu^{7} Pu^{8} Tj^{1} Tj^{2} Tr^{1} [*cor to sh*] Tr^{2} MTr^{3} [*Jolly* G R N Ku] *Bh Me* [*pāṭha*] *Nā Ku Rn Rc Mr Go Mandlik Jolly KSS* तमाद्यं; Hy *Dave* तस्माद्यं; Tj^{2} तण्डयेद्रजा; GMd^{5} दमयेद्रजा; TMd^{3} °द्राज्या — d) TMd^{3} यच्चाग्निं; BKt^{5} पञ्चाग्निं; Lo^{3} Tj^{1} यश्चाद्यं; wKt^{1} यश्चाग्निश्चोर°; oOr चौरये°; TMd^{3} चोदये°; Be^{3} स्तेनये°; Bo BKt^{5} sOx^{1} °येद्गृहान्

334. a) Pu^{7} यथाङ्गेषु — b) Lo^{3} स्तेने; GMd^{5} नृष्ववचक्षते; Be^{1} विचेष्टतं; Kt^{2} विचेष्टये; Be^{3} [*cor to*] Lo^{1} TMd^{4} NPu^{1} Tr^{1} [*but cor*] विचेष्टिते — c) TMd^{4} Tj^{1} तत्तदेवाहरे°; BCa wKt^{1} TMd^{3} GMd^{5} Tr^{1} MTr^{5} MTr^{6} हरेदस्य— d) TMd^{4} तत्रदेशाय; TMd^{3} पार्थिवं

335. Pādas c-d *ma* in Lo^{4}. Cited by *Lakṣ* 12.779; *Dev* 3.296; *Mādh* 1.391, 3.158 — a) Tj^{1} पितार्यः; TMd^{4} पिता भ्राता; wKt^{3} °चार्याः; wKt^{1} स्वकं माता — b) Kt^{2} TMd^{3} पुत्र — c) TMd^{3} [*Jolly* Nd] राज्ञास्ति — d) BKt^{5} Lo^{2} NNg [*ma as pāṭha*] *Dev Mādh* 2.158 धर्माद्विचलितः स्वकात् [BKt^{5} Lo^{2} स्वकान्]; Ho यस्त्वधर्मेण; Tj^{1} स्वधर्मे यो न; [*Jolly* R] यो न स्वधर्मे; Be^{1} Bo wKt^{3} La^{1} Lo^{1} TMd^{3} TMd^{4} GMd^{5} GMy NNg oOr sOx^{1} Ox^{2} NPu^{1} Pu^{2} Pu^{4} Tr^{2} *Mādh* 1.391 स्वधर्मेण तिष्ठति; Jm *om* न; Lo^{3} यो तिष्ठति

336. Cited by *Apa* 847; *Lakṣ* 12.799; *Dev* 3.298 — a) Tj^{1} कर्षापणं; Wa कार्पपणं; Be^{1} Be^{3} La^{1} sOx^{1} sPu^{6} MTr^{5} *Apa* भवेद्दण्डो — b) Tr^{2} यश्चान्यः; BBe^{2} यच्चान्यः; GMd^{5} यत्रान्यस्तु कृतो; TMd^{3} प्राकृते — c) Be^{3} TMd^{4} यत्र; *Dev* राज्ञो; *Lakṣ* राज्ञां; GMd^{5} राज्ञा; TMd^{3} राज्ञे; *Apa* विप्रो [vl विप्रोद्भवे°]; BBe^{2} *Dev Lakṣ* भवेद्दण्डः — d) NPu^{1} धारणं; TMd^{4} धारणः; La^{1} धारणात्

337. Pādas b-d *ma* in Lo^{4}. Cited by *Vij* 2.275; *Apa* 847; *Lakṣ* 12.551; *Mādh* 3.302 — a) GMy Ox^{2} Pu^{2} Pu^{4} अष्टपाद्यं; Ho Jo^{2} NKt^{4} Lo^{5} BKt^{5} NNg Pu^{7} Pu^{8} अष्टापद्यं; sOx^{1} sPu^{6} अष्टापादं;

ब्राह्मणस्य चतुःषष्टिः पूर्णं वापि शतं भवेत् ।
द्विगुणा वा चतुःषष्टिस्तद्दोषगुणविद्धि सः ॥३३८॥
वानस्पत्यं मूलफलं दार्वग्न्यर्थं तथैव च ।
तृणं च गोभ्यो ग्रासार्थमस्तेयं मनुरब्रवीत् ॥३३९॥
योऽदत्तादायिनो हस्ताल्लिप्सेत ब्राह्मणो धनम् ।
याजनाध्यापनेनापि यथा स्तेनस्तथैव सः ॥३४०॥
द्विजोऽध्वगः क्षीणवृत्तिर्द्वाविक्षू द्वे च मूलके ।
आददानः परक्षेत्रान्न दण्डं दातुमर्हति ॥३४१॥
असंदितानां संदाता संदितानां च मोक्षकः ।
दासाश्वरथहर्ता च प्राप्तः स्याच्चौरकिल्बिषम् ॥३४२॥

TMd[3] अष्टापात्रं; *Mādh* अष्टगुणं — b) Lo[3] Tj[1] स्तेयं; GMy तावति कि° — c) Lo[2] षोडशेव; Pu[8] वैश्य — d) sOx[1] sPu[6] द्वात्रिंशं; Be[1] BKt[5] La[1] Ox[2] Pu[2] द्वाविंशत्; Pu[4] द्वाविंशं; TMd[3] GMy द्विगुणं; Be[1] BBe[2] Hy Jm Jo[1] Kt[2] BKt[5] La[1] NNg oOr Ox[2] NPu[1] Pu[2] Pu[3] Pu[4] Pu[7] Tj[2] MTr[3] [*Jolly* G] *Mandlik Jha KSS Dave* च

338. Cited by *Vij* 2.275; *Apa* 848; *Lakṣ* 12.551; *Mādh* 3.303 — a) Tr[2] °षष्टीः; Lo[5] °षष्टी; Ho °षष्टिं; Be[1] NNg °षष्टि — b) Jo[2] पूर्णे; NKt[4] पूर्वं; Be[1] Ho Ox[2] चापि — c) La[1] द्विगुणां; Be[3] TMd[4] GMd[5] द्विगुणं; oOr द्विगुणो; wKt[1] त्रिगुणा; TMd[3] द्वितीयं; GMy द्वितीया; TMd[4] GMy च — d) oOr °षष्टिर्गुणविद्दोषविद्धि सः; GMy °स्तद्दोषविद्धि सः; *Mādh* °स्तद्दानगुण°; Be[1] *Apa* °गुणवद्धि सः; Lo[2] Pu[7] *Vij Mādh* °गुणवेदिनः; Tr[2] °गुणविद् द्विजः; GMd[1] °गुणवृद्धि सः; Bo °गुणवृद्धयः; NPu[1] °गुणवर्त्ति सः; *Lakṣ* °गुणविद्विषः; TMd[4] °गुणविद्धिदं

339. Omitted in Kt[2]. Cited by *Apa* 848; *Lakṣ* 2.321; *Dev* 2.467 — b) MTr[4] दार्व्यश्वर्थं; TMd[3] दाराग्न्यर्थं; TMd[4] दात्वग्न्यर्थं — c) GMd[1] त्रिंशं च गोभ्यां; MTr[4] गोप्यो; wKt[1] गोक्व्य; *Lakṣ* घासार्थ°; TMd[4] wKt[1] ग्रासात्रमस्तेयं

340. Pādas-d *ma* in Lo[4]. Cited by *Vij* 2.114 [intro.]; *Apa* 850; *Lakṣ* 12.549–50 — a) Pu[7] यादत्ता°; *Apa* अदत्ता° [*om* यो]; TMd[3] GMy योत्वादायिनो; NPu[1] योदेवादायिनो; GMd[1] °दयिनो; Be[3] दत्ताल्लि° — b) Kt[2] NNg °लिप्स्येत; GMd[1] °लिप्येत; Lo[1] ब्राह्मणं — c) GMy MTr[3] यजना°; BKt[5] °ध्याय-नैर्वापि; wKt[1] °ध्यापने वापि — d) GMy सा; Pu[4] चः; wKt[3] oOr च

341. Cited by *Vij* 2.275; *Har*-A 1.28.3; *Mādh* 3.304 — b) NPu[1] °विक्षु; Be[1] °विषू; BKt[5] *om* द्वे; TMd[3] त्वे; Hy मूलेके — c) GMd[1] आददाति; NPu[1] °क्षत्रान्न; TMd[3] °क्षेत्रे न — d) *Mādh* देयं दातुम°

Additional verses in BCa oOr; verses 1 and 3 in La[1]:

शालिव्रीहिमसूराणां मुष्टिग्राहे विधीयते ।
यवगोधूमयोर्वापि तथा च मुद्गमाषयोः ॥१॥
एतेषां शनकैर्मुष्टिर्गृहीतव्या पथच्छितैः[?]।
शाकं शानप्रमाणेन गृह्यमाणं न दुष्यति ॥२॥
ग्रहीतव्यानि पुष्पाणि देवतार्चनकारणात् ।
अदत्तादायिनं विद्यात्ततोऽधिकमिति स्थितिः ॥३॥

1. c) oOr °धूमयोश्चैव — d) oOr तथा वै; BCa °माखयोः

3. d) La[1] विंद्याद्यस्ततोधिकमृच्छति

342. Cited by *Lakṣ* 12.529 — a) Kt[2] Lo[3] Lo[5] Tj[1] [*Jolly* M] असंधितानां संधाता [Kt[2] संध्याता]; sOx[1] sPu[6] असादितानां; Jo[1] संध्याता; TMd[3] संधानां — b) Pu[4] संहितानां; Lo[5] संधितानां; Ho

अनेन विधिना राजा कुर्वाणः स्तेननिग्रहम् ।
यशोऽस्मिन्प्राप्नुयाल्लोके प्रेत्य चानुत्तमं सुखम् ॥३४३॥
ऐन्द्रं स्थानमभिप्रेप्सुर्यशश्चाक्षयमव्ययम् ।
नोपेक्षेत क्षणमपि राजा साहसिकं नरम् ॥३४४॥
वाग्दुष्टात्तस्कराच्चैव दण्डेनैव च हिंसतः ।
साहसस्य नरः कर्ता विज्ञेयः पापकृत्तमः ॥३४५॥
साहसे वर्तमानं तु यो मर्षयति पार्थिवः ।
स विनाशं व्रजत्याशु विद्वेषं चाधिगच्छति ॥३४६॥
न मित्रकारणाद्राजा विपुलाद्वा धनागमात् ।
समुत्सृजेत्साहसिकान् सर्वभूतभयावहान् ॥३४७॥
शस्त्रं द्विजातिभिर्ग्राह्यं धर्मो यत्रोपरुध्यते ।
द्विजातीनां च वर्णानां विप्लवे कालकारिते ॥३४८॥

om च; Lo^1 विमोक्षकः; Jm मोक्षदः; Lo^5 नोदकः; Be^1 भोक्षकः — c) Ho दाराश्च°; NPu^1 वासाश्च°; sOx^1 sPu^6 दासश्च रथहर्ता; Wa दासाश्च रत्नहर्ता; Pu^7 °हर्तारः [*om* च] — d) GMd^5 चोरः प्राप्नोति किल्बिषं; sOx^1 sPu^6 प्राप्ताश्चोर°; Pu^3 प्राप्नुयाच्चौर°; wKt^1 NKt^4 Lo^1 Lo^3 GMd^1 GMy NNg Tj^1 Tr^1 MTr^3 MTr^4 MTr^5 *Mandlik Jha KSS* स्याच्चोर°

343. Omitted in Wa — b) GMd^1 कुर्वत; TMd^4 कुर्वीत; oOr स्थेय°; Bo oOr °विग्रहं; Be^3 °विग्र-हान् — d) TMd^3 पित्र्यं; Bo वानुत्तमं; GMd^1 GMd^5 चानुत्तमां गतिं

344. a) Be^1 Lo^1 TMd^3 GMd^5 NNg Tj^1 ऐन्द्र; TMd^4 इन्द्र — b) GMd^1 °प्सुर्वशं चाक्षय°; Be^1 °श्चाक्षयमेव च; NNg °श्चाक्षयमक्षयं — c) Kt^2 नोपेक्षत; Lo^2 नाक्षेपेत; TMd^4 नोपिक्षेत — d) Bo राज्ञा; BBe^2 GMd^5 राज; Hy साहसिक; Lo^4 Lo^5 साहसिकान्नरान्; Lo^1 साहसिकान्तरं; Bo नरः; sOx^1 sPu^6 जनं

345. a) wKt^1 वाग्दुष्टाद्दुष्कराच्चैव; GMd^1 TMd^3 TMd^4 GMd^5 GMy NPu^1 Tj^1 MTr^5 Wa वाग्दुष्ट-स्तस्क°; Be^1 वाग्दुष्टः तस्क°; oOr Ox^2 Pu^2 वाग्दुष्टास्तस्क°; Be^3 La^1 Tr^2 वाग्दुष्टांस्तस्क°; Be^3 वाग्दुष्टां तस्क°; Be^1 Lo^3 GMd^1 TMd^3 TMd^4 GMd^5 GMy Pu^2 Tj^1 MTr^5 Wa °स्करश्चैव; oOr Pu^4 Pu^7 °स्करा-श्चैव; Be^3 La^1 Ox^2 Tr^2 °स्करांश्चैव; NPu^1 °स्करस्यैव — b) TMd^3 दण्डेनेव; La^1 °नैव निहिंसतः; Lo^4 Lo^5 °नैव विहिंसतः; Be^1 wKt^1 oOr Pu^3 Pu^8 Tr^2 तु; Be^1 Jo^2 TMd^3 GMd^5 GMy NPu^1 Pu^2 Pu^4 Tj^1 Wa [*Jolly* R Nd] हिंसकः; La^1 हिंसकाः; Ho sOx^1 sPu^6 Pu^7 Tr^1 [*Jolly* G Rā Nd] *Jolly* हिंसकात्; Be^3 हिंसयेत् — d) BKt^5 *om* पाप°; Wa पार°; wKt^1 Pu^7 [*Jolly* G] पापकृन्नरः; TMd^3 °कृत्तमं

346. a) Tr^2 साहसं; GMd^5 oOr वर्तमाने; Lo^4 Lo^5 °मानांस्तु — a-b) Jo^2 °मानं योवमर्षयति; BKt^5 °मानं यो हि मर्षयति — b) Tj^1 योवमर्षति; TMd^3 यो मर्षति — d) Tj^1 विद्वेषां; Lo^2 GMd^1 GMy वाधिगच्छति; TMd^4 च निगच्छति; Tr^1 MTr^4 MTr^5 MTr^6 वा निगच्छति; wKt^1 वा विगच्छति; NKt^4 La^1 Lo^3 Tj^1 वा नियच्छति; GMd^5 चैव गच्छति

347. a) NPu^1 Pu^2 Pu^4 निमित्तकार° [*om* न]; TMd^3 मित्राकार°; BKt^5 MTr^4 MTr^6 °कारणाद्वापि; sOx^1 sPu^6 °द्राजाद्विपु° — b) TMd^3 विपुलान्वा; BKt^5 प्रधानाद्वा — c) Be^1 Bo Lo^1 °त्साहसिकात्; wKt^3 BKt^5 °त्साहसिका — d) GMd^1 सर्वलोकभया°; Pu^4 °भयात्रहान्; Pu^2 °भयात्रहां; BKt^5 °भयापहत्; Bo °क्षयावहान्; Lo^1 °वहात्; TMd^4 Pu^3 °वहं

348. Cited by *Dev* 3.725; pādas a-b cited by *Vij* 2.21, 286; *Apa* 1043 — a) TMd^3 शस्त्रि-भिजातिभिर्धार्यं; Be^1 NKt^4 La^1 GMd^1 *Vij* 2.21 शास्त्रं; GMy °भिर्धार्यं — b) TMd^4 Pu^7 यत्राप°; Be^1 यत्रोपसाध्यते — c) MTr^6 जातीनां च स वर्णानां; GMd^5 द्वितीयायां; Ho La^1 sOx^1 sPu^6 तु; Pu^7 [*Jolly* G]

आत्मनश्च परित्राणे दक्षिणानां च संगरे ।
स्त्रीविप्राभ्युपपत्तौ च घ्नन्धर्मेण न दुष्यति ॥३४९॥
गुरुं वा बालवृद्धौ वा ब्राह्मणं वा बहुश्रुतम् ।
आततायिनमायान्तं हन्यादेवाविचारयन् ॥३५०॥
नाततायिवधे दोषो हन्तुर्भवति कश्चन ।
प्रकाशं वाप्रकाशं वा मन्युस्तन्मन्युमृच्छति ॥३५१॥

विप्राणां — d) Ho विप्लुवे; Bo विष्णवे; TMd^4 कारकारिते; NPu^1 कार्यकारिते; La^1 oOr कामकारिते; TMd^3 कायकारिते; Pu^7 [*Jolly* G] धर्मकारिते

349. Cited by *Vij* 2.21; *Dev* 3.725; pādas a-b cited by *Apa* 1043 — a) Kt^4 आत्मनञ्च; Tj^1 आत्मन [*om* च]; Li^1 Pu^2 Pu^4 आत्मनस्तु; NPu^1 आत्मनः स्वपरि°; TMd^3 परित्राणि; Lo^2 परिग्राणे — c) BKt^5 स्त्रीबालाद्यपत्तौ; Be^1 NNg Ox^2 NPu^1 Pu^2 Pu^4 Pu^7 Tr^1 Wa [*Jolly* M^{5-8-9} Nd] *Dev Bh* °प्राभ्यवपत्तौ; GMy °प्राभिविपत्तौ; TMd^3 °प्राभिवपेतौ; La^1 °प्राप्युपपत्तौ; Lo^3 Tj^1 [*Jolly* R] °प्राद्युपपत्तौ — d) TMd^3 GMd^5 GMy Tr^2 घ्नत्र धर्मेण दुष्यति [GMy तुष्यति]; Be^1 घ्नन् *mc sh* विघ्नन्; Ho घ्ननधर्मो न; Be^1 La^1 NNg [*but ma sh*] oOr NPu^1 *om* न; GMd^1 न दूपति; *Vij* न दण्डभाक्

350. Pādas c-d omitted in NKt^4. Cited by *Vij* 2.21; *Apa* 627, 1043; *Dev* 3.726 — a) GMy या बाल°; Lo^1 GMd^5 Pu^7 [*Jolly* G] °वृद्धं; Pu^2 Pu^4 °वृत्तौ; oOr °वृद्धौ च; Lo^4 *om second* वा *and* Lo^5 *the first* — b) Be^1 Hy ब्रह्मणं; GMd^5 *Apa* 627 श्रोत्रियं वा; TMd^4 *om* वा — d) Lo^4 Lo^5 °देवावधारयन्; Pu^7 °चारयेत्

Additional verse in wKt^3 NKt^4:

आततायिनमायान्तमपि वेदान्तगं रणे ।
जिघांसन्तं जिघांसीयात्र तेन ब्रह्महा भवेत् ॥

Additional half-verse in GMy [= 8.353 c-d].

Additional verses in NPu^1 Pu^2 Pu^4 *Mandlik* [क, ट, ठ] *Dave KSS:*

उद्यतासिर्विषासिश्च शापोद्यतकरस्तथा ।
आथर्वणेन हन्ता च पिशुनश्चैव राजनि ॥१॥
भार्यातिक्रमकारी च रन्ध्रान्वेषणतत्परः ।
एवमादीन्विजानीयात् सर्वानेवाततायिनः ॥२॥

1. a) *Mandlik KSS Dave* °सिर्विषाग्निभ्यां — c) Pu^2 Pu^4 आथर्वणमहन्ता — d) NPu^1 Pu^2 पिशुनाश्चैवद्यातमाः [Pu^4 °तमां]

2. a) *Mandlik KSS Dave* भर्यारिक्थापहारी च; Pu^2 Pu^4 दुष्टविक्रमकारी च — c) *Mandlik KSS Dave* एवमाद्यान्वि° — d) NPu^1 °तायिनं

Additional verses in BBe^2 [placed after 351b] TMd^3 [placed after verse 351d] *Mandlik* [क, ङ] *Dave KSS:*

अग्निदो गरदश्चैव शस्त्रपाणिर्धनापहः ।
क्षेत्रदारहरश्चैव षडेते आततायिनः ॥

c) BBe^2 °दारापहारी च — d) *Mandlik KSS Dave* पडेते ह्यात°

351.* Omitted in NKt^4 Lo^4 Lo^5; pādas a-b and c-d transposed in TMd^3. Cited by *Vij* 2.21, 286; *Dev* 3.728 — a) Be^1 Pu^2 Pu^4 आततायि° [*om* न]; Ho Lo^3 °वधो; Hy °वध; TMd^4 °वधाद्दोषो; La^1 दोषे — b) Kt^2 कञ्चन — c) *Vij* 2.21 प्रच्छन्नं वा प्रकाशं वा — d) NPu^1 मन्युस्तं दोषमृच्छति; BKt^5 Pu^2 Pu^4 मनयुस्तं मृत्युमृच्छति [BKt^5 °स्तन्मृत्यु°]; Be^1 Jo^2 Lo^1 Lo^2 TMd^4 GMd^5 NNg Ox^2 Pu^2 Pu^4 Pu^7 Pu^8 Tr^1 Tr^2 Wa [*Jolly* M] *Vij Dev Bh Mandlik Jha KSS Dave* मन्युस्तं मन्यु°; Jm GMd^1 TMd^3 GMy MTr^4 MTr^5 MTr^6 मन्युस्तम्मन्युं

परदाराभिमर्शेषु प्रवृत्तान्नृन्महीपतिः ।
उद्वेजनकरैर्दण्डैश्चिह्नयित्वा प्रवासयेत् ॥३५२॥
तत्समुत्थो हि लोकस्य जायते वर्णसंकरः ।
येन मूलहरोऽधर्मः सर्वनाशाय कल्पते ॥३५३॥
परस्य पत्न्या पुरुषः संभाषां योजयन् रहः ।
पूर्वमाक्षारितो दोषैः प्राप्नुयात्पूर्वसाहसम् ॥३५४॥
यस्त्वनाक्षारितः पूर्वमभिभाषेत कारणात् ।
न दोषं प्राप्नुयात्किंचिन्न हि तस्य व्यतिक्रमः ॥३५५॥
परस्त्रियं योऽभिवदेत् तीर्थेऽरण्ये वनेऽपि वा ।
नदीनां वापि संभेदे स संग्रहणमाप्नुयात् ॥३५६॥

Additional verse in oOr:

साहसं च समाख्यातं यथावदनुपूर्वशः ।
अत ऊर्ध्वं प्रवक्ष्यामि स्त्रीणां संग्रहणं परम् ॥

352. *ma* in Lo^{4}; pādas c-d omitted in NKt^{4}. Cited by *Apa* 853; *Lakṣ* 12.584 — a) TMd^{3} GMy [*Jolly* Nd] °दारोपसेवायां; GMd^{5} °दारोपसेवां च; Lo^{4} Lo^{5} Ox^{2} Pu^{8} *Jolly* °मर्षेषु; Pu^{2} Pu^{4} Tj^{1} Tr^{2} °मर्शे तु; wKt^{1} wKt^{1} °हर्षेषु — b) GMd^{1} TMd^{3} TMd^{4} GMy Tr^{1} [*ma*] MTr^{4} MTr^{6} [*Jolly* Nd] चेष्टमानान्नरान्नृपः; GMd^{5} चेष्टमानं नराधिपः; *Apa* प्रवृत्तेषु मही°; sOx^{1} sPu^{6} प्रवृत्तान्न मही°; Tr^{2} °पती — c) Lo^{2} °कारैर्द°; Ho °दण्डश्चि° — d) TMd^{3} TMd^{4} GMd^{5} GMy Tr^{1} [*ma sh*] [*Jolly* Nd] °दण्डैः परिचिह्नय प्रवा°; GMd^{1} °दण्डैः परिचिह्नं प्रवा°; MTr^{4} MTr^{6} °दण्डैर्गृहीत्वा परिवासयेत्

353. Omitted in NKt^{4}. Cited by *Apa* 854; *Lakṣ* 12.584 — a) TMd^{3} तत्समृद्धो; Be^{1} तत्समर्थो; Pu^{8} तत्समुच्छो; Tj^{1} तत्समुथ्यो; La^{1} तत्समुत्था — a-b) Pu^{7} [*Jolly* Nd] हि जायेत लोकानां वर्ण° [Nd जायते] — b) GMy जायते येन साहसं; TMd^{4} जायन्ते; Pu^{2} Pu^{4} ज्ञायते; Ho La^{1} Pu^{4} °शंकरः; MTr^{6} °संकरं; TMd^{3} °संस्कारः — c) Kt^{2} मूलधरो; wKt^{3} मूलहतो; Pu^{2} Pu^{4} शूलहरो; Be^{1} °धर्म्यः — c-d) GMy यस्त्वनाक्षारितः पूर्वमभिभाषेत कारणात् [= 8.355 a-b] — d) La^{1} कल्पयेत्; TMd^{4} कल्पति

354.* Pādas a-b omitted in NKt^{4}. Cited by *Apa* 854; *Lakṣ* 12.581 — a) Lo^{1} BCa पत्न्यां; GMd^{1} TMd^{4} पत्न्याः; Ho GMd^{1} पुरुषं — a-b) *Apa* पत्न्या संभाषं पुरुषो योजयन् — b) Be^{1} Lo^{4} Lo^{5} Ox^{2} NPu^{1} Pu^{2} Pu^{4} Pu^{7} MTr^{5} MTr^{6} *Go* संभाषं; *Me* appears to support the masculine; TMd^{4} संभाषे; Jo^{1} सभाषां; Lo^{2} संभीषं; oOr संभव्यान्योज°; GMd^{1} भाषयन्योज°; Lo^{1} Lo^{2} TMd^{3} GMy [*Jolly* Nd] योजयेद्रहः; Be^{1} wKt^{1} BKt^{5} GMd^{5} NNg oOr Ox^{2} Wa [*Jolly* M Me] *Apa Jolly* योजयन्सह; MTr^{5} योजयेत्सह; TMd^{4} योजंत्यह; La^{1} sOx^{1} NPu^{1} Pu^{2} Pu^{4} sPu^{6} Pu^{7} MTr^{4} MTr^{6} *Go* [*Jolly* G] योजयेत्सह; NPu^{1} योजयत्सह; Ho योजयेद्धनः; Tr^{2} योजयनहः; Hy योजयन्वहः; Bo योजयन्सहः; Kt^{2} योजयन्हरः — c) BKt^{5} NPu^{1} सर्वमारक्षितो; La^{1} सर्वमाक्षारिको; Pu^{2} Pu^{4} सर्वमाक्षापितो; TMd^{3} सर्वमक्षातितो — d) Pu^{2} Pu^{4} सर्वमाप्नोति साहसं; NKt^{4} °यात्सर्वसाहसं; MTr^{6} °साहसैः

355. Omitted in wKt^{1} [haplo]. Cited by *Vij* 2.284; *Apa* 854; *Lakṣ* 12.581 — a) NKt^{4} La^{1} Tr^{1} यस्तु नाक्षा°; TMd^{4} °नाक्षारतं; TMd^{3} °नाकारितः; BKt^{5} Lo^{4} Lo^{5} *Apa* °रितो दोषैरभिभा°; NKt^{4} सर्वमभिभा° — b) Ho °भाषेतु; TMd^{4} °भाषित कारिणा — c) NNg °यात्कंचिन्न — d) GMd^{1} TMd^{3} GMd^{5} GMy Tr^{1} MTr^{4} MTr^{6} तस्मिन्व्यतिक्रमः

356. Omitted in wKt^{1}; placed after 358 in TMd^{3} GMy Tr^{1} [*Jolly* Nd] — a) GMd^{1} TMd^{3} TMd^{4} GMd^{5} GMy Tr^{2} [*but cor sh*] MTr^{6} परस्त्रीं योभिभाषेत; Tr^{2} परां; sOx^{1} sPu^{6} °भिवादेत्; Lo^{2} °भिवदत् — b) BBe^{2} Ho wKt^{3} Lo^{4} Lo^{5} TMd^{3} GMd^{5} GMy sOx^{1} Ox^{2} NPu^{1} Pu^{3} sPu^{6} Tr^{1} Tr^{2} MTr^{4}

उपकारक्रिया केलिः स्पर्शो भूषणवाससाम् ।
सहखट्वासनं चैव सर्वं संग्रहणं स्मृतम् ॥३५७॥
स्त्रियं स्पृशेददेशे यः स्पृष्टो वा मर्षयेत्तया ।
परस्परस्यानुमते सर्वं संग्रहणं स्मृतम् ॥३५८॥
अब्राह्मणः संग्रहणे प्राणान्तं दण्डमर्हति ।
चतुर्णामपि वर्णानां दारा रक्ष्यतमाः सदा ॥३५९॥
भिक्षुका बन्दिनश्चैव दीक्षिताः कारवस्तथा ।
संभाषणं सह स्त्रीभिः कुर्युरप्रतिवारिताः ॥३६०॥
न संभाषां सह स्त्रीभिः प्रतिषिद्धः समाचरेत् ।
निषिद्धो भाषमाणस्तु सुवर्णं दण्डमर्हति ॥३६१॥

mTr^{6} [*Jolly* Nd]*Rn* [pāṭha] गृहेपि वा; Ho च — c) tMd^{4} नदीनामपि; Lo^{1} Ox^{2} Pu^{7} Tr^{2} चापि; bBe^{2} tMd^{3} gMd^{5} gMy Tr^{1} mTr^{4} mTr^{6} चैव; sOx^{1} sPu^{6} संनेदे — d) wKt^{3} *om* स; tMd^{3} न संग्र°; gMd^{1} सुसंग्र°; Tr^{2} सत्यं ग्रहण°; Lo^{4} Lo^{5} संग्रहमवाप्नुयात्

357. Pādas a-b omitted in wKt^{1} — a) Bo Ho Hy Jo^{1} Jo^{2} wKt^{3} La^{1} Ox^{2} Pu^{3} Tj^{1} mTr^{3} Wa [*Jolly* N Ku R] *Go Nā Ku Rn Rc Mr Mandlik KSS* उपचार°; bBe^{2} उपचारः; Lo^{1} Tr^{2} उपचारि°; sOx^{1} sPu^{6} उपचारिकया; Jm कलिः; tMd^{3} केचि — b) tMd^{4} स्पर्श; bKt^{5} °वाससा — c) Bo Pu^{7} सहषद्वा°; tMd^{3} °खद्वायनं; Pu^{2} Pu^{4} °सनं केलिः — d) wKt^{1} Kt^{2} gMd^{1} sOx^{1} सर्व; mTr^{6} सप्त; Tj^{2} सर्वं ग्रहणं

358. Pādas c-d omitted in gMd^{5}. Cited by *Vij* 2.284; *Mādh* 3.317 — a) Lo^{2} °देषे च; nKt^{4} स्पृशेददेषेपु — a-b) gMy स्पृशेददेषेन यः स्पृष्ट्वो मार्षयेत वा — b) sOx^{1} sPu^{6} स्पृष्टं; nKt^{4} वो; tMd^{4} हर्पये°; La^{1} °येत्तुया; Be^{1} nKt^{4} gMd^{1} °येत्तदा; Bo Kt^{2} bKt^{5} Lo^{2} Lo^{3} oOr nPu^{1} Tj^{1} *Vij* °येत्तथा — c) Pu^{7} [*Jolly* G] °मतेः; Tj^{2} °मते *add* तस्यां — d) Hy *om* सर्वं; Be^{1} Bo Kt^{2} nKt^{4} Lo^{1} सर्व; nNg सर्वं ग्रहणं; tMd^{3} तच्च संग्रहणं

Additional verse in Pu^{2} Pu^{4} *Mandlik* [ट, ठ] *Dave KSS:*

कामाभिपातिनी या तु नरं स्वयमुपव्रजेत् ।
राज्ञा दास्ये नियोज्या सा कृत्वा तद्दोषघोषणम् ॥

a) Pu^{2} कामाणिपातिनी — c) Pu^{2} राजा

359. Pādas c-d omitted in Lo^{2} [haplo]. Cited by *Lakṣ* 12.584; pādas c-d cited by *Apa* 855 — a) sOx^{1} sPu^{6} अब्राह्मण; La^{1} अब्राह्मणं; tMd^{3} अब्राह्मणा; Be^{1} संग्रहेण; tMd^{4} संग्रहणः — d) Kt^{2} bKt^{5} Lo^{1} nNg sOx^{1} sPu^{6} रक्षतमाः; tMd^{4} मताः; Be^{1} Jo^{2} Lo^{1} gMd^{1} tMd^{3} gMd^{5} gMy nNg Pu^{2} Pu^{4} Pu^{7} Tr^{1} [*but mc sh*] Tr^{2} mTr^{4} mTr^{6} [*Jolly* G Nd] *Go Lakṣ* स्मृताः; Wa यतः; oOr नृपः

360. Omitted in Lo^{2}; pādas c-d omitted in mTr^{6}. Cited by *Apa* 855; *Lakṣ* 12.582 — a) Tr^{1} भिक्षुकं वादिनश्चैव; mTr^{5} भिक्षुांश्चैव [as the full pāda]; Tj^{1} वन्धनश्चैव; tMd^{3} *Jolly* वन्दिनश्चैव — b) Kt^{1} कारुकास्तथा — c) gMd^{1} संभाषणे; gMd^{1} tMd^{4} mTr^{5} *Lakṣ* गृहे स्त्रीभिः; wKt^{1} La^{1} परस्त्रीभिः — d) Tj^{1} °रमतिवारिताः; tMd^{3} mTr^{4} °वादिताः

361. Omitted in Lo^{2}; pādas a-b omitted in mTr^{6}; pādas a-b and c-d transposed in mTr^{4}. Cited by *Apa* 855; *Lakṣ* 12.582 — a) gMd^{1} संभाषणं गृहे स्त्रीभिः [cf. 360c]; *Lakṣ* न भाषणं; tMd^{4} संभाष्यं; nKt^{4} Ox^{2} nPu^{1} Pu^{4} Pu^{7} *Go* संभाषं; bKt^{5} Tr^{2} संभाषणं; bCa Jm Jo^{1} Jo^{2} wKt^{1} Kt^{2} wKt^{3} La^{1} Lo^{3} tMd^{4} Tj^{1} Tj^{2} *Lakṣ Bh Mandlik Jolly Jha KSS Dave* परस्त्रीभिः — b) Ox^{2} nPu^{1} °षिद्धं; gMd^{5} समाचरन् — c) tMd^{4} निषेधो; wKt^{3} भाष्यमाणस्तु

नैष चारणदारेषु विधिर्नात्मोपजीविषु ।
सज्जयन्ति हि ते नारीर्निगूढाश्चारयन्ति च ॥३६२॥
किंचिदेव तु दाप्यः स्यात् संभाषां ताभिराचरन् ।
प्रेष्यासु चैकभक्तासु रहः प्रव्रजितासु च ॥३६३॥
योऽकामां दूषयेत्कन्यां स सद्यो वधमर्हति ।
सकामां दूषयंस्तुल्यो न वधं प्राप्नुयान्नरः ॥३६४॥
कन्यां भजन्तीमुत्कृष्टं न किंचिदपि दापयेत् ।
जघन्यं सेवमानां तु संयतां वासयेद्गृहे ॥३६५॥
उत्तमां सेवमानस्तु जघन्यो वधमर्हति ।
शुल्कं दद्यात्सेवमानः समामिच्छेत्पिता यदि ॥३६६॥

362. Cited by *Vij* 2.285; *Apa* 856; *Lakṣ* 12.583 — a) Ho Pu[2] नैषा; La[1] Pu[2] Pu[4] चारेण°; gMy धारण°; tMd[3] वारण° — b) Pu[7] विधिनाल्पोपजीविषु; Be[1] wKt[1] विधिनात्मो°; Tr[2] विधिं नात्मो°; gMy विधिरात्मो°; Pu[2] Pu[4] विधिमात्मो°; tMd[3] विधिरात्माप°; Ox[2] विधिर्नाम्नोप°; *Lakṣ* [vl] विधिर्नान्योप° — c) mTr[3] सज्जयति; Be[1] संजयन्ति; tMd[4] सङ्गयन्ति; Bo मज्जयन्ति; Jo[2] °यन्तीह; La[1] tMd[4] mTr[3] ह; nKt[4] च; Be[1] Ho nKt[4] tMd[4] Tj[1] नारी निगू°; Jo[2] La[1] Lo[3] Lo[4] Lo[5] nNg oOr sOx[1] Pu[2] sPu[6] Pu[7] Tr[1] *Vij Apa* नारीं निगू°; tMd[3] नारिं निगू°; gMy [*Jolly* Nd] दारान्निगू° — d) nPu[1] °रीर्निर्गूढाश्चा°; Be[1] tMd[4] sOx[1] sPu[6] °गूढा चार°; tMd[3] °गूढां चार°; Pu[2] Pu[4] °रूढाश्चार°; wKt[1] °गूत्राश्चार°; Hy °गूढीश्चार°; Jo[2] wKt[3] nPu[1] Tj[1] हि

363. Cited by *Apa* 856; *Lakṣ* 12.583 — a) La[1] °चिदेवपि; Jo[2] Lo[3] tMd[3] gMd[5] Tj[1] *Apa* हि; tMd[4] तु देव; Bo दाप्या; tMd[3] दाप्यस्यां — b) Pu[5] Pu[7] [*Jolly* G] रहः संभाषणं चरन्; gMd[1] भाषान्ताभिराचरन्; tMd[4] संभाषाभिचारयन्; Be[1] nKt[4] bKt[5] Lo[4] tMd[3] gMd[5] nNg Ox[2] nPu[1] Pu[2] Pu[4] mTr[6] *Apa Nā* संभाषं; bBe[2] La[1] ताभिचारयन्; nPu[1] तापिचारयन्; Bo °चरत्; Wa mTr[6] °चरेत् — c) Jo[1] La[1] Lo[1] Pu[3] *Jolly* प्रैष्यासु; tMd[4] प्राष्यासु; Tj[2] प्राष्याशु; Pu[2] Pu[4] प्रेक्षासु; Pu[8] प्रोष्यासु; bBe[2] La[1] gMd[5] nNg चैव भक्तासु; bKt[5] चापि भक्तासु; gMy °भक्तृषु; tMd[3] °भर्त्रेषु; nNg °भक्त्यासु; *Apa* °भक्तास्तु; oOr °कर्तासु — d) Tr[2] प्रवृत्तिजासु; wKt[1] प्रजिवितासु; Ho प्रपूजितासु; Lo[2] tMd[3] प्रजितासु; tMd[4] प्रविजातासु

364. Cited by *Vij* 2.288; *Apa* 858; *Mādh* 3.321 — a) gMy येकामां; tMd[4] अकामां; gMd[1] यः कामाद्दूष°; gMd[5] ये कामाद्दूष°; mTr[6] दोपये° — b) gMd[1] स समो; tMd[4] संसद्यो; Pu[5] Pu[7] समानां वध° — c) gMd[1] सकामं; tMd[4] Pu[7] दूषयन्तुल्यो; Hy दूषयस्तुल्यो; oOr दूषयेस्तुल्यो; Lo[1] दूषयेत्तुल्यो; Pu[5] दूषयन्कुल्यो; tMd[3] दूषयेद्यस्तु; wKt[1] दूषयंस्त्वन्यो — c-d) Be[1] सकामां दूषयाणस्त्वङ्गुलिच्छेदमवाप्नुयात् [cf. 368 a-b] — d) Tr[2] वधां; Lo[4] Lo[5] gMd[1] tMd[3] tMd[4] gMd[5] Tr[1] mTr[4] mTr[6] [*Jolly* M Nd Gr] प्राप्नुमर्हति

365. Pāda-d omitted in wKt[1]; [*Jolly* M[3–4]] place verses 365–390 after verse 148. Cited by *Apa* 858; *Lakṣ* 12.597 — a) Be[1] La[1] Lo[4] कन्या; Hy कन्यामजन्ती°; gMd[1] भजन्तमु°; Lo[5] tMd[3] भजन्तिमु°; Be[1] bBe[2] gMd[5] sOx[1] °मुत्कृष्टां; mTr[4] °मुत्कृष्टात्र — b) gMd[1] किंचिद्दापयेत् गतं; Tj[1] कंचि°; gMy किंचिद्दापयेत् [lacuna]; Be[1] दापेत्; tMd[4] दापयत्; Lo[2] दापयन्; Ho पादयेत्; tMd[3] धारयेत् — c) Be[1] gMd[5] Pu[5] Pu[7] जघन्यां; Bo nKt[4] जघन्य; nKt[4] sOx[1] Pu[3] sPu[6] सेवमाना; wKt[1] La[1] tMd[3] oOr Tr[2] सेवमानं; bCa सेव्यमानां; tMd[4] सेविनीं त्वेनां; Ho °मानात्तु — d) nKt[4] Lo[1] संयता; Be[1] संयत्तां; gMd[5] संगतां; Jo[2] वारये°; gMd[1] वासवोगृहे; Jo[2] Lo[3] tMd[4] Tj[1] °येद्गृहात्; Ho mTr[4] mTr[6] °येद्गृही; Tr[1] °येद्गृहा [*ma* न्]

366. Pāda-a omitted in wKt[1]. Cited by *Vij* 2.288; *Apa* 859; *Lakṣ* 12.595; *Mādh* 3.321 —

अभिषह्य तु यः कन्यां कुर्याद्दर्पेण मानवः ।
तस्याशु कर्त्ये अङ्गुल्यौ दण्डं चार्हति षट्शतम् ॥३६७॥
सकामां दूषयंस्तुल्यो नाङ्गुलिच्छेदमाप्नुयात् ।
द्विशतं तु दमं दाप्यः प्रसङ्गविनिवृत्तये ॥३६८॥
कन्यैव कन्यां या कुर्यात् तस्याः स्याद् द्विशतो दमः ।
शुल्कं च त्रिगुणं* दद्याच्छिफाश्चैवाप्नुयाद्दश ॥३६९॥
या तु कन्यां प्रकुर्यात्स्त्री सा सद्यो मौण्ड्यमर्हति ।
अङ्गुल्योरेव वा छेदं खरेणोद्वहनं तथा ॥३७०॥

a) wKt^{3} Pu^{4} उत्तमा; Lo^{1} उन्मार्गसेव°; GMy oOr °मानं तु — b) Pu^{2} Pu^{4} जघन्या — c) Ox^{3} शुल्कां; Bo Lo^{5} Tj^{1} शुक्कं; Pu^{5} Pu^{7} [*Jolly* G] दाप्यः सेव°; NKt^{4} °त्सेव्यमानः; BBe^{2} °माना; *Apa* [vl] °मानात् — d) wKt^{1} समानिच्छता यदि; BKt^{5} La^{1} GMd^{5} सममि°; Be^{1} शममि°; TMd^{4} °च्छेत वा यदि; TMd^{3} यति

367. Cited by *Vij* 2.288; *Apa* 858; *Lakṣ* 12.597; *Mādh* 3.321 — a) GMy अभिषह्यां; Tr^{1} अभिषह्यां *mc sh* अभिषज्य; Lo^{1} Tj^{1} अभिसह्य; GMd^{5} अविषह्य; TMd^{3} MTr^{6} अविषह्यं; *Nd Bh* [pāṭha] अविषह्यां [Nd gloss: भार्यत्वेन वोढुमशक्यां]; Ox^{3} अभिषत्य; *Lakṣ* अभिषज्य; wKt^{1} अभिसय्य; TMd^{4} अभिषक्तां; GMd^{1} विषह्यन्यान्तु; La^{1} °षह्यं भूयः; TMd^{3} कन्या — b) GMd^{5} ब्रूयाद्द°; Tr^{1} कुर्याद् द्वेषेण; NKt^{4} Pu^{7} °द्दर्प्येण; TMd^{3} °द्र्वेण; Lo^{3} Tj^{1} मानितः — c) TMd^{3} GMy [*Jolly* Nd] छेत्तव्यावङ्गुली तस्य; GMd^{5} छेत्तव्ये त्वङ्गुली तस्य; NPu^{1} छेत्तव्ये अङ्गुलीस्तस्य; GMd^{1} छेत्तव्यस्त्वङ्गुलिस्तस्य; MTr^{4} MTr^{6} छेत्तव्यस्त्वङ्गुली तस्य; Tr^{1} छेत्तव्येत्यंगुरुं तस्य [*but mc sh*]; La^{1} तस्याशु छिद्यादङ्गुल्यो; wKt^{1} Pu^{5} Pu^{7} कर्त्यौ; Kt^{2} कर्त्ते; Tr^{2} *Nā* [with gloss कर्त्ये] *Lakṣ* कल्प्ये; NNg कल्पे; sOx^{1} Pu^{2} Pu^{3} Pu^{4} sPu^{6} कर्त्यावङ्गुल्यौ; MTr^{5} कल्प्यावङ्गुल्यौ; BKt^{5} कार्तेताङ्गुल्यौ; Lo^{4} Lo^{5} कृन्तेदङ्गुल्यौ; oOr कृन्तादङ्गुल्यां; *Me Jha Dave* कर्त्या अङ्गुल्यो; TMd^{4} अङ्गुष्ठो — d) Jo^{2} Lo^{3} Tj^{1} [*Jolly* R] दण्डमर्हति; Ox^{3} Pu^{2} [*Jolly* M] वार्हति; TMd^{3} षट्छतं; TMd^{4} षट्पदं; La^{1} षट्श्रुतं

368. Cited by *Vij* 2.288; *Apa* 858; *Lakṣ* 12.597; *Mādh* 3.321 — a) wKt^{1} La^{1} Tj^{1} MTr^{6} सकामं; *Nā* दूषयन्तुल्यो; La^{1} दूषयंस्तुल्ये; Lo^{1} दूषयेत्तुल्यो; Tj^{2} दूषयेस्तुल्यो; Be^{1} Ho NNg Ox^{3} Ox^{2} Pu^{7} MTr^{5} Wa *Lakṣ* दूषयाणस्तु; Tr^{2} दूषयानतु; BKt^{5} दूषमानस्तु; NKt^{4} GMd^{1} TMd^{3} TMd^{4} GMy La^{1} Pu^{2} Pu^{3} Pu^{4} Tr^{1} MTr^{6} [*Jolly* N Gr] दूषयेद्यस्तु; *Vij* दूषयन्कन्यां; wKt^{1} दूषयंस्त्वन्यो; Lo^{2} दुषयन्सोपि; *Go Rn Ku* नाशयन्तुल्यो — b) BBe^{2} GMd^{1} TMd^{3} TMd^{4} GMd^{5} GMy oOr Tr^{1} MTr^{4} MTr^{6} [*Jolly* N Gr] *Vij Apa Mādh* °च्छेदमर्हति — c) GMd^{5} द्विशतं दमनं; BBe^{2} तु शतं; oOr दमो; La^{1} Lo^{3} Tj^{1} प्राप्यः; TMd^{4} दास्यं — d) BCa wKt^{1} La^{1} sOx^{1} Pu^{2} Pu^{4} sPu^{6} प्रसङ्गं विनिवर्तयेत्; GMy प्रसङ्गे; Lo^{3} प्रसङ्गो; Tr^{2} °वर्त्तये; BKt^{5} Lo^{1} TMd^{3} °वर्तये

369.* Cited by *Apa* 859; *Lakṣ* 12.597; *Mādh* 3.321; pādas a-b cited by *Vij* 2.288 — a) GMd^{1} TMd^{4} Ox^{3} MTr^{6} कन्येव; Be^{1} GMd TMd^{3} कन्या या; TMd^{4} कन्या कुर्याच्च; Jm GMd^{1} TMd^{3} GMy MTr^{4} यः; BKt^{5} यो — b) TMd^{3} TMd^{4} Pu^{7} MTr^{6} तस्य; *Vij* तस्यास्तु द्वि°; Tj^{2} तस्योस्तु द्वि°; BKt^{5} तस्या द्वि°; TMd^{3} TMd^{4} Tr^{1} [*mc to*] द्विशतं; TMd^{4} दमं; GMd^{5} दशः — c) Bo Lo^{5} Tj^{1} शुक्कं; GMd^{5} शुक्कं शतगुणं; Be^{1} Ox^{2} Wa हि; Bo Hy Jm Jo^{1} Jo^{2} wKt^{1} Kt^{2} wKt^{3} BKt^{5} La^{1} Lo^{1} Lo^{3} Lo^{4} Lo^{5} TMd^{3} Pu^{8} Tj^{1} Tj^{2} MTr^{5} *Bh Ku Mr Rc Mandlik Jolly Jha Dave* द्विगुणं; Pu^{4} त्रिगुणां — c-d) TMd^{4} शुल्कं च दद्यात्त्रिगुणं शिक्षा वै वाप्नुयाद्दश — d) GMd^{1} GMd^{5} GMy NNg Ox^{2} NPu^{1} Pu^{5} Pu^{7} *Go Nd* °च्छिखाश्चै°; La^{1} °च्छिखाच्चै°; TMd^{3} °ज्जङ्घाश्चै°; Pu^{2} °च्छिफां चैवा°; MTr^{5} *Lakṣ* °फाश्च प्राप्नुयाद्दश; TMd^{4} Tj^{1} °याद्दशा; La^{1} °यात्तदा

370. Omitted in Ox^{3}. Cited by *Vij* 2.288; *Apa* 859; *Lakṣ* 12.597; *Mādh* 3.321 — a) Lo^{4} Lo^{5} NNg [*Jolly* M] कन्यां प्रकुर्याद्या तु स्त्री; BKt^{5} कन्यां प्रकुर्यात्तु स्त्री; Pu^{5} Pu^{7} [*Jolly* G] *Jolly* या च;

भर्तारं लङ्घयेद्या तु ज्ञातिस्त्रीगुणदर्पिता ।
तां श्वभिः खादयेद्राजा संस्थाने बहुसंस्थिते ॥३७१॥
पुमांसं दाहयेत्पापं शयने तप्त आयसे ।
अभ्यादध्युश्च काष्ठानि तत्र दह्येत पापकृत् ॥३७२॥
संवत्सराभिशस्तस्य दुष्टस्य द्विगुणो दमः ।
व्रात्यया सह संवासे चाण्डाल्या तावदेव तु ॥३७३॥
शूद्रो गुप्तमगुप्तं वा द्वैजातं वर्णमावसन् ।
अगुप्त अङ्गसर्वस्वी गुप्ते सर्वेण हीयते* ॥३७४॥

TMd^3 या तं; WKt^1 कन्या; La^1 प्रकुर्वीत सा — b) Be^1 GMd^1 स; TMd^4 दद्ययो; La^1 मूलमर्हति; oOr दण्डमर्हति — c) Lo^1 sOx^1 Pu^3 sPu^6 Pu^8 Tr^2 अङ्गुल्योश्छेदनं चैव; Ox^2 अङ्गुल्यादेरेव छेदं; BCa Hy Tj^2 Wa [*Jolly* Ku] च; BBe^2 चा; Bo व; oOr तच्छेदं; Ho विछेदं; BKt^5 Lo^4 Lo^5 Tj^1 MTr^6 छेदः — d) GMd^1 शिखारेणोद्वहन्तथा; Pu^2 Pu^4 वरेणो°; BKt^5 oOr MTr^6 °द्वाहनं; WKt^3 °द्वहनस्तथा; GMy °द्वहनोस्तथा; TMd^3 °द्वहतोस्तथा; oOr यथा

371.* Cited by *Viś* 3.264; *Lakṣ* 12.593; *Dev* 3.749; *Mādh* 1.119 — a) Ox^3 लङ्घवद्या; TMd^3 °येद्भूतं; GMy °येद्यास्तु; GMd^1 °येद्या स्त्री; Pu^8 *om* तु — b) MTr^6 ज्ञातुज्ञस्त्रीगुणादपि; *Mādh* जातिस्त्री°; TMd^4 जातस्त्री°; Bo जातुस्त्री°; Be^1 BCa Hy Jm Jo^1 Kt^2 WKt^3 Lo^1 Lo^3 Lo^4 Lo^5 GMy Pu^2 Pu^4 Pu^8 Tj^2 MTr^3 Wa [*Jolly* Ku] *Lakṣ* स्त्री ज्ञाति°; TMd^3 स्त्री जातेगुण°; Lo^2 ज्ञातिश्रीबल°; BBe^2 Ho Jo^2 WKt^1 BKt^5 La^1 sOx^1 oOr NPu^1 sPu^6 Tj^1 Tr^1 [*mc sh to*] [*Jolly* R] स्त्री ज्ञातिबल°; *Nā* बल as pāṭha; WKt^3 °दर्पिशा; TMd^3 GMy °गर्विता — c) Pu^5 Pu^7 पाधये°; Lo^4 [*but mc*] पन्दये — d) TMd^3 GMy संस्थाने जनसंनिधौ; GMd^1 संस्थाने संस्थिते सति; Pu^2 Pu^4 संस्थासु; GMd^5 बहुभिस्थिते; *Mādh* °स्थितः; NPu^1 °स्थिता; Pu^8 °स्थितो; Jo^1 °स्थितिः; Wa °स्थिति

372. Cited by *Apa* 857; *Lakṣ* 12.587 — a) Pu^5 Pu^7 पुरुषं; Be^1 oOr दापये° — b) oOr शयानं; TMd^4 शय्याने; BBe^2 तप्तमायसे; Ox^3 ताम्रआयसो; Pu^5 Pu^7 आयसि; Jo^2 GMd^1 आयते; TMd^4 NPu^1 आसने; MTr^4 MTr^6 तपने — c) Pu^5 Pu^7 तत्रादध्यस्तु; Bo Pu^2 Pu^4 °दधुश्च; *Apa* °दद्युश्च; Kt^2 °दध्युञ्च; NNg °दध्याच्च; Hy °दध्युः [*om* च] — d) BKt^5 NPu^1 Pu^2 Pu^4 [*Jolly* M^{4-5-9}] तावद्यावदसौ मृतः; Ho Lo^2 NNg Tj^2 यावद्दह्येत; Bo यावद्दण्डयेत; Pu^5 Pu^7 यावद्दह्येत्स; oOr दहेत; WKt^3 दह्येच्च; BBe^2 La^1 Ox^2 Tj^1 दह्येत्स; Be^1 Wa दाह्यः स पापकृत्; Tr^2 दह्येत्पापकृत्; *Apa* [vl] पातकं

373. Cited by *Lakṣ* 12.589 — a) BKt^5 NNg MTr^4 MTr^6 *Me* संवत्सरेभि°; *Me* recognizes the compounded form: समासपाठे कथंचिद्योजना; Ox^3 संवत्सरोभि° — b) Tr^2 द्रिष्टस्य; oOr कृष्टस्य; Ox^3 द्विगुणा — c) GMd^1 व्रात्याया; Lo^5 व्रात्ययो; NNg साह; WKt^3 संभाषे; La^1 संवासो — d) Be^1 Bo WKt^3 NKt^4 BKt^5 Lo^3 Lo^4 Lo^5 GMd^1 TMd^3 TMd^4 GMd^5 GMy NNg sOx^1 sPu^6 Tj^1 Tr^1 Tr^2 चण्डाल्या; Pu^2 Pu^4 चण्डाला; Pu^5 Pu^7 तावदेव तत्

374.* Cited by *Vij* 2.286; *Apa* 857; *Lakṣ* 12.590; *Dev* 3.746; *Mādh* 3.318 — a) Lo^1 शूद्र; TMd^4 शूद्रा; Lo^2 °गुप्तां वा — b) TMd^3 GMy द्वैजात्यं; NPu^1 द्वैजातीं; Lo^2 द्वेजातं; TMd^4 द्विजाति; Bo °मावसत्; NKt^4 GMy MTr^4 MTr^6 °मावसेत्; Pu^3 °माविशन्; Tr^2 °माविशत्; Lo^1 °माचरेत् — c) TMd^4 अङ्गुष्ठेकाङ्गसर्वसव; WKt^3 अगुप्तमङ्गं सर्वस्व; Pu^5 Pu^7 [*Jolly* G Nd] *Jolly* अगुप्ते चाङ्ग°; WKt^1 BKt^5 Lo^2 GMd^1 TMd^3 GMd^5 GMy NNg Pu^2 Pu^3 Pu^4 Pu^8 Tr^1 Tr^2 MTr^4 MTr^5 MTr^6 *Apa Mādh* अगुप्तैकाङ्ग°; BKt^5 अगुप्तैकाङ्गं; BBe^2 Bo Ho Hy Jm Jo^1 Jo^2 Kt^2 NKt^4 Lo^1 Lo^3 Lo^4 Lo^5 oOr sOx^1 Ox^2 Ox^3 NPu^1 sPu^6 Tj^1 Tj^2 Wa [*Jolly* M R] *Vij Lakṣ Dev Mandlik Jha KSS Dave* अगुप्तमङ्ग°; Be^1 अगुप्तसंग°; La^1 अगुप्तकैकाङ्ग°; NPu^1 अगुप्तमर्द्धसर्व°; Lo^3 GMd^1 TMd^3 GMy sOx^1 sPu^6 Tj^1 Tr^1 [*Jolly* M G R Nd] °सर्वस्वं; WKt^3 °सर्वस्य; Be^1 Jm Jo^1 Jo^2 Kt^2 Lo^4 Lo^5 Pu^5 Pu^7 NNg Wa *Mandlik Jolly KSS* °सर्व-

वैश्यः सर्वस्वदण्ड्यः स्यात् संवत्सरनिरोधतः ।
सहस्रं क्षत्रियो दण्ड्यो मौण्ड्यं मूत्रेण चार्हति ॥३७५॥
ब्राह्मणीं यद्यगुप्तां तु गच्छेतां वैश्यपार्थिवौ ।
वैश्यं पञ्चशतं कुर्यात् क्षत्रियं तु सहस्रिणम् ॥३७६॥
उभावपि तु तावेव ब्राह्मण्या गुप्तया सह ।
विप्लुतौ शूद्रवद्दण्ड्यौ दग्धव्यौ वा कटाग्निना ॥३७७॥
सहस्रं ब्राह्मणो दण्ड्यो विप्रां गुप्तां बलाद्व्रजन् ।
शतानि पञ्च दण्ड्यः स्यादिच्छन्त्या सह संगतः ॥३७८॥
मौण्ड्यं प्राणान्तिको दण्डो ब्राह्मणस्य विधीयते ।
इतरेषां तु वर्णानां दण्डः प्राणान्तिको भवेत् ॥३७९॥

स्वैर्गुप्ते; nKt[4] °सर्वश्चाद्गुप्ते — d) *Mādh* गुप्तौ; bBe[2] Bo Hy Jm Jo[1] Jo[2] Kt[2] wKt[3] nKt[4] Lo[1] Lo[3] Lo[4] Lo[5] oOr Ox[2] nPu[1] Pu[8] Tj[1] Tj[2] mTr[3] *Vij Dev* [*Jolly* M G R] *Mandlik Jha KSS Dave* गुप्तं; Ox[3] गुप्त; Pu[5] Pu[7] गुप्तैः; wKt[1] bKt[5] गुप्तः

375. Omitted in mTr[3]; pāda-d omitted in Tj[2]. Cited by *Lakṣ* 12.591; *Dev* 3.747 — a) Lo[4] Lo[5] वैश्ये; tMd[4] वैश्यस्य सर्वदण्डः; Lo[1] tMd[3] gMd[5] सर्वस्यद°; Tj[1] °दण्ड्यं; Be[1] bBe[2] Hy Jm Jo[1] Kt[2] tMd[3] gMd[5] Ox[3] Tj[2] mTr[3] mTr[4] *Dev Mandlik Jha KSS Dave* °दण्डः — b) bBe[2] La[1] sPu[6] *Dev* °निरोधितः; nKt[4] °निरोधनः; gMd[1] °निरोधिणः; gMd[5] gMy °निरोधकः; tMd[4] °निरोधिकः; Be[1] Wa °निरोधकृत्; tMd[3] °निरोषतः; bKt[5] °निरोधः — c) gMy सहसा क्षत्रियाप्यायां; tMd[4] सहस्र; tMd[3] सहसा; oOr दण्डा — d) wKt[1] मौण्ड्य; oOr मौण्ड्या; Be[1] Hy Kt[2] सूत्रेण; bBe[2] Lo[5] Pu[2] Pu[4] शूद्रेण; Ox[3] Pu[2] Pu[4] mTr[4] mTr[6] वार्हति

376. Omitted in Ox[3] Tj[2]; pādas a-b omitted in mTr[3]. Cited by *Vij* 2.286; *Apa* 857; *Lakṣ* 12.591; *Dev* 3.747; *Mādh* 3.318 — a) *Dev* ब्राह्मणीं तु यदागुप्तां; tMd[3] ब्राह्मणी; wKt[1] यदि गुप्तां; bBe[2] यश्च गुप्तां; Lo[4] °गुप्तौ; Pu[5] Pu[7] [*Jolly* G] °गुप्तायां गच्छे° — b) *Lakṣ* सेवेयातामिति स्थितिः; *Mādh* सेवेतान्यः पुमान्यदि; *Vij* सेवेतां वैश्य°; Kt[2] वेश्य°; nKt[4] °पार्थिवो — c) Be[1] पञ्चाशतं; tMd[3] tMd[4] पञ्चदशं; Tr[2] °शतं दण्ड्यः — d) tMd[4] क्षत्रियस्य सहस्रकं; Lo[3] oOr Tj[1] च; Ho Lo[2] gMd[1] सहस्रकं; Pu[8] सहस्रिकं

377. Cited by *Vij* 2.286; *Apa* 857; *Lakṣ* 12.591; *Dev* 3.747; *Mādh* 3.318 — a) wKt[3] च; mTr[5] *Mādh Vij* हि; *Apa* तु भावेन: Pu[2] Pu[4] तावैव; wKt[3] तामिव — b) Bo ब्रह्मण्या; La[1] ब्राह्मणा — c) tMd[4] विपृतौ; Kt[2] सूर्यव°; mTr[6] शूद्रवच्छिष्यौ — d) wKt[1] gMy च; gMd[1] वा अग्निनादिना

378.* Pādas b-d omitted in Lo[1] [haplo]. Cited by *Vij* 2.286; *Lakṣ* 12.588; *Mādh* 3.317; pādas a-b cited by *Vij* 2.81; *Dev* 3.741; andpādas c-d by *Dev* 3.745 — a) nKt[4] mTr[3] ब्राह्मणं; wKt[3] ब्राह्म; Jo[2] *om* दण्ड्यो; tMd[4] दण्ड्या — b) Be[1] bBe[2] Bo Hy Jm Jo[1] Jo[2] wKt[1] Kt[2] wKt[3] La[1] Lo[2] Lo[3] nNg sOx[1] nPu[1] Pu[2] Pu[4] Pu[5] sPu[6] Pu[7] Pu[8] Tj[1] Tj[2] Tr[2] mTr[3] Wa *Mandlik Jolly KSS Dave* गुप्तां विप्रां; Ho गुप्तं विप्रं; Tj[2] गुप्तं; gMd[5] व्रजन्बलात्; Be[1] Wa बलाद्व्रजन्; Ox[3] Tr[2] mTr[6] °द्व्रजेत्; tMd[4] °द्व्ररन् — c) Pu[4] दण्ड्याः; La[1] Tr[2] दण्डः — c-d) tMd[4] दण्ड्यस्तु कामयन्त्या समागतः — d) Tr[2] स्यादगुप्तं सह; La[1] संगमे

379. Pāda-a omitted in Lo[1]. Cited by *Apa* 681; *Lakṣ* 12.588; *Dev* 3.293; *Mādh* 1.399 — a) tMd[3] oOr प्राणान्तिकं; wKt[3] प्राणान्तिके; bKt[5] *Me Jha Dave* प्राणान्तको; La[1] प्राणान्तके; *Me* gives प्राणान्तिको as *pāṭhāntara*; bBe[2] Bo [*but cor*] Jm wKt[1] gMd[1] tMd[4] gMd[5] दण्ड्यो; Tr[2] दण्ड्या; Pu[2]

न जातु ब्राह्मणं हन्यात् सर्वपापेष्वपि स्थितम् ।
राष्ट्रादेनं बहिः कुर्यात् समग्रधनमक्षतम् ॥३८०॥
न ब्राह्मणवधाद्भूयानधर्मो विद्यते भुवि ।
तस्मादस्य वधं राजा मनसापि न चिन्तयेत् ॥३८१॥
वैश्यश्चेत् क्षत्रियां गुप्तां वैश्यां वा क्षत्रियो व्रजेत् ।
यो ब्राह्मण्यामगुप्तायां तावुभौ दण्डमर्हतः ॥३८२॥
सहस्रं ब्राह्मणो दण्डं दाप्यो गुप्ते तु ते व्रजन् ।
शूद्रायां क्षत्रियविशोः साहस्रो वै भवेद्दमः ॥३८३॥

Pu^4 दण्ड्यौ; MTr^3 दण्डे — c-d) *Mādh* gives instead 8.323a-b — d) oOr *Jha Dave* प्राणान्तको; GMd^5 °न्तको वय:

380.* Cited by *Apa* 842; *Lakṣ* 12.783; *Dev* 3.291; pādas a-b cited by *Vij* 2.81, 3.257; *Apa* 1079 — a) TMd^3 जातुं; TMd^4 जातं; Pu^2 Pu^4 ब्राह्मणान् — b) Ox^2 °पापेषु संस्थितं; Be^1 Bo Ho Jo^2 BKt^5 Lo^1 Lo^4 Lo^5 GMd^1 TMd^4 GMd^5 oOr sOx^1 Ox^3 Pu^2 Pu^5 sPu^6 Pu^7 Tr^1 MTr^4 MTr^5 MTr^6 *Apa* 1079 *Lakṣ Dev* °पापेष्ववस्थितं; TMd^3 °पापेष्वपेस्थितं; Wa °पापे व्यवस्थितं; GMy स्थितः; the reading अपि is supported by *Me Nd Go Ku* — c) Ho sOx^1 sPu^6 Pu^7 [*Jolly* M] राष्ट्राच्चैनं; BKt^5 TMd^3 GMd^5 NNg MTr^5 [*Jolly* Nd Gr]राष्ट्रात्त्वेनं; NKt^4 राष्ट्रौ त्वेनं; Lo^1 राष्ट्रात्तं हि; GMd^1 राष्ट्रार्थेन; Pu^5 राष्टाद्यैनं; wKt^3 °देवं; Bo बर्हिः — d) TMd^3 समग्रं; Wa समस्तधन°; Pu^5 Pu^7 °मक्षितं; Ho Lo^2 sOx^1 sPu^6 °मक्षयं; MTr^6 °मक्षमं; Tr^2 °मिच्छतं

381. Cited by *Vij* 2.81; *Lakṣ* 12.783; *Dev* 3.294 — a) Pu^8 ब्राह्मणाद्वधा°; TMd^3 GMy °वधात्कश्चिदधर्मो; MTr^5 °द्भूयादधर्मो Bo °द्भीतानधर्मो — a-b) *Dev* °वधात्पापात् नाधर्मो; GMd^1 NNg Lo^1 °द्भूयात् न धर्मो; Be^1 °द्भूयो न धर्मो; Pu^5 Pu^7 °द्भूयोन्नधर्मो; La^1 Ox^2 °द्भूयो नाधर्मो; TMd^4 °द्भूयो ह्यधर्मो — b) BBe^2 Kt^2 wKt^3 °द्भूयान्नधर्मो; Hy °यानधर्मौ; Ox^3 °यानधर्मा; La^1 GMd^1 TMd^3 TMd^4 GMd^5 GMy Pu^3 Pu^8 Tr^1 Tr^2 MTr^6 [*Jolly* Nd] *Dev* विद्यते क्वचित्; BKt^5 *Lakṣ* भुवि विद्यते; wKt^3 तु विविद्ययते — c) GMd^5 *Dev* तस्मात्तस्य — d) oOr मनसा न विचिन्तयेत्; NKt^4 मनसा नापि चिन्तयेत्; TMd^4 मनसा तेन

382. Cited by *Vij* 2.286; *Apa* 857; *Lakṣ* 12.588; *Dev* 3.747; *Mādh* 3.319 — a) La^1 वैश्यांश्चेत्; TMd^4 वैश्यश्च; Be^1 गुप्ता — b) La^1 वैश्यो; NPu^1 वैश्याश्च; TMd^4 वै; wKt^3 च; La^1 क्षत्रियां; GMd^1 भवेत् — c) NKt^4 Pu^5 Pu^7 *om* यो; Hy यौ — d) Bo तामुभौ; *Lakṣ* तत्समं दण्ड°; wKt^1 La^1 Wa °मर्हति

Additional verse in Be^1 NKt^4 La^1 NNg Ox^2 NPu^1 Pu^2 Pu^3 Pu^4 Pu^8 *Mandlik* [क, ख, ग च, ज, ट, ड, ण, य, र, ल] *KSS Dave;* commented by *Nā Rc;* pādas a-b in Wa:

क्षत्रियां चैव वैश्यां च गुप्तां ब्राह्मणो व्रजन् ।
न मूत्रमुण्डः कर्तव्यो दाप्यस्तूत्तमसाहसम् ॥

a) NNg NPu^1 Pu^2 Pu^4 Wa वैश्यां वा; Be^1 Pu^8 वैश्यायां — b) La^1 *om* ब्राह्मणो; Be^1 Ox^2 व्रजेत् — c) Pu^2 Pu^4 स मूत्र°; Ox^2 न तत्र दण्डः; Be^1 मूत्रदण्डः

383. Verses 383 and 384 transposed in Lo^1 oOr; pādas a-b omitted in Wa. Cited by *Vij* 2.286; *Apa* 856; *Lakṣ* 12.588; *Mādh* 3.318; pādas a-b cited by *Dev* 3.746 — a) TMd^4 ब्राह्मणं; NKt^4 दण्डो; GMy दण्ड; La^1 दण्ड्य; Lo^3 GMd^1 oOr Tj^1 दण्ड्यो — a-b) Ho sOx^1 sPu^6 दाप्यो दण्डं — b) Pu^2 Pu^4 न दाप्यो; Be^1 NKt^4 गुप्ते उभे; TMd^4 गुप्ते तथा; GMd^5 गुप्तेतरां; Tr^1 [*but mc sh*] गुप्ते कृते; BBe^2 *om* ते; Bo Lo^5 GMd^5 MTr^4 व्रजेत्; Lo^2 व्रजेन् — c) *Jha* शूद्राया; *Dave* शूद्रायाः; Ox^2 शूद्राणां; NKt^4 क्षत्रिया°; NNg NPu^1 Pu^2 Pu^4 क्षत्रियो वैश्योः; NNg क्षत्रियो वैश्यो; TMd^4 °विशा; Pu^7 °विशौ — d) BBe^2 GMd^1 GMd^5 oOr sOx^1 Pu^5 sPu^6 Pu^7 सहस्रो; wKt^1 साहस्रं; TMd^3 GMy [*Jolly* Nd] *Vij Mādh* सहस्रं; Tr^2 साहसे; TMd^4 सहस्रा वा; *Vij Mādh* तु; Tj^2 वै दमः स्मृतः; TMd^3 GMy भवेद्दमं

क्षत्रियायामगुप्तायां वैश्ये पञ्चशतो दमः ।
मूत्रेण मौण्ड्यमृच्छेत्तु क्षत्रियो दण्डमेव वा ॥३८४॥
अगुप्ते वैश्यराजन्ये शूद्रां वा ब्राह्मणो व्रजन् ।
शतानि पञ्च दण्ड्यः स्यात् सहस्रं त्वन्त्यजस्त्रियम् ॥३८५॥
यस्य स्तेनः पुरे नास्ति नान्यस्त्रीगो न दुष्टवाक् ।
न साहसिकदण्डघ्नौ स राजा शक्रलोकभाक् ॥३८६॥
एतेषां निग्रहो राज्ञः पञ्चानां विषये स्वके ।

384.* Omitted in NKt^{4} Lo^{2} Ox^{2} Ox^{3} Pu^{5} Pu^{7} MTr^{5} Wa; the verse is not commented by *Nā Bh* — a) GMd^{5} क्षत्रियायां तु गुप्तायां; TMd^{3} °गुप्ताया — b) Be^{1} BCa Jo^{2} GMy oOr Tj^{1} Tr^{1} MTr^{3} वैश्यः; La^{1} वैश्यं; TMd^{4} वैश्य; Pu^{2} वैश्यै; BBe^{2} विशः; La^{1} °शते; Jm Jo^{1} Jo^{2} Kt^{2} Lo^{3} oOr Tj1 MTr^{3} *Mandlik Jolly Jha KSS Dave* °शतं; Pu^{2} Pu^{4} Tr^{1} MTr^{6} °दशो; Jo^{2} oOr Tj^{1} दमं; Pu^{8} द्रमः — c) La^{1} मौत्रेण; Be^{1} सूत्रेण; BBe^{2} wKt^{1} शूद्रेण; NPu^{1} मुण्ड्य°; oOr दण्डमन्विच्छेत्; Bo Ho Hy Jm Jo^{1} wKt^{1} Kt^{2} Lo^{4} Lo^{5} GMd^{1} GMd^{5} oOr Tj^{2} MTr^{3} *Mandlik Jolly KSS* °मिच्छेत्तु; BCa °मिच्छेत; Be^{1} Lo^{3} sOx^{1} sPu^{6} Tj^{1} *Rn* °मन्विच्छेत्; TMd^{4} °मृच्छेद [*om* तु] — d) GMd^{1} क्षत्रियं; Lo^{5} क्षत्रिये; Pu^{3} Pu^{4} दण्ड एव; NPu^{1} दण्ड्य एव; TMd^{4} दश्यमेव; La^{1} दण्डमर्हति; Bo Lo^{5} sOx^{1} NPu^{1} sPu^{6} Pu^{8} च; Ho तु; Be^{1} हि; GMy ह

385. Omitted in Lo^{4}. Cited by *Apa* 856; *Lakṣ* 12.589; *Dev* 3.745; pāda-d cited in *Vij* 2.294 — a) wKt^{1} आगुप्ते; Bo Lo^{1} Tr^{1} *Apa* [vl] अगुप्त; BBe^{2} Hy Jm Jo^{1} Kt^{2} wKt^{3} oOr Tj^{2} MTr^{3} *Lakṣ Mandlik Jolly Jha Dave KSS* क्षत्रियावैश्ये; oOr sOx^{1} sPu^{6} °राजन्यो — a-b) GMd^{1} TMd^{4} [*Jolly* M] विप्रक्षत्रियविट्शूद्रः स्त्रीरगुप्ताः परिव्रजन् [TMd^{4} °व्रजेत्] — b) Bo शूद्र्यां; Ox^{2} *Apa* [vl] शूद्रायां ब्रा°; Jo^{2} wKt^{1} NKt^{4} BKt^{5} La^{1} Lo^{2} Lo^{3} NNg Pu^{3} Pu^{5} Pu^{7} Tj^{1} Tr^{1} Tr^{2} MTr^{4} MTr^{5} MTr^{6} Wa च; BCa Ho oOr sOx^{1} sPu^{6} तु; TMd^{3} GMy चेद्ब्राह्मणो; TMd^{3} GMy Pu^{4} Tr^{1} MTr^{4} MTr^{6} *Dev* व्रजेत् — c) Tj^{1} दण्ड्या; sOx^{1} sPu^{6} दण्डः; TMd^{3} MTr^{6} दण्ड; BCa NKt^{4} La^{1} Lo^{1} NNg Pu^{3} Pu^{8} Tr^{2} MTr^{5} *Apa* दाप्यः; GMd^{1} दण्ड्याः स्युः — d) *Dev* सहस्रं चान्त्यजे स्मृतं; oOr साहसं; GMd^{5} चान्त्यज°; La^{1} Pu^{3} Tr^{2} त्वन्त्यजां स्त्रियं; Lo^{1} Pu^{4} त्वन्त्यजे स्त्रियं; GMd^{1} त्वन्त्यजा स्त्रियः; TMd^{4} त्वन्त्यजा स्त्रियं; Bo त्वन्त्यजः स्मृतं; Pu^{5} Pu^{7} [*Jolly* G] °स्त्रियः; Tj^{2} °स्त्रियां

Between pādas a-b and c-d, BKt^{5} adds: विप्रक्षत्रियविट्शूद्रः स्त्रीरगुप्ताश्च परिव्रजन् [see above variant for 385 pādas a-b].

Additional verses in Pu^{2} [omits last half verse] Pu^{4} *Mandlik* [ट, ठ] *KSS Dave:*

शूद्रोत्पन्नांशपापीयानेवं मुच्येत किल्बिषात् ।
तेभ्यो दण्डाद्धृतं द्रव्यं न कोशे संप्रवेशयेत् ॥१॥
अयाजिकं तु तद्राजा दद्याद्धृतकवेतनम् ।
यथा दण्डगतं वित्तं ब्राह्मणेभ्यस्तु लंभयेत् ॥२॥
भार्यापुरोहितस्तेना ये चान्ये तद्विधा द्विजाः ॥३॥

1. b) *KSS* °पीयान्न वै — c) Pu^{2} Pu^{4} दण्डाद्हृतं
2. c) तथा दण्डाद्धृतं द्रव्यं

386. Cited by *Lakṣ* 12.600 — a) oOr यस्या; Be^{1} Ox^{2} स्तेनो यस्य; Tr^{2} स्तेनो; Wa स्तेनां; Bo BCa La^{1} MTr^{6} पुरो — b) GMy देशे चोरो न विद्यते; Pu^{5} Pu^{7} °स्त्रीणो; TMd^{3} GMd^{5} °स्त्रीको; MTr^{4} MTr^{6} दुष्टभाक्; oOr दुष्टवान् — c) GMy lacuna for whole pāda; TMd^{3} न सामासेरधं दण्डं; GMd^{1} न सान्नसी-केदण्डघ्नो; GMd^{5} नासाह°; Lo^{1} sOx^{1} Pu^{4} Wa *Jha Dave* °दण्डघ्नो; GMd^{5} °दण्डघ्नं; MTr^{6} °दण्डघ्ना; TMd^{4} °दण्डघ्नस्स — d) BKt^{5} राज; TMd^{4} चक्रलो°; GMy शकलो°; wKt^{3} सकलो°

साम्राज्यकृत् सजात्येषु लोके चैव यशस्करः ॥३८७॥
ऋत्विजं यस्त्यजेद्याज्यो याज्यं चर्त्विक् त्यजेद्यदि ।
शक्तं कर्मण्यदुष्टं च तयोर्दण्डः शतं शतम् ॥३८८॥
न माता न पिता न स्त्री न पुत्रस्त्यागमर्हति ।
त्यजन्नपतितानेतान् राज्ञा दण्ड्यः शतानि षट् ॥३८९॥
आश्रमेषु द्विजातीनां कार्ये विवदतां मिथः ।
न विब्रूयान्नृपो धर्मं चिकीर्षन्हितमात्मनः ॥३९०॥
यथार्हमेतानभ्यर्च्य ब्राह्मणैः सह पार्थिवः ।
सान्त्वेन प्रशमय्यादौ स्वधर्मं प्रतिपादयेत् ॥३९१॥
प्रातिवेश्यानुवेश्यौ च कल्याणे विंशतिद्विजे ।
अर्हाविभोजयन्विप्रो दण्डमर्हति माषकम् ॥३९२॥

387. Pādas c-d *ma* in Lo^{4}. Cited by *Lakṣ* 12.600 — a) GMd^{1} TMd^{4} एषां तु निग्रहे; BBe^{2} La^{1} GMd^{5} oOr निग्रहे; Ox^{2} निग्रहाद्राज्ञा; Ho sOx^{1} Pu^{3} sPu^{6} Pu^{8} Tr^{2} निग्रहाद्राजा; Tj^{1} राज्ञा; MTr^{4}MTr^{6} राज्ञां — b) Bo विषयं स्वरं; Pu^{3} स्वकैः — c) La^{1} Tr^{2} साम्राज्यं कृत्स्नमाप्नोति; Pu^{3} साम्राज्यं कृत्स्नराज्ये; BBe^{2} BKt^{5} साम्राज्यंकृत्; GMy साम्राज्यक; Hy साजात्येषु; BKt^{5} Wa स्वजात्येषु; Bo sOx^{1} sPu^{6} Tj^{1} स्वजातेषु; Lo^{5} नजात्येषु; GMd^{1} TMd^{3} GMd^{5} GMy [*Jolly* Nd Gr] स्वराज्येषु; BBe^{2} Pu^{8} सराज्येषु; MTr^{4} MTr^{6} स्वराज्ये च; Tr^{1} स्वराष्ट्रेषु; Be^{1} सुकृत्येषु — d) Ho La^{1} यशःकरं

388. Cited by *Apa* 837; *Lakṣ* 12.368 — a) GMy यास्त्यजे°; wKt^{1} °जेत्स्वाज्यो; wKt^{3} *om* याज्यो — b) TMd^{3} याज्यं ऋत्विग्यजेद्यदि; MTr^{5} याज्यं वत त्यजेद्यदि; La^{1} याज्यं वा ऋत्विजो यदि; Pu^{3} याज्यांश्चर्त्विक्; BBe^{2} wKt^{3} Lo^{5} GMd^{1} [*Jolly* M] याज्यमृत्विक्; wKt^{1} याज्ञमृत्विक्; Tj^{1} [*Jolly* R] त्वर्त्विक्; GMy [*Jolly* Nd]*Jolly* वर्त्विक्; Pu^{7} चर्त्विजो; Ho Tr^{1} च ऋत्विक्; Pu^{5} Pu^{7} *om* त्यजेद्यदि — c) GMd^{5} शक्तिं; TMd^{3} GMy [*Jolly* Nd] क्षान्तमदुष्टं [GMy शान्त°]; TMd^{4} °दूष्टं; wKt^{1} वा — d) GMy MTr^{6} तयोर्दण्डं; BBe^{2} oOr तयोर्दण्ड्यः; wKt^{1} भयोर्दण्डां; *final* शतम् *om in* BKt^{5} and *ma in* Lo^{4} NNg

389. Cited by *Apa* 823 — b) TMd^{4} *om* अर्हति — c) Tj^{1} त्यजंति तानेतान्; TMd^{3} त्यजेन्नप°; TMd^{4} अजानन्नप° — d) Pu^{5} Pu^{7} राज्ञा पञ्च शतानि षट्; BBe^{2} Bo NNg Tj^{1} राजा; BBe^{2} दण्ड्योः; Bo Tr^{2} दण्डः; *Lakṣ Apa* दाप्यः; TMd^{3} GMy शतानि च

390. b) Be^{1} Bo BKt^{5} GMy Tj^{2} कार्यो; NKt^{4} GMd^{5} *Me* कार्यं; oOr कार्येषु वदतां; GMd^{5} संवदतां — c) TMd^{4} नाविब्रूयनृपाधर्म; sOx^{1} sPu^{6} न ब्रूया°; NKt^{4} न विक्रयान्नृपा; BKt^{5} न विक्रीयतां नृपो; Lo^{4} Lo^{5} धर्मा; Tr^{1} धर्मान्; TMd^{3} GMd^{5} GMy दण्डं — d) Pu^{7} [*Jolly* G] चिकीर्षन्नात्मनो हितं; TMd^{3} चिर्कीपंनहितात्मनः; BBe^{2} न चिकी°; GMy चिकीर्षान्हित°; Ho चिकीर्षुर्हित°; NKt^{4} Lo^{2} GMd^{1} Wa °मात्मने

Addtional verse in Lo^{4} Lo^{5}:

चौरदण्डेन तं पापं दण्डयेत्पृथिवीपतिः ।
भोगं केवलतो यस्तु कीर्तयेतागमं क्वचित् ।।

d) Lo^{5} कीर्तयेन्नागमं

391. a) Jo^{1} यथोर्ह°; TMd^{4} °मेनानभ्यर्च्य; Lo^{2} °मेतान्यभ्यर्च्य; Lo^{5} °मेतान्यभ्यर्चा — c) Be^{1} सात्वेन; BCa wKt^{3} शान्त्वेन; La^{1} शांत्वैनं; Jo^{2} Lo^{3} साम्नैव; Tj^{1} साम्नेव; NKt^{4} NPu^{1} प्रशमस्यादौ; TMd^{4} प्रशमंन्यादौ; Tr^{2} प्रसमयादौ; MTr^{4} MTr^{6} प्रशमय्येतान्; TMd^{3} GMy प्रथमं याप्य; GMd^{5} प्रथमं चैतान् — d) Lo^{5} प्रतिपादयत्

392.* Cited by *Apa* 835; *Lakṣ* 12.562 — a) Ho wKt^{3} BKt^{5} Lo^{1} Lo^{3} GMd^{1} TMd^{4} GMd^{5} Ox^{2}

श्रोत्रियः श्रोत्रियं साधुं भूतिकृत्येष्वभोजयन् ।
तदन्नं द्विगुणं दाप्यो हैरण्यं चैव माषकम् ॥३९३॥
अन्धो जडः पीठसर्पी सप्तत्या स्थविरश्च यः ।
श्रोत्रियेषूपकुर्वंश्च न दाप्याः केनचित्करम् ॥३९४॥
श्रोत्रियं व्याधितार्तौ च बालवृद्धावकिंचनम् ।
महाकुलीनमार्यं च राजा संपूजयेत्सदा ॥३९५॥
शाल्मलीफलके श्लक्ष्णे नेनिज्यान्नेजकः शनैः ।
न च वासांसि वासोभिर्निर्हरेन्न च वासयेत् ॥३९६॥

Pu^{8} Tj^{1} Tr^{2} MTr^{4} MTr^{5} MTr^{6} Wa *Me Jha Dave* प्रतिवेश्या° ; oOr प्रीतिवेश्या° ; GMy प्रतिवैश्यानुवैश्यौ; BKt^{5} La^{1} Lo^{3} °नुवैश्यौ; Lo^{2} °नुवेश्यो; TMd^{4} °नुवेश्यं; GMd^{5} °नुवेश्या; BBe^{2} तु — b) Pu^{7} कल्याणं; TMd^{4} कल्याणी; GMd^{1} प्रसवे विंशति° ; NPu^{1} विंशतिं; Pu^{3} Tr^{2} विंशतिर्द्विजे; Bo विंशतिद्वये; NNg शंसति द्विजैः — c) Be^{1} अर्हावेतौ यजन्विप्रो; Lo^{1} अर्हौ उभौ जयन्विप्रो; Lo^{4} अर्थानभोज° ; TMd^{4} अनावभोज° ; Pu^{2} अर्हनभोज° ; TMd^{3} GMy आहूयाभोज° ; GMd^{1} °भाजय° ; Tr^{2} °भोजये विप्रो; BKt^{5} °भोजन्विप्रो; [*Jolly* M$^{8-9}$ G Ku] *Jolly* °यन्विप्रौ; Ox^{2} °यन्विप्रं — d) NNg माषिकं; oOr मासकः; La^{1} नासकं

393. Omitted in sOx^{1} [haplo]. Cited by *Lakṣ* 12.562 — a) Lo^{1} श्रोत्रियं श्रोत्रियः; Bo श्रोत्रियः श्रोत्रियः — b) GMy *om* भूति; Bo Ho भूत° ; NKt^{4} Pu^{2} भूमि° ; TMd^{3} मृत° ; GMy मृति° ; wKt^{1} NKt^{4} °कृत्येषु भोजयन्; La^{1} Lo^{1} TMd^{3} GMy °कृत्येषु भोजयेत्; wKt^{3} °भोजयत्; Pu^{2} Pu^{4} Pu^{5} sPu^{6} Pu^{7} Tr^{1} MTr^{5} °भोजयेत्; Bo NNg °योजयन् — c) wKt^{3} तदर्थं; Lo^{5} तद्धनं; La^{1} द्विगुणो; Bo दाप्यौ; TMd^{3} दाप्यं; Lo^{3} Tj^{1} देयं — d) TMd^{3} GMy [*Jolly* Nd] दण्डं चैव समाषकं; MTr^{5} हैरण्यश्चैव माषकः; BCa Hy Jo^{1} wKt^{1} Lo^{1} Lo^{4} Lo^{5} NNg oOr Pu^{5} Pu^{7} Tj^{2} MTr^{3} [*Jolly* M G] हिरण्यं; Lo^{2} हैरण्यो; Kt^{2} हैरण्यश्चैव; BBe^{2} चैकमासकं; La^{1} वार्षिकं

394. Pāda-d *ma* in Lo^{4}. Cited by *Lakṣ* 11.91 — a) GMy जलः; Tr^{1} MTr^{5} जळः; BKt^{5} जनः; GMd^{1} जखुः पीरुसर्पः; Be^{1} पीट° ; TMd^{3} °सर्पि; NKt^{4} °सर्प्या; BBe^{2} °शर्पा — b) Pu^{3} सप्तत्यां; *Lakṣ* सप्तत्याः; Kt^{2} सद्मत्या; wKt^{1} स्थविरं तु; TMd^{3} सविरश्च; Pu^{5} Pu^{7} स्थविजश्च; oOr स्थविरस्थ; Tr^{2} *om* यः — c) GMd^{1} श्रोत्रियेष्वप्यकुर्वंश्च; *Lakṣ* श्रोत्रियेषु प्रकुर्वंश्च; TMd^{3} श्रोत्रियेषु च कुर्वश्च; wKt^{1} श्रोत्रिषूपकुर्वाणश्च; Bo श्रोत्रियेषूपकुर्वन्ति — d) GMd^{1} तद्दाप्यः; Be^{1} BCa Jo^{2} NKt^{4} Lo^{1} TMd^{3} GMd^{5} GMy Pu^{2} Pu^{4} Tj^{1} Tr^{1} दाप्यः; MTr^{5} MTr^{6} दाप्यां; Tr^{2} दाप्ये; TMd^{4} दाप्यं तेनचि° ; *Me Ku Nd Rc* support the plural; *Rn Mr Go* support the singular; TMd^{3} GMy [*Jolly* Nd] केनचिद्दमं; GMd^{5} केनचित्परं; Bo केनवित्परं; wKt^{3} °त्करां; BBe^{2} °त्करान्

395. a) BKt^{5} श्रोत्रियंश्चाधितार्तौ च; wKt^{3} श्रोत्रिय; [*Jolly* M G] व्याधितार्तं; Pu^{5} Pu^{7} व्याधिनार्तं; TMd^{4} व्याधितर्ता — b) [*Jolly* M$^{8-9}$] बालवृद्धयाद्यकिंचनं; Tr^{2} °वृद्धानकिं° ; GMd^{5} °वृत्तावकिं° ; TMd^{3} °वृद्धौ च किंचन; wKt^{1} BKt^{5} Lo^{1} TMd^{4} GMd^{5} NPu^{1} °किंचन; Pu^{2} Pu^{4} °किंचनः; GMy °कंचनं — c) Tr^{2} महाकुलमयं चासौ; Hy माहा° ; Lo^{1} °कुलिन° ; La^{1} °लीनं चार्तं; TMd^{3} °कुलिनकार्यं — d) Bo संपूज्य सर्वदा

396.* Omitted in Tj^{2}. Cited by *Vij* 2.238; *Apa* 823; *Lakṣ* 12.526; *Mādh* 3.311 — a) GMy शल्मली° ; TMd^{3} शल्मलि° ; Pu^{2} Pu^{4} शाल्मल° ; Be^{1} Bo Ho NKt^{4} Lo^{2} GMd^{1} TMd^{4} NNg oOr sOx^{1} NPu^{1} Pu^{5} sPu^{6} Pu^{7} Wa [*Jolly* M G] *Apa Lakṣ Mādh* °शाल्मले; sOx^{1} sPu^{6} °केफले; NKt^{4} °हलके; MTr^{4} MTr^{6} °फलकैः श्लक्ष्णैर्नेनि° ; Ho श्लक्ष्णौ — a-b) Lo^{1} शाल्मे फले श्लक्ष्णमेव ज्यान्नेजक शनेन च — b) GMd^{1} TMd^{3} TMd^{4} GMd^{5} GMy La^{1} Ox^{2} NPu^{1} Tr^{1} Tr^{2} MTr^{4} MTr^{5} MTr^{6} [*Jolly* M Gr Nd] *Vij Apa Mādh* निज्याद्वासांसि नेजकः [GMd^{1} निज्यान्वा° ; NPu^{1} निर्ज्याद्वा° ; MTr^{4} MTr^{6} निध्याद्वा° ; TMd^{3} नेजकं]; BBe^{2} Pu^{2} Pu^{4} Wa निर्निज्या° ; Bo नेनित्या° ; Tj^{1} नेमिन्या° ; NKt^{4} नेनिष्ठा° ; Pu^{3} नेजिष्टा° ; Hy लेनिज्याद्रजकः — c) Jo^{2} Tj^{1} नापि; Be^{1} नैव — d) La^{1} oOr Pu^{2} Pu^{4} °भिर्नहरेन्न; GMd^{5} °भिर्नाहरेन्न; Tr^{2}

तन्तुवायो दशपलं दद्यादेकपलाधिकम् ।
अतोऽन्यथा वर्तमानो दाप्यो द्वादशकं दमम् ॥३९७॥
शुल्कस्थानेषु कुशलाः सर्वपण्यविचक्षणाः ।
कुर्युरर्घं यथापण्यं ततो विंशं नृपो हरेत् ॥३९८॥
राज्ञः प्रख्यातभाण्डानि प्रतिषिद्धानि यानि च ।
तानि निर्हरतो लोभात् सर्वहारं हरेन्नृपः ॥३९९॥
शुल्कस्थानं परिहरन्नकाले क्रयविक्रयी ।
मिथ्यावादी च संख्याने दाप्योऽष्टगुणमत्ययम् ॥४००॥
आगमं निर्गमं स्थानं तथा वृद्धिक्षयावुभौ ।
विचार्य सर्वपण्यानां कारयेत्क्रयविक्रयौ ॥४०१॥
पञ्चरात्रे पञ्चरात्रे पक्षे पक्षेऽथ वा गते ।
कुर्वीत चैषां प्रत्यक्षमर्घसंस्थापनं नृपः ॥४०२॥

°हरेत न; Lo² °हरित्र; GMd¹ TMd⁴ *Lakṣ* °रेत्र विवासयेत्; Ox² °रेत्रापि वासयेत्

397. Pādas c-d omitted in BKt⁵. Cited by *Apa* 785; *Lakṣ* 12.524 — a) Pu⁵ Pu⁷ [*Jolly* G] तन्तुवोयोः पलं दत्त्वा [*Jolly* G °वायः]; Bo *om* तन्तु; La¹ नंद्रवायो; Jo² Lo³ Tj¹ °वायौ; La¹ Lo¹ [*but cor*] TMd⁴ GMy MTr³ [*Jolly* Nd]दशफलं; TMd³ दशफला; Bo शतफलं — b) Pu⁵ Pu⁷ दध्यादेक-पलात्मिकं; TMd³ दद्यावेक°; TMd³ GMy oOr sOx¹ sPu⁶ MTr³ *Nd* °फलाधिकं; Lo¹ TMd⁴ °पलादिकं; [*Jolly* Nd] °फलादिकं; wKt³ °पराधिकं — c) oOr अथो; TMd⁴ ततो; Lo⁵ वर्तमानं — d) Tr² दाप्यौ; Lo³ Tj¹ दाप्या; Pu² Pu⁴ दद्याद्; Pu⁵ Pu⁷ द्वादशिकं; GMd¹ दमः; Bo धनं

398. Pādas a-b omitted in BKt⁵. Cited by *Apa* 833; *Lakṣ* 12.518 — a) Bo Lo⁵ Tj¹ शुल्क°; Lo¹ °स्थाने तु; Tr² °स्थाने कुशलाः; Be¹ कुशलः — b) TMd³ सर्वविद्या°; TMd⁴ °पण°; TMd⁴ Wa °विचक्षणः; Pu⁸ °विचक्षर्णः; Tj² °विचक्षूणः; Jo² *Lakṣ* °विशारदाः — c) Be¹ Lo³ TMd⁴ GMd⁵ Tj¹ कुर्युरर्घ्यं; Ho कुर्युरर्धं; Lo² कुर्युरर्थं; Pu⁸ कुर्युरर्यं; GMd⁵ यदापण्यं — d) TMd⁴ तथा; Jo² Lo³ Tj¹ [*Jolly* R] हरेन्नृपः

399. Omitted in GMy Pu⁸. Cited by *Lakṣ* 12.516 — a) Be¹ GMd¹ राज्ञा; wKt¹ प्रक्षात°; Lo¹ प्रस्थान°; Bo प्रख्यातानि भाण्डानि — b) TMd⁴ प्रतिषेद्धानि; Pu⁵ Pu⁷ *om* च; NPu¹ Pu² Pu⁴ तु — c) sOx¹ sPu⁶ तानि हरतो; TMd³ GMd⁵ तानिर्हरतो; La¹ TMd⁴ निर्हरते; BBe² BKt⁵ निर्हतो; oOr निर्दहतो — d) TMd³ sOx¹ Ox² sPu⁶ सर्वाहारं; Tr¹ [*but mc sh*]सर्वपापं; wKt¹ भवेन्नृपः; Be¹ Pu² Pu³ Pu⁴ Tr² Wa [*Jolly* G] नृपो हरेत्; Pu⁷ नृपो भवेत्

400. Omitted in Pu⁵; pādas c-d omitted in GMd¹ [haplo] — a) Bo Lo⁵ Tj¹ शुल्क°; GMd⁵ शुष्क°; Ox² Pu² Pu⁴ °स्थने; La¹ °स्थान; TMd³ परीह° — b) TMd⁴ GMd⁵ GMy °न्नकाल; GMd¹ *om* विक्रयी [jumps to 401d, haplo]; Be¹ °विक्रये; NNg °विक्रयौ; BKt⁵ °विक्रयं; TMd³ °विक्रया — c) BKt⁵ संख्यानं; wKt¹ संस्थाने — d) Be¹ BBe² TMd³ °गुणमव्ययं; Pu⁷ °गुणमन्यजं; oOr °गुणमक्षयं; Pu² Pu⁴ °गुणं दमं; GMd⁵ °गुणकं दमं

401. Omitted in GMd¹ [up to कारयेत्क्रय°]. Cited by *Apa* 827; *Lakṣ* 12.516 — a) BKt⁵ अगमं; GMy *om* निर्गमं; Lo¹ GMd⁵ निर्गम; BBe² sOx¹ Pu⁵ sPu⁶ *Apa* निगमं — b) Ho वृद्ध° — c) Pu⁵ Pu⁷ [*Jolly* G] विज्ञाय; oOr निर्वाय — d) BBe² Tr² °विक्रयो; wKt¹ Tj² °विक्रयी; TMd³ °विक्रये

402. Omitted in Lo⁴ Lo⁵ [*Jolly* M⁴⁻⁵]. Cited by *Vij* 2.251; *Apa* 827; *Lakṣ* 12.517; *Mādh* 3.315 — a) *Apa Mādh* पञ्चरात्रे सप्तरात्रे; TMd³ °रात्रिपञ्च° — b) *Vij Apa Mādh* पक्षे मासे तथा गते;

तुला मानं प्रतीमानं सर्वं तत्स्यात्सुलक्षितम् ।
षट्सु षट्सु च मासेषु पुनरेव परीक्षयेत् ॥४०३॥
पणं यानं तरे दाप्यं पौरुषोऽर्धपणं तरे ।
पादं पशुश्च योषिच्च पादार्धं रिक्तकः पुमान् ॥४०४॥
भाण्डपूर्णानि यानानि तार्यं दाप्यानि सारतः ।
रिक्तभाण्डानि यत्किंचित् पुमांसश्चापरिच्छदाः ॥४०५॥
दीर्घाध्वनि यथादेशं यथाकालं तरो भवेत् ।
नदीतीरेषु तद्विद्यात् समुद्रे नास्ति लक्षणम् ॥४०६॥

Ho sOx[1] sPu[6] तथा पक्षे तथा गते; TMd[4] पञ्चपक्षेथ; BBe[2] Bo wKt[1] BKt[5] TMd[3] TMd[4] GMy NNg oOr Ox[2] NPu[1] Pu[5] Pu[7] MTr[5] MTr[6] [*Jolly* M Nd] पक्षे तथा गते; Pu[2] Pu[3] Pu[4] तथागमे; *Lakṣ* गतौ — c) La[1] कुर्वन्ति; GMd[1] चेमां; MTr[5] चैतां; TMd[3] चैव; NNg तथैषां; wKt[1] प्रत्यहम° — d) Pu[5] Pu[7] [*mc to*] °क्षं मूल्यसंस्था°; Tr[2] °क्षं सर्वसंस्था°; Tj[1] °मर्घ्यं संस्था°; MTr[4] MTr[6] °मस्वसंस्था°; Ox[2] °मर्थसंस्था°; TMd[3] GMy °मर्घस्य स्थापनं; BKt[5] °मर्घस्थानं; GMd[5] °स्थापकं

403. *Omitted in Lo[4] Lo[5] [*Jolly* M[4-5]]. Cited by *Apa* 825; *Lakṣ* 12.517 — a) TMd[3] तुलामांसं प्रतिमांसं; Be[1] NKt[4] GMd[1] GMd[5] GMy Pu[5] Pu[7] तुलामान; La[1] तुलामाने; NKt[4] NPu[1] प्रति° — b) Lo[2] GMd[1] TMd[3] TMd[4] GMd[5] GMy Tr[1] MTr[4] MTr[5] MTr[6] [*Jolly* Nd] *Nā* सर्वं पार्थिवलक्षितं [TMd[3] सर्व; TMd[4] सर्वे; GMd[5] GMy °रक्षितं], gloss of *Bh* राजमुद्राङ्कितं supports this reading; Jo[2] Lo[3] Tj[1] Tj[2] [*Jolly* R] सर्वं स्यात्सुपरीक्षितं; oOr [*Jolly* M[8]] सर्वतः स्यात्सु°; Be[1] Ho BKt[5] sOx[1] Ox[2] NPu[1] Pu[2] Pu[4] sPu[6] तु स्यात्सु°; BBe[2] Bo Hy Jm Jo[1] wKt[1] Kt[2] wKt[3] NKt[4] NNg Pu[8] Tr[2] MTr[3] *Mandlik Jha KSS Dave* च स्यात्सु°; Lo[1] च स्यात्स्वल°; La[1] स्यात्तत्सुल°; *Apa Lakṣ* °त्सुरक्षितं; sOx[1] sPu[6] °त्सलक्षितं; Lo[1] °त्स्वलक्षितं; Hy °त्परीक्षितं — c) Tr[2] *om* च — d) GMd[5] पुनरेव च कारयेत्; Pu[5] Pu[7] पौनःपुण्यं परीक्षणं; BBe[2] Ho wKt[1] NKt[4] La[1] sOx[1] sPu[6] MTr[5] पुनरेतत्परी°

404. Omitted in Lo[4] Lo[5] [*Jolly* M[4-5]]. Cited by *Vij* 2.263; *Apa* 834; *Lakṣ* 12.789 — a) Bo Ho NKt[4] Lo[1] यान; Be[1] TMd[4] Pu[5] Pu[7] यानां; Pu[8] जानं; BBe[2] GMd[1] GMy यानान्तरे; Be[1] तरो; sOx[1] sPu[6] तरी; Hy Pu[2] Pu[4] Pu[5] Pu[7] Tj[2] तरं; Be[1] Ho NKt[4] La[1] GMd[1] GMd[5] GMy oOr sOx[1] sPu[6] MTr[6] *Rc* दाप्यः; MTr[3] याप्यं; TMd[3] वाप्यः — b) Lo[1] रूपोर्धं पणमुत्तमं; TMd[4] पारुषार्धं पणं हरेत्; Be[1] wKt[1] GMd[1] *Vij Apa* पुरुषो; Pu[5] Pu[7] परुषो; BBe[2] Bo Ho Jo[2] NKt[4] BKt[5] La[1] Lo[3] TMd[3] GMy sOx[1] sPu[6] Tj[1] Wa [*Jolly* R N Nd] *Rc Jolly* पौरुषे; TMd[3] पारुषार्ध°; Ox[2] Pu[7] °पणां; Bo Jo[2] BKt[5] La[1] Lo[2] Lo[3] Pu[5] Pu[7] Pu[8] [*Jolly* G] *Lakṣ Apa* तरं; oOr Pu[3] Tr[2] Wa तरः; GMd[1] MTr[5] भरः; GMy भरं; MTr[4] MTr[6] परः; TMd[3] धरः; Be[1] [*Jolly* M] नरः; Ho NKt[4] करः; sOx[1] sPu[6] कराः; GMd[5] हरः; Pu[2] Pu[4] हरेत्; [*Jolly* Nd[1]] हरे — c) Jo[2] Lo[3] Tj[1] पादं पशुषु योषित्सु; Pu[3] Tr[2] पादं च पशुयोषिच्च; *Jha Dave* पादे; Pu[4] पादां; La[1] पशुं च; Kt[2] पशुञ्च; oOr पशुषु; TMd[3] GMy योषिश्च — d) Bo GMd[5] पादार्ध; GMd[1] रिक्तकं; NPu[1] Pu[4] रिक्ततः; Tr[1] रिक्थिकः; TMd[4] भुक्तकः; *Apa* द्विकरः पुमान्

405. Omitted in Lo[4] Lo[5] [*Jolly* M[4-5]]. Cited by *Vij* 2.263; *Lakṣ* 12.789 — a) Lo[1] °पूर्णनिपातानि; Pu[5] *om* यानानि; TMd[3] यायानि; Pu[2] Pu[4] मानानि — b) TMd[4] पर्यायस्यानि सारतः; sOx[1] sPu[6] तातीप्यानि सारतः; Jo[2] Lo[3] TMd[3] Tj[1] तारं; La[1] तार्यां; BBe[2] तार्या; wKt[1] भार्यां; GMd[1] दायं; Ho oOr सारितः; BKt[5] सर्वतः; GMy रङ्गनाः; TMd[3] रङ्गनः — c) Tj[2] Tr[2] रक्त°; BBe[2] रिक्थ°; TMd[4] भुक्त° — d) oOr पुमांसः सपरि°; GMd[1] TMd[4] Ox[2] Pu[3] Tr[2] पुमांसश्च परि°; Be[1] Hy Lo[1] °च्छदः

406. Omitted in Lo[4] Lo[5] [*Jolly* M[4-5]]. Cited by *Lakṣ* 12.789 — a) Kt[2] Lo[1] Pu[4] दीर्घध्वनि; La[1] MTr[5] दीर्घेध्वनि; Lo[2] दीर्घाच्चनि; TMd[4] दीर्घानि तु; TMd[3] GMy यथादेयं; Bo °देशे — a-b) MTr[5] यथाकालं यथादेशान्तरो भवेत् — b) Ho La[1] Lo[1] GMd[1] TMd[3] TMd[4] GMd[5] GMy sOx[1] Ox[2] Pu[2] Pu[4]

गर्भिणी तु द्विमासादिस्तथा प्रव्रजितो मुनिः ।
ब्राह्मणा लिङ्गिनश्चैव न दाप्यास्तारिकं तरे ॥४०७॥
यन्नावि किंचिद्दाशानां विशीर्येतापराधतः ।
तद्दाशैरेव दातव्यं समागम्य स्वतोऽंशतः ॥४०८॥
एष नौयायिनामुक्तो व्यवहारस्य निर्णयः ।
दाशापराधतस्तोये दैविके नास्ति निग्रहः ॥४०९॥
वाणिज्यं कारयेद्वैश्यं कुसीदं कृषिमेव च ।
पशूनां रक्षणं चैव दास्यं शूद्रं द्विजन्मनाम् ॥४१०॥
क्षत्रियं चैव वैश्यं च ब्राह्मणो वृत्तिकर्शितौ ।
बिभृयादानृशंस्येन स्वानि कर्माणि कारयेत् ॥४११॥

Pu^{5} sPu^{6} Pu^{7} MTr^{4} यथाकालान्तरो; MTr^{6} यथाकालान्तरे; BKt^{5} oOr यथाकालान्तरं; Pu^{2} Pu^{4} तरं; Be^{1} नरो — c) NNg नदीतीरेष्वेतदेव; wKt^{1} GMd^{1} नदीतरेषु; BKt^{5} नदीतीरे तद्वि°; wKt^{3} La^{1} GMd^{5} Pu^{5} Pu^{7} Tr^{2} MTr^{6} यद्विद्यात् — d) oOr समुद्रो; TMd^{4} नापि लक्षणं; GMd^{5} भक्षणं

407. *ma* in Lo^{4}. Cited by *Vij* 2.263; *Lakṣ* 12.789 — a) NPu^{1} गुर्विणी; Be^{1} Bo La^{1} Lo^{4} Lo^{5} GMd^{1} TMd^{3} TMd^{4} GMd^{5} GMy Pu^{2} Pu^{4} Tj^{1} द्विमासादि तथा; Pu^{7} प्रवासादि तथा [*mc* द्विमासादि]; Tr^{1} द्विमासादिं तथा; oOr द्विमासाद्यस्तथा — b) GMd^{1} प्रव्राजितो; TMd^{3} GMd^{5} प्रव्रजतो; Tr^{2} प्रवृतितो — c) TMd^{4} ब्राह्मणो — d) Be^{1} TMd^{4} Pu^{4} दाप्यस्ता°; GMd^{1} TMd^{3} Tr^{2} °स्तारिकां; wKt^{1} °स्तरिकं; Bo °स्तारिणं; NKt^{4} °स्वारिकन्; MTr^{5} °स्तारिकान्तरे; Pu^{7} करे; Pu^{5} [*Jolly* G] करं; *Vij* नराः

408. Cited by *Lakṣ* 12.790 — a) TMd^{4} या नावि; oOr यन्नास्य; BBe^{2} यद्वारि; MTr^{4} MTr^{6} यन्नाद्धि किंचि°; TMd^{3} GMd^{5} GMy यच्चापि किंचि°; Be^{1} [*but mc*] BCa Ho Jo^{1} Kt^{2} BKt^{5} La^{1} Lo^{1} GMd^{5} NNg sOx^{1} NPu^{1} Pu^{3} Pu^{4} Pu^{5} sPu^{6} Pu^{7} [*Jolly* M$^{8-9}$ Nd] °द्दासानां; GMd^{1} °द्दानानां; TMd^{4} °द्रासानां — b) wKt^{1} विशीर्यता°; BKt^{5} च्यशीर्येता°; TMd^{3} विशिध्येता°; Tr^{2} °राधताः; TMd^{3} °राधितः — c) Pu^{7} [*Jolly* G] नावारूढैः प्रदेयं तत्; Be^{1} BCa Ho Kt^{2} BKt^{5} La^{1} NNg NPu^{1} Pu^{2} Pu^{4} [*Jolly* M$^{8-9}$ Nd] तद्दासैरेव; MTr^{5} तद्दाशैवै; TMd^{4} तथा तैरेव; sOx^{1} sPu^{6} तादृशैरेव; Tr^{2} दासीरेव तु; oOr प्रदातव्यं — d) GMd^{5} स्वमागम्य; wKt^{3} स्वशोंशतः; wKt^{1} La^{1} सुतोंशतः; Be^{1} स्वतोंशकः; TMd^{3} ततोंशवः

409. Cited by *Lakṣ* 12.790 — a) Lo^{5} एवं नौ°; wKt^{3} Lo^{1} NPu^{1} नौयानिना°; GMy नावायिना°; TMd^{4} कायायिना° — b) Bo व्यवहारश्च; *Lakṣ* °हारविनिर्णयः; Wa °हारनिर्णयः — c) BCa Ho Jo^{1} BKt^{5} La^{1} Lo^{2} NNg sOx^{1} NPu^{1} Pu^{5} sPu^{6} Pu^{7} [*Jolly* M$^{8-9}$ Nd] दासा°; BBe^{2} TMd^{3} दशा°; TMd^{4} देशा°; Pu^{2} Pu^{4} दोषोपरा°; La^{1} °राधजस्तोये; Pu^{2} °राधनस्तोये; GMd^{1} TMd^{3} GMy °राधात्तोयेषु; Kt^{2} °स्तोयै; TMd^{4} °स्तोय — d) wKt^{3} Lo^{2} दैवके; TMd^{4} देवके; Tj^{2} देविके; Be^{1} Bo Ho wKt^{1} Kt^{2} TMd^{4} विग्रहः

410. Pādas c-d omitted in BKt^{5}. Cited by *Lakṣ* 12.776 — a) GMd^{1} MTr^{6} °द्वैश्यः — b) Ho wKt^{1} Kt^{2} La^{1} Pu^{5} Pu^{7} कुशीदं; BBe^{2} कुषीदं; NPu^{1} कुलीदं; Be^{1} कृषमेव; Pu^{5} Pu^{7} कृषिरेव; BKt^{5} sOx^{1} sPu^{6} Tr^{2} वा — c) Tr^{2} रक्षणे; GMd^{1} रक्षणश्चैव — d) La^{1} अनुवृत्तिं द्विजन्मनां; wKt^{1} दाश्यं; TMd^{3} GMd^{5} GMy Tr^{1} *Lakṣ* शूद्रं दास्यं; MTr^{4} MTr^{6} शूद्रो दास्यं; Hy wKt^{3} Pu^{5} शूद्र; GMd^{1} TMd^{4} शूद्रो; Be^{1} द्विजन्मना

411.* Omitted in BKt^{5}. Cited by *Apa* 789; *Lakṣ* 12.397; *Dev* 3.462; *Mādh* 3.244 — a) sPu^{6} *om* च — b) *Mādh* ब्राह्मणोऽवृत्तिकर्षितं; GMd^{1} ब्राह्मणौ; Be^{1} BBe^{2} Bo Ho Hy Jm Jo^{1} wKt^{1} Kt^{2} wKt^{3} oOr sOx^{1} Pu^{3} sPu^{6} Pu^{8} *Lakṣ Mādh Jolly* °कर्षितौ; La^{1} TMd^{4} GMd^{5} °कर्षितः — c) GMd^{1} Tj^{2} Tr^{2} °शंसेन — d) GMd^{1} Pu^{2} Pu^{4} स्वामि; GMd^{5} कार्याणि; Bo Jm Jo^{1} Jo^{2} wKt^{3} NKt^{4} Lo^{2} Lo^{4} [*cor to*] Lo^{5} GMd^{1} GMd^{5} Pu^{8} Tj^{1} Tr^{1} [*Jolly* Go M^{4} Ku R] *Ku Nd Mandlik KSS Dave* कारयन्; Tj^{2} कारयत्; MTr^{5} कारयः

दास्यं तु कारयंल्लोभाद् ब्राह्मणः संस्कृतान्द्विजान् ।
अनिच्छतः प्राभवत्याद् राज्ञा दण्ड्यः शतानि षट् ॥४१२॥
शूद्रं तु कारयेद्दास्यं क्रीतमक्रीतमेव वा ।
दास्यायैव हि सृष्टोऽसौ ब्राह्मणस्य स्वयंभुवा ॥४१३॥
न स्वामिना निसृष्टोऽपि शूद्रो दास्याद्विमुच्यते ।
निसर्गजं हि तत्तस्य कस्तस्मात्तदपोहति ॥४१४॥
ध्वजाहृतो भक्तदासो गृहजः क्रीतदत्त्रिमौ ।
पैत्रिको दण्डदासश्च सप्तैते दासयोनयः ॥४१५॥
भार्या पुत्रश्च दासश्च त्रय एवाधनाः स्मृताः ।

412. Omitted in bKt^{5}. Cited by *Apa* 789; *Lakṣ* 12.397; *Dev* 3.463; *Mādh* 3.244 — a) Pu^{5} Pu^{7} [*Jolly* G] यो दास्यं कारयेल्लोभाद्; wKt^{1} दाश्यं; Tr^{2} दास्यां; mTr^{3} लास्यं; Tj^{1} च; Be^{1} Kt^{2} कारयल्लोभाद्; bBe^{2} Bo Ho Hy Jo^{2} La^{1} Lo^{1} Lo^{2} Lo^{3} Lo^{5} tMd^{4} nNg oOr sOx^{1} Ox^{2} nPu^{1} Pu^{2} Pu^{4} sPu^{6} Pu^{8} Tj^{1} Tr^{2} Wa कारयेल्लोभाद्; tMd^{3} gMd^{5} gMy *Dev Lakṣ Mādh Apa* कारयेन्मोहाद्; mTr^{5} कारयन्मोहाद्; Bo °ल्लोभान्; mTr^{3} °ल्लोहाद् — b) tMd^{3} ब्राह्मणं संस्कृतां द्विजाः; Wa ब्राह्मणो — c) La^{1} सोर्हति प्रभुत्वेन; sOx^{1} sPu^{6} अनिच्छन्तः; Pu^{3} अनिक्षितः; *Nā* [pāṭha] प्राभावत्याद्; gMd^{1} Tj^{1} प्राभावत्या; gMy प्रभावत्या; Pu^{5} Pu^{7} प्रभावत्वां; mTr^{5} प्रभावत्वाद्; gMd^{5} mTr^{6} प्रभवता; nPu^{1} Pu^{2} Pu^{4} प्रभवतो; tMd^{3} प्रभावेन; tMd^{4} Tr^{1} प्रभावाद्यो; Be^{1} प्रभुत्वेतद्; bBe^{2} Ho wKt^{1} nKt^{4} oOr sOx^{1} Ox^{2} Pu^{3} sPu^{6} Tr^{2} *Nā* प्रभुत्वेन; Wa प्राभुतवेन — d) nNg Tr^{1} [*but cor sh*] राज्ञो; Tj^{1} राजा; Bo mTr^{6} दण्डः; wKt^{1} nKt^{4} Lo^{1} gMd^{1} nNg Pu^{8} mTr^{5} *Lakṣ Dev* दाप्यः; Tr^{2} वाप्यः

413. Omitted in Tj^{2}; pādas a-b omitted in bKt^{5}. Cited by *Apa* 789; *Lakṣ* 12.397; *Dev* 3.463; *Mādh* 3.244 — a) bBe^{2} mTr^{4} शूद्रस्तु; gMd^{5} *om* तु; Tj^{1} °द्दास्ये; mTr^{4} °द्दण्डं — b) tMd^{3} क्रीत-विक्रीतमेव; Be^{1} Bo च — c) tMd^{3} दास्यायैन सृष्टो हि ब्राह्म°; La^{1} *om* हि; gMy हि सृष्टोहि; mTr^{3} दृष्टो; sOx^{1} sPu^{6} सृष्टस्तु — d) Be^{1} bKt^{5} La^{1} Lo^{4} Lo^{5} gMd^{1} gMd^{5} nNg Ox^{2} Wa [*Jolly* M] *Lakṣ Dev Mādh* स्वयमेव स्वयंभुवा; Jo^{2} wKt^{1} Lo^{3} ब्राह्मणानां

414. Cited by *Apa* 786; *Lakṣ* 12.389 — a) gMd^{1} स्वामिना चैव निर्दिष्टो [*om* न]; Tr^{2} नास्य भिन्नानिसृ°; Pu^{4} *Apa* °मिनातिसृष्टोपि; bKt^{5} निसृष्टो वा; Be^{1} bCa wKt^{1} wKt^{3} La^{1} oOr Pu^{5} Pu^{7} mTr^{4} mTr^{6} [*Jolly* G] विसृष्टोपि; tMd^{3} विपृष्टोपि; Tj^{1} निकृष्टोपि; Lo^{1} तु सृष्टोसौ — b) bKt^{5} यास्याद्वि°; La^{1} oOr दास्यात्प्रमुच्यते — c) bCa Ho nKt^{4} sOx^{1} sPu^{6} निसर्गजं तद्धि तस्य; bKt^{5} निसजनं; Tr^{2} *om* हि; Be^{1} Pu^{3} Tr^{2} तं तस्य; Tj^{1} तस्तस्य; Pu^{8} तद्दास्य — d) gMd^{1} tMd^{3} tMd^{4} gMd^{5} gMy mTr^{4} mTr^{6} कस्तं तस्माद्विमोचयेत्; mTr^{5} कस्तन्तस्मादपोहति; oOr कर्तव्यात् व्यपोहति; *Lakṣ* °स्मादव्यपोहति; nKt^{4} La^{1} sOx^{1} sPu^{6} °त्तमपोहति; nPu^{1} °त्तद्व्यपोहति; *Apa* °त्तं व्यपोहति

415. Cited by *Vij* 2.181; *Apa* 789; *Mādh* 3.240 — a) wKt^{1} Lo^{4} ध्वजाकृतो; wKt^{3} ध्वजाधृतो; Bo Pu^{5} Pu^{7} ध्वजाहतो; gMy ध्वजमृतो; tMd^{3} ध्वजाभ्यतो; sOx^{1} sPu^{6} धनाहृतो; Lo^{1} व्याजाहृतो; nKt^{4} पूजाहृतो; wKt^{1} मुक्तदासो; Be^{1} °दासौ; bKt^{5} °दास्यो — a-b) gMd^{1} अपोहति द्विजो भृत्यो भक्तदासौ गृहं द्विजः — b) Pu^{5} Pu^{7} Tj^{1} गृहज; tMd^{3} गूढजः; bKt^{5} कृतदत्तृमौ; wKt^{3} कृतविक्रिमौ; Lo^{2} प्रीतदात्तृमौ; tMd^{4} gMd^{5} nPu^{1} Pu^{4} °दात्त्रिमौ; Pu^{5} Pu^{7} °दातृमौ; Bo Lo^{1} tMd^{3} °दत्तिमौ — c) bBe^{2} Bo Jo^{2} wKt^{1} wKt^{3} Lo^{1} tMd^{3} nNg nPu^{1} Tj^{1} Tr^{1} mTr^{6} *Vij Apa* पैतृको; Ho sOx^{1} sPu^{6} पौत्रिको; Be^{1} पौतृको; bKt^{5} पतृको; oOr पौरको; wKt^{1} La^{1} °दाशश्च; *Apa* °दासस्तु; bKt^{5} °दासस्यो — c-d) gMd^{1} क्रीतदासश्रीमन्तवै त्रिदण्ड-दासं च सप्ततेः — d) Bo sOx^{1} sPu^{6} *Apa* सप्तैता; nKt^{4} दासयो नृपः

यत्ते समधिगच्छन्ति यस्य ते तस्य तद्धनम् ॥४१६॥
विश्रब्धं ब्राह्मणः शूद्राद् द्रव्योपादानमाचरेत् ।
न हि तस्यास्ति किंचित्स्वं भर्तृहार्यधनो हि सः ॥४१७॥
वैश्यशूद्रौ प्रयत्नेन स्वानि कर्माणि कारयेत् ।
तौ हि च्युतौ स्वकर्मभ्यः क्षोभयेतामिदं जगत् ॥४१८॥
अहन्यहन्यवेक्षेत कर्मान्तान्वाहनानि च ।
आयव्ययौ च नियतावाकरान्कोशमेव च ॥४१९॥
एवं सर्वानिमान् राजा व्यवहारान्समापयन् ।
व्यपोह्य किल्बिषं सर्वं प्राप्नोति परमां गतिम् ॥४२०॥

416. Omitted in Lo^5. Cited by *Śab* 6.1.12 — a) wKt^1 भार्या दासश्च शूद्रश्च; sOx^1 sPu^6 भार्याः; Jo^2 Lo^3 Tj^1 *Śab* दासश्च पुत्रश्च — b) *Śab* निर्धनाः सर्व एव ते; Lo^1 यत्र एवा°; Be^1 TMd^4 एवधनाः; La^1 GMy Pu^2 Pu^3 एवधना; wKt^3 एतद्धनाः; NNg [*but cor fh*] एवाधनौ — c) Lo^1 एते सम°; Be^1 वृत्ते सम°; Lo^3 समाधि° — d) Jo^2 Lo^3 GMd^1 TMd^3 TMd^4 GMd^5 GMy Tj^1 Tr^1 MTr^6 यस्यैते; Hy यस्य तेनास्य; TMd^3 यस्य ते यस्य

417. Cited by *Lakṣ* 12.393 — a) TMd^4 विसृष्टो ब्राह्मणाच्छूद्रो; Be^1 Bo Ho Jo^1 Kt^2 wKt^3 Lo^3 GMd^1 sOx^1 sPu^6 Tj^1 MTr^5 *Mandlik Jha KSS Dave* विस्रब्धं; TMd^3 GMd^5 GMy Tr^1 [*but cor sh*] MTr^4 MTr^6 [*Jolly* Nd] विस्रब्धो; Pu^3 निःशंकं; BKt^5 GMd^1 TMd^3 शूद्रा; Lo^3 शूद्राः; MTr^6 शूद्रः — b) TMd^3 व्रात्योपा°; Jo^2 Lo^3 Ox^2 Tj^1 °माहरेत्; Wa °मर्हति — c) TMd^4 कस्यास्ति — d) wKt^1 भरहार्य°; NKt^4 MTr^4 MTr^6 भर्तृभार्य°; TMd^3 GMd^5 तत्रभार्याधनो; GMd^1 °हार्याधनो

418. Cited by *Lakṣ* 12.776 — a) Bo Lo^2 Wa °शूद्रो; wKt^3 °शूद्रा; TMd^4 °शूद्राः; NNg तु यत्नेन — b) Lo^5 GMy स्वामि — c) Lo^3 Tj^1 तौ च्युतौ तु स्व°; Tr^2 तौ च्युतौ हि स्व°; Bo च्युतो; TMd^4 sOx^1 स्वकर्मेभ्यः; wKt^1 स्वधमभ्यः; MTr^4 च कर्मभ्यः— d) Jo^1 क्षेभये°; Pu^5 Pu^7 [*Jolly* G] क्षोभयन्ताविदं; TMd^4 क्रोधयेतामिदं

419. a) Tr^2 अहन्यहर्वृत्तिवीक्षेत — b) Lo^4 Lo^5 TMd^3 TMd^4 GMy कर्मान्तं वाह°; Tr^2 कर्माणि वाह°; Bo कर्मत्तं वाह°; wKt^1 कर्मार्थं ताहनानि — c) Tj^1 अयव्य°; Be^1 BKt^5 Lo^4 Lo^5 NNg Wa च सततमाक° [BKt^5 हि]; La^1 नियतानाक°; Tj^2 नियताक°; TMd^4 नियतौ आक°; Tr^2 निहतावाक° — d) La^1 नियतौ प्रकारा°; GMy °वाकारं को°; GMd^1 MTr^6 °वाकारान्क्रोशमेव°; La^1 Tr^2 °न्कोषमेव; NNg °न्कोश एव

420. Not commented by *Rc*. Cited by *Mādh* 3.396 — a) Jo^1 राज्या — b) Bo NPu^1 °न्समापयत्; Lo^4 Lo^5 TMd^3 GMd^5 Pu^5 Pu^7 °न्समापयेत्; BKt^5 °न्समापये; BBe^2 °न्समाचरन्; BCa °न्समाचरेत्; GMy MTr^4 MTr^6 °न्समं नयन्; TMd^4 °न्समानयेत् — c) La^1 व्यपेतकल्मषौ नित्यं; Be^1 Lo^1 व्यपोहि; wKt^3 BKt^5 Lo^4 Lo^5 GMd^1 TMd^3 GMd^5 NNg Ox^2 NPu^1 Pu^2 Pu^4 Pu^5 Pu^7 Tr^1 MTr^4 MTr^6 Wa *Go* कल्मषं; GMy कलुषं — d) TMd^3 GMd^5 GMy Tr^1 [*but mc sh*] MTr^4 MTr^6 [*Jolly* Nd Gr] ब्रह्मलोके महीयते; La^1 स प्राप्नोति परां गतिं

इति मानवे धर्मशास्त्रे भृगुप्रोक्तायां संहितायामष्टमोऽध्यायः ॥

Colophon: Be^{1} Lo^{1} Lo^{3} TMd^{3} oOr sOx^{1} Ox^{2} sPu^{6} इति श्रीमानवे; wKt^{3} भृगुप्रोक्ते; BKt^{5} GMd^{1} TMd^{3} GMy MTr^{4} MTr^{6} *om* भृगुप्रोक्तायां संहितायां; Lo^{1} °प्रोक्तसंहि°; wKt^{3} *om* संहितायां; wKt^{1} Lo^{1} संहितायां व्यवहारो नामाष्टमो; NNg संहितायां कार्याणां निर्णयः साक्षिप्रश्नविधानं च अष्टमोध्यायः समाप्तः; Be^{1} °शास्त्रे व्यवहाराध्यायोष्टमः

[नवमोऽध्यायः]

पुरुषस्य स्त्रियाश्चैव धर्म्ये वर्त्मनि तिष्ठतोः ।
संयोगे विप्रयोगे च धर्मान्वक्ष्यामि शाश्वतान् ॥१॥
अस्वतन्त्राः स्त्रियः कार्याः पुरुषैः स्वैर्दिवानिशम् ।
विषये सज्जमानाश्च संस्थाप्या ह्यात्मनो वशे ॥२॥
पिता रक्षति कौमारे भर्ता रक्षति यौवने ।
रक्षन्ति स्थविरे पुत्रा न स्त्री स्वातन्त्र्यमर्हति ॥३॥
कालेऽदाता पिता याप्यो याप्यश्चानुपयन्पतिः ।
मृते भर्तरि पुत्रस्तु याप्यो मातुररक्षिता ॥४॥

1.* Cited by *Lakṣ* 12.601; *Dev* 3.561 — a) Lo^1 TMd^4 oOr NPu^1 Pu^2 Pu^4 पुरुषश्च; BKt^5 Tr^2 पुरुषस्त्रि°; La^1 Lo^3 TMd^4 GMy sOx^1 sPu^6 Tj^1 Tr^2 MTr^6 स्त्रियश्चैव; Lo^2 °श्चैवं — b) Ho wKt^1 Kt^2 wKt^3 BKt^5 Lo^1 Lo^2 Lo^3 Lo^4 TMd^3 TMd^4 GMd^5 sOx^1 Ox^2 NPu^1 Pu^2 Pu^4 Pu^5 sPu^6 Pu^7 Tj^1 Tr^1 Tr^2 MTr^4 MTr^{5}MTr^6 *KSS* धर्मे; NKt^4 GMd^1 GMy Tj^2 धर्म्मे; Wa धर्म; sOx^1 sPu^6 तिष्ठता; TMd^4 तिष्ठतः; oOr तिष्ठते — c) BCa wKt^1 संयोगे च वियोगे च; Tr^2 संयोगे प्रयोगे; GMd^1 विप्रयोगेन [*om* च] — d) Lo^4 TMd^4 NNg [*Jolly* M] धर्मं वक्ष्यामि शाश्वतं

2.* Cited by *Vij* 2.295 [intro.]; *Lakṣ*12.601; *Dev* 3.562; *Mādh* 3.322 — a) MTr^6 °तन्त्र्यः; Tj^1 स्त्रियाः — b) Lo^2 पुरुषः; TMd^4 पुरुषे; TMd^3 पुरुष स्याद्दिवा° — c) Be^1 BBe^2 Bo Hy Jm Jo^1 Jo^2 Kt^2 BKt^5 Lo^2 Lo^3 Lo^4 NNg NPu^1 Pu^2 Pu^4 Pu^5 Pu^7 Pu^8 Tj^1 Tj^2 Tr^2 Wa *Vij Lakṣ Mandlik Jolly Jha KSS Dave* विषयेषु च सज्जन्त्यः [BKt^5 विषयेष्वपि; Jo^2 Lo^3 Tj^1 प्रसज्जन्त्यः]; wKt^3 विषय; MTr^4 सज्य°; wKt^3 °मानस्य; GMd^1 °मानांश्च; GMd^5 GMy °मानं च; Ox^2 °मानास्ताः — d) Lo^1 संस्थाप्य; BBe^2 Ho Jo^2 La^1 sOx^1 sPu^6 *Lakṣ* °प्याश्चात्मनो; [*Jolly* Nd] स्वात्मनो; Hy Kt^2 NNg Pu^5 Pu^7 MTr^3 *Mandlik Jha KSS Dave* आत्मनो; Pu^4 वशो; TMd^4 वशात्

3. Cited by *Lakṣ* 12.602; *Dev* 3.564; *Mādh* 2.286; pādas a-b cited by *Dev* 3.574, and pāda-d by *Vij* 2.136 — a) Lo^2 Wa कोमारे; TMd^4 कामारि — c) Jo^2 wKt^3 Lo^3 TMd^3 GMd^5 GMy Tj^1 Tr^1 MTr^4 MTr^5 MTr^6 [*Jolly* R Nd] *Lakṣ Mādh* पुत्रास्तु स्थविरे भावे [MTr^5 पुत्रस्तु; wKt^3 स्थविर; TMd^3 GMy Tr^1 MTr^6 स्थविरी; MTr^4 स्थावरी]; Kt^2 Lo^2 Lo^4 Wa स्थाविरे; La^1 Pu^5 Pu^7 Tr^2 स्थावरे; NKt^4 स्थविरे भावे

4.* Cited by *Lakṣ* 12.604 — a) Kt^2 कालि; wKt^3 कालः; BKt^5 कालेतदा; Hy *om* याप्यो; Be^1 याव्यो; BBe^2 Bo BCa Ho Jo^1 Jo^2 wKt^1 Kt^2 wKt^3 wKt^5 Lo^1 Lo^2 Lo^3 TMd^3 sOx^1 Ox^2 Pu^2 Pu^3 Pu^4 Pu^5 sPu^6 Pu^7 Pu^8 Tj^1 Tj^2 Tr^2 Wa *Lakṣ Mandlik Jolly KSS Dave* वाच्यो; oOr वाक्यो; La^1 कन्यो — b) Be^1 याव्यश्चा°; Lo^4 याम्यश्चा°; BBe^2 Bo BCa Ho Hy Jo^1 Jo^2 wKt^1 Kt^2 wKt^3 wKt^5 Lo^1 Lo^2 Lo^3 TMd^3 sOx^1 Ox^2 Pu^2 Pu^3 Pu^4 Pu^5 sPu^6 Pu^7 Pu^8 Tj^1 Tj^2 Tr^2 Wa *Lakṣ Mandlik Jolly KSS Dave* वाच्यश्चा°; wKt^1 वाप्यश्चा°; oOr वाक्यस्यानु°; Lo^2 °नुपयश्छति; wKt^1 °नुगयत्पतिः; Pu^8 °पयन्पक्षतिः; TMd^3 °पयन्पितुः — d) Be^1 याव्यो मातुश्च रक्षिता; La^1 याच्यो; BBe^2 Bo BCa Ho Hy Jo^1 Jo^2 wKt^1 Kt^2 wKt^3 wKt^5 Lo^1 Lo^2 Lo^3 TMd^3 sOx^1 Ox^2 Pu^2 Pu^3 Pu^4 Pu^5 sPu^6 Pu^7 Pu^8 Tj^1 Tj^2 Tr^2 Wa *Lakṣ Mandlik*

सूक्ष्मेभ्योऽपि प्रसङ्गेभ्यः स्त्रियो रक्ष्या विशेषतः ।
द्वयोर्हि कुलयोः शोकमावहेयुररक्षिताः ॥५॥
इमं हि सर्ववर्णानां पश्यन्तो धर्ममुत्तमम् ।
यतन्ते रक्षितुं भार्यां भर्तारो दुर्बला अपि ॥६॥
स्वां प्रसूतिं चरित्रं च कुलमात्मानमेव च ।
स्वं च धर्मं प्रयत्नेन जायां रक्षन्हि रक्षति ॥७॥
पतिर्भार्यां संप्रविश्य गर्भो भूत्वेह जायते ।
जायायास्तद्धि जायात्वं यदस्यां जायते पुनः ॥८॥
यादृशं भजते हि स्त्री सुतं सूते तथाविधम् ।
तस्मात् प्रजाविशुद्ध्यर्थं स्त्रियं रक्षेत् प्रयत्नतः ॥९॥
न कश्चिद्योषितः शक्तः प्रसह्य परिरक्षितुम् ।

Jolly KSS Dave वाच्यो; oOr वाक्यो; Lo^1 मातूरक्षिता; GMd^1 oOr मातरि रक्षितः; MTr^6 °रक्षितः; Pu^2 Pu^3 Pu^4 °रक्षिताः; TMd^3 °रक्षकः; TMd^4 °गंक्षिता [?]

5. Cited by *Lakṣ* 12.603; *Dev* 3.562; *Mādh* 3.323 — a) TMd^4 माक्ष्मिभ्यो; BKt^5 La^1 °भ्यो हि; Jo^1 *om* पि — b) Jm Kt^2 wKt^3 La^1 Lo^2 NNg Pu^4 Pu^5 Pu^7 रक्षा; BKt^5 विशेषितः; BCa *Lakṣ* प्रयत्नतः — c) Lo^3 Tj^1 शोकामा° — d) GMd^1 sOx^1 sPu^6 °मवहेयु°; Tj^2 °माहवेयु°; TMd^4 °मावहीयु°; GMd^5 °मावहेयुः सुरक्षिताः; Hy °युरारक्षिताः; GMd^1 NPu^1 Pu^2 Tj^1 °रक्षिता

Additional verse in Bo sOx^1 sPu^6 Tr^2 *Mandlik* [ख, ज, झ, ण, ट, ठ] *KSS:*

भार्यायां रक्ष्यमाणायां प्रजा भवति रक्षिता ।
प्रजायां रक्ष्यमाणायामात्मा भवति रक्षितः ॥

a) Bo sPu^6 रक्षमा° — b) Tr^2 रक्षिताः — c) Bo sOx^1 sPu^6 रक्षमा° — d) Tr^2 रक्षिताः

6. Cited by *Lakṣ* 12.603; *Dev* 3.562; *Mādh* 3.323 — a) Ho इयं; GMd^1 इदं; MTr^6 इदः — c) BBe^2 यतस्ते रक्षितां; Pu^3 यतेरन्रक्षितुं; TMd^3 रक्षितं; oOr रक्षतं; wKt^3 लक्षितुं; Pu^5 Pu^7 भर्या — d) Pu^2 Pu^4 दुर्बलापि वा; BKt^5 La^1 दुर्बलास्वपि; TMd^3 sOx^1 sPu^6 रक्षिता अपि

7. Cited by *Viś* 1.80; *Lakṣ* 12.603; *Dev* 3.563; *Mādh* 3.323 — a) Lo^1 GMd^5 स्व; Tr^2 स्वयं; Bo प्रसूतां; BKt^5 सुप्रतिः; wKt^1 प्रसूतिं च वित्तं च; GMy प्रसूतिं च रात्रिं च; Kt^2 चरित्रश्च; TMd^4 *om* च — b) MTr^3 तुलमा°; GMy मूलमा° — c) Lo^4 स्वयं च; Pu^3 Pu^8 Tr^2 स्वं स्वं धर्मं; wKt^1 Lo^3 Tj^1 *Lakṣ* स्वधर्मं च [*Lakṣ* हि]; wKt^1 तु; GMd^1 TMd^3 GMd^5 Tr^1 [*but cor sh*] MTr^4 MTr^6 धर्मं प्रजाश्चैव; TMd^4 [*Jolly* Nd] धर्मं प्रजां चैव — d) TMd^3 GMd^5 जाया; Jm wKt^3 Lo^1 Lo^2 भार्यां; *Dev* रक्षन्स; Tr^2 हि रक्षन्रक्षति; Pu^8 रक्षसि

8. Cited by *Lakṣ* 12.609 — a) GMd^1 TMd^3 TMd^4 GMd^5 GMy Tr^1 MTr^4 MTr^6 [*Jolly* G] पतिर्भार्यां प्रविश्य स्वां [TMd^3 पतिभार्यां]; Hy Kt^2 Lo^2 Tj^1 [*cor to*] पतिभार्यां — b) TMd^3 गर्भे; Bo Tr^2 भूत्वेहि; GMd^1 भूत्वा हि; Kt^2 भूतोह; GMy भूत्वानुजायते; TMd^4 भूत्वाद्विजायते; Tr^1 भूत्वाभिजायते; Tr^2 जायति — c) NPu^1 जायास्तद्वद्विजायत्वं; Tj^1 जायया°; TMd^4 जायायां तच्च; GMy °यास्तद्ध; La^1 Pu^2 °यास्तद्विजायात्वं; Jo^1 Lo^1 TMd^3 जायत्वं — d) BKt^5 यदस्या

9. Cited by *Lakṣ* 12.607; *Dev* 3.565 — a) GMd^1 तादृपं; Ox^2 लभते — b) *Lakṣ* सूतेपत्यं तथाविधं; Lo^4 तं प्रसूते; NPu^1 MTr^6 °विधिं — c) GMy प्रविश्यवृध्यर्थं; GMd^1 °विवृद्ध्यर्थं — d) wKt^3 TMd^3 स्त्रिया; La^1 GMy MTr^4 MTr^6 [*Jolly* Nd] *Lakṣ* स्त्रियो; BBe^2 BKt^5 रक्षेत यत्नतः

एतैरुपाययोगैस्तु शक्यास्ताः परिरक्षितुम् ॥१०॥
अर्थस्य संग्रहे चैनां व्यये चैव नियोजयेत् ।
शौचे धर्मेऽन्नपक्त्यां च पारिणाह्यस्य चेक्षणे ॥११॥
अरक्षिता गृहे रुद्धाः पुरुषैराप्तकारिभिः ।
आत्मानमात्मना यास्तु रक्षेयुस्ताः सुरक्षिताः ॥१२॥
पानं दुर्जनसंसर्गः पत्या च विरहोऽटनम् ।
स्वप्नोऽन्यगेहवासश्च नारीसंदूषणानि षट् ॥१३॥
नैता रूपं परीक्षन्ते नासां वयसि संस्थितिः ।
सुरूपं वा विरूपं वा पुमानित्येव भुञ्जते ॥१४॥

10. Placed after verse 12 in Bo; pādas c-d omitted in Be^1 wKt^1 [haplo]. Cited by *Lakṣ* 12.608; *Dev* 3.565; *Mādh* 3.323 — a) GMd^5 न किंचित्प्रेषिताः; TMd^4 शक्ताः — b) GMy स प्रसह्य प्ररिक्षितुं; NNg oOr MTr^6 °रक्षितं; Pu^2 Pu^4 °रक्षणे — c) Lo^1 oOr Pu^2 Pu^4 Wa एतैरुपायैर्योगैस्तु [oOr °र्योगस्तु]; TMd^4 युपायंयोगेरेतास्तु; wKt^3 एतैरुपाधि°; wKt^3 TMd^3 GMy sOx^1 NPu^1 Pu^4 sPu^6 Wa °योगैश्च — d) TMd^3 न शक्यास्युः परिक्षितुं; Ho Lo^1 शक्तास्ताः; *Dev* शक्तस्ताः; GMd^1 TMd^4 GMd^5 GMy Tr^1 MTr^5 शक्याः स्युः; BBe^2 NNg °रक्षितं; TMd^4 °रक्षिताः

11. Cited by *Lakṣ* 12.608; *Dev* 3.566; *Mādh* 3.323 — a) sOx^1 sPu^6 MTr^5 अर्थसंग्रहणे; GMy आयस्याहरणे; NPu^1 Pu^3 चैतां; Pu^2 Pu^4 चैमां; Pu^7 [*but cor*] चैव — b) Lo^4 [*Jolly* M] व्यये वा विनियोजयेत्; NNg चापि; Lo^1 चैनां — c) Pu^5 Pu^7 धर्म्ये; Be^1 GMd^5 Ox^2 धर्मे च पत्त्यां; Hy धर्मेनुपत्त्यां; Lo^1 धर्मेनपत्त्यां; La^1 धर्मेतुपंत्या — d) GMd^1 GMd^5 GMy Tr^1 MTr^6 *Dev* पारिणह्यस्य; Ho TMd^4 NNg [*Jolly* M] परिणाह्यस्य; BKt^5 Pu^7 [*Jolly* G] पारीणह्यस्य; Bo Hy Lo^1 परिणह्यस्य; BBe^2 परिणय्यस्य; [*Jolly* R N] *Nā Mādh* पारिणय्यस्य; wKt^3 पारिणाव्यस्य; Tr^2 परिणस्य; Pu^3 Pu^4 *Nā* [pāṭha] पारिणाहस्य; Lo^4 पराणाद्यस्य; NKt^4 पारिणह्य; TMd^3 वारिणान्यस्य; Bo sOx^1 sPu^6 चेक्षते; wKt^3 चेतणे; Be^1 Hy Lo^1 oOr Pu^2 Pu^4 Pu^8 Tr^2 *Ku Jha KSS Dave* वेक्षणे; NPu^1 वीक्षणे; GMy Ox^2 *Mādh* रक्षणे; Pu^7 रक्षणे *mc sh to* वेक्षणे; TMd^4 भक्षणे

12. Cited by *Lakṣ* 12.608; pādas a-b cited by *Dev* 3.567, 745 and pādas c-d by *Dev* 3.566 — a) Jo^1 अरक्षितो; La^1 सुरक्षिता; GMd^1 गृहै; GMy गृह; NNg Tr^1 ग्रहे; GMd^1 Pu^5 Pu^7 रुद्धा; GMy रुद्धां; La^1 गुप्ताः — b) Ho पौरुषै°; Jo^2 Tj^1 पुरुषैश्चाप्त°; NKt^4 पुरुषैः स्वाप्त°; Bo °हारिभिः — c) GMy यस्तु; TMd^4 Tr^1 या तु — c-d) MTr^6 आत्मानं यस्तु रक्षेयुः रक्षेयुस्ताः सुरक्षिताः — d) GMd^1 TMd^4 GMd^5 रक्षेत्सा स्यात्सुरक्षिता

13. Cited by *Viś* 1.83; *Apa* 108; *Lakṣ* 12.622; *Dev* 3.567 — a) Tr^2 पनं; TMd^3 पातं; sOx^1 sPu^6 °सर्गाः; GMd^1 TMd^4 MTr^6 °सर्गं — b) GMd^5 स्वपत्या विरहोटनं; Be^1 सत्याच्च; *Apa* [vl] विरहे; Lo^2 विरहाटनं; TMd^3 वरिहोगतं; TMd^4 विरवद्धनं; wKt^1 °टना — c) La^1 स्वप्नमन्यगृहे वासो; NPu^1 सुप्तो; Pu^4 स्पान्यो; Be^1 Ho TMd^3 GMd^5 GMy Tr^1 *Apa Dev* °गेहे; sOx^1 sPu^6 °गृह°; BKt^5 °गेहेनवासश्च; Lo^4 °वाग्रश्च — d) Be^1 BBe^2 Bo Ho Hy wKt^1 La^1 TMd^3 oOr NPu^1 Pu^5 Pu^7 Pu^8 Tr^1 Tr^2 MTr^6 Wa [*Jolly* G] *Rc Dev* नारीणां दूषणानि; sOx^1 sPu^6 स्त्रीणां वै दूषणानि; MTr^3 °दूषणादि

14. Omitted in Jm. Cited by *Lakṣ* 12.604; *Dev* 3.563 — a) Lo^4 नैनां; Bo रूपं रक्षिते; La^1 sOx^1 sPu^6 परीक्ष्यन्ते; TMd^3 प्रतीक्षन्ते — b) La^1 NPu^1 तासां; Ho नासा; sOx^1 sPu^6 नाशौ; BKt^5 Lo^4 संस्थितः; GMd^1 TMd^4 संशयः; BBe^2 Jo^2 La^1 Lo^3 Tj^1 [*Jolly* R] *Lakṣ* निश्चयः — c) NKt^4 La^1 GMd^1 TMd^3 TMd^4 GMd^5 Tr^1 MTr^5 *Lakṣ* विरूपं रूपवन्तं वा; GMy [*Jolly* Nd] रूपवन्तमरूपं वा; MTr^4 MTr^6 रूपवन्तं विरूपं वा; BBe^2 Lo^4 स्वरूपं; Ho sOx^1 sPu^6 वा कुरूपं वा [supported by *Go* and *Ku*] — d)

पौंश्चल्याच्चालचित्त्याच्च नैःस्नेह्याच्च स्वभावतः ।
रक्षिता यत्नतोऽपीह भर्तृष्वेता विकुर्वते ॥१५॥
एवं स्वभावं ज्ञात्वासां प्रजापतिनिसर्गजम् ।
परमं यत्नमातिष्ठेत् पुरुषो रक्षणं प्रति ॥१६॥
शय्यासनमलंकारं कामं क्रोधमनार्यताम् ।
द्रोहभावं कुचर्यां च स्त्रीभ्यो मनुरकल्पयत् ॥१७॥
नास्ति स्त्रीणां क्रिया मन्त्रैरिति धर्मो व्यवस्थितः ।
निरिन्द्रिया ह्यमन्त्राश्च स्त्रियोऽनृतमिति स्थितिः ॥१८॥
तथा च श्रुतयो बह्वचो निगीता निगमेष्वपि ।
स्वालक्षण्यपरीक्षार्थं तासां च शृणुताकृतिम्* ॥१९॥

BKt[5] भुञ्जिते; Hy भुजते

Additional verses in La[1]:

यास्तु शश्वत् बहुमता रक्षन्ते दयितौ स्त्रियः ।
अपि ताः संप्रयुज्यन्ते कुब्जान्धजडमानवैः ॥
अनर्थित्वान्मनुष्याणां भयात्परिजनस्य च ।
मर्यादायाममर्यादाः स्त्रियस्तिष्ठन्ति भर्तृषु ॥

15. Omitted in Jm. Cited by *Lakṣ* 12.604; *Dev* 3.563 — a) Tj[1] पूंश्चल्यश्चलचित्ताश्च; Ho पौंश्चाल्या°; Hy wKt[3] पौशल्या°; Be[1] NPu[1] Pu[5] Pu[7] पुंश्चल्या°; Lo[3] पौंश्चल्यश्चा°; MTr[6] °च्चलचित्त्याच्च; Lo[1] Ox[2] Pu[3] °च्चलचित्याच्च; Lo[4] Tr[2] °च्चलचैत्याच्च; Be[1] °च्चालचिन्त्याच्च; wKt[1] BKt[5] NPu[1] °च्चाल-चित्ताच्च; sOx[1] sPu[6] °च्चालविद्याच्च; GMy °च्चालतीत्याश्च; Pu[2] °च्चालवत्याच्च; BBe[2] °च्चालयित्वाच्च; Hy Jo[1] Jo[2] Kt[2] Lo[3] GMd[1] TMd[4] MTr[3] MTr[4] [*Jolly* R] *Mandlik Jha KSS Dave* °च्चलचित्ताच्च; Tj[2] °च्चल्यचित्ताच्च; Bo °च्चलवित्ताच्च; Pu[5] Pu[7] [*Jolly* G Me] *Me Go Rn Dev Lakṣ Jolly* °च्चल-चित्तत्वान्नैःस्ने° — b) GMd[5] स्नेहाच्चैव स्वभावतः; BBe[2] नैसृज्याच्च; Lo[3] Tj[1] निस्नेहाश्च; La[1] नैम्लेपाच्च; Be[1] Ho TMd[3] °स्नेहाच्च; GMy NPu[1] °स्नैह्याश्च; BKt[5] °स्नेह्याश्च; Tj[1] स्वभावता — c) Pu[2] Pu[4] रक्षिताप्यन्नतो; Tj[1] यत्नता; GMy *om* °पीह — d) Jo[2] भर्तृष्वेव; La[1] °ष्वेतावकुर्वते; TMd[4] °ष्वेतानिकुर्वते; Pu[5] Pu[7] [*but cor*] विकुर्वति

16. Omitted in Jm. Cited by *Lakṣ* 12.605; *Dev* 3.563 — a) NKt[4] तु भावं; La[1] प्रभावान्; GMy दृष्ट्वासां — b) TMd[4] °विसर्गजं; wKt[1] °सर्गजां; La[1] °सर्गजान्; Wa °सर्गाजं; Bo °सर्जनं — c) GMd[5] परं प्रयत्नमातिष्ठेत् — d) wKt[1] रमणीं प्रति

17. Omitted in Jm GMy. Cited by *Lakṣ* 12.604; *Dev* 3.563 — a) La[1] शय्याशन° — b) GMd[1] TMd[4] GMd[5] काम; GMd[1] TMd[4] °मनार्यता; NKt[4] °मनार्यत; Lo[1] °मनार्यवं; Tj[2] °मनार्य्यवं; Be[1] Bo Ho Hy Jo[1] Kt[2] BKt[5] Lo[4] NNg MTr[3] [*Jolly* M Ku] *Mandlik KSS Dave* °मनार्जवं; sOx[1] sPu[6] Tr[2] °मनार्जतां — c) Wa द्रोहि°; La[1] कुचर्याश्च; GMd[1] वर्णचर्यां स्त्री° — d) NPu[1] Pu[2] स्त्रीणां; Wa °कल्पयेत्

18. Omitted in Jm; pādas c-d omitted in BKt[5] TMd[4] [haplo]. Cited by *Lakṣ* 12.605 — a) BKt[5] स्त्रियाणां; Pu[5] Pu[7] क्रियां; wKt[3] यन्त्रै°; TMd[4] तन्त्रै°; MTr[4] मात्रै° — a-b) GMy क्रिया काचित्क्रिया-धर्मो — b) TMd[4] धर्म; wKt[3] धर्मा; Jo[1] Kt[2] BKt[5] GMd[5] Tr[2] MTr[4] MTr[5] *Mandlik Jha KSS Dave* धर्मे; BKt[5] TMd[3] TMd[4] GMd[5] *Mandlik Jha KSS Dave* व्यवस्थितिः; Ho °स्थितं — c) NKt[4] °न्द्रियाश्चामन्त्रा-श्च; Tj[1] हि मन्त्राश्च; GMd[1] ह्यात्मजाश्च — d) Tr[2] स्त्रिये; Pu[2] Pu[4] °वृत्तमिति; Lo[4] °वृत्तं व्यस्थिताः; Bo स्थितः

19.* Cited by *Lakṣ* 12.605 — a) Lo[1] तथा च श्रुतिवाक्यानि [श्रुतयो *cor to* श्रुति]; Bo Jo[2] Lo[3]

यन्मे माता प्रलुलुभे विचरन्त्यपतिव्रता ।
तन्मे रेतः पिता वृङ्क्तामित्यस्यैतन्निदर्शनम् ॥२०॥
ध्यायत्यनिष्टं यत्किंचित् पाणिग्राहस्य चेतसा ।
तस्यैष व्यभिचारस्य निह्नवः सम्यगुच्यते ॥२१॥
यादृग्गुणेन भर्त्रा स्त्री संयुज्येत यथाविधि ।
तादृग्गुणा सा भवति समुद्रेणेव निम्नगा ॥२२॥
अक्षमाला वसिष्ठेन संयुक्ताधमयोनिजा ।
शार्ङ्गी च मन्दपालेन जगामाभ्यर्हणीयताम् ॥२३॥

Lo[4] GMd[1] Tj[1] *Rn* यथा; NNg तस्याश्च; TMd[3] तथा विश्रुतयो; BBe[2] *Lakṣ* हि; La[1] Pu[2] Pu[3] Pu[4] बाह्वयो; Be[1] बाह्यो; wKt[1] सन्यो — b) Lo[1] गीतानि च ममैष्वपि; Be[1] La[1] GMd[1] TMd[3] GMd[5] GMy Tr[1] MTr[4] MTr[5] MTr[6] [*Jolly* Nd Gr]*Nd* गदिता; TMd[4] कथिता; *Me* [pāṭha] निगदा [explained as मन्त्रविशेषाः] — c) Be[1] Jo[2] Lo[4] स्वल°; Pu[5] Pu[7] [*but cor*] स्वल्पल°; TMd[4] तं लक्षण्यं; MTr[6] °लाक्षण्य°; Be[1] Ho BKt[5] La[1] Lo[4] °लक्षण°; wKt[1] °रक्षण°; wKt[3] BKt[5] °परीतार्थं; GMd[1] °क्षार्थ — d) GMy तासां च शृण्वतां गतिं; TMd[3] तस्यां; TMd[4] श्रुणुयताकृतिः; Hy Jo[1] Jo[2] wKt[1] La[1] Lo[2] Lo[4] NNg oOr Pu[5] Pu[7] Wa [*Jolly* M G N Nd] *Nā Lakṣ Jolly* तासां शृणुत निष्कृतिं [wKt[1] निष्कृतीं; Hy निष्कृतः; Jo[1] निष्कृतिः]; Be[1] BBe[2] Bo Ho Jm Kt[2] wKt[3] NKt[4] BKt[5] Lo[1] Lo[3] sOx[1] Ox[2] NPu[1] Pu[2] Pu[3] Pu[4] sPu[6] Pu[8] Tj[1] Tj[2] Tr[2] MTr[3] [*Jolly* R Ku] *Ku Rc Mr Mandlik Jha KSS Dave* तासां शृणुत निष्कृतीः [Lo[1] शृण्वन्ति; BKt[5] NPu[1] निःकृती; Pu[2] Tr[2] निर्निती:]

20. Omitted in GMy; verses 20 and 21 transposed in [*Jolly* N]. Cited by *Lakṣ* 12.605 — a) sOx[1] sPu[6] तन्मे; wKt[3] यत्ने; La[1] यत्नेन माता; La[1] Pu[2] Pu[4] प्रलुभे; Be[1] Tr[1] [*but cor*] प्रलुलोभे; GMd[1] TMd[3] TMd[4] GMd[5] प्रलुलोभ; Tr[2] प्रालुलभे; wKt[1] प्रलुनुते; MTr[4] ललुलोभ; MTr[6] च लुलोभ— b) GMd[1] Tr[1] MTr[4] MTr[6] विचरन्त्यननुव्रता; TMd[4] विचरत्यननुव्रता; TMd[3] यचरत्यननुव्रता; GMd[5] चरत्यननुव्रता; Be[1] विचरत्य° — c) Be[1] यन्मे [*but mc*]; Tr[2] रेता; Bo [*Jolly* M[1–3–8–9]] वृक्तामि°; NPu[1] वृंत्त्यमि°; wKt[1] वृत्यामि°; Pu[5] Pu[7] पंक्तामि°; La[1] युक्तामि° — d) Lo[1] वृङ्क्त इत्येतच्च निदर्शनं; Be[1] °त्यस्यैव निदर्शनं; GMd[5] °तन्निर्दिशति

21. Cited by *Lakṣ* 12.605 — a) TMd[3] GMy किंचिद्ध्यायत्यनिष्टं यत्; Jo[2] Lo[3] Tj[1] Tr[1] [*mc to*] [*Jolly* R]यच्च ध्यायत्यनिष्ट स्त्री [Jo[2] यत्र]; La[1] यत्किंदिद्ध्यात्यनित्यं स्त्री; Be[1] Ho Pu[4] Pu[8] ध्यायन्त्य°; GMd[1] Tr[2] ध्यायन्तिनिष्टं; wKt[3] °त्यनित्यं; Tr[2] यत्किंच; GMd[1] *om* यत्किं ... चेतसा — b) Bo TMd[4] °ग्रहस्य; GMy °ग्राह्यस्य चेतसि; TMd[4] चेतना — c) GMy Wa तस्यैषा; BBe[2] BKt[5] Lo[3] Pu[2] Tj[2] तस्यैव; TMd[4] तस्मै च; Ho व्यवहारस्य — d) La[1] निह्नुवः; NNg निह्नयः; TMd[4] नह्नतः; wKt[3] चिह्नवः; wKt[1] निक्रयः

22. Cited by *Lakṣ* 12.609; *Dev* 3.567— a) sOx[1] sPu[6] MTr[6] यादृग्गुणे; Be[1] भर्त्ता; TMd[3] भर्ता; TMd[4] नर्ता — b) GMd[1] संयुज्येते; NNg तथाविधि; Lo[4] °विधा — c) TMd[4] यादृग्गुणां संभवति; BBe[2] यादृग्गुणा; Pu[4] तावग्गुणा — d) TMd[4] Pu[5] Pu[7] सामु°; Be[1] Tr[1] Tr[2] समुद्रेणैव; oOr NPu[1] Pu[4] Pu[7] निम्नगाः

23. Cited by *Lakṣ* 12.609 — a) GMd[1] क्षमालापविनिष्ठेना; wKt[1] अरक्षमा; TMd[3] अरुन्धती; GMd[5] oOr Tr[2] Wa वशि°; Pu[4] वासि°; BBe[2] wKt[1] Pu[5] Pu[7] विशिष्ठेन — b) Tj[2] *om* सं°; Bo La[1] GMd[1] GMd[5] Pu[2] Pu[4] MTr[3] संयुक्ताधर्मयोनिजा [Pu[2] Pu[4] संयुक्तो]; TMd[3] संयुक्तावरयोनिजा; Ho °योनिजाः — c) Ho वह्लामन्दश्चपालेन; sOx[1] sPu[6] Tr[2] शार्ङ्गं च; Lo[2] शाङ्गी च; Ox[2] शार्ङ्गीव; TMd[3] शार्बे च; Lo[4] शाडी च; GMd[1] शान्तो च; BBe[2] *om* च; Hy Jm Jo[1] wKt[1] Kt[2] wKt[3] Lo[3] Pu[3] Tj[2] MTr[3] *Lakṣ Mandlik KSS Jha Dave* शारङ्गी मन्द°; Jo[2] Tj[1] *Nā Rn* सारङ्गी मन्द° — d) Tr[1] जगाम ह्यर्हणी°; NPu[1] Pu[2] Pu[4] °मात्यर्ह°; Tj[1] °णीयतं; Hy °णीतां

एताश्चान्याश्च लोकेऽस्मिन्नवकृष्टप्रसूतयः ।
उत्कर्षं योषितः प्राप्ताः स्वैः स्वैर्भर्तृगुणैः शुभैः ॥२४॥
एषोदिता लोकयात्रा नित्यं स्त्रीपुंसयोः शुभा ।
प्रेत्येह च सुखोदर्कान् प्रजाधर्मान्निबोधत ॥२५॥
प्रजनार्थं महाभागाः पूजार्हा गृहदीप्तयः ।
स्त्रियः श्रियश्च गेहेषु न विशेषोऽस्ति कश्चन ॥२६॥
उत्पादनमपत्यस्य जातस्य परिपालनम् ।
प्रत्यहं लोकयात्रायाः प्रत्यक्षं स्त्री निबन्धनम् ॥२७॥
अपत्यं धर्मकार्याणि शुश्रूषा रतिरुत्तमा ।
दाराधीनस्तथा स्वर्गः पितॄणामात्मनश्च ह ॥२८॥
पतिं या नाभिचरति मनोवाग्देहसंयता ।
सा भर्तृलोकानाप्नोति सद्भिः साध्वीति चोच्यते ॥२९॥

24.* Cited by *Lakṣ* 12.609 — a) Ho एतांश्चा° — b) Bo Hy Jm Jo^1 Jo^2 Kt^2 Lo^2 Lo^3 GMd^1 GMd^5 GMy Tj^1 Tj^2 Tr^1 MTr^3 MTr^4 MTr^5 *Rc Lakṣ Mandlik Jolly KSS Dave* °न्नपकृष्ट°; La^1 °न्नप्रकृष्ट°; TMd^4 °न्नतकृष्ट°; wKt^1 °न्नवदृष्टि°; GMd^1 °कृष्टाः; MTr^6 °सूतकः — c) Ho उत्कर्ष; Tr^1 उत्कृष्टं; GMd^1 उत्कृष्ट; *Lakṣ* योषिताश्चाप्ताः; oOr प्राप्तां — d) Lo^4 Pu^5 Pu^7 [*Jolly* G] तैस्तैर्भर्तृ°; Lo^4 स्वैर्भर्तुर्गुणैः; NKt^4 स्वैर्भर्त्यगुणैः; Bo Ho °गणैः; Tr^2 शुभा

25. a) Jo^2 Tj^1 एषोचिता; Lo^4 °यात्राभिद्ये — b) wKt^1 नित्य; Pu^4 नित्यां; wKt^1 Kt^2 wKt^3 NPu^1 sPu^6 MTr^3 शुभाः; Pu^5 Pu^7 शुभः; NNg सदा — c) Lo^4 GMd^1 GMy Pu^7 प्रत्येह; Lo^1 प्रेतेह; La^1 Lo^3 sOx^1 Ox^2 sPu^6 Tj^1 प्रेत्य चेह; Ho सुखोत्कर्षान्; wKt^1 °दर्कात्; Lo^4 °दर्का; La^1 TMd^4 °दर्कं — d) Lo^2 प्रजा-न्ध°; La^1 °धर्मं निबो°; Jo^1 Wa °बोधते

26. Cited by *Lakṣ* 12.609; *Dev* 3.570 — a) Ho La^1 TMd^4 NNg Pu^2 Pu^4 प्रजानार्थं; *Lakṣ* प्रजनार्था; GMd^1 प्रजानर्था; La^1 TMd^3 GMy MTr^6 प्रजानार्था; Lo^4 पूजनार्थं; Bo Lo^4 °भाग — b) TMd^3 पूजार्ह; Lo^2 GMy पूजार्था; BKt^5 NPu^1 Pu^2 Pu^4 गृहमेधिनः — c) [*Jolly* R] श्रियः स्त्रियश्च; Tj^2 *om* स्त्रियः; Lo^1 स्त्रियः स्त्रियाश्च; La^1 स्त्रियः स्त्रियश्च; Pu^2 Pu^4 श्रियाः स्वगेहेषु; BKt^5 गेहेस्मिन् — d) Be^1 NNg oOr NPu^1 Pu^2 Pu^4 Wa विशेषो नास्ति कश्चन; GMd^5 Tj^1 किंचन

27. Cited by *Lakṣ* 12.609 — a) TMd^3 उत्पातन° — b) Tr^2 पातस्य; GMd^1 [*Jolly* Nd] परिरक्षणं — c) sOx^1 sPu^6 प्रत्ययं; NKt^4 Lo^2 Lo^4 NNg MTr^6 [*Jolly* M N] *Me Nā* [pāṭha] *Jolly Jha* प्रत्यर्थं; MTr^5 प्रत्यर्धं; BKt^5 NNg [*cor to sh*] NPu^1 Pu^5 Pu^7 Tr^2 Wa [*Jolly* G] *Nā Go Rc* प्रीत्यर्थं; MTr^4 वृत्त्यर्थं; GMd^1 प्रत्यक्षं; GMd^5 °यात्राय; MTr^6 °यात्रा च — d) Be^1 NNg Pu^5 Pu^7 प्रत्यहं; GMd^1 प्रेक्षणं; Lo^4 निबन्ध-नात्

28. Cited by *Lakṣ* 12.609 — a) wKt^1 TMd^3 sOx^1 sPu^6 अपत्य; oOr धर्मकर्माणि; TMd^3 कर्मकार्याणि — b) Bo Pu^5 Pu^7 °रुत्तमाः; GMd^1 °रुत्तरा — c) GMd^5 °धीनास्तथा; wKt^3 °धीनं तथा; GMd^1 °नस्तदा स्वर्ग्यः; Wa स्वर्गाः; Bo सर्जः — d) Pu^5 Pu^7 *Go* [*Jolly* G] °त्मनस्सदा; GMd^1 TMd^3 GMd^5 GMy Tr^1 MTr^4 MTr^6 हि; Be^1 वै; Ho यः

29. [= 5.165] Pāda-d omitted in Bo Pu^2 Pu^4 and *ma* in Lo^4. Cited by *Dev* 3.567 — a) NNg प्रत्यहं या नाभिचर; Ho पतिं न यातिचरति; Tr^2 पतिं या न व्यभिचरति; Pu^8 पतिं जाय नाभिचरति; NKt^4 Lo^4 GMd^1 TMd^3 GMd^5 GMy Tr^1 MTr^4 MTr^6 *Dev* नातिचरति — b) Tr^2 मनोकायकर्मभिः; Be^1 Bo Ho NKt^4 BKt^5 Lo^1 Lo^2 Lo^4 TMd^4 NNg oOr Pu^2 Pu^5 Pu^7 Pu^8 [*Jolly* M N] *Dev* °वाक्कायसंयता;

व्यभिचारात्तु भर्तुः स्त्री लोके प्राप्नोति निन्द्यताम् ।
सृगालयोनिं चाप्नोति पापरोगैश्च पीड्यते ॥३०॥
पुत्रं प्रत्युदितं सद्भिः पूर्वजैश्च महर्षिभिः ।
विश्वजन्यमिमं पुण्यमुपन्यासं निबोधत ॥३१॥
भर्तुः पुत्रं विजानन्ति श्रुतिद्वैधं तु कर्तरि* ।
आहुरुत्पादकं केचिदपरे क्षेत्रिणं विदुः ॥३२॥
क्षेत्रभूता स्मृता नारी बीजभूतः स्मृतः पुमान् ।
क्षेत्रबीजसमायोगात् संभवः सर्वदेहिनाम् ॥३३॥
विशिष्टं कुत्रचिद्बीजं स्त्रीयोनिस्त्वेव कुत्रचित् ।
उभयं तु समं यत्र सा प्रसूतिः प्रशस्यते ॥३४॥
बीजस्य चैव योन्याश्च बीजमुत्कृष्टमुच्यते ।
सर्वभूतप्रसूतिर्हि बीजलक्षणलक्षिता ॥३५॥
यादृशं तूप्यते बीजं क्षेत्रे कालोपपादिते ।

Ox^2 Pu^3 °वाक्कायकर्मभिः; MTr^4 MTr^6 °संयुता; Pu^5 Pu^7 [*Jolly* G] °संवृता; Bo °संमिता; Wa °संभवा — c) Bo sOx^1 sPu^6 स; Jo^2 La^1 Lo^4 NPu^1 Pu^2 Pu^4 Tj^1 Wa °लोकमाप्नोति; Lo^1 °लोकान्प्राप्नोति — d) Pu^7 सा सुसाध्वीति; La^1 साध्वीव सोच्यते

30. Verses 30 and 31 transposed in Ho. Omitted in Bo BKt^5 Pu^2 Pu^4; pādas a-b *ma* in Lo^4. Cited by *Lakṣ* 12.630; *Dev* 3.568 — a) TMd^4 °चाराश्च; TMd^3 भर्तृ — b) Ho Lo^4 लोकान्नाप्नोति निन्दितान्; GMd^1 लोके भवति निन्दिता; Be^1 लोकं; NPu^1 लोकः; La^1 प्राप्नोत्यनिन्दितां; Be^1 निन्दितं — c) BBe^2 Ho Hy Jm Jo^2 wKt^1 wKt^3 NKt^4 Lo^1 Lo^2 Lo^4 NNg oOr Ox^2 Pu^5 Pu^7 Pu^8 Tj^2 Tr^2 MTr^4 Wa *Lakṣ Mandlik Jha KSS Dave* शृगाल°; GMy °योनिश्चाप्नोति; Be^1 Lo^1 Lo^4 TMd^3 TMd^4 GMd^5 oOr sOx^1 Ox^2 sPu^6 Tr^2 *Lakṣ Dev* प्राप्नोति; La^1 चाभ्येति — d) Pu^5 Pu^7 पापैश्च परिपीड्यते; BBe^2 विद्यते

31. a) Be^1 पत्युदितं — b) Ho सर्वज्ञैश्च — c) wKt^3 °जन्यामिमं; Be^1 °जन्यममुं; Ho Lo^4 TMd^4 GMd^5 MTr^6 °जन्यमिदं; TMd^4 पुण्यामुप° — d) TMd^3 °पन्यायं; Hy निबोधता

32.* a) BKt^5 तु जानन्ति — b) Tj^2 च; Be^1 BBe^2 Bo Ho Hy Jm Jo^1 Jo^2 wKt^1 Kt^2 wKt^3 La^1 Lo^1 Lo^2 Lo^3 NNg sOx^1 Ox^2 NPu^1 Pu^2 Pu^3 Pu^4 Pu^5 sPu^6 [*cor to sh*] Pu^7 Pu^8 Tj^1 Tj^2 MTr^3 [*Jolly* G Ku] *Ku Nd Mr Mandlik KSS Dave* भर्तरि — c) TMd^4 आहुः पत्यातकं; TMd^4 oOr किंचिदपरे — d) BKt^5 °परं; GMd^5 °परो; NNg क्षेत्रिणां; oOr क्षत्रिणं; Tr^2 क्षणिणं; Ho विदः

33. Pādas a-b omitted in TMd^4 — a) Ho तथा नारी — b) Pu^2 Pu^4 पुमान्स्मृतः — d) Jo^2 °देहिनः

34. a) GMd^1 TMd^4 MTr^5 MTr^6 विशिष्टं तु क्वचिद्बीजं — b) Ho wKt^1 wKt^3 क्वचिद्योनिर्गरीयसी; TMd^4 MTr^4 MTr^6 क्वचित्स्त्रीयोनिरेव तु; GMd^1 क्वचित्स्त्रीयोनि कुत्रचित्; BBe^2 Bo BCa Jo^2 BKt^5 Lo^1 Lo^3 oOr sOx^1 Ox^2 Pu^4 sPu^6 Pu^8 Tj^1 Tj^2 Tr^1 Wa °योनिश्चैव; Lo^4 °योनिष्वेव; La^1 °योनिश्च कुत्र°; GMd^5 °योनिश्चैव तु क्वचित् — c) GMy तत्समं; TMd^4 Tr^2 समा — d) Ho Lo^4 प्रसूतिः सा; GMd^1 MTr^5 विशिष्यते

35. Omitted in Tr^2; pādas a-b *ma* in Lo^4. Cited by *Jmv* 113.3; *Lakṣ* 12.737 — a) oOr बीजश्च; BBe^2 बीजस्यैव तु; *Jmv* चैवं; Wa योनेश्च — c) NKt^4 सर्वं; Jm NKt^4 °भूतिप्रसू°; GMd^1 °प्रभृतिर्हि — d) NKt^4 °लक्षिताः

तादृग्रोहति तत्तस्मिन् बीजं स्वैर्व्यञ्जितं गुणैः ॥३६॥
इयं भूमिर्हि भूतानां शाश्वती योनिरुच्यते ।
न च योनिगुणान्कांश्चिद् बीजं पुष्यति पुष्टिषु ॥३७॥
भूमावप्येककेदारे कालोप्तानि कृषीवलैः ।
नानारूपाणि जायन्ते बीजानीह स्वभावतः ॥३८॥
व्रीहयः शालयो मुद्गास्तिला माषास्तथा यवाः ।
यथाबीजं प्ररोहन्ति लशुनानीक्षवस्तथा ॥३९॥
अन्यदुप्तं जातमन्यदित्येतन्नोपपद्यते ।
उप्यते यद्धि यद्बीजं तत्तदेव प्ररोहति ॥४०॥
तत्प्राज्ञेन विनीतेन ज्ञानविज्ञानवेदिना ।
आयुष्कामेन वप्तव्यं न जातु परयोषिति ॥४१॥
अत्र गाथा वायुगीताः कीर्तयन्ति पुराविदः ।
यथा बीजं न वप्तव्यं पुंसा परपरिग्रहे ॥४२॥

36. Cited by *Lakṣ* 12.737 — a) Lo[4] [*Jolly* M[4–5]] यादृशमुप्यते; Ho तूर्प्यते; NKt[4] तप्यते; BBe[2] Pu[2] Pu[4] तृप्यते; Pu[5] Pu[7] [*Jolly* G] वाप्यते; BKt[5] Ox[2] रूप्यते — b) NNg कालौपपादिकं; TMd[4] GMy *Lakṣ* °पादितं; Lo[2] °पाद्यते; Tr[2] °पद्यते — c) GMy तादृशोर्हन्ति; Wa °ग्रोहन्ति; Pu[5] Pu[7] [*Jolly* G] तत्क्षिप्रं — d) Lo[1] बीजमुत्कृष्टमुच्यते; TMd[3] बीज; Be[1] स्वैर्व्याजितं; GMd[1] स्वव्यञ्जितं; Bo स्वैर्योजितं; GMy स्वैर्यन्त्रितं; TMd[3] स्वैर्वर्णितं; sOx[1] sPu[6] स्वैर्विजितं; wKt[1] स्वैर्वाञ्चतं गनैः; La[1] Lo[3] Pu[5] Pu[7] Tj[1] [*Jolly* G] स्वैर्व्यञ्जितैर्गुणैः

37. Pādas a-b omitted in Lo[1] — a) GMd[5] जन्मभूमिर्हि; Tr[2] *om* भूमिर्हि — c) Tj[1] योनिर्गुणा°; Bo Lo[1] GMd[1] TMd[3] GMd[5] MTr[4] MTr[6] भूमिगुणा°; GMy °गुणं किंचिद्; TMd[3] °गुणान्किंचिद्; Tr[2] °गुणान्कस्मिन् — d) MTr[6] पुष्यन्ति; GMd[1] पुष्टिषु पुष्यति; La[1] पुष्यति पादपः; sOx[1] sPu[6] Pu[8] पुष्पिषु

38. a) Lo[4] भूमावेषैककेदारे; BKt[5] °केदाने — b) Be[1] wKt[1] कालोप्राणि; Jo[2] Tj[1] Tr[1] [*cor to*] सहोप्तानि; TMd[3] नालोप्तानि; Lo[3] वहोमानि; NNg Pu[5] Pu[7] °बलैः; BKt[5] °विशैः — d) Wa स्वभावजः

39. a) BKt[5] व्रीहयः स्वभावयोः मुग्दास्तिला; Tj[1] व्रीहियः; Wa व्रीहयो; GMd[1] शालवो — a-b) GMy [*Jolly* Nd] शालयो वापि तिलमाषयवास्तथा; TMd[3] शालयो माषास्तिला मुद्गा तथा यवाः — b) GMd[5] मुद्गा यवा माषास्तिलास्तथा; MTr[4] MTr[6] मुद्गा यवा माषास्तथा तिलाः; TMd[4] Tr[1] मुद्गा यवमाषास्तिलास्तथा; La[1] मुद्गा यवा माखास्तिलास्तथा; BCa Jo[2] wKt[1] Lo[3] GMd[1] TMd[3] Tj[1] माषा यवास्तथा — c) sOx[1] sPu[6] MTr[6] तथा°; Pu[5] Pu[7] [*Jolly* G] प्ररोहन्ते; Tr[2] प्ररोहं च

40. a) TMd[3] TMd[4] GMd[5] GMy MTr[6] अन्यदुप्तमन्यज्जातमित्ये°; NNg अन्यदुप्तां; wKt[1] अन्यसूप्तं; Kt[2] अन्यगुप्तं — b) Bo °न्यदुप्ते तन्नोप°; Tr[1] °दित्येवं नोप° — c) wKt[3] oOr Tr[1] [*cor to sh*] यद्यदेवोप्यते बीजं; MTr[6] उप्येत; Pu[5] Pu[7] यद्धि बीजं तु; Tj[1] यदि; Pu[3] यत्र; TMd[3] TMd[4] तद्बीजं — d) TMd[3] तद्वदेव

41. Cited by *Lakṣ* 12.737 — a) BKt[5] तत्प्रज्ञेन; TMd[4] यत्प्राज्ञेन; GMy तत्प्राज्ञेति; Lo[1] तत्प्रागेव; Ho विधीतेन — b) GMd[5] धर्मार्थज्ञानवेदिना; Lo[2] *om* विज्ञान; Lo[4] °विज्ञानचेतसा; GMy °विज्ञानशालिना; Pu[2] Pu[4] °विज्ञानकोविदा — c) GMd[1] वप्तव्या; GMd[5] वाप्तव्यं; Bo Lo[2] TMd[4] वक्तव्यं — d) Lo[1] oOr Pu[3] यातु; Bo °योषिता

42. a) Be[1] BBe[2] GMd[1] GMd[5] oOr sOx[1] NPu[1] Pu[2] Pu[4] sPu[6] Tr[1] MTr[5] MTr[6] Wa गाथां; BKt[5] वाथा; La[1] गव्यां पुरागीतां; Pu[8] गायुगीता; MTr[5] यमोद्गीतां; GMd[1] यमोन्नीतां; Be[1] BBe[2] oOr sOx[1] NPu[1]

नश्यतीषुर्यथा क्षिप्तः खे विद्धमनुविध्यतः ।
तथा नश्यति वै क्षिप्तं बीजं परपरिग्रहे ।४३॥
पृथोरपीमां पृथिवीं भार्यां पूर्वविदो विदुः ।
स्थाणुच्छेदस्य केदारमाहुः शल्यवतो मृगम् ॥४४॥
एतावानेव पुरुषो यज्जायात्मा प्रजेति ह ।
विप्राः प्राहुस्तथा चैतद्यो भर्ता सा स्मृताङ्गना ॥४५॥
न निष्क्रयविसर्गाभ्यां भर्तुर्भार्या विमुच्यते ।
एवं धर्मं विजानीमः प्राक्प्रजापतिनिर्मितम् ॥४६॥
सकृदंशो निपतति सकृत्कन्या प्रदीयते ।
सकृदाह ददानीति त्रीण्येतानि सकृत्सकृत् ॥४७॥

Pu² Pu⁴ sPu⁶ Tr¹ Tr² °गीतां; Lo¹ TMd³ Pu⁵ Pu⁷ °गीता; GMd⁵ °गतां — b) NPu¹ पुराविदुः — c) GMd⁵ Tr² वाप्तव्यं; TMd⁴ वक्तव्यं — d) La¹ Lo⁴ GMd⁵ GMy sOx¹ sPu⁶ [*Jolly* M⁴⁻⁵⁻⁹ R G Nd] *Jolly* पुंसां; wKt³ °ग्रहः; TMd⁴ °ग्रह

43.* Omitted in Be¹ BKt⁵ GMy [haplo]; versess 43 and 44 transposed in Wa — a) La¹ नश्यन्तीषु°; Lo¹ नश्यन्विदुर्यथा; oOr Wa क्षिप्तं; BBe² Ho Hy Jm Jo¹ Kt² NKt⁴ Lo² Lo³ GMd¹ TMd⁴ GMd⁵ Pu² Pu⁴ Tr¹ [*but cor sh*] MTr³ MTr⁴ MTr⁵ MTr⁶ [*Jolly* Ku Nd] *Nd Mandlik Jha KSS Dave* विद्धः; TMd³ विद्धं — b) BBe² खे; oOr यो विद्ध°; Lo⁴ वेध्यमनु — c) sOx¹ sPu⁶ नश्यन्ति; BBe² नश्यते; Lo⁴ GMd¹ TMd³ TMd⁴ GMd⁵ NNg Tr¹ [*Jolly* M] निक्षिप्तं; wKt¹ MTr³ [*Jolly* Go Ku] *Mandlik KSS Dave* क्षिप्रं — d) sPu⁶ परिपरिग्रहे

44. a) Tr² °रथीमां; wKt¹ °रुपामां; wKt³ °रपामां; Ho पृथिवी — b) Ho भार्या; GMd¹ adds at end: यथा बीजन्न वप्तव्यं — c) Lo¹ स्थाणुछन्दस्य — d) wKt¹ °माहुर्गन्यवतो; Pu² Pu⁴ °माहुराप्तवतो; Tj¹ शैलवतो

45. Cited by *Lakṣ* 12.738 — a) TMd³ GMd⁵ ऐतावद्देव; Lo³ एतामेव; TMd⁴ यातानेव; GMd¹ सृतावानेव; TMd⁴ पुरीषं — b) Be¹ यज्ञायात्मा प्रजायते; Tr² *om* यज्; TMd⁴ यज्ञानात्मा; NKt⁴ यक्रायात्मा; GMy [*Jolly* Nd] प्रजेह च; TMd³ GMd⁵ प्रजेदिह; Jo¹ हे; BBe² Bo Lo¹ oOr Pu³ Pu⁸ Tj² MTr⁶ *Lakṣ* च; Ho व — c) Be¹ Bo विप्रा; MTr⁶ विप्रान्; Lo¹ विप्रा ह्याहुस्तथा; TMd⁴ विप्रा आहुस्तथा; TMd³ प्राहांस्तथा; MTr⁴ प्रोचुस्तथा; oOr °स्तथाप्येतद्यो; wKt¹ °स्तथैवेतं यो; NPu¹ °स्तथैवैते भर्ता; Lo⁴ *Lakṣ* चैव यो — c-d) Lo¹ चैव सो — d) TMd³ चैतद्या; Ho wKt¹ Lo¹ GMd¹ GMd⁵ oOr MTr⁴ MTr⁶ साङ्गना स्मृता; TMd³ GMy सामृताङ्गना

46. Omitted in Pu⁵. Cited by *Lakṣ* 12.738 — a) Be¹ Tj¹ Tr¹ निष्क्रिय°; Tr² निक्रिय°; BBe² निष्क्रम°; Jo² Lo³ विक्रय°; MTr⁴ °निसर्गाभ्यां — b) NKt⁴ भर्ता भार्या; wKt¹ तत्तु भार्या; Lo³ Tj¹ Tr¹ [*mc to*] MTr⁶ वियुज्यते; Ho विविच्यते — c) NKt⁴ एतद्धर्मे प्रजानीमः; GMy एनं; BCa Hy BKt⁵ La¹ Lo⁴ Tj² *Bh* एतद्धर्मं; Ho विजानीयाः; La¹ विजानीयुः; Pu⁷ [*Jolly* G] विजानीत; Tr¹ [*Jolly* Gr] विजानीध्वं; Lo⁴ GMd¹ न जानीमः; Ox² NPu¹ Pu² Pu⁴ Tr² विजानीयात्; NNg विजानीतत् — d) Ho TMd⁴ प्रजापतिविनिर्मितं [*om* प्राक्]; Tr² प्रजापतिविनीवितं [*om* प्राक्]; Lo³ Tj¹ °निर्मितः; La¹ °निर्मिताः

47.* Omitted in Pu⁵; *ma* in Lo⁴. Cited by *Lakṣ* 2.56; *Dev* 1.218, 3.720; *Mādh* 1.490 — a) Kt² निपातति — b) Tr² सकृत्वकन्या; Hy प्रदीयेते — c) La¹ सकृज्जलपंति राजानस्; Lo¹ सकृद्दानं; Tj¹ सकृदाहुर्ददा°; Lo¹ Tr¹ ददातीति; GMy तदानीति; Jo² Kt² NNg [*cor to*] Ox² NPu¹ Pu² Pu⁴ sPu⁶ [*but cor*] Pu⁷ [*cor to*] MTr³ Wa [*Jolly* M¹⁻⁵⁻⁸⁻⁹ G R²] *Jolly Jha* ददामीति — d) Bo Ho Hy Jm Jo¹ Kt² NKt⁴ BKt⁵ Lo² NPu¹ Pu² Pu³ Pu⁸ Tj² Tr² MTr³ MTr⁵ [*Jolly* Ku] *Mandlik Jha KSS Dave* सतां

यथा गोऽश्वोष्ट्रदासीषु महिष्यजाविकासु च ।
नोत्पादकः प्रजाभागी तथैवान्याङ्गनास्वपि ॥४८॥
येऽक्षेत्रिणो बीजवन्तः परक्षेत्रप्रवापिणः ।
ते वै सस्यस्य जातस्य न लभन्ते फलं क्वचित् ॥४९॥
यद्यन्यगोषु वृषभो वत्सानां जनयेच्छतम् ।
गोमिनामेव ते वत्सा मोघं स्कन्दितमार्षभम् ॥५०॥
तथैवाक्षेत्रिणो बीजं परक्षेत्रप्रवापिणः ।
कुर्वन्ति क्षेत्रिणामर्थं न बीजी लभते फलम् ॥५१॥
फलं त्वनभिसंधाय क्षेत्रिणां बीजिनां तथा ।
प्रत्यक्षं क्षेत्रिणामर्थो बीजाद्योनिर्बलीयसी ॥५२॥

सकृत् [supported by *Bh Go Ku*]; Pu⁴ सतां सतां; NNg सकृत् *ma sh* सतां

48. Omitted in Pu⁵. Cited by *Lakṣ* 12.738; *Mādh* 2.37 — a) Tr² °दार्शीषु — b) MTr⁵ *Lakṣ* त्वजाविमहिषीषु च; *Mādh* महिषीष्वाविकासु च; Ho Kt² wKt³ La¹ Lo³ Lo⁴ GMd⁵ sOx¹ NPu¹ Pu² Pu⁴ sPu⁶ Tj¹ Tr¹ Tr² MTr⁶ महिष्याजावि°; NKt⁴ GMd¹ TMd⁴ महिषाजावि°; Bo मनुष्याजावि° — c) TMd⁴ प्रजागारी; NPu¹ °भोगी — d) BKt⁵ तथा नैवाङ्ग°; La¹ °न्यांगतास्वपि; Be¹ BBe² wKt³ Lo² Ox² °ङ्गनासु च

49. Cited by *Lakṣ* 12.738; *Mādh* 2.37 — a) Jm यो; Ho oOr बीजवतः; NPu¹ बीजमन्तः — b) Ho Pu⁵ Pu⁷ Tr¹ *Mādh* परक्षेत्रे; Be¹ °क्षेत्रेषु वापिनः; GMd¹ °क्षेत्रे तु वापिनः; Lo¹ °वापिताः — c) TMd³ GMd⁵ तेनैव सस्यजातस्य; Jm तेन वै तस्य जातस्य; TMd⁴ तेपि वै सस्यजातस्य; BCa wKt¹ BKt⁵ NPu¹ शस्यस्य; Be¹ Ox² जातस्य सस्यस्य; Lo⁴ सस्यप्रजातस्य; NKt⁴ सस्यस्य जायन्ते — d) Lo¹ क्वचिन्न लभते फलं; Pu⁵ Pu⁷ लभन्ति; Tr² भयंते

50. Pādas a-b omitted in Bo; verse 50 is placed after 52 in GMd¹ GMd⁵ TMd⁴. Cited by *Lakṣ* 12.738; *Mādh* 2.37 — a) Be¹ BBe² Ho Hy Jm Jo¹ Kt² Lo¹ oOr Ox² NPu¹ [*Jolly* Ku] *Mandlik Jha KSS Dave* यदन्य°; GMd¹ TMd³ GMy Tr¹ [*Jolly* Nd] यस्त्वन्य°; *Mādh* यथान्य°; Pu² Pu⁴ यथान्यणासु; sOx¹ sPu⁶ वृषभा — b) wKt³ वर्त्मना; Be¹ जायते शतं — c) TMd³ गोस्वामिनां ते वत्सा स्युर्; NKt⁴ NPu¹ गोपिनामेव; Ho *Go* स्वामिनामेव; La¹ गोस्वामिनामेव; TMd⁴ °नामिव; MTr⁵ ते सर्वे — d) La¹ मोघं बीजमिहार्षभं; GMd¹ TMd³ TMd⁴ GMd⁵ GMy Tr¹ [*but cor sh*] MTr⁴ MTr⁵ MTr⁶ [*Jolly* G Nd] मोघं वृषभचेष्टितं; sOx¹ sPu⁶ स्कन्दत°; BKt⁵ स्कन्दिति°; NKt⁴ oOr स्यन्दित°; Ho °मार्षभे; MTr³ °मार्षहं; Lo³ Tj¹ °मार्षकं

51. Cited by *Lakṣ* 12.738 — a) TMd³ GMy Tr¹ [*but cor sh*] MTr⁴ MTr⁶ *Nd* अक्षेत्रिणो बीजवन्तः [MTr⁴ °वन्तं]; Be¹ Lo⁴ GMd¹ GMd⁵ Ox² Ox³ तथैवक्षे°; MTr⁵ यथा चाक्षे°; Kt² oOr Tj¹ °क्षत्रिणो; Pu² Pu⁴ °क्षेत्रिणां; GMd⁵ °क्षेत्रिणे; BKt⁵ बीजा — b) Ox³ परं; GMd¹ NNg Tr¹ [*cor to sh*] °क्षेत्रे; GMy °क्षेत्रि°; Be¹ Ox² °क्षेत्रेषु वापिनः; Lo⁴ °क्षेत्रवापिणः; GMd⁵ °क्षेत्रस्य वापिनः; Bo °वापणः — c) Bo किर्वति; TMd⁴ MTr⁵ करोति; Kt² क्षत्रि° — d) GMd⁵ न बीजी फलमर्हति; TMd⁴ बीजाद्योनिर्बलीयसी [cf. 8.52d]; NKt⁴ BKt⁵ Lo¹ TMd³ NNg sOx¹ Ox³ NPu¹ Pu² Pu⁴ sPu⁶ Pu⁸ Tr¹ [*but cor sh*] Tr² MTr⁶ बीजी न; GMy बीजं न

52.* Omitted in TMd⁴; verses 52 and 53 are transposed in GMd¹ TMd³ GMd⁵ Tr¹ MTr⁴ MTr⁶ *Mādh*. Cited by *Vij* 2.127; *Lakṣ* 12.738; *Mādh* 3.350 — b) Kt² क्षत्रिणां; Bo Tj¹ क्षेत्रिणं; GMd¹ बीजिनां क्षेत्रिणां; Bo बीजिनं; Tj¹ बीजिना; Pu⁷ Pu⁵ बीजिनस्तथा — c) BKt⁵ प्रत्यक्षः; TMd³ प्रत्यक्ष; Pu⁵ Pu⁷ प्रत्यर्थं; Be¹ प्रत्यहं; Pu² Pu⁴ प्रत्ययं; Kt² क्षत्रि°; NPu¹ क्षेत्रिणामुत्तं; Be¹ °मर्थे; NKt⁴ La¹ GMd⁵ GMy MTr⁶ °मर्थं; TMd³ Pu² Pu⁴ मर्थ; GMd¹ °मर्थात् — d) Be¹ BBe² Bo Ho Hy Jm Jo¹ wKt¹ Kt²

क्रियाभ्युपगमात्त्वेतद् बीजार्थं यत्प्रदीयते ।
तस्येह भागिनौ दृष्टौ बीजी क्षेत्रिक एव च ॥५३॥
ओघवाताहृतं बीजं यस्य क्षेत्रे प्ररोहति ।
तज्ज्ञेयं क्षेत्रिकस्यैव न वप्ता लभते फलम् ॥५४॥
एष धर्मो गवाश्वस्य दास्युष्ट्राजाविकस्य च ।
विहंगमहिषीणां च विज्ञेयः प्रसवं प्रति ॥५५॥
एतद्वः सारफल्गुत्वं बीजयोन्योः प्रकीर्तितम् ।
अतः परं प्रवक्ष्यामि योषितां धर्ममापदि ॥५६॥
भ्रातुर्ज्येष्ठस्य या भार्या गुरुपत्न्यनुजस्य सा ।
यवीयसस्तु या भार्या स्नुषा ज्येष्ठस्य सा स्मृता ॥५७॥

wKt^{3} NKt^{4} BKt^{5} La^{1} Lo^{1} Lo^{3} NNg oOr sOx^{1} Ox^{2} Pu^{3} sPu^{6} Pu^{8} Tj^{1} Tj^{2} Tr^{1} Tr^{2} MTr^{3} [*Jolly* R^{1}] *Nā Rn Rc Mandlik KSS Dave* °निर्गरीयसी

53. Omitted in TMd^{4}. Cited by *Vij* 2.127; *Lakṣ* 12.722; *Mādh* 3.350 — a) La^{1} क्रियाप्युप°; Ox^{3} °गमस्त्वेद्; NKt^{4} NNg Pu^{2} Pu^{4} Tr^{1} MTr^{5} Wa °गमात्त्वेव; GMd^{5} NPu^{1} °गमात्त्वेवं; *Lakṣ* °गमादेतद्; wKt^{1} La^{1} GMd^{1} °गमादेव; Ho °गमाच्चैव; Lo^{4} [*Jolly* M] °गमाच्चैवं; Lo^{1} Lo^{3} Tj^{1} °गमत्वेन; BKt^{5} °गमत्वेन तद्; MTr^{4} °गमार्थं च; MTr^{6} °गमार्थे च; oOr °गमार्थेन; TMd^{3} °गमेप्येव; *Vij* °गमात्क्षेत्रं — b) GMd^{1} यद्वै बीजं प्रकीर्यते; wKt^{3} तत्प्र°; MTr^{5} यत्प्रकीर्यते; TMd^{3} sOx^{1} sPu^{6} यत्प्रतीयते; *Lakṣ* यत्र दीयते — c) Be^{1} तस्यैव; Lo^{4} Lo^{5} GMd^{1} Ox^{3} तस्यैह; Tr^{2} यस्येह; NKt^{4} BKt^{5} भागिनो; TMd^{3} भानौ दृष्टे च; BKt^{5} दृष्टो; Lo^{1} Pu^{5} दष्टौ — d) GMd^{1} बीजीकक्षेत्रिणावुभौ; TMd^{3} GMy NNg oOr बीज; BKt^{5} GMd^{5} Tj^{1} क्षेत्रक; Hy क्षेत्रिय; Kt^{2} क्षत्रिक; Ho wKt^{1} NKt^{4} Tj^{2} एव वा; BCa एव तु

54.* Pādas c-d *ma* in Lo^{4}. Cited by *Lakṣ* 12.739 — a) Pu^{2} Pu^{4} उघवता°; Lo^{1} ओड्यवता°; Ox^{2} उप्यवाता°; sOx^{1} sPu^{6} यद्यवाता°; NKt^{4} तप्यवाता°; La^{1} उदवातहतं; Bo Ho Kt^{2} Pu^{5} Pu^{7} °हतं — b) NKt^{4} क्षेत्रे यस्य; TMd^{4} विरोहति — c) Be^{1} Ox^{2} तत्क्षेत्रिकस्य विज्ञेयं; Pu^{5} Pu^{7} तत्क्षेमं क्षेत्रिकस्येह; BCa wKt^{1} तद्बीजं क्षेत्रिकस्यैव; BBe^{2} Bo Ho Hy Jm Jo^{1} Jo^{2} Kt^{2} BKt^{5} Lo^{1} Lo^{2} Lo^{3} Lo^{4} oOr sOx^{1} Ox^{3} NPu^{1} Pu^{2} Pu^{3} Pu^{4} sPu^{6} Pu^{8} Tj^{1} Tj^{2} Tr^{2} MTr^{3} Wa *Mandlik Jolly Jha KSS Dave* क्षेत्रिकस्यैव तद्बीजं [Lo^{4} Lo^{5} Ox^{3} क्षत्रकस्य तु; Tj^{1} क्षेत्रिकस्येव]; NKt^{4} तं ज्ञेयं; TMd^{4} क्षेत्रिणं चैव — d) Be^{1} Bo BCa Jo^{2} wKt^{1} BKt^{5} Lo^{1} Lo^{2} Lo^{3} Lo^{4} Lo^{5} NNg oOr sOx^{1} Ox^{3} NPu^{1} Pu^{2} Pu^{3} Pu^{4} Pu^{5} sPu^{6} Pu^{7} Pu^{8} Tj^{1} Tr^{2} Wa [*Jolly* M G R] *Lakṣ Me Jolly Jha* न बीजी

55. Cited by *Lakṣ* 12.739 — a) MTr^{4} MTr^{6} गजाश्वस्य— b) wKt^{1} दास्योष्ट्रा°; Pu^{3} दाशोष्ट्रा°; Be^{1} TMd^{3} °जाविकासु च; Bo °जाबीजकस्य च; Jo^{2} Lo^{3} Tj^{1} तु — c) wKt^{1} wKt^{3} BKt^{5} Lo^{2} GMd^{1} TMd^{4} GMy Tr^{1} MTr^{5} MTr^{6} °महिषाणां; GMd^{5} °महिषां च; Lo^{1} *om* च — d) GMy विज्ञेयाः; TMd^{4} विज्ञेया; BKt^{5} La^{1} विज्ञेयं

56. Omitted in Pu^{5} — a) sPu^{6} [*but cor*] साधुफल्गुत्वं; TMd^{4} सादफल्गुत्वं; Ho °फाल्गुत्वं — b) La^{1} बीजि°; Pu^{4} °योन्याः; Lo^{3} GMd^{5} प्रकीर्तितः; GMy प्रकल्पितं; Ox^{2} प्रकाशितं — c) BCa अत ऊर्ध्वं; Tj^{2} परं वक्ष्यामि — d) TMd^{4} योषिता

57. Pādas c-d omitted in Lo^{5} Ox^{3}; pādas b-d *ma sh* in Tr^{1} — a) Be^{1} Ho भ्रातुज्ये°; wKt^{3} °ष्ठस्य भार्यस्य; Be^{1} Bo Ho Hy Jm Jo^{1} Kt^{2} BKt^{5} La^{1} Lo^{1} Lo^{4} TMd^{3} Ox^{2} Ox^{3} Pu^{8} Tj^{2} MTr^{3} Wa *Mandlik Jolly Jha KSS Dave* भार्या या— b) GMd^{5} Pu^{7} °पत्न्यानुजस्य; NNg *ma fh* सा; TMd^{3} या; Pu^{5} Pu^{7} Tj^{1} वा; La^{1} sOx^{1} sPu^{6} MTr^{4} MTr^{6} च— c) TMd^{3} यवीयसश्च; La^{1} यवीयशश्च; Wa यवीयसीस्तु; TMd^{4} कवीयसस्तु; GMd^{1} अनुजस्य च या; BCa La^{1} Lo^{1} oOr NPu^{1} भार्या या; NNg *om* या

ज्येष्ठो यवीयसो भार्यां यवीयान्वाग्रजस्त्रियम् ।
पतितौ भवतो गत्वा नियुक्तावप्यनापदि ॥५८॥
देवराद्वा सपिण्डाद्वा स्त्रिया सम्यङ् नियुक्तया ।
प्रजेप्सिताधिगन्तव्या संतानस्य परिक्षये ॥५९॥
विधवायां नियुक्तस्तु घृताक्तो वाग्यतो निशि ।
एकमुत्पादयेत्पुत्रं न द्वितीयं कथंचन ॥६०॥
द्वितीयमेके प्रजनं मन्यन्ते स्त्रीषु तद्विदः ।
अनिवृत्तं नियोगार्थं पश्यन्तो धर्मतस्तयोः ॥६१॥
विधवायां नियोगार्थे निवृत्ते तु यथाविधि ।
गुरुवच्च स्नुषावच्च वर्तेयातां परस्परम् ॥६२॥
नियुक्तौ यौ विधिं हित्वा वर्तेयातां तु कामतः ।
तावुभौ पतितौ स्यातां स्नुषागगुरुतल्पगौ ॥६३॥
नान्यस्मिन्विधवा नारी नियोक्तव्या द्विजातिभिः ।
अन्यस्मिन्हि नियुञ्जाना धर्मं हन्युः सनातनम् ॥६४॥

58. Pāda-a *ma* in Tr[1]. Pādas c-d cited by *Viś* 1.69 — a) BBe[2] ज्येष्ठ; Jo[1] Lo[4] Lo[5] भार्या — b) BBe[2] यवीयांश्चाग्र°; Be[1] Lo[4] Lo[5] Ox[3] यवीयांस्त्वग्र°; Pu[5] यवीयसाग्र°; Pu[7] यवीयस्याग्र°; GMy oOr Tr[1] यवीयानग्र°; TMd[3] यवीयां चाग्र°; Lo[5] Bo °स्त्रियां — c) GMd[5] पतितौ तावुभौ स्यातां; Lo[4] पतितौ तावुभौ गत्वा; Be[1] GMy MTr[6] पतितो — d) Pu[2] नियुक्तावनापदि; GMy Tr[2] नियुक्तौ वाप्य° [Tr[2] °क्तो]

59. Pādas a-b omitted in Lo[4]. Cited by *Viś* 1.69; *Vij* 2.127; *Lakṣ* 12.639; *Dev* 1.224; *Mādh* 3.350 — b) *Mādh* सद्भिः नियुक्तया — c) TMd[4] प्रजेप्सिता निगन्तव्या; GMd[1] प्रजेप्सुतां तु गन्तव्या; La[1] प्रजेप्सयाधि°; Tj[2] प्रजेप्सियाधि°; Be[1] प्रजेप्सयाभि°; GMy प्रजेच्छयाधि°; *Mādh* बीजेप्सिताधि°; oOr °प्सित्यातिगन्तव्या; wKt[3] °ताभिगन्तव्या; TMd[3] °धिगत्या वा — d) GMd[1] सन्तानपरिरक्षये

60. Omitted in Lo[4]. Cited by *Vij* 2.127; *Dev* 1.225; *Mādh* 3.350; pādas a-b cited by *Viś* 1.69 — a) *Mādh* विधवायां नियोगार्थं; GMd[5] विधवानां निषक्तस्तु; Lo[3] विधवायाः; NNg नियुक्तास्तु — b) Tj[1] वाग्यतेशनि — c) Tr[2] एवमुत्पा° — d) BCa Pu[8] Tr[2] द्वितीयं न; TMd[4] कदाचन

61. Omitted in Lo[4]. Cited by *Dev* 1.225 — a) oOr द्वितीययैके; La[1] °मेको; TMd[3] GMd[5] °मेक; GMd[1] GMy प्रजननं — b) TMd[4] स्त्रीष्वभार्यासु चक्षते; Be[1] मन्यते; Pu[2] Pu[4] त्रिपु; oOr तेपु — c) La[1] अनिवृत्ता; Hy Jm Jo[1] Kt[2] Lo[3] NNg Pu[8] Tj[1] Tj[2] Tr[1] MTr[5] Wa *Mandlik Jha KSS Dave* अनिर्वृत्तं; Ho अनिर्वृत्त; wKt[5] TMd[3] *Dev* अनिर्वृतं; MTr[6] अनिवृत्ति; MTr[4] अनिर्वृत्ति — d) Ho पश्यन्ता; MTr[3] पश्यन्ते; Kt[2] Lo[1] GMd[1] TMd[3] पश्यतो

62. NKt[4] gives an additional half-verse at the beginning: विधवायां नियोगार्थं प्रपश्यन्तो धर्मतस्तयोः — a) Lo[1] विधवाया; GMd[5] विधवानां; Kt[2] °गार्थो; Lo[4] TMd[4] °गार्थी; Jm °गार्थं; GMy °गार्थ — b) Ho TMd[3] Pu[3] Pu[4] Tj[1] *Mandlik KSS Dave* निर्वृत्ते; Be[1] निवृत्तो; wKt[1] निवर्तेत यथा°; Pu[5] *om* तु; La[1] च; GMy ह; Be[1] °विधिः; MTr[6] °विधिं — d) TMd[3] oOr वर्तयेतां; BBe[2] परस्परः

63. a) oOr नियुक्तो यो; TMd[4] नियुक्तयो; BBe[2] Pu[2] Pu[4] *om* यौ; La[1] विधिर्हित्वा; Bo Ox[2] हत्वा — b) GMd[1] TMd[3] TMd[4] GMd[5] प्रवर्तेतां; GMy प्रपद्येतां; MTr[4] MTr[6] प्रवर्तेताशु का°; TMd[4] कामुकं — c) Wa पतितो; Bo तपतौ — d) Pu[2] Pu[4] स्नुषायागुरु°

64. Cited by *Viś* 1.69; *Vij* 2.127, 136; *Dev* 1.226; *Mādh* 3.351 — b) NPu[1] नियुक्तव्या; Pu[5]

नोद्वाहिकेषु मन्त्रेषु नियोगः कीर्त्यते क्वचित् ।
न विवाहविधावुक्तं विधवावेदनं पुनः ॥६५॥
अयं द्विजैर्हि विद्वद्भिः पशुधर्मो विगर्हितः ।
मनुष्याणामपि प्रोक्तो वेने राज्यं प्रशासति ॥६६॥
स महीमखिलां भुञ्जन् राजर्षिप्रवरः पुरा ।
वर्णानां संकरं चक्रे कामोपहतचेतनः ॥६७॥
तदा प्रभृति यो मोहात् प्रमीतपतिकां स्त्रियम् ।
नियोजयत्यपत्यार्थे तं विगर्हन्ति साधवः ॥६८॥
यस्या म्रियेत कन्याया वाचा सत्ये कृते पतिः ।
तामनेन विधानेन निजो विन्देत देवरः ॥६९॥
यथाविध्यधिगम्यैनां शुक्लवस्त्रां शुचिव्रताम् ।
मिथो भजेता प्रसवात् सकृत्सकृदृतावृतौ ॥७०॥

Pu[7] °क्तव्या कदाचन — c) Jo[2] Lo[3] OOr Tj[1] *Dev* अन्यस्मिन्विनियुञ्जाना; MTr[3] अन्यस्मिन्विधियुञ्जाना; SOx[1] SPu[6] प्रयुञ्जाना — d) MTr[6] धर्म्यं; Ho GMd[5] Tr[1] हन्यात्सना°

65.* Cited by *Vij* 2.127; *Mādh* 3.351; pādas c-d cited by *Viś* 1.66 — a) BBe[2] Hy NNg OOr Tj[2] Wa *Jolly* नौद्वाहि°; Ho °हकेपु; TMd[4] °हिके तु — b) Hy निर्योगः; TMd[3] नियोगा; TMd[4] नियोगं — c) TMd[4] विवासंविदामुक्तं; GMy °विधायुक्तं; *Mādh* °विधौ युक्तं — d) NPu[1] °देवनं; OOr MTr[4] °वेतनं; *Viś* °वेदनं क्वचित्; TMd[3] °वेदनं प्रति

66. Verses 66–75 placed after 84b in TMd[4]. Cited by *Viś* 1.69; *Vij* 2.127; *Mādh* 3.351 — a) BKt[5] द्विजैश्च; TMd[3] धर्मो हि; Wa द्विजैर्विद्वद्भिः; GMd[1] Pu[2] Pu[4] द्विजैरविद्वद्भिः; *Me* supports अविद्वद्भिः and he give विद्वद्भिः as a pāṭha; *Nd* and *Mr* support हि — b) TMd[3] निगर्हितः — c) Pu[2] Pu[4] °णामनुप्रोक्तो; OOr प्राप्तो — d) Kt[2] WKt[3] Lo[1] SOx[1] SPu[6] [*Jolly* Ku] वेणे; La[1] वेनो; GMd[5] वैने; Jo[1] वेन; Be[1] वने; Tr[2] वैन्ये; Ho वैणै; TMd[4] विशे; BKt[5] La[1] NNg प्रशास्यति

67. Cited by *Vij* 2.127; *Mādh* 3.351 — a) Hy *om* स; Tr[2] °खिलं — b) Tr[2] °प्रवरं; Jm °प्रवरः प्रभु — d) Lo[3] कामाप°; Tr[2] कार्योप°; GMy मोहोप°

68. Cited by *Vij* 2.127; *Mādh* 3.351 — a) TMd[3] तथा; BBe[2] Bo Ho Hy Jm Jo[1] WKt[1] Kt[2] Lo[1] Tj[2] MTr[3] *Vij Mandlik Jha KSS Dave* ततः; Lo[1] Ox[2] प्रभृतयो — b) Lo[1] °पतिकः; GMy °प्रतिकां; WKt[1] °परिकां; La[1] °मतिकां; Lo[4] [*Jolly* M] °पतिकाः स्त्रियः — c) WKt[1] Ox[2] नियोजयन्त्यप°; BKt[5] La[1] नियोजयेदप°; Hy Jm Jo[1] Kt[2] BKt[5] La[1] SOx[1] NPu[1] SPu[6] Pu[8] Tj[2] MTr[3] *Mandlik Jha KSS Dave* °पत्यार्थं — d) Lo[1] विगर्हन्ति च साधवः [*om* तं]; BBe[2] Jo[2] Lo[3] Tj[1] *Vij* गर्हन्ते तं हि साधवः; Be[1] तां; Be[1] Pu[5] Pu[7] विगहर्ति

69. Pādas b-d omitted in BKt[5]. Cited by *Viś* 1.69; *Vij* 1.68–9, 2.127; *Apa* 78; *Mādh* 3.351 — a) Bo यस्य; TMd[3] TMd[4] GMd[5] यस्यां; NKt[4] म्रियते; La[1] Pu[5] Pu[7] Pu[8] Tr[1] मृयेत; Pu[2] Pu[4] कन्याय; GMd[5] कन्यायां; BKt[5] कन्या — b) GMd[1] पापा सत्ये; GMy पत्यकृते पतिं; Lo[1] कृतः — d) MTr[6] निजां; *Apa* [vl] न द्विजो; GMd[1] विन्दत; Wa विन्देते; Tr[2] देवराः

70. Pādas a-b omitted in BKt[5]. Cited by *Vij* 2.127; *Jmv* 9.28; *Mādh* 3.351 — a) NPu[1] °विध्यभिग°; Tr[2] °विध्याभिग°; Tj[1] °विध्यभ्यग°; GMd[5] Tr[1] °विध्यनुग°; *Jmv* °विध्युपग°; WKt[3] °गम्यैना; NPu[1] °गम्यैतां — b) Tr[2] शुक्लवस्त्रं; Tr[2] शुचिवृतां; GMd[1] शुचिस्मितां; Pu[5] Pu[7] पतिव्रतां — c) Bo भजेत; BBe[2] GMd[1] भजेदा; BKt[5] Lo[1] Lo[3] OOr Tj[1] भजेतां; SOx[1] SPu[6] भयेता; Tr[2] प्रसवां; BKt[5] Tj[1] प्रसवा;

न दत्त्वा कस्यचित्कन्यां पुनर्दद्याद्विचक्षणः ।
दत्त्वा पुनः प्रयच्छन्हि प्राप्नोति पुरुषानृतम् ॥७१॥
विधिवत्प्रतिगृह्यापि त्यजेत्कन्यां विगर्हिताम् ।
व्याधितां विप्रदुष्टां वा छद्मना चोपपादिताम् ॥७२॥
यस्तु दोषवतीं कन्यामनाख्याय प्रयच्छति ।
तस्य तद्वितथं कुर्यात् कन्यादातुर्दुरात्मनः ॥७३॥
विधाय वृत्तिं भार्यायाः प्रवसेत्कार्यवान्नरः ।
अवृत्तिकर्शिता हि स्त्री प्रदुष्येत्स्थितिमत्यपि ॥७४॥
विधाय प्रोषिते वृत्तिं जीवेन्नियममास्थिता ।
प्रोषिते त्वविधायैव जीवेच्छिल्पैरगर्हितैः ॥७५॥
प्रोषितो धर्मकार्यार्थं प्रतीक्ष्योऽष्टौ नरः समाः ।
विद्यार्थं षड् यशोऽर्थं वा कामार्थं त्रींस्तु वत्सरान् ॥७६॥

TMd^{4} प्रसवं; Lo^{1} प्रभवात्; GMd^{5} सवनात् — d) Pu^{2} *om first* सकृत्; Lo^{1} °कृदनावृतौ; Jo^{1} La^{1} °कृद्वतावुभौ

71. Pādas c-d omitted in Ho Lo^{4}. Cited by *Lakṣ* 2.57; *Dev* 1.220 — a) Be^{1} TMd^{4} °चित्कन्या — b) sOx^{1} sPu^{6} पुनर्दत्वाविचक्षणः; Wa °चक्षिणः — c) BBe^{2} BCa La^{1} oOr प्रयच्छन्ति; GMd^{1} प्रयच्छन्यः; *Lakṣ* प्रयच्छंस्तु; *Dev* प्रयच्छेद्यः; Bo प्रशंसन्हि — d) NPu^{1} प्राप्नोतु; Be^{1} Lo^{2} TMd^{3} sOx^{1} Ox^{2} sPu^{6} [*Jolly* M^{9}] पुरुषोनृतं

72. *Go*'s commentary on the rest of Ch. 9 is missing. Cited by *Apa* 95; *Dev* 1.221; *Mādh* 1.492 — b) Pu^{4} त्यजेत्पुनर्दद्याद्धि च; *Apa* °त्कन्यामनिन्दितां; Tr^{2} प्रगर्हितां; Pu^{5} Pu^{7} [*Jolly* G] पतिव्रतां — c) MTr^{6} व्याथितां; MTr^{4} MTr^{6} विप्रकृष्टां; Pu^{2} Pu^{4} वा प्रदुष्टां वा; GMd^{1} TMd^{4} *Apa* च — d) Hy TMd^{3} छद्मनो; Bo छनाना; GMd^{1} चिद्रना; Pu^{8} MTr^{6} चोपपादितं; Lo^{3} Tj^{1} वोपपादितां; sOx^{1} sPu^{6} वोपपादिता

73.* Verses 73 and 75 transposed in Jm — b) BCa Hy Jm Jo^{1} Kt^{2} Lo^{4} GMd^{1} TMd^{4} Ox^{2} NPu^{1} Pu^{2} Pu^{4} Tj^{2} MTr^{3} [*Jolly* M] *Mandlik Jha KSS Dave* °ख्यायोपपादयेत्; La^{1} °ख्यायोपपादितां — c) [*Jolly* Nd G R] तस्यापि वितथं; La^{1} तस्य तद्विगुणं; Ho Jo^{2} wKt^{1} NKt^{4} La^{1} Lo^{3} NNg oOr sOx^{1} Pu^{5} sPu^{6} Pu^{7} Tj^{1} Tr^{1} [*cor to*] [*Jolly* G R] कार्यं; TMd^{3} विध्यात् — d) Lo^{2} GMd^{1} TMd^{3} TMd^{4} GMd^{5} GMy Pu^{8} Tr^{1} MTr^{5} MTr^{6} [*Jolly* Nd] कन्यादानं दुरा°; Tr^{2} °दातुरनात्मनः; NPu^{1} °रात्मनां

74.* TMd^{3} [*Jolly* Nd] inserts verses 95–6 after 74. Cited by *Lakṣ* 12.611; *Dev* 3.571 — a) TMd^{3} sOx^{1} sPu^{6} भार्यायां; Bo भार्यायात् — b) Be^{1} प्रसेवेत्का°; Bo wKt^{1} La^{1} GMd^{1} oOr प्रसवेत्का°; GMd^{5} व्यसवेत्का°; GMy [*Jolly* Nd] °वान्द्विजः — c) Pu^{5} Pu^{7} प्रवृत्ति°; GMd^{1} वृत्त्याप्रकर्शिता; Be^{1} BBe^{2} Ho Hy Jm Jo^{1} wKt^{1} Kt^{2} wKt^{3} La^{1} Lo^{1} Lo^{3} oOr sOx^{1} Ox^{2} sPu^{6} Pu^{8} Tj^{1} Tj^{2} *Mandlik Jolly KSS* °कर्पिता — d) TMd^{4} न दुश्येत्पतिमत्यपि; GMd^{1} प्रदुष्यात्स्थितिमित्यपि; Pu^{4} प्रग्रष्येत्स्थि°; Ho °ष्येत्स्थितमत्यपि

75. Cited by *Lakṣ* 12.631; *Dev* 3.592 — a) GMd^{5} प्रोषितो; NKt^{4} प्रोषित; Jo^{1} प्रोषितं; MTr^{6} प्रेषिते; TMd^{3} प्रापिते; GMy प्रोक्षिते; Lo^{2} शेषिते — b) La^{1} TMd^{4} जीवन्नि°; Lo^{1} °यतमास्थिता; Bo GMd^{5} GMy oOr Pu^{4} °स्थितः; Lo^{1} °स्थितिं — c) TMd^{3} प्रोषिते अविधा°; wKt^{1} तु विधायैव; wKt^{3} त्वभिधायैव; TMd^{3} त्वपिधायैव — d) oOr °च्छिल्पैश्च गर्हितैः; GMd^{5} °गर्हितः

76. a) TMd^{4} Tr^{2} प्रोषिते; NKt^{4} प्रोपिता; MTr^{6} प्रोपितं; Hy प्रपितो; NPu^{1} योषिता; GMd^{5} Tr^{1} [*Jolly*

संवत्सरमुदीक्षेत द्विषन्तीं योषितं पतिः ।
ऊर्ध्वं संवत्सरात्त्वेनां दायं हृत्वा न संवसेत् ॥७७॥
अतिक्रामेत् प्रमत्तं या मत्तं रोगार्तमेव वा ।
सा त्रीन्मासान्परित्याज्याविभूषणपरिच्छदा ॥७८॥
उन्मत्तं पतितं क्लीबमबीजं पापरोगिणम् ।
न त्यागोऽस्ति द्विषाणाया न च दायापवर्तनम् ॥७९॥
मद्यपासत्यवृत्ता च प्रतिकूला च या भवेत् ।
व्याधिता चाधिवेत्तव्या हिंस्रार्थघ्नी च सर्वदा ॥८०॥

Gr] धर्महेतोस्तु; GMd[1] धर्मसेतोस्तु; TMd[4] धर्महेतुस्थं; Lo[3] Tj[1] °कामार्थं — b) MTr[3] प्रतीच्यो; Lo[3] प्रतिष्ठो; Lo[1] *om* °ष्टौ; Be[1] नराः; TMd[4] नरः पुमान्; Bo Hy समः — c) GMd[1] विद्यार्था; Ho षड् यशोर्थे; Lo[1] NPu[1] यद्यशोर्थं — d) BKt[5] Lo[4] कार्यार्थं; Lo[1] TMd[3] GMy Ox[2] Pu[5] Pu[7] कामार्थंस्त्रींस्तु; MTr[4] तांस्तु; TMd[4] त्रीस्तु वत्सराः

77. Cited by *Lakṣ* 12.615; *Dev* 3.571 — a) Ho Hy Jm Jo[1] wKt[1] Kt[2] wKt[3] La[1] Lo[2] GMy Pu[5] Pu[7] Tj[2] MTr[3] [*Jolly* G R Nd Ku] *Ku Mandlik Jha KSS Dave* संवत्सरं प्रतीक्षेत;Be[1] संवत्सरं प्रतीक्ष्येत; TMd[4] संवत्सरं तु वेक्षेत — b) Lo[3] तद् द्विषन्तीं; Be[1] wKt[1] TMd[4] द्विषतीं; Bo Hy sOx[1] sPu[6] द्विषन्ती; BBe[2] Tr[2] द्विषती; wKt[3] द्विषत्रीं; NKt[4] wKt[5] Lo[4] NNg [*Jolly* M] *Me Jolly Jha*द्विषाणां [cf. 9.79]; Be[1] योषितां; TMd[4] योषितः; Lo[2] योद्विषं; TMd[3] पति; oOr NPu[1] प्रति — c) Lo[1] ऊर्ध्वं; NNg °त्सरात्त्वेतां; Ho wKt[3] Lo[1] Lo[2] sOx[1] sPu[6] Pu[8] °त्सराच्चैनां; Jo[2] wKt[1] Lo[3] Lo[4] Ox[2] Tj[1] °त्सरादेनां; La[1] °त्सरां त्वेनां; NPu[1] °त्सरं त्वेतां; MTr[6] °त्सरान्त्वेनां; Be[1] °त्सरामेनां — d) TMd[4] दायां; Tj[1] दयां; Wa दायं गृह्य; Bo Ho हत्वा; NKt[4] दत्वा; wKt[1] La[1] Tj[1] *Lakṣ* कृत्वा; BCa Jo[2] Pu[2] Pu[4] संविशेत्

78.* Pādas a-b and c-d transposed in MTr[6]. Cited by *Lakṣ* 12.615 — a) oOr अतिक्रामेत मत्तं वा; GMy नाति°; wKt[1] Lo[4] [*Jolly* M] °क्रमेत्; Lo[1] °क्रान्ते; BBe[2] BKt[5] Lo[4] GMy sOx[1] Ox[2] sPu[6] Tr[2] MTr[3] MTr[4] MTr[6] [*Jolly* M] प्रमत्तं वा; Wa प्रमत्तं वा या— a-b) GMd[1] TMd[3] TMd[4] GMd[5] Tr[1] MTr[5] मत्तं वा या प्रमत्तं वा रोगार्तं वातिवर्तते [TMd[3] मत्तं वाथ; TMd[3] वानिवर्तते]; NKt[4] *om* या मत्तं — b) Be[1] Kt[2] Lo[4] [*Jolly* M] च— c) oOr या; GMy यास्त्रीन्यासान्परि°; TMd[3] त्रीन्मासान्सा परि°; MTr[5] सा त्रिमासान्परि°; NKt[4] °रित्यज्या°; GMd[1] TMd[4] °त्यज्य° — d) GMd[1] TMd[4] sOx[1] sPu[6] °परिच्छदैः

79. Cited by *Lakṣ* 12.615; *Dev* 3.572— a) MTr[5] पतितं व्यङ्गम्° — b) Pu[5] Pu[7] क्लीबमुन्मत्तं पापरोगिणीं; HoTMd[3] क्लीबं बीजं; TMd[3] पापं च रोगिणां; *Dev* वापि रोगिणं — c) GMd[5] *Lakṣ* न च द्विषन्त्यास्त्यागोस्ति; GMd[1] Tr[1] [*but cor*] न प्रद्विषन्त्यास्त्यागोस्ति; BBe[2] द्विष [lacuna] न च; Tj[1] द्विषाणायां; Bo Tr[2] MTr[6] द्विषणाया; Lo[3] TMd[3] द्विषाणाय; sOx[1] sPu[6] द्विषाणायै; wKt[3] Pu[5] Pu[7] द्विषाणायो; Wa द्विषोनार्या; TMd[4] Be[1] प्रद्विषन्त्या; La[1] न द्विषन्त्या; Ho Hy Jm Kt[2] Jo[1] Tj[2] MTr[3] [*Jolly* Ku N] *Nā Rc Mr Mandlik Jha KSS Dave* द्विषन्त्याश्च; wKt[1] द्विषन्त्या वा; Lo[2] Pu[3] Pu[8] द्विषन्त्यास्तु — c-d) GMy न त्यागोस्ति द्विषायान्या वादया पापवर्त्तिनां [sic] — d) Tr[2] य च; wKt[3] न चा; Pu[8] दार्यपवर्तनं; GMd[5] दायापहर्तनं; Bo दास्याप्रवर्तनं; sOx[1] sPu[6] °पवार्धनं; Jo[2] wKt[3] Lo[3] Tj[1] °पवर्जनं; Wa °पवर्तते

80. Cited by *Apa* 100; *Lakṣ* 2.102; *Dev* 3.572; *Mādh* 1.507; pādas a-c cited by *Apa* 77 — a) TMd[4] pāda illegible; TMd[3] मद्यपासह्यवृत्ता; GMy मद्यपादासवृत्ता; BBe[2] Ho Hy Jm Jo[1] Kt[2] Lo[3] Tj[1] Tj[2] Tr[1] [*mc sh to*] MTr[3] [*Jolly* Ku R] *Mādh Ku Mandlik KSS* मद्यपासाधुवृत्ता [BBe[2] °वृत्त्या]; [*Jolly* M[4–5–9]] *Rn Jolly* मद्यपासत्प्रवृत्ता; *Dev* मद्यपासभ्यवृत्ता; Be[1] Lo[1] °वृत्त्या; wKt[1] वृत्ताया [*om* च]; wKt[3] वा — b) Bo प्रत्यकूला या; *Apa*77 [vl] प्रतिकूलाशया; Tr[2] °कूलां; Hy °कुला; Tj[1] यो; MTr[3] सा — c) *Lakṣ* व्याधिताप्यधि°; Jm Jo[1] Kt[2] wKt[3] Pu[2] Tr[2] MTr[3] [*Jolly* Ku] *Mandlik Jha KSS Dave*वाधि°; Ho Pu[5] Pu[7] [*Jolly* G] साधि°; wKt[1] नाधि°; GMd[1] चापि वेत्तव्या; wKt[3] °वेत्तस्या — d) GMy

वन्ध्याष्टमेऽधिवेद्याब्दे दशमे तु मृतप्रजा ।
एकादशे स्त्रीजननी सद्यस्त्वप्रियवादिनी ॥८१॥
या रोगिणी स्यात्तु हिता संपन्ना चैव शीलतः ।
सानुज्ञाप्याधिवेत्तव्या नावमान्या च कर्हिचित् ॥८२॥
अधिविन्ना तु या नारी निर्गच्छेद्रुषिता गृहात् ।
सा सद्यः संनिरोद्धव्या त्याज्या वा कुलसंनिधौ ॥८३॥
प्रतिषिद्धा पिबेद्या तु मद्यमभ्युदयेष्वपि ।
प्रेक्षासमाजौ गच्छेद्वा सा दण्ड्या कृष्णलानि षट् ॥८४॥
यदि स्वाश्चापराश्चैव विन्देरन् योषितो द्विजाः ।
तासां वर्णक्रमेण स्याज्ज्यैष्ठ्यं पूजा च वेश्म च ॥८५॥

हिंस्रार्थंवचनी सदा; Pu⁴ MTr³ हिंसा°; wKt¹ हिंस्रार्थिघ्नी; Lo⁴ हिंस्रार्थघ्ना; TMd³ हिंस्रार्थघ्नो; BBe² हिंस्रानर्थी; BKt⁵ च या सदा

81. Cited by *Apa* 100; *Dev* 3.574; *Mādh* 1.508 — a) GMd¹ वन्ध्याष्टमेब्दे कुर्वीत; Pu⁴ Pu⁵ Pu⁷ विन्ध्या°; BCa Ho Jo² Lo³ GMd⁵ GMy oOr Tr¹ [*cor sh to*] Tj¹ *Apa* °धिवेत्तव्या; Wa °धिवेद्योब्दे; NNg °धिवेद्यान्दे; wKt¹ °धिवेद्यज्ञे — b) BBe² Ho sOx¹ Ox² च; GMd⁵ Pu⁵ Pu⁷ °प्रजाः; Pu⁸ °प्रज — c) Be¹ एकादशी; wKt¹ एकदशे; Pu² Pu⁴ °जनसी; *Apa* [vl] °जनने — d) Tj² °प्रितंवादिनी

82. Cited by *Apa* 100; *Dev* 3.573 — a) wKt¹ सा; Kt² Tr² रोहिणी; GMy रागिणी; BKt⁵ योगिनी; wKt¹ Lo³ स्याद्दुहिता; GMd¹ स्यात्तद्दुहिता; sOx¹ sPu⁶ हिंसा — b) BKt⁵ सीलतः; TMd³ शीलतां; Lo³ Tj¹ शक्तितः; TMd⁴ निश्चला — c) MTr⁶ समनुज्ञाप्याधिवक्तव्या; BKt⁶ वन्ध्याष्टमेधिवेद्या [cf. 9.81a]; Tj¹ सातुज्ञा°; wKt³ °वेत्तस्या — d) *Apa* नावज्ञेया कथंचन; Be¹ BBe² Bo BCa NKt⁴ La¹ GMd¹ GMy sOx¹ NPu¹ Pu² Pu⁴ Pu⁵ sPu⁶ Pu⁷ Tj¹ MTr⁶ नावमन्या; wKt¹ नात्तव्याना; BBe² wKt¹ GMd¹ तु

83. Cited by *Apa* 101; *Dev* 3.574; *Mādh* 2.288 — a) NKt⁴ sOx¹ Ox² Pu³ sPu⁶ अधिवित्ता; wKt¹ अधिभिन्ना; La¹ आवविन्ना; Lo⁴ नु; Be¹ BBe² GMd¹ NPu¹ MTr⁴ MTr⁶ च — b) Lo⁴ न गच्छे°; Tr¹ [*but cor sh*] °च्छेद्रोषिता; Wa °च्छेद्रुखिता; Lo⁴ °च्छेद्रुदिता; TMd³ Pu⁵ Pu⁷ °च्छेद्रूषिता; Tr² °च्छेदुषिता; Ho Kt² Pu³ °च्छेद्रुःखिता; *Mādh* °च्छेद् द्वेषिता — c) GMd¹ न सद्यः — d) La¹ योज्या; GMd¹ चाकुल°; Hy व्याकुल°; *Mādh* °संनिधी

84. Cited by *Lakṣ* 12.630 — a) TMd³ प्रतिविध्या तु वैद्या तु; Pu⁵ Pu⁷ प्रतिषिद्धो; GMd¹ TMd⁴ प्रतिषिद्धं; *Me Jha Dave* प्रतिषेधे; Lo³ Tj¹ °षिद्धाधिवेद्या; NPu¹ °षिद्धानिवेद्या; [*Jolly* R] °षिद्धादिवेद्या; Jm Jo¹ GMy Ox² Pu³ MTr³ MTr⁵ *Mandlik KSS* [*Jolly* Nd] °षिद्धापि चेद्या; BKt⁵ भवेद्या; BCa NKt⁴ पिबेद्यापि; Ho पिबेद्वापि — b) La¹ सभ्यमभ्युद° — c) GMy Tj¹ प्रेक्षां; BKt⁵ प्रेक्ष्य°; Ho TMd³ प्रेष्या°; Tj² प्रेष्वा°; Lo⁴ प्रेक्ष्ये समाजे; Tr¹ [*but cor sh*] °समाजो; NNg *Lakṣ* °समाजे; NNg °समाजा; Hy Jm Jo¹ Kt² Lo³ Pu³ Tj¹ MTr³ [*Jolly* R] *Mr Mandlik Jha Dave KSS* °समाजं; GMd¹ °समाञ्च — d) GMd⁵ sOx¹ स; wKt¹ MTr⁴ MTr⁶ दाप्या

85. Cited by *Jmv* 11.1.47; *Lakṣ* 12.611; *Mādh* 1.509 — a) Tr¹ स्वाश्चापराश्चापि; Bo Ho wKt¹ Lo¹ Lo² NNg Pu³ *Nā* स्वाश्चावराश्चैव; Hy Lo⁴ GMd¹ TMd³ TMd⁴ GMd⁵ GMy *Jmv* स्वाश्च पराश्चैव; Be¹ स्वाश्च वराश्चैव; BKt⁵ *Lakṣ* स्वा च स्वावराश्चैव; sOx¹ sPu⁶ स्वास्वावराश्चैव; Pu⁵ Pu⁷ स्यात्स्वापराश्चैव; MTr⁶ स्वाश्चापराधैश्चैव — b) Bo विवरेद्; TMd⁴ योषित; MTr⁶ योषिता; Ho द्विजा; TMd³ द्विजः; GMy द्विषाः — c) GMy दास्यवर्ण°; *Jmv Lakṣ* °क्रमेणैव ज्यै° — d) wKt³ Pu² °ज्येष्ठ्यं; NKt⁴ MTr⁵ °ज्येष्ठ्यां; GMy °ज्यैष्ठं; Bo °ज्येष्ठं; La¹ °ज्येष्ठा; wKt¹ Pu³ पूज्यं; GMd¹ TMd³ TMd⁴ GMd⁵ GMy Tr¹ MTr⁴ MTr⁵ MTr⁶ Wa [*Jolly* Nd] *Mādh* च वेश्मनि; oOr च वेश्मनः

भर्तुः शरीरशुश्रूषां धर्मकार्यं च नैत्यकम् ।
स्वा स्वैव कुर्यात्सर्वेषां नासजातिः कथंचन ॥८६॥
यस्तु तत्कारयेन्मोहात् स्वजात्या स्थितयान्यया ।
यथा ब्राह्मणचण्डालः पूर्वदृष्टस्तथैव सः ॥८७॥
उत्कृष्टायाभिरूपाय वराय सदृशाय च ।
अप्राप्तामपि तां तस्मै कन्यां दद्याद्यथाविधि ॥८८॥

86. *ma fh* in NNg. Cited by *Jmv* 11.1.47; *Lakṣ* 12.611; *Mādh* 1.509 — a) TMd3 °श्रूषा — b) Pu3 धर्मं; Tr2 नैत्तिकं; BBe2 Ho Kt2 नैत्यिकं — c) Be1 Ox2 Pu3 Pu8 Tr2 स्वाश्चैव कुर्युः सर्वेषां; Lo3 स्वस्वैव; BBe2 Bo Hy Jo1 wKt1 BKt5 Lo1 TMd3 Pu2 Pu4 Tj2 MTr3 Wa *LakṣJmv* [vl as in ed] *Mandlik KSS Dave* स्वा चैव; Pu2 Pu3 Pu4 स्वां चैव; Be1 BKt5 TMd3 Ox2 Pu3 Pu8 Tr2 स्वाश्चैव; Ho स्वा चैक; La1 स्वयैव; Pu5 Pu7 [*Jolly* G]स्वस्यैव — d) TMd3 नासतिश्च कथंचन; GMd1 NNg नसजातिः; Lo4 Pu5 Pu7 [*Jolly* M G]नासजातिं; TMd3 नासांजातिः; Hy Jm Jo1 Kt2 NKt4 [*Jolly* Nd] *Mandlik Jha KSS Dave* नास्वजातिः; sOx1 sPu6 MTr6 नस्वजातिः; GMy नास्वाजातिः; NPu1 तासांजातिः; Ox2 नासूजातिः; wKt3 La1 नामजातिः; Bo Lo1 MTr4 *Jmv Lakṣ Mādh*नान्यजातिः; wKt1 न विजातिः; Tr1 नासवर्णा; wKt1 oOr कदाचन

87.* Cited by *Jmv* 11.1.47; *Lakṣ* 12.611 — a) Wa *om* तत्; sOx1 sPu6 यत्कार°; Pu2 Pu4 तस्करये°; La1 तत्करयन्मोहात्; Be1 Lo1 तत्कारणान्मोहात्; Tj1 °न्मोहान् — b) TMd3 स्वजाति; Pu2 Pu4 स्वाजात्या; Bo Jm Jo1 Jo2 Kt2 BKt5 Lo2 Pu3 Pu8 Tj2 MTr3 *Me Rc Mandlik Jolly Jha KSS Dave* सजात्या; Tr2 सयायात्या; Hy Lo3 NNg Tr2 *Lakṣ* स्थितयान्यथा; Be1 स्थितयोन्यथा; Ox2 स्थितया यथा; wKt1 स्थितया तया; Pu8 स्थितयानय — c) Ho ब्राह्मणश्चाण्डालः; Bo Ho Hy Jm Jo1 wKt1 Kt2 wKt3 La1 Lo1 sOx1 Ox2 Pu5 sPu6 Pu7 Pu8 Tj2 Tr1 Tr2 *Mandlik Jha KSS Dave* °चाण्डालः; Lo4 GMd1 GMd5 GMy °चण्डालाः; TMd3 °चाण्डाल्यः; [*Jolly* G Ku] °चाण्डाल — d) Lo2 पूर्वेदृ°; NKt4 सर्वदृ°; Lo1 °दिष्ट-स्त°; TMd3 °दुष्टस्त°; Lo1 Lo2 TMd4 GMy Wa °स्तथैव च

88. Cited by *Mādh* 1.481 — a) Ho उत्कृष्टाय स्वरूपाय; wKt3 GMd1 Tj1 उत्कृष्टया°; GMd1 °रूपाया — b) NKt4 धराय; BKt5 सदशाय; NKt4 TMd3 Pu5 Pu7 MTr4 MTr5 MTr6 वा — c) TMd3 तंप्राप्ता-मपि; Tr2 अप्रत्यामपि; Be1 तामस्मै — c-d) BBe2 तां कन्यां तस्मै दद्या° — d) wKt3 दद्यात्कन्यां यथा°; BKt5 *om* दद्यात्; TMd4 दद्यां यथा°; TMd3 *Mādh* दद्याद्विचक्षणः; NNg °विधिः

After the first half-verse an additional verse in Be1 NPu1 Pu2 Pu4 Wa; it is given after verse 88 in La1 *Mandlik* [ट, ठ, ड, ण] *KSS Dave* [= *VaDh* 17.70]:

प्रयच्छेन्नग्निकां कन्यामृतुकालभयात्पिता ।
ऋतुमत्यां हि तिष्ठन्त्यामेनो दातारमृच्छति ॥

a) Be1 Wa °च्छेन्मतिमान्कन्या° — b) La1 °काले तया तदा; NPu1 Pu2 Pu4 °भयान्वितः; Be1 °भयान्वितां — c) NPu1 वितिष्ठन्स्यादेनो; Pu2 Pu4 नितिष्ठन्त्यादेनो

Further additional verses in La1:

तस्मात्रग्नां प्रयच्छेत सदा दुहितरं पिता ।
श्रेयोन्यः सदृशेभ्यश्च जयनेभ्यो रजस्वलाम् ॥
यस्य परा वाक्कन्यायामृतुनैन्द्रियमश्नुते ।
प्रात्सुयविधवाया वा भ्रूणहा स न संशयः ॥
न तेन भोगं कुर्वीत यथा वै भ्रूणहा तथा ।
न च प्रतिष्ठां प्राप्नोति प्रायश्चित्तकृतो भवेत् ॥
तस्मात्प्रागृतुकाले तु दद्याद्दुहितरं पिता ।
परशो मुच्यते तस्मात्प्रेत्य स्वर्गं च गच्छति॥

काममा मरणात्तिष्ठेद् गृहे कन्यर्तुमत्यपि ।
न चैवैनां प्रयच्छेत्तु गुणहीनाय कर्हिचित् ॥८९॥
त्रीणि वर्षाण्युपासीत कुमार्यृतुमती सती ।
ऊर्ध्वं तु कालादेतस्माद्विन्देत सदृशं पतिम् ॥९०॥
अदीयमाना भर्तारमधिगच्छेद्यदि स्वयम् ।
नैनः किंचिदवाप्नोति न च यं साधिगच्छति ॥९१॥
अलंकारं नाददीत पित्र्यं कन्या स्वयंवरा ।
मातृकं भ्रातृदत्तं वा स्तेयं स्याद्यदि तं हरेत् ॥९२॥
पित्रे न दद्याच्छुल्कं तु कन्यामृतुमतीं हरन् ।
स च स्वाम्याददतिक्रामेदृतूनां प्रतिरोधनात् ॥९३॥
त्रिंशद्वर्षो वहेत्कन्यां हृद्यां द्वादशवार्षिकीम् ।

89. Cited by *Apa* 93; *Lakṣ* 2.33; *Hem* 3/3.804; *Dev* 1.216 — a) GMd^1 कामादा; Tr^2 मरणं तिष्ठेतु — b) Ho गेहे — c) wKt^1 न चैव यच्छेत्तु गुरोर्गुण°; GMd^1 चवैनां; TMd^3 NNg चैवेनां; Bo Lo^3 NPu^1 Pu^2 Pu^4 Tj^1 Wa *Apa Lakṣ Dev* त्वेवैनां; Lo^4 Pu^2 Pu^3 Pu^4 Pu^5 Pu^7 Tr^2 Wa [*Jolly* M G] *Lakṣ Hem Dev Jolly* प्रयच्छेत — d) Pu^4 गुणदीनाय; La^1 °हीना हि

90. Omitted in MTr^3. Cited by *Lakṣ* 2.48; *Hem* 3/3.805; *Dev* 1.217; *Mādh* 1.484 — a) *Ku Mr* त्रीणि वर्षाणि प्रतीक्षेत; NKt^4 BKt^5 oOr °ण्युदासीत; BBe^2 Bo Ho Hy Jm Jo^1 Jo^2 wKt^1 Kt^2 wKt^3 Lo^1 Lo^2 Lo^3 Pu^3 Pu^8 Tj^1 Tr^1 [*cor to sh*] Tr^2 Wa *Nā Rn Rc Mandlik Jha KSS Dave* °ण्युदीक्षेत; Tj^2 °ण्युपेक्षेत — b) Pu^8 Tr^2 *Dev* कुमार्यर्तु°; Pu^5 Pu^7 कन्या ऋतु°; TMd^3 क्रमादृतु° — c) wKt^3 La^1 *om* तु; Pu^5 Pu^7 कालाच्चैतस्मा°

91. Pādas a-c *ma* in Lo^4; pādas b-d omitted in wKt^1. Cited by *Lakṣ* 2.48; *Hem* 3/3.805; *Dev* 1. 217; *Mādh* 1.484 — a) sOx^1 sPu^6 अधीय°; wKt^1 अविद्यमाना; Be^1 Tj^1 °मानं — b) GMd^1 °मपिगच्छे°; Ho La^1 NNg °गच्छेत्स्वयं यदि; *Lakṣ* °गच्छेत्स्वयं तथा; BKt^5 °द्यदि प्रियं — c) NNg नैनं; TMd^4 न किंचि°; wKt^3 °चिदाप्नोति — d) GMd^1 GMd^5 Tr^1 MTr^6 स च यं; BBe^2 NKt^4 Tr^2 चायं; Lo^3 चेयं; Ox^2 चैनं; Lo^1 च संभाहमृच्छति; Tr^1 [*but cor*] सोधि°; GMd^1 साभिगच्छति

92.* Omitted in wKt^1. Cited by *Apa* 93; *Lakṣ* 2.48; *Dev* 1.217 — a) TMd^4 नाददीत त्वलंकारं; MTr^6 अलंकारान्; La^1 °कारे; Lo^1 वाददीत; TMd^3 नादधीत — b) *Lakṣ* पितृदत्तं स्वयंवरा; Pu^5 Pu^7 पैत्र्यं; Jm पित्रं; Hy पित्रां — c) *Lakṣ* मातृतो; Be^1 पितृकं; Ho GMd^5 MTr^4 MTr^6 भ्रातृकं दत्तं [*om* वा]; NNg भ्रातृकं वापि; TMd^4 °दत्तां — d) Hy NKt^4 स्तेन; Tr^1 स्ते [*ma sh* न]; Be^1 BBe^2 Bo BCa Ho Hy Jm Jo^1 Jo^2 Kt^2 wKt^3 Lo^1 Lo^2 Lo^3 sOx^1 Ox^2 Pu^3 sPu^6 Pu^8 Tj^1 Tj^2 Tr^2 MTr^3 [*Jolly* Ku R] *Dev Rn Rc Mandlik Jha KSS Dave* स्तेना; *Bh* [pāṭha] *Me* [pāṭha] स्तेनः; GMy विद्यात्तु तं; GMd^1 स्याद्यद्धि तं; GMd^5 स्यादिति तं; MTr^5 स्याद्यदिदं हरेत्; TMd^3 स्यादिति तास्वरेत्; BBe^2 तां; wKt^3 कं

93.* Omitted in wKt^1 Pu^4. Cited by *Apa* 93; *Lakṣ* 2.48 — a) NKt^4 Lo^4 Pu^2 पित्र्ये; Tr^2 पित्रो; oOr sOx^1 sPu^6 पित्रे तु; Lo^2 पित्रेण; BKt^5 La^1 पित्र्येण; GMd^5 Pu^3 *om* न; BCa °च्छुल्कस्तु; BKt^5 *om* तु; BBe^2 sOx^1 sPu^6 हि; Ho La^1 NNg च — b) Tr^2 °तुमता; BKt^5 °तुमहीं; wKt^3 La^1 MTr^4 Wa हरेत् — c) Pu^2 पितृस्वाम्याददतिक्रामेदृ°; Be^1 Lo^4 न च; BBe^2 BCa Ho Hy Jm Jo^1 wKt^3 La^1 Tj^2 Tr^1 [*mc sh to*] MTr^3 Wa [*Jolly* Ku] *Apa Lakṣ Rn Mr Jolly* स हि; oOr स सर्वस्वाददति°; TMd^3 काम्याददति°; Bo °दतिक्राम्ये°; sOx^1 sPu^6 °दपक्रामे° — d) GMy पतिरो°; BKt^5 पविरो°; Tj^1 °बोधनात्; Pu^5 Pu^7 °चोधनात्; TMd^3 °रोधकः

त्र्यष्टवर्षोऽष्टवर्षां वा धर्मे सीदति सत्वरः ॥९४॥
देवदत्तां पतिर्भार्यां विन्दते नेच्छयात्मनः ।
तां साध्वीं बिभृयान्नित्यं देवानां प्रियमाचरन् ॥९५॥
प्रजनार्थं स्त्रियः सृष्टाः संतानार्थं च मानवाः ।
तस्मात्साधारणो धर्मः श्रुतौ पत्न्या सहोदितः ॥९६॥
कन्यायां दत्तशुल्कायां म्रियेत यदि शुल्कदः ।
देवराय प्रदातव्या यदि कन्यानुमन्यते ॥९७॥
आददीत न शूद्रोऽपि शुल्कं दुहितरं ददत् ।
शुल्कं हि गृह्णन्कुरुते छन्नं दुहितृविक्रयम् ॥९८॥
एतत्तु न परे चक्रुर्नापरे जातु साधवः ।
यदन्यस्याभ्यनुज्ञाय पुनरन्यस्य दीयते ॥९९॥

94. Omitted in wKt^1 Kt^2 Pu^4. Cited by *Jmv* 1.39; *Hem* 3/3.802; *Dev* 1.212, 213; *Mādh* 1.474, 2.121 — a) Hy Lo^3 NPu^1 Pu^2 Pu^3 Pu^5 Pu^7 Tj^1 *Mandlik KSS* °द्वर्षोद्वहे° [supported by *Bh Ku Mr*]; La^1 °द्वर्षाद्वहे°; GMd^1 हरेत्कन्यां; *Jmv* [vl] वहेद्भार्यां — b) NPu^1 °वार्षिकी; Kt^2 °वार्षिकिं; BBe^2 °वार्षिकां — c) Bo NNg Tj^1 अष्टवर्षो; NNg °ष्टमां वर्षां BBe^2 °ष्टवर्षायां धर्मे; TMd^3 तु — d) NNg चाधर्मे; Pu^5 Pu^7 धर्मो; TMd^4 सिध्यति तत्परं; sOx^1 sPu^6 सत्वरा; BBe^2 GMd^1 सत्वरं; *Jmv* [vl] सत्वरे; TMd^3 सर्वशः

95. Omitted in wKt^1 Pu^4; placed after 9.74 in TMd^3 GMy. Cited by *Lakṣ* 12.611; *Dev* 3.568 — a) Lo^1 देवताप्रतिमाया वा; TMd^3 Tj^2 पतिभार्यां; Pu^5 Pu^7 °भार्या — b) Be^1 Lo^4 Pu^2 Pu^3 Pu^5 Pu^7 Tr^2 Wa [*Jolly* M G] *Jolly* विन्देतानिच्छयात्मनः; sOx^1 sPu^6 GMy विन्देते; NNg विन्देत; GMd^5 विन्दन्नेच्छ°; TMd^3 नेच्छया पतिः — d) Ox^2 हितमाचरन्; La^1 GMd^1 TMd^3 GMy sOx^1 sPu^6 °माचरेत्

96. Omitted in wKt^1; placed after 9.74 in TMd^3 GMy. Cited by *Lakṣ* 12.611 — a) Hy Pu^5 Pu^7 [*but cor*] प्रजानार्थं; Bo °नार्थे; TMd^3 Tj^1 °नार्थ — b) TMd^4 तु; BKt^5 GMy NPu^1 मानवः — d) GMd^5 श्रुतः; NKt^4 कृतौ; GMy sOx^1 sPu^6 पत्न्यां; GMd^1 पत्न्यौ; TMd^3 Wa पत्या; TMd^4 सहोदिताः

97. Omitted in wKt^1 Pu^4; pāda-b omitted in Pu^5. Cited by *Viś* 1.69; *Lakṣ* 2.61; *Dev* 1.219 — a) Be^1 Bo BKt^5 Lo^4 GMy Ox^2 [*Jolly* M^{4-5-9} Nd] शुल्कदत्तायां — b) Be^1 Ho Lo^2 Lo^3 Lo^4 GMd^1 GMd^5 NNg oOr NPu^1 Pu^7 Tj^1 म्रियते; Lo^1 म्रीयते; NKt^4 BKt^5 sOx^1 sPu^6 Tr^1 [*but cor sh*] मृयेत; La^1 मृयते; TMd^3 क्रियते — d) wKt^3 कन्यामनुमन्यते; Be^1 TMd^3 *Lakṣ* कन्या तु मन्यते; GMd^5 कन्या न मन्यते; Lo^1 कन्या तु मुच्यते; Jo^2 °नुविन्द्यते

98. Omitted in wKt^1; *Nd* has the following sequence of verses: 98, 100, 99, 101 — a) Ho आददाति — b) Jo^1 NKt^4 La^1 GMd^1 TMd^3 GMy Pu^7 Tj^1 Tj^2 MTr^5 *Mandlik Jha KSS Dave* ददन्; Be^1 वदन् — c) La^1 गृह्णन्हि शुल्कं कुरुते; Tr^1 [in addition after 3.51] शुल्कं हि द्रविणं कृत्वा; GMd^5 *om* हि — d) Ho छिन्नं; Ho °विक्रयः; Pu^2 Pu^4 °विक्रयां; Tr^2 °विक्रियं

99. Omitted in wKt^1 oOr; pādas c-d omitted in BKt^5; verses 99 and 100 transposed in GMy. Cited by *Lakṣ* 2.57–8; *Dev* 1.218 — a) NNg एतच्च; Pu^5 Pu^7 एवं तु; *Lakṣ* एवं च; GMy पुरे; Lo^2 पुरा; Pu^5 Pu^7 कुर्युर्नापरे; NPu^1 वक्तुं नापरे — a-b) Lo^4 तत्तु न परे जातु साधवः कुर्वते ध्रुवं — b) GMy चक्रुर्नापुरे; sOx^1 sPu^6 जात; GMd^5 चापि साधवः; NPu^1 साधनः; Pu^2 Pu^4 माधवः — c) TMd^4 GMd^5 यद्यन्य°; GMd^5 °न्यस्याप्यनुज्ञाय; Hy Jm Jo^1 Kt^2 wKt^3 sOx^1 Ox^2 sPu^6 Tj^2 MTr^3 [*Jolly* Ku] *Mandlik Jha KSS Dave* °न्यस्य प्रतिज्ञाय — d) Tr^2 पुनरन्ये प्रदीयते; GMd^1 पुनरन्यत्प्रदीयते

नानुशुश्रुम जात्वेतत् पूर्वेष्वपि हि जन्मसु ।
शुल्कसंज्ञेन मूल्येन छन्नं दुहितृविक्रयम् ॥१००॥
अन्योन्यस्याव्यभीचारो भवेदामरणान्तिकः ।
एष धर्मः समासेन ज्ञेयः स्त्रीपुंसयोः परः ॥१०१॥
तथा नित्यं यतेयातां स्त्रीपुंसौ तु कृतक्रियौ ।
यथा नातिचरेतां तौ वियुक्तावितरेतरम् ॥१०२॥
एष स्त्रीपुंसयोरुक्तो धर्मो वो रतिसंहितः ।
आपद्यपत्यप्राप्तिश्च दायधर्मं निबोधत ॥१०३॥
ऊर्ध्वं पितुश्च मातुश्च समेत्य भ्रातरः समम् ।
भजेरन्पैतृकं रिक्थमनीशास्ते हि जीवतोः ॥१०४॥

100. Omitted in wKt^{1} BKt^{5} oOr. Cited by *Dev* 1.232 — a) TMd^{3} तां न शुश्रम; Be^{1} नापि शुश्रुम; TMd^{4} नाशुश्रुम; Bo °श्रुश्रुत; wKt^{3} °शुश्रुपा; Lo^{1} °शुश्रुमो; Bo जात्वेनन् — a-b) GMd^{5} नैतच्छुश्रुम जात्वेतत्पुरुषेपु त्रिजन्मसु — b) GMd^{1} पूर्वेपु जन्मसु; Ho NKt^{4} ह; GMd^{5} GMy च — c) Ho शुल्कजज्ञेन; Pu^{4} मूलेन; GMd^{5} [in add after 3.51] मौल्येन; Wa स्वल्पेन — d) Pu^{5} Pu^{7} छिन्नं; Tr^{1} [in addition after 3.51] पापं; Ho °विक्रयः; TMd^{3} °विक्रीयं

Additional half-verse in TMd^{3}:

अयशो महदाप्नोति कुर्वन्निह च नित्यताम् ॥

101. Omitted in wKt^{1}; pādas c-d omitted in BKt^{5}, and pāda-d in Lo^{3}. Cited by *Apa* 101; *Lakṣ* 12.613; *Dev* 3.581 — a) TMd^{4} अन्योन्यस्मादाभीचारो; La^{1} अन्योन्याभिचारो; Lo^{3} अन्यान्य°; GMd^{1} Ox^{2} Pu^{2} Pu^{4} Tr^{2} °न्यस्यव्य°; Be^{1} Hy Jm Jo^{1} Jo^{2} Kt^{2} wKt^{5} Lo^{1} [*but cor*] Lo^{4} TMd^{3} GMy NPu^{1} Tr^{2} Wa [*Jolly* M Nd] *Apa KSS* °भिचारो; Pu^{2} Pu^{4} °चारौ — b) Ho °णान्तकः; TMd^{3} TMd^{4} GMd^{5} °णान्तिकं; Pu^{8} °णाङ्कितः — c) wKt^{3} TMd^{4} धर्मं — d) GMd^{5} *om* परः; Be^{1} समः; T Md^{3} MTr^{4} MTr^{5} MTr^{6} शुभः; GMyशुभं

102.* Omitted in wKt^{1}; pādas a-b omitted in Pu^{4} and pāda-a in Lo^{3}. Cited by *Lakṣ* 12.613; *Dev* 3.581 — a)oOr यथा; BKt^{5} नित्यं तथा; Tr^{2} यतेयात्सं — b) BBe^{2} पुमांसौ कृतविक्रयौ; TMd^{4} स्त्रीपुंसा तं कृतक्रिया; Lo^{2} °पुंसो; BCa HowKt^{3} °पुमांसौ कृत°; BKt^{5} °पुंसां संक्रितकरयौ; Tj^{1} तु यतौ क्रियौ; La^{1} हृतक्रियौ — c) Pu^{4} तथा; Be^{1} Bo Hy Jm Jo^{1} Jo^{2} Kt^{2} La^{1} Lo^{1} Lo^{2} Lo^{3} NNg Ox^{2} NPu^{1} Pu^{2} Pu^{3} Pu^{4} Pu^{5} Pu^{7} Pu^{8} Tj^{1} Tj^{2} Tr^{2} MTr^{3} [*Jolly* G Ku R] *Mandlik KSS* नाभिचरेतां; Ho नाभिचरेयातां तौ; sOx^{1} sPu^{6} नाभिचरेयातां [*om* तौ]; *Dev* नातिचरेयातां वियु° — d) Ho NKt^{4} Lo^{2} Lo^{4} TMd^{3} NNg oOr sOx^{1} NPu^{1} Pu^{2} Pu^{4} sPu^{6} Tr^{2} Wa [*Jolly* M] *Me Rc* नियुक्ता°; BBe^{2} Hy Jo^{2} Lo^{3} Tj^{1} Tj^{2} विमुक्ता°; MTr^{4} MTr^{6} संयुक्ता°; BKt^{5} GMd^{1} °रेतरौ

103. Omitted in wKt^{1}; pāda-d omitted in NKt^{4}. Cited by *Jmv* 1.3; *Dev* 3.597 — a) Lo^{3} एत — b) Be^{1} Bo TMd^{4} Pu^{2} Pu^{4} वा; Pu^{2} Pu^{4} रवि°; Tj^{2} रसि°; GMd^{5} रक्षति संहिताः; TMd^{3} °संहितं; NNg Wa *Jmv* [vl] °संज्ञितः; *Jmv* [vl] °संस्थितः; Be^{1} Ox^{2} °संग्रहः — c) TMd^{3} TMd^{4} °प्राप्तेश्च; MTr^{6} °प्राप्तिं च; Pu^{4} °प्रदानिश्च; Be^{1} °प्राप्तिश्चेद् — d) Be^{1} आपद्धर्मान्निबोधत; BBe^{2} Jo^{1} Kt^{2} wKt^{3} Pu^{3} Tj^{2} MTr^{3} *Mandlik KSS Dave* दायभागं [supported by *Ku Rn Mr*]; Pu^{2} *om* °धर्मं; Tr^{2} °धर्मो; Tj^{1} °धर्मां; sOx^{1} °कर्मं; Hy Jo^{2} Pu^{8} *Nā Rc* °धर्मान्निबोधत; wKt^{3} नियोधतः

104. Omitted in wKt^{1}; pāda-a omitted in NKt^{4}. Cited by *Apa* 718; *Jmv* 1.14; *Lakṣ* 12.648; *Dev* 3.599; pāda-a cited by *Vij* 2.117 and pāda-d by *Jmv* 2.7 — a) Lo^{2} *om* and Lo^{4} *ma* मातुश्च; Lo^{3} Tj^{1} भ्रातुश्च — b) BKt^{5} समेता; Wa समन्ये; Pu^{5} Pu^{7} भ्रातरं; NKt^{4} GMd^{1} GMd^{5} GMy Pu^{5} Pu^{7} Tr^{1}

ज्येष्ठ एव तु गृह्णीयात् पित्र्यं धनमशेषतः ।
शेषास्तमुपजीवेयुर्यथैव पितरं तथा ॥१०५॥
ज्येष्ठेन जातमात्रेण पुत्री भवति मानवः ।
पितॄणामनृणश्चैव स तस्मात्सर्वमर्हति ॥१०६॥
यस्मिन्नृणं संनयति येन चानन्त्यमश्नुते ।
स एव धर्मजः पुत्रः कामजानितरान्विदुः ॥१०७॥
पितेव पालयेत्पुत्राञ्ज्येष्ठो भ्राता यवीयसः ।
पुत्रवच्चापि वर्तेरञ्ज्येष्ठे भ्रातरि धर्मतः ॥१०८॥
ज्येष्ठः कुलं वर्धयति विनाशयति वा पुनः ।
ज्येष्ठः पूज्यतमो लोके ज्येष्ठः सद्भिरगर्हितः ॥१०९॥
यो ज्येष्ठो ज्येष्ठवृत्तिः स्यान्मातेव स पितेव सः ।
अज्येष्ठवृत्तिर्यस्तु स्यात् स संपूज्यस्तु बन्धुवत् ॥११०॥

mTr[4] mTr[5] mTr[6] [*Jolly* Nd Gr] सह; tMd[3] स्वयं — c) Tj[1] सजेर°; bKt[5] La[1] Lo[4] nPu[1] °न्मैत्रिकं; gMd[1] Ox[2] °तृकमृक्थम°; Be[1] रित्तम°; Wa रिच्छम°; La[1] शक्तम°; Hy खिप्यम° — d) Hy °नाशास्ते; tMd[4] °नीशास्ति; gMd[1] °नीगास्ते; bKt[5] °शास्तेषु जीवतोः; sOx[1] जीवतः; Lo[1] जीवते; Lo[2] जीवतौ; Hy जीवतीः

105. Omitted in wKt[1] Pu[5]; pādas c-d omitted in Pu[8]. Cited by *Vij* 2.117; *Apa* 722; *Jmv* 1.36, 3.15; *Lakṣ* 12.649; *Dev* 3.615; *Mādh* 3.334 — a) bKt[5] ज्येष्ठमेव; Be[1] Hy Jo[2] Lo[3] nNg Tj[1] हि — b) Ox[2] पैत्र्यं; Hy पित्रां; gMy °शेषतं — c) nPu[1] °मनुजीवेयु°; Tr[2] °जीवेषु यथैव — d) Bo °वेयुस्तथैव; bKt[5] La[1] पितरस्तथा

106. Omitted in wKt[1]. Cited by *Jmv* 1.36, 11.1.32; *Lakṣ* 12.650; *Dev* 1.43; *Mādh* 1.502; pādas a-b cited by *Vij* 2.130and pādas c-d by *Jmv* 11.6.31 — b) gMy मानवा — c) bKt[5] °नृणं चैव — d) Ho तस्मात्स सर्व°; *Jmv* 1.36 तस्माल्लुब्धमर्हति; *Jmv* 11.1.32, 11.6.31 तस्माल्लब्धुमर्हति

107. Omitted in wKt[1]; pādas c-d omitted in nKt[4]. Cited by *Jmv* 1.36; *Lakṣ* 12.650; *Dev* 1.48; *Mādh* 1.502 — a) Tj[1] संनयत्; Lo[1] सनयति — b) oOr चानन्तम°; La[1] nNg चात्यन्तमश्नुते; Hy Lo[2] gMd[1] tMd[3] tMd[4] gMd[5] gMy mTr[4] mTr[6] चामृतमश्नुते; Jo[2] Tj[1] वामृतमश्नुते; Bo Tr[1] चानृतमश्नुते; *Jmv* °मश्नोति — c) Tj[1] एवं; Lo[1] Lo[4] oOr Pu[5] Pu[7] [*Jolly* M[4–5–9] G] *Jolly* एष; gMd[1] [*Jolly* M[8] R Ku Nd] धर्मतः — d) nPu[1] °जानपरान्विदुः

108.* Omitted in wKt[1] nKt[4]; verses 108 and 109 transposed in gMy [*Jolly* Nd]. Cited by *Jmv* 6.1.54; *Lakṣ* 12.650; pādas a-b cited by *Apa* 433 — a) *Apa* पुत्रवत्पालयेच्चैनाञ्ज्ये°; Tr[2] पितैव; gMy °त्पुत्रा ज्ये°; mTr[4] mTr[6] °त्पुत्रो ज्ये° — b) wKt[3] °ञ्ज्येष्ठे; Be[1] Bo Jm Jo[1] Kt[2] bKt[5] Lo[1] Lo[2] Lo[4] gMy oOr Ox[2] Pu[8] Tj[2] Tr[2] mTr[3] *Lakṣ Mandlik Jolly Jha KSS Dave* भ्रातॄन्यवी°; Ho भ्रातॄन्यवीयवः; Pu[3] भ्रातॄनशेषतः — c) Ho wKt[3] nNg Pu[8] पुत्रवत्तेपि; tMd[3] °वच्चातिवर्ते°; *Jmv* [vl as in ed] °वच्चा-नुवर्ते°; mTr[5] वर्तेत ज्ये° — d) La[1] Tj[2] °ञ्ज्येष्ठो; Bo gMd[5] °ञ्ज्येष्ठ; mTr[3] संमतः

109. Omitted in wKt[1] nKt[4]. Cited by *Lakṣ* 12.650 — a) gMy ज्येष्ठा; Pu[3] Tr[2] वर्धयते — b) gMy °शयति चेतरः — c) bKt[5] ज्येष्ठः स पूज्य°; Tj[1] पूज्यतमा — d) Tj[1] ज्येष्ठ

110. Omitted in nKt[4]; pādas a-c omitted in wKt[1]. Cited by *Lakṣ* 12.650 — a) Wa *om* ज्येष्ठो; nPu[1] °वृद्धिः — b) Be[1] स्वपितेव; Lo[4] gMy च पितेव; gMy mTr[5] *Lakṣ* पितेव च — c) La[1] ज्येष्ठवृत्तिस्तयोर्न स्यात्; Pu[5] Pu[7] [*Jolly* G] अज्येष्ठ एव यस्तु; gMy °वृत्तिर्यस्य; Pu[2] °वृत्तिं यस्तु — d) oOr संपूज्यस्तु स बन्धुवत्; bBe[2] संपूज्यश्च; Wa °स्तु संबन्धु°; bKt[5] बन्धुभिः

एवं सह वसेयुर्वा पृथग्वा धर्मकाम्यया ।
पृथग्विवर्धते धर्मस्तस्माद्धर्म्या पृथक्क्रिया ॥१११॥
ज्येष्ठस्य विंश उद्धारः सर्वद्रव्याच्च यद्वरम् ।
ततोऽर्धं मध्यमस्य स्यात् तुरीयं तु यवीयसः ॥११२॥
ज्येष्ठश्चैव कनिष्ठश्च संहरेतां यथोदितम् ।
येऽन्ये ज्येष्ठकनिष्ठाभ्यां तेषां स्यान्मध्यमं धनम् ॥११३॥
सर्वेषां धनजातानामाददीताग्र्यमग्रजः ।
यच्च सातिशयं किंचिद्दशतश्चाप्नुयाद्वरम् ॥११४॥
उद्धारो न दशस्वस्ति संपन्नानां स्वकर्मसु ।
यत्किंचिदेव देयं तु ज्यायसे मानवर्धनम् ॥११५॥
एवं समुद्धृतोद्धारे समानंशान्प्रकल्पयेत् ।
उद्धारेऽनुद्धृते त्वेषामियं स्यादंशकल्पना ॥११६॥

111. Cited by *Apa* 719, 722; *Jmv* 1.37; *Lakṣ* 12.651; pādas a-b cited by *Jmv* 1.27 — b) TMd^{3} °काम्ययं; *Apa* °काङ्क्षया — c) GMd^{1} पृथक्प्रवर्धते; GMd^{5} पृथग्वावर्धते; *Apa* 722 [vl] पृथग्विभज्यते — d) Be^{1} °द्धर्म्याः; Wa °द्धर्म्य; BKt^{5} Pu^{5} Pu^{7} °द्धर्मा; TMd^{3} GMd^{5} °द्धर्मः; oOr °द्धर्म; Ho wKt^{3} Tr^{2} °द्धर्मात्पृथ°; *Apa* 719 °द्धर्मा: पृथ°; Lo^{2} Tr^{2} पृथक्क्रयां; MTr^{3} प्रतिक्रिया— NPu^{1} inserts here 9.213.

112. Cited by *Vij* 2.114, 117; *Jmv* 2.37; *Lakṣ* 12.655; *Dev* 3.619; *Mādh* 3.334 — a) Pu^{5} Pu^{7} [*Jolly* G] ज्येष्ठः समुद्धरेदंशं; La^{1} ज्येष्ठस्तु; Be^{1} TMd^{3} GMy sOx^{1} MTr^{4} वंश; TMd^{4} विंशमुद्धारं; wKt^{1} विंशतिद्वारः; Lo^{1} [*cor to*] उद्धारं — b) *Bh* [pāṭha] द्रव्येभ्यश्च वरं वरं; *Me* [pāṭha] द्रव्येष्वपि परं वरं; Be^{1} सर्वत्र स्याच्च यद्वरं; BKt^{5} °यज्ञाच्च; Hy °द्रव्येषु; Pu^{2} Pu^{4} °द्रव्याच्चराचरं; GMd^{1} GMy यद्वरः; Lo^{1} यद्धरेत् — c) Be^{1} La^{1} Lo^{2} Lo^{4} GMd^{1} NNg NPu^{1} Pu^{2} Pu^{4} Pu^{5} Pu^{7} Tr^{1} [*but cor sh*] MTr^{4} अतो; Pu^{8} अथो; Wa अंतोधं; Ox^{2} तदर्धं; Tr^{2} मध्यस्य; Pu^{5} Pu^{7} मध्यमस्तस्य — d) Hy सर्वद्रव्येपु यद्वरां [cf. 8.112b]; Pu^{5} Pu^{7} [*Jolly* G] तृतीयं; TMd^{4} MTr^{6} तुरीयस्तु; BKt^{5} TMd^{3} च; BBe^{2} यवीयसे; Ho sOx^{1} sPu^{6} कनीयसः

113. Cited by *Lakṣ* 12.656 — a) NPu^{1} ज्येष्ठस्यैव; Lo^{4} [*ma* धनं] ज्येष्ठं कनि°; sOx^{1} sPu^{6} कनीयांश्च; Pu^{2} Pu^{4} कनिष्ठस्तु; oOr कनिष्ठस्य — b) Lo^{3} यथोदितः; Hy यथोदिता; oOr यथोदितां; GMy [*Jolly* Nd] मिथो यदि — c) Tr^{1} यो; Lo^{3} Tj^{1} ये ये; TMd^{3} वन्ये; Jm येने; Lo^{1} येन; Hy TMd^{4} ज्येष्ठा° — d) *Lakṣ* येषां; Wa °न्मध्यमे; Lo^{2} °न्मध्यकं; Lo^{1} °न्मध्यगं

114. Omitted in sOx^{1}. Cited by *Lakṣ* 12.656 — a) GMy जनजाताना°; La^{1} धनदानाना°; Ho °जातीनामा° — b) wKt^{1} BKt^{5} La^{1} Pu^{2} Pu^{4} Pu^{5} sPu^{6} Pu^{7} Tj^{2} Tr^{2} Wa [*Jolly* M G] *Jolly* °ताग्रमग्रजः; Kt^{2} °ताग्रमग्रतः; Tr^{1} [*but cor sh*] °ताग्रमात्मजः — d) Pu^{5} Pu^{7} °शतस्राप्नु°; Hy Jo^{2} Lo^{3} TMd^{3} Pu^{3} Tj^{1} Tr^{2} *Lakṣ* °शतः प्राप्नु°; BKt^{5} °याद्वनं; Be^{1} wKt^{1} °याद्धनं; Lo^{1} °याद्धरं; *Bh* [pāṭha] °याद्वरान् commenting: अपरे तु दशतश्चाप्नुयाद्वरानिति द्वितीयाबहुवचनं पठन्ति

115. Cited by *Jmv* 2.45; *Lakṣ* 12.659; *Dev* 3.619 — a) sOx^{1} sPu^{6} उद्धारो दनशस्वस्ति [metathesis]; GMd^{1} उधारोतिशयस्वस्ति; GMy दशस्वेति — b) TMd^{4} सप्तनानानुकर्मसु; La^{1} Tr^{2} सुकर्मसु; Pu^{5} Pu^{7} [*Jolly* G] स्वधर्मतः — c) Lo^{2} °चिदेवादेयं तु; Pu^{5} Pu^{7} *Jmv Lakṣ Dev* देयं स्याज्ज्यायसे — d) MTr^{4} MTr^{6} ज्यायसो; Pu^{2} Pu^{4} °वार्धनं

116. Cited by *Jmv* 2.37; *Lakṣ* 12.660; *Dev* 3.620; pādas c-d cited by *Vij* 2.117; *Mādh* 3.334 — a) wKt^{1} समृद्धितोद्धारे; Pu^{4} समुद्धृतेद्वारे; Bo La^{1} GMd^{5} °द्धारो — b) Bo समाशा प्रविलङ्घयेत्; BBe^{2} GMd^{1} समानांशा°; TMd^{3} समांशांश्च प्रक° — c) Lo^{1} उद्धारोनधृते; GMy मुद्धारेण युते; Tj^{2}

एकाधिकं हरेज्ज्येष्ठः पुत्रोऽध्यर्धं ततोऽनुजः ।
अंशमंशं यवीयांस इति धर्मो व्यवस्थितः ॥११७॥
स्वेभ्योंऽशेभ्यस्तु कन्याभ्यः प्रदद्युर्भ्रातरः पृथक् ।
स्वात्स्वादंशाच्चतुर्भागं पतिताः स्युरदित्सवः ॥११८॥
अजाविकं चैकशफं न जातु विषमं भजेत् ।
अजाविकं तु विषमं ज्येष्ठस्यैव विधीयते ॥११९॥
यवीयाञ्ज्येष्ठभार्यायां पुत्रमुत्पादयेद्यदि ।
समस्तत्र विभागः स्यादिति धर्मो व्यवस्थितः ॥१२०॥
उपसर्जनं प्रधानस्य धर्मतो नोपपद्यते ।
पिता प्रधानं प्रजने तस्माद्धर्मेण तं भजेत् ॥१२१॥
पुत्रः कनिष्ठो ज्येष्ठायां कनिष्ठायां च पूर्वजः ।
कथं तत्र विभागः स्यादिति चेत्संशयो भवेत् ॥१२२॥

उद्धारेचोद्धृते; Lo^{4} उद्धारे उद्धृते; Ho उद्धारे च धृते; Be^{1} °द्धृते एषामियं; wKt^{1} त्वैषामियं; Be^{1} Ho Hy Jm Jo^{2} La^{1} Lo^{1} Lo^{3} Lo^{4} GMy NNg Pu^{5} Pu^{7} Tr^{2} [*Jolly* M G Nd] *Rc Mādh Jolly* तेषामियं; Tr^{1} चैषामियं — d) Lo^{1} °षामिदं; oOr स्यादर्थकल्पना; Lo^{1} °कल्पनं

117. Cited by *Vij* 2.117; *Lakṣ* 12.661; *Dev* 3.620; *Mādh* 3.334 — a) BKt^{5} एकादिकं; Bo एकाहिकं; MTr^{6} हरेत्पूज्यः — a-b) TMd^{4} एकाधिकां हरेत्पुत्रा ज्येष्ठाध्यर्धं ततोनुजः — b) Tr^{2} पुत्रोधर्मं; Hy °ध्यर्ध्यं; Tj^{1} °ध्यर्थं; TMd^{3} °त्यर्धं — c) Tr^{2} अंशमंशां; Lo^{1} TMd^{4} असमांशं; oOr Tr^{1} [*but mc sh*] °यांसमिति — d) Lo^{4} व्यवक्षितः; Lo^{1} °स्थितिः

118.* Cited by *Vij* 2.124; *Apa* 731; *Jmv* 3.36; *Lakṣ* 12.671; *Dev* 3.626; *Mādh* 3.345 — a) BKt^{5} स्वेभ्यः स्वेभ्यः स्वकन्याभ्यः; La^{1} येभ्यो; *Mādh* तेभ्यो; Lo^{4} TMd^{4} Wa [*Jolly* M] *Me* स्वाभ्यः स्वाभ्यस्तु; *Lakṣ* स्वेभ्यः स्वेभ्यस्तु; Tr^{2} स्वेभ्योस्वेभ्यस्तु; Be^{1} Pu^{5} Pu^{7} °भ्यश्च — b) *Mādh* स्वं दद्युर्भ्रा°; TMd^{4} प्रदद्याद्भ्रातरं — c) TMd^{3} *om first* स्वात्; MTr^{4} °शात्तुरीयांशं; Pu^{7} °च्चतुर्थांशं — d) Lo^{1} परिदद्युरुद्दित्सवः

119. Cited by *Vij* 2.118–9; *Apa* 723; *Lakṣ* 12.674 — a) Bo अजाविशं; NPu^{1} अजातिकं; wKt^{1} प्रजाविकं; Be^{1} °विकमेकशफं; Jm Jo^{1} Jo^{2} NKt^{4} Lo^{2} Tj^{2} MTr^{3} [*Jolly* Ku] *Vij Rn Mandlik KSS Dave* सैकशफं [supported by *Ku*]; Hy सेकशफं ; Kt^{2} सैकशसं; BKt^{5} शैफलकं; *Apa* त्वेकशफं; wKt^{3} चैवकफं — b) BCa BKt^{5} Lo^{1} Lo^{3} GMd^{1} NPu^{1} Tj^{2} भवेत्; GMy MTr^{4} MTr^{6} हरेत्; wKt^{1} त्यजेत् — c) *Vij* अजाविकं सैकशफं; Hy अजाविके

120. Cited by *Vij* 2.136; *Lakṣ* 12.708; *Mādh* 3.357 — a) *Vij Mādh* कनीयाञ्ज्ये°; GMd^{5} °भार्यायाः — b) BKt^{5} °दयेत्क्वचित् — c) Bo GMd^{5} NNg समस्तस्य; Tr^{2} विभागं — d) TMd^{3} °स्थितिः

121. Omitted in BKt^{5}. Cited by *Lakṣ* 12.709 — a) Lo^{4} उपसर्जन; wKt^{3} उपसज्जनं; TMd^{4} MTr^{6} उत्सर्जनं; Ho उपसर्जन्प्र° — b) Be^{1} ह्युपपद्यते — c) MTr^{4} विधा प्रधानं; TMd^{3} sOx^{1} sPu^{6} MTr^{4} MTr^{5} MTr^{6} *Bh* प्रधानः; Lo^{4} प्रजनं; wKt^{1} प्रसने; Ho जनने; GMd^{5} भजने — d) *Bh* [pāṭha] तस्मादर्धेन; TMd^{3} तस्माद्यत्नेन; Lo^{4} तां; sOx^{1} sPu^{6} Tj^{2} संभजेत्; Tr^{2} संभवेत्; GMd^{5} तत् भवेत्; Ox^{2} MTr^{3} व्रजेत्; *Me* [pāṭha; rejected by *Me*] त्यजेत्

122. Pādas a-b omitted in BKt^{5}. Cited by *Lakṣ* 12.658 — a) Lo^{4} अपुत्रः; Lo^{3} कविष्ठो; GMd^{5} GMy MTr^{4} MTr^{6} ज्येष्ठायाः; Lo^{2} ज्येष्ठां — b) NKt^{4} Tj^{2} *om* कनिष्ठायां; GMy MTr^{4} MTr^{6} कनिष्ठायाश्च; BCa Ho wKt^{1} wKt^{3} La^{1} NNg Pu^{3} Pu^{7} तु — c) GMd^{1} तस्य — d) wKt^{3} भजेत्

एकं वृषभमुद्धारं संहरेत स पूर्वजः ।
ततोऽपरेऽज्येष्ठवृषास्तदूनानां स्वमातृतः ॥१२३॥
ज्येष्ठस्तु जातो ज्येष्ठायां हरेद्वृषभषोडशाः ।
ततः स्वमातृतः शेषा भजेरन्निति धारणा ॥१२४॥
सदृशस्त्रीषु जातानां पुत्राणामविशेषतः ।
न मातृतो ज्यैष्ठ्यमस्ति जन्मतो ज्यैष्ठ्यमुच्यते ॥१२५॥
जन्मज्येष्ठेन चाह्वानं सुब्रह्मण्यास्वपि स्मृतम् ।
यमयोश्चैकगर्भेऽपि* जन्मतो ज्येष्ठता स्मृता ॥१२६॥
अपुत्रोऽनेन विधिना सुतां कुर्वीत पुत्रिकाम् ।
यदपत्यं भवेदस्यां तन्मम स्यात्स्वधाकरम् ॥१२७॥

123.* Cited by *Lakṣ* 12.658 — a) Tj^2 एक; wKt^1 La^1 एवं — b) wKt^1 Pu^5 Pu^7 [*Jolly* G] संहरेत्सर्वपूर्वजः [wKt^1 आहरेत्सर्व]; BCa संहरेत्तत्र पूर्वजः; Lo^2 संहारेत; wKt^3 Pu^8 संहरेत्तु; BKt^5 स तु प्रजः — c) Be^1 इत्थं तत्र विभागः स्यात्तदू°; MTr^6 ततोपरो; Ho °श्रेष्ठवृ°; TMd^3 °वृषां तदू°; GMd^5 °वृषात्तदू° — c-d) wKt^1 °वृशात्तद्धूतानां; GMy °वृषास्तदूना वै — d) Pu^5 Pu^7 °पास्तद्धनानां; Pu^2 Pu^4 °वृषास्तदूढायां; BBe^2 °वृशास्तामृशानां; TMd^3 °वृशां समाना वै; BBe^2 MTr^3 समातृतः

124. Omitted in oOr; pādas c-d *ma* in Lo^4. Cited by *Lakṣ* 12.658, 782 — a) Jo^1 जाता; GMy ज्येष्ठाया — b) Tr^2 हारयेद्वृषषोडशं; Tj^1 हरद्वृष°; Be^1 GMy NNg Pu^4 MTr^5 °षोडशः; Ho Jo^1 Kt^2 NKt^4 BKt^5 Lo^1 GMd^1 TMd^4 sOx^1 Pu^5 sPu^6 Pu^7 °षोडश; BBe^2 La^1 Lo^4 TMd^3 NPu^1 Pu^2 Wa [*Jolly* M Nd] °षोडशं; MTr^6 °षोडशान् — c) Lo^4 *om* स्वमातृतः; BBe^2 समातृतः; MTr^6 स्वमातृकाः; Ho स्वमातः शेषाश्च; Wa स्वमातृशेषो — d) NKt^4 La^1 Lo^4 GMd^5 NNg Tr^1 [*but mc sh*] हरेरन्निति; TMd^4 हरेदन्निति; GMd^1 TMd^3 MTr^4 MTr^6 हरेयुरिति; Lo^4 धारण; TMd^3 धारुणा; TMd^4 कारण

125. a) Be^1 सदृशः; BKt^5 जातायां; *Bh* [ad 8.126] gives a pāṭha, असदृश, which he rejects — b) GMd^1 °णां विशेषतः; Tj^1 °णामिव शेषतः; NKt^4 °णामपि शेषतः — c) oOr अमातृतो; TMd^3 समापृतो; NKt^4 मातृदो; TMd^4 मातृते; Tj^1 मावृतो; Lo^3 Pu^2 Wa ज्येष्ठ्यम°; BBe^2 wKt^1 wKt^3 Lo^2 TMd^3 TMd^4 oOr sOx^1 Pu^5 sPu^6 Pu^7 Tr^2 ज्येष्ठम°; Lo^4 ज्येष्ठ इति — d) TMd^3 जन्मनो; wKt^3 Lo^4 Pu^5 Pu^7 Tj^2 ज्यैष्ठमु°; BBe^2 NKt^4 sOx^1 sPu^6 ज्येष्ठमु°

126.* a) Ox^2 जन्मतो ज्यैष्ठ्यमाह्वानं; NKt^4 अजन्म°; Be^1 Ho GMd^1 Pu^2 Pu^4 MTr^6 Wa °ज्यैष्ठेन; Bo GMd^5 NNg Pu^8 °ज्यैष्ठ्येन; TMd^3 °ज्येष्ठ्येन; wKt^1 चाह्वानां — b) BBe^2 Kt^2 Tj^2 MTr^3 [*Jolly* R Ku] स्वब्रह्म°; Jo^1 स्वब्राह्म°; Pu^5 Pu^7 [*Jolly* G] सुब्रह्मण्या इति; GMd^5 °ह्मण्यासु च स्मृतं; GMd^1 TMd^4 स्मृतः; NNg Wa श्रुतं; La^1 स्थितं — c) TMd^3 यमयोरेकगर्भेपि; BBe^2 Hy Jo^2 wKt^1 La^1 Lo^2 Lo^3 oOr Pu^2 Pu^4 Pu^8 Tj^1 यमयोश्चैकगर्भेपु; GMd^5 यमयोश्चैव गर्भेपि; Be^1 Bo BCa Ho Jm Jo^1 Kt^2 wKt^3 NKt^4 BKt^5 Lo^1 Lo^4 NNg sOx^1 Ox^2 NPu^1 Pu^3 Pu^5 sPu^6 Pu^7 Tj^2 Tr^2 MTr^3 Wa *Mandlik Jolly Jha KSS Dave* यमयोश्चैव गर्भेषु [Be^1 यमयोश्चापि] — d) GMd^1 ज्येष्ठ्यता; Be^1 MTr^6 ज्यैष्ठता; TMd^3 ज्यैष्ठ्यता; oOr ज्येष्ठतः; La^1 GMd^1 स्मृताः; Wa स्मृतः

127. Pādas a-c omitted in Pu^2 Pu^4. Cited by *Jmv* 10.2; *Lakṣ* 12.726 — a) GMd^5 अपुत्रो येन; TMd^3 अपुत्रो केन — b) Pu^5 Pu^7 सुतं; wKt^1 शुभां; TMd^4 पुत्रिकाः — c) TMd^3 भवेदस्य; oOr *Jmv* [vl] भवेत्तस्यां; Be^1 Ho NNg MTr^6 भवेदस्यास्तन्मम; TMd^4 भवेदस्यात्तन्मम — d) Lo^3 Tj^1 जन्मतः स्या°; Lo^1 तन्मे स्यात्तु स्व°; GMd^1 स्याच्च स्व°; Be^1 GMd^1 TMd^3 GMd^5 NPu^1 MTr^4 स्यात्स्वधारकं; Ho °करः; Lo^2 °कारं

Additional verse in NPu^1 Pu^3 Tr^2 *Mandlik* [ख, ण, ल] *Dave KSS;* pādas c-d cited by *Apa*

अनेन तु विधानेन पुरा चक्रेऽथ पुत्रिकाः ।
विवृद्ध्यर्थं स्ववंशस्य स्वयं दक्षः प्रजापतिः ॥१२८॥
ददौ स दश धर्माय कश्यपाय त्रयोदश ।
सोमाय राज्ञे सत्कृत्य प्रीतात्मा सप्तविंशतिम् ॥१२९॥
यथैवात्मा तथा पुत्रः पुत्रेण दुहिता समा ।
तस्यामात्मनि तिष्ठन्त्यां कथमन्यो धनं हरेत् ॥१३०॥
मातुस्तु यौतकं यत्स्यात् कुमारीभाग एव सः ।
दौहित्र एव च हरेदपुत्रस्याखिलं धनम् ॥१३१॥
दौहित्रो ह्यखिलं रिक्थमपुत्रस्य पितुर्हरेत् ।
स एव दद्याद् द्वौ पिण्डौ पित्रे मातामहाय च ॥१३२॥
पौत्रदौहित्रयोर्लोके विशेषो नास्ति धर्मतः ।

80 [cf. *VaDh* 17.17]:

अभ्रातृकां प्रदास्यामि तुभ्यं कन्यामलंकृताम् ।
अस्यां यो जायते पुत्रः स मे पुत्रो भवेदिति ॥

d) *Apa* भविष्यति

128.* Pādas a-b omitted in Hy. Cited by *Lakṣ* 12.726 — a) TMd^{3} GMy अनेनैव; GMd^{5} च — b) MTr^{6} पुरो; Ho दुरा; Bo स्वधा; TMd^{3} चक्रे तु; GMd^{5} चक्रे च; MTr^{4} MTr^{6} चक्रेस्म; TMd^{4} चक्रेस्य; [*Jolly* Nd] *Jolly* चक्रे स; GMy Tr^{1} चक्रे सुपुत्रि°; Lo^{4} NPu^{1} Pu^{2} Pu^{4} Wa [*Jolly* M] चक्रे स्वपुत्रि°; Pu^{5} Pu^{7} [*Jolly* G] चक्रेप्यपुत्रि°; Tj^{2} चक्रेप्ठपुत्रि°; Bo [*cor to*] WKt^{1} La^{1} TMd^{3} GMd^{5} GMy NPu^{1} Pu^{2} Pu^{4} Tr^{1} [*but cor sh*] MTr^{6} [*Jolly* Nd] *Lakṣ* पुत्रिकां; BKt^{5} GMd^{1} Pu^{5} Pu^{7} पुत्रिका — c) WKt^{1} विशुद्ध्यर्थं; Lo^{4} [*ma* सं]वृद्ध्यर्थं — d) BBe^{2} Pu^{5} Pu^{7} दक्ष; Tr^{2} दत्तः

129. a) Tr^{2} ददौ दश च; GMy Tr^{1} ददौ सदृश; TMd^{3} ददौ सुदर्श; Pu^{2} Pu^{4} ददौ सतिदश — b) GMd^{1} GMd^{5} GMy MTr^{5} MTr^{6} काश्यपाय; TMd^{3} कार्यपाय — c) Hy राज्ञे सस्तुत्य — d) TMd^{4} पीतात्मा; Be^{1} Hy WKt^{1} La^{1} Lo^{1} Pu^{2} Pu^{4} °विंशति; GMy NPu^{1} °विंशतिः; TMd^{3} °विंशकं

130. Cited by *Jmv* 11.2.1; *Lakṣ* 12.708, 747; *Dev* 3.683 — a) TMd^{3} Tj^{1} पुत्रं — b) Hy La^{1} समः — c) Jo^{2} Tj^{1} तस्यात्मात्मनि; Lo^{3} तस्यात्मनि; MTr^{4} MTr^{6} निष्ठन्त्यां; *Jmv* जीवन्त्यां — d) Pu^{8} कथमन्यं; Wa कथं चमन्यो; Ho कथनमो; Hy Jo^{2} BKt^{5} Lo^{3} Pu^{5} Pu^{7} Tj^{1} *Jmv* हरेद्धनं

131. Cited by *Mādh* 3.372; pādas a-b cited by *Apa* 721; *Jmv* 4.2.13; *Lakṣ* 12.689 and pādas c-d by *Lakṣ* 12.724 — a) Pu^{2} Pu^{4} *Jmv* [vl] मातुश्च; Ho Bo La^{1} Lo^{4} NNg Pu^{5} Pu^{7} Wa [*Jolly* M$^{3-4}$ G] *Jolly* यौतुकं [but at 9.214 Jolly adopts यौतकं]; Pu^{2} MTr^{6} यौनकं; Hy यौतिकं; Pu^{8} यौतृकं — b) Bo कुमारोभाग; Hy कुमाराभाग; TMd^{3} एव तत् — c) La^{1} दौहित्र्य; Be^{1} Hy BKt^{5} La^{1} Lo^{2} GMd^{5} SOx^{1} SPu^{6} MTr^{5} *Lakṣ* एव तु; Bo एव हि; GMd^{1} एवापहरे° — d) WKt^{1} हरेत्पुत्रस्याखिलबन्धनं; TMd^{3} °खलं; Hy Jo^{2} Lo^{3} Tj^{1} [*Jolly* R] °खिलं वसु

132. Cited by *Jmv* 11.2.19; *Hem* 3/1.87; *Dev* 4.14; pādas c-d cited by *Lakṣ* 12.724 — a) GMd^{1} TMd^{4} GMd^{5} GMy MTr^{4} MTr^{6} दौहित्रोप्यखिलं; BCa Ox^{2} °खिलमृक्थ°; Lo^{2} रिक्थाम°; TMd^{4} निक्षम° — b) Pu^{3} पितुर्हरेन्; Tr^{2} पितुर्हरन्; OOr कथं हरेत्; *Jmv* [vl] हरेत्पितुः; BBe^{2} BKt^{5} Pu^{5} Pu^{7} MTr^{5} [*Jolly* G] *Bh Me* [pāṭha] हरेद्यदि — c) GMd^{1} स एष; TMd^{3} GMy MTr^{5} [*Jolly* Nd] दद्यात्तत्पिण्डं; NKt^{4} दद्यात्तत्पिण्डे; Lo^{2} दद्यात्तं पिण्डं; La^{1} Pu^{2} Pu^{4} दद्यात्पिण्डं तु; GMd^{1} Tr^{1} [*but mc sh*] MTr^{6} दद्यात्पिण्डं च; TMd^{4} Tr^{2} *om* द्वौ; OOr पिण्डं — d) TMd^{3} पित्रोर्माता°

तयोर्हि मातापितरौ संभूतौ तस्य देहतः ॥१३३॥
पुत्रिकायां कृतायां तु यदि पुत्रोऽनुजायते ।
समस्तत्र विभागः स्याज्ज्येष्ठता नास्ति हि स्त्रियाः ॥१३४॥
अपुत्रायां मृतायां तु पुत्रिकायां कथंचन ।
धनं तत्पुत्रिकाभर्ता हरेतैवाविचारयन् ॥१३५॥
अकृता वा कृता वापि यं विन्देत्सदृशात्सुतम् ।
पौत्री मातामहस्तेन दद्यात्पिण्डं हरेद्धनम् ॥१३६॥
पुत्रेण लोकाञ्जयति पौत्रेणानन्त्यमश्नुते ।
अथ पुत्रस्य पौत्रेण ब्रध्नस्याप्नोति विष्टपम् ॥१३७॥
पुन्नाम्नो नरकाद्यस्मात् पितरं त्रायते सुतः ।
तस्मात्पुत्र इति प्रोक्तः स्वयमेव स्वयंभुवा ॥१३८॥

133.* Pādas c-d omitted in gMy oOr. Cited by *Jmv* 11.2.19 — a) Lo^{3} Pu^{5} Pu^{7} पुत्र° ; gMd^{5} यौतौदौहित्र° ; gMd^{1} Tr^{1} [*but mc sh*] °त्रयोराप्ये; mTr^{5} °त्रयोरास्ये; tMd^{4} °त्रयोगाप्ते; mTr^{4} mTr^{6} *Nd* °त्रयोः कार्ये — b) Jm Jo^{1} Kt^{2} gMd^{1} tMd^{4} gMy Ox^{2} Tj^{2} mTr^{3} mTr^{4} mTr^{5} mTr^{6} *Mandlik Jolly Jha KSS Dave* न विशेषोस्ति; Pu^{2} Pu^{4} नास्ति कंचन [cf. 9.139] — d) wKt^{3} संभूतं; Tr^{2} यस्य; Bo तु स्वदेहतः

134. Omitted in Hy oOr. Cited by *Vij* 2.132; *Apa* 739; *Jmv* 2.39, 10.2; *Mādh* 3.347 — a) bBe^{2} *Jmv* 2.39 च — b) Lo^{3} Tj^{1} पिण्डोनुजा° ; nNg °भिजायते; Be^{1} nKt^{4} Lo^{1} sOx^{1} न जायते; tMd^{3} °पि जायते; Tj^{2} Tr^{2} °नुमन्यते — c) Be^{1} gMd^{1} gMd^{5} gMy nNg समस्तस्य; tMd^{3} विभागस्य ज्ये° — d) nNg Tr^{2} स्त्रियां; Ho nKt^{4} La^{1} Lo^{3} gMd^{5} sOx^{1} nPu^{1} Pu^{2} Pu^{3} Pu^{4} Pu^{5} sPu^{6} Pu^{7} स्त्रियः; Lo^{1} क्रियाः

135. Omitted in oOr. Cited by *Apa* 754; *Jmv* 11.2.16; *Lakṣ* 12.691; *Mādh* 3.374 — a) Kt^{2} wKt^{3} अपुत्राया; *Apa* अप्रजायां; Lo^{4} पुत्रिकायां मृ° ; Ho मृताया — b) mTr^{6} पुत्रिकायाः — d) gMy हरेतैववि° ; Lo^{4} tMd^{4} हरेतेवा° ; bKt^{5} हरेतवा° ; wKt^{3} tMd^{3} *Apa* हरेदेवा° ; Bo wKt^{1} *Mādh* हरेच्चैवा° ; Pu^{7} °वावधारयन्; Tr^{2} °वाभिचारयन्

Additional verse in tMd^{3}:

द्व्यामुष्यायणका दद्युर्द्वाभ्यां पिण्डोदरे पृथक् ।
रिक्थस्यार्थं समादद्याद्बीजक्षेत्रिकयोस्तथा ॥

136. Pādas a-b omitted in oOr. Cited by *Vij* 2.136; *Apa* 435; *Jmv* 10.3, 11.2.20 — a) Pu^{4} अकृत्वा; tMd^{4} अकृतो वा कृतो; gMd^{1} व; Tr^{2} या; nKt^{4} व्यकृता — a-b) gMy अकृता वापि यं विन्देत्सदृशात्सदृशं सुतं — b) nKt^{4} य; wKt^{3} यद्विन्दे° ; gMd^{1} विन्देत्संसुतं; Ho Lo^{4} gMd^{5} sOx^{1} Ox^{2} nPu^{1} Pu^{2} Pu^{4} Pu^{5} sPu^{6} Pu^{7} Tr^{1} Tr^{2} mTr^{4} mTr^{6} Wa [*Jolly* M G Nd] *Jolly* °त्सदृशं सुतं; bKt^{5} °त्सदृशान्सुतं; tMd^{3} °त्सदृशासुतं; mTr^{4} mTr^{6} °त्सदृशं पतिं — c) gMd^{1} tMd^{3} tMd^{4} gMy पुत्री; *Apa* पितामह° — d) *Jmv* 10.3 [vl] पिण्डं दद्याद्धरेद्धनं

137. Omitted in gMy. Cited by *Apa* 103; *Jmv* 11.1.31; *Lakṣ* 2.432 — a) Pu^{8} mTr^{5} लोकं जयति — b) Be^{1} Pu^{5} Pu^{7} *Lakṣ* पौत्रेणात्यन्तम° ; tMd^{4} पौत्रेणानन्तम° — c) Pu^{2} पुत्रस्यैव तु पौत्रेण; Bo La^{1} Lo^{2} पुत्रस्येह च पौत्रेण [Bo La^{1} तु]; Lo^{4} Pu^{5} Pu^{7} Pu^{8} Wa [*Jolly* M G] पौत्रस्येह तु पुत्रेण; nKt^{4} पौत्रस्य ह तु पुत्रेण; Pu^{3} अपि पुत्रस्य; Be^{1} [*cor to*] bCa wKt^{3} पौत्रस्य *for* पुत्रस्य; Be^{1} bCa *Apa* [vl] पुत्रेण — d) bKt^{5} नाकपृष्ठे महीयते; *Jmv* व्रध्न° ; Hy बध्न° ; nKt^{4} ब्रह्मस्या° ; bBe^{2} *Jmv* पिष्टपं

138. Pādas a-b omitted in gMy. Cited by *Jmv* 11.1.31; *Lakṣ* 12.741; pāda-a cited by *Jmv* 5.6 — b) Hy Jm Jo^{1} Pu^{2} Pu^{4} Tj^{2} mTr^{3} *Mandlik Jolly Jha KSS Dave* त्रायते पितरं; Kt^{2} प्रीयते

पौत्रदौहित्रयोर्लोके विशेषो नोपपद्यते ।
दौहित्रोऽपि ह्यमुत्रैनं संतारयति पौत्रवत् ॥१३९॥
मातुः प्रथमतः पिण्डं निर्वपेत्पुत्रिकासुतः ।
द्वितीयं तु पितुस्तस्यास्तृतीयं तु पितुः पितुः ॥१४०॥
उपपन्नो गुणैः सर्वैः पुत्रो यस्य तु दत्त्रिमः ।
स हरेतैव तद्रिक्थं संप्राप्तोऽप्यन्यगोत्रतः ॥१४१॥
गोत्ररिक्थे जनयितुर्न हरेद्दत्त्रिमः क्वचित् ।
गोत्ररिक्थानुगः पिण्डो व्यपैति ददतः स्वधा ॥१४२॥
अनियुक्तासुतश्चैव पुत्रिण्याप्तश्च देवरात् ।
उभौ तौ नार्हतो भागं जारजातककामजौ ॥१४३॥

पितरं; Ho sOx^1 sPu^6 तारयेत्सुतः; NPu^1 सुताः — c) Lo^1 Lo^3 Tj^1 इति ख्यातः — d) Kt^2 *om* स्वयमेव

139. Pādas c-d cited by *Jmv* 4.2.10, 11.6.9, 31 — a) BKt^5 Ox^3 NPu^1 Pu^2 Pu^3 Pu^4 Tr^2 पुत्रदौहि° — b) La^1 विशेपे; Lo^2 विशेषा; Bo Lo^2 Pu^8 नोपलभ्यते — c) Ox^3 दौहित्रौप्यपुत्रैनं; Pu^8 दौहित्रापि; *Jmv* दौहित्रेपि; GMd^1. हामुत्रैनं; TMd^3 Ox^3 Pu^5 Pu^7 ह्यपुत्रैनं; oOr ह्यपुत्रं तं; NKt^4 ह्यपुत्रेण; TMd^4 ह्यमन्त्रैव — d) wKt^3 संस्तार°; Lo^1 पौत्रवान्; wKt^1 Lo^4 GMy NNg Tr^2 पुत्रवत्; Pu^5 Pu^7 [*Jolly* G] पूर्वजान्

140. Pādas c-d omitted in Ho. Cited by *Apa* 435; *Lakṣ* 12.728; *Hem* 3/1.123; *Dev* 4.14 — a) TMd^3 मातुः पिण्डं तथा पूर्वं; Tr^1 माता — c) sOx^1 sPu^6 च; Be^1 TMd^3 *Me* [pāṭha] पितुस्तस्य तृती°; BKt^5 *Bh* [pāṭha] पितुः स्वस्य तृती° — d) Pu^2 Pu^4 *om* तु; Hy Jm Jo^1 Kt^2 Lo^2 Lo^3 Ox^2 Tj^2 Tr^1 MTr^3 *Mandlik Jolly Jha KSS Dave* तत्पितुः पितुः; GMy पितुः पिता

141. Cited by *Lakṣ* 12.731; *Dev* 3.671 — a) GMy गुणैः स्वैः स्वैः — a-b) TMd^4 gives instead 192a-b — b) Wa पुत्रा; Bo Lo^2 NNg यस्यास्ति; Ox^3 Pu^5 GMd^5 MTr^4 MTr^6 दात्त्रिमः; Bo Lo^1 MTr^3 दत्तिमः; Lo^2 दन्त्रिमः; Wa दातृमः; NPu^1 दातृनः — c) Be^1 GMy NNg Tj^1 Tr^2 संहरेतैव; TMd^3 संहरेरेव; BBe^2 संहरेच्चैव; wKt^1 हरेदेतद्रिक्थं; BBe^2 La^1 Ox^2 NPu^1 Pu^2 Pu^7 Wa तद्रुक्थं — d) GMy [*Jolly* Nd] संप्राप्तोस्य न पुत्रकः; sOx^1 sPu^6 स प्राप्तो; TMd^4 सप्राज्ञात्यन्य°; GMd^5 MTr^4 ह्यन्य°; Jo^2 °त्यन्य°; GMd^1 °प्यसगोत्रकः; BKt^5 °प्यस्यगोत्रतः; wKt^3 °प्यगोत्रतः; oOr Pu^7 MTr^4 MTr^6 °गोत्रजः; Tr^1 °गोत्रगः

142. Cited by *Vij* 2.132; *Lakṣ* 12.731; *Dev* 3.671; *Mādh* 3.351 — a) GMd गोत्रिरिक्थो; Be^1 La^1 °रिक्थ; wKt^1 TMd^3 sOx^1 sPu^6 °रिक्थं; Lo^2 °रिक्थो; BCa Ox^2 Tj^2 °ऋक्थे; La^1 Tr^2 जनयतुर्न; wKt^1 Tr^1 जनयितुं न — b) NKt^4 °तुर्नाहरे°; Hy हरद्द°; TMd^4 *Vij Mādh* भजेद्द°; GMd^1 NNg Pu^5 Pu^7 MTr^4 MTr^6 °द्दात्त्रिमः; Ho °द्दत्त्रिनः; Lo^2 °द्दन्त्रिमः; NPu^1 Pu^2 Pu^4 °द्दातृमः; Tr^2 °द्दत्त्रितः; Bo Lo^1 MTr^3 °द्दत्तिमः; NKt^4 °द्दतिमे; Jm Jo^2 TMd^3 TMd^4 GMd^5 GMy Tr^1 MTr^5 [*Jolly* Nd Gr] *Vij Dev Mādh* °द्दत्त्रिमः सुतः — c) BBe^2 Ox^2 °ऋक्थानुगः; TMd^4 °रिक्थेनुगः; Ho °रिक्ष्यानुगः; NKt^4 °नुगं; Be^1 पिण्डे — d) MTr^5 व्यपेति; GMd^1 ददता; GMd^5 स्वधां; sOx^1 sPu^6 स्वधी; TMd^4 स्वेधा

143. Cited by *Lakṣ* 12.744; *Dev* 3.630; *Mādh* 3.368 — a) GMy नियुक्तायासुताश्चैव; BKt^5 La^1 MTr^6 अनुयुक्ता°; GMd^1 अनुयुक्तो°; Lo^1 अवियुक्ता°; TMd^4 NNg अनियुक्तसु°; sOx^1 Pu^5 sPu^6 Pu^7 [*Jolly* G] अनियुक:सु°; NKt^4 °सुतश्चैवं; TMd^3 °सुतस्तेव — b) TMd^4 पुत्रिण्याश्चैव दैवरात्; sOx^1 °ण्याप्तदेवरात्; TMd^3 °ण्यापतदेवरात्; Pu^2 Pu^4 देवरान्; GMd^1 देवरां; NNg देवराट् — c) Jo^2 La^1 oOr उभौ तु; wKt^3 तावुभौ; GMd^1 उभौ नाहततो; Tj^1 Tr^2 नार्हतौ; Pu^7 नार्हते; TMd^4 नार्हतौ भागौ; TMd^3 भाग — d) GMd^5 जरजाज्जातकामजौ; Hy *om* जार; Be^1 जारजातज°; TMd^3 जारजातर°; oOr °जातिककर्मजौ; Tr^2 °कामतौ; TMd^4 °मामजौ

नियुक्तायामपि पुमान्नार्यां जातोऽविधानतः ।
नैवार्हः पैतृकं रिक्थं पतितोत्पादितो हि सः ॥१४४॥
हरेत्तत्र नियुक्तायां पुत्रो जातो यथौरसः ।
क्षेत्रिकस्य तु तद्बीजं धर्मतः प्रसवश्च सः ॥१४५॥
धनं यो बिभृयाद्भ्रातुर्मृतस्य स्त्रियमेव च ।
सोऽपत्यं भ्रातुरुत्पाद्य दद्यात्तस्यैव तद्धनम् ॥१४६॥
यानियुक्तान्यतः पुत्रं देवराद्वाप्यवाप्नुयात् ।
तं कामजमरिक्थीयं मिथ्योत्पन्नं प्रचक्षते ॥१४७॥
एतद्विधानं विज्ञेयं विभागस्यैकयोनिषु ।
बह्वीषु चैकजातानां नानास्त्रीषु निबोधत ॥१४८॥
ब्राह्मणस्यानुपूर्व्येण चतस्रस्तु यदि स्त्रियः ।
तासां पुत्रेषु जातेषु विभागेऽयं विधिः स्मृतः ॥१४९॥

144. Omitted in GMy [*Jolly* Nd[1] Nd[2]]. Cited by *Lakṣ* 12.744 — a) TMd[4] नियुक्तायामदे — b) Pu[7] °न्नार्या; La[1] °न्नार्यं; TMd[4] °न्नाराज्ञातौ विधानतः — c) Tr[2] न चार्हः; wKt[1] Pu[5] Pu[7] नैवार्हेत्पै°; Ho NKt[4] BKt[5] Lo[4] Pu[5] Pu[7] पैत्रिकं; Be[1] पैतृके; La[1] sOx[1] sPu[6] पौत्रिकं; BCa Hy oOr Ox[2] ऋक्थं; Be[1] रिक्थे — d) Bo GMd[1] °त्पातितो

145.* Omitted in GMy [*Jolly* Nd[1] Nd[2]] — a) GMd[1] TMd[3] TMd[4] GMd[5] Tr[1] MTr[4] MTr[5] MTr[6] हरेदेव; wKt[3] La[1] Lo[1] Pu[8] हरेतैव; Pu[3] Tr[2] हरेदथ; wKt[1] हरेत्कथं; Tr[1] MTr[5] नियुक्तायाः; wKt[3] GMd[1] नियुक्तानां — b) TMd[4] पुत्रे जाते यथौरसः; oOr पुत्रो जातस्तथौरसः; TMd[3] पुत्रौ जातौ; Be[1] BBe[2] Ho Hy Jm Jo[1] Kt[2] Lo[1] Lo[3] Ox[2] NPu[1] Pu[8] Tj[2] Tr[2] MTr[3] Wa *Mandlik Jolly Jha KSS Dave* जातः पुत्रो; sOx[1] sPu[6] यातः पुत्रो; wKt[3] जाता; BKt[5] यथोरसः — c) wKt[1] oOr क्षेत्रियस्य; Jo[2] Lo[1] Lo[3] Tj[1] Tr[1] MTr[6] [*Jolly* R] क्षेत्रिकस्यैव; Wa क्षेत्रियस्यैव; Be[1] BBe[2] GMd[1] Ox[2] Pu[5] Pu[7] [*Jolly* G] हि; GMd[5] च; TMd[4] तद्बीजे — d) GMd[5] धर्मजः; Lo[4] प्रसवो हि सः; Pu[5] Pu[7] प्रभवश्च सः; Pu[8] प्रसवस्तथा; MTr[3] यः

146. Omitted in GMy MTr[5] [*Jolly* Nd[1]]. Cited by *Vij* 2.136; *Apa* 742; *Lakṣ* 12.709; *Mādh* 3.357 — a) TMd[4] या — b) BKt[5] TMd[4] स्त्रिय एव; Be[1] BCa Jo[2] wKt[1] wKt[3] Lo[1] Lo[2] Lo[3] Lo[4] TMd[4] oOr sOx[1] Ox[2] sPu[6] Pu[8] Tj[1] Tr[1] Tr[2] Wa [*Jolly* M R Nd Gr] *Vij Apa* वा — c) TMd[4] Wa सापत्यं; Ho °रुत्पद्य — d) NPu[1] दत्वा तस्यैव

147.* Omitted in GMy [*Jolly* Nd[1] Nd[2]]; placed after 9.144 in Tr[1] — b) Lo[1] देवरादथ वाप्नुयात् — c) oOr काममतिरिक्थीयं; TMd[3] कामजं न रिक्थार्हं; Ho °रिक्थायं; GMd[5] Tr[1] MTr[4] MTr[6] °रिक्थार्हं; Lo[1] °रिक्थं; TMd[4] °रिक्षयं — d) Be[1] BKt[5] Pu[5] Pu[7] Tr[2] Wa मिथोत्पन्नं; TMd[4] मथ्योत्पन्नं; Tr[1] मध्योत्पन्नं; Hy Jm Jo[1] Kt[2] Tj[2] MTr[3] [*Jolly* G] *Mandlik KSS Dave* वृथोत्पन्नं; Hy NNg प्रचक्ष्यते

148. Omitted in [*Jolly* Nd[2]]. Cited by *Lakṣ* 12.696 — a) GMd[5] *Lakṣ* एतद्विभागं — c) NKt[4] BKt[5] Lo[1] Pu[3] Pu[5] चैव जातानां; Pu[7] [*Jolly* G] त्वेव जातानां; Lo[4] Pu[4] [*Jolly* M] °जातीनां — d) BBe[2] विधानतः

149. Cited by *Lakṣ* 12.696; *Mādh* 3.343 — a) Pu[5] Wa ब्रह्मण°; Be[1] BBe[2] Ho wKt[1] wKt[3] NKt[4] BKt[5] La[1] Lo[1] GMy NNg sOx[1] Pu[2] Pu[3] Pu[4] sPu[6] Tj[1] Tr[1] °पूवेण — b) wKt[1] Tr[1] चतस्रः स्युर्यदि; Lo[4] यदा — c) NPu[1] पुत्रेण; NNg जातेपु पुत्रेषु; Ho पुत्रेषु पौत्रेषु; Tr[2] पुत्रेषु रिक्थस्य — d) Be[1] BBe[2] NKt[4] La[1] Lo[4] TMd[4] GMy oOr Tr[2] MTr[6] विभागो; Hy स्मृताः

कीनाशो गोवृषो यानमलंकारश्च वेश्म च ।
विप्रस्यौद्धारिकं देयमेकांशश्च प्रधानतः ॥१५०॥
त्र्यंशं दायाद्धरेद्विप्रो द्वावंशौ क्षत्रियासुतः ।
वैश्याजोऽध्यर्धमेवांशमंशं शूद्रासुतो हरेत् ॥१५१॥
सर्वं वा रिक्थजातं तद् दशधा परिकल्पयेत् ।
धर्म्यं विभागं कुर्वीत विधिनानेन धर्मवित् ॥१५२॥
चतुरोऽंशान्हरेद्विप्रस्त्रीनंशान्क्षत्रियासुतः ।
वैश्यापुत्रो हरेद् द्व्यंशमंशं शूद्रासुतो हरेत् ॥१५३॥
यद्यपि स्यात्तु सत्पुत्रो यद्यपुत्रोऽपि वा भवेत् ।
नाधिकं दशमाद्दद्याच्छूद्रापुत्राय धर्मतः ॥१५४॥

150. Cited by *Lakṣ* 12.697 — a) NPu^{1} कीनाशौ; Pu^{2} Pu^{4} कनाशो; Lo^{1} विनाशो; TMd^{4} गोवृषा; Pu^{2} गावृषो; wKt^{1} नावृषो; Ox^{2} वृषभो — b) Be^{1} TMd^{4} Ox^{2} °कारं च; Pu^{5} Pu^{7} °कारस्य; TMd^{3} °कारस्तथैव च; TMd^{4} GMd^{1} वेश्मनि; NNg वेश्मसु — c) Be^{1} Ho wKt^{1} Lo^{2} Lo^{4} GMd^{1} TMd^{4} GMd^{5} GMy NNg Pu^{5} Pu^{7} Pu^{8} MTr^{6} Wa विप्रस्योद्धा°; Pu^{3} विप्रस्यौद्वारिकं; Pu^{2} Pu^{4} विप्रस्योद्वारिकं; La^{1} विप्रस्योद्वाहिको; BKt^{5} विप्रस्योधिकं; GMd^{5} °द्धारकं; Lo^{1} ज्ञेयमे° — d) Pu^{5} Pu^{7} देयं एकांशस्वविधानतः; Bo Lo^{1} Tj^{1} °मेकोंशश्च; Wa प्रधावतः; MTr^{3} प्रयत्नतः; [*Jolly* G] विधानतः

151. Pādas c-d omitted in NKt^{4}. Cited by *Jmv* 9.12; *Lakṣ* 12.697 — a) Pu^{3} Pu^{8} त्रीनंशानाहरेद्विप्रो; wKt^{1} त्र्यंशान्शयात्वरं प्रोक्तो; NPu^{1} अंशं; sOx^{1} sPu^{6} त्र्यंशाद्दाया° — b) Jo^{1} wKt^{1} Wa द्वावंशो; La^{1} NPu^{1} Tj^{1} Tr^{1} [*but mc sh*] द्वाविंशौ; GMd^{1} द्वौवंशौ; Lo^{2} Pu^{7} [*but cor*] क्षेत्रिया°; BKt^{5} क्षत्रियः सुतः; NKt^{4} क्षत्रियानुतः — c) Hy Jm Jo^{1} Kt^{2} Tj^{2} MTr^{3} *Ku Mandlik Jha Dave KSS* वैश्याजः सार्धमेवांशमंशं; BBe^{2} wKt^{3} Lo^{3} TMd^{3} Tj^{1} *Jmv* वैश्याजः सार्धमेकांशमंशं; oOr वैश्यासुतोध्यर्धमंशंशं; Lo^{1} हरेद्वैश्यासुतोध्यर्धमंशं; NKt^{4} GMd^{5} वैश्यापुत्रो हरेद् द्विंशमंशं; Bo wKt^{1} wKt^{3} TMd^{3} Ox^{2} GMy Tr^{2} वैश्यजो; GMd^{1} वैश्यजे; Be^{1} MTr^{4} MTr^{6} वैश्याजो द्व्यर्धमे°; Lo^{4} वैश्याप्यध्यर्धमे°; wKt^{1} wKt^{3} °प्यर्धमे°; Ox^{2} ह्यर्धमे° — d) GMd^{1} TMd^{4} MTr^{5} °वांशं शूद्रापुत्रोर्धमेव तु; TMd^{3} GMy MTr^{6} °वांशं शूद्रापुत्रोंशमेव च; GMd^{5} NPu^{1} °वांशमर्धं शूद्रा°; Wa °सुते; NNg [*but cor fh*] °सुतौ

152.* Cited by *Jmv* 9.12; *Lakṣ* 12.697; *Mādh* 3.343 — a) Lo^{4} [*Jolly* M^{4-5-9}] सर्वथा रिक्थजातं; GMd^{1} सर्वं वापि प्रजातं; BBe^{2} BCa Hy Lo^{4} Ox^{2} ऋक्थजातं; Lo^{3} Jo^{2} Tj^{1} [*Jolly* R] धनजातं; Be^{1} BBe^{2} BCa Jo^{2} wKt^{1} NKt^{4} BKt^{5} La^{1} Lo^{3} TMd^{4} Ox^{2} NPu^{1} Pu^{3} Pu^{4} Pu^{8} Tj^{1} Tr^{2} Wa [*Jolly* R] *Jmv Lakṣ Mādh* °जातं तु — b) Ho sOx^{1} sPu^{6} दशधापि प्रकल्पयेत्; NKt^{4} दशधा तत्प्रकल्पयेत्; La^{1} शतधा; Jo^{2} La^{1} Lo^{3} Tj^{1} [*Jolly* R] परिकल्पितं; BCa Hy Jm Jo^{1} Kt^{2} wKt^{3} BKt^{5} Ox^{2} Tj^{2} MTr^{3} Wa [*Jolly* Ku] *Jmv Mandlik Jha KSS Dave* परिकल्प्य च [BCa Wa तु; wKt^{3} वै; *Jmv* तत्]; GMd^{1} TMd^{4} GMd^{5} GMy Tr^{1} MTr^{4} MTr^{6} [*Jolly* Gr Nd] *Lakṣ Mādh* प्रविभज्य तु [MTr^{4} *om* प्र; TMd^{4} विप्रभज्य]; TMd^{3} संविसृज्य तु; MTr^{5} प्रतिविभतु — c) wKt^{3} BKt^{5} Lo^{1} धर्मं; wKt^{1} धर्म — d) GMy तद्विधानेन; BKt^{5} NPu^{1} Pu^{2} Pu^{3} Pu^{4} Pu^{8} Tr^{2} Wa धर्मतः [cf. 8.154d]; Be^{1} Ho sOx^{1} sPu^{6} तत्त्वतः; Lo^{4} दर्शितः

153. Omitted in BKt^{5} [haplo]. Cited by *Jmv* 9.12; *Lakṣ* 12.697; *Mādh* 3.343; pāda-a cited by *Vij* 2.124 — a) Pu^{5} Pu^{7} चतुरंशा°; Lo^{3} NNg चतुरांशा°; Wa चतुरोंशो हरे°; Be^{1} °शाद्धरेद्वि° — b) GMy °शात्क्षत्रिया° — c) Be^{1} wKt^{1} NPu^{1} वैश्यासुतो; Bo हरेदंशमंशं; TMd^{3} द्व्यंशानंशं — d) GMd^{5} *Mādh* द्व्यंशमेकं शूद्रा°; Bo शूद्रसुतो; TMd^{3} °सुतं; wKt^{3} भवेत्

154. Omitted in BKt^{5}. Cited by *Vij* 2.133; *Apa* 740; *Jmv* 9.27; *Lakṣ* 12.703; *Mādh* 3.344 — a) TMd^{4} स्यात्स; Tr^{1} [*but mc sh*] स्यात्सपुत्रस्तु [*Nd* calls this *samyakpāṭhaḥ*]; TMd^{3} सत्पुत्र; Be^{1}

ब्राह्मणक्षत्रियविशां शूद्रापुत्रो न रिक्थभाक् ।
यदेवास्य पिता दद्यात् तदेवास्य धनं भवेत् ॥१५५॥
समवर्णासु वा जाताः सर्वे पुत्रा द्विजन्मनाम् ।
उद्धारं ज्यायसे दत्त्वा भजेरन्नितरे समम् ॥१५६॥
शूद्रस्य तु सवर्णैव नान्या भार्या विधीयते ।
तस्यां जाताः समांशाः स्युर्यदि पुत्रशतं भवेत् ॥१५७॥
पुत्रान्द्वादश यानाह नृणां स्वायंभुवो मनुः ।
तेषां षड् बन्धुदायादाः षडदायादबान्धवाः ॥१५८॥
औरसः क्षेत्रजश्चैव दत्तः कृत्रिम एव च ।
गूढोत्पन्नोऽपविद्धश्च दायादा बान्धवाश्च षट् ॥१५९॥
कानीनश्च सहोढश्च क्रीतः पौनर्भवस्तथा ।

La^{1} TMd^{4} GMd^{5} oOr तत्पुत्रो; Ho सपुत्रो — b) Jo^{1} Kt^{2} Lo^{1} Lo^{2} MTr^{3} [*Jolly* Ku]*Lakṣ Mandlik Jha KSS Dave* सत्पुत्रोप्यसत्पुत्रोपि [*KSS* °पुत्रापि]; TMd^{4} यद्यपुत्रो हि; Pu^{5} Pu^{7} [*Jolly* G] यद्यत्पुत्रोपि; wKt^{3} यद्यपित्रापि; Lo^{1} ह्यपुत्रो ह्यपि वा; BBe^{2} wKt^{1} °पुत्रः पिता भवेत्; Pu^{3} °पुत्रोपि भावयेत्; GMd^{1} वा पुनः — c) TMd^{3} दशमां दद्या°; NPu^{1} दशमादंशाच्छू° — c-d) *Apa* नाधिकं दशमादंशाल्लभेच्छूद्रासुतोर्थतः — d) TMd^{3} °द्राधर्माय धर्मतः; oOr Tr^{1} धर्मवित्

155. Cited by *Vij* 2.125; *Jmv* 9.27; *Lakṣ* 12.704; *Mādh* 3.343; pādas a-b cited by *Dev* 3.614 — a) BKt^{5} ब्राह्मणात्क्षत्रियकाणां; TMd^{4} NNg ब्राह्मणः; Bo °क्षत्रियोवैश्यां; Pu^{2} Pu^{4} °क्षत्रियोविश्यां — b) GMd^{5} °पुत्रो निरर्थभाक्; GMy *om* न; GMd^{1} न कृत् भवेत्; BBe^{2} Jo^{1} BKt^{5} Ox^{2} ऋक्थ°; Lo^{3} Tj^{1} [*Jolly* R] दायभाक्; Ho शाच्छुभाक्— c) Be^{1} यदेवास्मै; wKt^{1} यदि वास्य — d) GMd^{1} हरेत्

156.* Pādas c-d omitted in Pu^{2} Pu^{4}. Cited by *Jmv* 2.43; *Lakṣ* 12.701 — a) Tr^{2} सवर्णायास्तु; Jo^{2} Lo^{3} Tj^{1} सवर्णासु च; NKt^{4} °वर्णास्तु; NPu^{1} °वर्णाः सुता जाताः; BBe^{2} Hy Jm Jo^{1} Jo^{2} wKt^{1} Kt^{2} wKt^{3} La^{1} Lo^{1} Lo^{3} TMd^{3} GMd^{5} GMy Tj^{1} Tj^{2} Tr^{1} Tr^{2} MTr^{4} MTr^{6} *Jmv Mandlik Jolly KSS Dave* ये जाताः; Bo Lo^{2} Pu^{8} जाता ये; TMd^{4} स जताः — b) NPu^{1} सर्वे वर्णा; BKt^{5} पुत्रे; MTr^{5} पुत्रास्सुजन्मनां; Ho °जन्मनी — c) wKt^{1} तद्धारं; Lo^{1} जायसे; Lo^{3} Tj^{1} चाग्रजे — d) NKt^{4} °न्नितरत्समं

157. Pādas a-b omitted in Pu^{2} Pu^{4}. Cited by *Lakṣ* 12.701 — a) sOx^{1} sPu^{6} शूद्रस्यैव; GMd^{1} शूद्रस्येव; wKt^{1} शुद्रा सा तु; BKt^{5} स शूद्रस्य सव°; GMd^{1} सवर्णेव; MTr^{4} MTr^{6} स्ववर्णैव; Bo समर्थैव — a-b) La^{1} शूद्रस्य सवर्णैकान्या भार्या विधीयते — b) Lo^{1} GMd^{5} Pu^{5} नान्य; wKt^{1} भार्योपदिश्यते — c) Wa तस्या; *Lakṣ* तत्र; wKt^{1} समानाः — d) TMd^{3} पुत्रोशतं

158. Cited by *Apa* 734; *Lakṣ* 12.714 — a) BKt^{5} Wa Tr^{1} [*but mc sh*]पुत्रा द्वा°; GMy पुत्रद्वा°; TMd^{3} पुत्रां द्वा°; wKt^{1} TMd^{3} °दशधानाह; BBe^{2} °दशानाह; TMd^{4} तानाह; MTr^{4} MTr^{6} यानार्हं; NPu^{1} Pu^{4} यानाहुर्नृणां — b) *Lakṣ* मनुः स्वयंभुवो नृणां — c) Pu^{5} Pu^{7} यद्बन्धु° — d) GMy षडदायादा ह्यबान्धवाः; wKt^{1} षड् दायादा अबान्धवाः; Lo^{1} षड् दायादास्वबान्धवाः; Lo^{3} Tj^{1} षट् च दाया°; Be^{1} पडादाया°; sOx^{1} sPu^{6} °बान्धवः

159. Verses 159 and 160 transposed in Jm. Cited by *Vij* 2.132; *Apa* 734; *Lakṣ* 12.714; *Mādh* 2.37, 3.349 — a) Lo^{2} NPu^{1} Pu^{2} Pu^{4} अरसः; GMy औरजः — b) Be^{1} दत्रिमः कृत्रिम; La^{1} GMd^{5} sOx^{1} sPu^{6} वा — c) Lo^{3} °न्नश्च विद्धश्च; NPu^{1} Tr^{2} °विद्धस्तु; TMd^{4} °विद्धस्य; Tr^{2} °विश्यश्च — d) BKt^{5} lacuna for the pāda; sOx^{1} sPu^{6} बान्धवश्च; Tj^{1} बान्धवास्तु; TMd^{4} बान्धवास्वषत्

स्वयंदत्तश्च शौद्रश्च षडदायादबान्धवाः ॥१६०॥
यादृशं गुणमाप्नोति कुप्लवैः संतरञ्जलम् ।
तादृशं गुणमाप्नोति कुपुत्रैः संतरंस्तमः ॥१६१॥
यद्येकरिक्थिनौ स्यातामौरसक्षेत्रजौ सुतौ ।
यस्य यत्पैतृकं रिक्थं तत्स गृह्णीत नेतरः ॥१६२॥
एक एवौरसः पुत्रः पित्र्यस्य वसुनः प्रभुः ।
शेषाणामानृशंस्यार्थं प्रदद्यात्तु प्रजीवनम् ॥१६३॥
षष्ठं तु क्षेत्रजस्यांशं प्रदद्यात्पैतृकाद्धनात् ।
औरसो विभजन्दायं पित्र्यं पञ्चममेव वा ॥१६४॥
औरसक्षेत्रजौ पुत्रौ पितृरिक्थस्य भागिनौ ।
दशापरे तु क्रमशो गोत्ररिक्थांशभागिनः ॥१६५॥

160. Cited by *Vij* 2.132; *Apa* 734; *Lakṣ* 12.714 [transposes pādas a-b and c-d]; *Mādh* 2.37, 3.349 — a) sOx[1] कानीनाश्च; Pu[7] सहाढश्च; TMd[4] सहेद्धाश्च — b) Lo[1] कृतः — c) TMd[4] °दत्तः पारशाश्च; La[1] Lo[2] Lo[4] NNg Ox[2] NPu[1] Pu[2] Pu[4] [*Jolly* G] शूद्रश्च; BKt[5] शौण्डश्च; GMd[5] *Apa* [vl] शौद्रिश्च — d) wKt[1] षड् दायादा अबान्धवाः; GMy षडदायादा ह्यबान्धवाः; Lo[3] Tj[1] षट् स्युर्दाया°; oOr °बान्धवः

161. Pādas b-c omitted in TMd[3] GMd[5] [haplo] — a) Hy Jm Jo[1] Jo[2] Kt[2] wKt[3] Lo[1] Lo[3] Tj[1] Tj[2] Tr[1] [*mc sh to*] MTr[3] [*Jolly* Ku] *Ku Rn Nd Mandlik Jha KSS Dave* फलमाप्नोति— b) TMd[4] कुधरैस्सततं जलं; sOx[1] sPu[6] [*but cor*] कुलवैः; oOr शुल्कं वै संतर°; Lo[4] सत्वरं जलं — c) Bo यादृशं; Hy Jm Jo[1] Jo[2] Kt[2] wKt[3] Lo[1] Lo[3] Tj[1] Tj[2] Tr[1] [*mc sh to*] MTr[3] [*Jolly* R Nd[1] Ku] *Ku Rn Nd Mandlik Jha KSS Dave* फलमाप्नोति; Pu[5] Pu[7] [*Jolly* G] कुलमाप्नोति — d) TMd[4] कुपुत्रसततं तमः; oOr संतरंस्तमं

162.* Cited by *Apa* 739; *Jmv* 10.15; *Lakṣ* 12.709 — a) Lo[1] Pu[2] Pu[4] यदेक°; BBe[2] BCa Jo[1] Ox[2] °कऋक्थिनौ; Pu[2] Pu[4] °रिक्थिनो; TMd[4] °रिक्थिना; BKt[5] °रिक्थिकौ — b) TMd[3] NPu[1] Pu[2] Pu[4] Pu[5] Pu[7] °मौरसः; GMy °मौरज° — c) La[1] तयोर्यद्यस्य पित्र्यं स्यात्; GMd[1] यस्यैतत्पैतृकं; GMd[5] *Apa Jmv* यद्यस्य पैतृकं; sOx[1] Pu[3] sPu[6] तत्पै°; NKt[4] BKt[5] sOx[1] Pu[5] sPu[6] Pu[7] यत्पैत्रिकं; BBe[2] BCa Jo[1] BKt[5] Ox[2] °कमृक्थं — d) MTr[4] MTr[6] तत्समं गृह्णते नरः; Bo BCa wKt[3] NKt[4] Lo[1] GMd[1] TMd[3] TMd[4] GMy NPu[1] Pu[2] Tr[2] तत्संगृह्णीत; Be[1] BBe[2] Hy Jm Jo[1] Jo[2] Kt[2] BKt[5] La[1] Lo[3] sOx[1] sPu[6] Tj[1] Tj[2] MTr[3] MTr[5] Wa *Jmv* [vl] *Lakṣ Mandlik Jolly Jha KSS Dave* स तद्गृह्णीत; sOx[1] sPu[6] नेतरत्; TMd[4] नेतरं

163. Cited by *Jmv* 10.13; *Lakṣ* 12.708; *Mādh* 3.348; pādas a-b cited by *Vij* 2.132; *Dev* 3.667 — a) wKt[3] एष; wKt[1] श्रेष्ठ एवौरसः — b) Ho sOx[1] sPu[6] प्रभुः पित्र्यस्य वस्तुनः; TMd[3] पित्र्यस्यैव सुतः प्रभुः; GMy पित्रस्य; NPu[1] पित्रोस्य — c) wKt[3] शेषामानृ°; Bo Tr[2] °मनृशं°; TMd[4] °मनुशासार्थं; Pu[3] Pu[4] °स्यार्थे — d) TMd[3] प्रदद्यात्तूपजीवनं; *Mādh* प्रदद्यात्तत्प्रजीवनं; NPu[1] प्रदद्याच्च; Lo[1] प्रवेशनं

164. Cited by *Vij* 2.132; *Apa* 733; *Jmv* 10.11; *Lakṣ* 12.710 — a) Be[1] षष्ठ्यं; Ho षष्ठां; wKt[1] शेषं; Pu[5] *om* तु; La[1] NNg च — b) wKt[3] BKt[5] La[1] NPu[1] sPu[6] °त्पैत्रिका°; TMd[3] MTr[4] MTr[6] °त्पैतृकं धनं — c) Tr[1] औरसोपि भजन्दायं; BCa औरसं; Tr[2] औरसान्; La[1] NPu[1] Pu[2] Pu[4] अरसो; Jo[1] आरेसो; GMy विभजेद्दायं; BKt[5] विभवन्दायं; Bo विभवं दायं; Ho विभजक्षायं; wKt[1] °न्दाया — d) Bo Ho Pu[3] Pu[5] Pu[7] Pu[8] Tr[2] Wa च

165. Omitted in BKt[5]. Cited by *Apa* 733; *Lakṣ* 12.710 — a) Bo Lo[1] oOr Pu[5] Pu[7] औरसः;

स्वे क्षेत्रे संस्कृतायां तु स्वयमुत्पादयेद्धि यम् ।
तमौरसं विजानीयात् पुत्रं प्राथमकल्पिकम् ॥१६६॥
यस्तल्पजः प्रमीतस्य क्लीबस्य व्याधितस्य वा ।
स्वधर्मेण नियुक्तायां स पुत्रः क्षेत्रजः स्मृतः ॥१६७॥
माता पिता वा दद्यातां यमद्भिः पुत्रमापदि ।
सदृशं प्रीतिसंयुक्तं स ज्ञेयो दत्त्रिमः सुतः ॥१६८॥
सदृशं तु प्रकुर्याद्यं गुणदोषविचक्षणम् ।
पुत्रं पुत्रगुणैर्युक्तं स विज्ञेयस्तु कृत्रिमः ॥१६९॥
उत्पद्यते गृहे यस्तु न च ज्ञायेत कस्य सः ।

Pu^2 Pu^4 अरसं; La^1 औरसक्षैत्रिजौ — b) Pu^3 NNg Tr^2 पितृरिक्थांशभागिनौ; Lo^4 [*Jolly* M] पित्र्यरिक्थस्य; BBe^2 Jo^1 Ox^2 पितृऋक्थस्य; La^1 पित्र्यशक्थस्य — c) TMd^4 तं क्रमशो; Ho क्रमतो — d) Lo^1 गोत्ररिक्थाः सभागिनः; BBe^2 BCa Jo^1 Ox^2 गोत्रऋक्थांश°; oOr °रुक्तस्य भाविनः; Lo^4 °भागिनौ

166. Cited by *Lakṣ* 12.719; *Mādh* 2.38 — a) Be^1 Ho Jm Jo^1 Jo^2 Lo^2 Lo^4 TMd^3 NNg Ox^2 Pu^5 Pu^7 Pu^8 Tj^2 Tr^2 MTr^3 Wa [*Jolly* M$^{4-8}$] *Mandlik Jha KSS Dave* स्वक्षेत्रे; TMd^4 सक्षेत्र; MTr^6 स्वक्षेत्र; GMd^5 क्षेत्र; TMd^3 संस्कृतेयस्तु — b) wKt^3 यमुत्पादयीत स्वयं; Lo^4 [*Jolly* M] पुत्रमुत्पा°; Tr^1 *Mādh* [*Jolly* Gr] °त्पादितश्च यः; BBe^2 La^1 GMd^1 GMy Pu^8 °दयेत्तु यं; wKt^1 °दयेच्च यं; Jo^2 Lo^3 NNg Tj^1 °दयेत यं; Lo^1 °दयेदिमं; NKt^4 Lo^4 Tr^2 [*Jolly* M] °दयेद् द्विजं — c) BKt^5 तयोरेव संविजानीयात्; Lo^1 तयोरंशं विजानीयात्; TMd^4 विजानीयं — d) TMd^4 पुत्रः प्रथमकल्पितः; BBe^2 Bo Hy Jm Jo^1 Jo^2 Kt^2 NKt^4 BKt^5 GMd^1 TMd^3 GMd^5 GMy Ox^2 Pu^2 Pu^3 Pu^4 Pu^8 Tj^2 Tr^1 [*but mc sh*] Tr^2 MTr^3 MTr^4 MTr^6 [*Jolly* Nd] *Nd Rc Mandlik KSS Dave* प्रथम°; Pu^2 Pu^4 °कल्पकं; Be^1 BBe^2 Jm Jo^1 Kt^2 wKt^3 BKt^5 La^1 GMd^1 TMd^3 GMd^5 GMy Ox^2 Pu^8 Tr^2 MTr^3 MTr^4 MTr^6 [*Jolly* Nd] *Nd Rc Mandlik KSS Dave* °कल्पितं

167. Cited by *Lakṣ* 12.721; *Dev* 3.667; *Mādh* 2.38 — a) wKt^1 Pu^5 Pu^7 यस्तल्पज; BKt^5 यस्तल्पगः; Be^1 Lo^2 यस्तुल्पजः; Pu^4 यस्तल्पतः; Tj^1 यस्त्वन्यजः; GMd^5 यस्त्वप्रजः; TMd^3 GMy Tr^1 यस्त्वप्रज; TMd^4 शयस्त्वजः; BBe^2 प्रणीतस्य — b) GMd^1 TMd^3 TMd^4 GMd^5 Tr^1 *Dev Mādh* पतितस्य वा; Ho wKt^3 Ox^2 Pu^8 Wa च — c) La^1 °धर्मे च; Pu^2 Pu^4 नियुक्तानां; Be^1 हि युक्तायां — d) oOr तत्पुत्रः; NPu^1 पुत्रो दातृमः

168. Omitted in Tr^2. Cited by *Vij* 2.130; *Apa* 736; *Lakṣ* 12.731; *Dev* 3.667–8; *Mādh* 2.38 — a) Pu^2 Pu^4 GMd^1 TMd^3 GMy Wa [*Jolly* M Nd] *Bh* च; commentators prefer the copula: *Bh* ये तु माता पिता वा दद्यातामिति पठन्ति [तदयुक्त]मुच्यते, and *Me* चशब्दः पठितुं युक्तः; Be^1 दद्यात्तं; GMd^5 Tr^1 [*but cor sh*] MTr^4 MTr^6 दद्यात्तु — b) oOr नामतः पुत्र° — c) GMd^5 प्रतिसं°; Ho NKt^4 oOr sOx^1 NPu^1 Pu^3 sPu^6 Pu^7 [*but cor*] Pu^8 Wa *Apa* °युक्तौ; GMd^1 °युक्तो — d) TMd^3 संज्ञेयो; wKt^3 BKt^5 विज्ञेयो; wKt^1 स पुत्रो दत्त्रिमः; Pu^7 MTr^4 MTr^6 दात्त्रिमः; Lo^2 दन्त्रिमः; Bo Lo^1 MTr^3 दत्तिमः; La^1 NPu^1 दातृमः; Pu^2 Pu^4 दादमः; Hy wKt^1 NNg स्मृतः

169. Cited by *Apa* 738; *Lakṣ* 12.734; *Dev* 3.668; *Mādh* 2.38 — a) *Lakṣ* सदृशं यं प्रकुर्यातां; *Apa* [vl]प्रकुर्याद्यो; Be^1 प्रकुर्यात्तु — a-b) Pu^2 Pu^4 सदृशं तु प्रकुर्वीत प्रकुर्याद्यं विचक्षणं — b) oOr °दोषे; wKt^1 °दोषौ; wKt^1 NPu^1 Pu^2 Pu^3 Pu^4 *Nā* [pāṭha] °विचक्षणः; Hy °विचक्षुणं — c) Lo^1 पुत्रं गुणैर्युक्ततरं; GMd^5 पुत्रगुणोपेतं; BKt^5 पुत्रविनिर्युक्तं — d) Hy Jm Jo^1 Kt^2 Pu^3 Tj^2 MTr^3 *Mandlik Jha KSS Dave* विज्ञेयश्च; TMd^4 कृत्रिमं; BBe^2 दत्रिमः

स गृहे गूढ उत्पन्नस्तस्य स्याद्यस्य तल्पजः ॥१७०॥
मातापितृभ्यामुत्सृष्टं तयोरन्यतरेण वा ।
यं पुत्रं परिगृह्णीयादपविद्धः स उच्यते ॥१७१॥
पितृवेश्मनि कन्या तु यं पुत्रं जनयेद्रहः ।
तं कानीनं वदेन्नाम्ना वोढुः कन्यासमुद्भवम् ॥१७२॥
या गर्भिणी संस्क्रियते ज्ञाताज्ञातापि वा सती ।
वोढुः स गर्भो भवति सहोढ इति चोच्यते ॥१७३॥
क्रीणीयाद्यस्त्वपत्यार्थं मातापित्रोर्यमन्तिकात् ।
स क्रीतकः सुतस्तस्य सदृशोऽसदृशोऽपि वा ॥१७४॥
या पत्या वा परित्यक्ता विधवा वा स्वयेच्छया ।

170.* Cited by *Lakṣ* 12.730; *Dev* 3.668; *Mādh* 2.38 — a) Pu^{2} Pu^{4} उत्पाद्यते; La^{1} GMd^{1} GMy Tr^{1} MTr^{6} उत्पद्येत; TMd^{3} उत्पाद्येत; Tr^{1} यश्च; BBe^{2} Bo BCa Ho Hy Jm Jo^{1} wKt^{1} Kt^{2} NKt^{4} BKt^{5} La^{1} Lo^{1} GMd^{1} TMd^{3} TMd^{4} GMd^{5} NNg sOx^{1} NPu^{1} Pu^{3} sPu^{6} Pu^{8} Tj^{2} Tr^{2} MTr^{3} MTr^{4} MTr^{5}MTr^{6} Wa [*Jolly* Nd Ku R] *Ku Mr Mandlik KSS* यस्य; wKt^{3} तस्य; GMy torn here — b) Ho न विभायेच्च तस्य सः; TMd^{4} स च; BBe^{2} Bo Jo^{2} wKt^{1} wKt^{3} BKt^{5} Lo^{1} Lo^{3} oOr sOx^{1} Ox^{2} Pu^{2} Pu^{3} Pu^{5} sPu^{6} Pu^{7} Pu^{8} Tj^{1} Tr^{2} [*Jolly* G R] *Dev* न विज्ञायेत; Pu^{4} न विज्ञातस्य; NNg ज्ञायेते [*but cor fh*] BKt^{5} यस्य; Be^{1} कस्य स्वः [*cor to* तस्य]; BCa Lo^{4} GMy Tr^{1} MTr^{4} MTr^{6} [*Jolly* M Nd] *Dev* कस्यचित्; Lo^{2} साः — c) TMd^{4} गृहे गूढसमुत्पन्नो यस्य; Lo^{4} TMd^{3} Pu^{4} [*Jolly* M] स्वगृहे; Be^{1} Bo Ho wKt^{1} wKt^{3} NKt^{4} La^{1} GMd^{1} TMd^{3} GMy oOr Ox^{2} NPu^{1} Pu^{2} Pu^{3} Pu^{8} Tr^{1} Tr^{2} MTr^{5} MTr^{6} Wa *Rn* गूढमुत्प° — d) BBe^{2} °न्नस्तस्माद्यस्तस्य तल्पजः; BKt^{5} GMy TMd^{3} TMd^{4} Tr^{1} MTr^{4} MTr^{6} °त्पन्नो यस्य स्यात्तस्य; Lo^{3} तल्पगः

171. Cited by *Apa* 739; *Dev* 3.668; *Mādh* 2.38 — a) Lo^{4} GMy °मुत्सृष्टस्तयो°; La^{1} °मुत्सृज्यस्तयो° — b) Be^{1} Ho NKt^{4} sOx^{1} Pu^{2} Pu^{4} sPu^{6} ताभ्यामन्यत°; Pu^{7} नरमन्यत° — c) BCa oOr *Apa* प्रतिगृ° — d) wKt^{1} °यात्परिविद्धः; TMd^{3} GMy *Dev* °विद्धस्तु स स्मृतः

172. Cited by *Vij* 2.129; *Apa* 736; *Dev* 3.668; *Mādh* 2.38 — a-b) *Dev* पितृवेश्मनि यं पुत्रं जनयेत्कन्यका रहः — b) Tr^{2} पुत्रः; BKt^{5} जनयेदहः; wKt^{1} जनयेत्त्वहः; TMd^{3} जनयेद्रहः — c) *Mādh* तं कानीनं विजानीयाद्; La^{1} GMd^{1} कानीनं तं; Tr^{2} कानिनं; Bo Lo^{1} कनीनं — d) GMd^{1} वोढुं; Tj^{1} कन्यां; Ho TMd^{3} GMd^{5} sOx^{1} sPu^{6} °समुद्भवः

173. Omitted in Lo^{4} [*Jolly* M]; pādas c-d omitted in Pu^{4}. Cited by *Apa* 738; *Lakṣ* 3.731; *Dev* 3.668; *Mādh* 2.38 — a) Pu^{4} यो; Bo संस्क्रियेत; Tr^{2} संस्कृत्यते; Ho BKt^{5} TMd^{3} sOx^{1} Pu^{5} sPu^{6} Pu^{7} संस्कृयते — b) *Mādh* ज्ञाताज्ञाततया सती; GMy *om first* ज्ञाता; La^{1} सा सती; Pu^{7} ता सती; Pu^{5} ना सती; Lo^{3} Tr^{1} [*but cor*] सति — c) TMd^{4} वोढुं; Be^{1} NKt^{4} Lo^{1} sOx^{1} sPu^{6} गर्भा; wKt^{1} गर्भ; GMd^{1} गर्भ्यो; GMd^{5} वहति — d) Tj^{2} सवोढ; BKt^{5} इति स चोच्यते; La^{1} सोच्यते; Be^{1} चोद्यते

174. Omitted in Lo^{4} [*Jolly* M]. Cited by *Vij* 2.131; *Apa* 738; *Lakṣ* 12.732; *Dev* 3.668; *Mādh* 2.38 — a) Tj^{1} क्रीणीयाद्यद्यपत्यार्थं; La^{1} स्त्रीणामाद्यस्त्वपत्यार्थं; GMd^{1} क्रीणाया°; Tr^{1} [*but mc sh*] विक्रीया°; GMd^{5} °याद्यदपत्यार्थे; Bo Hy wKt^{1} La^{1} GMy NNg oOr Tr^{1} MTr^{5} *Apa* °त्यार्थे — b) sOx^{1} sPu^{6} मातापुत्रो°; TMd^{4} °पित्रोन्यमन्तिकात्; La^{1} °त्रोर्यदन्तिकं; Pu^{5} Pu^{7} °मन्त्रिकात्; Pu^{2} Pu^{4} °न्तिकान् — c) TMd^{3} स च क्रीतसुतः पुत्रः; Lo^{1} कृतकः; La^{1} क्रीतस्तु सुत°; oOr सुतस्तस्याः — d) Jo^{2} Lo^{3} wKt^{3} Tj^{1} सदृशोसदृशो गुणैः [wKt^{3} तुलैः]

उत्पादयेत्पुनर्भूत्वा स पौनर्भव उच्यते ॥१७५॥
सा चेदक्षतयोनिः स्याद्गतप्रत्यागतापि वा ।
पौनर्भवेन भर्त्रा सा पुनः संस्कारमर्हति ॥१७६॥
मातापितृविहीनो यस्त्यक्तो वा स्यादकारणात् ।
आत्मानं स्पर्शयेद्यस्मै स्वयंदत्तस्तु स स्मृतः ॥१७७॥
यं ब्राह्मणस्तु शूद्रायां कामादुत्पादयेत्सुतम् ।
स पारयन्नेव शवस्तस्मात् पारशवः स्मृतः ॥१७८॥
दास्यां वा दासदास्यां वा यः शूद्रस्य सुतो भवेत् ।
सोऽनुज्ञातो हरेदंशमिति धर्मो व्यवस्थितः ॥१७९॥
क्षेत्रजादीन् सुतानेतानेकादश यथोदितान् ।
पुत्रप्रतिनिधीनाहुः क्रियालोपान्मनीषिणः ॥१८०॥

175. Omitted in Lo^4 [*Jolly* M]. Cited by *Lakṣ* 12.728; *Dev* 3.668; *Mādh* 2.38 — a) Ho Lo^1 Pu^3 Tj^2 Tr^2 *Lakṣ* या तु पत्या परि°; TMd^4 च — b) Jo^2 Lo^3 Tj^1 [*Jolly* R] विधवा स्वेच्छयापि वा; GMd^1 TMd^3 TMd^4 GMd^5 GMy Tr^1 MTr^4 MTr^5 MTr^6 [*Jolly* Nd] *Dev* विधवा वेच्छयात्मनः [MTr^5 विधिस्वेच्छ°; TMd^4 MTr^6 चेच्छ°; (*Jolly* Nd) स्वेच्छ°]; NPu^1 Pu^2 Pu^4 विधवा स्वेच्छया पुनः; Hy *om* वा; BKt^5 lacuna for वा; sOx^1 sPu^6 [*but cor*] या; BBe^2 wKt^1 Ox^2 वापि स्वेच्छया; Lo^1 वापि सेक्षया; Ho sOx^1 Pu^5 sPu^6 Pu^7 [*Jolly* G] यथेच्छया — d) oOr पुनर्भव

176. Omitted in Lo^4 [*Jolly* M]. Cited by *Viś* 1.66; *Apa* 96 — b) Bo TMd^4 MTr^6 °गतोपि; Ho sOx^1 sPu^6 Pu^8 च — c) Bo भर्ता; Pu^5 Pu^7 सा भर्त्रा; TMd^3 पत्या सा; Lo^3 Tj^1 भार्या सा; oOr भर्त्रा स्यात्; *Apa* भर्त्रासौ — d) Pu^3 °मर्हसि

Additional half-verse in NPu^1:

तस्यां पौनर्भवो जातो व्यक्तमुत्पादकस्य सः ॥

177. Omitted in Lo^4 [*Jolly* M]. Cited by *Apa* 738; *Lakṣ* 12.733; *Dev* 3.668; *Mādh* 2.38 — a) GMd^5 °पित्रोर्विहीनो; Be^1 °पितृभ्यां हीनो — b) GMd^1 GMy Tr^1 MTr^5 स्यादकारणे — c) oOr *Lakṣ* दर्शये°; TMd^3 संस्पृशये°; Be^1 oOr NPu^1 Pu^2 Wa °येद्यस्तु; TMd^4 °येद्यस्मात् — d) sOx^1 sPu^6 स्वयंदस्तु; NPu^1 Pu^2 Wa °दत्तश्च; Lo^2 °दत्तस्तु तस्य सः; Bo NKt^4 Lo^3 GMd^5 MTr^6 संस्मृतः

178. Omitted in Lo^4 [*Jolly* M]. Cited by *Jmv* 9.28; *Dev* 3.668; *Mādh* 2.38; pādas c-d cited by *Viś* 1.90 — a) Pu^5 Pu^7 [*Jolly* G] ब्राह्मणो यस्तु शूश्रायां; La^1 यो; Be^1 ब्रह्म°; GMd^5 भद्रायां — b) Tr^1 काममुत्पा° — c) Lo^1 पारयन्नेष; TMd^3 पारयेन्नेव; GMd^5 यशस्तस्मात्; oOr भवस्तस्मात्; TMd^4 वशं तस्मात् — d) Ho परशवः; oOr Pu^5 Pu^7 पारसवः; TMd^4 पारवश; wKt^1 पारसरः; TMd^3 पादशव; GMd^5 पारयश; BKt^5 पारशवो मतः

179. Cited by *Jmv* 9.29; *Lakṣ* 12.704 — a) Bo दास्यं वा दासदास्यं वा; GMd^1 अदास्यां वा सदास्यां वा; wKt^1 वा चादसलं वा; Tj^2 वा सदास्यां वा; Lo^1 वा यद्यदास्यां वा — b) MTr^5 शूद्रो यस्य सुतो भवेत्; GMd^1 योशूद्रस्य; Jo^1 सुतौ; Tr^2 हरेत् — c) Wa सानुज्ञातो; NKt^4 °ज्ञातां — d) GMd^1 धर्मे; Be^1 [*mc sh to*] व्यवस्थितिः

180. Cited by *Vij* 3.259; *Apa* 97, 735; *Lakṣ* 12.735; *Dev* 3.668 — a) *Apa* 735 क्षेत्रजादि; TMd^4 MTr^4 MTr^6 क्षेत्रजातान् — b) wKt^3 Tr^2 °तानैकादश; Pu^5 Pu^7 °तानेकंदश; Pu^8 °तानेवादश; Ho °दश शतोदितान्; [*Jolly* G] यथोदितं; La^1 *Vij* यथोचितान् — c) GMd^1 GMy पुत्रान्प्रति°; wKt^1 Tr^2 °विधानाहुः — d) TMd^3 °लोभान्मनी°; Bo °लोकान्मनी°

य एतेऽभिहिताः पुत्राः प्रसङ्गादन्यबीजजाः ।
यस्य ते बीजतो जातास्तस्य ते नेतरस्य तु ॥१८१॥
भ्रातृणामेकजातानामेकश्चेत्पुत्रवान्भवेत् ।
सर्वे ते तेन पुत्रेण पुत्रिणो मनुरब्रवीत् ॥१८२॥
सर्वासामेकपत्नीनामेका चेत्पुत्रिणी भवेत् ।
सर्वास्तास्तेन पुत्रेण प्राह पुत्रवतीर्मनुः ॥१८३॥
श्रेयसः श्रेयसोऽलाभे पापीयान् रिक्थमर्हति ।
बहवश्चेत्तु सदृशाः सर्वे रिक्थस्य भागिनः ॥१८४॥
न भ्रातरो न पितरः पुत्रा रिक्थहराः पितुः ।
पिता हरेदपुत्रस्य रिक्थं भ्रातर एव वा ॥१८५॥

181. Cited by *Apa* 97; *Lakṣ* 12.735; pādas c-d cited by *Apa* 81 — a) [*Jolly* Nd] यस्यैते; GMd^{5} यथा ते; wKt^{1} Lo^{4} [*Jolly* M] एते विहिताः; TMd^{3} TMd^{4} °भिहताः — b) GMd^{1} °दस्य बीजजाः; wKt^{1} °न्यजन्तुजाः; Kt^{2} °बीजनाः — c) wKt^{1} GMy Tr^{1} MTr^{4} MTr^{6} यस्यैते; Tr^{2} पश्यते; *Apa* जातस्तस्य — d) wKt^{1} Lo^{1} MTr^{6} °स्तस्यैते; Ho *om* ते; Lo^{3} वेतरस्य; TMd^{4} जनकस्य तु; NKt^{4} sOx^{1} sPu^{6} च; Lo^{4} [*Jolly* M] तत्

182. Omitted in Lo^{4} [*Jolly* M]; pādas c-d omitted in Be^{1} [haplo]. Cited by *Kum* 1.3.7; *Viś* 1.69; *Vij* 2.132; *Apa* 433; *Lakṣ* 12.740; *Hem* 3/1.99; pāda-c cited by *Jmv* 11.5.7 — a) Ho °जातीनामे° — b) Jo^{2} Lo^{3} Tj^{1} [*Jolly* R] *Viś* °जातानां यद्येकः पुत्र°; BKt^{5} °मान्भवेत् — c) Ox^{2} *Kum* सर्वे तेनैव पुत्रेण; NKt^{4} तेन पुत्रेण ते सर्वे; Lo^{1} तेन पुत्रेण तान्सर्वान्; BKt^{5} सर्वे तेनैव पुत्रेण; NPu^{1} ते सर्वे तेन; BBe^{2} BCa Hy Jm Jo^{1} Jo^{2} wKt^{1} wKt^{3} Lo^{2} Lo^{3} GMd^{1} TMd^{4} Tj^{1} Tj^{2} MTr^{3} MTr^{5} *Mandlik Jolly Jha KSS Dave* सर्वांस्तांस्तेन; Kt^{2} सर्वास्तास्तेन

183. Omitted in Lo^{4} TMd^{4} [*Jolly* M]; pādas a-b omitted in Be^{1} Pu^{4}. Cited by *Apa* 433; *Jmv* 4.3.32; *Lakṣ* 12.740; *Hem* 3/1.97, 101 — a) Tj^{2} सर्वासामेके; Bo La^{1} सर्वासामेव; GMd^{1} GMd^{5} GMy MTr^{4} MTr^{5} MTr^{6} बह्वीनामेक°; TMd^{3} बह्वीनां चैक°; Bo °पत्न्याना° — b) wKt^{1} oOr °त्नीनां यद्येका पुत्रिणी; TMd^{3} °त्रिणे — c) Be^{1} सर्वास्तेनैव पुत्रेण — d) Jo^{2} BKt^{5} La^{1} Lo^{3} GMy NNg Pu^{5} Pu^{7} Tj^{1} [*Jolly* G R Nd] *Jolly* पुत्रिण्यो मनुरब्रवीत् [Pu^{5} Pu^{7} पुत्रिणा]; TMd^{3} प्राहुः; Wa प्राप्त; TMd^{3} °वतीन्मनुः; Be^{1} Tj^{2} °वती मनुः

184. Omitted in Lo^{4} [*Jolly* M]. Cited by *Lakṣ* 12.717 — a) GMd^{1} TMd^{3} TMd^{4} GMd^{5} GMy Tr^{1} MTr^{4} MTr^{5} MTr^{6} [*Jolly* Nd] श्रेयसोभावे; wKt^{1} श्रेयसोयाते — b) GMd^{1} GMd^{5} NNg यवीयान्; Bo पापीयात्तीर्थम°; Pu^{5} Pu^{7} °यान्निष्ठमर्हति; BBe^{2} BCa Jo^{1} BKt^{5} GMy Ox^{2} *Lakṣ* ऋक्थम°; Lo^{2} रिक्थाम°; La^{1} रिक्थभागिनः; BKt^{5} °मर्पति — c) wKt^{1} °वश्चेत्र; BBe^{2} *om* तु; NNg सदृश्याः — d) TMd^{4} NNg सर्वे ते रिक्थभागिनः; Ho sOx^{1} sPu^{6} सर्व; BBe^{2} BCa Jo^{1} Ox^{2} *Lakṣ* ऋक्थस्य; TMd^{3} रिक्थार्धभागिनः; oOr रिक्थांशभागिनः

185. Omitted in Lo^{4} oOr [*Jolly* M]. Cited by *Apa* 653; *Lakṣ* 12.717; *Dev* 3.672, 691; pādas a-b cited by *Vij* 2.132; *Jmv* 11.1.40; *Dev* 3.667; *Mādh* 3.349, 356; pādas c-d by *Vij* 2.136; *Jmv* 11.5.5; *Lakṣ* 12.748; and pāda-c by *Vij* 2.136 — b) GMy पुत्रो रिक्थं हरेत्पितुः; Bo पित्रा; *Apa* पुत्रो रिक्थहरः; GMd^{1} रिक्थं; BBe^{2} Jo^{1} Ox^{2} *Lakṣ* ऋक्थ°; wKt^{3} *Lakṣ* °हराः स्मृताः; GMd^{5} °हराः पृथक् — c) Ho पितामह हरे°; NKt^{4} पितरा हरे° — d) BBe^{2} BCa Jo^{1} BKt^{5} Ox^{2} ऋक्थं; Lo^{3} रिक्थां; Be^{1} Jm Jo^{1} Kt^{2} Lo^{3} NNg Pu^{3} Pu^{8} MTr^{3} MTr^{5} *Mandlik Jha KSS Dave* एव च; *Rn* [pāṭha] अत्र च

त्रयाणामुदकं कार्यं त्रिषु पिण्डः प्रवर्तते ।
चतुर्थः संप्रदातैषां पञ्चमो नोपपद्यते ॥१८६॥
अनन्तरः सपिण्डाद्यस्तस्य तस्य धनं भवेत् ।
अत ऊर्ध्वं सकुल्यः स्यादाचार्यः शिष्य एव वा ॥१८७॥
सर्वेषामप्यभावे तु ब्राह्मणा रिक्थभागिनः ।
त्रैविद्याः शुचयो दान्तास्तथा धर्मो न हीयते ॥१८८॥
अहार्यं ब्राह्मणद्रव्यं राज्ञा नित्यमिति स्थितिः ।
इतरेषां तु वर्णानां सर्वाभावे हरेन्नृपः ॥१८९॥
संस्थितस्यानपत्यस्य सगोत्रात्पुत्रमाहरेत् ।
तत्र यद्रिक्थजातं स्यात् तत्तस्मिन् प्रतिपादयेत् ॥१९०॥

Additional verse in NPu[1]:

पत्नी दुहितरश्चैव पितरौ भ्रातरस्तथा ।
तत्सुतो गोत्रजो बन्धुः शिष्यः सब्रह्मचारिणः ॥

186. Omitted in Lo[4] [*Jolly* M]. Cited by *Apa* 744; *Jmv* 11.1.40, 11.6.7, 17; *Lakṣ* 12.748; pādas a-b cited by *Jmv* 4.3.36 — a) Tr[1] कुर्यात्; TMd[3] ग्राह्यं — b) Ho म्रितपिण्डः; Pu[5] Pu[7] पिण्डं; TMd[3] दण्डः — c) sOx[1] sPu[6] चतुर्थं; Ho Kt[2] wKt[3] BKt[5] GMd[5] sOx[1] NPu[1] Pu[5] Pu[7] संप्रदातेषां; wKt[1] संप्रदास्तेषां; *Apa* संप्रदस्तेषां; Tj[1] संप्रदानैषां— d) GMd[5] पञ्चमे; GMd[1] पञ्चानान्नोप°; *Apa* [vl] नोपलभ्यते

Additional verse in *Mandlik* [ग] *Dave KSS:*

असुतास्तु पितुः पत्न्यः समानांशाः प्रकीर्तिताः ।
पितामह्यश्च ताः सर्वाः मातृकल्पाः प्रकीर्तिताः ॥

187. Omitted in Lo[4] [*Jolly* M]. Cited by *Vij* 2.136; *Dev* 3.696; *Mādh* 3.354; pādas a-b cited by *Apa* 744; *Jmv* 11.6.17, and pādas c-d by *Lakṣ* 12.748; *Jmv* 11.6.14, 21 — a) wKt[1] अनन्तरा यः सपिण्डात्तस्य; GMd[1] अनन्तरस्तु यः पिण्डात्तस्य; *Dev Mādh* यो यो ह्यनन्तरः पिण्डात्तस्य; oOr यो यो हि पितर [*rest damaged*]; Be[1] आनन्तरः; La[1] अनन्तरं; Ox[2] Pu[3] MTr[6] सपिण्डो यस्तस्य; Pu[2] सपिण्डाश्च तस्य; Tr[2] सपिण्डात्तत्तस्य — b) Be[1] BKt[5] NNg Tj[2] हरेत् — c) *Jmv* 11.6.21 तदभावे सकुल्यः; NKt[4] ऊर्धमकुलाः; Lo[1] सकल्पः; GMd[1] TMd[3] TMd[4] GMd[5] GMy NPu[1] Tr[1] MTr[4] MTr[5] MTr[6] *Dev* सकुल्याः स्युराचार्यः — d) Be[1] Ho Pu[3] Pu[8] एव च

Additional half-verse in Tr[2] *Mandlik* [ख, ण] *KSS Dave:*

हरेरन्नृत्विजो वापि न्यायवृत्ताश्च याः स्त्रियः ॥

188. Omitted in Lo[4] [*Jolly* M]. Cited by *Vij* 2.136; *Jmv* 11.6.26; *Dev* 3.698; *Mādh* 3.355 — a) wKt[1] एतेषाम°; Tr[2] °भावेन — b) BBe[2] BCa Jo[1] BKt[5] oOr Ox[2] Pu[5] Pu[7] ऋक्थ°; *Jmv* [vl] °हारिणः — c) Lo[1] GMd[1] त्रिविद्याः; Tr[2] सुचये; TMd[4] शुचदा — d) GMy दान्ता यथा; TMd[4] दान्तास्सदा; Tj[2] दान्तास्तस्माद्धर्मो; *Jmv* दान्ता एवं धर्मो; Bo धर्मे; GMd[5] Tr[1] धर्मो विधीयते

189. Omitted in Lo[4] [*Jolly* M]. Cited by *Vij* 2.136; *Jmv* 11.6.34; *Dev* 3.698; *Mādh* 3.355 — a) Be[1] Ho La[1] Tj[1] आहार्यं; GMd[5] न हार्यं — b) Ho राजा; Be[1] [*but cor*] Ho स्थितः

190. Omitted in Lo[4] [*Jolly* M]. Cited by *Apa* 742; *Lakṣ* 12.745 — a) GMy संस्थितानपत्यस्य — b) Ho TMd[3] TMd[4] NNg Pu[5] Pu[7] MTr[4] MTr[6] [*Jolly* G Nd] *Lakṣ* सगोत्रात्तन्तुमाहरेत्; GMd[1] सगोत्रस्तन्तुमाहरेत्; GMd[5] सगोत्रां तन्तुमाहरेत्; *Apa* गोत्रात्तन्तुं समाहरेत्; Tj[2] सगोत्रात्सुतमाहरेत्; NKt[4] BKt[5] Ox[2] सगोत्राद्रिक्थमाहरेत्; GMy सगोत्रो रिक्थमाहरेत्; Be[1] सगोत्रोर्थं तमाहरेत्; NPu[1] Pu[4] Pu[8] सगोत्रस्तत्समाहरेत्; Pu[3] सगोत्रा तं समाहरेत्; La[1] सगोत्रस्तु धनं हरेत्; Tr[2] सगोत्रात्तु तमाहरेत्; oOr

द्वौ तु यौ विवदेयातां द्वाभ्यां जातौ स्त्रिया धने ।
तयोर्यद्यस्य पित्र्यं स्यात् तत्स गृह्णीत नेतरः ॥१९१॥
जनन्यां संस्थितायां तु समं सर्वे सहोदराः ।
भजेरन्मातृकं रिक्थं भगिन्यश्च सनाभयः ॥१९२॥
यास्तासां स्युर्दुहितरस्तासामपि यथार्हतः ।
मातामह्या धनात्किंचित् प्रदेयं प्रीतिपूर्वकम् ॥१९३॥
अध्यग्न्यध्यावाहनिकं दत्तं च प्रीतिकर्मणि ।
भ्रातृमातृपितृप्राप्तं षड्विधं स्त्रीधनं स्मृतम् ॥१९४॥
अन्वाधेयं च यद्दत्तं पत्या प्रीतेन चैव यत् ।
पत्यौ जीवति वृत्तायाः प्रजायास्तद्धनं भवेत् ॥१९५॥

°त्रमर्हति — c) Be[1] BCa oOr Tj[2] MTr[4] यत्र; Tr[1] तस्य; BBe[2] Jo[1] BKt[5] Ox[2] यद्वक्थ°; *Apa* यो रिक्थभागः; Pu[2] Pu[4] °क्थभागं — d) Ho NNg *om* तत्; *Apa* तं तस्मिन्; Be[1] Bo wKt[3] La[1] Lo[1] GMd[1] TMd[3] GMy oOr Ox[2] Pu[3] Pu[8] Tr[2] MTr[4] MTr[6] *LakṣApa* तत्तस्मै; [*Jolly* Nd] तत्तस्य; GMd[5] प्रतिदापयेत्

191. Omitted in Lo[4] [*Jolly* M]. Cited by *Jmv* 10.16; *Lakṣ* 12.745 — a) *Jmv* द्वौ सुतौ; BBe[2] La[1] यौ तु द्वौ; oOr यौतुकौ; Pu[5] Pu[7] [*Jolly* G] द्वौ चैव; BKt[5] GMy तौ; NNg विवि [*ma sh* दे] यातां; Wa विवहेयातां — b) Be[1] ज्ञातौ; Tr[2] ययौ; La[1] Pu[3] Tr[2] *Lakṣ* स्त्रियां; TMd[3] स्त्रियं; GMd[5] स्त्रियो; Be[1] धनं — c) GMd[1] तयोर्यदस्य; MTr[4] MTr[6] पुत्रस्स्यात्; GMd[5] रिक्थ्यं स्यात् — d) MTr[4] स तं; BBe[2] तु स; BBe[2] BCa Ho wKt[1] BKt[5] La[1] GMd[1] GMd[5] oOr sOx[1] Pu[5] sPu[6] Pu[7] MTr[5] तत्संगृह्णीत; TMd[3] TMd[4] GMy Tr[1] MTr[6] *Jmv* [vl] स तद्गृह्णीत; Be[1] नेतराः; oOr sPu[6] [*but cor*] MTr[5] Wa नेतरत्; La[1] नेतरान् [cf. 9.162]

Additional verse in NPu[1] Pu[2]; truncated citation in Pu[4]; cited by *Vij* 2.136:

अपुत्रा शयनं पत्युः पालयन्ती गुरौ स्थिता ।
भुञ्जीता मरणाच्छांता दायादश्चार्द्धमाहरेत् ॥

a) *Vij* भ्रातुः — a-b) Pu[4] [half-verse reads] अपुत्राः शयनं पद्ममहरेत् — b) *Vij* व्रते स्थिता — c-d) *Vij* पत्न्येव दद्यात्तत्पिण्डं कृत्स्नमंशं लभेत च — d) Pu[2] दायादाश्चार्द्धमाहरेत्

192. Omitted in Lo[4] [*Jolly* M]. Cited by *Vij* 2.145; *Apa* 721; *Jmv* 4.2.1; *Lakṣ* 12.688; *Mādh* 3.371 — b) oOr सर्व; GMd[1] सहोदरः — c) Lo[2] °रन्मातृकां; Be[1] °रन्भ्रातृकं; BCa Jo[1] BKt[5] Ox[2] °तृकमृक्थं — d) GMd[5] sOx[1] [*but cor*] sPu[6] [*but cor*] MTr[4] भगिन्याश्च; Tr[2] भगिन्योस्य

193. Omitted in Lo[4] [*Jolly* M]. Cited by *Vij* 2.145; *Lakṣ* 12.688; *Dev* 3.661; *Mādh* 3.371 — a) La[1] MTr[6] यस्तासां; BBe[2] wKt[3] यास्तु तासां दुहि° — b) Hy यथार्हसः; Be[1] यथार्थतः; TMd[3] यथाहतः — c) oOr मातामहाद्धनं किंचित्; GMd[1] मातामहा; Lo[1] Pu[5] Pu[7] मातामह्याद्धना°; TMd[4] मातामहाद्धना°; Be[1] TMd[3] GMd[5] NPu[1] धनं किंचित् — d) Be[1] TMd[4] प्रदीयं

194. Omitted in Lo[4] [*Jolly* M]. Cited by *Vij* 2.136, 143; *Jmv* 4.1.4; *Hem* 1.51; *Dev* 3.651 — a) BKt[5] °ध्याहनिकं; Be[1] Bo Ho Lo[2] TMd[3] TMd[4] GMd[5] GMy NNg sOx[1] NPu[1] Pu[3] Pu[4] Pu[5] sPu[6] Pu[7] Pu[8] Tr[2] Wa *Vij Dev* °वहनिकं; La[1] °वहिनिकं; Pu[2] °वहानिकं; Lo[1] °वाहनिके; TMd[4] °वहोनिकं; Jo[2] GMd[1] Ox[2] Tr[1] °हवनिकं — b) *Jmv* दत्तं च प्रीतितः स्त्रियै; TMd[3] TMd[4] दत्तश्च; Be[1] यत्प्रीति° — c) Lo[1] मातृभ्रातृप्रीतिप्राप्तं; Jo[2] GMd[1] GMy Tj[1] Tr[1] MTr[6] [*Jolly* Nd] मातृभ्रातृपितृ°

195. Omitted in Lo[4] [*Jolly* M]. Cited by *Lakṣ* 12.688; *Dev* 3.660 — a) La[1] अथाधेयेन यद्दत्तं; GMd[1] अन्ववायेन यद्दत्तं; Be[1] MTr[6] अन्वादेयं; NKt[4] अथाधेयं; TMd[4] अन्वादयं; Bo च दत्तं च — b) Be[1] TMd[3] पत्न्या; Pu[2] प्रात्या; NPu[1] प्रीत्येन; Jo[2] Lo[3] Tj[1] प्रीतेन वा पुनः; Lo[1] वापि तत् — c) Be[1] पत्न्यौ; NNg जीविति; Pu[4] वृत्तस्याः; BKt[5] वृत्तयाः; Bo wKt[1] GMd[1] TMd[3] TMd[4] GMy MTr[4] MTr[5] MTr[6] [*Jolly*

ब्राह्मदैवार्षगान्धर्वप्राजापत्येषु यद्धनं ।
अतीतायामप्रजसि भर्तुरेव तदिष्यते ॥१९६॥
यत्त्वस्याः स्याद्धनं दत्तं विवाहेष्वासुरादिषु ।
अतीतायामप्रजसि मातापित्रोस्तदिष्यते ॥१९७॥
स्त्रियास्तु यद्भवेद्वित्तं पित्रा दत्तं कथंचन ।
ब्राह्मणी तद्धरेत्कन्या तदपत्यस्य वा भवेत् ॥१९८॥
न निर्हारं स्त्रियः कुर्युः कुटुम्बाद्बहुमध्यगात् ।
स्वकादपि च वित्ताद्धि स्वस्य भर्तुरनाज्ञया ॥१९९॥
पत्यौ जीवति यः स्त्रीभिरलंकारो धृतो भवेत् ।
न तं भजेरन्दायादा भजमानाः पतन्ति ते ॥२००॥
अनंशौ क्लीबपतितौ जात्यन्धबधिरौ तथा ।

Nd] *Dev* वृत्तायां — d) BKt^{5} प्रजायास्तद्भवेद्धनं; Be^{1} La^{1} Pu^{2} Pu^{4} MTr^{6} हरेत्

196.* Omitted in Lo^{4} [*Jolly* M]; pādas-d omitted in NKt^{4} [haplo]. Cited by *Apa* 753; *Jmv* 4.2.27; *Lakṣ* 12.690; *Dev* 3.664; *Mādh* 3.373 — a) Tj^{1} ब्राह्मे; Pu^{2} ब्राह्मय°; BKt^{5} Lo^{3} GMd^{1} °देवार्ष°; TMd^{3} TMd^{4} OOr °गन्धर्व° — b) GMd^{1} MTr^{6} °प्रजापत्येपु; WKt^{3} Lo^{1} TMd^{4} तद्धनं; Be^{1} Hy Jm Jo^{1} Kt^{2} Lo^{2} Ox^{2} Pu^{8} Tj^{2} MTr^{3} *Mandlik Jha KSS Dave* यद्दसु; *Apa* यद्भवेत् — c) Be^{1} GMd^{1} *Jmv* अतीतायामप्रजायां; BBe^{2} Hy Jm Jo^{1} Jo^{2} WKt^{1} Kt^{2} WKt^{3} BKt^{5} La^{1} Lo^{3} TMd^{3} TMd^{4} GMd^{5} GMy NNg Ox^{2} NPu^{1} Pu^{2} Pu^{4} Pu^{5} Pu^{7} Pu^{8} Tj^{1} Tj^{2} Tr^{1} MTr^{3} MTr^{4} MTr^{5} MTr^{6} Wa *Mandlik Jolly Jha KSS Dave* अप्रजायामतीतायां — d) La^{1} GMd^{1} Pu^{4} मातापित्रोस्तु तद्धनं; WKt^{1} पत्युरेव

197.* Omitted in La^{1} Lo^{4} GMd^{1} Pu^{4} [*Jolly* M]; pādas a-c omitted in NKt^{4}. Cited by *Apa* 753; *Jmv* 4.2.27; *Lakṣ* 12.690; *Mādh* 3.373 — a) GMd^{5} यत्त्वस्य; Tr^{1} यत्त्वस्यै; Be^{1} Jo^{2} Lo^{3} Tj^{1} यत्तस्याः; TMd^{3} GMy MTr^{4} MTr^{6} [*Jolly* Nd] *Apa Mādh* यत्तस्यै; MTr^{5} यत्तत् वै; Pu^{2} Pu^{5} Pu^{7} [*Jolly* G] यत्तु तस्या धनं; NPu^{1} यत्तस्यां धनं; SOx^{1} SPu^{6} साधनं; BBe^{2} BCa WKt^{1} Lo^{2} Pu^{2} स्याद्धनं किंचिद् — c) BBe^{2} TMd^{3} GMd^{5} NNg Ox^{2} NPu^{1} Pu^{2} Pu^{5} Pu^{7} Pu^{8} MTr^{6} Wa [*Jolly* G] *Jmv Mādh* अतीतायामप्रजायां; Hy Jm Jo^{1} Jo^{2} WKt^{1} Kt^{2} WKt^{3} Lo^{1} Lo^{3} TMd^{4} GMy OOr Tj^{1} Tj^{2} MTr^{3} MTr^{4} MTr^{5} *Mandlik Jolly Jha KSS Dave* अप्रजायामतीतायां

198. Omitted in Lo^{4} [*Jolly* M]. Cited by *Vij* 2.145; *Apa* 721, 753; *Jmv* 4.2.16; *Lakṣ* 12.689; *Dev* 3.666; *Mādh* 3.372 — a) BBe^{2} Jo^{2} Lo^{3} Tj^{1} स्त्रियाश्च; GMd^{1} TMd^{4} स्त्रियांस्तु; Pu^{5} Pu^{7} Tj^{2} स्त्रियस्तु; BCa Hy Jm Jo^{1} WKt^{1} WKt^{3} Lo^{2} Ox^{2} MTr^{3} [*Jolly* Ku] *KSS* स्त्रियां तु; Kt^{2} *Mandlik Jha Dave* स्त्रियान्तु; NNg स्त्रियासु; Be^{1} स्त्रियाः स्युर्यद्ध°; Jo^{2} तद्भवे°; Pu^{5} Pu^{7} °वेद्दत्तं — b) Lo^{1} वृत्तं — c) La^{1} ब्राह्मणी उद्धरे°; *Apa* [vl] तद्धरतोविकन्या; Ho La^{1} Wa °त्कन्यां — d) La^{1} MTr^{4} °पत्यस्य भावयेत्; Ox^{2} या भवेत्

199. Omitted in Lo^{4} [*Jolly* M]. Cited by *Lakṣ* 12.683; *Dev* 3.654 — a) OOr *om* न; NKt^{4} नाभिर्हारं; TMd^{3} निर्हारः; GMd^{5} निर्हरं; WKt^{3} निर्दारं; Pu^{5} Pu^{7} Tr^{2} स्त्रियं; Ho स्त्रिया कार्यं — b) WKt^{1} °म्बादुत्तमध्य°; MTr^{5} °द्वाहुमध्य°; GMd^{1} NPu^{1} Pu^{2} Pu^{4} °मध्यमात्; Ho °मध्यमान् — c) La^{1} स्वकादस्येव वित्ताद्धि — d) Ho *Dev* स्वस्या; Be^{1} MTr^{6} तस्य; GMd^{1} °रनज्ञया; La^{1} Tr^{1} Tr^{2} °रनुज्ञया

200. Omitted in Lo^{4} [*Jolly* M]. Cited by *Vij* 2.118–9, 147; *Apa* 752; *Lakṣ* 12.683; *Dev* 3.659 — a) GMd^{1} Tr^{2} या; TMd^{3} GMy MTr^{6} यत्स्त्री° — b) La^{1} Tj^{1} °लंकारोद्धृतो; TMd^{3} भवेद्धृतः — c) NKt^{4} *om* न; BBe^{2} न ते; Tj^{1} न तद्भजे°; Lo^{3} तत्तद्भजे°; Bo °न्दायादां — d) Ho भजमानः; WKt^{3} पतन्ति च; *Dev* पतन्त्यधः

उन्मत्तजडमूकाश्च ये च केचिन्निरिन्द्रियाः ॥२०१॥
सर्वेषामपि तु न्याय्यं दातुं शक्त्या मनीषिणा ।
ग्रासाच्छादनमत्यन्तं पतितो ह्यददद्भवेत् ॥२०२॥
यद्यर्थिता तु दारैः स्यात् क्लीबादीनां कथंचन ।
तेषामुत्पन्नतन्तूनामपत्यं दायमर्हति ॥२०३॥
यत्किंचित्पितरि प्रेते धनं ज्येष्ठोऽधिगच्छति ।
भागो यवीयसां तत्र यदि विद्यानुपालिनः ॥२०४॥
अविद्यानां तु सर्वेषामीहातश्चेद्धनं भवेत् ।
समस्तत्र विभागः स्यादपित्र्य इति धारणा ॥२०५॥
विद्याधनं तु यद्यस्य तत्तस्यैव धनं भवेत् ।
मैत्रमौद्वाहिकं चैव माधुपर्किकमेव च ॥२०६॥
भ्रातॄणां यस्तु नेहेत धनं शक्तः स्वकर्मणा ।

201. Omitted in Lo^4 [*Jolly* M]. Cited by *Vij* 2.140; *Apa* 750; *Jmv* 5.7; *Lakṣ* 12.666; *Dev* 3.629; *Mādh* 3.201, 366 — a) GMd^1 क्लीबबधिरौ; Lo^1 °पतिजौ — b) GMd^5 Pu^5 Pu^7 जात्यान्ध°; wKt^1 जातान्धवालवौ; MTr^6 °बधिरा; GMd^1 Tr^1 [*but mc sh*] °पतितौ; *Apa* °बधिरावपि — c) Tr^1 °जळ°; Be^1 °मूकश्च; *Lakṣ* °मूकास्तु — d) TMd^4 *om* च; wKt^1 Tr^2 किंचिन्नि°; Pu^2 कंचिन्नि°; NPu^1 केच निरिन्द्रियाः

202. Pādas a-b omitted in Pu^4. Cited by *Vij* 2.140; *Lakṣ* 12.666; *Dev* 3.631; *Mādh* 3.366 — a) Lo^4 [*Jolly* M] च; *Lakṣ* तन्नयाय्यं; Tr^1 यौ न्याय्यं; Be^1 Bo Pu^2 न्यायं; GMy न्याया — b) Bo sOx^1 Ox^2 Pu^3 sPu^6 Pu^8 Tr^2 देयं; wKt^1 वित्तं; NKt^4 शक्ता; Lo^1 GMd^5 शक्या; *Dev* शक्यं; Ox^2 NPu^1 Pu^2 Pu^3 Pu^8 Tr^2 Wa मनीषिभिः; Ho TMd^4 *Mādh* मनीषिणः; Be^1 NNg मनीषिणाः; GMd^1 महर्षिणा — c) Jo^2 Tj^1 [*Jolly* R] ग्रासाच्छादनमात्रं तु; GMd^1 TMd^3 GMd^5 GMy Tr^1 [*but mc sh*] MTr^4 MTr^6 [*Jolly* Nd] °दनमभ्यङ्गं — d) GMd^1 अददन्पतितो भवेत्; Tr^2 पतितौ; Hy पतिता; GMy ह्यददद्धि चेत्

203. Cited by *Apa* 750; *Jmv* 5.17; *Lakṣ* 12.667 — a) La^1 या दारैः — b) Kt^2 कञ्चन — c) Be^1 तासामु°; Lo^4 GMd^5 Ox^2 Pu^2 Pu^4 Tj^1 Tr^1 Wa °जन्तूनाम° — d) GMy [*Jolly* Nd] दातुमर्हति

204. Cited by *Vij* 2.118-9; *Jmv* 6.1.54; *Lakṣ* 12.682 — a) Be^1 Ho °त्पितरे; Lo^3 Tj^1 प्राप्ते — b) Tr^2 Lo^1 ज्येष्ठे; La^1 श्रेष्ठो — c) Pu^2 Pu^4 भागौ; Lo^1 [*cor to*] यवीयसस्तत्र; BBe^2 यवीयसास्तत्र — d) Be^1 °पालिनं; BKt^5 GMd^5 Tj^1 *Mandlik KSS* °पालितः; [*Jolly* Nd] *Rn* [pāṭha] *Dave* °पालिनां; wKt^1 °शालिनः

205. Verses 205–25 are placed after 9.247 in TMd^3. Cited by *Apa* 727; *Lakṣ* 12.682 — a) BBe^2 Lo^1 Lo^4 Pu^8 च — b) NPu^1 सर्वेषां तत्तस्यैव धनं; Be^1 BBe^2 GMd^5 Pu^2 Pu^4 °मीहतश्चे°; Pu^5 Pu^7 °मीहतांश्चे°; GMd^1 °मीहायाश्चे°; TMd^4 °मीहातचे°; *Apa* [vl] °मीक्षतश्चे°; Lo^4 °महश्चे°; Tj^1 Wa °मीहेतश्च धनं; Lo^3 Tj^1 Tr^1 °श्चेद्भवेद्धनं; wKt^1 °श्चेद् द्वयं हरेत् — c) Lo^3 Tj^1 समं तत्र; Bo GMd^5 GMy NNg oOr समस्तस्य — d) *Apa* [vl] °पित्र्या; Lo^1 °पित्र्यमिति; TMd^4 °पित्र्यन्नितीतवान्; sOx^1 sPu^6 रतिधारणा; Lo^4 धारणात्

206. Lacuna for pādas a-b in wKt^1. Cited by *Apa* 724; *Jmv* 6.1.9, 31; *Lakṣ* 12.674 — a) TMd^4 दद्याद्धनं तु यद्यस्यात्; Tr^2 तु यस्य स्यात् — b) Lo^1 तस्यैव च धनं; BKt^5 *om* तत्; BKt^5 भवेद्धनं — c) Jo^1 Kt^2 La^1 Lo^1 Pu^5 Pu^7 *Mandlik Jha KSS Dave* मैत्र्यमौ° [for मैत्र see 8.118, 120]; Tj^1 मैत्रीमौ°; La^1 °मुद्वाहिकं; Lo^1 °द्वारिकं; Kt^2 TMd^3 °हिकश्चैव — d) GMd^5 GMy मधु°; TMd^3 °पर्कक°; TMd^4 °पर्केक°; *Jmv* °पार्किक°; Jo^2 wKt^1 La^1 TMd^3 GMd^5 Ox^2 Pu^4 Pu^5 Pu^7 वा

स निर्भाज्यः स्वकादंशात् किंचिद्दत्त्वोपजीवनम् ॥२०७॥
अनुपघ्नन्पितृद्रव्यं श्रमेण यदुपार्जितम् ।
स्वयमीहितलब्धं तन्नाकामो दातुमर्हति ॥२०८॥
पैतृकं तु पिता द्रव्यमनवाप्तं यदाप्नुयात् ।
न तत्पुत्रैर्भजेत्सार्धमकामः स्वयमर्जितम् ॥२०९॥
विभक्ताः सहजीवन्तो विभजेरन्पुनर्यदि ।
समस्तत्र विभागः स्याज्ज्यैष्ठ्यं तत्र न विद्यते ॥२१०॥
येषां ज्येष्ठः कनिष्ठो वा हीयेतांशप्रदानतः ।
म्रियेतान्यतरो वापि तस्य भागो न लुप्यते ॥२११॥
सोदर्या विभजेरंस्तं समेत्य सहिताः समम् ।
भ्रातरो ये च संसृष्टा भगिन्यश्च सनाभयः ॥२१२॥

207. Cited by *Jmv* 3.28; *Lakṣ* 12.665 — a) Bo NKt^{4} यत्तु; NNg यश्च; TMd^{4} यस्य; Bo नेहेतु; NKt^{4} मेहेत — b) GMd^{1} धनश्शक्तः; BKt^{5} शक्तिः; Tr^{1} शक्तं; wKt^{3} MTr^{4} MTr^{6} स्वधर्मणा — c) Pu^{2} स्वनिर्भाग्यः स्वकानंशात्; wKt^{1} सा; La^{1} संविभाग्यः; TMd^{4} निर्भाज्य; Lo^{2} विभाज्यः; Lo^{3} निर्भाव्यः; TMd^{3} निर्हस्य — d) La^{1} Lo^{1} TMd^{4} किंचिद्दत्तोप°; TMd^{3} किंचिदर्थोप°; BBe^{2} wKt^{3} BKt^{5} MTr^{6} °जीविनं

208. Cited by *Vij* 2.118–9; *Apa* 723; *Jmv* 6.1.3, 31; *Lakṣ* 12.676; *Mādh* 3.377 — a) NPu^{1} अन्वपघ्नन् पितृन् द्रव्यं; Bo अनुत्पन्नं पितुर्द्रव्यं; Lo^{4} अनपघ्न°; wKt^{1} अन्वपघ्न°; BKt^{5} अथपघ्न°; Be^{1} NKt^{4} BKt^{5} Lo^{2} TMd^{3} TMd^{4} sOx^{1} Pu^{4} Pu^{5} sPu^{6} Pu^{7} [*Jolly* G] °न्पितुर्द्रव्यं; Pu^{8} MTr^{3} MTr^{6} °न्पितुद्रव्यं — b) BKt^{5} क्रमेण; BBe^{2} BCa wKt^{1} Lo^{1} Lo^{3} GMd^{1} TMd^{3} TMd^{4} GMd^{5} NPu^{1} Pu^{5} Pu^{7} Tj^{1} Tr^{1} MTr^{5} Wa *Apa Jmv* [vl as in ex] यदुपार्जयेत्; MTr^{5} यदपार्जयेत्; wKt^{3} यदुपार्जयत्; Bo यदुपाययेत् — c) GMd^{1} TMd^{3} °मीहत°; Lo^{1} Lo^{3} GMd^{5} Tj^{1} °मीहेत; wKt^{1} °लब्धकान्नाकामो; TMd^{4} तान्नाकामो; NKt^{4} Pu^{8} वा नाकामो; Pu^{5} Pu^{7} Wa तु नाकामो; La^{1} *Apa Lakṣ* च नाकामो; Lo^{2} च तु नाकामो — c-d) *Vij Mādh* दायादेभ्यो न तद्दद्यात् विद्यया लब्धमेव च

209. Cited by *Vij* 2.121; *Jmv* 2.21, 6.2.32 — a) BKt^{5} पैत्रिकं; Lo^{4} TMd^{3} MTr^{4} [*Jolly* M] तु यदा — b) Tj^{1} °मानवाप्तं; TMd^{3} °मनुवाप्तं; Be^{1} *Jmv* [pāṭha] °मनवाप्यं; *Jmv* [pāṭha] °मनवाप्य [both rejected by *Jmv*]; NKt^{4} °मनवायं; Lo^{4} [*Jolly* M] °मनुपघ्नन्यदाप्नुयात्; GMy °वाप्तमवाप्नुयात् — c) GMd^{5} तत्पुनर्भजे° — d) Ho °त्सार्धं स्वकामः; Lo^{4} °त्सार्धं कामतः; TMd^{3} GMd^{5} °त्सार्धं कामं यत्स्वयम°; BKt^{5} °मकामं; La^{1} Lo^{2} GMd^{1} TMd^{3} TMd^{4} Pu^{5} Pu^{7} Tj^{1} °यमार्जितं; wKt^{1} °यमर्जितः; Lo^{3} °यमार्जिते; Pu^{2} Pu^{4} °यमार्जनं

210. Cited by *Apa* 748; *Jmv* 12.1; *Lakṣ* 12.754; *Dev* 3.700; *Mādh* 3.360; pādas a-b cited by *Vij* 2.139 — a) Pu^{5} Pu^{7} विभक्तो; Tr^{2} स्वयंजी° — b) wKt^{1} विभवेर°; *Jmv* [vl] °नर्यदा — c) MTr^{6} समास्तत्र; GMd^{1} समस्तस्य; wKt^{1} समौ तत्र; GMy MTr^{6} विभागस्य ज्यै° — d) Kt^{2} °ज्यैष्ठां; wKt^{3} °ज्यैष्ठं; La^{1} TMd^{4} NPu^{1} °ज्येष्ठं; NKt^{4} °ज्येष्ठ्यस्तत्र; Lo^{4} [*Jolly* M] °ज्येष्ठस्तत्र; TMd^{3} °ज्येष्ठ्यमत्र; Lo^{2} GMd^{1} TMd^{4} GMy MTr^{4} MTr^{6} [*Jolly* Nd] ह्यत्र

211. Cited by *Lakṣ* 12.754; *Dev* 3.703; *Mādh* 3.362 — a) NPu^{1} तेषां; TMd^{3} TMd^{4} एषां; Ho ज्येष्ठ — b) sOx^{1} sPu^{6} जाहीतांशं प्रधानतः; wKt^{1} हीयेतां च सदारतः; GMd^{5} हीयेतांशं; Be^{1} हीयेतांशः; MTr^{6} °प्रधानतः — c) Ox^{2} प्रियेता°; TMd^{3} दीयेता°; wKt^{1} म्रियेतामितरो; Ho म्रियेतात्पितरो; sOx^{1} sPu^{6} °तरोपि वा; oOr °तरोपि स्यात् — d) Wa भागोनुलुप्यते; MTr^{4} MTr^{6} भागो विलुप्यते; La^{1} लिप्यते

212. Cited by *Vij* 2.139; *Jmv* 11.5.32; *Lakṣ* 12.754; *Dev* 3.703; *Mādh* 3.362 — a) Bo

योो ज्येष्ठो विनिकुर्वीत लोभाद्भ्रातॄन्यवीयसः ।
सोऽज्येष्ठः स्यादभागश्च नियन्तव्यश्च राजभिः ॥२१३॥
सर्व एव विकर्मस्था नार्हन्ति भ्रातरो धनम् ।
न चादत्त्वा कनिष्ठेभ्यो ज्येष्ठः कुर्वीत यौतकम् ॥२१४॥
भ्रातॄणामविभक्तानां यद्युत्थानं भवेत्सह ।
न पुत्रभागं विषमं पिता दद्यात्कथंचन ॥२१५॥
ऊर्ध्वं विभागाज्जातस्तु पित्र्यमेव हरेद्धनम् ।
संसृष्टास्तेन वा ये स्युर्विभजेत स तैः सह ॥२१६॥
अनपत्यस्य पुत्रस्य माता दायमवाप्नुयात् ।
मातर्यपि च वृत्तायां पितुर्माता हरेद्धनम् ॥२१७॥
ऋणे धने च सर्वस्मिन् प्रविभक्ते यथाविधि ।
पश्चाद्दृश्येत यत्किंचित् तत्सर्वं समतां नयेत् ॥२१८॥

सोदर्य; Pu⁵ Pu⁷ Tr² Wa सौदर्या; Ho सौन्दर्या; Hy सदर्या; ᴛMd⁴ सोदर्यो; *Vij Jmv* विभजेयुस्तं; ʙBe² La¹ ᴛMd⁴ Tr² °जेरंस्तु; ᴛMd³ ɢMd⁵ ɢMy ɴNg ᴍTr⁶ °जेरंस्तत्; ʙKt⁵ Lo⁴ Pu⁵ Pu⁷ Tr¹ [*cor to sh*] °जेरंस्ते — b) wKt¹ विभजेरन्नपत्य सहिताः; Pu⁵ Pu⁷ सममेत्य समाहिताः; ɢMd¹ समाः — c) ɢMy भ्रातारश्चैव; Lo¹ भ्रातरो एव; Be¹ येत्र; Lo² येत — d) ɢMd⁵ sOx¹ भगिन्याश्च; Lo³ भागिन्यश्च

213. Cited by *Vij* 2.126; *Lakṣ* 12.660; *Mādh* 3.383 — a) Lo³ Tj¹ ज्येष्ठो यो; Tr² विकुर्वीत — b) Tj¹ लोभान्भ्रा°; ɢMd⁵ लोभाद्भ्रातृयवी° — c) Bo ज्येष्ठस्यादग्रभागश्च; Be¹ सज्येष्ठो; Be¹ °भागस्तु; *Lakṣ* °भगी च; ʙKt⁵ Pu⁵ Pu⁷ °भागः स्यान्निय° — c-d) wKt¹ सोपि ज्येष्ठस्य भागश्च निन्दितव्यश्च राजभिः — d) Kt² नियन्तव्यं च

214. Pāda-d omitted in ɢMd¹. Cited by *Lakṣ* 12.666; *Dev* 3.621; pādas a-b cited by *Apa* 720, 749; *Jmv* 5.6 — a) ᴛMd³ सर्वा — b) Be¹ Bo नार्हति; Jo¹ नार्हन्ती; Lo² भ्रातारा; Ho मातरो — c) La¹ नादत्त्वा च कनि°; Bo Ho sOx¹ sPu⁶ वादत्त्वा; wKt¹ चदत्त्वा; ᴛMd³ कनिष्ठिभ्यो; ᴛMd⁴ कनिष्ठाभ्यां — d) ɴNg oOr [*Jolly* G] यौतुकं; Ho Tj¹ योतकं; Pu² ᴍTr⁶ यौनकं; ᴛMd⁴ यौतदं; Bo पौतृकं

215. Omitted in ɢMd¹. Cited by *Apa* 727; *Jmv* 2.86; *Lakṣ* 12.655 — a) Ox² °वभक्तानां; Pu⁸ °विभागानां — b) ɢMy सहोत्थानं; wKt³ भवेत्सदा — c) ᴛMd⁴ *Jmv* [vl] *Lakṣ* न तत्र विषमं भागं; Lo² ᴛMd³ ɢMd⁵ ɢMy Tr¹ ᴍTr⁴ ᴍTr⁶ ᴍTr⁵ *Apa Jmv* न तत्र भागं; Bo Lo¹ °भाग; Be¹ Bo विषयं

216. Pādas a-b omitted in ɢMd¹. Cited by *Vij* 2.122; *Apa* 729; *Jmv* 7.1; *Dev* 3.711; *Mādh* 3.340 — a) wKt¹ विभागो जातस्तु; ᴛMd⁴ विभक्ता ज्ञातस्तु; La¹ Pu⁴ °ज्जातास्तु; ɴNg oOr °ज्जातश्च; Pu² °ज्जानश्च — b) ʙBe² पित्रमेव; Pu⁵ Pu⁷ पितामेव; Wa हारद्धनं; Jo² wKt¹ Lo³ Lo⁴ Pu² Pu⁴ Tj¹ *Lakṣ* धनं हरेत् — c) ᴍTr⁶ संसृष्टं तेन; wKt¹ ʙKt⁵ Lo³ ɴPu¹ ये वा; Bo वा यास्तु विभ°; Lo⁴ [*Jolly* M] वा यैस्तु विभ° — d) Pu⁵ Pu⁷ °भजेरन्स; Tr² शतैः सह; ᴛMd⁴ सुतैस्त्विह

217. Cited by *Vij* 2.136; *Apa* 744; *Jmv* 11.3.2; *Lakṣ* 12.748; *Dev* 3.691; pādas c-d cited by *Jmv* 11.4.4 — a) Tj² पुत्रस्तु — b) wKt¹ ɴKt⁴ ɢMd¹ ɴNg ɴPu¹ Pu² Pu⁴ Pu⁵ Pu⁷ Tr² ᴍTr⁵ ᴍTr⁶ Wa *Lakṣ* दायादमाप्नुयात् — c) ᴛMd⁴ तु; Ho वृत्तानां — d) Tr² पितृमाता; Lo⁴ *Apa Dev* धनं हरेत्

218. Omitted in ɢMy Pu² Pu⁴; pādas c-d omitted in ɢMd⁵ [haplo]; verses 218 and 219 transposed in [*Jolly* Nd]. Cited by *Jmv* 13.1; *Lakṣ* 12.695; *Dev* 3.713; *Mādh* 3.382 — a) ɢMd¹ रणे; Lo⁴ ऋणं धनं; sOx¹ sPu⁶ सर्वेस्मिन् — b) ᴛMd³ विभक्ते च यथाविधि; ɢMd¹ °भक्तैर्यथाविधि — c) sOx¹ पश्चाद्दृश्यते

वस्त्रं पत्त्रमलंकारं कृतान्नमुदकं स्त्रियः ।
योगक्षेमप्रचारं च न विभाज्यं प्रचक्षते ॥२१९॥
अयमुक्तो विभागो वः पुत्राणां च क्रियाविधिः ।
क्रमशः क्षेत्रजादीनां द्यूतधर्मं निबोधत ॥२२०॥
द्यूतं समाह्वयं चैव राजा राष्ट्रे निवारयेत् ।
राज्यान्तकरणावेतौ द्वौ दोषौ पृथिवीक्षिताम् ॥२२१॥
प्रकाशमेतत्तास्कर्यं यद्देवनसमाह्वयौ ।
तयोर्नित्यं प्रतीघाते नृपतिर्यत्नवान्भवेत् ॥२२२॥
अप्राणिभिर्यत्क्रियते तल्लोके द्यूतमुच्यते ।
प्राणिभिः क्रियते यस्तु स विज्ञेयः समाह्वयः ॥२२३॥

219.* Omitted in GMd^{5}. Cited by *Vij* 2.118–9; *Apa* 725; *Jmv* 6.2.23; *Lakṣ* 12.678; *Dev* 3.643; *Mādh* 3.380 — a) Lo^{1} NNg वस्त्र; TMd^{4} वस्त्रशस्त्रम°; GMd^{1} TMd^{3} GMy Ox^{2} MTr^{6} [*Jolly* Nd] *Nd* पात्रम°; Hy °लंकार; BKt^{5} *Lakṣ* °लंकारः — a-b) *Jmv* [vl as in ed] °लंकारोकृता° — b) GMd^{1} कृतानामु°; TMd^{3} °मुदयं; GMy स्त्रियाः — c) Be^{1} BBe^{2} Bo Ho Hy Jo^{1} Kt^{2} NKt^{4} wKt^{5} Lo^{1} Lo^{2} NNg sOx^{1} Ox^{2} NPu^{1} Pu^{2} Pu^{5} sPu^{6} Pu^{7} Pu^{8} Tj^{1} Tr^{2} MTr^{4} MTr^{6} Wa *Vij Apa Mandlik Jolly Jha KSS Dave* योगक्षेमं प्रचारं [in Tr^{1} the *anusvāra* is given and crossed out]; La^{1} °क्षेमः; wKt^{1} योगक्षेमं प्रतारं; TMd^{3} TMd^{4} योगक्षेमप्रकारं [TMd^{4} °क्षेमं] — d) Lo^{3} Tj^{1} विभज्यन्त्र प्र°; *Apa* विभाज्यं न प्र°; La^{1} GMd^{1} Ox^{2} MTr^{6} विभज्यं; oOr विभक्तं; wKt^{1} Tr^{2} विभाव्यं; Lo^{4} प्रचक्ष्यते

220. Omitted in Lo^{4} [*Jolly* M]; pādas a-b omitted in GMd^{5} — a) La^{1} स्वयमुक्तो; MTr^{5} एष गुप्तो विभागो; [*Jolly* Nd] हि भागो; TMd^{4} विभागे; TMd^{4} sOx^{1} Pu^{3} वा; TMd^{3} Pu^{2} Pu^{4} Tr^{2} यः — b) BKt^{5} यथाविधि — c) Be^{1} wKt^{3} TMd^{3} Pu^{5} Pu^{7} MTr^{4} MTr^{6} क्षेत्रजातीनां; GMd^{5} क्षेत्रजातानां; *R n* appears to read औरसादीनां — d) GMd^{5} °कर्म; Jo^{2} Lo^{3} Tj^{1}Tr^{2} °धर्मान्निबोधत

221.* Omitted in NKt^{4} [haplo] in Lo^{4} [*Jolly* M]. Cited by *Lakṣ* 12.762; *Mādh* 3.393 — a) wKt^{1} समार्गयंश्चैव; Kt^{2} °ह्वयश्चैव — b) TMd^{3} राज; Wa राष्ट्र निवा°; Tj^{1} राष्ट्रा निवा°; Bo राज्यां निवा°; Be^{1} BBe^{2} Ho Hy Jm Jo^{1} Jo^{2} wKt^{1} Kt^{2} wKt^{3} wKt^{5} Lo^{1} Lo^{3} TMd^{3} sOx^{1} Ox^{2} sPu^{6} Pu^{8} Tj^{2} Tr^{2} *Lakṣ* [but vl as in ed.] *Mandlik Jolly Jha KSS Dave* राष्ट्रान्निवा°; *Lakṣ* [but vl as in ed.] राष्ट्राद्विवासयेत्; Lo^{3} Tj^{1} [*Jolly* R] निवासयेत् — c) GMd^{5} राज्यस्यान्तकरावेतौ; Be^{1} BBe^{2} Jm Jo^{1} Kt^{2} [*but cor*] Lo^{1} Lo^{3} MTr^{3} *Mandlik Jha KSS* राजान्तकर°; sOx^{1} sPu^{6} राज्यान्तचार°; Tj^{2} राजान्तिकर°; Hy राजंतिकर°; GMd^{1} °करणौ तौ; TMd^{4} MTr^{4} MTr^{6} °करणौ ह्येतौ — d) TMd^{4} द्वौ द्वौ दाप्यौ पृथिवीक्षिता; TMd^{3} °क्षितः

222. Omitted in Lo^{4} NKt^{4} [*Jolly* M]. Cited by *Mādh* 3.393 — a) TMd^{4} प्रकाशयेत तास्कर्यं; wKt^{3} °मेतत्तत्कार्यं — b) TMd^{4} तस्माद् द्यूतसमाह्वये; TMd^{3} यद्दैवन°; wKt^{3} यद्देवल°; wKt^{1} °समार्गजौ; BKt^{5} °ह्वयं — c) Hy तयोर्नित्य; Be^{1} प्रतीघातं; Tj^{1} प्रतिघ्राते; Pu^{8} समाघाते; Hy प्रजीघाते; Pu^{2} Pu^{4} प्रद्याते — c-d) Tr^{1} [*but cor*] प्रतीघातैर्नृपतेर्यत्न°

223. Omitted in Lo^{4} NKt^{4} [*Jolly* M]. Cited by *Vij* 2.199 [intro.]; *Apa* 804; *Lakṣ* 12.761; *Dev* 3.19; *Mādh* 3.388 — a) Tr^{2} °त्क्रीयते; TMd^{4} °त्कृते — c) Jm *Vij Dev* प्राणिभिः क्रियमानस्तु; BCa प्राणिभिर्विविधैर्यस्तु; NNg यत्तु — d) wKt^{1} समार्गयः

Additional verse in La^{1}:

पुरे जनपदे चैव राजा राष्ट्रे निवारयेत् ।
द्यूताद्धि संप्रवर्तन्ते प्रजानां बहुलानयाः ॥

द्यूतं समाह्वयं चैव यः कुर्यात्कारयेत वा ।
तान्सर्वान् घातयेद्राजा शूद्रांश्च द्विजलिङ्गिनः ॥२२४॥
कितवान् कुशीलवान् केरान्* पाषण्डस्थांश्च मानवान् ।
विकर्मस्थान् शौण्डिकांश्च क्षिप्रं निर्वासयेत्पुरात् ॥२२५॥
एते राष्ट्रे वर्तमाना राज्ञः प्रच्छन्नतस्कराः ।
विकर्मक्रियया नित्यं बाधन्ते भद्रिकाः प्रजाः ॥२२६॥
द्यूतमेतत्पुराकल्पे दृष्टं वैरकरं महत् ।
तस्माद् द्यूतं न सेवेत हास्यार्थमपि बुद्धिमान् ॥२२७॥
प्रच्छन्नं वा प्रकाशं वा तन्निषेवेत यो नरः ।
तस्य दण्डविकल्पः स्याद् यथेष्टं नृपतेस्तथा ॥२२८॥
क्षत्रविट्शूद्रयोनिस्तु दण्डं दातुमशक्नुवन् ।
आनृण्यं कर्मणा गच्छेद् विप्रो दद्याच्छनैः शनैः ॥२२९॥

224. Omitted in Lo[4] [*Jolly* M]. Cited by *Vij* 2.202; *Apa* 804; *Lakṣ* 12.762; *Mādh* 3.392; pādas c-d cited by *Apa* 865 — a) wKt[1] समार्गयं — b) gMd[1] tMd[3] gMy Tr[1] mTr[6] [*Jolly* Nd] *Apa Lakṣ* यः कुर्याद्यश्च कारयेत् [tMd[3] यत्कुर्या°; gMd[1] Tr[1] ये कुर्युर्यश्च; (*Jolly* Nd) कुर्याद्यच्च]; wKt[3] mTr[4] यत्कु°; gMd[5] ये कुर्युः कार°; Lo[1] nPu[1] Pu[2] Pu[4] °रयेत्तथा; wKt[3] °रयेत्तु वा; tMd[4] °रयन्ति ये — c) tMd[3] यातये°; tMd[4] वान्तये° — d) Bo शूद्राश्च; wKt[1] mTr[6] Wa शूद्रांस्तु

225.* Omitted in Lo[4] [*Jolly* M]. Cited by *Lakṣ* 12.527; *Mādh* 3.393 — a) Pu[2] Pu[4] कितकान्; tMd[3] कुतवान्; sOx[1] sPu[6] शठान्कुशी°; [*Jolly* Nd] कितवाञ्छीलवान्; gMd[1] कितवान्कुलिवान्; Jm शीलवान्; Be[1] *om* केरान्; nKt[4] tMd[3] tMd[4] [*Jolly* Gr] *Bh* [pāṭha] *Nd* केलान्; gMd[1] gMd[5] gMy [*Jolly* Nd] कैलान्; *Mādh* कौलान्; Jm Jo[1] Kt[2] Ox[2] Pu[5] Pu[7] [*Jolly* G Ku] *Nā Bh Mandlik Jolly Jha KSS* क्रूरान्; Ho bKt[5] La[1] Lo[1] Lo[2] nPu[1] Pu[2] Pu[3] Pu[4] Pu[8] Tr[2] *Rc* चौरान्; sOx[1] sPu[6] Tj[2] चोरान्; Bo चारान् — b) nKt[4] bKt[5] sOx[1] Ox[2] nPu[1] Pu[3] sPu[6] Pu[8] पाखण्ड°; wKt[3] Lo[3] gMd[5] gMy oOr Tj[1] Tr[1] पाषण्डांश्चैव; Lo[1] पाखण्डांश्चापि; Bo पाखण्डश्चैव; *Mādh* पाषण्डानपि; Jo[2] पाखण्डस्थैव; Hy °स्थाश्च — c) Pu[7] सौण्डि°; gMd[5] चौण्डि°; bKt[5] शौण्डिकाश्च; tMd[4] काण्डिकांश्च — d) Hy sOx[1] sPu[6] निवासये°; bKt[5] gMd[1] gMd[5] निर्वापये°; Ox[2] निष्काशये°; Bo wKt[3] °त्पुरान्; Tj[2] °त्पुरां; gMd[5] nNg °त्पुरा; sOx[1] sPu[6] °त्पुमान्

226. Omitted in Lo[4] [*Jolly* M]; pādas b-d omitted in Pu[4]. Cited by *Lakṣ* 12.527 — a) La[1] ते राष्ट्रे वर्तमाना हि; nPu[1] एतै राष्ट्रे; Pu[4] राष्ट्रं; Tr[1] राज्ये; Tj[1] विद्यमाना — b) Hy प्रच्छन्नः; Bo gMy °तस्करः — c) gMy °क्रियाय; mTr[4] °क्रियवान्नित्यं — d) gMd[5] Pu[5] बाधते; Ho वधन्ते; Be[1] tMd[4] भद्रिका; Lo[1] भद्रिकां; tMd[3] भर्तृकाः; wKt[1] तन्त्रिकाः

227. Omitted in Lo[4] [*Jolly* M]; pāda-a omitted in Pu[4]. Cited by *Lakṣ* 12.762 — a) Hy °कल्पं; tMd[4] °कल्प — b) Hy दृष्ट; nKt[4] सृष्टं; gMy दुष्टं; bKt[5] चैवकरै सह — d) Be[1] हास्यार्थ्यमपि

228. Cited by *Lakṣ* 12.762 — b) Pu[5] Pu[7] यो निषेवेत मानवः — c) Tr[1] दण्डि°; Lo[1] Pu[5] Pu[7] [*but cor*] दण्डो विकल्प्यः; sOx[1] sPu[6] °प्रकल्पः; gMd[1] °विकारः; oOr °विकल्पस्तु — d) Pu[2] Pu[4] याव्यष्टं; Lo[4] नृपतेर्यथा; Be[1] नृपतेः सदा

229. Cited by *Lakṣ* 12.802; *Dev* 3.292; *Mādh* 3.159 — b) tMd[4] दण्डो; oOr दामं; Bo वातुम°; sOx[1] sPu[6] यातुम°; Bo Ho Pu[7] °क्नुवत् — c) Lo[1] Tj[1] अनृण्यं; wKt[3] आनृणं; Lo[1] mTr[6] कर्मणां — d) tMd[3] oOr *Dev* विप्रो गच्छेच्छनैः शनैः [tMd[3] द्विजो]; Lo[2] विप्रो शनैः शनैः [*om* दद्यात्]

स्त्रीबालोन्मत्तवृद्धानां दरिद्रानाथरोगिणाम् ।
शिफाविदलरज्ज्वाद्यैर्विदध्यान्नृपतिर्दमम् ॥२३०॥
ये नियुक्तास्तु कार्येषु हन्युः कार्याणि कार्यिणाम् ।
धनोष्मणा पच्यमानास्तान्निःस्वान्कारयेन्नृपः ॥२३१॥
कूटशासनकर्तॄंश्च प्रकृतीनां च दूषकान् ।
स्त्रीबालब्राह्मणघ्नांश्च हन्याद् द्विट्सेविनस्तथा ॥२३२॥
तीरितं चानुशिष्टं च यत्र क्वचन यद्भवेत् ।
कृतं तद्धर्मतो विद्यान्न तद्भूयो निवर्तयेत् ॥२३३॥
अमात्यः प्राड्विवाको वा यत्कुर्यात्कार्यमन्यथा ।
तत्स्वयं नृपतिः कुर्यात् तं सहस्रं च दण्डयेत् ॥२३४॥

230.* Cited by *Lakṣ* 12.802; *Dev* 3.292; *Mādh* 3.159 — a) Lo^{4} °वृत्तानां — b) Tr^{2} दरिद्राणाथिनां तथा; Be^{1} Ho Jm Jo^{1} Jo^{2} wKt^{1} Kt^{2} wKt^{3} NKt^{4} BKt^{5} Lo^{1} Lo^{2} Lo^{3} TMd^{4} GMd^{5} sOx^{1} Ox^{2} Pu^{2} Pu^{4} Pu^{5} sPu^{6} Pu^{7} Tj^{1} MTr^{3} [*Jolly* G Ku R] *Lakṣ Mādh Mandlik Jha KSS Dave* दरिद्राणां च रोगिणां — c) BKt^{5} शिफवि°; NPu^{1} Pu^{2} Pu^{4} Pu^{5} Pu^{7} *Dev* शफावि°; Jo^{1} निफावि°; La^{1} oOr शिकावि°; Lo^{2} लतावि°; TMd^{3} शिफाविदश°; *Mādh* शिथिलाविलरज्ज्वा°; Tr^{1} °विदळ°; Pu^{2} Pu^{4} °विदल्य° — d) wKt^{1} °पतिर्गमं; Lo^{4} °पतिर्ध्रुवं

231. a) Lo^{1} वियुक्तास्तेषु कार्येपु; Ho Pu^{4} यो; *Me* [pāṭha] येऽनियुक्तास्तु [*Me* comments: इत्यकारप्रश्लेषः पठन्ति]; GMd^{1} नियुक्तेषु कार्येषु — b) Bo कार्यिणं; GMd^{1} TMd^{3} GMd^{5} Tr^{1} [*but mc sh*] MTr^{6} कारिणां; Be^{1} कार्याणां; GMy कारणात् — c) TMd^{3} धनुष्मणा; MTr^{3} दवोष्मणा; GMy पाच्यमा°; Pu^{2} Pu^{4} मध्यमा°; BCa Lo^{1} TMd^{4} GMy Ox^{2} °मानांस्ता°; Tj^{1} Tr^{1} °मानान्ता°; Bo TMd^{3} NPu^{1} Pu^{2} Pu^{4} °मानंता° — d) Be^{1} Bo Hy Kt^{2} wKt^{3} BKt^{5} Lo^{1} Pu^{7} °स्तान्निस्वा°; TMd^{3} °स्तांस्तुत्त्वान्का°; oOr Pu^{2} Pu^{4} °स्तान्निस्कान्का°; Lo^{4} [*Jolly* M] °रयेद्बुधः

232. Cited by *Apa* 862; *Lakṣ* 12.570; *Dev* 3.752— a) NPu^{1} कूटसाक्षिण°; Bo Pu^{2} Pu^{4} °कर्तृश्च — b) Be^{1} Ho^{1} Wa दूषिकान् — d) Lo^{1} द्विट्वेषिन°

233. Cited by *Vij* 2.306; *Lakṣ* 12.266; *Mādh* 3.161 — a) Tr^{2} तीर्तितं; wKt^{1} GMd^{1} Tj^{1} तारितं; [*Jolly* Nd] निर्णीतं; MTr^{4} नीरितं; TMd^{3} ईरितं; TMd^{4} दीवितं; NPu^{1} मरितं; GMd^{1} चानुतिष्टं; oOr *om* च; La^{1} वा — b) *Vij* क्वचन विद्यते; TMd^{3} क्वचन संवसेत्; Kt^{2} GMd^{1} तद्भवेत् — c) Kt^{2} कृतां; GMy प्रकृतं धर्मतो; TMd^{4} यद्धर्मतो; *Dev* तद्धर्मयोर्वि°; Be^{1} विद्वान्न; TMd^{3} विद्यां न; *Vij* ज्ञेयं न — d) Pu^{2} Pu^{4} विद्यात्तत्तद्भूयो; *Vij* तत्प्राज्ञो; *Mādh* तद्भूयोपि वर्तयेत्; Lo^{4} TMd^{3} Tj^{1} [*Jolly* M] निवर्तते; Lo^{3} NPu^{1} न वर्तयेत्

Additional verse in NPu^{1} Pu^{2} Pu^{4} *Mandlik* [ट, ठ] *Dave KSS:*

तीरितं चानुशिष्टं च यो मन्येत विकर्मणा ।
द्विगुणं दण्डमास्थाय तत्कार्यं पुनरुद्धरेत् ॥

a) Pu^{4} तीरितां; Pu^{2} Pu^{4} वा

234.* Omitted in BKt^{5}. Cited by *Lakṣ* 12.269; *Dev* 3.304— a) BCa Hy Jm Jo^{1} wKt^{1} Kt^{2} wKt^{3} GMd^{1} TMd^{3} TMd^{4} GMd^{5} GMy Pu^{8} Tr^{1} MTr^{3} MTr^{4} MTr^{5} MTr^{6} [*Jolly* Nd] *Lakṣ Nā Ku Mandlik KSS Jha Dave* अमात्याः; Lo^{3} आमात्यः; GMd^{1} TMd^{3} GMy [*Jolly* Nd] *Bh* प्राड्विवाका; Pu^{7} [*but cor*] Pu^{5} प्राक्विवाको — b) TMd^{3} यत्कुर्युस्तच्च कारयेत्; Be^{1} Bo Ho Jo^{2} La^{1} Lo^{4} NNg NPu^{1} Pu^{2} Pu^{3} Pu^{4} Pu^{5} Pu^{7} Tj^{1} Tr^{2} Wa [*Jolly* M G] *Dev* यः कुर्या°; GMd^{1} GMd^{5} Pu^{8} *Lakṣ* ये कुर्युः कार्य°; BCa wKt^{3} य कुर्युः कार्य°; Hy Jm Jo^{1} Kt^{2} Lo^{2} GMd^{1} TMd^{3} TMd^{4} GMd^{5} GMy Pu^{8} Tj^{2} Tr^{1} MTr^{3}

ब्रह्महा च सुरापश्च तस्करो गुरुतल्पगः ।
एते सर्वे पृथग्वेद्या महापातकिनो नराः ॥२३५॥
चतुर्णामपि चैतेषां प्रायश्चित्तमकुर्वताम् ।
शरीरधनसंयुक्तं दण्डं धर्म्यं प्रकल्पयेत् ॥२३६॥
गुरुतल्पे भगः कार्यः सुरापाने सुराध्वजः ।
स्तेये तु श्वपदं कार्यं ब्रह्महण्यशिराः पुमान् ॥२३७॥
असंभोज्या ह्यसंयाज्या असंपाठ्याविवाहिनः ।
चरेयुः पृथिवीं दीनाः सर्वधर्मबहिष्कृताः ॥२३८॥
ज्ञातिसंबन्धिभिस्त्वेते त्यक्तव्याः कृतलक्षणाः ।

MTr⁴ MTr⁵ MTr⁶ *Mandlik KSS Jha Dave* [*Jolly* Ku] यत्कुर्युः कार्य° — c) GMy तत्सर्वं; oOr पश्येत् — d) GMy सहस्रं तांश्च दण्डयेत्; Pu⁵ Pu⁷ [*Jolly* G]सहस्रं चैव दण्डयेत्; Be¹ BBe² BCa Hy Jm Jo¹ GMd¹ TMd³ GMd⁵ sOx¹ NPu¹ Pu² Pu⁴ sPu⁶ Pu⁸ Tj² Tr¹ MTr⁴ MTr⁵ MTr⁶ *Bh Ku Mandlik KSS Dave* तान्; oOr तत्; NKt⁴ यत्; Lo¹ तैः; TMd⁴ तांत्सहस्रं; Be¹ तु दण्ड°

235.* Omitted in La¹. Cited by *Lakṣ* 12.784; *Dev* 3.753 — a-d) for this verse *Bh* gives the following as a pāṭha: ब्राह्मणघ्नं सुरापं च तस्करं गुरुतल्पगं । एतान्विद्यात्पृथक्सर्वान्महापातकिनो नरान् ॥ — a) Hy सुरापाश्च — b) Hy Jm Jo¹ Kt² Ox² Pu⁵ Pu⁷ Tj² Tr² MTr³ [*Jolly* G]*Rc Mandlik KSS* स्तेयी च गुरु° — c) NPu¹ ते सर्वे; Lo² एतान्सर्वान्पृ°; *Dev* पृथग्वध्या; BBe² पृथग्विद्या; Jo² Lo¹ Lo³ Lo⁴ NNg Ox² NPu¹ Pu⁵ Pu⁷ Tj¹ पृथग्दण्ड्या; Be¹ Bo Ho Hy Jm Jo¹ Kt² sOx¹ Pu² Pu³ Pu⁴ sPu⁶ Pu⁸ Tj² Tr² MTr³ Wa *Lakṣ Mandlik Jolly Jha KSS Dave* पृथग्ज्ञेया; Lo² पृथग्विद्यान्महा° — d) wKt³ सदा पात°; TMd³ नरः; Lo² नरान्

236.* Omitted in La¹. Cited by *Vij* 2.81; *Apa* 843; *Lakṣ* 12.784; *Dev* 3.291 — a) Lo³ Tj¹ चैवेषां; GMd¹ *Vij Dev* वर्णानां — b) Hy °कुर्वता — c) Be¹ Lo¹ TMd³ oOr Ox² Pu² Pu⁴ शरीरं; BBe² Hy Jm Jo¹ Jo² Kt² Lo³ Tj² MTr³ Wa *Vij Lakṣ Dev Mandlik Jolly Jha KSS Dave* शारीरं; wKt³ शारीषं; Lo⁴ Lo⁵ sOx¹ sPu⁶ °युक्त — d) GMy दण्डं राजा प्रकल्पयेत्; GMd⁵ दण्ड्यं; Lo⁵ दण्डान्धर्म्यान्; BCa wKt¹ Lo³ Pu⁷ Tj¹ *Lakṣ* धर्म्यं दण्डं; oOr धर्मदण्डं; Pu² Pu⁴ धर्मा दण्डं; Be¹ Bo wKt³ धर्मं; Tr² प्रकल्पते; *Apa* प्रकल्पितं; TMd³ च कल्पयेत्; Be¹ प्रचक्षते

237. Cited by *Vij* 2.270; *Apa* 842; *Lakṣ* 12.784; *Mādh* 3.304 — a) La¹ °तल्पो; BKt⁵ °तल्प; wKt¹ भागं; TMd⁴ यवः; wKt¹ TMd⁴ कार्यं — b) Ho सुरापान; GMd⁵ सुरापेन; TMd³ चनूध्वजः; wKt¹ °ध्वजं — c) GMd⁵ स्तेने; TMd⁴ *Jha* तस्करे श्व°; Be¹ Hy Jm Jo1 wKt¹ Kt² Lo³ Tj² MTr³ MTr⁵ *Vij Mandlik KSS Dave* च; Pu⁵ Pu⁷ MTr⁵ श्वपदः कार्यो; wKt¹ वपनं कार्यं — d) *Nā* अब्रह्मण्येशिराः and gives the reading of ed. as *kvacit pāṭhaḥ*; Be¹ wKt³ BKt⁵ Lo¹ ब्रह्महत्यशिराः [BKt⁵ °गिराः]; Ox² Pu⁵ Pu⁷ °शिरः; Ho °सुराः

238.* Pāda-c omitted in Pu⁴. Cited by *Apa* 843; *Lakṣ* 12.784; *Dev* 3.753 — a) TMd³ असंभाष्या ह्यसंभोज्या; BKt⁵ असंभाष्यास्त्वसंयाज्या; Lo⁵ GMd¹ Ox³ MTr⁴ MTr⁵ MTr⁶ °भोग्या; TMd⁴ °भोग्यं; Lo¹ *Apa* °भोज्यास्त्वसं°; La¹ °भोज्याश्चासं°; Hy wKt³ Lo⁴ NNg Ox² Ox³ Pu⁵ Pu⁷ Tj² Tr² Wa °भोज्या असं°; Lo⁴ TMd⁴ Ox³ Tj¹ MTr⁵ [*Jolly* M]ह्यसंयोज्या; Lo⁵ असंयोज्या; Bo ह्यसंयष्टा; MTr⁴ MTr⁶ ह्यसंभोज्या — b) *Dev* अपाठ्याश्चाविवाहिनः; TMd³ GMy [*Jolly* R Nd] ह्यसंपाठ्या°; Be¹ असंयाच्या°; Lo⁵ sOx¹ sPu⁶ MTr⁴ असंपाद्या°; Tj¹ ह्यसंपद्या°; Ox² असंवाद्या°; NPu¹ Pu² Pu⁴ असंवाह्या°; Pu³ असंपाक्या°; TMd⁴ असंबन्ध्या°; Tr² असंपंत्त्या°; Bo असंपत्त्य°; Lo¹ असंपाला°; *Apa* °विवाहिकाः Pu² °विवादनिः; TMd³ °विवादनाः; Pu⁴ °विवांदांनाः; MTr⁴ °विवापिनः; Lo⁴ *Me Jha* °विगर्हिताः — c) Lo⁵ Tj¹ Tr² पृथिवी; Tr² दीनां; *Dev* सर्वा — d) NPu¹ सर्वे; Bo °बहिष्कृतः

निर्दया निर्नमस्कारास्तन्मनोरनुशासनम् ॥२३९॥
प्रायश्चित्तं तु कुर्वाणाः पूर्वे वर्णा यथोदितम् ।
नाङ्क्या राज्ञा ललाटे स्युर्दाप्यास्तूत्तमसाहसम् ॥२४०॥
आगःसु ब्राह्मणस्यैषु कार्यो मध्यमसाहसः ।
विवास्यो वा भवेद्राष्ट्रात् सद्रव्यः सपरिच्छदः ॥२४१॥
इतरे कृतवन्तस्तु पापान्येतान्यकामतः ।
सर्वस्वहारमर्हन्ति कामतस्तु प्रवासनम् ॥२४२॥
नाददीत नृपः साधुर्महापातकिनो धनम् ।
आददानस्तु तल्लोभात् तेन दोषेण लिप्यते ॥२४३॥

239. Cited by *Lakṣ* 12.785; *Dev* 3.753 — a) Pu[2] Pu[4] जाति° ; Lo[4] *Dev* °बन्धिभिश्चैते; gMd[5] °बन्धिभिश्चैव; bCa Tr[2] °बन्धिनस्त्वेते; Lo[2] °बन्धिस्त्वेते; [*Jolly* M] °बन्धिनश्चैते; tMd[4] Pu[4] °बन्धिनश्चैव; Pu[2] °बन्धिश्चैव — b) *Dev* कर्तव्याः; Bo Pu[3] Wa °लक्षणः — c) Bo निर्दयां; tMd[4] निर्दाया; wKt[1] निर्दशा; Be[1] निष्क्रिया; oOr निर्वाण; *Dev* निर्वाच्या; Bo °मस्कारांस्त° ; nPu[1] °मस्कार्यास्त° — d) wKt[1] °नोरपि शासनं

240. Cited by *Vij* 2.270, 3.259; *Apa* 843; *Lakṣ* 12.785; *Dev* 3.754; *Mādh* 3.305 — a) bBe[2] tMd[3] tMd[4] gMy *Mādh* °श्चित्तमकुर्वाणाः; Bo bKt[5] Lo[5] Ox[2] कुर्वाणः — b) tMd[4] mTr[6] पूर्व; mTr[4] पूर्ण; Be[1] bBe[2] bCa Ho Jm Jo[2] wKt[1] Kt[2] wKt[3] La[1] Lo[3] sOx[1] Ox[2] nPu[1] Pu[2] Pu[3] Pu[4] sPu[6] Pu[8] Tj[1] [*Jolly* R Ku] *Vij Mādh* सर्वे; Jo[1] wKt[1] bKt[5] mTr[3] *Mandlik KSS* सर्ववर्णा; *Apa* त्रयो वर्णा; Kt[2] सवर्णा; Pu[5] Pu[7] mTr[5] यथोदिताः; Pu[2] Pu[4] यथोदितः; bKt[5] *Apa* यथोचितं — c) wKt[1] नाङ्का; nKt[4] नाक्या; *Mādh* अङ्क्या; tMd[3] नान्ता; Tj[1] नाभ्या; Lo[3] नाभ्यां; gMy अन्या; tMd[3] राज्ञो; gMd[1] राज्ञोपलाभेषु दाप्या° ; La[1] Lo[4] gMd[5] gMy Tr[1] mTr[5] Wa [*Jolly* M Nd] *Lakṣ* ललाटेषु दाप्या° ; bCa Jo[2] Lo[1] tMd[3] oOr Tj[1] [*Jolly* R] *Vij Dev* तु दाप्या° — d) *Mādh* °प्याश्चोत्तम° ; gMd[1] tMd[3] Tr[2] °साहसाः; oOr °साहसां

241. Omitted in Lo[4]. Cited by *Lakṣ* 12.785; *Dev* 3.754 — a) Pu[5] Pu[7] कृतागस्सु ब्राह्मणेषु; Lo[3] Tj[1] अगःसु; Lo[1] अगस्सु; Lo[4] Ox[3] आगत्सु; Pu[2] Pu[4] आतःसु; Bo अघस्त्यु; nKt[4] आवाःसु; wKt[1] आगस्त्व; gMd[1] gMd[5] Pu[2] Pu[4] Tj[1] °णस्येषु; Be[1] La[1] gMy [*Jolly* Nd R] °णस्यैष; Wa °णस्यैषा; Bo tMd[4] °णेष्वेषु; Hy Jm Jo[1] Kt[2] wKt[3] bKt[5] Tj[2] mTr[3] *Dev Mandlik Jolly Jha KSS Dave* °णस्यैव; nPu[1] °णश्चैव — b) tMd[4] कार्यं; gMd[1] °साहसाः; tMd[4] Pu[2] Pu[4] °साहसं — c) Tr[2] विवासो; bBe[2] Bo bCa Ho wKt[1] La[1] Lo[1] Lo[3] Tj[1] Tj[2] निर्वास्यो; Jo[2] sOx[1] sPu[6] [*mc sh*] निवास्यो; tMd[4] विवास्यश्च; wKt[3] oOr *om* वा; Bo भवेद्राष्ट्राः — d) tMd[4] प्रष्टव्यः; tMd[3] सद्रव्यस्यपरि° ; Lo[1] °रिच्छेदः

242. Omitted in Lo[4]. Cited by *Lakṣ* 12.785; *Dev* 3.754 — a) wKt[3] nPu[1] Pu[2] Pu[4] Wa °वन्तश्च — b) bBe[2] °तानकामतः; Be[1] tMd[3] °तानि कामतः; *Lakṣ* °तानि धर्मतः — c) gMd[1] ते सर्वहारम° ; Bo सर्वहारम° ; nKt[4] gMy Pu[3] mTr[6] °स्वाहारम° ; tMd[4] °स्वंहारम° ; Lo[4] °हानम° ; *Lakṣ* °हानीम° ; Be[1] Pu[5] Pu[7] °रमिच्छन्ति — d) Tj[1] सकामस्तु; gMd[5] काममस्तु; nKt[4] प्रभासनं; *Dev* प्रमापणं

Additional verse in bCa La[1] tMd[4] Tr[2]:

एवं विद्वान्ननुशासन् राजा धर्मेण युज्यते ।
लोकांश्च पुण्यानाप्नोति तन्मनोरनुशासनम् ॥

a) bCa एवंविधा° ; La[1] धर्माननुशा° ; tMd[4] °नुशासद्; Tr[2] °नूशासद् — c) tMd[4] पुण्यं जयति

243. Omitted in Pu[5]. Cited by *Lakṣ* 12.787 — a) Pu[4] Tr[2] नददीत; tMd[3] नादधीत; Lo[4] नावदीत; Bo नृपं — b) Lo[3] Tj[1] Tr[1] mTr[4] mTr[5] mTr[6] [*Jolly* Nd R] °पातकिनां; Hy gMd[1] °पातकिना — c) Tj[2] आददानस्स; Hy *om* तु — c-d) Lo[4] Ox[3] आददानस्तु वर्णेभ्यो तेनादोपैर्विकल्प्यते [Ox[3] °कल्पते]

अप्सु प्रवेश्य तं दण्डं वरुणायोपपादयेत् ।
श्रुतवृत्तोपपन्ने वा ब्राह्मणे प्रतिपादयेत् ॥२४४॥
ईशो दण्डस्य वरुणो राज्ञां दण्डधरो हि सः ।
ईशः सर्वस्य जगतो ब्राह्मणो वेदपारगः ॥२४५॥
यत्र वर्जयते राजा पापकृद्भ्यो धनागमम् ।
तत्र कालेन जायन्ते मानवा दीर्घजीविनः ॥२४६॥
निष्पद्यन्ते च सस्यानि यथोप्तानि विशां पृथक् ।
बालाश्च न प्रमीयन्ते विकृतं च न जायते ॥२४७॥
ब्राह्मणान्बाधमानं तु कामादवरवर्णजम् ।
हन्याच्चित्रैर्वधोपायैरुद्वेजनकरैर्नृपः ॥२४८॥
यावानवध्यस्य वधे तावान्वध्यस्य मोक्षणे ।

— d) Be^{1} Bo Ho Lo^{1} *Lakṣ* तेनाधर्मेण; BCa wKt^{1} BKt^{5} La^{1} Lo^{2} Lo^{3} Lo^{4} oOr sOx^{1} Ox^{2} NPu^{1} Pu^{2} Pu^{3} Pu^{4} sPu^{6} Pu^{8} Tj^{1} Tr^{2} [*Jolly* M R] *Jolly* पापेन; MTr^{5} तप्यते

244. Pādas c-d omitted in GMd^{1} TMd^{4} [haplo]. Cited by *Lakṣ* 12.787 — a) Lo^{4} प्रावेश्य; TMd^{4} प्रविश्य; Pu^{5} Pu^{7} प्रवेश्य दण्डं वा; Lo^{4} Lo^{5} [*but cor sh*] Ox^{3} तां; La^{1} TMd^{3} TMd^{4} GMd^{5} GMy *Lakṣ* तद्दण्डं — c) *Lakṣ* श्रुतिविद्योपसंपन्ने; Tr^{2} सुत°; Pu^{5} Pu^{7} °वृद्धोप°; TMd^{3} °वित्तोप°; MTr^{4} MTr^{5} MTr^{6} °पन्नं; wKt^{3} La^{1} GMy oOr Pu^{2} Pu^{4} [*Jolly* Nd] °पसंपन्ने ब्राह्म°; Be^{1} °पन्नो; GMd^{5} च — c-d) Lo^{4} आददानस्तु वर्णेभ्यो तेनादोषैर्विकल्प्यते [cf. 9.243] — d) MTr^{4} MTr^{6} ब्राह्मणं; MTr^{5} ब्राह्मणः; La^{1} Pu^{2} Pu^{4} चोपपादयेत्

245. Omitted in Pu^{4}. Cited by *Lakṣ* 12.787 — a) GMd^{1} अंशो; TMd^{4} पाशो; sPu^{6} देशो; sOx^{1} देशे; Lo^{4} दण्ड्यस्य — b) Be^{1} Lo^{4} Lo^{5} GMd^{5} Ox^{3} Pu^{5} Pu^{7} *Lakṣ* राज्ञो; Bo TMd^{3} राज्ञा; BKt^{5} Lo^{1} राजा; TMd^{4} हितः — c) Pu^{2} ईशश्च सर्वजगतो

246. Pāda-a omitted in Pu^{4}. Cited by *Lakṣ* 12.787 — a) Lo^{4} [*Jolly* M] यत्र च नियते; GMd^{1} वर्ज्यस्वतो — b) wKt^{1} पापकृत्यो; TMd^{4} पापकृत्स्या; Pu^{5} Pu^{7} °गमः — c) Lo^{1} यत्र; oOr अत्र; Be^{1} GMd^{5} Pu^{2} Pu^{4} काले तु; GMy [*Jolly* Nd] लोके तु; Lo^{4} Lo^{5} Ox^{3} लोके च; Wa जायेते — d) GMd^{1} दीर्घदर्शिनः

247.* Cited by *Lakṣ* 12.787 — a) NNg निःपाद्यन्ते; Be^{1} निःपीड्यन्ते; Jo^{2} wKt^{1} Lo^{3} TMd^{3} Tj^{1} उत्पद्यन्ते; Pu^{5} Pu^{7} [*but cor*] °द्यन्ति; Tr^{1} तु — b) oOr यथोप्तानि कृपीवलैः; Jo^{2} Lo^{3} Tj^{1} कालोप्तानि; Be^{1} Ho wKt^{1} NKt^{4} Lo^{2} GMd^{1} TMd^{3} GMy Ox^{3} NPu^{1} Pu^{5} Pu^{7} Pu^{8} Tr^{1} [*but cor*] MTr^{4} MTr^{5} MTr^{6} *Lakṣ* यथोक्तानि — c) TMd^{4} बालश्च; NKt^{4} Tj^{1} प्रमीयते; BKt^{5} प्रदीयन्ते — d) oOr सकृतं; Pu^{8} विकृतश्च; TMd^{3} Tr^{1} विकृतिश्च; Be^{1} BBe^{2} Hy Jm Jo^{1} Kt^{2} sOx^{1} Ox^{2} Ox^{3} NPu^{1} sPu^{6} Tj^{2} MTr^{3} [*Jolly* K] *Mandlik Jolly Jha KSS Dave* विकृतं न च; BKt^{5} Lo^{1} Lo^{4} [*Jolly* M] विकृतिर्न च; Bo Ho Pu^{2} Pu^{4} विकृतं नैव; Be^{1} राजते

Additional half-verse in TMd^{3}:

ब्राह्मणाश्च समाधिं तु करिष्यन्ति सुधार्मिकाः ॥

248. Omitted in oOr. Cited by *Dev* 3.754; *Mādh* 3.396 — a) Ho Lo^{1} TMd^{4} ब्राह्मणं बाध°; MTr^{6} ब्राह्मणं वध्यमानं; *Mādh* °णान्बाध्यमानं; Tr^{1} [*but cor*] °न्बाधमानां; Bo GMd^{1} sOx^{1} sPu^{6} °न्बाधमानस्तु — b) GMd^{1} sOx^{1} sPu^{6} °वर्णजः — c) BBe^{2} wKt^{1} GMd^{5} हन्याच्छिद्रै°; GMd^{1} *Dev* हन्याच्चित्रवधो°; wKt^{1} °त्रैर्वरोपा°

अधर्मो नृपतेर्दृष्टो धर्मस्तु विनियच्छतः ॥२४९॥
उदितोऽयं विस्तरशो मिथो विवदमानयोः ।
अष्टादशसु मार्गेषु व्यवहारस्य निर्णयः ॥२५०॥
एवं धर्म्याणि कार्याणि कुर्वन्सम्यङ्महीपतिः ।
देशानलब्धाँल्लिप्सेत लब्धांश्च परिपालयेत् ॥२५१॥
सम्यङ्निविष्टदेशस्तु कृतदुर्गश्च शास्त्रतः ।
कण्टकोद्धरणे नित्यमातिष्ठेद्यत्नमुत्तमम् ॥२५२॥
रक्षणादार्यवृत्तानां कण्टकानां च शोधनात् ।
नरेन्द्रास्त्रिदिवं यान्ति प्रजापालनतत्पराः ॥२५३॥
अशासंस्तस्करान्यस्तु बलिं गृह्णाति पार्थिवः ।
तस्य प्रक्षुभ्यते राष्ट्रं स्वर्गाच्च परिहीयते ॥२५४॥

249. Cited by *Lakṣ* 12.796 — a) Lo^1 यावान्वध्यस्य च वधे; Tr^2 यावान्वध्यस्य वध्ये तु; GMy °वद्धस्य; BKt^5 वधो; Pu^5 Pu^7 वधस्तावा° — c) TMd^3 अधर्मो धर्मवद्दृष्ट्वा; GMy °तेर्दुष्टो — d) BKt^5 Pu^2 Pu^4 Pu^5 Pu^7 धर्मस्य विनि°; TMd^4 विधियच्छतः; Lo^4 °यच्छति

250. Cited by *Lakṣ* 12.770 — a) Tr^2 उदितं यं; Lo^4 उक्तो [*ma* र्थो] यं; Be^1 उक्तो यः; Pu^5 Pu^7 उक्तो यो; GMd^1 *om* यं; Lo^1 Lo^4 NNg GMd^5 Ox^2 Wa विस्तरतो — c) GMd^1 अस्मादशेषमार्गेषु — d) *Lakṣ* व्यवहारविनिर्णयः; Be^1 GMd^1 व्यवहारेषु

251. Cited by *Lakṣ* 12.770 — a) NNg [*but cor fh*] एकं; BKt^5 TMd^4 Pu^2 Pu^4 BBe^2 धर्माणि; Be^1 Bo BCa Ho Jo^2 wKt^3 NKt^4 La^1 Lo^1 Lo^2 Lo^3 Lo^4 oOr sOx^1 sPu^6 Pu^8 Tj^1 Tj^2 Tr^1 [*Jolly* M] कार्याणि धर्म्याणि [Ho Pu^8 धर्माणि]; GMy सर्वाणि कार्याणि; MTr^5 *Lakṣ* कार्याणि सर्वाणि; GMd^5 कार्याणि कर्माणि; BKt^5 *om* कार्याणि; Pu^2 Pu^4 कर्माणि — b) TMd^4 कुर्वन्सर्वं मही°; Bo Ho Hy Jm Jo^1 wKt^1 Kt^2 Lo^1 Lo^4 Ox^2 NPu^1 Pu^2 Pu^3 Pu^4 Tj^2 Tr^2 MTr^3 *Mandlik Jolly Jha KSS Dave* सम्यक्कुर्वन्मही° — c) La^1 देशान्लब्धात्र लिप्सेत; GMy देशादल°; Tj^2 *om* अलब्धाँल्लिप्सेत; Lo^1 °लब्धांश्च लिप्सेरन् — d) oOr प्रतिपालयेत्; Wa परिकल्पयेत्

252. a) Be^1 सम्यक्विनष्ट°; TMd^4 सम्यगाविष्ट°; Tj^2 सम्यगाश्रित°; Lo^4 [*Jolly* M] °देशेषु — b) Ho कृतवर्गश्च; TMd^3 कृतवर्यश्च; Be^1 BCa wKt^1 Lo^4 TMd^4 GMd^5 oOr Tr^1 MTr^6 [*Jolly* M Nd] °दुर्गस्तु; Bo Tr^1 MTr^4 MTr^6 शाश्वतः; Lo^2 शास्त्रश्वतः — c) GMd^5 Tr^1 °द्धारणे; TMd^4 °द्धरणं — c-d) Wa नित्ययत्नमातिष्ठेदुत्तमं; Be^1 NNg Pu^5 Pu^7 यत्नमातिष्ठेन्नित्यमुत्तमं [Be^1 नित्यमाति°]; Jm Pu^2 Pu^4 यत्नमातिष्ठेद्यत्नमुत्तमं

253. a) TMd^3 रक्षणावार्य°; Tr^2 °वृत्तीनां — b) Bo शोधने; wKt^3 शोधयेत् — c) Bo नरेन्द्रस्त्रि° — d) Bo °तत्परं; Jm °तत्परान्

Additional verse in La^1 [quite illegibly written]:

समभर्ता जनपदे प्राणिदेय्यादिशांक्रमात् ।
क्रान्तान्तिकप्रव्रजितान्मौद्वत्तिकचिकित्सकान् ॥
वैदेहकानचरांश्च काष्टग्निकृतारणाम् ।
सिद्धनैमित्तिकोन्मत्तवैश्यान्वणिकशौंडिकान् ॥
वैश्यजानपराध्यन्क्षान् सृद्धिपाजीवचेष्टितैः ।
व्रघ्नाव्रुमुः समाहर्त्ते संविदध्यात्ततः परम् ॥

254. a) GMd^1 अशासन्तस्तस्करान्ये; Tr^1 अशासन्तस्क°; Be^1 Lo^1 Lo^4 आशासन्तस्क°; Lo^4 आशासंस्तस्क°; wKt^3 अशासस्तस्क°; TMd^4 अशासुस्तस्क°; wKt^1 अशास्य तस्क°; TMd^3 कशासंतस्क° — b) TMd^4

निर्भयं तु भवेद्यस्य राष्ट्रं बाहुबलाश्रितम् ।
तस्य तद्वर्धते नित्यं सिच्यमान इव द्रुमः ॥२५५॥
द्विविधांस्तस्करान्विद्यात् परद्रव्यापहारकान् ।
प्रकाशांश्चाप्रकाशांश्च चारचक्षुर्महीपतिः ॥२५६॥
प्रकाशवञ्चकास्तेषां नानापण्योपजीविनः ।
प्रच्छन्नवञ्चकास्त्वेते स्तेनाटव्यादयो जनाः ॥२५७॥
उत्कोचकाश्चौपधिका वञ्चकाः कितवास्तथा ।
मङ्गलादेशवृत्ताश्च भद्रप्रेक्षणिकैः* सह ॥२५८॥

बलं; GMd^1 पार्थिवाः — c) Be^1 Bo Ho Jo^2 Lo^3 Tj^1 तस्य क्षुभ्यति तद्राष्ट्रं; Lo^4 यस्य क्षुभ्यति वै राष्ट्रं; [*Jolly* M] यस्य; GMd^1 तत्र; wKt^3 तस्य क्षुभ्यते; Tr^2 प्रक्षुभते — d) BKt^5 स्वर्गाश्च; Lo^4 [*Jolly* M] स्वर्गात्स; GMy परिणीयते; TMd^4 परिजायते

255. Cited by *Lakṣ* 12.511 — a) GMd^1 TMd^3 MTr^4 MTr^6 निर्भयं यस्य वसति; Lo^3 निर्भवो हि; BBe^2 BCa NKt^4 Lo^1 Lo^4 GMd^5 GMy Pu^5 Pu^7 Tj^1 Tr^1 [*Jolly* Nd R] हि; NNg *Lakṣ* वा — b) Lo^1 MTr^4 MTr^6 राष्ट्रं वा बहुलाश्रितं [MTr^4 MTr^6 °लार्थितं]; NPu^1 राष्ट्रं राजबलान्वितं; GMd^5 राज्यं; Bo °बलाश्रुतं; Ox^2 °बलाश्रयात्; BCa Lo^4 °बलाश्रयं — c) Lo^4 [*Jolly* M] तस्याभिवर्धते; GMd^1 NNg oOr तद्वर्धते राष्ट्रं — d) Ho सिञ्च्यमाने; Kt^2 सिंच्यमान; Lo^4 [*Jolly* M] सेव्यमान; TMd^3 सिच्छमान; Tj^1 इति; Tr^2 दुमाः

256. Cited by *Lakṣ* 12.256; *Dev* 3.735 — a) La^1 TMd^3 विविधांस्तस्क°; Be^1 Lo^4 विविधान्तस्क°; Be^1 Bo La^1 Pu^2 Pu^7 Tr^1 °रान्विन्द्यात् — b) Tr^2 परराष्ट्राप°; Lo^2 TMd^3 TMd^4 GMy Pu^8 MTr^4 MTr^5 MTr^6 Wa [*Jolly* Nd] *LakṣNSm* 19.1 °हारिणः — c) TMd^4 प्रकाशाश्चाप्रकाशाश्च; wKt^3 Lo^4 Lo^5 TMd^3 प्रकाशांश्चप्रकाशांश्च; Tj^2 *om* अप्रकाशांश्च — d) NKt^4 भावचक्षु°; Be^1 चारवर्जमही°; MTr^6 °चक्षुर्महीयते

257.* a) GMy Tj^1 प्रकाशं; Bo GMy sOx^1 sPu^6 MTr^5 [*Jolly* M Nd] °कास्त्वेषां — b) Tr^2 °जीविनां — c) Be^1 BBe^2 BCa Ho wKt^3 NKt^4 La^1 GMd^5 oOr Ox^2 NPu^1 Pu^8 MTr^4 °वञ्चकास्तेषां; BKt^5 sOx^1 sPu^6 °वञ्चकास्त्वेषां; Pu^2 Pu^4 °वञ्चकाश्चेते; Lo^1 °वञ्चकास्ते च; Jo^2 [*ma fh*] wKt^1 Lo^3 Tj^1 [*Jolly* R] °वञ्चकाश्चैव; Bo NNg Pu^5 Pu^7 Wa °वञ्चकास्त्वेव; Lo^4 [*Jolly* M G] *Jolly* °वञ्चकास्त्वेवं; *Lakṣ* °वञ्चका ज्ञेया — d) Jo^2 wKt^1 Lo^3 Tj^1 [*Jolly* R] स्तेना आटविका जनाः [Tj^1 स्तेषमाट°]; GMd^5 Tr^1 स्तेनाटव्योपजीविनः; wKt^3 स्तेनकाटविका जनाः; BBe^2 Hy Jm Jo^1 Kt^2 Lo^2 sOx^1 Ox^2 Pu^3 sPu^6 Pu^8 Tj^2 Tr^2 MTr^3 *Rn* [pāṭha] *Rc Mandlik Jha KSS Dave* ये स्तेनाटविकादयः; Lo^1 नानापण्यादयो जनाः; TMd^3 नाप्यनिन्दितयोजनाः; GMd^1 नराः

258.* Cited by *Lakṣ* 12.508 — a) Pu^5 Pu^7 उत्कोचिकांश्चौपविका; MTr^5 उत्कोटका औपधिका; Lo^1 औत्काचका औषधिका; Bo उत्कौच°; Ho sOx^1 sPu^6 उत्कोचिका°; Wa औत्कोचिताश्चौप°; MTr^4 उत्कोटकांश्चौप°; La^1 Lo^4 °चकांश्चौप°; Be^1 [*Jolly* M] °चकांश्चौपधिकान्; NPu^1 Pu^2 Pu^4 °चकानौपधिकान्; GMd^5 Tr^1 MTr^5 °चका औपधिका; NKt^4 °चका अपविका; *Lakṣ* °चकाः सोपधिकाः; Jo^1 Jo^2 Lo^3 GMd^1 oOr Tj^1 MTr^6 Wa °श्चोपधिका; Lo^4 °श्चोपधिकान्; MTr^3 °श्चौपयिका; La^1 °पधिकां — b) Lo^4 NPu^1 Pu^2 Pu^4 [*Jolly* M] वञ्चकान्कितवांस्तथा; *Lakṣ* कितवा वञ्चकास्तथा; Be^1 Pu^5 Pu^7 वञ्चकान्कितवान्शठान् [Pu^5 Pu^7 °न्शवान्]; sOx^1 sPu^6 बन्धकाः कितवः शठाः; Ox^2 Pu^3 Pu^8 Tr^2 कितवाः शठाः; BKt^5 *om* तथा — c) GMd^1 माङ्गला°; NPu^1 मङ्गली°; Be^1 La^1 NPu^1 Pu^2 Pu^4 Pu^5 Pu^7 °वृत्तांश्च; Lo^4 °वृत्तीश्च; GMd^1 °वक्षाश्च — d) GMy [*Jolly* Nd] भद्राश्चैक्षणिकास्तथा; GMd^5 भद्राश्चैक्षणिकास्सह; Lo^4 *Rc* भद्राः प्रेक्ष°; Pu^2 Pu^4 भद्रान्प्रेक्ष°; Jo^2 भद्रकेक्ष°; Bo Hy Jm Jo^1 Kt^2 wKt^3 NKt^4 BKt^5 Lo^2 Lo^3 TMd^3 TMd^4 oOr Ox^2 Pu^3 Pu^8 Tj^1 Tr^1 MTr^3 MTr^4 MTr^5 Wa [*Jolly* G Ku R] *Mandlik Jha KSS Dave* भद्राश्चेक्ष°; Be^1 Pu^5 Pu^7 भद्राश्चैक्ष°; Pu^2 Pu^4 भद्रान्चेक्ष°; La^1 भद्रांश्चेक्ष°; NPu^1 Tr^2 MTr^6 भद्राश्चक्ष°; GMd^1 भद्रांश्चो-

असम्यक्कारिणश्चैव महामात्राश्चिकित्सका: ।
शिल्पोपचारयुक्ताश्च निपुणा: पण्ययोषित: ॥२५९॥
एवमाद्यान्विजानीयात् प्रकाशाँल्लोककण्टकान् ।
निगूढचारिणश्चान्याननार्यानार्यलिङ्गिन: ॥२६०॥
तान्विदित्वा सुचरितैर्गूढैस्तत्कर्मकारिभि: ।
चारैश्चानेकसंस्थानै: प्रोत्साह्य वशमानयेत् ॥२६१॥
तेषां दोषानभिख्याप्य स्वे स्वे कर्मणि तत्त्वत: ।
कुर्वीत शासनं राजा सम्यक्सारापराधत: ॥२६२॥
न हि दण्डादृते शक्य: कर्तुं पापविनिग्रह: ।
स्तेनानां पापबुद्धीनां निभृतं चरतां क्षितौ ॥२६३॥
सभाप्रपापूपशाला वेशमद्यान्नविक्रया: ।
चतुष्पथाश्चैत्यवृक्षा: समाजा: प्रेक्षणानि च ॥२६४॥

त्क्षेणिकै:; Ho Tj[2] Lo[1] NNg sOx[1] sPu[6] भद्राश्चेक्षणकै:; wKt[1] भद्राश्चैक्षलकै:; BBe[2] भद्राश्चेक्षासकै:

259. Cited by *Lakṣ* 12.508 — a) *Lakṣ* असभ्यकारि°; Pu[2] °रिणां चैव — b) sOx[1] sPu[6] °मात्रश्चि°; wKt[1] wKt[3] °मात्राचि°; La[1] Lo[4] Pu[2] Pu[4] Pu[5] Pu[7] °मात्रांश्चि°; TMd[3] °मन्त्राश्चि°; La[1] Lo[4] NPu[1] Pu[2] Pu[4] Pu[5] Pu[7] °कित्सकान्; Hy °कित्सक: — c) Lo[4] शिल्पोपश्चार°; TMd[3] GMd[5] [*Jolly* N Nd] शिल्पोपकार°; Be[1] La[1] Lo[4] NPu[1] Pu[2] Pu[4] Pu[7] °युक्तांश्च — d) TMd[4] MTr[6] निपुण:; TMd[3] निपुणां; Bo wKt[1] Pu[8] पुण्य°; NNg पूण्य°

260. After pāda-b Lo[1] places verse 262. Cited by *Lakṣ* 12.509 — a) Hy Jm Jo[1] Kt[2] Tj[2] MTr[3] *Mandlik KSS* एवमादीन्विजा°; sOx[1] sPu[6] [*Jolly* N Nd] °जानीयान् — b) wKt[1] °वञ्चकान् — c) Be[1] Lo[2] GMd[1] TMd[3] TMd[4] GMy NNg Pu[5] Pu[7] Wa *Nā* °कारिणश्चा°; MTr[6] °कारिणांश्चा°; NPu[1] °कारिणश्चैव अनार्या°

261. a) TMd[3] °दित्वापचरि°; wKt[3] स्वचरि°; GMd[5] MTr[4] MTr[6] तु चरि° — b) wKt[1] MTr[6] °गूढस्त°; NPu[1] °स्तत्करचारिभि:; oOr °स्तत्कामकारिभि:; BKt[5] °कारिण: — c) Pu[3] चारैरनेक°; Tr[2] चौरैरेक°; Lo[4] चामरैरनेक°; GMd[1] चारैस्थानैक°; TMd[4] °श्चानेनसंस्थानै: — d) La[1] Lo[4] [*Jolly* M] प्रोच्छाद्य; Tr[2] प्रोत्सात्य; BKt[5] GMy [*Jolly* Nd] प्रोत्सार्य; Wa प्रोक्ताह्य; MTr[6] प्रसंह्य; Hy Jm Jo[1] Kt[2] wKt[3] Lo[2] Ox[2] Pu[2] Pu[3] Pu[4] MTr[3] *Ku Mandlik KSS Jha Dave* [*Jolly* Ku] प्रोत्साद्य

262. a) Pu[5] Pu[7] भेदानभि°; GMd[5] sOx[1] sPu[6] °विख्याप्य; Pu[8] °भिकार्य; Lo[4] °भिव्याप्य — b) Lo[2] *om one* स्वे; Pu[5] Pu[7] स्वै: स्वै:; wKt[3] तिष्ठत: — d) TMd[4] °क्साकोपरा°; BKt[5] °क्चाराप्रसाधन:; sOx[1] sPu[6] °राधित:

263. Omitted in Lo[4] [*Jolly* M]; not commented by *Me*. Cited by *Lakṣ* 12.511 — a) TMd[3] शक्यं; BKt[5] सम्यक्कर्तुं — b) *Lakṣ* न्यायविनि°; TMd[3] °निग्रहं — c) Pu[2] Pu[4] स्तैनानां; wKt[1] wKt[3] Ox[2] पापवृत्तीनां; GMd[5] GMy पापबन्धूनां — d) TMd[4] चरतां निभृतिं क्षितौ; GMd[1] निग्रथं; TMd[3] GMy Tr[1] [*Jolly* Nd] निगूढं; wKt[3] चरता; Ho चरणं

264. Omitted in Lo[4] [*Jolly* M]; not commented by *Me*. Cited by *Apa* 841; *Lakṣ* 12.545 — a) NKt[4] La[1] सभा:; Lo[3] MTr[5] सभाप्रभा°; GMd[1] °प्रयाप्रपाशाला; NPu[1] °पौपशाला; GMd[5] MTr[5] °पूगशाला; Bo Pu[2] Pu[4] Pu[5] Pu[7] °यूपशाला; NNg °पूवशाला; TMd[4] °कूपशाला; NKt[4] °शूपशाला; Ox[2] °द्यूतशाला; Hy °शीला; *Mandlik Jha KSS Dave* °शालावेश° as a compound — b) Jo[2] Pu[7] वेशमन्त्राद्यविक्रया:; Ox[2] NPu[1] वेश्या°; La[1] वैश्या°; Pu[2] Pu[4] वेश्य°; Wa वेशो°; Lo[1] TMd[3] वेश्म°; La[1]

जीर्णोद्यानान्यरण्यानि कारुकावेशनानि च ।
शून्यानि चाप्यगाराणि वनान्युपवनानि च ॥२६५॥
एवंविधान्नृपो देशान् गुल्मैः स्थावरजङ्गमैः ।
तस्करप्रतिषेधार्थं चारैश्चाप्यनुचारयेत् ॥२६६॥
तत्सहायैरनुगतैर्नानाकर्मप्रवेदिभिः ।
विद्यादुत्साहयेच्चैव निपुणैः पूर्वतस्करैः ॥२६७॥
भक्ष्यभोज्यापदेशैश्च ब्राह्मणानां च दर्शनैः ।
शौर्यकर्मापदेशैश्च कुर्युस्तेषां समागमम् ॥२६८॥
ये तत्र नोपसर्पेयुर्मूलप्रणिहिताश्च ये ।
तान्प्रसह्य नृपो हन्यात् समित्रज्ञातिबान्धवान् ॥२६९॥

°मद्यानुविक्रयाः; Bo La[1] sOx[1] Ox[2] sPu[6] Tj[2] °क्रयः; wKt[1] °क्रया; GMy °क्रयान्; Lo[1] Pu[5] Pu[7] [*but cor*] MTr[6] °क्रियाः; NPu[1] °क्रियः; GMd[1] °क्रिया — c) TMd[3] GMd[5] GMy चतुष्पथांश्चैत्यवृक्षान् — d) TMd[3] TMd[4] GMd[5] GMy oOr समाज

265. Omitted in Lo[4] [*Jolly* M]; not commented by *Me*; *ma* in Lo[1]. Cited by *Apa* 841; *Lakṣ* 12.545 — a) *Apa* शीर्णो° — b) wKt[1] कारुणा°; Be[1] °वेशतानि; Ho °वेशमानि; oOr °वेश्मकानि — c) La[1] पशूनाचाप्यगा°; Bo *Apa* वाप्यगा°; Pu[3] चाप्यरण्यानि

Additional half-verse in NPu[1]:

तथा सलिलबन्धानि चत्वारापवनानि च ।

266. Omitted in Lo[4] [*Jolly* M]; not commented by *Me*. Cited by *Apa* 841; *Lakṣ*12.546 — a) GMd[5] एवंविधो नृपो; BKt[5] °न्नृपं; TMd[3] TMd[4] °न्नृपा; Tj[1] देशा — b) TMd[3] गूल्मैः; GMd[1] °जङ्गमात् — c) Ho तस्करं; wKt[1] °प्रतिरोधार्थं — d) La[1] GMd[1] चोरैश्चा°; *Apa* चारैरप्य°; oOr °प्युपचारयेत्; GMd[1] °चालयेत्; Lo[1] °चोदयेत्; BKt[5] °धारयेत्; GMy °चारयोः

267. Omitted in Lo[4] [*Jolly* M]; not commented by *Me*. Cited by *Apa* 841 — a) Lo[1] तत्साहा°; NKt[4] सत्सहा°; MTr[5] *Apa* तान्सहा°; Be[1] TMd[3] उत्सहा°; Tj[1] तत्साहसैर°; BKt[5] GMy Pu[5] Pu[7] MTr[4] MTr[6] [*Jolly* Nd] °हायैः स्वानु°; wKt[1] °हायैः स्वनु°; NNg °हायैस्वनु°; Bo Ho Pu Pu[3] Pu[8] °हायैश्चानु°; BBe[2] NKt[4] La[1] Lo[1] GMd[1] TMd[4] GMd[5] Ox[2] Pu[4] MTr[5] Wa °हायैस्त्वनु°; Tr[2] °हायैश्चानुगतिर्नाना°; Wa °नुमतैर्नाना° — b) GMy °र्नाकर्मप्रतिवादिभिः; Hy BCa BKt[5] GMd[1] TMd[3] TMd[4] Tj[2] MTr[4] MTr[6] [*Jolly* Nd] *Apa* °प्रवादिभिः; Be[1] Lo[2] Wa °प्रतारिभिः; sOx[1] sPu[6] °प्रवासिभिः; BBe[2] wKt[1] NNg Tr[2] *Me* [pāṭha] °प्रचारिभिः; Ox[2] °प्रवेशिभिः; GMd[5] °प्रदेशिभिः — c) Tr[2] विद्यात्सहायतश्चैव; wKt[1] विद्यामुत्सा°; Jm Jo[1] Kt[2] Lo[1] sOx[1] sPu[6] MTr[3] [*Jolly* Ku] *Ku Mandlik Jha KSS Dave* °दुत्सादये° [cf. 9.261]; TMd[4] °येच्चैवं — d) BBe[2] निपुणः

268. Omitted in Lo[4] [*Jolly* M]; not commented by *Me*; pādas a-b and c-d transposed in Lo[3] Tj[1]; pādas b-c omitted in TMd[4] [haplo]. Cited by *Apa* 841 — a) BBe[2] Bo Ho wKt[3] भक्ष°; GMd[5] भक्ष्यैर्भो°; sOx[1] sPu[6] °भोज्यप्रदेशैश्च; BBe[2] Jm Jo[1] Kt[2] MTr[3] *Mandlik KSS Jha* °भोज्योपदेशैश्च; La[1] °देशैस्तु — c) wKt[3] La[1] Pu[2] Pu[3] Pu[4] सौर्य°; TMd[3] GMy Tr[1] चौर्य°; La[1] sOx[1] NPu[1] sPu[6] °कर्मोपदे°; La[1] °देशैस्तु — d) TMd[3] GMd[5] कुर्यात्तेषां; MTr[5] तेषां कुर्यात्समा°; wKt[1] Lo[1] °गमः; NNg °गतं

269. Omitted in Lo[4] [*Jolly* M]; not commented by *Me*. Cited by *Apa* 841 — a) Tr[2] यत्र; GMd[1] चोपस° — b) *Apa* °सर्पेयुश्चारैः प्रणिहितैरपि [vl प्राणि°]; Tr[1] °युर्मौल°; Tr[2] °प्राणिहि° — c) *Apa* तेपि स्युः संग्रहीतव्याः — d) TMd[4] हन्यात्र मित्र°; Jo[2] Lo[3] GMy NNg NPu[1] Pu[5] Pu[7] Tj[1] Tr[1] [*but cor*]

न होढेन विना चौरं घातयेद्धार्मिको नृपः ।
सहोढं सोपकरणं घातयेदविचारयन् ॥२७०॥
ग्रामेष्वपि च ये केचिच्चौराणां भक्तदायकाः ।
भाण्डावकाशदाश्चैव सर्वांस्तानपि घातयेत् ॥२७१॥
राष्ट्रेषु रक्षाधिकृतान् सामन्तांश्चैव चोदितान् ।
अभ्याघातेषु मध्यस्थाञ्छिष्याच्चौरानिव द्रुतम् ॥२७२॥
यश्चापि धर्मसमयात् प्रच्युतो धर्मजीवनः ।
दण्डेनैव तमप्योषेत् स्वकाद्धर्माद्धि विच्युतम् ॥२७३॥
ग्रामघाते हिडाभङ्गे पथि मोषाभिदर्शने ।
शक्तितो नाभिधावन्तो निर्वास्याः सपरिच्छदाः ॥२७४॥

Wa [*Jolly* Nd R] सपुत्रज्ञाति°; *Apa* °बान्धवाः

270. Omitted in Lo[4] [*Jolly* M]; not commented by *Me*. Cited by *Apa* 849— a) Lo[3] NPu[1] Pu[4] Pu[5] Pu[7] Tj[1] सहोढेन; Bo NKt[4] होटेन; Lo[2] हेढेन; Pu[8] ह्युढेन; TMd[3] ह्यूढेन; Lo[2] GMd[5] GMy Tj[1] Tr[1] MTr[5] MTr[6] चोरं; GMd[1] TMd[4] चारं — b) TMd[4] घातविद्धा° — c) Tj[2] सहोढ; Lo[1] नहोढं; TMd[4] सकोधं; BKt[5] नोपकरणं; Pu[5] Pu[7] °करणे — d) Lo[1] MTr[5] हन्यादेवाविचा°; Wa °चारयेत्; Hy °चारयेन्; *Apa* [vl] °चारणं

271. Omitted in Lo[4] [*Jolly* M]; not commented by *Me*. Cited by *Apa* 849; *Lakṣ* 12.548 — a) BKt[5] *om* च; NKt[4] तु; Ho *om* ये; Bo Ox[2] किंचि°; TMd[4] कंचि° — b) Lo[1] GMd[5] GMd[1] GMy NNg Tj[1] Tr[1] MTr[5] MTr[6] °च्चोराणां; Hy °णामुक्तदायकाः; Bo Ho भक्ति°; TMd[4] भय°; Bo °दायकः; MTr[5] °दायकां — c) Jo[2] Lo[1] TMd[3] °काशदांश्चैव; sOx[1] sPu[6] °काशदश्चैव — d) GMd[5] सर्वांश्चैव विघातयेत्; sOx[1] sPu[6] MTr[4] MTr[6] *Lakṣ* °स्तानभिघातयेत्; GMd[1] °स्तानुपघातयेत्; TMd[4] °स्तानभिवादयेत्

272. Omitted in Lo[4] Pu[5] Pu[7] [*Jolly* M]; not commented by *Me*. Cited by *Apa* 850; *Lakṣ* 12.550 — a) GMy [*Jolly* Nd] राष्ट्रे पुरे वाधिकृतान्; wKt[1] रक्षाविकृतान्; La[1] Lo[1] Lo[3] GMd[1] GMd[5] oOr NPu[1] Tj[1] Tr[1] *Apa* राष्ट्राधिकृतान्; TMd[4] राष्ट्रविकृतान्; TMd[3] राजाधिगतान् — b) wKt[3] Pu[8] सामन्तांश्च यथोदितान्; Pu[3] सामन्तांश्चापि; TMd[4] यत्समांश्चैव; NNg NPu[1] नोदितान्; GMd[1] वन्दितान् — c) Tr[2] अत्याघातेषु; Be[1] अभ्यायातेषु; TMd[4] अध्यासूतेषु; GMd[1] अभ्यासान्तेषु — d) MTr[6] °ञ्छिन्द्या°; Lo[3] TMd[3] GMd[5] GMy NNg Tj[1] Tr[1] MTr[6] °च्चोरानिव; sOx[1] sPu[6] द्रुतान्

273. Omitted in Lo[4] [*Jolly* M]; not commented by *Me*. Cited by *Lakṣ* 12.776 — a) Pu[2] Pu[4] ये चापि — b) TMd[4] प्रत्युतो; sOx[1] sPu[6] °जीवतः; BCa [*but cor*] Ho wKt[1] NKt[4] La[1] TMd[4] oOr Ox[2] NPu[1] Pu[2] Pu[4] Tr[2] Wa °जीविनः; BKt[5] °जीवनं; GMd[1] °जीवनात् — c) wKt[1] NPu[1] Pu[2] Pu[4] शास्ये-त्तमपि दण्डेन [wKt[1] शिष्यात्तमपि]; wKt[3] ओपत्तमपि दण्डेन; La[1] °नैव तु तां शिष्यान्; Be[1] तमन्विपेत्; TMd[3] तमाघापेत्; Ox[2] तमूहेत् — c-d) oOr दण्डेनैव तत्सप्याच्चौरात्मनि इवेश्वरः — d) BBe[2] sOx[1] Ox[2] sPu[6] °द्धर्मात्प्रविच्युतं; wKt[1] wKt[3] La[1] °द्धर्मात्परिच्युतं; Tr[2] °द्धर्मादिव च्युतं; Pu[5] Pu[7] विच्युतः; Jo[2] Lo[3] Tj[1] निश्च्युतं

274.* Omitted in Lo[4] [*Jolly* M]. Cited by *Apa* 850; *Lakṣ* 12.550 — a) Ho La[1] ग्रामे; NPu[1] ग्रामभागे; TMd[3] TMd[4] ग्रामदाहे; Lo[3] Tj[1] °घात; GMy Pu[5] Pu[7] [*Jolly* G Nd] *Jolly* °घात इडा°; *Lakṣ* हिळा°; Jm Jo[1] wKt[1] Kt[2] wKt[3] wKt[5] oOr [*Jolly* Ku] *Nā* [pāṭha] *Ku Rn Rc Mr Mandlik KSS Jha Dave* हिता°; *Apa* [vl] हिड्न°; *Nā* तटा°; TMd[3] तडी°; Pu[3] दंडा°; sOx[1] sPu[6] Wa *Nd* सेतु°; GMd[1] सभा°; Pu[2] हिभंगे; [*Jolly* N] तडागभंगे; MTr[6] °भागे — b) TMd[4] पति; Tj[2] Wa *Lakṣ* मोषादि°; Lo[1] मेपादि°; NKt[4] रोषाभि°; BBe[2] Bo Ho Jo[2] La[1] TMd[3] NPu[1] Pu[2] Pu[3] Pu[4] Pu[8] MTr[4] चौराभि°; Lo[3] GMd[5]

राज्ञः कोशापहर्तृंश्च प्रतिकूलेषु च स्थितान् ।
घातयेद्विविधैर्दण्डैररीणां चोपजापकान् ॥२७५॥
संधिं छित्त्वा तु ये चौर्यं रात्रौ कुर्वन्ति तस्कराः ।
तेषां छित्त्वा नृपो हस्तौ तीक्ष्णे शूले निवेशयेत् ॥२७६॥
अङ्गुली ग्रन्थिभेदस्य छेदयेत् प्रथमे ग्रहे ।
द्वितीये हस्तचरणौ तृतीये वधमर्हति ॥२७७॥
अग्निदान्भक्तदांश्चैव तथा शस्त्रावकाशदान् ।
संनिधातृंश्च मोषस्य शिष्याच्चौरानिवेश्वरः ॥२७८॥

GMy Tj[1] Tr[1] MTr[6] चोराभि°; wKt[1] wKt[3] चौरादि°; GMd[1] MTr[5] चोरादि°; MTr[3] योषाभि°; Ho Jo[2] NKt[4] Lo[3] TMd[3] GMy NPu[1] Pu[2] Pu[4] Pu[8] *Nā Rc* °मर्शने; Wa °मर्पने — c) GMd[1] TMd[4] Tr[1] MTr[5] MTr[6] शक्तास्त्वनभिधावन्तो; Be[1] BCa Ho BKt[5] GMd[5] NNg शक्तितोनभि°; NKt[4] नाविधा°; Bo ननिधा°; wKt[3] न हि धाव°; Lo[1] नेविधन्तो *cor to* नेनविधिना; TMd[4] °धावन्ता — d) BKt[5] निवास्याः; Bo La[1] सपरिच्छदः; TMd[4] सपरिच्छदा

275.* Cited by *Vij* 2.302; *Apa*864; *Lakṣ* 12.568; *Mādh* 3.395 — a) La[1] GMd[5] राज्ञा; GMd[1] राजः; Be[1] TMd[3] TMd[4] GMy MTr[5] राजकोशा°; La[1] Pu[3] Pu[4] कोपा°; BBe[2] शेषाप°; Pu[5] Pu[7] कोशाभिह°; TMd[4] °हर्ताश्च — b) BBe[2] Ho Ox[2] Pu[3] Tr[2] प्रतिकूले च संस्थितान्; Bo wKt[1] La[1] Lo[1] Lo[3] Lo[4] sOx[1] sPu[6] Pu[8] Wa *Rn Lakṣ* प्रतिकूलेष्ववस्थितान् [Bo °स्थितं]; Jo[2] wKt[3] GMd[1] Tj[1] [*Jolly* Nd R] *Jolly Jha* प्रातिकूल्येष्ववस्थितान्; TMd[4] प्रतिकुल्येपिचेरितान् [?]; oOr प्रातिकूलेपु; GMd[5] GMy MTr[5] प्रातिकूल्येपु; TMd[3] प्रातिकूल्येपि; Pu[5] Pu[7] [*Jolly* G] °कूलेपु वा स्थितान् — c) Lo[1] पातये° — c-d) GMd[1] TMd[3] TMd[4] GMy MTr[4] MTr[5] MTr[6] [*Jolly* Nd] अरीणामुपजप्यांश्च घातयेद्विविधैर्वधैः [GMy °पजापांश्च; MTr[4] MTr[5] °पजघृंश्च; TMd[4] °पजिघ्रांश्च; [*Jolly* Nd] °पधावतो] — d) *Mādh* °ण्डैर्हरेत्सर्वस्वमेव च; Ox[2] °ण्डैश्चौराणां; La[1] चोपयापकान्; Be[1] चोपभेदकान्; wKt[1] sOx[1] sPu[6] *Vij* चोपकारकान्

276. Cited by *Vij* 2.275; *Apa* 845; *Lakṣ*12.527; *Dev* 3.738 — a) Pu[5] Pu[7] *Vij Dev* भित्त्वा; wKt[3] BKt[5] Lo[3] oOr Tj[1] [*Jolly* R] *Lakṣ* कृत्वा; MTr[4] MTr[6] जित्वा; Hy छिकृत्वा; TMd[3] oOr Wa च; BKt[5] यो; TMd[4] य; La[1] चोर्यं; TMd[4] चौरं; BKt[5] चौरा — a-b) oOr रात्रौ चौर्यं — b) TMd[4] कुर्वन्तु — c) *Apa* भित्त्वा; Wa नृपौ; Pu[5] Pu[7] करौ हस्तौ; TMd[4] हस्ता; Tr[1] हस्तं — d) Tr[2] तीक्ष्णौ; GMy दीक्ष्णे; La[1] Lo[4] GMd[1] Wa [*Jolly* Nd] *Vij* तीक्ष्णशूले; TMd[3] शीले; NKt[4] मूले; La[1] न्यवेशयेत्; Lo[3] नावेशयेत्

277. Cited by *Vij* 2.274; *Apa* 845; *Lakṣ* 12.532; *Dev* 3.738; *Mādh* 3.302 — a) GMy NNg Pu[2] Pu[4] अङ्गुलीं; Bo Lo[3] TMd[3] Ox[2] अङ्गुलि; BKt[5] अङ्गुलिं; Jm Jo[1] Ox[2] MTr[3] *Mandlik Jha KSS Dave* अङ्गुलीर्ग्रन्थि°; BCa Ox[2] ग्रन्थ°; La[1] पथ्वि°; BKt[5] °भेदश्च; NPu[1] Pu[2] Pu[4] °भेदे च; TMd[4] °भेदं च — b) TMd[4] छेदयत्; GMd[1] प्रथमो; sOx[1] प्रसवे; oOr प्रथमेहनि; Bo TMd[3] MTr[6] गृहे — c) Bo Wa द्वितीय; Lo[4] हस्ते; NPu[1] Pu[2] Pu[4] हस्तपादौ तु; GMd[1] °चरणे; MTr[6] °चरणं — d) Ho तृतीयं; NNg तृतीयो; GMd[1] MTr[4] MTr[6] वधमाप्नुयात्

278. Cited by *Apa* 849; *Lakṣ* 12.548 — a) Wa अग्नीदा°; BBe[2] Bo °दान्भक्ति°; Bo °दाश्चैव — b) NPu[1] वस्त्राव°; GMd[1] GMd[5] GMy oOr शास्त्राव°; Be[1] °वकाशकान्; GMd[1] °वघातकान् — c) Bo संविधातृंश्च तोषश्च; wKt[3] सान्निधा°; TMd[4] संसधा°; Wa संधिधा°; wKt[1] संनिधावस्य; Pu[5] Pu[7] मोषश्च; TMd[4] नोपश्च; MTr[3] मोहस्य; Pu[2] Pu[4] दोषस्य; BBe[2] घोषस्य; GMd[5] Lo[4] [*Jolly* M Nd] मोक्षस्य — d) Tr[2] शिष्यांचौ°; TMd[3] शिप्यांश्चो°; TMd[4] शिक्ष्याश्चौ°; Be[1] Hy Jm Jo[1] Kt[2] Lo[1] Lo[2] Lo[4] sOx[1] Ox[2] sPu[6] Tj[2] MTr[3] *Apa Lakṣ Mandlik Jolly Jha KSS Dave* हन्याच्चौ°; GMd[5] Tr[1] हन्याच्चो°; Lo[3] GMd[1] TMd[3] GMy NNg Tj[1] MTr[4] MTr[5] °च्चोरानि°; Hy Jm Jo[1] Kt[2] Lo[3] MTr[3] *Mandlik Jha KSS Dave* [*Jolly* G] °च्चौरमि; Lo[2] GMd[5] °च्चोरमि°; MTr[6] °च्चारानि°

तडागभेदकं हन्यादप्सु शुद्धवधेन वा ।
तद्वापि प्रतिसंस्कुर्याद् दद्याच्चोत्तमसाहसम् ॥२७९॥
कोष्ठागारायुधागारदेवतागारभेदकान् ।
हस्त्यश्वरथहर्तॄंश्च हन्यादेवाविचारयन् ॥२८०॥
यस्तु पूर्वनिविष्टस्य तडागस्योदकं हरेत् ।
आगमं वाप्यपां भिन्द्यात् स दाप्यः पूर्वसाहसम् ॥२८१॥
समुत्सृजेद्राजमार्गे यस्त्वमेध्यमनापदि ।
स द्वौ कार्षापणौ दद्यादमेध्यं चाशु शोधयेत् ॥२८२॥
आपद्गतोऽथ वा वृद्धो गर्भिणी बाल एव वा ।
परिभाषणमर्हन्ति तच्च शोध्यमिति स्थितिः ॥२८३॥

279.* Pāda-d omitted in Pu[4]. Cited by *Lakṣ* 12.566; *Dev* 3.757 — a) NKt[4] Lo[3] MTr[6] [*Jolly* Nd R] तडाक°; GMd[1] TMd[3] TMd[4] GMd[5] GMy Tj[1] Tr[1] MTr[5] *Dev* तटाक°; Tr[2] °भेदकां; TMd[3] °भेदिकं; BCa GMy NPu[1] Pu[2] Pu[4] [*Jolly* Nd] °भेदकान्; sOx[1] sPu[6] °भेदनं; GMd[5] Tr[1] °भेदिनं — b) Lo[1] Pu[8] हन्यादश्वशुद्ध°; Tj[2] °दप्स्वशुद्ध°; Tj[1] शुद्धा°; NPu[1] शूद्रवधेन; Lo[2] त्वन्यवधेन; Ho Lo[4] Tr[2] [*Jolly* M Nd] च — c) Ho La[1] Lo[1] sOx[1] NPu[1] Pu[3] sPu[6] Pu[8] Tr[2] *Dev Nā Rc* तच्चापि; Jo[1] wKt[1] *Ku Mandlik Jha KSS Dave* यद्वापि; Ox[2] तं चापि; GMd[5] न चापि; Lo[4] [*Jolly* M]तथापि; Pu[2] Pu[4] तत्त्वोपि; Bo यच्चापि; *Rn* यदि वा; MTr[5] तद्वा प्रति°; NKt[4] °स्कुर्युर् — d) Be[1] BBe[2] Bo Ho Jo[2] NKt[4] Lo[1] Lo[3] Lo[4] NNg oOr Pu[5] Pu[7] Pu[8] Tj[1] Wa *Jolly* [*Jolly* M G R Nd] दाप्यश्चोत्तम°; BCa Hy Jm Jo[1] Kt[2] wKt[5] Ox[2] Tj[2] Tr[2] MTr[3] *Mandlik KSS Jha Dave* दाप्यस्तूत्तम°; Lo[2] दिद्याश्चोत्तम°; *Dev* दद्याद्वोत्तम°; wKt[3] °साहसान्

280. Omitted in Lo[4] [*Jolly* M]; not commented by *Me*. Cited by *Vij* 2.273; *Apa* 845; *Lakṣ* 12.530 — a) Lo[3] काष्ठा°; TMd[3] TMd[4] GMd[5] GMy Tr[1] MTr[6] गोष्ठा°; oOr कोषागा°; *Apa* अग्र्यागा°; Be[1] कोष्ठाकारा° — b) Tr[2] °दैवता°; GMd[1] TMd[3] TMd[4] MTr[4] MTr[6] *Lakṣ* °भेदिनः — c) Lo[1] °भर्तॄंश्च; *Apa* °हन्तॄंश्च — d) Wa °विचारयेत्; NNg °विधारयन्

281. Omitted in Lo[4] [*Jolly* M]; not commented by *Me*. Cited by *Lakṣ* 12.566; *Dev* 3.757 — a) Pu[3] पूर्वं; Be[1] पूर्वा°; TMd[3] °विनिष्टस्य; wKt[1] °निवीजस्य — b) NKt[4] sOx[1] sPu[6] MTr[6] [*Jolly* Nd] तडाक°; GMd[1] TMd[3] TMd[4] GMd[5] GMy Tj[1] Tr[1] MTr[5] *Dev* तटाक° — c) NNg आगमां; BKt[5] NPu[1] Pu[4] *Lakṣ* चाप्यपां; *Dev* वाप्युपरुन्ध्यात्; Bo Ho Hy Jm Jo[1] Kt[2] Lo[1] Tj[2] Tr[1] *Nā* [pāṭha] *Rn Mandlik Jha KSS Dave* भिद्यात्; BKt[5] भिन्द्यां; TMd[3] भिद्यान्; BCa Jo[2] La[1] wKt[1] Wa *Nā* रुन्ध्यात्; Lo[3] Tj[1] रुध्यात्; BBe[2] कन्ध्यात् — d) sOx[1] sPu[6] °साहसः

282. Cited by *Apa* 765; *Lakṣ* 12.455; *Dev* 3.552; *Mādh* 3.279 — a) Wa °मार्गो — b) Tr[2] वस्तुमेध्य° — c) wKt[3] *om* स; Tr[2] य; La[1] GMd[1] कार्षपणौ; Lo[3] Tj[1] कार्षपणं; Wa कार्षपणो; Tr[1] कार्षापणाद् — c-d) Be[1] Bo Ho Lo[1] BKt[5] Ox[2] Tr[2] कार्षापणौ दण्ड्यस्तदमेध्यं च शोधयेत् [Be[1] दाप्यस्तद°; BKt[5] दद्यात्तद°] — d) Pu[3] दद्यात्तन्मेध्यं; sOx[1] sPu[6] °मेध्यानां च शोधनं; wKt[1] °ध्यमपि शोध°; Lo[2] चापि शोध°; *Lakṣ* स च शोध°; Pu[2] Pu[4] च विशोध°; Lo[4] [*Jolly* M] च प्रशोध°; Jm योधयेत्

283. Omitted in Jm La[1]. Cited by *Apa* 765; *Lakṣ* 12.455; *Dev* 3.553; *Mādh* 3.279 — a) Lo[3] Lo[4] TMd[4] NNg NPu[1] Pu[2] Pu[4] Pu[5] Pu[7] Tj[1] Wa [*Jolly* M R] आपद्गतो वा वृद्धो वा; BCa Jo[2] आपद्गतोथ वृद्धो वा; Lo[2] आपद्गतौ; oOr आपद्गते; TMd[3] आपद्गतोपि वा; BKt[5] आपद्गतो यथा; *Apa Lakṣ Dev Mādh* आपद्गतस्तथा; MTr[3] *Mandlik Jha KSS Dave* वृद्धा — b) TMd[3] गर्भिणे; Be[1] Bo Ho TMd[4] sOx[1] sPu[6] च — d) sOx[1] sPu[6] तच्छोध्य°; *Apa* न तु शोध्य°; GMy न द्वौ शोध्य°; *Apa* [vl] न त्वशोध्य°

चिकित्सकानां सर्वेषां मिथ्या प्रचरतां दमः ।
अमानुषेषु प्रथमो मानुषेषु तु मध्यमः ॥२८४॥
संक्रमध्वजयष्टीनां प्रतिमानां च भेदकः ।
प्रतिकुर्याच्च तत्सर्वं पञ्च दद्याच्छतानि च ॥२८५॥
अदूषितानां द्रव्याणां दूषणे भेदने तथा ।
मणीनामपवेधे च दण्डः प्रथमसाहसः ॥२८६॥
समैर्हि विषमं यस्तु चरेद्वै मूल्यतोऽपि वा ।
स प्राप्नुयाद्दमं पूर्वं नरो मध्यममेव वा ॥२८७॥
बन्धनानि च सर्वाणि राजमार्गे निवेशयेत् ।
दुःखिता यत्र दृश्येरन् विकृताः पापकारिणः ॥२८८॥
प्राकारस्य च भेत्तारं परिखाणां च पूरकम् ।
द्वाराणां चैव भङ्क्तारं क्षिप्रमेव प्रवासयेत् ॥२८९॥

284. Omitted in Jm GMd^1 — b) Bo Ho Pu^8 मिथ्योपचरतां; Lo^1 मिथ्यापचरतां; TMd^3 मिथ्याचारवतां; wKt^3 प्रवचतां; Pu^5 Pu^7 प्रवदतां; La^1 प्रभवतां; Pu^5 Pu^7 दमाः — c) Be^1 आमानु°; Pu^4 आमनु°; Pu^2 अमनु°; Pu^5 Pu^7 अमानुषे तु; Be^1 प्रथमौ; TMd^4 प्रथमा — d) Pu^5 Pu^7 मानुषे मध्यमः स्मृतः; GMy मनुष्येषु; La^1 Lo^1 TMd^3 GMd^5 Pu^3 Tr^1 Tr^2 च

285. Omitted in Jm. Cited by *Apa* 822; *Lakṣ* 12.565 — a) GMd^1 यस्तु संक्रमयष्टीनां; TMd^4 संक्रमद्वयषष्ठीनां — b) TMd^3 °ष्टीनामप्रमानां; TMd^4 प्रतिष्ठानां; Lo^2 भेदकाः — c) Bo तत्सर्वे — d) GMy पञ्चादद्या°; NPu^1 पञ्च दण्ड्यः शतानि; Pu^2 ददात्पञ्च शतानि; Tr^2 वा

286. Folio containing verses 286–99 is missing in Ho; pāda-d omitted in BKt^5. Cited by *Apa* 821; *Lakṣ* 12.565 — a) TMd^3 अदूषकानां — c) TMd^4 *Apa* [vl] मुनीना°; GMd^1 GMy Tj^1 [*Jolly* M Nd] °नामपि वेधे; NKt^4 La^1 GMd^5 NNg Pu^2 Pu^4 Tr^1 MTr^5 Wa *Bh* °नामप्यवेधे; TMd^4 °नामप्यवेदे; *Apa* [vl] °नामपवेदे; Be^1 °नामप्यभेदे; sOx^1 sPu^6 °नामपभेदे; BCa wKt^1 Ox^2 Pu^5 Pu^7 °नामपिभेदे; MTr^6 °नामप्यबोधे; NPu^1 °नामप्याबाधे; *Lakṣ* °नामवबाधेपु दण्डः; oOr °नामपवेधेन दण्डः; TMd^3 °नामपि भेदेन दण्डः; *Apa* तु; GMd^1 यद्दण्डः — d) GMd^1 TMd^4 दण्डं; Bo प्रयतसा°; Lo^4 GMd^1 TMd^4 °साहसं

287. Omitted in BKt^5; pādas c-d omitted in wKt^1. Cited by *Lakṣ* 12.513; *Apa* 825 — a) GMd^1 TMd^4 Tr^1 MTr^4 MTr^6 समैस्तु; TMd^3 MTr^5 समैश्च; Lo^1 समं हि; Pu^2 Pu^4 सचमं हि; MTr^5 विषमः; GMd^5 विषमान्यस्तु; Lo^2 विषमैर्यस्तु; GMd^1 TMd^4 MTr^5 MTr^6 Wa यश्च; TMd^3 यच्च — b) Wa विचरेन्मूल्यतो; GMd^1 TMd^4 GMy MTr^6 प्रचरेन्मूल्यतो; MTr^5 प्रकरेन्मूल्यतो; TMd^3 प्रचरेज्ञाप्यतो; Jo^2 Lo^3 Tj^1 कारयेन्मूल्यतो; Lo^2 °पि वै — c) Jo^2 GMd^1 sOx^1 sPu^6 Tr^2 संप्राप्नुया°; BBe^2 Jo^1 MTr^3 *Mandlik Jha KSS Dave* समाप्नु°; Hy पूर्व — d) GMd^5 दमं मध्य°; NKt^4 मध्यमेव; La^1 TMd^4 NNg [*Jolly* M] मध्यम एव; wKt^3 च

288. Omitted in Tr^2; pāda-a omitted in BKt^5. Cited by *Lakṣ* 12.782 — a) GMd^1 बान्धनानि; NKt^4 वचनानि; GMd^5 पिधनानि; Pu^2 Pu^4 तु; TMd^3 GMy MTr^4 MTr^6 [*Jolly* Nd] च कष्टानि — b) Jo^1 Tr^1 राजा मार्गे; MTr^4 MTr^6 प्रवेशयेत् — c) wKt^1 दुःकृता यदि दृश्येह; GMy [*Jolly* Nd] दुष्कृता; GMd^1 दुःखितान्यत्र; NPu^1 यस्य; wKt^3 दृश्येन्; GMd^1 दृश्यानि — d) Tj^1 विकृतां; GMd^1 धिक्क्वताः; GMd^5 पापकर्मणः

289. *ma* in Lo^1. Cited by *Apa* 853; *Lakṣ* 12.567 — a) BKt^5 TMd^3 प्रकारस्य; Tr^1 प्राकाराणां; *Lakṣ* °रस्यावभेत्तारं; Pu^5 Pu^7 *om* च; wKt^1 TMd^3 भेत्तारः — b) Bo La^1 Lo^2 NPu^1 Pu^2 Pu^4 Pu^5 Pu^7

अभिचारेषु सर्वेषु कर्तव्यो द्विशतो दमः ।
मूलकर्मणि चानाप्तैः कृत्यासु विविधासु च ॥२९०॥
अबीजविक्रयी चैव बीजोत्क्रष्टा तथैव च ।
मर्यादाभेदकश्चैव विकृतं प्राप्नुयाद्वधम् ॥२९१॥
सर्वकण्टकपापिष्ठं हेमकारं तु पार्थिवः ।
प्रवर्तमानमन्याये छेदयेल्लवशः क्षुरैः ॥२९२॥
सीताद्रव्यापहरणे शस्त्राणामौषधस्य च ।
कालमासाद्य कार्यं च राजा दण्डं प्रकल्पयेत् ॥२९३॥
स्वाम्यमात्यौ पुरं राष्ट्रं कोशदण्डौ सुहृत्तथा ।
सप्त प्रकृतयो ह्येताः समस्तं राज्यमुच्यते ॥२९४॥

परिषाणां; GMd^1 TMd^3 TMd^4 GMd^5 GMy Tj^1 Tr^1 परिघानां; Lo^3 परिदानां; GMd^1 च भेदकं — c) Be^1 Bo WKt^3 Pu^5 Pu^7 भक्तारं; La^1 TMd^3 TMd^4 GMy oOr SOx^1 NPu^1 SPu^6 Tj^1 *Apa Lakṣ* भेत्तारं — d) oOr Ox^2 Pu^3 Tr^2 क्षिप्रं निर्वासयेत्पुरात्; GMy प्रवादयेत् *cor to* प्रपादयेत्; *Apa Lakṣ* प्रमापयेत्; BBe^2 NKt^4 प्रकाशयेत्; TMd^3 प्रचाधयेत्

290. Cited by *Apa* 821; *Lakṣ* 12.565 — a) GMd^1 अभिसारेपु — c) Lo^4 °कर्माणि; Be^1 WKt^1 Lo^1 GMd^1 वानाप्तैः; Jm Jo^1 Kt^2 WKt^3 La^1 MTr^3 *Mandlik KSS* चानाप्तेः; TMd^3 TMd^4 GMy MTr^4 MTr^6 [*Jolly* Nd] चानाप्ते; SOx^1 SPu^6 वानाप्ते [*Nā Nd* support the locative]; Pu^5 Pu^7 [*Jolly* Ku R^2] *Jolly* चानाप्तौ; NPu^1 चाप्तेषु; [*Jolly* M^9] चानाप्तिः; *Apa* विद्वेपे; NKt^4 वानायैः; Pu^2 Pu^4 चान्प्रापौ — d) Pu^2 Pu^4 कृत्यास्तु; TMd^4 GMd^5 GMy विविधानि; NKt^4 वा

291. Cited by *Apa* 825; *Lakṣ* 12.513 — a) La^1 स्वबीज°; GMd^1 अवीच°; MTr^6 अजीव°; WKt^1 °विक्रयं; GMy °विक्रयश्चैव; TMd^3 °विक्रयायश्च; MTr^5 *Apa Lakṣ* °क्रयी यश्च; WKt^1 *om* चैव — b) GMd^1 बीजोत्कर्षकथैव च; oOr सर्वोकृष्टं; TMd^3 बीजात्कृष्टास्तथैव; Be^1 BBe^2 Bo Hy WKt^3 Tj^1 Tj^2 Tr^2 °त्कृष्टा; Jm Jo^1 Kt^2 Lo^2 MTr^3 [*Jolly* Ku] *KSS* °त्कृष्टं; GMd^5 °त्कृष्टे; NPu^1 Pu^2 Pu^4 °त्कृष्टी; BKt^5 °त्कर्ष्टा; Pu^2 Pu^4 °त्कर्षी; [*Jolly* M^1] °त्कृस्यः; [*Jolly* M^4] °त्क्रुष्टं; *Apa* [vl] °त्कुष्टा and °त्क्रुष्टं; Jo^2 Lo^1 Lo^4 TMd^4 GMy Pu^5 Pu^7 °त्कृष्टस्तथैव; WKt^1 La^1 [*Jolly* G Nd^2] °त्कृष्टास्तथैव; Pu^8 °त्कृष्टात्तथैव — c) SOx^1 SPu^6 मर्याद°; TMd^3 मर्याद्या°; WKt^1 सर्वदा°; Lo^4 NPu^1 °भेदकाश्चैव; *Apa* °भेदनाच्चैव — d) *Apa* [vl] विक्रयं; TMd^3 TMd^4 GMy [*Jolly* Nd] विविधं; GMy WKt^1 °याद्वधः; WKt^3 BKt^5 TMd^3 °याद्धनं; *Apa* °याद्दमं

292. Cited by *Vij* 2.297; *Apa* 862; *Lakṣ* 12.522 — a) WKt^3 °कण्ठक°; Be^1 °कन्दक°; GMd^1 °पापिष्ठौ — b) Pu^2 Pu^4 हेमंकारं; WKt^3 दमकारं; La^1 °कारं नराधिपः; WKt^1 TMd^4 NPu^1 Pu^2 Pu^4 Tr^2 च — c) TMd^4 Pu^2 Pu^4 प्रवृत्तमा°; TMd^3 प्रवर्तकारम°; NPu^1 °मन्यायो; Lo^3 °मन्योये; La^1 °मन्यायेन; NNg °मन्यायैश्छेद° — d) NPu^1 °येत्तवशः; *Dave Jha* °येत्खण्डशः [supported by *Me Ku*]; Be^1 शतैः

293. Pādas c-d omitted in Pu^5 — a) Be^1 La^1 सीमा°; Be^1 WKt^1 GMd^5 GMy °द्रव्यापहारेण — b) La^1 TMd^4 GMy शास्त्राणा° — c) SOx^1 SPu^6 कार्यमासाद्य कालं च; GMd^1 तु — d) TMd^4 GMy राज; Be^1 Bo WKt^1 WKt^3 NKt^4 BKt^5 Lo^1 Lo^2 Lo^4 NNg NPu^1 Pu^2 Pu^3 Pu^4 Pu^8 Tr^2 Wa दण्डं राजा; MTr^6 दण्डः; Lo^3 Tj^1 [*Jolly* R] प्रवर्तयेत्; after this verse GMy Tr^1 [*Jolly* Nd Gr] insert 9.312

294. a) Lo^3 Tj^1 °मात्याः; Be^1 °मात्यं; Pu^5 Pu^7 Tr^2 °मात्य; Tr^2 सुराराष्ट्रं; GMd^1 राष्ट्रौ — b) La^1 कोष°; Lo^4 कोशा°; Wa °दण्डो; Ox^2 °दण्डः; TMd^3 °दण्डा; BKt^5 TMd^4 Tr^2 °दण्डं; BKt^5 सुकृत्तथा; WKt^3 सुहृत्तम; GMd^1 TMd^4 GMy MTr^5 MTr^6 तथा सुहृत्; TMd^3 तदा सुहृत् — c) Pu^2 Pu^4 प्रकृततो — c-d) GMd^1 TMd^3 TMd^4 MTr^4 MTr^6 सप्तैतानि समस्तानि लोकेस्मिन्राज्यमुच्यते [GMd^1 समानानि] — d) Jo^2 Lo^3

सप्तानां प्रकृतीनां तु राज्यस्यासां यथाक्रमम् ।
पूर्वं पूर्वं गुरुतरं जानीयाद् व्यसनं महत् ॥२९५॥
सप्ताङ्गस्येह राज्यस्य विष्टब्धस्य त्रिदण्डवत् ।
अन्योन्यगुणवैशेष्यान्न किंचिदतिरिच्यते ॥२९६॥
तेषु तेषु हि कृत्येषु तत्तदङ्गं विशिष्यते ।
येन यत्साध्यते कार्यं तत्तस्मिञ्छ्रेष्ठमुच्यते ॥२९७॥
चारेणोत्साहयोगेन क्रिययैव च कर्मणाम् ।
स्वशक्तिं परशक्तिं च नित्यं विद्यात्परात्मनोः ॥२९८॥
पीडनानि च सर्वाणि व्यसनानि तथैव च ।
आरभेत ततः कार्यं संचिन्त्य गुरुलाघवम्* ॥२९९॥
आरभेतैव कर्माणि श्रान्तः श्रान्तः पुनः पुनः ।
कर्माण्यारभमाणं हि पुरुषं श्रीर्निषेवते ॥३००॥

Tj[1] [*Jolly* R Nd] समग्रं; Hy Jm Jo[1] Kt[2] GMd[5] oOr Tj[2] Tr[1] MTr[3] *Ku Mandlik Jha KSS Dave* सप्ताङ्गं; Lo[4] सप्तमं; oOr राज्यमिष्यते

295. Cited by *Lakṣ* 11.97 — a) Be[1] La[1] GMy Ox[2] NPu[1] Pu[2] Pu[4] *Lakṣ* च— b) TMd[4] राजस्यासां; Lo[1] TMd[3] Pu[3] Tr[1] Tr[2] राज्यस्यास्य; wKt[1] राज्यस्यांशं; Lo[4] राज्यस्यायं; GMy राजस्याहं; Lo[4] GMd[1] °क्रमः — c) Pu[3] पूर्वेपूर्वं; Pu[4] पूर्वपूर्वं; La[1] पूर्वपूर्व — d) wKt[1] वासनं; Bo वसनं; NKt[4] वाससं; *Lakṣ* व्यसनं नृपः; GMd[1] TMd[4] MTr[4] MTr[5] MTr[6] व्यसने नृपः

296. Cited by *Lakṣ* 11.97 — a) GMd[1] TMd[4] GMd[5] GMy oOr Tr[1] MTr[4] MTr[5] MTr[6] [*Jolly* Nd] *Lakṣ* सप्ताङ्गस्यास्य; TMd[3] सप्तकस्यास्य; Hy °ङ्गस्य ह — b) Lo[4] Ox[2] [*Jolly* M] विश्रब्धस्य; Be[1] विसृब्धस्य — c) Be[1] wKt[1] °वैशिष्ट्यान्न; wKt[3] Lo[1] NNg Pu[5] Pu[7] Tr[1] [*but cor*] Tr[2] °वैशिष्यान्न; Tj[1] °वैशम्यान्न — d) Jo[1] °चिदतिरेच्यते; BKt[5] GMy °चिदितिरिच्यते; wKt[1] °चिदिति चोच्यते

297. Cited by *Lakṣ* 11.97 — a) NNg Tj[2] MTr[4] *Nd* च; Bo Hy Jm Jo[1] Kt[2] Lo[2] Pu[3] Pu[8] Tr[2] MTr[3] MTr[6] *Mandlik Jha KSS Dave* तु; GMd[1] TMd[3] TMd[4] GMy MTr[5] MTr[6] कार्येषु — b) Tr[2] तेतदङ्गं; GMd[1] तत्तद्दण्डं — c) GMd[1] तेन; Be[1] तत्साध्यते; sOx[1] sPu[6] यत्सिध्यते; Lo[1] यत्साधने; GMd[1] यत्साधृते; *Lakṣ* तत्स्थाप्यते; TMd[3] कर्म — d) Pu[5] Pu[7] तत्तस्मिन्नेवमुच्यते; GMd[1] °ञ्छ्रैष्ठ्यमु°; GMy °ज्ज्येष्ठमु°; Lo[4] °ञ्श्लिष्टमु; [*Jolly* M] °न्शिष्टमु°; Be[1] °ञ्छ्रेष्ठ उच्यते; wKt[1] °न्योज्यमुच्यते

298. Omitted in MTr[5]. Cited by *Lakṣ* 11.113–4 — a) wKt[1] चारेणसाहयोगेन; BCa चरेणो°; Hy TMd[4] Tj[1] चारणो°; Lo[1] चोरेणो°; TMd[3] चोरोणो°; NNg चारेण्यो°; Tj[2] चौरेणो°; NKt[4] भारेणो°; Lo[2] °हया-गेन; Jo[2] Lo[3] Ox[2] Tj[1] Tr[1] [*but cor*] °हयुक्तेन — b) wKt[3] TMd[3] GMy क्रियया चैव; NPu[1] क्रियया वैव; wKt[1] GMd[1] TMd[4] sOx[1] sPu[6] कर्मणा; TMd[3] GMy [*Jolly* Nd] केवलं — c) Tj[2] परिशक्तिं — d) GMy विद्यान्नित्यं परात्मनोः; La[1] Lo[4] TMd[4] Pu[2] विन्द्या°; Lo[4] Pu[8] [*Jolly* M Gr] विद्यात्परात्मनः; BBe[2] Hy Jm Jo[1] Jo[2] wKt[1] Kt[2] wKt[3] Lo[1] Lo[3] Tj[1] Tj[2] MTr[3] [*Jolly* R Ku] *Mandlik Jolly KSS* विद्यान्महीपतिः

299. Pādas a-b and c-d transposed in Be[1]. Cited by *Lakṣ* 11.114 — a) Tr[1] पीडनादि; BCa तु — b) TMd[3] GMy व्यसनानि महीपतिः — c-d) GMd[1] TMd[3] TMd[4] GMy MTr[4] MTr[5] MTr[6] [*Jolly* Nd] *Bh* गुरुलाघवतो ज्ञात्वा ततः कार्यं समाचरेत् [GMy °लाघतो; GMd[1] GMy °लाघवतां; GMy (*Jolly* Nd) कर्म; TMd[3] समारभेत्] — d) Be[1] संत्यज्य; Lo[4] *ma* विचिन्त्य

300. Omitted in Lo[4]. Cited by *Lakṣ* 11.114 — a) TMd[4] आरभेत च; BKt[5] sOx[1] sPu[6] कार्याणि — b) TMd[4] श्रान्तोश्रान्तः — c) BKt[5] TMd[4] कर्मण्यार°; GMy sOx[1] sPu[6] °रम्भमाणं; GMd[1] °रभमाणां;

कृतं त्रेतायुगं चैव द्वापरं कलिरेव च ॥
राज्ञो वृत्तानि सर्वाणि राजा हि युगमुच्यते ॥३०१॥
कलिः प्रसुप्तो भवति स जाग्रद् द्वापरं युगम् ।
कर्मस्वभ्युद्यतस्त्रेता विचरंस्तु कृतं युगम् ॥३०२॥
इन्द्रस्यार्कस्य वातस्य यमस्य वरुणस्य च ।
चन्द्रस्याग्नेः पृथिव्याश्च तेजोवृत्तं नृपश्चरेत् ॥३०३॥
वार्षिकांश्चतुरो मासान् यथेन्द्रोऽभिप्रवर्षति ।
तथाभिवर्षेत्स्वं राष्ट्रं कामैरिन्द्रव्रतं चरन् ॥३०४॥
अष्टौ मासान्यथादित्यस्तोयं हरति रश्मिभिः ।
तथा हरेत्करं राष्ट्रान्नित्यमर्कव्रतं हि तत् ॥३०५॥

TMd^4 °रम्भमानां; Be^1 °रभाणं; Jo^2 wKt^3 Lo^1 GMd^5 NPu^1 Pu^2 Pu^4 तु; GMy तं — d) Bo पुरुषः; TMd^4 पुरुष; GMd^1 पुरुषान्; Lo^3 श्रीर्निषेविते; GMd^5 श्रीर्हि सेवते

301. Pādas a-b omitted in GMd^1 — a) TMd^4 GMd^5 GMy Tj^1 कृत; NPu^1 कृतां; GMy °युगे — b) Ho wKt^3 sOx^1 Pu^2 Pu^4 sPu^6 कलिमेव; GMd^5 वा — c) Lo^4 राजा; TMd^4 राज्ञा युक्तानि; wKt^1 La^1 वृत्तानि चत्वारि — d) TMd^3 राजं; GMd^1 राजापि

302. Pādas c-d omitted in wKt^1 [haplo] — b) Be^1 भवति जाग्रत; Lo^4 भवति जग्राह; Pu^2 Pu^4 भवति प्रजास्त; BKt^5 La^1 NPu^1 संजाग्रद्; Ox^2 जागृद्; Lo^4 द्वापर; Hy Tj^2 MTr^4 द्वापरं स्मृतं — c) Pu^5 Pu^7 कर्माण्यभ्यु°; Tr^1 कर्मस्त्वभ्यु°; Lo^4 NPu^1 [*Jolly* M] कर्मस्थोभ्यु°; Be^1 BCa Jo^2 NKt^4 BKt^5 Lo^1 Lo^3 Lo^4 TMd^3 GMd^5 Ox^2 NPu^1 Pu^5 Pu^7 Wa [*Jolly* M] °भ्युदितस्त्रेता; La^1 °भ्युदितास्त्रेता; TMd^4 °भ्युदिता त्रेता; GMy °भ्युत्थितस्त्रेता; MTr^6 °भ्युत्थितं त्रेता; Lo^2 °भ्युच्छितस्त्रेता; Pu^2 Pu^4 °भ्युच्छ्रितं त्रेता; Tr^2 °भ्युदितं प्रेता; GMd^1 °तस्त्रेतां — d) Lo^4 [*Jolly* M] विकृतं सुकृतं युगं; Tr^1 [*but cor*] विचारंस्तु; BKt^5 विचारं तु; TMd^4 विचरस्तु; Wa विचरं सुकृतं; GMd^1 विचारंस्कृतं

303.* Cited by *Lakṣ* 11.3 — a) sOx^1 sPu^6 रुद्रस्यार्कस्य; Wa °स्यार्कश्च; Hy Jm Jo^1 Kt^2 NKt^4 Lo^4 TMd^3 TMd^4 GMy NNg Pu^4 Pu^8 Tj^2 MTr^3 Wa *Mandlik Jolly Jha KSS Dave* वायोश्च — b) Jo^2 Lo^3 Tj^1 वरुणस्य यमस्य च; TMd^3 वा — c) TMd^4 sOx^1 Pu^5 sPu^6 Pu^7 MTr^5 इन्द्रस्याग्नेः; BKt^5 इन्द्रश्चाग्नेः; *Lakṣ* सोमस्याग्नेः — d) BKt^5 °वृत्तिं; TMd^3 °वृत्तजपश्चरेत्; Pu^5 Pu^7 नृपस्य तत्; Lo^2 नभश्चरेत्

304. Cited by *Lakṣ* 11.3 — a) GMy वार्ष°; BKt^5 वार्षिकीं चतुरो° — b) Jo^2 Lo^3 Tj^1 यथा चन्द्रोभिवर्षति; BBe^2 यथा चेन्द्रोभिवर्षति; Lo^2 यथैवेन्द्रोभिवर्षति; Bo Ho Lo^1 wKt^1 sOx^1 Pu^5 sPu^6 Pu^7 Pu^8 Tr^1 यथेन्द्रोद्भिः प्रवर्षति [wKt^1 प्रकर्षति]; GMd^5 यथेन्द्रोस्याभिवर्षति; TMd^3 यथैन्द्रो; NNg °न्द्रो ह्यभि°; Be^1 GMd^1 °न्द्रोपि प्रवर्षति; TMd^3 GMy NPu^1 Pu^2 Pu^4 °न्द्रो हि प्रवर्षति; BKt^5 °न्द्रोभिवर्षति; TMd^4 °न्द्रोभिप्रवर्तते — c) Bo NPu^1 यथा°; GMd^1 तथाविव°; GMy तथापिव°; TMd^3 तथा हि वर्षे°; La^1 तथा वर्षेत्स्वकं; BBe^2 तथा चरेत्स्वकं; wKt^1 °भिवर्षयेत्स्वं; Ho °भिवर्षन्स्वं; NKt^4 °भिवर्षस्वं; Lo^4 °भिवर्षैः स्वं; sOx^1 Ox^2 NPu^1 sPu^6 °र्षेत्स्वे राष्ट्रे; Lo^1 °र्षेत्स्वराष्ट्रं; BCa °र्षेत्स्वराष्टैः; *Lakṣ* °र्षेत्तद्राष्ट्रं — d) TMd^3 राजा चन्द्रव्रतं चरन्; Be^1 Ho Jo^2 wKt^1 La^1 Lo^3 Lo^4 GMd^5 Ox^2 Pu^2 Pu^4 Tj^1 Wa [*Jolly* M R Nd^2] चरेत्

305. *ma* in Lo^4 — a) GMd^1 अष्ट — b) Bo °त्यस्तपं; GMy °त्यस्तोरं; Lo^2 GMy हरेति; Pu^2 Pu^4 चरति — c) Pu^2 Pu^4 तथा चोर्यं हरेत्रष्ट्रान्नि°; NPu^1 तथारेन्नृपो राष्ट्रां नि°; TMd^4 ततो; wKt^1 हरेत्करे; BKt^5 *om* करं; La^1 राष्ट्रां नि°; Lo^4 [*Jolly* M] राज्यान्नि° — d) GMd^1 TMd^3 TMd^4 GMy MTr^4 MTr^5 MTr^6 [*Jolly* Nd] राष्ट्रात्सम्यगर्क°; Jo^1 Lo^3 Tj^1 Tr^2 °न्नित्यकर्मव्रतं; MTr^4 °मर्थव्रतं; TMd^4 Ox^2 Pu^3 Tr^2 °व्रतं चरेत्; GMd^1 NNg Pu^2 Pu^4 MTr^5 °व्रतं चरन्; NKt^4 हि तं; Tr^1 च तत्

प्रविश्य सर्वभूतानि यथा चरति मारुतः ।
तथा चारैः प्रवेष्टव्यं व्रतमेतद्धि मारुतम् ॥३०६॥
यथा यमः प्रियद्वेष्यौ प्राप्ते काले नियच्छति ।
तथा राज्ञा नियन्तव्याः प्रजास्तद्धि यमव्रतम् ॥३०७॥
वरुणेन यथा पाशैर्बद्ध एव हि दृश्यते ।
तथा पापान्निगृह्णीयाद् व्रतमेतद्धि वारुणम् ॥३०८॥
परिपूर्णं यथा चन्द्रं दृष्ट्वा हृष्यन्ति मानवाः ।
तथा प्रकृतयो यस्मिन् स चन्द्रव्रतिको नृपः ॥३०९॥
प्रतापयुक्तस्तेजस्वी नित्यं स्यात्पापकर्मसु ।
दुष्टसामन्तहिंस्रश्च तदाग्नेयं व्रतं स्मृतम् ॥३१०॥
यथा सर्वाणि भूतानि धरा धारयते समम् ।
तथा सर्वाणि भूतानि बिभ्रतः पार्थिवं व्रतम् ॥३११॥
एतैरुपायैरन्यैश्च युक्तो नित्यमतन्द्रितः ।

306. b) GMy यथा चन्द्रोयमारुतः — c) Bo यथा कालै; Lo^{4} GMy चरैः; sOx^{1} sPu^{6} चारौ; MTr^{6} चोरैः; Lo^{2} Lo^{3} प्रविष्टव्यं — d) TMd^{3} दूतमेनद्धि; Be^{1} मारुतः

307. Omitted in Be^{1}; verses 307 and 308 transposed in Pu^{5} Pu^{7}, and 307a-b and 308a-b in Bo — a) oOr तथा; NPu^{1} यमं; BKt^{5} प्रियः; La^{1} प्रियं द्वेष्यं; Tr^{2} °द्वैष्यौ; Lo^{1} [*but cor*] °द्विष्यौ; wKt^{1} GMy sOx^{1} sPu^{6} °द्वेषौ — b) Jo^{1} GMy NNg Pu^{3} प्राप्त; TMd^{4} नयच्छति — c) BKt^{5} यथा; Pu^{2} राजा; Pu^{5} Pu^{7} नियन्तव्यं — d) BBe^{2} प्रजांस्तद्धि; GMd^{1} TMd^{3} TMd^{4} GMd^{5} GMy Tr^{1} [*but mc sh*] MTr^{4} MTr^{6} [*Jolly* Nd Gr] सर्वे तद्धि; Pu^{5} Pu^{7} सर्वं तद्धि; GMy °द्धि व्रतं यथा; GMd^{1} यमं; BBe^{2} यमप्रजाः; TMd^{3} यमप्रभं

308. Pāda-d omitted in TMd^{3} [haplo] — a) GMy [*Jolly* Nd] वरुणेन तु पाशैश्च [*Jolly* Nd वरुणेनापि]; Ox^{2} वारुणेन; Jo^{2} Tj^{1} वरुणैस्तु; La^{1} वारुणेत्तु; oOr पाशोबद्ध — a-b) TMd^{4} पालैबुद्ध — b) TMd^{3} GMd^{5} GMy MTr^{4} [*Jolly* Nd] °र्बध्यते वरुणैर्नरः; Tr^{1} °र्बध्यते पापकृन्नरः; Lo^{1} °र्बध्यते न हि दृश्यते; Pu^{5} Pu^{7} MTr^{6} °र्बद्धमेवाभिदृश्यते; Bo sOx^{1} sPu^{6} °शैर्वध; Tr^{2} एवं; Be^{1} एव प्रदृश्यते; Hy Jm Jo^{1} Kt^{2} wKt^{3} GMd^{1} TMd^{4} Pu^{3} Tj^{2} MTr^{3} Wa *Mandlik Jolly Jha KSS Dave* एवाभिदृश्यते; MTr^{5} च; Jo^{2} Lo^{3} Tj^{1} तु — c) Bo BKt^{5} यथा; TMd^{3} तदा; Bo Pu^{3} पापं निगृ°; Be^{1} wKt^{1} पाशान्निगृ°; MTr^{5} °न्निबध्नीयाद्; Pu^{3} Tr^{2} °गृह्णीत

309. Omitted in TMd^{3}; pādas c-d omitted in Pu^{4} — b) Bo Ho wKt^{1} wKt^{3} GMy हृष्यति; TMd^{4} हृष्टन्ति; Pu^{5} Pu^{7} निर्यान्ति; Bo GMy sOx^{1} sPu^{6} मानवः — c) Bo BKt^{5} NPu^{1} यथा; Lo^{2} °तयोन्यस्मिन्; sOx^{1} sPu^{6} तस्मिन्; Kt^{2} रश्मिन् — d) BBe^{2} Hy Jm Jo^{1} Kt^{2} Ox^{2} Pu^{4} MTr^{3} *Mandlik Jolly Jha KSS Dave* चान्द्रव्रतिको

310. Omitted in TMd^{3} — a) Pu^{7} °युक्ततेज°; Pu^{5} °युक्तातेज° — c) GMy दृष्ट°; Jo^{2} Lo^{3} Tj^{1} °हिंस्रस्तु; TMd^{4} °हिंस्रस्य; BKt^{5} Pu^{2} Pu^{4} °हिंस्रेषु — d) Lo^{1} Lo^{4} GMd^{5} Pu^{8} तदाग्नेयव्रतं; TMd^{4} तथाग्नेय-व्रतं; Tj^{2} *om* स्मृतं

311. Omitted in TMd^{3}; pādas b-c omitted in GMd^{1} — a) Lo^{4} Pu^{2} Pu^{4} [*Jolly* M] भूतानि सर्वाणि — b) Ho NKt^{4} Tj^{1} धारा; TMd^{4} धरयते; Wa धारये — c) BKt^{5} यथा — d) Ox^{2} बिभृतः; GMd^{1} बिभ्रतं; La^{1} विधतः; Lo^{1} Tj^{1} पार्थिव; TMd^{4} प्रार्थितं

स्तेनान् राजा निगृह्णीयात् स्वराष्ट्रे पर एव च ॥३१२॥
परामप्यापदं प्राप्तो ब्राह्मणान्न प्रकोपयेत् ।
ते ह्येनं कुपिता हन्युः सद्यः सबलवाहनम् ॥३१३॥
यैः कृतः सर्वभक्षोऽग्निरपेयश्च महोदधिः ।
क्षयी चाप्यायितश्चेन्दुः को न नश्येत्प्रकोप्य तान् ॥३१४॥
लोकानन्यान्सृजेयुर्ये लोकपालांश्च कोपिताः ।
देवान्कुर्युरदेवांश्च कः क्षिण्वंस्तान्समृध्नुयात् ॥३१५॥
यान्समाश्रित्य तिष्ठन्ति लोका देवाश्च सर्वदा ।
ब्रह्म चैव धनं येषां को हिंस्यात्ताञ्जिजीविषुः ॥३१६॥
अविद्वांश्चैव विद्वांश्च ब्राह्मणो दैवतं महत् ।

312. Omitted in GMy; pādas a-c omitted in TMd^{3} — a) Lo^{4} °पायैरन्येभ्यो युक्तो — b) BKt^{5} नित्ययुक्तमतन्द्रितः; GMd^{5} नित्यो युक्तमतन्द्रितः; [*Jolly* M] युतो; Tj^{2} °तान्द्रितः; Pu^{8} °तन्द्रिवः — c) Be^{1} Lo^{1} स्तेनाद्राजा; TMd^{4} स्तेनान् राष्ट्रे; Be^{1} विगृह्णीयात्; BKt^{5} नगृह्णीयात् — d) Be^{1} Ho Lo^{3} Pu^{5} Pu^{7} Tj^{1} Tr^{1} Wa स्वे राष्ट्रे; BKt^{5} Lo^{2} GMd^{5} GMy oOr Ox^{2} NPu^{1} Pu^{2} Pu^{4} Tj^{1} Tr^{2} MTr^{4} MTr^{6} [*Jolly* R] वा

313. Omitted in GMy; verses 313–4 placed after 319 in [*Jolly* Nd] — a) GMd^{1} परम°; Pu^{2} °प्यापरं; Pu^{4} °भ्यापरं; Lo^{4} *om* प्राप्तो; GMd^{5} प्राप्तं; oOr Ox^{2} Tj^{1} Tr^{2} प्राप्य — b) TMd^{4} ब्राह्मणानां न कोपयेत्; Pu^{5} MTr^{6} ब्रह्म°; GMd^{5} ब्राह्मणं न — c) wKt^{1} ते येन ज्ञापिता हन्युः — d) Lo^{4} [*Jolly* M] सभृत्यबल°; wKt^{3} ससैन्यबल°

314.* Omitted in GMy; pādas c-d omitted in BKt^{5} Pu^{4} — a) oOr कृतं; BBe^{1} Ho Hy Jm Jo^{1} Jo^{2} wKt^{3} Lo^{3} Lo^{4} sOx^{1} Ox^{2} sPu^{6} Tj^{1} Tr^{2} Wa [*Jolly* M^{4} R Ku] *Mandlik KSS Dave* °भक्ष्यो; [*Jolly* M^{9}] °भक्षाग्नि° — b) sOx^{1} sPu^{6} °ग्निर्यैर्यैश्च महो° — c) Lo^{4} क्षयी [*ma* च] वृद्धिमांश्चेन्दुः; Bo वाप्यायि°; TMd^{3} चाप्यधिकश्चेन्दुः; Pu^{5} Pu^{7} चाप्यकृतश्चन्द्रः; BCa wKt^{1} La^{1} Lo^{1} NNg oOr sOx^{1} sPu^{6} Wa °यित-श्चन्द्रः; Be^{1} BBe^{2} Bo Ho Hy Jm Jo^{1} Kt^{2} wKt^{3} Lo^{2} Ox^{2} NPu^{1} Pu^{2} Pu^{3} Pu^{8} Tj^{2} Tr^{2} MTr^{3} *Rc Mandlik Jha KSS Dave* °यितः सोमः — d) Pu^{5} Pu^{7} वेनो नष्टो प्रकोप्य तान्; Ho *om* न; Lo^{4} नश्यत्प्र°; Be^{1} °कोपयेत् [*om* तान्]; Lo^{3} Tj^{1} °कोपितान्; Bo La^{1} °कोपतात्; TMd^{3} °कोपितैः; TMd^{4} °कुप्यतात्

Additional verse in TMd^{4}:

ब्राह्मणो देवता लोके ब्राह्मणे दिवि देवताः ।
ब्राह्मणानां प्रभावेन मान्वो दिवि विराजिते ॥

315. Pādas a-b *ma sh* in Tr^{1}; pāda-a omitted in BKt^{5}. Cited by *Lakṣ* 11.174 — a) *Lakṣ* लोकानलोकान्कुर्युस्ते; Pu^{8} °जेयुर्यं; Lo^{1} °जेयुस्ते; GMd^{5} °जेयुर्हि — b) BKt^{5} *om* ये लोकपालांश्च; Kt^{2} NPu^{1} °पालाश्च; Bo कोपितः; GMy कोविदाः — c) Pu^{5} Pu^{7} कुर्याद्देवानदेवांश्च; Lo^{3} Tj^{1} लोकान्कु°; Pu^{8} °न्कुर्युर्नृदेवांश्च; Kt^{2} wKt^{3} °देवाश्च — d) Pu^{5} Pu^{7} MTr^{6} कं भूतमधिकं ततः; NNg कस्तान्क्षिण्वन्समृ°; Wa क्षिण्वन्कः तान्समृ°

316. Cited by *Lakṣ* 11.174 — a) GMy [*Jolly* Nd] तान्समा°; Hy Jm Jo^{1} Kt^{2} GMd^{5} NPu^{1} Pu^{2} Pu^{4} Pu^{5} Pu^{7} Tj^{2} MTr^{3} [*Jolly* G Ku] *Lakṣ Mandlik Jolly Jha KSS Dave* यानुपाश्रित्य; NKt^{4} यानपाश्रित्य — b) Be^{1} लोकाः सर्वाश्च देवताः; Pu^{5} Pu^{7} देवा लोकांश्च सर्वशः; BCa La^{1} GMd^{1} TMd^{3} TMd^{4} Pu^{3} MTr^{5} MTr^{6} *Lakṣ* देवा लोकाश्च; GMy वेदा लोकाश्च; BBe^{2} देवांश्च; BKt^{5} GMd^{5} वेदाश्च; oOr सर्वशः — c) TMd^{4} ब्रह्मचर्यपथं येषां; Be^{1} ब्रह्मा; *Lakṣ* ब्रह्मैव च धनं; Bo वैव; GMy धनमेषां; wKt^{1} [*Jolly* M] तेषां; Pu^{5} Pu^{7} ह्येषां — d) Jo^{2} Lo^{3} Tj^{1} हन्यात्ताञ्जि°

प्रणीतश्चाप्रणीतश्च यथाग्निर्दैवतं महत् ॥३१७॥
श्मशानेष्वपि तेजस्वी पावको नैव दुष्यति ।
हूयमानश्च यज्ञेषु भूय एवाभिवर्धते ॥३१८॥
एवं यद्यप्यनिष्टेषु वर्तन्ते सर्वकर्मसु ।
सर्वथा ब्राह्मणाः पूज्याः परमं दैवतं हि तत् ॥३१९॥
क्षत्रस्यातिप्रवृद्धस्य ब्राह्मणान्प्रति सर्वशः ।
ब्रह्मैव संनियन्तृ स्यात् क्षत्रं हि ब्रह्मसंभवम् ॥३२०॥
अद्भ्योऽग्निर्ब्रह्मतः क्षत्रमश्मनो लोहमुत्थितम् ।
तेषां सर्वत्रगं तेजः स्वासु योनिषु शाम्यति ॥३२१॥
नाब्रह्म क्षत्रमृध्नोति नाक्षत्रं ब्रह्म वर्धते ।
ब्रह्म क्षत्रं च संपृक्तमिह चामुत्र वर्धते ॥३२२॥

317. Pādas a-b and c-d transposed in Be^{1} *Lakṣ*. Cited by *Lakṣ* 11.174 — a) *Lakṣ* अविद्वांश्च विद्वांश्चैव; NNg विद्वांश्चैवाप्यविद्वांश्च; Be^{1} एवं विद्वानविद्वांश्च; TMd^{4} विद्वांसः — b) TMd^{3} GMd^{5} ब्राह्मणं; Be^{1} TMd^{4} ब्रह्मणो; Be^{1} देवतं; Bo जीवितं; Wa नातितो महान् — c) TMd^{4} प्रणीतांश्चाप्रणीतांश्च — d) NPu^{1} तथा°; Be^{1} BKt^{5} sOx^{1} sPu^{6} °ग्निदैवतं; Tr^{1} °ग्निर्देवतं; BKt^{5} °वतं तथा

318. Omitted in MTr^{5}. Cited by *Lakṣ* 11.174 — a) MTr^{4}MTr^{6} श्मशाने ह्यपि; wKt^{3} श्मशानेपि हि; oOr श्मशाने नैव; Lo^{3} Tj^{1} Tr^{1}[*cor sh to*] श्मशानेषु च; Jo^{2} श्मशानेषु तु; TMd^{3} तेजस्वि — b) sOx^{1} sPu^{6} पाचको; TMd^{4} नेव — c) Lo^{2} Pu^{5} Pu^{7} Pu^{8} हूयमानेषु यज्ञेषु; TMd^{3} भूयमानश्च; BBe^{2} La^{1} NPu^{1} °मानस्तु; BKt^{5} °मानस्य — d) GMd^{1} TMd^{3} TMd^{4} GMd^{5} GMy MTr^{6} *Lakṣ* [*Jolly* Nd] एवाभिपूज्यते; Tr^{1} एव हि पूज्यते

319. Omitted in MTr^{5}. Cited by *Lakṣ* 11.174 — b) Lo^{1} TMd^{3} TMd^{4} GMd^{5} sOx^{1} Pu^{7} Tr^{1} MTr^{6} वर्तते; Tj^{2} वर्तन्ति; Be^{1} वर्तने — c) BKt^{5} Tr^{2} ब्रह्मणाः; GMd^{1} TMd^{3} GMd^{5} GMy NPu^{1} Tr^{1} MTr^{6} ब्राह्मणः पूज्यः; NNg पूज्या; NKt^{4} सज्याः — d) *Lakṣ* दैवतं परमं; La^{1} oOr Pu^{5} Pu^{7} सर्वथा दैवतं; Tj^{2} देवतं; Be^{1} BCa La^{1} Lo^{1} Lo^{4} GMd^{1} sOx^{1} NPu^{1} Pu^{2} Pu^{4} Pu^{5} sPu^{6} Pu^{7} Pu^{8} [*Jolly* M G] *Jolly* दैवतं महत्; wKt^{3} हि यत्; BKt^{5} Ox^{2} Pu^{3} Tr^{2} हि ते; TMd^{3} TMd^{4} GMd^{5} GMy Tr^{1} MTr^{4} MTr^{6} [*Jolly* Nd] हि सः

320. Pādas c-d omitted in Tr^{1}. Cited by *Lakṣ* 11.174 — a) Jo^{2} oOr Pu^{2} Pu^{4} Tj^{1} क्षत्रियस्यातिवृद्धस्य; Lo^{4} क्षत्रियस्यापि वृद्धस्य; Tj^{2} क्षत्रियस्याधिवृद्धस्य; NNg क्षत्रस्याप्रवृत्तस्य; BBe^{2} Wa क्षेत्रस्याभिप्र°; Hy La^{1} GMy Pu^{8} Tr^{2} *Lakṣ* क्षत्रास्यापि प्रवृ°; GMd^{5} क्षत्रियोपि प्रवृ°; TMd^{3} GMy °प्रवृत्तस्य — b) Tr^{1} ब्राह्मणान्सर्वतः प्रति; Lo^{4} ब्रह्म°; Be^{1} NPu^{1} Pu^{2} Pu^{4} ब्राह्मणं प्रति; wKt^{1} Lo^{4} GMd^{1} TMd^{3} GMd^{5} GMy NNg MTr^{4}MTr^{5} MTr^{6} Wa [*Jolly* Nd M] *Lakṣ* सर्वतः — c) GMd^{5} ब्रह्मेव; NKt^{4} संनियन्त्री; TMd^{3} संनियन्त्र — d) Wa क्षेत्रं

321. Omitted in GMy — a) Hy TMd^{3} GMd^{5} °ग्निर्ब्रह्मणः; BBe^{2} Hy Wa क्षेत्रम°; sOx^{1} sPu^{6} [*but ma sh*] *lacuna for* क्षत्रम् — b) oOr क्षत्रमश्मितो; TMd^{3} क्षत्रमग्नितो; Lo^{1} क्षत्रमशनो; GMd^{1} क्षत्रमष्टतो; Kt^{2} क्षत्रमश्मनोर्लोह°; BBe^{2} क्षत्रमश्वनोमोहमु°; TMd^{3} °मुद्धितः — c) Be^{1} wKt^{1} एषां; Hy सर्वत्रग; Lo^{1} TMd^{3} NNg सर्वगतं — d) BKt^{5} स्वस्वयोनिषु; BBe^{2} स्वानुयोनिषु; Lo^{4} प्रशाम्यति; Be^{1} मज्जति

322. Omitted in GMy. Cited by *Lakṣ* 11.173 — a) Lo^{4} नब्रह्म; GMd^{1} नृब्रह्म; Lo^{4} NPu^{1} Pu^{2} Pu^{4} Tr^{2} क्षत्रमृध्नाति — b) Lo^{4} TMd^{4} Pu^{2} Pu^{4} नक्षत्रं; wKt^{1} वर्तते — c) Tr^{2} सब्रह्म; Be^{1} ब्राह्म; Lo^{2} TMd^{4} GMd^{5} Tr^{1} MTr^{5} क्षत्रे च; GMd^{1} TMd^{3} MTr^{4} MTr^{6} क्षत्रे तु; sOx^{1} sPu^{6} क्षत्रेषु; La^{1} क्षत्रेण; Bo व; BCa BKt^{5} NNg oOr हि; Lo^{4} [*Jolly* M] तु; GMd^{1} TMd^{3} TMd^{4} GMd^{5} Tr^{1} MTr^{6} संपृक्ते इह; MTr^{5} संपृक्ते

दत्त्वा धनं तु विप्रेभ्यः सर्वदण्डसमुत्थितम् ।
पुत्रे राज्यं समासज्य कुर्वीत प्रायणं रणे ॥३२३॥
एवं चरन्सदा युक्तो राजधर्मेषु पार्थिवः ।
हितेषु चैव लोकस्य सर्वान्भृत्यान्नियोजयेत् ॥३२४॥
एषोऽखिलः कर्मविधिरुक्तो राज्ञः सनातनः ।
इमं कर्मविधिं विद्यात् क्रमशो वैश्यशूद्रयोः ॥३२५॥
वैश्यस्तु कृतसंस्कारः कृत्वा दारपरिग्रहम् ।
वार्त्तायां नित्ययुक्तः स्यात् पशूनां चैव रक्षणे ॥३२६॥
प्रजापतिर्हि वैश्याय सृष्ट्वा परिददे पशून् ।
ब्राह्मणाय च राज्ञे च सर्वाः परिददे प्रजाः ॥३२७॥
न च वैश्यस्य कामः स्यान्न रक्षेयं पशूनिति ।
वैश्ये चेच्छति नान्येन रक्षितव्याः कथंचन ॥३२८॥

इवा; Ox^{2} NPu^{1} Pu^{2} Pu^{4} *Lakṣ* संयुक्तमिह; BKt^{5} संपूज्याविह — d) TMd^{3} °मिहामुत्र च धर्मतः; Lo^{3} Tj^{1} [*Jolly* R] °मिहामुत्र च; sOx^{1} Pu^{5} sPu^{6} वामुत्र; BKt^{5} NNg MTr^{6} वर्धतः; Wa वर्द्धुतः; MTr^{5} च ध्रुतः; Tr^{1} चार्धुतः; TMd^{4} चाधृवं

323. Omitted in GMy — a) wKt^{3} हत्वा; Tr^{2} च; Lo^{2} सुविप्रेभ्यः — b) Pu^{5} सर्वे; BBe^{2} NKt^{4} MTr^{6} *Jolly* सर्वं; Pu^{2} Pu^{4} सर्वधर्म°; sOx^{1} sPu^{6} °समुत्थिते; TMd^{4} °समुत्थितः; Tr^{2} °समन्वितं; Pu^{8} °समुद्भवं; Ox^{2} °समुच्छ्रितं — c) [*Jolly* Nd] सुतं राज्ये समावेश्य; Lo^{1} पुत्रो; MTr^{5} पुत्रे सर्वं; Lo^{2} GMd^{5} राज्ये; Lo^{4} Pu^{2} Pu^{4} *Me Jha* [*Jolly* M] समासाद्य; Jm Jo^{1} Kt^{2} Lo^{2} Ox^{2} Pu^{3} MTr^{3} *Mandlik KSS Dave* समासृज्य; La^{1} विनिक्षिप्य — d) Be^{1} Ox^{2} प्रापणं; *Rn* [pāṭha] वने

324. Omitted in GMy — a) TMd^{4} एवं च न सदा; Ox^{2} Pu^{2} चरेत्सदा; Jo^{2} wKt^{1} wKt^{3} La^{1} GMd^{1} sOx^{1} Pu^{5} sPu^{6} Pu^{7} Pu^{8} MTr^{4} MTr^{6} [*Jolly* G R^{2}] चरन्समायुक्तो — b) BKt^{5} Pu^{2} Pu^{4} Tr^{1} राजा; NPu^{1} राज्य°; Pu^{5} Pu^{7} °धर्मेण — c) Be^{1} हिते च सर्वलोकस्य — d) TMd^{3} ब्रह्माप्येति सनातनं; Be^{1} Lo^{4} NNg MTr^{5} Wa सर्वभृत्या°

325. Omitted in GMy — a) Kt^{2} °खिल; BCa wKt^{1} Lo^{3} TMd^{3} GMd^{5} oOr Pu^{5} Pu^{7} Tj^{1} Tr^{1} °खिलो धर्मविधि°; GMd^{1} °खिलो राजधर्म उक्तो; Tj^{2} कामविधि° — a-b) Pu^{2} Pu^{4} °खिलेनाभिहितो राज्ञो धर्मः सनातनः — b) Lo^{2} राज्ञां — c) oOr एवं; wKt^{1} Lo^{4} GMd^{1} धर्मविधिं; NNg धर्मविधं; Be^{1} La^{1} NPu^{1} विन्द्यात्; oOr कुर्यात्; wKt^{3} दद्यात्

326. Cited by *Lakṣ* 2.255; *Mādh* 1.417 — a) TMd^{4} वैश्यस्त्वकृत° — b) Lo^{3} Tj^{1} कृतदार°; Jo^{2} wKt^{1} Lo^{3} Tj^{1} °परिग्रहः

327. Pādas c-d *ma sh* in Pu^{7}. Cited by *Lakṣ* 2.255 pādas a-b cited by *Mādh* 1.417 — a) GMy वैश्यायां; TMd^{4} वैश्याया; Pu^{5} वैश्यं; Pu^{7} वैश्यां — b) GMy सृष्टा; Lo^{2} TMd^{3} Tr^{1} परिददौ; NNg [*but cor*] परिदापयेत् — c) Be^{1} ब्राह्मणा च — d) Be^{1} सर्वा; NNg सृष्ट्वा; TMd^{4} प्रतिपदे; Lo^{2} TMd^{3} Pu^{2} Pu^{4} Tr^{1} परिददौ; Lo^{3} °ददे पशून्

328. Pādas c-d *ma sh* in Pu^{7}. Cited by *Lakṣ* 2.256; *Mādh* 1.417 — a) Lo^{1} GMy न तु; NPu^{1} Pu^{2} वैश्यः सकामः; wKt^{3} Lo^{4} [*Jolly* M] कामं; GMy कामि; TMd^{4} नाम — b) Be^{1} स्यादरक्षेयं; Tr^{1} रक्षेयः — c) GMy वैश्यश्चेच्छति; La^{1} वैश्ये तिष्ठति; TMd^{3} नेच्छति; MTr^{5} नेच्छेति; Pu^{5} Pu^{7} चान्येन; Lo^{1} मान्येन — d) GMd^{1} °तव्यः; TMd^{4} °तव्यं; sOx^{1} sPu^{6} °तव्याः प्रयत्नतः

मणिमुक्ताप्रवालानां लोहानां तान्तवस्य च ।
गन्धानां च रसानां च विद्यादर्घबलाबलम् ॥३२९॥
बीजानामुप्तिविच्च स्यात् क्षेत्रदोषगुणस्य च ।
मानयोगांश्च जानीयात् तुलायोगांश्च सर्वशः ॥३३०॥
सारासारं च भाण्डानां देशानां च गुणागुणम् ।
लाभालाभं च पण्यानां पशूनां च विवर्धनम् ॥३३१॥
भृत्यानां च भृतिं विद्याद् भाषाश्च विविधा नृणाम् ।
द्रव्याणां स्थानयोगांश्च क्रयविक्रयमेव च ॥३३२॥
धर्मेण च द्रव्यवृद्धावातिष्ठेद्यत्नमुत्तमम् ।
दद्याच्च सर्वभूतानामन्नमेव प्रयत्नतः ॥३३३॥
विप्राणां वेदविदुषां गृहस्थानां यशस्विनाम् ।
शुश्रूषैव तु शूद्रस्य धर्मो नैःश्रेयसः परः ॥३३४॥

329. Bo places 329c-d and 330a-b after 332b. Cited by *Lakṣ* 2.256; *Mādh* 1.417 — a) Be^{1} TMd^{4} °मुक्तप्र°; Tr^{1} MTr^{5} °प्रवाळानां; BKt^{5} °प्रवालादिना — b) *Lakṣ* लौहानां; TMd^{3} लोहनां; Pu^{2} Pu^{4} तान्तकस्य; GMd^{1} GMy धान्तवस्य; TMd^{4} कनकस्य — c) GMy गन्धर्वाणां रसानां — d) Bo La^{1} Lo^{4} NPu^{1} Tj^{1} विन्द्याद°; NKt^{4} °दर्घ्यबलाबलं; Be^{1} Ox^{2} °दर्थबलाबलं; TMd^{4} Pu^{3} °दर्घं बलाबलं; La^{1} Pu^{5} Pu^{7} °दर्थं बलाबलं; GMy °दश्वबलाबलं

330. Pādas c-d omitted in Pu^{5}. Cited by *Lakṣ* 2.256; *Mādh* 1.417 — a) Pu^{5} Pu^{7} उत्पत्तिं चैव बीजानां; Lo^{1} जीवानामुप्तिपिप्सुः स्यात्; GMd^{5} °मुप्तविच्च; Pu^{3} °प्तिवृद्धि स्यात्; Ox^{2} °मुप्तिवीर्यस्य — b) GMd^{1} TMd^{3} TMd^{4} GMd^{5} GMy Tr^{1} [*but mc sh*] MTr^{4} MTr^{5} MTr^{6} *Nd Lakṣ* क्षेत्रबीजगुणस्य — c) GMy [*Jolly* Nd]जनयोगांश्च; MTr^{5} °योगाश्च; Jm Jo^{1} Kt^{2} MTr^{3} *Mandlik Jha KSS Dave* °योगं च; wKt^{1} La^{1} °योगाच्च; sOx^{1} sPu^{6} जानीयांस्तुला° — d) TMd^{4} कुलयो°; wKt^{3} तुलायांश्च; NPu^{1} °योगाश्च; GMd^{1} °योगं च; Be^{1} Jo^{2} Lo^{3} GMd^{5} sOx^{1} sPu^{6} सर्वतः

331. Cited by *Lakṣ* 2.256; *Mādh* 1.417 — a) Bo BKt^{5} °सारां च; La^{1} °सारौ च; BBe^{2} °सारांश्च — b) TMd^{4} गुणेगुणं; Hy Jm Jo^{1} Kt^{2} La^{1} NNg Ox^{2} Pu^{8} MTr^{3} *Mandlik Jha KSS Dave* गुणागुणान् — c) TMd^{4} लोभालोभं च पुण्यानां; Be^{1} °लाभाश्च; BKt^{5} La^{1} sOx^{1} sPu^{6} °लाभौ च; Wa *om* पण्यानां; TMd^{3} पश्यानां — d) Bo Ho Hy Jm Jo^{1} wKt^{1} Kt^{2} wKt^{3} Lo^{1} Ox^{2} NPu^{1} Pu^{2} Pu^{3} Pu^{4} Pu^{8} Tj^{2} Tr^{2} MTr^{3} *Mandlik Jha KSS Dave* पशूनां परिवर्धनं; TMd^{3} कालयोगांस्तथैव च

332. Pādas c-d omitted in Bo. Cited by *Lakṣ* 2.256; *Mādh* 1.417 — a) NKt^{4} GMd^{1} TMd^{4} भृतानां; TMd^{3} भ्रातानां; GMy भूतानां; Tr^{2} भृती; MTr^{6} भृतं; TMd^{3} धृतिं; GMy मृतिं; La^{1} भूतिं; Bo Pu^{3} भृतीर्विद्याद्; La^{1} Lo^{1} Lo^{4} विन्द्याद्; NPu^{1} Pu^{2} Pu^{4} दद्याद् — b) BKt^{5} [*but cor*] La^{1} Lo^{1} भाषां च; TMd^{3} भाषांश्च; La^{1} Tr^{2} विविधां; NKt^{4} नृणं — c) Lo^{4} द्रव्यस्थानयोगश्च; TMd^{3} Pu^{2} Pu^{4} °योगं च; La^{1} °योगां च — d) MTr^{5} *Mādh* क्रयं विक्र°; BKt^{5} TMd^{3} Pu^{2} Pu^{4} °विक्रय एव

333. Cited by *Lakṣ* 2.256; *Mādh* 1.417 — a) Jo^{2} Lo^{3} Tj^{1} धर्मेण द्रव्यवृद्ध्यर्थमाति°; TMd^{4} GMd^{5} Pu^{2} Pu^{4} *om* च; GMd^{1} प्रजावृद्धा°; TMd^{4} धर्मवृद्धा°; Pu^{2} Pu^{4} °वृद्धानाति° — b) Be^{1} °वृद्धौ चातिष्ठे°; GMy oOr °वृद्धौ वातिष्ठे°; oOr °ष्ठेद्धर्ममुत्तमं; TMd^{3} °ष्ठेद् द्रव्यमुत्तमं; TMd^{4} °त्नमनुत्तमं — c) wKt^{1} प्रीत्या च — d) TMd^{3} °भूतानां दानमेव; GMd^{1} °न्नमेव च प्रय°; BKt^{5} °न्नमेतत्प्रय°

334. Pād- d omitted in TMd^{4}. Cited by *Lakṣ* 2.265; *Mādh* 1.417 — a) sOx^{1} sPu^{6} देवविदुषां — b) sOx^{1} sPu^{6} Tr^{2} तपस्विनां; NKt^{4} °स्विनः — c) TMd^{3} Tj^{2} शुश्रूषेव; Be^{1} शुश्रूषायेव; NKt^{4} शुश्रूषयो;

शुचिरुत्कृष्टशुश्रूषुर्मृदुवागनहंकृतः ।
ब्राह्मणापाश्रयो नित्यमुच्छ्रितिं जातितोऽश्नुते ॥३३५॥
एषोऽनापदि वर्णानामुक्तः कर्मविधिः शुभः ।
आपद्यपि हि यस्तेषां क्रमशस्तं निबोधत ॥३३६॥

॥ इति मानवे धर्मशास्त्रे भृगुप्रोक्तायां संहितायां नवमोऽध्यायः ॥

La^1 शुश्रूषयैव तु; Bo शुश्रूषुवै तु; bBe^2 wKt^3 Pu^2 Pu^4 च; wKt^1 हि — d) La^1 oOr sOx^1 sPu^6 धर्मः श्रेयस्करः परः; Bo Pu^5 धर्मे; Be^1 bKt^5 Lo^4 gMd^5 Pu^5 Pu^7 Pu^8 Wa निःश्रेयसः; bBe^2 wKt^1 wKt^3 Lo^2 Lo^3 gMd^1 nNg Tj^1 निश्रेयसः; nKt^4 निश्रेयसं परं; gMd^5 *Dave Jha* परं

335.* Omitted in Lo^4 tMd^4; pāda-d too faint to read in wKt^5. Cited by *Lakṣ* 2.265; *Mādh* 1.417 — a) Hy °त्कृष्टः; *Lakṣ* °त्कृष्टवर्णेषु मृदु°; Jo^1 bKt^5 °शुश्रूषुमृद्व°; Kt^2 °शुश्रूषमृदु°; Tj^1 °शुश्रूषःमृदु° — b) bBe^2 °पुर्मृद्धवाग°; Pu^8 °पुर्मदुवाग°; wKt^1 °पुः शुद्धवाग°; nKt^4 bKt^5 °पुर्मृदुवाचानहं°; *Mādh* °पुर्मृदुः शान्तोनहं°; gMy °कृतिः; wKt^3 °कृतं — c) Bo Ho Hy Jo^1 Kt^2 bKt^5 Lo^2 Lo^3 Tr^2 [*Jolly* R^1] ब्राह्मणायाश्रयो; Tj^2 ब्राह्मणायाश्रितो; sOx^1 sPu^6 ब्रह्मण्यसाश्रयो; bBe^2 gMy ब्राह्मणानाश्रयो; [*Jolly* Nd] ब्राह्मणानां श्रयं [Nd^2 श्रेयः]; Ox^2 ब्राह्मणस्याश्रयो; Be^1 Jm wKt^1 Pu^3 mTr^3 *Mandlik KSS Dave* ब्राह्मणाद्याश्रयो; La^1 Tj^1 ब्राह्मणाश्रयो; gMy °श्रयं — d) Hy Jm Jo^1 Kt^2 gMd^1 tMd^3 gMd^5 gMy Tj^2 mTr^3 mTr^4 mTr^6 *Mandlik Jolly Jha KSS Dave* मुत्कृष्टां जातिमश्नुते; Be^1 °मुच्छ्रिति; Bo wKt^1 wKt^3 Lo^3 Ox^2 nPu^1 Pu^2 Pu^4 Tj^1 Tr^2 °मुच्छ्रितं; *Nā* °मुच्छ्रितां; wKt^1 wKt^3 °मुत्थितं; Pu^5 Pu^7 °मुत्सृतिं; mTr^5 °मुत्सृप्तिं; Lo^2 °मुत्सृष्टिं; nKt^4 °मुत्सृपि; nNg sOx^1 sPu^6 Wa °मुत्कर्षं; Pu^2 Pu^4 Pu^5 Pu^7 ज्ञातितोश्नुते; Ox^2 जातिसोश्नुते

336. Pādas a-b omitted in tMd^4 — a) bKt^5 Pu^2 धर्माणा° — b) gMd^1 tMd^3 gMd^5 gMy Pu^2 Pu^4 Tr^1 mTr^4 mTr^5 mTr^6 °मुक्तो धर्मविधिः; Be^1 सर्वविधिः; nNg °विधिं; nPu^1 शुभाः; wKt^3 शुभं; bBe^2 परः; Jo^2 Lo^3 Tj^1 पुनः — c) bCa आपद्यपि विधिस्तेषां; tMd^4 *om* आपद्यपि हि; wKt^3 आपद्यतु; gMd^1 *om* हि; gMd^5 oOr Pu^2 Pu^4 Pu^5 Pu^7 Tr^1 mTr^5 च; Be^1 bBe^2 nKt^4 La^1 Lo^4 tMd^3 gMy mTr^6 तु; Lo^4 तु सर्वेषां; nKt^4 Lo^1 gMd^1 nNg sOx^1 nPu^1 sPu^6 Tj^1 mTr^5 mTr^6 यस्त्वेषां; La^1 Ox^2 यत्तेषां — d) Lo^3 Tj^1 क्रमतः संनिबोधत [Tj^1 क्रमस्त]; bBe^2 Bo Hy Jm Jo^1 Jo^2 Kt^2 wKt^3 nKt^4 Lo^1 Lo^4 wKt^5 tMd^3 gMd^5 gMy sOx^1 Ox^2 Pu^2 Pu^4 sPu^6 Tr^2 mTr^3 mTr^4 mTr^6 *Mandlik Jha KSS Dave* °शस्तन्निबोधत

Colophon: Be^1 Lo^1 tMd^3 nNg Ox^2 Tr^1 इति श्रीमानवे; Lo^3 इति श्रीमानवीये; Be^1 bKt^5 gMd^1 gMy sOx^1 mTr^6 *om* भृगुप्रोक्तायां संहितायां; oOr कण्ठकशोधनो नाम नवमो

[दशमोऽध्यायः]

अधीयीरंस्त्रयो वर्णाः स्वकर्मस्था द्विजातयः ।
प्रब्रूयाद्ब्राह्मणस्त्वेषां नेतराविति निश्चयः ॥१॥
सर्वेषां ब्राह्मणो विद्याद् वृत्त्युपायान्यथाविधि ।
प्रब्रूयादितरेभ्यश्च स्वयं चैव तथा भवेत् ॥२॥
वैशेष्यात्प्रकृतिश्रैष्ठ्यान्नियमस्य च धारणात् ।
संस्कारस्य विशेषाच्च वर्णानां ब्राह्मणः प्रभुः ॥३॥
ब्राह्मणः क्षत्रियो वैश्यस्त्रयो वर्णा द्विजातयः ।
चतुर्थ एकजातिस्तु शूद्रो नास्ति तु पञ्चमः ॥४॥
सर्ववर्णेषु तुल्यासु पत्नीष्वक्षतयोनिषु ।
आनुलोम्येन संभूता जात्या ज्ञेयास्त एव ते ॥५॥

Before the first verse [*Jolly* M] adds:

अतः परं प्रवक्ष्यामि अध्येतव्यस्य यो विधिः ॥

1. Pādas c-d omitted in Pu[4] [haplo]. Cited by *Dev* 1.143 — a) Lo[1] अतः परंस्त्रयो — a-b) TMd[3] अधीयीरन्स्वकर्मस्थास्त्रयो वर्णा द्विजातयः — b) Pu[5] Pu[7] सकर्म° ; sOx[1] sPu[6] °कर्मस्या — c) GMd[1] प्रब्रूयान्नेतरस्त्वेषां; Be[1] BBe[2] wKt[1] BKt[5] La[1] Lo[1] Lo[2] Lo[4] TMd[4] GMy NPu[1] Pu[2] Pu[10] Tr[2] *Dev* °णस्तेषां — d) GMy प्रब्रूयान्नेतराविति; oOr नेतरानिति; Lo[2] GMd[1] TMd[4] Pu[3] MTr[4] MTr[6] °विति धारणा

In place of verse 1 MTr[5] gives the following verse:

यस्मिन्नहनि संक्रान्ते परं मध्यन्दिनं भवेत् ।
आव्दिकं तत्र कर्तव्यं पूर्वस्मिन्नुभयोर्यदि ॥

2. Pādas a-b omitted in Pu[4]. Cited by *Viś* 1.197 — a) wKt[1] ब्रह्मणो; GMd[1] ब्राह्मणश्रेष्ठः; Bo La[1] Pu[2] विन्द्याद् — b) TMd[3] प्रीत्युपाया° ; MTr[6] प्रत्युपाया° — c) NKt[4] प्रकुर्युरितरेभ्यश्च — d) BKt[5] TMd[3] यथा; GMd[5] Tr[1] तदाचरेत्

3. Cited by *Lakṣ* 12.811 — a) wKt[1] GMd[1] GMd[5] GMy Tr[1] MTr[4] MTr[6] वैशिष्यां°; Pu[4] वैशैष्या° ; La[1] °त्प्रकृतिः; Ox[2] °त्प्रकृते; Be[1] BBe[2] Jo[1] Kt[2] Lo[2] TMd[4] NNg Pu[8] Tr[2] MTr[6] °श्रेष्ठ्या° ; wKt[1] °प्रैष्यान्नि° — b) GMy °न्निर्गमस्य; TMd[3] °न्निगमस्य; BKt[5] °न्नियम्य च; Ho NNg *om* च; sOx[1] sPu[6] तु; wKt[1] वारणात् — c) La[1] TMd[4] GMy NPu[1] संस्कारश्च; Tj[2] प्रवेषाच्च — d) GMd[1] TMd[4] GMd[5] Tr[1] MTr[4] MTr[6] [*Jolly* Gr]सर्वेषां ब्राह्मणः; Tj[2] ब्राह्मणो गुरुः

4. Omitted in Pu[10]. Cited by *Lakṣ* 12.811; *Dev* 2.407; pādas c-d referred to by *Śaṃ* on *VeS* 1.3.36— a) La[1] ब्राह्मणं; Jo[1] BKt[5] वैश्यास्त्रयो — c) GMd[1] चतुर्था; Pu[2] Pu[4] चतुर्थे; wKt[1] एवजातिस्तु; GMd[1] TMd[4] MTr[4] MTr[6] एकजातीयश्शूद्रो; Pu[2] Pu[4] °जातीस्तु; Be[1] °जातिः च; GMd[5] °जातस्तु — d) Be[1] नास्त्यत्र; Ox[2] नान्योस्ति; Pu[2] *om* तु

5*. Pādas c-d omitted in Pu[4]. Cited by *Dev* 4.180; *Mādh* 1.511 — a) wKt[1] ब्राह्मणादिष्वतुल्यासु; Pu[3] तुल्यास्तु; TMd[3] तुल्यास्युः — b) BKt[5] पत्नीपु तु योनिषु; La[1] GMy NPu[1] पत्नीपु क्षत° ; pāṭha

स्त्रीष्वनन्तरजातासु द्विजैरुत्पादितान्सुतान् ।
सदृशानेव तानाहुर्मातृदोषविगर्हितान् ॥६॥
अनन्तरासु जातानां विधिरेष सनातनः ।
द्व्येकान्तरासु जातानां धर्म्यं विद्यादिमं विधिम् ॥७॥
ब्राह्मणाद्वैश्यकन्यायामम्बष्ठो नाम जायते ।
निषादः शूद्रकन्यायां यः पारशव उच्यते ॥८॥
क्षत्रियाच्छूद्रकन्यायां क्रूराचारविहारवान् ।
क्षत्रशूद्रवपुर्जन्तुरुग्रो नाम प्रजायते ॥९॥
विप्रस्य त्रिषु वर्णेषु नृपतेर्वर्णयोर्द्वयोः ।
वैश्यस्य वर्णे चैकस्मिन् षडेतेऽपसदाः स्मृताः ॥१०॥
क्षत्रियाद्विप्रकन्यायां सूतो भवति जातितः ।
वैश्यान्मागधवैदेहौ राजविप्राङ्गनासुतौ ॥११॥

in *Bh* and *Me* नारीष्वक्षत°; Pu⁴ *om* अक्षतयोनिषु; Hy °योनिषु च — c) ʙKt⁵ sOx¹ sPu⁶ आनुलोम्ये संभूता; Hy ᴛMd³ Tj¹ अनुलो°; ɢMd¹ Tr² आनुलोमेन; — d) Be¹ Jo² ʙKt⁵ ᴛMd⁴ ɴPu¹ Pu⁵ Pu⁷ Wa *Dev* ज्ञेयास्तथैव ते

6. Omitted in Pu¹⁰; pādas a-b omitted in Pu⁴. Cited by *Lakṣ* 12.812; *Mādh* 1.511 — a) ɢMd⁵ स्त्रीष्वान°; ɴPu¹ Pu³ °जातास्तु — b) Bo द्विजादुत्पा°; ᴛMd³ °रुत्सादिता°; ɴPu¹ °तान्सुरान् — c) Tr² भवतः सदृशानेव मातृ°; Pu⁴ *om* सदृशान्; ᴛMd³ सदृशानिव; Be¹ सदृश्यानेव; wKt¹ तादृशानेव — d) Tj¹ °दोषाद्विग°; Jo² Lo³ °दोषाविग°; ɴNg °गर्हतान्

ɢMy inserts verses 10.14 and then 10.9, Tr¹ inserts verses 10.14–5, and ᴛMd³ verse 10.14 [ᴛMd³ also gives it at the proper place]

7. Omitted in Pu¹⁰. Cited by *Lakṣ* 12.812 — b) Tj¹ विधिरेषां; ʙKt⁵ विधिरेव; Pu² Pu⁴ समानतः — c) Tr² द्वन्तारसुतजातानां; ɢMd¹ तदद्व्यन्त°; Jo¹ द्व्यैकान्त°; wKt¹ ᴛMd³ एकान्त°; Ox² अन्तरासु [*om* द्व्येक]; Be¹ ɴKt⁴ ʙKt⁵ La¹ ᴛMd⁴ ɢMy ɢMd⁵ ɴPu¹ Pu² Pu³ Pu⁴ Tr¹ ᴍTr⁴ ᴍTr⁶ Wa द्व्यन्तरासु च [La¹ Pu² Pu³ *om* च; ɴKt⁴ ɢMd⁵ ɴPu¹ Pu⁴ तु; omitting of एक supported by *Nd Rc*]; reading of edition supported by *Bh Me Go Ku Rn* — d) ɢMd¹ धर्म्यां; Bo wKt¹ ʙKt⁵ Lo¹ Ox² Pu⁸ Tr² ᴍTr⁴ ᴍTr⁶ धर्मं; Tr¹ कर्मं; La¹ ɴPu¹ Tr¹ विन्द्या°; ɢMd¹ विद्यादिमां; Be¹ विद्यादमुं; ɴNg विद्यादनुं; Wa *om* इमं विधिं; sOx¹ Pu² Pu⁴ विधिः

8. Omitted in ᴛMd³; *ma* in Lo¹; pādas b-c omitted in ᴛMd⁴, and pāda-d in La¹ sOx¹ [haplo]. Cited by *Lakṣ* 12.812 — a) ʙKt⁵ °कन्यामम्बष्ठो — b) ʙBe² °म्बष्ठौ; Lo² नेव जायते — c) ʙBe² निषाधः — d) Lo¹ परशव; Pu¹⁰ परेशव; Be¹ पाराशर; wKt¹ पारसर; Pu² Pu⁴ पारसव; Tr² परःस

9. Omitted in ᴛMd³; *ma* in Lo¹; pādas b-d omitted in ɢMd⁵ oOr. Cited by *Lakṣ* 12.812 — a) Ho क्षत्रियाशूद्र°; Lo³ °कन्यायाः; Be¹ °कन्यानां — b) ᴛMd⁴ क्रूरोचार°; ɢMd¹ °विहीनवान्; Lo² °विकारवान् — c) Pu² Pu⁴ क्षेत्र°; Wa °वपुर्जन्तोरुग्री — d) Pu² Pu⁴ °न्तुरग्रो; ɢMd¹ °रुग्रनामा

10. Omitted in ɢMd⁵ oOr. Cited by *Lakṣ* 12.812; *Mādh* 1.512 — a) ʙCa विप्रेषु — b) Kt² Pu⁵ Tj¹ Tj² Tr² नृपते वर्ण°; ɢMd¹ नृपयोर्वर्ण° — c) Pu³ Pu⁴ वैश्यस्य एकस्मिन्; wKt¹ विशश्च; ɴKt⁴ वैश्यवर्णस्य; Bo ʙCa Jo² wKt¹ wKt³ La¹ Lo³ ᴛMd³ ɢMy Ox² Pu³ Tj¹ Tr¹ Tr² ᴍTr⁶ *Mādh* वर्ण एकस्मिन् — d) Lo¹ षडैते; ɢMd¹ ɢMy Pu³ Tr¹ ᴍTr⁵ *Bh* °पशदाः; ɴNg °पसदः; ᴛMd³ दशधा स्मृताः

11. Pāda-a omitted in ɢMd⁵ oOr. Cited by *Mādh* 1.513 — c) wKt¹ °न्मगध°; ɴNg Tj²

शूद्रादायोगवः क्षत्ता चण्डालश्चाधमो नृणाम् ।
वैश्यराजन्यविप्रासु जायन्ते वर्णसंकराः ॥१२॥
एकान्तरे त्वानुलोम्यादम्बष्ठोग्रौ यथा स्मृतौ ।
क्षत्तृवैदेहकौ तद्वत् प्रातिलोम्येन जन्मनि ॥१३॥
पुत्रा येऽनन्तरस्त्रीजाः क्रमेणोक्ता द्विजन्मनाम् ।
ताननन्तरनाम्नस्तु मातृदोषात्प्रचक्षते ॥१४॥
ब्राह्मणादुग्रकन्यायामावृतो नाम जायते ।
आभीरोऽम्बष्ठकन्यायामायोगव्यां तु धिग्वणः ॥१५॥
आयोगवश्च क्षत्ता च चण्डालश्चाधमो नृणाम् ।
प्रातिलोम्येन जायन्ते शूद्रादपसदास्त्रयः ॥१६॥

°वैदेहो; Pu^{10} °वेदेहौ; oOr °वेदेहा — d) nKt^{4} राज्ञीवि°; La^{1} राजपुत्राङ्ग°; tMd^{4} °ङ्गनासु च; Hy Pu^{10} °सुतो

12. Pādas c-d omitted in Tr^{1}. Cited by *Mādh* 1.513 — a) [*Jolly* N] शूद्रादयोगवः; Ho sOx^{1} sPu^{6} शूद्राच्चायोगवः; bKt^{5} शूद्रायायोगवः; Bo शूद्रादौयोगव; tMd^{4} °योगवं; oOr Pu^{5} Pu^{7} क्षत्ताश्चण्डा°; Tr^{2} क्षत्ताश्चाण्डा°; Tj^{1} Tr^{1} क्षाताश्चण्डा°; bKt^{5} tMd^{4} क्षत्राच्चण्डा° — b) wKt^{3} La^{1} Ox^{2} nPu^{1} Pu^{3} Tr^{2} [*Jolly* Ku] चाण्डा°; Bo Tj^{1} चण्डालाश्चा°; tMd^{4} चण्डालस्याधमो; nKt^{4} °धवो; Hy नृणं — d) gMd^{5} जायते; Ho nKt^{4} °शंकराः; Be^{1} gMd^{5} Pu^{10} Tr^{2} [*Jolly* Nd] °संकरः; Pu^{5} Pu^{7} °संकरो; La^{1} Lo^{2} gMd^{1} tMd^{4} nNg nPu^{1} Pu^{2} Pu^{4} Wa [*Jolly* M G] *Jolly* °संकरे; oOr °संकरेः

13.* Omitted in Pu^{5} Tr^{1} — a) nPu^{1} एकान्तरा; tMd^{4} ह्यानु°; bCa Jo^{2} Lo^{3} gMy Tj^{1} Wa चानु° — b) Jo^{2} Lo^{3} Tj^{1} °म्यादुग्राम्बष्ठौ; mTr^{4} oOr °ष्ठोग्रो; Pu^{7} [*Jolly* G] तथा; tMd^{4} स्मृते; mTr^{4} स्मृतः; La^{1} सुतौ — c) Be^{1} bCa wKt^{1} nKt^{4} Lo^{4} tMd^{4} nPu^{1} Pu^{2} Pu^{3} Pu^{4} Pu^{7} mTr^{6} Wa क्षत्र°; bBe^{2} Pu^{8} क्षत्रि°; bBe^{2} nPu^{1} Pu^{3} Pu^{4} Wa °वैदेहिकौ; Lo^{2} °वैदेहको; tMd^{4} तत्त्वात् — d) Tr^{2} प्रतिलोमेन; Pu^{8} प्रातिलोम्येनु; nPu^{1} प्रतिलोमेनु; Ho प्रातिलोमनि; bCa Lo^{4} gMy oOr Pu^{7} Wa [*Jolly* M G Nd] *Jolly* प्रातिलोम्ये तु; Pu^{10} प्रतिलोम्ये तु; bKt^{5} Pu^{2} Pu^{4} mTr^{5} प्रतिलोमे तु; bBe^{2} Hy Jm Jo^{1} wKt^{3} Kt^{2} Lo^{2} Tj^{2} mTr^{3} mTr^{4} mTr^{6} *Mandlik Jha KSS Dave* प्रातिलोम्येपि; Lo^{1} प्रातिलोम्येति; Bo Pu^{3} nKt^{4} प्रतिलोमेपि; Be^{1} प्रातिलोम्येषु; nNg प्रातिलोम्येत्रनन्मनि

14. Cited by *Viś* 1.1; pāda-a cited by *Viś* 1.14 — a) oOr Wa पुत्रो; tMd^{4} पुत्र एकान्तर°; bBe^{2} Tr^{1} येनान्तर°; sOx^{1} sPu^{6} Tr^{2} येनन्तरा°; bBe^{2} tMd^{3} [at 14 but not in addition after 6] Tr^{1} mTr^{4} °स्त्रीषु क्रमे° — b) Tr^{2} °णोक्तो; bKt^{5} °णोक्त; Ho द्विजन्मनी; tMd^{3} [at 14 but not in addition after 6] द्विजन्मनः — c) Pu^{5} Pu^{7} °नन्तरजातास्तु; Pu^{2} Pu^{4} °नन्तरजातांस्तु; tMd^{3} [at 14 but not in addition after 6] Tj^{1} °नाम्नास्तु; tMd^{4} °नाम्यस्तु — d) Lo^{1} gMd^{1} tMd^{3} [at 14] tMd^{4} Pu^{5} Pu^{7} mTr^{5} °दोषान्प्र°; tMd^{3} [at 6] °दोषो प्र°; bCa °त्प्रचक्ष्यते; Bo °त्प्रशस्यते; gMy °त्प्रमुच्यते

15. Verses 15 and 16 transposed in gMy Pu^{2}; [*Jolly* Nd] places verse 15 after 17; not commented by *Me*; pādas c-d omitted in bKt^{5}. Cited by *Lakṣ* 12.820 — b) Pu^{2} Pu^{4} °मावृत्तो; gMd^{5} °मवृतो; gMy °मावितो; Lo^{3} Tj^{1} °मातृतो; Tr^{1} °माप्रीतो — c) Bo Ho अभीरो; tMd^{3} अन्निरो; mTr^{6} °कन्ययामायो°; Lo^{1} °कन्याया आयो° — d) bBe^{2} °योगय्यां; Lo^{1} °गव्या; Pu^{10} °गव्यं; tMd^{4} °गवां; Bo °गव्यात्तु; oOr च; bBe^{2} gMd^{1} tMd^{3} gMy धिग्वनः; Bo धिग्विणः; Ox^{2} धिग्बलः; nPu^{1} धीगुणः; Pu^{10} धिगुणः; Tr^{1} धन्विनः; Be^{1} दिग्गुणः; Tj^{1} दिग्बणः; La^{1} विग्रणः; tMd^{4} निस्वनः

16. Omitted in bKt^{5}; not commented by *Me*. Cited by *Mādh* 1.513 — a) Pu^{4} अयोग°; Bo प्रायोग°; tMd^{4} °गवं च; Tj^{1} °गवस्तु; Pu^{10} वा — b) Jm Jo^{1} wKt^{3} Lo^{1} Lo^{4} oOr Ox^{2} Pu^{5} Pu^{7} Pu^{10} Tr^{2} चाण्डा° — c) Pu^{2} Pu^{4} प्रतिलो°; Tj^{2} जायन्त — d) nPu^{1} जायन्तेपरेप्यपसदास्त्रयः; gMy Pu^{3} mTr^{3} mTr^{4}

वैश्यान्मागधवैदेहौ क्षत्रियात्सूत एव तु ।
प्रतीपमेते जायन्ते परेऽप्यपसदास्त्रयः ॥१७॥
जातो निषादाच्छूद्रायां जात्या भवति पुल्कसः ।
शूद्राज्जातो निषाद्यां तु स वै कुक्कुटकः स्मृतः ॥१८॥
क्षत्तुर्जातस्तथोग्र्यां तु श्वपाक इति कीर्त्यते ।
वैदेहकेन त्वम्बष्ठ्यामुत्पन्नो वेण उच्यते ॥१९॥
द्विजातयः सवर्णासु जनयन्त्यव्रतांस्तु यान् ।
तान्सावित्रीपरिभ्रष्टान् व्रात्यानित्यभिनिर्दिशेत् ॥२०॥
व्रात्यात्तु जायते विप्रात् पापात्मा भृज्जकण्टकः* ।
आवन्त्यवाटधानौ च पुष्पधः शैख* एव च ॥२१॥

MTr[5] MTr[6] °पशदा°; sOx[1] sPu[6] °प्रसदा°; Bo °पहता°; GMd[1] °पशदास्त्रियः; Tr[1] °पशतस्त्रियः; TMd[3] °पदिदास्त्रियः

17. Omitted in Lo[3] GMy Tj[1] [haplo]; not commented by *Me*; pādas c-d omitted in wKt[1]; sequence of verses in Jm is 19, 18, 17. Pādas a-b cited by *Mādh* 2.56 — a) Tr[1] वैश्याः माग°; TMd[3] वैश्यां मगध°; Bo NKt[4] Lo[1] Wa °वैदेहो — b) TMd[3] °यात्सन्त; BBe[2] Jo[2] wKt[1] La[1] Lo[1] Lo[4] NNg oOr NPu[1] Pu[2] Pu[4] Pu[5] Pu[7] Pu[10] Wa च; [*Jolly* M] वा — c) BBe[2] प्रातिलोम्येन जायन्ते; Be[1] Ho NKt[4] GMd[1] TMd[3] TMd[4] sOx[1] NPu[1] sPu[6] MTr[5] प्रतीपमेव; Pu[3] Pu[4] प्रतीपमेवं — d) Jm Kt[2] शूद्रादपसदा°; TMd[4] परस्यपसदा°; NKt[4] GMd[1] TMd[3] GMd[5] Pu[3] Tr[1] MTr[3] MTr[4] MTr[6] °पशदा°

18* Omitted in GMy. Cited by *Lakṣ* 12.820 — a) Tr[1] निषादाः शूद्रायां; oOr निषादः शूद्रायां — b) sOx[1] sPu[6] जात्यां; Tr[2] जात्यो; wKt[3] जाति; Be[1] पुःकसः; BBe[2] BCa Jm Jo[1] wKt[1] Kt[2] NKt[4] La[1] NNg oOr sOx[1] Ox[2] sPu[6] Tj[2] [*Jolly* Ku]*Mandlik Jha KSS* पुक्कसः; wKt[1] wKt[3] पुक्कशः; Bo Jo[2] Lo[2] Lo[4] TMd[4] NPu[1] Pu[2] Pu[3] Pu[4] Pu[5] Pu[7] Pu[8] Pu[10] Tr[2] Wa [*Jolly* M G] पुष्कसः; Hy युक्कसः; BKt[5] तस्करः — c) Pu[2] Pu[4] शूद्राज्जातस्तु मैषद्यां; La[1] शूद्राज्जायते निषाद्यां तु; BKt[5] GMd[1] निषाद्यायां [*om* तु]; NKt[4] TMd[4] NPu[1] MTr[4] MTr[6] निषाद्यां यः — d) Tr[1] सर्वे कुक्कु°; Pu[2] Pu[4] कुकुटकः; Tj[1] स्मृताः

19 Cited by *Lakṣ* 12.820; *Mādh* 2.248 — a) TMd[3] GMy GMd[5] Tr[1] MTr[4] MTr[6] [*Jolly* Nd] उग्रात्तु जातः क्षत्तायां; TMd[4] उग्राज्जातः क्षत्रियायां; oOr क्षतृजात°; wKt[1] °स्तथाग्र्यास्तु; NKt[4] °स्तथाग्रातु; BBe[2] °स्तथोग्रां तु; Hy Jm Jo[1] Jo[2] Kt[2] Lo[3] Tj[1] Tj[2] MTr[3] [*Jolly* R Ku]*Rc Mandlik Jha KSS Dave* °स्तथोग्रायां [*om* तु]; Be[1] sOx[1] sPu[6] *om* तु — b) Ho भूपाक; Tj[1] विपाक — c) NPu[1] Pu[4] Pu[5] Pu[7] Tr[1] वैदेहिकेन; Pu[2] Pu[4] °केन अम्ब° — d) Bo Ho Lo[4] GMd[1] GMy NNg sOx[1] NPu[1] Pu[2] Pu[3] Pu[5] sPu[6] Pu[7] Tr[1] MTr[4] MTr[6] [*Jolly* G Nd] वेन; Tr[2] वेनं; Be[1] वेर; TMd[4] मेव; Pu[10] व्रिण

20. Cited by *Lakṣ* 12.826 — a) TMd[4] द्विजातयस्तु सर्वासु; TMd[3] द्विजातस्सव°; oOr द्विजातयो-सव°; Be[1] सवर्णांस्तु; Tr[2] सुवर्णासु — b) TMd[4] जनयन्ति व्रतांस्तु; BKt[5] °व्रतास्तु; Lo[3] Pu[2] Pu[4] Tj[1] °व्रतांश्च; TMd[3] GMd[5] GMy Pu[5] Pu[7] Tr[1] [*Jolly* G N] °व्रतान्सुतान्; Bo °व्रतात्सुयान्; Be[1] BBe[2] BKt[5] तान् — c) GMd[5] सावित्र्या च परिभ्रष्टान् — c-d) *Me* [pāṭha rejected by him] अव्रतायां जनयन्ति तान्व्रात्यान्विनिर्दिशेत्; TMd[3] °भ्रष्टा व्रात्या इत्य° — d) Hy Jm Jo[1] Kt[2] Tj[2] MTr[3] *Mr Mandlik Jha KSS Dave* °त्यानिति विनिर्दिशेत्; wKt[3] °त्यानित्यतिनिर्दिशेत्; Lo[3] °त्यानित्यपि निर्दिशेत्; MTr[6] °त्यानित्यभि-धीयते

21* Pādas c-d omitted in Tr[1]. Cited by *Lakṣ* 12.826 — a) Wa विप्रात्तु जायते व्रात्यात्; La[1] Tr[1] व्रात्यांतु; Be[1] व्रात्यास्तु; oOr व्रात्यस्तु; Pu[2] Pu[4] व्रात्या तु; TMd[4] व्रात्यांतो; NPu[1] व्रात्यायां; Be[1] विप्रान्; GMd[1] विप्र्यां — b) Pu[8] भृर्ज्ज°; Tj[2] भज्ज°; Be[1] भृज°; GMy भृज्य°; NKt[4] नृज्ज°; GMd[5] Tr[1] MTr[4] MTr[6]

झल्लो मल्लश्च राजन्याद् व्रात्याल्लिच्छिविरेव च ।
नटश्च करणश्चैव खसो द्रविड एव च ॥२२॥
वैश्यात्तु जायते व्रात्यात् सुधन्वाचार्य एव च ।
कारुषश्च विजन्मा च मैत्रः सात्वत एव च ॥२३॥
व्यभिचारेण वर्णानामवेद्यावेदनेन च ।
स्वकर्मणां च त्यागेन जायते वर्णसंकरः ॥२४॥
संकीर्णयोनयो ये तु प्रतिलोमानुलोमजाः ।
अन्योन्यव्यतिषक्ताश्च तान्प्रवक्ष्याम्यशेषतः ॥२५॥

भृत्य°; gMd^1 tMd^4 भ्रज्य°; [*Jolly* Nd Gr] भूत्य°; mTr^5 हुज्ज°; bBe^2 Bo bCa Ho Hy Jm Jo^1 Jo^2 wKt^1 Kt^2 wKt^3 Lo^4 oOr Pu^3 Tj^1 Tr^2 mTr^3 [*Jolly* Ku R] *Mandlik KSS Jha Dave* भूर्ज°; Lo^3 भुर्ज°; tMd^3 हृद्य° — c) nKt^4 Pu^5 आवन्त्या°; sBe^2 आयन्त्य°; bKt^5 अवर्श्र्व°; Be^1 °वटधानौ; Jo^2 °पाटधनौ; Lo^2 °वाटेधानौ; Pu^2 Pu^4 °वाटध्मानौ; sOx^1 sPu^6 °वाढधानौ; La^1 °वाढत्तानौ; Ho °वादधानौ; tMd^3 °पागयानौ — d) Tr^2 पुष्पवत्शेख भूयसः; Pu^5 Pu^7 [*Jolly* G] पुष्पं शैखकस्तथा [*Jolly* G पुष्यः]; sOx^1 sPu^6 पुष्प [lacuna] खरस्तथा; Ho पुष्पवध्रैषरस्तथा; Be^1 La^1 nPu^1 पुष्पवः; oOr पुष्पकः; Pu^2 Pu^4 पुष्पक; mTr^4 पुष्पलः; mTr^6 पुष्पवन्; gMd^1 पुष्पवं; bKt^5 पुष्करः; bBe^2 पत्र्यौधः; tMd^3 पुष्पकश्शैच; Lo^4 [*Jolly* M^4] *Jolly* पुष्पशैखर; [*Jolly* M^{1-2-5}] पुष्पशेखर; [*Jolly* M^3] पुष्पशखर; [*Jolly* M^9] पुष्परेषर; nKt^4 पुस्यवः शैत्व; [*Jolly* Nd] पुष्पशीबक; nNg Wa पुष्पशेषर; bBe^2 Pu^8 Pu^{10} शेख; La^1 शैथ; Kt^2 wKt^3 nPu^1 Pu^3 शैष; Lo^2 शैषा; wKt^1 bKt^5 शेष; wKt^1 nPu^1 Pu^2 Pu^4 उच्यते *for* एव च

22. Omitted in gMd^1 Pu^5 Tr^1; not commented by *Me*; pādas b-d omitted in Lo^2. Cited by *Lakṣ* 12.826 — a) Jo^2 रल्लो; Lo^3 Tj^1 कल्लो; nKt^4 La^1 mTr^4 सल्लो; Pu^2 Pu^4 शल्लो; Bo मल्लो; Lo^1 Ox^2 भल्लो; nPu^1 भिल्लो; Be^1 झलो मलश्च; gMd^5 मल्लाश्च; tMd^3 मल्लिश्च; La^1 Tr^2 राजन्या; Tj^1 राजन्यान् — b) La^1 व्रात्याछिल्लिवि°; Be^1 Ho nKt^4 sPu^6 Pu^7 mTr^5 व्रात्याल्लिच्छवि°; mTr^4 mTr^6 व्रात्याल्लच्छवि°; tMd^3 व्रात्याद्विछिचि°; bBe^2 bCa Hy Jm Jo^1 wKt^1 Kt^2 bKt^5 Lo^3 Lo^4 Pu^8 Tj^1 mTr^3 *Mandlik KSS Dave* व्रात्यान्निच्छिवि°; sOx^1 sPu^6 Tr^2 व्रात्यान्निच्छवि°; gMy [*Jolly* Nd] °च्छिखिरेव — c) mTr^6 नटश्चैव करणश्च; gMy नटकश्चारणश्चैव; La^1 मठश्च करकश्चैव; tMd^3 तटश्च; Bo करणे चैव; wKt^3 करणैश्चैव; Tj^2 करुणश्चैव — d) Be^1 bCa wKt^1 wKt^3 gMd^5 खशो; nKt^4 gMy mTr^4 खषो; nPu^1 Pu^4 खखो; Bo क्षसो; bKt^5 वेषो; tMd^3 घोषो; Ox^2 श्वशो; La^1 यशो; gMd^5 द्रविळ; nKt^4 mTr^4 द्रमिड; tMd^3 द्रमिळ; Be^1 nNg Pu^7 Tj^1 द्रविण; Pu^7 वा

23* Omitted in gMd^1 nNg; pāda-a omitted in Lo^2. Cited by *Lakṣ* 12.826 — a) Wa व्रात्यात्तु जायते वैश्यात्; bKt^5 वैश्यान्तु; nKt^4 वैश्यं तु; Pu^2 Pu^4 वैश्य तु; La^1 वैश्यायां जा°; nKt^4 जायन्ते; Be^1 nPu^1 व्रात्यां; Bo gMy Pu^2 Pu^4 mTr^6 व्रात्या — b) *Jolly* सुधन्वा चार्य; bCa एव तु — c) La^1 कारुष एवानिजन्मा च; tMd^3 भातुषश्च निजंघुश्च; Pu^8 कारूषश्च; bBe^2 कारुषाश्च; gMy [*Jolly* Nd] कारुजश्च; Lo^3 कारूपश्च; tMd^4 sOx^1 sPu^6 पारुषश्च; bKt^5 मारुषश्च; nKt^4 Tr^2 mTr^5 Wa भारुषश्च; nKt^4 निजन्मा च; gMy निजयाश्च; tMd^4 gMd^5 mTr^4 mTr^{5}mTr^6 [*Jolly* Nd] निजङ्घश्च; Tr^1 निजंयश्च — d) Pu^2 Pu^4 मित्रः; sOx^1 nPu^1 sPu^6 Wa सान्त्वत; Ho gMy mTr^6 सत्वत; nKt^4 स्वात्वत; Lo^2 सात्वेत; wKt^1 साद्वित; bKt^5 शाद्वत; Be^1 साभृत; tMd^3 वा

24. Omitted in Pu^5 [*Jolly* Nd] — a) Tr^2 अभिचा°; gMd^5 °चार्येण — b) Tr^1 °नां वेद्यावेदकुलेन च; tMd^4 gMd^5 sOx^1 Ox^2 sPu^6 °मावेद्या°; Ho Pu^7 °माविद्या°; nKt^4 °नां प्रवेद्या° — c) Bo सवर्णानां — d) Bo Ho Hy Jm Jo^1 wKt^1 Kt^2 bKt^5 tMd^4 gMy sOx^1 Ox^2 Pu^3 sPu^6 Pu^8 Tj^2 Tr^2 mTr^3 mTr^4 *Rc Mandlik Jha KSS Dave* जायन्ते वर्णसंकराः

25. Cited by *Lakṣ* 12.820 — a) tMd^4 संकीर्णवर्णयो; bCa Pu^4 Tr^1 ये च; bKt^5 यस्तु; Pu^{10} येपु

सूतो वैदेहकश्चैव चण्डालश्च नराधमः ।
मागधः क्षत्तृजातिश्च तथायोगव एव च ॥२६॥
एते षट् सदृशान्वर्णाञ्जनयन्ति स्वयोनिषु ।
मातृजात्या प्रसूयन्ते प्रवरासु च योनिषु ॥२७॥
यथा त्रयाणां वर्णानां द्वयोरात्मास्य जायते ।
आनन्तर्यात्स्वयोन्यां तु तथा बाह्येष्वपि क्रमः ॥२८॥
ते चापि बाह्यान्सुबहूंस्ततोऽप्यधिकदूषितान् ।
परस्परस्य दारेषु जनयन्ति विगर्हितान् ॥२९॥
यथैव शूद्रो ब्राह्मण्यां बाह्यं जन्तुं प्रसूयते ।
तथा बाह्यतरं बाह्यश्चातुर्वर्ण्ये प्रसूयते ॥३०॥

— b) Be[1] °लोमतः; TMd[3] °लोमयोः — c) NPu[1] °वृतिषक्ताश्च; Be[1] °व्यभिशस्ताश्च; GMd[1] TMd[3] GMd[5] Pu[5] Pu[7] MTr[6] °षिक्ताश्च; BBe[2] °षक्तास्तु; BKt[5] °षिक्तास्य; wKt[3] °सक्ताश्च; Lo[1] °षक्तांश्च; Tr[2] °व्याक्ताश्च — d) BBe[2] तान्विवक्षा°; BKt[5] तान्प्रचक्षस्यशे°

26. Cited by *Lakṣ* 12.821 — a) Pu[2] Pu[4] सूतौ; BBe[2] Pu[7] Wa वैदेहिक° — b) Jm Lo[1] oOr Pu[5] Pu[7] [*Jolly* G R] चाण्डा°; Bo GMd[1] Tr[1] चण्डालाश्च; *Lakṣ* °लश्चाधमो नृणां; Bo GMd[1] Tr[2] °धमाः — c) Be[1] La[1] मागधश्चैव क्षत्ता च [Be[1] क्षत्ताश्च]; GMd[5] मागधाः; Lo[2] क्षात्तृ°; BCa BKt[5] Lo[1] Pu[2] Pu[4] Pu[5] Pu[7] Tj[1] Tr[2] MTr[6] क्षत्र°; Bo क्षत्रि°; Hy Lo[3] TMd[3] Tr[1] क्षत्त°; BBe[2] °जातिस्तु; Bo Jo[2] Lo[3] TMd[4] Ox[2] Tj[1] °जातश्च — d) Bo तथायोगं च एव च; Lo[2] *om* एव च; La[1] वा

27* Pādas c-d omitted in BKt[5] Tj[1]. Cited by *Lakṣ* 12.821 — a) Lo[3] Tj[1] एतान्षट्; Tr[1] एतेषां सदृ°; NKt[4] सदृशात्कर्णा°; NNg *om* वर्णान्; T Md[4] °शान्वर्णं जन° — b) GMd[5] Tr[1] [*Jolly* Gr] °नयन्ति विगर्हितान्; Tj[2] स्वजातिषु; Be[1] च योनिषु — c) Pu[4] भ्रातृ°; *Me Jha* °जात्याः; BBe[2] Bo Ho Hy Jm Jo[1] Jo[2] wKt[1] Kt[2] wKt[3] La[1] Lo[3] GMd[1] NNg sOx[1] sPu[6] Tj[2] Tr[1] MTr[5] Wa [*Jolly* N Ku R] *Lakṣ Go Nā Nd* °जात्यां; Lo[1] °जात्यं; Lo[2] Ox[2] Pu[5] Pu[7] Pu[8] *Bh Me* [pāṭha] *RcJolly* °जातौ; oOr प्रजायन्ते; Tr[2] प्रहीयन्ते — c-d) Be[1] NKt[4] Lo[2] Ox[2] Pu[5] Pu[7] [*Jolly* G] मातृजातौ स्वयोन्यां तु सदृशं जनयन्ति वै [Be[1] NKt[4] °जात्यां; Lo[2] च]

28. Cited by *Lakṣ* 12.821 — a) Lo[1] TMd[4] तथा — b) GMy द्वयोराजा प्रजायते; Pu[3] Tr[2] °रात्मैव; NPu[1] °रात्माश्च; TMd[3] GMd[5] Ox[2] Pu[8] Tr[1] °रात्मा प्रजायते — c) Bo La[1] Tj[1] अनन्त°; Tr[2] आनन्त्ययात्स्व°; wKt[1] GMy आनन्तर्यां स्व°; TMd[3] आनन्तर्या स्व°; BBe[2] °योन्यास्तु; Pu[3] °योन्याश्च; TMd[3] TMd[4] GMd[5] °योन्यासु; Be[1] Lo[1] Lo[4] GMy NNg Pu[5] Pu[7] Pu[10] Tr[1] Tr[2] Wa [*Jolly* M G Nd] *Go Lakṣ Jolly* च — d) Tj[1] यथा; Be[1] Pu[5] Pu[7] [*Jolly* G] बाह्येष्वयं; wKt[1] बाह्येष्वपक्रमः; BKt[5] बाह्येष्वनुक्रमः; Lo[1] बाह्येष्वविक्रमः; MTr[4] MTr[6] बाह्येषु विक्रमः; GMy क्रमं; TMd[4] क्रयः; Hy Jm Jo[1] Kt[2] MTr[3] *Mandlik KSS Dave* क्रमात्

29. Pādas c-d omitted in Pu[2] Pu[4]. Cited by *Lakṣ* 12.821 — a) GMd[1] तेषां विवाह्यान्सुब°; Pu[7] [*but mc*] बाह्यापिसुब; TMd[3] GMy बाह्या सुब° — b) Jo[1] °स्तप्तो; Lo[2] °स्स्वतो; Ho Lo[4] sOx[1] Ox[2] sPu[6] Pu[10] Tr[2] MTr[5] *Bh* °भ्यधिक°; BBe[2] °दोषितान्; TMd[3] °मोहितान् — c) Be[1] परस्परेषु; NNg परस्परदारेषु; Kt[2] परस्परपदारेषु — d) BBe[2] प्रगर्हितान्

30. Omitted in Pu[10]; pādas a-b omitted in Bo and pādas c-d in TMd[4]. Cited by *Lakṣ* 12.821 — a) GMd[1] GMd[5] sOx[1] sPu[6] Tj[2] तथैव; Jo[2] wKt[1] wKt[3] Lo[3] Tj[1] यथा हि; GMd[1] शूद्रे; Tj[1] ब्राह्मण्या — b) TMd[3] बाह्यकरं तु प्रजायते; GMd[5] GMy Pu[4] बाह्य; Ox[2] बाह्यान्; Tj[1] जन्तुः; BKt[5] La[1] NPu[1] Pu[4] जन्तु; Pu[8] प्रजायते — c) BBe[2] यथा; Tr[1] Tr[2] बाह्यान्तरं; Tj[1] बाह्यंतरं; TMd[3] बाह्यतरो; sOx[1]

प्रतिकूलं वर्तमाना बाह्या बाह्यतरान्पुनः ।
हीना हीनान् प्रसूयन्ते वर्णान्पञ्चदशैव तु ॥३१॥
प्रसाधनोपचारज्ञमदासं दास्यजीवनम् ।
सैरन्ध्रं वागुरावृत्तिं सूते दस्युरयोगवे ॥३२॥
मैत्रेयकं तु वैदेहो माधूकं संप्रसूयते ।
नॄन् प्रशंसत्यजस्रं यो घण्टाताडोऽरुणोदये ॥३३॥
निषादो मार्गवं सूते दाशं नौकर्मजीविनम्
कैवर्तमिति यं प्राहुरार्यावर्तनिवासिनः ॥३४॥

sPu6 बाह्याश्चा°; wKt3 BKt5 Lo2 Lo4 Ox2 Pu2 Pu4 बाह्याच्चा°; Ho NNg बाह्यच्चा°; La1 Tj1 बाह्या चा°; BBe2 oOr बाह्यचा° — c-d) Be1 Pu5 Pu7 *Go* तथा बाह्यतरं बाह्याद्बाह्यो वर्णः प्रसूयते — d) NKt4 sOx1 sPu6 °श्चतु°; NPu1 °तुर्वर्ण्यं; Ho °तुर्वर्ण्यां; NNg °तुर्वर्ण्या; sOx1 sPu6 °तुर्वर्ण्यात्; Bo wKt1 NKt4 Pu4 Tr1 °तुर्वर्णे; La1 °तुर्वर्णं; BKt5 °तुर्वर्णान्; Pu3 Tr2 °तुर्वर्णेषु सूयते; GMd1 प्रकीर्त्यते

31. Cited by *Lakṣ* 12.821 — a) sOx1 sPu6 Tr2 °कूल; GMd1 °कूले; BBe2 Tr1 वर्तमानो; Tr2 वर्तमानान्; TMd4 वर्तमनां; Pu2 Pu4 व्रतमाना — b) Tj1 बाह्य; Be1 GMd5 Pu5 Pu7 बाह्यान्; Tr1 बाह्यान्तराः पुनः; Ho NKt4 sOx1 Pu5 sPu6 Pu7 °तरात्पुनः; TMd4 °तरत्पुनः; Bo La1 GMd5 °तरं पुनः; Pu2 Pu4 °तरां पुनः; BKt5 Ox2 NPu1 °तराः पुनः; GMd1 °तरान्वह — c) GMd5 GMy Pu2 Pu4 MTr4 MTr6 Wa हीना हीनाः; wKt3 Tj1 हीना हीना; Ox2 हीनान्हीनान्; GMy BKt5 Lo4 हीनहीनात्; oOr हीनान्हीनः; TMd3 हीनास्वनाः; La1 हीनाधीनाः; MTr4 हीनाद्धीनाः; Tr2 हीनानुसूयन्ते; Lo2 संसूयन्ते; Lo4 प्रसूते; TMd4 प्रयन्त्येव; GMd5 GMy MTr4 प्रजायन्ते — d) NKt4 वर्णानां च दशैव तु; Ho Tj1 वर्णात्पञ्च°; La1 GMy NPu1 Pu2 Pu4 वर्णाः पञ्च°; BKt5 वर्णा पञ्च°; sOx1 sPu6 °दशैव तत्

32. Cited by *Lakṣ* 12.821 — a) Be1 Lo3 प्रसादनो° — a-b) Pu2 Pu4 °चारज्ञः सदासं [Pu4 °ज्ञाः] — b) TMd3 °चारज्ञमत्स्यादं; Tr1 °मादासं; Be1 BCa wKt3 Lo1 sOx1 NPu1 sPu6 °दास्यं; Jo2 °दाशं; Hy Jm Jo1 Jo2 Kt2 wKt3 Lo1 Lo3 oOr Pu3 MTr3 *Mandlik KSS* दासजी°; Lo1 दास्यजी°; Lo2 °जीवनां; BCa Jm Jo2 wKt1 Lo3 Lo4 sOx1 Ox2 Pu2 Pu4 sPu6 Pu8 MTr3 MTr4 MTr6 °जीविनं; NKt4 °जीवितं — c) TMd3 सैरन्ध्रकं गुरावृत्तिं; sOx1 sPu6 सैरध्र; Ho सैरन्ध्रे; Tr2 सैरध्रं; Jm Jo1 Jo2 Kt2 wKt3 Ox2 MTr3 [*Jolly* Ku] *Mandlik KSS Dave* सैरिन्ध्रं; Hy सौरिध्रं; wKt1 सैवन्ध्रं; BKt5 सैरन्द्रां; Pu3 शौरन्द्रं — d) Pu2 Pu4 प्रसूते दस्युयागतिः; Be1 La1 GMd5 सुतो; GMd1 TMd3 TMd4 GMd5 GMy MTr4 MTr6 दस्युमयोगवः [GMd1 MTr6 दस्यम°; MTr4 दास्यम°; TMd4 दस्सुम°; GMd5 °गवैः; GMy °गवेः; MTr6 °गवं]; Wa °योगवः

33. Pādas c-d *ma* in Lo1. Cited by *Lakṣ* 12.821 — a) Pu4 मित्रेयकं; BKt5 मैत्रयकं; *Bh* [pāṭha] मैरेयकं; TMd4 मैत्रत्वकं; GMd5 मैत्रेयाणां; BBe2 *om* तु; Bo वेदेहो; BBe2 वैदेहौ; oOr वैदेहान् — a-b) BKt5 माधुकं वैदेहः — b) Be1 Bo La1 Lo3 GMd1 GMy Pu2 Pu4 MTr4 MTr6 माधुकं; GMd1 TMd3 TMd4 मधुकं; Pu10 मधूकं; Tr1 माधूरं; *Nd* माधुर; Jm मागधं; Ox2 संप्रजायते — c) La1 त्रीणि प्रशस्यं प्रजस्रं; BBe2 Pu2 Pu3 त्रीन्; Pu2 Pu4 प्रशंसन्त्य°; MTr6 प्रशस्यत्य°; wKt3 °जस्रं स — d) sOx1 sPu6 °ताण्डो; Ox2 °ताड्ये; Pu5 Pu7 °वादो; Bo Pu3 °नादो; BKt5 °तनो; MTr4 MTr6 °काडो; TMd3 GMd5 °ताळो; Tr1 °तार्थो

34* Pādas a-b *ma* in Lo1; lacuna for whole verse after निषाद in GMy; pādas c-d omitted in Pu2 Pu4. Cited by *Lakṣ* 12.822 — a) GMd5 GMy निषाद; La1 विषादो; Ho मार्गावं; GMd1 GMd5 Pu2 Pu4 Tr1 MTr4 MTr5 MTr6 *Bh* मार्गरं; TMd3 मार्गकं; NPu1 मार्गसं; BKt5 मार्दवं; sOx1 Ox2 Pu5 sPu6 Pu7 [*Jolly* G] मागधं; Tr2 माकुरं; La1 Tr1 सूतो — b) Tr1 दश; GMd1 दौशं; Be1 BBe2 Bo Ho Jo1 Kt2 Lo1 Lo4 [*but cor*] NNg oOr sOx1 NPu1 Pu2 Pu4 sPu6 Pu10 Tr2 Wa *Mandlik Jha KSS Dave* दासं; Lo2 दासां; BKt5 दास; Pu5 Pu7 दासो; TMd4 कोनं; Be1 शैकर्म°; Bo दौकर्म°; TMd4 नाकर°; NPu1 °जीविनां; Be1 BBe2 Bo Hy wKt1 wKt3 Lo1 Tj1 Tr2 °जीवनं; MTr4 °जीवनः; NKt4 °जीविजं — c) Be1

मृतवस्त्रभृत्स्वनार्यासु गर्हितान्नाशनासु च ।
भवन्त्यायोगवीष्वेते जातिहीनाः पृथक् त्रयः ॥३५॥
कारावरो निषादात्तु चर्मकारः प्रसूयते ।
वैदेहकादन्ध्रमेदौ बहिर्ग्रामप्रतिश्रयौ ॥३६॥
चण्डालात्पाण्डुसोपाकस्त्वक्सारव्यवहारवान् ।
आहिण्डिको निषादेन वैदेह्यामेव जायते ॥३७॥
चण्डालेन तु सोपाको मूलव्यसनवृत्तिमान् ।
पुल्कस्यां जायते पापः सदा सज्जनगर्हितः ॥३८॥

Bo Ho Jo^2 wKt^3 Lo^1 Lo^2 Lo^3 tMd^3 sOx^1 Pu^5 sPu^6 Pu^7 Tj^1 Tr^1 Wa कैवर्त इति; nNg कैवर्त इत्ययं; mTr^4 य:

35. Pādas a-b omitted in Pu^2 Pu^4; pādas c-d omitted in gMd^1. Cited by *Lakṣ* 12.822 — a) Hypermetric pāda; Jo^2 tMd^3 gMd^5 [*Jolly* R^2] मृतवस्त्रास्वनार्यासु; Bo Pu^5 Pu^7 मृतवस्त्रस्त्वनार्यासु [Bo °वस्त्रा°]; Tr^2 मृतवत्सास्वनार्यासु; Be^1 हतवस्त्रासु नार्यासु; bBe^2 मृतचर्मभृ°; Lo^1 °वस्त्रास्यनार्यासु; Tj^2 °भृत्स्वनायीषु; nPu^1 °भृत्स्वभार्यासु; Hy wKt^1 Lo^1 mTr^3 °भृत्सु नार्यासु; *KSS* °भृत्सु नारीषु; Kt^2 °हृत्सु नारीषु; Jo^1 *Mandlik* °भृत्सु नारी — b) La^1 °नार्यास्वगर्हिता°; Bo °तान्नासनासु; bKt^5 Lo^4 °तान्नादनासु; nNg °शनाय च — c) Bo भवत्या°; Tr^1 °गविष्वेते; tMd^3 °गवेष्वेत — d) Pu^4 ज्ञाति°; Bo जातो°; Pu^{10} Tr^2 Wa पृथक्त्रियः; nKt^4 bKt^5 gMd^5 Pu^2 Pu^3 Pu^4 Pu^5 Pu^7 [*Jolly* G] पृथक्क्रियाः; tMd^3 nPu^1 पृथ-क्क्रिया; La^1 oOr Ox^2 पृथक्क्रियः; Be^1 पृथक्क्रयः

36. Cited by *Lakṣ* 12.822 — a) tMd^4 काराधर्मो निषाध्यां तु; Be^1 La^1 nPu^1 कारावारो; Jo^2 कारवरो; Pu^2 Pu^4 कारावारे; Tr^2 कारोवरो; Tj^1 करारवो; Bo कारांबरो; gMd^1 कारापरे; tMd^3 कारावका; wKt^1 कारागवो [*mc sh to* °गिवो]; Lo^1 निषादस्तु; La^1 gMd^5 nPu^1 Pu^2 Pu^4 निषाद्यां तु; bKt^5 निषाद्यान्तु; tMd^3 निषाद्यां [*om* तु] — b) bKt^5 La^1 tMd^4 gMd^5 gMy Pu^3 Pu^{10} *Jha Dave* °कारं; sOx^1 sPu^6 °कारत्प्रसू°; Lo^1 °कारात्प्रसू°; Jo^2 Lo^3 Tj^1 प्रजायते; Tr^2 प्रशस्यते — c) Be^1 Hy Jo^1 wKt^1 Kt^2 Lo^2 Lo^3 Lo^4 Ox^2 Pu^2 Pu^4 Pu^{10} Tj^2 Tr^1 mTr^3 [*Jolly* M] *Bh Go Mr Mandlik Jha KSS Dave* वैदेहिका°; Pu^{10} वेदेहिका°; Tj^1 वैदेकादन्ध्र°; nKt^4 °कादप्रमदौ; gMd^5 Wa °मेदो; tMd^4 °मेदा; bBe^2 °मेधौ — d) mTr^4 mTr^6 बहिर्ग्रामप्रदूश्ययोः; gMy mTr^4 बहिर्ग्रामात्प्रति°; nPu^1 बहिर्ग्रामं प्रति°; Jm °श्रियौ; tMd^4 °श्रयोः; nPu^1 °श्रुतौ

37. Pādas a-b omitted in Pu^{10}; pādas b-d omitted in Pu^4 [haplo]; pādas a-b and c-d transposed in gMy Tr^1. Cited by *Lakṣ* 12.822 — a) bCa Ho La^1 gMd^5 Ox^2 Pu^5 Pu^7 Tr^2 चाण्डा°; tMd^3 चण्डालान्पा°; Pu^4 चण्डाल्यात्पा°; nKt^4 °शोपाक°; wKt^1 °शोपाद°; Bo Pu^3 °सौपाक°; tMd^3 °सोपर्क°; Tr^1 °लोपाक°; gMd^5 °सोपाकत्व°; bKt^5 °शोपाकत्व°; bBe^2 °शोकस्त्व°; gMd^1 °सोपाकौ त्व° — c) tMd^3 Pu^3 Tr^2 अहिण्डिको; sOx^1 sPu^6 आहिण्डको; Lo^4 अहिण्डको; Be^1 *mc to* आहिण्डिका; Lo^2 आहेण्डिको; Tj^1 आहिंविको; Tr^1 mTr^6 आभिण्डिको; La^1 आहितुण्डिको; Tr^1 निषाद्यां तु — c-d) gMd^1 निषादेन च वैदेह्याज्जायते वर्णसंकरः — d) Pu^2 वैदेह्यां नाम जायते; Jo^2 वेदेह्यामेव; Tr^1 वेदेहादेव; Tj^1 जायतौ

38. Omitted in Pu^5; pāda-a omitted in Pu^4. Cited by *Lakṣ* 12.822 — a) La^1 चण्डालेन स्वपाकस्तु; bKt^5 चण्डालो [*ma* पा] ण्डुशोपाको; Ho Jm wKt^1 Lo^1 Ox^2 Pu^{10} Tr^2 [*Jolly* MG] *Jolly* चाण्डा°; Tj^1 चण्डालोन; La^1 *om* तु; gMd^1 Pu^7 [*Jolly* G] च; sOx^1 sPu^6 सापाको; Pu^3 सौपाको — b) nKt^4 मौल°; gMd^1 tMd^4 mTr^4 mTr^6 Wa °वृत्तिकः; oOr °मूर्तिमान् — c) Bo Jo^2 bKt^5 Lo^2 Pu^2 Pu^4 Pu^7 Pu^8 Pu^{10} Tj^2 Tr^2 Wa [*Jolly* M] पुष्कस्यां; Ho Hy Jm Jo^1 wKt^1 Kt^2 La^1 oOr sOx^1 Ox^2 sPu^6 mTr^3 [*Jolly* Ku] *Mandlik KSS* पुक्कस्यां [see 10.18b note]; Lo^4 पुक्कस्या; wKt^3 पुक्कष्यां; Be^1

निषादस्त्री तु चण्डालात् पुत्रमन्त्यावसायिनम् ।
श्मशानगोचरं सूते बाह्यानामपि गर्हितम् ॥३९॥
संकरे जातयस्त्वेताः पितृमातृप्रदर्शिताः ।
प्रच्छन्ना वा प्रकाशा वा वेदितव्याः स्वकर्मभिः ॥४०॥
स्वजातिजानन्तरजाः षट् सुता द्विजधर्मिणः ।
शूद्राणां तु सधर्माणः सर्वेऽपध्वंसजाः स्मृताः ॥४१॥
तपोबीजप्रभावैश्च ते गच्छन्ति युगे युगे ।
उत्कर्षं चापकर्षं च मनुष्येष्विह जन्मतः ॥४२॥
शनकैस्तु क्रियालोपादिमाः क्षत्रियजातयः ।
वृषलत्वं गता लोके ब्राह्मणादर्शनेन च ॥४३॥

पु:कस्यां; NKt^{4} पुक्वस्यां; NNg पुंस्यां; Lo^{1} जप्यते; wKt^{1} पादः; TMd^{3} जन्तुः — d) TMd^{3} पापसज्जन°; NPu^{1} °वर्जितः

39. Cited by *Lakṣ* 12.822 — a) BBe^{2} निषाधस्त्री; Pu^{2} Pu^{10} °स्त्रीषु; BKt^{5} *om* तु; BBe^{2} Bo BCa Ho Jm wKt^{3} BKt^{5} Lo^{1} oOr Ox^{2} NPu^{1} Pu^{3} Pu^{4} Pu^{5} Pu^{7} Tr^{2} चाण्डालात् — b) Pu^{7} °मन्त्यवसा°; TMd^{3} GMy MTr^{6} °मन्तावसा°; GMd^{1} °मान्तवसा°; Be^{1} [*but cor*] °सायनं; GMd^{5} °सायिनः; wKt^{1} °सायिनां — c) TMd^{4} श्मशानं; wKt^{1} °गोचरः; wKt^{3} °गोचर; Ho °गोवरं — c-d) GMd^{1} श्मशानवासी गर्ह्यानां गह्यानपि गर्हितं — d) sOx^{1} sPu^{6} बाह्यामपि; TMd^{4} MTr^{4} MTr^{6} गर्हितः

Pu^{4} replaces pāda-d with 9.142 c-d; thereafter Pu^{4} replaces 40–47 with 9.143–150, verse 48 with 9.151 a-b, 152 c-d; verses 49–51 with 9.153–155; verse 52 with 9.156 a-b; and omits verses 53 and 54 a-b.

40. Pādas a-b omitted in La^{1}; pāda-d lacuna in MTr^{6}. Cited by *Lakṣ* 12.822 — a) Be^{1} संकीर्णयोनयस्त्वेताः; wKt^{1} Tj^{1} जायतस्त्वेताः; BKt^{5} जातयोस्त्वेताः; TMd^{3} जातवस्त्वेताः — b) GMd^{1} माता-पितृनिदर्शिताः; Tr^{2} मातृपितृ°; Hy *om* °मातृ°; GMd^{5} °प्रदर्शनाः; oOr Tr^{1} °विगर्हिताः — c) Ox^{2} प्रच्छन्ना-श्चाप्र°; Tr^{2} प्रकाशो; wKt^{1} प्रकाशाद्वा — d) Be^{1} वेदितव्यः; Bo TMd^{4} वेदितव्य; Be^{1} सुकर्मभिः

41. Omitted in Tj^{2} MTr^{6}. Cited by *Lakṣ* 12.824 — a) Be^{1} द्विजाति°; BBe^{2} Hy Jm Jo^{1} Kt^{2} MTr^{3} [*Jolly* G Ku] *Mandlik KSS Dave* सजाति°; Bo सजाती°; TMd^{3} GMd^{5} °न्तरजान्षट् — b) Pu^{10} षड्गुणा; MTr^{3} भूता; wKt^{1} तद्विधर्मिणः; GMd^{5} sOx^{1} sPu^{6} °धर्मणः; oOr Be^{1} [*but cor*] °कर्मिणः — c) NKt^{4} La^{1} Lo^{3} Tj^{1} MTr^{5} *Bh* शूद्रायां; wKt^{1} Pu^{8} च; BBe^{2} BKt^{5} MTr^{4} स्वधर्माणः; TMd^{4} स्वधर्माणां — d) NKt^{4} सर्वपर्व्वसमा स्मृताः; Ox^{2} सर्वे षड्वंसजाः; NNg *om* स्मृताः; La^{1} सुताः

42 Pāda-a omitted in MTr^{6}. Cited by *Lakṣ* 12.824 — a) La^{1} Tr^{2} तयोर्बीज°; MTr^{4} तपोजीव°; Be^{1} BBe^{2} Hy Jm Jo^{1} Jo^{2} Kt^{2} La^{1} Lo^{3} GMd^{1} NNg Ox^{2} Pu^{2} Pu^{4} Tj^{1} Tj^{2} MTr^{3} [*Jolly* R] *Mandlik Jolly Jha KSS Dave* °भावैस्तु; NKt^{4} oOr Pu^{5} Pu^{7} Wa [*Jolly* G Nd] *Nā Go* °भावेन; Pu^{8} °भावेग — b) GMy Tr^{1} MTr^{4} गच्छन्तीह युगे युगे; TMd^{3} गच्छन्ति ह युगे युगे; NKt^{4} तेन गच्छन्ति — c) MTr^{4} उत्कर्षश्चापकर्षश्च; Tr^{1} उत्कर्षे चापकर्षे च; La^{1} उत्कर्षश्चाप°; Ho वापकर्षं; GMd^{1} चानकर्षं; Ox^{2} तु — d) GMd^{1} TMd^{4} MTr^{6} मनुष्येषु न जन्मतः; BBe^{2} sOx^{1} Ox^{2} sPu^{6} मानुष्ये°; Lo^{1} Pu^{2} Pu^{3} Pu^{8} Tr^{1} Tr^{2} मानुषे°; Bo Ho GMd^{5} NPu^{1} Pu^{3} Pu^{5} Pu^{7} Tj^{1} जन्मनः; Be^{1} wKt^{3} Lo^{1} GMy sOx^{1} Ox^{2} Pu^{2} sPu^{6} Tr^{1} जन्मसु; Pu^{8} जन्मतु

43 Cited by *Lakṣ* 12.828 — a) wKt^{1} शनकैश्च; Ho °कैस्त्वक्रिया° — b) GMd^{1} °पादपीमाः क्षत्रजातयः; TMd^{4} °पादिति क्षत्रियजातयः; NKt^{4} क्षत्रियाः जातयः; Kt^{2} °जातितः — c) NNg गतो — d) GMd^{1} ब्राह्मणाः क्षत्रियास्तथा; La^{1} NNg NPu^{1} Pu^{2} Pu^{5} Pu^{7} Wa [*Jolly* G] *Me Jolly Jha* ब्राह्मणातिक्रमेण

पुण्ड्रकाश्चोडद्रविडाः काम्बोजा यवनाः शकाः ।
पारदाः पह्लवाश्चीनाः किराता दरदास्तथा ॥४४॥
मुखबाहूरुपज्जानां या लोके जातयो बहिः ।
म्लेच्छवाचोऽर्यवाचो वा सर्वे ते दस्यवः स्मृताः ॥४५॥
ये द्विजानामपसदा ये चापध्वंसजाः स्मृताः ।
ते निन्दितैर्वर्तयेयुर्द्विजानामेव कर्मभिः ॥४६॥
सूतानामश्वसारथ्यमम्बष्ठानां चिकित्सितम् ।
वैदेहकानां स्त्रीकार्यं मागधानां वणिक्पथः ॥४७॥
मत्स्यघातो निषादानां त्वष्टिस्त्वायोगवस्य च ।

44* Omitted in Pu[5]; pādas c-d omitted in ᴍTr[6]. Cited by *Lakṣ* 12.828 — a) ɢMd[1] आन्द्राश्च चोलद्रमिडाः; Lo[2] पूण्ड्रका°; ʙBe[2] Bo ʙCa Ho Hy Jo[1] wKt[1] Kt[2] wKt[3] ʙKt[5] La[1] Lo[1] Ox[2] Pu[3] Pu[8] Tj[2] ᴍTr[3] *Go Ku Rn Nd Rc Mandlik Bühler KSS* पौण्ड्रका°; Jm Pu[2] Pu[3] पौंड्रका°; wKt[1] पौंडका°; Pu[5] Pu[7] [*Jolly* G] पौष्ड्रका°; Tr[2] पौंड्यका°; Be[1] पौण्ड्रकांश्चौ°; ɴPu[1] पाण्डुकाश्चौमुद्र°; ᴛMd[3] ɢMd[5] Tr[1] ᴍTr[5] °श्चोळ°; [*Jolly* Gr] °श्चचौल°; [*Jolly* Nd] °श्चोल°; Ho ɴNg Pu[2] Tj[1] [*Jolly* M[2–3]] °श्चोंड्र°; ɴKt[4] La[1] Lo[4] sOx[1] sPu[6] Wa [*Jolly* M[1–4]] °श्चोड्र°; ʙBe[2] ʙCa Jm Jo[1] Kt[2] wKt[3] Ox[2] Tj[2] *Mandlik KSS Dave* °श्चौड्र°; Be[1] Hy Pu[8] °श्चौंड्र°; [*Jolly* M[9]] °श्चाड्र°; Bo °श्चौंड°; *Lakṣ* °श्चौद्र°; Tr[2] °श्चैंद्र°; wKt[1] °श्चौद्र°; Jo[2] °श्चोध्र°; Tj[1] °श्चोंध्र°; Lo[1] Lo[3] Pu[7] [*Jolly* M[8] R] °श्चान्ध्र°; ɴKt[4] ᴍTr[4] °द्रमिडाः; wKt[3] °द्रविताः; ᴍTr[5] °द्रमिलाः; ɢMd[5] Tr[1] ᴍTr[5] °द्रमिळाः — b) ᴛMd[3] Tj[1] काम्भोजा; Hy जवनाः; Tj[2] द्रविडाः; ʙBe[2] जवना नराः; La[1] शकः; ʙKt[5] सकाः; Tr[2] शिकाः; ᴛMd[3] ᴛMd[3] शुकाः — c) ᴛMd[4] पारशदाः प्रताश्चीनाः; wKt[1] wKt[3] Lo[1] ɢMy Tr[2] परदाः; Ho Jo[1] Kt[2] Lo[4] ɴNg sOx[1] sPu[6] Pu[8] Pu[10] ᴍTr[3] *Mandlik Jha KSS Dave* पारदा; oOr पाह्लवाश्चीना; Pu[7] ᴍTr[5] *Lakṣ* पल्लवाश्चीनाः; ᴛMd[3] पल्लवाश्चैन्दाः; Tj[1] प्रह्लदाश्चीनाः; Tr[2] पह्लवाश्चीनाः; wKt[3] Lo[1] [*mc to*] Lo[4] पह्नवाश्चीनाः; ɢMd[5] पप्लवाश्चीनाः; Bo Lo[3] पह्लदाश्चीनाः; ɴKt[4] प्लह्वयाश्चीनाः; La[1] पाहुवाश्चीनाः; ɴNg बाह्लिकाश्चीनाः; ɴPu[1] °श्चैनाः; ʙKt[5] °श्चीराः — d) Bo किरादा; Wa दारदास्तथा; ᴛMd[3] दरदाश्च ये; Hy Jm Jo[1] Jo[2] wKt[1] Kt[2] wKt[3] La[1] Lo[1] Lo[3] Lo[4] Ox[2] ɴPu[1] Pu[3] Tj[1] Tj[2] Tr[2] ᴍTr[3] [*Jolly* R] *Mandlik Jha KSS Dave* दरदाः खशाः; ʙCa Ox[2] दरदाः खसाः; ʙBe[2] दरदाः शनाः; Pu[2] दरदाः पसाः; Pu[8] दरदाः श्वसाः; Ho दरदाः श्वखाः

45. Omitted in Jm ᴍTr[6]. pādas a-b omitted in Pu[10] — a) ɢMd[1] °पाज्जानां — b) ᴛMd[4] Ox[2] ये; wKt[3] Pu[3] लोके या; ɢMd[1] ᴛMd[4] sOx[1] sPu[6] जायते — c) ɢMy म्लेच्छवाक् चार्यवाचो; oOr म्लेच्छवाचोजिवागवाः; ʙCa wKt[1] ʙKt[5] ᴛMd[4] °वाचार्यवाचा; ɢMd[1] ᴛMd[3] Tr[1] Wa °वाचौर्यवाचो [Wa °चोर्य°; ɢMd[1] °वाचा; ᴛMd[3] °जातो]; Jo[1] Kt[2] ᴍTr[3] ᴍTr[5] *Mandlik Jolly Jha KSS Dave* °वाचश्चार्य-वाचः सर्वे; ɴKt[4] °वाचआर्यवाचः सर्वे

46. Omitted in Jm ɢMy. Cited by *Lakṣ* 12.829 — a) ɢMd[1] ये पापा येपदा ये च; ʙKt[5] य; ᴛMd[3] ɢMd[5] Pu[2] Pu[3] Tr[1] ᴍTr[3] ᴍTr[4] ᴍTr[5] ᴍTr[6] °पशदा; ɴKt[4] °पशादा — b) ʙKt[5] ये वाप°; ᴛMd[3] सर्वेवध्वंसजा; Ho वाध्वंसजाः; ɢMd[1] °ध्वंशकाः; Tj[2] °ध्वंसनाः; Lo[2] सुताः — c) oOr तैर्निन्दि°; ᴛMd[3] °तैर्विवर्तेयुर्द्वि° — d) Be[1] °जानामिव; oOr °जानामेक

47. Omitted in Jm. Cited by *Apa* 119; *Lakṣ* 12.829 — a) Lo[2] °सारस्यम° — b) sOx[1] sPu[6] चिकित्सितां; wKt[1] ʙKt[5] चिकित्सता; La[1] oOr Pu[2] चिकित्सतं; Be[1] ɢMd[1] ᴛMd[3] चिकित्सकं; Hy Jo[1] Kt[2] ɢMy Tj[2] ᴍTr[3] *Mandlik Jha KSS Dave* चिकित्सनं — c) ʙBe[2] ᴛMd[4] Ox[2] Pu[2] Pu[5] Pu[7] वैदेहिकानां; Ox[2] स्त्रियां कार्यं; ʙKt[5] sOx[1] sPu[6] °कार्य — d) ᴛMd[3] मागदानां; Jo[2] La[1] ᴛMd[3] oOr ɴPu[1] Pu[2] Tj[1] वनिक्पथं; ɢMd[1] वणिक्तथा; wKt[3] वणिष्कथं

मेदान्ध्रचुञ्चुमद्गूनामारण्यपशुहिंसनम् ॥४८॥
क्षत्तुग्रपुल्कसानां तु बिलौकोवधबन्धनम् ।
धिग्वणानां चर्मकार्यं वेणानां भाण्डवादनम् ॥४९॥
चैत्यद्रुमश्मशानेषु शैलेषूपवनेषु च ।
वसेयुरेते विज्ञाता वर्तयन्तः स्वकर्मभिः ॥५०॥
चण्डालश्वपचानां तु बहिर्ग्रामात्प्रतिश्रयः ।
अपपात्राश्च कर्तव्या धनमेषां श्वगर्दभम् ॥५१॥

48. Omitted in Jm; pādas a-b and c-d transposed in Pu[8]. Cited by *Lakṣ* 12.829; pādas a-b cited by *Apa* 119 — a) Ox[2] मत्स्याघातो; Bo °घाते; Pu[10] °घाता; Ho निषादीनां; bBe[2] निषाधानां — b) *Apa* °दानामायोगव्यस्य लक्षणं [vl काक्षणं]; mTr[4] mTr[6] कृष्टरायोगपाण्डवः; Pu[5] Pu[7] तक्षिस्त्वायो°; La[1] तुष्टिस्त्वायो°; nNg Pu[10] Wa तष्टिस्त्वायो°; gMy तष्टारायो°; mTr[5] तष्टिरायो°; *Lakṣ* त्वष्टिरायो°; sOx[1] sPu[6] त्वष्टिश्चायो°; Lo[1] त्वष्टित्वायो°; tMd[3] gMd[5] तुष्ठिरायो°; Tr[1] तष्टिरायो°; tMd[4] gMd[5] तुष्टिरायो°; Lo[3] यष्टिस्त्वायो°; Tj[1] यष्टित्वायो°; Bo bCa wKt[1] nKt[4] Lo[2] tMd[4] gMd[5] gMy nNg sOx[1] Ox[2] Pu[3] Pu[5] sPu[6] Pu[7] Tr[1] Tr[2] mTr[5] Wa [*Jolly* G] तु — c) Be[1] मेधान्धचूहमांगाना°; bBe[2] मेधान्तचञ्चुजन्तूना°; nPu[1] भेदांचभूचमंडूकाना°; La[1] मेदांधवृन्कमद्गूना°; Pu[2] मेदान्ध्रयुयुमंशूना°; gMd[1] मेदान्द्रमक्षमत्गूना°; gMy मोदान्ध्रचुञ्चुमंगूना°; wKt[1] मेदोन्द्रिचुञ्चु°; Tr[1] वेनान्द्रचूचु°; Jo[1] Tj[1] °चञ्चु°; Pu[10] °चुञ्च°; Bo Jo[2] Lo[2] mTr[4] mTr[5] [*Jolly* G N Nd] *Jolly* °चूचु°; Lo[1] mTr[6] °चुचु°; Tr[2] Wa °चूच°; Pu[3] °चुचू°; [*Jolly* M [4-8-9]] °वूच°; Lo[4] [*Jolly* M[5]] °भूभु°; Ox[2] °कृच° — d) nKt[4] Ox[2] Tj[1] mTr[6] °मरण्य°; tMd[3] °मारुण्य°; wKt[1] °हिंसकं

49. Omitted in Jm gMy Pu[5] [*Jolly* Nd]. Cited by *Lakṣ* 12.829 — a) tMd[4] क्षत्तूग्र°; Tj[1] क्षत्र्युग्र°; tMd[3] gMd[5] Ox[2] Pu[7] Tr[1] mTr[4] mTr[6] क्षत्तोग्र°; Be[1] क्षत्रोग्र°; gMd[1] क्षमाल्ग°; Lo[1] क्षत्रग्रह°; Ho Jo[2] Lo[2] Lo[4] nPu[1] Pu[7] Pu[8] Pu[10] Tj[2] Tr[2] Wa [*Jolly* M G] °पुष्कसानां; Be[1] Bo °पुःकसानां; bBe[2] Hy Jo[1] wKt[1] Kt[2] nKt[4] bKt[5] La[1] oOr sOx[1] Ox[2] sPu[6] *Mandlik Jha KSS Dave* °पुक्कसानां [see 10.18b note]; wKt[3] °पुक्कशानां; Lo[1] *om* तु; wKt[1] wKt[3] bKt[5] nPu[1] Tr[2] च — b) wKt[1] बहिर्ग्रामिः प्रतिश्रयः [cf. 51b]; Kt[2] nKt[4] Lo[1] Lo[2] Pu[10] Wa बिलो°; mTr[6] विलौ°; Bo La[1] Pu[2] Pu[7] विलो°; mTr[5] बिलौक°; Be[1] La[1] gMd[1] mTr[4] विलोक°; tMd[3] बिल्लोक°; tMd[4] बिकोन°; bKt[5] धनौको°; nPu[1] विलोकौ°; gMd[5] वकोट° — c) tMd[3] Tr[1] धीवराणां तु कर्मार्यं; Lo[3] दिग्वणा°; Be[1] bBe[2] gMd[1] tMd[4] mTr[5] धिग्वनानां; Tj[1] धिग्बणानां; nKt[4] धिग्वभानां; La[1] धिग्वलानां; Lo[2] चिग्रणानां; Tr[2] च कर्मकार्यं; gMd[5] mTr[5] तु कर्मार्यं; La[1] कर्मकार्यं — d) Be[1] bBe[2] Lo[4] tMd[3] tMd[4] nNg Pu[7] Tr[1] mTr[4] mTr[6] वेनानां; Jo[1] Kt[2] Lo[1] वैणानां; sOx[1] sPu[6] वैनानां; Ho वनानां; tMd[4] भाण्डवादानं; nKt[4] भाण्डवादजं; Tr[1] mTr[4] mTr[6] भाण्डवाहनं

50. Omitted in Jm mTr[6]; placed after verse 52 in gMd[1] tMd[4] gMy [*Jolly* Nd]. Cited by *Lakṣ* 12.829, 832 — a) bKt[5] Lo[2] tMd[3] चैत्र°; Tr[2] त्रैत्र°; La[1] चैत्युद्रुम°; mTr[4] °श्मशाने तु — b) Lo[1] mTr[4] शैलेषु च वनेषु च; Jo[2] Lo[3] Pu[2] Pu[3] Tj[1] वनेषूपवनेषु च — c) gMd[5] वसेयुस्तेप्यविज्ञाता; Pu[5] Pu[7] वशेयु°; Wa वासयु°; bBe[2] वसेयुरिति; Jo[1] Kt[2] nNg Ox[2] mTr[3] *Mandlik KSS Dave* विज्ञाना

51. Cited by *Lakṣ* 12.832 — a) oOr चण्डालपुक्कसानां च; Ho bKt[5] La[1] Lo[1] Ox[2] nPu[1] Pu[8] चाण्डाल°; La[1] चण्डालं; wKt[1] चाण्डालः; nPu[1] °श्वपदानां; Tj[1] °स्वपजानां; nKt[4] °श्वपभावानां; wKt[1] Ho bKt[5] sOx[1] Ox[2] Pu[5] sPu[6] Pu[7] च — a-b) gMd[1] यनानां तु भूतानां निग्रामस्यात्प्रतिश्रयं — b) nKt[4] Lo[4] Pu[5] Pu[7] Tr[1] mTr[4] mTr[5] mTr[6] निर्ग्रामः स्यात्प्रति° [mTr[6] निर्ग्रामे]; oOr बहिर्ग्रामे प्रति°; wKt[1] बहिर्ग्रामः प्रति°; bKt[5] La[1] बहिर्ग्रामप्रति°; tMd[4] °तिश्रयं; Bo °तिशमः; bKt[5] °तिश्रवाः — c) Lo[2] Lo[4] Pu[10] Tj[1] [*Jolly* M N R Nd] *Nā Jolly* अवपात्राश्च [editions of *Me* give both अवपात्र and अपपात्र]; Ox[2] Pu[5] Pu[7] [*Jolly* G] अयःपात्राश्च; Tr[2] अथपात्राश्च; La[1] nPu[1] आमपात्राश्च; Be[1] अवपाशश्च; Bo tMd[4] °पात्रश्च;

वासांसि मृतचेलानि भिन्नभाण्डे च भोजनम् ।
कार्ष्णायसमलंकारः परिव्रज्या च नित्यशः ॥५२॥
न तैः समयमन्विच्छेत् पुरुषो धर्ममाचरन् ।
व्यवहारो मिथस्तेषां विवाहः सदृशैः सह ॥५३॥
अन्नमेषां पराधीनं देयं स्याद्भिन्नभाजने ।
रात्रौ न विचरेयुस्ते ग्रामेषु नगरेषु च ॥५४॥
दिवा चरेयुः कार्यार्थं चिह्निता राजशासनैः ।
अबान्धवं शवं चैव निर्हरेयुरिति स्थितिः ॥५५॥
वध्यांश्च हन्युः सततं यथाशास्त्रं नृपाज्ञया ।
वध्यवासांसि गृह्णीयुः शय्याश्चाभरणानि च ॥५६॥
वर्णपेतमविज्ञातं नरं कलुषयोनिजम् ।
आर्यरूपमिवानार्यं कर्मभिः स्वैर्विभावयेत् ॥५७॥

GMy °पात्रंश्च; TMd³ °पात्रं च; Lo¹ °पात्रास्ते; Wa °पात्राः प्रकर्तव्या; Be¹ TMd³ कर्तव्यं; NKt⁴ GMy कर्तव्य — d) Ox² यानमेषां; GMd⁵ वनमेषां; sOx¹ sPu⁶ *om* श्व; Pu⁵ Pu⁷ तु गर्दभं; Ho Lo² GMd¹ Ox² NPu¹ MTr⁴ च गर्दभं; Lo¹ Tr² °गर्धभं; BKt⁵ Ox² °गर्धभः; Jo² °गर्दभे; Pu¹⁰ °गर्दभी; TMd³ °गर्दभान्

52.* Cited by *Lakṣ* 12.832 — a) GMd¹ वासांस्यमृत°; GMy मृदुचेलानि; Be¹ Bo Ho Jo² La¹ Lo¹ Lo² Lo⁴ NNg sOx¹ Ox² NPu¹ Pu² Pu³ Pu⁵ sPu⁶ Pu⁷ Pu⁸ Pu¹⁰ Tr² Wa [*Jolly* M G] *Jolly Jha Dave* °चैलानि — b) La¹ भिन्नैर्भाण्डे; TMd³ हीनभाण्डे; Be¹ BBe² Hy Jm Jo¹ Kt² NKt⁴ GMd¹ GMd⁵ GMy Ox² NPu¹ Pu² Pu⁴ Pu⁵ Pu⁷ Pu⁸ Tj² [*Jolly* G Ku Nd] *Mandlik KSS Jha Dave* °भाण्डेषु — c) Lo¹ °यसम [*cor to* यसो] लंकारश्च; Ho BKt⁵ °यसश्चालंकारः; Lo² °यसस्त्वलंकारः; BBe² °कार; Be¹ La¹ Lo³ TMd⁴ oOr NPu¹ Pu² Pu⁵ Pu⁷ Tj¹ °कारं — d) Be¹ Tj¹ परिव्राज्या; Tr² परिवाज्या; sPu⁶ परिव्रज्यः; Bo परिवर्ज्या; Pu⁵ Pu⁷ परिव्रज्याच्च; BBe² sOx¹ Tr¹ परिव्रज्याश्च; oOr सर्वशः; after this verse MTr⁴ MTr⁶ insert verse 10.50.

53. Omitted in Pu⁴. Cited by *Lakṣ* 12.832 — a) Bo नेति समयमिच्छेद्धि; Jo² Lo³ नैतैः — c) BKt⁵ व्यवहारे; BKt⁵ Lo³ Tj¹ [*Jolly* R] मिथश्चैषां — d) oOr विवाहैः; Lo³ Tj¹ विवादः; TMd³ समा

54. Omitted in Pu¹⁰; pādas a-b omitted in Pu⁴. Cited by *Lakṣ* 12.832 — a) NPu¹ अर्थमेषां; NKt⁴ भिन्नमेषां; TMd⁴ Tr¹ °मेषा; GMd¹ परान्निन्द्यं; oOr °धीनां; Bo GMy °धीन — b) GMd¹ पेयं; TMd³ स्याद्भिन्नहारते; TMd⁴ °भाजनं; BBe² °भोजने — c) Lo⁴ विहरेयु°; oOr वितरेयु°; Bo Jo² wKt¹ NKt⁴ Lo³ GMd¹ TMd³ TMd⁴ GMd⁵ GMy oOr NPu¹ Pu³ Tj¹ Tr¹ Tr² MTr⁴ MTr⁶ °रेयुश्च; La¹ *om* ते — d) NKt⁴ वा

55. Cited by *Lakṣ* 12.832 — b) Pu⁴ Tj¹ चिह्नता; GMy °शासनात्; Ho °शासनः — c) Tr¹ अवालपशवश्चैव; Tj¹ आबान्धवं; GMd¹ °न्धवश्शवं; TMd³ GMy °न्धवशवं; GMd⁵ °न्धवशतं; Ox² °न्धवान्शवं; Kt² BKt⁵ TMd⁴ शवश्चैव; Ox² शवांश्चैव; wKt³ चैवं — d) Bo निर्धरेयु°

56. GMy places pādas c-d after verse 58. Cited by *Lakṣ* 12.832 — a) BKt⁵ वध्याश्च; Kt² Tr² वन्ध्यांश्च; Bo बन्ध्यांश्च; BCa वध्यांतु; Pu¹⁰ वेध्यांश्च; GMd¹ हन्युस्ते सर्वे — c) GMd¹ MTr⁶ °वासांस्याददीरन्; MTr⁴ गृह्णीरन् — d) GMy MTr⁶ शस्त्राण्याभर°; *Lakṣ* शय्याद्याभर°; GMd¹ शय्यांश्चाभर°; Hy शय्याभर°; Jo² wKt³ Tj¹ [*Jolly* R]शय्यां चाभर°; Lo¹ शय्या चाभर°; GMd⁵ शय्यास्त्वाभर°; Pu⁴ *om* चाभरणानि

57. Pādas c-d omitted in wKt¹ [haplogaphy] — a) Pu¹⁰ Tj¹ °विज्ञानं; MTr⁶ °विज्ञायं — b)

अनार्यता निष्ठुरता क्रूरता निष्क्रियात्मता ।
पुरुषं व्यञ्जयन्तीह लोके कलुषयोनिजम् ॥५८॥
पित्र्यं वा भजते शीलं मातुर्वोभयमेव वा ।
न कथंचन दुर्योनिः प्रकृतिं स्वां नियच्छति ॥५९॥
कुले मुख्येऽपि जातस्य यस्य स्याद्योनिसंकरः ।
संश्रयत्येव तच्छीलं नरोऽल्पमपि वा बहु ॥६०॥
यत्र त्वेते परिध्वंसा जायन्ते वर्णदूषकाः ।
राष्ट्रियैः सह तद्राष्ट्रं क्षिप्रमेव विनश्यति ॥६१॥
ब्राह्मणार्थे गवार्थे वा देहत्यागोऽनुपस्कृतः ।
स्त्रीबालाभ्यवपत्तौ च बाह्यानां सिद्धिकारणम् ॥६२॥
अहिंसा सत्यमक्रोधः शौचमिन्द्रियनिग्रहः ।
एतं सामासिकं धर्मं चातुर्वर्ण्येऽब्रवीन्मनुः ॥६३॥

gMd[1] Pu[4] कल्मष°; gMd[1] gMd[5] °योनिजः; Tr[2] °योनिनं; tMd[3] °योषितं — c) sOx[1] sPu[6] आर्यत्वमपि चानार्यं; Tj[2] °पमेवानार्यं; wKt[3] °मिवाकार्यं — d) tMd[4] °भावयत्

58. Omitted in wKt[1] — a) tMd[4] अनार्यतो — b) Pu[2] Pu[4] सततं निष्क्रि°; La[1] निःकृतात्मता; nPu[1] °यात्मका; Pu[4] °यात्मना — c) bKt[5] व्यञ्जतीह; gMd[5] व्यञ्जन्ति हि — d) Ox[2] नरं कलुष°; Be[1] कल्मष°

59. Cited by *Lakṣ* 12.828; *Mādh* 1.478 — a) gMd[1] tMd[3] tMd[4] gMd[5] gMy Tr[1] mTr[4] mTr[6] *Lakṣ Mādh* पितुर्वा — b) Be[1] gMy च — c) wKt[1] कथंचन तयोर्योनिः [*om* न]; bKt[5] *om* न; tMd[3] दुर्योनिं — d) tMd[4] प्रकृतिस्थानिगच्छति; gMd[1] स्वकीयं स्वां; tMd[3] gMy Tr[1] mTr[4] mTr[6] निगच्छति; gMd[5] च गच्छति; *Mādh* विमुञ्चति

60. a) gMd[1] gMd[5] sOx[1] sPu[6] कुल; nKt[4] मुखोपि; gMd[1] मुख्ये हि — b) tMd[3] tMd[4] gMd[5] gMy Tr[1] [*Jolly* Gr]यदि स्या°; gMy स्याद्वर्णसंकरः; bBe[2] wKt[3] bKt[5] La[1] °शंकरः — c) Lo[1] संप्रयत्येव; tMd[3] संश्रुत्यैव — d) wKt[3] नलो; Bo नराल्प°; wKt[1] नवाल्प°; bKt[5] °ल्पमथ वा; gMd[5] °ल्पमति वा; Be[1] gMd[5] बहुः; gMd[1] पुनः

61 Cited by *Lakṣ* 12.828 — a) gMd[5] Tr[1] यत्र चैते; Pu[2] यत्राच्चते; Pu[4] यत्राचते; Ox[2] परिध्वस्ता; Bo La[1] परिभ्रंशा; Tr[2] परिभ्रांशाः; wKt[1] वहुध्यंसा; Ho Jm Jo[1] nKt[4] gMd[5] sOx[1] sPu[6] mTr[3] *Lakṣ Mandlik Jha KSS* परिध्वंसाज्जाय° — b) Bo sOx[1] sPu[6] जायते; Pu[10] ज्ञायते; Tr[1] Tr[2] वर्णसंकरः; wKt[1] bKt[5] tMd[3] gMd[5] gMy Ox[2] Pu[3] Pu[8] *Nā Ku Mr* वर्णसंकराः; mTr[6] वर्णसंदूषकाः; oOr वर्णध्वंसकाः; nPu[1] °दूषकः — c) Lo[3] Tj[1] *Jha* राष्ट्रीयैः; Hy Jm Jo[1] Kt[2] mTr[3] *Mandlik KSS* राष्ट्रिकैः; gMd[1] gMy Tr[1] mTr[4] mTr[6] राष्ट्रेशैः; tMd[3] राष्ट्रेषैः; tMd[4] राष्ट्रैः; Pu[10] राष्ट्रिको; bKt[5] राष्ट्रिभिः; Pu[2] Pu[4] राष्ट्रजैः; tMd[3] तद्राज्यं — d) La[1] oOr प्रणश्यति

62.* Cited by *Apa* 119; *Lakṣ* 12.833 — a) Ho गवार्थं; Be[1] गवामर्थे देह°; nNg Wa [*Jolly* M] च — b) tMd[4] देहत्यागो नृ [lacuna] स्मृतः; Tj[1] °पस्कृतं; *Apa* [vl as in ed] °पस्कृतेः — c) bBe[2] Bo Ho Hy Jm Jo[1] Jo[2] wKt[1] Kt[2] wKt[3] La[1] Lo[1] Lo[3] Lo[4] [*cor to*] gMd[1] oOr sOx[1] Ox[2] sPu[6] Pu[8] Tj[1] Tj[2] Wa *Mandlik Jolly KSS Dave* °भ्युपपत्तौ; [*Jolly* M[1–2–8–9]] °ध्यवपत्तौ; Lo[2] °भ्यपपत्तौ; mTr[6] °भ्युपपत्तिश्च; gMd[1] वा — d) nKt[4] वाद्यानां; tMd[3] बाह्यतां; La[1] राज्यानां; gMd[5] सिद्ध°; wKt[3] °कारिणं

63* Cited by *Viś* 1.8; *Lakṣ* 12.834 — a) bBe[2] Hy Jm Jo[1] Jo[2] wKt[1] Kt[2] wKt[3] Lo[1] Lo[2] Lo[3] Ox[2] Pu[5] Pu[7] Tj[1] Tj[2] Tr[1] Tr[2] mTr[3] [*Jolly* G Ku R] *Viś* [vl] *Lakṣ Go Nā Ku Mandlik Jolly Jha*

शूद्रायां ब्राह्मणाज्जातः श्रेयसा चेत्प्रजायते ।
अश्रेयाञ्छ्रेयसीं जातिं गच्छत्या सप्तमाद्युगात् ॥६४॥
शूद्रो ब्राह्मणतामेति ब्राह्मणश्चैति शूद्रताम् ।
क्षत्रियाज्जातमेवं तु विद्याद्वैश्यात्तथैव च ॥६५॥
अनार्यायां समुत्पन्नो ब्राह्मणात्तु यदृच्छया ।
ब्राह्मण्यामप्यनार्यात्तु श्रेयस्त्वं क्वेति चेद्भवेत् ॥६६॥

KSS Dave सत्यमस्तेयं — a-b) GMd^{1} TMd^{4} MTr^{6} अहिंसा चानृशंस्यं च सत्यमस्तेयमार्जवं; NKt^{4} Lo^{2} Pu^{8} °न्द्रियसंयमः — c) Lo^{1} एनं; BBe^{2} BCa WKt^{1} WKt^{3} BKt^{5} La^{1} GMd^{5} OOr Tr^{1} एतत्; Ox^{2} Pu^{2} Pu^{4} Tr^{2} इमं; Pu^{3} इदं; Be^{1} Lo^{4} GMy Pu^{8} Tj^{2} [*Jolly* M Nd] एवं; SOx^{1} SPu^{6} एकं; Pu^{10} पञ्चं; WKt^{1} सामानिकं; Be^{1} GMd^{1} TMd^{4} NPu^{1} Pu^{2} Pu^{3} MTr^{4} MTr^{6} साधारणं; TMd^{3} सामाजिकं; Pu^{10} [*Jolly* M] स्वाभाविकं; Bo सामासितत्कर्मं; Kt^{2} OOr धर्मं; GMd^{5} MTr^{6} धर्म्यं — c-d) *Viś* एष साधारणो धर्मश्चातुर्वर्ण्ये प्रकीर्तितः — d) Be^{1} BBe^{2} Bo WKt^{1} WKt^{3} BKt^{5} La^{1} GMd^{1} TMd^{4} NPu^{1} Tj^{1} चातुर्वर्णे; GMy [*Jolly* Nd] सर्ववर्णे; Lo^{1} Tr^{1} चातुर्वर्ण्यं ब्रवी°

Between pādas a-b and c-d the following verse is added in Be^{1} GMd^{1} TMd^{4} NNg NPu^{1} Pu^{2} Pu^{4} MTr^{4} MTr^{6} *Mandlik*[क, च] *KSS*; the second half-verse is added in GMd^{5} GMy; this verse is given by *Go* at the beginning of his commentary on verse 63:

श्राद्धकर्मातिथेयं च दानमस्तेयमार्जवम् ।
प्रजनं स्वेषु दारेषु तथा चैवानसूयता ॥

a) MTr^{6} ° तिथेयस्त्वं दान° — a-b) MTr^{4} श्राद्धकर्मातिथेयत्वमानृशंस्यमथार्जवं — b) GMd^{1} विषयेन्द्रियनिग्रहः; TMd^{4} MTr^{6} दानमिन्द्रियनिग्रहः — d) GMd^{1} GMd^{5} GMy MTr^{4} MTr^{6} शौचं नित्यानसूयता; Pu^{2} Pu^{4} °सूयका

64. Omitted in Wa. Cited by *Lakṣ* 12.825 — a) La^{1} ब्राह्मणो जातः; NNg °णाज्जाताः — b) La^{1} श्रेयस्यां; Pu^{10} श्रेयस; TMd^{4} श्रेयसे तत्प्रजा°; Pu^{4} श्रेयसात्प्रजा°; Lo^{4} यत्प्रजा°; NNg च प्रजा°; WKt^{1} च प्रजापतेः; GMd^{5} च प्रजापते; OOr चेत्पतीयते — c) TMd^{4} श्रेयांछ्रेयसी ज्ञातिं च; BKt^{5} Pu^{5} Pu^{7} अश्रेयाच्छ्रे°; BBe^{2} °यसी जाति — c-d) GMd^{1} [half-verse reads] अश्रेयसी जातिमाचारात्समाद्यगात् — d) Hy La^{1} Tr^{2} गच्छन्त्या; OOr गच्छतः सप्त°; Lo^{1} सप्तमायुगात्; WKt^{1} TMd^{3} सप्तमश्चगत्; La^{1} सप्तमागमा; TMd^{3} GMd^{5} MTr^{4} सप्तमात्कुलात्; BCa [*but cor*] पञ्चमाद्युगात्

65. Omitted in Pu^{10}. Cited by *Lakṣ* 12.825 — a) Bo ब्राह्मतामेति — b) NPu^{1} ब्राह्मणाश्चैति; WKt^{1} ब्राह्मणाश्चैव; Jo^{2} Lo^{3} Tj^{1} ब्राह्मणो याति; Be^{1} Kt^{2} La^{1} Lo^{1} OOr Tr^{1} MTr^{6} °णश्चेति; GMd^{1} °णश्चाति; BBe^{2} Bo WKt^{1} WKt^{3} Ox^{2} Tr^{2} °णश्चैव — c) NKt^{4} Pu^{4} °ज्जातमेव; Tr^{1} °ज्जातमेवं चेद्; Jo^{2} GMd^{1} Lo^{3} Tj^{1} MTr^{6} °ज्जातमप्येवं विद्या° [Tj^{1} °प्येव]; TMd^{4} °ज्जातमध्येवं विद्या°; La^{1} TMd^{3} GMd^{5} GMy OOr MTr^{5} च; WKt^{1} हि — d) GMd^{1} TMd^{3} TMd^{4} GMd^{5} GMy Tr^{1} MTr^{4} MTr^{6} विद्यात्क्षत्रियतां गतं; La^{1} विंद्याद्वैश्यं तथैव; OOr NPu^{1} विद्याद्वैश्यस्तथैव; Jo^{2} Lo^{3} विद्याच्छूद्रात्तथैव; Tj^{1} विंध्याछूद्रा तथैव; Lo^{4} [*Jolly* M] तु

66. Pādas c-d omitted in Pu^{4} and *ma* in Lo^{1}. Cited by *Lakṣ* 12.823 — a) GMy अनार्याणां; TMd^{4} अनार्याय; Tj^{1} समुत्पन्नौ; BKt^{5} Pu^{10} समुत्पन्ने — b) NKt^{4} ब्रह्मणास्तु; MTr^{4} MTr^{6} ब्राह्यणस्तु; TMd^{4} ब्रह्मणातु — c) La^{1} TMd^{4} MTr^{6} अनार्यतो वा ब्राह्मण्यां; NPu^{1} ब्राह्मण्यम°; Pu^{5} Pu^{7} °मप्यनार्यायां; TMd^{3} °मप्यकाराद्वा; Pu^{2} °नार्यातु; Jo^{2} WKt^{1} WKt^{3} NKt^{4} Lo^{3} Tj^{1} °नार्याच्च; GMd^{5} GMy Tr^{1} MTr^{4} °नार्याद्वा; Lo^{1} OOr °नार्यां तु; BBe^{2} °नार्यत्व — c-d) GMd^{1} अनार्यतो वा जातस्तु न यस्त्वं केतिचेद्भवेत् — d) GMy श्रेयस्वं चेद्भवेदिति; La^{1} श्रेयात्र केनचिद्भवेत्; OOr श्रेयस्त्वेकेन च भवेत्; Hy Jo^{2} WKt^{3} Lo^{3} Tj^{1} [*Jolly* R] श्रेयान्कस्त्वनार्यो भवेत् [WKt^{3} °नार्याद्भ°; [*Jolly* R] °नार्योर्भ°]; [*Jolly* Nd] *om* क्वेति; Be^{1} WKt^{1} Lo^{4} कस्य चेद्भ°; [*Jolly* M^{4}] कस्य चिद्भ°; NPu^{1} Pu^{2} केनचिद्भ°; Pu^{5} Pu^{7} [*Jolly* G] नेति चेद्भ°; TMd^{3} Tr^{1}

जातो नार्यामनार्यायामार्यादार्यो भवेद्गुणैः ।
जातोऽप्यनार्यादार्यायामनार्य इति निश्चयः ॥६७॥
तावुभावप्यसंस्कार्याविति धर्मो व्यवस्थितः ।
वैगुण्याज्जन्मनः पूर्व उत्तरः प्रतिलोमतः ॥६८॥
सुबीजं चैव सुक्षेत्रे जातं संपद्यते यथा ।
तथार्याज्जात आर्यायां सर्वं संस्कारमर्हति ॥६९॥
बीजमेके प्रशंसन्ति क्षेत्रमेके मनीषिणः ।
बीजक्षेत्रे तथैवान्ये तत्रेयं तु व्यवस्थितिः ॥७०॥
अक्षेत्रे बीजमुत्सृष्टमन्तरैव विनश्यति ।
अबीजकमपि क्षेत्रं केवलं स्थण्डिलं भवेत् ॥७१॥
यस्माद्बीजप्रभावेण तिर्यग्जा ऋषयोऽभवन् ।

mTr[4] चेति चेद्ध° ; gMd[5] चैति चेद्ध° ; Ox[2] [*Jolly* M[9]] चिद्धवेत्

67. Omitted in Pu[10]; *ma* in Lo[1]; omitted up to इति in Pu[4]; pādas b-c omitted in bKt[5]; pādas a-b and c-d transposed in mTr[4]. Cited by *Lakṣ* 12.824 — a) Jo[2] Lo[3] Tj[1] अर्याज्जातस्त्वनार्यायामा° ; tMd[4] Tr[1] नार्यमनार्या° ; bBe[2] gMd[5] Pu[7] mTr[6] नार्यादनार्या° ; Lo[1] नार्योप्यनार्या° — b) wKt[3] gMy °मार्यानर्यो; Pu[8] °दार्यां भवे° — c) Lo[2] जातस्त्वनार्या° ; Be[1] °ह्यनार्या° ; Ox[2] Tr[1] [*but cor*] °प्यार्यादनार्यायाम° — d) wKt[1] इति स्थितिः

68. Omitted in wKt[1]; *ma sh* in sPu[6]. Cited by *Lakṣ* 12.824 — a) gMd[1] mTr[6] *Lakṣ* उभावपि त्वसंस्कायाविति° — b) gMd[1] °विति शास्त्रविदो विदुः; wKt[3] Tr[2] धर्मे; Tr[2] °स्थितिः — c) Lo[3] tMd[3] gMy sOx[1] sPu[6] Pu[10] Tr[1] Tr[2] *Lakṣ Me Jha Dave* °ज्जन्मतः; bBe[2] Bo Lo[3] tMd[3] tMd[4] nPu[1] Pu[5] Pu[7] mTr[6] Wa पूर्वमुत्तरः; bKt[5] पूवदुत्तरः — c-d) gMd[1] न वैगुण्याज्जनः पूर्व उत्तरप्रतिलोमकः — d) tMd[3] उतचः प्रयतोमतः; bBe[2] उत्तर; nPu[1] उत्ततं; bCa उत्तमः; oOr प्रतिलोमजः

69. Omitted in wKt[1]; *ma* in sPu[6]. Cited by *Lakṣ* 12.824 — a) bBe[2] bKt[5] स्वबीजं; tMd[3] gMd[5] gMy Tr[1] mTr[5] *Bh* [ad 10.70] सुबीजमेव; gMd[1] सुबीजस्त्वेव; La[1] सुवीर्यन्तेव; tMd[4] सतबीजमेव; *Lakṣ* त्वेव; Be[1] Ho tMd[3] सुक्षेत्रं; tMd[4] सुक्षेत्र; bBe[2] bKt[5] स्वक्षेत्रे — b) tMd[3] जातु; gMd[1] जातस्संप° ; Tr[1] संपाद्यते; Tj[1] संपद्यतं; Lo[1] तथा — c) mTr[5] तथार्यजातंस्त्वार्यायां; Pu[8] आर्याज्जातस्तथार्यायां; gMd[5] तथा जातमनार्यायां; bKt[5] यथा° ; tMd[4] तथान्याज्यात; bBe[2] Jo[2] La[1] Lo[3] oOr nPu[1] Pu[2] Pu[4] Pu[5] Pu[7] Tj[1] °ज्जातमार्या° ; Wa आचार्यायां — d) bCa Ho bKt[5] tMd[4] Pu[5] Pu[7] Wa सर्व; gMy सर्वस्संका° ; gMd[1] जातस्संका° ; Bo स वै संस्का°

70. Pādas c-d omitted in Pu[4]. Cited by *Lakṣ* 12.824 — a) nKt[4] gMy बीजमेव; Pu[4] क्षेत्रमेके; gMd[1] °मेके वदन्त्येव — b) bCa Hy Jm Jo[1] Jo[2] wKt[1] Kt[2] wKt[3] Lo[3] Tj[1] Tj[2] mTr[3] *Mandlik Jolly Jha KSS Dave* क्षेत्रमन्ये — c) Pu[5] Pu[7] °क्षेत्रं; Be[1] tMd[4] तथा चान्ये; Lo[1] तथा वान्ये; gMy तथान्ये तु — d) Tr[1] तत्रैवं; gMd[5] तत्रैव च; gMy तत्र यत्तु; Jo[2] तत्रैवेयं व्यव° ; wKt[1] *mc to* च; Tj[1] °स्थितीः; bKt[5] La[1] °स्थितः

71. Pādas c-d up to स्थण्डिलं omitted in Pu[4]; pādas a-b omitted in Pu[10]. Cited by *Lakṣ* 12.824 — a) oOr sOx[1] sPu[6] अक्षेत्र; La[1] वीर्यमुत्सृ° ; Lo[3] Tj[1] °मुत्पन्नम° ; gMd[1] Pu[7] Pu[8] °मुत्कृष्टम° — b) Be[1] Hy wKt[3] Lo[3] tMd[3] gMd[5] Pu[8] Tr[1] °मन्तरेव; bKt[5] °मन्तरे च; La[1] oOr nPu[1] Pu[2] °मन्तरिक्षे; wKt[1] °मन्तरिक्ष — c) gMy °जकमिव — d) gMd[1] tMd[3] tMd[4] gMd[5] Tr[1] निष्फलं भवेत्

पूजिताश्च प्रशस्ताश्च तस्माद्बीजं प्रशस्यते ॥७२॥
अनार्यमार्यकर्माणमार्यं चानार्यकर्मिणम् ।
संप्रधार्याब्रवीद्धाता न समौ नासमाविति ॥७३॥
ब्राह्मणा ब्रह्मयोनिस्था ये स्वकर्मव्यवस्थिताः ।
ते सम्यगुपजीवेयुः षट्कर्माणि यथाक्रमम् ॥७४॥
अध्यापनमध्ययनं यजनं याजनं तथा ।
दानं प्रतिग्रहश्चैव षट्कर्माण्यग्रजन्मनः ॥७५॥
षण्णां तु कर्मणामस्य त्रीणि कर्माणि जीविका ।
याजनाध्यापने चैव विशुद्धाच्च प्रतिग्रहः ॥७६॥
त्रयो धर्मा निवर्तन्ते ब्राह्मणात् क्षत्रियं प्रति ।
अध्यापनं याजनं च तृतीयश्च प्रतिग्रहः ॥७७॥
वैश्यं प्रति तथैवैते निवर्तेरन्निति स्थितिः ।

72. Omitted in Pu[1]. Cited by *Lakṣ* 12.824 — a) GMd[1] सदाचारानुभावेन; TMd[4] NNg oOr Pu[5] Pu[7] Tr[1] तस्माद्बीज° — b) GMd[1] TMd[3] °ज्जासूपयो; BKt[5] °ज्जानूपयो; NKt[4] Tj[1] भवान्; Be[1] Bo WKt[3] Lo[2] Pu[10] भवेत्; Tr[1] भवत् — c) TMd[3] °ताश्च सुरक्ताश्च — d) Bo NKt[4] विशिष्यते

73. Omitted in Pu[1]. Cited by *Lakṣ* 2.272, 826 — b) Be[1] Lo[1] वानार्य°; Lo[2] TMd[4] MTr[4] °कर्मकं; oOr °कर्मणं; *Lakṣ* 2.272 °कर्मिणः — c) Wa संप्रधाया°; TMd[3] संप्रदार्या° — d) BKt[5] नासमौ न समाविति; GMy Wa न समो; TMd[3] न समा; GMd[1] GMy Tj[1] नसमाविति; Jo[1] नासमाहितौ; Pu[10] नासमा गतिः; [*Jolly* M] तमसा गतिः; Tr[2] °मावपि

74. Omitted in NPu[1] Pu[10] — a) Lo[2] *om* ब्राह्मणा; TMd[4] ब्राह्मणां; MTr[6] ब्रह्मण; GMd[1] ये नरा ब्रह्मयोनि°; TMd[3] Tr[1] ब्राह्मयोनि° — b) La[1] °निस्थाः स्वकर्मे च व्यवस्थिताः; WKt[1] सुकर्मण्यव°; Bo Lo[3] Tj[1] MTr[4] *Bh* स्वकर्मस्ववस्थिताः; BBe[2] Hy Jm Jo[1] Jo[2] WKt[1] Kt[2] WKt[3] Lo[4] Pu[2] Pu[4] Pu[8] Tj[2] MTr[3] *Mandlik Jha KSS Dave* स्वकर्मण्यवथिताः [Ho *om* स्व°; TMd[3] स्वे; WKt[1] सुकर्माण्य°]; Ox[2] स्वधर्मव्यवस्थिताः — d) BKt[5] Wa यथाविधि; BBe[2] °क्रमः; Pu[3] °क्रमात्

75. Omitted in NPu[1]; pāda-d omitted in Pu[4]. Cited by *Lakṣ* 2.168; *Dev* 2.449; *Mādh* 1.135 — a) GMd[1] TMd[4] Tr[1] *Dev Mādh* °पनं चाध्ययनं — b) Jo[2] Lo[3] Tj[1] [*Jolly* G R] याजनं यजनं — c) Ho Jo[2] Lo[3] GMy Tj[1] °ग्रहश्चेति; BKt[5] La[1] TMd[3] TMd[4] Tr[1] MTr[6] °ग्रहं चैव; sOx[1] sPu[6] °ग्रहं चेति — d) GMd[1] °कर्माणि यथाक्रमं

76. Omitted in Pu[1]; pādas a-b omitted in Pu[4]. Cited by *Vij* 1.117; *Lakṣ* 2.167; *Mādh* 1.140 — a) GMd[1] कर्मणां यस्य; TMd[3] TMd[4] कर्मणां मध्ये — b) sOx[1] sPu[6] स्त्रीणि; BBe[2] TMd[4] Pu[2] Pu[4] जीविकाः; TMd[3] जीविता — c) GMd[1] sOx[1] sPu[6] यजना°; Bo °नाध्ययने; GMd[5] °नाध्यायने; BBe[2] Tj[1] °ध्यापना — d) WKt[1] विशुद्धाद्धि; BBe[2] GMy sOx[1] sPu[6] विशुद्धाश्च; *Lakṣ* विशुद्धश्च; *Dev* विशिष्टाच्च; TMd[4] विशिष्टस्य; NKt[4] °ग्रहाः

77. Omitted in Hy Pu[1]. Cited by *Lakṣ* 2.251; *Dev* 2.449; *Mādh* 1.308 — a) BKt[5] कर्मा; WKt[1] वर्णा; Be[1] Ho Pu[10] धर्माणि वर्तन्ते [Pu[10] वर्तात]; Jo[2] Tj[1] [*Jolly* R] *Mādh* निवर्तेरन् — b) [*Jolly* N] ब्राह्मणः; TMd[4] Tr[2] ब्रह्मणः; Lo[4] ब्राह्मणा; Lo[1] ब्राह्मणाः; *Lakṣ* ब्रह्मणाः; GMd[1] ब्राह्मं वै क्षत्रि°; MTr[4] MTr[6] ब्रह्म वै क्षत्रि°; GMy [*Jolly* Nd] ब्रह्मा वै क्षत्रि°; Tr[1] ब्राह्मा वै क्षत्रि°; Ho sOx[1] sPu[6] क्षत्रियान्प्रति — c) WKt[1] *om* च — d) Kt[2] BKt[5] Tr[1] तृतीयं च; Be[1] परिग्रहः

न तौ प्रति हि तान्धर्मान् मनुराह प्रजापतिः ॥७८॥
शस्त्रास्त्रभृत्त्वं क्षत्रस्य वणिक्पशुकृषी विशः ।
आजीवनार्थं धर्मस्तु दानमध्ययनं यजिः ॥७९॥
वेदाभ्यासो ब्राह्मणस्य क्षत्रियस्य तु रक्षणम् ।
वार्त्ताकर्मैव वैश्यस्य विशिष्टानि स्वकर्मसु ॥८०॥
अजीवंस्तु यथोक्तेन ब्राह्मणः स्वेन कर्मणा ।
जीवेत्क्षत्रियधर्मेण स ह्यस्य प्रत्यनन्तरः ॥८१॥
उभाभ्यामप्यजीवंस्तु कथं स्यादिति चेद्भवेत् ।
कृषिगोरक्षमास्थाय जीवेद्वैश्यस्य जीविकाम् ॥८२॥
वैश्यवृत्त्यापि जीवंस्तु ब्राह्मणः क्षत्रियोऽपि वा ।
हिंसाप्रायां पराधीनां कृषिं यत्नेन वर्जयेत् ॥८३॥
कृषिं साध्विति मन्यन्ते सा वृत्तिः सद्विगर्हिता ।

78. Omitted in Pu^{1}. Cited by *Lakṣ* 2.251; pādas a-b cited by *Dev* 2.449; *Mādh* 1.308 — a) Pu^{5} Pu^{7} यथैवैते; BKt^{5} Lo^{1} GMy NNg तथैवेते; BBe^{2} Lo^{4} Pu^{10} [*Jolly* M] तथैतानि — a-b) Pu^{2} प्रति निवर्तन्ते तथैवैते इति — c) GMy एतौ प्रति; Lo^{2} ततो प्रति; GMd^{5} प्रतिगृहाद्धर्मान्; MTr^{6} प्रतिग्रहान्धर्मान्; BKt^{5} *om* हि; GMy ह

79.* Omitted in Pu^{1}. Cited by *Dev* 2.449; *Mādh* 1.397; pādas a-b cited by *Vij* 1.119; *Mādh* 1.308 — a) Pu^{10} °भृत्यं; NNg क्षत्रियस्य — b) Pu^{5} Pu^{7} वणिक्पथ°; Kt^{2} sOx^{1} sPu^{6} MTr^{4} °कृषि; Be^{1} BBe^{2} Bo WKt^{3} BKt^{5} Lo^{1} TMd^{4} NNg oOr Pu^{2} Pu^{4} Pu^{5} Pu^{7} Pu^{8} Pu^{10} Tj^{2} *Nā* °कृषीर्विषः; Ho Jm Jo^{1} WKt^{1} NKt^{4} La^{1} Lo^{4} GMd^{5} Ox^{2} Tr^{1} MTr^{5} MTr^{6} *Dev Mandlik Jha KSS Dave* °कृषिर्विशः; GMy °यजीर्विशः; Tj^{1} Tr^{2} वशः — c) Tj^{1} अजीव°; Lo^{4} GMy आजीविनार्थं; Pu^{10} त्वधर्मस्तु; WKt^{3} धर्मास्तु; BKt^{5} oOr धर्मश्च — d) Pu^{10} यजति; *Mādh* जगुः; GMy रतिः

80. Omitted in NPu^{1} MTr^{5}; pāda-b from तु until the end of pāda-c omitted in Tj^{1} — a) Ho sOx^{1} sPu^{6} °भ्यासो हि विप्रस्य — b) Jm Jo^{1} Jo^{2} Kt^{2} Lo^{3} Lo^{4} sOx^{1} sPu^{6} Pu^{10} Tr^{2} MTr^{3} *Mandlik Jolly Jha KSS Dave* च; Ho व; WKt^{3} लक्षणं; NNg रक्षिणं; Lo^{4} संरक्षं — c) WKt^{1} वार्तान्नेव; GMd^{1} TMd^{4} Pu^{8} °कर्मेव; Tr^{1} Pu^{4} °कर्म च — d) WKt^{3} विशिप्टा हि; TMd^{4} निर्दिप्टासु

81. Omitted in Pu^{1}; verses 81 and 82 transposed in Wa. Cited by *Dev* 2.469 — a) Be^{1} Bo GMd^{5} GMy Ox^{2} MTr^{3} आजीवंस्तु; BKt^{5} TMd^{3} आजीवस्तु; TMd^{4} गोजीवन्त्य यथो° — b) BKt^{5} La^{1} ब्राह्मणाः — d) Tr^{2} प्रात्य°; GMy °नन्तरं

82. Omitted in Pu^{1}; pāda-b omitted in Pu^{10}; pādas b-d *ma* Lo^{1} [haplo]. Cited by *Vij* 3.35; *Dev* 2.470 — a) *Vij* °मप्याजीवंस्तु; Be^{1} °मुपजीवंस्तु; Bo GMd^{5} °मपिजीवंस्तु; Tr^{2} °मपिजीवस्तु; Hy °जीवस्तु — b) TMd^{4} चेद्विजः — c) WKt^{3} Pu^{5} Pu^{7} कृषिं; WKt^{3} GMd^{1} TMd^{4} GMy NNg *Dev* °रक्ष्यमा°; BBe^{2} °रक्षणास्थाय — d) Bo NKt^{4} Lo^{1} Lo^{4} GMd^{5} oOr Pu^{3} Pu^{10} Tr^{1} MTr^{4} MTr^{5} MTr^{6} स जीवेद्वैश्यजीविकां [MTr^{5} जीवितां]; Tj^{1} चरेदद्वैश्यजीविकां; Jo^{2} Lo^{3} चरेद्वैश्यस्य; Ox^{2} °द्वैश्यश्च; Pu^{4} वृत्तिकां; TMd^{3} जीवरां

83. Omitted in BKt^{5} NPu^{1} MTr^{5}. Cited by *Apa* 936; *Dev* 2.470; *Mādh* 1.426 — a) TMd^{4} *Mādh* °वृत्त्या तु; GMd^{5} °वृत्त्या हि; La^{1} °वृत्तेपि; TMd^{3} °वृत्तं हि; WKt^{1} Tr^{2} °वृत्त्याप्यजीवंस्तु; Tr^{1} °वृत्त्याभिजीवंस्तु — b) Jo^{1} *om* वा — c) oOr हिंसाप्रियं; Tr^{2} हिंसनिप्रायां; Lo^{1} हिंसायां च; NNg °प्रायं पराधीनं — d) Be^{1} कृपिर्यत्नेन; GMy यत्नेव

भूमिं भूमिशयांश्चैव हन्ति काष्ठमयोमुखम् ॥८४॥
इदं तु वृत्तिवैकल्यात् त्यजतो धर्मनैपुणम् ।
विट्पण्यमुद्धृतोद्धारं विक्रेयं वित्तवर्धनम् ॥८५॥
सर्वान् रसानपोहेत कृतान्नं च तिलैः सह ।
अश्मनो लवणं चैव पशवो ये च मानुषाः ॥८६॥
सर्वं च तान्तवं रक्तं शाणक्षौमाविकानि च ।
अपि चेत्स्युररक्तानि फलमूले तथौषधीः ॥८७॥
अपः शस्त्रं विषं मांसं सोमं गन्धांश्च सर्वशः ।
क्षीरं क्षौद्रं दधि घृतं तैलं मधु गुडं कुशान् ॥८८॥
आरण्यांश्च पशून्सर्वान् दंष्ट्रिणश्च वयांसि च ।
मद्यं नीलीं च लाक्षां च सर्वांश्चैकशफांस्तथा ॥८९॥

84. Omitted in NPu^{1} Pu^{5}. Cited by *Apa* 936; *Dev* 2.470; *Mādh* 1.426 — a) Ox^{2} Pu^{2} Pu^{4} Pu^{7} *Go* कृषिः; BKt^{5} कृषी; BKt^{5} Pu^{2} Tj^{1} Wa साध्वीति; Lo^{1} साध्वी मन्यते *cor to* साध्वीममन्यन्ते — b) Bo मा; Tr^{2} स्याद्विगर्हिता; oOr साधुगर्हिताः; GMd^{1} TMd^{3} MTr^{4} MTr^{5} MTr^{6} सर्वगर्हिता— c) Pu^{10} *om* भूमिं; Bo °शयाश्चैव — d) Tr^{1} MTr^{3} °मधोमुखं

Additional verse in Be^{1} TMd^{4}:

संवत्सरेण यत्पापं मत्स्यघाती समाप्नुयात् ।
एकाहात्तदवाप्नोति लाङ्गली कृपिजीवकः ॥

b) TMd^{4} मत्स्यबंधीरवाप्नुयात्

85. Omitted in Pu^{1}. Cited by *Lakṣ* 2.199 — a) oOr इमं; Lo^{2} इदं निवृत्ति°; oOr Tr^{2} वृत्त°; NKt^{4} GMd^{1} TMd^{3} TMd^{4} NNg MTr^{4} MTr^{5} MTr^{6} Wa वित्त°; *Lakṣ* धर्म°; Pu^{2} Pu^{4} °वैगुण्यात् — b) sOx^{1} sPu^{6} त्यजन्तो; TMd^{4} Pu^{3} त्यजता; Pu^{10} Tr^{1} त्यजते; wKt^{3} यजतो; MTr^{4} MTr^{6} वित्तनैपुणं; Pu^{10} °नेपुण्यं — c) Pu^{2} विपण्ये नु वृतोद्धारं; Lo^{2} विट्पाण्य°; La^{1} Lo^{1} विपण्य°; Pu^{4} विपण्य तु [*rest om*]; Lo^{1} GMy °मुद्धतो°; Pu^{10} °तोद्धरणं — d) TMd^{4} sOx^{1} Pu^{10} विक्रियं; GMy Pu^{2} विक्रयं; La^{1} विक्रया; Lo^{3} Tj^{1} विज्ञेयं

86. Omitted in Pu^{1}; pādas a-b omitted in Pu^{4}. Cited by *Har*-A 1.20.12; *Lakṣ* 2.199 — a) Pu^{2} रसान्व्यपोहेत; sOx^{1} sPu^{6} °पोहते; BKt^{5} °पोहेतु — b) *Lakṣ* तु — c) Be^{1} Lo^{4} अश्मानो; TMd^{4} अशनो — d) Ox^{2} ये न; Bo मानुपः; BBe^{2} *Lakṣ* मानवाः

87. Omitted in Pu^{1}. Cited by *Vij* 3.36–8; *Har*-A 1.20.12 — a) BKt^{5} सर्वे; Pu^{2} तु; Bo नक्तं; TMd^{4} वस्त्रं — b) Bo शण°; Ho Pu^{4} Tj^{1} शाणं; TMd^{4} शान°; Hy शाम°; BKt^{5} Lo^{4} Pu^{10} MTr^{5} °क्षौमाजिनानि — c) BKt^{5} Lo^{1} अपि च स्युर°; Hy चेत्साररक्तानि; Pu^{5} Pu^{7} °रत्नानि — d) Tj^{1} °मूल; La^{1} Pu^{2} Pu^{4} °मूलं; Pu^{2} Pu^{4} तथौषधी; La^{1} तथौषधं

88. Omitted in Pu^{1}. Cited by *Har*-A 1.20.12; pādas c-d cited by *Vij* 3.36–8; *Dev* 2.479 — a) Hy Lo^{1} Pu^{2} Pu^{4} आपः; TMd^{3} शस्त्रिं; Pu^{4} विप — b) TMd^{4} oOr सोम; GMy गोमं; Wa सामं; wKt^{3} Tj^{1} गन्धाश्च; BBe^{2} गन्धां सर्वशः; Wa सर्वतः — c) *Nā* क्षारं and as pāṭha क्षीरं; Pu^{4} क्षीरक्षौद्र; Pu^{10} जरिजौद्रं; Tr^{1} क्षारं क्षीरं दधि; Kt^{2} क्षौरं; GMd^{5} GMy MTr^{5} MTr^{6} [*Jolly* Nd] क्षारं दधि; Hy Tr^{1} घृत; BKt^{5} घृते — c-d) GMd^{1} क्षीरं क्षारं दधि मधु घृतं शुद्धोदकं कुशान् — d) BKt^{5} तैलमज्जान्कुशान्गुणं; Pu^{3} Tr^{2} मज्जा गुडं; Pu^{5} Pu^{7} Tr^{1} गुडां; MTr^{5} गुळं; TMd^{4} गुडे

89. Cited by *Har*-A 1.20.12; pādas a-b cited by *Vij* 3.36–8; *Apa* 931 — a) BCa La^{1} GMd^{1} Tj^{1} Tr^{1} अरण्यांश्च — b) Be^{1} वा — c) GMd^{5} मद्यान्; [*Jolly* Nd] मज्जां नीलीं; Hy नीलिं; Bo NKt^{4} BKt^{5}

काममुत्पाद्य कृष्या तु स्वयमेव कृषीवलः ।
विक्रीणीत तिलाञ्छुद्धान् धर्मार्थमचिरस्थितान् ॥९०॥

भोजनाभ्यञ्जनाद्दानाद् यदन्यत्कुरुते तिलैः ।
कृमिभूतः श्वविष्ठायां पितृभिः सह मज्जति ॥९१॥

सद्यः पतति मांसेन लाक्षया लवणेन च ।
त्र्यहेण शूद्रो भवति ब्राह्मणः क्षीरविक्रयात् ।९२॥

इतरेषां तु पण्यानां विक्रयादिह कामतः ।
ब्राह्मणः सप्तरात्रेण वैश्यभावं निगच्छति* ॥९३॥

TMd^3 TMd^4 GMd^5 sOx^1 Ox^2 Tj^1 MTr^6 नीलं; Tr^2 नीलां; Tr^1 तिलं; La^1 Pu^5 Pu^7 *om first* च; TMd^3 GMd^5 Tr^1 MTr^6 लाक्षं; La^1 Lo^1 oOr sOx^1 लाक्षांश्च; Lo^4 लाक्षाश्च — d) Hy सर्वाश्चैक°; Ho Jo^2 Lo^2 Lo^3 GMd^1 TMd^3 TMd^4 sOx^1 Pu^5 sPu^6 Pu^7 Tj^1 MTr^6 [*Jolly* G R]सर्वानेक°; BBe^2 सर्वानैक°; GMy सर्वा-ङ्गैक°; Bo °शफां तथा; Kt^2 wKt^3 °शफास्तथा; GMd^1 MTr^4 MTr^6 *Bh* [pāṭha]*Me* [pāṭha] °शफान्बहून्; TMd^3 GMd^5 GMy Tr^1 [*Jolly* Nd] *Har*-A°शफान्पशून्

Additional verse in Be^1 BCa GMd^1 TMd^4 GMy oOr Tr^1 MTr^4 MTr^6 [*Jolly* Gr Nd] *Mandlik* [क] *KSS Dave;* cited by *Lakṣ* 2.199:

त्रपुसीसे तथा लोहं तैजसानि च सर्वशः ।
वालांश्चर्म तथास्थीनि वसास्नायूनि रोचनाम् ॥

a) Be^1 °सीसं; BCa °शीषं; GMy °सीसं च लोहं च; *Lakṣ* लौहं; Tr^1 लोह — b) TMd^3 रजतं चैव सर्वशः — c) GMy चर्माणि च तथास्थीनि; Tr^1 [*Jolly* Gr Nd] पाशाश्चर्म; Be^1 तथास्थानि — d) Be^1 सस्नायूनि च वर्जयेत्; oOr °यूनि वर्जयेत्

90* Cited by *Vij* 3.39; *Apa* 933; *Har*-A 1.20.13; *Dev* 2.480; *Mādh* 1.431 — a) TMd^3 कामादुत्पाद्य; [*Jolly* M$^{4-5}$] हस्तमुत्पाद्य; Pu^{10} कामहस्तमुत्पाद्य; Tr^2 °मुत्पद्य; Jo^1 कृष्याः; Lo^1 कृष्यं *cor to* कृष्णं; Bo Jm BKt^5 La^1 Lo^3 GMd^1 NNg oOr Pu^5 Pu^7 Pu^8 Pu^{10} Tj^1 Tj^2 MTr^3 *Apa Har-A Dev Mandlik Jha KSS Dave* कृष्यां; Be^1 sOx^1 NPu^1 sPu^6 कृष्यांस्तु; Wa कृष्यास्तु; Ho GMd^5 *Vij* कृष्यात्तु; Kt^2 *Mādh Nd* कृष्यान्तु; TMd^3 तुष्यात्तु; BKt^5 च — c) Lo^1 विक्रीणति; oOr NPu^1 Tr^1 विक्रीणीते; La^1 Pu^8 विक्रीणीयात्; Ox^2 तिलान्सर्वान् — d) Tr^2 धर्मामचिरोस्थितान्; Ho धर्मार्थाम°; NKt^4 धर्मार्थायचिर°; Lo^3 °माचिरास्थितान्; GMd^1 °चिरात्स्थितान्; Pu^2 Pu^4 °चिरंस्थितान्

91. Omitted in Pu^{10} [*Jolly* M$^{8-9}$]. Cited by *Vij* 3.39; *Apa* 933; *Dev* 2.480; *Mādh* 1.431–2 — b) NKt^4 GMd^1 MTr^6 कुरुतेन्यत्तिलैस्तु यः [MTr^6 °लैस्तु यद्]; Hy Wa यत्त्वन्यत्कु°; NNg यस्त्वन्यत्कु°; Lo^2 °त्क्रियते — c) BKt^5 TMd^3 GMy Tr^1 [*Jolly* Nd] कृमिभूतश्च विष्ठायां; Tr^2 क्रमि°; NNg *Apa* क्रिमि°; Hy wKt^1 कृमी°; TMd^3 क्रिमी°; Be^1 BKt^5 NPu^1 कृमिर्भूतः; NKt^4 कृमिर्भूत; Ho Jo^2 Lo^3 TMd^4 GMd^5 oOr sOx^1 sPu^6 Tj^1 [*Jolly* R] *Vij Dev Mādh* कृमिर्भूत्वा [Lo^3 GMd^5 Tj^1 कृमि]; Be^1 BBe^2 wKt^1 NNg oOr sOx^1 sPu^6 [*Jolly* M^4 sh] *Dev Mādh* स विष्ठायां; [*Jolly* M^5]स्वविष्ठायां — c-d) GMd^1 कृमिभूतस्स घोरेषु नरकेषु हि मज्जति — d) La^1 पत्यते कृमिभिः सह; Lo^1 पितृभ्यां

92. Omitted in Pu^{10} [*Jolly* M$^{8-9}$]. Cited by *Vij* 3.40; *Apa* 934, 1046; *Dev* 2.480; *Mādh* 1.422 — a) La^1 MTr^6 पतित; Be^1 तपति; BKt^5 मासेन — b) Bo La^1 GMd^1 MTr^6 लाक्षाया; TMd^4 लाक्षयां; BBe^2 लाक्षयो; Tr^2 वा — c) TMd^3 त्र्येहेण; Lo^1 Pu^5 Pu^7 [*Jolly* G] शूद्री — d) [*Jolly* Gr] क्षार°; Tr^2 रसविक्र°; GMd^1 GMd^5 GMy Tr^1 MTr^4 MTr^5 MTr^6 °विक्रयी; TMd^3 °विक्रय

93* Omitted in Pu^{10} [*Jolly* M$^{8-9}$]. Cited by *Vij* 3.40; *Apa* 934; *Dev* 2.480 — a) TMd^4 GMy *Vij Apa Dev* [vl] इतरेषामपण्यानां; Lo^4 च; NNg Tr^1 Wa त्वपण्यानां; Tj^1 पुण्यानां — d) Bo GMy वैश्याभावं; GMd^1 *Vij* च गच्छति; BBe^2 Bo BCa Ho Hy Jm Jo^1 Jo^2 wKt^1 Kt^2 wKt^3 NKt^4 BKt^5 La^1

रसा रसैर्निमातव्या न त्वेव लवणं रसैः ।
कृतान्नं चाकृतान्नेन तिला धान्येन तत्समाः ॥९४॥
जीवेदेतेन राजन्यः सर्वेणाप्यनयं गतः ।
न त्वेव ज्यायसीं वृत्तिमभिमन्येत कर्हिचित् ॥९५॥
यो लोभादधमो जात्या जीवेदुत्कृष्टकर्मभिः ।
तं राजा निर्धनं कृत्वा क्षिप्रमेव प्रवासयेत् ॥९६॥
वरं स्वधर्मो विगुणो न पारक्यः स्वनुष्ठितः ।
परधर्मेण जीवन्हि सद्यः पतति जातितः ॥९७॥
वैश्योऽजीवन्स्वधर्मेण शूद्रवृत्त्यापि वर्तयेत् ।
अनाचरन्नकार्याणि निवर्तेत च शक्तिमान् ॥९८॥

Lo[1] Lo[2] Lo[3] sOx[1] Ox[2] NPu[1] Pu[2] Pu[3] Pu[4] Pu[5] sPu[6] Pu[7] Pu[8] Tj[1] Tj[2] Tr[2] MTr[3] Wa *Dev Mandlik Jha KSS Dave* नियच्छति; Be[1] *Apa* प्रयच्छति

94. Omitted in Pu[10] [*Jolly* M[8–9]]; pādas c-d omitted in Pu[2] Pu[4]. Cited by *Vij* 3.39; *Apa* 932–3; *Dev* 2.481; *Har*-A 1.20.15; *Mādh* 1.431 — a) Pu[5] Pu[7] रसैर्मिमातव्या; MTr[6] रसैर्नमातव्या; Tr[2] रसैर्निर्मातव्या; Bo °मान्तव्या; La[1] °मांडव्या; Be[1] *Apa* °पातव्या; BBe[2] °तव्यः; TMd[4] °तव्य — b) GMd[1] स त्वेव; La[1] न द्वेव; wKt[1] न द्वे लवणं; BKt[5] त्वेतन्लवणं; Tj[2] रसे; NKt[4] La[1] GMd[1] GMd[5] GMy Tr[1] MTr[4] MTr[5] MTr[6] [*Jolly* Nd Gr] *Me* [pāṭha] *Bh* तिलैः — c) Jo[2] Lo[3] Tj[1] कृतान्नमकृतान्नेन; Ho wKt[1] NKt[4] NPu[1] sOx[1] sPu[6] Tj[2] [*see* GDh 7.21] वाकृता°; Be[1] Lo[1] Lo[2] Lo[4] [*cor to*] MTr[3] [*Jolly* M Nd] *Jha* च कृतान्नेन [Jo[2] *om* च]; wKt[1] च कृतार्थेन — d) Be[1] Bo NKt[4] Lo[1] MTr[5] तिल; GMd[1] तिलो; MTr[5] तत्समं; NKt[4] तत्समं; GMd[1] तत्समान्

95. Pādas a-b omitted in Pu[2] Pu[4]. Cited by *Apa* 934; *Dev* 2.473 — a) TMd[3] जीवेदेकेन; oOr राजन्यं — b) La[1] सर्वेण व्यत्ययं गतः; GMd[1] TMd[4] Ox[2] Tj[1] *Apa* [vl] °प्ययनं; Pu[10] °प्यपनं; Tr[1] °प्यधनं; Lo[3] BBe[2] °प्यापदं; sOx[1] sPu[6] Pu[10] गताः — c) BBe[2] GMd[5] त्वेवं; Ox[2] त्वेनां; BKt[5] Pu[5] Pu[7] ज्यायसी — d) Be[1] वृत्तिं नाभि°; NPu[1] Pu[4] °मनुमन्येत

96. Omitted in Pu[10]; pādas c-d omitted in BBe[2]; the following sequence of verses in [*Jolly* M[1–2–8]] 96, 105–109, 114, 97–104, 115. Cited by *Apa* 822, 865; *Lakṣ* 12.565 — a) La[1] TMd[3] ये; wKt[3] लोभावधमो; GMy लाभादधमो; GMd[1] GMd[5] NPu[1] Pu[2] Pu[4] Pu[8] Tr[1] [*Jolly* G] मोहादधमो; *Apa* 822 [vl] लोकादधमो; Lo[4] लोभादवमो — b) wKt[1] जीवेद्वा कृष्णकर्मभिः — c) TMd[4] oOr निधनं — d) GMd[1] Pu[2] Pu[4] Tj[1] *Apa* 822 विवासयेत्; TMd[4] प्रकाशयेत्

97.* Omitted in BBe[2] Pu[10] [*Jolly* Nd]. Cited by *Vij* 3.41; *Apa* 935; *Dev* 2.466, 475 — a) TMd[3] परः स्वधर्मो निपुणः; TMd[4] श्रेयान्स्वधर्माद्विगुणः; GMy वर; GMd[1] TMd[4] GMd[5] Tr[1] MTr[4] [*Jolly* Gr] श्रेयान्स्वधर्मो; GMd[5] Tr[1] द्विगुणः; NKt[4] विमुखो — b) BKt[5] GMd[1] TMd[3] TMd[4] GMd[5] NNg Ox[2] Pu[3] Pu[8] Tr[1] Tr[2] MTr[4] Wa परधर्मात्स्वनुष्ठितात् [Tr[2] °निष्ठि°]; [*Jolly* M] *Jolly Jha Dave* परधर्मात्स्वधिष्ठितात्; GMy परधर्मान्स्वनुष्ठितान्; Lo[4] *ma* न; MTr[3] तार्क्यः; La[1] सुनिष्ठितः — c) TMd[4] *Vij* परधर्माश्रयाद्विप्रः; wKt[1] जीवन्तु; Be[1] जीवन्सः; GMy जीवन्यः — d) Tj[1] MTr[6] पतित

98. Omitted in Pu[10]; pādas a-b omitted in BBe[2]. Cited by *Apa* 934; *Dev* 2.473 — a) MTr[3] °जीवेत्स्व°; NKt[4] °जीवत्स्व°; Pu[7] °न्सधर्मेण; oOr °न्स्ववृत्तेन — b) GMd[1] वर्तयन्; Bo GMd[5] वर्जयेत् — c) MTr[6] अनाचाराद्यकार्याणि; BKt[5] GMd[1] GMy Tr[1] अनाचाराणि कार्याणि [GMy कर्माणि]; Bo TMd[3] अनाचारं न कार्याणि; sOx[1] अनाचारेण कार्याणि; Be[1] GMd[5] Pu[5] Pu[7] अनाचार° — d) TMd[3] न वर्तेत; NKt[4] वर्तेत [*om* नि°]; wKt[1] La[1] निवर्तेतैव; GMy निवर्त्येतैव; GMd[1] °र्तेत प्रयत्नतः; Be[1] स्वशक्तिमान्

अशक्नुवंस्तु शुश्रूषां शूद्रः कर्तुं द्विजन्मनाम् ।
पुत्रदारात्ययं प्राप्तो जीवेत्कारुककर्मभिः ॥९९॥
यैः कर्मभिः प्रचरितैः शुश्रूष्यन्ते द्विजातयः ।
तानि कारुककर्माणि शिल्पानि विविधानि च ॥१००॥
वैश्यवृत्तिमनातिष्ठन् ब्राह्मणः स्वे पथि स्थितः ।
अवृत्तिकर्शितः सीदन्निमं धर्मं समाचरेत् ॥१०१॥
सर्वतः प्रतिगृह्णीयाद् ब्राह्मणस्त्वनयं गतः ।
पवित्रं दुष्यतीत्येतद् धर्मतो नोपपद्यते ॥१०२॥
नाध्यापनाद्याजनाद्वा गर्हिताद्वा प्रतिग्रहात् ।
दोषो भवति विप्राणां ज्वलनाम्बुसमा हि ते ॥१०३॥
जीवितात्ययमापन्नो योऽन्नमत्ति यतस्ततः ।
आकाशमिव पङ्केन न स दोषेण लिप्यते ॥१०४॥
अजीगर्तः सुतं हन्तुमुपासर्पद् बुभुक्षितः ।

99. Omitted in Pu^{10}. Cited by *Apa* 162; *Mādh* 1.423 — a) oOr Pu^{3} Tr^{2} अशक्नुवंश्च; NPu^{1} अशुश्रुवंश्च — b) Lo^{3} Tj^{1} कुर्वन्द्विज°; Bo °जन्मनः — c) TMd^{4} °त्यये; Lo^{4} [*Jolly* M] *Apa* °त्यये पाप्ते — d) NKt^{4} TMd^{3} जीवत्कारुकर्मभिः; BKt^{5} जीवेत्सः कारुकर्मभिः; BBe^{2} जीवेच्च कारुकर्मभिः; Bo °त्कातुक°; NKt^{4} °त्कारुंकर्मभिः; Ho °कर्मिभिः; Ox^{2} °कर्मणा

100. Omitted in Pu^{10}. Cited by *Vij* 3.35; *Dev* 2.456,474; *Mādh* 1.423 — a) La^{1} कर्मभिस्तु चरितैः; BCa GMd^{1} TMd^{3} GMd^{5} GMy oOr Tj^{1} Tr^{1} [*Jolly* R Gr] *Mādh* सुचरितैः; Lo^{3} सुरचितैः — b) sOx^{1} sPu^{6} Tj^{1} शुश्रूपन्ते — c) TMd^{4} दारुककर्माणि

101.* Omitted in Pu^{10}; pādas a-b omitted in Pu^{4}. Cited by *Apa* 935; *Dev* 2.464 — a) NPu^{1} Pu^{2} °वृत्तिं समाति°; BKt^{5} °वृत्तिं त्वानाति°; GMd^{5} °तिष्ठेत्; TMd^{4} °तिष्ठे — b) TMd^{4} ब्राह्मणश्चापथि; Ho BKt^{5} sOx^{1} sPu^{6} Pu^{8} *Apa* स्वपथि; Lo^{1} पथे — c) La^{1} अवृत्तिं; *Apa* स्ववृत्ति°; Be^{1} BBe^{2} Bo Hy Jm Jo^{1} wKt^{1} Kt^{2} wKt^{3} BKt^{5} La^{1} oOr Ox^{2} Tj^{2} *Mandlik Jolly Jha KSS Dave* °कर्षितः; MTr^{6} °कृततस् — d) GMd^{1} TMd^{3} Ox^{2} NPu^{1} Pu^{4} Tr^{1} °न्निदं; wKt^{1} °न्निमान्धर्मान्समा°; Be^{1} धर्म्यं; Ox^{2} समारभेत्

102. Omitted in Pu^{10}. Cited by *Apa* 935; *Dev* 2.464; *Mādh* 2.326; pādas a-b cited by *Dev* 2.457 — a) *Apa* संप्रगृह्णीयाद् — b) Bo ब्राह्मणस्त्वनपण्डितः; Tj^{2} ब्राह्मण्यस्त्वनयं; MTr^{4} MTr^{6} ब्राह्मणोप्यनयं; Be^{1} ब्राह्मणस्त्वापदं; NPu^{1} ब्राह्मणः स्वापदं; Lo^{2} GMd^{1} Tj^{1} ब्राह्मणस्त्वयनं; Tr^{1} ब्राह्मणस्त्वधनं — c) TMd^{4} पवित्र्यं; GMd^{1} दुष्यतेत्येतद्; Pu^{3} दुःखतीत्येतद्; Tr^{2} दुष्यतीव त्वेतद्; BBe^{2} °तीत्येव — d) wKt^{1} धर्मतः प्रतिपद्यते

103. Omitted in Pu^{10} MTr^{5}. Cited by *Apa* 935; *Dev* 2.464; *Mādh* 2.326 — d) TMd^{4} लोलनाम्बुसमाहितः; Be^{1} Bo Jo^{2} wKt^{1} wKt^{3} La^{1} Lo^{3} TMd^{3} Ox^{2} Pu^{2} Pu^{3} Pu^{4} Pu^{5} Pu^{7} Tj^{1} Tr^{2} [*Jolly* G R Nd] *Rn Rc* ज्वलनार्कसमा; Hy ज्वलनाङ्कसमा; oOr Tj^{2} °समो; GMy °समो हि सः

104.* Omitted in Pu^{10} Wa. Cited by *Apa* 935; *Har*-A 1.213; *Mādh* 2.326 — a) GMd^{1} जीवतोत्यय°; TMd^{3} जीवतात्यय°; MTr^{5} जीविकात्यय° — b) *Me Jha Dave* ततस्ततः — c) GMy आकाश इव — d) GMd^{1} स दोषेण न लिप्यते; *Apa* न पापेन स लिप्यते; BCa स पापेन न लिप्यते; Tj^{1} *om* स; all NT mss. and all editions read न स पापेन लिप्यते; NPu^{1} पापैर्विलिप्यते

न चालिप्यत दोषेण क्षुत्प्रतीकारमाचरन् ॥१०५॥
श्वमांसमिच्छन्नार्तोऽत्तुं धर्माधर्मविचक्षणः ।
प्राणानां परिरक्षार्थं वामदेवो न लिप्तवान् ॥१०६॥
भरद्वाजः क्षुधार्तस्तु सपुत्रो विजने वने ।
बह्वीर्गाः प्रतिजग्राह बृबोस्तक्ष्णो* महातपाः ॥१०७॥
क्षुधार्तश्चात्तुमभ्यागाद् विश्वामित्रः श्वजाघनीम् ।
चण्डालहस्तादादाय धर्माधर्मविचक्षणः ॥१०८॥
प्रतिग्रहाद्याजनाद्वा तथैवाध्यापनादपि ।
प्रतिग्रहः प्रत्यवरः प्रेत्य विप्रस्य गर्हितः ॥१०९॥

105* Omitted in Pu^{10}; pādas a-b *ma* in Lo^4; pādas c-d omitted in Pu^4. Cited by *Apa* 935; *Dev* 2.465; *Mādh* 2.326 — a) GMy आजिगर्तिः; Tr^1 अजीगर्तुः; $_TMd^4$ अजीगर्तं — b) Be^1 °पसर्पाद्; $_wKt^3$ Pu^5 Pu^7 Pu^8 °पासर्प्यद्; $_NKt^4$ °पसर्प्यद्; $_GMd^1$ °पसर्पन्; Lo^4 °पागच्छद्; $_NPu^1$ °पातिष्ठद्; Tr^1 °क्षिताः — c) $_NPu^1$ नालिप्यत; GMy Tr^2 चालिप्यति; Lo^1 [*but cor*] $_TMd^3$ $_GMd^5$ oOr चालिप्येत; $_TMd^4$ दोषेवा; Be^1 $_BBe^2$ Bo BCa Ho Hy Jm Jo^1 $_wKt^1$ Kt^2 $_BKt^5$ Lo^1 Lo^2 Lo^4 NNg $_sOx^1$ Ox^2 $_NPu^1$ Pu^2 $_sPu^6$ Pu^8 Tj^2 $_MTr^3$ Wa [*Jolly* M] *Go Ku Mandlik KSS Jha Dave* पापेन — d) Ox^2 तत्प्रती°; $_wKt^1$ Wa क्षुत्प्रतिकारमा°; Ho $_wKt^3$ $_BKt^5$ Ox^2 Pu^3 Pu^8 Tr^2 °तीघातमा°

106 Omitted in Pu^4 [*Jolly* M^9]. Cited by *Apa* 935; *Dev* 2.465; *Mādh* 2.326 — a) La^1 Lo^2 $_TMd^3$ $_NPu^1$ स्वमांस°; $_wKt^1$ पुमांस°; $_MTr^5$ °न्नार्तस्तु; Be^1 Tj^1 °न्नार्तोतु; Bo °न्नार्तौतु; Lo^2 °न्नार्तेपि — b) Hy °विचारणः — c) $_GMd^1$ $_TMd^3$ $_GMd^5$ GMy Tr^1 प्राणानां रक्षणार्थाय; $_TMd^4$ प्राणापानपरिरक्षार्थं

107* Omitted in [*Jolly* M^9]. Cited by *Apa* 935; *Dev* 2.465; *Mādh* 2.326 — a) Bo Hy $_wKt^1$ La^1 Lo^3 Ox^2 Pu^5 Pu^7 Tr^1 $_MTr^5$ *Apa* भारद्वाजः; Bo BCa Ho La^1 $_TMd^4$ $_sOx^1$ $_sPu^6$ $_MTr^4$ $_MTr^5$ $_MTr^6$ क्षुधार्तश्च; Ox^2 क्षुधार्तोपि; *Apa* क्षुधं हन्तुं — b) $_GMd^1$ $_GMd^5$ oOr Tr^1 निर्जने; $_TMd^3$ GMy निर्जनो; $_TMd^4$ जीवने — c) GMy Pu^{10} बहिर्गाः; Pu^3 °जग्रहि — d) Pu^5 Pu^7 बृबुत°; BCa Hy Jm Jo^1 Jo^2 $_wKt^1$ Kt^2 $_NKt^4$ Lo^1 Lo^2 Lo^3 Lo^4 $_TMd^4$ NNg Pu^4 $_sPu^6$ Pu^8 Tj^2 $_MTr^3$ Wa [*Jolly* M^{3-4-5} Ku R] *Rn Mr Mandlik KSS Jha Dave* वृधोस्त°; $_BKt^5$ La^1 $_GMd^1$ GMy Pu^2 Pu^3 Tr^1 $_MTr^4$ $_MTr^5$ $_MTr^6$ [*Jolly* N Nd] *Nā Rc* बृहत्त°; Ox^2 Wa वृहत्त°; Tr^2 वृहत°; $_NPu^1$ वृहन्त°; Be^1 वृधुत°; $_BBe^2$ [*Jolly* M^{1-2-8}] वृद्धस्त°; $_sOx^1$ वृद्धास्त°; $_wKt^3$ वृध्रधोस्त°; Bo वुदोत्त°; *Dev* पृथोस्त°; oOr वृहतप्तो; Tj^1 पृथोस्तीक्ष्णो; *Apa* शिघुतीक्ष्णो; *Mādh* वृहत्प्राज्ञो; $_GMd^5$ बहदश्वो; Pu^{10} वृधस्तंभो; Ho वुद्धतक्षोर्महा°; $_TMd^3$ भृहतकोर्महा°; Hy La^1 NNg Ox^2 Pu^2 Pu^4 Pu^7 Tj^2 Tr^2 *Go Mr* °क्ष्णोर्महा°; $_GMd^1$ Tr^1 महत्तपाः; Pu^2 महायशाः; $_NKt^4$ $_BKt^5$ Lo^2 $_TMd^4$ NNg Ox^2 Pu^5 Pu^7 Pu^{10} $_MTr^4$ $_MTr^6$ *Go* महामनाः; Tr^2 *Apa* महात्मनः

108. Omitted in [*Jolly* M^9]. Cited by *Apa* 935; *Dev* 2.465; *Mādh* 2.326 — a) Tj^1 Tr^1 °श्चार्तुम°; $_wKt^1$ °श्चादुमत्यादाद्; NNg °भ्यगाद् — b) $_sOx^1$ $_sPu^6$ विश्वामित्रश्च जानुनी; $_TMd^3$ विश्वामित्रश्च जाघ्निः; Pu^5 Pu^7 श्वजाघृतं; $_wKt^1$ श्वजापनः; Tr^1 °जाघिनीं; Kt^2 °जाघनौ; $_BKt^5$ $_NPu^1$ °जाघनं — c) Bo Ho La^1 Lo^1 Ox^2 चाण्डाल° — d) La^1 $_MTr^4$ $_MTr^6$ विद्वानपि महातपाः

After चण्डालहस्ता $_TMd^4$ jumps to 11.190 and gives the omitted verses after 12.24; probably the exemplar the scribe was using had folios misplaced.

109. Omitted in [*Jolly* M^9]; pādas a-b omitted in Pu^2 Pu^4. Cited by *Apa* 935; *Dev* 2.476 — a) $_GMd^1$ °ग्रहाद्ध्यापनाद्वा; Ho $_NKt^4$ NNg $_sOx^1$ Pu^3 $_sPu^6$ Tr^1 Tr^2 $_MTr^4$ $_MTr^5$ $_MTr^6$ Wa °जनाच्च — b) $_TMd^3$ $_GMd^5$ तथैवाध्ययनादपि; *Apa* तथा वाध्या°; GMy °ध्यायनादपि — c) $_MTr^6$ °ग्रहं; Bo प्रेत्यवरः; *Apa* [vl] प्रतिवरः — d) Lo^3 Tj^1 प्रेत्य चेह च गर्हितः; *Dev* स तु विप्रस्य; La^1 गर्हिताः

याजनाध्यापने नित्यं क्रियेते संस्कृतात्मनाम् ।
प्रतिग्रहस्तु क्रियते शूद्रस्याप्यन्त्यजन्मनः ॥११०॥
जपहोमैरपैत्येनो याजनाध्यापनैः कृतम् ।
प्रतिग्रहनिमित्तं तु त्यागेन तपसैव च ॥१११॥
शिलोञ्छमप्याददीत विप्रोऽजीवन्यतस्ततः ।
प्रतिग्रहाच्छिलः श्रेयांस्ततोऽप्युञ्छः प्रशस्यते ॥११२॥
सीदद्भिः कुप्यमिच्छद्भिर्धनं वा पृथिवीपतिः ।
याच्यः स्यात्स्नातकैर्विप्रैरदित्संस्त्यागमर्हति ॥११३॥
अकृतं च कृतात्क्षेत्राद् गौरजाविकमेव च ।
हिरण्यं धान्यमन्नं च पूर्वं पूर्वमदोषवत् ॥११४॥
सप्त वित्तागमा धर्म्या दायो लाभः क्रयो जयः ।
प्रयोगः कर्मयोगश्च सत्प्रतिग्रह एव च ॥११५॥

110. Omitted in [*Jolly* M^9]; pādas b-d omitted in nKt^4. Cited by *Apa* 936; *Dev* 2.476 — a) Bo nKt^4 °ध्यापनैर्नित्यं; Tr^2 नित्ये — b) Lo^1 क्रीयेते संक्रियात्मनां; Be^1 bBe^2 Ho Hy bKt^5 La^1 gMd^1 tMd^3 gMy nNg sOx^1 Pu^2 Pu^5 sPu^6 [*but mc sh*] Pu^7 Tr^2 क्रियते; wKt^3 Lo^1 Tr^2 °त्मना — c) bKt^5 °ग्रहश्च; tMd^3 °ग्राहस्तु; gMd^1 °ग्रहस्य; mTr^6 क्रियेते — c-d) La^1 प्रतिग्रहस्य शूद्रस्य क्रियतेप्यन्त्यजन्मतः — d) Bo bCa Ho Jm Jo^1 Jo^2 Kt^2 Lo^1 Lo^3 Lo^4 tMd^3 gMd^5 sOx^1 Ox^2 sPu^6 Tj^1 Tj^2 Tr^2 mTr^3 mTr^5 [*Jolly* Ku] *Apa Me Go Ku Nā Mandlik Jha KSS Dave* शूद्रादप्यन्त्य°; Ho bKt^5 Pu^{10} Tj^2 °प्यन्तजन्मनः; Jo^1 Kt^2 °प्यान्त्यजन्मनः; Pu^2 °जन्मना

111. Omitted in [*Jolly* M^9]; pādas a-b omitted in nKt^4 and pādas c-d in Wa. Cited by *Vij* 3.35; *Apa* 936; *Dev* 2.476; *Mādh* 1.183-4 — a) wKt^1 La^1 gMd^1 tMd^3 Ox^2 Pu^{10} Tj^1 Tj^2 °मैरपे-त्येनो; sOx^1 sPu^6 °मैर्व्रजत्येनो; Ho °मैर्व्रजेत्येनो; nPu^1 °त्यैनो — b) bKt^5 जापनाध्या°; Ho sOx^1 sPu^6 °ध्यापनं; Bo °ध्ययनैः; *Apa* °ध्यापनात्कृतं — c) gMy °निमित्तेन त्या°; bKt^5 nPu^1 Tj^2 च — d) Pu^{10} तपसेव; bBe^2 Hy Jo^2 wKt^1 La^1 Lo^3 Ox^2 Pu^2 Pu^4 Pu^8 Tj^1 *Vij* तु; oOr Tr^2 वा; Pu^5 Pu^7 हि; tMd^4 तत्

112. Omitted in [*Jolly* M^9]; pādas a-b omitted in Wa and pādas c-d in oOr — a) tMd^3 सिलो°; Pu^5 Pu^7 °ञ्छमाददीतापि — b) tMd^3 gMd^5 Pu^5 Pu^7 Tr^1 °जीवन्नितस्ततः — c) gMd^1 °ग्रहा-त्शिलः; Tr^1 nKt^4 °ग्रहान्सिलिः; tMd^3 °ग्रहात्सिलं श्रेयस्ततो; La^1 °ग्रहश्छिन्नश्रेयान्ततो; Tr^2 °च्छिलं; gMd^1 gMy Pu^7 Tj^1 श्रेयान्ततो; Tr^1 श्रेयांततो — d) Tr^2 °प्युञ्छं; tMd^3 ह्युञ्छः

113. Omitted in oOr [*Jolly* M^9] — a) Kt^2 शीदद्भिः; Lo^2 सीसद्भिः; Tr^1 जीवद्भः; Pu^4 कुप्यनिच्छ° — b) tMd^3 gMy °द्भिर्धान्यं; tMd^3 वास्य पृथि° — c) sOx^1 याच्या; wKt^1 याज्यः; gMd^5 mTr^3 वाच्यः; Lo^1 याञ्च्यः — d) Jo^2 Lo^3 Tj^1 °प्रैरदित्सुस्त्याग°; tMd^4 °प्रैरधित्यत्याग°; gMd^1 °प्रैरपित्वंत्याग°; tMd^4 °मर्हतः

114. Omitted in gMy oOr [*Jolly* M^9]. Cited by *Dev* 2.477 — a) La^1 सुकृतं च कृतं क्षेत्रं; Jo^2 Lo^3 Tj^1 तु; gMd^1 चाकृतं क्षेत्रं; bKt^5 tMd^3 tMd^4 gMd^5 Tr^1 कृतं क्षेत्रं — b) La^1 tMd^4 nPu^1 *Dev* गोर°; bKt^5 °जादिकमेव; bCa wKt^1 bKt^5 Lo^1 Pu^8 वा — c) Ho sOx^1 sPu^6 धान्यमन्नं हिरण्यं च; La^1 gMd^1 tMd^4 हिरण्य; Ox^2 °मन्नांश्च — d) Hy Lo^4 Tj^1 पूर्वपूर्वम°; tMd^3 पूर्वः पूर्वम°; Pu^{10} पूर्वे पूर्वम°; tMd^4 पूर्व च दोपवत्; Lo^3 Tj^1 पूर्वं सदोपवत्; Be^1 Ox^2 Tj^2 °दोषकृत्; gMd^1 gMd^5 Tr^1 °दोषकं; Pu^8 °दोषयन्

115. Omitted in [*Jolly* M^9]; pādas c-d omitted in tMd^4. Cited by *Vij* 2.114 [intro.]; *Hem*

विद्या शिल्पं भृतिः सेवा गोरक्ष्यं विपणिः कृषिः ।
धृतिर्भैक्षं कुसीदं च दश जीवनहेतवः ॥११६॥
ब्राह्मणः क्षत्रियो वापि वृद्धिं नैव प्रयोजयेत् ।
कामं तु खलु धर्मार्थं दद्यात्पापीयसेऽल्पिकाम् ॥११७॥
चतुर्थमाददानोऽपि क्षत्रियो भागमापदि ।
प्रजा रक्षन्परं शक्त्या किल्बिषात्प्रतिमुच्यते ॥११८॥
स्वधर्मो विजयस्तस्य न भये स्यात्पराङ्मुखः ।
शस्त्रेण वैश्यान् रक्षित्वा धर्म्यमाहारयेद्बलिम् ॥११९॥
धान्येऽष्टमं विशां शुल्कं विंशं कार्षापणावरम् ।
कर्मोपकरणाः शूद्राः कारवः शिल्पिनस्तथा ॥१२०॥

1.41, 3/1.525; *Dev* 2.450; *Mādh* 1.309, 3.330 — a) Bo वित्ताङ्गमा; Lo[1] विभागमधर्म्या; wKt[3] TMd[4] Ox[2] धर्मा — b) Lo[3] दाया; T Md[3] योयो; MTr[6] लाभं; Jm लोभः; MTr[4] MTr[6] क्रिया; Kt[2] जया — c) La[1] प्रायोगः; Pu[7] सर्वयोगश्च; oOr कर्मजश्चैव; Kt[2] °योगञ्च — d) MTr[6] °ग्राह

116. Cited by *Vij* 3.42; *Apa* 936; *Lakṣ* 2.222; *Dev* 2.475 — a) GMy विद्यां; Tj[1] भृतः; Pu[10] घृतिः; GMd[1] भृतिस्त्वैव — b) Hy Lo[2] Tj[2] *Apa* गौर°; La[1] NPu[1] Pu[2] Pu[5] Pu[7] MTr[3] *Lakṣ* गोरक्षं; TMd[3] [*but cor*] गोरक्षणं; BKt[5] *Vij* गोरक्षा; TMd[4] गारक्ष्यं; wKt[1] गोलक्ष; GMd[1] Pu[3] विपणः; Pu[7] विपणिं — c) Ho Pu[2] Pu[4] Pu[5] Pu[7] Pu[8] Wa धृतिर्भैक्ष्यं; Pu[3] धृतिर्भिक्षा; Tr[2] धृतिर्भिक्ष्या; TMd[4] *Vij Apa* गिरिर्भैक्षं; TMd[3] MTr[3] भृतिर्भैक्षं; BBe[2] wKt[1] Kt[2] NNg कुशीदं; BKt[5] कुसीदश्च — d) MTr[3] जीवितहेतवः

117. Cited by *Dev* 2.472 — b) MTr[4] MTr[6] वृत्तिं; Tj[2] वृद्धिं च प्रयो°; Ox[2] नैवापि योजयेत् — c) Pu[10] *om* तु; Lo[3] TMd[4] Tj[1] च; GMy धर्मार्थाद् — d) Tr[1] °पीयसेविकां; TMd[4] °पीयसाल्पिकां; Pu[10] °ल्पिकाः; Jo[2] NKt[4] BKt[5] La[1] oOr Ox[2] NPu[1] [*Jolly* G N] °ल्पिकं; wKt[3] °ल्पिकान्; Be[1] sOx[1] sPu[6] °ल्पकां; Bo Ho NNg Pu[7] Tr[2] °ल्पकं

118. Omitted in MTr[3]. Cited by *Lakṣ* 11.89 — a) Pu[5] Pu[7] *Lakṣ* °दानो हि — a-b) Tr[2] क्षत्रियो चतुर्थमाददानोपि भागमापदि — b) wKt[1] क्षत्रिय; TMd[3] क्षेत्रियो; sOx[1] sPu[6] भागमर्हति; La[1] भागमत्यपि — c) wKt[1] परिरक्षन्प्रजाः सर्वाः; Jo[2] BKt[5] GMd[1] Pu[10] प्रजां; GMd[1] रक्षंपरं; La[1] रक्षन्परः; GMd[5] रक्षापरो भक्त्या; oOr रक्षन्यथाशक्त्या — d) La[1] किल्बिपाच्च प्रमुच्यते; TMd[3] किल्बिपान्प्रति°; Pu[4] किल्बिषां प्रति°; TMd[4] °षात्परिमुच्यते

119.* Cited by *Lakṣ* 11.89 — a) Be[1] Ox[2] स्वधर्मे; GMd[1] स्वधर्मा; Pu[10] सधर्मो; *Lakṣ* विजये तस्य — b) Pu[2] नाभये; BKt[5] स भये; BBe[2] Hy Jm Jo[1] Jo[2] wKt[1] Kt[2] wKt[3] BKt[5] La[1] Lo[3] Lo[4] [*mc to*] Pu[10] Tj[1] Tj[2] Tr[2] MTr[3] MTr[4] MTr[6] [*Jolly* M R] *Nd Mandlik Jha KSS Dave* नाहवे; GMd[1] न हये; [*Jolly* Nd] भवे; TMd[4] भव; GMd[5] भवेत्; TMd[3] भवेच्च परा°; sOx[1] sPu[6] स्वात्परा°; Tr[1] °राङ्मुखं — c) GMy अस्त्रेण; TMd[3] शास्त्रेण; BKt[5] वैश्यं; Tr[2] वैश्यो; Lo[1] वैश्यान्भक्षेत; TMd[4] क्षत्रियान् रक्ष — d) Bo GMy Tr[1] धर्म्यामा°; BKt[5] धर्मामा°; GMd[1] GMd[5] Pu[5] Pu[7] Pu[10] धर्ममा°; Bo BKt[5] Lo[1] TMd[3] sOx[1] °माहरये°; Pu[2] Pu[4] °येद्बलिः; GMy °येद्बलं

120. a) Ho °ष्टम; oOr °ष्टमे; Tj[1] °ष्टक; wKt[3] विशा; TMd[4] विना; Lo[1] शुक्लं — b) Tr[1] विंशत्कायणमावरं; GMy विंश; Pu[10] विशः; BBe[2] BKt[5] La[1] TMd[3] TMd[4] GMd[5] Pu[5] Pu[7] [*Jolly* N Nd] विंशत्कार्षा°; Tr[2] *Nā* [pāṭha] त्रिंशत्कार्षा°; GMd[1] निपोत्कर्पा°; La[1] कार्षप°; TMd[3] कर्पाप°; BKt[5] TMd[3] TMd[4] Ox[2] °पणं वरं; Jo[2] °पणेवरे; Lo[3] Tj[1] °पणावरे; [*Jolly* Nd] °पणापरं; Pu[3] °पणां वरं; Jo[2] °पणे वरं; Lo[2] °पणाधरं; Pu[7] °पणाद्धरन् — c) wKt[1] धर्मोप°; Lo[4] °पकारिणः; Pu[10] °पकारिणा तु शूद्राः; GMd[5] °रणश्शूद्रः; NKt[4] °रणश्चैव; sOx[1] sPu[6] °रणश्छूद्रक्कार° — d) wKt[1] GMd[1] TMd[3] GMd[5] GMy Pu[2] Pu[4] Tr[1]

शूद्रस्तु वृत्तिमाकाङ्क्षन् क्षत्रमाराधयेद्यदि ।
धनिनं वाप्युपाराध्य वैश्यं शूद्रो जिजीविषेत् ॥१२१॥
स्वर्गार्थमुभयार्थं वा विप्रानाराधयेत्तु सः ।
जातब्राह्मणशब्दस्य सा ह्यस्य कृतकृत्यता ॥१२२॥
विप्रसेवैव शूद्रस्य विशिष्टं कर्म कीर्त्यते ।
यदतोऽन्यद्धि कुरुते तद्भवत्यस्य निष्फलम् ॥१२३॥
प्रकल्प्या तस्य तैर्वृत्तिः स्वकुटुम्बाद्यथार्हतः ।
शक्तिं चावेक्ष्य दाक्ष्यं च भृत्यानां च परिग्रहम् ॥१२४॥
उच्छिष्टमन्नं दातव्यं जीर्णानि वसनानि च ।
पुलाकाश्चैव धान्यानां जीर्णाश्चैव परिच्छदाः ॥१२५॥

शिल्पिनः कारवस्तथा; Jo[2] Lo[3] कारुकाः; Tj[1] कारुकां

121.* Omitted in GMy [*Jolly* Nd]. Cited by *Apa* 161; *Lakṣ* 2.266; *Mādh* 1.421 — a) Pu[5] Pu[7] शूद्रश्च; La[1] शूद्रस्ववृत्ति°; Jo[2] वृत्तिकमाकाङ्क्षन्; MTr[5] वृत्तिं काङ्क्षन्; Ho °काङ्क्षत् — b) Tr[2] क्षमामारा°; Lo[1] क्षेत्रमारव्धये°; La[1] °माधारये°; GMd[1] Tr[1] [*Jolly* Gr] *Nd* °धयेदपि; Lo[4] TMd[3] Pu[10] [*Jolly* M[1–2–5–8–9]] *Jolly* °धयेदिति; NKt[4] TMd[4] MTr[4] MTr[6] °येद्यतः — c) Pu[2] Pu[4] धनिकं; *Apa* चाप्यु°; Tr[2] °पाराध्यं; Jo[2] °पारुध्य; GMd[5] °पाध्याय — d) Be[1] वैश्यां; Ho वैश्य; WKt[3] La[1] शूद्रं; GMd[1] शूद्रे; Ho NKt[4] La[1] SOx[1] NPu[1] Pu[2] Pu[4] SPu[6] [*Jolly* M] *Apa Jolly* जिजीविषुः; TMd[4] जिजीविघः; *Me Go Ku* support the active verb.

122. Omitted in GMy [*Jolly* Nd]. Cited by *Apa* 161; *Lakṣ* 2.266; *Mādh* 1.421 — a) GMd[1] °र्थमभयार्थं; *Lakṣ* च — b) Tr[2] *Apa* ब्राह्मणं न विरोधयेत्; NKt[4] La[1] GMd[1] TMd[3] TMd[4] GMd[5] Tr[1] MTr[4] MTr[6] *Lakṣ* ब्राह्मणानेव धारयेत् [NKt[4] राधयेत्; La[1] वाजयेत्]; MTr[5] ब्राह्मणानभिधारयेत्; *Nā* [pāṭha] विप्रानेवाभिवाचयेत् — c) TMd[4] जातं; MTr[4] MTr[6] जातु ब्राह्म°; *Apa* या तु ब्राह्म°; NNg जातब्राह्मणस्य [*om* शव्द]; TMd[3] GMd[5] °ह्मणकृत्यस्य; Pu[8] °शब्दश्च; Bo *Lakṣ* °शव्दो हि; *Mādh* °शव्दः स्यात्सा — d) Pu[3] स; Bo साध्यस्य; La[1] सास्वस्य; TMd[4] साहसं कृत°

123. Pādas c-d omitted in Pu[4] MTr[3]. Cited by *Apa* 161; *Lakṣ* 2.266; *Mādh* 1.421; pādas a-b cited by *Vij* 1.120; *Dev* 2.455— a) BKt[5] °सेवैश्च; Bo °सेवी च — b) Jo[2] Lo[3] Tj[1] केवलं कर्म; BBe[2] धर्म; Tr[2] ब्रह्म; BBe[2] WKt[3] कथ्यते; NPu[1] कुर्वते — c) GMd[5] यत्ततो; TMd[4] यदैतेन्यद्धि; Pu[10] यदन्यतो हि; Pu[5] Pu[7] यदन्यद्धि; OOr यतस्तथान्यद्धि; Lo[3] Tj[1] °न्यद्वै कुरुते; GMd[1] °न्यद्विकुरुते — d) Be[1] तद्भवत्वस्य; BBe[2] Lo[1] OOr तद्भवेदस्य; WKt[3] तद्भवदस्य; Ho SOx[1] NPu[1] Pu[2] SPu[6] *Apa* तद्भवेत्तस्य

124. Cited by *Apa* 161; *Lakṣ* 2.267; *Mādh* 1.420— a) Ox[2] प्रकल्प्य; SOx[1] Pu[5] SPu[6] Pu[7] प्रकल्पा; Ho Pu[2] प्रकल्प्यात्तस्य; GMy *Apa* प्रकल्प्यतेस्य; NPu[1] प्रकल्पातेस्य; *Lakṣ* प्रकल्पितास्य; WKt[1] चास्य; Ho BKt[5] SOx[1] SPu[6] *Mādh* तस्य वै वृत्तिः; Tr[1] तैर्वृत्तिं — b) GMd[5] स्वकुडु°; NKt[4] सकुटु°; GMy °टुम्बान्यथा°; TMd[3] °टुम्बां महीपतिः; OOr °टुम्बसमाहितः; NKt[4] °थाहतः; Pu[10] °थार्थतः; Ho SOx[1] Ox[2] SPu[6] °थाविधि — c) Tj[2] चावेक्ष्यं; Lo[1] वावेक्ष्य; Wa चोवेक्ष्य; Jo[2] NKt[4] La[1] Lo[3] Lo[4] Pu[10] Tj[1] चापेक्ष्य; Bo BKt[5] La[1] Pu[10] दाक्षं; Ho दात्त्यं; Lo[1] दाक्षण्यं [*om* च]; GMd[1] TMd[3] GMd[5] GMy Tr[1] MTr[4] MTr[6] भक्तिं च; TMd[4] भक्तं च — d) BBe[2] परिग्रहः; Wa परिच्छदाः [cf. 125d]; NNg परिच्छदं

125. Verses 125 and 126 transposed in Wa. Cited by *Apa* 162; *Lakṣ* 2.266; *Dev* 2.456; *Mādh* 1.420 — a) Pu[2] Pu[4] उच्छिष्टान्नं च दातव्यं; WKt[1] उच्छिष्टमपि दातव्यं — c) Lo[4] पुलाकांश्चैव; TMd[3] पुलकांश्चैव; NKt[4] Lo[1] GMd[1] GMy Ox[2] Tj[1] MTr[6] पुलकाश्चैव; Ho पुलाकश्चैव; SOx[1] SPu[6] पुलाकः

न शूद्रे पातकं किंचिन्न च संस्कारमर्हति ।
नास्याधिकारो धर्मेऽस्ति न धर्मात्प्रतिषेधनम् ॥१२६॥
धर्मेप्सवस्तु धर्मज्ञाः सतां वृत्तमनुष्ठिताः ।
मन्त्रवर्जं न दुष्यन्ति प्रशंसां प्राप्नुवन्ति च ॥१२७॥
यथा यथा हि सद्वृत्तमातिष्ठत्यनसूयकः ।
तथा तथेमं चामुं च लोकं प्राप्नोत्यनिन्दितः ॥१२८॥
शक्तेनापि हि शूद्रेण न कार्यो धनसंचयः ।
शूद्रो हि धनमासाद्य ब्राह्मणानेव बाधते ।१२९॥
एते चतुर्णां वर्णानामापद्धर्माः प्रकीर्तिताः ।
यान्सम्यगनुतिष्ठन्तो व्रजन्ति परमां गतिम् ॥१३०॥
एष धर्मविधिः कृत्स्नश्चातुर्वर्ण्यस्य कीर्तितः ।
अतः परं प्रवक्ष्यामि प्रायश्चित्तविधिं शुभम् ॥१३१॥

चैव; Pu^2 Pu^4 पुलाकोश्चैव — d) GMd^1 जीर्णश्चैव; TMd^3 जीर्णं चैव; BKt^5 जीर्णानांश्चैव; Bo परिच्छदः; oOr परिच्छान्

126. Cited by *Śaṃ* on *VeS* 1.3.36 — a) BBe^2 शूद्रो; oOr पातकः — b) GMd^5 किंचिन्नापि — c) BKt^5 धर्मे नास्याधिकारोस्ति; NKt^4 नास्याविकामे धर्मेस्ति; BBe^2 Bo TMd^3 GMd^5 NPu^1 Tj^1 धर्मोस्ति; TMd^4 *om* धर्मेस्ति; Wa *om* स्ति — d) La^1 TMd^3 GMd^5 Tr^1 नाधर्मा°; GMd^1 TMd^4 धर्मप्रति°; oOr धर्मात्प्रतिपादनं

127.* Pādas b-d omitted in Pu^4. Cited by *Lakṣ* 2.271 — a) La^1 धर्मेप्सुरस्वधर्मज्ञाः; GMd^1 धर्मेप्सुस्तु न धर्मज्ञाः; Tr^1 धर्मेप्लुवस्तु; wKt^1 Pu^2 Pu^4 °प्सवश्च; Bo धर्मज्ञः; Lo^4 धर्मन्ताः — b) BBe^2 Jo^2 wKt^3 La^1 Lo^1 Lo^3 GMd^1 TMd^3 TMd^4 GMd^5 GMy NPu^1 Tj^1 Tr^1.MTr^5 वृत्तिमनु°; Pu^2 वृत्तिरनु°; BCa wKt^1 BKt^5 Lo^4 NNg Ox^2 Pu^{10} Tr^2 [*Jolly* M] *Lakṣ Me Rn Jha Dave* धर्ममनु°; oOr धर्ममवस्थिताः — c) GMd^1 GMd^5 °वर्ज्यं; Tr^1 °वर्ज्यात्र; GMd^1 दुष्यति; GMd^5 दुष्याश्च — d) oOr प्रशंसामाप्नुवन्ति हि; MTr^6 प्रावान्यं प्रा°; GMy °वन्ति ते

128. Omitted in Lo^1; pāda-a omitted in Pu^4 — a) Jo^1 यथा हि यथा; BKt^5 यथा हि यथा हि; TMd^3 यथा यथाथ; GMd^1 ह; GMd^5 GMy Tr^1 सद्वृत्तिमा°; Tr^2 यद्वृत्तमा° — b) BBe^2 °तिष्ठन्ननसू°; BCa La^1 Tj^1 °नुसूयकः; Lo^1 °सूयकाः; GMd^1 MTr^4 °सूयतः — c) GMd^1 तथेमां; NKt^4 तथेयं; Tr^1 तथैमं; Ho La^1 TMd^3 oOr तथेमुं; Tj^1 *om* चामुं — d) oOr लोकः प्राप्नोति निन्दितः; Be^1 लोके; GMd^1 लोकानाप्नो°; BKt^5 °त्यनुत्तमं; Ho °निन्दिता; Hy NNg Pu^2 Pu^3 °निन्दितं; GMd^5 °निन्दकः

129. a) NPu^1 शक्तिनापि; Pu^{10} *om* हि; GMd^1 ह; TMd^4 च; BKt^5 [*but cor*] GMd^1 शूद्रस्य — b) Lo^4 Pu^2 Pu^3 Pu^4 Pu^5 Pu^7 [*cor to*] Tr^2 Wa धनसंग्रः — d) NKt^4 ब्रह्म°; MTr^4 ब्राह्मणेनैव; TMd^3 ब्राह्मणादेव; Ho °णानवभाधते; Ox^2 बाधयेत्; Tr^2 वर्धते

130. In wKt^3 folio missing containing 10.13b to 11.19c — a) MTr^6 चतुर्णामपि वर्णाना°; Pu^{10} [*Jolly* M] एवं; sOx^1 sPu^6 एतैश्चतुर्णां; BKt^5 धर्माणमा° — b) GMd^1 वर्णानामेव धर्माः — c) Tr^2 ये सम्य°; TMd^3 यां सम्य°; MTr^4 MTr^6 यान्धर्ममनु° — d) Ox^2 [*but cor*] Pu^3 Tr^2 व्रजन्तीह परां गतिं

131. a) Lo^4 एवं; BBe^2 TMd^3 कृत्स्नचातु° — b) BBe^2 Ho Pu^2 Pu^4 Pu^5 Pu^7 °तुर्वर्णस्य; Lo^4 [*Jolly* M$^{4-5}$] °तुर्वर्ण्ये प्रकीर्तितः; Pu^3 Pu^{10} Tr^2 [*Jolly* M^{2-8-9}] °तुर्वर्ण्यः प्रकीर्तितः [M^8 °र्तिताः]; TMd^4 °तुर्वर्णात्प्रकीर्तितं; La^1 °तुर्वर्णब्रवीन्मनुः; Tr^1 कीर्त्यतः — c) wKt^1 Pu^3 Tr^2 अत ऊर्ध्वं [Pu^3 Tr^2 अतः]; BKt^5 प्रवक्षामि — d) NPu^1 प्रायश्चित्तं; La^1 °विधिं शृणु

॥ इति मानवे धर्मशास्त्रे भृगुप्रोक्तायां संहितायां दशमोऽध्यायः ॥

Colophon: Lo^{1} TMd^{3} NNg sOx^{1} Ox^{2} sPu^{6} इति श्रीमानवे; Lo^{3} इति श्रीमानवीये; Be^{1} BKt^{5} Lo^{1} Lo^{2} GMd^{1} TMd^{3} GMy NNg Tr^{1} MTr^{6} *om* भृगुप्रोक्तायां संहितायां; wKt^{1} आपद्धर्मो नाम दशमो; oOr वर्णसंकरो नाम दशमो; NNg संकीर्णसंभवआपद्धर्मश्च दशमो; Pu^{5} Pu^{7} प्रतिलोमानुलोमजातवृत्तिनिरूपणं नाम दशमो; Tj^{1} वर्णानामापद्धर्मकथनं नाम दशमो

[एकादशोऽध्यायः]

सांतानिकं यक्ष्यमाणमध्वगं सार्ववेदसम् ।
गुर्वर्थं पितृमात्रर्थं स्वाध्यायार्थ्युपतापिनः ॥१॥
नवैतान् स्नातकान् विद्याद् ब्राह्मणान् धर्मभिक्षुकान् ।
निःस्वेभ्यो देयमेतेभ्यो दानं विद्याविशेषतः ॥२॥
एतेभ्यो हि द्विजाग्रेभ्यो देयमन्नं सदक्षिणम् ।
इतरेभ्यो बहिर्वेदि कृतान्नं देयमुच्यते ॥३॥
सर्वरत्नानि राजा तु यथार्हं प्रतिपादयेत् ।
ब्राह्मणान्वेदविदुषो यज्ञार्थं चैव दक्षिणाम् ॥४॥
कृतदारोऽपरान्दारान् भिक्षित्वा योऽधिगच्छति ।

1.* Cited by *Apa* 77, 263, 294; *Hem* 1.30, 3/1.354; *Mādh* 1.429 — a) Hy wKt^{1} BKt^{5} Lo^{1} Pu^{8} संता°; Tj^{1} साता°; Kt^{2} BKt^{5} *Apa* यक्षमा°; Pu^{10} वक्ष्यमा°; TMd^{4} °माणाम° — b) BBe^{2} Bo BCa Jm Jo^{1} La^{1} Lo^{1} Lo^{2} GMd^{1} oOr sOx^{1} Pu^{2} Pu^{3} Pu^{4} sPu^{6} Tj^{1} Tr^{2} [*Jolly* G R Ku Nd] *Mādh Mandlik Jolly KSS* सर्व°; TMd^{3} TMd^{4} सर्ववेदनं — c) MTr^{4} MTr^{5} MTr^{6} गुर्वम्बापितृभृत्यार्थं; *Apa* 294 गुर्वर्थि; Be^{1} BKt^{5} Lo^{2} *Apa* 263, 294 [vl] गुर्वर्थ; Pu^{5} गुर्वर्थी; TMd^{3} गुर्वर्थे; oOr गुर्वत्रं; Be^{1} BKt^{5} Pu^{10} *Apa* 77, 263, 294 [vl] °मात्रर्थ; Pu^{10} *Apa* 294 °मात्रर्थि; TMd^{3} °मात्रर्थे — d) GMd^{1} स्वाध्यार्थे उपतापिनं; Be^{1} °यार्थोपपातिनः; Ho sOx^{1} Ox^{2} sPu^{6} °यार्थोपतापिनं; BBe^{2} Lo^{3} oOr Pu^{10} Tj^{1} [*Jolly* R] °याद्युपतापिनं; NNg °याध्युपतापिनं; BKt^{5} °यार्थ्यपतापिनं; Tr^{1} °यार्थवतापिनं; BBe^{2} Bo Lo^{1} oOr °तापिनौ; GMd^{5} NNg Pu^{2} Pu^{10} Wa *Hem Mādh* °तापिनं; Lo^{4} °तापिनां

2. Cited by *Apa* 294; *Hem* 1.30;pādas a-b cited by *Apa* 77, 263 — a) MTr^{4} MTr^{5} MTr^{6} दशैतान्; Tr^{2} नवतान्; Be^{1} Tj^{1} नैव तान्; BKt^{5} Lo^{2} sOx^{1} sPu^{6} नचैतान्; Be^{1} सात्विकन्विद्याद्; Kt^{2} विद्या; Pu^{5} Pu^{7} विद्यान् — b) Hy ब्राह्मण; GMd^{1} सर्वभि°; Be^{1} *Apa* °भैक्षुकान्; *Apa* [vl] °भैक्षकान्; MTr^{6} °भिक्षुभिः — c) NKt^{4} BKt^{5} La^{1} Lo^{1} Pu^{3} निस्वेभ्यो; Tr^{2} नस्वेंभ्यो; Lo^{2} देवमे° — d) Hy TMd^{4} दान; NPu^{1} विद्यां; BBe^{2} GMd^{1} विद्याद्विशेषतः

3.* Pādas c-d omitted in Pu^{4}. Cited by *Apa* 294; *Hem* 1.30 — a) GMd^{1} GMd^{5} Tr^{1} [*Jolly* Nd] एतेभ्योपि; GMy एतेह्यापि; TMd^{3} एभ्यो हि; GMd^{1} Wa *Apa* द्विजाग्र्येभ्यो; TMd^{4} द्विजातिभ्यो; Lo^{1} द्विजातेभ्यो; Ox^{2} द्विजातभ्यो — b) Ho सदाक्षिणं — c) Lo^{1} बहिर्वेद्याः; TMd^{4} बहिर्वेना — d) Jo^{2} NKt^{4} La^{1} Lo^{3} TMd^{4} oOr Tj^{1} *Hem* कृतान्नं तु विधीयते [La^{1} कृतार्थं; TMd^{4} कृतान्नं न]; GMd^{1} TMd^{3} GMd^{5} GMy Tr^{1} MTr^{4} MTr^{5} MTr^{6} नाकृतान्नं विधीयते[TMd^{3} नाकृत्वान्नं]; *Apa* भुवि दीयते

4. Omitted in Pu^{5} TMd^{4}; pādas a-b omitted in Pu^{4} — a) oOr राज्ञा — b) Pu^{2} यथार्थं — c) Lo^{2} Lo^{4} Pu^{2} Pu^{3} Pu^{4} Pu^{10} [*Jolly* M] ब्राह्मणे वेदविदुषि [Lo^{4} Pu^{10} (*Jolly* M) विदुषे]; Ho sOx^{1} Ox^{2} sPu^{6} ब्राह्मणेभ्यश्च विद्वद्धो; wKt^{1} ब्राह्मणार्थेन विदुषो; NNg ब्राह्मणा वेद°; NPu^{1} °विदुषे — d) Pu^{2} यथार्थं; TMd^{3} च सदक्षिणां; Be^{1} Bo Ho NKt^{4} La^{1} Lo^{2} GMy NNg sOx^{1} Pu^{3} sPu^{6} Tr^{1} Tr^{2} MTr^{6} Wa दक्षिणाः; Pu^{7} Pu^{10} [*Jolly* M$^{1-2-3-5-9}$] दक्षिणा; wKt^{1} दक्षिणान्; GMd^{1} रक्षणं

रतिमात्रं फलं तस्य द्रव्यदातुस्तु संततिः ॥५॥
यस्य त्रैवार्षिकं भक्तं पर्याप्तं भृत्यवृत्तये ।
अधिकं वापि विद्येत स सोमं पातुमर्हति ॥७॥
अतः स्वल्पीयसि द्रव्ये यः सोमं पिबति द्विजः ।
सोऽपीतसोमपूर्वोऽपि* न तस्याप्नोति तत्फलम् ॥८॥
शक्तः परजने दाता स्वजने दुःखजीविनि ।
मध्वापातो विषास्वादः स धर्मप्रतिरूपकः ॥९॥

5.* Omitted in tMd^4; pādas a-b omitted in Pu^5 — a) tMd^3 कृतंदारोधिकं वारं; oOr कृतदारः परान्दारान्; Wa °परो दारान्; Tr^1 °परं दारं; Bo °न्दारा; Lo^3 °न्दारां; Lo^1 Lo^2 °न्दारे — b) gMd^1 gMd^5 gMy Tr^1 यो भिक्षित्वाधिगच्छति [gMd^1 °त्वा हि गच्छति]; bBe^2 भिक्षिता; Lo^4 भिक्षित्वान्यो; Lo^1 योवगच्छति — c) mTr^4 रतिस्तत्र फलं; gMd^1 tMd^3 Tr^1 °मात्र; oOr °मात्रः; mTr^6 तस्य फलं — d) sOx^1 sPu^6 वित्तदातु°; Be^1 wKt^1 gMd^1 tMd^3 gMd^5 nNg Tj^2 Tr^1 Wa °दातुश्च

An additional verse is given in the vulgate editions and Bühler as verse 6; it is found in the following mss: Be^1 Ho Jm Jo^1 Jo^2 Kt^2 nKt^4 La^1 gMd^1 tMd^3 oOr nPu^1 Pu^2 Pu^3 Pu^4 Tj^2 Tr^1 mTr^3 mTr^4 mTr^6; pādas c-d in Md^4. Verse number 6 is eliminated from the critical edition.

धनानि तु यथाशक्ति विप्रेषु प्रतिपादयेत् ।
वेदवित्सु विविक्तेषु प्रेत्य स्वर्गं समश्नुते ॥

a) Ho mTr^4 mTr^6 धनान्यपि; gMd^1 tMd^3 oOr Tr^1 nPu^1 Pu^2 Pu^4 रत्नानि तु [gMd^1 च; nPu^1 Pu^2 Pu^4 हि]; La^1 रत्नान्यपि; nKt^4 वित्तानि तु; Tj^2 धनधान्यं यथा° — b) tMd^3 विप्रेभ्यः — c) nPu^1 Pu^2 Pu^4 °वित्सु विधिज्ञेषु — d) gMd^1 प्राप्य; Ho gMd^1 tMd^3 tMd^4 nPu^1 Pu^2 Pu^4 Tr^1 mTr^4 mTr^6 स्वर्गे महीयते

Additional verse: gMd^1 tMd^3 gMd^5 Tr^1 [*Jolly* Gr]; given after 11.10 in Ox^2 nPu^1 Pu^2 Pu^3 [*but erased*] Pu^4 *Mandlik* [ट, ठ, ण, य, ल] *KSS Dave;* cited by *Mādh* 2.384; *Vij* 1.224, 2.175:

वृद्धौ च मातापितरौ साध्वी भार्या सुतः शिशुः ।
अप्यकार्यशतं कृत्वा भर्तव्या मनुरब्रवीत् ॥

b) Ox^2 *Vij* 2.175 शिशुः सुतः — c) [*Jolly* Gr] अपकार्य°

7. Omitted in Pu^5. Cited by *Apa* 165; *Lakṣ* 2.132–3; *Dev* 2.418; *Mādh* 1.157— a) Bo gMd^1 °वर्षिकं; Lo^4 °वार्षकं; Ox^2 *Mādh* वित्तं; La^1 gMd^1 mTr^4 mTr^6 धान्यं — b) La^1 विहितं भृत्य°; gMd^1 °वृद्धये; gMy °वर्तये; *Apa* °तृप्तये; Be^1 °गुप्तये — c) gMy [*Jolly* Nd] अतोधिकं वा विद्येत; Be^1 Bo Lo^2 Pu^2 Pu^7 चापि

8.* Pādas a-b omitted in oOr. Cited by *Apa* 165; *Lakṣ* 2.133; *Dev* 2.418; pādas a-b cited by *Vij* 1.124 — a) tMd^3 tMd^4 Ox^2 Pu^3 *Apa Lakṣ* अतस्त्वल्पीयसि; Bo स्वल्पीयसी; gMy द्रव्य — b) tMd^4 ये; gMd^1 पिबते; tMd^3 पातुमिच्छसि; nKt^4 पातुमर्हति [cf 11.7d] — c) Be^1 Be^2 Bo Hy Jm Jo^1 Jo^2 wKt^1 Kt^2 La^1 Lo^1 Lo^3 Lo^4 Ng oOr Ox^1 Ox^2 Pu^1 Pu^2 Pu^5 Pu^6 Pu^7 Pu^8 Pu^{10} Tj^1 Wa *Apa Lakṣ Mandlik Jolly Jha KSS Dave* स पीत°; Tj^2 नापीत; Ho nKt^4 Lo^2 gMd^1 tMd^3 gMd^5 gMy Tr^1 *Dev Bh Rc* अपीत° [*om* स]; bKt^5 आपीत — d) La^1 न तत्फलमवाप्नुयात्; nKt^4 gMd^1 tMd^3 gMd^5 gMy *Dev* न स प्राप्नोति [*Dev* स न]; Tr^1 न संप्राप्नोति; Bo यत्फलं; Pu^5 Pu^7 वै फलं

9. Pādas c-d omitted in gMd^5. Cited by *Apa* 283; *Hem* 1.44 — a) Tr^2 सक्तः; La^1 पराजने; gMy Pu^2 Pu^4 परिजने; mTr^5 परे जने; tMd^3 Wa °जनो — a-b) gMd^1 °जनैर्दाता स्वजनैर्दुःख° — b) Lo^3 स्वं; Pu^5 Pu^7 [*Jolly* G] दुःखपीडिते; gMd^1 Tr^1 °जीवनि; Ho °जीविति; wKt^1 °जीवति — c) *Bh* [ad 11.10 as pāṭha of some] मध्वास्वादो विपापातः; Ox^2 मध्वपातो; Wa मध्वापाता; Be^1 bKt^5 Lo^1 tMd^3

भृत्यानामुपरोधेन यः करोत्यौर्ध्वदेहिकम् ।
तद्भवत्यसुखोदर्कं जीवतोऽस्य मृतस्य च ॥१०॥
यज्ञश्चेत्प्रतिरुद्धः स्यादेकेनाङ्गेन यज्वनः ।
ब्राह्मणस्य विशेषेण धार्मिके सति राजनि ॥११॥
यो वैश्यः स्याद्बहुपशुर्हीनक्रतुरसोमपः ।
कुटुम्बात्तस्य तद्द्रव्यमाहरेद्यज्ञसिद्धये ॥१२॥
आहरेत् त्रीणि वा द्वे वा कामं शूद्रस्य वेश्मनः ।
न हि शूद्रस्य यज्ञेषु कश्चिदस्ति परिग्रहः ॥१३॥
योऽनाहिताग्निः शतगुरयज्वा च सहस्रगुः ।
तयोरपि कुटुम्बाभ्यामाहरेदविचारयन् ॥१४॥
आदाननित्याच्चादातुराहरेदप्रयच्छतः ।
तथा यशोऽस्य प्रथते धर्मश्चैव विवर्धते ॥१५॥

Tr^1 mTr^4 mTr^6 *Hem* मध्वापानो; tMd^4 मध्वपानो; oOr मध्वापितो; Lo^3 Tj^1 मध्वास्वादो विपा° — d) bBe^2 Lo^1 gMd^1 tMd^3 tMd^4 Tr^1 स्वधर्म°; oOr स्वधर्मः; Tj^1 [*Jolly* M^{1-8-9} R] स धर्मः; sOx^1 °प्रत्यरूपकः; mTr^4 °प्रतिकूलकः; gMd^1 °प्रतिकारकः; mTr^3 °रूपतः

10. Omitted in gMd^5. Cited by *Apa* 283; *Dev* 2.596 — a) gMy °नामनुपरो°; Lo^2 °रोधे च — b) Bo Hy Jm Jo^1 Kt^2 Lo^1 Tj^2 mTr^3 mTr^4 mTr^5 mTr^6 [*Jolly* Ku] *Mandlik Jha KSS Dave* यत्करो° [*Bh* gloss यदन्यत् supports यत्]; nKt^4 nNg Pu^2 Pu^4 Pu^{10} °त्यूर्ध्व°; Lo^3 Ox^2 nPu^1 Pu^2 Pu^4 mTr^6 Wa [*Jolly* R] *Dev* °दैहिकं — c) tMd^3 °सुरोदर्कं — d) Jm Jo^1 La^1 Lo^4 oOr जीवतस्य; bCa tMd^3 tMd^4 nPu^1 Pu^{10} mTr^6 जीवितस्य; Hy Kt^2 gMy Pu^3 Tj^2 Tr^1 mTr^3 mTr^4 Tr^5 mTr^6 *Dev Mandlik Jha KSS Dave* जीवतश्च; gMd^1 जीवन्तश्च; nKt^4 जीविश्चदतस्य; La^1 Tr^2 वा

11. Omitted in gMd^5. Cited by *Lakṣ* 2.162; *Dev* 2.422 — a) Lo^3 tMd^4 Tj^1 यज्ञश्च प्रति°; Bo °रुद्ध्यः; bKt^5 °रद्धः; nKt^4 tMd^4 mTr^4 mTr^5 °बद्धः; mTr^6 °बन्धः — b) mTr^6 °देकोनांगेन; Tr^2 °केनांशेन; bCa °कानांगेन; sOx^1 sPu^6 यज्वानः; nPu^1 यज्विनः; Tj^1 यज्वसः; Lo^2 यज्ञिनः — d) gMy धार्मिकस्यापरोधने

12. Cited by *Lakṣ* 2.162–3; *Dev* 2.422 — a) gMy यो वैश्यात् बहुपशोर्हीन°; Tj^1 या; Ox^2 स्यात्पशुबहुर्हीन°; Wa °पशुहीन° — b) bKt^5 °क्रतुसायकः; gMy °सोमपाः; tMd^4 °सोदवः — c) gMd^5 कुडुंबा°; Be^1 कुटुंबार्त्तस्य; *Lakṣ* कुटुम्बार्तस्य; gMd^1 करम्बात्तस्य — d) wKt^1 तद्द्रव्यं हरेद्यज्ञस्य सिद्धये; bKt^5 °रेद्यस्तु सिद्धये

13. Cited by *Dev* 2.422 — b) bKt^5 भागान्शूद्रस्य; bKt^5 tMd^4 nNg Pu^3 वेश्मतः — c) Lo^1 यज्ञस्य; wKt^1 यज्ञे तु — d) bKt^5 यश्चि°; tMd^4 प्रतिग्रहः

14. Cited by *Lakṣ* 2.162; *Dev* 2.422 — b) *Me Jha Dave* °गुरयज्ञश्च; tMd^4 °गुरयज्ञो वा; gMd^1 सहस्रगः — c) Jo^2 Lo^3 Tj^1 [*Jolly* R] द्वयोरपि; gMd^5 gMy कुडु° — d) Bo °विचारयेत्; Tr^2 °विचक्षणः

15. Cited by *Lakṣ* 2.162 — a) Hy Lo^3 gMd^1 Tj^1 अदान°; gMy आदना°; Be^1 bBe^2 °नित्याश्चा°; Pu^{10} °नितयाददातु° — b) Tr^1 °दातुर्नाहरेत प्रयत्नतः; gMd^5 °हरेच्च प्रयत्नतः; Pu^5 Pu^7 °हरेदप्रयत्नतः; Pu^{10} °प्रयस्त्वतः — c) Tr^2 यथा यथास्य प्रथते; Ho Lo^4 tMd^3 Ox^2 mTr^4 [*Jolly* M^{4-5-9}] *Lakṣ* यथा; tMd^4 यत; Pu^2 प्रथतो; sOx^1 sPu^6 mTr^3 प्रयते; Kt^2 प्रश्रते; Jo^1 प्रथसे; Pu^{10} प्रथमे — d) bKt^5 यज्ञश्चैवाभिवर्धते; Tr^1 स्वयं धर्मश्च वर्धते; bBe^2 धर्मश्चैवं; gMd^1 tMd^3 tMd^4 gMy mTr^4 mTr^6 स्वधर्मश्च; gMd^5

तथैव सप्तमे भक्ते भक्तानि षडनश्नता ।
अश्वस्तनविधानेन हर्तव्यं हीनकर्मणः ॥१६॥
खलात् क्षेत्रादगाराद्वा यतो वाप्युपलभ्यते ।
आख्यातव्यं तु तत्तस्मै पृच्छते यदि पृच्छति ॥१७॥
ब्राह्मणस्वं न हर्तव्यं क्षत्रियेण कदाचन ।
दस्युनिष्क्रिययोस्तु स्वमजीवन्हर्तुमर्हति ॥१८॥
योऽसाधुभ्योऽर्थमादाय साधुभ्यः संप्रयच्छति ।
स कृत्वा प्लवमात्मानं संतारयति तावुभौ ॥१९॥
यद्धनं यज्ञशीलानां देवस्वं तद्विदुर्बुधाः ।
अयज्वनां तु यद्वित्तमासुरस्वं तदुच्यते ॥२०॥
न तस्मिन्धारयेद्दण्डं धार्मिकः पृथिवीपतिः ।
क्षत्रियस्य हि बालिश्याद् ब्राह्मणः सीदति क्षुधा ॥२१॥
तस्य भृत्यजनं ज्ञात्वा स्वकुटुम्बान्महीपतिः ।

स्वकर्मश्च; Be^1 Ho Hy Jm Jo^1 Kt^2 GMd^5 Pu^3 Pu^8 Tj^2 MTr^3 *Mandlik Jha KSS Dave* प्रवर्धते; BBe^2 sOx^1 sPu^6 प्रवर्तते

16. Cited by *Vij* 3.43; *Apa* 938; *Dev* 2.466; *Mādh* 3.304 — a) *Apa* सप्तमं भक्तं — b) Pu^8 Tr^1 °नश्नतः — c) GMd^5 GMy Tr^1 °विधानाय; MTr^4 °निधानेन; GMd^1 TMd^3 MTr^5 MTr^6 *Bh* °निधानाय — d) Be^1 oOr Tr^2 कर्तव्यं; Kt^2 °कर्मणाः; TMd^4 °कर्मणा

17. Cited by *Vij* 3.43; *Apa* 938; *Dev* 2.467 — a) Wa खेलात्; BKt^5 खडात्; Tr^2 बलात्; sOx^1 sPu^6 स्वत्रात्क्षे°; TMd^4 खगाक्षे°; BBe^2 La^1 °दागाराद्वा; Jo^2 Lo^3 Tj^1 °गाराच्च — b) TMd^3 यत्नतोभ्युपलभ्यते; Tj^1 वाभ्युप°; GMy MTr^4 MTr^6 °पपद्यते — c) Bo अख्या°; BKt^5 °तव्यस्तु; TMd^4 °तव्यं ततस्तस्यै; NNg oOr Pu^{10} च; Lo^2 तु तस्मै

18. Omitted in Tj^1 [haplo]. Cited by *Apa* 938; *Lakṣ* 2.225; *Dev* 2.467 — a) Ox^2 ब्रह्मस्वं नैव; *Lakṣ* ब्रह्मस्वं न च; BKt^5 *om* न; La^1 oOr Tr^2 कर्तव्यं — b) BBe^2 कथंचन — c) TMd^4 तस्य निष्क्रि°; BKt^5 La^1 TMd^3 GMd^5 Pu^2 °निष्क्रय°; *Apa* °ययोश्च; GMy °ययोवस्तु स्वजीव°; GMd^1 स्वाम° — d) Pu^{10} °जीवे हर्तु°; wKt^1 TMd^3 °वन्हन्तु°; La^1 °वन्दत्तमर्हति; Jo^2 *Apa* (vl) °र्तुमिच्छति

19. Omitted in GMy; pādas a-b omitted in Tj^1; not commented by *Nd* — a) GMd^1 ये; wKt^1 °भ्यः स्वमादाय — b) Hy °दायासाधु°; TMd^4 साधुभ्यश्च प्रय° — c) Lo^1 सत्कृत्वा — d) Pu^{10} तंतार°; Tj^1 तानुभौ; Lo^1 ता उभौ; wKt^1 साधुतौ

20. Omitted in GMy; not commented by *Nd*; in place of verse 20, Jo^1 gives 10.125. Cited by *Viś* 3.252 — a) Pu^2 Pu^4 न धनं; Bo Ho Lo^2 sOx^1 Ox^2 Pu^3 Pu^5 sPu^6 Pu^7 Pu^8 Tj^2 Tr^2 [*Jolly* G] *Viś* धनं यद्यज्ञ°; Lo^1 वित्तं यद्यज्ञ°; TMd^3 °शालानां — b) Bo तं विदु° — c) Be^1 अयज्वानां; Jo^2 अयज्विनां; Bo Ho Lo^4 GMd^5 Pu^2 Pu^4 अयज्ञानां; Lo^2 अयज्ञिनां; Tr^2 अजज्ञानां; Lo^3 oOr Tj^1 च; GMd^1 तद्वित्त°; wKt^1 MTr^4 MTr^6 यद्द्रव्यमासु° — d) Bo Jo^2 wKt^1 NKt^4 Lo^2 TMd^4 NNg oOr sOx^1 Pu^2 Pu^3 sPu^6 Tr^1 *Viś* °मसुरस्वं; Ox^2 Tj^1 °मासुरं स्वं; wKt^3 °मासुरत्वं; Tr^2 °मसुराणां

21. Omitted in GMy; pādas c-d omitted in TMd^3 NPu^1; not commented by *Nd* — a) MTr^6 °येद्दण्डान् — c) Lo^4 क्षत्रियस्वं हि; Jo^2 wKt^3 Lo^4 Lo^3 GMd^5 Pu^{10} MTr^6 तु; Be^1 बालिशाद्; GMd^5 MTr^3 बालस्याद्; NNg [*but cor sh*] बालिस्याद्; TMd^4 वारिस्याद

श्रुतशीले च विज्ञाय वृत्तिं धर्म्यां प्रकल्पयेत् ॥२२॥
कल्पयित्वास्य वृत्तिं च रक्षेदेनं समन्ततः ।
राजा हि धर्मषड्भागं तस्मात्प्राप्नोति रक्षितात् ॥२३॥
न यज्ञार्थं धनं शूद्राद् विप्रो भिक्षेत धर्मवित् ।
यजमानो हि भिक्षित्वा चण्डालः प्रेत्य जायते ॥२४॥
यज्ञार्थमर्थं भिक्षित्वा यो न सर्वं प्रयच्छति ।
स याति भासतां विप्रः काकतां वा शतं समाः ॥२५॥
देवस्वं ब्राह्मणस्वं च लोभेनोपहिनस्ति यः ।
स पापात्मा परे लोके गृध्रोच्छिष्टेन जीवति ॥२६॥
इष्टिं वैश्वानरीं नित्यं निर्वपेदब्दपर्यये ।
क्लृप्तानां पशुसोमानां निष्कृत्यर्थमसंभवे ॥२७॥
आपत्कल्पेन यो धर्मं कुरुतेऽनापदि द्विजः ।

22. Pādas a-b omitted in TMd^{3} NPu^{1} — a) Pu^{3} अस्य; Pu^{10} [*Jolly* M^{2-8-9}] तस्माद्धृत्य° — b) GMd^{5} स्वकुडु°; GMy सकुडु°; MTr^{4} MTr^{6}सकुटु°; La^{1} स्वकुटुम्बं मही°; Ox^{2} स्वं कुटुम्बं मही°; wKt^{1} कुटुम्बं स्वं मही° — c) Tr^{2} श्रुति°; TMd^{4} ततश्शीले; wKt^{3} Pu^{2} Pu^{4} °शीले विदित्वास्य; Lo^{3} TMd^{4} विज्ञेय; Lo^{4} विज्ञान — d) Be^{1} La^{1} Lo^{4} Pu^{2} Pu^{4} धर्म्यां वृत्तिं; TMd^{4} धर्मा वृत्तिं; Pu^{10} धर्मो वृत्तिं; MTr^{6} धर्म्यं; Pu^{5} Pu^{7} [*Jolly* G] च पालयेत्

23. a) Be^{1} Lo^{1} sOx^{1} sPu^{6} °यित्वा च; BKt^{5} °यित्वा स; TMd^{3} वृत्तिश्च; Lo^{1} सद्वृत्तिं रक्षे°; BBe^{2} Jo^{2} wKt^{3} Lo^{4} Tj^{1} तु — c) Lo^{1} राज्ञा; Lo^{4} Pu^{10} राजापि; TMd^{3} TMd^{4} GMd^{5} GMy Tr^{1} फलषड्भागं — d) wKt^{1} GMd^{1} TMd^{3} GMy oOr Tr^{1} MTr^{5} तस्मादाप्नोति; sOx^{1} sPu^{6} रक्षतात्; Bo wKt^{3} NKt^{4} La^{1} Pu^{2} Pu^{4} रक्षितान्; BCa wKt^{1} Wa रक्षणात्; TMd^{3} TMd^{4} रक्षिता

24. Cited by *Apa* 168; *Hem* 1.60; *Dev* 2.421; *Mādh* 1.185 — a) Ho यज्ञार्थे — b) GMy विप्रे; *Hem* भिक्षुर्भिक्षेत; BBe^{2} भक्षेत; Lo^{1} कर्मवित्; BBe^{2} Bo Hy Jm Jo^{1} Kt^{2} Tj^{2} MTr^{3} *Hem Mandlik Jolly Jha KSS Dave* कर्हिचित् — c) *Hem* भिक्षित्वा यजमानो हि; *Dev* °मानस्तु; GMd^{5} °मानोपि — d) Bo Ho Jm La^{1} Lo^{1} Ox^{2} Pu^{10} *Mādh* चाण्डालः

25. Omitted in BKt^{5}. Cited by *Vij* 1.127; *Apa* 168; *Dev* 2.421 — a) Ho wKt^{3} यज्ञार्थमत्रं; Bo यज्ञार्थं भिक्षि° — b) *Vij* यः सर्वं न — c) GMd^{1} प्रयाति; Kt^{2} सज्ञाति; BBe^{2} सजाति; sOx^{1} sPu^{6} भासते; BBe^{2} wKt^{1} wKt^{3} भाषतां; La^{1} भवतां — c-d) GMd^{1} TMd^{3} GMd^{5} Tr^{1} भासतां विप्रः काकतां — d) BBe^{2} काकतां काकतां समाः; GMy कामतां

26. Omitted in Pu^{10}; pāda-a omitted in BKt^{5}. Cited by *Hem* 3/2.1035 — a) wKt^{3} देवब्राह्म°; Tj^{2} ब्राह्मणस्वे; Be^{1} Bo Hy Jm Jo^{1} Kt^{2} NKt^{4} La^{1} Lo^{2} Lo^{4} oOr Ox^{2} Pu^{3} Pu^{5} Pu^{7} Pu^{8} Tj^{2} Tr^{2} MTr^{3} [*Jolly* G] *Mandlik Jha KSS Dave* वा — b) NNg °भेनापहि°; Jo^{2} Tj^{1} °नोपहरेत्तु; BBe^{2} BCa Lo^{3} [*Jolly* R] °नापहरेत्तु — c) Tr^{2} दुरात्मा; Be^{1} पर — d) Bo शूद्रोच्छिष्टेन

27. Cited by *Vij* 3.265; *Apa* 167; *Dev* 2.415 — a) Hy इष्टि; Pu^{10} वैश्वानरं; Bo °नरीं विप्र; *Vij* °नरीं चैव; Lo^{2} *om* नित्यं — b) Tj^{1} °दष्टपर्यये; sOx^{1} sPu^{6} °पर्यया; Lo^{2} °पर्यय; BBe^{2} °वर्जये; NPu^{1} °पर्वणि — c) TMd^{3} क्लिप्तानां; TMd^{4} क्षिप्तानां; Tj^{2} क्लृप्ताच; Pu^{10} कप्तानां; *Vij* लुप्तानां; GMy गुप्तोनां; oOr पशुलोमानां — d) GMd^{1} निष्कृत्येषामसंभवे; BKt^{5} °र्थसंभवे; Bo GMd^{5} °र्थसमं भवेत्

स नाप्नोति फलं तस्य परत्रेत्यविचारितम् ॥२८॥
विश्वैश्च देवैः साध्यैश्च ब्राह्मणैश्च महर्षिभिः ।
आपत्सु मरणाद्भीतैर्विधेः प्रतिनिधिः कृतः ॥२९॥
प्रभुः प्रथमकल्पस्य योऽनुकल्पेन वर्तते ।
न सांपरायिकं तस्य दुर्मतेर्विद्यते फलम् ॥३०॥
न ब्राह्मणो वेदयीत किंचिद्राजनि धर्मवित् ।
स्ववीर्येणैव ताञ्छिष्यान्मानवानपकारिणः ॥३१॥
स्ववीर्याद्राजवीर्याच्च स्ववीर्यं बलवत्तरम् ।
तस्मात्स्वेनैव वीर्येण निगृह्णीयादरीन्द्विजः ॥३२॥
श्रुतीरथर्वाङ्गिरसीः कुर्यादित्यविचारितम् ।
वाक्शास्त्रं वै ब्राह्मणस्य तेन हन्यादरीन्द्विजः ॥३३॥

28.* Cited by *Apa* 167; *Dev* 2.415 — a) Be[1] *Apa* [vl] आपत्कालेन; BBe[2] यं; NKt[4] यद्धर्मं — c) NKt[4] Lo[4] समाप्नोति; Tr[1] *Apa* [vl] स प्राप्नोति — d) all NT mss. [except Pu[2]] *Apa Dev Mandlik Jolly Jha KSS Dave* परत्रेति विचारितं

29. Cited by *Apa* 167; *Dev* 2.415 — a) Lo[4] Tr[2] विश्वैर्देवैश्च; Lo[1] विश्वेदेवैश्च; Ho [*Jolly* M[2-8-9]] विश्वेदेवैः; Pu[10] वैश्वदेवः; Pu[10] [*Jolly* M[2-8-9]] स्वसाध्यैश्च; BKt[5] साध्यैः [*om* च] — b) GMd[1] ब्राह्मणश्च; Be[1] बाह्मणैर्वा; MTr[4] MTr[6] °णैः स महर्षिभिः; Wa °णैश्च बहुश्रुतैः — d) Ho Lo[4] TMd[3] SOx[1] SPu[6] MTr[5] °तैर्विधैः; GMy Ox[2] NPu[1] Pu[2] Pu[3] Pu[4] Pu[7] Pu[10] *Apa* [vl] °तैर्विधिः; WKt[3] °तैर्निधि; Lo[4] Pu[2] Pu[4] प्रतिनिधी; Pu[5] Pu[7] प्रतिनिधेः; Wa कृते; Lo[2] कृताः; GMd[1] TMd[3] GMd[5] GMy Tr[1] MTr[4] स्मृतः

30. Cited by *Apa* 168; *Hem* 1.88, 2/132, 3/1.452; *Dev* 4.160; *Mādh* 1.684; pādas a-b cited by *Viś* 1.38 — a) TMd[4] प्रभुं; Hy पशुः; Lo[4] प्रलयकल्पस्य — b) MTr[4] योनुकूल्येन; Lo[4] °कल्पे तु; GMd[1] °कल्पे स; *Apa* °कल्पेनुवर्तते; TMd[3] वर्तयेत् — c) TMd[3] न सांपरायिकस्यास्य; Tj[1] सांपारयिकं; Lo[4] सांपारयकं; Bo सापारयिकं; NNg Pu[2] °रायकं; Tr[2] °रायितुं — d) Be[1] OOr SOx[1] SPu[6] Tj[1] दुर्मते विद्यते; Pu[5] Pu[7] दुर्मतेर्वर्तते

31.* a) Lo[4] ब्राह्मणे; TMd[4] ब्राह्मण; TMd[3] Tr[1] वेदधीत; BCa वेदयिते; Be[1] वेदयते; Jo[1] Kt[2] वेदयत; BKt[5] वेदयेत्; TMd[4] वेदयति; Jm WKt[1] NKt[4] WKt[3] Lo[1] NNg Pu[5] Pu[7] Pu[8] Pu[10] Tj[2] MTr[3] Wa *Mandlik Jolly Jha KSS Dave* वेदयेत — b) Lo[1] न किंचिद्राजधर्मवित्; Lo[3] Tj[1] किंचिद्ब्राह्मण; TMd[4] किंशिद्राजान; Jo[1] किंशिद्राजने — c) SOx[1] SPu[6] सुवीर्ये°; GMy तच्छि°; Pu[5] Pu[7] तान्शिक्षेन्मा°; Bo तान्श्लिष्यान्मा°

32. Cited by *Apa* 232 — a) GMy °द्राजवीर्याद्धि — d) TMd[3] NPu[1] °यादरिं द्विजः

33.* Omitted in Lo[4] Tj[2]; verses 33 and 34 transposed in Bo — a) TMd[3] GMy Tr[1] श्रुतिर्ह्यथर्वशिरसि [TMd[3] GMy श्रुतिह्य°; GMy °गिरसी]; BKt[5] Wa श्रुतिर°; MTr[6] श्रुतिर्ह्यथर्वाङ्गि°; Ho WKt[1] BKt[5] Tj[1] °रसी; Kt[2] °रसोः; TMd[4] OOr Pu[10] °रसः — b) Jm प्रकुर्यादवि°; BBe[2] कुर्यादप्यवि°; Lo[2] कुर्यादेवावि°; Be[1] BBe[2] Bo BCa Hy Jm Jo[1] Jo[2] Kt[2] WKt[3] WKt[5] Lo[1] Lo[2] Lo[3] NNg OOr SOx[1] Ox[2] NPu[1] Pu[2] Pu[5] SPu[6] Pu[7] Pu[8] Pu[10] Tj[1] Tr[2] MTr[3] *Mandlik Jolly Jha KSS Dave* °विचारयन्; Pu[3] °विचारकं; Ho °विचारयत्; WKt[1] Wa [*Jolly* N] *Nā* °भिचारयन्; *Nd* reads अभिचारितं — c) Be[1] OOr Pu[4] वाक्शास्त्रं; WKt[1] वागस्त्रं; GMy वाग्वै शस्त्रं; Lo[1] °स्त्रं ब्राह्मणस्यैव; Be[1] °स्त्रं ब्राह्मणस्य वै; Lo[3] Ox[2] *om* वै; BKt[5] ब्राह्मणस्तेन — c-d) Tr[2] तद्धि कुरवन्यथाशक्ति प्राप्नोति परमां गतिं [see added verse] — d) MTr[4] MTr[6] तेन शस्त्रो विषं हरेत्; Pu[10] हन्यमरी°; TMd[3] दद्यादरिं द्विजः

Additional verse in La[1] [repeated after 34a-b] GMd[1] TMd[4] Ox[2] [pādas c-d given after

क्षत्रियो बाहुवीर्येण तरेदापदमात्मनः ।
धनेन वैश्यशूद्रौ तु जपहोमैर्द्विजोत्तमः ॥३४॥
विधाता शासिता वक्ता मैत्रो ब्राह्मण उच्यते ।
तस्मै नाकुशलं ब्रूयान्न शुक्तां गिरमीरयेत् ॥३५॥
नैव कन्या न युवतिर्नाल्पविद्यो न बालिशः ।
होता स्यादग्निहोत्रस्य नार्तो नासंस्कृतस्तथा ॥३६॥
नरकं हि पतन्त्येते जुह्वतः स च यस्य तत् ।
तस्माद्वैतानकुशलो होता स्याद्वेदपारगः ॥३७॥
प्राजापत्यमदत्त्वाश्वमग्न्याधेयस्य दक्षिणाम् ।
अनाहिताग्निर्भवति ब्राह्मणो विभवे सति ॥३८॥

34d] *Mandlik* [ट] *KSS;* given after 33 a-b in Tr^1 MTr^4 MTr^6:

तद्धि कुर्वन्यथाशास्त्रं प्राप्नोति परमां गतिम् ।
तच्चोग्रं सर्वशास्त्राणामनिवार्यं च शत्रुभिः ॥

a) Ox^2 °थाशक्ति — a-b) Omitted in TMd^4; *Mandlik KSS Dave* तदस्त्रं सर्वशास्त्राणामनिवार्यं च शक्तितः — c) Ox^2 यद्धयग्र्यं सर्व° — c-d) Omitted in La^1; *Mandlik KSS Dave* तपोवीर्यप्रभावेण अवध्यानपि बाधते — d) Tr^1 शक्तिभिः; La^1 GMd^1 शक्तितः

Half-verse added in TMd^4:

ब्राह्मणादुद्धितो मन्युः केनोपायेन शाम्यति ।

34. Cited by *Apa* 232 — a) Lo^4 बहुवीर्येण; TMd^3 ब्राह्मवीर्येण — b) wKt^1 तरेदपीदमा°; sOx^1 sPu^6 °त्मना — c) GMd^1 GMd^5 Tr^1 च — d) sOx^1 sPu^6 Pu^{10} MTr^4 Wa [*Jolly* M$^{2-9}$] °जोत्तमाः; Lo^3 [*Jolly* R] °जोत्तमैः

35. a) Hy रक्ता — b) [*Jolly* Ku] मैत्री; BKt^5 ब्राह्मणमुच्यते — c) GMd^5 तस्मान्नाकु°; GMy कुर्यान्नाकु°; wKt^1 वाकुशलं; Ho Tj^2 नाकुलं; Jo^2 wKt^1 Lo^3 TMd^4 GMd^5 Tj^1 Tr^1 MTr^4 MTr^6 [*Jolly* R N] *Bh* कुर्यान्न; NKt^4 क्रयान्न; Pu^5 Pu^7 ब्रूयुर्न — c-d) La^1 कुर्यानानुक्तां — d) oOr सूक्तामीरयेत् गिरं; [*Jolly* N] शुक्तं; Tj^2 मुक्तां; Pu^2 शुल्कां; Be^1 Bo Lo^2 [*Jolly* M$^{3-5}$] शुक्लां; Tr^2 शुकां; Jm Jo^1 Jo^2 Kt^2 BKt^5 Lo^1 Lo^4 Ox^2 Pu^1 Pu^5 Pu^7 Pu^{10} Wa *Mandlik Jha KSS Dave* शुष्कां; Tr^2 शुंकां

36.* Pāda-d omitted in Pu^8. Cited by *Apa* 125; *Lakṣ* 2.126; *Dev* 1.66, 2.423 — a) *Lakṣ* न च; Be^1 BBe^2 Ho Hy Jm Jo^1 wKt^1 Kt^2 wKt^3 NKt^4 BKt^5 La^1 Lo^1 Lo^2 sOx^1 NPu^1 Pu^2 Pu^5 sPu^6 Pu^7 Pu^8 Tj^2 Tr^2 MTr^3 Wa *Mandlik Jolly Jha KSS Dave* न वै; GMy नैकन्या; Pu^5 Pu^7 Tr^1 Tr^2 युवती नाल्प°; BBe^2 युवति नाल्प°; GMy युवतिभिर्नाल्प° — a-b) Bo नैव कन्या युवतिनानल्पविद्यो — b) GMd^1 °विद्या; Ox^2 बालशः — d) GMd^1 न संस्कृत°; MTr^3 नासंस्मृतस्तथा; *Dev* 1.66 °संस्कृतोपि च

37. Pādas a-b omitted in Pu^8 and pādas c-d in GMy. Cited by *Dev* 2.423 — a) Ho Jm Jo^1 wKt^1 Kt^2 TMd^4 sOx^1 sPu^6 Pu^{10} MTr^3 *Dev Mandlik Jolly Jha KSS Dave* नरके; Bo पतत्येते; Lo^1 पतन्तेते; Lo^4 पतन्त्यन्त्ये — b) wKt^1 दुर्गतः समयस्य यत्; La^1 Pu^2 *Dev* जुह्वन्तः; Pu^{10} सुहृदं स; Lo^2 यस्य तु — c) TMd^4 °कुशला — d) La^1 स्याद्वेगपारगः

38. Cited by *Dev* 2.420 — a) La^1 Lo^4 प्रजा°; Be^1 °दत्त्वास्वम°; Pu^{10} °देत्वास्वाम°; Lo^1 °दत्त्वासम°; Pu^2 Pu^4 °दत्त्वास्यम°; TMd^3 °दत्त्वार्थम° — b) TMd^4 °ग्रादानस्य; wKt^3 °ध्येयस्य; Bo wKt^1 °धेयश्च; Ho TMd^4 NPu^1 दक्षिणं — d) MTr^6 ब्राह्मणा; Jo^2 वैभवे; BKt^5 सती

After verse 38 Wa inserts 11.48–9

पुण्यान्यन्यानि कुर्वीत श्रद्दधानो जितेन्द्रियः ।
न त्वल्पदक्षिणैर्यज्ञैर्यजेतेह कथंचन ॥३९॥
इन्द्रियाणि यशः स्वर्गमायुः कीर्तिं प्रजां पशून् ।
हन्त्यल्पदक्षिणो यज्ञस्तस्मान्नाल्पधनो यजेत् ॥४०॥
अग्निहोत्र्यपविध्याग्नीन् ब्राह्मणः कामकारतः ।
चान्द्रायणं चरेन्मासं वीरहत्यासमं हि तत् ॥४१॥
ये शूद्रादधिगम्यार्थमग्निहोत्रमुपासते ।
ऋत्विजस्ते हि शूद्राणां ब्रह्मवादिषु गर्हिताः ॥४२॥
तेषां सततमज्ञानां वृषलाग्न्युपसेविनाम् ।
पदा मस्तकमाक्रम्य दाता दुर्गाणि संतरेत् ॥४३॥

39. Cited by *Dev* 2.419; *Mādh* 1.158 — a) NKt[4] पञ्चान्य° ; oOr पुण्यान्यगुणानि; Pu[10] कुर्वति — c) wKt[1] यस्त्वल्प° ; GMd[1] °क्षिणैर्यस्तु यजे° — d) Tj[1] Wa °ज्ञैर्यजन्तेह; Lo[1] ° ज्ञैर्यजतेहं; Lo[2] Pu[10] °ज्ञैर्यजतेह; NPu[1] °ज्ञैर्यजनेह; GMd[1] Tr[1] °ज्ञैर्यजतेहि; oOr °ज्ञैर्यजेत ह; *Mādh* °ज्ञैर्यजेताह; wKt[1] °ज्ञैर्न जयेत; Tr[2] °ज्ञैर्यन्नेहेत; BBe[2] wKt[1] La[1] कदाचन

40.* Cited by *Dev* 2.419 — a) Tr[1] स्वर्ग्यमायुः; Lo[4] स्वर्ग आयुः — b) Be[1] कीर्तिः; Hy NKt[4] La[1] Lo[4] sOx[1] Pu[10] कीर्ति; BBe[2] Jm Jo[2] wKt[1] Kt[2] wKt[3] BKt[5] Lo[1] Lo[4] oOr MTr[3] *Dev Mandlik Jolly Jha KSS Dave* प्रजाः; Hy Jo[1] La[1] Lo[1] Lo[3] Lo[4] प्रजा; Pu[5] Pu[7] पशुं — c) BBe[2] GMd[1] °दक्षिणा; GMd[1] NNg यज्ञास्तस्मा° ; Lo[1] यज्ञे तस्मा° ; BBe[2] यज्ञ तस्मा° — d) TMd[3] GMy MTr[4] MTr[5] MTr[6] यज्ञो न यजेताधनस्त्वतः [MTr[4] MTr[5] MTr[6] °धनस्ततः]; Lo[4] °धना; Pu[5] Pu[7] यजेत; BKt[5] Lo[4] MTr[3] जयेत्; Tr[2] व्रजेत्; sOx[1] Pu[2] Pu[3] sPu[6] भवेत्

Additional verse in Be[1] La[1] TMd[4] NPu[1] Pu[2] Pu[4] *Mandlik* [ञ, ट, ठ, ड, य, ल] *KSS Dave:*

अन्नहीनो दहेद्राष्ट्रं मन्त्रहीनस्तु ऋत्विजः ।
दीक्षितं दक्षिणाहीनो नास्ति यज्ञसमो रिपुः ॥

a) La[1] अर्थहीनो; TMd[4] हरेद्राष्ट्रं — b) La[1] TMd[4] ऋत्विजं — c) NPu[1] Pu[2] Pu[4] यजमानमदाक्षिण्यो — d) TMd[4] यज्ञवरो

41. Cited by *Apa* 1154; *Mādh* 2.425 — a) TMd[4] अग्निहोत्री हविर्योन्न; Be[1] Jo[1] °होत्रापवि° ; Tr[1] °होत्र्युपवि° ; BKt[5] °होत्राण्यपवि° ; wKt[1] °होत्रेपवि° ; NPu[1] °होत्रापवित्राग्नीन्; Be[1] Bo GMd[1] °विद्धाग्नीन्; Ho La[1] sOx[1] sPu[6] °विद्धाग्निः; Tr[2] °वीह्याग्नीन् — b) GMd[1] ब्राह्मणाः; Tj[1] °कातरः; NNg NPu[1] °कारकः; Be[1] BBe[2] oOr Pu[5] Pu[7] °चारतः — c) Hy चन्द्रा° ; Lo[1] चरेन्नित्यं; Bo हरेन्मासं — d) wKt[1] °समं महि; Bo ह तत्; TMd[4] हितः

42. Cited by *Apa* 168; *Hem* 1.60; *Dev* 2.420 — a) Pu[2] Pu[4] यः; Hy य; TMd[4] यच्छूद्राद° ; Kt[2] शून्याद° ; wKt[1] *Apa* °दभिगम्या° ; Tr[1] °गत्यार्थ° — b) *Apa* °म्यार्थं ह्यग्नि° — c) TMd[4] MTr[4] MTr[5] MTr[6] ऋत्विजस्ते भवन्त्यस्य; *Hem* सर्वे ते ब्राह्मणा निन्द्या; GMy ऋत्विजस्येहि; Lo[3] Tj[1] ऋत्विजस्तेपि; oOr ऋत्विजस्तेषु; GMd[1] GMy Tr[1] *Apa* शूद्रस्य; TMd[3] GMd[5] शूद्रास्स्युर्ब्रह्म° — d) GMy ब्रह्मवादिविगर्हिताः; Pu[10] गर्हितः; wKt[1] वेदिताः

43. Cited by *Apa* 168; *Dev* 2.420 — a) Tr[1] येषां; Lo[1] *Apa* सततयज्ञानां; Tj[1] °माज्ञानां; BBe[2] °ज्ञानं — a-b) GMy MTr[6] [*Jolly* Nd]पापानां सततं तेषामग्निं शूद्रस्य जुह्वतां [Tr[1] adds this half-verse after the regular 43a-b] — b) GMd[1] °ज्ञानामग्निं शूद्रस्य जुह्वतां; wKt[1] °ज्ञानां स्वाम्युपसेविनां; Ox[2] *Apa* [vl as in ed] वृषलानुपसे° ; TMd[4] °पजीविनां; NNg °सेवितां; TMd[3] °सेवतां — c) sOx[1] sPu[6] यदा; La[1] सदा — d) Kt[2] दातु; Lo[1] Tr[1] स्वर्गाणि; MTr[4] MTr[6] निस्तरेत्; Lo[1] संचरेत्

अकुर्वन्विहितं कर्म निन्दितं च समाचरन् ।
प्रसजंश्चेन्द्रियार्थेषु प्रायश्चित्तीयते नरः ॥४४॥
अकामतः कृते पापे प्रायश्चित्तं विदुर्बुधाः ।
कामकारकृतेऽप्याहुरेके श्रुतिनिदर्शनात् ॥४५॥
अकामतः कृतं पापं वेदाभ्यासेन शुध्यति ।
कामतस्तु कृतं मोहात् प्रायश्चित्तैः पृथग्विधैः ॥४६॥
प्रायश्चित्तीयतां प्राप्य दैवात्पूर्वकृतेन वा ।
न संसर्गं व्रजेत्सद्भिः प्रायश्चित्तेऽकृते द्विजः ॥४७॥
इह दुश्चरितैः केचित् केचित्पूर्वकृतैस्तथा ।
प्राप्नुवन्ति दुरात्मानो नरा रूपविपर्ययम् ॥४८॥
सुवर्णचौरः कौनख्यं सुरापः श्यावदन्तताम् ।
ब्रह्महा क्षयरोगित्वं दौश्चर्म्यं गुरुतल्पगः ॥४९॥

44.* Cited by *Viś* 3.210; *Vij* 3.219–20; *Mādh* 2.6; pāda-a cited as *pratīka* by *Kum* 3.6.43; *Śaṃ* on *TU* 1.1.1 [intro.] — a) Pu^{10} अकुर्वतिहितं; sPu^{6} अकुर्वन्निहितं — b) Kt^{2} mTr^{6} निन्दितश्च; Jo^{2} Lo^{3} Tj^{1} निषिद्धं च; Ho समाचरत् — c) Pu^{3} Tj^{2} प्रसज्जंश्चेन्द्रि° ; Pu^{8} प्रसजच्चैन्द्रि° ; bKt^{5} Lo^{1} oOr प्रसज्ज-श्चेन्द्रि° ; Tr^{2} प्रसंजंश्चेन्द्रि° ; wKt^{3} tMd^{4} प्रसज्जंचेन्द्रि° ; Pu^{5} Pu^{7} *Go* प्रसज्जंस्त्वेन्द्रि° ; mTr^{5} प्रसजश्चेन्द्रि° ; *Jha Dave* प्रसज्जन्निन्द्रि° ; Jm Jo^{1} Kt^{2} Kt^{4} Lo^{2} Lo^{3} Ox^{2} Pu^{2} Pu^{4} Pu^{10} Tj^{1} Wa *Vij Mandlik Jolly KSS* प्रसक्तश्चेन्द्रि° ; Jo^{2} प्रसक्तश्चेन्द्रि° *mc to* प्रसजन्निन्द्रि° ; tMd^{3} प्रशंसंश्चेन्द्रि° ; wKt^{1} सप्रजश्चेन्द्रि° — d) Lo^{1} प्रायश्चित्ती पतेन्नरः; tMd^{3} प्रायश्चित्तयते हि सः

45. Omitted in Wa; verses 45 and 46 transposed in Hy. Cited by *Vij* 3.226; *Mādh* 2.152 — c) nNg [*but mc sh*] धर्मकार° ; oOr Pu^{5} Pu^{7} कामचार° ; wKt^{1} nKt^{4} °कृते प्राहु° — d) Be^{1} Pu^{5} °हुरेक; gMd^{1} gMd^{5} °हुरेते; tMd^{3} °निर्दर्शनात्; Lo^{1} °निदर्शनाः; bKt^{5} °निबोधनात्

46. Cited by *Viś* 3.212, 226; *Apa* 1040 — b) Pu^{4} शुच्यति; bCa *Apa* नश्यति — c) bKt^{5} कामकारकृतं; Bo कृत; oOr *Apa* कृतं पापं — d) bKt^{5} पृथग्विधेः

47. a) Hy Lo^{1} °श्चित्तियतां; tMd^{4} °श्चित्तंयतां; sOx^{1} °श्चित्तेयतां; tMd^{3} °श्चित्तयतां — b) bKt^{5} gMd^{1} Pu^{5} Pu^{10} देवा° ; pāṭha in both *Bh Me* मोहात्पूर्व° [ad 11.90 *Bh* gives this as his own reading]; gMd^{5} °त्कामकृतेन; [*Jolly* R] °कृते सति; Ho च — c) wKt^{1} संसर्गं व्रजेत्सर्गं; tMd^{4} भवेत्सद्भिः — d) Be^{1} bBe^{2} wKt^{3} Lo^{2} Lo^{3} nNg oOr nPu^{1} Pu^{2} Pu^{4} Tj^{1} Wa *Bh* [ad 11.189] °कृते सति; Tj^{2} नरः

Additional verse in Ox^{2} Tr^{2} *Mandlik* [ख] *KSS Dave:*

प्रायो नाम तपः प्रोक्तं चित्तं निश्चय उच्यते ।
तपोनिश्चयसंयुक्तं प्रायश्चित्तमिति स्मृतम् ॥

c) Ox^{2} तयोर्निश्चय°

48. a) bBe^{2} इदं चरितैः — a-b) Lo^{1} कैश्चित्कैश्चित्पू° — b) Be^{1} Jm °त्पूर्वकृतेन वा [cf. 11.47b]; Wa °कृतैर्मघा — c) Pu^{4} आप्नुवन्ति; Lo^{2} दुरात्मने; mTr^{4} महात्मानो; Lo^{4} Pu^{10} [*Jolly* M] दुराचारा — d) Ox^{2} नानारूप° ; tMd^{3} इह रूप°

49. a) Lo^{3} gMd^{1} tMd^{4} gMd^{5} gMy Pu^{8} Tj^{1} Tr^{1} mTr^{5} mTr^{6} °चोरः; sOx^{1} sPu^{6} Tj^{1} कोनख्यं; tMd^{4} कौनखं — b) gMy सुरापाश्श्याव° ; Be^{1} शाव° ; tMd^{4} स्याव° ; Bo Pu^{2} Pu^{4} श्याम° ; gMd^{1} श्याप° ; wKt^{1} Pu^{5} Pu^{7} [*Jolly* G] °दन्तकः — c) bKt^{5} °योगित्वं; tMd^{3} क्षयरोगी स्याद्दौश्चर्म्यं — d) tMd^{4} दौश्चर्यं; Pu^{4} °तल्पकः

पिशुनः पूतिनासत्वं सूचकः पूतिवक्त्रताम् ।
धान्यचौरोऽङ्गहीनत्वमातिरैक्यं तु मिश्रकः ॥५०॥
अन्नहर्तामयावित्वं मौक्यं वागपहारकः ।
वस्त्रापहारकः श्वैत्र्यं पङ्गुतामश्वहारकः ॥५१॥
एवं कर्मविशेषेण जायन्ते सद्विगर्हिताः ।
जडमूकान्धबधिरा विकृताकृतयस्तथा ॥५३॥
चरितव्यमतो नित्यं प्रायश्चित्तं विशुद्धये ।
निन्द्यैर्हि लक्षणैर्युक्ता जायन्तेऽनिष्कृतैनसः ॥५४॥

50.* a) Be^{1} पिशुना; [*Jolly* M$^{2-5-8-9}$ Nd] पूतिनासत्त्वं; NKt^{4} La^{1} पूतिनाशत्वं; GMd^{5} पूतिनासित्वं; TMd^{3} पूतिनासित्यं; TMd^{4} पूतिनाशित्यं; Lo^{2} प्रतिनासत्वं; Be^{1} Bo BCa Ho Lo^{3} Lo^{4} sOx^{1} Ox^{2} NPu^{1} Pu^{2} Pu^{3} Pu^{4} sPu^{6} Pu^{8} Tj^{1} [*Jolly* M^{4} R] पूतिनासिक्यं; Kt^{2} Tr^{2} पूतिनाशिक्यं; NNg पूतनासिक्यं; oOr पूतिनासक्तं; Be^{2} Hy Jm Jo^{1} Jo^{2} wKt^{1} wKt^{3} BKt^{5} Lo^{1} Tj^{2} MTr^{3} [*Jolly* G] *Mandlik Jha KSS Dave* पौतिमासिक्यं; Pu^{5} Pu^{7} पौतिमाशिक्यं — b) NNg सूचकं; sOx^{1} sPu^{6} सूचिकः; NKt^{4} BKt^{5} शूचिकः; TMd^{4} माचकः; Be^{1} पौति°; Tr^{2} पूतिगन्धतां — c) Bo Ho Lo^{3} GMd^{1} TMd^{4} GMy Tj^{1} Tr^{1} MTr^{5} MTr^{6} °चोरो°; Lo^{4} Pu^{5} Pu^{10} Wa °चौरा°; Lo^{2} °चोरा°; Pu^{4} °हीनतश्चातिरैक्यं — d) TMd^{4} °त्वमातुरत्वं; BBe^{2} Ho Jo^{2} Lo^{2} TMd^{3} sOx^{1} sPu^{6} Tr^{1} °तिरेक्यं; GMd^{1} MTr^{6} °तिरिक्यं; Wa °तिरिक्तं; GMy °तिरत्त्वं; Hy °तिवैक्यं; wKt^{1} Tr^{2} च; MTr^{6} मिश्रिकः; Pu^{5} Pu^{7} मिश्रयः

51. Pādas c-d omitted in wKt^{1} TMd^{4} [haplo]. Cited by *Mādh* 2.251 — a) BKt^{5} °मायावित्वं; Pu^{2} Pu^{4} °मयाचित्रं — b) TMd^{3} मूकं गावापहारिकः; GMd^{5} मूको; BBe^{2} वाक्यं वाग° — c) NKt^{4} वस्त्रापंकारकश्वैन्यं; Pu^{8} वस्त्राग्रहारकः; Ho °हारकं; Be^{1} °हारकश्चैत्र्यं; Bo °हारकश्चैवैत्र्यं; BBe^{2} BCa श्वैत्रं; BKt^{5} Lo^{3} TMd^{3} Tr^{1} श्वैत्यं — d) GMd^{1} GMd^{5} GMy पङ्कुताम°; Ho खञ्जतामश्व°

Additional verse in Be^{1} BCa wKt^{3} La^{1} TMd^{4} NNg oOr Ox^{2} NPu^{1} Pu^{2} Pu^{4} [*Jolly* M R Ku] *Mandlik KSS Dave;* pādas a-b in Tr^{2}; given within brackets by *Jolly* [cf. ViDh 45.20–1]; *Rn* gives this as क्वचित्पाठः; commented by *Rc:*

दीपहर्ता भवेदन्धः काणो निर्वापकस्तथा ।
हिंसया व्याधिभूयिष्ठमरोगित्वमहिंसया ॥

a) NPu^{1} दीपकहर्ता; La^{1} भवत्यन्धः — b) NPu^{1} निर्वाणक°; La^{1} निर्वातक°; NNg Ox^{2} Tr^{2} [*Jolly* M R] *Mandlik Jolly KSS* निर्वापको भवेत्; TMd^{4} °पकः स्मृतः — c) wKt^{3} La^{1} [*Jolly* R] *Rn* हिंसारतः सदा रोगी [La^{1} भोगी]; Ox^{2} हिंसायां; Pu^{2} Pu^{4} °भूमिष्ट°; NNg [*Jolly* M] *Mandlik Jolly KSS* °भूयस्त्व° — d) *Rn* षण्ढश्च पारदारिकः; [*Jolly* R] स षण्ढः पारदारिकः; La^{1} वातांडः पारदारिकः; Bühler reads: वाताङ्गः पारदारिकः; BCa wKt^{3} पशुः स्यात्पारदायिकः [BCa पत्तः]; Ox^{2} अहिंसया तु नीरुजः; NPu^{1} °मारोगि°; Pu^{2} Pu^{4} °मारागित्वमहिंसकः

The above verse is given as verse 52 in Bühler's translation. To maintain the traditional numbering, I have eliminated the verse number 52.

53.* Omitted in Tr^{2} — a) Jm एतत्; w Kt^{3} एकं; Ox^{2} कर्मापशेषेण *cor to* कर्मविशेषेण; Bo BCa Hy Jm Jo^{1} Jo^{2} wKt^{1} Kt^{2} BKt^{5} La^{1} Lo^{1} Lo^{2} Lo^{3} Lo^{4} TMd^{3} TMd^{4} oOr NPu^{1} Pu^{3} Pu^{4} Pu^{5} Pu^{7} Pu^{8} Pu^{10} Tj^{1} Tj^{2} MTr^{3} [*Jolly* M G] *ViDh* 45.32 *Mandlik Jha KSS Dave* कर्मविशेपेण; Pu^{2} कर्माविशेपेण — b) Lo^{4} TMd^{3} जायते; TMd^{4} देयन्ते; Pu^{5} Pu^{7} वाद्विग°; BKt^{5} यद्विग°; oOr हि विग° — c) TMd^{3} GMd^{5} Tr^{1} MTr^{5} जळ°; GMy जडान्धमूक°; TMd^{4} GMd^{5} °बधिर

54. Omitted in Ox^{2}. Cited by *Vij* 3.219–20; *Mādh* 2.3 — a) TMd^{3} चरितं प्रयतो; Be^{1}

ब्रह्महत्या सुरापानं स्तेयं गुर्वङ्गनागमः ।
महान्ति पातकान्याहुः संयोगश्चैव तैः सह ॥५५॥
अनृतं च समुत्कर्षे राजगामि च पैशुनम् ।
गुरोश्चालीकनिर्बन्धः समानि ब्रह्महत्यया ॥५६॥
ब्रह्मोज्झता वेदनिन्दा कौटसाक्ष्यं सुहृद्वधः ।
गर्हितानाद्ययोर्जग्धिः सुरापानसमानि षट् ॥५७॥
निक्षेपस्यापहरणं नराश्वरजतस्य च ।
भूमिवज्रमणीनां च रुक्मस्तेयसमं स्मृतम् ॥५८॥
रेतःसेकः स्वयोन्यासु कुमारीष्वन्त्यजासु च ।
सख्युः पुत्रस्य च स्त्रीषु गुरुतल्पसमं विदुः ॥५९॥
गोवधोऽयाज्यसंयाज्यं पारदार्यात्मविक्रयौ ।

°व्यमथो — b) Tr^1 प्रायश्चित्त; Pu^2 Pu^4 च शुद्धये — c) bBe^2 निन्द्यैश्च; Ho निन्द्यैर्ह; Bo Jo^2 Lo^3 gMy oOr Tj^1 निन्दितैर्लक्ष°; mTr^4 mTr^6 ये निन्द्यैर्लक्ष°; La^1 °णैर्मुक्ता — d) nNg Pu^5 Pu^7 °निकृतै°; tMd^4 °निष्कृतैर्नरः; nKt^4 °निःशतेजसः; Tr^1 ननिष्कृतेनसः; wKt^3 Lo^3 Lo^4 gMd^1 tMd^3 gMy °तेनसः

55.* Only pratīka in Lo^4. Cited by *Apa* 1044 — a) Lo^2 gMy mTr^6 °हत्यां; tMd^4 gMd^5 °पान — b) bKt^5 Lo^1 Lo^2 gMd^5 gMy oOr Tr^2 *Apa* °नागमं— c) Bo Tr^1 महाति — d) Be^1 संयोगं दैवतैः सह; Lo^1 [*but cor illegibly*] संयोगंसहतैः सह; Lo^3 संसर्गश्च पतितैः सह; Tr^1 संयोग चैव; bBe^2 Hy Jo^1 Jo^2 wKt^1 Kt^2 wKt^3 La^1 Lo^3 Tj^1 Tj^2 mTr^3 [*Jolly* Ku] *Mandlik Jha KSS Dave* संसर्गश्चापि; Bo Lo^2 tMd^3 tMd^4 oOr nNg Pu^5 Pu^7 Pu^{10} Tr^2 mTr^5 mTr^6 Wa [Jolly M G]संयोगं चैव; Ho sOx^1 sPu^6 *Apa* संसर्गं चैव; Jm संसर्गैश्चापि

56. Cited by *Apa* 1047; *Har*-A1.24.23; *Mādh* 2.419 — a)gMy [*Jolly* Nd] अनृतं स्वयमु-त्कर्पे; gMd^1 अनृता; Tj^1 Wa °त्कर्षो; tMd^4 °त्कर्पा — b) nKt^4 राजगामिनि पैःशुनां; tMd^3 °गामिं; Tr^1 °गामी; gMy न पैशुनं; Pu^{10} पैशुनां; Be^1 पैश्वनं; Lo^2 मैथुनं — c) gMd^5 Tr^1 °ळीक°; Lo^1 °लिक°; Be^1 °निबन्धः; bKt^5 °संबन्धः — d) gMy सामानि

57. Cited by *Śaṃ* on *BU* 1.5.1; *Viś* 3.223; *Vij* 3.231; *Apa* 1047, 1157; *Mādh* 2.293; 2.419 — a) gMd^1 tMd^4 gMd^5 gMy Pu^2 Tr^1 mTr^4 mTr^6 *Śaṃ Viś Apa* ब्रह्मोज्झं वेदनिन्दा च [*Viś* °ज्झो; mTr^4 mTr^6 °ज्झा; gMd^1 देव°]; tMd^3 ब्रह्मेरुं वेदनिन्दा च; Be^1 ब्रह्मोज्झिता; bBe^2 ब्रह्महत्या; Bo ब्रह्मोदृता; Kt^2 ब्रह्मोद्धृता; nKt^4 ब्रह्मोष्टनं — b) bKt^5 Lo^4 gMd^1 tMd^3 nPu^1 Pu^2 Pu^4 Pu^{10} *Apa* कूट°; Kt^2 °साक्षां; wKt^3 °साक्षं; gMd^1 महद्वधः — c) Lo^1 गर्हितान्नादिजग्धिश्च; Tj^1 गर्हितानां च या जग्धिः; Bo गर्धिता°; wKt^3 La^1 nPu^1 Pu^5 Pu^7 Lo^4 gMd^1 gMd^5 gMy Ox^2 Tr^1 [*Jolly* M] *Apa* 1157गर्हितान्नाद्य°; tMd^3 *Vij* गर्हितान्नाज्ययो°; bKt^5 गर्हितानार्ययो°

58. Omitted in Pu^{10}. Cited by *Viś* 3.225; *Vij* 3.265; *Apa* 1048, 1110; *Mādh* 2.419 — a) Bo °पाहरणं; *Vij* °हरणे — b) Bo नराश्च°; gMd^5 रक्ताश्व° — c) wKt^1 भूमीचत्र°; tMd^4 भूमिप्रजा°; *Viś* भूमिवस्त्र° [but vl as ed]; Pu^5 Pu^7 वज्रभूमिमणीनां — d) tMd^4 रुक्मस्तेयं च संमतं; sOx^1 mTr^4 mTr^6 रुग्म°; nKt^4 रुक्ष°; tMd^3 रुक्त°; gMd^1 स्मृतः; wKt^1 Tr^2 विदुः; La^1 नृपं; bBe^2 द्विजः

59.* Omitted in bBe^2; pādas c-d omitted in gMy. Cited by *Vij* 3.231; *Apa* 1048 — a) Hy °सेकैः; mTr^6 °सेकं; La^1 Pu^8 स्वयोन्यां तु; Ho Jm Jo^1 Kt^2 Lo^2 gMd^1 Ox^2 Tr^2 mTr^3 [*Jolly* G M^3 Nd] *Apa Vij Mandlik Jolly Jha KSS Dave* स्वयोनीषु; Lo^3 Tj^1 [*Jolly* R] *Apa* [vl]स्वयोनिषु; tMd^3 Tr^1 त्वयोन्यासु; tMd^4 त्वयोन्यां तु — b) Ho Tj^1 °ष्वन्तजासु

गुरुमातृपितृत्यागः स्वाध्यायाग्न्योः सुतस्य च ॥६०॥
परिवित्तितानुजेन परिवेदनमेव च ।
तयोर्दानं च कन्यायास्तयोरेव च याजनम् ॥६१॥
कन्याया दूषणं चैव वार्धुषित्वं व्रताच्च्युतिः ।
तडागारामदाराणामपत्यस्य च विक्रयः ॥६२॥
व्रात्यता बान्धवत्यागो भृताध्यापनमेव च ।
भृताच्चाध्ययनादानमपण्यानां च विक्रयः ॥६३॥
सर्वाकरेष्वधीकारो महायन्त्रप्रवर्तनम् ।
हिंसौषधीनां स्त्र्याजीवोऽभिचारो मूलकर्म च ॥६४॥

60.* Omitted in GMy. Cited by *Mādh* 2.13 — a) Pu[10] गौवधो; GMd[1] गोर्थो; NKt[4] °याप्यसंयाप्यं; BBe[2] Hy Jm Jo[1] Kt[2] La[1] GMd[1] TMd[4] MTr[3] MTr[5] [*Jolly* M[2]] *Mandlik KSS* °संयाज्य — b) *Me* [pāṭha] पारदार्यमविक्रयं; NPu[1] Pu[2] पर°; Be[1] Pu[4] MTr[4] MTr[6] परदारात्मवि°; La[1] परदार्यार्थवि°; wKt[1] °दार्यासुविक्रमै; oOr °विक्रयोः; Bo °विक्रयैः; Lo[4] Pu[10] MTr[3] [*Jolly* M[2-3-4-5-8-9]] °विक्रयं; Be[1] BBe[2] Ho BKt[5] La[1] Lo[2] GMd[1] GMd[5] sOx[1] NPu[1] Pu[2] Pu[3] Pu[4] Pu[5] sPu[6] Pu[7] Tr[1] Tr[2] MTr[4] MTr[6] [*Jolly* G Nd]*Mādh Nā* °विक्रयः; Hy Jm Jo[1] Jo[2] Kt[2] Md[4] *Mandlik Jha KSS Dave* °विक्रयाः — c) Bo मातापितृगुरुत्यागः; NPu[1] Tr[2] गुरुमातृपरित्यागः; Tr[1] पितृमातृपरित्यागः — d) MTr[6] °ध्यायाग्नेः; oOr °ध्यायोग्नौ

61. Pādas a-b omitted in GMy. Cited by *Mādh* 2.13 — a) Pu[2] Pu[4] परित्तितानुजेनैव; NPu[1] परिवेत्तानुजेनैव; Ho Lo[1] TMd[3] GMd[5] Tj[2] Tr[1] MTr[5] MTr[6] [*Jolly* Nd Gr] परिवित्तिता चानुजेन [Tr[1] परिवित्तता; TMd[3] GMd[5] परिवित्ता]; sOx[1] sPu[6] परिवेत्तिता चानुजेन [sOx[1] परिवेत्ता]; Hy Jm Jo[1] Kt[2] Lo[2] MTr[3] *Mandlik KSS Jha Dave* परिवित्तितानुजेनूढे [Jm Jo[1] Kt[2] °नोढे; Jo[1] नोधे]; Lo[4] परिवेत्तानुजेनूढे — d) TMd[3] °स्तयोर्याजनमेव च; Pu[10] °योरेव प्रयोजनं; TMd[4] याजनः; Lo[4] योजनं

62.* Cited by *Mādh* 2.13 — a) sOx[1] sPu[6] कन्यायां — b) GMd[1] वार्धुषितं; BBe[2] Bo Hy Jm Jo[1] Kt[2] wKt[3] Lo[1] Lo[2] Lo[4] NNg Ox[2] Pu[5] Pu[7] Pu[8] Pu[10] Tj[2] Tr[2] MTr[3] Wa *Mandlik Jolly Jha KSS Dave* वार्धुष्यं; Be[1] Pu[3] वार्धुष्य; sOx[1] sPu[6] वार्धुषं; BKt[5] वार्धुकं; Lo[3] TMd[3] TMd[4] GMy Tj[1] Tr[1] व्रता-च्युतिः; La[1] व्रताच्युत; Ho wKt[1] NKt[4] NPu[1] Pu[2] Pu[4] [*Jolly* R Nd] *Me Mādh* व्रतच्युतिः; GMd[1] पुरा-च्युतिः; MTr[4] MTr[6] प्रजाच्युतिः; Be[1] BBe[2] Bo Hy Jm Jo[1] Kt[2] wKt[3] BKt[5] Lo[1] Lo[2] Lo[4] NNg sOx[1] Ox[2] Pu[5] sPu[6] Pu[7] Pu[8] Pu[10] Tj[2] Tr[2] MTr[3] Wa *Nā Rn* [pāṭha] *Rc Mr Mandlik Jolly Jha KSS Dave* व्रतलोपनं — c) GMd[1] TMd[3] TMd[4] GMd[5] GMy Tj[1] Tr[1] MTr[5] MTr[6] *Mādh* तटाक°; Lo[3] तडाका°; sOx[1] sPu[6] °रामपूराणाम° — d) BBe[2] *om* च; GMd[5] विक्रयं; sOx[1] विक्रियः; La[1] NPu[1] विक्रमः

63. Omitted in Pu[2] Pu[4]. Cited by *Mādh* 2.13 — a) Lo[1] व्रात्यानां; GMd[1] व्रात्यतौ; TMd[4] व्रात्यत्वं; BBe[2] °त्यागे — b) BBe[2] BCa Ho Jo[2] wKt[3] Lo[3] sOx[1] sPu[6] Tj[1] [*Jolly* R] *Rn ViDh* 37.20 भृतकाध्यापनं तथा [wKt[3] °पनस्तथा]; GMd[5] भृतकाध्यापनमेव च; Be[1] Jo[1] Kt[2] La[1] Pu[3] Pu[5] Pu[7] Pu[8] Tj[2] MTr[3] [*Jolly* M G Nd] *Mandlik Jha KSS Dave* भृत्याध्या°; Jm भृत्योध्या°; Lo[1] भृत्याध्ययनमेव — c) oOr भृतकाध्यापनादानम°; BBe[2] Ho Lo[1] NNg sOx[1] sPu[6] Tr[2] भृत्याच्चा°; Ho Lo[4] Ox[2] Pu[10] भृताद्वाध्य°; Jo[2] Lo[3] Tj[1] [*Jolly* R] भृतादध्य°; GMd[5] °ध्यापना°; Kt[2] °ध्ययना°; Bo °यनाद्दानम° — d) La[1] °दानं पण्यानां चैव विक्रयः; Be[1] °मरण्यानां; Pu[5] Pu[7] Pu[10] °मपत्यानां; TMd[3] °मपश्यानां; GMy विक्रयं; sOx[1] विक्रियः; Kt[2] विक्रमः

64. Cited by *Mādh* 2.13; pādas c-d cited by *Apa* 15 — a) Bo सर्वाकरे अधीकारो; TMd[3] सर्वागारेष्वपीकारो; Be[1] GMd[1] GMd[5] sOx[1] Pu[5] sPu[6] Pu[7] Tj[1] *Mādh* सर्वाकारे°; Jm सर्वाकरीष्व°; GMd[1]

इन्धनार्थमशुष्काणां द्रुमाणामवपातनम् ।
आत्मार्थं च क्रियारम्भो निन्दितान्नादनं तथा ॥६५॥
अनाहिताग्निता स्त्रैण्यम्* ऋणानां चानपक्रिया ।
असच्छास्त्राधिगमनं कौशील्यं व्यसनक्रिया* ॥६६॥
धान्यकुप्यपशुस्तेयं मद्यपस्त्रीनिषेवणम् ।
स्त्रीशूद्रविट्क्षत्रवधो नास्तिक्यं चोपपातकम् ॥६७॥
ब्राह्मणस्य रुजःकृत्यं घ्रातिरघ्रेयमद्ययोः ।
जैह्म्यं पुंसि च मैथुन्यं जातिभ्रंशकरं स्मृतम् ॥६८॥
खराश्वोष्ट्रमृगेभानामजाविकवधस्तथा ।
संकरीकरणं ज्ञेयं मीनाहिमहिषस्य च ॥६९॥

°धीकारा — b) Tr^{1} महायज्ञ°; TMd^{3} °प्रवर्तनः; Pu^{10} °प्रवर्तते — c) GMd^{1} GMd^{5} GMy MTr^{4} Tr^{1} *Nd* हिंसौषधिस्त्र्युपाजीवो [GMd^{5} °पजीवो]; TMd^{3} हिंस्राषड्युपजीवो वा; TMd^{4} हिंस्रोषधास्त्र्युपजीवो; Pu^{10} Tj^{1} हिंस्रौ°; Lo^{3} Pu^{5} Pu^{7} हिंस्रो° — c-d) MTr^{6} स्त्रीणां च जीवनं मूलं° — d) Pu^{10} °भिचारं; GMd^{1} विवाहो मूल°; BKt^{5} *om* मूल; Be^{1} °कर्मसु [*om* च]

65. Cited by *Mādh* 2.13; pādas c-d cited by *Mādh* 2.293 — b) Ho sOx^{1} sPu^{6} वृक्षाणामव°; Jo^{2} Tj^{1} तरूणामव°; Bo Lo^{1} °माणां चैव पातनं; BCa La^{1} °णामेव पातनं; BKt^{5} °वपीडनं — c) Hy आत्मार्थं च शीकरणं क्रियारम्भो; GMd^{5} क्रियाभोगो — d) MTr^{4} MTr^{6} निन्दितान्नस्य चादनं; Ox^{2} निन्दितान्नोपजीवनं; TMd^{3} निन्दितानाधनं तथा; Pu^{5} Pu^{7} °दनस्तथा

66.* Pāda-c omitted in GMd^{1}. Cited by *Mādh* 2.13 — a) Tr^{1} °ग्निका; Bo °ग्निस्तेयम्; Jo^{2} Lo^{3} Tj^{1} [*Jolly* R Nd] स्तैन्यम्; all other NT mss., *Mandlik Jolly Jha KSS Dave* स्तेयम् — b) Hy Jm Jo^{1} Kt^{2} Lo^{3} Tj^{2} MTr^{3} *Mandlik Jha KSS Dave* ऋणानामनप°; Ho NKt^{4} Pu^{2} Pu^{3} Pu^{4} Pu^{5} Pu^{7} *Nd* वानप°; NPu^{1} चानुप° — c) BBe^{2} BCa Jo^{2} La^{1} Lo^{1} Lo^{3} TMd^{3} GMd^{5} Pu^{10} Tj^{1} Tr^{2} MTr^{4} MTr^{6} °स्त्राभिगमनं; Ox^{2} °स्त्रार्थगमनं — d) BBe^{2} Bo BCa Ho Hy Jm Jo^{1} Jo^{2} wKt^{1} Kt^{2} wKt^{3} NKt^{4} BKt^{5} Lo^{2} Lo^{3} NNg sOx^{1} Pu^{3} sPu^{6} Pu^{8} Tj^{1} Tj^{2} Tr^{2} MTr^{3} Wa [*Jolly* Me Go R Ku] *Mandlik Jolly Jha KSS Dave* कौशीलव्यस्य च क्रिया [Bo कुशील°; NNg कौशल°]; Lo^{1} कौशील्यव्ययहोः क्रिया; TMd^{4} कौशील्य; TMd^{3} कौशीलं; Be^{1} La^{1} Pu^{5} Pu^{7} Pu^{10} [*Jolly* M] कौशील; [*Jolly* Nd] कौशल्यं; Lo^{4} कौशीत; MTr^{5} कौटिल्यं; GMd^{5} कौटिल्य; GMy [*Jolly* Nd] वसन°; Pu^{2} Pu^{4} व्यसनं तथा

67. Cited by *Mādh* 2.13 — a) Lo^{1} धान्यं; TMd^{3} GMy Tr^{1} MTr^{4} MTr^{5} MTr^{6} [*Jolly* Nd Gr] धान्यरूप्य° — b) Pu^{5} Pu^{7} Pu^{10} मद्यपास्त्री°; Bo °निवेपणं — c) MTr^{4} MTr^{6} स्त्रीशूद्राणां क्षत्रवधो; Jo^{2} °शूद्रक्षत्रियवधो; NNg *ma sh* °विट्°; MTr^{3} °क्षत्रबन्धो — d) TMd^{3} नास्तित्वं; Tj^{1} चोपपापकं

68.* Cited by *Vij* 3.234–42; *Apa* 1183; *Mādh* 2.14 — a) Be^{1} रुजा°; NPu^{1} रुजुः°; wKt^{1} wKt^{3} रजः°; MTr^{5} रुजं°; Be^{1} Bo BCa Hy Jo^{1} Jo^{2} wKt^{1} Kt^{2} wKt^{3} La^{1} Lo^{2} NPu^{1} Pu^{2} Pu^{4} Tj^{1} Wa *Vij Apa Mādh Nā Rc Mr Mandlik* °कृत्या; BBe^{2} Jm NKt^{4} BKt^{5} Lo^{3} Ox^{2} Pu^{3} Tr^{2} MTr^{3} [*Jolly* R] *KSS* कृत्वा — b) sOx^{1} sPu^{6} घ्रातिं चाघ्रे°; Ho Ox^{2} घ्राणं चाघ्रे°; MTr^{4} °मन्ययोः — c) Be^{1} BBe^{2} Ho Hy Jm Jo^{1} Kt^{2} wKt^{3} BKt^{5} Lo^{4} NNg sOx^{1} Pu^{3} sPu^{6} Pu^{8} Pu^{10} Tj^{2} MTr^{3} *Mandlik Jolly Jha KSS Dave* जैह्म्यं च मैथुनं पुंसि; TMd^{3} Ox^{2} च पुंसि; Tj^{1} पैशुन्यं — d) La^{1} NPu^{1} ज्ञाति°

69. Pāda-d *ma* in Be^{1}. Cited by *Vij* 3.234–42; *Apa* 1183; *Mādh* 2.14 — a) *Apa* खरोष्ट्रमृगबाणानाम°; Pu^{5} Pu^{7} खरोश्वो°; Jo^{2} Lo^{4} TMd^{3} GMd^{5} GMy Pu^{10} Tj^{2} MTr^{6} खरोष्ट्राश्व°; Lo^{1} खरौष्ट्राश्व°; Ox^{2} श्वखरोष्ट्र°; MTr^{5} खरोष्ट्रोश्व मृगे° — b) La^{1} °नां गोजाविकवधं तथा; Hy °विकबन्ध°; Tj^{1} °वधास्तथा; TMd^{3} °वधं तथा — c) MTr^{5} संकीर्णकरं संज्ञेयं; BKt^{5} शंकरी°; MTr^{3} संकली°; GMd^{1} TMd^{3}

निन्दितेभ्यो धनादानं वाणिज्यं शूद्रसेवनम् ।
अपात्रीकरणं ज्ञेयमसत्यस्य च भाषणम् ॥७०॥
कृमिकीटवयोहत्या मद्यानुगतभोजनम् ।
फलैधःकुसुमस्तेयमधैर्यं च मलावहम् ॥७१॥
एतान्येनांसि सर्वाणि यथोक्तानि पृथक्पृथक् ।
यैर्यैर्व्रतैरपोह्यन्ते तानि सम्यङ् निबोधत ॥७२॥
ब्रह्महा द्वादशाब्दानि कुटीं कृत्वा वने वसेत् ।
भैक्षाश्यात्मविशुद्ध्यर्थं कृत्वा शवशिरोध्वजम् ॥७३॥
लक्ष्यं शस्त्रभृतां वा स्याद् विदुषामिच्छयात्मनः ।
प्रास्येदात्मानमग्नौ वा समिद्धे त्रिरवाक्शिराः ॥७४॥
यजेत वाश्वमेधेन स्वर्जिता गोसवेन वा ।
अभिजिद्विश्वजिद्भ्यां वा त्रिवृताग्निष्टुतापि वा ॥७५॥

GMd^{5} GMy Tr^{1} MTr^{4} MTr^{6} संकीर्णकरणं; Lo^{1} °करणी — d) Tr^{2} असत्यस्य च भाषणं [cf. 70d]; TMd^{4} मीनाहे°; Tr^{1} मीनाभिर्महि°; Be^{1} °महिष्यस्य

70. Pādas a-c *ma* in Be^{1}. Cited by *Vij* 3.234–42; *Apa* 1183; *Mādh* 2.14 — a) TMd^{4} धनंदानं; Kt^{2} धमादानं — d) GMd^{1} ज्ञेयमसद्भिश्चैव भाषणं; NKt^{4} ज्ञेयं समसस्य च; Be^{1} TMd^{3} Tr^{1} MTr^{5} MTr^{6} *Apa* °सभ्यस्य च

71. Cited by *Vij* 3.234–42; *Apa* 1129, 1183; *Mādh* 2.14 — a) Lo^{3} TMd^{3} TMd^{4} GMd^{5} NNg Tr^{1} Tr^{2} *Apa* क्रिमि°; Hy °कीटं; TMd^{3} °वधोहत्या; wKt^{1} Lo^{1} °हत्वा; Pu^{10} °कन्या — b) Bo °भाजनं — c) wKt^{3} BKt^{5} GMd^{5} NNg *Apa* फलैधकु°; Kt^{2} फलैःधःकु°; Tr^{1} फलैःयःकु°; Bo फलैश्वकु°; TMd^{4} फलैपुकु°; Lo^{1} °कुशुमास्तेय° — d) wKt^{1} °मधैर्यमालावहं; TMd^{3} °मवैर्यं; GMy °मधैर्यश्च; Pu^{5} Pu^{7} मलापहं; GMd^{1} मवाचहं; MTr^{6} फलावहं

72. c) La^{1} NPu^{1} Pu^{2} Pu^{4} ययैर्व्र°; Lo^{3} *om first* यैर्; GMd^{1} °पोह्येत; BBe^{2} °पोहेत

73. Cited by *Apa* 1060; pādas a-b cited by *Vij* 3.243, and pāda-a by *Viś* 3.244 — a) BBe^{2} द्वादशाहानि; Hy Jm Jo^{1} Kt^{2} BKt^{5} Lo^{2} Lo^{4} Ox^{2} Pu^{8} Pu^{10} Tj^{2} Tr^{2} MTr^{3} Wa [*Jolly* M] *Me Mr Mandlik Jha KSS Dave* द्वादश समाः — c) Jo^{2} Lo^{3} Lo^{4} भैक्ष्याश्यात्म°; TMd^{3} भिक्षाह्यात्म°; Ho La^{1} sOx^{1} sPu^{6} MTr^{4} MTr^{5} MTr^{6} भक्ष्यं चात्म° [La^{1} चार्थ]; Pu^{10} भैक्षाशाश्चात्म°; MTr^{5} °त्मनिवृत्त्यर्थं — d) oOr शिवशिरो°; Lo^{3} °शिरौ°; Be^{1} °शरो°; TMd^{3} °शिरोर्ध्वजं; GMd^{5} °ध्वजः

74. Cited by *Viś* 3.243; *Mādh* 2.155, 405; pādas a-b cited by *Vij* 3.248; *Apa* 1060; pādas a and c by *Vij* 3.244; and pādas c-d by *Vij* 3.247; *Apa* 1059 — a) Bo wKt^{1} NKt^{4} Lo^{2} GMd^{5} NNg Pu^{3} Pu^{5} Pu^{7} लक्षं; Be^{1} शास्त्र°; Tr^{1} शर°; TMd^{3} °भृतं — b) GMd^{5} विदुषां चेच्छयात्मनः; wKt^{1} विद्विषा°; MTr^{4} इषूनामि°; GMy विषयामि°; oOr °यात्मनि — c) BBe^{2} BKt^{5} प्राश्येदा°; Lo^{1} प्रासेदा°; sOx^{1} प्रास्ये चात्मा° — d) Tr^{2} समृद्धे त्रीणि वाक्शिरः; GMy समिद्ध्ये; BKt^{5} निरवाक्शिराः; *Mādh* त्ववाक्शिराः; Lo^{2} °वाक्शिरः; Pu^{5} Pu^{7} °वाग्शिरः; sOx^{1} sPu^{6} °वाच्छिराः; NKt^{4} °वाङ्गिराः; MTr^{4} MTr^{6} °वाङ्मुखाः

75. Cited by *Vij* 3.248; *Mādh* 2.405; pāda-a cited by *Viś* 3.237 — a) sOx^{1} यजते; BBe^{2} La^{1} यजेद्वाश्व°; Lo^{2} सजेत विश्व°; TMd^{4} *om* वाश्व; Bo Pu^{10} याश्व° — b) TMd^{3} स्वार्जिता; TMd^{4} स्वर्जितं; GMd^{1} *Vij* च — c) GMd^{5} °श्वजिद्वापि — d) Tr^{2} त्रिवृताग्निश्वतापिता; GMd^{1} °ग्नेष्टुतापि; La^{1} °ग्निष्टुभापि; Lo^{4} °ग्निप्युतापि; TMd^{3} Pu^{10} °ग्निपुचापि

जपन्वान्यतमं वेदं योजनानां शतं व्रजेत् ।
ब्रह्महत्यापनोदाय मितभुङ्‍ नियतेन्द्रियः ॥७६॥
सर्वस्वं वा वेदविदे ब्राह्मणायोपपादयेत् ।
धनं वा जीवनायालं गृहं वा सपरिच्छदम् ॥७७॥
हविष्यभुग्वानुसरेत् प्रतिस्रोतः सरस्वतीम् ।
जपेद्वा नियताहारस्त्रिर्वै वेदस्य संहिताम् ॥७८॥
कृतवापनो निवसेद् ग्रामान्ते गोव्रजेऽपि वा ।
आश्रमे वृक्षमूले वा गोब्राह्मणहिते रतः ॥७९॥
ब्राह्मणार्थे गवार्थे वा सम्यक्प्राणान्परित्यजेत् ।
मुच्यते ब्रह्महत्याया गोप्ता गोब्राह्मणस्य च ॥८०॥

76. Cited by *Mādh* 2.406; pādas a-b cited by *Vij* 3.279 — a) *Vij* जपित्वान्यतमं; Lo^{4} वेद; Tr^{2} चेदं — b) wKt^{1} याजयनानां शतं व्रतं; wKt^{3} भवेत् — c) wKt^{1} °हत्यापनुत्यर्थं; Bo °नोदार्थं — d) Be^{1} BBe^{2} Lo^{4} Pu^{10} मितभुग्विजितेन्द्रियः

77. Cited by *Vij* 3.250; *Apa* 294, 1061; *Mādh* 2.399, 406 — a) GMd^{5} सर्वं च वा वेदविदे; Hy Jm Jo^{1} Kt^{2} Tj^{2} MTr^{3} *Mandlik Jha KSS Dave* सर्वस्वं वेदविदुषे; TMd^{4} वेदविदि — c) TMd^{4} वनं; BBe^{2} Ho NKt^{4} BKt^{5} Lo^{2} Lo^{4} *Jha Dave* हि; TMd^{4} ह; GMy जीवितायालं; Pu^{10} जीवनाचालं — d) Pu^{10} गृह; TMd^{4} नासपरि°; Lo^{4} GMy Pu^{10} *Me Rn Jha Dave* वासः परिच्छदं

78. Pādas c-d omitted in Lo^{4}. Cited by *Apa* 1060; *Mādh* 2.406; pādas a-b cited by *Vij* 3.249; pādas c-d by *Viś* 3.242; and pāda-c by *Viś* 3.244 — a) Lo^{2} GMy Pu^{2} Pu^{4} *Vij* [*Jolly* Nd] °भुग्वानुचरेत्; GMd^{1} GMd^{5} Tr^{1} MTr^{4} °भुग्वानुतरेत्; TMd^{3} °भुक्चाशुतरेत्; Lo^{3} [*Jolly* R] °भुग्वानुवसेत्; Lo^{1} °भुग्वा प्रसरेत्; Tj^{1} °भुग्वा तु वसेत् — b) BCa wKt^{1} oOr Tr^{2} °श्रोतः; TMd^{3} GMd^{5} GMy Tr^{1} °स्रोतां; GMd^{1} °स्रोषां — c) Pu^{2} Pu^{4} जपेद्वै; La^{1} अपि वा निय° — c-d) TMd^{4} MTr^{6} अपि वा नियतोरण्ये त्रिर्जपेद्वेदसंहितां [Tr^{1} add this after pāda-b] — d) Bo Ho Jo^{2} Lo^{3} GMd^{5} Ox^{2} sOx^{1} Pu^{3} sPu^{6} Tj^{1} Tr^{2} [*Jolly* R] °हारस्त्रिःकृत्वो वेदसीहितां [Lo^{3} Tj^{1} °स्त्रिः कृत्वा; sOx^{1} sPu^{6} °कृत्यो]; GMy °हारस्त्रिर्वेदस्य च संहितां; La^{1} °हारस्त्रिजये वेदसीहितां; BKt^{5} °हारस्त्रिर्वा

Additional verse in Pu^{2}; cited by *Mādh* 2.402:

विधेः प्राथमिकादस्माद् द्वितीये द्विगुणं भवेत् ।
तृतीये त्रिगुणं प्रोक्तं चतुर्थे नास्ति निष्कृतिः ॥

b) *Mādh* चरेत् — c) *Mādh* त्रिगुणं चैव — d) *om in* Pu^{2}

79. Cited by *Viś* 3.239, 244; *Vij* 3.243; *Apa* 1053; pāda-a cited by *Vij* 3.244 — a) MTr^{6} निवसेत्कृतवापो वा; *Apa* कृतवासो वसेद्गोष्ठे; Jo^{2} कृतवापोथ; GMd^{1} कृतवापोपि; Lo^{3} कृतपापोथ; Pu^{10} कृतवामनो; Tj^{1} कृतषापोथ; wKt^{1} NNg कृतवापो वा; GMy कृत्वापनो वा; sOx^{1} sPu^{6} कृतवासो वा; TMd^{3} कृतोपवासो; GMd^{5} कृतांचनो वा; Lo^{1} °वापनो *cor to* वाप्ये; Kt^{2} °वासनो; [*Jolly* M$^{1-2-5-9}$] °वपनो; BBe^{2} BCa Ho TMd^{4} Pu^{2} *Viś Vij Mādh* °वापनो वा नि°; Jm °वापनी वा नि°; NPu^{1} °वपनो वा नि°; La^{1} °वपनो वा वसेद्; oOr °वापनोपवसेद्; Pu^{3} °वापो निवसेद्; GMy निविशेद् — b) Pu^{10} गोव्रजो; Lo^{3} Tj^{1} गोव्रजेथ वा; Jo^{2} TMd^{3} गोव्रजे तथा — c) BKt^{5} गोवृक्षमूले — d) *Apa* सर्वभूतहिते; Pu^{10} [*Jolly* M$^{1-2-5-9}$] °हितेन वा; Pu^{2} Pu^{4} रसः

80.* After मुच्यते in pāda-c NKt^{4} jumps to 82d ब्रह्महत्यां [haplo]. Cited by *Viś* 3.239, 244; *Vij* 3.244 [twice]; *Apa* 1058 — a) Lo^{4} Pu^{5} Pu^{7} Pu^{10} गवार्थे ब्राह्मणार्थे वा; Lo^{3} NPu^{1} °णार्थं; Tj^{1} °णार्थ; Ho *om* गावर्थे; Lo^{3} Tj^{1} गवार्थं; Wa गवामर्थे [*om* वा]; Be^{1} *om* वा; sOx^{1} च — b) BBe^{2} Bo Ho

त्र्यवरं प्रतिरोद्धा वा सर्वस्वमवजित्य वा ।
विप्रस्य तन्निमित्ते वा प्राणालाभे विमुच्यते ॥८१॥
एवं दृढव्रतो नित्यं ब्रह्मचारी समाहितः ।
समाप्ते द्वादशे वर्षे ब्रह्महत्यां व्यपोहति ॥८२॥
शिष्ट्वा वा भूमिदेवानां नरदेवसमागमे ।
स्वमेनोऽवभृथस्नातो हयमेधे विमुच्यते ॥८३॥
धर्मस्य ब्राह्मणो मूलमग्रं राजन्य उच्यते ।
तस्मात्समागमे तेषामेनो विख्याप्य शुध्यति ॥८४॥
ब्राह्मणः संभवेनैव देवानामपि दैवतम् ।
प्रमाणं चैव लोकस्य ब्रह्मात्रैव हि कारणम् ॥८५॥
तेषां वेदविदो ब्रूयुस्त्रयोऽप्येनःसु निष्कृतिम् ।
सा तेषां पावनाय स्यात् पवित्रं विदुषां हि वाक् ॥८६॥

Hy Jm Jo^{1} Jo^{2} wKt^{1} Kt^{2} wKt^{3} La^{1} Lo^{3} tMd^{4} oOr sOx^{1} Ox^{2} Pu^{5} sPu^{6} Pu^{7} Pu^{10} Tj^{1} Tj^{2} Tr^{2} mTr^{3} mTr^{5} *Viś Vij Nā Mandlik Jolly KSS* सद्यः प्राणा°; Bo La^{1} Lo^{4} *Viś Vij* °त्यजन् — c) Lo^{1} मुच्यन्ते — d) mTr^{6} *om* गोप्ता; Kt^{2} nNg Ox^{2} *Go Ku Mr Mandlik Jha KSS Dave* गोर्ब्राह्म°; *Viś* वा

81.* Omitted in nKt^{4} gMy. Cited by *Viś* 3.244; *Vij* 3.245–6 — a) Lo^{2} त्र्यवारं; Jo^{1} mTr^{3} *Mandlik KSS* त्रिवारं [supported by *Ku*]; La^{1} त्रिवरं; tMd^{4} त्रवरं; Be^{1} Lo^{1} Pu^{8} अवरं; Ox^{2} अवारं; Lo^{3} °रोद्ध; Tr^{1} *Viś* [vl as in ed] °रोद्धो; mTr^{4} mTr^{6} °रुद्धो; Kt^{2} °रोधा; Lo^{4} °रोधो; gMd^{5} °विद्धो; [*Jolly* R Ku] °योद्धा — b) gMd^{5} Ox^{2} °विजित्य; gMd^{1} °विचित्य; Pu^{10} °पजित्य; Lo^{4} tMd^{3} [*Jolly* M] °पिजित्य; tMd^{4} °पहत्य; Pu^{5} Pu^{7} च; Tr^{1} या — c) Ox^{2} तु निमित्तं; Lo^{2} तन्निमित्तो; Tr^{2} तुन्निमित्ते — d) bBe^{2} Bo Lo^{4} tMd^{3} mTr^{6} *Vij* प्राणलाभे [supported by *Rn Nd*]; gMd^{1} प्राणलोभे; *Mandlik Jha Dave* °लाभेपि मुच्यते; Be^{1} nPu^{1} Pu^{2} Pu^{4} विशुध्यति; Lo^{2} विशुच्यते

82. Omitted in mTr^{5}. Cited by *Viś* 3.244; *Vij* 3.244— a) Bo wKt^{3} दृढं — c) Lo^{1} समासे; mTr^{4} mTr^{6} पूर्णे तु द्वादशे; wKt^{1} पूर्णे द्वादशमे — d) tMd^{4} mTr^{4} mTr^{6} मुच्यते ब्रह्महत्यया; Lo^{1} °हत्या; Tj^{2} °हत्यं; Be^{1} °हत्यामपोहति

83. Cited by *Vij* 3.244; *Apa* 1057 — a) Lo^{1} mTr^{4} mTr^{6} शिष्टा; gMd^{1} tMd^{3} gMd^{5} इष्ट्वा; Pu^{10} तिष्ट्वा; Hy शिस्था; tMd^{4} वसिष्टो वा; Ox^{2} शिष्ट्वानां भूमि°; tMd^{3} सर्वदेवानां — b) Tr^{2} नरं — c) bBe^{2} स्वात्मनोवभृ°; Tr^{1} स्वमेनावभृ°; Bo Lo^{1} °भृथः; Ho sOx^{1} Pu^{2} sPu^{6} Tj^{1} [*Jolly* G R] *Vij Apa* °भृथे; Jo^{2} Lo^{3} Tj^{1} [*Jolly* R] *Vij Apa* स्नात्वा; tMd^{4} °स्नाने — d) bBe^{2} °मेधेन मुच्यते; Wa °मेधेन शुध्यति; Lo^{1} °मेधाद्विमुच्यते; bCa La^{1} विमुच्यति; nKt^{4} gMd^{1} nPu^{1} Pu^{2} Pu^{4} विशुध्यति; Lo^{2} विशुध्यते

84. a) La^{1} धर्मस्य मूलं ब्राह्मणोग्रं — b) tMd^{3} मूलं समग्रं राज उच्यते; bBe^{2} Hy °मग्र; bCa Lo^{2} °मग्र्यं; Lo^{1} °मग्रे; gMd^{1} °मुग्रं; La^{1} राजानमुच्यते; Bo Lo^{3} Pu^{5} राजन्यमुच्यते — c) wKt^{1} °मागमं; oOr °मागमस्तेषा° — d) Wa °मेना विख्याता; Tr^{1} विज्ञाप्य; Ho शुध्यते

85. *ma* in Lo^{1} — a) wKt^{1} ब्रह्मणः; Kt^{2} ब्रह्मणाः; mTr^{3} स्वंभवे°; gMd^{5} संभवेनापि; Pu^{2} Pu^{4} Pu^{5} Pu^{7} सभावे चैव — b) bKt^{5} देवतं — c) Pu^{2} ब्रह्माणं चैव; Pu^{4} ब्राह्मणं चैव — d) Lo^{3} ब्रह्महा चैव कारणं; Tr^{2} ब्रह्म चात्रैव कारणं; bCa ब्रह्म चैवात्र कारणं; wKt^{1} nKt^{4} Tj^{1} ब्रह्म चैव हि [nKt^{4} ब्रह्मा]; bBe^{2} gMd^{5} Wa *om* हि

86. a) Tr^{1} एषां; mTr^{4} mTr^{6} ते यां; tMd^{4} तयोर्वेदविद्यो; Tr^{1} [*but cor*] ज्ञेयस्त्रयो — b) Tr^{2} ब्रूयुः श्रेयो; oOr ब्रूयुस्त्रयोरेनसि; Be^{1} °प्येनस्य; gMy निष्कृतिः; Be^{1} nNg tMd^{4} निष्कृतं; gMd^{5} दुष्कृतिं — c)

अतोऽन्यतममास्थाय विधिं विप्रः समाहितः ।
ब्रह्महत्याकृतं पापं व्यपोहत्यात्मवत्तया ॥८७॥
हत्वा गर्भमविज्ञातमेतदेव व्रतं चरेत् ।
राजन्यवैश्यौ चेजानावात्रेयीमेव च स्त्रियम् ॥८८॥
उक्त्वा चैवानृतं साक्ष्ये प्रतिरभ्य गुरुं तथा ।
अपहृत्य च निक्षेपं कृत्वा च स्त्रीसुहृद्वधम् ॥८९॥
इयं विशुद्धिरुदिता प्रमाप्याकामतो द्विजम् ।
कामतो ब्राह्मणवधे निष्कृतिर्न विधीयते ॥९०॥
सुरां पीत्वा द्विजो मोहादग्निवर्णां सुरां पिबेत् ।
तया स काये निर्दग्धे मुच्यते किल्बिषात्ततः ॥९१॥

Tr^{2} स; Pu^{5} Pu^{7} Tj^{1} [*Jolly* G R] पावनीय; Pu^{10}पाविनीय; GMd^{1} हवनाय — d) Be^{1} wKt^{1} Lo^{1} Lo^{2} Pu^{2} Pu^{3} पवित्रा; Lo^{1} विदुषा; Lo^{4} हि वा

87. Cited by *Vij* 3.244 — a) Lo^{1} अतोन्यतः समास्थाय; MTr^{3} ततो; Jm अन्योन्यतम°; Lo^{2} °माच्छ्राय — b) Lo^{4} विधिः; MTr^{4} MTr^{6} सिद्धिं — c) Wa *om* पापं — d) oOr पापमपोह°; La^{1} °पापमापह-त्यात्म°; MTr^{4} MTr^{6} व्यपोहेतात्म°; BBe^{2} oOr NPu^{1} Pu^{2} Pu^{4} Pu^{5} Pu^{7} °त्मवित्तया; Be^{1} °त्मचिन्तया; NNg Tr^{2} °त्मवत्तथा; Lo^{1} °त्मवत्यया; BKt^{5} °त्मवर्तया; *Vij* °त्मशुद्धये

88. Cited by *Apa* 1063; *Mādh* 2.32; pāda-a cited by *Vij* 3.251, pādas a-b by *Viś* 3.244 [twice], and pāda-c by *Viś* 3.245 — a) wKt^{1} हित्वा; sOx^{1} sPu^{6} गर्भं च विज्ञा°; TMd^{3} ग्रहमविज्ञा°; NNg [*but mc sh*] गर्भमज्ञात; Bo °विज्ञान°; Lo^{1} °भिज्ञात° — b) GMd^{1} व्रतश्चरेत्; BKt^{5} समः चरेत्; NKt^{4} चवं धरेत् — c) Tr^{2} राजन्यवैश्यबीजानामात्रेयी°; wKt^{3} Lo^{2} Pu^{10} °वैश्यो; Lo^{1} TMd^{3} °वैश्य; *Apa* °वैश्या-वीजाना°; NNg °वैश्यौ ईजानौ वात्रे°; Pu^{2} Pu^{4} °वैश्यो वेद्यावात्रे°; TMd^{3} वैजाना°; TMd^{4} MTr^{6} चाजाना°; Be^{1} चेजानो चात्रे°; Lo^{2} चेजानौ चात्रे°; GMd^{1} चेजानामात्रे°; Ox^{2} चेज्यायामात्रे°; Lo^{1} खेजानां वात्रे° — d) Bo °त्रेयी वापि च; Jo^{2} तु

Additional verse in Be^{1} *Mandlik* [र] *KSS Dave:*

जन्मप्रभृति संस्कारैः संस्कृता मन्त्रवाचया ।
गर्भिणी त्वथ वा या स्यात्तामात्रेयीं विदुर्बुधाः ॥

c-d) *Mandlik KSS Dave* वा स्यात्तामात्रेयीं च विदु°

89. Cited by *Viś* 3.246; *Vij* 3.251; *Apa* 1063 — a) Bo Lo^{4} Tj^{1} Tr^{1} उक्ता; MTr^{4} कृत्वा; Pu^{2} वैवा°; TMd^{4} साक्ष्यं — b) Be^{1} NKt^{4} Tr^{2} *Apa* परिरभ्य; oOr Tr^{1} *Rn Nd* प्रतिलभ्य; La^{1} प्रतिरख्य; wKt^{1} Lo^{2} प्रतिरुभ्य; Lo^{4} प्रतितुभ्य; BBe^{2} Hy Jm Jo^{1} Jo^{2} Kt^{2} wKt^{3} Lo^{1} Lo^{3} TMd^{3} Ox^{2} Pu^{5} Pu^{7} Pu^{8} Tj^{1} Tj^{2} MTr^{3} MTr^{6} *Vij Nā Rc Mandlik Jolly KSS* प्रतिरुध्य; wKt^{3} गुरुस्त्था — c) La^{1} अपकृत्य; Bo अपहत्य; Hy अपत्य; GMd^{1} तु; Be^{1} Bo Hy Jm Jo^{1} Kt^{2} BKt^{5} La^{1} Tj^{2} *Mandlik KSS Jha Dave* निःक्षेपं — d) Ho *om* च; wKt^{3} *om* च स्त्री; GMd^{1} चैव सुहृद्वधं; La^{1} °हृद्धनं; BBe^{2} °हृद्वरं

90. Cited by *Viś* 3.212; *Vij* 2.21, 3.226, 243; *Mādh* 2.11, 402; pādas a-b cited by *Vij* 3.254, 258 — a) Lo^{2} Lo^{4} [*Jolly* M] °रुद्दिष्टा — b) Lo^{2} प्रथमाकामतो द्विजः; wKt^{1} प्रमाण्या°; MTr^{6} द्विजः — c) Bo क्रामतो; NNg [*but mc sh*] ब्राह्मवधे; Tr^{2} °वधा — d) BKt^{5} निकृतिर्न; Pu^{10} निष्कृतीर्न

91. Pādas a-b cited by *Viś* 3.247; *Vij* 3.253 — a) MTr^{6} द्विजा; *Nd* prefers to read द्विजोऽमो-हात् with the comment: अमोहान्मतिपूर्वकमेवं व्याख्याने स्मृत्यन्तराणि संगच्छन्ते — b) Pu^{2} °हादाग्नि° — c) GMy तथा ये निर्दग्धे; NPu^{1} तयो; NKt^{4} GMd^{5} Pu^{4} तथा; Jo^{2} Pu^{5} Pu^{7} Tj^{1} [*Jolly* R^{2}] तयास्य; Bo तपांसि काये; GMd^{1} TMd^{3} Tr^{1} [*Jolly* G R^{1}] स्वकाये; Be^{1} BBe^{2} कायो — d) Ho sOx^{1} sPu^{6} मुच्यते

गोमूत्रमग्निवर्णं वा पिबेदुदकमेव वा ।
पयो घृतं वा मरणाद् गोशकृद्रसमेव वा ॥९२॥
कणान्वा भक्षयेदब्दं पिण्याकं वा सकृन्निशि ।
सुरापानापनुत्त्यर्थं वालवासा जटी ध्वजी ॥९३॥
सुरा वै मलमन्नानां पाप्मा च मलमुच्यते ।
तस्माद्ब्राह्मणराजन्यौ वैश्यश्च न सुरां पिबेत् ॥९४॥
गौडी पैष्टी च माध्वी च विज्ञेया त्रिविधा सुरा ।
यथैवैका तथा सर्वा न पातव्या द्विजोत्तमैः ॥९५॥
यक्षरक्षःपिशाचान्नं मद्यं मांसं सुरासवम् ।
तद्ब्राह्मणेन नात्तव्यं देवानामश्नता हविः ॥९६॥
अमेध्ये वा पतेन्मत्तो वैदिकं वाप्युदाहरेत् ।
अकार्यमन्यत्कुर्याद्वा ब्राह्मणो मदमोहितः ॥९७॥

सर्वकिल्बिपात्; Lo[2] °पात्तमः; TMd[3] °पात्स्वयं

92. Omitted in GMy; pādas c-d omitted in BKt[5] sOx[1] [haplo]. Cited by *Mādh* 2.412 — a) La[1] Lo[1] [*but cor*] °वणां; Be[1] वर्णा; Kt[2] °वर्णे — b) BCa Pu[3] च — d) BBe[2] oOr गोसकृद्रस°; Pu[2] Pu[4] गोत्राकृद्रस°; GMd[5] गोशकृद्यवमेव; wKt[1] गोशकृत्कुशमेव; Ho च

93. Pādas a-b omitted in oOr. Cited by *Viś* 3.248; *Vij* 3.254; *Mādh* 2.412 — a) Bo कणं वा; Hy Lo[4] करणात्वा; Ho sOx[1] Pu[3] sPu[6] कणान्नं भक्ष°; Be[1] °येदब्दः; Pu[4] °येदष्टं; Lo[1] °येद्वापि; Lo[2] °येद्दृष्ट्वा — b) Lo[2] GMd[1] पिण्याकं पापकृन्निशि — c) Be[1] Lo[4] NNg Pu[5] Pu[7] सुरापाणा°; *Mādh* °पानाघनुत्त्यर्थं; GMd[1] °पानविशुध्यर्थं — d) wKt[1] वने वा जटिलो ध्वजी; Wa *om* वाल°; La[1] वनवासा; Ox[2] मालवासा; Ho sOx[1] sPu[6] चीरवासा; Kt[2] जडी; *Viś* ध्वजी जटी; TMd[3] ध्वजी तजी; sOx[1] sPu[6] जपेद्यज

94. Verses 94 and 95 transposed by some according to *Bh,* but he prefers the normal sequence. Cited by *Viś* 3.247, 253; *Apa* 1044; *Lakṣ* 3.330; pādas a-b cited by *Vij* 3.253; pādas c-d by *Kum* 1.3.7 — a) La[1] Pu[2] Pu[3] Pu[4] सुरां; Pu[10] सुरायै; TMd[3] वै स मलं नाम — b) GMd[1] हि; NPu[1] Pu[2] Pu[4] वै; Hy *om* मलम्; BKt[5] मम उच्यते — c) Lo[2] °राजन्यो; Tj[1] °राजानौ — d) Kt[2] वैश्यैश्च; BKt[5] GMd[1] TMd[4] GMy न पिबेत्सुरां [GMy °त्सुराः; BKt[5] °त्सुरा]; Hy पिबत्

95. Cited by *Kum* 1.3.7; *Vij* 3.253 [twice]; *Apa* 1044; *Lakṣ* 3.330; *Har*-A 1.17.21, 1.21.8; *Mādh* 2.411; pādas a-b cited by *Har*-A 1.25.3 — a) TMd[3] GMd[5] Tr[1] गौळी; TMd[4] गौरी; Bo गुडिं पैषिं; BBe[2] sOx[1] sPu[6] पौष्टी; GMd[1] पैष्टे; sPu[6] *om* first च; BKt[5] TMd[4] GMd[5] NPu[1] Tr[1] MTr[4] MTr[6] *Vij* माध्वी च पैप्टी च — b) sOx[1] sPu[6] विज्ञेयस्त्रि°; La[1] त्रिविधाः; La[1] Pu[2] Pu[4] MTr[6] सुराः — c) BBe[2] तथै°; *Apa* यथा चैका; GMd[1] °वैकौ; La[1] °वैक — c-d) TMd[3] TMd[4] GMy Tr[1] *Har*-A *Mādh* यथैवैका न पातव्या तथा सर्वा द्विजोत्तमैः [TMd[3] यथा वैका; TMd[4] सर्वैर्द्विजो°] — d) Lo[2] NPu[1] Pu[2] Pu[4] Wa *Apa* [vl] द्विजातिभिः; *Kum* ब्रह्मवादिभिः

96. Cited by *Viś* 3.250; *Vij* 3.253; *Apa* 1069; *Lakṣ* 3.330–1 — a) sOx[1] यदारक्षः°; Ho NKt[4] GMd[5] GMd[1] sOx[1] sPu[6] Tj[1] Tr[1] MTr[4] MTr[6] [*Jolly* Nd] *Apa* [vl] °पिशाचानां; Ox[2] °पिशाचानं; La[1] °पिशाचार्थं — b) Lo[1] GMd[5] NNg मद्य; NKt[4] मैद्यं; BBe[2] Tj[1] Tr[1] मासं; GMy सुरासवः; Tr[2] सुरशवं; wKt[1] सुरावधं; Lo[2] TMd[4] सुरासमं — c) Ox[2] न ब्राह्मणेन पातव्यं; Lo[1] तद्ब्राह्मणो न पातव्यं *cor to* °ह्मणा; GMd[1] तथा ब्राह्म°; Tj[2] तद्ब्राह्मेन; sOx[1] sPu[6] न दातव्यं — d) Be[1] GMd[5] *Apa* °श्नतां; BBe[2] Bo Lo[4] °श्नुता

97. Cited by *Lakṣ* 3.331; pādas a-b cited by *Viś* 3.250, and pādas c-d by *Kum* 1.3.7 — a)

यस्य कायगतं ब्रह्म मद्येनाप्लाव्यते सकृत् ।
तस्य व्यपैति ब्राह्मण्यं शूद्रत्वं च स गच्छति ॥९८॥
एषा विचित्राभिहिता सुरापानस्य निष्कृतिः ।
अत ऊर्ध्वं प्रवक्ष्यामि सुवर्णस्तेयनिष्कृतिम् ॥९९॥
सुवर्णस्तेयकृद्विप्रो राजानमभिगम्य तु ।
स्वकर्म ख्यापयन्ब्रूयान्मां भवाननुशास्त्विति ॥१००॥
गृहीत्वा मुसलं राजा सकृद्धन्यात्तु तं स्वयम् ।
वधेन शुध्यति स्तेनो ब्राह्मणस्तपसैव वा ॥१०१॥
तपसापनुनुत्सुस्तु सुवर्णस्तेयजं मलम् ।
चीरवासा द्विजोऽरण्ये चरेद्ब्रह्महणो व्रतम् ॥१०२॥

Ho अमेध्यो; NKt[4] अमेध्यं; wKt[1] अमेध्ये निपते°; Lo[2] वै; Ho पतेन्मत्तौ; TMd[3] पतोन्मत्तो; Ox[2] परोन्मत्तो — b) *Rn* appears to read अवैदिकं commenting म्लेच्छभाषितं; TMd[3] वैदिकावाप्यु°; Bo BKt[5] NNg sOx[1] Pu[2] Pu[4] sPu[6] चाप्यु°; Pu[10] नाप्यु°; Lo[2] NPu[1] *Nā* वाप्युपाहरेत्; Pu[2] वाप्यपाहरेत्; Pu[4] वाप्यपांहरेत् — c) Bo sOx[1] sPu[6] अकार्यमन्यद्वा कुर्याद्; *Kum* °त्कुर्याद्धि; MTr[4] MTr[6] °त्कार्याद्वा; Tj[2] *om* वा

98. Omitted in Lo[4]. Cited by *Viś* 3.250; *Lakṣ* 3.331 — a)GMd[5] सर्वकाय°; Be[1] कायमतं; La[1] देहगतं — b) GMd[1] मेध्येनाप्लाव्यते शुभं; *Viś* मद्येनोत्प्ला°; Pu[8] भयेनाप्ला°; NNg °प्लावते — c) BBe[2] Tr[2] चापैति; GMd[1] TMd[3] GMd[5] GMy Tr[1] तद्ब्रह्म शूद्र° — d) Pu[5] Pu[7] अवगच्छति शूद्रतां; Ho हि स; GMy MTr[6] चाधिगच्छति; La[1] GMd[1] TMd[3] GMd[5] Tr[1] *Viś* स निगच्छति; Ho Jo[2] w Kt[1] NKt[4] Lo[2] Lo[3] oOr sOx[1] Ox[2] sPu[6] Tj[1] Wa च नियच्छति [sOx[1] sPu[6] हि]

99. Pādas a-b omitted in oOr — a) BKt[5] एषा मित्राभि°; Pu[10] वैचित्रा°; Ho La[1] Lo[2] Lo[4] TMd[3] sOx[1] sPu[6] Tj[1] Wa [*Jolly* M] °त्राविहिता — c) BKt[5] GMd[1] GMd[5] Tr[1] अतः परं प्रव°; BKt[5] °वक्षामि — d) wKt[1] GMd[5] Pu[5] Pu[7] Tr[1] स्वर्णस्तेयस्य निष्कृतिं [Pu[5] Pu[7] सुवर्ण°]; Bo °निष्कृतिः

100. Cited by *Viś* 3.251; *Apa* 1079; *Mādh* 2.414; pāda-a cited by *Vij* 3.257; *Apa* 1082 — a) GMd[5] स्वर्णस्तेयस्यकृद्विप्रो — b) TMd[3] GMy Wa °धिगम्य; Ho Jo[2] wKt[3] Lo[1] sOx[1] Ox[2] Pu[3] sPu[6] Tj[1] Tr[2] [*Jolly* R] च — c) MTr[6] व्याख्याप्य कर्म स्वं ब्रूया°; *Apa* गृहीत्वा मुसलं ब्रूया°; Tr[2] स्वकर्माख्याप°; MTr[4] ख्यापयेद्ब्रूया°; Ho La[1] sOx[1] Ox[2] sPu[6] Tj[1] ख्यापनं ब्रूया°; TMd[3] ख्यापयंस्तेनो मां — d) Lo[1] TMd[3] Tr[1] *Viś* °यान्मा; Tr[2] °नुशाश्विति; wKt[1] °नुशासति

101. Cited by *Viś* 3.251; *Vij* 3.257 (twice); *Mādh* 2.414; pādas a-b cited by *Apa* 1079 — a) *Viś Vij* (once) ततो मुसलमादाय; La[1] गृहीत्वार्थफलं राजा; Ho Jo[2] NKt[4] BKt[5] Lo[1] Lo[2] Lo[4] Ox[2] NPu[1] Pu[3] Pu[5] Pu[7] Pu[10] Tr[2] Wa मुशलं; Be[1] मुसुलं; BCa Hy wKt[1] wKt[3] मुषलं — b) *Viś* स्वयं हन्यात्तु तं नृपः; GMd[1] pāda reads: तन्निहन्यस्तुत्स्वयं; *Mādh* सकृत्कुर्यात् हतं स्वयं — c) NNg वध्येन; sOx[1] Ox[2] sPu[6] शुध्यते; Ho मुच्यते — d) Tr[1] ब्रह्म°; BBe[2] °णस्तपसेन; Jm Jo[1] Kt[2] Lo[4] Ox[2] Pu[2] Pu[3] Pu[4] Pu[10] MTr[3] [*Jolly* M Me] *Mandlik Jha KSS Dave* तु; Bo La[1] NPu[1] Pu[3] च; GMd[1] सा

102. Pāda-d omitted in Pu[10] and *ma* in Lo[4]. Cited by *Apa* 1080; *Mādh* 2.415 — a) Lo[1] तपसानुप्तिपत्सुश्च; GM d[1] तपसावापनुत्रस्तु; Pu[5] Pu[7] तपसापनुत्तुमिच्छुः; Bo तपसाचनु°; Tr[1] तपसापानु°; wKt[3] °नुत्स्वस्तु — b) GMy °स्तेयमज्जलं — c) Bo वीरवसा; oOr चीरवासो; GMd[5] *Mādh* बालवासा; Lo[3] द्विजारण्ये — d) oOr चरेद्वै बह्महि व्रतं; La[1] MTr[6] ब्रह्मघ्नव्रतमाचरेत्; TMd[4] ब्रह्महणो व्रतमाचरेत्; *Mādh* चरेद्ब्रह्मबधव्रतं; Pu[5] Pu[7] चरन्ब्रह्म°; TMd[3] GMd[5] चरेत्तु ब्राह्मणो; NKt[4] चरेदब्राह्मणो; wKt[3] चरेद्ब्रह्मणो; Be[1] Bo Ho Hy Jo[2] BKt[5] Lo[1] Lo[3] NNg Pu[3] Pu[5] Pu[7] Tj[1] Wa [*Jolly* G R] *Me Go Nā Ku* °हणि [cf. 11.128]; sOx[1] sPu[6] °हति; Ox[2] Tr[2] °हणं; Tj[2] °हण

एतैर्व्रतैरपोहेत पापं स्तेयकृतं द्विजः ।
गुरुस्त्रीगमनीयं तु व्रतैरेभिरपानुदेत् ॥१०३॥
गुरुतल्पोऽभिभाष्यैनस्तप्ते स्वप्यादयोमये ।
सूर्मीं ज्वलन्तीं वाश्लिष्येन्मृत्युना स विशुध्यति ॥१०४॥
स्वयं वा शिश्नवृषणावुत्कृत्याधाय चाञ्जलौ ।
नैर्ऋतीं दिशमातिष्ठेदा निपातादजिह्मगः ॥१०५॥
खट्वाङ्गी चीरवासा वा श्मश्रुलो निर्जने वने ।
प्राजापत्यं चरेत्कृच्छ्रमब्दमेकं समाहितः ॥१०६॥
चान्द्रायणं वा त्रीन्मासानभ्यसेन्नियतेन्द्रियः ।
हविष्येण यवाग्वा वा गुरुतल्पापनुत्तये ॥१०७॥

103. Omited in Pu^{10}; pādas a-b omitted in GMy — a) Tr^{1} °पोह्येत — b) Lo^{1} सुवर्णस्तेयकृद् द्विजः; BBe^{2} स्तेयद्विजः कृतं; sOx^{1} °कृते; Bo °कृतिं; MTr^{5} नरः — c) Bo °गमनीयात्तु; GMd^{1} °गमनेयंस्तु; TMd^{3} °गमनीयस्तु; Pu^{5} Pu^{7} [*Jolly* G] °गमनं चैव — d) BCa Ho TMd^{3} oOr sOx^{1} Pu^{2} Pu^{4} Pu^{5} sPu^{6} Pu^{7} Tj^{2} MTr^{6} व्रतैरेतैरपानुदेत् [cf. 11. 170]; GMd^{5} °भिरुपानुदेत्

104.* Cited by *Vij* 3.259; *Apa* 1083; *Mādh* 2.255 — a) Wa °तल्पेभिभा°; GMd^{1} TMd^{3} GMy MTr^{4} MTr^{5} MTr^{6} *Bh* °तल्पगोभिभा°; GMd^{5} °तल्पगभिभा°; BBe^{2} Bo Hy Jm Jo^{1} wKt^{1} Kt^{2} BKt^{5} Lo^{1} Lo^{4} TMd^{4} oOr Pu^{5} Pu^{7} Tj^{2} Tr^{2} [*Jolly* G] *Vij Mādh Me* [pāṭha] *Mandlik Jha KSS Dave* °तल्प्यभिभा° — b) Bo Tr^{2} *Rc Jha Dave* °नस्तल्पे; Lo^{3} Tj^{1} °नस्सुप्ते; BKt^{5} °नस्सुप्तो; Be^{1} °नस्स्वप्ने; Be^{1} Bo wKt^{1} wKt^{3} Lo^{2} Lo^{3} Lo^{4} GMy NPu^{1} Pu^{2} Pu^{4} Pu^{5} Pu^{7} Pu^{8} Pu^{10} Tj^{1} [*Jolly* M G R] *Jolly* सुप्याद°; oOr पुप्याद°; NPu^{1} सुप्ताद°; Ox^{2} शायाद°; Lo^{1} सूर्म्याद्ययोमये; Tr^{1} °धोमये — c) Ho BKt^{5} शूर्मीं; oOr शूर्मिं; wKt^{1} शूल्मीं; Wa सूमीं; Lo^{2} गुर्वीं; Hy Tj^{2} Tr^{1} ज्वलन्ती; Lo^{3} ज्वलन्तो; Lo^{4} TMd^{3} [*Jolly* M^{3-4-5} Me] °न्तीमाश्लिष्य मृत्यु°; [*Jolly* M^{8}] °न्तीमालिङ्गय मृत्यु°; Lo^{2} sOx^{1} sPu^{6} चाश्लि°; Hy MTr^{5} *Vij* स्वाश्लि°; Bo Tj^{1} वाशिष्ये°; NKt^{4} वाश्लिष्य मृत्यु°; Ox^{2} चाश्लिष्य मृत्यु°; [*Jolly* M^{1-2-9}]स्मालिङ्गय मृत्यु° — d) Pu^{5} Pu^{7} [*Jolly* G] °न्मृत्युर्भवति शुद्धये; MTr^{4} न विशु°; wKt^{3} विशुध्यते

105. Pāda-d omitted in Pu^{2} Pu^{4}. Cited by *Vij* 3.259;*Apa* 1083; *Mādh* 2.253, 255 — a) TMd^{3} च; Pu^{5} Pu^{7} श्लिष्य°; Tj^{1} °वृषणानुत्कृ° — b) Tr^{1} °णावुत्पत्याधाय; TMd^{4} °णावुद्धत्याधाय; Be^{1} sOx^{1} Pu^{5} sPu^{6} Pu^{7} Pu^{10} *Apa* °त्यादाय; TMd^{3} GMd^{5} वाञ्जलौ; Tr^{1} वाञ्जलिं — c) La^{1} TMd^{3} Tr^{1} नैर्ऋतिं; Be^{1} नैऋति; Pu^{10} निर्कृतीं; Be^{1} La^{1} दिशिमा°; TMd^{3} दशमा°

106.* Omitted in BKt^{5}; pāda-a omitted in Pu^{2} Pu^{4}. Cited by *Viś* 3.254; *Vij* 3.260— a) Bo खड्वाङ्गी; Kt^{2} खट्वाङ्गो;Lo^{2} Pu^{10} षट्वागी; Be^{1} चार°; NPu^{1} धीर°; Lo^{1} GMy °वासाश्च; GMd^{1} Pu^{5} Pu^{7} *om* वा; Be^{1} Bo Lo^{1} sOx^{1} sPu^{6} च — b) Be^{1} Bo Hy Jm Jo^{1} Jo^{2} Kt^{2} Lo^{1} Lo^{2} Lo^{3} Lo^{4} GMd^{1} NNg oOr Ox^{2} NPu^{1} Pu^{5} Pu^{7} Pu^{8} Tj^{1} Tj^{2} MTr^{3} *Vij Mandlik Jolly Jha KSS Dave* विजने — c)MTr^{4} MTr^{6} जपेत्कृच्छ्रम°

107. Cited by *Mādh* 2.264; pādas a-b cited by *Vij* 3.260 — a) Hy चन्द्रा°; Tr^{2} °यणैर्वा — b) TMd^{3} °सान्व्यवस्येन्निय°; BCa °सान्निवासान् यतेन्द्रियः; wKt^{1} °भ्यसन्निय°; GMd^{5} NNg °भ्यसेद्विजितेन्द्रियः; MTr^{4} MTr^{6} °भ्यसेद्वेदसंहितां; Bo °न्नियतव्रतः — c) NKt^{4} हविष्यं सुरवाम्वाथ; TMd^{4} हविष्येवं; La^{1} यवाग्रा — d) GMy °तल्पानुपत्तये; wKt^{1} °नुत्तयेत्

Additional verse in TMd^{4}:

ब्राह्मणस्तु सुरां पीत्वा गुरुतल्पं निवेश्य च ।
विप्राद्धुत्वा सुवर्णं च ब्रह्महत्यां विनैनसा [?] ।।

एतैर्व्रतैरपोहेयुर्महापातकिनो मलम् ।
उपपातकिनस्त्वेवमेभिर्नानाविधैर्व्रतैः ।१०८॥
उपपातकसंयुक्तो गोघ्नो मासं यवान्पिबेत् ।
कृतवापो वसेद्गोष्ठे चर्मणा तेन संवृतः ॥१०९॥
चतुर्थकालमश्नीयादक्षारलवणं मितम् ।
गोमूत्रेणाचरन् स्नानं द्वौ मासौ नियतेन्द्रियः ॥११०॥
दिवानुगच्छेत्ता गास्तु तिष्ठन्नूर्ध्वं रजः पिबेत् ।
शुश्रूषित्वा नमस्कृत्य रात्रौ वीरासनं वसेत् ॥१११॥
तिष्ठन्तीष्वनुतिष्ठेत्तु व्रजन्तीष्वप्यनुव्रजेत् ।
आसीनासु तथासीत नियतो वीतमत्सरः ॥११२॥

108. Cited by *Viś* 3.262 — a) Lo[1] एतैर्नियमैरिमैः अपोहेयु°; Bo nKt[4] tMd[4] Pu[10] एभिर्व्रत° — b) gMd[1] °पातकिनां; wKt[3] nKt[4] Lo[4] gMd[1] gMd[5] Ox[2] Pu[2] Pu[4] Pu[8] Pu[10] Tr[1] Tr[2] mTr[4] mTr[5] mTr[6] *Viś* मलान्; Lo[2] tMd[3] मलात्; tMd[4] मलाः — c) Tr[1] °नस्त्वेनमेभि° — c-d) Lo[2] sOx[1] sPu[6] °नस्त्वेव विविधैर्नियमैरिमैः [sOx[1] sPu[6] °यमैस्समैः]; Ho °नस्त्वेतैर्विविधैर्नियमैरिमैः; Pu[8] °नश्चैव विविधैर्नियमैरिमैः; bCa nKt[4] La[1] oOr Ox[2] nPu[1] Pu[2] Pu[3] Pu[4] Pu[5] Pu[7] mTr[5] [*Jolly* G]*Nā* विविधैर्नियमैरिमैः — d) gMd[1] °विधैर्व्रतः; gMy °विधैर्व्रतं

109. Pādas c-d placed after 110b in oOr. Cited by *Viś* 3.262; *Vij* 3.263–4; *Apa* 1101; *Mādh* 2.191 — b) Hy गोघ्ना; Tj[2] मोघ्नो; mTr[4] यथापिबेत् — c) Ox[2] Tr[1] Tr[2] कृतपापो; gMd[1] कृतवानो; Lo[2] *Viś* कृतवापनो; oOr Wa कृतवासो; Lo[1] वृत्तवापौ; tMd[4] वसन्गोष्ठे; nKt[4] भवेद्गोष्ठे; bKt[5] चरेद्गोष्ठे; Lo[2] वसेद्गोष्ठं — d) Tj[1] वर्मणा; *Vij* चर्मणाद्रेण; bBe[2] संव्रतः; tMd[4] संयुतः

110.* Cited by *Viś* 3.262; *Vij* 3.263–4; *Apa* 1101; *Mādh* 2.191 — a) Tj[1] mTr[6] चतुर्थं; gMd[5] चतुष्कालमनश्नी°; nNg °काले चाश्नी°; Pu[10] °कालीयाश्नी°; Pu[5] Pu[7] °कालं प्राश्नी°; bKt[5] Lo[4] °कालं वाश्नी° — b) Pu[5] Pu[7] mTr[6] °क्षारालवणं; Pu[10] °लवणां; oOr °लवणान्वितं; gMd[1] मतं; bKt[5] Lo[2] सितं — c) bKt[5] gMd[1] tMd[3] tMd[4] gMy Tr[1] गोमूत्रेण चरन्; bBe[2] bCa Jm wKt[1] Lo[1] Lo[3] oOr Tj[1] *Vij* °मूत्रेण चरेत्; nKt[4] °मूत्राचरेत्; Ho °चरत्; Be[1] Bo Hy Jo[1] Kt[2] wKt[3] La[1] Lo[4] nNg Ox[2] Pu[8] Tj[1] Tj[2] Tr[2] mTr[3] mTr[4] mTr[6] [*Jolly* R Ku] *Vij Apa Mādh Mandlik Jha KSS Dave* °चरेत् — d) Ox[2] मासौ सुसमाहितः; *Apa* [vl] नियतव्रतः

111. Omitted in Pu[10]; Jm gives 107–9 again in place of 111–3; pāda-d omitted in Ho. Cited by *Viś* 3.262; *Vij* 3.263–4; *Apa* 1101; *Mādh* 2.191 — a) Bo दिवा निगच्छेत्तां गास्तु; bKt[1] °गच्छेत्तदा गास्तु; mTr[3] °गच्छेद्रास्तासां; Hy Jo[1] Kt[2] Lo[3] Tj[1] Tj[2] *Mandlik Jolly Jha KSS Dave* °गच्छद्रास्तास्तु; Lo[2] गांस्तु — b) Pu[5] Pu[7] तिष्ठन्भूमि — c) Tr[2] शुश्रूषेत; bBe[2] शुश्रुयित्वा; Tj[1] शुश्रूषयित्वा; Pu[2] Pu[4] °षेत्वा; Ho नमस्कृत्यं; wKt[3] tMd[4] gMy °कृत्या; nKt[4] bBe[2] bCa Lo[3] gMd[1] Tj[1] Tr[1] mTr[5] *Viś* °कृत्वा — d) tMd[3] tMd[4] mTr[4] mTr[5] mTr[6] *Viś Mādh* वीरासनी; Lo[4] *Me Jha Dave* वीरासनो; [*Jolly* M] वीरासने; sOx[1] sPu[6] चीरासनं; tMd[3] tMd[4] gMy sOx[1] sPu[6] mTr[4] mTr[5] mTr[6] *Viś* [vl] *Mādh* भवेत्; Lo[1] विशेत्; Lo[2] व्रजेत्

112.* Omitted in Pu[10] mTr[5]. Cited by *Viś* 3.262; *Vij* 3.263–4; *Apa* 1101; *Mādh* 2.191; cf. *Raghuvaṃśa* 1.89 — a) gMd[1] tMd[4] mTr[6] *Viś Mādh* तिष्ठन्तीषु च तिष्ठेत [mTr[6] तिष्ठेच्च; *Mādh* तिष्ठेत्तु]; Lo[1] gMy Pu[5] तिष्ठतीष्व°; sOx[1] sPu[6] तिष्ठन्तीमनु°; nKt[4] bKt[5] La[1] Lo[2] oOr Pu[2] Pu[4] Tr[1] °तिष्ठेत; tMd[3] °तिष्ठेच्च; gMy °तिष्ठश्च — b) tMd[4] व्रजन्त्येष्व°; tMd[3] °न्तीष्वनु तां व्रजेत् — c) *Mādh* आसीनास्वपि चासीनो; bBe[2] Bo bCa gMd[5] तथासीन; Hy Jo[1] Kt[2] La[1] Pu[2] Pu[3] Pu[4] Tj[2] Tr[2] mTr[3]

आतुरामभिषक्तां वा चौरव्याघ्रादिभिर्भयैः ।
पतितां पङ्कलग्नां वा सर्वप्राणैर्विमोक्षयेत् ॥११३॥
उष्णे वर्षति शीते वा मारुते वाति वा भृशम् ।
न कुर्वीतात्मनस्त्राणं गोरकृत्वा तु शक्तितः ॥११४॥
आत्मनो यदि वान्येषां गृहे क्षेत्रेऽथ वा खले
भक्षयन्तीं न कथयेत् पिबन्तं चैव वत्सकम् ॥११५॥
अनेन विधिना यस्तु गोघ्नो गा अनुगच्छति ।
स गोहत्याकृतं पापं त्रिभिर्मासैर्व्यपोहति ॥११६॥
वृषभैकादशा गाश्च दद्यात्सुचरितव्रतः ।
अविद्यमाने सर्वस्वं वेदविद्भ्यो निवेदयेत् ॥११७॥
एतदेव व्रतं कुर्युरुपपातकिनो द्विजाः ।

[*Jolly* M$^{1-2-3-5-8-9}$ Rā] *Vij Mandlik Jolly Jha KSS Dave* तथासीनो — d) Tj^{1} नियतौ

113.* Omitted in mTr^{5}; pādas c-d omitted in La^{1}. Cited by *Viś* 3.262; *Vij* 3.263–4; *Apa* 1101; *Mādh* 2.191 — a) La^{1} °रामशस्तां; Bo bKt^{5} Lo^{2} tMd^{3} tMd^{4} gMy nNg nPu^{1} Pu^{2} Pu^{4} Pu^{5} sPu^{6} Pu^{7} Tr^{1} Tr^{2} Wa [*Jolly* G Nd] °भिषिक्तां; bBe^{2} Hy Jo^{1} Jo^{2} wKt^{1} Kt^{2} wKt^{3} Lo^{3} Tj^{1} Tj^{2} mTr^{3} [*Jolly* R Ku] *Vij Mandlik Jolly Jha KSS Dave* °भिशस्तां; *Mādh* °भियुक्तां; Pu^{10} °भिभक्तां; Be^{1} nKt^{4} bKt^{5} Lo^{4} gMd^{1} tMd^{3} tMd^{4} gMd^{5} gMy Pu^{10} Tr^{1} mTr^{4} mTr^{6} *Viś* च; Wa गो — b) Lo^{2} Lo^{3} gMd^{1} gMy nNg Tj^{1} Tr^{1} mTr^{6} *Viś* चोर° — c) gMy पतिताः; Be^{1} wKt^{1} nNg Ox^{2} Tj^{1} [*Jolly* R] °मग्नां; gMd^{5} °लग्नां गां; Be^{1} gMd^{1} Pu^{5} Pu^{7} Tr^{1} mTr^{4} mTr^{6} *Viś* च — d) Jo^{1} Kt^{2} mTr^{3} [*Jolly* G] *Vij Nā Mandlik KSS* सर्वोपायैर्वि°; Hy सवपापैर्वि°; nNg °प्राणैः समुद्धरेत्; bBe^{2} Ho Hy Jo^{1} Jo^{2} Kt^{2} wKt^{3} bKt^{5} Lo^{4} tMd^{3} gMd^{4} gMd^{5} sOx^{1} Pu^{5} sPu^{6} Pu^{7} Pu^{10} Tj^{2} Tr^{1} mTr^{3} *Vij Mandlik Jolly Jha KSS Dave* °र्विमोचयेत्

114. Omitted in La^{1}. Cited by *Viś* 3.262; *Vij* 3.263–4; *Apa* 1101; *Mādh* 2.191 — a) Pu^{10} उष्मे; Pu^{10} शीतो; wKt^{3} शीले — b) Pu^{10} मारुतो; Lo^{2} माक्षते; Pu^{10} Tr^{2} वापि वा; Pu^{2} Pu^{4} वातिवायति — c) mTr^{4} mTr^{6} न कुर्यादात्म°; Be^{1} Pu^{10} °त्मनः स्त्रीणां— d) Lo^{2} Pu^{10} गोरक्षित्वा; wKt^{3} °कृत्वाथ; tMd^{3} gMd^{5} gMy Tr^{1} [*Jolly* Nd] स्वशक्तितः

115. Cited by *Viś* 3.262; *Vij* 3.263–4; *Apa* 1101; *Mādh* 2.191 — a) bKt^{5} चान्येषां — b) Jo^{2} La^{1} gMd^{1} tMd^{3} tMd^{4} gMd^{5} gMy Pu^{5} Tj^{1} mTr^{6} गेहे; *Viś* क्षेत्रे गेहेथ; bBe^{2} Bo bKt^{5} gMy क्षेत्रे तथा खले; nNg क्षेत्रे वाथ वा खले; nKt^{4} Wa *Mādh* क्षेत्रे खलेपि वा; *Apa* क्षेत्रे खलेथ वा — c) nKt^{4} चैव वाथयेत् — d) wKt^{1} bKt^{5} Tj^{1} [*Jolly* M^{4-5-9} Nd R] पिबन्तीं; gMy पिबतिं; Jm पिबन्तंश्चैव; *Apa* नैव; Ho Jo^{2} sOx^{1} sPu^{6} वापि; Lo^{3} Tj^{1} चापि; wKt^{1} Pu^{8} वत्सकां

116.* Pādas c-d omitted in bKt^{5} Tr^{2}. Cited by *Viś* 3.262; *Vij* 3.263–4; *Apa* 1101; *Mādh* 2.191 — b) bBe^{2} Bo bCa Ho Hy Jm Jo^{1} Jo^{2} wKt^{1} Kt^{2} wKt^{3} bKt^{5} La^{1} Lo^{1} oOr sOx^{1} Ox^{2} Pu^{2} Pu^{4} Pu^{5} sPu^{6} Pu^{7} Tj^{2} Tr^{2} mTr^{3} Wa *Mandlik Jha KSS Dave* गामनु°; Lo^{2} गापनु°; bBe^{2} अनुतिष्ठति — c) tMd^{4} °हत्यकृतं; Tr^{1} °हत्या तु तं — d) *Bh* [pāṭha which he rejects] त्रिभिर्वर्षैर्व्यपोहति

117. Cited by *Vij* 3.263–4; *Apa* 1101; *Mādh* 2.191 — a) nKt^{4} tMd^{4} Tr^{1} mTr^{4} mTr^{6} ऋषभै°; gMd^{5} °दश; tMd^{3} °दशं; Tr^{1} °दशास्ताश्च; gMy °दशाङ्गं गां च; Tr^{2} °दशास्तु दद्या°; Bo Ho wKt^{1} wKt^{3} bKt^{5} Lo^{1} Lo^{4} oOr sOx^{1} Ox^{2} nPu^{1} Pu^{3} sPu^{6} Pu^{10} Tr^{2} *Jolly* गास्तु; Tj^{2} याश्च — b) Be^{1} स दद्याच्चरितव्रतः; Pu^{3} Tr^{2} °व्रती — c) Tr^{2} °मानो — d) nNg ब्राह्मणेभ्यो

अवकीर्णिवर्जं शुद्ध्यर्थं चान्द्रायणमथापि वा ॥११८॥
अवकीर्णी तु काणेन गर्दभेन चतुष्पथे ।
पाकयज्ञविधानेन यजेत निर्ऋतिं निशि ॥११९॥
हुत्वाग्नौ विधिवद्धोमानन्ततश्च समित्यृचा ।
वातेन्द्रगुरुवह्नीनां जुहुयात्सर्पिषाहुतीः ॥१२०॥
कामतो रेतसः सेकं व्रतस्थस्य द्विजन्मनः ।
अतिक्रमं व्रतस्याहुर्धर्मज्ञा ब्रह्मवादिनः ॥१२१॥
मारुतं पुरुहूतं च गुरुं पावकमेव च ।
चतुरो व्रतिनोऽभ्येति ब्राह्मं तेजोऽवकीर्णिनः ॥१२२॥
एतस्मिन्नेनसि प्राप्ते वसित्वा गर्दभाजिनम् ।
सप्तागारं चरेद्भैक्षं स्वकर्म परिकीर्तयन् ॥१२३॥

118. Cited by *Vij* 3.265; *Apa* 1105 — b) Jo^1 Pu^{10} द्विजः; Ho sOx^1 sPu^6 नराः — c) hypermetric pāda; Lo^1 TMd^3 TMd^4 sOx^1 Tr^1 MTr^4 अवकीर्णी च शुद्ध्यर्थं [sOx^1 °कीर्णि; TMd^4 °कीर्णेव; Ox^2 °कीर्णीव; Lo^1 तु]; Pu^5 Pu^7 [*Jolly* G] अवकीर्णिविशुद्ध्यर्थं; Lo^2 अवकीर्णे व्रते शुध्येच्च; La^1 NPu^1 Pu^2 Pu^3 Pu^4 *Bh Vij* °वर्ज्यं; Wa °वर्जां; MTr^6 °वर्जश्शुद्ध्यर्थं; MTr^5 °वर्जं च शुद्ध्यर्थं

119. Cited by *Vij* 3.280; *Apa* 1140; *Har*-A 1.26.8; *Mādh* 2.436 — a) Tr^1 °कीर्णि; NKt^4 Lo^2 °कीर्णा; sOx^1 °कीर्णं; La^1 च; Ho काष्णेन; BBe^2 oOr कामेन; Hy NKt^4 Ox^2 NPu^1 कालेन; GMy गाणेन; Jo^1 केणेन; La^1 काशेन — b) BBe^2 गर्धभेन; *Vij* रासभेन; oOr चतुष्पथैः — c) GMd^1 TMd^4 MTr^4 MTr^6 [*Jolly* Gr] *Mādh* स्थालीपाकविधानेन; GMy उपायज्ञविधानेन; TMd^3 पाकविधानेन — d) sOx^1 sPu^6 MTr^6 यजते; Pu^2 Pu^3 यज्ञेन; TMd^3 यजेन्निर्ऋतिं; Be^1 यजन्ता नैर्ऋतिः; Pu^{10} यजेनैकृतं; *Apa* नैर्ऋतं यजते; BBe^2 Hy wKt^3 La^1 oOr नैर्ऋतिं; Lo^4 नैर्ऋतं; NKt^4 निर्ऋत्यां; GMd^5 निर्जिते दिशि; BBe^2 NKt^4 La^1 GMd^1 TMd^4 Tr^1 दिशि; Be^1 Lo^2 oOr दिशं

120.* Cited by *Apa* 1140; *Mādh* 2.436 — a) Tr^2 हुत्वाग्निं; BBe^2 wKt^3 Lo^4 [*Jolly* M] कृत्वाग्नौ; NKt^4 La^1 Lo^2 Pu^2 विविधान्होमा°; TMd^3 Tr^1 [*Jolly* M$^{1-2-8-9}$ Nd] °वद्धोममन्त° — a-b) TMd^4 °वद्धोममुत्तरधसमिधचा [?]; GMd^1 GMy °वद्धोमं सततं च; GMd^5 MTr^6 °वद्धोमं सन्नतं च; Tr^1 °द्धोमं सगतं च; wKt^1 °वद्धोमांस्ततश्च — b) NKt^4 °द्धोमाननन्तश्च; BBe^2 Ho wKt^3 sOx^1 sPu^6 °न्ततस्तु; La^1 °न्तरश्च; Tr^1 सनित्यृचा; BBe^2 समिदृचा; wKt^1 समिदित्यृचा; Jm Jo^1 Kt^2 Lo^2 Ox^2 MTr^3 *Mandlik Jolly Jha KSS Dave* समेत्यृचा; Pu^{10} [*Jolly* M^{2-8-9}] समृतस्य च; BKt^5 समत्यृचा — c) GMd^1 TMd^3 TMd^4 GMd^5 GMy Tr^1 MTr^4 MTr^6 वाय्विन्द्र° — d) Lo^2 °हुतिं

121. *ma* in Lo^4. Cited by *Apa* 1140 — a) Jo^2 Lo^3 Tj^1 कामात्तु; BBe^2 कामको; BKt^5 सेके — b) GMd^5 द्विजन्मनां — c) wKt^1 °क्रामं — d) Pu^{10} °हुर्धर्मज्ञानै; GMd^1 Wa °हुर्ब्रह्मज्ञा; TMd^4 सत्यवादिनः; NNg [*but mc sh*] °वादिभिः

122. *ma* in Lo^4 [*Jolly* M^8] — a) wKt^1 La^1 Pu^3 मरुतं; Lo^2 NNg sOx^1 Ox^2 Pu^4 sPu^6 Tj^2 Wa मारुतः; Bo Ho NKt^4 BKt^5 Lo^1 NPu^1 Pu^5 Pu^7 Pu^{10} Tr^2 [*Jolly* M G] *Jolly* मरुतः; Hy मारुत; NKt^4 °हूते; Lo^2 °हूतन् — b) GMd^1 TMd^4 MTr^4 MTr^6 बृहस्पतिमथानलं; BBe^2 wKt^1 oOr गुरु; Bo पापक° — c) Pu^{10} चतुराव्रतिने; Tr^1 वृत्तिनो; Ho MTr^5 ह्येति; sOx^1 sPu^6 ह्येते; GMy °प्येति; Pu^2 °पैति — d) BCa Ho ब्राह्मयं; TMd^4 Tr^2 ब्रह्म; BBe^2 तेजोतिकीर्तनः; GMy °वकीर्णिना; Tr^2 °विकीर्णिनः; NKt^4 °वकीर्तितः; Pu^{10} °वकीर्तिवः

123. *ma* in Lo^4 [*Jolly* M^8]. Cited by *Vij* 3.280; *Apa* 1141; *Mādh* 2.436 — a) TMd^4 तस्मिनेनतु — b) sOx^1 sPu^6 गार्दभा°; BBe^2 गर्धभा°; Pu^5 Pu^7 °भाजिने; wKt^3 Tj^1 °भाजनं — c) BKt^5

तेभ्यो लब्धेन भैक्षेण वर्तयन्नेककालिकम् ।
उपस्पृशंस्त्रिषवणमब्देन स विशुध्यति ॥१२४॥
जातिभ्रंशकरं कर्म कृत्वान्यतममिच्छया ।
चरेत्सांतपनं कृच्छ्रं प्राजापत्यमनिच्छया ॥१२५॥
संकरापात्रकृत्यासु मासं शोधनमैन्दवम् ।
मलिनीकरणीयेषु तप्तः स्याद्यावकस्त्र्यहम् ॥१२६॥
तुरीयो ब्रह्महत्यायाः क्षत्रियस्य वधे स्मृतः ।
वैश्येऽष्टमांशो वृत्तस्थे शूद्रे ज्ञेयस्तु षोडशः ॥१२७॥
अकामतस्तु राजन्यं विनिपात्य द्विजोत्तमः ।
वृषभैकसहस्रा गा दद्याच्छुद्ध्यर्थमात्मनः ॥१२८॥

सप्तरात्रे; BBe^2 BCa Hy Jo^1 Kt^2 wKt^3 Pu^2 Pu^4 Tj^2 MTr^3 *Mandlik Jha KSS Dave* °गारांश्चरे°; Lo^4 *Mādh* °गारान्चरे; Be^1 Bo BCa Ho Jo^2 wKt^1 Kt^2 NKt^4 Lo^3 NNg oOr Ox^2 sPu^6 Pu^7 °द्वैक्ष्यं — d) NKt^4 स्वं; Be^1 परिवर्तयन्; TMd^4 परिवर्तयेत्

124. *ma* in Lo^4 [*Jolly* M^8]; pāda-d omitted in Pu^{10}. Cited by *Vij* 3.280; *Apa* 1141; *Mādh* 2.436 — a) GMd^1 एभ्यो; Be^1 Bo Ho Jo^2 Lo^3 Ox^2 Pu^2 Pu^3 Pu^5 Pu^7 Pu^8 भैक्ष्येण— b) Be^1 वर्तयेन्नेक°; TMd^3 *Apa* वर्तयेन्नैक°; Tj^2 वर्तेयन्नेक°; sOx^1 sPu^6 वर्तयेदेक°; Be^1 wKt^3 Lo^4 NNg °यन्नैक° — c) sOx^1 sPu^6 उपस्पृश्य त्रिषव°; Lo^3 Tj^1 °षवणाम° — d) GMd^1 TMd^3 TMd^4 GMd^5 GMy oOr MTr^4 MTr^5 MTr^6 °मव्देनैकेन शुध्यति [oOr °मर्थेनैकेन]; Jo^1 [*Jolly* G] °षवणं त्वव्देन

125. *ma* in Lo^4; pādas c-d omitted in Tj^1. Cited by *Vij* 3.254, 289; *Apa* 1183; *Mādh* 2.441 — a) BKt^5 °भ्रंशकृतं — b) Tr^2 कृत्वा तु भृशमिच्छया; NPu^1 Pu^2 Pu^4 °न्यतमदिच्छया; GMd^1 TMd^3 GMd^5 GMy Tr^1 MTr^6 °न्यतरदिच्छया; TMd^4 MTr^4 [*Jolly* Gr] °न्यतरमिच्छया; Pu^{10} °न्यतथमिच्छया; wKt^3 sOx^1 sPu^6 °च्छता — d) BKt^5 प्रजापत्य°

126.* *ma* in Lo^4. Cited by *Vij* 3.289; *Apa* 1183; pādas c-d cited by *Vij* 3.269; *Apa* 1128 — a) TMd^4 सकरात्रकृत्योसु; Lo^3 संकरी°; Be^1 संकरो°; sOx^1 sPu^6 सकरा°; TMd^3 सुकरा°; GMd^1 सत्कारपात्र°; NKt^4 संकराप्यत्र°; BBe^2 °पात्रं कृत्वाशु; Ho °कृत्येषु — b) GMd^1 मामासश्शोधनेन्दवः; NNg मास; Ho wKt^1 NKt^4 BKt^5 La^1 Lo^2 oOr Ox^2 Pu^5 Pu^7 Wa *Apa Me* मासः; TMd^3 TMd^4 GMd^5 GMy Tr^1 मांस; MTr^6 मांसं; Ho wKt^1 NKt^4 BKt^5 NNg Pu^5 Pu^7 Tr^2 Wa *Apa Me Jha Dave* °मैन्दवः — c) MTr^4 मैथुनी°; MTr^6 मिथुनी°; La^1 °कारिणीयेषु; TMd^4 °करिणीयेषु; sOx^1 Pu^{10} °णेयेषु; Lo^1 Pu^3 Pu^5 Pu^7 Tr^2 °णीये तु; Bo °णाये तु; *Apa* [vl] °णेयेन — d) wKt^1 तप्तस्यांवाचकस्त्र्यहं; Jo^2 GMy Tj^1 MTr^6 [*Jolly* R Nd] *Nd* तप्तं; BKt^5 सप्त; Jo^2 स्याद्यावकं त्र्यहं; Jm Jo^1 wKt^1 Kt^2 MTr^3 *Nā Jha KSS Dave* स्याद्यावकैस्त्र्यहं; *Mandlik* स्याद्यवकत्र्यहं; BKt^5 स्याद्याककस्त्र्यहं; La^1 स्यात्स्वाधिकस्त्र्यहं; Jo^2 Lo^3 TMd^4 GMy Tj^1 [*Jolly* R Nd] *Nd* स्याद्यावकं त्र्यहं ; Bo स्याद्याचकस्त्र्यहं; GMd^1 स्याद्यत्ते त्र्यहं

127. *ma* in Lo^4; pādas c-d omitted in BKt^5. Cited by *Viś* 3.244; *Vij* 3.266–7; *Apa* 1105; pādas a-b cited by *Vij* 3.285 — a) NKt^4 BKt^5 sOx^1 तुरीयं; Tr^2 तुरीया; GMd^5 तृतीयो — b) Jm वधेः; TMd^4 Tr^2 वध; La^1 Lo^1 वधः; Be^1 Tr^1 विधे; BKt^5 धधे; GMy स्मृतं; Lo^3 Tj^1 [*Jolly* R] स्थितः — c) BBe^2 Lo^2 वैश्याष्ट°; Hy TMd^3 TMd^4 NNg Ox^2 Pu^2 Pu^4 MTr^5 *Viś Apa* °ष्टमोंशो; Tr^1 °ष्टमेंशो; GMy °ष्टमांशे; GMd^5 °ष्टमेंशे; Be^1 NNg [*but cor fh*] वत्तस्थो; TMd^4 वत्तस्था; *Rn* appears to read व्रतस्थ — d) BBe^2 शूद्रो; Pu^{10} ज्ञेयास्तु; NNg ज्ञेयश्च; wKt^1 Kt^2 GMd^1 TMd^3 GMy NNg Pu^2 Pu^5 Pu^7 षोडश; Lo^1 षोडशं

128. Omitted in BKt^5; pādas c-d omitted in BBe^2 TMd^3. Cited by *Viś* 3.244, 263–4; *Har*-A 1.244; *Mādh* 2.73; pādas a-b cited by *Vij* 3.266–7; *Apa* 1105 — a) Bo आकाम°; La^1

त्र्यब्दं चरेद्वा नियतो जटी ब्रह्महणो व्रतम् ।
वसन्दूरतरे ग्रामाद् वृक्षमूलनिकेतनः ॥१२९॥
एतदेव चरेदब्दं प्रायश्चित्तं द्विजोत्तमः ।
प्रमाप्य वैश्यं वृत्तस्थं दद्याद्वैकशतं गवाम् ॥१३०॥
एतदेव व्रतं कृत्स्नं षण्मासाञ्छूद्रहा चरेत् ।
वृषभैकादशा वापि दद्याद्विप्राय गाः सिताः ॥१३१॥
मार्जारनकुलौ हत्वा चाषं मण्डूकमेव च ।
श्वगोधोलूककाकांश्च शूद्रहत्याव्रतं चरेत् ॥१३२॥
पयः पिबेत् त्रिरात्रं वा योजनं वाध्वनो व्रजेत् ।
उपस्पृशेत् स्रवन्त्यां वा सूक्तं वाब्दैवतं जपेत् ॥१३३॥

स्वकाम°; Pu^{10} अकामकस्तु; Tj^{2} अकामस्तु; Tr^{2} Wa राजन्यां — b) Be^{1} विनिपात्या; Wa विनीपत्य; GMy विनिपाद्य; Pu^{10} [*Jolly* M] विनिहत्य; Pu^{2} द्विजोत्तमाः; Tr^{1} द्विजोत्तमैः — c) *Viś* ऋपभै°; GMd^{5} GMy °सहस्रां; TMd^{4} Pu^{2} Pu^{4} °सहस्रं; GMd^{1} °सहस्राणि [*om* गा]; GMd^{5} गां — d) Hy Jm Jo^{1} Kt^{2} Tj^{2} MTr^{3} *Mandlik Jha KSS Dave* दद्यात्सुचरितव्रतः [cf. 11.116d]

129. Omitted in BKt^{5} Lo^{2} TMd^{3}. Cited by *Viś* 3.244; *Har*-A 1.24.4; *Mādh* 2.73 — a) [*Jolly* Nd] द्व्यब्दं; Be^{1} [*but cor*] wKt^{1} Lo^{1} Lo^{4} अब्दं; *Bh* [ad 11.131 as pāṭha of some] चरेच्च; La^{1} वा चरेन्नियतो; Pu^{2} Pu^{4} नियता; GMd^{5} निगतो — b) GMd^{1} TMd^{4} oOr MTr^{4} MTr^{5} MTr^{6} *Viś* जटिलो ब्रह्महव्रतं [TMd^{4} MTr^{4} MTr^{6} ब्रह्महा; oOr ब्रह्मणो]; Be^{1} जटी च ब्रह्मणि व्रतं; Pu^{10} यदि ब्रह्मणव्रतं; Tr^{2} ब्राह्म°; sOx^{1} sPu^{6} ब्रह्महतिव्रतं; Bo NNg Ox^{2} Pu^{3} Pu^{5} Pu^{7} Wa *Ku* °हणि; GMy °हणे — c) Pu^{5} Pu^{7} वसन्नदूरे ग्रामस्य; Ho Jo^{2} sOx^{1} sPu^{6} Tj^{1}[*Jolly* R] वसेद्दूर°; NKt^{4} °रतरा; Jo^{2} Lo^{4} Pu^{10} Tj^{2} °रतरं; *Mādh* ग्रामे — d) GMy वृक्षमूले

130. Pādas a-b omitted in Lo^{2} TMd^{3} oOr. Cited by *Har*-A 1.24.4; *Mādh* 2.73; pādas c-d cited by *Apa* 1105 — a) GMd^{1} तत्तदेव — b) Pu^{8} °श्चित्तमनुत्तमं; BKt^{5} द्विजन्मनः — c) BBe^{2} प्रमाप्याब्रह्मवृत्तिस्थं; TMd^{3} Pu^{5} Pu^{7} प्रमाद्य; Tr^{2} प्रभाप्य; wKt^{1} प्रसाम्य; GMd^{5} समाप्य; Pu^{3} Pu^{4} वैश्य; TMd^{4} वैश्या; TMd^{3} वृत्तं वैश्यस्थं; Pu^{2} Pu^{4} वृत्तिस्थं; Be^{1} व्रतस्थं — d) La^{1} Tj^{1} *Nā* [pāṭha] *Bh* [ad 11.131 as pāṭha of some] दद्याच्चैक°; Pu^{10} [*Jolly* M] दद्यात्त्वेक°; Lo^{1} TMd^{4} NPu^{1} Pu^{2} Pu^{4} दद्यादेक°; oOr दद्यादैक°

131. Pādas c-d omitted in sOx^{1} sPu^{6} [haplo]. Cited by *Viś* 3.262; *Apa* 1105; *Har*-A 1.24.4; *Mādh* 2.72 — a) NKt^{4} विधिं कृत्स्नं; BKt^{5} कृतं कृत्स्नं; BCa TMd^{3} कृछ्रं — a-b) Ho La^{1} GMd^{1} TMd^{4} sOx^{1} sPu^{6} MTr^{5} MTr^{6} *Mādh* प्रमाप्य शूद्रं षण्मासानेतदेव व्रतं चरेत्[sOx^{1} sPu^{6} °मासएत°; Ho °मासमेत°] — b) Lo^{1} GMy षण्मासं शूद्रहा; wKt^{3} भवेत्; NKt^{4} भजेत् — c) TMd^{4} GMd^{5} Tr^{1} MTr^{4} MTr^{6} *Viś* ऋपभैका°; TMd^{3} °दशं; Wa °दशी; La^{1} °दशा गास्तु — d) Pu^{10} तथा विप्राय; Tr^{1} °प्राय तास्तु गाः; GMd^{1} TMd^{3} स्थिताः; wKt^{1} शतं

132. Omitted in sOx^{1} sPu^{6}. Cited by *Viś* 3.266; *Vij* 3.270; *Apa* 1130; *Mādh* 2.68 — a) BKt^{5} मर्जार°; Lo^{4} Pu^{10} [*Jolly* M] मार्जारं नकुलं — b) BBe^{2} wKt^{1} चासं; Pu^{2} Pu^{4} चापं; Pu^{10} वार्षं; MTr^{3} चाष्ट; Lo^{1} मण्डुक°; BKt^{5} मण्डूष°; Be^{1} Kt^{2} Lo^{2} NNg NPu^{1} Pu^{2} Pu^{3} Pu^{4} वा — c) MTr^{4} MTr^{6} °गोधूलू°; TMd^{4} °लूखलाकांश्च; Tr^{1} °लूककांश्चैव; oOr °काकश्च — d) BKt^{5} चरेच्छूद्रहनि व्रतं; GMd^{1} शूद्रघातव्रतं; MTr^{4} MTr^{6} शूद्रघाती व्रतं

133. Cited by *Viś* 3.266; *Vij* 3.270; *Apa* 1131; *Mādh* 2.68 — a) Ho त्रिशतं — b) Lo^{1} योजनो; oOr योजनमध्वनो; NPu^{1} Pu^{10} वाध्वना; wKt^{1} वाध्वनं; Lo^{2} चाध्वनौ; BCa चाध्वनो; Pu^{5} Pu^{7} वाध्वजो — c) Lo^{3} उपस्पृश्य; Lo^{4} Pu^{10} [*Jolly* M] *Vij* अपः स्पृशेत्; Lo^{2} °स्पृशेत् त्रिरात्रं वा; Lo^{1} Tr^{1}

अभ्रिं कार्ष्णायसीं दद्यात् सर्पं हत्वा द्विजोत्तमः ।
पलालभारकं षण्ढे सैसकं चैव माषकम् ॥१३४॥
घृतकुम्भं वराहे तु तिलद्रोणं तु तित्तिरौ ।
शुके द्विहायनं वत्सं क्रौञ्चं हत्वा त्रिहायनम् ॥१३५॥
हत्वा हंसं बलाकां च बकं बर्हिणमेव च ।
वानरं श्येनभासौ च स्पर्शयेद्ब्राह्मणाय गाम् ॥१३६॥
वासो दद्याद्धयं हत्वा पञ्च नीलान् वृषान् गजम् ।
अजमेषावनड्वाहं खरं हत्वैकहायनम् ॥१३७॥
क्रव्यादांस्तु मृगान्हत्वा धेनुं दद्यात्पयस्विनीम् ।
अक्रव्यादान् वत्सतरीमुष्ट्रं हत्वा तु कृष्णलम् ॥१३८॥

स्रवन्त्या; Pu[8] स्रवन्तीं; Be[1] स्रवत्यां च — c-d) wKt[1] अपः स्पृशेत्सरस्वत्या मन्त्रं वाग्दैवतं जपेत् — d) Pu[2] सूत्रकं दैवतं; NKt[4] वाग्दैवतं; Be[1] Bo BKt[5] sOx[1] *Mādh* वा दैवतं; La[1] वै दैविकं; Tr[1] वाद्यैवतं; Pu[3] जयेत्; Lo[2] चरेत्; oOr व्रजेत्

134. Cited by *Vij* 3.273; *Apa*1132; *Mādh* 2.67 — a) TMd[3] क्वचित्काष्ठायसीं दद्यात्; Jo[2] Lo[2] Lo[3] Pu[3] Pu[5] Tr[2] अभ्रीं; GMd[5] अभ्रिः; Bo GMy अभ्रं; wKt[1] अद्रिं; Pu[2] Pu[4] अग्रि; BBe[2] अतिकार्ष्णायसीं; Tr[1] कृष्णायसीं; Tj[2] °यसी; oOr °यसं — b) wKt[1] Lo[1] Tj[2] सर्वं — c) La[1] पलालभारं वानं वा; Tr[2] पालाल°; Lo[2] TMd[4] पलालं; TMd[3] Tr[1] °हारकं; Kt[2] TMd[4] GMd[5] GMy षण्ढं; Lo[4] Pu[5] Pu[7] Tj[1] षण्डे; TMd[3] oOr Tr[1] षण्डं; Lo[1] खण्डे; GMd[1] भाण्डं — c-d) Pu[2] Pu[4] पलालभारकं प्रसीसकं चैव समाषकं — d) *Apa* माषकं चैव सीसकं; Bo BCa Jo[2] wKt[1] La[1] Lo[2] Lo[3] Lo[4] GMd[5] NPu[1] Pu[5] Pu[7] Tj[1] Tr[1] MTr[4] [*Jolly* G] *Ku Go* सीसकं; TMd[3] सीसतं; Tr[2] शैसाकं; BKt[5] शोशतं; GMd[1] सैसवं; oOr सैन्दवं; Hy Jo[1] Kt[2] Lo[3] Lo[4] NNg Tj[2] MTr[3] *Mandlik Jha KSS Dave* चैकमाषकं; NKt[4] माषकान्; Hy La[1] Tj[2] मासकं; TMd[3] मापकं

135. Cited by *Mādh* 2.64 — a) NNg °कुम्भ; Tj[2] °कुम्भे कराहे; GMd[1] TMd[3] TMd[4] GMd[5] Tr[1] MTr[4] MTr[6] वराहं; Jo[2] Lo[3] Tj[1] च — b) GMd[5] °द्रोणे; BKt[5] La[1] च; NKt[4] NNg sOx[1] Pu[2] Pu[4] Pu[5] sPu[6] Pu[7] Pu[8] तित्तिरे; TMd[3] TMd[4] GMd[5] GMy Tr[1] MTr[5] तित्तिरिं; MTr[4] MTr[6] तित्तिरीं — c) GMd[1] शुक; La[1] TMd[3] TMd[4] GMd[5] Tr[1] MTr[4] MTr[5] MTr[6] शुकं; MTr[5] द्विहायनः — d) BBe[2] हित्वा; wKt[3] Lo[4] त्रिहायणं; Bo La[1] TMd[3] Pu[4] त्र्यहायनं

136. Cited by *Vij* 3.272; *Apa*1132; *Mādh* 2.62 — a) Pu[2] Tj[1] हंस; Be[1] हंसा; NKt[4] BKt[5] TMd[3] GMy oOr Pu[2] Pu[4] Tr[1] MTr[6] बलाकं; MTr[5] बलाहं; Pu[5] Pu[7] [*Jolly* G] बलाकांश्च; wKt[1] sOx[1] sPu[6] वा — b) Kt[2] बक; Pu[2] Pu[4] बक्तं; Bo वर्षिणमेव; wKt[1] वा — c) BBe[2] wKt[3] °भाषौ; TMd[3] °हासौ — d) Lo[1] संस्पर्शाद्ब्राह्म°; TMd[4] स्पर्शाया ब्राह्म°; Tr[2] गाः

137. Cited by *Vij* 3.271; *Mādh* 2.69 — a) GMd[5] वासो हत्वा हयं दद्यात्; *Mādh* दद्याद्रयं; Bo दद्याद्धनं; BBe[2] La[1] NNg दद्याद्वयं; Pu[2] Pu[4] दत्वा — b) Lo[4] नीला; Pu[2] Pu[4] नीलवृष; NNg वृषानाजं; Pu[10] MTr[4] [*Jolly* M[1–2–9]] गजान् — c) TMd[4] Tr[2] अजामेषा°; Pu[10] गजमेषा°; Lo[2] अजं मेखमन°; Lo[3] TMd[3] TMd[4] °मेषामन°; NKt[4] La[1] Pu[2] Pu[4] °मेषमन° — d) Pu[8] खरं चैवैकं हायनं; TMd[4] खर; Lo[3] Pu[10] हत्वेक°; wKt[3] °हायणं; TMd[4] °हयनं

138. Omitted in TMd[4]. Cited by *Vij* 3.272; *Apa* 1132— a) Be[1] BBe[2] क्रव्यादास्तु; *Vij Apa* [vl as in ed] क्रव्यादस्तु; sOx[1] sPu[6] Pu[8] Tj[2] क्रव्यादांश्च; wKt[1] क्रव्यादं तु — b) BCa दद्याद्धेनुं पय°; sOx[1] sPu[6] दद्यः पय°; Pu[10] दत्वा पय°; Wa °यस्विनिं; Lo[4] °यस्विनी — c) wKt[1] Lo[4] Pu[10] GMd[5] GMy Tr[1] MTr[6] *Vij Apa* अक्रव्यादो; Tr[2] अक्रव्यादी; BBe[2] wKt[3] अक्रव्यादा; GMd[1] NNg Wa अक्रव्यादे; Lo[2] अकृव्या-

जीलकार्मुकबस्तावीन् पृथग्दद्याद्विशुद्धये ।
चतुर्णामपि वर्णानां नारीर्हत्वानवस्थिताः ॥१३९॥
दानेन वधनिर्णेकं सर्पादीनामशक्नुवन् ।
एकैकशश्चरेत्कृच्छ्रं द्विजः पापापनुत्तये ॥१४०॥
अस्थन्वतां तु सत्त्वानां सहस्रस्य प्रमापणे ।
पूर्णे चानस्थनस्थ्नां तु शूद्रहत्याव्रतं चरेत् ॥१४१॥
किंचिदेव तु विप्राय दद्यादस्थिमतां वधे ।
अनस्थ्नां चैव हिंसायां प्राणायामेन शुध्यति ॥१४२॥
फलदानां तु वृक्षाणां छेदने जप्यमृक्शतम् ।

देव; TMd[3] अकव्याष्टौ; Lo[1] क्रव्यादास्तु; La[1] क्रव्यादौ — d) Be[1] च; Be[1] Pu[5] Tr[2] *Apa* कृष्णलां; *Apa* [vl] वत्सलां

139.* Omitted in TMd[4]. Cited by *Apa* 1128; *Mādh* 2.76 — a) Tr[1] जलकूर्मकमुस्तावीः; wKt[3] NNg Pu[10] Wa [*Jolly* M Nd] *Jolly* जाल°; Ho जालं; GMy जल°; TMd[3] जला°; Be[2] Hy Jm Jo[1] Jo[2] wKt[1] Kt[2] La[1] Tj[1] Tr[2] [*Jolly* G Ku R] *Jha KSS Dave* जीन°; Lo[3] *Mandlik* जिन°; BKt[5] जन°; Bo Lo[1] Pu[3] Pu[8] *Apa* जीर्ण°; Ox[2] जीर्णं; sOx[1] sPu[6] जात°; GMd[1] चीर°; GMd[5] चेल°; Be[1] Pu[2] Pu[4] नील°; Lo[2] दति°; Tj[2] वीर्य°; wKt[1] °कामुक°; Be[1] NKt[4] Ox[2] Pu[2] Pu[3] Pu[4] MTr[6] *Apa* °बस्तावीः; Tj[2] Tr[2] °बस्तावी; TMd[3] °बस्ताविः; GMd[5] °बस्ताविं; Jo[2] Lo[3] La[1] sOx[1] sPu[6] Tj[1] [*Jolly* R] °बस्तादीन्; GMd[1] °बस्तापि — b) *Mādh* दद्यादघविशुद्धये; oOr पृथग्विद्याद्वि° — d) Be[1] NKt[4] Pu[5] Tj[1] Tj[2] नारी हत्वा°; BCa Ho wKt[1] wKt[3] BKt[5] oOr sOx[1] Pu[2] sPu[6] Pu[7] Pu[10] Tr[1] Tr[2] [*Jolly* M G] नारीं हत्वा°; Lo[1] नारो हत्वा°; NPu[1] नारीहत्या°; *Me* [pāṭha which he rejects] नारीर्गत्वा°; BKt[5] °त्वाव्यवस्थितां; Lo[1] Tr[1] °स्थितः; BCa Ho wKt[3] La[1] oOr sOx[1] Ox[2] NPu[1] Pu[2] sPu[6] [*Jolly* M G] °स्थितां; Tr[2] °स्थितिं

Additional verse in Be[1] BKt[5] La[1] NNg oOr *Mandlik* [क, ग, ञ, ठ, ड] *KSS Dave:*

वर्णानामानुपूर्वेण त्रयाणामविशेषतः ।
अमत्यैव प्रमाप्य स्त्रीं शुद्रहत्याव्रतं चरेत् ॥

a) BKt[5] oOr चतुर्णामानु° — c) La[1] अविपद्यां तु स्त्रियं हत्वा; NNg अमत्या च

140. Cited by *Viś* 3.270 — a) Lo[4] विध°; TMd[3] विधिनिर्मोकं; Pu[2] Pu[4] विधिनोर्नकं; TMd[4] तेन निर्णेकं; BKt[5] °निर्नेय; GMd[1] °निर्णेकस्सर्पा° — b) BKt[5] कार्पासादीनामनुस्मरन्; Lo[3] Tj[1] वस्त्रादीनाम°; Lo[1] सम्पादीनाम°; Bo Ho NPu[1] °शक्नुवत्; NKt[4] °शक्नवन् — c) GMd[1] GMy एकैकशं चरे°; Tr[2] एकैकः चरे°; Lo[4] TMd[4] oOr Pu[10] [*Jolly* M] एकैकस्य चरे° [TMd[4] हरे°]; TMd[3] एतैःकृशश्चरे°; Tr[1] एतैःकृशंश्चरे°; NKt[4] एकैकं संचरे°; Pu[5] Pu[7] °रेत्कृत्स्नं — d) *Viś* प्राजापत्यं विशुद्धये; Tr[1] पापविशुद्धये

141* Cited by *Mādh* 2.66; pādas c-d cited by *Vij* 3.243, and pāda-c by *Viś* 3.265 — a) Be[1] Jo[2] TMd[4] Pu[5] Pu[7] [*Jolly* G] *Go* अस्थ्यन्वितानां सत्त्वानां [TMd[4] *om* सत्त्वानां]; GMy अस्थ्यन्वतां; NNg Pu[10] [*Jolly* M] अस्थिन्वतां; Pu[4] अस्थिभृतां; BBe[2] Bo Ho Hy Jm Jo[1] wKt[1] Kt[2] wKt[3] NKt[4] BKt[5] La[1] Lo[1] Lo[2] Lo[3] Lo[4] sOx[1] Ox[2] NPu[1] Pu[2] Pu[3] sPu[6] Pu[8] Tj[1] Tj[2] MTr[3] Wa [*Jolly* Ku R] *Bh* [ad 11.131] *Mandlik Jha KSS Dave* अस्थिमतां; Pu[2] *om* तु; BKt[5] Lo[2] GMd[1] च; Lo[2] सत्यानां — b) NNg Tr[2] प्रमापणं; wKt[1] प्रमापयेत्; Ho प्रमापरे; Pu[4] प्रमाणये; NNg निपातने — c) MTr[5] पूर्वे; GMd[5] पूवे; BKt[5] NNg MTr[4] वानस्य°; TMd[4] Tr[1] चोनस्य°; Be[1] TMd[3] TMd[4] °नस्थ्रा; wKt[1] °नस्थां; NKt[4] °नस्था; GMd[1] °नास्था; Tr[1] °नस्थौ — d) TMd[4] शूद्रहर्ता व्रतं; Tj[2] चरत्

142. Cited by *Mādh* 2.66–7 — b) Pu[10] दद्याम°; oOr भवेदस्थि°; Hy °स्थिमता; sOx[1] °स्थिवतां — c) TMd[3] अनस्थितायां च हिंसायां; NKt[4] Pu[5] Pu[7] अनस्था; wKt[3] अनस्थां; Ho अनस्नां; Pu[10] अनस्थ्नश्चैव

गुल्मवल्लीलतानां च पुष्पितानां च वीरुधाम् ॥१४३॥
अन्नाद्यजानां सत्त्वानां रसजानां च सर्वशः ।
फलपुष्पोद्भवानां च घृतप्राशो विशोधनम् ॥१४४॥
कृष्टजानामोषधीनां जातानां च स्वयं वने ।
वृथारम्भेऽनुगच्छेद्गां दिनमेकं पयोव्रतः ॥१४५॥
एतैर्व्रतैरपोह्यं स्यादेनो हिंसासमुद्भवम् ।
ज्ञानाज्ञानकृतं कृत्स्नं शृणुतानाद्यभक्षणे ॥१४६॥
अज्ञानाद्वारुणीं पीत्वा संस्कारेणैव शुध्यति ।
मतिपूर्वमनिर्देश्यं प्राणान्तिकमिति स्थितिः ॥१४७॥
अपः सुराभाजनस्था मद्यभाण्डस्थितास्तथा ।
पञ्चरात्रं पिबेत्पीत्वा शङ्खपुष्पीशृतं पयः ॥१४८॥

143. Omitted in Pu^{10} Tj^{2}. Cited by *Vij* 3.276; *Apa* 1134; *Mādh* 2.434 — a) wKt^{3} nKt^{4} Lo^{2} gMy °दानं; nPu^{1} °दानांस्तु — b) wKt^{1} जप्यते शतं; Ho gMd^{5} °मृक्छतं; tMd^{3} Pu^{5} Pu^{7} °मृच्छतं; bKt^{5} °मृच्छति — c) nKt^{4} मुस्यवल्ली°; tMd^{4} तु; Hy *om* च पुष्पितानां— d) Tr^{2} विरुध्यतां

144. Cited by *Apa* 1138 — a) gMd^{1} अन्नाद्यानां चैव सत्त्वानां; La^{1} अनद्य°; wKt^{1} अर्थाद्य° — b) Tr^{2} रजतानां; oOr Tr^{1} [*Jolly* Gr] राजसानां; Pu^{2} Pu^{4} स्थलजानां; gMd^{1} रसानां चैव; bCa wKt^{1} La^{1} °जानां तथैव च; Ox^{2} पूर्वशः — d) oOr *Apa* घृतं प्राश्य; Pu^{10} [*Jolly* M^{2-8-9}] °प्राशोशु शोधनं; *Apa* विशुध्यति

145.* Omitted in Lo^{2}. Cited by *Apa* 1138; *Mādh* 2.434–5 — a) gMd^{5} कृष्टजामोषधीनां च; Be^{1} wKt^{3} °जातामोष°; Be^{1} Bo Ho Lo^{1} nNg sOx^{1} nPu^{1} Pu^{2} Pu^{4} Pu^{5} Pu^{7} sPu^{6} Wa °मौषधीनां; Tr^{1} °धीना; Pu^{8} °धानां — b) Tr^{2} *om* च; Tj^{2} वधे; Pu^{10} धने — c) Pu^{2} Pu^{4} वृथारम्भेण हिंसायां; nNg मृषारम्भे; tMd^{3} धृढारम्भो; bKt^{5} वृथाछेदे; gMy Tr^{1} °रम्भो; bBe^{2} Bo Hy Jm Jo^{1} Jo^{2} wKt^{1} Kt^{2} wKt^{3} La^{1} Lo^{1} Lo^{3} Ox^{2} Lo^{3} gMd^{5} Pu^{3} Pu^{5} Pu^{7} Pu^{8} Tj^{1} Tj^{2} Tr^{2} mTr^{3} [*Jolly* G R] *Mandlik Jha KSS Dave* °लम्भे; bKt^{5} Lo^{1} Lo^{3} gMd^{1} nNg Tj^{1} [*Jolly* M R] तु गच्छे°; Be^{1} nKt^{4} tMd^{3} nNg °गच्छेद्रा; tMd^{4} °गच्छाद्राः; wKt^{1} °गच्छेद्रा — d) gMy दिनमेकः; Ox^{2} दममेकं; Be^{1} bBe^{2} bCa La^{1} gMd^{1} tMd^{3} gMd^{5} nNg Pu^{5} Pu^{7} Tr^{1} पयोव्रतं

146. Pādas c-d omited in bKt^{5} — a) gMd^{5} एभिर्व्रतै°; Lo^{1} °पोह्या — b) Tj^{1} स्यादेना; Pu^{10} स्यादेने; tMd^{3} हिंसां; gMd^{1} °द्भवः; Pu^{4} °द्भवां — c) Pu^{2} Pu^{4} °कृत; bBe^{2} Lo^{4} Pu^{10} [*Jolly* M] कृच्छ्रं; gMy nPu^{1} [*Jolly* Nd]सर्वं; Jo^{2} wKt^{1} Lo^{3} tMd^{4} Tj^{1} [*Jolly* R]पापं — c-d) oOr °ज्ञानकृतं पापं कृच्छ्रं तान्नाद्यभक्षणे — d) Pu^{8} शृणुताभक्ष्यभक्षणे; bBe^{2} La^{1} शृण्वता°; Be^{1} tMd^{3} tMd^{4} gMy nPu^{1} Pu^{2} Pu^{4} Pu^{5} Pu^{7} [*Jolly* G] श्रुणुतान्नाद्य° [Pu^{7} (*Jolly* G) °न्नादि; Pu^{5} °न्नाद°]; Lo^{1} nNg sOx^{1} sPu^{6} Tj^{1} [*Jolly* M^{2-8-9} R] शृणुतान्नाद्य°

147. Omitted in bKt^{5}; pādas c-d omitted in Pu^{10} and *ma* in Lo^{4}. Cited by *Viś* 3.249; *Apa* 1074; pādas a-b cited by *Vij* 3.255, and pādas c-d by *Apa* 1069, 1210 — a) wKt^{3} अज्ञात्वाद्वा° — b) gMy *Vij* संस्कारेण विशुध्यति; oOr *Apa* पुनःसंस्कारमर्हति; gMd^{5} संस्कारैरेव — c) tMd^{3} मतिं; gMd^{5} °पूर्वाम°; Pu^{5} Pu^{7} °निर्देशां — d) mTr^{6} प्राणान्येनेति [?] धारणा; tMd^{4} प्राणामेकमिति स्थितः; Tr^{2} प्राणीतिक°; nKt^{4} °स्थिते:

148. *ma* in Lo^{4}. Cited by *Vij* 3.254; *Apa* 1074, 1160; *Mādh* 2.349 — a) *Bh* [ad 11.97] appears to read: सुराभाण्डस्थितास्त्वापः; bKt^{5} *om* अपः; Be^{1} bBe^{2} bCa Hy La^{1} Lo^{2} Lo^{3} Lo^{4} oOr

स्पृष्ट्वा दत्त्वा च मदिरां विधिवत्प्रतिगृह्य च ।
शूद्रोच्छिष्टाश्च पीत्वापः कुशवारि पिबेत् त्र्यहम् ॥१४९॥
ब्राह्मणस्तु सुरापस्य गन्धमाघ्राय सोमपः ।
प्राणानप्सु त्रिरायम्य घृतं प्राश्य विशुध्यति ॥१५०॥
अज्ञानात् प्राश्य विण्मूत्रं सुरासंस्पृष्टमेव च ।
पुनःसंस्कारमर्हन्ति त्रयो वर्णा द्विजातयः ॥१५१॥
वपनं मेखला दण्डो भैक्षचर्या व्रतानि च ।
निवर्तन्ते द्विजातीनां पुनःसंस्कारकर्मणि ॥१५२॥
अभोज्यानां तु भुक्तान्नं स्त्रीशूद्रोच्छिष्टमेव च ।
जग्ध्वा मांसमभक्ष्यं च सप्तरात्रं यवान्पिबेत् ॥१५३॥
शुक्तानि च कषायांश्च पीत्वा मेध्यान्यपि द्विजः ।
तावद्भवत्यप्रयतो यावत्तन्न व्रजत्यधः ॥१५४॥

NPu^{1} Pu^{2} Pu^{4} Pu^{5} Pu^{7} *Apa* 1074 [vl] आपः; BKt^{5} *om* °स्था — b) TMd^{4} मद्ये; Kt^{2} °भाण्डास्थि°; Bo °स्थितस्तथा; GMy °स्थितंस्तथा; Be^{1} °स्थिततथा; La^{1} °स्थितातथा; sOx^{1} sPu^{6} Pu^{7} °स्थिता अपि; oOr °स्थिा यथा; BCa °स्थिाश्च यः; Ho *om* तथा — c) Jo^{2} La^{1} Lo^{3} Tj^{1} [*Jolly* R] पिबेदुष्णं; TMd^{4} घृतं पीत्वा — d) BBe^{2} मुखंपुष्पीश्रतं; TMd^{3} °पुष्पि°; Tr^{1} MTr^{4} MTr^{6} °पुष्पश्रितं; GMd^{5} °पुष्पाश्रितं; Ox^{2} °पुष्पास्रितं; TMd^{4} °पुष्पश्रुतं; GMd^{1} NPu^{1} Pu^{2} Pu^{4} Pu^{10} °पुष्पीघृतं

149. *ma* in Lo^{4}. Cited by *Apa* 1164; *Mādh* 2.313 — a) Pu^{2} Pu^{4} सृष्ट्वा; Tr^{1} स्पृष्ट्वा दृष्ट्वा च; GMy पृष्ट्वा स्पृष्ट्वा च; *Apa* तु; Tj^{2} त्वमदिरं — b) Lo^{2} तु — c) Tr^{2} द्रोणोछिष्ट्वांश्च; Pu^{10} शूद्राश्लिष्टां च; Lo^{1} Tr^{1} °च्छिष्टांश्च; BKt^{5} °च्छिष्टां च; TMd^{4} *Mādh* °च्छिष्टं च; Ox^{2} °च्छिष्टो च; TMd^{3} *Apa* [vl] °च्छिष्टाच्च; *Apa* °च्छिष्टास्तु; Bo Lo^{1} पीत्वा यः; *Mādh* पीत्वा तु — d) La^{1} त्र्यहं पिबेत्

150. *ma* in Lo^{4}. Cited by *Vij* 3.254; *Apa* 1164; *Mādh* 2.349 — a) Jm BKt^{5} TMd^{3} Pu^{10} Tr^{2} [*Jolly* M] ब्राह्मणस्य सुरा° — b) *Mādh* मुखमाघ्राय; BKt^{5} GMd^{1} TMd^{4} Pu^{2} Pu^{4} Tr^{1} सोमपाः — c) Tr^{2} प्राणानस्पु; TMd^{4} त्रीनायम्य; Be^{1} BBe^{2} Bo NPu^{1} oOr Pu^{2} Pu^{4} Pu^{5} Pu^{7} Tr^{1} Tr^{2} त्रिराचम्य; Tj^{2} त्रिराषम्य — d) BKt^{5} Pu^{5} प्रास्य; Bo प्राप्य

151. Omitted in GMy [*Jolly* Nd]; *ma* in Lo^{4}. Cited by *Viś* 3.249; *Vij* 3.254; *Apa* 1074, 1164; *Mādh* 2.298 — a) wKt^{1} सज्ञानात्; GMd^{1} ज्ञानात् प्राश्य तु; Tr^{2} प्रास्य; Bo प्राप्य — b) oOr सुरापः स्पृष्टमेव; Tr^{1} °संपृष्टमेव; wKt^{1} wKt^{3} TMd^{3} °संसृष्टमेव; GMd^{5} °संसर्गमेव; BBe^{2} BCa Jo^{2} Lo^{3} Pu^{10} Tj^{1} Tr^{2} [*Jolly* M^{2-8-9} R] वा

152. *ma* in Lo^{4}. Cited by *Apa* 1075 — a) Lo^{2} वपनो; BKt^{5} Ox^{2} पवनं; Pu^{4} स्वपनं; TMd^{4} अननं; Pu^{2} Pu^{4} मेखलां; Hy मेखलो; BKt^{5} NNg Pu^{10} मेषला; Pu^{10} दण्डं — b) NNg भैक्षा°; Pu^{10} भक्ष°; Be^{1} BBe^{2} Bo BCa Ho Hy Jm Jo^{1} Kt^{2} La^{1} oOr sOx^{1} Ox^{2} Pu^{2} Pu^{4} Pu^{5} sPu^{6} Pu^{7} Pu^{8} Tr^{2} *Mandlik Jolly Jha KSS Dave* भैक्ष्य°; BBe^{2} भैक्ष्या°; wKt^{1} Kt^{2} °चर्य; Pu^{8} °चर्यां — c) GMd^{1} Tj^{1} निवर्तते — d) La^{1} GMd^{1} TMd^{4} Tr^{2} °संस्कारमर्हति; BKt^{5} °कर्मणा

153. *ma* in Lo^{4}. Cited by *Mādh* 2.313; *Apa* 1167; pādas c-d cited by *Vij* 3.289 — a) Jm oOr Pu^{8} च; Bo सु; Ho Tj^{1} भुक्तान्नं; Bo Pu^{5} Pu^{7} भुक्तानां — b) Tr^{2} वा — c) GMd^{5} मासमभक्ष्यं; wKt^{1} NKt^{4} BKt^{5} TMd^{3} TMd^{4} Pu^{5} Pu^{7} °भक्षं; Bo °भक्षाच्च; La^{1} °भक्ष्याणां सप्त°; *Vij* तु — d) Be^{1} °रात्रान्

154. Cited by *Vij* 3.289 — a) Pu^{5} Pu^{7} Tj^{1} Tr^{2} सुक्तानि; Bo सुक्तानी; wKt^{1} शक्तानि; MTr^{3} शुल्कानि; Pu^{2} शुक्ल्कानि; Lo^{1} शुष्कानि; GMy भुक्तानि; BKt^{5} कषायं च; Pu^{10} कृषायांश्च; TMd^{3} कृपामाश्च;

विड्वराहखरोष्ट्राणां गोमायोः कपिकाकयोः ।
प्राश्य मूत्रपुरीषाणि द्विजश्चान्द्रायणं चरेत् ॥१५५॥
शुष्काणि जग्ध्वा मांसानि भौमानि कवकानि च ।
अज्ञातं चैव सूनास्थमेतदेव व्रतं चरेत् ॥१५६॥
क्रव्यादसूकरोष्ट्राणां कुक्कुटानां च भक्षणे ।
नरकाकखराणां च तप्तकृच्छ्रं विशोधनम् ॥१५७॥
मासिकान्नं तु योऽश्नीयादसमावृत्तको द्विजः ।
स त्रीण्यहान्युपवसेदेकाहं चोदके वसेत् ॥१५८॥
व्रतचारी तु योऽश्नीयान्मधुमांसं कथंचन ।
स कृत्वा प्राकृतं कृच्छ्रं व्रतशेषं समापयेत् ॥१५९॥

TMd⁴ कपालां च — b) *Vij* [ed] पीत्वाऽमेध्या° [*Nd* reads अमेध्यानि]; TMd³ भुक्त्वा मेध्या°; Tr¹ भुक्ता मेध्या°; Lo³ Tj¹ मेध्यान्यथ — d) Pu¹⁰ यावत्यन्नं भवत्यधः; Tr² यावद्यन्न; Pu⁵ Pu⁷ यावन्न व्रज°; oOr Tr¹ यावदन्नं व्रज°; TMd⁴ यावत्यन्नं व्रज°; NNg पतत्यधः

155. *ma* in Lo⁴. Cited by *Apa* 1164; *Mādh* 2.296 — a) Lo¹ विड्वराहस्य चोष्ट्राणां — b) BBe² Pu⁵ गोमयो; oOr गोमयः; BKt⁵ कपिनाकयोः; Tr¹ पिककाकयोः; TMd³ °काययोः — c) Pu⁵ Pu¹⁰ प्रास्य; *Mādh* मूत्रं पुरीषं वा

156.* Omitted in BBe² BKt⁵; verses 156 and 157 transposed in Tj²; verse 156 placed after 162 in Bo. Cited by *Apa* 1166 — a) TMd³ TMd⁴ MTr⁴ MTr⁶ जग्ध्वा तु शुष्कमांसानि [MTr⁴ MTr⁶ शुल्कं]; Be¹ Bo Ho Hy Jm Jo¹ Kt² Lo¹ sOx¹ Ox² Pu³ Pu⁵ sPu⁶ Pu⁷ Pu⁸ Tj² Tr² MTr³ MTr⁵ *Mandlik Jolly Jha KSS Dave* भुक्त्वा; Lo⁴ भुक्ता; Pu¹⁰ भुक्त — b) TMd³ भणंननिकृणानि च; TMd⁴ कलिङ्गकतकानि च; Lo² *om* कवकानि; MTr⁶ कबकानि; Be¹ कविकानि; Hy करकानि — c) GMd¹ TMd⁴ अज्ञानं; La¹ अज्ञातश्चैव; GMd¹ sOx¹ सूनस्थ°; wKt¹ Kt² oOr शूनास्थ°; wKt³ शुनास्थ°; GMy सुनास्थि°; TMd³ सूतस्थ°; TMd⁴ सूनार्थ°; MTr⁴ सूतानामेत°; La¹ Pu¹⁰ सूनास्थामेत° — d) *Apa* °स्थं मांसमेतद्व्रतं

157. Cited by *Vij* 3.289; *Apa* 1166— a) Tr² क्राव्या°; wKt¹ *Vij Apa* क्रव्याद्विट्शूकरो° [wKt¹ क्रव्यादवि°]; BBe² Bo BCa Ho Kt² wKt³ BKt⁵ Lo¹ Lo² Lo⁴ Ox² Pu⁵ Pu⁷ Pu¹⁰ Tr² °शूकरो° — b) La¹ कुक्कुटीनां; TMd⁴ भक्षणात् — c) Pu² Pu⁴ °काकहावराणां तप्त°; La¹ oOr Wa °काकखरेभाणां तप्त°; *Vij* °काकखराश्वानां तप्त°; wKt¹ °खलानां — d) Lo¹ सप्त°; Lo² NNg sOx¹ Ox² Pu² Pu⁴ sPu⁶ MTr⁴ MTr⁵ MTr⁶ Wa *Apa* °कृच्छ्रो [cf. note to 11.209c]; La¹ विशोधयेत्

158.* Omitted in [*Jolly* M]; *ma* in Lo¹. Cited by *Apa* 1144 — a) Pu² Pu⁴ नासिकान्नं; NKt⁴ TMd³ TMd⁴ GMd⁵ GMy Pu⁵ Pu⁷ Tr¹ Tr² MTr⁴ MTr⁶ *Nā Rc Go* मासिकार्थं; Bo La¹ *om* तु; BBe² BCa Jm Jo² wKt¹ BKt⁵ Lo³ GMd¹ NNg oOr Pu² Pu⁴ Tj¹ च — b) Ox² Pu² Pu⁴ °यादासमा°; wKt¹ °यादसद्वृत्तिको; TMd⁴ °यात्वधसावर्तको; [*Jolly* M⁸] °शमावृको; Jo² BKt⁵ Lo² [*Jolly* R²] *Jolly* °वृत्तिको; BBe² Ho Hy Jm Jo¹ Kt² wKt³ Lo¹ GMd¹ GMy Ox² Pu⁵ Pu⁷ Tj² Tr¹ Tr² MTr⁴ MTr⁵ MTr⁶ [*Jolly* M³] *Mandlik Jha KSS Dave* °वर्तको; Lo³ TMd³ Pu² Pu⁴ Tj¹ [*Jolly* R²] °वर्तिको; Bo °वत्तको — d) Pu³ चोदकं; Ox² Tr² चोदकं पिबेत्; GMd¹ च जले वसेत्

159.* Cited by *Viś* 3.278 — a) BBe² Bo BCa Ho Hy Jm Jo¹ Jo² wKt¹ Kt² wKt³ Lo¹ [*ma*] Lo³ sOx¹ Ox² NPu¹ Pu² Pu³ Pu⁴ sPu⁶ Pu⁸ Pu¹⁰ Tj¹ Tj² MTr³ *Mandlik KSS* ब्रह्मचारी; Lo² च — b) Pu¹⁰ °न्मद्यमांसं; oOr कदाचन — c) La¹ स च कृत्वा व्रतं कृच्छ्रं; Pu¹⁰ प्रकृतं; Lo¹ प्राक्कृतं; Ho प्राकृतं शेषं; Pu² Pu⁴ कृप्द्रं — d) Ox² व्रतं; La¹ व्रतमशेषं; BCa La¹ oOr Pu¹⁰ Tr² समाचरेत्; Lo¹ समाहरेत्

बिडालकाकाखूच्छिष्टं जग्ध्वा श्वनकुलस्य च ।
केशकीटावपन्नं च पिबेद् ब्रह्मसुवर्चलाम् ॥१६०॥
अभोज्यमन्नं नात्तव्यमात्मनः शुद्धिमिच्छता ।
अज्ञातभुक्तमुत्तार्यं शोध्यं वाप्याशु शोधनैः ॥१६१॥
एषोऽनाद्यादनस्योक्तो व्रतानां विविधो विधिः ।
स्तेयदोषापहर्तॄणां व्रतानां श्रूयतां विधिः ॥१६२॥
धान्यान्नधनचौर्याणि कृत्वा कामाद् द्विजोत्तमः ।
स्वजातीयगृहादेव कृच्छ्राब्देन विशुध्यति ॥१६३॥
मनुष्याणां तु हरणे स्त्रीणां क्षेत्रगृहस्य च ।
कूपवापीजलानां च शुद्धिश्चान्द्रायणं स्मृतम् ॥१६४॥
द्रव्याणामल्पसाराणां स्तेयं कृत्वान्यवेश्मनः ।

160. *ma* in Lo^{4}. Cited by *Vij* 3.289; *Apa* 1167 — a) Lo^{2} बिडालकाकर्करिनां; NNg बिडाकाक-करिनां; GMd^{5} बिडाळ°; Tr^{1} बिलाळ° — c) Ho °कौटाव°; BBe^{2} MTr^{4} MTr^{6} °कीटोपपत्रं; sOx^{1} sPu^{6} °केटोपपत्रं; La^{1} °कीटपतंगां च; Lo^{4} *om* च — d) GMd^{5} पिबेच्च ब्रह्मवर्चलां; Hy ब्रह्मी°; Pu^{5} [*Jolly* R] ब्राह्मी°; Jo^{2} NKt^{4} Lo^{2} Lo^{3} Lo^{4} GMd^{1} NNg NPu^{1} Pu^{2} Pu^{4} Pu^{7} Tj^{1} Tr^{1} *Vij* ब्राह्मीं; sOx^{1} sPu^{6} [*Jolly* M] °सुवर्चलं; Wa °सुवर्चसं; MTr^{4} MTr^{6} °सुवर्चसां

161.* *ma* in Lo^{4}; pādas c-d omitted in GMy — b) Lo^{1} सिद्धि°; Lo^{2} शुचि°; oOr शुभमि°; Be^{1} °च्छतां; Tr^{2} °च्छत; Kt^{2} °च्छया; GMy °च्छतेति — c) BCa Ho Jm Jo^{1} sOx^{1} NPu^{1} sPu^{6} Tj^{1} *Mandlik Jolly Jha KSS Dave* अज्ञान°; BKt^{5} अज्ञातं; Bo BCa Ho Hy Jm Jo^{1} Tj^{2} Tr^{2} *Mandlik Jolly Jha KSS Dave* °भुक्तं तूत्तार्यं; TMd^{3} GMd^{5} Tr^{1} °भुक्तमुद्रार्यं; [*Jolly* Gr] °भुक्तं तूद्रार्यं; GMd^{1} TMd^{3} MTr^{4} MTr^{5} MTr^{6} °जग्धमुद्रार्यं; sOx^{1} sPu^{6} °भुक्तमुद्रीहं; [*Jolly* Nd] °भुक्तं तूच्चार्यं; NPu^{1} Wa °भुक्तमुद्धार्यं; Lo^{2} °भुक्तमुद्वार्यं; NNg °भुक्तमुद्वार्या; NKt^{4} °भुक्तमद्वार्यं; Pu^{5} Pu^{7} भुक्तं यद्वान्यं; [*Jolly* G] भुक्तं यद्वाम्नयं; Ox^{2} Pu^{2} Pu^{4} Pu^{10} °भुक्तशुद्ध्यर्थं; Tj^{1} °भुक्तार्य — d) BBe^{2} साधवोप्यात्मशोधनं; TMd^{4} शोद्धं; Pu^{2} Pu^{4} शाध्यं; Be^{1} wKt^{1} Lo^{1} Lo^{2} NNg Pu^{2} Pu^{4} चाप्याशु; sOx^{1} वाशु; La^{1} वाप्यास्थिशो°; BKt^{5} शोधने; wKt^{1} साधनैः

162. *ma* in Lo^{4} — a) GMd^{1} एष; Tr^{1} एषोनद्याद°; Bo La^{1} Lo^{1} Lo^{2} NPu^{1} Pu^{3} Pu^{5} Pu^{7} Tr^{2} एषोन्नाद्याद°; Lo^{4} MTr^{4} MTr^{6} °नाद्याशनस्योक्तो; BBe^{2} °नाद्यनस्योक्तो; Be^{1} sOx^{1} sPu^{6} °दन्नस्योक्तो; Lo^{2} °दनशक्तो; Tr^{2} °दरस्योक्तो; Ho °स्योक्त; La^{1} °स्योक्तानां — b) Pu^{2} Pu^{4} विविधौ; Tr^{1} विविधा — c) Pu^{10} तपदोषापहार्हाणां; La^{1} स्तेयो°; sOx^{1} sPu^{6} स्तेयदोषायह°; TMd^{3} °दोपोपह° — d) Pu^{10} क्रियतां — After verse 162 Bo adds verse 11.155

163. *ma* in Lo^{4}; pādas c-d omitted in Lo^{2}; the ms of MTr^{3} ends after कृत्वा का. Cited by *Vij* 3.265; *Apa* 1109; *Mādh* 2.427 — a) Pu^{2} Pu^{4} धान्यानांधन°; NPu^{1} धान्यानिधन°; Ho °धनश्चैर्याणि; Tj^{1} °चौरेण — b) GMd^{1} कृत्वा नाम; Pu^{2} Pu^{4} कृत्वा कर्म; Kt^{2} कस्माद्; Tr^{1} द्विजोत्तमाः — c) Be^{1} BBe^{2} Lo^{4} TMd^{4} sOx^{1} [*Jolly* M$^{3-4}$] *Vij* सजातीय° — d) oOr कृच्छ्राव्देव; Tj^{1} कृच्छ्रादद्वेन; Be^{1} Lo^{1} NNg Pu^{2} Pu^{3} Pu^{4} *Vij* कृच्छ्रार्धेन; TMd^{4} कृच्छ्रार्थेन; Bo कृच्छ्रादेव; BBe^{2} विशुध्यते

164. Omitted in Lo^{2}. Cited by *Vij* 3.265; *Apa* 1110; *Mādh* 2.427 — a) Hy *om* तु; Be Ho BKt^{5} Lo^{4} NNg sOx^{1} NPu^{1} sPu^{6} Pu^{8} Pu^{10} [*Jolly* M R] *Apa* च; TMd^{4} Tj^{1} हरणं — b) BKt^{5} क्षेत्रं; Lo^{1} तु — c) NPu^{1} Wa वापीकूप°; BBe^{2} Jm wKt^{1} wKt^{3} Lo^{1} तु — d) Bo oOr Tr^{1} शुद्धिं चान्द्रा°; Pu^{5} Pu^{7} शुद्धो चान्द्रा°; [*Jolly* G] शुद्धौ चान्द्रा°; Jm °यणंश्चरेत्; Tr^{2} °यणे चरेत्; GMd^{5} °यणं व्रतं; Tr^{1} °यणव्रतं; *Vij Apa* °यणेन तु

चरेत्सांतपनं कृच्छ्रं तन्निर्यात्यात्मशुद्धये ॥१६५॥
भक्ष्यभोज्यापहरणे यानशय्यासनस्य च ।
पुष्पमूलफलानां च पञ्चगव्यं विशोधनम् ॥१६६॥
तृणकाष्ठद्रुमाणां च शुष्कान्नस्य गुडस्य च ।
चेलचर्मामिषाणां च त्रिरात्रं स्यादभोजनम् ॥१६७॥
मणिमुक्ताप्रवालानां ताम्रस्य रजतस्य च ।
अयःकांस्योपलानां च द्वादशाहं कणान्नता ॥१६८॥
कार्पासकीटजोर्णानां द्विखुरैकखुरस्य च ।
पक्षिगन्धौषधीनां च रज्ज्वाश्चैव त्र्यहं पयः ॥१६९॥
एतैर्व्रतैरपोहेत पापं स्तेयकृतं द्विजः ।
अगम्यागमनीयं तु व्रतैरेभिरपानुदेत् ॥१७०॥
गुरुतल्पव्रतं कुर्याद्रेतः सिक्त्वा स्वयोनिषु ।

165.* Cited by *Vij* 3.235; *Apa* 1110; *Mādh* 2.427; pādas c-d cited by *Vij* 3.257— a) wKt^{3} *mc to* °ल्पमूलानां — b) Lo^{3} Tj^{1} कृत्वा च वेश्मनः; TMd^{4} GMd^{5} Tr^{1} *Me Jha Dave* °वेश्मनि; Bo BCa Ho Hy Jm Jo^{1} Jo^{2} wKt^{1} Kt^{2} wKt^{3} Kt^{4} La^{1} Lo^{1} Lo^{4} Ng oOr Ox^{2} Pu^{1} Pu^{5} Pu^{7} Pu^{8} Pu^{10} Tr^{2} Tr^{5} Wa *Vij Mandlik Jolly KSS* °वेश्मतः — c) GMd^{5} °त्सांतापनं; Pu^{10} °त्सांपवनं — d) La^{1} निर्यात्यात्म-विशद्धये; sOx^{1} sPu^{6} तत्पापस्य विशुद्धये; GMd^{1} तन्निर्याद्यात्म°

166. Cited by *Vij* 3.235; *Apa* 1110; *Mādh* 2.427 — a) BBe^{2} wKt^{1} भक्ष°; *Apa* पञ्चभोज्या°; Pu^{5} Pu^{7} °हरणं; Lo^{1} [*but cor*] GMd^{1} °हारेण — b) NKt^{4} Pu^{10} °शनस्य च — c) *Apa* [vl] पञ्चमूल°; NNg *om* च; GMd^{5} Tr^{1} तु — d) La^{1} विशोषणं

167. Omitted in Ho; pādas b-d omitted in BBe^{2}, and pādas c-d in Tr^{2}. Cited by *Vij* 3.235; *Apa* 1110; *Mādh* 2.427 — a) Lo^{3} Tj^{1} °गुडानां च; Bo NKt^{4} TMd^{4} GMd^{5} Tr^{1} MTr^{4} तु — b) TMd^{3} शुल्कान्नस्य; Bo शुष्कानां च; oOr शुष्कानां स; NKt^{4} गुदस्य; Pu^{4} वा — c) Hy Jo^{2} Kt^{2} La^{1} Lo^{1} Lo^{2} Lo^{4} Ng Ox^{1} Ox^{2} Pu^{1} Pu^{2} Pu^{4} Pu^{5} Pu^{6} Pu^{7} Pu^{8} Wa [*Jolly* M G] *Jolly* चैल°; wKt^{3} °कर्मामिषाणां; Lo^{3} Tj^{1} °चर्मविषाणां

168. Pādas a-b omitted in Tr^{2} and pādas a-c in BBe^{2}. Cited by *Vij* 3.265; *Apa* 1111; *Mādh* 2.427 — a) Be^{1} oOr °मुक्त°; GMd^{5} Tr^{1} °वाळानां — c) TMd^{4} °फलानां — c-d) Lo^{3} Tj^{1} [*Jolly* R] °पलादीनां हरणे च कणान्नता — d) oOr द्वादशानां; GMy कणान्नतः; GMd^{1} कणान्नकाः; BKt^{5} कणान्तता; wKt^{1} कणासिता; Tr^{2} करान्नता; *Vij* कदन्नता

169.* Cited by *Vij* 3.265; *Apa* 1110; *Mādh* 2.427 — a) NKt^{4} कर्प्यस्कीटायंजोर्णानां; NPu^{1} Pu^{2} Pu^{4} Tr^{2} कर्पास°; wKt^{1} कपिस°; Lo^{2} NNg Wa *Vij* °जौर्णानां; Ox^{2} जैर्णानां; Be^{1} wKt^{1} °जार्णानां; Pu^{10} °कोर्णानां — b) Be^{1} Bo BCa Ho Hy Jm Jo^{1} wKt^{1} Kt^{2} BKt^{5} Lo^{1} Lo^{2} Lo^{4} NNg oOr Ox^{2} Pu^{5} Pu^{7} Pu^{8} Pu^{10} Tj^{2} Tr^{2} *Apa Mādh Go Nā Ku Rn Mandlik Jolly KSS* द्विशफैकशफस्य; *Me Dave Jha* द्विशफैकखुरस्य — c) BKt^{5} पक्ष°; Lo^{4} Pu^{5} Pu^{10} °गन्धोष°; BCa तु — d) Bo रक्ताश्चैव; GMd^{5} रज्ज्वा चैव; TMd^{3} Tr^{1} रज्ज्वा च; wKt^{1} द्विजश्चैव; TMd^{4} रज्ज्वाश्च त्र्यहं

170. a) Bo NKt^{4} एभिर्व्रतैर°; Lo^{2} °तैरुपोहेत; NKt^{4} *om* अपोहेत — b) Lo^{1} स्तेयकृद् द्विजः; GMd^{1} Pu^{5} Pu^{7} [*Jolly* G] नरः — c) Bo °गमनीयत्तु; sOx^{1} sPu^{6} °गमनं चैव; wKt^{1} BKt^{5} Ox^{2} Pu^{10} च — d) wKt^{3} Lo^{2} GMd^{1} NNg oOr sOx^{1} sPu^{6} Tr^{1} Wa व्रतैरेतैरपानु°; Pu^{10} °भिरुपानुदेत्; Lo^{2} °भिरुपनुदेत्

सख्युः पुत्रस्य च स्त्रीषु कुमारीष्वन्त्यजासु च ॥१७१॥
पैतृष्वसेयीं भगिनीं स्वस्रीयां मातुरेव च ।
मातुश्च भ्रातुराप्तस्य गत्वा चान्द्रायणं चरेत् ॥१७२॥
एतास्तिस्रस्तु भार्यार्थे नोपयच्छेत बुद्धिमान् ।
ज्ञातित्वेनानुपेयास्ताः पतति ह्युपयन्नधः ॥१७३॥
अमानुषीषु पुरुष उदक्यायामयोनिषु ।
रेतः सिक्त्वा जले चैव कृच्छ्रं सांतपनं चरेत् ॥१७४॥
मैथुनं तु समासेव्य पुंसि योषिति वा द्विजः ।
गोयानेऽप्सु दिवा चैव सवासाः स्नानमाचरेत् ॥१७५॥

171. Cited by *Apa* 1118; *Mādh* 2.252, 264 — a) GMd^{1} °तल्पं व्रतं — b) Bo Tj^{1} Tr^{1} सिक्ता; BKt^{5} सक्त्विाश्च योनिषु — c) TMd^{3} पुत्रिषु; TMd^{4} पुत्रस्य भर्तृषु; Tr^{1} पुत्रस्य पत्नीषु; oOr पुत्रस्य च तथा — d) BKt^{5} °ष्वन्तजासु

172. Omitted in Hy; pādas a-b omitted in BBe^{2}. Cited by *Viś* 3.254; *Apa* 1118; *Lakṣ* 2.10; *Dev* 1.187, 189; *Mādh* 1.470 — a) *Lakṣ* पितृ°; Tr^{2} पैत्र°; NKt^{4} पैत्रि°; sOx^{1} पैतृस्वस्रीयीं; sPu^{6} पैतृश्वश्रेयीं; BCa पैतृस्वस्रेयीं; Bo पैतृव्यसेयीं; La^{1} पैतृस्वश्रीयां; Lo^{1} NPu^{1} Pu^{5} Pu^{7} पितृष्वस्रेयीं; Lo^{2} पितृस्वस्रेयीं; oOr Pu^{2} Pu^{4} पितृष्वस्तेयीं; Be^{1} पितृष्वस्रेय; NKt^{4} भगिनीं च — b) Bo स्वस्रीयं; Tr^{1} स्वस्रियं; Tr^{2} स्वस्रियां; Lo^{2} oOr स्वस्रेयां; Be^{1} NNg स्वस्रेयीं; wKt^{3} स्वस्रयीं; MTr^{4} स्वस्रयां; Pu^{5} Pu^{7} स्वश्रीयां; Ox^{2} श्वश्रेयीं; GMd^{5} स्वस्त्रीया; GMy स्वस्त्रियं; wKt^{1} स्वप्रीयां; Lo^{2} वा — c) MTr^{6} मातुश्च मातुराप्तस्य; TMd^{3} मातृश्च; NKt^{4} oOr Pu^{5} Pu^{7} [*Jolly* G] भ्रातुराप्तश्च; TMd^{3} GMy Tr^{1} MTr^{4} [*Jolly* Nd Gr] *Apa Nd* भ्रातुराप्तां च; La^{1} भ्रातुराप्रांश्च; Jm Jo^{1} Kt^{2} *Mandlik KSS* भ्रातुस्तनयां

173. Omitted in GMd^{1} [haplo]. Cited by *Apa* 1118; *Lakṣ* 2.10; *Dev* 1.187, 189, 190; pādas a-b cited by *Mādh* 1.470, and pādas c-d by *Apa* 79 — a) Be^{1} Pu^{10} एताः स्त्रियस्तु; TMd^{3} एतास्सर्वास्तु; Be^{1} BBe^{2} BCa wKt^{1} wKt^{3} La^{1} TMd^{4} Pu^{2} Pu^{4} Pu^{5} Pu^{7} Pu^{10} भार्यार्थं — b) Be^{1} नोपगच्छेत्सुबुद्धिमान्; Tr^{2} °यच्छेत्; Hy Jm Jo^{1} Kt^{2} Tj^{2} *Mandlik Jha KSS Dave* °यच्छेत्तु; BKt^{5} °गच्छेत; BBe^{2} La^{1} °गच्छेत्तु; oOr °सर्पेत — c) Be^{1} BBe^{2} wKt^{1} Lo^{3} Tj^{1} ज्ञातेयेनानु°; wKt^{3} ज्ञातयेनानु°; Tr^{1} ज्ञातेयानानु°; GMy ज्ञातिर्येनानु°; Pu^{5} Pu^{7} ज्ञातयोनानु°; TMd^{3} ज्ञातेयोनानु°; MTr^{4} MTr^{6} ज्ञातयोनुपे°; BKt^{5} ज्ञातित्वेचात्वपे°; *Apa* 79 °त्वेनाभ्युपे°; Lo^{1} °त्वेनावरोधेयास्ताः; *Apa* 79 [vl] °त्वेनान्वयेयास्ताः — d) GMy पतन्ति ह्युभयन्नरः; Tj^{1} पतितस्त्वपयन्नधः; BKt^{5} Lo^{2} Ox^{2} पतन्ति; Lo^{1} पतत्युपय°; NNg ह्यपय°; Lo^{3} त्वापय°; Be^{1} ह्यपयत्रधः; *Lakṣ* ह्युपयन्निमाः; Pu^{10} ह्युभयादधः

174. Omitted in GMd^{1}. Cited by *Apa* 1149; *Mādh* 2.272 — a) NNg Pu^{5} Pu^{7} अमानुषीष्वनङ्गेषु; *Me* [pāṭha] पीत्वाधरं पुरुष; Be^{1} TMd^{4} अमानुषेषु; GMd^{5} अमानुषुषु; TMd^{4} पुरुषे; Tr^{1} पुरुषं; *Mādh* गोवर्जम् — a-b) *Bh* [pāṭha] अमानुषीष्वनग्रे च पैशाच्यां चैव योषिति — b) Lo^{3} उदक्यानाम° — c) Wa रेतसः; Bo Ho Tj^{1} Tr^{1} सिक्ता; oOr तले; [*Jolly* M] कुले; *Bh* [pāṭha] *Me* [pāṭha] जले खे च [cf. *ViDh* 53.4]; wKt^{3} चैवं — d) GMd^{5} सांतापनं; GMy तरेत्; La^{1} स्मृतः

175. Omitted in NNg Tr^{2} [haplo]. Cited by *Mādh* 2.276 — a) Be^{1} Lo^{2} च; wKt^{1} समासेव्यं; Ho समासेद्य; Lo^{2} समासज्य; TMd^{4} समासीन्य; *Mādh* समारोप्य; Be^{1} समाख्येयं — b) Pu^{5} Pu^{7} पुंस; Bo पुंस्त्री; Pu^{10} योक्षिति; TMd^{4} वो — c) Pu^{10} गोयानेस्तु दिवा यैव; oOr योऽकालेप्सु; Be^{1} दिवा रात्रौ; GMd^{1} दिवापि वा — d) Hy सवाप्ताः; Bo La^{1} सर्वासां

GMd^{1} MTr^{6} omit pādas b and d making a half-verse of pādas a and c and gives the following as the second half-verse:

स्नात्वा वस्त्रैर्जपित्वाप्याः प्राणायामेन शुध्यति ॥

चण्डालान्त्यस्त्रियो गत्वा भुक्त्वा च प्रतिगृह्य च ।
पतत्यज्ञानतो विप्रो ज्ञानात्साम्यं तु गच्छति ॥१७६॥
विप्रदुष्टां स्त्रियं भर्ता निरुन्ध्यादेकवेश्मनि ।
यत्पुंसः परदारेषु तच्चैनां चारयेद्व्रतम् ॥१७७॥
सा चेत्पुनः प्रदुष्येत सदृशेनोपमन्त्रिता ।
कृच्छ्रं चान्द्रायणं चैव तदस्याः पावनं स्मृतम् ॥१७८॥
यत्करोत्येकरात्रेण वृषलीसेवनाद् द्विजः ।
तद्भैक्षभुग्जपन्नित्यं त्रिभिर्वर्षैर्व्यपोहति ॥१७९॥

176. Cited by *Viś* 3.257; *Vij* 3.260; *Apa* 1046, 1121; *Har*-A 1.28.11; *Mādh* 2.88 — a) BBe[2] Bo Hy Jm Jo[2] wKt[1] wKt[3] Lo[1] Lo[2] Lo[3] Lo[4] oOr Ox[2] Pu[3] Pu[10] Tj[1] [*Jolly* M[2-4-5] G R] *Vij* चाण्डा°; Tr[2] चाण्डालोत्य°; Ho चाण्डालानां स्त्रियो; Pu[5] Pu[7] चाण्डालस्य स्त्रियं; Tr[1] चण्डालायास्त्रियो; Wa °स्त्रियं — b) Bo Ho sOx[1] Tj[1] Tr[1] भुक्ता; TMd[3] कृत्वा; Bo भुक्त्वा प्रति° — c) GMd[1] °ज्ञानतो गत्वा — d) GMd[5] GMy °त्सम्यं; Ho Pu[2] Pu[5] Pu[7] च; Lo[2] यच्छति

177. Verses 177 and 178 placed afer 179 in GMy; pāda-d omitted in oOr. Cited by *Viś* 3.254; *Apa* 98, 1124; pādas a-b cited by *Dev* 3.569; *Mādh* 2.176, and pādas c-d by *Viś* 3.256; *Vij* 1.70, 3.275 — a) Pu[2] Pu[4] प्रदुष्यन्ति स्त्रियं — b) Be[1] Bo Tj[1] निरुध्या°; Wa निरध्या°; TMd[4] निरुन्ध्यामेक°; TMd[3] °देव वेश्मनि — c) Bo TMd[3] यः पुंसः; sOx[1] sPu[6] यत्पुंसं; NKt[4] पारदा°; oOr परदारे च — d) Lo[1] न चैनां; GMy चोरये°; BBe[2] wKt[3] Lo[4] कारये°; Pu[10] वरये°; Hy चारद्व्रतं

Two additonal verses in NPu[1] [for first verse see under 178]:

प्रायश्चित्तार्धमर्हन्ति स्त्रियो रोगिण एव च ।
बालाश्च षोडशाद्वर्षादशीतिपरतः पुमान् ॥

178. Pāda-a omitted in oOr. Cited by *Viś* 3.250, 254; *Apa* 1125 — a) La[1] या; Be[1] Hy Jm Jo[1] Kt[2] wKt[3] Lo[4] Ox[2] Tj[2] Tr[2] [*Jolly* Nd M[4]] *Mandlik Jha KSS Dave* प्रदुष्येत्तु; BBe[2] प्रनश्येत्तु; TMd[3] GMd[5] GMy Tr[1] MTr[4] संप्रदुष्येत् — b) Be[1] सदृशो°; Pu[10] सदृश्ये°; Pu[10] [*Jolly* M[1-2-5-9]] °नानुमन्त्रिता; MTr[4] °मन्त्रिताः; TMd[3] °मन्त्रितः; *Apa* °मन्त्रितं; BBe[2] Bo BCa Ho Hy Jm Jo[1] Jo[2] wKt[1] Kt[2] La[1] Lo[3] Lo[4] [*but cor*] GMy sOx[1] Ox[2] sPu[6] Pu[8] Tj[1] Tj[2] Tr[2] [*Jolly* M[4] Nd R] *Nd Rn Rc Mandlik KSS* °यन्त्रिता; Lo[1] °यन्त्रितां; BKt[5] °यन्तृणा — c) Bo wKt[3] कृच्छ्र; Lo[2] °यणे चैते — d) TMd[3] पावनिं; GMd[1] पावनं भवेत्

Additional verse in Be[1] *Mandlik* [ञ, ट, ड] *KSS Dave;* given after 176 in NPu[1]; cited by *Vij* 1.72:

ब्राह्मणक्षत्रियविशां भार्याः शूद्रेण संगताः ।
अप्रजाता विशुध्येयुः प्रायश्चित्तेन नेतराः ॥

b) NPu[1] *Mandlik KSS Dave* स्त्रियः शूद्रेण; *Mandlik KSS Dave* शूद्रेपसङ्गताः — c) *Vij* विशुध्यन्ति

Additional verses in Pu[1]:

माता मातृस्वसा स्वश्रू मातुलाणी पितृष्वसा ।
पितृव्यसखिशिष्यस्त्री भगिनी त [?] सखी स्नुषा ॥
दुहिता चार्यभार्या च सगोत्रा शरणागता ।
राज्ञी प्रव्रजिता साध्वी धात्री वर्णोत्तमा तु या ॥

179. Cited by *Mādh* 2.251 — a) BBe[2] Bo GMd[1] TMd[3] MTr[4] MTr[6] यः करो° — b) BKt[5] Lo[1] GMd[1] TMd[3] TMd[4] sOx[1] sPu[6] Tr[2] MTr[4] MTr[6] *Mādh*° सेवनं; GMd[5] °सवनाद्; GMy °संगतं; Tr[1]

एषा पापकृतामुक्ता चतुर्णामपि निष्कृतिः ।
पतितैः संप्रयुक्तानामिमाः शृणुत निष्कृतीः ॥१८०॥
संवत्सरेण पतति पतितेन सहाचरन् ।
याजनाध्यापनाद्यौनान्न तु यानासनाशनात् ॥१८१॥
यो येन पतितेनैषां संसर्गं याति मानवः ।
स तस्यैव व्रतं कुर्यात् तत्संसर्गविशुद्धये ॥१८२॥
पतितस्योदकं कार्यं सपिण्डैर्बान्धवैः सहः ।
निन्दितेऽहनि सायाह्ने ज्ञात्यृत्विग्गुरुसंनिधौ ॥१८३॥
दासी घटमपां पूर्णं पर्यस्येत् प्रेतवत्पदा ।
अहोरात्रमुपासीरन्नशौचं बान्धवैः सह ॥१८४॥
निवर्तेरंश्च तस्मात्तु संभाषणसहासने ।

°संगमा; Pu^{3} द्विजा: — c) Be^{1} BKt^{5} Ox^{2} Pu^{2} Pu^{4} Pu^{5} Pu^{7} तद्भैक्ष्य°; Tr^{2} तद्भैक्षे°; Bo Pu^{10} तद्भक्ष°; TMd^{3} *Mādh* स भैक्ष°; Wa °भुज्जपेन्नित्यं; Pu^{10} °भुज्जपं नित्यं; GMd^{1} MTr^{4} MTr^{6} °भुज्जपात्राप्यास्त्रिभि°; GMy °भुज्जपत्राप्यस्त्रिभि° — d) Tj^{2} *Bh* [pāṭha] त्रिभिर्मासैर्व्य°; GMd^{1} °पैरपोहति; *Mādh* °पोहिति

180. Verses 180 and 181 transposed in Wa — a) Jo^{1} Kt^{2} एषां; Lo^{2} NNg NPu^{1} Pu^{2} Pu^{4} Pu^{5} Pu^{7} MTr^{4} MTr^{6} Wa [*Jolly* M^{3-4-5}] एता:; GMd^{1} [*but cor*] Tr^{2} एता; NKt^{4} एतै:; Lo^{1} °वृतामुक्ता; BBe^{2} °कृतां युत्त्या; NKt^{4} NNg NPu^{1} Pu^{5} Pu^{7} Pu^{10} MTr^{4} MTr^{6} Wa °मुक्ताश्चतु° — b) sOx^{1} sPu^{6} चातुर्वर्ण्यस्य निष्कृति:; TMd^{3} चतुर्णामिह; Bo NKt^{4} Lo^{2} Pu^{5} Pu^{7} Wa निष्कृती:; NNg नि:कृती:; Tr^{2} नि:कृता:; Pu^{10} निष्कृतां — d) BBe^{2} GMd^{1} TMd^{3} GMd^{5} GMy oOr Tr^{1} MTr^{4} MTr^{6} [*Jolly* Nd] °नामिमां शृणुत निष्कृतिं; TMd^{4} °नामिहेमां श्रुणु निष्कृतिं; Be^{1} Pu^{10} Wa निष्कृति:

181. Cited by *Viś* 3.257; *Vij* 3.261; *Apa* 1087; *Har*-A 1.21.5; pādas a-b cited by *Viś* 3.257 — b) NNg पतितै: सह संचरन्; Bo GMd^{1} GMd^{5} sOx^{1} Tr^{1} MTr^{4} MTr^{6} [*Jolly* Gr Nd] *Viś GDh* 21.3 *BDh* 2.2.35 समाचरन्; BKt^{5} समं चरन्; GMy समाचरेत् — c) sOx^{1} sPu^{6} °ध्यापनीयौ°; TMd^{4} °पनात्सर्वा न; Be^{1} Pu^{5} Wa °द्योनान्न — d) BBe^{2} °द्यौनादेकशय्याशयाशनात्; Ox^{2} च; Be^{1} Bo Ho sOx^{1} Pu^{5} sPu^{6} Pu^{7} MTr^{5} MTr^{6} यानाशनासनात्; wKt^{1} NKt^{4} Lo^{1} यानासनासनात्; Lo^{4} यानाशनाशनात्; Tr^{2} यानासनातात्; Jo^{2} Lo^{3} TMd^{3} Ox^{2} Tj^{1} Tr^{1} शय्यासनाशनात् [TMd^{3} °नासनात्]

182. Cited by *Viś* 3.257 [twice]; *Vij* 3.261; *Mādh* 2.23 — a) wKt^{3} योगेन पति°; TMd^{4} °तेनैषा — c) TMd^{3} तस्यैप; Tr^{2} तु तं कुर्यात् — d) Bo Lo^{4} Pu^{5} Pu^{7} [*Jolly* M$^{4-5}$] तत्संसर्गस्य शुद्धये; BKt^{5} TMd^{3} TMd^{4} GMy Tr^{1} संसर्गस्य विशुद्धये; GMd^{5} संसर्गस्य च शुद्धये; Tj^{1} तत्संसर्गं

183.* Pādas b-d omitted in Lo^{4}. Cited by *Vij* 3.294; *Apa* 1206 — a) MTr^{6} °स्योदकं दद्यात् — b) GMy सापिण्डै°; Be^{1} BBe^{2} BCa Hy Jm Jo^{1} Jo^{2} wKt^{1} Kt^{2} wKt^{3} Lo^{1} Lo^{3} GMd^{1} NPu^{1} Pu^{2} Pu^{3} Pu^{4} Pu^{8} Tj^{1} Tj^{2} Wa *Vij Apa Mandlik Jha KSS Dave* °र्बान्धवैर्बहि:; wKt^{1} °र्ब्राह्मणैर्बहि:; Lo^{2} °र्बान्धवै: समं — c) TMd^{3} निर्हृतेहनि — d) *Apa* ज्ञातर्त्विग्गुरु°

184. Cited by *Vij* 3.294 — a) wKt^{3} चूर्णं — b) BCa पर्यसेत्; NKt^{4} पर्यस्यान्; GMd^{5} Tr^{1} MTr^{4} प्रास्य तु; TMd^{3} MTr^{6} प्राश्य तु; Lo^{2} *Nā* प्रेत्यव° [*Nā* pāṭha as in ed.]; Be^{1} Ho Lo^{3} TMd^{3} TMd^{4} GMy oOr Ox^{2} Pu^{8} Tj^{1} Tr^{2} [*Jolly* R] °वत्सदा; Jm BKt^{5} GMd^{1} NPu^{1} Pu^{2} Pu^{4} Pu^{5} Pu^{7} Wa [*Jolly* M^{2-8-9}] *Nā* °वत्तदा; Bo °वद्यदा — c) Bo Tr^{2} °पासीनन्न° — c-d) sOx^{1} sPu^{6} °मुपासीत न शौचं; NKt^{4} Lo^{3} Tj^{1} °मुपासीनं नाशौचं [Lo^{3} °पासीरं] — d) La^{1} GMd^{5} NNg oOr NPu^{1} Pu^{5} Pu^{7} Tr^{1} Wa *Vij* °रन्नाशौचं

दायाद्यस्य प्रदानं च यात्रा चैव हि लौकिकी ॥१८५॥
ज्येष्ठता च निवर्तेत ज्येष्ठावाप्यं च यद्धनम् ।
ज्येष्ठांशं प्राप्नुयाच्चास्य यवीयान् गुणतोऽधिकः ॥१८६॥
प्रायश्चित्ते तु चरिते पूर्णकुम्भमपां नवम् ।
तेनैव सार्धं प्रास्येयुः स्नात्वा पुण्ये जलाशये ॥१८७॥
स त्वप्सु तं घटं प्रास्य प्रविश्य भवनं स्वकम् ।
सर्वाणि ज्ञातिकार्याणि यथापूर्वं समाचरेत् ॥१८८॥
एतमेव विधिं कुर्याद् योषित्सु पतितास्वपि ।
वस्त्रान्नपानं देयं तु वसेयुश्च गृहान्तिके ॥१८९॥

185.* Omitted in Tr^{2}; pādas a-b omitted in GMy. Cited by *Vij* 3.294; *Lakṣ* 2.424— a) Ho TMd^{4} sOx^{1} sPu^{6} *Vij* निवर्तेरंस्ततस्तस्मात् [preferred by Bühler]; TMd^{3} निवृत्तेरंश्च; [*Jolly* M$^{8-9}$] निवर्तयेरंश्च; *Nā* [pāṭha] न कुर्वीत for निवर्तेरन्; Be^{1} BKt^{5} Lo^{3} Lo^{4} GMd^{5} NNg oOr Tj^{1} [*Jolly* M$^{4-5}$] °रंस्तु; BKt^{5} तस्माच्च; Lo^{4} [*Jolly* M$^{4-5}$] तस्मात्तत्; Ox^{2} Pu^{10} तस्मात् [*om* तु] — b) Ox^{2} NPu^{1} Pu^{3} Pu^{8} Pu^{10} Wa °सहासनैः; sOx^{1} sPu^{6} °सहायने — c) NNg प्रदानां; wKt^{1} प्रदोषं; oOr प्रदानं स्याद्; wKt^{1} हि — d) Be^{1} Bo Ho BKt^{5} La^{1} Lo^{4} TMd^{3} GMd^{5} GMy sOx^{1} Ox^{2} Pu^{5} sPu^{6} Pu^{7} Pu^{10} Tr^{1} MTr^{4} MTr^{6} Wa [*Jolly* M G N Nd] *Vij Jolly* यात्रामेव च लौकिकीं [Wa हि; TMd^{3} GMy लौकिकं; Pu^{10} लौकिकिं]; *Lakṣ* पात्रमेव च लौकिकी; oOr यात्रा एव च; wKt^{3} यात्रावहि; Lo^{1} चैवेह; GMd^{1} चैव च; TMd^{4} चैव तु; Tj^{1} लौकिकि; GMd^{1} लौकिकीं

186. Folios containing 11.186–229 missing in Tr^{1}. Omitted in Bo Pu^{10} — a) TMd^{3} तु BKt^{5} त; Tr^{2} चानिव°; Pu^{5} Pu^{7} [*Jolly* G] न निव°; TMd^{4} तन्निव°; NPu^{1} Pu^{4} विनिव°; Kt^{2} GMy निवर्तेते; NKt^{4} निर्वर्तन्त — b) Pu^{3} जैष्ठा°; Lo^{1} ज्येष्ठवाप्यं; Pu^{5} Pu^{7} ज्येष्ठंप्राप्यं; GMd^{1} ज्येष्ठभाव्यं; MTr^{6} ज्येष्ठभावं; Be^{1} ज्येष्ठेणाप्यं; Tr^{2} ज्यैष्ठ्यावाप्यं; Ox^{2} ज्यैष्ठ्याद्वाप्यं; Lo^{1} Tr^{2} तु; La^{1} MTr^{6} तद्धनं; Be^{1} wKt^{3} Lo^{4} sOx^{1} Ox^{2} Pu^{3} sPu^{6} Pu^{8} Tr^{2} [*Jolly* M G] *Me Jolly Jha Dave* यद्वसु; Pu^{5} Pu^{7} तद्वसु; TMd^{3} बन्धनं — c) Pu^{3} ज्यैष्ठांशं; Ox^{2} ज्यैष्ठ्यांशं; GMd^{1} ज्येष्ठता प्रा°; Tr^{2} ज्येष्ठ्यं प्रा°; BBe^{2} wKt^{3} चाप्नुया°; BKt^{5} नाप्नुया°; Jo^{2} Lo^{3} TMd^{3} GMy Tj^{1} [*Jolly* M^{2} Nd R Gr] *Jolly* °यात्तस्य; TMd^{4} °यादस्य; Ox^{2} °याद्वास्य; Pu^{3} Tr^{2} °याच्चैव — d) wKt^{1} यवीयांस्तु गुणाधिकः; oOr °गुणोगुणाः; GMy °धिकं

187. Cited by *Viś* 3.291; *Vij* 3.295; *Lakṣ* 2.424 — a) *Viś* चरितव्रत आयते; Pu^{2} °श्चित्तेनुचरिते; oOr च — b) wKt^{1} कुम्भं पूणमपां नवं; NNg Pu^{5} Pu^{7} *Vij* पूर्णं; La^{1} नवां; Pu^{2} Pu^{4} नवः — c) BBe^{2} La^{1} Lo^{1} Lo^{4} Tj^{1} प्राश्येयुः; TMd^{3} प्राश्चयेयुः; *Lakṣ* प्राश्यश्च; Be^{1} प्रापयेयुः; Bo प्राणेयुः — d) Bo BCa Jo^{2} Lo^{1} Lo^{2} Lo^{3} Pu^{5} Pu^{7} Tj^{1} पुण्य; Pu^{5} Pu^{7} जलाशयो

188. Omitted in Pu^{10}. Cited by *Lakṣ* 2.424 — a) wKt^{3} स तं त्वप्सु घटं प्रास्य; Ox^{2} सत्स्वप्सु; La^{1} सर्वेप्सु; BBe^{2} *om* तं; BBe^{2} BKt^{5} La^{1} GMd^{5} Pu^{2} Pu^{4} Pu^{5} Pu^{7} प्राश्य — b) Pu^{2} Pu^{4} भुवनं प्रविश्य; Bo विप्रस्य भवनं; Ox^{2} विप्रस्तु भवनं; sOx^{1} Pu^{5} sPu^{6} Pu^{7} भुवनं; Jm सुकं; BBe^{2} सुखं— c) GMd^{5} सर्वाणीति च कार्याणि; GMd^{1} ज्ञात°; Lo^{1} ज्ञान°; *Lakṣ* प्रेतकर्माणि

189. Omitted in BKt^{5} [haplo]. Cited by *Viś* 3.250, 292; *Apa* 99; *Lakṣ* 2.424; *Dev* 3.579, 680 — a) *Viś* एप एव विधिः कार्यो; Be^{1} BCa Ho Lo^{1} Lo^{4} NPu^{1} Wa [*Jolly* M^{3-4-5} Ku] *Dev* एवमेव; Jm Jo^{1} TMd^{3} TMd^{4} GMd^{5} oOr sOx^{1} Pu^{5} sPu^{6} Pu^{7} [*Jolly* G] *Viś* 3.250 *Vij* एतदेव; Jm TMd^{3} TMd^{4} GMd^{5} GMy oOr Pu^{5} Pu^{7} MTr^{4} *Viś* 3.250 *Vij* व्रतं कुर्याद्; *Vij* 3.260 कार्यं — b) *Lakṣ* योषित्स्वपतितास्वपि; NPu^{1} पापित्सु; Ox^{2} पतितासु च — c) GMd^{5} GMy MTr^{4} MTr^{6} *Viś Apa Lakṣ Dev* वस्त्रान्नमासां देयं तु; Lo^{2} NNg देयं तासां तु वस्त्रान्नं; TMd^{4} वस्त्रान्नंपानं; GMd^{1} TMd^{3} °न्नमांसं; La^{1} °न्नमासा;

एनस्विभिरनिर्णिक्तैर्नार्थं किंचित्समाचरेत् ।
कृतनिर्णेजनांश्चैनान्न जुगुप्सेत कर्हिचित् ॥१९०॥
बालघ्नांश्च कृतघ्नांश्च विशुद्धानपि धर्मतः ।
शरणागतहन्तॄंश्च स्त्रीहन्तॄंश्च न संवसेत् ॥१९१॥
येषां द्विजानां सावित्री नानूच्येत यथाविधि ।
तांश्चारयित्वा त्रीन्कृच्छ्रान् यथाविध्युपनाययेत् ॥१९२॥
प्रायश्चित्तं चिकीर्षन्ति विकर्मस्थास्तु ये द्विजाः ।
ब्रह्मणा च परित्यक्तास्तेषामप्येतदादिशेत् ॥१९३॥
यद्गर्हितेनार्जयन्ति कर्मणा ब्राह्मणा धनम् ।
तस्योत्सर्गेण शुध्यन्ति जप्येन तपसैव च ॥१९४॥

Pu^{2} Pu^{4} °न्नपावनं; Pu^{5} Pu^{7} °पान; sOx^{1} sPu^{6} °पानमादेयं वसे°; Ox^{2} Pu^{3} Tr^{2} च — d) NNg वासयेयुर्गृहान्तिके; *Apa* वसेयुस्तु; Lo^{4} विशेयुश्च; Ox^{2} गृहान्तिकं

190.* Pādas a-b omitted in BKt^{5}. Cited by *Lakṣ* 2.424; pādas a-b cited by *Vij* 3.261 — a) GMy एनस्वभि°; Tr^{2} एवमेभि°; Lo^{1} *cor to* एतैः स्वैःभि°; Bo Lo^{3} Tj^{1} एतस्त्रिभि°; TMd^{4} सस्त्वेभि°; wKt^{1} °नियुक्तै°; BBe^{2} °निर्युक्तै°; Pu^{4} °निर्णिक्तं नार्थं — b) Pu^{5} Pu^{7} °र्नार्यं; Lo^{3} °र्नाक्तं; oOr °र्नान्यं; Be^{1} Lo^{1} NNg sOx^{1} Pu^{4} sPu^{6} Wa [*Jolly* G R M^{4}] *Vij ViDh*54.31 कंचि°; GMy कश्चि°; GMd^{1} MTr^{6} °चिच्चरेत्सह; Hy Jo^{1} Kt^{2} NPu^{1} Pu^{3} Tj^{2} [*Jolly* Nd Ku] *Go Ku Lakṣ Mandlik Jha KSS Dave* °चित्सहाचरेत्; Ox^{2} °चित्समाश्रयेत् — c) Pu^{4} °जकांश्चैनान्न; Pu^{2} °जकां चैनान्न; Be^{1} Bo Ho Jo^{2} Lo^{1} NNg sOx^{1} Ox^{2} Pu^{3} sPu^{6} Tr^{2} Wa [*Jolly* M R Nd] *Jolly Jha Dave ViDh* 54.32 °जनांश्चैतान्न; NKt^{4} Lo^{4} Pu^{10} GMd^{5} GMy MTr^{4} MTr^{5} MTr^{6} °जनांश्चैनां न; GMd^{1} °जकांस्त्वेतान्न; *Lakṣ* °जतांस्त्वेतान्न; BCa Hy Jm Jo^{1} wKt^{1} Kt^{2} oOr Pu^{5} Pu^{7} Tj^{2} [*Jolly* G] *Mandlik KSS* °जनांश्चैव न — c-d) Tj^{1} °जनांश्चैव तान्जुगुप्सेत; BKt^{5} °जनांश्चैव जुगुप्सेत न — d) Jm गुप्सेत न कर्हिचित्; TMd^{4} जुगुप्सित

191. Cited by *Apa* 1209; *Mādh* 2.155— a) GMy [*Jolly* Nd] बालघ्नं च कृतघ्नं च; GMd^{5} बालश्च कृतघ्नश्च; TMd^{3} TMd^{4} बालघ्नां च कृतघ्नां च; MTr^{4} MTr^{6} ब्रह्मघ्नांश्च; Pu^{5} Tr^{2} *om* कृतघ्नांश्च — b) La^{1} विशुद्धांश्चापि; TMd^{4} GMd^{5} [*Jolly* Nd] विशुद्धावपि; TMd^{3} विशुध्यादपि — c) TMd^{3} GMy °हर्तांश्च — d) NNg *ma sh* स्त्रीहन्तृंश्च; GMy स्त्रीहरुंश्च; TMd^{3} स्त्रीहर्तृंश्च; wKt^{1} संवदेत्; Lo^{2} संविशेत्; *Apa* [vl] संपिबेत्

192. Pādas a-b omitted in oOr. Cited by *Viś* 3.262; *Vij* 3.265; *Apa* 1107; *Mādh* 2.433 — a) Lo^{1} Lo^{3} TMd^{3} GMd^{5} GMy Tj^{1} एषां; Tj^{1} सावित्रीं — b) Lo^{1} Ox^{2} नानूचेत; BKt^{5} नाद्युचेत; Bo NKt^{4} *Apa* [vl] नानूद्येत; BBe^{2} नानूत्येत; Pu^{2} Pu^{4} नावाह्येत; Lo^{2} नातन्येत; wKt^{1} नानृत्येत; TMd^{3} कास्यच्येत — c) Lo^{1} तांश्चरित्वा; TMd^{3} त्रीन्कृच्छ्रं — d) Pu^{2} Pu^{4} °विध्यापना°; NKt^{4} Lo^{1} °नापयेत्; Lo^{4} oOr Tj^{1} °नानयेत्; Bo °नोपयेत्; Tr^{2} °नायते — TMd^{4} jumps here to 12.25, and 11.193 to 12.24 are omitted

193. Cited by *Viś* 3.262; *Apa* 1107 — a) Tr^{2} °र्षन्ती — b) Be^{1} BBe^{2} BKt^{5} La^{1} Lo^{1} oOr Ox^{2} NPu^{1} Pu^{2} Pu^{4} Pu^{8} *Apa* °स्थाश्च; GMy °स्थायास्तु; TMd^{3} °स्था तु यो; BKt^{5} द्विजः — c) Bo La^{1} Lo^{2} TMd^{3} NPu^{1} ब्राह्मणा; MTr^{4} MTr^{6} ब्राह्मण्ये; Tr^{2} ब्रह्मणश्च; oOr ब्राह्मणाश्च; GMd^{5} ब्राह्मण्याच्च; Pu^{5} Pu^{7} ब्राह्मणाच्च; Pu^{2} Pu^{4} कर्मणा च; TMd^{3} हि; Pu^{10} ते परि° — d) Pu^{2} Pu^{4} °स्तेषामाद्यदमाविशेत्; TMd^{4} °दादिशत्; BBe^{2} TMd^{3} oOr °दाविशेत्; MTr^{6} °दाचरेत्

194. Cited by *Vij* 3.289; *Apa* 929, 1150 — a) Wa य गर्हि°; Ox^{2} ये गर्हि°; Ox^{2} NPu^{1} °र्हितेनार्चयन्ति; Lo^{1} °र्हितेनार्थयन्ति; TMd^{4} °र्हितेन जायन्ते; Jo^{1} °र्हितेनार्जयं; Bo GMy °र्जयति — a-b) Tr^{2} यद्गर्हिते कर्मणा च ब्राह्मणा यद्यमस्मृतं — b) La^{1} ब्राह्मणाः कर्मसाधनं; Ho sOx^{1} sPu^{6} ब्राह्मणाः कर्मणा; wKt^{3} ब्राह्मणा ब्राह्मणा; BKt^{5} Lo^{4} ब्रह्मणा; wKt^{1} ब्राह्मणो; NKt^{4} धना — c) *Apa* 1150 तदुत्सर्गेण — d)

जपित्वा त्रीणि सावित्र्याः सहस्राणि समाहितः ।
मासं गोष्ठे पयः पीत्वा मुच्यतेऽसत्प्रतिग्रहात् ॥१९५॥
उपवासकृशं तं तु गोव्रजात्पुनरागतम् ।
प्रणतं परिपृच्छेयुः साम्यं सौम्येच्छसीति किम् ॥१९६॥
सत्यमुक्त्वा तु विप्रेषु विकिरेद्यवसं गवाम् ।
गोभिः प्रवर्तिते तीर्थे कुर्युस्तस्य परिग्रहम् ॥१९७॥
व्रात्यानां याजनं कृत्वा परेषामन्त्यकर्म च ।
अभिचारमहीनं च त्रिभिः कृच्छ्रैर्विशुध्यति ॥१९८॥
शरणागतं परित्यज्य वेदं विप्लाव्य च द्विजः ।
संवत्सरं यवाहारस्तत्पापमपसेधति ॥१९९॥
श्वसृगालखरैर्दष्टो ग्राम्यैः क्रव्याद्भिरेव च ।
नराश्वोष्ट्रवराहैश्च प्राणायामेन शुध्यति ॥२००॥

NKt[4] Pu[5] Pu[7] जाप्येन; Lo[2] NNg Pu[4] MTr[4] *Apa* [vl at 929as in ed] जपेन; TMd[3] जपेति; BBe[2] तपसेन; oOr तपसापि; BKt[5] GMd[1] oOr वा; BCa wKt[1] Pu[8] तु

195. Cited by *Viś* 3.284; *Vij* 3.289; *Mādh* 2.430 — a) *Viś* जप्त्वा तु त्रीणि — b) La[1] समाहिताः — c) Pu[2] Pu[4] मांसं; Be[1] सायं; Jm गोष्ठी — d) Wa मुच्यन्ते; Be[1] TMd[3] °सत्परिग्रहात्

196. a) Lo[1] Wa उपवासं; Lo[1] TMd[3] sOx[1] Pu[2] Pu[4] sPu[6] Pu[10] °कृतं; GMy °कृशागं तु; TMd[4] °कृशं संतो; TMd[3] *om* तं — b) Pu[5] Pu[7] गोव्रजात्समुपागतं; GMy नगंव्रजा°; Lo[3] गोत्रजात्पुन°; Tj[1] गोत्रजाः पुन°; MTr[5] गोव्रतात्पुन°; TMd[4] गोव्रजान्पुन°; Be[1] oOr °त्पुनरागमं; Ho °त्पुनागतं — c) Pu[10] प्रणतं स परिच्छेयुः; Kt[2] प्रणतां; oOr ब्राह्मणाः परि°; BBe[2] प्रविपृच्छेयुः; Hy Jm Jo[1] Kt[2] *Mandlik KSS Jha Dave* प्रतिपृच्छेयुः — d) Pu[4] साम्ये सौ°; Tr[2] सौम्ये सौ°; Bo oOr Ox[2] सौम्यं सौ°; TMd[4] सौम्य सौ°; NNg [*but cor fh*] सोम्यं सौ°; NKt[4] स्वाम्यं सौ°; Lo[2] सोम्येच्छ°; GMd[1] साम्येच्छ°; GMd[1] Tj[1] कं

197. Omitted in Be[1]; pādas a-b omitted in Tj[1] — a) La[1] सम्यगुप्ता; Ho Pu[4] °मुक्ता; BBe[2] सुविप्रेषु; Lo[4] GMd[5] GMy Pu[4] Pu[10] विप्रेभ्यो; BKt[5] विप्रोप्या — a-b) Jo[2] तु विकिरेद्विप्रेषु यवसं — b) La[1] विकरेशुवशंगवं; sOx[1] विकेरद्य°; TMd[3] विकीर्यद्य°; TMd[4] विकिर्येद्य°; Tr[2] व्यकरे यवसं; Ho विदिरे यवसं; Tr[2] गवं — c) wKt[1] TMd[4] प्रवर्तते; GMd[5] प्रवृत्तिते; Pu[10] प्रवर्तेत; GMy प्रकीर्तिते; NNg पवित्रिते — d) Tj[1] [*Jolly* R] कुर्यात्तस्य; Lo[3] कुर्यास्तस्य; Pu[5] Pu[7] [*Jolly* G] कुर्युस्तेस्य; GMd[5] GMy MTr[4] प्रतिग्रहं

198. Cited by *Vij* 3.288; *Apa* 1152; *Mādh* 2.429 — a) TMd[4] भ्रात्रंनां जायिनं; TMd[3] यजनं; BKt[5] याजकं; Pu[10] योजनं; BKt[5] *om* कृत्वा — b) BBe[2] परेषां नित्यकर्म — c) Pu[2] Pu[4] अभीचा°; TMd[3] TMd[4] oOr °महीनां; Tj[1] °महिम्नैति; Lo[3] °महीम्नैति — d) Hy Jm Jo[1] Kt[2] GMd[1] NPu[1] Pu[5] Pu[7] Pu[8] Pu[10] [*Jolly* M[1-2-8-9] G] *Vij Mādh ViDh* 54.25 *Mandlik Jha KSS Dave* कृच्छ्रैर्व्यपोहति; sOx[1] *om* विशुध्यति

199. Cited by *Apa* 1152; *Mādh* 2.442 — a) Pu[5] Pu[7] शरणो°; Ox[2] °गतमुत्सृज्य; TMd[4] °गतं तु संत्यज्य — b) NKt[4] *om* च; Ho Ox[2] *Apa* वा; sOx[1] तु; GMd[5] तद् द्विजः — c) Ho संवत्सर; Hy यवहार°; MTr[4] MTr[6] यवाहारात्तत्पाप° — d) wKt[1] °त्पापं परासधति; Pu[5] Pu[7] °मपपेधति; BBe[2] °मपसेधते; Be[1] Lo[3] Ox[2] Tj[1] Wa °मवसेधति; BCa °मपसेवति; BKt[5] NPu[1] °मपशोधति; NKt[4] °मवशोधति; Pu[2] Pu[4] °मपमार्जति; *Apa* °मपकर्षति

200. Cited by *Vij* 3.277; *Apa* 1135; *Mādh* 2.54 — a) wKt[3] °खलैर्दष्टो; Ox[2] NPu[1] MTr[4] MTr[6] Wa °खरैर्दृष्टो; La[1] °खरैर्दुप्तो — b) [*Jolly* Nd] °ष्टोऽग्राम्यैः [supported by *Nā*]; Lo[2] ग्राम्ये — c) Be[1] Ho

षष्ठान्नकालता मासं संहिताजप एव च ।
होमाश्च शाकला नित्यमपाङ्क्त्यानां विशोधनम् ॥२०१॥
उष्ट्रयानं समारुह्य खरयानं च कामतः ।
स्नात्वा च विप्रो दिग्वासाः प्राणायामेन शुध्यति ॥२०२॥
विनाद्भिरप्सु वाप्यार्तः शारीरं संनिषेव्य तु ।
सचैलो बहिराप्लुत्य गामालभ्य विशुध्यति ॥२०३॥
वेदोदितानां नित्यानां कर्मणां समतिक्रमे ।
स्नातकव्रतलोपे च प्रायश्चित्तमभोजनम् ॥२०४॥
हुंकारं ब्राह्मणस्योक्त्वा त्वंकारं च गरीयसः ।

Lo^4 GMd^1 TMd^3 GMd^5 GMy NNg Pu^3 Pu^5 Pu^7 Pu^{10} Wa °श्चोष्ट्रैर्वरा°; Bo °श्चोष्ट्रौवरा°; Tr^2 °श्चष्ट्रेविहारैश्च — d) Jo^2 Lo^3 Tj^1 °यामैर्विशुध्यति

Additional verse in NNg *Mandlik* [क] *KSS Dave:*

शुनाघ्रातोपलीढस्य दन्तैर्विदलितस्य च ।
अद्भिः प्रक्षालनं प्रोक्तमग्निना चोपचूलनम् ॥

d) NNg वोपचूलनं

201. Omitted in BBe^2 BKt^5 GMd^5 [haplo]. Cited by *Vij* 3.286, 288; *Apa* 1153 — a) Bo षष्ठ्या°; TMd^4 °कातलो; Tj^1 °कानना; La^1 °सनता; La^1 NNg मांसं; Tr^2 मासि — b) sOx^1 °जपमेव; Hy Jm Jo^1 Kt^2 wKt^3 Pu^2 Pu^3 Pu^4 Tj^2 *Vij* 3.286 *Mandlik Jha KSS Dave* वा — c) Pu^7 Pu^{10} होमांश्च; MTr^6 होमश्च; TMd^3 Tr^2 शकला; TMd^4 MTr^6 शाकलो; Tj^1 शाकलान्; Lo^3 शकलान्; Ho शाकल्य; La^1 शषलो; Hy wKt^1 Kt^2 wKt^3 NKt^4 oOr *Mandlik* साकला; Jo^1 *KSS* सकला; MTr^4 साकालो; Pu^2 Pu^4 कालता; Hy नित्यामपा° — d) La^1 TMd^3 Wa °मपङ्क्त्यानां; *Vij* 3.286 °मपाङ्क्तानां; TMd^4 °मपांज्ञाना; MTr^4 MTr^6 °मपज्यानां; Lo^1 °मपांत्याग

202. Omitted in BBe^2 BKt^5 GMd^5. Cited by *Vij* 3.290; *Apa* 1184; *Mādh* 2.443 — a) Tr^2 उष्ट्रायानं; GMd^1 °याने — b) wKt^1 खल°; Pu^5 Pu^7 नर°; sOx^1 sPu^6 खराटनां; TMd^3 खरभानां; oOr चीरयानं; Hy Jm Jo^1 Kt^2 Tj^2 *Mandlik Jha KSS Dave* तु — c) Lo^3 Tj^1 स्नात्वा विप्रो विदिग्वासाः; MTr^4 MTr^6 स्नात्वा सचेलो दिग्वासाः; *Vij Apa Mādh* सवासा जलमाप्लुत्य [*Apa* विवासा]; wKt^3 ज्ञात्वा; Bo Hy Jm Jo^1 Kt^2 NPu^1 Pu^2 Pu^3 Pu^4 Pu^8 Tj^2 Wa *Mandlik Jha KSS Dave* तु; TMd^4 विप्रा दिग्वासः — d) Lo^3 GMd^1 MTr^6 प्राणायामं चरेत्सकृत्; TMd^4 प्राणायामं च; Lo^3 °यामे च

203.* Omitted in wKt^3 Lo^2; page containing verses 202b–205c missing in sPu^6. Cited by *Vij* 3.292; *Apa* 1188; *Mādh* 2.443 — a) Pu^{10} [*Jolly* M] °द्भिरथवाप्यार्तः; BKt^5 चाप्यार्तः; Bo चाप्यार्ताः; oOr वाप्यार्ताः; MTr^4 वाह्यार्तः; MTr^5 MTr^6 वानार्तः; Pu^5 Pu^7 *Apa* वाप्यन्तः; NNg चाप्यन्तः; GMd^1 वात्यन्तं; TMd^3 वाप्युक्त — b) sOx^1 Ox^2 Pu^2 Pu^4 sPu^6 शरीरं; MTr^6 शारीरस्; BCa Jm Jo^1 Jo^2 Kt^2 Lo^3 Tj^1 Tj^2 *Mandlik Jolly KSS* संनिवेश्य; Hy सन्निवेस्य; Tr^2 संनिखव्य; NKt^4 संनिपेप्य; Be^1 Hy Jm Jo^1 Jo^2 Kt^2 wKt^3 Lo^3 Pu^2 Pu^4 Tj^1 Tj^2 [*Jolly* R] *Mandlik KSS Jha Dave* च — c) Hy wKt^1 BKt^5 La^1 Lo^3 TMd^3 TMd^4 GMd^5 GMy oOr Tj^1 Tj^2 MTr^4 MTr^5 MTr^6 [*Jolly* R] *Mādh* सचेलो; Wa सचलो; *Apa* सचैलं; *Mādh* बहुधाप्लुत्य; TMd^4 बहिरावृत्य; MTr^5 जलमाप्लुत्य — d) GMy गामालिङ्गन्य; TMd^3 गामालङ्गन्य; TMd^4 विशुध्यते

204. Omitted in Pu^{10}. Cited by *Vij* 3.292; *Apa* 1188; *Mādh* 2.443; pādas c-d cited by *Har*-A 1.11.17; *Vij* 3.234–42 — a) Tj^1 विद्यानां; wKt^1 सर्वेषां — a-b) GMd^1 कर्मणां नित्यानां — b) Hy कर्मणी; GMd^1 °णामतिवर्तने — c) Ho स्नातकं; TMd^3 °लोपैश्च; GMd^5 °लोपेन; Hy Tj^2 तु

स्नात्वानश्नन्नहः शेषमभिवाद्य प्रसादयेत् ॥२०५॥
ताडयित्वा तृणेनापि कण्ठे वाबध्य वाससा ।
विवादे वा विनिर्जित्य प्रणिपत्य प्रसादयेत् ॥२०६॥
अवगूर्य त्वब्दशतं सहस्रमभिहत्य तु ।
जिघांसया ब्राह्मणस्य नरकं प्रतिपद्यते ॥२०७॥
शोणितं यावतः पांसून् संगृह्णाति द्विजन्मनः ।
तावन्त्यब्दसहस्राणि तत्कर्ता नरके वसेत् ॥२०८॥
अवगूर्य चरेत्कृच्छ्रमतिकृच्छ्रं निपातने ।
कृच्छ्रातिकृच्छ्रौ कुर्वीत विप्रस्योत्पाद्य शोणितम् ।२०९॥
अनुक्तनिष्कृतीनां तु पापानामपनुत्तये ।
शक्तिं चावेक्ष्य पापं च प्रायश्चित्तं प्रकल्पयेत् ॥२१०॥

205. Verses 205 and 206 transposed in Lo^{1}; pāda-d omitted in GMd^{5}. Cited by *Apa* 1185; *Mādh* 2.355 — a) BKt^{5} Lo^{1} हुंकारो; Hy हूकारं; GMd^{5} धिक्कारं; GMd^{1} ब्राह्मणे कृत्वा; BBe^{2} Bo Ho °स्योक्ता — b) Bo तुंकारं; Lo^{1} oOr तु; Tj^{1} गरीयसां; Lo^{3} गरीयसीं; MTr^{6} गरीयसं — c) BBe^{2} °श्नन्त्वहः

206. Pādas a-c omitted in GMd^{5}. Cited by *Apa* 1185 — b) Be^{1} Lo^{1} कण्ठे बध्वा च वाससा; Pu^{10} चाबध्य त्वाचवाससा [*om* कण्ठे]; GMy sOx^{1} चाबध्य; Ho चावध्य; Bo GMd^{5} नाबध्य; Ox^{2} बध्य च; BBe^{2} वामध्य; [*Jolly* Nd] चासज्य; TMd^{3} TMd^{4} वासज्य; BCa Pu^{8} बध्वापि; Tr^{2} वध्यापि; TMd^{3} वाससं — c) Be^{1} Pu^{5} Pu^{7} *Go* विवादेनापि निर्जित्व; Lo^{4} विवादिनाभिनिर्जित्य; wKt^{1} वारिवापि विनि°; Tj^{2} च; BCa Ho sOx^{1} Ox^{2} sPu^{6} Pu^{10} वापि निर्जित्य [BCa चापि; Ox^{2} नापि; Pu^{10} नाभि] — d) BBe^{2} प्रसाधयेत्; Jo^{2} Lo^{1} विसर्जयेत्

207. Omitted in BKt^{5} GMd^{5} Tr^{2}; pādas a-b and c-d transposed in TMd^{4}. Cited by *Apa* 223; *Lakṣ* 2.394; *Mādh* 2.358 — a) La^{1} अवगूर्ज्य; TMd^{3} अघूर्य; *Lakṣ* अवगूर्यस्त्वब्द°; Pu^{2} Pu^{4} त्वष्टशतं — b) wKt^{1} wKt^{3} La^{1} Lo^{1} Pu^{2} Pu^{3} Pu^{4} Pu^{7} *Apa* °भिहन्य; Lo^{2} °हन्यत [*om* च]; Be^{1} Hy Jm Jo^{1} Kt^{2} wKt^{3} Lo^{2} sOx^{1} Ox^{2} sPu^{6} Pu^{8} Tj^{2} *Mandlik Jha KSS Dave* च — c) Be^{1} जिघांसया च विप्रस्य

208. Verses 208 and 209 transposed in TMd^{3} TMd^{4} MTr^{4} MTr^{6}; pādas a-b omitted in BKt^{5}. Cited by *Apa* 223; *Lakṣ* 2.394–5; *Mādh* 2.358 — a) Lo^{1} यावतः शोणितं; MTr^{4} MTr^{6} यावत्तच्छोणितं; TMd^{4} यावता; BBe^{2} BCa Ho wKt^{1} Kt^{2} wKt^{3} NKt^{4} La^{1} Lo^{1} Lo^{4} oOr NPu^{1} Pu^{2} Pu^{4} Pu^{5} Pu^{7} *Mādh Jolly* पांशून् — b) GMy *Mādh* संगृह्णीयाद्; Wa संगृह्णीति; [*Jolly* Gr] द्विजन्मनां; Ox^{2} द्विजन्मनं; BBe^{2} Hy Jm Jo^{1} Kt^{2} Tj^{2} *Mandlik Jha KSS Dave* महीतले; Bo BCa Ho *ma* [as pāṭha] wKt^{1} La^{1} Lo^{1} oOr Pu^{8} *Apa* महीतलात् — c) Bo तावत्य°; Jo^{2} Lo^{3} तावदव्द°; *Lakṣ* तावद्यव्द°; Lo^{1} तावद्वर्षसह°; TMd^{4} तावन्त्यपिसह° — d) BCa Ho wKt^{3} Lo^{1} Lo^{2} GMd^{1} TMd^{4} GMy NNg Pu^{2} Pu^{4} Pu^{5} Pu^{7} Tr^{2} Wa नरकं; Lo^{1} TMd^{4} GMy NPu^{1} Wa *Me Jha Dave* व्रजेत्

209.* Pādas a-c omitted in GMd^{5} and pādas c-d in Be^{1}. Cited by *Vij* 3.280; *Mādh* 2.358 — b) Bo Lo^{1} TMd^{3} °कृच्छ्र; MTr^{4} MTr^{6} निपातते; Pu^{10} निपातनो — c) Wa कृत्स्नातिकृछ्रे; BBe^{2} Bo BCa Ho Jo^{2} NKt^{4} BKt^{5} Lo^{1} Lo^{3} Lo^{4} [*ma*] oOr Pu^{5} Pu^{7} Pu^{8} Pu^{10} Tj^{1} [*Jolly* M G R] *Jolly ViDh* 54.30 °तिकृच्छ्रं; Pu^{2} Tr^{2} °तिकृच्छ्र — c-d) *Vij* कृच्छ्रातिकृच्छ्रोऽसृक्पाते कृच्छ्रोऽभ्यन्तरशोणिते

210. Cited by *Mādh* 2.360 — a) NNg °निकृतीनां; TMd^{4} sOx^{1} sPu^{6} च — b) GMy °मनुपत्तये — c) wKt^{1} पापं चावेक्ष्य शक्तिं च; Jo^{2} La^{1} NKt^{4} NPu^{1} Pu^{2} Pu^{4} चापेक्ष्य; Tj^{1} *om last* च — d) BBe^{2} Ox^{2} *Bh* [ad 11.85] विकल्पयेत्; *Bh* [ad 11.209] reads प्रकल्पयेत्

यैरभ्युपायैरेनांसि मानवो व्यपकर्षति ।
तान्वोऽभ्युपायान्वक्ष्यामि देवर्षिपितृसेवितान् ॥२११॥
त्र्यहं प्रातस्त्र्यहं सायं त्र्यहमद्यादयाचितम् ।
त्र्यहं परं च नाश्नीयात् प्राजापत्यं चरन्द्विजः ॥२१२॥
गोमूत्रं गोमयं क्षीरं दधि सर्पिः कुशोदकम् ।
एकरात्रोपवासश्च कृच्छ्रं सांतपनं स्मृतम् ॥२१३॥
एकैकं ग्रासमश्नीयात् त्र्यहाणि त्रीणि पूर्ववत् ।
त्र्यहं चोपवसेदन्त्यमतिकृच्छ्रं चरन्द्विजः ॥२१४॥
तप्तकृच्छ्रं चरन्विप्रो जलक्षीरघृतानिलान् ।
प्रतित्र्यहं पिबेदुष्णान् सकृत्स्नायी समाहितः ॥२१५॥
यतात्मनोऽप्रमत्तस्य द्वादशाहमभोजनम् ।
पराको नाम कृच्छ्रोऽयं सर्वपापापनोदनः ॥२१६॥

211. Omitted in Lo^{2} — a) Jo^{2} Lo^{1} Lo^{4} oOr Pu^{10} Tj^{1} MTr^{5} यैर्यैरुपायै° ; GMd^{5} यैरप्युपायै° ; Pu^{10} °पायैरेजास्य; TMd^{3} °पायैरेकांसि — b) Pu^{5} Pu^{7} [*Jolly* G] मानवोभ्युपकर्षति; Tr^{2} मानवा; MTr^{6} मानव्यो; oOr मानिनो; NPu^{1} Pu^{2} Pu^{4} ह्यपकर्षति; Pu^{3} वापकर्षति — c) Pu^{10} तान्नो; TMd^{4} तान्व; MTr^{5} तान्वो ह्युपा° ; GMd^{5} तानप्युपा° ; Be^{1} °भ्युपेया° — d) Lo^{1} °पितृसंचितान्; Be^{1} °सेवितां

212. Cited by *Vij* 3.319; *Apa* 1236; *Mādh* 2.25 — c) *Vij* परं त्र्यहं च नाश्नीयात्; MTr^{4} त्र्यहात्परं; Lo^{2} *om* च; Lo^{4} GMd^{1} TMd^{3} TMd^{4} GMy Pu^{3} Pu^{5} Pu^{7} Pu^{10} MTr^{6} *Mādh* तु — d) Pu^{5} Pu^{7} [*but mc*] प्राजापत्योयमुच्यते; Lo^{1} TMd^{4} GMd^{5} NPu^{1} [*Jolly* Nd] चरेद् द्विजः

213. b) Be^{1} TMd^{3} sPu^{6} Tj^{1} सर्पि; TMd^{4} कुशोदनं — c) GMd^{5} °रात्र्योप° ; TMd^{3} °वासं च — d) Be^{1} NKt^{4} Lo^{2} NNg NPu^{1} Pu^{2} Pu^{4} Pu^{5} Pu^{7} Pu^{10} Wa [*Jolly* M$^{1-2-8-9}$ G] *Go BDh* 4.5.11 कृच्छ्रः सांतपनः स्मृतः; GMd^{5} सांतापनं; Ox^{2} Pu^{3} Tr^{2} °पनं चरेत्

214. Cited by *Vij* 3.319; *Apa* 1238; pāda-a cited by *Viś* 3.315 — a) BKt^{5} Lo^{1} TMd^{3} एकैक; Lo^{3} ग्रामम° ; TMd^{3} ग्रानम° — b) wKt^{1} अहानि; TMd^{3} त्रीणपूर्वकं; La^{1} पूर्वतः — c) Be^{1} Pu^{3} Tr^{2} तूपवसेद° ; wKt^{1} °वसेन्त्रित्यम° ; BKt^{5} °वसेदन्तेमति° ; GMy Pu^{8} °सेदन्यमति° — c-d) MTr^{4} °सेदन्यदितिकृच्छ्रं — d) Tr^{2} चरेन्द्विजः; TMd^{4} चरान्द्विजः; TMd^{3} चरं द्विजः; Pu^{3} चरेद् द्विजः

215. *ma* in Lo^{4}. Cited by *Vij* 3.317; *Apa* 1235 — a) GMy चरेद् विप्रो — b) Lo^{4} घृतक्षीरजलानिलान्; Lo^{3} TMd^{3} Tj^{1} दधिक्षीर° ; Pu^{4} नलक्षीर° ; Tr^{2} °घृतानि च — c) Ho °दुष्णात्; Pu^{10} °दुष्मान्; MTr^{6} °दुष्णे — d) TMd^{4} सकृष्णाया समन्वितः; Jo^{2} sOx^{1} sPu^{6} सकृत्स्नायात्; GMd^{1} सकृत्सायं; Pu^{4} सप्तसायी

Additional verse in NPu^{1} *Mandlik* [ग] *KSS Dave* [taken from *Me*'s com., where it has the ascription क्वचित्परिमाणं पठ्यन्ते]:

अपां पिबेच्च त्रिपलं पलमेकं च सर्पिषः ।
पयः पिबेत्तु त्रिपलं त्रिमात्रं चोक्तमानतः ॥

216. Omitted in Pu^{10}; bottom of folio containing verses 216c to 223d torn in sPu^{6}. Cited by *Vij* 3.326; *Mādh* 2.26 — a) TMd^{4} यदात्मनोप्रमत्तस्याद्; Be^{1} BKt^{5} Pu^{5} Pu^{7} यतात्मानो; oOr यत्रात्मनो; TMd^{3} तयोत्मानो; Pu^{5} Pu^{7} °प्रमत्तस्तु; BKt^{5} NNg °प्रमत्तश्च [NNg *ma sh*श्च]; BBe^{2} °प्रवर्तस्य; Lo^{2} °प्रमेयस्य — c) GMd^{5} NNg Pu^{2} Pu^{4} Pu^{5} Pu^{7} पाराको; La^{1} पारको — d) TMd^{4} GMd^{5} °पापप्रणोदनः; wKt^{1} NKt^{4} Pu^{2} Pu^{4} °पापापनोदकः; wKt^{3} °पापापनोदमः; NPu^{1} °पापापचोदनः; GMd^{1} TMd^{3} MTr^{4} MTr^{6} °पापप्रणाशनं; GMy [*Jolly* Nd Gr] *Mādh BDh* 4.5.15 °पापप्रणाशनः

एकैकं ह्रासयेत्पिण्डं कृष्णे शुक्ले च वर्धयेत् ।
उपस्पृशंस्त्रिषवणमेतच्चान्द्रायणं स्मृतम् ॥२१७॥
एतमेव विधिं कृत्स्नमाचरेद्यवमध्यमे ।
शुक्लपक्षादिनियतश्चरंश्चान्द्रायणं व्रतम् ॥२१८॥
अष्टावष्टौ समश्नीयात् पिण्डान्मध्यंदिने स्थिते ।
नियतात्मा हविष्यस्य यतिचान्द्रायणं चरन् ॥२१९॥
चतुरः प्रातरश्नीयात् पिण्डान्विप्रः समाहितः ।
चतुरोऽस्तमिते सूर्ये शिशुचान्द्रायणं स्मृतम् ॥२२०॥
यथाकथंचित्पिण्डानां तिस्रोऽशीतीः समाहितः ।
मासेनाश्नन्हविष्यस्य चन्द्रस्यैति सलोकताम् ॥२२१॥

217. *ma* in Lo[4]. Cited by *Apa* 1243; *Mādh* 2.240 — a) NKt[4] एकैनं; Lo[2] हांसये°; Tj[1] हासये°; BBe[2] TMd[3] TMd[4] sOx[1] sPu[6] Pu[8] MTr[4] [*Jolly* Nd] ग्रासये°; Pu[3] प्रासये°; GMd[1] °त्पिण्डान् — b) NNg *ma sh* कृष्णे; TMd[4] Ox[2] Pu[5] Pu[7] Tr[2] *Apa* शुक्ले कृष्णे; TMd[3] तु; Lo[2] वर्धयन्; *Apa* [vl] वर्जयेत् — c) TMd[4] अपस्पृ°; sOx[1] उपस्पृश्यंत्रि°; Ox[2] Pu[3] Pu[7] उपस्पृश्यत्रि°; wKt[1] Lo[4] TMd[3] GMd[5] उपस्पृशेत्रि° — d) *Apa* °णमतश्चान्द्रायणं व्रतं; *Mādh* °यणव्रतं; Lo[3] °यणं व्रतं; La[1] TMd[4] °यणं चरेत्; BKt[5] °यणं चरन्

218. Omitted in oOr. Cited by *Mādh* 2.241 — a) BKt[5] एतदेव; Lo[1] [*Jolly* Nd] एकमेव; Be[1] Ho Jo[2] wKt[3] Lo[3] Lo[4] TMd[3] NPu[1] Pu[3] Pu[5] Pu[7] Pu[10] Tj[1] Tr[2] Wa [*Jolly* M R G] एवमेव; TMd[4] Tr[2] कृत्स्नामा°; TMd[3] कृच्छ्रमा° — b) Pu[5] Pu[7] °चरन्यव°; wKt[1] La[1] °चरेयुरमध्यमं [La[1] °ध्यमे]; TMd[4] °मध्यमः — c) Lo[3] Tj[1] कृष्णपक्षा°; wKt[1] °पक्षाभिनिय°; Ho °पक्षयिनिय°; BCa wKt[3] BKt[5] La[1] MTr[6] °नियतं चरं°; GMd[5] °निरतश्चरं° — d) [*Jolly* Nd] °नियतश्चान्द्रायणमथापरं; Bo wKt[3] Tj[1] °तश्चरंचान्द्रा°; BBe[2] BKt[5] °तश्चरन्चान्द्रा°; Pu[5] Pu[7] [*Jolly* M G] *Jolly* °तश्चरेच्चान्द्रा°; Lo[4] Pu[10] °तश्चरेत् चान्द्रा°; Kt[2] La[1] NNg *Mādh* °यणव्रतं; GMy °यणमपरं; Ho Lo[1] TMd[3] Tr[2] स्मृतं

219. Omitted in oOr; the following order in Lo[1] 221a-b, 220a-b, 219, 220c-d, 221c-d; verses 218 and 219 transposed in NKt[4]; pādas c-d omitted in BKt[5]. Cited by *Vij* 3.324; *Apa* 1243 — a) TMd[3] अष्टौ ग्रासान्समश्नीयात्; La[1] Lo[1] समाश्नीयात्; GMy समाश्नीयान्; MTr[4] MTr[6] मासमाद्यात् — b) BKt[5] MTr[5] [haplo] after पिण्डान् jumps to विप्रः in 220b; Tj[1] °न्मध्यदिने; GMd[1] स्थितान् — c) GMy नियतात्म; Lo[1] यतात्मना; TMd[3] हविष्याश; Hy Jm Jo[1] Kt[2] *Nā Mandlik Jha KSS Dave* हविष्याशी; Tj[2] हविष्यासी [for reading adopted see 11.221c] — d) TMd[3] चान्द्रायणव्रतं चरन्; GMd[5] NNg NPu[1] यतिश्चान्द्रा°; Ho wKt[1] La[1] TMd[4] Pu[10] Wa *Vij* चरेत्; Be[1] Jo[2] Lo[1] Lo[3] sOx[1] Ox[2] NPu[1] Pu[2] Pu[8] Tj[1] MTr[4] MTr[6] स्मृतं

220. Omitted in oOr MTr[4] MTr[6]; pādas a-b omitted in Pu[4], and pādas c-d in BBe[2]. Cited by *Vij* 3.324; *Apa* 1243 — b) GMd[1] TMd[3] GMy NPu[1] Pu[2] Wa पिण्डान्विप्रः कृताह्निकः; TMd[4] विप्रः पिण्डां कृताह्निकः; La[1] विप्रः पिण्डान्कृतक्रियः; wKt[3] *om* पिण्डान् — c) NKt[4] °स्तं गते — d) TMd[3] GMd[5] NPu[1] शिशुश्चान्द्रा°; GMd[5] Pu[5] Pu[7] [*Jolly* G[2]] *Vij BDh* 4.5.18 °यणं चरेत्; La[1] GMd[1] TMd[3] TMd[4] GMy Pu[3] Tr[2] [*Jolly* G[1] Nd] °यणं चरन्; wKt[3] °यणं चर

221. Pādas a-b omitted in BBe[2]. Cited by *Vij* 3.324; *Hem* 3/3.23 — a) Bo यथाकालं च पिण्डानां; GMd[1] °चिद्विप्राणां — b) Ox[2] Pu[10] Tr[2] °शीतिः; Bo °शीतिं; *Hem* °शीति; wKt[1] °शीताः; Tj[2] °शीतः; Pu[5] Pu[7] °शीती समाहिताः — c) La[1] मासमश्न° — d) MTr[6] स चन्द्रस्येति लोकतां; BBe[2] wKt[1] NKt[4] GMd[1] TMd[3] oOr Pu[5] Pu[7] Tj[1] Tr[2] चन्द्रस्येति

एतद्रुद्रास्तथादित्या वसवश्चाचरन्व्रतम् ।
सर्वाकुशलमोक्षाय मरुतश्च महर्षिभिः ॥२२२॥
महाव्याहृतिभिर्होमः कर्तव्यः स्वयमन्वहम् ।
अहिंसासत्यमक्रोधमार्जवं च समाचरेत् ॥२२३॥
त्रिरह्नस्त्रिर्निशायाश्च सवासा जलमाविशेत् ।
स्त्रीशूद्रपतितांश्चैव नाभिभाषेत कर्हिचित् ॥२२४॥
स्थानासनाभ्यां विहरेदशक्तोऽधः शयीत वा ।
ब्रह्मचारी व्रती च स्याद् गुरुदेवद्विजार्चकः ॥२२५॥
सावित्रीं च जपेन्नित्यं पवित्राणि च शक्तितः ।
सर्वेष्वेव व्रतेष्वेवं प्रायश्चित्तार्थमादृतः ॥२२६॥
एतैर्द्विजातयः शोध्या व्रतैराविष्कृतैनसः ।
अनाविष्कृतपापांस्तु मन्त्रैर्होमैश्च शोधयेत् ॥२२७॥

222. b) GMy वसवाश्च परसृतं; BKt[5] Tr[2] °वश्च चरन्व्रतं; TMd[4] °वश्चावसन्व्रतं; MTr[6] °वश्चारयन्व्रतं; Jo[2] °चरन्द्विजाः — c) TMd[4] ससर्वकुलमोक्षाय; Lo[1] GMd[5] Ox[2] Pu[3] Tr[2] MTr[4] MTr[6] सर्वेकु°; Bo Pu[2] Pu[4] Pu[7] सर्वान्कु°; Pu[5] सर्वानकु°; Pu[2] Pu[4] °कुशलो; TMd[3] °मोक्षाच — d) NPu[1] मारुतश्च; Be[1] Ho GMd[1] TMd[3] TMd[4] GMd[5] GMy Ox[2] महर्षयः; Pu[5] Pu[7] MTr[4] MTr[6] सहर्षिभिः

223. Cited by *Apa* 1230; pādas a-b cited by *Vij* 3.325; *Apa* 1246, and pādas c-d by *Vij* 3.313; *Mādh* 2.459 — a) Ho °भिर्होमाः; oOr MTr[6] °भिर्होमैः; TMd[3] °भिर्होतुः — b) MTr[6] कर्तव्यं — c) BKt[5] Pu[5] Wa *Mādh* अहिंसां; wKt[1][*mc to*] GMd[5] Ox[2] Pu[3] Tr[2] सत्यमस्तेयमार्जवं — d) Ox[2] वा; NKt[4] समाचरत्; TMd[4] [*Jolly* G] समाचरन्; Tr[2] समाश्रयेत्

224.* Cited by *Apa* 1230; *Mādh* 2.459 — a) TMd[4] त्रिरह्नास्त्रि°; GMd[1] GMd[5] GMy Pu[8] MTr[4] MTr[5] MTr[6] [*Jolly* Nd] *Ku Apa Mādh* त्रिरह्नि त्रि°; Jo[1] Kt[2] Ox[2] *Mandlik KSS* त्रिरहस्त्रि°; La[1] त्रिवर्गस्त्रि°; Ho Pu[3] °निशायांश्च; Be[1] BCa Jm Jo[1] Jo[2] wKt[1] Kt[2] NKt[4] BKt[5] La[1] Lo[1] Lo[3] Lo[4] GMd[1] TMd[4] GMd[5] GMy sOx[1] Ox[2] NPu[1] Pu[2] Pu[4] Pu[8] Pu[10] Tj[1] MTr[4] MTr[5] MTr[6] [*Jolly* M R Nd] *Apa Mādh Me Rn Rc Mandlik KSS Jha Dave* °निशायां च; oOr °निशायां तु — b) oOr सवासाः स्नानमाचरेत्; Tj[1] सवासां; Bo NKt[4] स्नानमाचरेत्; TMd[4] °मावसेत्; sOx[1] °मावशेत्; BBe[2] °माप्नुयात् — c) BKt[5] Pu[2] Pu[4] °पतिताश्चैव; sOx[1] sPu[6] °पतितैश्चैव; TMd[4] °पतितां चैव; TMd[3] °पतितस्यैव — d) sOx[1] sPu[6] नाभ्यभाषेत; Tr[2] नाभिनाषेत; Jo[2] न संभाषेत; BKt[5] °भाषेत्कर्हिचित्

225. Cited by *Apa* 1230; *Mādh* 2.459 — a) BKt[5] °सनानां; GMd[1] विचरे°; oOr विरहे° — b) NKt[4] °रेदाशक्तो; La[1] °रेदसक्तो; Pu[8] °रेदशक्तोयः; Lo[1] °रेद्देशं क्रोधः *cor to* °रेदशक्तो वा; *Mādh* °रेदक्रोधोधः; BKt[5] °धश्चरेत वा; Lo[2] °धः शयी भवेत्; Bo Tr[2] च — c) Tj[1] व्रती न; oOr व्रती तस्य गुरु° — d) Lo[4] गुरुवेद°; Pu[5] Pu[7] °देवर्त्विजार्चकः; Tj[1] °द्विजार्चिकः; MTr[4] MTr[6] °द्विजाचितः; oOr °द्विजार्चनः; Pu[2] Pu[4] °द्विजार्वजः

226. Pādas c-d omitted in Tj[1]. Cited by *Apa* 1231; *Mādh* 2.459; pādas a-b cited by *Vij* 3.325 — a) wKt[3] NKt[4] Tr[2] सावित्री; Pu[3] Tr[2] तु; TMd[4] GMy जपन्नित्यं — b) Tr[2] पवित्राणां; GMd[1] सावित्राणि; TMd[3] स्वशक्तितः; BCa च सर्वशः — c) TMd[4] सर्वेष्वेवं [lacuna rest of pāda]; GMd[1] सर्वेष्वेष; NNg Ox[2] NPu[1] Pu[2] Wa सर्वेष्वेषु; BBe[2] सर्वेषु च; wKt[1] TMd[3] NNg NPu[1] Pu[2] व्रतेष्वेव; Lo[2] व्रतेष्वेषु; Bo व्रजेष्वेवं; wKt[3] कृतेष्वेवं — d) GMd[5] *Mādh* °र्थमादृताः; NKt[4] °र्थमादिते; Pu[2] °र्थमाहृतः

227. Cited by *Viś* 3.296; *Mādh* 2.451 — b) NKt[4] GMd[1] °विष्कृतेनसः — c) wKt[1] NKt[4] BKt[5]

ख्यापनेनानुतापेन तपसाध्ययनेन च ।
पापकृन्मुच्यते पापात् तथा दानेन चापदि ॥२२८॥
यथा यथा नरोऽधर्मं स्वयं कृत्वानुभाषते ।
तथा तथा त्वचेवाहिस्तेनाधर्मेण मुच्यते ॥२२९॥
यथा यथा मनस्तस्य दुष्कृतं कर्म गर्हति ।
तथा तथा शरीरं तत् तेनाधर्मेण मुच्यते ॥२३०॥
कृत्वा पापं हि संतप्य तस्मात्पापात्प्रमुच्यते ।
नैवं कुर्यां पुनरिति निवृत्त्या पूयते नरः ॥२३१॥
एवं संचिन्त्य मनसा प्रेत्य कर्मफलोदयम् ।
मनोवाङ्मूर्तिभिर्नित्यं शुभं कर्म समाचरेत् ॥२३२॥

[*Jolly* Nd] °पापास्तु; TMd[4] °पापस्तु; Be[1] Lo[2] GMd[1] Pu[5] Pu[7] °पापांश्च; TMd[3] °पापानां — d) MTr[5] मन्त्रैर्होमैर्विशोधनैः; BKt[5] व्रतैरेभिश्च; Lo[1] Lo[2] NNg Pu[3] °र्होमैस्तु; NKt[4] BKt[5] La[1] [*Jolly* Nd] *Viś* शोधनैः

228. Omitted in Hy. Cited by *Viś* 3.296; *Apa*1231; *Mādh* 2.336 — a) BKt[5] ख्यापनेनार्थतातेन; TMd[3] ख्यापितेनानुपापेन; Lo[1] [*cor to*]ख्यापने तु तापेन; Ho ख्यापनेन तोयेन — b) Ho oOr Ox[2] °ध्यापनेन; TMd[3] GMy °ध्यायनेन; Lo[2] NNg oOr वा — c) TMd[4] तापकृ° — d) BKt[5] यथा; GMy वापदि

229. Omitted in Hy; verses 229 and 230 transposed in Ho. Cited by *Apa* 1231 — a) TMd[3] यथा नरोधर्मं कर्म — b) Pu[5] Pu[7] [*Jolly* G] कृत्वा प्रभाषते; Bo कृत्वा तु भाषते; wKt[3] कृत्वा च भाषते; oOr Pu[2] Pu[4] कृत्वा न भाषते — c) Bo GMy Wa त्वचैवा°; Pu[10] त्वमेवा°; TMd[4] त्वचेवाह्नि° — d) GMd[1] oOr °हिस्तेन धर्मेण

230. Omitted in BCa Hy BKt[5] Pu[5] Pu[7] Tr[2] MTr[5] [haplo]; placed before 227 in MTr[4] MTr[6]. Cited by *Apa* 1231 — a) *Apa* पुनस्तस्य; Lo[4] Pu[10] [*Jolly* M]नरः स्वस्य — b) Ho दुष्कृत; Pu[8] दुष्कृते; TMd[4] दुष्करं; MTr[6] गर्हते; w Kt[1] TMd[3] TMd[4] GMd[5] GMy [*Jolly* Nd] *Apa* निन्दति; Lo[3] कर्षति — c) Jm NKt[4] शरीरं तं; BBe[2] Bo Jo[2] wKt[1] wKt[3] La[1] TMd[4] oOr sOx[1] Ox[2] sPu[6] Pu[8] Tj[1] शरीरं तु; GMd[5] शरीरस्तु; TMd[3] शरीरं हि; GMy शरीरी हि; Lo[2] शरीरस्थस्तेना° — d) sOx[1] sPu[6] स्तेना°; oOr Tr[1] तेन धर्मेण; wKt[3] उच्यते

231.* Omitted in Hy; pādas a-b omitted in BKt[5]. Cited by *Apa* 1231 — a) NPu[1] Pu[2] Pu[4] पापं कृत्वाभिसंतप्य; TMd[4] कृत्वा हि पापं संतप्य; Be[1] Lo[2] NNg sOx[1] Pu[5] sPu[6] Pu[7] Wa *Go Ku* पापं कृत्वा; Jo[2] La[1] Tj[1] पापानि संतप्य; Tr[2] सताप्य; Ox[2] संतप्येत्; NKt[4] संतप्यस्; BBe[2] संतर्प्य — b) wKt[1] °पात्स मुच्यते — c) Be[2] Jm नैव; sOx[1] sPu[6] नैनं; Tr[2] नैनां; [*Jolly* N]नैनः; Be[1] wKt[3] BKt[5] La[1] GMd[1] GMy oOr Pu[5] Pu[7] Pu[8] MTr[4] MTr[6] [*Jolly* M[1-2-5-8-9] G Nd] *Apa Jolly* नैतत्; Lo[3] कुर्या; Be[1] wKt[1] NKt[4] Lo[2] GMd[1] GMd[5] Pu[2] Pu[4] Pu[5] Pu[7] Tr[1] MTr[4] MTr[5] MTr[6] [*Jolly* M[1-2-5-8-9] G Nd] *Jolly* कुर्यात्; La[1] कुर्युः; oOr कार्यं; sOx[1] पुनरेति; Be[1]पुनरपि — d) GMd[1] TMd[4] MTr[4] MTr[6] निवृत्त्या च विशुध्यति [TMd[4] निवृत्य; MTr[4] *om* च]; MTr[5] निवृत्त्या शुध्यते नरः;NKt[4] निवृश्चाप्तयते नरः; Tj[1] निर्वृत्त्या; wKt[1] निवृत्तः; Tr[1] गीर्वृत्त्या; TMd[3] GMd[5] GMy Ox[2] Tr[1] [*Jolly* Nd] पूयते ततः; MTr[5] शुध्यते नरः; Bo Ho Jm Jo[1] Kt[2] Lo[2] oOr Pu[5] Pu[7] Pu[8] Tj[2] Tr[2] *Mandlik Jha KSS Dave* पूयते तु सः; Be[1] BKt[5] Lo[1] Pu[4] *Apa* पूयते हि सः; Wa पूयते च सः

232. Verses 232 and 233 transposed in GMy — a) Jm कथं संचि°; TMd[3] Pu[2] Pu[5] Pu[7] संचित्य — c) Ox[2] Pu[10] [*Jolly* M[1-2-8-9] R] *Jolly* मनोवाक्कर्मभिः° [for मूर्ति see parallel at 11.242] — d) TMd[4] शुभ; BKt[5] समाचरन्

अज्ञानाद्यदि वा ज्ञानात् कृत्वा कर्म विगर्हितम् ।
तस्माद्विमुक्तिमन्विच्छन् द्वितीयं न समाचरेत् ॥२३३॥
यस्मिन्कर्मण्यस्य कृते मनसः स्यादलाघवम् ।
तस्मिंस्तावत्तपः कुर्याद् यावत्तुष्टिकरं भवेत् ॥२३४॥
तपोमूलमिदं सर्वं दैवमानुषकं सुखम् ।
तपोमध्यं बुधैः प्रोक्तं तपोऽन्तं वेददर्शिभिः ॥२३५॥
ब्राह्मणस्य तपो ज्ञानं तपः क्षत्रस्य रक्षणम् ।
वैश्यस्य तु तपो वार्त्ता तपः शूद्रस्य सेवनम् ॥२३६॥
ऋषयः संशितात्मानः फलमूलानिलाशनाः ।
तपसैव प्रपश्यन्ति त्रैलोक्यं सचराचरम् ॥२३७॥
औषधान्यगदा विद्या दैवी च विविधा स्थितिः ।
तपसैव प्रसिध्यन्ति तपस्तेषां हि साधनम् ॥२३८॥
यद्दुस्तरं यद्दुरापं यद्दुर्गं यच्च दुष्करम् ।

233. Omitted in BCa GMd^{5} sOx^{1} sPu^{6} Pu^{10} Wa [haplo]; Kt^{2} repeats 231c-d in place of 233c-d — b) Kt^{2} कृत्वा कर्मफलोदयं [cf. 11.232b] — c) Lo^{1} TMd^{4} तस्माद्विमुक्तम° ; Bo Ho BKt^{5} La^{1} MTr^{4} MTr^{6} तस्माद्विशुद्धिम° ; Pu^{5} Pu^{7} °मुक्तिमिच्छन्; wKt^{1} Lo^{1} MTr^{4} °मुक्तिमन्विच्छेद्; La^{1} Pu^{4} *om* न; oOr च समा° ; Pu^{2} स समा°

234. a) MTr^{6} तस्मिन्क° ; wKt^{1} sOx^{1} sPu^{6} °न्कर्मण्यपि; Be^{1} Lo^{2} Ox^{2} NPu^{1} Pu^{2} Pu^{4} Pu^{5} Pu^{7} Tr^{2} *Go Rc* °न्कर्मण्यसुकृते; Tj^{2} °न्कर्मण्यकृते — c) wKt^{1} यस्मिं° ; Tr^{1} °स्तावर्तवः — d) wKt^{3} तावत्तु° ; GMd^{1} यावत्पुष्टि° ; BKt^{5} °ष्टिकमं

235. Pādas a-b omitted in Ca and pāda-d in wKt^{1} — a) Bo °मूलकरं सर्वं; Be^{1} सर्व — b) MTr^{4} MTr^{6} सुखं यद्देवमानुषं; GMy Tr^{1} Wa देव° ; wKt^{1} GMd^{1} GMd^{5} sOx^{1} Ox^{2} Pu^{5} sPu^{6} Pu^{7} Pu^{8} Tj^{1} [*Jolly* G M^{1-8-9}] दैवं; Be^{1} Bo wKt^{3} NKt^{4} BKt^{5} La^{1} Lo^{1} Lo^{3} GMd^{1} NNg sOx^{1} Ox^{2} NPu^{1} Pu^{2} sPu^{6} Pu^{8} Tj^{1} Wa °मानुष्यकं; Jo^{2} Pu^{5} Pu^{7} °मानुपिकं — c) Lo^{2} Wa तु वै प्रोक्तं — d) Lo^{4} देवदर्शिभिः; Wa °दर्शभिः; NKt^{4} La^{1} GMd^{1} MTr^{4} MTr^{5} MTr^{6} °दर्शनात्; GMy °दर्शितं

236. Omitted in Pu^{5}; pāda-a omitted in wKt^{1} — b) NNg [*but cor fh*] क्षत्रियस्य; TMd^{3} कारणं — c) Ho La^{1} *om* तु; BBe^{2} Bo wKt^{3} sOx^{1} sPu^{6} Pu^{7} [*Jolly* G] च

237.* *ma* in NPu^{1} — a) BCa ऋषयः पितरो देवाः; Lo^{2} TMd^{4} Pu^{2} Pu^{4} Pu^{8} Tj^{1} Wa शंसितात्मानः; NPu^{1} शंशितात्मानः; wKt^{1} wKt^{3} NKt^{4} Lo^{3} sOx^{1} sPu^{6} संसितात्मानः; Be^{1} BBe^{2} Bo Ho Hy Jm Jo^{1} Kt^{2} Lo^{1} Lo^{4} GMy Ox^{2} Pu^{3} Pu^{5} Pu^{7} Pu^{10} Tj^{2} Tr^{2} *Mandlik Jolly Jha KSS Dave* संयतात्मानः — b) GMd^{1} °मूल्या° ; Tr^{2} °मूलाशिलाशिनः; TMd^{4} °मूलनिशा तथा; Ho NNg Pu^{3} Tr^{1} °निलाशिनः; Lo^{2} °शनः — c) BKt^{5} तपसेव; wKt^{1} BKt^{5} sOx^{1} sPu^{6} प्रशंसन्ति; NKt^{4} प्रणस्यति; GMd^{5} प्रविश्यन्ति

238.* a) BBe^{2} Bo Hy Jm Jo^{1} wKt^{1} Kt^{2} wKt^{3} NKt^{4} BKt^{5} La^{1} Lo^{1} Lo^{4} TMd^{4} sOx^{1} Ox^{2} sPu^{1} Pu^{2} Pu^{3} Pu^{4} Pu^{6} Pu^{8} Tj^{1} Tj^{2} [*Jolly* R Ku] *Ku Rn Nd Mr Mandlik KSS* °न्यगदो; TMd^{3} °न्यगता; Pu^{2} Pu^{4} वैद्या — b) sOx^{1} दैवीं; NKt^{4} TMd^{3} Pu^{5} Pu^{7} Wa देवी; BBe^{2} दैवे; GMd^{5} स्थिता; BKt^{5} गतिः — c) TMd^{3} तपसैवं; TMd^{3} प्रसिधानि; wKt^{1} च सिध्यन्ति; NNg Tr^{1} हि सिध्यन्ति; Kt^{2} Tj^{1} प्रपश्यन्ति — d) Tj^{1} [*Jolly* R] तपस्त्वेषां; BKt^{5} तप एषां; GMd^{1} ततस्तेषां; wKt^{1} च

तत्सर्वं तपसा साध्यं तपो हि दुरतिक्रमम् ॥२३९॥
महापातकिनश्चैव शेषाश्चाकार्यकारिणः ।
तपसैव सुतप्तेन मुच्यन्ते किल्बिषात्ततः ॥२४०॥
कीटाश्चाहिपतंगाश्च पशवश्च वयांसि च ।
स्थावराणि च भूतानि दिवं यान्ति तपोबलात् ॥२४१॥
यत्किंचिदेनः कुर्वन्ति मनोवाङ्मूर्तिभिर्जनाः ।
तत्सर्वं निर्दहन्त्याशु तपसैव तपोधनाः ॥२४२॥
तपसैव विशुद्धस्य ब्राह्मणस्य दिवौकसः ।
इज्याश्च प्रतिगृह्णन्ति कामान्संवर्धयन्ति च ॥२४३॥
प्रजापतिरिदं शास्त्रं तपसैवासृजत्प्रभुः ।
तथैव वेदानृषयस्तपसा प्रतिपेदिरे ॥२४४॥
इत्येतत्तपसो देवा महाभाग्यं प्रचक्षते ।

239. Omitted in [*Jolly* Nd]; bottom of folio containing verses 239–43c torn off in sPu^{6} — a) BKt^{5} यद्दुष्करं यद्दुरापं; Be^{1} यद्दुस्तरं दुस्तरापं; TMd^{4} यद्दुस्तरं दुरालापं — a-b) WKt^{1} यत्तुस्तवं यत्तुवापं यत्त्वर्गं यच्च दुष्करं — b) NKt^{4} यद्दुर्गे; NPu^{1} Pu^{2} यद्दूरं; TMd^{3} यद्दुस्तं; Wa यद्दुरं; GMd^{1} यद्दुस्तरं यच्च; BKt^{5} sOx^{1} यच्च दुस्तरं; Lo^{1} TMd^{3} दुष्कृतं — c) Bo La^{1} Lo^{1} Lo^{4} Ox^{2} Pu^{3} Pu^{5} Pu^{7} Pu^{8} Pu^{10} [*Jolly* M G Ku] *Jolly Jha Dave ViDh* 95.17 सर्वं तत्तपसा; Tr^{2} सर्वं तं तपसा; BCa Hy Jm Jo^{1} Kt^{2} BKt^{5} Lo^{4} Ox^{2} Tj^{2} *Mandlik KSS* सर्वं तु तपसा; GMd^{1} TMd^{3} GMd^{5} Tr^{1} शक्यं — d) TMd^{3} तपोभिर्दुरति°; La^{1} Pu^{5} Pu^{7} Tr^{1} °क्रमः

240. Omitted in [*Jolly* Nd]. Cited by *Viś* 3.270; *Mādh* 2.454 — b) WKt^{3} sOx^{1} ये चान्ये कामकारिणः [WKt^{3} चान्य°]; BKt^{5} विशेषाकार्य°; Lo^{1} GMy °श्चकार्य°; TMd^{3} GMy °कारणः — d) Bo BCa NKt^{4} TMd^{3} GMd^{5} sOx^{1} Tr^{1} MTr^{4} MTr^{6} मुच्यते; TMd^{4} इष्यते; GMd^{1} Pu^{2} °षात्तमः

241. Omitted in [*Jolly* Nd] — a) TMd^{3} कीटश्चाहि°; WKt^{1} कीटास्वाहि°; TMd^{3} कीटाश्चाभि°; Be^{1} कीटाः श्वाहि°; GMd^{5} सर्पाश्चाहि°; [*Jolly* Nd] श्वानश्चाहि°; GMy कीटाश्चापि पतं°; Ho कीटश्चापि पतं°; sOx^{1} कीटाचापि पतं°; MTr^{5} कीताश्चैव पतं° — b) Bo पशुवद्यवयांसि; BKt^{5} गवांसि; Tr^{1} ध्वांसि — c) MTr^{4} MTr^{6} च सर्वाणि — d) sOx^{1} याति

242. Omitted in [*Jolly* Nd]. Cited by *Mādh* 2.454 — a) BBe^{2} यत्केचि° — b) BKt^{5} GMd^{5} GMy [*Jolly* Nd] *Jolly Jha Dave* मनोवाक्कर्मभिर्जनाः [cf. 11.232]; Lo^{4} GMd^{1} TMd^{3} Ox^{2} Pu^{10} Tr^{1} [*Jolly* M Gr] मनोवाक्कायकर्मभिः [*om* जनाः]; Pu^{3} मनोवाक्कायभिर्जनाः; Bo °भिर्जिताः — c) NKt^{4} Pu^{5} Pu^{7} निर्णुदन्त्याशु; Be^{1} Pu^{4} निर्णुदत्याशु; Bo निनुदन्त्याशु; TMd^{4} निर्गुदन्त्याशु; MTr^{4} निर्गदन्त्याशु; Tr^{1} तु दहन्त्याशु; La^{1} च निहत्याशु

243. Omitted in Kt^{2} [*Jolly* Nd] — a) Ho Tr^{2} तपसैवं; GMd^{5} विशुध्यन्ति; sOx^{1} सुतप्तस्य — c) Tr^{1} MTr^{4} MTr^{6} इज्यां च; Pu^{10} इज्याद्यां; TMd^{3} यज्ञांश्च; Lo^{4} [*but mc*] इष्टाश्च; oOr इज्यां संप्रति°; NKt^{4} प्रतिगृह्णं — d) WKt^{1} कामं संव°; Bo कामा संव°; NKt^{4} कानान्संव°; WKt^{3} कामान्वर्ध°; sOx^{1} sPu^{6} कामं संपादयन्ति; Bo °न्संबहुयन्ति

244. a) GMy °तिरिदं सर्वं — b) Tr^{1} °सैव सृजत्प्रभुः; TMd^{3} °वासृजन्प्रभुः; NPu^{1} °सृजद्विभुः — c) Ho वेदेरुप°; GMd^{5} Pu^{4} Tj^{2} देवानृष°; TMd^{3} देवा ऋष° — d) Lo^{3} TMd^{3} GMy Pu^{2} Pu^{4} Tj^{1} °यस्तपसैव प्रपेदिरे; Tj^{2} °यस्तपसैव्यतिपेदिरे

सर्वस्यास्य प्रपश्यन्तस्तपसः पुण्यमुद्भवम् ॥२४५॥
वेदाभ्यासोऽन्वहं शक्त्या महायज्ञक्रिया क्षमा ।
नाशयन्त्याशु पापानि महापातकजान्यपि ॥२४६॥
यथैधस्तेजसा वह्निः प्राप्तं निर्दहति क्षणात् ।
तथा ज्ञानाग्निना पापं कृत्स्नं दहति वेदवित् ॥२४७॥
सव्याहृतिकाः सप्रणवाः प्राणायामास्तु षोडश ।
अपि भ्रूणहणं मासात् पुनन्त्यहरहः कृताः ॥२४९॥

245. a) TMd[3] Tr[1] MTr[5] [*Jolly* G] इत्येवं तपसो; NKt[4] इत्येवं तत्तपसो; Ho इत्येतं तपसो; Pu[5] इत्येकं तपसो; *Me Jha Dave* यदेतत्तपसो; TMd[4] अत्यन्ततपसो; Lo[1] GMy Pu[5] Pu[7] °तपसा — b) Ho La[1] NPu[1] प्रचक्ष्यते — c) oOr सर्वस्यापि प्रपश्यन्ति; Ox[2] सर्वे तपः प्रशंसन्ति; Bo प्रशंसन्त°; BKt[5] प्रशस्यन्त°; Hy NNg प्रपश्यन्त तपसः [NNg तपसा]; BBe[2] La[1] °पश्यन्ति तपसः — d) Bo GMd[5] °स्तपसा; BKt[5] La[1] Ox[2] Tr[2] पुण्यसमुद्भवं; wKt[1] Lo[3] Tj[1] पुण्यसंभवं; TMd[3] पुण्यमुद्भवत्; Bo पुण्यमुद्वहं; BBe[2] Jm Jo[1] Kt[2] BKt[5] *Mandlik KSS* पुण्यमुत्तमं

Additional verse in Be[1] BCa La[1] Pu[3] Tr[2] *Mandlik* [क, ल] *KSS Dave;* given after verse 246 in BKt[5] oOr; commented by *Rc*:

ब्रह्मचर्यं तपो होमः काले शुद्धाल्पभोजनम् ।
अरागद्वेषलोभाश्च तप उक्तं स्वयंभुवा ॥

a) BCa जपो — b) La[1] शुद्धयल्प°; Be[1] शुद्धान्नभोजनं — c) Be[1] BCa oOr °लोभश्च

246. Cited by *Mādh* 2.172, 379, 451 — b) GMd[1] महायज्ञः क्षमा क्रिया; GMy °यज्ञाक्रिया; Ho Lo[4] TMd[3] sOx[1] Pu[3] sPu[6] [*Jolly* M] °यज्ञक्रियाः; Lo[1] °यज्ञकृपा; wKt[3] Lo[1] Lo[4] TMd[3] sOx[1] Pu[2] sPu[6] [*Jolly* M] क्षमाः; BKt[5] TMd[4] MTr[4] MTr[6] क्षमः — c) TMd[4] नाशयत्याशु; Tr[2] नाशयेत्यासु; Ox[2] शामयत्याशु; BKt[5] शोधयन्त्याशु — d) Lo[1] माहा°; Be[1] °जानि च; Jm °जान्प्रति

247.* Cited by *Mādh* 2.172, 451 — a) Bo NKt[4] sOx[1] NPu[1] Pu[2] Pu[4] sPu[6] Wa यथैधांसि समिद्धोग्निः; BBe[2] Jo[2] wKt[1] Lo[1] Lo[3] Pu[8] oOr Tj[1] Tj[2] यथाग्निस्तेजसैधांसि; Hy तथैध°; Be[1] Ho wKt[3] Lo[2] Lo[4] [*ma*] GMd[1] GMd[5] GMy NNg Ox[2] Pu[5] Pu[7] Tr[1] *Rc Go* यथैधांस्तेजसा; Tr[2] यथैधन्तेजसा; BKt[5] यथैधोस्तेजसा; Pu[10] [*Jolly* M]यथैव तेजसा; TMd[3] यथैवयांस्तेजसा; Pu[3] यथैधांस्यंजसा; wKt[3] °स्तैजसा; Tr[1] °स्तेजसां; TMd[3] NNg वह्नि — b) Ox[2] Tr[1] प्राप्तां; BBe[2] Hy wKt[3] Tr[2] प्राप्ता; NPu[1] Pu[2] Pu[4] प्रास्ता; BCa काष्ठं: Be[1] Bo GMd[1] TMd[3] GMd[5] Pu[3] Pu[5] Pu[7] प्राप्तान्निर्द°; NNg प्रास्नान्निर्द°; Ho Jo[2] wKt[1] NKt[4] BKt[5] Lo[1] Lo[2] sOx[1] sPu[6] Tj[1] Tj[2] प्राप्तानि दहति; Wa प्रास्तानि दहति; BBe[2] पापानि दहति; Tr[1] क्षणं — c) *Mādh* ज्ञानकृतं पापं — c-d) Lo[4] Pu[10] कृत्स्नं पापं — d) Hy Jm Jo[1] Kt[2] Pu[5] Pu[7] Pu[8] Tj[2] [*Jolly* G] *Go Ku Mandlik Jha KSS Dave* सर्वं; Jo[1] *om* वेदवित्; Jo[2] धर्मवित्

*Additional verse in most mss. and all editions [see note] as verse 248, which number is omitted in the edition:

इत्येतदेनसामुक्तं प्रायश्चित्तं यथाविधि ।
अत ऊर्ध्वं रहस्यानां प्रायश्चित्तं निबोधत ॥

a) *Rn* [pāṭha] इत्येषामेन°; BKt[5] °नसमुक्तं; wKt[1] °नसायुक्तं — a-b) Jo[2] Lo[3] Tj[1] इत्येषो विहितः कृत्स्नः प्रायश्चित्तस्य वो विधिः [Jo[2] °षोभिहितः] — b) Ox[2] Pu[3] Tr[2] °श्चित्तं विशुद्धये — c) BKt[5] अथ; oOr रजसानां

Verse numer 248 has been eliminated from the critical edition.

249.* Cited by *Vij* 3.301; *Apa* 1216; *Dev*2.368 — a) Hypermetric pāda; BBe[2] Hy wKt[1] wKt[3] BKt[5] La[1] Lo[1] Lo[3] NPu[1] Pu[2] Pu[3] Pu[4] Tj[1] Tj[2] MTr[4] Wa [*Jolly* R] *Nā* सव्याहृतीः सप्रणवाः

कौत्सं जप्त्वाप इत्येतद् वासिष्ठं च तृचं प्रति ।
माहित्रं शुद्धवत्यश्च सुरापोऽपि विशुध्यति ॥२५०॥
सकृज्जप्त्वास्यवामीयं शिवसंकल्पमेव च ।
अपहृत्य सुवर्णं तु क्षणाद्भवति निर्मलः ॥२५१॥
हविष्पान्तीयमभ्यस्य न तमंह इतीति च ।
जप्त्वा च पौरुषं सूक्तं मुच्यते गुरुतल्पगः ॥२५२॥
एनसां स्थूलसूक्ष्माणां चिकीर्षन्नपनोदनम् ।

[BBe² Hy La¹ Lo³ NPu¹ Pu² Pu³ Pu⁴ °हृतिः; BKt⁵ Wa °हृति]; Jm Jo¹ Kt² oOr Pu⁸ *Vij Dev Mandlik Jolly Jha KSS Dave* सव्याहृतिप्रणवकाः [oOr °हृतिः]; Pu¹⁰ सव्याहृदिकास्तु प्रणवाः; Be¹ NKt⁴ Tr² °हृतिकप्रणवाः; Lo² °हृतीकप्रणवाः; TMd⁴ संप्रणवाः; GMy सणवाः; Bo Ox² *Rc* प्रणवाः — b) Ho GMd⁵ GMy NPu¹ Tr¹ °यामस्तु; Hy °यामांस्तु; BBe² °यामाश्च; TMd⁴ °यामासु; Ho Tr¹ षोडशः — c) Ox² Tj² ब्रह्महणं; TMd³ GMy Tj¹ Tr¹ °हनं; Lo¹ °हनो; TMd⁴ °हतो; BBe² Bo मासान्; Lo³ [*Jolly* R] साक्षात्; Ox² पापात् — d) Bo पुनात्य°; Tj¹ कृता; BBe² कृतान्

250.* Pādas c-d omitted in Tj². Cited by *Vij* 3.303; *Apa* 1216; *Mādh* 2.457— a) TMd³ कौत्स्यं; Wa कोत्सं; Pu² कौशं; GMy कौसं; Pu⁴ कशं; La¹ कौछं; Tr¹ जप्त्वा त्वपेत्येतद्; *Mādh* जपित्वापैत्येनो वासि°; Jo² Pu⁵ Pu⁷ जप्त्वापन इति वासि°; La¹ इत्येता — b) TMd⁴ वासिष्ठं चैव तृचं प्रति; Be¹ NKt⁴ NPu¹ Pu² Pu⁴ Pu⁵ Pu⁷ [*Jolly* G] वासिष्ठं प्रति च त्र्यृचं [Be¹ (*Jolly* G) प्रति वत्यृचं; NKt⁴ तृचं]; Ho Tj¹ वाशिष्ठं; *Mādh* चेत्यृचं प्रति; Wa चापि च तृचं; Pu¹⁰ चापिचह्यचं; BKt⁵ *om* च; Ho *Jolly* त्र्यृचं प्रति; Bo Tr² त्यृचं प्रति; GMd¹ GMd⁵ GMy Tr¹ [*Jolly* Nd] त्रिचं प्रति; Lo¹ Ox² ऋचं प्रति; BCa Hy Jm Jo¹ wKt¹ Kt² Lo³ Lo⁴ [*Jolly* R Ku] *Vij Mr Mandlik Jha KSS Dave* प्रतीत्यृचं; Lo² प्रतिरित्यृचं; wKt³ प्रति त्र्यचं; Jo² प्रति त्र्यृचं; Pu⁸ Tj¹ Tj² प्रति त्यृचं; sOx¹ sPu⁶ प्रति तृचं; Pu² प्रति वत्र्यृचं; Lo² प्रतिरिचं; BKt⁵ प्रतिवद्गृच; La¹ प्रति प्रत्युच; Pu³ प्रत्र्यवं प्रति; BBe² प्रतित्युतं — c) Tr² माहित्यं; Bo माहित्यां; *Apa* साहित्यं; wKt¹ Lo² Lo⁴ GMd¹ oOr sOx¹ Ox² NPu¹ Pu² Pu⁴ Pu⁵ sPu⁶ Pu⁷ [*Jolly* M G N] *Bh Me* [pāṭha] *Go Nā* माहेन्द्रं; Pu¹⁰ माहेन्द्र; La¹ महेन्द्रं; TMd³ GMy Tr¹ MTr⁶ शुद्धलिङ्गं च; MTr⁴ शुद्धलिङ्गश्च; GMd⁵ शुचिलङ्गं च; La¹ स्वदुपत्यश्च; Ho Ox² °वन्त्यश्च; sOx¹ sPu⁶ °वत्यस्तु; wKt¹ °यत्यश्च — d) Lo¹ *cor to* सुरापश्च; wKt³ सुरापो विशु°

251. Pādas a-b omitted in Tj²; too blurred to be read in GMd⁵. Cited by *Vij* 3.303; *Apa* 1216 — a) sOx¹ sPu⁶ °स्यचापीयं; TMd³ °स्यवमिधं — b) Lo¹ Tr¹ शिवं; Pu¹⁰ [*Jolly* M] वा — c) NKt⁴ TMd³ GMy *Vij* सुवर्णमपहृत्यापि; TMd⁴ Tr¹ हिरण्यमपहृत्यापि; wKt³ La¹ अपकृत्य; Bo BCa Ho BKt⁵ La¹ Lo² GMd¹ NNg oOr sOx¹ NPu¹ sPu⁶ MTr⁴ MTr⁶ Wa हिरण्यं तु; Bo BCa Ho La¹ Ox² Pu³ Pu⁵ Pu⁷ Tr² च; Hy तत् — d) NNg निर्मलाः; Pu² Pu⁴ निर्मलं; BKt⁵ कर्मणः

252.* Cited by *Vij* 3.304; *Apa* 1216; *Mādh* 2.458 — a) wKt¹ wKt³ Lo¹ NPu¹ Pu² Pu⁴ Tr² हविष्पन्तीयम°; Jo² NKt⁴ TMd³ sOx¹ sPu⁶ Pu⁵ Pu⁷ Tj¹ Tr¹ हविष्यान्तीयम°; Be¹ हविष्मान्तीयम°; NNg हविष्मन्तीयम°; Ox² हविष्मतीयम°; TMd⁴ हविष्योकेत्यम°; Be² Hy Jm Jo¹ Kt² Wa *Mādh Mandlik Jolly Jha KSS Dave* हविष्यन्तीयम°; La¹ हविष्हतीयम°; Lo² हविभतीहम°; oOr भविष्यन्तीयम° — b) BKt⁵ स मम ह इतीत्यच; Tr¹ तमंग; Ho तमंति; BBe² तमंमहतीति; Pu³ वा; oOr ह — c) TMd⁴ MTr⁴ MTr⁶ जप्त्वा पुरुषसूक्तं च [MTr⁶ तथा पु°]; Be¹ Bo BCa Ho wKt¹ BKt⁵ La¹ GMd⁵ GMy NNg Ox² Pu³ Pu⁵ Pu⁷ Tr¹ Tr² [*Jolly* Nd] *Vij* जप्त्वा तु; Jo² Lo³ Tj¹ जप्त्वापि; MTr⁴ जप्त्वा; Hy Jm Jo¹ Jo² Kt² Lo⁴ GMy NPu¹ Pu⁸ Pu¹⁰ Tj² [*Jolly* M] *Mandlik Jolly Jha KSS Dave* जपित्वा पौरुषं; NPu¹ MTr⁴ पुरुषं — d) Wa मुच्यन्ते; TMd⁴ MTr⁴ MTr⁶ पूयते

अवेत्यृचं जपेदब्दं यत्किंचेदमितीति च ॥२५३॥
प्रतिगृह्याप्रतिग्राह्यं भुक्त्वा चान्नं विगर्हितम् ।
जपंस्तरत्समन्दीयं पूयते मानवस्त्र्यहात् ॥२५४॥
सोमारौद्रं तु बह्वेना मासमभ्यस्य शुध्यति ।
स्रवन्त्यामाचरन् स्नानमर्यम्णामिति च तृचम् ॥२५५॥
अब्दार्धमिन्द्रमित्येतदेनस्वी सप्तकं जपेत् ।
अप्रशस्तं तु कृत्वाप्सु मासमासीत भैक्षभुक् ॥२५६॥
मन्त्रैः शाकलहोमीयैरब्दं हुत्वा घृतं द्विजः ।
सुगुर्वप्यपहन्त्येनो जप्त्वा वा नम इत्यृचम् ॥२५७॥

253. Pādas c-d *ma* in Lo^{4}. Cited by *Vij* 3.305; *Apa* 1217; *Mādh* 2.459 — a) TMd^{4} °सूक्ष्माणि — b) BBe^{2} चिकीर्षादपनो° ; Bo Pu^{10} °न्नापनो° ; TMd^{4} °नोदकं — c) GMd^{1} Pu^{2} Pu^{4} अपेत्यृचं; Pu^{10} अवत्यृचं Be^{1} अवेतृचं; Tr^{2} अपेतृच; Lo^{2} अवेयचं; TMd^{3} अव्येतृचं; Tr^{1} अवेतिच; La^{1} अधित्यृचं; Pu^{4} Pu^{5} जपेदष्टं; Lo^{1} जपेद्विप्रो — d) oOr यत्किंचिदिदमब्रवीत्; Hy °चैदमितीति; wKt^{1} Kt^{2} wKt^{3} NKt^{4} Lo^{1} Lo^{2} Lo^{4} GMy Ox^{2} Tr^{2} [*Jolly* M G] °चिदमितीति; BCa Pu^{10} °चिदिदमितीति; Be^{1} Pu^{5} Pu^{7} °चिदिमीति च [Be^{1} °मिति]; TMd^{4} °चेदमितियचः; Hy Jm Jo^{1} Kt^{2} wKt^{3} NKt^{4} NMd^{3} GMy NNg *Vij Ku Rn Nd Mr Mandlik Jolly Jha KSS Dave* वा

254. Cited by *Vij* 3.306; *Apa* 1217; *Mādh* 2.174 — a) Bo °प्रतिग्राह्या; La^{1} °प्रतिगृह्यं — b) Bo Ho Tj^{1} Tr^{1} भुक्ता; NKt^{4} भुङ्क्ता; wKt^{3} गुत्वा; La^{1} भुक्त्वाप्यन्नं; Pu^{5} वान्नं; Tr^{1} चाहं — c) wKt^{1} जपं चरेत्स-मन्दीयं; Bo जपस्तर° ; MTr^{6} जपेत्तर° ; BKt^{5} समस्तर° ; Be^{1} °मन्देयं; BKt^{5} °मन्दायं — d) *Apa* मानवो मुच्यते त्र्यहात्; Lo^{1} पुनते; Bo Ho wKt^{1} La^{1} Lo^{4} Pu^{10} मुच्यते; Bo मानवा त्र्यहात्; La^{1} मानसस्त्र्यहात्; Tr^{1} [*but cor fh*] °स्त्र्यहं; Wa °स्त्र्यहन्तं

255. Pādas b-d torn in GMy. Cited by *Apa* 1217 — a) *Apa* [vl] सौमारौद्रेण बह्वेनाः; Pu^{10} सौम्यारुद्रं रुचाह्वानां; Be^{1} La^{1} Lo^{2} TMd^{3} *Apa* सौमा° ; Tr^{2} सोम° ; NPu^{1} साम° ; GMy सोमं; Pu^{2} Pu^{4} सोम्यं; Ox^{2} सौम्यं; Jo^{2} Lo^{3} Tj^{1} सोमरुद्रं; Bo °रुद्रं; GMd^{1} °रौद्रे; Pu^{2} Pu^{4} च; Bo Lo^{4} NNg Ox^{2} Tj^{1} बह्वेनां; TMd^{3} बह्वीना; TMd^{4} Tr^{1} बह्वीनां; Pu^{2} Pu^{4} बह्वीयं; Pu^{5} Pu^{7} बह्व्येन; BKt^{5} बह्वानां; wKt^{1} वर्गेनाः — b) NNg *Me Jha Dave* बह्वेनाः समामभ्यस्य; NKt^{4} समभ्यस्य; BBe^{2} विशुध्यति — c) wKt^{1} NKt^{4} Lo^{2} Tr^{2} श्रवन्त्या° ; BBe^{2} अवन्त्या° ; MTr^{4} MTr^{6} °न्त्यां वाचरेत्; Be^{1} oOr sOx^{1} Ox^{2} sPu^{6} Wa °चरेत्; Bo wKt^{1} °चरत् — d) NKt^{4} Lo^{1} Pu^{8} °मर्यम्णमिति; Be^{1} °मर्यम्यामिति; GMd^{1} Pu^{5} Pu^{7} °मर्यम्यमिति; wKt^{3} °मर्यमा-मिति; MTr^{4} °मयम्यमिति; Tr^{1} *Apa* °मर्यम्यमपि; TMd^{4} TMd^{3} °म्णामपि वा ऋचं; BBe^{2} *om* च; Be^{1} wKt^{3} Lo^{3} Lo^{4} oOr Ox^{2} NPu^{1} Pu^{2} Pu^{3} Pu^{4} Pu^{5} Pu^{7} Pu^{8} Tj^{1} MTr^{5} Wa [*Jolly* M Nd] वा; Lo^{2} चेत्तृचं; BKt^{5} GMd^{1} MTr^{4} MTr^{6} चाप्यृचं; La^{1} GMd^{5} Tr^{1} *Apa* वाप्यृचं; Tr^{2} यात्यृचं; Hy Kt^{2} Lo^{4} sOx^{1} Ox^{2} Pu^{2} sPu^{6} *Jolly* त्र्यृचं; Be^{1} Bo Ho wKt^{1} wKt^{3} NPu^{1} Pu^{5} Pu^{7} त्यृचं

256. Omitted in BKt^{5} GMd^{1}; page containing 255d to 260d damaged in sPu^{6}. Cited by *Apa* 1217; pādas c-d cited by *Vij* 3.306 — a) Hy अव्दाद्धमि° ; Lo^{2} अर्धाव्दमि° ; Bo Lo^{3} *Jha Dave* अव्दार्थमि° — b) GMd^{5} °त्येतन्मनस्वी; Be^{1} व्रजेत्; Tr^{2} त्यजेत् — c) Pu^{2} Pu^{4} अपशस्तं; NNg sOx^{1} Ox^{2} sPu^{6} Tr^{2} अप्रकाशं; TMd^{3} अप्रशत्त्यं; TMd^{4} अप्रमानस्तु; BBe^{2} च; NNg Ox^{2} Pu^{3} Tr^{2} कृत्वैनो — d) Lo^{1} °मासैत; Bo °मासैक; Ho Lo^{4} TMd^{3} NNg Ox^{2} Pu^{3} Pu^{5} Pu^{7} *Vij* भैक्ष्यभुक्

257. Omitted in BKt^{5} GMd^{1}. Cited by *Vij* 3.303; *Apa* 1217; *Mādh* 2.457 — a) TMd^{3} शकल° ; wKt^{3} सकल° ; La^{1} शाकम° ; GMy शाकं च होमी° — b) TMd^{3} GMd^{5} MTr^{6} कृत्वा; MTr^{6} व्रतं द्विजः — c) Lo^{1} सुगुर्वमप्यहत्येनो; TMd^{3} स्वगुरुर्वाप्यहतैनो; NNg Pu^{3} Tj^{1} स्वगु° ; La^{1} Ox^{2} Tj^{2} *Vij* सगु° ;

महापातकसंयुक्तोऽनुगच्छेद्गाः समाहितः ।
अभ्यस्याब्दं पावमानीर्भैक्षाहारो विशुध्यति ॥२५८॥
अरण्ये वा त्रिरभ्यस्य प्रयतो वेदसंहिताम् ।
मुच्यते पातकैः सर्वैः पराकैः शोधितस्त्रिभिः ॥२५९॥
त्र्यहं तूपवसेद्युक्तस्त्रिरह्नोऽभ्युपयन्नपः ।
मुच्यते पातकैः सर्वैर्जप्त्वा त्रिरघमर्षणम् ॥२६०॥
यथाश्वमेधः क्रतुराट् सर्वपापापनोदनः ।
तथाघमर्षणं सूक्तं सर्वपापापनोदनम् ॥२६१॥
हत्वा लोकानपीमांस्त्रीनश्नन्नपि यतस्ततः ।
ऋग्वेदं धारयन्विप्रो नैनः प्राप्नोति किंचन ॥२६२॥
ऋक्संहितां त्रिरभ्यस्य यजुषां वा समाहितः ।
साम्नां वा सरहस्यानां सर्वपापैः प्रमुच्यते ॥२६३॥
यथा महाह्रदं प्राप्य क्षिप्रं लोष्टो विनश्यति ।

Pu^{2} Pu^{4} सर्वं गुर्व° — d) Pu^{5} Pu^{7} जपित्वा नम; MTr^{4} MTr^{6} जपित्वा मन;WKt^{1} च; TMd^{3} TMd^{4} Pu^{2} Wa *Bh* [pāṭha] मन; Lo^{2} मनः;Lo^{4} नस; Tr^{2} मन त्रिचं; *Mādh* नमदित्यृचं

258. Pādas a-b omitted in GMd^{1}, and pādas c-d in MTr^{6}. Cited by *Apa* 1218; *Mādh* 2.458 — a) Be^{1} NNg SOx^{1} Ox^{2} Pu^{3} उपपातक° — b) TMd^{3} °सुगच्छेद्गाः; Lo^{1} न गच्छेद्गाः; NNg Pu^{10} [*Jolly* M^{9}] °च्छेद्गां; Lo^{2} °च्छेद्गा; Be^{1} BKt^{5} समाहिताः — c) GMd^{1} अव्दार्धं पावमानीश्च भैक्षा°; TMd^{4} अव्दस्याव्दं; Pu^{2} Pu^{4} °मानीयैर्भै°; Be^{1} Bo WKt^{1} NKt^{4} TMd^{4} Pu^{5} Tj^{1} °मानी भै°; BBe^{2} BCa WKt^{3} °मानीं भै°; Ox^{2} °मानं भै° — d) Be^{1} Bo Ho La^{1} Ox^{2} Pu^{3} Pu^{5} °नीर्भैक्ष्याहारो; WKt^{1} °नीर्भिक्षाहारो; TMd^{4} °हारैर्विशुध्यति

259. Pādas a-b omitted in MTr^{6}, pādas b-c in Ho, and pāda-d in BKt^{5}; 257c-d given in place of 259c-d in Jm. Cited by *Vij* 3.301; *Apa* 1218; *Mādh* 2.456 — a) Lo^{4} आरण्ये; Lo^{1} च — b) Jo^{1} प्रयता; *Apa* प्रसन्नो; Be^{1} °संहिता; BBe^{2} °संहितान् — d) La^{1} Lo^{2} NNg NPu^{1} Pu^{2} Pu^{5} Pu^{7} पाराकैः; BBe^{2} पराकैश्च; TMd^{4} Tr^{1} शोधितैस्त्रिभिः

260. Pādas a-c omitted in Ho BKt^{5}. Cited by *Apa* 1218 — a) GMy त्रियहं; MTr^{4} त्र्यहन्युपव°; Jo^{2} Lo^{1} NPu^{1} MTr^{6} चोपव°; Bo नोपव°; TMd^{4} Tr^{1} °सेद्युक्तं त्रिर°; MTr^{6} °सेन्नक्तस्त्रिर° — b) TMd^{4} °रह्ना; GMd^{1} °रह्नेप्यपय°; TMd^{3} °प्युपयन्नपः; La^{1} °भ्युपपन्नतः; Lo^{3} °पयन्पयः; Tr^{1} °पयं तपः — c) Tr^{1} सर्वे जह्वा — d) Be^{1} Hy Jm Jo^{1} Kt^{2} Lo^{4} TMd^{3} Ox^{2} Pu^{10} Tj^{2} [*Jolly* M] *Mandlik Jolly Jha KSS Dave* सर्वैस्त्रिर्जपित्वाघमर्षणं; TMd^{4} तमघम°

261. Verse 261 placed after 263 in GMy — a) Bo क्रतुराः — b) GMd^{1} TMd^{3} TMd^{4} GMd^{5} GMy Tr^{1} MTr^{4}MTr^{6} °पापप्रणोदनः; [*Jolly* Nd] °पापप्रणोदनं; WKt^{3} °नोदतः; Pu^{2} Pu^{4} °नोदकः; [*Jolly* R] *ViDh* 55.7 °नोदकं — c) BKt^{5} यथा° — d) GMd^{1} TMd^{3} TMd^{4} GMd^{5} GMy Tr^{1} MTr^{4}MTr^{6} °पापप्रणोदनं [GMy °दनः]; La^{1} OOr Pu^{2} Pu^{4} °पापप्रणाशनं; BKt^{5} °नोदनः; Jo^{2} Tj^{1} °नोदकं

262. Cited by *Lakṣ* 1.174; *Mādh* 2.174 — a) Lo^{4} हुत्वा; OOr कामानपी°; TMd^{3} लोकमिमांस्त्री° — a-b) MTr^{4} MTr^{6} हत्वापि त्रीनिमान्लोकान्भुञ्जानोपि यतस्ततः — b) TMd^{3} °स्त्रीनन्नश्ननपि यत्नतः; *Lakṣ* °स्त्रीन्जपेच्चिरघमर्पणं — c) Lo^{1} GMd^{5} Tr^{2} धारयेद्विप्रो; BBe^{2} वादयन्विप्रो — d) Tr^{1} नैनं

263. Cited by *Apa* 1218 — c) Ho साम्ना; Tr^{2} सामां; TMd^{4} समां — d) Tj^{1} प्रमुच्येते

तथा दुश्चरितं सर्वं वेदे त्रिवृति मज्जति ॥२६४॥
ऋचो यजूंषि चाद्यानि सामानि विविधानि च ।
एष ज्ञेयस्त्रिवृद्वेदो यो वेदैनं स वेदवित् ॥२६५॥
आद्यं यत् त्र्यक्षरं ब्रह्म त्रयी यस्मिन्प्रतिष्ठिता ।
सो गुह्योऽन्यस्त्रिवृद्वेदो यस्तं वेद स वेदवित् ॥२६६॥

264.* Cited by *Apa* 1218 — a) TMd[4] *om* महा; Ho महाहृदं; GMy लोप्य — b) wKt[1] लोष्टो नश्यति च द्रुतं; Lo[1] Tj[1] क्षिप्र; Hy विक्षिप्रं; Jo[1] Kt[2] w Kt[3] Lo[3] Lo[4] NNg sOx[1] sPu[6] [*mc sh to*] Pu[10] [*Jolly* M R] *Mandlik Jolly Jha KSS Dave* क्षिप्तं; wKt[3] लोष्टा; BBe[2] Bo Hy Jm Jo[1] Jo[2] Kt[2] BKt[5] Lo[1] Lo[4] [*cor to*] GMd[1] GMy oOr sOx[1] Ox[2] NPu[1] Pu[5] sPu[6] Pu[7] Pu[8] Tj[2] *Mandlik Jolly Jha KSS Dave* लोष्टं; Lo[1] प्रनश्यति; Tr[1] निमज्जति — c) Hy सर्वे — d) Tr[1] वेदे प्रति निमज्जति; TMd[3] TMd[4] GMy Pu[5] वेद; *Apa* त्रिर्वृति; TMd[4] त्रिवृत मज्ज च

265.* Cited by *Apa* 1218 — a) BKt[5] ऋचौ; *Apa* [vl] दशयजूंषि; Be[1] BCa Ho Jm Jo[1] wKt[1] Kt[2] wKt[3] La[1] Lo[3] TMd[3] TMd[4] GMd[5] GMy oOr sOx[1] Ox[2] sPu[6] Tj[1] Tj[2] Tr[1] MTr[4] MTr[6] Wa [*Jolly* R Ku Nd] *Me* [pāṭha] *Nā Ku Rn Nd Mr Mandlik KSS* चान्यानि; Hy वान्यानि; Lo[1] GMd[1] [*but cor*] सामानि; *Apa* चाग्र्याणि; Bo तागानि — a-b) BBe[2] यजूंषि सामानि चान्यानि; Lo[1] Tr[2] यजूंषि सामानि साङ्गानि [Lo[1] चाङ्गानि]— b) TMd[3] समानि — c) TMd[4] *om* एष; BKt[5] °द्वेष्टो — d) Kt[2] Lo[2] NNg Pu[2] Pu[4] Tr[1] Wa यस्तं वेद स; sOx[1] sPu[6] यस्तु वेद स; wKt[1] वेदेनं यः स; wKt[3] वेदेनैनं स; Hy *om* वेदवित्; La[1] सर्ववेदवित्

266. Omitted in Lo[2] sOx[1] sPu[6] — a) TMd[3] GMd[5] Tr[1] तु त्र्यक्षरं; Be[1] Lo[1] य अक्षरं; Ho wKt[1] wKt[3] यदक्षरं; La[1] यास्त्र्यक्षरं — b) MTr[4] MTr[6] तस्मि°; wKt[1] TMd[4] Pu[2] Pu[4] यत्र प्रति°; Lo[3] °तिष्ठितां; TMd[3] °तिष्ठति — c) MTr[4] गुह्योग्निस्त्रि°; wKt[3] °वृद्देशो — d) MTr[4] MTr[6] यस्त्वं; La[1] यस्तु; BKt[5] यो वेदेन स; Be[1] Bo Jo[2] wKt[1] Lo[4] GMd[5] My oOr Pu[5] Pu[7] Pu[10] Tr[1] Wa [*Jolly* M G Nd] *Go Nā Nd Jolly* यो वेदैनं स; [*Jolly* Gr] यो वेद तं स; BBe[2] वेदं; Tr[2] *om* वेद स

Additional verse in Ho La[1] Lo[3] TMd[4] GMd[5] oOr sOx[1] NPu[1] Pu[2] Pu[4] sPu[6] Tj[1] MTr[4] MTr[6] [*Jolly* Nd R] *Mandlik* [क, ट, ड] *KSS Dave;* commented by *Rn;* pādas a-b given in TMd[3] GMy:

इत्येषोऽभिहितः कृत्स्नः प्रायश्चित्तविनिर्णयः ।
नैःश्रेयसं कर्मविधिं विप्रस्येमं निबोधत ॥

a) Lo[3] Tj[1] [*Jolly* N R] *Mandlik KSS Dave* एष वोभिहितः कृत्स्नः; sOx[1] sPu[6] एष वो विहितः सर्वः — b) Ho TMd[3] *Mandlik KSS Dave* प्रायश्चित्तस्य निर्णयः [TMd[3] निर्णयं]; GMy प्रायश्चित्तस्सुनिश्चितः — c) NPu[1] Pu[2] Pu[4] *KSS Dave* निःश्रेयसं; *Mandlik* निश्रेयसं; MTr[6] नैःश्रेयसीं; TMd[4] *Mandlik KSS Dave* धर्मविधिं — d) Ho विप्रस्येह निबोधत; sOx[1] sPu[6] विप्रस्यैतान्निबोधत; La[1] विप्रस्येनं; [*Jolly* Nd R] विप्रस्यैनं

Additional half-verse in TMd[3] GMy sOx[1] sPu[6]:

अतः परं प्रवक्ष्यामि संसारविधिमुत्तमम् ।

b) TMd[3] नैश्रेसविधिं शुभं

Additional half-verse in La[1] Pu[2] Pu[4] *Mandlik* [ट, ड] *KSS Dave:*

पृथग्ब्राह्मणकल्पाभ्यां स हि वेदस्त्रिवृत्स्मृतः ।

॥ इति मानवे धर्मशास्त्रे भृगुप्रोक्तायां संहितायामेकादशोऽध्यायः ॥

Colophon: Be^{1} Lo^{1} Lo^{2} Lo^{3} TMd^{3} NNg oOr sOx^{1} sPu^{6} Tr^{1} इति श्रीमानवे; wKt^{3} भृगुप्रोक्ते; Be^{1} BKt^{5}. GMd^{1} TMd^{3} sOx^{1} sPu^{6} *om* भृगुप्रोक्तायां संहितायां; Lo^{1} Lo^{2} Lo^{3} भृगुप्रोक्तसंहितायां; wKt^{3} *om* संहितायां; sOx^{1} sPu^{6} प्रायश्चित्ताध्याय एकादशः; wKt^{1} प्रायश्चित्तनिर्णयो नामैकादशोध्यायः; Ho प्रायश्चित्ताख्यो नामैकादशोध्यायः; Lo^{1} प्रायश्चित्तविधिर्नामैकादशोध्यायः

[द्वादशोऽध्यायः]

चातुर्वर्ण्यस्य कृत्स्नोऽयमुक्तो धर्मस्त्वयानघ ।
कर्मणां फलनिर्वृत्तिं शंस नस्तत्त्वतः पराम् ॥१॥
स तानुवाच धर्मात्मा महर्षीन्मानवो भृगुः ।
अस्य सर्वस्य शृणुत कर्मयोगस्य निर्णयम् ॥२॥
शुभाशुभफलं कर्म मनोवाग्देहसंभवम् ।
कर्मजा गतयो नृणामुत्तमाधममध्यमाः ॥३॥
तस्येह त्रिविधस्यापि त्र्यधिष्ठानस्य देहिनः ।
दशलक्षणयुक्तस्य मनो विद्यात्प्रवर्तकम् ॥४॥
परद्रव्येष्वभिध्यानं मनसानिष्टचिन्तनम् ।
वितथाभिनिवेशश्च त्रिविधं कर्म मानसम् ॥५॥
पारुष्यमनृतं चैव पैशुन्यं चैव सर्वशः ।

Before verse 1 GMd[5] oOr add ऋषय ऊचुः

1. Cited by *Mādh* 2.484-5 — a) La[1] चतुर्वर्ण्यस्य; wKt[1] wKt[3] BKt[5] La[1] GMd[1] oOr NPu[1] Pu[2] Pu[4] Tr[2] चातुर्वर्णस्य; Ho चातुर्वर्ण्य; Be[1] कृच्छ्रो; NKt[4] कृष्णो — b) TMd[3] धर्मस्सनातनः — c) wKt[1] Tr[2] कर्मणा; BBe[2] wKt[1] BKt[5] °निष्पत्तिं — d) Tr[1] शंसि; GMd[1] °त्वतश्शुभां; Be[1] Bo Ho Lo[1] TMd[3] GMd[5] NNg NPu[1] Pu[3] Pu[10] Tr[2] Wa परं; BKt[5] परान्; here GMd[5] adds भृगुरुवाच

2. Omitted in Wa. Cited by *Mādh* 2.485 — b) GMd[1] महर्षीम्मानवो; Tr[2] गुरुः — c) wKt[3] अस्य धर्मस्य — d) wKt[3] कर्मदोषस्य; GMd[1] सर्वयोगस्य; TMd[4] निर्णयः; BBe[2] निश्चयं

3. Cited by *Mādh* 2.485 — a) GMy शुभाशुभं — b) sOx[1] sPu[6] °वाक्कायसंभवं; MTr[4] MTr[6] °संश्रयं — c) TMd[3] कर्मणा; Tr[1] कर्मजन्मर्क्षयो; TMd[4] तन्तुयो — d) Tr[2] °मध्यमः; Ho °मध्यमा; TMd[4] °मध्यमं

4. Cited by *Mādh* 2.485 — a) Lo[3] यस्येह; MTr[4] MTr[6] कस्येह; Hy Lo[3] Tj[1] °धस्यास्य — b) Ho Jm wKt[1] MTr[5] अधिष्ठा° [*om* त्रि]; *Mādh* ह्यधिष्ठा°; oOr °ष्ठानं च; GMy [*Jolly* Nd] देहिनां; La[1] MTr[4] MTr[6] देहिषु — c) GMd[5] °क्षणस्य युक्तस्य; TMd[3] °युक्तस्सन्मनो — d) La[1] Lo[1] GMd[1] TMd[4] विद्याप्रव°; La[1] °त्प्रमत्तकं; BKt[5] °वर्तकः; Lo[2] oOr °वर्तनं

Additional verse in Pu[2]; pādas a-b given after verse 5 in NKt[4] [cf. addition at 12.8]:

मानसं त्रिविधं कर्म वाचिकं तु चतुर्विधम् ।
त्रिविधं चैव शारीरं दशकर्मपथं व्रजेत् ।

a-b) NKt[4] त्रिविधं तु शरीरेण वाचा चैव चतुर्विधं

5. Cited by *Apa* 997; *Mādh* 2.485 — a) Tj[2] °भिध्यामं; Lo[2] °पध्यानं; TMd[3] °भिज्ञानं — b) Bo °चेतनं — c) TMd[4] विक्रिदाभि°; Ox[2] Tr[1] °निवेशं च; Be[1] TMd[4] °निवेशस्य — d) Lo[3] धर्म; Ho मानसः

अनिबद्धप्रलापश्च वाङ्मयं स्याच्चतुर्विधम् ॥६॥
अदत्तानामुपादानं हिंसा चैवाविधानतः ।
परदारोपसेवा च शारीरं त्रिविधं स्मृतम् ॥७॥
मानसं मनसैवायमुपभुङ्क्ते शुभाशुभम् ।
वाचा वाचा कृतं कर्म कायेनैव तु कायिकम् ॥८॥
शरीरजैः कर्मदोषैर्याति स्थावरतां नरः ।
वाचिकैः पक्षिमृगतां मानसैरन्त्यजातिताम् ॥९॥
वाग्दण्डोऽथ मनोदण्डः कर्मदण्डस्तथैव च ।
यस्यैते नियता बुद्धौ त्रिदण्डीति स उच्यते ॥१०॥

6.* Page containing verses 5c to 12b torn in sPu6. Cited by *Apa* 998; *Hem* 3/3.632; *Mādh* 2.485 — b) Lo2 *om* चैव पैशुन्यं; *Apa* पैशुन्यमपि; BBe2 Hy Jm Jo1 Jo2 wKt1 Kt2 La1 Lo1 Lo3 GMd1 TMd4 Ox2 Pu8 Tj1 Tj2 MTr6 [*Jolly* R Nd]*Mandlik Jha KSS Dave* चापि; sOx1 वापि; Pu5 Pu7 Pu10 Wa [*Jolly* M] *Apa* सर्वतः; Tr2 सर्वदा — c) GMd5 अनिर्बद्ध°; TMd3 अतबंध°; Be1 Pu2 Pu4 अनिरुद्ध°; Hy असंबद्धः; Bo Ho wKt1 असंबंध°; BBe2 Jm Jo1 Jo2 Kt2 wKt3 Lo1 Lo3 Ox2 Tj1 Tj2 *Lakṣ Mandlik Jha KSS Dave* असंबद्ध°; Tr1 °प्रलापं च — d) wKt1 वाचिकं; wKt3 स्याच्चतुर्गुणं; La1 स्याच्चतुर्थकं

7. Omitted in Pu10. Cited by *Hem* 3/3.632; *Mādh* 2.485 — b) Be1 TMd4 GMy Tj1 चैव विधानतः; La1 चैवभिधानतः; Tr2 चैव निशानतः — c) Ho °पसेवी; oOr °पवासे — d) Pu4 शरीरं; Jo2 wKt1 Lo3 Ox2 Tj1 *Hem* कायिकं

8. Cited by *Mādh* 2.485 — a) Tj1 मानसैवा°; Tr1 मानसेवा°; oOr °सैवेयमुप° — b) GMy °भुङ्क्त; [*Jolly* M] °युङ्क्ते — c) NKt4 वाचा वाचं; Ox2 वाचा वाचि; GMd5 GMy Tr1 MTr4 MTr6 *Mādh* वाचैव वाक्कृतं; TMd3 वाचिकं वाक्कृतं; Jo2 Pu3 Tj1 कृतं सर्वं; Tr2 *om* कर्म — d) wKt1 कायेनैकं; GMd1 Tj2 कार्येनैव; Be1 Bo Hy Jm Jo1 Jo2 Kt2 BKt5 Lo1 Lo2 Lo3 Pu3 Pu5 Pu7 Pu10 Tj1 Tj2 MTr5 *Mandlik Jolly Jha KSS Dave* च; Pu8 कायिकां; Lo2 कायकं

After pāda-b additional half-verse in TMd3:

मनसा यत्कृतं कर्म मानसं तदिहोच्यते ।

Additional verse in NNg oOr Ox2 *Mandlik* [क] *Dave KSS;* pādas c-d in NKt4 [see 12.5]:

त्रिविधं तु शरीरेण वाचा चैव चतुर्विधम् ।
मनसा त्रिविधं कर्म दशधर्मपथांस्त्यजेत् ॥

a) oOr Ox2 च — c) NNg Ox2 मानसं; NKt4 oOr त्रिविधं चैव — d) Ox2 दशकर्म नरस्त्यजेत्

9. Cited by *Apa* 996; *Mādh* 2.485; pādas c-d cited by *Vij* 3.68 — a) Tr2 शारीरैः कर्मदोषैश्च याति; Be1 GMd1 Pu5 Pu7 शारीरजैः; Tr1 वीरीरजैः — b) wKt1 जनः — c) oOr वाचकैः; Ho sOx1 Pu10 पक्ष°; MTr6 °मृगतो— d) Bo मारिनैरल्पजातितां; sOx1 °जाततां; NKt4 °जात्यतां; TMd3 °जातिमां

Additional verses in NNg *Mandlik* [numerous mss.] *Dave KSS:*

शुभैः प्रयोगैर्देवत्वं व्यामिश्रैर्मानुषो भवेत् ।
अशुभैः केवलैश्चैव तिर्यग्योनिषु जायते ॥

NNg adds two more verse [same as 1-2 after verse 10]; *Mandlik Dave KSS* add three more verses [same as 1-3 after verse 10]

10. Verses 10 and 11 transposed in TMd3. Cited by *Apa* 951; *Lakṣ* 14.42; *Mādh* 1.549 —

त्रिदण्डमेतन्निक्षिप्य सर्वभूतेषु मानवः ।
कामक्रोधौ च संयम्य ततः सिद्धिं नियच्छति ॥११॥
योऽस्यात्मनः कारयिता तं क्षेत्रज्ञं प्रचक्षते ।
यः करोति तु कर्माणि स भूतात्मोच्यते बुधैः ॥१२॥
जीवसंज्ञोऽन्तरात्मान्यः सहजः सर्वदेहिनाम् ।
येन वेदयते सर्वं सुखं दुःखं च जन्मसु ॥१३॥

a) Jo[2] Lo[3] Tj[1] *Apa* वाग्दण्डश्च; BKt[5] वाग्दण्डोग्र — b) BBe[2] Hy Jm Jo[1] Jo[2] wKt[1] Kt[2] wKt[3] Lo[1] Lo[3] Pu[3] Tj[1] Tj[2] [*Jolly* Ku] *Go Ku Rn Mr Mandlik Jha KSS Dave* कायदण्ड°; Bo Jo[2] La[1] Lo[3] GMd[1] TMd[4] GMy Tj[1] Tr[1] MTr[4] MTr[5] MTr[6] [*Jolly* Nd R]*Apa* °दण्डश्च ते त्रयः [*Apa* °दण्डोथ] — c) Bo तस्यैते; TMd[4] यस्य ते; Bo Ho Hy Jm Jo[1] Kt[2] Lo[1] Pu[8] Tj[2] *Me Rn Mr Mandlik Jolly Jha KSS Dave* निहिता; Be[1] NPu[1] Pu[3] Pu[4] Pu[10] Tr[2] [*Jolly* M]*Apa Rc* नियता दण्डाः; TMd[4] नियता शुद्धा; La[1] sOx[1] Ox[2] नियता नित्यं; NKt[4] बुद्धी — d) Tr[2] त्रिदण्डीत्युच्यते बुधैः; Jo[2] wKt[3] La[1] Lo[3] sOx[1] Ox[2] NPu[1] Pu[4] Pu[10] Tj[1] Wa [*Jolly* M] स त्रिदण्डी व्यवस्थितः; *Rn* स त्रिदण्डीति स्तूयते; *Apa* स त्रिदण्डीति कथ्यते; BKt[5] त्रिदण्डी स; Ho *om* स

Additional verses in Be[1] La[1]; they are given after 12.9 in NPu[1] *Mandlik KSS Dave*, and after 12.12 in Pu[2] Pu[4]; first two verse given after 12.9 in NNg; the second only after 12.10 and the first after 12.11 in Ox[2]; all three cited after 12.11 by *Go*; verse 2 cited by *Apa* 951:

वाग्दण्डो हन्ति विज्ञानं मानोदण्डः परां गतिम् ।
कर्मदण्डस्तु लोकांस्त्रीन्हन्यादपरिरक्षितः ।।१।।
वाग्दण्डो मौनमातिष्ठेत् कर्मदण्डे त्वनाशनम् ।
मानसस्य तु दण्डस्य प्राणायामो विधीयते ।।२।।
त्रिदण्डं धारयेद्योगी शारीरं न तु वैणवं ।
वाचिकं कायिकं चैव मानसं च यथाविधि ।।३।।

1. a) Ox[2] वै ज्ञानं — c) La[1] कर्मदण्डश्च

2. a) NNg NPu[1] *Mandlik KSS* वाग्दण्डोथ भवेन्मौनं; Ox[2] *Dave* वाग्दण्डे — b) NPu[1] मनोदण्डस्त्वनाशनं; *Apa* कर्मदण्डस्त्वहिंसनं; Be[1] त्वनाशकं; La[1] Pu[2] Pu[4] *Dave* त्वनश्नतां; Ox[2] त्वभोजनं — c) Ox[2] मानसे दाण्डनीये तु; NNg NPu[1] *Mandlik KSS* शारीरस्य हि दण्डस्य; Be[1] मानसे च तथा दण्डे — d) Ox[2] प्राणायामो विशोधनं

3. b) Be[1] Pu[4] शारीरेण तु — c-d) La[1] मानसं वाचिकं चैव कायिकं विजितेन्द्रियः

11. * Verses 11 and 12 transposed in Jm. Cited by *Lakṣ* 14.43; *Mādh* 1.549 — a) La[1] °मेतान्निक्षिप्य; TMd[3] °मेनं निक्षिप्य; Tr[1] °मेतं निक्षिप्य — b) Tj[1] मानवाः — c) BKt[5] °क्रोधो; TMd[3] °क्रोधा; La[1] °क्रोधं; *Lakṣ* °क्रोधौ वशे यस्य; BBe[2] Bo Ho Hy Jm Jo[1] Jo[2] Kt[2] GMd[1] TMd[3] GMy sOx[1] NPu[1] Pu[2] Pu[8] Tj[1] Tj[2] Tr[2] *Mādh Mandlik Jolly KSS* तु; *Dave Jha* सुसंयम्य — d) Kt[2] GMd[1] TMd[3] TMd[4] GMy Tr[1] MTr[5] *Mādh Bh Me Rn Rc Jolly Jha Dave* निगच्छति

12. Cited by *Lakṣ* 14.113 — a) Lo[2] Tj[1] यस्यात्मनः; *Lakṣ* अस्यात्मनः; Tr[1] योस्यान्मानः; Ho कारयता; sOx[1] sPu[6] कारयतः; GMd[1] कारयित्वा — b) BKt[5] Lo[1] क्षत्रज्ञं तं; TMd[4] च रक्षते — d) wKt[1] स दूतार्थोवृते; Jo[2] भूतात्मेत्युच्यते; Pu[5] Pu[7] भूतात्मोत्युच्यते

13. Cited by *Lakṣ* 14.113 — a) Pu[5] Pu[7] जीवः; TMd[3] MTr[6] °संज्ञान्त°; Be[1] NNg °रात्मा यः; Lo[2] Ox[2] °रात्मानः — b) Hy *om* सहजः; TMd[4] °देहिना — c) TMd[3] एवं वेद°; Pu[10] वेदयति; oOr sOx[1] sPu[6] वेदयते कर्म — d) GMd[1] TMd[3] TMd[4] sOx[1] sPu[6] सुखदुःखं; MTr[4] MTr[6] दुःखादिजन्मसु; Ho sOx[1] sPu[6] कर्मसु; NNg जन्म तु

तावुभौ भूतसंपृक्तौ महान्क्षेत्रज्ञ एव च ।
उच्चावचेषु भूतेषु स्थितं तं व्याप्य तिष्ठतः ॥१४॥
असंख्या मूर्त्तयस्तस्य निष्पतन्ति शरीरतः ।
उच्चावचानि भूतानि सततं चेष्टयन्ति याः ॥१५॥
पञ्चभ्य एव मात्राभ्यः प्रेत्य दुष्कृतिनां नृणाम् ।
शरीरं यातनार्थीयमन्यदुत्पद्यते दृढम् ॥१६॥
तेनानुभूय ता यामीः शरीरेणेह यातनाः ।
तास्वेव भूतमात्रासु प्रलीयन्ते विभागशः ॥१७॥
सोऽनुभूयासुखोदर्कान् दोषान्विषयसङ्गजान् ।
व्यपेतकल्मषोऽभ्येति तावेवोभौ महौजसौ ॥१८॥
तौ धर्मं पश्यतस्तस्य पापं चातन्द्रितौ सह ।
याभ्यां प्राप्नोति संपृक्तः प्रेत्येह च सुखासुखम् ॥१९॥

14. a) TMd^{3} ता उभौ; BBe^{2} °संप्रोक्तौ; NNg °संयुक्तौ; Tr^{1} °संवृत्तौ — b) Be^{1} BKt^{5} TMd^{4} NNg महाक्षे°; sPu^{6} °क्षेत्र एव; TMd^{4} NNg °त्रज्ञ उच्यते; Ox^{2} एव तु — d) wKt^{1} स्थितिं; NPu^{1} Pu^{2} Pu^{4} स्थितौ तौ; BKt^{5} [*Jolly* M] तौ; Pu^{5} Pu^{7} संव्याप्य; Ho La^{1} Lo^{2} MTr^{4} MTr^{6} तिष्ठति

Additional verse in NPu^{1} Pu^{2} Pu^{4} *Mandlik* [ट, ठ, ड] *KSS;* given after 14b in Be^{1}:

उत्तमः पुरुषस्त्वन्यः परमात्मेत्युदाहृतः ।
यो लोकत्रयमाविश्य बिभर्त्यव्ययमीश्वरः ॥

d) NPu^{1} Pu^{2} बिभर्ति त्रयमीश्वरः; Pu^{4} बिभर्ति स्वयमीश्वरः; *Mandlik* °व्यय ईश्वरः

15. a) NNg असंख्यया; TMd^{4} °यस्तस्या; GMd^{1} °यस्सर्वा — b) NKt^{4} निःपतति; BKt^{5} निपतन्ति; Tr^{2} शरीरितः; Ho शरीरिणः — d) GMy चेष्टयति; GMd^{1} चेष्टयत्प्रजाः; Ho या; Pu^{2} Pu^{4} Pu^{10} यः; MTr^{6} ताः; Pu^{8} तः

16.* a) wKt^{1} पञ्चेभ्यो द्रवमात्राभ्यः; Ho पञ्चेभ्य; GMd^{1} TMd^{3} GMd^{5} GMy MTr^{4} MTr^{5} MTr^{6} पञ्चानामेव; TMd^{4} पञ्चाने मात्रा°; Ho Lo^{3} मात्रेभ्यः; *Me Ku Dave Jha* भूतेभ्यः — b) TMd^{3} दुष्कृतिनो; GMd^{1} निष्कृतिनो — c) BBe^{2} याचनार्थी°; GMd^{1} यातनार्थाय अन्य°; Pu^{5} Pu^{7} यातनार्थाय वान्य°; [*Jolly* Nd] यातनात्मीयमन्य° — d) La^{1} GMy °न्यमुत्प°; Be^{1} BBe^{2} Bo Hy Jm Jo^{1} wKt^{1} Kt^{2} wKt^{3} NKt^{4} BKt^{5} La^{1} Lo^{1} Lo^{3} NNg oOr sOx^{1} Ox^{2} sPu^{6} Pu^{8} Pu^{10} Tj^{1} Tj^{2} Tr^{2} MTr^{5} [*Jolly* M Nd R^{1} Ra$^{1-3}$] *Mandlik Jolly Jha KSS Dave* ध्रुवं; Pu^{5} दण्डं

17. a) Pu^{3} ततोनुभूय; GMd^{1} °भूय ते यानि; Tj^{2} सा; NNg तां; Lo^{1} यामीस्ता; Ho oOr यामीं; TMd^{4} याविं; wKt^{1} चामीः — b) MTr^{5} शरीरेण तु; GMd^{1} यातना — c) wKt^{1} तान्येव; Pu^{4} तास्तेव; GMd^{1} तावेव; NKt^{4} तदेवं; BBe^{2} भूतमायासु; TMd^{4} °मात्रे तु; Tr^{2} °मात्राश्च — d) GMd^{1} MTr^{4} MTr^{6} तद्विहाय प्रलीयते

18. Pādas b-d omitted in Tr^{1} — a) Ho wKt^{3} TMd^{4} GMy NNg oOr sOx^{1} Pu^{5} sPu^{6} Pu^{7} Tj^{1} MTr^{6} [*Jolly* Go R] °भूय सुखो°; BKt^{5} Lo^{1} °भूयात्सुखो°; wKt^{1} °भूयाद्यथोदर्कान्; TMd^{3} °भूयादिवोदर्कं; Pu^{10} °खोदर्कां — b) NKt^{4} शेषान्वि°; Lo^{3} Tj^{1} लोकान्वि°; Lo^{3} °न्विषयमागतान्; Be^{1} Hy Lo^{1} oOr Tj^{1} Tj^{2} Tr^{2} °सङ्गतान्; TMd^{3} °सङ्गकान् — c) GMy व्यतीत°; Tr^{2} सपेत°; wKt^{1} व्यपेनि°; Be^{1} °कलुषो; TMd^{3} °प्येति — d) Jo^{2} La^{1} oOr Pu^{8} Tj^{2} महोजसौ; GMy NPu^{1} महाजसौ

19. Pāda-a omitted in Tr^{1}; page containing verses 19–21 missing in Pu^{10} — a) Pu^{5} Pu^{7}

यद्याचरति धर्मं स प्रायशोऽधर्ममल्पशः ।
तैरेव चावृतो भूतैः स्वर्गे सुखमुपाश्नुते ॥२०॥
यदि तु प्रायशोऽधर्मं सेवते धर्ममल्पशः ।
तैर्भूतैः स परित्यक्तो यामीः प्राप्नोति यातनाः ॥२१॥
यामीस्ता यातनाः प्राप्य स जीवो वीतकल्मषः ।
तान्येव पञ्च भूतानि पुनरभ्येति भागशः ॥२२॥
एता दृष्ट्वास्य जीवस्य गतीः स्वेनैव चेतसा ।
धर्मतोऽधर्मतश्चैव धर्मे दध्यात्सदा मनः ॥२३॥
सत्त्वं रजस्तमश्चैव त्रीन्विद्यादात्मनो गुणान् ।
यैर्व्याप्येमान्स्थितो भावान् महान्सर्वानशेषतः ॥२४॥
यो यदैषां गुणो देहे साकल्येनातिरिच्यते ।

द्वौ; TMd^3 तद्धर्मं; BKt^5 धर्मौं — b) Bo चातन्दृतौ; NKt^4 चातन्द्रितैः; Tr^1 चातन्द्रिणौ; TMd^3 च तन्द्रितौ — c) Ho NNg ताभ्यां; Lo^3 Tj^1 चाप्नोति; Bo Ho Jo^2 Lo^3 TMd^3 Tj^1 Tr^2 संयुक्तः — d) La^1 Lo^2 oOr sOx^1 Pu^3 sPu^6 Tr^2 प्रेत्य चेह; GMd^1 TMd^3 TMd^4 GMy Tr^1 सुखासुखे; Bo Ho BKt^5 La^1 Lo^3 oOr sOx^1 Ox^2 NPu^1 Pu^2 Pu^4 sPu^6 Tj^1 MTr^5 [*Jolly* R Nd] शुभाशुभं [Bo Ho Ox^2 °शुभे]

20. Pādas c-d omitted in BKt^5 — a) Ox^2 Pu^5 Pu^7 [*Jolly* M G R] *Nd Jolly Jha Dave* यथाचरति; NPu^1 Pu^2 Pu^4 Tr^1 यदाचरति; Be^1 यद्याचरसि; MTr^4 यः — b) TMd^4 °धर्मकल्पशः — c) Tr^2 तेनैव; Pu^5 Pu^7 तैरव्यापृतो; Ho प्रावृतो; wKt^3 चावृतैर्भूतैः; Tj^2 *om* भूतैः — d) wKt^1 स्वर्गेषु सुखमश्नुते; Ho स्वर्गं; La^1 सुखमपाश्नुते; Ox^2 सुखमश्नुते

21. Pādas a-b omitted in BKt^5, and pādas c-d in Pu^2 Pu^4 — a) TMd^3 यदि तं; oOr यदिति — b) Ho सेव्यते; GMy सेचन्ते; Pu^2 Pu^4 धर्मकल्मशः — c) Jo^1 शतैर्भूतैः; Jo^2 GMd^5 NNg Pu^5 Pu^7 Tr^1 Tr^2 [*Jolly* G R Nd M^3] संपरि°; GMd^1 GMy संपरिश्चक्तो; NKt^4 °त्यक्ते — d) BBe^2 Ho Pu^5 Pu^7 यामी; TMd^3 यामि; NKt^4 वामी; TMd^4 प्राप्या; TMd^3 यातना; Tr^2 नित्यशः

22.* Pādas a-b omitted in Pu^2 Pu^4 — a) La^1 Lo^1 Ox^2 [*Jolly* M] यामीस्तु; Wa यामी तु; TMd^4 यामीश्च; Tj^2 यातनामाप्य — b) wKt^1 शारीरो वीत°; Bo वात°; Be^1 [*but cor*] °कलुषः — c) TMd^4 एतानि पञ्च; MTr^5 सर्वभूतानि — d) Hy Jm Jo^1 wKt^1 Kt^2 NKt^4 GMd^1 TMd^3 TMd^4 Pu^5 Pu^7 Tj^2 Tr^1 MTr^4 MTr^6 [*Jolly* G Nd] *GoRn Nd Mandlik Jha KSS Dave* पुनरप्येति

23. Page containing verses 23c–28d torn in sPu^6 — a) Ox^2 एतास्तु दृष्ट्वा जीवस्य; NKt^4 BKt^5 La^1 GMd^1 TMd^3 GMd^5 GMy Tr^1 MTr^4 एतां; MTr^4 यः दृष्ट्वास्य; wKt^1 दृष्ट्वा च; Lo^3 Pu^3 Tj^1 दृष्टास्तु; TMd^3 दृष्टास्स; NNg *om* जीवस्य — b) La^1 GMd^1 TMd^3 GMd^5 GMy Tr^1 MTr^4 MTr^5 MTr^6 गतिं; NKt^4 गति; Tj^2 गतिः; Lo^3 गतोः; Ho गताः; Pu^5 Pu^7 गतः; TMd^4 गतिस्तेनैव; Ho स्वेनेव; Pu^5 Pu^7 स्वेनेह; GMy चेतसाः; Pu^2 चेतसः; TMd^3 चेतनं; Be^1 BBe^2 Ho GMd^1 Ox^2 Tr^1 तेजसा — d) BBe^2 Bo Hy Jm Jo^1 Kt^2 NKt^4 Ox^2 Pu^5 Pu^7 Tj^2 [*Jolly* G] *Mandlik Jha KSS Dave* दध्यात्सदा; GMd^1 दद्यान्मनस्सदा; sOx^1 °त्सनातनः; Bo MTr^4 °त्सदात्मनः; La^1 मतः

24. *ma* in Pu^7. Cited by *Lakṣ* 14126; *Mādh* 2.487 — a) GMd^1 TMd^3 GMd^5 TMd^4 GMy *Mādh* °मश्चेति — b) Bo La^1 Ox^2 त्रीन्विन्द्या°; wKt^3 गुणात्; La^1 गुणाः; TMd^4 गुणः; Ho गुणैः *cor to* गुणः — c) Tr^2 भवान्; wKt^1 भावा; Ho धर्मान्; La^1 लोकान् — d) Lo^3 महाशेपानशेपतः

स तदा तद्गुणप्रायं तं करोति शरीरिणम् ॥२५॥
सत्त्वं ज्ञानं तमोऽज्ञानं रागद्वेशौ रजः स्मृतम् ।
एतद्व्याप्तिमदेतेषां सर्वभूताश्रितं वपुः ॥२६॥
तत्र यत्प्रीतिसंयुक्तं किंचिदात्मनि लक्षयेत् ।
प्रशान्तमिव शुद्धाभं सत्त्वं तदुपधारयेत् ॥२७॥
यत्तु दुःखसमायुक्तमप्रीतिकरमात्मनः ।
तद्रजोऽप्रतिघं विद्यात् सततं हारि देहिनाम् ॥२८॥
यत्तु स्यान्मोहसंयुक्तमव्यक्तविषयात्मकम् ।
अप्रतर्क्यमविज्ञेयं तमस्तदुपधारयेत् ॥२९॥
त्रयाणामपि चैतेषां गुणानां यः फलोदयः ।
अग्र्यो मध्यो जघन्यश्च तं प्रवक्ष्याम्यशेषतः ॥३०॥
वेदाभ्यासस्तपो ज्ञानं शौचमिन्द्रियनिग्रहः ।

25. Omitted in Pu^{5}. Cited by *Lakṣ* 14.126; *Mādh* 2.487 — a) Ho योपदेषां; Be^{1} BBe^{2} Lo^{2} Lo^{3} TMd^{3} NNg oOr sOx^{1} Pu^{10} Tj^{1} Tr^{2} यदेषां; BKt^{5} यद्येषां; wKt^{1} यदैव; Lo^{3} गुणा; Hy देह — b) BKt^{5} शाकल्ये° — c) Lo^{2} °प्रायस्तं — d) BBe^{2} wKt^{3} TMd^{3} GMd^{5} Pu^{4} Pu^{7} शरीरिणां; wKt^{1} शरीरिणः

26. Cited by *Lakṣ* 14.126; *Mādh* 2.487 — a) oOr सत्त्व; Tr^{2} सत्त्वो; BKt^{5} सत्यं; La^{1} सर्वं; Bo सत्त्वज्ञान; Ho तपोज्ञानं — b) Lo^{3} GMd^{1} Wa °द्वेषो; Pu^{10} °द्वैषो; TMd^{4} °द्वेषि तमस्स्मृतौ; Lo^{3} Tj^{1} तमः स्मृतं; La^{1} Pu^{5} Pu^{7} स्मृतः; wKt^{1} oOr स्मृतौ; Lo^{3} स्मृती — c) Lo^{2} एतद्व्याप्तिः सदैतेषां; Ox^{2} एतद्व्याप्तमिदं तेषां; Pu^{2} स तद्व्या°; sOx^{1} °प्तिमहत्तेषां — d) GMy [*Jolly* Nd] °भूताश्रयं; Lo^{1} °भूतावितं

27. *ma* in wKt^{1}; pādas c-d omitted in BKt^{5} GMd^{1} [haplo]. Cited by *Apa* 999; *Lakṣ* 14.126 — a) Bo यत्र; TMd^{3} अत्र; Be^{1} य प्रीति°; NPu^{1} यः प्रीति°; BBe^{2} यत्प्रति° — b) Lo^{3} लक्षये — c) *Apa* प्रभातमिव; Wa शुद्धाभां; GMy शुद्धांभं; Tr^{2} शुद्धान्तं; TMd^{3} शुधाहं — d) Lo^{3} Pu^{5} Pu^{7} Tj^{1} तत्सत्त्वमुप°; Jo^{2} तत्सर्वमुप°; GMy तमुपधा°; BBe^{2} Bo Ho Jo^{2} Lo^{3} Ox^{2} Tj^{1} तदवधारयेत्; Pu^{8} °धारये; wKt^{1} °चारयेत्

28 Omitted in GMd^{1} TMd^{4}; pāda-a *ma* in wKt^{1}; pādas a-b omitted in Pu^{2}. Cited by *Lakṣ* 14.126 — a) Bo Lo^{1} यत्त; Jo^{2} Lo^{3} Tj^{1} *Lakṣ* यच्च; Pu^{10} [*Jolly* M] दुःखे; BKt^{5} दुष्यसमा° — a-b) Pu^{4} यत्तु स्यान्मोहसंयुक्तव्यकां विषयात्मकं — b) Lo^{2} °युक्तं किंचिदात्मनि लक्षयेत्; TMd^{3} °युक्तं प्रीतिकारकमात्मनः; Ho °युक्तं यत्प्रीति°; Lo^{3} Tj^{1} °युक्तं न प्रीति°; Pu^{5} Pu^{7} °कारमा°; GMy °मात्मनि — c) TMd^{3} तद्राजो; Be^{1} तद्रजो; NPu^{1} तद्यजो; sOx^{1} तत्तमो; NNg तद्रजः प्रतिघं; wKt^{1} तत्र यो प्रतिघं; La^{1} °प्रतिघ्नं; sOx^{1} Pu^{2} Pu^{4} °प्रतिजं; [*Jolly* M] *Me Mandlik Jha KSS Dave* °प्रतिपं; Pu^{5} Pu^{7} °प्रतिशं; NPu^{1} °प्रतिसं; Jo^{1} °प्रतियं; Ho Ox^{2} °प्रतिमं; Lo^{2} °प्रतिमँ; Tr^{2} °प्रथितं; Lo^{1} °प्रति विद्यात्; Ho Ox^{2} विन्द्यात् — d) Wa हारी; *Me Jha Dave* हर्तृ; Ho भर्तृ; Tr^{2} हरिणां मनः; Ox^{2} देहिनं

29.* Omitted in GMd^{1} TMd^{4}; Cited by *Lakṣ* 14.126 — a) NNg यस्तु; Tr^{1} यत्त — b) Tr^{2} °संयुक्तविषयात्मकं; *Lakṣ* °युक्तं स व्यक्त°; Jm Jo^{1} wKt^{1} Kt^{2} BKt^{5} Lo^{1} TMd^{3} GMd^{5} GMy oOr Ox^{2} NPu^{1} Pu^{2} Pu^{3} Pu^{4} Tr^{1} MTr^{4} MTr^{5} MTr^{6} [*Jolly* Nd] *Mandlik Jha KSS Dave* °मव्यक्तं; Pu^{5} Pu^{7} °विषयान्वितं — c) wKt^{3} °विज्ञेयस्तम° — d) Bo °स्तमुपधा°; BBe^{2} Jo^{2} Lo^{3} Tj^{1} °स्तदवधा°

30. Cited by *Lakṣ* 14.127 — a) Lo^{1} वैतेषां — b) Pu^{10} ये गुणानां फलोदयाः; GMy स्वफलोदयं — c) BBe^{2} wKt^{1} BKt^{5} अग्रो; Tr^{2} अग्र्ये मध्ये; Lo^{1} जघन्यश्चेत्; BKt^{5} जघन्यस्य — d) Pu^{5} Pu^{7} तत्प्रव°

धर्मक्रियात्मचिन्ता च सात्त्विकं गुणलक्षणम् ॥३१॥
आरम्भरतिता धैर्यमसत्कार्यपरिग्रहः ।
विषयोपसेवा चाजस्रं राजसं गुणलक्षणम् ॥३२॥
लोभः स्वप्नोऽधृतिः क्रौर्यं नास्तिक्यं भिन्नवृत्तिता ।
याचिष्णुता प्रमादश्च तामसं गुणलक्षणम् ॥३३॥
त्रयाणामपि चैतेषां गुणानां त्रिषु तिष्ठताम् ।
इदं सामासिकं ज्ञेयं क्रमशो गुणलक्षणम् ॥३४॥
यत्कर्म कृत्वा कुर्वंश्च करिष्यंश्चैव लज्जते ।
तज्ज्ञेयं विदुषा सर्वं तामसं गुणलक्षणम् ॥३५॥
येनास्मिन्कर्मणा लोके ख्यातिमिच्छति पुष्कलाम् ।
न च शोचत्यसंपत्तौ तद्विज्ञेयं तु राजसम् ॥३६॥
यत्सर्वेणेच्छति ज्ञातुं यन्न लज्जति चाचरन् ।

31. Pādas c-d omitted in Lo^{1} Pu^{5}. Cited by *Apa* 999; *Lakṣ* 14.127 — a) MTr^{4} MTr^{6} विद्याभ्या°; Ho TMd^{4} °भ्यासं तपो; Wa °भ्यासस्तमो; GMy Tr^{1} °स्तपो यज्ञाः; BBe^{2} °स्तपो दानं — b) Ox^{2} सत्यमिन्द्रि°; GMy °निग्रहं — c) Tr^{2} कर्मक्रिया°; sOx^{1} °क्रिया च चिन्ता; La^{1} °क्रिया चात्मचिन्ता [*om* च]; Wa °चिन्ता सा; TMd^{3} °चिन्ता न — d) BKt^{5} गुणं; wKt^{3} °लक्षकं

32 * Omitted in wKt^{3} Tj^{2}; pādas a-b omitted in Lo^{1} sOx^{1} sPu^{6}; verses 32 and 33 transposed in Lo^{2}. Cited by *Lakṣ* 14.127 — a) Hy Jm Jo^{1} Jo^{2} Kt^{2} Lo^{3} Pu^{3} Tj^{1} [*Jolly* R] *Rn Nd Rc Mandlik Jha KSS Dave* आरम्भरुचिता [wKt^{1} °रुचति]; oOr °रतितां; *Lakṣ* °रतितो; TMd^{3} °युतिता; oOr °तिताधर्मम°; TMd^{4} धीर्यम° — b) Ho धैर्यं सत्कार्यस्य परिग्रहः; oOr °मसत्कार्यं प्रतिग्रहः; Lo^{3} °प्रतिग्रहः — c) hypermetric pāda; TMd^{3} विषयोपवशाजस्रं; Lo^{1} [*cor to*] GMy विषयोपरिसेवा च; TMd^{4} विषयसेवा; Be^{1} GMd^{5} NPu^{1} Pu^{2} Pu^{3} Pu^{4} °सेवाजस्रं; BKt^{5} °सेवाजस्रं च; Tr^{2} °सेवाश्रयित्वं

33. Omitted in GMd^{1} MTr^{6} [haplo]. Cited by *Lakṣ* 14.127 — a) GMy [*Jolly* Nd] °धृतिर्धैर्यं — b) Tr^{1} हीनवृत्तिता — c) wKt^{1} याचितास्तु प्रमादस्तु; Bo यातिष्णुत्वा; oOr प्रमादाश्च; Ho प्रपातश्च; sOx^{1} sPu^{6} प्रमाद्यत्वं [*om* च]

34. *ma* in Lo^{1}. Cited by *Lakṣ* 14.127 — a) TMd^{4} यात्राणामपि — b) Lo^{2} गुणानामपि तिष्ठतां; La^{1} गुणानां च प्रतिष्ठितां; TMd^{3} नृणां च नृषि तिष्ठतां; Lo^{3} Tj^{1} त्रिष्वतिष्ठतां; TMd^{4} Ox^{2} Tr^{1} MTr^{4} MTr^{6} [*Jolly* Nd] नृषु तिष्ठतां — c) Pu^{2} Pu^{4} इदमासासिकं; TMd^{3} सामासिक; Ho समासिकं; TMd^{4} सामाविकं; GMd^{1} श्रेष्ठं — d) TMd^{4} MTr^{6} क्रमशस्तु स्वलक्षणं

35. Omitted in BKt^{5} Lo^{2} Tr^{2} [haplo]. Cited by *Lakṣ* 14.127 — a) Bo कुर्वंस्तु — b) Lo^{3} लज्यते; Hy Jm Jo^{1} Kt^{2} NKt^{4} Pu^{3} Pu^{10} Tj^{2} [*Jolly* M] *Nā Mandlik Jha KSS Dave* लज्जति; wKt^{1} लक्षते; La^{1} लक्ष्यते; wKt^{3} लभ्यते; Ox^{2} मज्जति — c) Be^{1} Bo Ho Pu^{3} तत्सर्वं विदुषा ज्ञेयं; GMd^{1} तददेयं; TMd^{4} तदेयं; TMd^{3} GMy sOx^{1} Tr^{1} विदुषां; Tj^{1} विदुषात्सर्वं; BBe^{2} सर्व

36. Omitted in Tj^{1} [haplo]. Cited by *Lakṣ* 14.127 — a) GMd^{1} नास्मिंश्च कर्मणां; TMd^{3} °न्कर्मणां; Lo^{2} °न्कर्मगोलोके — b) La^{1} Lo^{1} [*Jolly* Nd] ख्यातिमृच्छति; *Lakṣ* ख्यातिं गच्छति; BBe^{2} °च्छते; BBe^{2} Kt^{2} NKt^{4} Lo^{1} पुष्कलं — c) TMd^{4} न शोचयत्वसंपृत्तौ; wKt^{1} स च; GMd^{1} स न; sOx^{1} sPu^{6} नैव शोच°; Lo^{2} शोभ्यत्य°; Tr^{1} शोचेत्य°; Be^{1} शोचति संपत्तौ; BKt^{5} °संपत्तुः; MTr^{6} °संपत्त्यौ — d) GMd^{5} तद्धि ज्ञेयं; Lo^{2} च

येन तुष्यति चास्यात्मा तत्सत्त्वगुणलक्षणम् ॥३७॥
तमसो लक्षणं कामो रजसस्त्वर्थ उच्यते ।
सत्त्वस्य लक्षणं धर्मः श्रैष्ठ्यमेषां यथाक्रमम् ॥३८॥
येन यांस्तु गुणेनैषां संसारान्प्रतिपद्यते ।
तान्समासेन वक्ष्यामि सर्वस्यास्य यथाक्रमम् ॥३९॥
देवत्वं सात्त्विका यान्ति मनुष्यत्वं तु राजसाः ।
तिर्यक्त्वं तामसा नित्यमित्येषा त्रिविधा गतिः ॥४०॥
त्रिविधा त्रिविधैषा तु विज्ञेया गौणिकी गतिः ।
अधमा मध्यमाग्र्या च कर्मविद्याविशेषतः ॥४१॥
स्थावराः कृमिकीटाश्च मत्स्याः सर्पाः सरीसृपाः ।
पशवश्च सृगालाश्च जघन्या तामसी गतिः ॥४२॥

37. Omitted in Tj[1]. Cited by *Apa* 999; *Lakṣ* 14.126–7 — a) GMd[1] TMd[3] TMd[4] GMd[5] GMy Tr[1] MTr[4] [*Jolly* Nd] सर्वं येनेच्छति ज्ञातुं [TMd[4] GMy GMd[5] ज्ञानं; TMd[3] ज्ञेयं]; Lo[2] यत्सर्वेण तु विज्ञातुं; NPu[1] तत्सर्वे°; sOx[1] sPu[6] Pu[10] [*Jolly* M] यः सर्वे°; Ho *Lakṣ* यत्सर्वं नेच्छति — b) *Lakṣ* लज्जते न यदाचरन्; MTr[6] *Apa* लज्जते यत्र चाचरन्; BKt[5] यत्र; Lo[1] लज्जीत; Lo[3] लज्यति; TMd[4] लज्जेत; wKt[1] रक्षति चावरं; La[1] Lo[3] वाचरन्; Tr[2] चावसन्; MTr[4] चापरन्; BKt[5] नाचरन् — c) TMd[4] तुष्यति तत्सर्वं; TMd[3] Pu[2] Pu[10] वास्यात्मा; GMd[1] चाप्यात्मा; sOx[1] वा चात्मा; Hy Jm Jo[1] wKt[1] Kt[2] wKt[3] Pu[8] Tj[2] [*Jolly* G] *Mandlik Jha KSS Dave* चात्मास्य; Ox[2] चात्मास्यात्मा — d) TMd[4] सात्त्विकं गुणलक्षणं; GMd[5] तत्सत्त्वं; Tr[2] तत्वस्यगुण°; Bo TMd[3] oOr तत्सर्वं गुण°

38. Cited by *Apa* 999; *Lakṣ* 14.127 — a) MTr[6] तामसो; Tr[1] लक्षणा; Pu[5] Pu[7] कामं — b) MTr[6] राजस°; wKt[1] °स्त्वत्र; Pu[5] Pu[7] °स्त्वर्थमुच्यते — c) TMd[3] GMd[5] sOx[1] sPu[6] Tr[1] धर्मं — d) Jo[1] Lo[2] GMd[1] Tr[1] Tr[2] MTr[6] श्रेष्ठ्यमेषां; Ho wKt[3] La[1] TMd[4] श्रेष्ठमेषां; Pu[3] श्रैष्ठमेषां; wKt[1] प्रैष्यमेषां; *Apa* श्रेष्ठमेतद्यथा°; Wa यथाक्रमात्; Lo[3] यथातुमं; Ho Hy Jm Jo[1] Kt[2] Tj[2] [*Jolly* Ku] *Mandlik Jha KSS Dave* यथोत्तरं

39. Omitted in Tj[1] Tr[2] [haplo] — a) GMd[1] TMd[3] TMd[4] GMd[5] GMy Tr[1] येन येन गुणेनेमान्; [*Jolly* Nd] येन येन तु गुणेन; Be[1] Pu[2] Pu[4] यास्तु; oOr यस्तु; Pu[5] Pu[7] गुणानेषां — b) GMd[5] सदाचारान्प्रपद्यते; Ho NNg Pu[2] संसारात्प्रति°; NKt[4] संसारं प्रति°; TMd[3] संस्कारान्प्रति° — c) sOx[1] sPu[6] तत्समा°; GMd[1] तास्समा°; wKt[3] प्रवक्ष्यामि — d) MTr[4] सर्वं चास्य; TMd[3] सर्वस्य च

40. Pādas c-d omitted in TMd[4]. Cited by *Mādh* 2.488 — a) wKt[3] सात्त्विकं; NKt[4] याति — b) Lo[2] मानुषत्वं; Tr[2] मानुष्यंत्वं; sOx[1] sPu[6] हि; Hy Jm Jo[1] Jo[2] wKt[1] Kt[2] BKt[5] La[1] Lo[3] NNg oOr Ox[2] Pu[3] Pu[5] Pu[7] Tj[1] Tj[2] *Mandlik Jolly Jha KSS Dave* च; Ho राजसां; Lo[1] राजसा — c) NNg तिर्यक्तां; GMy Pu[2] Pu[3] Pu[4] Tr[2] तामसा यान्ति इत्येषा [Tr[2] याति]; GMd[1] GMd[5] Tr[1] MTr[4] तामसप्राया इत्येषा; MTr[6] तामसा इत्येषा — d) Bo Lo[1] TMd[3] sOx[1] sPu[6] °त्येषां; Jo[1] त्रिधा; Ox[2] विविधा

41.* Omitted in TMd[4]; pādas a-b omitted in sOx[1] [haplo]; page containing verses 41c to 46b torn in sPu[6]. Cited by *Mādh* 2.488 — a) Lo[2] विविधा त्रिवि°; Bo GMd[5] त्रिविधास्त्रिवि°; Be[1] BBe[2] Jo[2] BKt[5] La[1] Lo[2] Lo[3] NNg oOr Ox[2] NPu[1] Pu[7] [*but cor*] Tj[1] MTr[5] MTr[6] Wa [*Jolly* M[1] G Nd] *Jolly* त्रिविधैषां; Pu[2] Pu[4] विधिषां; GMy त्रिविधैवेषा विज्ञेया; wKt[3] च — b) Pu[3] सर्वेषां गौणिकी; Be[1] GMd[1] NNg Tr[2] गौणकी; La[1] त्रिविधा गतिः — c) Pu[7] मध्यमा चाग्र्या कर्म°; BBe[2] wKt[1] °माग्रा; Pu[8] तु — d) TMd[3] क्रमं विद्याद्विशेषतः; MTr[4] MTr[6] कर्म वक्ष्याम्यशेषतः; BBe[2] धर्मविद्या°; Lo[1] Tr[1] °विद्याद्विशेषतः

42.* Cited by *Apa* 1000; *Mādh* 2.488 — a) Lo[3] TMd[3] NNg Tj[1] Tr[1] Tr[2] क्रिमि°; Bo Ho oOr

हस्तिनश्च तुरंगाश्च शूद्रा म्लेच्छाश्च गर्हिताः ।
सिंहा व्याघ्रा वराहाश्च मध्यमा तामसी गतिः ॥४३॥
चारणाश्च सुपर्णाश्च पुरुषाश्चैव दाम्भिकाः ।
रक्षांसि च पिशाचाश्च तामसीषूत्तमा गतिः ॥४४॥
झल्ला मल्ला नटाश्चैव पुरुषाश्च कुवृत्तयः ।
द्यूतपानप्रसक्ताश्च प्रथमा राजसी गतिः ॥४५॥
राजानः क्षत्रियाश्चैव राज्ञां चैव पुरोहिताः ।
वादयुद्धप्रधानाश्च मध्यमा राजसी गतिः ॥४६॥
गन्धर्वा गुह्यका यक्षा विबुधानुचराश्च ये ।
तथैवाप्सरसः सर्वा राजसीषूत्तमा गतिः ॥४७॥

Ox^2 कृमयः कीटा मत्स्याः [oOr क्रिमयः] — b) Pu^3 Tr^2 मत्स्याः चापि सरीसृपाः; Ox^2 मत्स्याः नक्राः; BBe^2 सर्पा मत्स्याः; oOr नक्रा मत्स्याः; sOx^1 *om* सर्पाः; BKt^5 सर्प; Lo^1 सर्पाश्च कच्छपाः; TMd^3 GMy सरिसृपाः; NKt^4 सरीसृपं; Be^1 BBe^2 Bo^2 Ho Hy Jm Jo^1 Jo^2 wKt^1 Kt^2 wKt^3 Lo^1 Lo^2 Lo^3 NNg oOr Pu^5 Pu^7 Pu^8 Tj^2 [*Jolly* G Ku R] *Mandlik Jolly Jha KSS Dave* सकच्छपाः — c) Be^1 Hy Jm Jo^1 Kt^2 Lo^2 NNg Pu^5 Pu^7 Tj^2 *Go Ku Rc Mandlik Jha KSS Dave* मृगाश्चैव — d) Pu^5 Pu^7 जघन्यास्ताम° ; BKt^5 TMd^3 तमसी; TMd^4 तामसे; Pu^5 Pu^7 गतीः

43. Verse 43 placed after 45 in BBe^2. Cited by *Apa* 1000; *Mādh* 2.488 — a) Bo हस्तिरश्वतुरंगाश्च — b) Be^1 शूद्रो; wKt^1 म्लेच्छाः शूद्राश्च; TMd^4 म्लेच्छा च; wKt^3 मूर्च्छाश्च; *Apa* म्लेच्छा विगर्हिताः; Lo^3 गर्हितः; GMy गर्धभाः; TMd^3 गायकाः — c) BBe^2 Bo Ho wKt^3 La^1 Lo^3 GMd^1 TMd^4 GMd^5 GMy oOr sOx^1 Tj^1 [*Jolly* M Nd R G] *Jolly* सिंहव्याघ्रवराहाश्च; BKt^5 Tr^1 सिंह; TMd^3 सिंह्व; Pu^{10} व्याघ्र; TMd^3 वराहश्च

44 * Cited by *Apa* 1000; *Mādh* 2.488 — a) Ho चारणांश्च सुपर्णांश्च; Bo वारणाश्च; Jo^1 सुवर्णाश्च; Bo सुवर्णश्च — b) wKt^1 मनुष्याश्चैव; Bo दम्भिकाः; GMy धाम्भिकाः; TMd^3 Tr^1 डाम्भिकाः — c) Lo^1 Tj^1 पिशाचांश्च — d) Be^1 Bo NKt^4 BKt^5 La^1 Lo^1 Lo^2 Lo^3 GMd^1 TMd^3 GMd^5 NNg sOx^1 Ox^2 NPu^1 Pu^2 Pu^3 Pu^4 Pu^5 Pu^7 Tj^1 Tr^1 Tr^2 MTr^4 MTr^5 MTr^6 Wa [*Jolly* G] *Apa Mādha Go* तामसेपूत्तमा; BBe^2 TMd^4 तामसी तूत्तमा

45. Omitted in Lo^1. Cited by *Apa* 1000; *Mādh* 2.488 — a) GMd^5 oOr MTr^6 झल्ल; Lo^3 Ox^2 भल्ला मल्ला; MTr^5 सल्ला मल्ला; Ho झलमल्ला; *Apa* कल्ला मल्ला; La^1 नटीश्चैव — b) BBe^2 Ho Hy Jm Jo^1 Jo^2 wKt^1 Kt^2 wKt^3 Lo^1 Lo^3 Pu^3 Tj^2 [*Jolly* Ku] *Mādh Ku Mandlik Jha KSS Dave* पुरुषाः शस्त्रवृत्तयः; NKt^4 sOx^1 पुरुषाश्शक्तवृत्तयः; Lo^3 Tj^1 [*Jolly* R] पुरुषाः शस्त्रपाणयः; NKt^4 GMy पुरुषाश्चक्रवृत्तयः; GMd^1 पुरुषाश्चत्रवत्तयः — c) BBe^2 दूत° ; GMy द्यूता° ; Lo^2 °पानादिसक्ताश्च; BBe^2 NKt^4 La^1 °प्रशक्ताश्च; Ho Pu^{10} [*Jolly* M] °प्रयुक्ताश्च; Be^1 °सक्ता च — d) Hy Jm Jo^1 Kt^2 Lo^1 Tj^2 *Mandlik Jha KSS Dave* जघन्या; BKt^5 अधमा; Tj^1 मध्यमा; Lo^2 तामसी

46. Omitted in Pu^{10} Tj^1 [haplo]; pāda-c omitted in Pu^5. Cited by *Apa* 1000; *Mādh* 2.488 — a) sOx^1 *Apa* क्षत्रियश्चैव; MTr^5 क्षत्रिया वैश्याः — b) oOr ये राज्ञां पुरोहिताः; Tr^2 *om* राज्ञां चैव; wKt^1 राज्ञश्चैव; Pu^2 Pu^4 [*Jolly* Nd] राज्ञाश्चैव; Bo La^1 TMd^4 पुरोहितः — c) BKt^5 दानयुक्तप्रयुक्ताश्च; La^1 TMd^4 GMy Pu^3 Tr^1 Tr^2 MTr^4 MTr^6 *Rc* [*Jolly* Nd] दानयुद्ध° ; oOr वानयुद्ध° ; TMd^3 नागयुद्ध° ; NPu^1 चाटयुद्ध° ; Hy Jo^2 wKt^1 oOr sOx^1 sPu^6 Pu^8 Tj^2 [*Jolly* R] *Rn* °प्रसक्ताश्च; La^1 °प्रशक्ताश्च — d) Pu^5 रजसी गतिर्मध्यमाः; *Apa* द्वितीया; sPu^6 तामसी

47. Pāda-d omitted in oOr. Cited by *Apa* 1000; *Mādh* 2.488 — a) BKt^5 sOx^1 sPu^6 गन्धर्व;

तापसा यतयो विप्रा ये च वैमानिका गणाः ।
नक्षत्राणि च दैत्याश्च प्रथमा सात्त्विकी गतिः ॥४८॥
यज्वान ऋषयो देवा वेदा ज्योतींषि वत्सराः ।
पितरश्चैव साध्याश्च द्वितीया सात्त्विकी गतिः ॥४९॥
ब्रह्मा विश्वसृजो धर्मो महानव्यक्तमेव च ।
उत्तमां सात्त्विकीमेतां गतिमाहुर्मनीषिणः ॥५०॥
एष सर्वः समुद्दिष्टस्त्रिप्रकारस्य कर्मणः ।
त्रिविधस्त्रिविधः कृत्स्नः संसारः सार्वभौतिकः ॥५१॥
इन्द्रियाणां प्रसङ्गेन धर्मस्यासेवनेन च ।
पापान्संयान्ति संसारानविद्वांसो नराधमाः ॥५२॥
यां यां योनिं तु जीवोऽयं येन येनेह कर्मणा ।

Apa गुह्यकाश्चैव; oOr यक्षका गुह्या; wKt^{3} रक्षा — b) TMd^{3} विबुद्धानु° BBe^{2} wKt^{3} BKt^{5} GMd^{1} Pu^{10} [*Jolly* M] *Mādh* विविधानुचराश्च; sOx^{1} sPu^{6} विविधा [lacuna] चराश्च; *Apa* विविधा भूचराश्च — c) sOx^{1} sPu^{6} तथैवासरसः; TMd^{4} °प्सरसं; Be^{1} Lo^{2} Pu^{8} °रसः सिद्धा; GMy °रसश्चैव सर्वा; BBe^{2} GMd^{5} MTr^{6} सर्वे — d) BBe^{2} राजसी तूत्तमा स्मृताः; NNg उत्तमा राजसी गतिः; Be^{1} Bo NKt^{4} BKt^{5} La^{1} Lo^{2} GMd^{1} TMd^{3} GMd^{5} sOx^{1} Ox^{2} Pu^{3} Pu^{4} sPu^{6} Pu^{7} Tr^{1} Tr^{2} MTr^{4} MTr^{6} Wa *Apa Mādh Go* राजसेषूत्तमा [see 12.44d note]; TMd^{4} राजसी चोत्तमा

48. Pāda-a omitted in oOr. Cited by *Mādh* 2.488 — a) TMd^{3} तपसा यत्र ये विप्रा; TMd^{4} तापसाश्चैव ये विप्रा — b) GMy *om* च; Be^{1} wKt^{1} वैमाणिका; Pu^{2} Pu^{4} गणीः; oOr MTr^{5} गुणाः — c) TMd^{3} गृहनक्षत्रदैत्याश्च; Ho दैवत्याश्च; BKt^{5} *Nā* [pāṭha] सिद्धाश्च; MTr^{6} वेदस्य — d) BKt^{5} अधमा; Lo^{1} मध्यमा; Ox^{2} जघन्या; Ho सात्त्वकी

49. Omitted in Lo^{2} TMd^{4} sOx^{1} sPu^{6} [haplo]; pādas c-d omitted in oOr. Cited by *Mādh* 2.488 — a) Tr^{2} यज्वाना; Tj^{1} यज्वानः; La^{1} Lo^{1} TMd^{3} GMy oOr यज्वानो; NKt^{4} यज्ञानः — a-b) wKt^{1} ऋषयो वेदास्तथा ज्योतींषि; Bo GMd^{1} GMd^{5} oOr Tr^{1} *Mādh* वेदा देवा — b) La^{1} वासराः; Wa वत्सगाः — d) Be^{1} BBe^{2} Ho [*cor to*] Jo^{2} wKt^{1} NKt^{4} BKt^{5} La^{1} Lo^{1} NNg Ox^{2} Pu^{2} Pu^{4} Tj^{1} Tr^{2} [*Jolly* R] *Go Ku* मध्यमा; GMy गतिं

50. Cited by *Śaṃ* on *BU* 1.4.6, 3.1.1[intro.]; *Mādh* 2.488 — a) Lo^{3} GMd^{1} ब्रह्म; BBe^{2} विश्वस्रजो; Pu^{8} धर्मां — b) Be^{1} BBe^{2} La^{1} oOr sOx^{1} Pu^{2} Pu^{3} Pu^{4} Pu^{5} sPu^{6} Pu^{7} Pu^{8} Pu^{10} Tr^{2} *Go* [*Jolly* M G] *Jolly* महानव्यक्त एव; *Mādh* महदव्यक्तमेव; BKt^{5} महान्प्रव्यक्त एव; wKt^{1} वा — c) Ho सात्त्वकी°; wKt^{3} सात्त्विकमेतां; TMd^{4} तामसीमेतां; BKt^{5} °कीमेनां; oOr °कीमेषां; Pu^{2} Pu^{4} °कीमन्तां — c-d) TMd^{3} सात्त्विकीं विद्यामेतामाहुर्मनीषिणः — d) NNg [*but cor*] °नीषिभिः

51. Cited by *Mādh* 2.488 — a) Bo सर्वं; wKt^{1} oOr Tr^{2} सर्गः; Ho [*cor to*] BKt^{5} La^{1} Lo^{1} GMd^{1} TMd^{4} sOx^{1} NPu^{1} sPu^{6} Pu^{10} MTr^{4} MTr^{6} Wa [*Jolly* M] धर्मः — b) NNg °स्त्रिःप्रका° — c) TMd^{3} TMd^{4} त्रिविधं त्रिविधं; oOr सर्वः — d) TMd^{4} संसारं सार्वभौतिकं; La^{1} सर्व°

TMd^{3} GMy [*Jolly* Nd] places vers 12.81 after verse 51

52. a) sOx^{1} प्रसाथेन — b) Pu^{3} Tr^{2} धर्मस्यातिक्रमेण; Ox^{2} तु — c) TMd^{3} GMd^{5} GMy MTr^{5} पापास्सं°; NPu^{1} Pu^{2} Tr^{1} पापाः सं°; Tr^{2} पाराः सं°; Ho Kt^{2} TMd^{4} sOx^{1} sPu^{6} पापात्सं°; Bo La^{1} Lo^{1} GMy Pu^{2} Pu^{4} Tj^{1} Tr^{1} °याति — c-d) TMd^{4} °यान्ति पद्यन्ते न विद्वांसो — d) Be^{1} °रात्राविद्वांसो; wKt^{1} °रान्विद्वांसोपि; Tj^{2} °रान्विद्वांसो; BBe^{2} Tr^{2} नराधमः

क्रमशो याति लोकेऽस्मिंस्तत्तत्सर्वं निबोधत ॥५३॥
बहून्वर्षगणान्घोरान् नरकान् प्राप्य तत्क्षयात् ।
संसारान्प्रतिपद्यन्ते महापातकिनस्त्विमान् ॥५४॥
श्वसूकरखरोष्ट्राणां गोऽजाविमृगपक्षिणाम् ।
चण्डालपुल्कसानां च ब्रह्महा योनिमृच्छति ॥५५॥
कृमिकीटपतङ्गानां विड्भुजां चैव पक्षिणाम् ।
हिंस्राणां चैव सत्त्वानां सुरापो ब्राह्मणो व्रजेत् ॥५६॥
लूताहिसरटानां च तिरश्चां चाम्बुचारिणाम् ।
हिंस्राणां च पिशाचानां स्तेनो विप्रः सहस्रशः ॥५७॥
तृणगुल्मलतानां च क्रव्यादां दंष्ट्रिणामपि ।
क्रूरकर्मकृतां चैव शतशो गुरुतल्पगः ॥५८॥

53. Cited by *Mādh* 2.502 — a) GMy जीवे; NKt^4 *om* °यं — b) oOr Pu^3 Tr^2 Wa येन हि; wKt^1 येन तु — c) GMy कर्मशो; TMd^3 TMd^4 sOx^1 Tr^2 यान्ति; Tj^1 यानि — c-d) *Mādh* क्रमशोऽश्नाति लोकेऽस्मिन्नेतत्सर्वं निबोधत — d) Ox^2 °स्मिंस्तत्सर्वं तन्निबोधत; TMd^4 °स्मिन्न तत्सर्गं; sOx^1 sPu^6 °स्मिंस्तत्तु नि°; Tr^1 हि बोधत

54. Cited by *Mādh* 2.502 — a) Lo^1 °गतान्घोरान् — b) Tr^1 °राननेकान्; La^1 Ox^2 नरकं; Lo^3 Tj^1 [*Jolly* G R] प्राप्यते क्षयात्; Bo प्रथमान्क्षयात्; Be^1 Lo^1 GMd^1 TMd^4 oOr Ox^2 [*Jolly* M] तत्क्षणात्; sOx^1 sPu^6 तत्क्षणं; BKt^5 तत्क्षणान्त — c) TMd^4 संसारा इतिपद्यन्ते; Ho संसारात्प्रति°; wKt^3 GMy संसारा प्रति°; Tj^2 °पद्यन्त— d) TMd^3 GMd^5 °नस्त्विह

55. Cited by *Vij* 3.207–8; *Mādh* 2.502 — b) TMd^3 GMd^5 Pu^3 गोमायुमृग°; NKt^4 गोजाश्वमृग°; TMd^4 गोजातिमृग° — c) BBe^2 Bo Ho Jm wKt^1 La^1 Lo^1 Ox^2 Pu^3 *Vij* चाण्डाल°; Jo^1 wKt^3 NKt^4 oOr Ox^2 [*Jolly* Ku] *Mandlik Jha KSS Dave* °पुक्कसानां [see 10.18b note]; Hy Kt^2 °पुक्कशानां; Be^1 °पुःकसानां; Ho Jm Jo^2 La^1 Lo^2 NPu^1 Pu^5 Pu^7 Pu^8 Pu^{10} Tj^2 Tr^2 [*Jolly* G] °पुष्कसानां; BKt^5 °पुष्कलानां; Bo °पुष्पसानां; wKt^1 °पुष्कशादीनां; wKt^3 TMd^3 TMd^4 GMd^5 oOr तु — d) Ho oOr योनिमिच्छति

56. Pādas c-d *ma* in Lo^1 [haplo]. Cited by *Vij* 3.207–8; *Mādh* 2.510— a) TMd^3 NNg sOx^1 Tj^1 Tr^1 Tr^2 क्रिमि°; Be^1 क्रमि°; Pu^5 *om* कृमिकीट; La^1 कृमिकोटि°; Pu^{10} [*Jolly* M] °भुजंगानां — b) TMd^3 विड्फुक्तां; GMy विभुजां; TMd^4 विरुजां; GMd^1 विट्भूमिश्चैव; Pu^8 पक्षिणं — c) La^1 हिंसानां; TMd^4 चैव वस्यानां; Pu^2 Pu^4 च सत्त्वानां; MTr^6 चैव दस्यूनां; Ho sOx^1 sPu^6 च पिशाचानां — d) Tr^2 सुरापो योनिमाव्रजेत्; BKt^5 TMd^4 ब्रह्मणो; GMd^1 TMd^3 GMd^5 GMy Tr^1 MTr^4 MTr^5 MTr^6 ब्राह्मणोसकृत्; Hy व्रजत्; Lo^3 व्रजन्; Be^1 Lo^2 sOx^1 Pu^5 sPu^6 Pu^7 भवेत्; NPu^1 भजेत्

57. Omitted in sOx^1 sPu^6; pādas a-b *ma* in Lo^1. Cited by *Vij* 3.207–8; *Mādh* 2.511 — a) Lo^3 Tj^1 [*Jolly* R] लूतादि°; MTr^6 चूताहि°; BKt^5 लूतानां सरटानां; *Vij* °सरठानां; BBe^2 wKt^1 wKt^3 La^1 Ox^2 Pu^2 Pu^4 Tj^2 °शरटानां; GMd^1 °सरखाणां; MTr^5 °सरळानां — b) GMd^1 तिरश्चाम्बुनिचारिणां; oOr तिरश्चानां च जम्बुकां; GMd^5 दिशश्चां; wKt^1 चाभ्युचारिणां; NNg वायुचारिणां; Pu^{10} [*Jolly* M] वारिचारिणां; Ho Pu^2 चञ्चुचारिणां— c) La^1 हिंसानां; Jo^1 *om* च; *Mādh* सपिशाचानां — d) MTr^6 विप्राः; TMd^4 सहस्रः

58. Folios containing 58b to 84a missing in La^1 — b) GMy क्रव्यादानां च दंष्ट्रिणां [*om* अपि]; wKt^1 Tj^1 क्रव्यादा; oOr क्रव्याद; Bo दंष्ट्रिकामपि — c) Ho Pu^5 Pu^7 Pu^8 Pu^{10} MTr^4 °कृतानां च; TMd^3 TMd^4 GMd^5 GMy Tr^1 °रतानां च; Bo °गतां चैव — d) oOr Tr^1 MTr^4 क्रमशो

हिंस्रा भवन्ति क्रव्यादाः कृमयोऽभक्ष्यभक्षिणः ।
परस्परादिनः स्तेनाः प्रेतान्त्यस्त्रीनिषेविणः ॥५९॥
संयोगं पतितैर्गत्वा परस्यैव च योषितम् ।
अपहृत्य च विप्रस्वं भवति ब्रह्मराक्षसः ॥६०॥
मणिमुक्ताप्रवालानि हृत्वा लोभेन मानवः ।
विविधानि च रत्नानि जायते हेमकर्तृषु ॥६१॥
धान्यं हृत्वा भवत्याखुः कांस्यं हंसो जलं प्लवः ।
मधु दंशः पयः काको रसं श्वा नकुलो घृतम् ॥६२॥
मांसं गृध्रो वसां मद्गुस्तैलं तैलपकः खगः ।
चीरीवाकस्तु लवणं बलाका शकुनिर्दधि ॥६३॥

59 * Verses 59 and 60 transposed in wKt^{3} gMy — a) Bo भवति; Be^{1} क्रव्यादः; Ho wKt^{1} bKt^{5} Lo^{1} sOx^{1} क्रव्यादा — b) nKt^{4} Lo^{3} tMd^{3} nNg Pu^{10} Tj^{1} Tr^{1} क्रिमयो; Be^{1} Bo Tj^{2} क्रमयो; wKt^{1} क्रिययो; tMd^{4} क्रियाया; Hy Lo^{3} Pu^{10} Tj^{2} °भक्षभक्षिणः; Bo °भस्मभक्षिणः; *Me Dave Jha* °मेध्यभक्षिणः; Tj^{1} °भक्षणः; gMd^{1} gMd^{5} Pu^{2} Pu^{4} °भक्षणाः; oOr °भक्षणात् — c) Lo^{1} परस्यपादिन; bBe^{2} °रादिना; mTr^{4} mTr^{6} °रादिनो मत्स्याः; Be^{1} bBe^{2} Lo^{1} nNg स्तेना; Tr^{1} स्तेन — c-d) gMd^{1} mTr^{5} अन्यस्त्रीसेविनः प्रेताः स्तेनस्त्वन्योन्यघातिनः [gMd^{1} स्तेनाश्चान्योन्यपातिनः] — d) Tr^{2} प्रेत्यतां स्त्रीनिषेधिनः; nKt^{4} bKt^{5} प्रेतोन्त्य-स्त्री°; Ho Pu^{3} प्रेतान्यस्त्री°; Be^{1} Tr^{1} प्रेत्यान्यस्त्री°; tMd^{3} प्रेत्यानन्त्यस्त्री°; Tj^{2} प्रेतान्तःस्त्री°; nNg प्रेत्यस्त्री°; Hy °निषेविणाः; Pu^{2} Pu^{4} °निषेवणः; gMd^{5} °निषेवणाः; nKt^{4} tMd^{3} gMy Tr^{1} mTr^{4} °निषेवकाः; Lo^{1} °निषेविताः

60. Omitted in sOx^{1} sPu^{6}. Cited by *Mādh* 2.492, 511 — a) bKt^{5} संयोगैः; tMd^{4} पतितं गत्वा — b) bKt^{5} gMy nNg Ox^{2} Pu^{5} Pu^{7} तु; bBe^{2} bKt^{5} योषितां; Ho gMd^{1} oOr Tr^{1} योषितः — c) gMd^{1} tMd^{3} gMd^{5} mTr^{6} ब्रह्मस्वमपहृत्वापि [gMd^{5} °हृत्वा च; tMd^{3} °हृत्या च; mTr^{6} °हृत्यापि]; Pu^{4} अपकृत्य; gMy Pu^{5} Pu^{7} [*Jolly* G] तु; Tr^{2} य; Ho Pu^{2} Pu^{4} Pu^{8} Pu^{10} Wa [*Jolly* M] *YDh* 3.212 ब्रह्मस्वं; Lo^{1} [*but cor*] ब्रह्मत्वं — d) Be^{1} Hy bKt^{5} Lo^{1} gMd^{1} tMd^{3} gMd^{5} gMy Tr^{1} mTr^{5} भवन्ति; Be^{1} Bo wKt^{1} bKt^{5} Lo^{1} gMd^{1} tMd^{3} gMd^{5} gMy nPu^{1} Tr^{1} mTr^{5} °राक्षसाः

61. Pādas a-b omitted in Pu^{5}; section containing verses 61c to 66c torn in sPu^{6}. Cited by *Viś* 3.204; *Vij* 3.213; *Mādh* 2.511 — a) gMy °प्रवालांश्च; nKt^{4} Tr^{1} [*Jolly* M Nd] °प्रवालं च — b) Be^{1} हत्वा; wKt^{1} लोभेन यो नरः; bKt^{5} tMd^{3} gMd^{5} Pu^{4} *Viś* मानवाः; Tr^{1} मानवा — c) Pu^{5} Pu^{7} नानाविधानि रत्नानि; bBe^{2} *om* च; gMd^{1} यत्नाति; Lo^{2} सत्वानि — d) wKt^{1} wKt^{3} bKt^{5} tMd^{4} gMd^{5} Tj^{1} Tr^{1} mTr^{4} mTr^{6} Wa जायन्ते; tMd^{3} gMd^{5} *Mādh* लोहकर्तृषु

62. Cited by *Mādh* 2.511 — a) sOx^{1} धान्ये; tMd^{4} हत्वा; Hy कृत्वा; wKt^{1} Pu^{8} भवेदाखुः; bBe^{2} भवत्याखुं; wKt^{1} bKt^{5} भवत्याषुः; gMd^{1} भवत्यापुः — b) bBe^{2} कांश्यं; gMd^{1} हंस्यो; bKt^{5} हि हंसो; Lo^{2} ह्रासो; gMd^{1} tMd^{3} gMd^{5} gMy जल; mTr^{4} mTr^{6} जले; Bo ज्वलं; oOr जन — c) Lo^{2} दंशो; tMd^{3} दंशाक — d) mTr^{6} रसं च नकुलो; Lo^{2} श्वतुकुलो; Lo^{1} नकुलं; bKt^{5} खानपो घृतं

63 Cited by *Mādh* 2.511–2 — a) Bo घृधां; Tr^{1} गृद्धो; bKt^{5} वसा; bBe^{2} Bo Ho Hy Jm Jo^{1} wKt^{1} Kt^{2} wKt^{3} nKt^{4} Lo^{1} Lo^{2} tMd^{4} nNg Pu^{8} Tj^{2} [*Jolly* Ku] *Mandlik Jha KSS Dave* वपां; Lo^{3} Tj^{1} [*Jolly* R] रसान्मद्गु°; Lo^{2} पङ्गु° — b) nNg sOx^{1} nPu^{1} Pu^{2} Wa °स्तैलं स्यात्तैलपायिकः [Pu^{2} °पायिका; sOx^{1} °पायकः]; gMd^{1} Pu^{10} mTr^{5} [*Jolly* M Ku] *Jolly ViDh* 44.23 °स्तैलं वै तैलपायिकः [mTr^{5} °स्तैलः; gMd^{1} °पायिका]; Ho mTr^{4} mTr^{6} °स्तिलं; Kt^{2} °स्तेलं; oOr °स्तैलं च तैलपः; Ox^{2} तैलापकः; wKt^{1}

कौशेयं तित्तिरिर्हृत्वा क्षौमं हृत्वा तु दर्दुरः ।
कार्पासतान्तवं क्रौञ्चो गोधा गां वाग्गुदो गुडम् ॥६४॥
छुच्छुन्दरिः शुभान्गन्धान् पत्रशाकं तु बर्हिणः ।
श्वावित्कृतान्नं विविधमकृतान्नं तु शल्यकः ॥६५॥
बको भवति हृत्वाग्निं गृहकारी ह्युपस्करम् ।
रक्तानि हृत्वा वासांसि जायते जीवजीवकः ॥६६॥
वृको मृगेभं व्याघ्रोऽश्वं फलपुष्पं तु मर्कटः ।
स्त्रीमृक्षः स्तोकको वारि यानान्युष्ट्रः पशूनजः ॥६७॥

तेलपकः; GMd^5 MTr^4 MTr^6 तैलबकः; TMd^3 तैलबकं; TMd^4 तैलंबकः; GMy [*Jolly* Nd] तैलवकः; Bo Ho Jo^2 Lo^1 Pu^3 तैलपिबः; Tj^2 तैलपिवः; Be^1 तैलपयः; NKt^4 Lo^3 Tj^1 [*Jolly* R] तैलपगः; Tr^2 तैलापगः; BKt^5 तैलापगं; Pu^5 Pu^7 तैलपायः; Tr^1 तैलसकः; Lo^2 टौलपपः — c) NKt^4 MTr^4 *Nā* चीरवाक°; Bo चीरीकार°; BKt^5 सीरीवाक°; wKt^3 चीरीवाप°; Lo^1 चिरीकाख्य°; GMd^1 चीरपाक°; MTr^6 चीरराक°; NNg चीरीवाच°; TMd^3 GMy oOr Ox^2 [*Jolly* Nd] चक्रवाक°; *Mādh* क्षीरवास°; Tr^1 वीराणक°; [*Jolly* Rā^1] वीचीवाक°; [*Jolly* Rā^3] वीचीवाचकः; GMd^5 क्रकवाक° — d) Tr^2 बलका; BKt^6 बलाकः; TMd^3 बलाक; GMd^5 बलाकाश्शकु°; Tr^1 शकुनिं दधि

64. Cited by *Mādh* 2.512 — a) Be^1 कौशीयं; Be^1 BBe^2 TMd^3 Tj^1 तित्तिरि हृत्वा; Tr^2 तित्तिरी हृत्वा; Pu^{10} Tr^1 तित्तिरिं हृत्वा; BBe^2 Lo^3 °रिर्हत्वा— b) Pu^5 Pu^7 दौमं; wKt^3 कृत्वा; Lo^2 हन्त्वा; Jo^2 wKt^3 Lo^3 oOr sOx^1 NPu^1 Pu^4 Pu^7 Tj^1 च; Ho स; GMy त्वदर्दुरः; Be^1 BBe^2 दुर्दरः; Lo^2 दुदरः; Jo^2 Lo^3 NPu^1 Pu^4 दुर्दुरः — c) BBe^2 BKt^5 Lo^2 GMd^1 TMd^3 TMd^4 NPu^1 Pu^2 Pu^3 Pu^4 Pu^5 Pu^7 Tj^1 Tr^1 MTr^5 MTr^6 *Mādh* कार्पासं; NKt^4 कार्प्यासं; GMy काघासं; Ho °तान्तवो; TMd^3 तान्तव; GMd^1 °ताम्रकं; sOx^1 क्रौञ्चं — d) GMy [*Jolly* Nd] गोधा गव्यंददो गुडं; [*Jolly* M] गोधा मासाखुवल्गुतिः; GMd^5 गोधा च सरसं गुडं; Tr^1 गोधां; Lo^2 गोवा; BKt^5 *om* गां; Lo^1 Lo^3 Tj^1 गा; wKt^1 वागुदो; BKt^5 वाङ्गुदो; Tr^1 पशुदो गळं; Wa वलुलिर्गुडं; GMd^1 वाग्मुदो शखं

65. Placed after 66b in GMd^1; pādas 65c-d and 66a-b transposed in Tr^1 MTr^4 MTr^6. Cited by *Mādh* 2.512 — a) Bo *Mādh* छुच्छुंदरी; Pu^{10} *Jha Dave* छुच्छुंदरीः; Lo^3 छुच्छुंदरि; NKt^4 Tr^2 छुंछुंदरिः; Tj^1 छुंछुंदरि; GMd^5 छुंछुंदनी; Wa छंछंदटिः; TMd^3 TMd^4 चुंचुंदरि; GMd^5 चुञ्चुंदनि — b) *Mādh* पत्रं; Be^1 Ho Lo^2 oOr NPu^1 च; GMy Pu^5 बर्हिणं; Pu^7 बर्हिणां — c) TMd^3 MTr^5 श्वाविट्कृ°; oOr श्वाकृतान्नं च; Ho °त्कृतानां; Be^1 BBe^2 विविधाम° — d) Pu^{10} °धमनुकृतान्नं; BBe^2 wKt^1 °कृतार्थं; oOr Pu^2 Pu^4 Pu^5 Pu^7 च; Ox^2 Pu^2 Pu^4 Pu^5 Pu^7 शल्लकः; wKt^1 Pu^3 Tr^2 शल्यिकः; Lo^1 शल्यकं; MTr^6 शल्यतः; Tr^1 कुल्यकः

66. Folios containing verses 66–126 missing in Jm. Cited by *Mādh* 2.512 — a) TMd^3 शुको; GMd^5 बका भवन्ति — b) Pu^{10} गृध्रकार उप°; Ho NKt^4 BKt^5 oOr Pu^5 Pu^7 °कारी उप°; Lo^1 Ox^2 Pu^3 Pu^4 Tr^1 °कारिरुप°; Bo GMd^1 TMd^3 GMd^5 GMy Pu^2 Pu^8 MTr^6 °कारीरुप°; BBe^2 wKt^1 wKt^3 sOx^1 Wa °कार उप°; TMd^4 ह्युपस्करः; Kt^2 ह्यपस्करं — c) Lo^2 हृत्वा रक्तानि वासांसि; wKt^1 हृत्वा वासांसि रक्तानि; Be^1 हृत्वा रत्नानि वासांसि — d) GMd^1 जायन्ते जीवविक्रयः; TMd^3 जायन्ते जीवजीविताः; GMd^5 Tr^1 जायन्ते जीवजीविकाः [Tr^1 °जीवकाः]; sOx^1 *om* जायते; Ho जीविजीविकः

67. Cited by *Mādh* 2.512 — a) Hy मृगेभ; Tj^1 मृगेभ्यं; GMd^1 मृगोभं; TMd^3 मृगोहिव्याघ्रे; GMd^5 मृगेभिर्व्याघ्रांशं; Lo^3 व्याघ्रे; oOr व्याघाश्वं — b) sOx^1 Pu^2 Pu^4 sPu^6 फलं; BBe^2 Bo Ho Hy Jo^1 wKt^1 Kt^2 wKt^3 Lo^1 GMd^1 oOr Ox^2 Pu^5 Pu^7 Pu^8 Tj^2 MTr^4 MTr^5 MTr^6 [*Jolly* G Ku] *Go Ku Mandlik Jha KSS Dave* फलमूलं; NNg फलमूले; Be^1 wKt^1 Lo^2 Ox^2 Pu^2 च; Ho wKt^1 कर्कटः; TMd^3 नुत्कुटः — c) sOx^1 sPu^6 स्त्रीमृक्षां; Ox^2 स्त्रियमृक्षा; Lo^3 Tj^1 Pu^4 Tj^1 Tr^1 स्त्रीं वृक्षः; GMd^1 स्त्रीं वृक्षं; TMd^4 स्त्रीं पक्ष;

यद्वा तद्वा परद्रव्यमपहृत्य बलान्नरः ।
अवश्यं याति तिर्यक्त्वं जग्ध्वा चैवाहुतं हविः ॥६८॥
स्त्रियोऽप्येतेन कल्पेन हृत्वा दोषमवाप्नुयुः ।
एतेषामेव जन्तूनां भार्यात्वमुपयान्ति ताः ॥६९॥
स्वेभ्यः स्वेभ्यस्तु कर्मभ्यश्च्युता वर्णा ह्यनापदि ।
पापान्संसृत्य संसारान् प्रेष्यतां यान्ति दस्युषु ॥७०॥
वान्ताश्युल्कामुखः प्रेतो विप्रो भवति विच्युतः ।
अमेध्यकुणपाशी तु क्षत्रियः कटपूतनः ॥७१॥
मैत्राक्षज्योतिकः प्रेतो वैश्यो भवति पूयभुक् ।
चैलाशकस्तु भवति शूद्रो धर्मात्स्वकाच्च्युतः ॥७२॥

TMd3 हस्तिमृक्षः; Bo स्त्री मृगश्वातको; NPu1 स्त्रीं वृक्षश्वातको; Tr1 स्तोकरो; Pu5 Pu7 श्वोकको; NKt4 स्तेकको; Ho Jo2 Lo1 [*mc to*] Lo3 Tj1 Tr2 Wa चातको; wKt1 सृतिको वह्निं; MTr4 MTr6 चारि— d) Tr1 धातान्युष्टः पुरूनज; wKt3 oOr यानमुष्ट्रः; Lo1 यानान्मुपः; Tr2 यानान्युष्ट्रान्; BKt5 पशून्यजः; Lo2 पशूनजाः

68. Cited by *Viś* 3.221; *Vij* 3.210–1; *Mādh* 2.512 — a) Tr2 यद्वा यद्वा परं द्रव्य°; TMd3 यद्वा हृत्वा पर° — b) Ho बलवान्नरः; MTr4 MTr6 पशून्नरः — c) GMd5 वश्यं याति तु; Ho TMd4 जाति; sOx1 sPu6 तिर्यश्चं; Tr2 तिकृत्वं; Lo1 निर्यक्तं — d) TMd4 चैव हुतं

69. Omitted in TMd3 GMd5. Cited by *Vij* 3.216; *Mādh* 2.512 — b) GMd1 TMd4 MTr5 चोरत्वं याः प्रकुर्वते [TMd4 यः]; oOr *Vij* कृत्वा; sOx1 sPu6 दत्वा; Bo °वाप्नुयात् — c) Bo oOr एतेपामपि — d) GMy [*Jolly* Nd] पत्नीत्वमु°; Tr1 पतित्वमु°; Tr2 पत्नीत्वमपि यान्ति; GMd1 sOx1 sPu6 °मुपयाति; MTr4 °मुपयन्ति

70. Omitted in wKt1 — a) Ho Jo2 Lo1 [*mc to*] Lo3 Tj1 Tr1 स्वेभ्यश्च; Lo3 GMd1 oOr [*but cor*] कर्मेभ्य°; TMd4 MTr4 MTr6 धर्मेभ्यं° — b) BKt5 कर्मभ्यः श्वेता; oOr वाला; GMd5 वर्णास्त्वनापदि; Ho TMd4 GMy Tr1 वर्णा अनापदि; BKt5 वर्णाश्चानापदि; GMd1 धर्मादनापदि — c) GMd5 पापाः संस्कृत्य संस्काराः; BKt5 पापा संयान्ति संचारान्; NKt4 Ox2 पापात्सं°; sOx1 Pu2 Pu4 sPu6 Tr1 [*Jolly* Nd] पापाः सं°; GMd1 यावत्सं°; Ho °न्संसृज्य; NPu1 °न्संशृत्य; wKt3 °न्संश्रित्य; MTr4 MTr6 °न्संस्मृत्य; Pu10 °न्संवृत्य; TMd4 °न्विसृत्य; Tj2 *om* संसृत्य; Bo NKt4 Ox2 संसारात् — d) Lo1 प्रेक्ष्यतां; Tr1 MTr6 [*Jolly* Nd] प्रेततां; GMd5 प्रेत्यतां; Pu10 [*Jolly* M] भृत्यतां; BKt5 Lo2 GMd1 जन्तुषु; BBe2 Hy Jo1 wKt1 Kt2 Tj2 *Ku Go Mandlik KSS* शत्रुषु

71. Omitted in Hy. Cited by *Vij* 3.219–20 — a) Lo1 °ल्कमुखः; GMd1 TMd3 °मुखः प्रोक्तो — b) BBe2 Jo1 wKt1 Kt2 Tj2 [*Jolly* Nd R] *Vij Mandlik Jha KSS Dave* विप्रो धर्मात्स्वकाच्च्युतः [cf. 72d]; Lo1 ब्राह्मणो भवति च्युतः — c) wKt1 °पाशं; Be1 BBe2 Jo1 Jo2 Kt2 Kt2 wKt3 BKt5 Lo2 Lo3 Ox2 NPu1 Pu3 Pu5 Pu7 Tj1 Tj2 Tr2 *Mandlik Jolly Jha KSS Dave* च — d) BKt5 च न क्षत्रि°; MTr6 क्षत्रियं; NKt4 lacuna for कटपूतनः; Pu5 Pu7 [*Jolly* G] कठपूतनः; Pu10 MTr4 MTr6 कुटपूतनः; TMd3 Tr1 MTr5 *Me Jha Dave* [*Jolly* M] कूटपूतनः; Tr2 कातपूतनः; TMd4 कूटघातकः

72. Cited by *Vij* 3.219–20 — a) GMd1 MTr5 MTr6 मैत्राक्षो; NKt4 [lacuna]त्राक्षो; sOx1 sPu6 [*Jolly* M] मैत्राक्षि°; BBe2 मैत्राक्ष्य°; Hy Tj1 Tj2 Tr2 Wa मैत्राख्य°; Pu2 Pu4 Pu5 Pu7 मैत्राख्यो; wKt1 त्रैतामुज्यो°; oOr मैत्रेयोज्यो°; Tr1 मैत्राक्षिः द्यौतिकः; NPu1 मैत्राख्याज्योतिषः; Be1 मैत्राख्यज्योतिषः; GMd5 मैत्राविद्योतकः; TMd3 °ज्योतक; GMd1 sOx1 sPu6 Pu3 Tr2 Wa °ज्योतिष; Jo2 °ज्योतिनः; [*Jolly* Nd] °द्योतनः — b) TMd3 वैश्ये; sOx1 पूर्वभुक्; Bo पापभुक् — c) GMd1 GMd5 NKt4 Lo2 Tr1 MTr4 MTr5

यथा यथा निषेवन्ते विषयान्विषयात्मकाः ।
तथा तथा कुशलता तेषां तेषूपजायते ॥७३॥
तेऽभ्यासात्कर्मणां तेषां पापानामल्पबुद्धयः ।
संप्राप्नुवन्ति दुःखानि तासु तास्विह योनिषु ॥७४॥
तामिस्रादिषु चोग्रेषु नरकेषु विवर्तनम् ।
असिपत्त्रवनादीनि बन्धनच्छेदनानि च ॥७५॥
विविधाश्चैव संपीडाः काकोलूकैश्च भक्षणम् ।
करम्भवालुकातापान् कुम्भीपाकांश्च दुःसहान् ॥७६॥
संभवांश्च वियोनीषु दुःखप्रायासु नित्यशः ।
शीतातपाभिघातांश्च विविधानि भयानि च ॥७७॥
असकृद्गर्भवासेषु वासं जन्म च दारुणम् ।
बन्धनानि च कष्टानि परप्रेष्यत्वमेव च ॥७८॥

MTr^{6} [*Jolly* G N Nd] चेलाशकस्तु; NNg चैलाशिकस्तु; Hy Jo^{1} Kt^{2} Tj^{2} चैलाशकश्च; Tr^{2} चेलाशकश्च; Pu^{8} चैलाश्नस्तु; BKt^{5} सैलासक्तस्तु; Pu^{10} [*Jolly* M] तैलाशकस्तु; BBe^{2} तैलासकस्तु; Be^{1} वेलाशकस्तु; NPu^{1} Pu^{2} Pu^{4} बलाहकस्तु; TMd^{4} श्लेष्माशनस्तु; TMd^{3} चेलाशस्तु — d) GMd^{5} धर्मात्स्वकादपि; BBe^{2} धर्मात्सकामतः; Tr^{1} धर्मात्स्वकामतः

73. a) Be^{1} MTr^{5} यथा तथा; Wa निपेवन्ति — b) Pu^{5} Pu^{7} °षयात्मिकाः; BKt^{5} GMy °षयात्मकः; WKt^{1} °षयान्त्रिकाः; TMd^{4} °तयात्मनः; Pu^{10} [*Jolly* M] °षयैषिणः — c) Pu^{2} Pu^{4} कुशलतां; OOr कुशलिना — d) GMd^{1} कुलतामेषां; TMd^{4} तेषां तेषां प्रजायते; TMd^{3} GMy तेषु तेपूप°

74. Pādas c-d omitted in OOr — a) TMd^{4} GMy अभ्यासा° [*om* ते]; GMd^{5} तेभ्योसत्कर्मणां; Pu^{5} Pu^{7} ततश्च कर्मणां; OOr तेभ्यः सकर्मणा; GMy °त्कर्मण; BBe^{2} शेषां — b) SOx^{1} SPu^{6} पापासाम° — c) BBe^{2} संप्लुवन्ति च दुःखानि; SOx^{1} SPu^{6} समाप्नुवन्ति; GMd^{1} प्राप्य तप्यन्ति — d) GMd^{5} तासु तास्वखिलासु च; MTr^{6} तस्मात्तास्विह; BBe^{2} तास्वेतानिह

75. a) Ho Lo^{1} NPu^{1} Pu^{2} Pu^{4} Pu^{5} Pu^{7} Tr^{2} तामिश्रादिषु; TMd^{3} तामिस्रादिह; TMd^{4} चाग्रेषु; Jo^{2} SOx^{1} SPu^{6} घोरेषु; Pu^{5} Pu^{7} भूतेषु — b) NKt^{4} *om* नरकेषु; GMd^{1} नक्रकेषु; BKt^{5} विवर्तिनं; BBe^{2} NPu^{1} Pu^{2} Pu^{4} Pu^{5} Pu^{7} MTr^{6} निवर्तनं; Pu^{10} [*Jolly* M] प्रवर्तनं; Bo विवर्तते; NKt^{4} विवर्धनं — c) Bo असीपत्र°; Tj^{1} असपत्र° — d) Tr^{1} संधन°; Tr^{2} बन्धने च्छैदनानि; Lo^{2} बन्धनाच्छादनानि; OOr °च्छेदितानि

76. Omitted in GMd^{1} — a) Tr^{1} °धाश्चोपसंपिण्डाः; TMd^{4} °धाश्चायनः पीडान्; Tr^{2} °धाश्चैनसंवीजः; BKt^{5} TMd^{3} Pu^{5} Pu^{7} संपीडा — b) Bo °लूकश्च; BBe^{2} °लोकैश्च — c) GMd^{5} कारम्भ°; Ho करम्भा°; WKt^{1} कलम्भ°; Be^{1} °वालुवातापान्; TMd^{3} °वालुकानातान्; NPu^{1} Pu^{2} Pu^{4} Pu^{10} [*Jolly* M] °वालुकास्तप्ताः; BKt^{5} °वामुकास्तप्ता; GMd^{5} °कापातान्; Tr^{1} °तापात् — d) Hy कुम्भिपाकाश्च; Tj^{1} कुम्भीतापांश्च; TMd^{4} °पाकांस्तु; Hy Jo^{1} Kt^{2} Ox^{2} Pu^{2} Pu^{4} Pu^{8} Tj^{2} *Mandlik Jha KSS Dave* दारुणान्

77. Omitted in GMd^{1} — a) Kt^{2} BKt^{5} Pu^{5} Pu^{7} संभवाश्च; Tj^{1} संभावांश्च; Tr^{1} संभारांश्च; TMd^{3} GMd^{5} °वांश्चैव योनिषु; BKt^{5} वियोनिषु; Lo^{1} वियोन्यां तु — b) Lo^{1} °प्रायांस्तु; TMd^{4} °प्रायाश्च; BKt^{5} °प्रायातस्य नि°; OOr °प्रायासु योनिषु; TMd^{4} GMd^{5} NPu^{1} Pu^{2} Pu^{4} MTr^{4} MTr^{6} Wa सर्वशः; SOx^{1} SPu^{6} सर्वतः; TMd^{3} रुर्वशः — c) MTr^{6} शीततापाभि°; Tr^{1} शतातपाभि°; BKt^{5} GMy शीतवाताभि°; Ho °तपापघाताश्च; WKt^{1} °तपातिवाताश्च; BBe^{2} °यातांश्च — d) TMd^{4} त्रिविधानि

78. Omitted in Pu^{5} Wa; folio containing 78 to 83a torn in SPu^{6} — a) TMd^{4} असक्तगर्भवासिप्य; NPu^{1} Pu^{2} Pu^{4} °द्गर्भवासं च — b) NPu^{1} Pu^{2} Pu^{4} जन्म चैव हि दारुणं [*om* वासं]; TMd^{4} वसन्जन्म;

बन्धुप्रियवियोगांश्च संवासं चैव दुर्जनैः ।
द्रव्यार्जनं च नाशं च मित्रामित्रस्य चार्जनम् ॥७९॥
जरां चैवाप्रतीकारां व्याधिभिश्चोपपीडनम् ।
क्लेशांश्च विविधांस्तांस्तान् मृत्युमेव च दुर्जयम् ॥८०॥
यादृशेन तु भावेन यद्यत्कर्म निषेवते ।
तादृशेन शरीरेण तत्तत्फलमुपाश्नुते ॥ ८१॥
एष सर्वः समुद्दिष्टः कर्मणां वः फलोदयः ।
नैःश्रेयसं कर्मविधिं विप्रस्येमं निबोधत ॥८२॥
वेदाभ्यासस्तपो ज्ञानमिन्द्रियाणां च संयमः ।
अहिंसा गुरुसेवा च निःश्रेयसकरं परम् ॥८३॥
सर्वेषामपि चैतेषां शुभानामिह कर्मणाम् ।

Ox^{2} जन्म सुदारुणं; Pu^{10} जननदारुणं; BKt^{5} *om* च — c) Pu^{8} वा; Ho Pu^{10} Tr^{2} काष्टानि; NKt^{4} sOx^{1} *Mandlik KSS* काष्ठानि; Jo^{1} Pu^{7} कष्ठानि; Bo कर्पाणि; BBe^{2} वष्ठानि; Be^{1} Lo^{2} सर्वाणि — d) Pu^{7} पार°; Lo^{1} °प्रेक्ष्यत्वमेव; Ho °प्रेक्षात्वमेव; wKt^{3} °प्रेत्यत्वमेव

79. Omitted in Wa — a) TMd^{3} TMd^{4} oOr sOx^{1} बन्धुप्रियं वियोगं च; MTr^{6} बन्धुभिर्विप्रयोगांश्च; GMy °प्रिया°; NKt^{4} GMd^{5} NPu^{1} Pu^{2} Pu^{4} °वियोगं च; wKt^{1} °वियोगाश्च — b) TMd^{3} संसर्गं चाप्रियैः शुभैः; GMd^{5} GMy Tr^{1} MTr^{4} MTr^{6} संवासांश्चाप्रियैर्जनैः [Tr^{1} °वासं चा°]; Ox^{2} संयोगं चाप्रियैः सह; Tj^{2} विविधानि भयानि च [=12.77d]; Bo संवासां; wKt^{1} संवासश्चैव; Pu^{7} चातिदुर्जनैः; BKt^{5} स *for* चैव — c) GMd^{1} MTr^{5} द्रव्यार्जनविनाशं च — d) TMd^{3} मित्रामित्रविवेचनं; Tj^{1} चार्जुनं; Lo^{1} चार्चनं — NKt^{4} adds here a half-verse which is nearly identical to 12.77 a-b

80. Verses 80 and 81 transposed in Lo^{3} Tj^{1} — a) [*Jolly* Nd] जराश्चैवाप्रतीकाराः; Pu^{10} [*Jolly* M] राज्ञां चैव प्रतीकारं [Pu^{10} °कारां]; Bo Ho NKt^{4} जरा; Tj^{1} राजां; NKt^{4} TMd^{4} GMy oOr Tj^{1} Tr^{2} चैव प्रती°; wKt^{1} BKt^{5} GMd^{1} °प्रतीकारान्; Pu^{2} Pu^{4} °प्रतीकाशं — c) Ho क्लेशान्तु; Be^{1} शोकांश्च; Lo^{2} कोशांश्च; NKt^{4} शाकांश्च; BKt^{5} श्लेशांश्च — d) Pu^{2} Pu^{4} मृत्युरेव; Tj^{1} तु; BKt^{5} स; Jo^{2} Lo^{3} सुदुर्जयं; wKt^{3} MTr^{5} दुर्जनं

81. Placed after 12.51 in TMd^{3} GMy — a) Be^{1} wKt^{3} Lo^{2} oOr Pu^{5} Pu^{7} यादृशेनैव भावेन; TMd^{3} GMd^{5} यादृशेनापि भावेन; Ox^{2} यादृशेनानुभावेन; GMd^{1} यादृशेन शरीरेण; wKt^{1} च; TMd^{3} GMy Tr^{1} हि — b) Pu^{5} Pu^{7} [*but cor*] निषेवति — c) TMd^{3} यादृशेन — d) Pu^{10} [*Jolly* M] स तत्तत्फलमश्नुते; NKt^{4} *om one* तत्; Ho wKt^{1} sOx^{1} °लमवाप्नुयात्

82. a) Bo एतत्सर्वं; oOr सर्वं; Jo^{2} wKt^{3} BKt^{5} Lo^{3} Tj^{1} [*Jolly* R] धर्मः; NNg Pu^{10} [*Jolly* M] सर्गः — b) Kt^{2} wKt^{3} कर्मणा; GMd^{1} oOr यः; BKt^{5} स; sOx^{1} वा; Ho Lo^{1} NNg Ox^{2} Pu^{10} Wa च — c) Hy Jo^{1} Kt^{2} Tj^{2} *Mandlik KSS Jha Dave* नैःश्रेयसकरं कर्म; NNg Pu^{10} निश्रेयसं — d) Jo^{1} Jo^{2} Kt^{2} Tj^{2} *Mandlik Jha KSS Dave* विप्रस्येदं; NNg विप्रस्येव; [*Jolly* M] विप्रस्यैवं; GMd^{1} द्विजस्येमं

83. a) MTr^{4} MTr^{6} विद्याभ्या°; Bo *Bh* [pāṭha] ध्यानमिन्द्रि°; GMd^{1} *Bh* [pāṭha] दानमिन्द्रि° — b) Bo तु; wKt^{1} संयतः; Pu^{5} Pu^{7} [*Jolly* G] संग्रहः; Lo^{1} TMd^{3} GMd^{5} Tr^{1} [*Jolly* Gr] निग्रहः — c) wKt^{1} अहिंसा साग्नेश्च सेवा च; NKt^{4} गुरुपूजा; Pu^{10} गुरुमेव च; Lo^{3} °सेवां; BKt^{5} °सेवा स — d) BBe^{2} NKt^{4} Lo^{1} NNg Tj^{1} निश्रे°; BKt^{5} TMd^{3} GMd^{5} GMy नैश्रे°; Pu^{8} नैःश्रे°

किंचिच्छ्रेयस्करतरं कर्मोक्तं पुरुषं प्रति ॥८४॥
सर्वेषामपि चैतेषामात्मज्ञानं परं स्मृतम् ।
तद्ध्यग्र्यं सर्वविद्यानां प्राप्यते ह्यमृतं ततः ॥८५॥
षण्णामेषां तु पूर्वेषां कर्मणां प्रेत्य चेह च ।
श्रेयस्करतरं ज्ञेयं सर्वदा कर्म वैदिकम् ॥८६॥
वैदिके कर्मयोगे तु सर्वाण्येतान्यशेषतः ।
अन्तर्भवन्ति क्रमशस्तस्मिंस्तस्मिन्क्रियाविधौ ॥८७॥
सुखाभ्युदयिकं चैव नैःश्रेयसिकमेव च ।
प्रवृत्तं च निवृत्तं च द्विविधं कर्म वैदिकम् ॥८८॥

84. Omitted in BKt^{5} TMd^{3} GMd^{5} Pu^{10} [*Jolly* M]; pādas a-b omitted in Lo^{2}, and pādas b-c in Be^{1} — a) Pu^{8} सर्वेषामेव; Tr^{1} सर्वेषामिह; NKt^{4} °षामपि तु त्वेषां — b) wKt^{1} Pu^{3} °नामपि; Pu^{8} °नामेव — c) NKt^{4} GMd^{1} Pu^{3} Pu^{8} किंस्विच्छ्रेय° ; GMy NPu^{1} Pu^{2} Pu^{4} Tr^{1} MTr^{4} MTr^{6} Wa किं स्याच्छ्रेय° ; wKt^{1} La^{1} oOr किं तु श्रेय° ; Lo^{3} Tj^{1} किं निश्रेय°; NKt^{4} Lo^{1} °यस्करतमं; Pu^{8} °यस्करं चैव; MTr^{6} °यस्करं कर्म — d) Ho कर्मोक्तं प्रति दृश्यते

Additional verses in Ox^{2} Pu^{1}:

विधिना सर्वकर्माणि यज्ञदानतपांसि च ।
निषेवितानि सिध्यन्ति फलदानि भवन्ति च ॥१॥
विधिहीनं तु यत्कर्म तन्न सिद्ध्यति कर्हिचित् ।
सिद्धं चापि ह्यविधिना मूलान्यपि निकृन्तति ॥२॥

1. c) Ox^{2} निषेवति तानसिध्यन्ति
2. Pādas a-b omitted in NPu^{1} — c) Ox^{2} चाप्यन्यविधिना

85. Pāda-a omitted in Be^{1}. Pādas c-d cited by *Śaṃ* on *BU* 1.4.7 — b) BKt^{5} स्मृतिं — c) BKt^{5} तदर्थं सर्वविज्ञानं ; La^{1} TMd^{3} तद्ध्यग्रं; BBe^{2} तद्ध्यग्र; Be^{1} Jo^{2} sOx^{1} sPu^{6} Tr^{2} तदग्र्यं; oOr तदग्रं; Lo^{2} तद्यत्र सर्व° ; Wa °विद्यासु — d) wKt^{1} चामृतं; Ho स्वमृतं; MTr^{6} तपः

86.* a) BKt^{5} कन्यामेषां; Lo^{1} TMd^{4} Pu^{5} Pu^{7} Wa षण्णामेव तु; sOx^{1} *om* तु; BBe^{2} Hy Jo^{1} Kt^{2} wKt^{3} La^{1} sOx^{1} Pu^{3} Pu^{5} sPu^{6} Pu^{7} Tj^{2} Tr^{2} [*Jolly* G] *Go Rc Mandlik KSS* सर्वेषां — b) BKt^{5} प्रेत्य चाहतः; NPu^{1} Pu^{2} वेह; Pu^{4} वाह — c) Pu^{5} Pu^{7} श्रेयस्करं तं विज्ञेयं; GMy श्रेयस्करं ज्ञेयं; Be^{1} NKt^{4} Lo^{1} NNg श्रेयस्करतमं; Wa ज्ञानं — d) wKt^{3} BKt^{5} सर्वथा; [*Jolly* M] सर्वं वा कर्म; Lo^{2} *om* वैदिकं; Ho वैदिकां; Lo^{3} वेदिकं

87. a) TMd^{3} GMd^{5} वैदिकैः कर्मयोगैर्वा [GMd^{5} °योगैर्हि]; BKt^{5} *om* वैदिके; GMy वैदिकं; GMd^{1} धर्मयोगे; wKt^{3} *om* तु; Ho GMd^{1} sOx^{1} sPu^{6} MTr^{4} MTr^{6} हि; wKt^{1} La^{1} Pu^{3} Tr^{2} च — b) BKt^{5} वर्तन्ते तान्यशेषतः — c) sOx^{1} sPu^{6} अन्तर्भवति कर्माणि; oOr भवति तानि क्रमशस्त° ; wKt^{1} °र्भवति — d) GMy Tr^{1} [*Jolly* Nd] क्रमशो यस्मिन्कस्मि° ; TMd^{3} GMd^{5} क्रमशो यस्मिन्यस्मि° ; wKt^{1} Tr^{2} *om* क्रमशस्तस्मि-न्क्रिया° ; sOx^{1} sPu^{6} °स्मिन्यथाविधौ

88. Cited by *Vij* 3.58; *Apa* 1033; *Lakṣ* 14.146–7; pāda-d cited by *Śaṃ* on *BU* 1.1.1 — a) TMd^{3} GMd^{5} सुखार्थमाभ्युदयिकं [*om* चैव]; Ho °दयकं; wKt^{3} °दयितं; Lo^{2} °यिकं कर्म; wKt^{1} चैवं; *Apa* चैतन् — b) NKt^{4} BKt^{5} TMd^{3} La^{1} Lo^{1} MTr^{5} *Vij* नैश्रे°; BBe^{2} Pu^{4} Tj^{1} निश्रे° ; Ox^{2} Pu^{2} निःश्रे° ; GMy °यसकमेव; Wa °यसिमेव; Tj^{2} °यस्करमेव — c) GMd^{1} GMd^{5} Pu^{5} Pu^{7} प्रवृत्तिं च निवृत्तिं; NKt^{4} *om* निवृत्तं च — d) Pu^{5} Pu^{7} [*Jolly* G] द्विविधं कर्मणः फलं

इह वामुत्र वा काम्यं प्रवृत्तं कर्म कीर्त्यते ।
निष्कामं ज्ञानपूर्वं तु निवृत्तमुपदिश्यते ॥८९॥
प्रवृत्तं कर्म संसेव्य देवानामेति सार्ष्टिताम् ।
निवृत्तं सेवमानस्तु भूतान्यत्येति पञ्च वै ॥९०॥
सर्वभूतेषु चात्मानं सर्वभूतानि चात्मनि ।
समं पश्यन्नात्मयाजी स्वाराज्यमधिगच्छति ॥९१॥
यथोक्तान्यपि कर्माणि परिहाप्य द्विजोत्तमः ।
आत्मज्ञाने शमे च स्याद् वेदाभ्यासे च यत्नवान् ॥९२॥

89.* Pādas a-b torn in gMy. Cited by *Vij* 3.58; *Apa* 1033; *Lakṣ* 14.147 — a) La^1 इद्दृशंमुत्र; wKt^1 अहं वा अत्र वा; Be^1 bBe^2 Hy Jo^1 Jo^2 Kt^2 wKt^3 nKt^4 bKt^5 Lo^1 Lo^2 gMd^1 nNg sOx^1 Ox^2 Pu^2 Pu^3 Pu^4 sPu^6 Pu^{10} Tj^2 Tr^2 Wa [*Jolly* M] *Lakṣ Mandlik Jha KSS Dave* चामुत्र; oOr चामुत्र काम्यं तु; Bo Ho चामुत्र चाम्यं; tMd^3 चामुत्र चाकार्यं; nPu^1 Pu^2 Pu^4 कामं — b) Ho Jo^1 प्रवृत्त्यं; Pu^{10} च वृत्तं; Ho [*cor to*] कीर्तिते — c) Jo^2 bKt^5 Lo^1 Lo^3 Tj^1 ज्ञानपूर्वं तु निष्कामं; tMd^4 Pu^7 निष्काम; Pu^{10} *om* तु; bBe^2 wKt^1 Lo^2 sOx^1 sPu^6 च — d) oOr निवृत्तं कर्म दृश्यते; Lo^3 Tj^1 [*Jolly* R]प्रवृत्तमुप; La^1 sOx^1 sPu^6 Tr^2 °पदृश्यते

Additional verse in nKt^4 mTr^4 mTr^6 *Mandlik* [ग] *KSS Dave;* commented on by *Rn;* pādas a-b given after verse 88 in Pu^2 Pu^4:

अकामोपहतं नित्यं निवृत्तमभिधीयते ।
कामतस्तु कृतं कर्म प्रवृत्तमुपदिश्यते ॥

a) Pu^2 Pu^4 स्वकर्मोपहतं — b) *Mandlik KSS Dave* निवृत्तं च विधीयते

90.* Omitted in Pu^{10}. Cited by *Apa* 1033; *Lakṣ* 14.147 — a) Pu^8 प्रवृत्तं च हि संसेव्य; Lo^1 प्रवृत्त; Ox^2 निवृत्तं; tMd^4 कर्मणासद्य; Ho wKt^1 Lo^1 Ox^2 mTr^6 *Jha Dave* संसेव्यं; bKt^5 संसेव्यः; gMd^5 Pu^5 Pu^7 संसेवन्; tMd^3 संसेवं; Tr^1 संसेव; oOr संभाव्य — b) oOr देवानामात्मसात्मतां; Lo^2 देवानांप्रोति; Lo^3 देवानामिति; Kt^2 सेवानामेति; gMy °नामेव साक्षितां; tMd^4 °नामेति आत्मता; Ho Lo^2 Pu^5 Pu^7 साष्ट्र्यतां; Bo साष्ट्यतां; tMd^3 Tr^1 सष्टितां; Be^1 साष्ट्रतां; wKt^1 सार्ष्णितां; Jo^1 Kt^2 wKt^3 sOx^1 Ox^2 nPu^1 Pu^2 Pu^4 sPu^6 Pu^8 Tj^2 Tr^2 [*Jolly* K] *Me Rn* [pāṭha] *Mandlik Jha KSS Dave* साम्यतां; Pu^3 [*Jolly* M] *Apa* सात्म्यतां; Jo^2 La^1 nNg *Lakṣ* सात्मतां; Hy सास्मतां; bKt^5 साम्यतः — c) Pu^8 निवृत्तं कर्म संसेव्य; sOx^1 sPu^6 निवृत्त; gMd^1 निवृत्तान्; bBe^2 bKt^5 La^1 tMd^4 सेव्यमानस्तु; wKt^1 सेवमानं तु; nNg nPu^1 Pu^2 Pu^4 सेवमानश्च — d) gMd^1 भूतानत्येति; tMd^3 भूतानन्त्येति; Be^1 bKt^5 La^1 Lo^2 Ox^2 nPu^1 Pu^4 Wa [*Jolly* M] *Me* [pāṭha] *Nā* भूतान्यभ्येति; gMd^1 Tr^2 [*Jolly* G] *Me* [pāṭha but rejected] भूतान्यप्येति; Tr^1 भूतान्यप्यैति; Lo^1 भूतान्येतीति; *Apa* भूतान्पश्यति; tMd^3 gMd^5 पञ्च तु; Bo पञ्चकैः; *Lakṣ* पञ्चमे; bKt^5 वः

91. Verses 91 and 92 transposed in Pu^7. *Śaṃ* on *BU* 3.1.1[intro.] refers to this verse, cited by *Lakṣ* 14.147 — a) Pu^3 Pu^8 Tr^2 सर्वभूतस्थमात्मानं; bKt^5 सर्वभूतानि — b) oOr Pu^2 Pu^4 Pu^{10} सर्वभूतेषु — c) wKt^1 gMd^1 gMy Pu^2 Pu^4 संपश्यन्नात्मयाजी वै [Pu^2 Pu^4 च; gMd^1 त; wKt^1 सन्]; tMd^3 gMd^5 Tr^1 संपश्यन्नात्मवां जीवैः; La^1 संपश्यन्नानुयाजी च; Lo^1 संपश्यन्नात्मनात्मानं; Pu^{10} शमं; tMd^4 समुपश्यन्नात्म° — d) Be^1 bKt^5 Lo^1 Pu^{10} स्वराज्य°; Ho स्वं राज्य°; bBe^2 सराज्य°; wKt^1 सुराज्य°; tMd^3 gMd^5 समग्रमधि°; Pu^5 Pu^7 °धितिष्ठति; Ho Pu^{10} [*Jolly* M] °भिगच्छति

92. Cited by *Lakṣ* 14.147 — b) wKt^3 परिहार्य; Pu^2 परिहाये; Pu^4 परिहायो; bBe^2 Hy Jo^1 Kt^2 nNg Ox^2 Tr^2 *Me Rn Mandlik KSS Jha Dave* परिहाय; mTr^6 परिगृह्य; tMd^4 द्विजोत्तम — c) Pu^{10}

एतद्धि जन्मसामग्र्यं ब्राह्मणस्य विशेषतः ।
प्राप्यैतत्कृतकृत्यो हि द्विजो भवति नान्यथा ॥९३॥
पितृदेवमनुष्याणां वेदश्चक्षुः सनातनम् ।
अतर्क्यं चाप्रमेयं च वेदशास्त्रमिति स्थितिः ॥९४॥
या वेदबाह्याः श्रुतयो याश्च काश्च कुदृष्टयः ।
सर्वास्ता निष्फलाः प्रेत्य तमोनिष्ठा हि ताः स्मृताः ॥९५॥
उत्पद्यन्ते व्यथन्ते च यान्यतोऽन्यानि कानिचित् ।
तान्यर्वाक्कालिकतया निष्फलान्यनृतानि च ॥९६॥
चातुर्वर्ण्यं त्रयो लोकाश्चत्वारश्चाश्रमाः पृथक् ।
भूतं भव्यं भविष्यं च सर्वं वेदात्प्रसिध्यति ॥९७॥

[*Jolly* M] आत्मज्ञाने समावेश्य; Be¹ आत्मज्ञान; Lo¹ °ज्ञाने यत्नवान्स्याद्; BBe² Ho wKt¹ BKt⁵ Lo³ NNg NPu¹ Pu² Pu³ sPu⁶ Tj¹ समे; Wa साम; Be¹ Lo² क्रमे; BBe² oOr शमे तस्य; wKt¹ तु; Bo Lo² TMd³ GMd⁵ वा; Tr¹ व; BKt⁵ स — d) Tj¹ Tr¹ Tr² TMd³ TMd⁴ GMd⁵ °भ्यासेन यत्नवान्; GMd¹ °भ्यासेन यत्भवान्; Ho °भ्यासे प्रयत्नवान्; Pu² Pu⁴ Pu¹⁰ °भ्यासेत यत्नवान्

93. Omitted in [*Jolly* Nd]. Cited by *Śaṃ* on *BhG* 15.20; *Lakṣ* 14.147 — a) Be¹ NPu¹ एतद् द्विजन्मनामग्र्यं; TMd⁴ एतद् द्विजानामग्र्यं च; NNg sOx¹ Ox² Pu² Pu⁴ sPu⁶ Tr² जन्मनामग्र्यं; BBe² Bo Ho Hy Jo¹ Jo² wKt¹ Kt² Lo¹ Lo³ Pu⁸ Tj¹ Tj² [*Jolly* R] *Go Ku Mandlik Jha KSS Dave* जन्मसाफल्यं; BKt⁵ Pu⁵ Pu⁷ °सामाग्र्यं — b) TMd³ GMd⁵ ब्राह्मणस्य महात्मनः — c) Ho °कृत्ये; La¹ °कृत्योपि; Bo Ox² वै

94.* Omitted in Pu¹⁰. Cited by *Apa* 12; pādas a-b cited by *Dev* 1.129 — a) *Dev* [vl] ऋषिदेव° — b) TMd⁴ oOr वेदचक्षुः; La¹ देवश्चक्षुः; BKt⁵ देवचक्षुः; TMd⁴ Pu⁵ Pu⁷ *Dev* सनातनः — c) NPu¹ Pu² Pu⁴ अचिन्त्यं; BKt⁵ अनन्तं; BBe² Bo Ho Hy Jo¹ Jo² wKt¹ Kt² wKt³ La¹ Lo¹ Lo² Lo³ NNg Pu⁵ Pu⁷ Pu⁸ Tj¹ Tj² *Go Ku Rn Mandlik Jolly Jha KSS Dave* अशक्यं; TMd⁴ अवात्यं; NKt⁴ असत्यं; Be¹ अतर्क्यमप्रमेयं; TMd³ चाप्रतर्क्यं

95.* Folio containing verses 95c to 100d torn in sPu⁶. Cited by *Kum* 1.3.5; *Apa* 14; *Lakṣ* 1.262 — a) TMd³ Tr¹ [*but cor*] Wa यो; GMd¹ ये; MTr⁴ MTr⁶ °बाह्यः; BBe² Bo Ho Hy Jo¹ Jo² wKt¹ Kt² wKt³ Lo¹ Lo³ GMd⁵ sOx¹ Ox² sPu⁶ Pu⁸ Tj¹ Tj² Tr² MTr⁶ [*Jolly* Nd] *Kum Bh Ku Rc Mandlik KSS* स्मृतयो; MTr⁴ स्मृतं — b) Be¹ याश्चित्काश्चित्कु°; BBe² Ho NKt⁴ Lo¹ Lo³ oOr sOx¹ Pu⁵ sPu⁶ Pu⁷ Pu⁸ Pu¹⁰ Wa *Kum Apa* काश्चित्कु°; Tj¹ काचित्कु°; Pu² Pu⁴ कुदृष्टतः; GMd¹ नदृष्टयः; TMd³ सुदृष्टयः — c) oOr समस्ता; Bo सर्वास्तान्नि°; GMy निष्फलां; *Kum Apa Lakṣ* प्रोक्तास्तमो° — d) Lo³ Tj¹ *Apa* तमोभूता; TMd³ तमोनित्या; wKt³ °निष्ठान्विताः; GMd¹ य ता; MTr⁶ यतस्स्मृताः; Pu⁴ हि तानसः

96. Cited by *Apa* 12; *Lakṣ* 1.262 — a) Bo उत्पद्यते; wKt³ उपपद्यन्ते; GMd¹ MTr⁴ उत्पाद्यन्ते; Hy wKt³ Lo² TMd⁴ NNg NPu¹ Pu² Pu⁵ Pu⁷ *Apa* व्ययन्ते; Be¹ oOr कथन्ते; Tr¹ प्यनंते; BBe² Jo¹ Jo² wKt¹ Kt² Lo³ Pu⁸ Tj¹ MTr⁵ Wa [*Jolly* R] *Lakṣ Mandlik KSS* च्यवन्ते; La¹ व्यपद्यन्ते यान्य°; *Jha Dave* विनश्यन्ति यान्य°; TMd³ GMd⁵ विनश्यन्ते यान्य°; Ox² *Rc* विलीयन्ते यान्य° — a-b) Tr² ये च यान्यतोन्यानि तानि कानि च कर्हिचित् — b) Pu⁷ यानि तान्यन्यानि कानि च; GMd⁵ कानि च — c) BKt⁵ तान्यर्वाक्कालीनतया; La¹ तान्यर्वाक्कानितकया; NPu¹ सर्वाण्याकालिकतया; Ox² तान्यल्पकालि°; GMd⁵ Tr² °क्कालितया — d) GMd¹ NPu¹ °न्यमृतानि

97. Verses 97–112 illegible in TMd⁴. Cited by *Dev* 1.128 — a) Pu⁴ चतु°; BBe² BKt⁵

शब्दः स्पर्शश्च रूपं च रसो गन्धश्च पञ्चमः ।
वेदादेव प्रसिध्यन्ति प्रसूतिर्गुणकर्मतः ॥९८॥
बिभर्ति सर्वभूतानि वेदशास्त्रं सनातनम् ।
तस्मादेतत्परं मन्ये यज्जन्तोरस्य साधनम् ॥९९॥
सेनापत्यं च राज्यं च दण्डनेतृत्वमेव च ।
सर्वलोकाधिपत्यं च वेदशास्त्रविदर्हति ॥१००॥
यथा जातबलो वह्निर्दहत्यार्द्रानपि द्रुमान् ।
तथा दहति वेदज्ञः कर्मजं दोषमात्मनः ॥१०१॥
वेदशास्त्रार्थतत्त्वज्ञो यत्र तत्राश्रमे वसन् ।
इहैव लोके तिष्ठन्स ब्रह्मभूयाय कल्पते ॥१०२॥

चातुर्वर्ण्यं; GMd^{5} ततो; GMd^{1} लोकांश्च°; MTr^{6} धर्माश्च° — b) Pu^{10} [*Jolly* M] लोकाः स्मृतिश्चत्वारश्चाश्रमाः; wKt^{1} BKt^{5} Lo^{1} sOx^{1} °काश्चत्वारः पृथगाश्रमाः; oOr °काश्चत्वार आश्रमाः — c) Ho भूयं भवद्भविष्यश्च; Bo भूवभवद्भविष्यच्च; BBe^{2} NKt^{4} oOr Tr^{1} भूत; GMd^{1} sOx^{1} *Jha Dave* भवद्भविष्यं; BBe^{2} Hy NKt^{4} Lo^{3} GMd^{5} NNg Tj^{1} Tr^{1} [*Jolly* R^{1} Nd] *Dev* भविष्यच्च — d) Lo^{3} oOr सर्व

98.* Ms of Tr^{1} ends at pāda-c — a) TMd^{3} शब्दस्पर्शरूपं च; Lo^{1} Tj^{1} शब्द; Hy शब्दाः; Bo Ho NKt^{4} La^{1} MTr^{6} स्पर्शं च; Hy *om* रूपं च — b) wKt^{1} गन्धं च पञ्च वै; Pu^{5} Pu^{7} गन्धस्तथैव च; TMd^{3} पञ्चमं; GMd^{1} पश्चिमः — c) Hy wKt^{3} Pu^{8} प्रसिध्यति; Jo^{1} Kt^{2} Tj^{2} *Mandlik Jha KSS Dave* प्रसूयन्ते — d) Be^{1} Lo^{2} प्रसूतेर्गु°; Lo^{2} प्रसूतेगु°; Bo प्रसूतीगु°; BBe^{2} Hy Jo^{1} Jo^{2} wKt^{1} Kt^{2} wKt^{3} NKt^{4} Lo^{1} Lo^{3} GMd^{1} TMd^{3} GMy oOr sOx^{1} Pu^{2} Pu^{3} Pu^{4} Pu^{8} Tj^{2} Tr^{2} MTr^{4} MTr^{5} MTr^{6} [*Jolly* Ku R N] *Bh Ku Rn Rc Mandlik KSS* प्रसूतिगु°; Pu^{2} Pu^{4} प्रभूतिगु°; Pu^{5} Pu^{7} *Go* प्रभूतगु°; BKt^{5} प्रसूगु°; GMy °कर्मभिः; wKt^{1} °कर्म च; MTr^{4} MTr^{6} °कर्मणः; Ox^{2} °कर्मणोः; BKt^{5} TMd^{3} GMd^{5} sOx^{1} Pu^{3} Tr^{2} Wa [*Jolly* N] *Me* [pāṭha] *Nā* °धर्मतः

99. Pādas c-d omitted in wKt^{3}. Arrangement of verses in [*Jolly* M] is 99, 106–8, 100–5, 109–122, 126 — a) TMd^{3} Pu^{3} Tr^{2} सर्वशास्त्राणि — b) Ox^{2} वेदः — d) Pu^{10} जायन्ते चास्य साधनं; Bo यजन्तो°; NNg Wa जन्तो° [*om* यज्]; Lo^{1} GMd^{5} °न्तोरन्य; Wa °रस्य स्वसाधनं; NKt^{4} NPu^{1} शासनं; TMd^{3} दाधनं

100. Omitted in Pu^{5} Pu^{10} — a) Jo^{2} Lo^{3} Tj^{1} सैनाधिपत्यं राज्यं च; Hy wKt^{1} Kt^{2} wKt^{3} NKt^{4} Pu^{8} Tr^{2} Wa *Jolly Jha Dave* सैना°; BBe^{2} शैना°; GMd^{5} सेनापतिं — b) Pu^{7} दण्डं; Ho TMd^{3} °नेत्रत्वमेव; BBe^{2} °नेकृत्यमेव — d) Bo °शास्त्रविधिर्हितः; Tr^{2} °शास्त्रविगर्हितं

101. Omitted in Pu^{10}. Cited by *Dev* 1.129; *Mādh* 2.172 — a) Be^{1} Lo^{2} जातविदो; Tr^{2} यावतबलो — b) Pu^{2} Pu^{4} वह्निर्हन्यादार्द्रानपि; BKt^{5} °त्यार्द्रानमपि; Be^{1} °त्यार्द्रान्नपि; oOr °त्यार्द्रान्द्रुमान्महान् — c) Pu^{2} Pu^{4} वेदज्ञाः; Lo^{2} वैदत्तः

Additional verse in NPu^{1} Pu^{2} Pu^{4} *Mandlik* [क, ट, ठ] *KSS Dave:*

न वेदबलमाश्रित्य पापकर्मरुचिर्भवेत् ।
अज्ञानात्तु प्रमादाच्च दहते कर्म नेतरत् ॥

b) Pu^{2} Pu^{4} °कर्मरतिर्भवेत् — c) *Mandlik KSS Dave* अज्ञानाच्च; Pu^{4} प्रसादाच्च

102. Omitted in Pu^{10}; pādas c-d omitted in GMd^{1}. Cited by *Dev* 1.132 — a) Tr^{2} °तत्त्वज्ञे — b) Tr^{2} तत्र तत्रा°; Bo TMd^{3} *Dev* यत्र यत्रा°; Be^{1} °श्रमं; Bo GMd^{1} Pu^{2} Pu^{4} *Dev* वसेत्; Wa वसेन् — c) *Dev* इहैव तिष्ठन्लोके स; wKt^{3} NKt^{4} तिष्ठत्स; GMy तस्मिन्स — d) BKt^{5} °भूताय; NKt^{4} GMy कल्प्यते

अज्ञेभ्यो ग्रन्थिनः श्रेष्ठा ग्रन्थिभ्यो धारिणो वराः ।
धारिभ्यो ज्ञानिनः श्रेष्ठा ज्ञनिभ्यो व्यवसायिनः ॥१०३॥
तपो विद्या च विप्रस्य निःश्रेयसकरं परम् ।
तपसा कल्मषं हन्ति विद्ययामृतमश्नुते ॥१०४॥
प्रत्यक्षं चानुमानं च शास्त्रं च विविधागमम् ।
त्रयं सुविदितं कार्यं धर्मशुद्धिमभीप्सता ॥१०५॥
आर्षं धर्मोपदेशं च वेदशास्त्राविरोधिना ।
यस्तर्केणानुसंधत्ते स धर्मं वेद नेतरः ॥१०६॥
नैःश्रेयसमिदं कर्म यथोदितमशेषतः ।
मानवस्यास्य शास्त्रस्य रहस्यमुपदिश्यते ॥१०७॥
अनाम्नातेषु धर्मेषु कथं स्यादिति चेद्भवेत् ।
यं शिष्टा ब्राह्मणा ब्रूयुः स धर्मः स्यादशङ्कितः ॥१०८॥
धर्मेणाधिगतो यैस्तु वेदः सपरिबृंहणः ।

103. Omitted in Pu[10] — a) BKt[5] La[1] Tj[1] अग्रेभ्यो; NNg अग्रेभ्यो; Kt[2] ग्रन्थितः; BBe[2] गृहिनिनः श्रेष्ठो — b) TMd[3] पराः; NKt[4] वशः — d) Be[1] ज्ञातिभ्यो; Pu[4] *Bh* °भ्योध्यवसायिनः

104. Omitted in Pu[10]. Cited by *Apa* 960; *Dev* 1.144 — a) Lo[1] विद्याश्च; *Dev* विद्यापि; BKt[5] विप्राश्च — b) BBe[2] NKt[4] Tj[1] निश्रे°; wKt[1] wKt[3] La[1] sOx[1] sPu[6] नैश्रे°; GMy NPu[1] Pu[2] Pu[4] Pu[8] नैःश्रे°; TMd[3] GMd[5] तेजःश्रेयस्करं — c) oOr तापसा; BKt[5] तमसा; Hy Jo[1] Kt[2] sOx[1] sPu[6] Tj[2] *Mandlik Jha KSS Dave* किल्बिषं — d) BKt[5] विद्यायामृतम°; Pu[8] विविधयामृतम°; oOr विनयामृतम°

105. Omitted in Pu[10]; verses 105–26 omitted in wKt[1]. Cited by *Śaṃ* on *VeS* 2.1.11; *Kum* 1.3.2; *Lakṣ* 1.32; *Hem* 21.22 — a) La[1] GMd[1] Pu[8] *Śaṃ Kum Lakṣ Hem* प्रत्यक्षमनुमानं च; Be[1] प्रत्यक्ष्यं — b) Bo Tr[2] *Lakṣ* शब्दं च; NPu[1] Pu[2] Pu[3] Pu[4] *Kum* शाब्दं च; Be[1] द्विविधा°; MTr[6] विधिं स्मृतं; GMd[5] °धागमः — c) Lo[2] *om* त्रयं; Ho संविदितं; BKt[5] चाविदितं; Lo[1] NPu[1] तु विदितं — d) GMd[5] आत्मशुद्धिमीप्सता; Bo GMy NNg Pu[2] Pu[4] Tr[2] [*Jolly* Nd] धर्मसिद्धि°; BBe[2] MTr[4] MTr[6] कर्मशुद्धि°; wKt[3] Pu[3] कर्मसिद्धि°; [*Jolly* M] कर्मबुद्धि°; TMd[3] आत्मशुद्धि°; Ho GMd[1] Tr[2] °भीप्सिता; Pu[2] Pu[4] °भीप्सतः; *Kum* [*Jolly* M] °भीप्सतां; Bo °नीप्सता

106. Cited by *Śaṃ* on *VeS* 2.1.11; *Apa* 22; *Lakṣ* 1.32; *Hem* 21.22; pādas c-d cited by *Kum* 1.3.2 — a) Ho NKt[4] Lo[1] Pu[2] Pu[4] Pu[10] [*Jolly* M] आर्षं; GMd[1] एष; Ho Pu[10] [*Jolly* M] धर्मोपदेशेन [*om* च; Pu[10] धर्मोप°]; GMd[1] °देशश्च — b) Bo Hy TMd[3] GMd[5] NNg °शास्त्रविरो°; Pu[2] Pu[4] °शास्त्रंविरो°; Wa °शास्त्रांविरो°; NNg Ox[2] °विरोधना; TMd[3] °विरोधिनः; wKt[3] °विरोधिता — c) *Hem* यस्तर्केण तु संधत्ते — d) TMd[3] GMd[5] धर्मान्वेद; NPu[1] वद; La[1] नेतराः; Ho नेतरं; *Lakṣ* नापरः

107. Pādas c-d omitted in oOr — a) BKt[5] La[1] Lo[1] sOx[1] sPu[6] नैश्रे°; NNg Ox[2] NPu[1] Pu[2] Pu[3] Tr[2] निःश्रे°; NKt[4] निश्रे°; Be[1] Pu[3] Tr[2] °यसकरं कर्म — c) Pu[2] Pu[4] °वस्यास्य कथितं; BKt[5] La[1] धर्मस्य रह° — d) Pu[5] Pu[7] °स्यमुपेक्षते; wKt[3] GMd[1] NNg sOx[1] sPu[6] Pu[10] MTr[6] [*Jolly* M G] °पदेक्ष्यते; Lo[2] °पदिक्ष्यते; Tr[2] °पदृश्यते

108. Cited by *Lakṣ* 1.35; *Dev* 1.7 — a) La[1] अनाख्यातेषु; *Lakṣ* अनाज्ञातेषु; TMd[3] °म्नामेषु; BKt[5] धर्मेण; GMy सर्वेषु — a-b) Pu[2] Pu[4] अनाम्नातेषु कथं स्यादिति चेत्संशयो भवेत् — b) TMd[3] GMd[5] चेन्मतिः — c) Hy TMd[3] ये; GMd[1] शिष्ट; BKt[5] ब्रह्मणा

ते शिष्टा ब्राह्मणा ज्ञेयाः श्रुतिप्रत्यक्षहेतवः ॥१०९॥
दशावरा वा परिषद्यं धर्मं परिकल्पयेत् ।
त्र्यवरा वापि वृत्तस्था तं धर्मं न विचारयेत् ॥११०॥
त्रैविद्यो हेतुकस्तर्की नैरुक्तो धर्मपाठकः ।
त्रयश्चाश्रमिणः पूर्वे परिषत्स्याद्दशावरा ॥१११॥
ऋग्वेदविद्यजुर्विच्च सामवेदविदेव च ।
त्र्यवरा परिषज्ज्ञेया धर्मसंशयनिर्णये ॥११२॥
एकोऽपि वेदविद्धर्मं यं व्यवस्येद् द्विजोत्तमः ।
स विज्ञेयः परो धर्मो नाज्ञानामुदितोऽयुतैः ॥११३॥

109. Cited by *Apa* 82; *Dev* 1.6 — a) TMd^3 धर्मणाधि°; *Apa* न्यायेनाधि°; Be^1 °णापिगतो; oOr Wa °णावगतो; BKt^5 °गतं; BBe^2 यस्तु — b) MTr^4 MTr^6 वेदस्य परि°; La^1 वेदस्तु परि°; Pu^{10} °वृंहिणः; GMd^1 °बर्हणः; BKt^5 °बृंहिताः — c) Lo^3 शिष्ट; Tr^2 ब्रह्मणा; BKt^5 Ox^2 ब्रूयुः — d) BBe^2 श्रुतिः; Be^1 Lo^2 °प्रत्ययहेतवः

110. a) BBe^2 देशावरा; GMd^1 दशावारा; La^1 MTr^5 *Bh*[ad 11.85] दशापरा; Pu^{10} दशावरीया परि°; Be^1 GMd^1 sOx^1 sPu^6 Tj^2 *om* वा; Pu^5 Pu^7 तु; NNg NPu^1 Pu^2 च; Pu^4 Tr^2 व; Wa च या पर्षद्यं; Lo^1 पारिषद्यं; NPu^1 Pu^2 Pu^4 पर्षद्यं; sOx^1 sPu^6 परिश्छदं; Ho परिषधं; Lo^2 *om* परिषद्यं धर्मं — a-b) Lo^3 Tj^1 परिषद्धर्मं यं परि° — b) Lo^1 परिषद्धर्मं च परिकल्पयेत्; TMd^3 °षद्ये धर्मं परिभाषते; GMd^5 परिरक्षते; NNg Pu^3 °कल्पते — c) BBe^2 त्रिवरा; BKt^5 त्रिवरापि; TMd^3 त्र्यवराण्यपि; Lo^1 Tr^2 त्वरापि च [Lo^1 व]; Pu^3 त्र्यवरापि वृ°; NNg sOx^1 sPu^6 चापि; Bo यापि; GMd^5 ह्यपि; Be^1 वृत्तस्थ; wKt^3 वृत्तस्थं; BKt^5 वृत्तिस्था; sOx^1 sPu^6 वृत्तस्या; Ho oOr धर्मस्था; La^1 GMy Ox^2 Pu^2 Pu^3 Pu^4 Pu^8 वृत्तस्थास्तं; Tr^2 वृक्षस्थास्तं; Lo^1 वृत्तास्यात्तं — d) BBe^2 Bo Hy Jo^1 Jo^2 Kt^2 Lo^1 Lo^2 Lo^3 GMy oOr sOx^1 Ox^2 NPu^1 Pu^2 Pu^3 Pu^4 sPu^6 Pu^8 Tj^1 Tj^2 [*Jolly* R Nd] *Rn Rc Mandlik Jha KSS Dave* विचालयेत्

Additional verse in NPu^1 Pu^2 Pu^4 *Mandlik* [क, ग, ट, ठ] *KSS Dave:*

पुराणं मानवो धर्मः साङ्गो वेदश्चिकित्सितम् ।
आज्ञासिद्धानि चत्वारि न हन्तव्यानि हेतुभिः ॥

b) *Mandlik KSS Dave* साङ्गोपाङ्गचिकित्सकः

111. Cited by *Apa* 22; folio containing verses 111c to 117c torn in sPu^6 — a) Be^1 Bo GMd^1 TMd^3 GMd^5 MTr^6 त्रैविद्या; BBe^2 त्रैवेद्या; Ho Jo^2 La^1 Lo^1 Lo^3 NNg NPu^1 Pu^2 Pu^3 Pu^4 Pu^5 Pu^7 Pu^8 Tj^1 *Jolly* हैतुक°; TMd^3 हेतुकसुखी; NPu^1 °कस्तार्की; sPu^6 °कस्तर्कः; sOx^1 Pu^5 °कस्तर्क; BBe^2 GMd^5 Pu^2 Pu^4 °कस्तर्कं — b) oOr नैरुपे; sPu^6 °पाठतः — c) TMd^3 तृचश्चामित्रिणः; Pu^8 यश्चाश्रमिणः; Be^1 पूर्वं; Pu^{10} सर्वे; BKt^5 मुख्या — d) Bo TMd^3 GMd^5 GMy NNg NPu^1 Pu^2 Pu^3 Pu^4 Pu^{10} Tr^2 MTr^4 MTr^6 Wa *Apa* पर्षदेषा दशावरा [TMd^3 परिष°]; BBe^2 परिषः स्या°; Be^1 °वराः; GMd^1 °वरान्

112. Cited by *Vij* 3.299; *Apa* 21; *Dev* 1.8 — a) Ho ऋग्वेदयुजुर्विच्च; TMd^4 Ox^2 Pu^5 Pu^7 °विद्यजुर्वेदसाम°; BKt^5 °विद्यजुर्वेदस्साम° — a-b) Wa °विद्यजुर्वेदविच्च सामविदेव च — c) wKt^3 La^1 GMd^1 Pu^2 Pu^4 त्र्यवराः; BKt^5 GMd^5 त्रिवरा; *Apa* अवरा; *Vij* अपरा; NPu^1 *Vij* पर्षद्विज्ञेया; Pu^2 Pu^4 Wa पर्षदो ज्ञेया; TMd^4 पर्षदा ज्ञेया; La^1 पर्हता ज्ञेयाः; GMd^1 °ज्ज्ञेयाः — d) Ho °निर्णयोः

113. Cited by *Vij* 3.299; pādas a-b cited by *Viś* 1.9 — a) Lo^2 वेदार्थं यं — b) *Vij* यं व्यवस्येत्समाहितः; BKt^5 oOr यो; GMy संव्य°; BBe^2 GMd^1 विवस्येद्; NNg व्यवसेद्; Lo^3 व्यवस्यो; Lo^1 विवक्षेद्; GMd^1 sOx^1 द्विजन्मनः; BBe^2 La^1 TMd^3 GMd^5 GMy oOr MTr^4 MTr^6 विचक्षणः — c) La^1 स हि ज्ञेयः; Be^1 Lo^2 oOr Pu^2 Pu^4 *Vij* स ज्ञेयः परमो — d) TMd^3 MTr^6 नाज्ञानमु°; Tr^2 नज्ञायामु°; Lo^1

अव्रतानाममन्त्राणां जातिमात्रोपजीविनाम् ।
सहस्रशः समेतानां परिषत्त्वं न विद्यते ॥११४॥
यं वदन्ति तमोभूता मूर्खा धर्ममतद्विदः ।
तत्पापं शतधा भूत्वा तद्वक्तॄननुगच्छति ॥११५॥
एतद्वोऽभिहितं सर्वं निःश्रेयसकरं परम् ।
अस्मादप्रच्युतो विप्रः प्राप्नोति परमां गतिम् ॥११६॥
एवं स भगवान्देवो लोकानां हितकाम्यया ।
धर्मस्य परमं गुह्यं ममेदं सर्वमुक्तवान् ॥११७॥
सर्वमात्मनि संपश्येत् सच्चासच्च समाहितः ।
सर्वं ह्यात्मनि संपश्यन् नाधर्मे कुरुते मनः ॥११८॥
आत्मैव देवताः सर्वाः सर्वमात्मन्यवस्थितम् ।
आत्मा हि जनयत्येषां कर्मयोगं शरीरिणाम् ॥११९॥

नाज्ञानानु°; BBe[2] °मुदिते; Lo[1] SOx[1] °मुदितायुतैः; Lo[3] Tj[1] °मयुतायुतैः;Ho °युतेः; MTr[4] °यतैः

114. a) Lo[1] अयुतानाम° — b) BBe[2] °जीवनां; TMd[3] °सेवनां — c) Lo[2] Tr[2] सहस्रः — d) GMd[1] परिशिवं; TMd[4] NPu[1] Pu[2] Pu[4] MTr[6] Wa पर्षत्त्वं नैव [MTr[6] न हि]; Lo[2] °षत्त्वमविद्यते; BKt[5] वर्तते

115. Omitted in GMd[1] — a) Pu[8] य; Ho NKt[4] La[1] TMd[3] TMd[4] NNg NPu[1] Pu[2] Pu[3] Pu[4] Tj[1] Tr[2] Wa [*Jolly* R Nd Gr] *BDh* 1.1.11; *VaDh* 3.6 यद्वदन्ति; Lo[2] संवदन्ति; Lo[1] Wa तमो भूत्वा; BBe[2] WKt[3] La[1] TMd[4] GMy NNg NPu[1] Pu[2] Pu[4] [*Jolly* Nd] तमोमूढा — b) BKt[5] मूर्खाभिर्ममतद्विदः; TMd[4] धर्माधर्ममजानतः; TMd[3] GMd[5] मृषावादास्सभासदः; Tr[2] मूर्ख; Bo Ho NPu[1] Pu[2] Pu[4] Pu[5] Pu[7] Pu[10] मूर्पा; Bo °मविद्वदः; NPu[1] Pu[2] Pu[4] MTr[4] MTr[6] Wa °मजानतः; Pu[10] °मतन्द्रितः — c) TMd[3] तत्पादं; Lo[1] तत्पाशं; NNg [*but cor fh*] भूता; WKt[3] कृत्वा — d) TMd[3] वक्तॄनेवापगच्छति; GMd[5] वक्तॄनेव स गच्छति; GMy Pu[2] Pu[4] Pu[5] Pu[7] [*Jolly* G] वक्तारमनुगच्छति; MTr[4] MTr[6] तान्वक्तॄननु°; NPu[1] तद्वक्त्रमनु°; NNg तद्वक्त्रेणानु°; La[1] तद्वहूननु°; WKt[3] °क्तॄनधिरोहति

116. Omitted in GMd[1]. Cited by *Apa* 1027 — a) BBe[2] °विहितं; Be[1] °निहितं; SOx[1] °विदितं; NKt[4] धर्मं; Pu[2] Pu[4] Pu[5] Pu[7] शास्त्रं — b) NKt[4] BKt[5] SOx[1] Tj[1] निश्रे°; BBe[2] GMy NPu[1] Pu[3] Pu[8] Tr[2] नैःश्रे°; TMd[3] GMd[5] नैश्रे° — c) TMd[3] TMd[4] GMd[5] OOr [*Jolly* R] तस्मादप्रच्युतो; GMy [*Jolly* Nd] तस्मादविच्युतो; Lo[3] अस्मादप्यच्युतो; Hy अस्मादच्युतो; BBe[2] WKt[3] °विच्युतो; OOr वीरः

117. Cited by *Apa* 1027 — a) GMy एवं हि; TMd[4] Wa देवो भगवान् — d) OOr पूर्वमुक्तवान्

118. Omitted in Pu[5]; pāda-d omitted in GMd[1]; ms. of WKt[3] ends after pāda-b. Cited by *Apa* 1027; *Lakṣ* 14.201 — b) Pu[2] Pu[4] सदा सत्वस्य नित्यतां; BKt[5] समुच्चयं — c) GMd[1] GMy *Lakṣ* *Apa* सर्वमात्मनि; TMd[4] धर्मं ह्यात्मनि; Ho Jo[2] Lo[3] Tj[1] चात्मनि; La[1] स्वात्मनि; Lo[2] GMd[1] TMd[4] MTr[4] MTr[6] संपश्येन्; TMd[3] GMd[5] संपश्य — d) Pu[8] न पापे कुरुते मनः; BKt[5] Wa नाधर्मं; TMd[4] सुगते मतिः; TMd[3] GMd[5] Wa मतिं; BBe[2] नरः

119. Pāda-a omitted in GMd[1]. Cited by *Apa* 1027; *Lakṣ* 14.201 — b) TMd[4] Wa °त्मनि संस्थितं; BBe[2] Tr[2] °स्थितः — c) Ho आत्मा एव हि जानन्ति; Be[1] Lo[1] Lo[2] Pu[5] Pu[7] आत्मैव; Pu[5] Pu[7] जनयेत्तेषां — d) Lo[3] Tj[1] शरीरिणं

Additional verse in Ox[2]:

वेदविद्यां विदित्वादौ याथातथ्येन वेदवित् ।

खं संनिवेशयेत् खेषु चेष्टनस्पर्शनेऽनिलम् ।
पक्तिदृष्ट्योः परं तेजः स्नेहेऽपो गां च मूर्तिषु ॥१२०॥
मनसीन्दुं दिशः श्रोत्रे क्रान्ते विष्णुं बले हरिम् ।
वाच्यग्निं मित्रमुत्सर्गे प्रजने च प्रजापतिम् ॥१२१॥
प्रशासितारं सर्वेषामणीयांसमणोरपि ।
रुक्माभं स्वप्नधीगम्यं विद्यात्तं पुरुषं परम् ॥१२२॥
एतमेके वदन्त्यग्निं मनुमन्ये प्रजापतिम् ।
इन्द्रमेकेऽपरे प्राणमपरे ब्रह्म शाश्वतम् ॥१२३॥
एष सर्वाणि भूतानि पञ्चभिर्व्याप्य मूर्तिभिः ।
जन्मवृद्धिक्षयैर्नित्यं संसारयति चक्रवत् ॥१२४॥

य एवं विन्दते वेदं स वेदविदुषां मनः ॥

120. Omitted in Ho; mss. of sOx[1] sPu[6] end after pāda-a. Cited by *Apa* 1027; *Lakṣ* 14.201 — a) BBe[2] MTr[6] खं खं निवेदयेत्खेषु [MTr[6] संखं]; NKt[4] योगिनः संसयेत्खेषु; Ox[2] स्वं संनि°; TMd[3] °शयत्; Bo °शवत्; *Apa* खेतु; BKt[5] खेनुं; NNg स्वेषु — b) BBe[2] चेष्टनः; Pu[10] °स्पर्शनेति च; BKt[5] °नलं — c) BBe[2] GMy Pu[5] Pu[7] Pu[10] Wa *Apa* पङ्क्ति°; TMd[3] पंह्निंदृष्टेः; BKt[5] पक्वत्रिष्टो; Tr[2] यत्किंदृष्ट्यो; NKt[4] °दृष्टोः; BBe[2] Pu[10] °दृष्टो; GMd[1] °दृष्योत्; *Apa* °दृष्ट्रोः; Lo[2] Pu[2] Pu[4] °दृष्ट्यै; La[1] °दृष्ट्ये; NKt[4] पर; Lo[1] [*but cor*] परां — d) MTr[4] MTr[6] स्नेहो भोगाश्च कीर्त्तिषु; Be[1] Lo[2] Pu[2] Pu[4] *Apa* स्नेहो; GMd[1] स्नेह; Bo La[1] Ox[2] NPu[1] Pu[2] Pu[4] Pu[5] Pu[7] Pu[8] Pu[10] Tj[1] *Lakṣ* स्नेहे योगां च [La[1] NPu[1] Pu[8] योगं; Ox[2] Pu[5] Pu[7] Pu[10] योगांश्च]; GMd[1] स्नेहे वेगां च; Lo[3] °पा गां; Lo[2] Wa गांश्च; La[1] तु

121 * Omitted in NKt[4] TMd[4]; not commented by *Go*. Cited by *Apa* 1027; *Lakṣ* 14.201 — a) Bo मनसेन्दु; Pu[3] °सीन्दुः; *Apa* °सीन्द्रं; TMd[3] °सीन्दुर्जनश्रोत्रे; GMd[1] दृशो श्रोत्रा — b) Hy क्रान्ता; BKt[5] क्रान्तं; Bo कान्ते; TMd[3] कान्ता; GMd[5] कान्तौ; Ox[2] काष्ठे; *Lakṣ* पादे; Tr[2] विष्टं बले; MTr[6] पिण्डं बले; TMd[3] बलं; Pu[5] Pu[7] चले; La[1] कलेवरं; Pu[10] हरिः; BBe[2] Bo Hy Jo[1] Kt[2] Lo[1] Lo[3] BKt[5] GMd[1] GMd[5] NNg NPu[1] Pu[8] Tj[1] Tr[2] MTr[5] MTr[6] [*Jolly* Ku] *Apa Lakṣ Mandlik Jha KSS Dave* हरं; Wa हरत्; GMd[1] वरं — c) GMy Tr[2] वाच्याग्निं; Ho वायव्यग्निं; Pu[10] °ग्निमिंदुमुत्सर्गे; Pu[3] Wa °मुत्सर्गो — d) Tj[1] प्रजाने; Lo[2] Pu[2] Pu[4] प्रजनेश्च

122. Omitted in NKt[4] TMd[4]; not commented by *Go*. Cited by *Apa* 1027; *Lakṣ* 14.201 — a) Ho प्रशासितारः; Lo[1] प्रशसितारं; oOr Tr[2] प्रशंसितारं; *Lakṣ Apa* °तारमेतेषाम° — b) Bo °णीयानमणो°; GMy °णीयसामणो° — c) Bo रुक्मभं; MTr[4] MTr[6] रुग्माभं; Pu[10] स्वप्रयागम्यं — d) Pu[7] विन्द्यात्तं; Be[1] Lo[2] GMd[1] TMd[3] NNg NPu[1] Pu[2] Pu[4] MTr[6] Wa विद्यात्तु; BKt[5] तद्विद्यात्पुरुषं; *Lakṣ* पुरुषोत्तमं

123 * Omitted in NKt[4] TMd[4] [*Jolly* M]; not commented by *Go*. Cited by *Apa* 1027; *Lakṣ* 14.201; pādas a-b cited by *Śaṃ* on *BU* 1.4.6 — a) Pu[7] एनमेकं वदत्यग्नि; La[1] Lo[2] oOr Pu[4] MTr[4] MTr[6] एनमेके; NNg Pu[2] एतमेकं; BKt[5] एतमेव; TMd[3] एवमेके; La[1] वदत्य° — b) GMd[1] अन्ये चाहुः प्रजापतिं; BBe[2] Hy Lo[3] NNg oOr NPu[1] Pu[5] Pu[7] Tj[1] *Lakṣ* मनुमेके; Wa मनुमेक; Tr[2] मनुमेते; Lo[1] मन्युमन्ये; GMy TMd[3] GMd[5] MTr[4] MTr[6] मरुतोन्ये— c) Hy Jo[2] Lo[3] Tj[1] इन्द्रमन्ये; TMd[3] प्राणानपरे; BKt[5] प्राप्तमपरे

124. Omitted in NKt[4] [*Jolly* M]; not commented by *Go*. Cited by *Apa* 1027; *Lakṣ* 14.201 — b) Tr[2] °भिर्वाप्य; TMd[3] °भिर्व्यवतिष्ठति — c) GMy जन्मवृत्ति°; TMd[4] °विद्धिक्षयो नित्यं; Lo[1] °क्षयं नित्यं; GMd[1] Pu[7] *Apa* °क्षये नित्यं — d) Ho संसारपरिचक्रवत्; GMy संधारयति; BKt[5] संचारयति; Hy संसारे याति; NNg °रयति च ध्रुवं; La[1] चक्रवान्

एवं यः सर्वभूतेषु पश्यत्यात्मानमात्मना ।
स सर्वसमतामेत्य ब्रह्माभ्येति परं पदम् ॥१२५॥
इत्येतन्मानवं शास्त्रं भृगुप्रोक्तं पठन्द्विजः ।
भवत्याचारवान्नित्यं यथेष्टां प्राप्नुयाद्गतिम् ॥१२६॥

॥ इति मानवे धर्मशास्त्रे भृगुप्रोक्तायां संहितायां द्वादशोऽध्यायः ॥

125. Omitted in NKt^4 [*Jolly* M]; not commented by *Go*. Cited by *Apa* 1028; *Lakṣ* 14.201 — a) *Apa* य एवं; TMd^4 NNg °भूतानि — b) Hy NNg Tr^2 °नमात्मनि; oOr °नमव्ययं — c) GMd^1 स सर्वधर्मतामेत्य; Tj^2 सर्वत्र समतामेत्य; BBe^2 °तामेति — d) GMd^1 TMd^3 GMd^5 GMy Pu^5 Pu^7 ब्रह्माप्येति; Jo^2 BKt^5 Lo^1 Lo^3 TMd^3 GMd^5 GMy Ox^2 Pu^3 Tj^1 Tr^2 [*Jolly* R Nd Gr] *Lakṣ* °ति सनातनं

Additional verse in Hy Lo^3 Tj^1 *Mandlik* [ड, थ, न, श] *Dave KSS:*

चतुर्वेदसमं पुण्यमस्य शास्त्रस्य धारणात् ।
भूयो वाप्यतिरिच्येत पापनिर्यातनं महत् ।।

126. Omitted in NKt^4 Lo^2 Pu^5; not commented by *Go* — a) Lo^1 इति तन्मानवं; Hy Jo^2 BKt^5 La^1 Lo^3 GMd^5 Tj^1 MTr^4 MTr^6 इत्येवं मानवं — b) Lo^3 oOr Ox^2 Tj^1 पठेद् द्विजः; BKt^5 पठेत्तु यः — c) Be^1 Pu^2 Pu^4 आचारान्बोधयन्नित्यं; GMd^1 भवत्यानन्दभाग्नित्यं; BKt^5 भवेदाचार° — d) TMd^4 GMy MTr^6 यथेष्टं; TMd^3 यथेष्टादाप्नुया°; GMd^1 GMy MTr^5 MTr^6 [*Jolly* Nd] चाप्नुयाद्गितिं; Lo^1 गतिमाप्नुयात्

Additional verses in *Mandlik* [क] *KSS Dave:*

मनुः स्वायंभुवो देवः सर्वशास्त्रार्थपारगः ।
तस्यास्य निर्गतं धर्मं विचार्य बहुविस्तरम् ।।
ये पठन्ति द्विजाः केचित्सर्वपापोपशान्तिदम् ।
ते गच्छन्ति परं स्थानं ब्रह्मणः सद्म शाश्वतम् ।।

Colophon: Lo^1 Lo^2 TMd^3 NNg sOx^1 sPu^6 इति श्रीमानवे; Lo^3 इति श्रीमानवीये; GMd^1 भृगुप्रोक्ते and *om* संहितायां; Lo^1 Lo^2 भृगुप्रोक्तसंहितायां; Lo^3 *om* भृगुप्रोक्तायां संहितायां

NOTES TO THE CRITICAL EDITION

CHAPTER ONE

1.1 The initial invocatory verse before the first verse must be quite old, because it is commented by Govinda and found in 18 northern mss. It is, however, clearly spurious. The verse is not recorded in any ST ms., making it likely that it was a northern interpolation Medhātithi commenting on 1.2 calls it *dvitīyaḥ ślokaḥ* ("the second verse"); if he accepted the invocatory verse, 1.2 would have been the third verse. The invocatory verse must have been inserted into the text, therefore, sometime after Medhātithi.

1.2 The additional verses were probably interpolated at an early date, because they are found in several mss. of the ST (both Malayalam and Grantha), in the Kashmiri Śāradā ms., in *Nd*, and in many NT mss. They are ignored by *Me*, however, and missing is most ST and NT mss.

1.6c *Me*, *Rn*, and *Nd* take *pāda*-c as a single Bahuvrīhi compound *mahābhūtādivṛttaujāḥ* qualifying *svayambhūḥ*. The explanation of *Go* could go both ways, although Bühler, in his note to this verse, thinks that he takes *mahābhūtādi* as a separate compound qualifying *idam* of *pāda*-b. This is also the interpretation of *Ku* and *Mr*. On the other hand, *Rc* appears to read *mahābhūtādiḥ* in the masculine qualifying *svayambhūḥ*. It is difficult to determine who is right. Converting the entire *pāda* into a single compound makes it clumsy but keeps the *pāda* as a meaningful unit. My inclination is to go with *Ku*, because his interpretation makes a more natural division of the compound.

1.7a I have adopted the reading *atīndriyo 'grāhyaḥ*, although it is supported by only a few mss.: Ho Jo² NKt⁴ La¹ Ox² Ox³ Tj¹ Tr² Wa. The reading is, therefore, somewhat conjectural. It is supported, moreover, by *BhP* 2.11 and the citation in Śaṃkara's commentary on *BU* 1.4.6; it is also so understood by Ānandagiri in his sub-commentary on Śaṃkara. My reading is also supported by *Nā*. Most mss. and commentators, however, compound the two expressions: *atīndriyagrāhyaḥ*. Medhātithi interprets *atīndriya* ("what is beyond the senses") as the mind (*manas*), and takes the compound to mean that the creator is to be grasped by the mind. This interpretation is accepted by most other commentators. A slightly different interpretation is given by *Go*, who reads *atīndriyāgrāhyaḥ:* he cannot be grasped by the mind (*atīndriyeṇa manasā grahītum aśakyaḥ*). I think the traditional reading and interpretation is awkward and forced. The word *agrāhyaḥ* at the end of *pāda*-a nicely parallels the other negative with a similar meaning, *acintyaḥ*, at the same final position in *pāda*-c; note the parallel *-ndriyo* and *-mayo* in both with the elision of the initial *a* of the following word.

1.7d Although mss. are divided over the two readings *eṣa* and *eva*, it is clear that the former is far superior; it is represented in the broadest spectrum of ST and NT mss. and parallels nicely the correlative *yo 'sau* in *pāda*-a. The particle *eva*, furthermore, is pleonastic in conjunction with *svayam*. The adopted reading is found in: Be^{1} bBe^{2} Jo^{2} wKt^{1} wKt^{3} nKt^{4} bKt^{5} La^{1} La^{2} Lo^{1} Lo^{2} Lo^{3} Lo^{4} Lo^{5} gMd^{1} sOx^{1} Ox^{2} Ox^{3} sPu^{6} Pu^{8} Pu^{10} Tj^{1} Tr^{2} mTr^{4} mTr^{6} Wa*BhP* 2.11 *Nd Śaṃ* [vl in 6 mss; but edition gives *eva*] *Jha Dave*.

1.10a There is some question as to whether the reading is *nārāḥ* or *narāḥ*. *Ku* says that *Go* reads *narāḥ* and offers an explanation of it. *Ku* may have made a mistake here. It is *Me* (and not *Go*) who explains the term, saying that children are given the name of the father: thus children of Vasiṣṭha are called *vasiṣṭhāḥ* and the children of Bhṛgu *bhṛgavaḥ*. In both we see that the initial letter does not take *vṛddhi*. The preponderance of mss. evidence, however, supports *nārāḥ*.

1.13a There is strong manuscript support for both *tu* and *ca*. I have adopted *tu*, which is found in Be^{1} Bo Ho wKt^{1} nKt^{4} bKt^{5} La^{1} Lo^{1} Lo^{4} gMd^{1} tMd^{3} tMd^{4} gMd^{5} gMy Ox^{3} Pu^{2} Pu^{8} Pu^{10} Tr^{2} mTr^{3} mTr^{4}mTr^{6}. My choice is based on the unanimous support for*tu* in the mss. of ST, with strong support from many NT-x mss., whereas *ca* has the unanimous support of NT-y vulgate mss.

1.20 *Nd* places verse 27 before 20 and comments: "If some read it later on, it is due to the error of scribes." See Bühler 1886, 11; Jolly 1885–89, 17.

1.22a *Me* says that the particle *ca* is misplaced; its proper position should be after *devānām* at the end of the *pāda: karmātmanāṃ ca ity ayam adeśe caḥ paṭhitaḥ. tasya deśo devānām ity ato 'nantaram.*

1.44b There is strong manuscript support for both readings: *ca kacchapāḥ* and *sakacchapāḥ*. Commentaries do not offer any help. The latter is supported by bBe^{2} Jo^{2} nKt^{4} La^{1} Lo^{1} Lo^{3} Lo^{4} gMd^{1} tMd^{3} nNg oOr nPu^{1} Pu^{2} Pu^{4} Pu^{5} Pu^{7} Pu^{10} Tj^{1} Tr^{1} Tr^{2} mTr^{4} mTr^{6} Wa [*Jolly* M G R Nd] *BhP* 2.70 *Jolly*. I have adopted it because of support from most ST mss. However, some ST mss. also support the latter, and the reading here is clearly uncertain. For *sakacchapāḥ* at the end of a *pāda*-b, see 12.42 [critical apparatus], although there I have adopted the reading *sarīsṛpāḥ*.

1.45c *Me, Ku,* and *Rc* give the verb in the singular: *upajāyate*. With reference to the plural verb, *upajāyante*,*Me* observes: *upajāyante iti pāṭhe "ye cānye kecid īdṛśāḥ" iti paṭhitavyam*. He appears to connect *pādas* c-d syntactically, separating them from *pādas* a-b. I think the plural is justified without such textual emendation; along with*Sn* and *Rc*, I take *pāda*-c as syntactically connected to *pādas* a-b, with *pāda*-d forming a separate clause.

1.46a All the ST mss. contain the reading *sthāvarā* in place of *taravaḥ*. The reading is complicated by the sandhi with the previous word. Here, I think, the ST is wrong; I have adopted the latter reading, which is found in: Be^{1} bBe^{2} Ho Jo^{2} wKt^{1} bKt^{5} La^{2} Lo^{1} Lo^{2} Lo^{3} Lo^{4} nNg sOx^{1} Ox^{2} Ox^{3} nPu^{1} Pu^{2} Pu^{4} Pu^{5} sPu^{6} Pu^{7} Pu^{8} Pu^{10} Tj^{1} Tj^{2} Wa [*Jolly* M G R K] *Jolly*.

1.61d Both *amitaujasaḥ* (preferred by Jolly) and *mahaujasaḥ* have strong manuscript support. The commentators, except for *Rn*, are silent. I have adopted the latter principally because it is the near unanimous reading of the ST and in addition has backing from both NT-x and NT-y. It is found in: bBe^{2} Ho Hy Jm Jo^{1} Jo^{2} wKt^{1} Kt^{2} wKt^{3} bKt^{5} La^{1} Lo^{1} Lo^{3} Lo^{4} Lo^{5} gMd^{1} tMd^{3} gMd^{5} gMy oOr Pu^{5} Pu^{7} Tj^{1} Tj^{2} Tr^{1} mTr^{3} mTr^{4} mTr^{6}.

1.64c Jolly has preferred the instrumental singular *tāvatā*, but the vast majority of the mss. have the accusative plural *tāvataḥ*, and the commentators also support this reading.

The commentators, however, noticed the problem with the accusative in a nominal sentence and solved the problem by implying the verb *vidyāt*. Thus, *Ku* comments; *tāvata iti dvitīyānirdeśāt vidyād ity adhyāhāraḥ*. The reading adopted is found in: Be^{1} BBe^{2} Bo Hy Jm Jo^{1} Jo^{2} wKt^{1} Kt^{2} wKt^{3} NKt^{4} BKt^{5} La^{2} Lo^{1} Lo^{3} Lo^{4} TMd^{3} TMd^{4} Ox^{2} Ox^{3} NPu^{1} Pu^{5} Pu^{7} Pu^{8} Pu^{9} Pu^{10} Tj^{1} Tj^{2} Tr^{1} MTr^{4} Wa *Mandlik Jha KSS Dave*.

1.68c The particles *ca* and *tu* have strong manuscript support. I have adopted *ca* because it gives a better meaning connecting *pāda*-c with *pādas* a-b. Here the ST mss. go with the vulgate NT-y. It is found in Be^{1} Bo Ho wKt^{1} NKt^{4} La^{1} La^{2} Lo^{2} Lo^{4} Lo^{5} GMd^{1} oMd^{2} NNg oOr sOx^{1} Ox^{2} Ox^{3} NPu^{1} Pu^{2} Pu^{5} sPu^{6} Pu^{7} Pu^{8} Pu^{9} Pu^{10} Tr^{2} MTr^{6} Wa [*Jolly* M$^{1-2-7-8-9}$]; it is also supported in *Me, Go,* and *Ku*.

1.78 All editions have the redoing *rasaguṇāḥ smṛtāḥ;* Jolly does not even give any variants here. The manuscript support for this reading is limited; none of the ST mss. have *smṛtāḥ*. The adopted reading, *rasaguṇātmikāḥ* (supported also by mss. that have the readings *anvitāḥ* and *āśrayāḥ*) is found in Be^{1} Ho La^{1} La^{2} TMd^{4} GMy Ox^{2} Pu^{2} Pu^{4} Pu^{8} Tr^{1} Tr^{2} MTr^{4} MTr^{6} *Nā Rc*.

1.81d *Me, Nā,* and *Nd* support *upavartate*. The readings *prativartate* etc. may originate from commentarial glosses: *Rc Go*: *manuṣyān prati nopavartate* [or *na vartate*]; *Ku: manuṣyān prati saṃpadyate*.

1.97d The vulgate editions and many NT mss. read *brahmavedinaḥ*. All the ST mss. and the vast majority of the NT ones, however, have the correct reading *brahmavādinaḥ*. This term is used frequently by Manu with reference to persons with extraordinary knowledge (of either the Vedas or Brahman): see 2.113; 4.91, 199; 6.39; 11.42, 120. The form *brahmavedin* is found only here.

CHAPTER TWO

2.10c Although the preponderance of evidence favors *amīmāṃsye*, the positive alternative *mīmāṃsye* is noteworthy. It is found in both NT and ST mss. and is strongly supported by *Rn*, who argues against *Ku* on this point: *śrutismṛtī sarvārtheṣu jñātavyeṣu amīmāṃsye pratikūlatarkeṇa na vicārayitavye iti kullūkaḥ. tan na. sarvārtheṣu mīmāṃsye eva iti pāṭhaḥ*. The adopted reading, however, is supported by *Me, Go, Nā, Ku, Rc,* and *Mr*.

2.40d The reading adopted, *brāhmaṇaḥ saha*, is both the *lectio difficilior* and has the support of most mss. In the reading *brāhmaṇaiḥ saha*, the instrumental was clearly influenced by the proximity of *saha*, which actually governs the two words at the very beginning of the verse: *naitair apūtaiḥ*. The reading adopted is found in: Be^{1} BBe^{2} Bo BCa Ho Hy Jm^{1} Jo^{1} wKt^{1} Kt^{2} wKt^{3} BKt^{5} Lo^{2} GMd^{1} oMd^{2} oOr sOx^{1} Ox^{2} Ox^{3} sPu^{6} MTr^{4} Wa [*Jolly* G N Ku] *Apa Dev Mādh Nā Ku Rc Go Jolly KSS*.

2.44d The adopted reading, *sūtrikam*, is supported by Be^{1} Jo^{2} BKt^{5} Lo^{4} GMd^{1} TMd^{4} GMd^{5} Ox^{3} Pu^{2} Pu^{4} Pu^{8} Pu^{10} Tr^{2} MTr^{6} Wa [*Jolly* M N] *Apa Me Nd Jolly*, with numerous other mss. having the variant *sūtrakam*.

2.47d The mss. are evenly divided between *anagnidūṣitāḥ* and *nāgnidūṣitāḥ*. It is difficult to decide on the original; I have preferred the former, principally because it is the *lectio difficilior* with elision of the negative *a*, which many have prompted scribes to read the initial *na* as *na* + *a*, giving the reading *nāgni-*. The adopted reading, coming at the end of the second line, nicely parallels *anudvegakaraḥ* occurring at the beginning. This reading is favored also by *Me* and *Rc*, and appears to be supported also by the glosses of *Go* and *Ku*. The adopted reading is found in: BCa Jo^{1} BKt^{5} Lo^{2} Lo^{4} Lo^{5} GMd^{1} TMd^{4} NNg NPu^{1} Pu^{5} Pu^{7} Pu^{8} Pu^{9} Pu^{10} Tr^{1} MTr^{4} MTr^{6} Wa*Apa Mandlik Jha KSS Dave*.

2.50d The reading *nāvamānayet* is adopted by all editors, including Jolly's and has the support of *Go, Ku,* and *Mr*. The overwhelming majority of the mss., including all the ST ones, however, have the reading *na vimānayet*, which is also the *lectio difficilior*. This reading is supported by *Me*, who glosses *vimānanā avajñānam*, as also by *Rn* and *Nd*. It is found in: Be^{1} BCa Jo^{2} WKt^{1} WKt^{3} NKt^{4} BKt^{5} La^{1} Lo^{2} Lo^{3} Lo^{4} Lo^{5} GMd^{1} OMd^{2} TMd^{3} TMd^{4} GMd^{5} NNg Ox^{3} NPu^{1} Pu^{10} Tj^{1} Tr^{1} MTr^{4} MTr^{6} [*Jolly* M R Nd]*Apa*.

2.56b I have adopted the reading *nādyād etat* over *nādyādeva* both because of manuscript evidence and because it is the *lectio difficilior*. The referent of the pronoun *etat* is unclear, and this may have caused the emendation to *eva*. Most commentators do not comment on *etat*, and those who do are divided over the referent. *Nā* takes it to be *annam*, and *Nd*, with great probability, refers it to *ucchiṣṭam* of *pāda*-a and says that the student should not eat the leftovers given by his teacher between meals. I think that taking *ucchiṣṭa* as the referent is justified especially because this topic recurs in *pāda*-d, although the over-eating of *pāda*-c appears not to have anything to with *ucchiṣṭa*.

2.63c The reading of this *pāda* is quite uncertain, most mss. being divided over *prācīna āvītī* and *prācīnam āvītī*. Three commentators, *Me, Go,* and *Ku*, note that the correct form is *prācīnāvītī*. This compound has been dissolved for the sake of meter. The question is what the uncompounded form is. *Me* is silent; *Go* and *Ku* give it as *prācīna āvītī*. My better mss., however, prefer *prācīnam āvītī*, with the first member in the adverbial form. I have adopted this. The ST mss. have preserved the compounded form (also found in *Nd*) by inserting the particle *tu*, but this must be seen as a later innovation; it also violates the standard metrical form for the final four syllables of the *pāda* (all being long).

2.73 The reading I have adopted in *pāda*-a is supported by only a few mss. mostly from ST: BBe^{2} GMd^{1} TMd^{3} GMd^{5} Tr^{1} MTr^{4} Wa [*Jolly* N Nd]. It is clearly conjectural. The commonly accepted reading has the teacher as the subject of the verb *brūyāt* and the student intent on receiving instruction is the one to whom the teacher says these words. Medhātithi clearly states that it is the teacher who at the beginning of the lesson says "Recite" and at its conclusion (*pāda*-c) says "Stop" (*virāmo 'stu*). His interpretation is followed by *Go, Ku, Rn, Rc,* and *Mr*. The only commentators to dissent are *Nā* and *Nd;* both of them follow the reading I have adopted and take the pupil to be the subject. Several reasons prompt me to adopt this reading. First, the *GDh* (1.46) reads *adhīhi bho ity āmantrayed gurum*, where the subject is clearly the pupil and the words are addressed to the teacher. Now, Manu, as I have shown in the Introduction (p. 44), frequently follows Gautama and this verse, I think, is no exception, because none of the other *Dharmasūtras* says anything about the rites associated with the beginning and conclusion of instruction. We have an ambiguity similar to Manu's in *ŚāṅkGṛ* 2.5.10 and 4.8.12. Oldenberg (1886, 67) is correct in taking the words to be spoken by the pupil; this is confirmed by *Prātiśākya Sūtra* cited there by Oldenberg and *GobhGṛ* 2.10.38. In the TU (3.1–6) also these words are put in the mouth of the pupil. The request *adhīhi* (changed to the middle voice *adhīṣva* in Manu) is made by the pupil to the teacher in all these sources. Second, all the surrounding verses deal with things that the pupil must do; and the expression *adhyeṣyamāṇas tu* occurs at the very beginning of this section (verse 70). Third, if we take the teacher as the subject of the first sentence with *brūyāt*, then we have to abruptly change the subject in the sentence within *pāda-d* if, with most translators, we take the pupil to be the subject of *āramet*. I think the subject of *brūyāt* and *āramet* should be the same. With regard to the *iti* clause in *pāda*-d, *Nā* thinks that it is the pupil himself who says *virāmo 'stu* and then stops his recitation. I think this is erroneous, even though the natural reading of the text (with *iti* and then *iti ca*) suggests it. I think that this *ca* connects the two verbs rather than the *iti* clauses. Bühler is correct in taking the last quoted words as being said by the teacher, and this is supported by *ŚāṅkGṛ* 4.8.17.

2.75a Jolly adopts the conjectural reading *prāktūlān* in place of *prākkūlān* against the evidence of *all* his mss. His conjecture is based on B-R, which takes *prākkūla* as a wrong form of *prāktūla*, and on *GDh* 1.50. It may, indeed, be true that the former is an incorrect rendering; *prāktūla* is attested in several *sūtra* texts: *BauŚr* 2.1; *JaiGṛ* 2.8. Böhtlingk refers to *ĀśGṛ* 3.2.5 and *GobhGṛ* 4.5.11 [it should be 4.5.15; I have not been able to trace Böhtlingk's reference to the *Kauśika Sūtra* 11.25 in Whiney's edition]. The *ĀśGṛ* editions of Ānandāśrama Sanskrit Series 105 (Poona, 1936) and Adyar Library (Adyar, 1980), however, give the reading *prākkūla*. In *GDh* 1.50, the reading *prāktūla* in given in Stenzler's edition. Unfortunately, he provides no manuscript evidence or variant readings; it is thus unclear whether this reading was merely a "philological emendation" on the part of Stenzler or whether there was manuscript evidence for it. In the editions published subsequently with the commentaries of Haradatta and Maskarin, the reading is uniformly *prākkūla* (see my notes on this sūtra in Olivelle 2000). The conclusion one can draw from all this is that these two forms were used in the tradition probably from a very early date. It is difficult to decide which form was used by the author of the *MDh*. I have, therefore, retained the form *prākkūla*, attested to by all the mss. and the commentaries; "philological emendations" should be generally avoided in critical editions unless there is at least a modicum of manuscript support (see Olivelle 1988a and 1999a). Indeed, it is evident that *Me* read *kūla*, because he comments: *kūlaśabdo darbhāgravacanaḥ*; so also *Nā: kūlam agram*. Likewise, Devaṇṇabhaṭṭa (1.135) comments: *prākkūlān prāgagrān ity arthaḥ*.

2.80c All editions, including Jolly, read *brahma* for *vipra*. Surprisingly, Jolly does not give any variants, even though his own K ms. [= sPu^6] has *vipra*. The reading I have adopted is supported by all the ST mss. [except Tr^1] and by the vast majority of NT-x mss., as also by *Me, Nd,* and *Rc*. The gloss *brāhmaṇa* in *Go* and *Ku* may refer to either reading.

2.99c *Me* and *Ku* read *tato 'sya*, but it is unclear whether *tataḥ* is part of the commentary or a citation of the root text. The reading adopted, *tenāsya*, is supported by all the ST mss. and most NT ones.

2.101c Most NT mss. have the reading *samāsīnaḥ*. Only *Me* appears to read *sadāsīnaḥ;* and *sadā* here is certain, because he comments: *sadāśabdo nityatām āha, ubhayasaṃdhyāśeṣaḥ*. Only *Nā* clearly reads *samāsīta*, glossing it with *upaviśet*. Others, however, also support a finite verb here: *Ku: upaviṣṭaḥ syāt;* and *Rn: adhyāsīta upaviśya japed ity arthaḥ*. See the two finite verbs in verse 103. The original reading here is clearly uncertain. I have adopted *samāsīta*. The prefix *sam*-- is supported by all, whereas *sadā* is found only in *Me*. I have opted for the finite verb both because it is found in almost all ST mss., as well as in a few NT ones, and because it fits the syntax better paralleling *tiṣṭhet* of *pāda*-a. It is found, however, in only: La^{1} GMd^{1} TMd^{4} GMd^{5} sOx^{1} sPu^{6} Tr^{1} MTr^{4} MTr^{6} [*Jolly* N]*Nā*, and, therefore, should be considered conjectural.

2.101d Some mss. and *Nd* have the reading *samyagarkṣa-*, with "ā" inserted before *ṛkṣa*. That there should be an *ā* here is clear, but its absence was already noted by *Me*, who explains that this particle is implicitly taken over from *pāda*-b: *ārkadarśanād iti ya ākāraḥ sa ihānuṣaktavyaḥ*.

2.114a Quite a number of mss., including all of the ST, read *ityāha*. Because of the ambiguity of sandhi, this could be *iti āha* or *itya āha*. The latter would be an ungrammatical formation of the gerund, although such a formation from uncompounded verbs is occasionally encountered. Nevertheless, I think the original reading was *etyāha*. The parallel passages in *Nirukta* (2.4), *VaDh*(2.8), and *ViDh* (29.9) read *ājagāma*, and *Me, Go,* and *Ku* have the gloss *āgatya*. The adopted reading is found in: Be^{1} BBe^{2} Bo Ho Hy Jm Jo^{1} wKt^{1} Kt^{2} wKt^{3} BKt^{5} La^{2} Lo^{1} Lo^{2} Lo^{4} Lo^{5} sOx^{1} [*mc to*] Ox^{3} sPu^{6} [*mc to*] Tj^{2} MTr^{3} Wa [*Jolly* M$^{3-4}$] *Lakṣ Mandlik Jolly KSS Dave*.

2.115a Several mss. and editions have the reading *vidyān niyata-*, with the verb in the third person. The context of *vidyā* speaking to the Brahmin clearly calls for a verb in the 2nd person; and *vidyāḥ* (*vidyā* with the elision of the *visarga* through sandhi) parallels nicely *vidyā* personified who is speaking in the second person: *brūhi* (*pāda*-c) and *rakṣa* and *dāḥ* in the previous verse. The glosses of *Me* (*jānīthāḥ*) and *Ku* (*jānāsi*) are also in the second person, while *Go* has *jānīyāt* both in the editions and in my mss. The reading adopted is found in: BBe^{2} BCa Hy Kt^{2} wKt^{3} BKt^{5} Lo^{2} Lo^{3} Lo^{4} Lo^{5} TMd^{3} TMd^{4} GMy sOx^{1} Ox^{2} Ox^{3} oOr Pu^{2} Pu^{7} [but cor] Pu^{8} Tj^{2} Tr^{1} MTr^{4} Wa *Dave Jha Jolly*.

2.121c The reading *tasya vardhante* found in Jolly and other editions is attested by only a few mss. The vast majority has *vardhante* preceded by a word or prefix beginning with *sam*. The reading of *Me* appears to have been *sampravardhante*. Of the other commentators, only *Ku* notices this, and he reads *samyak vardhante*. Most ST mss., as well as the very old NKt^{4}, also have that reading, which I have adopted. The reading here, however, is uncertain. Jolly applies sandhi to the end of this *pāda* with the reading *vardhanta*. All but a few the mss., however, dispense with sandhi at the end of the *pāda* and read *vardhante*. The reading adopted is found in: La^{2} Lo^{2} TMd^{4} GMd^{5} GMy Pu^{2} Pu^{4} Pu^{8} Tj^{2} MTr^{4} MTr^{6} Wa *Ku BhP* 4.50, supported by other mss. with variants of this reading.

2.125d Jolly, following Bühler (see his long note to this verse), has adopted the reading *pūrvākṣaraplutaḥ* as a Bahuvrīhi compound. This reading is supported only by very few mss.; and even then we cannot be sure that this is not simply a scribal error, because *visargas* are often omitted in the mss. This reading is adopted only by *Nd* (who also explains the compound as Bahuvrīhi), and it is given as a variant by *Nā*. According to this reading, the letter "a" is added at the end of the name and the syllable preceding this addition is prolated. Thus, we have Devadattā(3)a. The majority of mss. and commentators read *pūrvākṣaraḥ plutaḥ*. This causes some grammatical problems, because *akṣara* is a neuter noun and the reading should be *pūrvākṣaraṃ plutam* (a reading suggested by some medieval authors of *Nibandhas*; see Jha 1999, Vol. 9, p. 100). *Nā* calls the masculine ending a vedic peculiarity: *liṅgavyatyayaś chāndasaḥ*. *Me* avoids this problem by giving the meaning of consonant to *akṣara*, thus taking *pūrvākṣaraḥ* as a Bahuvrīhi. He gives this rather complex and lengthy explanation: "The term *pūrvākṣaraḥ* qualifies the vowel 'a', which is to be lengthened; and *akṣara* here stands for the *consonant*; and the compound means 'that vowel of which the preceding syllable is a consonant,' i.e., the vowel occurring along with the consonant. What is meant is that it is the vowel 'a' already there that is to be lengthened, and not any such vowel as might be added." The interpretation offered by *Me* and others follows Pāṇini 8.2.83 and agrees broadly with *ĀpDh* 1.5.17; *VaDh* 13.46. I have provisionally adopted this reading. See the lengthy note to this verse given by Jha (1999, Vol. 9, pp. 100–05). According to this reading, the name is pronounced Devadattā(3).

2.129d Mss. are evenly divided over the two readings: *vā* and *ca*. I have opted for the former both because it make better sense within the context of an option between two forms of address and because most of the ST mss., including all the Malayalam ones, support it: Be^1 Be^3 Bo BCa Ho wKt^1 wKt^3 BKt^5 La^1 La^2 Lo^2 Lo^4 Lo^5 GMd^1 GMd^5 GMy NNg Ox^2 NPu^1 Pu^{10} Tr^1 Tr^2 MTr^4 MTr^6 *Dev*. It is also found in some mss. of the *Mādh* and supported by *Ku* and *Rc*.

2.135a-b The mss. are divided over the two reading in both *pādas*: *ca* and *tu*. I have opted for the former both because it fits the context better and because it is found in all but one of the ST mss. and a good number of NT-x ones: Be^3 Bo BCa Jo^2 BKt^5 La^2 Lo^2 Lo^3 GMd^1 TMd^3 GMd^5 GMy oOr Pu^8 Tj^1 Tr^1 MTr^4 MTr^6 Wa [*Jolly* R Nd] *BhP* 4.68. This reading is also found in the parallel passage in *ViDh* 32.17.

2.145 This is a problematic verse. The tradition is of many minds with regard to the grammatical case of the names for persons vis-à-vis whom others are more eminent: these are placed in the ablative singular (*upādhyāyāt, ācāryāt, pituḥ*), in the accusative plural (*upādhyāyān, pitṝn*), and in the genitive plural (*ācāryāṇām*). The ST mss. generally prefer the ablative, and it is clear from the manuscript evidence that this was the original reading in the case of *pituḥ*. In the case of *ācārya*, on the other hand, the ST mss. may have been seeking uniformity; the genitive plural is the best attested. In the case of *upādhyāya*, on the other hand, there is strong support for both the ablative and the accusative. I have adopted the former because it parallels the other ablative in *pāda*-c and is supported by all ST mss. and a good number of NT ones as well. Although the accusative and the ablative can be used with the verb *atiricyate*, I think the undisputed ablative of *pituḥ* in *pāda*-c supports a similar ablative in *pāda*-a. In *pāda*-c, the reading of *Me* is uncertain. Jha and Dave read *sahasraṃ pitṝn iti vacanam*, whereas Mandlik and my ms. Pu^{10} read instead *pitur iti vacanam*. In *pāda*-a, *upādhyāyāt* is found in: Be^1 Be^3 Bo Ho NKt^4 BKt^5 La^1 Lo^1 Lo^2 GMd^1 TMd^3 TMd^4 GMd^5 GMy sOx^1 Ox^2 NPu^1 sPu^6 Tr^1 Tr^2 MTr^6 *Rc Vij*. In *pāda*-c, *pituḥ* is found in: Be^1 BBe^2 Be^3 Bo BCa Ho Hy Jo^2 wKt^1 NKt^4 La^2 Lo^1 Lo^2 Lo^3 Lo^4 Lo^5 GMd^1 TMd^3 TMd^4 GMd^5 oOr sOx^1 Ox^2 Ox^3 NPu^1 Pu^5 sPu^6 Pu^7 Pu^9 Pu^{10} Tj^1 Tj^2 Tr^1 Tr^2 MTr^4 *Nā Nd* [pāṭha] *Ku Rc Mr Viś Dev* 3.688 *Mādh*, and this reading is supported by *Go*.

2.156a The reading *sthaviraḥ*, which I have adopted, in recorded in Be^1 BBe^2 Be^3 Bo BCa Ho Hy wKt^1 wKt^3 NKt^4 La^1 La^2 Lo^1 Lo^2 GMd^1 TMd^3 TMd^4 GMd^5 GMy sOx^1 Ox^2 sPu^6 Pu^8 Tj^2 Tr^1 MTr^4 MTr^6 *BhP* 4.100[*Jolly* Nd]. The commentators *Me, Go, Ku, Rc*, and *Mr* give *vṛddhaḥ*, although it is not altogether clear whether it is the reading of the root text or a gloss. I had adopted *sthaviraḥ* because it is the *lectio difficilior* and because it is found in all ST mss. and in quite a spectrum of NT ones; it also parallels the word in *pāda*-d. It is the *lectio difficilior* because it makes the *pāda* hypermetric with nine syllables. The way to make it scan is to read *bhavati* with the Prakrit pronunciation of *bhoti*, which is required also in other verses; for example, in 2.201 *pādas* a and c. It appears that *vṛddhaḥ* was substituted to restore the meter. However, *bhavati* does not give the regular cadence of the last four syllables, where as the reading *sthaviro bhoti* gives the regular cadence. Indeed, other scribes attempted other strategies, substituting *jñeyaḥ* and *bhūyāt* for *bhavati*. As in verse 201, this is probably a proverbial saying taken over by Manu; hence the Prakritic pronunciation.

2.190c Both the readings *eva* and *evam* have strong manuscript support. I have opted for the former because of strong manuscript evidence from both ST and NT: Hy Lo^{2} Lo^{3} GMd^{1} TMd^{3} GMy NNg Ox^{2} Pu^{2} Pu^{4} Pu^{5} Pu^{7} Pu^{10} Tj^{1} MTr^{6} [*Jolly* M G Ku R Nd] *Jolly*. See also other variant readings with *eva*. This reading also fits the context better.

2.190d The reading adopted, *pracakṣate*, is supported by most ST and NT mss: Be^{1} BBe^{2} Be^{3} Bo Ho wKt^{1} wKt^{3} NKt^{4} BKt^{5} La^{2} Lo^{1} Lo^{2} Lo^{3} Lo^{4} Lo^{5} TMd^{3} TMd^{4} GMd^{5} GMy sOx^{1} Ox^{2} Ox^{3} NPu^{1} Pu^{2} Pu^{5} sPu^{6} Pu^{7} Pu^{8} Pu^{10} Tj^{1} Tr^{1} MTr^{4} MTr^{6} Wa [*Jolly* M G Ku R Nd] *Jolly*.

2.191a-b Clearly, the reading *nodita/praṇodita* is the *lectio difficilior*. I have refrained from adopting it, however, because the overwhelming evidence of the mss., including all the ST ones and the citations of *Apa* and *Lakṣ*, support *codita:* NBe^{2} Bo BCa Ho Hy Jm^{1} Jo^{1} wKt^{1} Kt^{2} wKt^{3} NKt^{4} La^{2} Lo^{1} Lo^{2} GMd^{1} oMd^{2} TMd^{3} TMd^{4} GMd^{5} GMy NNg oOr sOx^{1} Ox^{2} NPu^{1} sPu^{6} Pu^{8} Pu^{10} Tj^{2} Tr^{1} MTr^{4} MTr^{6}. In Be^{1} *pāda*-a has *nodito* and *pāda*-b *apracodita*.

2.191c The vulgate has the reading *yatnam*. The source of this may be *Me*, who glosses *yogam* with *yatnam*, followed by *Go*.

2.193d Both readings, *abhimukhaḥ* and *abhimukham*, have strong manuscript support. I have chosen the former because it is the near unanimous reading of the ST and has strong support from NT mss. including the two Śāradā ones. My reading is supported by Ho Jo^{2} NKt^{4} BKt^{5} Lo^{2} Lo^{3} Lo^{4} Lo^{5} GMd^{1} TMd^{3} TMd^{4} GMy sOx^{1} Ox^{3} Pu^{2} Pu^{5} sPu^{6} Pu^{7} Pu^{10} Tj^{1} Tr^{1} MTr^{4} MTr^{6} Wa [*Jolly* M G R] *BhP* 4.164 [vl] *Lakṣ Jolly*.

2.198b The reading adopted, *nityaṃ syāt*, has overwhelming support: Be^{1} BBe^{2} BCa wKt^{1} wKt^{3} NKt^{4} wKt^{5} La^{1} Lo^{1} Lo^{4} Lo^{5} GMd^{1} oMd^{2} TMd^{3} TMd^{4} GMd^{5} GMy NNg sOx^{1} Ox^{3} NPu^{1} Pu^{2} Pu^{5} sPu^{6} Pu^{7} Pu^{9} Pu^{10} Tr^{1} Tr^{2} MTr^{4} MTr^{6} Wa *Me Ku Rc* Surprisingly, however, Jolly, who adopts this reading, gives no variants.

2.198c It is surprising that the reading *guros tu*, which has so little manuscript support, has been adopted by all the editions, including Jolly's, who gives no variants for this also.

2.201ac The *pādas* a and c of the verse are hypermetric, with nine syllables. As in verse 2.156, here also the word *bhavati* has to be pronounced as the Prakritic *bhoti*, which rectifies the meter and restores the proper cadence to the final four syllables of the *pāda*. Again like verse 2.156, this must have been a common proverb taken over by Manu; hence the Prakritic influence.

2.206a The mss. and commentators are divided over the two readings *evam* and *etat*. The former is supported by *Me* and *Go*, which lends it weight. I have gone with the latter, however, principally because it is found in all the ST mss. and a substantial number of NT-x and NT-y ones. According to Sanskrit grammar, the pronoun should agree with the noun to which it refers within the same sentence and not to its antecedent (Brereton 1986). Thus, the correct form should have been *eṣā* corresponding to *vṛttiḥ*. Yet, we must make allowances for later Sanskrit where this rule may not have been adhered to consistently. The adopted reading is found in: Be^{1} BBe^{2} BCa Hy Jm Jo^{1} Jo^{2} wKt^{1} Kt^{2} wKt^{3} La^{1} La^{2} Lo^{3} GMd^{1} oMd^{2} TMd^{3} TMd^{4} GMd^{5} GMy sOx^{1} sPu^{6} Pu^{8} Tj^{1} Tr^{2} MTr^{4} MTr^{6} *Nā Ku Mandlik Jolly KSS*.

2.220b Surprisingly all editions, including Jolly's, have the reading *kāmacārataḥ* even though it is supported by so few mss. The reading I have adopted, *kāmakārataḥ,* is supported by Be^{1} Bo BCa Ho Jo^{2} wKt^{1} NKt^{4} BKt^{5} wKt^{6} La^{1} La^{2} Lo^{2} Lo^{3} Lo^{4} Lo^{5} GMd^{1} TMd^{3} GMd^{5} GMy NNg oOr sOx^{1} Ox^{2} Ox^{3} NPu^{1} Pu^{2} Pu^{5} sPu^{6} Pu^{7} Pu^{8} Pu^{9} Pu^{10} Tj^{1} Tr^{1} Tr^{2} MTr^{4} MTr^{6} Wa |Jolly M G R Nd| *BhP* 4.189 *Nā Rn Rc.* Cf. *ViDh* 28.53. See the same form at 11.41, 45.

2.221a I have adopted the reading *abhinimluktaḥ.* It has only limited support: TMd^{3} TMd^{4} NNg Pu^{2} *BhP* 4.190 *Me Go Jolly Jha Dave*; but see the parallel *abhinimlocet* at 2.219. This word has been subject to many spellings, including *abhinimrukta* found in *ĀpDh* 2.12.22; *VaDh* 1.18. The most common form found in the mss., *abhinirmuktaḥ,* is clearly an error.

2.240c The mss. are divided between the two readings. The reading adopted, *vividhāni ca śilpāni,* is supported by Be^{3} Hy Jm Jo^{1} Kt^{2} NKt^{4} La^{1} Lo^{1} GMd^{1} oMd^{2} TMd^{3} GMd^{5} GMy NNg oOr sOx^{1} Ox^{2} Ox^{3} Pu^{2} Pu^{4} sPu^{6} Pu^{8} Tj^{2} Tr^{1} Tr^{2} MTr^{3} MTr^{4}MTr^{6} [*Jolly* Nd] *BhP* 4.209 *Mandlik Jha KSS Dave.* I have chosen this because it is supported by almost all ST mss., all NT-y mss., and a good number of NT-x ones, including the old NKt^{4} and the Śāradā mss. I also think it is the *lectio difficilior* in the sense that it would have been easier to change this general text (probably a well-known proverb) into the "theologically correct" alternative, rather than the other way round. Yet, the authority of *Me* and *Go* is behind the alternative, and the reading here must remain uncertain.

2.242c The reading *ca* is found in most mss., including all the NT-y mss. and most of the ST and NT-x ones.. The alternative reading *vā,* however, is the *lectio difficilior* and attested by both *Me* and *Go.* In fact, *Me* found the reading *vā* problematic and explained that it is used here with a copulative meaning: *vāśabdo 'py arthe.* Nevertheless, given the overwhelming manuscript support, I have gone with *ca,* which is found in: Be^{1} BBe^{2} BCa Hy Jo^{1} wKt^{1} Kt^{2} wKt^{3} NKt^{4} BKt^{5} wKt^{6} La^{1} La^{2} Lo^{1} Lo^{2} Lo^{3} oMd^{2} TMd^{3} GMd^{5} GMy Ox^{2} Pu^{7} Pu^{8} Tj^{1} Tr^{1} Tr^{2} MTr^{3} *BhP* 4.211 *Lakṣ Apa Mandlik Jolly KSS.*

CHAPTER THREE

3.5d The preponderance of manuscript evidence supports the reading *dārakarmaṇi maithune.* However, I have adopted the reading *dārakarmaṇy amaithunī.* This reading is supported by *Me* and *Nd* and is found in TMd^{3} GMd^{5} GMy Tr^{1} MTr^{4} MTr^{6} [*Jolly* Nd] *Jha Dave.* I take the reading *maithunī* in the sense of relationship by marriage as found in *PārGṛ* 3.10.13 and Pāṇini 4.3.125. Thus, *amaithunī* would mean "a woman unrelated by marriage." Given the context, this reading makes the best sense, and failure to detect this meaning may have led scribes and commentators to emend the text. *Nd* interprets *amaithunī* to mean a woman who is a virgin (*akṣatayoni*). *Me,* on the other hand, has an elaborate and unconvincing explanation, connecting the term with *pituḥ* and taking it to mean a girl who has not been born through the father's sexual union, i.e., a girl born from a leviratic union (*niyoga*). The meaning of the reading *maithune* is not altogether clear. Bühler, following most commentators, translates: "is recommended to twice-born men for wedlock and conjugal union." Why Manu should add that she is recommended for sex on top of marriage is unclear to me.

3.10c This *pāda* is hypermetric, containing nine syllables. A few mss. have attempted to correct this with the reading *-dantām* in place of *-daśanām*, and this is adopted by Jolly. It is clearly the *lectio facilior* and should be rejected.

3.12d Because of the ambiguous sandhi, it is unclear whether the reading is *varāḥ* or *avarāḥ;* most mss. do not write *avagrahas.* All editions, except Jolly's, adopt *avarāḥ* indicated by an *avagraha*, and so do the editors of *Vij Apa Jmv Dev Mādh*. Devaṇṇabhaṭṭa comments *avarā jaghaṇyā ity arthaḥ.* The commentators *Nd, Rn*, and *Rc* also support *avarāḥ* with their glosses: *hīnāḥ* and *hīnavarṇāḥ*. However, *Me, Go, Nā, Ku*, and *Mr* support *varāḥ*, which I have adopted, with their gloss: *śreṣṭhāḥ*.

3.13c Although there is support in the mss. for both readings *rājñas tu* and *rājñaś ca*, the prepondence of evidence supports the reading I have adopted: Bo BCa Ho Jo^{2} wKt^{3} NKt^{4} BKt^{5} wKt^{6} La^{2} Lo^{1} Lo^{2} Lo^{3} Lo^{4} Lo^{5} TMd^{4} GMd^{5} GMy NNg sOx^{1} Ox^{2} Ox^{3} NPu^{1} Pu^{2} sPu^{6} Pu^{8} Tj^{1} Tr^{1} Tr^{2} Wa *Apa Jmv* [vl] *Dev Mādh.*

3.18c The mss. are deeply divided over the two readings *adanti* and *aśnanti.* I have opted for the former, because it is found in almost all the ST mss. and a substantial number of NT-x ones: Bo Ho NKt^{4} wKt^{6} [*cor to*] La^{1} La^{2} Lo^{2} GMd^{1} TMd^{3} GMd^{5} GMy Ox^{3} Pu^{2} Pu^{7} Pu^{8} Pu^{10} Tr^{2} Tr^{1} Wa [*Jolly* M G Nd] *BhP* 7.12*Nā Nd Rc Jolly.* The reading of *Me* is unclear; the editions of Mandlik, Jha, and Dave read *aśnanti*, whereas in all my ms. (Lo^{4} Ox^{3} Pu^{10}; while Lo^{5} has the defective *nāti*) the reading is *nādanti.* The reading, however, remains uncertain.

3.23d There is uncertainty regarding the reading *na rākṣa-* and *arākṣa-*. The confusion is compounded because of the preceding word *dharmyān;* mss. sometimes tend to double a "n" before a vowel even though the doubling is supposed to take place only when the preceding vowel is short. Such a doubling would give rise to the form *dharmyānnarākṣa-*. I have adopted the reading *arākṣasān* because it has strong manuscript support and the Bahuvrīhi is syntactically more appropriate as qualifying *tān*. This reading is supported by BBe^{2} Ho Hy wKt^{3} NKt^{4} wKt^{5} La^{1} La^{2} Lo^{1} Lo^{2} Lo^{3} Lo^{4} GMd^{1} GMd^{5} sOx^{1} Ox^{2} Ox^{3} Pu^{2} sPu^{6} Pu^{8} Tj^{1} Tr^{1} Tr^{2} Wa *Me Ku Mr Apa Lakṣ Dev Mandlik KSS Dave*, as well as by the variant reading in Bo oMd^{2} TMd^{3} Ox^{2} Tr^{2} *BhP*.

3.25d The two readings, *kathaṃcana* and *kadācana*, have good manuscript support. Only two commentators, *Ku* and *Nd*, note the word, and they are divided. I have opted for the former reading because it has the unanimous support of the ST mss., as well as substantial support from mss. of NT-x. This reading is found in Ho Jo^{2} Lo^{1} Lo^{3} Lo^{4} Lo^{5} GMd^{1} TMd^{3} TMd^{4} GMd^{5} GMy Ox^{3} Pu^{2} Pu^{4} Tj^{1} Tr^{1} Tr^{2} MTr^{4} MTr^{6} Wa [*Jolly* R] *BhP* 7.19 *Mādh Nd.*

3.27a All editions, including Jolly's, read *arcayitvā*, even though it has very weak manuscript support. The reading adopted, *arhayitvā*, is found in Be^{1} Be^{3} Ho wKt^{3} NKt^{4} BKt^{5} wKt^{6} La^{1} La^{2} Lo^{1} Lo^{2} Lo^{3} GMd^{1} TMd^{3} TMd^{4} GMd^{5} GMy NNg oOr sOx^{1} Ox^{2} Ox^{3} NPu^{1} sPu^{6} Pu^{7} Pu^{8} Pu^{10} Tj^{1} Tr^{1} Tr^{2} MTr^{4} MTr^{6} [*Jolly* G]*Go Nā Rc Nd Dev Apa.* The editions of Jha and Dave give the reading of Medhātithi's commentary as *cārcayitvā*, whereas Mandlik and some of my mss. read *cārhayitvā*.

3.38d The short "a" in *kāyoḍhajaḥ* instead of *kāyoḍhājaḥ* is clearly due to metrical reasons. *Me*, however, and following him *Ku*, refers to Pāṇini 6.3.63, which permits the substitution of a short final "a" for the feminine long "ā" in the vedic language.

3.39c Most mss. record the usual form *varcasvinaḥ*, which is clearly the *lectio facilior*. The older and probably the original form *varcasinaḥ* is preserved mostly in the mss. of the ST. Using the principle of *lectio difficilior*, I have opted here to go with the minority reading with the strong and clear support of *Me: brahmavarcas tadvanto brahmavarcasinaḥ innanto 'yam*. The reading adopted is found in: Lo^2 GMd^1 TMd^3 GMy GMd^5 Tr^1 *Dev Me Rn Rc Mandlik Jha Dave*.

3.47b Note the double sandhi at *ninditaikādaśī* (for *ninditā ekādaśī*) clearly for metrical reasons. The only commentator to note this is *Rn*, who ascribes it to a vedic peculiarity: *sandhir ārṣaḥ*.

3.50b The reading *varjayet* is supported by most ST and NT-x mss. I have opted to go with the manuscript evidence, even though the participle *varjayan* fits the context better, coordinating with the other present participle *vasan* and leaving a single main clause with the finite verb *bhavati*. The participle *varjayan* is supported by *Me* and *Go* (both glossing with *pariharan*), *Nā* (glossing with *upgacchan*), *Ku*, *Rn*, and *Mr*, and has been adopted by all editions. The finite verb *varjayet*, which I have adopted, is found in: Be^3 Bo Ho wKt^3 BKt^5 wKt^6 La^1 La^2 Lo^3 GMd^1 TMd^4 GMd^5 GMy NNg oOr sOx^1 Ox^2 [*but cor sh*] NPu^1 Pu^2 Pu^4 Pu^5 sPu^6 Pu^7 Pu^{10} Tj^1 Tj^2 Tr^2 MTr^4 MTr^6 Wa *Viś Rc*.

3.53d The alternative reading, *tāvān eva sa vikrayaḥ*, has strong manuscript support and is the reading preferred by *Me*. The reading adopted, however, is supported by BBe^2 Be^3 Bo BCa Ho Hy Jm Jo^1 Kt^2 wKt^3 wKt^1 Kt^2 NKt^4 La^1 Lo^1 Lo^2 GMd^1 TMd^3 TMd^4 GMd^5 oOr NPu^1 Pu^3 Pu^5 Pu^7 Tj^2 Tr^1 MTr^3 MTr^4 MTr^6 *Dev Go Ku Mandlik Jolly KSS*. The support of the Malayalam and the Grantha mss. tilts the decision in favor of this reading, although the original is clearly uncertain.

3.59 Mss. give three readings: *sadābhyarcyāḥ*, *samabhyarcyāḥ*, and *sadā pūjyāḥ*. Most ST mss. record the second, while the NT-y vulgate has the third. I have opted for the first, with its two parts getting support from the other two readings. It is found in: BBe^2 Bo BCa Ho Jo^2 wKt^3 NKt^4 La^2 Lo^1 Lo^2 TMd^4 NNg oOr Ox^2 NPu^1 Pu^2 Pu^5 Pu^7 Pu^8 Tr^1 Tr^2 Wa [*Jolly* G Nd] *Lakṣ Go Mādh Jolly*.

3.63c, 65c There is much confusion on which of these *pādas* should read *kulāny āśu vinaśyanti* and which *kulāny akulatāṃ yānti*. All the editions, including Jolly's, as well as Bühler in his translation, have the latter in 63c and the former in 65c. I have inverted this order. That 65c should have the latter is clear from the manuscript evidence. All the ST mss. plus numerous NT-x ones have this reading: Be^3 Bo BCa Jo^2 wKt^1 NKt^4 La^1 Lo^2 Lo^3 GMd^1 TMd^3 TMd^4 GMd^5 GMy NNg oOr Ox^2 Pu^8 Tj^1 Tr^1 Tr^2 MTr^4 MTr^6 Wa [*Jolly* R N Nd] *Nd Dev*1.208[vl], *Lakṣ* 2.333; it is also supported by the parallel verse in *BDh* 1.10.28. It also fits nicely with the very next verse, which speaks of *kulasaṃkhyāṃ gacchanti*. The original reading of 63c, however, is not as certain. Here also I have gone with the unanimous ST reading, supported by several NT-x mss. including the important NKt^4 and the Śāradā mss.: Be^3 Kt^2 NKt^4 La^1 GMd^1 TMd^3 TMd^4 GMd^5 GMy NNg oOr sOx^1 Ox^2 NPu^1 sPu^6 Tr^1 Tr^2 MTr^4 MTr^6 Wa *Nā Nd*. The parallel verse in *BDh* 1.10.26, however, reads *kulāny akulatāṃ yānti*.

3.77b The reading I have adopted, *sarve jīvanti jantavaḥ*, has overwhelming manuscript support: Be^1 BBe^2 Be^3 Bo Ho Jo^2 wKt^1 BKt^5 wKt^6 La^2 Lo^1 Lo^2 Lo^3 Lo^4 Lo^5 oMd^2 TMd^3 TMd^4 GMd^5 NNg sOx^1 Ox^2 Ox^3 Pu^2 Pu^5 sPu^6 Pu^7 Pu^8 Pu^{10} Tj^1 Tr^1 MTr^4 MTr^6 Wa [*Jolly* M G R Nd] *Me Go Ku Jolly Jha Dave*.

3.79c Although the alternate reading adopted by Jolly and other editors has substantial manuscript support, the adopted reading, *atyantam*, is found in all ST mss. and in a majority of NT-x ones: Be^1 nKt^4 bKt^5 La^1 La^2 Lo^2 Lo^4 Lo^5 gMd^1 tMd^3 tMd^4 gMd^5 gMy nNg sOx^1 Ox^2 Pu^2 Pu^4 sPu^6 Pu^8 Pu^{10} Tr^1 Tr^2 mTr^4 mTr^6 Wa [*Jolly* M Nd]*Me Rc Dave Jha.*

3.82a, d The reading *dadyāt* in *pāda*-a, which I have adopted, has the overwhelming support of mss., commentators, and citations: Be^1 bBe^2 Bo bCa Ho Jo^2 mKt^1 bKt^5 mKt^6 La^1 La^2 Lo^3 tMd^3 tMd^4 gMd^5 oOr sOx^1 [*mc to*] Ox^3 nPu^1 sPu^6 [*mc to*] Pu^7 Pu^{10} Tj^1 Tr^1 Tr^2 mTr^4 mTr^6 [*Jolly* M G Nd R] *Me Go Rc Rn LakṣHem Dev Jolly Jha Dave.* The support for the adopted reading *āharan* in *pāda*-d is not as overwhelming but still very strong: Be^3 bCa Ho mKt^4 La^1 Lo^1 La^2 Lo^2 Lo^4 Lo^5 gMd^1 tMd^4 mNg oOr sOx^1 Ox^3 mPu^1 Pu^5 sPu^6 Pu^7 Pu^{10} Tr^2 mTr^4 mTr^6 Wa [*Jolly* M G] *Apa Hem Dev Jolly.*

3.83c It is unclear whether the original reading was *kaṃcit*, as all editions have it, or *kiṃcit*. The former has the support of only one ST ms., whereas all others read *kiṃcit*. However, the important and old nKt^4, as well as the Śāradā mss., also read *kaṃcit*. I have opted for *kaṃcit* mostly because it makes better sense, qualifying as it does *dvijam*, the former concluding *pāda*-c and the latter *pāda*-d. Because it is thus separated from its referent, *kaṃcit* is also the *lectio difficilior;* scribes may have been wanted to find a direct object for the adjacent verb. The reading of *Me* is unclear: Jha and Dave read *kaṃcit*, while Mandlik and my ms. Pu^{10} read *kiṃcit*; his explanation, however, indicates that his reading was indeed *kaṃcit*. Of the other commentators, *Nd* is the most clear, glossing *kiṃcid apy annam*, while *Go*'s gloss *anyaṃ brāhmaṇaṃ na kiṃcid bhojayet* also appears to support *kiṃcid*. *Ku*, on the other hand, supports the reading adopted: *na kaṃcid vaiśvadevārthaṃ brāhmaṇam atra bhojayet*, a reading found in Be^1 Bo bCa [*cor to*] wKt^3 nKt^4 Lo^1 Lo^2 gMd^5 nNg sOx^1 Pu^5 sPu^6 Pu^7 Pu^8 Tj^1 mTr^3 Wa [*Jolly* G Ku] *Hem Dev Ku Mandlik Jolly Jha KSS Dave.*

3.91b Most mss. are in error with regard to the unusual word *sarvānnabhūtaye*. It is found only in bKt^5 wKt^6 Lo^2 nNg Ox^3 nPu^1 Pu^2 Pu^7. It is unambiguously supported, however, by *Me, Go,* and *Rc*, and it is given as an alternate reading by *Nā*. See also *ŚāṅkhGṛ* 2.14.15, which gives the mantra to be recited on this occasion: *namaḥ sarvānnabhūtaye*. See Gopal 1962 for Manu's indebtedness to the *ŚāṅkhGṛ* in this passage.

3.92d It is difficult to decide which of the reading, *nikṣipet* or *nirvapet*, is the original. The former has broad support among both branches of the NT; it is also found in all the citations. I have opted for the latter principally because all but one of the ST mss. record it and it also has substantial support from the NT mss: bBe^2 bCa Jo^1 Kt^2 wKt^3 nKt^4 La^1 La^2 Lo^2 gMd^1 tMd^3 gMd^5 gMy nNg Ox^2 Pu^8 Tj^2 Tr^1 mTr^4 mTr^6 Wa [*Jolly* Nd] *Rc Mandlik Jolly Jha KSS Dave*. The reading, however, remains uncertain.

3.95b The traditional reading found in most mss. and all editions is *gāṃ dattvā vidhivad guroḥ*. Several mss., including the old nKt^4, as well as the Grantha and Śāradā mss., read *gāṃ dattvā tu yathāvidhi*. I think this is a variant of the original reading preserved in only the Malayalam and Telugu mss. *gāṃ dattvāgor yathāvidhi;* scribes probably did not understand *gor* (= *agor*) and changed it to *tu*. The word *agoḥ* (genitive of *aguḥ*, "a poor man") is somewhat rare and is clearly the *lectio difficilior*. This reading is supported by *Nd*, who glosses *agoḥ gohīnāya*, and by *Go*, who cites a *pratīka* from Yājñavalkya *alpaguḥ* (possibly a variant reading of *YDh* 1.204). It is easier to see how this difficult *pāda* was changed into the very common motif of giving a cow to a guru rather than the other way round. The adopted reading occurs in TMd^{3} TMd^{4} Tr^{1} MTr^{4} MTr^{6} [*Jolly* Nd]; it is also found in the Trivandrum ms. 22039, which was partially collated. A reading with the nominative *aguḥ* is given as a pāṭha by *Me*.

3.106d The alternate reading *atithibhojanam* has strong support. The verb *pūjayet*, however, with the meaning of feeding is found also at 3.243; 4.31. See also 3.117. I have adopted the reading *atithpūjanam*, because it is found in all but one of the ST mss. and a substantial number of NT ones: BCa Hy Jm Jo^{1} Kt^{2} wKt^{3} BKt^{5} wKt^{6} Lo^{4} Lo^{5} GMd^{1} TMd^{3} TMd^{4} GMd^{5} Pu^{2} Pu^{4} Tj^{1} Tj^{2} Tr^{1} MTr^{4} MTr^{6} [*JollyM*$^{3\text{-}4\text{-}6\text{-}9}$] *Mādh Nd Mandlik Jha KSS Dave*. Although *Me, Go,* and *Ku* have *bhojana* in their commentaries, it is unclear whether this reflects the reading of their root text or is simply a gloss.

3.108c The reading I have adopted, *tasmai cānnam*, occurs in Jo^{2} BKt^{5} wKt^{6} La^{1} Lo^{1} Lo^{3} Lo^{4} Lo^{5} sOx^{1} Ox^{2} NPu^{1} Pu^{2} Pu^{4} Pu^{5} sPu^{6} Pu^{7} Tj^{1} Tr^{2} MTr^{4}MTr^{6} Wa [Jolly G R M$^{3\text{-}4}$] *Me Go*. The reading is further supported by NKt^{4} Lo^{2} GMd^{5} Pu^{8} *Vij*, which also have *tasmai*, and by ST mss., which have *tasmād*. It is also partially supported by GMd^{1} TMd^{3} TMd^{4} GMy Tr^{1} which had *tasmād* and by Lo^{2} GMd^{5} Pu^{8} *Vij* that read *tasmā* [= *tasmai*] *annam*.

3.110a All editions, including Jolly's, have the reading *na brāhmaṇasya tv atithiḥ;* indeed, Jolly does not record any variants! The commentaries use the expression *na atithiḥ*, but it is unclear whether this is merely a gloss or reflects on the particle *na* in their root text. The vast majority of the mss., however, including all the ST ones, support the reading I have adopted: Be^{1} BBe^{2} Be^{3} Bo Jo^{2} wKt^{1} wKt^{3} NKt^{4} BKt^{5} wKt^{6} La^{1} La^{2} Lo^{1} Lo^{3} Lo^{4} Lo^{5} GMd^{1} TMd^{3} TMd^{4} GMd^{5} GMy NNg NPu^{1} Pu^{2} Pu^{4} Pu^{5} Pu^{7} Pu^{8} Tj^{1} Tr^{1} MTr^{4} MTr^{6} Wa *Dev* [vl in 2 of 3 mss.] *Mādh*.

3.114c It is remarkable that the original reading, *anvag eva*, attested by *Me, Go,* and *Nā*, is preserved only in the mss. of ST: GMd^{1} TMd^{3} TMd^{4} GMd^{5} GMy Tr^{1} MTr^{4} MTr^{6}. *Me* glosses *anvag evaitān anugatān eva bhojayet.* The gloss of *Go* also contains *anugatān*, clearly showing his dependence on *Me;* and *Nā* glosses *anvag agre*. It may well be that such a gloss that lies at the root of the NT reading *agre*. This reading is given by *Me, Go,* and *Nā* as an alternate reading preferred by some. *Me* says: *anye tv agra iti paṭhanti*. In this case Jolly does not follow the principle he himself articulated of adopting the reading of the old commentators such as *Me* and *Go*.

3.116a It is difficult to decide between the two readings *tu* and *ca*, both having equally strong mss. support. The commentators offer no help. I have gone with *tu*, because it is represented in Malayalam, Grantha, Telugu, and Old Nāgarī mss. The reading, however, remains uncertain.

3.120b The adopted reading, *upasthite*, is supported by Be^{3} BCa NKt^{4} Lo^{2} Lo^{4} Lo^{5} TMd^{4} sOx^{1} Ox^{3} NPu^{1} Pu^{5} sPu^{6} [*cor to*] Pu^{7} Pu^{10} Tr^{2} Wa [*Jolly* M G] *Jolly Jha Dave*. This *pāda* appears to have had several alternate readings even during the time of *Me*, who confesses: *iha dvitīye pāde 'nekadhā pāṭhapratipattiḥ*. And he states in the clearest terms that the reading I have adopted is the correct one: *ato 'yam eva pāṭho yuktaḥ yajñakarmaṇy upasthita iti*. The alternate reading, however, has the strong support of the ST mss., as well as a broad range of NT-x and NT-y mss.; it is also supported by *Go, Ku, Nā,* and *Rc*, who gloss *prāptau*. Yet, I think *upasthite* is the correct reading, especially in view of the identical reading at 3.187b, where this reading has unanimous support.

3.123a The reading *piṇḍānām* for *pitṝṇām* must be very old. It is attested in most ST mss., by *Go* and *Nd*, and given as an alternate reading by *Me*.

3.125a Although the alternate reading. *pitṛkārye,* has considerable manuscript support, I think the correct reading is *pitṛkṛtye,* which is supported by most commentators. It is found in: Be^{1} BBe^{2} Bo BCa Ho wKt^{1} wKt^{3} NKt^{4} BKt^{5} wKt^{6} La^{1} La^{2} Lo^{1} Lo^{2} Lo^{4} Lo^{5} GMd^{1} TMd^{4} oOr sOx^{1} Ox^{2} Ox^{3} NPu^{1} Pu^{2} Pu^{4} Pu^{5} sPu^{6} Pu^{7} Pu^{8} Tr^{2} Wa [*Jolly* M G] *Me Go Ku Rn Rc Dev Hem Apa Jolly Dave Jha;* cf. *VaDh* 11.27. See also *pretakṛtya* in 3.127.

3.133a The majority of the NT mss. and the commentators have the reading *grāsān,* as do all the editions. I have opted for *piṇḍān,* first because it is found in all ST mss. as well as a substantial number of NT-x ones (including the old NKt^{4} and the Śāradā mss.), and second because *piṇḍa* ("rice ball") makes a nice parallel to *ayoguḍa* ("iron ball") at the end of the verse. The reading adopted is found in BBe^{2} BCa wKt^{1} NKt^{4} wKt^{6} La^{1} Lo^{4} Lo^{5} GMd^{1} TMd^{3} TMd^{4} GMd^{5} GMy sOx^{1} Ox^{3} sPu^{6} [*mc to sh*] Pu^{10} Tr^{1} Tr^{2} MTr^{4} MTr^{6} [*Jolly* M Gr] *Apa Lakṣ Hem* .

3.151b Several readings are found in the mss.: *durvālam, durvalam, durbalam,* etc. The commentators gloss the word with *duścarma,* a man with bad skin or a skin disease. *Me* is the only commentator to give an alternate explanation: *skhalitalohitakeśo vikalendriyo vā.* The reading adopted in found only in Jo^{2} Lo^{4} Lo^{5} TMd^{3} GMd^{5} Ox^{3} Tr^{1} MTr^{4} MTr^{6}[*Jolly* M^{4} Me Nd] *Dev Mādh*; hence it is conjectural. The parallel passage in *GDh* 15.18, however, also reads *durvāla.* The list contains classes of people who are viewed as outside "good society"; within such a list, people who are weak or with bad skin seem incongruous. I think the term *durvāla* refers to "bald men" in the sense of heretical ascetics, parallel to *jaṭila.*

3.152a Numerous mss. read *cikitsakān devalakān* in the accusative plural; this is followed by Jolly. Then, we would have to connect *pādas* a-b syntactically with the preceding verse and the verb *na bhojayet.* It is more natural to take these *pādas* as forming a syntactic unit with the rest of this verse governed by *varjyāḥ syuḥ,* which would demand nominatives. Words in the nominative are also supported by *Me, Go, Ku, Rn, Rc,* and *Mr*; that is, all the commentators except *Nā.* The reading *cikitsakā devalakāḥ,* which I have adopted, is found in: Be^{1} Bo wKt^{1} wKt^{3} La^{2} Lo^{1} Lo^{2} GMd^{1} TMd^{3} Pu^{8} Tj^{1} Tr^{1} *Jha Dave.*

3.169c The reading *daive karmaṇi* has strong support from the ST mss. and those containing the commentary of *Me;* the latter must have been the reason for its adoption by Jolly. Yet, I think *daive haviṣi* is the correct reading because it has overwhelming manuscript support: Be^{1} BBe^{2} Be^{3} Bo BCa Ho Hy Jm Jo^{1} Jo^{2} wKt^{1} Kt^{2} wKt^{3} NKt^{4} BKt^{5} wKt^{6} La^{1} La^{2} Lo^{1} Lo^{2} Lo^{3} GMd^{1} oMd^{2} TMd^{4} oOr sOx^{1} Ox^{2} Pu^{2} Pu^{3} Pu^{5} sPu^{6} Pu^{7} Pu^{8} Tj^{1} Tj^{2} Tr^{2} Wa [*Jolly* R Ku] *Go Ku Mandlk KSS*. For the same expression where *haviṣi* has even greater manuscript and commentarial support, see 3.240c.

3.172a The reading *parivettā* has the broadest manuscript support, even though the short "i" violates the normal Pathyā form of the *śloka.* It appears that scribes attempted to correct this by either reading *parīvettā,* also adopted by Mandlik, Jolly, Jha, and Dave, or by adding a final *ca,* which, however, makes the *pāda* hypermetric.

3.175 The alternate reading in the plural, as opposed to the dual that I have opted for, is deliberately adopted by *Me,* who cites Pāṇini 1.2.58 (that a class name denoting the singular may optionally be used in the plural) in support: *jātyākhyāyām iti bahuvacanaṃ prāṇina iti.* The dual, however, has strong support from both NT and ST mss.: Be^{1} Be^{3} BCa Hy Jm Jo^{1} wKt^{1} Kt^{2} NKt^{4} BKt^{5} wKt^{6} La^{1} Lo^{1} Lo^{3} oMd^{2} TMd^{3} TMd^{4} GMd^{5} GMy oOr sOx^{1} Ox^{2} sPu^{6} Pu^{8} Tj^{1} Tj^{2} Tr^{1} Tr^{2} MTr^{3} MTr^{4} MTr^{6} *Mandlik Jolly KSS Nā Rc.*

3.178a Although the alternate reading *saṃspṛśati* has strong manuscript support, I have adopted *saṃspṛśet*. It is found in all ST mss. and a significant number of NT ones: BBe^2 Be^3 BCa Hy Jm Jo^1 wKt^1 NKt^4 Lo^1 Lo^3 GMd^1 TMd^3 TMd^4 GMd^5 GMy oOr Ox^2 NPu^1 Tj^1 Tj^2 Tr^1 MTr^4 MTr^6 and all editions. In the printed versions, *Me, Go, Ku,* and *Rc* read *saṃpraśati*, but these readings cannot be trusted without critical editions of these commentaries.

3.187c The alternate reading *nimantrayīta* must be very old; it is clearly the *lectio difficilior*. Nevertheless, I do not think it has the kind of manuscript support that would justify its adoption, as, for instance, *vācayīta* at 11.31. All the ST mss., for example, read *nimantrayeta*. Regarding the form *nimantrayīta* in the *Dharmasūtras,* see Bharadwaj 1982, 119–22. The adopted reading is found in Be^1 Ho Hy Jm Jo^1 Jo^2 Kt^2 NKt^4 La^1 La^2 Lo^2 Lo^3 GMd^1 oMd^2 TMd^3 GMd^5 GMy oOr sOx^1 Ox^2 Ox^3 Pu^2 sPu^6 Tj^1 Tj^2 Tr^1 Tr^2 MTr^4 MTr^6 Wa *Mandlik KSS;* see also *YDh* 1.225. The commentators *Me, Go, Ku,* and *Rc* have the reading *nimantrayet*. Even though there may be some orthographic confusion regarding "ī" and "e" in Devanāgarī, the two signs are quite distinct in the southern scripts and in old Nāgarī, Bengali, and Newari.

3.199a The reading of *pāda*-a is somewhat uncertain; mss. are divided between the two readings. The reading adopted, *anagnidagdhāgnidagdhān*, is found in NKt^4 Lo^2 Lo^4 Lo^5 GMd^1 TMd^4 sOx^1 NPu^1 Pu^2 Pu^5 sPu^6 [*Jolly* M] *Hem* [vl as in ed] *Me Go Jolly*, and has the support of BKt^5 wKt^6 Pu^7 Pu^{10} Tr^2 [*Jolly* G] *Jha Dave*.

3.204c The alternate reading is strongly supported by the ST mss.; the reading must, therefore, remain uncertain. The vast majority of the mss., however, have the reading I have adopted and it is supported also by *Me* and *Rc:* Be^1 Be^3 Bo BCa Ho Jo^2 BKt^5 wKt^6 La^1 La^2 Lo^2 Lo^3 Lo^4 Lo^5 TMd^4 NNg sOx^1 Ox^2 Ox^3 NPu^1 Pu^2 Pu^5 sPu^6 Pu^7 Pu^8 Pu^{10} Tj^1 Tj^2 Tr^2 Wa [*Jolly* M G R] *Me Rc Dev Apa Jolly Jha Dave*.

3.207b The reading I have adopted, *jalatīreṣu*, has the overwhelming support of the mss., including all the ST one: Ho NKt^4 BKt^5 wKt^6 La^1 Lo^1 Lo^2 Lo^4 Lo^5 GMd^1 TMd^3 TMd^4 GMd^5 GMy NNg oOr sOx^1 Ox^2 Ox^3 NPu^1 Pu^2 Pu^4 sPu^6 Pu^8 Tr^1 Tr^2 MTr^4 MTr^6 Wa [*Jolly* G] *Me Rc Apa Lakṣ Jha Dave*.

3.217d Most mss. of both the ST and NT have the reading *mantravit*, and this is followed by Mandlik and Bühler. All commentators, except *Rc*, support the reading I have adopted *mantravat*. Even when the editions read *mantravit*, as in the case of *Rn*, it is clear from the commentary itself that the commentator read *mantravat*, because they give the *mantra* that should be used in the rite. One possible reason for the alternate reading may be the frequent occurrence of *dharmavit* as the last word of a half-verse: 2.61, 128, 245; 3.149; 4.192; 5.167; 8.41, 265; 9.152; 11.31. The only occurrences of *mantravit* are at 3.131, 133, where the term appropriately refers to a learned man in general and not to the performer of a rite. The adopted reading is found in Be^3 wKt^1 Lo^1 GMd^5 Tr^1 and must be considered conjectural.

3.220c There is considerable manuscript support for the alternate reading *śrāddhe*, including several ST mss. Bühler also follows this reading. I have adopted *śrāddham* because it has the strong support of commentators. *Me*, for example, glosses: *śrāddhārtham annaṃ śrāddham*. Further, *śrāddham* is frequently used in the *MDh* as the direct object of eating: 3.146, 222, 247, 249 4.131; see also *śrāddhabhuk* at 3.250; 4.109. It is clearly the *lectio difficilior* here with the indirect object (one's own father) also in the accusative. In these usages, as *Me* notes, the term *śrāddha* refers specifically to the meal itself. The accusative reading is supported by Be^3 BCa BKt^5 wKt^6 Lo^4 Lo^5 GMd^1 TMd^3 TMd^4 Ox^3 Tr^1 MTr^4 MTr^6 *Dave Jha.*

3.221b The reading *jīvec cāpi* has the support of most ST mss. Nevertheless, I think *vāpi* is the original reading. *Nā*, for example, saw the problem of reading *vā* here and comments: *vāśabdaś cārthe*. Further, *Go* and *Ku* also have the gloss: *pitṛjīvanapakṣāpekṣo vāśabdaḥ*. This reading is found in Be^1 BBe^2 Be^1 Bo BCa Ho Jo^2 wKt^1 wKt^3 NKt^4 BKt^5 wKt^6 La^1 La^2 Lo^1 Lo^2 Lo^3 Lo^4 Lo^5 GMd^1 oMd^2 TMd^4 NNg oOr sOx^1 Ox^2 Ox^3 NPu^1 Pu^5 sPu^6 Pu^7 Pu^{10} Tj^1 Tr^2 Wa *Viś Vij Lakṣ Dev Nā Go Rc Jolly.*

3.226c The mss. of NT-y vulgate has the reading *pūrvam*, while those of the ST read *sarvam*. I have followed the reading of NT-x in this case, because it receives strong support from several commentators and from citations: Be^1 BBe^2 Be^3 Bo BCa Ho Jo^2 wKt^1 wKt^3 BKt^5 wKt^6 La^2 Lo^1 Lo^2 Lo^3 Lo^4 Lo^5 oMd^2 NNg sOx^1 Ox^2 Ox^3 NPu^1 Pu^2 Pu^3 Pu^5 sPu^6 Pu^7 Pu^8 Pu^9 Pu^{10} Tj^1 Tr^2 Wa [*Jolly* M G Ku Nd R] *Dev Hem Apa Go Ku Mr Jolly.*

3.228c The reading adopted, *pariveṣayet*, is found in BBe^2 Be^3 Bo BCa Ho Hy Jo^2 BKt^5 wKt^6 La^1 La^2 Lo^2 Lo^3 GMd^5 NNg oOr sOx^1 Ox^2 Ox^3 NPu^1 sPu^6 Pu^8 Tj^1 Tj^2 Tr^2 Wa *Me Go Nā Ku Jolly*. Most mss., however, have either *pariveṣayeta* or *pariveṣayec ca*. Both these would make the *pāda* hypermetric with 9 syllables. Jolly does not give any variants for this *pāda*. Given the divergence of the mss., the reading is uncertain.

3.233b The reading adopted has the support of mss. of ST and NT-x: Be^1 BBe^2 Be^3 BCa Ho Jo^2 wKt^1 BKt^5 wKt^6 La^2 Lo^1 Lo^2 Lo^4 Lo^5 GMd^1 TMd^4 GMd^5 GMy NNg oOr Ox^2 Ox^3 NPu^1 Pu^2 Pu^5 Pu^7 Pu^8 Pu^9 Pu^{10} MTr^4 Wa [*Jolly* M G Ku] *Hem Go Jolly.*

3.234c The alternate reading *āsane* has the unanimous support of the ST. The adopted reading, however, is the *lectio difficilior* and has the support of *Me, Go,* and *Rc*, who consider *āsanam* to be apposition to *kutapam*. The adopted reading is found in Be^1 BBe^2 Be^3 Bo BCa Ho Jo^2 NKt^4 BKt^5 wKt^6 La^1 La^2 Lo^1 Lo^2 Lo^3 Lo^4 Lo^5 NNg sOx^1 Ox^2 Pu^5 sPu^6 Pu^7 Pu^9 Pu^{10} Tj^1 Tj^2 Wa [*Jolly* M$^{1-2-4-5-8-9}$ Me G Ku R] *Apa Me Go Rc Jolly Jha Dave.*

3.236b The original reading here is quite uncertain. The mss. of NT-y vulgate read *te ca*, a reading followed by most editions. Many mss. of NT-x have the reading *te 'pi*. The reading I have adopted, *caiva*, is found in the mss. of ST and NT-x: BCa wKt^3 BKt^5 Lo^4 Lo^5 GMd^1 TMd^4 GMd^5 GMy NNg oOr sOx^1 Ox^2 Pu^2 sPu^6 Pu^8 Pu^{10} Tr^2 MTr^4 MTr^6 [*Jolly* M Nd] *Hem Jolly*. It is also supported by the variants in: TMd^3 Tr^1 *Dev Mādh*. The commentators offer no help on this.

3.237a The alternate reading *uṣṇaṃ bhavaty annam* has the support of some ST mss. The reading with *uṣmā*, however, has the support of *Me, Go,* and *Rc* and, I feel, is also the *lectio difficilior*. It is found in BBe^2 BCa Jo NKt^4 BKt^5 wKt^6 Lo^2 Lo^3 Lo^4 Lo^5 GMd^1 GMy NNg sOx^1 Ox^3 NPu^1 Pu^2 Pu^5 sPu^6 Pu^7 Pu^{10} Tj^1 Tr^2 [*Jolly* M G N R] *Apa Me Go Rc Jolly Jha Dave.*

3.240c Here the ST appears to go with the NT-y vulgate in reading *karmaṇi*, a reading not found in any commentary. The reading *haviṣi*, which I have adopted, has the support of most commentators and is found in Be^1 BBe^2 Bo BCa Ho Jo^2 wKt^1 wKt^3 NKt^4 BKt^5 wKt^6 La^1 La^2 Lo^1 Lo^2 Lo^3 Lo^4 Lo^5 sOx^1 Ox^2 Ox^3 NPu^1 Pu^2 Pu^5 sPu^6 Pu^7 Pu^8 Pu^9 Pu^{10} Tj^1 Tr^2 Wa [*Jolly* M G R] *Me Nā Ku Rn Rc Hem Jolly Jha Dave.*

3.247a The reading adopted, *asapiṇḍakriyākarma*, has the strong support of *Me*, who glosses:

prathamamṛtasya asapiṇḍakaraṇākhyaṃ karma kartavyam / sahapiṇḍadānaṃ pūrvābhyāṃ na kartavyam. The reading also has the support of *Go*, *Nā*, and *Rc*. This reading is found in Bo NKt^{4} La^{1} Lo^{2} Lo^{4} GMd^{1} TMd^{3} GMd^{5} NNg oOr sOx^{1} Ox^{3} NPu^{1} Pu^{2} Pu^{5} sPu^{6} Pu^{7} Pu^{9} Pu^{10} Tr^{1} Tr^{2} MTr^{4} MTr^{6} Wa [*Jolly* M G N Nd] *Viś Hem Go Nā Nd Rc Jolly*. For the problems of interpretation of this verse, see my note to the translation.

3.251d *Ku Rn Rc Mr* appear to read *bho abhiramyatām iti*. However, *Me* glosses *abhitaḥ* with *ubhayataḥ*, and explains: *ihaiva svagṛhe vā yatheṣṭam āsyatām ity arthaḥ*, and *Nā* and *Nd* have similar explanations of the term. *Go*'s explanation mirrors that of *Me*, while *Ku* gives *abhito* as a *pāṭha*.

3.254a *Me* takes the correct reading to be *svadadhvam* and rejects the reading *svaditam*. He also gives the alternate reading *svadatu*. Likewise, *Nā* gives the alternate reading *svadata*.

3.254d The reading adopted, *rocitam*, is found in Be^{1} BCa Ho Jo^{2} BKt^{5} wKt^{6} La^{2} Lo^{2} Lo^{3} Lo^{4} Lo^{5} NNg oOr sOx^{1} Ox^{2} Ox^{3} NPu^{1} Pu^{2} Pu^{5} sPu^{6} Pu^{7} Pu^{9} Pu^{10} Tj^{1} Tr^{2} Wa [*Jolly* M R G Nd] *Go Nā Rc Lakṣ Jolly*. The reading of the ST *rocata* also supports this reading over *rucitam*. However, *Me* appears to have had both readings in his sources, because he comments: *rucitaṃ rocitam iti vā*.

3.258b I have chosen *niyataḥ* over *prayataḥ;* the former is found in all ST mss., as well as in a substantial number of NT-x and NT-y ones, including the old NKt^{4} and the Śāradā mss. The adopted reading is found in: Be^{1} BBe^{2} Be^{3} BCa Ho Hy Jm Jo^{1} wKt^{1} Kt^{2} NKt^{4} La^{1} Lo^{1} GMd^{1} oMd^{2} TMd^{3} TMd^{4} GMd^{5} GMy NNg oOr sOx^{1} sPu^{6} Tj^{2} Tr^{1} Tr^{2} MTr^{3} MTr^{4} MTr^{6} [*Jolly* Ku R Nd] *Hem Rn Rc Mandlik KSS*.

3.261b Most editions, following the interpretation of most commentators, opt for the reading *parastāt*. They take the meaning to be that some prescribe the offering of the rice balls *after* the Brahmins have taken their meal. This stands in contrast to the provision at 3.215, where the balls are placed *before* the meal. The manuscript evidence for *parastāt*, however, is scant, as acknowledged by Bühler. I have adopted *purastāt*, because it is attested in mss. of ST and NT, as well as in all the citations: Be^{1} BBe^{2} Be^{3} Ho Hy Jm Jo^{1} Jo^{2} Kt^{2} wKt^{3} La^{1} La^{2} Lo^{2} Lo^{5} GMd^{1} TMd^{4} GMy NNg oOr sOx^{1} Ox^{2} Ox^{3} NPu^{1} Pu^{5} Pu^{7} Pu^{9} Pu^{10} Tj^{2} Tr^{1} Tr^{2} MTr^{3} MTr^{4} MTr^{6} Wa [*Jolly* M G N Nd] *Hem Dev Mādh Mandlik*. The editions of *Me* give his reading as *parastāt*, but all my mss. have the reading *purastāt*. For my interpretation of the term, see my note to the translation.

3.263d Even though all the editions read *sāttvikaṃ dhārmikam*, it is found in very few mss. Most mss. record the reading I have adopted: Be^{1} BBe^{2} Be^{3} Bo BCa Ho Jo^{2} wKt^{3} NKt^{4} BKt^{5} wKt^{6} La^{1} La^{2} Lo^{1} Lo^{2} Lo^{3} Lo^{4} Lo^{5} GMd^{1} oMd^{2} TMd^{3} TMd^{4} GMy NNg oOr sOx^{1} Ox^{2} Ox^{3} NPu^{1} Pu^{2} Pu^{4} Pu^{5} sPu^{6} Pu^{7} Pu^{8} Pu^{9} Tj^{1} Tr^{1} Tr^{2} MTr^{4} MTr^{6} Wa [*Jolly* G R] *Hem Lakṣ Dev Mādh*. This sequence is supported also by *Go*, *Ku*, and *Rn*.

3.267c All editions read *tṛpyanti*. The reading I have adopted, *prīyante*, however, is found in most mss. and in all citations: Be^{1} BBe^{2} Be^{3} Bo BCa Jo^{2} wKt^{1} wKt^{3} NKt^{4} BKt^{5} wKt^{6} La^{1} La^{2} Lo^{1} Lo^{2} Lo^{3} Lo^{4} Lo^{5} GMd^{1} oMd^{2} TMd^{3} TMd^{4} GMd^{5} GMy NNg oOr sOx^{1} Ox^{2} Ox^{3} NPu^{1} Pu^{5} sPu^{6} Pu^{7} Pu^{8} Pu^{9} Pu^{10} Tr^{1} Tr^{2} MTr^{4} MTr^{6} [*Jolly* M G R Nd] *Me Dev Lakṣ Mādh Hem Apa*; cf. *ViDh* 80.1. Both *Go* and *Ku* read *pitaras tṛpyanti*, but this may well be a gloss, because, in commenting on the following verse, both refer to the syntactic connection of that verse (268) with this, saying: *pitaraḥ prīyanta ity pūrveṇa saṃbandhaḥ*.

3.268b Both the readings, *iha* and *atha*, have strong manuscript support; the latter is found in most ST mss. including all the Malayalam ones. I have adopted the former, however, which is supported by all the medieval citations and found in Bo BCa Jo^2 La^1 La^2 Lo^1 Lo^2 Lo^3 GMd^1 oMd^2 GMy Ox^2 NPu^1 Pu^2 Pu^4 Pu^8 Pu^{10} Tj^1 Tr^2 Wa [*Jolly* M$^{1\text{-}2\text{-}8\text{-}9}$ R] *Rn* [*iha śrāddhe*] *Lakṣ Hem Dev Mādh Jolly*. This reading parallels *pārṣateneha* of 269b. The reading, nevertheless, remains uncertain.

3.270c The *pāda* is hypermetric, and this may have been the reason for scribes to attempt to correct it as reflected in the several variant readings, all restoring the meter. The reading adopted is found in a broad spectrum of mss. and is supported by all the medieval citations: Bo Hy Jm Jo^1 Jo^2 wKt^1 Kt^2 wKt^3 NKt^4 BKt^5 BKt^6 La^2 Lo^1 Lo^2 Lo^4 Lo^5 GMd^1 oMd^2 GMy Ox^2 NPu^1 Pu^8 Pu^{10} Tj^2 MTr^3 Wa [*Jolly* M$^{1-2-8-9}$] *Hem Dev Mādh Mandlik Jha KSS Dave*.

3.272a The reading *mahāśalkaḥ* is found in only a few mss: Jo^2 NNg sPu^6 Pu^{10} [*Jolly* M$^{2\text{-}8}$], and in *Hem* 3/1.586 *Jolly*. However, the singular is attested in more mss. than the plural *mahāśalkāḥ*, and the other items in this list are all in the singular..

3.273a The mss. are divided over the two readings, *madhunā miśram* and *madhusaṃmiśram*. I have opted for the former because it is represented in all but one of the ST mss., as well as in all the NT-y mss. and good number of NT-x ones. It is found in: Be^1 BBe^2 BCa Ho Hy Jm Jo^1 wKt^1 Kt^2 wKt^3 Lo^2 GMd^1 oMd^2 TMd^3 GMd^5 GMy oOr Tj^2 Tr^1 MTr^6 [*Jolly* Nd] *Mandlik Jha KSS Dave.*

3.274a The reading *bhūyāt* is found in Be^1 BBe^3 Bo BCa Jo^2 NKt^4 BKt^5 wKt^6 La^1 La^2 Lo^2 Lo^3 Lo^4 Lo^5 GMd^1 oMd^2 GMy NNg Ox^2 Ox^3 NPu^1 Pu^2 Pu^4 Pu^8 Pu^{10} Tj^1 Tr^2 MTr^4 MTr^6 [*Jolly* M R Ku] *Me Ku Go Lakṣ Hem Dev Jolly Jha Dave.*

3.275d The mss. are deeply divided over the two readings: *anantam* and *ānantyam*. I have opted for the latter mostly because it is represented by the largest number of ST mss. and a substantial number of ST-x ones. This reading is found in: Be^1 BBe^2 BCa Jo^2 wKt^1 wKt^3 NKt^4 La^1 La^2 Lo^1 Lo^2 TMd^3 GMd^5 GMy NNg Ox^2 NPu^1 Pu^2 Pu^4 Pu^5 Pu^7 Pu^8 Pu^9 Tr^1 Tr^2 MTr^6 [Jolly N Nd R]. The fact that *akṣaya* can be both an adjective and a substantive makes the choice harder, and the reading remains uncertain.

3.277 Verses 278 is placed before 277 in all editions, including Jolly's. I have followed the order of these verses found in all the ST mss., as well as in substantial number of NT-x mss., including the old NKt^4 and the Śāradā mss. This order is found in Be^1 BBe^2 Be^3 BCa Ho Jo^2 NKt^4 La^1 Lo^1 Lo^3 GMd^1 TMd^3 TMd^4 GMd^5 GMy NNg oOr sOx^1 Ox^2 NPu^1 Pu^2 Pu^4 sPu^6 Pu^8 Tj^1 Tr^1 MTr^4 MTr^6 Wa. In this order, verse 277concerning the two fortnights nicely connects with the matter dealt with in the preceding verse.

3.282a Both the readings, *paitṛyajñikaḥ* and *paitṛyajñiyaḥ*, have strong support. I have opted for the former because all the ST mss. have a form with "k." It is also supported by *Me, Go,* and *Nā*. See the parallel *pāñcayajñika* at 3.83, 281, 286.

3.284d There is strong manuscript support for both readings: *purātanī* and *sanātanī*. The latter is the reading of all but two ST mss. I have chosen the former, however, because it is found the most NT-x mss. and is the reading of *Me* and *Nā*, whereas the latter is supported by only *Rc*. The original reading, nevertheless, remains uncertain. The reading adopted is found in: BBe^2 BCa Jo^2 wKt^1 wKt^3 BKt^5 wKt^6 Lo^2 Lo^3 Lo^4 Lo^5 GMd^1 oMd^2 GMy oOr sOx^1 Ox^3 NPu^1 Pu^2 Pu^5 sPu^6 Pu^7 Pu^9 Pu^{10} Tj^1 Wa [*Jolly* M G N R] *Apa Me Nā Jolly*.

CHAPTER FOUR

4.4d The alternate reading, *kadācana*, is well represented in the mss. and appears to be supported by the glosses of *Go* [*kadācid api*] and *Ku* [*kadāpi*]. I have opted for *kathaṃcana*, however, which is found in all ST mss. and in most NT-x: Bo NKt^4 BKt^5 wKt^6 Lo^1 Lo^4 Lo^5 GMd^1 oMd^2 TMd^3 TMd^4 GMd^5 GMy NNg sOx^1 Ox^3 NPu^1 Pu^2 Pu^3 Pu^4 sPu^6 Pu^8 Pu^{10} Tr^1 Tr^2 MTr^4 MTr^6 Rc [*Jolly* M Nd].

4.10a I have adopted *vartayaṃs tu* because it is found in all the ST mss. as well and in several NT-x ones. All editions opt for *ca*, which is found only in the NT-y vulgate and in some NY-x ones, including the old NKt^4 and the Śāradā mss. The reading adopted is found in Be^1 Be^3 Ho Jo^2 wKt^1 La^2 Lo^3 GMd^1 TMd^3 TMd^4 GMd^5 GMy NNg NPu^1 Pu^2 Pu^4 Tj^1 Tr^1 MTr^4 MTr^6 Wa *Nd* [*Jolly* R].

4.17c The original reading here is clearly *yāpayan*, which is also the *lectio difficilior*. It was easy for a scribe to change this somewhat unusual word, meaning to support or make someone subsist, to the orthographically similar (in Devanāgarī) *dhyāpayan*, which when combined with the preceding *yathā* gives *adhyāpayan*, influenced no doubt by the *svādhyāya* mentioned in *pāda*-b. Significantly, this reading is absent in the mss. with southern scripts. The reading adopted is found in Bo wKt^1 wKt^3 NKt^4 BKt^5 wKt^6 La^2 Lo^2 GMd^1 TMd^3 TMd^4 GMd^5 GMy NNg Ox^3 Pu^2 Pu^4 Pu^7 [*but cor*] Tj^1 Tj^2 Tr^1 MTr^4 MTr^6 Wa *Nā Nd Go Dave Mandlik Jha*. This reading is also supported by the comments of *Me: kuṭumbakaṃ jīvayati*, and similar comments by *Ku, Rn*, and *Mr*.

4.26c This *pāda* has numerous variants. It is clear that that the original reading had *hy ayana-* rather than *tv ayana-*. The manuscripts and other sources are divided on the rest of the *pāda*. It is clear, however, that *ante* is the original reading, rather than *ādau*. The former is attested by *Me* and *Rc*, and found in most mss. including those of the ST. The latter is supported by *Nā, Go* and *Ku*. The reading adopted is found in BCa Jo^2 NKt^4 Lo^3 GMd^5 NNg Ox^3 NPu^1 Pu^2 Pu^4 Pu^{10} Tr^1 Wa [*Jolly* Me M$^{1\text{-}2\text{-}5\text{-}8\text{-}9}$ R Nd] *Me Rc Lakṣ Jolly Jha Dave*.

4.38d There is little to choose between *svaṃ rūpam* and *svarūpam*. I have chosen the former because it is found in most mss.: BBe^2 BCa Hy Jm Jo^1 Jo^2 wKt^3 NKt^4 BKt^5 wKt^6 La^1 La^2 Lo^4 GMd^1 oMd^2 sOx^1 Ox^2 Pu^2 Pu^3 Pu^4 sPu^6 Pu^7 Pu^8 Pu^9 Tj^2 MTr^3 MTr^4 MTr^6 Wa *Vij Mandlik Jolly KSS*.

4.42c The alternate reading *prajñā lakṣmī yaśaś cakṣuḥ* has much to commend itself; it is found in all the ST mss. and in several NT-x ones. I have, however, opted for the traditional reading; it is clearly possible that the change in the alternate reading was made deliberately so this *pāda* would not be identical to *pāda*-c of the previous verse.

4.49b There are quite a lot of variant readings here. It is clear that the original had *kāṣṭhaṃ loṣṭaṃ patraṃ* as separate words; the compounded form is found mostly in NT-y vulgate. The last two words, however, are less certain. I have opted for *tṛṇāni vā* because it has the best manuscript support, including most of the ST mss.: Be^1 BBe^2 Be^3 wKt^3 NKt^4 BKt^5 wKt^6 La^1 Lo^2 Lo^4 Lo^5 GMd^1 TMd^3 TMd^4 GMd^5 GMy NPu^1 Pu^5 Pu^7 Pu^8 Tr^1 MTr^4 MTr^6 Wa *Dev Apa*.

4.50 All the mss. containing *Me*'s commentary omit this verse. Yet, there is a brief comment: *mūtrotsargasamutsargaṃ tyāgam*, which appears to be a comment on the first words of this verse.

4.51d The reading *prāṇābādha* is found in BBe^{2} BCa Hy Jo^{1} wKt^{3} NKt^{4} TMd^{3} TMd^{4} GMd^{5} GMy NNg sOx^{1} Pu^{2} sPu^{6} Pu^{5} Pu^{7} Pu^{9} MTr^{4}MTr^{6} *Jolly*, and is supported by the parallel reading at verse 54d. In the Devanāgarī it is easy to drop the stroke for the long "ā" after a retroflex "ṇ".

4.52a, c Most mss. have the readings *pratyagnim* and *pratigām*, using the accusative with the particle *prati*. These forms may have been influenced by the a-stem neuters in the three other compounds: *pratisūryam*, *pratisomodakadvijam*, and *prativātam*. The original forms, however, were clearly the adverbial compounds *pratyagni* and *pratigu*. The former is found in Be^{3} Hy Jo^{2} wKt^{1} NKt^{4} Lo^{3} NNg Wa [*Jolly* M G N Nd R] *Jolly*, and the latter in Bo NKt^{4} wKt^{6} NNg Ox^{2} Pu^{2} Pu^{3} Pu^{5} Pu^{7} Pu^{9} Wa [*Jolly* G N] *Jolly Jha*, also supported by the mss. with the form *pratigum*. The reading *pratigu* is supported by *Nā* and *Rc*.

4.57a This *pāda* has a large number of variants, possibly because this was a well-known proverb with multiple readings. In attempting to come up with a plausible reading, I have tried to figure out first the form of the verb and second the position of the verb. The form *svapyāt* is the form found in most mss.; unfortunately the commentators do not bother with this *pāda*. The alternate form *supyāt* is found only in Bo Ho wKt^{1} La^{1} Lo^{1} Lo^{2} GMd^{1}. The position is less certain, but I think it should come at the third position, as in *pādas* b and c; that is, the verb comes after the initial "*na*" and the following word. The mss. also support this position; the verb in the last position is found only in La^{1} Jo Lo^{3} Lo^{4} Lo^{5} TMd^{4} NNg NPu^{1} Pu^{2} Pu^{4} Pu^{10} Wa.

4.57b The reading *śreyāṃsam* is clearly the original and the older reading attested by *MS* 3.4.5 and *KS* 22.2 (see the study by Jamison 2000). This reading is also presupposed by the comments of *Me, Go, Nā, Ku,* and *Rc*. It is found in Bo La^{2} Lo^{2} TMd^{3} GMd^{5} GMy Ox^{3} Pu^{8} Pu^{10} Tr^{1} Tr^{2} MTr^{4} MTr^{6}. There is some doubt as to the position of *na*, some placing it in the second position. The parallel with *pādas* a and c [see also the surrounding verses], as well as the manuscript evidence, makes it clear that its original position is at the beginning of the *pāda*.

4.61c The reading *-janākrānte* is supported by *Me* and is found in: Be^{1} BBe^{2} Bo Jo^{2} wKt^{3} BKt^{5} wKt^{6} La^{1} La^{2} Lo^{2} Lo^{3} TMd^{4} GMd^{5} NNg oOr sOx^{1} Ox^{2} NPu^{1} Pu^{3} Pu^{5} sPu^{6} Pu^{7} Pu^{8} Pu^{9} Pu^{10} Tj^{1} Tr^{2} MTr^{6} [*Jolly* M G R] *Lakṣ Me Rc Jolly*.

4.70a The editions of *Go* has the reading *gṛhṇīyāt*, but all three of my mss. with *Go*'s commentary read *mṛdnīyāt*. The gloss *vimardanam* by *Me* supports the adopted reading found in the vast majority of the mss.

4.74a Jha and Dave adopt the reading *dīvyet* following *Me*; but I think the word *dīvyet* is used by *Me* as a gloss on *krīḍet*, because *dīvyet* is not found in any ms. including those with *Me*'s commentary. It is difficult to choose between the alternate readings *kadācic ca* and *kadācit tu*. I have adopted the former, because it is found in most of the ST mss. and a good number of NT-x ones: Be^{1} Be^{3} BCa Jo^{2} NKt^{4} La^{2} Lo^{3} TMd^{3} GMd^{5} GMy oOr Pu^{5} Pu^{7} Pu^{9} Tr^{1} MTr^{4} MTr^{6} Wa *Jolly*.

4.75b The alternative reading, *astam ite ravau*, is supported by the comments of *Go, Ku, Rn,* and *Rc*. It is clear, however, that *Me* had the reading with *prati*, because he explains the accusative ending of *astamayam* with a reference to Pāṇini 1.4.90: *pratilakṣaṇe karmapravacanīyatvād dvitīyā*. The technical term *karmapravacanīya* (Pāṇini 1.4.83) refers to verbal prepositions that govern substantives. Here *prati* govern the accusative. The translation of Jha of this statement of *Me* is misleading; he appears to think that the explanation confirms the reading *astam ite ravau*. The reading adopted is found in BKt^5 wKt^6 La^2 Lo^2 GMd^1 TMd^3 TMd^4 GMd^5 GMy NNg oOr sOx^1 Ox^2 Ox^3 NPu^1 Pu^2 Pu^3 Pu^4 Pu^5 sPu^6 Pu^7 Pu^9 Pu^{10} Tr^2 MTr^4 MTr^6 Wa [*Jolly* M$^{1\text{-}2\text{-}8\text{-}9}$ G N Nd] *Nā Jolly*.

4.83c The reading adopted *snātas tu* is supported by most ST mss. and occurs in Be^1 BBe^2 Be^3 Bo Ho Jo^2 wKt^1 BKt^5 wKt^6 La^1 Lo^3 GMd^1 oMd^2 TMd^3 GMd^5 GMy NPu^1 Pu^2 Pu^4 Pu^5 Pu^7 Pu^9 Pu^{10} Tj^1 Tr^1 Tr^2 MTr^4 MTr^6 *RnLakṣ Hem*.

4.85cd The uncertainty of the reading—*veśa* or *veśyā*—is noted by *Ku*, who ascribes the former to *Me* and others and the latter to *Go*. *govindarājas tu daśaveśyāsamo nṛpa iti paṭhati / medhātithiprabhṛtayaḥ prāñco daśaveśasamo nṛpa iti paṭhanti*. The commentary of *Me* as we have it, however, does not contain this reading; his comments are very brief on this verse. The vast majority of mss., including almost all the ST ones, however, support the adopted reading: Be^3 Bo Ho wKt^1 NKt^4 BKt^5 wKt^6 La^1 Lo^2 Lo^3 Lo^4 Lo^5 GMd^1 TMd^3 TMd^4 GMd^5 GMy NNg oOr sOx^1 Ox^2 Ox^3 NPu^1 Pu^2 Pu^3 Pu^4 Pu^5 sPu^6 Pu^9 Pu^{10} Tj^1 Tr^1 Tr^2 Wa *Go Lakṣ Jolly*. The reading *veśyā* is also supported by *YDh* 1.141.

4.90c The reading *lohacāraka* is quite uncertain; there are numerous variants in the mss. and the commentators generally ignore the term. Competing readings are: *lohakāraka* found in most ST mss. (the reading of TMd^4 is unclear); *lohāṅgāraka*; and *lohadāraka*, which is the reading of most editions. The adopted reading is found in: Be^3 BCa wKt^1 Lo^2 Lo^4 Lo^5 GMd^1 NNg sOx^1 NPu^1 Pu^2 Pu^4 Pu^5 sPu^6 Pu^7 Pu^9 Tr^2 MTr^6 [*Jolly* M$^{3\text{-}4}$ G N Nd] *Apa Nā Jolly;* see also *ViDh* 43.22.

4.94 It is clear that the sense of the verse requires the verb to be in the past tense rather than in the optative. For this reason Jolly has adopted the reading *avāpnuvan*. It is, however, found in a very small number of mss. Even the ST mss. give the optative, but quite irregularly in the singular for a sentence with the subject in the plural. I have maintained the optative reading *avāpnuyuḥ* found in most mss., even though I am troubled by this reading.

4.123c It is surprising that all editions have adopted the reading *vāpy antam* when it has so little manuscript support. It is true that the distinction between "v" and "c" in northern scripts is often blurred. But mss. in southern scripts also favor "*ca*." The reading adopted in found in: BBe^2 Be^3 Bo Ho wKt^3 La^2 Lo^1 Lo^2 Lo^3 sOx^1 Ox^2 Ox^3 Pu^3 Pu^5 sPu^6 Pu^7 Pu^8 Pu^{10} Tj^1 Tr^2 Wa.

4.132d There are four alternate readings: *adhitiṣthec ca, adhitiṣṭed dhi, adhitiṣṭhet tu,* and *adhitiṣṭheta*, all with considerable manuscript support. Somewhat hesitantly I have gone with the first, mostly because it is strongly supported by most ST mss.: wKt^1 NKt^4 BKt^5 wKt^6 Lo^3 TMd^4 GMd^5 NNg Pu^5 Pu^7 Tr^1 MTr^4 MTr^6 [*Jolly* G K R]*Jolly*. The reading, however, remains uncertain.

4.141b The adopted reading, *vayo'dhikān*, has the unanimous support of the ST and NT-y mss., as well as a substantial number of NT-x ones: Be^1 BCa Ho Hy Jm Jo^1 Jo^2 wKt^3 La^1 Lo^1 Lo^3 GMd^1 oMd^2 TMd^3 TMd^4 GMd^5 GMy sOx^1 Ox^2 Pu^2 Pu^5 sPu^6 Pu^7 Tj^2 Tr^1 Tr^2 MTr^4 MTr^6 *MandlikJolly KSS*. The reading, nevertheless, is uncertain. In the southern mss. "g" may have been pronounced as "k" through Dravidian influence and then compensated by changing "ti" to "dhi." See the parallel at 7.149 where the reading is unmistakably *vayo'tigān*.

4.142d The plural reading *jyotirgaṇān* is supported by several ST mss. The reading adopted, *jyotirgaṇam*, however, has broader support: Be^{1} BBe^{2} Be^{3} Bo Ho Jo^{2} Kt^{2} wKt^{3} BKt^{5} wKt^{6} La^{1} La^{2} Lo^{2} Lo^{3} Lo^{4} Lo^{5} oMd^{2} TMd^{4} NNg Ox^{2} Ox^{3} NPu^{1} Pu^{2} Pu^{3} Pu^{4} Pu^{5} Pu^{7} Pu^{8} Pu^{10} Tr^{2} Wa [*Jolly* M G R]*Me Rc Jolly*. Likewise, *Go*'s gloss *samūham* also supports the singular.

4.144c All mss. read *rahasyāni*. The printed editions, however, give the reading *rahaḥsthāni* in several commentaries. Without critical editions of these commentaries it is impossible to determine the original readings. For example, in Mandlik and Dave *Me* reads *rahaḥsthāni*, but in Jha and my mss. *rahasyāni*. In Mandlik *Nā* and *Rn* (as also my ms.) read *rahasyāni*, but in Dave *rahaḥsthāni*. With either reading, however, the term refers to the "hidden" or the private parts of the body.

4.149b Although both readings, *dvijaḥ* and *punaḥ*, have substantial manuscript support, I have adopted the former because it is found in all the ST mss., as well as in a large number of NT-x ones and all the citations: Be^{1} Bo Ho NKt^{4} Lo^{2} Lo^{4} Lo^{5} GMd^{1} TMd^{3} GMd^{5} GMy Ox^{2} Ox^{3} Pu^{2} Pu^{8} Pu^{10} Tr^{1} MTr^{4} MTr^{6} [*Jolly* M Nd]*Lakṣ Dev Dave Jha*.

4.170c It is surprising that all editors, including Jolly, have adopted the reading *hiṃsāratah* when so few mss. record that reading. The reading of the commentators given in the editions cannot be trusted, because the stroke for "i" can be easily dropped.

4.176d The reading adopted, *lokasaṃkruṣṭam*, is found in Be^{3} Bo NKt^{4} La^{2} Lo^{2} Lo^{4} Lo^{5} GMd^{1} NNg sOx^{1} Ox^{3} Pu^{5} sPu^{6} Pu^{7} Tr^{1} Tr^{2} Wa [*Jolly* M G Nd] *Me Go Rc Jolly Jha Dave*. The prefix "*sam*," however, also has the support of a large number of other mss. with variant readings.

4.178d The reading adopted, *riṣyati*, is found in Be^{1} Be^{3} NKt^{4} La^{1} GMd^{1} TMd^{3} TMd^{4} GMd^{5} oOr sOx^{1} Ox^{2} Ox^{3} sPu^{6} Tr^{2} MTr^{4} MTr^{6} *Dev Me Nd Rn Rc Jha*. The Parasmaipada "ti" ending is also supported by other mss. with alternate readings. The reading *duṣyati* is clearly a very old variant, because it is found already in Kumārila.

4.181c The reading of the *pāda*, as also the meaning of the entire verse, is less than clear. The attempt to clarify the meaning may be the reason for many of the variant readings in this *pāda*, as also in *pāda*-a. The commentators *Me, Go, Ku*, and *Rc* appear to support the reading *etair jitaiḥ*. They appear to take the pronoun *etaiḥ*, however, as referring to the disputes rather than to the persons engaged in the dispute. This may be the reason why several mss. change *ebhiḥ* in *pāda*-a to *etān* referring to *vivādān*. I think the pronoun here and in *pāda*-a refer to the individuals listed in the previous verse. Within this context, I think the nominative *jitaḥ* makes much better sense. The parallel *etair adhikṣiptaḥ* in verse 185 also supports the nominative. Bühler (1886, 157) also thought that "this reading, though less well attested than the vulgata, is perhaps preferable." In fact, however, this reading is better attested and is the reading found in all the ST mss.: Be^{3} Bo BCa Ho Jm wKt^{3} NKt^{4} wKt^{5} La^{2} Lo^{3} GMd^{1} TMd^{3} GMd^{5} oOr Pu^{8} Tj^{2} Tr^{1} MTr^{4} MTr^{6} Wa [*Jolly* Nd] *Nā Rn Lakṣ Dave*.

4.183c All the editors have adopted the reading *apāṃ loke*, although it is found in only a few manuscripts. The reading adopted has broad manuscript support: Be^{1} Bo BCa wKt^{1} NKt^{4} wKt^{6} La^{2} Lo^{2} Lo^{4} Lo^{5} GMd^{1} TMd^{4} GMd^{5} oOr sOx^{1} Ox^{2} Ox^{3} NPu^{1} Pu^{2} Pu^{3} Pu^{4} Pu^{5} sPu^{6} Pu^{7} Pu^{10} Tr^{1} Tr^{2} MTr^{4} MTr^{6} Wa *Apa*. The commentators do not comment on this expression.

4.183d The genitive *lokasya* in *pāda*-c supports the adoption of *pṛthivyāḥ*, which becomes *pṛthivyā* due to sandhi. The orthographic distinction between that and the locative *pṛthivyāṃ* is slight. The reading adopted is found in Bo Jm La^2 Lo^1 GMd^1 TMd^3 GMd^5 sOx^1 Ox^2 Ox^3 NPu^1 Pu^2 Pu^3 Pu^4 Pu^5 sPu^6 Pu^7 Pu^{10} Tj^1 Tr^2 MTr^6 Wa *Apa Jha Dave.*

4.188c The reading adopted has the strong support of both ST and NT-x mss.: Be^1 BBe^2 Bo BCa Ho wKt^1 wKt^3 BKt^5 wKt^6 La^2 Lo^1 Lo^2 GMd^1 oMd^2 TMd^3 TMd^4 GMd^5 GMy sOx^1 Ox^2 NPu^1 Pu^3 Pu^5 sPu^6 Pu^7 Pu^8 Tj^1 Tr^1 Tr^2 MTr^4 MTr^6 [*Jolly* G Nd] *Rc Lakṣ Hem;* cf. *VaDh* 6.32 . Surprisingly all the editions adopt the alternate reading.

4.195b All three alternate readings have good manuscript support: *dambhikaḥ, dāmbhikaḥ,* and *dambhakaḥ.* The readings of the commentators are suspect, because it is unclear whether the editors have emended the text. In the editions, *Me Go Nā Ku* and *Mr* read *dambhakaḥ.* The reading adopted, *dambhikaḥ,* is found in Jo^2 NKt^4 Lo^4 Lo^5 oMd^2 TMd^3 GMd^5 Ox^3 Pu^2 Pu^4 Pu^5 Pu^7 Pu^{10} MTr^4 MTr^6 [Jolly M G Nd] *Jolly.* The original readings is uncertain.

4.196a Here again we have a problem with the readings found in the editions of the commentaries, which all read *naiṣkṛtikaḥ.* The overwhelming evidence of the mss. and all the medieval citations indicate that the editions are probably wrong and that the commentators also had the reading adopted: *naikṛtikaḥ.*

4.201b Again it is surprising that all editors (except Jha), including Jolly, adopt the reading *snāyāc ca* when it is found in so few mss. mostly belonging to NT-y vulgate. The reading adopted is found in Bo wKt^1 NKt^4 BKt^5 wKt^6 Lo^2 Lo^4 Lo^5 oMd^2 GMd^5 GMy NNg sOx^1 Ox^2 Ox^3 NPu^1 Pu^2 Pu^3 Pu^4 sPu^6 Pu^8 Pu^{10} Tj^1 Tr^1 Tr^2 MTr^4 MTr^6 [*Jolly* M Nd] *Apa Jha.* The commentaries offer no help.

4.202c The reading adopted *upayuñjāna* has overwhelming manuscript support: Bo BCa Jo^2 wKt^3 NKt^4 BKt^5 wKt^6 Lo^1 Lo^3 Lo^4 GMd^1 TMd^3 GMd^5 GMy Ox^3 Pu^2 Pu^5 Pu^7 Pu^8 Pu^{10} Tj^2 Tr^1 TTr^6 Wa [*Jolly* M G R Ku Nd] *Apa Me Ku Dave Jha Jolly.* Manuscripts frequently confuse formations from *yuj* and *bhuj.*

4.206a The three variant readings, *aślīkam, aśrīkam,* and *aślīlam,* have good manuscript support. It is clear that *Ku* and *Mr* read *aślīkam,* because they comment on the change of "r" to "l." It is simply a variant form of *aśrīkam,* and one or the other form is found in *Go, Ku, Rc,* and *Nd.* The reading of *Me* and *Nā* is unclear; the editions of these commentaries have *aślilam.* The gloss of *Me* is *aślaghyam,* and that of *Nā* is *pāpakaram.* The glosses can support either readings. I have adopted *aślīkam* because it, and the variant *aśrīkam,* have the broadest manuscript support. The reading adopted is found in Be^1 Bo Ho Hy Jo^1 Kt^2 BKt^5 La^1 Lo^1 Ox^2 NPu^1 Pu^3 Pu^8 MTr^3 MTr^4 MTr^6 *Lakṣ Jolly Mandlik KSS.*

4.214b There are three alternate readings: *-vikrayikasya, -vikrayakasya,* and *-vikrayiṇaḥ.* All have substantial manuscript support. At least in the printed editions, the first is supported by *Nā* and *Ku;* the second by *Me;* and the third by *Rn, Rc* and *Mr.* Given the slight difference between the first and the second, however, the editions cannot be trusted completely. Here even the ST mss. are divided. I have gone with the second, because it has the broadest manuscript support, including most of the ST ones: Ho NKt^4 Lo^2 Lo^3 Lo^4 Lo^5 GMd^1 TMd^3 GMy Ox^3 Pu^3 Pu^8 Pu^{10} Tr^1 MTr^4 MTr^6 [*Jolly* M $^{4\text{-}5\text{-}9}$ R] *Dave Jha.*

4.215b The reading *-avatārakasya* adopted by Jolly and others is found in only a small number of mss. Surprisingly, Jolly gives no variants even though his own Śāradā ms. has the reading I have adopted. This form has also entered into the Sanskrit dictionaries, probably via the previous editions of the *MDh*. The readings of the commentators are suspect because we have to depend on the imperfect editions. In them the above reading is found only in *Nā*. The reading adopted is found in Be^{1} Be^{3} Bo BCa Ho Hy Jo^{2} wKt^{3} NKt^{4} BKt^{5} wKt^{6} La^{2} Lo^{2} GMd^{1} TMd^{3} TMd^{4} GMd^{5} GMy NNg sOx^{1} Ox^{2} Ox^{3} Pu^{8} Pu^{10} Tj^{1} Tj^{2} Tr^{1} Tr^{2} MTr^{4} MTr^{6} Wa*Apa Hem Me Rn Rc Mr Dave Jha*.

4.216c Mandlik, Jolly, and KSS give the reading *rañjakasya*, meaning a dyer. This appears to be a silent editorial emendation; Jolly gives no variants when his own Śāradā ms. has the alternate reading. All but three of my mss. have the reading adopted, *rajakasya*; it is also the reading in *Vij, Apa*, and *Hem*. The problem is that this word generally means a washerman, who was already listed as *cailanirṇejaka* in *pāda*-b. It is evident that the meaning dyer was also attached to *rajaka*, for *Me* glosses it with *vāsasāṃ nīlādirāgakārakaḥ*. The various readings of the commentators for this word in the editions cannot be trusted.

4.223b All NT mss. have the reading *aśrāddhinaḥ* (with a few *aśrāddikaḥ*). It has been adopted in all editions. I have chosen to go with the ST and adopted the reading *aśraddhinaḥ* found in GMd^{1} TMd^{3} TMd^{4} GMy Tr^{1} MTr^{4}MTr^{6} [*Jolly* Nd]. It is given by *Me* as a *pāṭhāntara* with the following gloss: *aśraddhina iti vā pāṭhaḥ / aśraddhāvān ity arthaḥ / tathā cottaraśloke śraddhāyāḥ prādhānyam evāha vadānyasyeti*. I think *Me* is perceptive in pointing out the broader context in which this verse is placed, and that context deals with the importance of *śraddhā* (see verses 224–6). The same *pāṭhāntara* is given by *Hem* (3/1.785) with the same explanation. If we interpret the particle *vā* of *Me* as showing a preference ("or rather"; see note to the translation of 9.111), then I think we can assume that *Me* himself preferred this reading, which is also supported by his further remarks. This meaning of the expression is also supported by the comments of *Nā, Nd*, and *Rc*, although the latter also gives the alternate interpretation: a man who does not perform *śrāddhas*, which is the interpretation of *Go, Ku*, and *Rn*. In this case, I think, the ST has preserved the better and possibly original reading.

4.226 The additional three verses are commented by *Me*. It is probable that he took them to be authentic verse of the *MDh*. The fact that they are absent in almost all mss. indicates a) that *Me*'s influence on the establishment of the text was not as great as may be assumed, and b) that the mss. sometimes give better readings of the text than the commentators.

4.235b The mss. are equally divided between the two readings *eva ca* and *eva vā*. I have opted for the former both because the copulative makes better sense with *tav ubhau* in *pāda*-c. It is found in Be^{3} Ho Hy Jo^{1} wKt^{1} Kt^{2} BKt^{5} wKt^{6} La^{1} Lo^{1} GMd^{1} TMd^{3} GMy Pu^{2} Pu^{3} Tr^{2} MTr^{3} Wa*Mandlik Jolly KSS*.

4.237d Even though all editors have adopted the reading *ca*, most mss. including all the ST ones, as well as the citations, read *tu*, which I have adopted: Be^{1} BBe^{2} Bo wKt^{1} wKt^{3} NKt^{4} La^{1} La^{2} Lo^{1} Lo^{4} Lo^{5} GMd^{1} TMd^{3} TMd^{4} GMd^{5} GMy Ox^{3} Pu^{3} Pu^{8} Pu^{10} Tr^{1} MTr^{4} MTr^{6} Wa *Hem Apa*.

4.245b Even though the preponderance of manuscript evidence supports *varjayet*, I have adopted the minority reading *varjayan*, because the participle is clearly required by the syntax. The only commentator to note the word is *Go*, who clearly presupposes the participle. The reading adopted is found in BBe^{2} BCa Hy Jm Jo^{1} Jo^{2} Kt^{2} wKt^{3} NKt^{4} La^{2} oOr Ox^{2} Tj^{2} Tr^{1} MTr^{4} *Go Mandlik Jolly Jha KSS Dave*.

4.257d Both the alternate readings, *āsthitaḥ* and *āśritaḥ*, have strong manuscript support. Even the ST mss. are divided; so are the commentators. I have adopted the former, because its support is somewhat stronger both in the mss. and among commentators. It is found in Be^{3} Ho wKt^{1} NKt^{4} Lo^{2} Lo^{4} Lo^{5} GMd^{1} TMd^{4} NNg oOr sOx^{1} Ox^{2} Ox^{3} Pu^{3} Pu^{5} sPu^{6} Pu^{7} Pu^{8} Tj^{1} Tr^{2} [*Jolly* M G Nd] *Me Nā Rc Lakṣ Jolly Jha Dave*.

CHAPTER FIVE

5.11a The reading adopted, *kravyādaḥ*, with the consonant ending is the *lectio difficilior* and is found in Be^{3} BCa NKt^{4} BKt^{5} La^{1} Lo^{2} GMd^{1} GMd^{5} sOx^{1} Ox^{3} sPu^{6} Pu^{10} Tr^{1} Wa [*Jolly* M N Nd] *Hem Jha Dave*. This reading is supported by *Me Nā* and *Nd*. The alternate reading with the thematic ending, *kravyādān*, appears to have the support of *Ku, Rn* and *Rc*, although all give the nominative *kravyādāḥ* and we cannot trust the editions to be accurate here and the reading could as well be *kravyādaḥ*. The mss. that have the reading *kravyāda* may also support the reading adopted, because it is common to drop the *visarga* before a sibilant. It could also be the thematic stem form, however, compounding with *śakunīn*.

5.12c The two readings, *rajjuvālaṃ* and *rajjudālaṃ*, have strong manuscript support. I have gone with the latter because it is found in almost all NT-x mss., as well as in *ViDh* 51.29 and *YDh* 1.174. The former, nevertheless, has strong support and is found in almost all ST mss. The reading is clearly uncertain. The reading adopted is found in Be^{1} (*mc to*) Be^{3} Bo Ho Jo^{2} NKt^{4} BKt^{5} La^{2} Lo^{1} Lo^{4} NNg Ox^{3} NPu^{1} Pu^{2} Pu^{3} Pu^{4} Pu^{5} Pu^{7} Pu^{10} Tj^{2} Wa [*Jolly* M G N R] *Dev Jolly*. According to the printed editions, *Me, Go, Nā, Ku, Rc,* and *Mr* have *rajjuvālaṃ*, although such readings are not very trustworthy. My mss. of *Me*, for example, have the reading *rajjudālaṃ* in the commentary. Further, an animal name such as this may have had several regional variations.

5.16c-d In *pādas* c-d, most mss. give the accusative plural. This causes a problem of syntax. We have to either understand a finite verb or connect these accusatives with *na bhakṣayet* that begins the next verse. The latter alternative is given only by *Nd* and is unlikely, because verse 16 is meant to give exceptions to the blanket prohibition of fish in verse 14. The former is given by *Rc*. The best alternative, I think, is to take the words in *pādas* c-d as nominative, which is the reading of most commentators: *Me, Go, Nā, Ku, Rn,* and *Mr*. Although still problematic, then we can extend the past participle *ādyau* in the dual to these *pādas* by understanding it as plural, which appears to be the solution of the commentators. Although the edition has the accusatives, *Hem* also appears to read nominatives, because of his comment: *rājīvādyāḥ sarvaśo 'niyuktenāpi bhakṣyāḥ*. A similar explanation is given by *Dev*. The reading adopted is found in Jo^{2} Lo^{5} NNg NPu^{1} Pu^{5} Pu^{7} Wa [*Jolly* G] *Vij Dev*, while TMd^{3} has the nominatives in all but the first (*rājīvāṃ*), and MTr^{4} MTr^{6} have the nominative *siṃhatuṇḍāś ca*.

5.23c The reading *ṛṣiyajñeṣu* has the support of *Me, Nā, Ku, Rn,* and *Mr;* others do not comment. It is clearly the *lectio difficilior;* the change from *purāṇeṣv ṛṣi* to *purāṇeṣv api* requires only a slight emendation. The reading adopted is found in BBe^{2} Be^{3} Bo BCa Hy Jo^{2} wKt^{3} Lo^{2} Lo^{3} GMd^{1} TMd^{3} GMd^{5} NNg sOx^{1} Ox^{2} Ox^{3} Pu^{5} sPu^{6} Pu^{7} Pu^{8} Pu^{10} Tr^{1} MTr^{4} *Me Nā Ku Rn Mr Dave Jha Mandlik*. Quite surprisingly, Jolly adopts the alternate reading without giving any variants.

5.28c Both readings, *sthāvaraṃ jaṅgamam* and *jaṅgamaṃ sthāvaram*, have strong manuscript support. The word order of the reading adopted is supported by *Me, Rc*, and *Mr*, and it is found in Be^{3} Bo Hy Jm Jo^{1} Kt^{2} La^{1} Lo^{2} GMd^{1} GMd^{5} GMy NNg sOx^{1} Ox^{3} sPu^{6} Tj^{1} Tj^{2} Tr^{1} Tr^{2} MTr^{3} MTr^{4} MTr^{6}, as also in all the editions. Although the original reading is uncertain, my selection is influenced by the near unanimous reading of the ST mss.

5.33d The past participle *pretaḥ*, which I have adopted, is supported by *Me, Go*, and *Ku*. It is found in Be^{1} Lo^{1} Lo^{2} TMd^{3} GMd^{5} GMy NNg sOx^{1} Ox^{3} Pu^{5} sPu^{6} Pu^{7} Pu^{10} Tr^{1} MTr^{4} Wa [*Jolly* M G Nd] *Me Jolly Jha Dave*.

5.37d The reading adopted, *kathaṃcana*, is found in Be^{3} Bo Ho Jo^{2} Lo^{1} Lo^{3} GMd^{1} TMd^{3} TMd^{4} GMd^{5} GMy NNg Pu^{2} Pu^{3} Pu^{4} Pu^{8} Tj^{1} Tr^{1} MTr^{4} MTr^{6} [*Jolly* R Nd]*Lakṣ*.

5.38b The alternate reading, *tāvatkṛtvehe*, found in most ST mss. is probably derived from a different version of the verse found also in *ViDh* 51.60. In this version, *pāda*-d reads: *pretya ceha ca niṣkṛtim*. Thus, the object of the verb *prāpnoti* is *niṣkṛtim*. Then we can have the reading *kṛtvā iha* with the object *māraṇam*. The reading of the second half of the verse in the *MDh* makes it clear that the object of *prāpnoti* is *māraṇam*, making it certain that the reading should be *tāvatkṛtvo ha*.

5.50 It appears that some took this statement to be a negative one with reference to a persons who *does eat* meat, and not as a positive statement about someone who *does not eat* meat. Thus, *Lakṣ, Hem*, and several mss., especially ST ones, appear to read an *avagraha* before *priyatām*, thus making it a negative, and eliminate *na* in *pāda*-d.

5.61 Most mss. and commentators, as well as all editions, read here the two verses given in the critical apparatus. *Pādas* a-b of the first verse is clearly spurious. They are not commented by *Me* and *Go* and are absent in all ST mss. The citations by *Vij* 3.18, *Lakṣ* 10.17, and *Dev* 5.26 also omit these *pādas*. This causes the anomaly of a verse with six *pādas*. It is apparent that *pāda*-d of the first verse and *pāda*-a of the second verse are also later additions. The reading adopted in the critical edition follows BKt^{5} wKt^{6} Lo^{4} NNg Ox^{3} Pu^{5} Pu^{7} Pu^{9} [*Jolly* M G Gr] *Me Go*. Jolly also saw these *pādas* as spurious and placed them within brackets. He notes that the reading with a single verse is "probably the original reading." For further arguments in favor of the reading adopted in the critical edition, see the Introduction, pp. 44–46.

5.64a The alternate reading *rajanyāhnaiva caikena* has much to recommend it. All the ST mss. have it, as do the old NKt^{4}. It is also the *lectio difficilior* with the uncommon word *rajanī* for day. I have refrained from adopting it, however, because all the commentators (except for *Nd*), including *Me* and *Go*, have the other reading. Surprisingly, Jolly does not give any variants for this *pāda*.

5.64d All the editions have the reading *tryahād udakadāyinaḥ*, and Jolly does not record any variants here. The vast majority of the mss. and the citations, however, support the reading adopted, which is found in Be^{1} Be^{3} Bo Ho wKt^{3} BKt^{5} NKt^{4} La^{1} Lo^{1} Lo^{2} TMd^{3} TMd^{4} GMd^{5} GMy NNg sOx^{1} Ox^{2} Ox^{3} NPu^{1} Pu^{2} Pu^{3} Pu^{4} Pu^{5} sPu^{6} Pu^{7} Pu^{8} Pu^{9} Pu^{10} Tr^{1} Tr^{2} MTr^{4} MTr^{6} Wa *Vij Apa*.

5.65b All the editions have the participle *samācaran* in place of the finite verb; Jolly gives no variants. Within the syntax of the verse, the participle makes better sense, which also makes it the *lectio facilior*. The commentators *Me, Go, Nā, Ku*, and *Rn* imply a participle with their glosses *kurvan* and *kṛtvā*. However, it is unclear whether their root texts also had a participle or whether they were merely explaining the passage. The overwhelming majority of the mss., including all the ST ones, however has the reading adopted: Be^{1} Be^{3} wKt^{3} BKt^{5} wKt^{6} GMd^{1} TMd^{3} TMd^{4} GMd^{5} GMy NNg oOr sOx^{1} Ox^{2} NPu^{1} Pu^{2} Pu^{4} Pu^{5} sPu^{6} Pu^{7} Pu^{9} Tj^{1} Tj^{2} Tr^{1} Tr^{2} MTr^{4} MTr^{6} Wa *Vij Lakṣ Rc*. According to this reading, we have to understand either a correlative (*yaḥ* and *saḥ*) or a particle such as *yadi*.

5.65c The reading adopted, *pretāhāraiḥ*, is found in BBe^{2} Be^{3} BCa NKt^{4} BKt^{5} wKt^{6} La^{1} Lo^{2} Lo^{4} Lo^{5} GMd^{1} TMd^{3} GMd^{5} GMy NNg sOx^{1} Ox^{3} NPu^{1} Pu^{2} Pu^{3} Pu^{4} Pu^{5} sPu^{6} Pu^{7} Pu^{8} Pu^{9} Pu^{10} Tj^{1} Tj^{2} Tr^{1} MTr^{4} MTr^{6} *Vij Apa Dev Mādh Bh* (ad 11.197 in Derrett) *Jolly Jha*. Jolly gives no variants. It is unclear whether *āhāra* here is merely a variant of *hāra* found in the alternate reading. Devaṇṇabhaṭṭa in his gloss takes *āhāra* to mean food: *pretadravyopajīvinaḥ pretakuṭumbāntargatāḥ sapiṇḍā iti yāvat*. In any case, both forms imply a close relationship to the deceased and most commentators take the expression as referring to a *sapiṇḍa*.

5.67b All the editions read *viśuddhi*, and this reading appears to have the support of *Ku* and *Nd*. The vast majority of mss., including all the ST ones and the citations, however, support the negative *aśuddhi*, the reading adopted: Be^{1} Be^{3} Bo Ho Jo^{2} NKt^{4} BKt^{5} wKt^{6} Lo^{1} Lo^{3} TMd^{3} TMd^{4} GMy NNg sOx^{1} Ox^{2} Pu^{3} sPu^{6} Pu^{8} Tj^{1} Tr^{1} Tr^{2} MTr^{4} MTr^{6} *Vij Lakṣ*. This reading is also supported by GMd^{1} and Bo. Jolly, once again, gives no variants.

5.69b Even though all the editions read *na ca*, most mss. record the reading adopted: Be^{1} BBe^{2} BCa Jo^{2} wKt^{1} wKt^{3} NKt^{4} Lo^{1} Lo^{2} Lo^{3} TMd^{3} TMd^{4} GMy NNg oOr Ox^{2} NPu^{1} Pu^{5} Pu^{7} Pu^{8} Tj^{2} Tr^{1} Tr^{2} Wa [*Jolly* G] *Viś Vij Apa Dev Go Ku*. However, *Me* appears to support the reading with *ca*.

5.69d There are diverse readings for *kṣapeta* in the mss., and it is difficult to discern the original form. I have opted for the singular both because it is represented in the best mss. and because the singular is supported by *Me, Go, Ku,* and *Nd*. The reading adopted is found in: BCa NKt^{4} BKt^{5} Lo^{2} Ox^{3} sPu^{6} Pu^{10} MTr^{4} MTr^{6} [*Jolly* M$^{1\text{-}2\text{-}5\text{-}8\text{-}9}$; Me $^{1\text{-}2\text{-}5\text{-}8\text{-}9}$] *Dave Jha*. This reading, however, is quite uncertain. Mss. using the singular have other forms as well: *kṣapet tu, kṣapayet*. The final particle also has many variants: *tu, vā,* and *ca*. The reading adopted is found in: Be^{1} BBe^{2} Jo^{2} BKt^{5} wKt^{6} La^{1} Lo^{1} Lo^{2} Lo^{3} Lo^{4} Lo^{5} TMd^{3} TMd^{4} GMd^{5} GMy Ox^{2} Pu^{2} Pu^{8} Pu^{10} Tr^{1} Tr^{2} MTr^{4} MTr^{6} *Viś Vij Apa*.

5.82b All the editions read *sthitaḥ*. It has considerable manuscript support, and *Me* and *Ku* also have that reading, although we cannot trust the editions given the minor orthographic difference. I have adopted *sthitiḥ*, because the verb *syāt* would be somewhat superfluous with the participle *sthitaḥ*. The reading adopted is found in Be^{1} BBe^{2} Be^{3} Bo BCa Jm Jo^{2} BKt^{5} wKt^{6} Lo^{1} Lo^{3} Lo^{4} Lo^{5} GMd^{1} sOx^{1} sPu^{6} Tj^{1} Tj^{2} Tr^{2} MTr^{4} MTr^{6} Wa *Apa Rc Nd*.

5.108d The grammar of the verse with the *anuvṛtti* of *śudhyati* would require *dvijottamaḥ* to be in the singular. The mss. are divided. I have opted for the plural, first because it is the *lectio difficilior* (given the grammar of the verse); second because the plural is clearly the reading of both *Me* and *Go;* and third because a large plurality of the mss favor it. *Me* clearly states the plural: *tena dvijottamāḥ śuddhā bhavanti;* and *Go: brāhmaṇāś ca ṣaṣṭhādhyāyavakṣyamāṇena śudhyanti*. The singular is supported by *Nā Ku Rn*. The reading adopted in found in: Be^{1} BBe^{2} BCa Ho Jo^{2} wKt^{1} BKt^{5} wKt^{6} La^{1} Lo^{2} Lo^{3} TMd^{3} NNg oOr sOx^{1} Ox^{3} NPu^{1} Pu^{2} Pu^{3} Pu^{4} Pu^{5} sPu^{6} Pu^{7} Pu^{8} Pu^{10} Tj^{1} Tj^{2} MTr^{4} MTr^{6} Wa [*Jolly* M R] *Hem Me Go Jha Dave*, as well as in *ViDh* 22.91.

5.113a All the editions have the reading *apāṃ agneś ca.* The reading adopted is found in NKt^{4} La^{1} Lo^{4} Lo^{5} GMd^{1} GMd^{5} Ox^{3} NPu^{1} Pu^{10} Tr^{1} MTr^{4} MTr^{6} [*Jolly* M Gr] *Hem.* This reading is further supported by many other mss. that have variants of it and begin with *agneḥ.* Most commentators do not provide any clue as to the order of the two words. However, they refer to the vedic story about Agni copulating with water (Varuṇa) as the underlying myth behind Manu's statement. In the myth it is Agni who united with water, and having Agni first in this verse agrees with it.

5.118x The reading of the added verse is quite uncertain especially in *pāda*-a. For the most part I have followed the reading of the Malayalam mss., except that I have given the genitive plural conjecturally, following the majority of the mss. that have *śaucānām.*

5.122a The reading adopted, *-kāṣṭhāni,* is found in BCa wKt^{1} wKt^{3} NKt^{4} La^{1} Lo^{1} GMd^{1} TMd^{3} TMd^{4} GMd^{5} GMy oOr sOx^{1} Ox^{2} sPu^{6} Tr^{1} MTr^{4} MTr^{6} [*Jolly* Nd]. The commentators offer no help. The alternate reading has the strong support of NT mss. and is adopted by all editors. I have opted for the former because it is found in all the ST mss. with the support of several very old NT-x mss., including the old NKt^{4} and the Śāradā mss.

5.122b The reading adopted is found in Be^{1} BCa Ho wKt^{1} NKt^{4} BKt^{5} wKt^{6} La^{1} GMd^{1} TMd^{3} TMd^{4} GMd^{5} GMy NNg NPu^{1} Tr^{1} Tr^{2} MTr^{4} MTr^{6} Wa *Hem.* Again the commentators offer no help. All the editors have chosen the alternate reading, which is found in most NT mss. Once again my decision to go with the former is based on the fact that it is found in all ST mss. and several significant and old NT-x ones, including all three Old Nāgarī mss. and several Newari ones.

5.122x The verse excluded from the critical edition but included in all other editions is found in all but the following mss.: NKt^{4} BKt^{5} wKt^{6} [*but ma*] Lo^{4} Lo^{5} GMd^{1} TMd^{3} GMd^{5} GMy NNg Ox^{3} Pu^{10} Tr^{1} MTr^{4} MTr^{6} Wa [*Jolly* Nd]. The reasons for its exclusion are the following. At the manuscript level, it is omitted in all but one of the ST mss., as well in several NT-x ones, including the old NKt^{4}. It is not commented by *Me, Go, Nā, Nd,* and *Mr;* the only ones to comment on it are *Ku, Rn,* and *Rc.* The way this verse entered into the manuscript tradition is very clear. It is given at the very end of *Me*'s commentary on verse 122 with the introduction *yathoktam* and concluding with *iti,* clearly demarcating it as a citation. *Go* also gives it at the end of his commentary on verse 122 with the introduction *yathā ca vasiṣṭhaḥ* and concluding with *iti.* This verse is *VaDh* 3.59. Because the verse came at the very end of the commentary and right before the next *MDh* verse (124 in the critical edition), it was easy for copyists to mistake it for a verse of the *MDh.* In order to preserve the traditional verse numbering, I have eliminated the number 123 from my verse count. The inclusion of this verse in *MDh* mss. must have occurred early, because it is cited as a verse of Manu by both *Vij* and *Apa.*

5.137d I have opted for the reading *ca,* because most ST and NY-x mss. have this reading: Be^{1} Be^{3} Bo BCa Ho wKt^{3} La^{1} Lo^{2} Lo^{4} Lo^{5} TMd^{3} TMd^{4} oOr sOx^{1} Ox^{3} NPu^{1} Pu^{2} Pu^{5} sPu^{6} Pu^{7} Pu^{9} Pu^{10} Tj^{1} Tr^{2} MTr^{3} MTr^{4} MTr^{6} Wa [*Jolly* M] *Vij ApaDev.* The reading, however, is uncertain.

5.138a Here also I have opted for *ca* for the same reasons as in 137d. The adopted reading is found in: Be^{1} BBe^{2} Bo BCa wKt^{1} wKt^{3} NKt^{4} BKt^{5} wKt^{6} La^{1} Lo^{1} Lo^{2} Lo^{3} Lo^{4} Lo^{5} GMd^{1} GMd^{5} NNg oOr sOx^{1} Ox^{2} NPu^{1} Pu^{2} Pu^{3} Pu^{4} Pu^{5} sPu^{6} Pu^{7} Pu^{8} Pu^{9} Pu^{10} Tj^{1} Tr^{1} Wa [*Jolly* G] *Hem Me.*

5.139d The mss. have widely different readings of this *pāda.* Along with Jolly, I have opted for the neuter *strīśūdram* as a collective Dvandva; this is the *lectio difficilior.* It is supported by *Go* and *Nā*. Obviously the scribes had difficulty with this formation. The ST mss. along with the Śāradā and *Nd* have resolved the difficulty by using the dual. Others have split the compound into two nominatives: *strī* and *śūdraḥ*, many adding *ca* to connect the two. The reading adopted is found in: NKt^{4} NNg oOr Ox^{2} Lo^{2} Ox^{3} Pu^{10} [*Jolly* M$^{1-2-5-9}$] *Jolly*.

5.145b The reading adopted is found in Bo NKt^{4} Lo^{1} TMd^{3} GMd^{5} GMy NNg NPu^{1} Pu^{2} Pu^{4} Tj^{1} Tr^{1} Tr^{2} MTr^{4} MTr^{6} *Vij* 1.196 *Mādh* 1.224. I have opted for this reading, because it is found all the ST mss. and in several significant NT-x ones, including the three in Old Nāgarī, NKt^{4} NNg NPu^{1}. The reading, however, is uncertain.

5.146d I have adopted the singular *dharmam*, which is found in BBe^{2} Bo wKt^{1} NKt^{4} BKt^{5} wKt^{6} Lo^{2} Lo^{3} GMd^{5} GMy NNg oOr Ox^{2} Ox^{3} Tj^{1} Tr^{1} Tr^{2} MTr^{4} MTr^{6} [*Jolly* M$^{1-2-5-8-9}$ Me R Ku Nd] *Jolly*. This reading is found in some form in all the ST mss., as well as in several significant NT-x mss including the Old Nāgarī ones. The reading, once again, is uncertain. *Me* and *Go* appear to support the plural, whereas *Nā, Ku,* and *Rn* support the singular, although all these are glosses, and it is unclear what the readings of their root texts were.

5.150b I have adopted the singular reading *gṛhakārye ca*, which is supported by *Me, Go,* and *Ku*. Others do not comment. The reading adopted is found in Be^{1} BBe^{2} Be^{3} Bo BCa Ho wKt^{3} NKt^{4} BKt^{5} wKt^{6} La^{1} La^{2} Lo^{4} Lo^{5} GMd^{1} TMd^{4} GMy NNg oOr sOx^{1} Ox^{2} NPu^{1} Pu^{2} Pu^{4} Pu^{5} sPu^{6} Pu^{7} Pu^{8} Pu^{9} Pu^{10} Tj^{1} Tr^{1} MTr^{6} Wa [*Jolly* G] *Lakṣ Jha Dave.*

5.152d Several important mss., including most ST ones, have the reading *svāmi* in place of *svāmya*. I have, however, opted for the latter; it is the preferred reading of all the commentators and is clearly the *lectio difficilior*.

5.155b The support for both readings, *upoṣaṇam* and *upoṣitam*, is strong. I have opted for the former, which is found in Be^{3} wKt^{1} La^{2} Lo^{1} Lo^{3} TMd^{3} TMd^{4} GMd^{5} GMy sOx^{1} Ox^{2} NPu^{1} Pu^{2} Pu^{3} Pu^{5} sPu^{6} [*cor to*] Pu^{7} Pu^{8} Tr^{1} Tr^{2} MTr^{4} MTr^{6} [*Jolly* G R Nd N] *Lakṣ Hem Dev Nā Mandlik Jolly KSS Dave*. This reading has the support of all but one ST mss. The alternate reading is found in *Me* and *Rn;* most commentators simply gloss *upavāsam*, making it difficult to know the reading of their root text.

5.161d Although most mss. support the reading adopted, several commentators appear to presuppose the alternate reading *paralokāt*. This reading appears to be presupposed by *Me*'s gloss: *svargaṃ na prāpnoti*, and possibly also by *Go*'s gloss: *bhartrā sahārjitaṃ svargādilokaṃ na prāpnoti*. See the parallel at 5.166d.

5.163c The reading adopted has the overwhelming support of ST and NT-x mss. and is found in: BBe^{2} Be^{3} Bo Ho Jo^{2} wKt^{1} NKt^{4} BKt^{5} wKt^{6} Lo^{2} Lo^{3} Lo^{4} Lo^{5} GMd^{1} TMd^{3} TMd^{4} GMd^{5} GMy NNg oOr sOx^{1} Ox^{3} NPu^{1} Pu^{2} Pu^{3} Pu^{4} Pu^{5} sPu^{6} Pu^{7} Pu^{8} Pu^{9} Pu^{10} Tj^{1} Tr^{1} Tr^{2} MTr^{4} MTr^{6} [*Jolly* M R Nd] Wa *Lakṣ Mādh*. All the editions, however, adopt the alternate reading, probably because it restores the regular meter.

5.164a It is difficult to decide on the alternate spellings of *sṛgāla* and *śṛgāla*. See 9.30, 11.200 for similar confusion in the mss. I have adopted the former, which is found in: Be^{1} GMd^{1} TMd^{3} TMd^{4} GMd^{5} GMy sOx^{1} Pu^{3} Pu^{5} sPu^{6} Pu^{7} Pu^{9} Tj^{1} Tr^{1} MTr^{6} *Jolly*.

5.164c Although the alternate reading *prāpnoti* has considerable manuscript support, I think that the correct reading is *cāpnoti*, both because it provides a better sense and because it is the reading of most mss. in the parallel verse at 9.30.

5.166–7 These two verses are omitted in the mss. containing *Me*'s commentary. Jolly comments that they are superfluous, because they are also found at 9.29–30. They are, however, found in all other mss., including those of the ST. Medhātithi himself comments: *strīdharmopasaṃhāraślokā ṛjavaś ca strīdharmā ity ato mayātra vyākhyānādaraḥ kṛtaḥ*. It appears, then, that these verses were known to *Me*, although he did not think it necessary to comment on them.

CHAPTER SIX

6.4c The reading *niṣkramya* is found in all the ST mss., as well as in several NT-x ones, especially those containing the commentary of *Me*. Nevertheless, I have adopted the alternate reading found in most NT mss.; it is supported by the commentaries of *Go, Ku, Rn, Nd,* and *Rc*. The reading, however, is uncertain, with a third variant *nirgatya*.

6.7a I have adopted the reading *yadbhakṣaḥ* as a Bahuvrīhi. This is the reading in *Me* and *Go*, and it is also the *lectio difficilior* found in Ho NKt^{4} Lo^{4} Lo^{5} TMd^{3} GMy NNg NPu^{1} Pu^{2} Pu^{3} Pu^{4} Pu^{5} Pu^{7} Pu^{10} Tj^{1} Tr^{1} MTr^{4} MTr^{6} [*Jolly* M G Nd] *Me Go Dave Jha*. This reading is further supported by mss. that read *yadbhaikṣyaḥ*, as well as by those that read either *yadbhakṣa* or *yadbhaikṣa*, because manuscripts frequently drop the *visarga* before a sibilant. With regard to two correlatives, where the relative pronoun in the subordinate clause is within a compound, see Wackernagel II, 1: 32–3.

6.10c Many mss. have the reading *uttarāyaṇaṃ* in place of *turāyaṇaṃ*. That is clearly a mistake; possibly a commentarial gloss was taken over into the text. With this reading the *pāda* does not scan. The reading adopted is supported by *Me, Sn, Ku, Rn,* and *Nd*. The only commentators who appear to support the alternate reading are *Go* and *Mr*.

6.12a The mss. are divided over the readings *tu* and *ca*. I have opted for the latter, which is found in Be^{1} Bo BCa Jo^{2} WKt^{1} NKt^{4} La^{1} La^{2} Lo^{3} GMd^{1} TMd^{3} GMd^{5} GMy NNg Pu^{5} Pu^{7} Tj^{2} Tr^{1} Tr^{2} MTr^{4} MTr^{6} Wa [*Jolly* M$^{1-2-5-8-9}$ G Nd R] *Go Vij Lakṣ Jolly*. This reading is supported by most ST mss., as well as significant NT-x ones, including the old NKt^{4} and NNg. The commentators are silent, except for *Rc*, who clearly has the reading adopted and glosses: *ca punaḥ*.

6.16d The reading adopted, *puṣpāṇi*, has the support of all but one of the ST mss., as well as of many NT-x ones, including the old NKt^{4}. This reading is also supported by *Me, Go,* and *Rn*, whereas the alternate reading is given only by *Ku* and possibly by *Rn*, who says: *puṣpāṇīti medhātithiḥ*, indicating that he read otherwise. The adopted reading is found in: Be^{1} BBe^{2} Ho NKt^{4} BKt^{5} WKt^{6} Lo^{2} Lo^{4} Lo^{5} GMd^{1} TMd^{3} TMd^{4} GMd^{5} GMy Ox^{3} NPu^{1} Pu^{2} Pu^{4} Pu^{5} Pu^{7} Pu^{10} Tr^{2} MTr^{4} MTr^{6} Wa [*Jolly* M G Gr Nd] *Lakṣ Me Go Jolly*.

6.17d The reading *dantolūkhalikas tathā* has the support of the vast majority of NT-x mss. The commentators are silent on this reading. I have adopted the alternate reading, because it is found in all the ST and NT-y mss., as well as in a substantive minority of NT-x ones. The adopted reading is found in: BBe^{2} Bo BCa Ho Hy Jm Jo^{1} WKt^{1} WKt^{3} La^{2} Lo^{3} Lo^{5} GMd^{1} TMd^{3} TMd^{4} GMd^{5} GMy OOr Ox^{2} Pu^{2} Pu^{3} Pu^{4} Pu^{8} Tj^{2} Tr^{1} MTr^{3} MTr^{4} MTr^{6}.

6.19a The reading adopted, *vānnaṃ*, has the support of all ST mss. and numerous NT ones, including the old nKt^{4} and nNg. It is found in bBe^{2} Be^{3} bCa Hy nKt^{4} bKt^{5} Lo^{4} gMd^{1} tMd^{3} tMd^{4} gMd^{5} gMy nNg Ox^{2} nPu^{1} Tj^{1} Tr^{1} mTr^{4} mTr^{6} [*Jolly* M Nd] *Vij Jolly*.

6.25a The manuscripts are divided here with several readings: *cātmani, tvātmani, svātmani,* and simply *ātmani*. In this case, most ST mss. go with the NT-x vulgate. The commentators are silent. It is evident that some cluster of consonants preceded *ātmani;* thus the vulgate reading is erroneous. The reading I have adopted is found in: Be^{1} bBe^{2} Bo bCa Jo^{2} wKt^{3} bKt^{5} wKt^{6} La^{1} La^{2} Lo^{2} Lo^{3} Lo^{4} Lo^{5} nNg Ox^{2} Ox^{3} Pu^{5} Pu^{7} Pu^{9} Pu^{10} Tr^{2} Wa [*Jolly* M G] *Jolly*.

6.27b There is strong support for both readings: *ācaret* and *āharet*. The latter is given in all the editions. It also appears to be the readings of *Me, Go,* and *Ku*. However, these commentators give the persons from whom one begs in the ablative: e.g. *tāpasebhyaḥ, gṛhamedhibhyo vanavāsibhyaḥ*. It could well be, therefore, that *āharet* in the commentaries is merely a gloss and not the root. However, *āharet* is in one sense the *lectio difficilior*, because *bhaikṣam ācaret* is the more common expression. Nevertheless, I have opted for *ācaret*, because it is found in almost all ST mss. and a substantial number of NT ones: wKt^{1} La^{1} Lo^{3} gMd^{1} tMd^{3} gMd^{5} gMy nNg [*but mc*] sOx^{1} sPu^{6} Tj^{1} Tj^{2} Tr^{1} mTr^{3} mTr^{4} mTr^{6} [*Jolly* R Nd Gr] *Apa*. Further, *ācaret* is grammatically better with the locatives then *āharet*. The reading, however, is less than certain.

6.29d The two alternate readings have strong manuscript support. I have, however, opted for *saṃsiddaye*, because it is clearly supported by *Me, Nā, Ku,* and *Mr*. It is found in: bBe^{2} Be^{3} Bo Ho Hy Jm wKt^{1} Kt^{2} wKt^{3} nKt^{4} La^{1} [*but cor fh*] La^{2} Lo^{1} Lo^{2} Lo^{3} Lo^{4} Lo^{5} gMd^{1} tMd^{4} nNg nPu^{1} Pu^{2} Pu^{3} Pu^{4} Pu^{8} Pu^{10} Tj^{1} Tj^{2} mTr^{3} Wa *Vij Apa* and all the editions.

6.37b The mss. give three readings: *ātmajān, prajām,* and *sutān*. The commentators are silent on this word. I have adopted *ātmajān* because it is found in all but one ST mss. and in several NT-x ones, including the old nKt^{4} and the Śāradā mss. The reading, however, remains uncertain. The reading adopted is found in: Ho nKt^{4} Lo^{1} tMd^{3} tMd^{4} gMd^{5} gMy nNg oOr sOx^{1} Pu^{3} sPu^{6} Pu^{8} Tr^{1} Tr^{2} mTr^{4} mTr^{6} [*Jolly* Nd] *Lakṣ Mādh*.

6.43c The reading adopted, *asaṃcayikaḥ*, is attested in all the ST mss., as well as in a large number of NT-x ones and in the citations: Be^{1} nKt^{4} La^{1} Lo^{1} Lo^{2} gMd^{1} tMd^{3} tMd^{4} gMd^{5} gMy oOr sOx^{1} Ox^{2} Ox^{3} Pu^{2} Pu^{3} Pu^{4} sPu^{6} Pu^{8} Tj^{1} Tr^{1} Tr^{2} mTr^{4} mTr^{5} mTr^{6} Wa [*Jolly* N Nd Ku vl] *Rc Bh Lakṣ Apa*. This reading is supported also by *Bh, Nā,* and *Rc*. In addition, *Me* remarks that the alternate reading is preferred by some: *anye tv asaṃkusuka iti paṭhanti*, and gives the meaning of this unusual term. It is clear this was not *Me*'s own reading, which must have been *asaṃcayikaḥ*. The meaning of this word was so obvious that *Me* did not think it necessary to comment. *Rn*, likewise, ascribes the alternate reading to others: *kvacid saṃkusuka iti pāṭhaḥ*. Only *Go, Ku,* and *Mr* give the alternate reading; *Kū* gives the reading adopted as an alternate reading: *asāṃcayika ity anye paṭhante*. Even though I have adopted *asaṃcayika*, the alternate reading is clearly the *lectio difficilior*. It is easier to explain how the unusual *asaṃkusuka* was changed to the clear *asaṃcayika* than the other way round. Nevertheless, in this instance I think the manuscript and commentarial evidence outweighs the latter criterion.

6.43d The alternate reading has the unanimous support of all ST mss., plus several NY-x ones. Nevertheless, I think this is a later emendation from the more difficult *bhāvasamāhitaḥ*. This reading is given and explained by all the commentators, except *Nd;* both *Bh* and *Me* have the reading adopted.

6.45d The mss. are divided over the two readings *nirveśa* and *nirdeśa* (or *nideśa*). Only *Nā* clearly reads *nirdeśa* with the gloss *ājñā;* but he gives *nirveśa* as a *pāṭha*. All others, explain the word as *bhṛti* ("wages"), which would presuppose *nirveśa*. The old Kashmiri com. attached to sPu^{6} also contain the gloss *dhanakālam bhṛter upabhoga-kālam ity arthaḥ*. The reading *nirveśa* is attested in all but one of the ST mss. It is found in: Ho Lo^{2} Lo^{4} Lo^{5} GMd^{1} TMd^{4} GMd^{5} GMy Ox^{3} Pu^{2} Pu^{4} sPu^{6} [*cor to*] Pu^{10} Tr^{1} MTr^{4} MTr^{5}MTr^{6} [*Jolly* M] *Apa Me Jolly Bühler Jha*. See the parallel verse in *MBh* 12.237.15, where the Poona edition has *nideśam*, but it is given as doubtful; the Southern Recension of Telugu, Grantha, and Malayalam mss. all have *nirveśa*.

6.57b Even though all ST mss., except significantly MTr^{5} with Bhāruci's commentary, support the vulgate reading, I have adopted the alternate reading with the nominative *lābhaś cainam*. The latter is the *lectio difficilior*, because *lābhe* here may have been influenced by *alābhe* at the opening of *pāda*-b. The nominative also agrees better with the causative *harṣayet*, although dictionaries give also a non-causative meaning for it possibly depending on this verse of the *MDh*. The reading adopted is found in: Be^{1} Bo Jo^{2} wKt^{3} NKt^{4} La^{1} Lo^{4} Lo^{5} oOr sOx^{1} Ox^{3} NPu^{1} Pu^{2} Pu^{4} Pu^{5} Pu^{7} Pu^{9} Pu^{10} MTr^{5} Wa [*Jolly* M R] *Apa Go Rn Jolly*. It is also supported by the parallel reading in Be^{3} Lo^{1} sOx^{1} sPu^{6} Tj^{1}. The parallel verse in *MBh* 12.269.10 also has the reading adopted; and the editors do not give any variants for this *pāda*. Although Führer's edition of *VaDh* 10.22 reads *lābhe caiva* (which I followed in Olivelle 2000), I now think that the alternate reading *lābhaś cainam* found in the Ānandāśrama Sanskrit Series (48) Edition and some mss. (see my note to this verse) is preferable.

6.62b All the editions follow the alternative reading *saṃyogaṃ ca*. The commentators offer no help. I have adopted *saṃprayogam*, which parallels *viprayogam* of *pāda*-a, because it is found in all the ST mss., as well as several NT-x ones, including the old NKt^{4} and NNg. This reading is found in: Bo Jo^{2} wKt^{3} NKt^{4} Lo^{2} Lo^{3} Ox^{2} GMd^{1} TMd^{3} TMd^{4} GMd^{5} GMy NNg oOr NPu^{1} Pu^{4} Tj^{1} Tr^{1} MTr^{5} MTr^{4} MTr^{6} [*Jolly* Nd] *Apa*.

6.66a The reading adopted, *bhūṣito*, is attested in most NT-x mss., as well as a couple ST ones. It is also supported by the glosses of *Me* and *Nā*. This reading is found in: Be^{1} Be^{3} (*but cor sh*) Bo Ho wKt^{1} wKt^{3} NKt^{4} BKt^{5} wKt^{6} La^{1} La^{2} Lo^{1} Lo^{2} Lo^{4} Lo^{5} GMd^{1} TMd^{4} NNg oOr sOx^{1} Ox^{2} Ox^{3} NPu^{1} Pu^{2} Pu^{4} Pu^{5} sPu^{6} Pu^{7} Pu^{8} Pu^{9} Pu^{10} Tj^{1} Tj^{2} Wa [*Jolly* M G N] *Me Go Nā Dave Jha Jolly*.

6.66b The two alternative readings, *vasan* and *rataḥ*, have strong manuscript support. The commentators are by and large silent on this word, except for *Go* and *Ku*, and their gloss *sthitaḥ* appears to support the former. I have also gone with the former, because it is found in all but two ST mss., as well as in many NT-x ones and in the citations. It is found in: BBe^{2} Be^{3} Jo^{2} wKt^{1} La^{1} [*cor to sh*] Lo^{2} Lo^{3} TMd^{3} GMd^{5} GMy oOr sOx^{1} Ox^{2} Pu^{3} Pu^{5} sPu^{6} [*but cor*] Pu^{7} Pu^{9} Tj^{1} Tr^{1} MTr^{4} MTr^{6} [*Jolly* M^{1-2-9} G R Ku Nd] *Go Vij Apa*.

6.76a It is very difficult to choose between the two readings: *snāyubaddham* and *snāyu-yutam*. The latter appears to be the *lectio difficilior*, and it violates the meter; the Śloka does not permit short the sixth and seventh syllables. The parallel in *MBh* 12.316.42 also has this reading, although Telugu and Grantha mss. have the alternate reading. Nevertheless, I have adopted the former, principally because it is found in all the ST mss. and is presupposed by the glosses of *Me, Go,* and *Ku*. Even though *Me*'s comment *snāyunā baddham* may be simply a gloss on *yutam*, yet the parallel comment on *pāda*-c *dehacarmaṇā avanaddhaṃ* indicates that *Me* probably read *baddham*. The reading adopted is found in: Be^{1} Jo^{2} GMd^{1} TMd^{4} GMd^{5} GMy sOx^{1} Ox^{2} Pu^{5} sPu^{6} Pu^{7} Pu^{9} Tr^{1} Tr^{2} MTr^{4} MTr^{5}, and also supported by the variant in TMd^{3} MTr^{6}.

6.92c There is strong support for the alternate reading *hrīr vidyā* especially by the ST mss. and several commentators. Nevertheless, I think the correct reading is *dhīr vidyā*, because it is presupposed by the glosses of both *Bh* and *Me* and has the broadest manuscript support.

6.93a There are several variant readings of this *pāda* caused, I believe, by the fact that in the original reading the *pāda* is hypermetric. The most common correction is *daśalakṣaṇakaṃ dharmam*, which is the *lectio facilior* and influenced by the reading of *pāda*-a in the preceding and following verses. It is hard to see how such a reading would have been changed into the hypermetric *daśalakṣaṇāni dharmasya*. The other attempt at correction kept the plural and the genitive in place but changed *lakṣaṇāni* to *cihnāni*, thus restoring the meter. Two scribes appear to have restored the meter simply by omitting the plural ending and using *daśalakṣaṇa*, creating a grammatically impossible formation. The three mss. of *Go*, Pu^{5} Pu^{7} Pu^{9}, show the confusion created by the two readings; the scribes give both readings almost superimposed on each other: *daśalakṣaṇāni dharmasya ṇikaṃ dharmaṃ*. The scribe of Pu^{7} attempted to improve on this without much success: *daśalakaṇikaṃ dharmasya*, with a marginal notation giving the *pāṭha*: *lakṣaṇāni dharmasya*. The reading adopted is found in: BBe^{2} Ho Hy Jm Jo^{1} wKt^{1} Kt^{2} wKt^{3} BKt^{5} wKt^{6} Lo^{2} GMd^{1} TMd^{4} GMd^{5} NNg sOx^{1} NPu^{1} sPu^{6} Tj^{1} Tj^{2} MTr^{3} MTr^{4} MTr^{5}. The reading is supported by the glosses of *Go* and *Ku;* others are silent.

6.94c It is surprising that all editors, including Jolly, have adopted the singular *vedāntam* when the overwhelming manuscript evidence and the commentators support the plural. The glosses of *Me, Go, Nā,* and *Rn* presuppose the plural. The reading adopted is found in: Be^{1} BBe^{2} Bo BCa Ho Jo^{2} wKt^{3} NKt^{4} wKt^{6} La^{2} Lo^{1} Lo^{2} Lo^{3} Lo^{4} Lo^{5} TMd^{4} GMd^{5} NNg oOr Ox^{2} Ox^{3} NPu^{1} Pu^{2} Pu^{3} Pu^{4} Pu^{5} Pu^{7} Pu^{8} Pu^{9} Pu^{10} Tj^{1} Tr^{1} MTr^{4} MTr^{5} Wa [*Jolly* M] *Lakṣ*.

6.95c This is one instance that I have rejected the reading supported by a majority of the mss., including ST ones. I have adopted the present participle *abhyasyan* in preference to the gerund *abhyasya*. It makes better sense in the context and has the support of most commentators: *Me, Go, Nā,* and *Nd*. It appears that the source *Me* was using had the reading *abhyasya*. His gloss indicates that his preference was for the participle: *abhyasyann iti śatṛpratyayāntapāṭho vā*. Jha also interprets *vā* here as indicating *Me*'s preference. The reading adopted is found in: Jo^{2} Lo^{3} GMd^{5} oOr sOx^{1} Pu^{5} sPu^{6} Pu^{7} Pu^{8} Tj^{2} Tr^{1} [*Jolly* G N Nd R] *Jolly*.

CHAPTER SEVEN

7.6a The orthographic difference between *eva* and *eṣa*, especially in the northern scripts, is slight. Yet, I think the overwhelming manuscript evidence supports *eva*, even though all the editors opt for *eṣa*. Jolly gives no variants, and *Go* appears to support *eṣa*. The reading adopted is found in: Be^{1} Be^{3} Bo Ho wKt^{1} wKt^{3} NKt^{4} BKt^{5} wKt^{6} La^{2} Lo^{1} GMd^{1} TMd^{3} TMd^{4} GMy oOr sOx^{1} Ox^{2} Pu^{3} sPu^{6} Pu^{8} Tr^{1} Tr^{2} MTr^{3} MTr^{4} MTr^{5} MTr^{6} *Lakṣ Mādh*.

7.13b The reading *saṃvyavasyet* is attested in: Be^{3} BCa Hy Jo^{2} wKt^{1} wKt^{3} La^{1} Lo^{1} Lo^{2} Lo^{3} GMd^{5} GMy NNg sOx^{1} Ox^{2} NPu^{1} Pu^{2} Pu^{3} Pu^{4} sPu^{6} Pu^{8} Tj^{1} Tj^{2} Tr^{1} MTr^{4} MTr^{6} *Jolly*.

7.31c Three major readings are found in the mss.: (a) *daṇḍaḥ praṇayituṃ śakyaḥ*, (b) *daṇḍaḥ praṇetuṃ śakyas tu*, and (c) *praṇetuṃ śakyate daṇḍaḥ*. The second is a variant of the first and is found in all the ST mss. I have adopted the first, which is found in: BBe^{2} Ho Jo^{2} wKt^{1} wKt^{3} La^{1} Lo^{3} Lo^{4} NNg oOr sOx^{1} Ox^{3} NPu^{1} sPu^{6} Tj^{1} Tr^{2} MTr^{5} *Rc Lakṣ Jolly*.

7.32a There is strong manuscript support for both readings: *nyāyavṛttiḥ* and *nyāyavṛttaḥ*. I have adopted the former, however, because it is found in all the ST mss., as well as in many NT-x ones. The adopted reading is found in: Be^{1} wKt^{3} Lo^{4} Lo^{5} GMd^{1} TMd^{3} TMd^{4} GMd^{5} GMy NNg Ox^{3} Pu^{5} Pu^{7} Tr^{1} MTr^{4} Wa [*Jolly* M Me G Nd] *Lakṣ Me Jolly*. In his notes, Jolly indicates that this reading is found in *Me* and that the alternate reading is given as a *pāṭha* by *Me*. The editions of Jha and Dave give just the opposite. My own mss., however, support Jolly. The commentary of *Bh* also clearly supports *vṛttiḥ*, even though the root text gives *vṛttaḥ*.

7.54b The mss. are divided over the two readings *kulodgata* and *kulodbhava*, something encountered also at 7.62, 63, 141. In this verse, there is strong manuscript support for the latter reading also, but in the parallel verses the support is much less. I have opted for *kulodgata* in all the occurrences.

7.58c The mss. are divided over the readings *mantrayeta param* and *mantrayet paramam*. Although this verb generally takes the Ātmanepada, see the clearly Parasmaipada ending at 7.146. Commentators offer no help. *Me* has *param*, but it is unclear whether it is the root or a gloss. Although the reading is uncertain and editors have generally opted for the latter, I have gone with the former because it is found in the best and the widest array of mss., including most ST ones: Be^{1} wKt^{3} NKt^{4} BKt^{5} wKt^{6} La^{1} Lo^{1} Lo^{2} Lo^{4} Lo^{5} GMd^{1} TMd^{4} GMd^{5} NNg Ox^{3} NPu^{1} Pu^{2} Pu^{3} Pu^{4} Pu^{5} MTr^{5} Wa.

7.62ab There appears to be something amiss in this verse. See my note to the translation for a detailed analysis.

7.67d It is unclear whether the original reading in this *pāda* also was *kṛtyeṣu* as in *pāda*-a. It has the support of all the ST mss. and of several NT-x ones. I have decided to keep *bhṛtyeṣu* in this *pāda*, because of the broad manuscript support and because *kṛtyeṣu* here may have been influenced by the same word in *pāda*-a, and because the *ca* in this *pāda* calls for something different from *kṛtyeṣu*. The reading, however, is somewhat uncertain. See the note to the translation regarding the meaning of this verse.

7.70a, c In *pāda*-a the reading *ca* is found in: Be^{1} Bo BCa Ho Jo^{2} wKt^{3} La^{1} La^{2} Lo^{1} TMd^{3} GMd^{5} GMy Ox^{2} NPu^{1} Pu^{2} Pu^{3} Pu^{4} Pu^{5} Pu^{7} Tr^{1} Tr^{2} MTr^{4} MTr^{6} Wa *Viś* [*Jolly* G]; and in *pāda*-c it is found in: Be^{1} Bo BCa Ho Jo^{2} NKt^{4} BKt^{5} wKt^{6} La^{2} Lo^{1} Lo^{3} TMd^{3} GMy NNg sOx^{1} Ox^{2} Pu^{2} Pu^{4} Pu^{5} sPu^{6} Pu^{7} Tj^{1} Tr^{1} Tr^{2} MTr^{4} MTr^{6} Wa *Viś Vij Mādh*.

7.74d Even though all editions read *vidhīyate*, all the ST mss. and most NT ones record the reading *viśiṣyate*, which has been adopted. See the parallel use of *viśiṣyate* in verse 71. The use of this term is most appropriate if, as attested by several commentators, this verse is not a prescription of a fortress in general but a recommendation of a particular type of fortress, either one built with an earthen rampart [Bhāruci] or a hill fortress [Rāghavānanda]. See my comment in the note to the translation. The reading adopted is found in: Be^{3} Bo Ho Jm Jo^{2} wKt^{1} wKt^{3} La^{1} La^{2} Lo^{3} GMd^{1} TMd^{3} TMd^{4} GMd^{5} GMy oOr sOx^{1} Ox^{2} NPu^{1} Pu^{3} sPu^{6} Tj^{1} Tr^{1} Tr^{2} MTr^{4} MTr^{6} Wa [*Jolly* R Nd] *Lakṣ*.

7.85c I have constructed a conjectural reading for this *pāda*. I think the scribes and commentators tried to clarify and correct two problems with the original reading: the unusual word *prādhīta* and the final four syllables of the *pāda* which are all long and thus does not scan. For *prādhīta* there are two variants: *ācārya* and *śrotriya*. In the parallel passage of the *GDh* 5.20 the term is *śrotriya*. The term *ācārya* in this position is unlikely, both because Manu normally follows Gautama and because all the other terms indicate personal qualities rather than a relationship to the donor. I think *prādhīta* was the original in Manu, a term very rare and used only two other times in the Dharma literature, once in the *GDh* itself at 16.44 and once in *ViDh* 93.3, which is a citation of this very *pāda* and reads: *sahasraguṇaṃ prādhīte*, just as my conjectural reading. Another reason for the alterations may have been to restore the cadence to the *pāda*. This is especially true for the reading *prādhīte śatasāhasram*. Manu, however, has numerous verses which violate metrical principles, including hypermetric *pādas* (see Introduction, p. 37). Another reason favoring the conjectural reading is that all the other *pādas* open with a number, the second and third containing the word *guṇa* and bracketed by the first and the last having *sama* and *ananta*. The reading *ācārya* is supported by *Me* and *Nā*, and *prādhīte* by *Go*, *Ku*, and *Mr*. The reading *sahasraguṇam* has the support of *Nā*, all ST mss. and a substantial number of NT-x ones, whereas *Go* and *Ku* support *śatasāhasram*.

7.86b Even though a large group of mss. have the reading *tathaiva*, nevertheless it is evident that the correct reading should be the instrumental *śraddadhānatayaiva* paralleling *viśeṣeṇa* of *pāda*-a. The former is also the *lectio facilior*, and it is easy in the northern scripts to mistake *tha* for *ya*. The reading adopted is found in: BBe^{2} BCa Hy Jo^{1} Jo^{2} wKt^{1} Kt^{2} wKt^{3} NKt^{4} La^{1} Lo^{1} Lo^{2} Lo^{3} Lo^{4} Lo^{5} GMd^{1} TMd^{4} GMd^{5} sOx^{1} Ox^{2} sPu^{6} Tj^{2} Tr^{1} MTr^{3} MTr^{4} MTr^{5} MTr^{6} Wa.

7.86x The additional verse *deśe kāle* is accepted as part of the *MDh* by Jha and given within brackets after verse 85 by Jolly. It is clearly a spurious verse recorded in only three mss. Its claim to authenticity is the fact that *Me* comments on it. However, it appears that this verse is actually a citation by *Me* in his commentary on verse 86. This is demonstrated by the fact that, after he comments on this additional verse, *Me* returns to his commentary on 86 and completes it with his comments on the word *pretya*. Nowhere else does *Me* return to the previous verse after commenting on a subsequent verse of the *MDh*. Thus, the added verse must be an extraneous verse cited by *Me* in his elucidation of verse 86.

7.97a The reading here is uncertain. I have opted for *rājñe*, because it is attested in the best mss., including all but two of the ST and the old NKt^{4} and NNg. Further, the dative is supported by *Me*, *Go*, and *Ku*.

7.101c Scharfe (1993, 47, n. 20) suggests reading *buddhyā* for *vṛddhyā*. Although this reading is appealing, eliminating as it does the tautology (*vardhayed vṛddhyā*), it is found in very few mss. The reading *vṛddhyā* appears also to be the *lectio difficilior* because the commentators had to explain it. Bhāruci, for example, says: *atra vṛddhyartham upāyo vṛddhiśabdenocyate, prakaraṇasāmarthyāt*.

7.101d Even though all the editions have the reading *pātreṣu nikṣipet* (same as *pāda*-d of 99), the overwhelming majority of the mss. records the reading *dānena*, which I have adopted: BBe^{2} Be^{3} Bo BCa Jo^{1} Jo^{2} Ho Hy wKt^{1} Kt^{2} wKt^{3} NKt^{4} BKt^{5} wKt^{6} La^{1} Lo^{3} GMd^{1} TMd^{3} TMd^{4} GMd^{5} oOr Pu^{8} Tj^{1} Tj^{2} Tr^{1} MTr^{3} MTr^{4} MTr^{6} [*Jolly* M^{8}] *Mr*. I also think that this was the reading of most commentators. Bhāruci, for example, glosses: *dānena pātreṣu nikṣipet*. Here Derrett has taken *pātreṣu* as the root (so also the root in MTr^{5}), but I think Bhāruci saw *dānena* as the root and gave *pātreṣu* as a gloss because the object of the giving is left unstated in the root. At 99, for example, Bhāruci did not feel the need for a gloss because there the root was *pātreṣu*. Likewise, Kullūka: *vṛddhaṃ śāstrīyavibhāgena pātrebhyo dadyāt*. Here *śāstrīyavibhāgena* appears to gloss *dānena* with the addition, once again, of the object of the giving with *pātrebhyaḥ*. Kullūka also did not feel the need for such an explanation at 99 where the root is *pātreṣu*.

7.106 The vast majority of the mss., including several ST ones, transpose *pāda*-b and *pāda*-d. This order is supported by *Nā, Ku, Rn, Rd,* and *Rc*, and found also in the parallel verse of the *MBh* 12.138.25; the critical edition notes no variants, indicating that the *MBh* and the *MDh* traditions diverge markedly on this point. The commentators are of immense help here. All the ancient one—*Bh, Me,* and *Go*—support the order I have adopted, which is also found in the following mss.: Lo^{4} Lo^{5} GMd^{1} TMd^{3} TMd^{4} GMy Ox^{3} Pu^{2} Pu^{4} Pu^{5} Pu^{7} MTr^{5} MTr^{4} MTr^{6}. Note that most ST mss. and the ones with Medhātithi's commentary follow the order I have adopted. I think that this order also makes better sense. Running away goes well with the brooding mentioned in the first line, and attacking like a lion fits the tearing to pieces like a wolf in the second line.

7.114d All the NT mss., as well as two ST ones, read *saṃgram* in place of *guptaye*. I have conjecturally adopted the latter, a reading found in most ST mss. This also appears to have been the reading of *Bh*, who, in commenting on verses 113 and 114, makes a clear distinction between civil administration addressed in the 113 and public safety addressed in 114: *rājabhāvyasaṃgrahārthaṃ rakṣārthaṃ ca*. The distinction between *saṃgraha* and *gupti* is also clearly made in the parallel passage of *MBh* 12.88.1: *rāṣṭraguptiṃ ca me rājan rāṣṭrasyaiva ca saṃgraham / samyag jijñānamānāya prabrūhi bharatarṣabha* / The use of *saṃgraham* in verse 114 makes the syntax of the sentence impossible, with two separate objects (*gulmam* and *saṃgraham*) of the verb *kuryāt*. The commentators try to explain this with limited success. Several take *saṃgraha* to be a kind of a police station (*rakṣāsthāna*), but that is the meaning of *gulma* as attested in the *AŚ* 2.16.18 (with Kangle's note); 2.35.12; 3.20.14. We have parallel constructions with *guptaye* at the end of *pāda-d* in the *MDh* 1.94, 99. We also have frequently a dative of purpose at the end of the verse or half-verse: 6.30; 7.109, 167, 215; 8.368; 11.12, 53, 106, 138, 139, 164, 181, 209. The use of *saṃgraham* here may have been influenced by its use in the previous verse and the close presence of *kuryāt* in the same *pāda*. The reading adopted in supported by *Bh and Nd* and found in: GMd^{1} TMd^{4} MTr^{4} MTr^{5} MTr^{6}*Nd Lakṣ*. The dative is also supported by the variant reading in GMd^{5}. The reading of the *pāda*, nevertheless, remains uncertain. For a study of this verse, see Numata 1999. For the construction with *guptaye* at the end of the verse, see *YDh* 1.198, 321; *BṛSm* 1.28; *MBh* 12.69.24; 12.73.6, 7.

7.126b Most mss. and all editions have the reading *vetanam*, which is clearly the *lectio facilior*. All the ancient commentators support the reading *bhaktakam*. So, *Bh* comments on the two verses 126 and 127: *bhaktapraklptiḥ ślokadvayena*. Likewise *Me* comments: *bhaktārthaṃ paṇo deyaḥ;* and *Go: paṇo vakṣyamāṇaḥ sa jaghanyabhṛtakasya bhaktārthaṃ pratyahaṃ dātavyaḥ*. Similarly, *Nā* and *Rc* also support this reading with the gloss*: bhaktakaṃ bhṛtiḥ*. See also the parallel term *bhakta* in verse 127. See Introduction, p. 36 for further comments. The reading adopted has the unanimous support of the ST mss. and of several NT-x ones and is found in: Be^{3} NKt^{4} Lo^{2} GMd^{1} TMd^{3} TMd^{4} GMd^{5} GMy oOr Pu^{2} Pu^{4} Pu^{5} Pu^{7} Tr^{1} MTr^{4} MTr^{5} MTr^{6} Wa [*Jolly* G Nd] *Lakṣ*.

7.134d Even though all the editions have adopted the reading *acireṇaiva*, the overwhelming manuscript evidence, including most ST mss., is in favor of *acirād eva*. It is supported by *Go*, the only commentator to note the term. The adopted reading is found in: Be^{1} Be^{3} BCa Jo^{2} wKt^{1} wKt^{3} NKt^{4} La^{1} [*but cor sh*] Lo^{2} Lo^{3} GMd^{1} TMd^{3} GMd^{5} GMy oOr Pu^{2} Pu^{4} Tj^{1} Tr^{1} MTr^{4} MTr^{5} MTr^{6} Wa *Mādh*.

7.143d The mss. record a variety of readings, possibly because the scribes failed to understand the two pithy sentences within this *pāda*. I take *mṛtaḥ saḥ* as one sentence; and *na sa jīvati* as a second. The reading adopted is supported in various ways by several mss., especially the ST ones. It is found in Jo^{2} wKt^{1} La^{1} Lo^{2} Lo^{3} Ox^{3} Tj^{1} MTr^{5} [*Jolly* M] *Jolly*.

7.145c All editions have the Bahuvrīhi *hutāgniḥ*. The best mss., including all the ST ones, however, give the gerund *hutvā*, a reading I have adopted. It also accords well with the *ca* at *cārcya*. The reading adopted with the singular *agnim* is found in: Ho Jo^{2} wKt^{3} BKt^{5} Lo^{3} GMd^{1} TMd^{3} GMd^{5} GMy NNg Tj^{1} Tr^{1} MTr^{4} MTr^{6} Wa [*Jolly* R Nd] *Rn Dev*.

7.146a Several mss. have the plural *sthitāḥ* qualifying *prajāḥ*. Professor Wezler (personal communication) finds this quite an attractive interpretation. See, however, the similar expression at 8.2, where the one standing is clearly the king.

7.149b The reading adopted, *vayo'dhikān*, is found in: Be^{3} Hy Jo^{2} NKt^{4} BKt^{5} wKt^{6} Lo^{1} Lo^{3} TMd^{3} TMd^{4} GMd^{5} GMy Ox^{2} Pu^{3} Tj^{1} Tj^{2} Tr^{1} Tr^{2} MTr^{3} MTr^{4} MTr^{6} [*Jolly* R Nd]*Rn Mr*. See the note to 4.141 for further comments.

7.161b The reading adopted is found in all but one of the ST mss. and in most NT-x ones. It is supported by *Bh, Me,* and *Go.* It is also *the lectio difficilior*, the gerunds being changed to the substantives in imitation of the other terms of the sixfold strategy. See the usage of the gerunds in the parallel passage in *AŚ* 7.4.4. The reading adopted in found in: Be^{1} Bo BCa NKt^{4} La^{1} La^{2} Lo^{2} Lo^{4} Lo^{5} GMd^{1} TMd^{3} GMy NNg Ox^{3} Pu^{2} Pu^{4} Pu^{5} Pu^{7} Tr^{1} MTr^{4} MTr^{5} MTr^{6} [*Jolly* M^{4-5-9}G Nd Ku] *Nā* (pāṭha) *Lakṣ Jolly*.

7.163c Mandlik, Jolly, Jha, and KSS take *tadā* as a separate word: *tadā tvāyatisaṃyuktaḥ*. This is clearly an error. Bühler translates *tadātva* correctly: "An alliance which yields present and future advantages." This is also the clear understanding of *Bh, Go, Nā, Rn, Nd,* and *Mr*. Only *Rc* takes *tadā* as a separate word. See *tadātva* used again at 7.169.

7.164c I have adopted the reading *mitreṇa* even though the majority of the mss. and all the editions record *mitrasya*. The reading adopted is clearly the *lectio difficilior*, and it is attested by the all ST mss. plus a sizable number of NT-x ones. Even more importantly, it is the reading of *Bh, Go,* and *Nd,* and is given as an alternate reading by *Me*. It appears that the reading *mitrasya* gained popularity because of its adoption by *Me;* for example, *Ku* and *Rn* says that *Go* has the reading *mitreṇa*, but that they follow *Me* in reading *mitrasya*. We have a clear explanation of *mitreṇa* given by *Bh: yasya parasyāmitras tadvijigīṣor mitram. tena yadā parasyāpakriyate tadvijigīṣor mitreṇāpakṛte vyasanini pare viparīto vigrahaḥ*. This explanation is paraphrased by *Go*. See the construction with *mitreṇa* in the very next verse dealing with the two kinds of march into battle. The reading adopted is found in: Be^{1} NKt^{4} La^{1} Lo^{2} GMd^{1} TMd^{4} GMd^{5} oOr Pu^{2} Pu^{4} Pu^{5} Pu^{7} Tr^{1} MTr^{4} MTr^{5} MTr^{6} [*Jolly* G].

7.167b Although all the editions read *kāryārthasiddhaye,* the reading adopted is supported by all the ST mss., plus a large number of NT-x ones. The gloss of *Bh* also supports dropping *artha: svakāryasiddhiṃ kuryāt*. The reading adopted is found in: Bo Ho NKt^{4} La^{1} La^{2} Lo^{1} Lo^{2} Lo^{4} Lo^{5} GMd^{1} TMd^{3} TMd^{4} GMd^{5} GMy oOr sOx^{1} sPu^{6} Tr^{1} MTr^{4} MTr^{5} MTr^{6} *Lakṣ* [*Jolly* M^{4}].

7.168c I have adopted the reading *vyapadeśaś ca* even though it is found in a minority of mss. The major reason for adopting it is that it was probably the reading of the two oldest commentators, *Bh* and *Me*. The clearest is*Me*, who gives the reading of the majority as an alternate reading: *pāṭhāntaraṃ vyapadeśārtham iti*. In the commentary, *Me* explains: *vyapadeśaś cāpīḍite 'pi āgāmipīḍāparihārāya vyapadeśārtham anyaṃ saṃśrayet*. Here we have *vyapadeśārtham* used in explaining *vyapadeśaḥ*. This, I think, is true also of *Bh*, who comments: *sādhuṣv avyapadeśārtham*. Here also *-artham* is used in the gloss to explain the root text, which in *Bh* also is in the nominative. *Bh*'s use of the negative *avyapadeśa* is noteworthy, even though with just one extant ms. it is impossible to say whether this is merely a scribal error. I think that the reading of the glosses in these two ancient commentators may have influenced the alteration of the root text also to *vyapadeśārtham*, with the added influence of the parallel *arthasaṃpādanārtham* in *pāda*-a. The reading adopted is found in: Be^{3} Ho wKt^{3} NKt^{4} wKt^{5} TMd^{3} TMd^{4} GMd^{5} GMy *Lakṣ*, and is supported by La^{1} wKt^{6} NPu^{1} MTr^{5}.

7.170d All ST mss. and a large number of NT-x ones support *manyeta*, the reading adopted. The commentators gloss with *āśrayet* and *adhyavasyet*, but it is unclear what term they are glossing. The adopted reading is found in: Bo BCa NKt^{4} BKt^{5} wKt^{6} La^{2} Lo^{2} Lo^{4} Lo^{5} GMd^{1} TMd^{3} TMd^{4} GMd^{5} GMy sOx^{1} Ox^{3} Pu^{2} Pu^{4} Pu^{5} sPu^{6} Pu^{7} Tr^{1} Tr^{2} MTr^{4} MTr^{5} MTr^{6} [*Jolly* M G] *Rc Lakṣ*.

7.172d The reading of the last word is quite unclear; the mss. are divided over the singular and the plural, as well as the word: *ari* or *ripu*. Both the early commentators, *Bh* and *Me*, prefer the singular *arim*. The gloss *śatrūn* of *Go* and *Ku* supports the plural, leaving the term in the root unspecified. The evidence points in the direction of both the singular and the term *ari*. This is supported by *arim* in the very next verse; the surrounding verses also use the singular. The reading adopted is found in: BCa Jo^{2} Lo^{2} Lo^{5} GMd^{1} TMd^{3} TMd^{4} NNg oOr NPu^{1} Pu^{2} Pu^{4} MTr^{5} MTr^{6} [*Jolly* M$^{8-9}$ Me R Nd]*Jolly*.

7.176d Among the three major variants recorded in the mss., *nirvitarkaḥ* has the broadest support, including that of *Bh, Rn,* and *Rc* and of all ST mss. It is unclear what reading is supported by the gloss of *Me: nirvikāraḥ*. The reading adopted is found in: BBe^{2} Bo Ho wKt^{1} wKt^{3} La^{2} Lo^{3} GMd^{5} sOx^{1} sPu^{6} Tj^{1} Tj^{2} Tr^{1} MTr^{4} MTr^{5} MTr^{6} [*Jolly* M^{4} R Nd] *Bh Rn Rc Jolly*.

7.200c The reading adopted, *saṃyatto*, is clearly the *lectio difficilior* and is found in: Be^{1} Bo BCa Ho Hy Jo^{2} wKt^{1} wKt^{3} NKt^{4} La^{1} La^{2} Lo^{1} Lo^{3} GMd^{1} NNg sOx^{1} Pu^{3} Pu^{5} sPu^{6} Pu^{7} Pu^{8} Tj^{1} Tr^{2} MTr^{4} MTr^{6} [*Jolly* G R Nd]*Go Rc Mādh Jolly*. Note also the orthographic similarity between "p" and "y" and between "tt" and "nn" in northern scripts. Thus, *saṃyatta* can easily be read as *saṃpanna*.

7.213 Many mss., especially the ST ones, have gerundives in place of the finite verbs in *pādas* a-c. Derrett (1975, II: 83) supports the gerundive reading, referring among others to the ST reading of *MBh* 5.37.17 with the same reading. Although there is much to commend the gerundive readings, I have opted to keep the finite verbs. The main reason is that even the ST mss. are divided on this, TMd^{3}, GMd^{5}, and GMy giving the finite verbs always, while MTr^{4} has the finite verb in *pādas* a-b, and MTr^{6} in *pāda*-a. The overwhelming majority of the mss. support the reading adopted.

7.215d Even though all the editions read *arthasiddaye* (and Jolly surprisingly records no variants), the reading adopted has the overwhelming support of the ST and NT-x mss., as well as that of *Go* and *Rn*. The fragmentary gloss of *Bh* also appears to support it.

The adopted reading is found in: Be^{1} Be^{3} BCa Ho NKt^{4} BKt^{5} WKt^{6} La^{1} La^{2} Lo^{1} Lo^{2} GMd^{1} TMd^{3} GMd^{5} GMy NNg SOx^{1} Ox^{2} Ox^{3} NPu^{1} Pu^{2} Pu^{3} Pu^{4} SPu^{6} Pu^{7} Pu^{8} Tj^{2} Tr^{1} Tr^{2} MTr^{4} MTr^{5} MTr^{6} Wa *Lakṣ*.

7.216d All editions read *viśet*. However, all the ST mss. and a substantial number of NT-x ones have the reading *vrajet:* BBe^{2} Be^{3} BCa NKt^{4} La^{1} Lo^{4} Lo^{5} GMd^{1} TMd^{3} TMd^{4} GMd^{5} GMy NNg Ox^{3} NPu^{1} Tj^{2} Tr^{1} MTr^{4} MTr^{5}MTr^{6} *Lakṣ*. The gloss of *Me*, *yāyād*, is somewhat ambiguous, but probably supports *vrajet* more than *viśet*.

7.218a The reading *udakaiḥ* is found in all ST mss. It appears to be supported by *Me*, although the mss. simply give the *pāda* without comment; hence, it is unclear whether this is merely a scribal insertion or whether it was the reading of *Me*. The reading adopted is supported by *Go*, *Ku* (both with gloss *auṣadhaiḥ*), *Rn*, and *Rc*, and is found in almost all the NT mss.

7.218b Mss. are divided over the verb. I have adopted *nejayet*, which fits the context of sprinkling a liquid antidote better and is also supported by both ST and NT-x mss: WKt^{1} BKt^{5} WKt^{6} La^{1} Lo^{2} Lo^{4}GMd^{1} TMd^{3} GMd^{5} GMy Ox^{3} MTr^{4} MTr^{5}MTr^{6} [*Jolly* M G N Nd] *Nā Nd Rc Lakṣ Jolly*.

7.226a The reading adopted, *vṛttam*, is supported by *Me* and *Nā*, as well as all the ST mss. and a number of NT-x ones, including the old NKt^{4}. I also think that is fits the context better than *vidhānam*. The reading adopted in found in: Be^{3} NKt^{4} La^{1} Lo^{2} GMd^{1} TMd^{3} TMd^{4} GMd^{5} GMy Pu^{2} Pu^{4} Tr^{1} MTr^{4} MTr^{5} MTr^{6} [*Jolly* Nd] *Vij Lakṣ*.

CHAPTER EIGHT

8.11c The reading adopted is supported by *Bh*, *Me*, and *Nā*. The two latter commentators gloss *prakṛtaḥ* with *adhikṛtaḥ*, and this may have been the source of the reading introduced into the text. For the unusual term *prakṛta* found in the vocabulary of the *AŚ*, see my note to the translation of this verse. The adopted reading is found in: BBe^{2} Bo BCa Ho La^{1} Lo^{2} Lo^{5} GMd^{1} TMd^{3} TMd^{4} NNg SOx^{1} Ox^{2} NPu^{1} Pu^{3} Pu^{5} SPu^{6} Pu^{7} Pu^{8} Tr^{1} MTr^{4} MTr^{5} MTr^{6} Wa *Lakṣ Dev*.

8.13a The reading adopted is supported by *Me* and *Go*. The alternate is given by *Ku* and *Rn*, but *Ku* acknowledges the correctness of *Me*'s reading: *medhātithinā tu sabhā vā na praveṣṭavyā iti ṛjv eva paṭhitam*. This reading is found in: Bo Ho Hy Jo^{2} NKt^{4} Lo^{1} Lo^{3} GMd^{1} TMd^{3} GMd^{5} GMy SOx^{1} NPu^{1} Pu^{2} Pu^{4} Pu^{5} SPu^{6} Pu^{7} Pu^{8} Tj^{1} Tj^{2} Tr^{1} Tr^{2} MTr^{4}MTr^{5} MTr^{6} Wa [*Jolly* M G N R Nd] *Vij Apa Dev Jha Jolly*. Cf. *NSm Mā* 3.9.

8.16b Most mss., including all NT ones, have the reading *alam*. This is also the reading in *MBh* 12.91.13. Several ST mss., however, as well as many southern mss. of the *MBh*, record the reading *layam*. This reading fits nicely with the phonetic etymology of *vṛṣala*. Yet, I think, *alam* here is the *lectio difficilior* precisely because *layam* is more easily connected to the "la" of *vṛṣala*. All the commentators take the reading to be *alam*.

8.30a All the manuscripts have the compound *pranaṣṭasvāmikam*, and most commentators, including *Bh* and *Me*, explain it as a Bahuvrīhi compound. It is odd, however, to call the owner *pranaṣṭa;* this term is usually applied to lost property and not to a lost or absent owner (see the note to the translation of this verse for further details). Following the parallel passage in *GDh* 10.36, I propose that the original reading was *pranaṣṭam asvāmikaṃ riktham*, with a hypermetric *pāda*; or, perhaps, *pranaṣṭāsvāmikaṃ riktham*. This interpretation, where *pranaṣṭa* refers to lost property and *asvāmikam* to such property whose owner is unknown, appears to be supported by the commentary of *Go* (which is reproduced almost verbatim by *Ku*): *ajñāyamānasvāmikaṃ* [Ku *ajñātasvāmikaṃ*] *dhanaṃ rājā kasya kiṃ pranaṣṭam ity evaṃ paṭahādinākhyāya dvārādau varṣatrayaṃ sthāpayet.*

8.31b The alternate reading, *anuyojyaḥ*, is found in most mss.; it is also the reading of *Me, Go, Ku,* and *Rn.* Only *Nd* supports the reading I have adopted; *Bh*, unfortunately, does not comment. The adopted reading is found mostly in the ST mss., but with the support of the old nKt^4 and several other NT ones: wKt^1 nKt^4 La^1 [*but cor sh*] gMd^1 tMd^3 tMd^4 gMd^5 gMy oOr Tr^1 mTr^4 mTr^5 mTr^6, and the partial support of Pu^7. I think this is the correct reading. It fits the syntax better, with the main clause of the correlative construction containing a single verb *arhati*. With the gerundive *anuyojyaḥ*, which has to be taken as a verb substitute, we have to insert another pronoun as the subject of *saṃvādya* and *arhati*. As it is, the sentence moves smoothly: "He" — after he has been interrogated and identified the objects properly — "is (judged to be) the owner and deserves to get the article."

8.32a Although the reading *avedayāno naṣṭasya* is adopted in all the editions, the reading of the critical edition is supported by all the ST mss. and a considerable number of NT-x ones. The reading *praṇaṣṭasya*, moreover, fits with the use of the same word in the surrounding verses and is supported by the presence of *avedayan* in other variant readings. The reading adopted is found in: Ho La^1 [*cor to*] Lo^2 gMd^1 tMd^3 tMd^4 gMd^5 gMy sOx^1 Ox^2 Pu^3 sPu^6 Tr^1 Tr^2 mTr^4 mTr^6 Wa [*Jolly* Nd].

8.35b All the ST mss. have the reading *hetunā* or *hetutaḥ*. Even though mTr^5 has *mānavaḥ*, the commentary of *Bh* has the gloss *kāraṇataḥ*, which may at first sight support the southern reading. However, I think that the word *hetunā/hetutaḥ* may have entered the manuscript tradition precisely through such a gloss explaining *satyena*. We have in *Me* a similar gloss: *satyena pramāṇena*.

8.45b Both *Bh* and *Me* read *sākṣiṇam* in apposition to *ātmanam*. *Bh* comments: *paśyed ātmānaṃ sākṣiṇaṃ kṛtvā*. Likewise, *Me* using very similar words: *etac cātmānaṃ sākṣiṇaṃ kṛtvā gaveṣaṇīyam*. But *Me* recognizes the other reading taking *ātmānam* as a separate item, and comments: *asmin pakṣe sākṣiṇa iti svatantraṃ padam*. All other commentators opt for *sākṣiṇaḥ*, which is supported by the majority of both ST and NT mss.

8.51b, 52d In both these places *karaṇa* is clearly the correct reading and not *kāraṇa*, which was adopted by Jolly. For *karaṇa* as a legal instrument, see *NSm* 1.83, 117, 122, and *MDh* 8.57 (where most mss. read *karaṇa*), 154. This reading is also recorded in the B-R under *MDh* 8.51, 154.

8.52c Here and in the following verses, the reading *deśa* is clearly superior. It is found in the parallel passage in *AŚ* 3.1.19. For the meaning of *deśa* as documentary evidence, see my note to the translation of this verse. The change to *deśya* probably occurred because the original Arthaśāstric meaning of *deśa* had become obsolete. In this verse, the reading *deśa* is found in: Bo wKt^3 nKt^4 La^1 Lo^2 Lo^4 Lo^5 gMd^1 tMd^3 tMd^4 gMy nNg Ox^3 nPu^1 Pu^2 Pu^5 Pu^7 Tr^1 [*but cor sh*] mTr^4 mTr^6 Wa [*Jolly* M G N Nd] *Me Bh Nā Go Nd Jolly Jha Der* [not mTr^5].

8.57a The reading *sākṣiṇaḥ* is found in some NT mss. and is used in the vulgate editions. The overwhelming majority of mss. and all ancient commentators, however, have the reading *jñātāraḥ*, which is also the *lectio difficilior*. Medhātithi glosses *jñātāraḥ* with *sākṣiṇaḥ*, and that may have been the source of the vulgate reading. The reading *mety uktvā* contains a double sandhi [*me+iti* = *ma iti>mety*]. Kumārila (on *PMS* 1.3.24) notes this irregularity: *santi ma ity uktveti vaktavye vyākaraṇam anepekṣyaiva saṃhitā kṛtā.*

8.57d Most mss. of both the NT and the ST record the reading *hīnaṃ tam api*. Nevertheless, I think the correct reading is *hīnaṃ tam iti*. The grammatical problem in this construction was already noted by Medhātithi, who explains the irregularity of an accusative with *iti* by saying that *iti* here refers to the manner in which the decision should be made and is not used to mark a direct quote: *hīnaṃ tam iti dvitīyāntaḥ pāṭhaḥ / itiśabdaḥ prakārārtho draṣṭavyaḥ / ebhir uktaiḥ prakārair anyaiś caivaṃvidhair hīnaṃ taṃ nirdiśet.* He notes that if *iti* is taken in the normal sense, then the reading should have been *hīno 'sav iti*, which is the reading of *Dev*. Bhāruci likewise reads *iti* and explains it as having the meaning of *evam.* I think scribes and reader may have changed *iti* to *api* to "correct" the grammar of the sentence. The reading *iti* is supported by: BKt^{5} Lo^{2} GMd^{1} NPu^{1} Pu^{2} Pu^{4} Pu^{5} Pu^{7} MTr^{4} MTr^{5}MTr^{6} Wa [*Jolly* M G] *Bh Me Go Jolly Jha Dave*.

8.58b I have followed the reading of the overwhelming majority of mss. The orthographic distinction between "b" and "v," especially in northern scripts, is slight, however, and there appears to have been a confusion in the tradition as to the precise word and its meaning. Both *Bh* and *Me* gloss the word with *bandhana*, that is, imprisonment. They appear to assume the reading *bandhyaḥ*. The reading is uncertain, although the mss. in southern scripts, where the distinction between the two letters is clearer, support *vadhya*.

8.69d Even though all editions have *śarīrasyāpi*, the reading adopted, *śarīrasyaiva,* has broad support of both ST and NT-x mss.: Be^{1} BBe^{2} BCa Jo^{2} wKt^{1} wKt^{3} NKt^{4} La^{1} Lo^{2} Lo^{3} Lo^{4} Lo^{5} GMd^{1} TMd^{3} TMd^{4} GMd^{5} GMy sOx^{1} Ox^{2} sPu^{6} Tj^{1} Tr^{1} MTr^{4} MTr^{5} MTr^{6} [*Jolly* M^{4} R Nd].

8.77a The main question here is whether the readings should be (*a*)*lubdha* and *asākṣī*. One reading found in most NT mss. and several ST ones is (*a*)*lubdha* with the positive *sākṣī*. I have adopted this reading, which is also supported by Bhāruci. However, Medhātithi and Govinda prefer the positive reading *lubdha* and the negative *asākṣī*. Kullūka, who prefers the former, clearly states the position of his two predecessors: *medhātithigovindarājābhām eko lubdhas tv asākṣī syād iti paṭhitaṃ vyākhyātaṃ ca.* According to their interpretation, the prohibition of a single greedy individual implicitly permits a single individual free from greed to be a witness. This is a round about way of stating the obvious. The whole purpose of the verse is to contrast the preference of males over females when it comes to judicial testimony. Clearly, the thrust of the verse was lost on some readers. In *pāda*-b also, some mss. convert the negative to a positive: *śucyo 'pi ca striyaḥ*, implying that even women can testify if they are pure and honest.

8.80a I have adopted the reading *vittha*, which is obviously the correct one. The manuscript tradition, however, appears to have had a lot of trouble with this word; hence the numerous variants. See the parallel at 1.33. Besides being supported by many of the variants, the adopted reading is found in Be^{1} wKt^{3} Jo^{2} NKt^{4} La^{1} GMy Pu^{8} Tj^{1} *Dev Jolly*.

8.81b The original reading of this *pāda* is quite unclear. I have opted for *prāpnoti* over *āpnoti*, mostly because the Grantha and Telugu mss. (Be^{3} gMd^{1} tMd^{3} tMd^{4} gMd^{5} gMy) as well as several NT ones have this reading. The alternate reading, however, also has strong support, including the Malayam mss. With regard to *puṣkalān*, which I have adopted, and *anuttamān*, on the other hand, there is stronger support for the former. The latter is confined to some NT mss.

8.85c Although all the editions have adopted the reading *tāṃs tu*, all the ST mss. and a substantial number of NT-x ones record the reading adopted *tāṃś ca:* Be^{1} bBe^{2} Bo wKt^{3} nKt^{4} La^{1} Lo^{2} gMd^{1} tMd^{3} tMd^{4} gMy nNg Pu^{3} Pu^{5} Pu^{7} Tr^{1} mTr^{4} mTr^{5} mTr^{6} Wa*Go Lakṣ*.

8.88d Even though a plurality of the mss. have the reading *sarvais tu pātakaiḥ*, I think the ST mss. have retained the original reading *ebhis tu pātakaiḥ*. This reading is also supported by many important NT mss. such as the old nKt^{4} and nNg. A very similar verse is found at 8.113 where the reading is *sarvais tu.* In that verse (= *NSm* 1.181) this reading is appropriate and is supported by almost all the mss. It is possible that that reading may have influenced the reading in this verse. Here *ebhiḥ* is appropriate, because the consequences of perjury are enumerated in the subsequent verses. Medhātithi's gloss *vakṣyamāṇaiḥ pātakaiḥ* also supports the adopted reading, which is found in: Be^{3} nKt^{4} bKt^{5} Lo^{2} gMd^{1} tMd^{4} gMd^{5} gMy nNg Ox^{2} Pu^{2} Pu^{4} Pu^{5} Pu^{7} Tr^{1} [*but mc sh*] mTr^{5} Wa [*Jolly* Me M$^{8-9}$ G Nd] *Apa Me Go Jolly*. Medhātithi also cites this *pāda* in his commentary to 8.99 with precisely this reading.

8.93a There is strong manuscript support for both readings: *kapālī ca* and *kapālena*. I have opted for the latter, because it is found in most ST mss. and in the parallel passage at *VaDh* 16.33, and it fits with the surrounding adjectives describing the sinner. This reading appears to be supported by *Go* with the gloss *karpareṇa yuktaḥ* and by *Ku* with *karpareṇopalikṣitaḥ*. It is recorded in Be^{1} Be^{3} Bo Ho bKt^{5} Lo^{4} Lo^{5} tMd^{4} gMd^{5} Ox^{3} nPu^{1} Pu^{2} Pu^{3} Pu^{4} Pu^{8} Tr^{1} [*but mc sh*] Tr^{2} mTr^{4} mTr^{6} [*Jolly* M$^{4-5}$] *Rc Jha Dave*. The original reading, however, remains uncertain. Lariviere's critical edition of the parallel at *NSm* 1.183 has *kapālena*, although two mss. read *kapālī ca*.

8.100x The additional verse *paśuvat kṣaudra-* is found in all the ST mss., although only one NT ms. records it. Bhāruci apparently read this verse as an authentic part of his root text, because he comments *amī pañca ślokāḥ*, and we get five *ślokas* only by including this additional verse.

8.101d Although all editions give the reading *sarvam*, all the ST mss. and a large number of NT ones have the reading adopted *satyam:* Bo bCa Ho wKt^{3} bKt^{5} La^{1} Lo^{4} Lo^{5} gMd^{1} tMd^{3} tMd^{4} gMd^{5} gMy sOx^{1} Ox^{2} Pu^{3} sPu^{6} Pu^{8} Tr^{1} Tr^{2} mTr^{4} mTr^{5}mTr^{6} Wa [*Jolly* Nd] *Apa Dev*.

8.106d Jolly opts for the reading *tryṛcena*. See the *Vārttika* on Pāṇini 6.1.37 for the formation *tṛca*.

8.114a I follow Jolly in reading *vā hārayet*. All other editions read *vāhārayet* with sandhi [= *āhārayet*]. Only Kullūka has a comment showing that he accepted *āhārayet*.

8.124c All editions have the reading *yāni*, which is found in most NT mss. I have, however, adopted *tāni*, the reading in all the ST mss. and in several NT ones. I think *tāni* fits the syntax better; I take *pādas* a-b, *pāda*-c, and *pāda*-d as separate sentences. This reading is found in: Bo Ho La^{1} Lo^{2}gMd^{1} tMd^{3} tMd^{4} gMd^{5} gMy sOx^{1} Ox^{2} Pu^{3} Pu^{5} sPu^{6} Pu^{7} Pu^{8} Tr^{1} [*but* cor] Tr^{2} mTr^{4} mTr^{5} mTr^{6} [*Jolly* Nd Gr] *Dev Mādh*.

8.132 This verse is omitted in all but two of the ST mss., including all the Malayalam ones. It is omitted also in the ms. of Bhāruci's commentary. Medhātithi comments that this verse is omitted by some: *imaṃ ślokaṃ kecin nādhīyante trasareṇau vipratipattya-bhāvāt*. The authenticity of this verse is thus doubtful. Evidence, however, is insufficient to remove it from the critical edition. It is cited in several medieval sources.

8.133a This *pāda* is hypermetric, and several scribes have attempted to correct this by resorting to various strategies.

8.134b The alternate reading *eka* is found in all the citations and in many mss. The reading adopted, *eva*, however, is supported by all the ST mss., plus many NT ones, including the old NKt^{4} and NNg. The reading *tv eva kṛṣṇalam* is found only in Be^{1} NKt^{4} La^{1} sOx^{1} sPu^{6} Pu^{8} MTr^{5} *Jolly*, although *tu* here (as opposed to *ca*) has the support of all the mss. with the reading *eka*.

8.139 Jolly places this verse within brackets and doubts its authenticity. *Nā* also questions its authenticity with the comment: *ṛṇe deye pratijñāta iti ślokam atra kecit paṭhanti*. The context does make the verse suspect. However, it is found in all the mss. and both Bhāruci and Medhātithi comment on it.

8.149d Most mss. of NT-x have the reading *nopabhogena jīryati* [or *jīryate*], which is followed by Jolly. The reading adopted, however, is found in all the ST and NT-y mss., as well as in several NT-x ones.

8.151b The reading *āhṛtā* is supported by all ST mss. and a number of NT-x ones, as well as by Bhāruci and Medhātithi: Ho NKt^{4} BKt^{5} Lo^{2} GMd^{1} TMd^{3} GMd^{5} GMy Tr^{1} Tr^{2} MTr^{4} MTr^{5} MTr^{6} Wa *Bh Me Nā Vij Apa Dev Jha Dave*.

8.153b The mss. are deeply divided over the reading *vinirharet* and *punar haret*. I have opted for the latter principally because it is found in all the ST mss. The reading, however, is uncertain, especially because Medhātithi records the former. The adopted reading is found in: BBe^{2} BCa Ho Hy Jm Jo^{1} Jo^{2} Kt^{2} WKt^{3} NKt^{4} Lo^{3} GMd^{1} TMd^{3} TMd^{4} GMd^{5} GMy oOr Tj^{1} Tj^{2} Tr^{1} Tr^{2} MTr^{3} MTr^{4} MTr^{6} [*Jolly* Ku R Nd]*Rn Rc Nd Lakṣ Mandlik KSS*.

8.154d The correct reading is *karaṇaṃ*, i.e., a legal instrument or document. See note to 8.51.

8.158d The alternate reading, *yateta*, has broad but not unanimous support among the NT-x mss. I have adopted the reading *prayacchet*, which is found in all ST and NT-y mss., as well as in some NT-x ones: Hy Jm Jo^{1} Jo^{2} WKt^{1} Kt^{2} Lo^{2} Lo^{3} GMd^{1} TMd^{3} TMd^{4} GMd^{5} GMy Tj^{1} Tj^{2} Tr^{1} MTr^{3} MTr^{4} MTr^{5} MTr^{6} [*Jolly* R Nd]*Dev Mādh Nā Rc Mandlik KSS*. The reading, however, remains uncertain, especially because *yateta* is found in Medhātithi and is also the *lectio difficilior*.

8.166b The reading adopted, *kuṭumbe ca*, is found in Be^{1} Be^{3} BCa Ho NKt^{4} BKt^{5} Lo^{3} GMd^{1} TMd^{4} NNg oOr sOx^{1} NPu^{1} Pu^{2} Pu^{3} Pu^{4} Pu^{5} sPu^{6} Pu^{7} Pu^{8} Tj^{1} Tr^{1} Tr^{2} MTr^{4} MTr^{6} Wa [*Jolly* M G] *Me Nd Apa Lakṣ Dev Jolly Jha*. Although some ST mss. have the alternate reading, the adopted reading is favored by most ST mss. and our best NT-x mss.

8.181 The sequence of verses 181–99, but especially 181–4 in various mss. and commentaries is diverse. *Bh* and *Go* give the sequence 181, 183, 184, 182; the same sequence is found in Be^{1} Bo BCa NKt^{4} Lo^{2} NNg sOx^{1} Ox^{2} sPu^{6} Pu^{8} Tr^{2} MTr^{5}, whereas Wa transposes 182 and 183. The order in *Nā* is: 181, 183, 182, 184; in *Nd*: 180, 195, 188b, 185, 186, 189, 194, 187, 188a, 181–4, 196, 190–3, 197, 198. Medhātithi, however, makes it clear that the sequence should be 181ab, 182, and 181cd, and Bhāruci appears to agree with this. I have followed the latter sequence in the translation.

8.188a Most mss. support the alternate reading *eṣu*. The locative may have been influenced by the two surrounding locatives; scribes may have overlooked the syntactic connection of *eṣa* to *vidhiḥ* in the next *pāda*. I have, however, opted for the *lectio difficilior,* which is *eṣa*. This reading is supported by the glosses of Medhātithi (*anantaroktaḥ*), of Kullūka and Nandana (*pūrvoktaḥ*), and less clearly of Govinda. It is also supported by the mss. with the reading *eva*. The reading *eṣa* is found in only a small number of the mss.: wKt^3 NNg [*Jolly* G Me Ku] *Jolly*.

8.189b Even though all the editions have adopted the reading *vā*, the vast majority of both ST and NT mss. record *ca:* Be^1 BBe^2 Be^3 Bo BCa Jo^2 NKt^4 BKt^5 La^1 Lo^1 Lo^3 Lo^4 Lo^5 GMd^1 TMd^3 GMd^5 GMy NNg NPu^1 Pu^2 Pu^4 Pu^5 Pu^7 Tj^1 Tr^1 Tr^2 MTr^4 MTr^{5}MTr^6 Wa *Apa Lakṣ Dev*. This reading is also found in the vulgate of *NSm* (2.12; under 2.6 in Lariviere's critical edition).

8.199b The reading *krayo vikrayaḥ* is found in all the ST mss. and a good number of NT ones. However, the reading *kraya* may have been influenced by the following *vikraya*. I have adopted the *lectio difficilior*, which is supported by the commentators. Bhāruci's gloss *krayavikrayau* appears to support the alternate reading, but this may merely be a gloss on *vikaraya* which he sees as standing for both buying and selling. Further, it is difficult to see how a non-owner of an item can sell it!

8.199x The additional verse is found in all the ST mss. and many NT ones. This verse must have entered the manuscript tradition rather early. I have not adopted it, however, because it is ignored by all the ancient commentators, Bhāruci, Medhātithi, and Govinda.

8.202b The reading adopted, *-śodhitam*, is found in most mss.: BBe^2 Be^3 Bo BCa Ho Jo^2 wKt^3 NKt^4 BKt^5 La^1 Lo^1 Lo^2 Lo^3 Lo^4 Lo^5 TMd^3 TMd^4 GMy NNg oOr sOx^1 Ox^2 NPu^1 Pu^2 Pu^4 Pu^5 sPu^6 Pu^7 Pu^8 Tj^1 Tr^1 [*but cor sh*] Tr^2 MTr^4 MTr^{5}MTr^6 Wa [*Jolly* M G Nd] *Apa Lakṣ Dev Mādh Jolly*. The alternate reading, *-śodhitaḥ*, however, appears to be supported by *Bh, Me,* and *Go*. Under this interpretation, it is the person who is cleared of any wrongdoing by the public purchase of the article. But see *viśuddham* in the previous verse where the term refers to the clear legal title to the property purchased.

8.203ab All editions read *saṃsṛṣṭarūpam* as a compound. This is supported only by the NT-y (vulgate) mss. The commentators explain *rūpam* as a separate word referring to any article that is sold. *Nā* glosses: *rūpapadaṃ vikrītamātropalakṣaṇam*.

8.222cd *Bh* appears to have had the reading *so 'ntar daśāhāt tat sāmnā*, as in several other ST mss. He, however, rejects this reading as *apāṭha* and proposes the emendation: *so 'yaṃ dasāhāt tad dravyam*. He also gives an alternate reading that he found in his sources: *dānādāne daśāhaṃ tu syātām api nipātini*.

8.228d Numerous mss., including several ST ones, have the reading *dharme* or *dharmme*. The doubling of "m" may have contributed to the omission of "y" of *dharmye*, which I think is the correct reading. It is found in the following: Be^1 Hy Jm Jo^1 Jo^2 wKt^1 NKt^4 BKt^5 Lo^2 Pu^3 Pu^7 Pu^8 Tj^2 Tr^1 MTr^6 Wa *Lakṣ Dev Me Rn Mandlik Jolly* [without giving any variants] *Jha Dave*.

8.234c Here I have adopted the reading *paśuṣu svāminām dadyāt* against the testimony of the majority of mss. of both NT and ST. The adopted reading is found only in BCa Hy Jm Jo^1 Kt^2 wKt^3 Tj^2, with partial support from Lo^3 Tj^1. This reading, however, is clearly the *lectio difficilior;* the locative plural *paśuṣu* going with *mṛteṣu* of *pāda*-d to form a locative absolute. This connection, coming after the active verb *dadyāt*, may have been missed by scribes; hence, the "correction" found in most mss. The accepted reading is supported by the commentaries of *Me, Go, Ku,* and *Nd,* and by the reading of *Dev.* This reading has been adopted also by Mandlik, Jolly, Jha, KSS, and Dave.

8.234d I have adopted the reading *aṅkāṃś ca* against the testimony of the majority of mss. of both NT and ST. The reading adopted is found only in nKt^4 nNg nPu^1 Pu^7 mTr^5 [*Jolly* M G Ku] *Jolly Jha,* with some support from Lo^2 Lo^4 tMd^4 Pu^2 Pu^4 [here the mark for "e" may have been a mistake for the *anusvāra*]. The reading *aṅgāni* in this context makes little sense; what should be shown to the owner are not the limbs but the distinguishing marks of the dead animal. The reading *aṅka* is supported by the old commentators: Medhātithi: *aṅkāḥ karṇādayaḥ svāmiviśeṣajñānārthaṃ cihnāni;* Govinda: *cihnāni vadatā karṇatvagādīni;* Kullūka: *anyāni ca cihnāni śṛṅgakhurādīni.* Medhātithi's comment appears to indicate that owners branded their cattle with a marking on the ear, possibly a particular cut; by showing the ear the herdsman would be able to demonstrate to which owner the animal belonged, especially in the likely event that he herded cattle of more than one owner.

8.240a There is an ambiguity in the sandhi at *kṣetre parivṛte;* it could also be *aparivṛte* with the elision of "a." Derrett and Dave record an avagraha: *kṣetre 'parivṛte.* For reasons why I have adopted the positive *parivṛte,* see my note to the translation.

8.245c All but three mss. have the reading *jyeṣṭha.* Jolly has corrected this to the standard *jyaiṣṭha.* I see no reason to standardize this pronunciation against the near unanimous testimony of both ST and NT mss.

8.258b Although the mss. are evenly divided, I have opted for *grāmāḥ* because it is clearly the *lectio difficilior.* It is found in: Be^1 bBe^2 Be^3 Bo bCa Ho Hy Jm Jo^1 Jo^2 wKt^1 Kt^2 wKt^3 La^1 Lo^2 nNg oOr sOx^1 Ox^3 Pu^3 Pu^4 sPu^6 Pu^8 Tj^2 Tr^1 mTr^4 mTr^{5}mTr^6 [*Jolly* Ku N] *Rn Apa Mādh Mandlik KSS.* The difficulty of this unusual word with an older meaning may have caused scribes to change it to either the more usual *grāmyāḥ* or to compound it with the following with the result that *sāmanta* was changed to *sīmānta:* thus *grāmasīmāntavāsinaḥ.* Given the nature of the glosses, it is unclear which of these was the root reading of the ancient commentators. For *sāmanta,* see also verses 258, 262, and 263.

8.271c The adopted reading, *nikheyaḥ,* is supported by the parallel passages in *ViDh* 5.25 and *NSm* 15–16.23, as well as by a majority of the mss: Bo Ho Jo^2 nKt^4 bKt^5 Lo^2 Lo^3 gMd^1 tMd^4 gMd^5 nNg oOr Pu^3 Pu^5 Pu^7 Pu^8 Tj^1 Tr^1 Tr^2 mTr^4 mTr^5 [*Jolly* Me G R Nd].

8.279b The NT and ST are divided over the reading here. Only two NT mss. record the ST reading *hiṃsyāc chreyāṃsam.* I have followed here the NT reading; it is supported by the glosses of Bhāruci, Medhātithi, and Rāmacandra. The reading, however, remains somewhat uncertain.

8.281b Manuscripts are split over the readings *avakṛṣṭa* and *apakṛṣṭa.* Most ST mss. record the latter readings, although in tMd^3 tMd^4 the Telugu distinction between "v" and "p" being slight, the reading could be either. I have adopted *avakṛṣṭa* because most mss. have that reading: Be^1 bBe^2 Bo Ho Jo^2 wKt^3 nKt^4 bKt^5 La^1 Lo^1 Lo^3 Lo^4 Lo^5 tMd^3 tMd^4 nNg sOx^1 Ox^2 nPu^1 Pu^2 Pu^4 sPu^6 Pu^7 Pu^8 Tj^1 Tr^2 [*Jolly* M G R] *Apa Me Rc Jolly;* it is also supported by the reading in *NSm* 15–16.26. The reading, however, remains uncertain.

8.287a There is strong manuscript support for both major readings: the genitive *pīḍanānām* and the locative *pīḍanāyām.* The locative, however, is derived from the feminine noun *pīḍanā*, which is not attested in the dictionaries; the normal form is the neuter *pīḍanam*. I have, nevertheless, opted for the latter because the majority of the ST and NT mss., including all the Malayalam ones, support it. The genitive may have been created by scribes attempting the correct the grammatical irregularity. The locative is supported by: BBe² Bo BCa Ho Hy Jm Jo¹ Jo² wKt¹ Kt² wKt³ Lo¹ Lo³ TMd³ GMd⁵ sOx¹ sPu⁶ Pu⁸ Tj¹ Tj² Tr¹ MTr³ MTr⁴ MTr⁵ MTr⁶ [*Jolly* Me Ku R Nd]; this reading is supported by *Ku Nd*. Neuter verbal abstracts in *-ana* occur alongside feminine in *-anā* (see Wakernagel II.2, pp. 190f) especially in the early language. Manu may here be using an old form for the word that later scribes may have considered erroneous.

8.288d The mss. are divided over the genitive *rājñaḥ* and the dative *rājñe*. I have adopted the former principally because it is recorded in most ST mss., including all Malayalam ones, and in numerous NT mss.: BBe² Be³ Hy Jo¹ Jo² wKt¹ Kt² wKt³ NKt⁴ BKt⁵ La¹ Lo¹ Lo³ GMd¹ TMd³ TMd⁴ NPu¹ Pu² Tj¹ Tj² Tr¹ MTr³ MTr⁴ MTr⁶ Wa [*Jolly* Ku Nd R] *Ku Rn*. Even though the printed editions of *Me* and *Go* show the dative, it is unclear whether these old commentators themselves had that reading; they do not comment on the case. Manu uses both the dative (see 3.94, 99, 231; 4.80; 5.151 etc.) and the genitive (see 3.108; 8.184, 234, 275; 9.71, 155 etc.) with the verb √*dā*. The only other time the verb is used with the noun *rājan*, however, it is used in the genitive (7.97).

8.295d Opinion among commentators is divided over whether there is an elided "*a*" (= *avicāritam*) or if the term is the positive *vicāritam*. Mss. are of little help because they generally do not include *avagrahas* for elided "*a*." Bhāruci and Govinda take it to be the positive *vicāritaḥ*, which is given as an opinion by Medhātithi also. According to Bhāruci's explanation, *vicārita* here means that the punishment is determined according to the provisions of the following verses. All other commentators, however, follow Medhātithi in taking the term to be the negative *avicāritaḥ* (Bühler's comment on this verse erroneously takes *Rn*, *Nā*, and *Nd* as supporting the positive). Manu has similar constructions with *avicārayan* occupying the last place in a half-verse at 3.114; 7.212; 8.283; 8.250; 9.135, 170, 280; 11.14. In two other places Manu has *avicāritam* at the end of a half-verse: 11.29, 33. These parallels support my assumption that here also the negative is meant; nowhere else do we have the positive *vicāritam* in a similar context.

8.311a Even though all the editions read *hi*, it is found in only a small number of mss. The adopted reading *ca* is found in: Be¹ BBe² BCa Ho Jo² wKt¹ BKt⁵ La¹ Lo¹ Lo³ Lo⁴ Lo⁵ GMd¹ TMd³ TMd⁴ GMy NNg sOx¹ Ox² NPu¹ Pu² Pu⁴ sPu⁶ Pu⁸ Tj¹ Tj² Tr² MTr⁴ MTr⁵ Wa *Bh* [ad 8.306].

8.313a, c The mss. are divided over the appropriate relative pronoun at the beginning of the two *pādas*: *yat* or *yaḥ*. The grammar of the verse supports *yat*, which corresponds to *tena* of the main clauses. The change to *yaḥ* may have been prompted by mistaking *tena* for a masculine rather than a neuter instrumental. Kullūka, who reads *yaḥ*, is thus forced to add a second pronoun in the main clause: *duḥkhitair ākṣiptaḥ sahate yaḥ sa tena svargaloke pūjāṃ labhate*. The older commentators Medhātithi and Govinda have correctly adopted the reading *yat* (Bhāruci does not comment on the term). Some mss. have *yat* in *pāda*-a and *yaḥ* in *pāda*-c, although the latter reading is sometimes unclear because of the triple conjunct. The reading *yat* in *pāda*-a is found in: Be³ NKt⁴ BKt⁵ La¹ TMd³ TMd⁴ GMd⁵ GMy NNg NPu¹ Pu² Pu⁴ Pu⁵ Pu⁷ Tr¹ [*but cor sh*] MTr⁴ MTr⁵ [*Jolly* M 5–9 G Nd Me] *Me Rn Nd Go Dev Jolly*.

8.314b The vast majority of NT mss. and all editions have the reading *dhāvatā*. However, all the ST mss., as well as NT ones in old Nāgarī script, read *dhīmatā*, a reading supported by the two oldest commentators, Bhāruci and Medhātithi. The parallel passages in the *Dharmasūtras* (*GDh* 12.43; *BDh* 2.1.16) make no mention of running; only *VaDh* 20.41 has the reading *abhidhāvet*, which is also uncertain because several medieval citations (*Vij* 3.257; *Mādh* 2.416) give the reading *abhiyācet* (both Jolly and Bühler depend too heavily on the *VaDh* reading for their decision to adopt *dhāvatā*). The repetition of this provision by Manu at 11.100–1 also makes no reference to running. Bhāruci comments on the term: *dhīmatā "vividhena vadhena ca"* (*MDh* 8.310) *śuddhihetur idaṃ prāyaś-cittaśāstrasāmarthyād ity evaṃ jānatānena*. Medhātithi is more succinct: *dhīmatā dhairyavatā*. In the parallel passage of *NSm* (19.93) Lariviere has adopted the reading *dhāvatā;* however he used only northern mss. for the edition and the Trivandrum Sanskrit Series (no. 97 1929) edition of the *NSm* reads *dhīmatā.* In this case the southern mss. of the *MDh* and the *NSm* have preserved the original reading. The adopted reading is found in: NKt^4 BKt^5 GMd^1 TMd^3 TMd^4 GMd^5 GMy NNg NPu^1 Pu^2 Pu^4 MTr^4 MTr^5 [*Jolly* M Nd]*Bh Me Viś Jha Dave*.

8.322c Even though all the editions have the reading *śeṣe tv ekā-*, it is clear the reading should be *śeṣe 'py ekā-*. The latter reading is found in most mss., including all the ST ones. None of the commentators comment on the reading. The reading adopted is found in: BBe^2 Be^3 BCa Ho Jo^2 WKt^1 WKt^3 NKt^4 La^1 Lo^1 Lo^3 GMd^1 TMd^3 TMd^4 GMd^5 GMy OOr SOx^1 Ox^2 Pu^2 Pu^4 SPu^6 Pu^8 Tj^1 Tr^1 MTr^4 MTr^5 [*Jolly* Nd R]*Lakṣ*.

8.324d The sequence of *rājā daṇḍam* is unclear. All editions and some NT mss. read *daṇḍaṃ rājā*. I have adopted the sequence supported by the vast majority of mss. of both ST and NT: BBe^2 Bo BCa Ho Jo^2 WKt^1 WKt^3 NKt^4 La^1 GMd^1 TMd^3 TMd^4 GMd^5 GMy OOr SOx^1 Ox^2 Pu^5 SPu^6 Pu^7 Tr^1 MTr^4 MTr^5 MTr^6 Wa*Lakṣ Apa*. This sequence is supported by *Go, Ku,* and *Rc*.

8.325d The reading of this *pāda* is very uncertain. Most commentators did not quite understand the meaning of *sthūrikā;* hence the numerous readings of this word. Medhātithi gives no less than three opinions: goad, back side of the food, and a cow in the habit of running away. Bhāruci gives two meanings: barren cow and the area three inches above the heel. The correct meaning is clearly the second given by Bhāruci, i.e., the Achilles tendon. This meaning is also attested to by Medhātithi and Nandana (see my note to the translation of this verse). Mayrhofer (1999, III: 526) considers the term to be obscure, but accepts the meaning of ox and barren cow and refers to R. Hiersche, *Untersuchungen zur Frage der Tenues aspiratae im Indogermanischen* (Wiesbaden, 1964), p. 129 and note 44.

The last word of the *pāda* is even more problematic. All but one ms. (Wa) and all commentators read the locative *bhedane*. Given the history of interpretation of this verse, it is understandable that the tradition has preferred the locative *bhedane*, because this was thought to be a reference to one more crime. The *NSm* 19.40 points us in the right direction: *goṣu brāhmaṇasaṃsthāsu sthūrāyāś chedanaṃ bhavet*, "in the case of cows belonging to Brahmins, there should be the cleaving of the Achilles tendon." I have conjecturally adopted the accusative reading *bhedanam*. It is quite out of place for injury to an animal to occur here, given that the entire section deals with theft. It is clear that both punishments indicated in this verse—cleaving the heel and cutting half the foot—are for stealing livestock of Brahmins, the first for cows and the other for goats and the like.

8.329b The difference in the two readings *caivamādīnām adyānām*, which I have adopted, and *caivamādīnāṃ madyānām* is slight, simply the presence or the absence of the *anusvāra*. I think the term *evamādīnām* more properly relates to food items rather than to liquor. The adopted reading is found in: Be[3] BCa Ho Jm Jo[1] Kt[2] BKt[5] GMy NPu[1] Pu[2] Pu[4] MTr[3] MTr[5] *Mandlik Jha Dave*.

8.333c Most NT mss. have the reading *tam ādyam*. I have adopted the reading *taṃ śatam*, however, because it is recorded in all the ST mss. and a substantial number of NT ones. Further, this reading is supported by Medhātithi, who gives the alternate reading as a *pāṭha*. The reading is, nevertheless, uncertain, especially because Bhāruci's commentary is damaged at this crucial point; but later he mentions *ādyo daṇḍaḥ*, which supports the alternate reading.

8.351d For the reading *tan manyum* (as opposed to *taṃ manyum*), see parallels at *BDh* 1.18.13; *VaDh* 3.18; *ViDh* 5.191.

8.354b There is strong manuscript support for both *rahaḥ* and *saha*. The latter, indeed, could be seen as the *lectio difficilior*, because it is syntactically connected to *patnyā* occurring in the previous *pāda*. Nevertheless, I have adopted *rahaḥ* both because it fits the context better (secret conversation with a woman) and because it is supported by Medhātithi (Jolly is incorrect in assuming that *Me* reads *saha*). The reading adopted is found in: BBe[2] Jm Jo[1] Jo[2] WKt[3] Lo[1] Lo[2] Lo[3] GMd[1] TMd[3] GMy Pu[8] Tj[1] Tj[2] Tr[1] MTr[3] MTr[5] [*Jolly* Nd R] *Me Rc Mr*.

8.369c Manuscripts are divided over the readings *triguṇam* and *dviguṇam*. Among the older commentators, Bhāruci has *dviguṇam* and Medhātithi *triguṇam*. Neither, however, comment on the term, and given that we have a single ms. of Bhāruci and no critical edition of Medhātithi, it is difficult to know whether these were their own readings or later emendations. I have opted for *triguṇam* because it is recorded in most ST mss. and numerous NT-x ones: Be[1] BBe[2] Ho NKt[4] Lo[2] GMd[1] TMd[4] GMy NNg SOx[1] Ox[2] Ox[3] NPu[1] Pu[2] Pu[3] Pu[4] Pu[5] SPu[6] Pu[7] Tr[1] Tr[2] MTr[4] MTr[6] Wa [*Jolly* Nd[2]] *Lakṣ Apa Me Nd*.

8.371b It is unclear which sequence is original: *jñātistrīguṇa* or *strījñātiguṇa*. It is further unclear whether the latter is a compound or if *strī* should be construed separately with *yā tu* or the previous *pāda*. The commentators *Me*, *Nā*, and *Nd* gloss with *jñātiguṇa* and *strīguṇa* indicating that they read it as a Tatpuruṣa compound and that *jñāti* came before *strī*. Most of the medieval citations also support this sequence, which is found in: Bo NKt[4] Lo[2] GMd[1] TMd[4] GMd[5] NNg Ox[3] Pu[3] Pu[5] Pu[7] Tr[1] Tr[2] MTr[4] MTr[5]MTr[6] [*Jolly* M G N Nd] *Dev Mādh Viś Nd Jolly*.

8.374c-d This half-verse appears to have caused a lot of problems for commentators and scribes alike; hence the numerous variants. The uncertainties center around three times: *agupta*, *aṅgasarvasva*, and *gupta*. For the first, I have adopted conjecturally *agupta aṅga-*; this reading is not found in any ms. The problems here, I think, derive from this hiatus created by sandhi. Scribes appear to have resolved this in two ways: first, by adopting the accusative *aguptam aṅga-*, and second, by adding *eka* and adopting a double sandhi *aguptaikāṅga-*. A few mss. add a *ca* to eliminate the hiatus: *agupte cāṅga-*, which was adopted by Jolly. The reading *ekāṅga* is supported by *Bh*, *Nā*, and *Nd*. The unusual double sandi is explained by *Nd* thus: *aguptaikaṅgety atra śākalyamatena yakāralope kṛte chandonusārād yakāralopasya asiddhatvam anādṛtya vṛddhividhānam*. The addition of *eka* is probably a later formation; *Me*, *Go*, *Ku*, and *Rc* clearly state that the bodily part cut off is the part that was used to commit the crime, namely, the penis.

In the second compound there are three major readings: *aṅgasarvasvaiḥ, aṅgasarvasvam* and *aṅgasarvasvī*. There is scant manuscript support for the first; its introduction may have been influenced by the instrumental *sarveṇa* of *pāda*-d. The second is also represented by only a few mss.; the accusative also does not fit the syntax. The third appears to be an elliptical compound; *Me* and *Nā* clearly have this reading and have long explanations of its meaning. The meaning appears to be that a Śūdra who has sex with a guarded woman becomes "one having his penis and all his wealth (taken away)." I have adopted this reading, which is found also in all the medieval citations: BBe^{2} Bo Ho Hy La^{1} Lo^{1} Lo^{2} wKt^{1} BKt^{5} GMd^{5} oOr Ox^{3} NPu^{1} Pu^{2} Pu^{4} Pu^{8} Tj^{2} Tr^{2} MTr^{4} MTr^{5} MTr^{6} *Apa Lakṣ Mādh Me Nā Jha Dave*.

Finally, in *pāda*-d there are two readings: *gupte* and *guptam*. The former is clearly the correct reading; the latter may have been influenced by the "correction" introduced in *pāda*-c by some scribes. The reading adopted is found in: Be^{1} Ho La^{1} Lo^{2} GMd^{1} TMd^{3} TMd^{4} GMd^{5} GMy NNg sOx^{1} Pu^{2} Pu^{3} Pu^{4} sPu^{6} Tr^{1} Tr^{2} MTr^{4} MTr^{5} MTr^{6} Wa [*Jolly* N Nd] *Apa Lakṣ Bh Nd Rc Jolly*.

8.378b I have adopted the reading *viprāṃ guptām* first because it is found in all the ST mss. and a substantial number of NT-x ones, including the old NKt^{4}. Secondly, we see that *guptā* almost always follows the class name in all the surrounding verses (374–84). The only exception is verse 384, but the inversion of the order there may well be determined by the meter. The reading adopted in found in: BCa NKt^{4} BKt^{5} Lo^{4} Lo^{5} GMd^{1} TMd^{3} TMd^{4} GMd^{5} GMy oOr Ox^{2} Ox^{3} MTr^{5} MTr^{6}.

8.380b The mss. are divided over the two readings *api sthitam* and *vyavasthitam*. The context clearly favors *api*, and it is supported by the explicit statement of Medhātithi: *apiśabdo yugapatsarvapāpakārye 'pi brāhmaṇo na jātu kadācid dhantavyaḥ*. Similar support for *api* is given by *Go, Nd,* and *Ku*. The reading adopted is found in: BBe^{2} Hy Jm Jo^{1} wKt^{1} Kt^{2} wKt^{3} NKt^{4} La^{1} Lo^{2} Lo^{3} GMy NNg Ox^{2} NPu^{1} Pu^{3} Pu^{8} Tj^{1} Tj^{2} Tr^{2} MTr^{3} MTr^{4} *Vij Apa*.

8.384b Even though all the editions read *pañcaśataṃ*, this reading is supported by very few mss. The reading adopted is found in: Be^{1} BBe^{2} Bo BCa Ho Hy wKt^{1} wKt^{3} BKt^{5} Lo^{1} Lo^{4} Lo^{5} GMd^{1} TMd^{3} TMd^{4} GMd^{5} GMy NNg sOx^{1} NPu^{1} sPu^{6} Pu^{8} Tj^{2} Tr^{2} [*Jolly* M Nd]. The nominative masculine is also supported by other mss. that read *pañcadaśaḥ* and by the parallels at 8.264, 268, 297, 329, 369, 373. Only once is the accusative used: 8.331.

8.384c Although there is strong manuscript support for the reading *icchet*, it is clear that the original reading is *ṛcchet*. This reading is found in *Me*, who glosses it with *prāpnuyāt*, an explanation repeated by *Go* and *Ku*. No commentator permits the guilty Kṣatriya to exercise an option regarding his punishment. The reading adopted is found in: BBe^{2} Jo^{2} wKt^{3} La^{1} Lo^{1} TMd^{3} GMy NNg NPu^{1} Pu^{2} Pu^{3} Pu^{4} Pu^{8} Tr^{1} Tr^{2} MTr^{4} MTr^{6} *Me Rc Jha Dave*.

8.392a The reading with a short "a" *prati-* is explicitly given by Medhātithi; he gives *prāti* as an alternative: *ādidīrghapāṭhe svārthiko 'ṇ*. The former reading is found in most ST mss. I have, however, adopted *prāti*, because it has the broadest manuscript support. The proper reading in the parallel passage in *YDh* 2.263 (the short form is found in *Apa* and the long form in *Vij*) and in *Vidh* 5.94 is unclear. The reading adopted is found in: Be^{1} BBe^{2} Bo Hy Jm Jo^{1} Jo^{2} wKt^{1} Kt^{2} NKt^{4} La^{1} Lo^{2} Lo^{4} TMd^{3} NNg sOx^{1} NPu^{1} Pu^{2} Pu^{3} Pu^{4} Pu^{5} sPu^{6} Pu^{7} Tj^{2} MTr^{3} *Me* [pāṭha] *Go Nā Ku Rn Nd Rc Mr Mandlik Jolly KSS*. The reading, however, remains uncertain.

8.396b We have two distinct readings, the one in NT and the other in ST (also followed by 3 NT mss.). *Bh, Me,* and *Nd* do not comment on this *pāda*; all others support the NT reading, which I have adopted. The reading, however, is uncertain.

8.403a Jolly writes *tulāmānaṃ* as a compound. This is incorrect. Bhāruci clearly indicates three items in this list: *trayam apy etad rājamudrāṅkitam.*

8.403b The manuscripts have very divergent readings here: *ca syāt, tu syāt,* and *tat syāt.* Although the manuscript evidence is scant, I have adopted the last reading; it is found in the medieval citations and is attested by most commentators: *Me, Go, Ku, Rn,* and *Mr.*

8.411b Manuscripts and editions provide two readings: *karśitau* and *karṣitau.* Confusion between the palatal and retroflex sibilants is a common feature in mss., but here the palatal and the retroflex derive from two different roots √ *kṛś* and √ *kṛṣ*. In this compound, both makes sense. I have adopted the palatal form principally because it is attested to in most of the ST mss. and in numerous NT ones. It is found in: Jo^{2} NKt^{4} Lo^{1} Lo^{2} Lo^{3} Lo^{4} Lo^{5} TMd^{3} GMd^{5} GMy NNg Ox^{2} NPu^{1} Pu^{2} Pu^{4} Pu^{5} Pu^{7} Tj^{1} Tj^{2} Tr^{1} Tr^{2} MTr^{3} MTr^{4} MTr^{5} MTr^{6} Wa *Dev Mandlik Jha KSS Dave* [in GMd^{1} the palmleaf is damaged at this point]. See also 2.24d, 9.74c, 10.101c.

CHAPTER NINE

9.1b Most mss. of both ST and NT read *dharme.* Nevertheless, I have adopted what I believe is the correct form *dharmye,* which is found only in Be^{1} BBe^{2} Bo Hy Jm Jo^{1} Jo^{2} La^{1} NNg Pu^{8} MTr^{5} *Lakṣ Dev Mandlik Jolly Jha Dave.* The common form *dharme* is the *lectio facilior,* and the doubling of "m" (धर्म्मे) found in many mss. is very similar in Devanāgarī to (धर्म्ये).

9.2c The mss. are deeply divided over the reading of this verse. All the editions have the alternate reading, which is also supported by *Me, Nā, Rn,* and *Rc.* Even though there is uncertainly regarding the original reading, I have adopted the reading found in all the ST mss. and a large number of NT ones, including the old NKt^{4}. This reading is found in: BCa Ho wKt^{1} wKt^{3} NKt^{4} La^{1} GMd^{1} TMd^{3} TMd^{4} GMd^{5} GMy oOr sOx^{1} Ox^{2} sPu^{6} Tr^{1} MTr^{4} MTr^{5} MTr^{6} [*Jolly* Nd] *Dev Mādh.*

9.4 Most NT mss. have the reading *vācya* in *pādas* a, b, and d. This is the reading adopted in all the editions. I have adopted the reading *yāpya,* however, which is the *lectio difficilior* and the reading found in all but one ST mss., as well as in several NT ones: NKt^{4} Lo^{4} GMd^{1} TMd^{4} GMd^{5} GMy NNg NPu^{1} Tr^{1} MTr^{4} MTr^{5}MTr^{6} [*Jolly* M N Nd] *Nd.* This reading is also supported by the corrupt readings in Be^{1} La^{1}. Bhāruci is the only commentator to gloss this term (*yāpyā vacanīyāḥ*). Derrett here has emended the commentary to read *vācyā,* even though it would have been pointless for Bhāruci to gloss this term with *vacanīyāḥ.* For the meaning of the term *yāpya,* see Introduction, p. 36. For other occurrences of this term, see *GDh* 13.23; 19.2; *BDh* 3.10.2;*VaDh* 15.19.

9.19d The ST and NT diverge radically in the reading of this *pāda.* All the ST mss. have the reading I have adopted. I think *ākṛti* not only is the *lectio difficilior* but also makes far better sense and parallels *nidarśana* in the same position in the very next verse. Here the text is not dealing with expiatory rites or formulas but with the perverse nature of women. To prove this, Manu adduces a vedic text in verse 18, and goes on to say in the first half of verse 19 that there are numerous such texts in the Vedas. In the second half, he says that he will produce a sampling of these. The term *ākṛti* with the meaning of sample or specimen (cf. *ākṛtigaṇa* in grammar) is somewhat unusual, which may have led scribes and commentators to change it to *niṣkṛti*, especially in view of verse 21 that mentions an expiation (*nihnava*). I take *tāsām* in this *pāda* as referring to the vedic texts (*śruti*), here following Medhātithi; Bhāruci takes it as referring to women. Only Bhāruci and Nandana read *ākṛti*. It appears, however, that Bhāruci's commentary has been emended to read *vyabhicāraniṣkṛtim*, as pointed out by Derrett.

9.24b The reading *apakṛṣṭa* is found in most ST mss. and several NT ones and, therefore, should be a strong contender for adoption. I have adopted *avakṛṣṭa*, however, for several reasons. First, it is supported by Medhātithi; and, second, the parallel passages at 5.163; 7.126; 8.177, 281 all have *avakṛṣṭa*. The readings in several of these places, however, are somewhat uncertain, especially because of the confusion between "p" and "v" in many southern scripts.

9.32b Here we have a classic case of a *lectio difficilior*, in this case *kartari*, being changed to the easier *bhartari*, even though the latter reading causes a tautology. We see this process happening in sPu^{6}, where the original *kartari* has been corrected above the line by a later reader to *bhartari*, which reading is then reproduced in sOx^{1}, which is a copy of sPu^{6}. This *pāda* is also an example of the usual superiority of the ST; only a few NT mss. have preserved this original reading, which is supported by the clear gloss of Medhātithi. This reading is found in: NKt^{4} BKt^{5} Lo^{4} GMd^{1} TMd^{3} TMd^{4} GMd^{5} GMy sPu^{6} Tr^{1} Tr^{2} MTr^{4} MTr^{5} MTr^{6} Wa [*Jolly* Nd M N] *Me Nd* (pāṭha) *Jolly Jha*.

9.43a Normally I would have adopted the reading *viddhaḥ*, because it has the unanimous support of the ST mss. and is found in several NT ones. Yet, I think the original reading was *kṣiptaḥ*; it is supported by *Me, Go, Nā*, and *Ku*. The reading *viddhaḥ* may have been influenced by the repeated *viddham* and *vidhyataḥ* of the very next *pāda*. The reading *kṣiptaḥ* at the end of *pāda*-a nicely corresponds to *kṣiptam* in *pāda*-c; it also parallels *uptam* used with reference to the seed in earlier verses. The reading, however, is uncertain. The reading adopted is found in: Jo^{2} wKt^{1} wKt^{3} La^{1} Lo^{1} Lo^{4} NNg sOx^{1} Ox^{2} NPu^{1} Pu^{3} NPu^{6} Pu^{7} Pu^{8} Tj^{1} Tj^{2} Tr^{1} [*mc sh to*] Tr^{2} [*Jolly* M G N R] *Me Go Nā Ku Rc Mr Jolly*.

9.47d The reading adopted, *sakṛt sakṛt*, is found in: Be^{1} BBe^{2} BCa Jo^{2} wKt^{1} wKt^{3} La^{1} Lo^{1} Lo^{3} Lo^{4} GMd^{1} TMd^{3} TMd^{4} GMd^{5} GMy oOr sOx^{1} Ox^{2} sPu^{6} Pu^{7} Tj^{1} Tr^{1} MTr^{4} MTr^{6} Wa [*Jolly* M G R Nd] *Dev Lakṣ Mādh Rc Jolly*.

9.52d Manuscripts are divided over the two readings *balīyasī* and *garīyasī;* all ST mss., however, record the former. It is also supported by *Me, Go, Ku,* and *Nd*. This reading is found in: Jo^{2} Lo^{2} Lo^{4} GMd^{1} TMd^{3} GMd^{5} GMy Ox^{3} NPu^{1} Pu^{2} Pu^{4} Pu^{5} Pu^{7} MTr^{4} MTr^{5} MTr^{6} Wa [*Jolly* M G Ku Rd R^{2}] *Vij Mādh Jolly Jha*.

9.54c The reading of this *pāda* that has been adopted is found in all ST mss., and it is either found in or supported by several NT mss.: wKt^{3} NKt^{4} La^{1} GMd^{1} TMd^{3} TMd^{4} GMd^{5} GMy NNg Tr^{1} MTr^{4} MTr^{5} MTr^{6} [*Jolly* Nd] *Lakṣ*. The meaning of the *pāda* also supports this reading; it is not the seed (*bīja*) that belongs to the owner of the field but the crop. Commentators have wrongly interpreted *tat* in this *pāda* as referring to the seed; it refers instead to what has grown from the seed implied in the verb *prarohati* of the previous *pāda*.

9.54d The reading adopted, *vaptā*, is found in all the ST and several NT mss.: BBe^{2} Ho Hy Jm Jo^{1} Kt^{2} wKt^{3} NKt^{4} La^{1} GMd^{1} TMd^{3} TMd^{4} GMd^{5} GMy Ox^{2} Tj^{2} Tr^{1} MTr^{3} MTr^{4} MTr^{5}

mTr[6]. This reading also suits the context of a sower (probably of rice) whose seeds are carried to an adjoining farm by wind or water. The alternate reading may also be influenced by the identical reading of verse 51d.

9.65a Jolly has adopted the reading *naudvāhikeṣu*, and this parallels the form of the word at 9.206 [= *YDh* 2.118]. Only a few mss., however, support the *vṛddhi* for *audvāhika* here, although they adopt it at 9.206. Apparently, we have here two forms of the term with a very similar meaning.

9.73d The ST and the NT have two very different readings here: *kanyādānam* and *kanyādātur*. The former is at one level the easier reading, because the compound *kanyādāna* is so common. On the other hand, the genitive *kanyādātuḥ* may have been influenced by the other genitive compound in the same *pāda*. The reading *kanyādānam* has the advantage of providing a clear reference to the *tat* of the previous *pāda*.

9.74c On -*karśitā*, see note to 8.411. The palatal form *karśitā* is found in: Bo Jo[2] nKt[4] bKt[5] Lo[2] Lo[4] tMd[3] tMd[4] gMd[5] gMy nNg nPu[1] Pu[2] Pu[4] Pu[5] Pu[7] Tr[1] Tr[2] mTr[4] mTr[6] Wa *Jha Dave*.

9.78d *Mandlik*, *Jha*, *KSS*, and *Derrett* do not recognize the sandhi between *pādas* c and d, writing: *parityājyā vibhūṣaṇaparicchadā*. It is clear from both the context and the commentaries of *Me*, *Nā*, *Ku*, *Nd*, and *Rn* that the last compound is a negative one: *avibhūṣaṇaparicchadā*.

9.87b I have adopted *svajātyā* here, even though at 86d I adopted *nāsajātiḥ*. Numerous mss. that used *sajāti* in the previous verse give *svajāti* here. Both forms are correct and I see no reason to be consistent as to the spelling when the mss. are not. The reading *svajātyā* here has overwhelming manuscript support: Be[1] bBe[2] Ho wKt[1] wKt[3] nKt[4] La[1] Lo[1] Lo[3] Lo[4] gMd[1] tMd[4] gMd[5] gMy nNg sOx[1] Ox[2] nPu[1] Pu[5] sPu[6] Pu[7] Tj[1] Tr[1] mTr[4] mTr[5] mTr[6] Wa *Jmv Lakṣ Ku Nd*.

9.92d The mss. are divided over the readings *steyam* and *stenā*. I have adopted the former found in all the ST and numerous NT mss.: bKt[5] La[1] Lo[4] gMd[1] tMd[3] tMd[4] gMd[5] gMy nNg oOr nPu[1] Pu[2] Pu[4] Pu[5] Pu[7] Tr[1] mTr[4] mTr[5] mTr[6] Wa [*Jolly* M G Nd Gr] *Apa Lakṣ Jolly*. Bhāruci and Medhātithi also gives as a pāṭha the masculine *stenaḥ*. In this case, the one prohibited from taking the jewelry is the husband, as explained by Bhāruci: *evaṃ cāpāṭhe puruṣaviṣayaḥ śloko bhavati*.

9.93 Bhāruci comments that this verse belongs to some other *smṛti* and not to Manu: *smṛtyantareṣv ayaṃ śloko na tv atra samāmnāyate*. Medhātithi also records such a view: *kecid āhuḥ amānavo 'yaṃ ślokaḥ*.

9.102c Most NT mss. have the reading *abhicaretām*; this is, however, the easier reading because the term *vyabhicāra* for sexual transgression is a common term in the text. Medhātithi clearly reads *aticaretām*, because he comments: *aticāro 'tikramaḥ dharmārthakāmeṣv asahabhāvaḥ*. The reading adopted is found in all the ST mss. (gMd[1] is torn at this point) and in a few NT one: bBe[2] wKt[3] nKt[4] wKt[5] Lo[4] tMd[3] tMd[4] gMd[5] gMy oOr Tr[1] mTr[4] mTr[5] mTr[6] Wa[*Jolly* M N Nd] *Lakṣ Me Nā Mr Jolly Jha Dave*.

9.108b All editions have adopted the reading *bhrātṝn*. The majority of the mss., especially the ST ones, clearly support *bhrātā*: bBe[2] Hy Jo[2] wKt[3] La[1] Lo[3] gMd[1] tMd[3] tMd[4] gMd[5] nNg oOr sOx[1] nPu[1] Pu[2] Pu[4] Pu[5] sPu[6] Pu[7] Tj[1] Tr[1] mTr[6] Wa *Apa Jmv* [vl] *Ku*. This reading also parallels nicely *bhartari* in the same position in *pāda*-d.

9.118a Medhātithi appears to read: *svābhyaḥ svābhyaḥ kanyābhyaḥ*. This reading has considerable merit, because otherwise this *pāda* is simply repeating what is said in *pāda*-c; but it is supported by only a few mss. According to Medhātithi's reading, each brother is obliged to give a portion of his inheritance only to the sisters belonging to his own caste, that is, born to the same mother as he. This is also the interpretation of Nārāyaṇa and Rāghavānanda.

9.123c Editions are inconsistent with regard to the *avagraha* before*jyeṣṭha*. Mandlik, Jolly, and Jha put an *avagraha*, while KSS and Dave do not. Manuscripts usually omit all *avagrahas*; therefore, it is impossible to determine if a negative or a positive is intended. I follow Bhāruci and Medhātithi in reading here *(a)jyeṣṭhavṛṣāḥ*.

9.126c Once again the ST mss. give us a superior reading, *ekagarbhe 'pi*, which has been adopted. All but one of the ST mss. have this reading, and they are supported with regard to *eka* by 11NT mss. The reading adopted is supported by *Me* and *Nd* with respect to both *eka* and *api*, and by *Bh* and *Ku* with respect to *eka*.

9.128b The mss. are deeply divided over the word that comes after *cakre*. I have adopted *cakre 'tha*, which is found in the majority of mss.: Be^{1} bBe^{2} Bo Ho Jm Jo^{1} Jo^{2} wKt^{1} Kt^{2} wKt^{3} nKt^{4} bKt^{5} La^{1} Lo^{1} Lo^{2} Lo^{3} gMd^{1} nNg sOx^{1} Ox^{2} sPu^{6} Pu^{8} Tj^{1} Tr^{2} mTr^{3} mTr^{5}*Mandlik Jha KSS Dave*. No manuscript supports the reading *cakre sa* adopted by Jolly.

9.133b The reading is uncertain. Several ST mss. and a few NT ones have the reading adopted by all editions. The reading I have adopted, however, is found in three ST mss. and the vast majority of the NT ones. See also the parallel in verse 139b. The difference in the readings does not affect the meaning at all.

9.145b Although all editions read *jātaḥ putraḥ*, the sequence in inverted in all the ST and most of the NT mss.: Bo bCa Jo^{2} wKt^{1} wKt^{3} nKt^{4} bKt^{5} La^{1} Lo^{2} Lo^{4} gMd^{1} tMd^{3} tMd^{4} gMd^{5} nNg oOr Pu^{2} Pu^{4} Pu^{5} Pu^{7} Tj^{1} Tr^{1} mTr^{4} mTr^{5}mTr^{6}. This appears to be the sequence also of Bhāruci.

9.147a Mandlik, Derrett, and Dave give the positive reading *yā niyuktānyataḥ*. This reading is supported by the comments of *Ku* and *Nd*. I take the form to be *aniyuktā* and see a sandhi here as explicitly stated by *Me: aniyukteti praśleṣo draṣṭavyaḥ*. The negative meaning is supported also by *Nā*, *Rn*, and *Rc*.

9.152b The mss. present three major readings: *parikalpayet, parikalpya ca*, and *pravibhajya tu*. The two latter readings have the gerund, making the whole verse a syntactic unit; the first of these two is given in the NT-y [vulgate] mss., while the second is limited to the ST mss. I think that the gerund may have been introduced precisely to make the verse a single sentence; the reading adopted, which I think is the original, gives the verse two finite verbs. This reading is found in: Be^{1} bBe^{2} Bo wKt^{1} Lo^{1} Lo^{2} Lo^{4} oOr nPu^{1} Pu^{2} Pu^{3} Pu^{4} Pu^{5} Pu^{7} Pu^{8} Tr^{2} [*Jolly* M G] *Jolly*. I think the first half-verse ending with *parikalpayet* is an independent sentence providing an alternative to the complicated methods of partition given in the previous two verses. Then the second half-verse and verse 153 go on to state how the division is to be carried out among the sons from wives of different classes.

9.156a The mss. of both ST and NT are divided over *vā* and *ye*. I have adopted the former principally because it is attested to by *Bh* and *Me;* it is also found in a wide variety of mss., including the old nKt^{4}. This reading also makes better sense as this verse gives a simple alternative to the rather complex rules of partition outlined above (see the parallel in verse 152). Medhātithi is somewhat confused about this reading, because he apparently takes *vā* here as providing an alternative to the verse immediately preceding and feels that such an alternative is not possible: *vāśabdo dvitīyaṃ vikalpam antareṇānupapadyamānaḥ prakṛtam apekṣya nirākāṅkṣo bhavati* (Jha's translation of this is inaccurate). The reading adopted is found in: Be[1] Ho NKt[4] BKt[5] Lo[4] GMd[1] TMd[4] NNg oOr sOx[1] Ox[2] Pu[5] sPu[6] Pu[7] MTr[5] Wa [*Jolly* M G] *Bh Me Lakṣ Jha*.

9.162d The reading adopted here is found in Ho wKt[1] Lo[2] Lo[4] GMd[5] NNg Ox[2] Pu[3] Pu[7] Pu[8] *Apa Jmv*, but is also supported by the many mss. that read *tat saṃgṛhṇīta*. See, moreover, 9.191d where the same expression occurs; there the reading adopted here has greater manuscript support and is also adopted by all editions.

9.170a Here the majority of the mss. in both ST and NT have erred in reading *yasya* for *yas tu*. The latter reading is found in: Be[1] Jo[2] Lo[2] Lo[3] Lo[4] oOr Pu[2] Pu[4] Pu[5] Pu[7] Tj[1] [*Jolly* M G R] *Dev Jolly Jha Dave*. The person to whom the child belongs is not the person who owns the house but the person (i.e., the husband) to whom the mother of the child belongs. In a joint household, the owner of the house may be different from the husband of the woman who gives birth. Further, we would also expect a correlative for the *saḥ* of *pāda*-c, as we have in the surrounding verses.

9.196c The mss. are quite confused about the reading of this *pāda* and of 197b. Many have different readings here and in the parallel *pāda* at 197b. I have adopted the reading *atītāyām aprajasi*, which is clearly the *lectio difficilior* both because *aprajas* is a rare word in classical Sanskrit and because its adoption goes against the requirements of the standard Pathyā form of the *śloka*. These considerations may well have promoted scribes and commentators to change *aprajasi* to the more standard *aprajāyām*. Occurring at the end of the *pāda*, even this violates the normal *śloka*, which may have prompted others to move it to the beginning of the *pāda*, giving the reading found in the vulgate: *aprajāyām atītāyām*. The reading adopted is found in: Bo Ho NKt[4] Lo[1] Lo[2] oOr sOx[1] Pu[3] sPu[6] Tr[2], as well as in the citations of *Apa, Lakṣ,* and *Dev*. It is also supported by the reading in the parallel verse in *YDh* 2.144. The only commentator to note the term is *Nā*, who reads *aprajāyām*.

9.197c See the previous note for the reading adopted, *atītāyām aprajasi*, which is found in: Be[1] Bo Ho BKt[5] Lo[2] sOx[1] Pu[3] sPu[6] Tr[1] Tr[2] *Apa Lakṣ*.

9.219c Most mss. take *yogakṣema* and *pracāra* as two separate items. Only *Bh* and *Rn* take the three words as a single compound. Others take *pracāra* as a separate word, generally taking it to mean a pasture or a path. I have opted to see the three words as forming a single Tatpuruṣa compound, but this reading is found only in Jm Jo[2] wKt[3] Lo[3] GMd[1] TMd[3] GMy Tj[2] MTr[5] *Jmv Lakṣ Dev Mādh*. Bṛhaspati (1.26.52) and Kātyāyana (884), who can be regarded as early commentators of Manu, also divide the two terms, and Kātyāyana explicitly uses the expression *gopracāra*. Clearly, the older meaning of *pracāra* as "activities" became obsolete at an early date. Scharfe (1993, 195–200), in a close semantic study of the term *pracāra*, has clearly shown that it does not mean land or pasture but activities (see 7.153 n.). He says that this verse of Manu (9.219) may be the best candidate for the meaning of pasture. I think that even here the term refers to activity. The confusion is created by the fact that the term has been separated from the preceding word *yogakṣema*. The separation is created merely by the addition of an *anusvāra* at the end. At every other place in Manu, *pracāra* refers to some form of activity either within a Tatpuruṣa compound (*antaḥpurapracāram* 7.153; *udāsīnapracāram* 7.155) or with a genitive (*maṇḍalasya pracāram* 7.154; *madhyamasya pracāram* 7.155). It is, thus, always the *pracāra* of some place or person. I think the same is true here, and *pracāra* here refers to activities or measure taken to ensure safety. One can think of watchmen, fences, and the like. These must be continued undisturbed by the partition.

9.221b I have adopted the reading *rāṣṭre* in preference to *rāṣṭrāt*, which is found in all editions and most NT mss. The former, I think, makes better sense; the object is to suppress gambling activities within the kingdom, not to banish them from the kingdom (verse 224 tells him to execute gamblers; see the locatives in the additional verse in La^{1} after verse 223). This sense is made clear in the very next verse with the word *pratighāta*. This reading is also found in most ST mss. and is a good number of NT-x ones: La^{1} Lo^{2} gMd^{1} tMd^{4} gMd^{5} gMy nNg oOr nPu^{1} Pu^{2} Pu^{4} Pu^{5} Pu^{7} Tr^{1} mTr^{4} mTr^{6} *Mādh* (also vl in *Lakṣ*). Commentators offer no help with this reading.

9.225a The last word of this *pāda* is quite unclear; mss. give four major variants: *kera, kela, krūra*, and *caura*. I have adopted the first. The two last ones are probably attempts to find easier words for an obscure one; the "k" in *krūra* supports one of the first two, while the "r" of these two support *kera* over *kela*. The latter also may be an attempt to find an easier word; *Bh* explains it as *kelijīvinaḥ* and *Nd* as *keliśīlān*. The reading adopted is found in: bBe^{2} bCa Hy Jo^{2} wKt^{1} wKt^{3} Lo^{3} oOr Tj^{1} Tr^{1} mTr^{4} mTr^{5}mTr^{6} Wa [*Jolly* N R] *Nā Rn Mr Lakṣ Dave*.

9.230b The mss. are deeply divided over the reading of this *pāda*. I have gone with *daridrānātharogiṇām* both because it is probably the *lectio difficilior* and because the three-word compound nicely parallel *pāda*-a. This reading is found in: bBe^{2} Bo Hy La^{1} Lo^{4} gMd^{1} tMd^{3} gMy nNg oOr nPu^{1} Pu^{3} Pu^{8} Tj^{2} Tr^{1} mTr^{4} mTr^{5}mTr^{6} Wa [*Jolly* M Nd] *Dev Jolly*. This is supported by *Nā*, the only one to comment on this *pāda*.

9.234 The mss. and the commentators are deeply divided over whether the nouns, pronouns, and verbs are in the plural or the singular; several even give singulars in some and plurals in others. The central verb *kuryāt* in *pāda*-b is in the singular in most mss.; only the ST and vulgate mss. give the plural. I have opted for the singular throughout.

9.235c The reading adopted, *pṛthag vedyā*, is found in all the ST mss. and a good number of NT-x ones: wKt^{1} wKt^{3} nKt^{4} bKt^{5} Lo^{4} [after 8.46] gMd^{1} tMd^{3} tMd^{4} gMd^{5} gMy Ox^{3} Tr^{1} mTr^{4} mTr^{5} mTr^{6} [*Jolly* M Nd].

9.236c Even though all the editions have adopted the reading *śārīraṃ*, the overwhelming manuscript evidence points to the compound *śarīradhanasaṃyuktam*. This reading is supported by almost all ST mss., and it appears likely that the reading *śārīram* in several medieval texts is due to their modern editors using the vulgate *MDh* reading of this passage in their texts. The reading adopted is found in: Bo Ho wKt^{1} nKt^{4} bKt^{5} Lo^{2} Lo^{4} Lo^{5} gMd^{1} tMd^{4} gMd^{5} gMy nNg sOx^{1} Ox^{3} Pu^{3} Pu^{5} sPu^{6} Pu^{7} Pu^{8} Tj^{1} Tr^{1} Tr^{2} mTr^{4} mTr^{5} mTr^{6} *Apa Me Nā Rc*, with support from mss. with the reading *śarīraṃ*.

9.238b The sandhi between the two words has caused much difficulty to both scribes and commentators. *Me* tries to explain this by reading *vigarhita* and seeing the ensuing compound as a Dvandva [*asaṃpāṭhyāḥ* + *vigarhitāḥ*]. The most probable explanation is that here we have a case of double sandhi: *asaṃpāṭhyā avivāhinaḥ* being further combined to give *asaṃpāṭhyāvivāhinaḥ*.

9.247b Numerous mss., including most ST ones, have the reading *yathoktāni*. This is clearly a mistake; this expression is so frequent that the scribes may have unconsciously read it in place of the less common *yathoptāni*. The latter reading is found in: Bo Hy Jm Jo^1 Kt^2 wKt^3 bKt^5 La^1 Lo^1 Lo^4 Lo^5 tMd^4 nNg sOx^1 Ox^2 Pu^2 Pu^3 Pu^4 sPu^6 Tj^2 Tr^2 mTr^3 Wa, and supported by Jo^2 Lo^3 Tj^1.

9.257c The reading here is quite uncertain with no less than eight different versions. There is broadest support for *tv ete*, which is found in: Hy Jm Jo^1 Kt^2 Lo^2 gMd^1 tMd^3 tMd^4 gMy Pu^3 Tj^2 Tr^1 Tr^2 mTr^3 mTr^5 [*Jolly* Nd] *Mandlik Jha KSS Dave*.

9.258d The reading here is quite unclear, and so is the meaning. I have followed Jolly is adopting the reading *bhadraprekṣaṇika*, although it has very little manuscript support and must, therefore, be considered a conjecture. The only real support for this is provided by Medhātithi, whose root text clearly contained this reading and who provides the gloss: *sarvasya karavardhane bhadraprekṣaṇikāḥ praśaṃsipuruṣalakṣaṇāḥ.* Bhāruci does not comment on this verse; all others give some form of *īkṣaṇika*.

9.274a The reading here is very confused; scribes were clearly attempting to make sense of a very obscure word. Broadly we have three forms: *hiḍā*, *iḍā*, and *hitā*. None of these is a well-known term for a dike or dam. B-R and M-W give this meaning for *hitā*, but solely on the basis of its single occurrence in this verse. Other scribes have attempted to come up with easier terms, such as *taḍā*/*taṭā* [probably derived from *taḍāga*] and *setu*. Mainly on the basis of its frequency in the mss, I have chosen *hiḍā*, although with little certainty: Be^1 bBe^2 Bo bCa Ho Jo^2 nKt^4 La^1 Lo^1 Lo^2 Lo^3 tMd^3 gMd^5 nNg Ox^2 nPu^1 Pu^8 Tj^2 Tr^2 mTr^4 mTr^{5}mTr^6 [*Jolly* R] *Apa*. In Tr^1 the letter after *hi* has been erased and *ḍā* is written in the margin; it is impossible to make out the original letter, but it is probably *tā*, making its reading *hitā*.

9.275b The mss. are divided over the reading of this *pāda*. The reading adopted is found in bCa Hy Jm Jo^1 Kt^2 nKt^4 bKt^5 Lo^2 nNg oOr nPu^1 Pu^2 Pu^3 Pu^4 Pu^5 Pu^7 Tj^2 Tr^1 mTr^3 mTr^4 mTr^5 mTr^6 *Vij Apa Mādh Mandlik KSS Dave*.

9.279d The reading adopted, *dadyāc cottamasāhasam*, is found in wKt^1 wKt^3 La^1 gMd^1 tMd^3 tMd^4 gMd^5 gMy sOx^1 nPu^1 Pu^2 Pu^3 sPu^6 Tr^1 mTr^4 mTr^5 mTr^6 *Lakṣ*. The finite verb is supported by *Nā*.

9.303a All the editions read *vāyoś ca*, and this reading is found in an interesting group of mss. which normally do not contain identical readings, namely, several ST ones, the old nKt^4 and nNg, and the vulgate group of mss. Nevertheless, the manuscript support for the reading adopted is very strong: Be^1 bBe^2 Bo bCa Ho Jo^2 wKt^1 wKt^3 bKt^5 La^1 Lo^1 Lo^2 Lo^3 gMd^1 gMd^5 oOr sOx^1 Ox^2 nPu^1 Pu^2 Pu^3 sPu^6 Pu^7 Tj^1 Tr^1 Tr^2 mTr^4 mTr^5 mTr^6 [*Jolly* G R] *Lakṣ*.

9.314c Mss. give three readings: *indu*, *candra*, and *soma*. I have adopted the first, especially because, given the sandhi (*cenduḥ*), readings with *candra* also approximate it. The adopted reading is found in: Jo^2 nKt^4 Lo^3 gMd^1 tMd^3 tMd^4 gMd^5 Tj^1 Tr^1 mTr^4 mTr^6 [*Jolly* M G Nd R] *Jolly*.

9.335d Here all ST and NT-y (vulgate) mss. have the same reading, which is adopted by all editions. The reading *utkṛṣṭāṃ jātim* appears to be supported by *Me*, although it is unclear whether it is the original reading or merely a commentarial gloss. The reading *jātito 'śnute* is supported by all the NT-x mss., and it is also the *lectio difficilior* found in: Be^1 bBe^2 Bo Ho Jo^2 wKt^1 wKt^3 nKt^4 La^1 Lo^1 Lo^2 Lo^3 nNg oOr sOx^1 nPu^1 sPu^6 Pu^8 Tj^1 Tr^1 [*mc sh to*] Tr^2 Wa. The first word of this *pāda* is also unclear, the mss. giving several variants: *ucchritim*, *ucchritam*, *utsṛtim*, *utkarṣam*, and *utkṛṣṭām*. I have gone with the first even though it is found only in a few mss.: BBe^2 Ho Jo^2 Lo^1 Pu^8 and supported by *Rn*. It makes better grammatical sense than *ucchritam* and is supported by several variants ending in "i." The original reading of this *pāda*, however, remains uncertain.

CHAPTER TEN

10.5d The reading *tathaiva te* appears to have been the reading preferred by *Me*, who comments: *ye 'pi "ta eva te" iti paṭhanti teṣām api sa evārthas tajjātīyā iti*. The adopted reading, however, has the support of Bhāruci.

10.13d The original reading here is quite uncertain. Most mss. have the locative reading for *prātilomya* [or *pratiloma*] with the addition of the particle *tu* or *(a)pi*. The locative appears to be supported by *Bh*. This locative, however, may have been influenced by the proximity of *janmani*. I think *Nd* and *Rn* are correct in connecting *janmani* with *ekāntare*, the very first of the verse; these two locative thus bracket the entire statement. If that is the case, then the original reading probably was the instrumental *prātilomyena*, paralleling *ānulomyāt* of *pāda*-a. The reading adopted is found in: Jo^2 WKt^1 La^1 Lo^3 GMd^1 TMd^3 TMd^4 GMd^5 SOx^1 Ox^2 SPu^6 Tj^1 [*Jolly* R]; but the "n" of the instrumental is supported by variants in several mss.

10.18b The original reading of this caste name is unclear, and it is made more problematic because of the difficult orthography of the conjunct consonant. Jolly has preferred *pulkasa*, whereas the vulgate appears to read *pukkasa*. The same name occurs at 4.79; 10.38, 49; 12.55, and I have attempted to give consistency by adopting the form *pulkasa* everywhere. I think there is better evidence overall for this form than for the others, even though the reading remains uncertain. The adopted reading here is found in: Ho Lo^1 GMd^1 TMd^3 TMd^4 GMd^5 Tj^1 Tr^1 MTr^4 MTr^6 [*Jolly* R Nd Gr] *LakṣJolly Dave*. The readings found in the printed versions of the commentaries are unreliable, because each editor appears to have used his own preferred spelling.

10.21b, c As in verse 18, here also the spelling and pronunciation of the name is inconsistent. The reading I have adopted, *bhṛjjakaṇṭaka*, is found in: BKt^5 La^1 Lo^1 Lo^2 NNg SOx^1 Ox^2 NPu^1 Pu^2 Pu^4 Pu^5 SPu^6 Pu^7 Pu^{10}. This reading is supported by variants found in several mss., including ST ones. Likewise, the reading of *pāda*-c is quite unclear with regard to both *puṣpadhaḥ* and *śaikha*.

10.23b The sandhi here is unclear. Bühler takes the two words as *sudhanvā* + *ācārya*. This division with the sandhi of two *ā*'s is supported by *Go*, who also reads *ācārya*. Jolly, on the other hand, takes the two words to be *sudhanvā* and *cārya* without any sandhi, but he gives no reason for taking the latter term to be *cārya* rather than *ācārya*. From *Go*'s commentary it appears that both the Sātvata and the Ācārya earned their livelihood by functioning as temple or shrine priests (*devapūjana*). Although *Bh, Go, Rc*, and *Mr* take these as two separate names, *Nā* appears to take *sudhanvācārya* as a single term, because he sees only five names in the verse.

10.27cd Both the reading and the meaning of the second half-verse are quite unclear. There are four readings: *mātṛjātyāṃ* (locative), *mātṛjātyāḥ* (nominative plural), *mātṛjātyā* (instrumental), or *mātṛjātau* (locative). Most commentators support the locative. Only

Me prefers the nominative. Of the four forms, I think the least probable is the last; it must be construed as a Bahuvrīhi to obtain the masculine ending; I am unclear as to how that would fit with the syntax of the verse. I have also rejected the locative *mātṛjātyām*. This would force us to assume that the verse is speaking about three kinds of women; the clear parallel between *svayoniṣu* and *pravarāsu yoniṣu* makes it unlikely that a third category would be introduced with *jāti* in place of *yoni*. Further, this reading would also imply that *pratiloma* sexual unions as envisaged here would beget children who belong to the same class as the father. The reading preferred by *Me* is the nominative, but his explanation is labored with the introduction of a correlative *ye* and the assumption that *prasūyante* is passive (contrary to its use as an indicative in verses 30-1): *ye ca mātṛjātyāḥ prasūyante 'nulomā mātṛjātīyā . . . te 'pi svayoniṣu sadṛśān janayanti*. The parallel verse in *MBh* 13.48.14 reads: *mātṛjātyāṃ prasūyante pravarā hīnayoniṣu*, but this is clearly a *lectio facilior* and an attempt to resolve the difficulties of the original. I have adopted the instrumental *mātṛjātyā*, connecting it syntactically with *pravarāsu:* "in wombs that are higher by reason of the mother's caste." This corresponds to what will be said in the very next verse, namely, that a person begets children similar to him also from women of the class immediately below theirs also in the case of outcastes. Thus, a Vaidehika male (Vaiśya father and Kṣatriya mother) is one grade above a Māgadha female (Vaiśya father and Brahmin mother). In terms of the mother's *jāti*, hower, the Māgadha with a Brahmin mother is superior to the Vaidehika with a Kṣatriya mother. So, a Vaidehika begets children belonging to his own caste through a Māgadha woman. Granted, this is a somewhat elaborate explanation; but it appears to be the only plausible one, given the reading we have. The reading I have adopted is found in Lo^4 TMd^3 TMd^4 GMd^5 GMy NPu^1 Pu^2 Pu^3 Pu^4 Pu^{10} Tr^2 MTr^6 [*Jolly* M].

10.34b Although many mss. read *dāsa*, the correct spelling is clearly *dāśa*. The connection of this class of people with navigation is clearlly indicated in *MDh* 8.408–9. There is overwhelming manuscript support for the reading *-jīvinam*, but see 10.32b where the reading clearly is *-jīvanam*.

10.44 The ethnic names contained in this verse have a variety of readings, and it is impossible to determine the original forms. The readings given in the edition, therefore, are uncertain. In *pāda*-a the reading *puṇḍraka* is found in: Jo^2 NKt^4 Lo^3 Lo^4 TMd^3 TMd^4 GMd^5 GMy NNg sOx^1 sPu^6 Pu^{10} Tj^1 Tr^1 MTr^4 MTr^{5}MTr^6 Wa. In the last *pāda*, the reading adopted, *daradās tathā* is found in: Be^1 Bo NKt^4 BKt^5 Lo^2 GMd^1 TMd^4 GMd^5 NNg sOx^1 sPu^6 Pu^7 Pu^{10} Tr^1 MTr^4 MTr^{5}MTr^6 [*Jolly* M G Nd Gr], a reading adopted also by Jolly and Bühler.

10.52b The mss. are deeply divided over the reading. Even in the ST, the Grantha mss. read *bhāṇḍeṣu*, while the Telugu and Malayalam ones read *bhāṇḍe ca*, which I have adopted. This reading is found in: Bo BCa Ho Jo^2 wKt^1 wKt^3 BKt^5 La^1 Lo^1 Lo^3 Lo^4 TMd^3 TMd^4 NNg oOr sOx^1 Pu^3 sPu^6 Pu^{10} Tj^1 Tr^1 Tr^2 MTr^4 MTr^5 MTr^6 Wa [*Jolly* M Gr] *Jolly*.

10.62c The adopted the reading, *abhyavapattau,* is found in most of the ST mss. and a good number of NT-x ones: Be^1 NKt^4 BKt^5 Lo^4 TMd^3 TMd^4 GMd^5 GMy NNg NPu^1 Pu^2 Pu^4 Pu^5 Pu^7 Pu^{10} Tr^1 MTr^4 MTr^5 [*Jolly* M^5 G Nd] *Apa Me GoJha*. In *Lakṣ* the editor has adopted *upapattau* even though at least two mss. record the reading *avapattau*. The reading *avapatti* is also supported by the parallel in *ViDh* 16.18, which reads *strībālādyavapattau*. The word *abhyavapatti* or the verb *abhi-ava* √*pad* is not recorded in B-R or M-W dictionaries; Apte gives the verb as meaning "to protect."

10.63a I have adopted *akrodhaḥ* in place of *asteyam*, because it is found in most of the ST mss. and a large number of NT-x ones: Be^1 Bo Ho NKt^4 BKt^5 La^1 Lo^4 TMd^3 GMy NNg sOx^1 NPu^1 Pu^2 Pu^4 sPu^6 Pu^8 Pu^{10} MTr^5 Wa [*Jolly* M Nd] *Viś*. See also the parallel at 11.223. The reading *asteyam*, however, is found in the parallel verse in *YDh* 1.122. The reading here is clearly uncertain.

10.79b The mss. are divided over the three readings: *kṛṣī*, *kṛṣīḥ*, and *kṛṣiḥ*. The second is impossible as a feminine nominative plural; *Nā* is obliged to call it a Vedic form! I have opted for the first; the dual is the *lectio difficilior*, and I think *vaṇik* here stands outside the compound as a separate word for trade. The adopted reading is found in: Hy Jo^2 Lo^2 Lo^3 GMd^1 TMd^3 Tj^1 Tr^2 Wa [*Jolly* M G R Nd] *Vij Jolly*.

10.90a Most mss. and editions have the reading *kṛṣyām;* a few mss. record *kṛṣyāt*. This is clearly an error; scribes were influenced by the adjacent *utpādya* requiring an object in the accusative. There is no word *kṛṣyā* (fem.) or *kṛṣya* (mas./neuter). The term is *kṛṣi* and the correct reading here is *kṛṣyā* in the instrumental. This reading is found in BBe^2 Hy Jo^2 wKt^1 wKt^3 NKt^4 Lo^2 Lo^4 TMd^4 GMy Ox^2 Pu^2 Pu^4 Tr^1 Tr^2 MTr^4 MTr^6*Jolly*. The commentators *Me, Go, Ku, Nā*, and *Rn* support the instrumental.

10.93d All but two of the NT mss. have the reading *niyacchati*. Jolly appears to have adopted *nigacchati* conjecturally; all the mss. available to him read *niyacchati*. I also have adopted *nigacchati*, which gives a much better sense and is found, with a single variant, in all the ST mss.: Lo^4 TMd^3 TMd^4 GMd^5 GMy NNg Tr^1 MTr^4 MTr^5 MTr^6 *Jolly*. See the similar variants at 12.11.

10.97b The alternate reading, *paradharmāt svanuṣṭhitāt*, has strong manuscript support and is found in most ST mss. The ablative here, however, may have been influenced by *varam* of *pāda*-a. I have adopted the NT reading both because it is the *lectio difficilior* and because it is in several ways supported by many commentators. *Me, Go, Ku*, and *Rn* support the presence of the negative particle *na*, and *Go, Ku*, and *Rn* specifically comment on the term *pārakyaḥ*. This reading is also found in all the medieval citations. The original reading here, however, remains somewhat uncertain.

10.101c The reading adopted, *karśitaḥ*, is found in Ho Jo^{2}NKt^4 Lo^1 Lo^2 Lo^3 Lo^4 GMd^1 TMd^3 TMd^4 GMd^5 GMy NNg sOx^1 NPu^1 Pu^2 Pu^4 Pu^5 sPu^6 Pu^7 Pu^8 Tj^1 Tr^1 Tr^2 MTr^4 MTr^5 Wa. For this reading, see 8.411b note.

10.104d The reading adopted, *doṣeṇa*, is found in all the ST mss.: TMd^3 TMd^4 GMd^5 GMy Tr^1 MTr^4 MTr^6*Har*-A *Mādh*. Although the reading remains uncertain, I think the parallel in 105c favors *doṣeṇa* here also; see also *doṣa* in verse 103.

10.105c The reading adopted, *doṣeṇa*, is found in: Jo^2 wKt^3 NKt^4 La^1 Lo^3 GMd^1 TMd^3 GMd^5 GMy oOr Pu^3 Pu^5 Pu^7 Tj^1 Tr^1 Tr^2 MTr^4 MTr^5 MTr^6 [*Jolly* G R Nd] *Apa Mādh Rc Jolly*.

10.107d I have adopted the reading *bṛboḥ* conjecturally. The mss. present a wide variety of readings, a clear indication that the scribes did not know what to make of this word. Sāyaṇa in his commentary on *ṚV* 6.45.31 cites this verse with the reading *bṛboḥ* and gives the story behind the saying; interestingly, however, Mādhava, reputedly his brother, has a very different reading in his citation of this verse.

10.119b The adopted reading is found in: Be^1 Bo Ho NKt^4 Lo^1 Lo^2 TMd^1 GMy NNg sOx^1 Ox^2 NPu^1 Pu^3 Pu^4 Pu^5 sPu^6 Pu^7 Pu^8 Tr^1 MTr^5 Wa [*Jolly* G Ku] *Go Ku Lakṣ Jolly*. The reading of *Me* is unclear: *tathā cāhave na syāt parāṅmukhaḥ / bhaye upasthite parāṅmukho yuddhe na syād ity arthaḥ*. It is unclear whether *cāhave* is merely a gloss and *bhaye* is from the root text or vice versa. The fact that the text required such an explanation favors *bhaye* as the root; if it was *āhave* the text would have been clear. In *Go*, on the other hand, it is clear that his root had *bhaye*, for he comments: *prajārakṣaṇapravṛttasya ca yadi kutaścid bhayaṃ syāt tadā na yuddhaparāṅmukhaḥ syāt*. The same explanation is given by *Ku*.

10.121a-b The syntax of the first half-verse is turbid; *yadi* does not make much sense with the present participle *ākāṅkṣan*. The commentators *Me, Ku, Nd,* and *Mr* appear to read *ākāṅkṣet*, although it is unclear whether this is the root or a gloss. A finite verb would make better sense with *yadi*. On the other hand, *Go*, reading the present participle, provides the following explanation: *śūdro brāhmaṇaśuśrūṣayā ājīvan yadi vṛttyākāṅkṣī syāt tadā kṣatriyaṃ paricaret.* Jolly follows *Me* in substituting *iti* for *yadi*. This reading, however, has almost no manuscript support.

10.127b Mss. give three readings here: *vṛtta, vṛtti,* and *dharma*. The last has little support. There is little to choose between the other two. I have gone with the first principally because it parallels *sadvṛttam* of the very next verse, a reading supported by most mss. The reading adopted is found in : Be^1 Bo Ho Hy Jm Jo^1 Kt^2 NKt^4 sOx^1 Pu^5 sPu^6 Pu^7 Pu^8 Tj^2 MTr^4 MTr^6 Wa*Nā Rc Mandlik Jolly KSS.*

CHAPTER ELEVEN

11.1b The reading *sārvavedasam*, which I have adopted, is found in: Be^1 Ho Hy Jo^2 wKt^1 Kt^2 NKt^4 BKt^5 Lo^4 GMd^5 GMy NPu^1 Pu^5 Pu^7 Pu^8 Pu^{10} Tj^2 Tr^1 MTr^4 MTr^{5}MTr^6 Wa [*Jolly* M] *Apa Lakṣ Me Go Nā Nd Mr Jha Dave.*

11.3d Even though an alternate reading with *vidhīyate* is found in several significant mss., including all the ST ones, all the commentators favor the adopted reading.

11.5x The additional verse given as verse 6 in the vulgate editions is omitted in BBe^2 Bo Hy wKt^1 BKt^5 Lo^1 Lo^2 Lo^3 Lo^4 TMd^4 GMd^5 GMy NNg sOx^1 Ox^2 Pu^5 sPu^6 Pu^7 Pu^8 Pu^{10} Tj^1 Tr^2 MTr^5 Wa [*Jolly* M G N R]. This verse is also not commented by any commentator other than *Ku*. It is not notices by *Bh, Me,* and *Go*. Jolly gives the verse within brackets. This verse must have entered the text at a relatively early date, because it is found in several ST mss. and in the old NKt^4.

11.8c Two diametrically opposed interpretations of this *pāda* have produced two different readings: *sa pītasomapūrvaḥ* and *apītasomapūrvaḥ*. According to the first interpretation, even a man who has already performed a Soma sacrifice is deprived of the fruits of a Soma sacrifice he performs without the minimum wealth specified in the previous verse. Some, such as *Me* and, following him, *Vij* (on *YDh*1.124), consequently permit a man with lesser wealth to perform the sacrifice if it is the first time he is doing so. The implication is that the first Soma sacrifice is obligatory (*nitya*, hence the exception), whereas subsequent ones are optional (*kāmya*). This is unconvincing; if this were the case why would Manu put the particle *api* "even"? Others, such as *Ku*, draws an opposite conclusion: *a fortiori*, a person who has never performed a Soma sacrifice should not perform one without the minimum wealth. According to the second interpretation, even a man who has never performed a Soma sacrifice is forbidden to perform one without the minimum wealth; *a fortiori*, those who have already performed one are also forbidden, because such sacrifices are optional. The reading with the negative *apīta* is favored by *Bh, Go, Nd,* and *Rc.* I favor this interpretation, because it highlights the significance of the particle *api.* I think the original reading was *so (a)pītasomapūrvaḥ*, a reading that was misunderstood and changed to *sa pītasomapūrvaḥ* by some and to *apītasomapūrvaḥ* by others. The adopted reading is found, however, only in tMd^{4} Tr^{2} mTr^{4} mTr^{5} mTr^{6} *Bh* and must, therefore, be considered somewhat conjectural.

11.28d I have followed here the reading of the ST mss., all of which give the reading *avicāritam.* Of the NT mss., only Pu^{2} has this reading. For a detailed discussion of this reading, see note to 8.295.

11.31a The usual optative form *vedayeta* has been adopted by all the editions, even though it is found in a minority of mss. all belonging to NT. A broad range of mss., including most ST ones, have the adopted reading, *vedayīta:* bBe^{2} Bo Ho Hy Jo^{2} La^{1} Lo^{2} Lo^{3} Lo^{4} gMd^{1} gMd^{5} gMy oOr sOx^{1} Ox^{2} nPu^{1} Pu^{2} Pu^{3} Pu^{4} sPu^{6} Tj^{1} Tr^{2} mTr^{4} mTr^{6} [*Jolly* R]. The latter is clearly the *lectio difficilior*, a form of the optative that emerges in late Vedic texts and *sūtra* literature. It is easy to see how this unusual optative could have been changed to the more normal *vedayeta*, and very difficult to see how the latter could have been changed into the former in so many mss.

11.33b The presence of *iti* here makes it most probable that the term is *avicāritam* and not *avicārayan.* The former is found in all ST mss. but only in two NT ones. Here also the ST has proved to contain the superior reading. For *iti avicāritam*, see 11.28. The reading adopted is found in: nKt^{4} La^{1} gMd^{1} tMd^{3} tMd^{4} gMd^{5} gMy Tr^{1} mTr^{4} mTr^{5} mTr^{6} [*Jolly* G].

11.36a The reading adopted, *naiva*, is found in all the ST mss. and a good number of NT-x ones: Jo^{2} Lo^{3} Lo^{4} gMd^{1} tMd^{3} tMd^{4} gMd^{5} nNg oOr Ox^{2} Pu^{10} Tr^{1} mTr^{4} mTr^{5}mTr^{6} [*Jolly* R] *Apa Dev.*

11.40b All the editions read *prajāḥ*. The singular *prajām*, however, has broader manuscript support, including most mss. of the ST: Be^{1} Bo Ho nKt^{4} Lo^{1} Lo^{2} gMd^{1} tMd^{3} tMd^{4} gMd^{5} gMy nNg sOx^{1} Ox^{2} nPu^{1} Pu^{2} Pu^{3} Pu^{4} Pu^{5} sPu^{6} Pu^{7} Pu^{8} Pu^{10} Tr^{1} Tr^{2} mTr^{4} mTr^{5} mTr^{6} Wa.

11.44c The reading *prasajan*, possibly due to the sandhi creating *prasajaṃś*, has created problems for the scribes; hence the simplification to *prasaktaś* found in many mss. and adopted by some editors, including Jolly. The present participle here makes much better sense paralleling the participles in *pādas* a and b. The reading adopted is found in: Bo bCa Ho La^{1} Lo^{4} gMd^{5} gMy nNg sOx^{1} nPu^{1} sPu^{6} mTr^{4} mTr^{6}*Viś Mādh.* Derrett gives the reading *prasaktaś* both in the root and in the commentary of *Bh* without any note.

11.50a There are numerous variant readings, the three major ones being *pūtināsatva, pūtināsikya,* and *pautināsikya.* The last is found in only a few mss. mostly of NT-y and can be rejected. It is unclear whether the original was *nāsatva* or *nāsikya.* I have adopted the former both because it is represented (with many variants) of both the ST and the NT-x, and because the abstract noun parallels *pūtivakratām* of the next *pāda.* The adopted reading is found in: gMd^{1} gMy Pu^{10} Tr^{1} mTr^{4} mTr^{6} Wa *Jolly* [but see its many variants given in the critical apparatus]. The reading with *nāsikya*, however, is supported by the parallel in *YDh* 3.211 with *pūtināsikaḥ*.

11.53a Mss. of both ST and NT are deeply divided over the two readings, *karmāvaśeṣa* and *karmaviśeṣa.* I think both the manuscript evidence and the probable meaning of the verse favors the former, which is found in: Be^{1} bBe^{2} Ho wKt^{3} bKt^{4} gMd^{1} gMd^{5} gMy

NNg sOx^{1} sPu^{6} Tr^{1} MTr^{4} MTr^{5} MTr^{6} Wa *Jolly*. This reading is also supported by the commentaries of *Bh* [here and ad 8.66] *Me, Go, Ku,* and *Nā*.

11.55d The syntax calls for the nominative *saṃyogaḥ* rather than the accusative *saṃyogam*. The reading adopted is found in: NKt^{4} BKt^{5} GMd^{1} GMd^{5} GMy Ox^{2} NPu^{1} Pu^{2} Pu^{3} Pu^{4} Pu^{8} MTr^{4} [Jolly R Nd] *Me Jolly*.

11.59a The adopted reading, *svayonyāsu*, is attested (if we include the variants) in a large spectrum of mss. of both ST and NT. It is found in: Be^{1} Bo Hy Jo^{2} WKt^{1} WKt^{3} NKt^{4} BKt^{5} Lo^{1} Lo^{4} GMd^{5} GMy NNg sOx^{1} NPu^{1} Pu^{2} Pu^{4} Pu^{5} sPu^{6} Pu^{7} Pu^{10} Tj^{2} MTr^{4} MTr^{5} Wa [*Jolly* M$^{1\text{-}2\text{-}4\text{-}5\text{-}9}$] *Nd Go*. The grammatical form *yonyā*, however, is unusual, especially as a noun [see *R̥V* 8.45.30 for the adjective]. The form may also be influenced by the Prakrit formations in *-ya*, such as in *śriyā* and *striyā*. See Edgerton 1953, I: 10.6.

11.60b Although the majority of the mss. read *vikrayaḥ* and *vikrayāḥ*, it is clear that the dual is required here. The scribal confusion may have been created by the perception that *pāradāra* is a separate word and not part of the compound. The commentator *Nā* notes the abnormality of the singular masculine and ascribes it to a vedic peculiarity: *pāradāryātmavikraya ity ekavacanaṃ chāndhasam*. The adopted reading is found in: WKt^{1} WKt^{3} NKt^{4} Lo^{1} Lo^{3} NNg Ox^{2} Pu^{8} Tj^{1} Tj^{2} Wa [*Jolly* R] *Jolly*.

11.62b Two quite divergent readings are found in the mss. The reading *vārdhuṣitvam* is supported by all the ST mss. and a considerable number of NT ones. The exact form of the last portion of the *pāda* is, however, uncertain. Many have the compound *vratacyutiḥ*, while others have *vratācuytiḥ*. I think the latter must be actually *vratāc cyutiḥ*; scribes often fail to double the "c" especially before a conjunct consonant. The form *vratāc cyutiḥ* is found only in Jo^{2} MTr^{5} *Rn*.

11.66a All the NT mss., as well as *Me, Nā, Ku, Rn* and *Mr*, have the reading *steyam*, with the exception of a few that read *stainyam*. The NT reading is clearly the *lectio facilior*. All the ST mss. contain the more difficult *straiṇyam*, which I have adopted. This appears to be reading of *Bh*'s root text. Derrett (1975, I: 33) notes that Pandit Aithal examined 13 Malayalam manuscripts and found them all to read *straiṇyam*. It is also unclear why *steya* here should be mentioned without reference to the objects stolen, when specific forms of theft are referred to in verses 58, 67, and 71. Moreover, the three points in this half-verse go together: not establishing the fires, acting like a woman [perhaps homosexuality], and not paying the debts all imply refusal to get married.

11.66d The reading *vyasanakriyā* has broad mss. support, including all ST ones. It is found in: Be^{1} La^{1} Lo^{4} GMd^{1} TMd^{3} TMd^{4} GMd^{5} Ox^{2} NPu^{1} Pu^{5} Pu^{7} Pu^{10} Tr^{1} MTr^{4} MTr^{5} MTr^{6} [*Jolly* M]. This reading is supported by *Nd* and *Rc*. The previous word originally was some form of *kauśīlya*, because it is found in all the transmission lines. The reading *kauṭilya*, which Derrett (1975, I: 33) adopts, is clearly the *lectio facilior* and must have been introduced precisely because of the difficulty of *kauśīlya*.

11.68c The reading adopted, *puṃsi ca maithunyaṃ*, is found in: Bo Jo^{2} WKt^{1} NKt^{4} La^{1} Lo^{1} Lo^{2} Lo^{3} GMd^{1} TMd^{3} TMd^{4} GMd^{5} GMy oOr Ox^{2} NPu^{1} Pu^{2} Pu^{5} Pu^{7} Tj^{1} Tr^{1} Tr^{2} MTr^{4} MTr^{5} MTr^{6} Wa [*Jolly* R Nd] *Go Vij Apa*.

11.80b I have adopted *samyak* over *sadyaḥ* principally because it is represented in a wider range of mss., including all but two of the ST: Be^{1} NKt^{4} BKt^{5} Lo^{1} Lo^{2} Lo^{4} GMd^{1} TMd^{3} GMd^{5} GMy NNg NPu^{1} Pu^{2} Pu^{4} Pu^{8} Tr^{1} MTr^{4} MTr^{6} Wa [*Jolly* M$^{4\text{-}5}$ Nd] *Apa Me Dave Jha*.

11.81a In the parallel passages at *ĀpDh* 1.24.21; *GDh* 22.8; *VaDh* 20.28, the term used is *pratirāddha*. Manu appears to prefer *pratiroddha:* see also 3.153 and 9.93. In the parallel verse at *YDh* 3.246 the term is not used.

11.104a The reading adopted, *gurutalpo*, is found in Be^1 Ho Jo^2 wKt^3 NKt^4 La^1 Lo^2 Lo^3 NNg sOx^1 Ox^2 NPu^1 Pu^2 Pu^4 sPu^6 Pu^8 Pu^{10} Tj^1 Tr^1 [*Jolly* M R Nd] *Apa Nā Jolly*. Most ST mss. have the reading *gurutalpago*, which would make the *pāda* hypermetric. *Me* also appears to have the latter reading, giving the vulgate version as a *pāṭha*. The commentary of *Bh* also has *gurutalpagaḥ*, but in both cases it is unclear whether this reflects the reading of the root text or is simply a gloss.

11.106b The reading here is somewhat uncertain, but I have adopted *nirjane* because it is found in all but one ST mss., as well as in a number of NT ones: BCa Ho wKt^1 wKt^3 NKt^4 TMd^3 TMd^4 GMd^5 GMy sOx^1 sPu^6 Pu^{10} Tr^1 MTr^4 MTr^5 MTr^6 *Viś.*

11.110c I think the participle *ācaran* is better with the syntax. The participial form is also found in most ST mss. and a good number of NT ones. The reading adopted is found in Jo^2 BKt^5 Lo^2 GMd^5 sOx^1 NPu^1 Pu^2 Pu^4 Pu^5 sPu^6 Pu^7 Pu^{10} MTr^5 Wa [*Jolly* M G Nd Rā] *Viś Jolly*. See also all the mss. that read *caran*.

11.112c Even though all editors, including Jolly, have adopted the reading *āsīnaḥ*, it is found in only a few mss. The adopted reading, *āsīta*, is found in: Be^1 Ho Jo^2 wKt^1 wKt^3 NKt^4 wKt^5 Lo^1 Lo^2 Lo^3 Lo^4 GMd^1 TMd^3 TMd^4 GMy NNg oOr sOx^1 Ox^2 NPu^1 Pu^5 sPu^6 Pu^7 Pu^8 Tj^1 Tr^1 MTr^4 MTr^6 [*Jolly* M^4 R Nd Ku Gr] *Viś Apa.*

11.113a The reading adopted, *abhiṣaktām*, is found in Be^1 Ho NKt^4 Lo^1 Lo^4 GMd^1 sOx^1 Ox^2 Pu^8 MTr^4 MTr^6 *Viś Apa Nā*[*Jolly* M Me]. It is also supported, however, by the many mss. with the impossible reading *abhiṣiktām*. Even though the printed editions of *Me* has *abhiśastām*, the gloss *gṛhītām* goes better with *abhiṣaktām;* so also do the glosses of *Nā: parākṛtām*, of *Nd: pīḍitām*, and of *Rc: ākrāntām.*

11.113d The mss. are evenly divided between the equally possible readings: *vimokṣayet* and *vimocayet*. I have gone with the former principally because many ST mss. (especially the Malayalam ones) and significant NT-x ones, as well as three medieval citations support it: Be^1 Bo BCa wKt^1 NKt^4 Lo^1 Lo^2 Lo^3 GMd^1 TMd^4 Ox^2 NPu^1 Pu^2 Pu^3 Pu^4 Pu^8 Tj^1 Tr^2 MTr^4 MTr^6 Wa *Viś Apa Mādh*.The reading, however, remains uncertain.

11.116b Most NT mss. have the reading *gām* in the singular. This reading was probably influenced by the cow in the singular in the preceding verses 113–5. But this and the following verse conclude the description of the vow and picks up the theme of following cows (in the plural) that was the subject of the earlier verses 111–2. The reading adopted is found in: Be^1 NKt^4 Lo^3 Lo^4 GMd^1 TMd^3 TMd^4 GMd^5 GMy NNg NPu^1 Pu^8 Pu^{10} Tj^1 Tr^1 MTr^4 MTr^5 MTr^6 [*Jolly* M G Nd Ku R] *Viś Vij Apa Mādh Jolly.*

11.120b Even though all editors have adopted the reading *samety ṛcā*, it is supported by very few mss. *Me* clearly indicates that the *pratīka* intended here is simply *sam:* "*sam ity anayā.*" The formula is *TĀ* 2.1.8: *saṃ mā siñcantu marutaḥ*. The *pratīka* then should be either *sam iti* or *saṃ mety*. The reading adopted is found in: Be^1 Bo Ho Hy Jo^2 wKt^3 NKt^4 La^1 Lo^1 Lo^3 Lo^4 GMd^1 GMd^5 GMy NNg oOr sOx^1 NPu^1 Pu^2 Pu^3 Pu^4 Pu^5 sPu^6 Pu^7 Pu^8 Tj^1 Tj^2 Tr^2 MTr^6 [*Jolly* M$^{3\text{-}4\text{-}5}$ G R Nd] *Apa Mādh Me Rn.*

11.126b *Me* gives the reading in the nominative *aindavo māsaḥ*. This makes good sense, as it refers to the "lunar month," namely, the Cāndrāyaṇa fast. It appears that the presence of the neuter *śodhanam* has influenced the other two words. However, the manuscript evidence for the accusative endings is strong and I have retained them in the edition.

11.139a The original reading of the word is quite unclear, mss. giving *jīla, jāla, jīna,* and the like. Clearly this was a term that the scribes were unfamiliar with. The commentators unanimously explain the term as a "leather bag" (*carmapuṭa*), but it is unclear what the reading of their root text was; most editors use *jīna*, whose choice may have been influenced by the vulgate reading of Manu. The only other *Dharmaśāstra* to use the term is the *GDh* (22.26) in a parallel text giving the penance for killing a wanton Brahmin woman. In all likelihood, the term in the *GDh* reads *jīla*, which is Maskarin's reading. Haradatta, however, reads *nīla* both in the *GDh* and in *MDh* 11.139 that he cites. I think the evidence favors *jīla*, which is, however, found only in Be^{1} NKt^{4} Lo^{4} oOr NPu^{1} Pu^{5} Pu^{7} MTr^{4} MTr^{5}MTr^{6} *Bh*. The mss. with *jīna* supports the long "ī," while the "l" has the support of most ST mss. That this term, which may have been originally from a regional dialect, was obscure even by the time of Yājñavalkya is demonstrated by the fact that in the parallel verse (*YDh* 3.268) he substitutes the more common term for a leather bag, *dṛti*. Sanskrit dictionaries (B-R, M-W, Apte) depend solely on this verse of Manu to give the meaning of leather bag to the term *jīna*.

11.141a Most NT mss. have the reading *asthimatām*. I think this must have been a scribal change of the more difficult *asthanvatām*, which is retained in all the ST mss. and a few NT ones: GMd^{1} GMd^{5} Tr^{1} Tr^{2} MTr^{4} MTr^{5} MTr^{6} [*Jolly* Nd Gr] *Jolly*. See also the variant *asthinvatām*. Only *Nā* clearly supports this reading, glossing: *asthanvatām asthimatām*. See, however, *asthimatām* in 141b.

11.145c The "r" and "l" in the two readings *ārambe* and *ālambe* are clearly regional or dialectical variations. Although *ālamba* is viewed as the "correct" form, I have gone with the former because it is represented in a broad spectrum of mss.: Be^{1} Ho NKt^{4} Lo^{4} GMd^{1} TMd^{4} sOx^{1} NPu^{1} sPu^{6} Pu^{10} MTr^{4} MTr^{5}MTr^{6} Wa [*Jolly* M Nd] *Bh* [ad 11.143 in MTr^{5}] *Apa Jolly*.

11.156a All the ST mss., as well as quite a number of NT-x ones, read *jagdhvā*, which I have adopted: Jo^{2} wKt^{1} wKt^{3} NKt^{4} La^{1} Lo^{2} Lo^{3} GMd^{1} TMd^{3} TMd^{4} GMd^{5} GMy NNg oOr NPu^{1} Pu^{2} Pu^{4} Tj^{1} Tr^{1} MTr^{4} MTr^{6} Wa. See also the use of *jagdhvā* in preference to *bhuktvā* with regard to meat at 5.31, 33; 11.153. The term appears to have somewhat of a negative sense, similar to the English devour, and it is often used with reference to eating deplorable things: 4.112; 5.19, 20; 11.57, 160; 12.68.

11.158b There are widely different readings in the mss. I have opted for *samāvṛttakaḥ*, which is found in Be^{1} NKt^{4} La^{1} Lo^{4} GMd^{5} NNg oOr sOx^{1} NPu^{1} sPu^{6} Pu^{8} Pu^{10} [*Jolly* M$^{1\text{-}2\text{-}5\text{-}9}$] *Apa*. The reading here, however, is uncertain.

11.159a The mss. are evenly divided over the two readings, *vratacārī* and *brahmacārī*. I have opted for the former both because it is the *lectio difficilior* and because it is found in all the ST mss., as well as in a cross section of NT-x ones, especially the old NKt^{4} and NNg. This reading is found in: Be^{1} NKt^{4} BKt^{5} La^{1} Lo^{2} Lo^{4} GMd^{1} TMd^{3} TMd^{4} GMd^{5} GMy NNg Pu^{5} Pu^{7} Tr^{1} Tr^{2} MTr^{4}MTr^{5} MTr^{6} Wa [*Jolly* M^{4-5-9}G N Nd] *Viś Me Go Nā Nd Rc Jolly Jha Dave*.

11.161a Even though all the editors, including Jolly, have adopted the reading *ajñāna*, it is found in only few mss. The reading adopted *ajñāta* is found in: Be^{1} BBe^{2} Bo Hy Jo^{2} wKt^{3} NKt^{4} La^{1} GMd^{1} TMd^{3} TMd^{4} GMd^{5} NNg oOr Pu^{2} Pu^{4} Pu^{5} Pu^{7} Pu^{8} Pu^{10} Tj^{2} Tr^{1} Tr^{2} MTr^{4} MTr^{5} MTr^{6} Wa.

11.165b Mss. are divided over the two major readings: *veśmanaḥ* and *veśmataḥ*. I have gone *veśman* principally because all the ST mss., as well as several NT-y ones, support it. The reading adopted is found in Be^{1} bBe^{2} bKt^{5} Lo^{2} Lo^{3} gMd^{1} gMy sOx^{1} Pu^{2} Pu^{4} sPu^{6} Tj^{1} mTr^{4} mTr^{6} [*Jolly* Nd R]*Apa Mādh*. This reading with "n" in place of "t" is supported by the mss. with the reading *veśmani*, a reading also supported by *Me*.

11.169b The reading adopted with *khura* in place of *śapha* has the broadest manuscript support, including all the ST mss.: bBe^{2} Jo^{2} wKt^{3} nKt^{4} La^{1} Lo^{3} gMd^{1} tMd^{3} gMd^{5} gMy sOx^{1} nPu^{1} Pu^{2} Pu^{4} sPu^{6} Tj^{1} Tr^{1} mTr^{4} mTr^{5} mTr^{6} Wa [*Jolly* G R Nd] *Vij.*

11.183b One may argue that *bahiḥ* is the *lectio difficilior*, because *saha* may have been influenced by the instrumental. See also the parallel *bāndhavaiḥ saha* at 184d. Yet, I have opted for *saha* because of the overwhelming manuscript support from both the ST and the NT-x: Bo Ho nKt^{4} bKt^{5} La^{1} tMd^{3} tMd^{4} gMd^{5} gMy nNg oOr sOx^{1} Ox^{2} Pu^{5} sPu^{6} Pu^{7} Pu^{10} Tr^{1} Tr^{2} mTr^{4} mTr^{5} mTr^{6} [*Jolly* M G R] *Jolly.*

11.185d All but two ST mss. and numerous NT-x ones have the accusative reading *yātrāṃ laukikīm*. This, I think, goes against the grammar, the intransitive verb *nivarteran* requiring the nominative. The accusative may have been influenced by the presence of the neuter *pradānam* in *pāda*-c. The nominative reading that I have adopted is found in: bBe^{2} bCa Hy Jm Jo^{1} Jo^{2} wKt^{1} Kt^{2} wKt^{3} nKt^{4} Lo^{1} Lo^{2} Lo^{3} tMd^{4} nNg oOr nPu^{1} Pu^{2} Pu^{3} Pu^{4} Pu^{8} Tj^{1} Tj^{2} mTr^{5} [*Jolly* Ku R]*Mandlik Jha KSS Dave*. gMd^{1} gives the nominative of the first word and the accusative of the second.

11.190c Of the three major readings, *caināñ, caitān,* and *caiva*, I think, the manuscript evidence supports the first. It is found in bBe^{2} wKt^{3} La^{1} Lo^{2} Lo^{4} tMd^{3} tMd^{4} nPu^{1} Pu^{2} Pu^{4} Pu^{8} and is also supported by others with the variant *caināṃ*.

11.203b Although several editors, including Jolly, have adopted the reading *saṃniveśya*, the vast majority of the mss. record the reading adopted *saṃniṣevya:* Be^{1} bBe^{2} Bo Ho wKt^{1} nKt^{4} bKt^{5} La^{1} Lo^{1} Lo^{4} gMd^{1} tMd^{3} tMd^{4} gMd^{5} gMy nNg oOr sOx^{1} Ox^{2} nPu^{1} Pu^{2} Pu^{3} Pu^{4} Pu^{5} Pu^{7} mTr^{4} mTr^{5} mTr^{6} Wa *Me Rc Dave Jha.*

11.209c The question is whether Manu uses *kṛcchra* as a masculine or a neuter noun. Mss. are divided over this here and at verses 157 and 213. At verses 192 and 216, however, mss. are in agreement that the term is masculine. In several other verses where the term occurs in the nominative, it is placed in the neuter; but this may be because it is used adjectivally to qualify a neuter word such as *cāndrāyaṇa* and *sāntapana:* 11.178, 216. In all other occasions, *kṛcchram* is used in the accusative making it impossible to determine the gender. I think Manu generally uses *kṛcchra* as a masculine word.

11.224a The mss. are divided over the case of *ahar* and *niśā*. Most give the genitive *ahnaḥ*, and this is clearly the correct reading. With regard to *niśā*, on the other hand, most mss. of both ST and NT prefer the locative *niśāyāṃ* and this is also given by *Me*, although it is unclear whether it is the root or a gloss. I have opted for the genitive in both cases; it is somewhat anomalous for there to be a shift in the case between the two words, and orthographically याञ्च and याश्च in the mss. can be confusing. Some scribes, and even commentators, may have forgotten that the genitive is the preferred case with multiplicative numerals. The form *ahnaḥ* [see parallel at 11.260] is found in: Be^{1} bBe^{2} Bo bCa Ho Hy Jo^{2} wKt^{1} wKt^{3} nKt^{4} Lo^{1} Lo^{2} Lo^{3} Lo^{4} tMd^{3} tMd^{4} nNg oOr sOx^{1} nPu^{1} Pu^{2} Pu^{4} Pu^{5} Pu^{7} Pu^{10} Tj^{1} Tj^{2} Tr^{2} Wa [*Jolly* M G R] *Me Go Nā Rn Rc Mr Jolly Jha Dave*. The form *niśāyāḥ* is found in: Bo bBe^{2} Bo Hy wKt^{3} Lo^{2} nNg Pu^{5} Pu^{7} Tj^{2} Tr^{2} Wa [*Jolly* G] *Go Nā Mr Jolly.*

11.231c Mss. have differing readings of the two words here: *evam* and *etat*, and *kuryām* and *kuryāt*. In the case of the former, I think the preponderance of manuscript evidence supports *evam*, which is found in: Bo Ho Jo^1 Jo^2 wKt^1 Kt^2 NKt^4 Lo^1 Lo^2 Lo^3 Lo^4 TMd^3 TMd^4 GMd^5 NNg Ox^2 NPu^1 Pu^2 Pu^4 Pu^{10} Tj^1 Tj^2 Tr^1 Tr^2 [*Jolly* M$^{3-4}$ Ku R] *Nā Ku Mandlik Jha KSS Dave*. The decision is more difficult in the case of the latter, both readings having strong manuscript support from both ST and NT. I think we are here dealing not with an external prohibition: "Don't do this again!" implied by the third person *kuryāt*, but with an internal determination "I will not do this again!", which is supported by the very first statement of the next verse: *evaṃ saṃcintya*. The first person reading *kuryām* is found in: Bo Ho Jm Jo^1 Jo^2 Kt^2 wKt^3 BKt^5 Lo^1 Lo^4 TMd^3 TMd^4 GMy NNg oOr sOx^1 Ox^2 NPu^1 sPu^6 Pu^8 Tj^1 Tj^2 Tr^2 Wa [*Jolly* M$^{3-4}$ Ku R N] *Ku Rn Rc Go Mandlik Jha KSS Dave*. The reading, however, is uncertain.

11.231d *Me* appears to prefer the gerund *nivṛtya* He comments: *kriyābhedaṃ ca darśayati ktvāpratyayena saṃtapya nivṛtyeti*.

11.237a All editions read *saṃyata*. The correct reading is clearly *saṃśita*, which is found in the vast majority of the mss, especially the ST ones. Besides the ones with variants of the term recorded in the critical apparatus, the adopted reading is found in: BKt^5 La^1 GMd^1 TMd^3 GMd^5 NNg oOr sPu^6 Tr^1 MTr^4 MTr^5 MTr^6.

11.238a There is broad manuscript support for both the plural *agadāḥ* and the singular *agadaḥ*. The overwhelming support for the plural in most ST mss. prompts me to adopt it, although the reading remains uncertain. The adopted reading is found in: Be^1 Ho Jo^2 Lo^2 GMd^1 GMd^5 GMy NNg Pu^5 Pu^7 Pu^{10} Tr^1 Tr^2 MTr^4 MTr^6 Wa [*Jolly* M G N Nd] *Me Go Nā Jolly Jha Dave*.

11.247 After verse 247 most NT mss. add the verse given in the critical apparatus. Jolly also suspected this verse to be spurious and placed it within brackets in his edition. This verse in missing in all the ST mss., showing once again the general superiority of this line of transmission. It is also missing in Lo^2 Pu^{10}, and placed after 248 in Lo^4. This verse is not commented by *Bh, Go,* and *Nd*. It is given by *Me* with this introductory comment, which indicates that he himself did not accept the authenticity of this verse: *kecid atremaṃ ślokaṃ pūrvam adhīyate* (this comment is found in my ms. Pu^{10}, but omitted in the editions of Mandlik, Jha, and Dave).

11.249a This *pāda* has been subject to numerous emendations, probably because the original was hypermetric with nine syllables. This, I think, is the correct reading adopted in the edition and found in: Bo Ho Jo^2 Lo^4 GMd^1 TMd^3 TMd^4 GMd^5 GMy NNg sOx^1 Ox^2 Pu^5 sPu^6 Pu^7 Tr^1 MTr^5 MTr^6 [*Jolly* M G Nd] *Apa Rc*.This verse was probably a proverbial saying [hence the possibility of hypermeter] and found also in *BDh* 4.1.29 and *VaDh* 26.4 with the same reading. Several mss. attempt to restore the proper meter by deleting "ka" and reading *savyāhṛtīḥ*.

11.250b Mss. present widely varying readings of the final portion of this *pāda*. I think the preponderance of evidence suggests that *prati* is the final word of the *pāda*. I also think that the correct form of the other word is *tṛca* (a set of three verses) and not *tryṛca* (*tri* + *ṛca*) as assumed by Jolly (see 11.255d), or *trica* as found in several ST mss. The reading adopted is found in: TMd^3 TMd^4 NNg MTr^4 MTr^5 MTr^6 *Apa*. The reading, however, is uncertain.

11.252a The correct reading here must be *haviṣpāntīyam* [*ṚV* 10.88] The letter "p" after "ṣ" in Devanāgarī can look very much like "y," with several mss. reading *haviṣyāntīyam*. The adopted reading is found in: Bo Ho BKt^{5} Lo^{3} Lo^{4} GMd^{1} GMd^{5} GMy Pu^{5} Pu^{8} Pu^{10} MTr^{4} MTr^{5} MTr^{6} *Bh Vij Apa*, with the support of mss. reading *haviṣpantīyam*.

11.252c The reading adopted, *japtvā ca*, is found in: BBe^{2} wKt^{3} NKt^{4} Lo^{1} Lo^{2} GMd^{1} TMd^{3} oOr sOx^{1} NPu^{1} Pu^{2} Pu^{4} sPu^{6} MTr^{5} Wa [*Jolly* G] *Apa* (see *VaDh* 26.7). The reading is uncertain.

11.264b Even though all editors, including Jolly, have adopted the reading *kṣiptam*, it is found in only a very small number of mss. Although in Devanāgarī "pt" and "pr" can be orthographically confusing, in the southern scripts the two are quite distinct. The reading adopted, *kṣipram*, was also the reading preferred by Bühler. The noun *loṣṭa* can be either masculine or neuter. I have adopted the masculine, which is found in most ST mss.: Be^{1} Ho wKt^{3} NKt^{4} La^{1} Lo^{2} Lo^{3} Lo^{4} GMd^{1} TMd^{3} GMd^{5} NNg Pu^{2} Pu^{3} Pu^{4} Tj^{1} Tr^{1} Tr^{2} MTr^{4} MTr^{5} MTr^{6} Wa *Apa*.

11.265a All the ST mss. and a considerably number of NT ones have the reading *anyāni*. In spite of this strong manuscript support, I have opted for the reading *ādyāni*, principally because it is the preferred reading both of *Bh*, who comments: *yajūṃṣy ādyāni saṃhitāgatāni na tu brāhmaṇamadhye 'dhītāni padakramānvitāni* [which is repeated almost verbatim by *Go*], and of *Me*, who glosses *ādyāni mukhyānīty arthaḥ*. The adopted reading is found in: Jo^{2} NKt^{4} BKt^{5} Lo^{2} Lo^{4} NNg NPu^{1} Pu^{2} Pu^{4} Pu^{5} Pu^{7} Pu^{8} Pu^{10} MTr^{5} [*Jolly* M G] *Bh Me Go Jolly Jha Dave*.

CHAPTER TWELVE

12.6c The reading adopted, *anibaddha*, is found in: NKt^{4} BKt^{5} Lo^{2} GMd^{1} TMd^{4} GMy oOr NPu^{1} Pu^{3} Pu^{5} Pu^{7} Pu^{8} Pu^{10} Tr^{1} Tr^{2} MTr^{4} MTr^{5} MTr^{6} Wa [*Jolly* M G Nd] *Apa Mādh Jolly*. This is also the reading at *YDh* 3.135.

12.11d The reading *nigacchati* has the support of the old commentators *Bh* and *Me*. It has, however, weak manuscript support. The reading adopted *niyacchati* is found in: Be^{1} BBe^{2} Bo Ho Hy Jm Jo^{1} Jo^{2} wKt^{1} Kt^{2} wKt^{3} NKt^{4} BKt^{5} La^{1} Lo^{1} Lo^{2} Lo^{3} GMd^{5} NNg oOr sOx^{1} Ox^{2} NPu^{1} Pu^{2} Pu^{3} Pu^{4} Pu^{5} sPu^{6} Pu^{7} Pu^{8} Pu^{10} Tj^{1} Tj^{2} Tr^{2} MTr^{4} MTr^{6} Wa *Lakṣ Mandlik KSS*.

12.16d There is strong manuscript support for the two readings, *dṛḍham* and *dhruvam*. I have opted for the former because it is found in all the ST mss. and a good number of NT ones: Ho Jo^{2} Lo^{2} GMd^{1} TMd^{3} TMd^{4} GMd^{5} GMy NPu^{1} Pu^{2} Pu^{3} Pu^{4} Pu^{7} Tr^{1} MTr^{4} Wa [*Jolly* G Go R^{2} Rā^{2}].

12.22d There is good manuscript support for both readings *abhyeti* and*apyeti*. I have opted for the former, because it is found in a large number of reliable NT mss. and is supported by the reading in *Bh:* Be^{1} Bo Ho Jo^{2} wKt^{3} BKt^{5} La^{1} Lo^{1} Lo^{2} Lo^{3} GMd^{5} GMy NNg oOr sOx^{1} Ox^{2} NPu^{1} Pu^{2} Pu^{4} sPu^{6} Pu^{8} Pu^{10} Tj^{1} Tr^{2} MTr^{5} Wa [*Jolly* M R] *Bh Rc Jolly*. The reading, however, is uncertain.

12.29b All the ST mss. have the reading *avyaktam*, and this also appears to be the reading of *Me*. He explains *viṣayātmaka* as a separate compound. The meaning, however, suggests that the entire *pāda*-b is a single compound with *avyakta* in the stem form; attachment to senses is more a characteristic of *rajas* as indicated in verse 32. This is also the way *Go, Ku, Nā,* and *Rn* understand the verse. The adopted reading is found in: Be^{1} BBe^{2} Bo Ho Hy Jo^{2} wKt^{3} NKt^{4} La^{1} Lo^{2} Lo^{3} NNg sOx^{1} Pu^{5} sPu^{6} Pu^{7} Pu^{8} Pu^{10} Tj^{1} Tj^{2} Wa [*Jolly* M G N Ku R] *Jolly*. The compound form is found also in the parallel verse at *MBh* 12.239.22.

12.32a On the basis of the mss. it is impossible to decide whether the reading is (*a*)*dhairyam* in the negative or the positive *dhairyam*. All the commentators who note the term (*Me, Nā, Rn, Nd, Rc*) take it to be *adhairyam*. So do all the editors, who place an *avagraha* before *dhairyam* or simply connect it to the final -*tā* of the previous word. I have opted for the positive *dhairyam* mainly because in the context of *rajas* we should expect fortitude rather than its lack. Indeed, the lack of fortitude (*adhṛti*) is given in the very next verse as a characteristic of *tamas*. See also verses 36 and 46, where seeking fame and fortune and individuals such as kings, Kṣatriyas, soldiers, and debaters are connected to *rajas*, and verse 38 that relates *artha* to *rajas*.

12.41a Jolly has adopted the partitive genitive *eṣām*, but this reading has little manuscript support. No commentator notes it, and *Me, Nā,* and *Rc* explicitly presents *eṣā* as qualifying *gatiḥ*. The reading *eṣā* in the nominative is found in: Bo Ho Hy Jm Jo^{1} wKt^{1} wKt^{3} NKt^{4} Lo^{1} GMd^{1} TMd^{3} GMd^{5} Pu^{5} Pu^{7} [*cor to*] Pu^{8} Pu^{10} Tj^{2} Tr^{1} Tr^{2} MTr^{4} [*Jolly* M$^{2-3-8-9}$ R] *Mandlik Jha KSS Dave*.

12.42b All the editions have adopted the reading *sakacchapāḥ*, and it has good manuscript support. I have, however, opted for *sarīsṛpāḥ*, which is found in all the ST mss. and a large number of NT-x ones, as well as in the two medieval citations. The only other place that *kacchapa* occurs is at 1.44 and the reading of that *pāda* appears to have exerted influence on this verse; see, for example, the variant *nakra* in several mss. Only *Go* and *Ku* comment on this term and they gloss *kūrma*, which would support the alternate reading. The reading adopted is found in: BKt^{5} La^{1} GMd^{1} TMd^{4} GMd^{5} sOx^{1} Ox^{2} NPu^{1} Pu^{2} Pu^{3} Pu^{4} Pu^{10} Tr^{1} Tr^{2} MTr^{4} MTr^{5} MTr^{6} Wa [*Jolly* M Nd Gr] *Apa Mādh*.

12.44d The reading *tāmaseṣu* in the masculine locative plural has overwhelming manuscript support. According to this understanding, the reference is to the *tāmasa* kinds of species listed here; *Go* thus glosses *tāmaseṣu manuṣyeṣv uttamā gatiḥ*. I think, however, that this is a mistaken reading influenced by the several masculine nominatives in the list. These species rather constitute the highest *gati* among the *gatis* that are *tāmasa;* thus, I think, *tāmasīṣu* is the correct reading with the implied *gatiṣu*. The same is true of verse 47d where the correct reading should be *rājasīṣu*. The correctness of this reading is demonstrated by the parallel with reference to *sāttvika* in verse 50, where *sāttvikī* here in the singular qualifies *gati*. The reading *tāmasīṣu* is found in: Ho Hy Jm Jo^{1} Jo^{2} wKt^{1} Kt^{2} wKt^{3} GMy Pu^{8} Pu^{10} Tj^{2} *Ku Rc Mandlik Jolly Jha KSS Dave*.

12.59d Commentators note the irregular double sandhi here [*pretyā* + *antya*> *pretyāntya*], some calling this a vedic peculiarity.

12.86a The reading adopted, *pūrveṣām*, is found in all the ST mss. and a large number of NT-x one: Be^{1} Bo Ho Jo^{2} wKt^{1} NKt^{4} BKt^{5} Lo^{1} Lo^{2} Lo^{3} GMd^{1} TMd^{3} GMd^{5} GMy NNg oOr Ox^{2} NPu^{1} Pu^{2} Pu^{4} Pu^{8} Pu^{10} Tj^{1} Tr^{1} MTr^{4} MTr^{5} MTr^{6} Wa [*Jolly* M R Nd Ku] *Me Bh Nd Jolly Jha Dave*.

12.89a Even though most NT mss. read *cāmutra*, I think the context calls for *vā*. The reading adopted is found in: Lo^{3} TMd^{4} GMd^{5} NPu^{1} Pu^{5} Pu^{7} Pu^{8} Tj^{1} Tr^{1} MTr^{4} MTr^{5} MTr^{6} [*Jolly* Gr Nd] *Vij Apa Jolly*.

12.90b The *lectio difficilior* here is clearly *sārṣṭitām*, which is supported by several variants and found in: BBe^{2} NKt^{4} Lo^{1} Lo^{3} GMd^{1} GMd^{5} Tj^{1} MTr^{4} MTr^{5} MTr^{6} Wa [*Jolly* G R Nd] *Go Nā Rn Rc Jolly*.

12.94c The reading adopted, *atarkyam,* is found in all the ST mss. and in a number NT-x ones. GMd^{1} TMd^{3} GMd^{5} GMy oOr sOx^{1} Ox^{2} Pu^{3} sPu^{6} Tr^{1} Tr^{2} MTr^{4} MTr^{6} Wa *Nā Nd Rc Bh* [*Jolly* Nd] *Apa*.

12.95a The adopted reading, *śrutayaḥ*, is found in: Be^{1} NKt^{4} BKt^{5} La^{1} Lo^{2} GMd^{1} TMd^{3} TMd^{4} GMy NNg oOr NPu^{1} Pu^{2} Pu^{4} Pu^{5} Pu^{7} Pu^{10} Tr^{1} MTr^{5} Wa [*Jolly* M G] *Me Nā Apa Lakṣ Jolly Dave Jha*. The variant reading *smṛtayaḥ*, however, must have been very old, because it is found in Kumārila's citation.

12.98d Although the majority of the mss. gives the stem *prasūti*, thus forming a compound with the two next words, I think the correct reading is the nominative *prasūtiḥ*. The commentators *Me, Nā, Nd,* and *Rc* explain the *pāda* by taking *prasūtiḥ* as a nominative. Although *Bh* appears to base his first explanation on *prasūti* as forming a compound, his second explanation clearly takes it to be in the nominative. The nominative form is found in: Ho La^{1} GMd^{5} NNg Ox^{2} NPu^{1} Pu^{10} Tj^{1} [*Jolly* M] *Me Nā Nd Rc Jolly Jha Dave*.

12.121b I have adopted the reading *harim*, even though the alternate reading *haram* also has considerably manuscript support. The latter may have been, however, influenced by the proximity of *viṣṇum*, scribes desiring to bring Śiva into the picture. This reading is supported by *Nā*, who glosses *harim īśvaram*. The adopted reading is found in: Be^{1} Ho Jo^{2} Lo^{2} TMd^{3} GMy oOr Ox^{2} Pu^{2} Pu^{4} Pu^{5} Pu^{7} MTr^{4} [*Jolly* M G R Nd] *Rn Nd Jolly*. This reading is supported by *Nd* and *Rn*, both of whom interpret the term to mean Indra. *Rn* remarks on the alternate reading: *haram iti pramādapāṭhaḥ*.

12.123c The editions of *Mandlik, Jha, KSS,* and *Dave* read *pare* after *eke*, without an *avagraha*. It is impossible determine whether the reading should be *pare* or (*a*)*pare*, because the mss. almost never use *avagrahas*. Both *Ku* and *Rc*, however, explicitly give *apare* as the reading, and I have followed it. Jolly also gives the *avagraha*, whereas the editors of *Apa* and *Lakṣ* omit it and read *pare*.

APPENDICES

APPENDIX I

Fauna and Flora

Common fauna and flora that can be readily translated are not listed here; they are found in the Index. For further information on flora, see K. M. Nadkarni, *Indian Materia Medica*. Revised edition; 2 vols. Bombay: Popular Prakashan, 1976. For animals, see S. H. Prater, *The Book of Indian Animals*. Bombay Natural History Society. Reprint. Delhi: Oxford University Press, 1997. For birds, see K. N. Dave, *Birds in Sanskrit Literature*. Delhi: Motilal Banarsidass, 1985.

Aśmantaka. The plant *Bauhinia tomentosa*, whose fibers were used to make the girdle of a student.

Baka. This term is applied to a wide variety of water fowl, including heron, ibis, stork and the common flamingo.

Balāka. Flamingo; the term is sometimes applied to other water fowl, such as the egret.

Balvaja. A type of coarse grass: *Eleusine indica*.

Bel (Bilva). The tree *Aegle marmelos*, as also the fruits of this tree.

Bhāsa. The bearded vulture (*Gypaetus barbatus*), but often the term may refer to other kinds of vultures.

Bhūstṛṇa. The plant *Andropogon schoenanthus;* geranilum grass; *ruaghas* in Hindi. A fragrant grass native to central India.

Cakra. The ruddy sheldrake called the Brahmani Duck. The fidelity of a mated pair to each other and their grief when separated is celebrated in Indian poetry and folklore.

Darbha. A type of grass used for ritual purposes, most commonly the same as Kuśa; specifically the grass *Saccharum cylindricum*.

Dātyūha. The hawk cuckoo.

Eṇa. The Blackbuck (also called Kṛṣṇasāra: *MDh* 2.23), an antelope with black hair on the back and sides and white under the belly: *Antilope cervicapra*. About 32 inches at the shoulder and weighing about 90 lbs., with horns 20–5 inches long.

Haṃsa. The ruddy goose, the most celebrated species of Indian goose. The term is often applied to other large geese and swans.

Kākola. A kind of raven, although the term may have been used more widely for various species of ravens and crows.

Kālaśāka. The plant *Ocimum sanctum*, commonly referred to as holy basil or Tulasī plant.

Kalaviṅka. A species of sparrow, identified as the "village sparrow" by Vijñāneśvara on *YDh* 1.174. According to Dave (1985), the word is used for blackbirds, magpies, and finches.

Kataka. The fruit of the tree *Strychnos potatorum*, called "clearing nut tree"; Hindi *nirmalī*.

Khadira. The tree *Acacia catechu*, called "cutch tree"; Hindi *khair*.

Khañjarīṭaka. The yellow wagtail.

Kiṃśuka. The tree *Butea frondosa;* called "bastard teak"; Hindi *palas*.

Koyaṣṭhi. The lapwing, also called the paddy-bird. Dave (1985, 358) identifies these as "the smaller crested Herons and Bitterns which keep standing in shallow waters for hours for prey to come to them."

Krauñca. A species of large water bird, probably the common crane. Haradatta (on *ĀpDh* 1.17.36) says that they travel in pairs, and Bühler identifies the bird as the red-crested crane now called Sāras.

Kubjaka. The shrub *Rosa moschata;* called "musk-scented rose"; Hindi *kujai*.

Kuśa. The most common of the sacred grasses (see Darbha) used for rituals purposes. *Poa cynosuroides*.

Madgu. The snake fish or a cormorant.

Mahāśalka. A kind of large prawn.

Muñja. A species of rush belonging to the sugar-cane family and reaching about 10 feet in height and used for basket weaving: *Saccharum munja*. Its principal ritual use is in the manufacture of the girdle given to a Brahmin boy at his vedic initiation.

Mūrvā. A species of hemp used in the manufacture of bow strings and of the ritual girdle given to a Kṣatriya boy at his vedic initiation: *Sanseviera roxburghiana*.

Palāśa. A variety of fig tree called *dhak* with a beautiful trunk and abundant leaves: *Butea frondosa*. Incisions produce a red juice used as an astringent. The tree was viewed as sacred in ancient India and its wood used to make ritual implements.

Pāṭhīna. A kind of sheat-fish, *Silurus pelorius* or *boalis*.

Pīlu. The tree *Careya arborea;* Hindi *kumbi*.

Plava. A coot or cormorant.

Rājīva. Said to be a kind of lotus-colored fish, or one with stripes.

Rajjuvāla. A species of wild fowl.

Rohita. A kind of red fish said to feed on moss.

Ruru. A species of spotted antelope.

Sāla. The tree *Shorea robusta*, called the "Sal tree"; Hindi: *sakhu*, but in other languages *sal*.

Śāli. A variety of rice. Commentators call this red winter rice.

Śamī. The name covers two plants. First, *Mimosa suma* (Hindi: *chikkur*), a thorny shrub. Second, *Prosopis spicigera*.

Śaṅkhapuṣpī. The plant *Canscora decussata*.

Sārasa. A species of crane, *Ardea sibirica*.

Saśalka. Lit. "with scales," a kind of fish.

Śelu. The tree *Cordia myxa*.

Śigruka. The tree *Moringa oleifera* or *pterygosperma*, commonly called "drumstick" tree (Murunga), whose long pods are widely used as a vegetable.

Siṃhatuṇḍa. Lit. "lion-faced," a kind of fish.

Śleṣmātaka. Also called *śleṣmāta* and *śelu,* the fruit of this small tree is about the size of a cherry. Called *bhokar* in Marathi, it is used today for making pickles.

Śyena. A kind of hawk or falcon, although the term is used for any large bird of prey.

Udumbara. A type of fig tree whose wood is used for ritual purposes: *Ficus glomerata.*

Vārdhrīṇasa lit., "leather-snouted." This sometimes refers to the rhinoceros, but in these texts it refers to a type of bird, probably a hornbill. At *BDh* 1.12.6, however, it is classified as a bird that scratches with its feet in searching for food, which would argue against a waterbird.

Vrīhi. A variety of long-grained rice different from *śāli* and ripening, according to commentators, in 60 days.

APPENDIX II

Names of Gods, People, and Places

Ādityas. Literally the son(s) of Aditi, the term in the plural refers to a group of gods, including some prominent ones such as Varuṇa, Mitra, and Indra. Early texts give their number as eight, but the Brāhmaṇas already show their number as twelve, which has remained the norm ever since. Together with the Vasus and the Rudras, they constitute the three major classes of gods. In the singular, the term Āditya refers to the sun.

Agastya. The name of an ancient sage, said to be the son of Mitra and Varuṇa. In a later myth he is said to have instructed the Vindhya mountains to remain bowed (not to grow taller) until he turns from southern India.

Agni. Fire and the god of Fire.

Agnidagdha. The common designation of a class of ancestors (*pitṛ*) who maintained sacred fires while they were on earth.

Agniṣvātta. The common designation of a class of ancestors who maintained sacred fires but performed only domestic rites and not vedic sacrifices.

Ajīgarta. A sage famous for his story told in the *AitB* 7.13–16. He wanted to sacrifice his son, Śunaḥśepa, to appease the wrath of the god Varuṇa.

Ājyapa. Literally, "ghee drinkers," the name of a class of ancestors descendant from Pulastya. They are viewed as the ancestors of Vaiśyas.

All-gods (*viśvedeva*). The name of a class of gods. In the later Dharma texts they are listed as ten in five pairs: Kratu and Dakṣa, Vasu and Satya, Dhuri and Locana, Kāla and Kāma, and Purūravas and Ārdrava. See Kane 1962–75, IV. 457.

Anagnidagdha. The common designation of a class of ancestors distinguished from the *agnidagdha;* hence, possibly ancestors who did not maintin sacred fires on earth.

Andha-Tāmisra. One of the 21 hells. No light of the sun falls into this region. Suicides and adulterers are consigned to this hell.

Aṅgiras. Name of a sage. In later mythology, he is viewed as one of the ten mind-born sons of Brahmā.

Āṅgirasa. The name of a class of priests closely associated with another group called Atharvan. The name is also used with reference to a group of sundry divine beings and is an epithet of several gods, especially the fire god Agni.

Antyāvasāyin. A very low-caste person, even lower than a Cāṇḍāla. Explained as the offspring of a Niṣāda woman and a Cāṇḍāla man (*MDh* 10.39).

Apsaras. A class of female deities connected with water and often regarded as the wives of the Gandharvas.

Asaṃvṛta. A name of a hell.

Asipatravana. A hell where tree have leaves as sharp as knives. For further Purāṇic descriptions, see Mani 1975, 58.

Asura. Although in early Indo-Iranian mythology it was a divine epithet, in Indian myth *asuras* are viewed as demons and opponents of gods.

Aśvin. Twin deities described as young, beautiful, fond of honey, and expert in medical knowledge. They are the physicians of the gods.

Atri. A famous sage and author of many vedic hymns. Later mythology sees him as one of the ten mind-born sons of Brahmā.

Barhiṣad. Sons of Atri, they are the ancestors of various demonic classes of beings. For later descriptions, see Mani 1975, 108.

Bharadvāja. An ancient seer to whom the composition of the sixth book of the R̥gveda is ascribed.

Cailāśaka. An evil class of ghosts that feed on moths.

Cāṇḍāla. An outcaste person whose mere touch polutes. He is considered the offspring of a Śūdra father and a Brahmin mother.

Cāraṇa. This term can apply to bards, singers, and the like, and also to mythological beings connected with singing.

Daitya. A class of demons often associated with Dānavas.

Dakṣa. Name of a divine being associated with creation and one of the ten sons of Brahmā. For myths associated with him, see Mani 1975, 192.

Dānava. A class of demons often associated with the Daityas.

Dasyu. A generic name for degraded persons and outcastes. The name is also applied to ethinic groups outside the four major classes of society (see *MDh* 10.45).

Dhanvantari. A god produced at the cosmogonic churning of the ocean, he is the physician of the gods and the divine author of medical science.

Dr̥ṣadvatī. Name of a river flowing into the Sarasvatī from the east.

Gandharva. In the early vedic literature Gandharvas appear as a class of divine beings alongside the gods and the forefathers. They are associated with the Soma drink and are said to be fond of females. They are often associated with the celestial nymphs, Apsarases. In later literature, especially the epics, the Gandharvas are depicted as celestial singers and are associated with music.

Guhyaka. A class of divine beings; attendants fo Kubera.

Havirbhuj. Lit. "eaters of oblations," this class beings are regarded as the ancestors of Kṣatriyas.

Hiraṇyagarbha. Lit. "golden egg *or* foetus." In cosmology, the initial state of the cosmos in the form of an egg (*MDh* 1.9).

Indra. The most famous of the vedic gods, Indra is called the king of the gods. He is powerful and loves to drink Soma. His claim to fame is his victory over Vr̥tra, a combat that is given cosmogonic significance. Indra is closely associated with rain, and prominence is given to his weapon, the Vajra, conceived of as the thunderbolt in later tradition.

Kālasūtra. A hell depicted in the Purāṇas as extremely hot.

Kaśyapa. The name of an ancient sage.

Kaṭapūtana. An evil class of deceased persons (*preta*) or demons.

Kavi. An epithet of Bhr̥gu.

Kāvya. The name of a class of ancestors.

Kratu. One of the mind-born sons of Brahmā.

Kubera. God of riches and guardian of the northern quarter.

Kuru. Name of a tribe inhabiting the region of between the upper reaches of the Indus and Ganges rivers during vedic times. This tribe became allied with the Pañcālas, who occupied the land to the south-east of the Kurus.

Kurukṣetra. The land of the Kurus. In later times, this referred to a stretch of sacred land situated south of the river Sarasvatī and north of Dṛṣadvatī where the epic battle of the *Mahābhārata* took place.

Marīci. The first of the mind-born sons of Brahmā.

Maruts. A group of gods connected with the wind and the thunderstorm, and thus associated with Indra's exploits.

Matsya. Name of a region located to the west of the Pañcālas and south of the Kurus and of the people of that region.

Mitra. Name of a vedic god closely associated with Varuṇa.

Nāga. Serpent, especially mythical beings viewed as serpents.

Nārada. Well known in later literature as a famous sage, he is one of the sons of Brahmā. See Mani 1975, 526.

Nirṛti. Goddess personifying death, destruction, and adversity.

Niṣāda. A mixed caste considered to be the offspring of a Brahmin father and a Vaiśya mother.

Pañcāla. The name of a region in the upper reaches of the Ganges, to the south-east of the Kurus; also refers the people of this region.

Piśāca. An evil supernatural being; a goblin.

Pracetas. One of the sons of Brahmā.

Prajāpati. Literally "lord of creatures," he is the creator god *par excellence* in the Brāhmaṇas and the Upaniṣads. He is the father of the gods and the demons (*asura*), as well as of all creatures.

Prayāga. The sacred city at the confluence of the rivers Ganges and Yamunā; present-day Allahabad.

Pulkasa. An outcaste individual viewed as particularly impure; the son of a Niṣāda man and a Śūdra woman (*MDh* 10.38).

Rudra. Generally regarded as a storm god, Rudra has an ambivalent personality. He is fierce and feared. He is also a healer, the one who averts the anger of gods. In his benign aspect he is referred to as *śiva*, "the benign one," an epithet that becomes the name of the later god Śiva, with whom Rudra is identified.

Rudras. In the plural, the term refers to a group of eleven gods, who, together with the Ādityas and the Vasus, constitute the three classes of gods. The Rudras are associated with the Maruts; both of these groups are ruled by Rudra.

Sādhya. A group of somewhat ill-defined deities, said to occupy a region above that of the gods.

Sarasvatī. The most celebrated river of the vedic age, it is personified as a goddess. In the Brāhmaṇas she becomes identified with speech and the goddess of speech, and in later mythology Sarasvatī is the goddess of eloquence and wisdom. This river flowed between the Indus and Ganges river systems. Its disappearance in the desert became the focus of myths and folk tales.

Sarpa. A serpent; also mythical beings in the shape of serpents.

Saumya. A class of ancestors.

Śaunaka. A famous vedic sage to whom various vedic texts, as also works on Law, are ascribed.

Soma. A sacrificial drink pressed from a plant with apparently mind-altering qualities, it was personified as a god and later identified with the moon. Thus the term often simply means the moon.

Somapa. Lit. "Soma-drinker," a class of ancestors.

Somasad. A class of ancestors.

Sukālin. A class of ancestors.

Suparṇa. Generally referring to any large bird, the term is used with references to bird-shaped mythical beings.

Śūrasena(ka). The name of a region somewhat to the south of the Matya; also the appellation of the inhabitants of this region.

Ugra. A mixed class considered to be the offspring of a Vaiśya father and a Śūdra mother.

Utathya. Name of an authority on Law.

Varuṇa. One of the great gods in the early vedic literature, he is viewed as the grand sovereign and upholder of the natural and moral order. He becomes increasingly associated with the waters and the west, and his residence comes to be located within the ocean.

Vasiṣṭha. One of the most important seers of the Ṛgveda. May stories surround his personality, and he is credited with the authorship of numerous texts, including the seventh book of the Ṛgveda and a treatise on Law. His hostility to Viśvāmitra is a recurrent theme in the stories.

Vasus. A group of eight gods distinguished from the Ādityas and Rudras, although their general character and specific identities remain rather vague.

Vinaśana. The place where the river Sarasvatī is believed to disapper into the ground.

Vindhya. The major mountain range in north-central India dividing north India from the Deccan.

Virāj. Literally "the wide-ruling one," he is presented as the first creature in the Ṛgvedic creation story in the Puruṣa hymn (*ṚV* 10.90). In the *MDh* (1.32) also he is presented as the first creature to emerge from the union of the primeval pair.

Viṣṇu. The great god of later Hinduism. He is a somewhat minor solar deity in the vedic literature and is especially celebrated in his two human incarnations, Rāma and Kṛṣṇa.

Viśvāmitra. An important seer of the Ṛgveda. Stories depict his hostility towards Vasiṣṭha. In later legend, he is viewed as a Kṣatriya who transformed himself into a Brahmin by means of austerities.

Vrātya. The term is used in ancient literature to refer to groups of people, at least some of whom appear to have led a wandering or a nomadic life. Already in some vedic texts, however, the Vrātya is presented as a mysterious, powerful, and even divine person. In later times the term is used to refer to either mixed-caste people or to Brahmins who have not undergone vedic initiation.

Yama. The Indian god of death from the most ancient period of vedic mythology until contemporary times. In ancient myths he is called king and divine characteristics are ascribed to him, but he comes to be identified with death itself and many of the negative aspects of death become associated with Yama. Later myths associate him with judgment and punishment of the dead.

Yavana. The Indian designation of Greeks and Greek-speaking peoples in the northwestern parts of the subcontinent. A mixed class considered to be the offspring of a Kṣatriya father and a Śūdra mother.

APPENDIX III

Ritual Vocabulary

1. Names of Rites, Priests, and Ritual Objects

Abhijit. A particular sacrifice that is a component part of the major sacrificial session (*sattra*) lasting 12 months known as Gavāmayana.

Adhvaryu. One of the four principal priests at a vedic sacrifice. He belongs to the Yajurveda and is responsible for most of the sacrificial actions, including the offerings made in the sacred fire.

Agniṣṭut. A particular form of Soma sacrifice lasting a single day.

Ahīna. A particular kind of Soma sacrifice at which the pressing lasts between two and twelve days.

Bali. The offering of cooked food to various deities, spirits, and animals.

Brahman. One of the four principal priests at a vedic sacrifice.

Camasa. A square ladle made of banyan wood and used for a variety of purposes in a sacrifice, including serving as a container or a drinking vessel for Soma.

Caru. A porridge prepared from rice or barley and cooked in water with butter or milk.

Gosava. A one-day Soma sacrifice. It is recommended for people aspiring to sovereignty. See Kane 1962–75, ii. 1213.

Graha. A ladle used to take Soma out of a larger container.

Horse Sacrifice (*aśvamedha*). One of the most important vedic sacrifices, it is perfomed by a king to demonstrate his sovereignty and ritually to enhance his dominion. A horse is set free to roam at will for a whole year, during which time it is guarded by the king's troops. At the end of the year it is brought back and sacrificed.

Hotṛ. One of the four principal priests at a vedic sacrifice. He belongs to the Ṛgveda and is responsible for all the recitations during a sacrifice.

Sacrifice of first fruits. An oblation consisting of the first fruits of the harvest offered at the end of the rainy season.

Sacrificial cake (*puroḍāśa*). A cake made with rice or barley flour and baked in potsherds.

Śākalā. An oblation accompanied by the eight verses of *VS* 8.13.

Śakaṭa. A cart used to carry Soma plants and for other ritual purposes.

Sāvitra. Commentators take this to be an oblation offered to the god Savitṛ or an oblation using the Sāvitrī verse.

Seasonal sacrifice. Four sacrifices, each performed at the end of the four seasons.

Sphya. A wooden sword made of Khadira wood and used within the vedic ritual for a variety of ritual purposes.

Sruc. The common name for ladles (including Juhū, Upabhṛt, and Dhruvā) used for pouring ghee into the sacred fire.

Sruva. Distinguished from the Sruc-type ladles, this is a smaller spoon used mainly for spooning out ghee or milk into the Sruc. The Sruva has a long handle at the end of which there is a small globular spoon without a spout. It is made of Khadira wood.

Śūrpa. A winnowing basket made of bamboo or reed and used to winnow grain for the ritual.

Trivṛt. An oblation with the chanting in "triplicated" form of three verses, especially the verses of *ṚV* 9.11.

Udgātṛ. One of the four major priests in a vedic ritual. He Helongs to the Sāmaveda and performs the chanting of Sāmans.

Vaiśvānara. A sacrifice to the "Fire present in all men" generally cooked on twelve potsherds.

Viśvajit. A sacrifice at which one gives away all one's possessions. It is also a particular sacrifice that is a component part of the major sacrificial session (*sattra*) lasting 12 months known as Gavāmayana.

2. Names of Ritual Formulas and Texts

Aghamarṣaṇa. This is the hymn *ṚV* 10.190 used in a particular ritual to efface sins

Asyavāmīya. This the rather long hymn *ṚV* 1.164.

Calls. (*vyāhṛti*). These are the names of the seven worlds in ascending order: *bhur* (earth), *bhuvaḥ* (mid-space), *svar* (sky), *mahar* (great), *janas* (people), *tapas* (austerity), *satya* (truth). These names are considered sacred and powerful. The first three are generally referred to as simply Calls, whereas all seven are called Great Calls (*mahāvyāhṛti*).

Gāyatrī. Another name for Sāvitrī.

Great Calls. See Calls.

Haviṣpāntīya. This is the hymn *ṚV* 10.88.

Jyeṣṭha Sāmans. Haradatta (on *ĀpDh* 2.17.22; *GDh* 15.28) identifies this as *SV* 1.31 (= *ṚV* 1.24.15), while Govinda (on *BDh* 2.14.2) identifies it as *SV* 1.67 (= *ṚV* 6.7.1) and (on *BDh* 3.10.10) as *SV* 1.33 (= *ṚV* 10.9.4) and *ṚV* 1.115.1. Commentators of the *MDh* identify these as Sāmans sung in the wilderness. Obviously, there is a lot of confusion regarding these Sāmans.

Kūṣmāṇḍa. The four formulas *TĀ* 2.3; sometimes identified with the formulas at *TĀ* 2.6.

Kutsa's hymn. The hymn with eight verses *ṚV* 1.97.

Māhitra. The hymn *ṚV* 10.185.

Pāvavmānī. Opinions are divided about the identity of these verses. Some identify them as *ṚV* 9.67.21–27. Medhātithi (on *MDh* 11.258) takes them to be *ṚV* 9.1–114 (that is, the entire ninth Maṇḍala), whereas Bhāruci identifies them as *ṚV* 9.14—67.

Puruṣa hymn. The creation hymn *ṚV* 10.90.

Ṛc. The sacred verses found in the Ṛgveda.
Śākalahomīya. These are the eight verses of *VS* 8.13 = *TS* 3.2.5.7.
Sāman. A verse generally taken from the *ṚV* and sung to a particular melody. The Sāmans are contained in the Sāmaveda.
Sāvitrī. Also called Gāyatrī, this is the most sacred of ritual formulas: *ṚV* 3.62.10 (see App. III.3: "That excellent. . . ." Sometimes the term is used with reference to vedic initiation, because teaching this verse to the initiated boy forms a central part of that rite.
Śiras formula. "OṂ the Waters, the Light, the Taste, the Immortal, Brahman! Earth, Atmosphere, Sky! OṂ!" *Mahānārāyaṇa Upaniṣad* 342.
Śivasaṃkalpa. The first six verses of *VS* 34.
Solar formulas. According to Medhātithi (on *MDh* 5.86), they are the verses beginning with *ṚV* 1.50.1. According to Govinda (on *BDh* 3.8.14), *ṚV* 1.50.10; 1.50.1; 1.115.1.
Somāraudra. This is the hymn with four verses *ṚV* 6.74. Bhāruci (on *MDh* 11.255), however, identifies them as the verses to Rudra at *ṚV* 2.33.4 and to Soma at *ṚV* 9.96.5.
Śuddhavatī. The three verses *ṚV* 8.95.7–9.
Svadhā. The exclamation accompanying the offering of an oblation to ancestors.
Svāhā. The exclamation accompanying the offering of an oblation to gods.
Taratsamandī. The hymn *ṚV* 9.58.
Vaṣaṭ. A ritual exclamation uttered by the Hotṛ priest at the conclusion of the sacrificial verse as the Adhvaryu priest puts the oblation into the sacred fire.
Yajus. A ritual formula in prose contained in the Yajurveda. These formulas accompany the ritual offerings into the fire.

3. Formulas Cited in the Translations by the First Words

"Adoration . . .". Commentators identify this variously. Medhātithi and Bhāruci take it to be "Adoration to Rudra, to the strong one, to the one with braided hair. . . ." I have not been able to identify this verse.

"Aryaman, Varuṇa, and Mitra, Indra and Viṣṇu among these, Maruts and Aśvins. . . ." This is *ṚV* 4.2.4. Some commentators think that the three or two verses beginning with this are meant.

"Indra, Mitra, Varuṇa, Agni, the host of Maruts, and Aditi—we invoke for assistance. . ." The seven verses beginning with this are *ṚV* 1.106.1–7. Bhāruci (on *MDh* 256), however, take this to be *ṚV* 1.7.1.

"May the Maruts pour upon me, may Indra and Bṛhaspati; and may this fire pour upon me long life and strength. May they make me live long." *TĀ* 2.18.

"May the virile strength return again to me, may long life and prosperity. May goods return to me again, may the Brāhmaṇical state." *ĀśGṛ* 3.6.8. Variants of this verse are found in *AV* 7.67; *BṛU* 6.4.5.

"No anxiety, no danger, . . . " This is the hymn *ṚV* 10.126.

"That excellent glory of Savitṛ, the god, we meditate, that he may stimulate our thoughts." *ṚV* 3.62.10.

"This, yes, this is my inclination. . . ." This is the hymn *ṚV* 10.119.

"To welcome the Dawn the inspired Vasiṣṭhas did first awaken with songs and praises. . . ." This is the hymn *ṚV* 7.80, containing three verses.

"Untie, Varuṇa, from us the bond at the top, at the middle, and at the bottom, so that in your commandment, Āditya, we may remain sinless for Aditi." *ṚV* 1.24.15.

"Waters, you are refreshing. Further us to strength, to see great joy. The auspicious flavor that is yours, accord to us here, like eager mothers. To him may we come with satisfaction, to whose dwelling you quicken us, O waters, and propagate us." *TS* 4.1.5.1. These are the Abliṅga formulas.

"We placate your anger, Varuṇa, with obeisances, sacrifices, and oblations. Wise Lord, ruling king, loosen from us the sins we have committed." *ṚV* 1.24.14. Bhāruci, however, identifies this as *ṚV* 10.59.9.

"Whatever offense that we humans commit against the race of gods, Varuṇa, if by inattention we have violated your institutes, O god, may you not punish us because of that evil." *ṚV* 7.89.5.

APPENDIX IV

Weights, Measures, and Currency

NB: weights, measures, and coins have varied over time in India. The values given below are approximations. In coins the weight of each measurement differed for gold, silver, and copper. See *MDh* 8.132–37.

Aṅgula. A measurement of length (lit., a finger) approximately 2 cm.

Bow. A measurement of length; approximately 6 feet or 1.82 meters.

Dharaṇa. A measure of weight; approximately 377.6 grams; a silver *dharaṇa*, however, is said to weight only 3.776 grams.

Droṇa. A measurement of capacity especially of gains: probably about 5 liters. When it is a measure of weight, it is approximately 9.6 kg.

Finger. See Aṅgula.

Gaurasarṣapa. "White mustard seed"; a minute measure of weight equal to three Rājasarṣapas.

Kārṣāpaṇa. Also known as Paṇa, this basic copper coin weighed approximately 9.33 grams. A silver Kārṣāpaṇa weighed 3.76 grams.

Kārṣika. A copper coin, the same as Kārṣāpaṇa or Paṇa.

Kṛṣṇala. A measure of weight appliximately 0.118 grams.

Kumbha. A measure of capacity: about 105 liters.

Likṣā. "Egg of a louse"; a very minute measure of weight equal to eight Trasareṇus.

Māṣa. "A bean"; a measure of weight; approximately 0.59 grams.

Māṣaka. A silver Māṣaka weighed approximately 0.25 grams; a gold coin of this name is mentioned at 8.393.

Niṣka. A measurement of weight said to be four Suvarṇas, i.e., 37.76 grams.

Pala. A measure of weight; approximately 37.76 grams.

Paṇa. Same as Kārṣāpaṇa.

Purāṇa. A silver weight said to be sixteen silver Māṣakas, i.e., 3.776 grams.

Rājasarṣapa. "Black mustard seed"; a minute measure of weight equal to three Likṣās.

Rod's throw. It is unclear whether this is an actual measurement or the distance that a rod can be thrown.

Śatamāna. A silver Śatamāna weighed approximately 11.66 grams.

Suvarṇa. A measure of weight; approximately 9.44 grams.

Trasareṇu. A particle of dust seen in a sunbeam; smallest measure of weight.

Yava. A measurement of weight: 0.039 grams

BIBLIOGRAPHY

PRIMARY LITERATURE

Aparārka, *Aparāditya*, commentary on the *YDh*. 2 vols. Ānandāśrama Sanskrit Series, 46. Pune, 1903–04.

Āpastamba-Dharmasūtra. Ed. and tr. in Olivelle 2000.

Āpastamba-Gṛhyasūtra. Ed. by M. Winternitz. Vienna: Alfred Hölder, 1887. Tr. in Oldenberg 1886–92.

Baudhāyana-Dharmasūtra. Ed. and tr. in Olivelle 2000.

Bṛhaspati-Smṛti (Reconstructed). Ed. K. V. Rangaswami Aiyangar. Gaekwad's Oriental Series, 85. Baroda: Oriental Institute, 1941. Translated in Jolly 1889.

Devaṇabhaṭṭa, *Smṛticandrikā*. Government Oriental Library Series, 43, 44, 45, 48, 52, 56. Mysore: Government Oriental Library. Vol. 1, Saṃskārakāṇḍa, 1914; Vo. 2, Āhanikakāṇḍa, 1914; Vol. 3, Vyavahārakāṇḍa, 1914–16; Vol. 4, Śrāddhakāṇḍa, 1918; Vol. 5, Āśaucakāṇḍa, 1921.

Gautama-Dharmasūtra. Ed. and tr. in Olivelle 2000.

Gobhila-Gṛhyasūtra. Ed. with Bhaṭṭanārāyaṇa's commentary by C. Bhattacharya. Delhi: Munshiram Manoharlal, 1982. Tr. in Oldenberg 1886–92.

Jīmūtivāhana, *Dāyabhāga*. Ed. and tr. by L. Rocher. New York: Oxford University Press, 2002.

Kāmandaka, *Nītisāra* with Śaṅkarārya's commentary. Ed. T. Gaṇapati Śāstrī. Trivandrum Sanskrit Series, 14. Trivandrum: 1912.

Kātyāyana-Smṛti. Ed. P. V. Kane. Poona: Oriental Book Agency, n.d. Aiyangar, Rangaswami K. V. n.d. "Additional Verses of Kātyāyana on Vyavahāra." In *A Volume of Studies in Indology* (presented to P. V. Kane on his 61st birthday), ed. S. M. Katre and P. K. Goode (Poona: Oriental Book Agency), pp. 7–11.

Kautaḷya, *Arthaśāstra*. Ed. and tr. in Kangle 1965–72.

Lakṣmīdhara, *Kṛtyakalpataru*. Ed. by K. V. Rangaswami Aiyangar. Gaekwad's Oriental Series. 14 vols. Baroda: Oriental Institute, 1942–79.

Mādhava, *Parāśara-Mādhava*. 3 vols. Reprint. Calcutta: Asiatic Society, 1973–74.

Nārada-Smṛti. Ed. and tr. in Lariviere 2003.

Pañcatantra. Ed. and tr. by F. Edgerton. American Oriental Series 2–3. New Haven: American Oriental Society. Tr. by P. Olivelle. Oxford: Oxford University Press, 1997.

Pāraskara-Gṛhyasūtra. Ed. with five commentaries by M. G. Bakre. Bombay: Gujarati Printing Press, 1917. Tr. in Oldenberg 1886–92.

Patañjali, *Mahābhāṣya* on Pāṇini's *Aṣṭadhyāyī*. Ed. F. Kielhorn. 3rd revised edition by K. V. Abhyankar. Pune: Bhandarkar Oriental Research Institute, 1962–72.

Vaikhānasa-Dharmasūtra. Ed. by W. Caland. Calcutta: Asiactic Society, 1927. Tr. in Caland 1929.

Vaikhānasa-Gṛhyasūtra. Ed. by W. Caland. Calcutta: Asiactic Society, 1927. Tr. in Caland 1929.

Vasiṣṭha-Dharmasūtra. Ed. and tr. in Olivelle 2000.

Vijñāneśvara, *Mitākṣarā*, commentary on *YDh*. Ed. U. C. Pandey. Kashi Sanskrit Series, 178. Varanasi: Chowkhamba Sanskrit Series, 1967. Translated with Mitramiśra's *Vīramitrodaya* and Śūlapāṇi's *Dīpakalikā* by J. R. Gharpure. 3 vols. Bombay: 1936–38.

Viṣṇu-Dharmasūtra. Ed. with Nandapaṇḍita's commentary *Keśavavaijayantī* by V. Krishnamacharya. 2 vols. Madras: Adyar Library and Research Centre, 1964. Tr. in Jolly 1880.

Viśvarūpa, *Bālakrīḍā*, commentary on *YDh*. Ed. T. Ganapati Sastri. 1921–22. Reprint. New Delhi: Mushiram Manoharlal, 1982.

Yāska, *Nirukta*. Ed. V. K. Rajavade. Poona: Bhandarkar Oriental Research Institute, 1940.

EDITIONS AND TRANSLATIONS OF MANU

Bühler, G. Tr. *The Laws of Manu*. SBE 25. Oxford: Oxford University Press, 1886.

Burnell, A. C. Tr. *The Ordinances of Manu*. Completed and edited by E. W. Hopkins. 1884. Reprint. Delhi: Mushiram Manoharlal, 1995.

Dave, J. H. Ed. *Manu-Smṛti with Nine Commentaries by Medhātithi, Sarvajñanārāyaṇa, Kullūka, Rāghavānanda, Nandana, Rāmacandra, Maṇirāma, Govindarāja, and Bhāruci*. 6 volumes. Bombay: Bharatiya Vidya Bhavan, 1972–84.

Derrett, J. D. M. Ed. and Tr. *Bhāruci's Commentary on the Manusmṛti* (The Manu-Śāstra-Vivaraṇa, Books 6–12). 2 vols. Wiesbaden, 1975.

Deslongschamps, A. L. Ed. *Lois de Manou publié en Sanscrit avec des notes contenant un choix de variantes et de scholies*. Paris: Levrault, 1830.

_____. Tr. *Lois de Manou comprenant les institutions religieuses et civiles des Indiens*. Paris: de Crapelet, 1833.

Doniger, W. Tr. *The Laws of Manu*. London: Penguin, 1991.

Jha, G. Ed. and tr. *Manusmṛti with the 'Manubhāṣya' of Medhātithi*. 10 volumes. 1920–39. Reprint. Delhi: Motilal Banarsidass, 1999.

Jolly, J. Ed. *Mānava Dharma-śāstra: The Code of Manu. Original Sanskrit Text Critically Edited according to the Standard Sanskrit Commentaries*. London: Trübner, 1887.

Jones, W. Tr. *Institutes of Hindu Law or the Ordinences of Menu according to the Gloss of Cullúca*. Calcutta: 1794.

Kāvyatīrtha, N. R. A. Ed. *The Manusmṛti with the Commentary Manvarthamuktāvalī of Kullūka*. Bombay: Nirnaya Sagar Press, 1946.

Mandlik, V. N. Ed. *Mānava-Dharma Śāstra with the Commentaries of Medhātithi, Sarvajñanārāyaṇa, Kullūka, Rāghavānanda, Nandana, and Rāmachandra*. 2 volumes and a supplement containing the commentary of Govindarāja. Bombay: Ganpat Krishnaji's Press, 1886.

Menu Sanhita: the Institutes of Menu with the Commentary of Kullúka Bhatta. Calcutta: 1830.

Nene, G. S. Ed. *The Manusmṛti with the 'Manvartha-muktāvalī' Commentary of Kullūka Bhaṭṭa*. Kashi Sanskrit Series 114. Varanasi: Chowkhamba Sanskrit Series Office, 1970.

Strehly, G. Tr. *Les Lois de Manou*. Paris: Ernest Leroux, 1893.

SECONDARY LITERATURE AND TRANSLATIONS

Aktor, M. 1999. "*Smṛtis* and *Jātis:* The Ritualisation of Time and the Continuity of the Past." In *Invoking the Past: The Uses of History in South Asia*, ed. D. Ali, pp. 258–79. Delhi: Oxford University Press.

Altekar, A. S. 1952. *Sources of Hindu Dharma in its Socio-Religious Aspects*. Sholapur: Institute of Public Administration.

Ayyar, A. S. Nataraja. 1952. *Mīmāṃsā Jurispurdence: The Sources of Hindu Law*. Ganganatha Jha Research Institute Series, No. 2. Allahabad: Ganganatha Jha Research Institute.

Bailey, G. 1985. *Materials for the Study of Ancient Indian Ideologies: Pravṛtti and Nirtti*. Pubblicazioni di "Indologica Taurinensia". Turin.

Bandyopadhyaya, N. C. 1980. *Development of Hindu Polity and Political Theories*. New Delhi: Munshiram Manoharlal.

Banerjee, N. V. 1980. *Studies in the Dharmaśāstra of Manu*. New Delhi: Munshiram Manoharlal.

Banerji, S. C. 1972. *Smṛti Material in the Mahābhārata*. Calcutta: D. P. Mitra.

_____. 1999. *A Brief History of Dharmaśāstra*. Delhi: Abhinav Publications.

Beaman, G. B. 1895. *On the Sources of the Dharma-Śāstras of Manu and Yājñavalkya*. Leipzig: Harrassowitz.

Betai, R. S. 1962. "Textual Problems of the Manusmṛti." *Journal of the Gujarat Research Society* 24: 271–76.

_____. 1963. "Widowhood and Niyoga in the Arthaśāstra and the Manusmṛti." *Our Heritage* 11: 1–11.

_____. 1965–66. Revisions of the Manusmṛti and the Background of These—A Fresh Study." *Journal of the Ganganatha Jha Research Institute* 22: 193–201.

_____. 1968. "State of Criminal Law in Manusmṛti." *Ibid*. 24: 279–300.

_____. 1970. *A Reconstruction of the Original Interpretations of the Manusmṛti*. Gujarat University Theses Publication Series, 9. Ahmedabad: Gujarat University.

_____. 1973. "Criminal Law from Manu to Yājñavalkya to Nārada—A Positive Transition." *Journal of the Oriental Institute* (Baroda) 22: 265–89.

_____. 2003. *Evolution of Law of Crimes in Ancient India*. Delhi: Bharatiya Kala Prakashan.

Bharadwaj, S. K. 1982. *Linguistic Study of Dharmasūtras*. Rohtak (Haryana): Manthan Publications.

Bodewitz, H. W. 1973. *Jaiminīya Brāhmaṇa* I, 1–65: *Translation and Commentary with a Study Agnihotra and Prāṇāgnihotra*. Orientalia Rheno-Traiectina 17. Leiden: E. J. Brill.

_____. 1985. "Yama's Second Boon in the Kaṭha Upaniṣad." *WZKS* 29: 5–26.

Bongert, Y. 1963. "Réflexions sur le problème de l'esclavage dans l'Inde ancienne à propos de quelques ouvrages récents." *Bulletin de l'École Française d'extrême-orient*, LI: 143–94.

Bosch, L. P. van den. 1991. "The Marriage of the Dead in Ancient India: On the Interpretation of Vaikhānasasmārtasūtra V.9." In Leslie 1991, pp. 62–79.

Brereton, J. 1986. "'*Tat Tvam Asi*' in Context." *ZDMG* 136: 98–109.

Brinkhaus, H. 1978. *Die altindischen Mischkastensysteme*. Alt- und Neu-Indische Studien 19. Wiesbaden: Franz Steiner.

_____. 1980. "Zu J. D. M. Derretts Textausgabe und Übersetzung von Bhārucis Manuśāstra-vivaraṇa-fragment." *WZKS* 24: 147–80.

Bühler, G. (tr.) 1879–82. *Sacred Laws of the Āryas* [containing the Dharmasūtras of Āpastamba, Gautama, Vasiṣṭha, and Baudhāyana]. 2 vols. SBE 2, 14. Oxford: Oxford University Press.

_____. 1888. "Lexicographical Notes. 5. *Bhrūṇa, bhrūṇahan, bhrūṇahatyā, bhrūṇahanana*." *WZKM* 2: 182-85.

Burrow, T. 1975. "Two Śaka Loanwords in *Manusmṛti*." *Ural-Altaische Jahrbücher* 47: 30–34.

Caland, W. (tr.) 1929. *Vaikhānasasmārtasūtram*. Calcutta: Asiatic Society.

Chatterjee, H. 1971. *The Law of Debt in Ancient India*. Calcutta: Sanskrit College.

Chatterjee, H. 1972–74. *Forms of Marriage in Ancient India*. 2 vols. Calcutta: Sanskrit Pustak Bhandar.

Dallapiccola, A. L., and S. Zingel-Avé Lallemant, eds. 1989. *The Sastric Tradition in the Indian Arts*. Beiträge zur Südasienforschung. Wiesbaden: Steiner.

Das, R. M. 1962. *Women in Manu and His Seven Commentators*. Bodh Gaya: Kanchana Publications.

Das, S. 1977. *Crime and Punishment in Ancient India*. New Delhi: Abinav Publications.

Day, T. 1982. *The Conception of Punishment in Early Indian Literature*. Waterloo (Canada): Wilfrid Laurier University Press.

Derrett, J. D. M. 1964. "Bhāruci on the Royal Regulative Power in India." *JAOS* 84: 392–95.

_____. 1965. "A Newly-discovered Contact between Arthaśāstra and Dharmaśāstra." *ZDMG* 115: 134–52.

_____. 1967a. "A Jurist and His Sources: Medhātithi's Use of Bhāruci." *Adyar Library Bulletin* 30: 1-22.

_____. 1967b. "The Concept of Law according to Medhātithi, a Pre-Islamic Indian Jurist." In *Der Orient in der Forschung. Feshtschrift Otto Spies*, ed. W. Hoenerbach, pp. 18–41. Wiesbaden: Harrassowitz.

_____. 1968. *Religion, Law, and the State in India*. New York: Free Press.

_____. 1973. *Dharmaśāstra and Juridical Literature*. Wiesbaden: Harrassowitz.

_____. 1976–78. *Essays in Classical and Modern Hindu Law*. 4vols. Leiden: Brill.

_____. 1976. "Rājadharma." *Journal of Asian Studies* 35: 597–609.

Deshpande, M. M. 1999. "What to Do with the Anāryas? Dharmic Discourses of Inclusion and Exclusion." In *Aryan and Non-Aryan in South Asia: Evidence, Interpretation and Ideology*, ed. J. Bronkhorst and M. M. Deshpande, pp. 107–27. Harvard Oriental Series, Opera Minora, 3. Columbia, Missouri: South Asia Books.

Dirks, N. B. 2001. *Castes of Mind: Colonialism and the Making of Modern India*. Princeton: Princeton University Press.

Drekmeier, C. 1962. *Kingship and Community in Early India*. Stanford: Stanford Univ. Press.

Dutt, M. N. 1907. *The Dharma Śāstras*. Calcutta: Des Elysium Press.

Edgerton, F. 1953. *Buddhist Hybrid Sanskrit Grammar and Dictionary*. 2 vols. Reprint 1972. Delhi: Motilal Banarsidass.

Emeneau, M. B. 1962. "Barkcloth in India—Sanskrit *valkala*." *JAOS* 82:167–70.

Falk, H. 2001. "Suicidal Self-scorching in Ancient India." In *Vidyārṇavavandanam: Essays in Honour of Asko Parpola*, ed. K. Karttunen and P. Koskikallio, pp. 131–46. Studia Orientalia, 94. Helsinki: Finnish Oriental Society.

Fezas, J. 1996. "*śuśrūṣā* dans l'Arthaśāstra: obéissance, devoir conjugal ou maison du beau-père?" In *Langue, style et structure dans le monde indien: Centenaire de Louis Renou*, ed. N. Balbir and G-J. Pinault, pp. 385–412. Paris: Librairie Honoré Champion.

Fitzgerald, J. L. (tr.) 2004. *The Mahabharata: Book 11: The Book of the Women; Book 12: The Book of Peace, Part 1*. Chicago: University of Chicago Press.

Gharpure, J. R. 1943. *Sapiṇḍa or the Law of Sapiṇḍa Relationship*. Collection of Hindu Law Texts, 27. Bombay.

Ghosh, A. 1973. *The City in Early Historical India*. Simla: Indian Institute of Advanced Study.

Glucklich, A. 1982. "Karma and Social Justice in the Criminal Code of Manu." *Contributions to Indian Sociology* 16: 59–78.

_____. 1984. "Karma and Pollution in the Dharmasastra." *Ibid.*, 18: 25–43.

_____. 1988a. *Religious Jurisprudence in the Dharmasastras*. New York: Macmillan.

_____. 1988b. "The Royal Scepter (Daṇḍa) as Legal Punishment and Sacred Symbol." *History of Religions* 28: 97–122.

_____. 1990. "Images and Symbols in the Phenomenology of Dharma." *History of Religions* 29: 259–85.

Gonda, J. 1965. *Continuity and Change in Indian Religion*. The Hague: Mouton.

_____. 1966. *Ancient Indian Kingship from the Religius Viewpoint*. Leiden: Brill.

Gopal, R. 1962. "Manu's Indebtedness to Śāṅkhāyana." *Poona Orientalist* 27: 39–44.

Gupta, P. L. 1969. *Coins*. New Delhi: National Book Trust.

Hacker, P. 1959. "Two Accounts of Cosmogony." In *Jñānamuktāvali: Commemoration Volume in Honour of Joh. Nobel.* ed. C. Vogel, pp. 77–91. Sarasbati vihara series. v. 38. Delhi: International Academy of Indian Culture.

_____. 1961. "The Saṅkhyization of the Emanation Doctrine, Shown in a Critical Analysis of Texts." *WZKS* 5: 75–112.

Halbfass, W. 1991. "Homo Hierarchicus: The Conceptualization of the Varṇa System in Indian Thought." In *Tradition and Reflection*, ch. 10, pp. 347–405. Albany: State University of New York Press.

Hara, M. 1979. "*Śraddhāviveśa*." *Indologica Taurinensia* 7: 261–73.

_____. 1992. "Śraddhā in the Sense of Desire." *Asiatische Studien* 46: 180–94.

_____. 1994–95. "Bhartṛ-Piṇḍa-Niṣkraya—The Hindu Concept of Loyalty to the Kings." *Bulletin of the Deccan College Post-Graduate & Research Institute* 54–55: 299–311.

_____. 1997. "A Note on the *gṛhasthāśrama*." In Lienhard and Piovano 1997, 221–35.

Hazra, R. C. 1935. "Purāṇas in the History of Smṛti." *Indian Culture* 1:587–614.

Heesterman, J. C. 1968. "The Return of the Veda Scholar (samāvartana)." In *Pratidānam: Indian, Iranian and Indo-European Studies presented to Franciscus Bernardus Jacobus Kuiper on his Sixtieth Birthday*, ed. J. C. Heesterman et al., pp. 436–47. The Hague: Mouton.

Hiltebeitel, A. 2001. *Rethinking the Mahābhārata: A Reader's Guide to the Education of the Dharma King*. Chicago: University of Chicago Press.

Hopkins, E. 1881. *The Mutual Relation of the Four Castes According to the Mānavadhamaçâstram*. Leipzig: Breitkopf and Hartell.

_____. 1885. "On the Professed Quotations from Manu Found in the Mahābhārata." *JAOS* 11: 239–75.

Huxley, A. 1996. "When Manu met Mahāsammata." *JIP* 24: 593–621.

Jain, M. P. 1966. *Outlines of Indian Legal History*. Bombay: Tripathi.

Jamison, S. W. 1986. "Brāhmaṇa Syllable Counting, Vedic *Tvác* 'Skin', and the Sanskrit Expression for the Canoncial Creature." *Indo-Iranian Jouranl* 29: 161–81.

_____. 1991. *The Ravenous Hyenas and the Wounded Sun: Myth and Ritual in Ancient India*. Ithaca, NY: Cornell University Press.

_____. 1996. *Sacrificed Wife/Sacrificer's Wife: Women, Ritual, and Hospitality in Ancient India*. New York: Oxford University Press.

_____. 1997. "Sanskrit pāriṇāhya 'household goods': Semantic Evolution in Cultural Context." In *Festschrift Eric Hamp*, ed. D. Q. Adams. Vol. I. *Journal of Indo-European Studies Monograph* 23: 139–45.

_____. 1998. "Rhinoceros Toes: Manu 5.17–18 and the Development of the Dharma System." *JAOS* 118: 249–56.

_____. 2000. "A Sanskrit Maxim and Its Ritual and Legal Applications." In *Anusantatyai: Festschrift für Johanna Narten zum 70. Geburtstag*, ed. A. Hintze and E. Tichy, pp. 111–25. Münchener Studien zur Sprachwissenschaft, Beiheft 19.

Jayaswal, K. P. 1930. *Manu and Yājñavalkya: A Comparison and a Contrast, A Treatise on the Basic Hindu Law*. Calcutta: Butterworth.

Jha, Ganganatha. 1922–27. *Studies in Hindu Law*. The Princes of Wales Sarasvati Bhavana Series. 6 vols. Benares: Sarasvati Bhavana.

_____. 1930. *Hindu Law and Its Sources*. Delhi: Indian Press.

Jolly, J. (tr.) 1880. *The Institutes of Vishnu*. *SBE* 7. Oxford: Clarendon Press.

_____. 1885. *Outlines of an History of the Hindu Law of Partition, Inheritance, and Adoption*. Tagore Law Lectures 1883. Calcutta: Thacker, Spink, and Co.

_____. 1885–89. *Manuṭīkāsangraha: Being a Series of Copious Extracts from Six Unpublished Commentaries of the Code of Manu*. Calcutta: Asiatic Society.

_____. 1887. "Manu and Bṛhaspati." *WZKM* 1: 275–80 [expanded version in Jolly 1889].

_____. 1889. *The Minor Law-Books: Nārada, Brihaspati*. SBE 33. Oxford: Clarendon Press.

_____. 1913. "Arthaśāstra und Dharmaśāstra," *ZDMG* 67: 49–96.

Jong, J. W. de. 1988. "Buddhism and the Equality of the Four Castes." In *A Green Leaf: Papers in Honour of Professor Jes P. Asmussen*. Acta Iranica, 2nd Series, Vol. XII, pp. 424–31. Leiden: Brille.

Joshi, A. R. 1987–88. "Medhātithi and Other Commentators of Manusmṛti." *Journal of Manuscript Studies* 17–18: 153–71.

Kane, P. V. 1925. "The Tantravārttika and the Dharmaśāstra Literature," *Journal of the Bombay Branch of the Royal Asiatic Society*, N. S. 1: 95–102.

_____. 1962–75. *History of Dharmaśāstra*. 5 vols. Poona: Bhandarkar Oriental Research Institute.

Kangle, R. P. 1964. "Manu and Kauṭilya." *Indian Antiquary* (Third Series) I: 48–54.

_____. 1965–72. *The Kauṭilīya Arthaśāstra*. 3 vols. Bombay: University of Bombay.

Köhler, H. W. 1973. *Śrad-dhā in der vedischen und altbuddhistischen Literature*. Thesis Göttingen, 1948. Ed. K. L. Janert. Wiesbaden: Franz Steiner.

Konow, S. 1945. *Kautalya Studies*. Reprint. Delhi: Oriental Publishers.

Krishna, D. 1992. "The *varṇāśrama* Syndrome of Indian Sociology." *Contributions to Indian Sociology* 26, 2: 282–98.

Lane, J. W. 1981. "The Creation Account of *Manusmṛti*." *Annals of the Bhandarkar Oriental Research Institute* 62: 157–68.

Lariviere, R. W. 1982. "Coins in the Nāradasmṛti." *Journal of the Numismatic Society of India* 44: 108–13.

_____. 1983. "More Equine Lexicography: the Hamstring Is Not Connected to the Nose." *JAOS* 103: 421–22.

_____. 1989. "Justices and *Paṇḍitas:* Some Ironies in Contemporary Readings of the Hindu Legal Past." *Journal of Asian Studies* 48: 757–69.

_____. 1991. "Matrimonial Remedies for Women in Classical Hindu Law: Alternatives to Divorce." In Leslie 1991, pp. 37–45.

_____. 1997a. "Power and Authority: On the Interpretation of Indian Kingship from Sanskrit Sources." In Lienhard and Piovano 1997, pp. 313–27.

_____. 1997b. "Dharmaśāstra, Custom, 'Real Law' and 'Aprocryphal' Smṛtis." In *Recht, Staat, und Verwaltung im klassichen Indien*, ed. B. Koelver, pp. 97–110. Wiesbaden: Franz Steiner.

_____. (ed. and tr.) 2003. *The Nāradasmṛti*. 2nd ed. Delhi: Motilal Banarsidass.

Laszlo, F. 1971. *Die Parallelversion der Manusmṛti im Bhaviṣyapurāṇa*. Abhandlungen für die Kunde des Morgenlandes, XL, 2. Wiesbaden: Franz Steiner.

Leslie, J. 1991. *Rules and Remedies in Classical Indian Law*. Panels of the VIIth World Sanskrit Conference. Leiden: Brill.

Lienhard, S. and Piovano, I. ed. 1977. *Lex et Litterrae: Studies in Honour of Professor Oscar Botto*. Turin: Edizioni dell'Orso.

Lingat, R. 1962a. "Les quatre pieds du procès." *Journal Asiatique* 250: 489–503.

_____. 1962b. "Time and Dharma." *Contributions to Indian Sociology* 6:7–16.

_____. 1973. *The Classical Law of India*. Berkeley: University of California Press.

Losch, H. 1927. *Die Yājñavalkyasmṛti: Ein Beitrag zur Quellenkunde des indischen Rechts*. Leipzig: Harrassowitz.

Malamoud, C. 1972. "Obervations sur la notion de 'reste' dans le brāhmanisme." *WZKS* 16: 5–26.

_____. 1982. "On the Rhetoric and Semantics of puruṣārtha." In *Way of Life: King, Householder, Renouncer. Essays in Honour of Louis Dumont*, ed. T. N. Madan, pp. 33–54. New Delhi: Vikas.

Maxwell, T. S. 1989. "Śilpa versus Śāstra." In Dallapiccola 1989, pp. 5–15.

Mayrhofer, M. 1956–80. *Kurzgefasstes etymologisches Wörterbuch des Altindoarischen*. 4 Vols. Heidelberg: Carl Winter.

Meyer, J. J. 1927. *Über das Wesen der Altindischen Rechtsschriften und ihr Verhältnis zu einander und zu Kauṭilya*. Leipzig: Harrassowitz.

Mishra, S. C. 1993. *Evolution of Kautilya's Arthashastra: An Inscriptional Approach*. Delhi: Anamika Prakashan.

Numata, I. 1999. "Manusmṛti 7.114." *Journal of Indian and Buddhist Studies* (Indogaku Bukkyogaku Kenkyu) 47–2: 30–4.

O'Flaherty, W. (ed.) 1980. *Karma and Rebirth in Classical Indian Traditions*. Berkeley: University of California Press.

Oldenberg, H. 1886–92. *The Gṛhya-Sūtras: Rules of Vedic Domestic Ceremonies*. 2 parts. Oxford: Oxford University Press.

Olivelle, P. 1981. "Contributions to the Semantic History of *Saṃnyāsa*." *JAOS* 101: 265–74.

_____. 1986–87. *Renunciation in Hinduism: A Medieval Debate*. 2 vols. Vienna: Institute for Indology, University of Vienna.

_____. 1998a. "Unfaithful Transmitters: Philological Criticism and Critical Editions of the Upaniṣads." *JIP* 26: 173–87.

_____. 1998b. "Caste and Purity: A Study in the Language of the Dharma Literature." *Contributions to Indian Sociology* 32: 189–216.

_____. 1998c. *The Early Upaniṣads*. New York: Oxford University Press.

_____. 1993. *The Āśrama System: The History and Hermeneutics of a Religious Institution*. New York: Oxford University Press.

_____. 1999a. "Sanskrit Commentators and the Transmission of Texts: Haradatta on Āpastamba Dharmasūtra." *JIP* 27:551–74.

_____. (tr.) 1999b. *Dharmasūtras: The Law Codes of Ancient India*. Oxford: Oxford University Press.

_____. (ed. and tr.) 2000. *Dharmasūtras: The Law Codes of Āpastamba, Gautama, Baudhāyana, and Vasiṣṭha*. Delhi: Motilal Banarsidass.

_____. 2002a. "*Abhakṣya* and *abhojya:* An Exploration in Dietary Language." *JAOS* 122: 345–54.

_____. 2002b. "Food for Thought: Dietary Regulations and Social Organization in Ancient India." 2001 Gonda Lecture. Amsterdam: Royal Netherlands Academy of Arts and Sciences.

_____. 2004. *The Law Code of Manu*. Oxford World's Classics. Oxford: Oxford University Press.

_____. forthcoming-a. "Power of Words: The Ascetic Appropriation and the Semantic

Evolution of *dharma*." In *Asceticism and Power*, ed. Peter Flügel and Gustaaf Houtman. London: Curzon.

Olivelle, P. forthcoming-b. "Manu and Gautama: A Study in Śāstric Intertextuality." In *Wilhelm Halbfass Commemoration Volume*, ed. K. Preisendanz and E. Franco. Vienna: Verlag der Österreichischen Akademie der Wissenschaften.

_____. forthcoming-c. "Semantic History of *dharma:* The Middle and Late Vedic Periods." *JIP*.

Parasher, A. 1991. *Mlecchas in Early India: A Study in Attitudes towards Outsiders up to AD 600*. Delhi: Munshiram Manoharlal.

Patkar, M. M, 1978. *Nārada, Bṛhaspati and Kātyāyana: A Comparative Study in Judicial Procedure*. New Delhi: Munshiram Manoharlal.

Pollock, S. 1985. "The Theory of Practice and the Practice of Theory in Indian Intellectual History." *JAOS* 105: 499–519.

_____. 1989a. "The Idea of Śāstra in Traditional India." In Dallapiccola and Lallemant 1989, pp. 17–26.

_____. 1989b. "Playing by the Rules: Śāstra and Sanskrit Literature." In Dallapiccola and Lallemant 1989, pp. 301–12.

_____. 1990. "From Discoure of Ritual to Discourse of Power in Sanskrit Culture." *Journal of Ritual Studies* 4: 316–45.

_____. 1997. "The «Revelations» of «Tradition»: śruti, smṛti, and the Sanskrit Discourse of Power." In Lienhard and Piovano 1997, pp. 295–417.

Rau, W. 1957. *Staat und Gesellschaft im alten Indien nach den Brāhmaṇa-Texten dargestellt*. Wiesbaden: Harrassowitz.

Rocher, L. 1954. "The Technical Term '*anubandha*' in Sanskrit Legal Literature." *Annals of the Bhandarkar Oriental Research Institute* 35: 221–28.

_____. 1955. "Ancient Indian Criminal Law." *Journal of Oriental Research* 24: 15–34.

_____. 1964. "The Theory of Proof in Ancient Hindu Law." *Recueils de la Société Jean Bodin*, vol. XVIII, pp. 325–71. Brussells: Les Editions de la Librairie Encyclopedique.

_____. 1965. *Droit hindou ancient.* Introduction Bibliographique à l'Histoire du Droit et à l'Ethnologie Juridique, ed. J. Gilissen, vol. E/6. Brussels: Édition de l'Institut de Sociologie, Université Libre de Bruxelles.

_____. 1969. "'Lawyers' in Classical Hindu Law." *Law and Society Review* 3: 383–402.

_____. 1976a. "The Introduction of the Gautamadharmasūtra." *Adyar Library Bulletin* 39: 90–100.

_____. 1976b. "Notes on the Technical Term *Sāhasa* 'Fine, Pecuniary Penalgy'." In *V. Raghavan Commemoration Volume*, pp. 515–31. Delhi: Motilal Banarsidass.

_____. 1977–78. "The Purāṇa of Fate and Human Effort." *Annals of the Bhandarkar Oriental Research Institute* 58–59: 271–78.

_____. 1980. "Karma and Rebirth in the Dharmaśāstras." In O'Flaherty 1980, pp. 61–89.

_____. 1993. "Law Books in an Oral Culture: The Indian *Dharmaśāstras*." *Proceedings of the American Philosophical Society* 137: 254–67.

_____. 2002. "*Dāsadāsī*." *JAOS* 122: 374–80.

Samozvantsev, A. M. 1980–81. "Arthaśāstra and Dharmaśāstra—Two Traditions." *Indologica Taurinensia* 8–9: 353–63.

Sandahl, S. 2001. "Women One Should Not Marry—Some Comments on *Manusmṛti* 3.6–9, 11." *Acta Orientalia* 62: 166–76.

Sarkar, U. C. 1958. *Epochs in Hindu Legal History*. Hoshiarpur: Vishveshvaranand Vedic Research Institute.

Scharfe, H. 1993. *Investigations in Kauṭalya's Manual of Political Science*. Wiesbaden: Harrassowitz.

Schlingloff, D. 1965. "Arthaśāstra-Studien. Teil I: Kauṭilya und Medhātithi." *WZKS* 9: 1–38.

Schmidt, H.-P. 1987. *Some Women's Rites and Rights in the Veda*. Pune: Bhandarkar Oriental Research Institute.

Schmithausen, L. 1991. *The Problem of the Sentience of Plants in Earliest Buddhism*. Studia Philologica Buddhica, Monograph Series IV. Tokyo: International Institute for Buddhist Studies.

Sen, P. N. 1980. *Hindu Jurisprudence*. University of Calcutta Tagore Law Lectures, 1909. Calcutta: Saraswat Library.

Sen-Gupta, N. C. 1953. *Evolution of Ancient Indian Law*. University of Calcutta Tagore Law Lectures, 1950. London: Arthur Probsthain.

Sharma, R. S. 1990 (1958). *Śūdras in Ancient India: A Social History of the Lower Order Down to circa A. D. 600*. 3rd. ed. Delhi: Motilal Banarsidass.

Shastri, H. C. 1972–74. *Forms of Marriage in Ancient India*.2 vols. Calcutta: Sanskrit Pustak Bhandar.

Shastri, S. R. 1959. *Women in the Sacred Laws*. Bomay: Bharatiya Vidya Bhavan.

Silk, J. 1992. "A Bibligraphy of Ancient Indian Slavery." *Studien zur Indologie und Iranistik*, 16/17: 277–85.

Sircar, D. C. 1968. *Studies in Indian Coins*. Delhi: Motilal Banarsidass.

Smith, B. K. 1994. *Classifying the Universe: The Ancient Indian Varṇa System and the Origins of Caste*. New York: Oxford University Press.

Sprockhoff, J. F. 1987. "Kaṭhaśruti und Mānavaśrautasūtra: eine Nachlese zur Resignation." *Studien zur Indologie und Iranistik*, 13/14: 235–57.

Sternback, L. 1972. "Place and Time of King's Counsel with Ministers according to the Dharmaśāstra-s, Arthaśāstra-s and Subhāṣita-Saṃgraha-s." In *India Maior: Congratulatory Volume Presented to J. Gonda*, ed. J. Ensink and P. Gaeffke, pp. 200–7. Leiden: Brill.

_____. 1974. *The Mānava Dharmaśāstra I-III and the Bhaviṣya Purāṇa*. Varanasi: All India Kashi Raj Trust.

Stietencron, H. von 1997. "The Non-Existence of Impurity and the Legitimation of Kings." In Lienhard and Piovano 1997, pp. 487–508.

Thakur, A. 1933. *Hindu Law of Evidence; or, A Comparative Study of the Law of Evidence According to the Smṛtis*. Calcutta: University of Calcutta.

Thieme, P. 1931. "Grammatik und Sprache: eine Problem der altindischen Sprachwissenschaft," *Zeitschrift für Indologie und Iranistik* 8:23–32. *Kleine Schriften* 2:514–23.

_____. 1939. "Indische Wörter und Sitten," *ZDMG* 95: 219–221. *Kleine Schriften* 2: 343–70 [the section of Pūjā translated in *Journal of Oriental Research* 28(1960): 1–16].

_____. 1958. "Sanskrit *edhate*." *Indian Linguistics* 19: 149–58. *Kleine Schriften* 2:160–69.

_____. 1963. "'Jungfrauengatte': Sanskrit *kaumāraḥ patiḥ*." *Zeitschrift für vergleichende Sprachforschung auf dem Gebiete der indogermanischen Sprachen* 78:161–248. *Kleine Schriften* 2: 426–512.

_____. 1984. *Kleine Schriften*. Vol. 2. Wiesbaden: Franz Steiner.

Turner, R. L. 1966. *A Comparative Dictionary of Indo-Aryan Languages*. 4 vols. Reprint. Delhi: Motilal Banarsidass, 1999.

Wackernagel, J. 1957–78. *Altindische Grammatick*. 3 vols. Göttingen: Vandenhoeck & Ruprecht.

Watkins, C. 1994a. "Studies in Indo-European Legal Language, Institutions, and Mythology."

In *Selected Writings*, Vol. II, pp. 422–55. Innsbruck: Innsbrucker Beiträge zur Sprachwissenschaft.

_____. 1994b. "'In the Interstices of Procedure': Indo-European Legal Language and Comparative Law." *Ibid.*, pp. 718–27.

Wezler, A. 1982. "Manu's Omniscience: On the Interpretation of Manusmṛti II.7." In *Indology and Law: Studies in Honour of Professor J. Duncan M. Derrett.* ed. G. D. Sontheimer and P. K. Aithal, pp. 79-105. Wiesbaden: Steiner.

_____. 1986. "Cattle, Field and Barley: A Note on Mahābhāṣya I.337.24–27. *Adyar Library Bulletin* 50: 431–77.

_____. 1987. "On the Term *antaḥsaṃjña-*." *Annals of the Bhandarkar Oriental Institute* 58: 112–31.

_____. 1994. "A Note on Sanskrit *brūṇa* and *bhrūṇahatyā*." In *Festschrift Klaus Bruhn*, ed. N. Balbir and J. Bautze, pp. 623–46. Reinbek: Verlag für Orientalistische Fachpublikationen.

_____. 1995. "Der Tod als Mittel der Entsühnung." In *Im Tod gewinnt der Mensch sein Selbst: Das Phänomenon des Todes in asiatscher und abendländischer Religionstradition*, ed. G. Oberhammer, pp. 97–140. Vienna: Österreichischen Akademie der Wissenschaften.

_____. 1998a. "Medhātithi on the Role of Manu, the *Prayojana* of the Manusmṛti and the Inventive of the Brahmins to Study It." In *Sūryacandrāya: Essays in Honour of Akira Yuyama on the Occasion of His 65th Birthday*, ed. P. Harrison and G. Schopen, pp. 216–40. Göttingen: Swisttal-Odendorf.

_____. 1998b. "Should the Adopted Son Be a Close Relative? On the Interpretation of VasDhS 15.6 and 7." *Indologica Taurinensia* 17–18: 359–81.

_____. 1999a. "Methātithi on *sāmānyato dṛṣṭam [anumānam]*."*JIP* 27: 139–57.

_____. 1999b. "Über den sakramentalen Charakter des *dharma* nachsinnend." In *Raumzeitliche Vermittlung der Transzendenz*, ed. G. Oberhammer and M. Schmücker, pp. 63–113. Wien: Österreichischen Akademie der Wissenschaften.

_____. 2000. "Some Remarks on the 135th *Adhikaraṇa* of the 'Kauṭilīya' *Artha-śāstra* Entitled 'Policy towards *Saṁghas*'." *On the Understanding of Other Cultures*, ed. P. Balcerowicz and M. Mejor, pp. 489–503. Studia Indologiczne 7. Warsaw: Instytut Orientalistyczny.

Witzel, M. 1984. "Sur le chemin du ciel." *Bulletin D'Études Indiennes* 2: 213–79.

DHARMAŚĀSTRA PARALLELS

Chapter One

10	*MBh* 12.328.35
18	*MBh* 12.224.43
20	*MBh* 12.224.31
28	*MBh* 12.224.47
29	*MBh* 12.224.47
64	*MBh* 12.224.12–3
65	*MBh* 12.224.14
66	*MBh* 12.224.15
67	*MBh* 12.224.16
69	*MBh* 12.224.19
70	*MBh* 12.224.20
73	*MBh* 12.224.30
75	*MBh* 12.224.35
76	*MBh* 12.224.36
77	*MBh* 12.224.37
78	*MBh* 12.224.38
81	*MBh* 12.224.22
82	*MBh* 12.224.23
83	*MBh* 12.224.24
84	*MBh* 12.224.25
85	*MBh* 12.224.26
86	*MBh* 12.224.27
94	*YDh* 1.198–9

Chapter Two

6	*ĀpDh* 1 .1.1–3; *GDh* 1.1–3; *BDh* 1.1.1–6; *VaDh* 1.4–6
12	*YDh* 1.7
14	*ĀpDh* 1.30.9; *GDh* 1.4
22	*BDh* 1.2.9–10, *VaDh* 1.8–9
23	*BDh* 1.2.12; *VaDh* 1.13–5; *YDh* 1.2
24	*ĀpDh* 1.32.18; *BDh* 1.2.13–5; *ViDh* 84.2, 4
26	*YDh* 1.10
29	*MBh* 3.177.29; *ViDh* 27.4
30	*ViDh* 27.5
31	*ViDh* 27.6–9
34	*ViDh* 27.10–1; *YDh* 1.12
35	*ViDh* 27.12; *YDh* 1.12
36	*ĀpDh* 1.19; *GDh* 1.5–11; *BDh* 1.3.7–9; *VaDh* 11.49–51; *ViDh* 27.15–7; *YDh* 1.14
37	*ĀpDh* 1.1.20–6; *GDh* 1.6
38	*ĀpDh* 1.1.27; *GDh* 1.12–4; *BDh* 1.3.12; *ViDh* 27.26
39	*GDh* 21.11; *VaDh* 11.74–5; *ViDh* 27.27; *YDh* 1.38
40	*VaDh* 11.75
41	*ĀpDh* 1.2.39; 1.3.10; *GDh* 1.16–9; *BDh* 1.3.14; *VaDh* 11.61–7; *ViDh* 27.19–20; *YDh* 1.29
42	*ĀpDh* 1.2.33–7; *GDh* 1.15; *BDh* 1.3.13; *VaDh* 11.58–60; *ViDh* 27.18; *YDh* 1.29
44	*BDh* 1.8.5; *ViDh* 27.19; *YDh* 1.29
45	*ĀpDh* 1.2.38; *GDh* 1.22–4; *BDh* 1.3.15; *VaDh* 11.52–4; *ViDh* 27.21–3; *YDh* 1.29
46	*GDh* 1.26; *BDh* 1.3.15; *VaDh* 11.55–7; *ViDh* 27.22
47	*GDh* 1.25; *ViDh* 27.24
48	*ĀpDh* 1.3.25; *GDh* 2.8, 5; *YDh* 1.29
49	*ĀpDh* 1.3.28–30; *GDh* 2.36; *BDh* 1.3.16–7; *VaDh* 11.68–70; *ViDh* 27.25; *YDh* 1.30
51	*ĀpDh* 1.3.31–42; *GDh* 2.39–40; *ViDh* 68.40–1; *YDh* 1.31

52 *MBh* 13.107.25

53 *GDh* 2.41; *BDh* 2.5.21; 2.12.7; *VaDh* 3.28; *ViDh* 68.34–5

54 *BDh* 2.12.7; *VaDh* 3.69; *ViDh* 68.42–3; *YDh* 1.31

56 *ĀpDh* 2.1.2–3; *BDh* 2.12.9; *ViDh* 68.48; *YDh* 1.112

58 *BDh* 1.8.14; *VaDh* 3.26; *ViDh* 62.6; *YDh* 1.18

59 *BDh* 1.8.15–6; *VaDh* 3.26; *ViDh* 62.1–4; *YDh* 1.19

60 *ĀpDh* 1.16.2–10; *GDh* 1.36; *BDh* 1.8.19–21; *VaDh* 3.27–9; *ViDh* 62.6–8; *YDh* 1.20

61 *ĀpDh* 1.15.4–7; *BDh* 1.8.17; *VaDh* 3.31; *ViDh* 62.5; *YDh* 1.18,20

62 *GDh* 1.36; *BDh* 1.8.23; *VaDh* 3.31; *ViDh* 62.9; *YDh* 1.21

63 *ĀpDh* 1.6.18–9; *BDh* 1.8.5–10

64 *BDh* 1.6.6–9; *ViDh* 27.29

65 *GDh* 2.9; *YDh* 1.36

66 *ViDh* 27.13; *YDh* 1.13

67 *ViDh* 22.32; 27.14; *YDh* 1.13

69 *GDh* 2.6–10; *YDh* 1.15

71 *ĀpDh* 1.5.18–23; *BDh* 1.3.25–8; *ViDh* 30.32; *YDh* 1.26

72 *ĀpDh* 1.5.22; *GDh* 1.46; *BDh* 1.3.25; *ViDh* 30.32

73 *GDh* 1.46

74 *ĀpDh* 1.13.6–7; *GDh* 1.57; *ViDh* 30.33

75 *GDh* 1.48–51; *BDh* 2.7.5–7

76 *ViDh* 55.10

77 *ViDh* 55.11

78 *ViDh* 55.12

79 *VaDh* 26.4; *ViDh* 55.13

80 *ViDh* 55.14

81 *ViDh* 55.15

82 *ViDh* 55.16

83 *VaDh* 10.5; 25.11; *ViDh* 55.17

84 *ViDh* 55.18

85 *VaDh* 26.9; *ViDh* 55.19

86 *VaDh* 26.10; *ViDh* 55.20

87 *VaDh* 26.11; *ViDh* 55.21

101 *ĀpDh* 1.30.8; *GDh* 2.11; *BDh* 2.7.12–3; *VaDh* 7.16; *ViDh* 28.2–3; *YDh* 1.23–5

102 *BDh* 2.7.18–20; *VaDh* 26.2–3

103 *BDh* 2.7.15

105 *ĀpDh* 1.12.9

106 *ĀpDh* 1.12. 3–5

107 *ViDh* 30.34–8; *YDh* 1.41–6

108 *ĀpDh* 1.4.16, 23; 1.5.25; *GDh* 2.8,30; *BDh* 1.4. 4–8; *VaDh* 7.9, 15; *ViDh* 28.4, 7, 9, 12; *YDh* 1.25

109 *YDh* 1.28

110 *BDh* 1.4.2; *VaDh* 2.12

111 *ViDh* 29.7

112 *BDh* 1.4.1; *ViDh* 29.8

113 *BDh* 1.4.1

114 *Nirukta* 2.4; *VaDh* 2.8; *ViDh* 29.8

115 *Nirukta* 2.4; *VaDh* 29.9; *ViDh* 29.10

116 *ViDh* 30.41–2

117 *ĀpDh* 1.5.19–20; 1.14.7–9; *GDh* 6.1–3,5; *BDh* 1.3.25–8; *VaDh* 13.41–3; *ViDh* 30.43

119 *ĀpDh* 1.8.11; *GDh* 2.21, 25

120 *MBh* 13.107.32

121 *ĀpDh* 1.5.15; *BDh* 1.3.26; *MBh* 5.39.60

122 *ĀpDh* 1.5.12; *GDh* 6.5; *BDh* 1.3.27; *VaDh* 13.44; *ViDh* 28.17; *YDh* 1.26

123 *VaDh* 13.45

124 *ViDh* 28.17

125 *ĀpDh* 1.5.17; *VaDh* 13.46

127 *ĀpDh* 1.14.26–9; *GDh* 5.41–2

128 *GDh* 6.19

129 *ViDh* 32.7

130 *ĀpDh* 1.14.11; *GDh* 6.9; *BDh* 1.3.45; *VaDh* 13.41; *ViDh* 32.4

131 *GDh* 6.7; *ViDh* 32.2–3

132 *GDh* 6.7–8; *ViDh* 32.2

133 *ViDh* 32.3
134 *ĀpDh* 1.14.13; *GDh* 6.14–7
135 *ĀpDh* 1.14.25; *MBh* 13.8.20; *ViDh* 32.17
136 *GDh* 6.20; *VaDh* 13.56–7; *ViDh* 32.16; *YDh* 1.116
137 *GDh* 6.10; *YDh* 1.116
138 *GDh* 6.24; *BDh* 2.6.30; *VaDh* 13.58–60; *ViDh* 63.50; *YDh* 1.117
139 *GDh* 6.25; *VaDh* 13.59; *YDh* 1.117
140 *ĀpDh* 1.1.14; *GDh* 1.9–10; *VaDh* 3.21; *ViDh* 29.1; *YDh* 1.34
141 *VaDh* 3.22–3; *ViDh* 29.2; *YDh* 1.35
142 *YDh* 1.34
143 *ViDh* 29.3; *YDh* 1.35
144 *ĀpDh* 1.1.15; *Nirukta* 2.4; *VaDh* 2.10; *ViDh* 30.47
145 *VaDh* 13.48; *YDh* 1.35
146 *VaDh* 2.3–5; *ViDh* 30.44
147 *ĀpDh* 1.1.18; *ViDh* 30.45
148 *ĀpDh* 1.1.16–7; *GDh* 1.8; *ViDh* 30.46
151 *BDh* 1.3.47
154 *MBh* 3.133.12
155 *ViDh* 32.18
156 *MBh* 3.133.11
157 *BDh* 1.1.10; *VaDh* 3.11; *MBh* 12.37.39
158 *MBh* 12.37.40
159 *GDh* 2.42
166 *ĀpDh* 1.12.1–2; *YDh* 1.40
168 *VaDh* 3.2; *ViDh* 28.36
169 *VaDh* 2.3; *ViDh* 28.37; *YDh* 1.39
170 *VaDh* 2.3; *MBh* 3.177.29; *ViDh* 28.38
171 *GDh* 1.10; *BDh* 1.3.6; *VaDh* 2.4–6
172 *GDh* 2.4–5; *BDh* 1.3.6; *VaDh* 2.6; *MBh* 3.177.30
174 *ViDh* 27.28
176 *GDh* 2.8; *VaDh* 7.17; *YDh* 1.22
177 *ĀpDh* 1.2.23–6; *GDh* 2.13–20; *BDh* 1.3.23–4; *YDh* 1.33
178 *ĀpDh* 1.3.11, 7–24; 1.7.5; *GDh* 2.13; *BDh* 1.3.24; *VaDh* 7.15; *ViDh* 28.11; *YDh* 1.33
179 *ĀpDh* 1.3.12–3; 1.7.3, 8–10; *GDh* 2.13, 16–7; *BDh* 1.3.20; *ViDh* 28.11; *YDh* 1.33
180 *ViDh* 28.48
181 *ViDh* 28.51
182 *ĀpDh* 1.4.13–4; *BDh* 1.3.19
183 *ĀpDh* 1.3.25; *GDh* 2.35; *BDh* 1.3.18; *ViDh* 28.9; *YDh* 1.29
184 *GDh* 2.37–8
186 *ĀpDh* 1.4.16; *BDh* 1.3.19; *ViDh* 28.4
187 *ViDh* 28.52; *YDh* 3.281
188 *YDh* 1.32
189 *YDh* 1.32
190 *YDh* 1.32
191 *GDh* 2.29–30; *VaDh* 7.13; *ViDh* 28.6–7; *YDh* 1.27
192 *GDh* 2.22
193 *ĀpDh* 1.6.20
194 *ĀpDh* 1.4.22, 28; *GDh* 2.21; *BDh* 1.3.21; *ViDh* 28.13
195 *ĀpDh* 1.6.5; *GDh* 2.25; *ViDh* 28.18
196 *ĀpDh* 1.6.5–9; *GDh* 2.28; *BDh* 1.3.38; *VaDh* 7.12; *ViDh* 28.19
197 *ViDh* 28.20–2
198 *ĀpDh* 1.2.21; 1.6.14–7; *ViDh* 28.23
199 *ĀpDh* 1.8.15; *GDh* 2.18; *ViDh* 28.24–5
200 *ViDh* 28.26
203 *ĀpDh* 1.6.15, 23
204 *ĀpDh* 1.8.12–3; *BDh* 1.3.34; *ViDh* 28.27–8
205 *GDh* 6.3–4; *VaDh* 13.54; *ViDh* 28.29–30
206 *ĀpDh* 1.7.28–9
207 *ĀpDh* 1.7.30; *GDh* 2.31; *BDh* 1.3.44; *VaDh* 13.54; *ViDh* 32.1
208 *ViDh* 28.31

209 *ĀpDh* 1.7.30; *GDh* 2.32; *BDh* 1.3.36; *ViDh* 28.32–3

210 *ĀpDh* 1.7.27; *GDh* 2.31; *ViDh* 32.2.5

211 *ĀpDh* 1.7.27; *GDh* 2.32; *BDh* 1.3.37; *ViDh* 32.6

212 *GDh* 2.34; *BDh* 1.3.33; *ViDh* 32.13

213 *MBh* 13.48.37

214 *MBh* 13.48.36

215 *MBh* 13.48.37

216 *ViDh* 32.14

217 *ĀpDh* 1.14.8; *GDh* 2.33; 6.2–3; *ViDh* 32.15

219 *ĀpDh* 1.2.31–2; 1.30.8; *GDh* 1.27; *VaDh* 7.11; *ViDh* 28.41

220 *ĀpDh* 2.12.13–4; *GDh* 23.21; *BDh* 2.7.16; *VaDh* 20.4; *ViDh* 28.53

221 *ĀpDh* 2.12.22; *VaDh* 1.18

222 *GDh* 2.11; *BDh* 2.7.2; *ViDh* 28.2

223 *ĀpDh* 2.29.11; *MBh* 13.108.13

225 *ĀpDh* 1.14.6; *GDh* 21.15; *ViDh* 31.1–3

228 *ViDh* 31.5

229 *MBh* 12.109.5; *ViDh* 31.3,6

230 *MBh* 12.109.6; *ViDh* 31.7

231 *ĀpDh* 1.3.44; *MBh* 12.109.7; *ViDh* 31.8

232 *MBh* 12.109.8

233 *MBh* 12.109.8; *ViDh* 31.10

234 *MBh* 12.109.11; *ViDh* 31.9

235 *ViDh* 31.6

238 *ĀpDh* 2.29.11; *MBh* 12.159.29–30

239 *MBh* 12.159.29–30

241 *ĀpDh* 2.4.25; *GDh* 7.1–3; *BDh* 1.3.41–2

243 *ĀpDh* 2.21.6; *GDh* 3.5–6; *BDh* 2.11.13; *VaDh* 7.4; *ViDh* 28.43; *YDh* 1.49

244 *GDh* 3.9; *YDh* 1.50

245 *ĀpDh* 1.7.19; *GDh* 2.48–9; *ViDh* 28.42; *YDh* 1.51

247 *GDh* 3.7; *ViDh* 28.44–5; *YDh* 1.49

248 *GDh* 3.8; *VaDh* 7.5–6; *ViDh* 28.46; *YDh* 1.49

249 *ViDh* 28.47

Chapter Three

1 *ĀpDh* 1.2.12–6; *GDh* 2.45–7; *BDh* 1.3.1–4; *YDh* 1.36

2 *VaDh* 8.1; *YDh* 1.52

4 *GDh* 4.1; *VaDh* 8.1; *YDh* 1.52

5 *GDh* 4.2–5; *BDh* 2.1.37–8; *VaDh* 8.1–2; *MBh* 13.44.17; *ViDh* 24.9–10; *YDh* 1.53

7 *YDh* 1.54

8 *ViDh* 24.12–6; *YDh* 1.53

11 *YDh* 1.53

13 *BDh* 1.16.2–5; *VaDh* 1.24–5; *ViDh* 24.1–4; *YDh* 1.57

14 *VaDh* 1.26; *YDh* 1.56

15 *VaDh* 1.27; *ViDh* 26.6

16 *BDh* 2.2.7

17 *VaDh* 1.27

18 *VaDh* 14.11; *ViDh* 26.7

20 *MBh* 1.67.8

21 *BDh* 1.20.1; *VaDh* 1.29; *MBh* 1.67.8–9; *ViDh* 24.18

23 *GDh* 4.15; *MBh* 1.67.10

24 *ĀpDh* 2.12.3; *GDh* 4.14; *BDh* 1.20.10; *MBh* 1.67.10–1; *ViDh* 24.27–8

25 *MBh* 1.67.11–2

26` *BDh* 1.20.12; *MBh* 1.67.13

27 *ĀpDh* 2.11.17; *GDh* 4.6; *BDh* 1.20.2; *VaDh* 1.30; *ViDh* 24.19; *YDh* 1.58

28 *ĀpDh* 2.11.19; *GDh* 4.9; *BDh* 1.20.5; *VaDh* 1.31; *ViDh* 24.20; *YDh* 1.59

29 *ĀpDh* 2.11.18; *GDh* 4.8; *BDh* 1.20.4; *VaDh* 1.32; *ViDh* 24.21; *YDh* 1.59

30 *GDh* 4.7; *BDh* 1.20.3; *ViDh* 24.22; *YDh* 1.60

31 *ĀpDh* 2.12.1; *GDh* 4.11; *BDh* 1.20.6; *VaDh* 1.35; *ViDh* 24.24; *YDh* 1.61

32	*ĀpDh* 2.11.20; *GDh* 4.10; *BDh* 1.20.7; *VaDh* 1.33; *ViDh* 24.23; *YDh* 1.61
33	*ĀpDh* 2.12.2; *GDh* 4.12; *BDh* 1.20.8; *VaDh* 1.34; *ViDh* 24.25; *YDh* 1.61
34	*GDh* 4.13; *BDh* 1.20.9; *ViDh* 24.26; *YDh* 1.61
37	*GDh* 4.33; *ViDh* 24.29; *YDh* 1.58
38	*GDh* 4.29–32; *ViDh* 24.30–2; *YDh* 1.59–60
42	*ĀpDh* 2.12.4; *BDh* 1.21.1
43	*ViDh* 24.5; *YDh* 1.62
44	*ViDh* 24.6–8; *YDh* 1.62
45	*ĀpDh* 2.1.17–8; *GDh* 5.1–2; *BDh* 4.1.18–9; *VaDh* 12.21–4; *ViDh* 69.1; *YDh* 1.79–81
46	*YDh* 1.79
47	*YDh* 1.79
48	*YDh* 1.79
50	*YDh* 1.79
51	*ĀpDh* 2.13.11; *BDh* 1.21.2–3; 2.2.27; *VaDh* 1.37–8
53	*ĀpDh* 2.13.11; *VaDh* 1.36; *MBh* 13.45.21
54	*MBh* 13.46.1–2
55	*MBh* 13.46.3; *YDh* 1.82
56	*MBh* 13.46.5
57	*MBh* 13.46.5–6
58	*MBh* 13.46.6
61	*MBh* 13.46.4
63	*BDh* 1.10.26
64	*BDh* 1.10.28
65	*BDh* 1.10.28
66	*BDh* 1.10.29
67	*GDh* 5.7–8; *BDh* 2.4.22; *ViDh* 59.1–2; *YDh* 1.97
68	*ViDh* 59.19
69	*ViDh* 59.19–20
70	*GDh* 5.3–4, 9; *BDh* 2.5.11; 2.11.1; *ViDh* 59.20–4; *YDh* 1.102
72	*ViDh* 59.26
76	*MBh* 12.255.11
78	*VaDh* 8.14–6; *ViDh* 59.27–8
80	*ViDh* 59.29
81	*YDh* 1.104
82	*MBh* 13.100.8; *ViDh* 67.23–5
83–6	*ĀpDh* 2.3.12, 16–7; *GDh* 5.10; *BDh* 2.5.11–2; *VaDh* 11.3; *ViDh*
87–91	*ĀpDh* 2.3.12, 15, 18–23; 2.4.1–8; *GDh* 5.11–7; *VaDh* 11.4; *ViDh* 67.4–22
92	*ĀpDh* 2.9.5–6; *ViDh* 67.26; *YDh* 1.103
93	*ĀpDh* 2.4.9; *ViDh* 67.28, 32, 44, 46
94	*ĀpDh* 2.4.10–1; *BDh* 2.5.12–5; *VaDh* 11.5; *ViDh* 59.14; 67.27; *YDh* 1.108
96	*GDh* 5.18; *YDh* 1.108
97	*VaDh* 3.8
99	*ĀpDh* 2.4.13, 16; 2.6.7–15; *GDh* 5.31–4; *VaDh* 8.12; *ViDh* 67.45; *YDh* 1.107
100	*ViDh* 67.33
101	*ĀpDh* 2.4.14; *GDh* 5.35–6; *YDh* 1.107
102	*GDh* 5.40; *VaDh* 8.7; *ViDh* 67.34
103	*ŚāṅkhGṛ* 2.16.3; *ĀpDh* 2.6.5; *GDh* 5.40; *VaDh* 8.8; *ViDh* 67.35
104	*YDh* 1.112
105	*VaDh* 8.4–5, 8; *ViDh* 67.29–30; *YDh* 1.107
106	*ĀpDh* 2.8.2–4; *GDh* 5.38–9; *YDh* 1.104
107	*YDh* 1.107
108	*ĀpDh* 2.6.16–7; *VaDh* 11.12
110	*ŚāṅkhGṛ* 2.16.2; *GDh* 5.43
111	*GDh* 5.44; *ViDh* 67.36
112	*ĀpDh* 2.4.18–20; *GDh* 5.45; *BDh* 2.5.14; *ViDh* 67.37
113	*ViDh* 67.38; *YDh* 1.108
114	*ŚāṅkhGṛ* 2.14.21; *ĀpDh* 2.4.11–2; *GDh* 5.25; *BDh* 2.13.5; *ViDh* 67.39; *YDh* 1.105
115	*BDh* 2.5.18; 2.13.5; *ViDh* 67.40
116	*ĀpDh* 2.8.2; *ViDh* 67.41; *YDh* 1.105

117 *BDh* 2.13.6; *ViDh* 67.42
118 *BDh* 2.13.2; *ViDh* 67.43
119 *ĀpDh* 2.8.5–9; *GDh* 5.27–8; *BDh* 2.6.36–8; *VaDh* 11.1–2; *YDh* 1.109–10
120 *GDh* 5.29–30; *BDh* 2.6.37; *YDh* 1.110
122 *GDh* 15.2; *YDh* 1.217
125 *GDh* 15.21; *BDh* 2.15.10; *VaDh* 11.27; *ViDh* 73.3–4; *YDh* 1.228
126 *BDh* 2.15.11; *VaDh* 11.28
128 *VaDh* 3.8
129 *GDh* 15.21; *VaDh* 11.29
130 *MBh* 13.90.46; *ViDh* 82.2
134 *VaDh* 6.26; *MBh* 13.90.43; *ViDh* 83.9–13; *YDh* 1.221
135 *MBh* 13.90.44
138 *ĀpDh* 2.17.4; *GDh* 15.12; *BDh* 2.14.6; *VaDh* 11.17; *MBh* 13.90.36
139 *MBh* 13.90.34
140 *MBh* 13.90.35
141 *ĀpDh* 2.17.8; *MBh* 13.90.39
142 *MBh* 13.90.37
144 *ĀpDh* 2.17.5–6; *BDh* 2.14.4; *VaDh* 11.18
145 *BDh* 2.14.4
148 *GDh* 15.20; *ViDh* 83.17–8; *YDh* 1.220
149 *ViDh* 82.1–2
150 *GDh* 15.16; *VaDh* 11.19; *YDh* 1.223–4
151 *GDh* 15.16–8; *ViDh* 82.13
152 *GDh* 15.18; *ViDh* 82.8–9
153 *GDh* 15.16–8; *VaDh* 11.19; *ViDh* 82.26; *YDh* 1.222
154 *GDh* 15.16–8; *VaDh* 11.19; *YDh* 1.223
155 *GDh* 15.17–8; *YDh* 1.222
156 *ViDh* 82.20–1; *YDh* 1.222–3
157 *ViDh* 82.23, 29; *YDh* 1.22
158 *GDh* 15.18; *MBh* 13.90.7; *YDh* 1.223–4
159 *GDh* 15.19; *MBh* 13.90.8; *ViDh* 82.5, 28; *YDh* 1.222–3
160 *GDh* 15.18; *ViDh* 82.18; *YDh* 1.223
161 *ĀpDh* 2.17.21; *GDh* 15.18; *VaDh* 11.19; *ViDh* 82.19; *YDh* 1.222
162 *ĀpDh* 2.17.21; *ViDh* 82.7
164 *GDh* 15.18; *ViDh* 82.22; *YDh* 1.223
165 *YDh* 1.223
166 *GDh* 15.16; *YDh* 1.224
172 *BDh* 2.1.39; *MBh* 12.159.63
184 *ĀpDh* 2.17.22; *GDh* 15.28; *MBh* 13.90.19; *ViDh* 83.1–5; *YDh* 1.219
185 *ĀpDh* 2.17.22; *GDh* 15.28; *BDh* 2.14.2; *MBh* 13.90.20; *ViDh* 83.2–4, 15–6; *YDh* 1.219–21
186 *YDh* 1.219
187 *ĀpDh* 2.17.11–5; *BDh* 2.14.6; *VaDh* 11.17; *ViDh* 73.2; *YDh* 1.225
188 *GDh* 15.23; *YDh* 1.225
191 *GDh* 15.22
202 *ĀpDh* 2.19.3–4; *ViDh* 79.24; *YDh* 1.236
206 *ĀpDh* 2.18.6; *GDh* 15.25; *YDh* 1.227; *ViDh* 85.66
207 *ViDh* 85.54–65
208 *ViDh* 73.2; *YDh* 1.226
209 *BDh* 2.14.7; *ViDh* 73.12; *YDh* 1.231
210 *ĀpDh* 2.17.17–9; *BDh* 2.14.7; *ViDh* 73.12; *YDh* 1.235
211 *BDh* 2.14.7
215 *ViDh* 73.17–9; *YDh* 1.241
216 *ViDh* 73.22
218 *ViDh* 73.23
220 *ViDh* 75.1
221 *ViDh* 75.4
224 *VaDh* 11.26
225 *BDh* 2.15.3; *VaDh* 11.25
226–7 *ĀpDh* 2.16.23–4; 2.19.19–22; *ViDh* 73.21, 23–4
228 *ĀpDh* 2.17.4

229 *ĀpDh* 2.18.3; *ViDh* 79.19–21, 81.2
231 *BDh* 2.14.5; *ViDh* 79.5–15; *YDh* 1.239
232 *ViDh* 73.16
234 *ViDh* 79.16; 83.18
235 *VaDh* 11.35; *YDh* 1.235, 240
236 *ViDh* 81.11, 20
237 *VaDh* 11.32; *ViDh* 81.11, 20
238 *MBh* 13.90.13; *ViDh* 81.12–3
239 *ĀpDh* 2.17.20; *GDh* 15.24; *ViDh* 81.6–9
242 *ViDh* 81.15
243 *ViDh* 81.19
244 *ViDh* 81.22; *YDh* 1.241
245 *VaDh* 11.23; *ViDh* 81.23
246 *VaDh* 11.24; *ViDh* 81.24
247 *ViDh* 21.3
250 *VaDh* 11.37
251 *ViDh* 73.26; *YDh* 1.240
252 *YDh* 1.244–5
253 *YDh* 1.240
254 *VaDh* 3.69–71
258 *ViDh* 73.27
259 *ViDh* 73.28; *YDh* 1.246
260 *YDh* 1.257
261 *BDh* 2.14.9
265 *VaDh* 11.21–2; *YDh* 1.256–7
267 *GDh* 15.15; *MBh* 13.88.3; *ViDh* 80.1; *YDh* 1.258
268 *GDh* 15.15; *MBh* 13.88.5; *ViDh* 80.2–5; *YDh* 1.259
269 *GDh* 15.15; *MBh* 13.88.7; *ViDh* 80.6–9; *YDh* 1.259
270 *ĀpDh* 2.16.27; *GDh* 15.15; *ViDh* 80.10; *YDh* 1.259
271 *ĀpDh* 2.16.26; *GDh* 15.15; *MBh* 13.88.9; *ViDh* 80.11–2; *YDh* 1.260
272 *ĀpDh* 2.17.1–3; *GDh* 15.15; *ViDh* 80.14; *YDh* 1.260
273 *ĀpDh* 2.19.20; *MBh* 13.88.15; *YDh* 1.261
274 *VaDh* 11.39–40; *MBh* 13.88.12; *ViDh* 78.52–3
276 *ĀpDh* 2.16.5–6; *GDh* 15.3; *VaDh* 11.16
277 *ĀpDh* 2.16.8–22; *GDh* 15.2–4; *ViDh* 78.8–49; *YDh* 1.261–8
278 *ĀpDh* 2.16.5; *VaDh* 11.36; *ViDh* 73.2
279 *YDh* 1.232
280 *ĀpDh* 2.17.23; *ViDh* 77.8
283 *ĀpDh* 1.13.1; *BDh* 2.11.3
284 *YDh* 1.269
285 *MBh* 3.2.58; 12.235.11

Chapter Four

1 *MBh* 12.234.29, 235.1
2 *MBh* 12.254.6
7 *YDh* 1.128
8 *YDh* 1.128
12 *YDh* 1.129
14 *VaDh* 27.8
15 *YDh* 1.129
17 *BDh* 1.10.30; *ViDh* 71.4; *YDh* 1.129
18 *ViDh* 71.5–6; *YDh* 1.123
19 *ViDh* 71.8; *YDh* 1.99
21 *GDh* 5.3
25 *BDh* 2.4.23; *VaDh* 11.46; *ViDh* 59.4; *YDh* 1.124
26 *BDh* 2.4.23; *VaDh* 11.46; *ViDh* 59.5–7, 9; *YDh* 1.125
30 *YDh* 1.130
32 *ĀpDh* 2.4.13; *GDh* 5.22; *BDh* 2.5.19–20
33 *GDh* 9.63–4; *VaDh* 12.2; *ViDh* 63.1; *YDh* 1.130
34 *ĀpDh* 1.30.13; *GDh* 9.3; *VaDh* 12.4; *ViDh* 71.9
35 *ĀpDh* 1.30.10–2; *GDh* 9.4, 6–7, 71–2; *BDh* 1.5.7; *YDh* 1.131
36 *ĀpDh* 1.8.2; *BDh* 1.5.3–5; 1.6.1; 2.6.7; *VaDh* 12.14, 37–8; *ViDh* 71.13–6; *YDh* 1.133

37 *ĀpDh* 1.31.18; *BDh* 2.6.10; *VaDh* 12.10; *MBh* 13.107.17; *ViDh* 71.17–21; *YDh* 1.135

38 *ĀpDh* 1.31.13; *GDh* 9.52; *BDh* 2.6.15; *VaDh* 12.9; *ViDh* 63.42; 71.23

39 *GDh* 9.66; *ViDh* 63.25–30; *YDh* 1.133

40 *GDh* 9.29–30; *VaDh* 12.5; *ViDh* 69.11

43 *GDh* 9.32; *VaDh* 12.31; *ViDh* 68.46; 71.25; *YDh* 1.131

44 *GDh* 9.32, 48; *ViDh* 71.26; *YDh* 1.135

45 *ĀpDh* 1.30.18; *GDh* 9.40, 61; *BDh* 2.6.24; *VaDh* 6.12; 12.11; *ViDh* 60.11, 16, 19; 64.5; 68.14; *YDh* 1.131, 134

46 *ĀpDh* 1.30.18; *GDh* 9.40; *VaDh* 6.12; *ViDh* 60.4, 10, 21; *YDh* 1.134

47 *ViDh* 60.8–9, 15; *YDh* 1.134

48 *ĀpDh* 1.30.20; *GDh* 9.12; *ViDh* 60.22; *YDh* 1.134

49 *ĀpDh* 1.30.14–5; *GDh* 9.37–8; *BDh* 1.10.10; *VaDh* 12.13; *ViDh* 60.1, 3, 23; *YDh* 1.16

50 *ĀpDh* 1.31.1; *GDh* 9.41–3; *BDh* 1.10.10; *VaDh* 6.10; 12.13; *ViDh* 60.2; *YDh* 1.16

51 *VaDh* 6.13

52 *VaDh* 6.11

53 *ĀpDh* 1.15.20; 1.30.22; *GDh* 9.32; *VaDh* 12.27; *ViDh* 71.26, 32–34, 37; *YDh* 1.135, 137

54 *ĀpDh* 1.15.21; *GDh* 9.73; *ViDh* 71.36; *YDh* 1.137

55 *ViDh* 63.8; 68.12; 71.41, 55

56 *ĀpDh* 1.30.19; *ViDh* 71.32–5; *YDh* 1.137

57 *GDh* 9.54–5; *VaDh* 12.42; *ViDh* 70.13; 71.56, 58; *YDh* 1.138

58 *BDh* 2.6.38; *MBh* 12.186.19; 13.148.24; *ViDh* 71.60

59 *ĀpDh* 1.31.10, 16; *GDh* 9.22–4; *BDh* 2.6.11, 17; *VaDh* 12.32–3; *ViDh* 71.62; *YDh* 1.140

60–1 *ĀpDh* 1.15.22; 1.32.18; *GDh* 9.65; *BDh* 2.6.21; *ViDh* 63.2; 71.64–8

62 *GDh* 9.58; *ViDh* 68.27

63 *GDh* 9.9, 56; *BDh* 2.6.5; *ViDh* 68.21; 71.69

64 *ĀpDh* 2.20.13; *GDh* 9.51; *ViDh* 71.70–1

65 *ViDh* 68.20; 71.39

66 *GDh* 9.4; *ViDh* 71.47

67 *ViDh* 63.13–4

69 *ViDh* 71.44, 46; *YDh* 1.139

70 *ĀpDh* 1.32.28; *GDh* 9.51; *ViDh* 71.42–3

71 *MBh* 13.107.15

72 *ĀpDh* 1.32.5; *GDh* 9.32; *BDh* 2.6.9; *ViDh* 63.15

73 *GDh* 9.32; *BDh* 2.6.13; *YDh* 1.140

74 *GDh* 9.32; *BDh* 2.6.6; *VaDh* 12.36; *ViDh* 68.19, 23; 71.45; *YDh* 1.38

75 *GDh* 9.60; *ViDh* 68.29; 70.3

76 *ViDh* 68.34; 70.1

77 *GDh* 9.32; *BDh* 2.6.26; *VaDh* 12.45; *ViDh* 63.45; *YDh* 1.135

78 *ĀpDh* 2.20.11; *GDh* 9.15; *BDh* 2.6.16; *ViDh* 63.23–4; *YDh* 1.139

80 *ĀpDh* 1.31.22; *VaDh* 18.14; *ViDh* 71.48–52

81 *VaDh* 18.15

82 *ViDh* 68.38; 71.53

83 *ViDh* 64.12

84 *YDh* 1.140

85 *YDh* 1.141

87 *YDh* 1.140

88 *ViDh* 43.1–7

89 *ViDh* 43.8–15

90 *ViDh* 43.16–22

92 *VaDh* 12.47; *MBh* 13.107.16; *ViDh* 60.1

93 *ViDh* 71.77

94 *MBh* 13.107.18

95 *ĀpDh* 1.9.1, 3; *GDh* 16.1–2; *BDh* 1.12.16; *VaDh* 13.1–5; *ViDh* 30.1; *YDh* 1.142

96 *ĀpDh* 1.9.2; *BDh* 1.12.16; *ViDh* 30.2; *YDh* 1.143

97 *GDh* 16.40; *ViDh* 30.4

98 *VaDh* 13.6–7; *ViDh* 30.3

99 *ĀpDh* 1.9.9–11; *GDh* 16.19; *BDh* 1.21.15; *VaDh* 18.12–3; *ViDh* 30.14, 27; *YDh* 1.148

101 *VaDh* 13.8

102 *GDh* 16.5–6

103 *GDh* 16.22; *BDh* 1.21.6; *VaDh* 13.36–7; *ViDh* 30.8–9; *YDh* 1.145, 149

104 *ĀpDh* 1.11.8, 27–8, 31; *GDh* 16.10, 23

105 *ĀpDh* 1.11.30–1; *GDh* 16.15–6, 22; *BDh* 1.21.4; *VaDh* 13.32–3, 35; *ViDh* 30.9; *YDh* 1.145

106 *ĀpDh* 1.9.20–4; 1.11.29; *BDh* 1.21.7; *VaDh* 13.9; *YDh* 1.145

107 *ĀpDh* 1.10.24; 1.11.31; *GDh* 16.19, 45; *BDh* 1.21.4; *VaDh* 13.17; *YDh* 1.150

108 *ĀpDh* 1.9.14; 1.10.19; *GDh* 16.7, 19; *BDh* 1.21.5; *VaDh* 13.11; *ViDh* 30.10; *YDh* 1.148

109 *ĀpDh* 1.10.22; 1.11.17, 25–6; 1.32.12; *GDh* 16.11–2, 18, 34, 46; *BDh* 1.21.8, 21; *ViDh* 30.16; *YDh* 1.149

110 *ĀpDh* 1.11.30; *GDh* 16.22; *VaDh* 13.34; *ViDh* 30.5; *YDh* 1.146

111 *ĀpDh* 1.10.26; 1.11.25; *YDh* 1.146

112 *GDh* 16.17, 34; *VaDh* 13.14, 23; *ViDh* 13.17

113 *ĀpDh* 1.9.28; 1.11.15, 25, 31; *GDh* 16.7, 12, 35; *BDh* 1.21.4–5, 17, 22; *VaDh* 13.10, 21–2; *ViDh* 30.4; *YDh* 1.146, 148, 150

114 *BDh* 1.21.22

115 *ĀpDh* 1.10.19; 1.11.33; *GDh* 16.8; *BDh* 1.21.16; *VaDh* 13.35; *ViDh* 30.9, 12; *YDh* 1.148, 150

116 *ĀpDh* 1.9.6; 1.11.9; *GDh* 1.61; 16.18; *BDh* 1.21.8; *VaDh* 13.13, 26–7; *ViDh* 30.15; *YDh* 1.146, 148

117 *GDh* 16.48; *VaDh* 13.16; *BDh* 1.21.10–1

118 *GDh* 16.34; *BDh* 1.21.20

119 *ĀpDh* 1.10.1–2; *GDh* 16.36, 38; *ViDh* 30.5, 24–5; *YDh* 1.144, 146

120 *ĀpDh* 1.9.27; 1.11.16; *GDh* 16.17; *VaDh* 13.17–9; *ViDh* 30.18–21; *YDh* 1.151

121 *ĀpDh* 1.10.20; *GDh* 16.20, 34; *VaDh* 13.20, 28, 31; *ViDh* 30.11, 19–21; *YDh* 1.149

122 *ĀpDh* 1.11.8; *ViDh* 30.7; *YDh* 1.149

123 *ĀpDh* 1.10.17–8; *GDh* 16.21; *BDh* 1.21.5; *VaDh* 13.30; *ViDh* 30.26; *YDh* 1.145, 148

126 *GDh* 1.59; *ViDh* 30.22; *YDh* 1.147

127 *YDh* 1.149

128 *ĀpDh* 1.31.19; *BDh* 1.21.18; *VaDh* 12.21; *MBh* 13.107.54; *ViDh* 69.1; *YDh* 1.79

129 *ĀpDh* 1.32.8; *BDh* 2.6.25; *ViDh* 64.3–4, 6

130 *ViDh* 63.39; *YDh* 1.152

131 *MBh* 13.107.52; *ViDh* 63.19

132 *ViDh* 63.40; *YDh* 1.152

134 *MBh* 13.107.20

135 *YDh* 1.153

137 *ViDh* 71.76; *YDh* 1.153

138 *GDh* 9.68; *ViDh* 71.73–4; *YDh* 1.132

139 *ĀpDh* 1.31.12, 15; *GDh* 9.20, 32; *ViDh* 71.57; *YDh* 1.132

140 *BDh* 2.6.21–3; *VaDh* 12.43; *ViDh* 63.2, 4, 6–7, 9

141 *ViDh* 71.2

142 *ĀpDh* 1.15.18; *YDh* 1.155

143 *ĀpDh* 1.16.14

144 *ViDh* 71.79

146 *VaDh* 26.14

150 *ViDh* 71.86; 76.1; *YDh* 1.217

151 *ĀpDh* 1.31.2; *GDh* 9.39; *MBh* 13.107.48; *YDh* 1.154

152 *MBh* 13.107.21

154 *BDh* 2.6.35; *MBh* 13.107.33

155 *ViDh* 71.90; *YDh* 1.154

156 *VaDh* 6.7; *MBh* 13.107.6; *ViDh* 71.91

157 *VaDh* 6.6; *MBh* 13.107.7

158 *VaDh* 6.8; *MBh* 13.107.13; *ViDh* 71.92

162 *ĀpDh* 1.1.15; *GDh* 21.15

163 *ĀpDh* 1.31.23; *VaDh* 12.41; *ViDh* 71.83

164 *ViDh* 71.80–2

165 *GDh* 21.20

166 *GDh* 21.21

167–8 *GDh* 21.22

172 *MBh* 12.92.20

173 *MBh* 12.92.20

174 *MBh* 3.92.4

175 *GDh* 9.50, 68–70

176 *GDh* 9.73; *ViDh* 71.84–5; *YDh* 1.156

177 *VaDh* 6.42

179 *MBh* 12.235.12–3; *YDh* 1.157

180 *MBh* 12.235.13–4; *YDh* 1.158

181–5 *MBh* 12.235.14–9

186 *ViDh* 57.6–7

187 *ViDh* 57.8

188 *VaDh* 6.32; *YDh* 1.201–2

191 *YDh* 2.202

192 *ViDh* 93.7

195–200 *ViDh* 93.8–13

201 *BDh* 2.5.6; *ViDh* 64.1; *YDh* 1.159

202 *BDh* 2.6.29; *YDh* 1.160

203 *ViDh* 64.16; *YDh* 1.159

204 *YDh* 3.312–3

205 *ĀpDh* 1.18.27; *GDh* 17.17

207 *ĀpDh* 1.16.23–7; 1.19.1; *GDh* 17.9–10; *VaDh* 14.3, 22–3; *ViDh* 51.19; *YDh* 1.162, 167–8

208 *ĀpDh* 1.16.30; *GDh* 17.10–1; *ViDh* 51.17–8; *YDh* 1.167–8

209 *ĀpDh* 1.18.16–7; *GDh* 17.12, 17; *VaDh* 14.9–10; *ViDh* 51.7, 9, 17; *YDh* 1.161, 168

210 *ĀpDh* 1.18.18, 22–6; *GDh* 17.17–8; *VaDh* 14.2–3; *MBh* 12.37.22; *ViDh* 51.7–9; *YDh* 1.161

211 *ĀpDh* 1.17.17–20; 1.18.13; 1.19.14; *GDh* 17.14, 16–7; *VaDh* 14.2, 4, 20, 28–9; *ViDh* 51.9–10; *YDh* 1.161–2, 167

212 *ĀpDh* 1.16.19; 1. 7.3; 1.18.21; 1.19.14; *GDh* 17.17, 19; *VaDh* 14.2, 19; *ViDh* 51.10; *YDh* 1.162

213 *ĀpDh* 1.17.4; 2.6.19–20; *GDh* 17.17–21; *VaDh* 14.2; *ViDh* 51.11, 18, 20; *YDh* 1.162–4, 167

214 *ĀpDh* 1.18.30; *GDh* 17.18; *VaDh* 14.3; *ViDh* 51.12; *YDh* 1.161, 164–5

215 *ĀpDh* 1.18.19; *VaDh* 14.5; *ViDh* 51.14; *YDh* 1.161, 163

216 *GDh* 17.18; *VaDh* 14.3, 11; *ViDh* 51.15–6; *YDh* 1.163–4

217 *ĀpDh* 1.16.18; *GDh* 17.18; *VaDh* 14.6, 11; *MBh* 12.37.21; *YDh* 1.163

218 *VaDh* 14.2; *ViDh* 51.8

222 *GDh* 23.23–4

223 *ĀpDh* 1.18.3–8, 14

224 *BDh* 1.10.5; *VaDh* 14.17; *MBh* 12.256.9

225 *BDh* 1.10.5; *VaDh* 14.17; *MBh* 12.256.10

227 *YDh* 1.201

228 *YDh* 1.203

229 *VaDh* 29.8; *ViDh* 91.3, 15–6; 92.21, 23; *YDh* 1.210

230 *ViDh* 92.13–4; *YDh* 1.210

231 *ViDh* 92.5, 11–2; *YDh* 1.204–6, 210

232 *VaDh* 29.12; *ViDh* 92.22, 27; *YDh* 1.211

233 *VaDh* 29.19; *YDh* 1.212

240 *MBh* 13.112.11

241 *MBh* 13.112.10, 13

242 *MBh* 13.112.15

247 *ĀpDh* 1.18.1; *GDh* 17.3; *VaDh* 14.12; *ViDh* 57.10; *YDh* 1.214

248 *ĀpDh* 1.19.13; *VaDh* 14.16; *ViDh* 57.11; *YDh* 1.215

249 *ĀpDh* 1.19.14; *VaDh* 14.18; *ViDh* 57.12

250 *ĀpDh* 1.18.1; *GDh* 17.3; *BDh* 1.9.8; *VaDh* 14.12; *ViDh* 57.10; *YDh* 1.214

251 *ĀpDh* 1.7.20; *GDh* 17.4; *VaDh* 14.13; *ViDh* 57.13; *YDh* 1.216

252 *ViDh* 57.15

253 *GDh* 17.5–6; *ViDh* 57.16; *YDh* 1.166

260 *GDh* 9.74; *BDh* 2.3.1; *VaDh* 8.17

Chapter Five

5 *ĀpDh* 1.17.26, 28; *GDh* 17.32; *VaDh* 14.33; *ViDh* 51.3, 34, 36; *YDh* 1.171

6 *GDh* 17.32–3; *VaDh* 14.33; *ViDh* 51.36; *YDh* 1.171

7 *GDh* 17.31; *ViDh* 51.37; *YDh* 1.171, 173

8 *ĀpDh* 1.17.22–4; *GDh* 17.22–6; *BDh* 1.12.9–11; *VaDh* 14.34–5; *ViDh* 51.38–40; *YDh* 1.170

9 *ĀpDh* 1.17.18; *GDh* 17.14; *BDh* 1.12.15; *VaDh* 14.37–8; *ViDh* 51.38, 42; *YDh* 1.167, 170

10 *ĀpDh* 1.17.19; *GDh* 17.14; *BDh* 1.12.14; *ViDh* 51.42; *YDh* 1.169

11 *ĀpDh* 1.17.29, 34; *GDh* 17.28–29; *BDh* 1.12.1–2; *VaDh* 14.48; *ViDh* 51.28–30; *YDh* 1.172

12 *ĀpDh* 1.17.32–3; *GDh* 17.28–9; *BDh* 1.12.3; *VaDh* 14.48; *ViDh* 51.3, 29; *YDh* 1.172–4

13 *GDh* 17.35; *VaDh* 14.48; *ViDh* 51.27; *YDh* 1.172, 174–5

14 *GDh* 17.29, 34; *BDh* 1.12.3, 8; *VaDh* 14.48; *ViDh* 51.21, 29; *YDh* 1.173–5

16 *GDh* 17.36–7; *BDh* 1.12.8; *ViDh* 1.51.21; *YDh* 1.177–8

17 *ĀpDh* 1.17.37; *GDh* 17.27; *BDh* 1.12.5; *VaDh* 14.39, 44; *ViDh* 51.6, 27; *YDh* 1.174

18 *ĀpDh* 1.17.37; *GDh* 17.27; *BDh* 1.12.4–5; *VaDh* 14.39–40, 47; *ViDh* 51.6, 26; *YDh* 1.177

19 *GDh* 23.5; *ViDh* 51.3–4; *YDh* 1.176

20 *YDh* 1.176

22 *VaDh* 14.15

24–5 *ViDh* 51.35; *YDh* 1.169

26 *YDh* 1.178

27 *YDh* 1.179

28 *MBh* 12.10.6

29 *MBh* 12.100.15

34 *ViDh* 51.62

35 *VaDh* 11.34

36 *ViDh* 51.59

38 *ViDh* 51.60; *YDh* 1.180

39 *ViDh* 51.61

40 *ViDh* 51.63

41 *ŚāṅkhGṛ* 2.16.1; *VaDh* 4.6; *ViDh* 51.64

42 *ViDh* 51.65

43 *ViDh* 51.66

44 *ViDh* 51.67

45 *ViDh* 51.68

46 *ViDh* 51.69

47 *ViDh* 51.70; *YDh* 1.181

48 *VaDh* 4.7; *ViDh* 51.71

49 *ViDh* 51.72

50 *MBh* 13.116.12; *ViDh* 51.73

51 *ViDh* 51.74

52 *MBh* 13.116.14, 34; 13.117.10; *ViDh* 51.75

53 *MBh* 13.116.10, 16; *ViDh* 51.76; *YDh* 181

54 *ViDh* 51.77

55 *ViDh* 51.78

58 *ĀpDh* 2.15.2–4; *ViDh* 22.26–7; *YDh* 3.18, 23

59 *GDh* 14.1; *BDh* 1.11.1; *VaDh* 4.16;

	ViDh 22.1; *YDh* 3.18
60	*ĀpDh* 2.15.2–3; *GDh* 14.13; *BDh* 1.11.2; *VaDh* 4.17–8; *ViDh* 22.5
61	*GDh* 14.14–6; *BDh* 1.11.1, 19–23; *VaDh* 14.20–3; *YDh* 3.19
64	*GDh* 14.23–7
65	*ViDh* 22.85
66	*GDh* 14.17; *BDh* 1.11.31; *VaDh* 4.34; *ViDh* 22.72; *YDh* 3.20
67	*ViDh* 22.29–30; *YDh* 3.23
68	*BDh* 1.11.4; *YDh* 3.1
69	*ĀpDh* 2.15.3–4; *BDh* 1.11.4; *VaDh* 4.34; *ViDh* 22.28; *YDh* 3.1
71	*GDh* 14.20; *BDh* 1.11.30
72	*BDh* 1.11.8
73	*ĀpDh* 2.15.7–8; *GDh* 14.37–9; *BDh* 1.11.24; *YDh* 3.16
75	*GDh* 14.44; *ViDh* 22.39; *YDh* 3.21
76	*GDh* 14.19, 44; *VaDh* 4.36; *ViDh* 22.40–1; *YDh* 3.21
77	*YDh* 3.21
78	*GDh* 14.19, 44
79	*GDh* 14.6; *BDh* 1.11.17–8; *VaDh* 4.24; *ViDh* 22.35; *YDh* 3.20
80	*GDh* 14.28; *BDh* 1.11.28; *ViDh* 22.42–4; *YDh* 3.24
81	*GDh* 14.20, 22; *BDh* 1.11.29–30; *ViDh* 22.44; *YDh* 3.24
82	*ViDh* 22.45–6; *YDh* 3.24–5
83	*GDh* 14.2–5; *VaDh* 4.27–30; *ViDh* 22.1–4; *YDh* 3.22
85	*GDh* 14.30; *BDh* 1.9.5; 1.11.36; *VaDh* 4.38; *ViDh* 22.69; *YDh* 3.30
86	*BDh* 1.15.31
88	*ViDh* 22.87; *YDh* 3.5
89	*ViDh* 22.56; *YDh* 3.6
90	*YDh* 3.6
91	*ViDh* 22.86; *YDh* 3.15
93	*GDh* 14.1, 45–6; *BDh* 1.11.1; *VaDh* 19.48; *ViDh* 22.48–50; *YDh* 3.27–8
94	*VaDh* 19.47
95	*GDh* 14.9–11; *ViDh* 22.47, 52; *YDh* 3.21, 27
98	*YDh* 3.29
101	*BDh* 1.11.33
102	*ViDh* 22.8; *YDh* 3.15
103	*GDh* 14.31; *ViDh* 22.63–4; *YDh* 3.26
105	*BDh* 1.8.52; *ViDh* 22.88; *YDh* 1.194; 3.31
106	*ViDh* 22.89
107	*ViDh* 22.90; *YDh* 3.32–3
108	*VaDh* 3.58; *ViDh* 22.91; *YDh* 3.32
109	*BDh* 1.8.2; 3.1.27; *VaDh* 3.60; *ViDh* 22.92; *YDh* 3.33–4
110	*ViDh* 22.93
111	*ĀpDh* 1.17.11; *GDh* 1.29–30; *BDh* 1.8.32, 44; 1.14.4; *VaDh* 3.49–50
112	*BDh* 1.8.33; *VaDh* 3.61–2; *ViDh* 23.7; *YDh* 1.182–3
114	*BDh* 1.8.33; *VaDh* 3.58; *ViDh* 23.25–6; *YDh* 1.190
115	*ĀpDh* 1.17.12; *GDh* 1.29; *BDh* 1.8.35; 1.13.26–7; 1.14.16–7; *VaDh* 3.49; *ViDh* 23.27, 29–30; *YDh* 1.190
116	*ĀpDh* 1.17.13; *BDh* 1.8.50–1; 1.13.26, 29–32; *VaDh* 12.15–6; *ViDh* 23.8, 10; *YDh* 1.182–3
117	*ViDh* 23.9, 11; *YDh* 1.183–4
118	*GDh* 1.29; *BDh* 1.8.42; 1.13.11; 1.14.11–2; *VaDh* 3.49; *ViDh* 23.13–4, 18; *YDh* 1.184
119	*GDh* 1.33; *BDh* 1.8.36, 38, 43; 1.13.13; *VaDh* 3.53; *ViDh* 23.14–5, 18; *YDh* 1.182
120	*BDh* 1.8.39–42; *VaDh* 3.55; *ViDh* 23.19–22; *YDh* 1.186–7
121	*GDh* 1.30–1; *BDh* 1.8.45–7; *VaDh* 3.51–2; *ViDh* 23.23; *YDh* 1.185
122	*ĀpDh* 1.17.10; *GDh* 1.29; *BDh* 1.8.34; 1.13.21–5; 1.14.1–2; *VaDh* 3.49; *ViDh* 23.16, 18, 33, 56; *YDh* 1.187–8
123	*ViDh* 23.5
124	*GDh* 1.31–2; *BDh* 1.9.11; 1.13.16–20; *VaDh* 3.56–7; *YDh* 1.188

125 *VaDh* 14.23; *ViDh* 23.38; *YDh* 1.189
126 *GDh* 1.42; *VaDh* 3.48; *YDh* 1.191
127 *BDh* 1.9.9; *VaDh* 14.24; *ViDh* 23.47; *YDh* 1.191
128 *BDh* 1.9.10; *VaDh* 3.35–6, 47; *ViDh* 23.43; *YDh* 1.192
129 *BDh* 1.9.1; *VaDh* 3.46; *ViDh* 23.48; *YDh* 1.187
130 *BDh* 1.9.2; *VaDh* 3.45–6; 28.8; *ViDh* 23.49; *YDh* 1.187, 193
131 *VaDh* 3.45; *ViDh* 23.50; *YDh* 1.192
132 *ViDh* 23.51; *YDh* 1.194
133 *ViDh* 23.52; *YDh* 1.193
134 *GDh* 1.43; *BDh* 1.10.11–5; *ViDh* 60.24; *YDh* 1.17
135 *ViDh* 22.81
136 *BDh* 1.10.11–3; *VaDh* 6.18; *ViDh* 60.25
137 *VaDh* 6.19; *ViDh* 60.26
138 *ĀpDh* 1.16.7; *GDh* 1.36, 43–5; *BDh* 1.8.26; *VaDh* 3.26–9; *ViDh* 22.75; 62.8
139 *ĀpDh* 1.16.2–8; *GDh* 1.36; *BDh* 1.8.18–22; *VaDh* 3.26–34; *ViDh* 62.6–7; *YDh* 1.20,
140 *ĀpDh* 2.3.4–8
141 *ĀpDh* 1.16.11–3; *GDh* 1.38–41; *BDh* 1.8.24–5; *VaDh* 3.37; *ViDh* 23.53; *YDh* 1.195
142 *BDh* 1.10.34; *VaDh* 3.42; *ViDh* 23.54; *YDh* 1.195
143 *GDh* 1.28; *BDh* 1.8.27–9; *VaDh* 3.43; *ViDh* 23.55
144 *ĀpDh* 2.1.23; *ViDh* 22.67
145 *ĀpDh* 1.16.14; *GDh* 1.37; *VaDh* 3.38; *ViDh* 22.75; *YDh* 1.196
147 *GDh* 18.1; *BDh* 2.3.44; *VaDh* 5.1; *ViDh* 25.12
148 *BDh* 2.3.45; *VaDh* 5.3; *ViDh* 25.13; *YDh* 1.85
149 *YDh* 1.86
150 *ViDh* 25.4–6; *YDh* 1.83
151 *ViDh* 25.13–4; *YDh* 1.75, 83
154 *YDh* 1.77
155 *ViDh* 25.15; *YDh* 1.77
156–7 *YDh* 1.75
159 *ĀpDh* 2.23.5
160 *ViDh* 25.17; *YDh* 1.75
164 *VaDh* 21.14
166 *YDh* 1.87
167–8 *YDh* 1.89

Chapter Six

1–2 *ĀpDh* 2.21.1–5, 19; 2.22.6–7; *GDh* 3.1; *BDh* 2.17.2–5; *ViDh* 94.1–2; *YDh* 3.45
3 *ĀpDh* 2.21.9–10; *GDh* 3.26, 28; *BDh* 2.11.15; *ViDh* 94.3; *YDh* 3.45
4 *GDh* 3.26–7; *BDh* 2.11.15; *VaDh* 9.10; *ViDh* 94.4; *YDh* 3.45
5 *GDh* 3.26, 29; *BDh* 2.11.15; *VaDh* 9.4, 7, 12; *ViDh* 94.5; *YDh* 3.46
6 *ĀpDh* 2.22.1, 13–4, 17; *GDh* 3.34; *BDh* 2.11.15; 3.3.19; *VaDh* 9.1; *ViDh* 94.8–10; *YDh* 3.46
7 *ĀpDh* 2.22.7; *GDh* 3.29–30; *BDh* 2.11.15; 3.3.5–7, 20; *VaDh* 9.7
8 *ĀpDh* 2.21.21; 2.22.11; *BDh* 3.3.19; *VaDh* 9.8; *ViDh* 94.6; *YDh* 3.48
9 *ĀpDh* 2.22.12; *BDh* 3.3.5–7, 20; *VaDh* 9.10
11 *ĀpDh* 2.22.17–8
13 *ĀpDh* 2.22.2, 17; 2.23.2; *GDh* 3.26; *BDh* 2.11.15; *VaDh* 9.4; *ViDh* 95.7–11; *YDh* 3.49
15 *ĀpDh* 2.22.24; *ViDh* 94.12; *YDh* 3.47
16 *VaDh* 9.4; *YDh* 3.46
17 *BDh* 3.3.2, 9–12; *ViDh* 95.13–4; *YDh* 3.49
18 *ĀpDh* 2.23.1; *GDh* 3.35; *BDh* 2.11.15; 3.2.11; *ViDh* 94.11; *YDh* 3.47
19 *ViDh* 95.5–6; *YDh* 3.50
20 *ViDh* 95.11–2; *YDh* 3.50

21 *ĀpDh* 2.23.2; *BDh* 3.2.9, 11
22 *BDh* 2.11.15; *VaDh* 9.9; *ViDh* 94.10; *YDh* 3.48, 51
23 *ViDh* 95.1–4; *YDh* 3.52
25 *ĀpDh* 2.21.21; *VaDh* 9.11; *YDh* 3.54
26 *VaDh* 9.5, 11; *ViDh* 94.7; *YDh* 3.45, 51, 54
27 *YDh* 3.54
28 *ViDh* 94.13; *YDh* 3.55
31 *ĀpDh* 2.23.2, 4; *BDh* 3.3.9, 13–4; *YDh* 3.55
33 *BDh* 2.17.1–6; *ViDh* 96.1
34 *BDh* 2.17.15–6
35–7 *ĀpDh* 2.24.8; *BDh* 2.11.34; *YDh* 3.57
38 *BDh* 2.17.18–28; *ViDh* 96.1–2; *YDh* 3.56
39 *BDh* 2.17.29; *VaDh* 10.1; *MBh* 12.236.27; 12.269.20
40 *BDh* 2.17.30; *VaDh* 10.2–3
41 *GDh* 3.16; *BDh* 2.11.24; 2.17.31; *VaDh* 10.12, 28
42 *MBh* 12.237.4–5
43 *ĀpDh* 2.21.10; *GDh* 3.11, 14; *BDh* 2.11.16; *VaDh* 10.6; *MBh* 12.237.5; *ViDh* 96.2
44 *ĀpDh* 2.21.11; *GDh* 3.18–9, 24; *BDh* 2.11.19, 21; 2.17.44; *VaDh* 10.9–10, 13, 29; *MBh* 12.237.7; *ViDh* 96.10–11
45 *MBh* 12.237.15; *ViDh* 96.18
46 *BDh* 2.11.25; 2.17.43; 2.18.2; *ViDh* 96.14–7
47 *GDh* 3.24; *BDh* 2.11.23; *VaDh* 10.29; *MBh* 12.269.6; *ViDh* 96.19–20, 23
48 *BDh* 2.18.3; *MBh* 12.269.6
49 *ĀpDh* 2.21.13; *VaDh* 10.17, 20; *MBh* 12.317.25
50 *VaDh* 10.21
51 *ViDh* 96.5; *YDh* 3.59
52 *GDh* 3.22; *BDh* 2.11.18; 2.17.10–1; *VaDh* 10.6; *YDh* 3.58
53 *ViDh* 96.8; *YDh* 3.60
54 *ViDh* 96.7; *YDh* 3.60
55 *BDh* 2.18.12; *VaDh* 10.24–5; *ViDh* 96.3; *YDh* 3.59
56 *GDh* 3.15; *BDh* 2.11.22; 2.18.4–6; *VaDh* 10.7–8; *ViDh* 96.6; *YDh* 3.59
57 *VaDh* 10.22; *MBh* 12.269.10; *ViDh* 96.4
58 *MBh* 12.269.11; *ViDh* 96.9
59 *BDh* 2.18.10–3; *VaDh* 10.25
60 *BDh* 2.18.2–3; *YDh* 3.61
61 *ViDh* 96.36, 38; *YDh* 3.63–4
62 *ViDh* 96.27–9, 37; *YDh* 3.63–4
63 *ViDh* 96.39; *YDh* 3.63–4
64 *ViDh* 96.40–2; *YDh* 3.63–4
65 *VaDh* 10.14; *YDh* 3.63–4
66 *VaDh* 10.18; *YDh* 3.65
70 *VaDh* 10.5
71 *BDh* 4.1.24; *VaDh* 25.6
72 *ViDh* 96.24
73 *ViDh* 96.25
75 *ĀpDh* 2.21.14–6
76 *MBh* 12.316.42; *ViDh* 96.43–53
77 *MBh* 12.316.43; *ViDh* 96.43–53
83 *ĀpDh* 2.21.4; *BDh* 2.18.20–7; *VaDh* 10.4
87 *ĀpDh* 2.21.1; *GDh* 3.2–3; *BDh* 2.11.12
88 *ĀpDh* 2.21.2; *GDh* 3.1
89 *GDh* 3.36; *ViDh* 59.27–9
90 *VaDh* 8.14–6
92 *VaDh* 10.30; *YDh* 3.66
95 *VaDh* 10.26

Chapter Seven

8 *MBh* 12.68.40
14 *YDh* 1.353
16 *GDh* 12.51; *VaDh* 19.9; *ViDh* 3.91; *YDh* 1.367
18 *MBh* 12.15.2
19 *YDh* 1.355

22 *MBh* 12.15.34
25 *MBh* 12.15.11; *ViDh* 3.95
26 *GDh* 11.2–3; *YDh* 1.308–9
31 *GDh* 11.2–4
32 *ViDh* 3.96; *YDh* 1.333
33 *ViDh* 3.97
37 *ViDh* 3.76
38 *AŚ* 8.3.66; *ViDh* 3.76–7; *YDh* 1.309
43 *GDh* 11.3; *YDh* 1.310
44 *GDh* 11.4
45–7 *ViDh* 3.50
48 *ViDh* 3.51–2
54 *ViDh* 3.71; *YDh* 1.312
56 *YDh* 1.312
58 *YDh* 1.312
61–2 *ViDh* 3.16–21
63 *AŚ* 1.15.7–9
69 *ViDh* 3.4–5; *YDh* 1.321
70 *AŚ* 2.2.1–35; *MBh* 12.87.5; *ViDh* 3.6; *YDh* 1.321
76 *ĀpDh* 2.25.2–3
78 *GDh* 11.12–8; *BDh* 1.18.7–8; *VaDh* 19.3–6; *ViDh* 3.70; *YDh* 1.312–3
79 *ĀpDh* 2.26.1; *ViDh* 3.78, 81, 84; *YDh* 1.313
80 *YDh* 1.322
82–3 *YDh* 1.314
84 *VaDh* 30.7; *YDh* 1.315
85 *GDh* 5.20; *ViDh* 93.1–4
87 *GDh* 10.13–6; *BDh* 1.18.9; *ViDh* 3.43
88 *ViDh* 3.44; *YDh* 1.323
89 *ĀpDh* 2.26.2–3; *ViDh* 3.45; *YDh* 1.324
90 *BDh* 1.18.10; *YDh* 1.324
91–3 *ĀpDh* 2.10.11; *GDh* 10.18; *BDh* 1.18.11; *YDh* 1.325
94–5 *YDh* 1.325
96–8 *GDh* 10.20–3
99 *VaDh* 16.6; *YDh* 1.317; *Pañcatantra* I.2; *AŚ* 1.4.3
101 *YDh* 1.317; *AŚ* 1.4.3
102 *AŚ* 1.15.60; *MBh* 12.139.7
103 *MBh* 12.139.8
105 *MBh* 12.84.46; 12.139.24; *AŚ* 1.15.60
106 *MBh* 12.139.25
114 *AŚ* 2.1.4
115 *ĀpDh* 2.26.4–5; *MBh* 12.188.3; *ViDh* 3.7–10
116 *MBh* 12.88.4; *ViDh* 3.11–12
117 *MBh* 12.88.5; *ViDh* 3.13–5
118 *MBh* 12.88.6
119 *MBh* 12.88.6–8
120 *MBh* 12.88.9
121 *ĀpDh* 2.26.4; *MBh* 12.88.10
122 *MBh* 12.88.10; *YDh* 1.338
123 *YDh* 1.338
124 *YDh* 1.339
127 *MBh* 12.88.11
128 *ĀpDh* 2.26.9; *BDh* 1.18.15; *MBh* 12.88.15
130 *GDh* 10.24–5; *BDh* 1.18.1; *VaDh* 1.42; *ViDh* 3.22, 24
131 *GDh* 10.27; *VaDh* 1.42; *ViDh* 3.25
132 *GDh* 10.27; *ViDh* 3.23, 25
133 *ĀpDh* 2.26.10; *GDh* 10.11; *VaDh* 1.43; 19.23; *ViDh* 3.26
134 *ĀpDh* 2.25.11; *GDh* 10.9; *ViDh* 3.79
135 *YDh* 3.44
136 *VaDh* 1.44; *ViDh* 3.27
137 *VaDh* 19.26–7
138 *GDh* 10.31–2; *VaDh* 19.28; *ViDh* 3.32
141 *ViDh* 3.73; *YDh* 2.3
142 *ĀpDh* 2.10.6; *GDh* 10.7–8; *BDh* 1.18.1; *VaDh* 19.1; *ViDh* 3.2; *YDh* 1.335
147–8 *YDh* 1.344
155–8 *ViDh* 3.38; *YDh* 1.345
159 *ViDh* 3.39; *YDh* 1.346
160 *ViDh* 3.39; *YDh* 1.347

171 *YDh* 1.347

179 *MBh* 5.39.41

182 *ViDh* 3.40; *YDh* 1.347

183 *ViDh* 3.41

191 *MBh* 12.101.44

202 *ViDh* 3.47

203 *ViDh* 3.42; *YDh* 1.343

204 *AŚ* 6.2.6–12

205 *YDh* 1.349

208 *YDh* 1.352

213 *MBh* 5.37.17

216 *YDh* 1.327

218 *ViDh* 3.87

219 *ViDh* 3.88

221–2 *YDh* 1.329

223–4 *YDh* 1.330

225 *YDh* 1.331

Chapter Eight

1 *GDh* 13.26; *VaDh* 16.2; *ViDh* 3.72; *YDh* 1.359; 2.1

3 *GDh* 11.19–24; *VaDh* 1.17; 16.4–5

9 *GDh* 13.26; *VaDh* 16.2; *ViDh* 3.73; *YDh* 2.3

13 *NSm Mā* 3.9

16 *NSm Mā* 1.35; *MBh* 12.91.13

18 *GDh* 13.11; *BDh* 1.19.8

19 *BDh* 1.19.8

25–6 *YDh* 2.13–5

27 *GDh* 10.48; *VaDh* 16.8–9; *ViDh* 3.65

28 *ViDh* 3.65

30 *GDh* 10.36–8; *VaDh* 16.19–20; *YDh* 1.355; 2.33

31–2 *YDh* 2.33

35–6 *ViDh* 3.63–4; *YDh* 2.35

37 *GDh* 10.44; *VaDh* 3.14; *ViDh* 3.58; *YDh* 2.34

38 *GDh* 10.43; *ViDh* 3.56–7; *YDh* 2.34

39 *GDh* 10.45; *VaDh* 3.13; *ViDh* 3.58–62; *YDh* 2.35

40 *ĀpDh* 2.26.8; *GDh* 10.46–7; *ViDh* 3.66–7; *YDh* 2.36

41 *ĀpDh* 2.15.1; *GDh* 11.11, 20; *BDh* 1.2.1–8; *VaDh* 1.17; 19.7; *ViDh* 3.3; *YDh* 1.360

43 *GDh* 13.27

44 *ĀpDh* 2.29.6; *GDh* 11.23–4; *VaDh* 16.4–5

46 *ĀpDh* 2.15.1; *GDh* 11.20; *VaDh* 1.17

50 *ViDh* 6.18; *YDh* 2.40

52–7 *AŚ* 3.1.19

53–6 *YDh* 2.16

59 *YDh* 2.11

61 *GDh* 13.1

62 *BDh* 1.19.13; *ViDh* 8.8; *YDh* 2.68

63 *ĀpDh* 2.29.7; *GDh* 13.2; *VaDh* 16.28; *ViDh* 8.8; *YDh* 2.68

64 *GDh* 13.2; *ViDh* 8.3; *YDh* 2.70–1

65 *BDh* 1.19.13; *ViDh* 8.2; *YDh* 2.70

66 *BDh* 1.19.13; *ViDh* 8.2–3; *YDh* 2.70–1

67 *BDh* 1.19.13; *ViDh* 8.2; *YDh* 2.70

68 *VaDh* 16.30

69 *VaDh* 16.29; *YDh* 2.69

72 *GDh* 13.9; *ViDh* 8.6; *YDh* 2.72

73 *ViDh* 8.39; *YDh* 2.78, 80

74 *BDh* 1.19.7; *ViDh* 8.13–4

75 *ĀpDh* 2.29.9–10; *GDh* 13.7; *BDh* 1.19.14–5

76 *ViDh* 8.12

77 *YDh* 2.72

79 *ĀpDh* 2.29.7; *GDh* 13.5; *ViDh* 8.24; *YDh* 2.73

87 *ĀpDh* 2.29.7; *ViDh* 8.19

87–101 *AŚ* 3.11.34–7

88 *ViDh* 8.20–3

89 *ViDh* 8.25; *YDh* 2.73–4

90 *BDh* 1.19.10; *ViDh* 8.26; *YDh* 2.75

93 *VaDh* 16.33; *NSm* 1.183

97 *NSm* 1.188
98 *GDh* 13.14–5; *BDh* 1.19.12; *VaDh* 16.34; *NSm* 1.189
99 *GDh* 13.16; *BDh* 1.19.12; *NSm* 1.90
100 *GDh* 13.18–9
102 *BDh* 1.10.24
104 *GDh* 13.24–5; *VaDh* 16.36; *ViDh* 8.15; *YDh* 2.83
105 *YDh* 2.83
106 *BDh* 1.19.16; *ViDh* 8.16
107 *GDh* 13.6; *YDh* 2.76
108 *YDh* 2.113
109 *GDh* 13.12–3; *ViDh* 8.19
112 *GDh* 23.29; *VaDh* 16.36
113 *ViDh* 8.22–3
114–5 *ViDh* ch. 11–12; *YDh* 2.103–9
117 *ViDh* 8.40
119–23 *YDh* 2.81
124 *GDh* 12.46–7; *ViDh* 5.2–8
126 *GDh* 12.51; *YDh* 1.367
127–8 *VaDh* 19.43; *YDh* 1.356
129–30 *YDh* 1.366
131–7 *ViDh* 4.1–13; *YDh* 1.361–4
138 *ViDh* 4.14; *YDh* 1.365
139 *ViDh* 4.20–1; *YDh* 2.42
140 *GDh* 12.29; *VaDh* 2.50–1; *YDh* 2.37
141 *YDh* 2.37
142 *VaDh* 2.48; *ViDh* 6.2; *YDh* 2.37
143 *GDh* 12.32; *ViDh* 6.5
144 *ViDh* 6.6; *YDh* 2.59
145 *ViDh* 6.7–8; *YDh* 2.58
147–8 *GDh* 12.37; *VaDh* 16.16–7; *YDh* 2.24
149 *GDh* 12.38–9; *VaDh* 16.18; *YDh* 2.25
151 *GDh* 12.31, 36; *ViDh* 6.11–7; *YDh* 2.39
153 *GDh* 12.30, 34–5
158 *ViDh* 6.41; *YDh* 2.53
159 *GDh* 12.41; *VaDh* 16.31; *ViDh* 6.41; *YDh* 2.47, 53; *AŚ* 3.16.9
160 *YDh* 2.54
163 *YDh* 2.32
164 *ViDh* 7.11
165 *ViDh* 7.7; *YDh* 2.89
166 *ViDh* 6.39; *YDh* 2.45
168 *ViDh* 7.6; *YDh* 2.89
176 *ViDh* 6.19; *YDh* 2.40
180 *YDh* 2.65
189 *YDh* 2.66
191 *ViDh* 5.169–71
199 *YDh* 2.168
200 *NSm* 1.76
202 *YDh* 2.170
204 *YDh* 1.66
207 *YDh* 2.265
211 *YDh* 2.259
215–7 *ĀpDh* 2.28.2–3; *ViDh* 5.153–4; *YDh* 2.193
219 *ViDh* 5.168; *YDh* 2.187
222 *YDh* 2.177
224 *YDh* 1.66; *NSm* 12.33; *AŚ* 3.15.14
225 *YDh* 1.66; *NSm* 12.34
230 *ViDh* 5.138; *YDh* 2.164
231 *ViDh* 5.140
232 *ViDh* 5.138–9; *YDh* 2.164
233 *NSm* 6.18
235 *ViDh* 5.138–9; *NSm* 6.16
236 *NSm* 6.17
237 *YDh* 2.167
239 *NSm* 11.36
240 *ĀpDh* 2.28.5; *GDh* 12.19–21; *ViDh* 5.140–5; *YDh* 2.162
241 *GDh* 12.21–6; *ViDh* 5.146–7; *YDh* 2.161
242 *ViDh* 5.151; *YDh* 2.163; *AŚ* 3.10.24
243 *ĀpDh* 2.28.1
246–7 *YDh* 2.151
251 *YDh* 2.151
256 *YDh* 2.152

257 *YDh* 2.253
262 *VaDh* 16.13–5; *YDh* 2.154
263 *YDh* 2.153
265 *YDh* 2.153
267 *GDh* 12.1, 8, 10; *YDh* 2.207
268 *GDh* 12.11–4; *YDh* 2.207
269 *ViDh* 5.35–9; *YDh* 2.205–6
270 *ĀpDh* 2.27.14; *GDh* 12.1; *ViDh* 5.23
271 *ViDh* 5.25; *NSm* 15–16.23
272 *ViDh* 5.24; *NSm* 15–16.24
273 *ViDh* 5.26
274 *ViDh* 5.27; *YDh* 2.204
279 *GDh* 12.1; *ViDh* 5.19; *YDh* 2.215; *NSm* 15–16.25; *AŚ* 3.19.8
280 *YDh* 2.215
281 *ĀpDh* 2.27.15; *GDh* 12.7; *ViDh* 5.20; *NSm* 15–16.26
282 *ViDh* 5.21–2; *NSm* 15–16. 27
283 *ViDh* 5.65; *YDh* 2.217; *NSm* 15–16.28
284 *ViDh* 5.66–72; *YDh* 2.218–20
285 *ViDh* 5.55–9
286 *ViDh* 5.75–6
287 *ViDh* 5.75–6; *YDh* 2.222
291 *YDh* 2.299
292 *YDh* 2.298–9
297–8 *ViDh* 5.50–4
299–300 *ĀpDh* 1.8.28–9; *GDh* 2.42–4; *AŚ* 3.3.8–9
302 *ĀpDh* 2.25.15; *YDh* 1.336
304 *YDh* 1.335
305 *VaDh* 1.44; *MBh* 12.76.7
306 *YDh* 1.335
308 *YDh* 1.337
314–5 *ĀpDh*1.25.4; *GDh* 12.43; *BDh* 2.1.16–7; *VaDh* 20.41; *ViDh* 52.1; *YDh* 3.257
316 *ĀpDh* 1.25.4–5; *GDh* 12.44–5; *BDh* 2.1.17; *VaDh* 20.41; *ViDh* 52.2; *YDh* 3.257
317 *ĀpDh* 1.19.16; *VaDh* 19.44
318 *VaDh* 19.45
320 *ViDh* 5.12; *NSm* 19.33
321 *ViDh* 5.13; *NSm* 19.32, 34
322 *ViDh* 5.81–2
324–5 *ViDh* 5.77–8
326–1 *ViDh* 5.83–6
332 *YDh* 2.230; *AŚ* 3.17.1-1
335 *MBh* 12.121.57; *YDh* 1.358
337–8 *GDh* 12.15–7
339 *ĀpDh* 1.28.3; *GDh* 12.28; *YDh* 2.166
340 *GDh* 12.49–50
348 *BDh* 2.4.18; *VaDh* 3.24
349 *GDh* 7.25; *BDh* 2.4.18; *VaDh* 3.24
350 *BDh* 1.18.12–3; *VaDh* 3.15–7; *ViDh* 5.190
351 *BDh* 1.18.13; *VaDh* 3.17–8; *MBh* 12.15.55; 12.35.19; 12.56.30; *ViDh* 5.191
354 *ĀpDh* 2.26.19; *YDh* 2.285
355 *ĀpDh* 2.26.18
357–8 *YDh* 2.284
359 *ĀpDh* 2.26.20; *BDh* 2.4.1–2
361 *YDh* 2.285
362 *BDh* 2.4.3
363 *YDh* 2.293
364–7 *YDh* 2.287–8
367 *AŚ* 4.12.3
371 *GDh* 23.14; *MBh* 12.159.59; *ViDh* 5.18
372 *GDh* 23.15; *VaDh* 21.1–3; *MBh* 12.159.60
373 *MBh* 12.159.61
374 *ĀpDh* 2.27.9; *GDh* 12.2; *BDh* 2.3.52; *VaDh* 21.1, 5; *YDh* 2.286, 294
377 *ĀpDh* 2.26.20; *VaDh* 21.2–3; *YDh* 2.286
378 *ViDh* 5.40; *YDh* 2.286
380 *GDh* 8.13; *BDh* 1.18.17; *ViDh* 5.2
385 *ViDh* 5.41, 43; *YDh* 2.294
386 *ViDh* 5.197

389 *ViDh* 5.163; *YDh* 2.237
392 *ViDh* 5.94; *YDh* 2.263
394 *ĀpDh* 2.26.16
396 *YDh* 2.238
397 *YDh* 2.179
398 *YDh* 2.261
399 *ViDh* 5.130; *YDh* 2.261
400 *YDh* 2.262
401 *YDh* 2.252
402 *YDh* 2.251
403 *VaDh* 19.13
404–5 *AŚ* 2.28.21–21
407 *AŚ* 2.28.18; *ViDh* 5.132–3
416 *MBh* 1.77.22

Chapter Nine

2 *GDh* 18.1; *BDh* 2.3.44; *VaDh* 5.1; *ViDh* 25.12; *YDh* 1.85
3 *BDh* 2.3.45; *VaDh* 5.3; *MBh* 13.20.21; 13.46.13; *ViDh* 25.13; *YDh* 1.85; *NSm* 13.31
4 *GDh* 18.22; *BDh* 4.1.12, 17–9; *VaDh* 17.69–70; *YDh* 1.64
6 *MBh* 3.13.60
8 *YDh* 1.56
9 *YDh* 1.81
17 *MBh* 13.40.12
18 *BDh* 1.11.7; *MBh* 13.40.11
27 *MBh* 13.46.10
30 *VaDh* 21.14
32 *ĀpDh* 2.13.5–6; *GDh* 18.9–14; *VaDh* 17.6–9, 63–4
45 *ĀpDh* 2.14.16–20
47 *ViDh* 5.161; *YDh* 1.65
50 *VaDh* 17.8
59 *GDh* 18.4–5; *BDh* 2.4.9–10; *VaDh* 17.56; *YDh* 1.68
60 *VaDh* 17.61; *YDh* 1.68
61 *GDh* 18.8
62–3 *YDh* 1.69
71 *ViDh* 5.160–1; *YDh* 1.65
72–3 *ViDh* 5.162; *YDh* 1.66
75 *ViDh* 25.9–10; *YDh* 1.84
76 *GDh* 18.15–7; *VaDh* 17.75–80
80 *YDh* 1.73
81 *BDh* 2.4.6
86 *ViDh* 26.1; *YDh* 1.88
87 *MBh* 13.47.36; *ViDh* 26.2–3
88 *GDh* 18.21; *BDh* 4.1.11; *VaDh* 17.70
90 *GDh* 18.20; *BDh* 4.1.14; *VaDh* 17.67–8; *MBh* 13.44.15; *ViDh* 24.40; *YDh* 1.64
92 *GDh* 18.20
93 *ViDh* 24.41
94 *MBh* 13.44.13
95 *MBh* 13.44.26
98 *ĀpDh* 2.13.11
104 *GDh* 28.1; *BDh* 2.3.3, 8; *ViDh* 18.36; *YDh* 2.117
105 *ĀpDh* 2.14.6; *GDh* 28.3; *BDh* 2.3.13
107 *VaDh* 17.1; *ViDh* 15.45
109 *MBh* 13.108.6
111 *GDh* 28.4
112 *GDh* 28.5–7; *BDh* 2.3.4; *ViDh* 18.37; *YDh* 2.114
114 *GDh* 28.11–3; *BDh* 2.3.6; *VaDh* 17.43; *YDh* 2.114
115 *ĀpDh* 2.13.13
116 *GDh* 28.8
117 *GDh* 28.9–10; *VaDh* 17.42
118 *ViDh* 18.35; *YDh* 2.124
119 *BDh* 2.3.9
123–5 *GDh* 28.14–6
127 *GDh* 28.18; *BDh* 2.3.15; *VaDh* 17.15–7; *ViDh* 15.5
130 *BDh* 2.3.14; *MBh* 13.45.12
131 *GDh* 28.24; *BDh* 2.3.43; *VaDh* 17.46; *MBh* 13.45.13; *ViDh* 17.21
133 *MBh* 13.45.14; *YDh* 2.128
136 *GDh* 28.19

137 *BDh* 2.16.6; *VaDh* 17.5; *ViDh* 15.46; *YDh* 1.78

138 *ViDh* 15.44

139 *ViDh* 15.47

140 *BDh* 2.3.16

141 *VaDh* 15.9–10

143–4 *GDh* 28.23

149 *VaDh* 17.47

150 *MBh* 13.47.11

152 *ViDh* 18.1

153 *BDh* 2.3.10; *VaDh* 17.48–50; *ViDh* 18.2–5; *YDh* 2.125; *AŚ* 3.6.17

154 *ViDh* 18.32

155 *GDh* 28.39

156 *ViDh* 18.28–30, 36–7

157 *MBh* 13.47.56; *ViDh* 18.31

158 *ViDh* 15.1

159 *GDh* 28.33; *BDh* 2.3.32; *VaDh* 17.38

162 *ViDh* 17.23

163 *ViDh* 15.28–30

164 *BDh* 2.3.11

165 *GDh* 28.34; *YDh* 2.132

166 *ĀpDh* 2.13.1; *BDh* 2.3.14; *VaDh* 17.13; *MBh* 1.111.31; *ViDh* 15.2; *YDh* 2.128

167 *BDh* 2.3.17–8; *VaDh* 17.14; *ViDh* 15.3; *YDh* 1.69; 2.127–8

168 *BDh* 2.3.20; *VaDh* 17.29; *ViDh* 15.18–9; *YDh* 2.130

169 *BDh* 2.3.21; *YDh* 2.131

170 *BDh* 2.3.22; *VaDh* 17.24; *ViDh* 15.13–4; *YDh* 2.129

171 *BDh* 2.3.23; *VaDh* 17.37; *ViDh* 15.24–5; *YDh* 2.132

172 *BDh* 2.3.24; *VaDh* 17.22–3; *ViDh* 15.10–1; *YDh* 2.129

173 *BDh* 2.3.25; *VaDh* 17.26–7; *ViDh* 15.15–6; *YDh* 2.131

174 *BDh* 2.3.26; *VaDh* 17.30–2; *ViDh* 15.20–1; *YDh* 1.131

175 *BDh* 2.3.27; *VaDh* 17.18–9; *ViDh* 15.7–9; *YDh* 2.130

176 *BDh* 4.1.16; *VaDh* 17.74; *ViDh* 15.8

177 *BDh* 2.3.28; *VaDh* 17.33–5; *ViDh* 15.22–3; *YDh* 2.131

178 *BDh* 2.3.30; *VaDh* 17.38; *ViDh* 15.27

179 *YDh* 2.133

181 *ĀpDh* 2.13.6–10; *BDh* 2.3.33–5

182` *VaDh* 17.10; *ViDh* 15.42

183 *VaDh* 17.11; *ViDh* 15.41

184 *VaDh* 17.39, 81; *ViDh* 15.28–9

185 *ViDh* 17.6–8; *YDh* 2.135

186 *BDh* 1.11.9

187 *ĀpDh* 2.14.2–3; *GDh* 28.21; *BDh* 1.11.10–3; *VaDh* 17.81–2; *ViDh* 17.11; *YDh* 2.135

188 *GDh* 28.41; *BDh* 1.11.14; *VaDh* 17.84–6; *ViDh* 17.14

189 *ĀpDh* 2.14.5; *GDh* 28.42; *BDh* 1.11.15–6; *VaDh* 17.83; *ViDh* 17.13

192–3 *YDh* 2.117

194 *ViDh* 17.18; *YDh* 2.143

196 *ViDh* 17.19; *YDh* 2.145

197 *ViDh* 17.20; *YDh* 2.145

198 *MBh* 13.47.25

199 *MBh* 13.47.24

200 *ViDh* 17.22

201 *ĀpDh* 2.14.1; *GDh* 28.43; *BDh* 2.3.37–40; *VaDh* 17.52–3; *ViDh* 15.32; *YDh* 2.140

202 *GDh* 28.43; *BDh* 2.3.37–40; *VaDh* 17.54; *ViDh* 15.33; *YDh* 2.140

203 *GDh* 28.44; *ViDh* 15.34–6; *YDh* 2.141

205 *GDh* 28.31

206 *GDh* 28.30; *YDh* 2.118–9

207 *YDh* 2.116

208 *MBh* 13.108.11; *ViDh* 18.42

209 *ViDh* 18.43; *YDh* 2.119

210 *ViDh* 18.41; *YDh* 2.120

212 *ViDh* 17.17; *YDh* 2.138

213 *MBh* 13.108.7

214 *ĀpDh* 2.14.15; *GDh* 28.40; *BDh* 2.3.38; *MBh* 13.108.10
215 *MBh* 13.108.12; *YDh* 2.120
216 *GDh* 28.29; *ViDh* 17.3; *YDh* 2.122
217 *ViDh* 17.7; *YDh* 2.135; *AŚ* 4.11.9
218 *YDh* 2.126
219 *GDh* 28.46–7; *ViDh* 18.44
224 *YDh* 2.304
229 *YDh* 2.43
231 *ViDh* 5.180
232 *ViDh* 5.9, 11; *YDh* 2.240
234 *YDh* 2.305
237 *BDh* 1.18.18; *ViDh* 5.3–7
274 *ViDh* 5.74
276 *YDh* 2.273
277 *ViDh* 5.136; *AŚ* 4.10.1
278 *YDh* 2.276
279 *YDh* 2.279; *AŚ* 4.11.17
280 *YDh* 2.273
282 *ViDh* 5.106–7; *AŚ* 2.36.16–7
284 *ViDh* 5.175–7
285 *ViDh* 5.174
286 *ViDh* 5.124; *YDh* 2.245–6
292 *YDh* 2.297
294 *YDh* 1.352
294–5 *AŚ* 8.1.19
315 *MBh* 13.136.16
317 *MBh* 13.136.21
318 *MBh* 13.136.22
319 *MBh* 13.136.23
320 *MBh* 12.79.21
321 *MBh* 12.56.24; 12.79.22
322 *GDh* 11.14; *VaDh* 19.4
327 *MBh* 12.60.23
328` *MBh* 12.60.26

Chapter Ten

4 *ĀpDh* 1.1.3–5; *BDh* 1.16.1; *VaDh* 2.1–2; *MBh* 13.10.63; 13.47.7; *YDh* 1.10
5 *ĀpDh* 1.13.1; *ViDh* 16.1; *YDh* 1.90
6 *ĀpDh* 2.13.4–5; *BDh* 1.16.6
7 *GDh* 4.16; *BDh* 1.16.7; *VaDh* 18.8
8 *GDh* 4.16; *BDh* 1.16.7; 1.17.3; *VaDh* 18.8; *YDh* 1.91
9 *GDh* 4.16; *BDh* 1.16.7; 1.17.4; *VaDh* 18.8; *YDh* 1.92
11 *GDh* 4.17; *BDh* 1.16.8; 1.17.7–8; *VaDh* 18.6; *ViDh* 16.5–6; *YDh* 1.93–4
12 *GDh* 4.17; *BDh* 1.16.8; *ViDh* 16.4, 6; *YDh* 1.93–4
16 *BDh* 1.17.7; *VaDh* 18.1–3; *ViDh* 16.4; *YDh* 1.93–4
17 *BDh* 1.17.8; *ViDh* 16.5–6; *YDh* 1.93–4
18 *GDh* 4.19; *BDh* 1.16.8, 11–2; 1.17.13–4; *VaDh* 18.5; *ViDh* 16.5
19 *BDh* 1.16.8–10; 1.17.11–2; *VaDh* 18.2
20 *BDh* 1.16.16
21 *GDh* 4.20
22 *GDh* 4.21
24 *YDh* 1.96
27 *MBh* 13.48.14
28 *MBh* 13.48.15
29 *MBh* 13.48.16; *ViDh* 16.7
30 *MBh* 13.48.17
31 *MBh* 13.48.18
32 *MBh* 13.48.19–20
33 *MBh* 13.48.20
34 *MBh* 13.48.21
35 *MBh* 13.48.24–5
36 *MBh* 13.48.25–6
37 *MBh* 13.48.26–7
38 *MBh* 13.48.27
39 *VaDh* 18.3; *MBh* 13.48.28
40 *MBh* 13.48.29; *ViDh* 16.17
43 *MBh* 13.33.20–1; 13.35.17
44 *MBh* 13.35.18

47 *ViDh* 16.10–3
48 *ViDh* 16.8
49 *ViDh* 16.9
50 *MBh* 13.48.32
51 *ViDh* 16.14
52 *MBh* 13.48.32; *ViDh* 16.14
56 *ViDh* 16.11
57 *VaDh* 18.7; *ViDh* 16.17
58 *MBh* 13.48.40
59 *MBh* 13.48.41
60 *MBh* 13.48.43
62 *MBh* 13.48.34; *ViDh* 16.18
63 *ĀpDh* 1.23.6; *GDh* 8.23; *ViDh* 2.16–7; *YDh* 1.122
64 *GDh* 4.22; *YDh* 1.96
74 *VaDh* 2.13
75 *ĀpDh* 2.10.4; *GDh* 10.1–2; *BDh* 1.18.2; *VaDh* 2.13–4; *ViDh* 2.5, 9, 11; *YDh* 1.118
76 *ViDh* 2.11
77 *ĀpDh* 2.10.6; *GDh* 10.1; *BDh* 1.18.3; *VaDh* 2.15–6; *ViDh* 2.9; *YDh* 1.118
78 *ĀpDh* 2.10.7; *GDh* 10.1; *BDh* 1.18.4; *VaDh* 2.18; *ViDh* 2.9
79 *ĀpDh* 2.10.6–7; *GDh* 10.7, 15, 49; *BDh* 1.18.3–4; *VaDh* 2.17–9; *ViDh* 2.6–7, 12–3; *YDh* 1.119
81 *GDh* 7.6; *BDh* 2.4.16; *VaDh* 2.22; *ViDh* 2.15; *YDh* 3.35
82 *GDh* 7.7; *BDh* 2.4.19–21; *VaDh* 2.24, 32–6; *YDh* 3.35
84 *BDh* 2.4.20–1; *VaDh* 2.32–6; *MBh* 3.199.19; 12.254.44
85 *ĀpDh* 1.20.10–1; *GDh* 7.8; *YDh* 3.39
86 *ĀpDh* 1.20.12–3; *GDh* 7.9, 14–5; *BDh* 2.2.27; *VaDh* 2.24, 26, 29; *ViDh* 54.18, 21; *YDh* 3.36, 38
87 *GDh* 7.9–10; *VaDh* 2.24–6; *ViDh* 54.18, 20; *YDh* 3.36–8
88 *ĀpDh* 1.20.12–3; *GDh* 7.9–12; *VaDh* 2.26; *ViDh* 54.18–21; *YDh* 3.36–8
89 *ĀpDh* 1.20.12; *GDh* 7.13–5; *VaDh* 2.28; *ViDh* 54.21; *YDh* 3.37–8
90 *VaDh* 2.31; *YDh* 3.39
91 *BDh* 2.2.26; *VaDh* 2.30
92 *VaDh* 2.27; *YDh* 3.40
93 *YDh* 3.40
94 *ĀpDh* 1.20.15; *GDh* 7.16–7, 21; *VaDh* 2.37–9
95 *GDh* 7.26; *ViDh* 2.15
96 *VaDh* 2.23
98 *VaDh* 2.23; *ViDh* 2.15
99–100 *GDh* 10.57, 60; *ViDh* 2.14; *YDh* 1.120
102 *ĀpDh* 1.18.5–8, 14–5; *GDh* 7.4
103 *VaDh* 27.9
104 *YDh* 3.41
111 *ĀpDh* 1.28.11; *VaDh* 20.45–6; *ViDh* 54.28
114 *VaDh* 12.3
115 *GDh* 10.39–42
116 *YDh* 3.42
117 *VaDh* 2.40–3
119 *GDh* 10.16, 41
120 *VaDh* 19.37
121 *GDh* 10.56; *YDh* 1.120
124 *GDh* 10.61
125 *GDh* 10.58–9
126–7 *GDh* 10.64–5; *YDh* 1.121, 262
129 *GDh* 10.63

Chapter Eleven

1 *ĀpDh* 2.10.1–2; *GDh* 5.21; *BDh* 2.5.19; *MBh* 12.159.1
2 *MBh* 12.159.2
3 *GDh* 5.22; *BDh* 2.5.20; *MBh* 12.159.3
4 *MBh* 12.159.4
5 *ĀpDh* 2.10.3
7 *VaDh* 8.10; *MBh* 12.159.5; *ViDh* 59.8–9; *YDh* 1.124

11	*MBh* 12.159.6
12	*GDh* 18.25; *MBh* 12.159.7
13	*GDh* 18.24; *MBh* 12.159.8
14	*GDh* 18.26–7; *MBh* 159.9; *AŚ* 3.14.37
15	*MBh* 12.159.10
16	*GDh* 18.28–9; *MBh* 12.159.11; *YDh* 3.43
17	*GDh* 18.30; *MBh* 12.159.11–2; *YDh* 3.43
21	*GDh* 18.32; *MBh* 12.159.12–3
22	*GDh* 18.31; *MBh* 12.159.13; *YDh* 3.44
24	*ViDh* 59.11; *YDh* 1.127
25	*YDh* 1.127
27	*MBh* 12.159.14; *ViDh* 59.10; *YDh* 1.126
29	*MBh* 12.159.15
30	*MBh* 12.159.16
31	*MBh* 12.159.17
34	*VaDh* 26.16; *MBh* 12.159.19
35	*MBh* 12.159.18
36	*ĀpDh* 2.15.18–9; *GDh* 2.4; *VaDh* 2.6; *MBh* 12.159.20
37	*MBh* 12.159.20
38	*MBh* 12.159.21
39	*MBh* 12.159.22
40	*MBh* 12.159.23
41	*GDh* 22.34; *VaDh* 1.18; 21.27; *ViDh* 54.13
44	*GDh* 19.2; *BDh* 3.10.2; *VaDh* 22.1; *MBh* 12.35.2; *YDh* 3.219–20
45`	*GDh* 19.3–6; *BDh* 3.10.3–5; *VaDh* 20.1–2; 22.3–5; *YDh* 3.226
46	*YDh* 3.226
48	*VaDh* 20.43; *ViDh* 44.1
49	*VaDh* 1.18; 20.6, 44; *ViDh* 45.3–6; *YDh* 3.209
50	*ViDh* 45.7–10; *YDh* 3.211
51	*ViDh* 45.11–4; *YDh* 3.210
52	*ViDh* 45.20–1, 31
53	*ViDh* 44.32
54	*YDh* 3.220
55	*ĀpDh* 1.21.8; *GDh* 21.1; *VaDh* 1.19–21; *ViDh* 35.1–2; *YDh* 3.227
56	*GDh* 21.10; *ViDh* 36.1; 37.1–3; *YDh* 3.228
57	*ĀpDh* 1.21.8; *GDh* 21.1; *ViDh* 36.2; 37.4–5; *YDh* 3.228–9
58	*BDh* 2.2.3–4; *ViDh* 36.3; *YDh* 3.230
59	*ĀpDh* 1.21.8–9, 17–8; *GDh* 21.1; *BDh* 2.2.13; *ViDh* 36.4–7; *YDh* 3.231
60	*ĀpDh* 1.21.9–10; *GDh* 21.1, 11; *VaDh* 1.23; *ViDh* 37.6, 9–10, 13; *YDh* 3.234–5, 237, 239–40
61	*GDh* 21.11; *ViDh* 37.15–8; *YDh* 3.234–5, 238
62	*GDh* 21.11; *BDh* 2.2.13; *YDh* 3.236–8
63	*GDh* 21.11; *BDh* 2.2.5; *ViDh* 37.14, 19–21; *YDh* 3.234–5
64	*GDh* 21.11; *ViDh* 37.22–6; *YDh* 3.240, 242
65	*ĀpDh* 1.21.14–5; *GDh* 21.11; *ViDh* 37.7, 24, 27; *YDh* 3.239–40
66	*GDh* 21.11; *BDh* 2.2.13; *ViDh* 37.28–30, 32; *YDh* 3.234, 242
67	*GDh* 21.1, 11; *VaDh* 1.23; *ViDh* 37.13, 31, 33; *YDh* 3.236–7, 239
68	*ViDh* 38.1–6
69	*ViDh* 39.1
70	*BDh* 2.2.6; *ViDh* 40.1
71	*ĀpDh* 1.21.12–7; *BDh* 2.2.15–6; *ViDh* 41.1–4
72	*GDh* 22.1; *BDh* 2.1.1
73	*ĀpDh* 1.24.11–20; 1.28.21–9; *GDh* 22.4–6; *BDh* 2.1.2–3; *ViDh* 50.1–6, 15; *YDh* 3.243
74	*ĀpDh* 1.25.11; *GDh* 22.2–3; *YDh* 3.248
75	*GDh* 22.10; *BDh* 2.1.4
77	*YDh* 3.250
78	*YDh* 3.249
79	*ĀpDh* 1.24.18

80 *GDh* 22.7; *VaDh* 20.27; *YDh* 3.244–5

81 *ĀpDh* 1.24.21; *GDh* 22.8; *VaDh* 20.28; *YDh* 3.246

83 *ĀpDh* 1.24.22; *GDh* 22.9; *BDh* 2.1.5; *ViDh* 35.6; *YDh* 3.244

88 *ĀpDh* 1.24.6–9; *GDh* 22.12–3; *BDh* 2.1.12; *VaDh* 20.23–4, 34–6; *ViDh* 50.7–9; *YDh* 3.251

89 *ViDh* 50.10

90 *GDh* 21.7; *BDh* 2.1.6

91 *ĀpDh* 1.25.3; *GDh* 23.1; *BDh* 2.1.18; *VaDh* 20.22; *MBh* 12.159.45; *YDh* 3.253

92 *YDh* 3.253

93 *ViDh* 51.1; *YDh* 3.254

95 *ViDh* 22.82

102 *ĀpDh* 1.25.10; *ViDh* 52.3; *YDh* 3.258

104 *ĀpDh* 1.25.2; *GDh* 23.8–9; *BDh* 2.1.13–4; *VaDh* 20.14; *ViDh* 34.2; *YDh* 3.259

105 *ĀpDh* 1.25.1; *GDh* 23.10–1; *BDh* 2.1.15; *VaDh* 20.13; *MBh* 12.159.47; *YDh* 3.259

106 *ViDh* 53.1; *YDh* 3.260

107 *ViDh* 53.6; *YDh* 3.260

109 *ĀpDh* 1.26.1; *GDh* 22.18; *VaDh* 21.18; *ViDh* 50.16; *YDh* 3.263

110 *ViDh* 50.22

111 *ViDh* 50.16; *YDh* 3.263

112 *ViDh* 50.17–8

113 *ViDh* 50.19–20

114 *ViDh* 50.21

116 *ViDh* 50.24

117 *YDh* 3.263

118 *ViDh* 37.35

119 *ĀpDh* 1.26.8–9; *GDh* 23.17; *BDh* 2.1.31–3; *VaDh* 23.1–3; *YDh* 3.280

120 *GDh* 25.4; *BDh* 2.1.35

121 *BDh* 2.1.30; *VaDh* 23.4; *ViDh* 28.48

122 *GDh* 25.1–2

123 *GDh* 23.18; *ViDh* 28.49

124 *GDh* 23.19; *ViDh* 28.50

125 *ViDh* 28.7

126 *ViDh* 29.2; 40.2; 41.5

127 *GDh* 22.14–6; *BDh* 2.1.8–10; *VaDh* 20.31–3; *ViDh* 50.12–5; *YDh* 3.266–7

128 *ĀpDh* 1.24.14; *GDh* 22.14; *BDh* 1.19.1; *YDh* 3.266

129 *YDh* 3.266

130 *ĀpDh* 1.24.2, 4; *GDh* 22.15; *BDh* 1.19.2; *YDh* 3.267

131 *ĀpDh* 1.24.3–4; *GDh* 22.16; *BDh* 1.19.2; *YDh* 3.267

132 *ĀpDh* 1.25.13; *GDh* 22.19; *BDh* 1.19.6; *VaDh* 21.24; *ViDh* 50.30–2; *YDh* 3.270

133 *YDh* 3.270

134 *GDh* 22.23, 25; *ViDh* 50.34–5; *YDh* 3.273

135 *GDh* 22.24; *ViDh* 50.36–9; *YDh* 3.271, 273–4

136 *BDh* 1.19.6; *ViDh* 50.33; *YDh* 3.272

137 *BDh* 1.19.4; *ViDh* 50.25–8; *YDh* 3.271

138 *ViDh* 50.29, 40–1; *YDh* 3.272–3

139 *GDh* 22.26; *YDh* 3.268

140 *VaDh* 21.26; *YDh* 3.274

141 *ĀpDh* 1.26.2; *GDh* 22.20–1; *VaDh* 21.25; *ViDh* 50.46; *YDh* 3.269

142 *GDh* 22.22; *ViDh* 50.47; *YDh* 3.275

143 *ViDh* 50.48; *YDh* 3.276

144 *ViDh* 50.49; *YDh* 3.275

145 *ViDh* 50.50; *YDh* 3.276

147 *GDh* 23.2; *BDh* 2.1.19–21; *VaDh* 20.19; *ViDh* 51.4; *YDh* 3.255

148 *BDh* 2.1.22; *VaDh* 20.21; *ViDh* 51.23–4

150 *GDh* 23.6; *MBh* 12.159.71; *ViDh* 51.25

151 *GDh* 23.3; *VaDh* 20.20; *ViDh* 51.2; *YDh* 3.255

152 *BDh* 2.1.20; *VaDh* 20.18; *ViDh* 51.5

153 *VaDh* 14.33; *ViDh* 51.50, 54–6
156 *ViDh* 51.27.34
157 *GDh* 23.4–5; *VaDh* 23.30; *ViDh* 51.3–4
158 *VaDh* 23.12; *ViDh* 51.43–4
159 *VaDh* 23.11; *ViDh* 51.45; *YDh* 3.282
160 *VaDh* 23.11; *ViDh* 51.46–7
161 *GDh* 23.26
163 *ĀpDh* 1.25.10; *ViDh* 52.5
164 *ViDh* 52.6
165 *ViDh* 52.7
166 *ViDh* 52.8
167 *ViDh* 52.9
168 *ViDh* 52.10
169 *ViDh* 52.11, 13
171 *GDh* 23.12–3, 32; *BDh* 2.2.13–4; *VaDh* 20.15–6; *ViDh* 34.2; 53.1; *YDh* 3.233
173 *BDh* 2.1.37–8
174 *ĀpDh* 1.26.7; *GDh* 22.36, 23.34; *ViDh* 53.4, 7; *YDh* 3.288
175 *ViDh* 53.4; *YDh* 3.291
176 *BDh* 2.4.13–4; *VaDh* 23.41; *ViDh* 53.5–6
177 *MBh* 12.159.58; *ViDh* 53.8
179 *ĀpDh* 1.27.11; *BDh* 2.2.11; *ViDh* 53.9
181 *GDh* 21.3; *BDh* 2.2.35; *VaDh* 1.22; *MBh* 12.159.35; *ViDh* 35.3–5; *YDh* 3.261
182 *ViDh* 54.1
183 *GDh* 20.4–6; *BDh* 2.1.36; *VaDh* 15.12–3; *YDh* 3.295
184 *GDh* 20.4, 7; *VaDh* 15.12, 14; *ViDh* 22.57
185 *GDh* 20.8–9; *VaDh* 15.15–6; *YDh* 3.295
187 *GDh* 20.10; *BDh* 2.1.36; *VaDh* 15.17–21; *YDh* 3.296
188 *GDh* 20.11–4; *BDh* 2.1.36; *YDh* 3.296
189 *YDh* 3.297
190 *ViDh* 54.31
191 *ViDh* 54.32; *YDh* 3.299
192 *VaDh* 11.76–9; *ViDh* 54.26
193 *ViDh* 54.27
194 *ViDh* 54.28
195 *ViDh* 54.24; *YDh* 3.290
196–7 *BDh* 2.1.36; *YDh* 3.300
198 *ĀpDh* 1.26.7; *ViDh* 54.25; *YDh* 3.289
199 *YDh* 3.289
200 *GDh* 23.7; *VaDh* 23.31; *ViDh* 54.12; *YDh* 3.277
202 *YDh* 3.291
204 *ViDh* 54.29
205–6 *YDh* 3.292
208 *MBh* 12.159.43
209 *BDh* 2.1.7; *ViDh* 54.30; *YDh* 3.293
210 *ViDh* 54.34; *YDh* 3.294
212 *ĀpDh* 1.27.7; *GDh* 26.2–5; *BDh* 2.2.38; 4.5.6–7; *VaDh* 21.20; *ViDh* 46.10; *YDh* 3.320
213 *BDh* 4.5.11; *VaDh* 27.13; *ViDh* 54.19; *YDh* 3.315
214 *GDh* 26.18–9; *BDh* 2.2.40; 4.5.8; *VaDh* 24.1–2; *YDh* 3.320
215 *BDh* 2.2.37; 4.5.10; *VaDh* 21.21; *ViDh* 46.11; *YDh* 3.318
216 *BDh* 4.5.15; *ViDh* 46.18; *YDh* 3.321
217 *GDh* 27.12–3; *BDh* 3.8.10, 19–23; *VaDh* 23.45; 27.21; *ViDh* 47.4–5; *YDh* 3.324
218 *GDh* 27.14; *BDh* 3.8.26; 4.5.17; *VaDh* 27.21; *ViDh* 47.3, 6
219 *BDh* 4.5.19; *ViDh* 47.7
220 *BDh* 4.5.18; *ViDh* 47.8
221 *GDh* 27.18; *BDh* 3.8.31; 4.5.20; *ViDh* 47.9; *YDh* 3.325, 327
222 *BDh* 3.8.30; *ViDh* 47.10
223 *GDh* 26.1–6; 27.2; *BDh* 3.8.3, 7–9, 12–3
224 *BDh* 3.8.17; *YDh* 3.326

225 *BDh* 3.8.14–6
226 *VaDh* 24.46; *YDh* 3.309
227 *VaDh* 25.3
239 *ViDh* 95.17
246 *VaDh* 27.7; *YDh* 3.311
247 *VaDh* 27.1–2
249 *BDh* 4.1.29; *VaDh* 26.4; *ViDh* 55.2
250 *VaDh* 26.5; *ViDh* 55.4; *YDh* 3.304
251 *VaDh* 26.6; *YDh* 3.304
252 *VaDh* 26.7; *ViDh* 55.6; *YDh* 3.305
254 *GDh* 24.2–3; *BDh* 4.2.4–5
260 *GDh* 24.10–2; *BDh* 3.5.2–5; *VaDh* 26.8; *MBh* 12.148.26; 12.207.13; *YDh* 3.302
261 *BDh* 4.2.15; *MBh* 12.148.26; *ViDh* 55.7
262 *VaDh* 27.3
263 *BDh* 3.9.1–21; 4.5.29

Chapter Twelve

5 *YDh* 3.134
6 *YDh* 3.135
7 *YDh* 3.136
9 *YDh* 3.131, 134–6
24 *YDh* 3.182
27 *MBh* 12.187.30; 12.212.29; 12.239.20
28 *MBh* 12.187.31; 12.212.30; 12.239.21
29 *MBh* 12.187.32; 12.212.31; 12.239.22
31 *YDh* 3.137
32 *YDh* 3.138
33 *YDh* 3.139
40 *YDh* 3.137–9
52 *YDh* 3.219
55–6 *YDh* 3.207
57–8 *YDh* 3.208
60 *YDh* 3.212
61 *YDh* 3.213
62 *ViDh* 44.14–20; *YDh* 3.214–5
63 *ViDh* 44.21–5; *YDh* 3.211, 215
64 *ViDh* 44.26–30; *YDh* 3.215
65 *ViDh* 44.31–4; *YDh* 3.213
66 *ViDh* 44.35–7; *YDh* 3.214–5
67 *ViDh* 24.38–43; *YDh* 3.214
68 *ViDh* 44.44; *YDh* 3.217
69 *MBh* 13.112.110; *ViDh* 44.45
75–6 *YDh* 3.206
83 *YDh* 3.190
91 *ĀpDh* 1.23.1
101 *VaDh* 27.2
108 *GDh* 28.48; *VaDh* 1.5
109 *ĀpDh* 2.29.13–4; *BDh* 1.1.5–6; *VaDh* 1.6; 6.43
110 *GDh* 28.49; *BDh* 1.1.7, 9
111 *BDh* 1.1.8; *VaDh* 3.20
112 *YDh* 1.9
113 *GDh* 28.50
114 *BDh* 1.1.16; *VaDh* 3.5
115 *BDh* 1.1.11; *VaDh* 3.6

PĀDA INDEX

Note: The + sign indicates that the pāda is found in an additional verse given in the critial apparatus.

अ

आ

इ

ई

उ

ऐ

ओ

औ

क

ख

ग

घ

च

छ

ज

झ

ड

त

द

ध

न

प

फ

ब

भ

म

य

र

ल

व

श

INDEX TO THE TRANSLATION